THE NEW
COLLINS
THESAURUS

THE NEW
COLLINS
THESAURUS

MANAGING EDITOR
William T. McLeod

GUILD PUBLISHING LONDON

This edition published 1985 by
Book Club Associates
by arrangement with Wllm. Collins Sons & Co. Ltd

NOTE

Entered words that we have reason to believe
constitute trademarks have been designated as
such. However, neither the presence nor absence of
such designation should be regarded as affecting the
legal status of any trademark.

Computer typeset by C.R. Barber & Partners,
Wrotham, England.

Printed & Bound by
Brepols, Turnhout,
Belgium

Foreword

The *New Collins Thesaurus* gives practical and accessible help to the writer or speaker who wants to find a better word to replace one that is not quite right. Though a thesaurus can be used for a variety of purposes – to increase one's vocabulary, to track down a term that has been temporarily forgotten, or just for fun – its main use is to enable you to find just the right word for your purpose – a word that is more precise, or more vivid, or simpler, or more formal (or informal) than any you can call to mind unaided.

This being so, the best thesaurus is the one that enables you to find the most appropriate word quickly and easily on the largest possible number of occasions. The *New Collins Thesaurus* achieves this by arranging its material, like a dictionary, in a single alphabetical listing of main entry words.

A thesaurus in dictionary form has a big advantage: you go straight to the word that is your starting point and *there* are the synonyms. No matter how many meanings a word has, synonyms for all of them are found in the one entry. There is no need to consult several different locations to be sure of getting the full range of choices.

This thesaurus, however, has another distinct advantage: no synonym is entered unless it is *fully* substitutable for the headword in a sensible English sentence. Of course, not all items in a list are interchangeable – after all, some would claim that true synonyms, with *exactly* identical meanings, are rare things – but all are interchangeable in one context or another with the headword and often with each other. Because synonyms are chosen for inclusion with actual sentences in mind you can almost always find the better word that you are looking for.

A wide range of main entry words (totalling some 16000) has been included, the criterion for selection always being that the term in question is likely to be looked up as an entry in its own right. If the source word in mind does not occur as a main entry (say, *gallimaufry*) the synonyms can still be found by trying a simpler word of the same general meaning (say, *jumble* or *hotchpotch*). Obsolete words are not, in general, given as main entries though some may be included among the synonyms provided. Terms denoting concrete things are not included unless they have genuine synonyms or give rise to a figurative use. *Retina*, for example, is not a headword; but *eye* is entered with both literal and figurative senses, while *ear* is given figurative senses only.

A thesaurus lists synonyms; a dictionary lists meanings (among other things). They should be inseparable companions on any bookshelf. Further information on the range of meanings of words listed in this Thesaurus can be found in Collins English Dictionary or Collins Concise English Dictionary, together with information on pronunciation and etymology, style, grammar, syntax, and usage.

Wide coverage, clarity and ease of use, and the provision of true synonyms have been the priorities in the preparation of this volume. It is thus well equipped to be a regular and frequent source of *practical* help. Whether writing a letter, compiling a report, marshalling an argument, or solving a crossword, the owner of this volume need never again be at a loss for the best word.

W.T.M.

Explanatory Notes

1. Under each main entry word, the synonyms are arranged alphabetically. When a word has distinctly separate meanings, separate numbered lists are given for the different senses.

2. Where it is desirable to distinguish between different parts of speech, labels have been added as follows: *n.* (noun), *v.* (verb), *adj.* (adjective), *adv.* (adverb), *pron.* (pronoun), *conj.* (conjunction), *prep.* (preposition), *interj.* (interjection). See entries for *living, loaf, loan, lob, local.*

3. Usually the synonyms for a particular part of speech are grouped together. Thus, in the entry *catch* synonyms for all the verb senses are given first, followed by synonyms for all the noun senses. Sometimes, however, noun and verb functions are very closely associated in specific meanings, and where this is the case the synonyms are grouped by meanings, as in the entry for *cover.*

4. When a headword has more than one meaning *and* can function as more than one part of speech, a new part-of-speech function is shown by a large swung dash (~), as in the entry for *glance,* or *grasp.*

5. Much-used phrases appear as main entries; for instance, *act for* comes after *act*. Expressions such as *à la mode* or *en route* are also given as main entries within the alphabetical listing. Short idiomatic phrases are entered under their key word and are to be found either at the end of the entry or immediately following the sense with which they are associated. Thus, the phrase *take a dim view* appears as sense 7 of the entry *dim*, since the synonyms in sense 6 most closely approximate to the meaning of the phrase.

6. Plural forms that have a distinctly separate meaning, such as *provisions*, are entered at their own alphabetical position, while those with a less distinct difference, such as *appurtenances*, are given as a separate sense under the singular form, e.g. *appurtenance ... 2. Plural ...*

7. A label in brackets applies only to the synonym preceding it while one which is not bracketed relates to the whole of that particular sense. Labels have been abbreviated when a readily understandable shortened form exists, such as *Sl.* (Slang), *Inf.* (Informal), and *Fig.* (Figurative).

8. The small swung dash symbol (~) is used to show that a word has been broken merely because it happens to fall at the end of a line, while the conventional sign (-) is used to distinguish a word which is always written with a hyphen, as in *lifelong* and *deep-rooted* in the entry for *lasting*:

> **lasting** abiding, continuing, deep-rooted, durable, enduring, indelible, life~long, long-standing, ...

EDITORIAL STAFF

A

abaft *Nautical* aft, astern, behind

abandon v. **1.** desert, forsake, jilt, leave, leave behind **2.** evacuate, quit, vacate, withdraw from **3.** abdicate, cede, give up, relinquish, renounce, resign, surrender, waive, yield **4.** desist, discontinue, drop, forgo ~n. **5.** careless freedom, dash, recklessness, unrestraint, wantonness, wild impulse, wildness

abandoned 1. cast aside, cast away, cast out, derelict, deserted, discarded, dropped, forlorn, forsaken, jilted, left, neglected, outcast, rejected, relinquished, unoccupied, vacant **2.** corrupt, debauched, depraved, dissipated, dissolute, profligate, reprobate, sinful, wanton, wicked **3.** uncontrolled, uninhibited, unrestrained, wild

abandonment 1. dereliction, desertion, forsaking, jilting, leaving **2.** evacuation, quitting, withdrawal from **3.** abdication, cession, giving up, relinquishment, renunciation, resignation, surrender, waiver **4.** desistance, discontinuation, dropping

abase belittle, bring low, cast down, debase, degrade, demean, demote, depress, disgrace, dishonour, downgrade, humble, humiliate, lower, mortify, reduce

abasement belittlement, debasement, degradation, demotion, depression, disgrace, dishonour, downgrading, humbling, humiliation, lowering, mortification, reduction, shame

abash affront, astound, bewilder, chagrin, confound, confuse, discomfit, discompose, disconcert, discountenance, embarrass, humble, humiliate, mortify, perturb, shame

abashed affronted, ashamed, astounded, bewildered, chagrined, confounded, confused, discomfited, discomposed, disconcerted, discountenanced, dismayed, embarrassed, humbled, humiliated, mortified, perturbed, shamefaced, taken aback

abashment astonishment, bewilderment, chagrin, confusion, consternation, discomfiture, discomposure, disconcertion, dismay, embarrassment, humiliation, mortification, perturbation, shame

abate 1. alleviate, appease, attenuate, decline, decrease, diminish, dull, dwindle, ease, ebb, fade, lessen, let up, mitigate, moderate, quell, reduce, relieve, sink, slacken, slake, slow, subside, taper off, wane, weaken **2.** deduct, discount, subtract

abatement 1. alleviation, allowance, attenuation, cessation, decline, decrease, diminution, dulling, dwindling, easing, extenuation, fading, lessening, let-up (*Inf.*), mitigation, moderation, quelling, reduction, relief, remission, slackening, slaking, slowing, tapering off, waning, weakening **2.** deduction, discount, subtraction

abbey cloister, convent, friary, monastery, nunnery, priory

abbreviate abridge, abstract, clip, compress, condense, contract, curtail, cut, digest, epitomize, précis, reduce, shorten, summarize, trim, truncate

abbreviation abridgment, abstract, clipping, compendium, compression, condensation, conspectus, contraction, curtailment, digest, epitome, précis, reduction, résumé, shortening, summary, synopsis, trimming, truncation

abdicate abandon, abjure, abnegate, cede, forgo, give up, quit, relinquish, renounce, resign, retire, surrender, vacate, waive, yield

abdication abandonment, abjuration, abnegation, cession, giving up, quitting, relinquishment, renunciation, resignation, retiral (*esp. Scot.*), retirement, surrender, waiver, yielding

abdomen belly, breadbasket (*Sl.*), corporation (*Inf.*), guts (*Sl.*), midriff, midsection, paunch, pot, stomach, tummy (*Inf.*)

abdominal gastric, intestinal, stomachic, stomachical, visceral

abduct carry off, kidnap, make off with, run away with, run off with, seize, snatch (*Sl.*)

abduction carrying off, kidnapping, seizure

aberrant 1. abnormal, anomalous, defective, deviant, divergent, eccentric, irregular, odd, peculiar, queer, rambling, straying, untypical, wandering 2. delusive, delusory, disordered, hallucinatory, illusive, illusory, unstable 3. corrupt, corrupted, degenerate, depraved, deviant, erroneous, perverse, perverted, wrong

aberration 1. aberrancy, abnormality, anomaly, defect, deviation, divergence, eccentricity, irregularity, lapse, oddity, peculiarity, quirk, rambling, straying, wandering 2. delusion, hallucination, illusion, instability, mental disorder, vagary

abet 1. aid, assist, back, condone, connive at, help, promote, sanction, second, succour, support, sustain, uphold 2. egg on, encourage, incite, prompt, spur, urge

abettor 1. accessory, accomplice, assistant, associate, backer, confederate, conniver, cooperator, helper, henchman, second 2. encourager, fomenter, inciter, instigator, prompter

abeyance 1. adjournment, deferral, discontinuation, inactivity, intermission, postponement, recess, reservation, suspense, suspension, waiting 2. **in abeyance** hanging fire, on ice (*Inf.*), pending, shelved, suspended

abeyant adjourned, deferred, discontinued, dormant, inactive, intermitted, latent, postponed, put off, quiescent, reserved, shelved, suspended, waiting

abhor abominate, detest, execrate, hate, loathe, recoil from, regard with repugnance *or* horror, shrink from, shudder at

abhorrence abomination, animosity, aversion, detestation, disgust, distaste, enmity, execration, hate, hatred, horror, loathing, odium, repugnance, revulsion

abhorrent abominable, detestable, disgusting, distasteful, execrable, hated, hateful, heinous, horrible, horrid, loathsome, obnoxious, odious, offensive, repellent, repugnant, repulsive, revolting

abide 1. accept, bear, brook, endure, put up with, stand, stomach, submit to, suffer, tolerate 2. dwell, linger, live, lodge, reside, rest, sojourn, stay, stop, tarry, wait 3. continue, endure, last, persist, remain, survive

abide by 1. acknowledge, agree to, comply with, conform to, follow, obey, observe, submit to 2. adhere to, carry out, discharge, fulfil, hold to, keep to, persist in, stand by

abiding constant, continuing, durable, enduring, eternal, everlasting, fast, firm, immortal, immutable, indissoluble, lasting, permanent, persistent, persisting, steadfast, surviving, tenacious, unchanging, unending

ability adeptness, aptitude, capability, capacity, competence, competency, dexterity, endowment, energy, expertise, expertness, facility, faculty, flair, force, gift, knack, know-how (*Inf.*), potentiality, power, proficiency, qualification, skill, talent

abject 1. base, contemptible, cringing, debased, degraded, despicable, dishonourable, fawning, grovelling, humiliating, ignoble, ignominious, low, mean, servile, slavish, sordid, submissive, vile, worthless 2. deplorable, forlorn, hopeless, miserable, outcast, pitiable, wretched

abjectness 1. abjection, baseness, contemptibleness, debasement, degradation, dishonour, humbleness, humiliation, ignominy, lowness, meanness, servility, slavishness, sordidness, submissiveness, vileness, worthlessness 2. destitution, forlornness, hopelessness, misery, pitiableness, pitifulness, squalor, wretchedness

abjuration 1. denial, disavowal, disclaiming, disclamation, forswearing, recantation, renunciation, retraction 2. abnegation, abstention, eschewal, rejection, relinquishment, self-denial

abjure 1. deny, disavow, disclaim, forswear, recant, renege on, renounce, retract 2. abandon, abnegate, abstain from, eschew, forsake, give up, refrain from, reject, relinquish

ablaze 1. afire, aflame, alight, blazing, burning, fiery, flaming, ignited, lighted, on fire 2. aglow, brilliant, flashing, gleaming, glowing, illuminated, incandescent, luminous, radiant, sparkling 3. angry, aroused, enthusiastic, excited, fervent, frenzied, fuming, furious, impassioned, incensed, passionate, raging, stimulated

able accomplished, adept, adequate, adroit, capable, clever, competent, effective, efficient, experienced, expert, fit, fitted, gifted, highly endowed, masterful, masterly, powerful, practised, proficient, qualified, skilful, skilled, strong, talented

able-bodied firm, fit, hale, hardy, healthy, hearty, lusty, powerful, robust, sound, staunch, stout, strapping, strong, sturdy, vigorous

ablution bath, bathing, cleansing, lavation, purification, shower, wash, washing

abnegate abandon, abdicate, abjure, abstain from, concede, decline, deny, disallow, eschew, forbear, forgo, forsake, give up, refrain from, refuse, reject, relinquish, renounce, sacrifice, surrender, yield

abnegation abandonment, abjuration, abstinence, continence, disallowance, eschewal, forbearance, giving up, refusal, rejection, relinquishment, renunciation, sacrifice, self-denial, surrender, temperance

abnormal aberrant, anomalous, atypical, curious, deviant, eccentric, erratic, exceptional, extraordinary, irregular, monstrous, odd, peculiar, queer, singular, strange, uncommon, unexpected, unnatural, untypical, unusual, weird

abnormality aberration, anomaly, atypicalness, bizarreness, deformity, deviation, eccentricity, exception, extraordinariness, flaw, irregularity, monstrosity, oddity, peculiarity, queerness, singularity, strangeness, uncommonness, unexpectedness, unnaturalness, untypicalness, unusualness, weirdness

abode domicile, dwelling, dwelling-place, habitat, habitation, home, house, lodging, quarters, residence

abolish abrogate, annihilate, annul, blot out, cancel, destroy, do away with, eliminate, end, eradicate, expunge, exterminate, extinguish, extirpate, invalidate, nullify, obliterate, overthrow, overturn, put an end to, quash, repeal, repudiate, rescind, revoke, stamp out, subvert, suppress, terminate, vitiate, void, wipe out

abolition abrogation, annihilation, annulment, blotting out, cancellation, destruction, elimination, end, ending, eradication, expunction, extermination, extinction, extirpation, invalidation, nullification, obliteration, overthrow, overturning, quashing, repeal, repudiation, rescission, revocation, stamping out, subversion, suppression, termination, vitiation, voiding, wiping out, withdrawal

abominable abhorrent, accursed, atrocious, base, contemptible, despicable, detestable, disgusting, execrable, foul, hateful, heinous, hellish, horrible, horrid, loathsome, nauseous, obnoxious, odious, repellent, reprehensible, repugnant, repulsive, revolting, terrible, vile, villainous, wretched

abominate abhor, detest, execrate, hate, loathe, recoil from, regard with repugnance, shudder at

abomination 1. abhorrence, antipathy, aversion, detestation, disgust, distaste, execration, hate, hatred, horror, loathing, odium, repugnance, revulsion **2.** anathema, *bête noire*, bugbear, curse, disgrace, evil, horror, plague, shame, torment

aboriginal ancient, autochthonous, earliest, first, indigenous, native, original, primary, primeval, primitive, primordial, pristine

aborigine aboriginal, autochthon, indigene, native, original inhabitant

abort 1. miscarry, terminate (*a pregnancy*) **2.** arrest, call off, check, end, fail, halt, stop, terminate

abortion 1. aborticide, deliberate miscarriage, feticide, miscarriage, termination **2.** disappointment, failure, fiasco, misadventure, monstrosity, vain effort

abortive *adj.* **1.** bootless, failed, failing, fruitless, futile, idle, ineffectual, miscarried, unavailing, unsuccessful, useless, vain **2.** *Biol.* imperfectly developed, incomplete, rudimentary, stunted ~*n.* **3.** *Medical* abortifacient

abound be jammed with, be packed with, be plentiful, crowd, flourish, increase, infest, luxuriate, overflow, proliferate, superabound, swarm, swell, teem, thrive

abounding abundant, bountiful, copious, filled, flourishing, flowing, flush, full, lavish, luxuriant, overflowing, plenteous, plentiful, profuse, prolific, rank, replete, rich, superabundant, teeming

about *prep.* **1.** anent (*Scot.*), as regards, concerned with, concerning, connected with, dealing with, on, re, referring to, regarding, relating to, relative to, respecting, touching, with respect to **2.** adjacent, beside, circa (*used with dates*), close to, near, nearby **3.** around, encircling, on all sides, round, surrounding **4.** all over, over, through, throughout ~*adv.* **5.** almost, approaching, approximately, around, close to, more or less, nearing, nearly, roughly **6.** from place to place, here and there, hither and thither,

to and fro ~adj. **7.** active, around, astir, in motion, present, stirring
about to intending to, on the point of, on the verge or brink of, ready to
above prep. **1.** atop, beyond, exceeding, higher than, on top of, over, upon ~adv. **2.** atop, in heaven, on high, overhead ~adj. **3.** aforementioned, aforesaid, earlier, foregoing, preceding, previous, prior **4.** before, beyond, exceeding, prior to, superior to, surpassing
aboveboard 1. adv. candidly, forthrightly, frankly, honestly, honourably, openly, overtly, straightforwardly, truly, truthfully, uprightly, veraciously, without guile **2.** adj. candid, fair and square, forthright, frank, guileless, honest, honourable, legitimate, open, overt, square, straight, straightforward, true, trustworthy, truthful, upright, veracious
abracadabra 1. chant, charm, conjuration, hocus-pocus, incantation, invocation, magic, mumbo jumbo, sorcery, spell, voodoo, witchcraft **2.** babble, balderdash, blather, drivel, gibberish, gobbledegook, jabber, jargon, nonsense, twaddle
abrade erase, erode, file, grind, rub off, scour, scrape away, scrape out, wear away, wear down, wear off
abrasion 1. Medical chafe, graze, scrape, scratch, scuff, surface injury **2.** abrading, chafing, erosion, friction, grating, rubbing, scouring, scraping, scratching, scuffing, wearing away, wearing down
abrasive adj. **1.** chafing, erosive, frictional, grating, rough, scraping, scratching, scratchy, scuffing **2.** annoying, biting, caustic, cutting, galling, grating, hurtful, irritating, nasty, rough, sharp, unpleasant ~n. **3.** abradant, burnisher, grinder, scarifier, scourer
abreast 1. alongside, beside, level, shoulder to shoulder, side by side **2.** acquainted, au courant, au fait, conversant, familiar, informed, in touch, knowledgeable, up to date
abridge abbreviate, abstract, clip, compress, concentrate, condense, contract, curtail, cut, cut down, decrease, digest, diminish, epitomize, lessen, précis, reduce, shorten, summarize, synopsize (U.S.), trim
abridgment abbreviation, abstract, compendium, condensation, conspectus, contraction, curtailment, cutting, decrease, digest, diminishing, diminution, epitome, lessening, limitation, outline, précis, reduction, restraint, restriction, résumé, shortening, summary, synopsis
abroad 1. beyond the sea, in foreign lands, out of the country, overseas **2.** about, at large, away, circulating, current, elsewhere, extensively, far, far and wide, forth, in circulation, out, out-of-doors, outside, publicly, widely, without
abrogate abolish, annul, cancel, countermand, end, invalidate, nullify, override, quash, repeal, repudiate, rescind, retract, reverse, revoke, scrap (Inf.), set aside, void, withdraw
abrogation abolition, annulment, cancellation, countermanding, ending, invalidation, nullification, overriding, quashing, repeal, repudiation, rescission, retraction, reversal, revocation, scrapping (Inf.), setting aside, voiding, withdrawal
abrupt 1. blunt, brisk, brusque, curt, direct, discourteous, gruff, impolite, rough, rude, short, snappish, snappy, terse, unceremonious, uncivil, ungracious **2.** precipitous, sharp, sheer, steep, sudden **3.** hasty, headlong, hurried, precipitate, quick, sudden, surprising, swift, unanticipated, unexpected, unforeseen **4.** broken, disconnected, discontinuous, irregular, jerky, uneven
abscond bolt, clear out, decamp, disappear, do a bunk (Sl.), escape, flee, flit (Inf.), fly, make off, run off, slip away, sneak away, steal away
absence 1. absenteeism, nonappearance, nonattendance, truancy **2.** default, defect, deficiency, lack, need, nonexistence, omission, privation, unavailability, want **3.** absent-mindedness, abstraction, distraction, inattention, preoccupation, reverie
absent adj. **1.** away, elsewhere, gone, lacking, missing, nonattendant, nonexistent, not present, out, truant, unavailable, wanting **2.** absent-minded, absorbed, abstracted, bemused, blank, daydreaming, distracted, dreamy, empty, faraway, heedless, inattentive, musing, oblivious, preoccupied, unaware, unconscious, unheeding, unthinking, vacant, vague ~v. **3. absent oneself** abscond, depart, keep away, play truant, remove, stay away, truant, withdraw
absently absent-mindedly, abstractedly, bemusedly, blankly, distractedly,

dreamily, emptily, heedlessly, inattentively, obliviously, unconsciously, unheedingly, vacantly, vaguely

absent-minded absent, absorbed, abstracted, bemused, distracted, dreaming, dreamy, engrossed, faraway, forgetful, heedless, in a brown study, inattentive, musing, oblivious, preoccupied, unaware, unconscious, unheeding, unthinking

absolute 1. complete, consummate, downright, entire, out-and-out, outright, perfect, pure, sheer, thorough, total, unadulterated, unalloyed, unmitigated, unmixed, unqualified, utter **2.** actual, categorical, certain, conclusive, decided, decisive, definite, exact, genuine, infallible, positive, precise, sure, unambiguous, unequivocal, unquestionable **3.** absolutist, arbitrary, autarchical, autocratic, autonomous, despotic, dictatorial, full, peremptory, sovereign, supreme, tyrannical, unbounded, unconditional, unlimited, unqualified, unquestionable, unrestrained, unrestricted

absolutely 1. completely, consummately, entirely, fully, perfectly, purely, thoroughly, totally, unmitigatedly, utterly, wholly **2.** actually, categorically, certainly, conclusively, decidedly, decisively, definitely, exactly, genuinely, infallibly, positively, precisely, surely, truly, unambiguously, unequivocally, unquestionably **3.** arbitrarily, autocratically, autonomously, despotically, dictatorially, fully, peremptorily, sovereignly, supremely, tyrannically, unconditionally, unquestionably, unrestrainedly

absoluteness 1. consummateness, entirety, perfection, purity, thoroughness, totality, unmitigatedness, wholeness **2.** assuredness, certainty, certitude, conclusiveness, correctness, decidedness, decisiveness, definiteness, exactitude, genuineness, infallibility, positiveness, precision, sureness, surety, truth, unambiguousness, unequivocalness **3.** arbitrariness, autonomy, despotism, dictatorialness, fullness, peremptoriness, supremacy, tyranny, unboundedness, unquestionability, unrestrainedness, unrestrictedness

absolution acquittal, amnesty, deliverance, discharge, dispensation, exculpation, exemption, exoneration, forgiveness, freeing, indulgence, liberation, mercy, pardon, release, remission, setting free, shriving, vindication

absolutism absoluteness, arbitrariness, autarchy, authoritarianism, autocracy, despotism, dictatorship, totalitarianism, tyranny

absolutist arbiter, authoritarian, autocrat, despot, dictator, totalitarian, tyrant

absolve acquit, clear, deliver, discharge, exculpate, excuse, exempt, exonerate, forgive, free, let off, liberate, loose, pardon, release, remit, set free, shrive, vindicate

absorb 1. assimilate, consume, devour, digest, drink in, exhaust, imbibe, incorporate, ingest, osmose, receive, soak up, suck up, take in **2.** captivate, engage, engross, enwrap, fascinate, fill, fill up, fix, hold, immerse, monopolize, occupy, preoccupy, rivet

absorbed 1. captivated, concentrating, engaged, engrossed, fascinated, fixed, held, immersed, involved, lost, occupied, preoccupied, rapt, riveted, wrapped up **2.** assimilated, consumed, devoured, digested, exhausted, imbibed, incorporated, received

absorbent absorptive, assimilative, blotting, imbibing, penetrable, permeable, pervious, porous, receptive, spongy

absorbing arresting, captivating, engrossing, fascinating, gripping, interesting, intriguing, preoccupying, riveting, spellbinding

absorption 1. assimilation, consumption, digestion, exhaustion, incorporation, osmosis, soaking up, sucking up **2.** captivation, concentration, engagement, fascination, holding, immersion, intentness, involvement, occupation, preoccupation, raptness

abstain avoid, cease, decline, deny (oneself), desist, forbear, forgo, give up, keep from, refrain, refuse, renounce, shun, stop, withhold

abstemious abstinent, ascetic, austere, continent, frugal, moderate, self-denying, sober, sparing, temperate

abstention abstaining, abstinence, avoidance, desistance, eschewal, forbearance, nonindulgence, refraining, refusal, self-control, self-denial, self-restraint

abstinence abstemiousness, asceticism, avoidance, continence, forbearance, moderation, refraining, self-denial, self-restraint, soberness, sobriety, teetotalism, temperance

abstinent abstaining, abstemious, continent, forbearing, moderate, self-

controlled, self-denying, self-restraining, sober, temperate
abstract *adj.* **1.** abstruse, arcane, complex, conceptual, deep, general, generalized, hypothetical, indefinite, intellectual, nonconcrete, occult, philosophical, profound, recondite, separate, subtle, theoretic, theoretical, unpractical, unrealistic ~*n.* **2.** abridgment, compendium, condensation, digest, epitome, essence, outline, précis, recapitulation, résumé, summary, synopsis ~*v.* **3.** abbreviate, abridge, condense, digest, epitomize, outline, précis, shorten, summarize, synopsize (*U.S.*) **4.** detach, dissociate, extract, isolate, remove, separate, steal, take away, take out, withdraw
abstracted 1. absent, absent-minded, bemused, daydreaming, dreamy, faraway, inattentive, preoccupied, remote, withdrawn, woolgathering **2.** abbreviated, abridged, condensed, digested, epitomized, shortened, summarized, synopsized (*U.S.*)
abstraction 1. absence, absent-mindedness, bemusedness, dreaminess, inattention, pensiveness, preoccupation, remoteness, woolgathering **2.** concept, formula, generality, generalization, hypothesis, idea, notion, theorem, theory, thought
abstruse abstract, arcane, complex, dark, deep, enigmatic, esoteric, hidden, incomprehensible, mysterious, mystical, obscure, occult, perplexing, profound, puzzling, recondite, subtle, unfathomable, vague
abstruseness arcaneness, complexity, deepness, depth, esotericism, incomprehensibility, mysteriousness, obscurity, occultness, perplexity, profundity, reconditeness, subtlety, vagueness
absurd crazy (*Inf.*), daft (*Inf.*), farcical, foolish, idiotic, illogical, incongruous, irrational, laughable, ludicrous, meaningless, nonsensical, preposterous, ridiculous, senseless, silly, stupid, unreasonable
absurdity craziness (*Inf.*), daftness (*Inf.*), farce, farcicality, farcicalness, folly, foolishness, idiocy, illogicality, illogicalness, incongruity, irrationality, joke, ludicrousness, meaninglessness, nonsense, preposterousness, ridiculousness, senselessness, silliness, stupidity, unreasonableness
abundance 1. affluence, ampleness,

bounty, copiousness, exuberance, fullness, heap (*Inf.*), plenitude, plenteousness, plenty, profusion **2.** affluence, fortune, opulence, riches, wealth
abundant ample, bounteous, bountiful, copious, exuberant, filled, full, lavish, luxuriant, overflowing, plenteous, plentiful, profuse, rank, rich, teeming, well-provided, well-supplied
abuse *v.* **1.** damage, exploit, harm, hurt, ill-treat, impose upon, injure, maltreat, manhandle, mar, misapply, misuse, oppress, spoil, take advantage of, wrong **2.** calumniate, castigate, curse, defame, disparage, insult, inveigh against, libel, malign, revile, scold, slander, smear, swear at, traduce, upbraid, vilify, vituperate ~*n.* **3.** damage, exploitation, harm, hurt, ill-treatment, imposition, injury, maltreatment, manhandling, misapplication, misuse, oppression, spoiling, wrong **4.** blame, calumniation, castigation, censure, contumely, curses, cursing, defamation, derision, disparagement, insults, invective, libel, opprobrium, reproach, revilement, scolding, slander, swearing, tirade, traducement, upbraiding, vilification, vituperation **5.** corruption, crime, delinquency, fault, injustice, misconduct, misdeed, offence, sin, wrong, wrongdoing
abusive 1. calumniating, castigating, censorious, contumelious, defamatory, derisive, disparaging, insulting, invective, libellous, maligning, offensive, opprobrious, reproachful, reviling, rude, scathing, scolding, slanderous, traducing, upbraiding, vilifying, vituperative **2.** brutal, cruel, destructive, harmful, hurtful, injurious, rough
abut adjoin, border, impinge, join, meet, touch, verge
abutment brace, bulwark, buttress, pier, prop, strut, support
abutting adjacent, adjoining, bordering, contiguous, joining, meeting, next to, touching, verging
abysmal bottomless, boundless, complete, deep, endless, extreme, immeasurable, incalculable, infinite, profound, thorough, unending, unfathomable, vast
abyss abysm, bottomless depth, chasm, crevasse, fissure, gorge, gulf, pit, void
academic *adj.* **1.** bookish, campus, college, collegiate, erudite, highbrow, learned, lettered, literary, scholarly,

scholastic, school, studious, university 2. abstract, conjectural, hypothetical, impractical, notional, speculative, theoretical ~n. 3. academician, don, fellow, lecturer, master, professor, pupil, scholar, scholastic, schoolman, student, tutor
accede 1. accept, acquiesce, admit, agree, assent, comply, concede, concur, consent, endorse, grant, yield 2. assume, attain, come to, enter upon, inherit, succeed, succeed to (*as heir*)
accelerate advance, expedite, forward, further, hasten, hurry, pick up speed, precipitate, quicken, speed, speed up, spur, step up (*Inf.*), stimulate
acceleration expedition, hastening, hurrying, quickening, speeding up, spurring, stepping up (*Inf.*), stimulation
accent n. 1. beat, cadence, emphasis, force, pitch, rhythm, stress, timbre, tonality 2. articulation, enunciation, inflection, intonation, modulation, pronunciation, tone ~v. 3. accentuate, emphasize, stress, underline, underscore
accentuate accent, draw attention to, emphasize, highlight, stress, underline, underscore
accept 1. acquire, gain, get, have, obtain, receive, secure, take 2. accede, acknowledge, acquiesce, admit, adopt, affirm, agree to, approve, believe, concur with, consent to, cooperate with, recognize, swallow (*Inf.*) 3. bear, bow to, brook, defer to, put up with, stand, submit to, suffer, take, yield to 4. acknowledge, admit, assume, avow, bear, take on, undertake
acceptable 1. agreeable, delightful, grateful, gratifying, pleasant, pleasing, welcome 2. adequate, admissible, all right, fair, moderate, passable, satisfactory, so-so (*Inf.*), standard, tolerable
acceptance 1. accepting, acquiring, gaining, getting, having, obtaining, receipt, securing, taking 2. accedence, accession, acknowledgment, acquiescence, admission, adoption, affirmation, agreement, approbation, approval, assent, belief, compliance, concession, concurrence, consent, cooperation, credence, O.K. (*Inf.*), permission, recognition, stamp or seal of approval 3. deference, standing, submission, taking, yielding 4. acknowledgment, admission, assumption, avowal, taking on, undertaking
accepted acceptable, acknowledged, admitted, agreed, agreed upon, approved, authorized, common, confirmed, conventional, customary, established, normal, received, recognized, regular, sanctioned, standard, time-honoured, traditional, universal, usual
access 1. admission, admittance, approach, avenue, course, door, entering, entrance, entrée, entry, gateway, key, passage, passageway, path, road 2. *Medical* attack, fit, onset, outburst, paroxysm
accessibility 1. approachability, attainability, availability, handiness, nearness, obtainability, possibility, readiness 2. affability, approachability, conversableness, cordiality, friendliness, informality 3. exposedness, openness, susceptibility
accessible 1. achievable, at hand, attainable, available, get-at-able (*Inf.*), handy, near, nearby, obtainable, on hand, possible, reachable, ready 2. affable, approachable, available, conversable, cordial, friendly, informal 3. exposed, liable, open, subject, susceptible, vulnerable, wide-open
accession 1. addition, augmentation, enlargement, extension, increase 2. assumption, attaining to, attainment of, entering upon, succession (*to a throne, dignity, or office*), taking on, taking over 3. accedence, acceptance, acquiescence, agreement, concurrence, consent
accessory n. 1. abettor, accomplice, assistant, associate (*in crime*), colleague, confederate, helper, partner 2. accent, accompaniment, addition, adjunct, adornment, aid, appendage, attachment, component, convenience, decoration, extension, extra, frill, help, supplement, trim, trimming ~adj. 3. abetting, additional, aiding, ancillary, assisting in, auxiliary, contributory, extra, secondary, subordinate, supplemental, supplementary
accident 1. blow, calamity, casualty, chance, collision, crash, disaster, misadventure, mischance, misfortune, mishap, pile-up 2. chance, fate, fluke, fortuity, fortune, hazard, luck
accidental adventitious, casual, chance, contingent, fortuitous, haphazard, inadvertent, incidental, inessential, nonessential, random, uncalculated, uncertain, unessential, unexpected, unforeseen, unintended, unintentional,

unlooked-for, unplanned, unpremeditated, unwitting

accidentally adventitiously, by accident, by chance, by mistake, casually, fortuitously, haphazardly, inadvertently, incidentally, randomly, unconsciously, undesignedly, unexpectedly, unintentionally, unwittingly

acclaim 1. *v.* applaud, approve, celebrate, cheer, clap, commend, eulogize, exalt, extol, hail, honour, laud, praise, salute, welcome **2.** *n.* acclamation, applause, approbation, approval, celebration, cheering, clapping, commendation, eulogizing, exaltation, honour, laudation, plaudits, praise, welcome

acclamation acclaim, adulation, approbation, cheer, cheering, cheers, enthusiasm, laudation, loud homage, ovation, plaudit, praise, salutation, shouting, tribute

acclimatization acclimation, accommodation, acculturation, adaptation, adjustment, habituation, inurement, naturalization

acclimatize accommodate, acculture, accustom, adapt, adjust, become seasoned to, get used to, habituate, inure, naturalize

acclivity ascent, hill, rise, rising ground, steep upward slope

accommodate 1. billet, board, cater for, entertain, harbour, house, lodge, put up, quarter, shelter **2.** afford, aid, assist, furnish, help, oblige, provide, serve, supply **3.** accustom, adapt, adjust, comply, compose, conform, fit, harmonize, modify, reconcile, settle

accommodating complaisant, considerate, cooperative, friendly, helpful, hospitable, kind, obliging, polite, unselfish, willing

accommodation 1. adaptation, adjustment, compliance, composition, compromise, conformity, fitting, harmony, modification, reconciliation, settlement **2.** board, digs (*Inf.*), harbouring, house, housing, lodging(s), quartering, quarters, shelter, sheltering **3.** aid, assistance, help, provision, service, supply

accompany 1. attend, chaperon, conduct, convoy, escort, go with, squire, usher **2.** belong to, coexist with, coincide with, come with, follow, go together with, join with, occur with, supplement

accompanying accessory, added, additional, appended, associate, associated,

attached, attendant, complementary, concomitant, concurrent, connected, fellow, joint, related, supplemental, supplementary

accomplice abettor, accessory, ally, assistant, associate, coadjutor, collaborator, colleague, confederate, helper, henchman, partner

accomplish achieve, attain, bring about, bring off (*Inf.*), carry out, complete, conclude, consummate, do, effect, effectuate, execute, finish, fulfil, manage, perform, produce, realize

accomplished 1. achieved, attained, brought about, carried out, completed, concluded, consummated, done, effected, executed, finished, fulfilled, managed, performed, produced, realized **2.** adept, consummate, cultivated, expert, gifted, masterly, polished, practised, proficient, skilful, skilled, talented

accomplishment 1. achievement, attainment, bringing about, carrying out, completion, conclusion, consummation, doing, effecting, execution, finishing, fulfilment, management, performance, production, realization **2.** achievement, act, attainment, coup, deed, exploit, feat, stroke, triumph **3.** ability, achievement, art, attainment, capability, gift, proficiency, skill, talent

accord *v.* **1.** agree, assent, be in tune (*Inf.*), concur, conform, correspond, fit, harmonize, match, suit, tally **2.** allow, bestow, concede, confer, endow, give, grant, present, render, tender, vouchsafe ~*n.* **3.** accordance, agreement, concert, concurrence, conformity, congruence, correspondence, harmony, rapport, sympathy, unanimity

accordance 1. accord, agreement, assent, concert, concurrence, conformity, congruence, correspondence, harmony, rapport, sympathy, unanimity **2.** according, allowance, bestowal, concession, conferment, conferral, endowment, gift, giving, granting, presentation, rendering, tendering

accordingly 1. appropriately, correspondingly, fitly, properly, suitably **2.** as a result, consequently, ergo, hence, in consequence, so, therefore, thus

according to 1. commensurate with, in proportion, in relation **2.** as believed by, as maintained by, as stated by, in the light of, on the authority of, on the report of **3.** after, after the manner of, consistent with, in accordance with, in compliance with, in conformity with, in harmony with, in keeping with, in line with, in obedience to, in step with, in the manner of, obedient to

accost address, approach, buttonhole, confront, greet, hail, halt, salute, solicit (*as a prostitute*), stop

account *n.* **1.** chronicle, description, detail, explanation, history, narration, narrative, recital, record, relation, report, statement, story, tale, version **2.** *Commerce* balance, bill, book, books, charge, computation, inventory, invoice, ledger, reckoning, register, score, statement, tally **3.** advantage, benefit, consequence, distinction, esteem, honour, import, importance, merit, note, profit, rank, repute, significance, standing, use, value, worth **4.** basis, cause, consideration, ground, grounds, interest, motive, reason, regard, sake, score (*Inf.*) ~*v.* **5.** appraise, assess, believe, calculate, compute, consider, count, deem, esteem, estimate, explain, gauge, hold, judge, rate, reckon, regard, think, value, weigh

accountability 1. answerability, chargeability, culpability, liability, responsibility **2.** comprehensibility, explainability, explicability, intelligibility, understandability

accountable 1. amenable, answerable, charged with, liable, obligated, obliged, responsible **2.** comprehensible, explainable, explicable, intelligible, understandable

account for 1. answer for, clarify, clear up, elucidate, explain, illuminate, justify, rationalize **2.** destroy, incapacitate, kill, put out of action

accoutre adorn, appoint, array, bedeck, deck, decorate, equip, fit out, furnish, kit out, outfit, provide, supply

accoutrements adornments, appurtenances, array, clothing, decorations, dress, equipage, equipment, fittings, fixtures, furnishings, garb, gear, kit, ornamentation, outfit, paraphernalia, tackle, trappings, trimmings

accredit 1. appoint, authorize, certify, commission, depute, empower, endorse, entrust, guarantee, license, recognize, sanction, vouch for **2.** ascribe, assign, attribute, credit

accredited appointed, authorized, certified, commissioned, deputed, deputized, empowered, endorsed, guaranteed,

licensed, official, recognized, sanctioned, vouched for

accretion accumulation, addition, augmentation, enlargement, growth, increase, increment, supplement

accrue accumulate, amass, arise, be added, build up, collect, enlarge, ensue, flow, follow, grow, increase, issue, spring up

accumulate accrue, amass, build up, collect, cumulate, gather, grow, hoard, increase, pile up, stockpile, store

accumulation aggregation, augmentation, build-up, collection, conglomeration, gathering, growth, heap, hoard, increase, mass, pile, stack, stock, stockpile, store

accuracy accurateness, authenticity, carefulness, closeness, correctness, exactitude, exactness, faithfulness, faultlessness, fidelity, meticulousness, niceness, nicety, precision, strictness, truth, truthfulness, veracity, verity

accurate authentic, careful, close, correct, exact, faithful, faultless, just, meticulous, nice, precise, proper, regular, right, scrupulous, spot-on (*Inf.*), strict, true, truthful, unerring, veracious

accurately authentically, carefully, closely, correctly, exactly, faithfully, faultlessly, justly, meticulously, nicely, precisely, properly, regularly, rightly, scrupulously, strictly, truly, truthfully, unerringly, veraciously

accursed 1. bedevilled, bewitched, condemned, cursed, damned, doomed, hopeless, ill-fated, ill-omened, jinxed, luckless, ruined, undone, unfortunate, unlucky, wretched **2.** abominable, despicable, detestable, execrable, hateful, hellish, horrible

accusation allegation, arraignment, attribution, charge, citation, complaint, denunciation, impeachment, imputation, incrimination, indictment, recrimination

accuse allege, arraign, attribute, blame, censure, charge, cite, denounce, impeach, impute, incriminate, indict, recriminate, tax

accustom acclimatize, acquaint, adapt, discipline, exercise, familiarize, habituate, inure, season, train

accustomed 1. acclimatized, acquainted, adapted, disciplined, exercised, familiar, familiarized, given to, habituated, in the habit of, inured, seasoned, trained, used **2.** common, conventional, customary, established, everyday, expected, fixed, general, habitual, normal, ordinary, regular, routine, set, traditional, usual, wonted

ace *n*. **1**. *Cards, dice, etc.* one, single point **2**. *Inf.* adept, champion, dab hand (*Inf.*), expert, genius, master, star, virtuoso, winner, wizard (*Inf.*) ~*adj*. **3**. *Inf.* brilliant, champion, excellent, expert, fine, great, masterly, outstanding, superb, virtuoso

acerbic 1. acid, acrid, acrimonious, bitter, brusque, churlish, harsh, nasty, rancorous, rude, severe, sharp, stern, unfriendly, unkind **2**. acid, acidulous, acrid, astringent, bitter, harsh, sharp, sour, tart

acerbity 1. acrimony, asperity, bitterness, brusqueness, churlishness, harshness, nastiness, rancour, rudeness, severity, sharpness, sternness, unfriendliness, unkindness **2**. acidity, acidulousness, acridity, acridness, astringency, bitterness, sourness, tartness

ache *v*. **1**. hurt, pain, pound, smart, suffer, throb, twinge **2**. agonize, grieve, mourn, sorrow, suffer **3**. covet, crave, desire, hanker, hunger, long, need, pine, yearn ~*n*. **4**. hurt, pain, pang, pounding, smart, smarting, soreness, suffering, throb, throbbing **5**. anguish, grief, mourning, sorrow, suffering **6**. craving, desire, hankering, hunger, longing, need, pining, yearning

achievable accessible, accomplishable, acquirable, attainable, feasible, obtainable, possible, practicable, reachable, realizable, winnable, within one's grasp

achieve accomplish, acquire, attain, bring about, carry out, complete, consummate, do, earn, effect, execute, finish, fulfil, gain, get, obtain, perform, procure, reach, realize, win

achievement 1. accomplishment, acquirement, attainment, completion, execution, fulfilment, performance, production, realization **2**. accomplishment, act, deed, effort, exploit, feat, stroke

acid 1. acerbic, acidulous, acrid, biting, pungent, sharp, sour, tart, vinegarish, vinegary **2**. acerbic, acid, biting, bitter, caustic, cutting, harsh, hurtful, mordant, pungent, sharp, stinging, trenchant, vitriolic

acidity 1. acerbity, acidulousness, acridity, acridness, bitterness, pungency, sharpness, sourness, tartness, vinegari-

ness, vinegarishness **2**. acerbity, acridity, acridness, bitterness, causticity, causticness, harshness, hurtfulness, mordancy, pungency, sharpness, trenchancy

acidulous 1. acerbic, acid, bitter, harsh, sharp, sour, tart, vinegarish, vinegary **2**. acid, biting, bitter, caustic, cutting, harsh, pungent, sharp, sour

acknowledge 1. accede, accept, acquiesce, admit, allow, concede, confess, declare, grant, own, profess, recognize, yield **2**. address, greet, hail, notice, recognize, salute **3**. answer, notice, react to, recognize, reply to, respond to, return

acknowledged accepted, accredited, admitted, answered, approved, conceded, confessed, declared, professed, recognized, returned

acknowledgment 1. acceptance, accession, acquiescence, admission, allowing, confession, declaration, profession, realization, yielding **2**. addressing, greeting, hail, hailing, notice, recognition, salutation, salute **3**. answer, appreciation, credit, gratitude, reaction, recognition, reply, response, return, thanks

acme apex, climax, crown, culmination, height, high point, optimum, peak, pinnacle, summit, top, vertex, zenith

acolyte adherent, admirer, altar boy, assistant, attendant, follower, helper

acquaint advise, announce, apprise, disclose, divulge, enlighten, familiarize, inform, let (someone) know, notify, reveal, tell

acquaintance 1. associate, colleague, contact **2**. association, awareness, cognizance, companionship, conversance, conversancy, experience, familiarity, fellowship, intimacy, knowledge, relationship, social contact, understanding

acquainted alive to, apprised of, *au fait*, aware of, cognizant of, conscious of, conversant with, experienced in, familiar with, informed of, in on, knowledgeable about, privy to, versed in

acquiesce accede, accept, agree, allow, approve, assent, bow to, comply, concur, conform, consent, give in, go along with, submit, yield

acquiescence acceptance, accession, agreement, approval, assent, compliance, concurrence, conformity, consent, giving in, obedience, submission, yielding

acquiescent acceding, accepting, agreeable, agreeing, approving, assenting, compliant, concurrent, conforming, consenting, obedient, submissive, yielding

acquire achieve, amass, attain, buy, collect, earn, gain, gather, get, obtain, pick up, procure, realize, receive, secure, win

acquirement accomplishment, achievement, acquisition, attainment, gathering, knowledge, learning, mastery, mental gains, qualification, skill

acquisition 1. buy, gain, possession, prize, property, purchase 2. achievement, acquirement, attainment, gaining, learning, obtainment, procurement, pursuit

acquisitive avaricious, avid, covetous, grabbing, grasping, greedy, predatory, rapacious

acquisitiveness avarice, avidity, avidness, covetousness, graspingness, greed, predatoriness, rapaciousness, rapacity

acquit 1. absolve, clear, deliver, discharge, exculpate, exonerate, free, fulfil, liberate, release, relieve, vindicate 2. discharge, pay, pay off, repay, satisfy, settle 3. bear, behave, comport, conduct, perform

acquittal absolution, clearance, deliverance, discharge, exculpation, exoneration, freeing, liberation, release, relief, vindication

acquittance acknowledgment, discharge, payment, receipt, release, settlement, settling

acrid 1. acid, astringent, biting, bitter, burning, caustic, harsh, irritating, pungent, sharp, stinging 2. acrimonious, biting, bitter, caustic, cutting, harsh, mordant, nasty, sarcastic, sharp, trenchant, vitriolic

acrimonious acerbic, astringent, biting, bitter, caustic, censorious, churlish, crabbed, cutting, irascible, mordant, peevish, petulant, pungent, rancorous, sarcastic, severe, sharp, spiteful, splenetic, tart, testy, trenchant

acrimony acerbity, asperity, astringency, bitterness, churlishness, harshness, ill will, irascibility, mordancy, peevishness, rancour, sarcasm, spleen, tartness, trenchancy, virulence

act *n.* 1. accomplishment, achievement, action, blow, deed, doing, execution, exertion, exploit, feat, move, operation, performance, step, stroke, undertaking 2. bill, decree, edict, enactment, law, measure, ordinance, resolution, stat-

ute 3. affectation, attitude, counterfeit, dissimulation, fake, feigning, front, performance, pose, posture, pretence, sham, show, stance 4. performance, routine, show, sketch, turn ~*v.* 5. acquit, bear, behave, carry, carry out, comport, conduct, do, enact, execute, exert, function, go about, make, move, operate, perform, react, serve, strike, take effect, undertake, work 6. affect, assume, counterfeit, dissimulate, feign, imitate, perform, pose, posture, pretend, put on, seem, sham 7. act out, characterize, enact, impersonate, mime, mimic, perform, personate, personify, play, play *or* take the part of, portray, represent

act for cover for, deputize for, fill in for, function in place of, replace, represent, serve, stand in for, substitute for, take the place of

acting *adj.* 1. interim, *pro tem*, provisional, substitute, surrogate, temporary ~*n.* 2. characterization, dramatics, enacting, impersonation, performance, performing, playing, portrayal, portraying, stagecraft, theatre 3. assuming, counterfeiting, dissimulation, feigning, imitating, imitation, imposture, play-acting, posing, posturing, pretence, pretending, putting on, seeming, shamming

action 1. accomplishment, achievement, act, blow, deed, exercise, exertion, exploit, feat, move, operation, performance, stop, stroke, undertaking 2. activity, energy, force, liveliness, spirit, vigour, vim, vitality 3. activity, effect, effort, exertion, force, functioning, influence, motion, movement, operation, power, process, work, working 4. battle, combat, conflict, fighting, warfare 5. affray, battle, clash, combat, contest, encounter, engagement, fight, fray, skirmish, sortie 6. case, cause, lawsuit, litigation, proceeding, prosecution, suit

actions bearing, behaviour, comportment, conduct, demeanour, deportment, manners, ways

activate actuate, animate, arouse, energize, galvanize, impel, initiate, mobilize, motivate, move, prompt, propel, rouse, set going, set in motion, set off, start, stimulate, stir, switch on, trigger (off), turn on

active 1. acting, astir, at work, doing, effectual, functioning, in action, in force, in operation, live, moving, operative, running, stirring, working 2. bustling, busy, engaged, full, hard-working, involved, occupied, on the go (*Inf.*), on the move, strenuous **3**. alert, animated, diligent, energetic, industrious, lively, nimble, on the go (*Inf.*), quick, spirited, sprightly, spry, vibrant, vigorous, vital, vivacious **4**. activist, aggressive, ambitious, assertive, committed, devoted, energetic, engaged, enterprising, enthusiastic, forceful, forward, hard-working, industrious, militant, zealous

activity 1. action, activeness, animation, bustle, enterprise, exercise, exertion, hurly-burly, hustle, labour, life, liveliness, motion, movement, stir, work **2**. act, avocation, deed, endeavour, enterprise, hobby, interest, job, labour, occupation, pastime, project, pursuit, scheme, task, undertaking, venture, work

act on, act upon 1. act in accordance with, carry out, comply with, conform to, follow, heed, obey, yield to **2**. affect, alter, change, influence, modify, sway, transform

actor 1. actress, dramatic artist, leading man, performer, play-actor, player, Thespian, tragedian, trouper **2**. agent, doer, executor, factor, functionary, operative, operator, participant, participator, performer, perpetrator, practitioner, worker

actress actor, dramatic artist, leading lady, performer, play-actor, player, starlet, Thespian, tragedienne, trouper

actual 1. absolute, categorical, certain, concrete, corporeal, definite, factual, indisputable, indubitable, physical, positive, real, substantial, tangible, undeniable, unquestionable **2**. authentic, confirmed, genuine, real, realistic, true, truthful, verified **3**. current, existent, extant, live, living, present, present-day, prevailing

actuality 1. corporeality, factuality, materiality, reality, realness, substance, substantiality, truth, verity **2**. fact, reality, truth, verity

actually absolutely, as a matter of fact, de facto, essentially, indeed, in fact, in point of fact, in reality, in truth, literally, really, truly, veritably

actuate animate, arouse, cause, dispose, drive, excite, impel, incite, induce, influence, inspire, instigate, motivate, move, prompt, quicken, rouse, spur, stimulate, stir, urge

act up be naughty, carry on, cause trouble, give bother, give trouble, horse around (*Inf.*), malfunction, mess about, misbehave, play up (*Brit. inf.*)

act upon *see* ACT ON

acumen acuteness, astuteness, cleverness, discernment, ingenuity, insight, intelligence, judgment, keenness, penetration, perception, perspicacity, perspicuity, sagacity, sharpness, shrewdness, smartness, wisdom, wit

acute 1. astute, canny, clever, discerning, discriminating, incisive, ingenious, insightful, intuitive, keen, observant, penetrating, perceptive, perspicacious, piercing, sensitive, sharp, smart, subtle **2**. critical, crucial, dangerous, decisive, essential, grave, important, serious, severe, sudden, urgent, vital **3**. cutting, distressing, excruciating, exquisite, fierce, intense, overpowering, overwhelming, piercing, poignant, powerful, racking, severe, sharp, shooting, shrill, stabbing, sudden, violent **4**. cuspate, needle-shaped, peaked, pointed, sharp, sharpened

acuteness 1. acuity, astuteness, canniness, cleverness, discernment, discrimination, ingenuity, insight, intuition, intuitiveness, keenness, perception, perceptiveness, perspicacity, sensitivity, sharpness, smartness, subtleness, subtlety, wit **2**. criticality, criticalness, cruciality, danger, dangerousness, decisiveness, essentiality, gravity, importance, seriousness, severity, suddenness, urgency, vitalness **3**. distressingness, exquisiteness, fierceness, intenseness, intensity, poignancy, powerfulness, severity, sharpness, shrillness, suddenness, violence **4**. pointedness, sharpness

adage aphorism, apophthegm, axiom, by-word, dictum, maxim, motto, precept, proverb, saw, saying

adamant 1. determined, firm, fixed, immovable, inexorable, inflexible, insistent, intransigent, obdurate, resolute, rigid, set, stiff, stubborn, unbending, uncompromising, unrelenting, unshakable, unyielding **2**. adamantine, flinty, hard, impenetrable, indestructible, rock-hard, rocky, steely, stony, tough, unbreakable

adapt acclimatize, accommodate, adjust, alter, apply, change, comply, conform, familiarize, fashion, fit, habituate, harmonize, make, match, modify, prepare, qualify, remodel, shape, suit, tailor

adaptability adaptableness, adjustability, alterability, changeability, compliancy, convertibility, flexibility, malleability, modifiability, plasticity, pliability, pliancy, resilience, variability, versatility

adaptable adjustable, alterable, changeable, compliant, conformable, convertible, easy-going, flexible, malleable, modifiable, plastic, pliant, resilient, variable, versatile

adaptation 1. adjustment, alteration, change, conversion, modification, refitting, remodelling, reworking, shift, transformation, variation, version **2.** acclimatization, accustomedness, familiarization, habituation, naturalization

add 1. adjoin, affix, amplify, annex, append, attach, augment, enlarge by, include, increase by, supplement **2.** add up, compute, count up, reckon, sum up, total, tot up

addendum addition, adjunct, affix, appendage, appendix, attachment, augmentation, codicil, extension, extra, postscript, supplement

addict 1. dope-fiend (*Sl.*), fiend (*Inf.*), freak (*Sl.*), head (*Sl.*), junkie (*Sl.*), user (*Inf.*) **2.** adherent, buff (*Sl.*), devotee, enthusiast, fan, follower, freak (*Sl.*), nut (*Sl.*)

addicted absorbed, accustomed, dedicated, dependent, devoted, disposed, fond, habituated, hooked (*Sl.*), inclined, obsessed, prone

addiction craving, dependence, enslavement, habit, obsession

addition 1. accession, adding, adjoining, affixing, amplification, annexation, attachment, augmentation, enlargement, extension, inclusion, increasing **2.** addendum, additive, adjunct, affix, appendage, appendix, extension, extra, gain, increase, increment, supplement **3.** adding up, computation, counting up, reckoning, summation, summing up, totalling, totting up **4. in addition (to)** additionally, also, as well (as), besides, into the bargain, moreover, over and above, to boot, too, withal

additional added, affixed, appended, extra, fresh, further, increased, more, new, other, over-and-above, spare, supplementary

addle-brained *or* **addle-pated** befuddled, bewildered, confused, daft, dim-witted, dopey (*Sl.*), dozy (*Inf.*), flustered, foolish, halfwitted, mixed-up, muddled, muddleheaded, nonsensical, perplexed, silly, simple, simple-minded, stupid, thick, thickheaded, witless, woolly-minded

addled 1. befuddled, bewildered, confused, flustered, foolish, mixed-up, muddled, perplexed, silly **2.** bad, gone bad, off, rancid, rotten, turned

address *n.* **1.** abode, domicile, dwelling, home, house, location, lodging, place, residence, situation, whereabouts **2.** direction, inscription, superscription **3.** discourse, disquisition, dissertation, harangue, lecture, oration, sermon, speech, talk **4.** adroitness, art, dexterity, discretion, expertness, ingenuity, skilfulness, skill, tact ~*v.* **5.** accost, apostrophize, approach, greet, hail, invoke, salute, speak to, talk to **6.** discourse, give a speech, give a talk, harangue, lecture, orate, sermonize, speak, talk **7. address (oneself) to** apply (oneself) to, attend to, concentrate on, devote (oneself) to, engage in, focus on, knuckle down to, look to, take care of, take up, turn to, undertake

adduce advance, allege, cite, designate, mention, name, offer, present, quote

add up 1. add, compute, count, count up, reckon, sum up, total, tot up **2.** amount, come to, imply, indicate, mean, reveal, signify **3.** be plausible, be reasonable, hold water, make sense, ring true, stand to reason

adept 1. *adj.* able, accomplished, adroit, dexterous, expert, masterful, masterly, practised, proficient, skilful, skilled, versed **2.** *n.* dab hand (*Inf.*), expert, genius, master

adequacy capability, commensurateness, competence, fairness, requisiteness, satisfactoriness, sufficiency, suitability, tolerability

adequate capable, commensurate, competent, enough, fair, passable, requisite, satisfactory, sufficient, suitable, tolerable

adhere 1. attach, cement, cleave, cling, cohere, fasten, fix, glue, glue on, hold fast, paste, stick, stick fast, unite **2.** abide by, be attached, be constant, be devoted, be faithful, be loyal, be true, cleave to, cling, follow, fulfil, heed, keep, keep to, maintain, mind, obey, observe, respect, stand by, support

adherent 1. *n.* admirer, advocate, devotee, disciple, fan, follower, hanger-on, partisan, sectary, supporter, upholder, votary **2.** *adj.* adhering, adhesive, clinging, gluey, glutinous, gummy, holding, mucilaginous, sticking, sticky, tacky, tenacious
adhesion 1. adherence, adhesiveness, attachment, coherence, cohesion, grip, holding fast, sticking, union **2.** allegiance, attachment, constancy, devotion, faithfulness, fidelity, fulfilment, heed, loyalty, obedience, observation, respect, support
adhesive 1. *adj.* adhering, attaching, clinging, cohesive, gluey, glutinous, gummy, holding, mucilaginous, sticking, sticky, tacky, tenacious **2.** *n.* cement, glue, gum, mucilage, paste
adieu congé, farewell, goodbye, leave-taking, parting, valediction
adipose fat, fatty, greasy, obese, oily, oleaginous, sebaceous
adjacent abutting, adjoining, alongside, beside, bordering, close, contiguous, near, neighbouring, next door, touching
adjoin abut, add, affix, annex, append, approximate, attach, border, combine, communicate with, connect, couple, impinge, interconnect, join, link, neighbour, touch, unite, verge
adjoining abutting, adjacent, bordering, connecting, contiguous, impinging, interconnecting, joined, joining, near, neighbouring, next door, touching, verging
adjourn defer, delay, discontinue, interrupt, postpone, prorogue, put off, recess, stay, suspend
adjournment deferment, deferral, delay, discontinuation, interruption, postponement, prorogation, putting off, recess, stay, suspension
adjudge adjudicate, allot, apportion, assign, award, decide, declare, decree, determine, distribute, judge, order, pronounce
adjudicate adjudge, arbitrate, decide, determine, judge, referee, settle, umpire
adjudication adjudgment, arbitration, conclusion, decision, determination, finding, judgment, pronouncement, ruling, settlement, verdict
adjunct accessory, addendum, addition, appendage, appurtenance, auxiliary, complement, supplement

adjure 1. appeal to, beg, beseech, entreat, implore, invoke, pray, supplicate **2.** charge, command, direct, enjoin, order
adjust acclimatize, accommodate, accustom, adapt, alter, arrange, compose, dispose, fit, fix, harmonize, make conform, measure, modify, order, reconcile, rectify, redress, regulate, remodel, set, settle, suit, tune (up)
adjustable adaptable, alterable, flexible, malleable, modifiable, mouldable, movable, tractable
adjustment 1. adaptation, alteration, arrangement, arranging, fitting, fixing, modification, ordering, rectification, redress, regulation, remodelling, setting, tuning **2.** acclimatization, harmonization, orientation, reconciliation, settlement, settling in
ad-lib 1. *v.* extemporize, improvise, make up, speak extemporaneously, speak impromptu, speak off the cuff **2.** *adj.* extemporaneous, extempore, extemporized, impromptu, improvised, made up, off-the-cuff (*Inf.*), unprepared, unrehearsed **3.** *adv.* extemporaneously, extempore, impromptu, off the cuff, off the top of one's head (*Inf.*), without preparation, without rehearsal
administer 1. conduct, control, direct, govern, manage, oversee, run, superintend, supervise **2.** apply, contribute, dispense, distribute, execute, give, impose, mete out, perform, provide
administration 1. administering, application, conduct, control, direction, dispensation, distribution, execution, governing, government, management, overseeing, performance, provision, running, superintendence, supervision **2.** executive, governing body, government, management, ministry, term of office
administrative directorial, executive, governmental, gubernatorial (*Chiefly U.S.*), management, managerial, organizational, regulatory, supervisory
admirable choice, commendable, estimable, excellent, exquisite, fine, laudable, meritorious, praiseworthy, rare, superior, valuable, wonderful, worthy
admiration adoration, affection, amazement, appreciation, approbation, approval, astonishment, delight, esteem, pleasure, praise, regard, respect, surprise, veneration, wonder, wonderment
admire 1. adore, appreciate, approve, esteem, idolize, look up to, praise, prize,

respect, think highly of, value, venerate, worship **2.** appreciate, delight in, marvel at, take pleasure in, wonder at

admirer 1. beau, boyfriend, lover, suitor, sweetheart, wooer **2.** adherent, devotee, disciple, enthusiast, fan, follower, partisan, supporter, votary, worshipper

admissible acceptable, allowable, allowed, passable, permissible, permitted, tolerable, tolerated

admission 1. acceptance, access, admittance, entrance, entrée, entry, ingress, initiation, introduction **2.** acknowledgment, admitting, affirmation, allowance, avowal, concession, confession, declaration, disclosure, divulgence, profession, revelation

admit 1. accept, allow, allow to enter, give access, initiate, introduce, let in, receive, take in **2.** acknowledge, affirm, avow, concede, confess, declare, disclose, divulge, profess, reveal **3.** agree, allow, grant, let, permit, recognize

admittance acceptance, access, admitting, allowing, entrance, entry, letting in, passage, reception

admix add, alloy, amalgamate, blend, combine, commingle, commix, include, incorporate, intermingle, merge, mingle, mix, put in

admixture 1. alloy, amalgamation, blend, combination, compound, fusion, intermixture, medley **2.** component, constituent, element, ingredient

admonish advise, berate, caution, censure, check, chide, counsel, enjoin, exhort, forewarn, rebuke, reprimand, reprove, scold, tell off (*Inf.*), upbraid, warn

admonition advice, berating, caution, chiding, counsel, rebuke, remonstrance, reprimand, reproach, reproof, scolding, telling off (*Inf.*), upbraiding, warning

admonitory admonishing, advisory, cautionary, rebuking, reprimanding, reproachful, reproving, scolding, warning

ado agitation, bother, bustle, commotion, confusion, delay, disturbance, excitement, flurry, fuss, pother, stir, to-do, trouble

adolescence 1. boyhood, girlhood, juvenescence, minority, teens, youth **2.** boyishness, childishness, girlishness, immaturity, juvenility, puerility, youthfulness

adolescent 1. *adj.* boyish, girlish, growing, immature, juvenile, puerile,

teenage, young, youthful **2.** *n.* juvenile, minor, teenager, youngster, youth

adopt 1. accept, appropriate, approve, assume, choose, embrace, endorse, espouse, follow, maintain, ratify, select, support, take on, take over, take up **2.** foster, take in

adoption 1. acceptance, approbation, appropriation, approval, assumption, choice, embracing, endorsement, espousal, following, maintenance, ratification, selection, support, taking on, taking over, taking up **2.** adopting, fosterage, fostering, taking in

adorable appealing, attractive, captivating, charming, darling, dear, delightful, fetching, lovable, pleasing, precious

adoration admiration, esteem, estimation, exaltation, glorification, honour, idolatry, idolization, love, reverence, veneration, worship, worshipping

adore admire, bow to, cherish, dote on, esteem, exalt, glorify, honour, idolize, love, revere, reverence, venerate, worship

adorn array, beautify, bedeck, deck, decorate, embellish, emblazon, enhance, enrich, garnish, grace, ornament, trim

adornment 1. accessory, decoration, embellishment, frill, frippery, ornament, trimming **2.** beautification, decorating, decoration, embellishment, ornamentation, trimming

adrift 1. afloat, drifting, unanchored, unmoored **2.** aimless, directionless, goalless, purposeless **3.** amiss, astray, off course, wrong

adroit able, adept, apt, artful, clever, cunning, deft, dexterous, expert, ingenious, masterful, neat, nimble, proficient, quick-witted, skilful, skilled

adroitness ability, ableness, address, adeptness, aptness, artfulness, cleverness, cunning, deftness, dexterity, expertise, ingeniousness, ingenuity, masterfulness, mastery, nimbleness, proficiency, quick-wittedness, skilfulness, skill

adulation blandishment, bootlicking (*Inf.*), extravagant flattery, fawning, fulsome praise, servile flattery, sycophancy, worship

adulatory blandishing, bootlicking (*Inf.*), fawning, flattering, obsequious, praising, servile, slavish, sycophantic, worshipping

adult 1. *adj.* full grown, fully developed, fully grown, grown-up, mature, of age, ripe **2.** *n.* grown *or* grown-up person (man *or* woman), grown-up, person of mature age

adulterate 1. *v.* attenuate, bastardize, contaminate, corrupt, debase, depreciate, deteriorate, devalue, make impure, mix with, thin, vitiate, water down, weaken **2.** *adj.* adulterated, attenuated, bastardized, contaminated, corrupt, debased, depreciated, deteriorated, devalued, mixed, thinned, vitiated, watered down, weakened

adumbrate 1. delineate, indicate, outline, silhouette, sketch, suggest **2.** augur, forecast, foreshadow, foretell, portend, predict, prefigure, presage, prognosticate, prophesy **3.** bedim, darken, eclipse, obfuscate, obscure, overshadow

adumbration 1. delineation, draft, indication, outline, rough, silhouette, sketch, suggestion **2.** augury, forecast, foreshadowing, foretelling, omen, portent, prediction, prefiguration, prefigurement, presage, prognostication, prophecy, sign **3.** bedimming, cloud, darkening, darkness, eclipse, eclipsing, obfuscation, obscuring, overshadowing, shadow

advance *v.* **1.** accelerate, bring forward, bring up, come forward, elevate, go ahead, go forward, go on, hasten, move onward, move up, press on, proceed, progress, promote, send forward, send up, speed, upgrade **2.** benefit, further, grow, improve, multiply, prosper, thrive **3.** adduce, allege, cite, offer, present, proffer, put forward, submit, suggest **4.** increase (*price*), lend, pay beforehand, raise (*price*), supply on credit ~*n.* **5.** advancement, development, forward movement, headway, onward movement, progress **6.** advancement, amelioration, betterment, breakthrough, furtherance, gain, growth, improvement, progress, promotion, step **7.** appreciation, credit, deposit, down payment, increase (*in price*), loan, prepayment, retainer, rise (*in price*) **8.** advances approach, approaches, moves, overtures, proposals, proposition ~*adj.* **9.** beforehand, early, foremost, forward, in front, leading, prior **10. in advance** ahead, beforehand, earlier, in the forefront, in the lead, in the van, previously

advanced ahead, avant-garde, extreme, foremost, forward, higher, late, leading, precocious, progressive

advancement 1. advance, forward movement, headway, onward movement,

progress **2.** advance, amelioration, betterment, gain, growth, improvement, preferment, progress, promotion, rise

advantage aid, ascendancy, asset, assistance, avail, benefit, blessing, boon, convenience, dominance, edge, gain, good, help, interest, lead, precedence, pre-eminence, profit, service, start, superiority, sway, upper hand, use, utility, welfare

advantageous 1. dominant, dominating, favourable, superior **2.** beneficial, convenient, helpful, of service, profitable, useful, valuable, worthwhile

advent appearance, approach, arrival, coming, entrance, occurrence, onset, visitation

adventitious accidental, casual, chance, extraneous, foreign, fortuitous, incidental, nonessential, unexpected

adventure 1. *n.* chance, contingency, enterprise, experience, exploit, hazard, incident, occurrence, risk, speculation, undertaking, venture **2.** *v.* dare, endanger, hazard, imperil, jeopardize, risk, venture

adventurer 1. daredevil, hero, heroine, knight-errant, soldier of fortune, swashbuckler, traveller, venturer, voyager, wanderer **2.** charlatan, fortune-hunter, gambler, mercenary, opportunist, rogue, speculator

adventurous adventuresome, audacious, bold, dangerous, daredevil, daring, enterprising, foolhardy, hazardous, headstrong, intrepid, rash, reckless, risky, temerarious (*Rare*), venturesome

adversary antagonist, competitor, contestant, enemy, foe, opponent, opposer, rival

adverse antagonistic, conflicting, contrary, detrimental, disadvantageous, hostile, inexpedient, inimical, injurious, inopportune, negative, opposing, opposite, reluctant, repugnant, unfavourable, unfortunate, unfriendly, unlucky, unpropitious, unwilling

adversity affliction, bad luck, calamity, catastrophe, disaster, distress, hardship, hard times, ill-fortune, ill-luck, misery, misfortune, mishap, reverse, sorrow, suffering, trial, trouble, woe, wretchedness

advert *v.* allude, draw attention (to), mention, notice, observe, refer, regard, remark

advertise advise, announce, apprise,

blazon, declare, display, flaunt, inform, make known, notify, plug (*Inf.*), praise, proclaim, promote, promulgate, publicize, publish, puff, push (*Inf.*), tout **advertisement** ad (*Inf.*), advert (*Inf.*), announcement, bill, blurb, circular, commercial, display, notice, placard, plug (*Inf.*), poster, promotion, publicity, puff
advice 1. admonition, caution, counsel, guidance, help, injunction, opinion, recommendation, suggestion, view **2.** information, instruction, intelligence, notice, notification, warning, word
advisability appropriateness, aptness, desirability, expediency, fitness, judiciousness, profitability, propriety, prudence, seemliness, soundness, suitability, wisdom
advisable appropriate, apt, desirable, expedient, fit, fitting, judicious, politic, profitable, proper, prudent, recommended, seemly, sensible, sound, suggested, suitable, wise
advise 1. admonish, caution, commend, counsel, enjoin, recommend, suggest, urge **2.** acquaint, apprise, inform, make known, notify, report, tell, warn
adviser aide, authority, coach, confidant, consultant, counsel, counsellor, guide, helper, lawyer, mentor, right-hand man, solicitor, teacher, tutor
advisory advising, consultative, counselling, helping, recommending
advocacy advancement, argument for, backing, campaigning for, championing, defence, encouragement, justification, pleading for, promotion, promulgation, propagation, proposal, recommendation, spokesmanship, support, upholding, urging
advocate v. **1.** advise, argue for, campaign for, champion, countenance, defend, encourage, favour, hold a brief for (*Inf.*), justify, plead for, press for, promote, propose, recommend, speak for, support, uphold, urge ~n. **2.** apologist, apostle, backer, campaigner, champion, counsellor, defender, pleader, promoter, proponent, proposer, speaker, spokesman, supporter, upholder **3.** *Law.* attorney, barrister, counsel, lawyer, solicitor
aegis advocacy, auspices, backing, favour, guardianship, patronage, protection, shelter, sponsorship, support, wing
affability amiability, amicability, approachability, benevolence, benignity,

civility, congeniality, cordiality, courtesy, friendliness, geniality, good humour, good nature, graciousness, kindliness, mildness, obligingness, pleasantness, sociability, urbanity, warmth
affable amiable, amicable, approachable, benevolent, benign, civil, congenial, cordial, courteous, friendly, genial, good-humoured, good-natured, gracious, kindly, mild, obliging, pleasant, sociable, urbane, warm
affair 1. activity, business, circumstance, concern, episode, event, happening, incident, interest, matter, occurrence, proceeding, project, question, subject, transaction, undertaking **2.** amour, intrigue, liaison, relationship, romance
affect 1. act on, alter, bear upon, change, concern, impinge upon, influence, interest, involve, modify, prevail over, regard, relate to, sway, transform **2.** disturb, impress, move, overcome, perturb, stir, touch, upset **3.** adopt, aspire to, assume, contrive, counterfeit, feign, imitate, pretend, put on, sham, simulate
affectation act, affectedness, appearance, artificiality, assumed manners, façade, fakery, false display, insincerity, mannerism, pose, pretence, pretension, pretentiousness, sham, show, simulation, unnatural imitation
affected 1. afflicted, altered, changed, concerned, damaged, deeply moved, distressed, hurt, impaired, impressed, influenced, injured, melted, stimulated, stirred, touched, troubled, upset **2.** artificial, assumed, conceited, contrived, counterfeit, feigned, insincere, la-di-da (*Inf.*), mannered, mincing, phoney (*Inf.*), pompous, precious, pretended, pretentious, put-on, sham, simulated, spurious, stiff, studied, unnatural
affecting moving, pathetic, piteous, pitiable, pitiful, poignant, sad, saddening, touching
affection amity, attachment, care, desire, feeling, fondness, friendliness, good will, inclination, kindness, liking, love, passion, propensity, tenderness, warmth
affectionate attached, caring, devoted, doting, fond, friendly, kind, loving, tender, warm, warm-hearted
affiance betroth, bind, engage, pledge, promise
affiliate ally, amalgamate, annex, associate, band together, combine, confeder-

ate, connect, incorporate, join, unite

affiliation alliance, amalgamation, association, banding together, coalition, combination, confederation, connection, incorporation, joining, league, merging, relationship, union

affinity 1. alliance, analogy, closeness, compatibility, connection, correspondence, kinship, likeness, relation, relationship, resemblance, similarity **2.** attraction, fondness, inclination, leaning, liking, partiality, rapport, sympathy

affirm assert, asseverate, attest, aver, avouch, avow, certify, confirm, declare, maintain, pronounce, ratify, state, swear, testify

affirmation assertion, asseveration, attestation, averment, avouchment, avowal, certification, confirmation, declaration, oath, pronouncement, ratification, statement, testimony

affirmative agreeing, approving, assenting, concurring, confirming, consenting, corroborative, favourable, positive

affix add, annex, append, attach, bind, fasten, glue, join, paste, put on, stick, subjoin, tack, tag

afflict beset, burden, distress, grieve, harass, hurt, oppress, pain, plague, rack, smite, torment, trouble, try, wound

affliction adversity, calamity, cross, curse, depression, disease, distress, grief, hardship, misery, misfortune, ordeal, pain, plague, scourge, sickness, sorrow, suffering, torment, trial, tribulation, trouble, woe, wretchedness

affluence abundance, exuberance, fortune, opulence, plenty, profusion, prosperity, riches, wealth

affluent 1. loaded (*Sl.*), moneyed, opulent, prosperous, rich, wealthy, well-heeled (*Inf.*), well-off, well-to-do **2.** abundant, copious, exuberant, plenteous, plentiful

afford 1. bear, spare, stand, sustain **2.** bestow, furnish, give, grant, impart, offer, produce, provide, render, supply, yield

affray brawl, contest, disturbance, dogfight, encounter, feud, fight, fracas, free-for-all (*Inf.*), mêlée, outbreak, quarrel, scrap, scuffle, set-to (*Inf.*), tumult

affront 1. *v.* abuse, anger, annoy, displease, insult, offend, outrage, pique, provoke, slight, vex **2.** *n.* abuse, indignity, injury, insult, offence, outrage, provocation, slap in the face (*Inf.*),

slight, slur, vexation, wrong

afire 1. ablaze, aflame, alight, blazing, burning, fiery, flaming, ignited, lighted, lit, on fire **2.** aglow, aroused, excited, fervent, impassioned, passionate, stimulated

aflame 1. ablaze, afire, alight, blazing, burning, fiery, flaming, ignited, lighted, lit, on fire **2.** afire, aroused, excited, fervent, impassioned, passionate, stimulated **3.** aglow, flushed, inflamed, red, ruddy

afoot about, abroad, afloat, astir, brewing, circulating, current, going on, hatching, in preparation, in progress, in the wind, on the go (*Inf.*), operating, up (*Inf.*)

afraid 1. alarmed, anxious, apprehensive, cowardly, faint-hearted, fearful, frightened, intimidated, nervous, reluctant, scared, suspicious, timid, timorous **2.** regretful, sorry, unhappy

afresh again, anew, newly, once again, once more, over again

after afterwards, behind, below, following, later, subsequently, succeeding, thereafter

aftermath after-effects, consequences, effects, end, outcome, results, upshot

again 1. afresh, anew, another time, once more **2.** also, besides, furthermore, in addition, moreover, on the contrary, on the other hand

against 1. counter, hostile to, in contrast to, in defiance of, in opposition to, in the face of, opposed to, opposing, resisting, versus **2.** abutting, close up to, facing, fronting, in contact with, on, opposite to, touching, upon **3.** in anticipation of, in expectation of, in preparation for, in provision for

agape 1. gaping, wide, wide open, yawning **2.** agog, amazed, astonished, astounded, awestricken, dumbfounded, eager, expectant, flabbergasted, spellbound, surprised, thunderstruck

age *n.* **1.** date, day(s), duration, epoch, era, generation, lifetime, period, span, time **2.** advancing years, decline (*of life*), majority, maturity, old age, senescence, senility, seniority ~*v.* **3.** decline, deteriorate, grow old, mature, mellow, ripen

aged age-old, ancient, antiquated, antique, elderly, getting on, grey, hoary, old, senescent, superannuated

agency 1. action, activity, auspices,

efficiency, force, influence, instrumentality, intercession, intervention, means, mechanism, mediation, medium, operation, power, work **2**. bureau, business, department, office, organization

agenda calendar, diary, list, plan, programme, schedule, timetable

agent 1. advocate, deputy, emissary, envoy, factor, go-between, negotiator, rep (*Inf.*), representative, substitute, surrogate **2**. actor, author, doer, executor, mover, officer, operative, operator, performer, worker **3**. agency, cause, force, instrument, means, power, vehicle

agglomeration accumulation, clump, cluster, collection, heap, lump, mass, pile, stack

agglutinate adhere, attach, bond, cement, fasten, glue, gum, join, solder, stick, unite

aggrandize advance, amplify, augment, dignify, elevate, enlarge, ennoble, enrich, exaggerate, exalt, inflate, intensify, magnify, promote, widen

aggravate 1. exacerbate, exaggerate, heighten, increase, inflame, intensify, magnify, make worse, worsen **2**. *Inf.* annoy, exasperate, get on one's nerves (*Inf.*), irk, irritate, needle (*Inf.*), nettle, pester, provoke, tease, vex

aggravation 1. exacerbation, exaggeration, heightening, increase, inflaming, intensification, magnification, worsening **2**. *Inf.* annoyance, exasperation, irksomeness, irritation, provocation, teasing, vexation

aggregate 1. *v.* accumulate, amass, assemble, collect, combine, heap, mix, pile **2**. *n.* accumulation, agglomeration, amount, assemblage, body, bulk, collection, combination, heap, lump, mass, mixture, pile, sum, total, whole **3**. *adj.* accumulated, added, assembled, collected, collective, combined, composite, corporate, cumulative, mixed, total

aggression 1. assault, attack, encroachment, injury, invasion, offence, offensive, onslaught, raid **2**. aggressiveness, antagonism, belligerence, destructiveness, hostility, pugnacity

aggressive 1. belligerent, destructive, hostile, offensive, pugnacious, quarrelsome **2**. assertive, bold, dynamic, energetic, enterprising, forceful, militant, pushing, pushy (*Inf.*), vigorous, zealous

aggressor assailant, assaulter, attacker, invader

aggrieved afflicted, distressed, disturbed, harmed, hurt, ill-used, injured, peeved (*Inf.*), saddened, unhappy, woeful, wronged

aghast afraid, amazed, appalled, astonished, astounded, awestruck, confounded, frightened, horrified, horror-struck, shocked, startled, stunned, thunder-struck

agile active, acute, alert, brisk, clever, limber, lithe, lively, nimble, prompt, quick, quick-witted, sharp, sprightly, spry, supple, swift

agility activity, acuteness, alertness, briskness, cleverness, litheness, liveliness, nimbleness, promptitude, promptness, quickness, quick-wittedness, sharpness, sprightliness, spryness, suppleness, swiftness

agitate 1. beat, churn, convulse, disturb, rock, rouse, shake, stir, toss **2**. alarm, arouse, confuse, disconcert, disquiet, distract, disturb, excite, ferment, fluster, incite, inflame, perturb, rouse, ruffle, stimulate, trouble, upset, work up, worry **3**. argue, debate, discuss, dispute, examine, ventilate

agitation 1. churning, convulsion, disturbance, rocking, shake, shaking, stir, stirring, tossing, turbulence **2**. alarm, arousal, clamour, commotion, confusion, discomposure, disquiet, distraction, disturbance, excitement, ferment, flurry, fluster, incitement, lather (*Inf.*), outcry, stimulation, trouble, tumult, turmoil, upset, worry **3**. argument, controversy, debate, discussion, disputation, dispute, ventilation

agitator agent provocateur, demagogue, firebrand, inciter, instigator, rabble-rouser, revolutionary, troublemaker

agog avid, curious, eager, enthralled, enthusiastic, excited, expectant, impatient, in suspense, keen

agonize afflict, be in agony, be in anguish, distress, harrow, labour, pain, rack, strain, strive, struggle, suffer, torment, torture, worry, writhe

agony affliction, anguish, distress, misery, pain, pangs, suffering, throes, torment, torture, woe

agree 1. accede, acquiesce, admit, allow, assent, be of the same mind, comply, concede, concur, consent, engage, grant, permit, see eye to eye, settle **2**. accord, answer, chime, coincide, conform,

correspond, fit, get on (together), harmonize, match, square, suit, tally

agreeable 1. acceptable, delightful,
enjoyable, gratifying, pleasant, pleasing,
pleasurable, satisfying, to one's liking, to
one's taste **2**. appropriate, befitting,
compatible, consistent, fitting, in keeping, proper, suitable **3**. acquiescent, amenable, approving, complying, concurring,
consenting, in accord, responsive, sympathetic, well-disposed, willing

agreement 1. accord, accordance,
affinity, analogy, compatibility, compliance, concert, concord, concurrence, conformity, congruity, consistency, correspondence, harmony, similarity, suitableness, union **2**. arrangement, bargain,
compact, contract, covenant, deal (*Inf.*),
pact, settlement, treaty, understanding

agriculture agronomics, agronomy,
cultivation, culture, farming, husbandry,
tillage

aground ashore, beached, foundered,
grounded, high and dry, on the rocks,
stranded, stuck

ahead along, at an advantage, at the
head, before, forwards, in advance, in
front, in the foreground, in the lead, in
the vanguard, leading, on, onwards, to
the fore, winning

aid *v.* **1**. abet, assist, befriend, encourage, favour, help, promote, relieve, second, serve, subsidize, succour, support,
sustain ∼*n.* **2**. assistance, benefit, encouragement, favour, help, relief, service,
succour, support **3**. abettor, adjutant,
aide, aide-de-camp, assistant, helper,
second, supporter

ail 1. afflict, annoy, be the matter with,
bother, distress, irritate, pain, sicken,
trouble, upset, worry **2**. be ill, be indisposed, be *or* feel off colour, be sick, be
unwell, feel unwell

ailing debilitated, diseased, feeble, ill,
indisposed, infirm, invalid, off colour,
poorly, sick, sickly, suffering, under the
weather (*Inf.*), unsound, unwell, weak

ailment affliction, complaint, disease,
disorder, illness, infirmity, malady, sickness

aim 1. *v.* aspire, attempt, design, direct, draw a bead (on), endeavour, intend, level, mean, plan, point, propose,
purpose, resolve, seek, set one's sights
on, sight, strive, take aim (at), train, try,
want, wish **2**. *n.* ambition, aspiration,
course, design, desire, direction, end,
goal, intent, intention, mark, object, objective, plan, purpose, scheme, target,
wish

aimless chance, directionless, erratic,
frivolous, goalless, haphazard, pointless,
purposeless, random, stray, undirected,
unguided, unpredictable, vagrant, wayward

air *n.* **1**. atmosphere, heavens, sky **2**.
blast, breath, breeze, draught, puff, waft,
whiff, wind, zephyr **3**. ambience, appearance, atmosphere, aura, bearing, character, demeanour, effect, feeling, flavour,
impression, look, manner, mood, quality,
style, tone **4**. circulation, display, dissemination, exposure, expression, publicity, utterance, vent, ventilation **5**. aria,
lay, melody, song, tune ∼*v.* **6**. aerate, expose, freshen, ventilate **7**. circulate, communicate, declare, disclose, display, disseminate, divulge, exhibit, expose, express, give vent to, make known, make
public, proclaim, publicize, reveal, tell,
utter, ventilate, voice

airily 1. animatedly, blithely, breezily,
buoyantly, gaily, happily, high-
spiritedly, jauntily, light-heartedly **2**.
daintily, delicately, ethereally, gracefully, lightly

airiness 1. breeziness, draughtiness,
freshness, gustiness, lightness, openness,
windiness **2**. ethereality, immateriality,
incorporeality, insubstantiality, lightness, weightlessness **3**. animation,
blitheness, breeziness, buoyancy, gaiety,
happiness, high spirits, jauntiness, light-
heartedness, lightness of heart

airing 1. aeration, drying, freshening,
ventilation **2**. excursion, jaunt, outing,
promenade, stroll, walk **3**. circulation,
display, dissemination, exposure, expression, publicity, utterance, vent, ventilation

airless breathless, close, heavy, muggy,
oppressive, stale, stifling, stuffy, suffocating, sultry, unventilated

airs affectation, affectedness, arrogance, haughtiness, hauteur, pomposity,
pretensions, superciliousness, swank
(*Inf.*)

airy 1. blowy, breezy, draughty, fresh,
gusty, light, lofty, open, spacious, uncluttered, well-ventilated, windy **2**. aerial, delicate, ethereal, fanciful, flimsy, illusory, imaginary, immaterial, incorporeal, insubstantial, light, vaporous, visionary, weightless, wispy **3**. animated,

blithe, buoyant, cheerful, cheery, debonair, frolicsome, gay, graceful, happy, high-spirited, jaunty, light, light-hearted, lively, merry, nonchalant, sprightly

aisle corridor, gangway, lane, passage, passageway, path

ajar agape, gaping, open, partly open, unclosed

akin affiliated, alike, allied, analogous, cognate, comparable, congenial, connected, consanguineous, corresponding, kin, kindred, like, parallel, related, similar

alacrity alertness, avidity, briskness, cheerfulness, dispatch, eagerness, enthusiasm, gaiety, hilarity, joyousness, liveliness, promptness, quickness, readiness, speed, sprightliness, willingness, zeal

à la mode all the go (*Inf.*), all the rage (*Inf.*), chic, fashionable, in (*Inf.*), in fashion, in vogue, latest, modish, popular, stylish, the latest rage (*Inf.*), with it (*Inf.*)

alarm *v.* **1.** daunt, dismay, distress, frighten, give (someone) a turn (*Inf.*), panic, put the wind up (someone) (*Inf.*), scare, startle, terrify, unnerve **2.** alert, arouse, signal, warn ~*n.* **3.** anxiety, apprehension, consternation, dismay, distress, fear, fright, nervousness, panic, scare, terror, trepidation, unease, uneasiness **4.** alarm-bell, alert, bell, danger signal, distress signal, siren, tocsin, warning **5.** *Archaic* call to arms

alarming daunting, dismaying, distressing, disturbing, dreadful, frightening, scaring, shocking, startling, terrifying, unnerving

albeit although, even if, even though, notwithstanding that, though

alcoholic **1.** *adj.* brewed, distilled, fermented, hard, inebriant, inebriating, intoxicating, spirituous, strong, vinous **2.** *n.* bibber, boozer (*Inf.*), dipsomaniac, drunk, drunkard, hard drinker, inebriate, soak (*Inf.*), sot, sponge (*Inf.*), tippler, toper, tosspot (*Inf.*), wino (*Inf.*)

alcove bay, bower, compartment, corner, cubbyhole, cubicle, niche, nook, recess

alert **1.** *adj.* active, agile, attentive, brisk, careful, circumspect, heedful, lively, nimble, observant, on guard, on one's toes, on the ball (*Inf.*), on the lookout, on the watch, perceptive, quick, ready, spirited, sprightly, vigilant, wary, watchful, wide-awake **2.** *n.* alarm, signal, siren,

warning **3.** *v.* alarm, forewarn, inform, notify, signal, warn

alertness activeness, agility, attentiveness, briskness, carefulness, circumspection, heedfulness, liveliness, nimbleness, perceptiveness, promptitude, quickness, readiness, spiritedness, sprightliness, vigilance, wariness, watchfulness

alias **1.** *adv.* also called, also known as, otherwise, otherwise known as **2.** *n.* assumed name, *nom de guerre,* nom de plume, pen name, pseudonym, stage name

alibi defence, excuse, explanation, justification, plea, pretext, reason

alien **1.** *adj.* adverse, conflicting, contrary, estranged, exotic, foreign, inappropriate, incompatible, incongruous, not native, not naturalized, opposed, outlandish, remote, repugnant, separated, strange, unfamiliar **2.** *n.* foreigner, newcomer, outsider, stranger

alienate **1.** break off, disaffect, divert, divorce, estrange, make unfriendly, separate, set against, turn away, withdraw **2.** *Law* abalienate, convey, transfer

alienation **1.** breaking off, disaffection, diversion, divorce, estrangement, indifference, remoteness, rupture, separation, setting against, turning away, withdrawal **2.** *Law* abalienation, conveyance, transfer

alight[1] *v.* come down, come to rest, descend, disembark, dismount, get down, get off, land, light, perch, settle, touch down

alight[2] *adj.* **1.** ablaze, aflame, blazing, burning, fiery, flaming, flaring, ignited, lighted, lit, on fire **2.** bright, brilliant, illuminated, lit up, shining

align **1.** arrange in line, coordinate, even, even up, line up, make parallel, order, range, regulate, straighten **2.** affiliate, agree, ally, associate, cooperate, join, side, sympathize

alignment **1.** adjustment, arrangement, coordination, evening, evening up, line, lining up, order, ranging, regulating, sequence, straightening up **2.** affiliation, agreement, alliance, association, cooperation, sympathy, union

alike **1.** *adj.* akin, analogous, corresponding, duplicate, equal, equivalent, even, identical, parallel, resembling, similar, the same, uniform **2.** *adv.* analogously, correspondingly, equally, evenly, identically, similarly, uniformly

aliment fare, fodder, food, meat, nourishment, nutriment, nutrition, provender, sustenance

alimentary beneficial, nourishing, nutritional, nutritious, nutritive, sustaining, wholesome

alive 1. animate, breathing, having life, in the land of the living (*Inf.*), living, subsisting **2.** active, existent, existing, extant, functioning, in existence, in force, operative, unquenched **3.** active, alert, animated, awake, brisk, cheerful, eager, energetic, full of life, lively, quick, spirited, sprightly, spry, vigorous, vital, vivacious, zestful

alive to alert to, awake to, aware of, cognizant of, eager for, sensible of, sensitive to, susceptible to

alive with abounding in, bristling with, bustling with, buzzing with, crawling with, hopping with, infested with, jumping with, lousy with (*Sl.*), overrun by, packed with, swarming with, teeming with, thronged with

all *adj.* **1.** every bit of, the complete, the entire, the sum of, the totality of, the total of, the whole of **2.** each, each and every, every, every one of, every single **3.** complete, entire, full, greatest, perfect, total, utter ~*n.* **4.** aggregate, entirety, everything, sum, sum total, total, total amount, totality, utmost, whole, whole amount ~*adv.* **5.** altogether, completely, entirely, fully, totally, utterly, wholly

allay alleviate, appease, assuage, blunt, calm, check, compose, diminish, dull, ease, lessen, mitigate, moderate, mollify, pacify, quell, quiet, reduce, relieve, smooth, soften, soothe, subdue

allegation accusation, affirmation, assertion, asseveration, averment, avowal, charge, claim, declaration, deposition, plea, profession, statement

allege advance, affirm, assert, asseverate, aver, avow, charge, claim, declare, depose, maintain, plead, profess, put forward, state

alleged 1. affirmed, asserted, averred, declared, described, designated, stated **2.** doubtful, dubious, ostensible, professed, purported, so-called, supposed, suspect, suspicious

allegiance adherence, constancy, devotion, duty, faithfulness, fealty, fidelity, homage, loyalty, obedience, obligation

allegorical emblematic, figurative, parabolic, symbolic, symbolizing

allegory apologue, emblem, fable, myth, parable, story, symbol, symbolism, tale

allergic 1. affected by, hypersensitive, sensitive, sensitized, susceptible **2.** *Inf.* antipathetic, averse, disinclined, hostile, loath, opposed

allergy 1. antipathy, hypersensitivity, sensitivity, susceptibility **2.** *Inf.* antipathy, aversion, disinclination, dislike, hostility, loathing, opposition

alleviate abate, allay, assuage, blunt, check, diminish, dull, ease, lessen, lighten, mitigate, moderate, mollify, palliate, quell, quench, quiet, reduce, relieve, slacken, slake, smooth, soften, soothe, subdue

alleviation diminution, dulling, easing, lessening, lightening, mitigation, moderation, palliation, quelling, quenching, reduction, relief, slackening, slaking

alley alleyway, backstreet, lane, passage, passageway, pathway, walk

alliance affiliation, affinity, agreement, association, coalition, combination, compact, concordat, confederacy, confederation, connection, federation, league, marriage, pact, partnership, treaty, union

allied affiliated, amalgamated, associated, bound, combined, confederate, connected, hand in glove (*Inf.*), in cahoots (*U.S. inf.*), in league, joined, joint, kindred, leagued, linked, married, related, unified, united, wed

allocate allot, apportion, appropriate, assign, budget, designate, earmark, mete, set aside, share out

allocation allotment, allowance, apportionment, appropriation, grant, lot, measure, portion, quota, ration, share, stint

allot allocate, apportion, appropriate, assign, budget, designate, earmark, mete, set aside, share out

allotment 1. allocation, allowance, apportionment, appropriation, grant, lot, measure, portion, quota, ration, share, stint **2.** kitchen garden, patch, plot, tract

all-out complete, determined, exhaustive, full, full-scale, maximum, optimum, resolute, supreme, thorough, thoroughgoing, total, undivided, unlimited, unremitting, unrestrained, unstinted, utmost

allow 1. acknowledge, acquiesce, admit, concede, confess, grant, own **2.** approve, authorize, bear, brook, endure, give leave, let, permit, put up with (*Inf.*), sanction, stand, suffer, tolerate **3.** allocate, allot, assign, deduct, give, grant, provide, remit, spare

allowable acceptable, admissible, all right, appropriate, approved, permissible, sanctionable, sufferable, suitable, tolerable

allowance 1. allocation, allotment, amount, annuity, apportionment, grant, lot, measure, pension, portion, quota, ration, remittance, share, stint, stipend, subsidy **2.** admission, concession, sanction, sufferance, toleration **3.** concession, deduction, discount, rebate, reduction

allow for arrange for, consider, foresee, keep in mind, make allowances for, make concessions for, make provision for, plan for, provide for, set (something) aside for, take into account, take into consideration

alloy n. **1.** admixture, amalgam, blend, combination, composite, compound, hybrid, mixture ~v. **2.** admix, amalgamate, blend, combine, compound, fuse, mix **3.** adulterate, debase, devalue, diminish, impair

all right adj. **1.** acceptable, adequate, average, fair, O.K. (*Inf.*), passable, satisfactory, standard, unobjectionable **2.** hale, healthy, safe, sound, unharmed, unimpaired, uninjured, well, whole ~adv. **3.** acceptably, adequately, O.K. (*Inf.*), passably, satisfactorily, unobjectionably, well enough

allude advert, glance, hint, imply, insinuate, intimate, mention, refer, remark, speak of, suggest, touch upon

allure 1. v. attract, beguile, cajole, captivate, charm, coax, decoy, enchant, entice, inveigle, lead on, lure, persuade, seduce, tempt, win over **2.** n. appeal, attraction, charm, enchantment, enticement, glamour, lure, persuasion, seductiveness, temptation

alluring attractive, beguiling, bewitching, captivating, come-hither, enchanting, fascinating, fetching, intriguing, seductive, sexy, tempting

allusion casual remark, glance, hint, implication, indirect reference, innuendo, insinuation, intimation, mention, suggestion

ally 1. n. abettor, accessory, accomplice, associate, coadjutor, collaborator, colleague, confederate, co-worker, friend, helper, partner **2.** v. affiliate, associate, band together, collaborate, combine, confederate, connect, join, join forces, league, marry, unify, unite

almighty 1. absolute, all-powerful, invincible, omnipotent, supreme, unlimited **2.** *Inf.* awful, desperate, enormous, excessive, great, intense, loud, severe, terrible

almost about, all but, approximately, as good as, close to, just about, nearly, not far from, not quite, on the brink of, practically, virtually, well-nigh

alms benefaction, bounty, charity, donation, gift, relief

aloft above, heavenward, higher, high up, in the air, in the sky, on high, overhead, skyward, up, up above, upward

alone 1. abandoned, apart, by itself, by oneself, deserted, desolate, detached, forlorn, forsaken, isolated, lonely, lonesome, only, separate, single, single-handed, sole, solitary, unaccompanied, unaided, unassisted, unattended, uncombined, unconnected, unescorted **2.** incomparable, matchless, peerless, singular, unequalled, unique, unparalleled, unsurpassed

aloof 1. chilly, cold, cool, detached, distant, forbidding, formal, haughty, indifferent, remote, reserved, standoffish, supercilious, unapproachable, unfriendly, uninterested, unresponsive, unsociable, unsympathetic **2.** above, apart, at a distance, away, distanced, distant

aloud 1. audibly, clearly, distinctly, intelligibly, out loud, plainly **2.** clamorously, loudly, noisily, vociferously

already as of now, at present, before now, by now, by that time, by then, by this time, even now, heretofore, just now, previously

also additionally, along with, and, as well, as well as, besides, further, furthermore, in addition, including, into the bargain, moreover, on top of that, plus, to boot, too

alter adapt, adjust, amend, change, convert, diversify, metamorphose, modify, recast, reform, remodel, reshape, revise, shift, transform, transmute, turn, vary

alteration adaptation, adjustment, amendment, change, conversion, difference, diversification, metamorphosis, modification, reformation, remodelling, reshaping, revision, shift, transformation, transmutation, variance, variation

altercate argue, bicker, clash, contend, controvert, disagree, dispute, dissent, fall out (*Inf.*), quarrel, row, squabble, wrangle

altercation argument, bickering, clash, contention, controversy, disagreement, discord, dispute, dissension, quarrel, row, squabble, wrangle

alternate *v.* **1.** act reciprocally, alter, change, follow in turn, follow one another, interchange, intersperse, oscillate, rotate, substitute, take turns, vary ~*adj.* **2.** alternating, every other, every second, interchanging, rotating **3.** alternative, another, different, second, substitute

alternative **1.** *n.* choice, option, other (*of two*), preference, recourse, selection, substitute **2.** *adj.* alternate, another, different, other, second, substitute

alternatively as an alternative, by way of alternative, if not, instead, on the other hand, or, otherwise

although albeit, despite the fact that, even if, even supposing, even though, notwithstanding, though, while

altitude elevation, height, loftiness, peak, summit

altogether **1.** absolutely, completely, fully, perfectly, quite, thoroughly, totally, utterly, wholly **2.** all in all, all things considered, as a whole, collectively, generally, in general, *in toto*, on the whole **3.** all told, everything included, in all, in sum, *in toto*, taken together

altruistic benevolent, charitable, considerate, generous, humanitarian, philanthropic, public-spirited, self-sacrificing, unselfish

always consistently, constantly, continually, eternally, ever, everlastingly, evermore, every time, forever, *in perpetuum*, invariably, perpetually, repeatedly, unceasingly, without exception

amalgam admixture, alloy, amalgamation, blend, combination, composite, compound, fusion, mixture, union

amalgamate alloy, ally, blend, coalesce, combine, commingle, compound, fuse, incorporate, integrate, intermix, merge, mingle, unite

amalgamation admixture, alliance, alloy, amalgam, amalgamating, blend, coalition, combination, commingling, composite, compound, fusion, incorporation, integration, joining, merger, mingling, mixing, mixture, union

amass accumulate, aggregate, assemble, collect, compile, garner, gather, heap up, hoard, pile up, rake up, scrape together

amateur dabbler, dilettante, layman, nonprofessional

amateurish amateur, bungling, clumsy, crude, inexpert, unaccomplished, unprofessional, unskilful

amatory amorous, aphrodisiac, erotic, lascivious, libidinous, passionate, romantic, sensual, sexual, sexy

amaze alarm, astonish, astound, bewilder, bowl over (*Inf.*), confound, daze, dumbfound, electrify, flabbergast, shock, stagger, startle, stun, stupefy, surprise

amazement admiration, astonishment, bewilderment, confusion, marvel, perplexity, shock, stupefaction, surprise, wonder

ambassador agent, consul, deputy, diplomat, emissary, envoy, legate, minister, plenipotentiary, representative

ambience air, atmosphere, aura, character, complexion, feel, flavour, impression, milieu, mood, quality, setting, spirit, surroundings, temper, tenor, tone, vibes (*Inf.*), vibrations (*Inf.*)

ambiguity doubt, doubtfulness, dubiety, dubiousness, enigma, equivocacy, equivocality, equivocation, inconclusiveness, indefiniteness, indeterminateness, obscurity, puzzle, tergiversation, uncertainty, unclearness, vagueness

ambiguous cryptic, doubtful, dubious, enigmatic, enigmatical, equivocal, inconclusive, indefinite, indeterminate, obscure, puzzling, uncertain, unclear, vague

ambition **1.** aspiration, avidity, desire, drive, eagerness, enterprise, get-up-and-go (*Inf.*), hankering, longing, striving, yearning, zeal **2.** aim, aspiration, desire, dream, end, goal, hope, intent, objective, purpose, wish

ambitious **1.** aspiring, avid, desirous, driving, eager, enterprising, hopeful, intent, purposeful, striving, zealous **2.** arduous, bold, challenging, demanding, difficult, elaborate, energetic, exacting, formidable, grandiose, hard, impressive, industrious, pretentious, severe, strenuous

ambivalence clash, conflict, contradiction, doubt, equivocation, fluctuation, hesitancy, indecision, irresolution, opposition, uncertainty, vacillation, wavering

ambivalent clashing, conflicting,

contradictory, debatable, doubtful, equivocal, fluctuating, hesitant, inconclusive, in two minds, irresolute, mixed, opposed, uncertain, undecided, unresolved, unsure, vacillating, warring, wavering

amble dawdle, meander, mosey (*Inf.*), ramble, saunter, stroll, walk, wander

ambush 1. *n.* ambuscade, concealment, cover, hiding, hiding place, lying in wait, retreat, shelter, trap, waylaying **2.** *v.* ambuscade, bushwhack (*U.S.*), ensnare, surprise, trap, waylay

ameliorate advance, alleviate, amend, assuage, benefit, better, ease, elevate, improve, meliorate, mend, mitigate, promote, raise, reform, relieve

amenable 1. able to be influenced, acquiescent, agreeable, open, persuadable, responsive, susceptible, tractable **2.** accountable, answerable, chargeable, liable, responsible

amend alter, ameliorate, better, change, correct, enhance, fix, improve, mend, modify, rectify, reform, remedy, repair, revise

amendment 1. alteration, amelioration, betterment, change, correction, enhancement, improvement, mending, modification, rectification, reform, remedy, repair, revision **2.** addendum, addition, adjunct, alteration, attachment, clarification

amends apology, atonement, compensation, expiation, indemnity, recompense, redress, reparation, requital, restitution, restoration, satisfaction

amenity 1. advantage, comfort, convenience, facility, service **2.** affability, agreeableness, amiability, complaisance, courtesy, mildness, pleasantness (*of situation*), politeness, refinement, suavity

amiability affability, agreeableness, amiableness, attractiveness, benignity, charm, cheerfulness, delightfulness, engagingness, friendliness, friendship, geniality, good humour, good nature, kindliness, kindness, lovableness, pleasantness, pleasingness, sociability, sweetness, sweetness and light (*Inf.*), sweet temper, winsomeness

amiable affable, agreeable, attractive, benign, charming, cheerful, delightful, engaging, friendly, genial, good-humoured, good-natured, kind, kindly, lovable, obliging, pleasant, pleasing, sociable, sweet-tempered, winning, winsome

amicability amiability, amicableness, amity, brotherliness, civility, cordiality, courtesy, fraternity, friendliness, friendship, good will, harmony, kindliness, kindness, neighbourliness, peace, peaceableness, peacefulness, politeness, sociability

amicable amiable, brotherly, civil, cordial, courteous, fraternal, friendly, good-humoured, harmonious, kind, kindly, neighbourly, peaceable, peaceful, polite, sociable

amid amidst, among, amongst, in the middle of, in the midst of, in the thick of, surrounded by

amiss 1. *adj.* awry, confused, defective, erroneous, fallacious, false, faulty, improper, inaccurate, inappropriate, incorrect, mistaken, out of order, unsuitable, untoward, wrong **2.** *adv.* as an insult, as offensive, erroneously, faultily, improperly, inappropriately, incorrectly, mistakenly, out of turn, unsuitably, wrongly

amity accord, amicability, brotherhood, comity, comradeship, cordiality, fellowship, fraternity, friendliness, friendship, good will, harmony, kindliness, peace, peacefulness, tranquillity, understanding

ammunition armaments, cartridges, explosives, materiel, munitions, powder, rounds, shells, shot, shot and shell

amnesty absolution, condonation, dispensation, forgiveness, general pardon, immunity, oblivion, remission (*of penalty*), reprieve

amok *see* AMUCK

among, amongst 1. amid, in association with, in the middle of, in the midst of, in the thick of, midst, surrounded by, together with, with **2.** between, to each of **3.** in the class of, in the company of, in the group of, in the number of, out of **4.** by all of, by the joint action of, by the whole of, mutually, with one another

amorous affectionate, amatory, ardent, attached, doting, enamoured, erotic, fond, impassioned, in love, lovesick, loving, lustful, passionate, tender

amorphous characterless, formless, inchoate, indeterminate, irregular, nebulous, nondescript, shapeless, unformed, unshaped, unshapen, unstructured, vague

amount 1. bulk, expanse, extent, lot, magnitude, mass, measure, number, quantity, supply, volume **2.** addition, aggregate, entirety, extent, lot, sum, sum total, total, whole **3.** full effect, full value, import, result, significance

amount to add up to, aggregate, become, come to, develop into, equal, grow, mean, purport, total

amour affair, *affaire de coeur*, intrigue, liaison, love affair, relationship, romance

ample abounding, abundant, big, bountiful, broad, capacious, commodious, copious, enough and to spare, expansive, extensive, full, generous, great, large, lavish, liberal, plenteous, plentiful, plenty, profuse, rich, roomy, spacious, substantial, unrestricted, voluminous, wide

amplification augmentation, boosting, deepening, development, dilation, elaboration, enlargement, expansion, expatiation, extension, fleshing out, heightening, increase, intensification, lengthening, magnification, raising, rounding out, strengthening, stretching, supplementing, widening

amplify augment, boost, deepen, develop, dilate, elaborate, enlarge, expand, expatiate, extend, flesh out, go into detail, heighten, increase, intensify, lengthen, magnify, raise, round out, strengthen, stretch, supplement, widen

amplitude 1. bigness, breadth, bulk, capaciousness, compass, dimension, expanse, extent, greatness, hugeness, largeness, magnitude, mass, range, reach, scope, size, spaciousness, sweep, vastness, width **2.** abundance, ampleness, completeness, copiousness, fullness, plenitude, plethora, profusion, richness

amply abundantly, bountifully, capaciously, completely, copiously, extensively, fully, generously, greatly, lavishly, liberally, plenteously, plentifully, profusely, richly, substantially, thoroughly, unstintingly, well

amputate curtail, cut off, lop, remove, separate, sever, truncate

amuck, amok berserk, destructively, ferociously, frenziedly, in a frenzy, insanely, madly, maniacally, murderously, savagely, uncontrollably, violently, wildly

amulet charm, fetish, juju, periapt (*Rare*), talisman

amuse beguile, charm, cheer, delight, divert, enliven, entertain, gladden, gratify, interest, occupy, please, recreate, regale, tickle (*Inf.*)

amusement 1. beguilement, cheer, delight, diversion, enjoyment, entertainment, fun, gladdening, gratification, hilarity, interest, laughter, merriment, mirth, pleasing, pleasure, recreation, regalement, sport **2.** distraction, diversion, entertainment, game, hobby, joke, lark, pastime, prank, recreation, sport

amusing charming, cheerful, cheering, comical, delightful, diverting, droll, enjoyable, entertaining, facetious, funny, gladdening, gratifying, humorous, interesting, jocular, laughable, lively, merry, pleasant, pleasing, witty

anaemic ashen, bloodless, characterless, colourless, dull, enervated, feeble, frail, infirm, pale, pallid, sickly, wan, weak

anaesthetic 1. *n.* analgesic, anodyne, narcotic, opiate, painkiller, sedative, soporific, stupefacient, stupefactive **2.** *adj.* analgesic, anodyne, deadening, dulling, narcotic, numbing, opiate, painkilling, sedative, sleep-inducing, soporific, stupefacient, stupefactive

analogous agreeing, akin, alike, comparable, corresponding, equivalent, homologous, like, parallel, related, resembling, similar

analogy agreement, comparison, correlation, correspondence, equivalence, homology, likeness, parallel, relation, resemblance, similarity, similitude

analyse 1. assay, estimate, evaluate, examine, interpret, investigate, judge, test **2.** anatomize, break down, consider, dissect, dissolve, divide, resolve, separate, study, think through

analysis 1. anatomization, anatomy, assay, breakdown, dissection, dissolution, division, enquiry, examination, investigation, resolution, scrutiny, separation, sifting, test **2.** estimation, evaluation, finding, interpretation, judgment, opinion, reasoning, study

analytic, analytical detailed, diagnostic, discrete, dissecting, explanatory, expository, inquiring, inquisitive, interpretative, interpretive, investigative, logical, organized, problem-solving, questioning, rational, searching, studious, systematic, testing

anarchic chaotic, confused, disordered, disorganized, lawless, misgoverned, misruled, rebellious, revolutionary, rioting, riotous, ungoverned

anarchist insurgent, nihilist, rebel, revolutionary, terrorist

anarchy chaos, confusion, disorder, disorganization, lawlessness, misgovernment, misrule, rebellion, revolution, riot

anathema 1. ban, condemnation, curse, damnation, denunciation, excommunication, execration, imprecation, malediction, proscription, taboo **2.** abomination, bane, *bête noire*, bugbear, enemy, pariah

anathematize abominate, ban, condemn, curse, damn, denounce, excommunicate, execrate, imprecate, proscribe

anatomize analyse, break down, dissect, dissolve, divide, examine, resolve, scrutinize, separate, study

anatomy 1. analysis, dismemberment, dissection, division, enquiry, examination, investigation, study **2.** build, composition, frame, framework, make-up, structure

ancestor forebear, forefather, forerunner, precursor, predecessor, progenitor

ancestry ancestors, antecedents, blood, derivation, descent, extraction, family, forebears, forefathers, genealogy, house, line, lineage, origin, parentage, pedigree, progenitors, race, stock

anchorite eremite, hermit, recluse

ancient aged, age-old, antediluvian, antiquated, antique, archaic, bygone, early, hoary, obsolete, old, olden, old-fashioned, outmoded, out-of-date, primeval, primordial, superannuated, time-worn

ancillary accessory, additional, auxiliary, contributory, extra, secondary, subordinate, subsidiary, supplementary

and along with, also, as well as, furthermore, in addition to, including, moreover, plus, together with

androgynous bisexual, epicene, hermaphrodite, hermaphroditic

anecdote reminiscence, short story, sketch, story, tale, yarn

anew afresh, again, another time, from scratch, from the beginning, once again, once more, over again

angel 1. archangel, cherub, divine messenger, guardian spirit, seraph, spiritual being **2.** *Inf.* beauty, darling, dear, dream, gem, ideal, jewel, paragon, saint, treasure

angelic 1. celestial, cherubic, ethereal, heavenly, seraphic **2.** adorable, beatific, beautiful, entrancing, innocent, lovely, pure, saintly, virtuous

anger 1. *n.* annoyance, antagonism, choler, displeasure, exasperation, fury, ill humour, ill temper, indignation, ire, irritability, irritation, outrage, passion, pique, rage, resentment, spleen, temper, vexation, wrath **2.** *v.* affront, annoy, antagonize, displease, enrage, exasperate, excite, fret, gall, incense, infuriate, irritate, madden, nettle, offend, outrage, pique, provoke, rile, vex

angle *n.* **1.** bend, corner, crook, crotch, cusp, edge, elbow, intersection, knee, nook, point **2.** approach, aspect, outlook, perspective, point of view, position, side, slant, standpoint, viewpoint ~*v.* **3.** cast, fish

angle for aim for, be after (*Inf.*), cast about for, contrive, fish for, hunt, invite, look for, scheme, seek, solicit, try for

angry annoyed, antagonized, choleric, displeased, enraged, exasperated, furious, heated, hot, hot under the collar (*Inf.*), ill-tempered, incensed, indignant, infuriated, irascible, irate, ireful, irritable, irritated, mad (*Inf.*), nettled, outraged, passionate, piqued, provoked, raging, resentful, riled, splenetic, tumultuous, uptight (*Sl.*), wrathful

anguish agony, distress, grief, heartache, heartbreak, misery, pain, pang, sorrow, suffering, throe, torment, torture, woe

anguished afflicted, agonized, brokenhearted, distressed, grief-stricken, suffering, tormented, tortured, wounded, wretched

angular bony, gaunt, lank, lanky, lean, rangy, rawboned, scrawny, skinny, spare

animadversion blame, censure, comment, condemnation, criticism, knocking (*Inf.*), rebuke, reprehension, reproach, reproof, strictures

animal *n.* **1.** beast, brute, creature **2.** *Applied to a person* barbarian, beast, brute, monster, savage, wild man ~*adj.* **3.** bestial, bodily, brutish, carnal, fleshly, gross, physical, sensual

animate *v.* **1.** activate, embolden, encourage, energize, enliven, excite, fire, gladden, impel, incite, inspire, inspirit, instigate, invigorate, kindle, move, quicken, revive, rouse, spark, spur, stimulate, stir, urge, vitalize, vivify

~*adj.* **2.** alive, breathing, live, living, moving **3.** gay, lively, spirited, vivacious

animated active, airy, ardent, brisk, buoyant, dynamic, ebullient, elated, energetic, enthusiastic, excited, fervent, gay, lively, passionate, quick, spirited, sprightly, vibrant, vigorous, vital, vivacious, vivid, zealous, zestful

animation action, activity, airiness, ardour, briskness, buoyancy, dynamism, ebullience, elation, energy, enthusiasm, excitement, exhilaration, fervour, gaiety, high spirits, life, liveliness, passion, pep, sparkle, spirit, sprightliness, verve, vibrancy, vigour, vitality, vivacity, zeal, zest, zing (*Inf.*)

animosity acrimony, animus, antagonism, antipathy, bad blood, bitterness, enmity, hate, hatred, hostility, ill will, malevolence, malice, malignity, rancour, resentment, virulence

animus 1. acrimony, animosity, antagonism, antipathy, bad blood, bitterness, enmity, hate, hatred, hostility, ill will, malevolence, malice, malignity, rancour, resentment, virulence **2.** animating force, intention, motive, purpose, will

annals accounts, archives, chronicles, history, journals, memorials, records, registers

anneal case-harden, harden, indurate, steel, strengthen, temper, toughen

annex 1. add, adjoin, affix, append, attach, connect, fasten, join, subjoin, tack, unite **2.** acquire, appropriate, arrogate, conquer, expropriate, occupy, seize, take over

annexation annexing, appropriation, arrogation, conquest, expropriation, occupation, seizure, takeover

annexe 1. ell, extension, supplementary building, wing **2.** addendum, addition, adjunct, affix, appendix, attachment, supplement

annihilate abolish, destroy, eradicate, erase, exterminate, extinguish, extirpate, liquidate, nullify, obliterate, root out, wipe out

annihilation abolition, destruction, eradication, erasure, extermination, extinction, extinguishing, extirpation, liquidation, nullification, obliteration, rooting out, wiping out

annotate commentate, comment on, elucidate, explain, footnote, gloss, illustrate, interpret, make observations, note

annotation comment, commentary, elucidation, exegesis, explanation, explication, footnote, gloss, illustration, interpretation, note, observation

announce 1. advertise, broadcast, declare, disclose, divulge, give out, intimate, make known, proclaim, promulgate, propound, publish, report, reveal, tell **2.** augur, betoken, foretell, harbinger, herald, portend, presage, signal, signify

announcement advertisement, broadcast, bulletin, communiqué, declaration, disclosure, divulgence, intimation, proclamation, promulgation, publication, report, revelation, statement

announcer anchor man, broadcaster, commentator, master of ceremonies, newscaster, news reader, reporter

annoy anger, badger, bedevil, bore, bother, bug (*Inf.*), displease, disturb, exasperate, gall, get (*Inf.*), harass, harry, incommode, irk, irritate, madden, molest, needle (*Inf.*), nettle, peeve, pester, plague, provoke, rile, ruffle, tease, trouble, vex

annoyance 1. aggravation, anger, bedevilment, bother, displeasure, disturbance, exasperation, harassment, irritation, nuisance, provocation, trouble, vexation **2.** bind (*Inf.*), bore, bother, nuisance, pain (*Inf.*), pain in the neck (*Inf.*), pest, plague, tease

annoying aggravating, bedevilling, boring, bothersome, displeasing, disturbing, exasperating, galling, harassing, irksome, irritating, maddening, peeving (*Inf.*), provoking, teasing, troublesome, vexatious

annual once a year, yearlong, yearly

annually by the year, each year, every year, once a year, per annum, per year, year after year, yearly

annul abolish, abrogate, cancel, countermand, declare *or* render null and void, invalidate, negate, nullify, recall, repeal, rescind, retract, reverse, revoke, void

annulment abolition, abrogation, cancellation, countermanding, invalidation, negation, nullification, recall, repeal, rescindment, rescission, retraction, reversal, revocation, voiding

anodyne 1. *n.* analgesic, narcotic, painkiller, painreliever, palliative **2.** *adj.* analgesic, deadening, dulling, narcotic, numbing, pain-killing, pain-relieving, palliative

anoint 1. daub, embrocate, grease, oil, rub, smear, spread over **2.** anele (*Archaic*), bless, consecrate, hallow, sanctify

anomalous aberrant, abnormal, atypical, bizarre, deviating, eccentric, exceptional, incongruous, inconsistent, irregular, odd, peculiar, rare, unusual

anomaly aberration, abnormality, departure, deviation, eccentricity, exception, incongruity, inconsistency, irregularity, oddity, peculiarity, rarity

anon before long, betimes (*Archaic*), erelong (*Archaic*), forthwith, presently, promptly, shortly, soon

anonymous 1. incognito, innominate, nameless, unacknowledged, unattested, unauthenticated, uncredited, unidentified, unknown, unnamed, unsigned **2.** characterless, nondescript, unexceptional

answer *n.* **1.** acknowledgment, comeback, defence, explanation, plea, reaction, refutation, rejoinder, reply, report, resolution, response, retort, return, riposte, solution, vindication ~*v.* **2.** acknowledge, explain, react, refute, rejoin, reply, resolve, respond, retort, return, solve **3.** conform, correlate, correspond, do, fill, fit, fulfil, measure up, meet, pass, qualify, satisfy, serve, suffice, suit, work

answerable 1. accountable, amenable, chargeable, liable, responsible, subject, to blame **2.** explainable, refutable, resolvable, solvable

answer back argue, be cheeky, be impertinent, cheek (*Inf.*), contradict, disagree, dispute, rebut, retort, talk back

answer for 1. be accountable for, be answerable for, be chargeable for, be liable for, be responsible for, be to blame for, take the rap for (*Sl.*) **2.** atone for, make amends for, pay for, suffer for

answer to 1. be accountable to, be answerable to, be responsible to, be ruled by, obey **2.** agree, confirm, correspond, fit, match, meet

antagonism antipathy, competition, conflict, contention, discord, dissension, friction, hostility, opposition, rivalry

antagonist adversary, competitor, contender, enemy, foe, opponent, opposer, rival

antagonistic adverse, antipathetic, at odds, at variance, averse, conflicting, contentious, hostile, ill-disposed, incompatible, in dispute, inimical, opposed, unfriendly

antagonize 1. alienate, anger, annoy, disaffect, estrange, insult, irritate, offend, repel, rub (someone) up the wrong way (*Inf.*) **2.** contend with, counteract, neutralize, oppose, struggle with, work against

antecedent anterior, earlier, foregoing, former, preceding, precursory, preliminary, previous, prior

antecedents 1. ancestors, ancestry, blood, descent, extraction, family, forebears, forefathers, genealogy, line, progenitors, stock **2.** background, history, past

antedate anticipate, come first or before, forego, go before, precede, predate

antediluvian 1. prehistoric, primeval, primitive, primordial **2.** ancient, antiquated, antique, archaic, obsolete, old-fashioned, out-of-date, out of the ark (*Inf.*), passé

anterior 1. fore, forward, front, frontward **2.** antecedent, earlier, foregoing, former, introductory, preceding, previous, prior

anteroom antechamber, foyer, lobby, outer room, reception room, vestibule, waiting room

anthem 1. canticle, chant, chorale, hymn, psalm **2.** paean, song of praise

anthology analects, choice, collection, compendium, compilation, digest, garland, miscellany, selection, treasury

anticipate 1. apprehend, await, count upon, expect, forecast, foresee, foretell, hope for, look for, look forward to, predict, prepare for **2.** antedate, beat (someone) to it (*Inf.*), forestall, intercept, prevent

anticipation apprehension, awaiting, expectancy, expectation, foresight, foretaste, forethought, hope, preconception, premonition, prescience, presentiment

anticlimax bathos, comedown (*Inf.*), disappointment, letdown

antics buffoonery, capers, clowning, escapades, foolishness, frolics, larks, mischief, monkey tricks, playfulness, pranks, silliness, skylarking, stunts, tomfoolery, tricks

antidote antitoxin, antivenin, corrective, counteragent, countermeasure, cure, neutralizer, preventive, remedy, specific

antipathetic abhorrent, antagonistic, averse, disgusting, distasteful, hateful, hostile, incompatible, invidious, loathsome, obnoxious, odious, offensive, repellent, repugnant, repulsive, revolting

antipathy abhorrence, animosity, animus, antagonism, aversion, bad blood, contrariety, disgust, dislike, distaste, enmity, hatred, hostility, ill will, incompatibility, loathing, opposition, rancour, repugnance, repulsion

antiquated 1. antediluvian, antique, archaic, dated, obsolete, old-fashioned, old hat, outmoded, out-of-date, outworn, passé 2. aged, ancient, elderly, hoary, old, superannuated

antique *adj.* 1. aged, ancient, elderly, old, superannuated 2. archaic, obsolete, old-fashioned, outdated 3. antiquarian, classic, olden, vintage ~*n.* 4. bygone, heirloom, object of virtu, relic

antiquity 1. age, ancientness, elderliness, old age, oldness 2. ancient times, distant past, olden days, time immemorial 3. antique, relic, ruin

antiseptic 1. *adj.* aseptic, clean, germ-free, hygienic, pure, sanitary, sterile, uncontaminated, unpolluted 2. *n.* bactericide, disinfectant, germicide, purifier

antisocial 1. alienated, asocial, misanthropic, reserved, retiring, uncommunicative, unfriendly, unsociable, withdrawn 2. antagonistic, belligerent, disorderly, disruptive, hostile, menacing, rebellious

antithesis 1. antipode, contrary, contrast, converse, inverse, opposite, reverse 2. contradiction, contraposition, contrariety, contrast, inversion, opposition, reversal

antithetical, antithetic antipodal, contradictory, contrary, contrasted, contrasting, converse, counter, inverse, opposed, opposite, reverse

anxiety angst, apprehension, care, concern, disquiet, disquietude, distress, foreboding, fretfulness, misgiving, nervousness, restlessness, solicitude, suspense, tension, unease, uneasiness, watchfulness, worry

anxious 1. apprehensive, careful, concerned, disquieted, distressed, disturbed, fearful, fretful, in suspense, nervous, overwrought, restless, solicitous, taut, tense, troubled, uneasy, unquiet (*Chiefly literary*), watchful, worried 2. ardent, avid, desirous, eager, expectant, impatient, intent, itching, keen, yearning

apace at full speed, expeditiously, posthaste, quickly, rapidly, speedily, swiftly, with dispatch, without delay

apart 1. afar, alone, aloof, aside, away, by itself, by oneself, cut off, distant, distinct, divorced, excluded, independent, independently, isolated, piecemeal, separate, separated, separately, singly, to itself, to oneself, to one side 2. asunder, in bits, in pieces, into parts, to bits, to pieces 3. **apart from** aside from, besides, but, except for, excluding, not counting, other than, save

apartment accommodation, chambers, compartment, flat (*U.S.*), living quarters, penthouse, quarters, room, rooms, suite

apathetic cold, cool, emotionless, impassive, indifferent, insensible, listless, passive, phlegmatic, sluggish, stoic, stoical, torpid, unconcerned, unemotional, unfeeling, uninterested, unmoved, unresponsive

apathy coldness, coolness, emotionlessness, impassibility, impassivity, indifference, insensibility, listlessness, passiveness, passivity, phlegm, sluggishness, stoicism, torpor, unconcern, unfeelingness, uninterestedness, unresponsiveness

ape affect, caricature, copy, counterfeit, echo, imitate, mimic, mirror, mock, parody, parrot

aperture breach, chink, cleft, crack, eye, eyelet, fissure, gap, hole, interstice, opening, orifice, passage, perforation, rent, rift, slit, slot, space

apex acme, apogee, climax, crest, crown, culmination, height, high point, peak, pinnacle, point, summit, tip, top, vertex, zenith

aphorism adage, apothegm, axiom, dictum, gnome, maxim, precept, proverb, saw, saying

apiece each, for each, from each, individually, respectively, separately, severally, to each

apish affected, foolish, foppish, imitative, mimicking, silly, stupid, trifling

aplomb balance, calmness, composure, confidence, coolness, equanimity, level-headedness, poise, sang-froid, self-assurance, self-confidence, self-possession, stability

apocalyptic ominous, oracular, portentous, prophetic, revelational, vatic

apocryphal doubtful, dubious, equivocal, fictitious, legendary, mythical, questionable, spurious, unauthenticated, uncanonical, unsubstantiated, unverified

apogee acme, apex, climax, crest, crown, culmination, height, high point, peak, pinnacle, summit, tip, top, vertex, zenith

apologetic contrite, penitent, regretful, remorseful, rueful, sorry

apologist advocate, arguer, champion, defender, justifier, maintainer, pleader, spokesman, supporter, vindicator

apologize ask forgiveness, beg pardon, express regret, say one is sorry, say sorry

apologue allegory, fable, parable, story, tale

apology 1. acknowledgment, confession, defence, excuse, explanation, extenuation, justification, plea, vindication **2.** caricature, excuse, imitation, makeshift, mockery, stopgap, substitute, travesty

apostasy backsliding, defection, desertion, disloyalty, faithlessness, falseness, heresy, perfidy, recreance *or* recreancy (*Archaic*), treachery, unfaithfulness

apostate 1. *n.* backslider, defector, deserter, heretic, recreant (*Archaic*), renegade, traitor, turncoat **2.** *adj.* backsliding, disloyal, faithless, false, heretical, perfidious, recreant, traitorous, treacherous, unfaithful, untrue

apostatize backslide, defect, desert, renege, turn traitor

apostle 1. evangelist, herald, messenger, missionary, preacher, proselytizer **2.** advocate, champion, pioneer, propagandist, propagator, proponent

apothegm adage, aphorism, axiom, dictum, gnome, maxim, precept, proverb, saw, saying

apotheosis deification, elevation, exaltation, glorification, idealization, idolization

apotheosize deify, elevate, exalt, glorify, idealize, idolize

appal alarm, astound, daunt, dishearten, dismay, frighten, harrow, horrify, intimidate, outrage, petrify, scare, shock, terrify, unnerve

appalling alarming, astounding, awful, daunting, dire, disheartening, dismaying, dreadful, fearful, frightening, frightful, ghastly, grim, harrowing, hideous, horrible, horrid, horrific, horrifying, intimidating, petrifying, scaring, shocking, terrible, terrifying, unnerving

apparatus 1. appliance, contraption (*Inf.*), device, equipment, gear, implements, machine, machinery, materials, means, mechanism, outfit, tackle, tools, utensils **2.** bureaucracy, chain of command, hierarchy, network, organization, setup, structure, system

apparel accoutrements, array (*Poetic*), attire, clothes, clothing, costume, dress, equipment, garb, garments, gear (*Sl.*), habiliments, habit, outfit, raiment (*Archaic*), robes, trappings, vestments

apparent 1. clear, conspicuous, discernible, distinct, evident, indubitable, manifest, marked, obvious, open, overt, patent, plain, understandable, unmistakable, visible **2.** ostensible, outward, seeming, specious, superficial

apparently it appears that, it seems that, on the face of it, ostensibly, outwardly, seemingly, speciously, superficially

apparition 1. appearance, manifestation, materialization, presence, vision, visitation **2.** chimera, ghost, phantom, revenant, shade (*Literary*), spectre, spirit, spook (*Inf.*), visitant, wraith

appeal *n.* **1.** adjuration, application, entreaty, invocation, petition, plea, prayer, request, solicitation, suit, supplication **2.** allure, attraction, attractiveness, beauty, charm, engagingness, fascination, interestingness, pleasingness ~*v.* **3.** adjure, apply, ask, beg, beseech, call, call upon, entreat, implore, petition, plead, pray, refer, request, resort to, solicit, sue, supplicate **4.** allure, attract, charm, engage, entice, fascinate, interest, invite, please, tempt

appear 1. arise, arrive, attend, be present, come forth, come into sight, come into view, come out, come to light, crop up (*Inf.*), develop, emerge, issue, loom, materialize, occur, show (*Sl.*), show up (*Inf.*), surface, turn out, turn up **2.** look (like *or* as if), occur, seem, strike one as **3.** be apparent, be clear, be evident, be manifest, be obvious, be patent, be plain **4.** become available, be created, be developed, be invented, be published, come into being, come into existence, come out **5.** act, be exhibited, come on, come onstage, enter, perform, play, play a part, take part

appearance 1. advent, appearing, arrival, coming, debut, emergence, introduction, presence, showing up (*Inf.*), turning up **2.** air, aspect, bearing, demeanour, expression, face, figure, form, image, look, looks, manner, mien (*Literary*) **3**. front, guise, illusion, image, impression, outward show, pretence, semblance

appease allay, alleviate, assuage, blunt, calm, compose, conciliate, diminish, ease, lessen, lull, mitigate, mollify, pacify, placate, quell, quench, quiet, satisfy, soften, soothe, subdue, tranquillize

appeasement 1. acceding, accommodation, compromise, concession, conciliation, placation, propitiation **2**. abatement, alleviation, assuagement, blunting, easing, lessening, lulling, mitigation, mollification, pacification, quelling, quenching, quieting, satisfaction, softening, solace, soothing, tranquillization

appellation address, description, designation, epithet, name, sobriquet, style, term, title

append add, adjoin, affix, annex, attach, fasten, hang, join, subjoin, tack on, tag on

appendage 1. accessory, addendum, addition, adjunct, affix, ancillary, annexe, appendix, appurtenance, attachment, auxiliary, supplement **2**. *Zool.* extremity, limb, member, projection, protuberance

appendant *adj.* **1**. added, additional, adjoined, affixed, annexed, appended, attached, auxiliary, fastened, joined, subjoined, supplementary, tacked on, tagged on **2**. accompanying, associated, attendant, concomitant, connected, consequential, following, related, resulting ~*n*. **3**. addition, adjunct, affix, annexe, appendage, appendix, attachment, supplement

appendix addendum, addition, adjunct, appendage, codicil, postscript, supplement

appertain *Usually with* **to** apply, bear upon, be characteristic of, be connected, belong, be part of, be pertinent, be proper, be relevant, have to do with, inhere in, pertain, refer, relate, touch upon

appetence, appetency 1. appetite, craving, desire, hankering, hunger, longing, need, yearning **2**. bent, drive, inclination, instinct, leaning, penchant, propensity **3**. affection, affinity, allurement, attraction, fondness, liking, partiality

appetite appetence, appetency, craving, demand, desire, hankering, hunger, inclination, liking, longing, passion, proclivity, propensity, relish, stomach,

taste, willingness, yearning, zeal, zest

appetizer 1. antipasto, canapé, cocktail, hors d'oeuvre, titbit **2**. apéritif, cocktail **3**. foretaste, sample, taste

appetizing appealing, delicious, inviting, mouthwatering, palatable, savoury, scrumptious (*Inf.*), succulent, tasty, tempting

applaud acclaim, approve, cheer, clap, commend, compliment, encourage, eulogize, extol, laud, magnify (*Archaic*), praise

applause acclaim, acclamation, accolade, approbation, approval, cheering, cheers, commendation, eulogizing, hand, hand-clapping, laudation, ovation, plaudit, praise

appliance apparatus, device, gadget, implement, instrument, machine, mechanism, tool

applicable apposite, appropriate, apropos, apt, befitting, fit, fitting, germane, pertinent, relevant, suitable, suited, to the point, to the purpose, useful

applicant aspirant, candidate, claimant, inquirer, petitioner, postulant, suitor, suppliant

application 1. appositeness, exercise, function, germaneness, pertinence, practice, purpose, relevance, use, value **2**. appeal, claim, inquiry, petition, request, requisition, solicitation, suit **3**. assiduity, attention, attentiveness, commitment, dedication, diligence, effort, hard work, industry, perseverance, study **4**. balm, cream, dressing, emollient, lotion, ointment, poultice, salve, unguent

apply 1. administer, assign, bring into play, bring to bear, carry out, employ, engage, execute, exercise, implement, practise, put to use, use, utilize **2**. appertain, be applicable, be appropriate, bear upon, be fitting, be relevant, fit, pertain, refer, relate, suit **3**. anoint, bring into contact with, cover with, lay on, paint, place, put on, smear, spread on, touch to **4**. appeal, claim, inquire, make application, petition, put in, request, requisition, solicit, sue **5**. address, be assiduous, be diligent, be industrious, buckle down (*Inf.*), commit, concentrate, dedicate, devote, direct, give, make an effort, pay attention, persevere, study, try, work hard

appoint 1. allot, arrange, assign, choose, decide, designate, determine, establish, fix, set, settle **2**. assign, choose, commission, delegate, elect, install, name, nominate, select **3**. command, decree, direct, enjoin, ordain **4**. equip, fit out, furnish, provide, supply

appointed 1. allotted, arranged, assigned, chosen, decided, designated, determined, established, fixed, set, settled **2**. assigned, chosen, commissioned, delegated, elected, installed, named, nominated, selected **3**. commanded, decreed, directed, enjoined, ordained **4**. equipped, fitted out, furnished, provided, supplied

appointment 1. arrangement, assignation, consultation, date, engagement, interview, meeting, rendezvous, session, tryst (*Archaic*) **2**. allotment, assignment, choice, choosing, commissioning, delegation, designation, election, installation, naming, nomination, selection **3**. assignment, berth (*Inf.*), job, office, place, position, post, situation, station **4**. appointee, candidate, delegate, nominee, officeholder, representative **5**. *Usually plural* accoutrements, appurtenances, equipage, fittings, fixtures, furnishings, gear, outfit, paraphernalia, trappings

apportion allocate, allot, assign, deal, dispense, distribute, divide, dole out, measure out, mete out, parcel out, ration out, share

apportionment allocation, allotment, assignment, dealing out, dispensing, distribution, division, doling out, measuring out, meting out, parcelling out, rationing out, sharing

apposite appertaining, applicable, appropriate, apropos, apt, befitting, germane, pertinent, proper, relevant, suitable, suited, to the point, to the purpose

appraisal 1. assessment, estimate, estimation, evaluation, judgment, opinion, sizing up (*Inf.*) **2**. assay, pricing, rating, reckoning, survey, valuation

appraise assay, assess, estimate, evaluate, gauge, inspect, judge, price, rate, review, size up (*Inf.*), survey, value

appreciable ascertainable, clear-cut, considerable, definite, detectable, discernible, distinguishable, evident, marked, material, measurable, noticeable, obvious, perceivable, perceptible, pronounced, recognizable, significant, substantial, visible

appreciate 1. be appreciative, be grateful for, be indebted, be obliged, be thankful for, give thanks for **2**. acknowl-

edge, be alive to, be aware (cognizant, conscious) of, comprehend, estimate, know, perceive, realize, recognize, sympathize with, take account of, understand **3**. admire, cherish, enjoy, esteem, like, prize, rate highly, regard, relish, respect, savour, treasure, value **4**. enhance, gain, grow, improve, increase, inflate, raise the value of, rise

appreciation 1. acknowledgment, gratefulness, gratitude, indebtedness, obligation, thankfulness, thanks **2**. admiration, appraisal, assessment, awareness, cognizance, comprehension, enjoyment, esteem, estimation, knowledge, liking, perception, realization, recognition, regard, relish, respect, responsiveness, sensitivity, sympathy, understanding, valuation **3**. enhancement, gain, growth, improvement, increase, inflation, rise **4**. acclamation, criticism, critique, notice, praise, review, tribute

appreciative 1. beholden, grateful, indebted, obliged, thankful **2**. admiring, aware, cognizant, conscious, enthusiastic, in the know (*Inf.*), knowledgeable, mindful, perceptive, pleased, regardful, respectful, responsive, sensitive, supportive, sympathetic, understanding

apprehend 1. arrest, bust (*Inf.*), capture, catch, collar (*Inf.*), nab (*Inf.*), nick (*Sl.*), pinch (*Inf.*), run in (*Sl.*), seize, take, take prisoner **2**. appreciate, believe, comprehend, conceive, grasp, imagine, know, perceive, realize, recognize, think, understand **3**. be afraid of, dread, fear

apprehension 1. alarm, anxiety, apprehensiveness, concern, disquiet, doubt, dread, fear, foreboding, misgiving, mistrust, premonition, suspicion, unease, uneasiness, worry **2**. arrest, capture, catching, seizure, taking **3**. awareness, comprehension, grasp, intellect, intelligence, ken, knowledge, perception, understanding **4**. belief, concept, conception, conjecture, idea, impression, notion, opinion, sentiment, thought, view

apprehensive afraid, alarmed, anxious, concerned, disquieted, doubtful, fearful, foreboding, mistrustful, suspicious, uneasy, worried

apprentice beginner, learner, neophyte, novice, probationer, pupil, student, tyro

apprise acquaint, advise, communicate, enlighten, give notice, inform,

make aware, make cognizant, notify, tell, warn
approach v. **1.** advance, catch up, come close, come near, come to, draw near, gain on, meet, move towards, near, push forward, reach **2.** appeal to, apply to, broach the matter with, make advances to, make a proposal to, make overtures to, sound out **3.** begin, begin work on, commence, embark on, enter upon, make a start, set about, undertake **4.** approximate, be comparable to, be like, come close to, come near to, compare with, resemble ~n. **5.** access, advance, advent, arrival, avenue, coming, drawing near, entrance, nearing, passage, road, way **6.** approximation, likeness, semblance **7.** *Often plural* advance, appeal, application, invitation, offer, overture, proposal, proposition **8.** attitude, course, manner, means, method, mode, modus operandi, procedure, style, technique, way

approachable 1. accessible, attainable, come-at-able (*Inf.*), get-at-able (*Inf.*), reachable **2.** affable, congenial, cordial, friendly, open, sociable

approbation acceptance, acclaim, applause, approval, assent, commendation, congratulation, encouragement, endorsement, favour, laudation, praise, ratification, recognition, sanction, support

appropriate *adj.* **1.** adapted, applicable, apposite, appurtenant, apropos, apt, becoming, befitting, belonging, congruous, correct, felicitous, fit, fitting, germane, meet (*Archaic*), opportune, pertinent, proper, relevant, right, seemly, suitable, to the point, to the purpose, well-suited, well-timed ~v. **2.** allocate, allot, apportion, assign, devote, earmark, set apart **3.** annex, arrogate, assume, commandeer, confiscate, expropriate, impound, pre-empt, seize, take, take over, take possession of, usurp **4.** embezzle, filch, misappropriate, pilfer, pocket, steal

appropriateness applicability, appositeness, aptness, becomingness, congruousness, correctness, felicitousness, felicity, fitness, fittingness, germaneness, opportuneness, pertinence, properness, relevance, rightness, seemliness, suitability, timeliness, well-suitedness

appropriation 1. allocation, allotment, apportionment, assignment, earmarking, setting apart **2.** annexation, arrogation, assumption, commandeering, confiscation, expropriation, impoundment, pre-emption, seizure, takeover, taking, usurpation

approval 1. acquiescence, agreement, assent, authorization, blessing, compliance, concurrence, confirmation, consent, countenance, endorsement, imprimatur, leave, licence, mandate, O.K. (*Inf.*), permission, ratification, recommendation, sanction, the go-ahead (*Inf.*), the green light (*Inf.*), validation **2.** acclaim, admiration, applause, appreciation, approbation, commendation, esteem, favour, good opinion, liking, praise, regard, respect

approve 1. acclaim, admire, applaud, appreciate, be pleased with, commend, esteem, favour, have a good opinion of, like, praise, regard highly, respect, think highly of **2.** accede to, accept, advocate, agree to, allow, assent to, authorize, bless, concur in, confirm, consent to, countenance, endorse, give the go-ahead (*Inf.*), give the green light (*Inf.*), go along with, mandate, O.K. (*Inf.*), pass, permit, ratify, recommend, sanction, second, subscribe to, uphold, validate

approximate *adj.* **1.** almost accurate, almost exact, close, near **2.** estimated, inexact, loose, rough **3.** analogous, close, comparable, like, near, relative, similar, verging on **4.** adjacent, bordering, close together, contiguous, near, nearby, neighbouring ~v. **5.** approach, border on, come close, come near, reach, resemble, touch, verge on

approximately about, almost, around, circa (*used with dates*), close to, generally, in the neighbourhood of, in the region of, in the vicinity of, just about, loosely, more or less, nearly, not far off, relatively, roughly

approximation 1. conjecture, estimate, estimation, guess, guesswork, rough calculation, rough idea **2.** approach, correspondence, likeness, resemblance, semblance

appurtenance 1. accessory, accompaniment, adjunct, annexe, appendage, appurtenant, attachment, auxiliary, concomitant, incidental, piece of equipment, subordinate, subsidiary, supplement **2.** *Plural* accessories, accompaniments, accoutrements, appendages, equipment, impedimenta, paraphernalia, trappings

appurtenant accessory, appertaining, applicable, appropriate, belonging, concerned, connected, germane, incidental, pertaining, pertinent, proper, related, relating, relevant

a priori 1. deduced, deductive, from cause to effect, inferential **2.** conjectural, postulated, postulational, presumptive, self-evident, suppositional, theoretical

apron pinafore, pinny (*Inf.*)

apropos *adj.* **1.** applicable, apposite, appropriate, apt, befitting, belonging, correct, fit, fitting, germane, meet (*Archaic*), opportune, pertinent, proper, related, relevant, right, seemly, suitable, to the point, to the purpose ~*adv.* **2.** appropriately, aptly, opportunely, pertinently, relevantly, suitably, timely, to the point, to the purpose **3.** by the bye, by the way, incidentally, in passing, parenthetically, while on the subject

apropos of *prep.* in respect of, on the subject of, re, regarding, respecting, with reference to, with regard to, with respect to

apt 1. applicable, apposite, appropriate, apropos, befitting, correct, fit, fitting, germane, meet (*Archaic*), pertinent, proper, relevant, seemly, suitable, timely, to the point, to the purpose **2.** disposed, given, inclined, liable, likely, of a mind, prone, ready **3.** astute, bright, clever, expert, gifted, ingenious, intelligent, prompt, quick, sharp, skilful, smart, talented, teachable

aptitude 1. bent, disposition, inclination, leaning, predilection, proclivity, proneness, propensity, tendency **2.** ability, aptness, capability, capacity, cleverness, faculty, flair, gift, giftedness, intelligence, knack, proficiency, quickness, talent **3.** applicability, appositeness, appropriateness, fitness, relevance, suitability, suitableness

aptness 1. applicability, appositeness, appropriateness, becomingness, congruousness, correctness, felicitousness, felicity, fitness, fittingness, germaneness, opportuneness, pertinence, properness, relevance, rightness, seemliness, suitability, timeliness, well-suitedness **2.** aptitude, bent, disposition, inclination, leaning, liability, likelihood, likeliness, predilection, proclivity, proneness, propensity, readiness, tendency **3.** ability, capability, capacity, cleverness, faculty, fitness, flair, gift, giftedness, intelligence, knack, proficiency, quickness, suitability, talent

arable cultivable, farmable, fecund, fertile, fruitful, ploughable, productive, tillable

arbiter 1. adjudicator, arbitrator, judge, referee, umpire **2.** authority, controller, dictator, expert, governor, lord, master, pundit, ruler

arbitrariness 1. capriciousness, fancifulness, inconsistency, randomness, subjectivity, unreasonableness, whimsicality, wilfulness **2.** absoluteness, despotism, dictatorialness, dogmatism, domineeringness, high-handedness, imperiousness, magisterialness, overbearingness, peremptoriness, summariness, tyrannicalness, tyrannousness, tyranny, uncontrolledness, unlimitedness, unrestrainedness

arbitrary 1. capricious, chance, discretionary, erratic, fanciful, inconsistent, optional, personal, random, subjective, unreasonable, whimsical, wilful **2.** absolute, autocratic, despotic, dictatorial, dogmatic, domineering, high-handed, imperious, magisterial, overbearing, peremptory, summary, tyrannical, tyrannous, uncontrolled, unlimited, unrestrained

arbitrate adjudge, adjudicate, decide, determine, judge, pass judgment, referee, settle, sit in judgment, umpire

arbitration adjudication, arbitrament, decision, determination, judgment, settlement

arbitrator adjudicator, arbiter, judge, referee, umpire

arc arch, bend, bow, crescent, curve, half-moon

arcane cabbalistic, esoteric, hidden, mysterious, occult, recondite, secret

arch¹ *n.* **1.** archway, curve, dome, span, vault **2.** arc, bend, bow, curvature, curve, semicircle ~*v.* **3.** arc, bend, bow, bridge, curve, embow, span

arch² 1. accomplished, chief, consummate, expert, finished, first, foremost, greatest, highest, leading, main, major, master, pre-eminent, primary, principal, top **2.** artful, frolicsome, knowing, mischievous, pert, playful, roguish, saucy, sly, waggish, wily

archaic ancient, antiquated, antique, behind the times, bygone, obsolete, old, olden (*Archaic*), old-fashioned, old hat, outmoded, out of date, passé, primitive, superannuated

arched curved, domed, embowed, vaulted

archer bowman (*Archaic*), toxophilite (*Formal*)

archetype classic, exemplar, form, ideal, model, original, paradigm, pattern, prime example, prototype, standard

architect 1. designer, master builder, planner **2.** author, contriver, creator, deviser, engineer, founder, instigator, inventor, maker, originator, planner, prime mover, shaper

architecture 1. architectonics, building, construction, design, planning **2.** construction, design, framework, makeup, structure, style

archives 1. annals, chronicles, documents, papers, records, registers, rolls **2.** museum, record office, registry, repository

arctic 1. far-northern, hyperborean, polar **2.** *Inf.* chilly, cold, freezing, frigid, frost-bound, frosty, frozen, gelid, glacial, icy

ardent avid, eager, enthusiastic, fervent, fervid, fierce, fiery, hot, hot-blooded, impassioned, intense, keen, lusty, passionate, spirited, vehement, warm, warm-blooded, zealous

ardour avidity, devotion, eagerness, earnestness, enthusiasm, feeling, fervour, fierceness, fire, heat, intensity, keenness, passion, spirit, vehemence, warmth, zeal

arduous backbreaking, burdensome, difficult, exhausting, fatiguing, formidable, gruelling, hard, harsh, heavy, laborious, onerous, painful, punishing, rigorous, severe, steep, strenuous, taxing, tiring, toilsome, tough, troublesome, trying

area 1. district, domain, locality, neighbourhood, patch, plot, realm, region, sector, sphere, stretch, territory, tract, zone **2.** breadth, compass, expanse, extent, range, scope, size, width **3.** arena, department, domain, field, province, realm, sphere, territory **4.** part, portion, section, sector **5.** sunken space, yard

arena 1. amphitheatre, bowl, coliseum, field, ground, park (*Inf.*), ring, stadium, stage **2.** area, battlefield, battleground, domain, field, field of conflict, lists, province, realm, scene, scope, sector, sphere, territory, theatre

argot cant, dialect, idiom, jargon, lingo (*Inf.*), parlance, patois, slang, vernacular

argue 1. altercate, bandy words, bicker, disagree, dispute, fall out (*Inf.*), feud, fight, have an argument, quarrel, squabble, wrangle **2.** assert, claim, contend, controvert, debate, discuss, dispute, expostulate, hold, maintain, plead, question, reason, remonstrate **3.** convince, persuade, prevail upon, talk into, talk round **4.** demonstrate, denote, display, evince, exhibit, imply, indicate, manifest, point to, show, suggest

argument 1. altercation, barney (*Inf.*), bickering, clash, controversy, difference of opinion, disagreement, dispute, falling out (*Inf.*), feud, fight, quarrel, row, squabble, wrangle **2.** assertion, claim, contention, debate, discussion, dispute, expostulation, plea, pleading, questioning, remonstrance, remonstration **3.** argumentation, case, defence, dialectic, ground(s), line of reasoning, logic, polemic, reason, reasoning **4.** abstract, gist, outline, plot, story, story line, subject, summary, synopsis, theme

argumentative 1. belligerent, combative, contentious, contrary, disputatious, litigious, opinionated, quarrelsome **2.** contentious, controversial, disputed

arid 1. barren, desert, dried up, dry, moistureless, parched, sterile, waterless **2.** boring, colourless, dreary, dry, dull, flat, jejune, lifeless, spiritless, tedious, uninspired, uninteresting, vapid

aridity, aridness 1. barrenness, dryness, moisturelessness, parchedness, sterility, waterlessness **2.** boredom, colourlessness, dreariness, dryness, dullness, flatness, jejuneness, jejunity, lifelessness, spiritlessness, tediousness, tedium, uninspiredness, uninterestingness, vapidity, vapidness

aright accurately, appropriately, aptly, correctly, duly, exactly, fitly, in due order, justly, properly, rightly, suitably, truly, without error

arise 1. appear, begin, come into being, come to light, commence, crop up (*Inf.*), emanate, emerge, ensue, follow, happen, issue, occur, originate, proceed, result, set in, spring, start, stem **2.** get to one's feet, get up, go up, rise, stand up, wake up **3.** ascend, climb, lift, mount, move upward, rise, soar, tower

aristocracy body of nobles, elite, gentry, *haut monde*, nobility, noblesse (*Literary*), patricians, patriciate, peerage, ruling class, upper class, upper crust (*Inf.*)

aristocrat grandee, lady, lord, noble, nobleman, noblewoman, patrician, peer, peeress

aristocratic 1. blue-blooded, elite, gentle (*Archaic*), gentlemanly, highborn, lordly, noble, patrician, titled, upper-class, well-born **2.** courtly, dignified, elegant, fine, haughty, polished, refined, snobbish, stylish, well-bred

arm[1] *n.* **1.** appendage, limb, upper limb **2.** bough, branch, department, detachment, division, extension, offshoot, projection, section, sector **3.** branch, channel, estuary, firth, inlet, sound, strait, tributary **4.** authority, command, force, might, potency, power, strength, sway

arm[2] *v.* **1.** *Esp. with weapons* accoutre, array, deck out, equip, furnish, issue with, outfit, provide, rig, supply **2.** mobilize, muster forces, prepare for war, take up arms **3.** brace, equip, forearm, fortify, gird one's loins, guard, make ready, outfit, prepare, prime, protect, strengthen

armada fleet, flotilla, navy, squadron

armaments ammunition, arms, guns, materiel, munitions, ordnance, weaponry, weapons

armed accoutred, arrayed, carrying weapons, equipped, fitted out, forearmed, fortified, furnished, girded, guarded, in arms, prepared, primed, protected; provided, ready, rigged out, strengthened, supplied, under arms

armistice ceasefire, peace, suspension of hostilities, truce

armour armour plate, covering, protection, sheathing, shield

armoured armour-plated, bombproof, bulletproof, ironclad, mailed, protected, steel-plated

armoury ammunition dump, arms depot, arsenal, magazine, ordnance depot

arms 1. armaments, firearms, guns, instruments of war, ordnance, weaponry, weapons **2.** blazonry, crest, escutcheon, heraldry, insignia

army 1. armed force, host (*Archaic*), land forces, legions, military, military force, soldiers, soldiery, troops **2.** *Fig.* array, horde, host, multitude, pack, swarm, throng, vast number

aroma bouquet, fragrance, odour, perfume, redolence, savour, scent, smell

aromatic balmy, fragrant, odoriferous, perfumed, pungent, redolent, savoury, spicy, sweet-scented, sweet-smelling

around *prep.* **1.** about, encircling, enclosing, encompassing, environing, on all sides of, on every side of, surrounding **2.** about, approximately, circa (*used with dates*), roughly ~*adv.* **3.** about, all over, everywhere, here and there, in all directions, on all sides, throughout, to and fro **4.** at hand, close, close at hand, close by, near, nearby, nigh (*Archaic or dialect*)

arouse agitate, animate, awaken, call forth, enliven, excite, foment, foster, goad, incite, inflame, instigate, kindle, move, provoke, quicken, rouse, sharpen, spark, spur, stimulate, stir up, summon up, waken, wake up, warm, whet, whip up

arraign accuse, call to account, charge, complain about, denounce, impeach, incriminate, indict, prosecute, take to task

arraignment accusation, charge, complaint, denunciation, impeachment, incrimination, indictment, prosecution

arrange 1. align, array, class, classify, dispose, file, form, group, line up, marshal, order, organize, position, put in order, range, rank, set out, sort, sort out (*Inf.*), systematize, tidy **2.** adjust, agree to, come to terms, compromise, construct, contrive, determine, devise, fix up (*Inf.*), organize, plan, prepare, project, schedule, settle **3.** adapt, instrument, orchestrate, score

arrangement 1. alignment, array, classification, design, display, disposition, form, grouping, line-up, marshalling, order, ordering, organization, ranging, rank, setup (*Inf.*), structure, system **2.** *Often plural* adjustment, agreement, compact, compromise, construction, deal, devising, organization, plan, planning, preparation, provision, schedule, settlement, terms **3.** adaptation, instrumentation, interpretation, orchestration, score, version

arrant absolute, atrocious, blatant, complete, downright, egregious, extreme, flagrant, gross, infamous, monstrous, notorious, out-and-out, outright, rank, thorough, thoroughgoing, undisguised, unmitigated, utter, vile

array *n.* **1.** arrangement, collection, display, disposition, exhibition, formation, line-up, marshalling, muster, order, parade, show, supply **2.** *Poetic* apparel, attire, clothes, dress, finery, garb, garments, raiment (*Archaic*), regalia ~*v*. **3**. align, arrange, display, dispose, draw up, exhibit, form up, group, line up, marshal, muster, order, parade, place in order, range, set in line (*Military*), show **4**. accoutre, adorn, apparel (*Archaic*), attire, bedeck, caparison, clothe, deck, decorate, dress, equip, fit out, garb, outfit, robe, supply, wrap

arrest *v*. **1**. apprehend, bust (*Inf.*), capture, catch, collar (*Inf.*), detain, lay hold of, nab (*Inf.*), nick (*Sl.*), pinch (*Inf.*), run in (*Sl.*), seize, take, take into custody, take prisoner **2**. block, check, delay, end, halt, hinder, hold, inhibit, interrupt, obstruct, restrain, retard, slow, stall, stay, stop, suppress **3**. absorb, catch, engage, engross, fascinate, grip, hold, intrigue, occupy ~*n*. **4**. apprehension, bust (*Inf.*), capture, cop (*Sl.*), detention, seizure **5**. blockage, check, delay, end, halt, hindrance, inhibition, interruption, obstruction, restraint, stalling, stay, stoppage, suppression

arresting conspicuous, engaging, extraordinary, impressive, noticeable, outstanding, remarkable, striking, stunning, surprising

arrival **1**. advent, appearance, arriving, coming, entrance, happening, occurrence, taking place **2**. arriver, caller, comer, entrant, incomer, newcomer, visitant, visitor

arrive **1**. appear, attain, befall, come, enter, get to, happen, occur, reach, show up (*Inf.*), take place, turn up **2**. *Inf.* achieve recognition, become famous, make good, make it (*Inf.*), make the grade (*Inf.*), reach the top, succeed

arrogance bluster, conceit, conceitedness, contemptuousness, disdainfulness, haughtiness, hauteur, high-handedness, imperiousness, insolence, loftiness, lordliness, overweeningness, pomposity, pompousness, presumption, pretension, pretentiousness, pride, scornfulness, superciliousness, swagger, uppishness (*Brit. inf.*)

arrogant assuming, blustering, conceited, contemptuous, disdainful, haughty, high and mighty (*Inf.*), high-handed, imperious, insolent, lordly, overbearing, overweening, pompous, presumptuous, pretentious, proud, scornful, supercilious, swaggering, uppish (*Brit. inf.*)

arrogate appropriate, assume, claim

unduly, commandeer, demand, expropriate, presume, seize, usurp

arrogation appropriation, assumption, commandeering, demand, expropriation, presumption, seizure, usurpation

arrow **1**. bolt, dart, flight, quarrel, reed (*Archaic*), shaft (*Archaic*) **2**. indicator, pointer

arsenal ammunition dump, armoury, arms depot, magazine, ordnance depot, stock, stockpile, store, storehouse, supply

art **1**. adroitness, aptitude, artifice (*Archaic*), artistry, craft, craftsmanship, dexterity, expertise, facility, ingenuity, knack, knowledge, mastery, method, profession, skill, trade, virtuosity **2**. artfulness, artifice, astuteness, craftiness, cunning, deceit, duplicity, guile, trickery, wiliness

artful adept, adroit, clever, crafty, cunning, deceitful, designing, dexterous, foxy, ingenious, intriguing, masterly, politic, proficient, resourceful, scheming, sharp, shrewd, skilful, sly, smart, subtle, tricky, wily

article **1**. commodity, item, object, piece, substance, thing, unit **2**. composition, discourse, essay, feature, item, paper, piece, story, treatise **3**. branch, clause, count, detail, division, head, heading, item, matter, paragraph, part, particular, passage, piece, point, portion, section

articulate *adj.* **1**. clear, coherent, comprehensible, eloquent, expressive, fluent, intelligible, lucid, meaningful, understandable, vocal, well-spoken ~*v*. **2**. enounce, enunciate, express, pronounce, say, speak, state, talk, utter, verbalize, vocalize, voice **3**. connect, couple, fit together, hinge, join, joint

articulation **1**. delivery, diction, enunciation, expression, pronunciation, saying, speaking, statement, talking, utterance, verbalization, vocalization, voicing **2**. connection, coupling, hinge, joint, jointing, juncture

artifice **1**. contrivance, device, dodge, expedient, hoax, machination, manoeuvre, ruse, stratagem, subterfuge, tactic, trick, wile **2**. artfulness, chicanery, craft, craftiness, cunning, deception, duplicity, guile, scheming, slyness, trickery **3**. adroitness, cleverness, deftness, facility, finesse, ingenuity, invention, inventiveness, skill

artificer 1. artisan, craftsman, mechanic **2.** architect, builder, contriver, creator, designer, deviser, inventor, maker, originator

artificial 1. man-made, manufactured, non-natural, plastic, synthetic **2.** bogus, counterfeit, ersatz, fake, imitation, mock, phoney (*Inf.*), sham, simulated, specious, spurious **3.** affected, assumed, contrived, false, feigned, forced, hollow, insincere, meretricious, phoney (*Inf.*), pretended, spurious, unnatural

artillery battery, big guns, cannon, cannonry, gunnery, ordnance

artisan artificer, craftsman, handicraftsman, journeyman, mechanic, skilled workman, technician

artistic aesthetic, beautiful, creative, cultivated, cultured, decorative, elegant, exquisite, graceful, imaginative, ornamental, refined, sensitive, stylish, tasteful

artistry accomplishment, art, artistic ability, brilliance, craftsmanship, creativity, finesse, flair, genius, mastery, proficiency, sensibility, skill, style, talent, taste, touch, virtuosity, workmanship

artless 1. candid, direct, fair, frank, genuine, guileless, honest, open, plain, sincere, straightforward, true, undesigning **2.** humble, natural, plain, pure, simple, unadorned, unaffected, uncontrived, unpretentious **3.** awkward, bungling, clumsy, crude, incompetent, inept, maladroit, primitive, rude, unskilled, untalented **4.** childlike, ingenuous, innocent, jejune, naive, trustful, trusting, unsophisticated

as *conj.* **1.** at the time that, during the time that, just as, when, while **2.** in the manner that, in the way that, like **3.** that which, what **4.** because, considering that, seeing that, since **5.** in the same manner with, in the same way that, like **6.** for instance, like, such as ~*prep.* **7.** being, in the character of, in the role of, under the name of **8. as for** as regards, in reference to, on the subject of, with reference to, with regard to, with respect to **9. as it were** in a manner of speaking, in a way, so to say, so to speak

ascend climb, float up, fly up, go up, lift off, mount, move up, rise, scale, slope upwards, soar, take off, tower

ascendancy, ascendency authority, command, control, dominance, domination, dominion, hegemony, influence, mastery, power, predominance, preeminence, prevalence, reign, rule, sovereignty, superiority, supremacy, sway, upper hand

ascendant, ascendent *adj.* **1.** ascending, climbing, going upwards, mounting, rising **2.** authoritative, commanding, controlling, dominant, influential, powerful, predominant, preeminent, prevailing, ruling, superior, supreme, uppermost ~*n.* **3. in the ascendant** ascending, climbing, commanding, dominant, dominating, flourishing, growing, increasing, mounting, on the rise, on the way up, prevailing, rising, supreme, up-and-coming, uppermost, winning

ascension ascent, climb, mounting, moving upwards, rise, rising

ascent 1. ascending, ascension, clambering, climb, climbing, mounting, rise, rising, scaling, upward movement **2.** acclivity, gradient, incline, ramp, rise, rising ground, upward slope

ascertain confirm, determine, discover, establish, ferret out, find out, fix, identify, learn, make certain, settle, verify

ascetic 1. *n.* abstainer, anchorite, hermit, monk, nun, recluse, self-denier **2.** *adj.* abstemious, abstinent, austere, celibate, frugal, harsh, plain, puritanical, rigorous, self-denying, self-disciplined, severe, Spartan, stern

asceticism abstemiousness, abstinence, austerity, celibacy, frugality, harshness, mortification of the flesh, plainness, puritanism, rigorousness, rigour, self-abnegation, self-denial, self-discipline, self-mortification

ascribe assign, attribute, charge, credit, impute, put down, refer, set down

ashamed abashed, bashful, blushing, chagrined, conscience-stricken, crestfallen, discomfited, distressed, embarrassed, guilty, humbled, humiliated, mortified, prudish, reluctant, remorseful, shamefaced, sheepish, shy, sorry

ashen anaemic, ashy, colourless, grey, leaden, livid, pale, pallid, pasty, wan, white

ashore aground, landwards, on dry land, on land, on the beach, on the shore, shorewards, to the shore

aside 1. *adv.* alone, alongside, apart,

away, beside, in isolation, in reserve, on one side, out of mind, out of the way, privately, separately, to one side, to the side **2**. *n*. departure, digression, excursion, excursus, interpolation, interposition, parenthesis, tangent

asinine brainless, daft (*Inf.*), dunderheaded, fatuous, foolish, gormless (*Inf.*), halfwitted, idiotic, imbecile, imbecilic, inane, moronic, obstinate, senseless, silly, stupid, thickheaded, thick-witted

ask 1. inquire, interrogate, query, question, quiz **2**. appeal, apply, beg, beseech, claim, crave, demand, entreat, implore, petition, plead, pray, request, seek, solicit, sue, supplicate **3**. bid, invite, summon

askance 1. awry, indirectly, obliquely, out of the corner of one's eye, sideways, with a side glance **2**. disapprovingly, distrustfully, doubtfully, dubiously, mistrustfully, sceptically, suspiciously

askew *adv./adj*. aslant, awry, cock-eyed (*Inf.*), crooked, crookedly, lopsided, oblique, obliquely, off-centre, to one side

asleep crashed out (*Sl.*), dead to the world (*Inf.*), dormant, dozing, fast asleep, napping, sleeping, slumbering, snoozing (*Inf.*), sound asleep

aspect 1. air, appearance, attitude, bearing, condition, countenance, demeanour, expression, look, manner, mien (*Literary*) **2**. bearing, direction, exposure, outlook, point of view, position, prospect, scene, situation, view **3**. angle, facet, feature, side

asperity acerbity, acrimony, bitterness, churlishness, crabbedness, crossness, harshness, irascibility, irritability, moroseness, peevishness, roughness, ruggedness, severity, sharpness, sourness, sullenness

asperse abuse, calumniate, cast aspersions (on), defame, detract, disparage, reproach, slander, slur, smear, traduce, vilify, vituperate

aspersion abuse, calumny, censure, defamation, detraction, disparagement, obloquy, reproach, slander, slur, smear, traducement, vilification, vituperation

asphyxiate choke, smother, stifle, strangle, strangulate, suffocate, throttle

aspirant 1. *n*. applicant, aspirer, candidate, hopeful, postulant, seeker, suitor **2**. *adj*. ambitious, aspiring, eager, endeavouring, hopeful, longing, striving, wishful

aspiration aim, ambition, craving, desire, dream, eagerness, endeavour, goal, hankering, hope, longing, object, objective, wish, yearning

aspire aim, be ambitious, be eager, crave, desire, dream, hanker, hope, long, pursue, seek, wish, yearn

aspiring *adj*. ambitious, aspirant, eager, endeavouring, hopeful, longing, striving, wishful, would-be

ass 1. donkey, jennet, moke (*Sl.*) **2**. blockhead, bonehead (*Sl.*), dolt, dope (*Sl.*), dunce, fool, halfwit, idiot, jackass, nincompoop, ninny, nitwit, numskull, simpleton, twerp (*Inf.*), twit (*Inf.*)

assail 1. assault, attack, beset, charge, encounter, fall upon, invade, lay into, maltreat, set about, set upon **2**. abuse, berate, criticize, impugn, malign, revile, vilify

assailant aggressor, assailer, assaulter, attacker, invader

assassin eliminator (*Sl.*), executioner, hatchet man (*Sl.*), hit man (*Sl.*), killer, liquidator, murderer, slayer

assassinate eliminate (*Sl.*), hit (*U.S. sl.*), kill, liquidate, murder, slay

assault 1. *n*. aggression, attack, charge, incursion, invasion, offensive, onset, onslaught, storm, storming, strike **2**. *v*. assail, attack, beset, charge, fall upon, invade, lay into, set about, set upon, storm, strike at

assay *v*. **1**. analyse, appraise, assess, evaluate, examine, inspect, investigate, prove, test, try, weigh ~*n*. **2**. *Archaic* attempt, endeavour, essay, try, venture **3**. analysis, examination, inspection, investigation, test, trial

assemblage accumulation, aggregation, assembly, body, collection, company, conclave, congregation, convocation, crowd, flock, gathering, group, mass, meeting, multitude, rally, throng

assemble 1. accumulate, amass, bring together, call together, collect, come together, congregate, convene, convoke, flock, forgather, gather, marshal, meet, muster, rally, round up, summon **2**. build up, connect, construct, erect, fabricate, fit together, join, make, manufacture, piece together, put together, set up

assembly 1. accumulation, aggregation, assemblage, body, collection, company, conclave, conference, congregation, convocation, council, crowd, diet, flock, gathering, group, mass, meeting,

multitude, rally, synod, throng **2.** building up, connecting, construction, erection, fabrication, fitting together, joining, manufacture, piecing together, putting together, setting up
assent 1. *v.* accede, accept, acquiesce, agree, allow, approve, comply, concur, consent, fall in with, go along with, grant, permit, sanction, subscribe **2.** *n.* acceptance, accession, accord, acquiescence, agreement, approval, compliance, concurrence, consent, permission, sanction
assert 1. affirm, allege, asseverate, attest, aver, avouch (*Archaic*), avow, contend, declare, maintain, predicate, profess, pronounce, state, swear **2.** claim, defend, insist upon, press, put forward, stand up for, stress, uphold, vindicate **3.** **assert oneself** exert one's influence, make one's presence felt, put oneself forward
assertion 1. affirmation, allegation, asseveration, attestation, avowal, contention, declaration, predication, profession, pronouncement, statement **2.** defence, insistence, maintenance, stressing, vindication
assertive aggressive, confident, decided, decisive, demanding, dogmatic, domineering, emphatic, firm, forceful, forward, insistent, overbearing, positive, pushy (*Inf.*), self-assured, strong-willed
assess 1. appraise, compute, determine, estimate, evaluate, fix, gauge, judge, rate, size up (*Inf.*), value, weigh **2.** demand, evaluate, fix, impose, levy, rate, tax, value
assessment 1. appraisal, computation, determination, estimate, estimation, evaluation, judgment, rating, valuation **2.** charge, demand, duty, evaluation, fee, impost, levy, rate, rating, tariff, tax, taxation, toll, valuation
asset 1. advantage, aid, benefit, blessing, boon, help, resource, service **2.** *Plural* capital, estate, funds, goods, holdings, means, money, possessions, property, reserves, resources, valuables, wealth
asseverate affirm, assert, attest, aver, avouch (*Archaic*), avow, declare, maintain, predicate, profess, pronounce, protest, state, swear
asseveration affirmation, assertion, attestation, averment, avowal, declaration, predication, profession, pronouncement, protestation, statement, vow
assiduity application, assiduousness,

attentiveness, constancy, diligence, indefatigability, industriousness, industry, laboriousness, perseverance, persistence, sedulity, sedulousness, steadiness, studiousness, tirelessness
assiduous attentive, constant, diligent, hard-working, indefatigable, industrious, laborious, persevering, persistent, sedulous, steady, studious, unflagging, untiring, unwearied
assign 1. appoint, choose, delegate, designate, name, nominate, select **2.** allocate, allot, apportion, consign, distribute, give, give out, grant, make over **3.** appoint, appropriate, determine, fix, set apart, stipulate **4.** accredit, ascribe, attribute, put down
assignation 1. clandestine meeting, illicit meeting, rendezvous, secret meeting, tryst (*Archaic*) **2.** allocation, allotment, appointment, apportionment, appropriation, ascription, assignment, attribution, choice, consignment, delegation, designation, determination, distribution, giving, grant, nomination, selection, specification, stipulation
assignment 1. appointment, charge, commission, duty, job, mission, position, post, responsibility, task **2.** allocation, allotment, appointment, apportionment, appropriation, ascription, assignation (*Law, chiefly Scot.*), attribution, choice, consignment, delegation, designation, determination, distribution, giving, grant, nomination, selection, specification, stipulation
assimilate 1. absorb, digest, imbibe (*Literary*), incorporate, ingest, learn, take in **2.** acclimatize, accommodate, acculturate, accustom, adapt, adjust, become like, become similar, blend in, conform, fit, homogenize, intermix, mingle
assist abet, aid, back, benefit, boost, collaborate, cooperate, expedite, facilitate, further, help, reinforce, relieve, second, serve, succour, support, sustain, work for, work with
assistance abetment, aid, backing, benefit, boost, collaboration, cooperation, furtherance, help, helping hand, reinforcement, relief, service, succour, support, sustenance
assistant abettor, accessory, accomplice, aide, aider, ally, associate, auxiliary, backer, coadjutor (*Rare*), collaborator, colleague, confederate, cooperator, helper, helpmate, henchman, partner,

right-hand man, second, supporter

associate v. **1.** affiliate, ally, combine, confederate, conjoin, connect, correlate, couple, identify, join, league, link, lump together, mix, pair, relate, think of together, unite, yoke **2.** accompany, befriend, be friends, consort, fraternize, hang about, hang out (*Inf.*), hobnob, mingle, mix, run around (*Inf.*) ~n. **3.** ally, collaborator, colleague, companion, compeer, comrade, confederate, confrère, co-worker, follower, friend, mate, partner

association 1. affiliation, alliance, band, clique, club, coalition, combine, company, confederacy, confederation, cooperative, corporation, federation, fraternity, group, league, organization, partnership, society, syndicate, union **2.** companionship, comradeship, familiarity, fellowship, fraternization, friendship, intimacy, partnership, relations, relationship **3.** blend, bond, combination, concomitance, connection, correlation, identification, joining, juxtaposition, linkage, linking, lumping together, mixing, mixture, pairing, relation, tie, union, yoking

assort arrange, array, categorize, classify, dispose, distribute, file, grade, group, range, rank, sort, type

assorted 1. different, diverse, diversified, heterogeneous, miscellaneous, mixed, motley, sundry, varied, variegated, various **2.** arranged, arrayed, categorized, classified, disposed, filed, graded, grouped, ranged, ranked, sorted, typed

assortment 1. array, choice, collection, diversity, farrago, hotchpotch, jumble, medley, *mélange,* miscellany, mishmash, mixed bag (*Inf.*), mixture, potpourri, salmagundi, selection, variety **2.** arrangement, categorizing, classification, disposition, distribution, filing, grading, grouping, ranging, ranking, sorting, typing

assuage allay, alleviate, appease, calm, ease, lessen, lighten, lull, mitigate, moderate, mollify, pacify, palliate, quench, quiet, relieve, satisfy, soften, soothe, still, temper, tranquillize

assume 1. accept, believe, expect, fancy, guess (*Inf., chiefly U.S.*), imagine, infer, presume, presuppose, suppose, surmise, suspect, take for granted, think **2.** adopt, affect, counterfeit, feign, imitate, impersonate, mimic, pretend to, put on,

sham, simulate **3.** accept, acquire, attend to, begin, don, embark upon, embrace, enter upon, put on, set about, shoulder, take on, take over, take responsibility for, take up, undertake **4.** acquire, appropriate, arrogate, commandeer, expropriate, pre-empt, seize, take, take over, usurp

assumed 1. affected, bogus, counterfeit, fake, false, feigned, fictitious, imitation, made-up, make-believe, phoney (*Inf.*), pretended, pseudonymous, sham, simulated, spurious **2.** accepted, expected, hypothetical, presumed, presupposed, supposed, surmised, taken for granted **3.** appropriated, arrogated, pre-empted, seized, usurped

assuming adj. arrogant, bold, conceited, disdainful, domineering, egotistic, forward, haughty, imperious, overbearing, presumptuous, pushy (*Inf.*), rude

assumption 1. acceptance, belief, conjecture, expectation, fancy, guess, hypothesis, inference, postulate, postulation, premise, premiss, presumption, presupposition, supposition, surmise, suspicion, theory **2.** acceptance, acquisition, adoption, embracing, entering upon, putting on, shouldering, takeover, taking on, taking up, undertaking **3.** acquisition, appropriation, arrogation, expropriation, pre-empting, seizure, takeover, taking, usurpation **4.** arrogance, conceit, imperiousness, presumption, pride, self-importance

assurance 1. affirmation, assertion, declaration, guarantee, oath, pledge, profession, promise, protestation, vow, word, word of honour **2.** aggressiveness, assuredness, boldness, certainty, certitude, confidence, conviction, coolness, courage, faith, firmness, nerve, poise, positiveness, security, self-confidence, self-reliance, sureness **3.** arrogance, effrontery, gall (*Inf.*), impudence, nerve (*Inf.*), presumption

assure 1. comfort, convince, embolden, encourage, hearten, persuade, reassure, soothe **2.** affirm, attest, certify, confirm, declare confidently, give one's word to, guarantee, pledge, promise, swear, vow **3.** clinch, complete, confirm, ensure, guarantee, make certain, make sure, seal, secure

assured 1. beyond doubt, clinched, confirmed, dependable, ensured, fixed, guaranteed, indubitable, irrefutable, made certain, sealed, secure, settled, sure, unquestionable 2. assertive, audacious, bold, brazen, certain, complacent, confident, overconfident, poised, positive, pushy (*Inf.*), self-assured, self-confident, self-possessed, sure of oneself

astir active, afoot, awake, in motion, on the go (*Inf.*), on the move (*Inf.*), out of bed, roused, up and about, up and around

astonish amaze, astound, bewilder, confound, daze, dumbfound, flabbergast (*Inf.*), stagger, stun, stupefy, surprise

astonishing amazing, astounding, bewildering, breathtaking, impressive, staggering, striking, stunning, stupefying, surprising

astonishment amazement, awe, bewilderment, confusion, consternation, stupefaction, surprise, wonder, wonderment

astound amaze, astonish, bewilder, confound, daze, dumbfound, flabbergast (*Inf.*), overwhelm, stagger, stun, stupefy, surprise

astounding amazing, astonishing, bewildering, breathtaking, impressive, staggering, striking, stunning, stupefying, surprising

astray *adj./adv.* 1. adrift, afield, amiss, lost, off, off course, off the mark, off the right track, off the subject 2. into error, into sin, to the bad, wrong

astringent 1. acerbic, austere, caustic, exacting, grim, hard, harsh, rigid, rigorous, severe, stern, strict, stringent 2. contractile, contractive, styptic

astronaut cosmonaut, spaceman, space pilot, space traveller, spacewoman

astute adroit, artful, bright, calculating, canny, clever, crafty, cunning, discerning, foxy, insightful, intelligent, keen, knowing, penetrating, perceptive, politic, sagacious, sharp, shrewd, sly, subtle, wily

astuteness acumen, adroitness, artfulness, brightness, canniness, cleverness, craftiness, cunning, discernment, foxiness, insight, intelligence, keenness, knowledge, penetration, perceptiveness, sagacity, sharpness, shrewdness, slyness, subtlety, wiliness

asunder *adv./adj.* apart, in pieces, into pieces, rent, to bits, to pieces, torn, to shreds

asylum 1. harbour, haven, preserve, refuge, retreat, safety, sanctuary, shelter

2. *Old-fashioned* funny farm (*Sl.*), hospital, institution, loony bin (*Sl.*), madhouse (*Inf.*), mental hospital, nuthouse (*Sl.*), psychiatric hospital

atheism disbelief, freethinking, godlessness, heathenism, infidelity, irreligion, nonbelief, paganism, scepticism, unbelief

atheist disbeliever, freethinker, heathen, infidel, irreligionist, nonbeliever, pagan, sceptic, unbeliever

athlete competitor, contender, contestant, games player, gymnast, player, runner, sportsman, sportswoman

athletic 1. *adj.* able-bodied, active, brawny, energetic, fit, herculean, husky (*Inf.*), lusty, muscular, powerful, robust, sinewy, strapping, strong, sturdy, vigorous, well-proportioned 2. *pl. n.* contests, exercises, games of strength, gymnastics, races, sports, track and field events

atmosphere 1. aerosphere, air, heavens, sky 2. air, ambience, aura, character, climate, environment, feel, feeling, flavour, mood, quality, spirit, surroundings, tone

atom bit, crumb, dot, fragment, grain, iota, jot, mite, molecule, morsel, mote, particle, scintilla (*Rare*), scrap, shred, speck, spot, tittle, trace, whit

atone 1. *With* **for** answer for, compensate, do penance for, make amends for, make redress, make reparation for, make up for, pay for, recompense, redress 2. appease, expiate, make expiation for, propitiate, reconcile, redeem

atonement amends, compensation, expiation, payment, penance, propitiation, recompense, redress, reparation, restitution, satisfaction

atrocious 1. barbaric, brutal, cruel, diabolical, fiendish, flagrant, heinous, infamous, infernal, inhuman, monstrous, nefarious, ruthless, savage, vicious, villainous, wicked 2. appalling, detestable, execrable, grievous, horrible, horrifying, shocking, terrible

atrocity 1. abomination, act of savagery, barbarity, brutality, crime, cruelty, enormity, evil, horror, monstrosity, outrage, villainy 2. atrociousness, barbarity, barbarousness, brutality, cruelty, enormity, fiendishness, grievousness, heinousness, horror, infamy, inhumanity, monstrousness, nefariousness, ruthlessness, savagery, shockingness, viciousness, villainousness, wickedness

atrophy 1. *n.* decay, decaying, decline, degeneration, deterioration, diminution, shrivelling, wasting, wasting away, withering **2.** *v.* decay, decline, degenerate, deteriorate, diminish, dwindle, fade, shrink, shrivel, waste, waste away, wilt, wither

attach 1. add, adhere, affix, annex, append, bind, connect, couple, fasten, fix, join, link, make fast, secure, stick, subjoin, tie, unite **2.** accompany, affiliate, associate, become associated with, combine, enlist, join, join forces with, latch on to, sign on with, sign up with, unite with **3.** ascribe, assign, associate, attribute, connect, impute, invest with, lay, place, put **4.** allocate, allot, appoint, assign, consign, designate, detail, earmark, second, send

attached 1. affectionate towards, devoted, fond of, full of regard for, possessive **2.** accompanied, engaged, married, partnered, spoken for

attachment 1. adapter, bond, clamp, connection, connector, coupling, fastener, fastening, joint, junction, link, tie **2.** affection, affinity, attraction, bond, devotion, fidelity, fondness, friendship, liking, love, loyalty, partiality, possessiveness, predilection, regard, tenderness **3.** accessory, accoutrement, adapter, addition, adjunct, appendage, appurtenance, auxiliary, extension, extra, fitting, fixture, supplement, supplementary part

attack *n.* **1.** aggression, assault, charge, foray, incursion, inroad, invasion, offensive, onset, onslaught, raid, rush, strike **2.** abuse, blame, calumny, censure, criticism, denigration, impugnment, vilification **3.** access, bout, convulsion, fit, paroxysm, seizure, spasm, spell, stroke ~*v.* **4.** assail, assault, charge, fall upon, invade, lay into, raid, rush, set about, set upon, storm, strike (at) **5.** abuse, berate, blame, censure, criticize, impugn, malign, revile, vilify

attacker aggressor, assailant, assaulter, intruder, invader, raider

attain accomplish, achieve, acquire, arrive at, bring off, complete, earn, effect, fulfil, gain, get, grasp, obtain, procure, reach, realize, reap, secure, win

attainable accessible, accomplishable, achievable, at hand, feasible, gettable, graspable, likely, obtainable, possible, potential, practicable, probable, procurable, reachable, realizable, within reach

attainment 1. accomplishment, achievement, acquirement, acquisition, arrival at, completion, feat, fulfilment, gaining, getting, obtaining, procurement, reaching, realization, reaping, winning **2.** ability, accomplishment, achievement, art, capability, competence, gift, mastery, proficiency, skill, talent

attempt 1. *n.* assault, attack, bid, crack (*Inf.*), effort, endeavour, essay, experiment, go, shot (*Inf.*), trial, try, undertaking, venture **2.** *v.* endeavour, essay, experiment, have a crack (go, shot) (*Inf.*), seek, strive, tackle, take on, try, try one's hand at, undertake, venture

attend 1. appear, be at, be here, be present, be there, frequent, go to, haunt, make one (*Archaic*), put in an appearance, show oneself, show up (*Inf.*), turn up, visit **2.** care for, look after, mind, minister to, nurse, take care of, tend **3.** follow, hear, hearken (*Archaic*), heed, listen, look on, mark, mind, note, notice, observe, pay attention, pay heed, regard, take to heart, watch **4.** accompany, arise from, be associated with, be connected with, be consequent on, follow, go hand in hand with, issue from, occur with, result from **5.** *With* **to** apply oneself to, concentrate on, devote oneself to, get to work on, look after, occupy oneself with, see to, take care of **6.** accompany, chaperon, companion, convoy, escort, guard, squire, usher **7.** be in the service of, serve, wait upon, work for

attendance 1. appearance, attending, being there, presence **2.** audience, crowd, gate, house, number present, turnout

attendant 1. *n.* aide, assistant, auxiliary, chaperon, companion, custodian, escort, flunky, follower, guard, guide, helper, lackey, menial, servant, steward, underling, usher, waiter **2.** *adj.* accessory, accompanying, associated, concomitant, consequent, related

attention 1. concentration, consideration, contemplation, deliberation, heed, heedfulness, intentness, mind, scrutiny, thinking, thought, thoughtfulness **2.** awareness, consciousness, consideration, notice, observation, recognition, regard **3.** care, concern, looking after, ministration, treatment **4.** *Often plural* assiduities, care, civility, compliment, consideration, courtesy, deference, gallantry, mindfulness, politeness, regard, respect, service

attentive 1. alert, awake, careful, concentrating, heedful, intent, listening, mindful, observant, regardful, studious, watchful **2.** accommodating, civil, conscientious, considerate, courteous, devoted, gallant, gracious, kind, obliging, polite, respectful, thoughtful

attenuate v. **1.** adulterate, contract, decrease, devaluate, dilute, diminish, enervate, enfeeble, lessen, lower, reduce, sap, water down, weaken **2.** draw out, elongate, extend, lengthen, make fine, make slender, rarefy, refine, slim, spin out, stretch out, thin ~adj. also **attenuated 3.** adulterated, contracted, decreased, devalued, dilute, diluted, diminished, enervated, enfeebled, lessened, lowered, reduced, sapped, watered down, weakened **4.** drawn out, elongated, extended, lengthened, rarefied, refined, slender, slimmed, spun out, stretched out, thinned

attest adjure, affirm, assert, authenticate, aver, bear out, bear witness, certify, confirm, corroborate, declare, demonstrate, display, evince, exhibit, give evidence, invoke, manifest, prove, ratify, seal, show, substantiate, swear, testify, verify, vouch for, warrant, witness

attic[1] adj. chaste, classical, correct, elegant, graceful, polished, pure, refined, simple, tasteful

attic[2] n. garret, loft

attire 1. n. accoutrements, apparel, array (Poetic), clothes, clothing, costume, dress, garb, garments, gear (Sl.), habiliments, habit, outfit, raiment (Archaic), robes, uniform, vestment, wear **2.** v. accoutre, apparel (Archaic), array, clothe, costume, deck out, dress, equip, fit out, garb, rig out, robe, turn out

attitude 1. approach, disposition, frame of mind, mood, opinion, outlook, perspective, point of view, position, posture, stance, standing, view **2.** air, aspect, bearing, carriage, condition, demeanour, manner, mien (Literary), pose, position, posture, stance

attract allure, appeal to, bewitch, captivate, charm, decoy, draw, enchant, endear, engage, entice, fascinate, incline, induce, interest, invite, lure, pull (Inf.), tempt

attraction allure, appeal, attractiveness, bait, captivation, charm, come-on (Inf.), draw, enchantment, endearment, enticement, fascination, inducement, interest, invitation, lure, magnetism, pull (Inf.), temptation, temptingness

attractive agreeable, alluring, appealing, beautiful, captivating, charming, comely, engaging, enticing, fair, fascinating, fetching, good-looking, gorgeous, handsome, interesting, inviting, lovely, magnetic, pleasant, pleasing, prepossessing, pretty, seductive, tempting, winning, winsome

attribute 1. v. apply, ascribe, assign, blame, charge, credit, impute, lay at the door of, put down to, refer, set down to, trace to **2.** n. aspect, character, characteristic, facet, feature, idiosyncrasy, indication, mark, note, peculiarity, point, property, quality, quirk, sign, symbol, trait, virtue

attrition 1. abrasion, chafing, erosion, friction, grinding, rubbing, scraping, wear, wearing away, wearing down **2.** attenuation, debilitation, harassment, harrying, thinning out, weakening, wearing down

attune acclimatize, accord, accustom, adapt, adjust, coordinate, familiarize, harmonize, modulate, regulate, set, tune

auburn chestnut-coloured, copper-coloured, henna, nutbrown, reddish-brown, russet, rust-coloured, tawny, Titian red

au courant abreast of, acquainted, au fait, conversant, enlightened, in the know, in the swim, knowledgeable, up-to-date, well-informed, well up

audacious 1. adventurous, bold, brave, courageous, daredevil, daring, dauntless, death-defying, enterprising, fearless, intrepid, rash, reckless, risky, valiant, venturesome **2.** assuming, brazen, cheeky, defiant, disrespectful, forward, impertinent, impudent, insolent, pert, presumptuous, rude, shameless

audacity 1. adventurousness, audaciousness, boldness, bravery, courage, daring, dauntlessness, enterprise, fearlessness, guts (Sl.), intrepidity, nerve, rashness, recklessness, valour, venturesomeness **2.** audaciousness, brass neck (Inf.), cheek, defiance, disrespectfulness, effrontery, forwardness, gall (Inf.), impertinence, impudence, insolence, nerve, pertness, presumption, rudeness, shamelessness

audible clear, detectable, discernible, distinct, hearable, perceptible

audience 1. assemblage, assembly,

congregation, crowd, gallery, gathering, house, listeners, onlookers, spectators, turnout, viewers **2.** devotees, fans, following, market, public **3.** consultation, hearing, interview, meeting, reception

audit *Accounting* **1.** *n.* balancing, check, checking, examination, inspection, investigation, review, scrutiny, verification **2.** *v.* balance, check, examine, go over, go through, inspect, investigate, review, scrutinize, verify

au fait abreast of, *au courant,* clued up *(Sl.),* conversant, expert, familiar, fully informed, in the know, in touch, knowledgeable, on the ball *(Inf.),* well-acquainted, well up

augment add to, amplify, boost, build up, dilate, enhance, enlarge, expand, extend, grow, heighten, increase, inflate, intensify, magnify, multiply, raise, reinforce, strengthen, swell

augmentation accession, addition, amplification, boost, build-up, dilation, enhancement, enlargement, expansion, extension, growth, heightening, increase, inflation, intensification, magnification, multiplication, reinforcement, rise, strengthening, swelling

augur 1. *n.* auspex, diviner, haruspex, oracle, prophet, seer, soothsayer **2.** *v.* be an omen of, bespeak *(Archaic),* betoken, bode, foreshadow, harbinger, herald, portend, predict, prefigure, presage, promise, prophesy, signify

augury 1. divination, prediction, prophecy, soothsaying **2.** auspice, forerunner, forewarning, harbinger, herald, omen, portent, precursor, presage, prognostication, promise, prophecy, sign, token, warning

august dignified, exalted, glorious, grand, high-ranking, imposing, impressive, kingly, lofty, magnificent, majestic, monumental, noble, regal, solemn, stately, superb

aura air, ambience, aroma, atmosphere, emanation, feel, feeling, mood, odour, quality, scent, suggestion, tone, vibes *(Inf.),* vibrations *(Inf.)*

auspice *n.* **1.** *Usually plural* advocacy, aegis, authority, backing, care, championship, charge, control, countenance, guidance, influence, patronage, protection, sponsorship, supervision, support **2.** augury, indication, omen, portent, prognostication, prophecy, sign, token, warning

auspicious bright, encouraging, favourable, felicitous, fortunate, happy, hopeful, lucky, opportune, promising, propitious, prosperous, rosy, timely

austere 1. cold, exacting, forbidding, formal, grave, grim, hard, harsh, inflexible, rigorous, serious, severe, solemn, stern, stiff, strict, stringent, unfeeling, unrelenting **2.** abstemious, abstinent, ascetic, chaste, continent, economical, exacting, puritanical, rigid, self-denying, self-disciplined, sober, solemn, Spartan, strait-laced, strict, unrelenting **3.** bleak, economical, plain, severe, simple, spare, Spartan, stark, subdued, unadorned, unornamented

austerity 1. coldness, exactingness, forbiddingness, formality, gravity, grimness, hardness, harshness, inflexibility, rigour, seriousness, severity, solemnity, sternness, stiffness, strictness **2.** abstemiousness, abstinence, asceticism, chasteness, chastity, continence, economy, exactingness, puritanism, rigidity, self-denial, self-discipline, sobriety, solemnity, Spartanism, strictness **3.** economy, plainness, severity, simplicity, spareness, Spartanism, starkness

authentic accurate, actual, authoritative, bona fide, certain, dependable, factual, faithful, genuine, legitimate, original, pure, real, reliable, simon-pure *(Rare),* true, true-to-life, trustworthy, valid, veritable

authenticate attest, authorize, avouch, certify, confirm, endorse, guarantee, validate, verify, vouch for, warrant

authenticity accuracy, actuality, authoritativeness, certainty, dependability, factualness, faithfulness, genuineness, legitimacy, purity, realness, reliability, trustworthiness, truth, truthfulness, validity, veritableness, verity

author architect, composer, creator, designer, doer, fabricator, father, founder, framer, initiator, inventor, maker, mover, originator, parent, planner, prime mover, producer, writer

authoritarian 1. *adj.* absolute, autocratic, despotic, dictatorial, disciplinarian, doctrinaire, dogmatic, domineering, harsh, imperious, rigid, severe, strict, tyrannical, unyielding **2.** *n.* absolutist, autocrat, despot, dictator, disciplinarian, tyrant

authoritative 1. accurate, authentic,

definitive, dependable, factual, faithful, learned, reliable, scholarly, sound, true, trustworthy, truthful, valid, veritable **2.** assertive, autocratic, commanding, confident, decisive, dictatorial, dogmatic, dominating, imperative, imperious, imposing, lordly, masterly, peremptory, self-assured **3.** approved, authorized, commanding, legitimate, official, sanctioned, sovereign

authority 1. ascendancy, charge, command, control, domination, dominion, force, government, influence, jurisdiction, might, power, prerogative, right, rule, say-so, strength, supremacy, sway, weight **2. the authorities** administration, government, management, officialdom, police, powers that be, the establishment **3.** authorization, justification, licence, permission, permit, sanction, say-so, warrant **4.** arbiter, bible, connoisseur, expert, judge, master, professional, scholar, specialist, textbook **5.** attestation, avowal, declaration, evidence, profession, say-so, statement, testimony, word

authorization 1. ability, authority, power, right, say-so, strength **2.** approval, credentials, leave, licence, permission, permit, sanction, say-so, warrant

authorize 1. accredit, commission, empower, enable, entitle, give authority **2.** accredit, allow, approve, confirm, countenance, give authority for, give leave, license, permit, ratify, sanction, vouch for, warrant

autocracy absolution, despotism, dictatorship, tyranny

autocrat absolutist, despot, dictator, tyrant

autocratic absolute, all-powerful, despotic, dictatorial, domineering, imperious, tyrannical, tyrannous, unlimited

automatic 1. automated, mechanical, mechanized, push-button, robot, self-acting, self-activating, self-moving, self-propelling, self-regulating **2.** habitual, mechanical, perfunctory, routine, unconscious **3.** instinctive, instinctual, involuntary, mechanical, natural, reflex, spontaneous, unconscious, unwilled **4.** assured, certain, inescapable, inevitable, necessary, routine, unavoidable

autonomous free, independent, self-determining, self-governing, self-ruling, sovereign

autonomy freedom, home rule, independence, self-determination, self-government, self-rule, sovereignty

autopsy dissection, necropsy, postmortem, postmortem examination

auxiliary 1. *adj.* accessory, aiding, ancillary, assisting, back-up, emergency, helping, reserve, secondary, subsidiary, substitute, supplementary, supporting **2.** *n.* accessory, accomplice, ally, assistant, associate, companion, confederate, helper, partner, reserve, subordinate, supporter

avail *v.* **1.** aid, assist, be effective, benefit, be of advantage, be of use, be useful, help, profit, serve, work **2. avail oneself of** employ, exploit, have recourse to, make the most of, make use of, profit from, take advantage of, turn to account, use, utilize ~*n.* **3.** advantage, aid, assistance, benefit, effectiveness, efficacy, good, help, profit, purpose, service, use, usefulness, utility

available accessible, applicable, at hand, at one's disposal, attainable, convenient, free, handy, obtainable, on hand, on tap, ready, ready for use, to hand, vacant

avalanche 1. landslide, landslip, snow-slide, snow-slip **2.** barrage, deluge, flood, inundation, torrent

avant-garde *adj.* experimental, far-out (*Sl.*), innovative, innovatory, pioneering, progressive, unconventional, way-out (*Inf.*)

avarice acquisitiveness, close-fistedness, covetousness, cupidity, graspingness, greed, greediness, meanness, miserliness, niggardliness, parsimony, penny-pinching, penuriousness, rapacity, stinginess

avaricious acquisitive, close-fisted, covetous, grasping, greedy, mean, miserable, miserly, niggardly, parsimonious, penny-pinching, penurious, rapacious, stingy

avenge even the score for, get even for, punish, repay, requite, retaliate, revenge, take satisfaction for, take vengeance

avenue access, alley, approach, boulevard, channel, course, drive, driveway, entrance, entry, pass, passage, path, pathway, road, route, street, thoroughfare, way

aver affirm, allege, assert, asseverate, avouch, avow, declare, maintain, proclaim, profess, pronounce, protest, say, state, swear

average n. **1**. common run, mean, medium, midpoint, norm, normal, par, rule, run, run of the mill, standard **2. on average** as a rule, for the most part, generally, normally, typically, usually ~adj. **3**. common, commonplace, fair, general, indifferent, mediocre, middling, moderate, normal, not bad, ordinary, passable, regular, run-of-the-mill, so-so (Inf.), standard, tolerable, typical, undistinguished, unexceptional, usual **4**. intermediate, mean, median, medium, middle ~v. **5**. balance out to, be on average, do on average, even out to, make on average

averse antipathetic, backward, disinclined, hostile, ill-disposed, indisposed, inimical, loath, opposed, reluctant, unfavourable, unwilling

aversion abhorrence, animosity, antipathy, detestation, disgust, disinclination, dislike, distaste, hate, hatred, horror, hostility, indisposition, loathing, odium, opposition, reluctance, repugnance, repulsion, revulsion, unwillingness

avert 1. turn, turn aside, turn away **2**. avoid, fend off, forestall, frustrate, preclude, prevent, stave off, ward off

aviation aeronautics, flight, flying, powered flight

aviator aeronaut, airman, flier, pilot

avid 1. ardent, devoted, eager, enthusiastic, fanatical, fervent, intense, keen, passionate, zealous **2**. acquisitive, athirst, avaricious, covetous, grasping, greedy, hungry, insatiable, rapacious, ravenous, thirsty, voracious

avidity 1. ardour, devotion, eagerness, enthusiasm, fervour, keenness, zeal **2**. acquisitiveness, avarice, covetousness, cupidity, desire, graspingness, greediness, hankering, hunger, insatiability, longing, rapacity, ravenousness, thirst, voracity

avocation 1. diversion, hobby, occupation, pastime, recreation **2**. business, calling, employment, job, occupation, profession, pursuit, trade, vocation, work

avoid avert, bypass, circumvent, dodge, duck (out of) (Inf.), elude, escape, eschew, evade, fight shy of, keep aloof from, keep away from, prevent, refrain from, shirk, shun, sidestep, steer clear of

avoidance circumvention, dodging, eluding, escape, eschewal, evasion, keeping away from, prevention, refraining, shirking, shunning, steering clear of

avouch acknowledge, affirm, allege, assert, asseverate, aver, avow, declare, guarantee, maintain, proclaim, profess, pronounce, state, swear, vouch for

avow acknowledge, admit, affirm, allege, assert, asseverate, aver, confess, declare, maintain, own, proclaim, profess, recognize, state, swear

avowal acknowledgment, admission, affirmation, allegation, assertion, asseveration, averment, confession, declaration, maintenance, oath, owning, proclamation, profession, recognition, statement

avowed acknowledged, admitted, confessed, declared, open, professed, self-proclaimed, sworn

await 1. abide, anticipate, expect, look for, look forward to, stay for, wait for **2**. attend, be in readiness for, be in store for, be prepared for, be ready for, wait for

awake v. **1**. awaken, rouse, wake, wake up **2**. activate, alert, animate, arouse, awaken, call forth, enliven, excite, fan, incite, kindle, provoke, revive, stimulate, stir up, vivify ~adj. **3**. alert, alive, aroused, attentive, awakened, aware, conscious, heedful, not sleeping, observant, on guard, on the alert, on the lookout, vigilant, wakeful, waking, watchful, wide-awake

awaken activate, alert, animate, arouse, awake, call forth, enliven, excite, fan, incite, kindle, provoke, revive, rouse, stimulate, stir up, vivify, wake

awakening n. activation, animating, arousal, awaking, birth, enlivening, incitement, kindling, provocation, revival, rousing, stimulation, stirring up, vivification, waking, waking up

award v. **1**. accord, adjudge, allot, apportion, assign, bestow, confer, decree, distribute, endow, gift, give, grant, present, render ~n. **2**. adjudication, allotment, bestowal, conferment, conferral, decision, decree, endowment, gift, order, presentation **3**. decoration, gift, grant, prize, trophy, verdict

aware acquainted, alive to, appreciative, apprised, attentive, au courant, cognizant, conscious, conversant, enlightened, familiar, hip (Sl.), informed, knowing, knowledgeable, mindful, sensible, sentient, wise (Inf.)

awareness acquaintance, appreciation, attention, cognizance, consciousness, enlightenment, familiarity, knowledge, mindfulness, perception, realization, recognition, sensibility, sentience, understanding

away *adv.* **1.** abroad, elsewhere, from here, from home, hence, off **2.** apart, at a distance, far, remote **3.** aside, out of the way, to one side **4.** continuously, incessantly, interminably, relentlessly, repeatedly, uninterruptedly, unremittingly ~*adj.* **5.** abroad, absent, elsewhere, gone, not at home, not here, not present, not there, out ~*interj.* **6.** beat it (*Inf.*), begone, be off, get lost (*Inf.*), get out, go, go away, on your way

awe **1.** *n.* admiration, amazement, astonishment, dread, fear, horror, respect, reverence, terror, veneration, wonder **2.** *v.* amaze, astonish, cow, daunt, frighten, horrify, impress, intimidate, stun, terrify

awe-inspiring amazing, astonishing, awesome, breathtaking, daunting, fearsome, impressive, intimidating, magnificent, stunning (*Inf.*), wonderful, wondrous

awesome alarming, amazing, astonishing, awe-inspiring, awful, breathtaking, daunting, dreadful, fearful, fearsome, formidable, frightening, horrible, horrifying, imposing, impressive, intimidating, magnificent, majestic, overwhelming, redoubtable, shocking, solemn, stunning, stupefying, terrible, terrifying, wonderful, wondrous

awe-stricken, awe-struck afraid, amazed, astonished, awed, awe-inspired, cowed, daunted, dumbfounded, fearful, frightened, horrified, impressed, intimidated, shocked, struck dumb, stunned, terrified, wonder-stricken, wonderstruck

awful **1.** alarming, appalling, deplorable, dire, distressing, dreadful, fearful, frightful, ghastly, gruesome, harrowing, hideous, horrendous, horrible, horrific, horrifying, nasty, shocking, terrible, tremendous, ugly, unpleasant, unsightly **2.** *Archaic* amazing, awe-inspiring, awesome, dread, fearsome, majestic, portentous, solemn

awfully **1.** badly, disgracefully, disreputably, dreadfully, inadequately, reprehensibly, shoddily, unforgivably, unpleasantly, wickedly, woefully, wretch-

edly **2.** *Inf.* badly, dreadfully, exceedingly, exceptionally, excessively, extremely, greatly, immensely, quite, terribly, very, very much

awhile briefly, for a little while, for a moment, for a short time, for a while

awkward **1.** all thumbs, artless, blundering, bungling, clownish, clumsy, coarse, gauche, gawky, graceless, hamfisted, ham-handed, ill-bred, inelegant, inept, inexpert, lumbering, maladroit, oafish, rude, skill-less, stiff, uncoordinated, uncouth, ungainly, ungraceful, unpolished, unrefined, unskilful, unskilled **2.** cumbersome, difficult, inconvenient, troublesome, unhandy, unmanageable, unwieldy **3.** compromising, delicate, difficult, embarrassed, embarrassing, ill at ease, inconvenient, inopportune, painful, perplexing, sticky (*Inf.*), thorny, ticklish, troublesome, trying, uncomfortable, unpleasant, untimely **4.** annoying, bloody-minded (*Inf.*), difficult, disobliging, exasperating, hard to handle, intractable, irritable, perverse, prickly, stubborn, touchy, troublesome, trying, uncooperative, unhelpful, unpredictable, vexatious, vexing **5.** chancy (*Inf.*), dangerous, difficult, hazardous, perilous, risky

awkwardness **1.** artlessness, clownishness, clumsiness, coarseness, gaucheness, gaucherie, gawkiness, gracelessness, ill-breeding, inelegance, ineptness, inexpertness, maladroitness, oafishness, rudeness, skill-lessness, stiffness, uncoordination, uncouthness, ungainliness, unskilfulness, unskilledness **2.** cumbersomeness, difficulty, inconvenience, troublesomeness, unhandiness, unmanageability, unwieldiness **3.** delicacy, difficulty, discomfort, embarrassment, inconvenience, inopportuneness, painfulness, perplexingness, stickiness (*Inf.*), thorniness, ticklishness, unpleasantness, untimeliness **4.** bloody-mindedness (*Inf.*), difficulty, disobligingness, intractability, irritability, perversity, prickliness, stubbornness, touchiness, uncooperativeness, unhelpfulness, unpredictability **5.** chanciness (*Inf.*), danger, difficulty, hazardousness, peril, perilousness, risk, riskiness

awry *adv./adj.* amiss, askew, asymmetrical, cockeyed (*Inf.*), crooked, crookedly, misaligned, obliquely, off-centre, off course, out of line, out of true, skew-whiff (*Inf.*), to one side, twisted, uneven, unevenly, wrong

axe *n.* **1.** chopper, hatchet **2. an axe to grind** grievance, personal consideration, pet subject, private ends, private purpose, ulterior motive **3. the axe** *Inf.* cancellation, cutback, discharge, dismissal, termination, the boot (*Sl.*), the chop (*Sl.*), the sack (*Inf.*), wind-up ~*v.* **4.** chop, cut down, fell, hew **5.** *Inf.* cancel, cut back, discharge, dismiss, dispense with, eliminate, fire (*Inf.*), get rid of, remove, sack (*Inf.*), terminate, throw out, turn off (*Inf.*), wind up

axiom adage, aphorism, apophthegm, dictum, fundamental, gnome, maxim, postulate, precept, principle, truism

axiomatic 1. absolute, accepted, apodictic, assumed, certain, fundamental, given, granted, indubitable, manifest, presupposed, self-evident, understood, unquestioned **2.** aphoristic, apophthegmatic, epigrammatic, gnomic, pithy, terse

axis 1. axle, centre line, pivot, shaft, spindle **2.** alliance, bloc, coalition, compact, entente, league, pact

axle arbor, axis, mandrel, pin, pivot, rod, shaft, spindle

azure blue, cerulean, clear blue, sky-blue, sky-coloured, ultramarine

B

babble 1. v. blab, burble, cackle, chatter, gabble, gibber, gurgle, jabber, mumble, murmur, mutter, prate, prattle **2.** n. burble, clamour, drivel, gabble, gibberish, murmur

babe 1. baby, bairn (Scot.), child, infant, nursling, suckling **2.** babe in arms, ingénue, innocent

babel bedlam, clamour, confusion, din, disorder, hubbub, hullabaloo, hurlyburly, pandemonium, tumult, turmoil, uproar

baby 1. n. babe, bairn (Scot.), child, infant, newborn child **2.** adj. diminutive, dwarf, little, midget, mini, miniature, minute, pygmy, small, tiny, wee **3.** v. coddle, cosset, humour, indulge, mollycoddle, overindulge, pamper, pet, spoil, spoon-feed

babyish baby, childish, foolish, immature, infantile, juvenile, namby-pamby, puerile, silly, sissy, soft (Inf.), spoiled

bacchanal 1. carouser, debauchee, drunkard, reveller, roisterer, winebibber **2.** debauch, debauchery, orgy, revel, revelry

back v. **1.** abet, advocate, assist, champion, countenance, encourage, endorse, favour, finance, sanction, second, side with, sponsor, subsidize, support, sustain, underwrite **2.** backtrack, go back, move back, regress, retire, retreat, reverse, turn tail, withdraw ~n. **3.** backside, end, far end, hind part, hindquarters, posterior, rear, reverse, stern, tail end ~adj. **4.** end, hind, hindmost, posterior, rear, tail **5.** From an earlier time delayed, earlier, elapsed, former, overdue, past, previous **6. behind one's back** covertly, deceitfully, secretly, sneakily, surreptitiously

backbite abuse, calumniate, defame, denigrate, detract, libel, malign, revile, slander, traduce, vilify, vituperate

backbiting abuse, aspersion, bitchiness (Sl.), calumniation, calumny, cattiness (Inf.), defamation, denigration, detraction, disparagement, gossip, malice, scandalmongering, slander, spite, spitefulness, vilification, vituperation

backbone 1. Medical spinal column, spine, vertebrae, vertebral column **2.** bottle (Sl.), character, courage, determination, firmness, fortitude, grit, hardihood, mettle, moral fibre, nerve, pluck, resolution, resolve, stamina, steadfastness, strength of character, tenacity, toughness, will, willpower **3.** basis, foundation, mainstay, support

backbreaking arduous, crushing, exhausting, gruelling, hard, killing, laborious, punishing, strenuous, toilsome, wearing, wearying

back down accede, admit defeat, back-pedal, concede, give in, surrender, withdraw, yield

backer advocate, angel (Inf.), benefactor, patron, promoter, second, sponsor, subscriber, supporter, underwriter, well-wisher

backfire boomerang, disappoint, fail, flop, miscarry, rebound, recoil

background breeding, circumstances, credentials, culture, education, environment, experience, grounding, history, milieu, preparation, qualifications, tradition, upbringing

backhanded ambiguous, double-edged, equivocal, indirect, ironic, oblique, sarcastic, sardonic, two-edged

backing abetment, accompaniment, advocacy, aid, assistance, championing, encouragement, endorsement, funds, grant, moral support, patronage, sanction, seconding, sponsorship, subsidy, support

backlash backfire, boomerang, counteraction, counterblast, kickback, reaction, recoil, repercussion, resentment, resistance, response, retaliation, retroaction

backlog accumulation, excess, hoard, reserve, reserves, resources, stock, supply

back out abandon, cancel, chicken out (Inf.), give up, go back on, recant, renege, resign, retreat, withdraw

backslide fall from grace, go astray, go wrong, lapse, regress, relapse, renege, retrogress, revert, sin, slip, stray, weaken

backslider apostate, deserter, recidivist, recreant, renegade, reneger, turn-coat

back up aid, assist, bolster, confirm, corroborate, reinforce, second, stand by, substantiate, support

backward adj. 1. bashful, diffident, hesitating, late, reluctant, shy, sluggish, tardy, unwilling, wavering 2. behind, behindhand, dense, dull, retarded, slow, stupid, subnormal, underdeveloped, un-developed ~adv. 3. aback, behind, in re-verse, rearward

backwoods 1. adj. hick (Inf., chiefly U.S.), isolated, remote, rustic, uncouth 2. n. back of beyond, outback, sticks (Inf.)

bacteria bacilli, bugs (Sl.), germs, mi-crobes, microorganisms, pathogens, vi-ruses

bad 1. defective, deficient, erroneous, fallacious, faulty, imperfect, inadequate, incorrect, inferior, poor, substandard, unsatisfactory 2. damaging, dangerous, deleterious, detrimental, harmful, hurt-ful, injurious, ruinous, unhealthy 3. base, corrupt, criminal, delinquent, evil, immoral, mean, sinful, vile, villainous, wicked, wrong 4. disobedient, mischie-vous, naughty, unruly 5. decayed, mouldy, off, putrid, rancid, rotten, sour, spoiled 6. disastrous, distressing, grave, harsh, painful, serious, severe, terrible 7. ailing, diseased, ill, sick, unwell 8. apolo-getic, conscience-stricken, contrite, guilty, regretful, remorseful, sad, sorry, upset 9. adverse, discouraged, discourag-ing, distressed, distressing, gloomy, grim, melancholy, troubled, troubling, unfor-tunate, unpleasant 10. not bad all right, average, fair, fair to middling (Inf.), moderate, O.K. (Inf.), passable, respect-able, so-so (Inf.), tolerable

bad blood acrimony, anger, animos-ity, antagonism, dislike, enmity, feud, hatred, ill feeling, ill will, malevolence, malice, rancour, resentment

badge brand, device, emblem, identifi-cation, insignia, mark, sign, stamp, token

badger bully, chivvy, goad, harass, harry, hound, importune, nag, pester, plague, torment

badinage banter, chaff, drollery, mockery, persiflage, pleasantry, raillery, repartee, teasing, waggery, wordplay

badly 1. carelessly, defectively, erro-neously, faultily, imperfectly, inad-equately, incorrectly, ineptly, poorly,

shoddily, wrong, wrongly 2. unfavour-ably, unfortunately, unsuccessfully 3. criminally, evilly, immorally, improper-ly, naughtily, shamefully, unethically, wickedly 4. acutely, deeply, desperately, exceedingly, extremely, gravely, greatly, intensely, painfully, seriously, severely

baffle 1. amaze, astound, bewilder, confound, confuse, daze, disconcert, dumbfound, elude, flummox, mystify, nonplus, perplex, puzzle, stump, stun 2. balk, check, defeat, foil, frustrate, hin-der, thwart, upset

bag v. 1. balloon, bulge, droop, sag, swell 2. acquire, capture, catch, gain, get, kill, land, shoot, take, trap

baggage accoutrements, bags, belong-ings, equipment, gear, impedimenta, lug-gage, paraphernalia, suitcases, things

baggy billowing, bulging, droopy, flop-py, ill-fitting, loose, oversize, roomy, sag-ging, seated, slack

bail[1] n. bond, guarantee, guaranty, pledge, security, surety, warranty

bail[2], **bale** v. dip, drain off, ladle, scoop

bail out, bale out 1. aid, help, relieve, rescue 2. escape, quit, retreat, withdraw

bait n. 1. allurement, attraction, bribe, decoy, enticement, inducement, lure, snare, temptation ~v. 2. annoy, gall, harass, hound, irk, irritate, needle (Inf.), persecute, provoke, tease, torment 3. al-lure, beguile, entice, lure, seduce, tempt

baked arid, desiccated, dry, parched, scorched, seared, sun-baked

balance v. 1. level, match, parallel, poise, stabilize, steady 2. adjust, com-pensate for, counteract, counterbalance, counterpoise, equalize, equate, make up for, neutralize, offset 3. assess, compare, consider, deliberate, estimate, evaluate, weigh 4. calculate, compute, settle, square, tally, total ~n. 5. correspond-ence, equilibrium, equipoise, equity, equivalence, evenness, parity, symmetry 6. composure, equanimity, poise, self-control, self-possession, stability, steadi-ness 7. difference, remainder, residue, rest, surplus

balanced disinterested, equitable, even-handed, fair, impartial, just, unbi-ased, unprejudiced

balance sheet account, budget, cred-its and debits, ledger, report, statement

balcony 1. terrace, veranda 2. gallery, gods, upper circle

bald 1. baldheaded, baldpated, depilated, glabrous (*Biol.*), hairless **2.** barren, bleak, exposed, naked, stark, treeless, uncovered **3.** bare, blunt, direct, downright, forthright, outright, plain, severe, simple, straight, straightforward, unadorned, unvarnished

balderdash bunk (*Inf.*), bunkum, claptrap (*Inf.*), drivel, gibberish, nonsense, poppycock (*Inf.*), rot, rubbish, tommyrot, trash, twaddle

baldness 1. alopecia (*Pathology*), baldheadedness, baldpatedness, glabrousness (*Biol.*), hairlessness **2.** barrenness, bleakness, nakedness, sparseness, starkness, treelessness **3.** austerity, bluntness, plainness, severity, simplicity, spareness

bale *see* BAIL²

baleful calamitous, deadly, evil, harmful, hurtful, injurious, malevolent, malignant, menacing, mournful, noxious, ominous, pernicious, ruinous, sad, sinister, venomous, woeful

bale out *see* BAIL OUT

balk 1. demur, dodge, evade, flinch, hesitate, jib, recoil, refuse, resist, shirk, shrink from **2.** baffle, bar, check, counteract, defeat, disconcert, foil, forestall, frustrate, hinder, obstruct, prevent, thwart

balky intractable, obstinate, stubborn, uncooperative, unmanageable, unpredictable, unruly

ball 1. drop, globe, globule, orb, pellet, sphere, spheroid **2.** ammunition, bullet, grapeshot, pellet, shot, slug

ballast balance, counterbalance, counterweight, equilibrium, sandbag, stability, stabilizer, weight

balloon *v.* belly, billow, bloat, blow up, dilate, distend, enlarge, expand, inflate, puff out, swell

ballot election, poll, polling, vote, voting

ballyhoo 1. babble, commotion, fuss, hubbub, hue and cry, hullabaloo, noise, racket, to-do **2.** advertising, build-up, hype (*Sl.*), promotion, propaganda, publicity

balm 1. balsam, cream, embrocation, emollient, lotion, ointment, salve, unguent **2.** anodyne, comfort, consolation, curative, palliative, restorative, solace

balmy 1. clement, mild, pleasant, summery, temperate **2.** *Also* **barmy** crazy, daft, foolish, idiotic, insane, loony

(*Sl.*), nuts (*Sl.*), nutty (*Sl.*), odd, silly, stupid

bamboozle 1. cheat, con (*Sl.*), deceive, defraud, delude, dupe, fool, hoax, hoodwink, swindle, trick **2.** baffle, befuddle, confound, confuse, mystify, perplex, puzzle, stump

ban 1. *v.* banish, bar, debar, disallow, exclude, forbid, interdict, outlaw, prohibit, proscribe, restrict, suppress **2.** *n.* boycott, censorship, embargo, interdiction, prohibition, proscription, restriction, stoppage, suppression, taboo

banal clichéd, cliché-ridden, commonplace, everyday, hackneyed, humdrum, old hat, ordinary, pedestrian, platitudinous, stale, stereotyped, stock, threadbare, tired, trite, unimaginative, unoriginal, vapid

banality bromide (*Inf.*), cliché, commonplace, platitude, triteness, trite phrase, triviality, truism, vapidity

band¹ *n.* bandage, belt, binding, bond, chain, cord, fetter, fillet, ligature, manacle, ribbon, shackle, strap, strip, tie

band² *n.* **1.** assembly, association, body, clique, club, company, coterie, crew (*Inf.*), gang, horde, party, society, troop **2.** combo, ensemble, group, orchestra ~*v.* **3.** affiliate, ally, consolidate, federate, gather, group, join, merge, unite

bandage 1. *n.* compress, dressing, gauze, plaster **2.** *v.* bind, cover, dress, swathe

bandit brigand, crook, desperado, footpad, freebooter, gangster, gunman, highwayman, hijacker, marauder, outlaw, pirate, racketeer, robber, thief

bandy 1. *v.* barter, exchange, interchange, pass, shuffle, swap, throw, toss, trade **2.** *adj.* bandy-legged, bent, bowed, bow-legged, crooked, curved

bane affliction, *bête noire*, blight, burden, calamity, curse, despair, destruction, disaster, downfall, misery, nuisance, pest, plague, ruin, scourge, torment, trial, trouble, woe

baneful baleful, calamitous, deadly, deleterious, destructive, disastrous, fatal, harmful, hurtful, injurious, noxious, pernicious, pestilential, ruinous, venomous

bang *n.* **1.** boom, burst, clang, clap, clash, detonation, explosion, peal, pop, report, shot, slam, thud, thump **2.** blow, box, bump, cuff, hit, knock, punch, smack, stroke, wallop (*Inf.*), whack ~*v.*

3. bash (*Inf.*), beat, bump, clatter, crash, hammer, knock, pound, pummel, rap, slam, strike, thump **4**. boom, burst, clang, detonate, drum, echo, explode, peal, resound, thump, thunder ~*adv*. **5**. abruptly, hard, headlong, noisily, precisely, slap, smack, straight, suddenly

banish 1. deport, drive away, eject, evict, exclude, excommunicate, exile, expatriate, expel, ostracize, outlaw, shut out, transport **2**. ban, cast out, discard, dislodge, dismiss, dispel, eliminate, eradicate, get rid of, oust, remove, shake off

banishment deportation, exile, expatriation, expulsion, proscription, transportation

banisters balusters, balustrade, handrail, rail, railing

bank[1] **1**. *n*. accumulation, depository, fund, hoard, repository, reserve, reservoir, savings, stock, stockpile, store, storehouse **2**. *v*. deal with, deposit, keep, save, transact business with

bank[2] *n*. **1**. banking, embankment, heap, mass, mound, pile, ridge **2**. brink, edge, margin, shore, side ~*v*. **3**. amass, heap, mass, mound, pile, stack **4**. camber, cant, incline, pitch, slant, slope, tilt, tip

bank[3] *n*. array, file, group, line, rank, row, sequence, series, succession, tier, train

bank on assume, believe in, count on, depend on, lean on, look to, rely on, trust

bankrupt broke (*Inf.*), depleted, destitute, exhausted, failed, impoverished, insolvent, lacking, ruined, spent

bankruptcy disaster, exhaustion, failure, indebtedness, insolvency, lack, liquidation, ruin

banner banderole, burgee, colours, ensign, fanion, flag, gonfalon, pennant, pennon, standard, streamer

banquet dinner, feast, meal, repast, revel, treat

banter 1. *v*. chaff, deride, jeer, jest, joke, kid (*Inf.*), make fun of, rib (*Inf.*), ridicule, taunt, tease, twit **2**. *n*. badinage, chaff, chaffing, derision, jeering, jesting, joking, kidding (*Inf.*), mockery, persiflage, pleasantry, raillery, repartee, ribbing (*Inf.*), ridicule, wordplay

baptism 1. christening, immersion, purification, sprinkling **2**. beginning, debut, dedication, initiation, introduction, launching, rite of passage

baptize 1. besprinkle, cleanse, immerse, purify **2**. admit, enrol, initiate, recruit **3**. call, christen, dub, name, title

bar *n*. **1**. batten, crosspiece, paling, pole, rail, rod, shaft, stake, stick **2**. barricade, barrier, deterrent, hindrance, impediment, obstacle, obstruction, rail, railing, stop **3**. boozer (*Inf.*), canteen, counter, inn, lounge, pub (*Inf.*), public house, saloon, tavern **4**. bench, court, courtroom, dock, law court **5**. *Law* barristers, body of lawyers, counsel, court, judgment, tribunal ~*v*. **6**. barricade, bolt, fasten, latch, lock, secure **7**. ban, exclude, forbid, hinder, keep out, obstruct, prevent, prohibit, restrain

barb 1. bristle, point, prickle, prong, quill, spike, spur, thorn **2**. affront, cut, dig, gibe, insult, rebuff, sarcasm, scoff, sneer

barbarian *n*. **1**. brute, hooligan, lout, ruffian, savage, vandal, yahoo **2**. bigot, boor, ignoramus, illiterate, lowbrow, philistine ~*adj*. **3**. boorish, crude, lowbrow, philistine, primitive, uncouth, uncultivated, uncultured, unsophisticated, vulgar

barbaric 1. primitive, rude, uncivilized, wild **2**. barbarous, boorish, brutal, coarse, crude, cruel, fierce, inhuman, savage, uncouth, vulgar

barbarism 1. coarseness, crudity, savagery, uncivilizedness **2**. atrocity, barbarity, enormity, outrage **3**. corruption, misusage, misuse, solecism, vulgarism

barbarity brutality, cruelty, inhumanity, ruthlessness, savagery, viciousness

barbarous 1. barbarian, brutish, primitive, rough, rude, savage, uncivilized, uncouth, wild **2**. barbaric, brutal, cruel, ferocious, heartless, inhuman, monstrous, ruthless, vicious **3**. coarse, crude, ignorant, uncultured, unlettered, unrefined, vulgar

barbed 1. hooked, jagged, prickly, pronged, spiked, spiny, thorny, toothed **2**. acid, acrid, catty (*Inf.*), critical, cutting, hostile, hurtful, nasty, pointed, unkind

bare 1. denuded, exposed, naked, nude, peeled, shorn, stripped, unclad, unclothed, uncovered, undressed **2**. barren, blank, empty, lacking, mean, open, poor, scanty, scarce, unfurnished, vacant, void, wanting **3**. austere, bald, basic, cold, essential, hard, literal, plain, severe, sheer, simple, spare, stark, unadorned, unembellished, unvarnished

barefaced 1. audacious, bold, brash, brazen, impudent, insolent, shameless **2.** bald, blatant, flagrant, glaring, manifest, naked, obvious, open, palpable, patent, transparent, unconcealed

barely almost, hardly, just, only just, scarcely

bargain *n.* **1.** agreement, arrangement, business, compact, contract, convention, engagement, negotiation, pact, pledge, promise, stipulation, transaction, treaty, understanding **2.** (cheap) purchase, discount, giveaway, good buy, good deal, good value, reduction, snip (*Inf.*) ~*v.* **3.** agree, contract, covenant, negotiate, promise, stipulate, transact **4.** barter, buy, deal, haggle, sell, trade, traffic

bargain for anticipate, contemplate, expect, foresee, imagine, look for, plan for

bargain on assume, bank on, count on, depend on, plan on, rely on

barge canal boat, flatboat, lighter, narrow boat, scow

barge in break in, burst in, butt in, infringe, interrupt, intrude, muscle in (*Inf.*)

barge into bump into, cannon into, collide with, hit, push, shove

bark[1] **1.** *n.* casing, cortex (*Anat., bot.*), covering, crust, husk, rind, skin **2.** *v.* abrade, flay, rub, scrape, shave, skin, strip

bark[2] **1.** *n./v.* bay, growl, howl, snarl, woof, yap, yelp **2.** *v. Fig.* bawl, bawl at, berate, bluster, growl, shout, snap, snarl, yell

barmy 1. *Also* **balmy** crazy, daft, foolish, idiotic, insane, loony (*Sl.*), nuts (*Sl.*), nutty (*Sl.*), odd, silly, stupid **2.** fermenting, foamy, frothy, spumy, yeasty

baroque bizarre, convoluted, elaborate, extravagant, flamboyant, florid, grotesque, ornate, overdecorated

barracks billet, camp, cantonment, casern, encampment, garrison, quarters

barrage 1. battery, bombardment, cannonade, curtain of fire, fusillade, gunfire, salvo, shelling, volley **2.** assault, attack, burst, deluge, hail, mass, onslaught, plethora, profusion, rain, storm, stream, torrent

barred 1. banded, crosshatched, lined, marked, ribbed, ridged, streaked, striped, veined **2.** banned, excluded, forbidden, outlawed, prohibited, proscribed

barren 1. childless, infecund, infertile, sterile, unprolific **2.** arid, desert, desolate, dry, empty, unfruitful, unproductive, waste **3.** boring, dull, flat, fruitless, lacklustre, stale, uninformative, uninspiring, uninstructive, uninteresting, unrewarding, useless, vapid

barricade 1. *n.* barrier, blockade, bulwark, fence, obstruction, palisade, rampart, stockade **2.** *v.* bar, block, blockade, defend, fortify, obstruct, protect, shut in

barrier 1. bar, barricade, blockade, boundary, ditch, fence, fortification, obstacle, obstruction, railing, rampart, stop, wall **2.** *Fig.* check, difficulty, drawback, handicap, hindrance, hurdle, impediment, limitation, obstacle, restriction, stumbling block

barter bargain, exchange, haggle, sell, swap, trade, traffic

base[1] *n.* **1.** bed, bottom, foot, foundation, groundwork, pedestal, rest, stand, support **2.** basis, core, essence, essential, fundamental, heart, key, origin, principal, root, source **3.** camp, centre, headquarters, home, post, settlement, starting point, station ~*v.* **4.** build, construct, depend, derive, establish, found, ground, hinge, locate, station

base[2] **1.** abject, contemptible, corrupt, depraved, despicable, dishonourable, disreputable, evil, ignoble, immoral, infamous, scandalous, shameful, sordid, vile, villainous, vulgar, wicked **2.** downtrodden, grovelling, low, lowly, mean, menial, miserable, paltry, pitiful, poor, servile, slavish, sorry, subservient, worthless, wretched **3.** adulterated, alloyed, counterfeit, debased, fake, forged, fraudulent, impure, inferior, pinchbeck, spurious

baseless groundless, unconfirmed, uncorroborated, unfounded, ungrounded, unjustifiable, unjustified, unsubstantiated, unsupported

baseness 1. contemptibility, degradation, depravation, depravity, despicability, disgrace, ignominy, infamy, notoriety, obloquy, turpitude **2.** lowliness, meanness, misery, poverty, servility, slavishness, subservience, vileness, worthlessness, wretchedness **3.** adulteration, debasement, fraudulence, phoneyness (*Sl.*), pretence, speciousness, spuriousness

bash 1. *v.* biff (*Sl.*), break, crash, crush, hit, punch, slosh (*Sl.*), smash, sock (*Sl.*), strike, wallop (*Inf.*) **2.** *n.* attempt, crack, go, shot, stab, try

bashful abashed, blushing, confused, constrained, coy, diffident, easily embarrassed, nervous, overmodest, reserved, reticent, retiring, self-conscious, self-effacing, shamefaced, sheepish, shrinking, shy, timid, timorous

bashfulness constraint, coyness, diffidence, embarrassment, hesitation, modesty, reserve, self-consciousness, sheepishness, shyness, timidity, timorousness

basic central, elementary, essential, fundamental, indispensable, inherent, intrinsic, key, necessary, primary, underlying, vital

basically at bottom, at heart, *au fond*, essentially, firstly, fundamentally, inherently, in substance, intrinsically, mostly, primarily, radically

basics brass tacks (*Inf.*), core, essentials, facts, fundamentals, hard facts, necessaries, nitty-gritty (*Sl.*), nuts and bolts (*Inf.*), practicalities, principles, rudiments

basis 1. base, bottom, footing, foundation, ground, groundwork, support **2.** chief ingredient, core, essential, fundamental, heart, premise, principal element, principle, theory

bask 1. laze, lie in, loll, lounge, relax, sunbathe, swim in, toast oneself, warm oneself **2.** delight in, enjoy, indulge oneself, luxuriate, relish, revel, savour, take pleasure, wallow

bass deep, deep-toned, grave, low, low-pitched, resonant, sonorous

bastard 1. *n.* illegitimate (child), love child, natural child **2.** *adj.* adulterated, baseborn, counterfeit, false, illegitimate, imperfect, impure, inferior, irregular, misbegotten, sham, spurious

bastardize adulterate, cheapen, corrupt, debase, defile, degrade, demean, devalue, distort, pervert

bastion bulwark, citadel, defence, fastness, fortress, mainstay, prop, rock, stronghold, support, tower of strength

bat bang, hit, rap, smack, strike, swat, thump, wallop (*Inf.*), whack

batch accumulation, aggregation, amount, assemblage, bunch, collection, crowd, group, lot, pack, quantity, set

bath 1. *n.* ablution, cleansing, douche, douse, scrubbing, shower, soak, soaping, sponging, tub, wash, washing **2.** *v.* bathe, clean, douse, lave (*Archaic*), scrub down,

shower, soak, soap, sponge, tub, wash

bathe 1. *v.* cleanse, cover, dunk, flood, immerse, moisten, rinse, soak, steep, suffuse, wash, wet **2.** *n.* dip, swim

bathetic anticlimactic, mawkish, sentimental

bathing costume bathing suit, bikini, swimming costume, swimsuit, trunks

bathos anticlimax, false pathos, mawkishness, sentimentality

baton club, mace, rod, staff, stick, truncheon, wand

battalion army, brigade, company, contingent, division, force, horde, host, legion, multitude, regiment, squadron, throng

batten¹ board up, clamp down, cover up, fasten, fasten down, fix, nail down, secure, tighten

batten² fatten, flourish, gain, grow, increase, prosper, thrive, wax

batter 1. assault, bash, beat, belabour, break, buffet, dash against, lash, pelt, pound, pummel, smash, smite, thrash, wallop (*Inf.*) **2.** bruise, crush, deface, demolish, destroy, disfigure, hurt, injure, mangle, mar, maul, ruin, shatter, shiver

battered beaten, broken-down, bruised, crushed, damaged, dilapidated, injured, ramshackle, squashed, weather-beaten

battery 1. chain, ring, sequence, series, set, suite **2.** assault, attack, beating, mayhem, onslaught, physical violence, thumping **3.** artillery, cannon, cannonry, gun emplacements, guns

battle *n.* **1.** action, attack, combat, encounter, engagement, fight, fray, hostilities, skirmish, war, warfare **2.** agitation, campaign, clash, conflict, contest, controversy, crusade, debate, disagreement, dispute, strife, struggle ~*v.* **3.** agitate, argue, clamour, combat, contend, contest, dispute, feud, fight, strive, struggle, war

battle cry catchword, motto, slogan, war cry, war whoop, watchword

battlefield battleground, combat zone, field, field of battle, front

battlement barbican, bartizan, bastion, breastwork, bulwark, crenellation, fortification, parapet, rampart

battleship capital ship, gunboat, man-of-war, ship of the line, warship

batty barmy (*Sl.*), bats (*Sl.*), bonkers (*Sl.*), cracked (*Sl.*), crackers (*Sl.*), cranky (*Inf.*), crazy, daft, dotty (*Sl.*), eccentric, insane, loony (*Sl.*), lunatic, mad, nuts (*Sl.*), nutty (*Sl.*), odd, peculiar, potty (*Inf.*), queer, screwy (*Inf.*), touched

bauble bagatelle, gewgaw, gimcrack, kickshaw, knick-knack, plaything, toy, trifle, trinket

baulk *see* BALK

bawd brothel-keeper, madam, pimp, procuress, prostitute, whore

bawdy blue, coarse, dirty, erotic, gross, indecent, indecorous, indelicate, lascivious, lecherous, lewd, libidinous, licentious, lustful, obscene, prurient, ribald, risqué, rude, salacious, suggestive, vulgar

bawl 1. bellow, call, clamour, halloo, howl, roar, shout, vociferate, yell 2. blubber, cry, sob, squall, wail, weep

bay¹ bight, cove, gulf, inlet, natural harbour, sound

bay² alcove, compartment, embrasure, niche, nook, opening, recess

bay³ 1. bark, bell, clamour, cry, growl, howl, yelp 2. **at bay** caught, cornered, trapped

bayonet *v.* impale, knife, run through, spear, stab, stick, transfix

bays chaplet, garland, glory, laurel crown, praise, prize, renown, trophy

bazaar 1. exchange, market, marketplace, mart 2. bring-and-buy, fair, fête

be 1. be alive, breathe, exist, inhabit, live 2. befall, come about, come to pass, happen, occur, take place, transpire (*Inf.*) 3. abide, continue, endure, last, obtain, persist, prevail, remain, stand, stay, survive

beach coast, littoral, margin, sands, seaboard (*Chiefly U.S.*), seashore, seaside, shingle, shore, strand, water's edge

beachcomber forager, loafer, scavenger, scrounger, tramp, vagabond, vagrant, wanderer

beached abandoned, aground, ashore, deserted, grounded, high and dry, marooned, stranded, wrecked

beacon beam, bonfire, flare, lighthouse, pharos, rocket, sign, signal, signal fire, smoke signal, watchtower

bead blob, bubble, dot, drop, droplet, globule, pellet, pill, spherule

beads chaplet, choker, necklace, necklet, pearls, pendant, rosary

beak 1. bill, mandible, neb (*Archaic or dialect*), nib 2. nose, proboscis, snout 3. *Naut.* bow, prow, ram, rostrum, stem

beaked curved, hooked, pointed, sharp

beam *n.* 1. girder, joist, plank, rafter, spar, support, timber 2. bar, emission, gleam, glimmer, glint, glow, radiation, ray, shaft, streak, stream ~*v.* 3. broadcast, emit, glare, gleam, glitter, glow, radiate, shine, transmit 4. grin, laugh, smile

beaming 1. beautiful, bright, brilliant, flashing, gleaming, glistening, glittering, radiant, scintillating, shining, sparkling 2. cheerful, grinning, happy, joyful, smiling, sunny

bear 1. bring, carry, convey, move, take, tote, transport 2. cherish, entertain, exhibit, harbour, have, hold, maintain, possess, shoulder, support, sustain, uphold, weigh upon 3. abide, admit, allow, brook, endure, permit, put up with (*Inf.*), stomach, suffer, tolerate, undergo 4. beget, breed, bring forth, develop, engender, generate, give birth to, produce, yield

bearable admissible, endurable, manageable, passable, sufferable, supportable, sustainable, tolerable

beard 1. *n.* bristles, five-o'clock shadow, stubble, whiskers 2. *v.* brave, confront, dare, defy, face, oppose

bearded bewhiskered, bristly, bushy, hairy, hirsute, shaggy, stubbly, unshaven, whiskered

beardless 1. barefaced, clean-shaven, hairless, smooth, smooth-faced 2. callow, fresh, green, immature, inexperienced

bear down 1. burden, compress, encumber, press down, push, strain, weigh down 2. advance on, approach, attack, close in, converge on, move in

bearer 1. agent, carrier, conveyor, messenger, porter, runner, servant 2. beneficiary, consignee, payee

bearing 1. air, aspect, attitude, behaviour, carriage, demeanour, deportment, manner, mien, posture 2. *Naut.* course, direction, point of compass 3. application, connection, import, pertinence, reference, relation, relevance, significance

bearings aim, course, direction, location, orientation, position, situation, track, way, whereabouts

bearish 1. churlish, clumsy, gruff, rough, sullen, surly 2. *Stock Exchange* declining, falling, slumping

bear on affect, appertain to, belong to,

concern, involve, pertain to, **refer to**, relate to, touch upon

bear out confirm, corroborate, endorse, justify, prove, substantiate, support, uphold, vindicate

bear up bear the brunt, carry on, endure, grin and bear it (*Inf.*), persevere, suffer, withstand

bear with be patient, forbear, make allowances, put up with (*Inf.*), suffer, tolerate, wait

beast 1. animal, brute, creature **2.** barbarian, brute, fiend, monster, ogre, sadist, savage, swine

beastly 1. barbarous, bestial, brutal, brutish, coarse, cruel, depraved, inhuman, monstrous, repulsive, sadistic, savage **2.** awful, disagreeable, foul, mean, nasty, rotten, terrible, unpleasant

beat *v.* **1.** bang, batter, break, bruise, buffet, cane, cudgel, drub, flog, hit, knock, lash, maul, pelt, pound, punch, strike, thrash, thwack, whip **2.** best, conquer, defeat, excel, outdo, outrun, outstrip, overcome, overwhelm, subdue, surpass, vanquish **3.** fashion, forge, form, hammer, model, shape, work **4.** flap, flutter, palpitate, pound, pulsate, pulse, quake, quiver, shake, throb, thump, tremble, vibrate ~*n.* **5.** blow, hit, lash, punch, shake, slap, strike, swing, thump **6.** flutter, palpitation, pulsation, pulse, throb **7.** accent, cadence, measure, metre, rhythm, stress, time **8.** circuit, course, path, rounds, route, way ~*adj.* **9.** *Sl.* exhausted, fatigued, tired, wearied, worn out

beaten 1. baffled, cowed, defeated, disappointed, disheartened, frustrated, overcome, overwhelmed, thwarted, vanquished **2.** forged, formed, hammered, shaped, stamped, worked **3.** much travelled, trampled, trodden, well-trodden, well-used, worn **4.** blended, foamy, frothy, mixed, stirred, whipped, whisked

beatific blessed, blissful, divine, ecstatic, enraptured, exalted, glorious, heavenly, joyful, rapt, rapturous, serene, sublime

beating 1. belting (*Inf.*), caning, chastisement, corporal punishment, flogging, slapping, smacking, thrashing, whipping **2.** conquest, defeat, downfall, overthrow, rout, ruin

beatitude beatification, blessedness, bliss, ecstasy, exaltation, felicity, happiness, holy joy, saintliness

beat up assault, attack, batter, do over (*Sl.*), duff up (*Sl.*), fill in (*Sl.*), knock about *or* around, thrash

beau 1. admirer, boyfriend, escort, fiancé, lover, suitor, swain, sweetheart **2.** cavalier, coxcomb, dandy, fop, gallant, ladies' man, popinjay, swell (*Inf.*)

beautiful alluring, appealing, attractive, charming, comely, delightful, exquisite, fair, fine, good-looking, gorgeous, graceful, handsome, lovely, pleasing, radiant, ravishing, stunning (*Inf.*)

beautify adorn, array, bedeck, deck, decorate, embellish, enhance, garnish, gild, glamorize, grace, ornament

beauty 1. allure, attractiveness, bloom, charm, comeliness, elegance, exquisiteness, fairness, glamour, grace, handsomeness, loveliness, pulchritude, seemliness, symmetry **2.** belle, charmer, cracker (*Sl.*), goddess, good-looker, lovely (*Sl.*), stunner (*Inf.*), Venus **3.** advantage, asset, attraction, benefit, blessing, boon, excellence, feature, good thing

beaver away exert oneself, graft (*Inf.*), hammer away, peg away, persevere, persist, plug away (*Inf.*), slog, work

becalmed motionless, settled, still, stranded, stuck

because as, by reason of, in that, on account of, owing to, since, thanks to

beck gesture, nod, signal, summons, wave

beckon 1. bid, gesticulate, gesture, motion, nod, signal, summon, wave at **2.** allure, attract, call, coax, draw, entice, invite, lure, pull, tempt

becloud bedim, befog, complicate, confuse, darken, muddle, obfuscate, obscure, overcast, screen, veil

become 1. alter to, be transformed into, change into, develop into, evolve into, grow into, mature into, metamorphose into, ripen into **2.** embellish, enhance, fit, flatter, grace, harmonize, ornament, set off, suit

becoming 1. attractive, comely, enhancing, flattering, graceful, neat, pretty, tasteful **2.** appropriate, befitting, *comme il faut*, compatible, congruous, decent, decorous, fit, fitting, in keeping, meet (*Archaic*), proper, seemly, suitable, worthy

bed *n.* **1.** bedstead, berth, bunk, cot, couch, divan, pallet **2.** area, border, garden, patch, plot, row, strip **3.** base, bottom, foundation, groundwork, substratum ~*v.* **4.** base, embed, establish, fix, found, implant, insert, plant, settle, set up

bedaub besmear, smear, smirch, soil, spatter, splash, stain

bedazzle amaze, astound, bewilder, blind, captivate, confuse, daze, dazzle, dumbfound, enchant, overwhelm, stagger, stun

bedclothes bedding, bed linen, blankets, coverlets, covers, eiderdowns, pillowcases, pillows, quilts, sheets

bed down lie, retire, settle down, sleep, turn in (*Inf.*)

bedeck adorn, array, bedight (*Archaic*), bedizen (*Archaic*), decorate, embellish, festoon, garnish, ornament, trim

bedevil afflict, annoy, confound, distress, fret, frustrate, harass, irk, irritate, pester, plague, torment, torture, trouble, vex, worry

bedew besprinkle, dampen, drench, moisten, shower, soak, spray, sprinkle, water, wet

bedim becloud, bedarken, cloak, cloud, darken, dim, obscure, overcast, shade, shadow

bedlam chaos, clamour, commotion, confusion, furore, hubbub, madhouse (*Inf.*), noise, pandemonium, tumult, turmoil, uproar

bedraggled dirty, dishevelled, disordered, drenched, dripping, messy, muddied, muddy, sodden, soiled, stained, sullied, unkempt, untidy

bedridden confined, confined to bed, flat on one's back, incapacitated, laid up (*Inf.*)

bedrock **1.** bed, bottom, foundation, nadir, rock bottom, substratum, substructure **2.** basics, basis, core, essentials, fundamentals, roots

beef **1.** *Inf.* brawn, flesh, heftiness, muscle, physique, robustness, sinew, strength **2.** *Sl.* complaint, criticism, dispute, grievance, gripe (*Inf.*), grouse, grumble, objection, protestation

beefy *Inf.* **1.** brawny, bulky, burly, hulking, muscular, stalwart, stocky, strapping, sturdy **2.** chubby, corpulent, fat, fleshy, heavy, obese, overweight, paunchy, plump, podgy, portly, pudgy, rotund

beetle, beetling *adj.* jutting, leaning over, overhanging, pendent, projecting, protruding, sticking out, swelling over

befall bechance, betide, chance, come to pass, ensue, fall, follow, happen, materialize, occur, supervene, take place, transpire (*Inf.*)

befitting appropriate, becoming, fit, fitting, meet (*Archaic*), proper, right, seemly, suitable

befog becloud, blur, confuse, darken, fuzz, make hazy (indistinct, vague), muddle, obfuscate, obscure

befool bamboozle (*Inf.*), beguile, cheat, delude, dupe, fool, hoax, hoodwink, humbug, impose on, mislead, outwit, trick

before **1.** *adv.* ahead, earlier, formerly, in advance, in front, previously, sooner **2.** *prep.* earlier than, in advance of, in front of, in the presence of, prior to

beforehand ahead of time, already, before, before now, earlier, in advance, in anticipation, previously, sooner

befriend advise, aid, assist, back, benefit, encourage, favour, help, patronize, side with, stand by, succour, support, sustain, uphold, welcome

befuddle baffle, bewilder, confuse, daze, disorient, intoxicate, muddle, puzzle, stupefy

befuddled confused, dazed, fuddled, groggy (*Inf.*), inebriated, intoxicated, muddled, woozy (*Inf.*)

beg **1.** beseech, crave, desire, entreat, implore, importune, petition, plead, pray, request, solicit, supplicate **2.** cadge, call for alms, scrounge, seek charity, solicit charity, sponge on **3.** *As in* **beg the question** avoid, dodge, duck (*Inf.*), equivocate, eschew, evade, fend off, hedge, parry, shirk, shun, sidestep

beget **1.** breed, father, generate, get, procreate, propagate, sire **2.** bring, bring about, cause, create, effect, engender, give rise to, occasion, produce, result in

beggar *n.* **1.** cadger, mendicant, scrounger (*Inf.*), sponger (*Inf.*), supplicant, tramp, vagrant **2.** bankrupt, down-and-out, pauper, starveling ~*v.* **3.** *As in* **beggar description** baffle, challenge, defy, surpass

beggarly abject, base, contemptible, despicable, destitute, impoverished, inadequate, indigent, low, meagre, mean, miserly, needy, niggardly, pitiful, poor, poverty-stricken, stingy, vile, wretched

beggary bankruptcy, destitution, indigence, need, pauperism, poverty, vagrancy, wretchedness

begin 1. commence, embark on, inaugurate, initiate, instigate, institute, prepare, set about, set on foot, start **2.** appear, arise, be born, come into being, come into existence, commence, crop up (*Inf.*), dawn, emerge, happen, originate, spring, start

beginner amateur, apprentice, fledgling, freshman, greenhorn (*Inf.*), initiate, learner, neophyte, novice, recruit, starter, student, tenderfoot, trainee, tyro

beginning 1. birth, commencement, inauguration, inception, initiation, onset, opening, origin, outset, preface, prelude, rise, rudiments, source, start, starting point **2.** embryo, fountainhead, germ, root, seed

begrime besmirch, blacken, dirty, muddy, smear, smirch, soil, spatter, stain, sully, tarnish

begrudge be jealous, be reluctant, be stingy, envy, grudge, resent

beguile 1. befool, cheat, deceive, delude, dupe, fool, hoodwink, impose on, mislead, trick **2.** amuse, charm, cheer, delight, distract, divert, engross, entertain, occupy, solace

beguiling alluring, attractive, bewitching, captivating, charming, diverting, enchanting, entertaining, enthralling, interesting, intriguing

behalf account, advantage, benefit, defence, good, interest, part, profit, sake, side, support

behave 1. act, function, operate, perform, run, work **2.** act correctly, conduct oneself properly, mind one's manners

behaviour 1. actions, bearing, carriage, comportment, conduct, demeanour, deportment, manner, manners, ways **2.** action, functioning, operation, performance

behest bidding, charge, command, commandment, decree, dictate, direction, expressed desire, injunction, instruction, mandate, order, precept, wish

behind *prep.* **1.** after, at the back of, at the rear of, following, later than **2.** at the bottom of, causing, initiating, instigating, responsible for **3.** backing, for, in agreement, on the side of, supporting ~*adv.* **4.** after, afterwards, following, in the wake (of), next, subsequently **5.** behindhand, in arrears, in debt, overdue ~*n.* **6.** bottom, buttocks, posterior, rump, seat

behindhand backward, behind time,

dilatory, late, remiss, slow, tardy

behold 1. *v.* consider, contemplate, discern, eye, look at, observe, perceive, regard, scan, survey, view, watch, witness **2.** *interj.* lo, look, mark, observe, see, watch

beholden bound, grateful, indebted, obligated, obliged, owing, under obligation

behove be advisable, befit, be fitting, be incumbent upon, be necessary, benefit, be obligatory, beseem, be wise

beige biscuit, buff, *café au lait*, camel, cinnamon, coffee, cream, ecru, fawn, khaki, mushroom, neutral, oatmeal, sand, tan

being 1. actuality, animation, existence, life, living, reality **2.** entity, essence, nature, soul, spirit, substance **3.** animal, beast, body, creature, human being, individual, living thing, mortal, thing

belabour 1. batter, beat, flog, lambaste, thrash, whip **2.** attack, berate, castigate, censure, criticize, flay, lay into

belated behindhand, behind time, delayed, late, overdue, tardy

belch 1. burp (*Inf.*), eruct, eructate, hiccup **2.** discharge, disgorge, emit, erupt, give off, gush, spew forth, vent, vomit

beleaguer 1. assail, beset, besiege, blockade, encompass, environ, hem in, surround **2.** annoy, badger, bother, harass, pester, vex

beleaguered badgered, beset, besieged, bothered, harassed, nagged, persecuted, plagued, put upon, set upon, vexed

belie 1. confute, contradict, deny, disprove, gainsay, give the lie to, negate, repudiate **2.** conceal, deceive, disguise, falsify, gloss over, mislead, misrepresent

belief 1. admission, assent, assurance, confidence, conviction, credit, feeling, impression, judgment, notion, opinion, persuasion, presumption, reliance, theory, trust, view **2.** credence, credo, creed, doctrine, dogma, faith, ideology, principles, tenet

believable acceptable, authentic, credible, creditable, imaginable, likely, plausible, possible, probable, reliable, trustworthy

believe 1. accept, be certain of, be convinced of, count on, credit, depend on, have faith in, hold, place confidence

in, presume true, rely on, swear by, trust
2. assume, conjecture, consider, gather, guess, imagine, judge, maintain, postulate, presume, reckon, speculate, suppose, think

believer adherent, convert, devotee, disciple, follower, proselyte, supporter, upholder, zealot

belittle decry, deprecate, depreciate, deride, derogate, detract, diminish, disparage, downgrade, minimize, scoff at, scorn, sneer at, underestimate, underrate, undervalue

bellicose aggressive, antagonistic, belligerent, combative, defiant, hawkish, hostile, jingoistic, militaristic, provocative, pugnacious, quarrelsome, sabrerattling, warlike, warloving, warmongering

belligerence aggressiveness, animosity, antagonism, combativeness, hostility, pugnacity, unfriendliness

belligerent 1. adj. aggressive, antagonistic, argumentative, bellicose, combative, contentious, hostile, litigious, pugnacious, quarrelsome, unfriendly, warlike, warring **2.** n. combatant, fighter, warring nation

bellow bawl, call, clamour, cry, howl, roar, scream, shout, shriek, yell

belly 1. n. abdomen, breadbasket (Sl.), corporation (Inf.), gut, insides (Inf.), paunch, potbelly, stomach, tummy, vitals **2.** v. billow, bulge, fill, spread, swell, swell out

belong 1. With to be at the disposal of, be held by, be owned by, be the property of **2.** With to be affiliated to, be allied to, be a member of, be associated with, be included in **3.** attach to, be connected with, be fitting, be part of, fit, go with, have as a proper place, pertain to, relate to

belonging acceptance, affinity, association, attachment, fellowship, inclusion, kinship, loyalty, rapport, relationship

belongings accoutrements, chattels, effects, gear, goods, paraphernalia, personal property, possessions, stuff, things

beloved admired, adored, cherished, darling, dear, dearest, loved, pet, precious, prized, revered, sweet, treasured, worshipped

below adv. **1.** beneath, down, lower, under, underneath ~prep. **2.** inferior, lesser, lesser than, subject, subordinate,

unworthy of **3. below par** below average, imperfect, inferior, off colour, off form, poor, second-rate, unfit

belt 1. band, cincture, cummerbund, girdle, girth, sash, waistband **2.** Geog. area, district, layer, region, stretch, strip, tract, zone **3. below the belt** cowardly, foul, not playing the game (Inf.), unfair, unjust, unscrupulous, unsporting, unsportsmanlike

bemoan bewail, deplore, express sorrow, grieve for, lament, moan over, mourn, regret, rue, weep for

bemuse amaze, bewilder, confuse, daze, muddle, overwhelm, perplex, puzzle, stun

bemused absent-minded, bewildered, confused, dazed, engrossed, fuddled, half-drunk, muddled, perplexed, preoccupied, stunned, stupefied, tipsy

bench 1. form, pew, seat, settle, stall **2.** board, counter, table, trestle table, workbench, worktable **3.** court, courtroom, judge, judges, judiciary, magistrate, magistrates, tribunal

benchmark example, model, norm, reference, reference point, standard, touchstone, yardstick

bend v. **1.** bow, buckle, contort, crouch, curve, deflect, diverge, flex, incline, incurvate, lean, stoop, swerve, turn, twist, veer, warp **2.** compel, direct, influence, mould, persuade, shape, subdue, submit, sway, yield ~n. **3.** angle, arc, bow, corner, crook, curve, hook, loop, turn, twist, zigzag

beneath 1. adv. below, in a lower place, underneath **2.** prep. below, inferior to, less than, lower than, unbefitting, underneath, unworthy of

benediction beatitude, benedictus, benison, blessing, consecration, favour, grace, gratitude, invocation, orison, prayer, thankfulness, thanksgiving

benefaction 1. beneficence, benevolence, charity, generosity, liberality, munificence, philanthropy **2.** alms, bequest, boon, charity, contribution, donation, endowment, gift, grant, gratuity, legacy, offering, present

benefactor angel (Inf.), backer, contributor, donor, helper, patron, philanthropist, promoter, sponsor, subscriber, subsidizer, supporter, well-wisher

benefice Church living, emolument, office, prebend, preferment, sinecure, stipend

beneficence 1. altruism, benevolence, compassion, generosity, goodness, good will, helpfulness, kindness, liberality, love, unselfishness, virtue **2.** aid, benefaction, bestowal, donation, gift, largess, present, relief, succour

beneficent benevolent, benign, bounteous, bountiful, charitable, generous, helpful, kind, liberal, munificent, princely

beneficial advantageous, benign, favourable, gainful, healthful, helpful, profitable, salubrious, salutary, serviceable, useful, valuable, wholesome

beneficiary assignee, heir, inheritor, legatee, payee, receiver, recipient, successor

benefit 1. n. advantage, aid, asset, assistance, avail, betterment, blessing, boon, favour, gain, good, help, interest, profit, use **2.** v. advance, advantage, aid, ameliorate, assist, avail, better, enhance, further, improve, profit, promote, serve

benevolence altruism, charity, compassion, fellow feeling, generosity, goodness, good will, humanity, kindheartedness, kindness, sympathy

benevolent altruistic, beneficent, benign, bounteous, bountiful, caring, charitable, compassionate, considerate, generous, humane, humanitarian, kind, kindhearted, liberal, philanthropic, tenderhearted, warm-hearted, well-disposed

benighted backward, crude, ignorant, illiterate, primitive, uncivilized, uncultivated, unenlightened

benign 1. amiable, complaisant, friendly, generous, genial, gracious, kind, kindly, liberal, obliging, sympathetic **2.** balmy, gentle, healthful, mild, refreshing, temperate, warm, wholesome **3.** advantageous, auspicious, beneficial, encouraging, favourable, good, lucky, propitious, salutary **4.** Medical curable, harmless, limited, remediable, slight, superficial

bent adj. **1.** angled, arched, bowed, crooked, curved, hunched, stooped, twisted **2.** With on determined, disposed, fixed, inclined, insistent, predisposed, resolved, set ~n. **3.** ability, aptitude, facility, faculty, flair, forte, inclination, knack, leaning, penchant, preference, proclivity, propensity, talent, tendency

benumb anaesthetize, chill, deaden,

freeze, numb, paralyse, shock, stun, stupefy

benumbed anaesthetized, dazed, deadened, frozen, immobilized, insensible, insensitive, numb, paralysed, stunned, stupefied, unfeeling, unresponsive

bequeath bestow, commit, endow, entrust, give, grant, hand down, impart, leave to by will, pass on, transmit, will

bequest bequeathal, bestowal, dower, endowment, estate, gift, heritage, inheritance, legacy, settlement, trust

berate castigate, censure, chide, criticize, rail at, rebuke, reprimand, reproach, reprove, revile, scold, tell off (Inf.), upbraid, vituperate

bereave afflict, deprive of kindred, dispossess, divest, make destitute, strip, take away from, widow

bereavement affliction, death, deprivation, loss, misfortune, tribulation

bereft cut off, deprived, destitute, devoid, lacking, minus, parted from, shorn, wanting

berserk crazy, enraged, frantic, frenzied, insane, mad, maniacal, manic, rabid, raging, uncontrollable, violent, wild

berth n. **1.** bed, billet, bunk, cot (Naut.), hammock **2.** anchorage, dock, harbour, haven, pier, port, quay, slip, wharf **3.** appointment, employment, job, living, position, post, situation ~v. **4.** Naut. anchor, dock, drop anchor, land, moor, tie up

beseech adjure, ask, beg, call upon, crave, entreat, implore, importune, petition, plead, pray, solicit, sue, supplicate

beset 1. assail, attack, besiege, encircle, enclose, encompass, environ, hem in, surround **2.** Fig. badger, bedevil, embarrass, entangle, harass, perplex, pester, plague

besetting habitual, harassing, inveterate, persistent, prevalent, troublesome

beside 1. abreast of, adjacent to, alongside, at the side of, close to, near, nearby, neighbouring, next door to, next to, overlooking **2. beside oneself** apoplectic, berserk, crazed, delirious, demented, deranged, distraught, frantic, frenzied, insane, mad, out of one's mind, unbalanced, uncontrolled, unhinged

besides 1. adv. also, as well, further, furthermore, in addition, moreover, otherwise, too, what's more **2.** prep. apart from, barring, excepting, excluding, in addition to, other than, over and above, without

besiege 1. beleaguer, beset, blockade, confine, encircle, encompass, environ, hedge in, hem in, invest (*Rare*), lay siege to, shut in, surround **2.** badger, bother, harass, harry, hound, importune, nag, pester, plague, trouble

besmirch daub, defame, dishonour, slander, smear, soil, stain, sully, tarnish

besotted 1. befuddled, drunk, intoxicated, stupefied **2.** doting, hypnotized, infatuated, smitten, spellbound **3.** confused, foolish, muddled, witless

bespatter bedaub, befoul, begrime, besmirch, besprinkle, muddy, smear, spatter, splatter, sully

bespeak 1. engage, order beforehand, prearrange, solicit **2.** betoken, denote, display, evidence, evince, exhibit, foretell, imply, indicate, predict, proclaim, reveal, show, signify, suggest, testify to

best *adj.* **1.** chief, finest, first, first-class, first-rate, foremost, highest, leading, most excellent, outstanding, perfect, pre-eminent, principal, superlative, supreme, unsurpassed **2.** advantageous, apt, correct, golden, most desirable, most fitting, right **3.** greatest, largest, most ~*adv.* **4.** advantageously, attractively, excellently, most fortunately **5.** extremely, greatly, most deeply, most fully, most highly ~*n.* **6.** choice, cream, elite, favourite, finest, first, flower, pick, prime, top **7.** hardest, highest endeavour, utmost ~*v.* **8.** beat, conquer, defeat, get the better of, lick (*Inf.*), outclass, outdo, surpass, thrash, triumph over, trounce

bestial animal, barbaric, barbarous, beastlike, beastly, brutal, brutish, carnal, degraded, depraved, gross, inhuman, low, savage, sensual, sordid, vile

bestir activate, actuate, animate, awaken, exert, get going, incite, motivate, rouse, stimulate, stir up, trouble

bestow accord, allot, apportion, award, commit, confer, donate, entrust, give, grant, honour with, impart, lavish, present, render to

bestride bestraddle, bridge, dominate, extend, mount, span, step over, straddle, tower over

bet 1. *n.* ante, gamble, hazard, long shot, pledge, risk, speculation, stake, venture, wager **2.** *v.* chance, gamble, hazard, pledge, punt (*Brit.*), put money on, risk, speculate, stake, venture, wager

bête noire abomination, anathema, aversion, bugbear, pet hate

bethink cogitate, consider, ponder, recall, recollect, reconsider, reflect, remember, review, take thought

betide bechance, befall, chance, come to pass, crop up (*Inf.*), ensue, happen, occur, overtake, supervene, take place, transpire (*Inf.*)

betimes anon, beforehand, before long, early, first thing, in good time, punctually, seasonably, soon

betoken augur, bespeak, bode, declare, denote, evidence, indicate, manifest, mark, portend, presage, prognosticate, promise, represent, signify, suggest, typify

betray 1. be disloyal (treacherous, unfaithful), break one's promise, break with, double-cross (*Inf.*), inform on *or* against, sell down the river (*Inf.*), sell out (*Inf.*) **2.** blurt out, disclose, divulge, evince, expose, give away, lay bare, let slip, manifest, reveal, show, tell, tell on, uncover, unmask **3.** beguile, corrupt, deceive, delude, dupe, ensnare, entrap, lead astray, mislead, undo **4.** abandon, desert, forsake, jilt, walk out on

betrayal 1. deception, disloyalty, double-cross (*Inf.*), double-dealing, duplicity, falseness, perfidy, sell-out (*Inf.*), treachery, treason, trickery, unfaithfulness **2.** blurting out, disclosure, divulgence, giving away, revelation, telling

betrayer apostate, conspirator, deceiver, renegade, traitor

betroth affiance, contract, engage to marry, pledge in marriage, plight, plight one's troth, promise

betrothal affiancing, betrothing, engagement, espousal (*Archaic*), marriage compact, plight, promise, troth, vow

better *adj.* **1.** bigger, excelling, finer, fitter, greater, higher quality, larger, more appropriate (desirable, expert, fitting, suitable, useful, valuable), preferable, superior, surpassing, worthier **2.** cured, fitter, fully recovered, healthier, improving, less ill, mending, more healthy, on the mend (*Inf.*), progressing, recovering, stronger, well **3.** bigger, greater, larger, longer ~*adv.* **4.** in a more excellent manner, in a superior way, more advantageously (attractively, competently, completely, effectively, thoroughly), to a greater degree ~*v.* **5.** advance, ameliorate, amend, correct, enhance, forward, further, improve, meliorate, mend, promote, raise, rectify, reform **6**. beat, cap (*Inf.*), exceed, excel, improve on *or* upon, outdo, outstrip, surpass, top **7**. **get the better of** beat, best, defeat, get the upper hand, outdo, outsmart (*Inf.*), outwit, prevail over, score off, surpass, triumph over, worst

betterment amelioration, edification, improvement, melioration

between amidst, among, betwixt, halfway, in the middle of, mid

bevel 1. *n.* angle, bezel, cant, chamfer, diagonal, mitre, oblique, slant, slope **2**. *v.* cant, chamfer, cut at an angle, mitre

beverage draught, drink, libation (*Facetious*), liquid, liquor, potable, potation, refreshment

bevy 1. band, bunch (*Inf.*), collection, company, crowd, gathering, group, pack, troupe **2**. covey, flight, flock

bewail bemoan, cry over, deplore, express sorrow, grieve for, keen, lament, moan, mourn, regret, repent, rue, wail, weap over

beware avoid, be careful (cautious, wary), guard against, heed, look out, mind, refrain from, shun, steer clear of, take heed, watch out

bewilder baffle, befuddle, bemuse, confound, confuse, daze, mix up, mystify, perplex, puzzle, stupefy

bewildered awed, baffled, confused, disconcerted, dizzy, giddy, mystified, perplexed, puzzled, speechless, startled, stunned, surprised, taken aback, uncertain

bewitch allure, attract, beguile, captivate, charm, enchant, enrapture, entrance, fascinate, hypnotize, spellbind

bewitched charmed, enchanted, entranced, mesmerized, possessed, spellbound, transformed, under a spell, unrecognizable

beyond above, apart from, at a distance, away from, before, farther, out of range, out of reach, over, past, remote, superior to, yonder

bias *n.* **1**. bent, bigotry, favouritism, inclination, intolerance, leaning, narrow-mindedness, one-sidedness, partiality, penchant, predilection, predisposition, prejudice, proclivity, proneness, propensity, tendency, turn, unfairness **2**. angle, cross, diagonal line, slant ~*v.* **3**. distort,

influence, predispose, prejudice, slant, sway, twist, warp, weight

biased distorted, embittered, jaundiced, one-sided, partial, predisposed, prejudiced, slanted, swayed, twisted, warped, weighted

bicker argue, disagree, dispute, fight, quarrel, row (*Inf.*), scrap (*Inf.*), spar, squabble, wrangle

bid *v.* **1**. offer, proffer, propose, submit, tender **2**. call, greet, say, tell, wish **3**. ask, call, charge, command, desire, direct, enjoin, instruct, invite, require, solicit, summon, tell ~*n.* **4**. advance, amount, offer, price, proposal, proposition, submission, sum, tender **5**. attempt, crack (*Inf.*), effort, endeavour, try, venture

biddable amenable, complaisant, cooperative, docile, obedient, teachable

bidding 1. behest, call, charge, command, demand, direction, injunction, instruction, invitation, order, request, summons **2**. auction, offer, offers, proposal, tender

big 1. bulky, burly, colossal, considerable, enormous, extensive, gigantic, great, huge, hulking, immense, large, mammoth, massive, ponderous, prodigious, sizable, spacious, substantial, vast, voluminous **2**. eminent, important, influential, leading, main, momentous, paramount, powerful, prime, principal, prominent, serious, significant, valuable, weighty **3**. adult, elder, grown, grown-up, mature **4**. altruistic, benevolent, generous, gracious, heroic, magnanimous, noble, princely, unselfish **5**. arrogant, boastful, bragging, conceited, haughty, inflated, pompous, pretentious, proud

bigot dogmatist, fanatic, persecutor, sectarian, zealot

bigoted biased, dogmatic, illiberal, intolerant, narrow-minded, obstinate, opinionated, prejudiced, sectarian, twisted, warped

bigotry bias, discrimination, dogmatism, fanaticism, ignorance, injustice, intolerance, mindlessness, narrow-mindedness, prejudice, provincialism, racialism, racism, sectarianism, sexism, unfairness

bigwig big cheese (*Sl.*), big gun (*Sl.*), big noise (*Sl.*), big shot (*Sl.*, *chiefly U.S.*), celebrity, dignitary, heavyweight (*Inf.*), nob (*Sl.*), notability, notable, panjandrum, personage, somebody, V.I.P.

bile anger, bitterness, churlishness, ill

humour, irascibility, irritability, nastiness, peevishness, rancour, spleen

bilious 1. liverish, nauseated, out of sorts, queasy, sick **2.** bad-tempered, crabby, cross, crotchety, grouchy, grumpy, irritable, nasty, peevish, short-tempered, testy, touchy

bilk bamboozle, cheat, con (*Sl.*), deceive, defraud, do (*Sl.*), fleece, rook (*Sl.*), swindle, trick

bill[1] *n.* **1.** account, charges, invoice, note of charge, reckoning, score, statement, tally **2.** advertisement, broadsheet, bulletin, circular, handbill, handout, leaflet, notice, placard, playbill, poster **3.** agenda, card, catalogue, inventory, list, listing, programme, roster, schedule, syllabus **4.** measure, piece of legislation, projected law, proposal ~*v.* **5.** charge, debit, figure, invoice, reckon, record **6.** advertise, announce, give advance notice of, post

bill[2] beak, mandible, neb (*Archaic or dialect*), nib

billet 1. *n.* accommodation, barracks, lodging, quarters **2.** *v.* accommodate, berth, quarter, station

billow *n.* **1.** breaker, crest, roller, surge, swell, tide, wave **2.** cloud, deluge, flood, outpouring, rush, surge, wave ~*v.* **3.** balloon, belly, puff up, rise up, roll, surge, swell

billowy heaving, rippling, rolling, surging, swelling, swirling, undulating, waving, wavy

bind *v.* **1.** attach, fasten, glue, hitch, lash, paste, rope, secure, stick, strap, tie, tie up, truss, wrap **2.** compel, constrain, engage, force, necessitate, obligate, oblige, prescribe, require **3.** confine, detain, hamper, hinder, restrain, restrict **4.** bandage, cover, dress, encase, swathe, wrap **5.** border, edge, finish, hem, trim ~*n.* **6.** *Inf.* bore, difficulty, dilemma, nuisance, predicament, quandary

binding *adj.* compulsory, conclusive, imperative, indissoluble, irrevocable, mandatory, necessary, obligatory, unalterable

binge bender (*Sl.*), blind (*Sl.*), bout, fling, jag (*Sl.*), orgy, spree

biography account, life, life history, life story, memoir, profile

birth 1. childbirth, delivery, nativity, parturition, **2.** beginning, emergence, fountainhead, genesis, origin, rise, source **3.** ancestry, background, blood, breed-ing, derivation, descent, extraction, forebears, genealogy, line, lineage, nobility, noble extraction, parentage, pedigree, race, stock, strain

bisect bifurcate, cross, cut across, cut in half, cut in two, divide in two, halve, intersect, separate, split, split down the middle

bisexual AC/DC (*Sl.*), androgynous, epicene, gynandromorphic *or* gynandromorphous (*Entomology*), gynandrous, hermaphrodite, hermaphroditic, monoclinous (*Bot.*)

bishopric diocese, episcopacy, episcopate, primacy, see

bit[1] **1.** atom, chip, crumb, fragment, grain, iota, jot, mite, morsel, mouthful, part, piece, scrap, segment, slice, small piece, speck, tittle, whit **2.** instant, jiffy (*Inf.*), little while, minute, moment, period, second, spell, tick (*Inf.*), time

bit[2] **1.** brake, check, curb, restraint, snaffle **2. take the bit in** *or* **between one's teeth** defy, disobey, get stuck into (*Sl.*), get to grips with, rebel, resist, revolt, run amok, rush into, set about

bitchy catty (*Inf.*), cruel, malicious, mean, nasty, rancorous, snide, spiteful, venomous, vindictive, vixenish

bite *v.* **1.** champ, chew, clamp, crunch, crush, cut, gnaw, grip, hold, masticate, nibble, nip, pierce, pinch, rend, seize, snap, tear, wound **2.** burn, corrode, eat away, eat into, erode, smart, sting, tingle, wear away ~*n.* **3.** itch, nip, pinch, prick, smarting, sting, tooth marks, wound **4.** food, light meal, morsel, mouthful, piece, refreshment, snack, taste **5.** edge, kick (*Inf.*), piquancy, punch (*Inf.*), pungency, spice

biting 1. bitter, blighting, cold, cutting, freezing, harsh, nipping, penetrating, piercing, sharp **2.** caustic, cutting, incisive, mordant, sarcastic, scathing, severe, stinging, trenchant, withering

bitter 1. acid, acrid, astringent, sharp, sour, tart, unsweetened, vinegary **2.** acrimonious, begrudging, crabbed, embittered, hostile, morose, rancorous, resentful, sore, sour, sullen, with a chip on one's shoulder **3.** calamitous, cruel, dire, distressing, galling, grievous, harsh, heartbreaking, merciless, painful, poignant, ruthless, savage, vexatious **4.** biting, fierce, freezing, intense, severe, stinging

bitterness 1. acerbity, acidity, sharpness, sourness, tartness, vinegariness **2.**

animosity, grudge, hostility, pique, rancour, resentment **3.** acrimoniousness, asperity, sarcasm, venom, virulence

bizarre comical, curious, eccentric, extraordinary, fantastic, freakish, grotesque, ludicrous, odd, off-beat, outlandish, outré, peculiar, queer, ridiculous, strange, unusual, weird

blab blurt out, disclose, divulge, gossip, let slip, reveal, tattle, tell, tell on

blabber 1. *n.* busybody, gossip, informer, rumour-monger, scandalmonger, talebearer, tattler, telltale **2.** *v.* blather, blether (*Scot.*), chatter, gab (*Inf.*), jabber, prattle

blabbermouth bigmouth (*Sl.*), blatherskite, flibbertigibbet, gossip, loudmouth (*Inf.*)

black *adj.* **1.** coal-black, dark, dusky, ebony, inky, jet, murky, pitchy, raven, sable, starless, stygian, swarthy **2.** *Fig.* atrocious, depressing, dismal, distressing, doleful, foreboding, funereal, gloomy, hopeless, horrible, lugubrious, mournful, ominous, sad, sombre **3.** dingy, dirty, filthy, grimy, grubby, soiled, sooty, stained **4.** angry, furious, hostile, menacing, resentful, sullen, threatening **5.** bad, evil, iniquitous, nefarious, villainous, wicked ~*v.* **6.** ban, bar, blacklist, boycott **7. in the black** in credit, in funds, solvent, without debt

blackball *v.* ban, bar, blacklist, debar, drum out, exclude, expel, ostracize, oust, repudiate, snub, vote against

blacken 1. befoul, begrime, cloud, darken, grow black, make black, smudge, soil **2.** calumniate, decry, defame, defile, denigrate, dishonour, malign, slander, smear, smirch, stain, sully, taint, tarnish, traduce, vilify

blackguard bastard (*Offensive*), blighter (*Inf.*), bounder (*Brit. inf.*), miscreant, rascal, rogue, scoundrel, swine, villain, wretch

blacklist *v.* ban, bar, blackball, boycott, debar, exclude, expel, ostracize, preclude, proscribe, reject, repudiate, snub, vote against

black magic black art, diabolism, necromancy, sorcery, voodoo, witchcraft, wizardry

blackmail 1. *n.* bribe, exaction, extortion, hush money (*Sl.*), intimidation, milking, pay-off (*Inf.*), protection (*Inf.*), ransom, slush fund **2.** *v.* bleed (*Inf.*), bribe, coerce, compel, demand, exact, extort, force, hold to ransom, milk, squeeze, threaten

blackness darkness, duskiness, gloom, inkiness, melanism, murkiness, nigrescence, nigritude, swarthiness

blackout *n.* **1.** coma, faint, loss of consciousness, oblivion, swoon, syncope (*Pathology*), unconsciousness **2.** power cut, power failure **3.** censorship, noncommunication, radio silence, secrecy, suppression, withholding news

black out *v.* **1.** conceal, cover, darken, eclipse, obfuscate, shade **2.** collapse, faint, flake out (*Inf.*), lose consciousness, pass out, swoon

black sheep disgrace, ne'er-do-well, outcast, prodigal, renegade, reprobate, wastrel

blamable answerable, blameworthy, culpable, deserving of censure, faulty, guilty, in the wrong, liable, reprehensible, reproachable, reprovable, responsible

blame *n.* **1.** accountability, culpability, fault, guilt, incrimination, liability, onus, rap (*Inf.*), responsibility **2.** accusation, castigation, censure, charge, complaint, condemnation, criticism, recrimination, reproach, reproof ~*v.* **3.** accuse, admonish, censure, charge, chide, condemn, criticize, disapprove, express disapprobation, find fault with, hold responsible, reprehend, reproach, reprove, tax, upbraid

blameless above suspicion, clean, faultless, guiltless, immaculate, impeccable, innocent, in the clear, irreproachable, perfect, stainless, unblemished, unimpeachable, unoffending, unspotted, unsullied, untarnished, upright, virtuous

blameworthy discreditable, disreputable, indefensible, inexcusable, iniquitous, reprehensible, reproachable, shameful

blanch become *or* grow white, become pallid, bleach, blench, drain, fade, pale, turn pale, wan, whiten

bland 1. boring, dull, flat, humdrum, insipid, monotonous, tasteless, tedious, undistinctive, unexciting, uninspiring, uninteresting, unstimulating, vapid, weak **2.** affable, amiable, congenial, courteous, friendly, gentle, gracious, smooth, suave, unemotional, urbane **3.** balmy, calm, mild, mollifying, nonirritant *or* non-irritating (*Medical*), soft, soothing, temperate

blandishments blarney, cajolery, coaxing, compliments, fawning, flattery, ingratiation, inveiglement, soft soap (*Inf.*), soft words, sweet talk (*Inf., chiefly U.S.*), wheedling, winning caresses

blank *adj.* 1. bare, clean, clear, empty, plain, spotless, uncompleted, unfilled, unmarked, void, white 2. deadpan, dull, empty, expressionless, hollow, impassive, inane, lifeless, poker-faced (*Inf.*), vacant, vacuous, vague 3. at a loss, bewildered, confounded, confused, disconcerted, dumbfounded, muddled, nonplussed, uncomprehending 4. absolute, complete, outright, thorough, unqualified, utter ~*n.* 5. emptiness, empty space, gap, nothingness, space, tabula rasa, vacancy, vacuity, vacuum, void

blanket *n.* 1. afghan, cover, coverlet, rug 2. carpet, cloak, coat, coating, covering, envelope, film, layer, mantle, sheet, wrapper, wrapping ~*adj.* 3. across-the-board, all-inclusive, comprehensive, overall, sweeping, wide-ranging ~*v.* 4. cloak, cloud, coat, conceal, cover, eclipse, hide, mask, obscure, suppress, surround

blankness abstraction, fatuity, inanity, indifference, no recollection, obliviousness, vacancy, vacuity

blare blast, boom, clamour, clang, honk, hoot, peal, resound, roar, scream, sound out, toot, trumpet

blarney blandishment, cajolery, coaxing, exaggeration, flattery, honeyed words, overpraise, soft soap (*Inf.*), sweet talk (*Inf., chiefly U.S.*), wheedling

blasé apathetic, bored, cloyed, glutted, indifferent, jaded, lukewarm, nonchalant, offhand, satiated, surfeited, unconcerned, unexcited, uninterested, unmoved, weary, world-weary

blaspheme abuse, anathematize, curse, damn, desecrate, execrate, profane, revile, swear

blasphemous godless, impious, irreligious, irreverent, profane, sacrilegious, ungodly

blasphemy cursing, desecration, execration, impiety, impiousness, indignity (*to God*), irreverence, profanation, profaneness, profanity, sacrilege, swearing

blast *n./v.* 1. blare, blow, clang, honk, peal, scream, toot, wail ~*n.* 2. bang, blow-up, burst, crash, detonation, discharge, eruption, explosion, outburst, salvo, volley 3. gale, gust, squall, storm, strong breeze, tempest. ~*v.* 4. blow up, break up, burst, demolish, destroy, explode, ruin, shatter 5. blight, kill, shrivel, wither 6. attack, castigate, criticize, flay, rail at

blasted blighted, desolated, destroyed, devastated, ravaged, ruined, shattered, spoiled, wasted, withered

blastoff *n.* discharge, expulsion, firing, launch, launching, lift-off, projection, shot

blatant 1. bald, brazen, conspicuous, flagrant, flaunting, glaring, naked, obtrusive, obvious, ostentatious, outright, overt, prominent, pronounced, sheer, unmitigated 2. clamorous, deafening, ear-splitting, harsh, loud, noisy, piercing

blather claptrap (*Inf.*), drivel, gibberish, gobbledegook, jabber, jabbering, moonshine, twaddle

blaze *n.* 1. bonfire, conflagration, fire, flame, flames 2. beam, brilliance, flare, flash, glare, gleam, glitter, glow, light, radiance 3. blast, burst, eruption, flare-up, fury, outbreak, outburst, rush, storm, torrent ~*v.* 4. beam, burn, fire, flame, flare, flash, glare, gleam, glow, shine 5. boil, explode, flare up, fume, seethe

blazon broadcast, celebrate, flourish, make known, proclaim, renown, trumpet

bleach blanch, etiolate, fade, grow pale, lighten, peroxide, wash out, whiten

bleached achromatic, etiolated, faded, lightened, peroxided, stone-washed, washed-out

bleak 1. bare, barren, chilly, cold, desolate, exposed, gaunt, open, raw, unsheltered, weather-beaten, windswept, windy 2. cheerless, comfortless, depressing, discouraging, disheartening, dismal, dreary, gloomy, grim, hopeless, joyless, sombre, unpromising

bleary blurred, blurry, dim, fogged, foggy, fuzzy, hazy, indistinct, misty, murky, rheumy, watery

bleed 1. exude, flow, gush, lose blood, ooze, run, seep, shed blood, spurt, trickle, weep 2. deplete, drain, draw *or* take blood, exhaust, extort, extract, fleece, leech, milk, phlebotomize (*Medical*), reduce, sap, squeeze 3. ache, agonize, feel for, grieve, pity, suffer, sympathize

blemish 1. *n.* blot, blotch, blur, defect, disfigurement, disgrace, dishonour, fault, flaw, imperfection, mark, smudge, speck, spot, stain, taint 2. *v.* blot, blotch, blur, damage, deface, disfigure, flaw, impair, injure, mar, mark, smirch, smudge, spoil, spot, stain, sully, taint, tarnish

blench cower, cringe, falter, flinch, hesitate, quail, quake, quiver, recoil, shrink, shudder, shy, start, wince

blend v. 1. amalgamate, coalesce, combine, compound, fuse, intermix, merge, mingle, mix, synthesize, unite 2. complement, fit, go well, go with, harmonize, suit ~n. 3. alloy, amalgam, amalgamation, combination, composite, compound, concoction, fusion, mix, mixture, synthesis, union

bless 1. anoint, consecrate, dedicate, exalt, extol, give thanks to, glorify, hallow, invoke happiness on, magnify, ordain, praise, sanctify, thank 2. bestow, endow, favour, give, grace, grant, provide

blessed 1. adored, beatified, divine, hallowed, holy, revered, sacred, sanctified 2. endowed, favoured, fortunate, granted, lucky 3. blissful, contented, glad, happy, joyful, joyous

blessedness beatitude, bliss, blissfulness, content, felicity, happiness, heavenly joy, pleasure, sanctity, state of grace, *summum bonum*

blessing 1. benediction, benison, commendation, consecration, dedication, grace, invocation, thanksgiving 2. approbation, approval, backing, concurrence, consent, favour, good wishes, leave, permission, regard, sanction, support 3. advantage, benefit, boon, bounty, favour, gain, gift, godsend, good fortune, help, kindness, profit, service, windfall

blight n. 1. canker, decay, disease, fungus, infestation, mildew, pest, pestilence, rot 2. affliction, bane, contamination, corruption, curse, evil, plague, pollution, scourge, woe ~v. 3. blast, destroy, injure, nip in the bud, ruin, shrivel, taint with mildew, wither 4. *Fig.* annihilate, crush, dash, disappoint, frustrate, mar, nullify, ruin, spoil, wreck

blind adj. 1. destitute of vision, eyeless, sightless, stone-blind, unseeing, unsighted, visionless 2. *Fig.* careless, heedless, ignorant, inattentive, inconsiderate, indifferent, indiscriminate, injudicious, insensitive, morally darkened, neglectful, oblivious, prejudiced, thoughtless, unaware of, unconscious of, uncritical, undiscerning, unmindful of, unobservant, unreasoning 3. hasty, impetuous, irrational, mindless, rash, reckless, senseless, uncontrollable, uncontrolled, un-

thinking, violent, wild 4. closed, concealed, dark, dead-end, dim, hidden, leading nowhere, obscured, obstructed, without exit ~n. 5. camouflage, cloak, cover, façade, feint, front, mask, masquerade, screen, smoke screen

blindly 1. aimlessly, at random, confusedly, frantically, indiscriminately, instinctively, madly, purposelessly, wildly 2. carelessly, heedlessly, impulsively, inconsiderately, passionately, recklessly, regardlessly, senselessly, thoughtlessly, unreasonably, wilfully

blink 1. bat, flutter, glimpse, nictate, nictitate, peer, squint, wink 2. flash, flicker, gleam, glimmer, scintillate, shine, sparkle, twinkle, wink 3. *Fig.* condone, connive at, disregard, ignore, overlook, pass by, turn a blind eye to 4. **on the blink** *Inf.* faulty, malfunctioning, not working (properly), out of action, out of order, playing up

bliss beatitude, blessedness, blissfulness, ecstasy, euphoria, felicity, gladness, happiness, heaven, joy, paradise, rapture

blissful delighted, ecstatic, elated, enchanted, enraptured, euphoric, happy, heavenly (*Inf.*), in ecstasies, joyful, joyous, rapturous

blister abscess, blain, bleb, boil, bubble, canker, carbuncle, cyst, furuncle (*Pathology*), pimple, pustule, sore, swelling, ulcer, welt, wen

blithe 1. animated, buoyant, carefree, cheerful, cheery, debonair, gay, gladsome, happy, jaunty, light-hearted, merry, mirthful, sprightly, sunny, vivacious 2. careless, casual, heedless, indifferent, nonchalant, thoughtless, unconcerned, untroubled

blitz assault, attack, blitzkrieg, bombardment, offensive, onslaught, raid, strike

blizzard blast, gale, snowstorm, squall, storm, tempest

bloat balloon, blow up, dilate, distend, enlarge, expand, inflate, puff up, swell

blob ball, bead, bubble, dab, dewdrop, drop, droplet, glob, globule, lump, mass, pearl, pellet, pill

bloc alliance, axis, cabal, clique, coalition, combine, entente, faction, group, league, ring, union, wing

block n. 1. bar, brick, cake, chunk, cube, hunk, ingot, lump, mass, piece, square 2. bar, barrier, blockage, hindrance, impediment, jam, obstacle, obstruction, stoppage ~v. **3**. bung up (*Inf.*), choke, clog, close, obstruct, plug, stop up **4**. arrest, bar, check, deter, halt, hinder, impede, obstruct, stop, thwart

blockade barricade, barrier, closure, encirclement, hindrance, impediment, obstacle, obstruction, restriction, siege, stoppage

blockage block, blocking, impediment, obstruction, occlusion, stoppage, stopping up

blockhead bonehead (*Sl.*), dolt, dullard, dunce, fool, idiot, ignoramus, numskull

block out chart, map out, outline, plan, sketch

blond, blonde fair, fair-haired, fair-skinned, flaxen, golden-haired, light, light-coloured, light-complexioned, tow-headed

blood 1. gore, lifeblood, vital fluid **2**. ancestry, birth, consanguinity, descendants, descent, extraction, family, kindred, kinship, lineage, noble extraction, relations **3**. *Fig.* anger, disposition, feeling, passion, spirit, temper

bloodcurdling appalling, chilling, dreadful, fearful, frightening, hair-raising, horrendous, horrifying, scaring, spine-chilling, terrifying

bloodless 1. cold, languid, lifeless, listless, passionless, spiritless, torpid, unemotional, unfeeling **2**. anaemic, ashen, chalky, colourless, pale, pallid, pasty, sallow, sickly, wan

bloodshed blood bath, bloodletting, butchery, carnage, gore, killing, massacre, murder, slaughter, slaying

bloodthirsty barbarous, brutal, cruel, ferocious, inhuman, murderous, ruthless, savage, vicious, warlike

bloody 1. bleeding, blood-soaked, blood-spattered, bloodstained, gaping, raw, unstaunched **2**. cruel, ferocious, fierce, sanguinary, savage

bloom n. **1**. blossom, blossoming, bud, efflorescence, flower, opening (*of flowers*) **2**. *Fig.* beauty, blush, flourishing, flush, freshness, glow, health, heyday, lustre, perfection, prime, radiance, rosiness, vigour ~v. **3**. blossom, blow, bud, burgeon, open, sprout **4**. develop, fare well, flourish, grow, prosper, succeed, thrive, wax

blossom n. **1**. bloom, bud, floret, flower, flowers ~v. **2**. bloom, burgeon, flower **3**. *Fig.* bloom, develop, flourish, grow, mature, progress, prosper, thrive

blot n. **1**. blotch, mark, patch, smear, smudge, speck, splodge, spot **2**. blemish, blur, defect, disgrace, fault, flaw, spot, stain, taint ~v. **3**. bespatter, disfigure, disgrace, mark, smudge, spoil, spot, stain, sully, tarnish **4**. absorb, dry, soak up, take up **5. blot out** cancel, darken, destroy, efface, erase, expunge, obliterate, obscure, shadow

blotch blemish, blot, mark, patch, smudge, smutch, splash, splodge, spot, stain

blow¹ v. **1**. blast, breathe, exhale, fan, pant, puff, waft **2**. flow, rush, stream, whirl **3**. bear, buffet, drive, fling, flutter, sweep, waft, whirl, whisk **4**. blare, mouth, pipe, play, sound, toot, trumpet, vibrate ~n. **5**. blast, draught, flurry, gale, gust, puff, strong breeze, tempest, wind

blow² n. **1**. bang, bash (*Inf.*), belt (*Inf.*), buffet, clomp (*Sl.*), clout (*Inf.*), clump (*Sl.*), knock, punch, rap, slosh (*Sl.*), smack, sock (*Sl.*), stroke, thump, wallop (*Inf.*), whack **2**. *Fig.* affliction, bolt from the blue, bombshell, calamity, catastrophe, comedown (*Inf.*), disappointment, disaster, jolt, misfortune, reverse, setback, shock, upset

blowout 1. blast, detonation, eruption, explosion **2**. break, burst, escape, flat, flat tyre, fuse, leak, puncture, rupture, tear **3**. binge, feast, party, spree

blow out 1. extinguish, put out, snuff **2**. burst, erupt, explode, rupture, shatter

blow over be forgotten, cease, die down, disappear, end, finish, pass, pass away, subside, vanish

blow up 1. bloat, distend, enlarge, expand, fill, inflate, puff up, pump up, swell **2**. blast, bomb, burst, detonate, dynamite, explode, go off, rupture, shatter **3**. enlarge, enlarge on, exaggerate, heighten, magnify, overstate **4**. *Inf.* become angry, become enraged, erupt, go off the deep end (*Inf.*), hit the roof (*Inf.*), lose one's temper, rage

blowy blustery, breezy, draughty, exposed, fresh, stormy, well-ventilated, windy

blowzy, blowsy 1. bedraggled, dishevelled, frowzy, slatternly, slipshod, sloppy, slovenly, sluttish, tousled, unkempt, untidy **2**. florid, red-faced, ruddy

bludgeon n. **1**. club, cudgel, shillelagh, truncheon ~v. **2**. beat, beat up, club, cudgel, knock down, strike **3**. browbeat, bulldoze (*Inf.*), bully, coerce, force, hector, steamroller

blue 1. azure, cerulean, cobalt, cyan, navy, sapphire, sky-coloured, ultramarine 2. *Fig.* dejected, depressed, despondent, dismal, downcast, downhearted, down in the dumps (*Inf.*), fed up, gloomy, glum, low, melancholy, sad, unhappy 3. *Inf.* bawdy, dirty, indecent, lewd, naughty, near the knuckle (*Inf.*), obscene, risqué, smutty, vulgar

blueprint design, draft, layout, outline, pattern, pilot scheme, plan, project, prototype, scheme, sketch

blues dejection, depression, despondency, doldrums, dumps (*Inf.*), gloom, gloominess, glumness, low spirits, melancholy, moodiness

bluff¹ 1. *v.* deceive, defraud, delude, fake, feign, humbug, lie, mislead, pretend, sham 2. *n.* bluster, boast, braggadocio, bragging, bravado, deceit, deception, fake, feint, fraud, humbug, idle boast, lie, mere show, pretence, sham, show, subterfuge

bluff² *n.* 1. bank, cliff, crag, escarpment, headland, peak, precipice, promontory, ridge, scarp ~*adj.* 2. abrupt, blunt, blustering, downright, frank, genial, good-natured, hearty, open, outspoken, plain-spoken 3. abrupt, perpendicular, precipitous, sheer, steep, towering

blunder *n.* 1. error, fault, inaccuracy, mistake, oversight, slip, slip-up (*Inf.*) 2. boob (*Sl.*), clanger (*Inf.*), faux pas, gaffe, gaucherie, howler (*Inf.*), impropriety, indiscretion, mistake ~*v.* 3. botch, bungle, err, slip up (*Inf.*) 4. bumble, confuse, flounder, misjudge, stumble

blunt *adj.* 1. dull, dulled, edgeless, pointless, rounded, unsharpened 2. *Fig.* bluff, brusque, discourteous, explicit, forthright, frank, impolite, outspoken, plain-spoken, rude, straightforward, tactless, trenchant, uncivil, unpolished ~*v.* 3. dampen, deaden, dull, numb, soften, take the edge off, water down, weaken

blur *v.* 1. becloud, bedim, befog, cloud, darken, dim, fog, make hazy, make indistinct, make vague, mask, obscure, soften 2. blot, smear, smudge, spot, stain ~*n.* 3. blear, blurredness, cloudiness, confusion, dimness, fog, haze, indistinctness, obscurity 4. blot, smear, smudge, spot, stain

blurred bleary, blurry, faint, foggy, fuzzy, hazy, ill-defined, indistinct, lacking definition, misty, nebulous, out of focus, unclear, vague

blurt out babble, blab, cry, disclose, exclaim, gush, reveal, spill, spout (*Inf.*), sputter, tattle, utter suddenly

blush 1. *v.* colour, crimson, flush, redden, turn red, turn scarlet 2. *n.* colour, flush, glow, pink tinge, reddening, rosiness, rosy tint, ruddiness

bluster 1. *v.* boast, brag, bulldoze, bully, domineer, hector, rant, roar, roister, storm, swagger, swell, vaunt 2. *n.* bluff, boasting, boisterousness, bombast, bragging, bravado, crowing, swagger, swaggering

blustery blusterous, boisterous, gusty, squally, stormy, tempestuous, violent, wild

board *n.* 1. panel, piece of timber, plank, slat, timber 2. daily meals, food, meals, provisions, victuals 3. advisers, advisory group, committee, conclave, council, directorate, directors, panel, trustees ~*v.* 4. embark, embus, enplane, enter, entrain, mount 5. accommodate, feed, house, lodge, put up, quarter, room

boast *v.* 1. blow one's own trumpet, bluster, brag, crow, exaggerate, puff, strut, swagger, talk big (*Sl.*), vaunt 2. be proud of, congratulate oneself on, exhibit, flatter oneself, possess, pride oneself on, show off ~*n.* 3. avowal, brag, gasconade (*Rare*), rodomontade (*Literary*), swank (*Inf.*), vaunt 4. gem, joy, pride, pride and joy, source of pride, treasure

boastful bragging, cocky, conceited, crowing, egotistical, puffed-up, swaggering, swanky (*Inf.*), swollen-headed, vainglorious, vaunting

bob bounce, duck, hop, jerk, leap, nod, oscillate, quiver, skip, waggle, weave, wobble

bob up appear, arise, emerge, materialize, pop up, rise, spring up, surface, turn up

bode augur, betoken, forebode, foreshadow, foretell, forewarn, impart, omen, portend, predict, presage, prophesy, signify, threaten

bodiless disembodied, ghostly, immaterial, incorporeal, insubstantial, spectral, spiritual, supernatural

bodily 1. *adj.* actual, carnal, corporal, corporeal, fleshly, material, physical, substantial, tangible 2. *adv.* altogether, as a body, as a group, collectively, completely, en masse, entirely, fully, totally, wholly

body 1. build, figure, form, frame, physique, shape, torso, trunk **2.** cadaver, carcass, corpse, dead body, relics, remains, stiff (*Sl.*) **3.** being, creature, human, human being, individual, mortal, person **4.** bulk, essence, main part, mass, material, matter, substance **5.** association, band, bloc, collection, company, confederation, congress, corporation, society **6.** crowd, horde, majority, mass, mob, multitude, throng **7.** consistency, density, firmness, richness, solidity, substance

bog fen, marsh, marshland, mire, morass, moss (*Northern Eng. & Scot.*), peat bog, quagmire, slough, swamp, wetlands

bog down delay, halt, impede, sink, slow down, slow up, stall, stick

bogey 1. apparition, bogeyman, goblin, hobgoblin, imp, spectre, spirit, spook (*Inf.*), sprite **2.** bête noire, bugaboo, bugbear, nightmare

boggle 1. be alarmed (confused, surprised, taken aback), shy, stagger, startle, take fright **2.** demur, dither, doubt, equivocate, falter, hang back, hesitate, hover, jib, shillyshally (*Inf.*), shrink from, vacillate, waver

boggy fenny, marshy, miry, muddy, oozy, quaggy, soft, spongy, swampy, waterlogged, yielding

bogus artificial, counterfeit, dummy, fake, false, forged, fraudulent, imitation, phoney (*Sl.*), pseudo (*Inf.*), sham, spurious

bohemian 1. *adj.* alternative, artistic, arty (*Inf.*), avant-garde, eccentric, exotic, left bank, nonconformist, offbeat, unconventional, unorthodox, way-out (*Inf.*) **2.** *n.* beatnik, dropout, hippie, iconoclast, nonconformist

boil[1] *v.* **1.** agitate, bubble, churn, effervesce, fizz, foam, froth, seethe **2.** be angry, be indignant, foam at the mouth (*Inf.*), fulminate, fume, rage, rave, storm

boil[2] *n.* blain, blister, carbuncle, furuncle (*Pathology*), gathering, pustule, tumour, ulcer

boil down come down, condense, decrease, reduce, summarize

boiling 1. baking, blistering, hot, roasting, scorching, tropical, very hot **2.** angry, enraged, fuming, furious, incensed, indignant, infuriated

boisterous 1. bouncy, clamorous, disorderly, impetuous, loud, noisy, obstreperous, riotous, rollicking, rowdy, rumbustious, unrestrained, unruly, uproarious, vociferous, wild **2.** blustery, gusty, raging, rough, squally, stormy, tempestuous, tumultuous, turbulent

bold 1. adventurous, audacious, brave, courageous, daring, dauntless, enterprising, fearless, gallant, heroic, intrepid, lion-hearted, valiant, valorous **2.** barefaced, brash, brazen, cheeky, confident, forward, fresh (*Inf.*), impudent, insolent, pert, rude, saucy, shameless **3.** bright, colourful, conspicuous, eye-catching, flashy, forceful, lively, loud, prominent, pronounced, showy, spirited, striking, strong, vivid

bolster aid, assist, boost, brace, buoy up, buttress, cushion, help, hold up, maintain, pillow, prop, reinforce, shore up, stay, strengthen, support

bolt *n.* **1.** bar, catch, fastener, latch, lock, sliding bar **2.** peg, pin, rivet, rod **3.** bound, dart, dash, escape, flight, rush, spring, sprint **4.** arrow, dart, missile, projectile, shaft, thunderbolt ~*v.* **5.** bar, fasten, latch, lock, secure **6.** cram, devour, gobble, gorge, gulp, guzzle, stuff, swallow whole, wolf **7.** abscond, bound, dash, escape, flee, fly, hurtle, jump, leap, make a break (for it), run, run for it, rush, spring, sprint

bomb 1. *n.* bombshell, charge, device, explosive, grenade, mine, missile, projectile, rocket, shell, torpedo **2.** *v.* attack, blow up, bombard, destroy, shell, strafe, torpedo

bombard 1. assault, blast, blitz, bomb, cannonade, fire upon, open fire, pound, shell, strafe **2.** assail, attack, barrage, batter, beset, besiege, harass, hound, pester

bombardment assault, attack, barrage, blitz, bombing, cannonade, fire, flak, fusillade, shelling, strafe

bombast bluster, brag, braggadocio, extravagant boasting, fustian, gasconade (*Rare*), grandiloquence, grandiosity, magniloquence, pomposity, rant, rodomontade (*Literary*)

bombastic declamatory, fustian, grandiloquent, grandiose, high-flown, histrionic, inflated, magniloquent, pompous, ranting, turgid, verbose, windy, wordy

bona fide actual, authentic, genuine, honest, lawful, legal, legitimate, real, true

bond *n.* **1**. band, binding, chain, cord, fastening, fetter, ligature, link, manacle, shackle, tie **2**. affiliation, affinity, attachment, connection, link, relation, tie, union **3**. agreement, compact, contract, covenant, guarantee, obligation, pledge, promise, word ~*v.* **4**. bind, connect, fasten, fix together, fuse, glue, gum, paste

bondage captivity, confinement, duress, enslavement, enthralment, imprisonment, serfdom, servitude, slavery, subjection, subjugation, thraldom, vassalage, yoke

bonny 1. beautiful, comely, fair, handsome, lovely, pretty, sweet **2**. bouncing, buxom, chubby, fine, plump, rounded, shapely **3**. blithe, cheerful, cheery, gay, joyful, merry, sunny, winsome

bonus benefit, bounty, commission, dividend, extra, gift, gratuity, hand-out, honorarium, plus, premium, prize, reward

bony angular, emaciated, gangling, gaunt, lanky, lean, rawboned, scrawny, skinny, thin

booby blockhead, charlie (*Inf.*), dimwit (*Inf.*), duffer (*Inf.*), dunce, fool, goof (*Inf.*), idiot, muggins (*Sl.*), simpleton

book *n.* **1**. manual, publication, roll, scroll, textbook, tome, tract, volume, work **2**. album, diary, exercise book, jotter, notebook, pad ~*v.* **3**. arrange for, bill, charter, engage, line up, make reservations, organize, procure, programme, reserve, schedule **4**. enrol, enter, insert, list, log, mark down, note, post, put down, record, register, write down

bookish academic, donnish, erudite, intellectual, learned, literary, pedantic, scholarly, studious

boom *v.* **1**. bang, blast, crash, explode, resound, reverberate, roar, roll, rumble, thunder **2**. develop, expand, flourish, gain, grow, increase, intensify, prosper, spurt, strengthen, succeed, swell, thrive ~*n.* **3**. bang, blast, burst, clap, crash, explosion, roar, rumble, thunder **4**. advance, boost, development, expansion, gain, growth, improvement, increase, jump, push, spurt, upsurge, upswing, upturn

boomerang backfire, come back, come home to roost, rebound, recoil, return, reverse, ricochet

boon 1. *n.* advantage, benefaction, benefit, blessing, donation, favour, gift, godsend, grant, gratuity, present, windfall **2**. *adj.* close, intimate, special

boor barbarian, brute, bumpkin, churl, clodhopper (*Inf.*), clodpole, lout, oaf, peasant, philistine, vulgarian

boorish awkward, barbaric, bearish, churlish, clownish, coarse, crude, gross, gruff, ill-bred, loutish, lubberly, oafish, rude, rustic, uncivilized, uncouth, uneducated, unrefined, vulgar

boost *n.* **1**. encouragement, help, improvement, praise, promotion **2**. heave, hoist, lift, push, raise, shove, thrust **3**. addition, expansion, improvement, increase, increment, jump, rise ~*v.* **4**. advance, advertise, assist, encourage, foster, further, improve, inspire, plug (*Inf.*), praise, promote, support, sustain **5**. elevate, heave, hoist, lift, push, raise, shove, thrust **6**. add to, amplify, develop, enlarge, expand, heighten, hoick, increase, jack up, magnify, raise

boot *v.* **1**. drive, drop-kick, kick, knock, punt, shove **2**. *Inf.* dismiss, eject, expel, kick out, oust, sack (*Inf.*), throw out

bootless fruitless, futile, ineffective, profitless, unavailing, unsuccessful, useless, vain

bootlicker fawner, flatterer, flunky, lackey, spaniel, sycophant, toady, yes man

booty boodle (*Sl., chiefly U.S.*), gains, haul, loot, pillage, plunder, prey, spoil, spoils, swag (*Sl.*), takings, winnings

border *n.* **1**. bound, boundary, bounds, brim, brink, confine, confines, edge, hem, limit, limits, lip, margin, rim, skirt, verge **2**. borderline, boundary, frontier, line, march ~*v.* **3**. bind, decorate, edge, fringe, hem, rim, trim

borderline *adj.* ambivalent, doubtful, equivocal, indecisive, indefinite, indeterminate, inexact, marginal, unclassifiable

border on 1. abut, adjoin, connect, contact, impinge, join, march, neighbour, touch, verge on **2**. approach, approximate, be like, be similar to, come close to, come near, echo, match, parallel, resemble

bore¹ 1. *v.* burrow, drill, gouge out, mine, penetrate, perforate, pierce, sink, tunnel **2**. *n.* borehole, calibre, drill hole, hole, shaft, tunnel

bore² 1. *v.* annoy, be tedious, bother, exhaust, fatigue, jade, pall on, pester, send to sleep, tire, trouble, vex, wear out, weary, worry **2**. *n.* bother, drag (*Sl.*), dull person, headache (*Inf.*), nuisance, pain (*Inf.*), pain in the neck (*Inf.*), pest, tiresome person, wearisome talker

boredom apathy, doldrums, dullness, ennui, flatness, irksomeness, monotony, sameness, tedium, tediousness, weariness, world-weariness

boring dead, dull, flat, humdrum, insipid, monotonous, repetitious, routine, stale, tedious, tiresome, tiring, unexciting, uninteresting, unvaried, wearisome

borrow 1. cadge, scrounge (*Inf.*), take and return, take on loan, use temporarily **2.** acquire, adopt, appropriate, copy, filch, imitate, obtain, pilfer, pirate, plagiarize, simulate, steal, take, use, usurp

bosom *n*. **1.** breast, bust, chest **2.** affections, emotions, feelings, heart, sentiments, soul, spirit, sympathies **3.** centre, circle, core, midst, protection, shelter ~*adj.* **4.** boon, cherished, close, confidential, intimate, very dear

boss[1] **1.** *n.* administrator, chief, director, employer, executive, foreman, gaffer (*Inf.*), governor (*Inf.*), head, leader, manager, master, overseer, owner, superintendent, supervisor **2.** *v.* administrate, command, control, direct, employ, manage, oversee, run, superintend, supervise, take charge

boss[2] knob, nub, nubble, point, protuberance, stud, tip

boss around bully, dominate, domineer, oppress, order, overbear, push around (*Sl.*), put upon, tyrannize

bossy arrogant, authoritarian, despotic, dictatorial, domineering, highhanded, imperious, lordly, overbearing, tyrannical

botch 1. *v.* blunder, bungle, butcher, cobble, fumble, mar, mend, mess, mismanage, muff, patch, spoil **2.** *n.* blunder, bungle, bungling, failure, fumble, hash, mess, miscarriage

bother 1. *v.* alarm, annoy, concern, dismay, distress, disturb, harass, inconvenience, irritate, molest, nag, pester, plague, put out, trouble, upset, vex, worry **2.** *n.* aggravation, annoyance, bustle, difficulty, flurry, fuss, inconvenience, irritation, molestation, nuisance, perplexity, pest, problem, strain, trouble, vexation, worry

bothersome aggravating, annoying, distressing, exasperating, inconvenient, irritating, tiresome, troublesome, vexatious, vexing

bottleneck block, blockage, congestion, hold-up, impediment, jam, obstacle, obstruction

bottle up check, contain, curb, keep back, restrict, shut in, suppress, trap

bottom *n.* **1.** base, basis, bed, deepest part, depths, floor, foot, foundation, groundwork, lowest part, pedestal, support **2.** lower side, sole, underneath, underside **3.** backside, behind (*Inf.*), bum (*Sl.*), buttocks, fundament, posterior, rear, rear end, rump, seat, tail (*Inf.*) **4.** base, basis, cause, core, essence, ground, heart, mainspring, origin, principle, root, source, substance ~*adj.* **5.** base, basement, basic, fundamental, ground, last, lowest, undermost

bottomless boundless, deep, fathomless, immeasurable, inexhaustible, infinite, unfathomable, unlimited

bounce *v.* **1.** bob, bound, bump, jounce, jump, leap, rebound, recoil, resile, ricochet, spring, thump **2.** *Sl.* boot out (*Inf.*), eject, fire (*Inf.*), kick out (*Inf.*), oust, throw out ~*n.* **3.** bound, elasticity, give, rebound, recoil, resilience, spring, springiness **4.** animation, dynamism, energy, go (*Inf.*), life, liveliness, pep, vigour, vitality, vivacity, zip (*Inf.*)

bouncing blooming, bonny, healthy, robust, thriving, vigorous

bound[1] *adj.* **1.** cased, fastened, fixed, pinioned, secured, tied, tied up **2.** certain, destined, doomed, fated, sure **3.** beholden, committed, compelled, constrained, duty-bound, forced, obligated, obliged, pledged, required

bound[2] *v./n.* bob, bounce, caper, frisk, gambol, hurdle, jump, leap, pounce, prance, skip, spring, vault

bound[3] *n.* **1.** *Usually plural* border, boundary, confine, edge, extremity, fringe, limit, line, march, margin, pale, periphery, rim, termination, verge **2. out of bounds** banned, barred, forbidden, off-limits (*Chiefly U.S. military*), prohibited, taboo ~*v.* **3.** circumscribe, confine, define, delimit, demarcate, encircle, enclose, hem in, limit, restrain, restrict, surround, terminate

boundary barrier, border, borderline, bounds, brink, confines, edge, extremity, fringe, frontier, limits, march, margin, precinct, termination, verge

boundless endless, illimitable, immeasurable, immense, incalculable, inexhaustible, infinite, limitless, measureless, unbounded, unconfined, unending, unlimited, untold, vast

bountiful 1. abundant, ample, bounteous, copious, exuberant, lavish, luxuriant, plenteous, plentiful, prolific **2.** beneficent, bounteous, generous, liberal, magnanimous, munificent, open-handed, princely, unstinting

bounty 1. almsgiving, assistance, beneficence, benevolence, charity, generosity, kindness, liberality, open-handedness, philanthropy **2.** bonus, donation, gift, grant, gratuity, largess, premium, present, recompense, reward

bouquet 1. boutonniere, bunch of flowers, buttonhole, corsage, garland, nosegay, posy, spray, wreath **2.** aroma, fragrance, perfume, redolence, savour, scent

bourgeois conventional, hidebound, materialistic, middle-class, traditional

bourn 1. *Archaic* border, boundary, confine, destination, goal, limit **2.** *Chiefly southern Brit.* brook, burn, rill, rivulet, stream, torrent **3.** *Fig.* death

bout 1. course, fit, period, round, run, session, spell, spree, stint, stretch, term, time, turn **2.** battle, boxing match, competition, contest, encounter, engagement, fight, match, set-to, struggle

bovine dense, dull, slow, sluggish, stolid, stupid, thick

bow¹ *v.* **1.** bend, bob, droop, genuflect, incline, make obeisance, nod, stoop **2.** accept, acquiesce, comply, concede, defer, give in, kowtow, relent, submit, surrender, yield **3.** cast down, conquer, crush, depress, overpower, subdue, subjugate, vanquish, weigh down ~*n.* **4.** bending, bob, genuflexion, inclination, kowtow, nod, obeisance, salaam

bow² *Naut.* beak, fore, head, prow, stem

bowdlerize blue-pencil, censor, clean up, expurgate, mutilate

bowels 1. entrails, guts, innards (*Inf.*), insides (*Inf.*), intestines, viscera, vitals **2.** belly, core, deep, depths, hold, inside, interior **3.** *Archaic* compassion, mercifulness, mercy, pity, sympathy, tenderness

bower alcove, arbour, grotto, leafy shelter, shady recess, summerhouse

bowl 1. *n.* basin, deep dish, vessel **2.** *v.* fling, hurl, pitch, revolve, roll, rotate, spin, throw, trundle, whirl

bowl over 1. amaze, astonish,

astound, dumbfound, stagger, startle, stun, surprise **2.** bring down, fell, floor, knock down, overthrow, overturn

bow out abandon, back out, get out, give up, pull out, quit, resign, retire, step down, withdraw

box¹ **1.** *n.* carton, case, chest, container, pack, package, portmanteau, receptacle, trunk **2.** *v.* pack, package, wrap

box² *v.* **1.** exchange blows, fight, spar **2.** buffet, butt, clout (*Inf.*), cuff, hit, punch, slap, sock (*Sl.*), strike, thwack, wallop (*Inf.*), whack ~*n.* **3.** blow, buffet, clout (*Inf.*), cuff, punch, slap, stroke, thumping, wallop (*Inf.*)

boxer fighter, prizefighter, pugilist, sparrer, sparring partner

box in cage, confine, contain, coop up, enclose, hem in, isolate, shut in, surround, trap

boxing fisticuffs, prizefighting, pugilism, sparring, the fight game (*Inf.*), the ring

boy fellow, junior, lad, schoolboy, stripling, youngster, youth

boycott ban, bar, black, blackball, blacklist, embargo, exclude, ostracize, outlaw, prohibit, proscribe, refrain from, refuse, reject, spurn

boyfriend admirer, beau, date, follower, lover, man, steady, suitor, swain, sweetheart, young man

boyish adolescent, childish, immature, innocent, juvenile, puerile, young, youthful

brace 1. *n.* bracer, bracket, buttress, prop, reinforcement, stanchion, stay, strut, support, truss **2.** *v.* bandage, bind, bolster, buttress, fasten, fortify, hold up, prop, reinforce, shove, shove up, steady, strap, strengthen, support, tie, tighten

bracing brisk, chilly, cool, crisp, energizing, exhilarating, fortifying, fresh, invigorating, lively, refreshing, restorative, reviving, rousing, stimulating, tonic, vigorous

brackish bitter, briny, saline, salt, salty, undrinkable

brag blow one's own trumpet, bluster, boast, crow, swagger, talk big (*Sl.*), vaunt

braggart bigmouth (*Sl.*), bluffer, blusterer, boaster, brag, braggadocio, bragger, show-off, swaggerer, swashbuckler

braid entwine, interlace, intertwine, interweave, lace, plait, ravel, twine, weave

brain egghead (*Inf.*), genius, highbrow,

intellect, intellectual, mastermind, prodigy, pundit, sage, scholar

brainless foolish, idiotic, inept, mindless, senseless, stupid, thoughtless, unintelligent, witless

brains capacity, intellect, intelligence, mind, nous (*Sl.*), reason, sagacity, savvy (*Sl.*), sense, shrewdness, understanding, wit

brainwashing alteration, conditioning, indoctrination, persuasion, re-education

brainy bright, brilliant, clever, intelligent, smart

brake 1. *n.* check, constraint, control, curb, rein, restraint **2.** *v.* check, decelerate, halt, moderate, reduce speed, slacken, slow, stop

branch 1. arm, bough, limb, offshoot, prong, ramification, shoot, spray, sprig **2.** chapter, department, division, local office, office, part, section, subdivision, subsection, wing

branch out add to, develop, diversify, enlarge, expand, extend, increase, multiply, proliferate, ramify, spread out

brand *n.* **1.** cast, class, grade, kind, make, quality, sort, species, type, variety **2.** emblem, hallmark, label, mark, marker, sign, stamp, symbol, trademark **3.** blot, disgrace, infamy, mark, reproach, slur, smirch, stain, stigma, taint ~*v.* **4.** burn, burn in, label, mark, scar, stamp **5.** censure, denounce, discredit, disgrace, expose, mark, stigmatize

brandish display, exhibit, flaunt, flourish, parade, raise, shake, swing, wield

brash 1. audacious, foolhardy, hasty, impetuous, impulsive, indiscreet, precipitate, rash, reckless **2.** bold, brazen, cocky, forward, heedless, impertinent, impudent, insolent, rude

brass audacity, cheek, effrontery, gall, impertinence, impudence, insolence, nerve (*Inf.*), presumption, rudeness

brassy 1. barefaced, bold, brash, brazen, forward, impudent, insolent, loud-mouthed, pert, saucy **2.** blatant, flashy, garish, gaudy, hard, jazzy (*Inf.*), loud, obtrusive, showy, vulgar **3.** blaring, cacophonous, dissonant, grating, harsh, jangling, jarring, loud, noisy, piercing, raucous, shrill, strident

brat cub, guttersnipe, jackanapes, kid (*Inf.*), puppy (*Inf.*), rascal, spoilt child, urchin, whippersnapper, youngster

bravado bluster, boast, boastfulness, boasting, bombast, brag, braggadocio, fanfaronade (*Rare*), swagger, swaggering, swashbuckling, vaunting

brave 1. *adj.* bold, courageous, daring, dauntless, fearless, gallant, heroic, intrepid, plucky, resolute, undaunted, valiant, valorous **2.** *v.* bear, beard, challenge, confront, dare, defy, endure, face, stand up to, suffer, withstand

bravery boldness, courage, daring, dauntlessness, doughtiness, fearlessness, fortitude, gallantry, grit, guts (*Inf.*), hardihood, hardiness, heroism, indomitability, intrepidity, mettle, pluck, pluckiness, spirit, spunk (*Inf.*), valour

bravo assassin, bandit, brigand, cutthroat, desperado, hired killer, murderer, villain

bravura animation, audacity, boldness, brilliance, brio, daring, dash, display, élan, energy, exhibitionism, ostentation, panache, punch (*Inf.*), spirit, verve, vigour, virtuosity

brawl 1. *n.* affray (*Law*), altercation, argument, battle, broil, clash, disorder, dispute, donnybrook, fight, fracas, fray, free-for-all (*Inf.*), melee, punch-up (*Sl.*), quarrel, row (*Inf.*), ruckus (*Inf.*), rumpus, scrap (*Inf.*), scuffle, squabble, tumult, uproar, wrangle **2.** *v.* altercate, argue, battle, dispute, fight, quarrel, row (*Inf.*), scrap (*Inf.*), scuffle, tussle, wrangle, wrestle

brawn beef (*Inf.*), beefiness, brawniness, flesh, might, muscle, muscles, muscularity, power, robustness, strength, vigour

brawny athletic, beefy (*Inf.*), bulky, burly, fleshy, hardy, hefty (*Inf.*), herculean, husky (*Inf.*), muscular, powerful, robust, sinewy, stalwart, strapping, strong, sturdy, thewy, vigorous, well-knit

bray 1. *v.* blare, heehaw, hoot, roar, screech, trumpet **2.** *n.* bawl, bellow, blare, cry, harsh sound, heehaw, hoot, roar, screech, shout

brazen *adj.* **1.** audacious, barefaced, bold, brash, brassy (*Inf.*), defiant, forward, immodest, impudent, insolent, pert, saucy, shameless, unabashed, unashamed **2.** brass, brassy, bronze, metallic ~*v.* **3.** *With* **out** be impenitent, be unashamed, confront, defy, outface, outstare, persevere, stare out

breach 1. aperture, break, chasm, cleft, crack, fissure, gap, hole, opening, rent, rift, rupture, split **2**. contravention, disobedience, infraction, infringement, noncompliance, nonobservance, offence, transgression, trespass, violation **3**. alienation, difference, disaffection, disagreement, dissension, division, estrangement, falling-out (*Inf.*), parting of the ways, quarrel, schism, separation, severance, variance

bread 1. aliment, diet, fare, food, necessities, nourishment, nutriment, provisions, subsistence, sustenance, viands, victuals **2**. *Sl.* cash, dough (*Sl.*), finance, funds, money

breadth 1. beam (*of a ship*), broadness, latitude, span, spread, wideness, width **2**. amplitude, area, compass, comprehensiveness, dimension, expanse, extensiveness, extent, magnitude, measure, range, reach, scale, scope, size, space, spread, sweep, vastness **3**. broadmindedness, freedom, latitude, liberality, open-mindedness, openness, permissiveness

break *v.* **1**. batter, burst, crack, crash, demolish, destroy, disintegrate, divide, fracture, fragment, part, rend, separate, sever, shatter, shiver, smash, snap, splinter, split, tear **2**. breach, contravene, disobey, disregard, infract (*Law*), infringe, renege on, transgress, violate **3**. cow, cripple, demoralize, dispirit, enervate, enfeeble, impair, incapacitate, subdue, tame, undermine, weaken **4**. abandon, cut, discontinue, give up, interrupt, pause, rest, stop, suspend **5**. bust (*Inf.*), degrade, demote, discharge, dismiss, humiliate, impoverish, make bankrupt, reduce, ruin **6**. announce, come out, disclose, divulge, impart, inform, let out, make public, proclaim, reveal, tell **7**. *Of a record, etc.* beat, better, cap (*Inf.*), exceed, excel, go beyond, outdo, outstrip, surpass, top **8**. appear, burst out, come forth suddenly, emerge, erupt, happen, occur **9**. cut and run (*Inf.*), dash, escape, flee, fly, get away, run away **10**. cushion, diminish, lessen, lighten, moderate, reduce, soften, weaken ~*n.* **11**. breach, cleft, crack, division, fissure, fracture, gap, gash, hole, opening, rent, rift, rupture, split, tear **12**. breather (*Inf.*), halt, hiatus, interlude, intermission, interruption, interval, let-up (*Inf.*), lull, pause, recess, respite, rest, suspension **13**. alienation, breach, disaffection, dispute, divergence, estrangement, rift, rupture,

schism, separation, split **14**. *Inf.* advantage, chance, fortune, opening, opportunity, stroke of luck

breakable brittle, crumbly, delicate, flimsy, fragile, frail, frangible, friable

breakaway *adj.* dissenting, heretical, rebel, schismatic, seceding, secessionist

break away 1. decamp, escape, flee, fly, make a break for it, make a run for it (*Inf.*), make off, run away **2**. break with, detach, part company, secede, separate

breakdown 1. collapse, crackup (*Inf.*), disintegration, disruption, failure, mishap, stoppage **2**. analysis, categorization, classification, detailed list, diagnosis, dissection, itemization

break down be overcome, collapse, conk out (*Sl.*), crack up (*Inf.*), fail, give way, go kaput (*Sl.*), go to pieces, seize up, stop, stop working

breaker billow, comber, roller, wave, whitecap, white horse

break-in breaking and entering, burglary, invasion, robbery

break in 1. barge in, burst in, butt in, interfere, interject, interpose, interrupt, intervene, intrude **2**. break and enter, burgle, invade, rob **3**. accustom, condition, get used to, habituate, initiate, prepare, tame, train

break into begin, burst into, burst out, commence, dissolve into, give way to, launch into

break off 1. detach, divide, part, pull off, separate, sever, snap off, splinter **2**. cease, desist, discontinue, end, finish, halt, pause, stop, suspend, terminate

break out 1. appear, arise, begin, commence, emerge, happen, occur, set in, spring up, start **2**. abscond, bolt, break loose, burst out, escape, flee, get free **3**. burst out, erupt

breakthrough advance, development, discovery, find, finding, gain, improvement, invention, leap, progress, quantum leap, step forward

break through achieve, burst through, emerge, get past, pass, penetrate, shine forth, succeed

break-up breakdown, breaking, crackup (*Inf.*), disintegration, dispersal, dissolution, divorce, ending, parting, rift, separation, split, splitting, termination, wind-up (*Inf., chiefly U.S.*)

break up adjourn, disband, dismantle, disperse, disrupt, dissolve, divide, divorce, end, part, scatter, separate, sever, split, stop, suspend, terminate

breakwater groyne, jetty, mole, sea wall, spur

break with break away from, depart from, ditch (*Sl.*), drop (*Inf.*), jilt, part company, reject, renounce, repudiate, separate from

breast 1. boob (*Sl.*), bosom, bust, chest, front, teat, thorax, udder **2.** being, conscience, core, emotions, feelings, heart, seat of the affections, sentiments, soul, thoughts

breath 1. air, animation, breathing, exhalation, gasp, gulp, inhalation, pant, respiration, wheeze **2.** aroma, odour, smell, vapour, whiff **3.** break, breather, breathing-space, instant, moment, pause, respite, rest, second **4.** faint breeze, flutter, gust, puff, sigh, slight movement, waft, zephyr **5.** hint, murmur, suggestion, suspicion, undertone, whisper **6.** animation, energy, existence, life, lifeblood, life force, vitality

breathe 1. draw in, gasp, gulp, inhale and exhale, pant, puff, respire, wheeze **2.** imbue, impart, infuse, inject, inspire, instil, transfuse **3.** articulate, express, murmur, say, sigh, utter, voice, whisper

breather break, breathing space, breath of air, halt, pause, recess, respite, rest

breathless 1. choking, exhausted, gasping, gulping, out of breath, panting, short-winded, spent, wheezing, winded **2.** agog, anxious, astounded, avid, eager, excited, flabbergasted (*Inf.*), on tenterhooks, open-mouthed, thunderstruck, with bated breath

breathtaking amazing, astonishing, awe-inspiring, awesome, exciting, heart-stirring, impressive, magnificent, moving, overwhelming, stunning (*Inf.*), thrilling

breech backside (*Inf.*), behind (*Inf.*), buttocks, fundament, posterior, rump, seat

breed *v.* **1.** bear, beget, bring forth, engender, generate, hatch, multiply, originate, procreate, produce, propagate, reproduce **2.** bring up, cultivate, develop, discipline, educate, foster, instruct, nourish, nurture, raise, rear **3.** arouse, bring about, cause, create, generate, give rise to, induce, make, occasion, originate, produce, stir up ~*n.* **4.** brand, class, extraction, family, ilk, kind, line, lineage, pedigree, progeny, race, sort, species,

stamp, stock, strain, type, variety

breeding 1. ancestry, cultivation, development, lineage, nurture, raising, rearing, reproduction, training, upbringing **2.** civility, conduct, courtesy, cultivation, culture, gentility, manners, polish, refinement, urbanity

breeze 1. *n.* air, breath of wind, capful of wind, current of air, draught, flurry, gust, light wind, puff of air, waft, whiff, zephyr **2.** *v.* flit, glide, hurry, move briskly, pass, sail, sally, sweep, trip

breezy 1. airy, blowing, blowy, blusterous, blustery, fresh, gusty, squally, windy **2.** airy, animated, blithe, buoyant, carefree, casual, cheerful, debonair, easy-going, free and easy, informal, jaunty, light, light-hearted, lively, sparkling, spirited, sprightly, sunny, vivacious

brevity 1. conciseness, concision, condensation, crispness, curtness, economy, pithiness, succinctness, terseness **2.** briefness, ephemerality, impermanence, shortness, transience, transitoriness

brew *v.* **1.** boil, ferment, infuse (*tea*), make (*beer*), prepare by fermentation, seethe, soak, steep, stew **2.** breed, concoct, contrive, develop, devise, excite, foment, form, gather, hatch, plan, plot, project, scheme, start, stir up ~*n.* **3.** beverage, blend, concoction, distillation, drink, fermentation, infusion, liquor, mixture, preparation

bribe 1. *n.* allurement, backhander (*Sl.*), boodle (*Sl., chiefly U.S.*), corrupting gift, enticement, graft, hush money (*Sl.*), incentive, inducement, kickback (*U.S.*), pay-off (*Inf.*), payola (*Inf.*), reward for treachery **2.** *v.* buy off, corrupt, get at, grease the palm *or* hand of (*Sl.*), influence by gifts, lure, oil the palm of (*Inf.*), pay off (*Inf.*), reward, square, suborn

bribery buying off, corruption, graft, inducement, palm-greasing (*Sl.*), payola (*Inf.*), protection, subornation

bric-a-brac baubles, bibelots, curios, gewgaws, kickshaws, knick-knacks, objects of virtu, *objets d'art*, ornaments, trinkets

bridal bride's, conjugal, connubial, hymeneal, marital, marriage, matrimonial, nuptial, spousal, wedding

bridge *n.* **1.** arch, flyover, overpass, span, viaduct **2.** band, bond, connection, link, tie ~*v.* **3.** arch over, attach, bind, connect, couple, cross, cross over, extend across, go over, join, link, reach across, span, traverse, unite

bridle v. **1.** check, constrain, control, curb, govern, keep in check, master, moderate, repress, restrain, subdue **2.** be indignant, bristle, draw (oneself) up, get angry, get one's back up, raise one's hackles, rear up ~n. **3.** check, control, curb, restraint, trammels

brief adj. **1.** compendious, compressed, concise, crisp, curt, laconic, limited, pithy, short, succint, terse, thumbnail, to the point **2.** ephemeral, fast, fleeting, hasty, little, momentary, quick, short, short-lived, swift, temporary, transitory **3.** abrupt, blunt, brusque, curt, sharp, short, surly ~n. **4.** abridgment, abstract, digest, epitome, outline, précis, sketch, summary, synopsis **5.** argument, case, contention, data, defence, demonstration ~v. **6.** advise, explain, fill in (Inf.), gen up (Brit. inf.), give (someone) a rundown, give (someone) the gen (Brit. inf.), inform, instruct, prepare, prime, put (someone) in the picture (Inf.)

briefing conference, directions, guidance, information, instruction, instructions, meeting, preamble, preparation, priming, rundown

briefly abruptly, briskly, casually, concisely, cursorily, curtly, fleetingly, hastily, hurriedly, in a few words, in a nutshell, in brief, in outline, in passing, momentarily, precisely, quickly, shortly, temporarily

brigade band, body, company, contingent, corps, crew, force, group, organization, outfit, party, squad, team, troop, unit

brigand bandit, desperado, footpad (Archaic), freebooter, gangster, highwayman, marauder, outlaw, plunderer, robber, ruffian

bright **1.** beaming, blazing, brilliant, dazzling, effulgent, flashing, gleaming, glistening, glittering, glowing, illuminated, intense, lambent, luminous, lustrous, radiant, resplendent, scintillating, shimmering, shining, sparkling, twinkling, vivid **2.** clear, clement, cloudless, fair, limpid, lucid, pellucid, pleasant, sunny, translucent, transparent, unclouded **3.** acute, astute, aware, brainy, brilliant, clear-headed, clever, ingenious, intelligent, inventive, keen, quick, quick-witted, sharp, smart, wide-awake **4.** aus-

picious, encouraging, excellent, favourable, golden, good, hopeful, optimistic, palmy, promising, propitious, prosperous, rosy **5.** cheerful, gay, genial, glad, happy, jolly, joyful, joyous, light-hearted, lively, merry, vivacious **6.** distinguished, famous, glorious, illustrious, magnificent, outstanding, remarkable, splendid

brighten **1.** clear up, enliven, gleam, glow, illuminate, lighten, light up, make brighter, shine **2.** become cheerful, buck up (Inf.), buoy up, cheer, encourage, enliven, gladden, hearten, make happy, perk up

brilliance, brilliancy **1.** blaze, brightness, dazzle, effulgence, gleam, glitter, intensity, luminosity, lustre, radiance, refulgence, resplendence, sheen, sparkle, vividness **2.** acuity, aptitude, braininess, cleverness, distinction, excellence, genius, giftedness, greatness, inventiveness, talent, wisdom **3.** éclat, glamour, gorgeousness, grandeur, illustriousness, magnificence, splendour

brilliant **1.** ablaze, bright, coruscating, dazzling, glittering, glossy, intense, luminous, lustrous, radiant, refulgent, resplendent, scintillating, shining, sparkling, vivid **2.** celebrated, eminent, exceptional, famous, glorious, illustrious, magnificent, outstanding, splendid, superb **3.** accomplished, acute, astute, brainy, clever, discerning, expert, gifted, intellectual, intelligent, inventive, masterly, penetrating, profound, quick, talented

brim **1.** n. border, brink, circumference, edge, lip, margin, rim, skirt, verge **2.** v. fill, fill up, hold no more, overflow, run over, spill, well over

brimful brimming, filled, flush, full, level with, overflowing, overfull, packed, running over

brindled mottled, patched, speckled, spotted, streaked, tabby

brine pickling solution, saline solution, salt water, sea water, the sea

bring **1.** accompany, bear, carry, conduct, convey, deliver, escort, fetch, gather, guide, import, lead, take, transfer, transport, usher **2.** cause, contribute to, create, effect, engender, inflict, occasion, produce, result in, wreak **3.** compel, convince, dispose, force, induce, influence, make, move, persuade, prevail on or upon, prompt, sway **4.** command, earn, fetch, gross, net, produce, return, sell for, yield

bring about accomplish, achieve, bring to pass, cause, compass, create, effect, effectuate, generate, give rise to, make happen, manage, occasion, produce, realize

bring down abase, cut down, drop, fell, floor, lay low, level, lower, overthrow, overturn, pull down, reduce, shoot down, undermine, upset

bring in accrue, bear, be worth, fetch, gross, produce, profit, realize, return, yield

bring off accomplish, achieve, bring home the bacon (*Inf.*), bring to pass, carry off, carry out, discharge, execute, perform, pull off, succeed

bring up 1. breed, develop, educate, form, nurture, raise, rear, support, teach, train **2.** advance, allude to, broach, introduce, mention, move, propose, put forward, submit

brink border, boundary, brim, edge, fringe, frontier, limit, lip, margin, point, rim, skirt, threshold, verge

brisk 1. active, agile, alert, animated, bustling, busy, energetic, lively, nimble, no-nonsense, quick, speedy, sprightly, spry, vigorous, vivacious **2.** biting, bracing, crisp, exhilarating, fresh, invigorating, keen, nippy, refreshing, sharp, snappy, stimulating

briskly actively, brusquely, coolly, decisively, efficiently, energetically, firmly, incisively, nimbly, promptly, quickly, rapidly, readily, smartly, vigorously

bristle *n.* **1.** barb, hair, prickle, spine, stubble, thorn, whisker ~*v.* **2.** horripilate, prickle, rise, stand on end, stand up **3.** be angry, be infuriated, be maddened, bridle, flare up, get one's dander up (*Sl.*), rage, see red, seethe, spit (*Inf.*) **4.** *With* **with** abound, be alive, be thick, crawl, hum, swarm, teem

bristly bearded, bewhiskered, hairy, prickly, rough, stubbly, unshaven, whiskered

brittle 1. breakable, crisp, crumbling, crumbly, delicate, fragile, frail, frangible, friable, shatterable, shivery **2.** curt, edgy, irritable, nervous, prim, stiff, stilted, tense

broach 1. approach, bring up, hint at, introduce, mention, open up, propose, raise the subject, speak of, suggest, talk of, touch on **2.** crack, draw off, open,

pierce, puncture, start, tap, uncork

broad 1. ample, beamy (*of a ship*), capacious, expansive, extensive, generous, large, roomy, spacious, vast, voluminous, wide, widespread **2.** all-embracing, comprehensive, encyclopedic, far-reaching, general, inclusive, nonspecific, sweeping, undetailed, universal, unlimited, wide, wide-ranging **3.** *As in* **broad daylight** clear, full, obvious, open, plain, straightforward, undisguised **4.** broad-minded, liberal, open, permissive, progressive, tolerant, unbiased **5.** blue, coarse, gross, improper, indecent, indelicate, near the knuckle (*Inf.*), unrefined, vulgar

broadcast *v.* **1.** air, beam, cable, put on the air, radio, relay, show, televise, transmit **2.** advertise, announce, circulate, disseminate, make public, proclaim, promulgate, publish, report, spread ~*n.* **3.** programme, show, telecast, transmission

broaden augment, develop, enlarge, expand, extend, fatten, increase, open up, spread, stretch, supplement, swell, widen

broad-minded catholic, cosmopolitan, dispassionate, flexible, freethinking, indulgent, liberal, open-minded, permissive, responsive, tolerant, unbiased, unbigoted, undogmatic, unprejudiced

broadside abuse, assault, attack, battering, bombardment, censure, criticism, denunciation, diatribe, philippic

brochure advertisement, booklet, circular, folder, handbill, hand-out, leaflet, pamphlet

broil 1. *n.* affray, altercation, brawl, brouhaha, dispute, feud, fracas, fray, quarrel, scrimmage, strife, wrangle **2.** *v.* brawl, dispute, quarrel, scrimmage, wrangle

broke bankrupt, bust (*Inf.*), cleaned out (*Sl.*), flat broke (*Sl.*), impoverished, insolvent, on one's uppers, penniless, penurious, ruined, skint (*Brit. inf.*), stony-broke (*Sl.*)

broken 1. burst, demolished, destroyed, fractured, fragmented, rent, ruptured, separated, severed, shattered, shivered **2.** defective, exhausted, feeble, imperfect, kaput (*Inf.*), not functioning, out of order, ruined, run-down, spent, weak **3.** disconnected, discontinuous, disturbed, erratic, fragmentary, incomplete, intermittent, interrupted, spasmodic **4.** beaten, browbeaten, crippled, crushed, defeated, demoralized, humbled, oppressed, overpowered, subdued, tamed, vanquished **5.** dishonoured, disobeyed, disregarded, forgotten, ignored, infringed, isolated, retracted, traduced, transgressed **6.** disjointed, halting, hesitating, imperfect, stammering

broken-down collapsed, dilapidated, in disrepair, inoperative, kaput (*Sl.*), not functioning, not in working order, old, on the blink (*Inf.*), out of commission, out of order, worn out

brokenhearted crestfallen, desolate, despairing, devastated, disappointed, disconsolate, grief-stricken, heartbroken, heart-sick, inconsolable, miserable, mournful, prostrated, sorrowful, wretched

broker agent, dealer, factor, go-between, intermediary, middleman, negotiator

bromide banality, cliché, commonplace, hackneyed saying, platitude, stereotype, trite remark, truism

bronze brownish, chestnut, copper, copper-coloured, metallic brown, reddish-brown, reddish-tan, rust, tan

brood *v.* **1.** agonize, dwell upon, fret, meditate, mope, mull over, muse, ponder, repine, ruminate, think upon **2.** cover, hatch, incubate, set, sit upon ~*n.* **3.** breed, chicks, children, clutch, family, hatch, infants, issue, litter, offspring, progeny, young

brook[1] beck, burn, gill (*Dialect*), rill, rivulet, runnel (*Literary*), stream, streamlet, watercourse

brook[2] abide, accept, allow, bear, countenance, endure, put up with (*Inf.*), stand, stomach, suffer, support, swallow, thole (*Dialect*), tolerate, withstand

brothel bagnio, bawdy house (*Archaic*), bordello, house of ill fame, house of ill repute, house of prostitution, knocking shop (*Sl.*), red-light district, stews (*Archaic*), whorehouse

brother 1. blood brother, kin, kinsman, relation, relative, sibling **2.** associate, chum (*Inf.*), colleague, companion, compeer, comrade, confrère, fellow member, mate, pal (*Inf.*), partner **3.** cleric, friar, monk, regular, religious

brotherhood 1. brotherliness, camaraderie, companionship, comradeship, fellowship, friendliness, kinship **2.** alliance, association, clan, clique, commu-

nity, coterie, fraternity, guild, league, society, union

brotherly affectionate, altruistic, amicable, benevolent, cordial, fraternal, friendly, kind, neighbourly, philanthropic, sympathetic

brow 1. air, appearance, aspect, bearing, countenance, eyebrow, face, forehead, front, mien, temple **2.** brim, brink, crown, edge, peak, rim, summit, tip, top, verge

browbeat badger, bulldoze (*Inf.*), bully, coerce, cow, domineer, dragoon, hector, intimidate, lord it over, oppress, overawe, overbear, threaten, tyrannize

brown 1. *adj.* auburn, bay, brick, bronze, bronzed, browned, brunette, chestnut, chocolate, coffee, dark, donkey brown, dun, dusky, fuscous, ginger, hazel, nigger brown, rust, sunburnt, tan, tanned, tawny, toasted, umber **2.** *v.* cook, fry, grill, sauté, seal, sear

browned off cheesed off (*Brit. sl.*), discontented, discouraged, disgruntled, disheartened, fed up, weary

brown study absorption, abstractedness, abstraction, contemplation, meditation, musing, preoccupation, reflection, reverie, rumination

browse 1. dip into, examine cursorily, flip through, glance at, leaf through, look round, look through, peruse, scan, skim, survey **2.** crop, eat, feed, graze, nibble, pasture

bruise *v.* **1.** blacken, blemish, contuse, crush, damage, deface, discolour, injure, mar, mark, pound, pulverize **2.** displease, grieve, hurt, injure, insult, offend, pain, sting, wound ~*n.* **3.** black-and-blue mark, black mark, blemish, contusion, discoloration, injury, mark, swelling

brunt burden, force, full force, impact, pressure, shock, strain, stress, thrust, violence

brush[1] *n.* **1.** besom, broom, sweeper **2.** clash, conflict, confrontation, encounter, fight, fracas, scrap (*Inf.*), set-to (*Inf.*), skirmish, slight engagement, spot of bother (*Inf.*), tussle ~*v.* **3.** buff, clean, paint, polish, sweep, wash **4.** caress, contact, flick, glance, graze, kiss, scrape, stroke, sweep, touch

brush[2] *n.* brushwood, bushes, copse, scrub, shrubs, thicket, undergrowth, underwood

brush aside dismiss, disregard, have

no time for, ignore, override, sweep aside

brush-off *n.* cold shoulder, cut, dismissal, go-by (*Sl.*), rebuff, refusal, rejection, repudiation, repulse, slight, snub

brush off *v.* cold-shoulder, cut, deny, disdain, dismiss, disown, disregard, ignore, rebuff, refuse, reject, repudiate, scorn, slight, snub, spurn

brush up cram, go over, polish up, read up, refresh one's memory, relearn, revise, study

brusque abrupt, blunt, curt, discourteous, gruff, hasty, impolite, sharp, short, surly, tart, terse, unmannerly

brutal 1. barbarous, bloodthirsty, cruel, ferocious, heartless, inhuman, merciless, pitiless, remorseless, ruthless, savage, uncivilized, vicious **2.** beastly, bestial, brute, brutish, carnal, coarse, crude, sensual **3.** bearish, callous, gruff, harsh, impolite, insensitive, rough, rude, severe, uncivil, unfeeling, unmannerly

brutality atrocity, barbarism, barbarity, bloodthirstiness, brutishness, cruelty, ferocity, inhumanity, ruthlessness, savageness, savagery, viciousness

brutally barbarically, barbarously, brutishly, callously, cruelly, ferociously, fiercely, hardheartedly, heartlessly, in cold blood, inhumanly, meanly, mercilessly, murderously, pitilessly, remorselessly, ruthlessly, savagely, unkindly, viciously

brute *n.* **1.** animal, beast, creature, wild animal **2.** barbarian, beast, devil, fiend, monster, ogre, sadist, savage, swine ~*adj.* **3.** bodily, carnal, fleshly, instinctive, mindless, physical, senseless, unthinking **4.** bestial, coarse, depraved, gross, sensual

brutish barbarian, boorish, coarse, crass, crude, cruel, gross, loutish, savage, stupid, subhuman, swinish, uncouth, vulgar

bubble *n.* **1.** air ball, bead, blister, blob, drop, droplet, globule, vesicle **2.** bagatelle, delusion, fantasy, illusion, toy, trifle, vanity ~*v.* **3.** boil, effervesce, fizz, foam, froth, percolate, seethe, sparkle **4.** babble, burble, gurgle, murmur, purl, ripple, trickle, trill

bubbles effervescence, fizz, foam, froth, head, lather, spume, suds

bubbly 1. carbonated, curly, effervescent, fizzy, foamy, frothy, lathery, sparkling, sudsy **2.** animated, bouncy, elated, excited, happy, lively, merry

buccaneer corsair, freebooter, pirate, privateer, sea-rover

buck *n.* **1.** *Archaic* beau, blade, blood, coxcomb, dandy, fop, gallant, popinjay, spark ~*v.* **2.** bound, jerk, jump, leap, prance, spring, start, vault **3.** dislodge, throw, unseat **4.** *Inf.* cheer, encourage, gladden, gratify, hearten, inspirit, please

buckle *n.* **1.** catch, clasp, clip, fastener, hasp **2.** bulge, contortion, distortion, kink, warp ~*v.* **3.** catch, clasp, close, fasten, hook, secure **4.** bend, bulge, cave in, collapse, contort, crumple, distort, fold, twist, warp

buckle down apply oneself, exert oneself, launch into, pitch in, put one's shoulder to the wheel, set to

buck up 1. get a move on, hasten, hurry up, shake a leg, speed up **2.** brighten, cheer up, encourage, hearten, inspirit, perk up, rally, take heart

bucolic agrarian, agricultural, country, pastoral, rural, rustic

bud 1. *n.* embryo, germ, shoot, sprout **2.** *v.* burgeon, burst forth, develop, grow, pullulate, shoot, sprout

budding beginning, burgeoning, developing, embryonic, fledgling, flowering, germinal, growing, incipient, nascent, potential, promising

budge 1. dislodge, give way, inch, move, propel, push, remove, roll, shift, slide, stir **2.** bend, change, convince, give way, influence, persuade, sway, yield

budget 1. *n.* allocation, allowance, cost, finances, financial statement, fiscal estimate, funds, means, resources **2.** *v.* allocate, apportion, cost, cost out, estimate, plan, ration

buff¹ 1. *adj.* sandy, straw, tan, yellowish, yellowish-brown **2.** *n.* **in the buff** bare, in one's birthday suit (*Inf.*), in the altogether (*Inf.*), in the raw (*Inf.*), naked, nude, unclad, unclothed, with bare skin **3.** *v.* brush, burnish, polish, rub, shine, smooth

buff² addict, admirer, aficionado, connoisseur, devotee, enthusiast, expert, fan, fiend (*Inf.*), freak (*Sl.*)

buffer bulwark, bumper, cushion, fender, intermediary, safeguard, screen, shield, shock absorber

buffet¹ *n.* café, cafeteria, cold table, counter, cupboard, refreshment-counter, salad bar, sideboard, snack bar

buffet² 1. *v.* bang, batter, beat, box, bump, clobber (*Sl.*), cuff, flail, knock, pound, pummel, push, rap, shove, slap, strike, thump, wallop (*Inf.*) **2.** *n.* bang, blow, box, bump, cuff, jolt, knock, push, rap, shove, slap, smack, thump, wallop (*Inf.*)

buffoon clown, comedian, comic, droll, fool, harlequin, jester, joker, merry-andrew, silly billy (*Inf.*), wag

buffoonery clowning, drollery, jesting, nonsense, silliness, tomfoolery, waggishness

bug *n.* **1.** *Inf.* bacterium, disease, germ, infection, microorganism, virus **2.** craze, fad, mania, obsession, rage **3.** blemish, catch, defect, error, failing, fault, flaw, gremlin, imperfection, snarl-up (*Inf.*) ~*v.* **4.** *Inf.* annoy, badger, bother, disturb, get on (someone's) wick (*Sl.*), harass, irk, irritate, needle (*Inf.*), nettle, pester, plague, vex **5.** eavesdrop, listen in, spy, tap, wiretap

bugbear anathema, bane, *bête noire*, bogey, bugaboo, devil, dread, fiend, horror, nightmare, pet hate

build *v.* **1.** assemble, construct, erect, fabricate, form, make, put up, raise **2.** base, begin, constitute, establish, formulate, found, inaugurate, initiate, institute, originate, set up, start **3.** accelerate, amplify, augment, develop, enlarge, escalate, extend, improve, increase, intensify, strengthen ~*n.* **4.** body, figure, form, frame, physique, shape, structure

building 1. domicile, dwelling, edifice, fabric, house, pile, structure **2.** architecture, construction, erection, fabricating, raising

build-up 1. accumulation, development, enlargement, escalation, expansion, gain, growth, increase **2.** ballyhoo (*Inf.*), hype (*Sl.*), plug (*Inf.*), promotion, publicity, puff **3.** accretion, accumulation, heap, load, mass, stack, stockpile, store

build up 1. add to, amplify, develop, enhance, expand, extend, fortify, heighten, improve, increase, intensify, reinforce, strengthen **2.** advertise, boost, plug (*Inf.*), promote, publicize, spotlight

built-in essential, implicit, in-built, included, incorporated, inherent, inseparable, integral, part and parcel of

bulbous bloated, bulging, convex, rounded, swelling, swollen

bulge *n.* **1.** bump, lump, projection, protrusion, protuberance, swelling **2.** boost, increase, intensification, rise,

surge ~*v.* **3.** bag, dilate, distend, enlarge, expand, project, protrude, puff out, sag, stand out, stick out, swell, swell out

bulk 1. amplitude, bigness, dimensions, immensity, largeness, magnitude, massiveness, size, substance, volume, weight **2.** better part, body, generality, lion's share, main part, majority, major part, mass, most, nearly all, plurality, preponderance **3. bulk large** be important, carry weight, dominate, loom, loom large, preponderate, stand out, threaten

bulky big, colossal, cumbersome, enormous, heavy, huge, hulking, immense, mammoth, massive, massy, ponderous, substantial, unmanageable, unwieldy, very large, voluminous, weighty

bulldoze 1. demolish, flatten, level, raze **2.** drive, force, propel, push, shove, thrust **3.** browbeat, bully, coerce, cow, hector, intimidate

bullet ball, missile, pellet, projectile, shot, slug

bulletin account, announcement, communication, communiqué, dispatch, message, news flash, notification, report, statement

bull-headed headstrong, inflexible, mulish, obstinate, pig-headed, stiff-necked, stubborn, stupid, tenacious, uncompromising, unyielding, wilful

bullish assured, bold, confident, expectant, improving, positive, rising

bully 1. *n.* big bully, browbeater, bully boy, coercer, intimidator, oppressor, persecutor, ruffian, tormentor, tough **2.** *v.* bluster, browbeat, bulldoze (*Inf.*), bullyrag, coerce, cow, domineer, hector, intimidate, oppress, overbear, persecute, push around (*Sl.*), ride roughshod over, swagger, terrorize, tyrannize **3.** *adj.* admirable, excellent, fine, nifty (*Inf.*), very good **4.** *interj.* bravo, capital, good, grand, great, well done

bulwark 1. bastion, buttress, defence, embankment, fortification, outwork, partition, rampart, redoubt **2.** buffer, guard, mainstay, safeguard, security, support

bumbling awkward, blundering, botching, bungling, clumsy, incompetent, inefficient, inept, lumbering, maladroit, muddled, stumbling

bump *v.* **1.** bang, collide (with), crash, hit, knock, slam, smash into, strike **2.** bounce, jar, jerk, jolt, jostle, jounce, rattle, shake 3. budge, dislodge, displace, move, remove, shift ~n. 4. bang, blow, collision, crash, hit, impact, jar, jolt, knock, rap, shock, smash, thud, thump 5. bulge, contusion, hump, knob, knot, lump, node, nodule, protuberance, swelling

bumper *adj.* abundant, bountiful, excellent, exceptional, jumbo (*Inf.*), massive, prodigal, spanking (*Inf.*), teeming, unusual, whacking (*Inf.*), whopping (*Inf.*)

bump into chance upon, come across, encounter, happen upon, light upon, meet, meet up with, run across, run into

bumpkin boor, clodhopper, clown, country bumpkin, hick (*U.S. inf.*), hillbilly, lout, lubber, oaf, peasant, rustic, yokel

bump off assassinate, dispatch, do away with, do in (*Sl.*), eliminate, finish off, kill, knock off (*Sl.*), liquidate, murder, remove, wipe out (*Inf.*)

bumptious arrogant, boastful, brash, cocky, conceited, egotistic, forward, full of oneself, impudent, overbearing, overconfident, presumptuous, pushy (*Inf.*), self-assertive, showy, swaggering, vainglorious, vaunting

bumpy bone-breaking, bouncy, choppy, irregular, jarring, jerky, jolting, jolty, knobby, lumpy, pitted, potholed, rough, rutted, uneven

bunch *n.* 1. assortment, batch, bouquet, bundle, clump, cluster, collection, heap, lot, mass, number, parcel, pile, quantity, sheaf, spray, stack, tuft 2. band, crew (*Inf.*), crowd, flock, gang, gathering, group, knot, mob, multitude, party, swarm, team, troop ~v. 3. assemble, bundle, cluster, collect, congregate, cram together, crowd, flock, group, herd, huddle, mass, pack

bundle *n.* 1. accumulation, assortment, batch, bunch, collection, group, heap, mass, pile, quantity, stack 2. bag, bale, box, carton, crate, pack, package, packet, pallet, parcel, roll ~v. 3. bale, bind, fasten, pack, package, palletize, tie, tie together, tie up, truss, wrap 4. *With* out, off, into, *etc.* hurry, hustle, push, rush, shove, throw, thrust 5. *With* up clothe warmly, muffle up, swathe, wrap up

bungle blunder, bodge (*Inf.*), botch, butcher, cock up (*Sl.*), foul up, fudge, louse up (*Sl.*), make a mess of, mar, mess up, miscalculate, mismanage, muff, ruin, screw up (*Inf.*), spoil

bungler blunderer, botcher, butcher, butterfingers (*Inf.*), duffer (*Inf.*), fumbler, incompetent, lubber, muddler, muff

bungling awkward, blundering, botching, cack-handed (*Inf.*), clumsy, ham-fisted (*Inf.*), ham-handed (*Inf.*), incompetent, inept, maladroit, unskilful

bunk[1] *v.* abscond, beat it (*Sl.*), bolt, clear out (*Inf.*), cut and run (*Inf.*), decamp, do a bunk (*Brit. sl.*), flee, run for it (*Inf.*), scram (*Inf.*), skedaddle (*Inf.*)

bunk[2], **bunkum** balderdash, baloney (*Inf.*), bilge (*Inf.*), bosh (*Inf.*), garbage, havers (*Scot.*), hooey (*Sl.*), horsefeathers (*U.S. inf.*), nonsense, piffle (*Inf.*), poppycock (*Inf.*), rot, rubbish, stuff and nonsense, tarradiddle, tomfoolery, tommyrot, tosh (*Inf.*), trash, truck (*Inf.*), twaddle

buoy 1. *n.* beacon, float, guide, marker, signal 2. *v. With* up boost, cheer, cheer up, encourage, hearten, keep afloat, lift, raise, support, sustain

buoyancy 1. floatability, lightness, weightlessness 2. animation, bounce (*Inf.*), cheerfulness, cheeriness, good humour, high spirits, liveliness, pep, spiritedness, sunniness, zing (*Inf.*)

buoyant 1. afloat, floatable, floating, light, weightless 2. animated, blithe, bouncy, breezy, bright, carefree, cheerful, debonair, happy, jaunty, joyful, light-hearted, lively, peppy (*Inf.*), sunny, vivacious

burden *n.* 1. affliction, anxiety, care, clog, encumbrance, grievance, load, millstone, obstruction, onus, responsibility, sorrow, strain, stress, trial, trouble, weight, worry 2. *Naut.* cargo, freight, lading, tonnage ~v. 3. bother, encumber, handicap, load, oppress, overload, overwhelm, saddle with, strain, tax, weigh down, worry

burdensome crushing, difficult, exacting, heavy, irksome, onerous, oppressive, taxing, troublesome, trying, weighty

bureau 1. desk, writing desk 2. agency, branch, department, division, office, service

bureaucracy 1. administration, authorities, civil service, corridors of power, directorate, government, ministry, officials, officialdom, the system 2.

bumbledom, officialdom, officialese, red tape, regulations

bureaucrat administrator, apparatchik, civil servant, functionary, mandarin, minister, office-holder, officer, official, public servant

burglar cat burglar, filcher, housebreaker, picklock, pilferer, robber, sneak thief, thief

burglary break-in, breaking and entering, filching, housebreaking, larceny, pilferage, robbery, stealing, theft, thieving

burial burying, entombment, exequies, funeral, inhumation, interment, obsequies, sepulture

burial ground cemetery, churchyard, God's acre, golgotha (*Rare*), graveyard, necropolis

buried 1. coffined, consigned to the grave, entombed, interred, laid to rest **2.** dead and buried, dead and gone, in the grave, long gone, pushing up the daisies, six feet under **3.** covered, forgotten, hidden, repressed, sunk in oblivion, suppressed **4.** cloistered, concealed, hidden, private, sequestered, tucked away **5.** caught up, committed, concentrating, devoted, engrossed, immersed, intent, lost, occupied, preoccupied, rapt

burlesque 1. *n.* caricature, mock, mockery, parody, satire, send-up (*Brit. inf.*), spoof (*Inf.*), takeoff (*Inf.*), travesty **2.** *adj.* caricatural, comic, farcical, hudibrastic, ironical, ludicrous, mock, mock-heroic, mocking, parodic, satirical, travestying **3.** *v.* ape, caricature, exaggerate, imitate, lampoon, make fun of, mock, parody, ridicule, satirize, send up (*Brit. inf.*), spoof, (*Inf.*), take off (*Inf.*), travesty

burly beefy, big, brawny, bulky, hefty, hulking, muscular, powerful, stocky, stout, strapping, strong, sturdy, thickset, well-built

burn 1. be ablaze, be on fire, blaze, flame, flare, flash, flicker, glow, smoke **2.** brand, calcine, char, ignite, incinerate, kindle, light, parch, reduce to ashes, scorch, set on fire, shrivel, singe, toast, wither **3.** bite, hurt, pain, smart, sting, tingle **4.** be excited (angry, aroused, inflamed, passionate), blaze, desire, fume, seethe, simmer, smoulder, yearn **5.** consume, eat up, expend, use

burning 1. blazing, fiery, flaming, flashing, gleaming, glowing, hot, illumi-nated, scorching, smouldering **2.** all-consuming, ardent, eager, earnest, fervent, fervid, frantic, frenzied, impassioned, intense, passionate, vehement, zealous **3.** acrid, biting, caustic, irritating, painful, piercing, prickling, pungent, reeking, smarting, stinging, tingling **4.** acute, compelling, critical, crucial, essential, important, pressing, significant, urgent, vital

burnish 1. *v.* brighten, buff, furbish, glaze, polish, rub up, shine, smooth **2.** *n.* gloss, lustre, patina, polish, sheen, shine

burrow 1. *n.* den, hole, lair, retreat, shelter, tunnel **2.** *v.* delve, dig, excavate, hollow out, scoop out, tunnel

burst *v.* **1.** blow up, break, crack, disintegrate, explode, fly open, fragment, puncture, rend asunder, rupture, shatter, shiver, split, tear apart **2.** barge, break, break out, erupt, gush forth, run, rush, spout ~*n.* **3.** bang, blast, blasting, blowout, blow-up, breach, break, crack, discharge, explosion, rupture, split **4.** eruption, fit, gush, gust, outbreak, outburst, outpouring, rush, spate, spurt, surge, torrent ~*adj.* **5.** flat, punctured, rent, ruptured, split

bury 1. consign to the grave, entomb, inearth, inhume, inter, lay to rest, sepulchre **2.** conceal, cover, cover up, enshroud, hide, secrete, shroud, stow away **3.** drive in, embed, engulf, implant, sink, submerge **4.** absorb, engage, engross, immerse, interest, occupy

bush 1. hedge, plant, shrub, shrubbery, thicket **2.** backwoods, brush, scrub, scrubland, the wild, woodland

bushy bristling, bristly, fluffy, fuzzy, luxuriant, rough, shaggy, spreading, stiff, thick, unruly, wiry

busily actively, assiduously, briskly, carefully, diligently, earnestly, energetically, industriously, intently, purposefully, speedily, strenuously

business 1. calling, career, craft, employment, function, job, line, métier, occupation, profession, pursuit, trade, vocation, work **2.** company, concern, corporation, enterprise, establishment, firm, organization, venture **3.** bargaining, commerce, dealings, industry, manufacturing, merchandising, selling, trade, trading, transaction **4.** affair, assignment, concern, duty, function, issue, matter, point, problem, question, responsibility, subject, task, topic

businesslike correct, efficient, matter-of-fact, methodical, orderly, organized, practical, professional, regular, routine, systematic, thorough, well-ordered, workaday

businessman, businesswoman capitalist, employer, entrepreneur, executive, financier, industrialist, merchant, tradesman, tycoon

bust[1] bosom, breast, chest, torso

bust[2] v. **1.** break, burst, fracture, rupture **2.** bankrupt, break, crash, fail, impoverish, ruin **3.** arrest, catch, collar (Inf.), cop (Sl.), nab (Inf.), raid, search **4. go bust** become insolvent, be ruined, break, fail, go bankrupt ~n. **5.** arrest, capture, cop (Sl.), raid, search, seizure

bustle 1. v. bestir, dash, flutter, fuss, hasten, hurry, rush, scamper, scramble, scurry, scuttle, stir, tear **2.** n. activity, ado, agitation, commotion, excitement, flurry, fuss, haste, hurly-burly, hurry, pother, stir, to-do, tumult

bustling active, astir, busy, buzzing, crowded, energetic, eventful, full, humming, hustling, lively, rushing, stirring, swarming, teeming, thronged

busy adj. **1.** active, assiduous, brisk, diligent, employed, engaged, engrossed, hard at work, industrious, in harness, occupied, on duty, persevering, slaving, working **2.** active, energetic, exacting, full, hectic, hustling, lively, on the go (Inf.), restless, strenuous, tireless, tiring **3.** fussy, inquisitive, interfering, meddlesome, meddling, nosy, officious, prying, snoopy, stirring, troublesome ~v. **4.** absorb, employ, engage, engross, immerse, interest, occupy

busybody eavesdropper, gossip, intriguer, intruder, meddler, nosy parker (Inf.), pry, scandalmonger, snoop, snooper, troublemaker

but 1. sentence connector further, however, moreover, nevertheless, on the contrary, on the other hand, still, yet **2.** conj. bar, barring, except, excepting, excluding, notwithstanding, save, with the exception of **3.** adv. just, merely, only, simply, singly, solely

butcher n. **1.** destroyer, killer, murderer, slaughterer, slayer ~v. **2.** carve, clean, cut, cut up, dress, joint, prepare, slaughter **3.** assassinate, cut down, destroy, exterminate, kill, liquidate, massacre, put to the sword, slaughter, slay **4.**

bodge (Inf.), botch, destroy, mess up, mutilate, ruin, spoil, wreck

butchery blood bath, blood-letting, bloodshed, carnage, killing, massacre, mass murder, murder, slaughter

butt[1] **1.** haft, handle, hilt, shaft, shank, stock **2.** base, end, fag end (Inf.), foot, leftover, stub, tail, tip

butt[2] Aunt Sally, dupe, laughing stock, mark, object, point, subject, target, victim

butt[3] v./n. **1.** With or of the head or horns buck, buffet, bump, bunt, jab, knock, poke, prod, punch, push, ram, shove, thrust ~v. **2.** abut, join, jut, meet, project, protrude **3.** With **in** or **into** chip in (Inf.), cut in, interfere, interrupt, intrude, meddle, put one's oar in, stick one's nose in

butt[4] barrel, cask, pipe

butter up blarney, cajole, coax, fawn on or upon, flatter, honey up, oil one's tongue, soft-soap, suck up to (Inf.), wheedle

buttocks backside (Inf.), behind (Inf.), bottom, bum (Sl.), fundament, gluteus maximus (Anat.), haunches, hindquarters, nates (Technical name), posterior, rear, rump, seat

buttonhole v. Fig. accost, bore, catch, detain in talk, grab, importune, persuade importunately, take aside, waylay

buttress 1. n. abutment, brace, mainstay, pier, prop, reinforcement, shore, stanchion, stay, strut, support **2.** v. back up, bolster, brace, prop, prop up, reinforce, shore, shore up, strengthen, support, sustain, uphold

buxom ample, bosomy, busty, comely, debonair, fresh-looking, full-bosomed, healthy, hearty, jocund, jolly, lively, lusty, merry, plump, robust, sprightly, voluptuous, well-rounded, winsome

buy v. **1.** acquire, get, invest in, obtain, pay for, procure, purchase, shop for **2.** Often with **off** bribe, corrupt, fix (Inf.), grease someone's palm (Inf.), square, suborn ~n. **3.** acquisition, bargain, deal, purchase

buzz n. **1.** bombilation or bombination (Literary), buzzing, drone, hiss, hum, murmur, purr, ring, ringing, sibilation, susurration or susurrus (Literary), whir, whisper **2.** gossip, hearsay, news, report, rumour, scandal, whisper ~v. **3.** bombilate or bombinate (Literary), drone, fizzle, hum, murmur, reverberate, ring, sibilate, susurrate (*Literary*), whir, whisper, whizz **4**. chatter, gossip, natter, rumour, tattle

by *prep.* **1**. along, beside, by way of, close to, near, next to, over, past, via **2**. through, through the agency of, under the aegis of ~*adv.* **3**. aside, at hand, away, beyond, close, handy, in reach, near, past, to one side

by and by before long, eventually, in a while, in the course of time, one day, presently, soon

bygone ancient, antiquated, departed, erstwhile, extinct, forgotten, former, gone by, lost, of old, of yore, olden, onetime, past, past recall, previous, sunk in oblivion

bypass avoid, circumvent, depart from, detour round, deviate from, get round, go round, ignore, neglect, outflank, pass round

bystander eyewitness, looker-on, observer, onlooker, passer-by, spectator, viewer, watcher, witness

byword adage, aphorism, apophthegm, dictum, epithet, gnome, maxim, motto, precept, proverb, saw, saying, slogan

C

cab hackney, hackney carriage, mini-cab, taxi, taxicab

cabal caucus, clique, coalition, combination, conclave, confederacy, conspiracy, coterie, faction, intrigue, junta, league, machination, party, plot, scheme, set

cabbalistic cryptic, dark, esoteric, fanciful, mysterious, mystic, mystical, obscure, occult, secret

cabin 1. berth, bothy, chalet, cot, cottage, crib, hovel, hut, lodge, shack, shanty, shed **2.** berth, compartment, deckhouse, quarters, room

cabinet 1. case, chiffonier, closet, commode, cupboard, dresser, escritoire, locker **2.** administration, assembly, council, counsellors, ministry **3.** apartment, boudoir, chamber (*Archaic*)

cache 1. *n.* accumulation, fund, garner (*Archaic*), hiding place, hoard, nest egg, repository, reserve, stockpile, store, storehouse, supply, treasury **2.** *v.* bury, conceal, hide, put away, secrete, stash (*Inf.*), store

cackle babble, blather, chatter, chuckle, cluck, crow, gabble, gibber, giggle, jabber, prattle, snicker, snigger, titter

cacophonous discordant, dissonant, grating, harsh, inharmonious, jarring, raucous, strident

cacophony caterwauling, discord, disharmony, dissonance, stridency

cad bounder (*Brit. inf.*), churl, cur, dastard (*Archaic*), heel (*Sl.*), knave, rat (*Sl.*), rotter (*Sl.*)

cadaverous ashen, blanched, bloodless, corpselike, deathlike, deathly, emaciated, exsanguinous, gaunt, ghastly, haggard, hollow-eyed, pale, pallid, wan

caddish despicable, ill-bred, low, ungentlemanly, unmannerly

cadence 1. beat, lilt, measure, metre, pulse, rhythm, swing, tempo, throb **2.** accent, inflection, intonation, modulation

cadre core, framework, hard core, infrastructure, key group, nucleus

café cafeteria, coffee bar, coffee shop, lunchroom, restaurant, snack bar, tearoom

cage 1. *v.* confine, coop up, fence in, immure, impound, imprison, incarcerate, lock up, mew, restrain, shut up **2.** *n.* corral (*U.S.*), enclosure, pen, pound

cagey, cagy careful, cautious, chary, discreet, guarded, noncommittal, shrewd, wary, wily

caitiff 1. *n.* coward, knave, miscreant, rascal, rogue, scoundrel, traitor, vagabond, villain, wretch **2.** *adj.* base, cowardly, craven, dastardly, ignoble

cajole beguile, coax, decoy, dupe, entice, entrap, flatter, inveigle, lure, manoeuvre, mislead, seduce, sweet-talk (*U.S. inf.*), tempt, wheedle

cajolery beguilement, blandishments, blarney, coaxing, enticement, flattery, inducement(s), inveigling, persuasion, soft soap (*Inf.*), sweet talk (*Inf.*), wheedling

cake 1. *v.* bake, cement, coagulate, congeal, consolidate, dry, encrust, harden, inspissate (*Archaic*), ossify, solidify, thicken **2.** *n.* bar, block, cube, loaf, lump, mass, slab

calamitous blighting, cataclysmic, catastrophic, deadly, devastating, dire, disastrous, fatal, pernicious, ruinous, tragic, woeful

calamity adversity, affliction, cataclysm, catastrophe, disaster, distress, downfall, hardship, misadventure, mischance, misfortune, mishap, reverse, ruin, scourge, tragedy, trial, tribulation, woe, wretchedness

calculate 1. adjust, compute, consider, count, determine, enumerate, estimate, figure, gauge, judge, rate, reckon, value, weigh, work out **2.** aim, design, intend, plan

calculated considered, deliberate, intended, intentional, planned, premeditated, purposeful

calculating canny, cautious, contriving, crafty, cunning, designing, devious, Machiavellian, manipulative, politic, scheming, sharp, shrewd, sly

calculation 1. answer, computation, estimate, estimation, figuring, forecast, judgment, reckoning, result **2.** caution, circumspection, contrivance, deliberation, discretion, foresight, forethought, planning, precaution

calibre 1. bore, diameter, gauge, measure **2.** *Fig.* ability, capacity, distinction, endowment, faculty, force, gifts, merit, parts, quality, scope, stature, strength, talent, worth

call *v.* **1.** announce, arouse, awaken, cry, cry out, hail, halloo, proclaim, rouse, shout, waken, yell **2.** assemble, bid, collect, contact, convene, convoke, gather, invite, muster, phone, rally, ring up, summon, telephone **3.** christen, denominate, describe as, designate, dub, entitle, label, name, style, term **4.** announce, appoint, declare, decree, elect, ordain, order, proclaim, set apart **5.** consider, estimate, judge, regard, think ~*n.* **6.** cry, hail, scream, shout, signal, whoop, yell **7.** announcement, appeal, command, demand, invitation, notice, order, plea, request, ring (*Brit. inf.*), summons, supplication, visit **8.** cause, claim, excuse, grounds, justification, need, occasion, reason, right, urge

call for 1. demand, entail, involve, necessitate, need, occasion, require, suggest **2.** collect, fetch, pick up, uplift (*Scot.*)

calling business, career, employment, life's work, line, métier, mission, occupation, profession, province, pursuit, trade, vocation, walk of life, work

call on 1. drop in on, look in on, look up, see, visit **2.** appeal to, ask, bid, call upon, entreat, invite, invoke, request, summon, supplicate

callous apathetic, case-hardened, cold, hard-bitten, hard-boiled (*Inf.*), hardened, hardhearted, heartless, indifferent, indurated (*Rare*), insensate, insensible, insensitive, inured, obdurate, soulless, thick-skinned, torpid, uncaring, unfeeling, unresponsive, unsusceptible, unsympathetic

callow green, guileless, immature, inexperienced, jejune, juvenile, naive, puerile, raw, unfledged, unsophisticated, untried

calm *adj.* **1.** balmy, halcyon, mild, pacific, peaceful, placid, quiet, restful, serene, smooth, still, tranquil, windless **2.** collected, composed, cool, dispassionate, equable, impassive, imperturbable, relaxed, sedate, self-possessed, undisturbed, unemotional, unexcitable, unexcited, unflappable (*Inf.*), unmoved, unruffled ~*v.* **3.** hush, mollify, placate, quieten, relax, soothe ~*n.* **4.** calmness, hush, peace, peacefulness, quiet, repose, serenity, stillness

calmness 1. calm, composure, equability, hush, motionlessness, peace, peacefulness, placidity, quiet, repose, restfulness, serenity, smoothness, stillness, tranquillity **2.** composure, cool (*Sl.*), coolness, dispassion, equanimity, impassivity, imperturbability, poise, sang-froid, self-possession

calumniate asperse, backbite, blacken, defame, denigrate, detract, lampoon, libel, malign, misrepresent, revile, slander, stigmatize, traduce, vilify, vilipend (*Rare*)

calumnious abusive, aspersive, backbiting, defamatory, derogatory, detractive, insulting, libellous, lying, slanderous, vituperative

calumny abuse, aspersion, backbiting, calumniation, defamation, denigration, derogation, detraction, evil-speaking, insult, libel, lying, misrepresentation, obloquy, revilement, slander, smear, stigma, vilification, vituperation

camaraderie brotherhood, brotherliness, companionability, companionship, comradeship, esprit de corps, fellowship, fraternization, good-fellowship, togetherness

camouflage 1. *n.* blind, cloak, concealment, cover, deceptive markings, disguise, false appearance, front, guise, mask, masquerade, mimicry, protective colouring, screen, subterfuge **2.** *v.* cloak, conceal, cover, disguise, hide, mask, obfuscate, obscure, screen, veil

camp[1] bivouac, camping ground, camp site, cantonment (*Mil.*), encampment, tents

camp[2] affected, artificial, camped up, campy (*Inf.*), effeminate, mannered, ostentatious, poncy (*Sl.*), posturing

campaign attack, crusade, drive, expedition, jihad (*Rare*), movement, offensive, operation, push

canaille hoi polloi, masses, mob, plebs, populace, proletariat, rabble, ragtag, riffraff, scum, vulgar herd

cancel 1. abolish, abort, abrogate, annul, blot out, call off, countermand, cross out, delete, do away with, efface, eliminate, erase, expunge, obliterate, quash, repeal, repudiate, rescind, revoke **2.** balance out, compensate for, counterbalance, make up for, neutralize, nullify, offset, redeem

cancellation abandoning, abandonment, abolition, annulment, deletion, elimination, quashing, repeal, revocation

cancer blight, canker, carcinoma (*Pathol.*), corruption, evil, growth, malignancy, pestilence, rot, sickness, tumour

candid 1. blunt, fair, forthright, frank, free, guileless, impartial, ingenuous, just, open, outspoken, plain, sincere, straightforward, truthful, unbiased, unequivocal, unprejudiced **2.** impromptu, informal, uncontrived, unposed

candidate applicant, aspirant, claimant, competitor, contender, contestant, entrant, nominee, possibility, runner, solicitant, suitor

candour artlessness, directness, fairness, forthrightness, frankness, guilelessness, honesty, impartiality, ingenuousness, naïveté, openness, outspokenness, simplicity, sincerity, straightforwardness, truthfulness, unequivocalness

canker 1. *v.* blight, consume, corrode, corrupt, embitter, envenom, inflict, poison, pollute, rot, rust, waste away **2.** *n.* bane, blight, blister, cancer, corrosion, corruption, infection, lesion, rot, scourge, sore, ulcer

cannon 1. artillery piece, big gun (*Inf.*), field gun, gun, mortar **2.** *Plural* artillery, battery, big guns, cannonry, field guns, guns, ordnance

cannonade barrage, battery, bombardment, broadside, pounding, salvo, shelling, volley

canny acute, artful, astute, careful, cautious, circumspect, clever, judicious, knowing, perspicacious, prudent, sagacious, sharp, shrewd, subtle, wise, worldly-wise

canon catalogue, criterion, dictate, formula, list, precept, principle, regulation, roll, rule, standard, statute, yardstick

canonical accepted, approved, authoritative, authorized, orthodox, recognized, sanctioned

canopy awning, baldachin, covering, shade, sunshade, tester

cant *n.* **1.** affected piety, humbug, hypocrisy, insincerity, lip service, pious platitudes, pretence, pretentiousness, sanctimoniousness, sham holiness **2.** argot, jargon, lingo, slang, vernacular ~*v.*

3. angle, bevel, incline, rise, slant, slope, tilt

cantankerous bad-tempered, captious, choleric, contrary, crabby, cranky (*U.S. inf.*), crotchety (*Inf.*), crusty, difficult, disagreeable, grouchy (*Inf.*), grumpy, ill-humoured, irascible, irritable, peevish, perverse, quarrelsome, testy

canter *n.* amble, dogtrot, easy gait, jog, lope

canting hypocritical, insincere, Janusfaced, sanctimonious, two-faced

canvass *v.* **1.** analyse, campaign, electioneer, examine, inspect, investigate, poll, scan, scrutinize, sift, solicit, solicit votes, study, ventilate **2.** agitate, debate, discuss, dispute ~*n.* **3.** examination, investigation, poll, scrutiny, survey, tally

canyon coulee (*U.S.*), gorge, gulch (*U.S.*), gulf, gully, ravine

cap *v.* beat, better, complete, cover, crown, eclipse, exceed, excel, finish, outdo, outstrip, overtop, surpass, top, transcend

capability ability, capacity, competence, facility, faculty, means, potential, potentiality, power, proficiency, qualification(s), wherewithal

capable able, accomplished, adapted, adept, adequate, apt, clever, competent, efficient, experienced, fitted, gifted, intelligent, masterly, proficient, qualified, skilful, suited, susceptible, talented

capacious ample, broad, comfortable, commodious, comprehensive, expansive, extended, extensive, generous, liberal, roomy, sizable, spacious, substantial, vast, voluminous, wide

capacity 1. amplitude, compass, dimensions, extent, magnitude, range, room, scope, size, space, volume **2.** ability, aptitude, aptness, brains, capability, cleverness, competence, competency, efficiency, facility, faculty, forte, genius, gift, intelligence, power, readiness, strength **3.** appointment, function, office, position, post, province, role, service, sphere

cape chersonese (*Poetic*), head, headland, ness (*Archaic*), peninsula, point, promontory

caper 1. *v.* bounce, bound, cavort, dance, frisk, frolic, gambol, hop, jump, leap, romp, skip, spring **2.** *n.* antic, dido (*Inf.*), escapade, gambol, high jinks, hop, jape, jest, jump, lark (*Inf.*), leap, mischief, practical joke, prank, revel, shenanigan (*Inf.*), sport, stunt

capital *adj.* **1.** cardinal, central, chief, controlling, essential, foremost, important, leading, main, major, overruling, paramount, pre-eminent, primary, prime, principal, prominent, vital **2.** excellent, fine, first, first-rate, prime, splendid, superb ~*n.* **3.** assets, cash, finance, finances, financing, funds, investment(s), means, money, principal, property, resources, stock, wealth, wherewithal

capitalism free enterprise, *laissez faire*, private enterprise, private ownership

capitulate come to terms, give in, give up, relent, submit, succumb, surrender, yield

capitulation accedence, submission, surrender, yielding

caprice changeableness, fad, fancy, fickleness, fitfulness, freak, humour, impulse, inconstancy, notion, quirk, vagary, whim, whimsy

capricious changeful, crotchety (*Inf.*), erratic, fanciful, fickle, fitful, freakish, impulsive, inconstant, mercurial, odd, queer, quirky, unpredictable, variable, wayward, whimsical

capsize invert, keel over, overturn, tip over, turn over, turn turtle, upset

capsule 1. bolus, lozenge, pill, tablet, troche (*Medical*) **2.** case, pericarp (*Bot.*), pod, receptacle, seed vessel, sheath, shell, vessel

captain boss, chief, chieftain, commander, head, leader, master, number one (*Inf.*), officer, (senior) pilot, skipper

captious 1. carping, cavilling, censorious, critical, deprecating, disparaging, fault-finding, hypercritical, nagging, nit-picking (*Inf.*) **2.** acrimonious, cantankerous, crabbed, cross, irritable, peevish, testy, touchy

captivate allure, attract, beguile, bewitch, charm, dazzle, enamour, enchant, enrapture, enslave, ensnare, enthral, entrance, fascinate, hypnotize, infatuate, lure, mesmerize, seduce, win

captive 1. *n.* bondservant, convict, detainee, hostage, internee, prisoner, prisoner of war, slave **2.** *adj.* caged, confined, enslaved, ensnared, imprisoned, incarcerated, locked up, penned, restricted, subjugated

captivity bondage, confinement, custody, detention, durance (*Archaic*), duress, enthralment, imprisonment, incarceration, internment, restraint, servitude, slavery, thraldom, vassalage

capture 1. *v.* apprehend, arrest, bag, catch, collar (*Inf.*), lift (*Sl.*), nab (*Inf.*), secure, seize, take, take into custody, take prisoner **2.** *n.* apprehension, arrest, catch, imprisonment, seizure, taking, taking captive, trapping

car 1. auto (*U.S.*), automobile, jalopy (*Inf.*), machine, motor, motorcar, vehicle **2.** buffet car, cable car, coach, dining car, (railway) carriage, sleeping car, van

carafe decanter, flagon, flask, jug, pitcher

carcass body, cadaver (*Medical*), corpse, corse (*Archaic*), dead body, framework, hulk, remains, shell, skeleton

cardinal capital, central, chief, essential, first, foremost, fundamental, greatest, highest, important, key, leading, main, paramount, pre-eminent, primary, prime, principal

care 1. affliction, anxiety, burden, concern, disquiet, hardship, interest, perplexity, pressure, responsibility, solicitude, stress, tribulation, trouble, vexation, woe, worry **2.** attention, carefulness, caution, circumspection, consideration, direction, forethought, heed, management, meticulousness, pains, prudence, regard, vigilance, watchfulness **3.** charge, control, custody, guardianship, keeping, management, ministration, protection, supervision, ward

career *n.* **1.** calling, employment, life work, livelihood, occupation, pursuit, vocation **2.** course, passage, path, procedure, progress, race, walk ~*v.* **3.** bolt, dash, hurtle, race, rush, speed, tear

care for 1. attend, foster, look after, mind, minister to, nurse, protect, provide for, tend, watch over **2.** be fond of, desire, enjoy, find congenial, like, love, prize, take to, want

carefree airy, blithe, breezy, buoyant, careless, cheerful, cheery, easy-going, happy, happy-go-lucky, insouciant, jaunty, light-hearted, lightsome (*Archaic*), radiant, sunny, untroubled

careful 1. accurate, attentive, cautious, chary, circumspect, conscientious, discreet, fastidious, heedful, painstaking, precise, prudent, punctilious, scrupulous, thoughtful, thrifty **2.** alert, concerned, judicious, mindful, particular, protective, solicitous, vigilant, wary, watchful

careless 1. absent-minded, cursory, forgetful, hasty, heedless, incautious, inconsiderate, indiscreet, negligent, perfunctory, regardless, remiss, thoughtless, unconcerned, unguarded, unmindful, unthinking **2.** inaccurate, irresponsible, lackadaisical, neglectful, offhand, slapdash, slipshod, sloppy (*Inf.*) **3.** artless, casual, nonchalant, unstudied

carelessness inaccuracy, inattention, inconsiderateness, indiscretion, irresponsibility, neglect, negligence, omission, remissness, slackness, sloppiness (*Inf.*), thoughtlessness

caress 1. *v.* cuddle, embrace, fondle, hug, kiss, nuzzle, pet, stroke **2.** *n.* cuddle, embrace, fondling, hug, kiss, pat, stroke

caretaker 1. *n.* concierge, curator, custodian, janitor, keeper, porter, superintendent, warden, watchman **2.** *adj.* holding, interim, short-term, temporary

cargo baggage, consignment, contents, freight, goods, lading, load, merchandise, shipment, tonnage, ware

caricature 1. *n.* burlesque, cartoon, distortion, farce, lampoon, mimicry, parody, pasquinade, satire, send-up (*Brit. inf.*), takeoff (*Inf.*), travesty **2.** *v.* burlesque, distort, lampoon, mimic, mock, parody, ridicule, satirize, send up (*Brit. inf.*), take off (*Inf.*)

carnage blood bath, bloodshed, butchery, havoc, holocaust, massacre, mass murder, murder, shambles, slaughter

carnal 1. animal, erotic, fleshly, impure, lascivious, lecherous, lewd, libidinous, licentious, lustful, prurient, salacious, sensual, sensuous, unchaste, voluptuous, wanton **2.** corporeal, earthly, human, mundane, natural, physical, profane, secular, sublunary, temporal, unregenerate, unspiritual, worldly

carnality bestiality, corporeality, fleshliness, lechery, lust, lustfulness, prurience, salaciousness, sensuality, voluptuousness, worldliness

carnival celebration, fair, festival, fête, fiesta, gala, holiday, jamboree, jubilee, Mardi Gras, merrymaking, revelry

carol canticle, canzonet, chorus, ditty, hymn, lay, noel, song, strain

carouse booze (*Inf.*), drink, imbibe, make merry, quaff, roister, wassail

carp cavil, censure, complain, criticize, find fault, hypercriticize, knock (*Inf.*),

nag, pick holes (*Inf.*), quibble, reproach

carpenter cabinet-maker, joiner, woodworker

carping captious, cavilling, critical, fault-finding, grouchy (*Inf.*), hard to please, hypercritical, nagging, nit-picking (*Inf.*), picky (*Inf.*), reproachful

carriage 1. carrying, conveyance, conveying, delivery, freight, transport, transportation **2.** cab, coach, conveyance, vehicle **3.** *Fig.* air, bearing, behaviour, comportment, conduct, demeanour, deportment, gait, manner, mien, posture, presence

carry 1. bear, bring, conduct, convey, fetch, haul, lift, lug, move, relay, take, transfer, transmit, transport **2.** accomplish, capture, effect, gain, secure, win **3.** drive, impel, influence, motivate, spur, urge **4.** bear, hold up, maintain, shoulder, stand, suffer, support, sustain, underpin, uphold **5.** broadcast, communicate, display, disseminate, give, offer, publish, release, stock

carry on 1. continue, endure, keep going, last, maintain, perpetuate, persevere, persist **2.** administer, manage, operate, run **3.** *Inf.* create (*Sl.*), make a fuss, misbehave

carry out accomplish, achieve, carry through, consummate, discharge, effect, execute, fulfil, implement, perform, realize

carton box, case, container, pack, package, packet

cartoon animated cartoon, animated film, animation, caricature, comic strip, lampoon, parody, satire, sketch, takeoff

cartridge 1. capsule, case, cassette, container, cylinder, magazine **2.** charge, round, shell

carve chip, chisel, cut, divide, engrave, etch, fashion, form, grave, hack, hew, incise, indent, mould, sculpt, sculpture, slash, slice, whittle

cascade 1. *n.* avalanche, cataract, deluge, falls, flood, fountain, outpouring, shower, torrent, waterfall **2.** *v.* descend, flood, gush, overflow, pitch, plunge, pour, spill, surge, tumble

case 1. box, cabinet, canister, capsule, carton, cartridge, casket, chest, compact, container, crate, holder, receptacle, shell, suitcase, tray, trunk **2.** capsule, casing, cover, covering, envelope, folder, integument, jacket, sheath, wrapper, wrapping **3.** circumstance(s), condition, context, contingency, dilemma, event, plight, position, predicament, situation, state **4.** example, illustration, instance, occasion, occurrence, specimen **5.** *Law* action, cause, dispute, lawsuit, proceedings, process, suit, trial

cash banknotes, bread (*Sl.*), bullion, charge, coin, coinage, currency, dough (*Sl.*), funds, money, notes, payment, ready (*Inf.*), ready money, resources, specie, wherewithal

cashier 1. *n.* accountant, bank clerk, banker, bursar, clerk, purser, teller, treasurer **2.** *v.* break, cast off, discard, discharge, dismiss, drum out, expel

casket box, case, chest, coffer, jewel box, kist (*Scot.*)

cast *v.* **1.** chuck, drive, drop, fling, hurl, impel, launch, lob, pitch, project, shed, shy, sling, throw, thrust, toss **2.** bestow, deposit, diffuse, distribute, emit, give, radiate, scatter, shed, spread **3.** allot, appoint, assign, choose, name, pick, select **4.** add, calculate, compute, figure, forecast, reckon, total **5.** form, found, model, mould, set, shape ~*n.* **6.** fling, lob, throw, thrust, toss **7.** air, appearance, complexion, demeanour, look, manner, mien, semblance, shade, stamp, style, tinge, tone, turn **8.** actors, characters, company, dramatis personae, players, troupe

cast down deject, depress, desolate, discourage, dishearten, dispirit

caste class, estate, grade, lineage, order, race, rank, social order, species, station, status, stratum

castigate beat, berate, cane, censure, chasten, chastise, correct, criticize, discipline, dress down (*Inf.*), flail, flay, flog, haul over the coals (*Inf.*), lash, rebuke, reprimand, scold, scourge, whip

castle chateau, citadel, donjon, fastness, fortress, keep, mansion, palace, peel, stronghold, tower

castrate emasculate, geld, neuter, unman

casual 1. accidental, chance, contingent, fortuitous, incidental, irregular, occasional, random, serendipitous, uncertain, unexpected, unforeseen, unintentional, unpremeditated **2.** apathetic, blasé, cursory, indifferent, informal, insouciant, lackadaisical, nonchalant, offhand, perfunctory, relaxed, unconcerned

casualties dead, fatalities, losses, missing, wounded

casualty 1. loss, sufferer, victim **2.** accident, calamity, catastrophe, chance, contingency, disaster, misadventure, misfortune, mishap

casuistry chicanery, equivocation, oversubtleness, sophism, sophistry, speciousness

cat feline, grimalkin, malkin (*Archaic*), moggy (*Sl.*), mouser, puss (*Inf.*), pussy (*Inf.*), tabby

cataclysm calamity, catastrophe, collapse, convulsion, debacle, disaster, upheaval

catacomb crypt, ossuary, tomb, vault

catalogue 1. *n.* directory, gazetteer, index, inventory, list, record, register, roll, roster, schedule **2.** *v.* accession, alphabetize, classify, file, index, inventory, list, register

catapult 1. *n.* ballista, sling, slingshot (*U.S.*), trebuchet **2.** *v.* heave, hurl, hurtle, pitch, plunge, propel, shoot, toss

cataract 1. cascade, deluge, downpour, falls, Niagara, rapids, torrent, waterfall **2.** *Medical* opacity (*of the eye*)

catastrophe 1. adversity, affliction, blow, calamity, cataclysm, devastation, disaster, failure, fiasco, ill, mischance, misfortune, mishap, reverse, tragedy, trial, trouble **2.** conclusion, culmination, curtain, debacle, dénouement, end, finale, termination, upshot, winding-up

catcall 1. *v.* boo, deride, gibe, give the bird to (*Inf.*), hiss, jeer, whistle **2.** *n.* boo, gibe, hiss, jeer, raspberry, whistle

catch *v.* **1.** apprehend, arrest, capture, clutch, ensnare, entangle, entrap, grab, grasp, grip, lay hold of, nab (*Inf.*), seize, snare, snatch, take **2.** detect, discover, expose, find out, surprise, take unawares, unmask **3.** bewitch, captivate, charm, delight, enchant, enrapture, fascinate **4.** contract, develop, go down with, incur, succumb to, suffer from **5.** apprehend, discern, feel, follow, grasp, hear, perceive, recognize, sense, take in, twig (*Inf.*) ~*n.* **6.** bolt, clasp, clip, fastener, hasp, hook, hook and eye, latch, sneck, snib (*Scot.*) **7.** disadvantage, drawback, fly in the ointment, hitch, snag, stumbling block, trap, trick

catching 1. communicable, contagious, infectious, infective, transferable, transmittable **2.** attractive, captivating, charming, enchanting, fascinating, fetching, taking, winning

catch on comprehend, find out, grasp, see, see through, twig (*Inf.*), understand

catchword byword, motto, password, refrain, slogan, watchword

catchy captivating, haunting, memorable, popular

catechize cross-examine, drill, examine, grill (*Inf.*), interrogate, question

catechumen convert, disciple, initiate, learner, neophyte, novice, probationer, tyro

categorical absolute, direct, downright, emphatic, explicit, express, positive, unambiguous, unconditional, unequivocal, unqualified, unreserved

category class, classification, department, division, grade, grouping, head, heading, list, order, rank, section, sort, type

cater furnish, outfit, provide, provision, purvey, supply, victual

cater to coddle, gratify, humour, indulge, minister to, mollycoddle, pamper, pander to, spoil

caterwaul bawl, howl, scream, screech, shriek, squall, wail, yowl

catharsis abreaction, cleansing, lustration, purgation, purging, purification, release

catholic all-embracing, all-inclusive, broad-minded, charitable, comprehensive, eclectic, ecumenical, general, global, liberal, tolerant, unbigoted, universal, unsectarian, whole, wide, world-wide

cattle beasts, bovines, cows, kine (*Archaic*), livestock, neat (*Archaic*), stock

catty backbiting, bitchy (*Sl.*), ill-natured, malevolent, malicious, mean, rancorous, spiteful, venomous

caucus assembly, conclave, convention, get-together (*Inf.*), meeting, parley, session

cause n. **1.** agent, beginning, creator, genesis, mainspring, maker, origin, originator, prime mover, producer, root, source, spring **2.** account, agency, aim, basis, consideration, end, grounds, incentive, inducement, motivation, motive, object, purpose, reason **3.** attempt, belief, conviction, enterprise, ideal, movement, purpose, undertaking ~v. **4.** begin, bring about, compel, create, effect, engender, generate, give rise to, incite, induce, lead to, motivate, occasion, precipitate, produce, provoke, result in

caustic 1. acrid, astringent, biting, burning, corroding, corrosive, keen, mordant **2.** acrimonious, cutting, pungent, sarcastic, scathing, severe, stinging, trenchant, virulent

caution n. **1.** alertness, care, carefulness, circumspection, deliberation, discretion, forethought, heed, heedfulness, prudence, vigilance, watchfulness **2.** admonition, advice, counsel, injunction, warning ~v. **3.** admonish, advise, tip off, urge, warn

cautious alert, cagey (*Inf.*), careful, chary, circumspect, discreet, guarded, heedful, judicious, prudent, tentative, vigilant, wary, watchful

cavalcade array, march-past, parade, procession, spectacle, train

cavalier n. **1.** chevalier, equestrian, horseman, knight, royalist **2.** beau, blade (*Archaic*), escort, gallant, gentleman ~adj. **3.** arrogant, condescending, curt, disdainful, haughty, insolent, lofty, lordly, offhand, scornful, supercilious

cavalry horse, horsemen, mounted troops

cave cavern, cavity, den, grotto, hollow

caveat admonition, caution, warning

cavern cave, hollow, pothole

cavernous 1. concave, deep-set, hollow, sunken, yawning **2.** echoing, resonant, reverberant, sepulchral

cavil carp, censure, complain, find fault, hypercriticize, object, quibble

cavilling captious, carping, censorious, critical, fault-finding, hypercritical, nit-picking (*Inf.*), quibbling

cavity crater, dent, gap, hole, hollow, pit

cavort caper, caracole, frisk, frolic, gambol, prance, romp, sport

cease break off, bring *or* come to an end, conclude, culminate, desist, die away, discontinue, end, fail, finish, halt, leave off, refrain, stay, stop, terminate

ceaseless constant, continual, continuous, endless, eternal, everlasting, incessant, indefatigable, interminable, never-ending, nonstop, perennial, perpetual, unending, unremitting, untiring

cede abandon, abdicate, allow, concede, convey, grant, hand over, make over, relinquish, renounce, resign, surrender, transfer, yield

celebrate bless, commemorate, commend, drink to, eulogize, exalt, extol, glorify, honour, keep, laud, observe, perform, praise, proclaim, publicize, rejoice, reverence, solemnize, toast

celebrated acclaimed, distinguished, eminent, famed, famous, glorious, illustrious, lionized, notable, outstanding, popular, pre-eminent, prominent, renowned, revered, well-known

celebration 1. carousal, festival, festivity, gala, jollification, jubilee, junketing, merrymaking, party, revelry **2.** anniversary, commemoration, honouring, observance, performance, remembrance, solemnization

celebrity 1. big name, big shot (*Sl.*), bigwig (*Sl.*), dignitary, lion (*Inf.*), luminary, name, personage, personality, star, superstar, V.I.P. **2.** distinction, éclat, eminence, fame, glory, honour, notability, popularity, pre-eminence, prestige, prominence, renown, reputation, repute, stardom

celerity dispatch, expedition, fleetness, haste, promptness, quickness, rapidity, speed, swiftness, velocity, vivacity

celestial angelic, astral, divine, elysian, empyrean, eternal, ethereal, godlike, heavenly, immortal, seraphic, spiritual, sublime, supernatural

celibacy chastity, continence, purity, singleness, virginity

cell 1. cavity, chamber, compartment, cubicle, dungeon, stall **2.** caucus, coterie, group, nucleus, unit

cement 1. *v.* attach, bind, bond, cohere, combine, glue, gum, join, plaster, seal, solder, stick together, unite, weld **2.** *n.* adhesive, binder, glue, gum, paste, plaster, sealant

cemetery burial ground, churchyard, God's acre, graveyard, necropolis

censor blue-pencil, bowdlerize, cut, expurgate

censorious captious, carping, cavilling, condemnatory, disapproving, disparaging, fault-finding, hypercritical, severe

censurable at fault, blamable, blameworthy, chargeable, contemptible, culpable, faulty, guilty, reprehensible, scandalous

censure 1. *v.* abuse, berate, blame, castigate, chide, condemn, criticize, denounce, rebuke, reprehend, reprimand, reproach, reprove, scold, upbraid **2.** *n.* blame, castigation, condemnation, criticism, disapproval, dressing down (*Inf.*), obloquy, rebuke, remonstrance, reprehension, reprimand, reproach, reproof, stricture

central chief, essential, focal, fundamental, inner, interior, key, main, mean, median, mid, middle, primary, principal

centralize amalgamate, compact, concentrate, concentre, condense, converge, incorporate, rationalize, streamline, unify

centre 1. *n.* bull's-eye, core, crux, focus, heart, hub, mid, middle, midpoint, nucleus, pivot **2.** *v.* cluster, concentrate, converge, focus, revolve

centrepiece cynosure, epergne, focus, highlight, hub, star

centrifugal diffusive, divergent, diverging, efferent, radial, radiating

ceremonial 1. *adj.* formal, liturgical, ritual, ritualistic, solemn, stately **2.** *n.* ceremony, formality, rite, ritual, solemnity

ceremonious civil, courteous, courtly, deferential, dignified, exact, formal, precise, punctilious, ritual, solemn, starchy (*Inf.*), stately, stiff

ceremony 1. commemoration, function, observance, parade, rite, ritual, service, show, solemnities **2.** ceremonial, decorum, etiquette, form, formal courtesy, formality, niceties, pomp, propriety, protocol

certain 1. assured, confident, convinced, positive, satisfied, sure **2.** ascertained, conclusive, incontrovertible, indubitable, irrefutable, known, plain, true, undeniable, undoubted, unequivocal, unmistakable, valid **3.** bound, definite, destined, fated, ineluctable, inescapable, inevitable, inexorable, sure **4.** decided, definite, established, fixed, settled **5.** assured, constant, dependable, reliable, stable, steady, trustworthy, unfailing, unquestionable **6.** express, individual, particular, precise, special, specific

certainty 1. assurance, authoritativeness, certitude, confidence, conviction, faith, indubitableness, inevitability, positiveness, sureness, trust, validity **2.** fact, reality, sure thing (*Inf.*), surety, truth

certificate authorization, credential(s), diploma, document, licence, testimonial, voucher, warrant

certify ascertain, assure, attest, authenticate, aver, avow, confirm, corroborate, declare, endorse, guarantee, notify, show, testify, validate, verify, vouch, witness

certitude assurance, certainty, confidence, conviction

cessation abeyance, arrest, break, ceasing, discontinuance, ending, halt, halting, hiatus, intermission, interruption, interval, let-up (*Inf.*), pause, recess, remission, respite, rest, standstill, stay, stoppage, suspension, termination, time off

cession abandonment, abnegation, capitulation, ceding, conceding, concession, conveyance, grant, relinquishment, renunciation, surrender, yielding

chafe abrade, anger, annoy, exasperate, fret, fume, gall, grate, incense, inflame, irritate, offend, provoke, rage, rasp, rub, ruffle, scrape, scratch, vex, worry

chaff *n.* **1.** dregs, glumes, hulls, husks, refuse, remains, rubbish, trash, waste **2.** badinage, banter, joking, persiflage, raillery, teasing ~*v.* **3.** banter, deride, jeer, mock, rib (*Inf.*), ridicule, scoff, taunt, tease

chagrin 1. *n.* annoyance, discomfiture, discomposure, displeasure, disquiet, dissatisfaction, embarrassment, fretfulness, humiliation, ill-humour, irritation, mortification, peevishness, spleen, vexation **2.** *v.* annoy, discomfit, discompose, displease, disquiet, dissatisfy, embarrass, humiliate, irk, irritate, mortify, peeve, vex

chain *v.* **1.** bind, confine, enslave, fetter, gyve (*Archaic*), handcuff, manacle, restrain, shackle, tether, trammel, unite ~*n.* **2.** bond, coupling, fetter, link, manacle, shackle, union **3.** concatenation, progression, sequence, series, set, string, succession, train

chairman chairperson, chairwoman, director, master of ceremonies, president, presider, speaker, spokesman, toastmaster

chalk up accumulate, achieve, attain, credit, enter, gain, log, mark, record, register, score, tally, win

challenge 1. *v.* accost, arouse, beard, brave, call out, claim, confront, dare, defy, demand, dispute, impugn, investigate, object to, provoke, question, require, stimulate, summon, tax, test, throw down the gauntlet, try **2.** *n.* confrontation, dare, defiance, interrogation, provocation, question, summons to contest, test, trial, ultimatum

chamber 1. apartment, bedroom, cavity, compartment, cubicle, enclosure, hall, hollow, room **2.** assembly, council, legislative body, legislature

champion 1. *n.* backer, challenger, conqueror, defender, guardian, hero, nonpareil, patron, protector, title holder, upholder, victor, vindicator, warrior, winner **2.** *v.* advocate, back, defend, espouse, fight for, promote, support, uphold

chance *n.* **1.** liability, likelihood, occasion, odds, opening, opportunity, possibility, probability, prospect, scope, time **2.** accident, casualty, coincidence, contingency, destiny, fate, fortuity, fortune, luck, misfortune, peril, providence **3.** gamble, hazard, jeopardy, risk, speculation, uncertainty ~*v.* **4.** befall, betide, come about, come to pass, fall out, happen, occur **5.** endanger, gamble, go out on a limb (*Inf.*), hazard, jeopardize, risk, stake, try, venture, wager ~*adj.* **6.** accidental, casual, contingent, fortuitous, inadvertent, incidental, random, serendipitous, unforeseeable, unforeseen, unintentional, unlooked-for

chancy dangerous, dicey (*Sl.*), dodgy (*Inf.*), hazardous, problematical, risky, speculative, uncertain

change *v.* **1.** alter, convert, diversify, fluctuate, metamorphose, moderate, modify, mutate, reform, remodel, reorganize, restyle, shift, transform, transmute, vacillate, vary, veer **2.** alternate, barter, convert, displace, exchange, interchange, remove, replace, substitute, swap (*Inf.*), trade, transmit ~*n.* **3.** alteration, difference, innovation, metamorphosis, modification, mutation, permutation, revolution, transformation, transition, transmutation, vicissitude **4.** conversion, exchange, interchange, substitution, trade **5.** break (*Inf.*), diversion, novelty, variation, variety

changeable capricious, changeful, chequered, erratic, fickle, fitful, fluid, inconstant, irregular, kaleidoscopic, labile (*Chem.*), mercurial, mobile, mutable, protean, shifting, uncertain, unpredictable, unreliable, unsettled, unstable, unsteady, vacillating, variable, versatile, volatile, wavering

changeless abiding, consistent, constant, everlasting, fixed, immutable, permanent, perpetual, regular, reliable, resolute, settled, stationary, steadfast, steady, unalterable, unchanging, uniform, unvarying

channel n. 1. canal, chamber, conduit, duct, fluting, furrow, groove, gutter, main, passage, route, strait 2. Fig. approach, artery, avenue, course, means, medium, path, route, way ~v. 3. conduct, convey, direct, guide, transmit

chant 1. n. carol, chorus, melody, psalm, song 2. v. carol, chorus, croon, descant, intone, recite, sing, warble

chaos anarchy, bedlam, confusion, disorder, disorganization, entropy, lawlessness, pandemonium, tumult

chaotic anarchic, confused, deranged, disordered, disorganized, lawless, purposeless, rampageous, riotous, topsyturvy, tumultuous, uncontrolled

chap bloke (Inf.), character, cove (Sl.), customer, fellow, guy (Inf.), individual, person, sort, type

chaperon 1. n. companion, duenna, escort, governess 2. v. accompany, attend, escort, protect, safeguard, shepherd, watch over

chaplet bouquet, coronal, garland, wreath

chapter clause, division, episode, part, period, phase, section, stage, topic

char carbonize, cauterize, scorch, sear, singe

character 1. attributes, bent, calibre, cast, complexion, constitution, disposition, individuality, kidney, make-up, marked traits, nature, personality, quality, reputation, temper, temperament, type 2. honour, integrity, rectitude, strength, uprightness 3. card (Inf.), eccentric, oddball (Inf.), oddity, original, queer fish (Inf.) 4. cipher, device, emblem, figure, hieroglyph, letter, logo, mark, rune, sign, symbol, type 5. part, persona, portrayal, role 6. fellow, guy (Inf.), individual, person, sort, type

characteristic 1. adj. distinctive, distinguishing, idiosyncratic, individual, peculiar, representative, singular, special, specific, symbolic, symptomatic, typical 2. n. attribute, faculty, feature, idiosyncrasy, mark, peculiarity, property, quality, trait

characterize brand, distinguish, identify, indicate, inform, mark, represent, stamp, typify

charade fake, farce, pantomime, parody, pretence, travesty

charge v. 1. accuse, arraign, blame, impeach, incriminate, indict, involve ~n. 2. accusation, allegation, imputation, indictment ~v. 3. assail, assault, attack, rush, storm ~n. 4. assault, attack, onset, onslaught, rush, sortie ~v. 5. afflict, burden, commit, entrust, tax ~n. 6. burden, care, concern, custody, duty, office, responsibility, safekeeping, trust, ward 7. amount, cost, damage (Inf.), expenditure, expense, outlay, payment, price, rate ~v. 8. fill, instil, lade, load, suffuse 9. bid, command, enjoin, exhort, instruct, order, require ~n. 10. command, dictate, direction, exhortation, injunction, instruction, mandate, order, precept

charitable 1. beneficent, benevolent, bountiful, eleemosynary, generous, kind, lavish, liberal, philanthropic 2. broadminded, considerate, favourable, forgiving, gracious, humane, indulgent, kindly, lenient, magnanimous, sympathetic, tolerant, understanding

charity 1. alms-giving, assistance, benefaction, contributions, donations, endowment, fund, gift, hand-out, philanthropy, relief 2. affection, agape, altruism, benevolence, benignity, bountifulness, bounty, compassion, fellow feeling, generosity, goodness, good will, humanity, indulgence, love, tenderheartedness

charlatan cheat, con man (Inf.), fake, fraud, impostor, mountebank, phoney (Sl.), pretender, quack, sham, swindler

charm v. 1. allure, attract, beguile, bewitch, cajole, captivate, delight, enamour, enchant, enrapture, entrance, fascinate, mesmerize, please, win, win over ~n. 2. allure, allurement, appeal, attraction, desirability, enchantment, fascination, magic, magnetism, sorcery, spell 3. amulet, fetish, good-luck piece, lucky piece, periapt (Rare), talisman, trinket

charming appealing, attractive, bewitching, captivating, delectable, delightful, engaging, eye-catching, fetching, irresistible, lovely, pleasant, pleasing, seductive, winning, winsome

chart 1. n. blueprint, diagram, graph, map, plan, table, tabulation 2. v. delineate, draft, graph, map out, outline, plot, shape, sketch

charter 1. n. bond, concession, contract, deed, document, franchise, indenture, licence, permit, prerogative, privilege, right **2.** *v.* authorize, commission, employ, hire, lease, rent, sanction

chary 1. careful, cautious, circumspect, guarded, heedful, prudent, reluctant, scrupulous, slow, suspicious, uneasy, wary **2.** careful (*Brit.*), frugal, niggardly, parsimonious, thrifty

chase 1. *v.* course, drive, drive away, expel, follow, hound, hunt, pursue, put to flight, run after, track **2.** *n.* hunt, hunting, pursuit, race, venery (*Archaic*)

chasm abyss, alienation, breach, cavity, cleft, crater, crevasse, fissure, gap, gorge, gulf, hiatus, hollow, opening, ravine, rent, rift, split, void

chassis anatomy, bodywork, frame, framework, fuselage, skeleton, substructure

chaste austere, decent, decorous, elegant, immaculate, incorrupt, innocent, modest, moral, neat, pure, quiet, refined, restrained, simple, unaffected, uncontaminated, undefiled, unsullied, vestal, virginal, virtuous, wholesome

chasten afflict, castigate, chastise, correct, cow, curb, discipline, humble, humiliate, repress, soften, subdue, tame

chastise beat, berate, castigate, censure, correct, discipline, flog, lash, punish, scold, scourge, upbraid, whip

chastity celibacy, continence, innocence, maidenhood, modesty, purity, virginity, virtue

chat 1. *n.* chatter, chinwag (*Brit. inf.*), confab (*Inf.*), gossip, heart-to-heart, natter, talk, tête-à-tête **2.** *v.* chatter, chew the rag *or* fat (*Sl.*), gossip, jaw (*Sl.*), natter, rabbit (on) (*Brit. sl.*), talk

chatter *n./v.* babble, blather, chat, gab (*Inf.*), gossip, jabber, natter, prate, prattle, tattle, twaddle

chatty colloquial, familiar, friendly, gossipy, informal, newsy (*Inf.*), talkative

cheap 1. bargain, cut-price, economical, economy, inexpensive, keen, low-cost, low-priced, reasonable, reduced, sale **2.** common, inferior, paltry, poor, second-rate, shoddy, tatty, tawdry, worthless **3.** base, contemptible, despicable, low, mean, scurvy, sordid, vulgar

cheapen belittle, debase, degrade, demean, denigrate, depreciate, derogate, devalue, discredit, disparage, lower

cheat *v.* **1.** bamboozle (*Inf.*), beguile, bilk, con (*Sl.*), deceive, defraud, diddle (*Inf.*), do (*Sl.*), double-cross (*Inf.*), dupe,

finagle (*Inf.*), fleece, fool, gull (*Archaic*), hoax, hoodwink, mislead, rip off (*Sl.*), swindle, take for a ride (*Inf.*), take in (*Inf.*), trick, victimize **2.** baffle, check, defeat, deprive, foil, frustrate, prevent, thwart ~*n.* **3.** artifice, deceit, deception, fraud, imposture, rip-off (*Sl.*), swindle, trickery **4.** charlatan, cheater, con man (*Inf.*), deceiver, dodger, double-crosser (*Inf.*), impostor, knave (*Archaic*), rogue, shark, sharper, swindler, trickster

check *v.* **1.** compare, confirm, enquire into, examine, inspect, investigate, look at, look over, make sure, monitor, note, probe, scrutinize, study, test, tick, verify **2.** arrest, bar, bridle, control, curb, delay, halt, hinder, impede, inhibit, limit, nip in the bud, obstruct, pause, repress, restrain, retard, stop, thwart **3.** blame, chide, give (someone) a row (*Inf.*), rate, rebuff, rebuke, reprimand, reprove, scold, tell off (*Inf.*) ~*n.* **4.** examination, inspection, investigation, research, scrutiny, test **5.** constraint, control, curb, damper, hindrance, impediment, inhibition, limitation, obstruction, restraint, stoppage **6.** blow, disappointment, frustration, rejection, reverse, setback

cheek audacity, brass neck (*Inf.*), brazenness, disrespect, effrontery, gall (*Inf.*), impertinence, impudence, insolence, lip (*Sl.*), nerve, sauce (*Inf.*), temerity

cheeky audacious, disrespectful, forward, impertinent, impudent, insolent, insulting, pert, saucy

cheer *v.* **1.** animate, brighten, buoy up, cheer up, comfort, console, elate, elevate, encourage, enliven, exhilarate, gladden, hearten, incite, inspirit, solace, uplift, warm **2.** acclaim, applaud, clap, hail, hurrah ~*n.* **3.** animation, buoyancy, cheerfulness, comfort, gaiety, gladness, glee, hopefulness, joy, liveliness, merriment, merry-making, mirth, optimism, solace **4.** acclamation, applause, ovation, plaudits

cheerful animated, blithe, bright, bucked (*Inf.*), buoyant, cheery, contented, enlivening, enthusiastic, gay, glad, gladsome, happy, hearty, jaunty, jolly, joyful, light-hearted, lightsome (*Archaic*), merry, optimistic, pleasant, sparkling, sprightly, sunny

cheerfulness buoyancy, exuberance, gaiety, geniality, gladness, good cheer, good humour, high spirits, jauntiness, joyousness, light-heartedness

cheering auspicious, bright, comforting, encouraging, heartening, promising, propitious

cheerless austere, bleak, comfortless, dark, dejected, depressed, desolate, despondent, disconsolate, dismal, dolorous, drab, dreary, dull, forlorn, gloomy, grim, joyless, melancholy, miserable, mournful, sad, sombre, sorrowful, sullen, unhappy, woebegone, woeful

cheer up brighten, buck up (*Inf.*), comfort, encourage, enliven, gladden, hearten, jolly along, perk up, rally, take heart

cheery breezy, carefree, cheerful, good-humoured, happy, jovial, lively, pleasant, sunny

chef d'oeuvre brainchild, crowning achievement, *magnum opus*, masterpiece, masterwork

chemical compound, drug, potion, synthetic

cherish care for, cleave to, cling to, comfort, cosset, encourage, entertain, foster, harbour, hold dear, nourish, nurse, nurture, prize, shelter, support, sustain, treasure

cherubic adorable, angelic, heavenly, innocent, lovable, seraphic, sweet

chest box, case, casket, coffer, crate, strongbox, trunk

chew 1. bite, champ, crunch, gnaw, grind, masticate, munch 2. *Fig. Usually with* **over** consider, deliberate upon, meditate, mull (over), muse on, ponder, reflect upon, ruminate, weigh

chic elegant, fashionable, modish, smart, stylish, trendy (*Brit. inf.*)

chicanery artifice, cheating, chicane, deception, deviousness, dodge, double-dealing, duplicity, intrigue, sharp practice, skulduggery (*Inf.*), sophistry, stratagems, subterfuge, trickery, underhandedness, wiles, wire-pulling (*Chiefly U.S.*)

chide admonish, berate, blame, censure, check, criticize, find fault, give (someone) a row (*Inf.*), lecture, rebuke, reprehend, reprimand, reproach, reprove, scold, tell off (*Inf.*), upbraid

chief 1. *adj.* capital, cardinal, central, especial, essential, foremost, grand, highest, key, leading, main, most important, outstanding, paramount, predominant, pre-eminent, premier, prevailing, primary, prime, principal, superior, su-

preme, uppermost, vital 2. *n.* boss (*Inf.*), captain, chieftain, commander, director, governor, head, leader, lord, manager, master, principal, ringleader, ruler, superintendent, suzerain

chiefly above all, especially, essentially, in general, in the main, mainly, mostly, on the whole, predominantly, primarily, principally, usually

child babe, baby, bairn (*Scot.*), brat, chit, descendant, infant, issue, juvenile, kid (*Inf.*), little one, minor, nipper (*Inf.*), nursling, offspring, progeny, suckling, toddler, tot, wean (*Scot.*), youngster (*Inf.*)

childbirth accouchement, childbearing, confinement, delivery, labour, lying-in, parturition, travail

childhood boyhood, girlhood, immaturity, infancy, minority, schooldays, youth

childish boyish, foolish, frivolous, girlish, immature, infantile, juvenile, puerile, silly, simple, trifling, weak, young

childlike artless, credulous, guileless, ingenuous, innocent, naive, simple, trustful, trusting, unfeigned

chill *adj.* 1. biting, bleak, chilly, cold, freezing, frigid, raw, sharp, wintry 2. *Fig.* aloof, cool, depressing, distant, frigid, hostile, stony, unfriendly, ungenial, unresponsive, unwelcoming ~*v.* 3. congeal, cool, freeze, refrigerate 4. *Fig.* dampen, deject, depress, discourage, dishearten, dismay ~*n.* 5. bite, cold, coldness, coolness, crispness, frigidity, nip, rawness, sharpness

chilly 1. blowy, breezy, brisk, cool, crisp, draughty, fresh, nippy, penetrating, sharp 2. frigid, hostile, unfriendly, unresponsive, unsympathetic, unwelcoming

chime boom, clang, dong, jingle, peal, ring, sound, strike, tinkle, tintinnabulate, toll

chimera bogy, delusion, dream, fantasy, figment, hallucination, ignis fatuus, illusion, monster, monstrosity, snare, spectre, will-o'-the-wisp

chimerical delusive, fabulous, fanciful, fantastic, hallucinatory, illusive, illusory, imaginary, quixotic, unfounded, unreal, vain, visionary, wild

china ceramics, crockery, porcelain, pottery, service, tableware, ware

chink aperture, cleft, crack, cranny,

crevice, cut, fissure, flaw, gap, opening, rift

chip 1. *n.* dent, flake, flaw, fragment, nick, notch, paring, scrap, scratch, shard, shaving, sliver, wafer 2. *v.* chisel, damage, gash, nick, whittle

chip in contribute, donate, go Dutch (*Inf.*), interpose, interrupt, pay, subscribe

chirp cheep, chirrup, peep, pipe, tweet, twitter, warble

chivalrous bold, brave, courageous, courteous, courtly, gallant, gentlemanly, heroic, high-minded, honourable, intrepid, knightly, magnanimous, true, valiant

chivalry courage, courtesy, courtliness, gallantry, gentlemanliness, knight-errantry, knighthood, politeness

chivvy annoy, badger, harass, hassle (*Inf.*), hound, nag, pester, plague, pressure (*Inf.*), prod, torment

choice 1. *n.* alternative, discrimination, election, option, pick, preference, say, selection, variety 2. *adj.* best, dainty, elect, elite, excellent, exclusive, exquisite, hand-picked, nice, precious, prime, prize, rare, select, special, superior, uncommon, unusual, valuable

choke asphyxiate, bar, block, clog, close, congest, constrict, dam, obstruct, occlude, overpower, smother, stifle, stop, strangle, suffocate, suppress, throttle

choleric angry, bad-tempered, fiery, hasty, hot, hot-tempered, ill-tempered, irascible, irritable, passionate, petulant, quick-tempered, testy, touchy

choose adopt, cull, designate, desire, elect, espouse, fix on, opt for, pick, predestine, prefer, see fit, select, settle upon, single out, take, wish

choosy discriminating, exacting, faddy, fastidious, finicky, fussy, particular, selective

chop 1. *v.* axe, cleave, cut, fell, hack, hew, lop, sever, shear, slash, truncate 2. *n.* **the chop** *Sl.* dismissal, one's cards, sacking (*Inf.*), termination, the axe (*Inf.*), the boot (*Sl.*), the sack (*Inf.*)

choppy blustery, broken, rough, ruffled, squally, tempestuous

chop up cube, dice, divide, fragment, mince

chore burden, duty, errand, fag (*Inf.*), job, task

chortle cackle, chuckle, crow, guffaw

chorus 1. choir, choristers, ensemble, singers, vocalists 2. burden, refrain, response, strain 3. accord, concert, harmony, unison

christen baptize, call, designate, dub, name, style, term, title

chronic 1. confirmed, deep-rooted, deep-seated, habitual, incessant, incurable, ineradicable, ingrained, inveterate, persistent 2. *Inf.* appalling, atrocious, awful, dreadful

chronicle 1. *n.* account, annals, diary, history, journal, narrative, record, register, story 2. *v.* enter, narrate, put on record, record, recount, register, relate, report, set down, tell

chronicler annalist, diarist, historian, historiographer, narrator, recorder, reporter, scribe

chronological consecutive, historical, in sequence, ordered, progressive, sequential

chubby buxom, flabby, fleshy, plump, podgy, portly, rotund, round, stout, tubby

chuck cast, discard, fling, heave, hurl, pitch, shy, sling, throw, toss

chuckle chortle, crow, exult, giggle, laugh, snigger, titter

chum companion, comrade, crony, friend, mate (*Inf.*), pal (*Inf.*)

chummy affectionate, close, friendly, intimate, matey (*Inf.*), pally (*Inf.*), thick (*Inf.*)

chunk block, dollop (*Inf.*), hunk, lump, mass, piece, portion, slab, wad, wodge (*Inf.*)

chunky beefy (*Inf.*), dumpy, stocky, stubby, thickset

churl 1. boor, lout, oaf 2. bumpkin, clodhopper (*Inf.*), clown, hillbilly, peasant, rustic, yokel 3. curmudgeon, miser, niggard, skinflint

churlish 1. boorish, brusque, crabbed, harsh, ill-tempered, impolite, loutish, morose, oafish, rude, sullen, surly, uncivil, unmannerly, vulgar 2. close-fisted, illiberal, inhospitable, mean, miserly, niggardly, unneighbourly, unsociable

churlishness boorishness, crassness, crudeness, loutishness, oafishness, rudeness, surliness, uncouthness

churn agitate, beat, boil, convulse, foam, froth, seethe, stir up, swirl, toss

chute channel, gutter, incline, ramp, runway, slide, slope, trough

cicerone courier, escort, guide, mentor, pilot

cigarette cancer stick (*Sl.*), ciggy

(*Inf.*), coffin nail (*Sl.*), fag (*Sl.*), gasper (*Sl.*), smoke

cinema big screen (*Inf.*), films, flicks (*Sl.*), motion pictures, movies, pictures

cipher 1. nil, nothing, nought, zero **2.** nobody, nonentity **3.** character, digit, figure, number, numeral, symbol **4.** code, cryptograph **5.** device, logo, mark, monogram

circa about, approximately, around, in the region of, roughly

circle *n.* **1.** band, circumference, coil, cordon, cycle, disc, globe, lap, loop, orb, perimeter, periphery, revolution, ring, round, sphere, turn **2.** area, bounds, circuit, compass, domain, enclosure, field, orbit, province, range, realm, region, scene, sphere **3.** assembly, class, clique, club, company, coterie, crowd, fellowship, fraternity, group, school, set, society ~*v.* **4.** belt, circumnavigate, circumscribe, coil, compass, curve, encircle, enclose, encompass, envelop, gird, hem in, pivot, revolve, ring, rotate, surround, tour, whirl

circuit 1. area, compass, course, journey, orbit, perambulation, revolution, round, route, tour, track **2.** boundary, bounding line, bounds, circumference, compass, district, limit, range, region, tract

circuitous ambagious (*Archaic*), devious, indirect, labyrinthine, meandering, oblique, rambling, roundabout, tortuous, winding

circuitousness deviousness, indirectness, obliqueness, rambling, roundaboutness, tortuousness

circulate 1. broadcast, diffuse, disseminate, distribute, issue, make known, promulgate, propagate, publicize, publish, spread **2.** flow, gyrate, radiate, revolve, rotate

circulation 1. currency, dissemination, distribution, spread, transmission, vogue **2.** circling, flow, motion, rotation

circumference border, boundary, bounds, circuit, edge, extremity, fringe, limits, outline, perimeter, periphery, rim, verge

circumlocution beating about the bush (*Inf.*), diffuseness, discursiveness, euphemism, indirectness, periphrasis, prolixity, redundancy, wordiness

circumscribe bound, confine, define, delimit, delineate, demarcate, encircle, enclose, encompass, environ, hem in,

limit, mark off, restrain, restrict, surround

circumspect attentive, canny, careful, cautious, deliberate, discreet, discriminating, guarded, heedful, judicious, observant, politic, prudent, sagacious, sage, vigilant, wary, watchful

circumspection canniness, care, caution, chariness, deliberation, discretion, prudence, wariness

circumstance accident, condition, contingency, detail, element, event, fact, factor, happening, incident, item, occurrence, particular, position, respect, situation

circumstances life style, means, position, resources, situation, state, state of affairs, station, status, times

circumstantial conjectural, contingent, detailed, founded on circumstances, hearsay, incidental, indirect, inferential, particular, presumptive, provisional, specific

circumvent beguile, bypass, deceive, dupe, elude, ensnare, entrap, evade, hoodwink, mislead, outflank, outgeneral, outwit, overreach, sidestep, steer clear of, thwart, trick

circumvention chicanery, deceit, deception, dodge, duplicity, evasion, fraud, guile, imposition, imposture, trickery, wiles

cistern basin, reservoir, sink, tank, vat

citadel bastion, fastness, fortification, fortress, keep, stronghold, tower

citation 1. commendation, excerpt, illustration, passage, quotation, quote, reference, source **2.** award, commendation, mention

cite 1. adduce, advance, allude to, enumerate, evidence, extract, mention, name, quote, specify **2.** *Law* call, subpoena, summon

citizen burgess, burgher, denizen, dweller, freeman, inhabitant, ratepayer, resident, subject, townsman

city 1. *n.* conurbation, megalopolis, metropolis, municipality **2.** *adj.* civic, metropolitan, municipal, urban

civic borough, communal, community, local, municipal, public

civil 1. civic, domestic, home, interior, municipal, political **2.** accommodating, affable, civilized, complaisant, courteous, courtly, obliging, polished, polite, refined, urbane, well-bred, well-mannered

civility affability, amiability, breeding, complaisance, cordiality, courteousness, courtesy, good manners, graciousness, politeness, politesse, tact, urbanity

civilization 1. advancement, cultivation, culture, development, education, enlightenment, progress, refinement, sophistication **2.** community, nation, people, polity, society **3.** customs, mores, way of life

civilize cultivate, educate, enlighten, humanize, improve, polish, refine, sophisticate, tame

civilized cultured, educated, enlightened, humane, polite, sophisticated, tolerant, urbane

claim 1. v. allege, ask, assert, call for, challenge, collect, demand, exact, hold, insist, maintain, need, pick up, profess, require, take, uphold **2.** n. affirmation, allegation, application, assertion, call, demand, petition, pretension, privilege, protestation, request, requirement, right, title

claimant applicant, petitioner, pretender, suppliant, supplicant

clairvoyant 1. adj. extrasensory, fey, oracular, prescient, prophetic, psychic, second-sighted, sibylline, telepathic, vatic, visionary **2.** n. augur, diviner, fortune-teller, haruspex, oracle, prophet, prophetess, seer, sibyl, soothsayer, telepath, telepathist, visionary

clamber claw, climb, scale, scrabble, scramble, shin

clammy close, damp, dank, drizzly, moist, pasty, slimy, sticky, sweating, sweaty

clamorous blaring, deafening, insistent, lusty, noisy, riotous, tumultuous, uproarious, vehement, vociferous

clamour agitation, babel, blare, brouhaha, commotion, din, exclamation, hubbub, hullabaloo, noise, outcry, racket, shout, shouting, uproar, vociferation

clamp 1. n. bracket, fastener, grip, press, vice **2.** v. brace, clinch, fasten, fix, impose, make fast, secure

clan band, brotherhood, clique, coterie, faction, family, fraternity, gens, group, house, race, sect, sept, set, society, sodality, tribe

clandestine cloak-and-dagger, closet, concealed, covert, fraudulent, furtive, hidden, private, secret, sly, stealthy, surreptitious, underground, underhand, under-the-counter

clang 1. v. bong, chime, clank, clash, jangle, resound, reverberate, ring, toll **2.** n. clangour, ding-dong, knell, reverberation

clannish cliquish, exclusive, insular, narrow, sectarian, select, unfriendly

clap 1. acclaim, applaud, cheer **2.** bang, pat, slap, strike gently, thrust, thwack, wallop (Inf.), whack

claptrap affectation, blarney, bombast, bunk (Inf.), drivel, flannel (Inf.), guff (Sl.), hot air (Inf.), humbug, insincerity, nonsense, rodomontade, rubbish

clarification elucidation, explanation, exposition, illumination, interpretation, simplification

clarify 1. clear up, elucidate, explain, illuminate, make plain, resolve, simplify, throw or shed light on **2.** cleanse, purify, refine

clarion adj. blaring, clear, inspiring, loud, ringing, stirring, strident

clarity clearness, comprehensibility, definition, explicitness, intelligibility, limpidity, lucidity, obviousness, precision, simplicity, transparency

clash v. **1.** bang, clang, clank, clatter, crash, jangle, jar, rattle **2.** conflict, cross swords, feud, grapple, quarrel, war, wrangle ~n. **3.** brush, collision, conflict, confrontation, difference of opinion, disagreement, fight, showdown (Inf.)

clasp v. **1.** attack, clutch, concatenate, connect, embrace, enfold, fasten, grapple, grasp, grip, hold, hug, press, seize, squeeze ~n. **2.** brooch, buckle, catch, clip, fastener, fastening, grip, hasp, hook, pin, snap **3.** embrace, grasp, grip, hold, hug

class 1. n. caste, category, classification, collection, denomination, department, division, genre, genus, grade, group, grouping, kind, league, order, rank, set, sort, species, sphere, status, type, value **2.** v. brand, categorize, classify, codify, designate, grade, group, rank, rate

classic adj. **1.** best, consummate, finest, first-rate, masterly **2.** archetypal, definitive, exemplary, ideal, master, model, paradigmatic, quintessential, standard **3.** characteristic, regular, standard, time-honoured, typical, usual **4.** abiding, ageless, deathless, enduring, immortal, lasting, undying ~n. **5.** exemplar, masterpiece, masterwork, model, paradigm, prototype, standard

classical 1. chaste, elegant, harmonious, pure, refined, restrained, symmetrical, understated, well-proportioned **2**. Attic, Augustan, Grecian, Greek, Hellenic, Latin, Roman

classification analysis, arrangement, cataloguing, categorization, codification, grading, sorting, taxonomy

classify arrange, catalogue, categorize, codify, dispose, distribute, file, grade, pigeonhole, rank, sort, systematize, tabulate

classy elegant, exclusive, high-class, posh (*Inf.*), select, stylish, superior, swanky (*Inf.*), up-market

clause 1. article, chapter, condition, paragraph, part, passage, section **2**. heading, item, point, provision, proviso, specification, stipulation

claw 1. *n*. nail, nipper, pincer, talon, tentacle, unguis **2**. *v*. dig, graze, lacerate, mangle, maul, rip, scrabble, scrape, scratch, tear

clean *adj.* **1**. faultless, flawless, fresh, hygienic, immaculate, laundered, pure, sanitary, spotless, unblemished, unsoiled, unspotted, unstained, unsullied, washed **2**. antiseptic, clarified, decontaminated, natural, purified, sterile, sterilized, unadulterated, uncontaminated, unpolluted **3**. chaste, decent, exemplary, good, honourable, innocent, moral, pure, respectable, undefiled, upright, virtuous **4**. delicate, elegant, graceful, neat, simple, tidy, trim, uncluttered **5**. complete, conclusive, decisive, entire, final, perfect, thorough, total, unimpaired, whole ~*v*. **6**. bath, cleanse, deodorize, disinfect, do up, dust, launder, lave, mop, purge, purify, rinse, sanitize, scour, scrub, sponge, swab, sweep, vacuum, wash, wipe

clean-cut chiselled, clear, definite, etched, neat, outlined, sharp, trim, well-defined

cleanse absolve, clean, clear, lustrate, purge, purify, rinse, scour, scrub, wash

cleanser detergent, disinfectant, purifier, scourer, soap, soap powder, solvent

clear[1] *adj.* **1**. bright, cloudless, fair, fine, halcyon, light, luminous, shining, sunny, unclouded, undimmed **2**. apparent, audible, coherent, comprehensible, conspicuous, definite, distinct, evident, explicit, express, incontrovertible, intelligible, lucid, manifest, obvious, palpable, patent, perceptible, plain, pronounced, recognizable, unambiguous, unequivocal, unmistakable, unquestionable **3**. empty, free, open, smooth, unhampered, unhindered, unimpeded, unlimited, unobstructed **4**. crystalline, glassy, limpid, pellucid, see-through, transparent **5**. certain, convinced, decided, definite, positive, resolved, satisfied, sure **6**. clean, guiltless, immaculate, innocent, pure, sinless, stainless, unblemished, undefiled, untarnished, untroubled

clear[2] *v.* **1**. clean, cleanse, erase, purify, refine, sweep away, tidy (up), wipe **2**. break up, brighten, clarify, lighten **3**. absolve, acquit, excuse, exonerate, justify, vindicate **4**. emancipate, free, liberate, set free **5**. disengage, disentangle, extricate, free, loosen, open, rid, unblock, unclog, unload, unpack **6**. jump, leap, miss, pass over, vault **7**. acquire, earn, gain, make, reap, secure

clearance 1. authorization, consent, endorsement, go-ahead, green light, leave, O.K. (*Inf.*), permission, sanction **2**. allowance, gap, headroom, margin **3**. depopulation, emptying, evacuation, eviction, removal, unpeopling, withdrawal

clear-cut definite, explicit, plain, precise, specific, straightforward, unambiguous, unequivocal

clearing dell, glade

clearly beyond doubt, distinctly, evidently, incontestably, incontrovertibly, markedly, obviously, openly, seemingly, undeniably, undoubtedly

clearness audibility, brightness, clarity, coherence, distinctness, glassiness, intelligibility, lucidity, luminosity, transparency

clear out 1. empty, exhaust, get rid of, sort, tidy up **2**. beat it (*Sl.*), decamp, depart, leave, make oneself scarce, retire, take oneself off, withdraw

clear up 1. answer, clarify, elucidate, explain, resolve, solve, straighten out, unravel **2**. order, rearrange, tidy (up)

cleave[1] abide by, adhere, agree, attach, be true, cling, cohere, devoted to, hold, remain, stand by, stick

cleave[2] crack, dissever, disunite, divide, hew, open, part, rend, rive, sever, slice, split, sunder, tear asunder

cleft 1. *n*. breach, break, chasm, chink, crack, cranny, crevice, fissure, fracture, gap, opening, rent **2**. *adj.* cloven, parted, rent, riven, ruptured, separated, split, sundered, torn

clemency compassion, forbearance, forgiveness, humanity, indulgence, kindness, leniency, mercifulness, mercy, mildness, moderation, soft-heartedness, tenderness

clement 1. compassionate, forbearing, forgiving, gentle, humane, indulgent, kind, kind-hearted, lenient, merciful, mild, soft-hearted, tender **2.** balmy, calm, fair, fine, mild, temperate

clergy churchmen, clergymen, clerics, ecclesiastics, first estate, holy orders, ministry, priesthood, the cloth

clergyman chaplain, cleric, curate, divine, father, man of God, man of the cloth, minister, padre, parson, pastor, priest, rabbi, rector, reverend (*Inf.*), vicar

clerical 1. ecclesiastical, pastoral, priestly, sacerdotal **2.** book-keeping, clerkish, clerkly, office, secretarial, stenographic

clever able, adroit, apt, astute, brainy (*Inf.*), bright, canny, capable, cunning, deep, dexterous, discerning, expert, gifted, ingenious, intelligent, inventive, keen, knowing, knowledgeable, quick, quick-witted, rational, resourceful, sagacious, sensible, shrewd, skilful, smart, talented, witty

cleverness ability, adroitness, astuteness, brains, brightness, canniness, dexterity, flair, gift, gumption (*Inf.*), ingenuity, intelligence, nous (*Sl.*), quickness, quick wits, resourcefulness, sagacity, sense, sharpness, shrewdness, smartness, talent, wit

cliché banality, bromide, chestnut (*Inf.*), commonplace, hackneyed phrase, old saw, platitude, stereotype, truism

click *n./v.* **1.** beat, clack, snap, tick ~*v.* **2.** *Inf.* become clear, come home (to), fall into place, make sense **3.** *Sl.* be compatible, be on the same wavelength, feel a rapport, get on, go over (*Inf.*), hit it off (*Inf.*), make a hit, succeed, take to each other

client applicant, buyer, consumer, customer, dependant, habitué, patient, protégé, shopper

clientele business, clients, customers, following, market, patronage, regulars, trade

cliff bluff, crag, escarpment, face, overhang, precipice, rock face, scar, scarp

climactic climactical, critical, crucial, decisive, paramount, peak

climate 1. clime, country, region, temperature, weather **2.** ambience, disposition, feeling, mood, temper, tendency, trend

climax 1. *n.* acme, apogee, culmination, head, height, highlight, high spot (*Inf.*), ne plus ultra, pay-off (*Inf.*), peak, summit, top, zenith **2.** *v.* come to a head, culminate, peak

climb ascend, clamber, mount, rise, scale, shin up, soar, top

climb down 1. descend, dismount **2.** back down, eat crow (*U.S. inf.*), eat one's words, retract, retreat

clinch 1. assure, cap, conclude, confirm, decide, determine, seal, secure, set the seal on, settle, sew up (*Inf.*), verify **2.** bolt, clamp, fasten, fix, make fast, nail, rivet, secure **3.** clutch, cuddle, embrace, grasp, hug, squeeze

cling adhere, attach to, be true to, clasp, cleave to, clutch, embrace, fasten, grasp, grip, hug, stick, twine round

clinical analytic, antiseptic, cold, detached, disinterested, dispassionate, emotionless, impersonal, objective, scientific, unemotional

clip¹ 1. *v.* crop, curtail, cut, cut short, pare, prune, shear, shorten, snip, trim **2.** *n./v. Inf.* blow, box, clout (*Inf.*), cuff, knock, punch, skelp (*Dialect*), smack, thump, wallop (*Inf.*), whack **3.** *n. Inf.* gallop, lick (*Inf.*), rate, speed, velocity

**clip² ** *v.* attach, fasten, fix, hold, pin, staple

clipping cutting, excerpt, extract, piece

clique circle, clan, coterie, crew (*Inf.*), crowd, faction, gang, group, mob, pack, set

cloak 1. *v.* camouflage, conceal, cover, disguise, hide, mask, obscure, screen, veil **2.** *n.* blind, cape, coat, cover, front, mantle, mask, pretext, shield, wrap

clodhopper booby, boor, bumpkin, clown, galoot (*Sl., chiefly U.S.*), loon (*Inf.*), lout, oaf, yokel

clog 1. *v.* block, burden, congest, dam up, hamper, hinder, impede, jam, obstruct, occlude, shackle, stop up **2.** *n.* burden, dead weight, drag, encumbrance, hindrance, impediment, obstruction

cloistered cloistral, confined, hermitic, insulated, reclusive, restricted, secluded, sequestered, sheltered, shielded, shut off, withdrawn

close[1] *v.* **1.** bar, block, choke, clog, confine, cork, fill, lock, obstruct, plug, seal, secure, shut, shut up, stop up **2.** cease, complete, conclude, culminate, discontinue, end, finish, mothball, shut down, terminate, wind up (*Inf.*) **3.** come together, connect, couple, fuse, grapple, join, unite

close[2] **1.** adjacent, adjoining, approaching, at hand, handy, hard by, imminent, impending, near, nearby, neighbouring, nigh **2.** compact, congested, cramped, cropped, crowded, dense, impenetrable, jam-packed, packed, short, solid, thick, tight **3.** accurate, conscientious, exact, faithful, literal, precise, strict **4.** alert, assiduous, attentive, careful, concentrated, detailed, dogged, earnest, fixed, intense, intent, keen, minute, painstaking, rigorous, searching, thorough **5.** attached, confidential, dear, devoted, familiar, inseparable, intimate, loving **6.** airless, confined, frowsty, fuggy, heavy, humid, muggy, oppressive, stale, stifling, stuffy, suffocating, sweltering, thick, unventilated **7.** hidden, private, reticent, retired, secluded, secret, secretive, taciturn, uncommunicative, unforthcoming **8.** illiberal, mean, mingy (*Inf.*), miserly, near, niggardly, parsimonious, penurious, stingy, tight-fisted, ungenerous

close[3] cessation, completion, conclusion, culmination, denouement, end, ending, finale, finish, termination

closed 1. fastened, locked, out of business, out of service, sealed, shut **2.** concluded, decided, ended, finished, over, resolved, settled, terminated **3.** exclusive, restricted

closure 1. cessation, closing, conclusion, end, finish, stoppage **2.** cap, lid, plug, seal, stopper **3.** *In a deliberative assembly* cloture, guillotine

clot 1. clotting, coagulation, curdling, embolism, embolus, gob, lump, mass, occlusion, thrombus **2.** ass, buffoon, dolt, dope (*Sl.*), dunderhead, fathead (*Inf.*), fool, idiot, nincompoop, nit (*Inf.*), nitwit, numskull, twerp (*Inf.*) **3.** coagulate, coalesce, congeal, curdle, jell, thicken

cloth dry goods, fabric, material, stuff, textiles

clothe accoutre, apparel, array, attire, bedizen (*Archaic*), caparison, cover, deck, doll up (*Sl.*), drape, dress, endow, enwrap, equip, fit out, garb, habit, invest, outfit, rig, robe, swathe

clothes, clothing apparel, attire, clobber (*Brit. sl.*), costume, dress, duds (*Inf.*), ensemble, garb, garments, gear (*Inf.*), get-up (*Inf.*), habits, outfit, raiment, rigout (*Inf.*), togs (*Inf.*), vestments, vesture, wardrobe, wear

cloud *n.* **1.** billow, darkness, fog, gloom, haze, mist, murk, nebula, nebulosity, obscurity, vapour **2.** crowd, dense mass, flock, horde, host, multitude, shower, swarm, throng ~*v.* **3.** becloud, darken, dim, eclipse, obfuscate, obscure, overcast, overshadow, shade, shadow, veil **4.** confuse, disorient, distort, impair, muddle

cloudy blurred, confused, dark, dim, dismal, dull, dusky, emulsified, gloomy, hazy, indistinct, leaden, lowering, muddy, murky, nebulous, obscure, opaque, overcast, sombre, sullen, sunless

clout 1. *v.* box, clobber (*Sl.*), cuff, hit, skelp (*Dialect*), sock (*Sl.*), strike, thump, wallop (*Inf.*), wham **2.** *n.* authority, influence, power, prestige, pull, standing, weight

cloven bisected, cleft, divided, split

clown *n.* **1.** buffoon, comedian, dolt, fool, harlequin, jester, joker, merryandrew, mountebank, pierrot, prankster, punchinello **2.** boor, clodhopper (*Inf.*), hind, peasant, swain (*Archaic*), yahoo, yokel ~*v.* **3.** act the fool, act the goat, jest, mess about

clownish 1. comic, foolish, galumphing, nonsensical, slapstick, zany **2.** awkward, boorish, churlish, clumsy, ill-bred, rough, rude, rustic, uncivil, ungainly, vulgar

cloy disgust, glut, gorge, nauseate, sate, satiate, sicken, surfeit, weary

cloying excessive, nauseating, oversweet, sickly

club 1. *n.* bat, bludgeon, cosh, cudgel, stick, truncheon **2.** *v.* bash, baste, batter, beat, bludgeon, clobber (*Sl.*), clout (*Inf.*), cosh, hammer, pommel (*Rare*), pummel, strike **3.** *n.* association, circle, clique, company, fraternity, group, guild, lodge, order, set, society, sodality, union

clue evidence, hint, indication, inkling, intimation, lead, pointer, sign, suggestion, suspicion, tip, tip-off, trace

clump 1. *n.* bunch, bundle, cluster, mass, shock **2.** *v.* bumble, clomp, lumber, plod, stamp, stomp, stump, thud, thump, tramp

clumsy awkward, blundering, bumbling, bungling, cack-handed (*Inf.*), gauche, gawky, ham-fisted (*Inf.*), ham-handed (*Inf.*), heavy, ill-shaped, inept, inexpert, lumbering, maladroit, ponderous, uncoordinated, uncouth, ungainly, unhandy, unskilful, unwieldy

cluster 1. *n.* assemblage, batch, bunch, clump, collection, gathering, group, knot **2.** *v.* assemble, bunch, collect, flock, gather, group

clutch catch, clasp, cling to, embrace, fasten, grab, grapple, grasp, grip, seize, snatch

clutches claws, control, custody, grasp, grip, hands, keeping, possession, power, sway

clutter 1. *n.* confusion, disarray, disorder, hotchpotch, jumble, litter, mess, muddle, untidiness **2.** *v.* litter, scatter, strew

coach *n.* **1.** bus, car, carriage, charabanc, vehicle **2.** instructor, teacher, trainer, tutor ~*v.* **3.** cram, drill, instruct, prepare, train, tutor

coagulate clot, congeal, curdle, jell, thicken

coalesce amalgamate, blend, cohere, combine, come together, commingle, commix, consolidate, fraternize, fuse, incorporate, integrate, merge, mix, unite

coalition affiliation, alliance, amalgam, amalgamation, association, bloc, combination, compact, confederacy, confederation, conjunction, fusion, integration, league, merger, union

coarse 1. boorish, brutish, coarse-grained, foul-mouthed, gruff, loutish, rough, rude, uncivil **2.** bawdy, earthy, immodest, impolite, improper, impure, indelicate, inelegant, mean, offensive, ribald, rude, smutty, vulgar **3.** coarse-grained, crude, homespun, impure, rough-hewn, unfinished, unpolished, unprocessed, unpurified, unrefined

coarsen anaesthetize, blunt, callous, deaden, desensitize, dull, harden, indurate, roughen

coarseness bawdiness, boorishness, crudity, earthiness, indelicacy, offensiveness, poor taste, ribaldry, roughness, smut, smuttiness, uncouthness, unevenness

coast 1. *n.* beach, border, coastline, littoral, seaboard, seaside, shore, strand **2.**

v. cruise, drift, freewheel, get by, glide, sail, taxi

coat *n.* **1.** fleece, fur, hair, hide, pelt, skin, wool **2.** coating, covering, layer, overlay ~*v.* **3.** apply, cover, plaster, smear, spread

coating blanket, coat, covering, dusting, film, finish, glaze, lamination, layer, membrane, patina, sheet, skin, varnish, veneer

coax allure, beguile, cajole, decoy, entice, flatter, inveigle, persuade, prevail upon, soft-soap (*Inf.*), soothe, talk into, wheedle

cobble botch, bungle, clout, mend, patch, tinker

cock 1. *n.* chanticleer, cockerel, rooster **2.** *v.* perk up, prick, raise, stand up

cockeyed absurd, askew, asymmetrical, awry, crazy, crooked, lopsided, ludicrous, nonsensical, preposterous, skew-whiff (*Brit. inf.*), squint (*Inf.*)

cocksure arrogant, brash, bumptious, cocky, hubristic, overconfident, presumptuous

cocky arrogant, brash, cocksure, conceited, egotistical, lordly, swaggering, swollen-headed, vain

cocoon cushion, envelop, insulate, pad, protect, swaddle, swathe, wrap

coddle baby, cosset, humour, indulge, mollycoddle, nurse, pamper, pet, spoil

code 1. cipher, cryptograph **2.** canon, convention, custom, ethics, etiquette, manners, maxim, regulations, rules, system

codify catalogue, classify, collect, condense, digest, organize, summarize, systematize, tabulate

coerce browbeat, bulldoze (*Inf.*), bully, compel, constrain, dragoon, drive, force, intimidate, press-gang, pressurize

coercion browbeating, bullying, compulsion, constraint, duress, force, intimidation, pressure, strong-arm tactics (*Inf.*), threats

coeval coetaneous (*Rare*), coexistent, contemporaneous, contemporary, synchronous

coffer case, casket, chest, kist (*Scot.*), repository, strongbox, treasure chest, treasury

coffers assets, capital, finances, funds, means, reserves, treasury, vaults

cogency conviction, force, potency, power, strength

cogent compelling, conclusive, convincing, effective, forceful, forcible, influential, irresistible, potent, powerful, strong, urgent, weighty

cogitate consider, contemplate, deliberate, meditate, mull over, muse, ponder, reflect, ruminate, think

cogitation consideration, contemplation, deliberation, meditation, reflection, rumination, thought

cognate affiliated, akin, alike, allied, analogous, associated, connected, kindred, related, similar

cognition apprehension, awareness, comprehension, discernment, insight, intelligence, perception, reasoning, understanding

cognizance acknowledgment, apprehension, cognition, knowledge, notice, perception, percipience, recognition, regard

cognizant acquainted, aware, conscious, conversant, familiar, informed, knowledgeable, versed

cohere 1. adhere, bind, cling, coalesce, combine, consolidate, fuse, glue, hold, stick, unite 2. agree, be connected, be consistent, correspond, hang together, harmonize, hold good, hold water, square

coherence agreement, comprehensibility, concordance, congruity, connection, consistency, consonance, correspondence, intelligibility, rationality, union, unity

coherent articulate, comprehensible, consistent, intelligible, logical, lucid, meaningful, orderly, organized, rational, reasoned, systematic

cohort 1. band, company, contingent, legion, regiment, squadron, troop 2. *Chiefly U.S.* accomplice, assistant, comrade, follower, henchman, mate, myrmidon, partner, sidekick (*Sl.*), supporter

coil convolute, curl, entwine, loop, snake, spiral, twine, twist, wind, wreathe, writhe

coin 1. *v.* conceive, create, fabricate, forge, formulate, frame, invent, make up, mint, mould, originate, think up 2. *n.* cash, change, copper, money, silver, specie

coincide 1. be concurrent, coexist, occur simultaneously, synchronize 2. accord, harmonize, match, quadrate, square, tally 3. acquiesce, agree, concur, correspond

coincidence 1. accident, chance,

eventuality, fluke, fortuity, happy accident, luck, stroke of luck 2. concomitance, concurrence, conjunction, correlation, correspondence, synchronism

coincident coinciding, concomitant, concurring, consonant, contemporaneous, coordinate, correspondent, synchronous

coincidental 1. accidental, casual, chance, fluky (*Inf.*), fortuitous, unintentional, unplanned 2. coincident, concomitant, concurrent, simultaneous, synchronous

coitus coition, congress, copulation, coupling, mating, sexual intercourse, union

cold *adj.* 1. arctic, biting, bitter, bleak, brumal, chill, chilly, cool, freezing, frigid, frosty, frozen, gelid, icy, inclement, raw, wintry 2. benumbed, chilled, chilly, freezing, frozen to the marrow, numbed, shivery 3. aloof, apathetic, cold-blooded, dead, distant, frigid, glacial, indifferent, inhospitable, lukewarm, passionless, phlegmatic, reserved, spiritless, standoffish, stony, undemonstrative, unfeeling, unmoved, unresponsive, unsympathetic ~*n.* 4. chill, chilliness, coldness, frigidity, frostiness, iciness, inclemency

cold-blooded barbarous, brutal, callous, cruel, dispassionate, heartless, inhuman, merciless, pitiless, ruthless, savage, steely, stony-hearted, unemotional, unfeeling, unmoved

cold-hearted callous, detached, frigid, heartless, indifferent, inhuman, insensitive, stony-hearted, uncaring, unfeeling, unkind, unsympathetic

collaborate 1. cooperate, coproduce, join forces, participate, team up, work together 2. collude, conspire, cooperate, fraternize

collaboration alliance, association, concert, cooperation, partnership, teamwork

collaborator 1. associate, colleague, confederate, co-worker, partner, teammate 2. collaborationist, fraternizer, quisling, traitor, turncoat

collapse 1. *v.* break down, cave in, come to nothing, crack up (*Inf.*), crumple, fail, faint, fall, fold, founder, give way, subside 2. *n.* breakdown, cave-in, disintegration, downfall, exhaustion, failure, faint, flop (*Sl.*), prostration, subsidence

collar *v.* apprehend, appropriate, capture, catch, grab, lay hands on, seize

collate adduce, analogize, collect, compare, compose, gather (*Printing*)

collateral *n.* **1.** assurance, deposit, guarantee, pledge, security, surety ~*adj.* **2.** concurrent, confirmatory, corroborative, indirect, not lineal, parallel, related, supporting **3.** ancillary, auxiliary, secondary, subordinate

colleague aider, ally, assistant, associate, auxiliary, coadjutor (*Rare*), collaborator, companion, comrade, confederate, confrère, fellow worker, helper, partner, team-mate, workmate

collect 1. accumulate, aggregate, amass, assemble, gather, heap, hoard, save, stockpile **2.** assemble, cluster, congregate, convene, converge, flock together, rally **3.** acquire, muster, obtain, raise, secure, solicit

collected calm, composed, confident, cool, placid, poised, self-possessed, serene, together (*Sl.*), unperturbable, unperturbed, unruffled

collection 1. accumulation, anthology, compilation, congeries, heap, hoard, mass, pile, set, stockpile, store **2.** assemblage, assembly, assortment, cluster, company, congregation, convocation, crowd, gathering, group **3.** alms, contribution, offering, offertory

collective aggregate, combined, common, composite, concerted, cooperative, corporate, cumulative, joint, shared, unified, united

collide clash, come into collision, conflict, crash, meet head-on

collision 1. accident, bump, crash, impact, pile-up, prang (*Inf.*), smash **2.** clash, clashing, conflict, confrontation, encounter, opposition, skirmish

colloquial conversational, demotic, everyday, familiar, idiomatic, informal, vernacular

colloquy confabulation, conference, conversation, debate, dialogue, discourse, discussion, talk

collude abet, be in cahoots (*Inf.*), collaborate, complot, connive, conspire, contrive, intrigue, machinate, plot, scheme

collusion cahoots (*Inf.*), complicity, connivance, conspiracy, craft, deceit, fraudulent artifice, intrigue, secret understanding

colonist colonial, colonizer, frontiers-man, homesteader (*U.S.*), immigrant, pioneer, planter, settler

colonize open up, people, pioneer, populate, settle

colonnade arcade, cloisters, covered walk, peristyle, portico

colony community, dependency, dominion, outpost, possession, province, satellite state, settlement, territory

colossal Brobdingnagian, elephantine, enormous, gargantuan, gigantic, herculean, huge, immense, mammoth, massive, monstrous, monumental, mountainous, prodigious, titanic, vast

colour *n.* **1.** colorant, coloration, complexion, dye, hue, paint, pigment, pigmentation, shade, tincture, tinge, tint **2.** animation, bloom, blush, brilliance, flush, glow, liveliness, rosiness, ruddiness, vividness **3.** *Fig.* appearance, disguise, excuse, façade, false show, guise, plea, pretence, pretext, semblance ~*v.* **4.** colourwash, dye, paint, stain, tinge, tint **5.** *Fig.* disguise, distort, embroider, exaggerate, falsify, garble, gloss over, misrepresent, pervert, prejudice, slant, taint **6.** blush, burn, crimson, flush, go crimson, redden

colourful 1. bright, brilliant, intense, jazzy (*Sl.*), kaleidoscopic, motley, multicoloured, psychedelic, rich, variegated, vibrant, vivid **2.** characterful, distinctive, graphic, interesting, lively, picturesque, rich, stimulating, unusual, vivid

colourless 1. achromatic, achromic, anaemic, ashen, bleached, drab, faded, neutral, sickly, wan, washed out **2.** characterless, dreary, insipid, lacklustre, tame, uninteresting, unmemorable, vacuous, vapid

colours 1. banner, emblem, ensign, flag, standard **2.** *Fig.* aspect, breed, character, identity, nature, stamp, strain

coltish frisky, frolicsome, lively, playful, romping, skittish, sportive, unruly

column 1. cavalcade, file, line, list, procession, queue, rank, row, string, train **2.** caryatid, obelisk, pilaster, pillar, post, shaft, support, upright

columnist correspondent, critic, editor, gossip columnist, reporter, reviewer

coma drowsiness, insensibility, lethargy, oblivion, somnolence, stupor, torpor, trance, unconsciousness

comatose drowsy, drugged, insensible, lethargic, sleepy, sluggish, somnolent, soporose (*Medical*), stupefied, torpid, unconscious

comb v. **1**. arrange, curry, dress, groom, untangle **2**. *Of flax, wool, etc.* card, hackle, hatchel, heckle, tease, teasel, teazle **3**. *Fig.* go through with a fine-tooth comb, hunt, rake, ransack, rummage, scour, screen, search, sift, sweep

combat 1. *n*. action, battle, conflict, contest, encounter, engagement, fight, skirmish, struggle, war, warfare **2**. *v*. battle, contend, contest, cope, defy, do battle with, engage, fight, oppose, resist, strive, struggle, withstand

combatant 1. *n*. adversary, antagonist, belligerent, contender, enemy, fighter, fighting man, opponent, serviceman, soldier, warrior **2**. *adj*. battling, belligerent, combating, conflicting, contending, fighting, opposing, warring

combative aggressive, antagonistic, bellicose, belligerent, contentious, militant, pugnacious, quarrelsome, truculent, warlike

combination 1. amalgam, amalgamation, blend, coalescence, composite, connection, mix, mixture **2**. alliance, association, cabal, cartel, coalition, combine, compound, confederacy, confederation, consortium, conspiracy, federation, merger, syndicate, unification, union

combine amalgamate, associate, bind, blend, bond, compound, connect, co-operate, fuse, incorporate, integrate, join (together), link, marry, merge, mix, pool, put together, synthesize, unify, unite

combustible explosive, flammable, incendiary, inflammable

come 1. advance, appear, approach, arrive, become, draw near, enter, happen, materialize, move, move towards, near, occur, originate, show up (*Inf.*), turn out, turn up (*Inf.*) **2**. appear, arrive, attain, enter, materialize, reach, show up (*Inf.*), turn up (*Inf.*) **3**. fall, happen, occur, take place **4**. arise, emanate, emerge, end up, flow, issue, originate, result, turn out **5**. extend, reach **6**. be available (made, offered, on offer, produced)

come about arise, befall, come to pass, happen, occur, result, take place, transpire (*Inf.*)

come across bump into (*Inf.*), chance upon, discover, encounter, find, happen upon, hit upon, light upon, meet, notice, stumble upon, unearth

come along develop, improve, mend,

perk up, pick up, progress, rally, recover, recuperate

come apart break, come unstuck, crumble, disintegrate, fall to pieces, give way, separate, split, tear

come at 1. attain, discover, find, grasp, reach **2**. assail, assault, attack, charge, fall upon, fly at, go for (*Inf.*), light into, rush, rush at

comeback 1. rally, rebound, recovery, resurgence, return, revival, triumph **2**. rejoinder, reply, response, retaliation, retort, riposte

come back reappear, recur, re-enter, return

come between alienate, divide, estrange, interfere, meddle, part, separate, set at odds

come by acquire, get, lay hold of, obtain, procure, secure, take possession of, win

come clean acknowledge, admit, confess, make a clean breast, own up, reveal

comedian card (*Inf.*), clown, comic, funny man, humorist, jester, joker, laugh (*Inf.*), wag, wit

comedown anticlimax, blow, decline, deflation, demotion, disappointment, humiliation, letdown, reverse

come down 1. decline, degenerate, descend, deteriorate, fall, go downhill, reduce, worsen **2**. choose, decide, favour, recommend

come down on criticize, dress down (*Inf.*), jump on (*Inf.*), rebuke, reprimand

come down to amount to, boil down to, end up as, result in

come down with be stricken with, catch, contract, fall ill, fall victim to, sicken, take, take sick

comedy chaffing, drollery, facetiousness, farce, fun, hilarity, humour, jesting, joking, light entertainment, sitcom (*Inf.*), slapstick, wisecracking, witticisms

come forward offer one's services, present *or* proffer oneself, volunteer

come in appear, arrive, cross the threshold, enter, finish, reach, show up (*Inf.*)

come in for acquire, bear the brunt of, endure, get, receive, suffer

comely 1. attractive, beautiful, becoming, blooming, bonny, buxom, fair, good-looking, graceful, handsome, lovely, pleasing, pretty, wholesome, winsome **2**. *Archaic* decent, decorous, fit, fitting, proper, seemly, suitable

come off go off, happen, occur, succeed, take place, transpire

come on 1. advance, develop, improve, make headway, proceed, progress **2**. appear, begin, take place

come out 1. appear, be published (announced, divulged, issued, released, reported, revealed) **2**. conclude, end, result, terminate

come out with acknowledge, come clean, declare, disclose, divulge, lay open, own, own up, say

come round 1. accede, acquiesce, allow, concede, grant, mellow, relent, yield **2**. come to, recover, regain consciousness, revive **3**. call, drop in, pop in, stop by, visit

come through 1. accomplish, achieve, prevail, succeed, triumph **2**. endure, survive, weather the storm, withstand

come up arise, crop up, happen, occur, rise, spring up, turn up

comeuppance chastening, deserts, due reward, dues, merit, punishment, recompense, requital, retribution

come up to admit of comparison with, approach, compare with, equal, match, measure up to, meet, resemble, rival, stand *or* bear comparison with

come up with advance, create, discover, furnish, offer, present, produce, propose, provide, submit, suggest

comfort v. **1**. alleviate, assuage, cheer, commiserate with, compassionate (*Archaic*), console, ease, encourage, enliven, gladden, hearten, inspirit, invigorate, reassure, refresh, relieve, solace, soothe, strengthen ~n. **2**. aid, alleviation, cheer, compensation, consolation, ease, encouragement, enjoyment, help, relief, satisfaction, succour, support **3**. cosiness, creature comforts, ease, luxury, opulence, snugness, wellbeing

comfortable 1. adequate, agreeable, ample, commodious, convenient, cosy, delightful, easy, enjoyable, homely, loose, loose-fitting, pleasant, relaxing, restful, roomy, snug **2**. at ease, contented, gratified, happy, relaxed, serene **3**. affluent, prosperous, well-off, well-to-do

comforting cheering, consolatory, consoling, encouraging, heart-warming, inspiriting, reassuring, soothing

comfortless 1. bleak, cheerless, cold, desolate, dismal, dreary **2**. disconsolate, forlorn, inconsolable, miserable, sick at heart, woebegone, wretched

comic 1. *adj.* amusing, comical, droll, facetious, farcical, funny, humorous, jocular, joking, light, rich, waggish, witty **2**. *n.* buffoon, clown, comedian, funny man, humorist, jester, wag, wit

comical absurd, amusing, comic, diverting, droll, entertaining, farcical, funny, hilarious, humorous, laughable, ludicrous, priceless, ridiculous, risible, side-splitting, silly, whimsical

coming *adj.* **1**. approaching, at hand, due, en route, forthcoming, future, imminent, impending, in store, in the wind, near, next, nigh **2**. aspiring, future, promising, up-and-coming ~n. **3**. accession, advent, approach, arrival

command v. **1**. bid, charge, compel, demand, direct, enjoin, order, require **2**. control, dominate, govern, head, lead, manage, reign over, rule, supervise, sway ~n. **3**. behest, bidding, commandment, decree, direction, directive, edict, fiat, injunction, instruction, mandate, order, precept, requirement, ultimatum **4**. authority, charge, control, domination, dominion, government, grasp, management, mastery, power, rule, supervision, sway, upper hand

commandeer appropriate, confiscate, expropriate, hijack, requisition, seize, sequester, sequestrate, usurp

commander boss, captain, chief, C in C, C.O., commander-in-chief, commanding officer, director, head, leader, officer, ruler

commanding 1. advantageous, controlling, decisive, dominant, dominating, superior **2**. assertive, authoritative, autocratic, compelling, forceful, imposing, impressive, peremptory

commemorate celebrate, honour, immortalize, keep, memorialize, observe, pay tribute to, remember, salute, solemnize

commemoration ceremony, honouring, memorial service, observance, remembrance, tribute

commemorative celebratory, dedicatory, in honour, in memory, in remembrance, memorial

commence begin, embark on, enter upon, inaugurate, initiate, open, originate, start

commend 1. acclaim, applaud, approve, compliment, eulogize, extol, praise, recommend, speak highly of **2**.

commit, confide, consign, deliver, entrust, hand over, yield

commendable admirable, creditable, deserving, estimable, exemplary, laudable, meritorious, praiseworthy, worthy

commendation acclaim, acclamation, approbation, approval, credit, encomium, encouragement, good opinion, panegyric, praise, recommendation

commensurate adequate, appropriate, coextensive, comparable, compatible, consistent, corresponding, due, equivalent, fit, fitting, in accord, proportionate, sufficient

comment *v.* **1.** animadvert, interpose, mention, note, observe, opine, point out, remark, say **2.** annotate, criticize, elucidate, explain, interpret ~*n.* **3.** animadversion, observation, remark, statement **4.** annotation, commentary, criticism, elucidation, explanation, exposition, illustration, note

commentary analysis, critique, description, exegesis, explanation, narration, notes, review, treatise, voice-over

commentator 1. commenter, reporter, special correspondent, sportscaster **2.** annotator, critic, expositor, interpreter, scholiast

commerce 1. business, dealing, exchange, merchandising, trade, traffic **2.** communication, dealings, intercourse, relations, socializing

commercial 1. business, mercantile, profit-making, sales, trade, trading **2.** in demand, marketable, popular, profitable, saleable **3.** exploited, materialistic, mercenary, monetary, pecuniary, profit-making, venal

commingle amalgamate, blend, combine, commix, intermingle, intermix, join, mingle, unite

commiserate compassionate (*Archaic*), condole, console, feel for, pity, sympathize

commiseration compassion, condolence, consolation, fellow feeling, pity, sympathy

commission *n.* **1.** appointment, authority, charge, duty, employment, errand, function, mandate, mission, task, trust, warrant **2.** allowance, brokerage, compensation, cut, fee, percentage, rakeoff (*Sl.*) **3.** board, body of commissioners, commissioners, committee, delegation, deputation, representative ~*v.* **4.** appoint, authorize, contract, delegate,

depute, empower, engage, nominate, order, select, send

commit 1. carry out, do, enact, execute, perform, perpetrate **2.** commend, confide, consign, deliver, deposit, engage, entrust, give, hand over **3.** align, bind, compromise, endanger, make liable, obligate, pledge, rank **4.** confine, imprison, put in custody

commitment 1. duty, engagement, liability, obligation, responsibility, tie **2.** adherence, dedication, devotion, involvement, loyalty **3.** assurance, guarantee, pledge, promise, undertaking, vow, word

commodious ample, capacious, comfortable, convenient, expansive, extensive, large, loose, roomy, spacious

commodities goods, merchandise, produce, products, stock, wares

common 1. average, commonplace, conventional, customary, daily, everyday, familiar, frequent, general, habitual, humdrum, obscure, ordinary, plain, regular, routine, run-of-the-mill, simple, standard, stock, usual, workaday **2.** accepted, general, popular, prevailing, prevalent, universal, widespread **3.** collective, communal, community, popular, public, social **4.** coarse, hackneyed, inferior, low, pedestrian, plebeian, stale, trite, undistinguished, vulgar

commonplace 1. *adj.* common, customary, everyday, humdrum, obvious, ordinary, pedestrian, stale, threadbare, trite, uninteresting, widespread, worn out **2.** *n.* banality, cliché, platitude, truism

common-sense, common-sensical *adj.* astute, down-to-earth, hard-headed, judicious, level-headed, matter-of-fact, practical, realistic, reasonable, sane, sensible, shrewd, sound

common sense good sense, gumption (*Inf.*), horse sense, level-headedness, mother wit, native intelligence, nous (*Sl.*), practicality, prudence, reasonableness, sound judgment, soundness, wit

commotion ado, agitation, brouhaha, bustle, disorder, disturbance, excitement, ferment, furore, fuss, hubbub, hullabaloo, hurly-burly, perturbation, racket, riot, rumpus, to-do, tumult, turmoil, uproar

communal collective, communistic, community, general, joint, neighbourhood, public, shared

commune[1] *v.* **1.** communicate, confer,

confide in, converse, discourse, discuss, parley **2.** contemplate, meditate, muse, ponder, reflect

commune[2] *n.* collective, community, cooperative, kibbutz

communicable catching, contagious, infectious, taking, transferable, transmittable

communicate acquaint, announce, be in contact, be in touch, connect, convey, correspond, declare, disclose, disseminate, divulge, impart, inform, make known, pass on, phone, proclaim, publish, report, reveal, ring up, signify, spread, transmit, unfold

communication 1. connection, contact, conversation, correspondence, dissemination, intercourse, link, transmission **2.** announcement, disclosure, dispatch, information, intelligence, message, news, report, statement, word

communications 1. routes, transport, travel **2.** information technology, media, publicity, public relations, telecommunications

communicative candid, chatty, conversable, expansive, forthcoming, frank, informative, loquacious, open, outgoing, talkative, unreserved, voluble

communion 1. accord, affinity, agreement, closeness, communing, concord, converse, fellowship, harmony, intercourse, participation, rapport, sympathy, togetherness, unity **2.** *Church* Eucharist, Lord's Supper, Mass, Sacrament

communiqué announcement, bulletin, dispatch, news flash, official communication, report

communism Bolshevism, collectivism, Marxism, socialism, state socialism

communist Bolshevik, collectivist, Marxist, Red (*Inf.*), socialist

community 1. association, body politic, brotherhood, commonwealth, company, district, general public, locality, people, populace, population, public, residents, society, state **2.** affinity, agreement, identity, likeness, sameness, similarity

commute 1. barter, exchange, interchange, substitute, switch, trade **2.** *Law: of penalties, etc.* alleviate, curtail, mitigate, modify, reduce, remit, shorten, soften

commuter 1. *n.* daily traveller, straphanger, suburbanite **2.** *adj.* suburban

compact[1] *adj.* **1.** close, compressed, condensed, dense, firm, impenetrable, impermeable, pressed together, solid, thick **2.** brief, compendious, concise, epigrammatic, laconic, pithy, pointed, succinct, terse, to the point ~*v.* **3.** compress, condense, cram, pack down, stuff, tamp

compact[2] *n.* agreement, alliance, arrangement, bargain, bond, concordat, contract, covenant, deal, entente, pact, stipulation, treaty, understanding

companion 1. accomplice, ally, associate, buddy (*Inf.*), colleague, comrade, confederate, consort, crony, friend, mate (*Inf.*), partner **2.** aide, assistant, attendant, chaperon, duenna, escort, squire **3.** complement, counterpart, fellow, match, mate, twin

companionable affable, congenial, conversable, convivial, cordial, familiar, friendly, genial, gregarious, neighbourly, outgoing, sociable

companionship amity, camaraderie, company, comradeship, conviviality, esprit de corps, fellowship, fraternity, friendship, rapport, togetherness

company 1. assemblage, assembly, band, body, circle, collection, community, concourse, convention, coterie, crew, crowd, ensemble, gathering, group, league, party, set, throng, troop, troupe, turnout **2.** association, business, concern, corporation, establishment, firm, house, partnership, syndicate **3.** callers, companionship, fellowship, guests, party, presence, society, visitors

comparable 1. a match for, as good as, commensurate, equal, equivalent, in a class with, on a par, proportionate, tantamount **2.** akin, alike, analogous, cognate, corresponding, related, similar

comparative approximate, by comparison, qualified, relative

compare 1. *With* **with** balance, collate, contrast, juxtapose, set against, weigh **2.** *With* **to** correlate, equate, identify with, liken, parallel, resemble **3.** *Be the equal of* approach, approximate to, bear comparison, be in the same class as, be on a par with, come up to, compete with, equal, hold a candle to, match, vie

comparison 1. collation, contrast, distinction, juxtaposition **2.** analogy, comparability, correlation, likeness, resemblance, similarity

compartment 1. alcove, bay, berth,

booth, carrel, carriage, cell, chamber, cubbyhole, cubicle, locker, niche, pigeon-hole, section **2.** area, category, department, division, section, subdivision

compass n. **1.** area, bound, boundary, circle, circuit, circumference, enclosure, extent, field, limit, range, reach, realm, round, scope, sphere, stretch, zone ~v. **2.** beset, besiege, blockade, circumscribe, encircle, enclose, encompass, environ, hem in, invest (*Rare*), surround **3.** accomplish, achieve, attain, bring about, effect, execute, fulfil, perform, procure, realize

compassion charity, clemency, commiseration, compunction, condolence, fellow feeling, heart, humanity, kindness, mercy, ruth (*Archaic*), softheartedness, sorrow, sympathy, tenderheartedness, tenderness

compassionate benevolent, charitable, humane, humanitarian, indulgent, kind-hearted, kindly, lenient, merciful, pitying, sympathetic, tender, tender-hearted, understanding

compatibility affinity, agreement, amity, congeniality, empathy, harmony, like-mindedness, rapport, single-mindedness, sympathy

compatible accordant, adaptable, agreeable, congenial, congruent, congruous, consistent, consonant, harmonious, in harmony, in keeping, like-minded, reconcilable, suitable

compatriot countryman, fellow citizen, fellow countryman

compel bulldoze (*Inf.*), coerce, constrain, dragoon, drive, enforce, exact, force, hustle (*Sl.*), impel, make, necessitate, oblige, restrain, squeeze, urge

compelling 1. cogent, conclusive, convincing, forceful, irrefutable, powerful, telling, weighty **2.** enchanting, enthralling, gripping, hypnotic, irresistible, mesmeric, spellbinding **3.** binding, coercive, imperative, overriding, peremptory, pressing, unavoidable, urgent

compendious abbreviated, abridged, brief, comprehensive, concise, condensed, contracted, short, succinct, summarized, summary, synoptic

compensate 1. atone, indemnify, make good, make restitution, recompense, refund, reimburse, remunerate, repay, requite, reward, satisfy **2.** balance, cancel (out), counteract, counter-

balance, countervail, make amends, make up for, offset, redress

compensation amends, atonement, damages, indemnification, indemnity, payment, recompense, reimbursement, remuneration, reparation, requital, restitution, reward, satisfaction

compete be in the running, challenge, contend, contest, emulate, fight, pit oneself against, rival, strive, struggle, vie

competence ability, adequacy, appropriateness, capability, capacity, competency, expertise, fitness, proficiency, skill, suitability

competent able, adapted, adequate, appropriate, capable, clever, endowed, equal, fit, pertinent, proficient, qualified, sufficient, suitable

competition 1. contention, contest, emulation, one-upmanship (*Inf.*), opposition, rivalry, strife, struggle **2.** championship, contest, event, puzzle, quiz, tournament **3.** challengers, field, opposition, rivals

competitive aggressive, ambitious, antagonistic, at odds, combative, cut-throat, dog-eat-dog, emulous, opposing, rival, vying

competitor adversary, antagonist, challenger, competition, contestant, emulator, opponent, opposition, rival

compilation accumulation, anthology, assemblage, assortment, collection, treasury

compile accumulate, amass, anthologize, collect, cull, garner, gather, marshal, organize, put together

complacency contentment, gratification, pleasure, satisfaction, self-satisfaction, smugness

complacent contented, gratified, pleased, pleased with oneself, satisfied, self-assured, self-contented, self-righteous, self-satisfied, serene, smug, unconcerned

complain beef (*Sl.*), bellyache (*Sl.*), bemoan, bewail, bitch (*Sl.*), carp, deplore, find fault, fuss, grieve, gripe (*Inf.*), groan, grouse, growl, grumble, kick up a fuss (*Inf.*), lament, moan, whine

complaint 1. accusation, annoyance, beef (*Sl.*), bitch (*Sl.*), charge, criticism, dissatisfaction, fault-finding, grievance, gripe (*Inf.*), grouse, grumble, lament, moan, plaint, remonstrance, trouble, wail **2.** affliction, ailment, disease, disorder, illness, indisposition, malady, sickness, upset

complaisance accommodativeness, acquiescence, agreeableness, compliance, deference, obligingness

complaisant accommodating, amiable, compliant, conciliatory, deferential, obliging, polite, solicitous

complement n. 1. companion, completion, consummation, correlative, counterpart, finishing touch, rounding-off, supplement 2. aggregate, capacity, entirety, quota, total, totality, wholeness ~v. 3. cap (Inf.), complete, crown, round off, set off

complementary companion, completing, correlative, corresponding, fellow, interdependent, interrelating, matched, reciprocal

complete adj. 1. all, entire, faultless, full, intact, integral, plenary, unabridged, unbroken, undivided, unimpaired, whole 2. accomplished, achieved, concluded, ended, finished 3. absolute, consummate, dyed-in-the-wool, perfect, thorough, thoroughgoing, total, utter ~v. 4. accomplish, achieve, cap, close, conclude, crown, discharge, do, end, execute, fill in, finalize, finish, fulfil, perfect, perform, realize, round off, settle, terminate, wrap up (Inf.)

completely absolutely, altogether, down to the ground, en masse, entirely, from A to Z, from beginning to end, fully, heart and soul, hook, line and sinker, in full, in toto, perfectly, quite, root and branch, solidly, thoroughly, totally, utterly, wholly

completion accomplishment, attainment, close, conclusion, consummation, culmination, end, expiration, finalization, fruition, fulfilment, realization

complex adj. 1. circuitous, complicated, convoluted, Daedalian (Literary), intricate, involved, knotty, labyrinthine, mingled, mixed, tangled, tortuous 2. composite, compound, compounded, heterogeneous, manifold, multifarious, multiple ~n. 3. aggregate, composite, network, organization, scheme, structure, synthesis, system 4. fixation, fixed idea, idée fixe, obsession, phobia, preoccupation

complexion 1. colour, colouring, hue, pigmentation, skin, skin tone 2. appearance, aspect, cast, character, countenance, disposition, guise, light, look, make-up, nature, stamp

complexity complication, convolution, elaboration, entanglement, intricacy, involvement, multiplicity, ramification

compliance acquiescence, agreement, assent, complaisance, concession, concurrence, conformity, consent, deference, obedience, observance, passivity, submission, submissiveness, yielding

complicate confuse, entangle, interweave, involve, make intricate, muddle, snarl up

complicated 1. Byzantine (of attitudes, etc.), complex, convoluted, elaborate, interlaced, intricate, involved, labyrinthine 2. difficult, involved, perplexing, problematic, puzzling, troublesome

complication 1. combination, complexity, confusion, entanglement, intricacy, mixture, web 2. aggravation, difficulty, drawback, embarrassment, factor, obstacle, problem, snag

complicity abetment, collaboration, collusion, concurrence, connivance

compliment 1. n. admiration, bouquet, commendation, congratulations, courtesy, eulogy, favour, flattery, honour, praise, tribute 2. v. commend, congratulate, extol, felicitate, flatter, laud, pay tribute to, praise, salute, sing the praises of, speak highly of, wish joy to

complimentary 1. appreciative, approving, commendatory, congratulatory, eulogistic, flattering, laudatory, panegyrical 2. courtesy, donated, free, free of charge, gratis, gratuitous, honorary, on the house

compliments good wishes, greetings, regards, remembrances, respects, salutation

comply abide by, accede, accord, acquiesce, adhere to, agree to, conform to, consent to, defer, discharge, follow, fulfil, obey, observe, perform, respect, satisfy, submit, yield

component 1. n. constituent, element, ingredient, item, part, piece, unit 2. adj. composing, constituent, inherent, intrinsic

comport 1. accord, agree, coincide, correspond, fit, harmonize, square, suit, tally 2. acquit, act, bear, behave, carry, conduct, demean

compose 1. build, compound, comprise, constitute, construct, fashion, form, make, make up, put together **2.** contrive, create, devise, frame, imagine, indite, invent, produce, write **3.** adjust, arrange, reconcile, regulate, resolve, settle **4.** appease, assuage, calm, collect, control, pacify, placate, quell, quiet, soothe, still, tranquillize

composed at ease, calm, collected, confident, cool, imperturbable, level-headed, poised, relaxed, self-possessed, serene, together (*Sl.*), tranquil, unflappable, unruffled, unworried

composite 1. *adj.* blended, combined, complex, compound, conglomerate, mixed, synthesized **2.** *n.* amalgam, blend, compound, conglomerate, fusion, synthesis

composition 1. arrangement, configuration, constitution, design, form, formation, layout, make-up, organization, structure **2.** compilation, creation, fashioning, formation, formulation, invention, making, mixture, production **3.** creation, essay, exercise, literary work, opus, piece, study, work, writing **4.** arrangement, balance, concord, consonance, harmony, placing, proportion, symmetry

compost humus, mulch, organic fertilizer

composure aplomb, calm, calmness, collectedness, cool (*Sl.*), coolness, dignity, ease, equanimity, imperturbability, placidity, poise, sang-froid, sedateness, self-assurance, self-possession, serenity, tranquillity

compound *v.* **1.** amalgamate, blend, coalesce, combine, concoct, fuse, intermingle, mingle, mix, synthesize, unite **2.** add to, aggravate, augment, complicate, exacerbate, heighten, intensify, magnify, worsen **3.** *Used of a dispute, difference, etc.* adjust, arrange, compose, settle ~*n.* **4.** alloy, amalgam, blend, combination, composite, composition, conglomerate, fusion, medley, mixture, synthesis ~*adj.* **5.** complex, composite, conglomerate, intricate, multiple, not simple

comprehend 1. apprehend, assimilate, conceive, discern, fathom, grasp, know, make out, perceive, see, take in, understand **2.** comprise, contain, embody, embrace, enclose, encompass, include, involve, take in

comprehensible clear, coherent, conceivable, explicit, graspable, intelligible, plain, understandable

comprehension 1. conception, discernment, grasp, intelligence, judgment, knowledge, perception, realization, sense, understanding **2.** compass, domain, field, limits, province, range, reach, scope

comprehensive all-embracing, all-inclusive, blanket, broad, catholic, complete, encyclopedic, exhaustive, extensive, full, inclusive, sweeping, thorough, umbrella, wide

compress abbreviate, compact, concentrate, condense, constrict, contract, cram, crowd, crush, press, shorten, squash, squeeze, summarize, wedge

compressed abridged, compact, compacted, concentrated, concise, consolidated, constricted, flattened, reduced, shortened, squashed, squeezed

compression condensation, consolidation, constriction, crushing, pressure, squeezing, wedging

comprise 1. be composed of, comprehend, consist of, contain, embrace, encompass, include, take in **2.** compose, constitute, form, make up

compromise *v.* **1.** adjust, agree, arbitrate, compose, compound, concede, give and take, go fifty-fifty (*Inf.*), meet halfway, settle, strike a balance ~*n.* **2.** accommodation, accord, adjustment, agreement, concession, give-and-take, half measures, middle ground, settlement, trade-off ~*v.* **3.** discredit, dishonour, embarrass, expose, hazard, imperil, implicate, jeopardize, prejudice, weaken

compulsion 1. coercion, constraint, demand, duress, force, obligation, pressure, urgency **2.** drive, necessity, need, obsession, preoccupation, urge

compulsive besetting, compelling, driving, irresistible, obsessive, overwhelming, uncontrollable, urgent

compulsory binding, *de rigueur*, forced, imperative, mandatory, obligatory, required, requisite

compunction contrition, misgiving, penitence, qualm, regret, reluctance, remorse, repentance, sorrow, stab *or* sting of conscience

compute add up, calculate, cast up, cipher, count, enumerate, estimate, figure, figure out, measure, rate, reckon, sum, tally, total

comrade ally, associate, buddy (*Inf.*), colleague, companion, compatriot, compeer, confederate, co-worker, crony, fel-

low, friend, mate (*Inf.*), pal (*Inf.*),
partner

con 1. v. bamboozle (*Inf.*), bilk, cheat,
deceive, defraud, double-cross (*Inf.*),
dupe, gull (*Archaic*), hoax, hoodwink,
humbug, inveigle, mislead, rip off (*Sl.*),
rook (*Inf.*), swindle, trick **2.** n. bluff, deception, fraud, swindle, trick

concatenation chain, connection,
interlocking, linking, nexus, sequence,
series, succession

concave cupped, depressed, excavat-
ed, hollow, hollowed, incurved, indented,
scooped, sunken

conceal bury, camouflage, cover, disguise, dissemble, hide, keep dark, keep
secret, mask, obscure, screen, secrete,
shelter

concealed covered, hidden, inconspicuous, masked, obscured, screened,
secret, secreted, tucked away, unseen

concealment camouflage, cover, disguise, hideaway, hide-out, hiding, secrecy

concede 1. accept, acknowledge, admit, allow, confess, grant, own **2.** cede,
give up, hand over, relinquish, surrender, yield

conceit 1. amour-propre, arrogance,
complacency, egotism, narcissism, pride,
self-importance, self-love, swagger, vainglory, vanity **2.** *Archaic* belief, fancy,
fantasy, idea, image, imagination, judgment, notion, opinion, quip, thought, vagary, whim, whimsy

conceited arrogant, bigheaded (*Inf.*),
cocky, egotistical, immodest, narcissistic,
overweening, puffed up, self-important,
stuck up (*Inf.*), swollen-headed, vain,
vainglorious

conceivable believable, credible, imaginable, possible, thinkable

conceive 1. appreciate, apprehend,
believe, comprehend, envisage, fancy,
grasp, imagine, realize, suppose, understand **2.** contrive, create, design, develop, devise, form, formulate, produce,
project, purpose, think up **3.** become im-
pregnated, become pregnant

concentrate 1. be engrossed in, consider closely, focus attention on, give all
one's attention to, put one's mind to,
rack one's brains **2.** bring to bear, centre,
cluster, converge, focus **3.** accumulate,
cluster, collect, congregate, gather, huddle

concentrated 1. all-out (*Inf.*), deep,

hard, intense, intensive **2.** boiled down,
condensed, evaporated, reduced, rich,
thickened, undiluted

concentration 1. absorption, application, heed, single-mindedness **2.** bringing to bear, centralization, centring,
combination, compression, consolidation, convergence, focusing, intensification **3.** accumulation, aggregation, cluster, collection, convergence, horde, mass

concept abstraction, conception, con-
ceptualization, hypothesis, idea, image,
impression, notion, theory, view

conception 1. concept, design, idea,
image, notion, plan **2.** beginning, birth,
formation, inception, initiation, invention, launching, origin, outset **3.** appreciation, clue, comprehension, impression, inkling, perception, picture, understanding **4.** fertilization, germination,
impregnation, insemination

concern v. **1.** affect, apply to, bear on,
be relevant to, interest, involve, pertain
to, regard, touch ~n. **2.** affair, business,
charge, deportment, field, interest, involvement, job, matter, mission, occupation, responsibility, task, transaction **3.**
bearing, importance, interest, reference,
relation, relevance ~v. **4.** bother, disquiet, distress, disturb, make anxious, make
uneasy, perturb, trouble, worry ~n. **5.**
anxiety, apprehension, attention, burden, care, consideration, disquiet, disquietude, distress, heed, responsibility,
solicitude, worry **6.** business, company,
corporation, enterprise, establishment,
firm, house, organization

concerned 1. active, implicated, interested, involved, mixed up, privy to **2.**
anxious, bothered, distressed, disturbed,
exercised, troubled, uneasy, upset, worried **3.** attentive, caring, interested, solicitous

concerning about, anent (*Scot.*), apropos of, as regards, as to, in the matter
of, on the subject of, re, regarding, relating to, respecting, touching, with reference to

concert n. **1.** accord, agreement, concord, concordance, harmony, unanimity,
union, unison **2. in concert** concertedly,
in collaboration, in league, in unison,
jointly, shoulder to shoulder, together,
unanimously

concerted agreed upon, collaborative,
combined, coordinated, joint, planned,
prearranged, united

concession 1. acknowledgment, admission, assent, confession, surrender, yielding **2.** adjustment, allowance, boon, compromise, grant, indulgence, permit, privilege

conciliate appease, disarm, mediate, mollify, pacify, placate, propitiate, reconcile, restore harmony, soothe, win over

conciliation appeasement, disarming, mollification, pacification, placation, propitiation, reconciliation, soothing

conciliatory appeasing, disarming, irenic, mollifying, pacific, peaceable, placatory, propitiative

concise brief, compact, compendious, compressed, condensed, epigrammatic, laconic, pithy, short, succinct, summary, synoptic, terse, to the point

conclave assembly, cabinet, conference, council, parley, secret *or* private meeting, session

conclude 1. bring down the curtain, cease, close, come to an end, complete, draw to a close, end, finish, round off, terminate, wind up (*Inf.*) **2.** assume, decide, deduce, gather, infer, judge, reckon (*Inf.*), sum up, suppose, surmise **3.** accomplish, bring about, carry out, clinch (*Inf.*), decide, determine, effect, establish, fix, pull off, resolve, settle, work out

conclusion 1. close, completion, end, finale, finish, result, termination **2.** consequence, culmination, issue, outcome, result, upshot **3.** agreement, conviction, decision, deduction, inference, judgment, opinion, resolution, settlement, verdict **4. in conclusion** finally, in closing, lastly, to sum up

conclusive clinching, convincing, decisive, definite, definitive, final, irrefutable, ultimate, unanswerable, unarguable

concoct brew, contrive, cook up (*Inf.*), design, devise, fabricate, formulate, hatch, invent, make up, mature, plot, prepare, project, think up

concoction blend, brew, combination, compound, contrivance, creation, mixture, preparation

concomitant accompanying, associative, attendant, coexistent, coincidental, collateral, complementary, concurrent, contemporaneous, contributing, coterminous, synchronous

concord 1. accord, agreement, amity, concert, consensus, consonance, friendship, good understanding, good will, harmony, peace, rapport, unanimity, unison **2.** agreement, compact, concordat, convention, entente, protocol, treaty

concourse 1. assemblage, assembly, collection, confluence, convergence, crowd, crush, gathering, meeting, multitude, rout (*Archaic*), throng **2.** entrance, foyer, gathering *or* meeting place, hall, lounge, rallying point

concrete *adj.* **1.** actual, definite, explicit, factual, material, real, sensible, specific, substantial, tangible **2.** calcified, compact, compressed, conglomerated, consolidated, firm, petrified, solid, solidified ~*n.* **3.** cement (*Not in technical usage*), concretion

concubine courtesan, kept woman, leman (*Archaic*), mistress, odalisque, paramour

concupiscence appetite, desire, horniness (*Sl.*), lasciviousness, lechery, libidinousness, libido, lickerishness (*Archaic*), lust, lustfulness, randiness (*Sl.*)

concupiscent horny (*Sl.*), lascivious, lecherous, lewd, libidinous, lickerish (*Archaic*), lustful, randy (*Sl.*)

concur accede, accord, acquiesce, agree, approve, assent, coincide, combine, consent, cooperate, harmonize, join

concurrent 1. coexisting, coincident, concerted, concomitant, contemporaneous, simultaneous, synchronous **2.** confluent, convergent, converging, uniting **3.** agreeing, at one, compatible, consentient, consistent, cooperating, harmonious, in agreement, in rapport, like-minded, of the same mind

concussion clash, collision, crash, impact, jarring, jolt, jolting, shaking, shock

condemn 1. blame, censure, damn, denounce, disapprove, reprehend, reproach, reprobate, reprove, upbraid **2.** convict, damn, doom, pass sentence on, proscribe, sentence

condemnation 1. blame, censure, denouncement, denunciation, disapproval, reproach, reprobation, reproof, stricture **2.** conviction, damnation, doom, judgment, proscription, sentence

condemnatory accusatory, accusing, censorious, critical, damnatory, denunciatory, disapproving, proscriptive, reprobative

condensation 1. abridgment, contraction, digest, précis, synopsis **2.** condensate, deliquescence, distillation, liquefaction, precipitate, precipitation **3.**

compression, concentration, consolidation, crystallization, curtailment, reduction

condense 1. abbreviate, abridge, compact, compress, concentrate, contract, curtail, encapsulate, epitomize, précis, shorten, summarize **2**. boil down, coagulate, concentrate, decoct, precipitate (*Chem.*), reduce, solidify, thicken

condensed 1. abridged, compressed, concentrated, curtailed, shortened, shrunken, slimmed down, summarized **2**. boiled down, clotted, coagulated, concentrated, precipitated (*Chem.*), reduced, thickened

condescend 1. be courteous, bend, come down off one's high horse (*Inf.*), deign, humble *or* demean oneself, lower oneself, see fit, stoop, submit, unbend (*Inf.*), vouchsafe **2**. patronize, talk down to

condescending disdainful, lofty, lordly, patronizing, snobbish, snooty (*Inf.*), supercilious, superior, toffee-nosed (*Sl.*)

condescension 1. airs, disdain, haughtiness, loftiness, lordliness, patronizing attitude, superciliousness, superiority **2**. affability, civility, courtesy, deference, favour, graciousness, humiliation, obeisance

condign Used esp. of a punishment adequate, appropriate, deserved, fitting, just, meet (*Archaic*), merited, richly-deserved, suitable

condition n. **1**. case, circumstances, plight, position, predicament, shape, situation, state, state of affairs, status quo **2**. arrangement, article, demand, limitation, modification, prerequisite, provision, proviso, qualification, requirement, requisite, restriction, rule, stipulation, terms **3**. fettle, fitness, health, kilter, order, shape, state of health, trim **4**. ailment, complaint, infirmity, malady, problem, weakness **5**. caste, class, estate, grade, order, position, rank, status, stratum ~v. **6**. accustom, adapt, educate, equip, habituate, inure, make ready, prepare, ready, tone up, train, work out

conditional contingent, dependent, limited, provisional, qualified, subject to, with reservations

conditioned acclimatized, accustomed, adapted, adjusted, familiarized, habituated, inured, made ready, prepared, seasoned, trained, used

conditioning n. **1**. grooming, preparation, readying, training **2**. accustoming, familiarization, hardening, inurement, reorientation, seasoning ~adj. **3**. astringent, toning

conditions circumstances, environment, milieu, situation, surroundings, way of life

condole commiserate, compassionate (*Archaic*), console, feel for, sympathize

condolence commiseration, compassion, consolation, fellow feeling, sympathy

condone disregard, excuse, forgive, let pass, look the other way, make allowance for, overlook, pardon, turn a blind eye to, wink at

conduce advance, aid, avail, contribute, lead, promote, tend

conducive calculated to produce, contributive, contributory, favourable, helpful, leading, productive of, promotive, tending

conduct n. **1**. administration, control, direction, guidance, leadership, management, organization, running, supervision ~v. **2**. administer, carry on, control, direct, govern, handle, lead, manage, organize, preside over, regulate, run, supervise **3**. accompany, attend, chair, convey, escort, guide, pilot, preside over, steer, usher ~n. **4**. attitude, bearing, behaviour, carriage, comportment, demeanour, deportment, manners, mien (*Literary*), ways ~v. **5**. acquit, act, behave, carry, comport, deport

conduit canal, channel, duct, main, passage, pipe, tube

confab, confabulation n. chat, chinwag (*Brit. inf.*), conversation, discussion, gossip, natter, powwow, session, talk

confabulate v. chat, converse, discuss, gossip, natter, talk

confederacy alliance, bund, coalition, compact, confederation, conspiracy, covenant, federation, league, union

confederate 1. adj. allied, associated, combined, federal, federated, in alliance **2**. n. abettor, accessory, accomplice, ally, associate, colleague, partner **3**. v. ally, amalgamate, associate, band together, combine, federate, merge, unite

confer 1. accord, award, bestow, give, grant, present, vouchsafe **2**. consult, converse, deliberate, discourse, parley, talk

conference colloquium, congress, consultation, convention, convocation, discussion, forum, meeting, seminar, symposium, teach-in

confess 1. acknowledge, admit, allow, blurt out, come clean (*Inf.*), concede, confide, disclose, divulge, grant, make a clean breast of, own, own up, recognize **2.** affirm, assert, attest, aver, confirm, declare, evince, manifest, profess, prove, reveal

confession acknowledgment, admission, avowal, disclosure, divulgence, exposure, revelation, unbosoming

confidant, confidante alter ego, bosom friend, close friend, crony, familiar, intimate

confide 1. admit, breathe, confess, disclose, divulge, impart, reveal, whisper **2.** commend, commit, consign, entrust

confidence 1. belief, credence, dependence, faith, reliance, trust **2.** aplomb, assurance, boldness, courage, firmness, nerve, self-possession, self-reliance **3. in confidence** between you and me (and the gatepost), confidentially, in secrecy, privately

confident 1. certain, convinced, counting on, positive, satisfied, secure, sure **2.** assured, bold, dauntless, fearless, self-assured, self-reliant

confidential 1. classified, hush-hush (*Inf.*), intimate, off the record, private, privy, secret **2.** faithful, familiar, trusted, trustworthy, trusty

confidentially behind closed doors, between ourselves, in camera, in confidence, in secret, personally, privately, sub rosa

configuration arrangement, cast, conformation, contour, figure, form, outline, shape

confine 1. *v.* bind, bound, cage, circumscribe, enclose, hem in, hold back, immure, imprison, incarcerate, intern, keep, limit, repress, restrain, restrict, shut up **2.** *n.* border, boundary, frontier, limit, precinct

confined 1. enclosed, limited, restricted **2.** in childbed, in childbirth, lying-in

confinement 1. custody, detention, imprisonment, incarceration, internment **2.** *accouchement*, childbed, childbirth, labour, lying-in, parturition, time, travail

confines boundaries, bounds, circumference, edge, limits, precincts

confirm 1. assure, buttress, clinch, establish, fix, fortify, reinforce, settle, strengthen **2.** approve, authenticate, bear out, corroborate, endorse, ratify, sanction, substantiate, validate, verify

confirmation 1. authentication, corroboration, evidence, proof, substantiation, testimony, validation, verification **2.** acceptance, agreement, approval, assent, endorsement, ratification, sanction

confirmed chronic, dyed-in-the-wool, habitual, hardened, ingrained, inured, inveterate, long-established, rooted, seasoned

confiscate appropriate, commandeer, expropriate, impound, seize, sequester, sequestrate

confiscation appropriation, expropriation, forfeiture, impounding, seizure, sequestration, takeover

conflagration blaze, holocaust, inferno, wildfire

conflict *n.* **1.** battle, clash, collision, combat, contention, contest, encounter, engagement, fight, fracas, set-to (*Inf.*), strife, war, warfare **2.** antagonism, bad blood, difference, disagreement, discord, dissension, divided loyalties, friction, hostility, interference, opposition, strife, variance ~*v.* **3.** be at variance, clash, collide, combat, contend, contest, differ, disagree, fight, interfere, strive, struggle

conflicting antagonistic, clashing, contradictory, contrary, discordant, inconsistent, opposed, opposing, paradoxical

confluence 1. concurrence, conflux, convergence, junction **2.** assemblage, assembly, concourse, concurrence, crowd, host, meeting, multitude, union

conform 1. adapt, adjust, comply, fall in with, follow, follow the crowd, obey, run with the pack, yield **2.** accord, agree, assimilate, correspond, harmonize, match, square, suit, tally

conformation anatomy, arrangement, build, configuration, form, framework, outline, shape, structure

conformist *n.* Babbitt (*U.S.*), conventionalist, stick-in-the-mud (*Inf.*), traditionalist, yes man

conformity 1. allegiance, Babbittry (*U.S.*), compliance, conventionality, observance, orthodoxy **2.** affinity, agreement, conformance, congruity, consonance, correspondence, harmony, likeness, resemblance, similarity

confound 1. amaze, astonish, astound, baffle, bewilder, confuse, dumbfound, flabbergast (*Inf.*), mix up, mystify, nonplus, perplex, startle, surprise **2.** annihilate, contradict, demolish, destroy, explode, overthrow, overwhelm, refute, ruin

confront accost, beard, brave, bring face to face with, challenge, defy, encounter, face, face up to, oppose, stand up to

confrontation conflict, contest, crisis, encounter, set-to (*Inf.*), showdown (*Inf.*)

confuse 1. baffle, bemuse, bewilder, darken, mystify, obscure, perplex, puzzle **2.** blend, confound, disarrange, disorder, intermingle, involve, jumble, mingle, mistake, mix up, muddle, snarl up (*Inf.*), tangle **3.** abash, addle, demoralize, discomfit, discompose, disconcert, discountenance, disorient, embarrass, fluster, mortify, nonplus, rattle (*Inf.*), shame, throw off balance, upset

confused 1. at a loss, at sea, at sixes and sevens, baffled, bewildered, dazed, discombobulated (*Inf., chiefly U.S.*), disorganized, disorientated, flummoxed, muddled, muzzy (*U.S. inf.*), nonplussed, not with it (*Inf.*), perplexed, puzzled, taken aback, thrown off balance, upset **2.** at sixes and sevens, chaotic, disarranged, disordered, disorderly, disorganized, higgledy-piggledy (*Inf.*), huggermugger (*Archaic*), in disarray, jumbled, mistaken, misunderstood, mixed up, out of order, topsy-turvy, untidy

confusing ambiguous, baffling, complicated, contradictory, disconcerting, inconsistent, misleading, muddling, perplexing, puzzling, unclear

confusion 1. befuddlement, bemusement, bewilderment, disorientation, mystification, perplexity, puzzlement **2.** bustle, chaos, clutter, commotion, disarrangement, disorder, disorganization, hotchpotch, jumble, mess, muddle, shambles, tangle, turmoil, untidiness, upheaval **3.** abashment, chagrin, demoralization, discomfiture, distraction, embarrassment, fluster, perturbation

confute controvert, disprove, invalidate, oppugn, overthrow, prove false, rebut, refute, set aside

congeal benumb, clot, coagulate, condense, curdle, freeze, gelatinize, harden, jell, set, solidify, stiffen, thicken

congenial adapted, agreeable, companionable, compatible, complaisant, favourable, fit, friendly, genial, kindly,

kindred, like-minded, pleasant, pleasing, suitable, sympathetic, well-suited

congenital 1. constitutional, inborn, inbred, inherent, innate, natural **2.** *Inf.* complete, inveterate, thorough, utter

congested blocked-up, clogged, crammed, crowded, jammed, overcrowded, overfilled, overflowing, packed, stuffed, stuffed-up, teeming

congestion bottleneck, clogging, crowding, jam, mass, overcrowding, snarl-up (*Inf.*), surfeit

conglomerate 1. *adj.* amassed, clustered, composite, heterogeneous, massed **2.** *v.* accumulate, agglomerate, aggregate, cluster, coalesce, snowball **3.** *n.* agglomerate, aggregate, multinational

conglomeration accumulation, aggregation, assortment, combination, composite, hotchpotch, mass, medley, miscellany, mishmash, potpourri

congratulate compliment, felicitate, wish joy to

congratulations best wishes, compliments, felicitations, good wishes, greetings

congregate assemble, collect, come together, concentrate, convene, converge, convoke, flock, forgather, gather, mass, meet, muster, rally, rendezvous, throng

congregation assembly, brethren, crowd, fellowship, flock, host, laity, multitude, parish, parishioners, throng

congress assembly, chamber of deputies, conclave, conference, convention, convocation, council, delegates, diet, legislative assembly, legislature, meeting, parliament, representatives

congruence accord, agreement, coincidence, compatibility, concurrence, conformity, congruity, consistency, correspondence, harmony, identity

congruous appropriate, apt, becoming, compatible, concordant, congruent, consistent, consonant, correspondent, corresponding, fit, meet, seemly, suitable

conic, conical cone-shaped, conoid, funnel-shaped, pointed, pyramidal, tapered, tapering

conjectural academic, hypothetical, speculative, supposed, suppositional, surmised, tentative, theoretical

conjecture 1. *v.* assume, fancy, guess, hypothesize, imagine, infer, suppose, surmise, suspect, theorize **2.** *n.* assumption, conclusion, fancy, guess, guesstimate (*Inf.*), guesswork, hypothesis, inference, notion, presumption, shot in the dark, speculation, supposition, surmise, theorizing, theory

conjugal bridal, connubial, hymeneal, marital, married, matrimonial, nuptial, spousal, wedded

conjunction association, coincidence, combination, concurrence, juxtaposition, union

conjuncture combination, concurrence, connection, crisis, crossroads, crucial point, emergency, exigency, juncture, pass, predicament, stage, turning point

conjure 1. juggle, play tricks **2.** bewitch, call upon, cast a spell, charm, enchant, fascinate, invoke, raise, rouse, summon up **3.** adjure, appeal to, beg, beseech, crave, entreat, implore, importune, pray, supplicate

conjurer, conjuror magician, miracle-worker, sorcerer, thaumaturge (*Rare*), wizard

conjure up bring to mind, contrive, create, evoke, produce as by magic, recall, recollect

connect affix, ally, associate, cohere, combine, couple, fasten, join, link, relate, unite

connected 1. affiliated, akin, allied, associated, banded together, bracketed, combined, coupled, joined, linked, related, united **2.** *Of speech* coherent, comprehensible, consecutive, intelligible

connection 1. alliance, association, attachment, coupling, fastening, junction, link, tie, union **2.** affinity, association, bond, commerce, communication, correlation, correspondence, intercourse, interrelation, link, marriage, relation, relationship, relevance, tie-in **3.** context, frame of reference, reference **4.** acquaintance, ally, associate, contact, friend, sponsor **5.** kin, kindred, kinsman, kith, relation, relative

connivance abetment, abetting, collusion, complicity, conspiring, tacit consent

connive 1. cabal, collude, conspire, cook up (*Inf.*), intrigue, plot, scheme **2.** *With* at abet, aid, be an accessory to, be a party to, be in collusion with, blink at, disregard, lend oneself to, let pass, look the other way, overlook, pass by, shut one's eyes to, turn a blind eye to, wink at

connoisseur aficionado, appreciator,

arbiter, authority, buff (*Inf.*), cognoscente, devotee, expert, judge, savant, specialist

connotation association, colouring, implication, nuance, significance, suggestion, undertone

connote betoken, hint at, imply, indicate, intimate, involve, signify, suggest

connubial conjugal, marital, married, matrimonial, nuptial, wedded

conquer 1. beat, checkmate, crush, defeat, discomfit, get the better of, humble, master, overcome, overpower, overthrow, prevail, quell, rout, subdue, subjugate, succeed, surmount, triumph, vanquish **2.** acquire, annex, obtain, occupy, overrun, seize, win

conqueror champion, conquistador, defeater, hero, lord, master, subjugator, vanquisher, victor, winner

conquest 1. defeat, discomfiture, mastery, overthrow, rout, triumph, vanquishment, victory **2.** acquisition, annexation, appropriation, coup, invasion, occupation, subjection, subjugation, takeover **3.** captivation, enchantment, enthralment, enticement, seduction **4.** acquisition, adherent, admirer, catch, fan, feather in one's cap, follower, prize, supporter, worshipper

consanguinity affinity, blood-relationship, family tie, kin, kindred, kinship

conscience 1. moral sense, principles, scruples, sense of right and wrong, still small voice **2. in all conscience** assuredly, certainly, fairly, honestly, in truth, rightly, truly

conscience-stricken ashamed, compunctious, contrite, disturbed, guilty, penitent, remorseful, repentant, sorry, troubled

conscientious 1. careful, diligent, exact, faithful, meticulous, painstaking, particular, punctilious, thorough **2.** high-minded, high-principled, honest, honourable, incorruptible, just, moral, responsible, scrupulous, straightforward, strict, upright

conscious 1. alert, alive to, awake, aware, cognizant, percipient, responsive, sensible, sentient, wise to (*Sl.*) **2.** calculated, deliberate, intentional, knowing, premeditated, rational, reasoning, reflective, responsible, self-conscious, studied, wilful

consciousness apprehension, awareness, knowledge, realization, recognition, sensibility

consecrate dedicate, devote, exalt, hallow, ordain, sanctify, set apart, venerate

consecutive chronological, following, in sequence, in turn, running, sequential, seriatim, succeeding, successive, uninterrupted

consensus agreement, common consent, concord, concurrence, general agreement, harmony, unanimity, unity

consent 1. *v.* accede, acquiesce, agree, allow, approve, assent, comply, concede, concur, permit, yield 2. *n.* acquiescence, agreement, approval, assent, compliance, concession, concurrence, go-ahead (*Inf.*), O.K. (*Inf.*), permission, sanction

consequence 1. effect, end, event, issue, outcome, repercussion, result, upshot 2. account, concern, import, importance, interest, moment, note, portent, significance, value, weight 3. distinction, eminence, notability, rank, repute, standing, status 4. **in consequence** as a result, because, following

consequent ensuing, following, resultant, resulting, sequential, subsequent, successive

consequential 1. eventful, far-reaching, grave, important, momentous, serious, significant, weighty 2. arrogant, bumptious, conceited, inflated, pompous, pretentious, self-important, supercilious, vainglorious 3. consequent, indirect, resultant

consequently accordingly, ergo, hence, necessarily, subsequently, therefore, thus

conservation custody, economy, guardianship, husbandry, maintenance, preservation, protection, safeguarding, safekeeping, saving, upkeep

conservative 1. *adj.* cautious, conventional, die-hard, guarded, hidebound, middle-of-the-road, moderate, quiet, reactionary, right-wing, sober, tory, traditional 2. *n.* middle-of-the-roader, moderate, reactionary, right-winger, stick-in-the-mud (*Inf.*), tory, traditionalist

conservatory glasshouse, greenhouse, hothouse

conserve go easy on (*Inf.*), hoard, husband, keep, nurse, preserve, protect, save, store up, take care of, use sparingly

consider 1. chew over, cogitate, consult, contemplate, deliberate, discuss, examine, meditate, mull over, muse, ponder, reflect, revolve, ruminate, study, turn over in one's mind, weigh 2. believe, deem, hold to be, judge, rate, regard as, think 3. bear in mind, care for, keep in view, make allowance for, reckon with, regard, remember, respect, take into account

considerable 1. abundant, ample, appreciable, comfortable, goodly, great, large, lavish, marked, much, noticeable, plentiful, reasonable, sizable, substantial, tidy, tolerable 2. distinguished, important, influential, noteworthy, renowned, significant, venerable

considerably appreciably, greatly, markedly, noticeably, remarkably, significantly, substantially, very much

considerate attentive, charitable, circumspect, concerned, discreet, forbearing, kind, kindly, mindful, obliging, patient, tactful, thoughtful, unselfish

consideration 1. analysis, attention, cogitation, contemplation, deliberation, discussion, examination, reflection, regard, review, scrutiny, study, thought 2. concern, factor, issue, point 3. concern, considerateness, friendliness, kindliness, kindness, respect, solicitude, tact, thoughtfulness 4. fee, payment, perquisite, recompense, remuneration, reward, tip 5. **take into consideration** bear in mind, make allowance for, take into account, weigh

considering all in all, all things considered, insomuch as, in the light of, in view of

consign commend to, commit, convey, deliver, deposit with, entrust, hand over, relegate, ship (*cargo*), transfer, transmit

consignment 1. *Act of consigning* assignment, committal, dispatch, distribution, entrusting, handing over, relegation, sending, shipment, transmittal 2. *Something consigned* batch, delivery, goods, shipment

consist 1. *With* of be composed of, be made up of, amount to, comprise, contain, embody, include, incorporate, involve 2. *With* in be expressed by, be found or contained in, inhere, lie, reside

consistency 1. compactness, density, firmness, thickness, viscosity 2. accordance, agreement, coherence, compatibility, congruity, correspondence, harmony 3. constancy, evenness, regularity, steadfastness, steadiness, uniformity

consistent 1. constant, dependable, persistent, regular, steady, true to type, unchanging, undeviating 2. accordant, agreeing, all of a piece, coherent, compatible, congruous, consonant, harmonious, logical

consolation alleviation, assuagement, cheer, comfort, ease, easement, encouragement, help, relief, solace, succour, support

console assuage, calm, cheer, comfort, encourage, express sympathy for, relieve, solace, soothe

consolidate 1. amalgamate, cement, combine, compact, condense, conjoin, federate, fuse, harden, join, solidify, thicken, unite 2. fortify, reinforce, secure, stabilize, strengthen

consolidation alliance, amalgamation, association, compression, condensation, federation, fortification, fusion, reinforcement, strengthening

consonance accord, agreement, concord, conformity, congruence, congruity, consistency, correspondence, harmony, suitableness

consonant accordant, according, compatible, concordant, congruous, consistent, correspondent, harmonious, in agreement, suitable

consort n. 1. associate, companion, fellow, husband, partner, spouse (*of a reigning monarch*), wife ~v. 2. associate, fraternize, go around with, hang about *or* around with, keep company, mingle, mix 3. accord, agree, correspond, harmonize, square, tally

conspectus abstract, compendium, digest, epitome, outline, précis, résumé, summary, survey, syllabus, synopsis

conspicuous 1. apparent, clear, discernible, easily seen, evident, manifest, noticeable, obvious, patent, perceptible, visible 2. celebrated, distinguished, eminent, famous, illustrious, notable, outstanding, prominent, remarkable, signal, striking 3. blatant, flagrant, flashy, garish, glaring, showy

conspiracy cabal, collusion, confederacy, frame-up (*Sl.*), intrigue, league, machination, plot, scheme, treason

conspirator cabalist, conspirer, intriguer, plotter, schemer, traitor

conspire 1. cabal, confederate, contrive, devise, hatch treason, intrigue, machinate, manoeuvre, plot, scheme 2. combine, concur, conduce, contribute, cooperate, tend, work together

constancy decision, determination, devotion, fidelity, firmness, fixedness, permanence, perseverance, regularity, resolution, stability, steadfastness, steadiness, tenacity, uniformity

constant 1. continual, even, firm, fixed, habitual, immutable, invariable, permanent, perpetual, regular, stable, steadfast, steady, unalterable, unbroken, uniform, unvarying 2. ceaseless, continual, continuous, endless, eternal, everlasting, incessant, interminable, neverending, nonstop, perpetual, persistent, relentless, sustained, uninterrupted, unrelenting, unremitting 3. determined, dogged, persevering, resolute, unflagging, unshaken, unwavering 4. attached, dependable, devoted, faithful, loyal, staunch, tried-and-true, true, trustworthy, trusty, unfailing

constantly all the time, always, continually, continuously, endlessly, everlastingly, incessantly, interminably, invariably, morning, noon and night, night and day, nonstop, perpetually, relentlessly

consternation alarm, amazement, anxiety, awe, bewilderment, confusion, dismay, distress, dread, fear, fright, horror, panic, shock, terror, trepidation

constituent adj. 1. basic, component, elemental, essential, integral ~n. 2. component, element, essential, factor, ingredient, part, principle, unit 3. elector, voter

constitute 1. compose, comprise, create, enact, establish, fix, form, found, make, make up, set up 2. appoint, authorize, commission, delegate, depute, empower, name, nominate, ordain

constitution 1. composition, establishment, formation, organization 2. build, character, composition, disposition, form, habit, health, make-up, nature, physique, structure, temper, temperament

constitutional adj. 1. congenital, inborn, inherent, intrinsic, organic 2. chartered, statutory, vested ~n. 3. airing, stroll, turn, walk

constrain 1. bind, coerce, compel, drive, force, impel, necessitate, oblige, pressure, pressurize, urge 2. chain, check, confine, constrict, curb, hem in, restrain

constrained embarrassed, forced,

guarded, inhibited, reserved, reticent, subdued, unnatural

constraint 1. coercion, compulsion, force, necessity, pressure, restraint **2.** bashfulness, diffidence, embarrassment, inhibition, repression, reservation, restraint, timidity **3.** check, curb, damper, deterrent, hindrance, limitation, restriction

constrict choke, compress, contract, cramp, inhibit, limit, narrow, pinch, restrict, shrink, squeeze, strangle, strangulate, tighten

constriction blockage, compression, constraint, cramp, impediment, limitation, narrowing, pressure, reduction, restriction, squeezing, stenosis (*Pathology*), stricture, tightness

construct assemble, build, compose, create, design, elevate, engineer, erect, establish, fabricate, fashion, form, formulate, found, frame, make, manufacture, organize, put up, raise, set up, shape

construction 1. assembly, building, composition, creation, edifice, erection, fabric, fabrication, figure, form, formation, shape, structure **2.** explanation, inference, interpretation, reading, rendering

constructive helpful, positive, practical, productive, useful, valuable

construe analyse, deduce, explain, expound, interpret, parse, read, render, take, translate

consult 1. ask, ask advice of, commune, compare notes, confer, consider, debate, deliberate, interrogate, question, refer to, take counsel, turn to **2.** consider, have regard for, regard, respect, take account of, take into consideration

consultant adviser, authority, specialist

consultation appointment, conference, council, deliberation, dialogue, discussion, examination, hearing, interview, meeting, session

consume 1. absorb, deplete, dissipate, drain, eat up, employ, exhaust, expend, finish up, fritter away, lavish, lessen, spend, squander, use, use up, utilize, vanish, waste, wear out **2.** devour, eat, eat up, gobble (up), guzzle, polish off (*Inf.*), put away, swallow **3.** annihilate, decay, demolish, destroy, devastate, lay waste, ravage **4.** *Often passive* absorb, devour, dominate, eat up, engross, mo-

nopolize, obsess, preoccupy

consumer buyer, customer, purchaser, shopper, user

consuming absorbing, compelling, devouring, engrossing, excruciating, gripping, immoderate, overwhelming, tormenting

consummate 1. *v.* accomplish, achieve, carry out, compass, complete, conclude, crown, effectuate, end, finish, perfect, perform **2.** *adj.* absolute, accomplished, complete, conspicuous, finished, matchless, perfect, polished, practised, skilled, superb, supreme, total, transcendent, ultimate, unqualified, utter

consummation achievement, completion, culmination, end, fulfilment, perfection, realization

consumption 1. consuming, decay, decrease, depletion, destruction, diminution, dissipation, exhaustion, expenditure, loss, use, using up, utilization, waste **2.** *Medical* atrophy, emaciation, phthisis, T.B., tuberculosis

contact *n.* **1.** association, communication, connection **2.** approximation, contiguity, junction, juxtaposition, touch, union **3.** acquaintance, connection ~*v.* **4.** approach, call, communicate with, get *or* be in touch with, get hold of, phone, reach, ring (up), speak to, write to

contagion 1. contamination, corruption, infection, pestilence, plague, pollution, taint **2.** communication, passage, spread, transference, transmittal

contagious catching, communicable, epidemic, epizootic (*Veterinary medicine*), infectious, pestiferous, pestilential, spreading, taking (*Inf.*), transmissible

contain 1. accommodate, enclose, have capacity for, hold, incorporate, seat **2.** comprehend, comprise, embody, embrace, include, involve **3.** control, curb, hold back, hold in, repress, restrain, stifle

container holder, receptacle, repository, vessel

contaminate adulterate, befoul, corrupt, defile, deprave, infect, pollute, radioactivate, soil, stain, sully, taint, tarnish, vitiate

contamination adulteration, contagion, corruption, decay, defilement, dirtying, filth, foulness, impurity, infection, poisoning, pollution, radioactivation, rottenness, taint

contemn despise, disdain, disregard, hold cheap, neglect, scorn, slight, spurn, treat with contempt

contemplate 1. brood over, consider, deliberate, meditate, meditate on, mull over, muse over, observe, ponder, reflect upon, revolve *or* turn over in one's mind, ruminate (upon), study **2.** behold, examine, eye, gaze at, inspect, regard, scrutinize, stare at, survey, view **3.** aspire to, consider, design, envisage, expect, foresee, have in view *or* in mind, intend, mean, plan, propose, think of

contemplation 1. cogitation, consideration, deliberation, meditation, musing, pondering, reflection, reverie, rumination, thought **2.** examination, gazing at, inspection, looking at, observation, scrutiny, survey, viewing

contemplative deep *or* lost in thought, in a brown study, intent, introspective, meditative, musing, pensive, rapt, reflective, ruminative, thoughtful

contemporary *adj.* **1.** coetaneous (*Rare*), coeval, coexistent, coexisting, concurrent, contemporaneous, synchronous **2.** à la mode, current, in fashion, latest, modern, newfangled, present, present-day, recent, ultramodern, up-to-date, up-to-the-minute, with it (*Inf.*) ~*n.* **3.** compeer, fellow, peer

contempt 1. condescension, contumely, derision, despite (*Archaic*), disdain, disregard, disrespect, mockery, neglect, scorn, slight **2.** *A state of contempt* disgrace, dishonour, humiliation, shame

contemptible abject, base, cheap, degenerate, despicable, detestable, ignominious, low, low-down (*Inf.*), mean, paltry, pitiful, scurvy, shabby, shameful, vile, worthless

contemptuous arrogant, cavalier, condescending, contumelious, derisive, disdainful, haughty, high and mighty, insolent, insulting, scornful, sneering, supercilious

contend 1. clash, compete, contest, cope, emulate, grapple, jostle, litigate, skirmish, strive, struggle, vie **2.** affirm, allege, argue, assert, aver, avow, debate, dispute, hold, maintain

content¹ 1. *v.* appease, delight, gladden, gratify, humour, indulge, mollify, placate, please, reconcile, satisfy, suffice **2.** *n.* comfort, contentment, ease, gratification, peace, peace of mind, pleasure,

satisfaction **3.** *adj.* agreeable, at ease, comfortable, contented, fulfilled, satisfied, willing to accept

content² 1. burden, essence, gist, ideas, matter, meaning, significance, substance, text, thoughts **2.** capacity, load, measure, size, volume

contented at ease, at peace, cheerful, comfortable, complacent, content, glad, gratified, happy, pleased, satisfied, serene, thankful

contention 1. competition, contest, discord, dispute, dissension, enmity, feuding, hostility, rivalry, strife, struggle, wrangling **2.** affirmation, allegation, argument, assertion, asseveration, belief, claim, declaration, ground, idea, maintaining, opinion, position, profession, stand, thesis, view

contentious argumentative, bickering, captious, cavilling, combative, controversial, cross, disputatious, factious, litigious, peevish, perverse, pugnacious, quarrelsome, querulous, wrangling

contentment comfort, complacency, content, contentedness, ease, equanimity, fulfilment, gladness, gratification, happiness, peace, pleasure, repletion, satisfaction, serenity

contents 1. constituents, elements, ingredients, load **2.** chapters, divisions, subject matter, subjects, themes, topics

contest *n.* **1.** competition, game, match, tournament, trial **2.** affray, altercation, battle, combat, conflict, controversy, debate, discord, dispute, encounter, fight, shock, struggle ~*v.* **3.** compete, contend, fight, fight over, strive, vie **4.** argue, call in *or* into question, challenge, debate, dispute, doubt, litigate, object to, oppose, question

contestant aspirant, candidate, competitor, contender, entrant, participant, player

context 1. background, connection, frame of reference, framework, relation **2.** ambience, circumstances, conditions, situation

contiguous abutting, adjacent, adjoining, beside, bordering, conterminous, in contact, juxtaposed, juxtapositional, near, neighbouring, next, next door to, touching

continence abstinence, asceticism, celibacy, chastity, moderation, self-control, self-restraint, temperance

continent abstemious, abstinent, ascetic, austere, celibate, chaste, self-restrained, sober

contingency accident, chance, emergency, event, eventuality, fortuity, happening, incident, juncture, possibility, uncertainty

contingent adj. 1. With **on** or **upon** conditional, controlled by, dependent, subject to 2. accidental, casual, fortuitous, haphazard, random, uncertain ~n. 3. batch, body, bunch (Inf.), deputation, detachment, group, mission, quota, section, set

continual constant, continuous, endless, eternal, everlasting, frequent, incessant, interminable, oft-repeated, perpetual, recurrent, regular, repeated, repetitive, unceasing, uninterrupted, unremitting

continually all the time, always, constantly, endlessly, eternally, everlastingly, forever, incessantly, interminably, nonstop, persistently, repeatedly

continuance continuation, duration, period, protraction, term

continuation 1. addition, extension, furtherance, postscript, sequel, supplement 2. maintenance, perpetuation, prolongation, resumption

continue 1. abide, carry on, endure, last, live on, persist, remain, rest, stay, stay on, survive 2. go on, keep at, keep on, keep the ball rolling, keep up, maintain, persevere, persist in, prolong, pursue, stick at, stick to, sustain 3. draw out, extend, lengthen, project, prolong, reach 4. carry on, pick up where one left off, proceed, recommence, resume, return to, take up

continuing enduring, in progress, lasting, ongoing, sustained

continuity cohesion, connection, flow, interrelationship, progression, sequence, succession, whole

continuous connected, constant, continued, extended, prolonged, unbroken, unceasing, undivided, uninterrupted

contort convolute, deform, distort, gnarl, knot, misshape, twist, warp, wrench, writhe

contour curve, figure, form, lines, outline, profile, relief, shape, silhouette

contraband 1. n. black-marketing, bootlegging, moonshine (U.S.), rum-running, smuggling, trafficking 2. adj. banned, black-market, bootleg, bootlegged, forbidden, hot (Inf.), illegal, illic-it, interdicted, prohibited, smuggled, unlawful

contract v. 1. abbreviate, abridge, compress, condense, confine, constrict, curtail, dwindle, epitomize, lessen, narrow, purse, reduce, shrink, shrivel, tighten, wither, wrinkle 2. agree, arrange, bargain, clinch, close, come to terms, commit oneself, covenant, engage, enter into, negotiate, pledge, stipulate 3. acquire, be afflicted with, catch, develop, go down with (Inf.), incur ~n. 4. agreement, arrangement, bargain, bond, commission, commitment, compact, concordat, convention, covenant, deal (Inf.), engagement, pact, settlement, stipulation, treaty, understanding

contraction abbreviation, compression, constriction, diminution, drawing in, elision, narrowing, reduction, shortening, shrinkage, shrivelling, tensing, tightening

contradict be at variance with, belie, challenge, contravene, controvert, counter, counteract, deny, dispute, gainsay (Archaic), impugn, negate, oppose

contradiction conflict, confutation, contravention, denial, incongruity, inconsistency, negation, opposite

contradictory antagonistic, antithetical, conflicting, contrary, discrepant, incompatible, inconsistent, irreconcilable, opposed, opposite, paradoxical, repugnant

contraption apparatus, contrivance, device, gadget, mechanism, rig

contrary adj. 1. adverse, antagonistic, clashing, contradictory, counter, discordant, hostile, inconsistent, inimical, opposed, opposite, paradoxical 2. awkward, balky, cantankerous, cussed (Inf.), difficult, disobliging, froward, intractable, obstinate, perverse, stroppy (Brit. sl.), thrawn (Northern dialect), unaccommodating, wayward, wilful ~v. 3. antithesis, converse, opposite, reverse 4. **on the contrary** conversely, in contrast, not at all, on the other hand, quite the opposite or reverse

contrast 1. n. comparison, contrariety, difference, differentiation, disparity, dissimilarity, distinction, divergence, foil, opposition 2. v. compare, differ, differentiate, distinguish, oppose, set in opposition, set off

contravene 1. break, disobey, go against, infringe, transgress, violate 2.

conflict with, contradict, counteract, cross, go against, hinder, interfere, oppose, refute, thwart

contretemps accident, calamity, difficulty, misfortune, mishap, mistake, predicament

contribute 1. add, afford, bestow, chip in, donate, furnish, give, provide, subscribe, supply **2**. be conducive, be instrumental, be partly responsible for, conduce, help, lead, tend

contribution addition, bestowal, donation, gift, grant, input, offering, subscription

contributor 1. backer, bestower, conferrer, donor, giver, patron, subscriber, supporter **2**. correspondent, freelance, freelancer, journalist, reporter

contrite chastened, conscience-stricken, humble, in sackcloth and ashes, penitent, regretful, remorseful, repentant, sorrowful, sorry

contrition compunction, humiliation, penitence, remorse, repentance, self-reproach, sorrow

contrivance 1. artifice, design, dodge, expedient, fabrication, formation, intrigue, inventiveness, machination, measure, plan, plot, project, ruse, scheme, stratagem, trick **2**. apparatus, appliance, contraption, device, equipment, gadget, gear, implement, invention, machine, mechanism

contrive 1. concoct, construct, create, design, devise, engineer, fabricate, frame, improvise, invent, wangle (*Inf.*) **2**. arrange, bring about, effect, hit upon, manage, manoeuvre, plan, plot, scheme, succeed

contrived artificial, elaborate, forced, laboured, overdone, planned, recherché, strained, unnatural

control *v*. **1**. boss (*Inf.*), call the tune, command, conduct, direct, dominate, govern, have charge of, hold the purse strings, lead, manage, manipulate, oversee, pilot, reign over, rule, steer, superintend, supervise **2**. bridle, check, constrain, contain, curb, hold back, limit, master, rein in, repress, restrain, subdue **3**. *Used of a machine, an experiment, etc.* counteract, determine, monitor, regulate, verify ~*n*. **4**. authority, charge, command, direction, discipline, government, guidance, jurisdiction, management, mastery, oversight, rule, superintendence, supervision, supremacy **5**.

brake, check, curb, limitation, regulation, restraint

controls console, control panel, dashboard, dials, instruments

controversial at issue, contended, contentious, controvertible, debatable, disputable, disputed, open to question, under discussion

controversy altercation, argument, contention, debate, discussion, dispute, dissension, polemic, quarrel, squabble, strife, wrangle, wrangling

controvert 1. challenge, contradict, counter, deny, oppose, refute **2**. argue, contest, debate, discuss, dispute, wrangle

contumacious haughty, headstrong, insubordinate, intractable, intransigent, obdurate, obstinate, perverse, pig-headed, rebellious, recalcitrant, refractory, stiff-necked, stubborn

contumacy contempt, contrariety, delinquency, disobedience, haughtiness, insubordination, intransigence, obstinacy, perverseness, pig-headedness, rebelliousness, recalcitrance, refractoriness, stubbornness

contumelious contemptuous, disdainful, insolent, insulting, scornful, sneering, sniffy (*Inf.*), supercilious, withering

contumely abuse, affront, arrogance, contempt, derision, disdain, humiliation, indignity, insolence, insult, obloquy, opprobrium, rudeness, scorn, superciliousness

contusion bruise, discoloration, injury, knock, swelling

conundrum brain-teaser (*Inf.*), enigma, poser, problem, puzzle, riddle

convalescence improvement, recovery, recuperation, rehabilitation, return to health

convalescent *adj*. getting better, improving, mending, on the mend, recovering, recuperating

convene assemble, bring together, call, come together, congregate, convoke, gather, meet, muster, rally, summon

convenience 1. accessibility, appropriateness, availability, fitness, handiness, opportuneness, serviceability, suitability, usefulness, utility **2**. *A convenient time or situation* chance, leisure, opportunity, spare moment, spare time **3**. accommodation, advantage, benefit, comfort, ease, enjoyment, satisfaction, service, use **4**. *A useful device* amenity, appliance, comfort, facility, help, labour-saving device

convenient 1. adapted, appropriate, beneficial, commodious, fit, fitted, handy, helpful, labour-saving, opportune, seasonable, serviceable, suitable, suited, timely, useful, well-timed **2**. accessible, at hand, available, close at hand, handy, just round the corner, nearby, within reach

convent convent school, nunnery, religious community

convention 1. assembly, conference, congress, convocation, council, delegates, meeting, representatives **2**. code, custom, etiquette, formality, practice, propriety, protocol, tradition, usage **3**. agreement, bargain, compact, concordat, contract, pact, protocol, stipulation, treaty

conventional 1. accepted, common, correct, customary, decorous, expected, formal, habitual, normal, ordinary, orthodox, prevailing, prevalent, proper, regular, ritual, standard, traditional, usual, wonted **2**. bourgeois, commonplace, hackneyed, hidebound, pedestrian, prosaic, routine, run-of-the-mill, stereotyped, unoriginal

converge coincide, combine, come together, concentrate, focus, gather, join, meet, merge, mingle

convergence approach, blending, coincidence, concentration, concurrence, confluence, conflux, conjunction, junction, meeting, merging, mingling

conversant *Usually with* **with** acquainted, *au fait*, experienced, familiar, knowledgeable, practised, proficient, skilled, versed, well-informed, well up in (*Inf.*)

conversation chat, chinwag (*Brit. inf.*), colloquy, communication, communion, confab (*Inf.*), confabulation, conference, converse, dialogue, discourse, discussion, exchange, gossip, intercourse, powwow, talk, tête-à-tête

conversational chatty, colloquial, communicative, informal

converse[1] *v.* **1**. chat, commune, confer, discourse, exchange views **2**. *Obsolete* associate, consort ~*n.* **3**. chat, communication, conference, conversation, dialogue, talk

converse[2] **1**. *n.* antithesis, contrary, obverse, opposite, other side of the coin,

reverse **2**. *adj.* contrary, counter, opposite, reverse, reversed, transposed

conversion 1. change, metamorphosis, transfiguration, transformation, transmogrification (*Jocular*), transmutation **2**. adaptation, alteration, modification, reconstruction, remodelling, reorganization **3**. change of heart, proselytization, rebirth, reformation, regeneration

convert[1] *v.* **1**. alter, change, interchange, metamorphose, transform, transmogrify (*Jocular*), transmute, transpose, turn **2**. adapt, apply, appropriate, modify, remodel, reorganize, restyle, revise **3**. baptize, bring to God, convince, proselytize, reform, regenerate, save

convert[2] *n.* catechumen, disciple, neophyte, proselyte

convertible adaptable, adjustable, exchangeable, interchangeable

convex bulging, gibbous, outcurved, protuberant, rounded

convey 1. bear, bring, carry, conduct, fetch, forward, grant, guide, move, send, support, transmit, transport **2**. communicate, disclose, impart, make known, relate, reveal, tell **3**. *Law* bequeath, cede, deliver, demise, devolve, grant, lease, transfer, will

conveyance 1. carriage, movement, transfer, transference, transmission, transport, transportation **2**. transport, vehicle

convict 1. *v.* condemn, find guilty, imprison, pronounce guilty, sentence **2**. *n.* con (*Sl.*), criminal, culprit, felon, jailbird, malefactor, old lag (*Sl.*), prisoner

conviction 1. assurance, certainty, certitude, confidence, earnestness, fervour, firmness, reliance **2**. belief, creed, faith, opinion, persuasion, principle, tenet, view

convince assure, bring round, gain the confidence of, persuade, prevail upon, prove to, satisfy, sway, win over

convincing cogent, conclusive, credible, impressive, incontrovertible, likely, persuasive, plausible, powerful, probable, telling

convivial back-slapping, cheerful, festive, friendly, fun-loving, gay, genial, hearty, hilarious, jolly, jovial, lively, merry, mirthful, partyish (*Inf.*), sociable

conviviality bonhomie, cheer, cordiality, festivity, gaiety, geniality, good fellowship, jollification, jollity, joviality, liveliness, merrymaking, mirth, sociability

convocation assemblage, assembly, conclave, concourse, congregation, congress, convention, council, diet, meeting, synod

convoke assemble, call together, collect, convene, gather, muster, summon

convolution coil, coiling, complexity, contortion, curlicue, helix, intricacy, involution, loop, sinuosity, sinuousness, spiral, tortuousness, twist, undulation, winding

convoy 1. *n.* armed guard, attendance, attendant, escort, guard, protection **2.** *v.* accompany, attend, escort, guard, pilot, protect, shepherd, usher

convulse agitate, churn up, derange, disorder, disturb, shake, shatter, twist, work

convulsion 1. agitation, commotion, disturbance, furore, shaking, tumult, turbulence, upheaval **2.** contortion, contraction, cramp, fit, paroxysm, seizure, spasm, throe (*Rare*), tremor

convulsive churning, fitful, jerky, paroxysmal, spasmodic, sporadic, violent

cook up concoct, contrive, devise, fabricate, improvise, invent, plot, prepare, scheme

cool *adj.* **1.** chilled, chilling, chilly, coldish, nippy, refreshing **2.** calm, collected, composed, deliberate, dispassionate, imperturbable, level-headed, placid, quiet, relaxed, self-controlled, self-possessed, serene, together (*Sl.*), unemotional, unexcited, unruffled **3.** aloof, apathetic, distant, frigid, incurious, indifferent, lukewarm, offhand, reserved, standoffish, uncommunicative, unconcerned, unenthusiastic, unfriendly, uninterested, unresponsive, unwelcoming **4.** audacious, bold, brazen, cheeky, impertinent, impudent, presumptuous, shameless **5.** *Inf.* cosmopolitan, elegant, sophisticated, urbane ~*v.* **6.** chill, cool off, freeze, lose heat, refrigerate **7.** abate, allay, assuage, calm (down), dampen, lessen, moderate, quiet, temper ~*n.* **8.** *Sl.* calmness, composure, control, poise, self-control, self-discipline, self-possession, temper

coop 1. *n.* box, cage, enclosure, hutch, pen **2.** *v.* cage, confine, immure, imprison, pen, shut up

cooperate abet, aid, assist, collabo-

rate, combine, concur, conduce, conspire, contribute, coordinate, go along with, help, join forces, pitch in, play ball (*Inf.*), pool resources, pull together, work together

cooperation assistance, collaboration, combined effort, concert, concurrence, esprit de corps, give-and-take, helpfulness, participation, responsiveness, teamwork, unity

cooperative 1. accommodating, helpful, obliging, responsive, supportive **2.** coactive, collective, combined, concerted, coordinated, joint, shared, unified, united

coordinate 1. *v.* correlate, harmonize, integrate, match, mesh, organize, relate, synchronize, systematize **2.** *adj.* coequal, correlative, correspondent, equal, equivalent, parallel, tantamount

cope 1. carry on, get by (*Inf.*), hold one's own, make out (*Inf.*), make the grade, manage, rise to the occasion, struggle through, survive **2. cope with** contend, deal, dispatch, encounter, grapple, handle, struggle, tangle, tussle, weather, wrestle

copious abundant, ample, bounteous, bountiful, extensive, exuberant, full, generous, lavish, liberal, luxuriant, overflowing, plenteous, plentiful, profuse, rich, superabundant

copiousness abundance, amplitude, bountifulness, bounty, cornucopia, exuberance, fullness, horn of plenty, lavishness, luxuriance, plentifulness, plenty, richness, superabundance

cop-out alibi, dodge, fraud, pretence, pretext

cop out abandon, desert, dodge, quit, renege, renounce, revoke, skip, skive (*Sl.*), withdraw

copulation carnal knowledge, coition, coitus, congress, coupling, love, lovemaking, mating, sex, sex act, sexual intercourse, venery (*Archaic*)

copy *n.* **1.** archetype, carbon copy, counterfeit, duplicate, facsimile, forgery, image, imitation, likeness, model, pattern, photocopy, Photostat (*Trademark*), print, replica, replication, representation, reproduction, transcription, Xerox (*Trademark*) ~*v.* **2.** counterfeit, duplicate, photocopy, Photostat (*Trademark*), replicate, reproduce, transcribe, Xerox (*Trademark*) **3.** ape, echo, emulate, follow, follow suit, follow the example of, imitate, mimic, mirror, parrot, repeat, simulate

coquet dally, flirt, lead on, make eyes at, philander, tease, toy, trifle, vamp (*Inf.*)

coquettish amorous, arch, comehither (*Inf.*), coy, dallying, flighty, flirtatious, flirty, inviting, teasing

cord 1. line, rope, string, twine **2.** bond, connection, link, tie

cordial affable, affectionate, agreeable, cheerful, earnest, friendly, genial, heartfelt, hearty, invigorating, sociable, warm, warm-hearted, welcoming, wholehearted

cordiality affability, amiability, friendliness, geniality, heartiness, sincerity, warmth, wholeheartedness

cordon 1. *n.* barrier, chain, line, ring **2.** *v.* **cordon off** close off, encircle, enclose, fence off, isolate, picket, separate, surround

core centre, crux, essence, gist, heart, kernel, nub, nucleus, pith

corner *n.* **1.** angle, bend, crook, joint **2.** cavity, cranny, hideaway, hide-out, hidey-hole (*Inf.*), hole, niche, nook, recess, retreat **3.** hole (*Inf.*), pickle (*Inf.*), predicament, tight spot (*Inf.*) ~*v.* **4.** bring to bay, run to earth, trap **5.** *As in* **corner the market** engross, hog (*Sl.*), monopolize

cornerstone 1. quoin **2.** basis, bedrock, key, premise, starting point

corny banal, commonplace, dull, feeble, hackneyed, maudlin, mawkish, oldfashioned, old hat, sentimental, stale, stereotyped, trite

corollary conclusion, consequence, deduction, induction, inference, result, upshot

corporal anatomical, bodily, carnal, corporeal (*Archaic*), fleshly, material, physical, somatic

corporate allied, collaborative, collective, combined, communal, joint, merged, pooled, shared, united

corporation 1. association, corporate body, society **2.** civic authorities, council, municipal authorities, town council **3.** *Inf.* beer belly, paunch, pod, pot, potbelly, spare tyre

corporeal bodily, fleshly, human, material, mortal, physical, substantial

corps band, body, company, contingent, crew, detachment, division, regiment, squad, squadron, team, troop, unit

corpse body, cadaver, carcass, remains, stiff (*Sl.*)

corpulence blubber, burliness, *embonpoint*, fatness, fleshiness, obesity, plumpness, portliness, rotundity, stoutness, tubbiness

corpulent beefy (*Inf.*), bulky, burly, fat, fattish, fleshy, large, lusty, obese, overweight, plump, portly, roly-poly, rotund, stout, tubby, well-padded

corpus body, collection, compilation, complete works, entirety, *oeuvre*, whole

correct *v.* **1.** adjust, amend, cure, emend, improve, rectify, redress, reform, regulate, remedy, right **2.** admonish, chasten, chastise, chide, discipline, punish, reprimand, reprove ~*adj.* **3.** accurate, equitable, exact, faultless, flawless, just, O.K. (*Inf.*), precise, regular, right, strict, true **4.** acceptable, appropriate, diplomatic, fitting, O.K. (*Inf.*), proper, seemly, standard

correction 1. adjustment, alteration, amendment, improvement, modification, rectification, righting **2.** admonition, castigation, chastisement, discipline, punishment, reformation, reproof

corrective *adj.* **1.** palliative, rehabilitative, remedial, restorative, therapeutic **2.** disciplinary, penal, punitive, reformatory

correctly accurately, aright, perfectly, precisely, properly, right, rightly

correctness 1. accuracy, exactitude, exactness, faultlessness, fidelity, preciseness, precision, regularity, truth **2.** *bon ton*, civility, decorum, good breeding, propriety, seemliness

correlate associate, compare, connect, coordinate, correspond, equate, interact, parallel, tie in

correlation alternation, correspondence, equivalence, interaction, interchange, interdependence, interrelationship, reciprocity

correspond 1. accord, agree, be consistent, coincide, complement, conform, correlate, dovetail, fit, harmonize, match, square, tally **2.** communicate, exchange letters, keep in touch, write

correspondence 1. agreement, analogy, coincidence, comparability, comparison, concurrence, conformity, congruity, correlation, fitness, harmony, match, relation, similarity **2.** communication, letters, mail, post, writing

correspondent *n.* **1.** letter writer, pen

friend *or* pal **2.** contributor, gazetteer (*Archaic*), journalist, reporter, special correspondent ~*adj.* **3.** analogous, comparable, like, parallel, reciprocal, similar

corresponding analogous, answering, complementary, correlative, correspondent, equivalent, identical, interrelated, matching, reciprocal, similar, synonymous

corridor aisle, hallway, passage, passageway

corroborate authenticate, back up, bear out, confirm, document, endorse, establish, ratify, substantiate, support, sustain, validate

corrode canker, consume, corrupt, deteriorate, eat away, erode, gnaw, impair, oxidize, rust, waste, wear away

corrosive 1. acrid, biting, caustic, consuming, corroding, erosive, virulent, wasting, wearing **2.** caustic, cutting, incisive, mordant, sarcastic, trenchant, venomous

corrugated channelled, creased, crinkled, fluted, furrowed, grooved, puckered, ridged, rumpled, wrinkled

corrupt *adj.* **1.** bent (*Sl.*), bribable, crooked (*Inf.*), dishonest, fraudulent, rotten, shady (*Inf.*), unethical, unprincipled, unscrupulous, venal **2.** abandoned, debased, defiled, degenerate, demoralized, depraved, dishonoured, dissolute, profligate, vicious ~*v.* **3.** bribe, debauch, demoralize, deprave, entice, fix (*Inf.*), grease (someone's) palm (*Sl.*), lure, pervert, square (*Inf.*), suborn, subvert ~*adj.* **4.** adulterated, altered, contaminated, decayed, defiled, distorted, doctored, falsified, infected, polluted, putrescent, putrid, rotten, tainted ~*v.* **5.** adulterate, contaminate, debase, defile, doctor, infect, putrefy, spoil, taint, tamper with, vitiate

corruption 1. breach of trust, bribery, bribing, crookedness (*Inf.*), demoralization, dishonesty, extortion, fiddling (*Inf.*), fraud, fraudulency, graft, jobbery, profiteering, shadiness, shady dealings (*Inf.*), unscrupulousness, venality **2.** baseness, decadence, degeneration, degradation, depravity, evil, immorality, impurity, iniquity, perversion, profligacy, sinfulness, turpitude, vice, viciousness, wickedness **3.** adulteration, debasement, decay, defilement, distortion, doctoring, falsification, foulness, infection, pollu-

tion, putrefaction, putrescence, rot, rottenness

corsair buccaneer, freebooter, picaroon (*Archaic*), pirate, rover, sea rover

corset 1. belt, bodice, corselet, foundation garment, girdle, panty girdle, stays (*Rare*) **2.** *Fig.* check, curb, limitation, restriction

cortege cavalcade, entourage, procession, retinue, suite, train

cosmetic *adj.* beautifying, nonessential, superficial, surface, touching-up

cosmic grandiose, huge, immense, infinite, limitless, measureless, universal, vast

cosmonaut astronaut, spaceman, space pilot

cosmopolitan 1. *adj.* catholic, sophisticated, universal, urbane, well-travelled, worldly, worldly-wise **2.** *n.* cosmopolite, jetsetter, man *or* woman of the world, sophisticate

cosmos 1. creation, macrocosm, universe, world **2.** harmony, order, structure

cosset baby, coddle, cosher (*Irish*), mollycoddle, pamper, pet, wrap up in cotton wool (*Inf.*)

cost *n.* **1.** amount, charge, damage (*Inf.*), expenditure, expense, figure, outlay, payment, price, rate, worth **2.** damage, deprivation, detriment, expense, harm, hurt, injury, loss, penalty, sacrifice, suffering ~*v.* **3.** come to, command a price of, sell at, set (someone) back (*Inf.*) **4.** *Fig.* do disservice to, harm, hurt, injure, lose, necessitate

costly 1. dear, excessive, exorbitant, expensive, extortionate, highly-priced, steep (*Inf.*), valuable **2.** gorgeous, lavish, luxurious, opulent, precious, priceless, rich, splendid, sumptuous **3.** *Entailing loss or sacrifice* catastrophic, damaging, deleterious, disastrous, harmful, loss-making, ruinous, sacrificial

costs 1. budget, expenses, outgoings **2. at all costs** at any price, no matter what, regardless, without fail

costume apparel, attire, clothing, dress, ensemble, garb, get-up (*Inf.*), livery, national dress, outfit, robes, uniform

cosy comfortable, comfy (*Inf.*), cuddled up, homely, intimate, secure, sheltered, snug, snuggled down, tucked up, warm

coterie camp, circle, clique, gang, group, outfit (*Inf.*), set

cottage but-and-ben (*Scot.*), cabin,

chalet, cot, hut, lodge, shack

couch 1. *v.* express, frame, phrase, set forth, utter, word **2.** *n.* bed, chaise longue, chesterfield, daybed, divan, ottoman, settee, sofa

cough 1. *n.* bark, frog *or* tickle in one's throat, hack **2.** *v.* bark, clear one's throat, hack, hawk, hem

cough up ante up (*Inf.*), come across, deliver, fork out (*Sl.*), give up, hand over, shell out (*Inf.*), surrender

council assembly, board, cabinet, chamber, committee, conclave, conference, congress, convention, convocation, diet, governing body, ministry, panel, parliament, synod

counsel *n.* **1.** admonition, advice, caution, consideration, consultation, deliberation, direction, forethought, guidance, information, recommendation, suggestion, warning **2.** advocate, attorney, barrister, lawyer, legal adviser, solicitor ~*v.* **3.** admonish, advise, advocate, caution, exhort, instruct, recommend, urge, warn

count *v.* **1.** add (up), calculate, cast up, check, compute, enumerate, estimate, number, reckon, score, tally, tot up **2.** consider, deem, esteem, impute, judge, look upon, rate, regard, think **3.** carry weight, cut any ice (*Inf.*), enter into consideration, matter, rate, signify, tell, weigh **4.** include, number among, take into account *or* consideration ~*n.* **5.** calculation, computation, enumeration, numbering, poll, reckoning, sum, tally

countenance *n.* **1.** appearance, aspect, expression, face, features, look, mien, physiognomy, visage **2.** aid, approval, assistance, backing, endorsement, favour, sanction, support ~*v.* **3.** abet, aid, approve, back, champion, condone, encourage, endorse, help, sanction, support **4.** brook, endure, put up with (*Inf.*), stand for (*Inf.*), tolerate

counter 1. *adv.* against, at variance with, contrarily, contrariwise, conversely, in defiance of, versus **2.** *adj.* adverse, against, conflicting, contradictory, contrary, contrasting, obverse, opposed, opposing, opposite **3.** *v.* answer, hit back, meet, offset, parry, resist, respond, retaliate, return, ward off

counteract annul, check, contravene, counterbalance, countervail, cross, defeat, foil, frustrate, hinder, invalidate,

negate, neutralize, offset, oppose, resist, thwart

counterbalance balance, compensate, counterpoise, countervail, make up for, offset, set off

counterfeit 1. *v.* copy, fabricate, fake, feign, forge, imitate, impersonate, pretend, sham, simulate **2.** *adj.* bogus, copied, ersatz, faked, false, feigned, forged, fraudulent, imitation, phoney (*Sl.*), pseud (*Inf.*), pseudo (*Inf.*), sham, simulated, spurious, supposititious **3.** *n.* copy, fake, forgery, fraud, imitation, phoney (*Sl.*), reproduction, sham

countermand annul, cancel, override, repeal, rescind, retract, reverse, revoke

counterpane bedcover, bedspread, cover, coverlet, quilt

counterpart complement, copy, correlative, duplicate, equal, fellow, match, mate, opposite number, supplement, tally, twin

countless endless, immeasurable, incalculable, infinite, innumerable, legion, limitless, measureless, multitudinous, myriad, numberless, uncounted, untold

count on *or* **upon** bank on, believe (in), depend on, lean on, pin one's faith on, reckon on, rely on, take for granted, take on trust, trust

count out disregard, except, exclude, leave out, leave out of account, pass over

countrified Arcadian, bucolic, cracker-barrel (*U.S.*), homespun, idyllic, pastoral, picturesque, provincial, rural, rustic

country *n.* **1.** commonwealth, kingdom, nation, people, realm, sovereign state, state **2.** fatherland, homeland, motherland, nationality, native land, *patria* **3.** land, part, region, terrain, territory **4.** citizenry, citizens, community, electors, grass roots, inhabitants, nation, people, populace, public, society, voters **5.** backwoods, boondocks (*U.S. sl.*), countryside, farmland, green belt, outback (*Australian & New Zealand*), outdoors, provinces, rural areas, sticks (*Inf.*), the back of beyond, the middle of nowhere, wide open spaces (*Inf.*) ~*adj.* **6.** agrarian, Arcadian, bucolic, georgic (*Literary*), landed, pastoral, provincial, rural, rustic

countryman 1. bumpkin, country dweller, farmer, hayseed (*U.S. inf.*), hind, husbandman, peasant, provincial, rustic, swain, yokel **2.** compatriot, fellow citizen

countryside country, farmland, green belt, outback (*Australian & New Zealand*), outdoors, panorama, sticks (*Inf.*), view, wide open spaces (*Inf.*)

count up add, reckon up, sum, tally, total

county 1. *n.* province, shire **2.** *adj.* huntin', shootin', and fishin' (*Inf.*), plummy (*Inf.*), tweedy, upper-class, upper-crust (*Inf.*)

coup accomplishment, action, deed, exploit, feat, manoeuvre, masterstroke, stratagem, stroke, stroke of genius, stunt, *tour de force*

coup de grâce clincher (*Inf.*), comeuppance (*Sl.*), deathblow, final blow, kill, knockout blow, mercy stroke, mortal blow, quietus

coup d'état coup, overthrow, palace revolution, putsch, rebellion, seizure of power, takeover

couple 1. *n.* brace, duo, pair, span (*of horses or oxen*), twain (*Archaic*), twosome **2.** *v.* buckle, clasp, conjoin, connect, hitch, join, link, marry, pair, unite, wed, yoke

coupon card, certificate, detachable portion, slip, ticket, token, voucher

courage boldness, bottle (*Sl.*), bravery, daring, dauntlessness, fearlessness, firmness, fortitude, gallantry, grit, guts (*Inf.*), hardihood, heroism, intrepidity, lion-heartedness, mettle, nerve, pluck, resolution, spunk (*Inf.*), valour

courageous audacious, bold, brave, daring, dauntless, fearless, gallant, hardy, heroic, indomitable, intrepid, lionhearted, plucky, resolute, stouthearted, valiant, valorous

courier 1. bearer, carrier, emissary, envoy, herald, messenger, pursuivant (*Historical*), runner **2.** guide, representative

course *n.* **1.** advance, advancement, continuity, development, flow, furtherance, march, movement, order, progress, progression, sequence, succession, unfolding **2.** channel, direction, line, orbit, passage, path, road, route, tack, track, trail, trajectory, way **3.** duration, lapse, passage, passing, sweep, term, time **4.** behaviour, conduct, manner, method, mode, plan, policy, procedure, programme, regimen **5.** cinder track, circuit, lap, race, racecourse, round **6.** classes,

course of study, curriculum, lectures, programme, schedule, studies ~*v.* **7.** dash, flow, gush, move apace, race, run, scud, scurry, speed, stream, surge, tumble **8.** chase, follow, hunt, pursue **9. in due course** eventually, finally, in the course of time, in the end, in time, sooner or later **10. of course** certainly, definitely, indubitably, naturally, obviously, undoubtedly, without a doubt

court *n.* **1.** cloister, courtyard, piazza, plaza, quad (*Inf.*), quadrangle, square, yard **2.** hall, manor, palace **3.** attendants, cortege, entourage, retinue, royal household, suite, train **4.** bar, bench, court of justice, lawcourt, seat of judgment, tribunal **5.** addresses, attention, homage, respects, suit ~*v.* **6.** chase, date, go (out) with, go steady with (*Inf.*), keep company with, make love to, pay court to, pay one's addresses to, pursue, run after, serenade, set one's cap at, sue (*Archaic*), take out, walk out with, woo **7.** cultivate, curry favour with, fawn upon, flatter, pander to, seek, solicit **8.** attract, bring about, incite, invite, prompt, provoke, seek

courteous affable, attentive, ceremonious, civil, courtly, elegant, gallant, gracious, mannerly, polished, polite, refined, respectful, urbane, well-bred, well-mannered

courtesan call girl, demimondaine, *fille de joie*, harlot, hetaera, kept woman, mistress, paramour, prostitute, scarlet woman, whore

courtesy 1. affability, civility, courteousness, courtliness, elegance, gallantness, gallantry, good breeding, good manners, graciousness, polish, politeness, urbanity **2.** benevolence, consent, consideration, favour, generosity, indulgence, kindness

courtier attendant, follower, henchman, liegeman, pursuivant (*Historical*), squire, train-bearer

courtliness affability, ceremony, chivalrousness, correctness, courtesy, decorum, elegance, formality, gallantry, gentility, graciousness, politeness, politesse, propriety, refinement, stateliness, urbanity

courtly affable, aristocratic, ceremonious, chivalrous, civil, decorous, dignified, elegant, flattering, formal, gallant, highbred, lordly, obliging, polished, refined, stately, urbane

courtship courting, engagement, keeping company, pursuit, romance, suit, wooing

courtyard area, enclosure, peristyle, playground, quad, quadrangle, yard

cove[1] anchorage, bay, creek, firth *or* frith (*Scot.*), inlet, sound

cove[2] bloke, chap, character, customer, fellow, type

covenant *n.* **1.** arrangement, bargain, commitment, compact, concordat, contract, convention, pact, promise, stipulation, treaty, trust **2.** bond, deed ~*v.* **3.** agree, bargain, contract, engage, pledge, stipulate, undertake

cover *v.* **1.** camouflage, cloak, conceal, cover up, curtain, disguise, eclipse, enshroud, hide, hood, house, mask, obscure, screen, secrete, shade, shroud, veil ~*n.* **2.** cloak, cover-up, disguise, façade, front, mask, pretence, screen, smoke screen, veil, window-dressing ~*v.* **3.** defend, guard, protect, reinforce, shelter, shield, watch over ~*n.* **4.** camouflage, concealment, defence, guard, hiding place, protection, refuge, sanctuary, shelter, shield, undergrowth, woods ~*v.* **5.** canopy, clothe, coat, daub, dress, encase, envelop, invest, layer, mantle, overlay, overspread, put on, wrap ~*n.* **6.** binding, canopy, cap, case, clothing, coating, covering, dress, envelope, jacket, lid, sheath, top, wrapper ~*v.* **7.** comprehend, comprise, consider, contain, deal with, embody, embrace, encompass, examine, include, incorporate, involve, provide for, refer to, survey, take account of **8.** double for, fill in for, relieve, stand in for, substitute, take over, take the rap for (*Sl.*) **9.** describe, detail, investigate, narrate, recount, relate, report, tell of, write up **10.** balance, compensate, counterbalance, insure, make good, make up for, offset ~*n.* **11.** compensation, indemnity, insurance, payment, protection, reimbursement ~*v.* **12.** cross, pass through *or* over, range, travel over, traverse **13.** engulf, flood, overrun, submerge, wash over

coverage analysis, description, reportage, reporting, treatment

covering 1. *n.* blanket, casing, clothing, coating, cover, housing, layer, overlay, protection, shelter, top, wrap, wrapper, wrapping **2.** *adj.* accompanying, descriptive, explanatory, introductory

covert 1. *adj.* clandestine, concealed, disguised, dissembled, hidden, private, secret, stealthy, surreptitious, underhand, unsuspected, veiled **2.** *n.* brush (*Archaic*), bushes, coppice, shrubbery, thicket, undergrowth, underwood

cover-up complicity, concealment, conspiracy, front, smoke screen, whitewash (*Inf.*)

cover up 1. conceal, cover one's tracks, feign ignorance, hide, hush up, keep dark, keep secret, keep silent about, keep under one's hat (*Inf.*), repress, stonewall, suppress, whitewash (*Inf.*) **2.** coat, cover, encrust, envelop, hide, plaster, slather (*U.S. sl.*), swathe

covet aspire to, begrudge, crave, desire, envy, fancy (*Inf.*), hanker after, have one's eye on, long for, lust after, thirst for, yearn for

covetous acquisitive, avaricious, close-fisted, envious, grasping, greedy, jealous, mercenary, rapacious, yearning

covey bevy, brood, cluster, flight, flock, group, nye *or* nide (*of pheasants*)

cow awe, browbeat, bully, daunt, dishearten, dismay, frighten, intimidate, overawe, scare, subdue, terrorize, unnerve

coward caitiff (*Archaic*), craven, dastard (*Archaic*), faint-heart, funk (*Inf.*), poltroon, recreant (*Archaic*), renegade, scaredy-cat (*Inf.*), skulker, sneak, yellow-belly (*Sl.*)

cowardly base, caitiff (*Archaic*), chicken (*Sl.*), chicken-hearted, craven, dastardly, faint-hearted, fearful, gutless (*Inf.*), lily-livered, pusillanimous, recreant (*Archaic*), scared, shrinking, soft, spineless, timorous, weak, weak-kneed (*Inf.*), white-livered, yellow (*Inf.*)

cowboy broncobuster (*U.S.*), cattleman, cowhand, cowpuncher (*U.S. inf.*), drover, gaucho (*S American*), herder, herdsman, rancher, ranchero (*U.S.*), stockman, wrangler (*U.S.*)

cower cringe, crouch, draw back, fawn, flinch, grovel, quail, shrink, skulk, sneak, tremble, truckle

coxcomb beau, Beau Brummell, dandy, dude (*U.S.*), exquisite, fop, macaroni (*in the 18th century*), peacock, popinjay, poser (*Inf.*), prig, puppy, spark (*Rare*), swell (*Inf.*)

coy arch, backward, bashful, coquettish, demure, evasive, flirtatious, kittenish, modest, overmodest, prudish, reserved, retiring, self-effacing, shrinking, shy, skittish, timid

coyness affectation, archness, backwardness, bashfulness, coquettishness, demureness, diffidence, evasiveness, modesty, primness, prissiness (*Inf.*), prudery, prudishness, reserve, shrinking, shyness, skittishness, timidity

cozen bilk, cheat, circumvent, con (*Sl.*), deceive, diddle (*Inf.*), double-cross (*Inf.*), dupe, gull (*Archaic*), hoodwink, impose on, inveigle, swindle, take advantage of, take for a ride (*Inf.*), victimize

crabbed 1. acrid, acrimonious, captious, churlish, cross, cynical, difficult, fretful, harsh, ill-tempered, irritable, morose, perverse, petulant, prickly, sour, splenetic, surly, tart, testy, tough, trying **2.** *Of handwriting* awkward, cramped, hieroglyphical, illegible, indecipherable, laboured, squeezed, unreadable

crabby acid, awkward, bad-tempered, cross, crotchety (*Inf.*), grouchy, ill-humoured, irritable, mardy (*Dialect*), misanthropic, nasty-tempered, prickly, snappish, snappy, sour, surly, testy, unsociable

crack *v.* **1.** break, burst, chip, chop, cleave, crackle, craze, fracture, rive, snap, splinter, split ~*n.* **2.** breach, break, chink, chip, cleft, cranny, crevice, fissure, fracture, gap, interstice, rift ~*v.* **3.** burst, crash, detonate, explode, pop, ring, snap ~*n.* **4.** burst, clap, crash, explosion, pop, report, snap ~*v.* **5.** break down, collapse, give way, go to pieces, lose control, succumb, yield ~*v./n.* **6.** *Inf.* buffet, clip (*Inf.*), clout (*Inf.*), cuff, slap, thump, wallop (*Inf.*), whack ~*v.* **7.** decipher, fathom, get the answer to, solve, work out ~*n.* **8.** *Inf.* attempt, go, opportunity, stab, try **9.** *Sl.* dig, funny remark, gag, insult, jibe, joke, quip, smart-alecky remark, wisecrack, witticism ~*adj.* **10.** *Sl.* ace, choice, elite, excellent, first-class, first-rate, handpicked, superior

crackbrained cracked (*Sl.*), crackers (*Sl.*), crackpot (*Inf.*), crazy (*Inf.*), idiotic, insane, lunatic

crackdown clampdown, crushing, repression, suppression

cracked 1. broken, chipped, crazed, damaged, defective, faulty, fissured, flawed, imperfect, split **2.** *Sl.* bats (*Sl.*), batty (*Sl.*), crackbrained, crackpot (*Inf.*), crazy (*Inf.*), daft (*Sl.*), eccentric,

insane, loony (*Sl.*), nuts (*Sl.*), nutty (*Sl.*), off one's head *or* nut (*Sl.*), out of one's mind, round the bend (*Sl.*), touched

cracked up blown up, exaggerated, hyped up (*Sl.*), overpraised, overrated, puffed up

crack up break down, collapse, come apart at the seams (*Inf.*), freak out (*Inf.*), go crazy (*Inf.*), go off one's rocker (*Sl.*), go out of one's mind, go to pieces, have a breakdown

cradle *n.* **1.** bassinet, cot, crib, Moses basket **2.** *Fig.* beginning, birthplace, fount, fountainhead, origin, source, spring, wellspring ~*v.* **3.** hold, lull, nestle, nurse, rock, support **4.** nourish, nurture, tend, watch over

craft 1. ability, aptitude, art, artistry, cleverness, dexterity, expertise, expertness, ingenuity, knack, know-how (*Inf.*), skill, technique, workmanship **2.** artfulness, artifice, contrivance, craftiness, cunning, deceit, duplicity, guile, ruse, scheme, shrewdness, stratagem, subterfuge, subtlety, trickery, wiles **3.** business, calling, employment, handicraft, handiwork, line, occupation, pursuit, trade, vocation, work **4.** aircraft, barque, boat, plane, ship, spacecraft, vessel

craftiness artfulness, astuteness, canniness, cunning, deviousness, duplicity, foxiness, guile, shrewdness, slyness, subtlety, trickiness, wiliness

craftsman artificer, artisan, maker, master, skilled worker, smith, technician, wright

craftsmanship artistry, expertise, mastery, technique, workmanship

crafty artful, astute, calculating, canny, cunning, deceitful, designing, devious, duplicitous, foxy, fraudulent, guileful, insidious, knowing, scheming, sharp, shrewd, sly, subtle, tricksy, tricky, wily

crag aiguille, bluff, peak, pinnacle, rock, tor

craggy broken, cragged, jagged, jaggy (*Scot.*), precipitous, rock-bound, rocky, rough, rugged, stony, uneven

cram 1. compact, compress, crowd, crush, fill to overflowing, force, jam, overcrowd, overfill, pack, pack in, press, ram, shove, squeeze, stuff **2.** glut, gorge, gormandize, guzzle, overeat, overfeed, put *or* pack away, satiate, stuff **3.** *Inf.* con, grind, mug up (*Sl.*), revise, study, swot, swot up

cramp¹ *v.* check, circumscribe, clog,

confine, constrain, encumber, hamper, hamstring, handicap, hinder, impede, inhibit, obstruct, restrict, shackle, stymie, thwart

cramp² *n.* ache, contraction, convulsion, crick, pain, pang, shooting pain, spasm, stiffness, stitch, twinge

cramped 1. awkward, circumscribed, closed in, confined, congested, crowded, hemmed in, jammed in, narrow, overcrowded, packed, restricted, squeezed, uncomfortable **2.** *Esp. of handwriting* crabbed, indecipherable, irregular, small

cranky bizarre, capricious, eccentric, erratic, freakish, freaky (*Sl.*), funny (*Inf.*), idiosyncratic, odd, peculiar, queer, quirky, strange, wacky (*Sl.*)

cranny breach, chink, cleft, crack, crevice, fissure, gap, hole, interstice, nook, opening

crash *n.* **1.** bang, boom, clang, clash, clatter, clattering, din, racket, smash, smashing, thunder ~*v.* **2.** break, break up, dash to pieces, disintegrate, fracture, fragment, shatter, shiver, smash, splinter **3.** come a cropper (*Inf.*), dash, fall, fall headlong, give way, hurtle, lurch, overbalance, pitch, plunge, precipitate oneself, sprawl, topple **4.** bang, bump (into), collide, crash-land (*an aircraft*), drive into, have an accident, hit, hurtle into, plough into, run together, wreck ~*n.* **5.** accident, bump, collision, jar, jolt, pileup (*Inf.*), prang (*Inf.*), smash, smash-up, thud, thump, wreck **6.** bankruptcy, collapse, debacle, depression, downfall, failure, ruin, smash ~*v.* **7.** be ruined, collapse, fail, fold, fold up, go broke (*Inf.*), go bust (*Inf.*), go under, smash ~*adj.* **8.** *Of a course of studies, etc.* emergency, intensive, immediate, round-the-clock, speeded-up, telescoped, urgent

crass asinine, blundering, boorish, bovine, coarse, dense, doltish, gross, indelicate, insensitive, lumpish, oafish, obtuse, stupid, unrefined, witless

crassness asininity, boorishness, coarseness, denseness, doltishness, grossness, indelicacy, insensitivity, oafishness, stupidity, tactlessness, vulgarity

crate 1. *n.* box, case, container, packing case, tea chest **2.** *v.* box, case, encase, enclose, pack, pack up

crater depression, dip, hollow, shell hole

crave 1. be dying for, cry out for (*Inf.*), desire, fancy (*Inf.*), hanker after, hunger after, long for, lust after, need, pant for, pine for, require, sigh for, thirst for, want, yearn for **2.** ask, beg, beseech, entreat, implore, petition, plead for, pray for, seek, solicit, supplicate

craven 1. *adj.* caitiff (*Archaic*), chicken-hearted, cowardly, dastardly, fearful, lily-livered, mean-spirited, niddering (*Archaic*), pusillanimous, scared, timorous, weak, yellow (*Inf.*) **2.** *n.* base fellow (*Archaic*), caitiff (*Archaic*), coward, dastard (*Archaic*), niddering (*Archaic*), poltroon, recreant (*Archaic*), renegade, wheyface, yellow-belly (*Sl.*)

craving appetite, cacoethes, desire, hankering, hunger, longing, lust, thirst, urge, yearning, yen (*Inf.*)

craw crop, gizzard, gullet, maw, stomach, throat

crawl 1. advance slowly, creep, drag, go on all fours, inch, move at a snail's pace, move on hands and knees, pull *or* drag oneself along, slither, worm one's way, wriggle, writhe **2.** be overrun (alive, full of, lousy), swarm, teem **3.** abase oneself, cringe, fawn, grovel, humble oneself, toady, truckle

craze 1. *n.* enthusiasm, fad, fashion, infatuation, mania, mode, novelty, passion, preoccupation, rage, the latest (*Inf.*), thing, trend, vogue **2.** *v.* bewilder, confuse, dement, derange, distemper, drive mad, enrage, infatuate, inflame, madden, make insane, send crazy *or* berserk, unbalance, unhinge

crazy 1. *Inf.* a bit lacking upstairs (*Inf.*), barmy (*Sl.*), batty (*Sl.*), berserk, bonkers (*Sl.*), cracked (*Sl.*), crazed, cuckoo (*Inf.*), daft (*Sl.*), delirious, demented, deranged, idiotic, insane, lunatic (*Inf. or archaic*), mad, mad as a hatter, mad as a March hare, maniacal, mental (*Sl.*), not all there (*Inf.*), nuts (*Sl.*), nutty (*Sl.*), nutty as a fruitcake (*Inf.*), off one's head (*Sl.*), of unsound mind, potty (*Inf.*), round the bend (*Sl.*), touched, unbalanced, unhinged **2.** bizarre, eccentric, fantastic, odd, outrageous, peculiar, ridiculous, silly, strange, weird **3.** absurd, bird-brained (*Inf.*), cockeyed (*Inf.*), derisory, fatuous, foolhardy, foolish, half-baked (*Inf.*), idiotic, ill-conceived, impracticable, imprudent, inane, inappropriate, irresponsible, ludicrous, nonsensical, potty (*Inf.*), preposterous, puerile, quixotic, senseless, short-sighted, unrealistic, unwise, unworkable, wild **4**. *Inf.* ardent, beside oneself, devoted, eager, enamoured, enthusiastic, fanatical, hysterical, infatuated, mad, passionate, smitten, very keen, wild (*Inf.*), zealous

creak *v.* grate, grind, groan, rasp, scrape, scratch, screech, squeak, squeal

creaky creaking, grating, rasping, raspy, rusty, squeaking, squeaky, unoiled

cream *n.* **1**. cosmetic, emulsion, essence, liniment, lotion, oil, ointment, paste, salve, unguent **2**. best, *crème de la crème*, elite, flower, pick, prime ~*adj.* **3**. off-white, yellowish-white

creamy buttery, creamed, lush, milky, oily, rich, smooth, soft, velvety

crease 1. *v.* corrugate, crimp, crinkle, crumple, double up, fold, pucker, ridge, ruck up, rumple, screw up, wrinkle **2**. *n.* bulge, corrugation, fold, groove, line, overlap, pucker, ridge, ruck, tuck, wrinkle

create 1. beget, bring into being *or* existence, coin, compose, concoct, design, develop, devise, dream up (*Inf.*), form, formulate, generate, give birth to, give life to, hatch, initiate, invent, make, originate, produce, spawn **2**. appoint, constitute, establish, found, install, invest, make, set up **3**. bring about, cause, lead to, occasion

creation 1. conception, formation, generation, genesis, making, procreation, siring **2**. constitution, development, establishment, formation, foundation, inception, institution, laying down, origination, production, setting up **3**. achievement, brainchild (*Inf.*), *chef d'oeuvre*, concept, concoction, handiwork, invention, *magnum opus, pièce de résistance*, production **4**. all living things, cosmos, life, living world, natural world, nature, universe, world

creative artistic, clever, fertile, gifted, imaginative, ingenious, inspired, inventive, original, productive, stimulating, visionary

creativity cleverness, fecundity, fertility, imagination, imaginativeness, ingenuity, inspiration, inventiveness, originality, productivity, talent

creator architect, author, begetter, designer, father, framer, God, initiator, inventor, maker, originator, prime mover

creature 1. animal, beast, being, brute, critter (*U.S. dialect*), dumb animal, living thing, lower animal, quadruped **2**. body, character, fellow, human being, individual, man, mortal, person, soul, wight (*Archaic*), woman **3**. dependant, hanger-on, hireling, instrument (*Inf.*), lackey, minion, puppet, retainer, tool, wretch

credence acceptance, assurance, belief, certainty, confidence, credit, dependence, faith, reliance, trust

credentials attestation, authorization, card, certificate, deed, diploma, docket, letter of recommendation *or* introduction, letters of credence, licence, missive, passport, recommendation, reference(s), testament, testimonial, title, voucher, warrant

credibility believability, believableness, integrity, plausibility, reliability, tenability, trustworthiness

credible 1. believable, conceivable, imaginable, likely, plausible, possible, probable, reasonable, supposable, tenable, thinkable **2**. dependable, honest, reliable, sincere, trustworthy, trusty

credit *n.* **1**. acclaim, acknowledgment, approval, commendation, fame, glory, honour, kudos, merit, praise, recognition, thanks, tribute **2**. character, clout (*Inf.*), esteem, estimation, good name, influence, position, prestige, regard, reputation, repute, standing, status **3**. belief, confidence, credence, faith, reliance, trust **4**. *As in* **be a credit to** feather in one's cap, honour, source of satisfaction *or* pride **5**. **on credit** by deferred payment, by instalments, on account, on hire-purchase, on (the) H.P., on the slate (*Inf.*), on tick (*Inf.*) ~*v.* **6**. *With* **with** accredit, ascribe to, assign to, attribute to, chalk up to (*Inf.*), impute to, refer to **7**. accept, bank on, believe, buy (*Inf.*), depend on, fall for, have faith in, rely on, swallow (*Inf.*), trust

creditable admirable, commendable, deserving, estimable, exemplary, honourable, laudable, meritorious, praiseworthy, reputable, respectable, worthy

credulity blind faith, credulousness, gullibility, naiveté, silliness, simplicity, stupidity

credulous born yesterday (*Inf.*), dupable, green, gullible, naive, overtrusting, trustful, uncritical, unsuspecting, unsuspicious

creed articles of faith, belief, canon, catechism, confession, credo, doctrine, dogma, persuasion, principles, profession (*of faith*), tenet

creek 1. bay, bight, cove, firth *or* frith (*Scot.*), inlet **2.** *U.S., Canadian, & Australian* brook, rivulet, runnel, stream, streamlet, tributary, watercourse

creep *v.* **1.** crawl, crawl on all fours, glide, insinuate, slither, squirm, worm, wriggle, writhe **2.** approach unnoticed, skulk, slink, sneak, steal, tiptoe **3.** crawl, dawdle, drag, edge, inch, proceed at a snail's pace **4.** bootlick (*Inf.*), cower, cringe, fawn, grovel, kowtow, scrape, suck up to (*Inf.*), toady, truckle ~*n.* **5.** *Sl.* bootlicker (*Inf.*), sneak, sycophant, toady **6. give one the creeps** *or* **make one's flesh creep** disgust, frighten, horrify, make one flinch (quail, shrink, squirm, wince), make one's hair stand on end (*Inf.*), repel, repulse, scare, terrify, terrorize

creeper climber, climbing plant, rambler, runner, trailing plant, vine (*Chiefly U.S.*)

creepy awful, direful, disgusting, disturbing, eerie, frightening, ghoulish, goose-pimply (*Inf.*), gruesome, hair-raising, horrible, macabre, menacing, nightmarish, ominous, scary (*Inf.*), sinister, terrifying, threatening, unpleasant, weird

crepitate crack, crackle, rattle, snap

crescent *n.* **1.** half-moon, meniscus, new moon, old moon, sickle, sickle-shape ~*adj.* **2.** bow-shaped, curved, falcate, semicircular, sickle-shaped **3.** *Archaic* growing, increasing, waxing

Crescent, the Islam, Mohammedanism, Muslim Empire, Turkey

crest 1. apex, crown, head, height, highest point, peak, pinnacle, ridge, summit, top **2.** aigrette, caruncle (*Zoology*), cockscomb, comb, crown, mane, panache, plume, tassel, topknot, tuft **3.** *Heraldry* badge, bearings, charge, device, emblem, insignia, symbol

crestfallen chapfallen, dejected, depressed, despondent, disappointed, disconsolate, discouraged, disheartened, downcast, downhearted

crevasse abyss, bergschrund, chasm, cleft, crack, fissure

crevice chink, cleft, crack, cranny, fissure, fracture, gap, hole, interstice, opening, rent, rift, slit, split

crew 1. hands, (ship's) company, (ship's) complement **2.** company, corps,

gang, party, posse, squad, team, working party **3.** *Inf.* assemblage, band, bunch (*Inf.*), company, crowd, gang, herd, horde, lot, mob, pack, set, swarm, troop

crib *n.* **1.** bassinet, bed, cot **2.** bin, box, bunker, manger, rack, stall **3.** *Inf.* key, translation, trot (*U.S. sl.*) ~*v.* **4.** *Inf.* cheat, pass off as one's own work, pilfer, pirate, plagiarize, purloin, steal **5.** box up, cage, confine, coop, coop up, enclose, fence, imprison, limit, pen, rail, restrict, shut in

crick 1. *n.* convulsion, cramp, spasm, twinge **2.** *v.* jar, rick, wrench

crime 1. atrocity, fault, felony, malfeasance, misdeed, misdemeanour, offence, outrage, transgression, trespass, unlawful act, violation, wrong **2.** corruption, delinquency, guilt, illegality, iniquity, lawbreaking, malefaction, misconduct, sin, unrighteousness, vice, villainy, wickedness, wrong, wrongdoing

criminal *n.* **1.** con (*Sl.*), convict, crook (*Inf.*), culprit, delinquent, evildoer, felon, jailbird, lawbreaker, malefactor, offender, sinner, transgressor ~*adj.* **2.** bent (*Sl.*), corrupt, crooked (*Inf.*), culpable, felonious, illegal, illicit, immoral, indictable, iniquitous, lawless, nefarious, peccant (*Rare*), unlawful, unrighteous, vicious, villainous, wicked, wrong **3.** *Inf.* deplorable, foolish, preposterous, ridiculous, scandalous, senseless

criminality corruption, culpability, delinquency, depravity, guiltiness, illegality, sinfulness, turpitude, villainy, wickedness

cringe 1. blench, cower, dodge, draw back, duck, flinch, quail, quiver, recoil, shrink, shy, start, tremble, wince **2.** bend, bootlick (*Inf.*), bow, crawl, creep, crouch, fawn, grovel, kneel, kowtow, sneak, stoop, toady, truckle

crinkle *n./v.* **1.** cockle, crimp, crimple, crumple, curl, fold, pucker, ruffle, rumple, scallop, twist, wrinkle **2.** crackle, hiss, rustle, swish, whisper

crinkly buckled, cockled, curly, fluted, frizzy, furrowed, gathered, kinky, knit, puckered, ruffled, scalloped, wrinkled

cripple *v.* **1.** debilitate, disable, enfeeble, hamstring, incapacitate, lame, maim, mutilate, paralyse, weaken **2.** bring to a standstill, cramp, damage, destroy, halt, impair, put out of action, ruin, spoil, vitiate

crippled bedridden, deformed, disabled, enfeebled, handicapped, house-bound, incapacitated, laid up (*Inf.*), lame, paralysed

crisis 1. climacteric, climax, confrontation, critical point, crunch (*Inf.*), crux, culmination, height, moment of truth, point of no return, turning point 2. catastrophe, critical situation, dilemma, dire straits, disaster, emergency, exigency, extremity, mess, plight, predicament, quandary, strait, trouble

crisp 1. brittle, crispy, crumbly, crunchy, firm, fresh, unwilted 2. bracing, brisk, fresh, invigorating, refreshing 3. brief, brusque, clear, incisive, pithy, short, succinct, tart, terse 4. clean-cut, neat, orderly, smart, snappy, spruce, tidy, trig (*Dialect*), well-groomed, well-pressed

criterion bench mark, canon, gauge, measure, norm, principle, proof, rule, standard, test, touchstone, yardstick

critic 1. analyst, arbiter, authority, commentator, connoisseur, expert, expositor, judge, pundit, reviewer 2. attacker, carper, caviller, censor, censurer, detractor, fault-finder, knocker (*Inf.*), Momus, reviler, vilifier

critical 1. captious, carping, cavilling, censorious, derogatory, disapproving, disparaging, fault-finding, nagging, niggling, nit-picking (*Inf.*) 2. accurate, analytical, diagnostic, discerning, discriminating, fastidious, judicious, penetrating, perceptive, precise 3. all-important, crucial, dangerous, deciding, decisive, grave, hairy (*Sl.*), high-priority, momentous, perilous, pivotal, precarious, pressing, psychological, risky, serious, urgent, vital

criticism 1. animadversion, bad press, brickbats (*Inf.*), censure, critical remarks, disapproval, disparagement, fault-finding, flak (*Inf.*), knocking (*Inf.*), panning (*Inf.*), slam (*Sl.*), slating (*Inf.*), stricture 2. analysis, appraisal, appreciation, assessment, comment, commentary, critique, elucidation, evaluation, judgment, notice, review

criticize 1. animadvert on *or* upon, carp, censure, condemn, disapprove of, disparage, excoriate, find fault with, give (someone *or* something) a bad press, knock (*Inf.*), nag at, pan (*Inf.*), pass strictures upon, pick to pieces, slam (*Sl.*), slate (*Inf.*) 2. analyse, appraise, assess, comment upon, evaluate, give an

opinion, judge, pass judgment on, review

critique analysis, appraisal, assessment, commentary, essay, examination, review

croak *v.* 1. caw, gasp, grunt, squawk, utter *or* speak harshly (huskily, throatily), wheeze 2. *Inf.* complain, groan, grouse, grumble, moan, murmur, mutter, repine 3. *Sl.* die, expire, hop the twig (*Inf.*), kick the bucket (*Inf.*), pass away, perish

crone beldam (*Archaic*), gammer (*Dialect*), hag, old bag (*Derogatory sl.*), old bat (*Sl.*), witch

crony accomplice, ally, associate, buddy (*Inf.*), china (*Sl.*), chum (*Inf.*), colleague, companion, comrade, friend, mate (*Inf.*), pal (*Inf.*), sidekick (*Sl.*)

crook 1. *n. Inf.* cheat, criminal, knave (*Archaic*), racketeer, robber, rogue, shark, swindler, thief, villain 2. *v.* angle, bend, bow, curve, flex, hook

crooked 1. anfractuous, bent, bowed, crippled, curved, deformed, deviating, disfigured, distorted, hooked, irregular, meandering, misshapen, out of shape, tortuous, twisted, twisting, warped, winding, zigzag 2. angled, askew, asymmetric, at an angle, awry, lopsided, off-centre, slanted, slanting, squint, tilted, to one side, uneven, unsymmetrical 3. *Inf.* bent (*Sl.*), corrupt, crafty, criminal, deceitful, dishonest, dishonourable, dubious, fraudulent, illegal, knavish, nefarious, questionable, shady (*Inf.*), shifty, treacherous, underhand, unlawful, unprincipled, unscrupulous

croon breathe, hum, purr, sing, warble

crop *n.* 1. fruits, gathering, harvest, produce, reaping, season's growth, vintage, yield ~*v.* 2. clip, curtail, cut, lop, mow, pare, prune, reduce, shear, shorten, snip, top, trim 3. bring home, bring in, collect, garner, gather, harvest, mow, pick, reap 4. browse, graze, nibble

crop up appear, arise, emerge, happen, occur, spring up, turn up

cross *adj.* 1. angry, annoyed, cantankerous, captious, churlish, crotchety (*Inf.*), crusty, disagreeable, fractious, fretful, grouchy (*Inf.*), grumpy, ill-humoured, ill-tempered, impatient, in a bad mood, irascible, irritable, out of humour, peeved (*Inf.*), peevish, pettish, petulant, put out, querulous, shirty (*Sl.*), short, snappish, snappy, splenetic, sullen, surly, testy, vexed, waspish ~*v.* 2.

bridge, cut across, extend over, ford, meet, pass over, ply, span, traverse, zigzag **3.** crisscross, intersect, intertwine, lace, lie athwart of **4.** blend, crossbreed, cross-fertilize, cross-pollinate, hybridize, interbreed, intercross, mix, mongrelize **5.** block, deny, foil, frustrate, hinder, impede, interfere, obstruct, oppose, resist, thwart ~n. **6.** affliction, burden, grief, load, misery, misfortune, trial, tribulation, trouble, woe, worry **7.** crucifix, rood **8.** crossing, crossroads, intersection, junction **9.** amalgam, blend, combination, crossbreed, cur, hybrid, hybridization, mixture, mongrel, mutt (*Sl.*) ~adj. **10.** crosswise, intersecting, oblique, transverse **11.** adverse, contrary, opposed, opposing, unfavourable **12.** *Involving an interchange* opposite, reciprocal

cross-examine catechize, grill (*Inf.*), interrogate, pump, question, quiz

cross-grained awkward, cantankerous, crabby, difficult, disobliging, ill-natured, morose, peevish, perverse, refractory, stubborn, truculent, wayward

cross out *or* **off** blue-pencil, cancel, delete, eliminate, strike off *or* out

crosspatch bear, crank (*U.S. inf.*), curmudgeon, grump (*Inf.*), kill-joy, scold, shrew, sorehead (*Inf., chiefly U.S.*), sourpuss (*Inf.*)

crosswise, crossways across, aslant, at an angle, athwart, at right angles, awry, crisscross, diagonally, from side to side, on the bias, over, sideways, transversely

crotch crutch, groin

crotchet caprice, fad, fancy, quirk, vagary, whim, whimsy

crotchety awkward, bad-tempered, cantankerous, contrary, crabby, cross, crusty, curmudgeonly, difficult, disagreeable, fractious, grumpy, irritable, obstreperous, peevish, surly, testy

crouch 1. bend down, bow, duck, hunch, kneel, squat, stoop **2.** abase oneself, cower, cringe, fawn, grovel, truckle

crow bluster, boast, brag, exult, flourish, gloat, glory in, strut, swagger, triumph, vaunt

crowd n. **1.** army, assembly, company, concourse, flock, herd, horde, host, mass, mob, multitude, pack, press, rabble, swarm, throng, troupe **2.** bunch (*Inf.*), circle, clique, group, lot, set **3.** attendance, audience, gate, house, spectators ~v. **4.** cluster, congregate, cram, flock, forgather, gather, huddle, mass, muster, press, push, stream, surge, swarm, throng **5.** bundle, congest, cram, pack, pile, squeeze **6.** batter, butt, elbow, jostle, shove **7.** the crowd hoi polloi, masses, mob, people, populace, proletariat, public, rabble, rank and file, riffraff, vulgar herd

crowded busy, congested, cramped, crushed, full, huddled, jam-packed, mobbed, overflowing, packed, populous, swarming, teeming, thronged

crown n. **1.** chaplet, circlet, coronal (*Poetic*), coronet, diadem, tiara **2.** bays, distinction, garland, honour, kudos, laurels, laurel wreath, prize, trophy **3.** emperor, empress, king, monarch, monarchy, queen, *rex*, royalty, ruler, sovereign, sovereignty **4.** acme, apex, crest, head, perfection, pinnacle, summit, tip, top, ultimate, zenith ~v. **5.** adorn, dignify, festoon, honour, invest, reward **6.** be the climax *or* culmination of, cap, complete, consummate, finish, fulfil, perfect, put the finishing touch to, round off, surmount, terminate, top **7.** *Sl.* biff (*Sl.*), box, cuff, hit over the head, punch

crowning adj. climactic, consummate, culminating, final, paramount, sovereign, supreme, ultimate

crucial 1. central, critical, decisive, pivotal, psychological, searching, testing, trying **2.** *Inf.* essential, high-priority, important, momentous, pressing, urgent, vital

crucify 1. execute, harrow, persecute, rack, torment, torture **2.** *Sl.* lampoon, pan (*Inf.*), ridicule, tear to pieces, wipe the floor with (*Inf.*)

crude 1. boorish, coarse, crass, dirty, gross, indecent, lewd, obscene, smutty, tactless, tasteless, uncouth, vulgar **2.** natural, raw, unmilled, unpolished, unprepared, unprocessed, unrefined **3.** clumsy, makeshift, outline, primitive, rough, rough-hewn, rude, rudimentary, sketchy, undeveloped, unfinished, unformed, unpolished

crudely bluntly, clumsily, coarsely, impolitely, indecently, pulling no punches (*Inf.*), roughly, rudely, sketchily, tastelessly, vulgarly

crudity 1. coarseness, crudeness, impropriety, indecency, indelicacy, lewdness, loudness, lowness, obscenity, obtrusiveness, smuttiness, vulgarity **2.**

clumsiness, crudeness, primitiveness, roughness, rudeness

cruel 1. atrocious, barbarous, bitter, bloodthirsty, brutal, brutish, callous, cold-blooded, depraved, excruciating, fell (*Archaic*), ferocious, fierce, flinty, grim, hard, hard-hearted, harsh, heartless, hellish, implacable, inclement, inexorable, inhuman, inhumane, malevolent, painful, poignant, ravening, raw, relentless, remorseless, sadistic, sanguinary, savage, severe, spiteful, stony-hearted, unfeeling, unkind, unnatural, vengeful, vicious **2**. merciless, pitiless, ruthless, unrelenting

cruelly 1. barbarously, brutally, brutishly, callously, ferociously, fiercely, heartlessly, in cold blood, mercilessly, pitilessly, sadistically, savagely, spitefully, unmercifully, viciously **2**. bitterly, deeply, fearfully, grievously, monstrously, mortally, severely

cruelty barbarity, bestiality, bloodthirstiness, brutality, brutishness, callousness, depravity, ferocity, fiendishness, hardheartedness, harshness, heartlessness, inhumanity, mercilessness, murderousness, ruthlessness, sadism, savagery, severity, spite, spitefulness, venom, viciousness

cruise v. **1**. coast, sail, voyage **2**. coast, drift, keep a steady pace, travel along ~n. **3**. boat trip, sail, sea trip, voyage

crumb atom, bit, grain, mite, morsel, particle, scrap, shred, sliver, snippet, *soupçon*, speck

crumble 1. bruise, crumb, crush, fragment, granulate, grind, pound, powder, pulverize, triturate **2**. break up, collapse, come to dust, decay, decompose, degenerate, deteriorate, disintegrate, fall apart, go to pieces (*Inf.*), go to wrack and ruin, moulder, perish, tumble down

crumbly brashy, brittle, friable, powdery, rotted, short (*of pastry*)

crummy cheap, contemptible, half-baked (*Inf.*), inferior, lousy (*Sl.*), miserable, poor, rotten (*Inf.*), rubbishy, second-rate, shoddy, third-rate, trashy, useless, weak, worthless

crumple 1. crease, crush, pucker, rumple, screw up, wrinkle **2**. break down, cave in, collapse, fall, give way, go to pieces

crunch 1. v. champ, chew noisily, chomp, grind, masticate, munch **2**. n. *Inf.* crisis, critical point, crux, emergen-

cy, hour of decision, moment of truth, test

crusade campaign, cause, drive, holy war, jihad, movement, push

crusader advocate, campaigner, champion, reformer

crush v. **1**. bray, break, bruise, comminute, compress, contuse, crease, crumble, crumple, crunch, mash, pound, pulverize, rumple, smash, squeeze, wrinkle **2**. conquer, extinguish, overcome, overpower, overwhelm, put down, quell, stamp out, subdue, vanquish **3**. abash, browbeat, chagrin, dispose of, humiliate, mortify, put down (*Sl.*), quash, shame **4**. embrace, enfold, hug, press, squeeze ~n. **5**. crowd, huddle, jam, party

crust caking, coat, coating, concretion, covering, film, incrustation, layer, outside, scab, shell, skin, surface

crusty 1. brittle, crisp, crispy, friable, hard, short, well-baked, well-done **2**. brusque, cantankerous, captious, choleric, crabby, cross, curt, gruff, ill-humoured, irritable, peevish, prickly, short, short-tempered, snappish, snarling, splenetic, surly, testy, touchy

crux core, decisive point, essence, heart, nub

cry v. **1**. bawl, bewail, blubber, boohoo, greet (*Scot.*), howl one's eyes out, keen, lament, mewl, pule, shed tears, snivel, sob, wail, weep, whimper, whine, whinge (*Inf.*), yowl ~n. **2**. bawling, blubbering, crying, greet (*Scot.*), howl, keening, lament, lamentation, plaint (*Archaic*), snivel, snivelling, sob, sobbing, sorrowing, wailing, weep, weeping ~v. **3**. bawl, bellow, call, call out, ejaculate, exclaim, hail, halloo, holler (*Inf.*), howl, roar, scream, screech, shout, shriek, sing out, vociferate, whoop, yell ~n. **4**. bawl, bellow, call, ejaculation, exclamation, holler (*Inf.*), hoot, howl, outcry, roar, scream, screech, shriek, squawk, whoop, yell, yelp, yoo-hoo ~v. **5**. advertise, announce, bark (*Inf.*), broadcast, bruit, hawk, noise, proclaim, promulgate, publish, trumpet ~n. **6**. announcement, barking (*Inf.*), noising, proclamation, publication ~v. **7**. beg, beseech, clamour, entreat, implore, plead, pray ~n. **8**. appeal, entreaty, petition, plea, prayer, supplication

cry down belittle, decry, denigrate, disparage, run down

cry off back out, beg off, excuse oneself, quit, withdraw, withdraw from

crypt catacomb, tomb, undercroft, vault

cryptic abstruse, ambiguous, apocryphal, arcane, cabbalistic, dark, Delphic, enigmatic, equivocal, esoteric, hidden, mysterious, obscure, occult, oracular, perplexing, puzzling, recondite, secret, vague, veiled

crystallize appear, coalesce, form, harden, materialize, take shape

cub 1. offspring, whelp, young 2. babe (*Inf.*), beginner, fledgling, greenhorn (*Inf.*), lad, learner, puppy, recruit, tenderfoot, trainee, whippersnapper, youngster

cubbyhole 1. den, hideaway, hole, snug 2. compartment, niche, pigeonhole, recess, slot

cuddle canoodle (*Sl.*), clasp, cosset, embrace, fondle, hug, nestle, pet, snuggle

cuddly buxom, cuddlesome, curvaceous, huggable, lovable, plump, soft, warm

cudgel 1. *n.* bastinado, baton, bludgeon, club, cosh, shillelagh, stick, truncheon 2. *v.* bang, baste, batter, beat, bludgeon, cane, cosh, drub, maul, pound, pummel, thrash, thump, thwack

cue catchword, hint, key, nod, prompting, reminder, sign, signal, suggestion

cuff[1] 1. *v.* bat (*Inf.*), beat, belt (*Inf.*), biff (*Sl.*), box, buffet, clap, clobber (*Sl.*), clout (*Inf.*), knock, pummel, punch, slap, smack, thump, whack 2. *n.* belt (*Inf.*), biff (*Sl.*), box, buffet, clout (*Inf.*), knock, punch, rap, slap, smack, thump, whack

cuff[2] **off the cuff** ad lib, extempore, impromptu, improvised, offhand, off the top of one's head, on the spur of the moment, spontaneous, spontaneously, unrehearsed

cul-de-sac blind alley, dead end

cull 1. choose, pick, pluck, select, sift, thin, thin out, winnow 2. amass, collect, gather, glean, pick up

culminate climax, close, come to a climax, come to a head, conclude, end, end up, finish, rise to a crescendo, terminate, wind up (*Inf.*)

culmination acme, apex, apogee, climax, completion, conclusion, consummation, crown, crowning touch, finale, height, *ne plus ultra*, peak, perfection, pinnacle, punch line, summit, top, zenith

culpability answerability, blame, blameworthiness, fault, guilt, liability, responsibility

culpable answerable, at fault, blamable, blameworthy, censurable, found wanting, guilty, in the wrong, liable, reprehensible, sinful, to blame, wrong

culprit criminal, delinquent, evildoer, felon, guilty party, malefactor, miscreant, offender, person responsible, rascal, sinner, transgressor, wrongdoer

cult 1. body, church faction, clique, denomination, faith, following, party, religion, school, sect 2. admiration, craze, devotion, idolization, reverence, veneration, worship

cultivate 1. bring under cultivation, farm, fertilize, harvest, plant, plough, prepare, tend, till, work 2. ameliorate, better, bring on, cherish, civilize, develop, discipline, elevate, enrich, foster, improve, polish, promote, refine, train 3. aid, devote oneself to, encourage, forward, foster, further, help, patronize, promote, pursue, support 4. associate with, butter up, consort with, court, dance attendance upon, run after, seek out, seek someone's company or friendship, take trouble or pains with

cultivation 1. agronomy, farming, gardening, husbandry, planting, ploughing, tillage, tilling, working 2. breeding, civility, civilization, culture, discernment, discrimination, education, enlightenment, gentility, good taste, learning, letters, manners, polish, refinement, taste 3. advancement, advocacy, development, encouragement, enhancement, fostering, furtherance, help, nurture, patronage, promotion, support 4. devotion to, pursuit, study

cultural artistic, broadening, civilizing, developmental, edifying, educational, educative, elevating, enlightening, enriching, humane, humanizing, liberal, liberalizing

culture 1. civilization, customs, life style, mores, society, stage of development, the arts, way of life 2. accomplishment, breeding, education, elevation, enlightenment, erudition, gentility, good taste, improvement, polish, politeness, refinement, urbanity 3. agriculture, agronomy, cultivation, farming, husbandry

cultured accomplished, advanced, educated, enlightened, erudite, genteel, highbrow, knowledgeable, polished, refined, scholarly, urbane, versed, well-bred, well-informed, well-read

culvert channel, conduit, drain, gutter, watercourse

cumbersome awkward, bulky, burdensome, clumsy, cumbrous, embarrassing, heavy, hefty (*Inf.*), incommodious, inconvenient, oppressive, unmanageable, unwieldy, weighty

cumulative accruing, accumulative, aggregate, amassed, collective, heaped, increasing, snowballing

cunning adj. **1**. artful, astute, canny, crafty, devious, foxy, guileful, knowing, Machiavellian, sharp, shifty, shrewd, subtle, tricky, wily ~n. **2**. artfulness, astuteness, craftiness, deceitfulness, deviousness, foxiness, guile, shrewdness, slyness, trickery, wiliness ~adj. **3**. adroit, deft, dexterous, imaginative, ingenious, skilful ~n. **4**. ability, adroitness, art, artifice, cleverness, deftness, dexterity, finesse, ingenuity, skill, subtlety

cup beaker, cannikin, chalice, cupful, demitasse, draught, drink, goblet, potion, teacup, trophy

cupboard ambry (*Obsolete*), cabinet, closet, locker, press

Cupid amoretto, Eros, god of love, love

cupidity acquisitiveness, avarice, avidity, covetousness, graspingness, greed, greediness, hunger, itching, longing, rapaciousness, rapacity, voracity, yearning

cupola dome, onion dome

cur **1**. canine, hound, mongrel, mutt (*Sl.*), stray **2**. blackguard, coward, good-for-nothing, heel (*Inf.*), rat (*Sl.*), rotter (*Sl.*), scoundrel, villain, wretch

curative alleviative, corrective, healing, healthful, health-giving, medicinal, remedial, restorative, salutary, therapeutic, tonic

curb **1**. v. bite back, bridle, check, constrain, contain, control, hinder, impede, inhibit, moderate, muzzle, repress, restrain, restrict, retard, subdue, suppress **2**. n. brake, bridle, check, control, deterrent, limitation, rein, restraint

curdle clot, coagulate, condense, congeal, curd, thicken, turn sour

cure v. **1**. alleviate, correct, ease, heal, help, make better, mend, rehabilitate, relieve, remedy, restore, restore to health ~n. **2**. alleviation, antidote, corrective, healing, medicine, panacea, recovery,

remedy, restorative, specific, treatment ~v. **3**. dry, kipper, pickle, preserve, salt, smoke

cure-all catholicon, elixir, *elixir vitae*, nostrum, panacea

curio antique, bibelot, bygone, collector's item, knick-knack, trinket

curiosity **1**. inquisitiveness, interest, nosiness (*Inf.*), prying, snooping (*Inf.*) **2**. celebrity, freak, marvel, novelty, oddity, phenomenon, rarity, sight, spectacle, wonder **3**. bibelot, bygone, curio, knick-knack, *objet d'art*, trinket

curious **1**. inquiring, inquisitive, interested, puzzled, questioning, searching **2**. inquisitive, meddling, nosy (*Inf.*), peeping, peering, prying, snoopy (*Inf.*) **3**. bizarre, exotic, extraordinary, marvellous, mysterious, novel, odd, peculiar, puzzling, quaint, queer, rare, singular, strange, unconventional, unexpected, unique, unorthodox, unusual, wonderful

curl **1**. v. bend, coil, convolute, corkscrew, crimp, crinkle, crisp, curve, entwine, frizz, loop, meander, ripple, spiral, turn, twine, twirl, twist, wind, wreathe, writhe **2**. n. coil, curlicue, kink, ringlet, spiral, twist, whorl

curly corkscrew, crimped, crimpy, crinkly, crisp, curled, curling, frizzy, fuzzy, kinky, permed, spiralled, waved, wavy, winding

curmudgeon bear, bellyacher (*Sl.*), churl, crosspatch (*Inf.*), grouch (*Inf.*), grouser, grumbler, grump (*Inf.*), malcontent, sourpuss (*Inf.*)

currency **1**. bills, coinage, coins, medium of exchange, money, notes **2**. acceptance, circulation, exposure, popularity, prevalence, publicity, transmission, vogue

current adj. **1**. accepted, circulating, common, common knowledge, customary, general, going around, in circulation, in progress, in the air, in the news, ongoing, popular, present, prevailing, prevalent, rife, widespread **2**. contemporary, fashionable, in, in fashion, in vogue, now (*Inf.*), present-day, trendy (*Inf.*), up-to-date, up-to-the-minute ~n. **3**. course, draught, flow, jet, progression, river, stream, tide **4**. atmosphere, drift, feeling, inclination, mood, tendency, trend, undercurrent

curse n. **1**. blasphemy, expletive, oath, obscenity, swearing, swearword **2**. anathema, ban, denunciation, evil eye, excommunication, execration, imprecation, jinx, malediction, malison (*Archaic*) **3.** affliction, bane, burden, calamity, cross, disaster, evil, misfortune, ordeal, plague, scourge, torment, tribulation, trouble, vexation ~*v*. **4.** be foul-mouthed, blaspheme, cuss (*Inf.*), swear, take the Lord's name in vain, turn the air blue (*Inf.*), use bad language **5.** accurse, anathematize, damn, excommunicate, execrate, fulminate, imprecate **6.** afflict, blight, burden, destroy, doom, plague, scourge, torment, trouble, vex

cursed 1. accursed, bedevilled, blighted, cast out, confounded, damned, doomed, excommunicate, execrable, fey (*Scot.*), foredoomed, ill-fated, star-crossed, unholy, unsanctified, villainous **2.** abominable, damnable, detestable, devilish, fell (*Archaic*), fiendish, hateful, infamous, infernal, loathsome, odious, pernicious, pestilential, vile

cursory brief, careless, casual, desultory, hasty, hurried, offhand, passing, perfunctory, rapid, slapdash, slight, summary, superficial

curt abrupt, blunt, brief, brusque, concise, gruff, offhand, pithy, rude, sharp, short, snappish, succinct, summary, tart, terse, unceremonious, uncivil, ungracious

curtail abbreviate, abridge, contract, cut, cut back, cut short, decrease, dock, lessen, lop, pare down, reduce, retrench, shorten, trim, truncate

curtailment abbreviation, abridgment, contraction, cutback, cutting, cutting short, docking, retrenchment, truncation

curtain 1. *n.* drape (*Chiefly U.S.*), hanging **2.** *v.* conceal, drape, hide, screen, shroud, shut off, shutter, veil

curvaceous bosomy, buxom, comely, curvy, shapely, voluptuous, well-rounded, well-stacked (*Sl.*)

curvature arching, bend, curve, curving, curvity, deflection, flexure, incurvation

curve 1. *v.* arc, arch, bend, bow, coil, hook, inflect, spiral, swerve, turn, twist, wind **2.** *n.* arc, bend, camber, curvature, half-moon, loop, trajectory, turn

curved arced, arched, bent, bowed, crooked, humped, rounded, serpentine, sinuous, sweeping, turned, twisted

cushion 1. *n.* beanbag, bolster, hassock, headrest, pad, pillow, scatter cush-

ion, squab **2.** *v.* bolster, buttress, cradle, dampen, deaden, muffle, pillow, protect, soften, stifle, support, suppress

cushy comfortable, easy, jammy (*Sl.*), soft, undemanding

custodian caretaker, curator, guardian, keeper, overseer, protector, superintendent, warden, warder, watchdog, watchman

custody 1. aegis, auspices, care, charge, custodianship, guardianship, keeping, observation, preservation, protection, safekeeping, supervision, trusteeship, tutelage, ward, watch **2.** arrest, confinement, detention, durance (*Archaic*), duress, imprisonment, incarceration

custom 1. habit, habitude (*Rare*), manner, mode, procedure, routine, way, wont **2.** convention, etiquette, fashion, form, formality, matter of course, observance, observation, policy, practice, praxis, ritual, rule, style, unwritten law, usage, use **3.** customers, patronage, trade

customarily as a rule, commonly, generally, habitually, in the ordinary way, normally, ordinarily, regularly, traditionally, usually

customary accepted, accustomed, acknowledged, common, confirmed, conventional, established, everyday, familiar, fashionable, general, habitual, normal, ordinary, popular, regular, routine, traditional, usual, wonted

customer buyer, client, consumer, habitué, patron, prospect, purchaser, regular (*Inf.*), shopper

customs duty, import charges, tariff, taxes, toll

cut *v.* **1.** chop, cleave, divide, gash, incise, lacerate, nick, notch, penetrate, pierce, score, sever, slash, slice, slit, wound **2.** carve, chip, chisel, chop, engrave, fashion, form, saw, sculpt, sculpture, shape, whittle **3.** clip, dock, fell, gather, hack, harvest, hew, lop, mow, pare, prune, reap, saw down, shave, trim **4.** contract, cut back, decrease, ease up on, lower, rationalize, reduce, slash, slim (down) **5.** abbreviate, abridge, condense, curtail, delete, edit out, excise, precis, shorten **6.** *Often with* **through, off,** *or* **across** bisect, carve, cleave, cross, dissect, divide, interrupt, intersect, part, segment, sever, slice, split, sunder **7.** avoid, cold-shoulder, freeze (someone) out (*Inf., chiefly U.S.*), grieve, hurt, ignore, insult, look straight through (someone), pain, send to Coventry, slight, snub, spurn, sting, turn one's back on, wound ~*n.* **8.** gash, graze, groove, incision, laceration, nick, rent, rip, slash, slit, stroke, wound **9.** cutback, decrease, decrement, diminution, economy, fall, lowering, reduction, saving **10.** *Inf.* chop (*Sl.*), division, kickback (*Chiefly U.S.*), percentage, piece, portion, rake-off (*Sl.*), section, share, slice **11.** configuration, fashion, form, look, mode, shape, style **12. a cut above** *Inf.* better than, higher than, more efficient (capable, competent, reliable, trustworthy, useful) than, superior to **13. cut and dried** *Inf.* automatic, fixed, organized, prearranged, predetermined, settled, sorted out (*Inf.*)

cut along dash (off), fly, go, hurry (away), leave, press on

cutback cut, decrease, economy, lessening, reduction, retrenchment

cut back check, curb, decrease, economize, lessen, lower, prune, reduce, retrench, slash, trim

cut down 1. fell, hew, level, lop, raze **2.** *Sometimes with* **on** decrease, lessen, lower, reduce **3.** dispatch, kill, massacre, mow down, slaughter, slay (*Archaic*) **4. cut (someone) down to size** abash, humiliate, make (someone) look small, take the wind out of (someone's) sails

cut in break in, butt in, interpose, interrupt, intervene, intrude, move in

cut off 1. disconnect, intercept, interrupt, intersect **2.** bring to an end, discontinue, halt, obstruct, suspend **3.** isolate, separate, sever **4.** disinherit, disown, renounce

cut out 1. cease, delete, extract, give up, refrain from, remove, sever, stop **2.** *Inf.* displace, eliminate, exclude, oust, supersede, supplant

cut out for adapted, adequate, competent, designed, equipped, fitted, qualified, suitable, suited

cut-price bargain, cheap, cut-rate (*Chiefly U.S.*), reduced, sale

cutpurse footpad (*Archaic*), mugger, pickpocket, robber, thief

cut short abort, break off, bring to an end, check, halt, interrupt, leave unfinished, postpone, stop, terminate

cutthroat *n.* **1.** assassin, bravo, butcher, executioner, hit man (*Sl.*), homicide, killer, liquidator, murderer, slayer (*Archaic*), thug ~*adj.* **2.** barbarous, bloodthirsty, bloody, cruel, death-dealing, ferocious, homicidal, murderous, savage, thuggish, violent **3.** competitive, dog-eat-dog, fierce, relentless, ruthless, unprincipled

cutting *adj.* **1.** biting, bitter, chill, keen, numbing, penetrating, piercing, raw, sharp, stinging **2.** acid, acrimonious, barbed, bitter, caustic, hurtful, malicious, pointed, sarcastic, sardonic, scathing, severe, trenchant, wounding

cut up *v.* **1.** carve, chop, dice, divide, mince, slice **2.** injure, knife, lacerate, slash, wound **3.** *Inf.* criticize, crucify (*Sl.*), give (someone *or* something) a rough ride, pan (*Inf.*), ridicule, slate (*Inf.*), vilify ~*adj.* **4.** *Inf.* agitated, dejected, desolated, distressed, disturbed, heartbroken, stricken, upset, wretched

cycle aeon, age, circle, era, period, phase, revolution, rotation, round (*of years*)

cyclone hurricane, tempest, tornado, twister (*U.S. inf.*), typhoon, whirlwind

cynic doubter, misanthrope, misanthropist, pessimist, sceptic, scoffer

cynical contemptuous, derisive, distrustful, ironic, misanthropic, misanthropical, mocking, pessimistic, sarcastic, sardonic, sceptical, scoffing, scornful, sneering, unbelieving

cynicism disbelief, doubt, misanthropy, pessimism, sarcasm, sardonicism, scepticism

cynosure attraction, centre, centre of attention, focus, focus of attention, leading light (*Inf.*), point (of attraction), shining example

cyst bleb, blister, growth, sac, vesicle, wen

D

dab v. **1.** blot, daub, pat, stipple, swab, tap, touch, wipe ~n. **2.** bit, dollop (*Inf.*), drop, fleck, pat, smidgen (*Inf.*), smudge, speck, spot **3.** flick, pat, peck, smudge, stroke, tap, touch

dabble 1. dip, guddle (*Scot.*), moisten, paddle, spatter, splash, sprinkle, wet **2.** dally, dip into, play at, potter, tinker, trifle (with)

dabbler amateur, dilettante, potterer, tinkerer, trifler

dab hand ace (*Inf.*), adept, dabster (*Dialect*), expert, past master, wizard

daft 1. absurd, asinine, crazy, dopey (*Sl.*), foolish, giddy, idiotic, inane, scatty (*Inf.*), silly, simple, stupid, witless **2.** crackers (*Sl.*), crazy, demented, deranged, insane, lunatic, mental (*Inf.*), nuts (*Sl.*), nutty (*Sl.*), touched, unhinged **3.** *With* **about** besotted by, crazy (*Inf.*), doting, dotty (*Sl.*), infatuated by, mad, nuts (*Sl.*), nutty (*Inf.*), potty (*Inf.*), sweet on

dagger 1. bayonet, dirk, poniard, skean, stiletto **2.** **at daggers drawn** at enmity, at loggerheads, at odds, at war, on bad terms, up in arms **3.** **look daggers** frown, glare, glower, look black, scowl

daily adj. **1.** circadian, diurnal, everyday, quotidian **2.** common, commonplace, day-to-day, everyday, ordinary, quotidian, regular, routine ~adv. **3.** constantly, day after day, day by day, every day, often, once a day, per diem, regularly

dainty adj. **1.** charming, delicate, elegant, exquisite, fine, graceful, neat, petite, pretty **2.** choice, delectable, delicious, palatable, savoury, tasty, tender, toothsome **3.** choosy, fastidious, finical, finicky, fussy, mincing, nice, particular, refined, scrupulous ~n. **4.** *bonne bouche*, delicacy, fancy, sweetmeat, titbit

dale bottom, coomb, dell, dingle, glen, strath (*Scot.*), vale, valley

dalliance n. **1.** dabbling, dawdling, delay, dilly-dallying (*Inf.*), frittering, frivolling (*Inf.*), idling, loafing, loitering, playing, pottering, procrastination, toying, trifling **2.** *Archaic* amorous play, coquetry, flirtation

dally 1. dawdle, delay, dilly-dally (*Inf.*), fritter away, hang about, linger, loiter, procrastinate, tarry, waste time, while away **2.** *Often with* **with** caress, flirt, fondle, fool around, frivol (*Inf.*), lead on, play, play fast and loose (*Inf.*), tamper, tease, toy, trifle

dam 1. n. barrage, barrier, embankment, hindrance, obstruction, wall **2.** v. barricade, block, block up, check, choke, confine, hold back, hold in, obstruct, restrict

damage n. **1.** destruction, detriment, devastation, harm, hurt, impairment, injury, loss, mischief, mutilation, suffering **2.** *Inf.* bill, charge, cost, expense, total **3.** *Plural* compensation, fine, indemnity, reimbursement, reparation, satisfaction ~v. **4.** deface, harm, hurt, impair, incapacitate, injure, mar, mutilate, ruin, spoil, tamper with, weaken, wreck

damaging deleterious, detrimental, disadvantageous, harmful, hurtful, injurious, prejudicial, ruinous

dame baroness, dowager, *grande dame*, lady, matron (*Archaic*), noblewoman, peeress

damn v. **1.** blast, castigate, censure, condemn, criticize, denounce, denunciate, excoriate, inveigle against, pan (*Inf.*), slam (*Sl.*), slate (*Inf.*) **2.** abuse, anathematize, blaspheme, curse, execrate, imprecate, revile, swear **3.** condemn, doom, sentence ~n. **4.** brass farthing, hoot, iota, jot, tinker's damn (*Sl.*), two hoots, whit **5.** **not give a damn** be indifferent, not care, not mind

damnable abominable, accursed, atrocious, culpable, cursed, despicable, detestable, execrable, hateful, horrible, offensive, wicked

damnation anathema, ban, condemnation, consigning to perdition, damning, denunciation, doom, excommunication, objurgation, proscription, sending to hell

damned 1. accursed, anathematized, condemned, doomed, infernal, lost, reprobate, unhappy **2.** *Sl.* confounded, despicable, detestable, hateful, infamous, infernal, loathsome, revolting

damning accusatorial, condemnatory, damnatory, dooming, implicating, implicative, incriminating

damp *n.* **1.** clamminess, dampness, darkness, dew, drizzle, fog, humidity, mist, moisture, muzziness, vapour ~*adj.* **2.** clammy, dank, dewy, dripping, drizzly, humid, misty, moist, muggy, sodden, soggy, sopping, vaporous, wet ~*v.* **3.** dampen, moisten, wet **4.** *Fig.* allay, check, chill, cool, curb, dash, deaden, deject, depress, diminish, discourage, dispirit, dull, inhibit, moderate, restrain, stifle ~*n.* **5.** *Fig.* check, chill, cold water, curb, damper, discouragement, gloom, restraint, wet blanket

dampen **1.** bedew, besprinkle, make damp, moisten, spray, wet **2.** *Fig.* check, dash, deaden, depress, deter, dishearten, dismay, dull, lessen, moderate, muffle, reduce, restrain, smother, stifle

damper chill, cloud, cold water, curb, discouragement, gloom, hindrance, killjoy, pall, restraint, wet blanket

dance **1.** *v.* bob up and down, caper, frolic, gambol, hop, jig, prance, rock, skip, spin, sway, swing, whirl **2.** *n.* ball, dancing party, hop (*Inf.*), social

dandle amuse, caress, cradle, cuddle, dance, fondle, give a knee ride, pet, rock, toss, toy (with)

dandy **1.** *n.* beau, blade (*Archaic*), blood (*Rare*), buck (*Archaic*), coxcomb, exquisite (*Obsolete*), fop, macaroni (*Archaic*), man about town, peacock, popinjay, swell (*Inf.*), toff (*Sl.*) **2.** *adj. Inf.* capital, excellent, fine, first-rate, great, splendid

danger endangerment, hazard, insecurity, jeopardy, menace, peril, precariousness, risk, threat, venture, vulnerability

dangerous alarming, breakneck, chancy (*Inf.*), exposed, hairy (*Sl.*), hazardous, insecure, menacing, nasty, parlous (*Archaic*), perilous, precarious, risky, threatening, treacherous, ugly, unchancy (*Scot.*), unsafe, vulnerable

dangerously **1.** alarmingly, carelessly, daringly, desperately, harmfully, hazardously, perilously, precariously, recklessly, riskily, unsafely, unsecurely **2.** critically, gravely, seriously, severely

dangle *v.* **1.** depend, flap, hang, hang down, sway, swing, trail **2.** brandish, en-

tice, flaunt, flourish, lure, tantalize, tempt, wave

dangling disconnected, drooping, hanging, loose, swaying, swinging, trailing, unconnected

dank chilly, clammy, damp, dewy, dripping, moist, slimy, soggy

dapper active, brisk, chic, dainty, natty (*Inf.*), neat, nice, nimble, smart, spruce, spry, stylish, trig (*Archaic*), trim, well-groomed, well turned out

dapple *v.* bespeckle, dot, fleck, freckle, mottle, spot, stipple

dappled brindled, checkered, flecked, freckled, mottled, piebald, pied, speckled, spotted, stippled, variegated

dare *v.* **1.** challenge, defy, goad, provoke, taunt, throw down the gauntlet **2.** adventure, brave, endanger, gamble, hazard, make bold, presume, risk, stake, venture ~*n.* **3.** challenge, defiance, provocation, taunt

daredevil **1.** *n.* adventurer, desperado, exhibitionist, madcap, show-off (*Inf.*), stunt man **2.** *adj.* adventurous, audacious, bold, daring, death-defying, madcap, reckless

daring **1.** *adj.* adventurous, audacious, bold, brave, fearless, game (*Inf.*), impulsive, intrepid, plucky, rash, reckless, valiant, venturesome **2.** *n.* audacity, boldness, bottle (*Sl.*), bravery, courage, derring-do (*Archaic*), fearlessness, grit, guts (*Inf.*), intrepidity, nerve (*Inf.*), pluck, rashness, spirit, spunk (*Inf.*), temerity

dark *adj.* **1.** black, brunette, darkskinned, dusky, ebony, sable, swarthy **2.** cloudy, darksome (*Literary*), dim, dingy, indistinct, murky, overcast, pitch-black, pitchy, shadowy, shady, sunless, unlit **3.** abstruse, arcane, concealed, cryptic, deep, enigmatic, hidden, mysterious, mystic, obscure, occult, puzzling, recondite, secret **4.** bleak, cheerless, dismal, doleful, drab, gloomy, grim, joyless, morbid, morose, mournful, sombre **5.** benighted, ignorant, uncultivated, unenlightened, unlettered **6.** atrocious, damnable, evil, foul, hellish, horrible, infamous, infernal, nefarious, satanic, sinful, sinister, vile, wicked **7.** angry, dour, forbidding, frowning, glowering, glum, ominous, scowling, sulky, sullen, threatening ~*n.* **8.** darkness, dimness, dusk, gloom, murk, murkiness, obscurity, semidarkness **9.** evening, night, nightfall, night-time, twilight **10**. *Fig.* concealment, ignorance, secrecy

darken 1. becloud, blacken, cloud up *or* over, deepen, dim, eclipse, make dark, make darker, make dim, obscure, overshadow, shade, shadow **2**. become angry, become gloomy, blacken, cast a pall over, cloud, deject, depress, dispirit, grow troubled, look black, sadden

darkling 1. *adj.* black, dark, darksome (*Literary*), dim, dusky, gloomy, pitchy, shadowy, tenebrous **2**. *adv.* at *or* by night, in the dark, in the dead of night, in the night

darkness 1. blackness, dark, dimness, dusk, duskiness, gloom, murk, murkiness, nightfall, obscurity, shade, shadiness, shadows **2**. *Fig.* blindness, concealment, ignorance, mystery, privacy, secrecy, unawareness

darling *n.* **1**. beloved, dear, dearest, love, sweetheart, truelove **2**. apple of one's eye, blue-eyed boy, fair-haired boy (*U.S.*), favourite, pet, spoiled child ~*adj.* **3**. adored, beloved, cherished, dear, precious, treasured **4**. adorable, attractive, captivating, charming, enchanting, lovely, sweet

darn 1. *v.* cobble up, mend, patch, repair, sew up, stitch **2**. *n.* invisible repair, mend, patch, reinforcement

dart 1. bound, dash, flash, flit, fly, race, run, rush, scoot, shoot, spring, sprint, start, tear, whistle (*Inf.*), whiz **2**. cast, fling, hurl, launch, propel, send, shoot, sling, throw

dash *v.* **1**. break, crash, destroy, shatter, shiver, smash, splinter **2**. cast, fling, hurl, slam, sling, throw **3**. bolt, bound, dart, fly, haste, hasten, hurry, race, run, rush, speed, spring, sprint, tear **4**. abash, chagrin, confound, dampen, disappoint, discomfort, discourage **5**. blight, foil, frustrate, ruin, spoil, thwart ~*n.* **6**. bolt, dart, haste, onset, race, run, rush, sortie, sprint, spurt **7**. brio, élan, flair, flourish, panache, spirit, style, verve, vigour, vivacity **8**. bit, drop, flavour, hint, little, pinch, smack, *soupçon*, sprinkling, suggestion, tinge, touch

dashing 1. bold, daring, debonair, exuberant, gallant, lively, plucky, spirited, swashbuckling **2**. dapper, dazzling, elegant, flamboyant, jaunty, showy, smart, sporty, stylish, swish (*Inf.*)

dastard *n.* caitiff (*Archaic*), coward, craven, niddering (*Archaic*), poltroon, recreant (*Archaic*), renegade, sneak, traitor, worm

dastardly *adj.* base, caitiff (*Archaic*), contemptible, cowardly, craven, despicable, faint-hearted, low, mean, niddering (*Archaic*), recreant (*Archaic*), sneaking, sneaky, spiritless, underhand, vile, weakkneed (*Inf.*)

data details, documents, facts, figures, information, input, materials, statistics

date *n.* **1**. age, epoch, era, period, stage, time **2**. appointment, assignation, engagement, meeting, rendezvous, tryst **3**. escort, friend, partner, steady (*Inf.*) **4**. **out of date** antiquated, archaic, dated, obsolete, old, old-fashioned, passé **5**. **to date** now, so far, up to now, up to the present, up to this point, yet **6**. **up-to-date** à la mode, contemporary, current, fashionable, modern, trendy (*Inf.*), up-to-the-minute ~*v.* **7**. assign a date to, determine the date of, fix the period of, put a date on **8**. bear a date, belong to, come from, exist from, originate in **9**. become obsolete, be dated, obsolesce, show one's age

dated antiquated, archaic, démodé, obsolete, old-fashioned, old hat, out, outdated, outmoded, out of date, passé, unfashionable

daub *v.* **1**. coat, cover, paint, plaster, slap on (*Inf.*), smear **2**. bedaub, begrime, besmear, blur, deface, dirty, grime, smirch, smudge, spatter, splatter, stain, sully ~*n.* **3**. blot, blotch, smear, splodge, splotch, spot, stain

daunt 1. alarm, appal, cow, dismay, frighten, frighten off, intimidate, overawe, scare, subdue, terrify **2**. deter, discourage, dishearten, dispirit, put off, shake

daunted *adj.* alarmed, cowed, demoralized, deterred, discouraged, disillusioned, dismayed, dispirited, downcast, frightened, hesitant, intimidated, overcome, put off, unnerved

dauntless bold, brave, courageous, daring, doughty, fearless, gallant, heroic, indomitable, intrepid, lion-hearted, resolute, stouthearted, undaunted, unflinching, valiant, valorous

dawdle dally, delay, dilly-dally (*Inf.*), fritter away, hang about, idle, lag, loaf, loiter, potter, trail, waste time

dawdler laggard, lingerer, loiterer, slowcoach (*Inf.*), snail, tortoise

dawn *n.* **1**. aurora (*Literary*), cockcrow, crack of dawn, dawning, daybreak, daylight, dayspring (*Poetic*), morning, sunrise, sunup ~*v*. **2**. break, brighten, gleam, glimmer, grow light, lighten ~*n*. **3**. advent, beginning, birth, dawning, emergence, genesis, inception, onset, origin, outset, rise, start, unfolding ~*v*. **4**. appear, begin, develop, emerge, initiate, open, originate, rise, unfold **5**. come into one's head, come to mind, cross one's mind, flash across one's mind, hit, occur, register (*Inf*.), strike

day 1. daylight, daylight hours, daytime, twenty-four hours, working day **2**. age, ascendancy, cycle, epoch, era, generation, height, heyday, period, prime, time, zenith **3**. date, particular day, point in time, set time, time **4**. **call it a day** *Inf*. end, finish, knock off (*Inf*.), leave off, pack it in (*Sl*.), pack up (*Inf*.), shut up shop, stop **5**. **day after day** continually, monotonously, persistently, regularly, relentlessly **6**. **day by day** daily, gradually, progressively, steadily

daybreak break of day, cockcrow, crack of dawn, dawn, dayspring (*Poetic*), first light, morning, sunrise, sunup

daydream *n*. **1**. dream, imagining, musing, reverie, stargazing, vision, woolgathering **2**. castle in the air *or* in Spain, dream, fancy, fantasy, figment of the imagination, fond hope, pipe dream, wish ~*v*. **3**. dream, envision, fancy, fantasize, hallucinate, imagine, muse, stargaze

daydreamer castle-builder, dreamer, fantast, pipe dreamer, visionary, Walter Mitty, wishful thinker, woolgatherer

daylight 1. light of day, sunlight, sunshine **2**. broad day, daylight hours, daytime **3**. full view, light of day, openness, public attention

daze *v*. **1**. benumb, numb, paralyse, shock, stun, stupefy **2**. amaze, astonish, astound, befog, bewilder, blind, confuse, dazzle, dumbfound, flabbergast (*Inf*.), perplex, stagger, startle, surprise ~*n*. **3**. bewilderment, confusion, distraction, shock, stupor, trance, trancelike state

dazed baffled, bemused, bewildered, confused, disorientated, dizzy, dopey (*Sl*.), flabbergasted (*Inf*.), fuddled, groggy (*Inf*.), light-headed, muddled, nonplussed, numbed, perplexed, punch-drunk, shocked, staggered, stunned, stupefied, woozy (*Inf*.)

dazzle *v*. **1**. bedazzle, blind, blur, confuse, daze **2**. amaze, astonish, awe, bowl over (*Inf*.), fascinate, hypnotize, impress, overawe, overpower, overwhelm, strike dumb, stupefy ~*n*. **3**. brilliance, flash, glitter, magnificence, razzle-dazzle (*Sl*.), razzmatazz (*Sl*.), sparkle, splendour

dazzling brilliant, glittering, glorious, radiant, ravishing, scintillating, sensational, shining, sparkling, splendid, stunning, sublime, superb, virtuoso

dead *adj*. **1**. deceased, defunct, departed, extinct, gone, inanimate, late, lifeless, passed away, perished **2**. apathetic, callous, cold, dull, frigid, glassy, glazed, indifferent, inert, lukewarm, numb, paralysed, spiritless, torpid, unresponsive, wooden **3**. barren, inactive, inoperative, not working, obsolete, stagnant, sterile, still, unemployed, unprofitable, useless **4**. boring, dead-and-alive, dull, flat, insipid, stale, tasteless, uninteresting, vapid **5**. *Fig*. absolute, complete, downright, entire, outright, thorough, total, unqualified, utter **6**. *Inf*. dead beat (*Inf*.), exhausted, spent, tired, worn out ~*n*. **7**. depth, middle, midst ~*adv*. **8**. absolutely, completely, directly, entirely, exactly, totally

deaden abate, alleviate, anaesthetize, benumb, blunt, check, cushion, damp, dampen, diminish, dull, hush, impair, lessen, muffle, mute, numb, paralyse, quieten, reduce, smother, stifle, suppress, weaken

deadlock cessation, dead heat, draw, full stop, halt, impasse, stalemate, standoff, standstill, tie

deadly 1. baleful, baneful, dangerous, death-dealing, deathly, destructive, fatal, lethal, malignant, mortal, noxious, pernicious, poisonous, venomous **2**. cruel, grim, implacable, mortal, ruthless, savage, unrelenting **3**. ashen, deathlike, deathly, ghastly, ghostly, pallid, wan, white **4**. accurate, effective, exact, on target, precise, sure, true, unerring, unfailing **5**. *Inf*. boring, dull, monotonous, tedious, uninteresting, wearisome

deadpan blank, empty, expressionless, impassive, inexpressive, inscrutable, poker-faced, straight-faced

deaf *adj*. **1**. hard of hearing, stone deaf, without hearing **2**. indifferent, oblivious, unconcerned, unhearing, unmoved

deafen din, drown out, make deaf, split *or* burst the eardrums

deafening booming, dinning, earpiercing, ear-splitting, intense, overpowering, piercing, resounding, ringing, thunderous

deal *v.* **1.** *With* **with** attend to, cope with, handle, manage, oversee, see to, take care of, treat **2.** *With* **with** concern, consider, treat (of) **3.** *With* **with** act, behave, conduct oneself **4.** bargain, buy and sell, do business, negotiate, sell, stock, trade, traffic, treat (with) ~*n.* **5.** *Inf.* agreement, arrangement, bargain, buy (*Inf.*), contract, pact, transaction, understanding ~*v.* **6.** allot, apportion, assign, bestow, dispense, distribute, divide, dole out, give, mete out, reward, share ~*n.* **7.** amount, degree, distribution, extent, portion, quantity, share, transaction **8.** cut and shuffle, distribution, hand, round, single game

dealer chandler, marketer, merchandiser, merchant, trader, tradesman, wholesaler

dealings business, business relations, commerce, trade, traffic, transactions, truck

dear *adj.* **1.** beloved, cherished, close, darling, esteemed, familiar, favourite, intimate, precious, prized, respected, treasured **2.** at a premium, costly, expensive, high-priced, overpriced, pricey (*Inf.*) ~*n.* **3.** angel, beloved, darling, loved one, precious, treasure ~*adv.* **4.** at a heavy cost, at a high price, at great cost, dearly

dearly 1. extremely, greatly, profoundly, very much **2.** affectionately, devotedly, fondly, lovingly, tenderly **3.** at a heavy cost, at a high price, at great cost, dear

dearth absence, deficiency, exiguousness, famine, inadequacy, insufficiency, lack, need, paucity, poverty, scantiness, scarcity, shortage, sparsity, want

death 1. bereavement, cessation, curtains (*Inf.*), decease, demise, departure, dissolution, dying, end, exit, expiration, loss, passing, quietus, release **2.** annihilation, destruction, downfall, eradication, extermination, extinction, finish, grave, obliteration, ruin, ruination, undoing

deathless eternal, everlasting, immortal, imperishable, incorruptible, timeless, undying

deathly 1. cadaverous, deathlike, gaunt, ghastly, grim, haggard, pale, pallid, wan **2.** deadly, extreme, fatal, intense, mortal, terrible

debacle catastrophe, collapse, defeat, devastation, disaster, downfall, fiasco, havoc, overthrow, reversal, rout, ruin, ruination

debar bar, blackball, deny, exclude, hinder, keep out, obstruct, preclude, prevent, prohibit, refuse admission to, restrain, segregate, shut out, stop

debase 1. abase, cheapen, degrade, demean, devalue, disgrace, dishonour, drag down, humble, humiliate, lower, reduce, shame **2.** adulterate, bastardize, contaminate, corrupt, defile, depreciate, impair, pollute, taint, vitiate

debased 1. adulterated, depreciated, devalued, impure, lowered, mixed, polluted, reduced **2.** abandoned, base, corrupt, debauched, degraded, depraved, fallen, low, perverted, sordid, vile

debasement 1. adulteration, contamination, depreciation, devaluation, pollution, reduction **2.** abasement, baseness, corruption, degradation, depravation, perversion

debatable arguable, borderline, controversial, disputable, doubtful, dubious, in dispute, moot, open to question, problematical, questionable, uncertain, undecided, unsettled

debate *v.* **1.** argue, contend, contest, controvert, discuss, dispute, question, wrangle ~*n.* **2.** altercation, argument, contention, controversy, discussion, disputation, dispute, polemic ~*v.* **3.** cogitate, consider, deliberate, meditate upon, mull over, ponder, reflect, revolve, ruminate, weigh ~*n.* **4.** cogitation, consideration, deliberation, meditation, reflection

debauch *v.* **1.** corrupt, demoralize, deprave, lead astray, pervert, pollute, seduce, subvert, vitiate **2.** deflower, ravish, ruin, seduce, violate ~*n.* **3.** bacchanalia, bender (*Inf.*), binge (*Inf.*), bout, fling, orgy, saturnalia, spree

debauched abandoned, corrupt, debased, degenerate, degraded, depraved, dissipated, dissolute, immoral, licentious, perverted, profligate, wanton

debauchee libertine, Lothario, playboy, profligate, rake, roué, sensualist, wanton

debauchery carousal, depravity, dissipation, dissoluteness, excess, gluttony, incontinence, indulgence, intemperance, lewdness, licentiousness, lust, orgy, overindulgence, revel

debilitate devitalize, enervate, enfeeble, exhaust, incapacitate, prostrate, relax, sap, undermine, weaken, wear out

debility decrepitude, enervation, enfeeblement, exhaustion, faintness, feebleness, frailty, incapacity, infirmity, languor, malaise, sickliness, weakness

debonair affable, buoyant, charming, cheerful, courteous, dashing, elegant, jaunty, light-hearted, refined, smooth (*Inf.*), sprightly, suave, urbane, wellbred

debouch come forth, come out, come out in the open, disembogue, emerge, issue, sally, sortie

debrief 1. cross-examine, examine, interrogate, probe, question, quiz 2. describe, detail, report

debris bits, brash, detritus, dross, fragments, litter, pieces, remains, rubbish, rubble, ruins, waste, wreck, wreckage

debt 1. arrears, bill, claim, commitment, debit, due, duty, liability, obligation, score 2. **in debt** accountable, beholden, in arrears, in hock (*Inf., chiefly U.S.*), in the red (*Inf.*), liable, owing, responsible

debtor borrower, defaulter, insolvent, mortgagor

debunk cut down to size, deflate, disparage, expose, lampoon, mock, puncture, ridicule, show up

debut beginning, bow, coming out, entrance, first appearance, inauguration, initiation, introduction, launching, presentation

decadence corruption, debasement, decay, decline, degeneration, deterioration, dissipation, dissolution, fall, perversion, retrogression

decadent corrupt, debased, debauched, decaying, declining, degenerate, degraded, depraved, dissolute, immoral, self-indulgent

decamp 1. abscond, bolt, desert, do a bunk (*Sl.*), escape, flee, flit (*Inf.*), fly, hightail (*Inf., chiefly U.S.*), make off, run away, scarper (*Sl.*), skedaddle (*Inf.*), sneak off, steal away 2. break up camp, evacuate, march off, move off, strike camp, vacate

decant drain, draw off, pour out, tap

decapitate behead, execute, guillotine

decay *v.* 1. atrophy, crumble, decline, degenerate, deteriorate, disintegrate, dissolve, dwindle, moulder, shrivel, sink,

spoil, wane, waste away, wear away, wither 2. corrode, decompose, mortify, perish, putrefy, rot ~*n.* 3. atrophy, collapse, decadence, decline, degeneracy, degeneration, deterioration, dying, fading, failing, wasting, withering 4. caries, cariosity, decomposition, gangrene, mortification, perishing, putrefaction, putrescence, putridity, rot, rotting

decayed bad, carious, carrion, corroded, decomposed, perished, putrefied, putrid, rank, rotten, spoiled, wasted, withered

decaying crumbling, deteriorating, disintegrating, gangrenous, perishing, putrefacient, rotting, wasting away, wearing away

decease 1. *n.* death, demise, departure, dissolution, dying, release 2. *v.* cease, die, expire, pass away *or* on *or* over, perish

deceased *adj.* dead, defunct, departed, expired, finished, former, gone, late, lifeless, lost

deceit 1. artifice, cheating, chicanery, craftiness, cunning, deceitfulness, deception, dissimulation, double-dealing, duplicity, fraud, fraudulence, guile, hypocrisy, imposition, pretence, slyness, treachery, trickery, underhandedness 2. artifice, blind, cheat, chicanery, deception, duplicity, fake, feint, fraud, imposture, misrepresentation, pretence, ruse, sham, shift, stratagem, subterfuge, swindle, trick, wile

deceitful counterfeit, crafty, deceiving, deceptive, designing, dishonest, disingenuous, double-dealing, duplicitous, fallacious, false, fraudulent, guileful, hypocritical, illusory, insincere, knavish (*Archaic*), sneaky, treacherous, tricky, two-faced, underhand, untrustworthy

deceive 1. bamboozle (*Inf.*), beguile, betray, cheat, con (*Sl.*), cozen, delude, disappoint, double-cross (*Inf.*), dupe, ensnare, entrap, fool, hoax, hoodwink, impose upon, lead (someone) on (*Inf.*), mislead, outwit, pull a fast one (*Sl.*), pull the wool over (someone's) eyes, swindle, take for a ride (*Inf.*), take in (*Inf.*), trick 2. **be deceived by** be made a fool of, be taken in (by), be the dupe of, bite, fall for, fall into a trap, swallow, swallow hook, line, and sinker (*Inf.*), take the bait

deceiver betrayer, charlatan, cheat, con man (*Inf.*), cozener, crook (*Inf.*), deluder, dissembler, double-dealer, fake, fraud, hypocrite, impostor, inveigler, mountebank, pretender, sharper, swindler, trickster

decency appropriateness, civility, correctness, courtesy, decorum, etiquette, fitness, good form, good manners, modesty, propriety, respectability, seemliness

decent 1. appropriate, becoming, befitting, chaste, comely, *comme il faut*, decorous, delicate, fit, fitting, modest, nice, polite, presentable, proper, pure, respectable, seemly, suitable **2.** acceptable, adequate, ample, average, competent, fair, passable, reasonable, satisfactory, sufficient, tolerable **3.** accommodating, courteous, friendly, generous, gracious, helpful, kind, obliging, thoughtful

deception 1. craftiness, cunning, deceit, deceitfulness, deceptiveness, dissimulation, duplicity, fraud, fraudulence, guile, hypocrisy, imposition, insincerity, legerdemain, treachery, trickery **2.** artifice, bluff, cheat, decoy, feint, fraud, hoax, illusion, imposture, leg-pull (*Brit. inf.*), lie, ruse, sham, snare, stratagem, subterfuge, trick, wile

deceptive ambiguous, deceitful, delusive, dishonest, fake, fallacious, false, fraudulent, illusory, misleading, mock, specious, spurious, unreliable

decide adjudge, adjudicate, choose, come to a conclusion, commit oneself, conclude, decree, determine, elect, end, make a decision, make up one's mind, purpose, reach *or* come to a decision, resolve, settle

decided 1. absolute, categorical, certain, clear-cut, definite, distinct, express, indisputable, positive, pronounced, unambiguous, undeniable, undisputed, unequivocal, unquestionable **2.** assertive, decisive, deliberate, determined, emphatic, firm, resolute, strong-willed, unfaltering, unhesitating

decidedly absolutely, certainly, clearly, decisively, distinctly, downright, positively, unequivocally, unmistakably

deciding chief, conclusive, critical, crucial, decisive, determining, influential, prime, principal, significant

decipher construe, crack, decode, deduce, explain, figure out (*Inf.*), interpret, make out, read, reveal, solve, understand, unfold, unravel

decision 1. arbitration, conclusion,

finding, judgment, outcome, resolution, result, ruling, sentence, settlement, verdict **2.** decisiveness, determination, firmness, purpose, purposefulness, resoluteness, resolution, resolve, strength of mind *or* will

decisive 1. absolute, conclusive, critical, crucial, definite, definitive, fateful, final, influential, momentous, positive, significant **2.** decided, determined, firm, forceful, incisive, resolute, strong-minded, trenchant

deck *v.* **1.** adorn, apparel (*Archaic*), array, attire, beautify, bedeck, bedight (*Archaic*), bedizen (*Archaic*), clothe, decorate, dress, embellish, festoon, garland, grace, ornament, trim **2. deck up** *or* **out** doll up (*Sl.*), prettify, pretty up, prink, rig out, tog up *or* out, trick out

declaim 1. harangue, hold forth, lecture, orate, perorate, proclaim, rant, recite, speak, spiel (*Inf.*) **2. declaim against** attack, decry, denounce, inveigh, rail

declamation address, harangue, lecture, oration, rant, recitation, speech, tirade

declamatory bombastic, discursive, grandiloquent, high-flown, incoherent, inflated, magniloquent, orotund, pompous, rhetorical, stagy, stilted, theatrical, turgid

declaration 1. acknowledgment, affirmation, assertion, attestation, averment, avowal, deposition, disclosure, protestation, revelation, statement, testimony **2.** announcement, edict, manifesto, notification, proclamation, profession, promulgation, pronouncement, pronunciamento

declarative, declaratory affirmative, definite, demonstrative, enunciatory, explanatory, expository, expressive, positive

declare 1. affirm, announce, assert, attest, aver, avow, certify, claim, confirm, maintain, proclaim, profess, pronounce, state, swear, testify, validate **2.** confess, convey, disclose, make known, manifest, reveal, show

declension 1. decadence, decay, decline, degeneracy, descent, deterioration, diminution, fall **2.** inflection, variation

declination decline, declivity, descent, deviation, dip, divergence, inclination, obliquity, slope

decline *v.* **1.** avoid, deny, forgo, refuse, reject, say 'no', send one's regrets, turn down **2.** decrease, diminish, dwindle, ebb, fade, fail, fall, fall off, flag, lessen, shrink, sink, wane ~*n.* **3.** abatement, diminution, downturn, dwindling, falling off, lessening, recession, slump ~*v.* **4.** decay, degenerate, ˙deteriorate, droop, languish, pine, weaken, worsen ~*n.* **5.** decay, decrepitude, degeneration, deterioration, enfeeblement, failing, senility, weakening, worsening **6.** *Archaic* consumption, phthisis, tuberculosis ~*v.* **7.** descend, dip, sink, slant, slope ~*n.* **8.** declivity, hill, incline, slope

declivity brae (*Scot.*), declination, descent, incline, slant, slope

decompose 1. break up, crumble, decay, fall apart, fester, putrefy, rot, spoil **2.** analyse, atomize, break down, break up, decompound, disintegrate, dissect, dissolve, distil, separate

decomposition atomization, breakdown, corruption, decay, disintegration, dissolution, division, putrefaction, putrescence, putridity, rot

décor colour scheme, decoration, furnishing style, ornamentation

decorate 1. adorn, beautify, bedeck, deck, embellish, enrich, grace, ornament, trim **2.** colour, do up (*Inf.*), furbish, paint, paper, renovate, wallpaper **3.** cite, honour, pin a medal on

decoration 1. adornment, beautification, elaboration, embellishment, enrichment, garnishing, ornamentation, trimming **2.** arabesque, bauble, curlicue, falderal, flounce, flourish, frill, furbelow, garnish, ornament, scroll, spangle, trimmings, trinket **3.** award, badge, colours, emblem, garter, medal, order, ribbon, star

decorative adorning, arty-crafty, beautifying, enhancing, fancy, nonfunctional, ornamental, pretty

decorous appropriate, becoming, befitting, comely, *comme il faut*, correct, decent, dignified, fit, mannerly, polite, proper, refined, sedate, seemly, staid, suitable, well-behaved

decorum behaviour, breeding, courtliness, decency, deportment, dignity, etiquette, gentility, good grace, good manners, gravity, politeness, politesse, propriety, protocol, punctilio, respectability, seemliness

decoy 1. *n.* attraction, bait, ensnarement, enticement, inducement, lure, pretence, trap **2.** *v.* allure, bait, deceive, en-

snare, entice, entrap, inveigle, lure, seduce, tempt

decrease 1. *v.* abate, contract, curtail, cut down, decline, diminish, drop, dwindle, ease, fall off, lessen, lower, peter out, reduce, shrink, slacken, subside, wane **2.** *n.* abatement, contraction, cutback, decline, diminution, downturn, dwindling, ebb, falling off, lessening, loss, reduction, shrinkage, subsidence

decree 1. *n.* act, command, dictum, edict, enactment, law, mandate, order, ordinance, precept, proclamation, regulation, ruling, statute **2.** *v.* command, decide, determine, dictate, enact, lay down, ordain, order, prescribe, proclaim, pronounce, rule

decrepit 1. aged, crippled, debilitated, doddering, effete, feeble, frail, incapacitated, infirm, superannuated, wasted, weak **2.** antiquated, battered, broken-down, deteriorated, dilapidated, ramshackle, rickety, run-down, tumbledown, weather-beaten, worn-out

decrepitude 1. debility, dotage, feebleness, incapacity, infirmity, invalidity, old age, senility, wasting, weakness **2.** decay, degeneration, deterioration, dilapidation

decry abuse, belittle, blame, censure, condemn, criticize, cry down, denounce, depreciate, derogate, detract, devalue, discredit, disparage, rail against, run down, traduce, underestimate, underrate, undervalue

dedicate 1. commit, devote, give over to, pledge, surrender **2.** address, assign, inscribe, offer **3.** bless, consecrate, hallow, sanctify, set apart

dedicated committed, devoted, enthusiastic, given over to, purposeful, single-minded, sworn, wholehearted, zealous

dedication 1. adherence, allegiance, commitment, devotedness, devotion, faithfulness, loyalty, single-mindedness, wholeheartedness **2.** address, inscription, message **3.** consecration, hallowing, sanctification

deduce conclude, derive, draw, gather, glean, infer, reason, take to mean, understand

deducible derivable, inferable, to be inferred, traceable

deduct decrease by, knock off (*Inf.*), reduce by, remove, subtract, take away, take from, take off, take out, withdraw

deduction 1. assumption, conclusion,

consequence, corollary, finding, inference, reasoning, result **2.** abatement, allowance, decrease, diminution, discount, reduction, subtraction, withdrawal

deed 1. achievement, act, action, exploit, fact, feat, performance, reality, truth **2.** *Law* contract, document, indenture, instrument, title, title deed, transaction

deem account, believe, conceive, consider, esteem, estimate, hold, imagine, judge, reckon, regard, suppose, think

deep *adj.* **1.** abyssal, bottomless, broad, far, profound, unfathomable, wide, yawning **2.** abstract, abstruse, arcane, esoteric, hidden, mysterious, obscure, recondite, secret **3.** acute, discerning, learned, penetrating, sagacious, wise **4.** artful, astute, canny, cunning, designing, devious, insidious, knowing, scheming, shrewd **5.** extreme, grave, great, intense, profound **6.** absorbed, engrossed, immersed, lost, preoccupied, rapt **7.** *Of a colour* dark, intense, rich, strong, vivid **8.** *Of a sound* bass, booming, full-toned, low, low-pitched, resonant, sonorous ~*n.* **9.** *Usually preceded by* **the** briny (*Inf.*), high seas, main, ocean, sea **10.** culmination, dead, middle, mid point ~*adv.* **11.** deeply, far down, far into, late

deepen 1. dig out, dredge, excavate, hollow, scoop out, scrape out **2.** grow, increase, intensify, magnify, reinforce, strengthen

deeply 1. completely, gravely, profoundly, seriously, severely, thoroughly, to the heart, to the quick **2.** acutely, affectingly, distressingly, feelingly, intensely, mournfully, movingly, passionately, sadly

deep-rooted *or* **deep-seated** confirmed, entrenched, fixed, ineradicable, ingrained, inveterate, rooted, settled, subconscious, unconscious

deface blemish, deform, destroy, disfigure, impair, injure, mar, mutilate, obliterate, spoil, sully, tarnish, vandalize

defacement blemish, damage, destruction, disfigurement, distortion, impairment, injury, mutilation, vandalism

de facto 1. *adv.* actually, in effect, in fact, in reality, really **2.** *adj.* actual, existing, real

defalcation default, deficiency, deficit, embezzlement, fraud, misappropriation, shortage

defamation aspersion, calumny, character assassination, denigration, disparagement, libel, obloquy, opprobrium, scandal, slander, slur, smear, traducement, vilification

defamatory abusive, calumnious, contumelious, denigrating, derogatory, disparaging, injurious, insulting, libellous, slanderous, vilifying, vituperative

defame asperse, belie, besmirch, blacken, calumniate, cast a slur on, cast aspersions on, denigrate, detract, discredit, disgrace, dishonour, disparage, libel, malign, slander, smear, speak evil of, stigmatize, traduce, vilify, vituperate

default 1. *n.* absence, defect, deficiency, dereliction, failure, fault, lack, lapse, neglect, nonpayment, omission, want **2.** *v.* bilk, defraud, dodge, evade, fail, levant (*Brit.*), neglect, rat, swindle, welsh (*Sl.*)

defaulter delinquent, embezzler, levanter (*Brit.*), nonpayer, offender, peculator, welsher (*Sl.*)

defeat *v.* **1.** beat, conquer, crush, overpower, overthrow, overwhelm, quell, repulse, rout, subdue, subjugate, vanquish **2.** baffle, balk, confound, disappoint, discomfit, foil, frustrate, get the better of, ruin, thwart ~*n.* **3.** beating, conquest, debacle, overthrow, repulse, rout, trouncing, vanquishment **4.** disappointment, discomfiture, failure, frustration, rebuff, repulse, reverse, setback, thwarting

defeated balked, beaten, bested, checkmated, conquered, crushed, licked (*Inf.*), overcome, overpowered, overwhelmed, routed, thrashed, thwarted, trounced, vanquished, worsted

defeatist 1. *n.* pessimist, prophet of doom, quitter, submitter, yielder **2.** *adj.* pessimistic

defecate egest, empty, evacuate (*Physiol.*), excrete, move, open the bowels, pass a motion, void excrement

defecation egestion, elimination, emptying *or* opening of the bowels, evacuation (*Physiol.*), excrement, excretion, motion, movement, voiding excrement

defect *n.* **1.** blemish, blotch, error, failing, fault, flaw, foible, imperfection, mistake, spot, taint, want **2.** absence, default, deficiency, frailty, inadequacy, lack, shortcoming, weakness ~*v.* **3.** abandon, apostatize, break faith, change sides, desert, go over, rebel, revolt, tergiversate, walk out on (*Inf.*)

defection abandonment, apostasy, backsliding, dereliction, desertion, rebellion, revolt

defective 1. broken, deficient, faulty, flawed, imperfect, inadequate, incomplete, insufficient, not working, out of order, scant, short **2.** abnormal, mentally deficient, retarded, subnormal

defector apostate, deserter, rat (*Inf.*), recreant (*Archaic*), renegade, runagate (*Archaic*), tergiversator, turncoat

defence 1. armament, cover, deterrence, guard, immunity, protection, resistance, safeguard, security, shelter **2.** barricade, bastion, buckler, bulwark, buttress, fastness, fortification, rampart, shield **3.** apologia, apology, argument, excuse, exoneration, explanation, extenuation, justification, plea, vindication **4.** *Law* alibi, case, declaration, denial, plea, pleading, rebuttal, testimony

defenceless endangered, exposed, helpless, naked, powerless, unarmed, unguarded, unprotected, vulnerable, wide open

defend 1. cover, fortify, guard, keep safe, preserve, protect, safeguard, screen, secure, shelter, shield, ward off, watch over **2.** assert, champion, endorse, espouse, justify, maintain, plead, speak up for, stand by, stand up for, support, sustain, uphold, vindicate

defendant appellant, defence, litigant, offender, prisoner at the bar, respondent, the accused

defender 1. bodyguard, escort, guard, protector **2.** advocate, champion, patron, sponsor, supporter, vindicator

defensible 1. holdable, impregnable, safe, secure, unassailable **2.** justifiable, pardonable, permissible, plausible, tenable, valid, vindicable

defensive averting, defending, on the defensive, opposing, protective, safeguarding, uptight (*Sl.*), watchful, withstanding

defensively at bay, in defence, in self-defence, on guard, on the defensive, suspiciously

defer¹ adjourn, delay, hold over, postpone, procrastinate, prorogue, protract, put off, put on ice, set aside, shelve, suspend, table

defer² accede, bow, capitulate, comply, give in, give way to, respect, submit, yield

deference 1. acquiescence, capitulation, complaisance, compliance, obedience, obeisance, submission, yielding **2.** attention, civility, consideration, courtesy, esteem, homage, honour, obeisance, politeness, regard, respect, reverence, thoughtfulness, veneration

deferential civil, complaisant, considerate, courteous, dutiful, ingratiating, obedient, obeisant, obsequious, polite, regardful, respectful, reverential, submissive

deferment, deferral adjournment, delay, moratorium, postponement, putting off, stay, suspension

defiance challenge, confrontation, contempt, contumacy, disobedience, disregard, insolence, insubordination, opposition, provocation, rebelliousness, recalcitrance, spite

defiant aggressive, audacious, bold, challenging, contumacious, daring, disobedient, insolent, insubordinate, mutinous, provocative, rebellious, recalcitrant, refractory, truculent

deficiency 1. defect, demerit, failing, fault, flaw, frailty, imperfection, shortcoming, weakness **2.** absence, dearth, deficit, inadequacy, insufficiency, lack, scantiness, scarcity, shortage

deficient 1. defective, faulty, flawed, impaired, imperfect, incomplete, inferior, unsatisfactory, weak **2.** exiguous, inadequate, insufficient, lacking, meagre, scanty, scarce, short, skimpy, wanting

deficit arrears, default, deficiency, loss, shortage, shortfall

defile¹ *v.* **1.** befoul, contaminate, corrupt, dirty, make foul, pollute, smear, soil, taint, tarnish, vitiate **2.** besmirch, debase, degrade, disgrace, dishonour, stain, sully **3.** desecrate, profane, treat sacrilegiously **4.** abuse, deflower, molest, rape, ravish, seduce, violate

defile² *n.* gorge, gully, pass, passage, ravine, way through

defiled besmirched, desecrated, dishonoured, impure, polluted, profaned, ravished, spoilt, tainted, unclean

defilement contamination, corruption, debasement, degradation, depravity, desecration, disgrace, pollution, sullying, violation

definable apparent, definite, describable, determinable, explicable, perceptible, specific

define 1. characterize, describe, designate, detail, determine, explain, expound, interpret, specify, spell out **2.** bound, circumscribe, delimit, delineate, demarcate, limit, mark out, outline

definite 1. clear, clear-cut, clearly defined, determined, exact, explicit, express, fixed, marked, obvious, particular, precise, specific **2.** assured, certain, decided, guaranteed, positive, settled, sure

definitely absolutely, beyond any doubt, categorically, certainly, clearly, decidedly, easily, far and away, finally, indubitably, obviously, plainly, positively, surely, undeniably, unequivocally, unmistakably, unquestionably, without doubt, without fail, without question

definition 1. clarification, description, elucidation, explanation, exposition, statement of meaning **2.** delimitation, delineation, demarcation, determination, fixing, outlining, settling **3.** clarity, contrast, distinctness, focus, precision, sharpness

definitive absolute, authoritative, complete, conclusive, decisive, exhaustive, final, perfect, reliable, ultimate

deflate 1. collapse, contract, empty, exhaust, flatten, puncture, shrink, void **2.** chasten, dash, debunk (*Inf.*), disconcert, dispirit, humble, humiliate, mortify, put down (*Sl.*), squash, take the wind out of (someone's) sails **3.** *Economics* decrease, depreciate, depress, devalue, diminish, reduce

deflect bend, deviate, diverge, glance off, ricochet, shy, sidetrack, slew, swerve, turn, turn aside, twist, veer, wind

deflection aberration, bend, declination, deviation, divergence, drift, refraction, swerve, veer

deflower 1. assault, force, molest, rape, ravish, ruin, seduce, violate **2.** defile, desecrate, despoil, harm, mar, spoil, violate

deform 1. buckle, contort, distort, gnarl, malform, mangle, misshape, twist, warp **2.** cripple, deface, disfigure, injure, maim, mar, mutilate, ruin, spoil

deformed 1. bent, blemished, crippled, crooked, disfigured, distorted, maimed, malformed, mangled, marred, misbegotten, misshapen **2.** depraved, gross, offensive, perverted, twisted, warped

deformity 1. abnormality, defect, disfigurement, distortion, irregularity, malformation, misproportion, misshapenness, ugliness **2.** corruption, depravity, grossness, hatefulness, vileness

defraud beguile, bilk, cheat, con (*Sl.*), cozen, delude, diddle (*Inf.*), do (*Sl.*), dupe, embezzle, fleece, gull (*Archaic*), gyp (*Sl.*), outwit, pilfer, pull a fast one on (*Inf.*), rip off (*Sl.*), rob, rook (*Sl.*), swindle, trick

defray clear, cover, discharge, foot the bill, liquidate, meet, pay, settle

defrayal, defrayment clearance, discharge, liquidation, payment, settlement

deft able, adept, adroit, agile, clever, dexterous, expert, handy, neat, nimble, proficient, skilful

defunct 1. dead, deceased, departed, extinct, gone **2.** a dead letter, bygone, expired, inoperative, invalid, nonexistent, not functioning, obsolete, out of commission

defy 1. beard, brave, challenge, confront, contemn, dare, despise, disregard, face, flout, hurl defiance at, provoke, scorn, slight, spurn **2.** baffle, defeat, elude, foil, frustrate, repel, repulse, resist, thwart, withstand

degeneracy 1. corruption, decadence, degradation, depravity, dissoluteness, immorality, inferiority, meanness, poorness **2.** debasement, decay, decline, decrease, depravation, deterioration

degenerate 1. *adj.* base, corrupt, debased, debauched, decadent, degenerated, degraded, depraved, deteriorated, dissolute, fallen, immoral, low, mean, perverted **2.** *v.* decay, decline, decrease, deteriorate, fall off, lapse, regress, retrogress, rot, sink, slip, worsen

degeneration debasement, decline, degeneracy, descent, deterioration, dissipation, dissolution, regression

degradation 1. abasement, debasement, decadence, decline, degeneracy, degeneration, demotion, derogation, deterioration, downgrading, perversion **2.** discredit, disgrace, dishonour, humiliation, ignominy, mortification, shame

degrade 1. cheapen, corrupt, debase, demean, deteriorate, discredit, disgrace, dishonour, humble, humiliate, impair, injure, pervert, shame, vitiate **2.** break, cashier, demote, depose, downgrade, lower, reduce to inferior rank **3.** adulterate, dilute, doctor, mix, thin, water, water down, weaken

degraded abandoned, base, corrupt, debased, debauched, decadent, depraved, despicable, disgraced, disreputable, dissolute, low, mean, profligate, sordid, vicious, vile

degrading cheapening, contemptible, debasing, demeaning, disgraceful, dishonourable, humiliating, infra dig (*Inf.*), lowering, shameful, undignified, unworthy

degree 1. class, grade, level, order, position, rank, standing, station, status **2.** division, extent, gradation, grade, interval, limit, mark, measure, notch, point, rung, scale, stage, step, unit **3.** calibre, extent, intensity, level, measure, proportion, quality, quantity, range, rate, ratio, scale, scope, severity, standard **4. by degrees** bit by bit, gently, gradually, imperceptibly, inch by inch, little by little, slowly, step by step

dehydrate desiccate, drain, dry out, dry up, evaporate, exsiccate, parch

deification apotheosis, elevation, ennoblement, exaltation, glorification, idolization

deify apotheosize, elevate, ennoble, enthrone, exalt, extol, glorify, idealize, idolize, immortalize, venerate, worship

deign condescend, consent, deem worthy, lower oneself, see fit, stoop, think fit

deity celestial being, divine being, divinity, god, goddess, godhead, idol, immortal, supreme being

deject cast down, dampen, daunt, demoralize, depress, discourage, dishearten, dismay, dispirit

dejected blue, cast down, crestfallen, depressed, despondent, disconsolate, disheartened, dismal, doleful, down, downcast, downhearted, gloomy, glum, low, low-spirited, melancholy, miserable, morose, sad, woebegone, wretched

dejection blues, depression, despair, despondency, doldrums, downheartedness, dumps (*Inf.*), gloom, gloominess, heavy-heartedness, low spirits, melancholy, sadness, sorrow, unhappiness

de jure according to the law, by right, legally, rightfully

delay *v.* **1.** defer, hold over, postpone, procrastinate, prolong, protract, put off, shelve, stall, suspend, table, temporize ~*n.* **2.** deferment, postponement, procrastination, stay, suspension ~*v.* **3.** ar-

rest, bog down, check, detain, halt, hinder, hold back, hold up, impede, obstruct, retard, set back, slow up, stop ~*n.* **4.** check, detention, hindrance, hold-up, impediment, interruption, interval, obstruction, setback, stoppage, wait ~*v.* **5.** dawdle, dilly-dally (*Inf.*), drag, lag, linger, loiter, tarry ~*n.* **6.** dawdling, dilly-dallying (*Inf.*), lingering, loitering, tarrying

delectable adorable, agreeable, appetizing, charming, dainty, delicious, delightful, enjoyable, enticing, gratifying, inviting, luscious, lush, pleasant, pleasurable, satisfying, scrumptious (*Inf.*), tasty, toothsome, yummy (*Sl.*)

delectation amusement, delight, diversion, enjoyment, entertainment, gratification, happiness, pleasure, refreshment, relish, satisfaction

delegate *n.* **1.** agent, ambassador, commissioner, deputy, envoy, legate, representative, vicar ~*v.* **2.** accredit, appoint, authorize, commission, depute, designate, empower, mandate **3.** assign, consign, devolve, entrust, give, hand over, pass on, relegate, transfer

delegation 1. commission, contingent, deputation, embassy, envoys, legation, mission **2.** assignment, commissioning, committal, deputizing, devolution, entrustment, relegation

delete blot out, blue-pencil, cancel, cross out, cut out, dele, edit, edit out, efface, erase, expunge, obliterate, remove, rub out, strike out

deleterious bad, damaging, destructive, detrimental, harmful, hurtful, injurious, pernicious, prejudicial, ruinous

deliberate *v.* **1.** cogitate, consider, consult, debate, discuss, meditate, mull over, ponder, reflect, think, weigh ~*adj.* **2.** calculated, conscious, considered, designed, intentional, planned, prearranged, premeditated, purposeful, studied, thoughtful, wilful **3.** careful, cautious, circumspect, heedful, measured, methodical, ponderous, prudent, slow, thoughtful, unhurried, wary

deliberately by design, calculatingly, consciously, determinedly, emphatically, in cold blood, intentionally, knowingly, on purpose, pointedly, resolutely, studiously, wilfully, wittingly

deliberation 1. calculation, care, carefulness, caution, circumspection, cogitation, consideration, coolness, forethought, meditation, prudence, purpose, reflection, speculation, study, thought, wariness **2**. conference, consultation, debate, discussion

delicacy 1. accuracy, daintiness, elegance, exquisiteness, fineness, lightness, nicety, precision, subtlety **2**. debility, flimsiness, fragility, frailness, frailty, infirmity, slenderness, tenderness, weakness **3**. discrimination, fastidiousness, finesse, purity, refinement, sensibility, sensitiveness, sensitivity, tact, taste **4**. *bonne bouche*, dainty, luxury, relish, savoury, titbit, treat

delicate 1. ailing, debilitated, flimsy, fragile, frail, sickly, slender, slight, tender, weak **2**. choice, dainty, delicious, elegant, exquisite, fine, graceful, savoury, tender **3**. faint, muted, pastel, soft, subdued, subtle **4**. accurate, deft, detailed, minute, precise, skilled **5**. considerate, diplomatic, discreet, sensitive, tactful **6**. critical, difficult, precarious, sensitive, sticky (*Inf.*), ticklish, touchy **7**. careful, critical, discriminating, fastidious, prudish, pure, refined, scrupulous, squeamish

delicately carefully, daintily, deftly, elegantly, exquisitely, fastidiously, finely, gracefully, lightly, precisely, sensitively, skilfully, softly, subtly, tactfully

delicious 1. ambrosial, appetizing, choice, dainty, delectable, luscious, mouthwatering, nectareous, palatable, savoury, scrumptious (*Inf.*), tasty, toothsome, yummy (*Sl.*) **2**. agreeable, charming, delightful, enjoyable, entertaining, exquisite, pleasant, pleasing

delight *n*. **1**. ecstasy, enjoyment, felicity, gladness, gratification, happiness, joy, pleasure, rapture, transport ~*v*. **2**. amuse, charm, cheer, divert, enchant, gratify, please, ravish, rejoice, satisfy, thrill **3**. *With* in appreciate, enjoy, feast on, glory in, indulge in, like, love, luxuriate in, relish, revel in, savour

delighted captivated, charmed, ecstatic, elated, enchanted, gladdened, happy, joyous, jubilant, overjoyed, pleased, thrilled

delightful agreeable, amusing, captivating, charming, congenial, delectable, enchanting, engaging, enjoyable, entertaining, fascinating, gratifying, heavenly, pleasant, pleasing, pleasurable, rapturous, ravishing, thrilling

delimit bound, define, demarcate, determine, fix, mark (out)

delineate characterize, chart, contour, depict, describe, design, draw, figure, map out, outline, paint, picture, portray, render, sketch, trace

delineation account, chart, depiction, description, design, diagram, drawing, outline, picture, portrait, portrayal, representation, tracing

delinquency crime, fault, misbehaviour, misconduct, misdeed, misdemeanour, offence, wrongdoing

delinquent criminal, culprit, defaulter, juvenile delinquent, lawbreaker, malefactor, miscreant, offender, wrongdoer, young offender

delirious 1. crazy, demented, deranged, incoherent, insane, light-headed, mad, raving, unhinged **2**. beside oneself, carried away, corybantic, ecstatic, excited, frantic, frenzied, hysterical, wild

delirium 1. aberration, derangement, hallucination, insanity, lunacy, madness, raving **2**. ecstasy, fever, frenzy, fury, hysteria, passion, rage

deliver 1. bear, bring, carry, cart, convey, distribute, transport **2**. cede, commit, give up, grant, hand over, make over, relinquish, resign, surrender, transfer, turn over, yield **3**. acquit, discharge, emancipate, free, liberate, loose, ransom, redeem, release, rescue, save **4**. announce, declare, give, give forth, present, proclaim, pronounce, publish, read, utter **5**. administer, aim, deal, direct, give, inflict, launch, strike, throw **6**. discharge, dispense, feed, give forth, provide, release, supply

deliverance emancipation, escape, liberation, ransom, redemption, release, rescue, salvation

delivery 1. consignment, conveyance, dispatch, distribution, handing over, surrender, transfer, transmission, transmittal **2**. articulation, elocution, enunciation, intonation, speech, utterance **3**. *Medical* childbirth, confinement, labour, parturition **4**. deliverance, escape, liberation, release, rescue

delude bamboozle (*Inf.*), beguile, cheat, con (*Sl.*), cozen, deceive, dupe, fool, gull (*Archaic*), hoax, hoodwink, impose on, lead up the garden path (*Inf.*), misguide, mislead, take in (*Inf.*), trick

deluge *n*. **1**. cataclysm, downpour, flood, inundation, overflowing, spate, torrent **2.** *Fig.* avalanche, barrage, flood, rush, spate, torrent ~*v.* **3.** douse, drench, drown, flood, inundate, soak, submerge, swamp **4.** *Fig.* engulf, inundate, overload, overrun, overwhelm, swamp

delusion deception, error, fallacy, false impression, fancy, hallucination, illusion, misapprehension, misbelief, misconception, mistake, phantasm, self-deception

delusive chimerical, deceptive, fallacious, illusive, illusory, misleading, specious, spurious

de luxe choice, costly, elegant, exclusive, expensive, grand, luxurious, opulent, palatial, plush (*Inf.*), rich, select, special, splendid, sumptuous, superior

delve burrow, dig into, examine, explore, ferret out, investigate, look into, probe, ransack, research, rummage, search, unearth

demagogue agitator, firebrand, haranguer, rabble-rouser, soapbox orator

demand *v.* **1.** ask, challenge, inquire, interrogate, question, request **2.** call for, cry out for, involve, necessitate, need, require, take, want **3.** claim, exact, expect, insist on, order ~*n.* **4.** bidding, charge, inquiry, interrogation, order, question, request, requisition **5.** call, claim, necessity, need, requirement, want **6. in demand** fashionable, in vogue, needed, popular, requested, sought after

demanding 1. challenging, difficult, exacting, exhausting, exigent, hard, taxing, tough, trying, wearing **2.** clamorous, imperious, importunate, insistent, nagging, pressing, urgent

demarcate define, delimit, determine, differentiate, distinguish between, fix, mark, separate

demarcation 1. bound, boundary, confine, enclosure, limit, margin **2.** delimitation, differentiation, distinction, division, separation

demean abase, debase, degrade, descend, humble, lower, stoop

demeanour air, bearing, behaviour, carriage, comportment, conduct, deportment, manner, mien

demented crackbrained, crazed, crazy, daft (*Sl.*), deranged, distraught, dotty (*Sl.*), foolish, frenzied, idiotic, insane, lunatic, mad, maniacal, manic, *non compos mentis,* unbalanced, unhinged

demise *n.* **1.** death, decease, departure, expiration **2.** collapse, dissolution, downfall, end, failure, fall, ruin, termination **3.** *Law* alienation, conveyance, transfer, transmission ~*v.* **4.** *Law* bequeath, convey, grant, leave, transfer, will

democracy commonwealth, government by the people, representative government, republic

democratic autonomous, egalitarian, popular, populist, representative, republican, self-governing

demolish 1. bulldoze, destroy, dismantle, flatten, knock down, level, overthrow, pulverize, raze, ruin, tear down **2.** *Fig.* annihilate, defeat, destroy, overthrow, overturn, undo, wreck **3.** consume, devour, eat, gobble up, put away

demolition bulldozing, destruction, explosion, knocking down, levelling, razing, wrecking

demon 1. devil, evil spirit, fiend, goblin, malignant spirit **2.** *Fig.* devil, fiend, monster, rogue, villain **3.** ace (*Inf.*), addict, fanatic, fiend, go-getter (*Inf.*), master, wizard **4.** daemon, daimon, genius, guardian spirit, ministering angel, numen

demonic, demoniac, demoniacal 1. devilish, diabolic, diabolical, fiendish, hellish, infernal, satanic **2.** crazed, frantic, frenetic, frenzied, furious, hectic, like one possessed, mad, maniacal, manic

demonstrable attestable, axiomatic, certain, evident, evincible, incontrovertible, indubitable, irrefutable, obvious, palpable, positive, provable, self-evident, undeniable, unmistakable, verifiable

demonstrate 1. display, establish, evidence, evince, exhibit, indicate, manifest, prove, show, testify to **2.** describe, explain, illustrate, make clear, show how, teach **3.** march, parade, picket, protest, rally

demonstration 1. affirmation, confirmation, display, evidence, exhibition, expression, illustration, manifestation, proof, substantiation, testimony, validation **2.** description, explanation, exposition, presentation, test, trial **3.** march, mass lobby, parade, picket, protest, rally, sit-in

demonstrative 1. affectionate, effusive, emotional, expansive, expressive, gushing, loving, open, unreserved, unrestrained **2.** evincive, explanatory, expository, illustrative, indicative, symptomatic

demoralization 1. agitation, crushing, devitalization, discomfiture, enervation, lowering *or* loss of morale, panic, perturbation, trepidation, unmanning, weakening **2**. corruption, debasement, depravation, lowering, perversion, vitiation

demoralize 1. cripple, daunt, deject, depress, disconcert, discourage, dishearten, dispirit, enfeeble, rattle (*Inf.*), sap, shake, undermine, unnerve, weaken **2**. corrupt, debase, debauch, deprave, lower, pervert, vitiate

demoralized 1. broken, crushed, depressed, discouraged, disheartened, dispirited, downcast, subdued, unmanned, unnerved, weakened **2**. bad, base, corrupt, degenerate, depraved, dissolute, immoral, low, reprobate, sinful, wicked

demote declass, degrade, disrate (*Naval*), downgrade, kick downstairs (*Sl.*), lower in rank, relegate

demulcent calming, easing, emollient, lenitive, mild, mollifying, relieving, sedative, softening, soothing

demur 1. *v*. balk, cavil, disagree, dispute, doubt, hesitate, object, pause, protest, refuse, take exception, waver **2**. *n*. compunction, demurral, demurrer, dissent, hesitation, misgiving, objection, protest, qualm, scruple

demure 1. decorous, diffident, grave, modest, reserved, reticent, retiring, sedate, shy, sober, staid, unassuming **2**. affected, bashful, coy, priggish, prim, prissy (*Inf.*), prudish, strait-laced

den 1. cave, cavern, haunt, hide-out, hole, lair, shelter **2**. cloister, cubbyhole, hideaway, retreat, sanctuary, sanctum, snuggery, study

denial adjuration, contradiction, disavowal, disclaimer, dismissal, dissent, negation, prohibition, rebuff, refusal, rejection, renunciation, repudiation, repulse, retraction, veto

denigrate belittle, besmirch, blacken, calumniate, decry, defame, disparage, impugn, malign, revile, run down, slander, vilify

denigration aspersion, backbiting, defamation, detraction, disparagement, obloquy, scandal, scurrility, slander, vilification

denizen citizen, dweller, inhabitant, occupant, resident

denominate call, christen, designate, dub, entitle, name, phrase, style, term

denomination 1. belief, communion, creed, persuasion, religious group, school, sect **2**. grade, size, unit, value **3**. body, category, class, classification, group **4**. appellation, designation, label, name, style, term, title

denotation designation, indication, meaning, signification, specification

denote betoken, designate, express, imply, import, indicate, mark, mean, show, signify, typify

dénouement climax, conclusion, culmination, finale, outcome, resolution, solution, termination, upshot

denounce accuse, arraign, attack, brand, castigate, censure, condemn, declaim against, decry, denunciate, impugn, proscribe, revile, stigmatize, vilify

dense 1. close, close-knit, compact, compressed, condensed, heavy, impenetrable, opaque, solid, substantial, thick, thickset **2**. blockish, crass, dull, obtuse, slow, slow-witted, stolid, stupid, thick, thick-witted

density 1. body, bulk, closeness, compactness, consistency, crowdedness, denseness, impenetrability, mass, solidity, thickness, tightness **2**. crassness, dullness, obtuseness, slowness, stolidity, stupidity, thickness

dent 1. *n*. chip, concavity, crater, depression, dimple, dip, hollow, impression, indentation, pit **2**. *v*. depress, dint, gouge, hollow, imprint, make a dent in, make concave, press in, push in

denude bare, divest, expose, lay bare, strip, uncover

denunciate castigate, condemn, curse, damn, denounce, stigmatize, vituperate

denunciation accusation, castigation, censure, condemnation, criticism, denouncement, fulmination, incrimination, invective, obloquy, stigmatization

denunciatory accusatory, censorious, comminatory, condemnatory, fulminatory, incriminatory, recriminatory, reproachful

deny 1. contradict, disagree with, disprove, gainsay, oppose, rebuff, refute **2**. abjure, disavow, discard, disclaim, disown, recant, renounce, repudiate, revoke **3**. begrudge, decline, disallow, forbid, negative, refuse, reject, turn down, veto, withhold

deodorant air freshener, antiperspirant, deodorizer, disinfectant, fumigant

deodorize aerate, disinfect, freshen, fumigate, purify, refresh, ventilate

depart 1. absent (oneself), decamp, disappear, escape, exit, go, go away, leave, migrate, quit, remove, retire, retreat, set forth, start out, take (one's) leave, vanish, withdraw **2**. deviate, differ, digress, diverge, stray, swerve, turn aside, vary, veer

departed dead, deceased, expired, late

department 1. district, division, province, region, sector **2**. branch, bureau, division, office, section, station, subdivision, unit **3**. area, domain, function, line, province, realm, responsibility, speciality, sphere

departure 1. exit, exodus, going, going away, leave-taking, leaving, removal, retirement, withdrawal **2**. abandonment, branching off, deviation, digression, divergence, variation, veering **3**. branching out, change, difference, innovation, novelty, shift

depend 1. bank on, build upon, calculate on, confide in, count on, lean on, reckon on, rely upon, trust in, turn to **2**. be based on, be contingent on, be determined by, be subject to, be subordinate to, hang on, hinge on, rest on, revolve around

dependable faithful, reliable, responsible, steady, sure, trustworthy, trusty, unfailing

dependant n. child, client, hanger-on, henchman, minion, minor, protégé, relative, retainer, subordinate, vassal

dependence, dependency 1. assurance, belief, confidence, expectation, faith, hope, reliance, trust **2**. addiction, attachment, helplessness, need, subordination, subservience, vulnerability, weakness

dependent adj. **1**. counting on, defenceless, helpless, immature, reliant, relying on, vulnerable, weak **2**. conditional, contingent, depending, determined by, liable to, relative, subject to **3**. feudal, subject, subordinate, tributary

depict 1. delineate, draw, illustrate, limn, outline, paint, picture, portray, render, reproduce, sculpt, sketch **2**. characterize, describe, detail, narrate, outline, sketch

depiction delineation, description, drawing, illustration, image, likeness, outline, picture, portrayal, representation, sketch

deplete bankrupt, consume, decrease, drain, empty, evacuate, exhaust, expend, impoverish, lessen, milk, reduce, use up

depleted consumed, decreased, depreciated, devoid of, drained, emptied, exhausted, lessened, out of, reduced, short of, spent, used (up), wasted, weakened, worn out

depletion attenuation, consumption, decrease, deficiency, diminution, dwindling, exhaustion, expenditure, lessening, lowering, reduction, using up

deplorable 1. calamitous, dire, disastrous, distressing, grievous, heartbreaking, lamentable, melancholy, miserable, pitiable, regrettable, sad, unfortunate, wretched **2**. blameworthy, disgraceful, dishonourable, disreputable, execrable, opprobrious, reprehensible, scandalous, shameful

deplore 1. bemoan, bewail, grieve for, lament, mourn, regret, rue, sorrow over **2**. abhor, censure, condemn, denounce, deprecate, disapprove of, object to

deploy arrange, dispose, extend, position, redistribute, set out, set up, spread out, station, use, utilize

deport 1. banish, exile, expatriate, expel, extradite, oust **2**. Used reflexively acquit, act, bear, behave, carry, comport, conduct, hold

deportation banishment, eviction, exile, expatriation, expulsion, extradition, transportation

deportment air, appearance, aspect, bearing, behaviour, carriage, cast, comportment, conduct, demeanour, manner, mien, posture, stance

depose 1. break, cashier, degrade, demote, dethrone, dismiss, displace, downgrade, oust, remove from office **2**. Law avouch, declare, make a deposition, testify

deposit v. **1**. drop, lay, locate, place, precipitate, put, settle, sit down **2**. amass, bank, consign, entrust, hoard, lodge, save, store ~n. **3**. down payment, instalment, money (in bank), part payment, pledge, retainer, security, stake, warranty **4**. accumulation, alluvium, deposition, dregs, lees, precipitate, sediment, silt

depositary fiduciary (Law), guardian, steward, trustee

deposition 1. dethronement, dismissal, displacement, ousting, removal **2.** *Law* affidavit, declaration, evidence, sworn statement, testimony

depository depot, repository, safe-deposit box, store, storehouse, warehouse

depot 1. depository, repository, storehouse, warehouse **2.** *Military* arsenal, dump **3.** bus station, garage, terminus

deprave brutalize, corrupt, debase, debauch, degrade, demoralize, lead astray, pervert, seduce, subvert, vitiate

depraved abandoned, corrupt, debased, debauched, degenerate, degraded, dissolute, evil, immoral, lascivious, lewd, licentious, perverted, profligate, shameless, sinful, vicious, vile, wicked

depravity baseness, contamination, corruption, criminality, debasement, debauchery, degeneracy, depravation, evil, immorality, iniquity, profligacy, sinfulness, vice, viciousness, vitiation, wickedness

deprecate 1. condemn, deplore, disapprove of, frown on, object to, protest against, take exception to **2.** belittle, depreciate, detract, disparage

deprecatory 1. censuring, condemnatory, disapproving, opprobrious, reproachful **2.** apologetic, contrite, penitent, regretful, remorseful, rueful

depreciate 1. decrease, deflate, devaluate, devalue, lessen, lose value, lower, reduce **2.** belittle, decry, denigrate, deride, detract, disparage, look down on, ridicule, run down, scorn, sneer at, traduce, underestimate, underrate, undervalue

depreciation 1. deflation, depression, devaluation, drop, fall, slump **2.** belittlement, deprecation, derogation, detraction, disparagement, pejoration

depredation desolation, despoiling, destruction, devastation, harrying, laying waste, marauding, pillage, plunder, ransacking, rapine, ravaging, robbery, spoliation, theft

depredator despoiler, destroyer, looter, marauder, pillager, plunderer, raider, ransacker, ravager, rifler, sacker

depress 1. cast down, chill, damp, daunt, deject, desolate, discourage, dishearten, dispirit, make despondent, oppress, sadden, weigh down **2.** debilitate, devitalize, drain, enervate, exhaust, lower, sap, slow up, weaken, **3.** cheapen, depreciate, devaluate, devalue, diminish,

downgrade, impair, lessen, lower, reduce **4.** flatten, level, lower, press down, push down

depressed 1. blue, crestfallen, dejected, despondent, discouraged, dispirited, down, downcast, downhearted, fed up, glum, low, low-spirited, melancholy, moody, morose, pessimistic, sad, unhappy **2.** concave, hollow, indented, recessed, set back, sunken **3.** *Of an area, circumstances* distressed, deprived, destitute, disadvantaged, grey, needy, poor, poverty-stricken, run-down **4.** cheapened, depreciated, devalued, impaired, weakened

depressing black, bleak, daunting, dejecting, depressive, discouraging, disheartening, dismal, dispiriting, distressing, dreary, gloomy, heartbreaking, hopeless, melancholy, sad, saddening, sombre

depression 1. dejection, despair, despondency, dolefulness, downheartedness, dumps (*Inf.*), gloominess, hopelessness, low spirits, melancholia, melancholy, sadness, the blues **2.** *Commerce* dullness, economic decline, hard *or* bad times, inactivity, lowness, recession, slump, stagnation **3.** bowl, cavity, concavity, dent, dimple, dip, excavation, hollow, impression, indentation, pit, sag, sink, valley

deprivation 1. denial, deprival, dispossession, divestment, expropriation, removal, withdrawal, withholding **2.** destitution, detriment, disadvantage, distress, hardship, need, privation, want

deprive bereave, despoil, dispossess, divest, expropriate, rob, strip, wrest

deprived bereft, denuded, destitute, disadvantaged, forlorn, in need, in want, lacking, necessitous, needy, poor

depth 1. abyss, deepness, drop, extent, measure, profoundness, profundity **2.** *Fig.* astuteness, discernment, insight, penetration, profoundness, profundity, sagacity, wisdom **3.** abstruseness, complexity, obscurity, reconditeness **4.** intensity, richness, strength **5.** *Often plural* abyss, bowels of the earth, deepest (furthest, innermost, most intense, remotest) part, middle, midst, slough of despond **6. in depth** comprehensively, extensively, intensively, thoroughly

deputation 1. commission, delegates, delegation, deputies, embassy, envoys, legation **2.** appointment, assignment, commission, designation, nomination

depute *v.* accredit, appoint, authorize, charge, commission, delegate, empower, entrust, mandate

deputize 1. commission, delegate, depute **2.** act for, stand in for, take the place of, understudy

deputy 1. *n.* agent, ambassador, commissioner, delegate, legate, lieutenant, nuncio, proxy, representative, second-in-command, substitute, surrogate, vicegerent **2.** *adj.* assistant, depute (*Scot.*), subordinate

derange 1. confound, confuse, disarrange, disarray, discompose, disconcert, disorder, displace, disturb, ruffle, unsettle, upset **2.** craze, dement (*Rare*), drive mad, madden, make insane, unbalance, unhinge

deranged berserk, crazed, crazy, delirious, demented, distracted, frantic, frenzied, insane, irrational, lunatic, mad, maddened, unbalanced, unhinged

derangement 1. confusion, disarrangement, disarray, disorder, disturbance, irregularity, jumble, muddle **2.** aberration, alienation, delirium, dementia, hallucination, insanity, loss of reason, lunacy, madness, mania

derelict *adj.* **1.** abandoned, deserted, dilapidated, discarded, forsaken, neglected, ruined **2.** careless, irresponsible, lax, negligent, remiss, slack ~*n.* **3.** down-and-out, good-for-nothing, ne'er-do-well, outcast, tramp, vagrant, wastrel

dereliction 1. delinquency, evasion, failure, faithlessness, fault, neglect, negligence, nonperformance, remissness **2.** abandonment, abdication, desertion, forsaking, relinquishment, renunciation

deride chaff, contemn, detract, disdain, disparage, flout, gibe, insult, jeer, knock (*Inf.*), mock, pooh-pooh, ridicule, scoff, scorn, sneer, taunt

de rigueur comme il faut, conventional, correct, decent, decorous, done, fitting, necessary, proper, required, right, the done thing

derision contempt, contumely, disdain, disparagement, disrespect, insult, laughter, mockery, raillery, ridicule, satire, scoffing, scorn, sneering

derisive contemptuous, jeering, mocking, ridiculing, scoffing, scornful, taunting

derisory contemptible, insulting,

laughable, ludicrous, outrageous, preposterous, ridiculous

derivable attributable, deducible, determinable, extractable, inferable, obtainable, traceable

derivation 1. acquiring, deriving, extraction, getting, obtaining **2.** ancestry, basis, beginning, descent, etymology, foundation, genealogy, origin, root, source

derivative *adj.* **1.** acquired, borrowed, derived, inferred, obtained, procured, transmitted **2.** copied, imitative, plagiaristic, plagiarized, rehashed, secondary, second-hand, uninventive, unoriginal ~*n.* **3.** by-product, derivation, descendant, off-shoot, outgrowth, spin-off

derive 1. collect, deduce, draw, elicit, extract, follow, gain, gather, get, glean, infer, obtain, procure, receive, trace **2.** *With* **from** arise, descend, emanate, flow, issue, originate, proceed, spring from, stem from

derogate 1. cheapen, compromise, depreciate, detract, devaluate, diminish, disparage, lessen, run down **2.** *Of oneself* decline, degenerate, degrade, descend, deteriorate, deviate from, retrogress, stoop

derogatory belittling, damaging, defamatory, depreciative, detracting, discreditable, dishonouring, disparaging, injurious, offensive, slighting, uncomplimentary, unfavourable, unflattering

descant *v.* **1.** amplify, animadvert, comment on, dilate, discourse, discuss, enlarge, expatiate ~*n.* **2.** animadversion, commentary, criticism, discourse, discussion, dissertation **3.** counterpoint, decoration, melody, song, tune

descend 1. alight, dismount, drop, fall, go down, move down, plummet, plunge, sink, subside, tumble **2.** dip, gravitate, incline, slant, slope **3.** be handed down, be passed down, derive, issue, originate, proceed, spring **4.** abase oneself, condescend, degenerate, deteriorate, lower oneself, stoop **5.** *Often with* **on** arrive, assail, assault, attack, come in force, invade, pounce, raid, swoop

descent 1. coming down, drop, fall, plunge, swoop **2.** declination, declivity, dip, drop, incline, slant, slope **3.** ancestry, extraction, family tree, genealogy, heredity, lineage, origin, parentage **4.** debasement, decadence, decline, degradation, deterioration **5.** assault, attack, foray, incursion, invasion, pounce, raid, swoop

describe 1. characterize, define, depict, detail, explain, express, illustrate, narrate, portray, recount, relate, report, specify, tell **2.** delineate, draw, mark out, outline, trace

description 1. account, characterization, delineation, depiction, detail, explanation, narration, narrative, portrayal, report, representation, sketch **2.** brand, breed, category, class, genre, genus, ilk, kidney, kind, order, sort, species, type, variety

descriptive circumstantial, depictive, detailed, explanatory, expressive, graphic, illustrative, pictorial, picturesque, vivid

descry behold, detect, discern, discover, distinguish, espy, make out, mark, notice, observe, perceive, recognize, see, sight, spy out

desecrate abuse, blaspheme, commit sacrilege, contaminate, defile, despoil, dishonour, pervert, pollute, profane, violate

desecration blasphemy, debasement, defilement, impiety, profanation, sacrilege, violation

desert[1] **1.** *n.* solitude, waste, wasteland, wilderness, wilds **2.** *adj.* arid, bare, barren, desolate, infertile, lonely, solitary, uncultivated, uninhabited, unproductive, untilled, waste, wild

desert[2] *v.* abandon, abscond, betray, decamp, defect, forsake, give up, go over the hill (*Military sl.*), jilt, leave, leave high and dry, leave (someone) in the lurch, leave stranded, maroon, quit, rat (on), relinquish, renounce, resign, run out on (*Inf.*), strand, throw over, vacate, walk out on (*Inf.*)

desert[3] *n.* **1.** *Often plural* comeuppance (*Sl.*), due, guerdon (*Poetic*), meed (*Archaic*), payment, recompense, requital, retribution, return, reward, right **2.** excellence, merit (*or* demerit), virtue, worth

deserted abandoned, bereft, cast off, derelict, desolate, empty, forlorn, forsaken, godforsaken, isolated, left in the lurch, left stranded, lonely, neglected, solitary, unfriended, unoccupied, vacant

deserter absconder, apostate, defector, escapee, fugitive, rat (*Inf.*), renegade, runaway, traitor, truant

desertion abandonment, absconding, apostasy, betrayal, defection, departure, dereliction, escape, evasion, flight, forsaking, relinquishment, truancy

deserve be entitled to, be worthy of, earn, gain, justify, merit, procure, rate, warrant, win

deserved appropriate, condign, due, earned, fair, fitting, just, justifiable, justified, meet (*Archaic*), merited, proper, right, rightful, suitable, warranted, well-earned

deserving commendable, estimable, laudable, meritorious, praiseworthy, righteous, worthy

desiccate dehydrate, drain, dry, evaporate, exsiccate, parch

desiccated 1. dehydrated, dried, dry, powdered **2.** cold, dead, dry, dry-as-dust, dull, empty, inanimate, inert, lifeless, passionless, spiritless

desideratum aim, aspiration, dream, essential, goal, heart's desire, hope, ideal, lack, need, objective, *sine qua non*, want, wish

design *v.* **1.** delineate, describe, draft, draw, outline, plan, sketch, trace ~*n.* **2.** blueprint, delineation, draft, drawing, model, outline, plan, scheme, sketch ~*v.* **3.** conceive, create, fabricate, fashion, invent, originate, think up ~*n.* **4.** arrangement, configuration, construction, figure, form, motif, organization, pattern, shape, style ~*v.* **5.** aim, contrive, destine, devise, intend, make, mean, plan, project, propose, purpose, scheme, tailor ~*n.* **6.** enterprise, plan, project, schema, scheme, undertaking **7.** aim, end, goal, intent, intention, meaning, object, objective, point, purport, purpose, target, view **8.** *Often plural* conspiracy, evil intentions, intrigue, machination, plot, scheme

designate 1. call, christen, dub, entitle, label, name, nominate, style, term **2.** allot, appoint, assign, choose, delegate, depute, nominate, select **3.** characterize, define, denote, describe, earmark, indicate, pinpoint, show, specify, stipulate

designation 1. denomination, description, epithet, label, mark, name, title **2.** appointment, classification, delegation, indication, selection, specification

designedly by design, calculatedly, deliberately, intentionally, knowingly, on purpose, purposely, studiously, wilfully, wittingly

designer 1. architect, artificer, couturier, creator, deviser, inventor, originator, stylist 2. conniver, conspirator, intriguer, plotter, schemer

designing artful, astute, conniving, conspiring, crafty, crooked (*Inf.*), cunning, deceitful, devious, intriguing, Machiavellian, plotting, scheming, sharp, shrewd, sly, treacherous, tricky, unscrupulous, wily

desirability advantage, benefit, merit, profit, usefulness, value, worth

desirable 1. advantageous, advisable, agreeable, beneficial, covetable, eligible, enviable, good, pleasing, preferable, profitable, worthwhile 2. adorable, alluring, attractive, fascinating, fetching, seductive, sexy (*Inf.*)

desire v. 1. aspire to, covet, crave, desiderate, fancy, hanker after, long for, set one's heart on, want, wish for, yearn for ~n. 2. appetite, aspiration, craving, hankering, longing, need, want, wish, yearning, yen (*Inf.*) ~v. 3. ask, entreat, importune, petition, request, solicit ~n. 4. appeal, entreaty, importunity, petition, request, solicitation, supplication 5. appetite, concupiscence, lasciviousness, lechery, libido, lust, lustfulness, passion

desired accurate, appropriate, correct, exact, expected, express, fitting, necessary, particular, proper, required, right

desirous ambitious, anxious, aspiring, avid, craving, desiring, eager, hopeful, hoping, keen, longing, ready, willing, wishing, yearning

desist abstain, break off, cease, discontinue, end, forbear, give over (*Inf.*), give up, have done with, leave off, pause, refrain from, stop, suspend

desolate adj. 1. bare, barren, bleak, desert, dreary, ruined, solitary, unfrequented, uninhabited, waste, wild ~v. 2. depopulate, despoil, destroy, devastate, lay low, lay waste, pillage, plunder, ravage, ruin ~adj. 3. abandoned, bereft, cheerless, comfortless, companionless, dejected, depressing, despondent, disconsolate, dismal, downcast, forlorn, forsaken, gloomy, lonely, melancholy, miserable, wretched ~v. 4. daunt, deject, depress, discourage, dishearten, dismay, distress, grieve

desolation 1. destruction, devastation, havoc, ravages, ruin, ruination 2. barrenness, bleakness, desolateness, forlornness, isolation, loneliness, solitariness, solitude, wildness 3. anguish, dejection, despair, distress, gloom, gloominess, melancholy, misery, sadness, unhappiness, woe, wretchedness

despair v. 1. despond, give up, lose heart, lose hope ~n. 2. anguish, dejection, depression, desperation, despondency, disheartenment, gloom, hopelessness, melancholy, misery, wretchedness 3. burden, cross, ordeal, pain, trial, tribulation

despairing anxious, broken-hearted, dejected, depressed, desperate, despondent, disconsolate, downcast, frantic, grief-stricken, hopeless, inconsolable, melancholy, miserable, suicidal, wretched

despatch *see* DISPATCH

desperado bandit, criminal, cutthroat, gangster, gunman, hoodlum (*Chiefly U.S.*), lawbreaker, mugger, outlaw, ruffian, thug

desperate 1. audacious, dangerous, daring, death-defying, determined, foolhardy, frantic, furious, hasty, hazardous, headstrong, impetuous, madcap, precipitate, rash, reckless, risky, violent, wild 2. acute, critical, dire, drastic, extreme, great, urgent, very grave 3. despairing, despondent, forlorn, hopeless, inconsolable, irrecoverable, irremediable, irretrievable, wretched

desperately 1. badly, dangerously, gravely, perilously, seriously, severely 2. appallingly, fearfully, frightfully, hopelessly, shockingly

desperation 1. defiance, foolhardiness, frenzy, heedlessness, impetuosity, madness, rashness, recklessness 2. agony, anguish, anxiety, despair, despondency, distraction, heartache, hopelessness, misery, pain, sorrow, torture, trouble, unhappiness, worry

despicable abject, base, beyond contempt, cheap, contemptible, degrading, detestable, disgraceful, disreputable, hateful, ignominious, infamous, low, mean, pitiful, reprehensible, scurvy, shameful, sordid, vile, worthless, wretched

despise abhor, contemn, deride, detest, disdain, disregard, flout, loathe, look down on, neglect, revile, scorn, slight, spurn, undervalue

despite prep. against, even with, in contempt of, in defiance of, in spite of, in the face of, in the teeth of, notwithstanding, regardless of, undeterred by

despoil denude, deprive, destroy, devastate, dispossess, divest, loot, pillage, plunder, ravage, rifle, rob, strip, vandalize, wreak havoc upon, wreck

despoliation depredation, despoilment, destruction, devastation, havoc, looting, pillage, plunder, ruin, vandalism, wreckage

despond be cast down, be depressed, despair, give up, lose heart, lose hope, mourn, sorrow

despondency dejection, depression, despair, desperation, disconsolateness, discouragement, dispiritedness, downheartedness, gloom, hopelessness, low spirits, melancholy, misery, sadness, wretchedness

despondent blue, dejected, depressed, despairing, disconsolate, discouraged, disheartened, dispirited, doleful, down, downcast, downhearted, gloomy, glum, hopeless, in despair, low, low-spirited, melancholy, miserable, morose, sad, sorrowful, woebegone, wretched

despot autocrat, dictator, monocrat, oppressor, tyrant

despotic absolute, arbitrary, arrogant, authoritarian, autocratic, dictatorial, domineering, imperious, monocratic, oppressive, tyrannical, unconstitutional

despotism absolutism, autarchy, autocracy, dictatorship, monocracy, oppression, totalitarianism, tyranny

destination 1. harbour, haven, journey's end, landing-place, resting-place, station, stop, terminus **2.** aim, ambition, design, end, goal, intention, object, objective, purpose, target

destine allot, appoint, assign, consecrate, decree, design, devote, doom, earmark, fate, intend, mark out, ordain, predetermine, purpose, reserve

destined 1. bound, certain, designed, doomed, fated, foreordained, ineluctable, inescapable, inevitable, intended, meant, ordained, predestined, unavoidable **2.** assigned, booked, bound for, directed, en route, heading, on the road to, routed, scheduled

destiny cup, divine decree, doom, fate, fortune, karma, kismet, lot, portion

destitute 1. distressed, down and out, impecunious, impoverished, indigent, insolvent, moneyless, necessitous, needy, on one's uppers, on the breadline (*Inf.*),

penniless, penurious, poor, poverty-stricken **2.** bereft of, deficient in, depleted, deprived of, devoid of, drained, empty of, in need of, lacking, wanting, without

destitution beggary, dire straits, distress, impecuniousness, indigence, neediness, pauperism, pennilessness, penury, privation, utter poverty, want

destroy annihilate, blow to bits, break down, crush, demolish, desolate, devastate, dismantle, dispatch, eradicate, extinguish, extirpate, gut, kill, ravage, raze, ruin, shatter, slay, smash, torpedo, waste, wipe out, wreck

destruction annihilation, crushing, demolition, devastation, downfall, end, eradication, extermination, extinction, havoc, liquidation, massacre, overthrow, overwhelming, ruin, ruination, shattering, slaughter, undoing, wreckage, wrecking

destructive 1. baleful, baneful, calamitous, cataclysmic, catastrophic, damaging, deadly, deleterious, detrimental, devastating, fatal, harmful, hurtful, injurious, lethal, noxious, pernicious, ruinous **2.** adverse, antagonistic, contrary, derogatory, discouraging, discrediting, disparaging, hostile, invalidating, negative, opposed, undermining, vicious

desultory aimless, capricious, cursory, disconnected, discursive, disorderly, erratic, fitful, haphazard, inconsistent, inconstant, inexact, irregular, loose, maundering, off and on, rambling, random, roving, spasmodic, unmethodical, unsettled, unsystematic, vague

detach cut off, disconnect, disengage, disentangle, disjoin, disunite, divide, free, isolate, loosen, remove, segregate, separate, sever, tear off, uncouple, unfasten, unhitch

detached 1. disconnected, discrete, disjoined, divided, free, loosened, separate, severed, unconnected **2.** aloof, disinterested, dispassionate, impartial, impersonal, neutral, objective, reserved, unbiased, uncommitted, uninvolved, unprejudiced

detachment 1. aloofness, coolness, indifference, remoteness, unconcern **2.** disinterestedness, fairness, impartiality, neutrality, nonpartisanship, objectivity **3.** disconnection, disengagement, disjoining, separation, severing **4.** *Military* body, detail, force, party, patrol, squad, task force, unit

detail n. **1**. aspect, component, count, element, fact, factor, feature, item, particular, point, respect, specific, technicality **2**. *Plural* fine points, minutiae, niceties, particulars, parts, trivia, trivialities **3**. **in detail** comprehensively, exhaustively, inside out, item by item, point by point, thoroughly **4**. *Military* assignment, body, detachment, duty, fatigue, force, party, squad ~v. **5**. catalogue, delineate, depict, describe, enumerate, individualize, itemize, narrate, particularize, portray, recite, recount, rehearse, relate, specify **6**. allocate, appoint, assign, charge, commission, delegate, detach, send

detailed blow-by-blow, circumstantial, comprehensive, elaborate, exact, exhaustive, full, intricate, itemized, meticulous, minute, particular, particularized, specific, thorough

detain 1. check, delay, hinder, hold up, impede, keep, keep back, retard, slow up (or down), stay, stop **2**. arrest, confine, hold, intern, restrain

detect 1. ascertain, catch, descry, distinguish, identify, note, notice, observe, recognize, scent, spot **2**. catch, disclose, discover, expose, find, reveal, track down, uncover, unmask

detection discovery, exposé, exposure, ferreting out, revelation, tracking down, uncovering, unearthing, unmasking

detective C.I.D. man, constable, cop (*Sl.*), copper (*Sl.*), dick (*Sl., chiefly U.S.*), gumshoe (*U.S. sl.*), investigator, private eye, private investigator, sleuth (*Inf.*)

detention confinement, custody, delay, hindrance, holding back, imprisonment, incarceration, keeping in, quarantine, restraint, withholding

deter caution, check, damp, daunt, debar, discourage, dissuade, frighten, hinder, inhibit from, intimidate, prevent, prohibit, put off, restrain, stop, talk out of

detergent 1. n. cleaner, cleanser **2**. adj. abstergent, cleaning, cleansing, detersive, purifying

deteriorate 1. corrupt, debase, decline, degenerate, degrade, deprave, depreciate, go downhill (*Inf.*), go to pot, go to the dogs (*Inf.*), impair, injure, lower, spoil, worsen **2**. be the worse for wear

(*Inf.*), crumble, decay, decline, decompose, disintegrate, ebb, fade, fall apart, lapse, weaken, wear away

deterioration atrophy, corrosion, debasement, decline, degeneration, degradation, dégringolade, depreciation, descent, dilapidation, disintegration, downturn, drop, fall, lapse, retrogression, slump, vitiation, worsening

determinable answerable, ascertainable, assessable, definable, describable, discoverable

determinate absolute, certain, conclusive, decided, decisive, defined, definite, definitive, determined, distinct, established, explicit, express, fixed, limited, positive, precise, quantified, settled, specified

determination 1. backbone, constancy, conviction, dedication, doggedness, drive, firmness, fortitude, indomitability, perseverance, persistence, resoluteness, resolution, resolve, single-mindedness, steadfastness, tenacity, willpower **2**. conclusion, decision, judgment, purpose, resolve, result, settlement, solution, verdict

determine 1. arbitrate, conclude, decide, end, finish, fix upon, ordain, regulate, settle, terminate **2**. ascertain, certify, check, detect, discover, find out, learn, verify, work out **3**. choose, decide, elect, establish, fix, make up one's mind, purpose, resolve **4**. affect, condition, control, decide, dictate, direct, govern, impel, impose, incline, induce, influence, lead, modify, regulate, rule, shape

determined bent on, constant, dogged, firm, fixed, intent, persevering, persistent, purposeful, resolute, set on, single-minded, steadfast, strong-minded, strong-willed, tenacious, unflinching, unwavering

determining conclusive, critical, crucial, deciding, decisive, definitive, essential, final, important, settling

deterrent n. check, curb, defensive measures, determent, discouragement, disincentive, hindrance, impediment, obstacle, restraint

detest abhor, abominate, despise, dislike intensely, execrate, feel aversion (disgust, hostility, repugnance) towards, hate, loathe, recoil from

detestable abhorred, abominable, accursed, despicable, disgusting, execrable, hateful, heinous, loathsome, obnoxious,

detestation

detestation — devil

detestation 1. abhorrence, abomination, animosity, animus, antipathy, aversion, disgust, dislike, execration, hatred, hostility, loathing, odium, repugnance, revulsion **2.** abomination, anathema, bête noire, hate

dethrone depose, oust, uncrown, unseat

detonate blast, blow up, discharge, explode, fulminate, set off, touch off

detonation bang, blast, blow-up, boom, discharge, explosion, fulmination, report

detour bypass, byway, circuitous route, deviation, diversion, indirect course, roundabout way

detract 1. devaluate, diminish, lessen, lower, reduce, take away from **2.** deflect, distract, divert, shift

detraction abuse, aspersion, belittlement, calumny, defamation, denigration, deprecation, disparagement, innuendo, insinuation, misrepresentation, muckraking, running down, scandalmongering, scurrility, slander, traducement, vituperation

detractor backbiter, belittler, defamer, denigrator, derogator (*Rare*), disparager, muckraker, scandalmonger, slanderer, traducer

detriment damage, disadvantage, disservice, harm, hurt, impairment, injury, loss, mischief, prejudice

detrimental adverse, baleful, damaging, deleterious, destructive, disadvantageous, harmful, inimical, injurious, mischievous, pernicious, prejudicial, unfavourable

detritus debris, fragments, litter, remains, rubbish, waste

de trop in the way, redundant, superfluous, surplus, unnecessary, unwanted, unwelcome

devastate 1. demolish, desolate, despoil, destroy, lay waste, level, pillage, plunder, ravage, raze, ruin, sack, spoil, waste, wreck **2.** *Inf.* chagrin, confound, discomfit, discompose, disconcert, floor (*Inf.*), nonplus, overpower, overwhelm, take aback

devastating caustic, cutting, deadly, destructive, effective, incisive, keen, mordant, overpowering, overwhelming, ravishing, sardonic, satirical, savage, stunning, trenchant, withering

devastation demolition, depredation, desolation, destruction, havoc, pillage, plunder, ravages, ruin, ruination, spoliation

develop 1. advance, cultivate, evolve, flourish, foster, grow, mature, progress, promote, prosper, ripen **2.** amplify, augment, broaden, dilate upon, elaborate, enlarge, expand, unfold, work out **3.** acquire, begin, breed, commence, contract, establish, form, generate, invent, originate, pick up, start **4.** be a direct result of, break out, come about, ensue, follow, happen, result

development 1. advance, advancement, evolution, expansion, growth, improvement, increase, maturity, progress, progression, spread, unfolding, unravelling **2.** change, circumstance, event, happening, incident, issue, occurrence, outcome, phenomenon, result, situation, turn of events, upshot

deviant 1. *adj.* aberrant, abnormal, bent (*Sl.*), deviate, devious, freaky (*Sl.*), heretical, kinky (*Sl.*), perverse, perverted, queer (*Inf.*), twisted, wayward **2.** *n.* deviate, freak, misfit, odd type, pervert, queer (*Inf.*)

deviate avert, bend, deflect, depart, differ, digress, diverge, drift, err, part, stray, swerve, turn, turn aside, vary, veer, wander

deviation aberration, alteration, change, deflection, departure, digression, discrepancy, disparity, divergence, fluctuation, inconsistency, irregularity, shift, variance, variation

device 1. apparatus, appliance, contraption, contrivance, gadget, gimmick, implement, instrument, invention, tool, utensil **2.** artifice, design, dodge, expedient, gambit, improvisation, manoeuvre, plan, ploy, project, purpose, ruse, scheme, shift, stratagem, strategy, stunt, trick, wile **3.** badge, colophon, crest, design, emblem, figure, insignia, logo, motif, motto, symbol, token

devil 1. *Sometimes cap.* Apollyon, archfiend, Beelzebub, Belial, Clootie (*Scot.*), demon, fiend, Lucifer, Old Harry (*Inf.*), Old Nick (*Inf.*), Prince of Darkness, Satan **2.** beast, brute, demon, monster, ogre, rogue, savage, terror, villain **3.** imp, monkey (*Inf.*), rascal, rogue, scamp, scoundrel **4.** beggar, creature, thing, unfortunate, wretch **5.** demon, enthusiast, fiend, go-getter (*Inf.*)

devilish accursed, atrocious, damnable, detestable, diabolic, diabolical, execrable, fiendish, hellish, infernal, satanic, wicked

devil-may-care careless, casual, easy-going, flippant, happy-go-lucky, heedless, insouciant, nonchalant, reckless, swaggering, swashbuckling, unconcerned

devilment devilry, knavery, mischief, mischievousness, naughtiness, rascality, roguery, roguishness

devilry, deviltry 1. devilment, knavery, mischief, mischievousness, rascality, roguery **2**. cruelty, evil, malevolence, malice, vice, viciousness, villainy, wickedness **3**. black magic, diablerie, diabolism, sorcery

devious 1. calculating, crooked (Inf.), deceitful, dishonest, double-dealing, evasive, indirect, insidious, insincere, not straightforward, scheming, sly, surreptitious, treacherous, tricky, underhand, wily **2**. circuitous, confusing, crooked, deviating, erratic, excursive, indirect, misleading, rambling, roundabout, tortuous, wandering

devise arrange, conceive, concoct, construct, contrive, design, dream up, form, formulate, frame, imagine, invent, plan, plot, prepare, project, scheme, think up, work out

devitalize cripple, debilitate, enervate, enfeeble, exhaust, reduce, sap, undermine, weaken

devoid barren, bereft, deficient, denuded, destitute, empty, free from, lacking, sans (Archaic), unprovided with, vacant, void, wanting, without

devolution decentralization, delegation

devolve 1. be transferred, commission, consign, delegate, depute, entrust, fall upon or to, rest with, transfer **2**. Law alienate, be handed down, convey

devote allot, apply, appropriate, assign, commit, concern oneself, consecrate, dedicate, enshrine, give, occupy oneself, pledge, reserve, set apart

devoted ardent, caring, committed, concerned, constant, dedicated, devout, faithful, fond, loving, loyal, staunch, steadfast, true

devotee addict, adherent, admirer, aficionado, disciple, enthusiast, fan, fanatic, follower, supporter, votary

devotion 1. adherence, allegiance, commitment, consecration, constancy, dedication, faithfulness, fidelity, loyalty **2**. adoration, devoutness, godliness, holiness, piety, prayer, religiousness, reverence, sanctity, spirituality, worship **3**. affection, ardour, attachment, earnestness, fervour, fondness, intensity, love, passion, zeal **4**. Plural church service, divine office, prayers, religious observance

devotional devout, holy, pious, religious, reverential, sacred, solemn, spiritual

devour 1. bolt, consume, cram, dispatch, eat, gobble, gorge, gulp, guzzle, polish off (Inf.), stuff, swallow, wolf **2**. annihilate, consume, destroy, ravage, spend, waste, wipe out **3**. absorb, appreciate, be engrossed by, be preoccupied, delight in, drink in, enjoy, feast on, go through, read compulsively or voraciously, relish, revel in, take in

devouring consuming, excessive, insatiable, intense, overwhelming, passionate, powerful

devout 1. godly, holy, orthodox, pious, prayerful, pure, religious, reverent, saintly **2**. ardent, deep, devoted, earnest, fervent, genuine, heartfelt, intense, passionate, profound, serious, sincere, zealous

devoutly fervently, heart and soul, profoundly, sincerely, with all one's heart

dexterity 1. adroitness, artistry, deftness, effortlessness, expertise, facility, finesse, handiness, knack, mastery, neatness, nimbleness, proficiency, skill, smoothness, touch **2**. ability, address, adroitness, aptitude, aptness, art, cleverness, expertness, ingenuity, readiness, skilfulness, tact

dexterous able, active, acute, adept, adroit, agile, apt, clever, deft, expert, handy, ingenious, masterly, neat, nimble, nimble-fingered, proficient, prompt, quick, skilful

diabolic 1. demoniac, demonic, devilish, fiendish, hellish, infernal, satanic **2**. atrocious, cruel, evil, fiendish, monstrous, nefarious, vicious, villainous, wicked

diabolical appalling, atrocious, damnable, difficult, disastrous, dreadful, excruciating, fiendish, hellish, nasty, outrageous, shocking, tricky, unpleasant, vile

diadem circlet, coronet, crown, tiara

diagnose analyse, determine, distinguish, identify, interpret, investigate, pinpoint, pronounce, recognize

diagnosis 1. analysis, examination, investigation, scrutiny **2**. conclusion, interpretation, opinion, pronouncement

diagnostic demonstrative, distinctive, distinguishing, idiosyncratic, indicative, particular, peculiar, recognizable, symptomatic

diagonal *adj*. angled, cater-cornered (*U.S. inf*.), cornerways, cross, crossways, crosswise, oblique, slanting

diagonally aslant, at an angle, cornerwise, crosswise, obliquely, on the bias, on the cross

diagram chart, drawing, figure, layout, outline, plan, representation, sketch

dialect accent, idiom, jargon, language, lingo (*Inf*.), localism, patois, pronunciation, provincialism, speech, tongue, vernacular

dialectal dialect, idiomatic, local, nonstandard, regional, restricted, vernacular

dialectic 1. *adj*. analytic, argumentative, dialectical, logical, polemical, rational, rationalistic **2**. *n. Often plural* argumentation, contention, discussion, disputation, logic, polemics, ratiocination, reasoning

dialogue 1. colloquy, communication, confabulation, conference, conversation, converse, discourse, discussion, duologue, interlocution **2**. conversation, lines, script, spoken part

diametric, diametrical antipodal, antithetical, conflicting, contrary, contrasting, counter, opposed, opposite

diametrically absolutely, completely, entirely, utterly

diaphanous chiffon, clear, cobwebby, delicate, filmy, fine, gauzy, gossamer, light, pellucid, seethrough, sheer, thin, translucent, transparent

diary appointment book, chronicle, daily record, day-to-day account, engagement book, journal

diatribe abuse, castigation, criticism, denunciation, disputation, harangue, invective, philippic, reviling, stream of abuse, stricture, tirade, verbal onslaught, vituperation

dicey chancy (*Inf*.), dangerous, difficult, risky, ticklish, tricky

dicky *adj*. fluttery, queer, shaky, unreliable, unsound, unsteady, weak

dictate *v*. **1**. read out, say, speak, transmit, utter **2**. command, decree, direct, enjoin, impose, lay down, ordain,

order, prescribe, pronounce ~*n*. **3**. behest, bidding, command, decree, direction, edict, fiat, injunction, mandate, order, ordinance, requirement, statute, ultimatum, word **4**. code, dictum, law, precept, principle, rule

dictator absolute ruler, autocrat, despot, oppressor, tyrant

dictatorial 1. absolute, arbitrary, autocratic, despotic, totalitarian, tyrannical, unlimited, unrestricted **2**. authoritarian, bossy (*Inf*.), dogmatical, domineering, imperious, iron-handed, magisterial, oppressive, overbearing

dictatorship absolute rule, absolutism, authoritarianism, autocracy, despotism, reign of terror, totalitarianism, tyranny

diction 1. expression, language, phraseology, phrasing, style, usage, vocabulary, wording **2**. articulation, delivery, elocution, enunciation, fluency, inflection, intonation, pronunciation, speech

dictionary concordance, encyclopedia, glossary, lexicon, vocabulary, wordbook

dictum 1. command, decree, dictate, edict, fiat, order, pronouncement **2**. adage, axiom, gnome, maxim, precept, proverb, saw, saying

didactic edifying, educational, enlightening, homiletic, instructive, moral, moralizing, pedagogic, pedantic, preceptive

die 1. breathe one's last, decease, depart, expire, finish, give up the ghost, hop the twig (*Sl*.), kick the bucket (*Sl*.), pass away, perish, snuff it (*Sl*.) **2**. decay, decline, disappear, dwindle, ebb, end, fade, lapse, pass, sink, subside, vanish, wane, wilt, wither **3**. break down, fade out *or* away, fail, fizzle out, halt, lose power, peter out, run down, stop **4**. ache, be eager, desire, hunger, languish, long, pine for, swoon, yearn **5**. *Usually with* **of** be overcome, collapse, succumb to

die-hard 1. *n*. fanatic, intransigent, old fogy, reactionary, stick-in-the-mud (*Inf*.), ultraconservative, zealot **2**. *adj*. dyed-in-the-wool, immovable, inflexible, intransigent, reactionary, ultraconservative, uncompromising, unreconstructed (*Chiefly U.S*.)

diet[1] *n*. **1**. abstinence, dietary, fast, regime, regimen **2**. aliment, comestibles, commons, edibles, fare, food, nourishment, nutriment, provisions, rations, subsistence, sustenance, viands, victuals

~*v.* **3**. abstain, eat sparingly, fast, lose weight, reduce, slim

diet[2] chamber, congress, convention, council, legislative assembly, legislature, meeting, parliament, sitting

dieter calorie counter, faster, reducer, slimmer, weight watcher

differ 1. be dissimilar, be distinct, contradict, contrast, depart from, diverge, run counter to, stand apart, vary **2**. clash, contend, debate, demur, disagree, dispute, dissent, oppose, take issue

difference 1. alteration, change, contrast, deviation, differentiation, discrepancy, disparity, dissimilarity, distinction, distinctness, divergence, diversity, unlikeness, variation, variety **2**. distinction, exception, idiosyncrasy, particularity, peculiarity, singularity **3**. argument, clash, conflict, contention, contrariety, contretemps, controversy, debate, disagreement, discordance, dispute, quarrel, set-to (*Inf.*), strife, tiff, wrangle **4**. balance, remainder, rest, result

different 1. altered, at odds, at variance, changed, clashing, contrasting, deviating, discrepant, disparate, dissimilar, divergent, diverse, inconsistent, opposed, unlike **2**. another, discrete, distinct, individual, other, separate **3**. assorted, divers (*Archaic*), diverse, manifold, many, miscellaneous, multifarious, numerous, several, some, sundry, varied, various **4**. another story, atypical, bizarre, distinctive, extraordinary, out of the ordinary, peculiar, rare, singular, something else, special, strange, uncommon, unconventional, unique, unusual

differential 1. *adj.* diacritical, discriminative, distinctive, distinguishing **2**. *n.* amount of difference, difference, discrepancy, disparity

differentiate 1. contrast, discern, discriminate, distinguish, make a distinction, mark off, separate, set off *or* apart, tell apart **2**. adapt, alter, change, convert, make different, modify, transform

difficult 1. arduous, burdensome, demanding, formidable, hard, laborious, no picnic (*Inf.*), onerous, painful, strenuous, toilsome, uphill, wearisome **2**. abstract, abstruse, baffling, complex, complicated, delicate, enigmatical, intricate, involved, knotty, obscure, perplexing, problematical, thorny, ticklish **3**. demanding, fastidious, fractious, fussy, hard to please,

intractable, obstreperous, perverse, refractory, rigid, tiresome, troublesome, trying, unaccommodating, unamenable, unmanageable **4**. dark, full of hardship, grim, hard, straitened, tough, trying

difficulty 1. arduousness, awkwardness, hardship, laboriousness, labour, pain, painfulness, strain, strenuousness, tribulation **2**. deep water, dilemma, distress, embarrassment, fix (*Inf.*), hot water, jam (*Inf.*), mess, perplexity, pickle (*Inf.*), plight, predicament, quandary, spot (*Inf.*), straits, trial, trouble **3**. *Often plural* complication, hindrance, hurdle, impediment, objection, obstacle, opposition, pitfall, problem, protest

diffidence backwardness, bashfulness, constraint, doubt, fear, hesitancy, hesitation, humility, insecurity, lack of self-confidence, meekness, modesty, reluctance, reserve, self-consciousness, sheepishness, shyness, timidity, timidness, timorousness, unassertiveness

diffident backward, bashful, constrained, distrustful, doubtful, hesitant, insecure, meek, modest, reluctant, reserved, self-conscious, self-effacing, sheepish, shrinking, shy, suspicious, timid, timorous, unassertive, unassuming, unobtrusive, unsure, withdrawn

diffuse *adj.* **1**. circumlocutory, copious, diffusive, digressive, discursive, long-winded, loose, maundering, meandering, prolix, rambling, vague, verbose, waffling (*Inf.*), wordy **2**. dispersed, scattered, spread out, unconcentrated ~*v.* **3**. circulate, dispel, dispense, disperse, disseminate, dissipate, distribute, propagate, scatter, spread

diffusion 1. circulation, dispersal, dispersion, dissemination, dissipation, distribution, expansion, propaganda, propagation, scattering, spread **2**. circuitousness, diffuseness, digressiveness, discursiveness, long-windedness, prolixity, rambling, verbiage, verbosity, wandering, wordiness

dig *v.* **1**. break up, burrow, delve, excavate, gouge, grub, hoe, hollow out, mine, penetrate, pierce, quarry, scoop, till, tunnel, turn over **2**. drive, jab, poke, prod, punch, thrust **3**. delve, dig down, go into, investigate, probe, research, search **4**. *With* **out** *or* **up** bring to light, come across, come up with, discover, expose, extricate, find, retrieve, root (*Inf.*), rootle, uncover, unearth **5**. *Inf.* appreciate, enjoy, follow, groove (*Sl.*), like, under-stand ~*n.* **6.** jab, poke, prod, punch, thrust **7.** crack (*Sl.*), cutting remark, gibe, insult, jeer, quip, sneer, taunt, wise-crack (*Inf.*)

digest *v.* **1.** absorb, assimilate, concoct, dissolve, incorporate, macerate **2.** absorb, assimilate, con, consider, contemplate, grasp, master, meditate, ponder, study, take in, understand **3.** arrange, classify, codify, dispose, methodize, systematize, tabulate **4.** abridge, compress, condense, reduce, shorten, summarize ~*n.* **5.** abridgment, abstract, compendium, condensation, epitome, précis, résumé, summary, synopsis

digestion absorption, assimilation, conversion, incorporation, ingestion, transformation

dig in 1. defend, entrench, establish, fortify, maintain **2.** *Inf.* begin, set about, start eating, tuck in (*Inf.*)

dignified august, decorous, distinguished, exalted, formal, grave, honourable, imposing, lofty, lordly, noble, reserved, solemn, stately, upright

dignify adorn, advance, aggrandize, distinguish, elevate, ennoble, exalt, glorify, grace, honour, promote, raise

dignitary *n.* high-up (*Inf.*), notability, notable, personage, pillar of society (the church, the state), public figure, V.I.P., worthy

dignity 1. courtliness, decorum, grandeur, gravity, hauteur, loftiness, majesty, nobility, propriety, solemnity, stateliness **2.** elevation, eminence, excellence, glory, greatness, honour, importance, nobleness, rank, respectability, standing, station, status **3.** *amour-propre*, pride, self-esteem, self-importance, self-possession, self-regard, self-respect

digress be diffuse, depart, deviate, diverge, drift, expatiate, get off the point *or* subject, go off at a tangent, ramble, stray, turn aside, wander

digression apostrophe, aside, departure, detour, deviation, divergence, diversion, footnote, obiter dictum, parenthesis, straying, wandering

digressive anecdotal, circuitous, circumlocutory, diffuse, discursive, divergent, drifting, episodic, excursive, meandering, rambling

dilapidated battered, broken-down, crumbling, decayed, decaying, decrepit, fallen in, falling apart, gone to wrack and

ruin, in ruins, neglected, ramshackle, rickety, ruined, ruinous, run-down, shabby, shaky, tumble-down, uncared for, worn-out

dilapidation collapse, decay, demolition, destruction, deterioration, disintegration, disrepair, dissolution, downfall, ruin, waste, wear and tear

dilate 1. broaden, distend, enlarge, expand, extend, puff out, stretch, swell, widen **2.** amplify, be profuse, be prolix, descant, detail, develop, dwell on, enlarge, expand, expatiate, expound, spin out

dilation broadening, dilatation, distention, enlargement, expansion, extension, increase, spread

dilatory backward, behindhand, dallying, delaying, laggard, lingering, loitering, procrastinating, putting off, slack, slow, sluggish, snail-like, tardy, tarrying, time-wasting

dilemma 1. difficulty, embarrassment, fix (*Inf.*), jam (*Inf.*), mess, perplexity, pickle (*Inf.*), plight, predicament, problem, puzzle, quandary, spot (*Inf.*), strait, tight corner **2. on the horns of a dilemma** between Scylla and Charybdis, between the devil and the deep blue sea

dilettante aesthete, amateur, dabbler, nonprofessional, trifler

diligence activity, application, assiduity, assiduousness, attention, attentiveness, care, constancy, earnestness, heedfulness, industry, intentness, laboriousness, perseverance, sedulousness

diligent active, assiduous, attentive, busy, careful, conscientious, constant, earnest, hard-working, indefatigable, industrious, laborious, painstaking, persevering, persistent, sedulous, studious, tireless

dilly-dally dally, dawdle, delay, dither, falter, fluctuate, hesitate, hover, linger, loiter, potter, procrastinate, shilly-shally (*Inf.*), trifle, vacillate, waver

dilute *v.* **1.** adulterate, cut, make thinner, thin (out), water down, weaken **2.** *Fig.* attenuate, decrease, diffuse, diminish, lessen, mitigate, reduce, temper, weaken

diluted adulterated, cut, dilute, thinned, watered down, watery, weak, weakened, wishy-washy (*Inf.*)

dim *adj.* **1.** caliginous (*Archaic*), cloudy, dark, darkish, dusky, grey, overcast, poorly lit, shadowy, tenebrous, unilluminated **2.** bleary, blurred, faint, fuzzy, ill-defined, indistinct, obscured, shadowy, unclear **3.** dense, doltish, dull, dumb (*Inf.*), obtuse, slow, slow on the uptake (*Inf.*), stupid, thick **4.** confused, hazy, imperfect, indistinct, intangible, obscure, remote, shadowy, vague **5.** dingy, dull, feeble, lacklustre, muted, opaque, pale, sullied, tarnished, weak **6.** dashing, depressing, discouraging, gloomy, sombre, unfavourable, unpromising **7. take a dim view** be displeased, be sceptical, disapprove, look askance, reject, suspect, take exception, view with disfavour ~*v.* **8.** bedim, blur, cloud, darken, dull, fade, lower, obscure, tarnish, turn down

dimension *Often plural* **1.** amplitude, bulk, capacity, extent, measurement, proportions, size, volume **2.** bigness, extent, greatness, importance, largeness, magnitude, measure, range, scale, scope

diminish 1. abate, contract, curtail, cut, decrease, lessen, lower, reduce, retrench, shrink, weaken **2.** decline, die out, dwindle, ebb, fade away, peter out, recede, shrivel, slacken, subside, wane **3.** belittle, cheapen, demean, depreciate, devalue

diminution abatement, contraction, curtailment, cut, cutback, decay, decline, decrease, deduction, lessening, reduction, retrenchment, weakening

diminutive *adj.* bantam, Lilliputian, little, midget, mini, miniature, minute, petite, pocket(-sized), pygmy, small, tiny, undersized, wee

dimwit blockhead, bonehead (*Sl.*), booby, dullard, dunce, dunderhead, ignoramus, nitwit, numskull

din 1. *n.* babel, clamour, clangour, clash, clatter, commotion, crash, hubbub, hullabaloo, noise, outcry, pandemonium, racket, row, shout, uproar **2.** *v.* *Usually with* **into** drum into, go on at, hammer into, inculcate, instil, instruct, teach

dine 1. banquet, eat, feast, lunch, sup **2.** *Often with* **on, off** *or* **upon** consume, eat, feed on

dingle dale, dell, glen, hollow, vale, valley

dingy bedimmed, colourless, dark, dim, dirty, discoloured, drab, dreary, dull, dusky, faded, gloomy, grimy, murky, obscure, seedy, shabby, soiled, sombre, tacky

dinky dainty, mini, miniature, natty (*Inf.*), neat, petite, small, trim

dinner banquet, beanfeast (*Inf.*), blowout (*Sl.*), collation, feast, main meal, meal, refection, repast, spread

dint 1. *As in* **by dint of** force, means, power, use, virtue **2.** blow, dent, depression, indentation, stroke

dip *v.* **1.** bathe, douse, duck, dunk, immerse, plunge, rinse, souse **2.** decline, descend, disappear, droop, drop (down), fade, fall, lower, sag, set, sink, slope, slump, subside, tilt **3.** ladle, scoop, spoon **4.** *With* **in** *or* **into** browse, dabble, glance at, peruse, play at, run over, sample, skim, try **5.** *With* **in** *or* **into** draw upon, reach into ~*n.* **6.** douche, drenching, ducking, immersion, plunge, soaking **7.** bathe, dive, plunge, swim **8.** concoction, dilution, infusion, mixture, preparation, solution, suspension **9.** basin, concavity, depression, hole, hollow, incline, slope **10.** decline, fall, lowering, sag, slip, slump

diplomacy 1. international negotiation, statecraft, statesmanship **2.** artfulness, craft, delicacy, discretion, finesse, savoir faire, skill, subtlety, tact

diplomat conciliator, go-between, mediator, moderator, negotiator, politician, public relations expert, tactician

diplomatic adept, discreet, polite, politic, prudent, sensitive, subtle, tactful

dire 1. alarming, appalling, awful, calamitous, cataclysmic, catastrophic, cruel, disastrous, horrible, horrid, ruinous, terrible, woeful **2.** dismal, dreadful, fearful, gloomy, grim, ominous, portentous **3.** critical, crucial, crying, desperate, drastic, exigent, extreme, pressing, urgent

direct[1] *v.* **1.** administer, advise, conduct, control, dispose, govern, guide, handle, lead, manage, mastermind, oversee, preside over, regulate, rule, run, superintend, supervise **2.** bid, charge, command, dictate, enjoin, instruct, order **3.** guide, indicate, lead, point in the direction of, point the way, show **4.** address, aim, cast, fix, focus, intend, level, mean, point, train, turn **5.** address, label, mail, route, send, superscribe

direct[2] *adj.* **1.** candid, frank, honest, man-to-man, matter-of-fact, open, outspoken, plain-spoken, sincere, straight, straightforward **2.** absolute, blunt, categorical, downright, explicit, express, plain, point-blank, unambiguous, unequivocal **3**. nonstop, not crooked, shortest, straight, through, unbroken, undeviating, uninterrupted **4**. face-to-face, first-hand, head-on, immediate, personal

direction 1. administration, charge, command, control, government, guidance, leadership, management, order, oversight, superintendence, supervision **2**. aim, bearing, course, line, path, road, route, track, way **3**. bent, bias, current, drift, end, orientation, proclivity, tack, tendency, tenor, trend **4**. address, label, mark, superscription

directions briefing, guidance, guidelines, indication, instructions, plan, recommendation, regulations

directive *n*. charge, command, decree, dictate, edict, injunction, instruction, mandate, notice, order, ordinance, regulation, ruling

directly 1. by the shortest route, exactly, in a beeline, precisely, straight, unswervingly, without deviation **2**. as soon as possible, at once, dead, due, forthwith, immediately, in a second, instantaneously, instantly, presently, promptly, pronto (*Inf.*), quickly, right away, soon, speedily, straightaway **3**. candidly, face-to-face, honestly, in person, openly, personally, plainly, point-blank, straightforwardly, truthfully, unequivocally, without prevarication

directness bluntness, candour, forthrightness, frankness, honesty, outspokenness, sincerity, straightforwardness

director administrator, boss (*Inf.*), chairman, chief, controller, executive, governor, head, leader, manager, organizer, principal, producer, supervisor

direful appalling, awful, calamitous, dire, dreadful, fearful, ghastly, gloomy, horrible, horrid, shocking, terrible

dirge coronach (*Scot. & Irish*), dead march, elegy, funeral song, lament, requiem, threnody

dirt 1. dust, excrement, filth, grime, impurity, mire, muck, mud, slime, smudge, stain, tarnish **2**. clay, earth, loam, soil **3**. indecency, obscenity, pornography, smut

dirty *adj*. **1**. begrimed, filthy, foul, grimy, grubby, messy, mucky, muddy, nasty, polluted, soiled, sullied, unclean **2**. blue, indecent, obscene, off-colour, pornographic, risqué, salacious, smutty, vulgar **3**. clouded, dark, dull, miry, muddy, not clear **4**. corrupt, crooked, dishonest, fraudulent, illegal, treacherous, unfair, unscrupulous, unsporting **5**. base, beggarly, contemptible, cowardly, despicable, ignominious, low, low-down (*Inf.*), mean, nasty, scurvy, shabby, sordid, squalid, vile **6**. angry, annoyed, bitter, indignant, offended, resentful, scorching **7**. *Of weather* gusty, lowering, rainy, squally, stormy ~*v*. **8**. begrime, blacken, defile, foul, mess up, muddy, pollute, smear, smudge, soil, spoil, stain, sully

disability 1. affliction, ailment, complaint, defect, disablement, disorder, handicap, impairment, infirmity, malady **2**. disqualification, impotency, inability, incapacity, incompetency, unfitness, weakness

disable 1. cripple, damage, debilitate, enfeeble, hamstring, handicap, immobilize, impair, incapacitate, paralyse, prostrate, put out of action, render *hors de combat*, render inoperative, unfit, unman, weaken **2**. disenable, disqualify, invalidate, render *or* declare incapable

disabled bedridden, crippled, handicapped, incapacitated, infirm, lame, maimed, mangled, mutilated, paralysed, weak, weakened, wrecked

disabuse correct, enlighten, free from error, open the eyes of, set right, set straight, shatter (someone's) illusions, undeceive

disadvantage 1. damage, detriment, disservice, harm, hurt, injury, loss, prejudice **2**. *Often plural* burden, drawback, flaw, fly in the ointment (*Inf.*), handicap, hardship, hindrance, impediment, inconvenience, liability, minus (*Inf.*), nuisance, privation, snag, trouble, weakness, weak point **3**. **at a disadvantage** boxed in, cornered, handicapped, in a corner, vulnerable

disadvantaged deprived, discriminated against, handicapped, impoverished, struggling, underprivileged

disadvantageous adverse, damaging, deleterious, detrimental, harmful, hurtful, ill-timed, inconvenient, inexpedient, injurious, inopportune, prejudicial, unfavourable

disaffect alienate, antagonize, disunite, divide, estrange, repel

disaffected alienated, antagonistic, discontented, disloyal, dissatisfied, estranged, hostile, mutinous, rebellious, seditious, uncompliant, unsubmissive

disaffection alienation, animosity, antagonism, antipathy, aversion, breach, disagreement, discontent, dislike, disloyalty, dissatisfaction, estrangement, hostility, ill will, repugnance, resentment, unfriendliness

disagree 1. be discordant, be dissimilar, conflict, contradict, counter, depart, deviate, differ, diverge, run counter to, vary **2**. argue, bicker, clash, contend, contest, debate, differ (in opinion), dispute, dissent, fall out (*Inf.*), have words (*Inf.*), object, oppose, quarrel, take issue with, wrangle **3**. be injurious, bother, discomfort, distress, hurt, make ill, nauseate, sicken, trouble, upset

disagreeable 1. bad-tempered, brusque, churlish, contrary, cross, difficult, disobliging, ill-natured, irritable, nasty, peevish, rude, surly, unfriendly, ungracious, unlikable, unpleasant **2**. disgusting, displeasing, distasteful, nasty, objectionable, obnoxious, offensive, repellent, repugnant, repulsive, uninviting, unpalatable, unpleasant, unsavoury

disagreement 1. difference, discrepancy, disparity, dissimilarity, dissimilitude, divergence, diversity, incompatibility, incongruity, unlikeness, variance **2**. altercation, argument, clash, conflict, debate, difference, discord, dispute, dissent, division, falling out, misunderstanding, quarrel, squabble, strife, wrangle **3. in disagreement** at daggers drawn, at loggerheads, at odds, at variance, disunited, in conflict

disallow 1. abjure, disavow, disclaim, dismiss, disown, rebuff, refuse, reject, repudiate **2**. ban, cancel, embargo, forbid, prohibit, proscribe, veto

disappear 1. be lost to view, depart, drop out of sight, ebb, escape, evanesce, fade away, flee, fly, go, pass, recede, retire, vanish from sight, wane, withdraw **2**. cease, cease to be known, die out, dissolve, end, evaporate, expire, fade, leave no trace, melt away, pass away, perish, vanish

disappearance departure, desertion, disappearing, disappearing trick, eclipse, evanescence, evaporation, fading, flight, going, loss, melting, passing, vanishing, vanishing point

disappoint 1. chagrin, dash, deceive, delude, disenchant, disgruntle, dishearten, disillusion, dismay, dissatisfy, fail, let down, sadden, vex **2**. baffle, balk, defeat, disconcert, foil, frustrate, hamper, hinder, thwart

disappointed balked, cast down, depressed, despondent, discontented, discouraged, disenchanted, disgruntled, disillusioned, dissatisfied, distressed, downhearted, foiled, frustrated, let down, saddened, thwarted, upset

disappointing depressing, disagreeable, disconcerting, discouraging, failing, inadequate, inferior, insufficient, lame, pathetic, sad, second-rate, sorry, unexpected, unhappy, unsatisfactory, unworthy, upsetting

disappointment 1. chagrin, discontent, discouragement, disenchantment, disillusionment, displeasure, dissatisfaction, distress, failure, frustration, ill-success, mortification, regret, unfulfilment **2**. blow, calamity, disaster, failure, fiasco, letdown, miscarriage, misfortune, setback, washout (*Inf.*)

disapprobation blame, censure, condemnation, disapproval, disfavour, dislike, displeasure, dissatisfaction, reproof, stricture

disapproval censure, condemnation, criticism, denunciation, deprecation, disapprobation, displeasure, dissatisfaction, objection, reproach

disapprove 1. *Often with* of blame, censure, condemn, deplore, deprecate, discountenance, dislike, find unacceptable, frown on, look down one's nose at (*Inf.*), object to, reject, take exception to **2**. disallow, set aside, spurn, turn down, veto

disarm 1. disable, render defenceless, unarm **2**. deactivate, demilitarize, demobilize, disband **3**. persuade, set at ease, win over

disarmament arms limitation, arms reduction, de-escalation, demilitarization, demobilization

disarming charming, irresistible, likable, persuasive, winning

disarrange confuse, derange, discompose, disorder, disorganize, disturb, jumble (up), mess (up), scatter, shake (up), shuffle, unsettle, untidy

disarray 1. confusion, discomposure, disharmony, dismay, disorder, disorderliness, disorganization, disunity, indiscipline, unruliness, upset **2**. chaos, clutter, dishevelment, jumble, mess, mix-up, muddle, shambles, tangle, untidiness

disassemble deconstruct, dismantle, dismount, knock down, strike, take apart, take down

disaster accident, act of God, adversity, blow, calamity, cataclysm, catastrophe, misadventure, mischance, misfortune, mishap, reverse, ruin, ruination, stroke, tragedy, trouble

disastrous adverse, calamitous, cataclysmal, cataclysmic, catastrophic, destructive, detrimental, devastating, dire, dreadful, fatal, hapless, harmful, ill-fated, ill-starred, ruinous, terrible, tragic, unfortunate, unlucky, unpropitious, untoward

disavow abjure, contradict, deny, disclaim, disown, forswear, gainsay, reject, repudiate

disavowal abjuration, contradiction, denial, disclaimer, gainsaying, recantation, rejection, renunciation, repudiation, retraction

disband break up, demobilize, dismiss, disperse, dissolve, go (their) separate ways, let go, part company, scatter, send home, separate

disbelief distrust, doubt, dubiety, incredulity, mistrust, scepticism, unbelief

disbelieve discount, discredit, give no credence to, mistrust, not accept, not buy (*Inf.*), not credit, not swallow (*Inf.*), reject, repudiate, scoff at, suspect

disbeliever agnostic, atheist, doubter, doubting Thomas, questioner, sceptic, scoffer

disbelievingly askance, cynically, doubtingly, incredulously, mistrustfully, quizzically, sceptically, suspiciously, with a pinch of salt

disburden alleviate, diminish, discharge, disencumber, ease, free, relieve, take a load off one's mind, unburden, unload

disburse expend, fork out (*Sl.*), lay out, pay out, shell out (*Inf.*), spend

disbursement disposal, expenditure, outlay, payment, spending

discard abandon, cast aside, dispense with, dispose of, ditch (*Sl.*), drop, dump (*Inf.*), get rid of, jettison, reject, relinquish, remove, repudiate, scrap, shed, throw away *or* out

discern 1. behold, catch sight of, descry, discover, espy, make out, notice, observe, perceive, recognize, see **2.** detect, determine, differentiate, discriminate, distinguish, judge, make distinction, pick out

discernible apparent, appreciable, clear, detectable, discoverable, distinct, distinguishable, noticeable, observable, obvious, perceptible, plain, recognizable, visible

discerning acute, astute, clear-sighted, critical, discriminating, ingenious, intelligent, judicious, knowing, penetrating, perceptive, percipient, perspicacious, piercing, sagacious, sensitive, sharp, shrewd, subtle, wise

discernment acumen, acuteness, astuteness, awareness, clear-sightedness, cleverness, discrimination, ingenuity, insight, intelligence, judgment, keenness, penetration, perception, perceptiveness, percipience, perspicacity, sagacity, sharpness, shrewdness, understanding

discharge *v.* **1.** absolve, acquit, allow to go, clear, exonerate, free, liberate, pardon, release, set free ~*n.* **2.** acquittal, clearance, exoneration, liberation, pardon, release, remittance ~*v.* **3.** cashier, discard, dismiss, eject, expel, fire (*Inf.*), give (someone) the sack (*Inf.*), oust, remove, sack (*Inf.*) ~*n.* **4.** congé, demobilization, dismissal, ejection, the boot (*Sl.*), the sack (*Inf.*) ~*v.* **5.** detonate, explode, fire, let off, set off, shoot ~*n.* **6.** blast, burst, detonation, discharging, explosion, firing, fusillade, report, salvo, shot, volley ~*v.* **7.** disembogue, dispense, emit, empty, excrete, exude, give off, gush, leak, ooze, pour forth, release, void ~*n.* **8.** emission, emptying, excretion, flow, ooze, pus, secretion, seepage, suppuration, vent, voiding ~*v.* **9.** disburden, off-load, remove, unburden, unload ~*n.* **10.** disburdening, emptying, unburdening, unloading ~*v.* **11.** accomplish, carry out, do, execute, fulfil, observe, perform ~*n.* **12.** accomplishment, achievement, execution, fulfilment, observance, performance ~*v.* **13.** clear, honour, meet, pay, relieve, satisfy, settle, square up ~*n.* **14.** payment, satisfaction, settlement

disciple adherent, apostle, believer, catechumen, convert, devotee, follower, learner, partisan, proselyte, pupil, student, supporter, votary

disciplinarian authoritarian, despot, drill sergeant, hard master, martinet, stickler, strict teacher, taskmaster, tyrant

discipline n. 1. drill, exercise, method, practice, regimen, regulation, training 2. conduct, control, orderliness, regulation, restraint, self-control, strictness 3. castigation, chastisement, correction, punishment 4. area, branch of knowledge, course, curriculum, field of study, specialty, subject ~v. 5. break in, bring up, check, control, drill, educate, exercise, form, govern, instruct, inure, prepare, regulate, restrain, train 6. castigate, chasten, chastise, correct, penalize, punish, reprimand, reprove

disclaim abandon, abjure, abnegate, decline, deny, disaffirm, disallow, disavow, disown, forswear, reject, renounce, repudiate

disclaimer abjuration, contradiction, denial, disavowal, rejection, renunciation, repudiation, retraction

disclose 1. broadcast, communicate, confess, divulge, impart, leak, let slip, make known, make public, publish, relate, reveal, spill the beans about (Inf.), tell, unveil, utter 2. bring to light, discover, exhibit, expose, lay bare, reveal, show, uncover, unveil

disclosure acknowledgment, admission, announcement, broadcast, confession, declaration, discovery, divulgence, exposé, exposure, leak, publication, revelation, uncovering

discoloration blemish, blot, blotch, mark, patch, splotch, spot, stain

discolour fade, mar, mark, rust, soil, stain, streak, tarnish, tinge

discomfit 1. abash, confound, confuse, demoralize, discompose, disconcert, embarrass, faze (U.S. inf.), flurry, fluster, perplex, perturb, rattle (Inf.), ruffle, take aback, unsettle, worry 2. baffle, balk, beat, checkmate, defeat, foil, frustrate, outwit, overcome, thwart, trump, worst

discomfiture 1. abashment, chagrin, confusion, demoralization, discomposure, embarrassment, humiliation, shame, unease 2. beating, defeat, disappointment, failure, frustration, overthrow, rout, ruin, undoing

discomfort 1. n. ache, annoyance, disquiet, distress, hardship, hurt, inquietude, irritation, malaise, nuisance, pain, soreness, trouble, uneasiness, unpleasantness, vexation 2. v. discomfit, discompose, disquiet, distress, disturb, embarrass, make uncomfortable

discommode annoy, bother, burden, disquiet, disturb, harass, incommode, inconvenience, molest, put out, trouble

discompose agitate, annoy, bewilder, confuse, discomfit, disconcert, displease, disturb, embarrass, faze (U.S. inf.), flurry, fluster, fret, irritate, nettle, perplex, perturb, provoke, rattle (Inf.), ruffle, unsettle, upset, vex, worry

discomposure agitation, anxiety, confusion, discomfiture, disquiet, disquietude, distraction, disturbance, embarrassment, fluster, inquietude, malaise, nervousness, perturbation, uneasiness

disconcert 1. abash, agitate, bewilder, discompose, disturb, flurry, fluster, nonplus, perplex, perturb, put out of countenance, rattle (Inf.), ruffle, shake up (Inf.), take aback, throw off balance, trouble, unbalance, unsettle, upset, worry 2. baffle, balk, confuse, defeat, disarrange, frustrate, hinder, put off, thwart, undo

disconcerted annoyed, bewildered, caught off balance, confused, distracted, disturbed, embarrassed, fazed (U.S. inf.), flurried, flustered, mixed-up, nonplussed, out of countenance, perturbed, rattled (Inf.), ruffled, shook up (Inf.), taken aback, thrown (Inf.), troubled, unsettled, upset

disconcerting alarming, awkward, baffling, bewildering, bothersome, confusing, dismaying, distracting, disturbing, embarrassing, off-putting (Brit. inf.), perplexing, upsetting

disconnect cut off, detach, disengage, divide, part, separate, sever, take apart, uncouple

disconnected confused, disjointed, garbled, illogical, incoherent, irrational, jumbled, mixed-up, rambling, uncoordinated, unintelligible, wandering

disconnection cessation, cut-off, cutting off, discontinuation, discontinuity, interruption, separation, severance, stoppage, suspension

disconsolate crushed, dejected, desolate, despairing, forlorn, gloomy, grief-stricken, heartbroken, hopeless, inconsolable, melancholy, miserable, sad, unhappy, woeful, wretched

discontent n. discontentment, displeasure, dissatisfaction, envy, fretfulness, regret, restlessness, uneasiness, unhappiness, vexation

discontented brassed off (Sl.), cheesed off (Brit. sl.), complaining, disaffected, disgruntled, displeased, dissatisfied, exasperated, fed up, fretful, miserable, unhappy, vexed, with a chip on one's shoulder (*Inf.*)

discontinuance adjournment, cessation, discontinuation, disjunction, intermission, interruption, separation, stop, stoppage, stopping, suspension, termination

discontinue abandon, break off, cease, drop, end, finish, give up, halt, interrupt, leave off, pause, put an end to, quit, refrain from, stop, suspend, terminate

discontinued abandoned, ended, finished, given up *or* over, halted, no longer made, terminated

discontinuity disconnectedness, disconnection, disjointedness, disruption, disunion, incoherence, interruption, lack of coherence, lack of unity

discontinuous broken, disconnected, fitful, intermittent, interrupted, irregular, spasmodic

discord 1. clashing, conflict, contention, difference, disagreement, discordance, dispute, dissension, disunity, division, friction, incompatibility, lack of concord, opposition, rupture, strife, variance, wrangling 2. cacophony, din, disharmony, dissonance, harshness, jangle, jarring, racket, tumult

discordant 1. at odds, clashing, conflicting, contradictory, contrary, different, disagreeing, divergent, incompatible, incongruous, inconsistent, opposite 2. cacophonous, dissonant, grating, harsh, inharmonious, jangling, jarring, shrill, strident, unmelodious

discount *v.* 1. brush off, disbelieve, disregard, ignore, leave out of account, overlook, pass over 2. deduct, lower, mark down, rebate, reduce, take off ~*n.* 3. abatement, allowance, concession, cut, cut price, deduction, drawback, percentage (*Inf.*), rebate, reduction

discountenance *v.* 1. abash, chagrin, confuse, discompose, disconcert, embarrass, humiliate, put down (*Sl.*), shame 2. condemn, disapprove, discourage, disfavour, frown on, object to, oppose, resist, take exception to, veto

discourage 1. abash, awe, cast down, cow, damp, dampen, dash, daunt, deject, demoralize, depress, dishearten, dismay, dispirit, frighten, intimidate, overawe, put a damper on, scare, unman, unnerve 2. check, curb, deprecate, deter, discountenance, disfavour, dissuade, divert from, hinder, inhibit, prevent, put off, restrain, talk out of, throw cold water on (*Inf.*)

discouraged crestfallen, dashed, daunted, deterred, disheartened, dismayed, dispirited, downcast, down in the mouth, glum, pessimistic, put off

discouragement 1. cold feet (*Inf.*), dejection, depression, despair, despondency, disappointment, discomfiture, dismay, downheartedness, hopelessness, loss of confidence, low spirits, pessimism 2. constraint, curb, damper, deterrent, disincentive, hindrance, impediment, obstacle, opposition, rebuff, restraint, setback

discouraging dampening, daunting, depressing, disappointing, disheartening, dispiriting, off-putting (*Brit. inf.*), unfavourable, unpropitious

discourse *n.* 1. chat, communication, conversation, converse, dialogue, discussion, speech, talk 2. address, disquisition, dissertation, essay, homily, lecture, oration, sermon, speech, talk, treatise ~*v.* 3. confer, converse, debate, declaim, discuss, expatiate, hold forth, speak, talk

discourteous abrupt, bad-mannered, boorish, brusque, curt, disrespectful, ill-bred, ill-mannered, impolite, insolent, offhand, rude, uncivil, uncourteous, ungentlemanly, ungracious, unmannerly

discourtesy 1. bad manners, disrespectfulness, ill-breeding, impertinence, impoliteness, incivility, insolence, rudeness, ungraciousness, unmannerliness 2. affront, cold shoulder, insult, rebuff, slight, snub

discover 1. bring to light, come across, come upon, dig up, find, light upon, locate, turn up, uncover, unearth 2. ascertain, descry, detect, determine, discern, disclose, espy, find out, get wise to (*Inf.*), learn, notice, perceive, realize, recognize, reveal, see, spot, uncover 3. conceive, contrive, design, devise, invent, originate, pioneer

discoverer author, explorer, founder, initiator, inventor, originator, pioneer

discovery 1. ascertainment, detection, disclosure, espial, exploration, finding, introduction, locating, location, origination, revelation, uncovering 2. bonanza, breakthrough, coup, find, findings, godsend, innovation, invention, secret

discredit v. 1. blame, bring into disrepute, censure, defame, degrade, detract from, disgrace, dishonour, disparage, reproach, slander, slur, smear, vilify ~n. 2. aspersion, censure, disgrace, dishonour, disrepute, ignominy, ill-repute, imputation, odium, reproach, scandal, shame, slur, smear, stigma ~v. 3. challenge, deny, disbelieve, discount, dispute, distrust, doubt, mistrust, question ~n. 4. distrust, doubt, mistrust, question, scepticism, suspicion

discreditable blameworthy, degrading, disgraceful, dishonourable, humiliating, ignominious, improper, infamous, reprehensible, scandalous, shameful, unprincipled, unworthy

discredited brought into disrepute, debunked, discarded, exploded, exposed, obsolete, outworn, refuted, rejected

discreet careful, cautious, circumspect, considerate, diplomatic, discerning, guarded, judicious, politic, prudent, reserved, sagacious, sensible, tactful, wary

discrepancy conflict, contrariety, difference, disagreement, discordance, disparity, dissimilarity, dissonance, divergence, incongruity, inconsistency, variance, variation

discrepant at variance, conflicting, contradictory, contrary, differing, disagreeing, discordant, incompatible, incongruous, inconsistent

discrete detached, disconnected, discontinuous, distinct, individual, separate, unattached

discretion 1. acumen, care, carefulness, caution, circumspection, consideration, diplomacy, discernment, good sense, heedfulness, judgment, judiciousness, maturity, prudence, sagacity, tact, wariness 2. choice, disposition, inclination, liking, mind, option, pleasure, predilection, preference, responsibility, volition, will, wish

discretionary arbitrary (*Law*), elective, nonmandatory, open, open to choice, optional, unrestricted

discriminate 1. disfavour, favour, show bias, show prejudice, single out, treat as inferior, treat differently, victimize 2. assess, differentiate, discern, distinguish, draw a distinction, evaluate, segregate, separate, sift, tell the difference

discriminating acute, astute, critical, cultivated, discerning, fastidious, keen, particular, refined, selective, sensitive, tasteful

discrimination 1. bias, bigotry, favouritism, inequity, intolerance, prejudice, unfairness 2. acumen, acuteness, clearness, discernment, insight, judgment, keenness, penetration, perception, refinement, sagacity, subtlety, taste

discriminatory, discriminative 1. biased, favouring, inequitable, one-sided, partial, partisan, preferential, prejudiced, prejudicial, unjust, weighted 2. analytical, astute, differentiating, discerning, discriminating, perceptive, perspicacious

discursive circuitous, desultory, diffuse, digressive, erratic, long-winded, loose, meandering, prolix, rambling, roundabout, roving

discuss argue, confer, consider, consult with, converse, debate, deliberate, examine, exchange views on, get together (*Inf.*), go into, reason about, review, sift, talk about, thrash out, ventilate, weigh up the pros and cons

discussion analysis, argument, colloquy, confabulation, conference, consideration, consultation, conversation, debate, deliberation, dialogue, discourse, examination, exchange, review, scrutiny, symposium

disdain 1. v. belittle, contemn, deride, despise, disregard, look down on, look down one's nose at (*Inf.*), misprize, pooh-pooh, reject, scorn, slight, sneer at, spurn, undervalue 2. n. arrogance, contempt, contumely, derision, dislike, haughtiness, hauteur, indifference, scorn, sneering, snobbishness, superciliousness

disdainful aloof, arrogant, contemptuous, derisive, haughty, high and mighty (*Inf.*), hoity-toity (*Inf.*), insolent, proud, scornful, sneering, supercilious, superior

disease 1. affliction, ailment, complaint, condition, disorder, ill health, illness, indisposition, infection, infirmity, malady, sickness, upset 2. *Fig.* blight, cancer, canker, contagion, contamination, disorder, malady, plague

diseased ailing, infected, rotten, sick, sickly, tainted, unhealthy, unsound, unwell, unwholesome

disembark alight, arrive, get off, go ashore, land, step out of

disembodied bodiless, ghostly, immaterial, incorporeal, intangible, phantom, spectral, spiritual, unbodied

disembowel draw, eviscerate, gut, paunch

disenchant break the spell, bring (someone) down to earth, destroy (someone's) illusions, disabuse, disillusion, open (someone's) eyes, undeceive

disenchanted blasé, cynical, disappointed, disillusioned, indifferent, jaundiced, let down, out of love, sick of, soured, undeceived

disenchantment disappointment, disillusion, disillusionment, revulsion, rude awakening

disencumber disburden, discharge, disembarrass, disembroil, extricate, unburden, unhamper, unload

disengage 1. disentangle, ease, extricate, free, liberate, loosen, release, set free, unloose, untie **2.** detach, disconnect, disjoin, disunite, divide, separate, undo, withdraw

disengaged 1. apart, detached, free, loose, out of gear, released, separate, unattached, unconnected, uncoupled **2.** at ease, at leisure, free, not busy, uncommitted, unoccupied, vacant

disengagement detachment, disconnection, disentanglement, division, separation, withdrawal

disentangle 1. detach, disconnect, disengage, extricate, free, loose, separate, sever, unfold, unravel, unsnarl, untangle, untwist **2.** clarify, clear (up), resolve, simplify, sort out, work out

disfavour 1. disapprobation, disapproval, dislike, displeasure **2.** *As in* **fall into disfavour** bad books (*Inf.*), discredit, disesteem, disgrace, doghouse (*Inf.*), shame, unpopularity **3.** bad turn, discourtesy, disservice

disfigure blemish, damage, deface, deform, disfeature, distort, injure, maim, make ugly, mar, mutilate, scar

disfigurement blemish, defacement, defect, deformity, distortion, impairment, injury, mutilation, scar, spot, stain

disgorge 1. belch, discharge, eject, empty, expel, regurgitate, spew, spit up, spout, throw up, vomit **2.** cede, give up, relinquish, renounce, resign, surrender, yield

disgrace *n.* **1.** baseness, degradation, dishonour, disrepute, ignominy, infamy, odium, opprobrium, shame **2.** aspersion,

blemish, blot, defamation, reproach, scandal, slur, stain, stigma **3.** contempt, discredit, disesteem, disfavour, obloquy ∼*v.* **4.** abase, bring shame upon, defame, degrade, discredit, disfavour, dishonour, disparage, humiliate, reproach, shame, slur, stain, stigmatize, sully, taint

disgraced branded, degraded, discredited, dishonoured, humiliated, in disgrace, in the doghouse (*Inf.*), mortified, shamed, stigmatized

disgraceful blameworthy, contemptible, degrading, detestable, discreditable, dishonourable, disreputable, ignominious, infamous, low, mean, opprobrious, scandalous, shameful, shocking, unworthy

disgruntled annoyed, cheesed off (*Brit. sl.*), discontented, displeased, dissatisfied, grumpy, irritated, malcontent, peeved, peevish, petulant, put out, sulky, sullen, testy, vexed

disguise *v.* **1.** camouflage, cloak, conceal, cover, hide, mask, screen, secrete, shroud, veil **2.** deceive, dissemble, dissimulate, fake, falsify, fudge, gloss over, misrepresent ∼*n.* **3.** camouflage, cloak, costume, cover, get-up (*Inf.*), mask, screen, veil **4.** deception, dissimulation, façade, front, pretence, semblance, trickery, veneer

disguised camouflaged, cloaked, covert, fake, false, feigned, incognito, in disguise, masked, pretend, undercover, unrecognizable

disgust 1. *v.* cause aversion, displease, fill with loathing, nauseate, offend, outrage, put off, repel, revolt, sicken, turn one's stomach **2.** *n.* abhorrence, abomination, antipathy, aversion, detestation, dislike, distaste, hatefulness, hatred, loathing, nausea, repugnance, repulsion, revulsion

disgusted appalled, nauseated, offended, outraged, repelled, repulsed, scandalized, sick and tired of (*Inf.*), sickened, sick of (*Inf.*)

disgusting abominable, detestable, distasteful, foul, gross, hateful, loathsome, nasty, nauseating, nauseous, objectionable, obnoxious, odious, offensive, repellent, repugnant, revolting, shameless, sickening, stinking, vile, vulgar

dish *n.* **1.** bowl, plate, platter, salver **2.** fare, food, recipe ∼*v.* **3.** *Sl.* finish, muck up (*Sl.*), ruin, spoil, torpedo, wreck

disharmony clash, conflict, disaccord,

discord, discordance, dissonance, friction, inharmoniousness

dishearten cast down, crush, damp, dampen, dash, daunt, deject, depress, deter, discourage, dismay, dispirit, put a damper on

disheartened crestfallen, crushed, daunted, dejected, depressed, disappointed, discouraged, dismayed, dispirited, downcast, downhearted

dishevelled bedraggled, blowzy, disarranged, disordered, frowzy, hanging loose, messy, ruffled, rumpled, tousled, uncombed, unkempt, untidy

dishonest bent (*Sl.*), cheating, corrupt, crafty, crooked (*Inf.*), deceitful, deceiving, deceptive, designing, disreputable, double-dealing, false, fraudulent, guileful, knavish (*Archaic*), lying, mendacious, perfidious, shady (*Inf.*), swindling, treacherous, unfair, unprincipled, unscrupulous, untrustworthy, untruthful

dishonesty cheating, chicanery, corruption, craft, criminality, crookedness, deceit, duplicity, falsehood, falsity, fraud, fraudulence, graft, improbity, mendacity, perfidy, sharp practice, stealing, treachery, trickery, unscrupulousness, wiliness

dishonour *v.* 1. abase, blacken, corrupt, debase, debauch, defame, degrade, discredit, disgrace, shame, sully 2. defile, deflower, pollute, rape, ravish, seduce ~*n.* 3. abasement, degradation, discredit, disfavour, disgrace, disrepute, ignominy, infamy, obloquy, odium, opprobrium, reproach, scandal, shame 4. abuse, affront, discourtesy, indignity, insult, offence, outrage, slight

dishonourable 1. base, contemptible, despicable, discreditable, disgraceful, ignoble, ignominious, infamous, scandalous, shameful 2. blackguardly, corrupt, disreputable, shameless, treacherous, unprincipled, unscrupulous, untrustworthy

dish out allocate, distribute, dole out, hand out, inflict, mete out

dish-shaped concave, cupped, cup-shaped, depressed, hollow, hollowed out, incurvate, incurved, pushed in, scooped, scooped out, scyphiform, sunken

dish up ladle, prepare, present, produce, scoop, serve, spoon

disillusion *v.* break the spell, bring down to earth, disabuse, disenchant, open the eyes of, shatter one's illusions, undeceive

disillusioned disabused enlightened, disappointed, disenchanted, indifferent, out of love, sadder and wiser, undeceived

disincentive damper, determent, deterrent, discouragement, dissuasion, impediment

disinclination alienation, antipathy, aversion, demur, dislike, hesitance, lack of desire, lack of enthusiasm, loathness, objection, opposition, reluctance, repugnance, resistance, unwillingness

disinclined antipathetic, averse, balking, hesitating, indisposed, loath, not in the mood, opposed, reluctant, resistant, unwilling

disinfect clean, cleanse, decontaminate, deodorize, fumigate, purify, sanitize, sterilize

disinfectant antiseptic, germicide, sanitizer, sterilizer

disingenuous artful, cunning, deceitful, designing, dishonest, duplicitous, feigned, guileful, insidious, insincere, shifty, two-faced, uncandid, underhanded, unfair, wily

disinherit cut off, cut off without a penny, disown, dispossess, oust, repudiate

disintegrate break apart, break up, crumble, disunite, fall apart, fall to pieces, reduce to fragments, separate, shatter, splinter

disinter 1. dig up, disentomb, exhume, unearth 2. bring to light, disclose, discover, expose, uncover, unearth

disinterest candidness, detachment, disinterestedness, dispassionateness, equity, fairness, impartiality, justice, neutrality, unbiasedness

disinterested candid, detached, dispassionate, equitable, even-handed, free from self-interest, impartial, impersonal, neutral, outside, unbiased, uninvolved, unprejudiced, unselfish

disjointed 1. aimless, confused, disconnected, disordered, fitful, incoherent, loose, rambling, spasmodic, unconnected 2. disconnected, dislocated, displaced, disunited, divided, separated, split

dislikable detestable, displeasing, distasteful, hatable, nasty, objectionable, odious, unattractive, unlikable, unpleasant

dislike 1. *n.* animosity, animus, antagonism, antipathy, aversion, detestation, disapprobation, disapproval, disgust, disinclination, displeasure, distaste, enmity, hatred, hostility, loathing, repugnance 2. *v.* abhor, abominate, be averse to, despise, detest, disapprove, disfavour, disrelish, hate, have no taste *or* stomach for, loathe, not be able to bear *or* abide, object to, scorn, shun

dislocate 1. disorder, displace, disrupt, disturb, misplace, shift 2. disarticulate, disconnect, disengage, disjoint, disunite, luxate (*Medical*), put out of joint, unhinge

dislocation 1. disarray, disorder, disorganization, disruption, disturbance, misplacement 2. disarticulation, disconnection, disengagement, luxation (*Medical*), unhinging

dislodge dig out, disentangle, displace, disturb, eject, extricate, force out, knock loose, oust, remove, uproot

disloyal apostate, disaffected, faithless, false, perfidious, seditious, subversive, traitorous, treacherous, treasonable, two-faced, unfaithful, unpatriotic, untrustworthy

disloyalty betrayal of trust, breach of trust, breaking of faith, deceitfulness, double-dealing, falseness, falsity, inconstancy, infidelity, perfidy, Punic faith, treachery, treason, unfaithfulness

dismal black, bleak, cheerless, dark, depressing, despondent, discouraging, dolorous, dreary, forlorn, funereal, gloomy, gruesome, lonesome, lowering, lugubrious, melancholy, sad, sombre, sorrowful

dismantle demolish, disassemble, dismount, raze, strike, strip, take apart, take to pieces, unrig

dismay *v.* 1. affright, alarm, appal, distress, fill with consternation, frighten, horrify, paralyse, scare, terrify, unnerve 2. daunt, disappoint, discourage, dishearten, disillusion, dispirit, put off ~*n.* 3. agitation, alarm, anxiety, apprehension, consternation, distress, dread, fear, fright, horror, panic, terror, trepidation 4. chagrin, disappointment, discouragement, disillusionment, upset

dismember amputate, anatomize, cut into pieces, disjoint, dislimb, dislocate, dissect, divide, mutilate, rend, sever

dismiss 1. axe (*Inf.*), cashier, discharge, fire (*Inf.*), give notice to, lay off, oust, remove, sack (*Inf.*), send packing (*Inf.*) 2. disband, disperse, dissolve, free,

let go, release, send away 3. banish, discard, dispel, disregard, drop, lay aside, pooh-pooh, put out of one's mind, reject, relegate, repudiate, set aside, shelve, spurn

dismissal 1. adjournment, congé, end, freedom to depart, permission to go, release 2. discharge, expulsion, marching orders (*Inf.*), notice, one's cards, removal, the boot (*Sl.*), the push (*Sl.*), the sack (*Inf.*)

dismount alight, descend, get down, get off, light

disobedience indiscipline, infraction, insubordination, mutiny, noncompliance, nonobservance, recalcitrance, revolt, unruliness, waywardness

disobedient contrary, contumacious, defiant, disorderly, froward, insubordinate, intractable, mischievous, naughty, noncompliant, nonobservant, obstreperous, refractory, undisciplined, unruly, wayward, wilful

disobey contravene, defy, disregard, flout, go counter to, ignore, infringe, overstep, rebel, refuse to obey, resist, transgress, violate

disoblige 1. annoy, bother, discommode, disturb, inconvenience, put out, trouble, upset 2. affront, displease, insult, offend, slight

disobliging awkward, bloody-minded (*Inf.*), cussed (*Inf.*), disagreeable, discourteous, ill-disposed, rude, unaccommodating, uncivil, uncooperative, unhelpful, unobliging, unpleasant

disorder *n.* 1. chaos, clutter, confusion, derangement, disarray, disorderliness, disorganization, irregularity, jumble, mess, muddle, shambles, untidiness 2. brawl, clamour, commotion, disturbance, fight, fracas, hubbub, hullabaloo, quarrel, riot, rumpus, tumult, turbulence, turmoil, unrest, unruliness, uproar 3. *Medical* affliction, ailment, complaint, disease, illness, indisposition, malady, sickness ~*v.* 4. clutter, confound, confuse, derange, disarrange, discompose, disorganize, disturb, jumble, make hay of, mess up, mix up, muddle, scatter, unsettle, upset

disordered all over the place, confused, deranged, disarranged, dislocated, disorganized, displaced, higgledy-piggledy (*Inf.*), in a mess, in confusion, jumbled, misplaced, muddled, out of kelter, out of place, untidy

disorderly 1. chaotic, confused, disorganized, higgledy-piggledy (*Inf.*), indiscriminate, irregular, jumbled, messy, shambolic (*Inf.*), unsystematic, untidy **2.** boisterous, disruptive, indisciplined, lawless, obstreperous, rebellious, refractory, riotous, rowdy, stormy, tumultuous, turbulent, ungovernable, unlawful, unmanageable, unruly

disorganization chaos, confusion, derangement, disarray, disjointedness, disorder, disruption, incoherence, unconnectedness

disorganize break up, confuse, derange, destroy, disarrange, discompose, disorder, disrupt, disturb, jumble, make a shambles of, muddle, turn topsy-turvy, unsettle, upset

disorganized chaotic, confused, disordered, haphazard, jumbled, muddled, shuffled, unmethodical, unorganized, unsystematic

disorientate, disorient cause to lose one's bearings, confuse, dislocate, mislead, perplex, upset

disorientated, disoriented adrift, all at sea, astray, bewildered, confused, lost, mixed up, not adjusted, off-beam, off-course, out of joint, perplexed, unbalanced, unhinged, unsettled, unstable

disown abandon, abnegate, cast off, deny, disallow, disavow, disclaim, refuse to acknowledge *or* recognize, reject, renounce, repudiate

disparage belittle, criticize, decry, defame, degrade, denigrate, deprecate, depreciate, deride, derogate, detract from, discredit, disdain, dismiss, malign, minimize, ridicule, run down, scorn, slander, traduce, underestimate, underrate, undervalue, vilify

disparagement aspersion, belittlement, condemnation, contempt, contumely, criticism, debasement, degradation, denunciation, depreciation, derision, derogation, detraction, discredit, disdain, impairment, lessening, prejudice, reproach, ridicule, scorn, slander, underestimation

disparate at odds, at variance, contrary, contrasting, different, discordant, discrepant, dissimilar, distinct, diverse, unlike

disparity difference, discrepancy, disproportion, dissimilarity, dissimilitude, distinction, gap, imbalance, incongruity, inequality, unevenness, unlikeness

dispassion candidness, detachment, disinterestedness, impartiality, neutrality, objectivity

dispassionate 1. calm, collected, composed, cool, imperturbable, moderate, quiet, serene, sober, temperate, unemotional, unexcitable, unexcited, unmoved, unruffled **2.** candid, detached, disinterested, fair, impartial, impersonal, indifferent, neutral, objective, unbiased, uninvolved, unprejudiced

dispatch, despatch v. **1.** accelerate, consign, dismiss, express, forward, hasten, hurry, quicken, remit, send, transmit **2.** conclude, discharge, dispose of, expedite, finish, make short work of (*Inf.*), perform, settle **3.** assassinate, bump off (*Sl.*), butcher, eliminate (*Sl.*), execute, finish off, kill, murder, put an end to, slaughter, slay ~n. **4.** alacrity, celerity, expedition, haste, precipitateness, promptitude, promptness, quickness, rapidity, speed, swiftness **5.** account, bulletin, communication, communiqué, document, instruction, item, letter, message, missive, news, piece, report, story

dispel allay, banish, chase away, dismiss, disperse, dissipate, drive away, eliminate, expel, resolve, rout, scatter

dispensable disposable, expendable, inessential, needless, nonessential, superfluous, unnecessary, unrequired, useless

dispensation 1. allotment, appointment, apportionment, bestowal, conferment, consignment, dealing out, disbursement, distribution, endowment, supplying **2.** award, dole, part, portion, quota, share **3.** administration, direction, economy, management, plan, regulation, scheme, stewardship, system **4.** exception, exemption, immunity, indulgence, licence, permission, privilege, relaxation, relief, remission, reprieve

dispense 1. allocate, allot, apportion, assign, deal out, disburse, distribute, dole out, mete out, share **2.** measure, mix, prepare, supply **3.** administer, apply, carry out, direct, discharge, enforce, execute, implement, operate, undertake **4.** except, excuse, exempt, exonerate, let off (*Inf.*), release, relieve, reprieve **5.** *With* **with** abstain from, do without, forgo, give up, omit, relinquish, waive **6.** *With* **with** abolish, brush aside, cancel, dispose of, disregard, do away with, get rid of, ignore, pass over, render needless, shake off

disperse 1. broadcast, circulate, diffuse, disseminate, dissipate, distribute, scatter, spread, strew 2. break up, disappear, disband, dismiss, dispel, dissolve, rout, scatter, send off, separate, vanish

dispersion broadcast, circulation, diffusion, dispersal, dissemination, dissipation, distribution, scattering, spread

dispirit cast down, damp, dampen, dash, deject, depress, deter, discourage, dishearten, disincline, sadden

dispirited crestfallen, dejected, depressed, despondent, discouraged, disheartened, down, downcast, gloomy, glum, in the doldrums, low, morose, sad

displace 1. derange, disarrange, disturb, misplace, move, shift, transpose 2. cashier, depose, discard, discharge, dismiss, fire (*Inf.*), remove, sack (*Inf.*) 3. crowd out, oust, replace, succeed, supersede, supplant, take the place of 4. dislocate, dislodge, dispossess, eject, evict, force out, unsettle

display *v.* 1. betray, demonstrate, disclose, evidence, evince, exhibit, expose, manifest, open, open to view, present, reveal, show, unveil 2. expand, extend, model, open out, spread out, stretch out, unfold, unfurl 3. boast, flash (*Inf.*), flaunt, flourish, parade, show off, vaunt ~*n.* 4. array, demonstration, exhibition, exposition, exposure, manifestation, presentation, revelation, show 5. flourish, ostentation, pageant, parade, pomp, show, spectacle

displease aggravate (*Inf.*), anger, annoy, disgust, dissatisfy, exasperate, gall, incense, irk, irritate, nettle, offend, pique, provoke, put out, rile, upset, vex

displeasure anger, annoyance, disapprobation, disapproval, disfavour, disgruntlement, dislike, dissatisfaction, distaste, indignation, irritation, offence, pique, resentment, vexation, wrath

disport 1. amuse, beguile, cheer, delight, divert, entertain, make merry 2. caper, frisk, frolic, gambol, play, revel, romp, sport

disposable 1. biodegradable, compostable, decomposable, nonreturnable, paper, throwaway 2. at one's service, available, consumable, expendable, free for use, spendable

disposal 1. clearance, discarding,

dumping (*Inf.*), ejection, jettisoning, parting with, relinquishment, removal, riddance, scrapping, throwing away 2. arrangement, array, dispensation, disposition, distribution, grouping, placing, position 3. assignment, bequest, bestowal, consignment, conveyance, dispensation, gift, settlement, transfer 4. *As in* **at one's disposal** authority, conduct, control, determination, direction, discretion, government, management, ordering, regulation, responsibility

dispose 1. adjust, arrange, array, determine, distribute, fix, group, marshal, order, place, put, range, rank, regulate, set, settle, stand 2. actuate, adapt, bias, condition, incline, induce, influence, lead, motivate, move, predispose, prompt, tempt

disposed apt, given, inclined, liable, likely, minded, of a mind to, predisposed, prone, ready, subject, tending towards

dispose of 1. deal with, decide, determine, end, finish with, settle 2. bestow, give, make over, part with, sell, transfer 3. destroy, discard, dump (*Inf.*), get rid of, jettison, scrap, throw out *or* away, unload

disposition 1. character, constitution, make-up, nature, spirit, temper, temperament 2. bent, bias, habit, inclination, leaning, predisposition, proclivity, proneness, propensity, readiness, tendency 3. adjustment, arrangement, classification, disposal, distribution, grouping, ordering, organization, placement 4. control, direction, disposal, management, regulation

dispossess deprive, dislodge, divest, drive out, eject, evict, expel, oust, strip, take away, turn out

dispraise 1. *v.* animadvert on *or* upon, blame, censure, condemn, criticize, disapprove, disparage, reproach, reprove 2. *n.* blame, censure, depreciation, discredit, disgrace, dishonour, disparagement, opprobrium, reproach, shame

disproof confutation, counterargument, denial, disproval, invalidation, negation, rebuttal, refutation

disproportion asymmetry, discrepancy, disparity, imbalance, inadequacy, inequality, insufficiency, lopsidedness, unevenness, unsuitableness

disproportionate excessive, incommensurate, inordinate, out of proportion, too much, unbalanced, unequal, uneven, unreasonable

disprove confute, contradict, controvert, discredit, expose, give the lie to, invalidate, negate, prove false, rebut, refute

disputable arguable, controversial, debatable, doubtful, dubious, moot, open to discussion, questionable, uncertain

disputant adversary, antagonist, arguer, contender, contestant, debater, opponent

disputation argumentation, controversy, debate, dispute, dissension, polemics

disputatious argumentative, cantankerous, captious, cavilling, contentious, dissentious, litigious, polemical, pugnacious, quarrelsome

dispute v. **1.** altercate, argue, brawl, clash, contend, debate, discuss, quarrel, squabble, wrangle **2.** challenge, contest, contradict, controvert, deny, doubt, impugn, question ~n. **3.** altercation, argument, brawl, conflict, disagreement, discord, disturbance, feud, friction, quarrel, strife, wrangle **4.** argument, contention, controversy, debate, discussion, dissension

disqualification 1. disability, disablement, incapacitation, incapacity, unfitness **2.** debarment, disenablement, disentitlement, elimination, exclusion, incompetence, ineligibility, rejection

disqualified debarred, eliminated, ineligible, knocked out, out of the running

disqualify 1. disable, incapacitate, invalidate, unfit (*Rare*) **2.** debar, declare ineligible, disentitle, preclude, prohibit, rule out

disquiet 1. n. alarm, angst, anxiety, concern, disquietude, distress, disturbance, fear, foreboding, fretfulness, nervousness, restlessness, trouble, uneasiness, unrest, worry **2.** v. agitate, annoy, bother, concern, discompose, distress, disturb, fret, harass, incommode, make uneasy, perturb, pester, plague, trouble, unsettle, upset, vex, worry

disquieting annoying, bothersome, disconcerting, distressing, disturbing, irritating, perturbing, troubling, unnerving, unsettling, upsetting, vexing, worrying

disquisition discourse, dissertation, essay, exposition, lecture, paper, thesis, treatise

disregard v. **1.** brush aside or away, discount, disobey, ignore, laugh off, leave out of account, make light of, neglect, overlook, pass over, pay no attention to, pay no heed to, take no notice of, turn a blind eye to **2.** brush off (*Sl.*), coldshoulder, contemn, despise, disdain, disparage, slight, snub ~n. **3.** brushoff (*Sl.*), contempt, disdain, disrespect, heedlessness, ignoring, inattention, indifference, neglect, negligence, oversight, slight, the cold shoulder

disrelish 1. v. be averse to, be turned off by (*Sl.*), disfavour, dislike, loathe, regard with distaste **2.** n. antipathy, aversion, disfavour, disgust, disinclination, dislike, distaste, loathing, repugnance

disrepair 1. collapse, decay, deterioration, dilapidation, ruination **2. in disrepair** broken, bust (*Inf.*), decayed, decrepit, kaput (*Inf.*), not functioning, on the blink (*Sl.*), out of commission, out of order, worn out

disreputable 1. base, contemptible, derogatory, discreditable, disgraceful, dishonourable, disorderly, ignominious, infamous, louche, low, mean, notorious, opprobrious, scandalous, shady (*Inf.*), shameful, shocking, unprincipled, vicious, vile **2.** bedraggled, dilapidated, dingy, dishevelled, down at heel, scruffy, seedy, shabby, threadbare, worn

disrepute discredit, disesteem, disfavour, disgrace, dishonour, ignominy, ill favour, ill repute, infamy, obloquy, shame, unpopularity

disrespect contempt, discourtesy, dishonour, disregard, impertinence, impoliteness, impudence, incivility, insolence, irreverence, lack of respect, lese-majesty, rudeness, unmannerliness

disrespectful bad-mannered, cheeky, contemptuous, discourteous, ill-bred, impertinent, impolite, impudent, insolent, insulting, irreverent, misbehaved, rude, uncivil

disrobe bare, denude, divest, doff, remove, shed, strip, take off, unclothe, uncover, undress

disrupt 1. agitate, confuse, disorder, disorganize, disturb, spoil, throw into disorder, upset **2.** break up or into, interfere with, interrupt, intrude, obstruct, unsettle, upset

disruption confusion, disarray, disorder, disorderliness, disturbance, interference, interruption, stoppage

disruptive confusing, disorderly, distracting, disturbing, obstreperous, troublemaking, troublesome, unruly, unsettling, upsetting

dissatisfaction annoyance, chagrin, disappointment, discomfort, discontent, dislike, dismay, displeasure, distress, exasperation, frustration, irritation, regret, resentment, unhappiness

dissatisfied disappointed, discontented, disgruntled, displeased, fed up, frustrated, not satisfied, unfulfilled, ungratified, unhappy, unsatisfied

dissatisfy annoy, disappoint, discontent, disgruntle, displease, give cause for complaint, irritate, leave dissatisfied, not pass muster, not suffice, put out, vex

dissect 1. anatomize, cut up or apart, dismember, lay open **2.** analyse, break down, explore, inspect, investigate, scrutinize, study

dissection 1. anatomization, anatomy, autopsy, dismemberment, necropsy, postmortem (examination) **2.** analysis, breakdown, examination, inspection, investigation, scrutiny

dissemble 1. camouflage, cloak, conceal, cover up, disguise, dissimulate, hide, mask **2.** affect, counterfeit, falsify, feign, pretend, sham, simulate

dissembler charlatan, con man (*Inf.*), deceiver, dissimulator, feigner, fraud, hypocrite, impostor, pretender, trickster, whited sepulchre

disseminate broadcast, circulate, diffuse, disperse, dissipate, distribute, proclaim, promulgate, propagate, publicize, publish, scatter, sow, spread

dissemination broadcasting, circulation, diffusion, distribution, promulgation, propagation, publication, publishing, spread

dissension conflict, conflict of opinion, contention, difference, disagreement, discord, discordance, dispute, dissent, friction, quarrel, strife, variance

dissent 1. *v.* decline, differ, disagree, object, protest, refuse, withhold assent *or* approval **2.** *n.* difference, disagreement, discord, dissension, dissidence, nonconformity, objection, opposition, refusal, resistance

dissenter disputant, dissident, nonconformist, objector, protestant

dissentient *adj.* conflicting, differing,

disagreeing, dissenting, dissident, opposing, protesting

dissertation critique, discourse, disquisition, essay, exposition, thesis, treatise

disservice bad turn, disfavour, harm, ill turn, injury, injustice, unkindness, wrong

dissever cleave, disunite, divorce, part, rend, rift, separate, sever, sunder

dissidence difference of opinion, disagreement, discordance, dispute, dissent, feud, rupture, schism

dissident 1. *adj.* differing, disagreeing, discordant, dissentient, dissenting, heterodox, nonconformist, schismatic **2.** *n.* agitator, dissenter, protestor, rebel, recusant

dissimilar different, disparate, divergent, diverse, heterogeneous, mismatched, not alike, not capable of comparison, not similar, unlike, unrelated, various

dissimilarity difference, discrepancy, disparity, dissimilitude, distinction, divergence, heterogeneity, incomparability, nonuniformity, unlikeness, unrelatedness

dissimilitude difference, discrepancy, disparity, dissimilarity, diversity, heterogeneity, incomparability, nonuniformity, unlikeness, unrelatedness

dissimulate camouflage, cloak, conceal, disguise, dissemble, feign, hide, mask, pretend

dissimulation concealment, deceit, deception, dissembling, double-dealing, duplicity, feigning, hypocrisy, play-acting, pretence, sham, wile

dissipate 1. burn up, consume, deplete, expend, fritter away, indulge oneself, lavish, misspend, run through, spend, squander, waste **2.** disappear, dispel, disperse, dissolve, drive away, evaporate, scatter, vanish

dissipated 1. abandoned, debauched, dissolute, intemperate, profligate, rakish, self-indulgent **2.** consumed, destroyed, exhausted, scattered, squandered, wasted

dissipation 1. abandonment, debauchery, dissoluteness, drunkenness, excess, extravagance, indulgence, intemperance, lavishness, prodigality, profligacy, squandering, wantonness, waste **2.** amusement, distraction, diversion, entertainment, gratification **3.** disappearance, disintegration, dispersion, dissemination, dissolution, scattering, vanishing

dissociate 1. break off, disband, disrupt, part company, quit **2.** detach, disconnect, distance, divorce, isolate, segregate, separate, set apart

dissociation break, detachment, disconnection, disengagement, distancing, disunion, division, divorce, isolation, segregation, separation, severance

dissolute abandoned, corrupt, debauched, degenerate, depraved, dissipated, immoral, lax, lewd, libertine, licentious, loose, profligate, rakish, unrestrained, vicious, wanton, wild

dissolution 1. breaking up, disintegration, division, divorce, parting, resolution, separation **2.** death, decay, decomposition, demise, destruction, dispersal, extinction, overthrow, ruin **3.** adjournment, conclusion, disbandment, discontinuation, dismissal, end, ending, finish, suspension, termination **4.** corruption, debauchery, dissipation, intemperance, wantonness **5.** disappearance, evaporation, liquefaction, melting, solution

dissolve 1. deliquesce, flux, fuse, liquefy, melt, soften, thaw **2.** crumble, decompose, diffuse, disappear, disintegrate, disperse, dissipate, dwindle, evanesce, evaporate, fade, melt away, perish, vanish, waste away **3.** break up, destroy, discontinue, dismiss, end, overthrow, ruin, suspend, terminate, wind up **4.** break into *or* up, collapse, disorganize, disunite, divorce, loose, resolve into, separate, sever

dissonance 1. cacophony, discord, discordance, harshness, jangle, jarring, unmelodiousness, want of harmony **2.** difference, disagreement, discord, discrepancy, disparity, dissension, incongruity, inconsistency, variance

dissonant 1. cacophonous, discordant, grating, harsh, inharmonious, jangling, jarring, out of tune, raucous, strident, tuneless, unmelodious **2.** anomalous, at variance, different, differing, disagreeing, discrepant, dissentient, incompatible, incongruous, inconsistent, irreconcilable, irregular

dissuade advise against, deter, discourage, disincline, divert, expostulate, persuade not to, put off, remonstrate, talk out of, urge not to, warn

dissuasion caution, damper, deter-

ment, deterrence, deterrent, discouragement, disincentive, expostulation, hindrance, remonstrance, setback

dissuasive admonitory, cautionary, discouraging, disincentive, dissuading, monitory, off-putting (*Brit. inf.*), remonstrative, warning

distance *n.* **1.** absence, extent, gap, interval, lapse, length, range, reach, remoteness, remove, separation, space, span, stretch, width **2.** aloofness, coldness, coolness, frigidity, reserve, restraint, stiffness **3. go the distance** bring to an end, complete, finish, see through, stay the course **4. keep one's distance** avoid, be aloof (indifferent, reserved), keep (someone) at arm's length, shun **5. in the distance** afar, far away, far off, on the horizon, yonder ~*v.* **6.** dissociate oneself, put in proportion, separate oneself **7.** leave behind, outdistance, outdo, outrun, outstrip, pass

distant 1. abroad, afar, far, faraway, far-flung, far-off, outlying, out-of-the-way, remote, removed **2.** apart, disparate, dispersed, distinct, scattered, separate **3.** aloof, ceremonious, cold, cool, formal, haughty, reserved, restrained, reticent, standoffish, stiff, unapproachable, unfriendly, withdrawn **4.** faint, indirect, indistinct, obscure, slight, uncertain

distaste abhorrence, antipathy, aversion, detestation, disfavour, disgust, disinclination, dislike, displeasure, disrelish, dissatisfaction, horror, loathing, repugnance, revulsion

distasteful abhorrent, disagreeable, displeasing, loathsome, nauseous, objectionable, obnoxious, offensive, repugnant, repulsive, undesirable, uninviting, unpalatable, unpleasant, unsavoury

distend balloon, bloat, bulge, dilate, enlarge, expand, increase, inflate, puff, stretch, swell, widen

distended bloated, dilated, enlarged, expanded, inflated, puffy, stretched, swollen, tumescent

distension dilatation, dilation, enlargement, expansion, extension, inflation, intumescence, spread

distil condense, draw out, evaporate, express, extract, press out, purify, rectify, refine, sublimate, vaporize

distillation elixir, essence, extract, quintessence, spirit

distinct 1. apparent, clear, clear-cut,

decided, definite, evident, lucid, manifest, marked, noticeable, obvious, palpable, patent, plain, recognizable, sharp, unambiguous, unmistakable, well-defined 2. detached, different, discrete, dissimilar, individual, separate, unconnected

distinction 1. differentiation, discernment, discrimination, penetration, perception, separation 2. contrast, difference, differential, division, separation 3. characteristic, distinctiveness, feature, individuality, mark, particularity, peculiarity, quality 4. account, celebrity, consequence, credit, eminence, excellence, fame, greatness, honour, importance, merit, name, note, prominence, quality, rank, renown, reputation, repute, superiority, worth

distinctive characteristic, different, distinguishing, extraordinary, idiosyncratic, individual, original, peculiar, singular, special, typical, uncommon, unique

distinctly clearly, decidedly, definitely, evidently, manifestly, markedly, noticeably, obviously, palpably, patently, plainly, precisely, sharply

distinctness 1. clarity, lucidity, obviousness, plainness, sharpness, vividness 2. detachment, difference, discreteness, disparateness, dissimilarity, dissociation, distinctiveness, individuality, separation

distinguish 1. ascertain, decide, determine, differentiate, discriminate, judge, tell apart, tell between, tell the difference 2. categorize, characterize, classify, individualize, make distinctive, mark, separate, set apart, single out 3. discern, know, make out, perceive, pick out, recognize, see, tell 4. celebrate, dignify, honour, immortalize, make famous, signalize

distinguishable clear, conspicuous, discernible, evident, manifest, noticeable, obvious, perceptible, plain, recognizable, well-marked

distinguished 1. acclaimed, celebrated, conspicuous, eminent, famed, famous, illustrious, notable, noted, renowned, well-known 2. conspicuous, extraordinary, marked, outstanding, signal, striking

distinguishing characteristic, different, differentiating, distinctive, individualistic, marked, peculiar, typical

distort 1. bend, buckle, contort, de-

form, disfigure, misshape, twist, warp, wrench, wrest 2. bias, colour, falsify, garble, misrepresent, pervert, slant, twist

distortion 1. bend, buckle, contortion, crookedness, deformity, malformation, twist, twistedness, warp 2. bias, colouring, falsification, misrepresentation, perversion, slant

distract 1. divert, draw away, sidetrack, turn aside 2. amuse, beguile, engross, entertain, occupy 3. agitate, bewilder, confound, confuse, derange, discompose, disconcert, disturb, harass, madden, perplex, puzzle, torment, trouble

distracted 1. agitated, bemused, bewildered, confounded, confused, flustered, harassed, in a flap (*Inf.*), perplexed, puzzled, troubled 2. crazy, deranged, distraught, frantic, frenzied, grief-stricken, insane, mad, overwrought, raving, wild

distracting bewildering, bothering, confusing, disconcerting, dismaying, disturbing, off-putting (*Brit. inf.*), perturbing

distraction 1. abstraction, agitation, bewilderment, commotion, confusion, discord, disorder, disturbance 2. amusement, beguilement, diversion, divertissement, entertainment, pastime, recreation 3. disturbance, diversion, interference, interruption 4. aberration, alienation, delirium, derangement, desperation, frenzy, hallucination, incoherence, insanity, mania

distrait absent, absent-minded, abstracted, distracted, forgetful, inattentive, oblivious, preoccupied, unaware

distraught agitated, anxious, beside oneself, crazed, distracted, distressed, frantic, hysterical, mad, out of one's mind, overwrought, raving, wild, worked-up, wrought-up

distress *n.* 1. affliction, agony, anguish, anxiety, desolation, discomfort, grief, heartache, misery, pain, sadness, sorrow, suffering, torment, torture, woe, worry, wretchedness 2. adversity, calamity, destitution, difficulties, hardship, indigence, misfortune, need, poverty, privation, straits, trial, trouble ~*v.* 3. afflict, agonize, bother, disturb, grieve, harass, harrow, pain, perplex, sadden, torment, trouble, upset, worry, wound

distressed 1. afflicted, agitated, anxious, distracted, distraught, saddened, tormented, troubled, upset, worried, wretched **2**. destitute, indigent, needy, poor, poverty-stricken, straitened

distressing affecting, afflicting, distressful, disturbing, grievous, heartbreaking, hurtful, lamentable, nerveracking, painful, sad, upsetting, worrying

distribute 1. administer, allocate, allot, apportion, assign, deal, dispense, dispose, divide, dole out, give, measure out, mete, share **2**. circulate, convey, deliver, hand out, pass round **3**. diffuse, disperse, disseminate, scatter, spread, strew **4**. arrange, assort, categorize, class, classify, file, group

distribution 1. allocation, allotment, apportionment, dispensation, division, dole, partition, sharing **2**. circulation, diffusion, dispersal, dispersion, dissemination, propagation, scattering, spreading **3**. arrangement, assortment, classification, disposition, grouping, location, organization, placement **4**. *Commerce* dealing, delivery, handling, mailing, marketing, trading, transport, transportation

district area, community, locale, locality, neighbourhood, parish, quarter, region, sector, vicinity, ward

distrust 1. *v*. be sceptical of, be suspicious of, be wary of, disbelieve, discredit, doubt, misbelieve, mistrust, question, smell a rat (*Inf.*), suspect, wonder about **2**. *n*. disbelief, doubt, lack of faith, misgiving, mistrust, qualm, question, scepticism, suspicion, wariness

distrustful chary, cynical, disbelieving, distrusting, doubtful, doubting, dubious, mistrustful, sceptical, suspicious, uneasy, wary

disturb 1. bother, butt in on, disrupt, interfere with, interrupt, intrude on, pester, rouse, startle **2**. confuse, derange, disarrange, disorder, disorganize, muddle, unsettle **3**. agitate, alarm, annoy, confound, discompose, distract, distress, excite, fluster, harass, perturb, ruffle, shake, trouble, unsettle, upset, worry

disturbance 1. agitation, annoyance, bother, confusion, derangement, disorder, distraction, hindrance, interruption, intrusion, molestation, perturbation, upset **2**. bother (*Inf.*), brawl, commotion, disorder, fracas, fray, hubbub, riot, ruckus (*Inf.*), ruction (*Inf.*), tumult, turmoil, uproar

disturbed 1. *Psychiatry* disordered, maladjusted, neurotic, troubled, unbalanced, upset **2**. agitated, anxious, apprehensive, bothered, concerned, disquieted, troubled, uneasy, upset, worried

disturbing agitating, alarming, disconcerting, discouraging, dismaying, disquieting, distressing, frightening, perturbing, startling, threatening, troubling, unsettling, upsetting, worrying

disunion 1. abstraction, detachment, disconnection, disjunction, division, partition, separation, severance **2**. alienation, breach, disagreement, discord, dissension, dissidence, estrangement, feud, rupture, schism, split

disunite 1. detach, disband, disconnect, disengage, disjoin, disrupt, divide, part, segregate, separate, sever, split, sunder **2**. alienate, embroil, estrange, set at odds, set at variance

disunity alienation, breach, disagreement, discord, discordance, dissension, dissent, estrangement, rupture, schism, split, variance

disuse abandonment, decay, desuetude, discontinuance, idleness, neglect, non-employment, nonuse

ditch *n*. **1**. channel, drain, dyke, furrow, gully, moat, trench, watercourse ~*v*. **2**. dig, drain, excavate, gouge, trench **3**. *Sl*. abandon, discard, dispose of, drop, dump (*Inf.*), get rid of, jettison, scrap, throw out *or* overboard

dither 1. *v*. faff about (*Brit. inf.*), falter, haver, hesitate, oscillate, shillyshally (*Inf.*), swither (*Scot.*), teeter, vacillate, waver **2**. *n*. bother, flap (*Inf.*), fluster, flutter, pother, stew (*Inf.*), tiz-woz (*Inf.*), tizzy (*Inf.*), twitter

diurnal circadian, daily, daytime, everyday, quotidian, regular

dive *v*. **1**. descend, dip, disappear, drop, duck, fall, go underwater, jump, leap, nose-dive, pitch, plummet, plunge, submerge, swoop ~*n*. **2**. dash, header (*Inf.*), jump, leap, lunge, nose dive, plunge, spring **3**. *Sl*. honky-tonk (*U.S. sl.*), joint (*Sl.*), sleazy bar

diverge 1. bifurcate, branch, divaricate, divide, fork, part, radiate, separate, split, spread **2**. be at odds, be at variance, conflict, differ, disagree, dissent **3**. depart, deviate, digress, stray, turn aside, wander

divergence branching out, departure, deviation, difference, digression, disparity, divagation, ramification, separation deflection, varying

divergent conflicting, deviating, different, differing, disagreeing, dissimilar, diverging, diverse, separate, variant

divers different, manifold, many, multifarious, numerous, several, some, sundry, varied, various

diverse 1. assorted, diversified, miscellaneous, of every description, several, sundry, varied, various **2.** different, differing, discrete, disparate, dissimilar, distinct, divergent, separate, unlike, varying

diversify alter, assort, branch out, change, expand, mix, modify, spread out, transform, variegate, vary

diversion 1. alteration, change, deflection, departure, detour, deviation, digression, variation **2.** amusement, beguilement, delight, distraction, divertissement, enjoyment, entertainment, game, gratification, pastime, play, pleasure, recreation, relaxation, sport

diversity assortment, difference, dissimilarity, distinctiveness, divergence, diverseness, diversification, heterogeneity, medley, multiplicity, range, unlikeness, variance, variegation, variety

divert 1. avert, deflect, redirect, switch, turn aside **2.** amuse, beguile, delight, entertain, gratify, recreate, regale **3.** detract, distract, draw *or* lead away from, lead astray, sidetrack

diverted 1. changed, deflected, made use of, rebudgeted, rechannelled, reclassified, redirected, taken over, turned aside **2.** amused, entertained, taken out of oneself, tickled

diverting amusing, beguiling, enjoyable, entertaining, fun, humorous, pleasant

divest 1. denude, disrobe, doff, remove, strip, take off, unclothe, undress **2.** deprive, despoil, dispossess, strip

divide 1. bisect, cleave, cut (up), detach, disconnect, part, partition, segregate, separate, sever, shear, split, subdivide, sunder **2.** allocate, allot, apportion, deal out, dispense, distribute, divvy (up) (*Inf.*), dole out, measure out, portion, share **3.** alienate, break up, cause to disagree, come between, disunite, estrange, set *or* pit against one another, set at variance *or* odds, sow dissension, split **4.** arrange, categorize, classify, grade, group, put in order, separate, sort

dividend bonus, cut (*Inf.*), divvy (*Inf.*), extra, gain, plus, portion, share, surplus

divination augury, clairvoyance, divining, foretelling, fortune-telling, prediction, presage, prognostication, prophecy, soothsaying

divine *adj.* **1.** angelic, celestial, godlike, heavenly, holy, spiritual, superhuman, supernatural **2.** consecrated, holy, religious, sacred, sanctified, spiritual **3.** beatific, blissful, exalted, mystical, rapturous, supreme, transcendent, transcendental, transmundane **4.** *Inf.* beautiful, excellent, glorious, marvellous, perfect, splendid, superlative, wonderful ~*n.* **5.** churchman, clergyman, cleric, ecclesiastic, minister, pastor, priest, reverend ~*v.* **6.** apprehend, conjecture, deduce, discern, foretell, guess, infer, intuit, perceive, prognosticate, suppose, surmise, suspect, understand **7.** *Of water or minerals* dowse

diviner 1. astrologer, augur, oracle, prophet, seer, sibyl, soothsayer **2.** *Of water or minerals* dowser

divinity 1. deity, divine nature, godhead, godhood, godliness, holiness, sanctity **2.** daemon, deity, genius, god, goddess, guardian spirit, spirit **3.** religion, religious studies, theology

divisible dividable, fractional, separable, splittable

division 1. bisection, cutting up, detaching, dividing, partition, separation, splitting up **2.** allotment, apportionment, distribution, sharing **3.** border, boundary, demarcation, divide, divider, dividing line, partition **4.** branch, category, class, compartment, department, group, head, part, portion, section, sector, segment **5.** breach, difference of opinion, disagreement, discord, disunion, estrangement, feud, rupture, split, variance

divisive alienating, damaging, detrimental, discordant, disruptive, estranging, inharmonious, pernicious, troublesome, unsettling

divorce 1. *n.* annulment, breach, break, decree nisi, dissolution, disunion, rupture, separation, severance, split-up **2.** *v.* annul, disconnect, dissociate, dissolve (*marriage*), disunite, divide, part, separate, sever, split up, sunder

divulge betray, communicate, confess, declare, disclose, exhibit, expose, impart, leak, let slip, make known, proclaim, promulgate, publish, reveal, spill (*Inf.*), tell, uncover

divvy 1. *n.* cut (*Inf.*), dividend, percentage, portion, quota, share, whack (*Inf.*) **2.** *v. Sometimes with* **up** apportion, cut, distribute, divide, parcel out, share (out), split

dizzy 1. faint, giddy, light-headed, off balance, reeling, shaky, staggering, swimming, vertiginous, weak at the knees, wobbly, woozy (*Inf.*) **2.** befuddled, bemused, bewildered, confused, dazed, dazzled, muddled **3.** lofty, steep, vertiginous **4.** *Inf.* capricious, fickle, flighty, foolish, frivolous, giddy, light-headed, scatterbrained, silly

do *v.* **1.** accomplish, achieve, act, carry out, complete, conclude, discharge, end, execute, perform, produce, transact, undertake, work **2.** answer, be adequate, be enough, be of use, be sufficient, pass muster, satisfy, serve, suffice, suit **3.** arrange, be responsible for, fix, get ready, look after, make, make ready, organize, prepare, see to, take on **4.** decipher, decode, figure out, puzzle out, resolve, solve, work out **5.** adapt, render, translate, transpose **6.** bear oneself, behave, carry oneself, comport oneself, conduct oneself **7.** fare, get along, get on, make out, manage, proceed **8.** bring about, cause, create, effect, produce **9.** *Of a play, etc.* act, give, perform, present, produce, put on **10.** *Inf.* cover, explore, journey through *or* around, look at, stop in, tour, travel, visit **11.** *Sl.* cheat, con (*Sl.*), cozen, deceive, defraud, dupe, fleece, hoax, swindle, take (someone) for a ride (*Inf.*), trick ~*n.* **12.** *Inf.* affair, event, function, gathering, occasion, party **13. do's and don'ts** *Inf.* code, customs, etiquette, instructions, regulations, rules, standards

do away with 1. bump off (*Sl.*), destroy, do in (*Sl.*), exterminate, kill, liquidate, murder, slay **2.** abolish, discard, discontinue, eliminate, get rid of, put an end to, remove

docile amenable, biddable, compliant, ductile, manageable, obedient, pliant, submissive, teachable (*Rare*), tractable

docility amenability, biddableness, compliance, ductility, manageability, meekness, obedience, pliancy, submissiveness, tractability

dock[1] *n.* **1.** harbour, pier, quay, waterfront, wharf ~*v.* **2.** anchor, berth, drop

anchor, land, moor, put in, tie up **3.** *Of spacecraft* couple, hook up, join, link up, rendezvous, unite

dock[2] **1.** clip, crop, curtail, cut off, cut short, diminish, lessen, shorten **2.** decrease, deduct, diminish, lessen, reduce, subtract, withhold

docket 1. *n.* bill, certificate, chit, chitty, counterfoil, label, receipt, tab, tag, tally, ticket **2.** *v.* catalogue, file, index, label, mark, register, tab, tag, ticket

doctor *n.* **1.** general practitioner, G.P., medic (*Inf.*), medical practitioner, physician ~*v.* **2.** apply medication to, give medical treatment to, treat **3.** botch, cobble, do up (*Inf.*), fix, mend, patch up, repair **4.** alter, change, disguise, falsify, fudge, misrepresent, pervert, tamper with **5.** add to, adulterate, cut, dilute, mix with, spike, water down

doctrinaire *adj.* **1.** biased, dogmatic, fanatical, inflexible, insistent, opinionated, rigid **2.** hypothetical, ideological, impractical, speculative, theoretical, unpragmatic, unrealistic

doctrine article, article of faith, belief, canon, concept, conviction, creed, dogma, opinion, precept, principle, teaching, tenet

document 1. *n.* certificate, instrument, legal form, paper, record, report **2.** *v.* authenticate, back up, certify, cite, corroborate, detail, give weight to, instance, particularize, substantiate, support, validate, verify

dodder quake, quaver, quiver, shake, shamble, shiver, shuffle, stagger, sway, teeter, totter, tremble

doddering aged, decrepit, doddery, faltering, feeble, floundering, infirm, senile, shaky, shambling, tottery, trembly, unsteady, weak

doddle child's play (*Inf.*), cinch (*Sl.*), picnic (*Inf.*), piece of cake (*Inf.*), pushover (*Sl.*)

dodge *v.* **1.** dart, duck, shift, sidestep, swerve, turn aside **2.** avoid, deceive, elude, equivocate, evade, fend off, fudge, get out of, hedge, parry, shirk, shuffle, trick ~*n.* **3.** contrivance, device, feint, machination, ploy, ruse, scheme, stratagem, subterfuge, trick, wheeze (*Sl.*), wile

dodger evader, shifty so-and-so, shirker, slacker, slippery one, slyboots, trickster

dodgy chancy (*Inf.*), dangerous, delicate, dicey (*Sl.*), dicky (*Sl.*), difficult, problematical, risky, ticklish, tricky, uncertain, unreliable

doer achiever, active person, activist, bustler, dynamo, go-getter (*Inf.*), live wire (*Sl.*), organizer, powerhouse (*Sl.*), wheeler-dealer (*Inf.*)

doff 1. *Of a hat* lift, raise, remove, take off, tip, touch **2.** *Of clothing* cast off, discard, remove, shed, slip off, slip out of, take off, throw off, undress

do for defeat, destroy, finish (off), kill, ruin, shatter, slay

dog *n.* **1.** bitch, canine, cur, hound, man's best friend, mongrel, mutt (*Sl.*), pooch (*Sl.*), pup, puppy, tyke **2.** *Inf.* beast, blackguard, cur, heel (*Sl.*), knave (*Archaic*), scoundrel, villain **3. dog-eat-dog** cutthroat, ferocious, fierce, ruthless, vicious, with no holds barred **4. go to the dogs** *Inf.* degenerate, deteriorate, go down the drain, go to pot, go to ruin ~*v.* **5.** haunt, hound, plague, pursue, shadow, tail (*Inf.*), track, trail, trouble

dogged determined, firm, indefatigable, obstinate, persevering, persistent, pertinacious, resolute, single-minded, staunch, steadfast, steady, stubborn, tenacious, unflagging, unshakable, unyielding

doggedness bulldog tenacity, determination, endurance, obstinacy, perseverance, persistence, pertinacity, relentlessness, resolution, single-mindedness, steadfastness, steadiness, stubbornness, tenaciousness, tenacity

doggo lie doggo be in hiding, go to earth, keep a low profile, keep one's head down, keep out of the public eye, stay out of sight

dogma article, article of faith, belief, credo, creed, doctrine, opinion, precept, principle, teachings, tenet

dogmatic 1. arbitrary, arrogant, assertive, categorical, dictatorial, doctrinaire, downright, emphatic, imperious, magisterial, obdurate, opinionated, overbearing, peremptory **2.** authoritative, canonical, categorical, doctrinal, ex cathedra, oracular, positive

dogmatism arbitrariness, arrogance, dictatorialness, imperiousness, opinionatedness, peremptoriness, positiveness, presumption

dogsbody drudge, general factotum, man *or* maid of all work, menial, skivvy, slave

do in 1. butcher, dispatch, eliminate (*Sl.*), execute, kill, liquidate, murder, slaughter, slay **2.** exhaust, fag (*Inf.*), fatigue, shatter (*Inf.*), tire, wear out, weary

doing achievement, act, action, carrying out *or* through, deed, execution, exploit, handiwork, implementation, performance

doings actions, affairs, concerns, dealings, deeds, events, exploits, goings-on (*Inf.*), handiwork, happenings, proceedings, transactions

doldrums apathy, blues, boredom, depression, dullness, dumps (*Inf.*), ennui, gloom, inertia, lassitude, listlessness, malaise, stagnation, tedium, torpor

dole *n.* **1.** allowance, alms, benefit, donation, gift, grant, gratuity, modicum, parcel, pittance, portion, quota, share **2.** allocation, allotment, apportionment, dispensation, distribution, division ~*v.* **3.** *Usually with* **out** administer, allocate, allot, apportion, assign, deal, dispense, distribute, divide, give, hand out, mete, share

doleful cheerless, depressing, dismal, distressing, dolorous, down in the mouth, dreary, forlorn, funereal, gloomy, lugubrious, melancholy, mournful, painful, pitiful, rueful, sad, sombre, sorrowful, woebegone, woeful, wretched

doll up deck out, dress up (like a dog's dinner), gussy up (*Sl.*), preen, primp, prink, titivate, trick out

dolorous anguished, distressing, doleful, grievous, harrowing, heart-rending, melancholy, miserable, mournful, painful, rueful, sad, sorrowful, woebegone, woeful, wretched

dolour anguish, distress, grief, heartache, heartbreak, heaviness of heart, misery, ruth (*Archaic*), sadness, sorrow, suffering

dolt ass, blockhead, booby, chump (*Inf.*), clot (*Sl.*), dimwit (*Inf.*), dope (*Sl.*), dullard, dunce, fool, idiot, ignoramus, nitwit, simpleton, thickhead

doltish boneheaded (*Sl.*), brainless, clottish (*Inf.*), dense, dim-witted (*Inf.*), dopey (*Sl.*), dumb (*Inf.*), foolish, half-witted, idiotic, mindless, silly, stupid

domain 1. demesne, dominion, empire, estate, kingdom, lands, policies (*Scot.*), province, realm, region, territory **2.** area, authority, bailiwick, concern, department, discipline, field, jurisdiction, orbit, power, realm, scope, speciality, sphere, sway

domestic *adj.* **1.** domiciliary, family, home, household, private **2.** domesticated, home-loving, homely, housewifely, stay-at-home **3.** domesticated, house, house-trained, pet, tame, trained **4.** indigenous, internal, native, not foreign ~*n.* **5.** char (*Inf.*), charwoman, daily, daily help, help, maid, servant, woman (*Inf.*)

domesticate 1. break, gentle, house-train, tame, train **2.** acclimatize, accustom, familiarize, habituate, naturalize

domesticated 1. *Of plants or animals* broken (in), naturalized, tame, tamed **2.** *Of people* domestic, home-loving, homely, house-trained (*Jocular*), housewifely

domesticity domestication, home life, home-lovingness, homemaking, housekeeping, housewifery

domicile abode, dwelling, habitation, home, house, legal residence, mansion, residence, residency, settlement

dominance ascendancy, authority, command, control, domination, government, mastery, paramountcy, power, rule, supremacy, sway

dominant 1. ascendant, assertive, authoritative, commanding, controlling, governing, leading, presiding, ruling, superior, supreme **2.** chief, influential, main, outstanding, paramount, predominant, pre-eminent, prevailing, prevalent, primary, principal, prominent

dominate 1. control, direct, domineer, govern, have the upper hand over, have the whip hand over, keep under one's thumb, lead, lead by the nose (*Inf.*), master, monopolize, overbear, rule, tyrannize **2.** bestride, loom over, overlook, stand head and shoulders above, stand over, survey, tower above **3.** detract from, eclipse, outshine, overrule, overshadow, predominate, prevail over

domination 1. ascendancy, authority, command, control, influence, mastery, power, rule, superiority, supremacy, sway **2.** despotism, dictatorship, oppression, repression, subjection, subordination, suppression, tyranny

domineer bluster, boss around *or* about (*Inf.*), browbeat, bully, hector, intimidate, lord (it) over, menace, overbear, ride roughshod over, swagger, threaten, tyrannize

domineering arrogant, authoritarian, autocratic, bossy (*Inf.*), coercive, despotic, dictatorial, high-handed, imperious,

iron-handed, magisterial, masterful, oppressive, overbearing, tyrannical

dominion 1. ascendancy, authority, command, control, domination, government, jurisdiction, mastery, power, rule, sovereignty, supremacy, sway **2.** country, domain, empire, kingdom, province, realm, region, territory

don clothe oneself in, dress in, get into, pull on, put on, slip on *or* into

donate bequeath, bestow, chip in (*Inf.*), contribute, gift, give, make a gift of, present, subscribe

donation alms, benefaction, boon, contribution, gift, grant, gratuity, largess, offering, present, subscription

done *adj.* **1.** accomplished, completed, concluded, consummated, ended, executed, finished, over, perfected, realized, terminated, through **2.** cooked, cooked enough, cooked sufficiently, cooked to a turn, ready **3.** depleted, exhausted, finished, spent, used up **4.** acceptable, conventional, *de rigueur*, proper **5.** *Inf.* cheated, conned (*Sl.*), duped, taken for a ride (*Inf.*), tricked ~*interj.* **6.** agreed, it's a bargain, O.K. (*Inf.*), settled, you're on (*Inf.*) **7. done for** *Inf.* beaten, broken, dashed, defeated, destroyed, doomed, finished, foiled, lost, ruined, undone, wrecked **8. done in** *or* **up** *Inf.* all in (*Sl.*), bushed (*Inf.*), dead (*Inf.*), dead beat (*Inf.*), dog-tired (*Inf.*), exhausted, fagged out (*Inf.*), knackered (*Sl.*), on one's last legs, ready to drop, tired out, worn out, worn to a frazzle (*Inf.*) **9. have done with** be through with, desist, end relations with, finish with, give up, throw over, wash one's hands of

donnish bookish, erudite, formalistic, pedagogic, pedantic, precise, scholarly, scholastic

donor almsgiver, benefactor, contributor, donator, giver, grantor (*Law*), philanthropist

doom *n.* **1.** catastrophe, death, destiny, destruction, downfall, fate, fortune, lot, portion, ruin **2.** condemnation, decision, decree, judgment, sentence, verdict **3.** Armageddon, Doomsday, end of the world, Judgment Day, the Last Day, the Last Judgment, the last trump ~*v.* **4.** condemn, consign, damn, decree, destine, foreordain, judge, predestine, sentence, threaten

doomed bedevilled, bewitched, condemned, cursed, fated, hopeless, ill-fated, ill-omened, luckless, star-crossed

door 1. doorway, egress, entrance, entry, exit, ingress, opening **2. lay at the door of** blame, censure, charge, hold responsible, impute to **3. out of doors** alfresco, in the air, out, outdoors, outside **4. show someone the door** ask to leave, boot out (*Inf.*), bounce (*Sl.*), eject, oust, show out

do out of balk, bilk, cheat, con (*Sl.*), deprive, diddle (*Inf.*), swindle, trick

dope *n.* **1.** drugs, narcotic, opiate **2.** blockhead, dimwit (*Inf.*), dolt, dunce, fool, idiot, simpleton **3.** details, facts, gen (*Inf.*), info (*Inf.*), information, inside information, lowdown (*Inf.*), news, tip ~*v.* **4.** anaesthetize, doctor, drug, inject, knock out, narcotize, sedate, stupefy

dopey, dopy 1. dense, dozy (*Inf.*), dumb (*Inf.*), foolish, idiotic, senseless, silly, simple, slow, stupid, thick **2.** dazed, drowsy, drugged, groggy (*Inf.*), muzzy, stupefied, woozy (*Inf.*)

dormant asleep, comatose, fallow, hibernating, inactive, inert, inoperative, latent, quiescent, sleeping, sluggish, slumbering, suspended, torpid

dose dosage, draught, drench, measure, portion, potion, prescription, quantity

dot *n.* **1.** atom, circle, dab, fleck, full stop, iota, jot, mark, mite, mote, point, speck, spot **2. on the dot** exactly, on time, precisely, promptly, punctually, to the minute ~*v.* **3.** dab, dabble, fleck, spot, sprinkle, stipple, stud

dotage 1. decrepitude, feebleness, imbecility, old age, second childhood, senility, weakness **2.** doting, foolish fondness, infatuation

dote on *or* **upon** admire, adore, hold dear, idolize, lavish affection on, prize, treasure

doting adoring, devoted, fond, foolish, indulgent, lovesick

dotty 1. batty (*Sl.*), crazy, eccentric, feeble-minded, peculiar, potty (*Inf.*), touched **2.** *With* **about** crazy (*Inf.*), daft (*Inf.*), fond of, keen on

double *adj.* **1.** binate (*Botany*), coupled, doubled, dual, duplicate, in pairs, paired, twice, twin, twofold **2.** deceitful, dishonest, false, hypocritical, insincere, Janus-faced, knavish (*Archaic*), perfidious, treacherous, two-faced, vacillating ~*v.* **3.** duplicate, enlarge, fold, grow, increase, magnify, multiply, plait, repeat ~*n.* **4.** clone, copy, counterpart, dead ringer (*Sl.*), Doppelgänger, duplicate, fellow, impersonator, lookalike, mate, replica, ringer (*Sl.*), spitting image (*Inf.*), twin **5. at** *or* **on the double** at full speed, briskly, immediately, in double-quick time, p.d.q. (*Sl.*), posthaste, quickly, without delay

double back backtrack, circle, dodge, loop, retrace one's steps, return, reverse

double-cross betray, cheat, defraud, hoodwink, mislead, swindle, trick, two-time (*Inf.*)

double-dealer betrayer, cheat, con man (*Inf.*), deceiver, dissembler, double-crosser (*Inf.*), fraud, hypocrite, rogue, swindler, traitor, two-timer (*Inf.*)

double-dealing 1. *n.* bad faith, betrayal, cheating, deceit, deception, dishonesty, duplicity, foul play, hypocrisy, mendacity, perfidy, treachery, trickery, two-timing (*Inf.*) **2.** *adj.* cheating, crooked (*Inf.*), deceitful, dishonest, duplicitous, fraudulent, hypocritical, lying, perfidious, sneaky, swindling, treacherous, tricky, two-faced, two-timing (*Inf.*), underhanded, untrustworthy, wily

double entendre ambiguity, double meaning, innuendo, play on words, pun

doublet 1. jacket, jerkin, vest, waistcoat **2.** couple, pair, set, two

doubly again, as much again, even more, in double measure, once more, over again, twice, twofold

doubt *v.* **1.** discredit, distrust, fear, lack confidence in, misgive, mistrust, query, question, suspect ~*n.* **2.** apprehension, disquiet, distrust, fear, incredulity, lack of faith, misgiving, mistrust, qualm, scepticism, suspicion ~*v.* **3.** dubious, be uncertain, demur, fluctuate, hesitate, scruple, vacillate, waver ~*n.* **4.** dubiety, hesitancy, hesitation, indecision, irresolution, lack of conviction, suspense, uncertainty, vacillation **5.** ambiguity, confusion, difficulty, dilemma, perplexity, problem, quandary **6. no doubt** admittedly, assuredly, certainly, doubtless, doubtlessly, probably, surely

doubter agnostic, disbeliever, doubting Thomas, questioner, sceptic, unbeliever

doubtful 1. ambiguous, debatable, dubious, equivocal, hazardous, inconclusive, indefinite, indeterminate, obscure, precarious, problematic, questionable, unclear, unconfirmed, unsettled, vague

2. distrustful, hesitating, in two minds (*Inf.*), irresolute, perplexed, sceptical, suspicious, tentative, uncertain, unconvinced, undecided, unresolved, unsettled, unsure, vacillating, wavering **3**. disreputable, dubious, questionable, shady (*Inf.*), suspect, suspicious

doubtless **1**. assuredly, certainly, clearly, indisputably, of course, precisely, surely, truly, undoubtedly, unquestionably, without doubt **2**. apparently, most likely, ostensibly, presumably, probably, seemingly, supposedly

doughty bold, brave, courageous, daring, dauntless, fearless, gallant, hardy, heroic, intrepid, redoubtable, resolute, stouthearted, valiant, valorous

dour **1**. dismal, dreary, forbidding, gloomy, grim, morose, sour, sullen, unfriendly **2**. austere, hard, inflexible, obstinate, rigid, rigorous, severe, strict, uncompromising, unyielding

douse, dowse **1**. drench, duck, dunk, immerse, plunge into water, saturate, soak, souse, steep, submerge **2**. blow out, extinguish, put out, smother, snuff (out)

dovetail *v*. **1**. fit, fit together, interlock, join, link, mortise, tenon, unite **2**. accord, agree, coincide, conform, correspond, harmonize, match, tally

dowdy dingy, drab, frowzy, frumpish, frumpy, ill-dressed, old-fashioned, scrubby (*Inf.*), shabby, slovenly, tacky (*U.S. inf.*), unfashionable

dower **1**. dowry, inheritance, legacy, portion, provision, share **2**. endowment, faculty, gift, talent

do without abstain from, dispense with, forgo, get along without, give up, manage without

down *adj*. **1**. blue, dejected, depressed, disheartened, downcast, low, miserable, sad, unhappy ~*v*. **2**. bring down, fell, floor, knock down, overthrow, prostrate, subdue, tackle, throw, trip **3**. *Inf*. drain, drink (down), gulp, put away, swallow, toss off ~*n*. **4**. decline, descent, drop, dropping, fall, falling, reverse **5**. **have a down on** *Inf*. be antagonistic *or* hostile to, bear a grudge towards, be prejudiced against, be set against, feel ill will towards, have it in for (*Sl.*) **6**. **down with** away with, get rid of, kick out (*Inf.*), oust, push out

down and out **1**. *adj*. derelict, destitute, impoverished, penniless, ruined **2**. **down-and-out** *n*. beggar, derelict, dosser

(*Sl.*), loser, outcast, pauper, tramp, vagabond, vagrant

downcast cheerless, crestfallen, daunted, dejected, depressed, despondent, disappointed, disconsolate, discouraged, disheartened, dismayed, dispirited, miserable, sad, unhappy

downfall **1**. breakdown, collapse, comedown, comeuppance (*Sl.*), debacle, descent, destruction, disgrace, fall, overthrow, ruin, undoing **2**. cloudburst, deluge, downpour, rainstorm

downgrade **1**. degrade, demote, humble, lower *or* reduce in rank, take down a peg (*Inf.*) **2**. decry, denigrate, detract from, disparage, run down

downhearted blue, chapfallen, crestfallen, dejected, depressed, despondent, discouraged, disheartened, dismayed, dispirited, downcast, low-spirited, sad, sorrowful, unhappy

downpour cloudburst, deluge, flood, inundation, rainstorm, torrential rain

downright **1**. absolute, blatant, categorical, clear, complete, explicit, out-and-out, outright, plain, positive, simple, thoroughgoing, total, undisguised, unequivocal, unqualified, utter **2**. blunt, candid, forthright, frank, honest, open, outspoken, plain, sincere, straightforward, straight-from-the-shoulder

down-to-earth common-sense, hardheaded, matter-of-fact, mundane, nononsense, plain-spoken, practical, realistic, sane, sensible, unsentimental

downtrodden abused, afflicted, distressed, exploited, helpless, oppressed, subjugated, subservient, tyrannized

downward *adj*. declining, descending, earthward, heading down, sliding, slipping

downy feathery, fleecy, fluffy, plumate (*Zool., Bot.*), silky, soft, velvety, woolly

dowse *see* DOUSE

doze **1**. *v*. catnap, drop off (*Inf.*), drowse, kip (*Sl.*), nap, nod, nod off (*Inf.*), sleep, sleep lightly, slumber, snooze (*Inf.*), zizz (*Inf.*) **2**. *n*. catnap, forty winks (*Inf.*), kip (*Sl.*), little sleep, nap, shuteye (*Sl.*), siesta, snooze (*Inf.*)

dozy **1**. dozing, drowsy, half asleep, nodding, sleepy **2**. *Inf*. daft (*Sl.*), not all there, senseless, silly, simpie, slow, slowwitted, stupid, witless

drab cheerless, colourless, dingy, dismal, dreary, dull, flat, gloomy, grey, lacklustre, shabby, sombre, uninspired, vapid

draft v. **1.** compose, delineate, design, draw, draw up, formulate, outline, plan, sketch ~n. **2.** abstract, delineation, outline, plan, preliminary form, rough, sketch, version **3.** bill (of exchange), cheque, order, postal order

drag v. **1.** draw, hale, haul, lug, pull, tow, trail, tug, yank **2.** crawl, creep, go slowly, inch, limp along, shamble, shuffle **3.** dawdle, draggle, lag behind, linger, loiter, straggle, trail behind **4.** With on or out draw out, extend, keep going, lengthen, persist, prolong, protract, spin out, stretch out **5. drag one's feet** Inf. block, hold back, obstruct, procrastinate, stall ~n. **6.** Sl. annoyance, bore, bother, nuisance, pain (Inf.), pest

dragging boring, dull, going slowly, humdrum, monotonous, tedious, tiresome, wearisome

draggle 1. befoul, bemire, besmirch, drabble, trail **2.** dally, dawdle, dilly-dally (Inf.), lag, straggle, trail behind

dragoon v. browbeat, bully, coerce, compel, constrain, drive, force, impel, intimidate, strong-arm (Inf.)

drain v. **1.** bleed, draw off, dry, empty, evacuate, milk, pump off or out, remove, tap, withdraw **2.** consume, deplete, dissipate, empty, exhaust, sap, strain, tax, use up, weary **3.** discharge, effuse, exude, flow out, leak, ooze, seep, trickle, well out **4.** drink up, finish, gulp down, quaff, swallow ~n. **5.** channel, conduit, culvert, ditch, duct, outlet, pipe, sewer, sink, trench, watercourse **6.** depletion, drag, exhaustion, expenditure, reduction, sap, strain, withdrawal **7. down the drain** gone, gone for good, lost, ruined, wasted

drainage bilge (water), seepage, sewage, sewerage, waste

dram drop, glass, measure, shot (Inf.), slug, snort (Sl.), tot

drama 1. dramatization, play, show, stage play, stage show, theatrical piece **2.** acting, dramatic art, dramaturgy, stagecraft, theatre, Thespian art **3.** crisis, dramatics, excitement, histrionics, scene, spectacle, theatrics, turmoil

dramatic 1. dramaturgic, dramaturgical, theatrical, Thespian **2.** breathtaking, climactic, electrifying, emotional, exciting, melodramatic, sensational, startling, sudden, suspenseful, tense, thrilling **3.**

affecting, effective, expressive, impressive, moving, powerful, striking, vivid

dramatist dramaturge, playwright, scriptwriter

dramatize act, exaggerate, lay it on (thick) (Sl.), make a performance of, overdo, overstate, play-act, play to the gallery

drape 1. adorn, array, cloak, cover, fold, swathe, wrap **2.** dangle, droop, drop, hang, lean over, let fall, suspend

drastic desperate, dire, extreme, forceful, harsh, radical, severe, strong

draught 1. Of air current, flow, influx, movement, puff **2.** dragging, drawing, haulage, pulling, traction **3.** cup, dose, drench, drink, potion, quantity

draw v. **1.** drag, haul, pull, tow, tug **2.** delineate, depict, design, map out, mark out, outline, paint, portray, sketch, trace **3.** deduce, derive, get, infer, make, take **4.** allure, attract, bring forth, call forth, elicit, engage, entice, evoke, induce, influence, invite, persuade **5.** extort, extract, pull out, take out **6.** attenuate, elongate, extend, lengthen, stretch **7.** breathe in, drain, inhale, inspire, puff, pull, respire, suck **8.** compose, draft, formulate, frame, prepare, write **9.** choose, pick, select, single out, take ~n. **10.** Inf. attraction, enticement, lure, pull (Inf.) **11.** dead heat, deadlock, stalemate, tie

drawback defect, deficiency, detriment, difficulty, disadvantage, fault, flaw, fly in the ointment (Inf.), handicap, hindrance, hitch, impediment, imperfection, nuisance, obstacle, snag, stumbling block, trouble

draw back recoil, retract, retreat, shrink, start back, withdraw

drawing cartoon, delineation, depiction, illustration, outline, picture, portrayal, representation, sketch, study

drawl v. Of speech sounds drag out, draw out, extend, lengthen, prolong, protract

drawling dragging, drawly, droning, dull, twanging, twangy

drawn fatigued, fraught, haggard, harassed, harrowed, pinched, sapped, strained, stressed, taut, tense, tired, worn

draw on employ, exploit, extract, fall back on, have recourse to, make use of, rely on, take from, use

draw out drag out, extend, lengthen, make longer, prolong, prolongate, protract, spin out, stretch, string out

draw up 1. bring to a stop, halt, pull up, run in, stop, stop short **2**. compose, draft, formulate, frame, prepare, write out

dread 1. *v*. anticipate with horror, cringe at, fear, have cold feet (*Inf.*), quail, shrink from, shudder, tremble **2**. *n*. affright, alarm, apprehension, aversion, awe, dismay, fear, fright, funk (*Inf.*), heebie-jeebies (*Sl.*), horror, terror, trepidation **3**. *adj*. alarming, awe-inspiring, awful, dire, dreaded, dreadful, frightening, frightful, horrible, terrible, terrifying

dreadful alarming, appalling, awful, dire, distressing, fearful, formidable, frightful, ghastly, grievous, hideous, horrendous, horrible, monstrous, shocking, terrible, tragic, tremendous

dream *n*. **1**. daydream, delusion, fantasy, hallucination, illusion, imagination, pipe dream, reverie, speculation, trance, vagary, vision **2**. ambition, aspiration, design, desire, goal, hope, notion, wish **3**. beauty, delight, gem, joy, marvel, pleasure, treasure ~*v*. **4**. build castles in the air *or* in Spain, conjure up, daydream, envisage, fancy, fantasize, hallucinate, have dreams, imagine, stargaze, think, visualize

dreamer daydreamer, Don Quixote, fantasist, fantasizer, fantast, idealist, romancer, theorizer, utopian, visionary

dreamland cloud-cuckoo-land, cloudland, dream world, fairyland, fantasy, illusion, land of dreams, land of make-believe, land of Nod, never-never land (*Inf.*), sleep

dreamlike chimerical, hallucinatory, illusory, phantasmagoric, phantasmagorical, surreal, trancelike, unreal, unsubstantial, visionary

dream up concoct, contrive, cook up (*Inf.*), create, devise, hatch, imagine, invent, spin, think up

dreamy 1. fanciful, imaginary, impractical, quixotic, speculative, vague, visionary **2**. chimerical, dreamlike, fantastic, intangible, misty, phantasmagoric, phantasmagorical, shadowy, unreal **3**. absent, abstracted, daydreaming, faraway, in a reverie, musing, pensive, preoccupied, with one's head in the clouds **4**. calming, gentle, lulling, relaxing, romantic, soothing

dreary 1. bleak, cheerless, comfortless, depressing, dismal, doleful, downcast, drear, forlorn, gloomy, glum, joyless, lonely, lonesome, melancholy, mournful, sad, solitary, sombre, sorrowful, wretched **2**. boring, colourless, drab, dull, humdrum, lifeless, monotonous, routine, tedious, uneventful, uninteresting, wearisome

dredge up dig up, discover, drag up, draw up, fish up, raise, rake up, uncover, unearth

dreg bit, drop, mite, particle, piece, remnant, scrap

dregs 1. deposit, draff, dross, grounds, lees, residue, residuum, scourings, scum, sediment, trash, waste **2**. *Sl. canaille*, down-and-outs, good-for-nothings, outcasts, rabble, ragtag and bobtail, riffraff, scum

drench 1. drown, duck, flood, imbrue, inundate, saturate, soak, souse, steep, wet **2**. *Veterinary* dose, physic, purge

dress *n*. **1**. costume, ensemble, frock, garment, get-up (*Inf.*), gown, outfit, rig-out (*Inf.*), robe, suit **2**. apparel, attire, clothes, clothing, costume, garb, garments, gear (*Sl.*), guise, habiliment, raiment (*Archaic*), togs, vestment ~*v*. **3**. attire, change, clothe, don, garb, put on, robe, slip on *or* into **4**. adorn, apparel (*Archaic*), array, bedeck, deck, decorate, drape, embellish, furbish, ornament, rig, trim **5**. adjust, align, arrange, comb (out), dispose, do (up), fit, groom, prepare, set, straighten **6**. bandage, bind up, plaster, treat

dress down berate, carpet (*Inf.*), castigate, haul over the coals, rebuke, reprimand, reprove, scold, tear (someone) off a strip, tell off (*Inf.*), upbraid

dressmaker couturier, modiste, seamstress, sewing woman, tailor

dress up 1. doll up (*Sl.*), dress for dinner, dress formally, put on one's best bib and tucker (*Inf.*), put on one's glad rags (*Sl.*) **2**. disguise, play-act, put on fancy dress, wear a costume **3**. beautify, embellish, gild, improve, titivate, trick out *or* up

dressy classy (*Sl.*), elaborate, elegant, formal, ornate, ritzy (*Sl.*), smart, stylish, swish (*Inf.*)

dribble 1. drip, drop, fall in drops, leak, ooze, run, seep, trickle **2**. drip saliva, drivel, drool, slaver, slobber

driblet bit, dash, drop, droplet, fragment, gobbet, morsel, piece, scrap, speck, sprinkling

drift v. **1.** be carried along, coast, float, go (aimlessly), meander, stray, waft, wander **2.** accumulate, amass, bank up, drive, gather, pile up ~n. **3.** accumulation, bank, heap, mass, mound, pile **4.** course, current, direction, flow, impulse, movement, rush, sweep, trend **5.** *Fig.* aim, design, direction, gist, implication, import, intention, meaning, object, purport, scope, significance, tendency, tenor

drifter beachcomber, hobo (*U.S.*), itinerant, rolling stone, tramp, vagabond, vagrant, wanderer

drill v. **1.** discipline, exercise, instruct, practise, rehearse, teach, train ~n. **2.** discipline, exercise, instruction, practice, preparation, repetition, training ~v. **3.** bore, penetrate, perforate, pierce, puncture, sink in ~n. **4.** bit, borer, boring-tool, gimlet, rotary tool

drink v. **1.** absorb, drain, gulp, guzzle, imbibe, partake of, quaff, sip, suck, sup, swallow, swig, swill, toss off, wash down, wet one's whistle (*Inf.*) **2.** booze (*Inf.*), carouse, go on a binge *or* bender (*Inf.*), hit the bottle (*Inf.*), indulge, pub-crawl (*Chiefly Brit. sl.*), revel, tipple, tope, wassail ~n. **3.** beverage, liquid, potion, refreshment, thirst quencher **4.** alcohol, booze (*Inf.*), hooch (*Sl.*), liquor, spirits, the bottle (*Inf.*) **5.** cup, draught, glass, gulp, sip, swallow, swig (*Inf.*), taste **6. the drink** *Inf.* the briny (*Inf.*), the deep, the main, the ocean, the sea

drinkable drinking, fit to drink, potable

drinker alcoholic, bibber, boozer (*Inf.*), dipsomaniac, drunk, drunkard, guzzler, inebriate, lush (*Sl.*), soak (*Sl.*), sot, sponge (*Inf.*), tippler, toper, wino (*Sl.*)

drink in absorb, assimilate, be all ears (*Inf.*), be fascinated by, be rapt, hang on (someone's) words, hang on the lips of, pay attention

drinking bout bacchanalia, bender (*Inf.*), bevvy (*Dialect*), binge (*Inf.*), celebration, debauch, orgy, pub-crawl (*Chiefly Brit. sl.*), spree, wassail

drink to pledge, pledge the health of, salute, toast

drip v. **1.** dribble, drizzle, drop, exude, filter, plop, splash, sprinkle, trickle ~n. **2.** dribble, dripping, drop, leak, trickle **3.**

Inf. milksop, ninny, softy (*Inf.*), weakling, weed (*Inf.*), wet (*Inf.*)

drive v. **1.** herd, hurl, impel, propel, push, send, urge **2.** direct, go, guide, handle, manage, motor, operate, ride, steer, travel **3.** actuate, coerce, compel, constrain, force, goad, harass, impel, motivate, oblige, overburden, overwork, press, prick, prod, rush, spur **4.** dash, dig, plunge, hammer, ram, sink, stab, thrust ~n. **5.** excursion, hurl (*Scot.*), jaunt, journey, outing, ride, run, spin (*Inf.*), trip, turn **6.** action, advance, appeal, campaign, crusade, effort, push (*Inf.*), surge **7.** ambition, effort, energy, enterprise, get-up-and-go (*Inf.*), initiative, motivation, pressure, push (*Inf.*), vigour, zip (*Inf.*)

drive at aim, allude to, get at (*Inf.*), have in mind, hint at, imply, indicate, intend, intimate, mean, refer to, signify, suggest

drivel v. **1.** dribble, drool, slaver, slobber **2.** babble, blether, gab (*Inf.*), gas (*Inf.*), maunder, prate, ramble, waffle (*Inf.*) ~n. **3.** balderdash, blah (*Sl.*), bosh (*Inf.*), bunk (*Inf.*), bunkum, fatuity, gibberish, nonsense, poppycock (*Inf.*), prating, rot, rubbish, stuff, twaddle, waffle (*Inf.*) **4.** saliva, slaver, slobber

driveller 1. drooler, slaverer, slobberer, splutterer, sputterer **2.** babbler, blatherskite, prater, prattler, rambler, twaddler, waffler (*Inf.*), windbag (*Sl.*)

driving compelling, dynamic, energetic, forceful, galvanic, sweeping, vigorous, violent

drizzle 1. n. fine rain, Scotch mist **2.** v. mizzle (*Dialect*), rain, shower, spot *or* spit with rain, spray, sprinkle

droll amusing, clownish, comic, comical, diverting, eccentric, entertaining, farcical, funny, humorous, jocular, laughable, ludicrous, odd, quaint, ridiculous, risible, waggish, whimsical

drollery absurdity, archness, buffoonery, comicality, farce, fun, humour, jocularity, pleasantry, waggishness, whimsicality, wit

drone[1] n. idler, leech, loafer, lounger, parasite, scrounger (*Inf.*), sluggard, sponger (*Inf.*)

drone[2] v. **1.** buzz, hum, purr, thrum, vibrate, whirr **2.** *Often with* on be boring, chant, drawl, intone, prose about, speak monotonously, talk interminably ~n. **3.** buzz, hum, murmuring, purr, thrum, vibration, whirr, whirring

drool 1. *Often with* **over** dote on, fondle, gloat over, gush, make much of, pet, rave (*Inf.*), slobber over, spoil 2. dribble, drivel, salivate, slaver, slobber, water at the mouth

droop 1. bend, dangle, drop, fall down, hang (down), sag, sink 2. decline, diminish, fade, faint, flag, languish, slump, wilt, wither 3. despond, falter, give in, give up, give way, lose heart *or* hope

droopy 1. drooping, flabby, floppy, languid, languorous, lassitudinous, limp, pendulous, sagging, stooped, wilting 2. blue, dejected, disheartened, dispirited, doleful, downcast, down (in the dumps) (*Inf.*)

drop n. 1. bead, bubble, driblet, drip, droplet, globule, pearl, tear 2. dab, dash, mouthful, nip, pinch, shot (*Inf.*), sip, spot, taste, tot, trace, trickle 3. abyss, chasm, declivity, descent, fall, plunge, precipice, slope 4. cut, decline, decrease, deterioration, downturn, fall-off, lowering, reduction, slump ~v. 5. dribble, drip, fall in drops, trickle 6. decline, depress, descend, diminish, dive, droop, fall, lower, plummet, plunge, sink, tumble 7. abandon, cease, desert, discontinue, forsake, give up, kick (*Inf.*), leave, quit, relinquish, remit, terminate 8. *Inf.* disown, ignore, jilt, reject, renounce, repudiate, throw over 9. *Inf. Sometimes with* **off** deposit, leave, let off, set down, unload

drop in (on) blow in (*Inf.*), call, call in, go and see, look in (on), look up, pop in (*Inf.*), roll up (*Inf.*), stop, turn up, visit

drop off 1. decline, decrease, diminish, dwindle, fall off, lessen, slacken 2. allow to alight, deliver, leave, let off, set down 3. *Inf.* catnap, doze (off), drowse, fall asleep, have forty winks (*Inf.*), nod (off), snooze (*Inf.*)

drop out abandon, back out, forsake, give up, leave, quit, renege, stop, withdraw

dross crust, debris, dregs, impurity, lees, recrement, refuse, remains, scoria, scum, waste

drought 1. aridity, dehydration, drouth (*Archaic or Scot.*), dryness, dry spell, dry weather, parchedness 2. dearth, deficiency, insufficiency, lack, need, scarcity, shortage, want

drove collection, company, crowd, flock, gathering, herd, horde, mob, multitude, press, swarm, throng

drown 1. deluge, drench, engulf, flood, go down, go under, immerse, inundate, sink, submerge, swamp 2. *Fig.* deaden, engulf, muffle, obliterate, overcome, overpower, overwhelm, stifle, swallow up, wipe out

drowse 1. *v.* be drowsy, be lethargic, be sleepy, doze, drop off (*Inf.*), nap, nod, sleep, slumber, snooze (*Inf.*) 2. *n.* doze, forty winks (*Inf.*), nap, sleep, slumber

drowsy 1. comatose, dazed, dopey (*Sl.*), dozy, drugged, half asleep, heavy, lethargic, nodding, sleepy, somnolent, tired, torpid 2. dreamy, lulling, restful, sleepy, soothing, soporific

drub 1. bang, beat, birch, cane, club, cudgel, flog, hit, knock, pound, pummel, strike, thrash, thump, whack 2. beat, best, defeat, hammer (*Inf.*), lick (*Inf.*), outclass, overcome, rout, trounce, vanquish, worst

drubbing beating, clobbering (*Sl.*), defeat, flogging, hammering (*Inf.*), licking (*Inf.*), pounding, pummelling, thrashing, trouncing, walloping (*Inf.*), whipping

drudge 1. *n.* dogsbody (*Inf.*), factotum, hack, maid *or* man of all work, menial, plodder, scullion (*Archaic*), servant, skivvy, slave, toiler, worker 2. *v.* grind (*Inf.*), keep one's nose to the grindstone, labour, moil (*Archaic or dialect*), plod, plug away (*Inf.*), slave, toil, work

drudgery chore, donkey-work, fag (*Inf.*), grind (*Inf.*), hack work, hard work, labour, menial labour, skivvying, slavery, slog, sweat (*Inf.*), sweated labour, toil

drug n. 1. medicament, medication, medicine, physic, poison, remedy 2. dope (*Sl.*), narcotic, opiate ~v. 3. administer a drug, dope (*Sl.*), dose, medicate, treat 4. anaesthetize, deaden, knock out, numb, poison, stupefy

drugged comatose, doped (*Sl.*), dopey (*Sl.*), high (*Inf.*), on a trip (*Inf.*), spaced out (*Sl.*), stoned (*Sl.*), stupefied, turned on (*Sl.*), under the influence (*Inf.*), zonked (*Sl.*)

drum v. 1. beat, pulsate, rap, reverberate, tap, tattoo, throb 2. *With* **into** din into, drive home, hammer away, harp on, instil, reiterate

drum out cashier, discharge, dismiss, disown, drive out, expel, oust, outlaw

drum up attract, bid for, canvass, obtain, petition, round up, solicit

drunk 1. *adj.* bacchic, canned (*Sl.*), drunken, fu' (*Scot.*), fuddled, half seas over (*Inf.*), inebriated, intoxicated, maudlin, merry (*Inf.*), muddled, pie-eyed (*Sl.*), plastered (*Sl.*), sloshed (*Sl.*), soaked (*Inf.*), stewed (*Sl.*), stoned (*Sl.*), tiddly (*Sl.*), tight (*Inf.*), tipsy, tired and emotional (*Euphemistic*), under the influence (*Inf.*), well-oiled (*Sl.*) **2.** *n.* boozer (*Inf.*), drunkard, inebriate, lush (*Sl.*), soak (*Sl.*), sot, toper, wino (*Sl.*)

drunkard alcoholic, carouser, dipsomaniac, drinker, drunk, lush (*Sl.*), soak (*Sl.*), sot, tippler, toper, wino (*Sl.*)

drunken 1. bibulous, boozing (*Sl.*), drunk, (gin-)sodden, inebriate, intoxicated, red-nosed, sottish, tippling, toping, under the influence (*Inf.*) **2.** bacchanalian, bacchic, boozy (*Sl.*), debauched, dionysian, dissipated, orgiastic, riotous, saturnalian

drunkenness alcoholism, bibulousness, dipsomania, inebriety, insobriety, intemperance, intoxication, sottishness, tipsiness

dry *adj.* **1.** arid, barren, dehydrated, desiccated, dried up, juiceless, moistureless, parched, sapless, thirsty, torrid, waterless **2.** *Fig.* boring, dreary, dull, monotonous, plain, tedious, tiresome, uninteresting **3.** *Fig.* cutting, deadpan, droll, keen, low-key, quietly humorous, sarcastic, sharp, sly ∼*v.* **4.** dehumidify, dehydrate, desiccate, drain, make dry, parch, sear **5.** *With* **out** *or* **up** become dry, become unproductive, harden, mummify, shrivel up, wilt, wither, wizen

dryness aridity, aridness, dehumidification, dehydration, drought, thirst, thirstiness

dual binary, coupled, double, duplex, duplicate, matched, paired, twin, two-fold

duality biformity, dichotomy, doubleness, dualism, duplexity, polarity

dub 1. bestow, confer, confer knighthood upon, entitle, knight **2.** call, christen, denominate, designate, label, name, nickname, style, term

dubiety doubt, doubtfulness, dubiosity, incertitude, indecision, misgiving, mistrust, qualm, scepticism, uncertainty

dubious 1. doubtful, hesitant, iffy (*Inf.*), sceptical, uncertain, unconvinced, undecided, unsure, wavering **2.** ambiguous, debatable, doubtful, equivocal, indefinite, indeterminate, obscure, problematical, unclear, unsettled **3.** fishy (*Inf.*), questionable, shady (*Inf.*), suspect, suspicious, undependable, unreliable, untrustworthy

dubitable debatable, doubtable, doubtful, dubious, iffy (*Inf.*), in doubt, more than doubtful, open to doubt, problematic, problematical, questionable, unconvincing

duck 1. bend, bob, bow, crouch, dodge, drop, lower, stoop **2.** dip, dive, douse, dunk, immerse, plunge, souse, submerge, wet **3.** *Inf.* avoid, dodge, escape, evade, shirk, shun, sidestep

duct blood vessel, canal, channel, conduit, funnel, passage, pipe, tube

ductile 1. extensible, flexible, malleable, plastic, pliable, pliant **2.** amenable, biddable, compliant, docile, manageable, tractable, yielding

dud 1. *n.* failure, flop (*Inf.*), washout (*Inf.*) **2.** *adj.* broken, bust (*Inf.*), duff (*Sl.*), failed, inoperative, kaput (*Inf.*), not functioning, valueless, worthless

dudgeon 1. *Archaic* indignation, ire, resentment, umbrage, wrath **2. in high dudgeon** angry, fuming, indignant, offended, resentful, vexed

due *adj.* **1.** in arrears, outstanding, owed, owing, payable, unpaid **2.** appropriate, becoming, bounden, deserved, fit, fitting, just, justified, merited, obligatory, proper, requisite, right, rightful, suitable, well-earned **3.** adequate, ample, enough, plenty of, sufficient **4.** expected, expected to arrive, scheduled ∼*n.* **5.** comeuppance (*Sl.*), deserts, merits, prerogative, privilege, right(s) ∼*adv.* **6.** dead, direct, directly, exactly, straight, undeviatingly

duel *n.* **1.** affair of honour, single combat **2.** clash, competition, contest, encounter, engagement, fight, rivalry ∼*v.* **3.** clash, compete, contend, contest, fight, rival, struggle, vie with

dues charge, charges, contribution, fee, levy, membership fee

duff bad, counterfeit, dud (*Inf.*), fake, false, not working, useless, worthless

duffer blunderer, booby, bungler, clod, clot (*Sl.*), galoot (*Sl., chiefly U.S.*), lubber, lummox (*Inf.*), oaf

dulcet agreeable, charming, delightful, euphonious, harmonious, honeyed, mellifluent, mellifluous, melodious, musical, pleasant, pleasing, soothing, sweet

dull *adj.* **1**. dense, dim, dim-witted (*Inf.*), doltish, slow, stolid, stupid, thick, unintelligent **2**. apathetic, blank, callous, dead, empty, heavy, indifferent, insensible, insensitive, lifeless, listless, passionless, slow, sluggish, unresponsive, unsympathetic, vacuous **3**. boring, commonplace, dreary, dry, flat, humdrum, monotonous, plain, prosaic, run-of-the-mill, tedious, tiresome, unimaginative, uninteresting, vapid **4**. blunt, blunted, dulled, edgeless, not keen, not sharp, unsharpened **5**. cloudy, dim, dismal, gloomy, leaden, opaque, overcast, turbid **6**. depressed, inactive, slack, slow, sluggish, torpid, uneventful **7**. drab, faded, feeble, indistinct, lacklustre, muffled, murky, muted, sombre, subdued, subfusc, toned-down ~*v.* **8**. dampen, deject, depress, discourage, dishearten, dispirit, sadden **9**. allay, alleviate, assuage, blunt, lessen, mitigate, moderate, palliate, paralyse, relieve, soften, stupefy, take the edge off **10**. cloud, darken, dim, fade, obscure, stain, sully, tarnish

dullard blockhead, clod, dimwit (*Inf.*), dolt, dope (*Sl.*), dunce, nitwit, numskull, oaf

duly 1. accordingly, appropriately, befittingly, correctly, decorously, deservedly, fittingly, properly, rightfully, suitably **2**. at the proper time, on time, punctually

dumb 1. at a loss for words, inarticulate, mum, mute, silent, soundless, speechless, tongue-tied, voiceless, wordless **2**. *Inf.* dense, dim-witted (*Inf.*), dull, foolish, stupid, thick, unintelligent

dumbfound, dumfound amaze, astonish, astound, bewilder, bowl over (*Inf.*), confound, confuse, flabbergast (*Inf.*), nonplus, overwhelm, stagger, startle, stun, take aback

dumbfounded, dumfounded amazed, astonished, astounded, bewildered, bowled over (*Inf.*), breathless, confounded, confused, dumb, flabbergasted (*Inf.*), knocked for six (*Inf.*), knocked sideways (*Inf.*), nonplussed, overcome, overwhelmed, speechless, staggered, startled, stunned, taken aback, thrown, thunderstruck

dummy *n.* **1**. figure, form, lay figure, manikin, mannequin, model **2**. copy, counterfeit, duplicate, imitation, sham, substitute **3**. *Sl.* blockhead, dimwit

(*Inf.*), dolt, dullard, dunce, fool, numskull, simpleton ~*adj.* **4**. artificial, bogus, fake, false, imitation, mock, phoney (*Sl.*), sham, simulated **5**. mock, practice, simulated, trial

dump *v.* **1**. deposit, drop, fling down, let fall, throw down **2**., discharge, dispose of, ditch (*Sl.*), empty out, get rid of, jettison, scrap, throw away *or* out, tip, unload ~*n.* **3**. junkyard, refuse heap, rubbish heap, rubbish tip, tip **4**. *Inf.* hole (*Inf.*), hovel, joint (*Sl.*), mess, pigsty, shack, shanty, slum

dumps blues, dejection, depression, despondency, dolour, gloom, gloominess, low spirits, melancholy, mopes, sadness, unhappiness, woe

dumpy chubby, chunky, homely, plump, podgy, pudgy, roly-poly, short, squab, squat, stout, tubby

dun *v.* beset, importune, pester, plague, press, urge

dunce ass, blockhead, bonehead (*Sl.*), dimwit (*Inf.*), dolt, donkey, duffer (*Inf.*), dullard, dunderhead, goose (*Inf.*), halfwit, ignoramus, loon (*Inf.*), moron, nincompoop, numskull, simpleton, thickhead

dungeon cage, cell, donjon, lockup, oubliette, prison, vault

dupe *n.* **1**. fall guy (*Inf.*), gull, mug (*Sl.*), pigeon (*Sl.*), pushover (*Sl.*), sap (*Sl.*), simpleton, sucker (*Sl.*), victim **2**. cat's-paw, instrument, pawn, puppet, stooge (*Sl.*), tool ~*v.* **3**. bamboozle (*Inf.*), beguile, cheat, con (*Sl.*), cozen, deceive, defraud, delude, gull (*Archaic*), hoax, hoodwink, humbug, outwit, overreach, rip off (*Sl.*), swindle, trick

duplicate 1. *adj.* corresponding, identical, matched, matching, twin, twofold **2**. *n.* carbon copy, clone, copy, double, facsimile, likeness, lookalike, match, mate, photocopy, Photostat (*Trademark*), replica, reproduction, ringer (*Sl.*), twin, Xerox (*Trademark*) **3**. *v.* clone, copy, double, echo, photocopy, Photostat (*Trademark*), repeat, replicate, reproduce, Xerox (*Trademark*)

duplicity artifice, chicanery, deceit, deception, dishonesty, dissimulation, double-dealing, falsehood, fraud, guile, hypocrisy, perfidy

durability constancy, durableness, endurance, imperishability, lastingness, permanence, persistence

durable abiding, constant, dependable, enduring, fast, firm, fixed, hard-wearing, lasting, long-lasting, permanent, persistent, reliable, resistant, sound, stable, strong, sturdy, substantial, tough

duration continuance, continuation, extent, length, period, perpetuation, prolongation, span, spell, stretch, term, time

duress 1. coercion, compulsion, constraint, pressure, threat **2.** captivity, confinement, constraint, hardship, imprisonment, incarceration, restraint

dusk 1. dark, evening, eventide, gloaming, nightfall, sundown, sunset, twilight **2.** *Poetic* darkness, gloom, murk, obscurity, shade, shadowiness

dusky 1. dark, dark-complexioned, dark-hued, sable, swarthy **2.** caliginous (*Archaic*), cloudy, crepuscular, darkish, dim, gloomy, murky, obscure, overcast, shadowy, shady, tenebrous, twilight, twilit, veiled

dust *n.* **1.** fine fragments, grime, grit, particles, powder, powdery dirt **2.** dirt, earth, ground, soil **3.** *Inf.* commotion, disturbance, fuss, racket, row **4. bite the dust** *Inf.* die, drop dead, expire, fall in battle, pass away, perish **5. lick the dust** *Inf.* be servile, bootlick (*Inf.*), demean oneself, grovel, kowtow, toady **6. throw dust in the eyes of** con (*Sl.*), confuse, deceive, fool, have (someone) on, hoodwink, mislead, take in (*Inf.*) ~*v.* **7.** cover, dredge, powder, scatter, sift, spray, spread, sprinkle

dust-up argument, brush, conflict, encounter, fight, fracas, punch-up (*Sl.*), quarrel, scrap (*Inf.*), set-to (*Inf.*), shindig (*Sl.*), skirmish, tussle

dusty 1. dirty, grubby, sooty, unclean, undusted, unswept **2.** chalky, crumbly, friable, granular, powdery, sandy

dutiful compliant, conscientious, deferential, devoted, docile, duteous (*Archaic*), filial, obedient, punctilious, respectful, reverential, submissive

duty 1. assignment, business, calling, charge, engagement, function, mission, obligation, office, onus, province, responsibility, role, service, task, work **2.** allegiance, deference, loyalty, obedience, respect, reverence **3.** customs, due, excise, impost, levy, tariff, tax, toll **4. do duty for** stand in, substitute, take the place of **5. be the duty of** behove (*Archaic*), be incumbent upon, belong to, be (someone's) pigeon (*Inf.*), be up to (*Inf.*), devolve upon, pertain to, rest with **6. off duty** at leisure, free, off, off work, on holiday **7. on duty** at work, busy, engaged

dwarf *n.* **1.** bantam, homunculus, hopo'-my-thumb, Lilliputian, manikin, midget, pygmy, Tom Thumb **2.** gnome, goblin ~*adj.* **3.** baby, diminutive, dwarfed, Lilliputian, miniature, petite, pocket, small, tiny, undersized ~*v.* **4.** dim, diminish, dominate, minimize, overshadow, tower above *or* over **5.** check, cultivate by bonsai, lower, retard, stunt

dwarfish diminutive, dwarfed, low, miniature, minute, pint-size (*Inf.*), pygmaean, pygmy, runtish, runty, short, small, stunted, tiny, undersized

dwell abide, establish oneself, hang out (*Inf.*), inhabit, live, lodge, quarter, remain, reside, rest, settle, sojourn, stay, stop

dweller denizen, inhabitant, occupant, occupier, resident

dwelling abode, domicile, dwelling house, establishment, habitation, home, house, lodging, quarters, residence

dwell on *or* **upon** be engrossed in, continue, elaborate, emphasize, expatiate, harp on, linger over, tarry over

dwindle abate, contract, decay, decline, decrease, die away (down, out), diminish, ebb, fade, fall, grow less, lessen, peter out, pine, shrink, shrivel, sink, subside, taper off, wane, waste away, weaken, wither

dye 1. *n.* colorant, colour, colouring, pigment, stain, tinge, tint **2.** *v.* colour, pigment, stain, tincture, tinge, tint

dyed-in-the-wool complete, confirmed, deep-rooted, entrenched, established, inveterate, through-and-through

dying at death's door, ebbing, expiring, fading, failing, final, going, *in extremis*, moribund, mortal, passing, perishing, sinking

dynamic active, driving, electric, energetic, forceful, go-ahead, go-getting (*Inf.*), high-powered, lively, magnetic, powerful, vigorous, vital, zippy (*Inf.*)

dynamism drive, energy, enterprise, forcefulness, get-up-and-go (*Inf.*), go (*Inf.*), initiative, liveliness, pep, push (*Inf.*), vigour, zap (*Sl.*), zip (*Inf.*)

dynasty ascendancy, dominion, empire, government, house, regime, rule, sovereignty, sway

E

each 1. *adj.* every **2.** *pron.* each and every one, each one, every one, one and all **3.** *adv.* apiece, for each, from each, individually, per capita, per head, per person, respectively, singly, to each

eager agog, anxious, ardent, athirst, avid, earnest, enthusiastic, fervent, fervid, greedy, hot, hungry, impatient, intent, keen, longing, raring, vehement, yearning, zealous

eagerness ardour, avidity, earnestness, enthusiasm, fervour, greediness, heartiness, hunger, impatience, impetuosity, intentness, keenness, longing, thirst, vehemence, yearning, zeal

ear *Fig.* **1.** attention, consideration, hearing, heed, notice, regard **2.** appreciation, discrimination, musical perception, sensitivity, taste

early *adj.* **1.** advanced, forward, premature, untimely **2.** primeval, primitive, primordial, undeveloped, young ~*adv.* **3.** ahead of time, beforehand, betimes (*Archaic*), in advance, in good time, prematurely, too soon

earmark 1. *v.* allocate, designate, keep back, label, mark out, reserve, set aside, tag **2.** *n.* attribute, characteristic, feature, hallmark, label, quality, signature, stamp, tag, token, trademark, trait

earn 1. bring in, collect, draw, gain, get, gross, make, net, obtain, procure, realize, reap, receive **2.** acquire, attain, be entitled to, be worthy of, deserve, merit, rate, warrant, win

earnest *adj.* **1.** close, constant, determined, firm, fixed, grave, intent, resolute, resolved, serious, sincere, solemn, stable, staid, steady, thoughtful **2.** ardent, devoted, eager, enthusiastic, fervent, fervid, heartfelt, impassioned, keen, passionate, purposeful, urgent, vehement, warm, zealous ~*n.* **3.** determination, reality, resolution, seriousness, sincerity, truth **4.** assurance, deposit, down payment, earnest money (*Law*), foretaste, guarantee, pledge, promise, security, token

earnestness ardour, determination, devotion, eagerness, enthusiasm, fervour, gravity, intentness, keenness, passion, purposefulness, resolution, seriousness, sincerity, urgency, vehemence, warmth, zeal

earnings emolument, gain, income, pay, proceeds, profits, receipts, remuneration, return, reward, salary, stipend, takings, wages

earth 1. globe, orb, planet, sphere, terrestrial sphere, world **2.** clay, clod, dirt, ground, land, loam, mould, sod, soil, topsoil, turf

earthenware ceramics, crockery, crocks, pots, pottery, terra cotta

earthiness bawdiness, coarseness, crudeness, crudity, lustiness, naturalness, ribaldry, robustness, uninhibitedness

earthly 1. mundane, sublunary, tellurian, telluric, terrene, terrestrial, worldly **2.** human, material, mortal, nonspiritual, profane, secular, temporal, worldly **3.** base, carnal, fleshly, gross, low, materialistic, physical, sensual, sordid, vile **4.** *Inf.* conceivable, feasible, imaginable, likely, possible, practical

earthy bawdy, coarse, crude, down-to-earth, homely, lusty, natural, ribald, robust, rough, simple, uninhibited, unrefined, unsophisticated

ease *n.* **1.** affluence, calmness, comfort, content, contentment, enjoyment, happiness, leisure, peace, peace of mind, quiet, quietude, relaxation, repose, rest, restfulness, serenity, tranquillity **2.** easiness, effortlessness, facility, readiness, simplicity **3.** flexibility, freedom, informality, liberty, naturalness, unaffectedness, unconstraint, unreservedness **4.** aplomb, composure, insouciance, nonchalance, poise, relaxedness ~*v.* **5.** abate, allay, alleviate, appease, assuage, calm, comfort, disburden, lessen, lighten, mitigate, moderate, mollify, pacify, palliate, quiet, relax, relent, relieve, slacken, soothe, still, tranquillize **6.** aid, assist, expedite, facilitate, forward, further, lessen the labour of, make easier, simplify, smooth, speed up **7.** edge, guide, inch, manoeuvre, move carefully, slide, slip, squeeze, steer

easeful calm, comfortable, easy,

peaceful, quiet, reposeful, restful, soothing, tranquil

easily 1. comfortably, effortlessly, fac-
ilely, readily, simply, smoothly, with
ease, without difficulty, without trouble
2. absolutely, beyond question, by far,
certainly, clearly, definitely, doubtlessly,
far and away, indisputably, indubitably,
plainly, surely, undeniably, undoubtedly, unequivocally, unquestionably, without a doubt **3.** almost certainly, probably, well

easy 1. a piece of cake (*Inf.*), a pushover (*Sl.*), child's play (*Inf.*), clear,
effortless, facile, light, no bother, not
difficult, no trouble, painless, simple,
smooth, straightforward, uncomplicated,
undemanding **2.** calm, carefree, comfortable, contented, cushy (*Sl.*), easeful, leisurely, peaceful, pleasant, quiet, relaxed,
satisfied, serene, tranquil, undisturbed,
untroubled, unworried, well-to-do **3.**
flexible, indulgent, lenient, liberal, light,
mild, permissive, tolerant, unburden-
some, unoppressive **4.** affable, casual,
easy-going, friendly, gentle, graceful,
gracious, informal, mild, natural, open,
pleasant, relaxed, smooth, tolerant, unaffected, unceremonious, unconstrained,
undemanding, unforced, unpretentious
5. accommodating, amenable, biddable,
compliant, docile, gullible, manageable,
pliant, soft, submissive, suggestible, susceptible, tractable, trusting, yielding **6.**
comfortable, gentle, leisurely, light,
mild, moderate, temperate, undemanding, unexacting, unhurried

easy-going amenable, calm, carefree, casual, complacent, easy, even-
tempered, flexible, happy-go-lucky, indulgent, insouciant, laid-back (*Inf.*), lenient, liberal, mild, moderate, nonchalant, permissive, placid, relaxed, serene,
tolerant, unconcerned, uncritical, undemanding, unhurried

eat 1. chew, consume, devour, ingest,
munch, scoff (*Sl.*), swallow **2.** break
bread, dine, feed, have a meal, take food,
take nourishment **3.** corrode, crumble,
decay, dissolve, erode, rot, waste away,
wear away **4. eat one's words** abjure, recant, rescind, retract, take (statement)
back

eatable comestible (*Rare*), digestible,
edible, esculent, fit to eat, good, harmless, palatable, wholesome

eavesdrop bug (*Inf.*), listen in, monitor, overhear, snoop (*Inf.*), spy, tap (*Inf.*)

eavesdropper listener, monitor,
snooper (*Inf.*), spy

ebb *v.* **1.** abate, fall away, fall back,
flow back, go out, recede, retire, retreat,
retrocede, sink, subside, wane, withdraw
~*n.* **2.** ebb tide, going out, low tide, low
water, reflux, regression, retreat, retro-
cession, subsidence, wane, waning, withdrawal ~*v.* **3.** decay, decline, decrease,
degenerate, deteriorate, diminish, drop,
dwindle, fade away, fall away, flag, less-
en, peter out, shrink, sink, slacken,
weaken ~*n.* **4.** decay, decline, decrease,
degeneration, deterioration, diminution,
drop, dwindling, fading away, flagging,
lessening, petering out, shrinkage, sinking, slackening, weakening

ebullience 1. buoyancy, effervescence, effusiveness, elation, enthusiasm,
excitement, exhilaration, exuberance,
high spirits, vivacity, zest **2.** boiling,
bubbling, ebullition, effervescence, ferment, fermentation, foam, froth, frothing, seething

ebullient 1. buoyant, effervescent,
effusive, elated, enthusiastic, excited, exhilarated, exuberant, frothy, gushing, in
high spirits, irrepressible, vivacious,
zestful **2.** boiling, bubbling, effervescent,
foaming, frothing, seething

ebullition 1. boiling, bubbling, effervescence, fermentation, frothing, outburst, overflow, seething **2.** access, fit,
outbreak, outburst, overflow, paroxysm,
spasm, storm, throe (*Rare*)

eccentric 1. *adj.* aberrant, abnormal,
anomalous, bizarre, capricious, erratic,
freakish, idiosyncratic, irregular, odd,
outlandish, peculiar, queer (*Inf.*),
quirky, singular, strange, uncommon,
unconventional, weird, whimsical **2.** *n.*
case (*Inf.*), character (*Inf.*), crank (*Inf.*),
freak (*Sl.*), nonconformist, odd fish
(*Inf.*), oddity, weirdie *or* weirdo (*Inf.*)

eccentricity aberration, abnormality,
anomaly, bizarreness, caprice, capriciousness, foible, freakishness, idiosyncrasy, irregularity, nonconformity, oddity, oddness, outlandishness, peculiarity,
queerness (*Inf.*), quirk, singularity,
strangeness, unconventionality, waywardness, weirdness, whimsicality,
whimsicalness

ecclesiastic 1. *n.* churchman, clergyman, cleric, divine, holy man, man of the
cloth, minister, parson, priest **2.** *adj.*

Also **ecclesiastical** church, churchly, clerical, divine, holy, pastoral, priestly, religious, spiritual

echelon degree, grade, level, office, place, position, rank, tier

echo *v.* **1.** repeat, resound, reverberate **2.** ape, copy, imitate, mirror, parallel, parrot, recall, reflect, reiterate, reproduce, resemble, ring, second ~*n.* **3.** answer, repetition, reverberation **4.** copy, imitation, mirror image, parallel, reflection, reiteration, reproduction, ringing **5.** allusion, evocation, hint, intimation, memory, reminder, suggestion, trace **6.** *Often plural* aftereffect, aftermath, consequence, repercussion

echoic imitative, onomatopoeic

éclat 1. brilliance, effect, success **2.** display, lustre, ostentation, pomp, show, showmanship, splendour **3.** celebrity, distinction, fame, glory, renown **4.** acclaim, acclamation, applause, approval, plaudits

eclectic all-embracing, broad, catholic, comprehensive, dilettantish, diverse, diversified, general, heterogeneous, liberal, many-sided, multifarious, selective, varied, wide-ranging

eclipse *v.* **1.** blot out, cloud, darken, dim, extinguish, obscure, overshadow, shroud, veil **2.** exceed, excel, outdo, outshine, surpass, transcend ~*n.* **3.** darkening, dimming, extinction, obscuration, occultation, shading **4.** decline, diminution, failure, fall, loss

eclogue bucolic, georgic, idyll, pastoral

economic 1. business, commercial, financial, industrial, mercantile, trade **2.** money-making, productive, profitable, profit-making, remunerative, solvent, viable **3.** bread-and-butter (*Inf.*), budgetary, financial, fiscal, material, monetary, pecuniary **4.** *Inf. Also* **economical** cheap, fair, inexpensive, low, low-priced, modest, reasonable

economical 1. cost-effective, efficient, money-saving, sparing, time-saving, unwasteful, work-saving **2.** careful, economizing, frugal, prudent, saving, scrimping, sparing, thrifty **3.** *Also* **economic** cheap, fair, inexpensive, low, low-priced, modest, reasonable

economize be economical, be frugal, be sparing, cut back, husband, retrench, save, scrimp, tighten one's belt

economy frugality, husbandry, parsimony, providence, prudence, restraint, retrenchment, saving, sparingness, thrift, thriftiness

ecstasy bliss, delight, elation, enthusiasm, euphoria, exaltation, fervour, frenzy, joy, rapture, ravishment, rhapsody, seventh heaven, trance, transport

ecstatic blissful, delirious, elated, enraptured, enthusiastic, entranced, euphoric, fervent, frenzied, in exaltation, in transports of delight, joyful, joyous, on cloud nine (*Inf.*), overjoyed, rapturous, rhapsodic, transported

ecumenical catholic, general, unifying, universal, worldwide

eddy 1. *n.* counter-current, counterflow, swirl, vortex, whirlpool **2.** *v.* swirl, whirl

edge *n.* **1.** border, bound, boundary, brim, brink, contour, fringe, limit, line, lip, margin, outline, perimeter, periphery, rim, side, threshold, verge **2.** acuteness, animation, bite, effectiveness, force, incisiveness, interest, keenness, point, pungency, sharpness, sting, urgency, zest **3.** advantage, ascendancy, dominance, lead, superiority, upper hand **4.** **on edge** apprehensive, eager, edgy, excited, ill at ease, impatient, irritable, keyed up, nervous, on tenterhooks, tense, uptight (*Inf.*) ~*v.* **5.** bind, border, fringe, hem, rim, shape, trim **6.** creep, ease, inch, sidle, steal, work, worm **7.** hone, sharpen, strop, whet

edgy anxious, ill at ease, irascible, irritable, keyed up, nervous, on edge, restive, tense, touchy

edible comestible (*Rare*), digestible, eatable, esculent, fit to eat, good, harmless, palatable, wholesome

edict act, command, decree, dictate, dictum, enactment, fiat, injunction, law, mandate, manifesto, order, ordinance, proclamation, pronouncement, pronunciamento, regulation, ruling, statute, ukase (*Rare*)

edification education, elevation, enlightenment, guidance, improvement, information, instruction, nurture, schooling, teaching, tuition, uplifting

edifice building, construction, erection, fabric (*Rare*), habitation, house, pile, structure

edify educate, elevate, enlighten, guide, improve, inform, instruct, nurture, school, teach, uplift

edit 1. adapt, annotate, censor, check,

condense, correct, emend, polish, redact, rephrase, revise, rewrite **2.** assemble, compose, put together, rearrange, reorder, select

edition copy, impression, issue, number, printing, programme (*TV*, *Radio*), version, volume

educate civilize, coach, cultivate, develop, discipline, drill, edify, enlighten, exercise, foster, improve, indoctrinate, inform, instruct, mature, rear, school, teach, train, tutor

educated 1. coached, informed, instructed, nurtured, schooled, taught, tutored **2.** civilized, cultivated, cultured, enlightened, experienced, informed, knowledgeable, learned, lettered, literary, polished, refined, tasteful

education breeding, civilization, coaching, cultivation, culture, development, discipline, drilling, edification, enlightenment, erudition, improvement, indoctrination, instruction, knowledge, nurture, scholarship, schooling, teaching, training, tuition, tutoring

educational cultural, didactic, edifying, educative, enlightening, heuristic, improving, informative, instructive

educative didactic, edifying, educational, enlightening, heuristic, improving, informative, instructive

educator coach, edifier, educationalist *or* educationist, instructor, pedagogue, schoolmaster, schoolmistress, schoolteacher, teacher, trainer, tutor

educe 1. come out, develop, evolve **2.** bring forth, bring out, derive, draw out, elicit, evoke, extract **3.** *Logic* conclude, deduce, infer

eerie awesome, creepy (*Inf.*), eldritch (*Poetic*), fearful, frightening, ghostly, mysterious, scary (*Inf.*), spectral, spooky (*Inf.*), strange, uncanny, unearthly, weird

efface 1. annihilate, blot out, cancel, cross out, delete, destroy, dim, eradicate, erase, excise, expunge, extirpate, obliterate, raze, rub out, wipe out **2.** *Of oneself* be modest (bashful, diffident, retiring, timid, unassertive), humble, lower, make inconspicuous, withdraw

effect *n.* **1.** aftermath, conclusion, consequence, event, fruit, issue, outcome, result, upshot **2.** clout (*Inf.*), effectiveness, efficacy, efficiency, fact, force, influence, power, reality, strength, use, validity, vigour, weight **3.** drift, essence,

impact, import, impression, meaning, purport, purpose, sense, significance, tenor **4.** action, enforcement, execution, force, implementation, operation **5. in effect** actually, effectively, essentially, for practical purposes, in actuality, in fact, in reality, in truth, really, to all intents and purposes, virtually **6. take effect** become operative, begin, come into force, produce results, work ~*v.* **7.** accomplish, achieve, actuate, bring about, carry out, cause, complete, consummate, create, effectuate, execute, fulfil, give rise to, initiate, make, perform, produce

effective 1. able, active, adequate, capable, competent, effectual, efficacious, efficient, energetic, operative, productive, serviceable, useful **2.** cogent, compelling, convincing, emphatic, forceful, forcible, impressive, moving, persuasive, potent, powerful, striking, telling **3.** active, actual, current, in effect, in execution, in force, in operation, operative, real

effectiveness capability, clout (*Inf.*), cogency, effect, efficacy, efficiency, force, influence, potency, power, strength, success, use, validity, vigour, weight

effects belongings, chattels, furniture, gear, goods, movables, paraphernalia, possessions, property, things, trappings

effectual 1. capable, effective, efficacious, efficient, forcible, influential, potent, powerful, productive, serviceable, successful, telling, useful **2.** authoritative, binding, in force, lawful, legal, licit (*Rare*), sound, valid

effectuate accomplish, achieve, bring about, carry out *or* through, cause, complete, create, do, effect, execute, fulfil, make, perform, procure, produce

effeminacy delicacy, femininity, softness, tenderness, unmanliness, weakness, womanishness, womanliness

effeminate delicate, feminine, sissy, soft, tender, unmanly, weak, womanish, womanlike, womanly

effervesce bubble, ferment, fizz, foam, froth, sparkle

effervescence 1. bubbling, ferment, fermentation, fizz, foam, foaming, froth, frothing, sparkle **2.** animation, buoyancy, ebullience, enthusiasm, excitedness, excitement, exhilaration, exuberance, gaiety, high spirits, liveliness, vim (*Sl.*), vitality, vivacity, zing (*Inf.*)

effervescent 1. bubbling, bubbly, carbonated, fermenting, fizzing, fizzy, foaming, foamy, frothing, frothy, sparkling **2**. animated, bubbly, buoyant, ebullient, enthusiastic, excited, exhilarated, exuberant, gay, in high spirits, irrepressible, lively, merry, vital, vivacious, zingy (*Inf.*)

effete 1. corrupt, debased, decadent, decayed, decrepit, degenerate, dissipated, enervated, enfeebled, feeble, ineffectual, overrefined, spoiled, weak **2**. burnt out, drained, enervated, exhausted, played out, spent, used up, wasted, worn out **3**. barren, fruitless, infecund, infertile, sterile, unfruitful, unproductive, unprolific

efficacious active, adequate, capable, competent, effective, effectual, efficient, energetic, operative, potent, powerful, productive, serviceable, successful, useful

efficacy ability, capability, competence, effect, effectiveness, efficaciousness, efficiency, energy, force, influence, potency, power, strength, success, use, vigour, virtue, weight

efficiency ability, adeptness, capability, competence, economy, effectiveness, efficacy, power, productivity, proficiency, readiness, skilfulness, skill

efficient able, adept, businesslike, capable, competent, economic, effective, effectual, powerful, productive, proficient, ready, skilful, well-organized, workmanlike

effigy dummy, figure, guy, icon, idol, image, likeness, picture, portrait, representation, statue

effluence discharge, effluent, effluvium, efflux, emanation, emission, exhalation, flow, outflow, outpouring, secretion

effluent *n.* **1**. effluvium, pollutant, sewage, waste **2**. discharge, effluence, efflux, emanation, emission, exhalation, flow, outflow, outpouring ~*adj.* **3**. discharged, emanating, emitted, outflowing

effluvium exhalation, exhaust, fumes, mephitis, miasma, niff (*Sl.*), odour, pong (*Inf.*), reek, smell, stench, stink

effort 1. application, endeavour, energy, exertion, force, labour, pains, power, strain, stress, stretch, striving, struggle, toil, travail (*Literary*), trouble, work **2**. attempt, endeavour, essay, go, shot (*Inf.*), stab (*Inf.*), try **3**. accomplishment,

achievement, act, creation, deed, feat, job, product, production

effortless easy, facile, painless, simple, smooth, uncomplicated, undemanding, untroublesome

effrontery arrogance, assurance, audacity, boldness, brashness, brass (*Inf.*), brass neck (*Inf.*), brazenness, cheek (*Inf.*), cheekiness, disrespect, gall (*Inf.*), impertinence, impudence, incivility, insolence, nerve, presumption, rudeness, shamelessness, temerity

effulgence blaze, brightness, brilliance, dazzle, fire, flame, fluorescence, glow, incandescence, luminosity, lustre, radiance, refulgence (*Literary*), resplendence, shine, splendour, vividness

effulgent beaming, blazing, bright, brilliant, dazzling, flaming, fluorescent, fulgent (*Poetic*), glowing, incandescent, lucent, luminous, lustrous, radiant, refulgent (*Literary*), resplendent, shining, splendid, vivid

effusion 1. discharge, effluence, efflux, emission, gush, outflow, outpouring, shedding, stream **2**. address, outpouring, speech, talk, utterance, writing

effusive demonstrative, ebullient, enthusiastic, expansive, extravagant, exuberant, free-flowing, fulsome, gushing, lavish, overflowing, profuse, talkative, unreserved, unrestrained, wordy

egg on encourage, exhort, goad, incite, prod, prompt, push, spur, urge

egocentric egoistic, egoistical, egotistic, egotistical, self-centred, selfish

egoism egocentricity, egomania, egotism, narcissism, self-absorption, self-centredness, self-importance, self-interest, selfishness, self-love, self-regard, self-seeking

egoist egomaniac, egotist, narcissist, self-seeker

egoistic, egoistical egocentric, egomaniacal, egotistic, egotistical, narcissistic, self-absorbed, self-centred, self-important, self-seeking

egotism conceitedness, egocentricity, egoism, egomania, narcissism, self-admiration, self-centredness, self-conceit, self-esteem, self-importance, self-love, self-praise, superiority, vainglory, vanity

egotist bighead (*Inf.*), blowhard (*Inf.*), boaster, braggadocio, braggart, egoist, egomaniac, self-admirer, swaggerer

egotistic, egotistical boasting, bragging, conceited, egocentric, egoistic, egoistical, egomaniacal, narcissistic, opinionated, self-admiring, self-centred, self-important, superior, vain, vainglorious

egregious arrant, enormous, flagrant, glaring, grievous, gross, heinous, infamous, insufferable, intolerable, monstrous, notorious, outrageous, rank, scandalous, shocking

egress departure, emergence, escape, exit, exodus, issue, outlet, passage out, vent, way out, withdrawal

ejaculate 1. discharge, eject, emit, spurt **2.** blurt out, burst out, cry out, exclaim, shout

ejaculation 1. cry, exclamation, shout **2.** discharge, ejection, emission, spurt

eject 1. cast out, discharge, disgorge, emit, expel, spew, spout, throw out, vomit **2.** banish, boot out (*Inf.*), bounce (*Sl.*), deport, dispossess, drive out, evacuate, evict, exile, expel, oust, remove, throw out, turn out **3.** discharge, dislodge, dismiss, fire (*Inf.*), get rid of, kick out (*Inf.*), oust, sack (*Inf.*), throw out

ejection 1. casting out, disgorgement, expulsion, spouting, throwing out **2.** banishment, deportation, dispossession, evacuation, eviction, exile, expulsion, ouster (*Law*), removal **3.** discharge, dislodgement, dismissal, firing (*Inf.*), sacking (*Inf.*), the boot (*Sl.*), the sack (*Inf.*)

eke out 1. be economical with, be frugal with, be sparing with, economize on, husband, stretch out **2.** add to, enlarge, increase, make up (with), supplement

elaborate *adj.* **1.** careful, detailed, exact, intricate, laboured, minute, painstaking, perfected, precise, skilful, studied, thorough **2.** complex, complicated, decorated, detailed, extravagant, fancy, fussy, involved, ornamented, ornate, ostentatious, showy ~*v.* **3.** add detail, amplify, complicate, decorate, develop, devise, embellish, enhance, enlarge, expand (upon), flesh out, garnish, improve, ornament, polish, produce, refine, work out

élan animation, brio, dash, esprit, flair, impetuosity, panache, spirit, style, verve, vigour, vivacity, zest

elapse glide by, go, go by, lapse, pass, pass by, roll by, roll on, slip away, slip by

elastic 1. ductile, flexible, plastic, pliable, pliant, resilient, rubbery, springy, stretchable, stretchy, supple, yielding **2.** accommodating, adaptable, adjustable, complaisant, compliant, flexible, supple, tolerant, variable, yielding **3.** bouncy, buoyant, irrepressible, resilient

elasticity 1. ductileness, ductility, flexibility, give (*Inf.*), plasticity, pliability, pliancy, pliantness, resilience, rubberiness, springiness, stretch, stretchiness, suppleness **2.** adaptability, adjustability, complaisance, compliantness, flexibility, suppleness, tolerance, variability **3.** bounce (*Inf.*), buoyancy, irrepressibility, resilience

elated animated, blissful, cheered, delighted, ecstatic, elevated, euphoric, excited, exhilarated, exultant, gleeful, in high spirits, joyful, joyous, jubilant, overjoyed, proud, puffed up, roused

elation bliss, delight, ecstasy, euphoria, exaltation, exhilaration, exultation, glee, high spirits, joy, joyfulness, joyousness, jubilation, rapture

elbow *n.* **1.** angle, bend, corner, joint, turn **2. at one's elbow** at hand, close by, handy, near, to hand, within reach **3. out at elbow(s)** beggarly, down at heel, impoverished, in rags, ragged, seedy, shabby, tattered **4. rub elbows with** associate, fraternize, hang out (*Inf.*), hobnob, mingle, mix, socialize **5. up to the elbows** absorbed, busy, engaged, engrossed, immersed, occupied, tied up, up to the ears, wrapped up ~*v.* **6.** bump, crowd, hustle, jostle, knock, nudge, push, shoulder, shove

elbowroom freedom, latitude, leeway, play, room, scope, space

elder *adj.* **1.** ancient, earlier born, first-born, older, senior ~*n.* **2.** older person, senior **3.** *Presbyterianism* church official, office bearer, presbyter

elect 1. *v.* appoint, choose, decide upon, designate, determine, opt for, pick, pick out, prefer, select, settle on, vote **2.** *adj.* choice, chosen, elite, handpicked, picked, preferred, select, selected

election appointment, choice, choosing, decision, determination, judgment, preference, selection, vote, voting

elector chooser, constituent, selector, voter

electric *Fig.* charged, dynamic, exciting, rousing, stimulating, stirring, tense, thrilling

electrify *Fig.* amaze, animate, astonish, astound, excite, fire, galvanize, invigorate, jolt, rouse, shock, startle, stimulate, stir, take one's breath away, thrill

eleemosynary almsgiving, altruistic, benevolent, charitable, philanthropic

elegance, elegancy 1. beauty, courtliness, dignity, exquisiteness, gentility, grace, gracefulness, grandeur, luxury, polish, politeness, refinement, sumptuousness 2. discernment, distinction, propriety, style, taste

elegant 1. à la mode, artistic, beautiful, chic, choice, comely, courtly, cultivated, delicate, exquisite, fashionable, fine, genteel, graceful, handsome, luxurious, modish, nice, polished, refined, stylish, sumptuous, tasteful 2. appropriate, apt, clever, effective, ingenious, neat, simple

elegiac dirgeful, funereal, keening, lamenting, melancholy, mournful, nostalgic, plaintive, sad, threnodial, threnodic, valedictory

elegy coronach (*Scot., Irish*), dirge, keen, lament, plaint (*Archaic*), requiem, threnody

element 1. basis, component, constituent, essential factor, factor, feature, hint, ingredient, member, part, section, subdivision, trace, unit 2. domain, environment, field, habitat, medium, milieu, sphere

elemental 1. basic, elementary, essential, fundamental, original, primal, primitive, primordial 2. atmospheric, meteorological, natural

elementary 1. clear, easy, facile, plain, rudimentary, simple, straightforward, uncomplicated 2. basic, elemental, fundamental, initial, introductory, original, primary, rudimentary

elements 1. basics, essentials, foundations, fundamentals, principles, rudiments 2. atmospheric conditions, atmospheric forces, powers of nature, weather

elephantine bulky, clumsy, enormous, heavy, huge, hulking, immense, laborious, lumbering, massive, monstrous, ponderous, weighty

elevate 1. heighten, hoist, lift, lift up, raise, uplift, upraise 2. advance, aggrandize, exalt, prefer, promote, upgrade 3. animate, boost, brighten, buoy up, cheer, elate, excite, exhilarate, hearten, lift up, perk up, raise, rouse, uplift 4. augment, boost, heighten, increase, intensify, magnify, swell

elevated 1. dignified, exalted, grand, high, high-flown, high-minded, inflated, lofty, noble, sublime 2. animated, bright,

cheerful, cheery, elated, excited, exhilarated, gleeful, in high spirits, overjoyed

elevation 1. altitude, height 2. acclivity, eminence, height, hill, hillock, mountain, rise, rising ground 3. exaltedness, grandeur, loftiness, nobility, nobleness, sublimity 4. advancement, aggrandizement, exaltation, preferment, promotion, upgrading

elfin arch, charming, elfish, elflike, elvish, frolicsome, impish, mischievous, playful, prankish, puckish, sprightly

elicit bring forth, bring out, bring to light, call forth, cause, derive, draw out, educe, evoke, evolve, exact, extort, extract, give rise to, obtain, wrest

eligible acceptable, appropriate, desirable, fit, preferable, proper, qualified, suitable, suited, worthy

eliminate 1. cut out, dispose of, do away with, eradicate, exterminate, get rid of, remove, stamp out, take out 2. dispense with, disregard, drop, eject, exclude, expel, ignore, knock out, leave out, omit, put out, reject, throw out 3. *Sl.* annihilate, bump off (*Sl.*), kill, liquidate, murder, rub out (*U.S. sl.*), slay, terminate, waste (*U.S. sl.*)

elite 1. *n.* aristocracy, best, cream, *crème de la crème*, elect, flower, gentry, high society, nobility, pick, upper class 2. *adj.* aristocratic, best, choice, crack (*Sl.*), elect, exclusive, first-class, noble, pick, selected, upper-class

elixir 1. cure-all, nostrum, panacea, sovereign remedy 2. concentrate, essence, extract, pith, principle, quintessence 3. mixture, potion, solution, syrup, tincture

elliptical 1. oval 2. abstruse, ambiguous, concentrated, concise, condensed, cryptic, laconic, obscure, recondite, terse

elocution articulation, declamation, delivery, diction, enunciation, oratory, pronunciation, public speaking, rhetoric, speech, speechmaking, utterance, voice production

elongate draw out, extend, lengthen, make longer, prolong, protract, stretch

elope abscond, bolt, decamp, disappear, escape, leave, run away, run off, slip away, steal away

eloquence expression, expressiveness, fluency, forcefulness, oratory, persuasiveness, rhetoric, way with words

eloquent 1. articulate, fluent, forceful, graceful, moving, persuasive, silver-tongued, stirring, well-expressed **2.** expressive, meaningful, pregnant, revealing, suggestive, telling, vivid

elsewhere abroad, absent, away, hence (*Archaic*), in *or* to another place, not here, not present, somewhere else

elucidate annotate, clarify, clear up, explain, explicate, expound, gloss, illuminate, illustrate, interpret, make plain, shed *or* throw light upon, spell out, unfold

elucidation annotation, clarification, comment, commentary, explanation, explication, exposition, gloss, illumination, illustration, interpretation

elude 1. avoid, circumvent, dodge, duck (*Inf.*), escape, evade, flee, get away from, outrun, shirk, shun **2.** baffle, be beyond (someone), confound, escape, foil, frustrate, puzzle, stump, thwart

elusive 1. difficult to catch, shifty, slippery, tricky **2.** baffling, fleeting, indefinable, intangible, puzzling, subtle, transient, transitory **3.** ambiguous, deceitful, deceptive, elusory, equivocal, evasive, fallacious, fraudulent, illusory, misleading, unspecific

Elysian blessed, blissful, celestial, charming, delightful, enchanting, glorious, happy, heavenly, paradisiac, paradisiacal, ravishing, seraphic

emaciated atrophied, attenuate, attenuated, cadaverous, gaunt, haggard, lank, lean, meagre, pinched, scrawny, skeletal, thin, wasted

emaciation atrophy, attenuation, gauntness, haggardness, leanness, meagreness, scrawniness, thinness, wasting away

emanate 1. arise, come forth, derive, emerge, flow, issue, originate, proceed, spring, stem **2.** discharge, emit, exhale, give off, give out, issue, radiate, send forth

emanation 1. arising, derivation, emergence, flow, origination, proceeding **2.** discharge, effluent, efflux, effusion, emission, exhalation, radiation

emancipate deliver, discharge, disencumber, disenthral, enfranchise, free, liberate, manumit, release, set free, unchain, unfetter, unshackle

emancipation deliverance, discharge, enfranchisement, freedom, liberation, liberty, manumission, release

emasculate 1. castrate, geld **2.** crip-

ple, debilitate, deprive of force, enervate, impoverish, soften, weaken

embalm 1. mummify, preserve **2.** *Of memories* cherish, consecrate, conserve, enshrine, immortalize, store, treasure **3.** *Poetic* make fragrant, perfume, scent

embargo 1. *n.* ban, bar, barrier, blockage, check, hindrance, impediment, interdict, interdiction, prohibition, proscription, restraint, restriction, stoppage **2.** *v.* ban, bar, block, check, impede, interdict, prohibit, proscribe, restrict, stop

embark 1. board ship, go aboard, put on board, take on board, take ship **2.** *With on or upon* begin, broach, commence, engage, enter, initiate, launch, plunge into, set about, set out, start, take up, undertake

embarrass abash, chagrin, confuse, discomfit, discompose, disconcert, discountenance, distress, fluster, mortify, put out of countenance, shame, show up (*Inf.*)

embarrassing awkward, blushmaking, compromising, discomfiting, disconcerting, distressing, humiliating, mortifying, sensitive, shameful, shaming, touchy, tricky, uncomfortable

embarrassment 1. awkwardness, bashfulness, chagrin, confusion, discomfiture, discomposure, distress, humiliation, mortification, self-consciousness, shame, showing up (*Inf.*) **2.** bind (*Inf.*), difficulty, mess, pickle (*Inf.*), predicament, scrape (*Inf.*) **3.** excess, overabundance, superabundance, superfluity, surfeit, surplus

embed dig in, drive in, fix, hammer in, implant, plant, ram in, root, set, sink

embellish adorn, beautify, bedeck, deck, decorate, dress up, elaborate, embroider, enhance, enrich, exaggerate, festoon, garnish, gild, grace, ornament, varnish

embellishment adornment, decoration, elaboration, embroidery, enhancement, enrichment, exaggeration, gilding, ornament, ornamentation

embers ashes, cinders, live coals

embezzle abstract, appropriate, defalcate (*Law*), filch, have one's hand in the till (*Inf.*), misapply, misappropriate, misuse, peculate, pilfer, purloin, steal

embezzlement abstraction, appropriation, defalcation (*Law*), filching, fraud, larceny, misapplication, misap-

propriation, misuse, peculation, pilferage, pilfering, purloining, stealing, theft,
thieving

embitter 1. alienate, anger, disaffect,
disillusion, envenom, make bitter *or* resentful, poison, sour 2. aggravate, exacerbate, exasperate, worsen

emblazon 1. adorn, blazon, colour,
decorate, embellish, illuminate, ornament, paint 2. extol, glorify, laud (*Literary*), praise, proclaim, publicize, publish,
trumpet

emblem badge, crest, device, figure,
image, insignia, mark, representation,
sigil (*Rare*), sign, symbol, token, type

emblematic, emblematical figurative, representative, symbolic

embodiment 1. bodying forth, example, exemplar, exemplification, expression, incarnation, incorporation, manifestation, personification, realization,
reification, representation, symbol, type
2. bringing together, codification, collection, combination, comprehension, concentration, consolidation, inclusion, incorporation, integration, organization,
systematization

embody 1. body forth, concretize, exemplify, express, incarnate, incorporate,
manifest, personify, realize, reify, represent, stand for, symbolize, typify 2.
bring together, codify, collect, combine,
comprehend, comprise, concentrate,
consolidate, contain, include, incorporate, integrate, organize, systematize

embolden animate, cheer, encourage,
fire, hearten, inflame, inspirit, invigorate, nerve, reassure, rouse, stimulate,
stir, strengthen, vitalize

embrace *v.* 1. clasp, cuddle, encircle,
enfold, grasp, hold, hug, seize, squeeze,
take *or* hold in one's arms 2. accept,
adopt, avail oneself of, espouse, grab,
make use of, receive, seize, take up, welcome 3. comprehend, comprise, contain,
cover, deal with, embody, enclose, encompass, include, involve, provide for,
subsume, take in, take into account ~*n.*
4. clasp, clinch (*Sl.*), cuddle, hug,
squeeze

embroil complicate, compromise, confound, confuse, disorder, disturb, encumber, enmesh, ensnare, entangle, implicate, incriminate, involve, mire, mix
up, muddle, perplex, trouble

embryo beginning, germ, nucleus,
root, rudiment

embryonic beginning, early, immature, inchoate, incipient, primary, rudimentary, undeveloped

emend amend, correct, edit, improve,
rectify, redact, revise

emendation amendment, correction,
editing, improvement, rectification, re-
daction, revision

emerge 1. appear, arise, become visible, come forth, come into view, come
out, come up, emanate, issue, proceed,
rise, spring up, surface 2. become apparent, become known, come out, come to
light, crop up, develop, materialize, transpire, turn up

emergence advent, apparition, appearance, arrival, coming, dawn, development, disclosure, emanation, issue,
materialization, rise

emergency crisis, danger, difficulty,
exigency, extremity, necessity, pass,
pinch, plight, predicament, quandary,
scrape (*Inf.*), strait

emergent appearing, budding, coming, developing, rising

emetic vomitive, vomitory

emigrate migrate, move, move abroad,
remove

emigration departure, exodus, migration, removal

eminence 1. celebrity, dignity, distinction, esteem, fame, greatness, illustriousness, importance, notability, note,
pre-eminence, prestige, prominence,
rank, renown, reputation, repute, superiority 2. elevation, height, high ground,
hill, hillock, knoll, rise, summit

eminent celebrated, conspicuous, distinguished, elevated, esteemed, exalted,
famous, grand, great, high, high-ranking,
illustrious, important, notable, noted,
noteworthy, outstanding, paramount,
pre-eminent, prestigious, prominent, renowned, signal, superior, well-known

eminently conspicuously, exceedingly, exceptionally, extremely, greatly,
highly, notably, outstandingly, promi-
nently, remarkably, signally, strikingly,
surpassingly, well

emissary agent, ambassador, courier,
delegate, deputy, envoy, go-between,
herald, legate, messenger, representative, scout, secret agent, spy

emission diffusion, discharge, ejaculation, ejection, emanation, exhalation,
exudation, issuance, issue, radiation,

shedding, transmission, utterance, venting

emit breathe forth, cast out, diffuse, discharge, eject, emanate, exhale, exude, give off, give out, give vent to, issue, radiate, send forth, send out, shed, throw out, transmit, utter, vent

emollient 1. *adj.* assuaging, assuasive, balsamic, demulcent, lenitive, mollifying, softening, soothing **2.** *n.* balm, lenitive, liniment, lotion, moisturizer, oil, ointment, salve

emolument benefit, compensation, earnings, fee, gain, hire, pay, payment, profits, recompense, remuneration, return, reward, salary, stipend, wages

emotion agitation, ardour, excitement, feeling, fervour, passion, perturbation, sensation, sentiment, vehemence, warmth

emotional 1. demonstrative, excitable, feeling, hot-blooded, passionate, responsive, sensitive, sentimental, susceptible, temperamental, tender, warm **2.** affecting, emotive, exciting, heart-warming, moving, pathetic, poignant, sentimental, stirring, tear-jerking (*Inf.*), thrilling, touching **3.** ardent, enthusiastic, fervent, fervid, fiery, heated, impassioned, passionate, roused, stirred, zealous

emotionless blank, cold, cold-blooded, cool, detached, distant, frigid, glacial, impassive, indifferent, remote, toneless, undemonstrative, unemotional, unfeeling

emotive 1. argumentative, controversial, delicate, sensitive, touchy **2.** affecting, emotional, exciting, heart-warming, moving, pathetic, poignant, sentimental, stirring, tear-jerking (*Inf.*), thrilling, touching **3.** ardent, emotional, enthusiastic, fervent, fervid, fiery, heated, impassioned, passionate, roused, stirred, zealous

emphasis accent, accentuation, attention, decidedness, force, importance, impressiveness, insistence, intensity, moment, positiveness, power, pre-eminence, priority, prominence, significance, strength, stress, underscoring, weight

emphasize accent, accentuate, dwell on, give priority to, highlight, insist on, lay stress on, play up, press home, put the accent on, stress, underline, underscore, weight

emphatic absolute, categorical, certain, decided, definite, direct, distinct, earnest, energetic, forceful, forcible, important, impressive, insistent, marked, momentous, positive, powerful, pronounced, resounding, significant, striking, strong, telling, unequivocal, unmistakable, vigorous

empire 1. commonwealth, domain, imperium (*Rare*), kingdom, realm **2.** authority, command, control, dominion, government, power, rule, sovereignty, supremacy, sway

empirical, empiric experiential, experimental, observed, practical, pragmatic

emplace insert, place, position, put, put in place, set up, station

emplacement 1. location, lodgment, platform, position, site, situation, station **2.** placement, placing, positioning, putting in place, setting up, stationing

employ *v.* **1.** commission, engage, enlist, hire, retain, take on **2.** engage, fill, keep busy, make use of, occupy, spend, take up, use up **3.** apply, bring to bear, exercise, exert, make use of, ply, put to use, use, utilize ~*n.* **4.** employment, engagement, hire, service

employed active, busy, engaged, in a job, in employment, in work, occupied, working

employee hand, job-holder, staff member, wage-earner, worker, workman

employer boss (*Inf.*), business, company, establishment, firm, gaffer (*Inf., chiefly Brit.*), organization, outfit (*Inf.*), owner, patron, proprietor

employment 1. engagement, enlistment, hire, retaining, taking on **2.** application, exercise, exertion, use, utilization **3.** avocation (*Archaic*), business, calling, craft, employ, job, line, métier, occupation, profession, pursuit, service, trade, vocation, work

emporium bazaar, market, mart, shop, store

empower allow, authorize, commission, delegate, enable, entitle, license, permit, qualify, sanction, warrant

emptiness 1. bareness, blankness, desertedness, desolation, destitution, vacancy, vacuum, void, waste **2.** aimlessness, banality, barrenness, frivolity, futility, hollowness, inanity, ineffectiveness, meaninglessness, purposelessness, senselessness, silliness, unreality, unsatisfactoriness, unsubstantiality, vainness, valuelessness, vanity, worthlessness **3**. cheapness, hollowness, idleness, insincerity, triviality, trivialness **4**. absentness, blankness, expressionlessness, unintelligence, vacancy, vacantness, vacuity, vacuousness **5**. *Inf.* desire, hunger, ravening

empty *adj.* **1**. bare, blank, clear, deserted, desolate, destitute, hollow, unfurnished, uninhabited, unoccupied, untenanted, vacant, void, waste **2**. aimless, banal, bootless, frivolous, fruitless, futile, hollow, inane, ineffective, meaningless, purposeless, senseless, silly, unreal, unsatisfactory, unsubstantial, vain, valueless, worthless **3**. cheap, hollow, idle, insincere, trivial **4**. absent, blank, expressionless, unintelligent, vacant, vacuous **5**. *Inf.* famished, hungry, ravenous, starving (*Inf.*), unfed, unfilled ~*v.* **6**. clear, consume, deplete, discharge, drain, dump, evacuate, exhaust, gut, pour out, unburden, unload, use up, vacate, void

empty-headed brainless, dizzy (*Inf.*), featherbrained, flighty, frivolous, giddy, harebrained, inane, scatterbrained, silly, skittish, vacuous

empyrean, empyreal aerial, airy, celestial, ethereal, heavenly, refined, skylike, sublime

emulate challenge, compete with, contend with, copy, follow, follow suit, follow the example of, imitate, mimic, rival, take after, vie with

emulation challenge, competition, contention, contest, copying, envy, following, imitation, jealousy, mimicry, rivalry, strife

emulous aspiring, competitive, contending, imitative, vying

enable allow, authorize, capacitate, commission, empower, facilitate, fit, license, permit, prepare, qualify, sanction, warrant

enact **1**. authorize, command, decree, establish, legislate, ordain, order, pass, proclaim, ratify, sanction **2**. act, act out, appear as, depict, perform, personate, play, play the part of, portray, represent

enactment **1**. authorization, command, commandment, decree, dictate, edict, law, legislation, order, ordinance, proclamation, ratification, regulation, statute **2**. acting, depiction, performance, personation, play-acting, playing, portrayal, representation

enamour bewitch, captivate, charm, enchant, endear, enrapture, entrance, fascinate, infatuate

enamoured bewitched, captivated, charmed, crazy about (*Inf.*), enchanted, enraptured, entranced, fascinated, fond, infatuated, in love, nuts on *or* about (*Sl.*), smitten, swept off one's feet, taken, wild about (*Inf.*)

encampment base, bivouac, camp, camping ground, campsite, cantonment, quarters, tents

encapsulate, incapsulate abridge, compress, condense, digest, epitomize, précis, summarize, sum up

enchain bind, enslave, fetter, hold, hold fast, manacle, pinion, put in irons, shackle

enchant beguile, bewitch, captivate, cast a spell on, charm, delight, enamour, enrapture, enthral, fascinate, hypnotize, mesmerize, spellbind

enchanter conjurer, magician, magus, necromancer, sorcerer, spellbinder, warlock, witch, wizard

enchanting alluring, appealing, attractive, bewitching, captivating, charming, delightful, endearing, entrancing, fascinating, lovely, pleasant, ravishing, winsome

enchantment **1**. allure, allurement, beguilement, bliss, charm, delight, fascination, hypnotism, mesmerism, rapture, ravishment, transport **2**. charm, conjuration, incantation, magic, necromancy, sorcery, spell, witchcraft, wizardry

enchantress **1**. conjurer, lamia, magician, necromancer, sorceress, spellbinder, witch **2**. charmer, *femme fatale*, seductress, siren, vamp (*Inf.*)

encircle begird (*Poetic*), circle, circumscribe, compass, enclose, encompass, enfold, envelop, environ, gird in, girdle, hem in, ring, surround

enclose, inclose **1**. bound, circumscribe, cover, encase, encircle, encompass, environ, fence, hedge, hem in, pen, shut in, wall in, wrap **2**. include, insert, put in, send with **3**. comprehend, contain, embrace, hold, include, incorporate

encomium acclaim, acclamation, applause, compliment, eulogy, homage, laudation, panegyric, praise, tribute

encompass **1**. circle, circumscribe, encircle, enclose, envelop, environ, girdle, hem in, ring, surround **2**. bring about, cause, contrive, devise, effect, manage **3**.

admit, comprehend, comprise, contain, cover, embody, embrace, hold, include, incorporate, involve, subsume, take in

encounter v. **1.** bump into (Inf.), chance upon, come upon, confront, experience, face, happen on or upon, meet, run across, run into (Inf.) **2.** attack, clash with, combat, come into conflict with, contend, cross swords with, do battle with, engage, fight, grapple with, strive, struggle ~n. **3.** brush, confrontation, meeting **4.** action, battle, clash, collision, combat, conflict, contest, dispute, engagement, fight, run-in (Inf.), set to (Inf.), skirmish

encourage 1. animate, buoy up, cheer, comfort, console, embolden, hearten, incite, inspire, inspirit, rally, reassure, rouse, stimulate **2.** abet, advance, advocate, aid, boost, egg on, favour, forward, foster, further, help, promote, spur, strengthen, succour, support, urge

encouragement advocacy, aid, boost, cheer, consolation, favour, help, incitement, inspiration, inspiritment, promotion, reassurance, stimulation, stimulus, succour, support, urging

encouraging bright, cheerful, cheering, comforting, good, heartening, hopeful, promising, reassuring, rosy, satisfactory, stimulating

encroach appropriate, arrogate, impinge, infringe, intrude, invade, make inroads, overstep, trench, trespass, usurp

encroachment appropriation, arrogation, impingement, incursion, infringement, inroad, intrusion, invasion, trespass, usurpation, violation

encumber burden, clog, cramp, embarrass, hamper, handicap, hinder, impede, incommode, inconvenience, make difficult, obstruct, oppress, overload, retard, saddle, slow down, trammel, weigh down

encumbrance burden, clog, difficulty, drag, embarrassment, handicap, hindrance, impediment, inconvenience, liability, load, millstone, obstacle, obstruction

encyclopedic all-embracing, all-encompassing, all-inclusive, complete, comprehensive, exhaustive, thorough, universal, vast, wide-ranging

end n. **1.** bound, boundary, edge, extent, extreme, extremity, limit, point, terminus, tip **2.** attainment, cessation, close, closure, completion, conclusion, consequence, consummation, culmination, denouement, ending, expiration, expiry, finale, finish, issue, outcome, resolution, result, stop, termination, upshot, wind-up **3.** aim, aspiration, design, drift, goal, intent, intention, object, objective, point, purpose, reason **4.** part, piece, portion, responsibility, share, side **5.** bit, fragment, leftover, remainder, remnant, scrap, stub, tag end **6.** annihilation, death, demise, destruction, dissolution, doom, extermination, extinction, ruin, ruination **7. the end** Sl. beyond endurance, insufferable, intolerable, the final blow, the last straw, the limit (Inf.), the worst, too much (Inf.), unbearable, unendurable ~v. **8.** bring to an end, cease, close, complete, conclude, culminate, dissolve, expire, finish, resolve, stop, terminate, wind up **9.** abolish, annihilate, destroy, exterminate, extinguish, kill, put to death, ruin

endanger compromise, hazard, imperil, jeopardize, put at risk, put in danger, risk, threaten

endear attach, attract, bind, captivate, charm, engage, win

endearing adorable, attractive, captivating, charming, engaging, lovable, sweet, winning, winsome

endearment 1. affectionate utterance, loving word, sweet nothing **2.** affection, attachment, fondness, love

endeavour 1. n. aim, attempt, crack (Inf.), effort, enterprise, essay, go, shot (Inf.), stab (Inf.), trial, try, undertaking, venture **2.** v. aim, aspire, attempt, do one's best, essay, have a go (crack, shot, stab), labour, make an effort, strive, struggle, take pains, try, undertake

ending catastrophe, cessation, close, completion, conclusion, consummation, culmination, denouement, end, finale, finish, resolution, termination, wind-up

endless 1. boundless, ceaseless, constant, continual, eternal, everlasting, immortal, incessant, infinite, interminable, limitless, measureless, perpetual, unbounded, unbroken, undying, unending, uninterrupted, unlimited **2.** interminable, monotonous, overlong **3.** continuous, unbroken, undivided, whole

endorse, indorse 1. advocate, affirm, approve, authorize, back, champion, confirm, favour, ratify, recommend, sanction, subscribe to, support, sustain, vouch for, warrant **2**. countersign, sign, superscribe, undersign

endorsement, indorsement 1. comment, countersignature, qualification, signature, superscription **2**. advocacy, affirmation, approbation, approval, authorization, backing, championship, confirmation, favour, fiat, O.K. (*Inf.*), ratification, recommendation, sanction, seal of approval, subscription to, support, warrant

endow award, bequeath, bestow, confer, donate, endue, enrich, favour, finance, fund, furnish, give, grant, invest, leave, make over, provide, settle on, supply, will

endowment 1. award, benefaction, bequest. bestowal, boon, donation, fund, gift, grant, income, largess, legacy, presentation, property, provision, revenue **2**. *Often plural* ability, aptitude, attribute, capability, capacity, faculty, flair, genius, gift, power, qualification, quality, talent

endue, indue endow, fill, furnish, invest, provide, supply

end up 1. become eventually, finish as, finish up, turn out to be **2**. arrive finally, come to a halt, fetch up (*Inf.*), finish up, stop, wind up

endurable bearable, sufferable, supportable, sustainable, tolerable

endurance 1. bearing, fortitude, patience, perseverance, persistence, pertinacity, resignation, resolution, stamina, staying power, strength, submission, sufferance, tenacity, toleration **2**. continuation, continuity, durability, duration, immutability, lastingness, longevity, permanence, stability

endure 1. bear, brave, cope with, experience, go through, stand, stick it out (*Inf.*), suffer, support, sustain, take it (*Inf.*), thole (*Scot.*), undergo, weather, withstand **2**. abide, allow, bear, brook, countenance, permit, put up with, stand, stick (*Sl.*), stomach, submit to, suffer, swallow, take patiently, tolerate **3**. abide, be durable, continue, hold, last, live, live on, persist, prevail, remain, stand, stay, survive, wear well

enduring abiding, continuing, durable, eternal, firm, immortal, imperishable, lasting, living, long-lasting, perennial, permanent, persistent, persisting, prevailing, remaining, steadfast, steady, surviving, unfaltering, unwavering

enemy adversary, antagonist, competitor, foe, opponent, rival, the opposition, the other side

energetic active, animated, brisk, dynamic, forceful, forcible, high-powered, indefatigable, lively, potent, powerful, spirited, strenuous, strong, tireless, vigorous, zippy (*Inf.*)

energize 1. activate, animate, enliven, inspirit, invigorate, liven up, motivate, pep up, quicken, stimulate, vitalize **2**. activate, electrify, start up, switch on, turn on

energy activity, animation, ardour, *brio*, drive, efficiency, élan, exertion, fire, force, forcefulness, get-up-and-go (*Inf.*), go (*Inf.*), intensity, life, liveliness, pluck, power, spirit, stamina, strength, strenuousness, verve, vigour, vim (*Sl.*), vitality, vivacity, zeal, zest, zip (*Inf.*)

enervate 1. *v.* debilitate, devitalize, enfeeble, exhaust, fatigue, incapacitate, paralyse, prostrate, sap, tire, unnerve, wash out, weaken, wear out **2**. *adj.* debilitated, devitalized, done in (*Inf.*), enervated, enfeebled, exhausted, fatigued, feeble, incapacitated, limp, paralysed, prostrate, prostrated, run-down, sapped, spent, tired, undermined, unnerved, washed out, weak, weakened, worn out

enervation debilitation, debility, enfeeblement, exhaustedness, exhaustion, fatigue, feebleness, impotence, incapacity, infirmity, lassitude, paralysis, powerlessness, prostration, tiredness, weakening, weakness

enfeeble debilitate, deplete, devitalize, diminish, exhaust, fatigue, render feeble, sap, undermine, unhinge, unnerve, weaken, wear out

enfold, infold clasp, embrace, enclose, encompass, envelop, enwrap, fold, hold, hug, shroud, swathe, wrap, wrap up

enforce administer, apply, carry out, coerce, compel, constrain, exact, execute, implement, impose, insist on, oblige, prosecute, put in force, put into effect, reinforce, require, urge

enforced compelled, compulsory, constrained, dictated, imposed, involuntary, necessary, ordained, prescribed, required, unavoidable, unwilling

enforcement 1. administration, application, carrying out, exaction, execution, implementation, imposition, prosecution, reinforcement **2**. coercion, compulsion, constraint, insistence, obligation, pressure, requirement

enfranchise 1. give the vote to, grant suffrage to, grant the franchise to, grant voting rights to **2**. emancipate, free, liberate, manumit, release, set free

enfranchisement 1. giving the vote, granting suffrage or the franchise, granting voting rights **2**. emancipation, freedom, freeing, liberating, liberation, manumission, release, setting free

engage 1. appoint, commission, employ, enlist, enrol, hire, retain, take on **2**. bespeak, book, charter, hire, lease, prearrange, rent, reserve, secure **3**. absorb, busy, engross, grip, involve, occupy, preoccupy, tie up **4**. allure, arrest, attach, attract, captivate, catch, charm, draw, enamour, enchant, fascinate, fix, gain, win **5**. embark on, enter into, join, partake, participate, practise, set about, take part, undertake **6**. affiance, agree, betroth (Archaic), bind, commit, contract, covenant, guarantee, obligate, oblige, pledge, promise, undertake, vouch, vow **7**. Military assail, attack, combat, come to close quarters with, encounter, fall on, fight with, give battle to, join battle with, meet, take on **8**. activate, apply, bring into operation, energize, set going, switch on **9**. dovetail, interact, interconnect, interlock, join, mesh

engaged 1. affianced, betrothed (Archaic), pledged, promised, spoken for **2**. absorbed, busy, committed, employed, engrossed, in use, involved, occupied, preoccupied, tied up, unavailable

engagement 1. assurance, betrothal, bond, compact, contract, oath, obligation, pact, pledge, promise, troth (Archaic), undertaking, vow, word **2**. appointment, arrangement, commitment, date, meeting **3**. commission, employment, gig (Sl.), job, post, situation, stint, work **4**. action, battle, combat, conflict, confrontation, contest, encounter, fight

engaging agreeable, appealing, attractive, captivating, charming, enchanting, fascinating, fetching (Inf.), likable, lovable, pleasant, pleasing, winning, winsome

engender 1. beget, breed, bring about, cause, create, excite, foment, generate, give rise to, hatch, incite, induce, instigate, lead to, make, occasion, precipitate, produce, provoke **2**. beget, breed, bring forth, father, generate, give birth to, procreate, propagate, sire, spawn

engine 1. machine, mechanism, motor **2**. agency, agent, apparatus, appliance, contrivance, device, implement, instrument, means, tool, weapon

engineer 1. n. architect, contriver, designer, deviser, director, inventor, manager, manipulator, originator, planner, schemer **2**. v. bring about, cause, concoct, contrive, control, create, devise, effect, encompass, finagle (Inf.), manage, manoeuvre, mastermind, originate, plan, plot, scheme, wangle (Inf.)

engorge bolt, cram, devour, eat, fill, glut, gobble, gorge, gulp, guzzle, satiate, stuff, wolf

engraft, ingraft graft, implant, incorporate, inculcate, infix, infuse, ingrain, instil

engrain see INGRAIN

engrave 1. carve, chase, chisel, cut, enchase (Rare), etch, grave (Archaic), inscribe **2**. impress, imprint, print **3**. embed, fix, impress, imprint, infix, ingrain, lodge

engraving 1. carving, chasing, chiselling, cutting, dry point, enchasing (Rare), etching, inscribing, inscription **2**. block, carving, etching, inscription, plate, woodcut **3**. etching, impression, print

engross 1. absorb, arrest, engage, engulf, hold, immerse, involve, occupy, preoccupy **2**. corner, monopolize, sew up (U.S.)

engrossed absorbed, captivated, caught up, deep, enthralled, fascinated, gripped, immersed, intent, intrigued, lost, preoccupied, rapt, riveted

engrossing absorbing, captivating, compelling, enthralling, fascinating, gripping, interesting, intriguing, riveting

engulf, ingulf absorb, bury, consume, deluge, drown, encompass, engross, envelop, flood (out), immerse, inundate, overrun, overwhelm, plunge, submerge, swallow up, swamp

enhance add to, augment, boost, complement, elevate, embellish, exalt, heighten, improve, increase, intensify, lift, magnify, raise, reinforce, strengthen, swell

enigma conundrum, mystery, problem, puzzle, riddle

enigmatic, enigmatical ambiguous, cryptic, Delphic, doubtful, equivocal, incomprehensible, indecipherable, inexplicable, inscrutable, mysterious, obscure, perplexing, puzzling, recondite, sphinx-like, uncertain, unfathomable, unintelligible

enjoin 1. advise, bid, call upon, charge, command, counsel, demand, direct, instruct, order, prescribe, require, urge, warn **2**. *Law* ban, bar, disallow, forbid, interdict, place an injunction on, preclude, prohibit, proscribe, restrain

enjoy 1. appreciate, be entertained by, be pleased with, delight in, like, rejoice in, relish, revel in, take joy in, take pleasure in *or* from **2**. be blessed *or* favoured with, experience, have, have the benefit of, have the use of, own, possess, reap the benefits of, use **3**. **enjoy oneself** have a ball (*Inf.*), have a good time, have fun, make merry

enjoyable agreeable, amusing, delectable, delicious, delightful, entertaining, gratifying, pleasant, pleasing, pleasurable, satisfying, to one's liking

enjoyment 1. amusement, delectation, delight, diversion, entertainment, fun, gladness, gratification, gusto, happiness, indulgence, joy, pleasure, recreation, relish, satisfaction, zest **2**. advantage, benefit, exercise, ownership, possession, use

enkindle 1. fire, ignite, kindle, light, put a match to, put to the torch, set ablaze, set alight, set fire to, set on fire **2**. arouse, awake, excite, foment, incite, inflame, inspire, provoke, stir

enlarge 1. add to, amplify, augment, blow up (*Inf.*), broaden, diffuse, dilate, distend, elongate, expand, extend, grow, heighten, increase, inflate, lengthen, magnify, make *or* grow larger, multiply, stretch, swell, wax, widen **2**. amplify, descant, develop, dilate, elaborate, expand, expatiate, give details

enlighten advise, apprise, cause to understand, civilize, counsel, edify, educate, inform, instruct, make aware, teach

enlightened aware, broad-minded, civilized, cultivated, educated, informed, knowledgeable, liberal, literate, open-minded, reasonable, refined, sophisticated

enlightenment awareness, broad-mindedness, civilization, comprehension, cultivation, edification, education, information, insight, instruction, knowledge, learning, literacy, open-mindedness, refinement, sophistication, teaching, understanding, wisdom

enlist engage, enrol, enter (into), gather, join, join up, muster, obtain, procure, recruit, register, secure, sign up, volunteer

enliven animate, brighten, buoy up, cheer, cheer up, excite, exhilarate, fire, gladden, hearten, inspire, inspirit, invigorate, pep up, perk up, quicken, rouse, spark, stimulate, vitalize, vivify, wake up

en masse all at once, all together, as a group, as a whole, as one, ensemble, in a group (body, mass), together

enmesh catch, embroil, ensnare, entangle, implicate, incriminate, involve, net, snare, snarl, tangle, trammel, trap

enmity acrimony, animosity, animus, antagonism, antipathy, aversion, bad blood, bitterness, hate, hatred, hostility, ill will, malevolence, malice, malignity, rancour, spite, venom

ennoble aggrandize, dignify, elevate, enhance, exalt, glorify, honour, magnify, raise

ennui boredom, dissatisfaction, lassitude, listlessness, tedium, the doldrums

enormity 1. atrociousness, atrocity, depravity, disgrace, evilness, heinousness, monstrousness, nefariousness, outrageousness, turpitude, viciousness, vileness, villainy, wickedness **2**. abomination, atrocity, crime, disgrace, evil, horror, monstrosity, outrage, villainy **3**. *Inf.* enormousness, greatness, hugeness, immensity, magnitude, massiveness, vastness

enormous 1. astronomic, Brobdingnagian, colossal, excessive, gargantuan, gigantic, gross, huge, immense, jumbo (*Inf.*), mammoth, massive, monstrous, mountainous, prodigious, titanic, tremendous, vast **2**. *Archaic* abominable, atrocious, depraved, disgraceful, evil, heinous, monstrous, nefarious, odious, outrageous, vicious, vile, villainous, wicked

enough 1. *adj.* abundant, adequate, ample, plenty, sufficient **2**. *n.* abundance, adequacy, ample supply, plenty, right amount, sufficiency **3**. *adv.* abundantly, adequately, amply, fairly, moderately, passably, reasonably, satisfactorily, sufficiently, tolerably

enquire 1. ask, query, question, request information, seek information **2**. *Also* **inquire** conduct an inquiry, examine, explore, inspect, investigate, look into, make inquiry, probe, scrutinize, search

enquiry 1. query, question **2.** *Also in-quiry* examination, exploration, inquest, inspection, investigation, probe, re-search, scrutiny, search, study, survey

enrage aggravate (*Inf.*), anger, exas-perate, incense, incite, inflame, infuriate, irritate, madden, make one's blood boil, make one see red (*Inf.*), provoke

enraged aggravated (*Inf.*), angered, angry, boiling mad, exasperated, fuming, furious, incensed, inflamed, infuriated, irate, irritated, livid (*Inf.*), mad (*Inf.*), raging, raging mad, wild

enrapture beguile, bewitch, captivate, charm, delight, enamour, enchant, en-thral, entrance, fascinate, ravish, spell-bind, transport

enrich 1. make rich, make wealthy **2.** aggrandize, ameliorate, augment, culti-vate, develop, endow, enhance, improve, refine, supplement **3.** adorn, decorate, embellish, grace, ornament

enrol 1. chronicle, inscribe, list, note, record **2.** accept, admit, engage, enlist, join up, matriculate, recruit, register, sign up *or* on, take on

enrolment acceptance, admission, en-gagement, enlistment, matriculation, re-cruitment, registration

en route in transit, on *or* along the way, on the road

ensconce 1. curl up, establish, install, nestle, settle, snuggle up **2.** conceal, cov-er, hide, protect, screen, shelter, shield

ensemble *n.* **1.** aggregate, assemblage, collection, entirety, set, sum, total, total-ity, whole, whole thing **2.** costume, get-up (*Inf.*), outfit, suit **3.** band, cast, cho-rus, company, group, supporting cast, troupe ~*adv.* **4.** all at once, all together, as a group, as a whole, at once, at the same time, en masse, in concert

enshrine apotheosize, cherish, conse-crate, dedicate, embalm, exalt, hallow, preserve, revere, sanctify, treasure

enshroud cloak, cloud, conceal, cover, enclose, enfold, envelop, enwrap, hide, obscure, pall, shroud, veil, wrap

ensign badge, banner, colours, flag, jack, pennant, pennon, standard, streamer

enslave bind, dominate, enchain, en-thral, reduce to slavery, subjugate, yoke

ensnare catch, embroil, enmesh, en-tangle, entrap, net, snare, snarl, trap

ensue arise, attend, be consequent on, befall, come after, come next, come to pass (*Archaic*), derive, flow, follow, issue, proceed, result, stem, succeed, super-vene, turn out *or* up

ensure, insure 1. certify, confirm, effect, guarantee, make certain, make sure, secure, warrant **2.** guard, make safe, protect, safeguard, secure

entail bring about, call for, cause, de-mand, encompass, give rise to, impose, involve, lead to, necessitate, occasion, re-quire, result in

entangle 1. catch, compromise, em-broil, enmesh, ensnare, entrap, foul, im-plicate, involve, knot, mat, mix up, ravel, snag, snare, tangle, trammel, trap **2.** be-wilder, complicate, confuse, jumble, mix up, muddle, perplex, puzzle, snarl, twist

entanglement 1. complication, confu-sion, ensnarement, entrapment, imbro-glio (*Obsolete*), involvement, jumble, knot, mesh, mess, mix-up, muddle, snare, snarl-up (*Inf.*), tangle, toils, trap **2.** difficulty, embarrassment, imbroglio, involvement, liaison, predicament, tie

entente *Also* **entente cordiale** agree-ment, arrangement, compact, deal, friendship, pact, treaty, understanding

enter 1. arrive, come *or* go in *or* into, insert, introduce, make an entrance, pass into, penetrate, pierce **2.** become a mem-ber of, begin, commence, commit oneself to, embark upon, enlist, enrol, join, par-ticipate in, set about, set out on, sign up, start, take part in, take up **3.** inscribe, list, log, note, record, register, set down, take down **4.** offer, present, proffer, put forward, register, submit, tender

enterprise 1. adventure, effort, en-deavour, essay, operation, plan, pro-gramme, project, undertaking, venture **2.** activity, adventurousness, alertness, audacity, boldness, daring, dash, drive, eagerness, energy, enthusiasm, get-up-and-go (*Inf.*), gumption (*Inf.*), initiative, push (*Inf.*), readiness, resource, re-sourcefulness, spirit, vigour, zeal **3.** busi-ness, company, concern, establishment, firm, operation

enterprising active, adventurous, alert, audacious, bold, daring, dashing, eager, energetic, enthusiastic, go-ahead, intrepid, keen, ready, resourceful, spirit-ed, stirring, up-and-coming, venture-some, vigorous, zealous

entertain 1. amuse, charm, cheer, delight, divert, occupy, please, recreate (*Rare*), regale **2**. accommodate, be host to, harbour, have company, have guests *or* visitors, lodge, put up, show hospitality to, treat **3**. cherish, cogitate on, conceive, consider, contemplate, foster, harbour, hold, imagine, keep in mind, maintain, muse over, ponder, support, think about, think over

entertaining amusing, charming, cheering, delightful, diverting, funny, humorous, interesting, pleasant, pleasing, pleasurable, recreative (*Rare*), witty

entertainment amusement, cheer, distraction, diversion, enjoyment, fun, good time, leisure activity, pastime, play, pleasure, recreation, satisfaction, sport, treat

enthral beguile, captivate, charm, enchant, enrapture, entrance, fascinate, grip, hold spellbound, hypnotize, intrigue, mesmerize, rivet, spellbind

enthralling beguiling, captivating, charming, compelling, compulsive, enchanting, entrancing, fascinating, gripping, hypnotizing, intriguing, mesmerizing, riveting, spellbinding

enthusiasm 1. ardour, avidity, devotion, eagerness, earnestness, excitement, fervour, frenzy, interest, keenness, passion, relish, vehemence, warmth, zeal, zest **2**. craze, fad (*Inf.*), hobby, hobbyhorse, interest, mania, passion, rage

enthusiast admirer, aficionado, buff (*Inf.*), devotee, fan, fanatic, fiend (*Inf.*), follower, freak (*Sl.*), lover, supporter, zealot

enthusiastic ardent, avid, devoted, eager, earnest, ebullient, excited, exuberant, fervent, fervid, forceful, hearty, keen, lively, passionate, spirited, unqualified, unstinting, vehement, vigorous, warm, wholehearted, zealous

entice allure, attract, beguile, cajole, coax, decoy, draw, inveigle, lead on, lure, persuade, prevail on, seduce, tempt, wheedle

enticement allurement, attraction, bait, blandishments, cajolery, coaxing, come-on (*Inf.*), decoy, inducement, inveiglement, lure, persuasion, seduction, temptation

entire 1. complete, full, total, whole **2**. absolute, full, outright, thorough, total, undiminished, unmitigated, unreserved, unrestricted **3**. intact, perfect, sound, unbroken, undamaged, unmarked, un-

marred, whole, without a scratch **4**. continuous, integrated, unbroken, undivided, unified

entirely 1. absolutely, altogether, completely, fully, in every respect, perfectly, thoroughly, totally, unreservedly, utterly, wholly, without exception, without reservation **2**. exclusively, only, solely

entirety 1. absoluteness, completeness, fullness, totality, undividedness, unity, wholeness **2**. aggregate, sum, total, unity, whole

entitle 1. accredit, allow, authorize, empower, enable, enfranchise, fit for, license, make eligible, permit, qualify for, warrant **2**. call, characterize, christen, denominate, designate, dub, label, name, style, term, title

entity 1. being, body, creature, existence, individual, object, organism, presence, quantity, substance, thing **2**. essence, essential nature, quiddity (*Philosophy*), quintessence, real nature

entomb bury, inhume, inter, inurn, lay to rest, sepulchre

entombment burial, inhumation, interment, inurnment, sepulture

entourage 1. associates, attendants, companions, company, cortege, court, escort, followers, following, retainers, retinue, staff, suite, train **2**. ambience, environment, environs, milieu, surroundings

entrails bowels, guts, innards (*Inf.*), insides (*Inf.*), intestines, offal, viscera

entrance[1] *n*. **1**. access, avenue, door, doorway, entry, gate, ingress, inlet, opening, passage, portal, way in **2**. appearance, arrival, coming in, entry, ingress, introduction **3**. access, admission, admittance, entrée, entry, ingress, permission to enter **4**. beginning, commencement, debut, initiation, introduction, outset, start

entrance[2] *v*. **1**. bewitch, captivate, charm, delight, enchant, enrapture, enthral, fascinate, gladden, ravish, spellbind, transport **2**. hypnotize, mesmerize, put in a trance

entrant 1. beginner, convert, initiate, neophyte, newcomer, new member, novice, probationer, tyro **2**. candidate, competitor, contestant, entry, participant, player

entrap 1. capture, catch, ensnare, net, snare, trap **2**. allure, beguile, decoy, embroil, enmesh, ensnare, entangle, entice, implicate, inveigle, involve, lead on, lure, seduce, trick

entreat appeal to, ask, ask earnestly, beg, beseech, conjure, crave, enjoin, exhort, implore, importune, petition, plead with, pray, request, supplicate

entreaty appeal, earnest request, exhortation, importunity, petition, plea, prayer, request, solicitation, suit, supplication

entrench, intrench 1. construct defences, dig in, dig trenches, fortify **2.** anchor, dig in, embed, ensconce, establish, fix, implant, ingrain, install, lodge, plant, root, seat, set, settle **3.** encroach, impinge, infringe, interlope, intrude, make inroads, trespass

entrenched, intrenched deep-rooted, deep-seated, firm, fixed, indelible, ineradicable, ingrained, rooted, set, unshakable, well-established

entre nous between ourselves, between the two of us, between you and me, confidentially, in confidence, off the record, privately

entrust, intrust assign, authorize, charge, commend, commit, confide, consign, delegate, deliver, give custody of, hand over, invest, trust, turn over

entry 1. appearance, coming in, entering, entrance, initiation, introduction **2.** access, avenue, door, doorway, entrance, gate, ingress, inlet, opening, passage, passageway, portal, way in **3.** access, admission, entrance, entrée, free passage, permission to enter **4.** account, item, jotting, listing, memo, memorandum, minute, note, record, registration **5.** attempt, candidate, competitor, contestant, effort, entrant, participant, player, submission

entwine, intwine braid, embrace, encircle, entwist (*Archaic*), interlace, intertwine, interweave, knit, plait, surround, twine, twist, weave, wind

enumerate 1. cite, detail, itemize, list, mention, name, quote, recapitulate, recite, recount, rehearse, relate, specify, spell out, tell **2.** add up, calculate, compute, count, number, reckon, sum up, tally, total

enunciate 1. articulate, enounce, pronounce, say, sound, speak, utter, vocalize, voice **2.** declare, proclaim, promulgate, pronounce, propound, publish, state

envelop blanket, cloak, conceal, cover, embrace, encase, encircle, enclose, en-

compass, enfold, engulf, enwrap, hide, obscure, sheathe, shroud, surround, swaddle, swathe, veil, wrap

envelope case, casing, coating, cover, covering, jacket, sheath, shell, skin, wrapper, wrapping

envenom 1. contaminate, infect, poison, taint **2.** acerbate, aggravate (*Inf.*), embitter, enrage, exacerbate, exasperate, incense, inflame, irritate, madden, provoke, sour

enviable advantageous, blessed, covetable, desirable, favoured, fortunate, lucky, much to be desired, privileged

envious begrudging, covetous, green-eyed, green with envy, grudging, jaundiced, jealous, malicious, resentful, spiteful

environ beset, besiege, encircle, enclose, encompass, engird, envelop, gird, hem, invest (*Rare*), ring, surround

environment atmosphere, background, conditions, context, domain, element, habitat, locale, medium, milieu, scene, setting, situation, surroundings, territory

environs district, locality, neighbourhood, outskirts, precincts, purlieus, suburbs, surrounding area, vicinity

envisage 1. conceive (of), conceptualize, contemplate, fancy, imagine, picture, think up, visualize **2.** anticipate, envision, foresee, predict, see

envision anticipate, conceive of, contemplate, envisage, foresee, predict, see, visualize

envoy agent, ambassador, courier, delegate, deputy, diplomat, emissary, intermediary, legate, messenger, minister, plenipotentiary, representative

envy 1. *n.* covetousness, enviousness, grudge, hatred, ill will, jealousy, malice, malignity, resentfulness, resentment, spite, the green-eyed monster (*Inf.*) **2.** *v.* be envious (of), begrudge, be jealous (of), covet, grudge, resent

ephemeral brief, evanescent, fleeting, flitting, fugacious, fugitive, impermanent, momentary, passing, short, short-lived, temporary, transient, transitory

epicene *adj.* **1.** androgynous, bisexual, gynandrous, hermaphrodite, hermaphroditic **2.** asexual, neuter, sexless **3.** effeminate, unmanly, weak, womanish ~*n.* **4.** androgyne, bisexual, gynandromorph, hermaphrodite

epicure 1. *bon vivant*, epicurean, gastronome, gourmet **2**. glutton, gourmand, hedonist, sensualist, sybarite, voluptuary

epicurean 1. *adj.* gluttonous, gourmandizing, hedonistic, libertine, luscious, lush, luxurious, pleasure-seeking, self-indulgent, sensual, sybaritic, voluptuous **2**. *n.* bon vivant, epicure, gastronome, gourmet

epidemic 1. *adj.* general, pandemic, prevailing, prevalent, rampant, rife, sweeping, wide-ranging, widespread **2**. *n.* growth, outbreak, plague, rash, spread, upsurge, wave

epigram bon mot, quip, witticism

epigrammatic concise, laconic, piquant, pithy, pointed, pungent, sharp, short, succinct, terse, witty

epilogue afterword, coda, concluding speech, conclusion, postscript

episode 1. adventure, affair, business, circumstance, event, experience, happening, incident, matter, occurrence **2**. chapter, instalment, part, passage, scene, section

episodic anecdotal, digressive, disconnected, discursive, disjointed, intermittent, irregular, occasional, picaresque, rambling, sporadic, wandering

epistle communication, letter, message, missive, note

epithet appellation, description, designation, name, nickname, sobriquet, tag, title

epitome 1. archetype, embodiment, essence, exemplar, personification, quintessence, representation, type, typical example **2**. abbreviation, abridgment, abstract, compendium, condensation, conspectus, contraction, digest, précis, résumé, summary, syllabus, synopsis

epitomize 1. embody, exemplify, illustrate, incarnate, personify, represent, symbolize, typify **2**. abbreviate, abridge, abstract, condense, contract, curtail, cut, encapsulate, précis, reduce, shorten, summarize, synopsize

epoch age, date, era, period, time

equable 1. agreeable, calm, composed, easy-going, even-tempered, imperturbable, level-headed, placid, serene, temperate, unexcitable, unflappable (*Inf.*), unruffled **2**. consistent, constant, even, regular, smooth, stable, steady, temperate, tranquil, unchanging, uniform, unvarying

equal *adj.* **1**. alike, commensurate, equivalent, identical, like, one and the same, proportionate, tantamount, the same, uniform **2**. balanced, corresponding, egalitarian, even, evenly balanced, evenly matched, evenly proportioned, fifty-fifty (*Inf.*), level pegging (*Brit. inf.*), matched, regular, symmetrical, uniform, unvarying **3**. able, adequate, capable, competent, fit, good enough, ready, strong enough, suitable, up to **4**. egalitarian, equable, even-handed, fair, impartial, just, unbiased ~*n.* **5**. brother, compeer, counterpart, equivalent, fellow, match, mate, parallel, peer, rival, twin ~*v.* **6**. agree with, amount to, balance, be equal to, be even with, be level with, be tantamount to, come up to, correspond to, equalize, equate, even, level, match, parallel, rival, square with, tally with, tie with

equality balance, coequality, correspondence, egalitarianism, equal opportunity, equatability, equivalence, evenness, fairness, identity, likeness, parity, sameness, similarity, uniformity

equalize balance, equal, equate, even up, level, make equal, match, regularize, smooth, square, standardize

equanimity aplomb, calm, calmness, composure, coolness, imperturbability, level-headedness, peace, phlegm, placidity, poise, presence of mind, sang-froid, self-possession, serenity, steadiness, tranquillity

equate agree, balance, be commensurate, compare, correspond with *or* to, equalize, liken, make *or* be equal, match, offset, pair, parallel, square, tally, think of together

equation agreement, balancing, comparison, correspondence, equality, equalization, equating, equivalence, likeness, match, pairing, parallel

equestrian 1. *adj.* in the saddle, mounted, on horseback **2**. *n.* cavalier (*Archaic*), horseman, knight, rider

equilibrate balance, ballast, compensate (for), counterbalance, counterpoise, countervail, equipoise, even up, neutralize, offset

equilibrium 1. balance, counterpoise, equipoise, evenness, rest, stability, steadiness, symmetry **2**. calm, calmness, collectedness, composure, coolness, equanimity, poise, self-possession, serenity, stability, steadiness

equip accoutre, arm, array, attire,

deck out, dress, endow, fit out, fit up, furnish, kit out, outfit, prepare, provide, rig, stock, supply

equipage 1. carriage, coach **2.** accoutrements, apparatus, baggage, equipment, gear, materiel, munitions, stores

equipment accoutrements, apparatus, appurtenances, baggage, equipage, furnishings, furniture, gear, materiel, outfit, paraphernalia, rig, stuff, supplies, tackle, tools

equipoise *n.* **1.** balance, equilibrium, even balance, evenness, stability, steadiness, symmetry **2.** ballast, counterbalance, counterpoise, counterweight, offset ~*v.* **3.** balance, ballast, compensate (for), counterbalance, counterpoise, countervail, equilibrate, neutralize, offset

equitable candid, disinterested, dispassionate, due, even-handed, fair, honest, impartial, just, nondiscriminatory, proper, proportionate, reasonable, right, rightful, unbiased, unprejudiced

equity disinterestedness, equitableness, even-handedness, fair-mindedness, fairness, fair play, honesty, impartiality, integrity, justice, reasonableness, rectitude, righteousness, uprightness

equivalence agreement, alikeness, conformity, correspondence, equality, evenness, identity, interchangeableness, likeness, match, parallel, parity, sameness, similarity, synonymy

equivalent 1. *adj.* alike, commensurate, comparable, correspondent, corresponding, equal, even, homologous, interchangeable, of a kind, same, similar, synonymous, tantamount **2.** *n.* correspondent, counterpart, equal, match, opposite number, parallel, peer, twin

equivocal ambiguous, ambivalent, doubtful, dubious, evasive, indefinite, indeterminate, misleading, oblique, obscure, questionable, suspicious, uncertain, vague

equivocate avoid the issue, beat about the bush (*Inf.*), dodge, evade, fence, fudge, hedge, parry, prevaricate, pussyfoot (*Inf.*), quibble, shuffle, sidestep, tergiversate, waffle (*Inf.*)

equivocation ambiguity, double talk, doubtfulness, evasion, hedging, prevarication, quibbling, shuffling, tergiversation, waffle (*Inf.*), weasel words (*Inf., chiefly U.S.*)

era age, cycle, date, day *or* days, epoch, generation, period, stage, time

eradicate abolish, annihilate, deracinate, destroy, efface, eliminate, erase, expunge, exterminate, extinguish, extirpate, obliterate, remove, root out, stamp out, uproot, weed out, wipe out

eradication abolition, annihilation, deracination, destruction, effacement, elimination, erasure, expunction, extermination, extinction, extirpation, obliteration, removal

erase blot, cancel, delete, efface, expunge, obliterate, remove, rub out, scratch out, wipe out

erect *adj.* **1.** elevated, firm, perpendicular, pricked-up, raised, rigid, standing, stiff, straight, upright, vertical ~*v.* **2.** build, construct, elevate, lift, mount, pitch, put up, raise, rear, set up, stand up **3.** create, establish, form, found, initiate, institute, organize, set up

erection 1. assembly, building, construction, creation, elevation, establishment, fabrication, manufacture **2.** building, construction, edifice, pile, structure

erelong before long, early, quickly, shortly, soon, speedily

eremite anchorite, hermit, recluse, solitary

ergo accordingly, consequently, for that reason, hence, in consequence, so, then, therefore, thus

erode abrade, consume, corrode, destroy, deteriorate, disintegrate, eat away, grind down, spoil, wear down *or* away

erosion abrasion, attrition, consumption, corrasion, corrosion, destruction, deterioration, disintegration, eating away, grinding down, spoiling, wear, wearing down *or* away

erotic amatory, aphrodisiac, carnal, erogenous, rousing, seductive, sensual, sexy (*Inf.*), stimulating, suggestive, titillating, voluptuous

err 1. be inaccurate, be incorrect, be in error, blunder, go astray, go wrong, make a mistake, misapprehend, miscalculate, misjudge, mistake, slip up (*Inf.*) **2.** deviate, do wrong, fall, go astray, lapse, misbehave, offend, sin, transgress, trespass

errand charge, commission, job, message, mission, task

errant 1. *Archaic* itinerant, journeying, peripatetic, rambling, roaming, roving, wandering **2.** aberrant, deviant, erring, offending, sinning, straying, wrong

erratic 1. aberrant, abnormal, capricious, changeable, desultory, eccentric, fitful, inconsistent, irregular, shifting, unpredictable, unreliable, unstable, variable, wayward 2. directionless, meandering, planetary, wandering

erroneous amiss, fallacious, false, faulty, flawed, inaccurate, incorrect, inexact, invalid, mistaken, spurious, unfounded, unsound, untrue, wrong

error 1. bloomer (*Inf.*), blunder, boner (*Sl.*), boob (*Sl.*), delusion, erratum, fallacy, fault, flaw, howler (*Inf.*), inaccuracy, misapprehension, miscalculation, misconception, mistake, oversight, slip, solecism 2. delinquency, deviation, fault, lapse, misdeed, offence, sin, transgression, trespass, wrong, wrongdoing

ersatz artificial, bogus, counterfeit, fake, imitation, phoney (*Inf.*), pretended, sham, simulated, spurious, substitute, synthetic

erstwhile bygone, ex (*Inf.*), former, late, old, once, one-time, past, previous, quondam, sometime

erudite cultivated, cultured, educated, knowledgeable, learned, lettered, literate, scholarly, well-educated, well-read

erudition education, knowledge, learning, letters, lore, scholarship

erupt 1. be ejected, belch forth, blow up, break out, burst forth, burst into, burst out, discharge, explode, flare up, gush, pour forth, spew forth *or* out, spit out, spout, throw off, vent, vomit 2. *Medical* appear, break out

eruption 1. discharge, ejection, explosion, flare-up, outbreak, outburst, sally, venting 2. *Medical* inflammation, outbreak, rash

escalate amplify, ascend, be increased, enlarge, expand, extend, grow, heighten, increase, intensify, magnify, mount, raise, rise, step up

escapade adventure, antic, caper, fling, lark (*Inf.*), mischief, prank, romp, scrape (*Inf.*), spree, stunt, trick

escape *v.* 1. abscond, bolt, break free *or* out, decamp, do a bunk (*Sl.*), flee, fly, get away, make *or* effect one's escape, make one's getaway, run away *or* off, skip, slip away ~*n.* 2. bolt, break, breakout, decampment, flight, getaway ~*v.* 3. avoid, circumvent, dodge, duck, elude, evade, pass, shun, slip ~*n.* 4. avoidance, circumvention, elusion, evasion ~*v.* 5. discharge, drain, emanate, flow, gush, issue, leak, pour forth, seep, spurt ~*n.* 6.

discharge, drain, effluence, efflux, emanation, emission, gush, leak, leakage, outflow, outpour, seepage, spurt ~*v.* 7. baffle, be beyond (someone), be forgotten by, elude, puzzle, stump ~*n.* 8. distraction, diversion, pastime, recreation, relief

eschew abandon, abjure, abstain from, avoid, elude, fight shy of, forgo, forswear, give up, have nothing to do with, keep *or* steer clear of, refrain from, renounce, shun, swear off

escort *n.* 1. bodyguard, company, convoy, cortege, entourage, guard, protection, retinue, safeguard, train 2. attendant, beau, chaperon, companion, guide, partner, protector, squire (*Rare*) ~*v.* 3. accompany, chaperon, conduct, convoy, guard, guide, lead, partner, protect, shepherd, squire, usher

esculent eatable, edible, fit to eat, palatable, wholesome

esoteric abstruse, arcane, cabbalistic, cryptic, hidden, inner, inscrutable, mysterious, mystic, mystical, obscure, occult, private, recondite, secret

especial 1. chief, distinguished, exceptional, extraordinary, marked, notable, noteworthy, outstanding, principal, signal, special, uncommon, unusual 2. exclusive, express, individual, particular, peculiar, personal, private, singular, special, specific, unique

especially 1. chiefly, conspicuously, exceptionally, extraordinarily, mainly, markedly, notably, outstandingly, principally, remarkably, signally, specially, strikingly, supremely, uncommonly, unusually 2. exclusively, expressly, particularly, peculiarly, singularly, specifically, uniquely

espionage counter-intelligence, intelligence, spying, undercover work

espousal 1. adoption, advocacy, backing, championing, championship, defence, embracing, maintenance, support, taking up 2. *Archaic* affiancing, betrothal, betrothing (*Archaic*), engagement, espousing (*Archaic*), marriage, nuptials, plighting, wedding

espouse 1. adopt, advocate, back, champion, defend, embrace, maintain, stand up for, support, take up 2. *Archaic* betroth (*Archaic*), marry, take as spouse, take to wife, wed

esprit animation, brio, élan, liveliness, quickness, sparkle, spirit, sprightliness, verve, vitality, vivacity, wit, zest

espy behold, catch a glimpse of, catch sight of, descry, detect, discern, discover, glimpse, make out, notice, observe, perceive, sight, spot, spy

essay[1] article, composition, discourse, disquisition, dissertation, paper, piece, tract

essay[2] **1.** *n.* aim, attempt, bid, crack (*Inf.*), effort, endeavour, exertion, experiment, go, shot, struggle, test, trial, try, undertaking, venture **2.** *v.* aim, attempt, endeavour, have a go (bash (*Inf.*), crack (*Inf.*), shot), put to the test, strive, take on, test, try, try out, undertake

essence 1. being, core, crux, entity, heart, kernel, life, lifeblood, meaning, nature, pith, principle, quiddity, quintessence, significance, soul, spirit, substance **2.** concentrate, distillate, elixir, extract, spirits, tincture **3.** *Rare* cologne, fragrance, perfume, scent **4. in essence** basically, essentially, fundamentally, in effect, in substance, in the main, materially, substantially, to all intents and purposes, virtually **5. of the essence** crucial, essential, indispensable, of the utmost importance, vital, vitally important

essential *adj.* **1.** crucial, important, indispensable, necessary, needed, requisite, vital **2.** basic, cardinal, constitutional, elemental, elementary, fundamental, inherent, innate, intrinsic, key, main, principal **3.** absolute, complete, ideal, perfect, quintessential **4.** concentrated, distilled, extracted, rectified, refined, volatile ~*n.* **5.** basic, fundamental, must, necessity, prerequisite, principle, requisite, rudiment, *sine qua non*, vital part

establish 1. base, constitute, create, decree, enact, ensconce, entrench, fix, form, found, ground, implant, inaugurate, install, institute, organize, plant, root, secure, settle, set up, start **2.** authenticate, certify, confirm, corroborate, demonstrate, prove, ratify, show, substantiate, validate, verify

establishment 1. creation, enactment, formation, foundation, founding, inauguration, installation, institution, organization, setting up **2.** business, company, concern, corporation, enterprise, firm, house, institute, institution, organization, outfit (*Inf.*), setup (*Inf.*), structure, system **3.** building, factory, house, office, plant, quarters **4.** abode,

domicile, dwelling, home, house, household, residence **5. the Establishment** established order, institutionalized authority, ruling class, the powers that be, the system

estate 1. area, demesne, domain, holdings, lands, manor, property **2.** *Property law* assets, belongings, effects, fortune, goods, possessions, property, wealth **3.** caste, class, order, rank **4.** condition, lot, period, place, position, quality, rank, situation, standing, state, station, status

esteem *v.* **1.** admire, be fond of, cherish, honour, like, love, prize, regard highly, respect, revere, reverence, think highly of, treasure, value, venerate **2.** *Formal* account, believe, calculate, consider, deem, estimate, hold, judge, rate, reckon, regard, think, view ~*n.* **3.** admiration, consideration, credit, estimation, good opinion, honour, regard, respect, reverence, veneration

estimable admirable, esteemed, excellent, good, honourable, honoured, meritorious, reputable, respectable, respected, valuable, valued, worthy

estimate *v.* **1.** appraise, assess, calculate roughly, evaluate, gauge, guess, judge, number, reckon, value **2.** assess, believe, conjecture, consider, form an opinion, guess, judge, rank, rate, reckon, surmise, think ~*n.* **3.** appraisal, appraisement, approximate calculation, assessment, evaluation, guess, guesstimate (*Inf.*), judgment, reckoning, valuation **4.** appraisal, appraisement, assessment, belief, conjecture, educated guess, estimation, judgment, opinion, surmise, thought(s)

estimation 1. appraisal, appreciation, assessment, belief, consideration, considered opinion, estimate, evaluation, judgment, opinion, view **2.** admiration, credit, esteem, good opinion, honour, regard, respect, reverence, veneration

estrange alienate, antagonize, disaffect, disunite, divide, drive apart, lose *or* destroy the affection of, make hostile, part, separate, set at odds, withdraw, withhold

estrangement alienation, antagonization, breach, break-up, disaffection, dissociation, disunity, division, hostility, parting, separation, split, withdrawal, withholding

estuary creek, firth, fjord, inlet, mouth

et cetera and others, and so forth, and

so on, and the like, and the rest, et al.

etch carve, corrode, cut, eat into, engrave, furrow, impress, imprint, incise, ingrain, inscribe, stamp

etching carving, engraving, impression, imprint, inscription, print

eternal 1. abiding, ceaseless, constant, deathless, endless, everlasting, immortal, infinite, interminable, never-ending, perennial, perpetual, sempiternal (*Literary*), timeless, unceasing, undying, unending, unremitting, without end **2.** deathless, enduring, everlasting, immortal, immutable, imperishable, indestructible, lasting, permanent

eternity 1. age, ages, endlessness, for ever, immortality, infinitude, infinity, perpetuity, timelessness, time without end **2.** *Theology* heaven, paradise, the afterlife, the hereafter, the next world

ethereal 1. dainty, delicate, exquisite, fine, insubstantial, light, rarefied, refined, subtle, tenuous **2.** aerial, airy, fairy, impalpable, intangible, light, rarefied **3.** celestial, empyreal, heavenly, spiritual, sublime, unearthly, unworldly

ethical conscientious, correct, decent, fair, fitting, good, honest, honourable, just, moral, principled, proper, right, righteous, upright, virtuous

ethics conscience, moral code, morality, moral philosophy, moral values, principles, rules of conduct, standards

ethnic cultural, indigenous, national, native, racial, traditional

ethos attitude, beliefs, character, disposition, ethic, spirit, tenor

etiolated achromatic, blanched, bleached, colourless, faded, pale, wan, washed out, white, whitened

etiquette civility, code, convention, courtesy, customs, decorum, formalities, good *or* proper behaviour, manners, politeness, politesse, propriety, protocol, rules, usage

eulogize acclaim, applaud, commend, compliment, cry up, exalt, extol, glorify, laud, magnify (*Archaic*), panegyrize, pay tribute to, praise, sing *or* sound the praises of

eulogy acclaim, acclamation, accolade, applause, commendation, compliment, encomium, exaltation, glorification, laudation, paean, panegyric, plaudit, praise, tribute

euphonic, euphonious canorous (*Rare*), clear, consonant, dulcet, harmonious, mellifluous, mellow, melodic, melodious, musical, pleasing to the ear, silvery, sweet-toned, tuneful

euphony consonance, harmony, mellifluousness, mellowness, melodiousness, melody, music, musicality, tunefulness

euphoria bliss, ecstasy, elation, exaltation, exhilaration, exultation, glee, high spirits, intoxication, joy, joyousness, jubilation, rapture, transport

evacuate 1. abandon, clear, decamp, depart, desert, forsake, leave, move out, pull out, quit, relinquish, remove, vacate, withdraw **2.** defecate, discharge, eject, eliminate, empty, excrete, expel, void

evade 1. avoid, circumvent, decline, dodge, duck, elude, escape, escape the clutches of, get away from, shirk, shun, sidestep, steer clear of **2.** balk, circumvent, cop out (*Sl.*), equivocate, fence, fend off, fudge, hedge, parry, prevaricate, quibble, waffle (*Inf.*)

evaluate appraise, assay, assess, calculate, estimate, gauge, judge, rank, rate, reckon, size up (*Inf.*), value, weigh

evaluation appraisal, assessment, calculation, estimate, estimation, judgment, opinion, rating, valuation

evanesce clear, disappear, disperse, dissolve, evaporate, fade, melt, vanish

evanescence brevity, briefness, ephemerality, ephemeralness, fleetingness, fugaciousness, fugacity, impermanence, momentariness, transience, transitoriness

evanescent brief, ephemeral, fading, fleeting, fugacious, fugitive, impermanent, momentary, passing, short-lived, transient, transitory, vanishing

evangelical, evangelistic crusading, missionary, propagandizing, proselytizing, zealous

evaporate 1. dehydrate, desiccate, dry, dry up, vaporize **2.** dematerialize, disappear, dispel, disperse, dissipate, dissolve, evanesce, fade, fade away, melt, melt away, vanish

evaporation 1. dehydration, desiccation, drying, drying up, vaporization **2.** dematerialization, disappearance, dispelling, dispersal, dissipation, dissolution, evanescence, fading, fading away, melting, melting away, vanishing

evasion artifice, avoidance, circumvention, cop-out (*Sl.*), cunning, dodge, elusion, equivocation, escape, evasiveness, excuse, fudging, obliqueness, pretext, prevarication, ruse, shift, shirking, shuffling, sophism, sophistry, subterfuge, trickery, waffle (*Inf.*)

evasive cagey (*Inf.*), casuistic, casuistical, cunning, deceitful, deceptive, devious, dissembling, elusive, elusory, equivocating, indirect, misleading, oblique, prevaricating, shifty, shuffling, slippery, sophistical, tricky

eve 1. day before, night before, vigil **2**. brink, edge, point, threshold, verge

even *adj.* **1**. flat, flush, horizontal, level, parallel, plane, plumb, smooth, steady, straight, true, uniform **2**. constant, metrical, regular, smooth, steady, unbroken, uniform, uninterrupted, unvarying, unwavering **3**. calm, composed, cool, equable, equanimous, even-tempered, imperturbable, peaceful, placid, serene, stable, steady, tranquil, undisturbed, unexcitable, unruffled, well-balanced **4**. coequal, commensurate, comparable, drawn, equal, equalized, equally balanced, fifty-fifty (*Inf.*), identical, level, level pegging (*Brit. inf.*), like, matching, neck and neck, on a par, parallel, similar, square, the same, tied, uniform **5**. balanced, disinterested, dispassionate, equitable, fair, fair and square, impartial, just, unbiased, unprejudiced **6**. **get even (with)** *Inf.* be revenged *or* revenge oneself, even the score, give tit for tat, pay back, reciprocate, repay, requite, return like for like, settle the score, take an eye for an eye, take vengeance ∼*adv.* **7**. all the more, much, still, yet **8**. despite, disregarding, in spite of, notwithstanding **9**. **even as** at the same time as, at the time that, during the time that, exactly as, just as, while, whilst **10**. **even so** all the same, be that as it may, despite (that), however, in spite of (that), nevertheless, nonetheless, notwithstanding (that), still, yet ∼*v.* **11**. *Often followed by out or up* align, balance, become level, equal, equalize, flatten, level, match, regularize, smooth, square, stabilize, steady **12**. **even the score** be revenged *or* revenge oneself, equalize, get even (*Inf.*), give tit for tat, pay (someone) back, reciprocate, repay, requite, return like for like, settle the score, take an eye for an eye, take vengeance

even-handed balanced, disinterested, equitable, fair, fair and square, impartial, just, unbiased, unprejudiced

event 1. adventure, affair, business, circumstance, episode, experience, fact, happening, incident, matter, milestone, occasion, occurrence **2**. conclusion, consequence, effect, end, issue, outcome, result, termination, upshot **3**. bout, competition, contest, game, tournament **4**. **at all events** at any rate, come what may, in any case, in any event, regardless, whatever happens

even-tempered calm, composed, cool, cool-headed, equable, imperturbable, level-headed, peaceful, placid, serene, steady, tranquil, unexcitable, unruffled

eventful active, busy, consequential, critical, crucial, decisive, exciting, fateful, full, historic, important, lively, memorable, momentous, notable, noteworthy, remarkable, significant

eventual concluding, consequent, ensuing, final, future, later, overall, prospective, resulting, ultimate

eventuality case, chance, contingency, event, likelihood, possibility, probability

eventually after all, at the end of the day, finally, in the course of time, in the end, in the long run, one day, some day, some time, sooner or later, ultimately, when all is said and done

eventuate be a consequence, be consequent, come about, come to pass (*Archaic*), ensue, follow, issue, result

ever 1. at all, at any time (period, point), by any chance, in any case, on any occasion **2**. always, at all times, constantly, continually, endlessly, eternally, everlastingly, evermore, for ever, incessantly, perpetually, relentlessly, to the end of time, unceasingly, unendingly

everlasting 1. abiding, deathless, endless, eternal, immortal, imperishable, indestructible, infinite, interminable, never-ending, perpetual, timeless, undying **2**. ceaseless, constant, continual, continuous, endless, incessant, interminable, never-ending, unceasing, uninterrupted, unremitting

evermore always, eternally, ever, for ever, *in perpetuum*, to the end of time

every all, each, each one, the whole number

everybody all and sundry, each one, each person, everyone, every person, one and all, the whole world

everyday 1. daily, quotidian **2**. accustomed, common, common or garden

(*Inf.*), commonplace, conventional, customary, dull, familiar, frequent, habitual, informal, mundane, ordinary, routine, run-of-the-mill, stock, unexceptional, unimaginative, usual, wonted, workaday

everyone all and sundry, each one, each person, everybody, every person, one and all, the whole world

everything all, each thing, the aggregate, the entirety, the lot, the sum, the total, the whole caboodle (*Inf.*), the whole lot

everywhere all around, all over, far and wide *or* near, high and low, in each place, in every place, omnipresent, the world over, to *or* in all places, ubiquitous, ubiquitously

evict boot out (*Inf.*), chuck out (*Inf.*), dislodge, dispossess, eject, expel, kick out (*Inf.*), oust, put out, remove, show the door (to), throw on to the streets, throw out, turf out (*Inf.*), turn out

eviction clearance, dislodgement, dispossession, ejection, expulsion, ouster (*Law*), removal

evidence 1. *n.* affirmation, attestation, averment, confirmation, corroboration, data, declaration, demonstration, deposition, grounds, indication, manifestation, mark, proof, sign, substantiation, testimony, token, witness 2. *v.* demonstrate, denote, display, evince, exhibit, indicate, manifest, prove, reveal, show, signify, testify to, witness

evident apparent, clear, conspicuous, incontestable, incontrovertible, indisputable, manifest, noticeable, obvious, palpable, patent, perceptible, plain, tangible, unmistakable, visible

evidently 1. clearly, doubtless, doubtlessly, incontestably, incontrovertibly, indisputably, manifestly, obviously, patently, plainly, undoubtedly, unmistakably, without question 2. apparently, it seems, it would seem, ostensibly, outwardly, seemingly, to all appearances

evil *adj.* 1. bad, base, corrupt, depraved, heinous, immoral, iniquitous, maleficent, malevolent, malicious, malignant, nefarious, reprobate, sinful, vicious, vile, villainous, wicked, wrong ~*n.* 2. badness, baseness, corruption, curse, depravity, heinousness, immorality, iniquity, maleficence, malignity, sin, sinfulness, turpitude, vice, viciousness, villainy, wickedness, wrong, wrongdoing ~*adj.* 3. baneful (*Archaic*), calamitous,

catastrophic, deleterious, destructive, detrimental, dire, disastrous, harmful, hurtful, inauspicious, injurious, mischievous, painful, pernicious, ruinous, sorrowful, unfortunate, unlucky, woeful ~*n.* 4. affliction, calamity, catastrophe, disaster, harm, hurt, ill, injury, mischief, misery, misfortune, pain, ruin, sorrow, suffering, woe ~*adj.* 5. foul, mephitic, noxious, offensive, pestilential, putrid, unpleasant, vile

evince attest, bespeak, betoken, demonstrate, display, establish, evidence, exhibit, express, indicate, make clear, make evident, manifest, reveal, show, signify

evoke 1. arouse, awaken, call, excite, give rise to, induce, recall, rekindle, stimulate, stir up, summon up 2. call forth, educe (*Rare*), elicit, produce, provoke 3. arouse, call, call forth, conjure up, invoke, raise, summon

evolution development, enlargement, evolvement, expansion, growth, increase, maturation, progress, progression, unfolding, unrolling, working out

evolve develop, disclose, educe, elaborate, enlarge, expand, grow, increase, mature, open, progress, unfold, unroll, work out

exacerbate aggravate, embitter, enrage, envenom, exasperate, excite, inflame, infuriate, intensify, irritate, madden, provoke, vex, worsen

exact *adj.* 1. accurate, careful, correct, definite, explicit, express, faithful, faultless, identical, literal, methodical, orderly, particular, precise, right, specific, true, unequivocal, unerring, veracious, very 2. careful, exacting, meticulous, painstaking, punctilious, rigorous, scrupulous, severe, strict ~*v.* 3. call for, claim, command, compel, demand, extort, extract, force, impose, insist upon, require, squeeze, wrest, wring

exacting demanding, difficult, hard, harsh, imperious, oppressive, painstaking, rigid, rigorous, severe, stern, strict, stringent, taxing, tough, unsparing

exaction compulsion, contribution, demand, extortion, imposition, oppression, rapacity, requirement, requisition, squeeze (*Inf.*), tribute

exactitude accuracy, carefulness, correctness, exactness, faithfulness, faultlessness, nicety, orderliness, painstakingness, preciseness, precision, promptitude, regularity, rigorousness, rigour, scrupulousness, strictness, truth, unequivocalness, veracity

exactly *adv.* **1**. accurately, carefully, correctly, definitely, explicitly, faithfully, faultlessly, literally, methodically, precisely, rigorously, scrupulously, severely, strictly, truly, truthfully, unequivocally, unerringly, veraciously **2**. absolutely, bang, explicitly, expressly, indeed, in every respect, just, particularly, precisely, quite, specifically **3**. **not exactly** *Ironical* by no means, certainly not, hardly, in no manner, in no way, not at all, not by any means, not quite, not really ~*interj.* **4**. absolutely, assuredly, as you say, certainly, indeed, just so, of course, precisely, quite, quite so, spot-on (*Inf.*), truly

exactness accuracy, carefulness, correctness, exactitude, faithfulness, faultlessness, nicety, orderliness, painstakingness, preciseness, precision, promptitude, regularity, rigorousness, rigour, scrupulousness, strictness, truth, unequivocalness, veracity

exaggerate amplify, embellish, embroider, emphasize, enlarge, exalt, hyperbolize, inflate, lay it on thick (*Inf.*), magnify, overdo, overemphasize, overestimate, overstate

exaggerated amplified, exalted, excessive, extravagant, highly coloured, hyperbolic, inflated, overblown, overdone, overestimated, overstated, pretentious, tall (*Inf.*)

exaggeration amplification, embellishment, emphasis, enlargement, exaltation, excess, extravagance, hyperbole, inflation, magnification, overemphasis, overestimation, overstatement, pretension, pretentiousness

exalt **1**. advance, aggrandize, dignify, elevate, ennoble, honour, promote, raise, upgrade **2**. acclaim, apotheosize, applaud, bless, extol, glorify, idolize, laud, magnify (*Archaic*), pay homage to, pay tribute to, praise, reverence, set on a pedestal, worship **3**. animate, arouse, electrify, elevate, excite, fire the imagination (of), heighten, inspire, inspirit, stimulate, uplift **4**. delight, elate, exhilarate, fill with joy, thrill

exaltation **1**. advancement, aggrandizement, dignity, elevation, eminence, ennoblement, grandeur, high rank, hon-

our, loftiness, prestige, promotion, rise, upgrading **2**. acclaim, acclamation, apotheosis, applause, blessing, extolment, glorification, glory, homage, idolization, laudation, lionization, magnification, panegyric, plaudits, praise, reverence, tribute, worship **3**. animation, elevation, excitement, inspiration, stimulation, uplift **4**. bliss, delight, ecstasy, elation, exhilaration, exultation, joy, joyousness, jubilation, rapture, transport

exalted **1**. august, dignified, elevated, eminent, grand, high, high-ranking, honoured, lofty, prestigious **2**. elevated, high-minded, ideal, intellectual, lofty, noble, sublime, superior, uplifting **3**. *Inf.* elevated, exaggerated, excessive, inflated, overblown, pretentious **4**. animated, blissful, ecstatic, elated, elevated, excited, exhilarated, exultant, in high spirits, in seventh heaven, inspired, inspirited, joyous, jubilant, on cloud nine (*Inf.*), rapturous, stimulated, transported, uplifted

examination analysis, assay, catechism, checkup, exploration, inquiry, inquisition, inspection, interrogation, investigation, observation, perusal, probe, questioning, quiz, research, review, scrutiny, search, study, survey, test, trial

examine **1**. analyse, appraise, assay, check, check out, consider, explore, go over *or* through, inspect, investigate, look over, peruse, ponder, pore over, probe, review, scan, scrutinize, sift, study, survey, take stock of, test, vet, weigh **2**. catechize, cross-examine, grill (*Inf.*), inquire, interrogate, question, quiz

example **1**. case, case in point, exemplification, illustration, instance, sample, specimen **2**. archetype, exemplar, ideal, illustration, model, paradigm, paragon, pattern, precedent, prototype, standard **3**. admonition, caution, lesson, warning **4**. **for example** as an illustration, by way of illustration, e.g., *exempli gratia*, for instance, to cite an instance, to illustrate

exasperate aggravate (*Inf.*), anger, annoy, bug (*Inf.*), embitter, enrage, exacerbate, excite, gall, get (*Inf.*), incense, inflame, infuriate, irk, irritate, madden, needle (*Inf.*), nettle, peeve (*Inf.*), pique, provoke, rankle, rile (*Inf.*), rouse, try the patience of, vex

exasperation aggravation (*Inf.*), anger, annoyance, exacerbation, fury, ire (*Literary*), irritation, passion, pique, provocation, rage, vexation, wrath

excavate burrow, cut, delve, dig, dig out, dig up, gouge, hollow, mine, quarry, scoop, trench, tunnel, uncover, unearth

excavation burrow, cavity, cut, cutting, dig, diggings, ditch, dugout, hole, hollow, mine, pit, quarry, shaft, trench, trough

exceed 1. beat, be superior to, better, cap (*Inf.*), eclipse, excel, go beyond, outdistance, outdo, outreach, outrun, outshine, outstrip, overtake, pass, surmount, surpass, top, transcend **2.** go beyond the bounds of, go over the limit of, go over the top, overstep

exceeding enormous, exceptional, excessive, extraordinary, great, huge, preeminent, superior, superlative, surpassing, vast

exceedingly enormously, especially, exceptionally, excessively, extraordinarily, extremely, greatly, highly, hugely, inordinately, superlatively, surpassingly, unusually, vastly, very

excel 1. beat, be superior, better, cap (*Inf.*), eclipse, exceed, go beyond, outdo, outrival, outshine, pass, surmount, surpass, top, transcend **2.** be good, be master of, be proficient, be skilful, be talented, predominate, shine, show talent, take precedence

excellence distinction, eminence, fineness, goodness, greatness, high quality, merit, perfection, pre-eminence, purity, superiority, supremacy, transcendence, virtue, worth

excellent A1 (*Inf.*), admirable, capital, champion, choice, distinguished, estimable, exemplary, exquisite, fine, first-class, first-rate, good, great, meritorious, notable, noted, outstanding, prime, select, sterling, superb, superior, superlative, tiptop, top-notch (*Inf.*), worthy

except 1. *prep. Also* **except for** apart from, bar, barring, besides, but, excepting, excluding, exclusive of, omitting, other than, save (*Archaic*), saving, with the exception of **2.** *v.* ban, bar, disallow, exclude, leave out, omit, pass over, reject, rule out

exception 1. debarment, disallowment, excepting, exclusion, leaving out, omission, passing over, rejection **2.** anomaly, departure, deviation, freak, inconsistency, irregularity, oddity, peculi-

arity, quirk, special case **3. take exception** be offended, be resentful, demur, disagree, object, quibble, take offence, take umbrage

exceptionable disagreeable, inappropriate, objectionable, unacceptable, unbearable, undesirable, unsatisfactory, unwelcome

exceptional 1. aberrant, abnormal, anomalous, atypical, deviant, extraordinary, inconsistent, irregular, odd, peculiar, rare, singular, special, strange, uncommon, unusual **2.** excellent, extraordinary, marvellous, outstanding, phenomenal, prodigious, remarkable, special, superior

excerpt 1. *n.* citation, extract, fragment, part, passage, pericope, piece, portion, quotation, section, selection **2.** *v.* cite, cull, extract, pick out, quote, select, take

excess *n.* **1.** glut, leftover, overabundance, overdose, overflow, overload, plethora, remainder, superabundance, superfluity, surfeit, surplus, too much **2.** debauchery, dissipation, dissoluteness, exorbitance, extravagance, immoderation, intemperance, overindulgence, prodigality, unrestraint ~*adj.* **3.** extra, leftover, redundant, remaining, residual, spare, superfluous, surplus

excessive disproportionate, enormous, exaggerated, exorbitant, extravagant, extreme, immoderate, inordinate, intemperate, needless, overdone, overmuch, prodigal, profligate, superfluous, too much, unconscionable, undue, unreasonable

exchange *v.* **1.** bandy, barter, change, commute, convert into, interchange, reciprocate, swap (*Inf.*), switch, trade, truck ~*n.* **2.** barter, dealing, interchange, quid pro quo, reciprocity, substitution, swap (*Inf.*), switch, tit for tat, trade, traffic, truck **3.** Bourse, market

excise[1] customs, duty, impost, levy, surcharge, tariff, tax, toll

excise[2] **1.** cross out, cut, delete, destroy, eradicate, erase, expunge, exterminate, extirpate, strike out **2.** cut off *or* out, extract, remove

excision deletion, destruction, eradication, extermination, extirpation, removal

excitable edgy, emotional, hasty, highly strung, hot-headed, hot-tempered, irascible, mercurial, nervous, passionate, quick-tempered, sensitive, susceptible, temperamental, testy, touchy, violent, volatile

excite agitate, animate, arouse, awaken, discompose, disturb, electrify, elicit, evoke, fire, foment, galvanize, incite, inflame, inspire, instigate, kindle, move, provoke, quicken, rouse, stimulate, stir up, thrill, titillate, waken, whet

excited aflame, agitated, animated, aroused, awakened, discomposed, disturbed, enthusiastic, feverish, flurried, high (*Inf.*), hot and bothered (*Inf.*), moved, nervous, overwrought, roused, stimulated, stirred, thrilled, tumultuous, wild, worked up

excitement 1. action, activity, ado, adventure, agitation, animation, commotion, discomposure, elation, enthusiasm, ferment, fever, flurry, furore, heat, kicks (*Inf.*), passion, perturbation, thrill, tumult, warmth 2. impulse, incitement, instigation, motivation, motive, provocation, stimulation, stimulus, urge

exciting electrifying, exhilarating, inspiring, intoxicating, moving, provocative, rip-roaring (*Inf.*), rousing, sensational, stimulating, stirring, thrilling, titillating

exclaim call, call out, cry, cry out, declare, ejaculate, proclaim, shout, utter, vociferate, yell

exclamation call, cry, ejaculation, expletive, interjection, outcry, shout, utterance, vociferation, yell

exclude 1. ban, bar, blackball, debar, disallow, embargo, forbid, interdict, keep out, ostracize, prohibit, proscribe, refuse, shut out, veto 2. count out, eliminate, except, ignore, leave out, omit, pass over, preclude, reject, repudiate, rule out, set aside 3. bounce (*Sl.*), drive out, eject, evict, expel, force out, get rid of, oust, remove, throw out

exclusion 1. ban, bar, debarment, embargo, forbiddance, interdict, nonadmission, preclusion, prohibition, proscription, refusal, veto 2. elimination, exception, omission, rejection, repudiation 3. eviction, expulsion, removal

exclusive 1. absolute, complete, entire, full, only, private, single, sole, total, undivided, unique, unshared, whole 2. aristocratic, chic, choice, clannish, classy (*Sl.*), cliquish, closed, discriminative, elegant, fashionable, limited, narrow, posh (*Inf.*), private, restricted, restrictive, se-

lect, selfish, snobbish 3. confined, limited, peculiar, restricted, unique 4. debarring, except for, excepting, excluding, leaving aside, not counting, omitting, restricting, ruling out

excogitate conceive, contemplate, contrive, deliberate, devise, evolve, frame, invent, mull over, ponder, ruminate, think out *or* up, weigh, work out

excommunicate anathematize, ban, banish, cast out, denounce, eject, exclude, expel, proscribe, remove, repudiate, unchurch

excoriate 1. abrade, flay, gall, peel, scarify, scrape, scratch, skin, strip 2. attack, berate, castigate, censure, chastise, condemn, criticize, denounce, flay, lambaste, rebuke, reproach, reprove, revile, scold, upbraid, vilify

excrescence 1. *Medical* growth, lump, swelling, tumour, wart 2. knob, lump, outgrowth, process, projection, prominence, protrusion, protuberance

excrete defecate, discharge, egest, eject, eliminate, evacuate, expel, exude, void

excruciate afflict, agonize, harrow, rack, torment, torture

excruciating acute, agonizing, burning, exquisite, extreme, harrowing, insufferable, intense, piercing, racking, searing, severe, tormenting, torturous, unbearable, unendurable, violent

exculpate absolve, acquit, clear, discharge, dismiss, excuse, exonerate, free, justify, pardon, release, vindicate

excursion 1. airing, day trip, expedition, jaunt, journey, outing, pleasure trip, ramble, tour, trip 2. detour, deviation, digression, episode, excursus, wandering

excursive devious, diffusive, digressive, discursive, episodic, errant, rambling, roaming, roving, wandering

excusable allowable, defensible, forgivable, justifiable, minor, pardonable, permissible, slight, understandable, venial, warrantable

excuse v. 1. absolve, acquit, bear with, exculpate, exonerate, extenuate, forgive, indulge, make allowances for, overlook, pardon, pass over, tolerate, turn a blind eye to, wink at 2. apologize for, condone, defend, explain, justify, mitigate, vindicate 3. absolve, discharge, exempt, free, let off, liberate, release, relieve, spare ~n. 4. apology, defence, explanation, grounds, justification, mitigation, plea, pretext, reason, vindication **5.** cop-out (*Sl.*), disguise, evasion, expedient, makeshift, pretence, pretext, semblance, shift, subterfuge **6.** *Inf.* apology, makeshift, mockery, substitute, travesty

execrable abhorrent, abominable, accursed, atrocious, damnable, deplorable, despicable, detestable, disgusting, foul, hateful, heinous, horrible, loathsome, nauseous, obnoxious, odious, offensive, repulsive, revolting, sickening, vile

execrate abhor, abominate, anathematize, condemn, curse, damn, denounce, deplore, despise, detest, excoriate, hate, imprecate, loathe, revile, vilify

execration abhorrence, abomination, anathema, condemnation, contempt, curse, damnation, detestation, excoriation, hate, hatred, imprecation, loathing, malediction, odium, vilification

execute **1.** behead, electrocute, guillotine, hang, kill, put to death, shoot **2.** accomplish, achieve, administer, bring off, carry out, complete, consummate, discharge, do, effect, enact, enforce, finish, fulfil, implement, perform, prosecute, put into effect, realize, render **3.** *Law* deliver, seal, serve, sign, validate

execution **1.** accomplishment, achievement, administration, carrying out, completion, consummation, discharge, effect, enactment, enforcement, implementation, operation, performance, prosecution, realization, rendering **2.** capital punishment, hanging, killing **3.** delivery, manner, mode, performance, rendition, style, technique **4.** *Law* warrant, writ

executioner **1.** hangman, headsman **2.** assassin, hit man (*Sl.*), killer, murderer, slayer

executive *n.* **1.** administrator, director, manager, official **2.** administration, directorate, directors, government, hierarchy, leadership, management ~*adj.* **3.** administrative, controlling, decision-making, directing, governing, managerial

exemplar **1.** criterion, epitome, example, ideal, model, paradigm, paragon, pattern, standard **2.** example, exemplification, illustration, instance, prototype, specimen, type

exemplary **1.** admirable, commendable, correct, estimable, excellent, good, honourable, ideal, laudable, meritorious, model, praiseworthy, punctilious, ster-

ling **2.** admonitory, cautionary, monitory, warning **3.** characteristic, illustrative, representative, typical

exemplify demonstrate, depict, display, embody, evidence, exhibit, illustrate, instance, manifest, represent, serve as an example of, show

exempt **1.** *v.* absolve, discharge, except, excuse, exonerate, free, grant immunity, let off, liberate, release, relieve, spare **2.** *adj.* absolved, clear, discharged, excepted, excused, favoured, free, immune, liberated, not liable, not subject, privileged, released, spared

exemption absolution, discharge, dispensation, exception, exoneration, freedom, immunity, privilege, release

exercise *v.* **1.** apply, bring to bear, employ, enjoy, exert, practise, put to use, use, utilize, wield **2.** discipline, drill, habituate, inure, practise, train, work out **3.** afflict, agitate, annoy, burden, distress, disturb, occupy, pain, perturb, preoccupy, trouble, try, vex, worry ~*n.* **4.** action, activity, discipline, drill, drilling, effort, labour, toil, training, work, workout **5.** accomplishment, application, discharge, employment, enjoyment, exertion, fulfilment, implementation, practice, use, utilization **6.** drill, lesson, practice, problem, schooling, schoolwork, task, work

exert **1.** bring into play, bring to bear, employ, exercise, expend, make use of, put forth, use, utilize, wield **2. exert oneself** apply oneself, do one's best, endeavour, labour, make an effort, spare no effort, strain, strive, struggle, toil, try hard, work

exertion action, application, attempt, effort, employment, endeavour, exercise, industry, labour, pains, strain, stretch, struggle, toil, travail (*Literary*), trial, use, utilization

exhalation breath, breathing out, discharge, effluvium, emanation, emission, evaporation, exhaust, expiration, fog, fume, mist, smoke, steam, vapour

exhale breathe, breathe out, discharge, eject, emanate, emit, evaporate, expel, give off, issue, respire, steam

exhaust **1.** bankrupt, cripple, debilitate, disable, drain, enervate, enfeeble, fatigue, impoverish, prostrate, sap, tire, tire out, weaken, wear out **2.** consume, deplete, dissipate, expend, finish, run through, spend, squander, use up, waste

3. drain, dry, empty, strain, void **4**. be emitted, discharge, emanate, escape, issue

exhausted 1. all in (*Sl.*), beat (*Sl.*), crippled, dead (*Inf.*), dead beat (*Inf.*), dead tired, debilitated, disabled, dog-tired (*Inf.*), done in (*Inf.*), drained, enervated, enfeebled, fatigued, jaded, knackered (*Sl.*), out on one's feet, prostrated, ready to drop, sapped, spent, tired out, wasted, weak, worn out **2**. at an end, consumed, depleted, dissipated, done, expended, finished, gone, spent, squandered, used up, wasted **3**. bare, drained, dry, empty, void

exhausting arduous, backbreaking, crippling, debilitating, difficult, draining, enervating, fatiguing, gruelling, hard, laborious, punishing, sapping, strenuous, taxing, testing, tiring

exhaustion 1. debilitation, enervation, fatigue, feebleness, lassitude, prostration, tiredness, weariness **2**. consumption, depletion, emptying

exhaustive all-embracing, all-inclusive, all-out (*Inf.*), complete, comprehensive, encyclopedic, extensive, far-reaching, full, full-scale, in-depth, intensive, sweeping, thorough, thoroughgoing, total

exhibit 1. *v.* air, demonstrate, disclose, display, evidence, evince, expose, express, flaunt, indicate, make clear *or* plain, manifest, offer, parade, present, put on view, reveal, show **2**. *n.* display, exhibition, illustration, model, show

exhibition airing, demonstration, display, exhibit, expo (*Inf.*), exposition, fair, manifestation, performance, presentation, representation, show, showing, spectacle

exhilarate animate, cheer, delight, elate, enliven, exalt, gladden, inspirit, invigorate, lift, pep *or* perk up, rejoice, stimulate, thrill

exhilarating breathtaking, cheering, enlivening, exalting, exciting, exhilarant, exhilarative, exhilaratory, gladdening, invigorating, stimulating, thrilling, vitalizing

exhilaration animation, cheerfulness, delight, elation, exaltation, excitement, gaiety, gladness, gleefulness, high spirits, hilarity, joy, joyfulness, liveliness, mirth, sprightliness, vivacity

exhort admonish, advise, beseech, bid, call upon, caution, counsel, encourage,

enjoin, entreat, goad, incite, persuade, press, spur, urge, warn

exhortation admonition, advice, beseeching, bidding, caution, counsel, encouragement, enjoinder (*Rare*), entreaty, goading, incitement, lecture, persuasion, sermon, urging, warning

exhume dig up, disentomb, disinter, unbury, unearth

exigency, exigence 1. acuteness, constraint, criticalness, demandingness, difficulty, distress, emergency, imperativeness, necessity, needfulness, pressingness, pressure, stress, urgency **2**. constraint, demand, necessity, need, requirement, wont **3**. crisis, difficulty, emergency, extremity, fix (*Inf.*), hardship, jam (*Inf.*), juncture, pass, pickle (*Inf.*), pinch, plight, predicament, quandary, scrape (*Inf.*), strait

exigent 1. acute, constraining, critical, crucial, imperative, importunate, insistent, necessary, needful, pressing, urgent **2**. arduous, demanding, difficult, exacting, hard, harsh, rigorous, severe, stiff, strict, stringent, taxing, tough

exiguous bare, meagre, negligible, paltry, scanty, skimpy, slender, spare, sparse

exile *n.* **1**. banishment, deportation, expatriation, expulsion, ostracism, proscription, separation **2**. deportee, émigré, expatriate, outcast, refugee ~*v.* **3**. banish, deport, drive out, eject, expatriate, expel, ostracize, oust, proscribe

exist 1. abide, be, be extant, be living, be present, breathe, continue, endure, happen, last, live, obtain, occur, prevail, remain, stand, survive **2**. eke out a living, get along *or* by, stay alive, subsist, survive

existence 1. actuality, animation, being, breath, continuance, continuation, duration, endurance, life, subsistence, survival **2**. being, creature, entity, thing **3**. creation, life, reality, the world

existent abiding, around, current, enduring, existing, extant, in existence, living, obtaining, present, prevailing, remaining, standing, surviving

exit *n.* **1**. door, egress, gate, outlet, passage out, vent, way out **2**. adieu, departure, evacuation, exodus, farewell, going, goodbye, leave-taking, retirement, retreat, withdrawal **3**. death, decease, demise, expiry, passing away ~*v.* **4**. bid farewell, depart, go away, go offstage

(*Theatre*), go out, issue, leave, retire, retreat, say goodbye, take one's leave, withdraw

exodus departure, evacuation, exit, flight, going out, leaving, migration, retirement, retreat, withdrawal

exonerate 1. absolve, acquit, clear, discharge, dismiss, exculpate, excuse, justify, pardon, vindicate **2.** discharge, dismiss, except, excuse, exempt, free, let off, liberate, release, relieve

exoneration 1. absolution, acquittal, amnesty, discharge, dismissal, exculpation, justification, pardon, vindication **2.** deliverance, discharge, dismissal, exception, exemption, freeing, liberation, release, relief

exorbitance excess, excessiveness, extravagance, extremeness, immoderateness, immoderation, inordinateness, preposterousness, unreasonableness

exorbitant enormous, excessive, extortionate, extravagant, extreme, immoderate, inordinate, outrageous, preposterous, unconscionable, undue, unreasonable, unwarranted

exorcise adjure, cast out, deliver (from), drive out, expel, purify

exorcism adjuration, casting out, deliverance, driving out, expulsion, purification

exordium beginning, foreword, introduction, opening, opening remarks, preamble, preface, prelude, proem, prolegomenon, prologue

exotic 1. alien, external, extraneous, extrinsic, foreign, imported, introduced, naturalized, not native **2.** bizarre, colourful, curious, different, extraordinary, fascinating, glamorous, mysterious, outlandish, peculiar, strange, striking, unfamiliar, unusual

expand 1. amplify, augment, bloat, blow up, broaden, develop, dilate, distend, enlarge, extend, fatten, fill out, grow, heighten, increase, inflate, lengthen, magnify, multiply, prolong, protract, swell, thicken, wax, widen **2.** diffuse, open (out), outspread, spread (out), stretch (out), unfold, unfurl, unravel, unroll **3.** amplify, develop, dilate, elaborate, embellish, enlarge, expatiate, expound, flesh out, go into detail

expanse area, breadth, extent, field, plain, range, space, stretch, sweep, tract

expansion amplification, augmentation, development, diffusion, dilatation, distension, enlargement, expanse, growth, increase, inflation, magnification, multiplication, opening out, spread, swelling, unfolding, unfurling

expansive 1. dilating, distending, elastic, enlargeable, expanding, extendable, inflatable, stretching, stretchy, swelling **2.** all-embracing, broad, comprehensive, extensive, far-reaching, inclusive, thorough, voluminous, wide, wide-ranging, widespread **3.** affable, communicative, easy, effusive, free, friendly, garrulous, genial, loquacious, open, outgoing, sociable, talkative, unreserved, warm

expatiate amplify, descant, develop, dilate, dwell on, elaborate, embellish, enlarge, expound, go into detail

expatriate 1. *adj.* banished, emigrant, émigré, exiled, refugee **2.** *n.* emigrant, émigré, exile **3.** *v.* banish, exile, expel, ostracize, proscribe

expect 1. assume, believe, calculate, conjecture, forecast, foresee, imagine, presume, reckon, suppose, surmise, think, trust **2.** anticipate, await, bargain for, contemplate, envisage, hope for, look ahead to, look for, look forward to, predict, watch for **3.** call for, count on, demand, insist on, look for, rely upon, require, want, wish

expectancy 1. anticipation, assumption, belief, conjecture, expectation, hope, looking forward, prediction, presumption, probability, supposition, surmise, suspense, waiting **2.** likelihood, outlook, prospect

expectant 1. anticipating, anxious, apprehensive, awaiting, eager, expecting, hopeful, in suspense, ready, watchful **2.** enceinte, expecting (*Inf.*), gravid, pregnant

expectation 1. assumption, assurance, belief, calculation, confidence, conjecture, forecast, likelihood, presumption, probability, supposition, surmise, trust **2.** anticipation, apprehension, chance, expectancy, fear, hope, looking forward, outlook, possibility, prediction, promise, prospect, suspense **3.** demand, insistence, reliance, requirement, trust, want, wish

expecting enceinte, expectant, gravid, in the family way (*Inf.*), pregnant, with child

expediency, expedience 1. advantageousness, advisability, appropriateness, aptness, benefit, convenience, desirability, effectiveness, fitness, helpfulness, judiciousness, meetness, practicality, pragmatism, profitability, properness, propriety, prudence, suitability, usefulness, utilitarianism, utility **2.** contrivance, device, expedient, makeshift, manoeuvre, means, measure, method, resort, resource, scheme, shift, stopgap, stratagem, substitute

expedient 1. *adj.* advantageous, advisable, appropriate, beneficial, convenient, desirable, effective, fit, helpful, judicious, meet, opportune, politic, practical, pragmatic, profitable, proper, prudent, suitable, useful, utilitarian, worthwhile **2.** *n.* contrivance, device, expediency, makeshift, manoeuvre, means, measure, method, resort, resource, scheme, shift, stopgap, stratagem, substitute

expedite accelerate, advance, assist, dispatch, facilitate, forward, hasten, hurry, precipitate, press, promote, quicken, rush, speed (up), urge

expedition 1. enterprise, excursion, exploration, journey, mission, quest, safari, tour, trek, trip, undertaking, voyage **2.** company, crew, explorers, team, travellers, voyagers, wayfarers **3.** alacrity, celerity, dispatch, expeditiousness, haste, hurry, promptness, quickness, rapidity, readiness, speed, swiftness

expeditious active, alert, brisk, diligent, efficient, fast, hasty, immediate, instant, nimble, prompt, quick, rapid, ready, speedy, swift

expel 1. belch, cast out, discharge, dislodge, drive out, eject, remove, spew, throw out **2.** ban, banish, bar, blackball, discharge, dismiss, drum out, evict, exclude, exile, expatriate, oust, proscribe, send packing, throw out, turf out (*Inf.*)

expend consume, disburse, dissipate, employ, exhaust, fork out (*Sl.*), go through, lay out (*Inf.*), pay out, shell out (*Inf.*), spend, use (up)

expendable dispensable, inessential, nonessential, replaceable, unimportant

expenditure application, charge, consumption, cost, disbursement, expense, outgoings, outlay, output, payment, spending, use

expense charge, consumption, cost, disbursement, expenditure, loss, outlay, output, payment, sacrifice, spending, toll, use

expensive costly, dear, excessive, exorbitant, extravagant, high-priced, inordinate, lavish, overpriced, rich, steep (*Inf.*), stiff

experience *n.* **1.** contact, doing, evidence, exposure, familiarity, involvement, know-how (*Inf.*), knowledge, observation, participation, practice, proof, training, trial, understanding **2.** adventure, affair, encounter, episode, event, happening, incident, occurrence, ordeal, test, trial ~*v.* **3.** apprehend, become familiar with, behold, encounter, endure, face, feel, go through, have, know, live through, meet, observe, participate in, perceive, sample, sense, suffer, sustain, taste, try, undergo

experienced 1. accomplished, adept, capable, competent, expert, familiar, knowledgeable, master, practised, professional, qualified, seasoned, skilful, tested, trained, tried, veteran, well-versed **2.** knowing, mature, sophisticated, wise, worldly, worldly-wise

experiment 1. *n.* assay, attempt, examination, experimentation, investigation, procedure, proof, research, test, trial, trial and error, trial run, venture **2.** *v.* assay, examine, investigate, put to the test, research, sample, test, try, verify

experimental empirical, exploratory, pilot, preliminary, probationary, provisional, speculative, tentative, test, trial, trial-and-error

expert 1. *n.* ace (*Inf.*), adept, authority, connoisseur, dab hand (*Inf.*), master, past master, pro (*Inf.*), professional, specialist, virtuoso, wizard **2.** *adj.* able, adept, adroit, apt, clever, deft, dexterous, experienced, facile, handy, knowledgeable, master, masterly, practised, professional, proficient, qualified, skilful, skilled, trained, virtuoso

expertise ableness, adroitness, aptness, cleverness, command, deftness, dexterity, expertness, facility, judgment, knack, know-how (*Inf.*), knowledge, masterliness, mastery, proficiency, skilfulness, skill

expertness ableness, adroitness, aptness, command, deftness, dexterity, expertise, facility, judgment, know-how (*Inf.*), knowledge, masterliness, mastery, proficiency, skilfulness, skill

expiate atone for, do penance for, make amends for, redeem, redress

expiation amends, atonement, penance, redemption, redress, shrift (*Archaic*)

expiration 1. cessation, close, conclusion, end, expiry, finis, finish, termination **2.** death, decease, demise, departure

expire 1. cease, close, come to an end, conclude, end, finish, lapse, run out, stop, terminate **2.** breathe out, emit, exhale, expel **3.** decease, depart, die, kick the bucket (*Inf.*), pass away *or* on, perish

explain 1. clarify, clear up, define, demonstrate, describe, disclose, elucidate, explicate (*Formal*), expound, illustrate, interpret, make clear *or* plain, resolve, solve, teach, unfold **2.** account for, excuse, give an explanation for, give a reason for, justify

explanation 1. clarification, definition, demonstration, description, elucidation, explication, exposition, illustration, interpretation, resolution **2.** account, answer, cause, excuse, justification, meaning, mitigation, motive, reason, sense, significance, vindication

explanatory demonstrative, descriptive, elucidatory, explicative, expository, illuminative, illustrative, interpretive, justifying

explicable accountable, definable, explainable, intelligible, interpretable, justifiable, resolvable, understandable

explicate 1. clarify, clear up, elucidate, explain, expound, interpret, make clear *or* explicit, make plain, unfold, untangle **2.** construct, develop, devise, evolve, formulate, work out

explicit absolute, categorical, certain, clear, definite, direct, distinct, exact, express, frank, open, outspoken, patent, plain, positive, precise, specific, stated, straightforward, unambiguous, unequivocal, unqualified, unreserved

explode 1. blow up, burst, detonate, discharge, erupt, go off, set off, shatter, shiver **2.** belie, debunk, discredit, disprove, give the lie to, invalidate, refute, repudiate

exploit *n.* **1.** accomplishment, achievement, adventure, attainment, deed, feat, stunt ~*v.* **2.** abuse, impose upon, manipulate, milk, misuse, play on *or* upon, take advantage of **3.** capitalize on, cash in on (*Sl.*), make capital out of, make use of, profit by *or* from, put to use, turn to account, use, use to advantage, utilize

exploration 1. analysis, examination, inquiry, inspection, investigation, probe, research, scrutiny, search, study **2.** expedition, reconnaissance, survey, tour, travel, trip

exploratory analytic, experimental, fact-finding, investigative, probing, searching, trial

explore 1. analyse, examine, inquire into, inspect, investigate, look into, probe, prospect, research, scrutinize, search **2.** have *or* take a look around, range over, reconnoitre, scout, survey, tour, travel, traverse

explosion 1. bang, blast, burst, clap, crack, detonation, discharge, outburst, report **2.** eruption, fit, outbreak, outburst, paroxysm

explosive 1. unstable, volatile **2.** fiery, stormy, touchy, vehement, violent **3.** charged, dangerous, hazardous, overwrought, perilous, tense, ugly

exponent 1. advocate, backer, champion, defender, promoter, propagandist, proponent, spokesman, spokeswoman, supporter, upholder **2.** commentator, demonstrator, elucidator, expositor, expounder, illustrator, interpreter **3.** example, exemplar, illustration, indication, model, sample, specimen, type **4.** executant, interpreter, performer, player, presenter

expose 1. display, exhibit, manifest, present, put on view, reveal, show, uncover, unveil **2.** air, betray, bring to light, denounce, detect, disclose, divulge, lay bare, let out, make known, reveal, show up, smoke out, uncover, unearth, unmask **3.** endanger, hazard, imperil, jeopardize, lay open, leave open, make vulnerable, risk, subject **4.** *With* to acquaint with, bring into contact with, familiarize with, introduce to, make conversant with

exposé disclosure, divulgence, exposure, revelation, uncovering

exposed 1. bare, exhibited, laid bare, made manifest, made public, on display, on show, on view, revealed, shown, unconcealed, uncovered, unveiled **2.** open, open to the elements, unprotected, unsheltered **3.** in danger, in peril, laid bare, laid open, left open, liable, open, susceptible, vulnerable

exposition 1. account, commentary, critique, description, elucidation, exegesis, explanation, explication, illustration, interpretation, presentation **2.** demonstration, display, exhibition, expo (*Inf.*), fair, presentation, show

expository descriptive, elucidative, exegetic, explanatory, explicative, explicatory, hermeneutic, illustrative, interpretive

expostulate argue (with), dissuade, protest, reason (with), remonstrate (with)

exposure 1. baring, display, exhibition, manifestation, presentation, publicity, revelation, showing, uncovering, unveiling **2.** airing, betrayal, denunciation, detection, disclosure, divulgence, divulging, exposé, revelation, unmasking **3.** danger, hazard, jeopardy, risk, vulnerability **4.** acquaintance, contact, conversancy, experience, familiarity, introduction, knowledge **5.** aspect, frontage, location, outlook, position, setting, view

expound describe, elucidate, explain, explicate (*Formal*), illustrate, interpret, set forth, spell out, unfold

express *v.* **1.** articulate, assert, asseverate, communicate, couch, declare, enunciate, phrase, pronounce, put, put across, put into words, say, speak, state, tell, utter, verbalize, voice, word **2.** bespeak, convey, denote, depict, designate, disclose, divulge, embody, evince, exhibit, indicate, intimate, make known, manifest, represent, reveal, show, signify, stand for, symbolize, testify **3.** extract, force out, press out, squeeze out ~*adj.* **4.** accurate, categorical, certain, clear, definite, direct, distinct, exact, explicit, outright, plain, pointed, precise, unambiguous **5.** clearcut, especial, particular, singular, special **6.** direct, fast, high-speed, nonstop, quick, rapid, speedy, swift

expression 1. announcement, assertion, asseveration, communication, declaration, enunciation, mention, pronouncement, speaking, statement, utterance, verbalization, voicing **2.** demonstration, embodiment, exhibition, indication, manifestation, representation, show, sign, symbol, token **3.** air, appearance, aspect, countenance, face, look, mien (*Literary*) **4.** choice of words, delivery, diction, emphasis, execution, intonation, language, phraseology, phrasing, speech, style, wording **5.** idiom, locution, phrase, remark, set phrase, term, turn of phrase, word

expressionless blank, deadpan, dull, empty, inscrutable, poker-faced (*Inf.*), straight-faced, vacuous, wooden

expressive 1. eloquent, emphatic, energetic, forcible, lively, mobile, moving, poignant, striking, strong, sympathetic, telling, vivid **2.** allusive, demonstrative, indicative, meaningful, pointed, pregnant, revealing, significant, suggestive, thoughtful

expressly 1. especially, exactly, intentionally, on purpose, particularly, precisely, purposely, specially, specifically **2.** absolutely, categorically, clearly, decidedly, definitely, distinctly, explicitly, in no uncertain terms, manifestly, outright, plainly, pointedly, positively, unambiguously, unequivocally, unmistakably

expropriate appropriate, arrogate, assume, commandeer, confiscate, impound, requisition, seize, take, take over

expulsion banishment, debarment, discharge, dislodgment, dismissal, ejection, eviction, exclusion, exile, expatriation, extrusion, proscription, removal

expunge abolish, annihilate, annul, blot out, cancel, delete, destroy, efface, eradicate, erase, exterminate, extinguish, extirpate, obliterate, raze, remove, strike out, wipe out

expurgate blue-pencil, bowdlerize, censor, clean up (*Inf.*), cut, purge, purify

exquisite 1. beautiful, dainty, delicate, elegant, fine, lovely, precious **2.** attractive, beautiful, charming, comely, lovely, pleasing, striking **3.** admirable, choice, consummate, delicious, excellent, fine, flawless, incomparable, matchless, outstanding, peerless, perfect, rare, select, splendid, superb, superlative **4.** appreciative, consummate, cultivated, discerning, discriminating, fastidious, impeccable, meticulous, polished, refined, selective, sensitive **5.** acute, excruciating, intense, keen, piercing, poignant, sharp

extant existent, existing, in existence, living, remaining, subsisting, surviving, undestroyed

extemporaneous, extemporary 1. ad-lib, extempore, free, impromptu, improvisatory, improvised, made-up, offhand, off-the-cuff (*Inf.*), spontaneous, unplanned, unpremeditated, unprepared, unrehearsed **2.** expedient, improvised, makeshift, on-the-spot, temporary

extempore *adv./adj.* ad lib, extemporaneous, extemporary, freely, impromptu, improvised, offhand, off the cuff (*Inf.*), off the top of one's head, on the spot, spontaneously, unplanned, unpremeditated, unprepared

extemporize ad-lib, improvise, make up, play (it) by ear

extend 1. carry on, continue, drag out, draw out, elongate, lengthen, make longer, prolong, protract, spin out, spread out, stretch, unfurl, unroll **2.** carry on, continue, go on, last, take **3.** amount to, attain, go as far as, reach, spread **4.** add to, amplify, augment, broaden, develop, dilate, enhance, enlarge, expand, increase, spread, supplement, widen **5.** advance, bestow, confer, give, grant, hold out, impart, offer, present, proffer, put forth, reach out, stretch out, yield

extended 1. continued, drawn-out, elongated, enlarged, lengthened, long, prolonged, protracted, spread (out), stretched out, unfolded, unfurled, unrolled **2.** broad, comprehensive, enlarged, expanded, extensive, far-reaching, large-scale, sweeping, thorough, wide, widespread **3.** conferred, outstretched, proffered, stretched out

extension 1. amplification, augmentation, broadening, continuation, delay, development, dilatation, distension, elongation, enlargement, expansion, extent, increase, lengthening, postponement, prolongation, protraction, spread, stretching, widening **2.** addendum, addition, adjunct, annexe, appendage, appendix, branch, ell, supplement, wing

extensive all-inclusive, broad, capacious, commodious, comprehensive, expanded, extended, far-flung, far-reaching, general, great, huge, large, large-scale, lengthy, long, pervasive, prevalent, protracted, spacious, sweeping, thorough, universal, vast, voluminous, wholesale, wide, widespread

extent 1. bounds, compass, play, range, reach, scope, sphere, sweep **2.** amount, amplitude, area, breadth, bulk, degree, duration, expanse, expansion, length, magnitude, measure, quantity, size, stretch, term, time, volume, width

extenuate 1. decrease, diminish, excuse, lessen, make allowances for, minimize, mitigate, moderate, palliate, play down, qualify, reduce, soften, temper, weaken **2.** discount, make light of, underestimate, underrate, undervalue

extenuating justifying, mitigating, moderating, qualifying, serving as an excuse

exterior n. **1.** appearance, aspect, coating, covering, façade, face, finish, outside, shell, skin, surface ~adj. **2.** external, outer, outermost, outside, outward, superficial, surface **3.** alien, exotic, external, extraneous, extrinsic, foreign, outside

exterminate abolish, annihilate, destroy, eliminate, eradicate, extirpate

external 1. apparent, exterior, outer, outermost, outside, outward, superficial, surface, visible **2.** alien, exotic, exterior, extramural, extraneous, extrinsic, foreign, independent, outside

extinct 1. dead, defunct, gone, lost, vanished **2.** doused, extinguished, inactive, out, quenched, snuffed out **3.** abolished, defunct, ended, obsolete, terminated, void

extinction abolition, annihilation, death, destruction, dying out, eradication, excision, extermination, extirpation, obliteration, oblivion

extinguish 1. blow out, douse, put out, quench, smother, snuff out, stifle **2.** abolish, annihilate, destroy, eliminate, end, eradicate, erase, expunge, exterminate, extirpate, kill, obscure, remove, suppress, wipe out

extirpate abolish, annihilate, deracinate, destroy, eliminate, eradicate, erase, expunge, exterminate, extinguish, pull up by the roots, remove, root out, uproot, wipe out

extol acclaim, applaud, celebrate, commend, cry up, eulogize, exalt, glorify, laud, magnify (Archaic), panegyrize, pay tribute to, praise, sing the praises of

extort blackmail, bleed (Inf.), bully, coerce, exact, extract, force, squeeze, wrest, wring

extortion 1. blackmail, coercion, compulsion, demand, exaction, force, oppression, rapacity **2.** enormity, exorbitance, expensiveness, overcharging

extortionate 1. excessive, exorbitant, extravagant, immoderate, inflated, inordinate, outrageous, preposterous, sky-high, unreasonable **2.** blood-sucking (Inf.), exacting, grasping, hard, harsh, oppressive, rapacious, rigorous, severe, usurious

extra adj. **1.** accessory, added, additional, ancillary, auxiliary, fresh, further, more, new, other, supplemental, supplementary **2.** excess, extraneous, inessential, leftover, needless, redundant, re-

serve, spare, supererogatory, superfluous, supernumerary, surplus, unnecessary, unneeded, unused ~*n*. **3**. accessory, addendum, addition, adjunct, affix,
appendage, appurtenance, attachment,
bonus, complement, extension, supernumerary, supplement ~*adv*. **4**. especially,
exceptionally, extraordinarily, extremely, particularly, remarkably, uncommonly, unusually

extract *v*. **1**. draw, extirpate, pluck
out, pull, pull out, remove, take out, uproot, withdraw **2**. bring out, derive,
draw, elicit, evoke, exact, gather, get,
glean, obtain, reap, wrest, wring **3**. deduce, derive, develop, educe, elicit,
evolve **4**. distil, draw out, express, obtain, press out, separate out, squeeze,
take out **5**. abstract, choose, cite, copy
out, cull, cut out, quote, select ~*n*. **6**.
concentrate, decoction, distillate, distillation, essence, juice **7**. abstract, citation, clipping, cutting, excerpt, passage,
quotation, selection

extraction 1. drawing, extirpation,
pulling, removal, taking out, uprooting,
withdrawal **2**. derivation, distillation,
separation **3**. ancestry, birth, blood, derivation, descent, family, lineage, origin,
parentage, pedigree, race, stock

extraneous 1. accidental, additional,
adventitious, extra, incidental, inessential, needless, nonessential, peripheral,
redundant, superfluous, supplementary,
unessential, unnecessary, unneeded **2**.
beside the point, immaterial, impertinent, inadmissible, inapplicable, inapposite, inappropriate, inapt, irrelevant, off
the subject, unconnected, unrelated **3**.
adventitious, alien, exotic, external, extrinsic, foreign, out of place, strange

extraordinary amazing, bizarre, curious, exceptional, fantastic, marvellous,
odd, outstanding, particular, peculiar,
phenomenal, rare, remarkable, singular,
special, strange, surprising, uncommon,
unfamiliar, unheard-of, unique, unprecedented, unusual, unwonted, weird, wonderful

extravagance 1. improvidence, lavishness, overspending, prodigality,
profligacy, profusion, squandering,
waste, wastefulness **2**. absurdity, dissipation, exaggeration, excess, exorbitance, folly, immoderation, outrageousness, preposterousness, recklessness, unreasonableness, unrestraint, wildness

extravagant 1. excessive, improvident, imprudent, lavish, prodigal, profligate, spendthrift, wasteful **2**. absurd, exaggerated, excessive, exorbitant, fanciful, fantastic, foolish, immoderate, inordinate, outrageous, preposterous, reckless, unreasonable, unrestrained, wild **3**.
fancy, flamboyant, flashy, garish, gaudy,
grandiose, ornate, ostentatious, pretentious, showy **4**. costly, excessive, exorbitant, expensive, extortionate, inordinate,
overpriced, steep (*Inf.*), unreasonable

extravaganza display, flight of fancy,
pageant, show, spectacle, spectacular

extreme *adj*. **1**. acute, great, greatest,
high, highest, intense, maximum, severe,
supreme, ultimate, utmost, uttermost,
worst **2**. downright, egregious, exaggerated, exceptional, excessive, extraordinary,
extravagant, fanatical, immoderate, inordinate, intemperate, out-and-out, outrageous, radical, remarkable, sheer, uncommon, unconventional, unreasonable,
unusual, utter, zealous **3**. dire, Draconian, drastic, harsh, radical, rigid, severe, stern, strict, unbending, uncompromising **4**. faraway, far-off, farthest, final,
last, most distant, outermost, remotest,
terminal, ultimate, utmost, uttermost
~*n*. **5**. acme, apex, apogee, boundary,
climax, consummation, depth, edge, end,
excess, extremity, height, limit, maximum, minimum, nadir, pinnacle, pole,
termination, top, ultimate, zenith

extremely acutely, awfully (*Inf.*), exceedingly, exceptionally, excessively,
extraordinarily, greatly, highly, inordinately, intensely, markedly, quite, severely, terribly, to *or* in the extreme, ultra, uncommonly, unusually, utterly,
very

extremist die-hard, fanatic, radical,
ultra, zealot

extremity 1. acme, apex, apogee, border, bound, boundary, brim, brink, edge,
end, extreme, frontier, limit, margin,
maximum, minimum, nadir, pinnacle,
pole, rim, terminal, termination, terminus, tip, top, ultimate, verge, zenith **2**.
acuteness, climax, consummation, depth,
excess, height **3**. adversity, crisis, dire
straits, disaster, emergency, exigency,
hardship, pinch, plight, setback, trouble
4. *Plural* fingers and toes, hands and
feet, limbs

extricate clear, deliver, disembarrass,
disengage, disentangle, free, get out, get

(someone) off the hook (*Sl.*), liberate, release, relieve, remove, rescue, withdraw, wriggle out of

extrinsic alien, exotic, exterior, external, extraneous, foreign, imported, outside, superficial

extrude eject, expel, force out, press out, squeeze out, thrust out

exuberance 1. animation, buoyancy, cheerfulness, eagerness, ebullience, effervescence, energy, enthusiasm, excitement, exhilaration, high spirits, life, liveliness, spirit, sprightliness, vigour, vitality, vivacity, zest **2.** effusiveness, exaggeration, excessiveness, fulsomeness, lavishness, prodigality, superfluity **3.** abundance, copiousness, lavishness, lushness, luxuriance, plenitude, profusion, rankness, richness, superabundance, teemingness

exuberant 1. animated, buoyant, cheerful, eager, ebullient, effervescent, elated, energetic, enthusiastic, excited, exhilarated, high-spirited, in high spirits, lively, sparkling, spirited, sprightly, vigorous, vivacious, zestful **2.** effusive, exaggerated, excessive, fulsome, lavish, overdone, prodigal, superfluous **3.** abundant, copious, lavish, lush, luxuriant, overflowing, plenteous, plentiful, profuse, rank, rich, superabundant, teeming

exude 1. bleed, discharge, emanate, emit, excrete, filter through, issue, leak, ooze, secrete, seep, sweat, trickle, weep, well forth **2.** display, emanate, exhibit, manifest, radiate, show

exult 1. be delighted, be elated, be in high spirits, be joyful, be jubilant, be overjoyed, celebrate, jubilate, jump for joy, make merry, rejoice **2.** boast, brag, crow, gloat, glory (in), revel, take delight in, taunt, triumph, vaunt

exultant cock-a-hoop, delighted, elated, exulting, flushed, gleeful, joyful, joyous, jubilant, overjoyed, rejoicing, revelling, transported, triumphant

exultation 1. celebration, delight, elation, glee, high spirits, joy, joyousness, jubilation, merriness, rejoicing, transport **2.** boasting, bragging, crowing, gloating, glory, glorying, revelling, triumph

eye *n.* **1.** eyeball, optic (*Inf.*), orb (*Poetic*), peeper (*Sl.*) **2.** appreciation, discernment, discrimination, judgment, perception, recognition, taste **3.** *Often plural* belief, judgment, mind, opinion, point of view, viewpoint **4. keep an** *or* **one's eye on** guard, keep in view, keep tabs on (*Inf.*), keep under surveillance, look after, look out for, monitor, observe, pay attention to, regard, scrutinize, supervise, survey, watch, watch over **5. an eye for an eye** justice, reprisal, requital, retaliation, retribution, revenge, vengeance **6. lay, clap** *or* **set eyes on** behold, come across, encounter, meet, notice, observe, run into, see **7. see eye to eye** accord, agree, back, be in unison, coincide, concur, fall in, get on, go along, harmonize, jibe (*Inf.*), subscribe to **8. up to one's eyes** busy, caught up, engaged, flooded out, fully occupied, inundated, overwhelmed, up to here, up to one's elbows, wrapped up in ~*v.* **9.** contemplate, gaze at, glance at, have *or* take a look at, inspect, look at, peruse, regard, scan, scrutinize, stare at, study, survey, view, watch **10. eye up,** give (someone) the (glad) eye, leer at, make eyes at, ogle

eye-catching arresting, attractive, captivating, showy, spectacular, striking

eyeful 1. gaze, glance, look, sight, view **2.** beauty, dazzler, knockout (*Inf.*), show, spectacle, stunner (*Inf.*), vision

eyesight observation, perception, range of vision, sight, vision

eyesore atrocity, blemish, blight, blot, disfigurement, disgrace, horror, mess, monstrosity, sight (*Inf.*), ugliness

eyewitness bystander, looker-on, observer, onlooker, passer-by, spectator, viewer, watcher, witness

F

Fabian attritional, cautious, circumspect, cunctative or cunctatory (*Rare*), delaying, procrastinating

fable 1. allegory, apologue, legend, myth, parable, story, tale **2.** fabrication, fairy story (*Inf.*), falsehood, fantasy, fib, fiction, figment, invention, lie, romance, tall story (*Inf.*), untruth, white lie, yarn (*Inf.*)

fabled fabulous, famed, famous, fictional, legendary, mythical, storied

fabric 1. cloth, material, stuff, textile, web **2.** constitution, construction, foundations, framework, infrastructure, make-up, organization, structure

fabricate 1. assemble, build, construct, erect, fashion, form, frame, make, manufacture, shape **2.** coin, concoct, devise, fake, falsify, feign, forge, form, invent, make up, trump up

fabrication 1. assemblage, assembly, building, construction, erection, manufacture, production **2.** cock-and-bull story (*Inf.*), concoction, fable, fairy story (*Inf.*), fake, falsehood, fiction, figment, forgery, invention, lie, myth, untruth

fabulous 1. amazing, astounding, breathtaking, fictitious, immense, inconceivable, incredible, legendary, phenomenal, unbelievable **2.** *Inf.* fantastic (*Inf.*), marvellous, out-of-this-world (*Inf.*), spectacular, superb, wonderful **3.** apocryphal, fantastic, fictitious, imaginary, invented, legendary, made-up, mythical, unreal

façade appearance, exterior, face, front, frontage, guise, mask, pretence, semblance, show, veneer

face *n.* **1.** clock (*Sl.*), countenance, dial (*Sl.*), features, kisser (*Sl.*), lineaments, mug (*Sl.*), phiz or phizog (*Sl.*), physiognomy, visage **2.** appearance, aspect, expression, frown, grimace, look, *moue*, pout, scowl, smirk **3.** air, appearance, disguise, display, exterior, façade, front, mask, pretence, semblance, show **4.** authority, dignity, honour, image, prestige, reputation, self-respect, standing, status **5.** *Inf.* assurance, audacity, boldness, brass neck (*Inf.*), cheek (*Inf.*), confidence, effrontery, gall (*Inf.*), impudence, nerve, presumption, sauce (*Inf.*) **6.** aspect, cover, exterior, facet, front, outside, right side, side, surface **7. face to face** *à deux*, confronting, eyeball to eyeball, in confrontation, opposite, tête-à-tête, vis-à-vis **8. fly in the face of** act in defiance of, defy, disobey, go against, oppose, rebel against, snap one's fingers at (*Inf.*) **9. on the face of it** apparently, at first sight, seemingly, to all appearances, to the eye **10. pull** (or **make**) **a long face** frown, grimace, knit one's brows, look black (disapproving, displeased, put out, stern), lower, pout, scowl, sulk **11. show one's face** approach, be seen, come, put in or make an appearance, show up (*Inf.*), turn up **12. to one's face** directly, in one's presence, openly, straight ~*v.* **13.** be confronted by, brave, come up against, confront, cope with, deal with, defy, encounter, experience, meet, oppose **14.** be opposite, front onto, give towards or onto, look onto, overlook **15.** clad, coat, cover, dress, finish, level, line, overlay, sheathe, surface, veneer

face-lift 1. cosmetic surgery, plastic surgery **2.** renovation, restoration

facer difficulty, dilemma, how-do-you-do (*Inf.*), poser, problem, puzzle

facet angle, aspect, face, part, phase, plane, side, slant, surface

facetious amusing, comical, droll, flippant, frivolous, funny, humorous, jesting, jocose, jocular, merry, playful, pleasant, tongue in cheek, unserious, waggish, witty

face up to accept, acknowledge, come to terms with, confront, cope with, deal with, meet head-on

facile 1. adept, adroit, dexterous, easy, effortless, fluent, light, proficient, quick, ready, simple, skilful, smooth, uncomplicated **2.** cursory, glib, hasty, shallow, slick, superficial

facilitate assist the progress of, ease, expedite, forward, further, help, make easy, promote, smooth the path of, speed up

facility 1. ability, adroitness, dexterity, ease, efficiency, effortlessness, expertness, fluency, knack, proficiency, quickness, readiness, skilfulness, skill, smoothness **2**. *Often plural* advantage, aid, amenity, appliance, convenience, equipment, means, opportunity, resource

facing 1. *adj*. fronting, opposite, partnering **2**. *n*. cladding, coating, façade, false front, front, overlay, plaster, reinforcement, revetment, stucco, surface, trimming, veneer

facsimile carbon, carbon copy, copy, duplicate, photocopy, Photostat (*Trademark*), print, replica, reproduction, transcript, Xerox (*Trademark*)

fact 1. act, deed, event, *fait accompli*, happening, incident, occurrence, performance **2**. actuality, certainty, gospel (truth), naked truth, reality, truth **3**. circumstance, detail, feature, item, particular, point, specific **4. in fact** actually, indeed, in point of fact, in reality, in truth, really, truly

faction 1. bloc, cabal, camp, caucus, clique, coalition, combination, confederacy, contingent, division, gang, ginger group, group, junta, lobby, minority, party, pressure group, section, sector, set, splinter group **2**. conflict, disagreement, discord, disharmony, dissension, disunity, division, divisiveness, friction, infighting, rebellion, sedition, strife, tumult, turbulence

factious conflicting, contentious, disputatious, dissident, divisive, insurrectionary, litigious, malcontent, mutinous, partisan, rebellious, refractory, rival, sectarian, seditious, troublemaking, tumultuous, turbulent, warring

factitious affected, artificial, assumed, counterfeited, engineered, fabricated, fake, false, imitation, insincere, made-up, manufactured, mock, phoney (*Sl.*), pinchbeck, put-on, sham, simulated, spurious, synthetic, unnatural, unreal

factor 1. aspect, cause, circumstance, component, consideration, determinant, element, influence, item, part, point, thing **2**. *Scot.* agent, deputy, estate manager, middleman, reeve, steward

factory manufactory (*Obsolete*), mill, plant, works

factotum Girl Friday, handyman, jack of all trades, Man Friday, man of all work, odd job man

facts data, details, gen (*Inf.*), info (*Inf.*), information, the lowdown (*Inf.*), the score (*Inf.*), the whole story

factual accurate, authentic, circumstantial, close, correct, credible, exact, faithful, genuine, literal, matter-of-fact, objective, precise, real, sure, true, true-to-life, unadorned, unbiased, veritable

faculties capabilities, intelligence, powers, reason, senses, wits

faculty 1. ability, adroitness, aptitude, bent, capability, capacity, cleverness, dexterity, facility, gift, knack, power, propensity, readiness, skill, talent, turn **2**. branch of learning, department, discipline, profession, school, teaching staff (*Chiefly U.S.*) **3**. authorization, licence, prerogative, privilege, right

fad affectation, craze, fancy, fashion, mania, mode, rage, trend, vogue, whim

fade 1. blanch, bleach, blench, dim, discolour, dull, grow dim, lose colour, lose lustre, pale, wash out **2**. decline, die away, die out, dim, disappear, disperse, dissolve, droop, dwindle, ebb, etiolate, evanesce, fail, fall, flag, languish, melt away, perish, shrivel, vanish, vanish into thin air, wane, waste away, wilt, wither

faded bleached, dim, discoloured, dull, etiolated, indistinct, lustreless, pale, washed out

fading declining, decreasing, disappearing, dying, on the decline, vanishing

faeces bodily waste, droppings, dung, excrement, excreta, ordure, stools

fag *n*. bind (*Inf.*), bore, bother, chore, drag (*Sl.*), inconvenience, irritation, nuisance

fagged out all in (*Sl.*), beat (*Sl.*), exhausted, fatigued, jaded, jiggered (*Inf.*), knackered (*Sl.*), on one's last legs (*Inf.*), wasted, weary, worn out

fail 1. be defeated, be found lacking *or* wanting, be in vain, be unsuccessful, break down, come a cropper (*Inf.*), come to grief, come to naught, come to nothing, fall, fall short, fall short of, fall through, fizzle out (*Inf.*), flop (*Inf.*), founder, go astray, go down, go up in smoke (*Inf.*), meet with disaster, miscarry, misfire, miss, not make the grade (*Inf.*), run aground, turn out badly **2**. abandon, break one's word, desert, disappoint, forget, forsake, let down, neglect, omit **3**. be on one's last legs (*Inf.*), cease, conk out (*Inf.*), cut out, decline, die, disappear, droop, dwindle, fade, give out, give up, gutter, languish, peter out, sicken, sink, stop working, wane, weaken

4. become insolvent, close down, crash, fold (*Inf.*), go bankrupt, go broke (*Inf.*), go bust (*Inf.*), go into receivership, go out of business, go to the wall, go under, smash **5. without fail** conscientiously, constantly, dependably, like clockwork, punctually, regularly, religiously, without exception

failing 1. *n.* blemish, blind spot, defect, deficiency, drawback, error, failure, fault, flaw, foible, frailty, imperfection, lapse, miscarriage, misfortune, shortcoming, weakness **2.** *prep.* in default of, in the absence of, lacking

failure 1. abortion, breakdown, collapse, defeat, downfall, fiasco, frustration, lack of success, miscarriage, overthrow, wreck **2.** black sheep, dead duck (*Inf.*), disappointment, dud (*Inf.*), flop (*Inf.*), incompetent, loser, ne'er-do-well, no-good, no-hoper (*Chiefly Aust.*), nonstarter, washout (*Inf.*) **3.** default, deficiency, dereliction, neglect, negligence, nonobservance, nonperformance, nonsuccess, omission, remissness, shortcoming, stoppage **4.** breakdown, decay, decline, deterioration, failing, loss **5.** bankruptcy, crash, downfall, folding (*Inf.*), insolvency, ruin

fain *adv.* **1.** as lief, as soon, cheerfully, eagerly, gladly, willingly ~*adj.* **2.** anxious, eager, glad, well-pleased **3.** compelled, constrained, with no alternative but

faint *adj.* **1.** bleached, delicate, dim, distant, dull, faded, faltering, feeble, hazy, hushed, ill-defined, indistinct, light, low, muffled, muted, soft, subdued, thin, vague, whispered **2.** feeble, remote, slight, unenthusiastic, weak **3.** dizzy, drooping, enervated, exhausted, faltering, fatigued, giddy, languid, lethargic, light-headed, muzzy, vertiginous, weak, woozy (*Inf.*) **4.** faint-hearted, lily-livered, spiritless, timid, timorous ~*v.* **5.** black out, collapse, fade, fail, flake out (*Inf.*), keel over (*Inf.*), languish, lose consciousness, pass out, swoon (*Literary*), weaken ~*n.* **6.** blackout, collapse, swoon (*Literary*), syncope (*Medical*), unconsciousness

faint-hearted diffident, half-hearted, irresolute, timid, timorous, weak

faintly 1. feebly, in a whisper, indistinctly, softly, weakly **2.** a little, dimly, slightly, somewhat

faintness dimness, dizziness, feebleness, giddiness, indistinctness, languor, loss of strength, shakiness, weakness

fair[1] *adj.* **1.** above board, according to the rules, clean, disinterested, dispassionate, equal, equitable, even-handed, honest, honourable, impartial, just, lawful, legitimate, objective, on the level (*Inf.*), proper, square, trustworthy, unbiased, unprejudiced, upright **2.** blond, blonde, fair-haired, flaxen-haired, light, light-complexioned, tow-haired, tow-headed **3.** adequate, all right, average, decent, mediocre, middling, moderate, not bad, O.K. (*Inf.*), passable, reasonable, respectable, satisfactory, so-so (*Inf.*), tolerable **4.** beauteous, beautiful, bonny, comely, handsome, lovely, pretty, well-favoured **5.** bright, clear, clement, cloudless, dry, favourable, fine, sunny, sunshiny, unclouded

fair[2] *n.* bazaar, carnival, expo (*Inf.*), exposition, festival, fête, gala, market, show

fair-and-square above board, correct, honest, just, on the level (*Inf.*), straight

fairly 1. adequately, moderately, pretty well, quite, rather, reasonably, somewhat, tolerably **2.** deservedly, equitably, honestly, impartially, justly, objectively, properly, without fear or favour **3.** absolutely, in a manner of speaking, positively, really, veritably

fair-minded disinterested, even-handed, impartial, just, open-minded, unbiased, unprejudiced

fairness decency, disinterestedness, equitableness, equity, impartiality, justice, legitimacy, rightfulness, uprightness

fairy brownie, elf, hob, leprechaun, pixie, Robin Goodfellow, sprite

fairy tale *or* **fairy story 1.** folk tale, romance **2.** cock-and-bull story (*Inf.*), fabrication, fantasy, fiction, invention, lie, tall story, untruth

faith 1. assurance, confidence, conviction, credence, credit, dependence, reliance, trust **2.** belief, church, communion, creed, denomination, dogma, persuasion, religion **3.** allegiance, constancy, faithfulness, fealty, fidelity, loyalty, truth, truthfulness **4.** *As in* **keep faith, in good faith** honour, pledge, promise, sincerity, vow, word, word of honour

faithful 1. attached, constant, dependable, devoted, loyal, reliable, staunch, steadfast, true, true-blue, trusty, truthful, unswerving, unwavering **2**. accurate, close, exact, just, precise, strict, true **3. the faithful** adherents, believers, brethren, communicants, congregation, followers, the elect

faithfulness 1. adherence, constancy, dependability, devotion, fealty, fidelity, loyalty, trustworthiness **2**. accuracy, closeness, exactness, justice, strictness, truth

faithless disloyal, doubting, false, false-hearted, fickle, inconstant, perfidious, recreant (*Archaic*), traitorous, treacherous, unbelieving, unfaithful, unreliable, untrue, untrustworthy, untruthful

faithlessness betrayal, disloyalty, fickleness, inconstancy, infidelity, perfidy, treachery, unfaithfulness

fake 1. *v.* affect, assume, copy, counterfeit, fabricate, feign, forge, pretend, put on, sham, simulate **2**. *n.* charlatan, copy, forgery, fraud, hoax, imitation, impostor, mountebank, phoney (*Sl.*), reproduction, sham **3**. *adj.* affected, artificial, assumed, counterfeit, false, forged, imitation, mock, phoney (*Sl.*), pinchbeck, pseudo, reproduction, sham

faker fake, fraud, humbug, impostor, phoney (*Sl.*), pretender, sham

fall *v.* **1**. be precipitated, cascade, collapse, crash, descend, dive, drop, drop down, go head over heels, keel over, nose-dive, pitch, plummet, plunge, settle, sink, stumble, subside, topple, trip, trip over, tumble **2**. abate, become lower, decline, decrease, depreciate, diminish, dwindle, ebb, fall off, flag, go down, lessen, slump, subside **3**. be overthrown, be taken, capitulate, give in *or* up, give way, go out of office, pass into enemy hands, resign, succumb, surrender, yield **4**. be a casualty, be killed, be lost, be slain, die, meet one's end, perish **5**. become, befall, chance, come about, come to pass, fall out, happen, occur, take place **6. fall foul of** brush with, come into conflict with, cross swords with, have trouble with, make an enemy of **7. fall in love (with)** become attached to, become enamoured of, become fond of, become infatuated (with), be smitten by, conceive an affection for, fall (for), lose one's heart (to), take a fancy to **8**. fall away, incline, incline downwards, slope **9**. backslide, err, go astray, lapse, offend, sin, transgress, trespass, yield to temptation ~*n.* **10**. de-

scent, dive, drop, nose dive, plummet, plunge, slip, spill, tumble **11**. cut, decline, decrease, diminution, dip, drop, dwindling, falling off, lessening, lowering, reduction, slump **12**. capitulation, collapse, death, defeat, destruction, downfall, failure, overthrow, resignation, ruin, surrender **13**. declivity, descent, downgrade, incline, slant, slope **14**. degradation, failure, lapse, sin, slip, transgression

fallacious deceptive, delusive, delusory, erroneous, false, fictitious, illogical, illusory, incorrect, misleading, mistaken, sophistic, sophistical, spurious, untrue, wrong

fallacy casuistry, deceit, deception, delusion, error, falsehood, faultiness, flaw, illusion, inconsistency, misapprehension, misconception, mistake, sophism, sophistry, untruth

fall apart break up, crumble, disband, disintegrate, disperse, dissolve, fall to bits, go *or* come to pieces, lose cohesion, shatter

fall asleep doze off, drop off (*Inf.*), go to sleep, nod off (*Inf.*)

fall back draw back, recede, recoil, retire, retreat, withdraw

fall back on call upon, employ, have recourse to, make use of, press into service, resort to

fall behind be in arrears, drop back, get left behind, lag, lose one's place, trail

fall down disappoint, fail, fail to make the grade, fall short, go wrong, prove unsuccessful

fallen *adj.* **1**. collapsed, decayed, flat, on the ground, ruinous, sunken **2**. disgraced, dishonoured, immoral, loose, lost, ruined, shamed, sinful, unchaste **3**. dead, killed, lost, perished, slain, slaughtered

fall for 1. become infatuated with, desire, fall in love with, lose one's head over, succumb to the charms of **2**. accept, be deceived (duped, fooled, taken in) by, give credence to, swallow (*Inf.*)

fallible erring, frail, ignorant, imperfect, mortal, prone to error, uncertain, weak

fall in cave in, collapse, come down about one's ears, sink

falling off *n.* deceleration, decline, decrease, deterioration, downward trend, drop, slackening, slowing down, slump, waning, worsening

fall in with accept, agree with, assent, concur with, cooperate with, go along with, support

fall on or **fall upon** assail, assault, attack, descend upon, lay (pitch, tear) into, set upon or about, snatch

fall out 1. altercate, argue, clash, differ, disagree, fight, quarrel, squabble **2.** chance, come to pass, happen, occur, result, take place, turn out

fallow dormant, idle, inactive, inert, resting, uncultivated, undeveloped, unplanted, untilled, unused

falls cascade, cataract, force (*Northern dialect*), linn (*Scot.*), rapids, waterfall

fall short be deficient (lacking, wanting), fail, miss, prove inadequate

fall through come to nothing, fail, fizzle out (*Inf.*), miscarry

fall to 1. apply oneself to, begin, commence, set about, start **2.** be up to, come down to, devolve upon

false 1. concocted, erroneous, faulty, fictitious, improper, inaccurate, incorrect, inexact, invalid, mistaken, unfounded, unreal, wrong **2.** lying, mendacious, truthless, unreliable, unsound, untrue, untrustworthy, untruthful **3.** artificial, bogus, counterfeit, ersatz, fake, feigned, forged, imitation, mock, pretended, sham, simulated, spurious, synthetic **4.** deceitful, deceiving, deceptive, delusive, fallacious, fraudulent, hypocritical, misleading, trumped up **5.** dishonest, dishonourable, disloyal, double-dealing, duplicitous, faithless, false-hearted, hypocritical, perfidious, treacherous, treasonable, two-faced, unfaithful, untrustworthy **6. play (someone) false** betray, cheat, deceive, double-cross, give the Judas kiss to, sell down the river (*Inf.*), stab in the back

falsehood 1. deceit, deception, dishonesty, dissimulation, inveracity (*Rare*), mendacity, perjury, prevarication, untruthfulness **2.** fabrication, fib, fiction, lie, misstatement, story, untruth

falsification adulteration, deceit, dissimulation, distortion, forgery, misrepresentation, perversion, tampering with

falsify alter, belie, cook (*Sl.*), counterfeit, distort, doctor, fake, forge, garble, misrepresent, misstate, pervert, tamper with

falsity 1. deceit, deceptiveness, dishonesty, double-dealing, duplicity, fraudulence, hypocrisy, inaccuracy, mendacity, perfidy, treachery, unreality, untruth **2.** cheating, deception, fraud, lie

falter break, hesitate, shake, speak haltingly, stammer, stumble, stutter, totter, tremble, vacillate, waver

faltering broken, hesitant, irresolute, stammering, tentative, timid, uncertain, weak

fame celebrity, credit, eminence, glory, honour, illustriousness, name, prominence, public esteem, renown, reputation, repute, stardom

famed acclaimed, celebrated, recognized, renowned, widely-known

familiar 1. accustomed, common, common or garden (*Inf.*), conventional, customary, domestic, everyday, frequent, household, mundane, ordinary, recognizable, repeated, routine, stock, well-known **2. familiar with** abreast of, acquainted with, at home with, *au courant, au fait*, aware of, conscious of, conversant with, introduced, knowledgeable, no stranger to, on speaking terms with, versed in, well up in **3.** amicable, chummy (*Inf.*), close, confidential, cordial, easy, free, free-and-easy, friendly, hail-fellow-well-met, informal, intimate, near, open, relaxed, unceremonious, unconstrained, unreserved **4.** bold, disrespectful, forward, impudent, intrusive, overfree, presuming, presumptuous

familiarity 1. acquaintance, acquaintanceship, awareness, experience, grasp, understanding **2.** absence of reserve, closeness, ease, fellowship, freedom, friendliness, friendship, informality, intimacy, naturalness, openness, sociability, unceremoniousness **3.** boldness, disrespect, forwardness, liberties, liberty, presumption

familiarize accustom, bring into common use, coach, get to know (about), habituate, instruct, inure, make conversant, make used to, prime, school, season, train

family 1. brood, children, descendants, folk (*Inf.*), household, issue, kin, kindred, kinsmen, kith and kin, ménage, offspring, one's nearest and dearest, one's own flesh and blood, people, progeny, relations, relatives **2.** ancestors, ancestry, birth, blood, clan, descent, dynasty, extraction, forebears, forefathers, genealogy, house, line, lineage, parentage, pedigree, race, sept, stemma, stirps, strain, tribe **3.** class, classification, genre, group, kind, network, subdivision, system

family tree ancestry, extraction, genealogy, line, lineage, line of descent, pedigree, stemma, stirps

famine dearth, destitution, hunger, scarcity, starvation

famished ravening, ravenous, starved, starving, voracious

famous acclaimed, celebrated, conspicuous, distinguished, eminent, excellent, far-famed, glorious, honoured, illustrious, legendary, lionized, much-publicized, notable, noted, prominent, remarkable, renowned, signal, well-known

fan[1] v. **1.** Often fig. add fuel to the flames, agitate, arouse, enkindle, excite, impassion, increase, provoke, rouse, stimulate, stir up, whip up, work up **2.** air-condition, air-cool, blow, cool, refresh, ventilate, winnow (Rare) ~n. **3.** air conditioner, blade, blower, propeller, punkah (In India), vane, ventilator

fan[2] adherent, admirer, aficionado, buff (Inf.), devotee, enthusiast, fiend (Inf.), follower, freak (Sl.), lover, rooter (U.S.), supporter, zealot

fanatic n. activist, addict, bigot, devotee, enthusiast, extremist, militant, visionary, zealot

fanatical bigoted, burning, enthusiastic, extreme, fervent, frenzied, immoderate, mad, obsessive, overenthusiastic, passionate, rabid, visionary, wild, zealous

fanaticism bigotry, dedication, devotion, enthusiasm, extremism, immoderation, infatuation, madness, monomania, obsessiveness, overenthusiasm, single-mindedness, zeal, zealotry

fancier aficionado, amateur, breeder, connoisseur, expert

fanciful capricious, chimerical, curious, extravagant, fabulous, fairy-tale, fantastic, ideal, imaginary, imaginative, mythical, poetic, romantic, unreal, visionary, whimsical, wild

fancy v. **1.** be inclined to think, believe, conceive, conjecture, guess, imagine, infer, reckon, suppose, surmise, think, think likely **2.** be attracted to, crave, desire, dream of, hanker after, have a yen for, long for, relish, wish for, would like, yearn for **3.** Inf. be attracted to, be captivated by, desire, favour, go for (Inf.), have an eye for, like, lust after,

prefer, take a liking to, take to ~n. **4.** caprice, desire, humour, idea, impulse, inclination, notion, thought, urge, whim **5.** fondness, hankering, inclination, liking, partiality, predilection, preference, relish **6.** conception, image, imagination, impression **7.** chimera, daydream, delusion, dream, fantasy, nightmare, phantasm, vision ~adj. **8.** baroque, decorated, decorative, elaborate, elegant, embellished, extravagant, fanciful, intricate, ornamental, ornamented, ornate **9.** capricious, chimerical, delusive, fanciful, fantastic, far-fetched, illusory, whimsical

fanfare ballyhoo, fanfaronade, flourish, trump (Archaic), trumpet call, tucket (Archaic)

fang tooth, tusk

fan out disperse, lay out, open out, space out, spread, spread out, unfurl

fantastic 1. comical, eccentric, exotic, fanciful, freakish, grotesque, imaginative, odd, outlandish, peculiar, phantasmagorical, quaint, queer, rococo, strange, unreal, weird, whimsical **2.** ambitious, chimerical, extravagant, far-fetched, grandiose, illusory, ludicrous, ridiculous, unrealistic, visionary, wild **3.** absurd, capricious, implausible, incredible, irrational, mad, preposterous, unlikely **4.** Inf. enormous, extreme, great, overwhelming, severe, tremendous **5.** Inf. excellent, first-rate, marvellous, out of this world (Inf.), sensational, superb, wonderful

fantasize build castles in the air, daydream, dream, envision, give free rein to the imagination, hallucinate, imagine, invent, live in a dream world, romance, see visions

fantasy, phantasy 1. creativity, fancy, imagination, invention, originality **2.** apparition, daydream, delusion, dream, fancy, figment of the imagination, flight of fancy, hallucination, illusion, mirage, nightmare, pipe dream, reverie, vision

far adv. **1.** afar, a good way, a great distance, a long way, deep, miles **2.** considerably, decidedly, extremely, greatly, incomparably, much, very much **3. by far** by a long chalk (Inf.), by a long shot, by a long way, easily, far and away, immeasurably, incomparably, to a great degree, very much **4. far and wide** broadly, everywhere, extensively, far and near, here, there, and everywhere, widely, worldwide **5. so far** thus far, to date, until now, up to now, up to the present ~*adj.* **6.** distant, faraway, far-flung, far-off, far-removed, long, outlying, out-of-the-way, remote, removed

faraway 1. beyond the horizon, distant, far, far-flung, far-off, far-removed, outlying, remote **2.** absent, abstracted, distant, dreamy, lost

farce 1. broad comedy, buffoonery, burlesque, comedy, satire, slapstick **2.** absurdity, joke, mockery, nonsense, parody, ridiculousness, sham, travesty

farcical absurd, amusing, comic, custard-pie, derisory, diverting, droll, funny, laughable, ludicrous, nonsensical, preposterous, ridiculous, risible, slapstick

fare *n.* **1.** charge, passage money, price, ticket money, transport cost **2.** passenger, pick-up (*Inf.*), traveller **3.** commons, diet, eatables, food, meals, menu, provisions, rations, sustenance, table, victuals ~*v.* **4.** do, get along, get on, make out, manage, prosper **5.** *Used impersonally* go, happen, proceed, turn out

farewell adieu, adieux *or* adieus, departure, goodbye, leave-taking, parting, sendoff (*Inf.*), valediction

far-fetched doubtful, dubious, fantastic, hard to swallow (*Inf.*), implausible, improbable, incredible, preposterous, strained, unbelievable, unconvincing, unlikely, unnatural, unrealistic

farm 1. *n.* acreage, acres, croft (*Scot.*), farmstead, grange, holding, homestead, land, plantation, ranch (*Chiefly North American*), smallholding, station (*Aust. & New Zealand*) **2.** *v.* bring under cultivation, cultivate, operate, plant, practise husbandry, till the soil, work

farmer agriculturist, agronomist, husbandman, smallholder, yeoman

farming agriculture, agronomy, husbandry

far-out advanced, avant-garde, bizarre, outlandish, outré, unconventional, weird, wild

farrago gallimaufry, hash, hodgepodge, hotchpotch, jumble, medley, *mélange*, miscellany, mishmash, mixed bag, mixture, potpourri, salmagundi

far-reaching broad, extensive, important, momentous, pervasive, significant, sweeping, widespread

far-sighted acute, canny, cautious, discerning, far-seeing, judicious, politic,

prescient, provident, prudent, sage, shrewd, wise

fascinate absorb, allure, beguile, bewitch, captivate, charm, delight, enamour, enchant, engross, enrapture, enravish, enthral, entrance, hold spellbound, hypnotize, infatuate, intrigue, mesmerize, rivet, spellbind, transfix

fascinated absorbed, beguiled, bewitched, captivated, charmed, engrossed, enthralled, entranced, hooked on, hypnotized, infatuated, smitten, spellbound, under a spell

fascinating alluring, bewitching, captivating, compelling, enchanting, engaging, engrossing, enticing, gripping, intriguing, irresistible, ravishing, riveting, seductive

fascination allure, attraction, charm, enchantment, glamour, lure, magic, magnetism, pull, sorcery, spell

fashion *n.* **1.** convention, craze, custom, fad, latest, latest style, look, mode, prevailing taste, rage, style, trend, usage, vogue **2.** attitude, demeanour, manner, method, mode, style, way **3.** appearance, configuration, cut, figure, form, guise (*Archaic*), line, make, model, mould, pattern, shape **4.** description, kind, sort, type **5.** beau monde, fashionable society, high society, jet set **6. after a fashion** in a manner of speaking, in a way, moderately, somehow, somehow or other, to a degree, to some extent ~*v.* **7.** construct, contrive, create, design, forge, form, make, manufacture, mould, shape, work **8.** accommodate, adapt, adjust, fit, suit, tailor

fashionable à la mode, all the go (*Inf.*), all the rage, chic, current, customary, genteel, in (*Inf.*), in vogue, latest, modern, modish, popular, prevailing, smart, stylish, trendsetting, trendy (*Inf.*), up-to-date, up-to-the-minute, usual, with it (*Inf.*)

fast¹ *adj.* **1.** accelerated, brisk, fleet, flying, hasty, hurried, mercurial, nippy (*Inf.*), quick, rapid, speedy, swift, winged ~*adv.* **2.** apace, hastily, hell for leather, hurriedly, in haste, like a bat out of hell (*Inf.*), like a flash, like a shot (*Inf.*), posthaste, presto, quickly, rapidly, speedily, swiftly, with all haste ~*adj.* **3.** close, constant, fastened, firm, fixed, fortified, immovable, impregnable, lasting, loyal, permanent, secure, sound, staunch, steadfast, tight, unwavering ~*adv.* **4.**

deeply, firmly, fixedly, securely, soundly, tightly ~*adj.* **5.** dissipated, dissolute, extravagant, gadabout, giddy, immoral, intemperate, licentious, loose, profligate, promiscuous, rakish, reckless, self-indulgent, wanton, wild ~*adv.* **6.** extravagantly, intemperately, loosely, promiscuously, rakishly, recklessly, wildly **7. pull a fast one** bamboozle (*Inf.*), cheat, con (*Sl.*), deceive, defraud, hoodwink, put one over on (*Inf.*), swindle, take advantage of, take for a ride (*Inf.*), trick

fast[2] **1.** *v.* abstain, deny oneself, go hungry, go without food, practise abstention, refrain from food *or* eating **2.** *n.* abstinence, fasting

fasten 1. affix, anchor, attach, bind, bolt, chain, connect, fix, grip, join, lace, link, lock, make fast, make firm, seal, secure, tie, unite **2.** *Fig.* aim, bend, concentrate, direct, fix, focus, rivet

fastidious choosy, critical, dainty, difficult, discriminating, finicky, fussy, hard to please, hypercritical, meticulous, overdelicate, overnice, particular, pernickety, punctilious, squeamish

fat *adj.* **1.** beefy (*Inf.*), broad in the beam (*Inf.*), corpulent, elephantine, fleshy, gross, heavy, obese, overweight, plump, podgy, portly, roly-poly, rotund, solid, stout, tubby **2.** adipose, fatty, greasy, oily, oleaginous, suety **3.** affluent, cushy (*Sl.*), fertile, flourishing, fruitful, jammy (*Sl.*), lucrative, lush, productive, profitable, prosperous, remunerative, rich, thriving ~*n.* **4.** adipose tissue, blubber, bulk, cellulite, corpulence, fatness, flab, flesh, obesity, overweight, paunch, weight problem

fatal 1. deadly, destructive, final, incurable, killing, lethal, malignant, mortal, pernicious, terminal **2.** baleful, baneful, calamitous, catastrophic, disastrous, lethal, ruinous **3.** critical, crucial, decisive, destined, determining, doomed, fateful, final, foreordained, inevitable, predestined

fatalism acceptance, determinism, necessitarianism, passivity, predestinarianism, resignation, stoicism

fatality casualty, deadliness, death, disaster, fatal accident, lethalness, loss, mortality

fate 1. chance, destiny, divine will, fortune, kismet, nemesis, predestination, providence, weird (*Archaic*) **2.** cup, fortune, horoscope, lot, portion, stars **3.**
end, future, issue, outcome, upshot **4.** death, destruction, doom, downfall, end, ruin

fated destined, doomed, foreordained, ineluctable, inescapable, inevitable, marked down, predestined, pre-elected, preordained, sure, written

fateful 1. critical, crucial, decisive, important, portentous, significant **2.** deadly, destructive, disastrous, fatal, lethal, ominous, ruinous

Fates Providence, the Norns, the Three Sisters, the Weird Sisters

fathead ass, booby, dimwit, dope (*Sl.*), dunderhead, fool, goose, idiot, imbecile, jackass, nincompoop, nitwit, numskull, twerp (*Inf.*), twit (*Inf.*)

father *n.* **1.** begetter, dad (*Inf.*), daddy (*Inf.*), governor (*Inf.*), old boy (*Inf.*), old man (*Inf.*), pa (*Inf.*), pater, paterfamilias, patriarch, pop (*Inf.*), sire **2.** ancestor, forebear, forefather, predecessor, progenitor **3.** architect, author, creator, founder, inventor, maker, originator, prime mover **4.** city father, elder, leader, patriarch, patron, senator **5.** abbé, confessor, curé, padre (*Inf.*), pastor, priest ~*v.* **6.** beget, get, procreate, sire **7.** create, engender, establish, found, institute, invent, originate

fatherland homeland, land of one's birth, land of one's fathers, motherland, native land, old country

fatherly affectionate, benevolent, benign, forbearing, indulgent, kind, kindly, paternal, patriarchal, protective, supportive, tender

fathom 1. divine, estimate, gauge, measure, penetrate, plumb, probe, sound **2.** comprehend, get to the bottom of, grasp, interpret, understand

fathomless abysmal, bottomless, deep, immeasurable, impenetrable, incomprehensible, profound, unfathomable, unplumbed

fatigue 1. *v.* drain, drain of energy, exhaust, fag (out) (*Inf.*), jade, overtire, take it out of (*Inf.*), tire, weaken, wear out, weary, whack (*Inf.*) **2.** *n.* debility, ennui, heaviness, languor, lethargy, listlessness, overtiredness, tiredness

fatigued all in (*Sl.*), bushed (*Inf.*, *Chiefly North American*), dead beat (*Inf.*), exhausted, fagged (out) (*Inf.*), jaded, jiggered (*Inf.*), knackered (*Sl.*), overtired, tired, tired out, wasted, weary, whacked (*Inf.*)

fatness bulkiness, corpulence, *embonpoint*, flab, flesh, fleshiness, girth, grossness, heaviness, obesity, overweight, podginess, rotundity, size, stoutness, weight, weight problem

fatten 1. broaden, coarsen, expand, gain weight, grow fat, put on weight, spread, swell, thicken, thrive **2.** *Often with* **up** bloat, build up, cram, distend, feed, feed up, nourish, overfeed, stuff

fatty adipose, fat, greasy, oily, oleaginous, rich

fatuity absurdity, brainlessness, daftness (*Inf.*), denseness, fatuousness, folly, foolishness, idiocy, imbecility, insanity, ludicrousness, lunacy, mindlessness, stupidity

fatuous absurd, asinine, brainless, dense, dull, foolish, idiotic, inane, ludicrous, lunatic, mindless, moronic, puerile, silly, stupid, vacuous, weak-minded, witless

fault n. **1.** blemish, defect, deficiency, drawback, failing, flaw, imperfection, infirmity, lack, shortcoming, snag, weakness, weak point **2.** blunder, boob (*Sl.*), error, error of judgment, inaccuracy, indiscretion, lapse, mistake, negligence, offence, omission, oversight, slip, slip-up **3.** accountability, culpability, liability, responsibility **4.** delinquency, frailty, lapse, misconduct, misdeed, misdemeanour, offence, peccadillo, sin, transgression, trespass, wrong **5. at fault** answerable, blamable, culpable, guilty, in the wrong, responsible, to blame **6. find fault with** carp at, complain, criticize, pick holes in, pull to pieces, quibble, take to task **7. to a fault** excessively, immoderately, in the extreme, needlessly, out of all proportion, overly (*U.S.*), overmuch, preposterously, ridiculously, unduly ~v. **8.** blame, call to account, censure, criticize, find fault with, find lacking, hold (someone) accountable (responsible, to blame), impugn

fault-finding 1. *n.* carping, hairsplitting, nagging, niggling, nit-picking (*Inf.*) **2.** *adj.* captious, carping, censorious, critical, hypercritical, pettifogging

faultless 1. accurate, classic, correct, exemplary, faithful, flawless, foolproof, impeccable, model, perfect, unblemished **2.** above reproach, blameless, guiltless, immaculate, innocent, irreproachable, pure, sinless, spotless, stainless, unblemished, unspotted, unsullied

faulty bad, blemished, broken, damaged, defective, erroneous, fallacious, flawed, impaired, imperfect, imprecise, inaccurate, incorrect, invalid, malfunctioning, not working, out of order, unsound, weak, wrong

faux pas blunder, boob (*Sl.*), breach of etiquette, clanger (*Inf.*), gaffe, gaucherie, impropriety, indiscretion, solecism

favour n. **1.** approbation, approval, backing, bias, championship, esteem, favouritism, friendliness, good opinion, good will, grace, kindness, kind regard, partiality, patronage, support **2.** benefit, boon, courtesy, good turn, indulgence, kindness, obligement (*Scot. or Archaic*), service **3. in favour of** all for (*Inf.*), backing, for, on the side of, pro, supporting, to the benefit of **4.** gift, keepsake, love-token, memento, present, souvenir, token **5.** badge, decoration, knot, ribbons, rosette ~v. **6.** be partial to, esteem, have in one's good books, indulge, pamper, pull strings for (*Inf.*), reward, side with, smile upon, spoil, treat with partiality, value **7.** advocate, approve, back, be in favour of, champion, choose, commend, countenance, encourage, fancy, incline towards, like, opt for, patronize, prefer, single out, support **8.** abet, accommodate, advance, aid, assist, befriend, do a kindness to, facilitate, help, oblige, promote, succour **9.** *Inf.* be the image or picture of, look like, resemble, take after **10.** ease, extenuate, spare

favourable 1. advantageous, appropriate, auspicious, beneficial, convenient, encouraging, fair, fit, good, helpful, hopeful, opportune, promising, propitious, suitable, timely **2.** affirmative, agreeable, amicable, approving, benign, encouraging, enthusiastic, friendly, kind, positive, reassuring, sympathetic, understanding, welcoming, well-disposed

favourably 1. advantageously, auspiciously, conveniently, fortunately, opportunely, profitably, to one's advantage, well **2.** agreeably, approvingly, enthusiastically, genially, graciously, helpfully, in a kindly manner, positively, with approval (approbation, cordiality), without prejudice

favoured 1. best-liked, chosen, favourite, pet, preferred, recommended, selected, singled out **2.** advantaged, blessed, elite, lucky, privileged

favourite 1. *adj.* best-loved, choice, dearest, esteemed, preferred **2.** *n.* beloved, blue-eyed boy (*Inf.*), choice, darling, dear, idol, pet, pick, preference, teacher's pet, the apple of one's eye

favouritism bias, jobs for the boys (*Inf.*), nepotism, one-sidedness, partiality, partisanship, preference, preferential treatment

fawn[1] *adj.* beige, buff, greyish-brown, neutral

fawn[2] *v. Often with* **on** *or* **upon** be obsequious, be servile, bow and scrape, court, crawl, creep, cringe, curry favour, dance attendance, flatter, grovel, ingratiate oneself, kneel, kowtow, lick (someone's) boots, pay court, toady, truckle

fawning abject, bootlicking (*Inf.*), bowing and scraping, crawling, cringing, deferential, flattering, grovelling, obsequious, prostrate, servile, slavish, sycophantic

fealty allegiance, devotion, faith, faithfulness, fidelity, homage, loyalty, obeisance, submission

fear *n.* **1.** alarm, apprehensiveness, awe, blue funk (*Inf.*), consternation, cravenness, dismay, dread, fright, horror, panic, qualms, terror, timidity, tremors, trepidation **2.** *bête noire*, bogey, bugbear, horror, nightmare, phobia, spectre **3.** agitation, anxiety, apprehension, concern, disquietude, distress, doubt, foreboding(s), misgiving(s), solicitude, suspicion, unease, uneasiness, worry **4.** awe, reverence, veneration, wonder ~*v.* **5.** apprehend, be apprehensive (afraid, frightened, scared), be in a blue funk (*Inf.*), dare not, dread, have a horror of, have a phobia about, have butterflies in one's stomach (*Inf.*), have qualms, live in dread of, shake in one's shoes, shudder at, take fright, tremble at **6.** anticipate, apprehend, be afraid, expect, foresee, suspect **7.** *With* **for** be anxious (concerned, distressed) about, be disquieted over, feel concern for, tremble for, worry about **8.** respect, revere, reverence, stand in awe of, venerate

fearful 1. afraid, alarmed, anxious, apprehensive, diffident, faint-hearted, frightened, hesitant, intimidated, jittery (*Inf.*), jumpy, nervous, nervy, panicky, pusillanimous, scared, shrinking, tense, timid, timorous, uneasy **2.** appalling, atrocious, awful, dire, distressing, dreadful, frightful, ghastly, grievous, grim, gruesome, hair-raising, hideous, horrendous, horrible, horrific, monstrous, shocking, terrible, unspeakable

fearfully 1. apprehensively, diffidently, in fear and trembling, nervously, timidly, timorously, uneasily, with many misgivings *or* forebodings, with one's heart in one's mouth **2.** awfully, exceedingly, excessively, frightfully, terribly, tremendously, very

fearless bold, brave, confident, courageous, daring, dauntless, doughty, gallant, game (*Inf.*), gutsy (*Sl.*), heroic, indomitable, intrepid, lion-hearted, plucky, unabashed, unafraid, undaunted, unflinching, valiant, valorous

fearlessness boldness, bravery, confidence, courage, dauntlessness, guts (*Inf.*), indomitability, intrepidity, lion-heartedness, nerve, pluckiness

fearsome alarming, appalling, awe-inspiring, awesome, awful, daunting, dismaying, formidable, frightening, hair-raising, horrendous, horrifying, menacing, unnerving

feasibility expediency, practicability, usefulness, viability, workability

feasible achievable, attainable, likely, possible, practicable, realizable, reasonable, viable, workable

feast *n.* **1.** banquet, barbecue, beanfeast (*Brit. inf.*), beano (*Brit. sl.*), blowout (*Sl.*), carousal, carouse, dinner, entertainment, festive board, jollification, junket, repast, revels, slap-up meal (*Brit. inf.*), spread (*Inf.*), treat **2.** celebration, festival, fête, gala day, holiday, holy day, saint's day **3.** delight, enjoyment, gratification, pleasure, treat ~*v.* **4.** eat one's fill, eat to one's heart's content, fare sumptuously, gorge, gormandize, indulge, overindulge, stuff, stuff one's face (*Sl.*), wine and dine **5.** entertain, hold a reception for, kill the fatted calf for, regale, treat, wine and dine **6.** delight, gladden, gratify, rejoice, thrill

feat accomplishment, achievement, act, attainment, deed, exploit, performance

feathers down, plumage, plumes

feathery downy, feathered, fluffy, plumate *or* plumose (*Bot. & Zool.*), plumed, plumy, wispy

feature *n.* **1.** aspect, attribute, characteristic, facet, factor, hallmark, mark, peculiarity, point, property, quality, trait **2.** attraction, crowd puller (*Inf.*), draw, highlight, innovation, main item, special, special attraction, speciality, specialty **3.** article, column, comment, item, piece, report, story ~*v.* **4.** accentuate, call attention to, emphasize, give prominence to, give the full works (*Sl.*), headline, play up, present, promote, set off, spotlight, star

featured given prominence, headlined, highlighted, in the public eye, presented, promoted, recommended, specially presented, starred

features countenance, face, lineaments, physiognomy

featuring calling attention to, displaying, drawing attention to, giving a star role, giving prominence to, giving the full works (*Sl.*), highlighting, making the main attraction, presenting, promoting, pushing, recommending, showing, showing off, starring, turning the spotlight on

febrile delirious, fevered, feverish, fiery, flushed, hot, inflamed, pyretic (*Medical*)

feckless aimless, feeble, futile, hopeless, incompetent, ineffectual, irresponsible, shiftless, useless, weak, worthless

fecund fertile, fructiferous, fruitful, productive, prolific, teeming

fecundity fertility, fructiferousness, fruitfulness, productiveness

federate *v.* amalgamate, associate, combine, confederate, integrate, syndicate, unify, unite

federation alliance, amalgamation, association, *Bund*, coalition, combination, confederacy, copartnership, entente, federacy, league, syndicate, union

fed up (with) annoyed, blue, bored, brassed off (*Inf.*), browned-off (*Inf.*), depressed, discontented, dismal, dissatisfied, down, gloomy, glum, sick and tired of (*Inf.*), tired of, weary of

fee account, bill, charge, compensation, emolument, hire, honorarium, pay, payment, recompense, remuneration, reward, toll

feeble 1. debilitated, delicate, doddering, effete, enervated, enfeebled, etiolated, exhausted, failing, faint, frail, infirm, languid, powerless, puny, shilpit (*Scot.*), sickly, weak, weakened **2.** flat, flimsy, inadequate, incompetent, indecisive, ineffective, ineffectual, inefficient, insignificant, insufficient, lame, paltry, poor, slight, tame, thin, unconvincing, weak

feeble-minded addle-pated, bone-headed (*Sl.*), deficient, dim-witted (*Inf.*), dull, dumb (*Inf.*), half-witted, idiotic, imbecilic, lacking, moronic, retarded, simple, slow on the uptake, slow-witted, soft in the head (*Inf.*), stupid, vacant, weak-minded

feebleness 1. debility, delicacy, effeteness, enervation, etiolation, exhaustion, frailness, frailty, incapacity, infirmity, lack of strength, languor, lassitude, sickliness, weakness **2.** flimsiness, inadequacy, incompetence, indecisiveness, ineffectualness, insignificance, insufficiency, lameness, weakness

feed *v.* **1.** cater for, nourish, provide for, provision, supply, sustain, victual, wine and dine **2.** *Sometimes with* on devour, eat, exist on, fare, graze, live on, nurture, partake of, pasture, subsist, take nourishment **3.** augment, bolster, encourage, foster, fuel, minister to, strengthen, supply ~*n.* **4.** fodder, food, forage, pasturage, provender, silage **5.** *Inf.* feast, meal, nosh (*Sl.*), nosh-up (*Brit. sl.*), repast, spread (*Inf.*), tuck-in (*Inf.*)

feel *v.* **1.** caress, finger, fondle, handle, manipulate, maul, paw, run one's hands over, stroke, touch **2.** be aware of, be sensible of, endure, enjoy, experience, go through, have, have a sensation of, know, notice, observe, perceive, suffer, take to heart, undergo **3.** explore, fumble, grope, sound, test, try **4.** be convinced, feel in one's bones, have a hunch, have the impression, intuit, sense **5.** believe, be of the opinion that, consider, deem, hold, judge, think **6.** appear, resemble, seem, strike one as **7.** *With* **for** be moved by, be sorry for, bleed for, commiserate, compassionate, condole with, empathize, feel compassion for, pity, sympathize with **8.** **feel like** could do with, desire, fancy, feel inclined, feel the need for, feel up to, have the inclination, want ~*n.* **9.** finish, surface, texture, touch **10.** air, ambience, atmosphere, feeling, impression, quality, sense, vibes (*Inf.*)

feeler 1. antenna, tentacle, whisker **2.** advance, approach, probe, trial balloon

feeling 1. feel, perception, sensation, sense, sense of touch, touch **2.** apprehension, consciousness, hunch, idea, impression, inkling, notion, presentiment, sense, suspicion **3.** affection, ardour, emotion, fervour, fondness, heat, intensity, passion, sentiment, sentimentality, warmth **4**. appreciation, compassion, concern, empathy, pity, sensibility, sensitivity, sympathy, understanding **5**. inclination, instinct, opinion, point of view, view **6**. air, ambience, atmosphere, aura, feel, mood, quality **7**. **bad feeling** anger, dislike, distrust, enmity, hostility, upset

feelings ego, emotions, self-esteem, sensitivities, susceptibilities

feign act, affect, assume, counterfeit, devise, dissemble, fabricate, fake, forge, give the appearance of, imitate, make a show of, pretend, put on, sham, simulate

feigned affected, artificial, assumed, counterfeit, fabricated, fake, false, imitation, insincere, pretended, pseudo (*Inf.*), sham, simulated, spurious

feint *n*. artifice, blind, bluff, distraction, dodge, expedient, gambit, manoeuvre, mock attack, play, pretence, ruse, stratagem, subterfuge, wile

felicitate compliment, congratulate, wish joy to

felicitous apposite, appropriate, apropos, apt, fitting, happy, inspired, neat, opportune, pat, propitious, suitable, timely, well-chosen, well-timed

felicity 1. blessedness, bliss, blissfulness, delectation, ecstasy, happiness, joy **2**. applicability, appropriateness, aptness, becomingness, effectiveness, grace, propriety, suitability, suitableness

feline 1. catlike, leonine **2**. graceful, sinuous, sleek, slinky, smooth, stealthy

fell[1] *v*. cut, cut down, demolish, flatten, floor, hew, knock down, level, prostrate, raze, strike down

fell[2] *adj*. **1**. barbarous, bloody, cruel, ferocious, fierce, grim, implacable, inhuman, malicious, malignant, merciless, pitiless, relentless, ruthless, sanguinary, savage, vicious **2**. baneful, deadly, destructive, fatal, malign, mortal, noxious, pernicious, pestilential, ruinous

fellow *n*. **1**. bloke (*Inf.*), boy, chap (*Inf.*), character, customer (*Inf.*), guy (*Inf.*), individual, man, person **2**. associate, colleague, companion, compeer, comrade, co-worker, equal, friend, member, partner, peer **3**. brother, counterpart, double, duplicate, match, mate, twin ~*adj*. **4**. affiliated, akin, allied, associate, associated, co-, like, related, similar

fellow feeling compassion, empathy, sympathy, understanding

fellowship 1. amity, brotherhood, camaraderie, communion, companionability, companionship, familiarity, fraternization, intercourse, intimacy, kindliness, sociability **2**. association, brotherhood, club, fraternity, guild, league, order, sisterhood, society, sodality

feminine 1. delicate, gentle, girlish, graceful, ladylike, modest, soft, tender, womanly **2**. effeminate, effete, unmanly, unmasculine, weak, womanish

femininity delicacy, feminineness, gentleness, girlishness, muliebrity, softness, womanhood, womanliness

femme fatale charmer, Circe, enchantress, seductress, siren, vamp (*Inf.*)

fen bog, holm (*Dialect*), marsh, morass, moss (*Scot.*), quagmire, slough, swamp

fence *n*. **1**. barbed wire, barricade, barrier, defence, guard, hedge, paling, palisade, railings, rampart, shield, stockade, wall **2**. **on the fence** between two stools, irresolute, uncertain, uncommitted, undecided, vacillating ~*v*. **3**. *Often with* **in** *or* **off** bound, circumscribe, confine, coop, defend, encircle, enclose, fortify, guard, hedge, pen, protect, restrict, secure, separate, surround **4**. beat about the bush, cavil, dodge, equivocate, evade, hedge, parry, prevaricate, quibble, shift, stonewall, tergiversate

fencing *Fig.* beating about the bush, double talk, equivocation, evasiveness, hedging, parrying, prevarication, quibbling, stonewalling, tergiversation, weasel words (*Inf., chiefly U.S.*)

fend for look after, make do, make provision for, provide for, shift for, support, sustain, take care of

fend off avert, beat off, deflect, drive back, hold *or* keep at bay, keep off, parry, repel, repulse, resist, stave off, turn aside, ward off

feral 1. unbroken, uncultivated, undomesticated, untamed, wild **2**. bestial, brutal, fell, ferocious, fierce, savage, vicious

ferment *v*. **1**. boil, brew, bubble, concoct, effervesce, foam, froth, heat, leaven, rise, seethe, work ~*n*. **2**. bacteria, barm, fermentation agent, leaven, leavening, mother, mother-of-vinegar, yeast ~*v*. **3**. *Fig.* agitate, boil, excite, fester, foment, heat, incite, inflame, provoke, rouse, seethe, smoulder, stir up ~*n*. **4**. *Fig.* agitation, brouhaha, commotion, disruption, excitement, fever, frenzy, furore, glow, heat, hubbub, imbroglio, state of unrest, stew, stir, tumult, turbulence, turmoil, unrest, uproar

ferocious 1. feral, fierce, predatory, rapacious, ravening, savage, violent, wild **2.** barbaric, barbarous, bloodthirsty, brutal, brutish, cruel, merciless, pitiless, relentless, ruthless, tigerish, vicious

ferocity barbarity, bloodthirstiness, brutality, cruelty, ferociousness, fierceness, inhumanity, rapacity, ruthlessness, savageness, savagery, viciousness, wildness

ferret out bring to light, dig up, disclose, discover, drive out, elicit, get at, nose out, root out, run to earth, search out, smell out, trace, track down, unearth

ferry 1. *n.* ferryboat, packet, packet boat **2.** *v.* carry, chauffeur, convey, run, ship, shuttle, transport

fertile abundant, fat, fecund, flowering, flowing with milk and honey, fruit-bearing, fruitful, generative, luxuriant, plenteous, plentiful, productive, prolific, rich, teeming, yielding

fertility abundance, fecundity, fruitfulness, luxuriance, productiveness, richness

fertilization 1. implantation, impregnation, insemination, pollination, procreation, propagation **2.** dressing, manuring, mulching, top dressing

fertilize 1. fecundate, fructify, impregnate, inseminate, make fruitful, make pregnant, pollinate **2.** compost, dress, enrich, feed, manure, mulch, top-dress

fertilizer compost, dressing, dung, guano, manure, marl

fervent, fervid animated, ardent, devout, eager, earnest, ecstatic, emotional, enthusiastic, excited, fiery, heartfelt, impassioned, intense, perfervid (*Literary*), vehement, warm, zealous

fervour animation, ardour, eagerness, earnestness, enthusiasm, excitement, fervency, intensity, passion, vehemence, warmth, zeal

fester 1. become inflamed, decay, gather, maturate, putrefy, suppurate, ulcerate **2.** *Fig.* aggravate, chafe, gall, intensify, irk, rankle, smoulder

festering 1. gathering, inflamed, maturating, poisonous, purulent, pussy, septic, suppurating, ulcerated **2.** black-hearted, smouldering, venomous, vicious, virulent

festival 1. anniversary, commemoration, feast, fête, fiesta, holiday, holy day, saint's day **2.** carnival, celebration, entertainment, festivities, fête, field day, gala, jubilee, treat

festive back-slapping, carnival, celebratory, cheery, Christmassy, convivial, festal, gala, gay, gleeful, happy, hearty, holiday, jolly, jovial, joyful, joyous, jubilant, light-hearted, merry, mirthful, sportive

festivity 1. amusement, conviviality, fun, gaiety, jollification, joviality, joyfulness, merriment, merrymaking, mirth, pleasure, revelry, sport **2.** *Often plural* carousal, celebration, entertainment, festival, festive event, festive proceedings, fun and games, jollification, party

festoon 1. *n.* chaplet, garland, lei, swag, swathe, wreath **2.** *v.* array, bedeck, beribbon, deck, decorate, drape, garland, hang, swathe, wreathe

fetch 1. bring, carry, conduct, convey, deliver, escort, get, go for, lead, obtain, retrieve, transport **2.** draw forth, elicit, give rise to, produce **3.** bring in, earn, go for, make, realize, sell for, yield

fetching alluring, attractive, captivating, charming, cute, enchanting, enticing, fascinating, intriguing, sweet, taking, winsome

fetch up arrive, come, end up, finish up, halt, land, reach, stop, turn up

fête, fete 1. *n.* bazaar, fair, festival, gala, garden party, sale of work **2.** *v.* bring out the red carpet for (someone), entertain regally, hold a reception for (someone), honour, kill the fatted calf for (someone), lionize, make much of, treat, wine and dine

fetid corrupt, foul, malodorous, mephitic, noisome, noxious, offensive, rancid, rank, reeking, stinking

fetish 1. amulet, cult object, talisman **2.** fixation, *idée fixe*, mania, obsession, thing (*Inf.*)

fetter *v.* bind, chain, confine, curb, encumber, gyve (*Archaic*), hamper, hamstring, hobble, hold captive, manacle, put a straitjacket on, restrain, restrict, shackle, tie, tie up, trammel

fetters *n.* **1.** bilboes, bonds, chains, gyves (*Archaic*), irons, leg irons, manacles, shackles **2.** bondage, captivity, check, curb, hindrance, obstruction, restraint

feud 1. *n.* argument, bad blood, bickering, broil, conflict, contention, disagreement, discord, dissension, enmity, estrangement, faction, falling out, grudge, hostility, quarrel, rivalry, strife, vendetta **2.** *v.* be at daggers drawn, be at odds, bicker, brawl, clash, contend, dispute, duel, fall out, quarrel, row, squabble, war

fever *Fig.* agitation, delirium, ecstasy, excitement, ferment, fervour, flush, frenzy, heat, intensity, passion, restlessness, turmoil, unrest

fevered burning, feverish, flushed, hectic, hot, on fire, pyretic (*Medical*)

feverish 1. burning, febrile, fevered, flushed, hectic, hot, inflamed, pyretic (*Medical*) **2.** agitated, distracted, excited, frantic, frenetic, frenzied, impatient, obsessive, overwrought, restless

few *adj.* **1.** hardly any, inconsiderable, infrequent, insufficient, meagre, negligible, not many, rare, scant, scanty, scarce, scarcely any, scattered, sparse, sporadic, thin **2. few and far between** at great intervals, hard to come by, infrequent, in short supply, irregular, rare, scarce, scattered, seldom met with, uncommon, unusual, widely spaced ~*pron.* **3.** handful, scarcely any, scattering, small number, some

fiancé, fiancée betrothed, intended, prospective spouse, wife- *or* husband-to-be

fiasco catastrophe, debacle, disaster, failure, flap (*Inf.*), mess, rout, ruin, washout (*Inf.*)

fiat 1. authorization, permission, sanction, warrant **2.** command, decree, dictate, dictum, edict, mandate, order, ordinance, precept, proclamation, ukase

fib *n.* fiction, lie, prevarication, story, untruth, white lie, whopper (*Inf.*)

fibre 1. fibril, filament, pile, staple, strand, texture, thread **2.** *Fig.* essence, nature, quality, spirit, substance **3.** *Fig., as in* **moral fibre** resolution, stamina, strength, strength of character, toughness

fickle blowing hot and cold, capricious, changeable, faithless, fitful, flighty, inconstant, irresolute, mercurial, mutable, quicksilver, unfaithful, unpredictable, unstable, unsteady, vacillating, variable, volatile

fickleness capriciousness, fitfulness, flightiness, inconstancy, mutability, unfaithfulness, unpredictability, unsteadiness, volatility

fiction 1. fable, fantasy, legend, myth, novel, romance, story, storytelling, tale, work of imagination, yarn (*Inf.*) **2.** cock and bull story (*Inf.*), concoction, fabrication, falsehood, fancy, fantasy, figment of the imagination, imagination, improvisation, invention, lie, tall story, untruth

fictional imaginary, invented, legendary, made-up, nonexistent, unreal

fictitious apocryphal, artificial, assumed, bogus, counterfeit, fabricated, false, fanciful, feigned, imaginary, imagined, improvised, invented, made-up, make-believe, mythical, spurious, unreal, untrue

fiddle *v.* **1.** *Often with* **with** fidget, finger, interfere with, mess about *or* around, play, tamper with, tinker, toy, trifle **2.** *Inf.* cheat, cook the books, diddle (*Inf.*), finagle (*Inf.*), fix, gerrymander, graft, manoeuvre, racketeer, swindle, wangle (*Inf.*) ~*n.* **3.** violin **4. fit as a fiddle** blooming, hale and hearty, healthy, in fine fettle, in good form, in good shape, in rude health, in the pink, sound, strong **5.** *Inf.* fix, fraud, graft, piece of sharp practice, racket, swindle, wangle (*Inf.*)

fiddling futile, insignificant, pettifogging, petty, trifling, trivial

fidelity 1. allegiance, constancy, dependability, devotedness, devotion, faith, faithfulness, fealty, integrity, loyalty (*Archaic or Scot.*), loyalty, staunchness, true-heartedness, trustworthiness **2.** accuracy, adherence, closeness, correspondence, exactitude, exactness, faithfulness, preciseness, precision, scrupulousness

fidget 1. *v.* be like a cat on hot bricks (*Inf.*), bustle, chafe, fiddle, fret, jiggle, jitter (*Inf.*), move restlessly, squirm, twitch, worry **2.** *n. Usually* **the fidgets** fidgetiness, jitters (*Inf.*), nervousness, restlessness, unease, uneasiness

fidgety impatient, jerky, jittery (*Inf.*), jumpy, nervous, on edge, restive, restless, twitchy, uneasy

field *n.* **1.** grassland, green, greensward (*Archaic*), lea (*Literary*), mead (*Archaic*), meadow, pasture **2.** applicants, candidates, competition, competitors, con-

fiend

253

figure

testants, entrants, possibilities, runners **3.** area, bailiwick, bounds, confines, department, discipline, domain, environment, limits, line, metier, province, purview, range, scope, speciality, specialty, sphere of influence (activity, interest, study), territory ~v. **4.** catch, pick up, retrieve, return, stop **5.** *Fig.* deal with, deflect, handle, turn aside

fiend 1. demon, devil, evil spirit, hellhound **2.** barbarian, beast, brute, degenerate, monster, ogre, savage **3.** *Inf.* addict, enthusiast, fanatic, freak (*Sl.*), maniac

fiendish accursed, atrocious, blackhearted, cruel, demoniac, devilish, diabolical, hellish, implacable, infernal, inhuman, malevolent, malicious, malignant, monstrous, satanic, savage, ungodly, unspeakable, wicked

fierce 1. barbarous, brutal, cruel, dangerous, fell (*Archaic*), feral, ferocious, fiery, menacing, murderous, passionate, savage, threatening, tigerish, truculent, uncontrollable, untamed, vicious, wild **2.** blustery, boisterous, furious, howling, powerful, raging, stormy, strong, tempestuous, tumultuous, uncontrollable, violent **3.** cutthroat, intense, keen, relentless, strong

fiercely ferociously, frenziedly, furiously, in a frenzy, like cat and dog, menacingly, passionately, savagely, tempestuously, tigerishly, tooth and nail, uncontrolledly, viciously, with bared teeth, with no holds barred

fierceness 1. ferocity, fieriness, mercilessness, ruthlessness, savageness, viciousness, wildness **2.** bluster, destructiveness, roughness, storminess, tempestuousness, turbulence, violence **3.** avidity, fervidness, fervour, intensity, passion, relentlessness, strength

fiery 1. ablaze, afire, aflame, blazing, burning, flaming, glowing, in flames, on fire, red-hot **2.** choleric, excitable, fierce, hot-headed, impetuous, irascible, irritable, passionate, peppery, violent **3.** burning, febrile, fevered, feverish, flushed, heated, hot, inflamed

fight *v.* **1.** assault, battle, bear arms against, box, brawl, carry on war, clash, close, combat, come to blows, conflict, contend, cross swords, do battle, engage, engage in hostilities, exchange blows, feud, go to war, grapple, joust, scrap (*Inf.*), spar, struggle, take the field, take

up arms against, tilt, tussle, wage war, war, wrestle **2.** contest, defy, dispute, make a stand against, oppose, resist, stand up to, strive, struggle, withstand **3.** argue, bicker, dispute, fall out (*Inf.*), squabble, wrangle **4.** carry on, conduct, engage in, prosecute, wage **5. fight shy of** avoid, duck out of (*Inf.*), keep aloof from, keep at arm's length, shun, steer clear of ~*n.* **6.** action, affray (*Law*), altercation, battle, bout, brawl, brush, clash, combat, conflict, contest, dispute, dissension, dogfight, duel, encounter, engagement, exchange of blows, fracas, fray, free-for-all (*Inf.*), hostilities, joust, melee, passage of arms, riot, row, rumble (*U.S. sl.*), scrap (*Inf.*), scuffle, set-to (*Inf.*), skirmish, sparring match, struggle, tussle, war **7.** *Fig.* belligerence, gameness, mettle, militancy, pluck, resistance, spirit, will to resist

fight back 1. defend oneself, give tit for tat, put up a fight, reply, resist, retaliate **2.** bottle up, contain, control, curb, hold back, hold in check, restrain

fight down bottle up, control, curb, hold back, repress, restrain, suppress

fighter 1. fighting man, man-at-arms, soldier, warrior **2.** boxer, bruiser (*Inf.*), prize fighter, pugilist **3.** antagonist, battler, belligerent, combatant, contender, contestant, disputant, militant

fighting 1. *adj.* aggressive, argumentative, bellicose, belligerent, combative, contentious, disputatious, hawkish, martial, militant, pugnacious, sabre-rattling, truculent, warlike **2.** *n.* battle, bloodshed, blows struck, combat, conflict, hostilities, warfare

fight off beat off, keep *or* hold at bay, repel, repress, repulse, resist, stave off, ward off

figment creation, fable, fabrication, falsehood, fancy, fiction, improvisation, invention, production

figurative 1. allegorical, emblematical, metaphorical, representative, symbolical, typical **2.** descriptive, fanciful, florid, flowery, ornate, pictorial, poetical, tropical (*Rhetoric*)

figure *n.* **1.** character, cipher, digit, number, numeral, symbol **2.** amount, cost, price, sum, total, value **3.** form, outline, shadow, shape, silhouette **4.** body, build, chassis (*Sl.*), frame, physique, proportions, shape, torso **5.** depiction, design, device, diagram, drawing, emblem, illustration, motif, pattern, representation, sketch **6**. celebrity, character, dignitary, force, leader, notability, notable, personage, personality, presence, somebody, worthy ~*v*. **7**. *Often with* **up** add, calculate, compute, count, reckon, sum, tally, tot up, work out **8**. *Usually with* **in** act, appear, be conspicuous, be featured, be included, be mentioned, contribute to, feature, have a place in, play a part **9**. **it figures** it follows, it goes without saying, it is to be expected

figured adorned, decorated, embellished, marked, ornamented, patterned, variegated

figurehead cipher, dummy, front man (*Inf*.), leader in name only, man of straw, mouthpiece, name, nonentity, puppet, straw man (*Chiefly U.S.*), titular *or* nominal head, token

figure of speech conceit, image, trope, turn of phrase

figure out 1. calculate, compute, reckon, work out **2**. comprehend, decipher, fathom, make head or tail of (*Inf*.), make out, resolve, see, understand

filament cilium (*Biol. & Zool*.), fibre, fibril, pile, staple, strand, string, thread, wire

filch abstract, crib (*Inf*.), embezzle, half-inch (*Sl*.), lift (*Inf*.), misappropriate, nick (*Sl*.), pilfer, pinch (*Inf*.), purloin, rip off (*Sl*.), snaffle (*Inf*.), steal, swipe (*Sl*.), take, thieve, walk off with

file[1] *v*. abrade, burnish, furbish, polish, rasp, refine, rub, rub down, scrape, shape, smooth

file[2] *n*. **1**. case, data, documents, dossier, folder, information, portfolio ~*v*. **2**. document, enter, pigeonhole, put in place, record, register, slot in ~*n*. **3**. column, line, list, queue, row, string ~*v*. **4**. march, parade, troop

filibuster *n*. **1**. *Chiefly U.S., with reference to legislation* delay, hindrance, obstruction, postponement, procrastination ~*v*. **2**. *Chiefly U.S., with reference to legislation* delay, hinder, obstruct, prevent, procrastinate, put off ~*n*. **3**. adventurer, buccaneer, corsair, freebooter, pirate, sea robber, sea rover, soldier of fortune

filigree lace, lacework, lattice, tracery, wirework

fill 1. brim over, cram, crowd, furnish, glut, gorge, inflate, pack, pervade, replenish, sate, satiate, satisfy, stock, store, stuff, supply, swell **2**. charge, imbue, impregnate, overspread, pervade, saturate, suffuse **3**. block, bung, close, cork, plug, seal, stop **4**. assign, carry out, discharge, engage, execute, fulfil, hold, occupy, officiate, perform, take up **5**. **one's fill** all one wants, ample, a sufficiency, enough, plenty, sufficient

fill in 1. answer, complete, fill out (*U.S.*), fill up **2**. *Inf*. acquaint, apprise, bring up to date, give the facts *or* background, inform, put wise (*Sl*.) **3**. deputize, replace, represent, stand in, sub, substitute, take the place of

filling 1. *n*. contents, filler, innards (*Inf*.), inside, insides, padding, stuffing, wadding **2**. *adj*. ample, heavy, satisfying, square, substantial

fillip *n*. goad, incentive, prod, push, spice, spur, stimulus, zest

film *n*. **1**. coat, coating, covering, dusting, gauze, integument, layer, membrane, pellicle, scum, skin, tissue **2**. blur, cloud, haze, haziness, mist, mistiness, opacity, veil **3**. flick (*Sl*.), motion picture, movie (*U.S. inf*.) ~*v*. **4**. photograph, shoot, take **5**. *Often with* **over** blear, blur, cloud, dull, haze, mist, veil

filmy 1. chiffon, cobwebby, delicate, diaphanous, fine, finespun, flimsy, floaty, fragile, gauzy, gossamer, insubstantial, seethrough, sheer, transparent **2**. bleared, bleary, blurred, blurry, cloudy, dim, hazy, membranous, milky, misty, opalescent, opaque, pearly

filter *v*. **1**. clarify, filtrate, purify, refine, screen, sieve, sift, strain, winnow **2**. *Often with* **through** *or* **out** dribble, escape, exude, leach, leak, ooze, penetrate, percolate, seep, trickle, well ~*n*. **3**. gauze, membrane, mesh, riddle, sieve, strainer

filth 1. carrion, contamination, defilement, dirt, dung, excrement, excreta, faeces, filthiness, foul matter, foulness, garbage, grime, muck, nastiness, ordure, pollution, putrefaction, putrescence, refuse, sewage, slime, sludge, squalor, uncleanness **2**. corruption, dirtymindedness, impurity, indecency, obscenity, pornography, smut, vileness, vulgarity

filthy 1. dirty, faecal, feculent, foul, nasty, polluted, putrid, scummy, slimy, squalid, unclean, vile **2**. begrimed, black, blackened, grimy, grubby, miry, mucky, muddy, mud-encrusted, smoky, sooty, unwashed **3.** bawdy, coarse, corrupt, depraved, dirty-minded, foul, foul-mouthed, impure, indecent, lewd, licentious, obscene, pornographic, smutty, suggestive **4.** base, contemptible, despicable, low, mean, offensive, scurvy, vicious, vile

final 1. closing, concluding, end, eventual, last, last-minute, latest, terminal, terminating, ultimate **2.** absolute, conclusive, decided, decisive, definite, definitive, determinate, finished, incontrovertible, irrevocable, settled

finale climax, close, conclusion, crowning glory, culmination, dénouement, epilogue, finis, last act

finality certitude, conclusiveness, decidedness, decisiveness, definiteness, inevitableness, irrevocability, resolution, unavoidability

finalize agree, clinch (*Inf.*), complete, conclude, decide, settle, sew up (*Inf.*), tie up, work out, wrap up (*Inf.*)

finally 1. at last, at length, at long last, at the last, at the last moment, eventually, in the end, in the long run, lastly, ultimately, when all is said and done **2.** in conclusion, in summary, to conclude **3.** beyond the shadow of a doubt, completely, conclusively, convincingly, decisively, for all time, for ever, for good, inescapably, inexorably, irrevocably, once and for all, permanently

finance 1. *n.* accounts, banking, business, commerce, economics, financial affairs, investment, money, money management **2.** *v.* back, bankroll (*U.S.*), float, fund, guarantee, pay for, provide security for, set up in business, subsidize, support, underwrite

finances affairs, assets, capital, cash, financial condition, funds, money, resources, wherewithal

financial budgeting, economic, fiscal, monetary, money, pecuniary

financing *n.* costs, expenditure, expense(s), funding, operating expenses, outlay

find *v.* **1.** catch sight of, chance upon, come across, come up with, descry, discover, encounter, espy, expose, ferret out, hit upon, lay one's hand on, light upon, locate, meet, recognize, run to earth, spot, stumble upon, track down, turn up, uncover, unearth **2.** achieve, acquire, attain, earn, gain, get, obtain, procure, win **3.** get back, recover, regain, re-

possess, retrieve **4.** arrive at, ascertain, become aware, detect, discover, experience, learn, note, notice, observe, perceive, realise, remark **5.** be responsible for, bring, contribute, cough up (*Inf.*), furnish, provide, supply ~*n.* **6.** acquisition, asset, bargain, catch, discovery, good buy

finding award, conclusion, decision, decree, judgment, pronouncement, recommendation, verdict

find out 1. detect, discover, learn, note, observe, perceive, realize **2.** bring to light, catch, detect, disclose, expose, reveal, rumble (*Sl.*), suss out (*Sl.*), uncover, unmask

fine[1] *adj.* **1.** accomplished, admirable, beautiful, choice, excellent, exceptional, exquisite, first-class, first-rate, great, magnificent, masterly, ornate, outstanding, rare, select, showy, skilful, splendid, superior, supreme **2.** balmy, bright, clear, clement, cloudless, dry, fair, pleasant, sunny **3.** dainty, delicate, elegant, expensive, exquisite, fragile, quality **4.** abstruse, acute, critical, discriminating, fastidious, hairsplitting, intelligent, keen, minute, nice, precise, quick, refined, sensitive, sharp, subtle, tasteful, tenuous **5.** delicate, diaphanous, fine-grained, flimsy, gauzy, gossamer, light, lightweight, powdered, powdery, pulverized, sheer, slender, small, thin **6.** clear, pure, refined, solid, sterling, unadulterated, unalloyed, unpolluted **7.** attractive, bonny, good-looking, handsome, lovely, smart, striking, stylish, well-favoured **8.** acceptable, agreeable, all right, convenient, good, O.K. (*Inf.*), satisfactory, suitable **9.** brilliant, cutting, honed, keen, polished, razor-sharp, sharp

fine[2] **1.** *v.* amerce (*Archaic*), mulct, penalize, punish **2.** *n.* amercement (*Archaic*), damages, forfeit, penalty, punishment

finery best bib and tucker (*Inf.*), decorations, frippery, gear (*Inf.*), gewgaws, glad rags (*Sl.*), ornaments, showiness, splendour, Sunday best, trappings, trinkets

finesse *n.* **1.** adeptness, adroitness, artfulness, cleverness, craft, delicacy, diplomacy, discretion, know-how (*Inf.*), polish, quickness, savoir-faire, skill, sophistication, subtlety, tact **2.** artifice, bluff, feint, manoeuvre, ruse, stratagem, trick, wile ~*v.* **3.** bluff, manipulate, manoeuvre

finger *v.* **1.** feel, fiddle with (*Inf.*), handle, manipulate, maul, meddle with, paw (*Inf.*), play about with, touch, toy with **2.** **put one's finger on** bring to mind, discover, find out, hit the nail on the head, hit upon, identify, indicate, locate, pin down, place, recall, remember

finicky choosy (*Inf.*), critical, dainty, difficult, fastidious, finicking, fussy, hard to please, nit-picking (*Inf.*), overnice, overparticular, particular, scrupulous, squeamish

finish *v.* **1.** accomplish, achieve, bring to a close *or* conclusion, carry through, cease, close, complete, conclude, culminate, deal with, discharge, do, end, execute, finalize, fulfil, get done, get out of the way, make short work of, put the finishing touch(es) to, round off, settle, stop, terminate, wind up (*Inf.*), wrap up (*Inf.*) **2.** *Sometimes with* **up** *or* **off** consume, deplete, devour, dispatch, dispose of, drain, drink, eat, empty, exhaust, expend, spend, use, use up **3.** *Often with* **off** administer *or* give the coup de grâce, annihilate, best, bring down, defeat, destroy, dispose of, drive to the wall, exterminate, get rid of, kill, overcome, overpower, put an end to, rout, ruin, worst ~*n.* **4.** cessation, close, closing, completion, conclusion, culmination, dénouement, end, ending, finale, last stage(s), termination, winding up (*Inf.*), wind-up (*Inf., chiefly U.S.*) **5.** annihilation, bankruptcy, curtains (*Inf.*), death, defeat, end, end of the road, liquidation, ruin ~*v.* **6.** elaborate, perfect, polish, refine ~*n.* **7.** cultivation, culture, elaboration, perfection, polish, refinement ~*v.* **8.** coat, face, gild, lacquer, polish, smooth off, stain, texture, veneer, wax ~*n.* **9.** appearance, grain, lustre, patina, polish, shine, smoothness, surface, texture

finished 1. accomplished, classic, consummate, cultivated, elegant, expert, flawless, impeccable, masterly, perfected, polished, professional, proficient, refined, skilled, smooth, urbane **2.** accomplished, achieved, closed, complete, completed, concluded, done, ended, entire, final, finalized, full, in the past, over, over and done with, sewed up (*Inf.*), shut, terminated, through, tied up, wrapped up (*Inf.*) **3.** done, drained, empty, exhausted, gone, played out (*Inf.*),

spent, used up **4.** bankrupt, defeated, devastated, done for (*Inf.*), doomed, gone, liquidated, lost, ruined, through, undone, washed up (*Inf., chiefly U.S.*), wiped out, wound up, wrecked

finite bounded, circumscribed, conditioned, delimited, demarcated, limited, restricted, subject to limitations, terminable

fire *n.* **1.** blaze, combustion, conflagration, flames, inferno **2.** barrage, bombardment, cannonade, flak, fusillade, hail, salvo, shelling, sniping, volley **3.** *Fig.* animation, ardour, brio, burning passion, dash, eagerness, élan, enthusiasm, excitement, fervency, fervour, force, heat, impetuosity, intensity, life, light, lustre, passion, radiance, scintillation, sparkle, spirit, splendour, verve, vigour, virtuosity, vivacity **4.** **hanging fire** delayed, in abeyance, pending, postponed, put back, put off, shelved, suspended, undecided **5.** **on fire a.** ablaze, aflame, alight, blazing, burning, fiery, flaming, in flames **b.** ardent, eager, enthusiastic, excited, inspired, passionate ~*v.* **6.** enkindle, ignite, kindle, light, put a match to, set ablaze, set aflame, set alight, set fire to, set on fire **7.** detonate, discharge, eject, explode, hurl, launch, let off, loose, pull the trigger, set off, shell, shoot, touch off **8.** *Fig.* animate, arouse, electrify, enliven, excite, galvanize, impassion, incite, inflame, inspire, inspirit, irritate, quicken, rouse, stir **9.** *Inf.* cashier, discharge, dismiss, give marching orders, make redundant, sack (*Sl.*), show the door

firebrand *Fig.* agitator, demagogue, fomenter, incendiary, instigator, rabble-rouser, soapbox orator, tub-thumper

fireworks 1. illuminations, pyrotechnics **2.** *Fig.* fit of rage, hysterics, paroxysms, rage, rows, storm, temper, trouble, uproar

firm[1] *adj.* **1.** close-grained, compact, compressed, concentrated, congealed, dense, hard, inelastic, inflexible, jelled, jellified, rigid, set, solid, solidified, stiff, unyielding **2.** anchored, braced, cemented, embedded, fast, fastened, fixed, immovable, motionless, riveted, robust, rooted, secure, secured, stable, stationary, steady, strong, sturdy, taut, tight, unfluctuating, unmoving, unshakable **3.** adamant, constant, definite, fixed, inflexible, obdurate, resolute, resolved, set on, settled, staunch, steadfast, strict, true, unalterable, unbending, unfaltering, unflinching, unshakable, unshaken, unswerving, unwavering, unyielding

firm[2] n. association, business, company, concern, conglomerate, corporation, enterprise, house, organization, outfit (*Inf.*), partnership

firmament empyrean (*Literary*), heaven, heavens, sky, the blue, the skies, vault, vault of heaven, welkin (*Archaic*)

firmly 1. enduringly, immovably, like a rock, motionlessly, securely, steadily, tightly, unflinchingly, unshakably 2. determinedly, resolutely, staunchly, steadfastly, strictly, through thick and thin, unchangeably, unwaveringly, with a rod of iron, with decision

firmness 1. compactness, density, fixedness, hardness, inelasticity, inflexibility, resistance, rigidity, solidity, stiffness 2. immovability, soundness, stability, steadiness, strength, tautness, tensile strength, tension, tightness 3. constancy, fixedness, fixity of purpose, inflexibility, obduracy, resolution, resolve, staunchness, steadfastness, strength of will, strictness

first adj. 1. chief, foremost, head, highest, leading, pre-eminent, prime, principal, ruling 2. earliest, initial, introductory, maiden, opening, original, premier, primeval, primitive, primordial, pristine 3. basic, cardinal, elementary, fundamental, key, primary, rudimentary ~adv. 4. at the beginning, at the outset, before all else, beforehand, firstly, initially, in the first place, to begin with, to start with ~n. 5. As in **from the first** beginning, commencement, inception, introduction, outset, start, starting point, word 'go' (*Inf.*)

firsthand direct, straight from the horse's mouth

first-rate admirable, A-one (*Inf.*), crack (*Sl.*), elite, excellent, exceptional, exclusive, first class, outstanding, prime, second to none, superb, superlative, tiptop, top, topnotch (*Inf.*), tops (*Sl.*)

fiscal budgetary, economic, financial, monetary, money, pecuniary

fish for angle for, elicit, hint at, hope for, hunt for, invite, look for, search for, seek, solicit

fish out extract, extricate, find, haul out, produce, pull out

fishy 1. *Inf.* doubtful, dubious, funny (*Inf.*), implausible, improbable, odd, queer, questionable, suspect, suspicious, unlikely 2. blank, deadpan, dull, expressionless, glassy, glassy-eyed, inexpressive, lacklustre, lifeless, vacant, wooden 3. fishlike, piscatorial, piscatory, piscine

fission breaking, cleavage, division, parting, rending, rupture, schism, scission, splitting

fissure breach, break, chink, cleavage, cleft, crack, cranny, crevice, fault, fracture, gap, hole, interstice, opening, rent, rift, rupture, slit, split

fit[1] adj. 1. able, adapted, adequate, appropriate, apt, becoming, capable, competent, convenient, correct, deserving, equipped, expedient, fitted, fitting, good enough, meet (*Archaic*), prepared, proper, qualified, ready, right, seemly, suitable, trained, well-suited, worthy 2. able-bodied, hale, healthy, in good condition, in good shape, in good trim, robust, strapping, toned up, trim, well ~v. 3. accord, agree, be consonant, belong, concur, conform, correspond, dovetail, go, interlock, join, match, meet, suit, tally 4. *Often with* **out** *or* **up** accommodate, accoutre, arm, equip, fit out, kit out, outfit, prepare, provide, rig out 5. adapt, adjust, alter, arrange, dispose, fashion, modify, place, position, shape

fit[2] n. 1. attack, bout, convulsion, paroxysm, seizure, spasm 2. caprice, fancy, humour, mood, whim 3. bout, burst, outbreak, outburst, spell 4. **by fits and starts** erratically, fitfully, intermittently, irregularly, on and off, spasmodically, sporadically, unsystematically

fitful broken, desultory, disturbed, erratic, flickering, fluctuating, haphazard, impulsive, intermittent, irregular, spasmodic, sporadic, unstable, variable

fitfully desultorily, erratically, in fits and starts, in snatches, intermittently, interruptedly, irregularly, off and on, spasmodically, sporadically

fitness 1. adaptation, applicability, appropriateness, aptness, competence, eligibility, pertinence, preparedness, propriety, qualifications, readiness, seemliness, suitability 2. good condition, good health, health, robustness, strength, vigour

fitted 1. adapted, cut out for, equipped, fit, qualified, right, suitable, tailor-made 2. *Often with* **with** accoutred, appointed, armed, equipped, furnished, outfitted, provided, rigged out, set up, supplied **3.** built-in, permanent

fitting 1. *adj.* appropriate, becoming, *comme il faut*, correct, decent, decorous, desirable, meet (*Archaic*), proper, right, seemly, suitable **2.** *n.* accessory, attachment, component, connection, part, piece, unit

fittings accessories, accoutrements, appointments, appurtenances, conveniences, equipment, extras, furnishings, furniture, trimmings

fix *v.* **1.** anchor, embed, establish, implant, install, locate, place, plant, position, root, set, settle **2.** attach, bind, cement, connect, couple, fasten, glue, link, make fast, pin, secure, stick, tie **3.** agree on, appoint, arrange, arrive at, conclude, decide, define, determine, establish, limit, name, resolve, set, settle, specify **4.** adjust, correct, mend, patch up, put to rights, regulate, repair, see to, sort **5.** congeal, consolidate, harden, rigidify, set, solidify, stiffen, thicken **6.** direct, focus, level at, rivet **7.** *Inf.* bribe, fiddle, influence, manipulate, manoeuvre, pull strings (*Inf.*), rig **8.** *Sl.* cook (someone's) goose (*Inf.*), get even with, get revenge on, pay back, settle (someone's) hash (*Inf.*), sort (someone) out (*Inf.*), take retribution on, wreak vengeance on ~*n.* **9.** *Inf.* difficult situation, difficulty, dilemma, embarrassment, hole (*Sl.*), jam (*Inf.*), mess, pickle (*Inf.*), plight, predicament, quandary, spot (*Inf.*), ticklish situation

fixation complex, hang-up (*Inf.*), *idée fixe*, infatuation, mania, obsession, preoccupation, thing (*Inf.*)

fixed 1. anchored, attached, established, immovable, made fast, permanent, rigid, rooted, secure, set **2.** intent, level, resolute, steady, unbending, unblinking, undeviating, unflinching, unwavering **3.** agreed, arranged, decided, definite, established, planned, resolved, settled **4.** going, in working order, mended, put right, repaired, sorted **5.** *Inf.* framed, manipulated, packed, put-up, rigged

fixity doggedness, intentness, perseverance, persistence, stability, steadiness

fix up 1. agree on, arrange, fix, organize, plan, settle, sort out **2.** *Often with* **with** accommodate, arrange for, bring about, furnish, lay on, provide

fizz bubble, effervesce, fizzle, froth, hiss, sparkle, sputter

fizzle out abort, collapse, come to nothing, die away, end in disappointment, fail, fall through, fold (*Inf.*), miss the mark, peter out

fizzy bubbling, bubbly, carbonated, effervescent, gassy, sparkling

flab fat, flabbiness, flesh, fleshiness, heaviness, overweight, plumpness, slackness, weight

flabbergasted abashed, amazed, astonished, astounded, bowled over (*Inf.*), confounded, dazed, disconcerted, dumbfounded, nonplussed, overcome, overwhelmed, rendered speechless, speechless, staggered, struck dumb, stunned

flabbiness bloatedness, flaccidity, limpness, looseness, pendulousness, slackness

flabby 1. baggy, drooping, flaccid, floppy, hanging, lax, limp, loose, pendulous, sagging, slack, sloppy, toneless, unfit, yielding **2.** effete, enervated, feeble, impotent, ineffective, ineffectual, nerveless, spineless, weak

flaccid drooping, flabby, lax, limp, loose, nerveless, slack, soft, weak

flaccidity flabbiness, limpness, looseness, nervelessness, slackness, softness

flag[1] *v.* abate, decline, die, droop, ebb, fade, fail, faint, fall, fall off, feel the pace, languish, peter out, pine, sag, sink, slump, succumb, taper off, wane, weaken, weary, wilt

flag[2] *n.* **1.** banderole, banner, colours, ensign, gonfalon, jack, pennant, pennon, standard, streamer ~*v.* **2.** *Sometimes with* **down** hail, salute, signal, warn, wave **3.** docket, indicate, label, mark, note, tab

flagellate beat, castigate, chastise, flay, flog, lash, scourge, thrash, whip

flagellation beating, flogging, lashing, thrashing, whipping

flagging declining, decreasing, deteriorating, ebbing, fading, failing, faltering, giving up, sinking, slowing down, tiring, waning, weakening, wilting

flagrancy blatancy, enormity, heinousness, infamy, insolence, ostentation, outrageousness, public display, shamelessness

flagrant arrant, atrocious, awful, barefaced, blatant, bold, brazen, crying, dreadful, egregious, enormous, flagitious, flaunting, glaring, heinous, immodest, infamous, notorious, open, ostentatious, out-and-out, outrageous, scandalous, shameless, undisguised

flagstone block, flag, paving stone, slab

flail *v.* beat, thrash, thresh, windmill

flair 1. ability, accomplishment, aptitude, faculty, feel, genius, gift, knack, mastery, talent **2.** chic, dash, discernment, elegance, panache, style, stylishness, taste

flak *Fig.* abuse, bad press, brickbats (*Inf.*), censure, complaints, condemnation, criticism, disapprobation, disapproval, disparagement, fault-finding, hostility, opposition

flake 1. *n.* disk, lamina, layer, peeling, scale, shaving, sliver, squama (*Biol.*), wafer **2.** *v.* blister, chip, desquamate, peel (off), scale (off)

flake out collapse, faint, keel over, lose consciousness, pass out, swoon (*Literary*)

flamboyant 1. baroque, elaborate, extravagant, florid, ornate, ostentatious, rich, rococo, showy, theatrical **2.** brilliant, colourful, dashing, dazzling, exciting, glamorous, swashbuckling

flame *v.* **1.** blaze, burn, flare, flash, glare, glow, shine ~*n.* **2.** blaze, brightness, fire, light **3.** *Fig.* affection, ardour, enthusiasm, fervency, fervour, fire, intensity, keenness, passion, warmth **4.** *Inf.* beau, beloved, boyfriend, girlfriend, heart-throb (*Brit.*), ladylove, lover, sweetheart

flameproof fire-resistant, incombustible, nonflammable, non-inflammable

flaming 1. ablaze, afire, blazing, brilliant, burning, fiery, glowing, ignited, in flames, raging, red, red-hot **2.** angry, ardent, aroused, frenzied, hot, impassioned, intense, raging, scintillating, vehement, vivid

flammable combustible, ignitable, incendiary, inflammable

flank *n.* **1.** ham, haunch, hip, loin, quarter, side, thigh **2.** side, wing ~*v.* **3.** border, bound, edge, fringe, line, screen, skirt, wall

flannel *Fig.* **1.** *n.* baloney (*Inf.*), blarney, equivocation, flattery, hedging, prevarication, soft soap (*Inf.*), sweet talk (*U.S. inf.*), waffle (*Inf.*), weasel words (*Inf., chiefly U.S.*) **2.** *v.* blarney, butter up, equivocate, flatter, hedge, prevari-

cate, pull the wool over (someone's) eyes, soft-soap (*Inf.*), sweet-talk (*U.S. inf.*), waffle

flap *v.* **1.** agitate, beat, flail, flutter, shake, swing, swish, thrash, thresh, vibrate, wag, wave ~*n.* **2.** bang, banging, beating, flutter, shaking, swinging, swish, waving ~*v.* **3.** *Inf.* dither, fuss, panic ~*n.* **4.** *Inf.* agitation, commotion, fluster, panic, state (*Inf.*), stew (*Inf.*), sweat (*Inf.*), tizzy (*Inf.*), twitter **5.** apron, cover, fly, fold, lapel, lappet, overlap, skirt, tab, tail

flare *v.* **1.** blaze, burn up, dazzle, flicker, flutter, glare, waver **2.** *Often with* **out** broaden, spread out, widen ~*n.* **3.** blaze, burst, dazzle, flame, flash, flicker, glare

flare up blaze, blow one's top (*Inf.*), boil over, break out, explode, fire up, fly off the handle (*Inf.*), lose control, lose one's cool (*Inf.*), lose one's temper, throw a tantrum

flash *v.* **1.** blaze, coruscate, flare, flicker, glare, gleam, glint, glisten, glitter, light, scintillate, shimmer, sparkle, twinkle ~*n.* **2.** blaze, burst, coruscation, dazzle, flare, flicker, gleam, ray, scintillation, shaft, shimmer, spark, sparkle, streak, twinkle ~*v.* **3.** bolt, dart, dash, fly, race, shoot, speed, sprint, streak, sweep, whistle, zoom ~*n.* **4.** instant, jiffy (*Inf.*), moment, second, shake, split second, trice, twinkling, twinkling of an eye, two shakes of a lamb's tail (*Inf.*) ~*v.* **5.** display, exhibit, expose, flaunt, flourish, show ~*n.* **6.** burst, demonstration, display, manifestation, outburst, show, sign, touch ~*adj.* **7.** *Inf.* cheap, glamorous, ostentatious, tacky (*U.S. inf.*), tasteless, vulgar

flashy cheap, cheap and nasty, flamboyant, flaunting, garish, gaudy, glittery, glitzy, in poor taste, jazzy (*Inf.*), loud, meretricious, ostentatious, showy, snazzy (*Inf.*), tasteless, tawdry, tinselly

flat¹ *adj.* **1.** even, horizontal, level, levelled, low, planar, plane, smooth, unbroken **2.** laid low, lying full length, outstretched, prostrate, reclining, recumbent, supine **3.** boring, dead, dull, flavourless, insipid, jejune, lacklustre, lifeless, monotonous, pointless, prosaic, spiritless, stale, tedious, uninteresting, vapid, watery, weak **4.** absolute, categorical, direct, downright, explicit, final, fixed, out-and-out, peremptory, plain, positive, straight, unconditional, unequivocal, unmistakable, unqualified **5.** blown out, burst, collapsed, deflated, empty, punctured ~*n.* **6.** *Often plural* lowland, marsh, mud flat, plain, shallow, shoal, strand, swamp ~*adv.* **7.** absolutely, categorically, completely, exactly, point blank, precisely, utterly **8. flat out** all out, at full gallop, at full speed, at full tilt, for all one is worth, hell for leather, posthaste, under full steam

flat [2] apartment, rooms

flatly absolutely, categorically, completely, positively, unhesitatingly

flatness 1. evenness, horizontality, levelness, smoothness, uniformity **2.** dullness, emptiness, insipidity, monotony, staleness, tedium, vapidity

flatten 1. compress, even out, iron out, level, plaster, raze, roll, smooth off, squash, trample **2.** bowl over, crush, fell, floor, knock down, knock off one's feet, prostrate, subdue

flatter 1. blandish, butter up, cajole, compliment, court, fawn, flannel (*Inf.*), humour, inveigle, lay it on (thick) (*Sl.*), praise, puff, soft-soap (*Inf.*), sweet-talk (*U.S. inf.*), wheedle **2.** become, do something for, enhance, set off, show to advantage, suit

flattering 1. becoming, effective, enhancing, kind, well-chosen **2.** adulatory, complimentary, fawning, fulsome, gratifying, honeyed, honey-tongued, ingratiating, laudatory, sugary

flattery adulation, blandishment, blarney, cajolery, false praise, fawning, flannel (*Inf.*), fulsomeness, honeyed words, obsequiousness, servility, soft-soap (*Inf.*), sweet-talk (*U.S. inf.*), sycophancy, toadyism

flatulence 1. borborygmus (*Medical*), eructation, wind **2.** *Fig.* boasting, bombast, claptrap, empty words, fanfaronade (*Rare*), fustian, hot air (*Inf.*), pomposity, prolixity, rodomontade, twaddle

flatulent *Fig.* bombastic, inflated, long-winded, pompous, pretentious, prolix, swollen, tedious, turgid, wordy

flaunt boast, brandish, display, disport, exhibit, flash about, flourish, make a great show of, make an exhibition of, make a show of, parade, show off, sport, vaunt

flaunting brazen, flamboyant, gaudy, ostentatious, pretentious

flavour *n.* **1.** aroma, essence, extract, flavouring, odour, piquancy, relish, savour, seasoning, smack, tang, taste, zest, zing (*Inf.*) **2.** aspect, character, essence, feel, feeling, property, quality, soupçon, stamp, style, suggestion, tinge, tone, touch ~*v.* **3.** ginger up, imbue, infuse, lace, leaven, season, spice

flavouring essence, extract, spirit, tincture, zest

flaw 1. blemish, defect, disfigurement, failing, fault, imperfection, speck, spot, weakness, weak spot **2.** breach, break, cleft, crack, crevice, fissure, fracture, rent, rift, scission, split, tear

flawed blemished, broken, chipped, cracked, damaged, defective, erroneous, faulty, imperfect, unsound

flawless 1. faultless, impeccable, perfect, spotless, unblemished, unsullied **2.** intact, sound, unbroken, undamaged, whole

flay 1. excoriate, skin **2.** *Fig.* castigate, excoriate, execrate, give a tonguelashing, pull to pieces (*Inf.*), revile, tear a strip off, tear into (*Inf.*), upbraid

fleabite drop in the ocean, nothing, piddling amount, pinprick, trifle

flea-bitten crawling, decrepit, fetid, flea-ridden, frowsty, grotty (*Sl.*), grubby, infested, insalubrious, lousy, mean, mucky, pediculous (*Medical*), run-down, scabby, scruffy, scurfy, sleazy, slummy, sordid, squalid, tatty, unhygienic

fleck 1. *v.* bespeckle, besprinkle, dapple, dot, dust, mark, mottle, speckle, spot, stipple, streak, variegate **2.** *n.* dot, mark, pinpoint, speck, speckle, spot, streak

fledgling 1. chick, nestling **2.** apprentice, beginner, learner, neophyte, newcomer, novice, rookie (*Inf.*), trainee, tyro

flee abscond, avoid, beat a hasty retreat, bolt, cut and run (*Inf.*), decamp, depart, escape, fly, get away, leave, make a quick exit, make off, make oneself scarce (*Inf.*), make one's escape, make one's getaway, run away, scarper (*Sl.*), shun, skedaddle (*Inf.*), split (*Sl.*), take flight, take off (*Inf.*), take to one's heels, vanish

fleece 1. *Fig.* bleed (*Inf.*), cheat, con (*Sl.*), defraud, despoil, diddle (*Inf.*), mulct, overcharge, plunder, rifle, rip off (*Sl.*), rob, rook (*Sl.*), soak (*Sl., chiefly U.S.*), steal, swindle, take for a ride (*Inf.*), take to the cleaners (*Sl.*) **2.** clip, shear

fleecy downy, fluffy, shaggy, soft, woolly

fleet[1] n. argosy, armada, flotilla, naval force, navy, sea power, squadron, task force, vessels, warships

fleet[2] adj. fast, flying, mercurial, meteoric, nimble, nimble-footed, quick, rapid, speedy, swift, winged

fleeting brief, ephemeral, evanescent, flitting, flying, fugacious, fugitive, here today, gone tomorrow, momentary, passing, short, short-lived, temporary, transient, transitory

fleetness celerity, lightning speed, nimble-footedness, nimbleness, quickness, rapidity, speed, speediness, swiftness, velocity

flesh 1. beef (Inf.), body, brawn, fat, fatness, food, meat, tissue, weight 2. animality, body, carnality, flesh and blood, human nature, physicality, physical nature, sensuality 3. homo sapiens, humankind, human race, living creatures, man, mankind, mortality, people, race, stock, world 4. one's own flesh and blood blood, family, kin, kindred, kinsfolk, kith and kin, relations, relatives

fleshiness chubbiness, corpulence, flabbiness, heaviness, obesity, plumpness, stoutness

fleshly 1. animal, bodily, carnal, erotic, lascivious, lecherous, lustful, sensual 2. corporal, corporeal, earthly, human, material, mundane, of this world, physical, secular, terrestrial, worldly

fleshy ample, beefy (Inf.), brawny, chubby, chunky, corpulent, fat, hefty, meaty, obese, overweight, plump, podgy, stout, tubby, well-padded

flex v. angle, bend, contract, crook, curve, tighten

flexibility adaptability, adjustability, complaisance, elasticity, give (Inf.), pliability, pliancy, resilience, springiness, tensility

flexible 1. bendable, ductile, elastic, limber, lithe, mouldable, plastic, pliable, pliant, springy, stretchy, supple, tensile, whippy, willowy, yielding 2. adaptable, adjustable, discretionary, open, variable 3. amenable, biddable, complaisant, compliant, docile, gentle, manageable, responsive, tractable

flick v. 1. dab, fillip, flip, hit, jab, peck, rap, strike, tap, touch 2. With through browse, flip, glance, skim, skip, thumb ~n. 3. fillip, flip, jab, peck, rap, tap, touch

flicker v. 1. flare, flash, glimmer, gutter, shimmer, sparkle, twinkle 2. flutter, quiver, vibrate, waver ~n. 3. flare, flash, gleam, glimmer, spark 4. atom, breath, drop, glimmer, iota, spark, trace, vestige

flickering fitful, guttering, twinkling, unsteady, wavering

flight[1] 1. flying, mounting, soaring, winging 2. Of air travel journey, trip, voyage 3. aerial navigation, aeronautics, air transport, aviation, flying 4. cloud, flock, formation, squadron, swarm, unit, wing

flight[2] 1. departure, escape, exit, exodus, fleeing, getaway, retreat, running away 2. put to flight chase off, disperse, drive off, rout, scare off, scatter, send packing, stampede 3. take (to) flight abscond, beat a retreat, bolt, decamp, do a bunk (Sl.), flee, light out (Inf.), make a hasty retreat, run away or off, withdraw hastily

flightiness capriciousness, fickleness, flippancy, frivolity, giddiness, irresponsibility, levity, lightness, mercurialness, volatility

flighty capricious, changeable, dizzy, fickle, frivolous, giddy, harebrained, impetuous, impulsive, irresponsible, lightheaded, mercurial, scatterbrained, skittish, thoughtless, unbalanced, unstable, unsteady, volatile, wild

flimsy 1. delicate, fragile, frail, gimcrack, insubstantial, makeshift, rickety, shaky, shallow, slight, superficial, unsubstantial 2. chiffon, gauzy, gossamer, light, sheer, thin, transparent 3. feeble, frivolous, implausible, inadequate, poor, thin, transparent, trivial, unconvincing, unsatisfactory, weak

flinch baulk, blench, cower, cringe, draw back, duck, flee, quail, recoil, retreat, shirk, shrink, shy away, start, swerve, wince, withdraw

fling v. 1. cast, catapult, chuck (Inf.), heave, hurl, jerk, let fly, lob (Inf.), pitch, precipitate, propel, send, shy, sling, throw, toss ~n. 2. cast, lob, pitch, shot, throw, toss 3. binge, bit of fun, good time, indulgence, spree 4. attempt, bash (Inf.), crack (Inf.), gamble, go, shot, stab, trial, try, venture, whirl (Inf.)

flinty adamant, cruel, hard, hardhearted, heartless, inflexible, obdurate, pitiless, steely, stern, stony, unfeeling, unmerciful, unyielding

flip v./n. cast, flick, jerk, pitch, snap, spin, throw, toss, twist

flippancy cheek (*Inf.*), cheekiness, disrespectfulness, frivolity, impertinence, irreverence, levity, pertness, sauciness

flippant cheeky, disrespectful, flip (*Inf., chiefly U.S.*), frivolous, glib, impertinent, impudent, irreverent, offhand, pert, rude, saucy, superficial

flirt v. **1.** chat up (*Inf.*), coquet, dally, lead on, make advances, make eyes at, philander **2.** *Usually with* **with** consider, dabble in, entertain, expose oneself to, give a thought to, play with, toy with, trifle with ~n. **3.** coquette, heartbreaker, philanderer, tease, trifler, wanton

flirtation coquetry, dalliance, intrigue, philandering, teasing, toying, trifling

flirtatious amorous, arch, comehither, come-on (*Inf.*), coquettish, coy, enticing, flirty, provocative, sportive, teasing

flirting amorous play, chatting up (*Inf.*), coquetry, dalliance, sport

flit dart, flash, fleet, flutter, fly, pass, skim, speed, whisk, wing

float v. **1.** be *or* lie on the surface, be buoyant, displace water, hang, hover, poise, rest on water, stay afloat **2.** bob, drift, glide, move gently, sail, slide, slip along **3.** get going, launch, promote, push off, set up

floating 1. afloat, buoyant, buoyed up, nonsubmersible, ocean-going, sailing, swimming, unsinkable **2.** fluctuating, free, migratory, movable, unattached, uncommitted, unfixed, variable, wandering

flock v. **1.** collect, congregate, converge, crowd, gather, group, herd, huddle, mass, throng, troop ~n. **2.** colony, drove, flight, gaggle, herd, skein **3.** assembly, bevy, collection, company, congregation, convoy, crowd, gathering, group, herd, host, mass, multitude, throng

flog 1. beat, castigate, chastise, flagellate, flay, lash, scourge, thrash, trounce, whack, whip **2.** drive, oppress, overexert, overtax, overwork, punish, push, strain, tax

flogging beating, caning, flagellation, hiding (*Inf.*), horsewhipping, lashing,

scourging, thrashing, trouncing, whipping

flood v. **1.** brim over, deluge, drown, immerse, inundate, overflow, pour over, submerge, swamp **2.** engulf, flow, gush, overwhelm, rush, surge, swarm, sweep **3.** choke, fill, glut, oversupply, saturate ~n. **4.** deluge, downpour, flash flood, freshet, inundation, overflow, spate, tide, torrent **5.** abundance, flow, glut, multitude, outpouring, profusion, rush, stream, torrent

floor 1. n. level, stage, storey, tier **2.** v. *Fig.* baffle, beat, bewilder, bowl over (*Inf.*), bring up short, confound, conquer, defeat, discomfit, disconcert, dumbfound, knock down, nonplus, overthrow, perplex, prostrate, puzzle, stump, throw (*Inf.*)

flop v. **1.** collapse, dangle, droop, drop, fall, hang limply, sag, slump, topple, tumble **2.** *Inf.* bomb (*U.S. sl.*), close, come to nothing, fail, fall flat, fall short, fold (*Inf.*), founder, misfire ~n. **3.** *Inf.* cockup (*Brit. sl.*), debacle, disaster, failure, fiasco, loser, nonstarter, washout (*Inf.*)

floppy baggy, droopy, flaccid, flapping, flip-flop, hanging, limp, loose, pendulous, sagging, soft

floral flower-patterned, flowery

florescence blooming, blossoming, development, flourishing, flowering, fruition, maturity

florid 1. blowzy, flushed, highcoloured, high-complexioned, rubicund, ruddy **2.** baroque, busy, embellished, euphuistic, figurative, flamboyant, flowery, fussy, grandiloquent, high-flown, ornate, overelaborate

flossy downy, feathery, fluffy, satiny, silky, soft

flotsam debris, detritus, jetsam, junk, odds and ends, sweepings, wreckage

flounce v. bounce, fling, jerk, spring, stamp, storm, throw, toss

flounder v. be in the dark, blunder, fumble, grope, muddle, plunge, struggle, stumble, thrash, toss, tumble, wallow

flourish v. **1.** bear fruit, be in one's prime, be successful, be vigorous, bloom, blossom, boom, burgeon, develop, do well, flower, get ahead, get on, go great guns (*Sl.*), go up in the world, grow, grow fat, increase, prosper, succeed, thrive **2.** brandish, display, flaunt, flutter, shake, sweep, swing, swish, twirl, vaunt, wag, wave, wield ~n. **3.** brandishing, dash, display, fanfare, parade, shaking, show, showy gesture, twirling, wave **4.** curlicue, decoration, embellishment, ornamentation, plume, sweep

flourishing blooming, burgeoning, doing well, going strong, in the pink, in top form, lush, luxuriant, mushrooming, on the up and up (*Inf.*), prospering, rampant, successful, thriving

flout defy, deride, gibe at, insult, jeer at, laugh in the face of, mock, outrage, ridicule, scoff at, scorn, scout (*Archaic*), show contempt for, sneer at, spurn, taunt, treat with disdain

flow v. **1.** circulate, course, glide, gush, move, pour, purl, ripple, roll, run, rush, slide, surge, sweep, swirl, whirl **2.** cascade, deluge, flood, inundate, overflow, pour, run, run out, spew, spill, spurt, squirt, stream, teem, well forth **3.** arise, emanate, emerge, issue, pour, proceed, result, spring ~n. **4.** course, current, drift, flood, flux, gush, outflow, outpouring, spate, stream, tide **5.** abundance, deluge, effusion, emanation, outflow, outpouring, plenty, plethora, succession, train

flower n. **1.** bloom, blossom, efflorescence **2.** *Fig.* best, choicest part, cream, elite, freshness, greatest *or* finest point, height, pick, vigour ~v. **3.** bloom, blossom, blow, burgeon, effloresce, flourish, mature, open, unfold

flowering *adj.* abloom, blooming, blossoming, florescent, in bloom, in blossom, in flower, open, out, ready

flowery baroque, embellished, euphuistic, fancy, figurative, florid, high-flown, ornate, overwrought, rhetorical

flowing 1. falling, gushing, rolling, rushing, smooth, streaming, sweeping **2.** continuous, cursive, easy, fluent, smooth, unbroken, uninterrupted **3.** abounding, brimming over, flooded, full, overrun, prolific, rich, teeming

fluctuate alter, alternate, change, ebb and flow, go up and down, hesitate, oscillate, rise and fall, seesaw, shift, swing, undulate, vacillate, vary, veer, waver

fluctuation alternation, change, fickleness, inconstancy, instability, oscillation, shift, swing, unsteadiness, vacillation, variation, wavering

fluency articulateness, assurance, command, control, ease, facility, glib-ness, readiness, slickness, smoothness, volubility

fluent articulate, easy, effortless, facile, flowing, glib, natural, ready, smooth, smooth-spoken, voluble, well-versed

fluff 1. *n.* down, dust, dustball, fuzz, lint, nap, oose (*Scot.*), pile **2.** *v. Inf.* bungle, cock up (*Sl.*), foul up (*Inf.*), make a mess off, mess up (*Inf.*), muddle, screw up (*Inf.*), spoil

fluffy downy, feathery, fleecy, flossy, fuzzy, gossamer, silky, soft

fluid *adj.* **1.** aqueous, flowing, in solution, liquefied, liquid, melted, molten, running, runny, watery **2.** adaptable, adjustable, changeable, flexible, floating, fluctuating, indefinite, mercurial, mobile, mutable, protean, shifting **3.** easy, elegant, feline, flowing, graceful, sinuous, smooth ~n. **4.** liquid, liquor, solution

fluke accident, blessing, break, chance occurrence, fortuity, lucky break, quirk of fate, stroke of luck, windfall

fluky 1. accidental, coincidental, fortuitous, lucky **2.** at the mercy of events, chancy, incalculable, uncertain, variable

flummox baffle, bamboozle (*Inf.*), bewilder, bring up short, defeat, fox, mystify, nonplus, perplex, stump, stymie

flummoxed at a loss, at sea, baffled, bewildered, foxed, mystified, stumped, stymied

flunky 1. assistant, drudge, hanger-on, menial, minion, slave, toady, tool, underling, yes man **2.** footman, lackey, manservant, valet

flurry n. **1.** *Fig.* ado, agitation, bustle, commotion, disturbance, excitement, ferment, flap, fluster, flutter, furore, fuss, hurry, stir, to-do, tumult, whirl **2.** flaw, gust, squall **3.** burst, outbreak, spell, spurt ~v. **4.** agitate, bewilder, bother, bustle, confuse, disconcert, disturb, fluster, flutter, fuss, hassle (*Inf.*), hurry, hustle, rattle (*Inf.*), ruffle, unsettle, upset

flush[1] v. **1.** blush, burn, colour, colour up, crimson, flame, glow, go red, redden, suffuse ~n. **2.** bloom, blush, colour, freshness, glow, redness, rosiness ~v. **3.** cleanse, douche, drench, eject, expel, flood, hose down, rinse out, swab, syringe, wash out

flush[2] *adj.* **1.** even, flat, level, plane, square, true **2.** abundant, affluent, full, generous, lavish, liberal, overflowing, prodigal **3.** *Inf.* in funds, in the money

(*Inf.*), moneyed, rich, rolling (*Sl.*), wealthy, well-heeled, well-off, well-supplied ~*adv.* **4.** even with, hard against, in contact with, level with, squarely, touching

flush[3] *v.* discover, disturb, drive out, put to flight, rouse, start, uncover

flushed 1. blushing, burning, crimson, embarrassed, feverish, glowing, hot, red, rosy, rubicund, ruddy **2.** *Often with* **with** ablaze, animated, aroused, elated, enthused, excited, exhilarated, high (*Inf.*), inspired, intoxicated, thrilled

fluster 1. *v.* agitate, bother, bustle, confound, confuse, disturb, excite, flurry, hassle (*Inf.*), heat, hurry, make nervous, perturb, rattle (*Inf.*), ruffle, throw off balance, upset **2.** *n.* agitation, bustle, commotion, disturbance, dither, flap (*Inf.*), flurry, flutter, furore, perturbation, ruffle, state (*Inf.*), turmoil

fluted channelled, corrugated, furrowed, grooved

flutter *v.* **1.** agitate, bat, beat, flap, flicker, flit, flitter, fluctuate, hover, palpitate, quiver, ripple, ruffle, shiver, tremble, vibrate, waver ~*n.* **2.** palpitation, quiver, quivering, shiver, shudder, tremble, tremor, twitching, vibration **3.** agitation, commotion, confusion, dither, excitement, flurry, fluster, perturbation, state (*Inf.*), state of nervous excitement, tremble, tumult

flux alteration, change, flow, fluctuation, fluidity, instability, modification, motion, mutability, mutation, transition, unrest

fly[1] *v.* **1.** flit, flutter, hover, mount, sail, soar, take to the air, take wing, wing **2.** aviate, be at the controls, control, manoeuvre, operate, pilot **3.** display, flap, float, flutter, show, wave **4.** elapse, flit, glide, pass, pass swiftly, roll on, run its course, slip away **5.** be off like a shot (*Inf.*), bolt, career, dart, dash, hare (*Inf.*), hasten, hurry, race, rush, scamper, scoot, shoot, speed, sprint, tear, whiz (*Inf.*), zoom **6.** abscond, avoid, beat a retreat, clear out (*Inf.*), cut and run (*Inf.*), decamp, disappear, escape, flee, get away, hasten away, hightail (*Inf., chiefly U.S.*), light out (*Inf.*), make a getaway, make a quick exit, make one's escape, run, run for it, run from, show a clean pair of heels, shun, take flight, take off, take to one's heels **7. fly in the ointment** difficulty, drawback, flaw, hitch, prob-

lem, rub, small problem, snag **8. fly off the handle** blow one's top, explode, flip one's lid (*Sl.*), fly into a rage, have a tantrum, hit *or* go through the roof (*Inf.*), let fly (*Inf.*), lose one's cool (*Sl.*), lose one's temper **9. let fly a.** burst forth, give free reign, keep nothing back, lash out, let (someone) have it, lose one's temper, tear into (*Inf.*), vent **b.** cast, chuck, fire, fling, heave, hurl, hurtle, launch, let off, lob (*Inf.*), shoot, sling, throw

fly[2] *adj.* astute, canny, careful, knowing, nobody's fool, not born yesterday, on the ball (*Inf.*), sharp, shrewd, smart, wide-awake

fly at assail, assault, attack, fall upon, get stuck into (*Inf.*), go for, have a go at (*Inf.*), lay about, pitch into, rush at

fly-by-night *adj.* **1.** cowboy (*Inf.*), dubious, questionable, shady, undependable, unreliable, untrustworthy **2.** brief, here today, gone tomorrow, impermanent, short-lived

flying *adj.* **1.** brief, fleeting, fugacious, hasty, hurried, rushed, short-lived, transitory **2.** express, fast, fleet, mercurial, mobile, rapid, speedy, winged **3.** airborne, flapping, floating, fluttering, gliding, hovering, in the air, soaring, streaming, volitant, waving, wind-borne, winging

foam 1. *n.* bubbles, froth, head, lather, spray, spume, suds **2.** *v.* boil, bubble, effervesce, fizz, froth, lather

foamy bubbly, foaming, frothy, lathery, spumescent, sudsy

fob off 1. appease, deceive, equivocate with, give (someone) the run-around (*Inf.*), put off, stall **2.** dump, foist, get rid of, inflict, palm off, pass off, unload

focus *n.* **1.** bull's eye, centre, centre of activity, centre of attraction, core, cynosure, focal point, headquarters, heart, hub, meeting place, target **2. in focus** clear, distinct, sharp-edged, sharply defined **3. out of focus** blurred, fuzzy, ill-defined, indistinct, muzzy, unclear ~*v.* **4.** aim, bring to bear, centre, concentrate, converge, direct, fix, join, meet, pinpoint, rivet, spotlight, zero in (*Inf.*), zoom in

fodder feed, food, foodstuff, forage, provender, rations

foe adversary, antagonist, enemy, foeman (*Archaic*), opponent, rival

fog *n.* **1.** gloom, miasma, mist, murk, murkiness, peasouper (*Inf.*), smog **2.** *Fig.*

blindness, confusion, daze, haze, mist, obscurity, perplexity, stupor, trance ~v. **3**. becloud, bedim, befuddle, bewilder, blind, cloud, confuse, darken, daze, dim, muddle, obfuscate, obscure, perplex, stupefy **4**. cloud, mist over *or* up, steam up

foggy 1. blurred, brumous (*Rare*), cloudy, dim, grey, hazy, indistinct, misty, murky, nebulous, obscure, smoggy, soupy, vaporous **2**. *Fig.* befuddled, bewildered, clouded, cloudy, confused, dark, dazed, dim, indistinct, muddled, obscure, stupefied, stupid, unclear, vague

fogy, fogey anachronism, antique (*Inf.*), back number (*Inf.*), dodo (*Inf.*), fossil (*Inf.*), fuddy-duddy (*Inf.*), relic, square (*Inf.*), stick-in-the-mud (*Inf.*)

foible defect, failing, fault, idiosyncrasy, imperfection, infirmity, peculiarity, quirk, weakness, weak point

foil[1] *v.* baffle, balk, check, checkmate, circumvent, counter, defeat, disappoint, elude, frustrate, nip in the bud, nullify, outwit, put a spoke in (someone's) wheel (*Brit.*), stop, thwart

foil[2] antithesis, background, complement, contrast, setting

foist fob off, get rid of, impose, insert, insinuate, interpolate, introduce, palm off, pass off, put over, sneak in, unload

fold *v.* **1**. bend, crease, crumple, dog-ear, double, double over, gather, intertwine, overlap, pleat, tuck, turn under ~*n.* **2**. bend, crease, double thickness, folded portion, furrow, knife-edge, layer, overlap, pleat, turn, wrinkle ~*v.* **3**. do up, enclose, enfold, entwine, envelop, wrap, wrap up **4**. *Inf.* be ruined, close, collapse, crash, fail, go bankrupt, go bust (*Inf.*), go to the wall, go under (*Inf.*), shut down

folder binder, envelope, file, portfolio

folk clan, ethnic group, family, kin, kindred, people, race, tribe

follow 1. come after, come next, step into the shoes of, succeed, supersede, supplant, take the place of **2**. chase, dog, hound, hunt, pursue, run after, shadow, stalk, tail, track, trail **3**. accompany, attend, bring up the rear, come *or* go with, come after, escort, tag along, tread on the heels of **4**. act in accordance with, be guided by, comply, conform, give allegiance to, heed, mind, note, obey, observe, regard, watch **5**. appreciate, catch, catch on (*Inf.*), comprehend, fathom,

get, get the picture, grasp, keep up with, realize, see, take in, understand **6**. arise, be consequent, develop, emanate, ensue, flow, issue, proceed, result, spring, supervene **7**. adopt, copy, emulate, imitate, live up to, pattern oneself upon, take as example **8**. be a devotee *or* supporter of, be devoted to, be interested in, cultivate, keep abreast of, support

follower 1. adherent, admirer, apostle, backer, believer, convert, devotee, disciple, fan, fancier, habitué, partisan, pupil, representative, supporter, votary, worshipper **2**. attendant, companion, hanger-on, helper, henchman, lackey, minion, retainer (*History*), sidekick (*Sl.*)

following 1. *adj.* coming, consequent, consequential, ensuing, later, next, specified, subsequent, succeeding, successive **2**. *n.* audience, circle, clientele, coterie, entourage, fans, patronage, public, retinue, suite, support, supporters, train

follow through bring to a conclusion, complete, conclude, consummate, pursue, see through

follow up 1. check out, find out about, investigate, look into, make inquiries, pursue **2**. consolidate, continue, make sure, reinforce

folly absurdity, daftness, fatuity, foolishness, idiocy, imbecility, imprudence, indiscretion, irrationality, lunacy, madness, nonsense, preposterousness, rashness, recklessness, silliness, stupidity

foment abet, agitate, arouse, brew, encourage, excite, fan the flames, foster, goad, incite, instigate, promote, provoke, quicken, raise, sow the seeds of, spur, stimulate, stir up, whip up

fomenter agitator, demagogue, firebrand, incendiary, inciter, instigator, rabble-rouser, troublemaker

fond 1. *With of* addicted to, attached to, enamoured of, have a liking (fancy, taste) for, have a soft spot for, hooked on, keen on, partial to, predisposed towards **2**. adoring, affectionate, amorous, caring, devoted, doting, indulgent, loving, tender, warm **3**. absurd, credulous, deluded, delusive, delusory, empty, foolish, indiscreet, naive, overoptimistic, vain

fondle caress, cuddle, dandle, pat, pet, stroke

fondly 1. affectionately, dearly, indulgently, lovingly, possessively, tenderly, with affection 2. credulously, foolishly, naively, stupidly, vainly

fondness 1. attachment, fancy, liking, love, partiality, penchant, predilection, preference, soft spot, susceptibility, taste, weakness 2. affection, attachment, devotion, kindness, love, tenderness

food 1. aliment, board, bread, chow (*Inf.*), comestibles, commons, cooking, cuisine, diet, eatables (*Sl.*), eats (*Sl.*), edibles, fare, foodstuffs, grub (*Sl.*), larder, meat, menu, nosh (*Sl.*), nourishment, nutriment, nutrition, pabulum (*Rare*), provender, provisions, rations, refreshment, scoff (*Sl.*), stores, subsistence, sustenance, table, tuck (*Inf.*), viands, victuals 2. *Cattle, etc.* feed, fodder, forage, provender

fool *n.* 1. ass, bird-brain (*Inf.*), blockhead, bonehead (*Sl.*), chump (*Inf.*), clodpate (*Archaic*), clot (*Inf.*), dimwit (*Inf.*), dolt, dope (*Sl.*), dunce, dunderhead, fathead (*Inf.*), goose (*Inf.*), halfwit, idiot, ignoramus, illiterate, imbecile (*Inf.*), jackass, loon, mooncalf, moron, nincompoop, ninny, nit (*Inf.*), nitwit, numskull, sap (*Sl.*), silly, simpleton, twerp (*Inf.*), twit (*Inf.*) 2. butt, chump (*Inf.*), dupe, easy mark (*Sl.*), fall guy (*Inf., chiefly U.S.*), greenhorn (*Inf.*), gull (*Archaic*), laughing stock, mug (*Sl.*), stooge (*Sl.*), sucker (*Sl.*) 3. buffoon, clown, comic, harlequin, jester, merry-andrew, motley, pierrot, punchinello 4. **act** *or* **play the fool** act up, be silly, cavort, clown, cut capers, frolic, lark about (*Inf.*), mess about, play the goat, show off ~*v.* 5. bamboozle, beguile, bluff, cheat, con (*Sl.*), deceive, delude, dupe, gull (*Archaic*), have (someone) on, hoax, hoodwink, kid (*Inf.*), make a fool of, mislead, play a trick on, put one over on (*Inf.*), take in, trick 6. act the fool, cut capers, feign, jest, joke, kid (*Inf.*), make believe, pretend, tease 7. *With* **with, around with** *or* **about with** fiddle, meddle, mess, monkey, play, tamper, toy, trifle

fool around *or* **about** dawdle, footle (*Inf.*), hang around, idle, kill time, lark, mess about, play about, waste time

foolery antics, capers, carry-on (*Inf.*), childishness, clowning, folly, fooling, horseplay, larks, mischief, monkey tricks (*Inf.*), nonsense, practical jokes, pranks, shenanigans (*Inf.*), silliness, tomfoolery

foolhardy adventurous, bold, hotheaded, impetuous, imprudent, incautious, irresponsible, madcap, precipitate, rash, reckless, temerarious, venturesome, venturous

fooling *n.* bluffing, buffoonery, clownishness, farce, joking, kidding (*Inf.*), mockery, nonsense, pretence, shamming, skylarking (*Inf.*), teasing, tricks, trifling

foolish 1. absurd, ill-advised, ill-considered, ill-judged, imprudent, incautious, indiscreet, injudicious, nonsensical, senseless, short-sighted, silly, unintelligent, unreasonable, unwise 2. brainless, crazy, daft (*Inf.*), doltish, fatuous, half-baked (*Inf.*), half-witted, harebrained, idiotic, imbecilic, ludicrous, mad, moronic, potty (*Brit. inf.*), ridiculous, senseless, silly, simple, stupid, weak, witless

foolishly absurdly, idiotically, ill-advisedly, imprudently, incautiously, indiscreetly, injudiciously, like a fool, mistakenly, short-sightedly, stupidly, unwisely, without due consideration

foolishness 1. absurdity, folly, imprudence, inanity, indiscretion, irresponsibility, silliness, stupidity, weakness 2. bunk (*Inf.*), bunkum, carrying-on (*Inf.*), claptrap (*Inf.*), foolery, nonsense, rigmarole, rubbish

foolproof certain, guaranteed, infallible, never-failing, safe, sure-fire (*Inf.*), unassailable, unbreakable

footing 1. basis, establishment, foothold, foundation, ground, groundwork, installation, settlement 2. condition, grade, position, rank, relations, relationship, standing, state, status, terms

footling fiddling, fussy, hairsplitting, immaterial, insignificant, irrelevant, minor, niggly, petty, pointless, silly, time-wasting, trifling, trivial, unimportant

footslog hike, hoof it (*Sl.*), march, plod, tramp, trudge, yomp (*Sl.*)

footstep 1. footfall, step, tread 2. footmark, footprint, trace, track

fop beau, Beau Brummel, clothes-horse, coxcomb (*Archaic*), dandy, exquisite (*Obsolete*), fashion plate, macaroni (*in the C18*), peacock, popinjay, smoothie (*Sl.*), swell

foppish coxcombical, dandified, dandyish, dapper, dressy (*Inf.*), finical, natty (*Inf.*), preening, prinking, spruce, vain

forage 1. *n. Cattle, etc.* feed, fodder, food, foodstuffs, provender 2. *v.* cast about, explore, hunt, look round, plunder, raid, ransack, rummage, scour, scrounge (*Inf.*), search, seek

foray depredation, descent, incursion, inroad, invasion, irruption, raid, reconnaissance, sally, sortie, swoop

forbear abstain, avoid, cease, decline, desist, eschew, hold back, keep from, omit, pause, refrain, resist the temptation to, restrain oneself, stop, withhold

forbearance 1. indulgence, leniency, lenity, longanimity (*Rare*), long-suffering, mildness, moderation, patience, resignation, restraint, self-control, temperance, tolerance **2**. abstinence, avoidance, refraining

forbearing clement, easy, forgiving, indulgent, lenient, long-suffering, merciful, mild, moderate, patient, tolerant

forbid ban, debar, disallow, exclude, hinder, inhibit, interdict, outlaw, preclude, prohibit, proscribe, rule out, veto

forbidden banned, outlawed, out of bounds, prohibited, proscribed, taboo, *verboten*, vetoed

forbidding 1. abhorrent, disagreeable, odious, offensive, off-putting (*Inf.*), repellent, repulsive **2**. daunting, foreboding, frightening, grim, hostile, menacing, ominous, sinister, threatening, unfriendly

force *n*. **1**. dynamism, energy, impact, impulse, life, might, momentum, muscle, potency, power, pressure, stimulus, strength, stress, vigour **2**. arm-twisting (*Inf.*), coercion, compulsion, constraint, duress, enforcement, pressure, violence **3**. bite, cogency, effect, effectiveness, efficacy, influence, persuasiveness, power, punch (*Inf.*), strength, validity, weight **4**. drive, emphasis, fierceness, intensity, persistence, vehemence, vigour **5**. army, battalion, body, corps, detachment, division, host, legion, patrol, regiment, squad, squadron, troop, unit **6**. **in force a**. binding, current, effective, in operation, on the statute book, operative, valid, working **b**. all together, in full strength, in great numbers ~*v*. **7**. bring pressure to bear upon, coerce, compel, constrain, drive, impel, impose, make, necessitate, obligate, oblige, overcome, press, press-gang, pressure, pressurize, put the squeeze on (*Inf.*), strong-arm (*Inf.*), urge **8**. blast, break open, prise, propel, push, thrust, use violence on, wrench, wrest **9**. drag, exact, extort, wring

forced 1. compulsory, conscripted, en-

forced, involuntary, mandatory, obligatory, slave, unwilling **2**. affected, artificial, contrived, false, insincere, laboured, stiff, strained, unnatural, wooden

forceful cogent, compelling, convincing, dynamic, effective, persuasive, pithy, potent, powerful, telling, vigorous, weighty

forcible 1. active, cogent, compelling, effective, efficient, energetic, forceful, impressive, mighty, potent, powerful, strong, telling, valid, weighty **2**. aggressive, armed, coercive, compulsory, drastic, violent

forcibly against one's will, by force, by main force, compulsorily, under compulsion, under protest, willy-nilly

forebear ancestor, father, forefather, forerunner, predecessor, progenitor

forebode augur, betoken, foreshadow, foreshow, foretell, foretoken, forewarn, indicate, portend, predict, presage, prognosticate, promise, warn of

foreboding 1. anxiety, apprehension, apprehensiveness, chill, dread, fear, misgiving, premonition, presentiment **2**. augury, foreshadowing, foretoken, omen, portent, prediction, presage, prognostication, sign, token, warning

forecast 1. *v*. anticipate, augur, calculate, divine, estimate, foresee, foretell, plan, predict, prognosticate, prophesy **2**. *n*. anticipation, conjecture, foresight, forethought, guess, outlook, planning, prediction, prognosis, projection, prophecy

forefather ancestor, father, forebear, forerunner, predecessor, primogenitor, procreator, progenitor

forefront centre, fore, foreground, front, lead, prominence, spearhead, van, vanguard

forego *see* FORGO

foregoing above, antecedent, anterior, former, preceding, previous, prior

foreground centre, forefront, front, limelight, prominence

foreign 1. alien, borrowed, distant, exotic, external, imported, outlandish, outside, overseas, remote, strange, unfamiliar, unknown **2**. extraneous, extrinsic, incongruous, irrelevant, unassimilable, uncharacteristic, unrelated

foreigner alien, immigrant, incomer, newcomer, outlander, stranger

foreknowledge clairvoyance, foresight, forewarning, precognition, prescience, prevision, prior knowledge

foremost chief, first, front, headmost, highest, inaugural, initial, leading, paramount, pre-eminent, primary, prime, principal, supreme

foreordain doom, fate, foredoom, prearrange, predestine, predetermine, reserve

forerunner 1. ancestor, announcer, envoy, forebear, foregoer, harbinger, herald, precursor, predecessor, progenitor, prototype 2. augury, foretoken, indication, omen, portent, premonition, prognostic, sign, token

foresee anticipate, divine, envisage, forebode, forecast, foretell, predict, prophesy

foreshadow adumbrate, augur, betoken, bode, forebode, imply, indicate, portend, predict, prefigure, presage, promise, prophesy, signal

foresight anticipation, care, caution, circumspection, far-sightedness, forethought, precaution, premeditation, preparedness, prescience, prevision (*Rare*), provision, prudence

forestall anticipate, balk, circumvent, frustrate, head off, hinder, intercept, nip in the bud, obviate, parry, preclude, prevent, provide against, thwart

forestry arboriculture, dendrology (*Bot.*), silviculture, woodcraft, woodmanship

foretaste n. example, foretoken, indication, prelude, preview, sample, trailer, warning, whiff

foretell adumbrate, augur, bode, forebode, forecast, foreshadow, foreshow, forewarn, portend, predict, presage, prognosticate, prophesy, signify, soothsay

forethought anticipation, far-sightedness, foresight, precaution, providence, provision, prudence

foretoken v. augur, forebode, foreshadow, foreshow, give notice of, give warning of, portend, presage, signify, warn of

forever 1. always, evermore, for all time, for good and all (*Inf.*), for keeps, in perpetuity, till Doomsday, till the cows come home (*Inf.*), till the end of time, world without end 2. all the time, constantly, continually, endlessly, eternally, everlastingly, incessantly, interminably, perpetually, unremittingly

forewarn admonish, advise, alert, apprise, caution, dissuade, give fair warning, put on guard, put on the qui vive, tip off

foreword introduction, preamble, preface, preliminary, prolegomenon, prologue

forfeit 1. n. amercement (*Obsolete*), damages, fine, forfeiture, loss, mulct, penalty 2. v. be deprived of, be stripped of, give up, lose, relinquish, renounce, surrender

forfeiture confiscation, giving up, loss, relinquishment, sequestration (*Law*), surrender

forge v. 1. construct, contrive, create, devise, fabricate, fashion, form, frame, hammer out, invent, make, mould, shape, work 2. coin, copy, counterfeit, fake, falsify, feign, imitate

forger coiner, counterfeiter, falsifier

forgery 1. coining, counterfeiting, falsification, fraudulence, fraudulent imitation 2. counterfeit, fake, falsification, imitation, phoney (*Inf.*), sham

forget 1. consign to oblivion, dismiss from one's mind, let bygones be bygones, let slip from the memory 2. leave behind, lose sight of, omit, overlook

forgetful absent-minded, apt to forget, careless, dreamy, heedless, inattentive, lax, neglectful, negligent, oblivious, unmindful

forgetfulness absent-mindedness, abstraction, carelessness, dreaminess, heedlessness, inattention, lapse of memory, laxness, oblivion, obliviousness, woolgathering

forgive absolve, accept (someone's) apology, acquit, bear no malice, condone, excuse, exonerate, let bygones be bygones, let off (*Inf.*), pardon, remit

forgiveness absolution, acquittal, amnesty, condonation, exoneration, mercy, overlooking, pardon, remission

forgiving clement, compassionate, forbearing, humane, lenient, magnanimous, merciful, mild, soft-hearted, tolerant

forgo, forego abandon, abjure, cede, do without, give up, leave alone *or* out, relinquish, renounce, resign, sacrifice, surrender, waive, yield

forgotten blotted out, buried, bygone, consigned to oblivion, gone (clean) out of one's mind, left behind *or* out, lost, obliterated, omitted, past, past recall, unremembered

fork *v.* bifurcate, branch, branch off, diverge, divide, go separate ways, part, split

forked angled, bifurcate(d), branched, branching, divided, pronged, split, tined, zigzag

forlorn abandoned, bereft, cheerless, comfortless, deserted, desolate, destitute, disconsolate, forgotten, forsaken, friendless, helpless, homeless, hopeless, lonely, lost, miserable, pathetic, pitiable, pitiful, unhappy, woebegone, wretched

form[1] *v.* **1.** assemble, bring about, build, concoct, construct, contrive, create, devise, establish, fabricate, fashion, forge, found, invent, make, manufacture, model, mould, produce, put together, set up, shape **2.** arrange, combine, design, dispose, draw up, frame, organize, pattern, plan, think up **3.** accumulate, appear, become visible, come into being, crystallize, grow, materialize, rise, settle, show up, take shape **4.** acquire, contract, cultivate, develop, get into (*Inf.*), pick up **5.** compose, comprise, constitute, make, make up, serve as **6.** bring up, discipline, educate, instruct, rear, school, teach, train

form[2] *n.* **1.** appearance, cast, configuration, construction, cut, fashion, formation, model, mould, pattern, shape, structure **2.** anatomy, being, body, build, figure, frame, outline, person, physique, shape, silhouette **3.** arrangement, character, description, design, guise, kind, manifestation, manner, method, mode, order, practice, semblance, sort, species, stamp, style, system, type, variety, way **4.** format, framework, harmony, order, orderliness, organization, plan, proportion, structure, symmetry **5.** condition, fettle, fitness, good condition, good spirits, health, shape, trim **6.** off form below par, not in the pink (*Inf.*), not up to the mark, out of condition, stale, under the weather (*Inf.*), unfit **7.** behaviour, ceremony, conduct, convention, custom, done thing, etiquette, formality, manners, procedure, protocol, ritual, rule **8.** application, document, paper, sheet **9.** class, grade, rank

formal 1. approved, ceremonial, explicit, express, fixed, lawful, legal, methodical, official, prescribed, *pro forma*, regular, rigid, ritualistic, set, solemn, strict **2.** affected, aloof, ceremonious, conventional, correct, exact, precise, prim, punctilious, reserved, starched, stiff, unbending

formality 1. ceremony, convention, conventionality, custom, form, gesture, matter of form, procedure, red tape, rite, ritual **2.** ceremoniousness, correctness, decorum, etiquette, politesse, protocol, punctilio

format appearance, arrangement, construction, form, layout, look, make-up, plan, style, type

formation 1. accumulation, compilation, composition, constitution, crystallization, development, establishment, evolution, forming, generation, genesis, manufacture, organization, production **2.** arrangement, configuration, design, disposition, figure, grouping, pattern, rank, structure

formative 1. impressionable, malleable, mouldable, pliant, sensitive, susceptible **2.** determinative, developmental, influential, moulding, shaping

former 1. antecedent, anterior, *ci-devant*, earlier, erstwhile, ex-, late, one-time, previous, prior, quondam, whilom (*Archaic*) **2.** ancient, bygone, departed, long ago, long gone, of yore, old, old-time, past **3.** above, aforementioned, aforesaid, first mentioned, foregoing, preceding

formerly aforetime (*Archaic*), already, at one time, before, heretofore, lately, once, previously

formidable 1. appalling, dangerous, daunting, dismaying, dreadful, fearful, frightful, horrible, intimidating, menacing, shocking, terrifying, threatening **2.** arduous, challenging, colossal, difficult, mammoth, onerous, overwhelming, staggering, toilsome **3.** awesome, great, impressive, indomitable, mighty, powerful, puissant, redoubtable, terrific, tremendous

formless amorphous, disorganized, inchoate, incoherent, indefinite, nebulous, shapeless, unformed, vague

formula 1. form of words, formulary, rite, ritual, rubric **2.** blueprint, method, modus operandi, precept, prescription, principle, procedure, recipe, rule, way

formulate 1. codify, define, detail, express, frame, give form to, particularize, set down, specify, systematize **2.** coin, develop, devise, evolve, forge, invent, map out, originate, plan, work out

forsake 1. abandon, cast off, desert,

disown, jettison, jilt, leave, leave in the lurch, quit, repudiate, throw over **2**. abdicate, forgo, forswear, give up, have done with, relinquish, renounce, set aside, surrender, turn one's back on, yield

forsaken abandoned, cast off, deserted, destitute, disowned, forlorn, friendless, ignored, isolated, jilted, left behind, left in the lurch, lonely, marooned, outcast, solitary

forswear 1. abandon, abjure, drop (*Inf.*), forgo, forsake, give up, renounce, swear off **2**. deny, disavow, disclaim, disown, recant, reject, repudiate, retract **3**. lie, perjure oneself, renege, swear falsely

fort 1. blockhouse, camp, castle, citadel, fastness, fortification, fortress, garrison, redoubt, station, stronghold **2. hold the fort** carry on, keep things moving, keep things on an even keel, maintain the status quo, stand in, take over the reins

forte gift, long suit (*Inf.*), métier, speciality, strength, strong point, talent

forth ahead, away, forward, into the open, onward, out, out of concealment, outward

forthcoming 1. approaching, coming, expected, future, imminent, impending, prospective **2**. accessible, at hand, available, in evidence, obtainable, on tap (*Inf.*), ready **3**. chatty, communicative, expansive, free, informative, open, sociable, talkative, unreserved

forthright above-board, blunt, candid, direct, frank, open, outspoken, plainspoken, straightforward, straight from the shoulder (*Inf.*)

forthwith at once, directly, immediately, instantly, quickly, right away, straightaway, *tout de suite*, without delay

fortification 1. bastion, bulwark, castle, citadel, defence, fastness, fort, fortress, keep, protection, stronghold **2**. embattlement, reinforcement, strengthening

fortify 1. brace, buttress, embattle, garrison, protect, reinforce, secure, shore up, strengthen, support **2**. brace, cheer, confirm, embolden, encourage, hearten, invigorate, reassure, stiffen, strengthen, sustain

fortitude backbone, braveness, courage, dauntlessness, determination, endurance, fearlessness, firmness, grit, guts (*Inf.*), hardihood, intrepidity, patience, perseverance, pluck, resolution, staying power, stoutheartedness, strength, strength of mind, valour

fortress castle, citadel, fastness, fort, redoubt, stronghold

fortuitous 1. accidental, arbitrary, casual, chance, contingent, incidental, random, unforeseen, unplanned **2**. fluky (*Inf.*), fortunate, happy, lucky, providential, serendipitous

fortunate 1. born with a silver spoon in one's mouth, bright, favoured, golden, happy, having a charmed life, in luck, lucky, prosperous, rosy, sitting pretty (*Inf.*), successful, well-off **2**. advantageous, auspicious, convenient, encouraging, favourable, felicitous, fortuitous, helpful, opportune, profitable, promising, propitious, providential, timely

fortunately by a happy chance, by good luck, happily, luckily, providentially

fortune 1. affluence, gold mine, opulence, possessions, property, prosperity, riches, treasure, wealth **2**. accident, chance, contingency, destiny, fate, fortuity, hap (*Archaic*), hazard, kismet, luck, providence **3**. *Often plural* adventures, circumstances, destiny, doom, expectation, experience(s), history, life, lot, portion, star, success **4**. bomb (*Sl.*), bundle (*Sl.*), king's ransom, mint, packet (*Sl.*), pile (*Sl.*), wealth

forward *adj*. **1**. advanced, advancing, early, forward-looking, onward, precocious, premature, progressive, well-developed **2**. advance, first, fore, foremost, front, head, leading **3**. assuming, bare-faced, bold, brash, brass-necked (*Inf.*), brazen, brazen-faced, cheeky, confident, familiar, fresh (*Inf.*), impertinent, impudent, overassertive, overweening, pert, presuming, presumptuous, pushy (*Inf.*) ~*adv*. **4**. *Also* **forwards** ahead, forth, on, onward **5**. into consideration, into prominence, into the open, into view, out, to light, to the fore, to the surface ~*v*. **6**. advance, aid, assist, back, encourage, expedite, favour, foster, further, hasten, help, hurry, promote, speed, support **7**. *Commerce* dispatch, freight, post, route, send, send on, ship, transmit

forward-looking dynamic, enlightened, enterprising, go-ahead, go-getting (*Inf.*), liberal, modern, progressive, reforming

forwardness boldness, brashness, brazenness, cheek (*Inf.*), cheekiness, impertinence, impudence, overconfidence, pertness, presumption

fossilized 1. dead, dead as a dodo, extinct, inflexible, ossified, petrified, prehistoric **2.** anachronistic, antediluvian, antiquated, archaistic, behind the times, démodé, obsolete, out of the ark (*Inf.*), passé, superannuated

foster 1. cultivate, encourage, feed, foment, nurture, promote, stimulate, support, uphold **2.** bring up, mother, nurse, raise, rear, take care of **3.** accommodate, cherish, entertain, harbour, nourish, sustain

foul *adj.* **1.** contaminated, dirty, disgusting, fetid, filthy, impure, loathsome, malodorous, mephitic, nasty, nauseating, noisome, offensive, polluted, putrid, rank, repulsive, revolting, rotten, squalid, stinking, sullied, tainted, unclean **2.** abusive, blasphemous, blue, coarse, dirty, filthy, foul-mouthed, gross, indecent, lewd, low, obscene, profane, scatological, scurrilous, smutty, vulgar **3.** abhorrent, abominable, base, despicable, detestable, disgraceful, dishonourable, egregious, hateful, heinous, infamous, iniquitous, nefarious, notorious, offensive, scandalous, shameful, vicious, vile, wicked **4.** crooked, dirty, dishonest, fraudulent, inequitable, shady (*Inf.*), underhand, unfair, unjust, unscrupulous, unsportsmanlike **5.** bad, blustery, disagreeable, foggy, murky, rainy, rough, stormy, wet, wild ~*v.* **6.** begrime, besmear, besmirch, contaminate, defile, dirty, pollute, smear, soil, stain, sully, taint **7.** block, catch, choke, clog, ensnare, entangle, jam, snarl, twist

foul-mouthed abusive, blasphemous, coarse, Fescennine (*Rare*), obscene, offensive, profane

foul play chicanery, corruption, crime, deception, dirty work, doubledealing, duplicity, fraud, perfidy, roguery, sharp practice, skulduggery, treachery, villainy

foul up botch, bungle, make a mess of, mismanage, muck up (*Sl.*), put a spanner in the works (*Inf.*), spoil

found 1. bring into being, constitute, construct, create, endow, erect, establish, fix, inaugurate, institute, organize, originate, plant, raise, settle, set up, start **2.** base, bottom, build, ground, rest, root, sustain

foundation 1. base, basis, bedrock, bottom, footing, groundwork, substructure, underpinning **2.** endowment, establishment, inauguration, institution, organization, setting up, settlement

founder[1] *n.* architect, author, beginner, benefactor, builder, constructor, designer, establisher, father, framer, generator, initiator, institutor, inventor, maker, organizer, originator, patriarch

founder[2] *v.* **1.** be lost, go down, go to the bottom, sink, submerge **2.** *Fig.* abort, break down, collapse, come to grief, come to nothing, fail, fall through, miscarry, misfire **3.** collapse, fall, go lame, lurch, sprawl, stagger, stumble, trip

foundling orphan, outcast, stray, waif

fountain 1. font, fount, jet, reservoir, spout, spray, spring, well **2.** *Fig.* beginning, cause, commencement, derivation, fountainhead, genesis, origin, rise, source, wellhead, wellspring

fountainhead fons et origo, fount, inspiration, mainspring, origin, source, spring, well, wellspring

foursquare 1. *adv.* firmly, resolutely, squarely **2.** *adj.* firm, firmly-based, immovable, resolute, solid, steady, strong, unyielding

foxy artful, astute, canny, crafty, cunning, devious, guileful, knowing, sharp, shrewd, sly, tricky, wily

foyer antechamber, anteroom, entrance hall, lobby, reception area, vestibule

fracas affray (*Law*), aggro (*Sl.*), brawl, disturbance, donnybrook, fight, free-for-all (*Inf.*), melee, quarrel, riot, row, rumpus, scrimmage, scuffle, trouble, uproar

fractious awkward, captious, crabby, cross, fretful, froward, grouchy (*Inf.*), irritable, peevish, pettish, petulant, querulous, recalcitrant, refractory, testy, touchy, unruly

fracture 1. *n.* breach, break, cleft, crack, fissure, gap, opening, rent, rift, rupture, schism, split **2.** *v.* break, crack, rupture, splinter, split

fragile breakable, brittle, dainty, delicate, feeble, fine, flimsy, frail, frangible, infirm, slight, weak

fragility brittleness, delicacy, feebleness, frailty, frangibility, infirmity, weakness

fragment 1. *n.* bit, chip, fraction, morsel, part, particle, piece, portion, remnant, scrap, shiver, sliver 2. *v.* break, break up, come apart, come to pieces, crumble, disintegrate, disunite, divide, shatter, shiver, splinter, split, split up

fragmentary bitty, broken, disconnected, discrete, disjointed, incoherent, incomplete, partial, piecemeal, scattered, scrappy, sketchy, unsystematic

fragrance aroma, balm, bouquet, fragrancy, perfume, redolence, scent, smell, sweet odour

fragrant ambrosial, aromatic, balmy, odoriferous, odorous, perfumed, redolent, sweet-scented, sweet-smelling

frail breakable, brittle, decrepit, delicate, feeble, flimsy, fragile, frangible, infirm, insubstantial, puny, slight, tender, unsound, vulnerable, weak, wispy

frailty 1. fallibility, feebleness, frailness, infirmity, peccability, puniness, susceptibility, weakness 2. blemish, defect, deficiency, failing, fault, flaw, foible, imperfection, peccadillo, shortcoming, vice, weak point

frame *v.* 1. assemble, build, constitute, construct, fabricate, fashion, forge, form, institute, invent, make, manufacture, model, mould, put together, set up 2. block out, compose, conceive, concoct, contrive, cook up, devise, draft, draw up, form, formulate, hatch, map out, plan, shape, sketch 3. case, enclose, mount, surround ~*n.* 4. casing, construction, fabric, form, framework, scheme, shell, structure, system 5. anatomy, body, build, carcass, morphology, physique, skeleton 6. mount, mounting, setting 7. **frame of mind** attitude, disposition, fettle, humour, mood, outlook, spirit, state, temper

frame-up fabrication, fit-up (*Sl.*), put-up job, trumped-up charge

framework core, fabric, foundation, frame, frame of reference, groundwork, plan, schema, shell, skeleton, structure, the bare bones

franchise authorization, charter, exemption, freedom, immunity, prerogative, privilege, right, suffrage, vote

frank artless, blunt, candid, direct, downright, forthright, free, honest, ingenuous, open, outright, outspoken, plain, plain-spoken, sincere, straightforward, straight from the shoulder (*Inf.*), transparent, truthful, uncon-

cealed, undisguised, unreserved, unrestricted

frankly 1. candidly, honestly, in truth, to be honest 2. bluntly, directly, freely, openly, plainly, straight (*Inf.*), without reserve

frankness absence of reserve, bluntness, candour, forthrightness, ingenuousness, openness, outspokenness, plain speaking, truthfulness

frantic at one's wits' end, berserk, beside oneself, distracted, distraught, fraught (*Inf.*), frenetic, frenzied, furious, hectic, mad, overwrought, raging, raving, wild

fraternity association, brotherhood, camaraderie, circle, clan, club, companionship, company, comradeship, fellowship, guild, kinship, league, set, sodality, union

fraternize associate, concur, consort, cooperate, go around with, hang out (*Inf.*), hobnob, keep company, mingle, mix, socialize, sympathize, unite

fraud 1. artifice, cheat, chicane, chicanery, craft, deceit, deception, double-dealing, duplicity, guile, hoax, humbug, imposture, sharp practice, spuriousness, stratagems, swindling, treachery, trickery 2. bluffer, charlatan, cheat, counterfeit, double-dealer, fake, forgery, hoax, hoaxer, impostor, mountebank, phoney (*Inf.*), pretender, quack, sham, swindler

fraudulent counterfeit, crafty, criminal, crooked (*Inf.*), deceitful, deceptive, dishonest, double-dealing, duplicitous, false, knavish, phoney (*Inf.*), sham, spurious, swindling, treacherous

fraught 1. *With* **with** abounding, accompanied, attended, bristling, charged, filled, full, heavy, laden, replete, stuffed 2. *Inf.* agitated, anxious, difficult, distracted, distressed, distressing, emotionally charged, emotive, hag-ridden, strung-up, tense, tricky, trying, uptight (*Inf.*)

fray[1] *n.* affray (*Law*), battle, battle royal, brawl, broil, clash, combat, conflict, disturbance, donnybrook, fight, melee, quarrel, riot, row, ruckus (*Inf.*), rumble (*U.S. sl.*), rumpus, scuffle, set-to (*Inf.*)

fray[2] *v.* become threadbare, chafe, fret, rub, wear, wear away, wear thin

frayed frazzled, out at elbows, ragged, tattered, threadbare, worn

freak *n.* 1. aberration, abnormality,

abortion, anomaly, grotesque, malformation, monster, monstrosity, mutant, oddity, queer fish (*Inf.*), *rara avis*, sport, teratism, weirdo *or* weirdie (*Inf.*) **2.** caprice, crotchet, fad, fancy, folly, humour, irregularity, quirk, turn, twist, vagary, whim, whimsy **3.** *Sl.* addict, aficionado, buff, devotee, enthusiast, fan, fanatic, fiend (*Inf.*), nut (*Sl.*) ~*adj.* **4.** aberrant, abnormal, atypical, bizarre, erratic, exceptional, fluky (*Inf.*), fortuitous, odd, queer, unaccountable, unexpected, unforeseen, unparalleled, unpredictable, unusual

freakish 1. arbitrary, capricious, changeable, erratic, fanciful, fitful, humorous, odd, unpredictable, vagarious (*Rare*), wayward, whimsical **2.** aberrant, abnormal, fantastic, freaky (*Sl.*), grotesque, malformed, monstrous, odd, outlandish, *outré*, preternatural, strange, teratoid (*Biol.*), unconventional, weird

freaky abnormal, bizarre, crazy, far-out (*Sl.*), freakish, odd, queer, strange, unconventional, weird, wild

free *adj.* **1.** complimentary, for free (*Inf.*), for nothing, free of charge, gratis, gratuitous, on the house, unpaid, without charge **2.** at large, at liberty, footloose, independent, liberated, loose, off the hook (*Inf.*), on the loose, uncommitted, unconstrained, unengaged, unfettered, unrestrained **3.** able, allowed, clear, disengaged, loose, open, permitted, unattached, unengaged, unhampered, unimpeded, unobstructed, unregulated, unrestricted, untrammelled **4.** *With* **of** above, beyond, deficient in, devoid of, exempt from, immune to, lacking (in), not liable to, safe from, sans (*Archaic*), unaffected by, unencumbered by, untouched by, without **5.** autarchic, autonomous, democratic, emancipated, independent, self-governing, self-ruling, sovereign **6.** at leisure, available, empty, extra, idle, not tied down, spare, unemployed, uninhabited, unoccupied, unused, vacant **7.** casual, easy, familiar, forward, frank, free and easy, informal, laid-back (*Inf.*), lax, liberal, loose, natural, open, relaxed, spontaneous, unbidden, unceremonious, unconstrained, unforced, uninhibited **8.** big (*Inf.*), bounteous, bountiful, charitable, eager, generous, hospitable, lavish, liberal, munificent, open-handed, prodigal, unsparing, unstinting, willing **9. free and easy** casual, easy-going, informal,

laid-back (*Inf.*), lax, lenient, liberal, relaxed, tolerant, unceremonious ~*adv.* **10.** at no cost, for love, gratis, without charge **11.** abundantly, copiously, freely, idly, loosely ~*v.* **12.** deliver, discharge, disenthrall, emancipate, let go, let out, liberate, loose, manumit, release, set at liberty, set free, turn loose, uncage, unchain, unfetter, unleash, untie **13.** clear, cut loose, deliver, disengage, disentangle, exempt, extricate, ransom, redeem, relieve, rescue, rid, unburden, undo, unshackle

freebooter bandit, brigand, buccaneer, cateran (*Scot.*), highwayman, looter, marauder, pillager, pirate, plunderer, raider, reiver (*Dialect*), robber, rover

freedom 1. autonomy, deliverance, emancipation, home rule, independence, liberty, manumission, release, self-government **2.** exemption, immunity, impunity, privilege **3.** ability, carte blanche, discretion, elbowroom, facility, flexibility, free rein, latitude, leeway, licence, opportunity, play, power, range, scope **4.** abandon, candour, directness, ease, familiarity, frankness, informality, ingenuousness, lack of restraint *or* reserve, openness, unconstraint **5.** boldness, brazenness, disrespect, forwardness, impertinence, laxity, licence, overfamiliarity, presumption

free-for-all affray (*Law*), brawl, donnybrook, dust-up (*Inf.*), fight, fracas, melee, riot, row, shindy (*Sl.*)

free hand *n.* authority, carte blanche, discretion, freedom, latitude, liberty, scope

freely 1. of one's own accord, of one's own free will, spontaneously, voluntarily, willingly, without prompting **2.** candidly, frankly, openly, plainly, unreservedly, without reserve **3.** as you please, unchallenged, without let or hindrance, without restraint **4.** abundantly, amply, bountifully, copiously, extravagantly, lavishly, liberally, like water, open-handedly, unstintingly, with a free hand **5.** cleanly, easily, loosely, readily, smoothly

freethinker agnostic, deist, doubter, infidel, sceptic, unbeliever

freewheel coast, drift, float, glide, relax one's efforts, rest on one's oars

freeze 1. benumb, chill, congeal, glaciate, harden, ice over *or* up, stiffen **2.** fix, hold up, inhibit, peg, stop, suspend

freezing arctic, biting, bitter, chill,

chilled, cutting, frost-bound, frosty, glacial, icy, numbing, penetrating, polar, raw, Siberian, wintry

freight *n.* **1.** carriage, conveyance, shipment, transportation **2.** bales, bulk, burden, cargo, consignment, contents, goods, haul, lading, load, merchandise, payload, tonnage

French Gallic

frenetic demented, distraught, excited, fanatical, frantic, frenzied, hyped up (*Sl.*), insane, mad, maniacal, obsessive, overwrought, unbalanced, wild

frenzied agitated, all het up (*Inf.*), convulsive, distracted, distraught, excited, feverish, frantic, frenetic, furious, hysterical, mad, maniacal, rabid, uncontrolled, wild

frenzy 1. aberration, agitation, delirium, derangement, distraction, fury, hysteria, insanity, lunacy, madness, mania, paroxysm, passion, rage, seizure, transport, turmoil **2.** bout, burst, convulsion, fit, outburst, paroxysm, spasm

frequency constancy, frequentness, periodicity, prevalence, recurrence, repetition

frequent[1] *adj.* common, constant, continual, customary, everyday, familiar, habitual, incessant, numerous, persistent, recurrent, recurring, reiterated, repeated, usual

frequent[2] *v.* attend, be a regular customer of, be found at, hang out at (*Inf.*), haunt, patronize, resort, visit

frequenter client, fan, habitué, haunter, patron, regular, regular customer, regular visitor

frequently commonly, customarily, habitually, many a time, many times, much, not infrequently, oft (*Literary*), often, oftentimes (*Archaic*), over and over again, repeatedly, thick and fast, very often

fresh 1. different, latest, modern, modernistic, new, new-fangled, novel, original, recent, this season's, unconventional, unusual, up-to-date **2.** added, additional, auxiliary, extra, further, more, other, renewed, supplementary **3.** bracing, bright, brisk, clean, clear, cool, crisp, invigorating, pure, refreshing, spanking, sparkling, stiff, sweet, unpolluted **4.** alert, bouncing, bright, bright eyed and bushy tailed (*Inf.*), chipper (*Inf., chiefly U.S.*), energetic, full of vim and vigour (*Inf.*), invigorated, keen, like a new man,

lively, refreshed, rested, restored, revived, sprightly, spry, vigorous, vital **5.** blooming, clear, fair, florid, glowing, good, hardy, healthy, rosy, ruddy, wholesome **6.** dewy, undimmed, unfaded, unwearied, unwithered, verdant, vivid, young **7.** artless, callow, green, inexperienced, natural, new, raw, uncultivated, untrained, untried, youthful **8.** crude, green, natural, raw, uncured, undried, unprocessed, unsalted **9.** *Inf.* bold, brazen, cheeky, disrespectful, familiar, flip (*Inf., chiefly U.S.*), forward, impudent, insolent, pert, presumptuous, saucy, smart-alecky (*Inf.*)

freshen 1. enliven, freshen up, liven up, refresh, restore, revitalize, rouse, spruce up, titivate **2.** air, purify, ventilate

freshness 1. innovativeness, inventiveness, newness, novelty, originality **2.** bloom, brightness, cleanness, clearness, dewiness, glow, shine, sparkle, vigour, wholesomeness

fret[1] **1.** affront, agonize, anguish, annoy, brood, chagrin, goad, grieve, harass, irritate, lose sleep over, provoke, ruffle, torment, upset *or* distress oneself, worry **2.** agitate, bother, distress, disturb, gall, irk, nag, nettle, peeve (*Inf.*), pique, rankle with, rile, trouble, vex

fret[2] abrade, chafe, erode, fray, gall, rub, wear, wear away

fretful captious, complaining, cross, crotchety (*Inf.*), edgy, fractious, irritable, out of sorts, peevish, petulant, querulous, short-tempered, splenetic, testy, touchy, uneasy

friable brittle, crisp, crumbly, powdery, pulverizable

friction 1. abrasion, attrition, chafing, erosion, fretting, grating, irritation, rasping, resistance, rubbing, scraping, wearing away **2.** animosity, antagonism, bad blood, bad feeling, bickering, conflict, disagreement, discontent, discord, disharmony, dispute, dissension, hostility, incompatibility, opposition, resentment, rivalry, wrangling

friend 1. Achates, alter ego, boon companion, bosom friend, buddy (*Inf.*), china (*Sl.*), chum (*Inf.*), companion, comrade, confidant, crony, familiar, intimate, mate (*Inf.*), pal, partner, playmate, soul mate **2.** adherent, advocate, ally, associate, backer, benefactor, partisan, patron, supporter, well-wisher

friendless abandoned, alienated, all alone, alone, cut off, deserted, estranged, forlorn, forsaken, isolated, lonely, lonesome, ostracized, shunned, solitary, unattached, with no one to turn to, without a friend in the world, without ties

friendliness affability, amiability, companionability, congeniality, conviviality, geniality, kindliness, mateyness (*Brit. inf.*), neighbourliness, open arms, sociability, warmth

friendly affable, affectionate, amiable, amicable, attached, attentive, auspicious, beneficial, benevolent, benign, chummy (*Inf.*), close, clubby, companionable, comradely, conciliatory, confiding, convivial, cordial, familiar, favourable, fond, fraternal, genial, good, helpful, intimate, kind, kindly, matey (*Brit. inf.*), neighbourly, on good terms, on visiting terms, outgoing, peaceable, propitious, receptive, sociable, sympathetic, thick (*Inf.*), welcoming, well-disposed

friendship affection, affinity, alliance, amity, attachment, benevolence, closeness, concord, familiarity, fondness, friendliness, good-fellowship, good will, harmony, intimacy, love, rapport, regard

fright 1. alarm, apprehension, (blue) funk (*Inf.*), cold sweat, consternation, dismay, dread, fear, fear and trembling, horror, panic, quaking, scare, shock, terror, the shivers, trepidation **2.** *Inf.* eyesore, frump, mess (*Inf.*), scarecrow, sight (*Inf.*)

frighten affright (*Archaic*), alarm, appal, cow, daunt, dismay, freeze one's blood, intimidate, make one's blood run cold, make one's hair stand on end (*Inf.*), make (someone) jump out of his skin (*Inf.*), petrify, put the wind up (someone) (*Inf.*), scare, scare (someone) stiff, scare the living daylights out of (someone) (*Inf.*), shock, startle, terrify, terrorize, throw into a fright, throw into a panic, unman, unnerve

frightened abashed, affrighted (*Archaic*), afraid, alarmed, cowed, dismayed, frozen, in a cold sweat, in a panic, in fear and trepidation, numb with fear, panicky, petrified, scared, scared stiff, startled, terrified, terrorized, terror-stricken, unnerved

frightening alarming, appalling, bloodcurdling, daunting, dismaying, dreadful, fearful, fearsome, hair-raising, horrifying, intimidating, menacing, scary (*Inf.*), shocking, spooky (*Inf.*), terrifying, unnerving

frightful 1. alarming, appalling, awful, dire, dread, dreadful, fearful, ghastly, grim, grisly, gruesome, harrowing, hideous, horrendous, horrible, horrid, lurid, macabre, petrifying, shocking, terrible, terrifying, traumatic, unnerving, unspeakable **2.** annoying, awful, disagreeable, dreadful, extreme, great, insufferable, terrible, terrific, unpleasant

frigid 1. arctic, chill, cold, cool, frostbound, frosty, frozen, gelid, glacial, hyperborean, icy, Siberian, wintry **2.** aloof, austere, cold-hearted, forbidding, formal, icy, lifeless, passionless, passive, repellent, rigid, stiff, unapproachable, unbending, unfeeling, unloving, unresponsive

frigidity aloofness, austerity, chill, cold-heartedness, coldness, frostiness, iciness, impassivity, lack of response, lifelessness, passivity, touch-me-not attitude, unapproachability, unresponsiveness, wintriness

frill *n.* flounce, furbelow, gathering, purfle, ruche, ruching, ruff, ruffle, tuck

frills additions, affectation(s), bits and pieces, decoration(s), dressing up, embellishment(s), extras, fanciness, fandangles, finery, frilliness, frippery, fuss, gewgaws, jazz (*Sl.*), mannerisms, nonsense, ornamentation, ostentation, superfluities, tomfoolery, trimmings

frilly fancy, flouncy, frothy, lacy, ruched, ruffled

fringe *n.* **1.** binding, border, edging, hem, tassel, trimming **2.** borderline, edge, limits, march, marches, margin, outskirts, perimeter, periphery ~*adj.* **3.** unconventional, unofficial, unorthodox ~*v.* **4.** border, edge, enclose, skirt, surround, trim

fringed befringed, bordered, edged, margined, outlined, overhung

frippery 1. fanciness, finery, flashiness, foppery, frilliness, frills, fussiness, gaudiness, glad rags (*Sl.*), meretriciousness, nonsense, ostentation, pretentiousness, showiness, tawdriness **2.** adornment, bauble, decoration, fandangle, gewgaw, knick-knack, ornament, toy, trinket

frisk 1. bounce, caper, cavort, curvet, dance, frolic, gambol, hop, jump, play, prance, rollick, romp, skip, sport, trip **2.**

Inf. check, inspect, run over, search, shake down (*U.S. sl.*)

frisky bouncy, coltish, frolicsome, full of beans (*Inf.*), full of joie de vivre, high-spirited, in high spirits, kittenish, lively, playful, rollicking, romping, spirited, sportive

fritter (away) dally away, dissipate, fool away, idle (away), misspend, run through, spend like water, squander, waste

frivolity childishness, flightiness, flippancy, flummery, folly, frivolousness, fun, gaiety, giddiness, jest, levity, light-heartedness, lightness, nonsense, puerility, shallowness, silliness, superficiality, trifling, triviality

frivolous 1. childish, dizzy, empty-headed, flighty, flip (*Inf.*), flippant, foolish, giddy, idle, ill-considered, juvenile, light-minded, nonserious, puerile, silly, superficial 2. extravagant, impractical, light, minor, niggling, paltry, peripheral, petty, pointless, shallow, trifling, trivial, unimportant

frizzle crisp, fry, hiss, roast, scorch, sizzle, sputter

frizzy corrugated, crimped, crisp, frizzed, tight-curled, wiry

frolic *v.* 1. caper, cavort, cut capers, frisk, gambol, lark, make merry, play, rollick, romp, sport ~*n.* 2. antic, escapade, gambado, gambol, game, lark, prank, revel, romp, spree 3. amusement, drollery, fun, fun and games, gaiety, high jinks, merriment, skylarking (*Inf.*), sport

frolicsome coltish, frisky, gay, kittenish, lively, merry, playful, rollicking, sportive, sprightly, wanton (*Archaic*)

front *n.* 1. anterior, exterior, façade, face, facing, foreground, forepart, frontage, obverse 2. beginning, fore, forefront, front line, head, lead, top, van, vanguard 3. air, appearance, aspect, bearing, countenance, demeanour, expression, exterior, face, manner, mien, show 4. blind, cover, cover-up, disguise, façade, mask, pretext, show 5. **in front** ahead, before, first, in advance, in the lead, in the van, leading, preceding, to the fore ~*adj.* 6. first, foremost, head, headmost, lead, leading, topmost ~*v.* 7. face (onto), look over *or* onto, overlook

frontier borderland, borderline, bound, boundary, confines, edge, limit, marches, perimeter, verge

frost freeze, freeze-up, hoarfrost, Jack Frost, rime

frosty 1. chilly, cold, frozen, hoar (*Rare*), ice-capped, icicled, icy, rimy, wintry 2. discouraging, frigid, off-putting, standoffish, unenthusiastic, unfriendly, unwelcoming

froth 1. *n.* bubbles, effervescence, foam, head, lather, scum, spume, suds 2. *v.* bubble over, come to a head, effervesce, fizz, foam, lather

frothy 1. foaming, foamy, spumescent, spumous, spumy, sudsy 2. *Fig.* empty, frilly, frivolous, light, petty, slight, trifling, trivial, trumpery, unnecessary, unsubstantial, vain

frown 1. give a dirty look, glare, glower, knit one's brows, look daggers, lower, scowl 2. *With* **on** *or* **upon** disapprove of, discountenance, discourage, dislike, look askance at, not take kindly to, show disapproval *or* displeasure, take a dim view of, view with disfavour

frowsty close, fuggy, fusty, ill-smelling, musty, stale, stuffy

frowzy blowzy, dirty, draggletailed (*Archaic*), frumpish, messy, slatternly, sloppy, slovenly, sluttish, ungroomed, unkempt, untidy, unwashed

frozen 1. arctic, chilled, chilled to the marrow, frigid, frosted, icebound, ice-cold, ice-covered, icy, numb 2. fixed, pegged (*of prices*), petrified, rooted, stock-still, stopped, suspended, turned to stone

frugal abstemious, careful, cheese-paring, economical, meagre, niggardly, parsimonious, penny-wise, provident, prudent, saving, sparing, thrifty

frugality carefulness, conservation, economizing, economy, good management, husbandry, moderation, providence, thrift, thriftiness

fruit 1. crop, harvest, produce, product, yield 2. advantage, benefit, consequence, effect, outcome, profit, result, return, reward

fruitful 1. fecund, fertile, fructiferous 2. abundant, copious, flush, plenteous, plentiful, productive, profuse, prolific, rich, spawning 3. advantageous, beneficial, effective, gainful, productive, profitable, rewarding, successful, useful, well-spent, worthwhile

fruition actualization, attainment, completion, consummation, enjoyment, fulfilment, materialization, maturation, maturity, perfection, realization, ripeness

fruitless abortive, barren, bootless, futile, idle, ineffectual, in vain, pointless, profitless, to no avail, to no effect, unavailing, unfruitful, unproductive, unprofitable, unprolific, unsuccessful, useless, vain

fruity 1. full, mellow, resonant, rich **2.** *Inf.* bawdy, blue, hot, indecent, indelicate, juicy, near the knuckle (*Inf.*), racy, ripe, risqué, salacious, sexy, smutty, spicy (*Inf.*), suggestive, titillating, vulgar

frumpish, frumpy badly-dressed, dated, dingy, dowdy, drab, dreary, out of date

frustrate 1. baffle, balk, block, check, circumvent, confront, counter, defeat, disappoint, foil, forestall, inhibit, neutralize, nullify, render null and void, stymie, thwart **2.** depress, discourage, dishearten

frustrated carrying a chip on one's shoulder (*Inf.*), disappointed, discontented, discouraged, disheartened, embittered, foiled, irked, resentful

frustration 1. blocking, circumvention, contravention, curbing, failure, foiling, nonfulfilment, nonsuccess, obstruction, thwarting **2.** annoyance, disappointment, dissatisfaction, grievance, irritation, resentment, vexation

fuddled confused, drunk, inebriated, intoxicated, muddled, muzzy, sozzled (*Inf.*), stupefied, tipsy, woozy (*Inf.*)

fuddy-duddy *n.* back number (*Inf.*), conservative, dodo (*Inf.*), fossil, museum piece, (old) fogy, square (*Inf.*), stick-in-the-mud (*Inf.*), stuffed shirt (*Inf.*)

fudge *v.* avoid, cook (*Sl.*), dodge, equivocate, evade, fake, falsify, hedge, misrepresent, patch up, shuffle, slant, stall

fuel 1. *n. Fig.* ammunition, encouragement, fodder, food, incitement, material, means, nourishment, provocation **2.** *v.* charge, fan, feed, fire, incite, inflame, nourish, stoke up, sustain

fug fetidity, fetor, frowst, frowstiness, fustiness, reek, stale air, staleness, stink

fuggy airless, fetid, foul, frowsty, noisome, noxious, stale, stuffy, suffocating, unventilated

fugitive 1. *n.* deserter, escapee, refugee, runagate (*Archaic*), runaway **2.** *adj.* brief, ephemeral, evanescent, fleeing, fleeting, flitting, flying, fugacious, momentary, passing, short, short-lived, temporary, transient, transitory, unstable

fulfil accomplish, achieve, answer, bring to completion, carry out, complete, comply with, conclude, conform to, discharge, effect, execute, fill, finish, keep, meet, obey, observe, perfect, perform, realise, satisfy

fulfilment accomplishment, achievement, attainment, carrying out *or* through, completion, consummation, crowning, discharge, discharging, effecting, end, implementation, observance, perfection, realization

full 1. brimful, brimming, complete, entire, filled, gorged, intact, loaded, replete, sated, satiated, satisfied, saturated, stocked, sufficient **2.** abundant, adequate, all-inclusive, ample, broad, comprehensive, copious, detailed, exhaustive, extensive, generous, maximum, plenary, plenteous, plentiful, thorough, unabridged **3.** chock-a-block, chock-full, crammed, crowded, in use, jammed, occupied, packed, taken **4.** clear, deep, distinct, loud, resonant, rich, rounded **5.** baggy, balloonlike, buxom, capacious, curvaceous, large, loose, plump, puffy, rounded, voluminous, voluptuous **6. in full** completely, in its entirety, in total, *in toto*, without exception **7. to the full** completely, entirely, fully, thoroughly, to the utmost, without reservation

full-blooded gutsy (*Sl.*), hearty, lusty, mettlesome, red-blooded, vigorous, virile

full-bodied fruity, full-flavoured, heady, heavy, mellow, redolent, rich, strong, well-matured

full-grown adult, developed, full-fledged, grown-up, in one's prime, marriageable, mature, nubile, of age, ripe

fullness 1. abundance, adequateness, ampleness, copiousness, fill, glut, plenty, profusion, repletion, satiety, saturation, sufficiency **2.** broadness, completeness, comprehensiveness, entirety, extensiveness, plenitude, totality, vastness, wealth, wholeness **3.** clearness, loudness, resonance, richness, strength **4.** curvaceousness, dilation, distension, enlargement, roundness, swelling, tumescence, voluptuousness

full-scale all-encompassing, all-out, comprehensive, exhaustive, extensive, full-dress, in-depth, major, proper, sweeping, thorough, thoroughgoing, wide-ranging

fully 1. absolutely, altogether, completely, entirely, every inch, from first to last, heart and soul, in all respects, intimately, perfectly, positively, thoroughly, totally, utterly, wholly **2.** abundantly, adequately, amply, comprehensively, enough, plentifully, satisfactorily, sufficiently **3.** at least, quite, without (any) exaggeration, without a word of a lie (*Inf.*)

fully-fledged experienced, mature, professional, proficient, qualified, senior, time-served, trained

fulminate animadvert upon, berate, castigate, censure, criticize, curse, denounce, denunciate, execrate, fume, inveigh against, protest against, rage, rail against, reprobate, thunder, upbraid, vilify, vituperate

fulmination condemnation, denunciation, diatribe, invective, obloquy, philippic, reprobation, tirade

fulsome adulatory, cloying, excessive, extravagant, fawning, gross, immoderate, ingratiating, inordinate, insincere, nauseating, overdone, saccharine, sickening, smarmy (*Inf.*), sycophantic, unctuous

fumble 1. bumble, feel around, flounder, grope, paw (*Inf.*), scrabble **2.** botch, bungle, make a hash of (*Inf.*), mess up, misfield, mishandle, mismanage, muff, spoil

fume *Fig.* **1.** *v.* boil, chafe, champ at the bit (*Inf.*), get hot under the collar (*Inf.*), get steamed up about (*Sl.*), rage, rant, rave, seethe, smoulder, storm **2.** *n.* agitation, dither, fit, fret, fury, passion, rage, stew (*Inf.*), storm

fumes effluvium, exhalation, exhaust, gas, haze, miasma, pollution, reek, smog, smoke, stench, vapour

fumigate clean out *or* up, cleanse, disinfect, purify, sanitize, sterilize

fuming all steamed up (*Sl.*), angry, at boiling point (*Inf.*), enraged, foaming at the mouth, in a rage, incensed, raging, roused, seething, up in arms

fun *n.* **1.** amusement, cheer, distraction, diversion, enjoyment, entertainment, frolic, gaiety, good time, high jinks, jollification, jollity, joy, junketing, living it up, merriment, merrymaking, mirth, pleasure, recreation, romp, sport, treat, whoopee (*Inf.*) **2.** buffoonery,

clowning, foolery, game, horseplay, jesting, jocularity, joking, nonsense, play, playfulness, skylarking (*Inf.*), sport, teasing, tomfoolery **3. in** *or* **for fun** facetiously, for a joke, for a laugh, in jest, jokingly, light-heartedly, mischievously, playfully, roguishly, teasingly, tongue in cheek, with a gleam *or* twinkle in one's eye, with a straight face **4. make fun of** deride, hold up to ridicule, lampoon, laugh at, make a fool of, make game of, make sport of, make the butt of, mock, parody, poke fun at, rag, rib (*Inf.*), ridicule, satirize, scoff at, send up (*Brit. inf.*), sneer at, take off, taunt ~*adj.* **5.** amusing, convivial, diverting, enjoyable, entertaining, lively, witty

function *n.* **1.** activity, business, capacity, charge, concern, duty, employment, exercise, job, mission, occupation, office, operation, part, post, province, purpose, raison d'être, responsibility, role, situation, task ~*v.* **2.** act, act the part of, behave, be in commission, be in operation *or* action, be in running order, do duty, go, officiate, operate, perform, run, serve, serve one's turn, work ~*n.* **3.** affair, do (*Inf.*), gathering, reception, social occasion

functional hard-wearing, operative, practical, serviceable, useful, utilitarian, utility, working

functionary dignitary, employee, office bearer, office holder, officer, official

fund *n.* **1.** capital, endowment, foundation, kitty, pool, reserve, stock, store, supply **2.** hoard, mine, repository, reserve, reservoir, source, storehouse, treasury, vein ~*v.* **3.** capitalize, endow, finance, float, pay for, promote, stake, subsidize, support

fundamental 1. *adj.* basic, cardinal, central, constitutional, crucial, elementary, essential, first, important, indispensable, integral, intrinsic, key, necessary, organic, primary, prime, principal, rudimentary, underlying, vital **2.** *n.* axiom, basic, cornerstone, essential, first principle, law, principle, rudiment, rule, *sine qua non*

fundamentally at bottom, at heart, basically, essentially, intrinsically, primarily, radically

funds 1. bread (*Sl.*), capital, cash, dough (*Sl.*), finance, hard cash, money, ready money, resources, savings, the ready (*Inf.*), the wherewithal **2. in funds**

flush (*Inf.*), in the black, solvent, well-off, well-supplied

funeral burial, inhumation, interment, obsequies

funereal dark, deathlike, depressing, dirgelike, dismal, dreary, gloomy, grave, lamenting, lugubrious, mournful, sad, sepulchral, solemn, sombre, woeful

funk 1. *v.* chicken out of (*Inf.*), dodge, duck out of (*Inf.*), flinch from, recoil from, take fright, turn tail 2. **be in a (blue) funk** be in a cold sweat, be in a panic, be scared stiff, be sick with fear, cower, dread, fear, quail, quake, quiver, shake at the knees, shrink, tremble, tremble in one's boots

funnel *v.* channel, conduct, convey, direct, filter, move, pass, pour

funny *adj.* 1. absurd, amusing, a scream (card, caution) (*Inf.*), comic, comical, diverting, droll, entertaining, facetious, farcical, hilarious, humorous, jocose, jocular, jolly, killing (*Inf.*), laughable, ludicrous, rich, ridiculous, riotous, risible, side-splitting, silly, slapstick, waggish, witty 2. curious, dubious, mysterious, odd, peculiar, perplexing, puzzling, queer, remarkable, strange, suspicious, unusual, weird ~*n.* 3. *Inf.* crack (*Sl.*), jest, joke, play on words, pun, quip, wisecrack, witticism

furbish brighten, burnish, polish, renovate, restore, rub, shine, smarten up, spruce up

furious 1. angry, beside oneself, boiling, enraged, frantic, frenzied, fuming, incensed, infuriated, in high dudgeon, livid (*Inf.*), mad, maddened, on the warpath (*Inf.*), raging, up in arms, wrathful, wroth (*Archaic*) 2. agitated, boisterous, fierce, impetuous, intense, savage, stormy, tempestuous, tumultuous, turbulent, ungovernable, unrestrained, vehement, violent, wild

furnish 1. appoint, decorate, equip, fit (out, up), outfit, provide, provision, rig, stock, store, supply 2. afford, bestow, endow, give, grant, offer, present, provide, reveal, supply

furniture appliances, appointments, chattels, effects, equipment, fittings, furnishings, goods, household goods, movable property, movables, possessions, things (*Inf.*)

furore 1. commotion, disturbance, excitement, flap (*Inf.*), frenzy, fury, hullabaloo, outburst, outcry, stir, to-do, uproar 2. craze, enthusiasm, mania, rage

furrow 1. *n.* channel, corrugation, crease, crow's-foot, fluting, groove, hollow, line, rut, seam, trench, wrinkle 2. *v.* corrugate, crease, draw together, flute, knit, seam, wrinkle

further 1. *adj.* additional, extra, fresh, more, new, other, supplementary 2. *adv.* additionally, also, as well as, besides, furthermore, in addition, moreover, on top of, over and above, to boot, what's more, yet 3. *v.* advance, aid, assist, champion, contribute to, encourage, expedite, facilitate, forward, foster, hasten, help, lend support to, patronize, plug (*Inf.*), promote, push, speed, succour, work for

furtherance advancement, advocacy, backing, boosting, carrying-out, championship, promotion, prosecution, pursuit

furthermore additionally, as well, besides, further, in addition, into the bargain, moreover, not to mention, to boot, too, what's more

furthest extreme, farthest, furthermost, most distant, outermost, outmost, remotest, ultimate, uttermost

furtive clandestine, cloaked, conspiratorial, covert, hidden, secret, secretive, skulking, slinking, sly, sneaking, sneaky, stealthy, surreptitious, underhand, under-the-table

fury 1. anger, frenzy, impetuosity, ire, madness, passion, rage, wrath 2. ferocity, fierceness, force, intensity, power, savagery, severity, tempestuousness, turbulence, vehemence, violence 3. bacchante, hag, hellcat, shrew, spitfire, termagant, virago, vixen

fuse *v.* agglutinate, amalgamate, blend, coalesce, combine, commingle, dissolve, federate, integrate, intermingle, intermix, join, meld, melt, merge, run together, smelt, solder, unite, weld

fusillade barrage, broadside, burst, fire, hail, outburst, salvo, volley

fusion alloy, amalgam, amalgamation, blend, blending, coalescence, commingling, commixture, federation, integration, liquefaction, merger, merging, mixture, smelting, synthesis, union, uniting, welding

fuss *n.* 1. ado, agitation, bother, bustle, commotion, confusion, excitement, fidget, flap (*Inf.*), flurry, fluster, flutter, hurry, palaver, pother, stir, storm in a teacup (*Brit.*), to-do, upset, worry 2. altercation, argument, bother, complaint, difficulty, display, furore, hassle (*Inf.*), objection, row, squabble, trouble, unrest, upset ~*v.* **3**. bustle, chafe, fidget, flap (*Inf.*), fret, fume, get in a stew (*Inf.*), get worked up, labour over, make a meal of (*Inf.*), make a thing of (*Inf.*), niggle, take pains, worry

fusspot fidget, fussbudget (*U.S.*), nit-picker (*Inf.*), old woman, perfectionist, worrier

fussy 1. choosy (*Inf.*), dainty, difficult, discriminating, exacting, faddish, faddy, fastidious, finicky, hard to please, nit-picking (*Inf.*), old-maidish, old woman-ish, overparticular, particular, pernick-ety, squeamish **2**. busy, cluttered, over-decorated, overelaborate, overembel-lished, overworked, rococo

fustiness airlessness, dampness, frowstiness, fug, mouldiness, mustiness, smell of decay, staleness, stuffiness

fusty 1. airless, damp, frowsty, ill-smelling, malodorous, mildewed, mil-dewy, mouldering, mouldy, musty, rank, stale, stuffy **2**. antediluvian, antiquated, archaic, old-fashioned, old-fogyish, out-dated, out-of-date, out of the ark (*Inf.*), passé

futile 1. abortive, barren, bootless, empty, forlorn, fruitless, hollow, ineffec-tual, in vain, nugatory, profitless, sterile, to no avail, unavailing, unproductive, unprofitable, unsuccessful, useless, vain, valueless, worthless **2**. idle, pointless, tri-fling, trivial, unimportant

futility 1. bootlessness, emptiness, fruitlessness, hollowness, ineffectiveness, uselessness **2**. pointlessness, triviality, unimportance, vanity

future 1. *n.* expectation, hereafter, outlook, prospect, time to come **2**. *adj.* approaching, coming, destined, eventual, expected, fated, forthcoming, impend-ing, in the offing, later, prospective, sub-sequent, to be, to come, ultimate, un-born

fuzz down, fibre, floss, fluff, hair, lint, nap, pile

fuzzy 1. down-covered, downy, flossy, fluffy, frizzy, linty, napped, woolly **2**. bleary, blurred, distorted, faint, ill-defined, indistinct, muffled, out of focus, shadowy, unclear, unfocused, vague

G

gab 1. *v.* babble, blabber, blather, buzz, chatter, gossip, jabber, jaw (*Sl.*), prattle, talk, yak (*Sl.*) **2.** *n.* blab, blarney, blather, chat, chatter, chitchat, conversation, gossip, loquacity, palaver, small talk, talk, tête-à-tête, tittle-tattle, tongue-wagging, yackety-yak (*Sl.*), yak (*Sl.*)

gabble 1. *v.* babble, blab, blabber, cackle, chatter, gaggle, gibber, gush, jabber, prattle, rattle, splutter, spout, sputter **2.** *n.* babble, blabber, cackling, chatter, drivel, gibberish, jargon, prattle, twaddle, waffle (*Inf.*)

gabby chatty, effusive, garrulous, glib, gossiping, gushing, long-winded, loquacious, mouthy, prattling, prolix, talkative, verbose, voluble, windy, wordy

gad (about *or* **around)** gallivant, ramble, range, roam, rove, run around, stravaig (*Scot., & northern English dialect*), stray, traipse (*Inf.*), wander

gadabout gallivanter, pleasure-seeker, rambler, rover, wanderer

gadget appliance, contraption (*Inf.*), contrivance, device, gimmick, gizmo (*Sl., chiefly U.S.*), invention, novelty, thing, tool

gaffe bloomer (*Inf.*), blunder, boob (*Brit. sl.*), boo-boo (*Inf.*), clanger (*Inf.*), faux pas, gaucherie, howler, indiscretion, mistake, slip, solecism

gaffer 1. granddad, greybeard, old boy (*Inf.*), old fellow, old man, old-timer (*U.S.*) **2.** *Inf.* boss (*Inf.*), foreman, ganger, manager, overseer, superintendent, supervisor

gag[1] *v.* **1.** curb, muffle, muzzle, quiet, silence, stifle, still, stop up, suppress, throttle **2.** *Sl.* disgorge, heave, puke (*Sl.*), retch, spew, throw up (*Inf.*), vomit **3.** *Sl.* choke, gasp, pant, struggle for breath

gag[2] crack (*Sl.*), funny (*Inf.*), hoax, jest, joke, wisecrack (*Inf.*), witticism

gage *n.* **1.** bond, deposit, earnest, guarantee, pawn, pledge, security, surety, token **2.** challenge, dare, defiance, gauntlet, glove

gaiety 1. animation, blitheness, blithesomeness (*Literary*), cheerfulness, effervescence, elation, exhilaration, glee, good humour, high spirits, hilarity, *joie de vivre*, jollity, joviality, joyousness, lightheartedness, liveliness, merriment, mirth, sprightliness, vivacity **2.** celebration, conviviality, festivity, fun, jollification, merrymaking, revelry, revels **3.** brightness, brilliance, colour, colourfulness, gaudiness, glitter, show, showiness, sparkle

gaily 1. blithely, cheerfully, gleefully, happily, joyfully, light-heartedly, merrily **2.** brightly, brilliantly, colourfully, flamboyantly, flashily, gaudily, showily

gain *v.* **1.** achieve, acquire, advance, attain, bag, build up, capture, collect, enlist, gather, get, glean, harvest, improve, increase, net, obtain, pick up, procure, profit, realize, reap, secure, win, win over **2.** acquire, bring in, clear, earn, get, make, net, obtain, produce, realize, win, yield **3.** *Usually with* **on a.** approach, catch up with, close with, get nearer, narrow the gap, overtake **b.** draw *or* pull away from, get farther away, leave behind, outdistance, recede, widen the gap **4.** arrive at, attain, come to, get to, reach **5. gain time** delay, procrastinate, stall, temporize, use delaying tactics ~*n.* **6.** accretion, achievement, acquisition, advance, advancement, advantage, attainment, benefit, dividend, earnings, emolument, growth, headway, improvement, income, increase, increment, lucre, proceeds, produce, profit, progress, return, rise, winnings, yield

gainful advantageous, beneficial, fruitful, lucrative, moneymaking, paying, productive, profitable, remunerative, rewarding, useful, worthwhile

gains booty, earnings, gainings, pickings, prize, proceeds, profits, revenue, takings, winnings

gainsay contradict, contravene, controvert, deny, disaffirm, disagree with, dispute

gait bearing, carriage, pace, step, stride, tread, walk

gala 1. *n.* carnival, celebration, festival, festivity, fête, jamboree, pageant, party **2.** *adj.* celebratory, convivial, festal, festive, gay, jovial, joyful, merry

gale 1. blast, cyclone, hurricane, squall, storm, tempest, tornado, typhoon 2. *Inf.* burst, eruption, explosion, fit, howl, outbreak, outburst, peal, shout, shriek

gall[1] 1. *Inf.* brass (*Inf.*), brass neck (*Inf.*), brazenness, cheek (*Inf.*), effrontery, impertinence, impudence, insolence, nerve (*Inf.*), sauciness 2. acrimony, animosity, animus, antipathy, bad blood, bile, bitterness, enmity, hostility, malevolence, malice, malignity, rancour, sourness, spite, spleen, venom

gall[2] *n.* 1. abrasion, chafe, excoriation, raw spot, scrape, sore, sore spot, wound 2. aggravation (*Inf.*), annoyance, bother, botheration (*Inf.*), exasperation, harassment, irritant, irritation, nuisance, pest, provocation, vexation ~*v.* 3. abrade, bark, chafe, excoriate, fret, graze, irritate, rub raw, scrape, skin 4. aggravate (*Inf.*), annoy, bother, exasperate, fret, harass, irk, irritate, nag, nettle, peeve (*Inf.*), pester, plague, provoke, rankle, rile (*Inf.*), rub up the wrong way, ruffle, vex

gallant *adj.* 1. bold, brave, courageous, daring, dashing, dauntless, doughty, fearless, game (*Inf.*), heroic, high-spirited, honourable, intrepid, lion-hearted, manful, manly, mettlesome, noble, plucky, valiant, valorous 2. attentive, chivalrous, courteous, courtly, gentlemanly, gracious, magnanimous, noble, polite 3. august, dignified, elegant, glorious, grand, imposing, lofty, magnificent, noble, splendid, stately ~*n.* 4. admirer, beau, boyfriend, escort, lover, paramour, suitor, wooer 5. beau, blade (*Archaic*), buck (*Inf.*), dandy, fop, ladies' man, lady-killer (*Inf.*), man about town, man of fashion 6. adventurer, cavalier, champion, daredevil, hero, knight, man of mettle, *preux chevalier*

gallantry 1. audacity, boldness, bravery, courage, courageousness, daring, dauntlessness, derring-do (*Archaic*), fearlessness, heroism, intrepidity, manliness, mettle, nerve, pluck, prowess, spirit, valiance, valour 2. attentiveness, chivalry, courteousness, courtesy, courtliness, elegance, gentlemanliness, graciousness, nobility, politeness

galling aggravating (*Inf.*), annoying, bitter, bothersome, exasperating, harassing, humiliating, irksome, irritating, nettlesome, plaguing, provoking, rankling, vexatious, vexing

gallivant gad about, ramble, range, roam, rove, run around, stravaig (*Scot. & northern English dialect*), stray, traipse (*Inf.*), wander

gallop bolt, career, dart, dash, fly, hasten, hie (*Archaic*), hurry, race, run, rush, scud, shoot, speed, sprint, tear along, zoom

galore all over the place, aplenty, everywhere, in abundance, in great quantity, in numbers, in profusion, to spare

galvanize arouse, awaken, electrify, excite, fire, inspire, invigorate, jolt, move, provoke, quicken, shock, spur, startle, stimulate, stir, thrill, vitalize, wake

gamble *v.* 1. back, bet, game, have a flutter (*Inf.*), lay *or* make a bet, play, punt, stake, try one's luck, wager 2. back, chance, hazard, put one's faith *or* trust in, risk, speculate, stake, stick one's neck out (*Inf.*), take a chance, venture ~*n.* 3. chance, leap in the dark, lottery, risk, speculation, uncertainty, venture 4. bet, flutter (*Inf.*), punt, wager

gambol 1. *v.* caper, cavort, curvet, cut a caper, frisk, frolic, hop, jump, prance, rollick, skip 2. *n.* antic, caper, frolic, gambado, hop, jump, prance, skip, spring

game[1] *n.* 1. amusement, distraction, diversion, entertainment, frolic, fun, jest, joke, lark, merriment, pastime, play, recreation, romp, sport 2. competition, contest, event, match, meeting, round, tournament 3. adventure, business, enterprise, line, occupation, plan, proceeding, scheme, undertaking 4. chase, prey, quarry, wild animals 5. *Inf.* design, device, plan, plot, ploy, scheme, stratagem, strategy, tactic, trick 6. **make (a) game of** deride, make a fool of, make a laughing stock, make fun of, make sport of, mock, poke fun at, ridicule, send up (*Brit. inf.*)

game[2] *adj.* 1. bold, brave, courageous, dauntless, dogged, fearless, gallant, heroic, intrepid, persevering, persistent, plucky, resolute, spirited, unflinching, valiant, valorous 2. desirous, disposed, eager, inclined, interested, prepared, ready, willing

game[3] *adj.* bad, crippled, deformed, disabled, gammy (*Brit. sl.*), incapacitated, injured, lame, maimed

gamesome coltish, frisky, frolicsome, gay, lively, merry, playful, rollicking, sportive, vivacious

gamin guttersnipe, mudlark (*Sl.*), ragamuffin, street Arab, (street) urchin, waif

gammon 1. *v.* beguile, cheat, deceive, dupe, gull (*Archaic*), hoax, hoodwink, humbug, kid (*Inf.*), trick **2.** *n.* deceit, deception, humbug, imposition, nonsense, trick

gamut area, catalogue, compass, field, range, scale, scope, series, sweep

gang band, circle, clique, club, company, coterie, crew (*Inf.*), crowd, group, herd, horde, lot, mob, pack, party, ring, set, shift, squad, team, troupe

gangling, gangly angular, awkward, lanky, loose-jointed, rangy, rawboned, skinny, spindly, tall

gangster bandit, brigand, crook (*Inf.*), desperado, gang member, hood (*U.S. sl.*), hoodlum (*Chiefly U.S.*), mobster (*U.S. sl.*), racketeer, robber, ruffian, thug, tough

gaol *see* JAIL

gap 1. blank, breach, break, chink, cleft, crack, cranny, crevice, discontinuity, divide, hiatus, hole, interlude, intermission, interruption, interstice, interval, lacuna, lull, opening, pause, recess, rent, rift, space, vacuity, void **2.** difference, disagreement, disparity, divergence, inconsistency

gape 1. gawk, gawp (*Brit. sl.*), goggle, stare, wonder **2.** crack, open, split, yawn

gaping broad, cavernous, great, open, vast, wide, wide open, yawning

garb *n.* **1.** apparel, array, attire, clothes, clothing, costume, dress, garment, gear (*Sl.*), habiliment, habit, outfit, raiment (*Archaic*), robes, uniform, vestments, wear **2.** cut, fashion, look, mode, style **3.** appearance, aspect, attire, covering, guise, outward form ∼*v.* **4.** apparel, attire, clothe, cover, dress, rig out, robe

garbage 1. bits and pieces, debris, detritus, junk, litter, odds and ends, rubbish, scraps **2.** dross, filth, muck, offal, refuse, rubbish, scourings, slops, sweepings, swill, trash (*Chiefly U.S.*), waste

garble 1. confuse, jumble, mix up **2.** corrupt, distort, doctor, falsify, misinterpret, misquote, misreport, misrepresent, misstate, mistranslate, mutilate, pervert, slant, tamper with, twist

gargantuan big, Brobdingnagian, colossal, elephantine, enormous, giant, gigantic, huge, immense, mammoth, massive, monstrous, monumental, mountainous, prodigious, titanic, towering, tremendous, vast

garish brassy, brummagem, cheap, flash (*Inf.*), flashy, flaunting, gaudy, glaring, glittering, loud, meretricious, raffish, showy, tasteless, tawdry, vulgar

garland 1. *n.* bays, chaplet, coronal, crown, festoon, honours, laurels, wreath **2.** *v.* adorn, crown, deck, festoon, wreathe

garments apparel, array, articles of clothing, attire, clothes, clothing, costume, dress, duds (*Inf.*), garb, gear (*Sl.*), habiliment, habit, outfit, raiment (*Archaic*), robes, togs, uniform, vestments, wear

garner 1. *v.* accumulate, amass, assemble, collect, deposit, gather, hoard, husband, lay in *or* up, put by, reserve, save, stockpile, store, stow away, treasure **2.** *n.* *Literary* depository, granary, store, storehouse, vault

garnish 1. *v.* adorn, beautify, bedeck, deck, decorate, embellish, enhance, grace, ornament, set off, trim **2.** *n.* adornment, decoration, embellishment, enhancement, garniture, ornament, ornamentation, trim, trimming

garniture accessories, adornment, appendages, appurtenances, decoration, embellishment, furniture, garnish, ornamentation, ornaments, trimmings

garrison *n.* **1.** armed force, command, detachment, troops, unit **2.** base, camp, encampment, fort, fortification, fortress, post, station, stronghold ∼*v.* **3.** assign, mount, position, post, put on duty, station **4.** defend, guard, man, occupy, protect, supply with troops

garrulity 1. babble, babbling, chatter, chattering, chattiness, effusiveness, gabbiness (*Inf.*), garrulousness, gift of the gab (*Inf.*), glibness, loquacity, mouthiness, prating, prattle, talkativeness, verbosity, volubility **2.** diffuseness, longwindedness, prolixity, prosiness, verbosity, windiness, wordiness

garrulous 1. babbling, chattering, chatty, effusive, gabby (*Inf.*), glib, gossiping, gushing, loquacious, mouthy, prating, prattling, talkative, verbose, voluble **2.** diffuse, gassy (*Sl.*), long-winded, prolix, prosy, verbose, windy, wordy

gash 1. *v.* cleave, cut, gouge, incise, lacerate, rend, slash, slit, split, tear, wound **2.** *n.* cleft, cut, gouge, incision, laceration, rent, slash, slit, split, tear, wound

gasp 1. *v.* blow, catch one's breath, choke, fight for breath, gulp, pant, puff **2.** *n.* blow, ejaculation, exclamation, gulp, pant, puff

gate access, barrier, door, doorway, egress, entrance, exit, gateway, opening, passage, port (*Scot.*), portal

gather 1. accumulate, amass, assemble, bring *or* get together, collect, congregate, convene, flock, forgather, garner, group, heap, hoard, marshal, mass, muster, pile up, round up, stack up, stockpile **2.** assume, be led to believe, conclude, deduce, draw, hear, infer, learn, make, surmise, understand **3.** clasp, draw, embrace, enfold, hold, hug **4.** crop, cull, garner, glean, harvest, pick, pluck, reap, select **5.** build, deepen, enlarge, expand, grow, heighten, increase, intensify, rise, swell, thicken, wax **6.** fold, pleat, pucker, ruffle, shirr, tuck

gathering 1. assemblage, assembly, company, conclave, concourse, congregation, congress, convention, convocation, crowd, flock, get-together (*Inf.*), group, knot, meeting, muster, party, rally, throng, turnout **2.** accumulation, acquisition, aggregate, collecting, collection, concentration, gain, heap, hoard, mass, pile, procuring, roundup, stock, stockpile **3.** *Inf.* abscess, boil, carbuncle, pimple, pustule, sore, spot, tumour, ulcer

gauche awkward, clumsy, graceless, ignorant, ill-bred, ill-mannered, inelegant, inept, insensitive, lacking in social graces, maladroit, tactless, uncultured, unpolished, unsophisticated

gaucherie 1. awkwardness, bad taste, clumsiness, gaucheness, gracelessness, ignorance, ill-breeding, inelegance, ineptness, insensitivity, lack of polish, maladroitness, tactlessness, unsophisticatedness **2.** bloomer (*Inf.*), blunder, boob (*Sl.*), breach of etiquette, clanger (*Inf.*), faux pas, gaffe, indiscretion, mistake, slip, solecism

gaudy bright, brilliant, brummagem, flash (*Inf.*), flashy, florid, garish, gay, glaring, loud, meretricious, ostentatious, raffish, showy, tasteless, tawdry, vulgar

gauge *v.* **1.** ascertain, calculate, check, compute, count, determine, measure, weigh **2.** adjudge, appraise, assess, estimate, evaluate, guess, judge, rate, reckon, value ~*n.* **3.** basis, criterion, example, exemplar, guide, guideline, indicator, measure, meter, model, pattern, rule, sample, standard, test, touchstone, yardstick **4.** bore, capacity, degree, depth, extent, height, magnitude, measure, scope, size, span, thickness, width

gaunt 1. angular, attenuated, bony, cadaverous, emaciated, haggard, lank, lean, meagre, pinched, rawboned, scraggy, scrawny, skeletal, skinny, spare, thin, wasted **2.** bare, bleak, desolate, dismal, dreary, forbidding, forlorn, grim, harsh

gauzy delicate, diaphanous, filmy, flimsy, gossamer, insubstantial, light, see-through, sheer, thin, translucent, transparent

gawk 1. *n.* boor, churl, clod, clodhopper (*Inf.*), dolt, dunderhead, galoot (*Sl.*), ignoramus, lout, lubber, lummox (*Inf.*), oaf **2.** *v.* gape, gawp (*Sl.*), gaze open-mouthed, goggle, stare

gawky awkward, clownish, clumsy, gauche, loutish, lumbering, lumpish, maladroit, oafish, uncouth, ungainly

gay 1. animated, blithe, carefree, cheerful, debonair, glad, gleeful, happy, hilarious, insouciant, jolly, jovial, joyful, joyous, light-hearted, lively, merry, sparkling, sunny, vivacious **2.** bright, brilliant, colourful, flamboyant, flashy, fresh, garish, gaudy, rich, showy, vivid **3.** convivial, festive, frivolous, frolicsome, fun-loving, gamesome, merry, playful, pleasure-seeking, rakish, rollicking, sportive, waggish

gaze 1. *v.* contemplate, gape, look, look fixedly, regard, stare, view, watch, wonder **2.** *n.* fixed look, look, stare

gazette journal, newspaper, newssheet, organ, paper, periodical

gear *n.* **1.** cog, cogwheel, gearwheel, toothed wheel **2.** cogs, gearing, machinery, mechanism, works **3.** accessories, accoutrements, apparatus, equipment, harness, instruments, outfit, paraphernalia, rigging, supplies, tackle, tools, trappings **4.** baggage, belongings, effects, kit, luggage, stuff, things **5.** *Sl.* apparel, array, attire, clothes, clothing, costume, dress, garb, garments, habit, outfit, rigout (*Inf.*), togs, wear ~*v.* **6.** adapt, adjust, equip, fit, rig, suit, tailor

gelatinous gluey, glutinous, gummy, jelly-like, mucilaginous, sticky, viscid, viscous

gelid arctic, chilly, cold, freezing, frigid, frosty, frozen, glacial, ice-cold, icy, polar

gem 1. jewel, precious stone, semi-precious stone, stone 2. flower, jewel, masterpiece, pearl, pick, prize, treasure

genealogy ancestry, blood line, derivation, descent, extraction, family tree, line, lineage, pedigree, progeniture, stemma, stirps, stock, strain

general 1. accepted, broad, common, extensive, popular, prevailing, prevalent, public, universal, widespread 2. accustomed, conventional, customary, everyday, habitual, normal, ordinary, regular, typical, usual 3. approximate, ill-defined, imprecise, inaccurate, indefinite, inexact, loose, undetailed, unspecific, vague 4. across-the-board, all-inclusive, blanket, broad, catholic, collective, comprehensive, encyclopedic, generic, indiscriminate, miscellaneous, panoramic, sweeping, total, universal

generality 1. abstract principle, generalization, loose statement, sweeping statement, vague notion 2. acceptedness, commonness, extensiveness, popularity, prevalence, universality 3. approximateness, impreciseness, indefiniteness, inexactness, lack of detail, looseness, vagueness 4. breadth, catholicity, comprehensiveness, miscellaneity, sweepingness, universality

generally 1. almost always, as a rule, by and large, conventionally, customarily, for the most part, habitually, in most cases, mainly, normally, on average, on the whole, ordinarily, regularly, typically, usually 2. commonly, extensively, popularly, publicly, universally, widely 3. approximately, broadly, chiefly, for the most part, in the main, largely, mainly, mostly, on the whole, predominantly, principally

generate beget, breed, bring about, cause, create, engender, form, give rise to, initiate, make, originate, procreate, produce, propagate, spawn, whip up

generation 1. begetting, breeding, creation, engenderment, formation, genesis, origination, procreation, production, propagation, reproduction 2. age group, breed, crop 3. age, day, days, epoch, era, period, time, times

generic all-encompassing, blanket, collective, common, comprehensive, general, inclusive, sweeping, universal, wide

generosity 1. beneficence, benevolence, bounteousness, bounty, charity, kindness, liberality, munificence, open-handedness 2. disinterestedness, goodness, high-mindedness, magnanimity, nobleness, unselfishness

generous 1. beneficent, benevolent, bounteous, bountiful, charitable, free, hospitable, kind, lavish, liberal, munificent, open-handed, princely, ungrudging, unstinting 2. big-hearted, disinterested, good, high-minded, lofty, magnanimous, noble, unselfish 3. abundant, ample, copious, full, lavish, liberal, overflowing, plentiful, rich, unstinting

genesis beginning, birth, commencement, creation, dawn, engendering, formation, generation, inception, origin, outset, propagation, root, source, start

genial affable, agreeable, amiable, cheerful, cheery, congenial, convivial, cordial, easygoing, enlivening, friendly, glad, good-natured, happy, hearty, jolly, jovial, joyous, kind, kindly, merry, pleasant, sunny, warm, warm-hearted

geniality affability, agreeableness, amiability, cheerfulness, cheeriness, congenialness, conviviality, cordiality, friendliness, gladness, good cheer, good nature, happiness, heartiness, jollity, joviality, joy, joyousness, kindliness, kindness, mirth, pleasantness, sunniness, warm-heartedness, warmth

genius 1. adept, brain (Inf.), expert, intellect (Inf.), maestro, master, masterhand, mastermind, virtuoso 2. ability, aptitude, bent, brilliance, capacity, creative power, endowment, faculty, flair, gift, inclination, knack, propensity, talent, turn

genre brand, category, character, class, fashion, genus, group, kind, school, sort, species, style, type

genteel aristocratic, civil, courteous, courtly, cultivated, cultured, elegant, fashionable, formal, gentlemanly, ladylike, mannerly, polished, polite, refined, respectable, stylish, urbane, well-bred, well-mannered

gentility 1. civility, courtesy, courtliness, cultivation, culture, decorum, elegance, etiquette, formality, good breeding, good manners, mannerliness, polish, politeness, propriety, refinement, respectability, urbanity **2.** blue blood, gentle birth, good family, high birth, nobility, rank **3.** aristocracy, elite, gentlefolk, gentry, nobility, nobles, ruling class, upper class

gentle 1. amiable, benign, bland, compassionate, dove-like, humane, kind, kindly, lenient, meek, merciful, mild, pacific, peaceful, placid, quiet, soft, sweet-tempered, tender **2.** balmy, calm, clement, easy, light, low, mild, moderate, muted, placid, quiet, serene, slight, smooth, soft, soothing, temperate, tranquil, untroubled **3.** easy, gradual, imperceptible, light, mild, moderate, slight, slow **4.** biddable, broken, docile, manageable, placid, tame, tractable **5.** *Archaic* aristocratic, courteous, cultured, elegant, genteel, gentlemanlike, gentlemanly, high-born, ladylike, noble, polished, polite, refined, upper-class, well-born, well-bred

gentlemanly civil, civilized, courteous, cultivated, gallant, genteel, gentlemanlike, honourable, mannerly, noble, obliging, polished, polite, refined, reputable, suave, urbane, well-bred, well-mannered

gentry aristocracy, elite, gentility, gentlefolk, nobility, nobles, ruling class, upper class, upper crust (*Inf.*)

genuine 1. actual, authentic, bona fide, honest, legitimate, natural, original, pure, real, sound, sterling, true, unadulterated, unalloyed, veritable **2.** artless, candid, earnest, frank, heartfelt, honest, sincere, unaffected, unfeigned

genus breed, category, class, genre, group, kind, order, race, set, sort, type

germ 1. bacterium, bug (*Inf.*), microbe, microorganism, virus **2.** beginning, bud, cause, embryo, origin, root, rudiment, seed, source, spark **3.** bud, egg, embryo, nucleus, ovule, ovum, seed, spore, sprout

germane akin, allied, apposite, appropriate, apropos, apt, cognate, connected, fitting, kindred, material, pertinent, proper, related, relevant, suitable, to the point *or* purpose

germinate bud, develop, generate, grow, originate, pullulate, shoot, sprout, swell, vegetate

gestation development, evolution, incubation, maturation, pregnancy, ripening

gesticulate gesture, indicate, make a sign, motion, sign, signal, wave

gesture 1. *n.* action, gesticulation, indication, motion, sign, signal **2.** *v.* gesticulate, indicate, motion, sign, signal, wave

get 1. achieve, acquire, attain, bag, bring, come by, come into possession of, earn, fall heir to, fetch, gain, glean, inherit, make, net, obtain, pick up, procure, realize, reap, receive, secure, succeed to, win **2.** be afflicted with, become infected with, be smitten by, catch, come down with, contract, fall victim to, take **3.** arrest, capture, collar (*Inf.*), grab, lay hold of, seize, take, trap **4.** become, come to be, grow, turn, wax **5.** catch, comprehend, fathom, follow, hear, notice, perceive, see, take in, understand, work out **6.** arrive, come, make it (*Inf.*), reach **7.** arrange, contrive, fix, manage, succeed, wangle (*Inf.*) **8.** coax, convince, induce, influence, persuade, prevail upon, sway, talk into, wheedle, win over **9.** communicate with, contact, get in touch with, reach **10.** *Inf.* affect, arouse, excite, have an effect on, impress, move, stimulate, stir, touch **11.** *Inf.* annoy, bother, bug (*Inf.*), get (someone's) goat (*Sl.*), irk, irritate, pique, rub (someone) up the wrong way, upset, vex **12.** baffle, confound, mystify, nonplus, perplex, puzzle, stump

get across 1. cross, ford, negotiate, pass over, traverse **2.** bring home to, communicate, convey, get (something) through to, impart, make clear *or* understood, put over, transmit

get ahead 1. advance, be successful, do well, flourish, get on, make good, progress, prosper, succeed, thrive **2.** excel, leave behind, outdo, outmanoeuvre, overtake, surpass

get along 1. agree, be compatible, be friendly, get on, harmonize, hit it off (*Inf.*) **2.** cope, develop, fare, get by (*Inf.*), make out (*Inf.*), manage, progress, shift **3.** be off, depart, go, go away, leave, move off

get at 1. acquire, attain, come to grips with, gain access to, get, get hold of, reach **2.** hint, imply, intend, lead up to, mean, suggest **3.** annoy, attack, blame, carp, criticize, find fault with, irritate, nag, pick on, taunt **4.** bribe, buy off, corrupt, influence, suborn, tamper with

getaway break, break-out, decampment, escape, flight

get away break free, break out, decamp, depart, disappear, escape, flee, leave, make good one's escape

get back 1. recoup, recover, regain, repossess, retrieve **2.** arrive home, come back *or* home, return, revert, revisit **3.** *With* **at** be avenged, get even with, give tit for tat, retaliate, settle the score with, take vengeance on

get by 1. circumvent, get ahead of, go around, go past, overtake, pass, round **2.** *Inf.* contrive, cope, exist, fare, get along, make both ends meet, manage, subsist, survive

get down 1. alight, bring down, climb down, descend, disembark, dismount, get off, lower, step down **2.** bring down, depress, dishearten, dispirit

get in alight, appear, arrive, collect, come, embark, enter, include, infiltrate, insert, interpose, land, mount, penetrate

get off 1. alight, depart, descend, disembark, dismount, escape, exit, leave **2.** detach, remove, shed, take off

get on 1. ascend, board, climb, embark, mount **2.** advance, cope, fare, get along, make out (*Inf.*), manage, progress, prosper, succeed **3.** agree, be compatible, be friendly, concur, get along, harmonize, hit it off (*Inf.*)

get out alight, break out, clear out (*Inf.*), decamp, escape, evacuate, extricate oneself, free oneself, leave, vacate, withdraw

get out of avoid, dodge, escape, evade, shirk

get over 1. cross, ford, get across, pass, pass over, surmount, traverse **2.** come round, get better, mend, pull through, recover from, revive, survive **3.** defeat, get the better of, master, overcome, shake off **4.** communicate, convey, get *or* put across, impart, make clear *or* understood

get round 1. bypass, circumvent, edge, evade, outmanoeuvre, skirt **2.** *Inf.* cajole, coax, convert, persuade, prevail upon, talk round, wheedle, win over

get together accumulate, assemble, collect, congregate, convene, converge, gather, join, meet, muster, rally, unite

get up arise, ascend, climb, increase, mount, rise, scale, stand

gewgaw bagatelle, bauble, bijou, gaud, gimcrack, kickshaw, knick-knack, novelty, plaything, toy, trifle, trinket

ghastly ashen, cadaverous, deathlike, deathly pale, dreadful, frightful, grim, grisly, gruesome, hideous, horrendous, horrible, horrid, livid, loathsome, pale, pallid, repellent, shocking, spectral, terrible, terrifying, wan

ghost 1. apparition, manes, phantasm, phantom, revenant, shade (*Literary*), soul, spectre, spirit, spook (*Inf.*), wraith **2.** glimmer, hint, possibility, semblance, shadow, suggestion, trace

ghostly eerie, ghostlike, illusory, insubstantial, phantasmal, phantom, spectral, spooky (*Inf.*), supernatural, uncanny, unearthly, weird, wraithlike

ghoulish disgusting, grisly, gruesome, macabre, morbid, sick (*Inf.*), unwholesome

giant 1. *n.* behemoth, colossus, Hercules, leviathan, monster, titan **2.** *adj.* Brobdingnagian, colossal, elephantine, enormous, gargantuan, gigantic, huge, immense, jumbo (*Inf.*), large, mammoth, monstrous, prodigious, titanic, vast

gibber babble, blab, blabber, blather, cackle, chatter, gabble, jabber, prattle

gibberish babble, balderdash, blather, double talk, drivel, gabble, gobbledegook (*Inf.*), jabber, jargon, mumbo jumbo, nonsense, prattle, twaddle, yammer (*Inf.*)

gibbous bulging, convex, crookbacked, humpbacked, humped, hunchbacked, hunched, protuberant, rounded

gibe, jibe 1. *v.* deride, flout, jeer, make fun of, mock, poke fun at, ridicule, scoff, scorn, sneer, taunt, twit **2.** *n.* crack (*Sl.*), cutting remark, derision, dig, jeer, mockery, ridicule, sarcasm, scoffing, sneer, taunt

giddiness dizziness, faintness, lightheadedness, vertigo

giddy 1. dizzy, dizzying, faint, lightheaded, reeling, unsteady, vertiginous **2.** capricious, careless, changeable, changeful, erratic, fickle, flighty, frivolous, heedless, impulsive, inconstant, irresolute, irresponsible, reckless, scatterbrained, silly, thoughtless, unbalanced, unstable, unsteady, vacillating, volatile, wild

gift 1. benefaction, bequest, bonus, boon, bounty, contribution, donation, grant, gratuity, largess, legacy, offering, present **2.** ability, aptitude, attribute, bent, capability, capacity, endowment, faculty, flair, genius, knack, power, talent, turn

gifted able, accomplished, adroit, brilliant, capable, clever, expert, ingenious, intelligent, masterly, skilled, talented

gigantic Brobdingnagian, colossal, Cyclopean, elephantine, enormous, gargantuan, giant, herculean, huge, immense, mammoth, monstrous, prodigious, stupendous, titanic, tremendous, vast

giggle *v./n.* cackle, chortle, chuckle, laugh, snigger, te-hee, titter, twitter

gild adorn, beautify, bedeck, brighten, coat, deck, dress up, embellish, embroider, enhance, enrich, garnish, grace, ornament

gimcrack 1. *adj.* cheap, rubbishy, shoddy, tawdry, trashy 2. *n.* bauble, gewgaw, kickshaw, plaything, toy, trinket

gimmick contrivance, device, dodge, gadget, gambit, gizmo (*Sl., chiefly U.S.*), ploy, scheme, stratagem, stunt, trick

gingerly 1. *adv.* carefully, cautiously, charily, circumspectly, daintily, delicately, fastidiously, hesitantly, reluctantly, squeamishly, suspiciously, timidly, warily 2. *adj.* careful, cautious, chary, circumspect, dainty, delicate, fastidious, hesitant, reluctant, squeamish, suspicious, timid, wary

gird[1] 1. belt, bind, girdle 2. blockade, encircle, enclose, encompass, enfold, engird, environ, hem in, pen, ring, surround 3. brace, fortify, make ready, prepare, ready, steel

gird[2] deride, gibe, jeer, make fun of, mock, poke fun at, ridicule, scoff, scorn, sneer, taunt

girdle 1. *n.* band, belt, cincture, cummerbund, fillet, sash, waistband 2. *v.* bind, bound, encircle, enclose, encompass, engird, environ, gird, hem, ring, surround

girl bird (*Sl.*), chick (*Sl.*), colleen (*Irish*), damsel (*Archaic*), daughter, female child, lass, lassie (*Inf.*), maid (*Archaic*), maiden (*Archaic*), miss, wench

girth bulk, circumference, measure, size

gist core, drift, essence, force, idea, import, marrow, meaning, nub, pith, point, quintessence, sense, significance, substance

give 1. accord, administer, allow, award, bestow, commit, confer, consign, contribute, deliver, donate, entrust, furnish, grant, hand over *or* out, make over, permit, present, provide, supply, vouchsafe 2. announce, be a source of, communicate, emit, impart, issue, notify, pro-

nounce, publish, render, transmit, utter 3. demonstrate, display, evidence, indicate, manifest, offer, proffer, provide, set forth, show 4. allow, cede, concede, devote, grant, hand over, lend, relinquish, surrender, yield 5. cause, do, engender, lead, make, occasion, perform, produce 6. bend, break, collapse, fall, recede, retire, sink

give away betray, disclose, divulge, expose, inform on, leak, let out, let slip, reveal, uncover

give in admit defeat, capitulate, collapse, comply, concede, quit, submit, surrender, yield

given addicted, apt, disposed, inclined, liable, likely, prone

give off discharge, emit, exhale, exude, produce, release, send out, smell of, throw out, vent

give out 1. discharge, emit, exhale, exude, produce, release, send out, smell of, throw out, vent 2. announce, broadcast, communicate, disseminate, impart, make known, notify, publish, transmit, utter

give up abandon, capitulate, cease, cede, cut out, desist, despair, forswear, hand over, leave off, quit, relinquish, renounce, resign, stop, surrender, throw in the towel, waive

glacial 1. arctic, biting, bitter, chill, chilly, cold, freezing, frigid, frosty, frozen, gelid, icy, piercing, polar, raw, wintry 2. antagonistic, cold, frigid, hostile, icy, inimical, unfriendly

glad 1. blithesome (*Literary*), cheerful, chuffed (*Sl.*), contented, delighted, gay, gleeful, gratified, happy, jocund, jovial, joyful, overjoyed, pleased, willing 2. animated, cheerful, cheering, cheery, delightful, felicitous, gratifying, joyous, merry, pleasant, pleasing

gladden cheer, delight, elate, enliven, exhilarate, gratify, hearten, please, rejoice

gladly cheerfully, freely, gaily, gleefully, happily, jovially, joyfully, joyously, merrily, readily, willingly, with (a) good grace, with pleasure

gladness animation, blitheness, cheerfulness, delight, felicity, gaiety, glee, happiness, high spirits, hilarity, jollity, joy, joyousness, mirth, pleasure

glamorous alluring, attractive, beautiful, bewitching, captivating, charming, dazzling, elegant, enchanting, entrancing, exciting, fascinating, glittering, glossy, lovely, prestigious, smart

glamour allure, appeal, attraction, beauty, bewitchment, charm, enchantment, fascination, magnetism, prestige, ravishment, witchery

glance v. 1. gaze, glimpse, look, peek, peep, scan, view 2. flash, gleam, glimmer, glint, glisten, glitter, reflect, shimmer, shine, twinkle 3. bounce, brush, graze, rebound, ricochet, skim 4. *With* **over, through,** *etc.* browse, dip into, flip through, leaf through, riffle through, run over *or* through, scan, skim through, thumb through ~*n.* 5. brief look, dekko (*Sl.*), gander (*Inf.*), glimpse, look, peek, peep, quick look, squint, view 6. flash, gleam, glimmer, glint, reflection, sparkle, twinkle 7. allusion, passing mention, reference

glare v. 1. frown, give a dirty look, glower, look daggers, lower, scowl, stare angrily 2. blaze, dazzle, flame, flare ~*n.* 3. angry stare, black look, dirty look, frown, glower, lower, scowl 4. blaze, brilliance, dazzle, flame, flare, glow 5. flashiness, floridness, gaudiness, loudness, meretriciousness, showiness, tawdriness

glaring 1. audacious, blatant, conspicuous, egregious, flagrant, gross, manifest, obvious, open, outrageous, outstanding, overt, patent, rank, unconcealed, visible 2. blazing, bright, dazzling, flashy, florid, garish, glowing, loud

glassy 1. clear, glossy, icy, shiny, slick, slippery, smooth, transparent 2. blank, cold, dazed, dull, empty, expressionless, fixed, glazed, lifeless, vacant

glaze 1. v. burnish, coat, enamel, furbish, gloss, lacquer, polish, varnish 2. n. coat, enamel, finish, gloss, lacquer, lustre, patina, polish, shine, varnish

gleam n. 1. beam, flash, glimmer, glow, ray, sparkle 2. brightness, brilliance, coruscation, flash, gloss, lustre, sheen, splendour 3. flicker, glimmer, hint, inkling, ray, suggestion, trace ~v. 4. coruscate, flare, flash, glance, glimmer, glint, glisten, glitter, glow, scintillate, shimmer, shine, sparkle

glean accumulate, amass, collect, cull, garner, gather, harvest, learn, pick, pick up, reap, select

glee cheerfulness, delight, elation, exhilaration, exuberance, exultation, fun, gaiety, gladness, hilarity, jocularity, jollity, joviality, joy, joyfulness, joyousness,

liveliness, merriment, mirth, sprightliness, triumph, verve

gleeful cheerful, cock-a-hoop, delighted, elated, exuberant, exultant, gay, gratified, happy, jocund, jovial, joyful, joyous, jubilant, merry, mirthful, overjoyed, pleased, triumphant

glib artful, easy, fast-talking, fluent, garrulous, insincere, plausible, quick, ready, slick, slippery, smooth, smooth-tongued, suave, talkative, voluble

glide coast, drift, float, flow, fly, roll, run, sail, skate, skim, slide, slip, soar

glimmer v. 1. blink, flicker, gleam, glisten, glitter, glow, shimmer, shine, sparkle, twinkle ~*n.* 2. blink, flicker, gleam, glow, ray, shimmer, sparkle, twinkle 3. flicker, gleam, grain, hint, inkling, ray, suggestion, trace

glimpse 1. n. brief view, glance, look, peek, peep, quick look, sight, sighting, squint 2. v. catch sight of, descry, espy, sight, spot, spy, view

glint 1. v. flash, gleam, glimmer, glitter, shine, sparkle, twinkle 2. n. flash, gleam, glimmer, glitter, shine, sparkle, twinkle, twinkling

glisten coruscate, flash, glance, glare, gleam, glimmer, glint, glitter, scintillate, shimmer, shine, sparkle, twinkle

glitter v. 1. coruscate, flare, flash, glare, gleam, glimmer, glint, glisten, scintillate, shimmer, shine, sparkle, twinkle ~*n.* 2. beam, brightness, brilliance, flash, glare, gleam, lustre, radiance, scintillation, sheen, shimmer, shine, sparkle 3. display, gaudiness, glamour, pageantry, show, showiness, splendour, tinsel

gloaming dusk, eventide (*Archaic*), half-light, nightfall, twilight

gloat crow, exult, glory, relish, revel in, rub it in (*Inf.*), triumph, vaunt

global 1. international, pandemic, planetary, universal, world, worldwide 2. all-encompassing, all-inclusive, all-out, comprehensive, encyclopedic, exhaustive, general, thorough, total, unbounded, unlimited

globe ball, earth, orb, planet, round, sphere, world

globular globate, globelike, globoid, globose, globous, globulous, orbicular, round, spherical, spheroid

globule bead, bubble, drop, droplet, particle, pearl, pellet

gloom 1. blackness, cloud, cloudiness, dark, darkness, dimness, dullness, dusk, duskiness, gloominess, murk, murkiness, obscurity, shade, shadow, twilight **2.** blues, dejection, depression, desolation, despair, despondency, downheartedness, low spirits, melancholy, misery, sadness, sorrow, unhappiness, woe

gloomy 1. black, crepuscular, dark, dim, dismal, dreary, dull, dusky, murky, obscure, overcast, shadowy, sombre, Stygian, tenebrous **2.** bad, black, cheerless, comfortless, depressing, disheartening, dispiriting, dreary, joyless, sad, saddening, sombre **3.** blue, chapfallen, cheerless, crestfallen, dejected, despondent, dismal, dispirited, down, downcast, downhearted, down in the dumps (*Inf.*), down in the mouth, glum, in low spirits, melancholy, miserable, moody, morose, pessimistic, sad, saturnine, sullen

glorify 1. add lustre to, adorn, aggrandize, augment, dignify, elevate, enhance, ennoble, illuminate, immortalize, lift up, magnify, raise **2.** adore, apotheosize, beatify, bless, canonize, deify, enshrine, exalt, honour, idolize, pay homage to, revere, sanctify, venerate, worship **3.** celebrate, cry up (*Inf.*), eulogize, extol, hymn, laud, lionize, magnify, panegyrize, praise, sing *or* sound the praises of

glorious 1. celebrated, distinguished, elevated, eminent, excellent, famed, famous, grand, honoured, illustrious, magnificent, majestic, noble, noted, renowned, sublime, triumphant **2.** beautiful, bright, brilliant, dazzling, divine, effulgent, gorgeous, radiant, resplendent, shining, splendid, superb **3.** *Inf.* delightful, enjoyable, excellent, fine, great, heavenly (*Inf.*), marvellous, pleasurable, splendid, wonderful

glory *n.* **1.** celebrity, dignity, distinction, eminence, exaltation, fame, honour, illustriousness, immortality, kudos, praise, prestige, renown **2.** adoration, benediction, blessing, gratitude, homage, laudation, praise, thanksgiving, veneration, worship **3.** grandeur, greatness, magnificence, majesty, nobility, pageantry, pomp, splendour, sublimity, triumph **4.** beauty, brilliance, effulgence, gorgeousness, lustre, radiance, resplendence ~*v.* **5.** boast, crow, exult, gloat, pride oneself, relish, revel, take delight, triumph

gloss¹ *n.* **1.** brightness, brilliance, burnish, gleam, lustre, polish, sheen, shine, varnish, veneer **2.** appearance, façade, front, mask, semblance, show, surface ~*v.* **3.** burnish, finish, furbish, glaze, lacquer, polish, shine, varnish, veneer **4.** camouflage, conceal, cover up, disguise, hide, mask, smooth over, veil, whitewash (*Inf.*)

gloss² **1.** *n.* annotation, comment, commentary, elucidation, explanation, footnote, interpretation, note, scholium, translation **2.** *v.* annotate, comment, construe, elucidate, explain, interpret, translate

glossy bright, brilliant, burnished, glassy, glazed, lustrous, polished, sheeny, shining, shiny, silken, silky, sleek, smooth

glow *n.* **1.** burning, gleam, glimmer, incandescence, lambency, light, luminosity, phosphorescence **2.** brightness, brilliance, effulgence, radiance, splendour, vividness **3.** ardour, earnestness, enthusiasm, excitement, fervour, gusto, impetuosity, intensity, passion, vehemence, warmth **4.** bloom, blush, flush, reddening, rosiness ~*v.* **5.** brighten, burn, gleam, glimmer, redden, shine, smoulder **6.** be suffused, blush, colour, fill, flush, radiate, thrill, tingle

glower 1. *v.* frown, give a dirty look, glare, look daggers, lower, scowl **2.** *n.* angry stare, black look, dirty look, frown, glare, lower, scowl

glowing 1. aglow, beaming, bright, flaming, florid, flushed, lambent, luminous, red, rich, ruddy, suffused, vibrant, vivid, warm **2.** adulatory, complimentary, ecstatic, enthusiastic, eulogistic, laudatory, panegyrical, rave (*Inf.*), rhapsodic

glue 1. *n.* adhesive, cement, gum, mucilage, paste **2.** *v.* affix, agglutinate, cement, fix, gum, paste, seal, stick

glum chapfallen, churlish, crabbed, crestfallen, crusty, dejected, doleful, down, gloomy, gruff, grumpy, ill-humoured, low, moody, morose, pessimistic, saturnine, sour, sulky, sullen, surly

glut *n.* **1.** excess, overabundance, oversupply, saturation, superabundance, superfluity, surfeit, surplus ~*v.* **2.** cram, fill, gorge, overfeed, satiate, stuff **3.** choke, clog, deluge, flood, inundate, overload, oversupply, saturate

glutinous adhesive, cohesive, gluey,

gummy, mucilaginous, sticky, viscid, viscous

glutton gannet (*Sl.*), gobbler, gorger, gormandizer, gourmand, pig (*Inf.*)

gluttonous gormandizing, greedy, hoggish, insatiable, piggish, rapacious, ravenous, voracious

gluttony gormandizing, gourmandism, greed, greediness, piggishness, rapacity, voraciousness, voracity

gnarled contorted, knotted, knotty, knurled, leathery, rough, rugged, twisted, weather-beaten, wrinkled

gnaw 1. bite, chew, munch, nibble, worry **2.** consume, devour, eat away *or* into, erode, fret, wear away *or* down **3.** distress, fret, harry, haunt, nag, plague, prey on one's mind, trouble, worry

go *v.* **1.** advance, decamp, depart, fare (*Archaic*), journey, leave, make for, move, move out, pass, proceed, repair, set off, travel, withdraw **2.** function, move, operate, perform, run, work **3.** connect, extend, fit, give access, lead, reach, run, span, spread, stretch **4.** avail, concur, conduce, contribute, incline, lead to, serve, tend, work towards **5.** develop, eventuate, fall out, fare, happen, proceed, result, turn out, work out **6.** accord, agree, blend, chime, complement, correspond, fit, harmonize, jibe (*Inf.*), match, suit **7.** die, expire, give up the ghost, pass away, perish **8.** elapse, expire, flow, lapse, pass, slip away ~*n.* **9.** attempt, bid, crack (*Inf.*), effort, essay, shot (*Inf.*), stab, try, turn, whack (*Inf.*), whirl (*Inf.*) **10.** *Inf.* activity, animation, drive, energy, force, get-up-and-go (*Inf.*), life, oomph (*Inf.*), pep, spirit, verve, vigour, vitality, vivacity

go about 1. circulate, move around, pass around, wander **2.** approach, begin, set about, tackle, undertake **3.** busy *or* occupy oneself with, devote oneself to

goad 1. *n.* impetus, incentive, incitement, irritation, motivation, pressure, spur, stimulation, stimulus, urge **2.** *v.* annoy, arouse, drive, egg on, exhort, harass, hound, impel, incite, instigate, irritate, lash, prick, prod, prompt, propel, spur, stimulate, sting, urge, worry

go-ahead 1. *n. Inf.* assent, authorization, consent, green light, leave, O.K. (*Inf.*), permission **2.** *adj.* ambitious, enterprising, go-getting (*Inf.*), pioneering, progressive, up-and-coming

go ahead advance, begin, continue, go forward, go on, proceed, progress

goal aim, ambition, design, destination, end, intention, limit, mark, object, objective, purpose, target

go along 1. acquiesce, agree, assent, concur, cooperate, follow **2.** accompany, carry on, escort, join, keep up, move, pass, travel

go at argue, attack, blame, criticize, impugn, set about

go away decamp, depart, exit, leave, move out, recede, withdraw

gob blob, chunk, clod, gobbet, hunk, lump, piece, wad, wodge (*Brit. inf.*)

go back 1. return, revert **2.** change one's mind, desert, forsake, renege, repudiate, retract

gobble bolt, cram, devour, gorge, gulp, guzzle, stuff, swallow, wolf

gobbledegook babble, cant, double talk, gabble, gibberish, hocus-pocus, jabber, jargon, mumbo jumbo, nonsense, officialese, rigmarole, twaddle

go-between agent, broker, dealer, factor, intermediary, liaison, mediator, medium, middleman

go by 1. elapse, exceed, flow on, move onward, pass, proceed **2.** adopt, be guided by, follow, heed, judge from, observe, take as guide

godforsaken abandoned, backward, bleak, deserted, desolate, dismal, dreary, forlorn, gloomy, lonely, neglected, remote, wretched

godless atheistic, depraved, evil, impious, irreligious, profane, ungodly, unprincipled, unrighteous, wicked

godlike celestial, deific, deiform, divine, heavenly, superhuman, transcendent

godly devout, god-fearing, good, holy, pious, religious, righteous, saintly

go down 1. be beaten, collapse, decline, decrease, drop, fall, founder, go under, lose, set, sink, submerge, submit, suffer defeat **2.** be commemorated (recalled, recorded, remembered)

godsend blessing, boon, manna, stroke of luck, windfall

go far advance, be successful, do well, get ahead (*Inf.*), get on (*Inf.*), make a name for oneself, progress, succeed

go for 1. clutch at, fetch, obtain, reach, seek, stretch for **2.** admire, be attracted to, be fond of, choose, favour, hold with, like, prefer **3.** assail, assault, attack, launch oneself at, rush upon, set about *or* upon, spring upon

goggle gape, gawk, gawp (*Sl.*), peer, rubberneck (*Sl.*), stare

go in (for) adopt, embrace, engage in, enter, espouse, practise, pursue, take up, undertake

going-over 1. analysis, check, examination, inspection, investigation, review, scrutiny, study, survey **2.** beating, buffeting, doing (*Inf.*), drubbing, thrashing, thumping, whipping **3.** castigation, chastisement, chiding, dressing-down (*Inf.*), lecture, rebuke, reprimand, row, scolding, talking-to (*Inf.*), tongue-lashing

go into 1. begin, develop, enter, participate in, undertake **2.** analyse, consider, delve into, discuss, examine, inquire into, investigate, look into, probe, pursue, review, scrutinize, study

golden 1. blond *or* blonde, bright, brilliant, flaxen, resplendent, shining, yellow **2.** best, blissful, delightful, flourishing, glorious, happy, joyful, joyous, precious, prosperous, rich, successful **3.** advantageous, auspicious, excellent, favourable, opportune, promising, propitious, rosy, valuable

gone 1. elapsed, ended, finished, over, past **2.** absent, astray, away, lacking, lost, missing, vanished **3.** dead, deceased, defunct, departed, extinct, no more **4.** consumed, done, finished, spent, used up

good *adj.* **1.** acceptable, admirable, agreeable, capital, choice, commendable, excellent, fine, first-class, first-rate, great, pleasant, pleasing, positive, precious, satisfactory, splendid, super (*Inf.*), superior, tiptop, valuable, worthy **2.** admirable, estimable, ethical, exemplary, honest, honourable, moral, praiseworthy, right, righteous, upright, virtuous, worthy **3.** able, accomplished, adept, adroit, capable, clever, competent, dexterous, efficient, expert, first-rate, proficient, reliable, satisfactory, serviceable, skilled, sound, suitable, talented, thorough, trustworthy, useful **4.** adequate, advantageous, auspicious, beneficial, convenient, favourable, fit, fitting, healthy, helpful, opportune, profitable, propitious, salubrious, salutary, suitable, useful, wholesome **5.** eatable, fit to eat, sound, uncorrupted, untainted, whole **6.** altruistic, approving, beneficent, benevolent,

charitable, friendly, gracious, humane, kind, kind-hearted, kindly, merciful, obliging, well-disposed **7.** authentic, bona fide, dependable, genuine, honest, legitimate, proper, real, reliable, sound, true, trustworthy, valid **8.** decorous, dutiful, mannerly, obedient, orderly, polite, proper, seemly, well-behaved, well-mannered **9.** agreeable, cheerful, congenial, convivial, enjoyable, gratifying, happy, pleasant, pleasing, pleasurable, satisfying **10.** adequate, ample, complete, considerable, entire, extensive, full, large, long, sizable, solid, substantial, sufficient, whole **11.** best, fancy, finest, newest, nicest, precious, smartest, special, valuable **12.** *Of weather* balmy, bright, calm, clear, clement, cloudless, fair, halcyon, mild, sunny, sunshiny, tranquil ~*n.* **13.** advantage, avail, behalf, benefit, gain, interest, profit, service, use, usefulness, welfare, wellbeing, worth **14.** excellence, goodness, merit, morality, probity, rectitude, right, righteousness, uprightness, virtue, worth **15. for good** finally, for ever, irrevocably, never to return, once and for all, permanently, *sine die*

goodbye adieu, farewell, leave-taking, parting

good-for-nothing 1. *n.* black sheep, idler, layabout, ne'er-do-well, profligate, rapscallion, scapegrace, waster, wastrel **2.** *adj.* feckless, idle, irresponsible, useless, worthless

good-humoured affable, amiable, cheerful, congenial, genial, good-tempered, happy, pleasant

good-looking attractive, comely, fair, handsome, personable, pretty, well-favoured

goodly 1. ample, considerable, large, significant, sizable, substantial, tidy (*Inf.*) **2.** agreeable, attractive, comely, desirable, elegant, fine, good-looking, graceful, handsome, personable, pleasant, pleasing, well-favoured

good-natured agreeable, benevolent, friendly, good-hearted, helpful, kind, kindly, tolerant, warm-hearted, well-disposed, willing to please

goodness 1. excellence, merit, quality, superiority, value, worth **2.** beneficence, benevolence, friendliness, generosity, good will, graciousness, humaneness, kind-heartedness, kindliness, kindness, mercy, obligingness **3.** honesty, honour, integrity, merit, morality, probity, rectitude, righteousness, uprightness, virtue **4.** advantage, benefit, nourishment, nutrition, salubriousness, wholesomeness

goods 1. appurtenances, belongings, chattels, effects, furnishings, furniture, gear, movables, paraphernalia, possessions, property, things, trappings **2.** commodities, merchandise, stock, stuff, wares

good will amity, benevolence, favour, friendliness, friendship, heartiness, kindliness, zeal

gooey 1. gluey, glutinous, mucilaginous, soft, sticky, tacky, viscous **2.** maudlin, mawkish, sentimental, slushy (*Inf.*), syrupy (*Inf.*), tear-jerking (*Inf.*)

go off 1. blow up, detonate, explode, fire **2.** happen, occur, take place **3.** decamp, depart, go away, leave, move out, part, quit **4.** *Inf.* go bad, go stale, rot

go on 1. continue, endure, happen, last, occur, persist, proceed, stay **2.** blether, carry on, chatter, prattle, ramble on, waffle, witter (on) (*Inf.*)

go out 1. depart, exit, leave **2.** be extinguished, die out, expire, fade out

go over 1. examine, inspect, rehearse, reiterate, review, revise, study **2.** peruse, read, scan, skim

gore[1] *n.* blood, bloodshed, butchery, carnage, slaughter

gore[2] *v.* impale, pierce, spit, stab, transfix, wound

gorge[1] *n.* canyon, cleft, clough (*Dialect*), defile, fissure, pass, ravine

gorge[2] *v.* bolt, cram, devour, feed, fill, glut, gobble, gormandize, gulp, guzzle, overeat, raven, sate, satiate, stuff, surfeit, swallow, wolf

gorgeous 1. beautiful, brilliant, dazzling, elegant, glittering, grand, luxuriant, magnificent, opulent, ravishing, resplendent, showy, splendid, stunning (*Inf.*), sumptuous, superb **2.** *Inf.* attractive, bright, delightful, enjoyable, exquisite, fine, glorious, good, good-looking, lovely, pleasing

gory blood-soaked, bloodstained, bloodthirsty, bloody, ensanguined (*Literary*), murderous, sanguinary

gospel 1. certainty, fact, the last word, truth, verity **2.** credo, creed, doctrine, message, news, revelation, tidings

gossamer *adj.* airy, delicate, diaphanous, fine, flimsy, gauzy, light, sheer, silky, thin, transparent

gossip *n.* **1.** blether, chinwag (*Brit. inf.*), chitchat, clishmaclaver, (*Scot.*), hearsay, idle talk, jaw (*Sl.*), newsmongering (*Old-fashioned*), prattle, scandal, small talk, tittle-tattle **2.** babbler, blatherskite, blether, busybody, chatterbox (*Inf.*), chatterer, flibbertigibbet, gossipmonger, newsmonger (*Old-fashioned*), prattler, quidnunc, scandalmonger, tattler, telltale ~*v.* **3.** blather, blether, chat, gabble, jaw (*Sl.*), prate, prattle, tattle

go through 1. bear, brave, endure, experience, suffer, tolerate, undergo, withstand **2.** consume, exhaust, squander, use **3.** check, examine, explore, hunt, look, search

go together 1. accord, agree, fit, harmonize, make a pair, match **2.** *Inf.* court, date (*Inf., chiefly U.S.*), escort, go out with, go steady with (*Inf.*)

gouge 1. *v.* chisel, claw, cut, dig (out), gash, hollow (out), incise, scoop, score, scratch **2.** *n.* cut, furrow, gash, groove, hollow, incision, notch, scoop, score, scratch, trench

go under default, die, drown, fail, fold (*Inf.*), founder, go down, sink, submerge, succumb

gourmet *bon vivant*, connoisseur, epicure, gastronome

govern 1. administer, be in power, command, conduct, control, direct, guide, hold sway, lead, manage, order, oversee, pilot, reign, rule, steer, superintend, supervise **2.** bridle, check, contain, control, curb, direct, discipline, get the better of, hold in check, inhibit, master, regulate, restrain, subdue, tame **3.** decide, determine, guide, influence, rule, sway, underlie

government 1. administration, authority, dominion, execution, governance, law, polity, rule, sovereignty, state, statecraft **2.** administration, executive, ministry, powers-that-be, regime **3.** authority, command, control, direction, domination, guidance, management, regulation, restraint, superintendence, supervision, sway

governmental administrative, bureaucratic, executive, ministerial, official, political, sovereign, state

governor administrator, boss (*Inf.*), chief, commander, comptroller, controller, director, executive, head, leader,

manager, overseer, ruler, superintendent, supervisor

go with accompany, agree, blend,
complement, concur, correspond, fit,
harmonize, match, suit

go without abstain, be denied, be deprived of, deny oneself, do without, go
short, lack, want

gown costume, dress, frock, garb, garment, habit, robe

grab bag, capture, catch, catch *or* take
hold of, clutch, grasp, grip, latch on to,
nab (*Inf.*), pluck, seize, snap up, snatch

grace n. **1**. attractiveness, beauty,
charm, comeliness, ease, elegance, finesse, gracefulness, loveliness, pleasantness, poise, polish, refinement, shapeliness, tastefulness **2**. benefaction, beneficence, benevolence, favour, generosity,
goodness, good will, kindliness, kindness
3. breeding, consideration, cultivation,
decency, decorum, etiquette, mannerliness, manners, propriety, tact **4**. charity,
clemency, compassion, forgiveness, indulgence, leniency, lenity, mercy, pardon, quarter, reprieve **5**. benediction,
blessing, prayer, thanks, thanksgiving
~v. **6**. adorn, beautify, bedeck, deck,
decorate, dignify, distinguish, elevate,
embellish, enhance, enrich, favour, garnish, glorify, honour, ornament, set off

graceful agile, beautiful, becoming,
charming, comely, easy, elegant, fine,
flowing, gracile (*Rare*), natural, pleasing,
smooth, symmetrical, tasteful

graceless 1. barbarous, boorish,
coarse, crude, ill-mannered, improper,
indecorous, rude, shameless, unmannerly, unsophisticated, vulgar **2**. awkward,
clumsy, forced, gauche, gawky, inelegant, loutish, rough, uncouth, ungainly,
untutored

Graces, the Charities

gracious accommodating, affable,
amiable, beneficent, benevolent, benign,
benignant, charitable, chivalrous, civil,
compassionate, considerate, cordial,
courteous, courtly, friendly, hospitable,
indulgent, kind, kindly, lenient, loving,
merciful, mild, obliging, pleasing, polite,
well-mannered

gradation 1. array, progression, sequence, series, succession **2**. degree,
grade, level, mark, measurement, notch,
place, point, position, rank, stage, step **3**.
arrangement, classification, grouping, ordering, sorting

grade n. **1**. brand, category, class, condition, degree, echelon, group, level,
mark, notch, order, place, position, quality, rank, rung, size, stage, station, step
2. make the grade *Inf.* come through
with flying colours, come up to scratch
(*Inf.*), measure up, measure up to expectations, pass muster, prove acceptable,
succeed, win through **3**. acclivity, bank,
declivity, gradient, hill, incline, rise,
slope ~v. **4**. arrange, brand, class, classify, evaluate, group, order, range, rank,
rate, sort, value

gradient acclivity, bank, declivity,
grade, hill, incline, rise, slope

gradual continuous, even, gentle,
graduated, moderate, piecemeal, progressive, regular, slow, steady, successive, unhurried

gradually bit by bit, by degrees, drop
by drop, evenly, gently, little by little,
moderately, piece by piece, piecemeal,
progressively, slowly, steadily, step by
step, unhurriedly

graduate v. **1**. calibrate, grade, mark
off, measure out, proportion, regulate **2**.
arrange, classify, grade, group, order,
range, rank, sort

graft 1. *n*. bud, implant, scion, shoot,
splice, sprout **2**. *v*. affix, implant, ingraft,
insert, join, splice, transplant

grain 1. cereals, corn **2**. grist, kernel,
seed **3**. atom, bit, crumb, fragment, granule, iota, jot, mite, modicum, molecule,
morsel, mote, ounce, particle, piece, scintilla (*Rare*), scrap, scruple, spark, speck,
suspicion, trace, whit **4**. fibre, nap, pattern, surface, texture, weave **5**. character, disposition, humour, inclination,
make-up, temper

grand 1. ambitious, august, dignified,
elevated, eminent, exalted, fine, glorious,
grandiose, great, haughty, illustrious,
imposing, impressive, large, lofty, lordly,
luxurious, magnificent, majestic, monumental, noble, opulent, ostentatious, palatial, pompous, pretentious, princely,
regal, splendid, stately, striking, sublime, sumptuous **2**. admirable, excellent,
fine, first-class, first-rate, great (*Inf.*),
marvellous (*Inf.*), outstanding, smashing
(*Inf.*), splendid, super (*Inf.*), superb, terrific (*Inf.*), very good, wonderful **3**. chief,
head, highest, leading, main, pre-
eminent, principal, supreme

grandeur augustness, dignity, greatness, importance, loftiness, magnifi-

cence, majesty, nobility, pomp, splendour, state, stateliness, sublimity

grandiloquent bombastic, flowery, fustian, high-flown, high-sounding, inflated, magniloquent, orotund, pompous, pretentious, rhetorical

grandiose 1. affected, ambitious, bombastic, extravagant, flamboyant, high-flown, ostentatious, pompous, pretentious, showy **2.** ambitious, grand, imposing, impressive, lofty, magnificent, majestic, monumental, stately

grant v. **1.** accede to, accord, acknowledge, admit, agree to, allocate, allot, allow, assign, award, bestow, cede, concede, confer, consent to, donate, give, impart, permit, present, vouchsafe, yield **2.** Law assign, convey, transfer, transmit ~n. **3.** admission, allocation, allotment, allowance, award, benefaction, bequest, boon, bounty, concession, donation, endowment, gift, present, subsidy

granular crumbly, grainy, granulated, gravelly, gritty, rough, sandy

granulate crumble, crush, crystallize, grind, levigate (*Chemistry*), pound, powder, pulverize, triturate

granule atom, crumb, fragment, grain, iota, jot, molecule, particle, scrap, speck

graphic 1. clear, descriptive, detailed, explicit, expressive, forcible, illustrative, lively, lucid, picturesque, striking, telling, vivid, well-drawn **2.** delineated, diagrammatic, drawn, illustrative, pictorial, representational, seen, visible, visual

grapple 1. catch, clasp, clutch, come to grips, fasten, grab, grasp, grip, hold, hug, lay or take hold, make fast, seize, wrestle **2.** address oneself to, attack, battle, clash, combat, confront, contend, cope, deal with, do battle, encounter, engage, face, fight, struggle, tackle, take on, tussle, wrestle

grasp v. **1.** catch, clasp, clinch, clutch, grab, grapple, grip, hold, lay or take hold of, seize, snatch **2.** catch or get the drift of, catch on, comprehend, follow, get, realize, see, take in, understand ~n. **3.** clasp, clutches, embrace, grip, hold, possession, tenure **4.** capacity, compass, control, extent, mastery, power, range, reach, scope, sway, sweep **5.** awareness, comprehension, ken, knowledge, mastery, perception, realization, understanding

grasping acquisitive, avaricious, close-fisted, covetous, greedy, mean, miserly, niggardly, penny-pinching (*Inf.*), rapacious, selfish, stingy, tightfisted, usurious, venal

grate v. **1.** mince, pulverize, shred, triturate **2.** creak, grind, rasp, rub, scrape, scratch **3.** annoy, chafe, exasperate, fret, gall, get one down, get on one's nerves (*Inf.*), irk, irritate, jar, nettle, peeve, rankle, rub one up the wrong way, set one's teeth on edge, vex

grateful 1. appreciative, beholden, indebted, obliged, thankful **2.** acceptable, agreeable, favourable, gratifying, nice, pleasing, refreshing, restful, satisfactory, satisfying, welcome

gratification delight, enjoyment, fruition, fulfilment, glee, indulgence, joy, kick or kicks (*Inf.*), pleasure, recompense, relish, reward, satisfaction, thrill

gratify cater to, delight, favour, fulfil, give pleasure, gladden, humour, indulge, please, recompense, requite, satisfy, thrill

grating adj. annoying, disagreeable, discordant, displeasing, grinding, harsh, irksome, irritating, jarring, offensive, rasping, raucous, scraping, squeaky, strident, unpleasant, vexatious

gratis for nothing, free, freely, free of charge, gratuitously, on the house, unpaid

gratitude appreciation, gratefulness, indebtedness, obligation, recognition, sense of obligation, thankfulness, thanks

gratuitous 1. complimentary, free, spontaneous, unasked-for, unpaid, unrewarded, voluntary **2.** assumed, baseless, causeless, groundless, irrelevant, needless, superfluous, uncalled-for, unfounded, unjustified, unmerited, unnecessary, unprovoked, unwarranted, wanton

gratuity baksheesh, benefaction, bonus, boon, bounty, donation, gift, largess, perquisite, *pourboire*, present, recompense, reward, tip

grave[1] n. burying place, crypt, last resting place, mausoleum, pit, sepulchre, tomb, vault

grave[2] **1.** dignified, dour, dull, earnest, gloomy, grim-faced, heavy, leaden, long-faced, muted, quiet, sage (*Obsolete*), sedate, serious, sober, solemn, sombre, staid, subdued, thoughtful, unsmiling **2.** acute, critical, crucial, dangerous, exigent, hazardous, important, life-and-death, momentous, of great consequence, perilous, pressing, serious, severe, significant, threatening, urgent, vital, weighty

graveyard boneyard (*Inf.*), burial ground, cemetery, charnel house, churchyard, God's acre (*Literary*), necropolis

gravitate 1. *With* **to** *or* **towards** be influenced (attracted, drawn, pulled), incline, lean, move, tend **2**. be precipitated, descend, drop, fall, precipitate, settle, sink

gravity 1. acuteness, consequence, exigency, hazardousness, importance, moment, momentousness, perilousness, pressingness, seriousness, severity, significance, urgency, weightiness **2**. demureness, dignity, earnestness, gloom, grimness, reserve, sedateness, seriousness, sobriety, solemnity, thoughtfulness

graze¹ browse, crop, feed, pasture

graze² *v.* **1**. brush, glance off, kiss, rub, scrape, shave, skim, touch **2**. abrade, bark, chafe, scrape, scratch, skin ~*n.* **3**. abrasion, scrape, scratch

greasy 1. fatty, oily, slick, slimy, slippery **2**. fawning, glib, grovelling, ingratiating, oily, slick, smarmy (*Brit. inf.*), smooth, sycophantish, toadying, unctuous

great 1. big, bulky, colossal, enormous, extensive, gigantic, huge, immense, large, mammoth, prodigious, stupendous, tremendous, vast, voluminous **2**. extended, lengthy, long, prolonged, protracted **3**. capital, chief, grand, leading, main, major, paramount, primary, principal, prominent, superior **4**. considerable, decided, excessive, extravagant, extreme, grievous, high, inordinate, prodigious, pronounced, strong **5**. consequential, critical, crucial, grave, heavy, important, momentous, serious, significant, weighty **6**. celebrated, distinguished, eminent, exalted, excellent, famed, famous, glorious, illustrious, notable, noteworthy, outstanding, prominent, remarkable, renowned, superlative, talented **7**. august, chivalrous, dignified, distinguished, exalted, fine, glorious, grand, heroic, high-minded, idealistic, impressive, lofty, magnanimous, noble, princely, sublime **8**. active, devoted, enthusiastic, keen, zealous **9**. able, adept, adroit, crack (*Sl.*), expert, good, masterly, proficient, skilful, skilled **10**. *Inf.* admirable, excellent, fantastic (*Inf.*), fine, first-rate, good, marvellous (*Inf.*), terrific (*Inf.*),

tremendous (*Inf.*), wonderful **11**. absolute, arrant, complete, consummate, downright, egregious, flagrant, out-and-out, perfect, positive, thoroughgoing, thundering (*Inf.*), total, unmitigated, unqualified, utter

greatly abundantly, by leaps and bounds, by much, considerably, enormously, exceedingly, extremely, highly, hugely, immensely, markedly, mightily, much, notably, powerfully, remarkably, tremendously, vastly, very much

greatness 1. bulk, enormity, hugeness, immensity, largeness, length, magnitude, mass, prodigiousness, size, vastness **2**. amplitude, force, high degree, intensity, potency, power, strength **3**. gravity, heaviness, import, importance, moment, momentousness, seriousness, significance, urgency, weight **4**. celebrity, distinction, eminence, fame, glory, grandeur, illustriousness, lustre, note, renown **5**. chivalry, dignity, disinterestedness, generosity, grandeur, heroism, high-mindedness, idealism, loftiness, majesty, nobility, nobleness, stateliness, sublimity

greed, greediness 1. edacity, esurience, gluttony, gormandizing, hunger, insatiableness, ravenousness, voracity **2**. acquisitiveness, avidity, covetousness, craving, cupidity, desire, eagerness, graspingness, longing, rapacity, selfishness

greedy 1. edacious, esurient, gluttonous, gormandizing, hoggish, hungry, insatiable, piggish, ravenous, voracious **2**. acquisitive, avaricious, avid, covetous, craving, desirous, eager, grasping, hungry, impatient, rapacious, selfish

Greek 1. *n.* Hellene **2**. *adj.* Hellenic

green *adj.* **1**. blooming, budding, flourishing, fresh, grassy, leafy, new, undecayed, verdant, verdurous **2**. fresh, immature, new, raw, recent, unripe **3**. callow, credulous, gullible, ignorant, immature, inexperienced, inexpert, ingenuous, innocent, naive, new, raw, unpolished, unpractised, unskilful, unsophisticated, untrained, unversed, wet behind the ears (*Inf.*) **4**. covetous, envious, grudging, jealous, resentful **5**. ill, nauseous, pale, sick, unhealthy, wan **6**. immature, pliable, supple, tender, undried, unseasoned, young ~*n.* **7**. common, grassplot, lawn, sward, turf

greenhorn apprentice, beginner, ignoramus, ingénue, learner, naïf, neophyte, newcomer, novice, raw recruit, simpleton, tyro

green light approval, authorization, blessing, clearance, confirmation, goahead (*Inf.*), imprimatur, O.K. (*Inf.*), okay (*Inf.*), permission, sanction

greet accost, address, compliment, hail, meet, nod to, receive, salute, tip one's hat to, welcome

greeting 1. address, hail, reception, salutation, salute, welcome **2.** *Plural* best wishes, compliments, devoirs, good wishes, regards, respects, salutations

gregarious affable, companionable, convivial, cordial, friendly, outgoing, sociable, social

grey 1. ashen, bloodless, colourless, livid, pale, pallid, wan **2.** cheerless, cloudy, dark, depressing, dim, dismal, drab, dreary, dull, foggy, gloomy, misty, murky, overcast, sunless **3.** anonymous, characterless, colourless, dull, indistinct, neutral, unclear, unidentifiable **4.** aged, ancient, elderly, experienced, hoary, mature, old, venerable

grief 1. affliction, agony, anguish, bereavement, dejection, distress, grievance, heartache, heartbreak, misery, mournfulness, mourning, pain, regret, remorse, sadness, sorrow, suffering, trial, tribulation, trouble, woe **2. come to grief** *Inf.* come unstuck, fail, meet with disaster, miscarry

grief-stricken afflicted, agonized, broken, brokenhearted, crushed, desolate, despairing, devastated, heartbroken, inconsolable, overwhelmed, sorrowful, sorrowing, woebegone, wretched

grievance affliction, beef (*Sl.*), complaint, damage, distress, grief, gripe (*Inf.*), hardship, injury, injustice, resentment, sorrow, trial, tribulation, trouble, unhappiness, wrong

grieve 1. ache, bemoan, bewail, complain, deplore, lament, mourn, regret, rue, sorrow, suffer, wail, weep **2.** afflict, agonize, break the heart of, crush, distress, hurt, injure, make one's heart bleed, pain, sadden, wound

grievous 1. afflicting, calamitous, damaging, distressing, dreadful, grave, harmful, heavy, hurtful, injurious, lamentable, oppressive, painful, severe, wounding **2.** appalling, atrocious, deplorable, dreadful, egregious, flagrant, glaring, heinous, intolerable, lamentable,

monstrous, offensive, outrageous, shameful, shocking, unbearable **3.** agonized, grief-stricken, heart-rending, mournful, pitiful, sorrowful, tragic

grim cruel, ferocious, fierce, forbidding, formidable, frightful, ghastly, grisly, gruesome, harsh, hideous, horrible, horrid, implacable, merciless, morose, relentless, resolute, ruthless, severe, shocking, sinister, stern, sullen, surly, terrible, unrelenting, unyielding

grimace 1. *n.* face, frown, mouth, scowl, sneer, wry face **2.** *v.* frown, make a face *or* faces, mouth, scowl, sneer

grime dirt, filth, smut, soot

grimy begrimed, besmeared, besmirched, dirty, filthy, foul, grubby, smutty, soiled, sooty, unclean

grind *v.* **1.** abrade, comminute, crush, granulate, grate, kibble, mill, pound, powder, pulverize, triturate **2.** file, polish, sand, sharpen, smooth, whet **3.** gnash, grate, grit, scrape **4.** *With* **down** afflict, harass, hold down, hound, oppress, persecute, plague, trouble, tyrannize (over) ~*n.* **5.** *Inf.* chore, drudgery, hard work, labour, sweat (*Inf.*), task, toil

grip *n.* **1.** clasp, handclasp (*U.S.*), purchase **2.** clutches, comprehension, control, domination, grasp, hold, influence, keeping, mastery, perception, possession, power, tenure, understanding **3. come** *or* **get to grips (with)** close with, confront, contend with, cope with, deal with, encounter, face up to, grapple with, grasp, handle, meet, tackle, take on, undertake ~*v.* **4.** clasp, clutch, grasp, hold, latch on to, seize, take hold of **5.** catch up, compel, engross, enthral, entrance, fascinate, hold, involve, mesmerize, rivet, spellbind

gripe *v.* **1.** *Inf.* beef (*Sl.*), bellyache (*Sl.*), bitch (*Sl.*), carp, complain, groan, grouch (*Inf.*), grouse, grumble, moan, nag, whine **2.** ache, compress, cramp, hurt, pain, pinch, press, squeeze ~*n.* **3.** *Often plural* ache, aching, affliction, colic, cramps, distress, griping, pain, pang, pinching, stomachache, twinge **4.** *Inf.* beef (*Sl.*), complaint, grievance, groan, grouch (*Inf.*), grouse, grumble, moan, objection

gripping compelling, compulsive, engrossing, enthralling, entrancing, exciting, fascinating, riveting, spellbinding, thrilling, unputdownable (*Inf.*)

grisly abominable, appalling, awful,

dreadful, frightful, ghastly, grim, gruesome, hideous, horrible, horrid, macabre, shocking, sickening, terrible, terrifying

grit *n.* **1.** dust, gravel, pebbles, sand **2.** backbone, courage, determination, doggedness, fortitude, gameness, guts (*Inf.*), hardihood, mettle, nerve, perseverance, pluck, resolution, spirit, tenacity, toughness ~*v.* **3.** clench, gnash, grate, grind

gritty 1. abrasive, dusty, grainy, granular, gravelly, rasping, rough, sandy **2.** brave, courageous, determined, dogged, game, hardy, mettlesome, plucky, resolute, spirited, steadfast, tenacious, tough

grizzle fret, girn (*Scot.*), pule, snivel, whimper, whine, whinge (*Inf.*)

grizzled canescent, grey, grey-haired, grey-headed, greying, griseous, grizzly, hoary

groan *n.* **1.** cry, moan, sigh, whine **2.** *Inf.* beef (*Sl.*), complaint, gripe (*Inf.*), grouse, grumble, objection ~*v.* **3.** cry, moan, sigh, whine **4.** *Inf.* beef (*Sl.*), bemoan, bitch (*Sl.*), complain, gripe (*Inf.*), grouse, grumble, lament, object

groggy befuddled, confused, dazed, dizzy, faint, muzzy, punch-drunk, reeling, shaky, staggering, stunned, stupefied, unsteady, weak, wobbly, woozy (*Inf.*)

groom *n.* **1.** currier (*Rare*), hostler *or* ostler (*Archaic*), stableboy, stableman ~*v.* **2.** clean, dress, get up (*Inf.*), preen, primp, smarten up, spruce up, tidy, turn out **3.** brush, clean, curry, rub down, tend **4.** coach, drill, educate, make ready, nurture, prepare, prime, ready, train

groove channel, cut, cutting, flute, furrow, gutter, hollow, indentation, rebate, rut, score, trench

grope cast about, feel, finger, fish, flounder, fumble, grabble, scrabble, search

gross *adj.* **1.** big, bulky, corpulent, dense, fat, great, heavy, hulking, large, lumpish, massive, obese, overweight, thick **2.** aggregate, before deductions, before tax, entire, total, whole **3.** coarse, crude, improper, impure, indecent, indelicate, lewd, low, obscene, offensive, ribald, rude, sensual, smutty, unseemly, vulgar **4.** apparent, arrant, blatant, downright, egregious, flagrant, glaring, grievous, heinous, manifest, obvious, outrageous, plain, rank, serious, shameful, sheer, shocking, unmitigated, un-

qualified, utter **5.** boorish, callous, coarse, crass, dull, ignorant, imperceptive, insensitive, tasteless, uncultured, undiscriminating, unfeeling, unrefined, unsophisticated ~*v.* **6.** bring in, earn, make, rake in (*Inf.*), take

grossness 1. bigness, bulkiness, corpulence, fatness, greatness, heaviness, lumpishness, obesity, thickness **2.** bestiality, coarseness, crudity, impurity, indecency, indelicacy, licentiousness, obscenity, offensiveness, ribaldry, rudeness, sensuality, smut, smuttiness, unseemliness, vulgarity **3.** blatancy, egregiousness, flagrancy, grievousness, obviousness, rankness, seriousness, shamefulness **4.** coarseness, crassness, ignorance, insensitivity, lack of taste, tastelessness

grotesque absurd, bizarre, deformed, distorted, extravagant, fanciful, fantastic, freakish, incongruous, ludicrous, malformed, misshapen, odd, outlandish, preposterous, ridiculous, strange, unnatural, weird, whimsical

grouch *v.* **1.** beef (*Sl.*), bellyache (*Sl.*), bitch (*Sl.*), carp, complain, find fault, gripe (*Inf.*), grouse, grumble, moan, whine ~*n.* **2.** beef (*Sl.*), complaint, grievance, gripe (*Inf.*), grouse, grumble, moan, objection **3.** complainer, crab (*Inf.*), crosspatch (*Inf.*), curmudgeon, faultfinder, grouser, grumbler, malcontent, moaner, whiner

grouchy cantankerous, cross, discontented, grumbling, grumpy, illtempered, irascible, irritable, peevish, petulant, querulous, sulky, surly, testy

ground *n.* **1.** clod, dirt, dry land, dust, earth, field, land, loam, mould, sod, soil, terra firma, terrain, turf **2.** *Often plural* area, country, district, domain, estate, fields, gardens, habitat, holding, land, property, realm, terrain, territory, tract **3.** *Usually plural* account, argument, base, basis, call, cause, excuse, factor, foundation, inducement, justification, motive, occasion, premise, pretext, rationale, reason **4.** *Usually plural* deposit, dregs, grouts, lees, sediment, settlings **5.** arena, field, park (*Inf.*), pitch, stadium ~*v.* **6.** base, establish, fix, found, set, settle **7.** acquaint with, coach, familiarize with, inform, initiate, instruct, prepare, teach, train, tutor

groundless baseless, chimerical, empty, false, idle, illusory, imaginary, unauthorized, uncalled-for, unfounded, unjustified, unprovoked, unsupported, unwarranted

groundwork base, basis, cornerstone, footing, foundation, fundamentals, preliminaries, preparation, spadework, underpinnings

group *n.* **1.** aggregation, assemblage, association, band, batch, bunch, category, circle, class, clique, clump, cluster, collection, company, congregation, coterie, crowd, faction, formation, gang, gathering, organization, pack, party, set, troop ~*v.* **2.** arrange, assemble, associate, assort, bracket, class, classify, dispose, gather, marshal, order, organize, put together, range, sort **3.** associate, band together, cluster, congregate, consort, fraternize, gather, get together

grouse 1. *v.* beef (*Sl.*), bellyache (*Sl.*), bitch (*Sl.*), carp, complain, find fault, gripe (*Inf.*), grouch (*Inf.*), grumble, moan, whine **2.** *n.* beef (*Sl.*), complaint, grievance, gripe (*Inf.*), grouch (*Inf.*), grumble, moan, objection

grove brake, coppice, copse, covert, plantation, spinney, thicket, wood, woodland

grovel abase oneself, bootlick (*Inf.*), bow and scrape, cower, crawl, creep, cringe, crouch, demean oneself, fawn, flatter, humble oneself, kowtow, sneak, toady

grow 1. develop, enlarge, expand, extend, fill out, get bigger, get taller, heighten, increase, multiply, spread, stretch, swell, thicken, widen **2.** develop, flourish, germinate, shoot, spring up, sprout, vegetate **3.** arise, issue, originate, spring, stem **4.** advance, expand, flourish, improve, progress, prosper, succeed, thrive **5.** become, come to be, develop (into), get, turn, wax **6.** breed, cultivate, farm, nurture, produce, propagate, raise

grown-up 1. *adj.* adult, fully-grown, mature, of age **2.** *n.* adult, man, woman

growth 1. aggrandizement, augmentation, development, enlargement, evolution, expansion, extension, growing, heightening, increase, multiplication, proliferation, stretching, thickening, widening **2.** crop, cultivation, development, germination, produce, production, shooting, sprouting, vegetation **3.** advance, advancement, expansion, improvement, progress, prosperity, rise, success **4.** *Medicine* excrescence, lump, tumour

grub *v.* **1.** burrow, dig up, probe, pull up, root (*Inf.*), rootle (*Brit.*), search for, uproot **2.** ferret, forage, hunt, rummage, scour, search, uncover, unearth **3.** drudge, grind (*Inf.*), labour, plod, slave, slog, sweat, toil ~*n.* **4.** caterpillar, larva, maggot **5.** *Sl.* eats (*Sl.*), food, nosh (*Sl.*), rations, sustenance, victuals

grubby besmeared, dirty, filthy, frowzy, grimy, manky (*Scot. dialect*), mean, messy, mucky, scruffy, seedy, shabby, slovenly, smutty, soiled, sordid, squalid, unkempt, untidy, unwashed

grudge 1. *n.* animosity, animus, antipathy, aversion, bitterness, dislike, enmity, grievance, hard feelings, hate, ill will, malevolence, malice, pique, rancour, resentment, spite, venom **2.** *v.* begrudge, be reluctant, complain, covet, envy, hold back, mind, resent, stint

gruelling arduous, backbreaking, brutal, crushing, demanding, difficult, exhausting, fatiguing, fierce, grinding, hard, harsh, laborious, punishing, severe, stiff, strenuous, taxing, tiring, trying

gruesome abominable, awful, fearful, ghastly, grim, grisly, hideous, horrendous, horrible, horrid, horrific, horrifying, loathsome, macabre, repugnant, repulsive, shocking, spine-chilling, terrible

gruff 1. bad-tempered, bearish, blunt, brusque, churlish, crabbed, crusty, curt, discourteous, grouchy (*Inf.*), grumpy, ill-humoured, ill-natured, impolite, rough, rude, sour, sullen, surly, uncivil, ungracious, unmannerly **2.** croaking, guttural, harsh, hoarse, husky, low, rasping, rough, throaty

grumble *v.* **1.** beef (*Sl.*), bellyache (*Sl.*), bitch (*Sl.*), carp, complain, find fault, gripe (*Inf.*), grouch (*Inf.*), grouse, moan, repine, whine **2.** growl, gurgle, murmur, mutter, roar, rumble ~*n.* **3.** beef (*Sl.*), complaint, grievance, gripe (*Inf.*), grouch (*Inf.*), grouse, moan, objection **4.** growl, gurgle, murmur, muttering, roar, rumble

grumpy cantankerous, crabbed, cross, crotchety (*Inf.*), grouchy (*Inf.*), grumbling, ill-tempered, irritable, peevish, petulant, querulous, sulky, sullen, surly, testy

guarantee 1. *n.* assurance, bond, certainty, collateral, covenant, earnest, guaranty, pledge, promise, security, surety, undertaking, warranty, word, word of honour **2.** *v.* answer for, assure, certify, ensure, insure, maintain, make certain, pledge, promise, protect, secure, stand behind, swear, vouch for, warrant

guarantor backer, bailsman (*Rare*), bondsman (*Law*), guarantee, sponsor, supporter, surety, underwriter, voucher, warrantor

guaranty 1. agreement, assurance, bond, contract, covenant, guarantee, insurance, oath, pledge, promise, undertaking, warrant, warranty, word **2.** bail, bond, collateral, deposit, earnest, gage, pawn, pledge, security, token

guard v. **1.** cover, defend, escort, keep, mind, oversee, patrol, police, preserve, protect, safeguard, save, screen, secure, shelter, shield, supervise, tend, watch, watch over ~n. **2.** custodian, defender, lookout, picket, protector, sentinel, sentry, warder, watch, watchman **3.** convoy, escort, patrol **4.** buffer, bulwark, bumper, defence, pad, protection, rampart, safeguard, screen, security, shield **5.** attention, care, caution, heed, vigilance, wariness, watchfulness **6. off (one's) guard** napping, unprepared, unready, unwary, with one's defences down **7. on (one's) guard** alert, cautious, circumspect, on the alert, on the lookout, on the qui vive, prepared, ready, vigilant, wary, watchful

guarded cagey (*Inf.*), careful, cautious, circumspect, discreet, noncommittal, prudent, reserved, restrained, reticent, suspicious, wary

guardian attendant, champion, curator, custodian, defender, escort, guard, keeper, preserver, protector, trustee, warden, warder

guerrilla freedom fighter, irregular, member of the underground *or* resistance, partisan, underground fighter

guess v. **1.** conjecture, estimate, fathom, hypothesize, penetrate, predict, solve, speculate, work out **2.** believe, conjecture, dare say, deem, divine, fancy, hazard, imagine, judge, reckon, suppose, surmise, suspect, think ~n. **3.** conjecture, feeling, hypothesis, judgment, notion, prediction, reckoning, speculation, supposition, surmise, suspicion, theory

guesswork conjecture, estimation, presumption, speculation, supposition, surmise, suspicion, theory

guest boarder, caller, company, lodger, visitant, visitor

guff balderdash, bilge (*Inf.*), bosh (*Inf.*), drivel, empty talk, hot air (*Inf.*), humbug, nonsense, poppycock (*Inf.*), rot, rubbish

guidance advice, auspices, conduct, control, counsel, counselling, direction, government, help, instruction, intelligence, leadership, management, teaching

guide v. **1.** accompany, attend, conduct, convoy, direct, escort, lead, pilot, shepherd, show the way, steer, usher **2.** command, control, direct, handle, manage, manoeuvre, steer **3.** advise, counsel, educate, govern, influence, instruct, oversee, regulate, rule, superintend, supervise, sway, teach, train ~n. **4.** adviser, attendant, chaperon, cicerone, conductor, controller, counsellor, director, escort, leader, mentor, monitor, pilot, steersman, teacher, usher **5.** criterion, example, exemplar, ideal, inspiration, lodestar, master, model, paradigm, standard **6.** beacon, clue, guiding light, key, landmark, lodestar, mark, marker, pointer, sign, signal, signpost **7.** catalogue, directory, guidebook, handbook, instructions, key, manual, vade mecum

guild association, brotherhood, club, company, corporation, fellowship, fraternity, league, lodge, order, organization, society, union

guile art, artfulness, artifice, cleverness, craft, craftiness, cunning, deceit, deception, duplicity, gamesmanship (*Inf.*), knavery, ruse, sharp practice, slyness, treachery, trickery, trickiness, wiliness

guileful artful, clever, crafty, cunning, deceitful, duplicitous, foxy, sly, sneaky, treacherous, tricky, underhand, wily

guileless above-board, artless, candid, frank, genuine, honest, ingenuous, innocent, naive, natural, open, simple, simple-minded, sincere, straightforward, truthful, undesigning, unsophisticated

guilt 1. blame, blameworthiness, criminality, culpability, delinquency, guiltiness, iniquity, misconduct, responsibility, sinfulness, wickedness, wrong, wrongdoing **2.** bad conscience, contrition, disgrace, dishonour, guiltiness, guilty conscience, infamy, regret, remorse, self-condemnation, self-reproach, shame, stigma

guiltless blameless, clean (*Sl.*), clear, immaculate, impeccable, innocent, irreproachable, pure, sinless, spotless, unimpeachable, unsullied, untainted, untarnished

guilty 1. at fault, blameworthy, convicted, criminal, culpable, delinquent, erring, evil, felonious, iniquitous, offending, reprehensible, responsible, sinful, to blame, wicked, wrong **2.** ashamed, conscience-stricken, contrite, hangdog, regretful, remorseful, rueful, shamefaced, sheepish, sorry

guise air, appearance, aspect, behaviour, demeanour, disguise, dress, façade, face, fashion, form, front, mask, mode, pretence, semblance, shape, show

gulf 1. bay, bight, sea inlet **2.** abyss, breach, chasm, cleft, gap, opening, rent, rift, separation, split, void, whirlpool

gull 1. *n.* babe in arms (*Inf.*), chump (*Inf.*), dupe, easy mark (*Sl.*), fool, gudgeon (*Sl.*), mug (*Sl.*), sap (*Sl.*), simpleton, sucker (*Sl.*) **2.** *v.* beguile, cheat, con (*Sl.*), cozen, deceive, defraud, dupe, hoax, put one over on (*Inf.*), rook (*Sl.*), swindle, take in (*Inf.*), trick

gullet craw, crop, maw, oesophagus, throat

gullibility credulity, innocence, naiveté, simplicity, trustingness

gullible born yesterday, credulous, easily taken in, foolish, green, innocent, naive, silly, simple, trusting, unsceptical, unsophisticated, unsuspecting

gully channel, ditch, gutter, watercourse

gulp *v.* **1.** bolt, devour, gobble, guzzle, knock back (*Inf.*), quaff, swallow, swig (*Inf.*), swill, toss off, wolf **2.** choke, gasp, stifle, swallow ~*n.* **3.** draught, mouthful, swallow, swig (*Inf.*)

gum 1. *n.* adhesive, cement, exudate, glue, mucilage, paste, resin **2.** *v.* affix, cement, clog, glue, paste, stick, stiffen

gummy adhesive, gluey, sticky, tacky, viscid

gumption ability, acumen, astuteness, cleverness, common sense, discernment, enterprise, get-up-and-go (*Inf.*), horse sense, initiative, mother wit, nous (*Brit. sl.*), resourcefulness, sagacity, savvy (*Sl.*), shrewdness, spirit, wit(s)

gunman assassin, bandit, bravo, desperado, gangster, gunslinger (*U.S. sl.*), hit man (*Sl.*), killer, mobster (*U.S. sl.*), murderer, terrorist, thug

gurgle 1. *v.* babble, bubble, burble, crow, lap, murmur, plash, purl, ripple, splash **2.** *n.* babble, murmur, purl, ripple

guru authority, guiding light, leader, maharishi, master, mentor, sage, swami, teacher, tutor

gush *v.* **1.** burst, cascade, flood, flow, jet, pour, run, rush, spout, spurt, stream **2.** babble, blather, chatter, effervesce, effuse, enthuse, jabber, overstate, spout ~*n.* **3.** burst, cascade, flood, flow, jet, outburst, outflow, rush, spout, spurt, stream, torrent **4.** babble, blather, chatter, effusion, exuberance

gushy cloying, effusive, emotional, excessive, fulsome, gushing, mawkish, overdone, overenthusiastic, sentimental

gust *n.* **1.** blast, blow, breeze, flurry, gale, puff, rush, squall **2.** burst, eruption, explosion, fit, gale, outburst, paroxysm, passion, storm, surge ~*v.* **3.** blast, blow, puff, squall

gusto appetite, appreciation, brio, delight, enjoyment, enthusiasm, exhilaration, fervour, liking, pleasure, relish, savour, verve, zeal, zest

gusty blowy, blustering, blustery, breezy, squally, stormy, tempestuous, windy

gut *n.* **1.** *Often plural* belly, bowels, entrails, innards (*Inf.*), insides (*Inf.*), intestines, inwards, paunch, stomach, viscera **2.** *Plural. Inf.* audacity, backbone, boldness, bottle (*Sl.*), courage, daring, forcefulness, grit, hardihood, mettle, nerve, pluck, spirit, spunk (*Inf.*), willpower ~*v.* **3.** clean, disembowel, draw, dress, eviscerate **4.** clean out, despoil, empty, pillage, plunder, ransack, ravage, rifle, sack, strip ~*adj.* **5.** *Inf.* basic, deep-seated, emotional, heartfelt, innate, instinctive, intuitive, involuntary, natural, spontaneous, unthinking, visceral

gutless abject, chicken (*Sl.*), cowardly, craven, faint-hearted, feeble, irresolute, lily-livered, spineless, submissive, timid, weak

gutsy bold, brave, courageous, determined, gallant, game (*Inf.*), indomitable, mettlesome, plucky, resolute, spirited, staunch

gutter channel, conduit, ditch, drain, duct, pipe, sluice, trench, trough, tube

guttersnipe gamin, mudlark (*Sl.*), ragamuffin, street Arab, street urchin, waif

guttural deep, gravelly, gruff, hoarse, husky, low, rasping, rough, thick, throaty

guy 1. *n. Inf.* bloke (*Brit. inf.*), cat

(*Sl.*), chap, fellow, lad, man, person, youth **2**. *v*. caricature, make (a) game of, make fun of, mock, poke fun at, rib (*Inf.*), ridicule, send up (*Brit inf.*), take off (*Inf.*)

    guzzle bolt, carouse, cram, devour, drink, gobble, gorge, gormandize, knock back (*Inf.*), quaff, stuff (oneself), swill, tope, wolf

Gypsy, Gipsy Bohemian, nomad, rambler, roamer, Romany, rover, traveller, vagabond, vagrant, wanderer

    gyrate circle, pirouette, revolve, rotate, spin, spiral, twirl, whirl

    gyration convolution, pirouette, revolution, rotation, spin, spinning, spiral, whirl, whirling

H

habiliment apparel, array, attire, clothes, clothing, costume, dress, garb, garment, habit, raiment, robes, uniform, vestments

habit *n.* **1.** bent, custom, disposition, manner, mannerism, practice, proclivity, propensity, quirk, tendency, way **2.** convention, custom, mode, practice, routine, rule, second nature, usage, wont **3.** constitution, disposition, frame of mind, make-up, nature **4.** addiction, dependence, fixation, obsession, weakness **5.** apparel, dress, garb, garment, habiliment, riding dress ~*v.* **6.** array, attire, clothe, dress, equip

habitat abode, element, environment, home, home ground, locality, natural home, surroundings, terrain, territory

habitation 1. abode, domicile, dwelling, dwelling house, home, house, living quarters, lodging, quarters, residence **2.** inhabitance, inhabitancy, occupancy, occupation, tenancy

habitual 1. accustomed, common, customary, familiar, fixed, natural, normal, ordinary, regular, routine, standard, traditional, usual, wonted **2.** chronic, confirmed, constant, established, frequent, hardened, ingrained, inveterate, persistent, recurrent

habituate acclimatize, accustom, break in, condition, discipline, familiarize, harden, inure, make used to, school, season, train

habituated acclimatized, accustomed, adapted, broken in, conditioned, disciplined, familiarized, hardened, inured, schooled, seasoned, trained, used (to)

habitué constant customer, frequenter, frequent visitor, regular (*Inf.*), regular patron

hack[1] *v.* **1.** chop, cut, gash, hew, kick, lacerate, mangle, mutilate, notch, slash ~*n.* **2.** chop, cut, gash, notch, slash ~*v./n.* **3.** *Inf.* bark, cough, rasp

hack[2] *adj.* **1.** banal, mediocre, pedestrian, poor, stereotyped, tired, undistinguished, uninspired, unoriginal ~*n.* **2.** Grub Street writer, literary hack, penny-a-liner, scribbler **3.** drudge, plodder, slave **4.** crock, hired horse, horse, jade, nag, poor old tired horse

hackles make one's hackles rise anger, annoy, bridle at, cause resentment, get one's dander up (*Sl.*), make one see red (*Inf.*)

hackneyed banal, clichéd, common, commonplace, overworked, pedestrian, played out (*Inf.*), run-of-the-mill, stale, stereotyped, stock, threadbare, timeworn, tired, trite, unoriginal, worn-out

Hades hell, infernal regions, lower world, nether regions, realm of Pluto, (the) inferno, underworld

hag beldam (*Archaic*), crone, fury, harridan, Jezebel, shrew, termagant, virago, vixen, witch

haggard careworn, drawn, emaciated, gaunt, ghastly, hollow-eyed, pinched, shrunken, thin, wan, wasted, wrinkled

haggle 1. bargain, barter, beat down, chaffer, dicker (*Chiefly U.S.*), higgle, palter **2.** bicker, dispute, quarrel, squabble, wrangle

hail[1] *Fig.* **1.** *n.* barrage, bombardment, pelting, rain, shower, storm, volley **2.** *v.* barrage, batter, beat down upon, bombard, pelt, rain, rain down on, shower, storm, volley

hail[2] **1.** acclaim, acknowledge, applaud, cheer, exalt, glorify, greet, honour, salute, welcome **2.** accost, address, call, flag down, halloo, shout to, signal to, sing out, speak to, wave down **3.** *With* **from** be a native of, be born in, come from, originate in

hair 1. head of hair, locks, mane, mop, shock, tresses **2. by a hair** by a fraction of an inch, by a hair's-breadth, by a narrow margin, by a split second, by a whisker, by the skin of one's teeth **3. get in one's hair** annoy, exasperate, harass, irritate, pester, plague **4. let one's hair down** let it all hang out (*Inf.*), let off steam (*Inf.*), let oneself go, relax **5. not turn a hair** keep one's cool (*Sl.*), keep one's hair on (*Brit. inf.*), not bat an eyelid, remain calm **6. split hairs** cavil, find fault, overrefine, pettifog, quibble

hairdo coiffure, cut, haircut, hairstyle, style

hairless bald, baldheaded, beardless, clean-shaven, depilated, glabrous *or* glabrate (*Biol.*), shorn, tonsured

hair-raising alarming, bloodcurdling, breathtaking, creepy, exciting, frightening, horrifying, petrifying, scary, shocking, spine-chilling, startling, terrifying, thrilling

hair's-breadth 1. *n.* fraction, hair, jot, narrow margin, whisker 2. *adj.* close, hazardous, narrow

hairsplitting *adj.* captious, carping, cavilling, fault-finding, fine, finicky, nice, niggling, nit-picking (*Inf.*), overrefined, pettifogging, quibbling, subtle

hairy 1. bearded, bewhiskered, bushy, fleecy, furry, hirsute, pileous (*Biol.*), pilose (*Biol.*), shaggy, stubbly, unshaven, woolly 2. *Sl.* dangerous, difficult, hazardous, perilous, risky, scaring

halcyon 1. calm, gentle, mild, pacific, peaceful, placid, quiet, serene, still, tranquil, undisturbed, unruffled 2. *Fig.* carefree, flourishing, golden, happy, palmy, prosperous

hale able-bodied, blooming, fit, flourishing, healthy, hearty, in fine fettle, in the pink, robust, sound, strong, vigorous, well

half 1. *n.* bisection, division, equal part, fifty per cent, fraction, hemisphere, portion, section 2. *adj.* divided, fractional, halved, incomplete, limited, moderate, partial 3. *adv.* after a fashion, all but, barely, inadequately, incompletely, in part, partially, partly, pretty nearly, slightly 4. **by half** considerably, excessively, very much

half-baked 1. brainless, crazy, foolish, harebrained, senseless, silly, stupid 2. ill-conceived, ill-judged, impractical, poorly planned, short-sighted, unformed, unthought out *or* through

half-hearted apathetic, cool, indifferent, lacklustre, listless, lukewarm, neutral, passive, perfunctory, spiritless, tame, unenthusiastic, uninterested

halfway *adv.* 1. midway, to *or* in the middle, to the midpoint 2. incompletely, moderately, nearly, partially, partly, rather 3. **meet halfway** accommodate, come to terms, compromise, concede, give and take, strike a balance, trade off ~*adj.* 4. central, equidistant, intermediate, mid, middle, midway 5. imperfect, incomplete, moderate, partial, part-way

halfwit dimwit (*Inf.*), dolt, dullard,

dunce, dunderhead, fool, idiot, imbecile (*Inf.*), mental defective, moron, nitwit, simpleton

half-witted addle-brained, barmy (*Sl.*), batty (*Sl.*), crazy, doltish, dull, dull-witted, feeble-minded, foolish, idiotic, moronic, silly, simple, simple-minded, stupid

hall 1. corridor, entrance hall, entry, foyer, hallway, lobby, passage, passageway, vestibule 2. assembly room, auditorium, chamber, concert hall, meeting place

hallmark 1. authentication, device, endorsement, mark, seal, sign, stamp, symbol 2. badge, emblem, indication, sure sign, telltale sign

halloo call, cry, hail, holla, shout

hallow bless, consecrate, dedicate, devote, enshrine, glorify, magnify (*Archaic*), respect, revere, reverence, sanctify, venerate

hallowed beatified, blessed, consecrated, dedicated, holy, honoured, inviolable, revered, sacred, sacrosanct, sanctified

hallucinate daydream, envision, fantasize, freak out (*Inf.*), have hallucinations, imagine, trip (*Inf.*)

hallucination aberration, apparition, delusion, dream, fantasy, figment of the imagination, illusion, mirage, phantasmagoria, vision

halo aura, aureole *or* aureola, corona, halation (*Photog.*), nimbus, radiance, ring of light

halt[1] *v.* 1. break off, call it a day, cease, close down, come to an end, desist, draw up, pull up, rest, stand still, stop, wait 2. arrest, block, bring to an end, check, curb, cut short, end, hold back, impede, obstruct, stem, terminate ~*n.* 3. arrest, break, close, end, impasse, interruption, pause, stand, standstill, stop, stoppage, termination

halt[2] *v.* 1. be defective, falter, hobble, limp, stumble 2. be unsure, boggle, dither, haver, hesitate, pause, stammer, swither (*Scot. dialect*), think twice, waver ~*adj.* 3. *Archaic* crippled, lame, limping

halting awkward, faltering, hesitant, imperfect, laboured, stammering, stumbling, stuttering

halve 1. bisect, cut in half, divide equally, reduce by fifty per cent, share equally, split in two 2. **by halves** imperfectly, incompletely, scrappily, skimpily

hammer v. **1.** bang, beat, drive, hit, knock, strike, tap **2.** beat out, fashion, forge, form, make, shape **3.** *Often with into* din into, drive home, drub into, drum into, grind into, impress upon, instruct, repeat **4.** *Often with away (at)* beaver away (*Brit. inf.*), drudge, grind, keep on, peg away (*Chiefly Brit.*), persevere, persist, plug away (*Inf.*), pound away, stick at, work **5.** *Inf.* beat, clobber (*Sl.*), defeat, drub, slate (*Inf.*), thrash, trounce, worst

hammer out accomplish, bring about, come to a conclusion, complete, excogitate, finish, form a resolution, make a decision, negotiate, produce, settle, sort out, thrash out, work out

hamper v. bind, cramp, curb, embarrass, encumber, entangle, fetter, frustrate, hamstring, handicap, hinder, hold up, impede, interfere with, obstruct, prevent, restrain, restrict, slow down, thwart, trammel

hamstring 1. cripple, disable, hock, injure, lame **2.** balk, foil, frustrate, prevent, ruin, stop, thwart

hamstrung at a loss, crippled, disabled, helpless, *hors de combat*, incapacitated, paralysed

hand n. **1.** fist, mitt (*Sl.*), palm, paw (*Inf.*) **2.** agency, direction, influence, part, participation, share **3.** aid, assistance, help, support **4.** artificer, artisan, craftsman, employee, hired man, labourer, operative, worker, workman **5.** calligraphy, chirography, handwriting, longhand, penmanship, script **6.** clap, ovation, round of applause **7.** ability, art, artistry, skill **8.** *at or on hand* approaching, available, close, handy, imminent, near, nearby, on tap (*Inf.*), ready, within reach **9. from hand to mouth** by necessity, improvidently, in poverty, insecurely, on the breadline (*Inf.*), precariously, uncertainly **10. hand in glove** allied, in cahoots (*Inf.*), in league, in partnership **11. hand over fist** by leaps and bounds, easily, steadily, swiftly **12. in hand a.** in order, receiving attention, under control **b.** available for use, in reserve, put by, ready ~v. **13.** deliver, hand over, pass **14.** aid, assist, conduct, convey, give, guide, help, lead, present, transmit

handbook Baedeker, guide, guidebook, instruction book, manual, vade mecum

handcuff 1. v. fetter, manacle, shackle **2.** n. *Plural* bracelets (*Sl.*), cuffs (*Inf.*), fetters, manacles, shackles

hand down *or* **on** bequeath, give, grant, pass on *or* down, transfer, will

handful few, small number, small quantity, smattering, sprinkling

handicap n. **1.** barrier, block, disadvantage, drawback, encumbrance, hindrance, impediment, limitation, millstone, obstacle, restriction, shortcoming, stumbling block **2.** advantage, edge, head start, odds, penalty, upper hand **3.** defect, disability, impairment ~v. **4.** burden, encumber, hamper, hamstring, hinder, hold back, impede, limit, place at a disadvantage, restrict, retard

handicraft art, artisanship, craft, craftsmanship, handiwork, skill, workmanship

handily 1. adroitly, capably, cleverly, deftly, dexterously, expertly, proficiently, skilfully **2.** accessibly, advantageously, conveniently, helpfully, readily, suitably

handiness 1. accessibility, availability, closeness, convenience, practicality, proximity, usefulness, workability **2.** adroitness, aptitude, cleverness, deftness, dexterity, efficiency, expertise, knack, proficiency, skill

handiwork 1. craft, handicraft, handwork **2.** achievement, artefact, creation, design, invention, product, production, result

handle n. **1.** grip, haft, handgrip, helve, hilt, knob, stock ~v. **2.** feel, finger, fondle, grasp, hold, maul, paw (*Inf.*), pick up, poke, touch **3.** control, direct, guide, manage, manipulate, manoeuvre, operate, steer, use, wield **4.** administer, conduct, cope with, deal with, manage, supervise, take care of, treat **5.** discourse, discuss, treat **6.** carry, deal in, market, sell, stock, trade, traffic in

handling administration, approach, conduct, direction, management, manipulation, running, treatment

hand-me-down adj. handed down, inherited, passed on, second-hand, used, worn

hand-out 1. alms, charity, dole **2.** bulletin, circular, free sample, leaflet, literature (*Inf.*), press release

hand out deal out, disburse, dish out (*Inf.*), dispense, disseminate, distribute, give out, mete

hand over deliver, donate, fork out or up (Sl.), present, release, surrender, turn over, yield

hand-picked choice, chosen, elect, elite, recherché, select, selected

hands 1. authority, care, charge, command, control, custody, disposal, guardianship, keeping, possession, power, supervision **2. hands down** easily, effortlessly, with no contest

handsome 1. admirable, attractive, becoming, comely, elegant, fine, good-looking, graceful, majestic, personable, stately, well-proportioned **2.** abundant, ample, bountiful, considerable, generous, gracious, large, liberal, magnanimous, plentiful, sizable

handsomely abundantly, amply, bountifully, generously, liberally, magnanimously, munificently, plentifully, richly

handwriting calligraphy, chirography, fist, hand, longhand, penmanship, scrawl, script

handy 1. accessible, at or on hand, available, close, convenient, near, nearby, within reach **2.** convenient, easy to use, helpful, manageable, neat, practical, serviceable, useful **3.** adept, adroit, clever, deft, dexterous, expert, nimble, proficient, ready, skilful, skilled

hang 1. be pendent, dangle, depend, droop, incline, suspend **2.** execute, gibbet, send to the gallows, string up (Inf.) **3.** adhere, cling, hold, rest, stick **4.** attach, cover, deck, decorate, drape, fasten, fix, furnish **5.** be poised, drift, float, hover, remain, swing **6.** bend downward, bend forward, bow, dangle, drop, incline, lean over, let droop, loll, lower, sag, trail **7. hang fire** be slow, be suspended, delay, hang back, procrastinate, stall, stick, vacillate **8. get the hang of** comprehend, get the knack or technique, grasp, understand

hang about or **around 1.** dally, linger, loiter, roam, tarry, waste time **2.** associate with, frequent, haunt, resort

hang back be backward, be reluctant, demur, hesitate, hold back, recoil

hangdog adj. abject, browbeaten, cowed, cringing, defeated, downcast, furtive, guilty, shamefaced, sneaking, wretched

hanger-on dependant, follower, freeloader (Sl., chiefly U.S.), lackey, leech, minion, parasite, sponger (Inf.), sycophant

hanging adj. **1.** dangling, drooping, flapping, flopping, floppy, loose, pendent, suspended, swinging, unattached, unsupported **2.** undecided, unresolved, unsettled, up in the air (Inf.) **3.** beetle, beetling, jutting, overhanging, projecting

hang on 1. carry on, continue, endure, go on, hold on, hold out, persevere, persist, remain **2.** cling, clutch, grasp, grip, hold fast **3.** be conditional upon, be contingent on, be dependent on, be determined by, depend on, hinge, rest, turn on **4.** Also **hang onto, hang upon** be rapt, give ear, listen attentively **5.** Inf. hold on, hold the line, remain, stop, wait

hang-out den, dive (Sl.), haunt, home, joint (Sl.), resort

hangover aftereffects, crapulence, head (Inf.), morning after (Inf.)

hang over be imminent, impend, loom, menace, threaten

hang-up block, difficulty, inhibition, obsession, preoccupation, problem, thing (Inf.)

hank coil, length, loop, piece, roll, skein

hanker With **for** or **after** covet, crave, desire, hunger, itch, long, lust, pine, thirst, want, wish, yearn, yen (Inf.)

hankering craving, desire, hunger, itch, longing, pining, thirst, urge, wish, yearning, yen (Inf.)

hanky-panky chicanery, deception, devilry, funny business (Inf.), jiggery-pokery (Inf.), knavery, machinations, mischief, monkey business (Inf.), shenanigans (Inf.), subterfuge, trickery

haphazard 1. accidental, arbitrary, chance, fluky (Inf.), random **2.** aimless, careless, casual, disorderly, disorganized, hit or miss (Inf.), indiscriminate, slapdash, slipshod, unmethodical, unsystematic

hapless cursed, ill-fated, ill-starred, jinxed, luckless, miserable, unfortunate, unhappy, unlucky, wretched

happen 1. appear, arise, come about, come off (Inf.), come to pass, crop up (Inf.), develop, ensue, eventuate, follow, materialize, occur, present itself, result, take place, transpire (Inf.) **2.** become of, befall, betide **3.** chance, fall out, have the fortune to be, supervene, turn out

happening accident, adventure, affair, case, chance, episode, event, experience, incident, occasion, occurrence, phenomenon, proceeding, scene

happen on or **upon** chance upon, come upon, discover unexpectedly, find, hit upon, light upon, stumble on, turn up

happily 1. agreeably, contentedly, delightedly, enthusiastically, freely, gladly, heartily, willingly, with pleasure **2.** blithely, cheerfully, gaily, gleefully, joyfully, joyously, merrily **3.** auspiciously, favourably, fortunately, luckily, opportunely, propitiously, providentially, seasonably **4.** appropriately, aptly, felicitously, gracefully, successfully

happiness beatitude, blessedness, bliss, cheer, cheerfulness, cheeriness, contentment, delight, ecstasy, elation, enjoyment, exuberance, felicity, gaiety, gladness, high spirits, joy, jubilation, light-heartedness, merriment, pleasure, prosperity, satisfaction, wellbeing

happy 1. blessed, blest, blissful, blithe, cheerful, content, contented, delighted, ecstatic, elated, glad, gratified, jolly, joyful, joyous, jubilant, merry, overjoyed, over the moon (*Inf.*), pleased, sunny, thrilled, walking on air (*Inf.*) **2.** advantageous, appropriate, apt, auspicious, befitting, convenient, enviable, favourable, felicitous, fortunate, lucky, opportune, promising, propitious, satisfactory, seasonable, successful, timely, welltimed

happy-go-lucky blithe, carefree, casual, devil-may-care, easy-going, heedless, improvident, insouciant, irresponsible, light-hearted, nonchalant, unconcerned, untroubled

harangue 1. *n.* address, declamation, diatribe, exhortation, lecture, oration, philippic, screed, speech, spiel (*Inf.*), tirade **2.** *v.* address, declaim, exhort, hold forth, lecture, rant, spout (*Inf.*)

harass annoy, badger, bait, beleaguer, bother, chivvy (*Brit.*), devil (*Inf.*), disturb, exasperate, exhaust, fatigue, harry, hassle (*Inf.*), hound, perplex, persecute, pester, plague, tease, tire, torment, trouble, vex, weary, worry

harassed careworn, distraught, harried, hassled (*Inf.*), plagued, strained, tormented, troubled, under pressure, under stress, vexed, worried

harassment aggravation (*Inf.*), annoyance, badgering, bedevilment, bother, hassle (*Inf.*), irritation, molestation, nuisance, persecution, pestering, torment, trouble, vexation

harbinger forerunner, foretoken, herald, indication, messenger, omen, portent, precursor, sign

harbour *n.* **1.** anchorage, destination, haven, port **2.** asylum, covert, haven, refuge, retreat, sanctuary, sanctum, security, shelter ~*v.* **3.** conceal, hide, lodge, protect, provide refuge, relieve, secrete, shelter, shield **4.** believe, brood over, cherish, cling to, entertain, foster, hold, imagine, maintain, nurse, nurture, retain

hard *adj.* **1.** compact, dense, firm, impenetrable, inflexible, rigid, rocklike, solid, stiff, stony, strong, tough, unyielding **2.** arduous, backbreaking, burdensome, exacting, exhausting, fatiguing, formidable, Herculean, laborious, rigorous, strenuous, toilsome, tough, uphill, wearying **3.** baffling, complex, complicated, difficult, intricate, involved, knotty, perplexing, puzzling, tangled, thorny, unfathomable **4.** callous, cold, cruel, exacting, grim, hardhearted, harsh, implacable, obdurate, pitiless, ruthless, severe, stern, strict, stubborn, unfeeling, unjust, unkind, unrelenting, unsparing, unsympathetic **5.** calamitous, dark, disagreeable, disastrous, distressing, grievous, grim, intolerable, painful, unpleasant **6.** driving, fierce, forceful, heavy, powerful, strong, violent **7.** *Of feelings or words* acrimonious, angry, antagonistic, bitter, hostile, rancorous, resentful **8.** *Of truth or facts* actual, bare, cold, definite, indisputable, plain, undeniable, unvarnished, verified ~*adv.* **9.** energetically, fiercely, forcefully, forcibly, heavily, intensely, powerfully, severely, sharply, strongly, vigorously, violently, with all one's might, with might and main **10.** assiduously, determinedly, diligently, doggedly, earnestly, industriously, intently, persistently, steadily, strenuously, untiringly **11.** agonizingly, badly, distressingly, harshly, laboriously, painfully, roughly, severely, with difficulty **12.** bitterly, hardly, keenly, rancorously, reluctantly, resentfully, slowly, sorely

hard and fast binding, immutable, incontrovertible, inflexible, invariable, rigid, set, strict, stringent, unalterable

hard-bitten or **hard-boiled** casehardened, cynical, down-to-earth, hardheaded, hard-nosed (*Sl.*), matter-of-fact, practical, realistic, shrewd, tough, unsentimental

hard-core 1. dedicated, die-hard, dyed-in-the-wool, extreme, intransigent, obstinate, rigid, staunch, steadfast **2.** explicit, obscene

harden 1. anneal, bake, cake, freeze, set, solidify, stiffen **2.** brace, buttress, fortify, gird, indurate, nerve, reinforce, steel, strengthen, toughen **3.** accustom, brutalize, case-harden, habituate, inure, season, train

hardened 1. chronic, fixed, habitual, incorrigible, inveterate, irredeemable, reprobate, set, shameless **2.** accustomed, habituated, inured, seasoned, toughened

hard-favoured *or* **hard-featured** austere, coarse-featured, forbidding, grim visaged, ill-favoured, severe, ugly

hard-headed astute, cool, hard-boiled (*Inf.*), level-headed, practical, pragmatic, realistic, sensible, shrewd, tough, unsentimental

hardhearted callous, cold, cruel, hard, heartless, indifferent, inhuman, insensitive, intolerant, merciless, pitiless, stony, uncaring, unfeeling, unkind, unsympathetic

hard-hitting critical, no holds barred, pulling no punches, strongly worded, tough, unsparing, vigorous

hardihood 1. backbone, boldness, bottle (*Sl.*), bravery, courage, daring, determination, firmness, grit, guts (*Inf.*), intrepidity, mettle, nerve, pluck, resolution, spirit, spunk (*Inf.*), strength **2.** assurance, audacity, effrontery, foolhardiness, impertinence, impetuousness, rashness, recklessness, temerity

hardiness boldness, courage, fortitude, intrepidity, resilience, resolution, robustness, ruggedness, sturdiness, toughness, valour

hardline definite, inflexible, intransigent, tough, uncompromising, undeviating, unyielding

hardly almost not, barely, by no means, faintly, infrequently, just, not at all, not quite, no way, only, only just, scarcely, with difficulty

hard-pressed harried, hotly pursued, in difficulties, pushed (*Inf.*), under attack, under pressure, up against it (*Inf.*), with one's back to the wall

hardship adversity, affliction, austerity, burden, calamity, destitution, difficulty, fatigue, grievance, labour, misery,

misfortune, need, oppression, persecution, privation, suffering, toil, torment, trial, tribulation, trouble, want

hard up bankrupt, broke (*Inf.*), bust (*Inf.*), cleaned out (*Sl.*), impecunious, impoverished, in the red (*Inf.*), on one's uppers (*Inf.*), out of pocket, penniless, poor, short, short of cash *or* funds, skint (*Brit. sl.*)

hard-wearing durable, resilient, rugged, stout, strong, tough, well-made

hard-working assiduous, busy, conscientious, diligent, energetic, indefatigable, industrious, sedulous, zealous

hardy 1. firm, fit, hale, healthy, hearty, in fine fettle, lusty, robust, rugged, sound, stalwart, stout, strong, sturdy, tough, vigorous **2.** bold, brave, courageous, daring, heroic, intrepid, manly, plucky, resolute, stouthearted, valiant, valorous **3.** audacious, brazen, foolhardy, headstrong, impudent, rash, reckless

harebrained asinine, careless, empty-headed, flighty, foolish, giddy, half-baked (*Inf.*), harum-scarum, heedless, inane, mindless, rash, reckless, scatter-brained, unstable, unsteady, wild

hark attend, give ear, give heed, hear, hearken (*Archaic*), listen, mark, notice, pay attention

hark back look back, recall, recollect, regress, remember, revert, think back

harlot call girl, fallen woman, hussy, loose woman, pro (*Inf.*), prostitute, scrubber (*Sl.*), streetwalker, strumpet, tart (*Inf.*), tramp (*Sl.*), whore

harm *n.* **1.** abuse, damage, detriment, disservice, hurt, ill, impairment, injury, loss, mischief, misfortune **2.** evil, immorality, iniquity, sin, sinfulness, vice, wickedness, wrong ~*v.* **3.** abuse, blemish, damage, hurt, ill-treat, ill-use, impair, injure, maltreat, mar, molest, ruin, spoil, wound

harmful baleful, baneful, damaging, deleterious, destructive, detrimental, disadvantageous, evil, hurtful, injurious, noxious, pernicious

harmless gentle, innocent, innocuous, innoxious, inoffensive, nontoxic, not dangerous, safe, unobjectionable

harmonious 1. agreeable, compatible, concordant, congruous, consonant, coordinated, correspondent, dulcet, euphonious, harmonic, harmonizing, matching, mellifluous, melodious, musical, sweet-sounding, symphonious (*Literary*), tuneful **2.** agreeable, amicable, compatible, concordant, congenial, cordial, *en rapport*, fraternal, friendly, in accord, in harmony, in unison, of one mind, sympathetic

harmonize accord, adapt, agree, arrange, attune, be in unison, be of one mind, blend, chime with, cohere, compose, coordinate, correspond, match, reconcile, suit, tally, tone in with

harmony 1. accord, agreement, amicability, amity, compatibility, concord, conformity, consensus, cooperation, friendship, good will, like-mindedness, peace, rapport, sympathy, unanimity, understanding, unity **2.** balance, compatibility, concord, congruity, consistency, consonance, coordination, correspondence, fitness, parallelism, suitability, symmetry **3.** euphony, melodiousness, melody, tune, tunefulness

harness *n.* **1.** equipment, gear, tack, tackle, trappings **2. in harness** active, at work, busy, in action, working ~*v.* **3.** couple, hitch up, put in harness, saddle, yoke **4.** apply, channel, control, employ, exploit, make productive, mobilize, render useful, turn to account, utilize

harp *With* **on** *or* **upon** dwell on, go on, labour, press, reiterate, renew, repeat

harping *n.* nagging, reiteration, repetition

harridan battle-axe (*Inf.*), nag, scold, shrew, tartar, termagant, virago, witch, Xanthippe

harried agitated, anxious, beset, bothered, distressed, hag-ridden, harassed, hard-pressed, hassled (*Inf.*), plagued, tormented, troubled, worried

harrow *v. Fig.* agonize, distress, harass, lacerate, perturb, rack, rend, tear, torment, torture, vex, wound, wring

harrowing agonizing, alarming, chilling, distressing, disturbing, excruciating, frightening, heartbreaking, heartrending, nerve-racking, painful, racking, soaring, terrifying, tormenting, traumatic

harry 1. annoy, badger, bedevil, chivvy, disturb, fret, harass, hassle (*Inf.*), molest, persecute, pester, plague, tease, torment, trouble, vex, worry **2.** depredate (*Rare*), despoil, devastate, pillage, plunder, raid, ravage, rob, sack

harsh 1. coarse, croaking, crude, discordant, dissonant, glaring, grating, guttural, jarring, rasping, raucous, rough,

strident, unmelodious **2.** abusive, austere, bitter, bleak, brutal, comfortless, cruel, dour, Draconian, grim, hard, pitiless, punitive, relentless, ruthless, severe, sharp, Spartan, stern, stringent, unfeeling, unkind, unpleasant, unrelenting

harshly brutally, cruelly, grimly, roughly, severely, sharply, sternly, strictly

harshness acerbity, acrimony, asperity, austerity, bitterness, brutality, churlishness, coarseness, crudity, hardness, ill-temper, rigour, roughness, severity, sourness, sternness

harum-scarum careless, erratic, giddy, haphazard, harebrained, hasty, ill-considered, impetuous, imprudent, irresponsible, precipitate, rash, reckless, scatterbrained, scatty (*Brit. inf.*), wild

harvest *n.* **1.** harvesting, harvest-time, ingathering, reaping **2.** crop, produce, yield **3.** *Fig.* consequence, effect, fruition, product, result, return ~*v.* **4.** gather, mow, pick, pluck, reap **5.** accumulate, acquire, amass, collect, garner

hash 1. confusion, hotchpotch, jumble, mess, mishmash, mix-up, muddle, shambles **2. make a hash of** *Inf.* botch, bungle, jumble, mess up, mishandle, mismanage, mix, muddle

hassle *n.* **1.** altercation, argument, bickering, disagreement, dispute, fight, quarrel, squabble, tussle, wrangle **2.** bother, difficulty, inconvenience, problem, struggle, trial, trouble, upset ~*v.* **3.** annoy, badger, bother, bug (*Inf.*), harass, harry, hound, pester

haste 1. alacrity, briskness, celerity, dispatch, expedition, fleetness, nimbleness, promptitude, quickness, rapidity, rapidness, speed, swiftness, urgency, velocity **2.** bustle, hastiness, helter-skelter, hurry, hustle, impetuosity, precipitateness, rashness, recklessness, rush

hasten 1. bolt, dash, fly, haste, hurry (up), make haste, race, run, rush, scurry, scuttle, speed, sprint, step on it (*Inf.*), tear (along) **2.** accelerate, advance, dispatch, expedite, goad, hurry (up), precipitate, press, push forward, quicken, speed (up), step up (*Inf.*), urge

hastily 1. apace, double-quick, fast, posthaste, promptly, quickly, rapidly, speedily, straightaway **2.** heedlessly, hurriedly, impetuously, impulsively, on the spur of the moment, precipitately, rashly, recklessly, too quickly

hasty 1. brisk, eager, expeditious, fast, fleet, hurried, prompt, rapid, speedy, swift, urgent **2.** brief, cursory, fleeting, passing, perfunctory, rushed, short, superficial **3.** foolhardy, headlong, heedless, impetuous, impulsive, indiscreet, precipitate, rash, reckless, thoughtless, unduly quick **4.** brusque, excited, fiery, hot-headed, hot-tempered, impatient, irascible, irritable, passionate, quick-tempered, snappy

hatch 1. breed, bring forth, brood, incubate **2.** *Fig.* conceive, concoct, contrive, cook up (*Inf.*), design, devise, dream up (*Inf.*), plan, plot, project, scheme, think up

hatchet man assassin, bravo, calumniator, cutthroat, debunker, defamer, destroyer, detractor, gunman, hired assassin, hit man (*Sl.*), killer, murderer, smear campaigner, thug, traducer

hate *v.* **1.** abhor, abominate, be hostile to, be repelled by, be sick of, despise, detest, dislike, execrate, have an aversion to, loathe, recoil from **2.** be loath, be reluctant, be sorry, be unwilling, dislike, feel disinclined, have no stomach for, shrink from ~*n.* **3.** abhorrence, abomination, animosity, animus, antagonism, antipathy, aversion, detestation, dislike, enmity, execration, hatred, hostility, loathing, odium

hateful abhorrent, abominable, despicable, detestable, disgusting, execrable, forbidding, foul, heinous, horrible, loathsome, obnoxious, odious, offensive, repellent, repugnant, repulsive, revolting, vile

hatred abomination, animosity, animus, antagonism, antipathy, aversion, detestation, dislike, enmity, execration, hate, ill will, odium, repugnance, revulsion

haughtiness airs, aloofness, arrogance, conceit, contempt, contemptuousness, disdain, hauteur, insolence, loftiness, pomposity, pride, snobbishness, superciliousness

haughty arrogant, assuming, conceited, contemptuous, disdainful, high, high and mighty (*Inf.*), hoity-toity (*Inf.*), imperious, lofty, overweening, proud, scornful, snobbish, snooty (*Inf.*), stuck-up (*Inf.*), supercilious, uppish (*Brit. inf.*)

haul *v.* **1.** drag, draw, hale, heave, lug, pull, tow, trail, tug **2.** carry, cart, convey, hump (*Brit. sl.*), move, transport ~*n.* **3.** drag, heave, pull, tug **4.** booty, catch, find, gain, harvest, loot, spoils, takings, yield

haunt *v.* **1.** visit, walk **2.** beset, come back, obsess, plague, possess, prey on, recur, stay with, torment, trouble, weigh on **3.** frequent, hang around *or* about, repair, resort, visit ~*n.* **4.** den, gathering place, hangout (*Inf.*), meeting place, rendezvous, resort, stamping ground

haunted 1. cursed, eerie, ghostly, jinxed, possessed, spooky (*Inf.*) **2.** obsessed, plagued, preoccupied, tormented, troubled, worried

haunting disturbing, eerie, evocative, indelible, nostalgic, persistent, poignant, recurrent, recurring, unforgettable

hauteur affectedness, airs, arrogance, contempt, dignity, disdain, haughtiness, loftiness, pride, snobbishness, stateliness, superciliousness

have 1. hold, keep, obtain, occupy, own, possess, retain **2.** accept, acquire, gain, get, obtain, procure, receive, secure, take **3.** comprehend, comprise, contain, embody, include, take in **4.** endure, enjoy, experience, feel, meet with, suffer, sustain, undergo **5.** *Sl.* cheat, deceive, dupe, fool, outwit, swindle, take in (*Inf.*), trick **6.** *Usually* **have to** be bound, be compelled, be forced, be obliged, have got to, must, ought, should **7.** allow, consider, entertain, permit, put up with (*Inf.*), think about, tolerate **8.** bear, beget, bring forth, bring into the world, deliver, give birth to **9. have had it** *Inf.* be defeated, be exhausted, be finished, be out, be past it (*Inf.*)

haven 1. anchorage, harbour, port, roads (*Nautical*) **2.** *Fig.* asylum, refuge, retreat, sanctuary, sanctum, shelter

have on 1. be clothed in, be dressed in, wear **2.** be committed to, be engaged to, have on the agenda, have planned **3.** *Of a person* deceive, kid (*Inf.*), play a joke on, tease, trick

havoc 1. carnage, damage, desolation, despoliation, destruction, devastation, rack and ruin, ravages, ruin, slaughter, waste, wreck **2.** *Inf.* chaos, confusion, disorder, disruption, mayhem, shambles **3. play havoc (with)** bring into chaos, confuse, demolish, destroy, devastate, disorganize, disrupt, wreck

hawk *v.* **1.** bark (*Inf.*), cry, market, peddle, sell, tout (*Inf.*), vend **2.** *Often with* **about** bandy about (*Inf.*), bruit about (*Archaic*), buzz, noise abroad, put about, retail, rumour

hawker barrow boy (*Brit.*), cheap-jack (*Inf.*), colporteur, crier, huckster, pedlar, vendor

haywire 1. *Of things* chaotic, confused, disarranged, disordered, disorganized, mixed up, on the blink (*Inf.*), out of commission, out of order, shambolic (*Inf.*), tangled, topsy-turvy 2. *Of people* crazy, erratic, mad, wild

hazard n. 1. danger, endangerment, imperilment, jeopardy, peril, risk, threat 2. accident, chance, coincidence, fluke, luck, misfortune, mishap, stroke of luck ~v. 3. chance, dare, gamble, risk, stake 4. advance, conjecture, offer, presume, proffer, speculate, submit, suppose, throw out, venture, volunteer 5. endanger, expose, imperil, jeopardize, risk, threaten

hazardous 1. dangerous, dicey (*Sl., chiefly Brit.*), difficult, fraught with danger, hairy (*Sl.*), insecure, perilous, precarious, risky, unsafe 2. chancy (*Inf.*), haphazard, precarious, uncertain, unpredictable

haze cloud, dimness, film, fog, mist, obscurity, smog, smokiness, steam, vapour

hazy 1. blurry, cloudy, dim, dull, faint, foggy, misty, nebulous, obscure, overcast, smoky, veiled 2. *Fig.* fuzzy, ill-defined, indefinite, indistinct, loose, muddled, muzzy, nebulous, uncertain, unclear, vague

head n. 1. conk (*Sl.*), cranium, crown, loaf (*Sl.*), noddle (*Inf., chiefly Brit.*), nut (*Sl.*), pate, skull 2. boss (*Inf.*), captain, chief, chieftain, commander, director, headmaster, headmistress, head teacher, leader, manager, master, principal, superintendent, supervisor 3. apex, crest, crown, height, peak, pitch, summit, tip, top, vertex 4. first place, fore, forefront, front, van, vanguard 5. beginning, commencement, origin, rise, source, start 6. ability, aptitude, brain, brains (*Inf.*), capacity, faculty, flair, intellect, intelligence, mentality, mind, talent, thought, understanding 7. branch, category, class, department, division, heading, section, subject, topic 8. climax, conclusion, crisis, culmination, end, turning point 9. *Geog.* cape, foreland, headland, point, promontory 10. **go to one's head** dizzy, excite, intoxicate, make

conceited, puff up 11. **head over heels** completely, intensely, thoroughly, uncontrollably, utterly, wholeheartedly 12. **put (our, their, etc.) heads together** *Inf.* confab (*Inf.*), confabulate, confer, consult, deliberate, discuss, palaver, powwow, talk over ~adj. 13. arch, chief, first, foremost, front, highest, leading, main, pre-eminent, premier, prime, principal, supreme, topmost ~v. 14. be or go first, cap, crown, lead, lead the way, precede, top 15. be in charge of, command, control, direct, govern, guide, lead, manage, rule, run, supervise 16. *Often with* for aim, go to, make a beeline for, make for, point, set off for, set out, start towards, steer, turn

headache 1. cephalalgia (*Medical*), migraine, neuralgia 2. *Inf.* bane, bother, inconvenience, nuisance, problem, trouble, vexation, worry

headfirst 1. *adj./adv.* diving, headlong, head-on 2. *adv.* carelessly, hastily, head over heels, precipitately, rashly, recklessly

heading 1. caption, headline, name, rubric, title 2. category, class, division, section

headland bill, bluff, cape, cliff, foreland, head, mull (*Scot.*), point, promontory

headlong 1. *adj./adv.* headfirst, headforemost, head-on 2. *adj.* breakneck, dangerous, hasty, impetuous, impulsive, inconsiderate, precipitate, reckless, thoughtless 3. *adv.* hastily, heedlessly, helter-skelter, hurriedly, pell-mell, precipitately, rashly, thoughtlessly, wildly

head off 1. block off, cut off, deflect, divert, intercept, interpose, intervene 2. avert, fend off, forestall, parry, prevent, stop, ward off

headstrong contrary, foolhardy, froward, heedless, imprudent, impulsive, intractable, mulish, obstinate, perverse, pig-headed, rash, reckless, self-willed, stubborn, ungovernable, unruly, wilful

headway 1. advance, improvement, progress, progression, way 2. **make headway** advance, come or get on, cover ground, develop, gain, gain ground, make strides, progress

heady 1. inebriating, intoxicating, potent, spirituous, strong 2. exciting, exhilarating, intoxicating, overwhelming, stimulating, thrilling 3. hasty, impetuous, impulsive, inconsiderate, precipitate, rash, reckless, thoughtless

heal 1. cure, make well, mend, regenerate, remedy, restore, treat 2. alleviate, ameliorate, compose, conciliate, harmonize, patch up, reconcile, settle, soothe

healing 1. analeptic, curative, medicinal, remedial, restorative, restoring, sanative, therapeutic 2. assuaging, comforting, emollient, gentle, lenitive, mild, mitigative, palliative, soothing

health 1. fitness, good condition, haleness, healthiness, robustness, salubrity, soundness, strength, vigour, wellbeing 2. condition, constitution, fettle, form, shape, state, tone

healthful beneficial, bracing, good for one, health-giving, healthy, invigorating, nourishing, nutritious, salubrious, salutary, wholesome

healthy 1. active, blooming, fit, flourishing, hale, hale and hearty, hardy, hearty, in fine feather, in fine fettle, in fine form, in good condition, in good shape (*Inf.*), in the pink, physically fit, robust, sound, strong, sturdy, vigorous, well 2. beneficial, bracing, good for one, healthful, health-giving, hygienic, invigorating, nourishing, nutritious, salubrious, salutary, wholesome

heap *n.* 1. accumulation, aggregation, collection, hoard, lot, mass, mound, mountain, pile, stack, stockpile, store 2. *Often plural Inf.* abundance, a lot, great deal, lashings (*Brit. inf.*), load(s) (*Inf.*), lots (*Inf.*), mass, mint, ocean(s), oodles (*Inf.*), plenty, pot(s) (*Inf.*), quantities, stack(s), tons ~*v.* 3. accumulate, amass, augment, bank, collect, gather, hoard, increase, mound, pile, stack, stockpile, store 4. assign, bestow, burden, confer, load, shower upon

hear 1. attend, be all ears (*Inf.*), catch, eavesdrop, give attention, hark, hearken (*Archaic*), heed, listen in, listen to, overhear 2. ascertain, be informed, be told of, discover, find out, gather, get wind of (*Inf.*), hear tell (*Dialect*), learn, pick up, understand 3. *Law* examine, investigate, judge, try

hearing 1. audition, auditory, ear, perception 2. audience, audition, chance to speak, interview 3. auditory range, earshot, hearing distance, range, reach, sound 4. inquiry, investigation, review, trial

hearsay buzz, gossip, grapevine (*Inf.*), idle talk, mere talk, *on dit*, report, rumour, talk, talk of the town, tittle-tattle, word of mouth

heart 1. character, disposition, emotion, feeling, inclination, nature, sentiment, soul, sympathy, temperament 2. affection, benevolence, compassion, concern, humanity, love, pity, tenderness, understanding 3. boldness, bravery, courage, fortitude, guts (*Inf.*), mettle, mind, nerve, pluck, purpose, resolution, spirit, spunk (*Inf.*), will 4. central part, centre, core, crux, essence, hub, kernel, marrow, middle, nucleus, pith, quintessence, root 5. **at heart** *au fond*, basically, essentially, fundamentally, in essence, in reality, really, truly 6. **by heart** by memory, by rote, off pat, parrot-fashion (*Inf.*), pat, word for word 7 **eat one's heart out** agonize, brood, grieve, mope, mourn, pine, regret, repine, sorrow 8. **from (the bottom of) one's heart** deeply, devoutly, fervently, heart and soul, heartily, sincerely, with all one's heart 9. **heart and soul** absolutely, completely, devotedly, entirely, gladly, wholeheartedly 10. **take heart** be comforted, be encouraged, be heartened, brighten up, buck up (*Inf.*), cheer up, perk up, revive

heartache affliction, agony, anguish, bitterness, despair, distress, grief, heartbreak, heartsickness, pain, remorse, sorrow, suffering, torment, torture

heartbreak anguish, desolation, despair, grief, misery, pain, sorrow, suffering

heartbreaking agonizing, bitter, desolating, disappointing, distressing, grievous, heart-rending, pitiful, poignant, sad, tragic

heartbroken brokenhearted, crestfallen, crushed, dejected, desolate, despondent, disappointed, disconsolate, disheartened, dispirited, downcast, grieved, heartsick, miserable

hearten animate, assure, buck up (*Inf.*), buoy up, cheer, comfort, console, embolden, encourage, incite, inspire, inspirit, raise someone's spirits, reassure, revivify, rouse, stimulate

heartfelt ardent, cordial, deep, devout, earnest, fervent, genuine, hearty, honest, profound, sincere, unfeigned, warm, wholehearted

heartily 1. cordially, deeply, feelingly, genuinely, profoundly, sincerely, unfeignedly, warmly 2. eagerly, earnestly, enthusiastically, resolutely, vigorously, zealously **3.** absolutely, completely, thoroughly, totally, very

heartless brutal, callous, cold, cold-blooded, cold-hearted, cruel, hard, hard-hearted, harsh, inhuman, merciless, pitiless, uncaring, unfeeling, unkind

heart-rending affecting, distressing, harrowing, heartbreaking, moving, pathetic, piteous, pitiful, poignant, sad, tragic

heartsick dejected, despondent, dispirited, downcast, heartsore, heavy-hearted, sick at heart

heart-to-heart 1. *adj.* candid, intimate, open, personal, sincere, unreserved **2.** *n.* cosy chat, tête-à-tête

heart-warming 1. gratifying, pleasing, rewarding, satisfying **2.** affecting, cheering, encouraging, heartening, moving, touching, warming

hearty 1. affable, ardent, back-slapping, cordial, eager, ebullient, effusive, enthusiastic, friendly, generous, genial, jovial, unreserved, warm **2.** earnest, genuine, heartfelt, honest, real, sincere, true, unfeigned, wholehearted **3.** active, energetic, hale, hardy, healthy, robust, sound, strong, vigorous, well **4.** ample, filling, nourishing, sizable, solid, square, substantial

heat *n.* **1.** calefaction, fever, fieriness, high temperature, hotness, hot spell, sultriness, swelter, torridity, warmness, warmth **2.** *Fig.* agitation, ardour, earnestness, excitement, fervour, fever, fury, impetuosity, intensity, passion, vehemence, violence, warmth, zeal ~*v.* **3.** become warm, chafe, flush, glow, grow hot, make hot, reheat, warm up **4.** animate, excite, impassion, inflame, inspirit, rouse, stimulate, stir, warm

heated angry, bitter, excited, fierce, fiery, frenzied, furious, impassioned, intense, passionate, raging, stormy, tempestuous, vehement, violent

heathen *n.* **1.** idolater, idolatress, infidel, pagan, unbeliever **2.** barbarian, philistine, savage ~*adj.* **3.** godless, heathenish, idolatrous, infidel, irreligious, pagan **4.** barbaric, philistine, savage, uncivilized, unenlightened

heave 1. drag (up), elevate, haul (up), heft (*Inf.*), hoist, lever, lift, pull (up), raise, tug **2.** cast, fling, hurl, pitch, send, sling, throw, toss **3.** breathe heavily, groan, puff, sigh, sob, suspire (*Archaic*),

utter wearily **4.** billow, breathe, dilate, exhale, expand, palpitate, pant, rise, surge, swell, throb **5.** gag (*Sl.*), retch, spew, throw up (*Inf.*), vomit

heaven 1. abode of God, bliss, Elysium *or* Elysian fields (*Greek myth*), happy hunting ground (*Amerind legend*), hereafter, life everlasting, life to come, next world, nirvana (*Buddhism, Hinduism*), paradise, Valhalla (*Norse myth*), Zion (*Christianity*) **2.** *Usually plural* empyrean (*Poetic*), ether, firmament, sky, welkin (*Archaic*) **3.** *Fig.* bliss, dreamland, ecstasy, enchantment, felicity, happiness, paradise, rapture, seventh heaven, sheer bliss, transport, utopia

heavenly 1. *Inf.* alluring, beautiful, blissful, delightful, divine (*Inf.*), entrancing, exquisite, glorious, lovely, rapturous, ravishing, sublime, wonderful **2.** angelic, beatific, blessed, blest, celestial, cherubic, divine, empyrean, extraterrestrial, godlike, holy, immortal, paradisaical, seraphic, superhuman, supernal (*Literary*), supernatural

heavily 1. awkwardly, clumsily, ponderously, weightily **2.** laboriously, painfully, with difficulty **3.** completely, decisively, roundly, thoroughly, utterly **4.** dejectedly, dully, gloomily, sluggishly, woodenly **5.** closely, compactly, densely, fast, hard, thick, thickly **6.** deep, deeply, profoundly, sound, soundly **7.** a great deal, considerably, copiously, excessively, frequently, to excess, very much

heaviness 1. gravity, heftiness, ponderousness, weight **2.** arduousness, burdensomeness, grievousness, onerousness, oppressiveness, severity, weightiness **3.** deadness, dullness, languor, lassitude, numbness, sluggishness, torpor **4.** dejection, depression, despondency, gloom, gloominess, glumness, melancholy, sadness, seriousness

heavy 1. bulky, hefty, massive, ponderous, portly, weighty **2.** burdensome, difficult, grievous, hard, harsh, intolerable, laborious, onerous, oppressive, severe, tedious, vexatious, wearisome **3.** apathetic, drowsy, dull, inactive, indolent, inert, listless, slow, sluggish, stupid, torpid, wooden **4.** crestfallen, dejected, depressed, despondent, disconsolate, downcast, gloomy, grieving, melancholy, sad, sorrowful **5.** complex, deep, difficult, grave, profound, serious, solemn, weighty **6**. abundant, considerable, copious, excessive, large, profuse **7**. burdened, encumbered, laden, loaded, oppressed, weighted **8**. boisterous, rough, stormy, tempestuous, turbulent, violent, wild **9**. dull, gloomy, leaden, louring, lowering, overcast

heavy-handed 1. awkward, bungling, clumsy, graceless, ham-fisted (*Inf.*), ham-handed (*Inf.*), inept, inexpert, like a bull in a china shop (*Inf.*), maladroit, unhandy **2**. bungling, inconsiderate, insensitive, tactless, thoughtless **3**. autocratic, domineering, harsh, oppressive, overbearing

heavy-hearted crushed, depressed, despondent, discouraged, disheartened, downcast, downhearted, forlorn, heartsick, melancholy, miserable, morose, mournful, sad, sorrowful

heckle bait, barrack (*Inf.*), disrupt, interrupt, jeer, pester, shout down, taunt

hectic animated, boisterous, chaotic, excited, fevered, feverish, flurrying, flustering, frantic, frenetic, frenzied, furious, heated, riotous, rumbustious, tumultuous, turbulent, wild

hector bluster, boast, browbeat, bully, bullyrag, harass, huff and puff, intimidate, menace, provoke, ride roughshod over, roister, threaten, worry

hedge *n.* **1**. hedgerow, quickset **2**. barrier, boundary, screen, windbreak **3**. compensation, counterbalance, guard, insurance cover, protection ~*v.* **4**. border, edge, enclose, fence, surround **5**. block, confine, hem in (about, around), hinder, obstruct, restrict **6**. beg the question, be noncommittal, dodge, duck, equivocate, evade, prevaricate, pussyfoot (*Inf.*), quibble, sidestep, temporize, waffle (*Inf.*) **7**. cover, fortify, guard, insure, protect, safeguard, shield

hedonism 1. epicureanism, epicurism, sybaritism **2**. dolce vita, gratification, luxuriousness, pleasure-seeking, pursuit of pleasure, self-indulgence, sensualism, sensuality

hedonist 1. epicure, epicurean, sybarite **2**. *bon vivant*, pleasure seeker, sensualist, voluptuary

hedonistic 1. epicurean, sybaritic **2**. luxurious, pleasure-seeking, self-indulgent, voluptuous

heed 1. *n.* attention, care, caution, consideration, ear, heedfulness, mind, note, notice, regard, respect, thought,

watchfulness **2**. *v.* attend, bear in mind, be guided by, consider, follow, give ear to, listen to, mark, mind, note, obey, observe, pay attention to, regard, take notice of, take to heart

heedful attentive, careful, cautious, chary, circumspect, mindful, observant, prudent, vigilant, wary, watchful

heedless careless, foolhardy, imprudent, inattentive, incautious, neglectful, negligent, oblivious, precipitate, rash, reckless, thoughtless, unmindful, unobservant, unthinking

heel[1] *n.* **1**. crust, end, remainder, rump, stub, stump **2**. *Sl.* blackguard, bounder (*Brit. inf.*), cad (*Brit inf.*), rotter (*Sl., chiefly Brit.*), scoundrel, swine **3**. **down at heel** dowdy, impoverished, out at elbows, run-down, seedy, shabby, slipshod, slovenly, worn **4**. **take to one's heels** escape, flee, run away *or* off, show a clean pair of heels, skedaddle (*Inf.*), take flight, vamoose (*Sl., chiefly U.S.*) **5**. **well-heeled** affluent, flush (*Inf.*), moneyed, prosperous, rich, wealthy, well-off, well-to-do

heel[2] cant, careen, incline, keel over, lean over, list, tilt

hefty 1. beefy (*Inf.*), big, brawny, burly, hulking, husky (*Inf.*), massive, muscular, robust, strapping, strong **2**. forceful, heavy, powerful, thumping (*Sl.*), vigorous **3**. ample, awkward, bulky, colossal, cumbersome, heavy, large, massive, ponderous, substantial, tremendous, unwieldy, weighty

height 1. altitude, elevation, highness, loftiness, stature, tallness **2**. apex, apogee, crest, crown, elevation, hill, mountain, peak, pinnacle, summit, top, vertex, zenith **3**. acme, dignity, eminence, exaltation, grandeur, loftiness, prominence **4**. climax, culmination, extremity, limit, maximum, *ne plus ultra*, ultimate, utmost degree, uttermost

heighten 1. add to, aggravate, amplify, augment, enhance, improve, increase, intensify, magnify, sharpen, strengthen **2**. elevate, enhance, ennoble, exalt, magnify, raise, uplift

heinous abhorrent, abominable, atrocious, awful, evil, execrable, flagrant, grave, hateful, hideous, infamous, iniquitous, monstrous, nefarious, odious, outrageous, revolting, shocking, unspeakable, vicious, villainous

heir beneficiary, heiress (*Fem.*), inheritor, inheritress *or* inheritrix (*Fem.*), next in line, scion, successor

hell 1. Abaddon, abode of the damned, abyss, Acheron (*Greek myth*), bottomless pit, fire and brimstone, Gehenna (*New Testament, Judaism*), Hades (*Greek myth*), hellfire, infernal regions, inferno, lower world, nether world, Tartarus (*Greek myth*), underworld **2.** affliction, agony, anguish, martyrdom, misery, nightmare, ordeal, suffering, torment, trial, wretchedness **3. hell for leather** at the double, full-tilt, headlong, hotfoot, hurriedly, like a bat out of hell (*Inf.*), pell-mell, posthaste, quickly, speedily, swiftly

hellbent bent, determined, fixed, intent, resolved, set, settled

hellish 1. damnable, damned, demoniacal, devilish, diabolical, fiendish, infernal **2.** abominable, accursed, atrocious, barbarous, cruel, detestable, execrable, inhuman, monstrous, nefarious, vicious, wicked

helm 1. *Nautical* rudder, steering gear, tiller, wheel **2.** *Fig.* command, control, direction, leadership, rule **3. at the helm** at the wheel, directing, in charge, in command, in control, in the driving seat, in the saddle

help *v.* **1.** abet, aid, assist, back, befriend, cooperate, lend a hand, promote, relieve, save, second, serve, stand by, succour, support **2.** alleviate, ameliorate, cure, ease, facilitate, heal, improve, mitigate, relieve, remedy, restore **3.** abstain, avoid, control, eschew, forbear, hinder, keep from, prevent, refrain from, resist, shun, withstand ~*n.* **4.** advice, aid, assistance, avail, benefit, cooperation, guidance, helping hand, service, support, use, utility **5.** assistant, employee, hand, helper, worker **6.** balm, corrective, cure, relief, remedy, restorative, salve, succour

helper abettor, adjutant, aide, aider, ally, assistant, attendant, auxiliary, coadjutor, collaborator, colleague, deputy, helpmate, mate, partner, right-hand man, second, subsidiary, supporter

helpful 1. advantageous, beneficial, constructive, favourable, fortunate, practical, productive, profitable, serviceable, timely, useful **2.** accommodating, beneficent, benevolent, caring, considerate, cooperative, friendly, kind, neighbourly, supportive, sympathetic

helping *n.* dollop (*Inf.*), piece, plateful, portion, ration, serving

helpless 1. abandoned, defenceless, dependent, destitute, exposed, forlorn, unprotected, vulnerable **2.** debilitated, disabled, feeble, impotent, incapable, incompetent, infirm, paralysed, powerless, unfit, weak

helpmate assistant, associate, companion, consort, helper, helpmeet, husband, partner, spouse, support, wife

helter-skelter 1. *adv.* carelessly, hastily, headlong, hurriedly, pell-mell, rashly, recklessly, wildly **2.** *adj.* anyhow, confused, disordered, haphazard, higgledy-piggledy (*Inf.*), hit-or-miss, jumbled, muddled, random, topsy-turvy

hem 1. *n.* border, edge, fringe, margin, trimming **2.** *v. Usually with* **in** beset, border, circumscribe, confine, edge, enclose, environ, hedge in, restrict, shut in, skirt, surround

hem and haw falter, fumble, hesitate, pause, stammer, stutter

hence ergo, for this reason, on that account, therefore, thus

henceforth from now on, from this day forward, hence, hereafter, hereinafter, in the future

henchman aide, associate, attendant, bodyguard, cohort (*Chiefly U.S.*), crony, follower, heavy (*Sl.*), minder (*Sl.*), minion, myrmidon, right-hand man, satellite, sidekick (*Sl.*), subordinate, supporter

henpeck browbeat, bully, carp, cavil, chide, criticize, domineer, find fault, harass, hector, intimidate, nag, niggle, pester, pick at, scold, torment

henpecked browbeaten, bullied, cringing, dominated, led by the nose, meek, subject, subjugated, timid, treated like dirt

herald *n.* **1.** bearer of tidings, crier, messenger **2.** forerunner, harbinger, indication, omen, precursor, sign, signal, token ~*v.* **3.** advertise, announce, broadcast, proclaim, publicize, publish, trumpet **4.** foretoken, harbinger, indicate, pave the way, portend, precede, presage, promise, show, usher in

herculean 1. arduous, demanding, difficult, exhausting, formidable, gruelling, hard, heavy, laborious, onerous, prodigious, strenuous, toilsome, tough **2.** athletic, brawny, husky (*Inf.*), mighty, muscular, powerful, rugged, sinewy, stalwart, strapping, strong, sturdy **3**. colossal, enormous, gigantic, great, huge, large, mammoth, massive, titanic

herd *n*. **1**. assemblage, collection, crowd, crush, drove, flock, horde, mass, mob, multitude, press, swarm, throng **2**. mob, populace, rabble, riffraff, the hoi polloi, the masses, the plebs ~*v*. **3**. assemble, associate, collect, congregate, flock, gather, huddle, muster, rally **4**. drive, force, goad, guide, lead, shepherd, spur

herdsman cowherd, cowman, drover, grazier, stockman

hereafter 1. *adv*. after this, from now on, hence, henceforth, henceforward, in future **2**. *n*. afterlife, future life, life after death, next world, the beyond

hereditary 1. family, genetic, inborn, inbred, inheritable, transmissible **2**. ancestral, bequeathed, handed down, inherited, patrimonial, traditional, transmitted, willed

heredity congenital traits, constitution, genetic make-up, genetics, inheritance

heresy apostasy, dissidence, error, heterodoxy, iconoclasm, impiety, revisionism, schism, unorthodoxy

heretic apostate, dissenter, dissident, nonconformist, renegade, revisionist, schismatic, sectarian, separatist

heretical freethinking, heterodox, iconoclastic, idolatrous, impious, revisionist, schismatic, unorthodox

heritage bequest, birthright, endowment, estate, inheritance, legacy, lot, patrimony, portion, share, tradition

hermetic, hermetical airtight, sealed, shut

hermit anchoret, anchorite, eremite, monk, recluse, solitary, stylite

hero 1. celebrity, champion, conqueror, exemplar, great man, heart-throb (*Brit*.), idol, man of the hour, popular figure, star, superstar, victor **2**. lead actor, leading man, male lead, principal male character, protagonist

heroic 1. bold, brave, courageous, daring, dauntless, doughty, fearless, gallant, intrepid, lion-hearted, stouthearted, undaunted, valiant, valorous **2**. classical, Homeric, legendary, mythological **3**. classic, elevated, epic, exaggerated, extravagant, grand, grandiose, high-flown, inflated

heroine 1. celebrity, goddess, ideal,

woman of the hour **2**. diva, female lead, lead actress, leading lady, prima donna, principal female character, protagonist

heroism boldness, bravery, courage, courageousness, daring, fearlessness, fortitude, gallantry, intrepidity, prowess, spirit, valour

hero worship admiration, adoration, adulation, idealization, idolization, putting on a pedestal, veneration

hesitant diffident, doubtful, half-hearted, halting, hanging back, hesitating, irresolute, lacking confidence, reluctant, sceptical, shy, timid, uncertain, unsure, vacillating, wavering

hesitate 1. be uncertain, delay, dither, doubt, haver (*Brit*.), pause, shillyshally (*Inf*.), swither (*Scot. dialect*), vacillate, wait, waver **2**. balk, be reluctant, be unwilling, boggle, demur, hang back, scruple, shrink from, think twice **3**. falter, fumble, hem and haw, stammer, stumble, stutter

hesitation 1. delay, doubt, dubiety, hesitancy, indecision, irresolution, uncertainty, vacillation **2**. demurral, misgiving(s), qualm(s), reluctance, scruple(s), unwillingness **3**. faltering, fumbling, hemming and hawing, stammering, stumbling, stuttering

heterodox dissident, heretical, iconoclastic, revisionist, schismatic, unorthodox, unsound

heterogeneous assorted, contrary, contrasted, different, discrepant, disparate, dissimilar, divergent, diverse, diversified, incongruous, miscellaneous, mixed, motley, opposed, unlike, unrelated, varied

hew 1. axe, chop, cut, hack, lop, split **2**. carve, fashion, form, make, model, sculpt, sculpture, shape, smooth

heyday bloom, flowering, pink, prime, prime of life, salad days

hiatus aperture, blank, breach, break, chasm, discontinuity, gap, interruption, interval, lacuna, lapse, opening, rift, space

hibernate hole up, lie dormant, overwinter, remain torpid, sleep snug, vegetate, winter

hidden abstruse, clandestine, close, concealed, covered, covert, cryptic, dark, hermetic, hermetical, masked, mysterious, mystic, mystical, obscure, occult, recondite, secret, shrouded, ulterior, unrevealed, unseen, veiled

hide¹ 1. cache, conceal, go into hiding, go to ground, go underground, hole up, lie low, secrete, take cover **2.** blot out, bury, camouflage, cloak, conceal, cover, disguise, eclipse, mask, obscure, screen, shelter, shroud, veil **3.** hush up, keep secret, suppress, withhold

**hide² ** fell, pelt, skin

hideaway haven, hide-out, hiding place, nest, refuge, retreat, sanctuary, sequestered nook

hidebound brassbound, conventional, narrow, narrow-minded, rigid, set, set in one's ways, strait-laced, ultraconservative

hideous 1. ghastly, grim, grisly, grotesque, gruesome, monstrous, repulsive, revolting, ugly, unsightly **2.** abominable, appalling, awful, detestable, disgusting, dreadful, horrendous, horrible, horrid, loathsome, macabre, odious, shocking, sickening, terrible, terrifying

hide-out den, hideaway, hiding place, lair, secret place, shelter

hiding *n.* beating, caning, drubbing, flogging, larruping (*Brit. dialect*), lathering (*Inf.*), licking (*Inf.*), spanking, tanning (*Sl.*), thrashing, walloping (*Inf.*), whaling, whipping

hierarchy grading, pecking order, ranking

hieroglyphic *adj.* enigmatical, figurative, indecipherable, obscure, runic, symbolical

higgledy-piggledy 1. *adv.* all over the place, all over the shop (*Inf.*), anyhow, any old how, confusedly, disorderly, haphazard, helter-skelter, pell-mell, topsy-turvy **2.** *adj.* haphazard, helter-skelter, indiscriminate, jumbled, muddled, pell-mell, topsy-turvy

high *adj.* **1.** elevated, lofty, soaring, steep, tall, towering **2.** excessive, extraordinary, extreme, great, intensified, sharp, strong **3.** arch, chief, consequential, distinguished, eminent, exalted, important, influential, leading, powerful, prominent, ruling, significant, superior **4.** arrogant, boastful, bragging, despotic, domineering, haughty, lofty, lordly, ostentatious, overbearing, proud, tyrannical, vainglorious **5.** capital, extreme, grave, important, serious **6.** boisterous, bouncy (*Inf.*), cheerful, elated, excited, exhilarated, exuberant, joyful, light-hearted, merry, strong, tumultuous, turbulent **7.** *Inf.* delirious, euphoric,

freaked out (*Inf.*), hyped up (*Sl.*), inebriated, intoxicated, on a trip (*Inf.*), spaced out (*Sl.*), stoned (*Sl.*), tripping (*Inf.*), turned on (*Sl.*) **8.** costly, dear, exorbitant, expensive, high-priced, steep (*Inf.*), stiff **9.** acute, high-pitched, penetrating, piercing, piping, sharp, shrill, soprano, strident, treble **10.** extravagant, grand, lavish, luxurious, rich **11.** gamy, niffy (*Sl.*), pongy (*Brit. sl.*), strong-flavoured, tainted, whiffy (*Inf.*) **12. high and dry** abandoned, bereft, destitute, helpless, stranded **13. high and low** all over, everywhere, exhaustively, far and wide, in every nook and cranny **14. high and mighty** *Inf.* arrogant, cavalier, conceited, disdainful, haughty, imperious, overbearing, self-important, snobbish, stuck-up (*Inf.*), superior ~*adv.* **15.** aloft, at great height, far up, way up ~*n.* **16.** apex, height, peak, record level, summit, top **17.** *Inf.* delirium, ecstasy, euphoria, intoxication, trip (*Inf.*)

highborn aristocratic, blue-blooded, gentle (*Archaic*), noble, patrician, pedigreed, thoroughbred, well-born

highbrow 1. *n.* aesthete, Brahmin (*U.S.*), brain (*Inf.*), brainbox (*Sl.*), egghead (*Inf.*), intellectual, mastermind, savant, scholar **2.** *adj.* bookish, brainy (*Inf.*), cultivated, cultured, deep, highbrowed, intellectual, sophisticated

high-class A-one (*Inf.*), choice, classy (*Sl.*), elite, exclusive, first-rate, high-quality, posh (*Inf., chiefly Brit.*), select, superior, tip-top, top-flight, tops (*Sl.*), U (*Brit. inf.*), upper-class

highfalutin, highfaluting big, bombastic, florid, grandiose, high-flown, high-sounding, lofty, magniloquent, pompous, pretentious, supercilious, swanky (*Inf.*)

high-flown elaborate, exaggerated, extravagant, florid, grandiose, highfalutin (*Inf.*), inflated, lofty, magniloquent, overblown, pretentious

high-handed arbitrary, autocratic, bossy (*Inf.*), despotic, dictatorial, domineering, imperious, inconsiderate, oppressive, overbearing, peremptory, self-willed, tyrannical, wilful

high jinks fun and games, horseplay, jollity, junketing, merrymaking, revelry, skylarking (*Inf.*), sport, spree

highland *n.* heights, hill country, hills, mountainous region, plateau, tableland, uplands

highlight 1. *n.* best part, climax, feature, focal point, focus, high point, high spot, main feature, memorable part, peak **2.** *v.* accent, accentuate, bring to the fore, emphasize, feature, focus attention on, give prominence to, play up, set off, show up, spotlight, stress, underline

highly 1. decidedly, eminently, exceptionally, extraordinarily, extremely, greatly, immensely, supremely, tremendously, vastly, very, very much **2.** appreciatively, approvingly, enthusiastically, favourably, warmly, well

highly strung easily upset, edgy, excitable, irascible, irritable, nervous, nervy (*Brit. inf.*), neurotic, restless, sensitive, stressed, taut, temperamental, tense

high-minded elevated, ethical, fair, good, honourable, idealistic, magnanimous, moral, noble, principled, pure, righteous, upright, virtuous, worthy

high-powered aggressive, driving, dynamic, effective, energetic, enterprising, forceful, go-ahead, go-getting (*Inf.*), highly capable, vigorous

high-pressure *Of salesmanship* aggressive, bludgeoning, coercive, compelling, forceful, high-powered, importunate, insistent, intensive, persistent, persuasive, pushy (*Inf.*)

high-priced costly, dear, excessive, exorbitant, expensive, extortionate, high, steep (*Inf.*), stiff, unreasonable

high-sounding affected, artificial, bombastic, extravagant, flamboyant, florid, grandiloquent, grandiose, high-flown, imposing, magniloquent, ostentatious, overblown, pompous, pretentious, stilted, strained

high-speed brisk, express, fast, hotted-up (*Inf.*), quick, rapid, souped-up (*Inf.*), streamlined, swift

high-spirited animated, boisterous, bold, bouncy, daring, dashing, ebullient, effervescent, energetic, exuberant, frolicsome, full of life, fun-loving, gallant, lively, mettlesome, spirited, spunky (*Inf.*), vibrant, vital, vivacious

high spirits abandon, boisterousness, exhilaration, exuberance, good cheer, hilarity, *joie de vivre*, rare good humour

hijack commandeer, expropriate, seize, skyjack, take over

hike *v.* **1.** back-pack, hoof it (*Sl.*), leg it (*Inf.*), ramble, tramp, walk **2.** *Usually with* **up** hitch up, jack up, lift, pull up, raise ~*n.* **3.** journey on foot, march, ramble, tramp, trek, walk

hilarious amusing, comical, convivial, entertaining, exhilarated, funny, gay, happy, humorous, jolly, jovial, joyful, joyous, merry, mirthful, noisy, rollicking, side-splitting, uproarious

hilarity amusement, boisterousness, cheerfulness, conviviality, exhilaration, exuberance, gaiety, glee, high spirits, jollification, jollity, joviality, joyousness, laughter, levity, merriment, mirth

hill 1. brae (*Scot.*), down (*Archaic*), elevation, eminence, fell, height, hillock, hilltop, knoll, mound, mount, prominence, tor **2.** drift, heap, hummock, mound, pile, stack **3.** acclivity, brae (*Scot.*), climb, gradient, incline, rise, slope

hillock barrow, hummock, knap (*Dialect*), knoll, monticule, mound, tump (*Western Brit. dialect*)

hilt 1. grip, haft, handgrip, handle, helve **2. to the hilt** completely, entirely, fully, totally, wholly

hind after, back, caudal (*Anat.*), hinder, posterior, rear

hinder arrest, check, debar, delay, deter, encumber, frustrate, hamper, hamstring, handicap, hold up *or* back, impede, interrupt, obstruct, oppose, prevent, retard, slow down, stop, stymie, thwart, trammel

hindmost concluding, final, furthest, furthest behind, last, most remote, rearmost, terminal, trailing, ultimate

hindrance bar, barrier, check, deterrent, difficulty, drag, drawback, encumbrance, handicap, hitch, impediment, interruption, limitation, obstacle, obstruction, restraint, restriction, snag, stoppage, stumbling block, trammel

hinge *v.* be contingent, be subject to, depend, hang, pivot, rest, revolve around, turn

hint *n.* **1.** allusion, clue, implication, indication, inkling, innuendo, insinuation, intimation, mention, reminder, suggestion, tip-off, word to the wise **2.** advice, help, pointer, suggestion, tip, wrinkle (*Inf.*) **3.** breath, dash, *soupçon*, speck, suggestion, suspicion, taste, tinge, touch, trace, undertone, whiff, whisper ~*v.* **4.** allude, cue, imply, indicate, insinuate, intimate, let it be known, mention, prompt, suggest, tip off

hip *adj.* aware, fashionable, in, informed, in on, knowledgeable, onto, trendy, wise (*Sl.*), with it (*Inf.*)

hippie beatnik, bohemian, dropout, flower child

hire v. 1. appoint, commission, employ, engage, sign up, take on 2. charter, engage, lease, let, rent ~*n.* 3. charge, cost, fee, price, rent, rental

hirsute bearded, bewhiskered, bristly, hairy, hispid (*Biol.*), shaggy, unshaven

hiss n. 1. buzz, hissing, sibilance, sibilation 2. boo, catcall, contempt, derision, jeer, raspberry ~*v.* 3. rasp, shrill, sibilate, wheeze, whirr, whistle, whiz 4. blow a raspberry, boo, catcall, condemn, damn, decry, deride, hoot, jeer, mock, revile, ridicule

historian annalist, biographer, chronicler, historiographer, recorder

historic celebrated, consequential, epoch-making, extraordinary, famous, momentous, notable, outstanding, red-letter, remarkable, significant

historical actual, archival, attested, authentic, chronicled, documented, factual, real, verifiable

history 1. account, annals, autobiography, biography, chronicle, memoirs, narration, narrative, recapitulation, recital, record, relation, saga, story 2. ancient history, antiquity, bygone times, days of old, days of yore, olden days, the good old days, the old days, the past, yesterday, yesteryear

histrionic affected, artificial, bogus, dramatic, forced, insincere, melodramatic, sensational, theatrical, unnatural

histrionics dramatics, performance, scene, staginess, tantrums, temperament, theatricality

hit v. 1. bang, bash (*Inf.*), batter, beat, belt (*Sl.*), clip (*Sl.*), clobber (*Sl.*), clout (*Inf.*), cuff, flog, knock, lob, punch, slap, smack, smite (*Archaic*), sock (*Sl.*), strike, swat, thump, wallop (*Inf.*), whack 2. bang into, bump, clash with, collide with, crash against, meet head-on, run into, smash into 3. accomplish, achieve, arrive at, attain, gain, reach, secure, strike, touch 4. affect, damage, devastate, impinge on, influence, leave a mark on, make an impact *or* impression on, move, overwhelm, touch ~*n.* 5. blow, bump, clash, clout (*Inf.*), collision, cuff, impact, knock, rap, shot, slap, smack, stroke, swipe (*Inf.*), wallop (*Inf.*) 6. *Inf.*

sellout, sensation, smash (*Inf.*), success, triumph, winner

hitch v. 1. attach, connect, couple, fasten, harness, join, make fast, tether, tie, unite, yoke 2. *Often with* up hoick, jerk, pull, tug, yank 3. *Inf.* hitchhike, thumb a lift ~*n.* 4. catch, check, delay, difficulty, drawback, hindrance, hold-up, impediment, mishap, problem, snag, stoppage, trouble

hither close, closer, here, near, nearer, nigh (*Archaic*), over here, to this place

hitherto heretofore, previously, so far, thus far, till now, until now, up to now

hit off 1. capture, catch, impersonate, mimic, represent, take off (*Inf.*) 2. **hit it off** *Inf.* be on good terms, click (*Sl.*), get on (well) with, take to, warm to

hit on *or* **upon** arrive at, chance upon, come upon, discover, guess, invent, light upon, realize, strike upon, stumble on, think up

hit or miss aimless, casual, cursory, disorganized, haphazard, indiscriminate, perfunctory, random, undirected, uneven

hit out (at) assail, attack, castigate, condemn, denounce, inveigh against, lash out, rail against, strike out at

hive 1. cluster, colony, swarm 2. *Fig.* centre, heart, hub, powerhouse (*Sl.*)

hoard 1. *n.* accumulation, cache, fund, heap, mass, pile, reserve, stockpile, store, supply, treasure-trove 2. *v.* accumulate, amass, buy up, cache, collect, deposit, garner, gather, hive, lay up, put away, put by, save, stash away (*Inf.*), stockpile, store, treasure

hoarder collector, magpie (*Brit.*), miser, niggard, saver, squirrel (*Inf.*)

hoarse croaky, discordant, grating, gravelly, growling, gruff, guttural, harsh, husky, rasping, raucous, rough, throaty

hoary 1. frosty, grey, grey-haired, grizzled, hoar, silvery, white, white-haired 2. aged, ancient, antiquated, antique, old, venerable

hoax 1. *n.* cheat, con (*Sl.*), deception, fast one (*Inf.*), fraud, imposture, joke, practical joke, prank, ruse, spoof (*Inf.*), swindle, trick 2. *v.* bamboozle (*Inf.*), befool, bluff, con (*Sl.*), deceive, delude, dupe, fool, gammon (*Inf.*), gull, (*Archaic*), hoodwink, hornswoggle (*Sl.*), swindle, take in (*Inf.*), take (someone) for a ride (*Inf.*), trick

hoaxer bamboozler (*Inf.*), hoodwinker, humbug, joker, practical joker, prankster, spoofer (*Inf.*), trickster

hobble 1. dodder, falter, halt, limp, shamble, shuffle, stagger, stumble, totter **2.** clog, fasten, fetter, hamstring, restrict, shackle, tie

hobby diversion, favourite occupation, (leisure) activity, leisure pursuit, pastime, relaxation, sideline

hobgoblin apparition, bogey, goblin, hob, imp, spectre, spirit, sprite

hobnob associate, consort, fraternize, hang about, keep company, mingle, mix, socialize

hocus-pocus 1. artifice, cheat, chicanery, deceit, deception, delusion, hoax, humbug, imposture, swindle, trickery **2.** abracadabra, cant, gibberish, gobbledegook (*Inf.*), jargon, mumbo jumbo, nonsense, rigmarole **3.** conjuring, jugglery, legerdemain, prestidigitation, sleight of hand

hoggish brutish, dirty, filthy, gluttonous, greedy, gross, mean, piggish, rapacious, ravenous, selfish, sordid, squalid, swinish, unclean

hogwash balderdash, bilge (*Inf.*), bunk (*Inf.*), drivel, hooey (*Sl.*), nonsense, piffle (*Inf.*), rot, rubbish, tosh (*Brit. inf.*), trash, tripe (*Inf.*), twaddle

hoiden *see* HOYDEN

hoi polloi admass, *canaille*, commonalty, riffraff, the (common) herd, the common people, the great unwashed (*Inf. and derogatory*), the lower orders, the masses, the plebs, the populace, the proles (*Derogatory sl., chiefly Brit.*), the proletariat, the rabble, the third estate

hoist 1. *v.* elevate, erect, heave, lift, raise, rear, upraise **2.** *n.* crane, elevator, lift, tackle, winch

hoity-toity arrogant, conceited, disdainful, haughty, high and mighty (*Inf.*), lofty, overweening, proud, scornful, snobbish, snooty (*Inf.*), stuck-up (*Inf.*), supercilious, toffee-nosed (*Sl., chiefly Brit.*), uppish (*Brit. inf.*)

hold *v.* **1.** have, keep, maintain, occupy, own, possess, retain **2.** adhere, clasp, cleave, clinch, cling, clutch, cradle, embrace, enfold, grasp, grip, stick **3.** arrest, bind, check, confine, curb, detain, imprison, restrain, stay, stop, suspend **4.** assume, believe, consider, deem, entertain, esteem, judge, maintain, presume, reckon, regard, think, view **5.** continue, endure, last, persevere, persist, remain,

resist, stay, wear **6.** assemble, call, carry on, celebrate, conduct, convene, have, officiate at, preside over, run, solemnize **7.** bear, brace, carry, prop, shoulder, support, sustain, take **8.** accommodate, comprise, contain, have a capacity for, seat, take **9.** apply, be in force, be the case, exist, hold good, operate, remain true, remain valid, stand up **10. hold one's own** do well, hold fast, hold out, keep one's head above water, keep pace, keep up, maintain one's position, stand firm, stand one's ground, stay put, stick to one's guns (*Inf.*) ~*n.* **11.** clasp, clutch, grasp, grip **12.** anchorage, foothold, footing, leverage, prop, purchase, stay, support, vantage **13.** ascendancy, authority, clout (*Inf.*), control, dominance, dominion, influence, mastery, pull (*Inf.*), sway

hold back 1. check, control, curb, inhibit, repress, restrain, suppress **2.** desist, forbear, keep back, refuse, withhold

holder 1. bearer, custodian, incumbent, keeper, occupant, owner, possessor, proprietor, purchaser **2.** case, container, cover, housing, receptacle, sheath

hold forth declaim, descant, discourse, go on (*Inf.*), harangue, lecture, orate, preach, speak, speechify, spiel (*Inf.*), spout (*Inf.*)

holdings assets, estate, investments, land interests, possessions, property, resources, securities, stocks and shares

hold off 1. avoid, defer, delay, keep from, postpone, put off, refrain **2.** fend off, keep off, rebuff, repel, repulse, stave off

hold out 1. extend, give, offer, present, proffer **2.** carry on, continue, endure, hang on, last, persevere, persist, stand fast, withstand

hold over adjourn, defer, delay, postpone, put off, suspend, waive

hold-up 1. bottleneck, delay, difficulty, hitch, obstruction, setback, snag, stoppage, traffic jam, trouble, wait **2.** burglary, mugging (*Inf.*), robbery, stick-up (*Sl.*), theft

hold up 1. delay, detain, hinder, impede, retard, set back, slow down, stop **2.** brace, buttress, jack up, prop, shore up, support, sustain **3.** mug (*Inf.*), rob, stick up (*Sl.*), waylay **4.** display, exhibit, flaunt, present, show **5.** bear up, endure, last, survive, wear

hold with agree to *or* with, approve of,

be in favour of, countenance, subscribe to, support, take kindly to

hole 1. aperture, breach, break, crack, fissure, gap, opening, orifice, outlet, perforation, puncture, rent, split, tear, vent 2. cave, cavern, cavity, chamber, depression, excavation, hollow, pit, pocket, scoop, shaft 3. burrow, covert, den, earth, lair, nest, retreat, shelter 4. *Inf.* dive (*Sl.*), dump (*Inf.*), hovel, joint (*Sl.*), slum 5. *Inf.* cell, dungeon, oubliette, prison 6. defect, discrepancy, error, fallacy, fault, flaw, inconsistency, loophole 7. *Sl.* dilemma, fix (*Inf.*), imbroglio, jam (*Inf.*), mess, predicament, quandary, scrape (*Inf.*), tangle, (tight) spot (*Inf.*) 8. **pick holes in** cavil, crab (*Inf.*), criticize, denigrate, disparage, disprove, find fault, niggle, pull to pieces, run down, slate (*Inf.*)

hole-and-corner backstairs, clandestine, furtive, secret, secretive, sneaky (*Inf.*), stealthy, surreptitious, underhand, under the counter (*Inf.*)

hole up go to earth, hibernate, hide, shelter, take cover, take refuge

holiday 1. break, leave, recess, time off, vacation 2. anniversary, bank holiday, celebration, feast, festival, festivity, fête, gala, public holiday, saint's day

holier-than-thou goody-goody (*Inf.*), pietistic, pietistical, priggish, religiose, sanctimonious, self-righteous, self-satisfied, smug, unctuous

holiness blessedness, devoutness, divinity, godliness, piety, purity, religiousness, righteousness, sacredness, saintliness, sanctity, spirituality, virtuousness

holler *v./n.* bawl, bellow, call, cheer, clamour, cry, hail, halloo, hollo, hurrah, huzzah (*Archaic*), roar, shout, whoop, yell

hollow *adj.* 1. empty, not solid, unfilled, vacant, void 2. cavernous, concave, deep-set, depressed, indented, sunken 3. deep, dull, expressionless, flat, low, muffled, muted, reverberant, rumbling, sepulchral, toneless 4. empty, fruitless, futile, meaningless, pointless, Pyrrhic, specious, unavailing, useless, vain, worthless 5. empty, famished, hungry, ravenous, starved 6. artificial, cynical, deceitful, faithless, false, flimsy, hollow-hearted, hypocritical, insincere, treacherous, unsound, weak 7. **beat (someone) hollow** *Inf.* defeat, hammer (*Inf.*), outdo, overcome, rout, thrash,

trounce, worst ~*n.* 8. basin, bowl, cave, cavern, cavity, concavity, crater, cup, den, dent, depression, dimple, excavation, hole, indentation, pit, trough 9. bottom, dale, dell, dingle, glen, valley ~*v.* 10. channel, dig, dish, excavate, furrow, gouge, groove, pit, scoop

holocaust annihilation, carnage, conflagration, destruction, devastation, genocide, inferno, massacre, mass murder

holy 1. devout, divine, faithful, god-fearing, godly, hallowed, pious, pure, religious, righteous, saintly, sublime, virtuous 2. blessed, consecrated, dedicated, hallowed, sacred, sacrosanct, sanctified, venerable, venerated

homage 1. admiration, adoration, adulation, awe, deference, devotion, duty, esteem, honour, respect, reverence, worship 2. allegiance, devotion, faithfulness, fealty, fidelity, loyalty, obeisance, service, tribute

home *n.* 1. abode, domicile, dwelling, dwelling place, habitation, house, residence 2. birthplace, family, fireside, hearth, homestead, home town, household 3. abode, element, environment, habitat, habitation, haunt, home ground, range, stamping ground, territory 4. **at home** a. available, in, present b. at ease, comfortable, familiar, relaxed c. entertaining, giving a party, having guests, receiving d. *As a noun* party, reception, soirée 5. **at home in, on,** *or* **with** conversant with, familiar with, knowledgeable, proficient, skilled, well-versed 6. **bring home to** drive home, emphasize, impress upon, make clear, press home ~*adj.* 7. central, domestic, familiar, family, household, inland, internal, local, national, native

homeland country of origin, fatherland, mother country, motherland, native land

homeless 1. *adj.* abandoned, destitute, displaced, dispossessed, down-and-out, exiled, forlorn, forsaken, outcast, unsettled 2. *n.* **the homeless** dossers (*Sl.*), squatters, vagrants

homelike cheerful, comfortable, cosy, easy, familiar, homy, informal, intimate, relaxing, snug

homely comfortable, comfy (*Inf.*), cosy, domestic, everyday, familiar, friendly, homelike, homespun, homy, informal, modest, natural, ordinary, plain, simple, unaffected, unassuming, unpretentious, welcoming

Homeric epic, grand, heroic, imposing, impressive

homespun artless, coarse, homely, home-made, inelegant, plain, rough, rude, rustic, unpolished, unsophisticated

homicidal deadly, death-dealing, lethal, maniacal, mortal, murderous

homicide 1. bloodshed, killing, manslaughter, murder, slaying **2.** killer, murderer, slayer

homily address, discourse, lecture, preaching, preachment, sermon

homogeneity analogousness, comparability, consistency, correspondence, identicalness, oneness, sameness, similarity, uniformity

homogeneous akin, alike, analogous, cognate, comparable, consistent, identical, kindred, similar, uniform, unvarying

homologous analogous, comparable, correspondent, corresponding, like, parallel, related, similar

homosexual adj. bent (Sl.), camp (Inf.), gay (Inf.), homoerotic, lesbian, queer (Inf.), sapphic

homy comfortable, comfy (Inf.), congenial, cosy, domestic, familiar, friendly, informal, intimate, pleasant, warm

hone v. edge, file, grind, point, polish, sharpen, strop, whet

honest 1. conscientious, decent, ethical, high-minded, honourable, law-abiding, reliable, reputable, scrupulous, trustworthy, trusty, truthful, upright, veracious, virtuous **2.** above board, authentic, bona fide, genuine, honest to goodness, on the level (Inf.), on the up and up, proper, real, straight, true **3.** equitable, fair, fair and square, impartial, just **4.** candid, direct, forthright, frank, ingenuous, open, outright, plain, sincere, straightforward, undisguised, unfeigned

honestly 1. by fair means, cleanly, ethically, honourably, in good faith, lawfully, legally, legitimately, on the level (Inf.), with clean hands **2.** candidly, frankly, in all sincerity, in plain English, plainly, straight (out), to one's face, truthfully

honesty 1. faithfulness, fidelity, honour, incorruptibility, integrity, morality, probity, rectitude, reputability, scrupulousness, straightness, trustworthiness, truthfulness, uprightness, veracity, vir-

tue **2.** bluntness, candour, equity, even-handedness, fairness, frankness, genuineness, openness, outspokenness, plainness, sincerity, straightforwardness

honeyed agreeable, alluring, cajoling, dulcet, enticing, flattering, mellow, melodious, seductive, soothing, sweet, sweetened, unctuous

honorary complimentary, ex officio, formal, honoris causa, in name or title only, nominal, titular, unofficial, unpaid

honour n. **1.** credit, dignity, distinction, elevation, esteem, fame, glory, high standing, prestige, rank, renown, reputation, repute **2.** acclaim, accolade, adoration, commendation, deference, homage, kudos, praise, recognition, regard, respect, reverence, tribute, veneration **3.** decency, fairness, goodness, honesty, integrity, morality, principles, probity, rectitude, righteousness, trustworthiness, uprightness **4.** compliment, credit, favour, pleasure, privilege, source of pride or satisfaction **5.** chastity, innocence, modesty, purity, virginity, virtue ~v. **6.** admire, adore, appreciate, esteem, exalt, glorify, hallow, prize, respect, revere, reverence, value, venerate, worship **7.** be as good as (Inf.), be faithful to, be true to, carry out, discharge, fulfil, keep, live up to, observe **8.** acclaim, celebrate, commemorate, commend, compliment, decorate, dignify, exalt, glorify, laud, lionize, praise **9.** accept, acknowledge, cash, clear, credit, pass, pay, take

honourable 1. ethical, fair, high-minded, honest, just, moral, principled, true, trustworthy, trusty, upright, upstanding, virtuous **2.** distinguished, eminent, great, illustrious, noble, notable, noted, prestigious, renowned, venerable **3.** creditable, estimable, proper, reputable, respectable, respected, right, righteous, virtuous

honours adornments, awards, decorations, dignities, distinctions, laurels, titles

hoodwink bamboozle (Inf.), befool, cheat, con (Sl.), cozen, delude, dupe, fool, gull (Archaic), hoax, impose, lead up the garden path (Inf.), mislead, pull a fast one on (Inf.), rook (Sl.), swindle, trick

hook n. **1.** catch, clasp, fastener, hasp, holder, link, lock, peg **2.** noose, snare, springe, trap **3. by hook or by crook** by any means, by fair means or foul, somehow, somehow or other, someway **4. hook, line, and sinker** *Inf.* completely, entirely, thoroughly, through and through, totally, utterly, wholly **5. off the hook** *Sl.* acquitted, cleared, exonerated, in the clear, let off, under no obligation, vindicated ~*v.* **6.** catch, clasp, fasten, fix, hasp, secure **7.** catch, enmesh, ensnare, entrap, snare, trap

hooked 1. aquiline, beaked, beaky, bent, curved, falcate (*Biol.*), hamate (*Rare*), hooklike, hook-shaped, unciform (*Anat., etc.*), uncinate (*Biol.*) **2.** addicted to, devoted to, enamoured of, obsessed with, taken with, turned on (*Sl.*)

hooligan delinquent, hoodlum (*Chiefly U.S.*), rowdy, ruffian, tough, vandal, yob *or* yobbo (*Brit. sl.*)

hoop band, circlet, girdle, loop, ring, wheel

hoot *n.* **1.** call, cry, toot **2.** boo, catcall, hiss, jeer, yell **3.** *Inf.* card (*Inf.*), caution (*Inf.*), laugh (*Inf.*), scream (*Inf.*) ~*v.* **4.** boo, catcall, condemn, decry, denounce, execrate, hiss, howl down, jeer, yell at **5.** cry, scream, shout, shriek, toot, whoop, yell

hop 1. *v.* bound, caper, dance, jump, leap, skip, spring, vault **2.** *n.* bounce, bound, jump, leap, skip, spring, step, vault

hope 1. *n.* ambition, anticipation, assumption, belief, confidence, desire, dream, expectancy, expectation, faith, longing **2.** *v.* anticipate, aspire, await, believe, contemplate, count on, desire, expect, foresee, long, look forward to, rely, trust

hopeful 1. anticipating, assured, buoyant, confident, expectant, looking forward to, optimistic, sanguine **2.** auspicious, bright, cheerful, encouraging, heartening, promising, propitious, reassuring, rosy

hopefully 1. confidently, expectantly, optimistically, sanguinely **2.** *Inf.* all being well, conceivably, expectedly, feasibly, probably

hopeless 1. defeatist, dejected, demoralized, despairing, desperate, despondent, disconsolate, downhearted, forlorn, in despair, pessimistic, woebegone **2.** helpless, incurable, irremediable, irreparable, irreversible, lost, past remedy, remediless **3.** forlorn, futile, impossible, impracticable, pointless, unachievable, unattainable, useless, vain **4.** *Inf.*

inadequate, incompetent, ineffectual, inferior, no good, poor, useless (*Inf.*)

horde band, crew, crowd, drove, gang, host, mob, multitude, pack, press, swarm, throng, troop

horizon 1. field of vision, skyline, vista **2.** compass, ken, perspective, prospect, purview, range, realm, scope, sphere, stretch

horrible 1. abhorrent, abominable, appalling, awful, dreadful, fearful, frightful, ghastly, grim, grisly, gruesome, heinous, hideous, horrid, loathsome, repulsive, revolting, shameful, shocking, terrible, terrifying **2.** *Inf.* awful, beastly (*Inf.*), cruel, disagreeable, dreadful, ghastly (*Inf.*), mean, nasty, terrible, unkind, unpleasant

horrid 1. awful, disagreeable, disgusting, dreadful, horrible, nasty, offensive, terrible, unpleasant **2.** abominable, alarming, appalling, formidable, frightening, hair-raising, harrowing, hideous, horrific, odious, repulsive, revolting, shocking, terrifying, terrorizing **3.** *Inf.* beastly (*Inf.*), cruel, mean, nasty, unkind

horrific appalling, awful, dreadful, frightening, frightful, ghastly, grim, grisly, horrendous, horrifying, shocking, terrifying

horrify 1. affright, alarm, frighten, intimidate, petrify, scare, terrify, terrorize **2.** appal, disgust, dismay, outrage, shock, sicken

horror 1. alarm, apprehension, awe, consternation, dismay, dread, fear, fright, panic, terror **2.** abhorrence, abomination, antipathy, aversion, detestation, disgust, hatred, loathing, repugnance, revulsion

horror-struck *or* **horror-stricken** aghast, appalled, awe-struck, frightened to death, horrified, petrified, scared out of one's wits, shocked

horse around *or* **about** clown, fool about *or* around, misbehave, play the fool, roughhouse (*Sl.*)

horseman cavalier, cavalryman, dragoon, equestrian, horse-soldier, rider

horseplay buffoonery, clowning, fooling around, high jinks, pranks, romping, rough-and-tumble, roughhousing (*Sl.*), skylarking (*Inf.*)

horse sense common sense, gumption (*Inf.*), judgment, mother wit, nous (*Inf.*), practicality

hospitable 1. amicable, bountiful, cordial, friendly, generous, genial, gracious, kind, liberal, sociable, welcoming **2**. accessible, amenable, open-minded, receptive, responsive, tolerant

hospitality cheer, conviviality, cordiality, friendliness, heartiness, hospitableness, neighbourliness, sociability, warmth, welcome

host[1] *n*. **1**. entertainer, innkeeper, landlord, master of ceremonies, proprietor **2**. anchor man, compere (*Brit*.), presenter ∼*v*. **3**. compere (*Brit*.), introduce, present

host[2] army, array, drove, horde, legion, multitude, myriad, swarm, throng

hostage captive, gage, pawn, pledge, prisoner, security, surety

hostile 1. antagonistic, anti (*Inf*.), bellicose, belligerent, contrary, ill-disposed, inimical, malevolent, opposed, opposite, rancorous, unkind, warlike **2**. adverse, alien, inhospitable, unfriendly, unpropitious, unsympathetic, unwelcoming

hostilities conflict, fighting, state of war, war, warfare

hostility abhorrence, animosity, animus, antagonism, antipathy, aversion, detestation, enmity, hatred, ill will, malevolence, malice, opposition, resentment, unfriendliness

hot 1. blistering, boiling, burning, fiery, flaming, heated, piping hot, roasting, scalding, scorching, searing, steaming, sultry, sweltering, torrid, warm **2**. acrid, biting, peppery, piquant, pungent, sharp, spicy **3**. *Fig*. animated, ardent, excited, fervent, fervid, fierce, fiery, impetuous, inflamed, intense, irascible, lustful, passionate, raging, stormy, touchy, vehement, violent **4**. fresh, just out, latest, new, recent, up to the minute **5**. approved, favoured, in demand, in vogue, popular, sought-after **6**. close, following closely, in hot pursuit, near

hot air blather, blether, bombast, bosh (*Inf*.), bunkum, claptrap (*Inf*.), empty talk, gas (*Sl*.), guff (*Sl*.), rant, tall talk (*Inf*.), verbiage, wind

hotbed breeding ground, den, forcing house, nest, nursery, seedbed

hot-blooded ardent, excitable, fervent, fiery, heated, impulsive, passionate, rash, spirited, temperamental, wild

hotchpotch conglomeration, farrago, gallimaufry, hash, jumble, medley, *mélange*, mess, miscellany, mishmash, mixture, olio, olla podrida, potpourri

hotfoot hastily, helter-skelter, hurriedly, pell-mell, posthaste, quickly, speedily

hothead daredevil, desperado, hotspur, madcap, tearaway

hot-headed fiery, foolhardy, hasty, hot-tempered, impetuous, precipitate, quick-tempered, rash, reckless, unruly, volatile

hothouse 1. *n*. conservatory, glasshouse, greenhouse **2**. *adj*. coddled, dainty, delicate, exotic, fragile, frail, overprotected, pampered, sensitive

hound *v*. **1**. chase, drive, give chase, hunt, hunt down, pursue **2**. badger, goad, harass, harry, impel, persecute, pester, prod, provoke

house *n*. **1**. abode, building, domicile, dwelling, edifice, habitation, home, homestead, residence **2**. family, household, ménage **3**. ancestry, clan, dynasty, family tree, kindred, line, lineage, race, tribe **4**. business, company, concern, establishment, firm, organization, outfit (*Inf*.), partnership **5**. Commons, legislative body, parliament **6**. hotel, inn, public house, tavern **7**. **on the house** for nothing, free, gratis, without expense ∼*v*. **8**. accommodate, billet, board, domicile, harbour, lodge, put up, quarter, take in **9**. contain, cover, keep, protect, sheathe, shelter, store

household 1. *n*. family, home, house, ménage **2**. *adj*. domestic, domiciliary, family, ordinary, plain

householder homeowner, occupant, resident, tenant

housekeeping home economy, homemaking (*U.S*.), housecraft, household management, housewifery

housing 1. accommodation, dwellings, homes, houses **2**. case, casing, container, cover, covering, enclosure, sheath

hovel cabin, den, hole, hut, shack, shanty, shed

hover 1. be suspended, drift, float, flutter, fly, hang, poise **2**. hang about, linger, wait nearby **3**. alternate, dither, falter, fluctuate, haver (*Brit*.), oscillate, pause, seesaw, swither (*Scot. dialect*), vacillate, waver

however after all, anyhow, be that as it may, but, nevertheless, nonetheless, notwithstanding, on the other hand, still, though, yet

howl 1. *n*. bay, bellow, clamour, cry, groan, hoot, outcry, roar, scream, shriek, ululation, wail, yelp, yowl **2.** *v.* bellow, cry, cry out, lament, quest (*used of hounds*), roar, scream, shout, shriek, ululate, wail, weep, yell, yelp

howler bloomer (*Brit. inf.*), blunder, boner (*Sl.*), bull (*Sl.*), clanger (*Inf.*), error, malapropism, mistake, schoolboy howler

hoyden, hoiden romp (*Archaic*), tomboy

hoydenish, hoidenish boisterous, bold, ill-mannered, inelegant, rackety, uncouth, unfeminine, ungenteel, unladylike, unruly

hub centre, core, focal point, focus, heart, middle, nerve centre, pivot

hubbub babel, bedlam, brouhaha, clamour, confusion, din, disorder, disturbance, hue and cry, hullabaloo, hurly-burly, noise, pandemonium, racket, riot, ruckus (*Inf.*), ruction (*Inf.*), rumpus, tumult, uproar

huckster barker (*Inf.*), hawker, pedlar, pitchman (*U.S.*), salesman, vendor

huddle *n.* **1.** confusion, crowd, disorder, heap, jumble, mass, mess, muddle **2.** *Inf.* confab (*Inf.*), conference, discussion, meeting ~*v.* **3.** cluster, converge, crowd, flock, gather, press, throng **4.** crouch, cuddle, curl up, hunch up, make oneself small, nestle, snuggle

hue **1.** colour, dye, shade, tincture, tinge, tint, tone **2.** aspect, cast, complexion, light

hue and cry brouhaha, clamour, furore, hullabaloo, much ado, outcry, ruction (*Inf.*), rumpus, uproar

huff *n.* **1.** anger, bad mood, miff (*Inf.*), passion, pet, pique, rage, temper **2. in a huff** angered, annoyed, exasperated, hurt, in high dudgeon, irked, miffed (*Inf.*), nettled, peeved, piqued, provoked, put out (*Inf.*), riled (*Inf.*), vexed ~*v.* **3.** blow, exhale, puff

huffish, huffy angry, crabbed, cross, crotchety (*Inf.*), crusty, curt, disgruntled, grumpy, irritable, moody, moping, offended, peevish, pettish, petulant, querulous, resentful, shirty (*Sl., chiefly Brit.*), short, snappy, sulky, sullen, surly, testy, touchy, waspish

hug *v.* **1.** clasp, cuddle, embrace, enfold, hold close, squeeze, take in one's arms **2.** cling to, follow closely, keep close, stay near **3.** cherish, cling, hold onto, nurse, retain ~*n.* **4.** bear hug, clasp, clinch (*Sl.*), embrace, squeeze

huge Brobdingnagian, bulky, colossal, enormous, extensive, gargantuan, giant, gigantic, great, immense, jumbo (*Inf.*), large, mammoth, massive, monumental, mountainous, prodigious, stupendous, titanic, tremendous, vast

huggermugger confusion, disarray, disorder, disorganization, guddle (*Scot.*), huddle, jumble, mess, muddle, shambles

hulk **1.** derelict, frame, hull, shell, shipwreck, wreck **2.** lout, lubber, lump (*Inf.*), oaf

hulking awkward, bulky, clumsy, cumbersome, gross, lubberly, lumbering, lumpish, massive, oafish, overgrown, ponderous, ungainly, unwieldy

hull *n.* **1.** body, casing, covering, frame, framework, skeleton **2.** husk, peel, pod, rind, shell, shuck, skin ~*v.* **3.** husk, peel, shell, shuck, skin, trim

hullabaloo babel, bedlam, brouhaha, clamour, commotion, confusion, din, disturbance, furore, hubbub, hue and cry, hurly-burly, noise, outcry, pandemonium, racket, ruckus (*Inf.*), ruction (*Inf.*), rumpus, to-do, tumult, turmoil, uproar

hum **1.** bombinate *or* bombilate (*Literary*), buzz, croon, drone, mumble, murmur, purr, sing, throb, thrum, vibrate, whir **2.** be active, be busy, bustle, buzz, move, pulsate, pulse, stir, vibrate

human *adj.* **1.** anthropoid, fleshly, manlike, mortal **2.** approachable, compassionate, considerate, fallible, forgivable, humane, kind, kindly, natural, understandable, understanding, vulnerable ~*n.* **3.** body, child, creature, human being, individual, man, mortal, person, soul, wight (*Archaic*), woman

humane benevolent, benign, charitable, clement, compassionate, forbearing, forgiving, gentle, good, good-natured, kind, kind-hearted, kindly, lenient, merciful, mild, sympathetic, tender, understanding

humanitarian **1.** *adj.* altruistic, beneficent, benevolent, charitable, compassionate, humane, philanthropic, public-spirited **2.** *n.* altruist, benefactor, Good Samaritan, philanthropist

humanitarianism beneficence, benevolence, charity, generosity, good will, humanism, philanthropy

humanities classical studies, classics, liberal arts, literae humaniores

humanity **1.** flesh, Homo sapiens,

humankind, human race, man, mankind, men, mortality, people **2.** human nature, humanness, mortality **3.** benevolence, benignity, brotherly love, charity, compassion, fellow feeling, kind-heartedness, kindness, mercy, philanthropy, sympathy, tenderness, tolerance, understanding

humanize civilize, cultivate, educate, enlighten, improve, mellow, polish, reclaim, refine, soften, tame

humble *adj.* **1.** meek, modest, self-effacing, submissive, unassuming, unostentatious, unpretentious **2.** common, commonplace, insignificant, low, low-born, lowly, mean, modest, obscure, ordinary, plebeian, poor, simple, undistinguished, unimportant, unpretentious **3.** courteous, deferential, obliging, obsequious, polite, respectful, servile, subservient ~*v.* **4.** abase, abash, break, bring down, chagrin, chasten, crush, debase, degrade, demean, disgrace, humiliate, lower, mortify, put down (*Sl.*), reduce, shame, sink, subdue, take down a peg (*Inf.*) **5. humble oneself** abase oneself, eat crow (*U.S. inf.*), eat humble pie, go on bended knee, grovel, swallow one's pride

humbly cap in hand, deferentially, diffidently, meekly, modestly, obsequiously, on bended knee, respectfully, servilely, submissively, subserviently, unassumingly

humbug *n.* **1.** bluff, cheat, deceit, deception, dodge, feint, fraud, hoax, imposition, imposture, ruse, sham, swindle, trick, trickery, wile **2.** charlatan, cheat, con man (*Sl.*), faker, fraud, impostor, phoney (*Sl.*), quack, swindler, trickster **3.** baloney (*Inf.*), cant, charlatanry, claptrap (*Inf.*), eyewash (*Inf.*), gammon (*Brit. inf.*), hypocrisy, nonsense, quackery, rubbish ~*v.* **4.** bamboozle (*Inf.*), befool, beguile, cheat, cozen, deceive, delude, dupe, fool, gull (*Archaic*), hoax, hoodwink, impose, mislead, swindle, take in (*Inf.*), trick

humdrum boring, commonplace, dreary, dull, monotonous, mundane, ordinary, repetitious, routine, tedious, tiresome, uneventful, uninteresting, unvaried, wearisome

humid clammy, damp, dank, moist, muggy, steamy, sticky, sultry, watery, wet

humidity clamminess, damp, damp-ness, dankness, dew, humidness, moistness, moisture, mugginess, sogginess, wetness

humiliate abase, abash, bring low, chagrin, chasten, crush, debase, degrade, discomfit, disgrace, embarrass, humble, make (someone) eat humble pie, mortify, put down (*Sl.*), shame, subdue, take down a peg (*Inf.*)

humiliating crushing, degrading, disgracing, embarrassing, humbling, ignominious, mortifying, shaming

humiliation abasement, affront, chagrin, condescension, degradation, disgrace, dishonour, embarrassment, humbling, ignominy, indignity, loss of face, mortification, put-down, resignation, self-abasement, shame, submission, submissiveness

humility diffidence, humbleness, lack of pride, lowliness, meekness, modesty, self-abasement, servility, submissiveness, unpretentiousness

hummock hillock, hump, knoll, mound

humorist comedian, comic, droll, eccentric, funny man, jester, joker, wag, wit

humorous amusing, comic, comical, entertaining, facetious, farcical, funny, hilarious, jocose, jocular, laughable, ludicrous, merry, playful, pleasant, side-splitting, waggish, whimsical, witty

humour *n.* **1.** amusement, comedy, drollery, facetiousness, fun, funniness, jocularity, ludicrousness, wit **2.** comedy, farce, gags (*Sl.*), jesting, jests, jokes, joking, pleasantry, wisecracks (*Inf.*), wit, witticisms, wittiness **3.** disposition, frame of mind, mood, spirits, temper **4.** bent, bias, fancy, freak, mood, propensity, quirk, vagary, whim ~*v.* **5.** accommodate, cosset, favour, flatter, go along with, gratify, indulge, mollify, pamper, spoil

hump *n.* **1.** bulge, bump, knob, mound, projection, protrusion, protuberance, swelling **2. the hump** *Brit. inf.* megrims (*Rare*), the blues, the doldrums, the dumps (*Inf.*), the grumps (*Inf.*), the mopes, the sulks ~*v.* **3.** arch, curve, form a hump, hunch, lift, tense **4.** *Sl.* carry, heave, hoist, lug, shoulder

hunch **1.** *n.* feeling, idea, impression, inkling, intuition, premonition, presentiment, suspicion **2.** *v.* arch, bend, crouch, curve, draw in, huddle, hump, squat, stoop, tense

hunchback crookback (*Rare*), crouchback (*Archaic*), humpback, kyphosis (*Pathol.*), Quasimodo

hunchbacked gibbous, humpbacked, humped, malformed, misshapen, stooped

hunger n. **1.** appetite, emptiness, esurience, famine, hungriness, ravenousness, starvation, voracity **2.** appetence, appetite, craving, desire, greediness, itch, lust, yearning, yen (*Inf.*) ~v. **3.** crave, desire, hanker, itch, long, pine, starve, thirst, want, wish, yearn

hungry 1. empty, famished, famishing, hollow, peckish (*Inf., chiefly Brit.*), ravenous, sharp-set, starved, starving, voracious **2.** athirst, avid, covetous, craving, desirous, eager, greedy, keen, yearning

hunk block, chunk, gobbet, lump, mass, piece, slab, wedge, wodge (*Brit. inf.*)

hunt v. **1.** chase, gun for, hound, pursue, stalk, track, trail **2.** ferret about, forage, go in quest of, look, look high and low, rummage through, scour, search, seek, try to find ~n. **3.** chase, hunting, investigation, pursuit, quest, search

hunted careworn, desperate, distraught, gaunt, haggard, harassed, harried, persecuted, stricken, terror-stricken, tormented, worn

hurdle n. **1.** barricade, barrier, fence, hedge, wall **2.** barrier, complication, difficulty, handicap, hindrance, impediment, obstacle, obstruction, snag, stumbling block

hurl cast, chuck (*Inf.*), fire, fling, heave, launch, let fly, pitch, project, propel, send, shy, sling, throw, toss

hurly-burly bedlam, brouhaha, chaos, commotion, confusion, disorder, furore, hubbub, pandemonium, tumult, turbulence, turmoil, uproar

hurricane cyclone, gale, storm, tempest, tornado, twister (*U.S. inf.*), typhoon, willy-willy (*Aust.*), windstorm

hurried breakneck, brief, cursory, hasty, hectic, perfunctory, precipitate, quick, rushed, short, slapdash, speedy, superficial, swift

hurry v. **1.** dash, fly, get a move on (*Inf.*), lose no time, make haste, rush, scoot, scurry, step on it (*Inf.*) **2.** accelerate, expedite, goad, hasten, hustle, push

on, quicken, speed (up), urge ~n. **3.** bustle, celerity, commotion, dispatch, expedition, flurry, haste, precipitation, promptitude, quickness, rush, speed, urgency

hurt v. **1.** bruise, damage, disable, harm, impair, injure, mar, spoil, wound **2.** ache, be sore, be tender, burn, pain, smart, sting, throb **3.** afflict, aggrieve, annoy, cut to the quick, distress, grieve, pain, sadden, sting, upset, wound ~n. **4.** discomfort, distress, pain, pang, soreness, suffering **5.** bruise, sore, wound **6.** damage, detriment, disadvantage, harm, injury, loss, mischief, wrong ~adj. **7.** bruised, cut, damaged, grazed, harmed, injured, scarred, scraped, scratched, wounded **8.** aggrieved, crushed, injured, miffed (*Inf.*), offended, pained, piqued, rueful, sad, wounded

hurtful cruel, cutting, damaging, destructive, detrimental, disadvantageous, distressing, harmful, injurious, malicious, mean, mischievous, nasty, pernicious, prejudicial, spiteful, unkind, upsetting, wounding

hurtle charge, crash, fly, go hell for leather (*Inf.*), plunge, race, rush, rush headlong, scoot, scramble, shoot, speed, spurt, tear

husband v. budget, conserve, economize, hoard, manage thriftily, save, store, use sparingly

husbandry 1. agriculture, agronomy, cultivation, farming, land management, tillage **2.** careful management, economy, frugality, good housekeeping, thrift

hush v. **1.** mute, muzzle, quieten, shush, silence, still, suppress **2.** allay, appease, calm, compose, mollify, soothe ~n. **3.** calm, peace, peacefulness, quiet, silence, still (*Poetic*), stillness, tranquillity

hush-hush classified, confidential, restricted, secret, top-secret

hush up conceal, cover up, keep dark, keep secret, sit on (*Inf.*), smother, squash, suppress

husk bark, chaff, covering, glume, hull, rind, shuck

huskiness dryness, harshness, hoarseness, raspingness, roughness

husky 1. croaking, croaky, gruff, guttural, harsh, hoarse, rasping, raucous, rough, throaty **2.** *Inf.* beefy (*Inf.*), brawny, burly, hefty, muscular, powerful, rugged, stocky, strapping, thickset

hussy baggage (*Inf.*, *old-fashioned*), floozy (*Sl.*), jade, minx, quean (*Archaic*), scrubber (*Brit. sl.*), slut, strumpet, tart (*Inf.*), tramp (*Sl.*), trollop, wanton, wench (*Archaic*)

hustle bustle, crowd, elbow, force, haste, hasten, hurry, impel, jog, jostle, push, rush, shove, thrust

hut cabin, den, hovel, lean-to, refuge, shanty, shed, shelter

hybrid *n.* amalgam, composite, compound, cross, crossbreed, half-blood, half-breed, mixture, mongrel, mule

hygiene cleanliness, hygienics, sanitary measures, sanitation

hygienic aseptic, clean, disinfected, germ-free, healthy, pure, salutary, sanitary, sterile

hype ballyhoo (*Inf.*), brouhaha, build-up, plugging (*Inf.*), publicity, puffing, racket, razzmatazz (*Sl.*)

hyperbole amplification, enlargement, exaggeration, magnification, overstatement

hypercritical captious, carping, cavilling, censorious, fault-finding, finicky, fussy, hairsplitting, niggling, overcritical, overexacting, overscrupulous, pernickety (*Inf.*), strict

hypnotic mesmeric, mesmerizing, narcotic, opiate, sleep-inducing, somniferous, soothing, soporific, spellbinding

hypnotize 1. mesmerize, put in a trance, put to sleep 2. entrance, fascinate, magnetize, spellbind

hypochondria hypochondriasis, valetudinarianism

hypochondriac *adj./n.* valetudinarian

hypocrisy cant, deceit, deceitfulness, deception, dissembling, duplicity, falsity, imposture, insincerity, pharisaism, phariseeism, phoneyness (*Sl.*), pretence, sanctimoniousness, speciousness, two-facedness

hypocrite charlatan, deceiver, dissembler, fraud, Holy Willie, impostor, Pecksniff, pharisee, phoney (*Sl.*), pretender, Tartuffe, whited sepulchre

hypocritical canting, deceitful, deceptive, dissembling, duplicitous, false, fraudulent, hollow, insincere, Janus-faced, pharisaical, phoney (*Sl.*), sanctimonious, specious, spurious, two-faced

hypothesis assumption, postulate, premise, premiss, proposition, supposition, theory, thesis

hypothetical academic, assumed, conjectural, imaginary, putative, speculative, supposed, theoretical

hysteria agitation, delirium, frenzy, hysterics, madness, panic, unreason

hysterical 1. berserk, beside oneself, convulsive, crazed, distracted, distraught, frantic, frenzied, mad, overwrought, raving, uncontrollable 2. *Inf.* comical, farcical, hilarious, screaming, side-splitting, uproarious, wildly funny

I

ice 1. break the ice begin, initiate the proceedings, kick off (*Inf.*), lead the way, make a start, start *or* set the ball rolling (*Inf.*), take the plunge (*Inf.*) **2. on thin ice** at risk, in jeopardy, open to attack, out on a limb, sticking one's neck out (*Inf.*), unsafe, vulnerable

ice-cold arctic, biting, bitter, chilled to the bone *or* marrow, freezing, frozen, glacial, icy, raw, refrigerated, shivering

iconoclast critic, dissident, heretic, radical, rebel

iconoclastic denunciatory, dissentient, impious, innovative, irreverent, questioning, radical, rebellious, subversive

icy 1. arctic, biting, bitter, chill, chilling, chilly, cold, freezing, frost-bound, frosty, frozen over, ice-cold, raw **2.** glacial, glassy, like a sheet of glass, rimy, slippery, slippy (*Inf.*) **3.** *Fig.* aloof, cold, distant, forbidding, frigid, frosty, glacial, hostile, indifferent, steely, stony, unfriendly, unwelcoming

idea 1. abstraction, concept, conception, conclusion, fancy, impression, judgment, perception, thought, understanding **2.** belief, conviction, doctrine, interpretation, notion, opinion, teaching, view, viewpoint **3.** approximation, clue, estimate, guess, hint, impression, inkling, intimation, notion, suspicion **4.** aim, end, import, intention, meaning, object, objective, plan, purpose, *raison d'être*, reason, sense, significance **5.** design, hypothesis, plan, recommendation, scheme, solution, suggestion, theory **6.** archetype, essence, form, pattern

ideal *n.* **1.** archetype, criterion, epitome, example, exemplar, last word, model, nonpareil, paradigm, paragon, pattern, perfection, prototype, standard, standard of perfection **2.** *Often plural* moral value, principle, standard ~*adj.* **3.** archetypal, classic, complete, consummate, model, optimal, perfect, quintessential, supreme **4.** abstract, conceptual, hypothetical, intellectual, mental, theoretical, transcendental **5.** fanciful, imaginary, impractical, ivory-tower, unattainable, unreal, Utopian, visionary

idealist *n.* romantic, Utopian, visionary

idealistic impracticable, optimistic, perfectionist, quixotic, romantic, starry-eyed, Utopian, visionary

idealization ennoblement, exaltation, glorification, magnification, worship

idealize apotheosize, deify, ennoble, exalt, glorify, magnify, put on a pedestal, romanticize, worship

ideally all things being equal, if one had one's way, in a perfect world, under the best of circumstances

idée fixe bee in one's bonnet, fixation, fixed idea, hobbyhorse, monomania, obsession, one-track mind (*Inf.*), preoccupation, thing (*Inf.*)

identical alike, corresponding, duplicate, equal, equivalent, indistinguishable, interchangeable, like, matching, selfsame, the same, twin

identifiable ascertainable, detectable, discernible, distinguishable, known, noticeable, recognizable, unmistakable

identification 1. cataloguing, classifying, establishment of identity, labelling, naming, pinpointing, recognition **2.** association, connection, empathy, fellow feeling, involvement, rapport, relationship, sympathy **3.** credentials, ID, letters of introduction, papers

identify 1. catalogue, classify, diagnose, label, make out, name, pick out, pinpoint, place, put one's finger on (*Inf.*), recognize, single out, spot, tag **2.** *Often with* **with** ally, associate, empathize, feel for, put in the same category, put oneself in the place *or* shoes of, relate to, respond to, see through another's eyes, think of in connection (with)

identity 1. distinctiveness, existence, individuality, oneness, particularity, personality, self, selfhood, singularity, uniqueness **2.** accord, correspondence, empathy, rapport, sameness, unanimity, unity

ideology articles of faith, belief(s), creed, dogma, ideas, philosophy, principles, tenets, *Weltanschauung*, world view

idiocy abject stupidity, asininity, fatuity, fatuousness, foolishness, imbecility, inanity, insanity, lunacy, senselessness, tomfoolery

idiom 1. expression, locution, phrase, set phrase, turn of phrase **2**. jargon, language, mode of expression, parlance, style, talk, usage, vernacular

idiomatic dialectal, native, vernacular

idiosyncrasy affectation, characteristic, eccentricity, habit, mannerism, oddity, peculiarity, personal trait, quirk, singularity, trick

idiosyncratic distinctive, individual, individualistic, peculiar

idiot ass, blockhead, booby, cretin, dimwit (*Inf.*), dunderhead, fool, halfwit, imbecile, mooncalf, moron, nincompoop, nitwit, simpleton

idiotic asinine, crazy, daft (*Inf.*), dumb (*Inf.*), fatuous, foolhardy, foolish, halfwitted, harebrained, imbecile, imbecilic, inane, insane, lunatic, moronic, senseless, stupid, unintelligent

idle *adj.* **1**. dead, empty, gathering dust, inactive, jobless, mothballed, out of action *or* operation, out of work, redundant, stationary, ticking over, unemployed, unoccupied, unused, vacant **2**. indolent, lackadaisical, lazy, shiftless, slothful, sluggish **3**. frivolous, insignificant, irrelevant, nugatory, superficial, trivial, unhelpful, unnecessary **4**. abortive, bootless, fruitless, futile, groundless, ineffective, of no avail, otiose, pointless, unavailing, unproductive, unsuccessful, useless, vain, worthless ~*v*. **5**. *Often followed by* **away** dally, dawdle, fool, fritter, kill time, laze, loiter, lounge, potter, waste, while **6**. coast, drift, mark time, shirk, sit back and do nothing, skive (*Brit. sl.*), slack, slow down, take it easy (*Inf.*), vegetate

idleness 1. inaction, inactivity, leisure, time on one's hands, unemployment **2**. hibernation, inertia, laziness, shiftlessness, sloth, sluggishness, torpor, vegetating **3**. dilly-dallying (*Inf.*), lazing, loafing, pottering, skiving (*Brit. sl.*), time-wasting, trifling

idler clock-watcher, dawdler, deadbeat (*Inf.*), dodger, drone, laggard, layabout, lazybones, loafer, lounger, malingerer, shirker, slacker, sloth, slouch (*Inf.*), slugabed, sluggard, time-waster, Weary Willie (*Inf.*)

idling *adj.* dawdling, drifting, loafing, pottering, resting, resting on one's oars,

taking it easy (*Inf.*), ticking over

idol 1. deity, god, graven image, image, pagan symbol **2**. *Fig.* beloved, darling, favourite, hero, pet, pin-up (*Sl.*), superstar

idolater 1. heathen, idol-worshipper, pagan **2**. admirer, adorer, devotee, idolizer, votary, worshipper

idolatrous adoring, adulatory, reverential, uncritical, worshipful

idolatry adoration, adulation, apotheosis, deification, exaltation, glorification, hero worship, idolizing

idolize admire, adore, apotheosize, bow down before, deify, dote upon, exalt, glorify, hero-worship, look up to, love, revere, reverence, venerate, worship, worship to excess

idyllic arcadian, charming, halcyon, heavenly, ideal, idealized, out of this world, pastoral, peaceful, picturesque, rustic, unspoiled

if 1. *conj*. admitting, allowing, assuming, granting, in case, on condition that, on the assumption that, provided, providing, supposing, though, whenever, wherever, whether **2**. *n*. condition, doubt, hesitation, stipulation, uncertainty

iffy chancy (*Inf.*), conditional, doubtful, in the lap of the gods, problematical, uncertain, undecided, unpredictable, up in the air

ignis fatuus bubble, chimera, delusion, illusion, mirage, phantasm, self-deception, will-o'-the-wisp

ignite burn, burst into flames, catch fire, fire, flare up, inflame, kindle, light, put a match to (*Inf.*), set alight, set fire to, take fire, touch off

ignoble 1. abject, base, contemptible, craven, dastardly, degenerate, degraded, despicable, disgraceful, dishonourable, heinous, infamous, low, mean, petty, shabby, shameless, unworthy, vile, wretched **2**. baseborn (*Archaic*), common, humble, lowborn (*Rare*), lowly, mean, of humble birth, peasant, plebeian, vulgar

ignominious abject, despicable, discreditable, disgraceful, dishonourable, disreputable, humiliating, indecorous, inglorious, mortifying, scandalous, shameful, sorry, undignified

ignominy bad odour, contempt, discredit, disgrace, dishonour, disrepute, humiliation, infamy, mortification, obloquy, odium, opprobrium, reproach, shame, stigma

ignoramus ass, blockhead, bonehead (*Sl.*), dolt, donkey, duffer (*Inf.*), dullard, dunce, fool, illiterate, lowbrow, numskull, simpleton

ignorance 1. greenness, inexperience, innocence, nescience (*Literary*), oblivion, unawareness, unconsciousness, unfamiliarity **2.** benightedness, blindness, illiteracy, lack of education, mental darkness, unenlightenment, unintelligence

ignorant 1. benighted, blind to, inexperienced, innocent, in the dark about, oblivious, unaware, unconscious, unenlightened, uninformed, uninitiated, unknowing, unschooled, unwitting **2.** green, illiterate, naive, unaware, uncultivated, uneducated, unknowledgeable, unlearned, unlettered, unread, untaught, untrained, untutored **3.** crass, crude, gross, half-baked (*Inf.*), insensitive, rude, shallow, superficial, uncomprehending, unscholarly

ignore be oblivious to, bury one's head in the sand, cold-shoulder, cut (*Inf.*), disregard, give the cold shoulder to, neglect, overlook, pass over, pay no attention to, reject, send (someone) to Coventry, shut one's eyes to, take no notice of, turn a blind eye to, turn a deaf ear to, turn one's back on

ilk brand, breed, character, class, description, disposition, kidney, kind, sort, stamp, style, type, variety

ill *adj.* **1.** ailing, dicky (*Sl.*), diseased, funny (*Inf.*), indisposed, infirm, laid up (*Inf.*), not up to snuff (*Inf.*), off-colour, on the sick list (*Inf.*), out of sorts (*Inf.*), poorly (*Inf.*), queasy, queer, seedy (*Inf.*), sick, under the weather (*Inf.*), unhealthy, unwell, valetudinarian **2.** bad, damaging, deleterious, detrimental, evil, foul, harmful, iniquitous, injurious, ruinous, unfortunate, unlucky, vile, wicked, wrong **3.** acrimonious, adverse, antagonistic, cantankerous, cross, harsh, hateful, hostile, hurtful, inimical, malevolent, malicious, sullen, surly, unfriendly, unkind **4.** disturbing, foreboding, inauspicious, ominous, sinister, threatening, unfavourable, unhealthy, unlucky, unpromising, unpropitious, unwholesome ~*n.* **5.** affliction, harm, hurt, injury, misery, misfortune, pain, trial, tribulation, trouble, unpleasantness, woe **6.** ailment, complaint, disease, disorder, illness, in-

disposition, infirmity, malady, malaise, sickness **7.** abuse, badness, cruelty, damage, depravity, destruction, evil, ill usage, malice, mischief, suffering, wickedness ~*adv.* **8.** badly, hard, inauspiciously, poorly, unfavourably, unfortunately, unluckily **9.** barely, by no means, hardly, insufficiently, scantily **10.** *As in* **ill-gotten** criminally, dishonestly, foully, fraudulently, illegally, illegitimately, illicitly, unlawfully, unscrupulously

ill-advised foolhardy, foolish, ill-considered, ill-judged, impolitic, imprudent, inappropriate, incautious, indiscreet, injudicious, misguided, overhasty, rash, reckless, short-sighted, thoughtless, unseemly, unwise, wrong-headed

ill-assorted incompatible, incongruous, inharmonious, mismatched, uncongenial, unsuited

ill at ease anxious, awkward, disquieted, disturbed, edgy, faltering, fidgety, hesitant, nervous, on edge, on pins and needles (*Inf.*), on tenterhooks, out of place, restless, self-conscious, strange, tense, uncomfortable, uneasy, unquiet, unrelaxed, unsettled, unsure

ill-bred bad-mannered, boorish, churlish, coarse, crass, discourteous, ill-mannered, impolite, indelicate, rude, uncivil, uncivilized, uncouth, ungallant, ungentlemanly, unladylike, unmannerly, unrefined, vulgar

ill-considered careless, hasty, heedless, improvident, imprudent, injudicious, overhasty, precipitate, rash, unwise

ill-defined blurred, dim, fuzzy, indistinct, nebulous, shadowy, unclear, vague, woolly

ill-disposed against, antagonistic, anti (*Inf.*), antipathetic, averse, disobliging, down on (*Inf.*), hostile, inimical, opposed, uncooperative, unfriendly, unwelcoming

illegal actionable (*Law*), banned, black-market, bootleg, criminal, felonious, forbidden, illicit, lawless, outlawed, prohibited, proscribed, unauthorized, unconstitutional, under the counter, unlawful, unlicensed, unofficial, wrongful

illegality crime, criminality, felony, illegitimacy, illicitness, lawlessness, unlawfulness, wrong, wrongness

illegible crabbed, faint, hard to make out, hieroglyphic, indecipherable, obscure, scrawled, undecipherable, unreadable

illegitimacy 1. illegality, illicitness, irregularity, unconstitutionality, unlawfulness **2.** bastardism, bastardy

illegitimate 1. illegal, illicit, improper, unauthorized, unconstitutional, unlawful, unsanctioned **2.** baseborn (*Archaic*), bastard, born on the wrong side of the blanket, born out of wedlock, fatherless, misbegotten (*Literary*), natural, spurious (*Rare*) **3.** illogical, incorrect, invalid, spurious, unsound

ill-fated blighted, doomed, hapless, ill-omened, ill-starred, luckless, star-crossed, unfortunate, unhappy, unlucky

ill-favoured hideous, plain, repulsive, ugly, unattractive, unlovely, unprepossessing, unsightly

ill feeling animosity, animus, antagonism, bad blood, bitterness, disgruntlement, dissatisfaction, dudgeon (*Archaic*), enmity, frustration, hard feelings, hostility, ill will, indignation, offence, rancour, resentment

ill-founded baseless, empty, groundless, idle, unjustified, unproven, unreliable, unsubstantiated, unsupported

ill humour (bad) mood, (bad) temper, crabbiness, crossness, disagreeableness, grumpiness, irascibility, irritability, moodiness, moroseness, petulance, pique, sharpness, spleen, sulkiness, sulks, tartness, testiness

ill-humoured acrimonious, bad-tempered, crabbed, crabby, cross, disagreeable, grumpy, huffy, impatient, irascible, irritable, like a bear with a sore head (*Inf.*), mardy (*Dialect*), moody, morose, out of sorts, out of temper, petulant, sharp, snappish, snappy, sulky, sullen, tart, testy, thin-skinned, touchy, waspish

illiberal 1. bigoted, hidebound, intolerant, narrow-minded, prejudiced, reactionary, small-minded, uncharitable, ungenerous **2.** close-fisted, mean, miserly, niggardly, parsimonious, selfish, sordid, stingy, tight, tightfisted, ungenerous

illicit 1. black-market, bootleg, contraband, criminal, felonious, illegal, illegitimate, prohibited, unauthorized, unlawful, unlicensed **2.** clandestine, forbidden, furtive, guilty, immoral, improper, wrong

illimitable boundless, eternal, immeasurable, immense, infinite, limitless, unbounded, unending, unlimited, vast, without end

illiteracy benightedness, ignorance, illiterateness, lack of education

illiterate benighted, ignorant, uncultured, uneducated, unlettered, untaught, untutored

ill-judged foolish, ill-advised, ill-considered, injudicious, misguided, overhasty, rash, short-sighted, unwise, wrong-headed

ill-mannered badly behaved, boorish, churlish, coarse, discourteous, ill-behaved, ill-bred, impolite, insolent, loutish, rude, uncivil, uncouth, unmannerly

ill-natured bad-tempered, catty (*Inf.*), churlish, crabbed, cross, cross-grained, disagreeable, disobliging, malevolent, malicious, mean, nasty, perverse, petulant, spiteful, sulky, sullen, surly, unfriendly, unkind, unpleasant

illness affliction, ailment, attack, complaint, disability, disease, disorder, ill health, indisposition, infirmity, malady, malaise, poor health, sickness

illogical absurd, fallacious, faulty, inconclusive, inconsistent, incorrect, invalid, irrational, meaningless, senseless, sophistical, specious, spurious, unreasonable, unscientific, unsound

ill-starred doomed, ill-fated, ill-omened, inauspicious, star-crossed, unfortunate, unhappy, unlucky

ill temper annoyance, bad temper, crossness, curtness, impatience, irascibility, irritability, petulance, sharpness, spitefulness, tetchiness

ill-tempered annoyed, bad-tempered, choleric, cross, curt, grumpy, ill-humoured, impatient, irascible, irritable, sharp, spiteful, testy, tetchy, touchy

ill-timed awkward, inappropriate, inconvenient, inept, inopportune, unseasonable, untimely, unwelcome

ill-treat abuse, damage, handle roughly, harass, harm, harry, ill-use, injure, knock about, maltreat, mishandle, misuse, oppress, wrong

ill-treatment abuse, damage, harm, ill-use, injury, mistreatment, misuse, rough handling

illuminate 1. brighten, illumine (*Literary*), irradiate, light, light up **2.** clarify, clear up, elucidate, enlighten, explain, give insight into, instruct, make clear, shed light on **3.** adorn, decorate, illustrate, ornament

illuminating enlightening, explanatory, helpful, informative, instructive, revealing

illumination 1. beam, brightening, brightness, light, lighting, lighting up, lights, radiance, ray **2.** awareness, clarification, edification, enlightenment, insight, inspiration, instruction, perception, revelation, understanding

illuminations decorations, fairy lights, lights

illusion 1. chimera, daydream, fantasy, figment of the imagination, hallucination, ignis fatuus, mirage, mockery, phantasm, semblance, will-o'-the-wisp **2.** deception, delusion, error, fallacy, false impression, fancy, misapprehension, misconception

illusory *or* **illusive** apparent, Barmecide, beguiling, chimerical, deceitful, deceptive, delusive, fallacious, false, hallucinatory, misleading, mistaken, seeming, sham, unreal, untrue

illustrate 1. bring home, clarify, demonstrate, elucidate, emphasize, exemplify, exhibit, explain, instance, interpret, make clear, make plain, point up, show **2.** adorn, decorate, depict, draw, ornament, picture, sketch

illustrated decorated, embellished, graphic, illuminated, pictorial, picture, pictured, with illustrations

illustration 1. analogy, case, case in point, clarification, demonstration, elucidation, example, exemplification, explanation, instance, interpretation, specimen **2.** adornment, decoration, figure, picture, plate, sketch

illustrative delineative, descriptive, diagrammatic, explanatory, explicatory, expository, graphic, illustrational, interpretive, pictorial, representative, sample, typical

illustrious brilliant, celebrated, distinguished, eminent, exalted, famed, famous, glorious, great, noble, notable, noted, prominent, remarkable, renowned, resplendent, signal, splendid

ill will acrimony, animosity, animus, antagonism, antipathy, aversion, bad blood, dislike, enmity, envy, grudge, hard feelings, hatred, hostility, malevolence, malice, no love lost, rancour, resentment, spite, unfriendliness, venom

image 1. appearance, effigy, figure, icon, idol, likeness, picture, portrait, reflection, representation, statue **2.** chip off the old block (*Inf.*), counterpart, (dead) ringer (*Sl.*), Doppelgänger, double, facsimile, replica, similitude, spit (*Inf.*), spitting image *or* spit and image (*Inf.*) **3.** conceit, concept, conception, figure, idea, impression, mental picture, perception, trope

imaginable believable, comprehensible, conceivable, credible, likely, plausible, possible, supposable, thinkable, under the sun, within the bounds of possibility

imaginary assumed, chimerical, dreamlike, fancied, fanciful, fictional, fictitious, hallucinatory, hypothetical, ideal, illusive, illusory, imagined, invented, legendary, made-up, mythological, nonexistent, phantasmal, shadowy, supposed, suppositious, supposititious, unreal, unsubstantial, visionary

imagination 1. creativity, enterprise, fancy, ingenuity, insight, inspiration, invention, inventiveness, originality, resourcefulness, vision, wit, wittiness **2.** chimera, conception, idea, ideality, illusion, image, invention, notion, supposition, unreality

imaginative clever, creative, dreamy, enterprising, fanciful, fantastic, ingenious, inspired, inventive, original, poetical, visionary, vivid, whimsical

imagine 1. conceive, conceptualize, conjure up, create, devise, dream up (*Inf.*), envisage, fantasize, form a mental picture of, frame, invent, picture, plan, project, scheme, see in the mind's eye, think of, think up, visualize **2.** apprehend, assume, believe, conjecture, deduce, deem, fancy, gather, guess, infer, realize, suppose, surmise, suspect, take for granted, take it, think

imbalance bias, disproportion, inequality, lack of proportion, lopsidedness, partiality, top-heaviness, unevenness, unfairness

imbecile 1. *n.* bungler, cretin, dolt, dotard, fool, halfwit, idiot, moron, thickhead **2.** *adj.* asinine, fatuous, feebleminded, foolish, idiotic, imbecilic, inane, ludicrous, moronic, simple, stupid, thick, witless

imbecility asininity, childishness, cretinism, fatuity, foolishness, idiocy, inanity, incompetency, stupidity

imbibe 1. consume, drink, knock back

(*Inf.*), quaff, sink (*Inf.*), suck, swallow, swig (*Inf.*) 2. *Literary* absorb, acquire, assimilate, gain, gather, ingest, receive, take in

imbroglio complexity, complication, embarrassment, entanglement, involvement, misunderstanding, quandary

imbue 1. *Fig.* bathe, impregnate, inculcate, infuse, instil, permeate, pervade, saturate, steep 2. colour, dye, ingrain, stain, suffuse, tinge, tint

imitate affect, ape, burlesque, caricature, copy, counterfeit, do (*Inf.*), do an impression of, duplicate, echo, emulate, follow, follow in the footsteps of, follow suit, impersonate, mimic, mirror, mock, parody, personate, repeat, send up (*Brit. inf.*), simulate, spoof (*Inf.*), take a leaf out of (someone's) book, take off (*Inf.*), travesty

imitation *n.* 1. aping, copy, counterfeit, counterfeiting, duplication, echoing, likeness, mimicry, resemblance, simulation 2. fake, forgery, impersonation, impression, mockery, parody, reflection, replica, reproduction, sham, substitution, takeoff (*Inf.*), travesty ~*adj.* 3. artificial, dummy, ersatz, man-made, mock, phoney (*Inf.*), pseudo (*Inf.*), repro, reproduction, sham, simulated, synthetic

imitative copied, copycat (*Inf.*), copying, derivative, echoic, mimetic, mimicking, mock, onomatopoeic, parrotlike, plagiarized, pseudo (*Inf.*), put-on, secondhand, simulated, unoriginal

imitator aper, copier, copycat (*Inf.*), echo, epigone (*Rare*), follower, impersonator, impressionist, mimic, parrot, shadow

immaculate 1. clean, impeccable, neat, neat as a new pin, spick-and-span, spruce, trim, unexceptionable 2. above reproach, faultless, flawless, guiltless, incorrupt, innocent, perfect, pure, sinless, spotless, stainless, unblemished, uncontaminated, undefiled, unpolluted, unsullied, untarnished, virtuous

immanent congenital, inborn, indigenous, indwelling, inherent, innate, internal, intrinsic, mental, natural, subjective

immaterial 1. a matter of indifference, extraneous, impertinent, inapposite, inconsequential, inconsiderable, inessential, insignificant, irrelevant, of little account, of no consequence, of no im-

portance, trifling, trivial, unimportant, unnecessary 2. airy, disembodied, ethereal, ghostly, incorporeal, metaphysical, spiritual, unembodied, unsubstantial

immature 1. adolescent, crude, green, imperfect, premature, raw, undeveloped, unfinished, unfledged, unformed, unripe, unseasonable, untimely, young 2. babyish, callow, childish, inexperienced, infantile, jejune, juvenile, puerile, wet behind the ears (*Inf.*)

immaturity 1. crudeness, crudity, greenness, imperfection, rawness, unpreparedness, unripeness 2. babyishness, callowness, childishness, inexperience, juvenility, puerility

immeasurable bottomless, boundless, endless, illimitable, immense, incalculable, inestimable, inexhaustible, infinite, limitless, measureless, unbounded, unfathomable, unlimited, vast

immediate 1. instant, instantaneous 2. adjacent, close, contiguous, direct, near, nearest, next, primary, proximate, recent 3. actual, current, existing, extant, on hand, present, pressing, up to date, urgent

immediately 1. at once, before you could say Jack Robinson (*Inf.*), directly, forthwith, instantly, now, promptly, pronto (*Inf.*), right away, right now, straight away, this instant, this very minute, *tout de suite*, unhesitatingly, without delay, without hesitation 2. at first hand, closely, directly, nearly

immemorial age-old, ancient, archaic, fixed, long-standing, of yore, olden (*Archaic*), rooted, time-honoured, traditional

immense Brobdingnagian, colossal, elephantine, enormous, extensive, giant, gigantic, great, huge, illimitable, immeasurable, infinite, interminable, jumbo (*Inf.*), large, mammoth, massive, monstrous, monumental, prodigious, stupendous, titanic, tremendous, vast

immensity bulk, enormity, expanse, extent, greatness, hugeness, infinity, magnitude, massiveness, scope, size, sweep, vastness

immerse 1. bathe, dip, douse, duck, dunk, plunge, sink, submerge, submerse 2. *Fig.* absorb, busy, engage, engross, involve, occupy, take up

immersed *Fig.* absorbed, bound up, buried, busy, consumed, deep, engrossed, in a brown study, involved, mesmerized, occupied, rapt, spellbound, taken up, wrapped up

immersion 1. baptism, bathe, dip, dipping, dousing, ducking, dunking, plunging, submerging **2.** *Fig.* absorption, concentration, involvement, preoccupation

immigrant incomer, newcomer, settler

imminent at hand, brewing, close, coming, fast-approaching, forthcoming, gathering, impending, in the air, in the offing, looming, menacing, near, nigh (*Archaic*), on the horizon, on the way, threatening

immobile at a standstill, at rest, fixed, frozen, immobilized, immotile, immovable, like a statue, motionless, rigid, riveted, rooted, stable, static, stationary, stiff, still, stock-still, stolid, unmoving

immobility absence of movement, firmness, fixity, immovability, inertness, motionlessness, stability, steadiness, stillness

immobilize bring to a standstill, cripple, disable, freeze, halt, lay up (*Inf.*), paralyse, put out of action, render inoperative, stop, transfix

immoderate egregious, enormous, exaggerated, excessive, exorbitant, extravagant, extreme, inordinate, intemperate, over the odds (*Inf.*), profligate, steep (*Inf.*), uncalled-for, unconscionable, uncontrolled, undue, unjustified, unreasonable, unrestrained, unwarranted, wanton

immoderation excess, exorbitance, extravagance, intemperance, lack of restraint *or* balance, overindulgence, prodigality, unrestraint

immodest 1. bawdy, coarse, depraved, flirtatious, gross, immoral, improper, impure, indecent, indecorous, indelicate, lewd, obscene, revealing, titillating, unchaste **2.** bold, bold as brass, brassnecked (*Sl.*), brazen, forward, fresh (*Inf.*), impudent, pushy (*Inf.*), shameless, unblushing

immodesty 1. bawdiness, coarseness, impurity, indecorousness, indelicacy, lewdness, obscenity **2.** audacity, boldness, brass neck (*Sl.*), forwardness, gall (*Inf.*), impudence, shamelessness, temerity

immolate kill, sacrifice

immolation offering up, sacrifice, slaughter

immoral abandoned, bad, corrupt, debauched, degenerate, depraved, dishonest, dissolute, evil, impure, indecent, iniquitous, lewd, licentious, nefarious, obscene, of easy virtue, pornographic, profligate, reprobate, sinful, unchaste, unethical, unprincipled, vicious, vile, wicked, wrong

immorality badness, corruption, debauchery, depravity, dissoluteness, evil, iniquity, licentiousness, profligacy, sin, turpitude, vice, wickedness, wrong

immorally corruptly, degenerately, dishonestly, dissolutely, evilly, sinfully, unethically, unrighteously, wickedly

immortal *adj.* **1.** abiding, constant, death-defying, deathless, endless, enduring, eternal, everlasting, imperishable, incorruptible, indestructible, lasting, perennial, perpetual, sempiternal (*Literary*), timeless, undying, unfading ~*n.* **2.** god, goddess, Olympian **3.** genius, great (*Usually plural*), hero, paragon

immortality 1. deathlessness, endlessness, eternity, everlasting life, incorruptibility, indestructibility, perpetuity, timelessness **2.** celebrity, fame, glorification, gloriousness, glory, greatness, renown

immortalize apotheosize, celebrate, commemorate, enshrine, eternalize, eternize, exalt, glorify, memorialize, perpetuate, solemnize

immovable 1. fast, firm, fixed, immutable, jammed, rooted, secure, set, stable, stationary, stuck, unbudgeable **2.** adamant, constant, impassive, inflexible, obdurate, resolute, steadfast, stonyhearted, unchangeable, unimpressionable, unshakable, unshaken, unwavering, unyielding

immune clear, exempt, free, insusceptible, invulnerable, let off (*Inf.*), not affected, not liable, not subject, proof (against), protected, resistant, safe, unaffected

immunity 1. amnesty, charter, exemption, exoneration, franchise, freedom, indemnity, invulnerability, liberty, licence, prerogative, privilege, release, right **2.** immunization, protection, resistance

immunize inoculate, protect, safeguard, vaccinate

immure cage, cloister, confine, enclose, imprison, incarcerate, jail, shut in *or* up, wall up *or* in

immutability agelessness, changelessness, constancy, durability, invariability, permanence, stability, unalterableness, unchangeableness

immutable abiding, ageless, changeless, constant, enduring, fixed, fixed as the laws of the Medes and Persians, inflexible, invariable, permanent, perpetual, sacrosanct, stable, steadfast, unalterable, unchangeable

imp brat, demon, devil, gamin, minx, rascal, rogue, scamp, sprite, urchin

impact *n*. **1**. bang, blow, bump, collision, concussion, contact, crash, force, jolt, knock, shock, smash, stroke, thump **2**. brunt, burden, consequences, effect, full force, impression, influence, meaning, power, repercussions, significance, thrust, weight ~*v*. **3**. clash, collide, crash, crush, hit, strike

impair blunt, damage, debilitate, decrease, deteriorate, diminish, enervate, enfeeble, harm, hinder, injure, lessen, mar, reduce, spoil, undermine, vitiate, weaken, worsen

impaired damaged, defective, faulty, flawed, imperfect, unsound

impale lance, pierce, run through, skewer, spear, spike, spit, stick, transfix

impalpable airy, delicate, disembodied, fine, imperceptible, incorporeal, indistinct, insubstantial, intangible, shadowy, tenuous, thin, unsubstantial

impart **1**. communicate, convey, disclose, discover, divulge, make known, pass on, relate, reveal, tell **2**. accord, afford, bestow, confer, contribute, give, grant, lend, offer, yield

impartial detached, disinterested, equal, equitable, even-handed, fair, just, neutral, nondiscriminating, nonpartisan, objective, open-minded, unbiased, unprejudiced, without fear or favour

impartiality detachment, disinterest, disinterestedness, dispassion, equality, equity, even-handedness, fairness, lack of bias, neutrality, nonpartisanship, objectivity, open-mindedness

impassable blocked, closed, impenetrable, obstructed, pathless, trackless, unnavigable

impasse blind alley (*Inf.*), dead end, deadlock, stalemate, standoff, standstill

impassioned animated, ardent, blazing, excited, fervent, fervid, fiery, furious, glowing, heated, inflamed, inspired, intense, passionate, rousing, stirring, vehement, violent, vivid, warm, worked up

impassive aloof, apathetic, callous, calm, composed, cool, dispassionate, emotionless, impassible (*Rare*), imperturbable, indifferent, inscrutable, insensible, insusceptible, phlegmatic, pokerfaced (*Inf.*), reserved, self-contained, serene, stoical, stolid, unconcerned, unemotional, unexcitable, unfeeling, unimpressible, unmoved, unruffled

impassivity aloofness, calmness, composure, dispassion, impassiveness, imperturbability, indifference, inscrutability, insensibility, phlegm, stoicism, stolidity

impatience **1**. haste, hastiness, heat, impetuosity, intolerance, irritability, irritableness, quick temper, rashness, shortness, snappiness, vehemence, violence **2**. agitation, anxiety, avidity, disquietude, eagerness, edginess, fretfulness, nervousness, restiveness, restlessness, uneasiness

impatient **1**. abrupt, brusque, curt, demanding, edgy, hasty, hot-tempered, indignant, intolerant, irritable, quicktempered, snappy, sudden, testy, vehement, violent **2**. agog, athirst, chafing, eager, fretful, headlong, impetuous, like a cat on hot bricks (*Inf.*), restless, straining at the leash

impeach **1**. accuse, arraign, blame, censure, charge, criminate (*Rare*), denounce, indict, tax **2**. call into question, cast aspersions on, cast doubt on, challenge, disparage, impugn, question

impeachment accusation, arraignment, indictment

impeccable above suspicion, exact, exquisite, faultless, flawless, immaculate, incorrupt, innocent, irreproachable, perfect, precise, pure, sinless, stainless, unblemished, unerring, unimpeachable

impecunious broke (*Inf.*), cleaned out (*Sl.*), destitute, indigent, insolvent, penniless, poverty-stricken, skint (*Sl.*), stony (*Sl.*), strapped (*Sl.*)

impede bar, block, brake, check, clog, curb, delay, disrupt, hamper, hinder, hold up, obstruct, restrain, retard, slow (down), stop, throw a spanner in the works (*Inf.*), thwart

impediment bar, barrier, block, check, clog, curb, defect, difficulty, encumbrance, hindrance, obstacle, obstruction, snag, stumbling block

impedimenta accoutrements, baggage, belongings, effects, equipment, gear, junk (*Inf.*), luggage, movables, odds and ends, paraphernalia, possessions, stuff, things, trappings, traps

impel actuate, compel, constrain, drive, force, goad, incite, induce, influence, inspire, instigate, motivate, move, oblige, power, prod, prompt, propel, push, require, spur, stimulate, urge

impending approaching, brewing, coming, forthcoming, gathering, hovering, imminent, in the offing, looming, menacing, near, nearing, on the horizon, threatening

impenetrable 1. dense, hermetic, impassable, impermeable, impervious, inviolable, solid, thick, unpiercable **2.** arcane, baffling, cabbalistic, dark, enigmatic, enigmatical, hidden, incomprehensible, indiscernible, inexplicable, inscrutable, mysterious, obscure, unfathomable, unintelligible

impenitence hardheartedness, impenitency, incorrigibility, obduracy, stubbornness

impenitent defiant, hardened, hardhearted, incorrigible, obdurate, recidivistic, relentless, remorseless, unabashed, unashamed, uncontrite, unreformed, unrepentant

imperative 1. compulsory, crucial, essential, exigent, indispensable, insistent, obligatory, pressing, urgent, vital **2.** authoritative, autocratic, commanding, dictatorial, domineering, high-handed, imperious, lordly, magisterial, peremptory

imperceptible faint, fine, gradual, impalpable, inappreciable, inaudible, indiscernible, indistinguishable, infinitesimal, insensible, invisible, microscopic, minute, shadowy, slight, small, subtle, tiny, undetectable, unnoticeable

imperceptibly by a hair's-breadth, inappreciably, indiscernibly, invisibly, little by little, slowly, subtly, unnoticeably, unobtrusively, unseen

imperceptive impercipient, insensitive, obtuse, superficial, unappreciative, unaware, undiscerning, unobservant, unseeing

imperfect broken, damaged, defective, deficient, faulty, flawed, immature, impaired, incomplete, inexact, limited, partial, patchy, rudimentary, sketchy, undeveloped, unfinished

imperfection blemish, defect, defi-

ciency, failing, fallibility, fault, flaw, foible, frailty, inadequacy, incompleteness, infirmity, insufficiency, peccadillo, shortcoming, stain, taint, weakness, weak point

imperial 1. kingly, majestic, princely, queenly, regal, royal, sovereign **2.** august, exalted, grand, great, high, imperious, lofty, magnificent, noble, superior, supreme

imperil endanger, expose, hazard, jeopardize, risk

imperious arrogant, authoritative, autocratic, bossy (*Inf.*), commanding, despotic, dictatorial, domineering, exacting, haughty, high-handed, imperative, lordly, magisterial, overbearing, overweening, tyrannical, tyrannous

imperishable abiding, enduring, eternal, everlasting, immortal, indestructible, perennial, permanent, perpetual, undying, unfading, unforgettable

impermanent brief, elusive, ephemeral, evanescent, fleeting, fly-by-night (*Inf.*), flying, fugacious, fugitive, here today, gone tomorrow (*Inf.*), inconstant, momentary, mortal, passing, perishable, short-lived, temporary, transient, transitory

impermeable hermetic, impassable, impenetrable, impervious, nonporous, proof, resistant

impersonal bureaucratic, businesslike, cold, detached, dispassionate, formal, inhuman, neutral, remote

impersonate act, ape, do (*Inf.*), do an impression of, enact, imitate, masquerade as, mimic, pass oneself off as, personate, pose as (*Inf.*), take off (*Inf.*)

impersonation caricature, imitation, impression, mimicry, parody, takeoff (*Inf.*)

impertinence assurance, audacity, backchat (*Inf.*), boldness, brass neck (*Sl.*), brazenness, cheek (*Inf.*), disrespect, effrontery, forwardness, impudence, incivility, insolence, nerve (*Inf.*), pertness, presumption, rudeness, sauce (*Inf.*)

impertinent 1. bold, brazen, cheeky (*Inf.*), discourteous, disrespectful, flip (*Inf.*), forward, fresh (*Inf.*), impolite, impudent, insolent, interfering, pert, presumptuous, rude, saucy (*Inf.*), uncivil, unmannerly **2.** inapplicable, inappropriate, incongruous, irrelevant

imperturbable calm, collected, complacent, composed, cool, equanimous, nerveless, sedate, self-possessed, stoical, tranquil, undisturbed, unexcitable, unflappable (*Inf.*), unmoved, unruffled

impervious 1. hermetic, impassable, impenetrable, impermeable, imperviable, invulnerable, resistant, sealed **2.** closed to, immune, invulnerable, proof against, unaffected by, unmoved by, unreceptive, unswayable, untouched by

impetuosity haste, hastiness, impulsiveness, precipitancy, precipitateness, rashness, vehemence, violence

impetuous ardent, eager, fierce, furious, hasty, headlong, impassioned, impulsive, passionate, precipitate, rash, spontaneous, spur-of-the-moment, unbridled, unplanned, unpremeditated, unreflecting, unrestrained, unthinking, vehement, violent

impetuously helter-skelter, impulsively, in the heat of the moment, on the spur of the moment, passionately, rashly, recklessly, spontaneously, unthinkingly, vehemently, without thinking

impetus 1. catalyst, goad, impulse, impulsion, incentive, motivation, push, spur, stimulus **2.** energy, force, momentum, power

impiety godlessness, iniquity, irreligion, irreverence, profaneness, profanity, sacrilege, sinfulness, ungodliness, unholiness, unrighteousness, wickedness

impinge 1. encroach, invade, make inroads, obtrude, trespass, violate **2.** affect, bear upon, have a bearing on, influence, infringe, relate to, touch, touch upon **3.** clash, collide, dash, strike

impious blasphemous, godless, iniquitous, irreligious, irreverent, profane, sacrilegious, sinful, ungodly, unholy, unrighteous, wicked

impish devilish, elfin, mischievous, prankish, puckish, rascally, roguish, sportive, waggish

implacability implacableness, inexorability, inflexibility, intractability, mercilessness, pitilessness, relentlessness, ruthlessness, unforgivingness, vengefulness

implacable cruel, inexorable, inflexible, intractable, merciless, pitiless, rancorous, relentless, remorseless, ruthless, unappeasable, unbending, uncompromising, unforgiving, unrelenting, unyielding

implant 1. inculcate, infix, infuse, inseminate, instil, sow **2.** embed, fix, graft, ingraft, insert, place, plant, root, sow

implausible dubious, far-fetched, flimsy, improbable, incredible, suspect, unbelievable, unconvincing, unlikely, unreasonable, weak

implement 1. *n.* agent, apparatus, appliance, device, gadget, instrument, tool, utensil **2.** *v.* bring about, carry out, complete, effect, enforce, execute, fulfil, perform, put into action *or* effect, realize

implementation accomplishment, carrying out, discharge, effecting, enforcement, execution, fulfilment, performance, performing, realization

implicate associate, compromise, concern, embroil, entangle, imply, include, incriminate, inculpate, involve, mire, tie up with

implicated incriminated, involved, suspected, under suspicion

implication 1. association, connection, entanglement, incrimination, involvement **2.** conclusion, inference, innuendo, meaning, overtone, presumption, ramification, significance, signification, suggestion

implicit 1. contained, implied, inferred, inherent, latent, tacit, taken for granted, undeclared, understood, unspoken **2.** absolute, constant, entire, firm, fixed, full, steadfast, total, unhesitating, unqualified, unreserved, unshakable, unshaken, wholehearted

implicitly absolutely, completely, firmly, unconditionally, unhesitatingly, unreservedly, utterly, without reservation

implied hinted at, implicit, indirect, inherent, insinuated, suggested, tacit, undeclared, unexpressed, unspoken, unstated

implore beg, beseech, conjure, crave, entreat, go on bended knee to, importune, plead with, pray, solicit, supplicate

imply 1. connote, give (someone) to understand, hint, insinuate, intimate, signify, suggest **2.** betoken, denote, entail, evidence, import, include, indicate, involve, mean, point to, presuppose

impolite bad-mannered, boorish, churlish, discourteous, disrespectful, ill-bred, ill-mannered, indecorous, indelicate, insolent, loutish, rough, rude, uncivil, ungallant, ungentlemanly, ungracious, unladylike, unmannerly, unrefined

impoliteness bad manners, boorishness, churlishness, discourtesy, disrespect, incivility, indelicacy, insolence, rudeness, unmannerliness

impolitic ill-advised, ill-judged, imprudent, indiscreet, inexpedient, injudicious, maladroit, misguided, undiplomatic, untimely, unwise

import n. **1**. bearing, drift, gist, implication, intention, meaning, message, purport, sense, significance, thrust **2**. consequence, importance, magnitude, moment, significance, substance, weight ~v. **3**. bring in, introduce, land

importance 1. concern, consequence, import, interest, moment, momentousness, significance, substance, value, weight **2**. distinction, eminence, esteem, influence, mark, pre-eminence, prestige, prominence, standing, status, usefulness, worth

important 1. far-reaching, grave, large, material, meaningful, momentous, of substance, primary, salient, serious, signal, significant, substantial, urgent, weighty **2**. eminent, foremost, high-level, high-ranking, influential, leading, notable, noteworthy, of note, outstanding, powerful, pre-eminent, prominent, seminal **3**. *Usually with* **to** basic, essential, of concern *or* interest, relevant, valuable, valued

importunate burning, clamant, clamorous, demanding, dogged, earnest, exigent, insistent, persistent, pertinacious, pressing, solicitous, troublesome, urgent

importune badger, beset, besiege, dun, entreat, harass, hound, lay siege to, pester, plague, press, solicit

importunity cajolery, dunning, entreaties, insistence, persistence, pressing, solicitations, urging

impose 1. decree, establish, exact, fix, institute, introduce, lay, levy, ordain, place, promulgate, put, set **2**. appoint, charge with, dictate, enforce, enjoin, inflict, prescribe, saddle (someone) with **3**. *With* **on** *or* **upon** butt in, encroach, foist, force oneself, gate-crash (*Inf.*), horn in (*Inf.*), intrude, obtrude, presume, take liberties, trespass **4**. *With* **on** *or* **upon a.** abuse, exploit, play on, take advantage of, use **b.** con (*Inf.*), deceive, dupe, hoodwink, pull the wool over (somebody's) eyes, trick

imposing august, commanding, dignified, effective, grand, impressive, majestic, stately, striking

imposition 1. application, decree, introduction, laying on, levying, promulgation **2**. cheek (*Inf.*), encroachment, intrusion, liberty, presumption **3**. artifice, cheating, con (*Inf.*), deception, dissimulation, fraud, hoax, imposture, stratagem, trickery **4**. burden, charge, constraint, duty, levy, tax

impossibility hopelessness, impracticability, inability, inconceivability

impossible 1. beyond one, beyond the bounds of possibility, hopeless, impracticable, inconceivable, not to be thought of, out of the question, unachievable, unattainable, unobtainable, unthinkable **2**. absurd, inadmissible, insoluble, intolerable, ludicrous, outrageous, preposterous, unacceptable, unanswerable, ungovernable, unreasonable, unsuitable, unworkable

impostor charlatan, cheat, deceiver, fake, fraud, hypocrite, impersonator, knave (*Archaic*), phoney (*Sl.*), pretender, quack, rogue, sham, trickster

imposture artifice, cheat, con trick (*Inf.*), counterfeit, deception, fraud, hoax, impersonation, imposition, quackery, swindle, trick

impotence disability, enervation, feebleness, frailty, helplessness, inability, inadequacy, incapacity, incompetence, ineffectiveness, inefficacy, inefficiency, infirmity, paralysis, powerlessness, uselessness, weakness

impotent disabled, emasculate, enervated, feeble, frail, helpless, incapable, incapacitated, incompetent, ineffective, infirm, nerveless, paralysed, powerless, unable, unmanned, weak

impoverish 1. bankrupt, beggar, break, ruin **2**. deplete, diminish, drain, exhaust, pauperize, reduce, sap, use up, wear out

impoverished 1. bankrupt, destitute, distressed, impecunious, indigent, in reduced *or* straitened circumstances, necessitous, needy, on one's uppers, penurious, poverty-stricken, ruined, straitened **2**. barren, denuded, depleted, drained, empty, exhausted, played out, reduced, spent, sterile, worn out

impracticability futility, hopelessness, impossibility, impracticality, unsuitableness, unworkability, uselessness

impracticable 1. impossible, out of the question, unachievable, unattainable, unfeasible, unworkable **2**. awk-

ward, impractical, inapplicable, inconvenient, unserviceable, unsuitable, useless

impractical 1. impossible, impracticable, inoperable, nonviable, unrealistic,
unserviceable, unworkable, visionary,
wild **2.** idealistic, romantic, starry-eyed,
unbusinesslike, unrealistic, visionary

impracticality hopelessness, impossibility, inapplicability, romanticism,
unworkability

imprecation anathema, blasphemy,
curse, denunciation, execration, malediction, profanity, vilification

imprecise ambiguous, blurred round
the edges, careless, equivocal, estimated,
fluctuating, hazy, ill-defined, inaccurate,
indefinite, indeterminate, inexact, inex-
plicit, loose, rough, sloppy (*Inf.*), vague,
wide of the mark, woolly

impregnable immovable, impenetrable, indestructible, invincible, invulnerable, secure, strong, unassailable, unbeatable, unconquerable, unshakable

impregnate 1. fill, imbrue (*Rare*), imbue, infuse, percolate, permeate, pervade, saturate, soak, steep, suffuse **2.** fecundate, fertilize, fructify, get with
child, inseminate, make pregnant

impress 1. affect, excite, grab (*Sl.*), influence, inspire, make an impression,
move, stir, strike, sway, touch **2.** *Often
with* **on** *or* **upon** bring home to, emphasize, fix, inculcate, instil into, stress **3.**
emboss, engrave, imprint, indent, mark,
print, stamp

impression 1. effect, feeling, impact,
influence, reaction, sway **2. make an impression** arouse comment, be conspicuous, cause a stir, excite notice, find favour, make a hit (*Inf.*), make an impact,
stand out **3.** belief, concept, conviction,
fancy, feeling, funny feeling (*Inf.*),
hunch, idea, memory, notion, opinion,
recollection, sense, suspicion **4.** brand,
dent, hollow, impress, imprint, indentation, mark, outline, stamp, stamping **5.**
edition, imprinting, issue, printing **6.**
imitation, impersonation, parody, send-
up (*Brit. inf.*), takeoff (*Inf.*)

impressionability ingenuousness, receptiveness, receptivity, sensitivity, suggestibility, susceptibility, vulnerability

impressionable feeling, gullible, ingenuous, open, receptive, responsive,
sensitive, suggestible, susceptible, vulnerable

impressive affecting, exciting, forcible, moving, powerful, stirring, touching

imprint 1. *n.* impression, indentation,
mark, print, sign, stamp **2.** *v.* engrave,
establish, etch, fix, impress, print, stamp

imprison confine, constrain, detain,
immure, incarcerate, intern, jail, lock up,
put away, put under lock and key, send
down (*Inf.*), send to prison

imprisoned behind bars, captive, confined, immured, incarcerated, in irons, in
jail, inside (*Sl.*), interned, jailed, locked
up, put away, under lock and key

imprisonment confinement, custody,
detention, durance (*Archaic*), duress, incarceration, internment, porridge (*Sl.*)

improbability doubt, doubtfulness,
dubiety, uncertainty, unlikelihood

improbable doubtful, dubious, fanciful, far-fetched, implausible, questionable, unbelievable, uncertain, unconvincing, unlikely, weak

improbity chicanery, crookedness
(*Inf.*), dishonesty, faithlessness, fraud,
knavery, unfairness, unscrupulousness,
villainy

impromptu 1. *adj.* ad-lib, extemporaneous, extempore, extemporized, improvised, offhand, off the cuff (*Inf.*), spontaneous, unpremeditated, unprepared, unrehearsed, unscripted, unstudied **2.** *adv.*
ad lib, off the cuff (*Inf.*), off the top of
one's head (*Inf.*), on the spur of the moment, spontaneously, without preparation

improper 1. impolite, indecent, indecorous, indelicate, off-colour, risqué,
smutty, suggestive, unbecoming, unfitting, unseemly, untoward, vulgar **2.** ill-
timed, inapplicable, inapposite, inappropriate, inapt, incongruous, infelicitous,
inopportune, malapropos, out of place,
uncalled-for, unfit, unseasonable, unsuitable, unsuited, unwarranted **3.** abnormal, erroneous, false, inaccurate, incorrect, irregular, wrong

impropriety 1. bad taste, immodesty,
incongruity, indecency, indecorum, unsuitability, vulgarity **2.** blunder, faux
pas, gaffe, gaucherie, mistake, slip, solecism

improve 1. advance, ameliorate,
amend, augment, better, correct, help,
mend, polish, rectify, touch up, upgrade
2. develop, enhance, gain strength, increase, look up (*Inf.*), make strides, perk

up, pick up, progress, rally, reform, rise, take a turn for the better (*Inf.*), take on a new lease of life (*Inf.*) **3.** convalesce, gain ground, gain strength, grow better, make progress, mend, recover, recuperate, turn the corner

improvement 1. advancement, amelioration, amendment, augmentation, betterment, correction, gain, rectification **2.** advance, development, enhancement, furtherance, increase, progress, rally, recovery, reformation, rise, upswing

improvidence carelessness, extravagance, heedlessness, imprudence, negligence, prodigality, profligacy, shortsightedness, thriftlessness, wastefulness

improvident careless, heedless, imprudent, inconsiderate, negligent, prodigal, profligate, reckless, shiftless, shortsighted, spendthrift, thoughtless, thriftless, uneconomical, unthrifty, wasteful

improvisation ad-lib, ad-libbing, expedient, extemporizing, impromptu, invention, makeshift, spontaneity

improvise 1. ad-lib, coin, extemporize, invent, play it by ear (*Inf.*), speak off the cuff (*Inf.*) **2.** concoct, contrive, devise, make do, throw together

improvised ad-lib, extemporaneous, extempore, extemporized, makeshift, off the cuff (*Inf.*), spontaneous, spur-of-the-moment, unprepared, unrehearsed

imprudence carelessness, folly, foolhardiness, foolishness, heedlessness, improvidence, inadvisability, incaution, incautiousness, inconsideration, indiscretion, irresponsibility, rashness, recklessness, temerity

imprudent careless, foolhardy, foolish, heedless, ill-advised, ill-considered, ill-judged, impolitic, improvident, incautious, inconsiderate, indiscreet, injudicious, irresponsible, overhasty, rash, reckless, temerarious, unthinking, unwise

impudence assurance, audacity, backchat (*Inf.*), boldness, brass neck (*Sl.*), bumptiousness, cheek (*Inf.*), effrontery, face (*Inf.*), impertinence, insolence, lip (*Sl.*), nerve (*Inf.*), pertness, presumption, rudeness, sauciness, shamelessness

impudent audacious, bold, bold-faced, brazen, bumptious, cheeky (*Inf.*), cocky (*Inf.*), forward, fresh (*Inf.*), immodest, impertinent, insolent, pert, pre-

sumptuous, rude, saucy (*Inf.*), shameless

impugn assail, attack, call into question, cast aspersions upon, cast doubt upon, challenge, criticize, dispute, gainsay, oppose, question, resist, traduce

impulse 1. catalyst, force, impetus, momentum, movement, pressure, push, stimulus, surge, thrust **2.** *Fig.* caprice, drive, feeling, incitement, inclination, influence, instinct, motive, notion, passion, resolve, urge, whim, wish

impulsive devil-may-care, emotional, hasty, headlong, impetuous, instinctive, intuitive, passionate, precipitate, quick, rash, spontaneous, unconsidered, unpredictable, unpremeditated

impunity dispensation, exemption, freedom, immunity, liberty, licence, nonliability, permission, security

impure 1. admixed, adulterated, alloyed, debased, mixed, unrefined **2.** contaminated, defiled, dirty, filthy, foul, infected, polluted, sullied, tainted, unclean, unwholesome, vitiated **3.** carnal, coarse, corrupt, gross, immodest, immoral, indecent, indelicate, lascivious, lewd, licentious, lustful, obscene, prurient, ribald, salacious, smutty, unchaste, unclean

impurity 1. admixture, adulteration, mixture **2.** befoulment, contamination, defilement, dirtiness, filth, foulness, infection, pollution, taint, uncleanness **3.** *Often plural* bits, contaminant, dirt, dross, foreign body, foreign matter, grime, marks, pollutant, scum, spots, stains **4.** carnality, coarseness, corruption, grossness, immodesty, immorality, indecency, lasciviousness, lewdness, licentiousness, obscenity, prurience, salaciousness, smuttiness, unchastity, vulgarity

imputable accreditable, ascribable, attributable, chargeable, referable, traceable

imputation accusation, ascription, aspersion, attribution, blame, censure, charge, insinuation, reproach, slander, slur

impute accredit, ascribe, assign, attribute, credit, lay at the door of, refer, set down to

inability disability, disqualification, impotence, inadequacy, incapability, incapacity, incompetence, ineptitude, powerlessness

inaccessible impassable, out of reach, out of the way, remote, unapproachable, unattainable, un-get-at-able (*Inf.*), unreachable

inaccuracy 1. erroneousness, imprecision, incorrectness, inexactness, unfaithfulness, unreliability **2**. blunder, corrigendum, defect, erratum, error, fault, howler (*Inf.*), literal (*Printing*), miscalculation, mistake, slip, typo (*Inf., printing*)

inaccurate careless, defective, discrepant, erroneous, faulty, imprecise, incorrect, in error, inexact, mistaken, out, unfaithful, unreliable, unsound, wide of the mark, wild, wrong

inaccurately carelessly, clumsily, imprecisely, inexactly, unfaithfully, unreliably

inaction dormancy, idleness, immobility, inactivity, inertia, rest, torpidity, torpor

inactive 1. abeyant, dormant, idle, immobile, inert, inoperative, jobless, kicking one's heels, latent, mothballed, out of service, out of work, unemployed, unoccupied, unused **2**. dull, indolent, lazy, lethargic, low-key (*Inf.*), passive, quiet, sedentary, slothful, slow, sluggish, somnolent, torpid

inactivity 1. dormancy, hibernation, immobility, inaction, passivity, unemployment **2**. dilatoriness, *dolce far niente*, dullness, heaviness, indolence, inertia, inertness, lassitude, laziness, lethargy, quiescence, sloth, sluggishness, stagnation, torpor, vegetation

inadequacy 1. dearth, deficiency, inadequateness, incompleteness, insufficiency, meagreness, paucity, poverty, scantiness, shortage, skimpiness **2**. defectiveness, faultiness, inability, inaptness, incapacity, incompetence, incompetency, ineffectiveness, inefficacy, unfitness, unsuitableness **3**. defect, failing, imperfection, lack, shortage, shortcoming, weakness

inadequate 1. defective, deficient, faulty, imperfect, incommensurate, incomplete, insubstantial, insufficient, meagre, niggardly, scanty, short, sketchy, skimpy, sparse **2**. found wanting, inapt, incapable, incompetent, not up to scratch (*Inf.*), unequal, unfitted, unqualified

inadequately imperfectly, insufficiently, meagrely, poorly, scantily, sketchily, skimpily, sparsely, thinly

inadmissible immaterial, improper,

inappropriate, incompetent, irrelevant, unacceptable, unallowable, unqualified, unreasonable

inadvertence, inadvertency blunder, carelessness, error, heedlessness, inattention, inconsideration, inobservance, mistake, neglect, negligence, oversight, remissness, thoughtlessness

inadvertent accidental, careless, chance, heedless, negligent, thoughtless, unheeding, unintended, unintentional, unplanned, unpremeditated, unthinking, unwitting

inadvertently 1. carelessly, heedlessly, in an unguarded moment, negligently, thoughtlessly, unguardedly, unthinkingly **2**. accidentally, by accident, by mistake, involuntarily, mistakenly, unintentionally, unwittingly

inadvisable ill-advised, impolitic, imprudent, inexpedient, injudicious, unwise

inalienable absolute, entailed (*Law*), inherent, inviolable, non-negotiable, nontransferable, sacrosanct, unassailable, untransferable

inane asinine, daft (*Inf.*), devoid of intelligence, empty, fatuous, frivolous, futile, idiotic, imbecilic, mindless, puerile, senseless, silly, stupid, trifling, unintelligent, vacuous, vain, vapid, worthless

inanimate cold, dead, defunct, extinct, inactive, inert, insensate, insentient, lifeless, quiescent, soulless, spiritless

inanity asininity, bêtise (*Rare*), daftness (*Inf.*), emptiness, fatuity, folly, frivolity, imbecility, puerility, senselessness, silliness, vacuity, vapidity, worthlessness

inapplicable inapposite, inappropriate, inapt, irrelevant, unsuitable, unsuited

inapposite impertinent, inapplicable, inappropriate, infelicitous, irrelevant, out of place, unfit, unsuitable

inappreciable imperceptible, infinitesimal, insignificant, minuscule, negligible

inappropriate disproportionate, ill-fitted, ill-suited, ill-timed, improper, incongruous, malapropos, out of place, tasteless, unbecoming, unbefitting, unfit, unfitting, unseemly, unsuitable, untimely

inapt 1. ill-fitted, ill-suited, inapposite, inappropriate, infelicitous, unsuitable, unsuited **2**. awkward, clumsy, dull, gauche, incompetent, inept, inexpert, maladroit, slow, stupid

inaptitude awkwardness, clumsiness, incompetence, maladroitness, unfitness, unreadiness, unsuitableness

inarticulate 1. blurred, incoherent, incomprehensible, indistinct, muffled, mumbled, unclear, unintelligible **2.** dumb, mute, silent, speechless, tongue-tied, unspoken, unuttered, unvoiced, voiceless, wordless **3.** faltering, halting, hesitant, poorly spoken

inattention absent-mindedness, carelessness, daydreaming, disregard, forgetfulness, heedlessness, inadvertence, inattentiveness, indifference, neglect, preoccupation, thoughtlessness, woolgathering

inattentive absent-minded, careless, distracted, distrait, dreamy, heedless, inadvertent, neglectful, negligent, preoccupied, regardless, remiss, thoughtless, unheeding, unmindful, unobservant, vague

inaudible indistinct, low, mumbling, out of earshot, stifled, unheard

inaugural dedicatory, first, initial, introductory, maiden, opening

inaugurate 1. begin, commence, get under way, initiate, institute, introduce, kick off (*Inf.*), launch, originate, set in motion, set up, usher in **2.** induct, install, instate, invest **3.** commission, dedicate, open, ordain

inauguration 1. initiation, institution, launch, launching, opening, setting up **2.** induction, installation, investiture

inauspicious bad, black, discouraging, ill-omened, ominous, unfavourable, unfortunate, unlucky, unpromising, unpropitious, untoward

inborn congenital, connate, hereditary, inbred, ingrained, inherent, inherited, innate, instinctive, intuitive, native, natural

inbred constitutional, deep-seated, ingrained, inherent, innate, native, natural

incalculable boundless, countless, enormous, immense, incomputable, inestimable, infinite, innumerable, limitless, measureless, numberless, uncountable, untold, vast, without number

incandescent brilliant, glowing, luminous, phosphorescent, radiant, red-hot, shining, white-hot

incantation abracadabra, chant, charm, conjuration, formula, hex (*U.S. dialect*), invocation, spell

incapable 1. feeble, inadequate, incompetent, ineffective, inept, inexpert, insufficient, not equal to, not up to, unfit, unfitted, unqualified, weak **2.** helpless, impotent, powerless, unable, unfit **3.** *With* of impervious, not admitting of, not susceptible to, resistant

incapacitate cripple, disable, disqualify, immobilize, lay up (*Inf.*), paralyse, prostrate, put out of action (*Inf.*), scupper (*Brit. sl.*), unfit (*Rare*)

incapacitated disqualified, *hors de combat*, immobilized, indisposed, laid up (*Inf.*), out of action (*Inf.*), unfit

incapacity disqualification, feebleness, impotence, inability, inadequacy, incapability, incompetency, ineffectiveness, powerlessness, unfitness, weakness

incapsulate *see* ENCAPSULATE

incarcerate commit, confine, coop up, detain, gaol, immure, impound, imprison, intern, jail, lock up, put under lock and key, restrain, restrict, send down (*Brit.*), throw in jail

incarceration bondage, captivity, confinement, detention, imprisonment, internment, restraint

incarnate 1. in bodily form, in human form, in the flesh, made flesh **2.** embodied, personified, typified

incarnation avatar, bodily form, embodiment, exemplification, impersonation, manifestation, personification, type

incautious careless, hasty, heedless, ill-advised, ill-judged, improvident, imprudent, impulsive, inconsiderate, indiscreet, injudicious, negligent, precipitate, rash, reckless, thoughtless, unguarded, unthinking, unwary

incautiously imprudently, impulsively, indiscreetly, precipitately, rashly, recklessly, thoughtlessly, unthinkingly

incendiary *adj.* **1.** dissentious, inflammatory, provocative, rabble-rousing, seditious, subversive ~*n.* **2.** arsonist, firebug (*Inf.*), fire raiser, pyromaniac **3.** agitator, demagogue, firebrand, insurgent, rabble-rouser, revolutionary

incense[1] *v.* anger, enrage, exasperate, excite, get one's hackles up, inflame, infuriate, irritate, madden, make one's blood boil (*Inf.*), make one see red (*Inf.*), make one's hackles rise, provoke, raise one's hackles, rile (*Inf.*)

incense[2] *n.* aroma, balm, bouquet, fragrance, perfume, redolence, scent

incensed angry, enraged, exasperated,

fuming, furious, indignant, infuriated, irate, ireful (*Literary*), mad (*Inf.*), maddened, on the warpath (*Inf.*), steamed up (*Sl.*), up in arms, wrathful

incentive bait, carrot (*Inf.*), encouragement, enticement, goad, impetus, impulse, inducement, lure, motivation, motive, spur, stimulant, stimulus

inception beginning, birth, commencement, dawn, inauguration, initiation, kickoff (*Inf.*), origin, outset, rise, start

incessant ceaseless, constant, continual, continuous, endless, eternal, everlasting, interminable, never-ending, nonstop, perpetual, persistent, relentless, unbroken, unceasing, unending, unrelenting, unremitting

incessantly all the time, ceaselessly, constantly, continually, endlessly, eternally, everlastingly, interminably, nonstop, perpetually, persistently, without a break

inchoate 1. beginning, inceptive, incipient, nascent **2.** elementary, embryonic, formless, immature, imperfect, rudimentary, undeveloped, unformed

incidence amount, degree, extent, frequency, occurrence, prevalence, rate

incident 1. adventure, circumstance, episode, event, fact, happening, matter, occasion, occurrence **2.** brush, clash, commotion, confrontation, contretemps, disturbance, mishap, scene, skirmish

incidental 1. accidental, casual, chance, fortuitous, odd, random **2.** *With* to accompanying, attendant, by-the-way, concomitant, contingent, contributory, related **3.** ancillary, minor, nonessential, occasional, secondary, subordinate, subsidiary

incidentally 1. accidentally, by chance, casually, fortuitously **2.** by the bye, by the way, in passing, parenthetically

incidentals contingencies, extras, minutiae, odds and ends

incinerate burn up, carbonize, char, consume by fire, cremate, reduce to ashes

incipient beginning, commencing, developing, embryonic, inceptive, inchoate, nascent, originating, starting

incise carve, chisel, cut (into), engrave, etch

incision cut, gash, notch, opening, slash, slit

incisive 1. acute, keen, penetrating, perspicacious, piercing, trenchant **2.** acid, biting, caustic, cutting, mordant, sarcastic, sardonic, satirical, severe, sharp

incisiveness 1. keenness, penetration, perspicacity, sharpness, trenchancy **2.** acidity, pungency, sarcasm

incite agitate for *or* against, animate, drive, egg on, encourage, excite, foment, goad, impel, inflame, instigate, prompt, provoke, put up to, rouse, set on, spur, stimulate, stir up, urge, whip up

incitement agitation, encouragement, goad, impetus, impulse, inducement, instigation, motivation, motive, prompting, provocation, spur, stimulus

incivility bad manners, boorishness, discourteousness, discourtesy, disrespect, ill-breeding, impoliteness, rudeness, unmannerliness

inclemency 1. bitterness, boisterousness, rawness, rigour, roughness, severity, storminess **2.** callousness, cruelty, harshness, mercilessness, severity, tyranny, unfeelingness

inclement 1. bitter, boisterous, foul, harsh, intemperate, rigorous, rough, severe, stormy, tempestuous **2.** callous, cruel, draconian, harsh, intemperate, merciless, pitiless, rigorous, severe, tyrannical, unfeeling, unmerciful

inclination 1. affection, aptitude, bent, bias, desire, disposition, fancy, fondness, leaning, liking, partiality, penchant, predilection, predisposition, prejudice, proclivity, proneness, propensity, stomach, taste, tendency, turn, turn of mind, wish **2.** bending, bow, bowing, nod **3.** angle, bend, bending, deviation, gradient, incline, leaning, pitch, slant, slope, tilt

incline v. **1.** be disposed *or* predisposed, bias, influence, persuade, predispose, prejudice, sway, tend, turn **2.** bend, bow, lower, nod, stoop **3.** bend, bevel, cant, deviate, diverge, lean, slant, slope, tend, tilt, tip, veer ~n. **4.** acclivity, ascent, declivity, descent, dip, grade, gradient, ramp, rise, slope

inclined apt, disposed, given, liable, likely, minded, of a mind (*Inf.*), predisposed, prone, willing

inclose *see* ENCLOSE

include 1. comprehend, comprise, contain, cover, embody, embrace, encompass, incorporate, involve, subsume, take in, take into account **2.** add, allow for, build in, count, enter, insert, introduce, number among

including as well as, containing, counting, inclusive of, plus, together with, with

inclusion addition, incorporation, insertion

inclusive across-the-board, all-embracing, all in, all together, blanket, catch-all (*Chiefly U.S.*), comprehensive, full, general, *in toto*, overall, sweeping, umbrella, without exception

incognito disguised, in disguise, under an assumed name, unknown, unrecognized

incoherence disconnectedness, disjointedness, inarticulateness, unintelligibility

incoherent confused, disconnected, disjointed, disordered, inarticulate, inconsistent, jumbled, loose, muddled, rambling, stammering, stuttering, unconnected, uncoordinated, unintelligible, wandering, wild

incombustible fireproof, flameproof, noncombustible, nonflammable, noninflammable

income earnings, gains, interest, means, pay, proceeds, profits, receipts, revenue, salary, takings, wages

incoming approaching, arriving, entering, homeward, landing, new, returning, succeeding

incommensurate disproportionate, inadequate, inequitable, insufficient, unequal

incommode annoy, be a trouble to, bother, disturb, embarrass, give (someone) bother *or* trouble, hinder, impede, inconvenience, irk, put out, put (someone) to trouble, trouble, upset, vex

incommodious awkward, confined, cramped, inconvenient, narrow, restricted, small, uncomfortable

incommunicable indescribable, ineffable, inexpressible, unspeakable, unutterable

incomparable beyond compare, inimitable, matchless, paramount, peerless, superlative, supreme, transcendent, unequalled, unmatched, unparalleled, unrivalled

incomparably beyond compare, by far, easily, eminently, far and away, immeasurably

incompatibility antagonism, conflict, discrepancy, disparateness, incongruity, inconsistency, irreconcilability, uncongeniality

incompatible antagonistic, antipathetic, conflicting, contradictory, discordant, discrepant, disparate, ill-assorted, incongruous, inconsistent, inconsonant, irreconcilable, mismatched, uncongenial, unsuitable, unsuited

incompetence inability, inadequacy, incapability, incapacity, incompetency, ineffectiveness, ineptitude, ineptness, insufficiency, skill-lessness, unfitness, uselessness

incompetent bungling, floundering, incapable, incapacitated, ineffectual, inept, inexpert, insufficient, skill-less, unable, unfit, unfitted, unskilful, useless

incomplete broken, defective, deficient, fragmentary, imperfect, insufficient, lacking, partial, short, unaccomplished, undeveloped, undone, unexecuted, unfinished, wanting

incomprehensible above one's head, all Greek to (*Inf.*), baffling, beyond comprehension, beyond one's grasp, enigmatic, impenetrable, inconceivable, inscrutable, mysterious, obscure, opaque, perplexing, puzzling, unfathomable, unimaginable, unintelligible, unthinkable

inconceivable beyond belief, impossible, incomprehensible, incredible, mind-boggling (*Sl.*), not to be thought of, out of the question, staggering (*Inf.*), unbelievable, unheard-of, unimaginable, unknowable, unthinkable

inconclusive ambiguous, indecisive, indeterminate, open, uncertain, unconvincing, undecided, unsettled, up in the air (*Inf.*), vague

incongruity conflict, discrepancy, disparity, inappropriateness, inaptness, incompatibility, inconsistency, inharmoniousness, unsuitability

incongruous absurd, conflicting, contradictory, contrary, disconsonant, discordant, extraneous, improper, inappropriate, inapt, incoherent, incompatible, inconsistent, out of keeping, out of place, unbecoming, unsuitable, unsuited

inconsequential immaterial, inconsiderable, insignificant, minor, negligible, of no significance, paltry, petty, trifling, trivial, unimportant

inconsiderable exiguous, inconsequential, insignificant, light, minor, negligible, petty, slight, small, small-time (*Inf.*), trifling, trivial, unimportant

inconsiderate careless, indelicate, insensitive, intolerant, rude, self-centred, selfish, tactless, thoughtless, uncharitable, ungracious, unkind, unthinking

inconsistency 1. contrariety, disagreement, discrepancy, disparity, divergence, incompatibility, incongruity, inconsonance, paradox, variance 2. fickleness, instability, unpredictability, unreliability, unsteadiness

inconsistent 1. at odds, at variance, conflicting, contradictory, contrary, discordant, discrepant, incoherent, incompatible, in conflict, incongruous, irreconcilable, out of step 2. capricious, changeable, erratic, fickle, inconstant, irregular, unpredictable, unstable, unsteady, vagarious (*Rare*), variable

inconsistently contradictorily, differently, eccentrically, erratically, inequably, randomly, unequally, unfairly, unpredictably, variably

inconsolable brokenhearted, desolate, despairing, heartbroken, heartsick, prostrate with grief, sick at heart

inconspicuous camouflaged, hidden, insignificant, modest, muted, ordinary, plain, quiet, retiring, unassuming, unnoticeable, unobtrusive, unostentatious

inconstant blowing hot and cold (*Inf.*), capricious, changeable, changeful, erratic, fickle, fluctuating, inconsistent, irresolute, mercurial, mutable, uncertain, undependable, unreliable, unsettled, unstable, unsteady, vacillating, vagarious (*Rare*), variable, volatile, wavering, wayward

incontestable beyond doubt, beyond question, certain, incontrovertible, indisputable, indubitable, irrefutable, self-evident, sure, undeniable, unquestionable

incontinent 1. unbridled, unchecked, uncontrollable, uncontrolled, ungovernable, ungoverned, unrestrained 2. debauched, lascivious, lecherous, lewd, loose, lustful, profligate, promiscuous, unchaste, wanton

incontrovertible beyond dispute, certain, established, incontestable, indisputable, indubitable, irrefutable, positive, sure, undeniable, unquestionable, unshakable

inconvenience n. 1. annoyance, awkwardness, bother, difficulty, disadvantage, disruption, disturbance, drawback, fuss, hindrance, nuisance, trouble, uneasiness, upset, vexation 2. awkwardness, cumbersomeness, unfitness, unhandiness, unsuitableness, untimeliness, unwieldiness ∼v. 3. bother, discommode, disrupt, disturb, give (someone) bother *or* trouble, irk, make (someone) go out of his way, put out, put to trouble, trouble, upset

inconvenient 1. annoying, awkward, bothersome, disadvantageous, disturbing, embarrassing, inopportune, tiresome, troublesome, unseasonable, unsuitable, untimely, vexatious 2. awkward, cumbersome, difficult, unhandy, unmanageable, unwieldy

incorporate absorb, amalgamate, assimilate, blend, coalesce, combine, consolidate, embody, fuse, include, integrate, merge, mix, subsume, unite

incorporation absorption, amalgamation, assimilation, blend, coalescence, federation, fusion, inclusion, integration, merger, unifying

incorrect erroneous, false, faulty, flawed, improper, inaccurate, inappropriate, inexact, mistaken, out, specious, unfitting, unsuitable, untrue, wide of the mark (*Inf.*), wrong

incorrectness erroneousness, error, fallacy, faultiness, impreciseness, imprecision, impropriety, inaccuracy, inexactness, speciousness, unsoundness, unsuitability, wrongness

incorrigible hardened, hopeless, incurable, intractable, inveterate, irredeemable, unreformed

incorruptibility honesty, honour, integrity, justness, uprightness

incorruptible 1. above suspicion, honest, honourable, just, straight, trustworthy, unbribable, upright 2. everlasting, imperishable, undecaying

increase v. 1. add to, advance, aggrandize, amplify, augment, boost, build up, develop, dilate, enhance, enlarge, escalate, expand, extend, grow, heighten, inflate, intensify, magnify, mount, multiply, proliferate, prolong, raise, snowball, spread, step up (*Inf.*), strengthen, swell, wax ∼n. 2. addition, augmentation, boost, development, enlargement, escalation, expansion, extension, gain, growth, increment, intensification, rise, upsurge, upturn 3. on the increase developing, escalating, expanding, growing, increasing, multiplying, on the rise, proliferating, spreading

increasingly more and more, progressively, to an increasing extent

incredible 1. absurd, beyond belief, far-fetched, implausible, impossible, improbable, inconceivable, preposterous, unbelievable, unimaginable, unthinkable **2.** *Inf.* ace (*Inf.*), amazing, astonishing, astounding, awe-inspiring, extraordinary, far-out (*Sl.*), great, marvellous, prodigious, superhuman, wonderful

incredulity disbelief, distrust, doubt, scepticism, unbelief

incredulous disbelieving, distrustful, doubtful, doubting, dubious, mistrustful, sceptical, suspicious, unbelieving, unconvinced

increment accretion, accrual, accruement, addition, advancement, augmentation, enlargement, gain, increase, step (up)

incriminate accuse, arraign, blacken the name of, blame, charge, impeach, implicate, inculpate, indict, involve, point the finger at (*Inf.*), stigmatize

inculcate drill, drum into, hammer into (*Inf.*), implant, impress, indoctrinate, infuse, instil

inculpate accuse, blame, censure, charge, drag into (*Inf.*), impeach, implicate, incriminate, involve

incumbent binding, compulsory, mandatory, necessary, obligatory

incur arouse, bring (upon oneself), contract, draw, earn, expose oneself to, gain, induce, lay oneself open to, meet with, provoke

incurable *adj.* **1.** dyed-in-the-wool, hopeless, incorrigible, inveterate **2.** fatal, inoperable, irrecoverable, irremediable, remediless, terminal

incurious apathetic, indifferent, pococurante, unconcerned, uninquiring, uninterested

incursion foray, infiltration, inroad, invasion, irruption, penetration, raid

indebted beholden, grateful, in debt, obligated, obliged, under an obligation

indecency bawdiness, coarseness, crudity, foulness, grossness, immodesty, impropriety, impurity, indecorum, indelicacy, lewdness, licentiousness, obscenity, outrageousness, pornography, smut, smuttiness, unseemliness, vileness, vulgarity

indecent 1. blue, coarse, crude, dirty, filthy, foul, gross, immodest, improper, impure, indelicate, lewd, licentious, pornographic, salacious, scatological, smutty, vile **2.** ill-bred, improper, in bad taste, indecorous, offensive, outrageous, tasteless, unbecoming, unseemly, vulgar

indecipherable crabbed, illegible, indistinguishable, unintelligible, unreadable

indecision ambivalence, doubt, hesitancy, hesitation, indecisiveness, irresolution, shilly-shallying (*Inf.*), uncertainty, vacillation, wavering

indecisive 1. doubtful, faltering, hesitating, in two minds (*Inf.*), irresolute, pussyfooting (*Inf.*), tentative, uncertain, undecided, undetermined, vacillating, wavering **2.** inconclusive, indefinite, indeterminate, unclear, undecided

indecorous boorish, churlish, coarse, ill-bred, immodest, impolite, improper, indecent, rude, tasteless, uncivil, uncouth, undignified, unmannerly, unseemly, untoward

indeed actually, certainly, doubtlessly, in point of fact, in truth, positively, really, strictly, to be sure, truly, undeniably, undoubtedly, verily (*Archaic*), veritably

indefatigable assiduous, diligent, dogged, inexhaustible, patient, persevering, pertinacious, relentless, sedulous, tireless, unflagging, unremitting, untiring, unwearied, unwearying

indefensible faulty, inexcusable, insupportable, unforgivable, unjustifiable, unpardonable, untenable, unwarrantable, wrong

indefinable dim, hazy, impalpable, indescribable, indistinct, inexpressible, nameless, obscure, unrealized, vague

indefinite ambiguous, confused, doubtful, equivocal, evasive, general, ill-defined, imprecise, indeterminate, indistinct, inexact, loose, obscure, uncertain, unclear, undefined, undetermined, unfixed, unknown, unlimited, unsettled, vague

indefinitely continually, endlessly, for ever, *sine die*

indelible enduring, indestructible, ineffaceable, ineradicable, inexpungible, inextirpable, ingrained, lasting, permanent

indelicacy bad taste, coarseness, crudity, grossness, immodesty, impropriety, indecency, obscenity, offensiveness, rudeness, smuttiness, suggestiveness, tastelessness, vulgarity

indelicate blue, coarse, crude, embarrassing, gross, immodest, improper, indecent, indecorous, low, near the knuckle (*Inf.*), obscene, off-colour, offensive, risqué, rude, suggestive, tasteless, unbecoming, unseemly, untoward, vulgar

indemnify 1. endorse, guarantee, insure, protect, secure, underwrite 2. compensate, pay, reimburse, remunerate, repair, repay, requite, satisfy

indemnity 1. guarantee, insurance, protection, security 2. compensation, redress, reimbursement, remuneration, reparation, requital, restitution, satisfaction 3. *Law* exemption, immunity, impunity, privilege

indent *v.* 1. ask for, order, request, requisition 2. cut, dint, mark, nick, notch, pink, scallop, score, serrate

indentation bash (*Inf.*), cut, dent, depression, dimple, dip, hollow, jag, nick, notch, pit

independence autarchy, autonomy, freedom, home rule, liberty, self-determination, self-government, self-reliance, self-rule, self-sufficiency, separation, sovereignty

independent 1. absolute, free, liberated, separate, unconnected, unconstrained, uncontrolled, unrelated 2. autarchic, autarchical, autonomous, decontrolled, nonaligned, self-determining, self-governing, separated, sovereign 3. bold, individualistic, liberated, self-contained, self-reliant, self-sufficient, self-supporting, unaided, unconventional

independently alone, autonomously, by oneself, individually, on one's own, separately, solo, unaided

indescribable beggaring description, beyond description, beyond words, incommunicable, indefinable, ineffable, inexpressible, unutterable

indestructible abiding, durable, enduring, everlasting, immortal, imperishable, incorruptible, indelible, indissoluble, lasting, nonperishable, permanent, unbreakable, unfading

indeterminate imprecise, inconclusive, indefinite, inexact, uncertain, undefined, undetermined, unfixed, unspecified, unstipulated, vague

index 1. clue, guide, indication, mark, sign, symptom, token 2. director, fore-

finger, hand, indicator, needle, pointer

indicate 1. add up to (*Inf.*), bespeak, be symptomatic of, betoken, denote, evince, imply, manifest, point to, reveal, show, signify, suggest 2. designate, point out, point to, specify 3. display, express, mark, read, record, register, show

indicated advisable, called-for, desirable, necessary, needed, recommended, suggested

indication clue, evidence, explanation, forewarning, hint, index, inkling, intimation, manifestation, mark, note, omen, portent, sign, signal, suggestion, symptom, warning

indicative exhibitive, indicatory, indicial, pointing to, significant, suggestive, symptomatic

indicator display, gauge, guide, index, mark, marker, meter, pointer, sign, signal, signpost, symbol

indict accuse, arraign, charge, impeach, prosecute, serve with a summons, summon, summons, tax

indictment accusation, allegation, charge, impeachment, prosecution, summons

indifference 1. absence of feeling, aloofness, apathy, callousness, carelessness, coldness, coolness, detachment, disregard, heedlessness, inattention, lack of interest, negligence, stoicalness, unconcern 2. disinterestedness, dispassion, equity, impartiality, neutrality, objectivity 3. insignificance, irrelevance, triviality, unimportance

indifferent 1. aloof, apathetic, callous, careless, cold, cool, detached, distant, heedless, impervious, inattentive, regardless, uncaring, unconcerned, unimpressed, uninterested, unmoved, unresponsive, unsympathetic 2. immaterial, insignificant, of no consequence, unimportant 3. average, fair, mediocre, middling, moderate, ordinary, passable, perfunctory, so-so (*Inf.*), undistinguished, uninspired 4. disinterested, dispassionate, equitable, impartial, neutral, nonaligned, nonpartisan, objective, unbiased, uninvolved, unprejudiced

indigence destitution, distress, necessity, need, penury, poverty, privation, want

indigenous 1. aboriginal, autochthonous, home-grown, native, original 2. congenital, connate, inborn, inbred, inherent, innate

indigent destitute, impecunious, impoverished, in want, necessitous, needy, on one's uppers (*Inf.*), penniless, penurious, poor, poverty-stricken, straitened

indigestion dyspepsia, dyspepsy, upset stomach

indignant angry, annoyed, disgruntled, exasperated, fuming (*Inf.*), furious, heated, huffy (*Inf.*), in a huff, incensed, in high dudgeon, irate, livid (*Inf.*), mad (*Inf.*), miffed (*Inf.*), narked (*Sl.*), peeved (*Inf.*), provoked, resentful, riled, scornful, seeing red (*Inf.*), sore (*Inf.*), up in arms (*Inf.*), wrathful

indignation anger, exasperation, fury, ire (*Literary*), pique, rage, resentment, righteous anger, scorn, umbrage, wrath

indignity abuse, affront, contumely, dishonour, disrespect, humiliation, injury, insult, obloquy, opprobrium, outrage, reproach, slap in the face (*Inf.*), slight, snub

indirect 1. backhanded, circuitous, circumlocutory, crooked, devious, long-drawn-out, meandering, oblique, periphrastic, rambling, roundabout, tortuous, wandering, winding, zigzag 2. ancillary, collateral, contingent, incidental, secondary, subsidiary, unintended

indirectly by implication, circumlocutorily, in a roundabout way, obliquely, periphrastically, second-hand

indiscernible hidden, impalpable, imperceptible, indistinct, indistinguishable, invisible, unapparent, undiscernible

indiscreet foolish, hasty, heedless, ill-advised, ill-considered, ill-judged, impolitic, imprudent, incautious, injudicious, naive, rash, reckless, tactless, undiplomatic, unthinking, unwise

indiscretion error, faux pas, folly, foolishness, gaffe, gaucherie, imprudence, mistake, rashness, recklessness, slip, slip of the tongue, tactlessness

indiscriminate 1. aimless, careless, desultory, general, hit or miss (*Inf.*), random, sweeping, uncritical, undiscriminating, unmethodical, unselective, unsystematic, wholesale 2. chaotic, confused, haphazard, higgledy-piggledy (*Inf.*), jumbled, mingled, miscellaneous, mixed, mongrel, motley, promiscuous, undistinguishable

indispensable crucial, essential, imperative, key, necessary, needed, needful, requisite, vital

indisposed 1. ailing, confined to bed, ill, laid up (*Inf.*), on the sick list (*Inf.*), poorly (*Inf.*), sick, unwell 2. averse, disinclined, loath, reluctant, unwilling

indisposition 1. ailment, ill health, illness, sickness 2. aversion, disinclination, dislike, distaste, hesitancy, reluctance, unwillingness

indisputable absolute, beyond doubt, certain, evident, incontestable, incontrovertible, indubitable, irrefutable, positive, sure, unassailable, undeniable, unquestionable

indissoluble abiding, binding, enduring, eternal, fixed, imperishable, incorruptible, indestructible, inseparable, lasting, permanent, solid, unbreakable

indistinct ambiguous, bleary, blurred, confused, dim, doubtful, faint, fuzzy, hazy, ill-defined, indefinite, indeterminate, indiscernible, indistinguishable, misty, muffled, obscure, out of focus, shadowy, unclear, undefined, unintelligible, vague, weak

indistinguishable 1. alike, identical, like as two peas in a pod (*Inf.*), (the) same, twin 2. imperceptible, indiscernible, invisible, obscure

individual 1. *adj.* characteristic, discrete, distinct, distinctive, exclusive, identical, idiosyncratic, own, particular, peculiar, personal, personalized, proper, respective, separate, several, single, singular, special, specific, unique 2. *n.* being, body (*Inf.*), character, creature, mortal, party, person, personage, soul, type, unit

individualism egocentricity, egoism, freethinking, independence, originality, self-direction, self-interest, self-reliance

individualist freethinker, independent, loner, lone wolf, maverick, nonconformist, original

individualistic 1. characteristic, distinctive, idiosyncratic, individual, original, particular, special, typical, unique 2. egocentric, egoistic, independent, self-reliant

individuality character, discreteness, distinction, distinctiveness, originality, peculiarity, personality, separateness, singularity, uniqueness

individually apart, independently, one at a time, one by one, personally, separately, severally, singly

indoctrinate brainwash, drill, ground,

imbue, initiate, instruct, school, teach, train

indoctrination brainwashing, drilling, grounding, inculcation, instruction, schooling, training

indolence faineance, faineancy, heaviness, idleness, inactivity, inertia, inertness, languidness, languor, laziness, lethargy, shirking, skiving (*Brit. sl.*), slacking, sloth, sluggishness, torpidity, torpor

indolent fainéant, idle, inactive, inert, lackadaisical, languid, lazy, lethargic, listless, lumpish, slack, slothful, slow, sluggish, torpid, workshy

indomitable invincible, resolute, staunch, steadfast, unbeatable, unconquerable, unflinching, untameable, unyielding

indorse see ENDORSE

indorsement see ENDORSEMENT

indubitable certain, evident, incontestable, incontrovertible, indisputable, irrefutable, obvious, sure, unarguable, undeniable, undoubted, unquestionable, veritable

induce 1. actuate, convince, draw, encourage, get, impel, incite, influence, instigate, move, persuade, press, prevail upon, prompt, talk into **2.** bring about, cause, effect, engender, generate, give rise to, lead to, occasion, produce, set in motion

inducement attraction, bait, carrot (*Inf.*), cause, come-on (*Inf.*), consideration, encouragement, impulse, incentive, incitement, influence, lure, motive, reward, spur, stimulus, urge

induct inaugurate, initiate, install, introduce, invest, swear in

induction 1. inauguration, initiation, installation, institution, introduction, investiture **2.** conclusion, generalization, inference

indulge 1. cater to, give way to, gratify, pander to, regale, satiate, satisfy, treat oneself to, yield to **2.** *With* in bask in, give free rein to, give oneself up to, luxuriate in, revel in, wallow in **3.** baby, coddle, cosset, favour, foster, give in to, go along with, humour, mollycoddle, pamper, pet, spoil

indulgence 1. excess, fondness, immoderation, intemperance, intemperateness, kindness, leniency, pampering, partiality, permissiveness, profligacy, profligateness, spoiling **2.** appeasement, fulfilment, gratification, satiation, satisfaction **3.** extravagance, favour, luxury, privilege, treat **4.** courtesy, forbearance, good will, patience, tolerance, understanding

indulgent compliant, easy-going, favourable, fond, forbearing, gentle, gratifying, kind, kindly, lenient, liberal, mild, permissive, tender, tolerant, understanding

industrialist baron, big businessman, boss, capitalist, captain of industry, financier, magnate, manufacturer, producer, tycoon

industrious active, assiduous, busy, conscientious, diligent, energetic, hardworking, laborious, persevering, persistent, productive, purposeful, sedulous, steady, tireless, zealous

industriously assiduously, conscientiously, diligently, doggedly, hard, like a Trojan, nose to the grindstone (*Inf.*), perseveringly, sedulously, steadily, without slacking

industry 1. business, commerce, commercial enterprise, manufacturing, production, trade **2.** activity, application, assiduity, determination, diligence, effort, labour, perseverance, persistence, tirelessness, toil, vigour, zeal

inebriate *v.* **1.** intoxicate, make drunk, stupefy **2.** animate, arouse, carry away, excite, exhilarate, fire, stimulate ~*n.* **3.** alcoholic, boozer (*Inf.*), dipsomaniac, drunk, drunkard, heavy drinker, lush (*U.S. sl.*), soak (*Sl.*), sot, toper

inebriated befuddled, blind drunk, blotto (*Sl.*), drunk, fou *or* fu' (*Scot.*), half-cut (*Inf.*), half seas over (*Inf.*), high (*Inf.*), high as a kite (*Inf.*), inebriate, in one's cups, intoxicated, legless (*Inf.*), merry, paralytic (*Inf.*), pie-eyed (*Sl.*), plastered (*Sl.*), smashed (*Sl.*), sozzled (*Inf.*), stoned (*Sl.*), the worse for drink, three sheets in the wind (*Inf.*), tight (*Inf.*), tipsy, under the influence (*Inf.*), under the weather (*Inf.*)

inebriation crapulence, drunkenness, inebriety, insobriety, intemperance, intoxication, sottishness

ineffable beyond words, incommunicable, indefinable, indescribable, inexpressible, unspeakable, unutterable

ineffective barren, bootless, feeble, fruitless, futile, idle, impotent, inadequate, ineffectual, inefficacious, inefficient, unavailing, unproductive, useless, vain, weak, worthless

ineffectual abortive, bootless, emasculate, feeble, fruitless, futile, idle, impotent, inadequate, incompetent, ineffective, inefficacious, inefficient, inept, lame, powerless, unavailing, useless, vain, weak

inefficacious abortive, futile, ineffective, ineffectual, unavailing, unproductive, unsuccessful

inefficacy futility, inadequacy, ineffectiveness, ineffectuality, nonsuccess, unproductiveness, uselessness

inefficiency carelessness, disorganization, incompetence, muddle, slackness

inefficient disorganized, feeble, incapable, incompetent, ineffectual, inefficacious, inept, inexpert, slipshod, sloppy, wasteful, weak

inelegant awkward, clumsy, coarse, crass, crude, gauche, graceless, indelicate, laboured, rough, uncouth, uncultivated, ungainly, ungraceful, unpolished, unrefined

ineligible disqualified, incompetent (*Law*), objectionable, ruled out, unacceptable, undesirable, unequipped, unfit, unfitted, unqualified, unsuitable

inept 1. awkward, bumbling, bungling, cack-handed (*Inf.*), clumsy, gauche, incompetent, inexpert, maladroit, unhandy, unskilful, unworkmanlike **2**. absurd, improper, inappropriate, inapt, infelicitous, malapropos, meaningless, out of place, pointless, ridiculous, unfit, unsuitable

ineptitude 1. clumsiness, gaucheness, incapacity, incompetence, inexpertness, unfitness, unhandiness **2**. absurdity, inappropriateness, pointlessness, uselessness

inequality bias, difference, disparity, disproportion, diversity, imparity, irregularity, lack of balance, preferentiality, prejudice, unevenness

inequitable biased, discriminatory, one-sided, partial, partisan, preferential, prejudiced, unfair, unjust

inequity bias, discrimination, injustice, one-sidedness, prejudice, unfairness, unjustness

inert dead, dormant, dull, idle, immobile, inactive, inanimate, indolent, lazy, leaden, lifeless, motionless, passive, quiescent, slack, slothful, sluggish, slumberous (*Chiefly poetic*), static, still, torpid, unmoving, unreactive, unresponsive

inertia apathy, deadness, disinclina-

tion to move, drowsiness, dullness, idleness, immobility, inactivity, indolence, languor, lassitude, laziness, lethargy, listlessness, passivity, sloth, sluggishness, stillness, stupor, torpor, unresponsiveness

inescapable certain, destined, fated, ineluctable, ineludible (*Rare*), inevitable, inexorable, sure, unavoidable

inessential 1. *adj*. dispensable, extraneous, extrinsic, needless, optional, redundant, spare, superfluous, surplus, uncalled-for, unnecessary **2**. *n*. accessory, extra, extravagance, luxury, makeweight, superfluity, trimming

inestimable beyond price, immeasurable, incalculable, invaluable, precious, priceless, prodigious

inevitable assured, certain, decreed, destined, fixed, ineluctable, inescapable, inexorable, necessary, ordained, settled, sure, unavoidable, unpreventable

inevitably as a necessary consequence, as a result, automatically, certainly, necessarily, of necessity, perforce, surely, unavoidably, willy-nilly

inexact imprecise, inaccurate, incorrect, indefinite, indeterminate, off

inexcusable indefensible, inexpiable, outrageous, unforgivable, unjustifiable, unpardonable, unwarrantable

inexhaustible 1. bottomless, boundless, endless, illimitable, infinite, limitless, measureless, never-ending, unbounded **2**. indefatigable, tireless, undaunted, unfailing, unflagging, untiring, unwearied, unwearying

inexorable adamant, cruel, hard, harsh, immovable, implacable, ineluctable, inescapable, inflexible, merciless, obdurate, pitiless, relentless, remorseless, severe, unappeasable, unbending, unrelenting, unyielding

inexorably implacably, inevitably, irresistibly, relentlessly, remorselessly, unrelentingly

inexpedient disadvantageous, ill-advised, ill-considered, ill-judged, impolitic, impractical, improper, imprudent, inadvisable, inappropriate, indiscreet, injudicious, misguided, unadvisable, undesirable, undiplomatic, unsuitable, unwise

inexpensive bargain, budget, cheap, economical, low-cost, low-priced, modest, reasonable

inexperience callowness, greenness,

ignorance, newness, rawness, unexpert-ness, unfamiliarity

inexperienced amateur, callow, fresh, green, immature, new, raw, unaccus-tomed, unacquainted, unfamiliar, un-fledged, unpractised, unschooled, unsea-soned, unskilled, untrained, untried, un-used, unversed, wet behind the ears (*Inf.*)

inexpert amateurish, awkward, bun-gling, cack-handed (*Inf.*), clumsy, inept, maladroit, skill-less, unhandy, unprac-tised, unprofessional, unskilful, un-skilled, unworkmanlike

inexplicable baffling, beyond compre-hension, enigmatic, incomprehensible, inscrutable, insoluble, mysterious, mys-tifying, strange, unaccountable, unfath-omable, unintelligible

inexpressible incommunicable, inde-finable, indescribable, ineffable, un-speakable, unutterable

inexpressive bland, blank, cold, dead, deadpan, emotionless, empty, expres-sionless, impassive, inanimate, inscru-table, lifeless, stony, vacant

inextinguishable enduring, eternal, immortal, imperishable, indestructible, irrepressible, undying, unquenchable, unsuppressible

inextricably indissolubly, indistin-guishably, inseparably, intricately, irre-trievably, totally

infallibility 1. faultlessness, impec-cability, irrefutability, omniscience, per-fection, supremacy, unerringness 2. de-pendability, reliability, safety, sureness, trustworthiness

infallible 1. faultless, impeccable, om-niscient, perfect, unerring, unimpeach-able 2. certain, dependable, foolproof, reliable, sure, sure-fire (*Inf.*), trust-worthy, unbeatable, unfailing

infamous abominable, atrocious, base, detestable, disgraceful, dishonourable, disreputable, egregious, flagitious, hate-ful, heinous, ignominious, ill-famed, in-iquitous, loathsome, monstrous, nefari-ous, notorious, odious, opprobrious, out-rageous, scandalous, scurvy, shameful, shocking, vile, villainous, wicked

infamy abomination, atrocity, dis-credit, disgrace, dishonour, disrepute, ig-nominy, notoriety, obloquy, odium, op-probrium, outrageousness, scandal, shame, stigma, villainy

infancy 1. babyhood, early childhood

2. beginnings, cradle, dawn, early stages, emergence, inception, origins, outset, start

infant 1. *n.* babe, baby, bairn (*Scot.*), child, little one, neonate, newborn child, suckling, toddler, tot, wean (*Scot.*) 2. *adj.* baby, dawning, developing, early, emergent, growing, immature, initial, nascent, newborn, unfledged, young

infantile babyish, childish, immature, puerile, tender, weak, young

infatuate befool, beguile, besot, be-witch, captivate, delude, enchant, enrap-ture, enravish, fascinate, make a fool of, mislead, obsess, stupefy, sweep one off one's feet, turn (someone's) head

infatuated beguiled, besotted, be-witched, captivated, carried away, crazy about (*Inf.*), enamoured, enraptured, fascinated, head over heels in love with, inflamed, intoxicated, obsessed, pos-sessed, smitten (*Inf.*), spellbound, swept off one's feet, under the spell of

infatuation crush (*Inf.*), fixation, fol-ly, foolishness, madness, obsession, pas-sion, thing (*Inf.*)

infect affect, blight, contaminate, cor-rupt, defile, influence, poison, pollute, spread to *or* among, taint, touch, vitiate

infection contagion, contamination, corruption, defilement, poison, pollu-tion, septicity, virus

infectious catching, communicable, contagious, contaminating, corrupting, defiling, infective, pestilential, poison-ing, polluting, spreading, transmittable, virulent, vitiating

infelicity 1. inappropriateness, inapt-ness, incongruity, unsuitability, wrong-ness 2. bad luck, misery, misfortune, sadness, unhappiness, woe, wretched-ness

infer conclude, conjecture, deduce, de-rive, gather, presume, read between the lines, surmise, understand

inference assumption, conclusion, conjecture, consequence, corollary, de-duction, illation (*Rare*), presumption, reading, surmise

inferior *adj.* 1. junior, lesser, lower, menial, minor, secondary, subordinate, subsidiary, under, underneath 2. bad, imperfect, indifferent, low-grade, mean, mediocre, poor, poorer, second-class, second-rate, shoddy, substandard, worse ~*n.* 3. junior, menial, subordinate, underling

inferiority 1. badness, deficiency, imperfection, inadequacy, insignificance, meanness, mediocrity, shoddiness, unimportance, worthlessness **2.** abasement, inferior status *or* standing, lowliness, subordination, subservience

infernal 1. chthonian, Hadean, hellish, lower, nether, Plutonian, Stygian, Tartarean (*Literary*), underworld **2.** accursed, damnable, damned, demonic, devilish, diabolical, fiendish, hellish, malevolent, malicious, satanic

infertile barren, infecund, nonproductive, sterile, unfruitful, unproductive

infertility barrenness, infecundity, sterility, unfruitfulness, unproductiveness

infest beset, flood, invade, overrun, penetrate, ravage, swarm, throng

infested àlive, beset, crawling, lousy, overrun, pervaded, plagued, ravaged, ridden, swarming, teeming

infidel atheist, freethinker, Gentile, giaour (*Turkish*), heathen, heretic, pagan, sceptic, unbeliever

infidelity 1. adultery, bad faith, betrayal, cheating (*Inf.*), disloyalty, duplicity, faithlessness, false-heartedness, falseness, perfidy, unfaithfulness **2.** apostasy, disbelief, irreligion, scepticism, treachery, unbelief

infiltrate creep in, filter through, insinuate oneself, penetrate, percolate, permeate, pervade, sneak in (*Inf.*), work *or* worm one's way into

infinite absolute, all-embracing, bottomless, boundless, enormous, eternal, everlasting, illimitable, immeasurable, immense, inestimable, inexhaustible, interminable, limitless, measureless, never-ending, numberless, perpetual, stupendous, total, unbounded, uncounted, untold, vast, wide, without end, without number

infinitesimal atomic, inappreciable, insignificant, microscopic, minuscule, minute, negligible, teeny, tiny, unnoticeable, wee

infinity boundlessness, endlessness, eternity, immensity, infinitude, perpetuity, vastness

infirm 1. ailing, debilitated, decrepit, doddering, doddery, enfeebled, failing, feeble, frail, lame, weak **2.** faltering, indecisive, insecure, irresolute, shaky, unsound, unstable, vacillating, wavering, weak, wobbly

infirmity 1. debility, decrepitude, deficiency, feebleness, frailty, ill health, imperfection, sickliness, vulnerability **2.** ailment, defect, disorder, failing, fault, malady, sickness, weakness

infix 1. engraft, fasten, implant, insert, inset, introduce, place, set **2.** drum into, entrench, impress, inculcate, ingrain, instil

inflame 1. agitate, anger, arouse, embitter, enrage, exasperate, excite, fire, foment, heat, ignite, impassion, incense, infuriate, intoxicate, kindle, madden, provoke, rile, rouse, stimulate **2.** aggravate, exacerbate, exasperate, fan, increase, intensify, worsen

inflamed angry, chafing, festering, fevered, heated, hot, infected, red, septic, sore, swollen

inflammable combustible, flammable, incendiary

inflammation burning, heat, painfulness, rash, redness, sore, soreness, tenderness

inflammatory anarchic, demagogic, explosive, fiery, incendiary, inflaming, instigative, insurgent, intemperate, provocative, rabble-rousing, rabid, riotous, seditious

inflate aerate, aggrandize, amplify, balloon, bloat, blow up, boost, dilate, distend, enlarge, escalate, exaggerate, expand, increase, puff up *or* out, pump up, swell

inflated bombastic, exaggerated, grandiloquent, ostentatious, overblown, swollen

inflation aggrandizement, blowing up, distension, enhancement, enlargement, escalation, expansion, extension, increase, intensification, puffiness, rise, spread, swelling, tumefaction

inflect 1. intonate, modulate **2.** *Gram.* conjugate, decline **3.** arch, bend, bow, crook, curve, flex, round

inflection 1. accentuation, bend, bow, crook, curvature, intonation, modulation **2.** *Gram.* conjugation, declension **3.** angle, arc, arch

inflexibility 1. hardness, immovability, inelasticity, rigidity, stiffness, stringency **2.** fixity, intransigence, obduracy, obstinacy, steeliness

inflexible 1. adamant, brassbound, dyed-in-the-wool, firm, fixed, hard and fast, immovable, immutable, implacable, inexorable, intractable, iron, obdurate, obstinate, relentless, resolute, rigorous, set, set in one's ways, steadfast, steely, strict, stringent, stubborn, unadaptable, unbending, unchangeable, uncompromising, unyielding **2.** hard, hardened, inelastic, nonflexible, rigid, stiff, taut

inflict administer, apply, deliver, exact, impose, levy, mete *or* deal out, visit, wreak

infliction 1. administration, exaction, imposition, perpetration, wreaking **2.** affliction, penalty, punishment, trouble, visitation, worry

influence *n.* **1.** agency, ascendancy, authority, control, credit, direction, domination, effect, guidance, magnetism, mastery, power, pressure, rule, spell, sway, weight **2.** clout (*Inf.*), connections, good offices, hold, importance, leverage, power, prestige, pull (*Inf.*), weight ~*v.* **3.** act *or* work upon, affect, arouse, bias, control, count, direct, dispose, guide, impel, impress, incite, incline, induce, instigate, lead to believe, manipulate, modify, move, persuade, predispose, prompt, rouse, sway **4.** bring pressure to bear upon, carry weight with, make oneself felt, pull strings (*Inf.*)

influential authoritative, controlling, effective, efficacious, forcible, guiding, important, instrumental, leading, meaningful, momentous, moving, persuasive, potent, powerful, significant, telling, weighty

influx arrival, convergence, flow, incursion, inflow, inrush, inundation, invasion, rush

infold *see* ENFOLD

inform 1. acquaint, advise, apprise, communicate, enlighten, give (someone) to understand, instruct, leak to, let know, make conversant (with), notify, put (someone) in the picture (*Inf.*), send word to, teach, tell, tip off **2.** *Often with* **against** *or* **on** betray, blab, blow the whistle on (*U.S. inf.*), clype (*Scot.*), denounce, grass (*Brit. sl.*), incriminate, inculpate, nark (*Brit. sl.*), peach (*Sl.*), rat, snitch (*Sl.*), squeal (*Sl.*), tell on (*Inf.*) **3.** animate, characterize, illuminate, imbue, inspire, permeate, suffuse, typify

informal casual, colloquial, easy, familiar, natural, relaxed, simple, unceremonious, unconstrained, unofficial

informality casualness, ease, familiarity, lack of ceremony, naturalness, relaxation, simplicity

information advice, counsel, data, dope (*Sl.*), facts, gen (*Brit. inf.*), info (*Inf.*), inside story, instruction, intelligence, knowledge, lowdown (*Inf.*), material, message, news, notice, report, tidings, word

informative chatty, communicative, edifying, educational, enlightening, forthcoming, gossipy, illuminating, instructive, newsy, revealing

informed abreast, acquainted, *au courant*, *au fait*, briefed, conversant, enlightened, erudite, expert, familiar, genned up (*Brit. inf.*), in the know (*Inf.*), knowledgeable, learned, posted, primed, reliable, up, up to date, versed, well-read

informer accuser, betrayer, grass (*Brit. sl.*), Judas, nark (*Brit. sl.*), sneak, squealer (*Sl.*), stool pigeon

infraction breach, breaking, contravention, infringement, nonfulfilment, transgression, trespass, violation

infrequent few and far between, occasional, rare, sporadic, uncommon, unusual

infringe 1. break, contravene, disobey, transgress, violate **2.** *With* **on** *or* **upon** encroach, intrude, trespass

infringement breach, contravention, infraction, noncompliance, nonobservance, transgression, trespass, violation

infuriate anger, be like a red rag to a bull, enrage, exasperate, get one's back up (*Inf.*), get one's goat (*Sl.*), incense, irritate, madden, make one's blood boil, make one see red (*Inf.*), make one's hackles rise, provoke, raise one's hackles, rile

infuriating aggravating (*Inf.*), annoying, exasperating, galling, irritating, maddening, mortifying, pestilential, provoking, vexatious

infuse 1. breathe into, engraft, impart to, implant, inculcate, inspire, instil, introduce **2.** brew, macerate, soak, steep

ingenious adroit, bright, brilliant, clever, crafty, creative, dexterous, fertile, inventive, masterly, original, ready, resourceful, shrewd, skilful, subtle

ingenuity adroitness, cleverness, faculty, flair, genius, gift, ingeniousness, inventiveness, knack, originality, resourcefulness, sharpness, shrewdness, skill, turn

ingenuous artless, candid, childlike, frank, guileless, honest, innocent, naive, open, plain, simple, sincere, trustful, trusting, unreserved, unsophisticated, unstudied

ingenuousness artlessness, candour, frankness, guilelessness, innocence, naivety, openness, trustingness, unsuspiciousness

inglorious discreditable, disgraceful, dishonourable, disreputable, failed, humiliating, ignoble, ignominious, infamous, obscure, shameful, unheroic, unknown, unsuccessful, unsung

ingraft see ENGRAFT

ingrain embed, entrench, fix, imbue, implant, impress, imprint, instil, root

ingrained brassbound, constitutional, deep-rooted, deep-seated, fixed, fundamental, hereditary, inborn, inbred, inbuilt, indelible, ineradicable, inherent, in the blood, intrinsic, inveterate, rooted

ingratiate be a yes man, blandish, crawl, curry favour, fawn, flatter, get in with (*Inf.*), get on the right side of, grovel, insinuate oneself, lick (someone's) boots, play up to, rub (someone) up the right way (*Inf.*), seek the favour (of someone), suck up to (*Inf.*), toady, worm oneself into (someone's) favour

ingratiating bootlicking (*Inf.*), crawling, fawning, flattering, humble, obsequious, servile, sycophantic, timeserving, toadying, unctuous

ingratitude thanklessness, unappreciativeness, ungratefulness

ingredient component, constituent, element, part

ingress access, admission, admittance, door, entrance, entrée, entry, right of entry, way in

ingulf see ENGULF

inhabit abide, dwell, live, lodge, make one's home, occupy, people, populate, possess, reside, take up residence in, tenant

inhabitant aborigine, citizen, denizen, dweller, indigene, indweller, inmate, native, occupant, occupier, resident, tenant

inhabited colonized, developed, held, occupied, peopled, populated, settled, tenanted

inhalation breath, breathing, inhaling, inspiration

inhale breathe in, draw in, gasp, respire, suck in

inharmonious antipathetic, cacophonous, clashing, discordant, dissonant, grating, harsh, incompatible, inconsonant, jangling, jarring, strident, tuneless,

unharmonious, unmelodious, unmusical

inherent basic, congenital, connate, essential, hereditary, inborn, inbred, inbuilt, ingrained, inherited, innate, instinctive, intrinsic, native, natural

inherit accede to, be bequeathed, be left, come into, fall heir to, succeed to

inheritance bequest, birthright, heritage, legacy, patrimony

inheritor beneficiary, heir, legatee, recipient, successor

inhibit arrest, bar, bridle, check, constrain, cramp (someone's) style (*Inf.*), curb, debar, discourage, forbid, frustrate, hinder, hold back *or* in, impede, obstruct, prevent, prohibit, restrain, stop

inhibited constrained, frustrated, guarded, repressed, reserved, reticent, self-conscious, shy, subdued, uptight (*Inf.*), withdrawn

inhibition bar, check, embargo, hang-up (*Sl.*), hindrance, interdict, mental blockage, obstacle, prohibition, reserve, restraint, restriction, reticence, self-consciousness, shyness

inhospitable 1. cool, uncongenial, unfriendly, ungenerous, unkind, unreceptive, unsociable, unwelcoming, xenophobic **2.** bare, barren, bleak, desolate, empty, forbidding, hostile, lonely, sterile, unfavourable, uninhabitable

inhuman animal, barbaric, barbarous, bestial, brutal, cold-blooded, cruel, diabolical, fiendish, heartless, merciless, pitiless, remorseless, ruthless, savage, unfeeling, vicious

inhumane brutal, cruel, heartless, pitiless, uncompassionate, unfeeling, unkind, unsympathetic

inhumanity atrocity, barbarism, brutality, brutishness, cold-bloodedness, cold-heartedness, cruelty, hardheartedness, heartlessness, pitilessness, ruthlessness, unkindness, viciousness

inhumation burial, entombment, interment, sepulture

inhume bury, entomb, inter, lay to rest, sepulchre

inimical adverse, antagonistic, antipathetic, contrary, destructive, disaffected, harmful, hostile, hurtful, ill-disposed, injurious, noxious, opposed, oppugnant (*Rare*), pernicious, repugnant, unfavourable, unfriendly, unwelcoming

inimitable consummate, incomparable, matchless, nonpareil, peerless, supreme, unequalled, unexampled, unique, unmatched, unparalleled, unrivalled, unsurpassable

iniquitous abominable, accursed, atrocious, base, criminal, evil, heinous, immoral, infamous, nefarious, reprehensible, reprobate, sinful, unjust, unrighteous, vicious, wicked

iniquity abomination, baseness, crime, evil, evildoing, heinousness, infamy, injustice, misdeed, offence, sin, sinfulness, unrighteousness, wickedness, wrong, wrongdoing

initial adj. beginning, commencing, early, first, inaugural, inceptive, inchoate, incipient, introductory, opening, primary

initially at or in the beginning, at first, at the outset, at the start, first, firstly, in the early stages, originally, primarily, to begin with

initiate v. 1. begin, break the ice, commence, get under way, inaugurate, institute, kick off (Inf.), launch, lay the foundations of, open, originate, pioneer, set going, set in motion, set the ball rolling, start 2. coach, familiarize with, indoctrinate, induct, instate, instruct, introduce, invest, teach, train ~n. 3. beginner, convert, entrant, learner, member, novice, probationer, proselyte, tyro

initiation admission, commencement, debut, enrolment, entrance, inauguration, inception, induction, installation, instatement, introduction, investiture

initiative 1. advantage, beginning, commencement, first move, first step, lead 2. ambition, drive, dynamism, enterprise, get-up-and-go (Inf.), inventiveness, leadership, originality, push (Inf.), resource, resourcefulness

inject 1. inoculate, jab (Inf.), shoot (Inf.), vaccinate 2. bring in, infuse, insert, instil, interject, introduce

injection 1. inoculation, jab (Inf.), shot (Inf.), vaccination, vaccine 2. dose, infusion, insertion, interjection, introduction

injudicious foolish, hasty, ill-advised, ill-judged, ill-timed, impolitic, imprudent, incautious, inconsiderate, indiscreet, inexpedient, rash, unthinking, unwise

injunction admonition, command, dictate, exhortation, instruction, mandate, order, precept, ruling

injure abuse, blemish, blight, break,

damage, deface, disable, harm, hurt, impair, maltreat, mar, ruin, spoil, tarnish, undermine, vitiate, weaken, wound, wrong

injured 1. broken, disabled, hurt, lamed, undermined, weakened, wounded 2. cut to the quick, disgruntled, displeased, hurt, long-suffering, put out, reproachful, stung, unhappy, upset, wounded 3. abused, blackened, blemished, defamed, ill-treated, maligned, maltreated, offended, tarnished, vilified, wronged

injurious adverse, bad, baneful (Archaic), corrupting, damaging, deleterious, destructive, detrimental, disadvantageous, harmful, hurtful, iniquitous, mischievous, noxious, pernicious, ruinous, slanderous, unconducive, unhealthy, unjust, wrongful

injury abuse, damage, detriment, disservice, evil, grievance, harm, hurt, ill, injustice, mischief, ruin, wound, wrong

injustice bias, discrimination, favouritism, inequality, inequity, iniquity, onesidedness, oppression, partiality, partisanship, prejudice, unfairness, unjustness, unlawfulness, wrong

inkling clue, conception, faintest or foggiest idea, glimmering, hint, idea, indication, intimation, notion, suggestion, suspicion, whisper

inland adj. domestic, interior, internal, upcountry

inlet arm (of the sea), bay, bight, cove, creek, entrance, firth or frith (Scot.), ingress, passage, sea loch (Scot.)

inmost or **innermost** basic, buried, central, deep, deepest, essential, intimate, personal, private, secret

innards 1. entrails, guts, insides (Inf.), intestines, inwards, viscera, vitals 2. guts (Inf.), mechanism, works

innate congenital, connate, constitutional, essential, inborn, inbred, indigenous, ingrained, inherent, inherited, instinctive, intrinsic, intuitive, native, natural

inner 1. central, essential, inside, interior, internal, intestinal, inward, middle 2. esoteric, hidden, intimate, personal, private, repressed, secret, unrevealed 3. emotional, mental, psychological, spiritual

innkeeper host, hostess, hotelier, landlady, landlord, mine host, publican

innocence 1. blamelessness, chastity,

clean hands, guiltlessness, incorruptibility, probity, purity, righteousness, sinlessness, stainlessness, uprightness, virginity, virtue **2.** harmlessness, innocuousness, innoxiousness, inoffensiveness **3.** artlessness, credulousness, freshness, guilelessness, gullibility, inexperience, ingenuousness, naiveté, simplicity, unsophistication, unworldliness **4.** ignorance, lack of knowledge, nescience (*Literary*), unawareness, unfamiliarity

innocent *adj.* **1.** blameless, clear, faultless, guiltless, honest, in the clear, not guilty, uninvolved, unoffending **2.** chaste, immaculate, impeccable, incorrupt, pristine, pure, righteous, sinless, spotless, stainless, unblemished, unsullied, upright, virgin, virginal **3.** *With of* clear of, empty of, free from, ignorant, lacking, nescient, unacquainted with, unaware, unfamiliar with, untouched by **4.** harmless, innocuous, inoffensive, unmalicious, unobjectionable, well-intentioned, well-meant **5.** artless, childlike, credulous, frank, guileless, gullible, ingenuous, naive, open, simple, unsuspicious, unworldly, wet behind the ears (*Inf.*) ~*n.* **6.** babe (in arms) (*Inf.*), child, greenhorn (*Inf.*), ingénue (*fem.*)

innocuous harmless, innocent, innoxious, inoffensive, safe, unobjectionable

innovation alteration, change, departure, introduction, modernism, modernization, newness, novelty, variation

innuendo aspersion, hint, implication, imputation, insinuation, intimation, overtone, suggestion, whisper

innumerable beyond number, countless, incalculable, infinite, many, multitudinous, myriad, numberless, numerous, unnumbered, untold

inoffensive harmless, humble, innocent, innocuous, innoxious, mild, neutral, nonprovocative, peaceable, quiet, retiring, unobjectionable, unobtrusive, unoffending

inoperable impracticable, impractical, nonviable, unrealistic, unworkable

inoperative broken, broken-down, defective, *hors de combat*, ineffective, ineffectual, inefficacious, invalid, nonactive, null and void, out of action, out of commission, out of order, out of service, unserviceable, unworkable, useless

inopportune ill-chosen, ill-timed, inappropriate, inauspicious, inconvenient, malapropos, mistimed, unfavourable, unfortunate, unpropitious, unseasonable, unsuitable, untimely

inordinate disproportionate, excessive, exorbitant, extravagant, immoderate, intemperate, preposterous, unconscionable, undue, unreasonable, unrestrained, unwarranted

inorganic artificial, chemical, manmade, mineral

inquest inquiry, inquisition, investigation, probe

inquietude anxiety, apprehension, disquiet, disquietude, jumpiness, nervousness, restlessness, the jitters (*Inf.*), unease, uneasiness, worry

inquire 1. examine, explore, inspect, investigate, look into, make inquiries, probe, scrutinize, search **2.** *Also* **enquire** ask, query, question, request information, seek information

inquiring analytical, curious, doubtful, inquisitive, interested, investigative, outward-looking, probing, questioning, searching, wondering

inquiry 1. examination, exploration, inquest, interrogation, investigation, probe, research, scrutiny, search, study, survey **2.** *Also* **enquiry** query, question

inquisition cross-examination, examination, grilling (*Inf.*), inquest, inquiry, investigation, question, quizzing, third degree (*Inf.*)

inquisitive curious, inquiring, intrusive, nosy (*Inf.*), nosy-parkering (*Inf.*), peering, probing, prying, questioning, scrutinizing, snooping (*Inf.*), snoopy (*Inf.*)

inroad 1. advance, encroachment, foray, incursion, intrusion, invasion, irruption, onslaught, raid **2. make inroads upon** consume, eat away, eat up *or* into, encroach upon, use up

insalubrious injurious, insanitary, noxious, unhealthful, unhealthy, unwholesome

insane 1. crazed, crazy, demented, deranged, mad, mentally disordered, mentally ill, *non compos mentis*, of unsound mind, out of one's mind, unhinged **2.** barmy (*Sl.*), batty (*Sl.*), bonkers (*Sl.*), cracked (*Sl.*), crackers (*Sl.*), cuckoo (*Inf.*), loony (*Sl.*), loopy (*Inf.*), mental (*Sl.*), nuts (*Sl.*), nutty (*Sl.*), off one's chump (*Inf.*), off one's head (*Inf.*), off one's nut (*Inf.*), off one's rocker (*Inf.*), round the bend (*Inf.*), round the twist (*Inf.*), screwy (*Inf.*) **3.** bizarre, daft

(*Inf.*), fatuous, foolish, idiotic, impractical, irrational, irresponsible, lunatic (*Inf.*), preposterous, senseless, stupid

insanitary contaminated, dirtied, dirty, disease-ridden, feculent, filthy, impure, infected, infested, insalubrious, noxious, polluted, unclean, unhealthy, unhygienic

insanity 1. aberration, craziness, delirium, dementia, frenzy, madness, mental derangement, mental disorder, mental illness **2.** folly, irresponsibility, lunacy, preposterousness, senselessness, stupidity

insatiable gluttonous, greedy, insatiate, intemperate, quenchless, rapacious, ravenous, unappeasable, unquenchable, voracious

inscribe 1. carve, cut, engrave, etch, impress, imprint **2.** engross, enlist, enrol, enter, record, register, write **3.** address, dedicate

inscription dedication, engraving, label, legend, lettering, saying, words

inscrutable 1. blank, deadpan, enigmatic, impenetrable, poker-faced (*Inf.*), sphinxlike, unreadable **2.** hidden, incomprehensible, inexplicable, mysterious, undiscoverable, unexplainable, unfathomable, unintelligible

insecure 1. afraid, anxious, uncertain, unconfident, unsure **2.** dangerous, defenceless, exposed, hazardous, ill-protected, open to attack, perilous, unguarded, unprotected, unsafe, unshielded, vulnerable **3.** built upon sand, flimsy, frail, insubstantial, loose, on thin ice, precarious, rickety, rocky, shaky, unreliable, unsound, unstable, unsteady, weak, wobbly

insecurity 1. anxiety, fear, uncertainty, unsureness, worry **2.** danger, defencelessness, hazard, peril, risk, uncertainty, vulnerability, weakness **3.** dubiety, frailness, instability, precariousness, shakiness, uncertainty, unreliability, unsteadiness, weakness

insensate 1. anaesthetized, dead, inanimate, inert, insensible, insentient, lifeless, numbed, out (*Inf.*), unconscious **2.** hardened, imperceptive, impercipient, indifferent, insensitive, inured, obtuse, stolid, thick-skinned, thoughtless, unfeeling, unperceiving **3.** brainless, fatuous, foolish, mindless, senseless, stupid, thoughtless, unreasonable, witless

insensibility 1. apathy, callousness, dullness, indifference, insensitivity, lethargy, thoughtlessness, torpor **2.** inertness, numbness, unconsciousness

insensible 1. anaesthetized, benumbed, dull, inert, insensate, numbed, senseless, stupid, torpid **2.** apathetic, callous, cold, deaf, hard-hearted, impassive, impervious, indifferent, oblivious, unaffected, unaware, unconscious, unfeeling, unmindful, unmoved, unresponsive, unsusceptible, untouched **3.** imperceivable, imperceptible, minuscule, negligible, unnoticeable

insensibly by degrees, gradually, imperceptibly, invisibly, little by little, slightly, unnoticeably

insensitive 1. callous, crass, hardened, imperceptive, indifferent, obtuse, tactless, thick-skinned, tough, uncaring, unconcerned, unfeeling, unresponsive, unsusceptible **2.** *With* to dead to, immune to, impervious to, nonreactive, proof against, unaffected by, unmoved by

inseparable 1. conjoined, inalienable, indissoluble, indivisible, inseverable **2.** bosom, close, devoted, intimate

insert embed, enter, implant, infix, interject, interpolate, interpose, introduce, place, pop in (*Inf.*), put, set, stick in, tuck in, work in

insertion addition, implant, inclusion, insert, inset, interpolation, introduction, supplement

inside *n.* **1.** contents, inner part, interior **2.** *Often plural. Inf.* belly, bowels, entrails, gut, guts, innards (*Inf.*), internal organs, stomach, viscera, vitals ~*adv.* **3.** indoors, under cover, within ~*adj.* **4.** inner, innermost, interior, internal, intramural, inward **5.** classified, confidential, esoteric, exclusive, internal, limited, private, restricted, secret

insidious artful, crafty, crooked, cunning, deceitful, deceptive, designing, disingenuous, duplicitous, guileful, intriguing, Machiavellian, slick, sly, smooth, sneaking, stealthy, subtle, surreptitious, treacherous, tricky, wily

insight acumen, awareness, comprehension, discernment, intuition, intuitiveness, judgment, observation, penetration, perception, perspicacity, understanding, vision

insightful astute, discerning, knowledgeable, observant, penetrating, perceptive, perspicacious, sagacious, shrewd, understanding, wise

insignia badge, crest, decoration, distinguishing mark, earmark, emblem, ensign, symbol

insignificance immateriality, inconsequence, irrelevance, meaninglessness, negligibility, paltriness, pettiness, triviality, unimportance, worthlessness

insignificant flimsy, immaterial, inconsequential, inconsiderable, irrelevant, meagre, meaningless, minor, negligible, nondescript, nonessential, not worth mentioning, nugatory, of no account (consequence, moment), paltry, petty, scanty, trifling, trivial, unimportant, unsubstantial

insincere deceitful, deceptive, devious, dishonest, disingenuous, dissembling, dissimulating, double-dealing, duplicitous, evasive, faithless, false, hollow, hypocritical, Janus-faced, lying, mendacious, perfidious, pretended, two-faced, unfaithful, untrue, untruthful

insincerity deceitfulness, deviousness, dishonesty, disingenuousness, dissimulation, duplicity, faithlessness, hypocrisy, lip service, mendacity, perfidy, pretence, untruthfulness

insinuate 1. allude, hint, imply, indicate, intimate, suggest 2. infiltrate, infuse, inject, instil, introduce 3. curry favour, get in with (*Inf.*), ingratiate, worm *or* work one's way in

insinuation 1. allusion, aspersion, hint, implication, innuendo, slur, suggestion 2. infiltration, infusion, ingratiating, injection, instillation, introduction

insipid 1. anaemic, banal, bland, characterless, colourless, drab, dry, dull, flat, jejune, lifeless, limp, pointless, prosaic, prosy, spiritless, stale, stupid, tame, tedious, trite, unimaginative, uninteresting, vapid, weak, wearisome, wishy-washy (*Inf.*) 2. bland, flavourless, savourless, tasteless, unappetizing, watered down, watery, wishy-washy (*Inf.*)

insipidity, insipidness 1. banality, colourlessness, dullness, flatness, lack of imagination, pointlessness, staleness, tameness, tediousness, triteness, uninterestingness, vapidity 2. blandness, flavourlessness, lack of flavour, tastelessness

insist 1. be firm, brook no refusal, demand, lay down the law, not take no for an answer, persist, press (someone), require, stand firm, stand one's ground,

take *or* make a stand, urge 2. assert, asseverate, aver, claim, contend, hold, maintain, reiterate, repeat, swear, urge, vow

insistence assertion, contention, demands, emphasis, importunity, insistency, persistence, pressing, reiteration, stress, urging

insistent demanding, dogged, emphatic, exigent, forceful, importunate, incessant, peremptory, persevering, persistent, pressing, unrelenting, urgent

insobriety crapulence, drunkenness, inebriety, intemperance, intoxication

insolence abuse, audacity, backchat (*Inf.*), boldness, cheek (*Inf.*), chutzpah (*U.S. inf.*), contemptuousness, contumely, disrespect, effrontery, gall (*Inf.*), impertinence, impudence, incivility, insubordination, offensiveness, pertness, rudeness, sauce (*Inf.*), uncivility

insolent abusive, bold, brazen-faced, contemptuous, fresh (*Inf.*), impertinent, impudent, insubordinate, insulting, pert, rude, saucy, uncivil

insoluble baffling, impenetrable, indecipherable, inexplicable, mysterious, mystifying, obscure, unaccountable, unfathomable, unsolvable

insolvency bankruptcy, failure, liquidation, ruin

insolvent bankrupt, broke (*Inf.*), failed, gone bust (*Inf.*), gone to the wall (*Inf.*), in queer street (*Inf.*), in receivership, in the hands of the receivers, on the rocks (*Inf.*), ruined

insomnia sleeplessness, wakefulness

insouciance airiness, breeziness, carefreeness, jauntiness, light-heartedness, nonchalance

insouciant airy, breezy, buoyant, carefree, casual, free and easy, gay, happy-go-lucky, jaunty, light-hearted, nonchalant, sunny, unconcerned, untroubled, unworried

inspect check, examine, give (something *or* someone) the once-over (*Inf.*), go over *or* through, investigate, look over, oversee, scan, scrutinize, search, superintend, supervise, survey, vet

inspection check, checkup, examination, investigation, look-over, once-over (*Inf.*), review, scan, scrutiny, search, superintendence, supervision, surveillance, survey

inspector censor, checker, critic, examiner, investigator, overseer, scrutineer, scrutinizer, superintendent, supervisor

inspiration 1. arousal, awakening, encouragement, influence, muse, spur, stimulus **2**. afflatus, creativity, elevation, enthusiasm, exaltation, genius, illumination, insight, revelation, stimulation

inspire 1. animate, be responsible for, encourage, enliven, fire *or* touch the imagination of, galvanize, hearten, imbue, influence, infuse, inspirit, instil, spark off, spur, stimulate **2**. arouse, enkindle, excite, give rise to, produce, quicken, stir

inspired 1. brilliant, dazzling, enthralling, exciting, impressive, memorable, of genius, outstanding, superlative, thrilling, wonderful **2**. *Of a guess* instinctive, instinctual, intuitive **3**. aroused, elated, enthused, exalted, exhilarated, galvanized, possessed, stimulated, stirred up, uplifted

inspiring affecting, encouraging, exciting, exhilarating, heartening, moving, rousing, stimulating, stirring, uplifting

inspirit animate, cheer, embolden, encourage, enliven, exhilarate, fire, galvanize, give hope to, hearten, incite, inspire, invigorate, move, nerve, put (new) heart into, rouse, stimulate

instability capriciousness, changeableness, disequilibrium, fickleness, fitfulness, fluctuation, fluidity, frailty, imbalance, impermanence, inconstancy, insecurity, irresolution, mutability, oscillation, precariousness, restlessness, shakiness, transience, unpredictability, unsteadiness, vacillation, variability, volatility, wavering, weakness

install, instal 1. fix, lay, lodge, place, position, put in, set up, station **2**. establish, inaugurate, induct, instate, institute, introduce, invest, set up **3**. ensconce, position, settle

installation 1. establishment, fitting, instalment, placing, positioning, setting up **2**. inauguration, induction, instatement, investiture **3**. equipment, machinery, plant, system **4**. *Military* base, establishment, post, station

instalment chapter, division, episode, part, portion, repayment, section

instance *n*. **1**. case, case in point, example, illustration, occasion, occurrence, precedent, situation, time **2**. application, behest, demand, entreaty, importunity, impulse, incitement, insistence, instigation, pressure, prompting, request, so-

licitation, urging ~*v*. **3**. adduce, cite, mention, name, quote, specify

instant *n*. **1**. flash, jiffy (*Inf*.), moment, second, shake (*Inf*.), split second, tick (*Brit. inf*.), trice, twinkling, twinkling of an eye (*Inf*.), two shakes of a lamb's tail (*Inf*.) **2**. **on the instant** forthwith, immediately, instantly, now, right away, without delay **3**. juncture, moment, occasion, point, time ~*adj*. **4**. direct, immediate, instantaneous, on-the-spot, prompt, quick, split-second, urgent **5**. convenience, fast, precooked, ready-mixed **6**. burning, exigent, imperative, importunate, pressing, urgent

instantaneous direct, immediate, instant, on-the-spot

instantaneously at once, forthwith, immediately, in a fraction of a second, instantly, in the same breath, in the twinkling of an eye (*Inf*.), like greased lightning (*Inf*.), on the instant, on the spot, promptly, quick as lightning, straight away, then and there

instantly at once, directly, forthwith, immediately, instantaneously, instanter (*Law*), now, on the spot, pronto (*Inf*.), right away, right now, straight away, there and then, this minute, *tout de suite*, without delay

instate establish, inaugurate, induct, install, invest, put in office

instead 1. alternatively, in lieu, in preference, on second thoughts, preferably, rather **2**. *With* **of** as an alternative *or* equivalent to, in lieu of, in place of, rather than

instigate actuate, bring about, encourage, foment, impel, incite, influence, initiate, kindle, move, persuade, prompt, provoke, rouse, set on, spur, start, stimulate, stir up, urge, whip up

instigation behest, bidding, encouragement, incentive, incitement, prompting, urging

instigator agitator, firebrand, fomenter, goad, incendiary, inciter, leader, mischief-maker, motivator, prime mover, ringleader, spur, troublemaker

instil, instill engender, engraft, imbue, implant, impress, inculcate, infix, infuse, insinuate, introduce

instinct aptitude, faculty, feeling, gift, gut feeling (*Inf*.), gut reaction (*Inf*.), impulse, intuition, knack, natural inclination, predisposition, proclivity, sixth sense, talent, tendency, urge

instinctive automatic, inborn, inherent, innate, instinctual, intuitional, intuitive, involuntary, mechanical, native, natural, reflex, spontaneous, unlearned, unpremeditated, unthinking, visceral

instinctively automatically, by instinct, intuitively, involuntarily, naturally, without thinking

institute[1] *v.* appoint, begin, bring into being, commence, constitute, enact, establish, fix, found, induct, initiate, install, introduce, invest, launch, ordain, organize, originate, pioneer, put into operation, set in motion, settle, set up, start

institute[2] *n.* **1.** academy, association, college, conservatory, foundation, guild, institution, school, seat of learning, seminary, society **2.** custom, decree, doctrine, dogma, edict, law, maxim, precedent, precept, principle, regulation, rule, tenet

institution 1. constitution, creation, enactment, establishment, formation, foundation, initiation, introduction, investiture, investment, organization **2.** academy, college, establishment, foundation, hospital, institute, school, seminary, society, university **3.** convention, custom, fixture, law, practice, ritual, rule, tradition

institutional 1. accepted, bureaucratic, conventional, established, establishment (*Inf.*), formal, organized, orthodox, societal **2.** cheerless, clinical, cold, drab, dreary, dull, forbidding, formal, impersonal, monotonous, regimented, routine, uniform, unwelcoming

instruct 1. bid, charge, command, direct, enjoin, order, tell **2.** coach, discipline, drill, educate, enlighten, ground, guide, inform, school, teach, train, tutor **3.** acquaint, advise, apprise, brief, counsel, inform, notify, tell

instruction 1. apprenticeship, coaching, discipline, drilling, education, enlightenment, grounding, guidance, information, lesson(s), preparation, schooling, teaching, training, tuition, tutelage **2.** briefing, command, direction, directive, injunction, mandate, order, ruling

instructions advice, directions, guidance, information, key, orders, recommendations, rules

instructive cautionary, didactic, edifying, educational, enlightening, helpful, illuminating, informative, instructional, revealing, useful

instructor adviser, coach, demonstrator, exponent, guide, master, mentor, mistress, pedagogue, preceptor (*Rare*), schoolmaster, schoolmistress, teacher, trainer, tutor

instrument 1. apparatus, appliance, contraption (*Inf.*), contrivance, device, gadget, implement, mechanism, tool, utensil **2.** agency, agent, channel, factor, force, means, mechanism, medium, organ, vehicle **3.** *Inf.* cat's-paw, dupe, pawn, puppet, tool

instrumental active, assisting, auxiliary, conducive, contributory, helpful, helping, influential, involved, of help *or* service, subsidiary, useful

instrumentality agency, assistance, good offices, intercession, intervention, mediation, medium, vehicle

insubordinate contumacious, defiant, disobedient, disorderly, fractious, insurgent, mutinous, rebellious, recalcitrant, refractory, riotous, seditious, turbulent, undisciplined, ungovernable, unruly

insubordination defiance, disobedience, indiscipline, insurrection, mutinousness, mutiny, rebellion, recalcitrance, revolt, riotousness, sedition, ungovernability

insubstantial 1. feeble, flimsy, frail, poor, slight, tenuous, thin, weak **2.** chimerical, ephemeral, false, fanciful, idle, illusory, imaginary, immaterial, incorporeal, unreal

insufferable detestable, dreadful, enough to test the patience of a saint, enough to try the patience of Job, impossible, insupportable, intolerable, more than flesh and blood can stand, outrageous, past bearing, too much, unbearable, unendurable, unspeakable

insufficiency dearth, deficiency, inadequacy, inadequateness, lack, paucity, poverty, scantiness, scarcity, shortage, short supply, want

insufficient deficient, inadequate, incapable, incommensurate, incompetent, lacking, short, unfitted, unqualified

insular *Fig.* blinkered, circumscribed, closed, contracted, cut off, illiberal, inward-looking, isolated, limited, narrow, narrow-minded, parish-pump, parochial, petty, prejudiced, provincial

insulate *Fig.* close off, cocoon, cushion, cut off, isolate, protect, sequester, shield, wrap up in cotton wool

insult 1. *n.* abuse, affront, aspersion, contumely, indignity, insolence, offence, outrage, rudeness, slap in the face (*Inf.*), slight, snub **2.** *v.* abuse, affront, call names, give offence to, injure, miscall (*Dialect*), offend, outrage, revile, slag (*Sl.*), slander, slight, snub

insulting abusive, affronting, contemptuous, degrading, disparaging, insolent, offensive, rude, scurrilous, slighting

insuperable impassable, insurmountable, invincible, unconquerable

insupportable 1. insufferable, intolerable, past bearing, unbearable, unendurable **2.** indefensible, unjustifiable, untenable

insurance assurance, cover, coverage, guarantee, indemnification, indemnity, protection, provision, safeguard, security, something to fall back on (*Inf.*), warranty

insure assure, cover, guarantee, indemnify, underwrite, warrant

insurgent 1. *n.* insurrectionist, mutineer, rebel, resister, revolter, revolutionary, revolutionist, rioter **2.** *adj.* disobedient, insubordinate, insurrectionary, mutinous, rebellious, revolting, revolutionary, riotous, seditious

insurmountable hopeless, impassable, impossible, insuperable, invincible, overwhelming, unconquerable

insurrection coup, insurgency, mutiny, putsch, rebellion, revolt, revolution, riot, rising, sedition, uprising

insusceptible immovable, immune, indifferent, insensible, insensitive, proof against, unimpressible, unmoved, unresponsive

intact all in one piece, complete, entire, perfect, scatheless, sound, together, unbroken, undamaged, undefiled, unharmed, unhurt, unimpaired, uninjured, unscathed, untouched, unviolated, virgin, whole

intangible airy, dim, elusive, ethereal, evanescent, impalpable, imperceptible, incorporeal, indefinite, invisible, shadowy, unreal, unsubstantial, vague

integral 1. basic, component, constituent, elemental, essential, fundamental, indispensable, intrinsic, necessary, requisite **2.** complete, entire, full, intact, undivided, whole

integrate accommodate, amalgamate, assimilate, blend, coalesce, combine,

fuse, harmonize, incorporate, intermix, join, knit, merge, mesh, unite

integration amalgamation, assimilation, blending, combining, commingling, fusing, harmony, incorporation, mixing, unification

integrity 1. candour, goodness, honesty, honour, incorruptibility, principle, probity, purity, rectitude, righteousness, uprightness, virtue **2.** coherence, cohesion, completeness, soundness, unity, wholeness

intellect 1. brains (*Inf.*), intelligence, judgment, mind, reason, sense, understanding **2.** *Inf.* brain (*Inf.*), egghead (*Inf.*), genius, intellectual, intelligence, mind, thinker

intellectual 1. *adj.* bookish, cerebral, highbrow, intelligent, mental, rational, scholarly, studious, thoughtful **2.** *n.* academic, egghead (*Inf.*), highbrow, thinker

intelligence 1. acumen, alertness, aptitude, brain power, brains (*Inf.*), brightness, capacity, cleverness, comprehension, discernment, grey matter (*Inf.*), intellect, mind, nous (*Brit. sl.*), penetration, perception, quickness, reason, understanding **2.** advice, data, disclosure, facts, findings, gen (*Inf.*), information, knowledge, low-down (*Inf.*), news, notice, notification, report, rumour, tidings, tip-off, word

intelligent acute, alert, apt, brainy (*Inf.*), bright, clever, discerning, enlightened, instructed, knowing, penetrating, perspicacious, quick, quick-witted, rational, sharp, smart, thinking, well-informed

intelligentsia eggheads (*Inf.*), highbrows, illuminati, intellectuals, literati, masterminds, the learned

intelligibility clarity, clearness, comprehensibility, distinctness, explicitness, lucidity, plainness, precision, simplicity

intelligible clear, comprehensible, distinct, lucid, open, plain, understandable

intemperance crapulence, excess, extravagance, immoderation, inebriation, insobriety, intoxication, overindulgence, unrestraint

intemperate excessive, extravagant, extreme, immoderate, incontinent, inordinate, intoxicated, passionate, prodigal, profligate, self-indulgent, severe, tempestuous, unbridled, uncontrollable, ungovernable, unrestrained, violent, wild

intend 1. aim, be resolved *or* determined, contemplate, determine, have in mind *or* view, mean, meditate, plan, propose, purpose, scheme **2.** *Often with* **for** aim, consign, design, destine, earmark, mark out, mean, set apart

intended 1. *adj.* betrothed, destined, future, planned, proposed **2.** *n. Inf.* betrothed, fiancé, fiancée, future wife *or* husband, husband- *or* wife-to-be

intense 1. acute, agonizing, close, concentrated, deep, excessive, exquisite, extreme, fierce, forceful, great, harsh, intensive, powerful, profound, protracted, severe, strained **2.** ardent, burning, consuming, eager, earnest, energetic, fanatical, fervent, fervid, fierce, forcible, heightened, impassioned, keen, passionate, speaking, vehement

intensely deeply, extremely, fiercely, passionately, profoundly, strongly

intensify add fuel to the flames (*Inf.*), add to, aggravate, boost, concentrate, deepen, emphasize, enhance, escalate, exacerbate, heighten, increase, magnify, quicken, redouble, reinforce, set off, sharpen, step up (*Inf.*), strengthen, whet

intensity ardour, concentration, depth, earnestness, emotion, energy, excess, extremity, fanaticism, fervency, fervour, fierceness, fire, force, intenseness, keenness, passion, potency, power, severity, strain, strength, tension, vehemence, vigour

intensive all-out, comprehensive, concentrated, demanding, exhaustive, in-depth, thorough, thoroughgoing

intent *adj.* **1.** absorbed, alert, attentive, committed, concentrated, determined, eager, earnest, engrossed, fixed, industrious, intense, occupied, piercing, preoccupied, rapt, resolute, resolved, steadfast, steady, watchful, wrapped up **2.** bent, hellbent (*Inf.*), set ~*n.* **3.** aim, design, end, goal, intention, meaning, object, objective, plan, purpose **4. to all intents and purposes** as good as, practically, virtually

intention aim, design, end, end in view, goal, idea, intent, meaning, object, objective, point, purpose, scope, target, view

intentional calculated, deliberate, designed, done on purpose, intended, meant, planned, prearranged, preconcerted, premeditated, purposed, studied, wilful

intentionally by design, deliberately, designedly, on purpose, wilfully

intently attentively, closely, fixedly, hard, keenly, searchingly, steadily, watchfully

inter bury, entomb, inhume, inurn, lay to rest, sepulchre

intercede advocate, arbitrate, interpose, intervene, mediate, plead, speak

intercept arrest, block, catch, check, cut off, deflect, head off, interrupt, obstruct, seize, stop, take

intercession advocacy, entreaty, good offices, intervention, mediation, plea, pleading, prayer, solicitation, supplication

intercessor advocate, arbitrator, go-between, interceder, intermediary, mediator, middleman, negotiator, pleader

interchange 1. *v.* alternate, bandy, barter, exchange, reciprocate, swap (*Inf.*), switch, trade **2.** *n.* alternation, crossfire, exchange, give and take, intersection, junction, reciprocation

interchangeable commutable, equivalent, exchangeable, identical, reciprocal, synonymous, the same, transposable

intercourse 1. association, commerce, communication, communion, connection, contact, converse, correspondence, dealings, intercommunication, trade, traffic, truck **2.** carnal knowledge, coition, coitus, congress, copulation, intimacy, sex (*Inf.*), sexual act, sexual intercourse, sexual relations

interdict 1. *v.* ban, bar, debar, disallow, forbid, outlaw, prevent, prohibit, proscribe, veto **2.** *n.* ban, disallowance, interdiction, prohibition, taboo, veto

interest *n.* **1.** affection, attention, attentiveness, attraction, concern, curiosity, notice, regard, suspicion, sympathy **2.** concern, consequence, importance, moment, note, relevance, significance, weight **3.** activity, diversion, hobby, leisure activity, pastime, preoccupation, pursuit, relaxation **4.** advantage, benefit, gain, good, profit **5. in the interest of** for the sake of, on behalf of, on the part of, profitable to, to the advantage of **6.** authority, claim, commitment, influence, investment, involvement, participation, portion, right, share, stake **7.** *Often plural* affair, business, care, concern, matter ~*v.* **8.** amuse, arouse one's curiosity, attract, divert, engross, fascinate, hold the attention of, intrigue, move, touch **9.** affect, concern, engage, involve

interested 1. affected, attentive, attracted, curious, drawn, excited, fascinated, intent, keen, moved, responsive, stimulated **2.** biased, concerned, implicated, involved, partial, partisan, predisposed, prejudiced

interesting absorbing, amusing, appealing, attractive, compelling, curious, engaging, engrossing, entertaining, gripping, intriguing, pleasing, provocative, stimulating, suspicious, thought-provoking, unusual

interfere 1. butt in, get involved, intermeddle, intervene, intrude, meddle, poke one's nose in (*Inf.*), stick one's oar in (*Inf.*), tamper **2.** *Often with* **with** be a drag upon (*Sl.*), block, clash, collide, conflict, cramp, frustrate, get in the way of, hamper, handicap, hinder, impede, inhibit, obstruct, trammel

interference 1. intermeddling, intervention, intrusion, meddlesomeness, meddling, prying **2.** clashing, collision, conflict, impedance, obstruction, opposition

interim 1. *adj.* acting, caretaker, improvised, intervening, makeshift, pro tem, provisional, stopgap, temporary **2.** *n.* interregnum, interval, meantime, meanwhile

interior *adj.* **1.** inner, inside, internal, inward **2.** *Geog.* central, inland, remote, upcountry **3.** *Politics* domestic, home **4.** hidden, inner, intimate, mental, personal, private, secret, spiritual ~*n.* **5.** bosom, centre, contents, core, heart, innards (*Inf.*), inside **6.** *Geog.* centre, heartland, upcountry

interject interpolate, interpose, interrupt with, introduce, put in, throw in

interjection cry, ejaculation, exclamation, interpolation, interposition

interlace braid, cross, entwine, interlock, intersperse, intertwine, interweave, interwreathe, knit, plait, reticulate, twine

interlink interconnect, interlock, intertwine, interweave, knit, link, mesh

interloper gate-crasher (*Inf.*), intermeddler, intruder, meddler, trespasser, uninvited guest, unwanted visitor

interlude break, breathing space, delay, episode, halt, hiatus, intermission, interval, pause, respite, rest, spell, stop, stoppage, wait

intermediary *n.* agent, broker, entrepreneur, go-between, mediator, middleman

intermediate halfway, in-between (*Inf.*), intermediary, interposed, intervening, mean, mid, middle, midway, transitional

interment burial, burying, funeral, inhumation, sepulture

interminable boundless, ceaseless, dragging, endless, everlasting, immeasurable, infinite, limitless, long, long-drawn-out, long-winded, never-ending, perpetual, protracted, unbounded, unlimited, wearisome

intermingle amalgamate, blend, combine, commingle, commix, fuse, interlace, intermix, interweave, merge, mix

intermission break, cessation, entr'acte, interlude, interruption, interval, let-up (*Inf.*), lull, pause, recess, respite, rest, stop, stoppage, suspense, suspension

intermittent broken, discontinuous, fitful, irregular, occasional, periodic, punctuated, recurrent, recurring, spasmodic, sporadic, stop-go (*Inf.*)

intern confine, detain, hold, hold in custody

internal 1. inner, inside, interior, intimate, private, subjective **2.** civic, domestic, home, in-house, intramural

international cosmopolitan, ecumenical (*Rare*), global, intercontinental, universal, worldwide

internecine bloody, deadly, destructive, exterminating, exterminatory, fatal, mortal, ruinous

interplay give-and-take, interaction, meshing, reciprocation, reciprocity

interpolate add, insert, intercalate, introduce

interpolation addition, aside, insert, insertion, intercalation, interjection, introduction

interpose 1. come *or* place between, intercede, interfere, intermediate, intervene, intrude, step in **2.** insert, interject, interrupt (with), introduce, put forth

interpret adapt, clarify, construe, decipher, decode, define, elucidate, explain, explicate, expound, make sense of, paraphrase, read, render, solve, spell out, take, throw light on, translate, understand

interpretation analysis, clarification, construction, diagnosis, elucidation, exegesis, explanation, explication, exposition, meaning, performance, portrayal, reading, rendering, rendition, sense, signification, translation, understanding, version

interpreter annotator, commentator, exponent, scholiast, translator

interrogate ask, catechize, cross-examine, cross-question, enquire, examine, give (someone) the third degree (*Inf.*), grill (*Inf.*), inquire, investigate, pump, put the screws on (*Inf.*), question, quiz

interrogation cross-examination, cross-questioning, enquiry, examination, grilling (*Inf.*), inquiry, inquisition, probing, questioning, third degree (*Inf.*)

interrogative curious, inquiring, inquisitive, inquisitorial, questioning, quizzical

interrupt barge in (*Inf.*), break, break in, break off, break (someone's) train of thought, butt in, check, cut, cut off, cut short, delay, disconnect, discontinue, disjoin, disturb, disunite, divide, heckle, hinder, hold up, interfere (with), intrude, lay aside, obstruct, punctuate, separate, sever, stay, stop, suspend

interrupted broken, cut off, disconnected, discontinuous, disturbed, incomplete, intermittent, uneven

interruption break, cessation, disconnection, discontinuance, disruption, dissolution, disturbance, disuniting, division, halt, hiatus, hindrance, hitch, impediment, intrusion, obstacle, obstruction, pause, separation, severance, stop, stoppage, suspension

intersect bisect, crisscross, cross, cut, cut across, divide, meet

intersection crossing, crossroads, interchange, junction

intersperse bestrew, interlard, intermix, pepper, scatter, sprinkle

interstice aperture, chink, cleft, crack, cranny, crevice, fissure, gap, interval, opening, slit, space

intertwine braid, convolute, cross, entwine, interlace, interweave, interwreathe, inweave, link, reticulate, twist

interval break, delay, distance, gap, hiatus, interim, interlude, intermission, meantime, meanwhile, opening, pause, period, playtime, rest, season, space, spell, term, time, wait

intervene 1. arbitrate, intercede, interfere, interpose oneself, intrude, involve oneself, mediate, step in (*Inf.*), take a hand (*Inf.*) **2.** befall, come to pass, ensue, happen, occur, succeed, supervene, take place

intervention agency, intercession, interference, interposition, intrusion, mediation

interview 1. *n.* audience, conference, consultation, dialogue, evaluation, meeting, oral (examination), press conference, talk **2.** *v.* examine, interrogate, question, sound out, talk to

interviewer examiner, interlocutor, interrogator, investigator, questioner, reporter

interweave blend, braid, crisscross, cross, interlace, intertwine, interwreathe, inweave, reticulate, splice

interwoven blended, connected, entwined, inmixed, interconnected, interlaced, interlocked, intermingled, knit

intestinal abdominal, coeliac, duodenal, gut (*Inf.*), inner, stomachic, visceral

intestines bowels, entrails, guts, innards (*Inf.*), insides (*Inf.*), internal organs, viscera, vitals

intimacy closeness, confidence, confidentiality, familiarity, fraternization, understanding

intimate[1] *adj.* **1.** bosom, cherished, close, confidential, dear, friendly, near, nearest and dearest, thick (*Inf.*), warm **2.** confidential, personal, private, privy, secret **3.** deep, detailed, exhaustive, experienced, first-hand, immediate, in-depth, penetrating, personal, profound, thorough **4.** comfy (*Inf.*), cosy, friendly, informal, snug, tête-à-tête, warm ~*n.* **5.** bosom friend, buddy (*Inf.*), china (*Brit. sl.*), chum (*Inf.*), close friend, comrade, confidant, confidante, (constant) companion, crony, familiar, friend, mate (*Inf.*), mucker (*Brit. sl.*), pal

intimate[2] *v.* allude, announce, communicate, declare, drop a hint, give (someone) to understand, hint, impart, imply, indicate, insinuate, let it be known, make known, remind, state, suggest, tip (someone) the wink (*Brit. inf.*), warn

intimately 1. affectionately, closely, confidentially, confidingly, familiarly, personally, tenderly, very well, warmly **2.** fully, in detail, inside out, thoroughly, through and through, to the core, very well

intimation 1. allusion, hint, indication, inkling, insinuation, reminder, suggestion, warning **2.** announcement, communication, declaration, notice

intimidate affright (*Archaic*), alarm, appal, browbeat, bully, coerce, cow, daunt, dishearten, dismay, dispirit, frighten, lean on (*Inf.*), overawe, scare, scare off (*Inf.*), subdue, terrify, terrorize, threaten, twist someone's arm (*Inf.*)

intimidation arm-twisting (*Inf.*), browbeating, bullying, coercion, fear, menaces, pressure, terror, terrorization, threat(s)

intolerable beyond bearing, excruciating, impossible, insufferable, insupportable, more than flesh and blood can stand, not to be borne, painful, unbearable, unendurable

intolerance bigotry, chauvinism, discrimination, dogmatism, fanaticism, illiberality, impatience, jingoism, narrow-mindedness, narrowness, prejudice, racialism, racism, xenophobia

intolerant bigoted, chauvinistic, dictatorial, dogmatic, fanatical, illiberal, impatient, narrow, narrow-minded, one-sided, prejudiced, racialist, racist, small-minded, uncharitable, xenophobic

intonation 1. accentuation, cadence, inflection, modulation, tone **2.** chant, incantation

intone chant, croon, intonate, recite, sing

in toto as a whole, completely, entirely, in its entirety, totally, unabridged, uncut, wholly

intoxicate 1. addle, befuddle, fuddle, go to one's head, inebriate, put (someone) under the table (*Inf.*), stupefy **2.** *Fig.* elate, excite, exhilarate, inflame, make one's head spin, stimulate

intoxicated 1. blotto (*Sl.*), canned (*Sl.*), cut (*Brit. sl.*), drunk, drunken, fuddled, half seas over (*Brit. inf.*), high (*Inf.*), inebriated, in one's cups (*Inf.*), lit up (*Sl.*), plastered (*Sl.*), smashed (*Sl.*), sozzled (*Inf.*), stewed (*Sl.*), stiff (*Sl.*), stoned (*Sl.*), the worse for drink, three sheets in the wind (*Inf.*), tight (*Inf.*), tipsy, under the influence **2.** *Fig.* dizzy, elated, enraptured, euphoric, excited, exhilarated, high (*Inf.*), infatuated, sent (*Sl.*), stimulated

intoxicating 1. alcoholic, inebriant, intoxicant, spirituous, strong **2.** *Fig.* exciting, exhilarating, heady, stimulating, thrilling

intoxication 1. drunkenness, inebriation, inebriety, insobriety, tipsiness **2.** *Fig.* delirium, elation, euphoria, exaltation, excitement, exhilaration, infatuation

intractability awkwardness, cantankerousness, contrariness, incorrigibility, indiscipline, indocility, mulishness, obduracy, obstinacy, perverseness, perversity, pig-headedness, stubbornness, uncooperativeness, ungovernability, waywardness

intractable awkward, bull-headed, cantankerous, contrary, difficult, fractious, headstrong, incurable, insoluble, intransigent, obdurate, obstinate, perverse, pig-headed, refractory, self-willed, stubborn, unbending, uncooperative, undisciplined, ungovernable, unmanageable, unruly, unyielding, wayward, wild, wilful

intransigent hardline, immovable, intractable, obdurate, obstinate, stubborn, tenacious, tough, unbending, unbudgeable, uncompromising, unyielding

intrenched *see* ENTRENCHED

intrepid audacious, bold, brave, courageous, daring, dauntless, doughty, fearless, gallant, game (*Inf.*), heroic, lion-hearted, nerveless, plucky, resolute, stalwart, stouthearted, unafraid, undaunted, unflinching, valiant, valorous

intrepidity audacity, boldness, bravery, courage, daring, dauntlessness, doughtiness, fearlessness, fortitude, gallantry, guts (*Inf.*), heroism, lion-heartedness, nerve, pluck, prowess, spirit, stouteartedness, valour

intricacy complexity, complication, convolutions, elaborateness, entanglement, intricateness, involution, involvement, knottiness, obscurity

intricate baroque, Byzantine, complex, complicated, convoluted, daedal (*Literary*), difficult, elaborate, fancy, involved, knotty, labyrinthine, obscure, perplexing, rococo, sophisticated, tangled, tortuous

intrigue *v.* **1.** arouse the curiosity of, attract, charm, fascinate, interest, pique, rivet, tickle one's fancy, titillate **2.** connive, conspire, machinate, manoeuvre, plot, scheme ~*n.* **3.** cabal, chicanery, collusion, conspiracy, double-dealing, knavery, machination, manipulation, manoeuvre, plot, ruse, scheme, sharp practice, stratagem, trickery, wile **4.** affair, amour, intimacy, liaison, romance

intriguing beguiling, compelling, diverting, exciting, fascinating, interesting, tantalizing, titillating

intrinsic basic, built-in, central, congenital, constitutional, elemental, essential, fundamental, genuine, inborn, inbred, inherent, native, natural, real, true, underlying

intrinsically as such, at heart, basically, by definition, constitutionally, essentially, fundamentally, in itself, per se

introduce 1. acquaint, do the honours, familiarize, make known, make the introduction, present **2.** begin, bring in, commence, establish, found, inaugurate, initiate, institute, launch, organize, pioneer, set up, start, usher in **3.** advance, air, bring up, broach, moot, offer, propose, put forward, recommend, set forth, submit, suggest, ventilate **4.** announce, lead into, lead off, open, preface **5.** add, inject, insert, interpolate, interpose, put in, throw in (*Inf.*)

introduction 1. baptism, debut, establishment, first acquaintance, inauguration, induction, initiation, institution, launch, pioneering, presentation **2.** commencement, exordium, foreword, intro (*Inf.*), lead-in, opening, opening passage, opening remarks, overture, preamble, preface, preliminaries, prelude, proem, prolegomena, prolegomenon, prologue **3.** addition, insertion, interpolation

introductory early, elementary, first, inaugural, initial, initiatory, opening, precursory, prefatory, preliminary, preparatory, starting

introspection brooding, heart-searching, introversion, self-analysis, self-examination

introspective brooding, contemplative, inner-directed, introverted, inward-looking, meditative, pensive, subjective

introverted indrawn, inner-directed, introspective, inward-looking, self-centred, self-contained, withdrawn

intrude butt in, encroach, infringe, interfere, interrupt, meddle, obtrude, push in, thrust oneself in *or* forward, trespass, violate

intruder burglar, gate-crasher (*Inf.*), infiltrator, interloper, invader, prowler, raider, snooper (*Inf.*), squatter, thief, trespasser

intrusion encroachment, infringement, interference, interruption, invasion, trespass, violation

intrusive disturbing, forward, impertinent, importunate, interfering, invasive, meddlesome, nosy (*Inf.*), officious, presumptuous, pushy (*Inf.*), uncalled-for, unwanted

intrust *see* ENTRUST

intuition discernment, hunch, insight, instinct, perception, presentiment, sixth sense

intuitive innate, instinctive, instinctual, involuntary, spontaneous, unreflecting, untaught

intwine *see* ENTWINE

inundate deluge, drown, engulf, flood, glut, immerse, overflow, overrun, overwhelm, submerge, swamp

inundation deluge, flood, overflow, tidal wave, torrent

inure accustom, anneal, case-harden, desensitize, familiarize, habituate, harden, strengthen, temper, toughen, train

invade 1. assail, assault, attack, burst in, descend upon, encroach, infringe, make inroads, occupy, raid, violate **2.** infect, infest, overrun, overspread, penetrate, permeate, pervade, swarm over

invader aggressor, alien, attacker, looter, plunderer, raider, trespasser

invalid[1] **1.** *adj.* ailing, bedridden, disabled, feeble, frail, ill, infirm, poorly (*Inf.*), sick, sickly, valetudinarian, weak **2.** *n.* convalescent, patient, valetudinarian

invalid[2] *adj.* baseless, fallacious, false, ill-founded, illogical, inoperative, irrational, not binding, nugatory, null, null and void, unfounded, unscientific, unsound, untrue, void, worthless

invalidate abrogate, annul, cancel, nullify, overrule, overthrow, quash, render null and void, rescind, undermine, undo, weaken

invalidism chronic illness, valetudinarianism

invalidity fallaciousness, fallacy, falsity, illogicality, inconsistency, irrationality, sophism, speciousness, unsoundness

invaluable beyond price, costly, inestimable, precious, priceless, valuable

invariable changeless, consistent, constant, fixed, immutable, inflexible, regular, rigid, set, unalterable, unchangeable, unchanging, unfailing, uniform, unvarying, unwavering

invariably always, consistently, customarily, day in, day out, ever, every time, habitually, inevitably, on every occasion, perpetually, regularly, unfailingly, without exception

invasion 1. aggression, assault, attack, foray, incursion, inroad, irruption, offensive, onslaught, raid **2.** breach, encroachment, infiltration, infraction, infringement, intrusion, overstepping, usurpation, violation

invective abuse, berating, billingsgate, castigation, censure, contumely, denunciation, diatribe, obloquy, philippic(s), reproach, revilement, sarcasm, tirade, tongue-lashing, vilification, vituperation

inveigh berate, blame, castigate, censure, condemn, denounce, expostulate, lambaste (*Inf.*), rail, recriminate, reproach, sound off, tongue-lash, upbraid, vituperate

inveigle allure, bamboozle (*Inf.*), beguile, cajole, coax, con (*Sl.*), decoy, ensnare, entice, entrap, lead on, lure, manipulate, manoeuvre, persuade, seduce, sweet-talk (*Inf.*), wheedle

invent 1. coin, come up with (*Inf.*), conceive, contrive, create, design, devise, discover, dream up (*Inf.*), formulate, imagine, improvise, originate, think up **2.** concoct, cook up (*Inf.*), fabricate, feign, forge, make up, trump up

invention 1. brainchild (*Inf.*), contraption, contrivance, creation, design, development, device, discovery, gadget **2.** coinage, creativeness, creativity, genius, imagination, ingenuity, inspiration, inventiveness, originality, resourcefulness **3.** deceit, fabrication, fake, falsehood, fantasy, fib (*Inf.*), fiction, figment *or* product of (someone's) imagination, forgery, lie, prevarication, sham, story, tall story (*Inf.*), untruth, yarn

inventive creative, fertile, gifted, imaginative, ingenious, innovative, inspired, original, resourceful

inventor architect, author, coiner, creator, designer, father, framer, maker, originator

inventory *n.* account, catalogue, file, list, record, register, roll, roster, schedule, stock book

inverse *adj.* contrary, converse, inverted, opposite, reverse, reversed, transposed

inversion antipode, antithesis, contraposition, contrariety, contrary, opposite, reversal, transposal, transposition

invert capsize, introvert, intussuscept (*Pathol.*), invaginate (*Pathol.*), overset, overturn, reverse, transpose, turn inside out, turn turtle, turn upside down, upset, upturn

invest 1. advance, devote, lay out, put in, sink, spend **2.** endow, endue, provide, supply **3.** authorize, charge, empower, license, sanction, vest **4.** adopt, consecrate, enthrone, establish, inaugurate, induct, install, ordain **5.** *Mil.* beleaguer, beset, besiege, enclose, lay siege to, surround **6.** *Archaic* array, bedeck, bedizen (*Archaic*), clothe, deck, drape, dress, robe

investigate consider, enquire into, examine, explore, go into, inquire into, inspect, look into, make enquiries, probe, put to the test, scrutinize, search, sift, study

investigation analysis, enquiry, examination, exploration, fact finding, hearing, inquest, inquiry, inspection, probe, research, review, scrutiny, search, study, survey

investigative fact-finding, inspecting, investigating, research, researching

investigator dick (*Sl.*), examiner, gumshoe (*U.S. sl.*), inquirer, (private) detective, private eye (*Inf.*), researcher, reviewer, sleuth *or* sleuthhound (*Inf.*)

investiture admission, enthronement, inauguration, induction, installation, instatement, investing, investment, ordination

investment 1. asset, investing, speculation, transaction, venture **2.** ante (*Inf.*), contribution, stake **3.** *Mil.* beleaguering, besieging, blockading, siege, surrounding

inveterate chronic, confirmed, deepdyed, deep-rooted, deep-seated, dyed-in-the-wool, entrenched, established, habitual, hard-core, hardened, incorrigible, incurable, ineradicable, ingrained, long-standing, obstinate

invidious discriminatory, envious (*Obsolete*), hateful, obnoxious, odious, offensive, repugnant, slighting, undesirable

invigorate animate, brace, buck up (*Inf.*), energize, enliven, exhilarate, fortify, freshen (up), galvanize, harden, liven up, nerve, pep up, perk up, put new heart into, quicken, refresh, rejuvenate, revitalize, stimulate, strengthen

invigorating bracing, energizing, exhilarating, fresh, healthful, refreshing, rejuvenating, rejuvenative, restorative, salubrious, stimulating, tonic, uplifting

invincible impregnable, indestructible, indomitable, inseparable, insuperable, invulnerable, unassailable, unbeatable, unconquerable, unsurmountable, unyielding

inviolability holiness, inalienability, inviolacy, invulnerability, sacredness, sanctity

inviolable hallowed, holy, inalienable, sacred, sacrosanct, unalterable

inviolate entire, intact, pure, sacred, stainless, unbroken, undefiled, undisturbed, unhurt, unpolluted, unstained, unsullied, untouched, virgin, whole

invisible 1. imperceptible, indiscernible, out of sight, unperceivable, unseen **2**. concealed, disguised, hidden, inappreciable, inconspicuous, infinitesimal, microscopic

invitation 1. asking, begging, bidding, call, invite (*Inf.*), request, solicitation, summons, supplication **2**. allurement, challenge, come-on (*Inf.*), coquetry, enticement, glad eye (*Inf.*), incitement, inducement, open door, overture, provocation, temptation

invite 1. ask, beg, bid, call, request, request the pleasure of (someone's) company, solicit, summon **2**. allure, ask for (*Inf.*), attract, bring on, court, draw, encourage, entice, lead, leave the door open to, provoke, solicit, tempt, welcome

inviting alluring, appealing, attractive, beguiling, captivating, delightful, engaging, enticing, fascinating, intriguing, magnetic, mouthwatering, pleasing, seductive, tempting, warm, welcoming, winning

invocation appeal, beseeching, entreaty, petition, prayer, supplication

invoke 1. adjure, appeal to, beg, beseech, call upon, conjure, entreat, implore, petition, pray, solicit, supplicate **2**. apply, call in, have recourse to, implement, initiate, put into effect, resort to, use

involuntary 1. compulsory, forced, obligatory, reluctant, unwilling **2**. automatic, blind, conditioned, instinctive, instinctual, reflex, spontaneous, unconscious, uncontrolled, unintentional, unthinking

involve 1. entail, imply, mean, necessitate, presuppose, require **2**. affect, associate, compromise, concern, connect, draw in, implicate, incriminate, inculpate, mix up (*Inf.*), touch **3**. comprehend, comprise, contain, cover, embrace, include, incorporate, number among, take in **4**. absorb, bind, commit, engage, engross, grip, hold, preoccupy, rivet, wrap up **5**. complicate, embroil, enmesh, entangle, link, mire, mix up, snarl up, tangle

involved 1. Byzantine, complex, complicated, confusing, convoluted, difficult, elaborate, intricate, knotty, labyrinthine, sophisticated, tangled, tortuous **2**. caught (up), concerned, implicated, in on (*Inf.*), mixed up in or with, occupied, participating, taking part

involvement 1. association, commitment, concern, connection, dedication, interest, participation, responsibility **2**. complexity, complication, difficulty, embarrassment, entanglement, imbroglio, intricacy, problem, ramification

invulnerability impenetrability, inviolability, safety, security, strength, unassailability, untouchability

invulnerable impenetrable, indestructible, insusceptible, invincible, proof against, safe, secure, unassailable

inward *adj.* **1**. entering, inbound, incoming, inflowing, ingoing, inpouring, penetrating **2**. confidential, hidden, inmost, inner, innermost, inside, interior, internal, personal, private, privy, secret

inwardly at heart, deep down, in one's head, in one's inmost heart, inside, privately, secretly, to oneself, within

iota atom, bit, grain, hint, jot, mite, particle, scintilla (*Rare*), scrap, speck, tittle, trace, whit

irascibility asperity, bad temper, cantankerousness, choler, crossness, edginess, fieriness, ill temper, impatience, irritability, irritation, petulance, shortness, snappishness, testiness, touchiness, uncertain temper

irascible cantankerous, choleric, crabbed, cross, hasty, hot-tempered, irritable, narky (*Inf.*), peppery, petulant, quick-tempered, short-tempered, testy, touchy

irate angered, angry, annoyed, enraged, exasperated, fuming (*Inf.*), furious, incensed, indignant, infuriated, irritated, livid, mad (*Inf.*), piqued, provoked, riled, up in arms, worked up, wrathful, wroth (*Archaic*)

ire anger, annoyance, choler, displeasure, exasperation, fury, indignation, passion, rage, wrath

iridescent nacreous, opalescent, opaline, pearly, polychromatic, prismatic, rainbow-coloured, shimmering, shot

Irish Hibernian

irk aggravate (*Inf.*), annoy, bug (*Inf.*), gall, get on one's nerves (*Inf.*), irritate, miff (*Inf.*), nettle, peeve (*Inf.*), provoke, put one's nose out of joint (*Inf.*), put out (*Inf.*), rile, rub one up the wrong way (*Inf.*), ruffle, vex

irksome annoying, boring, bothersome, burdensome, disagreeable, exasperating, irritating, tedious, tiresome, troublesome, uninteresting, unwelcome, vexatious, vexing, wearisome

iron *adj.* **1.** chalybeate, ferric, ferrous, irony **2.** *Fig.* adamant, cruel, hard, heavy, immovable, implacable, indomitable, inflexible, obdurate, rigid, robust, steel, steely, strong, tough, unbending, unyielding

ironic, ironical 1. double-edged, mocking, sarcastic, sardonic, satirical, scoffing, sneering, wry **2.** incongruous, paradoxical

iron out clear up, eliminate, eradicate, erase, expedite, get rid of, harmonize, put right, reconcile, resolve, settle, simplify, smooth over, sort out, straighten out, unravel

irons bonds, chains, fetters, gyves (*Archaic*), manacles, shackles

irony 1. mockery, sarcasm, satire **2.** contrariness, incongruity, paradox

irradiate brighten, cast light upon, enlighten, illume (*Poetic*), illuminate, illumine, lighten, light up, shine upon

irrational 1. absurd, crazy, foolish, illogical, injudicious, nonsensical, preposterous, silly, unreasonable, unreasoning, unsound, unthinking, unwise **2.** aberrant, brainless, crazy, demented, insane, mindless, muddle-headed, raving, senseless, unstable, wild

irrationality absurdity, brainlessness, illogicality, insanity, lack of judgment, lunacy, madness, preposterousness, senselessness, unreasonableness, unsoundness

irreconcilable 1. hardline, implacable, inexorable, inflexible, intransigent, unappeasable, uncompromising **2.** clashing, conflicting, diametrically opposed, incompatible, incongruous, inconsistent, opposed

irrecoverable gone for ever, irreclaimable, irredeemable, irremediable, irreparable, irretrievable, lost, unregainable, unsalvageable, unsavable

irrefutable apodeictic, apodictic, beyond question, certain, incontestable, incontrovertible, indisputable, indubitable, invincible, irrefragable, irresistible, sure, unanswerable, unassailable, undeniable, unquestionable

irregular *adj.* **1.** desultory, disconnected, eccentric, erratic, fitful, fluctuating, fragmentary, haphazard, intermittent, nonuniform, occasional, out of order, patchy, random, shifting, spasmodic, sporadic, uncertain, unmethodical, unpunctual, unsteady, unsystematic, variable, wavering **2.** abnormal, anomalous, capricious, disorderly, eccentric, exceptional, extraordinary, immoderate, improper, inappropriate, inordinate, odd, peculiar, queer, quirky, unconventional, unofficial, unorthodox, unsuitable, unusual **3.** asymmetrical, broken, bumpy, craggy, crooked, elliptic, elliptical, holey, jagged, lopsided, lumpy, pitted, ragged, rough, serrated, unequal, uneven, unsymmetrical ∼*n.* **4.** guerrilla, partisan, volunteer

irregularity 1. asymmetry, bumpiness, crookedness, jaggedness, lack of symmetry, lopsidedness, lumpiness, patchiness, raggedness, roughness, unevenness **2.** aberration, abnormality, anomaly, breach, deviation, eccentricity, freak, malfunction, malpractice, oddity, peculiarity, singularity, unconventionality, unorthodoxy **3.** confusion, desultoriness, disorderliness, disorganization, haphazardness, lack of method, randomness, uncertainty, unpunctuality, unsteadiness

irregularly anyhow, by fits and starts, disconnectedly, eccentrically, erratically, fitfully, haphazardly, in snatches, intermittently, jerkily, now and again, occasionally, off and on, out of sequence, spasmodically, unevenly, unmethodically, unpunctually

irrelevance, irrelevancy inappositeness, inappropriateness, inaptness, inconsequence, non sequitur

irrelevant beside the point, extraneous, immaterial, impertinent, inapplicable, inapposite, inappropriate, inapt, inconsequent, neither here nor there, unconnected, unrelated

irreligious 1. agnostic, atheistic, freethinking, godless, pagan, sceptical, unbelieving **2.** blasphemous, iconoclastic, impious, irreverent, profane, sacrilegious, sinful, undevout, ungodly, unholy, unrighteous, wicked

irremediable beyond redress, deadly, fatal, final, hopeless, incurable, irrecoverable, irredeemable, irreparable, irreversible, mortal, remediless, terminal

irreparable beyond repair, incurable, irrecoverable, irremediable, irreplaceable, irretrievable, irreversible

irreplaceable indispensable, invaluable, priceless, unique, vital

irrepressible boisterous, bubbling over, buoyant, ebullient, effervescent, insuppressible, uncontainable, uncontrollable, unmanageable, unquenchable, unrestrainable, unstoppable

irreproachable beyond reproach, blameless, faultless, guiltless, impeccable, inculpable, innocent, irreprehensible, irreprovable, perfect, pure, unblemished, unimpeachable

irresistible 1. compelling, imperative, overmastering, overpowering, overwhelming, potent, urgent **2.** ineluctable, inescapable, inevitable, inexorable, unavoidable **3.** alluring, beckoning, enchanting, fascinating, ravishing, seductive, tempting

irresolute doubtful, fickle, halfhearted, hesitant, hesitating, indecisive, infirm, in two minds, tentative, undecided, undetermined, unsettled, unstable, unsteady, vacillating, wavering, weak

irresolution faint-heartedness, halfheartedness, hesitancy, hesitation, indecisiveness, infirmity (of purpose), shilly-shallying (*Inf.*), uncertainty, vacillation, wavering

irrespective of apart from, despite, discounting, in spite of, notwithstanding, regardless of, without reference to, without regard to

irresponsible careless, featherbrained, flighty, giddy, harebrained, harum-scarum, ill-considered, immature, reckless, scatter-brained, shiftless, thoughtless, undependable, unreliable, untrustworthy, wild

irreverence cheek (*Inf.*), cheekiness (*Inf.*), derision, disrespect, flippancy, impertinence, impudence, lack of respect, mockery, sauce (*Inf.*)

irreverent cheeky (*Inf.*), contemptuous, derisive, disrespectful, flip (*Inf.*), flippant, iconoclastic, impertinent, impious, impudent, mocking, saucy, tongue-in-cheek

irreversible final, incurable, irreparable, irrevocable, unalterable

irrevocable changeless, fated, fixed, immutable, invariable, irremediable, irretrievable, irreversible, predestined, predetermined, settled, unalterable, unchangeable, unreversible

irrigate flood, inundate, moisten, water, wet

irritability bad temper, ill humour, impatience, irascibility, peevishness, petulance, prickliness, testiness, tetchiness, touchiness

irritable bad-tempered, cantankerous, choleric, crabbed, crabby, cross, crotchety (*Inf.*), dyspeptic, exasperated, fiery, fretful, hasty, hot, ill-humoured, ill-tempered, irascible, narky (*Inf.*), out of humour, oversensitive, peevish, petulant, prickly, snappish, snappy, snarling, tense, testy, touchy

irritate 1. aggravate (*Inf.*), anger, annoy, bother, drive one up the wall (*Inf.*), enrage, exasperate, fret, get in one's hair (*Inf.*), get one's back up (*Inf.*), get one's hackles up, get on one's nerves (*Inf.*), harass, incense, inflame, infuriate, needle (*Inf.*), nettle, offend, pester, provoke, raise one's hackles, rankle with, rub up the wrong way (*Inf.*), ruffle, try one's patience, vex **2.** aggravate, chafe, fret, inflame, intensify, pain, rub

irritated angry, annoyed, bothered, cross, displeased, exasperated, flustered, harassed, impatient, irritable, nettled, out of humour, peeved (*Inf.*), piqued, put out, ruffled, vexed

irritating aggravating (*Inf.*), annoying, displeasing, disquieting, disturbing, galling, infuriating, irksome, maddening, nagging, pestilential, provoking, thorny, troublesome, trying, upsetting, vexatious, worrisome

irritation 1. anger, annoyance, crossness, displeasure, exasperation, ill humour, ill temper, impatience, indignation, irritability, resentment, shortness, snappiness, testiness, vexation, wrath **2.** aggravation (*Inf.*), annoyance, goad, irritant, nuisance, pain (*Inf.*), pain in the neck (*Inf.*), pest, provocation, tease, thorn in one's flesh

irrupt break in, burst in, crash in (*Inf.*), invade, rush in, storm in

irruption breaking in, foray, forcible entry, incursion, inroad, intrusion, invasion, raid

isolate cut off, detach, disconnect, divorce, insulate, quarantine, segregate, separate, sequester, set apart

isolated 1. backwoods, hidden, incommunicado, lonely, off the beaten track, outlying, out-of-the-way, remote, retired, secluded, unfrequented **2.** abnormal, anomalous, exceptional, freak, random, single, solitary, special, unique, unrelated, untypical, unusual

isolation aloofness, detachment, disconnection, exile, insularity, insulation, loneliness, quarantine, remoteness, retirement, seclusion, segregation, self-sufficiency, separation, solitude, withdrawal

issue *n.* **1.** affair, argument, concern, controversy, matter, matter of contention, point, point in question, problem, question, subject, topic **2. at issue** at variance, controversial, in disagreement, in dispute, to be decided, under discussion, unsettled **3. take issue** challenge, disagree, dispute, object, oppose, raise an objection, take exception **4.** conclusion, consequence, culmination, effect, end, finale, outcome, pay-off (*Inf.*), result, termination, upshot **5.** copy, edition, impression, instalment, number, printing **6.** circulation, delivery, dispersion, dissemination, distribution, granting, issuance, issuing, publication, sending out, supply, supplying **7.** children, descendants, heirs, offspring, progeny, scions, seed (*Biblical*) ~*v.* **8.** announce, broadcast, circulate, deliver, distribute,

emit, give out, promulgate, publish, put in circulation, put out, release **9.** arise, be a consequence of, come forth, emanate, emerge, flow, originate, proceed, rise, spring, stem

itch *v.* **1.** crawl, irritate, prickle, tickle, tingle **2.** ache, burn, crave, hanker, hunger, long, lust, pant, pine, yearn ~*n.* **3.** irritation, itchiness, prickling, tingling **4.** craving, desire, hankering, hunger, longing, lust, passion, restlessness, yearning, yen (*Inf.*)

itching agog, aquiver, atremble, avid, burning, consumed with curiosity, eager, impatient, inquisitive, longing, mad keen (*Inf.*), raring, spoiling for

itchy eager, edgy, fidgety, impatient, restive, restless, unsettled

item 1. article, aspect, component, consideration, detail, entry, matter, particular, point, thing **2.** account, article, bulletin, dispatch, feature, note, notice, paragraph, piece, report

itemize count, detail, document, enumerate, instance, inventory, list, number, particularize, record, set out, specify

iterate go over, recap (*Inf.*), recapitulate, reiterate, repeat, restate

itinerant *adj.* ambulatory, Gypsy, journeying, migratory, nomadic, peripatetic, roaming, roving, travelling, unsettled, vagabond, vagrant, wandering, wayfaring

itinerary 1. circuit, journey, line, programme, route, schedule, tour **2.** Baedeker, guide, guidebook

ivory tower cloister, refuge, remoteness, retreat, sanctum, seclusion, splendid isolation, unreality, world of one's own

ivory-towered 1. cloistered, far from the madding crowd, remote, retired, sequestered, sheltered, withdrawn **2.** academic, airy-fairy (*Inf.*), idealistic, quixotic, unrealizable, visionary

J

jab v./n. dig, lunge, nudge, poke, prod, punch, stab, tap, thrust

jabber babble, blather, blether, chatter, drivel, gabble, munble, prate, rabbit (*Sl.*), ramble, tattle, yap (*Inf.*)

jackass blockhead, dimwit (*Inf.*), dolt, fool, idiot, imbecile, lamebrain (*Inf.*), nincompoop, ninny, numskull, simpleton

jacket case, casing, coat, covering, envelope, folder, sheath, skin, wrapper, wrapping

jackpot award, bonanza, kitty, pool, pot, prize, reward, winnings

jack up 1. elevate, heave, hoist, lift, lift up, raise, rear **2.** accelerate, augment, boost, escalate, increase, inflate, put up, raise

jade harridan, hussy, nag, shrew, slattern, slut, trollop, vixen, wench

jaded 1. exhausted, fagged (out) (*Inf.*), fatigued, spent, tired, tired-out, weary **2.** bored, cloyed, dulled, glutted, gorged, sated, satiated, surfeited, tired

jag¹ notch, point, projection, protuberance, snag, spur, tooth

jag² binge (*Inf.*), bout, carouse, fit, orgy, period, spell, spree

jagged barbed, broken, cleft, craggy, denticulate, indented, notched, pointed, ragged, ridged, rough, serrated, snaggy, spiked, toothed, uneven

jail, gaol 1. n. borstal, brig (*Chiefly U.S.*), clink (*Sl.*), cooler (*Sl.*), inside (*Sl.*), jailhouse (*Southern U.S.*), jug (*Sl.*), lockup, nick (*Sl.*), penitentiary (*U.S.*), prison, quod (*Sl.*), reformatory, stir (*Sl.*) **2.** v. confine, detain, immure, impound, imprison, incarcerate, lock up, send down

jailer, gaoler captor, guard, keeper, screw (*Sl.*), turnkey (*Archaic*), warden, warder

jam v. **1.** cram, crowd, crush, force, pack, press, ram, squeeze, stuff, throng, wedge **2.** block, cease, clog, congest, halt, obstruct, stall, stick ~n. **3.** crowd, crush, horde, mass, mob, multitude, pack, press, swarm, throng **4.** bind, dilemma, fix (*Inf.*), hole (*Sl.*), pickle (*Inf.*), plight, predicament, quandary, scrape (*Inf.*), spot (*Inf.*), strait, trouble

jamboree carnival, carouse, celebration, festival, festivity, fête, frolic, jubilee, merriment, party, revelry, spree

jangle 1. v. chime, clank, clash, clatter, jingle, rattle, vibrate **2.** n. cacophony, clang, clangour, clash, din, dissonance, jar, racket, rattle, reverberation

janitor caretaker, concierge, custodian, doorkeeper, porter

jar¹ amphora, carafe, container, crock, flagon, jug, pitcher, pot, receptacle, urn, vase, vessel

jar² v. **1.** bicker, clash, contend, disagree, interfere, oppose, quarrel, wrangle **2.** agitate, convulse, disturb, grate, irritate, jolt, offend, rasp, rattle (*Inf.*), rock, shake, vibrate **3.** annoy, clash, discompose, grate, grind, irk, irritate, nettle ~n. **4.** agitation, altercation, bickering, disagreement, discord, grating, irritation, jolt, quarrel, rasping, wrangling

jargon 1. argot, cant, dialect, idiom, lingo (*Inf.*), parlance, patois, slang, tongue, usage **2.** balderdash, bunkum (*Inf.*), drivel, gabble, gibberish, gobbledegook, mumbo jumbo, nonsense, palaver, rigmarole, twaddle

jaundiced 1. cynical, preconceived, sceptical **2.** biased, bigoted, bitter, distorted, envious, hostile, jealous, partial, prejudiced, resentful, spiteful, suspicious

jaunt airing, excursion, expedition, outing, promenade, ramble, stroll, tour, trip

jaunty airy, breezy, buoyant, carefree, dapper, gay, high-spirited, lively, perky, self-confident, showy, smart, sprightly, spruce, trim

jaw v. **1.** babble, chat, chatter, gossip, lecture, talk **2.** abuse, censure, criticize, revile, scold ~n. **3.** chat, chinwag (*Brit. inf.*), conversation, gossip, natter, talk

jaws abyss, aperture, entrance, gates, ingress, maw, mouth, opening, orifice

jazz up animate, enhance, enliven, heighten, improve

jazzy animated, fancy, flashy, gaudy, lively, smart, snazzy (*Inf.*), spirited, vivacious, wild, zestful

jealous 1. covetous, desirous, emulous, envious, green, green-eyed, grudging, intolerant, invidious, resentful, rival **2.** anxious, apprehensive, attentive, guarded, mistrustful, protective, solicitous, suspicious, vigilant, wary, watchful, zealous

jealousy covetousness, distrust, envy, heart-burning, ill-will, mistrust, possessiveness, resentment, spite, suspicion

jeer 1. *v.* banter, barrack, cock a snook at (*Brit.*), contemn, deride, flout, gibe, heckle, hector, knock (*Sl.*), mock, ridicule, scoff, sneer, taunt **2.** *n.* abuse, aspersion, catcall, derision, gibe, hiss, hoot, obloquy, ridicule, scoff, sneer, taunt

jejune 1. childish, immature, juvenile, naive, pointless, puerile, senseless, silly, simple, unsophisticated **2.** banal, colourless, dry, dull, inane, insipid, prosaic, uninteresting, vapid, wishy-washy (*Inf.*)

jell 1. congeal, harden, set, solidify, thicken **2.** come together, crystallize, finalize, form, materialize, take shape

jeopardize chance, endanger, expose, gamble, hazard, imperil, risk, stake, venture

jeopardy danger, endangerment, exposure, hazard, insecurity, liability, peril, precariousness, risk, venture, vulnerability

jeremiad complaint, groan, keen, lament, lamentation, moan, plaint, wail

jerk *v./n.* jolt, lurch, pull, throw, thrust, tug, tweak, twitch, wrench, yank

jerky bouncy, bumpy, convulsive, fitful, jolting, jumpy, rough, shaky, spasmodic, tremulous, twitchy, uncontrolled

jerry-built cheap, defective, faulty, flimsy, ramshackle, rickety, shabby, slipshod, thrown together, unsubstantial

jest 1. *n.* banter, bon mot, crack (*Sl.*), fun, gag (*Sl.*), hoax, jape, joke, play, pleasantry, prank, quip, sally, sport, wisecrack (*Inf.*), witticism **2.** *v.* banter, chaff, deride, gibe, jeer, joke, kid (*Inf.*), mock, quip, scoff, sneer, tease

jester 1. comedian, comic, humorist, joker, quipster, wag, wit **2.** buffoon, clown, fool, harlequin, madcap, mummer, pantaloon, prankster, zany

jet[1] black, coal-black, ebony, inky, pitch-black, raven, sable

jet[2] *n.* **1.** flow, fountain, gush, spout, spray, spring, stream **2.** atomizer, nose, nozzle, rose, spout, sprayer, sprinkler ~*v.* **3.** flow, gush, issue, rush, shoot, spew, spout, squirt, stream, surge **4.** fly, soar, zoom

jettison abandon, discard, dump, eject, expel, heave, scrap, throw overboard, unload

jetty breakwater, dock, groyne, mole, pier, quay, wharf

jewel 1. brilliant, gemstone, ornament, precious stone, rock (*Sl.*), sparkler (*Inf.*), trinket **2.** charm, find, gem, humdinger (*Sl.*), masterpiece, paragon, pearl, prize, rarity, treasure (*Fig.*), wonder

jewellery finery, gems, jewels, ornaments, precious stones, regalia, treasure, trinkets

Jezebel harlot, harridan, hussy, jade, virago, wanton, witch

jib balk, recoil, refuse, retreat, shrink, stop short

jibe *see* GIBE

jiffy flash, instant, moment, second, split second, trice, twinkling

jig *v.* bob, bounce, caper, jiggle, jounce, prance, shake, skip, twitch, wiggle, wobble

jiggle agitate, bounce, fidget, jerk, jig, jog, joggle, shake, shimmy, twitch, wiggle

jilt *v.* abandon, betray, break with, coquette, deceive, desert, disappoint, discard, ditch (*Sl.*), drop, forsake, reject, throw over

jingle *v.* **1.** chime, clatter, clink, jangle, rattle, ring, tinkle, tintinnabulate ~*n.* **2.** clang, clangour, clink, rattle, reverberation, ringing, tinkle **3.** chorus, ditty, doggerel, limerick, melody, song, tune

jinx 1. *n.* black magic, curse, evil eye, hex (*U.S.*), nemesis, plague, voodoo **2.** *v.* bewitch, curse, hex (*U.S.*)

jitters anxiety, fidgets, nerves, nervousness, tenseness, the shakes (*Inf.*), the willies (*Inf.*)

jittery agitated, anxious, fidgety, jumpy, nervous, quivering, shaky, trembling

job 1. affair, assignment, charge, chore, concern, contribution, duty, enterprise, errand, function, pursuit, responsibility, role, stint, task, undertaking, venture, work **2.** activity, business, calling, capacity, career, craft, employment, function, livelihood, métier, occupation, office, position, post, profession, situation, trade, vocation **3.** allotment, assignment, batch, commission, consignment, contract, lot, output, piece, portion, product, share

jobless idle, inactive, out of work, unemployed, unoccupied

jockey 1. bamboozle, cheat, con (*Sl.*), deceive, dupe, fool, hoax, hoodwink, trick **2.** cajole, engineer, finagle (*Inf.*), ingratiate, insinuate, manage, manipulate, manoeuvre, negotiate, trim, wheedle

jocose blithe, comical, droll, facetious, funny, humorous, jesting, jocular, jovial, joyous, merry, mischievous, playful, pleasant, sportive, teasing, waggish, witty

jocular amusing, comical, droll, facetious, frolicsome, funny, humorous, jesting, jocose, jocund, joking, jolly, jovial, playful, roguish, sportive, teasing, waggish, whimsical, witty

jog 1. activate, arouse, nudge, prod, prompt, push, remind, shake, stimulate, stir, suggest **2.** bounce, jar, jerk, jiggle, joggle, jolt, jostle, jounce, rock, shake **3.** canter, dogtrot, lope, run, trot **4.** lumber, plod, traipse (*Inf.*), tramp, trudge

joie de vivre ebullience, enjoyment, enthusiasm, gaiety, gusto, joy, joyfulness, pleasure, relish, zest

join 1. accompany, add, adhere, annex, append, attack, cement, combine, connect, couple, fasten, knit, link, marry, splice, tie, unite, yoke **2.** affiliate with, associate with, enlist, enrol, enter, sign up **3.** adjoin, border, border on, butt, conjoin, extend, meet, reach, touch, verge on

joint *n.* **1.** articulation, connection, hinge, intersection, junction, juncture, knot, nexus, node, seam, union ~*adj.* **2.** collective, combined, communal, concerted, consolidated, cooperative, joined, mutual, shared, united ~*v.* **3.** connect, couple, fasten, fit, join, unite **4.** carve, cut up, dismember, dissect, divide, segment, sever, sunder

jointly as one, collectively, in common, in conjunction, in league, in partnership, mutually, together, unitedly

joke *n.* **1.** frolic, fun, gag (*Sl.*), jape, jest, lark, play, pun, quip, quirk, sally, sport, whimsy, wisecrack (*Inf.*), witticism, yarn **2.** buffoon, butt, clown, laughing stock, simpleton, target ~*v.* **3.** banter, chaff, deride, frolic, gambol, jest, kid (*Inf.*), mock, quip, ridicule, taunt, tease

joker buffoon, clown, comedian, comic, humorist, jester, kidder (*Inf.*), prankster, trickster, wag, wit

jolly blithesome, carefree, cheerful, convivial, festive, frolicsome, funny, gay, gladsome, hilarious, jocund, jovial, joyful, joyous, jubilant, merry, mirthful, playful, sportive, sprightly

jolt *v.* **1.** jar, jerk, jog, jostle, knock, push, shake, shove **2.** astonish, discompose, disturb, perturb, stagger, startle, stun, surprise, upset ~*n.* **3.** bump, jar, jerk, jog, jump, lurch, quiver, shake, start **4.** blow, bolt from the blue, bombshell, reversal, setback, shock, surprise, thunderbolt

jostle bump, butt, crowd, elbow, hustle, jog, joggle, jolt, press, push, scramble, shake, shove, squeeze, throng, thrust

jot 1. *n.* ace, atom, bit, detail, fraction, grain, iota, mite, morsel, particle, scintilla, scrap, smidgen (*U.S.*), speck, tittle, trifle, whit **2.** *v.* list, note, note down, record, register, scribble, tally

journal 1. chronicle, daily, gazette, magazine, monthly, newspaper, paper, periodical, record, register, review, tabloid, weekly **2.** chronicle, commonplace book, daybook, diary, log, record

journalist broadcaster, columnist, commentator, contributor, correspondent, hack, newsman, newspaperman, pressman, reporter, scribe (*Inf.*), stringer

journey 1. *n.* excursion, expedition, jaunt, odyssey, outing, passage, peregrination, pilgrimage, progress, ramble, tour, travel, trek, trip, voyage **2.** *v.* fare, fly, go, peregrinate, proceed, ramble, range, roam, rove, tour, travel, traverse, trek, voyage, wander, wend

joust 1. *n.* combat, duel, encounter, engagement, lists, match, passage of arms, set-to, tilt, tournament, tourney **2.** *v.* break a lance, cross swords, engage, enter the lists, fight, tilt, trade blows

jovial airy, animated, blithe, buoyant, cheery, convivial, cordial, gay, glad, happy, hilarious, jocose, jocund, jolly, jubilant, merry, mirthful

joviality fun, gaiety, glee, hilarity, jollity, merriment, mirth

joy 1. bliss, delight, ecstasy, elation, exaltation, exultation, felicity, festivity, gaiety, gladness, glee, hilarity, pleasure, rapture, ravishment, satisfaction, transport **2.** charm, delight, gem, jewel, pride, prize, treasure, treat, wonder

joyful blithesome, delighted, elated, enraptured, glad, gladsome, gratified, happy, jocund, jolly, jovial, jubilant, light-hearted, merry, pleased, satisfied

joyless cheerless, dejected, depressed, dismal, dispirited, downcast, dreary, gloomy, miserable, sad, unhappy

joyous cheerful, festive, heartening, joyful, merry, rapturous

jubilant elated, enraptured, euphoric, excited, exuberant, exultant, glad, joyous, overjoyed, rejoicing, rhapsodic, thrilled, triumphal, triumphant

jubilation celebration, ecstasy, elation, excitement, exultation, festivity, jamboree, joy, jubilee, triumph

jubilee carnival, celebration, festival, festivity, fête, gala, holiday

Judas betrayer, deceiver, renegade, traitor, turncoat

judge n. **1.** adjudicator, arbiter, arbitrator, moderator, referee, umpire **2.** appraiser, arbiter, assessor, authority, connoisseur, critic, evaluator, expert **3.** beak (*Brit. sl.*), justice, magistrate ~v. **4.** adjudge, adjudicate, arbitrate, ascertain, conclude, decide, determine, discern, distinguish, mediate, referee, umpire **5.** appraise, appreciate, assess, consider, criticize, esteem, estimate, evaluate, examine, rate, review, value **6.** adjudge, condemn, decree, doom, find, pass sentence, pronounce sentence, rule, sentence, sit, try

judgment 1. acumen, common sense, discernment, discrimination, intelligence, penetration, percipience, perspicacity, prudence, sagacity, sense, shrewdness, taste, understanding, wisdom **2.** arbitration, award, conclusion, decision, decree, determination, finding, order, result, ruling, sentence, verdict **3.** assessment, belief, conviction, deduction, diagnosis, estimate, finding, opinion appraisal, valuation, view **4.** damnation, doom, fate, misfortune, punishment, retribution

judicial 1. judiciary, juridical, legal, official **2.** discriminating, distinguished, impartial, judgelike, magisterial, magistral

judicious acute, astute, careful, cautious, circumspect, considered, diplomatic, discerning, discreet, discriminating, enlightened, expedient, informed, politic, prudent, rational, reasonable, sagacious, sage, sane, sapient, sensible, shrewd, skilful, sober, sound, thoughtful, well-advised, well-judged, wise

jug carafe, container, crock, ewer, jar, pitcher, urn, vessel

juggle alter, change, disguise, doctor (*Inf.*), falsify, fix (*Inf.*), manipulate, manoeuvre, misrepresent, modify, tamper with

juice extract, fluid, liquid, liquor, nectar, sap, secretion, serum

juicy 1. lush, moist, sappy, succulent, watery **2.** colourful, interesting, provocative, racy, risqué, sensational, spicy, suggestive, vivid

jumble 1. v. confound, confuse, disarrange, dishevel, disorder, disorganize, entangle, mistake, mix, muddle, shuffle, tangle **2.** n. chaos, clutter, confusion, disarrangement, disarray, disorder, farrago, gallimaufry, hodgepodge, hotchpotch, litter, medley, *mélange*, mess, miscellany, mishmash, mixture, muddle

jumbo giant, gigantic, huge, immense, large, oversized

jump v. **1.** bounce, bound, caper, clear, gambol, hop, hurdle, leap, skip, spring, vault **2.** flinch, jerk, recoil, start, wince **3.** avoid, digress, evade, miss, omit, overshoot, skip, switch **4.** advance, ascend, boost, escalate, gain, hike, increase, mount, rise, surge ~n. **5.** bound, buck, caper, hop, leap, skip, spring, vault **6.** barricade, barrier, fence, hurdle, impediment, obstacle, rail **7.** breach, break, gap, hiatus, interruption, lacuna, space **8.** advance, augmentation, boost, increase, increment, rise, upsurge, upturn **9.** jar, jerk, jolt, lurch, shock, start, swerve, twitch, wrench

jumper pullover, sweater, woolly

jumpy agitated, anxious, apprehensive, fidgety, jittery, nervous, on edge, restless, shaky, tense, timorous

junction alliance, combination, connection, coupling, joint, juncture, linking, seam, union

juncture 1. conjuncture, contingency, crisis, crux, emergency, exigency, moment, occasion, point, predicament, strait, time **2.** bond, connection, convergence, edge, intersection, junction, link, seam, weld

junior inferior, lesser, lower, minor, secondary, subordinate, younger

junk clutter, debris, leavings, litter, oddments, odds and ends, refuse, rubbish, rummage, scrap, trash, waste

junta assembly, cabal, clique, combination, confederacy, convocation, coterie, council, crew, faction, gang, league, party, ring, set

jurisdiction 1. authority, command, control, dominion, influence, power, prerogative, rule, say, sway **2.** area, bounds, circuit, compass, district, dominion, field, orbit, province, range, scope, sphere, zone

just *adj.* **1.** blameless, conscientious, decent, equitable, fair, fairminded, good, honest, honourable, impartial, lawful, pure, right, righteous, unbiased, upright, virtuous **2.** accurate, correct, exact, faithful, normal, precise, proper, regular, sound, true **3.** appropriate, apt, condign, deserved, due, fitting, justified, legitimate, merited, proper, reasonable, rightful, suitable, well-deserved ~*adv.* **4.** absolutely, completely, entirely, exactly, perfectly, precisely **5.** hardly, lately, only now, recently, scarcely **6.** at most, but, merely, no more than, nothing but, only, simply, solely

just about all but, almost, around, close to, nearly, not quite, practically, well-nigh

justice 1. equity, fairness, honesty, impartiality, integrity, justness, law, legality, legitimacy, reasonableness, rectitude, right **2.** amends, compensation, correction, penalty, recompense, redress, reparation **3.** judge, magistrate

justifiable acceptable, defensible, excusable, fit, lawful, legitimate, proper, reasonable, right, sound, tenable, understandable, valid, vindicable, warrantable, well-founded

justification 1. absolution, apology, approval, defence, exculpation, excuse, exoneration, explanation, extenuation, plea, rationalization, vindication **2.** basis, defence, grounds, plea, reason, warrant

justify absolve, acquit, approve, confirm, defend, establish, exculpate, excuse, exonerate, explain, legalize, legitimize, maintain, substantiate, support, sustain, uphold, validate, vindicate, warrant

justly accurately, correctly, equally, equitably, fairly, honestly, impartially, lawfully, properly

jut bulge, extend, impend, overhang, poke, project, protrude, stick out

juvenile 1. *n.* adolescent, boy, child, girl, infant, minor, youth **2.** *adj.* babyish, boyish, callow, childish, girlish, immature, inexperienced, infantile, jejune, puerile, undeveloped, unsophisticated, young, youthful

juxtaposition adjacency, closeness, contact, contiguity, nearness, propinquity, proximity, vicinity

K

kaleidoscopic 1. changeable, fluctuating, fluid, many-coloured, mobile, motley, mutable, unstable, variegated **2**. complex, complicated, confused, convoluted, disordered, intricate, jumbled, varied

kaput broken, dead, defunct, destroyed, extinct, finished, ruined, undone, wrecked

keel over black out (*Inf.*), capsize, collapse, faint, founder, overturn, pass out, swoon (*Literary*), topple over, upset

keen¹ 1. ardent, avid, devoted to, eager, earnest, ebullient, enthusiastic, fervid, fierce, fond of, impassioned, intense, zealous **2**. acid, acute, biting, caustic, cutting, edged, finely honed, incisive, penetrating, piercing, pointed, razorlike, sardonic, satirical, sharp, tart, trenchant **3**. astute, brilliant, canny, clever, discerning, discriminating, perceptive, perspicacious, quick, sagacious, sapient, sensitive, shrewd, wise

keen² 1. *v.* bewail, grieve, lament, mourn, wail, weep **2**. *n.* coronach (*Scot., Irish*), dirge, lament, lamentation, mourning, wailing, weeping

keenness 1. ardour, avidity, avidness, diligence, eagerness, earnestness, ebullience, enthusiasm, fervour, impatience, intensity, passion, zeal, zest **2**. acerbity, harshness, incisiveness, mordancy, penetration, pungency, rigour, severity, sharpness, sternness, trenchancy, unkindness, virulence **3**. astuteness, canniness, cleverness, discernment, insight, sagacity, sapience, sensitivity, shrewdness, wisdom

keep *v.* **1**. conserve, control, hold, maintain, possess, preserve, retain **2**. accumulate, amass, carry, deal in, deposit, furnish, garner, heap, hold, pile, place, stack, stock, store, trade in **3**. care for, defend, guard, look after, maintain, manage, mind, operate, protect, safeguard, shelter, shield, tend, watch over **4**. board, feed, foster, maintain, nourish, nurture, provide for, provision, subsidize, support, sustain, victual **5**. accompany, associate with, consort with, fraternize with **6**. arrest, block, check, con-

strain, control, curb, delay, detain, deter, hamper, hamstring, hinder, hold, hold back, impede, inhibit, keep back, limit, obstruct, prevent, restrain, retard, shackle, stall, withhold **7**. adhere to, celebrate, commemorate, comply with, fulfil, hold, honour, obey, observe, perform, respect, ritualize, solemnize ∼*n.* **8**. board, food, livelihood, living, maintenance, means, nourishment, subsistence, support **9**. castle, citadel, donjon, dungeon, fastness, stronghold, tower

keep at be steadfast, carry on, complete, continue, drudge, endure, finish, grind, labour, last, maintain, persevere, persist, remain, slave, stay, stick, toil

keep back 1. check, constrain, control, curb, delay, hold back, limit, prohibit, restrain, restrict, retard, withhold **2**. censor, conceal, hide, reserve, suppress, withhold

keeper attendant, caretaker, curator, custodian, defender, gaoler, governor, guard, guardian, jailer, overseer, preserver, steward, superintendent, warden, warder

keeping 1. aegis, auspices, care, charge, custody, guardianship, keep, maintenance, patronage, possession, protection, safekeeping, trust **2**. accord, agreement, balance, compliance, conformity, congruity, consistency, correspondence, harmony, observance, proportion

keep on carry on, continue, endure, last, persevere, persist, prolong, remain

keepsake emblem, favour, memento, relic, remembrance, reminder, souvenir, symbol, token

keep up balance, compete, contend, continue, emulate, keep pace, maintain, match, persevere, preserve, rival, sustain, vie

keg barrel, cask, drum, firkin, hogshead, tun, vat

ken 1. compass, field, range, scope, sight, view, vision **2**. acquaintance, awareness, cognisance, comprehension, knowledge, notice, understanding

kerchief babushka, headscarf, headsquare, scarf, square

kernel core, essence, germ, gist, grain, marrow, nub, pith, seed, substance

key n. **1.** latchkey, opener **2.** Fig. answer, clue, cue, explanation, guide, indicator, interpretation, lead, means, pointer, sign, solution, translation ~adj. **3.** basic, chief, crucial, decisive, essential, fundamental, important, leading, main, major, pivotal, principal

keynote centre, core, essence, gist, heart, kernel, marrow, pith, substance, theme

keystone basis, core, cornerstone, crux, fundament, ground, linchpin, mainspring, motive, principle, quoin, root, source, spring

kick v. **1.** boot, punt **2.** Fig. complain, gripe (Inf.), grumble, object, oppose, protest, rebel, resist, spurn **3.** Inf. abandon, desist from, give up, leave off, quit, stop ~n. **4.** force, intensity, pep, power, punch, pungency, snap (Inf.), sparkle, strength, tang, verve, vitality, zest **5.** buzz (Sl.), enjoyment, excitement, fun, gratification, pleasure, stimulation, thrill

kickback bribe, cut (Inf.), gift, graft, payment, payoff, recompense, reward, share

kickoff n. beginning, commencement, opening, outset, start

kick off v. begin, commence, get under way, initiate, open, start

kick out discharge, dismiss, eject, evict, expel, get rid of, oust, reject, remove, sack, toss out

kid 1. n. baby, bairn, boy, child, girl, infant, lad, little one, stripling, teenager, tot, youngster, youth **2.** v. bamboozle, beguile, cozen, delude, fool, gull (Archaic), hoax, hoodwink, jest, joke, mock, plague, pretend, rag (Sl.), ridicule, tease, trick

kidnap abduct, capture, hijack, hold to ransom, remove, seize, skyjack, steal

kill 1. annihilate, assassinate, bump off (Sl.), butcher, destroy, dispatch, do away with, do in (Sl.), eradicate, execute, exterminate, extirpate, knock off (Sl.), liquidate, massacre, murder, neutralize, obliterate, slaughter, slay, take (someone's) life, waste (Sl.) **2.** Fig. cancel, cease, deaden, defeat, extinguish, halt, quash, quell, ruin, scotch, smother, stifle, still, stop, suppress, veto

killer assassin, butcher, cutthroat, destroyer, executioner, exterminator, gun-

man, hit man (Sl.), liquidator, murderer, slaughterer, slayer

killing n. **1.** bloodshed, carnage, execution, extermination, fatality, homicide, manslaughter, massacre, murder, slaughter, slaying **2.** Inf. bomb (Sl.), bonanza, cleanup (Inf.), coup, gain, profit, success, windfall ~adj. **3.** deadly, death-dealing, deathly, fatal, lethal, mortal, murderous **4.** Inf. debilitating, enervating, exhausting, fatiguing, punishing, tiring **5.** Inf. absurd, amusing, comical, hilarious, ludicrous, uproarious

kill-joy dampener, damper, spoilsport, wet blanket (Inf.)

kin n. **1.** affinity, blood, connection, consanguinity, extraction, kinship, lineage, relationship, stock **2.** connections, family, kindred, kinsfolk, kinsmen, kith, people, relations, relatives ~adj. **3.** akin, allied, close, cognate, consanguine, consanguineous, kindred, near, related

kind[1] **1.** n. brand, breed, class, family, genus, ilk, race, set, sort, species, variety **2.** character, description, essence, habit, manner, mould, nature, persuasion, sort, style, temperament, type

kind[2] adj. affectionate, amiable, amicable, beneficent, benevolent, benign, bounteous, charitable, clement, compassionate, congenial, considerate, cordial, courteous, friendly, generous, gentle, good, gracious, humane, indulgent, kind-hearted, kindly, lenient, loving, mild, neighbourly, obliging, philanthropic, propitious, sympathetic, tender-hearted, thoughtful, understanding

kind-hearted altruistic, amicable, compassionate, considerate, generous, good-natured, gracious, helpful, humane, kind, sympathetic, tender-hearted

kindle 1. fire, ignite, inflame, light, set fire to **2.** Fig. agitate, animate, arouse, awaken, bestir, enkindle, exasperate, excite, foment, incite, induce, inflame, inspire, provoke, rouse, sharpen, stimulate, stir, thrill

kindliness amiability, beneficence, benevolence, benignity, charity, compassion, friendliness, gentleness, humanity, kind-heartedness, kindness, sympathy

kindly 1. adj. beneficial, benevolent, benign, compassionate, cordial, favourable, genial, gentle, good-natured, hearty, helpful, kind, mild, pleasant, polite, sympathetic, warm **2.** adv. agreeably, cordially, graciously, politely, tenderly, thoughtfully

kindness 1. affection, amiability, beneficence, benevolence, charity, clemency, compassion, decency, fellow-feeling, generosity, gentleness, goodness, good will, grace, hospitality, humanity, indulgence, kindliness, magnanimity, patience, philanthropy, tenderness, tolerance, understanding **2**. aid, assistance, benefaction, bounty, favour, generosity, good deed, help, service

kindred n. **1**. affinity, consanguinity, relationship **2**. connections, family, flesh, kin, kinsfolk, kinsmen, lineage, relations, relatives ~adj. **3**. affiliated, akin, allied, cognate, congenial, corresponding, kin, like, matching, related, similar

king crowned head, emperor, majesty, monarch, overlord, prince, ruler, sovereign

kingdom 1. dominion, dynasty, empire, monarchy, realm, reign, sovereignty **2**. commonwealth, county, division, nation, province, state, territory, tract **3**. area, domain, field, province, sphere, territory

kingly 1. imperial, monarchical, regal, royal, sovereign **2**. august, glorious, grand, grandiose, imposing, majestic, noble, splendid, stately

kink 1. bend, coil, corkscrew, crimp, entanglement, frizz, knot, tangle, twist, wrinkle **2**. cramp, crick, pang, pinch, spasm, stab, tweak, twinge **3**. complication, defect, difficulty, flaw, hitch, imperfection, knot, tangle **4**. crotchet, eccentricity, fetish, foible, idiosyncrasy, quirk, singularity, vagary, whim

kinky 1. bizarre, eccentric, odd, outlandish, peculiar, queer, quirky, strange, unconventional, weird **2**. degenerated, depraved, deviant, licentious, perverted, unnatural, warped **3**. coiled, crimped, curled, curly, frizzled, frizzy, tangled, twisted

kinsfolk connections, family, kin, kindred, kinsmen, relations, relatives

kinship 1. blood relationship, consanguinity, kin, relation, ties of blood **2**. affinity, alliance, association, bearing, connection, correspondence, relationship, similarity

kinsman blood relative, fellow clansman, fellow tribesman, relation, relative

kiosk bookstall, booth, counter, newsstand, stall, stand

kismet destiny, fate, fortune, karma, lot, portion, preordination, Providence

kiss v. **1**. buss (*Archaic*), canoodle (*Inf.*), greet, neck (*Inf.*), osculate, peck (*Inf.*), salute, smooch (*Inf.*) **2**. brush, caress, glance, graze, scrape, touch ~n. **3**. buss (*Archaic*), osculation, peck (*Inf.*), smacker (*Sl.*)

kit accoutrements, apparatus, effects, equipment, gear, impedimenta, implements, instruments, outfit, paraphernalia, provisions, rig, supplies, tackle, tools, trappings, utensils

kitchen cookhouse, galley, kitchenette

kit out or **up** accoutre, arm, deck out, equip, fit out, fix up, furnish, outfit, provide with, supply

kittenish coquettish, coy, flirtatious, frisky, frolicsome, funloving, playful, sportive

knack ability, adroitness, aptitude, bent, capacity, dexterity, expertise, expertness, facility, flair, forte, genius, gift, handiness, ingenuity, propensity, quickness, skilfulness, skill, talent, trick

knave blackguard, bounder (*Inf.*), cheat, rapscallion, rascal, reprobate, rogue, rotter (*Sl.*), scallywag (*Inf.*), scamp, scapegrace, scoundrel, swindler, varlet (*Archaic*), villain

knavery chicanery, corruption, deceit, deception, dishonesty, double-dealing, duplicity, fraud, imposture, rascality, roguery, trickery, villainy

knavish deceitful, deceptive, dishonest, dishonourable, fraudulent, lying, rascally, roguish, scoundrelly, tricky, unprincipled, unscrupulous, villainous

knead blend, form, manipulate, massage, mould, press, rub, shape, squeeze, stroke, work

kneel bow, bow down, curtsey, genuflect, get down on one's knees, kowtow, make obeisance, stoop

knell 1. v. announce, chime, herald, peal, resound, ring, sound, toll **2**. n. chime, peal, ringing, sound, toll

knickers bloomers, briefs, drawers, panties, smalls, underwear

knick-knack bagatelle, bauble, bibelot, bric-a-brac, gewgaw, gimcrack, kickshaw, plaything, trifle, trinket

knife 1. n. blade, cutter, cutting tool **2**. v. cut, impale, lacerate, pierce, slash, stab, wound

knightly chivalrous, courageous,

courtly, gallant, gracious, heroic, noble, valiant

knit 1. affix, ally, bind, connect, contract, fasten, heal, interlace, intertwine, join, link, loop, mend, secure, tie, unite, weave **2.** crease, furrow, knot, wrinkle

knob boss, bulk, bump, bunch, door-handle, knot, knurl, lump, nub, projection, protrusion, protuberance, snag, stud, swell, swelling, tumour

knock v. **1.** buffet, clap, cuff, hit, punch, rap, slap, smack, smite (Archaic), strike, thump, thwack ~n. **2.** blow, box, clip, clout, cuff, hammering, rap, slap, smack, thump ~v. **3.** Inf. abuse, belittle, carp, cavil, censure, condemn, criticize, deprecate, disparage, find fault, lambaste, run down, slam (Sl.) ~n. **4.** blame, censure, condemnation, criticism, defeat, failure, rebuff, rejection, reversal, setback, stricture

knock about or **around 1.** ramble, range, roam, rove, traipse, travel, wander **2.** abuse, batter, beat up (Inf.), bruise, buffet, damage, hit, hurt, maltreat, manhandle, maul, mistreat, strike, wound

knock down batter, clout (Inf.), demolish, destroy, fell, floor, level, pound, raze, smash, wallop (Inf.), wreck

knock off 1. clock off, clock out, complete, conclude, finish, stop work, terminate **2.** filch, nick (Sl.), pilfer, pinch, purloin, rob, steal, thieve **3.** assassinate, bump off (Sl.), do away with, do in (Sl.), kill, liquidate, murder, slay, waste (Sl.)

knockout 1. coup de grâce, kayo (Sl.), K.O. (Sl.) **2.** hit, sensation, smash, smash-hit, stunner (Inf.), success, triumph, winner

knoll barrow, hill, hillock, hummock, mound, swell

knot v. **1.** bind, complicate, entangle, knit, loop, secure, tether, tie, weave ~n. **2.** bond, bow, braid, connection, joint, ligature, loop, rosette, tie **3.** aggregation, bunch, clump, cluster, collection, heap, mass, pile, tuft **4.** assemblage, band, circle, clique, company, crew (Inf.), crowd, gang, group, mob, pack, set, squad

knotty 1. bumpy, gnarled, knobby, knotted, nodular, rough, rugged **2.** baffling, complex, complicated, difficult, hard, intricate, mystifying, perplexing, problematical, puzzling, thorny, tricky, troublesome

know 1. apprehend, comprehend, experience, fathom, feel certain, ken

(Scot.), learn, notice, perceive, realize, recognize, see, undergo, understand **2.** associate with, be acquainted with, be familiar with, fraternize with, have dealings with, have knowledge of, recognize **3.** differentiate, discern, distinguish, identify, make out, perceive, recognize, see, tell

know-how ability, adroitness, aptitude, capability, dexterity, experience, expertise, faculty, flair, ingenuity, knack, knowledge, proficiency, savoir-faire, skill, talent

knowing 1. astute, clever, competent, discerning, experienced, expert, intelligent, qualified, skilful, well-informed **2.** acute, cunning, eloquent, expressive, meaningful, perceptive, sagacious, shrewd, significant **3.** aware, conscious, deliberate, intended, intentional

knowingly consciously, deliberately, intentionally, on purpose, purposely, wilfully, wittingly

knowledge 1. education, enlightenment, erudition, instruction, intelligence, learning, scholarship, schooling, science, tuition, wisdom **2.** ability, apprehension, cognition, comprehension, consciousness, discernment, grasp, judgment, recognition, understanding **3.** acquaintance, cognizance, familiarity, information, intimacy, notice

knowledgeable 1. acquainted, au courant, au fait, aware, cognizant, conscious, conversant, experienced, familiar, in the know (Inf.), understanding, well-informed **2.** educated, erudite, intelligent, learned, lettered, scholarly

known acknowledged, admitted, avowed, celebrated, common, confessed, familiar, famous, manifest, noted, obvious, patent, plain, popular, published, recognized, well-known

knuckle under v. accede, acquiesce, capitulate, give in, give way, submit, succumb, surrender, yield

knurl bulb, bulge, burl, gnarl, knot, lump, node, protuberance, ridge

kowtow 1. bow, genuflect, kneel **2.** court, cringe, fawn, flatter, grovel, pander, suck up to (Sl.), toady, truckle

kudos acclaim, applause, distinction, esteem, fame, glory, honour, laudation, notability, plaudits, praise, prestige, regard, renown, repute

L

label *n.* **1.** docket (*Chiefly Brit.*), marker, sticker, tag, tally, ticket **2.** characterization, classification, description, epithet **3.** brand, company, mark, trademark ~*v.* **4.** docket (*Chiefly Brit.*), mark, stamp, sticker, tag, tally **5.** brand, call, characterize, class, classify, define, describe, designate, identify, name

laborious 1. arduous, backbreaking, burdensome, difficult, fatiguing, hard, herculean, onerous, strenuous, tiresome, toilsome, tough, uphill, wearing, wearisome **2.** assiduous, diligent, hardworking, indefatigable, industrious, painstaking, persevering, sedulous, tireless, unflagging **3.** *Of literary style, etc.* forced, laboured, not fluent, ponderous, strained

labour *n.* **1.** industry, toil, work **2.** employees, hands, labourers, workers, work force, workmen **3.** donkey-work, drudgery, effort, exertion, grind (*Inf.*), industry, pains, painstaking, sweat (*Inf.*), toil, travail **4.** chore, job, task, undertaking **5.** childbirth, contractions, delivery, labour pains, pains, parturition, throes, travail ~*v.* **6.** drudge, endeavour, grind (*Inf.*), peg along *or* away (*Chiefly Brit.*), plod, plug along *or* away (*Inf.*), slave, strive, struggle, sweat (*Inf.*), toil, travail, work **7.** *Usually with* **under** be a victim of, be burdened by, be disadvantaged, suffer **8.** dwell on, elaborate, overdo, overemphasize, strain **9.** *Of a ship* heave, pitch, roll, toss

laboured 1. awkward, difficult, forced, heavy, stiff, strained **2.** affected, contrived, overdone, overwrought, ponderous, studied, unnatural

labourer blue-collar worker, drudge, hand, labouring man, manual worker, navvy (*Brit. inf.*), unskilled worker, worker, working man, workman

labyrinth coil, complexity, complication, convolution, entanglement, intricacy, jungle, knotty problem, maze, perplexity, puzzle, riddle, snarl, tangle, windings

labyrinthine Byzantine, complex, confused, convoluted, Daedalian, Gordian, intricate, involved, knotty, maze-like, mazy, perplexing, puzzling, tangled, tortuous, winding

lace *n.* **1.** filigree, netting, openwork, tatting **2.** bootlace, cord, shoelace, string, thong, tie ~*v.* **3.** attach, bind, close, do up, fasten, intertwine, interweave, thread, tie, twine **4.** add to, fortify, mix in, spike

lace into assail, attack, belabour, berate, castigate, flay, lay into, light into (*Inf.*), set about, vituperate

lacerate 1. claw, cut, gash, jag, maim, mangle, rend, rip, slash, tear, wound **2.** *Fig.* afflict, distress, harrow, rend, torment, torture, wound

laceration cut, gash, injury, mutilation, rent, rip, slash, tear, wound

lachrymose crying, dolorous, lugubrious, mournful, sad, tearful, weeping, weepy (*Inf.*), woeful

lack 1. *n.* absence, dearth, deficiency, deprivation, destitution, insufficiency, need, privation, scantiness, scarcity, shortage, shortcoming, shortness, want **2.** *v.* be deficient in, be short of, be without, miss, need, require, want

lackadaisical 1. apathetic, dull, enervated, half-hearted, indifferent, languid, languorous, lethargic, limp, listless, spiritless **2.** abstracted, dreamy, idle, indolent, inert, lazy

lackey 1. creature, fawner, flatterer, flunky, hanger-on, instrument, menial, minion, parasite, pawn, sycophant, toady, tool, yes man **2.** attendant, flunky, footman, manservant, valet

lacking defective, deficient, flawed, impaired, inadequate, minus (*Inf.*), missing, needing, sans (*Archaic*), wanting, without

lacklustre boring, dim, drab, dry, dull, flat, leaden, lifeless, lustreless, muted, prosaic, sombre, unimaginative, uninspired, vapid

laconic brief, compact, concise, crisp, curt, pithy, sententious, short, succinct, terse, to the point

lacuna blank, break, gap, hiatus, omission, space, void

lacy delicate, filigree, fine, frilly, gauzy,

gossamer, lacelike, meshy, netlike, open, sheer

lad boy, chap (*Inf.*), fellow, guy (*Inf.*), juvenile, kid, laddie (*Scot.*), schoolboy, shaver (*Inf.*), stripling, youngster, youth

laden burdened, charged, encumbered, fraught, full, hampered, loaded, oppressed, taxed, weighed down, weighted

la-di-da affected, conceited, highfalutin (*Inf.*), mannered, mincing, overrefined, posh (*Inf., chiefly Brit.*), precious, pretentious, snobbish, snooty (*Inf.*), stuck-up (*Inf.*), toffee-nosed (*Sl., chiefly Brit.*), too-too

lady-killer Casanova, Don Juan, heartbreaker, ladies' man, libertine, Lothario, philanderer, rake, roué, wolf (*Inf.*), womanizer

ladylike courtly, cultured, decorous, elegant, genteel, modest, polite, proper, refined, respectable, well-bred

lag 1. be behind, dawdle, delay, drag (behind), drag one's feet, hang back, idle, linger, loiter, saunter, straggle, tarry, trail 2. decrease, diminish, ebb, fail, fall off, flag, lose strength, slacken, wane

laggard dawdler, idler, lingerer, loafer, loiterer, lounger, saunterer, slowcoach (*Brit. inf.*), sluggard, snail, straggler

laid-back at ease, casual, easy-going, free and easy, relaxed, unflappable (*Inf.*), unhurried

laid up bedridden, disabled, housebound, ill, immobilized, incapacitated, injured, on the sick list, out of action (*Inf.*), sick

lair 1. burrow, den, earth, form, hole, nest, resting place 2. *Inf.* den, hide-out, refuge, retreat, sanctuary

laissez faire *n.* free enterprise, free trade, individualism, live and let live, nonintervention

lam batter, beat, hit, knock, pelt, pound, strike, thrash

lambaste 1. beat, bludgeon, cudgel, drub, flog, strike, thrash, whip 2. berate, castigate, censure, flay, rebuke, reprimand, scold, upbraid

lambent 1. dancing, flickering, fluttering, licking, touching, twinkling 2. gleaming, glistening, glowing, luminous, lustrous, radiant, refulgent, shimmering 3. *Of wit or humour* brilliant, light, sparkling

lamblike 1. gentle, meek, mild, passive, peaceable, submissive 2. artless,

childlike, guileless, innocent, naive, simple, trusting

lame 1. crippled, defective, disabled, game, halt (*Archaic*), handicapped, hobbling, limping 2. *Fig.* feeble, flimsy, inadequate, insufficient, poor, thin, unconvincing, unsatisfactory, weak

lament *v.* 1. bemoan, bewail, complain, deplore, grieve, mourn, regret, sorrow, wail, weep ~*n.* 2. complaint, keening, lamentation, moan, moaning, plaint, ululation, wail, wailing 3. coronach (*Scot., Irish*), dirge, elegy, monody, requiem, threnody

lamentable 1. deplorable, distressing, grievous, mournful, regrettable, sorrowful, tragic, unfortunate, woeful 2. low, meagre, mean, miserable, pitiful, poor, unsatisfactory, wretched

lamentation dirge, grief, grieving, keening, lament, moan, mourning, plaint, sobbing, sorrow, ululation, wailing, weeping

laminate 1. coat, cover, face, foliate, layer, stratify, veneer 2. exfoliate, flake, separate, split

lampoon 1. *n.* burlesque, caricature, parody, pasquinade, satire, send-up (*Brit. inf.*), skit, squib, takeoff (*Inf.*) 2. *v.* burlesque, caricature, make fun of, mock, parody, pasquinade, ridicule, satirize, send up (*Brit. inf.*), squib, take off (*Inf.*)

land *n.* 1. dry land, earth, ground, terra firma 2. dirt, ground, loam, soil 3. countryside, farming, farmland, rural districts 4. acres, estate, grounds, property, real property, realty 5. country, district, fatherland, motherland, nation, province, region, territory, tract ~*v.* 6. alight, arrive, berth, come to rest, debark, disembark, dock, touch down 7. *Sometimes with* **up** arrive, bring, carry, cause, end up, lead, turn up, wind up 8. *Inf.* acquire, gain, get, obtain, secure, win

landlord 1. host, hotelier, hotelkeeper, innkeeper 2. freeholder, lessor, owner, proprietor

landmark 1. feature, monument 2. crisis, milestone, turning point, watershed 3. benchmark, boundary, cairn, milepost, signpost

landscape countryside, outlook, panorama, prospect, scene, scenery, view, vista

landslide 1. *n.* avalanche, landslip,

rockfall **2.** *adj.* decisive, overwhelming, runaway

language 1. communication, conversation, discourse, expression, interchange, parlance, speech, talk, utterance, verbalization, vocalization **2.** argot, cant, dialect, idiom, jargon, lingo (*Inf.*), lingua franca, patois, speech, terminology, tongue, vernacular, vocabulary **3.** diction, expression, phraseology, phrasing, style, wording

languid 1. drooping, faint, feeble, languorous, limp, pining, sickly, weak, weary **2.** indifferent, lackadaisical, languorous, lazy, listless, spiritless, unenthusiastic, uninterested **3.** dull, heavy, inactive, inert, lethargic, sluggish, torpid

languish 1. decline, droop, fade, fail, faint, flag, sicken, waste, weaken, wilt, wither **2.** *Often with* for desire, hanker, hunger, long, pine, sigh, want, yearn **3.** be abandoned, be disregarded, be neglected, rot, suffer, waste away **4.** brood, despond, grieve, repine, sorrow

languishing 1. declining, deteriorating, drooping, droopy, fading, failing, flagging, sickening, sinking, wasting away, weak, weakening, wilting, withering **2.** dreamy, longing, lovelorn, lovesick, melancholic, nostalgic, pensive, pining, soulful, tender, wistful, woebegone, yearning

languor 1. apathy, debility, enervation, ennui, faintness, fatigue, feebleness, frailty, heaviness, lassitude, lethargy, listlessness, torpor, weakness, weariness **2.** dreaminess, drowsiness, indolence, laziness, lotus-eating, relaxation, sleepiness, sloth **3.** calm, hush, lull, oppressiveness, silence, stillness

lank 1. dull, lifeless, limp, long, lustreless, straggling **2.** attenuated, emaciated, gaunt, lanky, lean, rawboned, scraggy, scrawny, skinny, slender, slim, spare, thin

lanky angular, bony, gangling, gaunt, loose-jointed, rangy, rawboned, scraggy, scrawny, spare, tall, thin, weedy (*Inf.*)

lap¹ 1. *n.* circle, circuit, course, distance, loop, orbit, round, tour **2.** *v.* cover, enfold, envelop, fold, swaddle, swathe, turn, twist, wrap

lap² 1. gurgle, plash, purl, ripple, slap, splash, swish, wash **2.** drink, lick, sip, sup

lapse *n.* **1.** error, failing, fault, indiscretion, mistake, negligence, omission, oversight, slip **2.** break, gap, intermission, interruption, interval, lull, passage, pause **3.** backsliding, decline, descent, deterioration, drop, fall, relapse ~*v.* **4.** decline, degenerate, deteriorate, drop, fail, fall, sink, slide, slip **5.** become obsolete, become void, end, expire, run out, stop, terminate

lapsed 1. discontinued, ended, expired, finished, invalid, out of date, run out, unrenewed **2.** backsliding, lacking faith, nonpractising

larceny burglary, misappropriation, pilfering, purloining, robbery, stealing, theft

large 1. big, bulky, colossal, considerable, enormous, giant, gigantic, goodly, great, huge, immense, jumbo (*Inf.*), king-size, man-size, massive, monumental, sizable, substantial, tidy (*Inf.*), vast **2.** abundant, ample, broad, capacious, comprehensive, copious, extensive, full, generous, grand, grandiose, liberal, plentiful, roomy, spacious, sweeping, wide **3. at large a.** at liberty, free, on the loose, on the run, roaming, unconfined **b.** as a whole, chiefly, generally, in general, in the main, mainly **c.** at length, considerably, exhaustively, greatly, in full detail

large-hearted big-hearted, compassionate, good, good-hearted, kind, kind-hearted, large-souled, magnanimous, sympathetic, understanding

largely as a rule, by and large, chiefly, considerably, extensively, generally, mainly, mostly, predominantly, primarily, principally, to a great extent, widely

large-scale broad, extensive, far-reaching, global, sweeping, vast, wholesale, wide, wide-ranging

largess 1. alms-giving, benefaction, bounty, charity, generosity, liberality, munificence, open-handedness, philanthropy **2.** bequest, bounty, donation, endowment, gift, grant, present

lark 1. *n.* antic, caper, escapade, fling, frolic, fun, gambol, game, jape, mischief, prank, revel, rollick, romp, skylark, spree **2.** *v.* caper, cavort, cut capers, frolic, gambol, have fun, make mischief, play, rollick, romp, sport

lascivious 1. horny (*Sl.*), lecherous, lewd, libidinous, licentious, lustful, prurient, randy (*Sl., chiefly Brit.*), salacious, sensual, unchaste, voluptuous, wanton **2.** bawdy, blue, coarse, crude, dirty, indecent, obscene, offensive, pornographic, ribald, scurrilous, smutty, suggestive, vulgar

lash[1] *n.* **1.** blow, hit, stripe, stroke, swipe (*Inf.*) ~*v.* **2.** beat, birch, chastise, flagellate, flog, horsewhip, lam (*Sl.*), scourge, thrash, whip **3.** beat, buffet, dash, drum, hammer, hit, knock, larrup (*Dialect*), pound, smack, strike **4.** attack, belabour, berate, castigate, censure, criticize, flay, lambaste, lampoon, ridicule, satirize, scold, tear into (*Inf.*), upbraid

lash[2] bind, fasten, join, make fast, rope, secure, strap, tie

lass bird (*Sl.*), chick (*Sl.*), colleen (*Irish*), damsel, girl, lassie (*Scot.*), maid, maiden, miss, schoolgirl, young woman

lassitude apathy, drowsiness, dullness, enervation, ennui, exhaustion, fatigue, heaviness, languor, lethargy, listlessness, prostration, sluggardliness, sluggishness, tiredness, torpor, weariness

last[1] *adj.* **1.** aftermost, at the end, hindmost, rearmost **2.** latest, most recent **3.** closing, concluding, extreme, final, furthest, remotest, terminal, ultimate, utmost ~*adv.* **4.** after, behind, bringing up the rear, in *or* at the end, in the rear ~*n.* **5.** close, completion, conclusion, end, ending, finale, finish, termination **6. at last** at length, eventually, finally, in conclusion, in the end, ultimately

last[2] *v.* abide, carry on, continue, endure, hold on, hold out, keep, keep on, persist, remain, stand up, survive, wear

last-ditch all-out (*Inf.*), desperate, final, frantic, heroic, straining, struggling

lasting abiding, continuing, deeprooted, durable, enduring, indelible, lifelong, long-standing, long-term, perennial, permanent, perpetual, unceasing, undying, unending

lastly after all, all in all, at last, finally, in conclusion, in the end, to conclude, to sum up, ultimately

last word, the 1. final say, finis, summation, ultimatum **2.** best, cream, *crème de la crème*, crown, epitome, *ne plus ultra*, perfection, quintessence, ultimate **3.** *dernier cri*, fashion, latest, newest, rage, vogue

latch 1. *n.* bar, bolt, catch, clamp, fastening, hasp, hook, lock, sneck (*Dialect*) **2.** *v.* bar, bolt, fasten, lock, make fast, secure, sneck (*Dialect*)

late *adj.* **1.** behind, behindhand, belat-

ed, delayed, last-minute, overdue, slow, tardy, unpunctual **2.** advanced, fresh, modern, new, recent **3.** dead, deceased, defunct, departed, ex-, former, old, past, preceding, previous ~*adv.* **4.** at the last minute, behindhand, behind time, belatedly, dilatorily, slowly, tardily, unpunctually

lately in recent times, just now, latterly, not long ago, of late, recently

lateness advanced hour, belatedness, delay, late date, retardation, tardiness, unpunctuality

latent concealed, dormant, hidden, inherent, invisible, lurking, potential, quiescent, secret, undeveloped, unexpressed, unrealized, unseen, veiled

later *adv.* after, afterwards, by and by, in a while, in time, later on, next, subsequently, thereafter

lateral edgeways, flanking, side, sideward, sideways

latest *adj.* current, fashionable, in, modern, most recent, newest, now, up-to-date, up-to-the-minute, with it (*Inf.*)

lather *n.* **1.** bubbles, foam, froth, soap, soapsuds, suds **2.** *Inf.* dither, fever, flap (*Inf.*), fluster, fuss, pother, state (*Inf.*), stew (*Inf.*), sweat, tizzy (*Inf.*), twitter ~*v.* **3.** foam, froth, soap **4.** *Inf.* beat, cane, drub, flog, lambaste, strike, thrash, whip

lathery bubbly, foamy, frothy, soapy, sudsy

latitude 1. breadth, compass, extent, range, reach, room, scope, space, span, spread, sweep, width **2.** elbowroom, freedom, indulgence, laxity, leeway, liberty, licence, play, unrestrictedness

latter closing, concluding, last, last-mentioned, later, latest, modern, recent, second

latterly hitherto, lately, of late, recently

lattice fretwork, grating, grid, grille, latticework, mesh, network, openwork, reticulation, tracery, trellis, web

laud acclaim, approve, celebrate, extol, glorify, honour, magnify (*Archaic*), praise, sing *or* sound the praises of

laudable admirable, commendable, creditable, estimable, excellent, meritorious, of note, praiseworthy, worthy

laudatory acclamatory, adulatory, approbatory, approving, commendatory, complimentary, eulogistic, panegyrical

laugh *v.* **1.** be convulsed (*Inf.*), be in

stitches, chortle, chuckle, crease up (*Inf.*), giggle, guffaw, roar with laughter, snigger, split one's sides, titter 2. **laugh at** belittle, deride, jeer, lampoon, make a mock of, make fun of, mock, ridicule, scoff at, take the mickey (out of) (*Inf.*), taunt ~*n.* 3. belly laugh (*Inf.*), chortle, chuckle, giggle, guffaw, roar *or* shriek of laughter, snigger, titter 4. *Inf.* card (*Inf.*), caution (*Inf.*), clown, comedian, comic, entertainer, hoot (*Inf.*), humorist, joke, lark, scream (*Inf.*), wag, wit

laughable 1. absurd, derisive, derisory, ludicrous, nonsensical, preposterous, ridiculous, worthy of scorn 2. amusing, comical, diverting, droll, farcical, funny, hilarious, humorous, mirthful, risible

laughing stock Aunt Sally (*Brit.*), butt, everybody's fool, fair game, figure of fun, target, victim

laugh off brush aside, dismiss, disregard, ignore, minimize, pooh-pooh, shrug off

laughter 1. cachinnation, chortling, chuckling, giggling, guffawing, laughing, tittering 2. amusement, glee, hilarity, merriment, mirth

launch 1. cast, discharge, dispatch, fire, project, propel, send off, set afloat, set in motion, throw 2. begin, commence, embark upon, inaugurate, initiate, instigate, introduce, open, start

laurels acclaim, awards, bays, commendation, credit, distinction, fame, glory, honour, kudos, praise, prestige, recognition, renown, reward

lavatory bathroom, bog (*Brit. sl.*), can (*U.S. sl.*), cloakroom (*Brit.*), Gents, head(s) (*Nautical sl.*), john (*U.S. sl.*), Ladies, latrine, loo (*Brit. inf.*), powder room, (public) convenience, toilet, washroom, water closet, W.C.

lavish *adj.* 1. abundant, copious, exuberant, lush, luxuriant, opulent, plentiful, profuse, prolific, sumptuous 2. bountiful, effusive, free, generous, liberal, munificent, open-handed, unstinting 3. exaggerated, excessive, extravagant, immoderate, improvident, intemperate, prodigal, thriftless, unreasonable, unrestrained, wasteful, wild ~*v.* 4. deluge, dissipate, expend, heap, pour, shower, spend, squander, waste

law 1. charter, code, constitution, jurisprudence 2. act, code, command, commandment, covenant, decree, edict, enactment, order, ordinance, rule, statute 3. axiom, canon, criterion, formula, precept, principle, regulation, standard 4. **lay down the law** dictate, dogmatize, emphasize, pontificate

law-abiding compliant, dutiful, good, honest, honourable, lawful, obedient, orderly, peaceable, peaceful

lawbreaker convict, criminal, crook (*Inf.*), culprit, delinquent, felon (*Formerly criminal law*), miscreant, offender, sinner, transgressor, trespasser, violater, wrongdoer

lawful allowable, authorized, constitutional, just, legal, legalized, legitimate, licit, permissible, proper, rightful, valid, warranted

lawless anarchic, chaotic, disorderly, insubordinate, insurgent, mutinous, rebellious, reckless, riotous, seditious, ungoverned, unrestrained, unruly, wild

lawlessness anarchy, chaos, disorder, mobocracy, mob rule, ochlocracy, reign of terror

lawsuit action, argument, case, cause, contest, dispute, litigation, proceedings, prosecution, suit, trial

lawyer advocate, attorney, barrister, counsel, counsellor, legal adviser, solicitor

lax 1. careless, casual, easy-going, lenient, neglectful, negligent, overindulgent, remiss, slack, slipshod 2. broad, general, imprecise, inaccurate, indefinite, inexact, nonspecific, shapeless, vague 3. flabby, flaccid, loose, slack, soft, yielding

laxative aperient, cathartic, physic (*Rare*), purgative, purge, salts

lay[1] 1. deposit, establish, leave, place, plant, posit, put, set, set down, settle, spread 2. arrange, dispose, locate, organize, position, set out 3. bear, deposit, produce 4. advance, bring forward, lodge, offer, present, put forward, submit 5. allocate, allot, ascribe, assign, attribute, charge, impute 6. concoct, contrive, design, devise, hatch, plan, plot, prepare, work out 7. apply, assess, burden, charge, encumber, impose, saddle, tax 8. bet, gamble, give odds, hazard, risk, stake, wager 9. allay, alleviate, appease, assuage, calm, quiet, relieve, soothe, still, suppress 10. **lay bare** disclose, divulge, explain, expose, reveal, show, unveil 11. **lay hands on a.** acquire, get, get hold of, grab, grasp, seize **b.** assault, attack, beat up, lay into, set on **c.** discover, find, unearth **d.** *Christianity* bless, confirm, consecrate, ordain **12. lay hold of** get, get hold of, grab, grasp, grip, seize, snatch

lay[2] **1.** laic, laical, nonclerical, secular **2.** amateur, inexpert, nonprofessional, nonspecialist

lay[3] ballad, lyric, ode, poem, song

layabout beachcomber, good-for-nothing, idler, laggard, loafer, lounger, ne'er-do-well, shirker, skiver (*Brit. sl.*), slubberdegullion (*Archaic*), vagrant, wastrel

lay aside abandon, cast aside, dismiss, postpone, put aside, put off, reject, shelve

lay away accumulate, collect, hoard, keep, lay aside, lay in, salt away, save, stash (*Inf.*), stockpile, store

lay down 1. discard, drop, give, give up, relinquish, surrender, yield **2.** affirm, assume, establish, formulate, ordain, postulate, prescribe, stipulate

layer 1. bed, ply, row, seam, stratum, thickness, tier **2.** blanket, coat, coating, cover, covering, film, mantle, sheet

lay in accumulate, amass, build up, collect, hoard, stockpile, stock up, store (up)

lay into assail, attack, belabour, hit out at, lambaste, let fly at, pitch into, set about

layman amateur, lay person, nonprofessional, outsider

lay-off discharge, dismissal, unemployment

lay off 1. discharge, dismiss, drop, let go, make redundant, oust, pay off **2.** *Inf.* cease, desist, give it a rest (*Inf.*), give over (*Inf.*), give up, leave alone, leave off, let up, quit, stop

lay on 1. cater (for), furnish, give, provide, supply **2. lay it on** *Sl.* butter up, exaggerate, flatter, overdo it, overpraise, soft-soap

layout arrangement, design, draft, formation, geography, outline, plan

lay out 1. arrange, design, display, exhibit, plan, spread out **2.** *Inf.* disburse, expend, fork out (*Sl.*), invest, pay, shell out (*Inf.*), spend **3.** *Inf.* kayo (*Sl.*), knock for six (*Inf.*), knock out, knock unconscious, KO (*Sl.*)

lay up 1. accumulate, amass, garner, hoard, keep, preserve, put away, save, store up, treasure **2.** *Inf.* confine (to bed), hospitalize, incapacitate

laze 1. hang around, idle, loaf, loll, lounge, stand around **2.** *Often with* **away** fool away, fritter away, kill time, pass time, waste time, while away the hours

laziness dilatoriness, do-nothingness, faineance, faineancy, idleness, inactivity, indolence, lackadaisicalness, slackness, sloth, slothfulness, slowness, sluggishness, tardiness

lazy 1. idle, inactive, indolent, inert, remiss, shiftless, slack, slothful, slow, workshy **2.** drowsy, languid, languorous, lethargic, sleepy, slow-moving, sluggish, somnolent, torpid

lazybones loafer, lounger, shirker, skiver (*Brit. sl.*), sleepyhead, slugabed, sluggard

leach drain, extract, filter, filtrate, lixiviate (*Chem.*), percolate, seep, strain

lead *v.* **1.** conduct, escort, guide, pilot, precede, show the way, steer, usher **2.** cause, dispose, draw, incline, induce, influence, persuade, prevail, prompt **3.** command, direct, govern, head, manage, preside over, supervise **4.** be ahead (of), blaze a trail, come first, exceed, excel, outdo, outstrip, surpass, transcend **5.** experience, have, live, pass, spend, undergo **6.** bring on, cause, conduce, contribute, produce, result in, serve, tend ~*n.* **7.** advance, advantage, edge, first place, margin, precedence, primacy, priority, start, supremacy, van, vanguard **8.** direction, example, guidance, leadership, model **9.** clue, guide, hint, indication, suggestion, tip, trace **10.** leading role, principal, protagonist, star part, title role ~*adj.* **11.** chief, first, foremost, head, leading, main, most important, premier, primary, prime, principal

leaden 1. burdensome, crushing, cumbersome, heavy, inert, lead, onerous, oppressive **2.** humdrum, laboured, plodding, sluggish, stiff, stilted, wooden **3.** dismal, dreary, dull, gloomy, languid, lifeless, listless, spiritless **4.** dingy, grey, greyish, lacklustre, lowering, lustreless, overcast, sombre

leader bellwether, boss (*Inf.*), captain, chief, chieftain, commander, conductor, counsellor, director, guide, head, number one, principal, ringleader, ruler, superior

leadership 1. administration, direction, directorship, domination, guidance, management, running, superintendency **2.** authority, command, control, influence, initiative, pre-eminence, supremacy, sway

leading chief, dominant, first, foremost, governing, greatest, highest, main, number one, outstanding, pre-eminent, primary, principal, ruling, superior

lead off begin, commence, get going, get under way, inaugurate, initiate, kick off (*Inf.*), open, set out, start, start the ball rolling (*Inf.*)

lead on beguile, deceive, draw on, entice, inveigle, lure, seduce, string along (*Inf.*), tempt

lead up to approach, intimate, introduce, make advances, make overtures, pave the way, prepare for, prepare the way, work round to

leaf *n.* **1.** blade, bract, flag, foliole, frond, needle, pad **2.** folio, page, sheet **3.** **turn over a new leaf** amend, begin anew, change, change one's ways, improve, reform ~*v.* **4.** bud, green, put out leaves, turn green **5.** browse, flip, glance, riffle, skim, thumb (through)

leaflet advert (*Brit. inf.*), bill, booklet, brochure, circular, handbill, pamphlet

leafy bosky (*Literary*), green, in foliage, leafed, leaved, shaded, shady, springlike, summery, verdant, wooded

league *n.* **1.** alliance, association, band, coalition, combination, combine, compact, confederacy, confederation, consortium, federation, fellowship, fraternity, group, guild, partnership, union **2.** ability group, category, class, level **3.** **in league (with)** allied, collaborating, hand in glove, in cahoots (*Inf.*), leagued ~*v.* **4.** ally, amalgamate, associate, band, collaborate, combine, confederate, join forces, unite

leak *n.* **1.** aperture, chink, crack, crevice, fissure, hole, opening, puncture **2.** drip, leakage, leaking, oozing, percolation, seepage **3.** disclosure, divulgence ~*v.* **4.** discharge, drip, escape, exude, ooze, pass, percolate, seep, spill, trickle **5.** disclose, divulge, give away, let slip, let the cat out of the bag, make known, make public, pass on, reveal, spill the beans (*Inf.*), tell

leaky cracked, holey, leaking, not watertight, perforated, porous, punctured, split, waterlogged

lean¹ *v.* **1.** be supported, prop, recline, repose, rest **2.** bend, incline, slant, slope, tilt, tip **3.** be disposed to, be prone to, favour, gravitate towards, have a propensity, prefer, tend **4.** confide, count on, depend, have faith in, rely, trust

lean² *adj.* **1.** angular, bony, emaciated, gaunt, lank, rangy, scraggy, scrawny, skinny, slender, slim, spare, thin, unfatty, wiry **2.** bare, barren, inadequate, infertile, meagre, pitiful, poor, scanty, sparse, unfruitful, unproductive

leaning aptitude, bent, bias, disposition, inclination, liking, partiality, penchant, predilection, proclivity, proneness, propensity, taste, tendency

leap *v.* **1.** bounce, bound, caper, cavort, frisk, gambol, hop, jump, skip, spring **2.** *Fig.* arrive at, come to, form hastily, hasten, hurry, jump, reach, rush **3.** clear, jump (over), vault **4.** advance, become prominent, escalate, gain attention, increase, rocket, soar, surge ~*n.* **5.** bound, caper, frisk, hop, jump, skip, spring, vault **6.** escalation, increase, rise, surge, upsurge, upswing

learn **1.** acquire, attain, become able, grasp, imbibe, master, pick up **2.** commit to memory, con (*Archaic*), get off pat, get (something) word-perfect, learn by heart, memorize **3.** ascertain, detect, determine, discern, discover, find out, gain, gather, hear, understand

learned academic, cultured, erudite, experienced, expert, highbrow, intellectual, lettered, literate, scholarly, skilled, versed, well-informed, well-read

learner apprentice, beginner, disciple, neophyte, novice, pupil, scholar, student, trainee, tyro

learning acquirements, attainments, culture, education, erudition, information, knowledge, letters, literature, lore, research, scholarship, schooling, study, tuition, wisdom

lease *v.* charter, hire, let, loan, rent

leash *n.* **1.** lead, rein, tether **2.** check, control, curb, hold, restraint ~*v.* **3.** fasten, secure, tether, tie up **4.** check, control, curb, hold back, restrain, suppress

least feeblest, fewest, last, lowest, meanest, minimum, minutest, poorest, slightest, smallest, tiniest

leathery coriaceous, durable, hard, hardened, leatherlike, leathern (*Archaic*), rough, rugged, tough, wrinkled

leave¹ *v.* **1.** abandon, decamp, depart, desert, disappear, do a bunk (*Brit. sl.*), exit, flit (*Inf.*), forsake, go, go away, move, pull out, quit, relinquish, retire, set out, take off (*Inf.*), withdraw **2.** forget, lay down, leave behind, mislay **3.** cause, deposit, generate, produce, result in **4**. abandon, cease, desert, desist, drop, evacuate, forbear, give up, refrain, relinquish, renounce, stop, surrender **5**. allot, assign, cede, commit, consign, entrust, give over, refer **6**. bequeath, demise, devise (*Law*), hand down, transmit, will

leave² n. **1**. allowance, authorization, concession, consent, dispensation, freedom, liberty, permission, sanction **2**. furlough, holiday, leave of absence, sabbatical, time off, vacation **3**. adieu, departure, farewell, goodbye, leave-taking, parting, retirement, withdrawal

leaven n. **1**. barm, ferment, leavening, yeast **2**. *Fig*. catalyst, influence, inspiration ~v. **3**. ferment, lighten, raise, work **4**. *Fig*. elevate, imbue, inspire, permeate, pervade, quicken, stimulate, suffuse

leave off abstain, break off, cease, desist, discontinue, end, give over (*Inf.*), give up, halt, knock off (*Inf.*), refrain, stop

leave out bar, cast aside, count out, disregard, except, exclude, ignore, neglect, omit, overlook, reject

leave-taking departure, farewell, going, goodbye, leaving, parting, sendoff (*Inf.*), valediction

leavings bits, dregs, fragments, leftovers, orts (*Archaic or dialect*), pieces, refuse, remains, remnants, residue, scraps, spoil, sweepings, waste

lecher adulterer, Casanova, debauchee, dirty old man (*Sl.*), Don Juan, fornicator, goat (*Inf.*), libertine, profligate, rake, roué, satyr, seducer, sensualist, wanton, wolf (*Inf.*), womanizer

lecherous carnal, concupiscent, goatish (*Archaic*), lascivious, lewd, libidinous, licentious, lubricous, lustful, prurient, randy (*Sl., chiefly Brit.*), raunchy (*U.S. Sl.*), ruttish, salacious, unchaste, wanton

lechery carnality, concupiscence, debauchery, lasciviousness, lecherousness, leching (*Inf.*), lewdness, libertinism, libidinousness, licentiousness, lubricity, lust, lustfulness, profligacy, prurience, rakishness, randiness (*Sl., chiefly Brit.*), salaciousness, sensuality, wantonness, womanizing

lecture n. **1**. address, discourse, disquisition, harangue, instruction, lesson, speech, talk ~v. **2**. address, discourse, expound, give a talk, harangue, hold forth, speak, talk, teach ~n. **3**. castigation, censure, chiding, dressing-down

(*Inf.*), going-over (*Inf.*), rebuke, reprimand, reproof, scolding, talking-to (*Inf.*), telling off (*Inf.*), wigging (*Brit. sl.*) ~v. **4**. admonish, berate, carpet (*Inf.*), castigate, censure, chide, rate, reprimand, reprove, scold, tell off (*Inf.*)

ledge mantle, projection, ridge, shelf, sill, step

lee cover, protection, refuge, screen, shade, shadow, shelter, shield

leech *Fig*. bloodsucker (*Inf.*), freeloader (*U.S. sl.*), hanger-on, parasite, sponger (*Inf.*), sycophant

leer n./v. eye, gloat, goggle, grin, ogle, smirk, squint, stare, wink

leery careful, cautious, chary, distrustful, doubting, dubious, on one's guard, sceptical, shy, suspicious, uncertain, unsure, wary

lees deposit, dregs, grounds, precipitate, refuse, sediment, settlings

leeway elbowroom, latitude, margin, play, room, scope, space

left adj. **1**. larboard (*Nautical*), left-hand, port, sinistral **2**. *Of politics* leftist, left-wing, liberal, progressive, radical, socialist

left-handed 1. awkward, cack-handed (*Inf.*), careless, clumsy, fumbling, gauche, maladroit **2**. ambiguous, back-handed, double-edged, enigmatic, equivocal, indirect, ironic, sardonic

leftover n. **1**. legacy, remainder, residue, surplus, survivor **2**. *Plural* leavings, oddments, odds and ends, remains, remnants, scraps ~adj. **3**. excess, extra, remaining, surplus, uneaten, unused, unwanted

leg 1. limb, lower limb, member, pin (*Inf.*), stump (*Inf.*) **2**. brace, prop, support, upright **3**. lap, part, portion, section, segment, stage, stretch **4**. **a leg up** assistance, boost, help, helping hand, push, support **5**. **not have a leg to stand on** *Inf.* be defenceless, be full of holes, be illogical, be invalid, be undermined, be vulnerable, lack support **6**. **on one's (its) last legs** about to break down, about to collapse, at death's door, dying, exhausted, failing, giving up the ghost, worn out **7**. **pull someone's leg** *Inf.* chaff, deceive, fool, make fun of, tease, trick **8**. **shake a leg** *Sl.* **a**. get a move on (*Inf.*), get cracking (*Inf.*), hasten, hurry, look lively (*Inf.*), rush, stir one's stumps **b**. dance, hoof it (*Sl.*), trip the light fantastic **9**. **stretch one's legs** exercise, go for a walk, legacy 390 lend

move about, promenade, stroll, take a walk, take the air **10. leg it** *Inf.* go on foot, hotfoot, hurry, run, skedaddle (*Inf.*), walk

legacy 1. bequest, devise (*Law*), estate, gift, heirloom, inheritance **2**. birthright, endowment, heritage, inheritance, patrimony, throwback, tradition

legal 1. allowable, allowed, authorized, constitutional, lawful, legalized, legitimate, licit, permissible, proper, rightful, sanctioned, valid **2**. forensic, judicial, juridical

legalistic contentious, disputatious, hairsplitting, literal, litigious, narrow, narrow-minded, polemical, strict

legality accordance with the law, admissibleness, lawfulness, legitimacy, permissibility, rightfulness, validity

legalize allow, approve, authorize, decriminalize, legitimate, legitimatize, license, permit, sanction, validate

legate ambassador, delegate, depute, deputy, emissary, envoy, messenger, nuncio

legatee beneficiary, heir, inheritor, recipient

legation consulate, delegation, diplomatic mission, embassy, envoys, ministry, representation

legend 1. fable, fiction, folk tale, myth, narrative, saga, story, tale **2**. celebrity, luminary, marvel, phenomenon, prodigy, spectacle, wonder **3**. caption, device, inscription, motto **4**. cipher, code, key, table of symbols

legendary 1. apocryphal, fabled, fabulous, fanciful, fictitious, mythical, romantic, storied, traditional **2**. celebrated, famed, famous, illustrious, immortal, renowned, well-known

legerdemain 1. prestidigitation, sleight of hand **2**. artfulness, artifice, chicanery, contrivance, craftiness, cunning, deception, feint, hocus-pocus, manipulation, manoeuvring, subterfuge, trickery

legibility clarity, decipherability, ease of reading, legibleness, neatness, plainness, readability, readableness

legible clear, decipherable, distinct, easily read, easy to read, neat, plain, readable

legion *n.* **1**. army, brigade, company, division, force, troop **2**. drove, horde, host, mass, multitude, myriad, number, throng ~*adj.* **3**. countless, multitudi-

nous, myriad, numberless, numerous, very many

legislate codify, constitute, enact, establish, make laws, ordain, pass laws, prescribe, put in force

legislation 1. codification, enactment, lawmaking, prescription, regulation **2**. act, bill, charter, law, measure, regulation, ruling, statute

legislative *adj.* congressional, judicial, juridical, jurisdictive, lawgiving, lawmaking, ordaining, parliamentary

legislator lawgiver, lawmaker, parliamentarian

legislature assembly, chamber, congress, diet, house, lawmaking body, parliament, senate

legitimate *adj.* **1**. acknowledged, authentic, authorized, genuine, lawful, legal, legit (*Sl.*), licit, proper, real, rightful, sanctioned, statutory, true **2**. admissible, correct, just, justifiable, logical, reasonable, sensible, valid, warranted, well-founded ~*v.* **3**. authorize, legalize, legitimatize, legitimize, permit, pronounce lawful, sanction

legitimatize, legitimize authorize, legalize, legitimate, permit, pronounce lawful, sanction

leisure 1. breathing space, ease, freedom, free time, holiday, liberty, opportunity, pause, quiet, recreation, relaxation, respite, rest, retirement, spare moments, spare time, time off, vacation **2**. **at leisure a.** available, free, not booked up, on holiday, unengaged, unoccupied **b.** *Also* **at one's leisure** at an unhurried pace, at one's convenience, deliberately, in one's own (good) time, unhurriedly, when it suits one, when one gets round to it (*Inf.*), without hurry

leisurely 1. *adj.* comfortable, easy, gentle, laid-back (*Inf.*), lazy, relaxed, restful, slow, unhurried **2**. *adv.* at one's convenience, at one's leisure, comfortably, deliberately, easily, indolently, lazily, lingeringly, slowly, unhurriedly, without haste

leitmotif *All with* **recurrent** *or* **recurring** air, convention, device, idea, melody, motif, phrase, strain, theme

lend 1. accommodate one with, advance, loan **2**. add, afford, bestow, confer, contribute, furnish, give, grant, impart, present, provide, supply **3**. **lend an ear** give ear, hearken (*Archaic*), heed, listen, take notice **4**. **lend a hand** aid, assist, give a (helping) hand, help, help out **5. lend itself to** be adaptable, be appropriate, be serviceable, fit, present opportunities of, suit **6. lend oneself to** agree, consent, cooperate, countenance, espouse, support

length 1. *Of linear extent* distance, extent, longitude, measure, reach, span **2.** *Of time* duration, period, space, span, stretch, term **3.** measure, piece, portion, section, segment **4.** elongation, extensiveness, lengthiness, protractedness **5. at length a.** completely, fully, in depth, in detail, thoroughly, to the full **b.** for ages, for a long time, for hours, interminably **c.** at last, at long last, eventually, finally, in the end

lengthen continue, draw out, elongate, expand, extend, increase, make longer, prolong, protract, spin out, stretch

lengthy diffuse, drawn-out, extended, interminable, lengthened, long, long-drawn-out, long-winded, overlong, prolix, prolonged, protracted, tedious, verbose, very long

leniency, lenience clemency, compassion, forbearance, gentleness, indulgence, lenity, mercy, mildness, moderation, tenderness, tolerance

lenient clement, compassionate, forbearing, forgiving, gentle, indulgent, kind, merciful, mild, sparing, tender, tolerant

lenitive alleviative, assuaging, calming, easing, mitigative, mollifying, palliative, relieving, soothing

leper lazar (*Archaic*), outcast, pariah, untouchable

lesbian 1. *n.* butch (*Sl.*), dyke (*Sl.*), sapphist, tribade **2.** *adj.* butch (*Sl.*), gay (*Inf.*), homosexual, sapphic, tribadic

lesion abrasion, bruise, contusion, hurt, impairment, injury, sore, trauma (*Pathol.*), wound

less *adj.* **1.** shorter, slighter, smaller **2.** inferior, minor, secondary, subordinate ~*adv.* **3.** barely, little, meagrely, to a smaller extent ~*prep.* **4.** excepting, lacking, minus, subtracting, without

lessen abate, abridge, contract, curtail, decrease, de-escalate, degrade, die down, diminish, dwindle, ease, erode, grow less, impair, lighten, lower, minimize, moderate, narrow, reduce, shrink, slacken, slow down, weaken, wind down

lessening abatement, contraction, curtailment, decline, decrease, de-escalation, diminution, dwindling, ebbing, erosion, let-up (*Inf.*), minimization, moderation, petering out, reduction, shrinkage, slackening, slowing down, waning, weakening

lesser inferior, less important, lower, minor, secondary, slighter, subordinate, under-

lesson 1. class, coaching, instruction, period, schooling, teaching, tutoring **2.** assignment, drill, exercise, homework, lecture, practice, reading, recitation, task **3.** deterrent, example, exemplar, message, model, moral, precept **4.** admonition, censure, chiding, punishment, rebuke, reprimand, reproof, scolding, warning

let[1] *v.* **1.** allow, authorize, give leave, give permission, give the go-ahead (green light, O.K.) (*Inf.*), grant, permit, sanction, suffer (*Archaic*), tolerate, warrant **2.** hire, lease, rent **3.** allow, cause, enable, grant, make, permit

let[2] *n.* constraint, hindrance, impediment, interference, obstacle, obstruction, prohibition, restriction

letdown anticlimax, bitter pill, blow, comedown (*Inf.*), disappointment, disgruntlement, disillusionment, frustration, setback, washout (*Inf.*)

let down disappoint, disenchant, disillusion, dissatisfy, fail, fall short, leave in the lurch, leave stranded

lethal baleful, dangerous, deadly, deathly, destructive, devastating, fatal, mortal, murderous, noxious, pernicious, poisonous, virulent

lethargic apathetic, comatose, debilitated, drowsy, dull, enervated, heavy, inactive, indifferent, inert, languid, lazy, listless, sleepy, slothful, slow, sluggish, somnolent, stupefied, torpid

lethargy apathy, drowsiness, dullness, hebetude (*Rare*), inaction, indifference, inertia, languor, lassitude, listlessness, sleepiness, sloth, slowness, sluggishness, stupor, torpidity, torpor

let in admit, allow to enter, give access to, greet, include, incorporate, receive, take in, welcome

let off 1. detonate, discharge, emit, explode, exude, fire, give off, leak, release **2.** absolve, discharge, dispense, excuse, exempt, exonerate, forgive, pardon, release, spare

let on 1. admit, disclose, divulge, give

away, make known, reveal, say **2**. act, counterfeit, dissemble, dissimulate, feign, make believe, make out, pretend, profess, simulate

let out 1. emit, give vent to, produce **2**. discharge, free, let go, liberate, release **3**. betray, disclose, leak, let fall, let slip, make known, reveal

letter 1. character, sign, symbol **2**. acknowledgment, answer, billet (*Archaic*), communication, dispatch, epistle, line, message, missive, note, reply **3. to the letter** accurately, exactly, literally, precisely, strictly, word for word

lettered accomplished, cultivated, cultured, educated, erudite, informed, knowledgeable, learned, literate, scholarly, versed, well-educated, well-read

letters belles-lettres, culture, erudition, humanities, learning, literature, scholarship

let-up abatement, break, cessation, interval, lessening, lull, pause, recess, remission, respite, slackening

let up abate, decrease, diminish, ease (up), moderate, slacken, stop, subside

levee ceremony, entertainment, gathering, party, reception

level *adj.* **1**. consistent, even, flat, horizontal, plain, plane, smooth, uniform **2**. aligned, balanced, commensurate, comparable, equivalent, even, flush, in line, neck and neck, on a line, on a par, proportionate **3**. calm, equable, even, even-tempered, stable, steady ~*v.* **4**. even off *or* out, flatten, make flat, plane, smooth **5**. bulldoze, demolish, destroy, devastate, equalize, flatten, knock down, lay low, pull down, raze, smooth, tear down, wreck **6**. aim, beam, direct, focus, point, train **7**. *Inf.* be above board, be frank, be honest, be open, be straightforward, be up front (*Sl.*), come clean (*Inf.*), keep nothing back ~*n.* **8**. altitude, elevation, height, vertical position **9**. achievement, degree, grade, position, rank, stage, standard, standing, status **10**. bed, floor, layer, storey, stratum, zone **11**. flat surface, horizontal, plain, plane **12. on the level** *Inf.* above board, fair, genuine, honest, open, sincere, square, straight, straightforward, up front (*Sl.*)

level-headed balanced, calm, collected, composed, cool, dependable, even-tempered, reasonable, sane, self-possessed, sensible, steady, together (*Sl., chiefly U.S.*), unflappable (*Inf.*)

lever 1. *n.* bar, crowbar, handle, handspike, jemmy **2**. *v.* force, jemmy, move, prise, pry (*U.S.*), purchase, raise

leverage ascendancy, authority, clout (*Inf.*), influence, pull (*Inf.*), purchasing power, rank, weight

leviathan behemoth, colossus, hulk, mammoth, monster, Titan, whale

levity buoyancy, facetiousness, fickleness, flightiness, flippancy, frivolity, giddiness, light-heartedness, light-mindedness, silliness, skittishness, triviality

levy *v.* **1**. charge, collect, demand, exact, gather, impose, tax **2**. call, call up, conscript, mobilize, muster, press, raise, summon ~*n.* **3**. assessment, collection, exaction, gathering, imposition **4**. assessment, duty, excise, fee, imposition, impost, tariff, tax, toll

lewd bawdy, blue, dirty, impure, indecent, lascivious, libidinous, licentious, loose, lustful, obscene, pornographic, profligate, salacious, smutty, unchaste, vile, vulgar, wanton, wicked

lewdness bawdiness, carnality, crudity, debauchery, depravity, impurity, indecency, lasciviousness, lechery, licentiousness, lubricity, obscenity, pornography, profligacy, salaciousness, smut, smuttiness, unchastity, vulgarity, wantonness

lexicon dictionary, glossary, vocabulary, wordbook, word list

liabilities accounts payable, debts, expenditure, obligations

liability 1. accountability, answerability, culpability, duty, obligation, onus, responsibility **2**. arrear, debit, debt, indebtedness, obligation **3**. burden, disadvantage, drag, drawback, encumbrance, handicap, hindrance, impediment, inconvenience, millstone, minus (*Inf.*), nuisance **4**. likelihood, probability, proneness, susceptibility, tendency

liable 1. accountable, amenable, answerable, bound, chargeable, obligated, responsible **2**. exposed, open, subject, susceptible, vulnerable **3**. apt, disposed, inclined, likely, prone, tending **4. render oneself liable to** expose oneself to, incur, lay oneself open to, run the risk of

liaison 1. communication, connection, contact, go-between, hook-up, interchange, intermediary **2**. affair, amour, entanglement, illicit romance, intrigue, love affair, romance

liar fabricator, falsifier, fibber, perjurer, prevaricator, storyteller (*Inf.*)

libel 1. *n.* aspersion, calumny, defamation, denigration, obloquy, slander, smear, vituperation **2.** *v.* blacken, calumniate, defame, derogate, drag (someone's) name through the mud, malign, revile, slander, slur, smear, traduce, vilify

libellous aspersive, calumniatory, calumnious, defamatory, derogatory, false, injurious, malicious, maligning, scurrilous, slanderous, traducing, untrue, vilifying, vituperative

liberal 1. advanced, humanistic, latitudinarian, libertarian, progressive, radical, reformist **2.** altruistic, beneficent, bounteous, bountiful, charitable, free-handed, generous, kind, open-handed, open-hearted, unstinting **3.** advanced, broad-minded, catholic, enlightened, high-minded, humanitarian, indulgent, magnanimous, permissive, tolerant, unbiased, unbigoted, unprejudiced **4.** abundant, ample, bountiful, copious, handsome, lavish, munificent, plentiful, profuse, rich **5.** broad, flexible, free, general, inexact, lenient, loose, not close, not literal, not strict

liberalism freethinking, humanitarianism, latitudinarianism, libertarianism, progressivism, radicalism

liberality 1. altruism, beneficence, benevolence, bounty, charity, freehandedness, generosity, kindness, largess, munificence, open-handedness, philanthropy **2.** breadth, broadmindedness, candour, catholicity, impartiality, latitude, liberalism, libertarianism, magnanimity, permissiveness, progressivism, toleration

liberalize ameliorate, broaden, ease, expand, extend, loosen, mitigate, moderate, modify, relax, slacken, soften, stretch

liberate deliver, discharge, disenthral, emancipate, free, let loose, let out, manumit, redeem, release, rescue, set free

liberation deliverance, emancipation, enfranchisement, freedom, freeing, liberating, liberty, manumission, redemption, release, unfettering, unshackling

liberator deliverer, emancipator, freer, manumitter, redeemer, rescuer, saviour

libertine 1. *n.* debauchee, lecher, loose liver, profligate, rake, reprobate, roué, seducer, sensualist, voluptuary, womanizer **2.** *adj.* abandoned, corrupt, debauched, decadent, degenerate, depraved, dissolute, immoral, licentious, profligate, rakish, reprobate, voluptuous, wanton

liberty 1. autonomy, emancipation, freedom, immunity, independence, liberation, release, self-determination, sovereignty **2.** authorization, carte blanche, dispensation, exemption, franchise, freedom, leave, licence, permission, prerogative, privilege, right, sanction **3.** *Often plural* disrespect, familiarity, forwardness, impertinence, impropriety, impudence, insolence, overfamiliarity, presumption, presumptuousness **4.** at liberty free, not confined, on the loose, unlimited, unoccupied, unrestricted

libidinous carnal, concupiscent, debauched, impure, incontinent, lascivious, lecherous, lickerish (*Archaic*), loose, lustful, prurient, randy (*Sl., chiefly Brit.*), ruttish, salacious, sensual, unchaste, wanton, wicked

libretto book, lines, lyrics, script, words

licence *n.* **1.** authority, authorization, carte blanche, certificate, charter, dispensation, entitlement, exemption, immunity, leave, liberty, permission, permit, privilege, right, warrant **2.** freedom, independence, latitude, liberty, self-determination **3.** abandon, anarchy, disorder, excess, immoderation, impropriety, indulgence, irresponsibility, lawlessness, laxity, profligacy, unruliness

license *v.* accredit, allow, authorize, certify, commission, empower, permit, sanction, warrant

licentious abandoned, debauched, disorderly, dissolute, immoral, impure, lascivious, lax, lewd, libertine, libidinous, lubricous, lustful, profligate, promiscuous, sensual, uncontrollable, uncontrolled, uncurbed, unruly, wanton

licentiousness abandon, debauchery, dissipation, dissoluteness, lechery, lewdness, libertinism, libidinousness, lubricity, lust, lustfulness, profligacy, promiscuity, prurience, salaciousness, salacity, wantonness

lick *v.* **1.** brush, lap, taste, tongue, touch, wash **2.** *Of flames* dart, flick, flicker, ignite, kindle, play over, ripple, touch **3.** *Inf.* **a.** defeat, overcome, rout, trounce, vanquish, wipe the floor with (*Inf.*) **b.**

beat, flog, slap, spank, strike, thrash, wallop (*Inf.*) **c.** beat, best, excel, outdo, outstrip, surpass, top ~*n.* **4.** bit, brush, dab, little, sample, speck, stroke, taste, touch **5.** *Inf.* clip (*Inf.*), pace, rate, speed

licking 1. beating, drubbing, flogging, hiding (*Inf.*), spanking, tanning (*Sl.*), thrashing, whipping **2.** beating, defeat, drubbing, trouncing

lie¹ 1. *v.* dissimulate, equivocate, fabricate, falsify, fib, forswear oneself, invent, misrepresent, perjure, prevaricate, tell a lie, tell untruths **2.** *n.* deceit, fabrication, falsehood, falsification, falsity, fib, fiction, invention, mendacity, prevarication, untruth, white lie

lie² 1. *v.* **1.** be prone, be prostrate, be recumbent, be supine, couch, loll, lounge, recline, repose, rest, sprawl, stretch out **2.** be, be buried, be found, be interred, be located, belong, be placed, be situated, exist, extend, remain **3.** *Usually with* **on** *or* **upon** burden, oppress, press, rest, weigh **4.** *Usually with* **in** be present, consist, dwell, exist, inhere, pertain **5. lie low** conceal oneself, go to earth, go underground, hide, hide away, hide out, hole up, keep a low profile, keep out of sight, lurk, skulk, take cover

liege chieftain, feudal lord, master, overlord, seigneur, sovereign, superior, suzerain

lieu place, room, stead

life 1. animation, being, breath, entity, growth, sentience, viability, vitality **2.** being, career, continuance, course, duration, existence, lifetime, span, time **3.** human, human being, individual, mortal, person, soul **4.** autobiography, biography, career, confessions, history, life story, memoirs, story **5.** behaviour, conduct, life style, way of life **6.** the human condition, the times, the world, this mortal coil, trials and tribulations, vicissitudes **7.** activity, animation, brio, energy, get-up-and-go (*Inf.*), go (*Inf.*), high spirits, liveliness, oomph (*Inf.*), sparkle, spirit, verve, vigour, vitality, vivacity, zest **8.** animating spirit, *élan vital*, essence, heart, lifeblood, soul, spirit, vital spark **9.** creatures, living beings, living things, organisms, wildlife **10. come to life** awaken, become animate, revive, rouse, show signs of life **11. for dear life** *Inf.* desperately, for all one is worth, intensely, quickly, urgently, vigorously

lifeblood animating force, driving

force, essence, guts (*Inf.*), heart, inspiration, life, stimulus, vital spark

lifeless 1. cold, dead, deceased, defunct, extinct, inanimate, inert **2.** bare, barren, desert, empty, sterile, uninhabited, unproductive, waste **3.** cold, colourless, dull, flat, heavy, hollow, lacklustre, lethargic, listless, passive, pointless, slow, sluggish, spent, spiritless, static, stiff, torpid, wooden **4.** comatose, dead to the world, in a faint, inert, insensate, insensible, out cold, out for six, unconscious

lifelike authentic, exact, faithful, graphic, natural, photographic, real, realistic, true-to-life, undistorted, vivid

lifelong constant, deep-rooted, enduring, for all one's life, for life, lasting, lifetime, long-lasting, long-standing, perennial, permanent, persistent

lifetime all one's born days, career, course, day(s), existence, life span, one's natural life, period, span, time

life work business, calling, career, interest, mission, occupation, profession, purpose, pursuit, vocation, work

lift *v.* **1.** bear aloft, buoy up, draw up, elevate, heft (*Inf.*), hoist, pick up, raise, raise high, rear, upheave, uplift, upraise **2.** advance, ameliorate, boost, dignify, elevate, enhance, exalt, improve, promote, raise, upgrade **3.** annul, cancel, countermand, end, relax, remove, rescind, revoke, stop, terminate **4.** ascend, be dispelled, climb, disappear, disperse, dissipate, mount, rise, vanish **5.** *Inf.* appropriate, copy, crib (*Inf.*), half-inch (*Brit. sl.*), nick (*Sl., chiefly Brit.*), pilfer, pinch (*Inf.*), pirate, plagiarize, pocket, purloin, steal, take, thieve ~*n.* **6.** car ride, drive, ride, run, transport **7.** boost, encouragement, fillip, pick-me-up, reassurance, shot in the arm (*Inf.*), uplift **8.** elevator (*Chiefly U.S.*)

ligature band, bandage, binding, bond, connection, ligament, link, tie

light¹ *n.* **1.** blaze, brightness, brilliance, effulgence, flash, glare, gleam, glint, glow, illumination, incandescence, lambency, luminescence, luminosity, lustre, phosphorescence, radiance, ray, refulgence, scintillation, shine, sparkle **2.** beacon, bulb, candle, flare, lamp, lantern, lighthouse, star, taper, torch, windowpane **3.** broad day, cockcrow, dawn, daybreak, daylight, daytime, morn (*Poetic*), morning, sun, sunbeam, sunrise, sunshine **4**. *Fig*. angle, approach, aspect, attitude, context, interpretation, point of view, slant, vantage point, viewpoint **5**. awareness, comprehension, elucidation, explanation, illustration, information, insight, knowledge, understanding **6**. example, exemplar, guiding light, model, paragon, shining example **7**. flame, lighter, match **8**. **bring to light** disclose, discover, expose, reveal, show, uncover, unearth, unveil **9**. **come to light** appear, be disclosed, be discovered, be revealed, come out, transpire, turn up **10**. **in (the) light of** bearing in mind, because of, considering, in view of, taking into account, with knowledge of **11**. **shed** *or* **throw light on** clarify, clear up, elucidate, explain, simplify ~*adj*. **12**. aglow, bright, brilliant, glowing, illuminated, luminous, lustrous, shining, sunny, well-lighted, well-lit **13**. bleached, blond, faded, fair, light-hued, light-toned, pale, pastel ~*v*. **14**. fire, ignite, inflame, kindle, set a match to **15**. brighten, clarify, floodlight, flood with light, illuminate, illumine, irradiate, lighten, light up, put on, switch on, turn on **16**. animate, brighten, cheer, irradiate, lighten

light² *adj*. **1**. airy, buoyant, delicate, easy, flimsy, imponderous, insubstantial, lightsome, lightweight, portable, slight, underweight **2**. faint, gentle, indistinct, mild, moderate, slight, soft, weak **3**. inconsequential, inconsiderable, insignificant, minute, scanty, slight, small, thin, tiny, trifling, trivial, unsubstantial, wee **4**. cushy (*Sl*.), easy, effortless, manageable, moderate, simple, undemanding, unexacting, untaxing **5**. agile, airy, graceful, light-footed, lithe, nimble, sprightly, sylphlike **6**. amusing, diverting, entertaining, frivolous, funny, gay, humorous, light-hearted, pleasing, superficial, trifling, trivial, witty **7**. airy, animated, blithe, carefree, cheerful, cheery, fickle, frivolous, gay, lively, merry, sunny **8**. dizzy, giddy, light-headed, reeling, unsteady, volatile **9**. digestible, frugal, modest, not heavy, not rich, restricted, small **10**. crumbly, friable, loose, porous, sandy, spongy ~*v*. **11**. alight, land, perch, settle **12**. *With* **on** *or* **upon** chance, come across, discover, encounter, find, happen upon, hit upon, stumble on

lighten¹ become light, brighten, flash,

gleam, illuminate, irradiate, light up, make bright, shine

lighten² **1**. disburden, ease, make lighter, reduce in weight, unload **2**. alleviate, ameliorate, assuage, ease, facilitate, lessen, mitigate, reduce, relieve **3**. brighten, buoy up, cheer, elate, encourage, gladden, hearten, inspire, lift, perk up, revive

light-fingered crafty, crooked (*Inf*.), dishonest, furtive, pilfering, pinching (*Inf*.), shifty, sly, stealing, thieving, underhand

light-footed agile, buoyant, graceful, lithe, nimble, sprightly, spry, swift, tripping, winged

light-headed **1**. bird-brained (*Inf*.), featherbrained, fickle, flighty, flippant, foolish, frivolous, giddy, inane, rattle-brained (*Inf*.), shallow, silly, superficial, trifling **2**. delirious, dizzy, faint, giddy, hazy, vertiginous, woozy (*Inf*.)

light-hearted blithe, blithesome (*Literary*), bright, carefree, cheerful, effervescent, frolicsome, gay, glad, gleeful, happy-go-lucky, insouciant, jocund, jolly, jovial, joyful, joyous, merry, playful, sunny, untroubled, upbeat (*Inf*.)

light into assail, attack, belabour, clobber (*Brit. sl*.), flail, flay, go at hammer and tongs, lambaste, lay into, let fly at, pitch into, sail into (*Inf*.), set about, tear into (*Inf*.)

lightless caliginous (*Archaic*), dark, dim, dusky, gloomy, inky, jet black, murky, pitch-black, pitch-dark, pitchy, Stygian, sunless, tenebrous, unilluminated, unlighted, unlit

lightly **1**. airily, delicately, faintly, gently, gingerly, slightly, softly, timidly **2**. moderately, sparingly, sparsely, thinly **3**. easily, effortlessly, readily, simply **4**. breezily, carelessly, flippantly, frivolously, heedlessly, indifferently, slightingly, thoughtlessly

light out abscond, depart, do a bunk (*Brit. sl*.), escape, make off, quit, run away, scarper (*Brit. sl*.)

lightweight **1**. *adj*. inconsequential, insignificant, of no account, paltry, petty, slight, trifling, trivial, unimportant, worthless

likable, likeable agreeable, amiable, appealing, attractive, charming, engaging, friendly, genial, nice, pleasant, pleasing, sympathetic, winning, winsome

like¹ **1**. *adj*. akin, alike, allied, analogous, approximating, cognate, corresponding, equivalent, identical, parallel, relating, resembling, same, similar **2.** *n.* counterpart, equal, fellow, match, parallel, twin

like² *v.* **1.** adore (*Inf.*), be fond of, be keen on, be partial to, delight in, dig (*Sl.*), enjoy, go for (*Sl.*), love, relish, revel in **2.** admire, appreciate, approve, cherish, esteem, hold dear, prize, take a shine to (*Inf.*), take to **3.** care to, choose, choose to, desire, fancy, feel inclined, prefer, select, want, wish ~*n.* **4.** *Usually plural* cup of tea (*Inf.*), favourite, liking, partiality, predilection, preference

likelihood chance, good chance, liability, likeliness, possibility, probability, prospect, reasonableness, strong possibility

likely *adj.* **1.** anticipated, apt, disposed, expected, in a fair way, inclined, liable, on the cards, possible, probable, prone, tending, to be expected **2.** **be** *or* **seem likely** be in the running for, bid fair, incline towards, promise, stand a good chance, suggest, tend **3.** believable, credible, feasible, plausible, reasonable, verisimilar **4.** acceptable, agreeable, appropriate, befitting, fit, pleasing, proper, qualified, suitable **5.** fair, favourite, hopeful, odds-on, promising, up-and-coming ~*adv.* **6.** doubtlessly, in all probability, like as not (*Inf.*), like enough (*Inf.*), no doubt, presumably, probably

like-minded agreeing, compatible, *en rapport*, harmonious, in accord, in harmony, of one mind, of the same mind, unanimous

liken compare, equate, juxtapose, match, parallel, relate, set beside

likeness 1. affinity, correspondence, resemblance, similarity, similitude **2.** copy, counterpart, delineation, depiction, effigy, facsimile, image, model, photograph, picture, portrait, replica, representation, reproduction, study **3.** appearance, form, guise, semblance

likewise 1. also, besides, further, furthermore, in addition, moreover, too **2.** in like manner, in the same way, similarly

liking affection, affinity, appreciation, attraction, bent, bias, desire, fondness, inclination, love, partiality, penchant, predilection, preference, proneness, propensity, soft spot, stomach, taste, tendency, weakness

Lilliputian 1. *n.* dwarf, homunculus, hop-o'-my-thumb, manikin, midget, pygmy, Tom Thumb **2.** *adj.* baby, bantam, diminutive, dwarf, little, mini, miniature, minuscule, petite, pocket-sized, pygmy, small, teeny, teeny-weeny, tiny, wee

lilt beat, cadence, rhythm, sway, swing

lily-livered chicken (*Sl.*), chicken-hearted, cowardly, craven, faint-hearted, fearful, gutless (*Inf.*), pusillanimous, scared, spineless, timid, timorous, yellow (*Inf.*), yellow-bellied (*Sl.*)

lily-white 1. milk-white, pure white, white, white as snow, white-skinned **2.** *Inf.* chaste, innocent, irreproachable, pure, spotless, unsullied, untainted, untarnished, virgin, virtuous

limb 1. appendage, arm, extension, extremity, leg, member, part, wing **2.** bough, branch, offshoot, projection, spur

limber *adj.* **1.** elastic, flexible, plastic, pliable, pliant, supple **2.** agile, graceful, lissom, lithe, loose-jointed, loose-limbed, supple ~*v.* **3.** *With* **up** exercise, get ready, loosen up, prepare, warm up

limelight attention, celebrity, fame, glare of publicity, prominence, public eye, publicity, public notice, recognition, stardom, the spotlight

limit *n.* **1.** bound, breaking point, cut-off point, deadline, end, end point, furthest bound, greatest extent, termination, the bitter end, ultimate, utmost **2.** *Often plural* border, boundary, confines, edge, end, extent, frontier, perimeter, periphery, precinct **3.** ceiling, check, curb, limitation, maximum, obstruction, restraint, restriction **4.** **the limit** *Inf.* enough, it (*Inf.*), the end, the last straw ~*v.* **5.** bound, check, circumscribe, confine, curb, delimit, demarcate, fix, hem in, hinder, ration, restrain, restrict, specify

limitation block, check, condition, constraint, control, curb, disadvantage, drawback, impediment, obstruction, qualification, reservation, restraint, restriction, snag

limited 1. bounded, checked, circumscribed, confined, constrained, controlled, curbed, defined, finite, fixed, hampered, hemmed in, restricted **2.** cramped, diminished, inadequate, insufficient, minimal, narrow, reduced, restricted, short, unsatisfactory

limitless boundless, countless, endless, illimitable, immeasurable, immense, inexhaustible, infinite, measureless, never-ending, numberless, unbounded, uncalculable, undefined, unending, unlimited, untold, vast

limp[1] 1. *v.* falter, halt (*Archaic*), hobble, hop, shamble, shuffle 2. *n.* hobble, lameness

limp[2] *adj.* 1. drooping, flabby, flaccid, flexible, floppy, lax, limber, loose, pliable, relaxed, slack, soft 2. debilitated, enervated, exhausted, lethargic, spent, tired, weak, worn out

limpid 1. bright, clear, crystal-clear, crystalline, pellucid, pure, translucent, transparent 2. clear, comprehensible, intelligible, lucid, perspicuous, unambiguous 3. calm, peaceful, placid, quiet, serene, still, tranquil, unruffled, untroubled

line[1] *n.* 1. band, bar, channel, dash, groove, mark, rule, score, scratch, streak, stripe, stroke, underline 2. crease, crow's foot, furrow, mark, wrinkle 3. border, borderline, boundary, demarcation, edge, frontier, limit, mark 4. configuration, contour, features, figure, outline, profile, silhouette 5. cable, cord, filament, rope, strand, string, thread, wire 6. axis, course, direction, path, route, track, trajectory 7. approach, avenue, belief, course, course of action, ideology, method, policy, position, practice, procedure, scheme, system 8. activity, area, business, calling, department, employment, field, forte, interest, job, occupation, profession, province, pursuit, specialization, trade, vocation 9. column, crocodile (*Brit.*), file, procession, queue, rank, row, sequence, series 10. ancestry, breed, family, lineage, race, stock, strain, succession 11. card, letter, message, note, postcard, report, word 12. clue, hint, indication, information, lead 13. *Military* disposition, firing line, formation, front, front line, position, trenches 14. **draw the line** lay down the law, object, prohibit, put one's foot down, restrict, set a limit 15. **in line a.** in alignment, in a row, plumb, straight, true **b.** in accord, in agreement, in conformity, in harmony, in step 16. **in line for** a candidate for, being considered for, due for, in the running for, next in succession to, on the short list for ~*v.* 17. crease, cut, draw, furrow, inscribe, mark, rule, score, trace, underline 18. border, bound, edge,

fringe, rank, rim, skirt, verge

line[2] *v.* ceil, cover, face, fill, interline

lineage ancestry, birth, breed, descendants, descent, extraction, family, forebears, forefathers, genealogy, heredity, house, line, offspring, pedigree, progeny, stirps, stock, succession

lineaments configuration, countenance, face, features, line, outline, phiz *or* phizog (*Sl., chiefly Brit.*), physiognomy, trait, visage

lined 1. feint, ruled 2. furrowed, wizened, worn, wrinkled

lines 1. appearance, configuration, contour, cut, outline, shape, style 2. convention, example, model, pattern, plan, principle, procedure 3. part, script, words

line-up arrangement, array, row, selection, team

line up 1. fall in, form ranks, queue up 2. assemble, come up with, lay on, obtain, organize, prepare, procure, produce, secure 3. align, arrange, array, marshal, order, range, regiment, straighten

linger 1. hang around, loiter, remain, stay, stop, tarry, wait 2. dally, dawdle, delay, idle, lag, procrastinate, take one's time 3. cling to life, die slowly, hang on, last, survive 4. abide, continue, endure, persist, remain, stay

lingering dragging, long-drawn-out, persistent, protracted, remaining, slow

lingo argot, cant, dialect, idiom, jargon, language, patois, speech, talk, tongue, vernacular

liniment balm, balsam, cream, embrocation, emollient, lotion, ointment, salve, unguent

link *n.* 1. component, constituent, division, element, member, part, piece 2. association, attachment, bond, connection, joint, knot, relationship, tie, tie-up, vinculum ~*v.* 3. attach, bind, connect, couple, fasten, join, tie, unite, yoke 4. associate, bracket, connect, identify, relate

lion *Fig.* 1. brave man, champion, conqueror, fighter, hero, warrior 2. big name, celebrity, idol, luminary, notable, prodigy, star, superstar, V.I.P., wonder 3. **beard the lion in his den** brave, confront, court destruction, defy danger, face, stand up to, tempt providence

lion-hearted bold, brave, courageous, daring, dauntless, heroic, intrepid, resolute, stalwart, valiant, valorous

lionize acclaim, adulate, aggrandize, celebrate, eulogize, exalt, fête, glorify, hero-worship, honour, idolize, make much of, mob, sing *or* sound the praises of

lip 1., brim, brink, edge, margin, rim **2.** *Sl.* backchat (*Inf.*), cheek (*Inf.*), effrontery, impertinence, insolence, rudeness, sauce (*Inf.*) **3.** *Music* control, embouchure **4. smack** *or* **lick one's lips** anticipate, delight in, drool over, enjoy, gloat over, relish, savour, slaver over

liquefaction deliquescence, dissolution, dissolving, fusion, melting, thawing

liquefy deliquesce, dissolve, flux, fuse, liquesce, liquidize, melt, run, thaw

liquid *n.* **1.** fluid, juice, liquor, solution ~*adj.* **2.** aqueous, flowing, fluid, liquefied, melted, molten, running, runny, thawed, wet **3.** bright, brilliant, clear, limpid, shining, translucent, transparent **4.** dulcet, fluent, mellifluent, mellifluous, melting, smooth, soft, sweet **5.** *Of assets* convertible, negotiable

liquidate 1. clear, discharge, honour, pay, pay off, settle, square **2.** abolish, annul, cancel, dissolve, terminate **3.** cash, convert to cash, realize, sell off, sell up **4.** annihilate, bump off (*Sl.*), destroy, dispatch, do away with, do in (*Sl.*), eliminate, exterminate, finish off, get rid of, kill, murder, remove, rub out (*U.S. sl.*), silence, wipe out (*Inf.*)

liquor 1. alcohol, booze (*Inf.*), drink, grog, hard stuff (*Inf.*), hooch (*Sl., chiefly U.S.*), intoxicant, juice (*Inf.*), spirits, strong drink **2.** broth, extract, gravy, infusion, juice, liquid, stock

lissom agile, flexible, graceful, light, limber, lithe, loose-jointed, loose-limbed, nimble, pliable, pliant, supple, willowy

list¹ 1. *n.* catalogue, directory, file, index, inventory, invoice, leet (*Scot.*), listing, record, register, roll, schedule, series, syllabus, tabulation, tally **2.** *v.* bill, book, catalogue, enrol, enter, enumerate, file, index, itemize, note, record, register, schedule, set down, tabulate, write down

list² 1. *v.* cant, careen, heel, heel over, incline, lean, tilt, tip **2.** *n.* cant, leaning, slant, tilt

listen 1. attend, be all ears, be attentive, give ear, hang on (someone's) words, hark, hear, hearken (*Archaic*), keep one's ears open, lend an ear, pin back one's ears (*Inf.*), prick up one's ears **2.** concentrate, do as one is told, give

heed to, heed, mind, obey, observe, pay attention, take notice

listless apathetic, enervated, heavy, impassive, inattentive, indifferent, indolent, inert, languid, languishing, lethargic, lifeless, limp, lymphatic, mopish, sluggish, spiritless, supine, torpid, vacant

listlessness apathy, enervation, ennui, inattention, indifference, indolence, languidness, languor, lethargy, lifelessness, sluggishness, spiritlessness, supineness, torpidity

litany 1. invocation, petition, prayer, supplication **2.** account, catalogue, enumeration, list, recital, recitation, refrain, repetition, tale

literacy ability, articulacy, articulateness, cultivation, education, knowledge, learning, proficiency, scholarship

literal 1. accurate, close, exact, faithful, strict, verbatim, word for word **2.** boring, colourless, down-to-earth, dull, factual, matter-of-fact, prosaic, prosy, unimaginative, uninspired **3.** actual, bona fide, genuine, gospel, plain, real, simple, true, unexaggerated, unvarnished

literally actually, exactly, faithfully, plainly, precisely, really, simply, strictly, to the letter, truly, verbatim, word for word

literary bookish, erudite, formal, learned, lettered, literate, scholarly, well-read

literate cultivated, cultured, educated, erudite, informed, knowledgeable, learned, lettered, scholarly, well-informed, well-read

literature 1. belles-lettres, letters, lore, writings, written works **2.** brochure, information, leaflet, pamphlet

lithe flexible, limber, lissom, loose-jointed, loose-limbed, pliable, pliant, supple

litigant claimant, contestant, disputant, litigator, party, plaintiff

litigate contest at law, file a suit, go to court, go to law, institute legal proceedings, press charges, prosecute, sue

litigation action, case, contending, disputing, lawsuit, process, prosecution

litigious argumentative, belligerent, contentious, disputatious, quarrelsome

litter 1. debris, detritus, fragments, muck, refuse, rubbish, shreds **2.** clutter, confusion, disarray, disorder, jumble, mess, scatter, untidiness **3.** brood, family, offspring, progeny, young **4.** bedding, couch, floor cover, mulch, straw-bed **5.** palanquin, stretcher ~*v.* **6.** clutter, derange, disarrange, disorder, mess up, scatter, strew

little *adj.* **1.** diminutive, dwarf, elfin, infinitesimal, Lilliputian, mini, miniature, minute, petite, pygmy, short, slender, small, tiny, wee **2.** babyish, immature, infant, junior, undeveloped, young **3.** hardly any, insufficient, meagre, scant, skimpy, small, sparse **4.** brief, fleeting, hasty, passing, short, short-lived **5.** inconsiderable, insignificant, minor, negligible, paltry, trifling, trivial, unimportant **6.** base, cheap, illiberal, mean, narrow-minded, petty, small-minded ~*adv.* **7.** barely, hardly, not much, not quite, only just **8.** hardly ever, not often, rarely, scarcely, seldom **9.** little by little bit by bit, by degrees, gradually, imperceptibly, piecemeal, progressively, slowly, step by step ~*n.* **10.** bit, dab, dash, fragment, hint, modicum, particle, pinch, small amount, snippet, speck, spot, taste, touch, trace, trifle

liturgical ceremonial, eucharistic, formal, ritual, sacramental, solemn

liturgy celebration, ceremony, form of worship, formula, rite, ritual, sacrament, service, services, worship

livable 1. adequate, comfortable, fit (for human habitation), habitable, inhabitable, satisfactory **2.** acceptable, bearable, endurable, passable, sufferable, supportable, tolerable, worth living, worthwhile **3.** *With* **with** companionable, compatible, congenial, easy, easy to live with, harmonious, sociable

live¹ *v.* **1.** be, be alive, breathe, draw breath, exist, have life **2.** be permanent, be remembered, last, persist, prevail, remain alive **3.** *Sometimes with* **in** abide, dwell, hang out (*Inf.*), inhabit, lodge, occupy, reside, settle, stay (*Chiefly Scot.*) **4.** abide, continue, earn a living, endure, fare, feed, get along, lead, make ends meet, pass, remain, subsist, support oneself, survive **5.** be happy, enjoy life, flourish, luxuriate, make the most of life, prosper, thrive **6. live it up** *Inf.* celebrate, enjoy oneself, have a ball (*Inf.*), have fun, make whoopee (*Inf.*), paint the town red, push the boat out (*Brit. inf.*), revel

live² *adj.* **1.** alive, animate, breathing,

existent, living, quick (*Archaic*), vital **2.** active, burning, controversial, current, hot, pertinent, pressing, prevalent, topical, unsettled, vital **3.** *Inf.* active, alert, brisk, dynamic, earnest, energetic, lively, vigorous, vivid, wide-awake **4.** active, alight, blazing, burning, connected, glowing, hot, ignited, smouldering, switched on

livelihood employment, job, living, maintenance, means, (means of) support, occupation, (source of) income, subsistence, sustenance, work

liveliness activity, animation, boisterousness, briskness, dynamism, energy, gaiety, quickness, smartness, spirit, sprightliness, vitality, vivacity

livelong complete, dragged out, entire, everlasting, full, long-drawn-out, unbroken, whole

lively 1. active, agile, alert, brisk, chipper (*Inf.*), chirpy, energetic, full of pep (*Inf.*), keen, nimble, perky, quick, sprightly, spry, vigorous **2.** animated, blithe, blithesome, cheerful, frisky, frolicsome, gay, merry, sparkling, spirited, vivacious **3.** astir, bustling, busy, buzzing, crowded, eventful, moving, stirring **4.** bright, colourful, exciting, forceful, invigorating, racy, refreshing, stimulating, vivid

liven animate, brighten, buck up (*Inf.*), enliven, hot up (*Inf.*), pep up, perk up, put life into, rouse, stir, vitalize, vivify

liverish 1. bilious, queasy, sick **2.** crotchety (*Inf.*), crusty, disagreeable, fratchy (*Inf.*), grumpy, ill-humoured, irascible, irritable, peevish, snappy, splenetic

livery attire, clothing, costume, dress, garb, raiment (*Poetic*), regalia, suit, uniform, vestments

live wire ball of fire (*Inf.*), dynamo, go-getter (*Inf.*), hustler (*U.S.*), life and soul of the party, self-starter

livid 1. angry, black-and-blue, bruised, contused, discoloured, purple **2.** ashen, blanched, bloodless, doughy, greyish, leaden, pale, pallid, pasty, wan, waxen **3.** *Inf.* angry, beside oneself, boiling, enraged, exasperated, fuming, furious, incensed, indignant, infuriated, mad (*Inf.*), outraged

living *adj.* **1.** active, alive, animated, breathing, existing, in the land of the living (*Inf.*), lively, quick (*Archaic*), strong, vigorous, vital **2**. active, contemporary, continuing, current, developing, extant, in use, ongoing, operative, persisting ~*n*. **3**. animation, being, existence, existing, life, subsistence **4**. life style, mode of living, way of life **5**. job, livelihood, maintenance, (means of) support, occupation, (source of) income, subsistence, sustenance, work **6**. *Church of England* benefice **7**. **the living** flesh and blood, the quick (*Archaic*)

load *n*. **1**. bale, cargo, consignment, freight, lading, shipment **2**. affliction, burden, encumbrance, incubus, millstone, onus, oppression, pressure, trouble, weight, worry ~*v*. **3**. cram, fill, freight, heap, lade, pack, pile, stack, stuff **4**. burden, encumber, hamper, oppress, saddle with, trouble, weigh down, worry **5**. *Of firearms* charge, make ready, prepare to fire, prime **6. load the dice** fix, rig, set up

loaded 1. burdened, charged, freighted, full, laden, weighted **2**. biased, distorted, weighted **3**. artful, insidious, manipulative, prejudicial, tricky **4**. at the ready, charged, primed, ready to shoot *or* fire **5**. *Sl.* affluent, flush (*Inf.*), moneyed, rich, rolling (*Sl.*), wealthy, well-heeled (*Sl.*), well off, well-to-do

loaf[1] *n*. **1**. block, cake, cube, lump, slab **2**. *Sl.* block (*Inf.*), chump (*Brit. sl.*), gumption (*Inf.*), head, noddle (*Inf., chiefly Brit.*), nous (*Brit. sl.*), sense

loaf[2] *v*. **1**. be indolent, idle, laze, lie around, loiter, loll, lounge around, take it easy (*Inf.*) **2**. *With* **away** fritter away, kill time, pass time, waste time, while away the hours

loafer bum (*Inf., chiefly U.S.*), drone (*Brit.*), idler, layabout, lazybones (*Inf.*), lounger, ne'er-do-well, shirker, skiver (*Brit. sl.*), time-waster, wastrel

loan 1. *n*. accommodation, advance, allowance, credit, mortgage, touch (*Sl.*) **2**. *v*. accommodate, advance, allow, credit, lend, let out

loath, loth against, averse, backward, counter, disinclined, indisposed, opposed, reluctant, resisting, unwilling

loathe abhor, abominate, despise, detest, dislike, execrate, feel repugnance towards, find disgusting, hate, have a strong aversion to, not be able to bear *or* abide

loathing abhorrence, abomination, antipathy, aversion, detestation, disgust,

execration, hatred, horror, odium, repugnance, repulsion, revulsion

loathsome abhorrent, abominable, detestable, disgusting, execrable, hateful, horrible, nasty, nauseating, obnoxious, odious, offensive, repugnant, repulsive, revolting, vile

lob *v*. fling, launch, lift, loft, pitch, shy (*Inf.*), throw, toss

lobby *n*. **1**. corridor, entrance hall, foyer, hall, hallway, passage, passageway, porch, vestibule **2**. pressure group ~*v*. **3**. bring pressure to bear, campaign for, exert influence, influence, persuade, press for, pressure, promote, pull strings (*Brit. inf.*), push for, solicit votes, urge

local *adj*. **1**. community, district, neighbourhood, parish, provincial, regional **2**. confined, limited, narrow, parish, parochial, provincial, pump, restricted, small-town ~*n*. **3**. character (*Inf.*), inhabitant, local yokel (*Disparaging*), native, resident

locale locality, location, locus, place, position, scene, setting, site, spot, venue

locality 1. area, district, neck of the woods (*Inf.*), neighbourhood, region, vicinity **2**. locale, location, place, position, scene, setting, site, spot

localize 1. circumscribe, concentrate, confine, contain, delimit, delimitate, limit, restrain, restrict **2**. ascribe, assign, narrow down, pinpoint, specify

locate 1. come across, detect, discover, find, lay one's hands on, pin down, pinpoint, run to earth, track down, unearth **2**. establish, fix, place, put, seat, set, settle, situate

location bearings, locale, locus, place, point, position, site, situation, spot, venue, whereabouts

lock[1] *n*. **1**. bolt, clasp, fastening, padlock ~*v*. **2**. bolt, close, fasten, latch, seal, secure, shut, sneck (*Dialect*) **3**. clench, engage, entangle, entwine, join, link, mesh, unite **4**. clasp, clutch, embrace, encircle, enclose, grapple, grasp, hug, press

lock[2] curl, ringlet, strand, tress, tuft

lock out ban, bar, debar, exclude, keep out, refuse admittance to, shut out

lockup cell, cooler (*Sl.*), gaol, jail, jug (*Sl.*), police cell

lock up cage, confine, detain, imprison, incarcerate, jail, put behind bars, shut up

locomotion action, headway, motion,

movement, moving, progress, progression, travel, travelling

locution 1. collocation, expression, idiom, phrase, term, turn of speech, wording **2.** accent, articulation, diction, inflection, intonation, manner of speech, phrasing, style

lodestar beacon, guide, model, pattern, signal, standard

lodestone beacon, focal point, focus, lodestar, magnet

lodge n. **1.** cabin, chalet, cottage, gatehouse, house, hunting lodge, hut, shelter **2.** assemblage, association, branch, chapter, club, group, society **3.** den, haunt, lair, retreat ~v. **4.** accommodate, billet, board, entertain, harbour, put up, quarter, room, shelter, sojourn, stay, stop **5.** become fixed, catch, come to rest, imbed, implant, stick **6.** deposit, file, lay, place, put, put on record, register, set, submit

lodger boarder, guest, paying guest, P.G., resident, roomer, tenant

lodging *Often plural* abode, accommodation, apartments, boarding, digs (*Brit. inf.*), dwelling, habitation, quarters, residence, rooms, shelter

lofty 1. elevated, high, raised, sky-high, soaring, tall, towering **2.** dignified, distinguished, elevated, exalted, grand, illustrious, imposing, majestic, noble, renowned, stately, sublime, superior **3.** arrogant, condescending, disdainful, haughty, high and mighty (*Inf.*), lordly, patronizing, proud, snooty (*Inf.*), supercilious, toffee-nosed (*Brit. sl.*)

log n. **1.** block, bole, chunk, piece of timber, stump, trunk ~v. **2.** chop, cut, fell, hew ~n. **3.** account, chart, daybook, journal, listing, logbook, record, tally ~v. **4.** book, chart, make a note of, note, record, register, report, set down, tally

loggerhead at loggerheads at daggers drawn, at each other's throats, at enmity, at odds, estranged, feuding, in dispute, opposed, quarrelling

logic 1. argumentation, deduction, dialectics, ratiocination, science of reasoning, syllogistic reasoning **2.** good reason, good sense, reason, sense, sound judgment **3.** chain of thought, coherence, connection, link, rationale, relationship

logical 1. clear, cogent, coherent, consistent, deducible, pertinent, rational, reasonable, relevant, sound, valid, well-organized **2.** judicious, most likely, nec-

essary, obvious, plausible, reasonable, sensible, wise

logistics coordination, engineering, management, masterminding, orchestration, organization, plans, strategy

loiter dally, dawdle, delay, dilly-dally (*Inf.*), hang about *or* around, idle, lag, linger, loaf, loll, saunter, skulk, stroll

loll 1. flop, lean, loaf, lounge, recline, relax, slouch, slump, sprawl **2.** dangle, droop, drop, flap, flop, hang, hang loosely, sag

lone by oneself, deserted, isolated, lonesome, one, only, separate, separated, single, sole, solitary, unaccompanied

loneliness aloneness, desertedness, desolation, dreariness, forlornness, isolation, lonesomeness, seclusion, solitariness, solitude

lonely 1. abandoned, destitute, estranged, forlorn, forsaken, friendless, lonesome, outcast **2.** alone, apart, by oneself, companionless, isolated, lone, single, solitary, withdrawn **3.** deserted, desolate, isolated, off the beaten track (*Inf.*), out-of-the-way, remote, secluded, sequestered, solitary, unfrequented, uninhabited

loner hermit, individualist, lone wolf, maverick, misanthrope, outsider, recluse, solitary

lonesome cheerless, companionless, deserted, desolate, dreary, forlorn, friendless, gloomy, isolated, lone, lonely

long¹ adj. **1.** elongated, expanded, extended, extensive, far-reaching, lengthy, spread out, stretched **2.** dragging, interminable, late, lengthy, lingering, long-drawn-out, prolonged, protracted, slow, sustained, tardy

long² v. covet, crave, desire, dream of, hanker, hunger, itch, lust, pine, want, wish, yearn

long-drawn-out dragged out, interminable, lengthy, marathon, overextended, overlong, prolonged, protracted, spun out

long-headed acute, astute, discerning, far-sighted, penetrating, perceptive, sagacious, shrewd, wise

longing 1. n. ambition, aspiration, coveting, craving, desire, hankering, hungering, itch, thirst, urge, wish, yearning, yen (*Inf.*) **2.** adj. anxious, ardent, avid, craving, desirous, eager, hungry, languishing, pining, wishful, wistful, yearning

long-lived enduring, full of years, longevous, long-lasting, old as Methuselah

long-standing abiding, enduring, established, fixed, hallowed by time, long-established, long-lasting, long-lived, time-honoured

long-suffering easygoing, forbearing, forgiving, patient, resigned, stoical, tolerant, uncomplaining

long-winded diffuse, discursive, garrulous, lengthy, long-drawn-out, overlong, prolix, prolonged, rambling, repetitious, tedious, verbose, wordy

look v. **1.** behold (*Archaic*), consider, contemplate, examine, eye, feast one's eyes upon, gaze, glance, inspect, observe, peep, regard, scan, scrutinize, see, study, survey, take a gander at (*Inf.*), view, watch **2.** appear, display, evidence, exhibit, look like, make clear, manifest, present, seem, seem to be, show, strike one as **3.** face, front, front on, give onto, overlook **4.** anticipate, await, expect, hope, reckon on **5.** forage, hunt, search, seek **6.** gape, gawk, gawp (*Brit. sl.*), glower, goggle, rubberneck (*Sl.*), ogle, stare **7.** **look like** be the image of, favour, make one think of, put one in mind of, remind one of, resemble, take after ~n. **8.** examination, eyeful (*Inf.*), gaze, glance, glimpse, inspection, look-see (*Sl.*), observation, once-over (*Inf.*), peek, review, sight, squint (*Inf.*), survey, view **9.** air, appearance, aspect, bearing, cast, complexion, countenance, demeanour, effect, expression, face, fashion, guise, manner, mien (*Literary*), semblance

look after attend to, care for, guard, keep an eye on, mind, nurse, protect, sit with, supervise, take care of, take charge of, tend, watch

lookalike clone, dead ringer (*Sl.*), double, exact match, living image, replica, ringer (*Sl.*), spit (*Inf.*), spit and image (*Inf.*), spitting image (*Inf.*), twin

look down on *or* **upon** contemn, despise, disdain, hold in contempt, look down one's nose at (*Inf.*), misprize, scorn, sneer, spurn, treat with contempt, turn one's nose up (at) (*Inf.*)

look forward to anticipate, await, count on, count the days until, expect, hope for, long for, look for, wait for

look into check out, delve into, examine, explore, follow up, go into, inquire about, inspect, investigate, look over, make enquiries, probe, research, scrutinize, study

lookout 1. guard, qui vive, readiness, vigil, watch **2.** guard, sentinel, sentry, vedette (*Military*), watchman **3.** beacon, citadel, observation post, post, tower, watchtower **4.** *Inf.* business, concern, funeral (*Inf.*), pigeon (*Brit. inf.*), worry **5.** chances, future, likelihood, outlook, prospect, view

look out be alert, be careful, be on guard, be on the qui vive, be vigilant, beware, keep an eye out, keep one's eyes open (peeled, skinned), pay attention, watch out

look over cast an eye over, check, examine, flick through, inspect, look through, monitor, peruse, scan, view

look up 1. find, hunt for, research, search for, seek out, track down **2.** ameliorate, come along, get better, improve, perk up, pick up, progress, shape up, show improvement **3.** *With* **to** admire, defer to, esteem, have a high opinion of, honour, regard highly, respect, revere **4.** call (on), drop in on (*Inf.*), go to see, look in on, pay a visit to, visit

loom 1. appear, become visible, be imminent, bulk, emerge, hover, impend, menace, take shape, threaten **2.** dominate, hang over, mount, overhang, overshadow, overtop, rise, soar, tower

loop 1. n. bend, circle, coil, convolution, curl, curve, eyelet, hoop, kink, loophole, noose, ring, spiral, twirl, twist, whorl **2.** v. bend, braid, circle, coil, connect, curl, curve round, encircle, fold, join, knot, roll, spiral, turn, twist, wind round

loophole 1. aperture, knothole, opening, slot **2.** *Fig.* avoidance, escape, evasion, excuse, let-out, means of escape, plea, pretence, pretext, subterfuge

loose adj. **1.** floating, free, insecure, movable, released, unattached, unbound, unconfined, unfastened, unfettered, unrestricted, unsecured, untied, wobbly **2.** baggy, easy, hanging, loosened, not fitting, not tight, relaxed, slack, slackened, sloppy **3.** diffuse, disconnected, disordered, ill-defined, imprecise, inaccurate, indefinite, indistinct, inexact, rambling, random, vague **4.** abandoned, debauched, disreputable, dissipated, dissolute, fast, immoral, lewd, libertine, licentious, profligate, promiscuous, unchaste, wanton **5.** careless, heedless, imprudent, lax, negligent, rash, thoughtless, unmindful ~*v*. **6**. detach, disconnect, disengage, ease, free, let go, liberate, loosen, release, set free, slacken, unbind, undo, unfasten, unleash, unloose, untie

loose-jointed *or* **loose-limbed** agile, elastic, flexible, limber, lissom, lithe, pliable, pliant, supple

loosen 1. detach, let out, separate, slacken, unbind, undo, unloose, unstick, untie, work free, work loose **2**. deliver, free, let go, liberate, release, set free **3**. *Often with* **up** ease up *or* off, go easy (*Inf.*), lessen, let up, mitigate, moderate, relax, soften, weaken

loot 1. *n*. booty, goods, haul, plunder, prize, spoils, swag (*Sl.*) **2**. *v*. despoil, pillage, plunder, raid, ransack, ravage, rifle, rob, sack

lop chop, clip, crop, curtail, cut, detach, dock, hack, prune, sever, shorten, trim, truncate

lope bound, canter, gallop, lollop, spring, stride

lopsided askew, asymmetrical, awry, cockeyed, crooked, disproportionate, off balance, one-sided, out of shape, out of true, squint, tilting, unbalanced, unequal, uneven, warped

loquacious babbling, blathering, chattering, chatty, gabby (*Inf.*), garrulous, gassy (*Sl.*), gossipy, talkative, voluble, wordy

loquacity babbling, chattering, chattiness, effusiveness, gabbling, garrulity, gassiness (*Sl.*), talkativeness, volubility

lord 1. commander, governor, king, leader, liege, master, monarch, overlord, potentate, prince, ruler, seigneur, sovereign, superior **2**. earl, noble, nobleman, peer, viscount **3. lord it over** act big (*Sl.*), be overbearing, boss around (*Inf.*), domineer, order around, play the lord, pull rank, put on airs, swagger

Lord, Our *or* **The** Christ, God, Jehovah, Jesus Christ, the Almighty

lordly 1. arrogant, condescending, despotic, dictatorial, disdainful, domineering, haughty, high and mighty (*Inf.*), high-handed, hoity-toity (*Inf.*), imperious, lofty, overbearing, patronizing, proud, stuck-up (*Inf.*), supercilious, toffee-nosed (*Sl., chiefly Brit.*), tyrannical **2**. aristocratic, dignified, exalted, gracious, grand, imperial, lofty, majestic, noble, princely, regal, stately

lore 1. beliefs, doctrine, experience, folk-wisdom, mythos, saws, sayings, teaching, traditional wisdom, traditions, wisdom **2**. erudition, knowhow (*Inf.*), knowledge, learning, letters, scholarship

lose 1. be deprived of, displace, drop, fail to keep, forget, mislay, misplace, miss, suffer loss **2**. capitulate, default, fail, fall short, lose out on (*Inf.*), miss, pass up (*Inf.*), yield **3**. be defeated, be the loser, be worsted, come a cropper (*Inf.*), come to grief, get the worst of, lose out, suffer defeat, take a licking (*Inf.*) **4**. consume, deplete, dissipate, drain, exhaust, expend, lavish, misspend, squander, use up, waste **5**. confuse, miss, stray from, wander from **6**. lap, leave behind, outdistance, outrun, outstrip, overtake, pass **7**. dodge, duck, elude, escape, evade, give someone the slip, shake off, slip away, throw off

loser also-ran, dud (*Inf.*), failure, flop (*Inf.*), lemon (*Sl.*), no-hoper (*Austral. sl.*), underdog, washout (*Inf.*)

loss 1. bereavement, deprivation, disappearance, failure, forfeiture, losing, misfortune, mislaying, privation, squandering, waste **2**. cost, damage, defeat, destruction, detriment, disadvantage, harm, hurt, impairment, injury, ruin **3**. *Plural* casualties, dead, death toll, fatalities, number killed (captured, injured, missing, wounded) **4**. *Sometimes plural* debit, debt, deficiency, deficit, depletion, losings, shrinkage **5. at a loss** at one's wits' end, baffled, bewildered, confused, helpless, nonplussed, perplexed, puzzled, stuck (*Inf.*), stumped

lost 1. disappeared, forfeited, mislaid, misplaced, missed, missing, strayed, vanished, wayward **2**. adrift, astray, at sea, disoriented, off-course, off-track **3**. baffled, bewildered, clueless (*Sl.*), confused, helpless, ignorant, mystified, perplexed, puzzled **4**. abolished, annihilated, demolished, destroyed, devastated, eradicated, exterminated, obliterated, perished, ruined, wasted, wiped out, wrecked **5**. absent, absorbed, abstracted, distracted, dreamy, engrossed, entranced, preoccupied, rapt, spellbound, taken up **6**. consumed, dissipated, frittered away, misapplied, misdirected, misspent, misused, squandered, wasted **7**. bygone, dead, extinct, forgotten, gone, lapsed, obsolete, out-of-date, past, unremembered **8**. abandoned, corrupt, damned, depraved, dissolute, fallen, irreclaimable, licentious, profligate, unchaste, wanton

lot 1. assortment, batch, bunch (*Inf.*), collection, consignment, crowd, group, quantity, set **2.** accident, chance, destiny, doom, fate, fortune, hazard, plight, portion **3.** allowance, cut (*Inf.*), parcel, part, percentage, piece, portion, quota, ration, share **4. a lot** *or* **lots** abundance, a great deal, heap(s), large amount, load(s) (*Inf.*), masses (*Inf.*), numbers, ocean(s), oodles (*Inf.*), piles, plenty, quantities, reams (*Inf.*), scores, stack(s) **5. draw lots** choose, cut for aces, cut straws (*Inf.*), decide, pick, select, spin a coin, toss up **6. throw in one's lot with** ally *or* align oneself with, join, join forces with, join fortunes with, make common cause with, support

loth *see* LOATH

lotion balm, cream, embrocation, liniment, salve, solution

lottery 1. draw, raffle, sweepstake **2.** chance, gamble, hazard, risk, toss-up (*Inf.*), venture

loud 1. blaring, blatant, boisterous, booming, clamorous, deafening, earpiercing, ear-splitting, forte (*Music*), high-sounding, noisy, obstreperous, piercing, resounding, rowdy, sonorous, stentorian, strident, strong, thundering, tumultuous, turbulent, vehement, vociferous **2.** *Fig.* brassy, flamboyant, flashy, garish, gaudy, glaring, lurid, ostentatious, showy, tasteless, tawdry, vulgar **3.** brash, brazen, coarse, crass, crude, loudmouthed (*Inf.*), offensive, raucous, vulgar

loudly at full volume, at the top of one's voice, clamorously, deafeningly, fortissimo (*Music*), lustily, noisily, shrilly, uproariously, vehemently, vigorously, vociferously

loudmouth bigmouth (*Sl.*), blowhard (*Inf.*), blusterer, brag, braggadocio, braggart, gasbag (*Sl.*), swaggerer, windbag (*Sl.*)

lounge *v.* **1.** laze, lie about, loaf, loiter, loll, recline, relax, saunter, sprawl, take it easy (*Inf.*) **2.** dawdle, fritter time away, idle, kill time, pass time idly, potter, waste time

lour *see* LOWER[2]

lousy 1. *Sl.* base, contemptible, despicable, dirty, hateful, low, mean, rotten (*Inf.*), vicious, vile **2.** *Sl.* awful, bad, infe-

rior, miserable, no good, poor, rotten (*Inf.*), second-rate, shoddy, slovenly, terrible **3.** lice-infected, lice-infested, lice-ridden, pedicular, pediculous **4. lousy with** *Sl.* **a.** amply supplied with, not short of, rolling in (*Sl.*), well-supplied with **b.** alive with, overrun by, swarming with, teeming with

lout bear, boor, bumpkin, churl, clod, clumsy idiot, dolt, gawk, lubber, lummox (*Inf.*), oaf, yahoo, yob *or* yobbo (*Brit. sl.*)

loutish boorish, bungling, churlish, clodhopping (*Inf.*), coarse, doltish, gawky, gross, ill-bred, ill-mannered, lubberly, lumpen (*Inf.*), lumpish, oafish, rough, stolid, swinish, uncouth, unmannerly

lovable adorable, amiable, attractive, captivating, charming, cuddly, delightful, enchanting, endearing, engaging, fetching (*Inf.*), likable, lovely, pleasing, sweet, winning, winsome

love *v.* **1.** adore, adulate, be attached to, be in love with, cherish, dote on, have affection for, hold dear, idolize, prize, think the world of, treasure, worship **2.** appreciate, delight in, desire, enjoy, fancy, have a weakness for, like, relish, savour, take pleasure in **3.** canoodle (*Sl.*), caress, cuddle, embrace, fondle, kiss, neck (*Inf.*), pet ~*n.* **4.** adoration, adulation, affection, amity, ardour, attachment, devotion, fondness, friendship, infatuation, liking, passion, rapture, regard, tenderness, warmth **5.** delight, devotion, enjoyment, fondness, inclination, liking, partiality, relish, soft spot, taste, weakness **6.** angel, beloved, darling, dear, dearest, dear one, inamorata, inamorato, loved one, lover, sweet, sweetheart, truelove **7. for love** for nothing, freely, free of charge, gratis, pleasurably, without payment **8. for love or money** by any means, ever, under any conditions **9. in love** besotted, charmed, enamoured, enraptured, infatuated, smitten **10. fall in love (with)** bestow one's affections on, be taken with, fall for, lose one's heart (to), take a shine to (*Inf.*)

love affair 1. affair, *affaire de coeur*, amour, intrigue, liaison, relationship, romance **2.** appreciation, devotion, enthusiasm, love, mania, passion

loveless 1. disliked, forsaken, friendless, lovelorn, unappreciated, uncherished, unloved, unvalued **2.** cold, coldhearted, frigid, hard, heartless, icy, insensitive, unfeeling, unfriendly, unloving, unresponsive

lovelorn crossed in love, jilted, languishing, lovesick, mooning, moping, pining, slighted, spurned, unrequited, yearning

lovely 1. admirable, adorable, amiable, attractive, beautiful, charming, comely, exquisite, graceful, handsome, pretty, sweet, winning **2.** agreeable, captivating, delightful, enchanting, engaging, enjoyable, gratifying, nice, pleasant, pleasing

lovemaking act of love, carnal knowledge, coition, coitus, copulation, intercourse, intimacy, mating, sexual intercourse, sexual relations, sexual union *or* congress

lover admirer, beau, beloved, boyfriend, fancy man (*Sl.*), fancy woman (*Sl.*), fiancé, fiancée, flame (*Inf.*), girlfriend, inamorata, inamorato, mistress, paramour, suitor, swain (*Archaic*), sweetheart

lovesick desiring, languishing, longing, lovelorn, pining, yearning

loving affectionate, amorous, ardent, cordial, dear, demonstrative, devoted, doting, fond, friendly, kind, solicitous, tender, warm, warm-hearted

low¹ 1. little, short, small, squat, stunted **2.** deep, depressed, ground-level, low-lying, shallow, subsided, sunken **3.** depleted, insignificant, little, meagre, paltry, reduced, scant, small, sparse, trifling **4.** deficient, inadequate, inferior, low-grade, mediocre, poor, puny, second-rate, shoddy, substandard, worthless **5.** coarse, common, crude, disgraceful, dishonourable, disreputable, gross, ill-bred, obscene, rough, rude, unbecoming, undignified, unrefined, vulgar **6.** humble, lowborn, lowly, meek, obscure, plain, plebeian, poor, simple, unpretentious **7.** blue, brassed off (*Inf.*), dejected, depressed, despondent, disheartened, down, downcast, down in the dumps (*Inf.*), fed up, forlorn, gloomy, glum, miserable, morose, sad, unhappy **8.** debilitated, dying, exhausted, feeble, frail, ill, prostrate, reduced, sinking, stricken, weak **9.** gentle, hushed, muffled, muted, quiet, soft, subdued, whispered **10.** cheap, economical, inexpensive, moderate, modest, reasonable **11.** abject, base, contemptible, dastardly, degraded, depraved, despicable, ignoble, mean, me-

nial, nasty, scurvy, servile, sordid, unworthy, vile, vulgar

low² 1. *v.* bellow, moo **2.** *n.* bellow, bellowing, lowing, moo, mooing

lowdown dope (*Sl.*), gen (*Brit. inf.*), info (*Inf.*), information, inside story, intelligence

low-down base, cheap (*Inf.*), contemptible, despicable, low, mean, nasty, reprehensible, scurvy, ugly, underhand

lower¹ *adj.* **1.** inferior, junior, lesser, low-level, minor, secondary, second-class, smaller, subordinate, under **2.** curtailed, decreased, diminished, lessened, pared down, reduced ~*v.* **3.** depress, drop, fall, let down, make lower, sink, submerge, take down **4.** abase, belittle, condescend, debase, degrade, deign, demean, devalue, disgrace, downgrade, humble, humiliate, stoop **5.** abate, curtail, cut, decrease, diminish, lessen, minimize, moderate, prune, reduce, slash **6.** soften, tone down

lower², lour 1. be brewing, blacken, cloud up *or* over, darken, loom, menace, threaten **2.** frown, give a dirty look, glare, glower, look daggers, look sullen, scowl

lowering 1. black, clouded, cloudy, dark, darkening, forbidding, foreboding, gloomy, grey, heavy, menacing, ominous, overcast, threatening **2.** brooding, frowning, glowering, grim, scowling, sullen, surly

low-grade bad, inferior, not good enough, not up to snuff (*Inf.*), poor, second-rate, substandard

low-key low-pitched, muffled, muted, played down, quiet, restrained, subdued, toned down, understated

lowly 1. ignoble, inferior, lowborn, mean, obscure, plebeian, proletarian, subordinate **2.** docile, dutiful, gentle, humble, meek, mild, modest, submissive, unassuming **3.** average, common, homespun, modest, ordinary, plain, poor, simple, unpretentious

low-minded coarse, crude, dirty, disgusting, filthy, foul, gross, indecent, obscene, rude, smutty, uncouth, vulgar

low-spirited apathetic, blue, brassed off (*Inf.*), dejected, depressed, despondent, down, down-hearted, down in the dumps (*Inf.*), fed up, gloomy, heavy-hearted, low, miserable, moody, sad, unhappy

loyal attached, constant, dependable,

devoted, dutiful, faithful, patriotic, staunch, steadfast, tried and true, true, true-blue, true-hearted, trustworthy, trusty, unswerving, unwavering

loyalty allegiance, constancy, dependability, devotion, faithfulness, fealty, fidelity, patriotism, reliability, staunchness, steadfastness, true-heartedness, trueness, trustiness, trustworthiness

lozenge cough drop, jujube, pastille, tablet, troche

lubberly adj. awkward, blundering, bungling, churlish, clodhopping (Inf.), clownish, clumsy, coarse, crude, doltish, gawky, heavy-handed, loutish, lumbering, lumpen (Inf.), lumpish, oafish, uncouth, ungainly

lubricate grease, make slippery, make smooth, oil, oil the wheels, smear, smooth the way

lucid 1. clear, clear-cut, comprehensible, crystal clear, distinct, evident, explicit, intelligible, limpid, obvious, pellucid, plain, transparent 2. beaming, bright, brilliant, effulgent, gleaming, luminous, radiant, resplendent, shining 3. clear, crystalline, diaphanous, glassy, limpid, pellucid, pure, translucent, transparent 4. all there, clear-headed, compos mentis, in one's right mind, rational, reasonable, sane, sensible, sober, sound

luck 1. accident, chance, destiny, fate, fortuity, fortune, hap (Archaic), hazard 2. advantage, blessing, break (Inf.), fluke, godsend, good fortune, good luck, prosperity, serendipity, stroke, success, windfall

luckily 1. favourably, fortunately, happily, opportunely, propitiously, providentially 2. as it chanced, as luck would have it, by chance, fortuitously

luckless calamitous, cursed, disastrous, doomed, hapless, hopeless, ill-fated, ill-starred, jinxed, star-crossed, unfortunate, unhappy, unlucky, unpropitious, unsuccessful

lucky 1. advantageous, blessed, charmed, favoured, fortunate, prosperous, serendipitous, successful 2. adventitious, auspicious, fortuitous, opportune, propitious, providential, timely

lucrative advantageous, fat, fruitful, gainful, high-income, money-making, paying, productive, profitable, remunerative, well-paid

lucre gain, mammon, money, pelf, profit, riches, spoils, wealth

lucubration 1. brainwork, grind (Inf.), meditation, study 2. dissertation, opus, production, treatise

ludicrous absurd, burlesque, comic, comical, crazy, droll, farcical, funny, incongruous, laughable, nonsensical, odd, outlandish, preposterous, ridiculous, silly, zany

lug carry, drag, haul, heave, hump (Brit. sl.), pull, tow, yank

luggage baggage, bags, cases, gear, impedimenta, paraphernalia, suitcases, things, trunks

lugubrious dirgelike, dismal, doleful, dreary, funereal, gloomy, melancholy, morose, mournful, sad, serious, sombre, sorrowful, woebegone, woeful

lukewarm 1. blood-warm, tepid, warm 2. Fig. apathetic, cold, cool, half-hearted, indifferent, laodicean, phlegmatic, unconcerned, unenthusiastic, uninterested, unresponsive

lull v. 1. allay, calm, compose, hush, lullaby, pacify, quell, quiet, rock to sleep, soothe, still, subdue, tranquillize 2. abate, cease, decrease, diminish, dwindle, ease off, let up, moderate, quieten down, slacken, subside, wane ~n. 3. calm, calmness, hush, let-up (Inf.), pause, quiet, respite, silence, stillness, tranquillity

lullaby berceuse, cradlesong

lumber[1] 1. n. castoffs, clutter, discards, jumble, junk, refuse, rubbish, trash, trumpery, white elephants 2. v. Brit. sl. burden, encumber, impose upon, land, load, saddle

lumber[2] v. clump, lump along, plod, shamble, shuffle, stump, trudge, trundle, waddle

lumbering awkward, blundering, bovine, bumbling, clumsy, elephantine, heavy, heavy-footed, hulking, lubberly, overgrown, ponderous, ungainly, unwieldy

luminary big name, celebrity, dignitary, leading light, lion, notable, personage, somebody, star, V.I.P., worthy

luminescent effulgent, fluorescent, glowing, luminous, phosphorescent, radiant, shining

luminous 1. bright, brilliant, glowing, illuminated, lighted, lit, luminescent, lustrous, radiant, resplendent, shining, vivid 2. clear, evident, intelligible, lucid, obvious, perspicuous, plain, transparent

lump[1] n. **1.** ball, bunch, cake, chunk, clod, cluster, dab, gob, gobbet, group, hunk, mass, nugget, piece, spot, wedge **2.** bulge, bump, growth, protrusion, protuberance, swelling, tumescence, tumour ~v. **3.** agglutinate, aggregate, batch, bunch, coalesce, collect, combine, conglomerate, consolidate, group, mass, pool, unite

lump[2] v. bear, brook, endure, put up with, stand, suffer, take, thole (*Northern dialect*), tolerate

lumpish awkward, bungling, clumsy, doltish, elephantine, gawky, heavy, lethargic, lumbering, oafish, obtuse, puddingy, stolid, stupid, ungainly

lumpy bumpy, clotted, curdled, full of lumps, grainy, granular, knobbly, uneven

lunacy 1. dementia, derangement, idiocy, insanity, madness, mania, psychosis **2.** aberration, absurdity, craziness, folly, foolhardiness, foolishness, idiocy, imbecility, madness, senselessness, stupidity, tomfoolery

lunatic 1. adj. barmy (*Sl.*), bonkers (*Sl.*), crackbrained, crazy, daft, demented, deranged, insane, irrational, mad, maniacal, nuts (*Sl.*), psychotic, unhinged **2.** n. loony (*Sl.*), madman, maniac, nut (*Sl.*), nutcase (*Sl.*), nutter (*Sl.*), psychopath

lunge 1. n. charge, cut, jab, pass, pounce, spring, stab, swing, swipe, thrust **2.** v. bound, charge, cut, dash, dive, fall upon, hit at, jab, leap, pitch into, plunge, poke, pounce, set upon, stab, strike at, thrust

lurch 1. heave, lean, list, pitch, rock, roll, tilt, wallow **2.** reel, stagger, stumble, sway, totter, weave

lure 1. v. allure, attract, beckon, decoy, draw, ensnare, entice, inveigle, invite, lead on, seduce, tempt **2.** n. allurement, attraction, bait, carrot (*Inf.*), come-on (*Inf.*), decoy, enticement, inducement, magnet, siren song, temptation

lurid 1. exaggerated, graphic, melodramatic, sensational, shocking, startling, unrestrained, vivid, yellow (*Of journalism*) **2.** disgusting, ghastly, gory, grim, grisly, gruesome, macabre, revolting, savage, violent **3.** ashen, ghastly, pale, pallid, sallow, wan **4.** bloody, fiery, flaming, glaring, glowering, intense, livid, overbright, sanguine

lurk conceal oneself, crouch, go furtively, hide, lie in wait, move with stealth, prowl, skulk, slink, sneak, snoop

luscious appetizing, delectable, delicious, honeyed, juicy, mouth-watering, palatable, rich, savoury, scrumptious (*Inf.*), succulent, sweet, toothsome, yummy (*Sl.*)

lush 1. abundant, dense, flourishing, green, lavish, overgrown, prolific, rank, teeming, verdant **2.** fresh, juicy, ripe, succulent, tender **3.** elaborate, extravagant, grand, lavish, luxurious, opulent, ornate, palatial, plush (*Inf.*), ritzy (*Sl.*), sumptuous

lust n. **1.** carnality, concupiscence, lasciviousness, lechery, lewdness, libido, licentiousness, pruriency, randiness (*Sl., chiefly Brit.*), salaciousness, sensuality, wantonness **2.** appetence, appetite, avidity, covetousness, craving, cupidity, desire, greed, longing, passion, thirst ~v. **3.** be consumed with desire for, covet, crave, desire, hunger for *or* after, lech after (*Inf.*), need, slaver over, want, yearn

lustful carnal, concupiscent, craving, hankering, horny (*Sl.*), hot-blooded, lascivious, lecherous, lewd, libidinous, licentious, passionate, prurient, randy (*Sl., chiefly Brit.*), raunchy (*U.S. sl.*), sensual, sexy (*Inf.*), unchaste, wanton

lustily forcefully, hard, loudly, powerfully, strongly, vigorously, with all one's might, with might and main

lustiness energy, hardihood, hardiness, healthiness, power, robustness, stoutness, strength, sturdiness, toughness, vigour, virility

lustre 1. burnish, gleam, glint, glitter, gloss, glow, sheen, shimmer, shine, sparkle **2.** brightness, brilliance, dazzle, lambency, luminousness, radiance, resplendence **3.** distinction, fame, glory, honour, illustriousness, prestige, renown

lustreless colourless, dingy, drab, dull, faded, flat, lacklustre, lifeless, matt, pale, tarnished, unburnished, unpolished, washed out

lustrous bright, burnished, dazzling, gleaming, glistening, glossy, glowing, luminous, radiant, shimmering, shining, shiny, sparkling

lusty brawny, energetic, hale, healthy, hearty, in fine fettle, powerful, red-blooded (*Inf.*), robust, rugged, stalwart, stout, strapping, strong, sturdy, vigorous, virile

luxuriance abundance, denseness, excess, exuberance, lavishness, lushness, profusion, rankness, richness, sumptuousness

luxuriant 1. abundant, ample, copious, excessive, lavish, plenteous, plentiful, prodigal, profuse, superabundant **2**. baroque, corinthian, decorated, elaborate, extravagant, fancy, festooned, flamboyant, florid, flowery, ornate, rococo, sumptuous **3**. dense, exuberant, fecund, fertile, flourishing, fruitful, lush, overflowing, productive, prolific, rank, rich, riotous, teeming, thriving

luxuriate 1. bask, delight, enjoy, flourish, indulge, relish, revel, wallow **2**. abound, bloom, burgeon, flourish, grow, prosper, thrive **3**. be in clover, have the time of one's life, live in luxury, live the life of Riley, take it easy, wanton

luxurious 1. comfortable, costly, de luxe, expensive, lavish, magnificent, opulent, plush (*Inf.*), rich, ritzy (*Sl.*), splendid, sumptuous, well-appointed **2**. epicurean, pampered, pleasure-loving, self-indulgent, sensual, sybaritic, voluptuous

luxury 1. affluence, hedonism, opulence, richness, splendour, sumptuousness, voluptuousness **2**. bliss, comfort, delight, enjoyment, gratification, indulgence, pleasure, satisfaction, wellbeing **3**. extra, extravagance, frill, indulgence, nonessential, treat

lying 1. *n*. deceit, dishonesty, dissimulation, double-dealing, duplicity, fabrication, falsity, fibbing, guile, mendacity, perjury, prevarication, untruthfulness **2**. *adj*. deceitful, dishonest, dissembling, double-dealing, false, guileful, mendacious, perfidious, treacherous, two-faced, untruthful

lyric *adj*. **1**. *Of poetry* expressive, lyrical, melodic, musical, songlike **2**. *Of a voice* clear, dulcet, flowing, graceful, light, silvery ~*n*. **3**. *Plural* book, libretto, text, the words, words of a song

lyrical carried away, ecstatic, effusive, emotional, enthusiastic, expressive, impassioned, inspired, poetic, rapturous, rhapsodic

M

macabre cadaverous, deathlike, deathly, dreadful, eerie, frightening, frightful, ghastly, ghostly, ghoulish, grim, grisly, gruesome, hideous, horrid, morbid, unearthly, weird

macerate mash, pulp, soak, soften, steep

machiavellian amoral, artful, astute, crafty, cunning, cynical, deceitful, designing, double-dealing, foxy, intriguing, opportunist, perfidious, scheming, shrewd, sly, underhand, unscrupulous, wily

machinate conspire, contrive, design, devise, engineer, hatch, intrigue, invent, manoeuvre, plan, plot, scheme

machination artifice, cabal, conspiracy, design, device, dodge, intrigue, manoeuvre, plot, ploy, ruse, scheme, stratagem, trick

machine 1. apparatus, appliance, contraption, contrivance, device, engine, instrument, mechanism, tool **2**. agency, machinery, organization, party, setup (*Inf.*), structure, system **3**. *Fig.* agent, automaton, mechanical man, puppet, robot, zombie

machinery 1. apparatus, equipment, gear, instruments, mechanism, tackle, tools, works **2**. agency, channels, machine, organization, procedure, structure, system

mad 1. aberrant, bananas (*Sl.*), barmy (*Sl.*), batty (*Sl.*), bonkers (*Sl.*), crackers (*Sl.*), crazed, crazy (*Inf.*), cuckoo (*Inf.*), delirious, demented, deranged, distracted, frantic, frenzied, insane, loony (*Sl.*), loopy (*Inf.*), lunatic, mental (*Sl.*), *non compos mentis*, nuts (*Sl.*), nutty (*Sl.*), off one's chump (*Sl.*), off one's head, off one's nut (*Sl.*), off one's rocker (*Sl.*), off one's trolley (*Sl.*), of unsound mind, out of one's mind, psychotic, rabid, raving, round the bend (*Brit. sl.*), round the twist (*Brit. sl.*), screwy (*Inf.*), unbalanced, unhinged, unstable **2**. absurd, daft (*Inf.*), foolhardy, foolish, imprudent, irrational, ludicrous, nonsensical, preposterous, senseless, unreasonable, unsafe, unsound, wild **3**. *Inf.* angry, berserk, enraged, exasperated, fuming, furi-

ous, in a wax (*Inf.*), incensed, infuriated, irate, irritated, livid (*Inf.*), raging, resentful, seeing red (*Inf.*), wild, wrathful **4**. ardent, avid, crazy, daft (*Inf.*), devoted, dotty (*Brit. sl.*), enamoured, enthusiastic, fanatical, fond, hooked (*Sl.*), impassioned, infatuated, in love with, keen, nuts (*Sl.*), wild, zealous **5**. abandoned, agitated, boisterous, ebullient, energetic, excited, frenetic, frenzied, gay, riotous, uncontrolled, unrestrained, wild **6**. **like mad** *Inf.* energetically, enthusiastically, excitedly, furiously, madly, quickly, rapidly, speedily, unrestrainedly, violently, wildly

madcap 1. *adj.* crazy, foolhardy, harebrained, heedless, hot-headed, ill-advised, imprudent, impulsive, lively, rash, reckless, thoughtless, wild **2**. *n.* daredevil, hothead, tearaway, wild man

madden annoy, craze, derange, drive one crazy (off one's head, out of one's mind, round the bend (*Brit. sl.*), round the twist (*Brit. sl.*), to distraction), enrage, exasperate, get one's hackles up, incense, inflame, infuriate, irritate, make one's blood boil, make one see red (*Inf.*), make one's hackles rise, provoke, raise one's hackles, unhinge, upset, vex

made-up fabricated, false, fictional, imaginary, invented, make-believe, mythical, specious, trumped-up, unreal, untrue

madhouse 1. funny farm (*Inf.*), insane asylum, loony bin (*Sl.*), lunatic asylum, mental hospital, mental institution, nuthouse (*Sl.*), psychiatric hospital **2**. Babel, bedlam, chaos, pandemonium, turmoil, uproar

madly 1. crazily, deliriously, dementedly, distractedly, frantically, frenziedly, hysterically, insanely, rabidly **2**. absurdly, foolishly, irrationally, ludicrously, nonsensically, senselessly, unreasonably, wildly **3**. energetically, excitedly, furiously, hastily, hurriedly, like mad, quickly, rapidly, recklessly, speedily, violently, wildly **4**. *Inf.* desperately, devotedly, exceedingly, excessively, extremely, intensely, passionately, to distraction

madman or **madwoman** loony (*Sl.*),

lunatic, maniac, mental case (*Sl.*), nut (*Sl.*), nutcase (*Sl.*), nutter (*Sl.*), psycho (*Sl.*), psychopath, psychotic

madness 1. aberration, craziness, delusion, dementia, derangement, distraction, insanity, lunacy, mania, mental illness, psychopathy, psychosis **2**. absurdity, daftness (*Inf.*), folly, foolhardiness, foolishness, nonsense, preposterousness, wildness **3**. anger, exasperation, frenzy, fury, ire, rage, raving, wildness, wrath **4**. ardour, craze, enthusiasm, fanaticism, fondness, infatuation, keenness, passion, rage, zeal **5**. abandon, agitation, excitement, frenzy, furore, intoxication, riot, unrestraint, uproar

maelstrom 1. vortex, whirlpool **2**. bedlam, chaos, confusion, disorder, pandemonium, tumult, turmoil, uproar

maestro expert, genius, master, virtuoso

magazine 1. journal, pamphlet, paper, periodical **2**. ammunition dump, arsenal, depot, powder-room (*Obsolete*), store, storehouse, warehouse

magic *n.* **1**. black art, enchantment, necromancy, occultism, sorcery, sortilege, spell, theurgy, witchcraft, wizardry **2**. conjuring, hocus-pocus, illusion, jiggery-pokery (*Inf., chiefly Brit.*), jugglery, legerdemain, prestidigitation, sleight of hand, trickery **3**. allurement, charm, enchantment, fascination, glamour, magnetism, power ~*adj.* **4**. *Also* **magical** bewitching, charismatic, charming, enchanting, entrancing, fascinating, magnetic, marvellous, miraculous, sorcerous, spellbinding

magician 1. archimage (*Rare*), conjurer, conjuror, enchanter, enchantress, illusionist, necromancer, sorcerer, thaumaturge (*Rare*), theurgist, warlock, witch, wizard **2**. genius, marvel, miracle-worker, spellbinder, virtuoso, wizard, wonder-worker

magisterial arrogant, assertive, authoritative, bossy (*Inf.*), commanding, dictatorial, domineering, high-handed, imperious, lordly, masterful, overbearing, peremptory

magistrate bailie (*Scot.*), J.P., judge, justice, justice of the peace, provost (*Scot.*)

magnanimity beneficence, big-heartedness, bountifulness, charitableness, generosity, high-mindedness, largess, munificence, nobility, open-handedness, selflessness, unselfishness

magnanimous beneficent, big, big-hearted, bountiful, charitable, free, generous, great-hearted, handsome, high-minded, kind, kindly, munificent, noble, open-handed, selfless, ungrudging, unselfish, unstinting

magnate 1. baron, big cheese (*Sl.*), big noise (*Sl.*), big shot (*Sl.*), big wheel (*Sl.*), bigwig (*Sl.*), captain of industry, chief, fat cat (*Sl.*), leader, mogul, Mr. Big (*Sl.*), nabob (*Inf.*), notable, plutocrat, tycoon, V.I.P. **2**. aristocrat, baron, bashaw, grandee, magnifico, merchant, noble, notable, personage, prince

magnetic alluring, attractive, captivating, charismatic, charming, enchanting, entrancing, fascinating, hypnotic, irresistible, mesmerizing, seductive

magnetism allure, appeal, attraction, attractiveness, captivatingness, charisma, charm, draw, drawing power, enchantment, fascination, hypnotism, magic, mesmerism, power, pull, seductiveness, spell

magnification aggrandizement, amplification, augmentation, blow-up (*Inf.*), boost, build-up, deepening, dilation, enhancement, enlargement, exaggeration, expansion, heightening, increase, inflation, intensification

magnificence brilliance, glory, gorgeousness, grandeur, luxuriousness, luxury, majesty, nobility, opulence, pomp, resplendence, splendour, stateliness, sublimity, sumptuousness

magnificent august, brilliant, elegant, elevated, exalted, excellent, fine, glorious, gorgeous, grand, grandiose, imposing, impressive, lavish, luxurious, majestic, noble, opulent, outstanding, princely, regal, resplendent, rich, splendid, stately, sublime, sumptuous, superb, superior, transcendent

magnifico 1. aristocrat, grandee, lord, magnate, noble, patrician, seigneur **2**. bashaw, big cheese (*Sl.*), big noise (*Sl.*), big shot (*Sl.*), big wheel (*Sl.*), bigwig (*Sl.*), mogul, nabob (*Inf.*), notable, personage, V.I.P.

magnify 1. aggrandize, amplify, augment, blow up (*Inf.*), boost, build up, deepen, dilate, enlarge, expand, heighten, increase, intensify **2**. aggravate, blow up, blow up out of all proportion, dramatize, enhance, exaggerate, inflate, make a mountain out of a molehill, overdo, overemphasize, overestimate, overplay, over-rate, overstate

magniloquence bombast, fustian, grandiloquence, loftiness, pomposity, pretentiousness, turgidity

magniloquent bombastic, declama-tory, elevated, exalted, grandiloquent, high-flown, high-sounding, lofty, oro-tund, overblown, pompous, pretentious, rhetorical, sonorous, stilted, turgid

magnitude 1. consequence, eminence, grandeur, greatness, importance, mark, moment, note, significance, weight 2. amount, amplitude, bigness, bulk, capac-ity, dimensions, enormity, expanse, ex-tent, hugeness, immensity, intensity, largeness, mass, measure, proportions, quantity, size, space, strength, vastness, volume

maid 1. damsel, girl, lass, lassie (*Inf.*), maiden, miss, nymph (*Poetic*), wench 2. abigail (*Archaic*), handmaiden (*Archa-ic*), housemaid, maid-servant, servant, serving-maid

maiden n. 1. damsel, girl, lass, lassie (*Inf.*), maid, miss, nymph, virgin, wench ~*adj.* 2. chaste, intact, pure, undefiled, unmarried, unwed, virgin, virginal 3. first, inaugural, initial, initiatory, intro-ductory 4. fresh, new, unbroached, un-tapped, untried, unused

maidenly chaste, decent, decorous, demure, gentle, girlish, modest, pure, re-served, undefiled, unsullied, vestal, vir-ginal, virtuous

mail n. 1. correspondence, letters, packages, parcels, post 2. post, postal service, postal system ~*v.* 3. dispatch, forward, post, send, send by mail *or* post

maim cripple, disable, hamstring, hurt, impair, incapacitate, injure, lame, mangle, mar, mutilate, put out of action, wound

main adj. 1. capital, cardinal, central, chief, critical, crucial, essential, fore-most, head, leading, necessary, outstand-ing, paramount, particular, predomi-nant, pre-eminent, premier, primary, prime, principal, special, supreme, vital 2. absolute, brute, direct, downright, en-tire, mere, pure, sheer, undisguised, ut-most, utter ~*n.* 3. cable, channel, con-duit, duct, line, pipe 4. effort, force, might, potency, power, puissance, strength 5. **in** (*or* **for**) **the main** for the most part, generally, in general, mainly, mostly, on the whole

mainly above all, chiefly, first and foremost, for the most part, generally, in general, in the main, largely, mostly, most of all, on the whole, overall, pre-dominantly, primarily, principally, sub-stantially, to the greatest extent, usually

mainspring cause, driving force, gen-erator, impulse, incentive, inspiration, motivation, motive, origin, prime mover, source

mainstay anchor, backbone, bulwark, buttress, chief support, linchpin, pillar, prop

maintain 1. care for, carry on, con-serve, continue, finance, keep, keep up, prolong, look after, nurture, perpetuate, preserve, provide, retain, supply, sup-port, sustain, take care of, uphold 2. affirm, allege, assert, asseverate, aver, avow, claim, contend, declare, hold, in-sist, profess, state 3. advocate, argue for, back, champion, defend, fight for, justi-fy, plead for, stand by, take up the cudg-els for, uphold, vindicate

maintenance 1. care, carrying-on, conservation, continuance, continuation, keeping, nurture, perpetuation, preser-vation, prolongation, provision, repairs, retainment, supply, support, sustain-ment, sustention, upkeep 2. aliment, ali-mony, allowance, food, keep, livelihood, living, subsistence, support, sustenance, upkeep

majestic august, awesome, dignified, elevated, exalted, grand, grandiose, im-perial, imposing, impressive, kingly, lofty, magnificent, monumental, noble, pompous, princely, regal, royal, splen-did, stately, sublime, superb

majesty augustness, awesomeness, dignity, exaltedness, glory, grandeur, im-posingness, impressiveness, kingliness, loftiness, magnificence, nobility, pomp, queenliness, royalty, splendour, state, stateliness, sublimity

major 1. better, bigger, chief, elder, greater, higher, larger, leading, main, most, senior, superior, supreme, upper-most 2. critical, crucial, grave, great, im-portant, notable, outstanding, pre-eminent, radical, serious, significant, vi-tal, weighty

majority 1. best part, bulk, greater number, mass, more, most, plurality, preponderance, superiority 2. adult-hood, manhood, maturity, seniority, womanhood

make v. 1. assemble, build, compose, constitute, construct, create, fabricate, fashion, forge, form, frame, manufacture, mould, originate, produce, put together, shape, synthesize 2. accomplish, beget, bring about, cause, create, effect, engender, generate, give rise to, lead to, occasion, produce 3. cause, coerce, compel, constrain, dragoon, drive, force, impel, induce, oblige, press, pressurize, prevail upon, require 4. appoint, assign, create, designate, elect, install, invest, nominate, ordain 5. draw up, enact, establish, fix, form, frame, pass 6. add up to, amount to, compose, constitute, embody, form, represent 7. act, carry out, do, effect, engage in, execute, perform, practise, prosecute 8. calculate, estimate, gauge, judge, reckon, suppose, think 9. acquire, clear, earn, gain, get, net, obtain, realize, secure, take in, win 10. arrive at, arrive in time for, attain, catch, get to, meet, reach 11. **make it** *Inf.* arrive (*Inf.*), be successful, come through, get on, get somewhere, prosper, pull through, succeed, survive ∼n. 12. brand, build, character, composition, constitution, construction, cut, designation, form, kind, make-up, mark, model, shape, sort, structure, style, type, variety 13. cast of mind, character, disposition, frame of mind, humour, kidney, make-up, nature, stamp, temper, temperament

make as if *or* **though** act as if *or* though, affect, feign, feint, give the impression that, make a show of, pretend

make away 1. abscond, beat a hasty retreat, clear out (*Inf.*), cut and run (*Inf.*), decamp, depart, flee, fly, make off, run away *or* off, run for it (*Inf.*), scoot, skedaddle (*Inf.*), take to one's heels 2. *With* **with** abduct, carry off, filch, kidnap, knock off (*Sl.*), make off with, nab (*Inf.*), nick (*Sl.*), pilfer, pinch (*Inf.*), purloin, steal, swipe (*Sl.*) 3. *With* **with** bump off (*Sl.*), destroy, dispose of, do away with, do in (*Sl.*), eliminate, get rid of, kill, murder

make-believe 1. *n.* charade, dream, fantasy, imagination, play-acting, pretence, unreality 2. *adj.* dream, fantasized, fantasy, imaginary, imagined, made-up, mock, pretend, pretended, sham, unreal

make believe act as if *or* though, dream, enact, fantasize, imagine, play, play-act, pretend

make do cope, get along *or* by, improvise, manage, muddle through, scrape along *or* by

make for 1. aim for, be bound for, head for *or* towards, proceed towards, steer (a course) for 2. assail, assault, attack, fall on, fly at, go for, have a go at (*Inf.*), lunge at, set upon 3. be conducive to, conduce to, contribute to, facilitate, favour, promote

make off 1. abscond, beat a hasty retreat, bolt, clear out (*Inf.*), cut and run (*Inf.*), decamp, flee, fly, make away, run away *or* off, run for it (*Inf.*), take to one's heels 2. *With* **with** abduct, carry off, filch, kidnap, knock off (*Sl.*), make away with, nab (*Inf.*), nick (*Sl.*), pilfer, pinch (*Inf.*), purloin, run away *or* off with, steal, swipe (*Sl.*)

make out 1. descry, detect, discern, discover, distinguish, espy, perceive, recognize, see 2. comprehend, decipher, fathom, follow, grasp, perceive, realize, see, understand, work out 3. complete, draw up, fill in *or* out, inscribe, write (out) 4. demonstrate, describe, prove, represent, show 5. assert, claim, let on, make as if *or* though, pretend 6. fare, get on, manage, prosper, succeed, thrive

maker author, builder, constructor, director, fabricator, framer, manufacturer, producer

Maker Creator, God

makeshift 1. *adj.* expedient, jury (*Chiefly nautical*), make-do, provisional, rough and ready, stopgap, substitute, temporary 2. *n.* expedient, shift, stopgap, substitute

make-up 1. cosmetics, face (*Inf.*), greasepaint (*Theatre*), *maquillage*, paint (*Inf.*), powder, war paint (*Inf., humorous*) 2. arrangement, assembly, composition, configuration, constitution, construction, form, format, formation, organization, structure 3. build, cast of mind, character, constitution, disposition, figure, frame of mind, make, nature, stamp, temper, temperament

make up 1. compose, comprise, constitute, form 2. coin, compose, concoct, construct, cook up (*Inf.*), create, devise, dream up, fabricate, formulate, frame, hatch, invent, originate, trump up, write 3. complete, fill, meet, supply 4. *With* **for** atone, balance, compensate, make amends, offset, recompense, redeem, redress, requite 5. bury the hatchet, call it quits, come to terms, compose, forgive and forget, make peace, mend, reconcile, settle, shake hands **6. make up one's mind** choose, come to a decision, decide, determine, make a decision, reach a decision, resolve, settle **7. make up to** *Inf.* chat up (*Inf.*), court, curry favour with, flirt with, make overtures to, woo

making 1. assembly, building, composition, construction, creation, fabrication, forging, manufacture, production **2. in the making** budding, coming, emergent, growing, nascent, potential

makings 1. beginnings, capability, capacity, ingredients, materials, potentiality, potential(s), qualities **2.** earnings, income, proceeds, profits, returns, revenue, takings

maladjusted alienated, disturbed, estranged, hung-up (*Sl.*), neurotic, unstable

maladministration blundering, bungling, corruption, dishonesty, incompetence, inefficiency, malfeasance (*Law*), malpractice, misgovernment, mismanagement, misrule

maladroit 1. awkward, bungling, cack-handed (*Inf.*), clumsy, hamfisted *or* -handed (*Inf.*), inept, inexpert, unhandy, unskilful **2.** gauche, inconsiderate, inelegant, insensitive, tactless, thoughtless, undiplomatic, untoward

malady affliction, ailment, complaint, disease, disorder, ill, illness, indisposition, infirmity, sickness

malaise angst, anxiety, depression, discomfort, disquiet, doldrums, enervation, illness, lassitude, melancholy, sickness, unease, weakness

malapropos 1. *adj.* ill-timed, impertinent, inapposite, inappropriate, inapt, inopportune, misapplied, out of place, unseemly, unsuitable **2.** *adv.* impertinently, inappositely, inappropriately, inaptly, inopportunely, out of turn, unseasonably, unsuitably, untimely **3.** *n.* blunder, faux pas, gaffe, malapropism, solecism

malcontent 1. *adj.* disaffected, discontented, disgruntled, disgusted, dissatisfied, dissentious, factious, ill-disposed, rebellious, resentful, restive, unhappy, unsatisfied **2.** *n.* agitator, complainer, fault-finder, grouch (*Inf.*), grouser, grumbler, mischief-maker, rebel, troublemaker

male manful, manlike, manly, masculine, virile

malediction anathema, curse, damnation, damning, denunciation, execration, imprecation, malison (*Archaic*)

malefactor convict, criminal, crook (*Inf.*), culprit, delinquent, evildoer, felon, lawbreaker, miscreant, offender, outlaw, transgressor, villain, wrongdoer

maleficent baleful, deleterious, destructive, detrimental, evil, harmful, hurtful, injurious, malign, malignant, noxious, pernicious

malevolence hate, hatred, ill will, malice, maliciousness, malignity, rancour, spite, spitefulness, vengefulness, vindictiveness

malevolent baleful, evil-minded, hateful (*Archaic*), hostile, ill-natured, malicious, malign, malignant, pernicious, rancorous, spiteful, vengeful, vicious, vindictive

malformation crookedness, deformity, distortion, misshape, misshapenness

malformed abnormal, contorted, crooked, deformed, distorted, irregular, misshapen, twisted

malfunction 1. *v.* break down, develop a fault, fail, go wrong **2.** *n.* breakdown, defect, failure, fault, flaw, impairment

malice animosity, animus, bad blood, bitterness, enmity, evil intent, hate, hatred, ill will, malevolence, maliciousness, malignity, rancour, spite, spitefulness, spleen, vengefulness, venom, vindictiveness

malicious baleful, bitchy (*Sl.*), bitter, catty (*Inf.*), evil-minded, hateful, ill-disposed, ill-natured, injurious, malevolent, malignant, mischievous, pernicious, rancorous, resentful, spiteful, vengeful, vicious

malign 1. *adj.* bad, baleful, baneful, deleterious, destructive, evil, harmful, hostile, hurtful, injurious, malevolent, malignant, pernicious, vicious, wicked **2.** *v.* abuse, blacken (someone's name), calumniate, defame, denigrate, derogate, disparage, do a hatchet job on (*Inf.*), harm, injure, libel, revile, run down, slander, smear, speak ill of, traduce, vilify

malignant 1. baleful, bitter, destructive, harmful, hostile, hurtful, inimical, injurious, malevolent, malicious, malign, of evil intent, pernicious, spiteful, vicious **2.** *Medical* cancerous, dangerous, deadly, evil, fatal, irremediable, metastatic, uncontrollable, virulent

malignity 1. animosity, animus, bad blood, bitterness, evil, hate, hatred, hostility, ill will, malevolence, malice, maliciousness, rancour, spite, vengefulness, venom, viciousness, vindictiveness, wickedness **2.** balefulness, deadliness, destructiveness, harmfulness, hurtfulness, perniciousness, virulence

malleable 1. ductile, plastic, soft, workable **2.** adaptable, biddable, compliant, governable, impressionable, manageable, pliable, tractable

malodorous evil-smelling, fetid, foul-smelling, mephitic, nauseating, niffy (*Brit. sl.*), noisome, offensive, putrid, rank, reeking, smelly, stinking

malpractice 1. abuse, dereliction, misbehaviour, misconduct, mismanagement, negligence **2.** abuse, misdeed, offence, transgression

maltreat abuse, bully, damage, handle roughly, harm, hurt, ill-treat, injure, mistreat

maltreatment abuse, bullying, harm, ill-treatment, ill-usage, injury, mistreatment, rough handling

mammoth Brobdingnagian, colossal, enormous, gargantuan, giant, gigantic, huge, immense, jumbo (*Inf.*), massive, mighty, monumental, mountainous, prodigious, stupendous, titanic, vast

man *n.* **1.** bloke (*Brit. inf.*), chap (*Inf.*), gentleman, guy (*Inf.*), male **2.** adult, being, body, human, human being, individual, one, person, personage, somebody, soul **3.** Homo sapiens, humanity, humankind, human race, mankind, mortals, people **4.** attendant, employee, follower, hand, hireling, manservant, retainer, servant, soldier, subject, subordinate, valet, vassal, worker, workman **5.** beau, boyfriend, husband, lover, partner, spouse **6. to a man** bar none, every one, one and all, unanimously, without exception ~*v.* **7.** crew, fill, furnish with men, garrison, occupy, people, staff

manacle 1. *n.* bond, chain, fetter, gyve (*Archaic*), handcuff, iron, shackle, tie **2.** *v.* bind, chain, check, clap *or* put in irons, confine, constrain, curb, fetter, hamper, handcuff, inhibit, put in chains, restrain, shackle, tie one's hands

manage 1. administer, be in charge

(of), command, concert, conduct, direct, govern, manipulate, oversee, preside over, rule, run, superintend, supervise **2.** accomplish, arrange, bring about *or* off, contrive, cope with, deal with, effect, engineer, succeed **3.** control, dominate, govern, guide, handle, influence, manipulate, operate, pilot, ply, steer, train, use, wield **4.** carry on, cope, fare, get along, get by, get on, make do, make out, muddle through, shift, survive

manageable amenable, compliant, controllable, convenient, docile, easy, governable, handy, submissive, tamable, tractable, wieldy

management 1. administration, board, bosses (*Inf.*), directorate, directors, employers, executive(s) **2.** administration, care, charge, command, conduct, control, governance, government, guidance, handling, manipulation, operation, rule, running, superintendence, supervision

manager administrator, boss (*Inf.*), comptroller, conductor, controller, director, executive, gaffer (*Inf.*), governor, head, organizer, overseer, proprietor, superintendent, supervisor

mandate authority, authorization, bidding, charge, command, commission, decree, directive, edict, fiat, injunction, instruction, order, precept, sanction, warrant

mandatory binding, compulsory, obligatory, required, requisite

manful bold, brave, courageous, daring, determined, gallant, hardy, heroic, indomitable, intrepid, manly, noble, powerful, resolute, stalwart, stout, stout-hearted, strong, valiant, vigorous

manfully boldly, bravely, courageously, desperately, determinedly, gallantly, hard, heroically, intrepidly, like a Trojan, like one possessed, like the devil, nobly, powerfully, resolutely, stalwartly, stoutly, strongly, to the best of one's ability, valiantly, vigorously, with might and main

mangle butcher, cripple, crush, cut, deform, destroy, disfigure, distort, hack, lacerate, maim, mar, maul, mutilate, rend, ruin, spoil, tear, wreck

mangy dirty, mean, moth-eaten, scabby (*Inf.*), scruffy, seedy, shabby, shoddy, squalid

manhandle 1. handle roughly, knock about, maul, paw (*Inf.*), pull, push, rough up **2**. carry, haul, heave, hump (*Brit. sl.*), lift, manoeuvre, pull, push, shove, tug

manhood bravery, courage, determination, firmness, fortitude, hardihood, manfulness, manliness, masculinity, maturity, mettle, resolution, spirit, strength, valour, virility

mania 1. aberration, craziness, delirium, dementia, derangement, disorder, frenzy, insanity, lunacy, madness **2**. cacoethes, craving, craze, desire, enthusiasm, fad (*Inf.*), fetish, fixation, obsession, partiality, passion, preoccupation, rage, thing (*Inf.*)

maniac 1. loony (*Sl.*), lunatic, madman, madwoman, nutcase (*Sl.*), nutter (*Brit. sl.*), psycho (*Sl.*), psychopath **2**. enthusiast, fan, fanatic, fiend (*Inf.*), freak (*Sl.*)

maniacal *or* **manic** berserk, crazed, crazy, demented, deranged, frenzied, insane, lunatic, mad, nutty (*Sl.*), psychotic, raving, unbalanced, wild

manifest 1. *adj.* apparent, clear, conspicuous, distinct, evident, glaring, noticeable, obvious, open, palpable, patent, plain, unmistakable, visible **2**. *v.* declare, demonstrate, display, establish, evince, exhibit, expose, express, make plain, prove, reveal, set forth, show

manifestation appearance, demonstration, disclosure, display, exhibition, exposure, expression, indication, instance, mark, materialization, revelation, show, sign, symptom, token

manifold abundant, assorted, copious, diverse, diversified, many, multifarious, multifold, multiple, multiplied, multitudinous, numerous, varied, various

manipulate 1. employ, handle, operate, ply, use, wield, work **2**. conduct, control, direct, engineer, guide, influence, manoeuvre, negotiate, steer

mankind Homo sapiens, humanity, humankind, human race, man, people

manliness boldness, bravery, courage, fearlessness, firmness, hardihood, heroism, independence, intrepidity, manfulness, manhood, masculinity, mettle, resolution, stoutheartedness, valour, vigour, virility

manly bold, brave, courageous, daring, dauntless, fearless, gallant, hardy, heroic, male, manful, masculine, muscular, noble, powerful, red-blooded (*Inf.*), resolute, robust, stout-hearted, strapping, strong, valiant, valorous, vigorous, virile, well-built

man-made artificial, ersatz, manufactured, plastic (*Sl.*), synthetic

manner 1. air, appearance, aspect, bearing, behaviour, comportment, conduct, demeanour, deportment, look, mien (*Literary*), presence, tone **2**. approach, custom, fashion, form, genre, habit, line, means, method, mode, practice, procedure, process, routine, style, tack, tenor, usage, way, wont **3**. brand, breed, category, form, kind, nature, sort, type, variety

mannered affected, artificial, posed, pretentious, pseudo (*Inf.*), put-on, stilted

mannerism characteristic, foible, habit, idiosyncrasy, peculiarity, quirk, trait, trick

mannerly civil, civilized, courteous, decorous, genteel, gentlemanly, gracious, ladylike, polished, polite, refined, respectful, well-behaved, well-bred, well-mannered

manners 1. bearing, behaviour, breeding, carriage, comportment, conduct, demeanour, deportment **2**. ceremony, courtesy, decorum, etiquette, formalities, good form, polish, politeness, politesse, proprieties, protocol, refinement, social graces, the done thing

manoeuvrable fast-moving, handleable, manipulatable, mobile, responsive, versatile

manoeuvre *n.* **1**. action, artifice, dodge, intrigue, machination, move, movement, plan, plot, ploy, ruse, scheme, stratagem, subterfuge, tactic, trick **2**. deployment, evolution, exercise, movement, operation ~*v.* **3**. contrive, devise, engineer, intrigue, machinate, manage, manipulate, plan, plot, pull strings, scheme, wangle (*Inf.*) **4**. deploy, exercise, move **5**. direct, drive, guide, handle, navigate, negotiate, pilot, steer

mansion abode, dwelling, habitation, hall, manor, residence, seat, villa

mantle *n.* **1**. *Archaic* cape, cloak, hood, shawl, wrap **2**. blanket, canopy, cloud, cover, covering, curtain, envelope, pall, screen, shroud, veil ~*v.* **3**. blanket, cloak, cloud, cover, disguise, envelop, hide, mask, overspread, screen, shroud, veil, wrap

manual 1. *adj.* done by hand, hand-operated, human, physical **2**. *n.* bible, enchiridion (*Rare*), guide, guidebook, handbook, instructions, workbook

manufacture *v.* **1.** assemble, build, compose, construct, create, fabricate, forge, form, make, mass-produce, mould, process, produce, put together, shape, turn out **2.** concoct, cook up (*Inf.*), devise, fabricate, hatch, invent, make up, think up, trump up ~*n.* **3.** assembly, construction, creation, fabrication, making, mass-production, produce, production

manufacturer builder, constructor, creator, fabricator, factory-owner, industrialist, maker, producer

manumission deliverance, emancipation, enfranchisement, freeing, liberation, release, unchaining

manumit deliver, emancipate, enfranchise, free, liberate, release, set free, unchain

manure compost, droppings, dung, muck, ordure

many *adj.* **1.** abundant, copious, countless, divers (*Archaic*), frequent, innumerable, manifold, multifarious, multifold, multitudinous, myriad, numerous, profuse, sundry, umpteen (*Inf.*), varied, various ~*n.* **2.** a horde, a lot, a mass, a multitude, a thousand and one, heaps (*Inf.*), large numbers, lots (*Inf.*), piles (*Inf.*), plenty, scores, tons (*Inf.*), umpteen (*Inf.*) **3. the many** crowd, hoi polloi, majority, masses, multitude, people, rank and file

mar blemish, blight, blot, damage, deface, detract from, disfigure, harm, hurt, impair, injure, maim, mangle, mutilate, ruin, scar, spoil, stain, sully, taint, tarnish, vitiate

maraud despoil, forage, foray, harry, loot, pillage, plunder, raid, ransack, ravage, reive (*Dialect*), sack

marauder bandit, brigand, buccaneer, cateran (*Scot.*), corsair, freebooter, mosstrooper, outlaw, pillager, pirate, plunderer, raider, ravager, reiver (*Dialect*), robber

march *v.* **1.** file, footslog, pace, parade, stalk, stride, strut, tramp, tread, walk ~*n.* **2.** hike, routemarch, tramp, trek, walk **3.** demo (*Inf.*), demonstration, parade, procession **4.** gait, pace, step, stride **5.** advance, development, evolution, progress, progression **6. on the march** advancing, afoot, astir, en route, marching,

on one's way, on the way, proceeding, progressing, under way

marches borderland, borders, boundaries, confines, frontiers, limits, marchlands

margin 1. border, bound, boundary, brim, brink, confine, edge, limit, perimeter, periphery, rim, side, verge **2.** allowance, compass, elbowroom, extra, latitude, leeway, play, room, scope, space, surplus

marginal 1. bordering, borderline, on the edge, peripheral **2.** insignificant, low, minimal, minor, negligible, slight, small

marijuana bhang, cannabis, charas, dope (*Sl.*), ganja, grass (*Sl.*), hash (*Sl.*), hashish, hemp, kif, leaf (*Sl.*), mary jane (*U.S. sl.*), pot (*Sl.*), smoke (*Inf.*), stuff (*Sl.*), tea (*U.S. sl.*), weed (*Sl.*)

marine maritime, nautical, naval, ocean-going, oceanic, pelagic, saltwater, sea, seafaring, seagoing, thalassic

mariner bluejacket, gob (*Inf.*), hand, Jack Tar, matelot (*Brit. sl.*), navigator, sailor, salt, sea dog, seafarer, seafaring man, seaman, tar

marital conjugal, connubial, married, matrimonial, nuptial, spousal, wedded

maritime 1. marine, nautical, naval, oceanic, sea, seafaring **2.** coastal, littoral, seaside

mark *n.* **1.** blemish, blot, blotch, bruise, dent, impression, line, nick, pock, scar, scratch, smudge, splotch, spot, stain, streak **2.** badge, blaze, brand, characteristic, device, earmark, emblem, evidence, feature, hallmark, impression, incision, index, indication, label, note, print, proof, seal, sign, stamp, symbol, symptom, token **3.** criterion, level, measure, norm, standard, yardstick **4.** aim, end, goal, object, objective, purpose, target **5.** consequence, dignity, distinction, eminence, fame, importance, influence, notability, note, notice, prestige, quality, regard, standing **6.** footmark, footprint, sign, trace, track, trail, vestige **7. make one's mark** achieve recognition, be a success, find a place in the sun, get on in the world, make a success of oneself, make good, make it (*Inf.*), make something of oneself, prosper, succeed ~*v.* **8.** blemish, blot, blotch, brand, bruise, dent, impress, imprint, nick, scar, scratch, smudge, splotch, stain, streak **9.** brand, characterize, identify, label, stamp **10.** betoken, denote, distinguish, evince, exemplify, illustrate, show **11**. attend, hearken (*Archaic*), mind, note, notice, observe, pay attention, pay heed, regard, remark, watch **12**. appraise, assess, correct, evaluate, grade

marked apparent, clear, considerable, conspicuous, decided, distinct, evident, manifest, notable, noted, noticeable, obvious, outstanding, patent, prominent, pronounced, remarkable, salient, signal, striking

markedly clearly, considerably, conspicuously, decidedly, distinctly, evidently, greatly, manifestly, notably, noticeably, obviously, outstandingly, patently, remarkably, signally, strikingly, to a great extent

market 1. *n*. bazaar, fair, mart **2**. *v*. offer for sale, retail, sell, vend

marketable in demand, merchantable, salable, sought after, vendible, wanted

marksman, -woman crack shot (*Inf.*), deadeye (*Inf., chiefly U.S.*), dead shot (*Inf.*), good shot, sharpshooter

maroon abandon, cast ashore, cast away, desert, leave, leave high and dry (*Inf.*), strand

marriage 1. espousal, match, matrimony, nuptial rites, nuptials, wedding, wedding ceremony, wedlock **2**. alliance, amalgamation, association, confederation, coupling, link, merger, union

married 1. hitched (*Inf.*), joined, one, spliced (*Inf.*), united, wed, wedded **2**. conjugal, connubial, husbandly, marital, matrimonial, nuptial, spousal, wifely

marrow core, cream, essence, gist, heart, kernel, pith, quick, quintessence, soul, spirit, substance

marry 1. become man and wife, espouse, get hitched (*Inf.*), get spliced (*Inf.*), take the plunge (*Inf.*), take to wife, tie the knot (*Inf.*), walk down the aisle (*Inf.*), wed, wive (*Archaic*) **2**. ally, bond, join, knit, link, match, merge, splice, tie, unify, unite, yoke

marsh bog, fen, morass, moss (*Scot., & northern English dialect*), quagmire, slough, swamp

marshal 1. align, arrange, array, assemble, collect, deploy, dispose, draw up, gather, group, line up, muster, order, organize, rank **2**. conduct, escort, guide, lead, shepherd, usher

marshy boggy, fenny, miry, quaggy, spongy, swampy, waterlogged, wet

martial bellicose, belligerent, brave, heroic, military, soldierly, warlike

martinet disciplinarian, drillmaster, stickler

martyrdom agony, anguish, ordeal, persecution, suffering, torment, torture

marvel 1. *v*. be amazed, be awed, be filled with surprise, gape, gaze, goggle, wonder **2**. *n*. genius, miracle, phenomenon, portent, prodigy, whiz (*Inf.*), wonder

marvellous 1. amazing, astonishing, astounding, breathtaking, extraordinary, miraculous, phenomenal, prodigious, remarkable, singular, spectacular, stupendous, wondrous **2**. difficult *or* hard to believe, fabulous, fantastic, implausible, improbable, incredible, surprising, unbelievable, unlikely **3**. *Inf.* colossal, excellent, fabulous (*Inf.*), fantastic (*Inf.*), glorious, great (*Inf.*), magnificent, sensational, smashing (*Inf.*), splendid, stupendous, super (*Inf.*), superb, terrific (*Inf.*), wonderful

masculine 1. male, manful, manlike, manly, mannish, virile **2**. bold, brave, gallant, hardy, muscular, powerful, red-blooded (*Inf.*), resolute, robust, stout-hearted, strapping, strong, vigorous, well-built

mask *n*. **1**. domino, false face, visor, vizard (*Archaic*) **2**. blind, camouflage, cloak, concealment, cover, cover-up, disguise, façade, front, guise, screen, semblance, show, veil, veneer ~*v*. **3**. camouflage, cloak, conceal, cover, disguise, hide, obscure, screen, veil

masquerade *n*. **1**. costume ball, fancy dress party, mask, masked ball, masked party, mummery, revel **2**. costume, disguise, domino **3**. cloak, cover, cover-up, deception, disguise, dissimulation, front (*Inf.*), guise, imposture, mask, pose, pretence, put-on (*Sl.*), screen, subterfuge ~*v*. **4**. disguise, dissemble, dissimulate, impersonate, mask, pass oneself off, pose, pretend (to be)

mass *n*. **1**. block, chunk, concretion, hunk, lump, piece **2**. aggregate, body, collection, entirety, sum, sum total, totality, whole **3**. accumulation, aggregation, assemblage, batch, bunch, collection, combination, conglomeration, heap, load, lot, pile, quantity, stack **4**. assemblage, band, body, bunch (*Inf.*), crowd, group, horde, host, lot, mob, number, throng, troop **5**. body, bulk, greater part, lion's share, majority, preponderance **6.** bulk, dimension, greatness, magnitude, size **7. the masses** commonalty, common people, crowd, hoi polloi, multitude ~*adj.* **8.** extensive, general, indiscriminate, large-scale, pandemic, popular, wholesale, widespread ~*v.* **9.** accumulate, amass, assemble, collect, congregate, forgather, gather, mob, muster, rally, swarm, throng

massacre 1. *n.* annihilation, blood bath, butchery, carnage, extermination, killing, mass slaughter, murder, slaughter **2.** *v.* annihilate, butcher, cut to pieces, exterminate, kill, mow down, murder, slaughter, slay, wipe out

massage 1. *n.* kneading, manipulation, rubbing, rub-down **2.** *v.* knead, manipulate, rub, rub down

massive big, bulky, colossal, enormous, extensive, gargantuan, gigantic, great, heavy, hefty, huge, hulking, immense, imposing, impressive, mammoth, monster, monumental, ponderous, solid, substantial, titanic, vast, weighty, whacking (*Inf.*), whopping (*Inf.*)

master *n.* **1.** boss (*Inf.*), captain, chief, commander, controller, director, employer, governor, head, lord, manager, overlord, overseer, owner, principal, ruler, skipper (*Inf.*), superintendent **2.** ace (*Inf.*), adept, dab hand (*Brit. inf.*), doyen, expert, genius, maestro, past master, pro (*Inf.*), virtuoso, wizard **3.** guide, guru, instructor, pedagogue, preceptor, schoolmaster, spiritual leader, swami, teacher, tutor ~*adj.* **4.** adept, crack (*Inf.*), expert, masterly, proficient, skilful, skilled **5.** chief, controlling, foremost, grand, great, leading, main, predominant, prime, principal ~*v.* **6.** acquire, become proficient in, get the hang of (*Inf.*), grasp, learn **7.** bridle, check, conquer, curb, defeat, overcome, overpower, quash, quell, subdue, subjugate, suppress, tame, triumph over, vanquish **8.** command, control, direct, dominate, govern, manage, regulate, rule

masterful 1. adept, adroit, clever, consummate, crack (*Inf.*), deft, dexterous, excellent, expert, exquisite, fine, finished, first-rate, masterly, skilful, skilled, superior, superlative, supreme **2.** arrogant, authoritative, bossy (*Inf.*), despotic, dictatorial, domineering, high-handed, imperious, magisterial, over-

bearing, overweening, peremptory, self-willed, tyrannical

masterly adept, adroit, clever, consummate, crack (*Inf.*), dexterous, excellent, expert, exquisite, fine, finished, first-rate, masterful, skilful, skilled, superior, superlative, supreme

mastermind 1. *v.* be the brains behind (*Inf.*), conceive, devise, direct, manage, organize, plan **2.** *n.* architect, authority, brain(s) (*Inf.*), director, engineer, genius, intellect, manager, organizer, planner, virtuoso

masterpiece *chef d'oeuvre*, classic, jewel, magnum opus, master work, *pièce de résistance, tour de force*

mastery 1. command, comprehension, familiarity, grasp, knowledge, understanding **2.** ability, acquirement, attainment, cleverness, deftness, dexterity, expertise, finesse, know-how (*Inf.*), proficiency, prowess, skill, virtuosity **3.** ascendancy, authority, command, conquest, control, domination, dominion, pre-eminence, rule, superiority, supremacy, sway, triumph, upper hand, victory, whip hand

masticate champ, chew, crunch, eat, munch

masturbation autoeroticism, onanism, playing with oneself (*Sl.*), self-abuse

match *n.* **1.** bout, competition, contest, game, test, trial **2.** competitor, counterpart, equal, equivalent, peer, rival **3.** companion, complement, counterpart, equal, equivalent, fellow, mate, tally **4.** copy, dead ringer (*Sl.*), double, duplicate, equal, lookalike, replica, ringer (*Sl.*), spit (*Inf.*), spit and image (*Inf.*), spitting image (*Inf.*), twin **5.** affiliation, alliance, combination, couple, duet, marriage, pair, pairing, partnership, union ~*v.* **6.** ally, combine, couple, join, link, marry, mate, pair, unite, yoke **7.** accompany, accord, adapt, agree, blend, coordinate, correspond, fit, go with, harmonize, suit, tally, tone with **8.** compare, compete, contend, emulate, equal, measure up to, oppose, pit against, rival, vie

matching analogous, comparable, coordinating, corresponding, double, duplicate, equal, equivalent, identical, like, paired, parallel, same, toning, twin

matchless consummate, exquisite, incomparable, inimitable, peerless, perfect, superlative, supreme, unequalled, unique, unmatched, unparalleled, unrivalled

mate n. **1.** better half (*Humorous*), husband, partner, spouse, wife **2.** *Inf.* buddy (*Inf.*), china (*Brit. sl.*), chum (*Inf.*), comrade, crony, friend, pal (*Inf.*) **3.** associate, colleague, companion, compeer, co-worker, fellow-worker **4.** assistant, helper, subordinate **5.** companion, double, fellow, match, twin ~v. **6.** breed, copulate, couple, pair **7.** marry, match, wed **8.** couple, join, match, pair, yoke

material n. **1.** body, constituents, element, matter, stuff, substance **2.** data, evidence, facts, information, notes, work **3.** cloth, fabric, stuff ~adj. **4.** bodily, concrete, corporeal, fleshly, nonspiritual, palpable, physical, substantial, tangible, worldly **5.** consequential, essential, grave, important, indispensable, key, meaningful, momentous, serious, significant, vital, weighty **6.** applicable, apposite, apropos, germane, pertinent, relevant

materialize appear, come about, come into being, come to pass, happen, occur, take place, take shape, turn up

materially considerably, essentially, gravely, greatly, much, seriously, significantly, substantially

materiel accoutrements, apparatus, equipment, gear, hardware, machinery, materials, stores, supplies, tackle, tools

maternal motherly

maternity motherhood, motherliness

matrimonial conjugal, connubial, hymeneal, marital, married, nuptial, spousal, wedded, wedding

matrimony marital rites, marriage, nuptials, wedding ceremony, wedlock

matrix forge, mould, origin, source, womb

matted knotted, tangled, tousled, uncombed

matter n. **1.** body, material, stuff, substance **2.** affair, business, concern, episode, event, incident, issue, occurrence, proceeding, question, situation, subject, thing, topic, transaction **3.** amount, quantity, sum **4.** argument, context, purport, sense, subject, substance, text, thesis **5.** consequence, import, importance, moment, note, significance, weight **6.** complication, difficulty, distress, problem, trouble, upset, worry **7.** *Medical* discharge, purulence, pus, secretion ~v. **8.** be important, be of consequence, carry weight, count, have influence, make a difference, mean something, signify

matter-of-fact deadpan, down-to-earth, dry, dull, emotionless, flat, lifeless, mundane, plain, prosaic, sober, unembellished, unimaginative, unsentimental, unvarnished

mature 1. *adj.* adult, complete, fit, full-blown, fully fledged, full-grown, grown, grown-up, matured, mellow, of age, perfect, prepared, ready, ripe, ripened, seasoned **2.** *v.* age, become adult, bloom, come of age, develop, grow up, maturate, mellow, perfect, reach adulthood, ripen, season

maturity adulthood, completion, experience, full bloom, full growth, fullness, majority, manhood, maturation, matureness, perfection, ripeness, wisdom, womanhood

maudlin lachrymose, mawkish, mushy (*Inf.*), overemotional, sentimental, slushy (*Inf.*), soppy (*Brit. inf.*), tearful, weepy (*Inf.*)

maul 1. abuse, handle roughly, ill-treat, manhandle, molest, paw **2.** batter, beat, beat up (*Inf.*), claw, knock about, lacerate, mangle, pummel, rough up, thrash

maunder 1. dawdle, dilly-dally (*Inf.*), drift, idle, loaf, meander, mooch (*Sl.*), potter, ramble, straggle, stray, traipse (*Inf.*) **2.** babble, blather, blether, chatter, gabble, prattle, rabbit (*Brit. sl.*), ramble, rattle on, witter (*Inf.*)

maw craw, crop, gullet, jaws, mouth, stomach, throat

mawkish 1. emotional, feeble, gushy (*Inf.*), maudlin, mushy (*Inf.*), schmaltzy (*Sl.*), sentimental, slushy (*Inf.*), soppy (*Brit. inf.*) **2.** disgusting, flat, foul, insipid, jejune, loathsome, nauseous, offensive, stale, vapid

maxim adage, aphorism, apophthegm, axiom, byword, gnome, motto, proverb, rule, saw, saying

maximum 1. *n.* apogee, ceiling, crest, extremity, height, most, peak, pinnacle, summit, top, upper limit, utmost, uttermost, zenith **2.** *adj.* greatest, highest, maximal, most, paramount, supreme, topmost, utmost

maybe it could be, mayhap (*Archaic*), peradventure (*Archaic*), perchance (*Archaic*), perhaps, possibly

mayhem chaos, commotion, confusion, destruction, disorder, fracas, havoc, trouble, violence

maze 1. convolutions, intricacy, labyrinth, meander **2**. *Fig.* bewilderment, confusion, imbroglio, mesh, perplexity, puzzle, snarl, tangle, uncertainty, web

mazy baffling, bewildering, confused, confusing, intricate, labyrinthine, perplexing, puzzling, serpentine, twisting, twisting and turning, winding

meadow field, grassland, lea (*Poetic*), ley, pasture

meagre 1. deficient, exiguous, inadequate, insubstantial, little, paltry, poor, puny, scanty, scrimpy, short, skimpy, slender, slight, small, spare, sparse **2**. bony, emaciated, gaunt, hungry, lank, lean, scraggy, scrawny, skinny, starved, thin, underfed **3**. barren, infertile, poor, unfruitful, unproductive, weak

mealy-mouthed afraid, equivocal, euphemistic, hesitant, indirect, mincing, overdelicate, prim, reticent

mean¹ *v.* **1**. betoken, connote, convey, denote, drive at, express, hint at, imply, indicate, purport, represent, say, signify, spell, stand for, suggest, symbolize **2**. aim, aspire, contemplate, design, desire, have in mind, intend, plan, propose, purpose, set out, want, wish **3**. design, destine, fate, fit, make, match, predestine, preordain, suit **4**. bring about, cause, engender, entail, give rise to, involve, lead to, necessitate, produce, result in **5**. adumbrate, augur, betoken, foreshadow, foretell, herald, portend, presage, promise

mean² **1**. *adj.* beggarly, close, mercenary, mingy (*Brit. inf.*), miserly, near (*Inf.*), niggardly, parsimonious, penny-pinching, penurious, selfish, stingy, tight, tight-fisted, ungenerous **2**. bad-tempered, cantankerous, churlish, disagreeable, hostile, ill-tempered, malicious, nasty, rude, sour, unfriendly, unpleasant **3**. abject, base, callous, contemptible, degenerate, degraded, despicable, disgraceful, dishonourable, hard-hearted, ignoble, low-minded, narrow-minded, petty, scurvy, shabby, shameful, sordid, vile, wretched **4**. beggarly, contemptible, down-at-heel, insignificant, miserable, paltry, petty, poor, run-down, scruffy, seedy, shabby, sordid, squalid, tawdry, wretched **5**. base, baseborn (*Archaic*), common, humble, ignoble, inferior, low, lowborn, lowly, menial, modest,

obscure, ordinary, plebeian, proletarian, servile, undistinguished, vulgar

mean³ **1**. *n.* average, balance, compromise, happy medium, median, middle, middle course *or* way, mid-point, norm **2**. *adj.* average, intermediate, medial, median, medium, middle, middling, normal, standard

meander 1. *v.* ramble, snake, stravaig (*Scot.*), stray, stroll, turn, wander, wind, zigzag **2**. *n.* bend, coil, curve, loop, turn, twist, zigzag

meandering anfractuous, circuitous, convoluted, indirect, roundabout, serpentine, snaking, tortuous, wandering, winding

meaning *n.* **1**. connotation, denotation, drift, explanation, gist, implication, import, interpretation, message, purport, sense, significance, signification, substance, upshot, value **2**. aim, design, end, goal, idea, intention, object, plan, point, purpose, trend **3**. effect, efficacy, force, point, thrust, use, usefulness, validity, value, worth ~*adj.* **4**. eloquent, expressive, meaningful, pointed, pregnant, speaking, suggestive

meaningful 1. important, material, purposeful, relevant, serious, significant, useful, valid, worthwhile **2**. eloquent, expressive, meaning, pointed, pregnant, speaking, suggestive

meaningless aimless, empty, futile, hollow, inane, inconsequential, insignificant, insubstantial, nonsensical, nugatory, pointless, purposeless, senseless, trifling, trivial, useless, vain, valueless, worthless

meanness 1. minginess (*Brit. inf.*), miserliness, niggardliness, parsimony, penuriousness, selfishness, stinginess, tight-fistedness **2**. bad temper, cantankerousness, churlishness, disagreeableness, hostility, ill temper, malice, maliciousness, nastiness, rudeness, sourness, unfriendliness, unpleasantness **3**. abjectness, baseness, degeneracy, degradation, despicableness, disgracefulness, dishonourableness, low-mindedness, narrow-mindedness, pettiness, scurviness, shabbiness, shamefulness, sordidness, vileness, wretchedness **4**. beggarliness, contemptibleness, insignificance, paltriness, pettiness, poorness, scruffiness, seediness, shabbiness, sordidness, squalor, tawdriness, wretchedness **5**. baseness, humbleness, lowliness, obscurity, servility

means 1. agency, avenue, channel, course, expedient, instrument, measure, medium, method, mode, process, way **2.** affluence, capital, estate, fortune, funds, income, money, property, resources, riches, substance, wealth, wherewithal **3. by all means** absolutely, certainly, definitely, doubtlessly, of course, positively, surely **4. by means of** by dint of, by way of, through, using, utilizing, via, with the aid of **5. by no means** absolutely not, definitely not, in no way, not at all, not in the least, not in the slightest, not the least bit, on no account

meantime at the same time, concurrently, for now, for the duration, for the moment, for then, in the interim, in the interval, in the intervening time, in the meantime, in the meanwhile, simultaneously

meanwhile at the same time, concurrently, for now, for the duration, for the moment, for then, in the interim, in the interval, in the intervening time, in the meantime, in the meanwhile, simultaneously

measly beggarly, contemptible, meagre, mean, mingy (*Brit. inf.*), miserable, miserly, niggardly, paltry, pathetic, petty, pitiful, poor, puny, scanty, skimpy, stingy, ungenerous

measurable assessable, computable, determinable, gaugeable, material, mensurable, perceptible, quantifiable, quantitative, significant

measure *n.* **1.** allotment, allowance, amount, amplitude, capacity, degree, extent, magnitude, portion, proportion, quantity, quota, range, ration, reach, scope, share, size **2.** gauge, metre, rule, scale, yardstick **3.** method, standard, system **4.** criterion, example, model, norm, standard, test, touchstone, yardstick **5.** bounds, control, limit, limitation, moderation, restraint **6.** act, action, course, deed, expedient, manoeuvre, means, procedure, proceeding, step **7.** act, bill, enactment, law, resolution, statute **8.** beat, cadence, foot, metre, rhythm, verse **9. for good measure** as a bonus, besides, in addition, into the bargain, to boot ~*v.* **10.** appraise, assess, calculate, calibrate, compute, determine, estimate, evaluate, gauge, judge, mark out, quantify, rate, size, sound, survey,

value, weigh **11.** adapt, adjust, calculate, choose, fit, judge, tailor

measured 1. exact, gauged, modulated, precise, predetermined, quantified, regulated, standard, verified **2.** dignified, even, leisurely, regular, sedate, slow, solemn, stately, steady, unhurried **3.** calculated, considered, deliberate, grave, planned, premeditated, reasoned, sober, studied, well thought-out

measureless beyond measure, boundless, endless, immeasurable, immense, incalculable, inestimable, infinite, limitless, unbounded, vast

measurement 1. appraisal, assessment, calculation, calibration, computation, estimation, evaluation, judgment, mensuration, metage, survey, valuation **2.** amount, amplitude, area, capacity, depth, dimension, extent, height, length, magnitude, size, volume, weight, width

measure off circumscribe, delimit, demarcate, determine, fix, lay down, limit, mark out, pace out

measure out allot, apportion, assign, deal out, dispense, distribute, divide, dole out, issue, mete out, parcel out, pour out, share out

measure up (to) be adequate, be capable, be equal to, be fit, be suitable, be suited, come up to scratch (*Inf.*), come up to standard, compare, cut the mustard (*U.S. sl.*), equal, fit *or* fill the bill, fulfil the expectations. make the grade (*Inf.*), match, meet, rival

meat 1. aliment, cheer, chow (*Inf.*), comestibles, eats (*Sl.*), fare, flesh, food, grub (*Inf.*), nourishment, nutriment, provender, provisions, rations, subsistence, sustenance, viands, victuals **2.** core, essence, gist, heart, kernel, marrow, nub, nucleus, pith, point, substance

meaty 1. hearty, nourishing, rich, substantial **2.** beefy (*Inf.*), brawny, burly, fleshy, heavily built, heavy, husky (*Inf.*), muscular, solid, strapping, sturdy **3.** interesting, meaningful, pithy, profound, rich, significant, substantial

mechanical 1. automated, automatic, machine-driven **2.** automatic, cold, cursory, dead, emotionless, habitual, impersonal, instinctive, involuntary, lacklustre, lifeless, machine-like, matter-of-fact, perfunctory, routine, spiritless, unconscious, unfeeling, unthinking

mechanism 1. apparatus, appliance, contrivance, device, instrument, machine, structure, system, tool **2.** action, components, gears, innards (*Inf.*), machinery, motor, workings, works **3.** agency, execution, functioning, means, medium, method, operation, performance, procedure, process, system, technique, workings

meddle butt in, interfere, intermeddle, interpose, intervene, intrude, pry, put one's oar in, stick one's nose in (*Inf.*), tamper

meddlesome interfering, intermeddling, intruding, intrusive, meddling, mischievous, officious, prying

mediate act as middleman, arbitrate, bring to an agreement, bring to terms, conciliate, intercede, interpose, intervene, make peace between, moderate, reconcile, referee, resolve, restore harmony, settle, step in (*Inf.*), umpire

mediation arbitration, conciliation, good offices, intercession, interposition, intervention, reconciliation

mediator advocate, arbiter, arbitrator, go-between, honest broker, interceder, intermediary, judge, middleman, moderator, negotiator, peacemaker, referee, umpire

medicable curable, healable, remediable, treatable

medicinal analeptic, curative, healing, medical, remedial, restorative, roborant, sanatory, therapeutic

medicine cure, drug, medicament, medication, physic, remedy

medieval 1. Gothic **2.** *Inf.* antediluvian, antiquated, antique, archaic, old-fashioned, primitive, unenlightened

mediocre average, commonplace, fair to middling (*Inf.*), indifferent, inferior, insignificant, mean, medium, middling, ordinary, passable, pedestrian, run-of-the-mill, second-rate, so-so (*Inf.*), tolerable, undistinguished, uninspired

mediocrity 1. commonplaceness, indifference, inferiority, insignificance, ordinariness, poorness, unimportance **2.** cipher, lightweight (*Inf.*), nobody, nonentity, second-rater

meditate 1. be in a brown study, cogitate, consider, contemplate, deliberate, muse, ponder, reflect, ruminate, study, think **2.** consider, contemplate, design, devise, have in mind, intend, mull over, plan, purpose, scheme, think over

meditation brown study, cerebration, cogitation, concentration, contempla-

tion, musing, pondering, reflection, reverie, ruminating, rumination, study, thought

meditative cogitative, contemplative, deliberative, pensive, reflective, ruminative, studious, thoughtful

medium *adj.* **1.** average, fair, intermediate, mean, medial, median, mediocre, middle, middling, midway ~*n.* **2.** average, centre, compromise, mean, middle, middle course (ground, path, way), midpoint **3.** agency, avenue, channel, form, instrument, instrumentality, means, mode, organ, vehicle, way **4.** atmosphere, conditions, element, environment, habitat, influences, milieu, setting, surroundings **5.** spiritist, spiritualist

medley assortment, confusion, farrago, gallimaufry, hodge-podge, hotchpotch, jumble, *mélange*, miscellany, mishmash, mixed bag (*Inf.*), mixture, olio, omnium-gatherum, pastiche, patchwork, potpourri, salmagundi

meek 1. deferential, docile, forbearing, gentle, humble, long-suffering, mild, modest, patient, peaceful, soft, submissive, unassuming, unpretentious, yielding **2.** acquiescent, compliant, resigned, spineless, spiritless, tame, timid, unresisting, weak, weak-kneed (*Inf.*)

meekness 1. deference, docility, forbearance, gentleness, humbleness, humility, long-suffering, lowliness, mildness, modesty, patience, peacefulness, resignation, softness, submission, submissiveness **2.** acquiescence, compliance, resignation, spinelessness, spiritlessness, tameness, timidity, weakness

meet 1. bump into, chance on, come across, confront, contact, encounter, find, happen on, run across, run into **2.** abut, adjoin, come together, connect, converge, cross, intersect, join, link up, touch, unite **3.** answer, carry out, come up to, comply, cope with, discharge, equal, fulfil, gratify, handle, match, measure up, perform, satisfy **4.** assemble, collect, come together, congregate, convene, forgather, gather, muster, rally **5.** bear, encounter, endure, experience, face, go through, suffer, undergo

meeting 1. assignation, confrontation, encounter, engagement, introduction, rendezvous, tryst (*Archaic*) **2.** assembly, audience, company, conclave, conference, congregation, convention, convocation, gathering, get-together (*Inf.*), meet, rally, reunion, session **3.** concourse, confluence, conjunction, convergence, crossing, intersection, junction, union

melancholy 1. *n.* blues, dejection, depression, despondency, gloom, gloominess, low spirits, pensiveness, sadness, sorrow, unhappiness, woe **2.** *adj.* blue, dejected, depressed, despondent, disconsolate, dismal, dispirited, doleful, down, downcast, downhearted, down in the dumps (*Inf.*), down in the mouth, gloomy, glum, heavy-hearted, joyless, low, low-spirited, lugubrious, melancholic, miserable, moody, mournful, pensive, sad, sombre, sorrowful, unhappy, woebegone, woeful

mélange assortment, confusion, farrago, gallimaufry, hodge-podge, hotchpotch, jumble, medley, miscellany, mishmash, mix, mixed bag (*Inf.*), mixture, olio, omnium-gatherum, pastiche, potpourri, salmagundi

melee affray, battle royal, brawl, broil, donnybrook, fight, fracas, fray, free-for-all (*Inf.*), ruckus (*Inf.*), ruction (*Inf.*), rumpus, scrimmage, scuffle, set-to (*Inf.*), stramash (*Scot.*), tussle

mellifluous, mellifluent dulcet, euphonious, honeyed, mellow, silvery, smooth, soft, soothing, sweet, sweet-sounding

mellow *adj.* **1.** delicate, full-flavoured, juicy, mature, perfect, rich, ripe, soft, sweet, well-matured **2.** dulcet, full, mellifluous, melodious, rich, rounded, smooth, sweet, tuneful, well-tuned **3.** cheerful, cordial, elevated, expansive, genial, half-tipsy, happy, jolly, jovial, merry (*Brit.inf.*), relaxed ~*v.* **4.** develop, improve, mature, perfect, ripen, season, soften, sweeten

melodious concordant, dulcet, euphonious, harmonious, melodic, musical, silvery, sweet-sounding, sweet-toned, tuneful

melodramatic blood-and-thunder, extravagant, hammy (*Inf.*), histrionic, overdramatic, overemotional, sensational, stagy, theatrical

melody 1. air, descant, music, refrain, song, strain, theme, tune **2.** euphony, harmony, melodiousness, music, musicality, tunefulness

melt 1. deliquesce, diffuse, dissolve, flux, fuse, liquefy, soften, thaw **2.** *Often with* **away** disappear, disperse, dissolve, evanesce, evaporate, fade, vanish **3.** dis-

arm, mollify, relax, soften, touch

member 1. associate, fellow, representative **2.** appendage, arm, component, constituent, element, extremity, leg, limb, organ, part, portion

membership 1. associates, body, fellows, members **2.** belonging, enrolment, fellowship, participation

memento keepsake, memorial, relic, remembrance, reminder, souvenir, token, trophy

memoir account, biography, essay, journal, life, monograph, narrative, record, register

memoirs 1. autobiography, diary, experiences, journals, life, life story, memories, recollections, reminiscences **2.** annals, chronicles, records, transactions

memorable catchy, celebrated, distinguished, extraordinary, famous, historic, illustrious, important, impressive, momentous, notable, noteworthy, remarkable, signal, significant, striking, unforgettable

memorial *adj.* **1.** commemorative, monumental ~*n.* **2.** cairn, memento, monument, plaque, record, remembrance, souvenir **3.** address, memorandum, petition, statement

memorize commit to memory, con (*Archaic*), get by heart, learn, learn by heart, learn by rote, remember

memory 1. recall, recollection, remembrance, reminiscence, retention **2.** commemoration, honour, remembrance **3.** celebrity, fame, glory, name, renown, reputation, repute

menace *v.* **1.** alarm, bode ill, browbeat, bully, frighten, impend, intimidate, loom, lour, lower, terrorize, threaten, utter threats to ~*n.* **2.** commination, intimidation, scare, threat, warning **3.** danger, hazard, jeopardy, peril **4.** *Inf.* annoyance, nuisance, pest, plague, troublemaker

menacing alarming, dangerous, frightening, intimidating, intimidatory, looming, louring, lowering, minacious, minatory, ominous, threatening

mend *v.* **1.** cure, darn, fix, heal, patch, rectify, refit, reform, remedy, renew, renovate, repair, restore, retouch **2.** ameliorate, amend, better, correct, emend, improve, rectify, reform, revise **3.** convalesce, get better, heal, recover, recuperate ~*n.* **4.** darn, patch, repair, stitch **5**. **on the mend** convalescent, convalescing, getting better, improving, recovering, recuperating

mendacious deceitful, deceptive, dishonest, duplicitous, fallacious, false, fraudulent, insincere, lying, perfidious, perjured, untrue, untruthful

mendacity deceit, deceitfulness, dishonesty, distortion, duplicity, falsehood, falsification, fraudulence, insincerity, inveracity, lie, lying, mendaciousness, misrepresentation, perfidy, perjury, untruth, untruthfulness

mendicant 1. *adj.* begging **2**. *n.* beggar, pauper

menial *adj.* 1. boring, dull, humdrum, low-status, routine, unskilled **2**. abject, base, degrading, demeaning, fawning, grovelling, humble, ignoble, ignominious, low, lowly, mean, obsequious, servile, slavish, sorry, subservient, sycophantic, vile ~*n*. **3**. attendant, dogsbody (*Inf.*), domestic, drudge, flunky, labourer, lackey, serf, servant, skivvy (*Brit.*), slave, underling

menstruation catamenia (*Physiology*), courses (*Physiology*), flow (*Inf.*), menses, menstrual cycle, monthly (*Inf.*), period, the curse (*Inf.*)

mensuration assessment, calculation, calibration, computation, estimation, measurement, measuring, metage, survey, surveying

mental 1. cerebral, intellectual **2**. deranged, disturbed, insane, lunatic, mad, mentally ill, psychiatric, psychotic, unbalanced, unstable

mentality 1. brainpower, brains, comprehension, grey matter (*Inf.*), intellect, intelligence quotient, I.Q., mental age, mind, rationality, understanding, wit **2**. attitude, cast of mind, character, disposition, frame of mind, make-up, outlook, personality, psychology, turn of mind, way of thinking

mentally in one's head, intellectually, in the mind, inwardly, psychologically, rationally, subjectively

mention *v*. 1. acknowledge, adduce, allude to, bring up, broach, call attention to, cite, communicate, declare, disclose, divulge, hint at, impart, intimate, make known, name, point out, recount, refer to, report, reveal, speak about *or* of, state, tell, touch upon **2**. **not to mention** as well as, besides, not counting, to say nothing of ~*n*. **3**. acknowledgment, cita-

tion, recognition, tribute **4**. allusion, announcement, indication, notification, observation, reference, remark

mentor adviser, coach, counsellor, guide, guru, instructor, teacher, tutor

menu bill of fare, carte du jour, tariff (*Chiefly Brit.*)

mephitic baleful, baneful, evil- *or* ill-smelling, fetid, foul, foul-smelling, malodorous, miasmal, miasmatic, miasmic, noisome, noxious, pestilential, poisonous, putrid, stinking

mercantile commercial, marketable, trade, trading

mercenary *adj.* 1. acquisitive, avaricious, bribable, covetous, grasping, greedy, money-grubbing (*Inf.*), sordid, venal **2**. bought, hired, paid, venal ~*n*. **3**. condottiere (*Hist.*), free companion (*Hist.*), freelance (*Hist.*), hireling, soldier of fortune

merchandise 1. *n.* commodities, goods, produce, products, staples, stock, stock in trade, truck, vendibles, wares **2**. *v.* buy and sell, deal in, distribute, do business in, market, retail, sell, trade, traffic in, vend

merchant broker, dealer, retailer, salesman, seller, shopkeeper, trader, tradesman, trafficker, vendor, wholesaler

merchantable marketable, salable, tradable, vendible

merciful beneficent, benignant, clement, compassionate, forbearing, forgiving, generous, gracious, humane, kind, lenient, liberal, mild, pitying, soft, sparing, sympathetic, tender-hearted

merciless barbarous, callous, cruel, fell (*Archaic*), hard, hard-hearted, harsh, heartless, implacable, inexorable, inhumane, pitiless, relentless, ruthless, severe, unappeasable, unfeeling, unforgiving, unmerciful, unpitying, unsparing, unsympathetic

mercurial active, capricious, changeable, erratic, fickle, flighty, gay, impulsive, inconstant, irrepressible, light-hearted, lively, mobile, quicksilver, spirited, sprightly, temperamental, unpredictable, unstable, variable, volatile

mercy 1. benevolence, charity, clemency, compassion, favour, forbearance, forgiveness, grace, kindness, leniency, pity, quarter **2**. benison (*Archaic*), blessing, boon, godsend, piece of luck, relief **3**. **at the mercy of** defenceless against, exposed to, in the clutches of, in the power of, naked before, open to, prey to, subject to, threatened by, unprotected against, vulnerable to

mere *adj.* absolute, bare, common, complete, entire, nothing more than, plain, pure, pure and simple, sheer, simple, stark, unadulterated, unmitigated, unmixed, utter

meretricious 1. flashy, garish, gaudy, plastic (*Sl.*), showy, tawdry, tinsel, trashy **2.** bogus, counterfeit, deceitful, false, hollow, insincere, phoney (*Inf.*), put-on, sham, specious, spurious

merge amalgamate, be swallowed up by, become lost in, blend, coalesce, combine, consolidate, converge, fuse, incorporate, intermix, join, meet, meld, melt into, mingle, mix, tone with, unite

merger amalgamation, coalition, combination, consolidation, fusion, incorporation, union

meridian acme, apex, apogee, climax, crest, culmination, high noon, highwater mark, peak, pinnacle, summit, zenith

merit *n.* **1.** advantage, asset, excellence, good, goodness, integrity, quality, strong point, talent, value, virtue, worth, worthiness **2.** claim, credit, desert, due, right ~*v.* **3.** be entitled to, be worthy of, deserve, earn, have a claim to, have a right to, have coming to one, incur, rate, warrant

merited appropriate, condign, deserved, earned, entitled, just, justified, rightful, rightly due, warranted

meritorious admirable, commendable, creditable, deserving, excellent, exemplary, good, honourable, laudable, praiseworthy, right, righteous, virtuous, worthy

merriment amusement, conviviality, festivity, frolic, fun, gaiety, glee, hilarity, jocularity, jollity, joviality, laughter, levity, liveliness, merry-making, mirth, revelry, sport

merry 1. blithe, blithesome, carefree, cheerful, convivial, festive, frolicsome, fun-loving, gay, glad, gleeful, happy, jocund, jolly, joyful, joyous, light-hearted, mirthful, rollicking, sportive, vivacious **2.** amusing, comic, comical, facetious, funny, hilarious, humorous, jocular, mirthful **3.** *Brit. inf.* elevated (*Inf.*), happy, mellow, squiffy (*Brit. inf.*), tiddly (*Brit. sl.*), tipsy **4. make merry** carouse, celebrate, enjoy oneself, feast, frolic,

have a good time, have fun, make whoopee (*Inf.*), revel

merrymaking carousal, carouse, celebration, conviviality, festivity, fun, gaiety, jollification, merriment, party, revelry

mesh *n.* **1.** net, netting, network, plexus, reticulation, tracery, web **2.** entanglement, snare, tangle, toils, trap, web ~*v.* **3.** catch, enmesh, ensnare, entangle, net, snare, tangle, trap **4.** combine, come together, connect, coordinate, dovetail, engage, fit together, harmonize, interlock, knit

mesmerize captivate, enthral, entrance, fascinate, grip, hold spellbound, hypnotize, magnetize, spellbind

mess *n.* **1.** botch, chaos, clutter, confusion, dirtiness, disarray, disorder, disorganization, hash (*Inf.*), jumble, litter, mishmash, shambles, turmoil, untidiness **2.** difficulty, dilemma, fine kettle of fish (*Inf.*), fix (*Inf.*), imbroglio, jam (*Inf.*), mix-up, muddle, perplexity, pickle (*Inf.*), plight, predicament, stew (*Inf.*) ~*v.* **3.** *Often with* **up** befoul, besmirch, botch, bungle, clutter, dirty, disarrange, dishevel, foul, litter, make a hash of (*Inf.*), muck up (*Brit. sl.*), muddle, pollute, scramble **4.** *Often with* **with** fiddle (*Inf.*), interfere, meddle, play, tamper, tinker

mess about *or* **around 1.** amuse oneself, dabble, footle (*Inf.*), muck about (*Inf.*), play about *or* around, potter, trifle **2.** fiddle (*Inf.*), interfere, meddle, play, tamper, tinker, toy

message 1. bulletin, communication, communiqué, dispatch, intimation, letter, memorandum, missive, note, notice, tidings, word **2.** idea, import, meaning, moral, point, purport, theme **3.** commission, errand, job, mission, task **4. get the message** catch on (*Inf.*), comprehend, get it (*Inf.*), get the point, see, take the hint, understand

messenger agent, bearer, carrier, courier, delivery boy, emissary, envoy, errand-boy, go-between, harbinger, herald, runner

messy chaotic, cluttered, confused, dirty, dishevelled, disordered, disorganized, grubby, littered, muddled, shambolic (*Inf.*), sloppy (*Inf.*), slovenly, unkempt, untidy

metamorphose alter, be reborn, change, convert, mutate, remake, remodel, reshape, transfigure, transform, translate, transmogrify (*Jocular*), transmute, transubstantiate

metamorphosis alteration, change, changeover, conversion, mutation, rebirth, transfiguration, transformation, translation, transmogrification (*Jocular*), transmutation, transubstantiation

metaphor allegory, analogy, emblem, figure of speech, image, symbol, trope

metaphorical allegorical, emblematic, emblematical, figurative, symbolic, tropical (*Rhetoric*)

metaphysical 1. basic, esoteric, essential, eternal, fundamental, general, ideal, intellectual, philosophical, profound, speculative, spiritual, subjective, universal 2. abstract, abstruse, deep, high-flown, oversubtle, recondite, theoretical, transcendental 3. immaterial, impalpable, incorporeal, intangible, spiritual, supernatural, unreal, unsubstantial

mete *v.* administer, allot, apportion, assign, deal, dispense, distribute, divide, dole, measure, parcel, portion, ration, share

meteoric brief, brilliant, dazzling, ephemeral, fast, flashing, fleeting, momentary, overnight, rapid, spectacular, speedy, sudden, swift, transient

method 1. approach, arrangement, course, fashion, form, manner, mode, modus operandi, plan, practice, procedure, process, programme, routine, rule, scheme, style, system, technique, way 2. design, form, order, orderliness, organization, pattern, planning, purpose, regularity, structure, system

methodical businesslike, deliberate, disciplined, efficient, meticulous, neat, ordered, orderly, organized, painstaking, planned, precise, regular, structured, systematic, tidy, well-regulated

meticulous detailed, exact, fastidious, fussy, microscopic, painstaking, particular, perfectionist, precise, punctilious, scrupulous, strict, thorough

métier 1. calling, craft, line, occupation, profession, pursuit, trade, vocation 2. forte, long suit (*Inf.*), speciality, specialty, strong point, strong suit

metropolis capital, city

mettle 1. ardour, boldness, bottle (*Brit. sl.*), bravery, courage, daring, fire, fortitude, gallantry, gameness, grit, guts (*Inf.*), hardihood, heart, indomitability, life, nerve, pluck, resolution, resolve,

spirit, spunk (*Inf.*), valour, vigour 2. calibre, character, disposition, kidney, make-up, nature, quality, stamp, temperament, temper

mettlesome ardent, bold, brisk, courageous, daring, dashing, fiery, frisky, game (*Inf.*), high-spirited, lively, mettled, plucky, sprightly, valiant, vigorous

mewl blubber, cry, grizzle (*Brit. inf.*), pule, snivel, whimper, whine, whinge (*Inf.*)

miasma effluvium, fetor, mephitis, odour, pollution, reek, smell, stench

miasmal fetid, foul, insalubrious, malodorous, mephitic, noisome, noxious, polluted, putrid, reeking, smelly, stinking, unwholesome

microbe bacillus, bacterium, bug (*Inf.*), germ, microorganism, virus

microscopic imperceptible, infinitesimal, invisible, minuscule, minute, negligible, tiny

midday noon, noonday, noontide, noontime, twelve noon, twelve o'clock

middle *adj.* 1. central, halfway, inner, inside, intermediate, intervening, mean, medial, median, medium, mid ~*n.* 2. centre, focus, halfway point, heart, inside, mean, midpoint, midsection, midst, thick 3. midriff, midsection, waist

middleman broker, distributor, entrepreneur, go-between, intermediary

middling adequate, all right, average, fair, indifferent, mediocre, medium, moderate, modest, O.K. (*Inf.*), okay (*Inf.*), ordinary, passable, run-of-the-mill, so-so (*Inf.*), tolerable, unexceptional, unremarkable

midget 1. *n.* dwarf, gnome, homuncule, homunculus, manikin, pygmy, shrimp (*Inf.*), Tom Thumb 2. *adj.* baby, dwarf, Lilliputian, little, miniature, pocket, pygmy, small, tiny

midnight dead of night, middle of the night, the witching hour, twelve o'clock (at night)

midst 1. bosom, centre, core, depths, heart, hub, interior, middle, thick 2. **in the midst of** among, during, enveloped by, in the middle of, in the thick of, surrounded by

midway betwixt and between, halfway, in the middle

mien air, appearance, aspect, aura, bearing, carriage, countenance, demeanour, deportment, look, manner, presence

miffed aggrieved, annoyed, displeased,

hurt, in a huff, irked, irritated, narked (*Brit. sl.*), nettled, offended, piqued, put out, resentful, upset, vexed

might 1. ability, capability, capacity, clout (*Sl.*), efficacy, efficiency, energy, force, potency, power, prowess, puissance, strength, sway, valour, vigour **2**. (**with**) **might and main** as hard as one can, as hard as possible, forcefully, full blast, full force, lustily, manfully, mightily, vigorously, with all one's might *or* strength

mightily 1. decidedly, exceedingly, extremely, greatly, highly, hugely, intensely, much, very, very much **2**. energetically, forcefully, lustily, manfully, powerfully, strongly, vigorously, with all one's might and main, with all one's strength

mighty 1. doughty, forceful, hardy, indomitable, lusty, manful, potent, powerful, puissant, robust, stalwart, stout, strapping, strong, sturdy, vigorous **2**. bulky, colossal, enormous, gigantic, grand, great, huge, immense, large, massive, monumental, prodigious, stupendous, titanic, towering, tremendous, vast

migrant 1. *n*. drifter, emigrant, gypsy, immigrant, itinerant, nomad, rover, tinker, transient, vagrant, wanderer **2**. *adj*. drifting, gypsy, immigrant, itinerant, migratory, nomadic, roving, shifting, transient, travelling, vagrant, wandering

migrate drift, emigrate, journey, move, roam, rove, shift, travel, trek, voyage, wander

migration emigration, journey, movement, roving, shift, travel, trek, voyage, wandering

migratory gypsy, itinerant, migrant, nomadic, peripatetic, roving, shifting, transient, travelling, unsettled, vagrant, wandering

mild 1. amiable, balmy, bland, calm, clement, compassionate, docile, easy, easy-going, equable, forbearing, forgiving, gentle, indulgent, kind, meek, mellow, merciful, moderate, pacific, peaceable, placid, pleasant, serene, smooth, soft, temperate, tender, tranquil, warm **2**. demulcent, emollient, lenitive, mollifying, soothing

mildness blandness, calmness, clemency, docility, forbearance, gentleness, indulgence, kindness, leniency, lenity, meekness, mellowness, moderation, placidity, smoothness, softness, temperateness, tenderness, tranquillity, warmth

milieu background, element, environment, locale, location, *mise en scène*, scene, setting, sphere, surroundings

militant *adj*. **1**. active, aggressive, assertive, combative, vigorous **2**. belligerent, combating, contending, embattled, fighting, in arms, warring ~*n*. **3**. activist, partisan **4**. belligerent, combatant, fighter, warrior

military 1. *adj*. armed, martial, soldierlike, soldierly, warlike **2**. *n*. armed forces, army, forces, services

militate 1. *With* **against** be detrimental to, conflict with, contend, count, counter, counteract, oppose, resist, tell, weigh **2**. *With* **for** advance, aid, further, help, promote

militia fencibles (*History*), National Guard (*U.S.*), reserve(s), Territorial Army (*Brit.*), trainband (*History*), yeomanry (*History*)

milk *v*. **1**. drain, draw off, express, extract, let out, press, siphon, tap **2**. bleed, drain, exploit, extract, impose on, pump, take advantage of, use, wring

milk-and-water feeble, innocuous, insipid, jejune, vapid, weak, wishy-washy (*Inf.*)

milksop chinless wonder (*Brit. inf.*), coward, dastard (*Archaic*), mollycoddle, namby-pamby, sissy, weakling

milky alabaster, clouded, cloudy, milk-white, opaque, white, whitish

mill *n*. **1**. factory, foundry, plant, shop, works **2**. crusher, grinder **3**. **run of the mill** average, commonplace, everyday, fair, middling, ordinary, routine, unexceptional, unremarkable ~*v*. **4**. comminute, crush, granulate, grate, grind, pound, powder, press, pulverize **5**. crowd, seethe, swarm, throng

millstone 1. grindstone, quernstone **2**. affliction, burden, dead weight, drag, encumbrance, load, weight

mime 1. *n*. dumb show, gesture, mummery, pantomime **2**. *v*. act out, gesture, pantomime, represent, simulate

mimic *v*. **1**. ape, caricature, imitate, impersonate, parody, take off (*Inf.*) **2**. echo, look like, mirror, resemble, simulate, take on the appearance of ~*n*. **3**. caricaturist, copycat (*Inf.*), imitator, impersonator, impressionist, parodist, parrot ~*adj*. **4**. echoic, imitation, imitative, make-believe, mimetic, mock, sham, simulated

mimicry apery, burlesque, caricature, copying, imitating, imitation, impersonation, impression, mimicking, mockery, parody, take-off (*Inf.*)

minatory dangerous, menacing, minacious, minatorial, threatening

mince 1. chop, crumble, cut, grind, hash **2.** diminish, euphemize, extenuate, hold back, moderate, palliate, soften, spare, tone down, weaken **3.** attitudinize, give oneself airs, ponce (*Sl.*), pose, posture

mincing affected, dainty, effeminate, foppish, lah-di-dah (*Inf.*), nice, niminy-piminy, poncy (*Sl.*), precious, pretentious, sissy

mind *n.* **1.** brain(s) (*Inf.*), grey matter (*Inf.*), intellect, intelligence, mentality, ratiocination, reason, sense, spirit, understanding, wits **2.** memory, recollection, remembrance **3.** brain, head, imagination, psyche **4.** brain (*Inf.*), genius, intellect, intellectual, thinker **5.** attitude, belief, feeling, judgment, opinion, outlook, point of view, sentiment, thoughts, view, way of thinking **6.** bent, desire, disposition, fancy, inclination, intention, leaning, notion, purpose, tendency, urge, will, wish **7.** attention, concentration, thinking, thoughts **8.** judgment, marbles (*Inf.*), mental balance, rationality, reason, sanity, senses, wits **9. in** *or* **of two minds** dithering, hesitant, shillyshallying (*Inf.*), swithering (*Scot.*), uncertain, undecided, unsure, vacillating, wavering **10. make up one's mind** choose, come to a decision, decide, determine, reach a decision, resolve **11. bear** *or* **keep in mind** be cognizant of, be mindful of, remember, take note of ~*v.* **12.** be affronted by, bothered, care, disapprove, dislike, look askance at, object, resent, take offence **13.** adhere to, attend, comply with, follow, heed, listen to, mark, note, notice, obey, observe, pay attention, pay heed to, regard, respect, take heed, watch **14.** be sure, ensure, make certain **15.** attend to, guard, have charge of, keep an eye on, look after, take care of, tend, watch **16.** be careful, be cautious, be on (one's) guard, be wary, take care, watch **17. never mind** disregard, do not concern yourself, don't bother, don't give (it) a second thought, forget (it), it does not matter, it's none of your business, it's nothing to do with you, pay no attention

mindful alert, alive to, attentive,

aware, careful, chary, cognizant, conscious, heedful, regardful, respectful, sensible, thoughtful, wary, watchful

mindless 1. asinine, brutish, careless, foolish, forgetful, gratuitous, heedless, idiotic, imbecilic, inattentive, moronic, neglectful, negligent, oblivious, obtuse, stupid, thoughtless, unintelligent, unmindful, unthinking, witless **2.** automatic, brainless, mechanical

mind out be careful, be on one's guard, beware, keep one's eyes open, look out, pay attention, take care, watch

mind's eye head, imagination, memory, mind, recollection, remembrance

mine *n.* **1.** coalfield, colliery, deposit, excavation, lode, pit, shaft, vein **2.** abundance, fund, hoard, reserve, source, stock, store, supply, treasury, wealth **3.** sap, trench, tunnel ~*v.* **4.** delve, dig for, dig up, excavate, extract, hew, quarry, unearth **5.** lay mines in *or* under, sow with mines **6.** sap, subvert, tunnel, undermine, weaken

miner coalminer, collier (*Brit.*), pitman (*Brit.*)

mingle 1. alloy, blend, coalesce, combine, commingle, compound, intermingle, intermix, interweave, join, marry, merge, mix, unite **2.** associate, circulate, consort, fraternize, hang about *or* around, hang out (*Inf.*), hobnob, rub shoulders (*Inf.*), socialize

miniature *adj.* baby, diminutive, dwarf, Lilliputian, little, midget, mini, minuscule, minute, pocket, pygmy, reduced, scaled-down, small, tiny, toy, wee

minimal least, least possible, littlest, minimum, nominal, slightest, smallest, token

minimize 1. abbreviate, attenuate, curtail, decrease, diminish, miniaturize, prune, reduce, shrink **2.** belittle, decry, deprecate, depreciate, discount, disparage, make light *or* little of, play down, underestimate, underrate

minimum 1. *n.* bottom, depth, least, lowest, nadir, slightest **2.** *adj.* least, least possible, littlest, lowest, minimal, slightest, smallest

minion bootlicker (*Inf.*), creature, darling, dependant, favourite, flatterer, flunky, follower, hanger-on, henchman, hireling, lackey, lickspittle, myrmidon, parasite, pet, sycophant, toady, underling, yes man

minister *n.* **1.** churchman, clergyman,

cleric, divine, ecclesiastic, parson, pastor, preacher, priest, vicar **2.** administrator, ambassador, cabinet member, delegate, diplomat, envoy, executive, office-holder, official, plenipotentiary **3.** agent, aide, assistant, lieutenant, servant, subordinate, underling ~v. **4.** accommodate, administer, answer, attend, be solicitous of, cater to, pander to, serve, take care of, tend

ministration aid, assistance, favour, help, patronage, relief, service, succour, support

ministry 1. administration, cabinet, council, government, holy orders, the church, the priesthood, the pulpit **2.** bureau, department, office

minor inconsequential, inconsiderable, inferior, insignificant, junior, lesser, light, negligible, paltry, petty, secondary, slight, small, smaller, subordinate, trifling, trivial, unimportant, younger

minstrel bard, harper, jongleur, musician, singer, troubadour

mint n. **1.** bomb (Brit. sl.), bundle (Sl.), fortune, heap (Inf.), King's ransom, million, packet (Sl.), pile (Inf.) ~adj. **2.** brand-new, excellent, first-class, fresh, perfect, unblemished, undamaged, untarnished ~v. **3.** cast, coin, make, produce, punch, stamp, strike **4.** coin, construct, devise, fabricate, fashion, forge, invent, make up, produce, think up

minuscule diminutive, fine, infinitesimal, Lilliputian, little, microscopic, miniature, minute, tiny, very small

minute[1] n. **1.** sixtieth of an hour, sixty seconds **2.** flash, instant, jiffy (Inf.), moment, second, shake (Inf.), tick (Inf.), trice **3. any minute** any moment, any second, any time, at any time, before long, very soon **4. up to the minute** all the rage, in, latest, modish, (most) fashionable, newest, now (Inf.), smart, stylish, trendiest, trendy, up to date, vogue, with it (Inf.)

minute[2] adj. **1.** diminutive, fine, infinitesimal, Lilliputian, little, microscopic, miniature, minuscule, slender, small, tiny **2.** inconsiderable, negligible, paltry, petty, picayune (U.S.), piddling (Inf.), puny, slight, trifling, trivial, unimportant **3.** close, critical, detailed, exact, exhaustive, meticulous, painstaking, precise, punctilious

minutely closely, critically, exactly,

exhaustively, in detail, meticulously, painstakingly, precisely, with a fine-tooth comb

minutes memorandum, notes, proceedings, record(s), transactions, transcript

minutiae details, finer points, niceties, particulars, subtleties, trifles, trivia

minx baggage (Inf.), coquette, flirt, hoyden, hussy, jade, tomboy, wanton

miracle marvel, phenomenon, prodigy, thaumaturgy, wonder

miraculous amazing, astonishing, astounding, extraordinary, incredible, inexplicable, magical, marvellous, phenomenal, preternatural, prodigious, superhuman, supernatural, thaumaturgic, unaccountable, unbelievable, wonderful, wondrous

mirage hallucination, illusion, optical illusion, phantasm

mire n. **1.** bog, marsh, morass, quagmire, swamp **2.** dirt, muck, mud, ooze, slime **3. in the mire** encumbered, entangled, in difficulties, in trouble ~v. **4.** bog down, flounder, sink, stick in the mud **5.** begrime, besmirch, bespatter, cake, dirty, muddy, soil **6.** catch up, enmesh, entangle, involve

mirror n. **1.** glass, looking-glass, reflector, speculum **2.** copy, double, image, likeness, reflection, replica, representation, twin ~v. **3.** copy, depict, echo, emulate, follow, reflect, represent, show

mirth amusement, cheerfulness, festivity, frolic, fun, gaiety, gladness, glee, hilarity, jocularity, jollity, joviality, joyousness, laughter, levity, merriment, merrymaking, pleasure, rejoicing, revelry, sport

mirthful amused, amusing, blithe, cheerful, cheery, festive, frolicsome, funny, gay, glad, gladsome (Archaic), happy, hilarious, jocund, jolly, jovial, laughable, light-hearted, merry, playful, sportive, uproarious, vivacious

misadventure accident, bad break (Inf.), bad luck, calamity, catastrophe, debacle, disaster, failure, ill fortune, ill luck, mischance, misfortune, mishap, reverse, setback

misanthrope cynic, egoist, egotist, mankind-hater, misanthropist

misanthropic antisocial, cynical, egoistic, inhumane, malevolent, unfriendly, unsociable

misanthropy cynicism, egoism, hatred of mankind, inhumanity, malevolence

misapply abuse, misappropriate, misemploy, misuse, pervert

misapprehend get the wrong idea *or* impression, misconceive, misconstrue, misinterpret, misread, mistake, misunderstand

misapprehension delusion, error, fallacy, false belief, false impression, misconception, misconstruction, misinterpretation, misreading, mistake, misunderstanding, wrong idea *or* impression

misappropriate defalcate (*Law*), embezzle, misapply, misspend, misuse, peculate, pocket, steal; swindle

misbegotten 1. dishonest, disreputable, ill-gotten, illicit, purloined, shady (*Inf.*), stolen, unlawful, unrespectable 2. abortive, hare-brained, ill-advised, ill-conceived, poorly thought-out 3. *Literary* bastard, born out of wedlock, illegitimate, natural, spurious (*Rare*)

misbehave act up (*Inf.*), be bad, be insubordinate, be naughty, carry on (*Inf.*), get up to mischief, muck about (*Brit. sl.*)

misbehaviour acting up (*Inf.*), bad behaviour, impropriety, incivility, indiscipline, insubordination, misconduct, misdeeds, misdemeanour, monkey business (*Inf.*), naughtiness, rudeness, shenanigans (*Inf.*)

misbelief delusion, error, fallacy, false belief, heresy, unorthodoxy

miscalculate blunder, calculate wrongly, err, get (it) wrong (*Inf.*), go wrong, make a mistake, misjudge, overestimate, overrate, slip up, underestimate, underrate

miscarriage 1. miss (*Inf.*), spontaneous abortion 2. botch (*Inf.*), breakdown, error, failure, misadventure, mischance, misfire, mishap, mismanagement, nonsuccess, perversion, thwarting, undoing

miscarry 1. abort 2. come to grief, come to nothing, fail, fall through, gang agley (*Scot.*), go amiss, go astray, go awry, go wrong, misfire

miscellaneous assorted, confused, diverse, diversified, farraginous, heterogeneous, indiscriminate, jumbled, many, mingled, mixed, motley, multifarious, multiform, promiscuous, sundry, varied, various

miscellany anthology, assortment,

collection, diversity, farrago, gallimaufry, hotchpotch, jumble, medley, *mélange*, mixed bag, mixture, omniumgatherum, potpourri, salmagundi, variety

mischance accident, bad break (*Inf.*), bad luck, calamity, contretemps, disaster, ill chance, ill fortune, ill luck, infelicity, misadventure, misfortune, mishap

mischief 1. devilment, impishness, misbehaviour, monkey business (*Inf.*), naughtiness, pranks, roguery, roguishness, shenanigans (*Inf.*), trouble, waywardness 2. devil, imp, monkey, nuisance, pest, rascal, rogue, scallywag (*Inf.*), scamp, tyke (*Inf.*), villain 3. damage, detriment, disadvantage, disruption, evil, harm, hurt, injury, misfortune, trouble

mischievous 1. arch, bad, badly behaved, exasperating, frolicsome, impish, naughty, playful, puckish, rascally, roguish, sportive, teasing, troublesome, vexatious, wayward 2. bad, damaging, deleterious, destructive, detrimental, evil, harmful, hurtful, injurious, malicious, malignant, pernicious, sinful, spiteful, troublesome, vicious, wicked

misconceive fail to understand, get the wrong idea (about), misapprehend, misconstrue, misjudge, mistake, misunderstand

misconception delusion, error, fallacy, misapprehension, misconstruction, mistaken belief, misunderstanding, wrong end of the stick (*Inf.*), wrong idea

misconduct 1. *n.* delinquency, dereliction, immorality, impropriety, malfeasance (*Law*), malpractice, malversation (*Rare*), misbehaviour, misdemeanour, mismanagement, naughtiness, rudeness, transgression, unethical behaviour, wrongdoing 2. *v.* behave badly, botch (up), bungle, err, make a mess of, misdirect, mismanage, sin

misconstruction false interpretation, misapprehension, misinterpretation, misreading, mistake, mistaken *or* false impression, misunderstanding, wrong idea

misconstrue get a false impression, make a wrong interpretation, misapprehend, misconceive, misinterpret, misjudge, misread, mistake, mistranslate, misunderstand, take the wrong way (*Inf.*)

miscreant 1. *n.* blackguard, caitiff

(*Archaic*), criminal, evildoer, knave (*Archaic*), malefactor, rascal, reprobate, rogue, scoundrel, sinner, vagabond, villain, wrongdoer **2.** *adj.* corrupt, criminal, depraved, evil, iniquitous, nefarious, rascally, reprehensible, reprobate, scoundrelly, unprincipled, vicious, villainous, wicked

misdeed crime, fault, misconduct, misdemeanour, offence, sin, transgression, trespass, villainy, wrong

misdemeanour fault, infringement, misbehaviour, misconduct, misdeed, offence, peccadillo, transgression, trespass

miser cheapskate (*Inf.*), churl, curmudgeon, hunks (*Rare*), niggard, pennypincher (*Inf.*), screw (*Sl.*), Scrooge, skinflint, tightwad (*U.S. sl.*)

miserable 1. afflicted, broken-hearted, crestfallen, dejected, depressed, desolate, despondent, disconsolate, distressed, doleful, down, downcast, down in the mouth (*Inf.*), forlorn, gloomy, heartbroken, melancholy, mournful, sorrowful, unhappy, woebegone, wretched **2.** destitute, impoverished, indigent, meagre, needy, penniless, poor, poverty-stricken, scanty **3.** abject, bad, contemptible, deplorable, despicable, detestable, disgraceful, lamentable, low, mean, pathetic, piteous, pitiable, scurvy, shabby, shameful, sordid, sorry, squalid, vile, worthless, wretched

miserliness avarice, cheeseparing, churlishness, close- *or* tightfistedness, covetousness, graspingness, meanness, minginess (*Brit. inf.*), nearness, niggardliness, parsimony, penny-pinching (*Inf.*), penuriousness, stinginess

miserly avaricious, beggarly, close, close-fisted, covetous, grasping, illiberal, mean, mingy (*Brit. inf.*), near, niggardly, parsimonious, penny-pinching (*Inf.*), penurious, sordid, stingy, tightfisted, ungenerous

misery 1. agony, anguish, depression, desolation, despair, discomfort, distress, gloom, grief, hardship, melancholy, sadness, sorrow, suffering, torment, torture, unhappiness, woe, wretchedness **2.** affliction, bitter pill (*Inf.*), burden, calamity, catastrophe, curse, disaster, load, misfortune, ordeal, sorrow, trial, tribulation, trouble, woe **3.** destitution, indigence, need, penury, poverty, privation, sordidness, squalor, want, wretchedness **4.**

Brit. inf. grouch (*Inf.*), killjoy, moaner, pessimist, prophet of doom, sourpuss (*Inf.*), spoilsport, wet blanket (*Inf.*)

misfire fail, fail to go off, fall through, go phut (*Inf.*), go wrong, miscarry

misfit eccentric, fish out of water (*Inf.*), nonconformist, square peg (in a round hole) (*Inf.*)

misfortune 1. bad luck, evil fortune, hard luck, ill luck, infelicity **2.** accident, adversity, affliction, blow, calamity, disaster, evil chance, failure, hardship, harm, loss, misadventure, mischance, misery, mishap, reverse, setback, stroke of bad luck, tragedy, trial, tribulation, trouble

misgiving anxiety, apprehension, distrust, doubt, hesitation, qualm, reservation, scruple, suspicion, uncertainty, unease, worry

misguided deluded, erroneous, foolish, ill-advised, imprudent, injudicious, labouring under a delusion *or* misapprehension, misled, misplaced, mistaken, uncalled-for, unreasonable, unwarranted, unwise

mishandle botch, bungle, make a hash of (*Inf.*), make a mess of, mess up (*Inf.*), mismanage, muff, screw (up) (*Inf.*)

mishap accident, adversity, bad luck, calamity, contretemps, disaster, evil chance, evil fortune, hard luck, ill fortune, ill luck, infelicity, misadventure, mischance, misfortune

mishmash farrago, gallimaufry, hash, hotchpotch, jumble, medley, potpourri, salmagundi

misinform deceive, give (someone) a bum steer (*Sl.*), give (someone) duff gen (*Brit. inf.*), misdirect, misguide, mislead

misinterpret distort, falsify, get wrong, misapprehend, misconceive, misconstrue, misjudge, misread, misrepresent, mistake, misunderstand, pervert

misjudge be wrong about, get the wrong idea about, miscalculate, overestimate, overrate, underestimate, underrate

mislay be unable to find, be unable to put *or* lay one's hand on, forget the whereabouts of, lose, lose track of, misplace, miss

mislead beguile, bluff, deceive, delude, fool, give (someone) a bum steer (*Sl.*), hoodwink, lead astray, misdirect, misguide, misinform, pull the wool over (someone's) eyes (*Inf.*), take in (*Inf.*)

misleading ambiguous, casuistical, confusing, deceitful, deceptive, delusive, delusory, disingenuous, evasive, false, sophistical, specious, spurious, tricky (*Inf.*), unstraightforward

mismanage be incompetent, be inefficient, botch, bungle, make a hash of (*Inf.*), make a mess of, maladminister, mess up, misconduct, misdirect, misgovern, mishandle

mismatched clashing, discordant, disparate, ill-assorted, incompatible, incongruous, irregular, misallied, unreconcilable, unsuited

misplace 1. be unable to find, be unable to put *or* lay one's hand on, forget the whereabouts of, lose, lose track of, misfile, mislay, miss, put in the wrong place **2.** place unwisely, place wrongly

misprint corrigendum, erratum, literal, mistake, printing error, typo (*Inf.*), typographical error

misprize disparage, fail to appreciate, hold cheap, look down on, set no store by, slight, underestimate, underrate, undervalue

misquote distort, falsify, garble, mangle, misreport, misrepresent, misstate, muddle, pervert, quote *or* take out of context, twist

misrepresent belie, disguise, distort, falsify, garble, misinterpret, misstate, pervert, twist

misrule 1. bad government, maladministration, misgovernment, mismanagement **2.** anarchy, chaos, confusion, disorder, lawlessness, tumult, turmoil

miss[1] *v.* **1.** avoid, be late for, blunder, err, escape, evade, fail, fail to grasp, fail to notice, forego, lack, leave out, let go, let slip, lose, miscarry, mistake, omit, overlook, pass over, pass up, skip, slip, trip **2.** feel the loss of, long for, need, pine for, want, wish, yearn for ~*n.* **3.** blunder, error, failure, fault, loss, mistake, omission, oversight, want

miss[2] damsel, girl, lass, lassie (*Inf.*), maid, maiden, schoolgirl, spinster, young lady

misshapen contorted, crippled, crooked, deformed, distorted, grotesque, ill-made, ill-proportioned, malformed, twisted, ugly, ungainly, unshapely, unsightly, warped, wry

missile projectile, rocket, weapon

missing absent, astray, gone, lacking,

left behind, left out, lost, mislaid, misplaced, not present, nowhere to be found, unaccounted-for, wanting

mission 1. aim, assignment, business, calling, charge, commission, duty, errand, goal, job, office, operation, purpose, pursuit, quest, task, trust, undertaking, vocation, work **2.** commission, delegation, deputation, embassy, legation, ministry, task force

missionary apostle, converter, evangelist, preacher, propagandist, proselytizer

missive communication, dispatch, epistle, letter, memorandum, message, note, report

misspent dissipated, idle, imprudent, misapplied, prodigal, profitless, squandered, thrown away, wasted

misstate distort, falsify, garble, give a false impression, misquote, misreport, misrepresent, pervert, twist

misstep bad move, blunder, error, false step, faux pas, gaffe, indiscretion, lapse, mistake, slip, slip-up (*Inf.*), stumble, trip, wrong move

mist 1. *n.* cloud, condensation, dew, drizzle, film, fog, haar (*Eastern Brit.*), haze, smog, smur *or* smir (*Scot.*), spray, steam, vapour **2.** *v.* becloud, befog, blur, cloud, film, fog, obscure, steam (up)

mistake *n.* **1.** bloomer (*Brit. inf.*), blunder, boob (*Brit. sl.*), boo-boo (*Inf.*), clanger (*Inf.*), erratum, error, error of judgment, false move, fault, faux pas, gaffe, goof (*Inf.*), howler (*Inf.*), inaccuracy, miscalculation, misconception, misstep, misunderstanding, oversight, slip, slip-up (*Inf.*), solecism ~*v.* **2.** get wrong, misapprehend, misconceive, misconstrue, misinterpret, misjudge, misread, misunderstand **3.** accept as, confound, confuse with, misinterpret as, mix up with, take for **4.** be wide of *or* be off the mark, be wrong, blunder, drop a clanger (*Inf.*), err, goof (*Inf.*), miscalculate, misjudge, put one's foot in it (*Inf.*), slip up (*Inf.*)

mistaken barking up the wrong tree (*Inf.*), erroneous, fallacious, false, faulty, inaccurate, inappropriate, incorrect, in the wrong, labouring under a misapprehension, misguided, misinformed, mislead, off target, off the mark, unfounded, unsound, wide of the mark, wrong

mistakenly by mistake, erroneously, fallaciously, falsely, inaccurately, inappropriately, incorrectly, in error, misguidedly, wrongly

mistimed badly timed, ill-timed, inconvenient, inopportune, unseasonable, unsynchronized, untimely

mistreat abuse, brutalize, handle roughly, harm, ill-treat, ill-use, injure, knock about (*Inf.*), maltreat, manhandle, maul, misuse, molest, rough up, wrong

mistreatment abuse, brutalization, harm, ill-treatment, ill-usage, injury, maltreatment, manhandling, mauling, misuse, molestation, rough handling, roughing up, unkindness

mistress concubine, doxy (*Archaic*), fancy woman (*Sl.*), girlfriend, inamorata, kept woman, ladylove (*Rare*), lover, paramour

mistrust 1. *v.* apprehend, beware, be wary of, distrust, doubt, fear, have doubts about, suspect 2. *n.* apprehension, distrust, doubt, dubiety, fear, misgiving, scepticism, suspicion, uncertainty, wariness

mistrustful apprehensive, cautious, chary, cynical, distrustful, doubtful, dubious, fearful, hesitant, leery (*Sl.*), sceptical, suspicious, uncertain, wary

misty bleary, blurred, cloudy, dark, dim, foggy, fuzzy, hazy, indistinct, murky, nebulous, obscure, opaque, overcast, unclear, vague

misunderstand get (it) wrong, get the wrong end of the stick (*Inf.*), get the wrong idea (about), misapprehend, misconceive, misconstrue, mishear, misinterpret, misjudge, misread, miss the point (of), mistake

misunderstanding 1. error, false impression, misapprehension, misconception, misconstruction, misinterpretation, misjudgment, misreading, mistake, mix-up, wrong idea 2. argument, breach, conflict, difference, difficulty, disagreement, discord, dissension, falling-out (*Inf.*), quarrel, rift, rupture, squabble, variance

misunderstood misconstrued, misheard, misinterpreted, misjudged, misread, unappreciated, unrecognized

misuse *n.* 1. abuse, barbarism, catachresis, corruption, desecration, dissipation, malapropism, misapplication, misemployment, misusage, perversion, profanation, solecism, squandering, waste 2. abuse, cruel treatment, exploitation, harm, ill-treatment, ill-usage, in-

humane treatment, injury, maltreatment, manhandling, mistreatment, rough handling ~*v.* 3. abuse, corrupt, desecrate, dissipate, misapply, misemploy, pervert, profane, prostitute, squander, waste 4. abuse, brutalize, exploit, handle roughly, harm, ill-treat, ill-use, injure, maltreat, manhandle, maul, mistreat, molest, wrong

mitigate abate, allay, appease, assuage, blunt, calm, check, diminish, dull, ease, extenuate, lessen, lighten, moderate, modify, mollify, pacify, palliate, placate, quiet, reduce the force of, remit, soften, soothe, subdue, take the edge off, temper, tone down, tranquillize, weaken

mitigation abatement, allaying, alleviation, assuagement, diminution, easement, extenuation, moderation, mollification, palliation, relief, remission

mix *v.* 1. alloy, amalgamate, associate, blend, coalesce, combine, commingle, commix, compound, cross, fuse, incorporate, intermingle, interweave, join, jumble, merge, mingle, put together, unite 2. associate, come together, consort, fraternize, hang out (*Inf.*), hobnob, join, mingle, socialize ~*n.* 3. alloy, amalgam, assortment, blend, combination, compound, fusion, medley, mixture

mixed 1. alloyed, amalgamated, blended, combined, composite, compound, fused, incorporated, joint, mingled, united 2. assorted, cosmopolitan, diverse, diversified, heterogeneous, miscellaneous, motley, varied 3. crossbred, hybrid, interbred, interdenominational, mongrel 4. ambivalent, equivocal, indecisive, uncertain

mixed-up bewildered, confused, distraught, disturbed, maladjusted, muddled, perplexed, puzzled, upset

mixture admixture, alloy, amalgam, amalgamation, association, assortment, blend, brew, combine, composite, compound, concoction, conglomeration, cross, fusion, hotchpotch, jumble, medley, *mélange*, miscellany, mix, potpourri, salmagundi, union, variety

mix-up confusion, disorder, fankle (*Scot.*), jumble, mess, mistake, misunderstanding, muddle, snarl-up (*Brit. inf.*), tangle

mix up 1. blend, combine, commix, mix 2. confound, confuse, muddle 3. bewilder, confuse, disturb, fluster, muddle, perplex, puzzle, throw into confusion, upset **4**. embroil, entangle, implicate, involve, rope in

moan *n*. **1**. groan, lament, lamentation, sigh, sob, sough, wail, whine **2**. *Inf.* beef (*Sl.*), bitch (*Sl.*), complaint, gripe (*Inf.*), grouse, grumble, whine, whinge ~*v.* **3**. bemoan, bewail, deplore, grieve, groan, keen, lament, mourn, sigh, sob, sough, whine **4**. *Inf.* beef (*Sl.*), bitch (*Sl.*), carp, complain, gripe (*Inf.*), groan, grouse, grumble, moan and groan, whine, whinge

mob *n*. **1**. assemblage, body, collection, crowd, drove, flock, gang, gathering, herd, horde, host, mass, multitude, pack, press, swarm, throng **2**. class, company, crew (*Inf.*), gang, group, lot, set, troop **3**. *canaille*, commonalty, great unwashed (*Inf.*), hoi polloi, masses, rabble, riffraff, scum ~*v.* **4**. crowd around, jostle, overrun, set upon, surround, swarm around **5**. cram into, crowd, crowd into, fill, fill to overflowing, jam, pack

mobile 1. ambulatory, itinerant, locomotive, migrant, motile, movable, moving, peripatetic, portable, travelling, wandering **2**. animated, changeable, ever-changing, expressive

mobilize activate, animate, call to arms, call up, get *or* make ready, marshal, muster, organize, prepare, put in motion, rally, ready

mock *v*. **1**. chaff, deride, flout, insult, jeer, laugh at, laugh to scorn, make fun of, poke fun at, ridicule, scoff, scorn, show contempt for, sneer, take the mickey (out of) (*Inf.*), taunt, tease **2**. ape, burlesque, caricature, counterfeit, imitate, lampoon, mimic, parody, satirize, send up (*Brit. inf.*), take off (*Inf.*), travesty **3**. belie, cheat, deceive, delude, disappoint, dupe, elude, fool, let down, mislead **4**. defeat, defy, disappoint, foil, frustrate, thwart ~*n.* **5**. banter, derision, gibe, jeering, mockery, ridicule, scorn, sneer, sneering **6**. Aunt Sally (*Brit.*), butt, dupe, fool, jest, laughing stock, sport, travesty **7**. counterfeit, fake, forgery, fraud, imitation, phoney (*Sl.*), sham ~*adj.* **8**. artificial, bogus, counterfeit, dummy, ersatz, fake, faked, false, feigned, forged, fraudulent, imitation, phoney (*Sl.*), pretended, pseudo (*Inf.*), sham, spurious

mockery 1. contempt, contumely, derision, disdain, disrespect, gibes, insults, jeering, ridicule, scoffing, scorn **2**. bur-

lesque, caricature, deception, farce, imitation, lampoon, laughing stock, mimicry, parody, pretence, send-up (*Brit. sl.*), sham, spoof (*Inf.*), take-off (*Inf.*), travesty **3**. apology, disappointment, farce, joke, letdown

mocking contemptuous, contumelious, derisive, derisory, disdainful, disrespectful, insulting, irreverent, sarcastic, sardonic, satiric, satirical, scoffing, scornful, taunting

mode 1. approach, condition, course, custom, fashion, form, manner, method, plan, practice, procedure, process, quality, rule, state, style, system, technique, vein, way **2**. craze, fashion, look, rage, style, trend, vogue

model *n*. **1**. copy, dummy, facsimile, image, imitation, miniature, mock-up, replica, representation **2**. archetype, design, epitome, example, exemplar, gauge, ideal, lodestar, mould, original, paradigm, paragon, pattern, prototype, standard, type **3**. poser, sitter, subject **4**. mannequin **5**. configuration, design, form, kind, mark, mode, style, type, variety, version ~*v.* **6**. base, carve, cast, design, fashion, form, mould, pattern, plan, sculpt, shape **7**. display, show off, sport (*Inf.*), wear ~*adj.* **8**. copy, dummy, facsimile, imitation, miniature **9**. archetypal, exemplary, ideal, illustrative, paradigmatic, perfect, standard, typical

moderate *adj*. **1**. calm, controlled, cool, deliberate, equable, gentle, judicious, limited, middle-of-the-road, mild, modest, peaceable, reasonable, restrained, sober, steady, temperate **2**. average, fair, fairish, fair to middling (*Inf.*), indifferent, mediocre, medium, middling, ordinary, passable, so-so (*Inf.*), unexceptional ~*v.* **3**. abate, allay, appease, assuage, calm, control, curb, decrease, diminish, lessen, mitigate, modulate, pacify, play down, quiet, regulate, repress, restrain, soften, soft pedal (*Inf.*), subdue, tame, temper, tone down **4**. arbitrate, chair, judge, mediate, preside, referee, take the chair

moderately fairly, gently, in moderation, passably, quite, rather, reasonably, slightly, somewhat, to a degree, tolerably, to some extent, within limits, within reason

moderation 1. calmness, composure, coolness, equanimity, fairness, judiciousness, justice, justness, mildness, moderateness, reasonableness, restraint, sedateness, temperance **2. in moderation** moderately, within limits, within reason

modern contemporary, current, fresh, late, latest, neoteric (*Rare*), new, newfangled, novel, present, present-day, recent, twentieth-century, up-to-date, up-to-the-minute, with-it (*Inf.*)

modernity contemporaneity, currency, freshness, innovation, newness, novelty, recentness

modernize bring into the twentieth century, bring up to date, rejuvenate, remake, remodel, renew, renovate, revamp, update

modest 1. bashful, blushing, coy, demure, diffident, discreet, humble, meek, quiet, reserved, reticent, retiring, self-conscious, self-effacing, shy, simple, unassuming, unpretentious **2.** fair, limited, middling, moderate, ordinary, small, unexceptional

modesty bashfulness, coyness, decency, demureness, diffidence, discreetness, humbleness, humility, lack of pretension, meekness, propriety, quietness, reserve, reticence, self-effacement, shyness, simplicity, timidity, unobtrusiveness, unpretentiousness

modicum atom, bit, crumb, dash, drop, fragment, grain, inch, iota, little, mite, ounce, particle, pinch, scrap, shred, small amount, speck, tinge, touch

modification adjustment, alteration, change, modulation, mutation, qualification, refinement, reformation, restriction, revision, variation

modify 1. adapt, adjust, alter, change, convert, recast, redo, refashion, reform, remodel, reorganize, reshape, revise, rework, transform, vary **2.** abate, lessen, limit, lower, moderate, qualify, reduce, restrain, restrict, soften, temper, tone down

modish à la mode, all the rage, chic, contemporary, current, fashionable, hip (*Sl.*), in, now (*Inf.*), smart, stylish, trendy (*Brit. inf.*), up-to-the-minute, vogue, voguish, with it (*Inf.*)

modulate adjust, attune, balance, harmonize, inflect, regulate, tone, tune, vary

modus operandi method, operation, practice, praxis, procedure, process, system, technique, way

mogul baron, bashaw, big cheese (*Sl.*), big gun (*Sl.*), big noise (*Brit. sl.*), big shot (*Sl.*), big wheel (*Sl.*), lord, magnate,

nabob (*Inf.*), notable, personage, potentate, tycoon, V.I.P.

moiety fifty percent, half, part, piece, portion, share

moist clammy, damp, dampish, dank, dewy, dripping, drizzly, humid, not dry, rainy, soggy, wet, wettish

moisten bedew, damp, dampen, humidify, lick, moisturize, soak, water, wet

moisture damp, dampness, dankness, dew, humidity, liquid, perspiration, sweat, water, wateriness, wetness

mole breakwater, dike, dyke, embankment, groyne, jetty, pier, sea wall

molecule atom, iota, jot, mite, mote, particle, speck

molest 1. abuse, afflict, annoy, badger, beset, bother, bug (*Inf.*), disturb, harass, harry, hector, irritate, persecute, pester, plague, tease, torment, upset, vex, worry **2.** abuse, accost, assail, attack, harm, hurt, illtreat, injure, interfere with, maltreat, manhandle

mollify 1. appease, calm, compose, conciliate, pacify, placate, propitiate, quell, quiet, soothe, sweeten **2.** abate, allay, assuage, blunt, curb, cushion, ease, lessen, lull, mitigate, moderate, modify, relieve, soften, temper, tone down, tranquillize

mollycoddle 1. *v.* baby, coddle, cosset, indulge, pamper, pet, ruin, spoil **2.** *n.* baby, chinless wonder (*Brit. inf.*), crybaby, milksop, milquetoast (*U.S.*), namby-pamby, sissy, weakling

moment 1. flash, instant, jiffy (*Inf.*), minute, no time, second, shake (*Inf.*), split second, tick (*Brit. inf.*), trice, twinkling, two shakes (*Inf.*), two shakes of a lamb's tail (*Inf.*) **2.** hour, instant, juncture, point, point in time, stage, time **3.** concern, consequence, gravity, import, importance, seriousness, significance, substance, value, weight, weightiness, worth

momentarily briefly, for a moment (little while, minute, second, short time, short while), for an instant, temporarily

momentary brief, ephemeral, evanescent, fleeting, flying, fugitive, hasty, passing, quick, short, short-lived, temporary, transitory

momentous consequential, critical, crucial, decisive, earth-shaking (*Inf.*), fateful, grave, historic, important, of moment, pivotal, serious, significant, vital, weighty

momentum drive, energy, force, impetus, power, propulsion, push, strength, thrust

monarch crowned head, emperor, empress, king, potentate, prince, princess, queen, ruler, sovereign

monarchy 1. absolutism, autocracy, despotism, kingship, monocracy, royalism, sovereignty **2.** empire, kingdom, principality, realm

monastery abbey, cloister, convent, friary, house, nunnery, priory, religious community

monastic ascetic, austere, celibate, cenobitic, cloistered, cloistral, coenobitic, contemplative, conventual, eremitic, hermit-like, monachal, monkish, recluse, reclusive, secluded, sequestered, withdrawn

monetary budgetary, capital, cash, financial, fiscal, pecuniary

money 1. banknotes, bread (*Sl.*), capital, cash, coin, currency, dough (*Sl.*), filthy lucre (*Facetious*), funds, gelt (*Sl.*), green (*Sl.*), hard cash, legal tender, lolly (*Brit. sl.*), loot (*Inf.*), mazuma (*Sl., chiefly U.S.*), moolah (*Sl.*), pelf (*Contemptuous*), readies (*Inf.*), riches, specie, spondulix (*Sl.*), the ready (*Inf.*), the wherewithal, wealth **2. in the money** affluent, flush (*Inf.*), in clover (*Inf.*), loaded (*Sl.*), on Easy Street (*Inf.*), prosperous, rich, rolling (*Sl.*), wealthy, well-heeled (*Sl.*), well-off, well-to-do

moneyed, monied affluent, flush (*Inf.*), loaded (*Sl.*), prosperous, rich, wealthy, well-heeled (*Sl.*), well-off, well-to-do

moneymaking *adj.* gainful, going, lucrative, paying, profitable, remunerative, successful, thriving

mongrel 1. *n.* bigener (*Biol.*), cross, crossbreed, half-breed, hybrid, mixed breed **2.** *adj.* bastard, crossbred, half-breed, hybrid, of mixed breed

monitor 1. *n.* guide, invigilator, overseer, prefect (*Brit.*), supervisor, watchdog **2.** *v.* check, follow, keep an eye on, keep track of, observe, oversee, record, scan, supervise, survey, watch

monitory admonishing, admonitory, cautionary, cautioning, reproving, warning

monk brother, friar (*loosely*), monastic, religious

monkey *n.* **1.** primate, simian **2.** devil, imp, mischief maker, rascal, rogue,

scamp **3.** *Sl.* ass, butt, dupe, fool, laughing stock **4. make a monkey of** make a fool of, make (someone) a laughing stock, make fun of, make (someone) look foolish (ridiculous, silly), play a trick on, ridicule ~*v.* **5.** fiddle, fool, interfere, meddle, mess, play, tamper, tinker, trifle

monkey business 1. carry-on (*Inf.*), clowning, mischief, monkey tricks, pranks, shenanigans (*Inf.*), skylarking (*Inf.*), tomfoolery **2.** chicanery, dishonesty, funny business, hanky-panky (*Inf.*), skulduggery (*Inf.*), trickery

monolithic colossal, giant, gigantic, huge, immovable, impenetrable, imposing, intractable, massive, monumental, solid, substantial, undifferentiated, undivided, unitary

monologue harangue, lecture, sermon, soliloquy, speech

monomania bee in one's bonnet (*Inf.*), fanaticism, fixation, hobbyhorse, *idée fixe*, obsession, one-track mind (*Inf.*)

monopolize control, corner, corner the market in, dominate, engross, exercise *or* have a monopoly of, hog (*Sl.*), keep to oneself, take over, take up

monotonous all the same, boring, colourless, droning, dull, flat, humdrum, plodding, repetitious, repetitive, samey (*Inf.*), soporific, tedious, tiresome, toneless, unchanging, uniform, uninflected, unvaried, wearisome

monotony boredom, colourlessness, dullness, flatness, humdrumness, monotonousness, repetitiveness, repetitiousness, routine, sameness, tediousness, tedium, tiresomeness, uniformity, wearisomeness

monster *n.* **1.** barbarian, beast, bogeyman, brute, demon, devil, fiend, ogre, savage, villain **2.** abortion, freak, lusus naturae, miscreation, monstrosity, mutant, teratism **3.** behemoth, Brobdingnagian, colossus, giant, leviathan, mammoth, titan ~*adj.* **4.** Brobdingnagian, colossal, enormous, gargantuan, giant, gigantic, huge, immense, jumbo (*Inf.*), mammoth, massive, monstrous, stupendous, titanic, tremendous

monstrosity 1. abortion, eyesore, freak, horror, lusus naturae, miscreation, monster, mutant, ogre, teratism **2.** abnormality, atrocity, dreadfulness, evil, frightfulness, heinousness, hellishness, hideousness, horror, loathsomeness, obscenity

monstrous 1. abnormal, dreadful, enormous, fiendish, freakish, frightful, grotesque, gruesome, hellish, hideous, horrendous, horrible, miscreated, obscene, teratoid, terrible, unnatural **2.** atrocious, cruel, devilish, diabolical, disgraceful, egregious, evil, fiendish, foul, heinous, horrifying, infamous, inhuman, intolerable, loathsome, odious, outrageous, satanic, scandalous, shocking, vicious, villainous **3.** colossal, elephantine, enormous, gargantuan, giant, gigantic, great, huge, immense, mammoth, massive, prodigious, stupendous, titanic, towering, tremendous, vast

month four weeks, moon, thirty days

monument 1. cairn, cenotaph, commemoration, gravestone, headstone, marker, mausoleum, memorial, obelisk, pillar, shrine, statue, tombstone **2.** memento, record, remembrance, reminder, testament, token, witness

monumental 1. awe-inspiring, awesome, classic, enduring, enormous, epoch-making, historic, immortal, important, lasting, majestic, memorable, outstanding, prodigious, significant, stupendous, unforgettable **2.** commemorative, cyclopean, funerary, memorial, monolithic, statuary **3.** *Inf.* catastrophic, colossal, egregious, gigantic, great, horrible, immense, indefensible, massive, staggering, terrible, tremendous, unforgivable, whopping (*Inf.*)

mood 1. disposition, frame of mind, humour, spirit, state of mind, temper, tenor, vein **2.** bad temper, blues, depression, doldrums, dumps (*Inf.*), fit of pique, grumps (*Inf.*), low spirits, melancholy, sulk, the sulks **3. in the mood** disposed (towards), eager, favourable, inclined, interested, in the (right) frame of mind, keen, minded, willing

moody 1. angry, broody, cantankerous, crabbed, crabby, crestfallen, cross, crotchety (*Inf.*), crusty, curt, dismal, doleful, dour, downcast, down in the dumps (*Inf.*), down in the mouth (*Inf.*), frowning, gloomy, glum, huffish, huffy, ill-humoured, ill-tempered, in a huff, in the doldrums, introspective, irascible, irritable, lugubrious, melancholy, miserable, mopish, mopy, morose, offended, out of sorts (*Inf.*), pensive, petulant, piqued, sad, saturnine, short-tempered,

splenetic, sulky, sullen, temperamental, testy, touchy, waspish, wounded **2.** capricious, changeable, erratic, faddish, fickle, fitful, flighty, impulsive, inconstant, mercurial, temperamental, unpredictable, unstable, unsteady, volatile

moon *n.* **1.** satellite **2. once in a blue moon** almost never, hardly ever, rarely, very seldom ~*v.* **3.** daydream, idle, languish, mooch (*Sl.*), mope, waste time

moonshine 1. moonbeams, moonlight **2.** *U.S.* bootleg, hooch *or* hootch (*U.S. sl.*), poteen **3.** blather, blether, bosh (*Inf.*), bunk (*Inf.*), bunkum, claptrap (*Inf.*), foolish talk, gas (*Sl.*), guff (*Sl.*), havers (*Scot.*), hogwash, hot air (*Inf.*), nonsense, piffle (*Inf.*), rubbish, stuff and nonsense, tarradiddle, tosh (*Inf.*), tripe (*Inf.*), twaddle

moor[1] fell (*Brit.*), heath, moorland, muir (*Scot.*)

moor[2] anchor, berth, dock, fasten, fix, lash, make fast, secure, tie up

moot 1. *adj.* arguable, at issue, contestable, controversial, debatable, disputable, doubtful, open, open to debate, undecided, unresolved, unsettled **2.** *v.* bring up, broach, introduce, propose, put forward, suggest, ventilate

mop *n.* **1.** sponge, squeegee, swab **2.** mane, shock, tangle, thatch ~*v.* **3.** clean, soak up, sponge, swab, wash, wipe

mope be apathetic, be dejected, be down in the mouth (*Inf.*), be gloomy, brood, fret, go about like a half-shut knife (*Inf.*), hang around, idle, languish, moon, pine, pout, sulk, waste time, wear a long face

mop up 1. clean up, mop, soak up, sponge, swab, wash, wipe **2.** *Military* account for, clean out, clear, eliminate, finish off, neutralize, pacify, round up, secure

moral *adj.* **1.** ethical **2.** blameless, chaste, decent, ethical, good, high-minded, honest, honourable, incorruptible, innocent, just, meritorious, noble, principled, proper, pure, right, righteous, upright, upstanding, virtuous ~*n.* **3.** lesson, meaning, message, point, significance **4.** adage, aphorism, apophthegm, epigram, gnome, maxim, motto, proverb, saw, saying

morale confidence, esprit de corps, heart, mettle, self-esteem, spirit, temper

morality 1. chastity, decency, ethicality, ethicalness, goodness, honesty, integ-

rity, justice, principle, rectitude, righteousness, rightness, uprightness, virtue
2. conduct, ethics, habits, ideals, manners, moral code, morals, mores, philosophy, principles, standards

morals behaviour, conduct, ethics,
habits, integrity, manners, morality, mores, principles, scruples, standards

morass 1. bog, fen, marsh, marshland,
moss (*Scot.*, & *northern English
dialect*), quagmire, slough, swamp **2**.
chaos, confusion, jam (*Inf.*), mess, mix-
up, muddle, quagmire, tangle

moratorium freeze, halt, postponement, respite, standstill, stay, suspension

morbid 1. brooding, ghoulish, gloomy,
grim, melancholy, pessimistic, sick, sombre, unhealthy, unwholesome **2**. dreadful, ghastly, grisly, gruesome, hideous,
horrid, macabre **3**. ailing, deadly, diseased, infected, malignant, pathological,
sick, sickly, unhealthy, unsound

mordant 1. acerbic, acid, acrimonious,
astringent, biting, caustic, cutting,
edged, harsh, incisive, pungent, sarcastic, scathing, sharp, stinging, trenchant,
venomous, waspish **2**. acid, acidic, caustic, corrosive, pungent

more 1. *adj.* added, additional, extra,
fresh, further, new, other, spare, supplementary **2**. *adv.* better, further, longer, to a greater extent

moreover additionally, also, as well,
besides, further, furthermore, in addition, into the bargain, likewise, to boot,
too, what is more, withal (*Literary*)

morgue mortuary

moribund 1. at death's door, breathing one's last, doomed, dying, fading
fast, failing, (having) one foot in the
grave, *in extremis*, near death, near the
end, on one's deathbed, on one's last legs
2. at a standstill, declining, forceless, obsolescent, on its last legs, on the way out,
stagnant, stagnating, standing still, waning, weak

morning a.m., break of day, dawn,
daybreak, forenoon, morn (*Poetic*), mor-
row (*Archaic*), sunrise

moron ass, blockhead, bonehead (*Sl.*),
cretin, dimwit (*Inf.*), dolt, dope (*Sl.*),
dummy (*Sl.*), dunce, dunderhead, fool,
halfwit, idiot, imbecile, mental defective,
muttonhead (*Sl.*), numskull, simpleton,
thickhead

moronic asinine, Boeotian, brainless,

cretinous, daft, dimwitted (*Inf.*), doltish,
foolish, gormless (*Inf.*), halfwitted, idiotic, imbecilic, mentally defective, mindless, muttonheaded (*Sl.*), retarded, simple, stupid, thick, unintelligent

morose blue, churlish, crabbed, crabby, cross, crusty, depressed, dour, down,
down in the dumps (*Inf.*), gloomy, glum,
grouchy (*Inf.*), gruff, ill-humoured, ill-
natured, ill-tempered, in a bad mood,
low, melancholy, moody, mournful, perverse, pessimistic, saturnine, sour, sulky,
sullen, surly, taciturn

morsel bit, bite, crumb, fraction, fragment, grain, mouthful, nibble, part,
piece, scrap, segment, slice, snack,
soupçon, taste, titbit

mortal *adj.* **1**. corporeal, earthly,
ephemeral, human, impermanent, passing, sublunary, temporal, transient,
worldly **2**. deadly, death-dealing, destructive, fatal, killing, lethal, murderous, terminal **3**. bitter, deadly, implacable, irreconcilable, out-and-out, remorseless, sworn, to the death, unrelenting **4**. agonizing, awful, dire, enormous,
extreme, grave, great, intense, severe,
terrible ~*n*. **5**. being, body, earthling,
human, human being, individual, man,
person, woman

mortality 1. ephemerality, humanity,
impermanence, temporality, transience
2. bloodshed, carnage, death, destruction, fatality, killing, loss of life

mortification 1. abasement, annoyance, chagrin, discomfiture, dissatisfaction, embarrassment, humiliation, loss of
face, shame, vexation **2**. abasement,
chastening, control, denial, discipline,
subjugation **3**. *Medical* corruption, festering, gangrene, necrosis, putrescence

mortified 1. abashed, affronted, annoyed, ashamed, chagrined, chastened,
confounded, crushed, deflated, discomfited, displeased, embarrassed, given a
showing up (*Inf.*), humbled, humiliated,
made to eat humble pie (*Inf.*), put down,
put out (*Inf.*), put to shame, rendered
speechless, shamed, vexed **2**. abased,
chastened, conquered, controlled,
crushed, disciplined, subdued **3**. *Of flesh*
decayed, gangrenous, necrotic, rotted

mortify 1. abase, abash, affront, annoy, chagrin, chasten, confound, crush,
deflate, disappoint, discomfit, displease,
embarrass, humble, humiliate, make
(someone) eat humble pie (*Inf.*), put

down, put to shame, shame, take (someone) down a peg (*Inf.*), vex **2**. abase, chasten, control, deny, discipline, subdue **3**. *Of flesh* become gangrenous, corrupt, deaden, die, fester, gangrene, necrose, putrefy

mortuary funeral parlour, morgue

mostly above all, almost entirely, as a rule, chiefly, customarily, for the most part, generally, largely, mainly, most often, on the whole, particularly, predominantly, principally, usually

mote atom, grain, mite, particle, speck, spot

moth-eaten antiquated, decayed, decrepit, dilapidated, obsolete, outdated, outworn, ragged, seedy, shabby, stale, tattered, threadbare, worn-out

mother *n*. **1**. dam, ma (*Inf.*), mater, mom (*U.S. inf.*), mum (*Brit. inf.*), mummy (*Brit. inf.*), old lady (*Inf.*), old woman (*Inf.*) ~*adj*. **2**. connate, inborn, innate, native, natural ~*v*. **3**. bear, bring forth, give birth to, produce **4**. care for, cherish, nurse, nurture, protect, raise, rear, tend **5**. baby, fuss over, indulge, pamper, spoil

motherly affectionate, caring, comforting, fond, gentle, kind, loving, maternal, protective, sheltering, tender, warm

mother wit brains, common sense, gumption (*Brit. inf.*), horse sense, judgment, native intelligence, savvy (*Sl.*)

motif 1. concept, idea, leitmotiv, subject, theme **2**. decoration, design, form, ornament, shape

motion *n*. **1**. action, change, flow, kinesics, locomotion, mobility, motility, move, movement, passage, passing, progress, travel **2**. gesticulation, gesture, sign, signal, wave **3**. proposal, proposition, recommendation, submission, suggestion **4**. in motion afoot, functioning, going, in progress, moving, on the go (*Inf.*), on the move (*Inf.*), operational, travelling, under way, working ~*v*. **5**. beckon, direct, gesticulate, gesture, nod, signal, wave

motionless at a standstill, at rest, calm, fixed, frozen, halted, immobile, inanimate, inert, lifeless, paralysed, standing, static, stationary, still, stock-still, transfixed, unmoved, unmoving

motivate actuate, arouse, bring, cause, draw, drive, give incentive to, impel, induce, inspire, inspirit, instigate, lead, move, persuade, prompt, provoke, set on, stimulate, stir, trigger

motivation 1. ambition, desire, drive, hunger, inspiration, interest, wish **2**. impulse, incentive, incitement, inducement, inspiration, instigation, motive, persuasion, reason, spur, stimulus

motive 1. *n*. cause, design, ground(s), incentive, incitement, inducement, influence, inspiration, intention, mainspring, motivation, object, occasion, purpose, rationale, reason, spur, stimulus, thinking **2**. *adj*. activating, driving, impelling, motivating, moving, operative, prompting

motley 1. assorted, disparate, dissimilar, diversified, heterogeneous, mingled, miscellaneous, mixed, unlike, varied **2**. chequered, multicoloured, particoloured, polychromatic, polychrome, polychromous, rainbow, variegated

mottled blotchy, brindled, chequered, dappled, flecked, freckled, marbled, piebald, pied, speckled, spotted, stippled, streaked, tabby, variegated

motto adage, byword, cry, formula, gnome, maxim, precept, proverb, rule, saw, saying, slogan, watchword

mould[1] *n*. **1**. cast, die, form, matrix, pattern, shape **2**. brand, build, configuration, construction, cut, design, fashion, form, format, frame, kind, line, make, pattern, shape, structure, style **3**. calibre, character, ilk, kidney, kind, nature, quality, sort, stamp, type ~*v*. **4**. carve, cast, construct, create, fashion, forge, form, make, model, sculpt, shape, stamp, work **5**. affect, control, direct, form, influence, make, shape

mould[2] blight, fungus, mildew, mouldiness, mustiness

mould[3] dirt, earth, humus, loam, soil

moulder crumble, decay, decompose, disintegrate, perish, rot, waste

mouldy bad, blighted, decaying, fusty, mildewed, musty, rotten, rotting, spoiled, stale

mound 1. bing (*Scot.*), drift, heap, pile, stack **2**. bank, dune, embankment, hill, hillock, knoll, rise **3**. *Archaeology* barrow, tumulus **4**. bulwark, earthwork, motte (*History*), rampart

mount *v*. **1**. ascend, clamber up, climb, escalade, go up, make one's way up, scale **2**. bestride, climb onto, climb up on, get astride, get (up) on, jump on **3**. arise, ascend, rise, soar, tower **4**. accumulate, build, escalate, grow, increase, intensify, multiply, pile up, swell **5**. display, frame, set, set off **6**. exhibit, get up (*Inf.*), prepare, produce, put on, stage **7**. *Military* deliver, launch, prepare, ready, set in motion, stage **8**. emplace, fit, install, place, position, put in place, set up ~*n*. **9**. backing, base, fixture, foil, frame, mounting, setting, stand, support **10**. horse, steed (*Literary*)

mountain 1. alp, ben (*Scot.*), elevation, eminence, fell (*Brit.*), height, mount, peak **2**. abundance, heap, mass, mound, pile, stack, ton

mountainous 1. alpine, high, highland, rocky, soaring, steep, towering, upland **2**. daunting, enormous, gigantic, great, huge, hulking, immense, mammoth, mighty, monumental, ponderous, prodigious

mountebank charlatan, cheat, confidence trickster, con man (*Inf.*), fake, fraud, impostor, phoney (*Sl.*), pretender, quack, rogue, swindler

mourn bemoan, bewail, deplore, grieve, keen, lament, miss, rue, sorrow, wail, wear black, weep

mournful 1. afflicting, calamitous, deplorable, distressing, grievous, lamentable, melancholy, painful, piteous, plaintive, sad, sorrowful, tragic, unhappy, woeful **2**. brokenhearted, cheerless, desolate, disconsolate, downcast, funereal, gloomy, grief-stricken, grieving, heartbroken, heavy, heavy-hearted, joyless, lugubrious, melancholy, rueful, sad, sombre, unhappy, woeful

mourning 1. bereavement, grief, grieving, keening, lamentation, weeping, woe **2**. black, sackcloth and ashes, weeds, widow's weeds

mousy, mousey 1. brownish, colourless, drab, dull, indeterminate, plain **2**. diffident, ineffectual, quiet, self-effacing, shy, timid, timorous, unassertive

mouth *n*. **1**. chops (*Sl.*), gob (*Sl.*), jaws, lips, maw, trap (*Sl.*), yap (*Sl.*) **2**. *Inf.* boasting, braggadocio, bragging, empty talk, gas (*Sl.*), hot air (*Sl.*), idle talk **3**. *Inf.* backchat (*Inf.*), cheek (*Inf.*), impudence, insolence, lip (*Sl.*), rudeness, sauce (*Inf.*) **4**. aperture, cavity, crevice, door, entrance, gateway, inlet, lips, opening, orifice, rim **5**. face, grimace, *moue*, pout, wry face **6**. **down in** *or* **at the mouth** blue, crestfallen, dejected, depressed, disheartened, dispirited, down, downcast, down in the dumps (*Inf.*), in low spirits, melancholy, sad, unhappy

mouthful bit, bite, drop, forkful, little, morsel, sample, sip, spoonful, sup, swallow, taste

mouthpiece 1. agent, delegate, representative, spokesman, spokeswoman **2**. journal, organ, periodical, publication

movable detachable, mobile, not fixed, portable, portative, transferable, transportable

movables belongings, chattels, effects, furniture, gear (*Inf.*), goods, possessions, property, stuff (*Inf.*), things (*Inf.*)

move 1. advance, budge, change position, drift, go, march, proceed, progress, shift, stir, walk **2**. carry, change, shift, switch, transfer, transport, transpose **3**. change residence, flit (*Scot., & northern English dialect*), go away, leave, migrate, move house, quit, relocate, remove **4**. activate, drive, impel, motivate, operate, propel, push, set going, shift, shove, start, turn **5**. actuate, affect, agitate, cause, excite, give rise to, impel, impress, incite, induce, influence, inspire, instigate, lead, make an impression on, motivate, persuade, prompt, rouse, stimulate, touch, urge **6**. advocate, propose, put forward, recommend, suggest, urge ~*n*. **7**. act, action, deed, manoeuvre, measure, motion, movement, ploy, shift, step, stratagem, stroke, turn **8**. change of address, flit (*Scot., & northern English dialect*), flitting (*Scot., & northern English dialect*), migration, relocation, removal, shift, transfer **9**. **get a move on** get cracking (*Inf.*), get going (*Inf.*), hurry (up), make haste, speed up, step on it (*Inf.*), stir oneself **10**. **on the move** *Inf.* **a**. in transit, journeying, moving, on the road (*Inf.*), on the run, on the wing, travelling, under way, voyaging **b**. active, advancing, astir, going forward, moving, progressing, stirring, succeeding

movement 1. act, action, activity, advance, agitation, change, development, displacement, exercise, flow, gesture, manoeuvre, motion, move, moving, operation, progress, progression, shift, steps, stir, stirring, transfer **2**. campaign, crusade, drive, faction, front, group, grouping, organization, party **3**. current, drift, flow, swing, tendency, trend **4**. action, innards (*Inf.*), machinery, mechanism, workings, works **5**. *Music* division, part, passage, section **6**. beat, cadence, measure, metre, pace, rhythm, swing, tempo

movie 1. feature, film, flick (*Sl.*), motion picture, moving picture (*U.S.*), picture **2.** *Plural* cinema, film, films, flicks (*Sl.*), pictures (*Inf.*), silver screen (*Inf.*)

moving 1. affecting, arousing, emotional, emotive, exciting, impelling, impressive, inspiring, pathetic, persuasive, poignant, stirring, touching **2.** mobile, motile, movable, portable, running, unfixed **3.** dynamic, impelling, inspirational, motivating, propelling, stimulating, stimulative

mow crop, cut, scythe, shear, trim

mow down butcher, cut down, cut to pieces, massacre, shoot down, slaughter

much 1. *adj.* abundant, a lot of, ample, considerable, copious, great, plenteous, plenty of, sizeable, substantial **2.** *adv.* a great deal, a lot, considerably, decidedly, exceedingly, frequently, greatly, indeed, often, regularly **3.** *n.* a good deal, a great deal, a lot, an appreciable amount, heaps (*Inf.*), loads (*Inf.*), lots (*Inf.*), plenty

muck 1. dung, manure, ordure **2.** dirt, filth, gunge (*Inf.*), gunk (*Inf.*), mire, mud, ooze, scum, sewage, slime, sludge **3. make a muck of** *Sl.* botch, bungle, make a mess of, mar, mess up, muff, ruin, screw up (*Inf.*), spoil

muck up botch, bungle, make a mess of, make a muck of (*Sl.*), mar, mess up, muff, ruin, screw up (*Inf.*), spoil

mucky begrimed, bespattered, dirty, filthy, grimy, messy, mud-caked, muddy, soiled, sticky

mucous glutinous, gummy, mucilaginous, slimy, viscid, viscous

mud clay, dirt, mire, ooze, silt, sludge

muddle *v.* **1.** confuse, disarrange, disorder, disorganize, jumble, make a mess of, mess, mix up, scramble, spoil, tangle **2.** befuddle, bewilder, confound, confuse, daze, disorient, perplex, stupefy ~*n.* **3.** chaos, clutter, confusion, daze, disarray, disorder, disorganization, fankle (*Scot.*), jumble, mess, mix-up, perplexity, plight, predicament, tangle

muddle along *or* **through** cope, get along, get by, make it, manage, manage somehow, scrape by

muddled 1. chaotic, confused, disarrayed, disordered, disorganized, higgledy-piggledy (*Inf.*), jumbled, messy, mixed-up, scrambled, tangled **2.** at sea,

befuddled, bewildered, confused, dazed, disoriented, perplexed, stupefied, vague **3.** confused, incoherent, loose, muddleheaded, unclear, woolly

muddy *adj.* **1.** bespattered, boggy, clarty (*Scot., & northern English dialect*), dirty, grimy, marshy, miry, mucky, mud-caked, quaggy, soiled, swampy **2.** blurred, dingy, dull, flat, lustreless, smoky, unclear, washed-out **3.** cloudy, dirty, foul, impure, opaque, turbid **4.** confused, fuzzy, hazy, indistinct, muddled, unclear, vague, woolly ~*v.* **5.** begrime, bespatter, cloud, dirty, smear, smirch, soil

muff *v.* botch, bungle, fluff (*Inf.*), make a mess of, make a muck of (*Inf.*), mess up, mismanage, screw up (*Inf.*), spoil

muffle 1. cloak, conceal, cover, disguise, envelop, hood, mask, shroud, swaddle, swathe, wrap up **2.** deaden, dull, gag, hush, muzzle, quieten, silence, soften, stifle, suppress

muffled dim, dull, faint, indistinct, muted, stifled, strangled, subdued, suppressed

mug[1] beaker, cup, flagon, jug, pot, tankard, toby jug

mug[2] clock (*Brit. sl.*), countenance, dial (*Sl.*), face, features, kisser (*Sl.*), mush (*Brit. sl.*), phiz *or* phizog (*Brit. sl.*), puss (*Sl.*), visage

mug[3] chump (*Inf.*) gull (*Archaic*), easy *or* soft touch (*Sl.*), fool, innocent, mark (*Sl.*), muggins (*Brit. sl.*), simpleton, sucker (*Sl.*)

muggy clammy, close, damp, humid, moist, oppressive, sticky, stuffy, sultry

mug up bone up (*Inf. chiefly U.S.*), burn the midnight oil (*Inf.*), cram (*Inf.*), get up (*Inf.*), study, swot (*Brit. inf.*)

mulish bull-headed, cross-grained, difficult, headstrong, inflexible, intractable, intransigent, obstinate, perverse, pig-headed, recalcitrant, refractory, rigid, self-willed, stiff-necked, stubborn, unreasonable, wilful

mull consider, contemplate, deliberate, examine, meditate, muse on, ponder, reflect on, review, ruminate, study, think about, think over, turn over in one's mind, weigh

multifarious different, diverse, diversified, legion, manifold, many, miscellaneous, multiform, multiple, multitudinous, numerous, sundry, varied, variegated

multiple collective, manifold, many, multitudinous, numerous, several, sundry, various

multiplicity abundance, array, diversity, heaps (*Inf.*), host, loads (*Inf.*), lot, lots (*Inf.*), mass, myriad, number, oodles (*Inf.*), piles, profusion, scores, stacks, tons, variety

multiply accumulate, augment, breed, build up, expand, extend, increase, proliferate, propagate, reproduce, spread

multitude 1. army, assemblage, assembly, collection, concourse, congregation, crowd, great number, horde, host, legion, lot, lots (*Inf.*), mass, mob, myriad, sea, swarm, throng 2. commonalty, common people, herd, hoi polloi, mob, populace, proletariat, public, rabble

multitudinous abounding, abundant, considerable, copious, countless, great, infinite, innumerable, legion, manifold, many, myriad, numerous, profuse, teeming, very numerous

mum 1. closemouthed, dumb, mute, quiet, secretive, silent, tight-lipped, uncommunicative, unforthcoming 2. **mum's the word** don't let on, don't tell a soul, keep quiet, keep silent, keep (something) secret, keep (something) to oneself, keep (something) under one's hat, play dumb, say nothing, tell no-one

mumbo jumbo 1. abracadabra, chant, charm, conjuration, hocus-pocus, incantation, magic, rite, ritual, spell, superstition 2. cant, claptrap (*Inf.*), double talk, gibberish, gobbledegook (*Inf.*), humbug, jargon, nonsense, rigmarole

munch champ, chew, chomp, crunch, masticate, scrunch

mundane 1. banal, commonplace, day-to-day, everyday, humdrum, ordinary, prosaic, routine, workaday 2. earthly, fleshly, human, material, mortal, secular, sublunary, temporal, terrestrial, worldly

municipal borough, city, civic, community, public, town, urban

municipality borough, burgh (*Scot.*), city, district, town, township, urban community

munificence beneficence, benevolence, big-heartedness, bounteousness, bounty, generosity, generousness, largess, liberality, magnanimousness, open-handedness, philanthropy

munificent beneficent, benevolent, big-hearted, bounteous, bountiful, free-handed, generous, lavish, liberal, magnanimous, open-handed, philanthropical, princely, rich, unstinting

murder n. 1. assassination, bloodshed, butchery, carnage, homicide, killing, manslaughter, massacre, slaying 2. *Inf.* agony, an ordeal, a trial, danger, difficulty, hell (*Inf.*), misery, trouble ∼v. 3. assassinate, bump off (*Inf.*), butcher, destroy, dispatch, do in (*Inf.*), do to death, eliminate (*Sl.*), hit (*U.S. sl.*), kill, massacre, rub out (*U.S. sl.*), slaughter, slay, take the life of, waste (*U.S. sl.*) 4. abuse, butcher, destroy, mangle, mar, misuse, ruin, spoil 5. *Inf.* beat decisively, defeat utterly, drub, hammer (*Inf.*), make mincemeat of (*Inf.*), slaughter, thrash

murderer assassin, butcher, cutthroat, hit man (*Sl.*), homicide, killer, slaughterer, slayer

murderous 1. barbarous, bloodthirsty, bloody, brutal, cruel, deadly, death-dealing, destructive, devastating, fatal, fell (*Archaic*), ferocious, internecine, lethal, sanguinary, savage, slaughterous, withering 2. *Inf.* arduous, difficult, exhausting, harrowing, hellish (*Inf.*), killing (*Inf.*), sapping, strenuous, unpleasant

murky cheerless, cloudy, dark, dim, dismal, dreary, dull, dusky, foggy, gloomy, grey, impenetrable, misty, nebulous, obscure, overcast

murmur n. 1. babble, buzzing, drone, humming, mumble, muttering, purr, rumble, susurrus (*Literary*), undertone, whisper, whispering ∼v. 2. babble, buzz, drone, hum, mumble, mutter, purr, rumble, speak in an undertone, whisper ∼n. 3. beef (*Sl.*), complaint, gripe (*Inf.*), grouse, grumble, moan (*Inf.*), word ∼v. 4. beef (*Sl.*), carp, cavil, complain, gripe (*Inf.*), grouse, grumble, moan (*Inf.*)

muscle n. 1. muscle tissue, sinew, tendon, thew 2. brawn, clout (*Sl.*), force, forcefulness, might, potency, power, stamina, strength, sturdiness, weight ∼v. 3. **muscle in** *Inf.* butt in, elbow one's way in, force one's way in, impose oneself

muscular athletic, beefy (*Inf.*), brawny, husky (*Inf.*), lusty, powerful, powerfully built, robust, sinewy, stalwart, strapping, strong, sturdy, vigorous, well-knit

muse be in a brown study, be lost in thought, brood, cogitate, consider, contemplate, deliberate, dream, meditate, mull over, ponder, reflect, ruminate, speculate, think, think over, weigh

mush 1. dough, mash, pap, paste, pulp **2.** *Inf.* corn (*Inf.*), mawkishness, schmaltz (*Sl.*), sentimentality, slush (*Inf.*)

mushroom *v.* boom, burgeon, expand, flourish, grow rapidly, increase, luxuriate, proliferate, shoot up, spread, spring up, sprout

mushy 1. doughy, pappy, paste-like, pulpy, semi-liquid, semi-solid, slushy, soft, squashy, squelchy, squidgy (*Inf.*) **2.** *Inf.* corny (*Inf.*), maudlin, mawkish, saccharine, schmaltzy (*Sl.*), sentimental, sloppy (*Inf.*), slushy (*Inf.*), sugary, syrupy, weepy, wet (*Inf.*)

musical dulcet, euphonious, harmonious, lilting, lyrical, melodic, melodious, sweet-sounding, tuneful

musing *n.* absent-mindedness, abstraction, brown study, cerebration, cogitation, contemplation, daydreaming, dreaming, introspection, meditation, reflection, reverie, rumination, thinking, woolgathering

must[1] *n.* duty, essential, fundamental, imperative, necessary thing, necessity, obligation, prerequisite, requirement, requisite, *sine qua non*

must[2] *n.* decay, fetor, fustiness, mildew, mould, mouldiness, mustiness, rot

muster *v.* **1.** assemble, call together, call up, collect, come together, congregate, convene, convoke, enrol, gather, group, marshal, meet, mobilize, rally, round up, summon ~*n.* **2.** assemblage, assembly, collection, concourse, congregation, convention, convocation, gathering, meeting, mobilization, rally, round-up **3. pass muster** be *or* come up to scratch, be acceptable, fill the bill (*Inf.*), make the grade, measure up, qualify

musty 1. airless, dank, decayed, frowsty, fusty, mildewed, mildewy, mouldy, old, smelly, stale, stuffy **2.** ancient, antediluvian, antiquated, banal, clichéd, dull, hackneyed, hoary, moth-eaten, obsolete, old-fashioned, stale, threadbare, trite, worn-out

mutability alteration, change, evolution, metamorphosis, transition, variation, vicissitude

mutable adaptable, alterable, change-able, changing, fickle, flexible, inconsistent, inconstant, irresolute, uncertain, undependable, unreliable, unsettled, unstable, unsteady, vacillating, variable, volatile, wavering

mutation 1. alteration, change, deviation, evolution, metamorphosis, modification, transfiguration, transformation, variation **2.** anomaly, deviant, mutant

mute 1. *adj.* aphasiac, aphasic, aphonic, dumb, mum, silent, speechless, unexpressed, unspeaking, unspoken, voiceless, wordless **2.** *v.* dampen, deaden, lower, moderate, muffle, soften, soft-pedal, subdue, tone down, turn down

mutilate 1. amputate, butcher, cripple, cut to pieces, cut up, damage, disable, disfigure, dismember, hack, injure, lacerate, lame, maim, mangle **2.** adulterate, bowdlerize, butcher, censor, cut, damage, distort, expurgate, hack, mar, spoil

mutinous bolshie (*Brit. inf.*), contumacious, disobedient, insubordinate, insurgent, rebellious, refractory, revolutionary, riotous, seditious, subversive, turbulent, ungovernable, unmanageable, unruly

mutiny 1. *n.* defiance, disobedience, insubordination, insurrection, rebellion, refusal to obey orders, resistance, revolt, revolution, riot, rising, strike, uprising **2.** *v.* be insubordinate, defy authority, disobey, rebel, refuse to obey orders, resist, revolt, rise up, strike

mutt 1. dolt, dunderhead, fool, idiot, ignoramus, imbecile (*Inf.*), moron, thick-head **2.** cur, dog, mongrel

mutter complain, grouch, grouse, grumble, mumble, murmur, rumble

mutual common, communal, correlative, interactive, interchangeable, interchanged, joint, reciprocal, reciprocated, requited, returned, shared

muzzle *n.* **1.** jaws, mouth, nose, snout **2.** gag, guard ~*v.* **3.** censor, choke, curb, gag (*Inf.*), restrain, silence, stifle, suppress

myopic near-sighted, short-sighted

myriad 1. *adj.* a thousand and one, countless, immeasurable, incalculable, innumerable, multitudinous, untold **2.** *n.* a million, army, a thousand, flood, horde, host, millions, mountain, multitude, scores, sea, swarm, thousands

mysterious abstruse, arcane, baffling, concealed, covert, cryptic, curious, dark, enigmatic, furtive, hidden, impenetrable, incomprehensible, inexplicable, inscrutable, insoluble, mystical, mystifying, obscure, perplexing, puzzling, recondite, secret, secretive, sphinxlike, strange, uncanny, unfathomable, unknown, veiled, weird

mystery conundrum, enigma, problem, puzzle, question, riddle, secrecy, secret

mystic, mystical abstruse, arcane, cabalistic, cryptic, enigmatical, esoteric, hidden, inscrutable, metaphysical, mysterious, nonrational, occult, otherworldly, paranormal, preternatural, supernatural, transcendental

mystify baffle, bamboozle (*Inf.*), beat (*Sl.*), befog, bewilder, confound, confuse, elude, escape, perplex, puzzle, stump

mystique awe, charisma, charm, fascination, glamour, magic, spell

myth 1. allegory, fable, fairy story, fiction, folk tale, legend, parable, saga, story, tradition **2**. delusion, fancy, fantasy, figment, illusion, imagination, superstition, tall story

mythical 1. allegorical, chimerical, fabled, fabulous, fairy-tale, legendary, mythological, storied **2**. fabricated, fanciful, fantasy, fictitious, imaginary, invented, made-up, make-believe, nonexistent, pretended, unreal, untrue

mythological fabulous, folkloric, heroic, legendary, mythic, mythical, traditional

mythology folklore, folk tales, legend, lore, mythos, myths, stories, tradition

N

nab apprehend, arrest, capture, catch, collar (*Inf.*), grab, seize, snatch

nabob billionaire, Croesus, millionaire, multimillionaire

nadir bottom, depths, lowest point, minimum, rock bottom, zero

nag[1] 1. *v.* annoy, badger, berate, chivvy, goad, harass, harry, henpeck, irritate, pester, plague, provoke, scold, torment, upbraid, vex, worry 2. *n.* harpy, scold, shrew, tartar, termagant, virago

nag[2] hack, horse, jade, plug (*U.S.*)

nagging continuous, critical, distressing, irritating, painful, persistent, scolding, shrewish, worrying

naiad nymph, sprite, undine, water nymph

nail *v.* attach, beat, fasten, fix, hammer, join, pin, secure, tack

naive 1. artless, candid, childlike, confiding, frank, guileless, ingenuous, innocent, jejune, natural, open, simple, trusting, unaffected, unpretentious, unsophisticated, unworldly 2. callow, credulous, gullible, green (*Inf.*), unsuspicious

naiveté 1. artlessness, candour, frankness, guilelessness, inexperience, ingenuousness, innocence, naturalness, openness, simplicity 2. callowness, credulity, gullibility

naked 1. bare, denuded, disrobed, divested, exposed, in one's birthday suit (*Inf.*), in the altogether (*Inf.*), in the buff (*Inf.*), nude, starkers (*Inf.*), stripped, unclothed, unconcealed, uncovered, undraped, undressed 2. blatant, evident, manifest, open, overt, patent, plain, simple, stark, unadorned, undisguised, unexaggerated, unmistakable, unqualified, unvarnished 3. defenceless, helpless, insecure, unarmed, unguarded, unprotected, vulnerable

nakedness 1. baldness, bareness, nudity, undress 2. openness, plainness, simplicity, starkness

namby-pamby anaemic, colourless, feeble, insipid, mawkish, prim, prissy (*Inf.*), sentimental, spineless, vapid, weak, wishy-washy (*Inf.*)

name *n.* 1. appellation, cognomen, denomination, designation, epithet, handle (*Sl.*), moniker (*Inf.*), nickname, sobriquet, term, title 2. distinction, eminence, esteem, fame, honour, note, praise, renown, repute 3. character, credit, reputation ~*v.* 4. baptize, call, christen, denominate, dub, entitle, label, style, term 5. appoint, choose, cite, classify, commission, designate, identify, mention, nominate, select, specify

named 1. baptized, called, christened, denominated, dubbed, entitled, known as, labelled, styled, termed 2. appointed, chosen, cited, classified, commissioned, designated, identified, mentioned, nominated, picked, selected, singled out, specified

nameless 1. anonymous, innominate, undesignated, unnamed, untitled 2. incognito, obscure, undistinguished, unheard-of, unknown, unsung 3. abominable, horrible, indescribable, ineffable, inexpressible, unmentionable, unspeakable, unutterable

namely i.e., specifically, that is to say, to wit, viz.

nap[1] 1. *v.* catnap, doze, drop off (*Inf.*), drowse, nod, nod off (*Inf.*), rest, sleep, snooze (*Inf.*) 2. *n.* catnap, forty winks (*Inf.*), rest, shuteye (*Sl.*), siesta, sleep

nap[2] down, fibre, grain, pile, shag, weave

narcissism egotism, self-admiration, self-love, vanity

narcotic 1. *n.* anaesthetic, analgesic, anodyne, drug, opiate, painkiller, sedative, tranquillizer 2. *adj.* analgesic, calming, dulling, hypnotic, Lethean, numbing, painkilling, sedative, somnolent, soporific, stupefacient, stupefactive, stupefying

narrate chronicle, describe, detail, recite, recount, rehearse, relate, repeat, report, set forth, tell, unfold

narration description, explanation, reading, recital, rehearsal, relation, storytelling, telling, voice-over (*in film*)

narrative account, chronicle, detail, history, report, statement, story, tale

narrator annalist, author, bard, chronicler, commentator, raconteur, reciter, relater, reporter, storyteller, writer

narrow *adj.* **1.** circumscribed, close, confined, constricted, contracted, cramped, incapacious, limited, meagre, near, pinched, restricted, scanty, straitened, tight **2.** biased, bigoted, dogmatic, illiberal, intolerant, narrow-minded, partial, prejudiced, reactionary, small-minded **3.** attenuated, fine, slender, slim, spare, tapering, thin **4.** exclusive, select **5.** *Inf.* avaricious, close (*Inf.*), mean, mercenary, niggardly, ungenerous ~*v.* **6.** circumscribe, constrict, diminish, limit, reduce, simplify, straiten, tighten

narrowly 1. barely, by a whisker *or* hair's-breadth, just, only just, scarcely **2.** carefully, closely, painstakingly, scrutinizingly

narrow-minded biased, bigoted, conservative, hidebound, illiberal, insular, intolerant, opinionated, parochial, petty, prejudiced, provincial, reactionary, short-sighted, small-minded, strait-laced

narrows channel, gulf, passage, sound, straits

nascent beginning, budding, dawning, developing, evolving, incipient

nastiness 1. defilement, dirtiness, filth, filthiness, foulness, impurity, pollution, squalor, uncleanliness **2.** indecency, licentiousness, obscenity, pollution, porn (*Inf.*), pornography, ribaldry, smuttiness **3.** disagreeableness, malice, meanness, offensiveness, spitefulness, unpleasantness

nasty 1. dirty, disagreeable, disgusting, filthy, foul, horrible, loathsome, malodorous, mephitic, nauseating, noisome, objectionable, obnoxious, odious, offensive, polluted, repellent, repugnant, sickening, unappetizing, unpleasant, vile **2.** blue, foul, gross, impure, indecent, lascivious, lewd, licentious, obscene, pornographic, ribald, smutty **3.** abusive, annoying, bad-tempered, despicable, disagreeable, distasteful, malicious, mean, spiteful, unpleasant, vicious, vile **4.** bad, critical, dangerous, painful, serious, severe

nation commonwealth, community, country, people, population, race, realm, society, state, tribe

national *adj.* **1.** civil, countrywide, governmental, nationwide, public, state, widespread **2.** domestic, internal, social ~*n.* **3.** citizen, inhabitant, native, resident, subject

nationalism allegiance, chauvinism, fealty, jingoism, loyalty, nationality, patriotism

nationalistic chauvinistic, jingoistic, loyal, patriotic, xenophobic

nationality birth, ethnic group, nation, race

nationwide countrywide, general, national, overall, widespread

native *adj.* **1.** built-in, congenital, endemic, hereditary, inborn, inbred, indigenous, ingrained, inherent, inherited, innate, instinctive, intrinsic, inveterate, natal, natural **2.** genuine, original, real **3.** domestic, home, home-grown, homemade, indigenous, local, mother, vernacular **4.** aboriginal, autochthonous ~*n.* **5.** aborigine, autochthon, citizen, countryman, dweller, inhabitant, national, resident

nativity 1. birth, delivery, parturition **2.** crèche, manger scene

natter 1. *v.* blather, blether, chatter, gabble, gossip, jabber, jaw (*Sl.*), palaver, prate, prattle, talk, talk idly, witter (*Inf.*) **2.** *n.* blather, blether, chat, chinwag (*Brit. inf.*), chitchat, confabulation, conversation, gab (*Inf.*), gabble, gossip, jabber, jaw (*Sl.*), palaver, prattle, talk

natty chic, dapper, elegant, fashionable, neat, smart, snazzy (*Inf.*), spruce, stylish, trim, well-dressed, well-turned-out

natural 1. common, everyday, legitimate, logical, normal, ordinary, regular, typical, usual **2.** characteristic, congenital, essential, inborn, indigenous, inherent, innate, instinctive, intuitive, natal, native **3.** artless, candid, frank, genuine, ingenuous, open, real, simple, spontaneous, unaffected, unpretentious, unsophisticated, unstudied **4.** organic, plain, pure, unbleached, unmixed, unpolished, unrefined, whole

naturalism factualism, realism, verisimilitude

naturalist 1. biologist, botanist, ecologist, zoologist **2.** factualist, realist

naturalistic factualistic, kitchen sink, lifelike, photographic, realistic, real-life, representational, true-to-life, warts and all (*Inf.*)

naturalize acclimate, acclimatize, acculturate, accustom, adapt, adopt, domesticate, enfranchise, familiarize, grant citizenship, habituate

naturally 1. *adv.* as anticipated, customarily, genuinely, informally, normally, simply, spontaneously, typically, unaffectedly, unpretentiously 2. *interj.* absolutely, as a matter of course, certainly, of course

naturalness 1. artlessness, candidness, frankness, genuineness, ingenuousness, openness, realism, simpleness, simplicity, spontaneousness, unaffectedness, unpretentiousness, unsophisticatedness, unstudiedness 2. plainness, pureness, purity, wholeness

nature 1. attributes, character, complexion, constitution, essence, features, make-up, quality, traits 2. category, description, kind, sort, species, style, type, variety 3. cosmos, creation, earth, environment, universe, world 4. disposition, humour, mood, outlook, temper, temperament 5. country, countryside, landscape, natural history, scenery

naturist nudist

naught nil, nothing, nothingness, nought, zero

naughty 1. annoying, bad, disobedient, exasperating, fractious, impish, misbehaved, mischievous, perverse, playful, refractory, roguish, sinful, teasing, wayward, wicked, worthless 2. bawdy, blue, improper, lewd, obscene, off-colour, ribald, risqué, smutty, vulgar

nausea 1. biliousness, qualm(s), queasiness, retching, sickness, squeamishness, vomiting 2. abhorrence, aversion, disgust, loathing, repugnance, revulsion

nauseate disgust, horrify, offend, repel, repulse, revolt, sicken

nauseous abhorrent, detestable, disgusting, distasteful, loathsome, nauseating, offensive, repugnant, repulsive, revolting, sickening

nautical marine, maritime, naval, oceanic, seafaring, seagoing, yachting

naval marine, maritime, nautical, oceanic

navel 1. bellybutton (*Inf.*), omphalos (*Literary*), umbilicus 2. central point, centre, hub, middle

navigable 1. clear, negotiable, passable, traversable, unobstructed 2. controllable, dirigible, sailable, steerable

navigate con (*Nautical*), cross, cruise, direct, drive, guide, handle, journey, manoeuvre, pilot, plan, plot, sail, skipper, steer, voyage

navigation cruising, helmsmanship, pilotage, sailing, seamanship, steering, voyaging

navigator mariner, pilot, seaman

navvy labourer

navy argosy (*Archaic*), armada, fleet, flotilla, warships

near *adj.* **1.** adjacent, adjoining, alongside, at close quarters, beside, bordering, close, close by, contiguous, nearby, neighbouring, nigh, touching 2. approaching, forthcoming, imminent, impending, in the offing, looming, near-at-hand, next, on the cards (*Inf.*) 3. akin, allied, attached, connected, dear, familiar, intimate, related 4. *Inf.* close-fisted, mean, miserly, niggardly, parsimonious, stingy, tightfisted, ungenerous

nearby 1. *adj.* adjacent, adjoining, convenient, handy, neighbouring 2. *adv.* at close quarters, close at hand, not far away, within reach

nearing advancing, approaching, approximating, coming, imminent, impending

nearly *adv.* about, all but, almost, approaching, approximately, as good as, closely, just about, not quite, practically, roughly, virtually, well-nigh

nearness 1. accessibility, availability, closeness, contiguity, handiness, juxtaposition, propinquity, proximity, vicinity 2. immediacy, imminence 3. dearness, familiarity, intimacy 4. *Inf.* meanness, niggardliness, parsimony, stinginess

near-sighted myopic, short-sighted

near thing close shave (*Inf.*), narrow escape, near miss

neat 1. accurate, dainty, fastidious, methodical, nice, orderly, shipshape, smart, spick-and-span, spruce, straight, systematic, tidy, trim, uncluttered 2. adept, adroit, agile, apt, clever, deft, dexterous, efficient, effortless, elegant, expert, graceful, handy, nimble, practised, precise, skilful, stylish, well-judged 3. *Of alcoholic drinks* pure, straight, undiluted, unmixed

neaten arrange, clean up, groom, put to rights, straighten out *or* up, tidy, tidy up, trim

neatly 1. accurately, daintily, fastidiously, methodically, nicely, smartly, sprucely, systematically, tidily 2. adeptly, adroitly, agilely, aptly, cleverly, deftly, dexterously, efficiently, effortlessly, elegantly, expertly, gracefully, handily, nimbly, precisely, skilfully, stylishly

neatness 1. accuracy, daintiness, fastidiousness, methodicalness, niceness, nicety, orderliness, smartness, spruceness, straightness, tidiness, trimness **2**. adeptness, adroitness, agility, aptness, cleverness, deftness, dexterity, efficiency, effortlessness, elegance, expertness, grace, gracefulness, handiness, nimbleness, preciseness, precision, skilfulness, skill, style, stylishness

nebulous ambiguous, amorphous, cloudy, confused, dim, hazy, imprecise, indefinite, indeterminate, indistinct, misty, murky, obscure, shadowy, shapeless, uncertain, unclear, unformed, vague

necessarily accordingly, automatically, axiomatically, by definition, certainly, compulsorily, consequently, incontrovertibly, ineluctably, inevitably, inexorably, irresistibly, naturally, *nolens volens*, of course, of necessity, perforce, undoubtedly, willy-nilly

necessary 1. compulsory, *de rigueur*, essential, imperative, indispensable, mandatory, needed, needful, obligatory, required, requisite, vital **2**. certain, fated, inescapable, inevitable, inexorable, unavoidable

necessitate call for, coerce, compel, constrain, demand, force, impel, make necessary, oblige, require

necessities essentials, fundamentals, indispensables

necessitous destitute, distressed, impecunious, impoverished, indigent, needy, penniless, penurious, poor, poverty-stricken

necessity 1. demand, exigency, indispensability, need, needfulness, requirement **2**. desideratum, essential, fundamental, necessary, need, prerequisite, requirement, requisite, *sine qua non*, want **3**. destitution, extremity, indigence, need, penury, poverty, privation **4**. compulsion, destiny, fate, inevitability, inexorableness, obligation

necromancer black magician, diviner, enchanter, enchantress, magician, sorcerer, sorceress, warlock, witch, wizard

necromancy black art, black magic, demonology, divination, enchantment, magic, sorcery, thaumaturgy (*Rare*), voodoo, witchcraft, witchery, wizardry

necropolis burial ground, cemetery, churchyard, God's acre, graveyard

need v. **1**. call for, demand, have occasion to *or* for, lack, miss, necessitate, require, want ~n. **2**. longing, requisite,

want, wish **3**. deprivation, destitution, distress, extremity, impecuniousness, inadequacy, indigence, insufficiency, lack, neediness, paucity, penury, poverty, privation, shortage **4**. emergency, exigency, necessity, obligation, urgency, want **5**. demand, desideratum, essential, requirement, requisite

needed called for, desired, lacked, necessary, required, wanted

needful essential, indispensable, necessary, needed, required, requisite, stipulated, vital

needle v. aggravate (*Inf.*), annoy, bait, goad, harass, irk, irritate, nag, nettle, pester, prick, prod, provoke, rile, ruffle, spur, sting, taunt

needless causeless, dispensable, excessive, expendable, gratuitous, groundless, nonessential, pointless, redundant, superfluous, uncalled-for, undesired, unnecessary, unwanted, useless

needlework embroidery, fancywork, needlecraft, sewing, stitching, tailoring

needy deprived, destitute, disadvantaged, impecunious, impoverished, indigent, on the breadline (*Inf.*), penniless, poor, poverty-stricken, underprivileged

ne'er-do-well black sheep, good-for-nothing, idler, layabout, loafer, loser, wastrel

nefarious abominable, atrocious, base, criminal, depraved, detestable, dreadful, evil, execrable, foul, heinous, horrible, infamous, infernal, iniquitous, monstrous, odious, opprobrious, shameful, sinful, vicious, vile, villainous, wicked

negate 1. abrogate, annul, cancel, countermand, invalidate, neutralize, nullify, repeal, rescind, retract, reverse, revoke, void, wipe out **2**. contradict, deny, disallow, disprove, gainsay, oppose, refute

negation 1. antithesis, antonym, contradiction, contrary, converse, counterpart, denial, disavowal, disclaimer, inverse, opposite, rejection, renunciation, reverse **2**. opposition, proscription, refusal, repudiation, veto **3**. cancellation, neutralization, nullification **4**. blank, nonexistence, nothingness, nullity, vacuity, void

negative adj. **1**. contradictory, contrary, denying, dissenting, opposing, recusant, refusing, rejecting, resisting **2**. annulling, counteractive, invalidating, neutralizing, nullifying **3**. antagonistic, colourless, contrary, cynical, gloomy, jaundiced, neutral, pessimistic, uncooperative, unenthusiastic, uninterested, unwilling, weak ~n. **4.** contradiction, denial, refusal

negativeness, negativity 1. contradiction, contradictoriness, contrariness, denial, dissent, opposition, recusancy, refusal, rejection, resistance **2.** antagonism, colourlessness, contrariness, cynicism, gloom, neutrality, pessimism, uncooperativeness, uninterestedness, unwillingness, weakness

neglect v. **1.** contemn, disdain, disregard, ignore, leave alone, overlook, pass by, rebuff, scorn, slight, spurn **2.** be remiss, evade, forget, let slide, omit, pass over, procrastinate, shirk, skimp ~n. **3.** disdain, disregard, disrespect, heedlessness, inattention, indifference, slight, unconcern **4.** carelessness, default, dereliction, failure, forgetfulness, laxity, laxness, neglectfulness, negligence, oversight, remissness, slackness, slovenliness

neglected 1. abandoned, derelict, overgrown **2.** disregarded, unappreciated, underestimated, undervalued

neglectful careless, disregardful, heedless, inattentive, indifferent, lax, negligent, remiss, thoughtless, uncaring, unmindful

negligence carelessness, default, dereliction, disregard, failure, forgetfulness, heedlessness, inadvertence, inattention, inattentiveness, indifference, laxity, laxness, neglect, omission, oversight, remissness, shortcoming, slackness, thoughtlessness

negligent careless, cursory, disregardful, forgetful, heedless, inadvertent, inattentive, indifferent, neglectful, nonchalant, offhand, regardless, remiss, slack, thoughtless, unmindful, unthinking

negligible imperceptible, inconsequential, insignificant, minor, minute, petty, small, trifling, trivial, unimportant

negotiable debatable, discussable, discussible, transactional, transferable, variable

negotiate 1. adjudicate, arbitrate, arrange, bargain, conciliate, confer, consult, contract, deal, debate, discuss, handle, manage, mediate, parley, settle, transact, work out **2.** clear, cross, get over, get past, get round, pass, pass through, surmount

negotiation arbitration, bargaining, debate, diplomacy, discussion, mediation, transaction

negotiator adjudicator, ambassador, arbitrator, delegate, diplomat, honest broker, intermediary, mediator, moderator

neighbourhood community, confines, district, environs, locale, locality, precincts, proximity, purlieus, quarter, region, surroundings, vicinity

neighbouring abutting, adjacent, adjoining, bordering, connecting, contiguous, near, nearby, nearest, next, surrounding

neighbourly amiable, civil, companionable, considerate, friendly, genial, harmonious, helpful, hospitable, kind, obliging, sociable, social, well-disposed

nemesis destiny, destruction, fate, retribution, vengeance

neologism buzz word (*Inf.*), coinage, new phrase, new word, nonce word, vogue word

neophyte amateur, apprentice, beginner, catechumen, disciple, learner, novice, novitiate, probationer, proselyte, pupil, recruit, student, trainee, tyro

ne plus ultra acme, culmination, extreme, perfection, the last word, ultimate, uttermost point

nerve n. **1.** bottle (*Brit. sl.*), bravery, coolness, courage, daring, determination, endurance, energy, fearlessness, firmness, force, fortitude, gameness, grit (*Inf.*), guts (*Inf.*), hardihood, intrepidity, mettle, might, pluck, resolution, spirit, spunk (*Inf.*), steadfastness, vigour, will **2.** *Inf.* audacity, boldness, brass (*Inf.*), brazenness, cheek (*Inf.*), effrontery, gall, impertinence, impudence, insolence, sauce (*Inf.*), temerity ~v. **3.** brace, embolden, encourage, fortify, hearten, invigorate, steel, strengthen

nerveless 1. calm, collected, composed, controlled, cool, impassive, imperturbable, self-possessed, unemotional **2.** afraid, cowardly, debilitated, enervated, feeble, nervous, spineless, timid, weak

nerve-racking annoying, difficult, distressing, frightening, harassing, harrowing, maddening, stressful, tense, trying, worrying

nerves anxiety, fretfulness, imbalance, nervousness, strain, stress, tension

nervous agitated, anxious, apprehensive, edgy, excitable, fearful, fidgety, flustered, hesitant, highly strung, hysterical, jittery (*Inf.*), jumpy, nervy (*Inf.*), neurotic, on edge, ruffled, shaky, tense, timid, timorous, uneasy, uptight (*Inf.*), weak, worried

nervous breakdown breakdown, collapse, crack-up (*Inf.*), nervous disorder, neurasthenia (*Obsolete*)

nervousness agitation, anxiety, disquiet, excitability, fluster, perturbation, tension, timidity, touchiness, tremulousness, worry

nervy agitated, anxious, excitable, fidgety, jittery (*Inf.*), jumpy, nervous, on edge, restless, tense

nescience 1. ignorance, lack of knowledge, obliviousness, unawareness, unconsciousness, unenlightenment 2. agnosticism, doubt, irreligion, unbelief

nescient 1. ignorant, oblivious, unaware, unconscious, unenlightened, unknowing, unknowledgeable 2. agnostic, doubting, irreligious, unbelieving

nest 1. den, haunt, hideaway, refuge, resort, retreat, snuggery 2. breeding-ground, den, hotbed

nest egg cache, deposit, fund(s), reserve, savings, store

nestle cuddle, curl up, huddle, nuzzle, snuggle

nestling 1. chick, fledgling 2. babe, babe in arms, baby, infant, suckling

net[1] 1. *n.* lacework, lattice, mesh, netting, network, openwork, reticulum, tracery, web 2. *v.* bag, capture, catch, enmesh, ensnare, entangle, nab (*Inf.*), trap

net[2], **nett** *adj.* 1. after taxes, clear, final, take-home 2. closing, conclusive, final ~*v.* 3. accumulate, bring in, clear, earn, gain, make, realize, reap

nether basal, below, beneath, bottom, inferior, lower, under, underground

nether world Avernus, Hades, hell, infernal regions, nether regions, underworld

nettle annoy, chafe, exasperate, fret, goad, harass, incense, irritate, pique, provoke, ruffle, sting, tease, vex

nettled aggrieved, angry, annoyed, chafed, cross, exasperated, galled, goaded, harassed, huffy, incensed, irritable, irritated, peeved, peevish, piqued, provoked, put out, riled, ruffled, stung, teased, touchy, vexed

network arrangement, channels, circuitry, complex, convolution, grid, grill, interconnections, labyrinth, maze, mesh, net, nexus, organization, plexus, structure, system, tracks, web

neurosis abnormality, affliction, derangement, deviation, instability, maladjustment, mental disturbance, mental illness, obsession, phobia, psychological *or* emotional disorder

neurotic abnormal, anxious, compulsive, deviant, disordered, distraught, disturbed, maladjusted, manic, nervous, obsessive, overwrought, unhealthy, unstable

neuter *v.* castrate, doctor (*Inf.*), dress, emasculate, fix (*Inf.*), geld, spay

neutral 1. disinterested, dispassionate, even-handed, impartial, indifferent, nonaligned, nonbelligerent, noncombatant, noncommittal, nonpartisan, sitting on the fence, unaligned, unbiased, uncommitted, undecided, uninvolved, unprejudiced 2. achromatic, colourless, dull, expressionless, indeterminate, indistinct, indistinguishable, intermediate, toneless, undefined

neutrality detachment, disinterestedness, impartiality, nonalignment, noninterference, noninterventionism, noninvolvement, nonpartisanship

neutralize cancel, compensate for, counteract, counterbalance, frustrate, invalidate, negate, nullify, offset, undo

never-ending boundless, ceaseless, constant, continual, continuous, eternal, everlasting, incessant, interminable, nonstop, perpetual, persistent, relentless, unbroken, unceasing, unchanging, uninterrupted, unremitting

never-never hire-purchase (*Brit.*), H.P. (*Brit.*)

nevertheless but, even so, however, nonetheless, notwithstanding, regardless, still, yet

new 1. advanced, contemporary, current, different, fresh, latest, modern, modernistic, modish, newfangled, novel, original, recent, topical, ultramodern, unfamiliar, unknown, unused, unusual, up-to-date, virgin 2. added, extra, more, supplementary 3. altered, changed, improved, modernized, redesigned, renewed, restored

newcomer alien, arrival, beginner, foreigner, immigrant, incomer, novice, outsider, settler, stranger

newfangled contemporary, fashionable, gimmicky, modern, new, new-fashioned, novel, recent

newly anew, freshly, just, lately, latterly, recently

newness freshness, innovation, novelty, oddity, originality, strangeness, unfamiliarity, uniqueness

news account, advice, bulletin, communiqué, disclosure, dispatch, exposé, gossip, hearsay, information, intelligence, leak, news flash, release, report, revelation, rumour, scandal, statement, story, tidings, word

newsworthy arresting, important, interesting, notable, noteworthy, remarkable, significant, stimulating

next adj. **1.** consequent, ensuing, following, later, subsequent, succeeding **2.** adjacent, adjoining, closest, nearest, neighbouring ~adv. **3.** afterwards, closely, following, later, subsequently, thereafter

next world afterlife, afterworld, heaven, hereafter, nirvana, paradise

nexus bond, connection, joining, junction, link, tie

nibble 1. n. bite, crumb, morsel, peck, snack, soupçon, taste, titbit **2.** v. bite, eat, gnaw, munch, nip, peck, pick at

nice 1. agreeable, amiable, attractive, charming, commendable, courteous, delightful, friendly, good, kind, likable, pleasant, pleasurable, polite, prepossessing, refined, well-mannered **2.** dainty, fine, neat, tidy, trim **3.** accurate, careful, critical, delicate, discriminating, exact, exacting, fastidious, fine, meticulous, precise, rigorous, scrupulous, strict, subtle **4.** cultured, genteel, refined, respectable, virtuous, well-bred

nicely 1. acceptably, agreeably, amiably, attractively, charmingly, commendably, courteously, delightfully, kindly, likably, pleasantly, pleasingly, pleasurably, politely, prepossessingly, well **2.** daintily, finely, neatly, tidily, trimly **3.** accurately, carefully, critically, delicately, exactingly, exactly, fastidiously, finely, meticulously, precisely, rigorously, scrupulously, strictly, subtly **4.** genteelly, respectably, virtuously

niceness 1. agreeableness, amiability, attractiveness, charm, courtesy, delightfulness, friendliness, good manners, goodness, kindness, likableness, pleasantness, pleasurableness, politeness, refinement **2.** daintiness, fineness, neatness, tidiness, trimness **3.** accuracy, care, carefulness, criticalness, delicacy, discrimination, exactingness, exactitude, exactness, fastidiousness, fineness, meticulosity, meticulousness, preciseness, precision, rigorousness, rigour, scrupulosity, scrupulousness, strictness, subtleness, subtlety **4.** gentility, good breeding, refinement, respectability, virtue

nicety 1. accuracy, exactness, fastidiousness, finesse, meticulousness, minuteness, precision **2.** daintiness, delicacy, discrimination, distinction, nuance, refinement, subtlety

niche 1. alcove, corner, hollow, nook, opening, recess **2.** calling, pigeonhole (Inf.), place, position, slot (Inf.), vocation

nick chip, cut, damage, dent, mark, notch, scar, score, scratch, snick

nickname diminutive, epithet, familiar name, handle (Sl.), label, pet name, moniker (Inf.), sobriquet

nifty agile, apt, attractive, chic, clever, deft, enjoyable, excellent, neat, pleasing, quick, sharp, smart, spruce, stylish

niggard cheapskate (Inf.), cheese-parer, churl, miser, penny-pincher (Inf.), screw (Sl.), Scrooge, skinflint

niggardliness 1. avarice, avariciousness, closeness, covetousness, frugality, grudgingness, meanness, mercenariness, miserliness, nearness (Inf.), parsimony, penuriousness, sordidness, sparingness, stinginess, thrift, tightfistedness, ungenerousness **2.** beggarliness, inadequacy, insufficiency, meagreness, meanness, miserableness, paltriness, scantiness, skimpiness, smallness, wretchedness

niggardly 1. avaricious, close, covetous, frugal, grudging, mean, mercenary, miserly, near (Inf.), parsimonious, penurious, Scroogelike, sordid, sparing, stinging, stingy, tightfisted, ungenerous **2.** beggarly, inadequate, insufficient, meagre, mean, miserable, paltry, scanty, skimpy, small, wretched

niggle 1. carp, cavil, criticize, find fault, fuss **2.** annoy, irritate, rankle, worry

niggler carper, caviller, fault-finder, fusspot (Brit. inf.), nag, nit-picker (Inf.), pettifogger, quibbler

niggling 1. cavilling, finicky, fussy, insignificant, minor, nit-picking (Inf.), pettifogging, petty, piddling (Inf.), quibbling, trifling, unimportant **2.** gnawing, irritating, persistent, troubling, worrying

nigh 1. *adj.* adjacent, adjoining, approximate, at hand, bordering, close, contiguous, imminent, impending, near, next **2.** *adv.* about, almost, approximately, close, near, practically

night dark, darkness, dead of night, hours of darkness, night-time, night watches

night and day all the time, ceaselessly, constantly, continually, continuously, day in, day out, endlessly, incessantly, interminably, unremittingly

nightfall crepuscule, dusk, eve (*Archaic*), evening, eventide, gloaming, sundown, sunset, twilight, vespers

nightly *adv./adj.* **1.** each night, every night, night after night, nights (*Inf.*) ~*adv.* **2.** after dark, at night, by night, in the night, nights (*Inf.*), nocturnally ~*adj.* **3.** night-time, nocturnal

nightmare 1. bad dream, hallucination, incubus, succubus **2.** horror, ordeal, torment, trial, tribulation

nightmarish agonizing, alarming, creepy (*Inf.*), disturbing, frightening, harrowing, horrible, Kafkaesque, scaring, terrifying, unreal

nihilism 1. abnegation, agnosticism, atheism, denial, disbelief, nonbelief, rejection, renunciation, repudiation, scepticism **2.** blank, emptiness, negation, nonexistence, nothingness, nullity, oblivion **3.** anarchy, disorder, lawlessness, terrorism

nihilist 1. agnostic, atheist, cynic, disbeliever, nonbeliever, pessimist, sceptic **2.** agitator, anarchist, extremist, revolutionary, terrorist

nil duck, love, naught, *nihil*, none, nothing, zero

nimble active, agile, alert, brisk, deft, dexterous, lively, nippy (*Brit. inf.*), proficient, prompt, quick, quick-witted, ready, smart, sprightly, spry, swift

nimbleness adroitness, agility, alacrity, alertness, dexterity, finesse, grace, lightness, nippiness (*Brit. inf.*), skill, smartness, sprightliness, spryness

nimbly actively, acutely, agilely, alertly, briskly, deftly, dexterously, easily, fast, fleetly, proficiently, promptly, quickly, quick-wittedly, readily, sharply, smartly, speedily, spryly, swiftly

nimbus ambience, atmosphere, aura, aureole, cloud, corona, glow, halo, irradiation

nincompoop blockhead, dimwit (*Inf.*), dolt, dunce, fool, idiot, ninny, nitwit, noodle, numskull, simpleton

nip[1] *v.* **1.** bite, catch, clip, compress, grip, nibble, pinch, snag, snap, snip, squeeze, tweak, twitch **2.** check, frustrate, thwart

nip[2] *n.* dram, draught, drop, finger, mouthful, peg (*Brit.*), portion, shot (*Inf.*), sip, snifter (*Inf.*), *soupçon*, sup, swallow, taste

nipper 1. claw, pincer **2.** *Inf.* baby, boy, child, girl, infant, kid (*Inf.*), little one, tot

nipple breast, dug, mamilla, pap, papilla, teat, tit, udder

nippy 1. biting, chilly, nipping, sharp, stinging **2.** *Brit. inf.* active, agile, fast, nimble, quick, spry

nirvana bliss, joy, paradise, peace, serenity, tranquillity

nit-picking captious, carping, cavilling, finicky, fussy, hairsplitting, pedantic, pettifogging, quibbling

nitty-gritty basics, brass tacks (*Inf.*), core, crux, essence, essentials, facts, fundamentals, gist, heart of the matter, reality, substance

nitwit dimwit (*Inf.*), dummy (*Sl.*), fool, halfwit, nincompoop, ninny, simpleton

nob big shot (*Sl.*), bigwig (*Sl.*), fat cat (*U.S. sl.*), nabob (*Inf.*), toff (*Brit. sl.*)

nobble 1. disable, handicap, incapacitate, weaken **2.** bribe, get at, influence, intimidate, outwit, win over **3.** filch, knock off (*Sl.*), nick (*Sl.*), pilfer, pinch (*Inf.*), purloin, snitch (*Sl.*), steal, swipe (*Sl.*) **4.** get hold of, grab, take

nobbly nubby, projecting, protruding, protuberant, ridged, rough

nobility 1. aristocracy, elite, high society, lords, nobles, patricians, peerage, ruling class, upper class **2.** dignity, eminence, excellence, grandeur, greatness, illustriousness, loftiness, magnificence, majesty, nobleness, stateliness, sublimity, superiority, worthiness **3.** honour, incorruptibility, integrity, uprightness, virtue

noble *n.* **1.** aristocrat, lord, nobleman, peer ~*adj.* **2.** aristocratic, blue-blooded, gentle (*Archaic*), highborn, lordly, patrician, titled **3.** august, dignified, distinguished, elevated, eminent, excellent, grand, great, imposing, impressive, lofty, splendid, stately **4.** generous, honourable, magnanimous, upright, virtuous, worthy

nobody 1. no-one 2. cipher, lightweight (*Inf.*), menial, nonentity, nothing (*Inf.*)

nocturnal night, nightly, night-time, of the night

nod *v.* 1. acknowledge, bob, bow, dip, duck, gesture, indicate, salute, signal 2. agree, assent, concur, show agreement 3. be sleepy, doze, droop, drowse, nap, sleep, slump ~*n.* 4. acknowledgment, beck, gesture, greeting, indication, salute, sign, signal

node bud, bump, burl, growth, knob, knot, lump, nodule, protuberance, swelling

noggin 1. gill, quarter-pint 2. cup, dram, mug, nip, tot 3. *Inf.* block (*Inf.*), bonce (*Brit. sl.*), conk (*Sl.*), dome (*Sl.*), head, napper (*Sl.*), noddle (*Inf.*), nut (*Sl.*)

no go futile, hopeless, impossible, not on (*Inf.*), vain

noise 1. *n.* babble, blare, clamour, clatter, commotion, cry, din, fracas, hubbub, outcry, pandemonium, racket, row, sound, talk, tumult, uproar 2. *v.* advertise, bruit (*Archaic*), circulate, gossip, publicize, repeat, report, rumour

noiseless hushed, inaudible, mute, muted, quiet, silent, soundless, still

noisome 1. bad, baneful (*Archaic*), deleterious, harmful, hurtful, injurious, mischievous, pernicious, pestiferous, pestilential, poisonous, unhealthy, unwholesome 2. disgusting, fetid, foul, malodorous, mephitic, noxious, offensive, putrid, reeking, smelly, stinking

noisy boisterous, cacophonous, chattering, clamorous, deafening, earsplitting, loud, obstreperous, piercing, riotous, strident, tumultuous, turbulent, uproarious, vociferous

nomad drifter, itinerant, migrant, rambler, rover, vagabond, wanderer

nomadic itinerant, migrant, migratory, pastoral, peripatetic, roaming, roving, travelling, vagrant, wandering

nom de plume alias, assumed name, nom de guerre, pen name, pseudonym

nomenclature classification, codification, locution, phraseology, taxonomy, terminology, vocabulary

nominal 1. formal, ostensible, pretended, professed, puppet, purported, self-styled, so-called, *soi-disant*, supposed, theoretical, titular 2. inconsiderable, insignificant, minimal, small, symbolic, token, trifling, trivial

nominate appoint, assign, choose, commission, designate, elect, elevate, empower, name, present, propose, recommend, select, submit, suggest, term

nomination appointment, choice, designation, election, proposal, recommendation, selection, suggestion

nominee aspirant, candidate, contestant, entrant, favourite, protégé, runner

nonaligned impartial, neutral, uncommitted, undecided

nonchalance calm, composure, cool (*Sl.*), equanimity, imperturbability, indifference, sang-froid, self-possession, unconcern

nonchalant airy, apathetic, blasé, calm, careless, casual, collected, cool, detached, dispassionate, indifferent, insouciant, offhand, unconcerned, unemotional, unperturbed

noncombatant civilian, neutral, non-belligerent

noncommittal ambiguous, careful, cautious, circumspect, discreet, equivocal, evasive, guarded, indefinite, neutral, politic, reserved, tactful, temporizing, tentative, unrevealing, vague, wary

non compos mentis crazy, deranged, insane, mentally ill, of unsound mind

nonconformist dissenter, dissentient, eccentric, heretic, iconoclast, individualist, maverick, protester, radical, rebel

nonconformity dissent, eccentricity, heresy, heterodoxy, unconventionality

nondescript characterless, common or garden (*Inf.*), commonplace, dull, featureless, indeterminate, mousy, ordinary, unclassifiable, unclassified, undistinguished, unexceptional, uninspiring, uninteresting, unmemorable, unremarkable, vague

none nil, nobody, no-one, no part, not a bit, not any, nothing, not one, zero

nonentity cipher, lightweight (*Inf.*), mediocrity, nobody, small fry, unimportant person

nonessential dispensable, excessive, expendable, extraneous, inessential, peripheral, superfluous, unimportant, unnecessary

nonetheless despite that, even so, however, in spite of that, nevertheless, yet

nonexistent chimerical, fancied, fictional, hallucinatory, hypothetical, illusory, imaginary, imagined, insubstantial, legendary, missing, mythical, unreal

nonpareil 1. *n.* ideal, nonesuch (*Archaic*), paragon, perfection 2. *adj.* incomparable, matchless, peerless, supreme, unequalled, unique, unmatched, unparalleled, unrivalled, unsurpassed

nonpartisan detached, impartial, independent, neutral, nonpolitical, objective, unaffiliated, unbiased, unprejudiced

nonplus astonish, astound, baffle, bewilder, confound, confuse, discomfit, disconcert, discountenance, dismay, dumbfound, embarrass, mystify, perplex, puzzle, stump, stun, take aback

nonsense absurdity, balderdash, blather, bombast, bunk (*Inf.*), claptrap (*Inf.*), double Dutch (*Brit. inf.*), drivel, fatuity, folly, foolishness, gibberish, inanity, jest, ludicrousness, ridiculousness, rot, rubbish, senselessness, silliness, stuff, stupidity, trash, twaddle, waffle (*Brit. inf.*)

nonsensical absurd, crazy, foolish, inane, incomprehensible, irrational, ludicrous, meaningless, ridiculous, senseless, silly

nonstop 1. *adj.* ceaseless, constant, continuous, direct, endless, incessant, interminable, relentless, steady, unbroken, unending, unfaltering, uninterrupted, unremitting 2. *adv.* ceaselessly, constantly, continuously, directly, endlessly, incessantly, interminably, relentlessly, steadily, unbrokenly, unendingly, unfalteringly, uninterruptedly, unremittingly, without stopping

nonviolent nonbelligerent, pacifist, peaceable, peaceful

nook alcove, cavity, corner, cranny, crevice, cubbyhole, hide-out, inglenook (*Brit.*), niche, opening, recess, retreat

noon high noon, midday, noonday, noontide, noontime, twelve noon

norm average, benchmark, criterion, mean, measure, model, pattern, rule, standard, type, yardstick

normal 1. accustomed, acknowledged, average, common, conventional, habitual, natural, ordinary, popular, regular, routine, run-of-the-mill, standard, typical, usual 2. rational, reasonable, sane, well-adjusted

normality 1. accustomedness, averageness, commonness, common-

placeness, conventionality, habitualness, naturalness, ordinariness, popularity, regularity, routineness, typicality, usualness 2. adjustment, balance, rationality, reason, sanity

normally as a rule, commonly, habitually, ordinarily, regularly, typically, usually

normative controlling, normalizing, prescriptive, regularizing, regulating, standardizing

north 1. *adj.* Arctic, boreal, northerly, northern, polar 2. *adv.* northerly, northward(s)

North Star lodestar, Polaris, Pole Star

nose *v.* 1. detect, scent, search (for), smell, sniff 2. ease forward, nudge, nuzzle, push, shove 3. meddle, pry, snoop (*Inf.*)

nose dive dive, drop, plummet, plunge

nosegay bouquet, posy

nosh 1. *n.* aliment, chow (*Inf.*), comestibles, eats (*Sl.*), fare, food, grub (*Sl.*), meal, repast, scoff (*Sl.*), sustenance, viands, victuals 2. *v.* consume, eat, scoff (*Sl.*)

nostalgia homesickness, longing, pining, regret, regretfulness, remembrance, reminiscence, wistfulness, yearning

nostalgic homesick, longing, regretful, sentimental, wistful

nostrum cure, cure-all, drug, elixir, medicine, panacea, patent medicine, potion, quack medicine, remedy, sovereign cure, specific, treatment

nosy, nosey curious, eavesdropping, inquisitive, interfering, intrusive, meddlesome, prying, snooping (*Inf.*)

notability 1. celebrity, distinction, eminence, esteem, fame, renown 2. celebrity, dignitary, notable, personage, V.I.P., worthy

notable 1. *adj.* celebrated, conspicuous, distinguished, eminent, evident, extraordinary, famous, manifest, marked, memorable, noteworthy, noticeable, notorious, outstanding, preeminent, pronounced, rare, remarkable, renowned, striking, uncommon, unusual, well-known 2. *n.* celebrity, dignitary, notability, personage, V.I.P., worthy

notably conspicuously, distinctly, especially, markedly, noticeably, outstandingly, particularly, remarkably, signally, strikingly, uncommonly

notation 1. characters, code, script,

signs, symbols, system **2**. jotting, notating, note, noting, record

notch *n*. **1**. cleft, cut, incision, indentation, mark, nick, score **2**. *Inf.* cut (*Inf.*), degree, grade, level, step ~*v*. **3**. cut, indent, mark, nick, score, scratch

notch up achieve, gain, make, register, score

note *n*. **1**. annotation, comment, communication, epistle, gloss, jotting, letter, memo, memorandum, message, minute, record, remark, reminder **2**. indication, mark, sign, symbol, token **3**. heed, notice, observation, regard **4**. celebrity, character, consequence, distinction, eminence, fame, prestige, renown, reputation ~*v*. **5**. denote, designate, indicate, mark, mention, notice, observe, perceive, record, register, remark, see

notebook commonplace book, diary, exercise book, jotter, journal, memorandum book, notepad, record book

noted acclaimed, celebrated, conspicuous, distinguished, eminent, famous, illustrious, notable, notorious, prominent, recognized, renowned, well-known

notes impressions, jottings, outline, record, report, sketch

noteworthy exceptional, extraordinary, important, notable, outstanding, remarkable, significant, unusual

nothing bagatelle, cipher, emptiness, naught, nobody, nonentity, nonexistence, nothingness, nought, nullity, trifle, void, zero

nothingness 1. nihility, nonbeing, nonexistence, nullity, oblivion **2**. insignificance, unimportance, worthlessness

notice *v*. **1**. detect, discern, distinguish, heed, mark, mind, note, observe, perceive, remark, see, spot ~*n*. **2**. cognizance, consideration, heed, note, observation, regard **3**. advice, announcement, communication, instruction, intelligence, intimation, news, notification, order, warning **4**. advertisement, comment, criticism, poster, review, sign **5**. attention, civility, respect

noticeable appreciable, clear, conspicuous, distinct, evident, manifest, observable, obvious, perceptible, plain, striking, unmistakable

notification advice, alert, announcement, declaration, information, intelligence, message, notice, notifying, publication, statement, telling, warning

notify acquaint, advise, alert, announce, apprise, declare, inform, publish, tell, warn

notion 1. apprehension, belief, concept, conception, idea, impression, inkling, judgment, knowledge, opinion, sentiment, understanding, view **2**. caprice, desire, fancy, impulse, inclination, whim, wish

notional abstract, conceptual, fanciful, hypothetical, ideal, imaginary, speculative, theoretical, unreal, visionary

notoriety dishonour, disrepute, infamy, obloquy, opprobrium, scandal

notorious 1. dishonourable, disreputable, infamous, opprobrious, scandalous **2**. blatant, flagrant, glaring, obvious, open, overt, patent, undisputed

notoriously 1. dishonourably, disreputably, infamously, opprobriously, scandalously **2**. blatantly, flagrantly, glaringly, notably, obviously, openly, overtly, particularly, patently, spectacularly, undisputedly

notwithstanding although, despite, however, nevertheless, nonetheless, though, yet

nought naught, nil, nothing, nothingness, zero

nourish 1. attend, feed, furnish, nurse, nurture, supply, sustain, tend **2**. comfort, cultivate, encourage, foster, maintain, promote, support

nourishing alimentative, beneficial, healthful, health-giving, nutritious, nutritive, wholesome

nourishment aliment, diet, food, nutriment, nutrition, sustenance, viands, victuals

nouveau riche arriviste, new-rich, parvenu, upstart

novel 1. *adj*. different, fresh, innovative, new, original, rare, singular, strange, uncommon, unfamiliar, unusual **2**. *n*. fiction, narrative, romance, story, tale

novelty 1. freshness, innovation, newness, oddity, originality, strangeness, surprise, unfamiliarity, uniqueness **2**. bagatelle, bauble, curiosity, gadget, gewgaw, gimcrack, gimmick, knick-knack, memento, souvenir, trifle, trinket

novice amateur, apprentice, beginner, convert, learner, neophyte, newcomer, novitiate, probationer, proselyte, pupil, tyro

novitiate 1. apprenticeship, probation, training 2. novice

now 1. at once, immediately, instanter (*Law*), instantly, presently (*Scot. & U.S.*), promptly, straightaway 2. any more, at the moment, nowadays, these days 3. **now and then** *or* **again** at times, from time to time, infrequently, intermittently, occasionally, on and off, once in a while, on occasion, sometimes, sporadically

nowadays any more, at the moment, in this day and age, now, these days, today

noxious baneful (*Archaic*), corrupting, deadly, deleterious, destructive, detrimental, foul, harmful, hurtful, injurious, insalubrious, noisome, pernicious, pestilential, poisonous, unhealthy, unwholesome

nuance degree, distinction, gradation, hint, nicety, refinement, shade, shadow, subtlety, suggestion, suspicion, tinge, touch, trace

nub 1. core, crux, essence, gist, heart, kernel, nucleus, pith, point 2. bulge, bump, knob, knot, lump, node, protuberance, swelling

nubile marriageable, ripe (*Inf.*)

nucleus basis, centre, core, focus, heart, kernel, nub, pivot

nude *au naturel*, bare, disrobed, exposed, in one's birthday suit (*Inf.*), in the altogether (*Inf.*), in the buff (*Inf.*), naked, starkers (*Inf.*), stark-naked, stripped, unclad, unclothed, uncovered, undraped, undressed

nudge *v.* bump, dig, elbow, jog, poke, prod, push, shove, touch

nudity bareness, nakedness, undress

nugatory 1. insignificant, trifling, trivial, valueless, worthless 2. bootless, futile, ineffectual, inoperative, invalid, null and void, unavailing, useless, vain

nugget chunk, clump, hunk, lump, mass, piece

nuisance annoyance, bore, bother, inconvenience, infliction, irritation, offence, pest, plague, problem, trouble, vexation

null characterless, ineffectual, inoperative, invalid, nonexistent, null and void, powerless, useless, vain, valueless, void, worthless

nullify abolish, abrogate, annul, bring to naught, cancel, counteract, countervail, invalidate, negate, neutralize, quash, render null and void, repeal, rescind, revoke, veto, void

nullity characterlessness, ineffectualness, invalidity, nonexistence, powerlessness, uselessness, valuelessness, voidness, worthlessness

numb 1. *adj.* benumbed, dead, deadened, frozen, immobilized, insensible, insensitive, paralysed, stupefied, torpid, unfeeling 2. *v.* benumb, deaden, dull, freeze, immobilize, paralyse, stun, stupefy

number *n.* 1. character, count, digit, figure, integer, numeral, sum, total, unit 2. aggregate, amount, collection, company, crowd, horde, many, multitude, quantity, throng 3. copy, edition, imprint, issue, printing ~*v.* 4. account, add, calculate, compute, count, enumerate, include, reckon, tell, total

numbered categorized, contained, counted, designated, fixed, included, limited, limited in number, specified, totalled

numberless countless, endless, infinite, innumerable, multitudinous, myriad, unnumbered, untold

numbness deadness, dullness, insensibility, insensitivity, paralysis, stupefaction, torpor, unfeelingness

numeral character, cipher, digit, figure, integer, number, symbol

numerous abundant, copious, many, plentiful, profuse, several

numinous awe-inspiring, divine, heavenly, holy, mysterious, religious, spiritual, supernatural

numskull blockhead, bonehead (*Sl.*), buffoon, clot (*Brit. sl.*), dimwit (*Inf.*), dolt, dope (*Sl.*), dullard, dummy (*Sl.*), dunce, dunderhead, fathead (*Inf.*), fool, simpleton, thickhead, twit (*Inf.*)

nuncio ambassador, envoy, legate, messenger

nunnery abbey, cloister, convent, house, monastery

nuptial *adj.* bridal, conjugal, connubial, hymeneal (*Poetic*), marital, matrimonial, wedded, wedding

nuptials espousal (*Archaic*), marriage, matrimony, wedding

nurse *v.* 1. care for, look after, minister to, tend, treat 2. breast-feed, feed, nourish, nurture, suckle, wet-nurse 3. *Fig.* cherish, cultivate, encourage, foster, harbour, keep alive, preserve, promote, succour, support

nurture *n.* **1.** diet, food, nourishment **2.** development, discipline, education, instruction, rearing, training, upbringing ~*v.* **3.** feed, nourish, nurse, support, sustain, tend **4.** bring up, cultivate, develop, discipline, educate, instruct, rear, school, train

nut 1. kernel, seed, stone **2.** *Sl.* brain, head, mind, reason, senses **3.** *Sl.* crackpot (*Inf.*), crank (*Inf.*), eccentric, loony (*Sl.*), lunatic, madman, maniac, nutcase (*Sl.*)

nutriment aliment, diet, food, foodstuff, nourishment, nutrition, subsistence, support, sustenance

nutrition food, nourishment, nutriment, sustenance

nutritious alimental, alimentative, beneficial, healthful, health-giving, invigorating, nourishing, nutritive, strengthening, wholesome

nuts bananas (*Brit. sl.*), batty (*Sl.*), crazy (*Inf.*), demented, deranged, eccentric, insane, irrational, loony (*Sl.*), loopy (*Inf.*), mad, nutty (*Sl.*)

nuts and bolts basics, details, essentials, fundamentals, nitty-gritty (*Sl.*), practicalities

nuzzle burrow, cuddle, fondle, nestle, nudge, pet, snuggle

nymph damsel, dryad, girl, hamadryad, lass, maid, maiden, naiad, oread, sylph

O

oaf blockhead, bonehead (*Sl.*), booby, brute, clod, dolt, dullard, dummy (*Sl.*), dunce, fool, galoot (*Sl.*), gawk, goon, gorilla (*Inf.*), halfwit, idiot, imbecile, lout, lummox (*Inf.*), moron, nincompoop, sap (*Sl.*), simpleton

oafish blockish, Boeotian, boneheaded (*Sl.*), bovine, brutish, dense, dim, dimwitted (*Inf.*), doltish, dull, dumb (*Inf., chiefly U.S.*), heavy, loutish, lubberly, lumbering, moronic, obtuse, slow on the uptake (*Inf.*), stupid, thick

oasis *Fig.* haven, island, refuge, resting place, retreat, sanctuary, sanctum

oath 1. affirmation, avowal, bond, pledge, promise, sworn statement, vow, word 2. blasphemy, curse, cuss (*Inf.*), expletive, imprecation, malediction, profanity, strong language, swearword

obdurate adamant, callous, dogged, firm, fixed, hard, hard-hearted, harsh, immovable, implacable, indurate (*Rare*), inexorable, inflexible, iron, mulish, obstinate, perverse, pig-headed, proof against persuasion, relentless, stiff-necked, stubborn, unbending, unfeeling, unimpressible, unrelenting, unshakable, unyielding

obedience accordance, acquiescence, agreement, compliance, conformability, deference, docility, dutifulness, duty, observance, respect, reverence, submission, submissiveness, subservience, tractability

obedient acquiescent, amenable, biddable, compliant, deferential, docile, duteous, dutiful, law-abiding, observant, regardful, respectful, submissive, subservient, tractable, under control, well-trained, yielding

obeisance bending of the knee, bow, curtsy *or* curtsey, deference, genuflection, homage, kowtow, respect, reverence, salaam, salutation

obelisk column, monolith, monument, needle, pillar, shaft

obese corpulent, Falstaffian, fat, fleshy, gross, heavy, outsize, overweight, paunchy, plump, podgy, portly, roly-poly, rotund, stout, tubby, well-upholstered (*Inf.*)

obesity bulk, corpulence, *embonpoint*, fatness, fleshiness, grossness, overweight, portliness, stoutness, tubbiness, weight problem

obey 1. abide by, act upon, adhere to, be ruled by, carry out, comply, conform, discharge, do what is expected, embrace, execute, follow, fulfil, heed, keep, mind, observe, perform, respond, serve 2. bow to, come to heel, do what one is told, get into line, give in, give way, knuckle under (*Inf.*), submit, surrender (to), take orders from, toe the line, yield

obfuscate befog, bewilder, cloud, confuse, darken, obscure, perplex

object[1] *n.* 1. article, body, entity, fact, item, phenomenon, reality, thing 2. aim, butt, focus, recipient, target, victim 3. design, end, end in view, end purpose, goal, idea, intent, intention, motive, objective, point, purpose, reason

object[2] *v.* argue against, demur, expostulate, oppose, protest, raise objections, take exception

objection cavil, censure, counter-argument, demur, doubt, exception, niggle (*Inf.*), opposition, protest, remonstrance, scruple

objectionable abhorrent, deplorable, disagreeable, dislikable, displeasing, distasteful, exceptionable, indecorous, insufferable, intolerable, noxious, obnoxious, offensive, regrettable, repugnant, unacceptable, undesirable, unpleasant, unseemly, unsociable

objective 1. *adj.* detached, disinterested, dispassionate, equitable, even-handed, fair, impartial, impersonal, judicial, just, open-minded, unbiased, uncoloured, unemotional, uninvolved, unprejudiced 2. *n.* aim, ambition, aspiration, design, end, end in view, goal, intention, mark, object, purpose, target

objectively disinterestedly, dispassionately, even-handedly, impartially, with an open mind, with objectivity *or* impartiality, without fear or favour

objectivity detachment, disinterest, disinterestedness, dispassion, equitableness, impartiality, impersonality

obligation 1. accountability, accountableness, burden, charge, compulsion, duty, liability, must, onus, requirement, responsibility, trust **2.** agreement, bond, commitment, contract, debt, engagement, promise, understanding **3. under an obligation** beholden, duty-bound, grateful, honour-bound, indebted, in (someone's) debt, obligated, obliged, owing a favour, thankful

obligatory binding, coercive, compulsory, *de rigueur*, enforced, essential, imperative, mandatory, necessary, required, requisite, unavoidable

oblige 1. bind, coerce, compel, constrain, force, impel, make, necessitate, obligate, require **2.** accommodate, benefit, do (someone) a favour *or* a kindness, favour, gratify, indulge, please, put oneself out for, serve

obliged 1. appreciative, beholden, grateful, gratified, indebted, in (someone's) debt, thankful **2.** bound, compelled, forced, required, under an obligation, under compulsion, without any option

obliging accommodating, agreeable, amiable, civil, complaisant, considerate, cooperative, courteous, eager to please, friendly, good-natured, helpful, kind, polite, willing

oblique 1. angled, aslant, at an angle, inclined, slanted, slanting, sloped, sloping, tilted **2.** backhanded, circuitous, circumlocutory, evasive, implied, indirect, roundabout, sidelong

obliquely 1. aslant, aslope, at an angle, diagonally, slantwise **2.** circuitously, evasively, in a roundabout manner *or* way, indirectly, not in so many words

obliterate annihilate, blot out, cancel, delete, destroy, destroy root and branch, efface, eradicate, erase, expunge, extirpate, root out, wipe off the face of the earth, wipe out

obliteration annihilation, deletion, effacement, elimination, eradication, erasure, expunction, extirpation, wiping (blotting, rooting, sponging) out

oblivion 1. abeyance, disregard, forgetfulness, insensibility, neglect, obliviousness, unawareness, unconsciousness, (waters of) Lethe **2.** blackness, darkness, eclipse, extinction, limbo, nothingness, obscurity, void

oblivious blind, careless, deaf, disregardful, forgetful, heedless, ignorant, inattentive, insensible, neglectful, negligent, regardless, unaware, unconcerned,

unconscious, unmindful, unobservant

obloquy 1. abuse, animadversion, aspersion, attack, bad press, blame, calumny, censure, contumely, criticism, defamation, detraction, invective, opprobrium, reproach, slander, vilification **2.** discredit, disfavour, disgrace, dishonour, humiliation, ignominy, ill fame, ill repute, infamy, odium, shame, stigma

obnoxious abhorrent, abominable, detestable, disagreeable, disgusting, dislikable, foul, hateful, hateful, horrid, insufferable, loathsome, nasty, nauseating, objectionable, odious, offensive, repellent, reprehensible, repugnant, repulsive, revolting, sickening, unpleasant

obscene 1. bawdy, blue, coarse, dirty, disgusting, Fescennine (*Rare*), filthy, foul, gross, immodest, immoral, improper, impure, indecent, lewd, licentious, loose, offensive, pornographic, prurient, ribald, salacious, scabrous, shameless, smutty, suggestive, unchaste, unwholesome **2.** *Fig.* atrocious, evil, heinous, loathsome, outrageous, shocking, sickening, vile, wicked

obscenity 1. bawdiness, blueness, coarseness, dirtiness, filthiness, foulness, grossness, immodesty, impurity, lewdness, licentiousness, pornography, prurience, salacity, smuttiness, suggestiveness, vileness **2.** four-letter word, impropriety, indecency, indelicacy, profanity, smut, swearword, vulgarism **3.** abomination, affront, atrocity, blight, evil, offence, outrage, vileness, wrong

obscure *adj.* **1.** abstruse, ambiguous, arcane, concealed, confusing, cryptic, deep, doubtful, enigmatic, esoteric, hazy, hidden, incomprehensible, indefinite, intricate, involved, mysterious, occult, opaque, recondite, unclear, vague **2.** blurred, clouded, cloudy, dim, dusky, faint, gloomy, indistinct, murky, obfuscated, shadowy, shady, sombre, tenebrous, unlit, veiled **3.** humble, inconspicuous, inglorious, little-known, lowly, minor, nameless, out-of-the-way, remote, undistinguished, unheard-of, unhonoured, unimportant, unknown, unnoted, unseen, unsung ~*v.* **4.** conceal, cover, disguise, hide, muddy, obfuscate, screen, throw a veil over, veil **5.** adumbrate, bedim, befog, block, block out, blur, cloak, cloud, darken, dim, dull, eclipse, mask, overshadow, shade, shroud

obscurity 1. abstruseness, ambiguity, complexity, impenetrableness, incomprehensibility, intricacy, reconditeness, vagueness **2.** darkness, dimness, dusk, duskiness, gloom, haze, haziness, indistinctness, murkiness, shadowiness, shadows **3.** inconspicuousness, ingloriousness, insignificance, lowliness, namelessness, nonrecognition, unimportance

obsequies burial, burial service, exequies, funeral, funeral rites, last offices

obsequious abject, cringing, deferential, fawning, flattering, grovelling, ingratiating, mealy-mouthed, menial, servile, slavish, smarmy (*Brit. inf.*), submissive, sycophantic, toadying, unctuous

obsequiously abjectly, cringingly, deferentially, fawningly, ingratiatingly, on one's knees, servilely, slavishly, smarmily (*Brit inf.*), sycophantically, unctuously

observable apparent, appreciable, clear, detectable, discernible, evident, noticeable, obvious, open, patent, perceivable, perceptible, recognizable, visible

observance 1. adherence to, attention, carrying out, celebration, compliance, discharge, fulfilment, heeding, honouring, notice, observation, performance **2.** ceremonial, ceremony, custom, fashion, form, formality, practice, rite, ritual, service, tradition

observant alert, attentive, eagle-eyed, heedful, mindful, obedient, perceptive, quick, sharp-eyed, submissive, vigilant, watchful, wide-awake

observation 1. attention, cognition, consideration, examination, experience, information, inspection, knowledge, monitoring, notice, review, scrutiny, study, surveillance, watching **2.** annotation, comment, finding, note, obiter dictum, opinion, pronouncement, reflection, remark, thought, utterance

observe 1. detect, discern, discover, espy, note, notice, perceive, see, spot, witness **2.** contemplate, keep an eye on (*Inf.*), keep under observation, look at, monitor, pay attention to, regard, scrutinize, study, survey, view, watch **3.** animadvert, comment, declare, mention, note, opine, remark, say, state **4.** abide by, adhere to, comply, conform to, follow, fulfil, heed, honour, keep, mind, obey, perform, respect **5.** celebrate, commemorate, keep, remember, solemnize

observer beholder, bystander, commentator, eyewitness, looker-on, onlooker, spectator, spotter, viewer, watcher, witness

obsess bedevil, be on one's mind, be uppermost in one's thoughts, consume, dominate, engross, grip, haunt, monopolize, plague, possess, preoccupy, prey on one's mind, rule, torment

obsessed beset, dominated, gripped, hag-ridden, haunted, hung up on (*Sl. chiefly U.S.*), immersed in, infatuated, in the grip of, preoccupied, troubled

obsession bee in one's bonnet (*Inf.*), complex, enthusiasm, fetish, fixation, hang-up (*Inf.*), *idée fixe*, infatuation, mania, phobia, preoccupation, ruling passion, thing (*Inf.*)

obsessive besetting, compulsive, consuming, fixed, gripping, haunting, tormenting, unforgettable

obsolescent ageing, declining, dying out, not with it (*Inf.*), on the decline, on the wane, on the way out, past its prime, waning

obsolete anachronistic, ancient, antediluvian, antiquated, antique, archaic, bygone, dated, *démodé*, discarded, disused, extinct, musty, old, old-fashioned, old hat, out, outmoded, out of date, out of fashion, out of the ark (*Inf.*), outworn, passé, superannuated, *vieux jeu*

obstacle bar, barrier, check, difficulty, hindrance, hitch, hurdle, impediment, interference, interruption, obstruction, snag, stumbling block

obstinacy doggedness, firmness, inflexibility, intransigence, mulishness, obduracy, perseverance, persistence, pertinacity, pig-headedness, resoluteness, stubbornness, tenacity, wilfulness

obstinate contumacious, determined, dogged, firm, headstrong, immovable, inflexible, intractable, intransigent, mulish, opinionated, persistent, pertinacious, perverse, pig-headed, recalcitrant, refractory, self-willed, steadfast, strongminded, stubborn, tenacious, unyielding, wilful

obstreperous boisterous, clamorous, disorderly, loud, noisy, out of control, out of hand, rackety, rambunctious (*Inf.*), rampaging, raucous, restive, riotous, rip-roaring (*Inf.*), roistering, roisterous, rough, rowdy, stroppy (*Brit. sl.*), tempestuous, tumultuous, turbulent, uncontrolled, undisciplined, unmanageable, unruly, uproarious, vociferous, wild

obstruct arrest, bar, barricade, block, bring to a standstill, check, choke, clog, cumber, curb, cut off, frustrate, get in the way of, hamper, hamstring, hide, hinder, hold up, impede, inhibit, interfere with, interrupt, mask, obscure, prevent, restrict, retard, shield, shut off, slow down, stop, thwart, trammel

obstruction bar, barricade, barrier, blockage, check, difficulty, hindrance, impediment, snag, stop, stoppage, trammel

obstructive awkward, blocking, delaying, hindering, inhibiting, preventative, restrictive, stalling, uncooperative, unhelpful

obtain 1. achieve, acquire, attain, come by, earn, gain, get, get hold of, get one's hands on, procure, secure 2. be in force, be prevalent, be the case, exist, hold, prevail, stand

obtainable achievable, at hand, attainable, available, on tap (*Inf.*), procurable, ready, realizable, to be had

obtrusive 1. forward, importunate, interfering, intrusive, meddling, nosy, officious, prying, pushy (*Inf.*) 2. noticeable, obvious, prominent, protruding, protuberant, sticking out

obtrusively blatantly, bluntly, boldly, crassly, importunately, obviously, officiously, pushily

obtuse 1. boneheaded (*Sl.*), dense, dopey (*Sl.*), dull, dull-witted, dumb (*Inf., chiefly U.S.*), heavy, imperceptive, insensitive, muttonheaded (*Sl.*), retarded, slow, slow on the uptake (*Inf.*), stolid, stupid, thick, thick-skinned, uncomprehending, unintelligent 2. blunt, rounded

obviate anticipate, avert, counter, counteract, do away with, preclude, prevent, remove, render unnecessary

obvious apparent, clear, clear as a bell, conspicuous, distinct, evident, indisputable, manifest, much in evidence, noticeable, open, overt, palpable, patent, perceptible, plain, plain as the nose on your face (*Inf.*), pronounced, recognizable, right under one's nose (*Inf.*), self-evident, self-explanatory, staring one in the face (*Inf.*), sticking out a mile (*Inf.*), straightforward, transparent, unconcealed, undeniable, undisguised, unmistakable, unsubtle, visible

obviously certainly, clearly, distinctly,

manifestly, of course, palpably, patently, plainly, undeniably, unmistakably, unquestionably, without doubt

occasion *n.* 1. chance, convenience, incident, moment, occurrence, opening, opportunity, time 2. affair, celebration, event, experience, occurrence 3. call, cause, excuse, ground(s), inducement, influence, justification, motive, prompting, provocation, reason ~*v.* 4. bring about, cause, create, effect, elicit, engender, evoke, generate, give rise to, induce, influence, inspire, lead to, move, originate, persuade, produce, prompt, provoke

occasional casual, desultory, incidental, infrequent, intermittent, irregular, odd, rare, sporadic, uncommon

occasionally at intervals, at times, (every) now and then, every so often, from time to time, irregularly, now and again, off and on, on and off, once in a while, on occasion, periodically, sometimes

occlude block, choke, clog, close, fill, hinder, obstruct, plug, seal, shut, stop up

occult abstruse, arcane, cabbalistic, concealed, esoteric, hidden, invisible, magical, mysterious, mystic, mystical, obscure, preternatural, recondite, secret, supernatural, unknown, unrevealed, veiled

occultism black magic, diabolism, magic, sorcery, supernaturalism, the black arts, witchcraft

occupancy habitation, holding, inhabitancy, occupation, possession, residence, tenancy, tenure, term, use

occupant addressee, denizen, holder, incumbent, indweller, inhabitant, inmate, lessee, occupier, resident, tenant, user

occupation 1. activity, business, calling, craft, employment, job, line (of work), post, profession, pursuit, trade, vocation, walk of life, work 2. control, holding, occupancy, possession, residence, tenancy, tenure, use 3. conquest, foreign rule, invasion, seizure, subjugation

occupied 1. busy, employed, engaged, hard at it (*Inf.*), tied up (*Inf.*), working 2. engaged, full, in use, taken, unavailable 3. full, inhabited, lived-in, peopled, settled, tenanted

occupy 1. *Often passive* absorb, amuse, busy, divert, employ, engage, engross, entertain, hold the attention of, immerse, interest, involve, keep busy or occupied, monopolize, preoccupy, take up, tie up **2.** be established in, be in residence in, dwell in, ensconce oneself in, establish oneself in, inhabit, live in, own, possess, reside in, stay in (*Scot.*), tenant **3.** cover, fill, hold, permeate, pervade, take up, use, utilize **4.** capture, garrison, hold, invade, keep, overrun, seize, take over, take possession of

occur 1. arise, befall, betide, chance, come about, come off (*Inf.*), come to pass (*Archaic*), crop up (*Inf.*), eventuate, happen, materialize, result, take place, turn up (*Inf.*) **2.** appear, be found, be met with, be present, develop, exist, manifest itself, obtain, show itself **3.** *With* **to** come to mind, come to one, cross one's mind, dawn on, enter one's head, spring to mind, strike one, suggest (offer, present) itself

occurrence 1. adventure, affair, circumstance, episode, event, happening, incident, instance, proceeding, transaction **2.** appearance, development, existence, manifestation, materialization

odd 1. abnormal, atypical, bizarre, curious, deviant, different, eccentric, exceptional, extraordinary, fantastic, freak, freakish, freaky (*Sl.*), funny, irregular, kinky (*Sl.*), outlandish, out of the ordinary, peculiar, quaint, queer, rare, remarkable, singular, strange, uncanny, uncommon, unconventional, unusual, weird, whimsical **2.** casual, fragmentary, incidental, irregular, miscellaneous, occasional, periodic, random, seasonal, sundry, varied, various **3.** leftover, lone, remaining, single, solitary, spare, surplus, unconsumed, uneven, unmatched, unpaired

oddity 1. abnormality, anomaly, eccentricity, freak, idiosyncrasy, irregularity, kink (*Sl.*), peculiarity, phenomenon, quirk, rarity **2.** card (*Inf.*), crank (*Inf.*), fish out of water, maverick, misfit, oddball (*Inf., chiefly U.S.*), odd bird (*Inf.*), odd fish (*Brit. inf.*), rara avis, screwball (*U.S. sl.*), weirdie or weirdo (*Inf.*) **3.** abnormality, bizarreness, eccentricity, extraordinariness, freakishness, incongruity, oddness, outlandishness, peculiarity, queerness, singularity, strangeness, unconventionality, unnaturalness

odd man out exception, freak, maverick, misfit, nonconformist, outsider

oddment bit, end, end of a line, fag end, fragment, leftover, off cut, remnant, scrap, shred, sliver, snippet

odds 1. advantage, allowance, edge, lead, superiority **2.** balance, chances, likelihood, probability **3.** *Brit.* difference, disparity, dissimilarity, distinction **4. at odds** at daggers drawn, at loggerheads, at sixes and sevens, at variance, in conflict, in disagreement, in opposition to, not in keeping, on bad terms, out of line

odds and ends bits, bits and pieces, debris, leavings, litter, oddments, remnants, rubbish, scraps, sundry or miscellaneous items

odious abhorrent, abominable, detestable, disgusting, execrable, foul, hateful, horrible, horrid, loathsome, obnoxious, offensive, repellent, repugnant, repulsive, revolting, unpleasant, vile

odium abhorrence, antipathy, censure, condemnation, detestation, disapprobation, disapproval, discredit, disfavour, disgrace, dishonour, dislike, disrepute, execration, hatred, infamy, obloquy, opprobrium, reprobation, shame

odorous aromatic, balmy, fragrant, odoriferous, perfumed, redolent, scented, sweet-smelling

odour 1. aroma, bouquet, essence, fragrance, perfume, redolence, scent, smell, stench, stink **2.** air, atmosphere, aura, emanation, flavour, quality, spirit

odyssey crusade, journey, peregrination, pilgrimage, quest, trek, voyage

off *adj.* **1.** absent, cancelled, finished, gone, inoperative, postponed, unavailable **2.** bad, below par, disappointing, disheartening, displeasing, low-quality, mortifying, poor, quiet, slack, substandard, unrewarding, unsatisfactory **3.** bad, decomposed, high, mouldy, rancid, rotten, sour, turned ~*adv.* **4.** apart, aside, away, elsewhere, out

off and on (every) now and again, every once in a while, from time to time, intermittently, now and then, occasionally, on and off, sometimes, sporadically

offbeat bizarre, Bohemian, eccentric, far-out (*Sl.*), freaky (*Sl.*), idiosyncratic, kinky (*Sl.*), novel, oddball (*Chiefly U.S. inf.*), outré, strange, uncommon, unconventional, unorthodox, unusual, way-out (*Inf.*), weird

off colour ill, not up to par, off form, out of sorts, peaky, poorly (*Inf.*), queasy, run down, sick, under the weather (*Inf.*), unwell, washed out

offence 1. breach of conduct, crime, delinquency, fault, lapse, misdeed, misdemeanour, peccadillo, sin, transgression, trespass, wrong, wrongdoing **2.** affront, displeasure, harm, hurt, indignity, injury, injustice, insult, outrage, put-down (*Sl.*), slight, snub **3.** anger, annoyance, displeasure, hard feelings, huff, indignation, ire (*Literary*), needle (*Sl.*), pique, resentment, umbrage, wounded feelings, wrath **4. take offence** be disgruntled, be offended, get riled, go into a huff, resent, take the huff, take the needle (*Brit. sl.*), take umbrage

offend 1. affront, annoy, disgruntle, displease, fret, gall, give offence, hurt (someone's) feelings, insult, irritate, miff (*Inf.*), outrage, pain, pique, provoke, put (someone's) back up (*Inf.*), rile, slight, snub, tread on (someone's) toes (*Inf.*), upset, vex, wound **2.** be disagreeable to, disgust, make (someone) sick, nauseate, repel, repulse, sicken, turn (someone) off (*Sl.*)

offended affronted, disgruntled, displeased, huffy, in a huff, miffed (*Inf.*), outraged, pained, piqued, put out (*Inf.*), resentful, smarting, stung, upset

offender criminal, culprit, delinquent, lawbreaker, malefactor, miscreant, sinner, transgressor, wrongdoer

offensive *adj.* **1.** abusive, annoying, detestable, discourteous, displeasing, disrespectful, embarrassing, impertinent, insolent, insulting, irritating, objectionable, rude, uncivil, unmannerly **2.** abominable, detestable, disagreeable, disgusting, grisly, loathsome, nasty, nauseating, noisome, obnoxious, odious, repellent, revolting, sickening, unpalatable, unpleasant, unsavoury, vile **3.** aggressive, attacking, invading ~*n.* **4.** attack, drive, onslaught, push (*Inf.*) **5. on the offensive** advancing, aggressive, attacking, invading, invasive, on the warpath (*Inf.*)

offer *v.* **1.** bid, extend, give, hold out, proffer, put on (*Inf.*), put on the market, put under the hammer, put up for sale, tender **2.** afford, furnish, make available, place at (someone's) disposal, present, provide, show **3.** advance, extend, move, propose, put forth, put forward, submit, suggest **4.** be at (someone's) service, come forward, offer one's services, volunteer ~*n.*

5. attempt, bid, endeavour, essay, overture, proposal, proposition, submission, suggestion, tender

offering contribution, donation, gift, oblation (*in religious contexts*), present, sacrifice, subscription, widow's mite

off form below par, having lost one's touch, not at one's best, not up to scratch (*Inf.*), on a bad day, out of practice, out of training, unpractised

offhand 1. *adj.* abrupt, aloof, brusque, careless, casual, cavalier, couldn't-careless, curt, glib, informal, offhanded, perfunctory, take-it-or-leave-it (*Inf.*), unceremonious, unconcerned, uninterested **2.** *adv.* ad lib, extempore, just like that (*Inf.*), off the cuff (*Inf.*), off the top of one's head (*Inf.*), without preparation

office 1. appointment, business, capacity, charge, commission, duty, employment, function, obligation, occupation, place, post, responsibility, role, service, situation, station, trust, work **2.** *Plural* advocacy, aegis, aid, auspices, backing, favour, help, intercession, intervention, mediation, patronage, recommendation, referral, support, word

officer agent, appointee, bureaucrat, dignitary, executive, functionary, office-holder, official, public servant, representative

official 1. *adj.* accredited, authentic, authoritative, authorized, bona fide, certified, endorsed, ex cathedra, ex officio, formal, legitimate, licensed, proper, sanctioned, straight from the horse's mouth (*Inf.*) **2.** *n.* agent, bureaucrat, executive, functionary, office bearer, officer, representative

officiate chair, conduct, emcee (*Inf.*), manage, oversee, preside, serve, superintend

officious bustling, dictatorial, forward, impertinent, inquisitive, interfering, intrusive, meddlesome, meddling, mischievous, obtrusive, opinionated, overbusy, overzealous, pragmatical (*Rare*), pushy (*Inf.*), self-important

offing in the offing close at hand, coming up, hovering, imminent, in prospect, in the immediate future, in the wings, on the horizon, on the way

off key discordant, dissonant, inharmonious, jarring, out of keeping, out of tune

off-load disburden, discharge, dump, get rid of, jettison, shift, take off, transfer, unburden, unload, unship

off-putting daunting, discomfiting, disconcerting, discouraging, dismaying, dispiriting, disturbing, formidable, frustrating, intimidating, unnerving, unsettling, upsetting

offset 1. *v.* balance out, cancel out, compensate for, counteract, counterbalance, counterpoise, countervail, make up for, neutralize 2. *n.* balance, compensation, counterbalance, counterweight, equipoise

offshoot adjunct, appendage, branch, by-product, development, limb, outgrowth, spin-off, sprout

offspring child, children, descendant, descendants, family, fry, heir, heirs, issue, kids (*Inf.*), progeny, scion, seed, spawn, successor, successors, young

often again and again, frequently, generally, many a time, much, oft (*Poetic*), oftentimes (*Archaic*), ofttimes (*Archaic*), over and over again, repeatedly, time after time, time and again

ogle eye up (*Inf.*), gawp at (*Brit. sl.*), give the glad eye (*Inf.*), give the once-over (*Inf.*), lech *or* letch after (*Inf.*), leer, make sheep's eyes at (*Inf.*)

ogre bogey, bogeyman, bugbear, demon, devil, giant, monster, spectre

oil *v.* grease, lubricate

oily 1. fatty, greasy, oiled, oleaginous, smeary, swimming 2. flattering, fulsome, glib, hypocritical, obsequious, plausible, servile, smarmy (*Brit. inf.*), smooth, unctuous

ointment balm, cerate, cream, embrocation, emollient, liniment, lotion, salve, unguent

O.K., okay 1. *adj.* acceptable, accurate, adequate, all right, approved, convenient, correct, fair, fine, good, in order, middling, not bad (*Inf.*), passable, permitted, satisfactory, so-so (*Inf.*), tolerable 2. *n.* agreement, approbation, approval, assent, authorization, consent, endorsement, go-ahead (*Inf.*), green light, permission, sanction, say-so (*Inf.*), seal of approval 3. *v.* agree to, approve, authorize, consent to, endorse, give one's consent to, give the go-ahead to (*Inf.*), give the green light to, give the thumbs up to, pass, rubber-stamp (*Inf.*), sanction, say yes to 4. *interj.* agreed, all right, right, very good, very well, yes

old 1. advanced in years, aged, ancient, decrepit, elderly, full of years, getting on

(*Inf.*), grey, grey-haired, grizzled, hoary, mature, over the hill (*Inf.*), past one's prime, patriarchal, senescent, senile, venerable 2. antediluvian, antiquated, antique, cast-off, crumbling, dated, decayed, done, hackneyed, obsolete, old-fashioned, outdated, outmoded, out of date, passé, stale, superannuated, timeworn, unfashionable, unoriginal, worn-out 3. aboriginal, antique, archaic, bygone, early, immemorial, of old, of yore, olden (*Archaic*), original, primeval, primitive, primordial, pristine, remote 4. age-old, experienced, familiar, hardened, long-established, of long standing, practised, skilled, time-honoured, traditional, versed, veteran, vintage 5. earlier, erstwhile, ex-, former, one-time, previous, quondam

old age advancing years, age, agedness, Anno Domini (*Inf.*), autumn *or* evening of one's life, declining years, dotage, senescence, senility

old-fashioned ancient, antiquated, archaic, behind the times, corny (*Sl.*), dated, dead, démodé, fusty, musty, not with it (*Inf.*), obsolescent, obsolete, old-fangled, (old-)fogyish, old hat, old-time, outdated, outmoded, out of date, out of style, out of the ark (*Inf.*), passé, past, square (*Inf.*), superannuated, unfashionable

old hand expert, old soldier, old-timer, one of the old school, past master, veteran

old man elder, elder statesman, father, gaffer, grandfather, greybeard, O.A.P. (*Brit.*), old codger (*Inf.*), old stager, oldster (*Inf.*), old-timer (*U.S.*), patriarch, senior citizen

old-time ancient, antique, bygone, former, old-fashioned, past, vintage

old womanish finicky, fussy, niggly, old-maidish (*Inf.*), overcautious, over-particular, pernickety (*Inf.*), prim, prudish, strait-laced, timid, timorous

old-world archaic, ceremonious, chivalrous, courtly, gallant, old-fashioned, picturesque, quaint, traditional

oleaginous adipose, fat, fatty, greasy, oily, sebaceous, unguinous (*Obsolete*)

Olympian elevated, exalted, glorious, godlike, lofty, majestic, rarefied, splendid, sublime

omen augury, foreboding, foretoken, indication, portent, premonition, presage, prognostic, prognostication, sign, straw in the wind, warning, writing on the wall

ominous baleful, dark, fateful, foreboding, inauspicious, menacing, minatory, portentous, premonitory, sinister, threatening, unpromising, unpropitious

omission default, exclusion, failure, forgetfulness, gap, lack, leaving out, neglect, noninclusion, oversight

omit disregard, drop, eliminate, exclude, fail, forget, give (something) a miss (*Inf.*), leave out, leave (something) undone, let (something) slide, miss (out), neglect, overlook, pass over, skip

omnipotence divine right, invincibility, mastery, sovereignty, supremacy, supreme power, undisputed sway

omnipotent all-powerful, almighty, supreme

omniscient all-knowing, all-seeing, all-wise

on and off discontinuously, (every) now and again, fitfully, from time to time, intermittently, now and then, off and on, on occasion, sometimes, spasmodically

once 1. at one time, formerly, in the old days, in the past, in times gone by, in times past, long ago, once upon a time, previously **2. at once a.** directly, forthwith, immediately, instantly, now, right away, straight away, straightway (*Archaic*), this (very) minute, without delay, without hesitation **b.** at *or* in one go (*Inf.*), at the same time, simultaneously, together **3. once and for all** conclusively, decisively, finally, for all time, for good, for the last time, permanently, positively, with finality **4. once in a while** at intervals, at times, every now and then, from time to time, now and again, occasionally, once in a blue moon (*Inf.*), on occasion, sometimes

oncoming advancing, approaching, forthcoming, imminent, impending, looming, onrushing

one-horse backwoods, inferior, minor, obscure, petty, quiet, sleepy, slow, small, small-time (*Inf.*), tinpot (*Brit. inf.*), unimportant

onerous backbreaking, burdensome, crushing, demanding, difficult, exacting, exhausting, exigent, formidable, grave, hard, heavy, laborious, oppressive, responsible, taxing, weighty

one-sided biased, coloured, discriminatory, inequitable, lopsided, partial, partisan, prejudiced, unequal, unfair, unjust

one-time erstwhile, ex-, former, late, previous, quondam, sometime

ongoing advancing, continuous, current, developing, evolving, extant, growing, in progress, progressing, successful, unfinished, unfolding

onlooker bystander, eyewitness, looker-on, observer, spectator, viewer, watcher, witness

only 1. *adv.* at most, barely, exclusively, just, merely, purely, simply **2.** *adj.* exclusive, individual, lone, one and only, single, sole, solitary, unique

onomatopoeic echoic, imitative, onomatopoetic

onrush charge, flood, flow, onset, onslaught, push, rush, stampede, stream, surge

onset 1. assault, attack, charge, onrush, onslaught **2.** beginning, inception, kick-off (*Inf.*), outbreak, start

onslaught assault, attack, blitz, charge, offensive, onrush, onset

onus burden, liability, load, obligation, responsibility, task

onward, onwards *adv.* ahead, beyond, forth, forward, in front, on

ooze 1. *v.* bleed, discharge, drain, dribble, drip, drop, emit, escape, exude, filter, leach, leak, overflow with, percolate, seep, strain, sweat, weep **2.** *n.* alluvium, mire, muck, mud, silt, slime, sludge

oozy dewy, dripping, miry, moist, mucky, slimy, sloppy, sludgy, sweaty, weeping

opacity cloudiness, density, dullness, filminess, impermeability, milkiness, murkiness, obscurity, opaqueness

opalescent iridescent, lustrous, nacreous, opaline, pearly, prismatic, rainbow-hued, shot

opaque 1. clouded, cloudy, dim, dull, filmy, hazy, impenetrable, lustreless, muddied, muddy, murky, obfuscated, turbid **2.** abstruse, baffling, cryptic, difficult, enigmatic, incomprehensible, obscure, unclear, unfathomable, unintelligible

open *adj.* **1.** agape, ajar, expanded, extended, gaping, revealed, spread out, unbarred, unclosed, uncovered, unfastened, unfolded, unfurled, unlocked, unobstructed, unsealed, yawning **2.** airy, bare, clear, exposed, extensive, free, navigable, not built-up, passable, rolling, spacious, sweeping, uncluttered, uncrowded, unenclosed, unfenced, unsheltered, wide, wide-open **3**. accessible, available, free, general, nondiscriminatory, public, unconditional, unengaged, unoccupied, unqualified, unrestricted, vacant **4**. apparent, avowed, barefaced, blatant, clear, conspicuous, downright, evident, flagrant, frank, manifest, noticeable, obvious, overt, plain, unconcealed, undisguised, visible **5**. arguable, debatable, moot, undecided, unresolved, unsettled, up in the air, yet to be decided **6**. disinterested, free, impartial, objective, receptive, unbiased, uncommitted, unprejudiced **7**. *With* to an easy target for, at the mercy of, defenceless against, disposed, exposed, liable, susceptible, vulnerable **8**. artless, candid, fair, frank, guileless, honest, ingenuous, innocent, natural, sincere, transparent, unreserved **9**. filigree, fretted, holey, honeycombed, lacy, loose, openwork, porous, spongy **10**. bounteous, bountiful, generous, liberal, munificent **11**. exposed, undefended, unfortified, unprotected ~*v.* **12**. begin, begin business, commence, get *or* start the ball rolling, inaugurate, initiate, kick off (*Inf.*), launch, put up one's plate, set in motion, set up shop, start **13**. clear, crack, throw wide, unbar, unblock, unclose, uncork, uncover, undo, unfasten, unlock, unseal, untie, unwrap **14**. expand, spread (out), unfold, unfurl, unroll **15**. come apart, crack, rupture, separate, split **16**. disclose, divulge, exhibit, explain, lay bare, pour out, show, uncover

open-air alfresco, outdoor

open-and-shut foregone, noncontroversial, obvious, simple, straightforward

open-handed bountiful, free, generous, lavish, liberal, munificent, unstinting

opening *n*. **1**. aperture, breach, break, chink, cleft, crack, fissure, gap, hole, interstice, orifice, perforation, rent, rupture, slot, space, split, vent **2**. break (*Inf.*), chance, look-in (*Inf.*), occasion, opportunity, place, vacancy **3**. beginning, birth, commencement, dawn, inauguration, inception, initiation, kickoff (*Inf.*), launch, launching, onset, outset, start ~*adj.* **4**. beginning, commencing, early, first, inaugural, initial, initiatory, introductory, maiden, primary

openly 1. candidly, face to face, forth-

rightly, frankly, plainly, straight from the shoulder (*Inf.*), unhesitatingly, unreservedly **2**. blatantly, brazenly, flagrantly, in full view, in public, publicly, shamelessly, unabashedly, unashamedly, wantonly, without pretence

open-minded broad, broad-minded, catholic, dispassionate, enlightened, free, impartial, liberal, reasonable, receptive, tolerant, unbiased, undogmatic, unprejudiced

operate 1. act, be in action, function, go, perform, run, work **2**. be in charge of, handle, manage, manoeuvre, use, work **3**. perform surgery

operation 1. action, affair, course, exercise, motion, movement, performance, procedure, process, use, working **2**. **in operation** effective, functioning, going, in action, in force, operative **3**. activity, agency, effect, effort, force, influence, instrumentality, manipulation **4**. affair, business, deal, enterprise, proceeding, transaction, undertaking **5**. assault, campaign, exercise, manoeuvre **6**. surgery

operational functional, going, in working order, operative, prepared, ready, usable, viable, workable, working

operative *adj.* **1**. active, current, effective, efficient, functional, functioning, in force, in operation, operational, serviceable, standing, workable **2**. crucial, important, indicative, influential, key, relevant, significant ~*n.* **3**. artisan, employee, hand, labourer, machinist, mechanic, worker

operator 1. conductor, driver, handler, mechanic, operative, practitioner, skilled employee, technician, worker **2**. administrator, contractor, dealer, director, manager, speculator, trader **3**. *Inf.* Machiavellian, machinator, manipulator, mover, punter, shyster (*Sl., chiefly U.S.*), smart aleck (*Inf.*), wheeler-dealer (*Inf.*), wirepuller, worker

opiate anodyne, bromide, downer (*Sl.*), drug, narcotic, nepenthe, pacifier, sedative, soporific, tranquillizer

opine believe, conceive, conclude, conjecture, declare, give as one's opinion, judge, presume, say, suggest, suppose, surmise, think, venture, volunteer, ween (*Poetic*)

opinion 1. assessment, belief, conception, conjecture, estimation, feeling, idea, impression, judgment, mind, notion, persuasion, point of view, sentiment, theory, view **2. be of the opinion** be convinced, believe, be under the impression, conclude, consider, hold, judge, reckon, suppose, surmise, think **3. matter of opinion** debatable point, matter of judgment, moot point, open question, open to debate, up to the individual

opinionated adamant, biased, bigoted, bull-headed, cocksure, dictatorial, doctrinaire, dogmatic, inflexible, obdurate, obstinate, overbearing, pig-headed, prejudiced, self-assertive, single-minded, stubborn, uncompromising

opponent adversary, antagonist, challenger, competitor, contestant, disputant, dissentient, enemy, foe, opposer, rival, the opposition

opportune advantageous, appropriate, apt, auspicious, convenient, favourable, felicitous, fit, fitting, fortunate, happy, lucky, proper, propitious, seasonable, suitable, timely, well-timed

opportunism expediency, exploitation, Machiavellianism, making hay while the sun shines (*Inf.*), pragmatism, realism, *Realpolitik*, striking while the iron is hot (*Inf.*), trimming, unscrupulousness

opportunity break (*Inf.*), chance, convenience, hour, look-in (*Inf.*), moment, occasion, opening, scope, time

oppose 1. bar, check, combat, confront, contradict, counter, counterattack, defy, face, fight, fly in the face of, hinder, obstruct, prevent, resist, speak against, stand up to, take a stand against, take issue with, take on, thwart, withstand **2.** compare, contrast, counterbalance, match, pit *or* set against, play off

opposed against, antagonistic, anti (*Inf.*), antipathetic, antithetical, at daggers drawn, clashing, conflicting, contrary, dissentient, hostile, incompatible, inimical, in opposition, opposing, opposite

opposing antagonistic, antipathetic, clashing, combatant, conflicting, contrary, enemy, hostile, incompatible, irreconcilable, opposed, opposite, rival, warring

opposite *adj.* **1.** corresponding, facing, fronting **2.** adverse, antagonistic, antithetical, conflicting, contradictory, contrary, contrasted, diametrically opposed, different, differing, diverse, hostile, inconsistent, inimical, irreconcilable, opposed, reverse, unlike ~*n.* **3.** antithesis, contradiction, contrary, converse, in-

verse, reverse, the other extreme, the other side of the coin (*Inf.*)

opposition 1. antagonism, competition, contrariety, counteraction, disapproval, hostility, obstruction, obstructiveness, prevention, resistance, unfriendliness **2.** antagonist, competition, foe, opponent, other side, rival

oppress 1. afflict, burden, depress, dispirit, harass, lie *or* weigh heavy upon, sadden, take the heart out of, torment, vex **2.** abuse, crush, harry, maltreat, overpower, overwhelm, persecute, rule with an iron hand, subdue, subjugate, suppress, trample underfoot, tyrannize over, wrong

oppressed abused, browbeaten, burdened, disadvantaged, downtrodden, enslaved, harassed, henpecked, maltreated, misused, prostrate, slave, subject, troubled, tyrannized, underprivileged

oppression abuse, brutality, calamity, cruelty, hardship, harshness, injury, injustice, iron hand, maltreatment, misery, persecution, severity, subjection, suffering, tyranny

oppressive 1. brutal, burdensome, cruel, despotic, grinding, harsh, heavy, inhuman, onerous, overbearing, overwhelming, repressive, severe, tyrannical, unjust **2.** airless, close, heavy, muggy, overpowering, stifling, stuffy, suffocating, sultry, torrid

oppressor autocrat, bully, despot, harrier, intimidator, iron hand, persecutor, scourge, slave-driver, taskmaster, tormentor, tyrant

opprobrious 1. abusive, calumniatory, contemptuous, contumelious, damaging, defamatory, hateful, insolent, insulting, invective, offensive, scandalous, scurrilous, vitriolic, vituperative **2.** abominable, contemptible, despicable, dishonourable, disreputable, hateful, ignominious, infamous, notorious, reprehensible, shameful

opprobrium calumny, censure, contumely, discredit, disfavour, disgrace, dishonour, disrepute, ignominy, ill repute, infamy, obloquy, odium, reproach, scurrility, shame, slur, stigma

oppugn argue, assail, attack, call into question, cast doubt on, combat, dispute, oppose, resist, withstand

opt (for) choose, decide (on), elect, exercise one's discretion (in favour of), go for (*Inf.*), make a selection, plump for, prefer

optimistic 1. disposed to take a favourable view, idealistic, seen through rose-coloured spectacles, Utopian **2**. assured, bright, buoyant, buoyed up, cheerful, confident, encouraged, expectant, hopeful, positive, sanguine

optimum *adj*. A1 (*Inf.*), best, choicest, flawless, highest, ideal, most favourable *or* advantageous, optimal, peak, perfect, superlative

option alternative, choice, election, preference, selection

optional discretionary, elective, extra, noncompulsory, open, possible, up to the individual, voluntary

opulence 1. affluence, easy circumstances, easy street (*Inf.*), fortune, lavishness, luxuriance, luxury, plenty, prosperity, riches, richness, sumptuousness, wealth **2**. abundance, copiousness, cornucopia, fullness, profusion, richness, superabundance

opulent 1. affluent, lavish, luxurious, moneyed, prosperous, rich, sumptuous, wealthy, well-heeled (*Sl.*), well-off, well-to-do **2**. abundant, copious, lavish, luxuriant, plentiful, profuse, prolific

opus composition, creation, *oeuvre*, piece, production, work

oracle 1. augur, Cassandra, prophet, seer, sibyl, soothsayer **2**. answer, augury, divination, divine utterance, prediction, prognostication, prophecy, revelation, vision **3**. adviser, authority, guru, high priest, horse's mouth, mastermind, mentor, pundit, source, wizard

oracular 1. auspicious, foreboding, haruspical, mantic, ominous, portentous, prescient, prophetic, pythonic, sibylline, vatic (*Rare*) **2**. authoritative, dictatorial, dogmatic, grave, positive, sage, significant, venerable, wise **3**. ambiguous, arcane, cryptic, Delphic, equivocal, mysterious, obscure, two-edged

oral spoken, verbal, viva voce, vocal

orate declaim, discourse, hold forth, make a speech, pontificate, speak, speechify, talk

oration address, declamation, discourse, harangue, homily, lecture, speech, spiel (*Inf.*)

orator Cicero, declaimer, lecturer, public speaker, rhetorician, speaker, spellbinder, spieler (*Inf.*)

oratorical bombastic, Ciceronian, declamatory, eloquent, grandiloquent, high-flown, magniloquent, rhetorical, silver-tongued, sonorous

oratory declamation, elocution, eloquence, grandiloquence, public speaking, rhetoric, speechifying, speechmaking, spieling (*Inf.*)

orb ball, circle, globe, ring, round, sphere

orbit *n*. **1**. circle, circumgyration, course, cycle, ellipse, path, revolution, rotation, track, trajectory **2**. *Fig.* ambit, compass, course, domain, influence, range, reach, scope, sphere, sphere of influence, sweep ~*v*. **3**. circle, circumnavigate, encircle, revolve around

orchestrate 1. arrange, score **2**. arrange, concert, coordinate, integrate, organize, present, put together, set up, stage-manage

ordain 1. anoint, appoint, call, consecrate, destine, elect, frock, invest, nominate **2**. fate, foreordain, intend, predestine, predetermine **3**. decree, dictate, enact, enjoin, fix, lay down, legislate, order, prescribe, pronounce, rule, set, will

ordeal affliction, agony, anguish, nightmare, suffering, test, torture, trial, tribulation(s), trouble(s)

order *n*. **1**. arrangement, harmony, method, neatness, orderliness, organization, pattern, plan, propriety, regularity, symmetry, system, tidiness **2**. arrangement, array, categorization, classification, codification, disposal, disposition, grouping, layout, line, line-up, ordering, placement, progression, sequence, series, setup (*Inf.*), structure, succession **3**. **in order** *a*. arranged, in sequence, neat, orderly, shipshape, tidy *b*. acceptable, appropriate, called for, correct, fitting, O.K. (*Inf.*), right, suitable **4**. **out of order** *a*. broken, broken-down, bust (*Sl.*), gone haywire (*Inf.*), gone phut (*Inf.*), in disrepair, inoperative, kaput (*Inf.*), nonfunctional, not working, on the blink (*Sl.*), out of commission, U/S (*Inf.*), wonky (*Brit. sl*) *b*. improper, indecorous, not cricket (*Inf.*), not done, not on (*Inf.*), out of place, out of turn, uncalled-for, wrong **5**. calm, control, discipline, law, law and order, peace, quiet, tranquillity **6**. caste, class, degree, grade, hierarchy, pecking order (*Inf.*), position, rank, status **7**. breed, cast, class, family, genre, genus, ilk, kind, sort, species, subclass, taxonomic group, tribe, type **8**. behest, command, decree, dictate, direction, directive, injunction, instruction, law, mandate, ordinance, precept, regulation, rule, say-so (*Inf.*), stipulation **9.** application, booking, commission, request, requisition, reservation **10.** association, brotherhood, community, company, fraternity, guild, league, lodge, organization, sect, sisterhood, society, sodality, union ~*v.* **11.** adjure, bid, charge, command, decree, direct, enact, enjoin, instruct, ordain, prescribe, require **12.** apply for, authorize, book, call for, contract for, engage, prescribe, request, reserve, send away for **13.** adjust, align, arrange, catalogue, class, classify, conduct, control, dispose, group, lay out, manage, marshal, neaten, organize, put to rights, regulate, set in order, sort out, systematize, tabulate, tidy

orderly *adj.* **1.** businesslike, in apple-pie order (*Inf.*), in order, methodical, neat, regular, scientific, shipshape, systematic, systematized, tidy, trim, well-organized, well-regulated **2.** controlled, decorous, disciplined, law-abiding, nonviolent, peaceable, quiet, restrained, well-behaved

ordinance **1.** canon, command, decree, dictum, edict, enactment, fiat, law, order, precept, regulation, rule, ruling, statute **2.** ceremony, institution, observance, practice, rite, ritual, sacrament, usage

ordinarily as a rule, commonly, customarily, generally, habitually, in general, in the general run (of things), in the usual way, normally, usually

ordinary **1.** accustomed, common, customary, established, everyday, habitual, humdrum, normal, prevailing, quotidian, regular, routine, settled, standard, stock, typical, usual, wonted **2.** common or garden (*Inf.*), conventional, familiar, homespun, household, humble, modest, plain, prosaic, run-of-the-mill, simple, unmemorable, unpretentious, unremarkable, workaday **3.** average, commonplace, fair, indifferent, inferior, mean, mediocre, pedestrian, second-rate, stereotyped, undistinguished, unexceptional, uninspired, unremarkable **4. out of the ordinary** atypical, distinguished, exceptional, exciting, extraordinary, high-calibre, imaginative, important, impressive, inspired, noteworthy, outstanding, rare, remarkable, significant, special,

striking, superior, uncommon, unusual

ordnance arms, artillery, big guns, cannon, guns, matériel, munitions, weapons

organ **1.** device, implement, instrument, tool **2.** element, member, part, process, structure, unit **3.** agency, channel, forum, journal, means, medium, mouthpiece, newspaper, paper, periodical, publication, vehicle, voice

organic **1.** animate, biological, biotic, live, living, natural **2.** integrated, methodical, ordered, organized, structured, systematic **3.** anatomical, constitutional, fundamental, inherent, innate, integral, structural

organism animal, being, body, creature, entity, living thing, structure

organization **1.** assembling, assembly, construction, coordination, disposal, formation, forming, formulation, making, management, methodology, organizing, planning, regulation, running, standardization, structuring **2.** arrangement, chemistry, composition, configuration, conformation, constitution, design, format, framework, grouping, make-up, method, organism, pattern, plan, structure, system, unity, whole **3.** association, body, combine, company, concern, confederation, consortium, corporation, federation, group, institution, league, outfit (*Inf.*), syndicate

organize arrange, be responsible for, catalogue, classify, codify, constitute, construct, coordinate, dispose, establish, form, frame, get going (*Inf.*), get together (*Sl.*), group, lay the foundations of, lick into shape, look after, marshal, pigeonhole, put in order, put together, run, see to (*Inf.*), set up, shape, straighten out, systematize, tabulate, take care of

orgiastic abandoned, bacchanalian, bacchic, debauched, depraved, Dionysian, dissolute, frenetic, riotous, Saturnalian, wanton, wild

orgy **1.** bacchanal, bacchanalia, debauch, revel, revelry, Saturnalia **2.** binge (*Inf.*), bout, excess, indulgence, overindulgence, splurge, spree, surfeit

orient *v.* acclimatize, adapt, adjust, align, familiarize, find one's feet (*Inf.*), get one's bearings, get the lie of the land, orientate

orientation **1.** bearings, coordination, direction, location, position, sense of direction **2**. acclimatization, adaptation, adjustment, assimilation, breaking in, familiarization, introduction, settling in

orifice aperture, cleft, hole, mouth, opening, perforation, pore, rent, vent

origin 1. base, basis, cause, derivation, *fons et origo*, font (*Poetic*), fountain, fountainhead, occasion, provenance, root, roots, source, spring, wellspring **2**. beginning, birth, commencement, creation, dawning, early stages, emergence, foundation, genesis, inauguration, inception, launch, origination, outset, start **3**. ancestry, beginnings, birth, descent, extraction, family, heritage, lineage, parentage, pedigree, stirps, stock

original *adj*. **1**. aboriginal, autochthonous, commencing, earliest, early, embryonic, first, infant, initial, introductory, opening, primary, primitive, primordial, pristine, rudimentary, starting **2**. creative, fertile, fresh, imaginative, ingenious, innovative, innovatory, inventive, new, novel, resourceful, seminal, unconventional, unprecedented, untried, unusual **3**. archetypal, authentic, first, first-hand, genuine, master, primary, prototypical ~*n*. **4**. archetype, master, model, paradigm, pattern, precedent, prototype, standard, type **5**. anomaly, card (*Inf.*), case (*Inf.*), character, eccentric, nonconformist, oddity, queer fish (*Brit. inf.*), weirdo (*Inf.*)

originality boldness, break with tradition, cleverness, creativeness, creative spirit, creativity, daring, freshness, imagination, imaginativeness, individuality, ingenuity, innovation, innovativeness, inventiveness, new ideas, newness, novelty, resourcefulness, unconventionality, unorthodoxy

originally at first, at the outset, at the start, by origin (birth, derivation), first, initially, in the beginning, in the first place, to begin with

originate 1. arise, be born, begin, come, derive, emanate, emerge, flow, issue, proceed, result, rise, spring, start, stem **2**. bring about, conceive, create, develop, discover, evolve, form, formulate, generate, give birth to, inaugurate, initiate, institute, introduce, invent, launch, pioneer, produce, set in motion, set up

originator architect, author, creator, father, founder, generator, innovator, inventor, maker, mother, pioneer, prime mover

ornament *n*. **1**. accessory, adornment, bauble, decoration, embellishment, frill, furbelow, garnish, gewgaw, knick-knack, trimming, trinket **2**. flower, honour, jewel, leading light, pride, treasure ~*v*. **3**. adorn, beautify, bedizen (*Archaic*), brighten, deck, decorate, dress up, embellish, festoon, garnish, gild, grace, prettify, prink, trim

ornamental attractive, beautifying, decorative, embellishing, for show, showy

ornamentation adornment, decoration, elaboration, embellishment, embroidery, frills, ornateness

ornate aureate, baroque, beautiful, bedecked, busy, convoluted, decorated, elaborate, elegant, fancy, florid, flowery, fussy, high-wrought, ornamented, over-elaborate, rococo

orthodox accepted, approved, conformist, conventional, correct, customary, doctrinal, established, official, received, sound, traditional, true, well-established

orthodoxy authenticity, authoritativeness, authority, conformism, conformity, conventionality, devotion, devoutness, faithfulness, inflexibility, received wisdom, soundness, traditionalism

oscillate fluctuate, seesaw, sway, swing, vacillate, vary, vibrate, waver

oscillation fluctuation, instability, seesawing, swing, vacillation, variation, wavering

ossified bony, fixed, fossilized, frozen, hardened, indurated (*Rare*), inflexible, petrified, rigid, rigidified, solid

ossify fossilize, freeze, harden, indurate (*Rare*), petrify, solidify, stiffen

ostensible alleged, apparent, avowed, exhibited, manifest, outward, plausible, pretended, professed, purported, seeming, so-called, specious, superficial, supposed

ostensibly apparently, for the ostensible purpose of, on the face of it, on the surface, professedly, seemingly, supposedly, to all intents and purposes

ostentation affectation, boasting, display, exhibitionism, flamboyance, flashiness, flaunting, flourish, pageantry, parade, pomp, pretension, pretentiousness, show, showiness, showing off (*Inf.*), swank (*Inf.*), vaunting, window-dressing

ostentatious boastful, conspicuous,

crass, dashing, extravagant, flamboyant, flash (*Inf.*), flashy, flaunted, gaudy, loud, obtrusive, pompous, pretentious, showy, swanky (*Inf.*), vain, vulgar

ostracism avoidance, banishment, boycott, cold-shouldering, exclusion, exile, expulsion, isolation, rejection

ostracize avoid, banish, blackball, blacklist, boycott, cast out, cold-shoulder, exclude, excommunicate, exile, expatriate, expel, give (someone) the cold shoulder, reject, send to Coventry, shun

other *adj.* **1.** added, additional, alternative, auxiliary, extra, further, more, spare, supplementary **2.** contrasting, different, dissimilar, distinct, diverse, remaining, separate, unrelated, variant

otherwise *adv.* **1.** if not, or else, or then **2.** any other way, contrarily, differently

ounce atom, crumb, drop, grain, iota, particle, scrap, shred, speck, trace, whit

oust depose, disinherit, dislodge, displace, dispossess, eject, evict, expel, throw out, topple, turn out, unseat

out *adj.* **1.** impossible, not allowed, not on (*Inf.*), ruled out, unacceptable **2.** abroad, absent, away, elsewhere, gone, not at home, outside **3.** antiquated, behind the times, dated, dead, *démodé*, old-fashioned, old hat, passé, square (*Inf.*), unfashionable **4.** at an end, cold, dead, doused, ended, exhausted, expired, extinguished, finished, used up

out-and-out absolute, complete, consummate, downright, dyed-in-the-wool, outright, perfect, thoroughgoing, total, unmitigated, unqualified, utter

outbreak burst, epidemic, eruption, explosion, flare-up, flash, outburst, rash, spasm, upsurge

outburst access, attack, discharge, eruption, explosion, fit of temper, flare-up, gush, outbreak, outpouring, paroxysm, spasm, storm, surge

outcast *n.* castaway, derelict, displaced person, exile, leper, pariah, *persona non grata*, refugee, reprobate, untouchable, vagabond, wretch

outclass be a cut above (*Inf.*), beat, eclipse, exceed, excel, leave *or* put in the shade, leave standing (*Inf.*), outdistance, outdo, outrank, outshine, outstrip, overshadow, surpass

outcome aftereffect, aftermath, conclusion, consequence, end, end result, issue, payoff (*Inf.*), result, upshot

outcry clamour, commotion, complaint, cry, exclamation, howl, hue and cry, hullaballoo, noise, outburst, protest, scream, screech, uproar, yell

outdated antiquated, antique, archaic, behind the times (*Inf.*), *démodé*, obsolete, old-fashioned, outmoded, out of date, out of style, passé, unfashionable

outdistance leave behind, leave standing (*Inf.*), lose, outrun, outstrip, shake off

outdo beat, be one up on, best, eclipse, exceed, excel, get the better of, go one better than (*Inf.*), outclass, outdistance, outfox, outjockey, outmanoeuvre, outshine, outsmart (*Inf.*), overcome, surpass, top, transcend

outdoor alfresco, open-air, out-of-door(s), outside

outer exposed, exterior, external, outlying, outside, outward, peripheral, remote, superficial, surface

outface beard, brave, confront, defy, look straight in the eye, outstare, square up to, stare down, stare out (of countenance)

outfit *n.* **1.** accoutrements, clothes, costume, ensemble, garb, gear, get-up (*Inf.*), kit, rigout (*Inf.*), suit, togs (*Inf.*), trappings **2.** *Inf.* clique, company, corps, coterie, crew, firm, *galère*, group, organization, set, setup (*Inf.*), squad, team, unit ~*v.* **3.** accoutre, appoint, equip, fit out, furnish, kit out, provision, stock, supply, turn out

outfitter clothier, costumier, couturier, dressmaker, haberdasher (*U.S.*), modiste, tailor

outflow discharge, drainage, ebb, effluence, efflux, effusion, emanation, emergence, gush, jet, outfall, outpouring, rush, spout

outgoing **1.** departing, ex-, former, last, leaving, past, retiring, withdrawing **2.** approachable, communicative, cordial, demonstrative, easy, expansive, extrovert, friendly, genial, gregarious, informal, open, sociable, sympathetic, unreserved, warm

outgoings costs, expenditure, expenses, outlay, overheads

outgrowth **1.** bulge, excrescence, node, offshoot, outcrop, process, projection, protuberance, shoot, sprout **2.** by-product, consequence, derivative, development, emergence, issue, product, result, spin-off, yield

outing excursion, expedition, jaunt, pleasure trip, spin (*Inf.*), trip

outlandish alien, barbarous, bizarre, eccentric, exotic, fantastic, far-out (*Sl.*), foreign, freakish, grotesque, *outré*, preposterous, queer, strange, unheard-of, weird

outlast endure beyond, outlive, outstay, outwear, survive

outlaw 1. *n.* bandit, brigand, desperado, fugitive, highwayman, marauder, outcast, pariah, robber **2.** *v.* ban, banish, bar, condemn, disallow, embargo, exclude, forbid, interdict, make illegal, prohibit, proscribe, put a price on (someone's) head

outlay *n.* cost, disbursement, expenditure, expenses, investment, outgoings, spending

outlet 1. avenue, channel, duct, egress, exit, means of expression, opening, orifice, release, safety valve, vent, way out **2.** market, shop, store

outline *n.* **1.** draft, drawing, frame, framework, layout, lineament(s), plan, rough, skeleton, sketch, tracing **2.** bare facts, main features, recapitulation, résumé, rough idea, rundown, summary, synopsis, thumbnail sketch **3.** configuration, contour, delineation, figure, form, profile, shape, silhouette ~*v.* **4.** adumbrate, delineate, draft, plan, rough out, sketch (in), summarize, trace

outlive come through, endure beyond, live through, outlast, survive

outlook 1. angle, attitude, frame of mind, perspective, point of view, slant, standpoint, viewpoint, views **2.** expectations, forecast, future, prospect **3.** aspect, panorama, prospect, scene, view, vista

outlying backwoods, distant, far-flung, outer, out-of-the-way, peripheral, provincial, remote

outmanoeuvre circumvent, get the better of, outdo, outflank, outfox, outgeneral, outjockey, outsmart (*Inf.*), outwit, run rings round (*Inf.*), steal a march on (*Inf.*)

outmoded anachronistic, antediluvian, antiquated, antique, archaic, behind the times (*Inf.*), bygone, dated, *démodé*, fossilized, obsolescent, obsolete, olden (*Archaic*), oldfangled, old-fashioned, old-time, out, out of date, out

of style, outworn, passé, square (*Inf.*), superannuated, superseded, unfashionable, unusable

out of date antiquated, archaic, dated, discarded, elapsed, expired, extinct, invalid, lapsed, obsolete, old-fashioned, outmoded, outworn, passé, stale, superannuated, superseded, unfashionable

out-of-the-way 1. distant, far-flung, inaccessible, isolated, lonely, obscure, off the beaten track, outlying, remote, secluded, unfrequented **2.** abnormal, curious, exceptional, extraordinary, odd, outlandish, out of the ordinary, peculiar, strange, uncommon, unusual

out of work idle, jobless, laid off, on the dole (*Brit.*), out of a job, redundant, unemployed

outpouring cascade, debouchment, deluge, effluence, efflux, effusion, emanation, flow, flux, outflow, spate, spurt, stream, torrent

output achievement, manufacture, outturn (*Rare*), product, production, productivity, yield

outrage *n.* **1.** atrocity, barbarism, enormity, evil, inhumanity **2.** abuse, affront, desecration, indignity, injury, insult, offence, profanation, rape, ravishing, shock, violation, violence **3.** anger, fury, hurt, indignation, resentment, shock, wrath ~*v.* **4.** affront, incense, infuriate, madden, make one's blood boil, offend, scandalize, shock **5.** abuse, defile, desecrate, injure, insult, maltreat, rape, ravage, ravish, violate

outrageous 1. abominable, atrocious, barbaric, beastly, egregious, flagrant, heinous, horrible, infamous, inhuman, iniquitous, nefarious, scandalous, shocking, unspeakable, villainous, violent, wicked **2.** disgraceful, excessive, exorbitant, extravagant, immoderate, offensive, preposterous, scandalous, shocking, steep (*Inf.*), unreasonable

outré bizarre, eccentric, extravagant, fantastic, freakish, freaky (*Sl.*), grotesque, indecorous, kinky (*Sl.*), odd, outlandish, unconventional, way-out (*Inf.*), weird

outrider advance guard, advance man, attendant, bodyguard, escort, guard, harbinger, herald, precursor, scout, squire

outright *adj.* **1.** absolute, arrant, complete, consummate, downright, out-and-out, perfect, pure, thorough, thoroughgoing, total, unconditional, undeniable, unmitigated, unqualified, utter, wholesale **2**. definite, direct, flat, straightforward, unequivocal, unqualified ~*adv.* **3**. absolutely, completely, explicitly, openly, overtly, straightforwardly, thoroughly, to the full, without hesitation, without restraint **4**. at once, cleanly, immediately, instantaneously, instantly, on the spot, straight away, there and then, without more ado

outrun beat, escape, exceed, excel, get away from, leave behind, lose, outdistance, outdo, outpace, outstrip, shake off, surpass

outset beginning, commencement, early days, inauguration, inception, kickoff (*Inf.*), onset, opening, start, starting point

outshine be head and shoulders above, be superior to, eclipse, leave *or* put in the shade, outclass, outdo, outstrip, overshadow, surpass, top, transcend, upstage

outside *adj.* **1**. exterior, external, extramural, extraneous, extreme, out, outdoor, outer, outermost, outward, surface **2**. distant, faint, marginal, negligible, remote, slight, slim, small, unlikely ~*n.* **3**. exterior, façade, face, front, skin, surface, topside

outsider alien, foreigner, incomer, interloper, intruder, newcomer, nonmember, odd man out, outlander, stranger

outskirts borders, boundary, edge, environs, faubourgs, periphery, purlieus, suburbia, suburbs, vicinity

outsmart deceive, dupe, get the better of, go one better than (*Inf.*), make a fool of (*Inf.*), outfox, outjockey, outmanoeuvre, outperform, outthink, outwit, pull a fast one on (*Inf.*), put one over on (*Inf.*), run rings round (*Inf.*), trick

outspoken abrupt, blunt, candid, direct, explicit, forthright, frank, free, free-spoken, open, plain-spoken, round, unceremonious, undissembling, unequivocal, unreserved

outspread **1**. *adj.* expanded, extended, fanlike, fanned out, flared, open, opened up, outstretched, unfolded, unfurled, wide-open **2**. *v.* expand, extend, fan out, open, open wide, outstretch, spread out, unfold, unfurl

outstanding **1**. celebrated, distinguished, eminent, excellent, exceptional, great, important, impressive, meritorious, pre-eminent, special, superior, superlative, well-known **2**. arresting, conspicuous, eye-catching, marked, memorable, notable, noteworthy, prominent, salient, signal, striking **3**. due, ongoing, open, owing, payable, pending, remaining, uncollected, unpaid, unresolved, unsettled

outstrip beat, better, eclipse, exceed, excel, get ahead of, leave behind, leave standing (*Inf.*), lose, outclass, outdistance, outdo, outpace, outperform, outrun, outshine, overtake, shake off, surpass, top, transcend

outward *adj.* apparent, evident, exterior, external, noticeable, observable, obvious, ostensible, outer, outside, perceptible, superficial, surface, visible

outwardly apparently, as far as one can see, externally, officially, on the face of it, on the surface, ostensibly, professedly, seemingly, superficially, to all appearances, to all intents and purposes, to the eye

outweigh cancel (out), compensate for, eclipse, make up for, outbalance, overcome, override, predominate, preponderate, prevail over, take precedence over, tip the scales

outwit cheat, circumvent, deceive, defraud, dupe, get the better of, gull (*Archaic*), make a fool *or* monkey of, outfox, outjockey, outmanoeuvre, outsmart (*Inf.*), outthink, put one over on (*Inf.*), run rings round (*Inf.*), swindle, take in (*Inf.*)

outworn abandoned, antiquated, behind the times (*Inf.*), defunct, discredited, disused, exhausted, hackneyed, obsolete, outdated, outmoded, out of date, overused, rejected, stale, superannuated, threadbare, tired, worn-out

oval *adj.* egg-shaped, ellipsoidal, elliptical, ovate, oviform, ovoid

ovation acclaim, acclamation, applause, cheering, cheers, clapping, laudation, plaudits, tribute

over *adj.* **1**. accomplished, ancient history (*Inf.*), at an end, by, bygone, closed, completed, concluded, done (with), ended, finished, gone, past, settled, up (*Inf.*) ~*adj./adv.* **2**. beyond, extra, in addition, in excess, left over, remaining, superfluous, surplus, unused ~*prep.* **3**. above, on, on top of, superior to, upon **4**. above, exceeding, in excess of, more than ~*adv.*

5. above, aloft, on high, overhead **6**. **over and above** added to, as well as, besides, in addition to, let alone, not to mention, on top of, plus **7**. **over and over (again)** ad nauseam, again and again, frequently, often, repeatedly, time and again

overabundance embarrassment of riches, excess, glut, oversupply, plethora, profusion, superabundance, superfluity, surfeit, surplus, too much of a good thing

overact exaggerate, ham *or* ham up (*Inf.*), overdo, overplay

overall 1. *adj.* all-embracing, blanket, complete, comprehensive, general, global, inclusive, long-range, long-term, total, umbrella **2**. *adv.* generally speaking, in general, in (the) large, in the long term, on the whole

overawe abash, alarm, browbeat, cow, daunt, frighten, intimidate, scare, terrify

overbalance capsize, keel over, lose one's balance, lose one's footing, overset, overturn, slip, take a tumble, tip over, topple over, tumble, turn turtle, upset

overbearing arrogant, autocratic, bossy (*Inf.*), cavalier, despotic, dictatorial, dogmatic, domineering, haughty, high-handed, imperious, lordly, magisterial, officious, oppressive, overweening, peremptory, supercilious, superior, tyrannical

overblown 1. disproportionate, excessive, fulsome, immoderate, inflated, overdone, undue **2**. aureate, bombastic, euphuistic, florid, flowery, fustian, grandiloquent, magniloquent, pompous, turgid, windy

overcast clouded, clouded over, cloudy, darkened, dismal, dreary, dull, grey, hazy, leaden, lowering, murky, sombre, sunless, threatening

overcharge 1. cheat, clip (*Sl.*), diddle (*Inf.*), do (*Sl.*), fleece, rip off (*Sl.*), rook (*Sl.*), short-change, sting (*Inf.*), surcharge **2**. burden, oppress, overburden, overload, overtask, overtax, strain, surfeit **3**. *Literary* embellish, embroider, exaggerate, hyperbolize, lay it on thick (*Inf.*), overstate

overcome 1. *v.* beat, best, be victorious, come out on top (*Inf.*), conquer, crush, defeat, get the better of, lick (*Inf.*), master, overpower, overthrow, overwhelm, prevail, render incapable (helpless, powerless), rise above, subdue, subjugate, surmount, survive, triumph over, vanquish, weather, worst **2**. *adj.*

affected, at a loss for words, bowled over (*Inf.*), overwhelmed, speechless, swept off one's feet, unable to continue, visibly moved

overconfident brash, cocksure, foolhardy, hubristic, overweening, presumptuous, riding for a fall (*Inf.*), uppish (*Brit. inf.*)

overcritical captious, carping, cavilling, fault-finding, hairsplitting, hard to please, hypercritical, nit-picking (*Inf.*), overparticular, pernickety (*Inf.*)

overcrowded choked, congested, crammed full, jam-packed, like the Black Hole of Calcutta, overloaded, overpopulated, packed (out), swarming

overdo 1. be intemperate, belabour, carry too far, do to death (*Inf.*), exaggerate, gild the lily, go overboard (*Inf.*), go to extremes, lay it on thick (*Inf.*), not know when to stop, overindulge, overplay, overreach, overstate, overuse, overwork, run riot **2**. **overdo it** bite off more than one can chew, burn the candle at both ends (*Inf.*), drive oneself, fatigue, go too far, have too many irons in the fire, overburden, overload, overtax one's strength, overtire, overwork, strain *or* overstrain oneself, wear oneself out

overdone 1. beyond all bounds, exaggerated, excessive, fulsome, immoderate, inordinate, overelaborate, preposterous, too much, undue, unnecessary **2**. burnt, burnt to a cinder, charred, dried up, overcooked, spoiled

overdue behindhand, behind schedule, behind time, belated, late, long delayed, not before time (*Inf.*), owing, tardy, unpunctual

overeat binge (*Inf.*), eat like a horse (*Inf.*), gorge, gormandize, guzzle, make a pig of oneself (*Inf.*), overindulge, pack away (*Sl.*), pig away (*Sl.*), stuff, stuff oneself

overemphasize belabour, blow up out of all proportion, lay too much stress on, make a big thing of (*Inf.*), make a mountain out of a molehill (*Inf.*), make something out of nothing, make too much of, overdramatize, overstress

overexert burn the candle at both ends (*Inf.*), do too much, drive (oneself), fatigue, knock (oneself) out, overstrain, overtax, overtire, overwork, push (oneself) too hard, strain, wear out, work to death

overflow *v.* **1**. bubble (brim, fall, pour,

run, slop, well) over, discharge, pour out, run with, shower, spill, spray, surge **2.** cover, deluge, drown, flood, inundate, soak, submerge, swamp ~*n.* **3.** discharge, flash flood, flood, flooding, inundation, overabundance, spill, spilling over, surplus

overflowing abounding, bountiful, brimful, copious, plentiful, profuse, rife, superabundant, swarming, teeming, thronged

overhang *v.* beetle, bulge, cast a shadow, extend, impend, jut, loom, project, protrude, stick out, threaten

overhaul *v.* **1.** check, do up (*Inf.*), examine, inspect, recondition, re-examine, repair, restore, service, survey ~*n.* **2.** check, checkup, examination, going-over (*Inf.*), inspection, reconditioning, service ~*v.* **3.** catch up with, draw level with, get ahead of, overtake, pass

overhead 1. *adv.* above, aloft, atop, in the sky, on high, skyward, up above, upward **2.** *adj.* aerial, overhanging, roof, upper

overheads burden, oncosts, operating cost(s), running cost(s)

overheated agitated, fiery, flaming, impassioned, inflamed, overexcited, roused

overindulge be immoderate *or* intemperate, drink *or* eat too much, have a binge (*Inf.*), live it up (*Inf.*), make a pig of oneself (*Inf.*), overdo it

overindulgence excess, immoderation, intemperance, overeating, surfeit

overjoyed delighted, deliriously happy, elated, euphoric, happy as a lark, in raptures, joyful, jubilant, on cloud nine (*Inf.*), only too happy, over the moon (*Inf.*), rapturous, thrilled, tickled pink, transported

overlay 1. *v.* adorn, blanket, cover, inlay, laminate, ornament, overspread, superimpose, veneer **2.** *n.* adornment, appliqué, covering, decoration, ornamentation, veneer

overload burden, encumber, oppress, overburden, overcharge, overtax, saddle (with), strain, weigh down

overlook 1. disregard, fail to notice, forget, ignore, leave out of consideration, leave undone, miss, neglect, omit, pass, slight, slip up on **2.** blink at, condone, disregard, excuse, forgive, let bygones be bygones, let one off with, let pass, let ride, make allowances for, pardon, turn a

blind eye to, wink at **3.** afford a view of, command a view of, front on to, give upon, have a view of, look over *or* out on

overly exceedingly, excessively, immoderately, inordinately, over, too, unduly, very much

overpower beat, conquer, crush, defeat, get the upper hand over, immobilize, knock out, master, overcome, overthrow, overwhelm, quell, subdue, subjugate, vanquish

overpowering compelling, extreme, forceful, invincible, irrefutable, irresistible, nauseating, overwhelming, powerful, sickening, strong, suffocating, telling, unbearable, uncontrollable

overrate assess too highly, exaggerate, make too much of, overestimate, overpraise, overprize, oversell, overvalue, rate too highly, think *or* expect too much of, think too highly of

overreach 1. overreach oneself be hoist with one's own petard, bite off more than one can chew, defeat one's own ends, go too far, have one's schemes rebound (backfire, boomerang) on one, try to be too clever **2.** cheat, circumvent, deceive, defraud, dupe, gull (*Archaic*), outsmart (*Inf.*), outwit, swindle, trick, victimize

override annul, cancel, countermand, disregard, ignore, nullify, outweigh, overrule, quash, reverse, ride roughshod over, set aside, supersede, take no account of, trample underfoot, upset, vanquish

overriding cardinal, compelling, determining, dominant, final, major, number one, overruling, paramount, pivotal, predominant, prevailing, primary, prime, ruling, supreme, ultimate

overrule 1. alter, annul, cancel, countermand, disallow, invalidate, make null and void, outvote, override, overturn, recall, repeal, rescind, reverse, revoke, rule against, set aside, veto **2.** bend to one's will, control, direct, dominate, govern, influence, prevail over, sway

overrun 1. cut to pieces, invade, massacre, occupy, overwhelm, put to flight, rout, swamp **2.** choke, infest, inundate, overflow, overgrow, permeate, ravage, spread like wildfire, spread over, surge over, swarm over **3.** exceed, go beyond, overshoot, run over *or* on

overseer boss (*Inf.*), chief, foreman, gaffer (*Inf.*), manager, master, super

(*Inf.*), superintendent, superior, supervisor

overshadow 1. dominate, dwarf, eclipse, excel, leave *or* put in the shade, outshine, outweigh, render insignificant by comparison, rise above, steal the limelight from, surpass, take precedence over, throw into the shade, tower above **2.** adumbrate, becloud, bedim, cloud, darken, dim, obfuscate, obscure, veil **3.** blight, cast a gloom upon, mar, ruin, spoil, take the edge off, take the pleasure *or* enjoyment out of, temper

oversight 1. blunder, carelessness, delinquency, error, fault, inattention, lapse, laxity, mistake, neglect, omission, slip **2.** administration, care, charge, control, custody, direction, handling, inspection, keeping, management, superintendence, supervision, surveillance

overt apparent, manifest, observable, obvious, open, patent, plain, public, unconcealed, undisguised, visible

overtake 1. catch up with, do better than, draw level with, get past, leave behind, outdistance, outdo, outstrip, overhaul, pass **2.** befall, catch unprepared, come upon, engulf, happen, hit, overwhelm, strike, take by surprise

overthrow *v.* **1.** abolish, beat, bring down, conquer, crush, defeat, depose, dethrone, do away with, master, oust, overcome, overpower, overwhelm, subdue, subjugate, topple, unseat, vanquish **2.** bring to ruin, demolish, destroy, knock down, level, overturn, put an end to, raze, ruin, subvert, upend, upset ~*n.* **3.** defeat, deposition, destruction, dethronement, discomfiture, disestablishment, displacement, dispossession, downfall, end, fall, ousting, prostration, rout, ruin, subjugation, subversion, suppression, undoing, unseating

overtone association, connotation, flavour, hint, implication, innuendo, intimation, nuance, sense, suggestion, undercurrent

overture 1. *Often plural* advance, approach, conciliatory move, invitation, offer, opening move, proposal, proposition, signal, tender **2.** *Music* introduction, opening, prelude

overturn 1. capsize, keel over, knock over *or* down, overbalance, reverse, spill, tip over, topple, tumble, upend, upset, upturn **2.** abolish, annul, bring down, countermand, depose, destroy, invali-

date, overthrow, repeal, rescind, reverse, set aside, unseat

overused cliché'd, hackneyed, platitudinous, played out, stale, stereotyped, threadbare, tired, unoriginal, worn (out)

overweening 1. arrogant, cavalier, cocksure, cocky, conceited, egotistical, haughty, high and mighty (*Inf.*), high-handed, insolent, lordly, opinionated, pompous, presumptuous, proud, self-confident, supercilious, uppish (*Brit. inf.*), vain, vainglorious **2.** blown up out of all proportion, excessive, extravagant, immoderate

overweight *adj.* ample, bulky, chubby, chunky, corpulent, fat, fleshy, gross, heavy, hefty, huge, massive, obese, on the plump side, outsize, plump, podgy, portly, stout, tubby (*Inf.*), well-padded (*Inf.*), well-upholstered (*Inf.*)

overwhelm 1. bury, crush, deluge, engulf, flood, inundate, snow under, submerge, swamp **2.** bowl over (*Inf.*), confuse, devastate, knock (someone) for six (*Inf.*), overcome, overpower, prostrate, render speechless, stagger **3.** crush, cut to pieces, destroy, massacre, overpower, overrun, rout

overwhelming breathtaking, crushing, devastating, invincible, irresistible, overpowering, shattering, stunning, towering, uncontrollable, vast, vastly superior

overwork be a slave-driver *or* hard taskmaster to, burden, burn the midnight oil, drive into the ground, exhaust, exploit, fatigue, oppress, overstrain, overtax, overuse, prostrate, strain, sweat (*Inf.*), wear out, weary, work one's fingers to the bone

overwrought 1. agitated, beside oneself, distracted, excited, frantic, in a state (tizzy, twitter) (*Inf.*), keyed up, on edge, overexcited, overworked, stirred, strung up (*Inf.*), tense, uptight (*Inf.*), worked up (*Inf.*), wound up (*Inf.*) **2.** baroque, busy, contrived, florid, flowery, fussy, overdone, overelaborate, overembellished, overornate, rococo

owe be beholden to, be in arrears, be in debt, be obligated *or* indebted, be under an obligation to

owing *adj.* due, outstanding, overdue, owed, payable, unpaid, unsettled

owing to *prep.* as a result of, because of, on account of

own *adj.* **1.** individual, particular, personal, private **2. on one's own** alone, by oneself, by one's own efforts, independently, isolated, left to one's own devices, off one's own bat, on one's tod (*Brit. sl.*), singly, (standing) on one's own two feet, unaided, unassisted **3. hold one's own** compete, keep going, keep one's end up, keep one's head above water, maintain one's position ~*v.* **4.** be in possession of, be responsible for, enjoy, have, hold, keep, possess, retain **5. own up (to)** admit, come clean (about) (*Inf.*), confess, make a clean breast of, tell the truth (about) **6.** acknowledge, admit, allow, allow to be valid, avow, concede, confess, disclose, go along with (*Inf.*), grant, recognize

owner holder, landlord, lord, master, mistress, possessor, proprietor, proprietress, proprietrix

ownership dominion, possession, proprietary rights, proprietorship, right of possession, title

P

pace *n.* **1.** gait, measure, step, stride, tread, walk **2.** clip (*Inf.*), lick (*Inf.*), momentum, motion, movement, progress, rate, speed, tempo, time, velocity ~*v.* **3.** march, patrol, pound, stride, walk back and forth, walk up and down **4.** count, determine, mark out, measure, step

pacific 1. appeasing, conciliatory, diplomatic, irenic, pacificatory, peacemaking, placatory, propitiatory **2.** dovelike, dovish, friendly, gentle, mild, nonbelligerent, nonviolent, pacifist, peaceable, peace-loving **3.** at peace, calm, halcyon, peaceful, placid, quiet, serene, smooth, still, tranquil, unruffled

pacifist conchie (*Inf.*), conscientious objector, dove, passive resister, peace lover, peacemonger, peacenik (*Inf.*), satyagrahi

pacify 1. allay, ameliorate, appease, assuage, calm, compose, conciliate, make peace, moderate, mollify, placate, pour oil on troubled waters, propitiate, quiet, restore harmony, smooth down *or* over, smooth one's ruffled feathers, soften, soothe, still, tranquillize **2.** chasten, crush, impose peace, put down, quell, repress, silence, subdue, tame

pack *n.* **1.** back pack, bale, bundle, burden, fardel (*Archaic*), kit, kitbag, knapsack, load, package, packet, parcel, rucksack, truss **2.** assemblage, band, bunch, collection, company, crew, crowd, deck, drove, flock, gang, group, herd, lot, mob, set, troop ~*v.* **3.** batch, bundle, burden, load, package, packet, store, stow **4.** charge, compact, compress, cram, crowd, fill, jam, mob, press, ram, stuff, tamp, throng, wedge **5.** *With* off bundle out, dismiss, hustle out, send someone about his business, send away, send packing (*Inf.*)

package *n.* **1.** box, carton, container, packet, parcel **2.** amalgamation, combination, entity, unit, whole ~*v.* **3.** batch, box, pack, packet, parcel (up), wrap, wrap up

packed brimful, chock-a-block, chockfull, congested, cram-full, crammed, crowded, filled, full, hoatching (*Scot.*), jammed, jam-packed, loaded *or* full to the gunwales, overflowing, overloaded, packed like sardines, seething, swarming

packet 1. bag, carton, container, package, parcel, poke (*Dialect*), wrapper, wrapping **2.** *Sl.* a bob or two (*Brit. inf.*), bomb (*Brit. sl.*), bundle (*Sl.*), fortune, king's ransom (*Inf.*), lot(s), mint, pile (*Inf.*), pot(s) (*Inf.*), pretty penny (*Inf.*), tidy sum (*Inf.*)

pack in 1. attract, cram, draw, fill to capacity, squeeze in **2.** *Brit. inf.* cease, chuck (*Inf.*), desist, give up *or* over, jack in, leave off, stop

pack up 1. put away, store, tidy up **2.** *Inf.* call it a day (*Inf.*), finish, give up, pack in (*Brit. inf.*) **3.** break down, conk out (*Inf.*), fail, give out, stall, stop

pact agreement, alliance, arrangement, bargain, bond, compact, concord, concordat, contract, convention, covenant, deal, league, protocol, treaty, understanding

pad[1] *n.* **1.** buffer, cushion, protection, stiffening, stuffing, wad **2.** block, jotter, notepad, tablet, writing pad **3.** foot, paw, sole **4.** *Sl.* apartment, flat, hang-out (*Inf.*), home, place, quarters, room ~*v.* **5.** cushion, fill, line, pack, protect, shape, stuff **6.** *Often with* out amplify, augment, eke, elaborate, fill out, flesh out, inflate, lengthen, protract, spin out, stretch

pad[2] *v.* **1.** creep, go barefoot, pussyfoot (*Inf.*), sneak, steal **2.** hike, march, plod, traipse (*Inf.*), tramp, trek, trudge, walk

padding 1. filling, packing, stuffing, wadding **2.** hot air (*Inf.*), prolixity, verbiage, verbosity, waffle (*Inf.*), wordiness

paddle[1] **1.** *n.* oar, scull, sweep **2.** *v.* oar, propel, pull, row, scull

paddle[2] dabble, plash, slop, splash (about), stir, wade

paddy fit of temper, paddywhack (*Inf.*), passion, rage, tantrum, temper, tiff, wax (*Inf.*)

paean 1. anthem, hymn, psalm, thanksgiving **2.** encomium, eulogy, hymn of praise, ovation, panegyric, rave review (*Inf.*)

pagan 1. *n.* Gentile, heathen, idolater, infidel, polytheist, unbeliever **2.** *adj.*

Gentile, heathen, heathenish, idolatrous, infidel, irreligious, polytheistic

page[1] n. **1.** folio, leaf, sheet, side **2.** chapter, episode, epoch, era, event, incident, period, phase, point, stage, time ~v. **3.** foliate, number, paginate

page[2] **1.** n. attendant, bellboy (U.S.), footboy, pageboy, servant, squire **2.** v. announce, call, call out, preconize, seek, send for, summon

pageant display, extravaganza, parade, procession, ritual, show, spectacle, tableau

pageantry display, drama, extravagance, glamour, glitter, grandeur, magnificence, parade, pomp, show, showiness, spectacle, splash (Inf.), splendour, state, theatricality

pain n. **1.** ache, cramp, discomfort, hurt, irritation, pang, smarting, soreness, spasm, suffering, tenderness, throb, throe (Rare), trouble, twinge **2.** affliction, agony, anguish, bitterness, distress, grief, heartache, misery, suffering, torment, torture, tribulation, woe, wretchedness **3.** Inf. aggravation, annoyance, bore, bother, drag (Sl.), headache (Inf.), irritation, nuisance, pain in the neck (Inf.), pest, vexation ~v. **4.** ail, chafe, discomfort, harm, hurt, inflame, injure, smart, sting, throb **5.** afflict, aggrieve, agonize, cut to the quick, disquiet, distress, grieve, hurt, sadden, torment, torture, vex, worry, wound **6.** Inf. annoy, exasperate, gall, harass, irritate, rile, vex

pained aggrieved, anguished, distressed, hurt, injured, miffed (Inf.), offended, reproachful, stung, unhappy, upset, worried, wounded

painful 1. afflictive, disagreeable, distasteful, distressing, grievous, saddening, unpleasant **2.** aching, agonizing, excruciating, harrowing, hurting, inflamed, raw, smarting, sore, tender, throbbing **3.** arduous, difficult, hard, laborious, severe, tedious, troublesome, trying, vexatious **4.** Inf. awful, dire, dreadful, excruciating, extremely bad, terrible

painfully alarmingly, clearly, deplorably, distressingly, dreadfully, excessively, markedly, sadly, unfortunately, woefully

painkiller anaesthetic, analgesic, anodyne, drug, palliative, remedy, sedative

painless easy, effortless, fast, no trouble, pain-free, quick, simple, trouble-free

pains 1. assiduousness, bother, care, diligence, effort, industry, labour, special attention, trouble **2.** birth-pangs, childbirth, contractions, labour

painstaking assiduous, careful, conscientious, diligent, earnest, exacting, hard-working, industrious, meticulous, persevering, punctilious, scrupulous, sedulous, strenuous, thorough, thoroughgoing

paint n. **1.** colour, colouring, dye, emulsion, pigment, stain, tint **2.** Inf. cosmetics, face (Inf.), greasepaint, make-up, maquillage, war paint (Inf.) ~v. **3.** catch a likeness, delineate, depict, draw, figure, picture, portray, represent, sketch **4.** apply, coat, colour, cover, daub, decorate, slap on (Inf.) **5.** bring to life, capture, conjure up a vision, depict, describe, evoke, make one see, portray, put graphically, recount, tell vividly **6. paint the town red** Inf. celebrate, go on a binge (Inf.), go on a spree, go on the town, live it up (Inf.), make merry, make whoopee (Inf.), revel

pair 1. n. brace, combination, couple, doublet, duo, match, matched set, span, twins, two of a kind, twosome, yoke **2.** v. bracket, couple, join, marry, match, match up, mate, pair off, put together, team, twin, wed, yoke

pal boon companion, buddy (Inf.), chum (Inf.), companion, comrade, crony, friend, mate (Inf.)

palatable 1. appetizing, delectable, delicious, luscious, mouthwatering, savoury, tasty, toothsome **2.** acceptable, agreeable, attractive, enjoyable, fair, pleasant, satisfactory

palate 1. appetite, heart, stomach, taste **2.** appreciation, enjoyment, gusto, liking, relish, zest

palatial de luxe, grand, grandiose, illustrious, imposing, luxurious, magnificent, majestic, opulent, plush (Inf.), regal, spacious, splendid, stately, sumptuous

palaver n. **1.** business (Inf.), carry-on (Inf.), performance (Inf.), procedure, rigmarole, song and dance (Brit. inf.), to-do **2.** babble, blather, blether, chatter, hubbub, natter (Brit.), prattle, tonguewagging, yak (Sl.) **3.** colloquy, confab (Inf.), conference, discussion, get-together (Inf.), parley, powwow, session ~v. **4.** confab (Inf.), confer, discuss, go into a huddle (Inf.), parley, powwow, put heads together **5.** blather, blether, chatter, gabble, jabber, jaw (*Sl.*), natter (*Brit.*), prattle, yak (*Sl.*)

pale[1] *adj.* **1.** anaemic, ashen, ashy, bleached, bloodless, colourless, faded, light, pallid, pasty, sallow, wan, washed-out, white, whitish **2.** dim, faint, feeble, inadequate, poor, thin, weak ~*v.* **3.** become pale, blanch, go white, lose colour, whiten **4.** decrease, dim, diminish, dull, fade, grow dull, lessen, lose lustre

pale[2] *n.* **1.** paling, palisade, picket, post, slat, stake, upright **2.** barricade, barrier, fence, palisade, railing **3.** border, boundary, bounds, confines, district, limits, region, territory **4. beyond the pale** barbaric, forbidden, improper, inadmissible, indecent, irregular, not done, out of line, unacceptable, unseemly, unspeakable, unsuitable

palisade bulwark, defence, enclosure, fence, paling, stockade

pall[1] *n.* **1.** cloud, mantle, shadow, shroud, veil **2.** check, damp, damper, dismay, gloom, melancholy

pall[2] *v.* become dull *or* tedious, bore, cloy, glut, jade, satiate, sicken, surfeit, tire, weary

palliate **1.** abate, allay, alleviate, assuage, diminish, ease, mitigate, moderate, mollify, relieve, soften, soothe, temper **2.** cloak, conceal, cover, excuse, extenuate, gloss over, hide, lessen, minimize, paper over the cracks (*Inf.*), varnish, whitewash (*Inf.*)

palliative **1.** *adj.* alleviative, anodyne, assuasive, calmative, calming, demulcent, lenitive, mitigative, mitigatory, mollifying, soothing **2.** *n.* analgesic, anodyne, calmative, demulcent, drug, lenitive, painkiller, sedative, tranquillizer

pallid **1.** anaemic, ashen, ashy, cadaverous, colourless, pale, pasty, sallow, wan, waxen, wheyfaced, whitish **2.** anaemic, bloodless, colourless, insipid, lifeless, spiritless, sterile, tame, tired, uninspired, vapid

pallor ashen hue, bloodlessness, lack of colour, paleness, pallidness, wanness, whiteness

pally affectionate, chummy (*Inf.*), close, familiar, friendly, intimate, thick as thieves (*Inf.*)

palm[1] **1.** hand, mitt (*Sl.*), paw (*Inf.*) **2. in the palm of one's hand** at one's mercy, in one's clutches (control, power) **3. grease someone's palm** *Sl.* bribe, buy, corrupt, fix (*Inf.*), give a backhander

(*Sl.*), induce, influence, pay off (*Inf.*), square, suborn

palm[2] *Fig.* bays, crown, fame, glory, honour, laurels, merit, prize, success, triumph, trophy, victory

palm off 1. *With* **on** *or* **with** fob off, foist off, pass off **2.** *With* **on** foist on, force upon, impose upon, take advantage of, thrust upon, unload upon

palmy flourishing, fortunate, glorious, golden, halcyon, happy, joyous, luxurious, prosperous, thriving, triumphant

palpable **1.** apparent, blatant, clear, conspicuous, evident, manifest, obvious, open, patent, plain, unmistakable, visible **2.** concrete, material, real, solid, substantial, tangible, touchable

palpitate beat, flutter, pitapat, pitter-patter, pound, pulsate, pulse, quiver, shiver, throb, tremble, vibrate

palsied arthritic, atonic (*Pathol.*), crippled, debilitated, disabled, helpless, paralysed, paralytic, rheumatic, sclerotic, shaking, shaky, spastic, trembling

palter **1.** be evasive, deceive, double-talk, equivocate, fudge, hedge, mislead, prevaricate, shuffle, tergiversate, trifle **2.** bargain, barter, chaffer, dicker (*Chiefly U.S.*), haggle, higgle

paltry base, beggarly, contemptible, derisory, despicable, inconsiderable, insignificant, low, meagre, mean, Mickey Mouse (*Sl.*), minor, miserable, petty, picayune (*U.S.*), piddling (*Inf.*), pitiful, poor, puny, slight, small, sorry, trifling, trivial, twopenny-halfpenny (*Brit. inf.*), unimportant, worthless, wretched

pamper baby, cater to one's every whim, coddle, cosset, fondle, gratify, humour, indulge, mollycoddle, pet, spoil

pamphlet booklet, brochure, circular, folder, leaflet, tract

pan[1] *n.* **1.** container, pot, saucepan, vessel ~*v.* **2.** look for, search for, separate, sift out, wash **3.** *Inf.* censure, criticize, flay, hammer (*Brit.*), knock (*Inf.*), roast (*Inf.*), rubbish (*Inf.*), slam (*Sl.*), slate (*Inf.*), throw brickbats at (*Inf.*)

pan[2] *v.* follow, move, scan, sweep, swing, track, traverse

panacea catholicon, cure-all, elixir, nostrum, sovereign remedy, universal cure

panache a flourish, *brio*, dash, élan, flair, flamboyance, spirit, style, swagger, verve

pandemonium babel, bedlam, chaos,

clamour, commotion, confusion, din, hubbub, hue and cry, hullabaloo, racket, ruckus (*Inf.*), ruction (*Inf.*), rumpus, tumult, turmoil, uproar

pander 1. *v. With* **to** cater to, gratify, indulge, play up to (*Inf.*), please, satisfy **2.** *n.* go-between, mack (*Sl.*), pimp, ponce (*Sl.*), procurer, white-slaver, whoremaster (*Archaic*)

panegyric accolade, commendation, encomium, eulogy, homage, paean, praise, tribute

panegyrical commendatory, complimentary, encomiastic, eulogistic, favourable, flattering, glowing, laudatory

pang ache, agony, anguish, discomfort, distress, gripe, pain, prick, spasm, stab, sting, stitch, throe (*Rare*), twinge, wrench

panic 1. *n.* agitation, alarm, consternation, dismay, fear, fright, horror, hysteria, scare, terror **2.** *v.* become hysterical, be terror-stricken, go to pieces (*Inf.*), lose one's bottle (*Sl.*), lose one's nerve, overreact **3.** alarm, put the wind up (someone) (*Inf.*), scare, startle, terrify, unnerve

panicky afraid, agitated, distressed, fearful, frantic, frenzied, frightened, hysterical, in a flap (*Inf.*), in a tizzy (*Inf.*), jittery (*Inf.*), nervous, windy (*Sl.*), worked up, worried

panic-stricken *or* **panic-struck** aghast, agitated, alarmed, appalled, fearful, frenzied, frightened, frightened out of one's wits, frightened to death, horrified, horror-stricken, hysterical, in a cold sweat (*Inf.*), panicky, petrified, scared, scared stiff, startled, terrified, terror-stricken, unnerved

panoply array, attire, dress, garb, getup (*Inf.*), insignia, raiment (*Archaic*), regalia, show, trappings, turnout

panorama 1. bird's-eye view, prospect, scenery, scenic view, view, vista **2.** overall picture, overview, perspective, survey

panoramic all-embracing, bird's-eye, comprehensive, extensive, far-reaching, general, inclusive, overall, scenic, sweeping, wide

pan out come out, come to pass (*Archaic*), culminate, eventuate, happen, result, turn out, work out

pant *v.* **1.** blow, breathe, gasp, heave, huff, palpitate, puff, throb, wheeze **2.** *Fig.* ache, covet, crave, desire, hanker after, hunger, long, pine, set one's heart on, sigh, thirst, want, yearn ~*n.* **3.** gasp, huff, puff, wheeze

panting *adj.* **1.** breathless, gasping, out of breath, out of puff, puffed, puffed out, puffing, short of breath, winded **2.** agog, all agog, anxious, champing at the bit (*Inf.*), eager, impatient, raring to go

pants 1. *Brit.* boxer shorts, briefs, drawers, knickers, panties, underpants, Y-fronts **2.** *U.S.* slacks, trousers

pap 1. baby food, mash, mush, pulp **2.** drivel, rubbish, trash, trivia

paper *n.* **1.** *Often plural* certificate, deed, documents, instrument, record **2.** *Plural* archive, diaries, documents, dossier, file, letters, records **3.** daily, gazette, journal, news, newspaper, organ, rag (*Inf.*) **4.** analysis, article, assignment, composition, critique, dissertation, essay, examination, monograph, report, script, study, thesis, treatise **5. on paper** ideally, in the abstract, in theory, theoretically ~*adj.* **6.** cardboard, disposable, flimsy, insubstantial, paper-thin, papery, thin ~*v.* **7.** cover with paper, hang, line, paste up, wallpaper

papery flimsy, fragile, frail, insubstantial, light, lightweight, paperlike, paper-thin, thin

par *n.* **1.** average, level, mean, median, norm, standard, usual **2.** balance, equal footing, equality, equilibrium, equivalence, parity **3. above par** excellent, exceptional, first-rate (*Inf.*), outstanding, superior **4. below par a.** below average, inferior, lacking, not up to scratch (*Inf.*), poor, second-rate, substandard, wanting **b.** not oneself, off colour (*Chiefly Brit.*), off form, poorly (*Inf.*), sick, under the weather (*Inf.*), unfit, unhealthy **5. par for the course** average, expected, ordinary, predictable, standard, typical, usual **6. on a par** equal, much the same, the same, well-matched **7. up to par** acceptable, adequate, good enough, passable, satisfactory, up to scratch (*Inf.*), up to the mark

parable allegory, exemplum, fable, lesson, moral tale, story

parabolic allegorical, figurative, metaphoric, symbolic

parade *n.* **1.** array, cavalcade, ceremony, column, march, pageant, procession, review, spectacle, train **2.** array, display, exhibition, flaunting, ostentation, pomp, show, spectacle, vaunting ~*v.* **3.** defile, march, process **4**. air, brandish, display, exhibit, flaunt, make a show of, show, show off (*Inf.*), strut, swagger, vaunt

paradigm archetype, example, exemplar, ideal, model, original, pattern, prototype

paradise 1. City of God, divine abode, Elysian fields, garden of delights (*Islam*), heaven, heavenly kingdom, Olympus (*Poetic*), Promised Land, Zion **2**. Eden, Garden of Eden **3**. bliss, delight, felicity, heaven, seventh heaven, utopia

paradisiacal blessed, blissful, celestial, divine, Elysian, glorious, golden, heavenly, out of this world (*Inf.*), utopian

paradox absurdity, ambiguity, anomaly, contradiction, enigma, inconsistency, mystery, oddity, puzzle

paradoxical absurd, ambiguous, baffling, confounding, contradictory, enigmatic, equivocal, illogical, impossible, improbable, inconsistent, puzzling, riddling

paragon apotheosis, archetype, criterion, cynosure, epitome, exemplar, ideal, jewel, masterpiece, model, nonesuch (*Archaic*), nonpareil, paradigm, pattern, prototype, quintessence, standard

paragraph clause, item, notice, part, passage, portion, section, subdivision

parallel adj. **1**. aligned, alongside, coextensive, equidistant, side by side **2**. akin, analogous, complementary, correspondent, corresponding, like, matching, resembling, similar, uniform ~n. **3**. analogue, complement, corollary, counterpart, duplicate, equal, equivalent, likeness, match, twin **4**. analogy, comparison, correlation, correspondence, likeness, parallelism, resemblance, similarity ~v. **5**. agree, be alike, chime with, compare, complement, conform, correlate, correspond, equal, keep pace (with), match

paralyse 1. cripple, debilitate, disable, incapacitate, lame **2**. anaesthetize, arrest, benumb, freeze, halt, immobilize, numb, petrify, stop dead, stun, stupefy, transfix

paralysis 1. immobility, palsy, paresis (*Pathol.*) **2**. arrest, breakdown, halt, shutdown, stagnation, standstill, stoppage

paralytic adj. **1**. crippled, disabled, immobile, immobilized, incapacitated,

lame, numb, palsied, paralysed **2**. *Inf.* canned (*Sl.*), drunk, inebriated, intoxicated, legless (*Inf.*), pie-eyed (*Sl.*), plastered (*Sl.*), sloshed (*Sl.*), smashed (*Sl.*), stewed (*Sl.*), stoned (*Sl.*)

parameter constant, criterion, framework, guideline, limit, limitation, restriction, specification

paramount capital, cardinal, chief, dominant, eminent, first, foremost, main, outstanding, predominant, preeminent, primary, prime, principal, superior, supreme

paramour beau, concubine, courtesan, fancy man (*Sl.*), fancy woman (*Sl.*), inamorata, inamorato, kept woman, lover, mistress

paraphernalia accoutrements, apparatus, appurtenances, baggage, belongings, clobber (*Brit. sl.*), effects, equipage, equipment, gear, impedimenta, material, stuff, tackle, things, trappings

paraphrase 1. n. interpretation, rehash, rendering, rendition, rephrasing, restatement, rewording, translation, version **2**. v. express in other words or one's own words, interpret, rehash, render, rephrase, restate, reword

parasite bloodsucker (*Inf.*), cadger, drone (*Brit.*), hanger-on, leech, scrounger (*Inf.*), sponge (*Inf.*), sponger (*Inf.*)

parasitic, parasitical bloodsucking (*Inf.*), cadging, leechlike, scrounging (*Inf.*), sponging (*Inf.*)

parcel n. **1**. bundle, carton, pack, package, packet **2**. band, batch, bunch, collection, company, crew, crowd, gang, group, lot, pack **3**. piece of land, plot, property, tract ~v. **4**. *Often with* **up** do up, pack, package, tie up, wrap **5**. *Often with* **out** allocate, allot, apportion, carve up, deal out, dispense, distribute, divide, dole out, mete out, portion, share out, split up

parch blister, burn, dehydrate, desiccate, dry up, evaporate, make thirsty, scorch, sear, shrivel, wither

parched arid, dehydrated, dried out or up, drouthy (*Scot.*), dry, scorched, shrivelled, thirsty, waterless, withered

parching adj. baking, blistering, burning, dry, drying, hot, roasting (*Inf.*), scorching, searing, sweltering, withering

pardon 1. v. absolve, acquit, amnesty, condone, exculpate, excuse, exonerate, forgive, free, let off (*Inf.*), liberate, overlook, release, remit, reprieve **2**. n. absolution, acquittal, allowance, amnesty, condonation, discharge, excuse, exoneration, forgiveness, grace, indulgence, mercy, release, remission, reprieve

pardonable allowable, condonable, excusable, forgivable, minor, not serious, permissible, understandable, venial

pare 1. clip, cut, peel, shave, skin, trim **2.** crop, cut, cut back, decrease, dock, lop, prune, reduce, retrench, shear

parent 1. begetter, father, guardian, mother, procreator, progenitor, sire **2.** architect, author, cause, creator, forerunner, origin, originator, prototype, root, source, wellspring

parentage ancestry, birth, derivation, descent, extraction, family, line, lineage, origin, paternity, pedigree, race, stirps, stock

parenthetic, parenthetical bracketed, by-the-way, explanatory, extraneous, extrinsic, incidental, in parenthesis, inserted, interposed, qualifying

parenthetically by the bye, by the way, by way of explanation, incidentally, in parenthesis, in passing

pariah exile, leper, outcast, outlaw, undesirable, unperson, untouchable

paring n. clipping, flake, fragment, peel, peeling, rind, shaving, shred, skin, slice, sliver, snippet

parish church, churchgoers, community, congregation, flock, fold, parishioners

parity 1. consistency, equality, equal terms, equivalence, par, parallelism, quits (*Inf.*), uniformity, unity **2.** affinity, agreement, analogy, conformity, congruity, correspondence, likeness, resemblance, sameness, similarity, similitude

park 1. n. estate, garden, grounds, parkland, pleasure garden, recreation ground, woodland **2.** v. leave, manoeuvre, position, station

parlance idiom, jargon, language, lingo (*Inf.*), manner of speaking, phraseology, -speak, speech, talk, tongue

parley 1. n. colloquy, confab (*Inf.*), conference, council, dialogue, discussion, meeting, palaver, powwow, talk(s) **2.** v. confabulate, confer, deliberate, discuss, negotiate, palaver, powwow, speak, talk

parliament 1. assembly, congress, convocation, council, diet, legislature, senate, talking shop (*Inf.*) **2. Parliament** Houses of Parliament, Mother of Parliaments, the House, the House of Com-

mons and the House of Lords, Westminster

parliamentary congressional, deliberative, governmental, lawgiving, lawmaking, legislative

parlour best room, drawing room, front room, lounge, reception room, sitting room

parlous chancy (*Inf.*), dangerous, desperate, difficult, dire, hairy (*Sl.*), hazardous, perilous, risky

parochial insular, inward-looking, limited, narrow, narrow-minded, parish-pump, petty, provincial, restricted, small-minded

parodist burlesquer, caricaturist, humorist, impressionist, ironist, lampooner, mimic, mocker, pasquinader, satirist

parody n. **1.** burlesque, caricature, imitation, lampoon, satire, send-up (*Brit. inf.*), skit, spoof (*Inf.*), takeoff (*Inf.*) **2.** apology, caricature, farce, mockery, travesty ~v. **3.** burlesque, caricature, do a takeoff of (*Inf.*), lampoon, mimic, poke fun at, satirize, send up (*Brit. inf.*), spoof (*Inf.*), take off (*Inf.*), travesty

paroxysm attack, convulsion, eruption, fit, flare-up (*Inf.*), outburst, seizure, spasm

parrot n. **1.** *Fig.* copycat (*Inf.*), imitator, (little) echo, mimic **2. parrot-fashion** *Inf.* by rote, mechanically, mindlessly ~v. **3.** copy, echo, imitate, mimic, reiterate, repeat

parry 1. block, deflect, fend off, hold at bay, rebuff, repel, repulse, stave off, ward off **2.** avoid, circumvent, dodge, duck (*Inf.*), evade, fence, fight shy of, shun, sidestep

parsimonious cheeseparing, close, close-fisted, frugal, grasping, mean, mingy (*Brit. inf.*), miserable, miserly, near (*Inf.*), niggardly, penny-pinching (*Inf.*), penurious, saving, scrimpy, skinflinty, sparing, stingy, stinting, tightfisted

parsimony frugality, meanness, minginess (*Brit. inf.*), miserliness, nearness (*Inf.*), niggardliness, penny-pinching (*Inf.*), stinginess, tightness

parson churchman, clergyman, cleric, divine, ecclesiastic, incumbent, man of God, man of the cloth, minister, pastor, preacher, priest, rector, reverend (*Inf.*), vicar

part n. **1.** bit, fraction, fragment, lot, particle, piece, portion, scrap, section, sector, segment, share, slice **2**. branch, component, constituent, department, division, element, ingredient, limb, member, module, organ, piece, unit **3**. behalf, cause, concern, faction, interest, party, side **4**. bit, business, capacity, charge, duty, function, involvement, office, place, responsibility, role, say, share, task, work **5**. *Theat.* character, lines, role **6**. *Often plural* airt (*Scot.*), area, district, neck of the woods (*Inf.*), neighbourhood, quarter, region, territory, vicinity **7. for the most part** chiefly, generally, in the main, largely, mainly, mostly, on the whole, principally **8. in good part** cheerfully, cordially, good-naturedly, well, without offence **9. in part** a little, in some measure, partially, partly, slightly, somewhat, to a certain extent, to some degree **10. on the part of** for the sake of, in support of, in the name of, on behalf of **11. take part in** associate oneself with, be instrumental in, be involved in, have a hand in, join in, partake in, participate in, play a part in, put one's twopenceworth in, take a hand in ~*v*. **12**. break, cleave, come apart, detach, disconnect, disjoin, dismantle, disunite, divide, rend, separate, sever, split, tear **13**. break up, depart, go, go away, go (their) separate ways, leave, part company, quit, say goodbye, separate, split up, take one's leave, withdraw **14. part with** abandon, discard, forgo, give up, let go of, relinquish, renounce, sacrifice, surrender, yield

partake 1. *With in* engage, enter into, participate, share, take part **2**. *With of* consume, eat, receive, share, take **3**. *With of* evince, evoke, have the quality of, show, suggest

partial 1. fragmentary, imperfect, incomplete, limited, uncompleted, unfinished **2**. biased, discriminatory, influenced, interested, one-sided, partisan, predisposed, prejudiced, tendentious, unfair, unjust **3. be partial to** be fond of, be keen on, be taken with, care for, have a liking (soft spot, weakness) for

partiality 1. bias, favouritism, partisanship, predisposition, preference, prejudice **2**. affinity, fondness, inclination, liking, love, penchant, predilection, predisposition, preference, proclivity, taste, weakness

partially fractionally, halfway, incompletely, in part, moderately, not wholly,

partly, piecemeal, somewhat, to a certain extent *or* degree

participant associate, contributor, member, partaker, participator, party, shareholder

participate be a participant, be a party to, engage in, enter into, get in on the act, have a hand in, join in, partake, perform, share, take part

participation assistance, contribution, involvement, joining in, partaking, partnership, sharing in, taking part

particle atom, bit, crumb, grain, iota, jot, mite, molecule, mote, piece, scrap, shred, speck, tittle, whit

particular *adj.* **1**. distinct, exact, express, peculiar, precise, special, specific **2**. especial, exceptional, marked, notable, noteworthy, remarkable, singular, uncommon, unusual **3**. blow-by-blow, circumstantial, detailed, itemized, minute, painstaking, precise, selective, thorough **4**. choosy (*Inf.*), critical, dainty, demanding, discriminating, exacting, fastidious, finicky, fussy, meticulous, nice (*Rare*), overnice, pernickety (*Inf.*), picky (*Inf.*) ~*n*. **5**. *Usually plural* circumstance, detail, fact, feature, item, specification **6. in particular** distinctly, especially, exactly, expressly, particularly, specifically

particularity 1. *Often plural* circumstance, detail, fact, instance, item, point **2**. carefulness, choosiness (*Inf.*), fastidiousness, fussiness, meticulousness **3**. accuracy, detail, precision, thoroughness **4**. characteristic, distinctiveness, feature, idiosyncrasy, individuality, peculiarity, property, singularity, trait

particularize detail, enumerate, itemize, specify, spell out, stipulate

particularly 1. decidedly, especially, exceptionally, markedly, notably, outstandingly, peculiarly, singularly, surprisingly, uncommonly, unusually **2**. distinctly, especially, explicitly, expressly, in particular, specifically

parting *n*. **1**. adieu, departure, farewell, going, goodbye, leave-taking, valediction **2**. breaking, detachment, divergence, division, partition, rift, rupture, separation, split ~*adj.* **3**. departing, farewell, final, last, valedictory

partisan *n*. **1**. adherent, backer, champion, devotee, disciple, follower, stalwart, supporter, upholder, votary ~*adj.* **2**. biased, factional, interested, one-sided, partial, prejudiced, sectarian, tendentious ~n. **3.** guerrilla, irregular, resistance fighter, underground fighter ~adj. **4.** guerrilla, irregular, resistance, underground

partition n. **1.** dividing, division, segregation, separation, severance, splitting **2.** barrier, divider, room divider, screen, wall **3.** allotment, apportionment, distribution, portion, rationing out, share ~v. **4.** apportion, cut up, divide, parcel out, portion, section, segment, separate, share, split up, subdivide **5.** divide, fence off, screen, separate, wall off

partly halfway, incompletely, in part, in some measure, not fully, partially, relatively, slightly, somewhat, to a certain degree or extent, up to a certain point

partner 1. accomplice, ally, associate, bedfellow, collaborator, colleague, companion, comrade, confederate, copartner, helper, mate, participant, teammate **2.** bedfellow, consort, helpmate, husband, mate, spouse, wife

partnership 1. companionship, connection, cooperation, copartnership, fellowship, interest, participation, sharing **2.** alliance, association, combine, company, conglomerate, cooperative, corporation, firm, house, society, union

parts 1. ability, accomplishments, attributes, calibre, capabilities, endowments, faculties, genius, gifts, intellect, intelligence, talents **2.** bits and pieces, components, spare parts, spares

party 1. at-home, bash (*Inf.*), celebration, do (*Inf.*), festivity, function, gathering, get-together (*Inf.*), knees-up (*Brit. inf.*), rave-up (*Brit. sl.*), reception, shindig (*Sl.*), social, social gathering, soirée **2.** band, body, bunch (*Inf.*), company, crew, detachment (*Military*), gang, gathering, group, squad, team, unit **3.** alliance, association, cabal, clique, coalition, combination, confederacy, coterie, faction, grouping, league, set, side **4.** individual, person, somebody, someone **5.** *Law* contractor (*Law*), defendant, litigant, participant, plaintiff

parvenu 1. n. arriviste, *nouveau riche*, social climber, upstart **2.** adj. *nouveau riche*, upstart

pass¹ v. **1.** depart, elapse, flow, go, go by or past, lapse, leave, move, move onwards, proceed, roll, run **2.** beat, exceed, excel, go beyond, outdistance, outdo,

outstrip, surmount, surpass, transcend **3.** answer, come up to scratch (*Inf.*), do, get through, graduate, pass muster, qualify, succeed, suffice, suit **4.** beguile, devote, employ, experience, fill, occupy, spend, suffer, undergo, while away **5.** befall, come up, develop, fall out, happen, occur, take place **6.** convey, deliver, exchange, give, hand, kick, let have, reach, send, throw, transfer, transmit **7.** accept, adopt, approve, authorize, decree, enact, establish, legislate, ordain, ratify, sanction, validate **8.** declare, deliver, express, pronounce, utter **9.** disregard, ignore, miss, neglect, not heed, omit, overlook, skip (*Inf.*) **10.** defecate, discharge, eliminate, empty, evacuate, excrete, expel, void **11.** blow over, cease, die, disappear, dissolve, dwindle, ebb, end, evaporate, expire, fade, go, melt away, terminate, vanish, wane **12.** *With* **for** or **as** be accepted as, be mistaken for, be regarded as, be taken for, impersonate, serve as

pass² n. **1.** canyon, col, defile, gap, gorge, ravine **2.** authorization, identification, licence, passport, permission, permit, safe-conduct, ticket, warrant **3.** *Inf.* advances, approach, overture, play (*Inf.*), proposition, suggestion **4.** condition, juncture, pinch, plight, predicament, situation, stage, state, state of affairs, straits **5.** feint, jab, lunge, push, swing, thrust

passable 1. acceptable, adequate, admissible, allowable, all right, average, fair, fair enough, mediocre, middling, moderate, not too bad, ordinary, presentable, so-so (*Inf.*), tolerable, unexceptional **2.** clear, crossable, navigable, open, traversable, unobstructed

passably after a fashion, fairly, moderately, pretty much, rather, relatively, somewhat, tolerably, well enough

passage 1. avenue, channel, course, lane, opening, path, road, route, thoroughfare, way **2.** corridor, doorway, entrance, entrance hall, exit, hall, hallway, lobby, passageway, vestibule **3.** clause, excerpt, extract, paragraph, piece, quotation, reading, section, sentence, text, verse **4.** crossing, journey, tour, trek, trip, voyage **5.** advance, change, conversion, flow, motion, movement, passing, progress, progression, transit, transition **6.** allowance, authorization, freedom, permission, right, safe-conduct, visa, warrant **7.** acceptance, enactment, establishment, legalization, legislation, passing, ratification

passageway aisle, alley, corridor, cut, entrance, exit, hall, hallway, lane, lobby, passage, wýnd (*Scot.*)

pass away croak (*Sl.*), decease, depart (this life), die, expire, pass on, pass over, peg out (*Inf.*), shuffle off this mortal coil, snuff it (*Inf.*)

pass by 1. go past, leave, move past, pass **2.** disregard, miss, neglect, not choose, overlook, pass over

passé antiquated, dated, *démodé*, obsolete, old-fashioned, old hat, outdated, outmoded, out-of-date, outworn, unfashionable

passenger fare, hitchhiker, pillion rider, rider, traveller

passer-by bystander, onlooker, witness

passing adj. **1.** brief, ephemeral, fleeting, momentary, short, short-lived, temporary, transient, transitory **2.** casual, cursory, glancing, hasty, quick, shallow, short, slight, superficial **3. in passing** accidentally, by the bye, by the way, en passant, incidentally, on the way ~n. **4.** death, decease, demise, end, finish, loss, termination

passion 1. animation, ardour, eagerness, emotion, excitement, feeling, fervour, fire, heat, intensity, joy, rapture, spirit, transport, warmth, zeal, zest **2.** adoration, affection, ardour, attachment, concupiscence, desire, fondness, infatuation, itch, keenness, love, lust **3.** bug (*Inf.*), craving, craze, enthusiasm, fancy, fascination, idol, infatuation, mania, obsession **4.** anger, fit, flare-up (*Inf.*), frenzy, fury, indignation, ire, outburst, paroxysm, rage, resentment, storm, vehemence, wrath

passionate 1. amorous, ardent, aroused, desirous, erotic, hot, loving, lustful, sensual, sexy (*Inf.*), wanton **2.** animated, ardent, eager, emotional, enthusiastic, excited, fervent, fervid, fierce, frenzied, heartfelt, impassioned, impetuous, impulsive, intense, strong, vehement, warm, wild, zealous **3.** choleric, excitable, fiery, hot-headed, hot-tempered, irascible, irritable, peppery, quick-tempered, stormy, tempestuous, violent

passionless 1. apathetic, cold, cold-blooded, cold-hearted, emotionless, frigid, icy, indifferent, uncaring, unfeeling, unloving, unresponsive **2.** calm, de-

tached, dispassionate, impartial, impassive, neutral, restrained, unemotional, uninvolved

passive acquiescent, compliant, docile, enduring, inactive, inert, lifeless, long-suffering, nonviolent, patient, quiescent, receptive, resigned, submissive, unassertive, uninvolved, unresisting

pass off 1. counterfeit, fake, feign, make a pretence of, palm off **2.** come to an end, die away, disappear, fade out, vanish **3.** emit, evaporate, give off, send forth, vaporize **4.** be completed, go off, happen, occur, take place, turn out **5.** dismiss, disregard, ignore, pass by, wink at

pass out 1. *Inf.* become unconscious, black out (*Inf.*), drop, faint, flake out (*Inf.*), keel over (*Inf.*), lose consciousness, swoon (*Literary*) **2.** deal out, distribute, dole out, hand out

pass over disregard, forget, ignore, not dwell on, omit, overlook, pass by, take no notice of

pass up decline, forgo, give (something) a miss (*Inf.*), ignore, let go, let slip, miss, neglect, refuse, reject

password countersign, key word, open sesame, signal, watchword

past adj. **1.** accomplished, completed, done, elapsed, ended, extinct, finished, forgotten, gone, over, over and done with, spent **2.** ancient, bygone, early, erstwhile, foregoing, former, late, long-ago, olden, preceding, previous, prior, quondam, recent ~n. **3. the past** antiquity, days gone by, days of yore, former times, good old days, history, long ago, olden days, old times, times past, yesteryear (*Literary*) **4.** background, experience, history, life, past life ~adv. **5.** across, beyond, by, on, over ~prep. **6.** after, beyond, farther than, later than, outside, over, subsequent to

paste 1. *n.* adhesive, cement, glue, gum, mucilage **2.** *v.* cement, fasten, fix, glue, gum, stick

pastel adj. delicate, light, muted, pale, soft, soft-hued

pastiche blend, farrago, gallimaufry, hotchpotch, medley, *mélange*, miscellany, mixture, motley

pastille cough drop, jujube, lozenge, tablet, troche (*Medical*)

pastime activity, amusement, distraction, diversion, entertainment, game, hobby, leisure, play, recreation, relaxation, sport

past master ace (*Inf.*), artist, dab hand (*Brit. inf.*), expert, old hand, virtuoso, wizard

pastor churchman, clergyman, divine, ecclesiastic, minister, parson, priest, rector, vicar

pastoral *adj.* **1.** Arcadian, bucolic, country, georgic (*Literary*), idyllic, rural, rustic, simple **2.** clerical, ecclesiastical, ministerial, priestly

pasture grass, grassland, grazing, grazing land, lea (*Poetic*), meadow, pasturage, shieling (*Scot.*)

pasty *adj.* **1.** doughy, glutinous, mucilaginous, starchy, sticky **2.** anaemic, pale, pallid, sallow, sickly, unhealthy, wan, wheyfaced

pat[1] *v.* **1.** caress, dab, fondle, pet, slap, stroke, tap, touch ~*n.* **2.** clap, dab, light blow, slap, stroke, tap **3.** cake, dab, lump, portion, small piece

pat[2] *adv.* **1.** exactly, faultlessly, flawlessly, off pat, perfectly, precisely **2.** aptly, bang, dead on, fittingly, just right, opportunely, plumb (*Inf.*), relevantly, seasonably ~*adj.* **3.** apposite, apropos, apt, felicitous, fitting, happy, neat, pertinent, relevant, spot-on (*Brit. inf.*), suitable, to the point **4.** automatic, easy, facile, glib, ready, simplistic, slick, smooth

patch *n.* **1.** piece of material, reinforcement **2.** bit, scrap, shred, small piece, spot, stretch **3.** area, ground, land, plot, tract ~*v.* **4.** cover, fix, mend, reinforce, repair, sew up **5.** *With* **up** bury the hatchet, conciliate, make friends, placate, restore, settle, settle differences, smooth

patchwork confusion, hash, hotchpotch, jumble, medley, mishmash, mixture, pastiche

patchy bitty, erratic, fitful, irregular, random, sketchy, spotty, uneven, variable, varying

patent 1. *adj.* apparent, blatant, clear, conspicuous, downright, evident, flagrant, glaring, indisputable, manifest, obvious, open, palpable, transparent, unconcealed, unequivocal, unmistakable **2.** *n.* copyright, invention, licence

paternal 1. benevolent, concerned, fatherlike, fatherly, protective, solicitous, vigilant **2.** patrilineal, patrimonial

paternity 1. fatherhood, fathership **2.** descent, extraction, family, lineage, parentage **3.** authorship, derivation, origin, source

path 1. footpath, footway, pathway, towpath, track, trail, walkway (*Chiefly U.S.*) **2.** avenue, course, direction, passage, procedure, road, route, track, walk, way

pathetic 1. affecting, distressing, heartbreaking, heart-rending, melting, moving, pitiable, plaintive, poignant, sad, tender, touching **2.** deplorable, feeble, inadequate, lamentable, meagre, miserable, paltry, petty, pitiful, poor, puny, sorry, wet (*Brit. inf.*), woeful **3.** *Sl.* crummy (*Sl.*), rubbishy, trashy, uninteresting, useless, worthless

pathfinder discoverer, explorer, guide, pioneer, scout, trailblazer

pathless impassable, impenetrable, trackless, uncharted, unexplored, untrodden, waste, wild

pathos pitiableness, pitifulness, plaintiveness, poignancy, sadness

patience 1. calmness, composure, cool (*Sl.*), equanimity, even temper, forbearance, imperturbability, restraint, serenity, sufferance, tolerance, toleration **2.** constancy, diligence, endurance, fortitude, long-suffering, perseverance, persistence, resignation, stoicism, submission

patient *adj.* **1.** calm, composed, enduring, long-suffering, persevering, persistent, philosophical, quiet, resigned, self-possessed, serene, stoical, submissive, uncomplaining, untiring **2.** accommodating, even-tempered, forbearing, forgiving, indulgent, lenient, mild, tolerant, understanding ~*n.* **3.** case, invalid, sick person, sufferer

patois 1. dialect **2.** argot, cant, jargon, lingo (*Inf.*), patter, slang, vernacular

patriarch 1. father, paterfamilias, sire **2.** elder, grandfather, greybeard, old man

patrician 1. *n.* aristocrat, noble, nobleman, peer **2.** *adj.* aristocratic, blue-blooded, gentle (*Archaic*), highborn, high-class, lordly, noble

patrimony bequest, birthright, heritage, inheritance, legacy, portion, share

patriot chauvinist, flag-waver (*Inf.*), jingo, lover of one's country, loyalist, nationalist

patriotic chauvinistic, flag-waving (*Inf.*), jingoistic, loyal, nationalistic

patriotism flag-waving (*Inf.*), jingoism, love of one's country, loyalty, nationalism

patrol *n.* **1.** guarding, policing, protecting, rounds, safeguarding, vigilance, watching **2.** garrison, guard, patrolman, sentinel, watch, watchman ~*v.* **3.** cruise, guard, inspect, keep guard, keep watch, make the rounds, police, pound, range, safeguard, walk the beat

patron 1. advocate, angel (*Inf.*), backer, benefactor, champion, defender, friend, guardian, helper, philanthropist, protector, sponsor, supporter **2.** buyer, client, customer, frequenter, habitué, shopper

patronage 1. aid, assistance, backing, benefaction, championship, encouragement, help, promotion, sponsorship, support **2.** business, clientele, commerce, custom, trade, trading, traffic **3.** condescension, deigning, disdain, patronizing, stooping

patronize 1. be lofty with, look down on, talk down to, treat as inferior, treat condescendingly, treat like a child **2.** assist, back, befriend, foster, fund, help, maintain, promote, sponsor, subscribe to, support **3.** be a customer *or* client of, buy from, deal with, do business with, frequent, shop at, trade with

patronizing condescending, contemptuous, disdainful, gracious, haughty, lofty, snobbish, stooping, supercilious, superior, toffee-nosed (*Sl.*)

patter[1] *v.* **1.** scurry, scuttle, skip, tiptoe, trip, walk lightly **2.** beat, pat, pelt, pitapat, pitter-patter, rat-a-tat, spatter, tap ~*n.* **3.** pattering, pitapat, pitter-patter, tapping

patter[2] *n.* **1.** line, monologue, pitch, spiel (*Inf.*) **2.** chatter, gabble, jabber, nattering, prattle, yak (*Sl.*) **3.** argot, cant, jargon, lingo (*Inf.*), patois, slang, vernacular ~*v.* **4.** babble, blab, chatter, hold forth, jabber, prate, rattle off, rattle on, spiel (*Inf.*), spout (*Inf.*), tattle

pattern *n.* **1.** arrangement, decoration, decorative design, design, device, figure, motif, ornament **2.** arrangement, method, order, orderliness, plan, sequence, system **3.** kind, shape, sort, style, type, variety **4.** design, diagram, guide, instructions, original, plan, stencil, template **5.** archetype, criterion, cynosure, example, exemplar, guide, model, norm, original, paradigm, paragon, prototype, sample, specimen, standard ~*v.* **6.** copy,

emulate, follow, form, imitate, model, mould, order, shape, style **7.** decorate, design, trim

paucity dearth, deficiency, fewness, insufficiency, lack, meagreness, paltriness, poverty, rarity, scantiness, scarcity, shortage, slenderness, slightness, smallness, sparseness, sparsity

paunch abdomen, beer-belly (*Sl.*), belly, corporation (*Brit. inf.*), pot, potbelly

pauper bankrupt, beggar, down-and-out, have-not, indigent, insolvent, mendicant, poor person

pauperism beggary, destitution, impecuniousness, indigence, mendicancy, need, neediness, pennilessness, penury, poverty, privation, want

pauperize bankrupt, beggar, break, bust (*Inf.*), cripple financially, impoverish, reduce to beggary, ruin

pause 1. *v.* break, cease, delay, deliberate, desist, discontinue, halt, have a breather (*Inf.*), hesitate, interrupt, rest, stop briefly, take a break, wait, waver **2.** *n.* break, breather (*Inf.*), caesura, cessation, delay, discontinuance, gap, halt, hesitation, interlude, intermission, interruption, interval, let-up (*Inf.*), lull, respite, rest, stay, stoppage, wait

pave asphalt, concrete, cover, flag, floor, macadamize, surface, tar, tile

paw *v.* grab, handle roughly, manhandle, maul, molest

pawn[1] **1.** *v.* deposit, gage (*Archaic*), hazard, hock (*Inf., chiefly U.S.*), mortgage, pledge, pop (*Inf.*), stake, wager **2.** *n.* assurance, bond, collateral, gage, guarantee, guaranty, pledge, security

pawn[2] *n.* cat's-paw, creature, dupe, instrument, plaything, puppet, stooge (*Sl.*), tool, toy

pay *v.* **1.** clear, compensate, cough up (*Inf.*), discharge, foot, give, honour, liquidate, meet, offer, recompense, reimburse, remit, remunerate, render, requite, reward, settle, square up **2.** be advantageous, benefit, be worthwhile, repay, serve **3.** bestow, extend, give, grant, present, proffer, render **4.** *Often with* **for** answer for, atone, be punished, compensate, get one's deserts, make amends, suffer, suffer the consequences **5.** bring in, produce, profit, return, yield **6.** be profitable, be remunerative, make a return, make money, provide a living **7.** avenge oneself for, get even with (*Inf.*), get revenge on, pay back, punish, reciprocate, repay, requite, settle a score ~*n.* **8.** allowance, compensation, earnings, emoluments, fee, hire, income, payment, recompense, reimbursement, remuneration, reward, salary, stipend, takings, wages

payable due, mature, obligatory, outstanding, owed, owing, receivable, to be paid

pay back 1. get even with (*Inf.*), get one's own back, reciprocate, recompense, retaliate, settle a score **2.** refund, reimburse, repay, return, settle up, square

payment 1. defrayal, discharge, outlay, paying, remittance, settlement **2.** advance, deposit, instalment, portion, premium, remittance **3.** fee, hire, remuneration, reward, wage

payoff *n.* **1.** conclusion, day of reckoning, final reckoning, judgment, retribution, reward, settlement **2.** *Inf.* climax, clincher (*Inf.*), consequence, culmination, finale, moment of truth, outcome, punch line, result, the crunch (*Inf.*), upshot

pay off 1. discharge, dismiss, fire, lay off, let go, sack (*Inf.*) **2.** clear, discharge, liquidate, pay in full, settle, square **3.** be effective (profitable, successful), succeed, work **4.** get even with (*Inf.*), pay back, retaliate, settle a score **5.** *Inf.* bribe, buy off, corrupt, get at, grease the palm of (*Sl.*), oil (*Inf.*), suborn

pay out 1. cough up (*Inf.*), disburse, expend, fork out *or* over *or* up (*Sl.*), lay out (*Inf.*), shell out (*Inf.*), spend **2.** get even with (*Inf.*), pay back, retaliate, settle a score

peace 1. accord, agreement, amity, concord, harmony **2.** armistice, cessation of hostilities, conciliation, pacification, treaty, truce **3.** calm, composure, contentment, placidity, relaxation, repose, serenity **4.** calm, calmness, hush, peacefulness, quiet, quietude, repose, rest, silence, stillness, tranquillity

peaceable 1. amiable, amicable, conciliatory, dovish, friendly, gentle, inoffensive, mild, nonbelligerent, pacific, peaceful, peace-loving, placid, unwarlike **2.** balmy, calm, peaceful, quiet, restful, serene, still, tranquil, undisturbed

peaceful 1. amicable, at peace, free from strife, friendly, harmonious, nonviolent, on friendly *or* good terms, without hostility **2.** calm, gentle, placid, qui-

et, restful, serene, still, tranquil, undisturbed, unruffled, untroubled **3.** conciliatory, irenic, pacific, peaceable, peace-loving, placatory, unwarlike

peacemaker appeaser, arbitrator, conciliator, mediator, pacifier, peacemonger

peak *n.* **1.** aiguille, apex, brow, crest, pinnacle, point, summit, tip, top **2.** acme, apogee, climax, crown, culmination, high point, maximum point, *ne plus ultra*, zenith ~*v.* **3.** be at its height, climax, come to a head, culminate, reach its highest point, reach the zenith

peaky emaciated, ill, in poor shape, off colour, pale, peelie-wally (*Scot.*), pinched, poorly (*Inf.*), sick, sickly, under the weather (*Inf.*), unwell, wan

peal 1. *n.* blast, carillon, chime, clamour, clang, clap, crash, resounding, reverberation, ring, ringing, roar, rumble, sound, tintinnabulation **2.** *v.* chime, crack, crash, resonate, resound, reverberate, ring, roar, roll, rumble, sound, tintinnabulate, toll

peasant 1. churl (*Archaic*), countryman, hind (*Archaic*), rustic, son of the soil, swain (*Archaic*) **2.** *Inf.* boor, churl, country bumpkin, lout, provincial, yokel

peccadillo error, indiscretion, infraction, lapse, misdeed, misdemeanour, petty offence, slip, trifling fault

peck *v./n.* bite, dig, hit, jab, kiss, nibble, pick, poke, prick, strike, tap

peculate appropriate, defalcate (*Law*), defraud, embezzle, misapply, misappropriate, pilfer, purloin, rob, steal

peculiar 1. abnormal, bizarre, curious, eccentric, exceptional, extraordinary, far-out (*Sl.*), freakish, funny, odd, offbeat, outlandish, out-of-the-way, quaint, queer, singular, strange, uncommon, unconventional, unusual, weird **2.** appropriate, characteristic, distinct, distinctive, distinguishing, endemic, idiosyncratic, individual, local, particular, personal, private, restricted, special, specific, unique

peculiarity 1. abnormality, bizarreness, eccentricity, foible, freakishness, idiosyncrasy, mannerism, oddity, odd trait, queerness, quirk **2.** attribute, characteristic, distinctiveness, feature, mark, particularity, property, quality, singularity, speciality, trait

pecuniary commercial, financial, fiscal, monetary

pedagogue dogmatist, dominie (*Scot.*), educator, instructor, master, mistress, pedant, schoolmaster, schoolmistress, teacher

pedant casuist, doctrinaire, dogmatist, hairsplitter, literalist, nit-picker (*Inf.*), pedagogue, pettifogger, precisian, quibbler, scholastic, sophist

pedantic abstruse, academic, bookish, didactic, donnish, erudite, formal, fussy, hairsplitting, nit-picking (*Inf.*), overnice, particular, pedagogic, pompous, precise, priggish, punctilious, scholastic, schoolmasterly, sententious, stilted

pedantry bookishness, finicality, hairsplitting, overnicety, pedagogism, pettifoggery, pomposity, punctiliousness, quibbling, sophistry, stuffiness

peddle flog (*Sl.*), hawk, huckster, market, push (*Inf.*), sell, sell door to door, trade, vend

pedestal 1. base, dado (*Architect.*), foot, foundation, mounting, pier, plinth, socle, stand, support 2. **put on a pedestal** apotheosize, deify, dignify, ennoble, exalt, glorify, idealize, worship

pedestrian 1. *n.* footslogger, foot-traveller, walker 2. *adj.* banal, boring, commonplace, dull, flat, humdrum, mediocre, mundane, ordinary, plodding, prosaic, run-of-the-mill, unimaginative, uninspired, uninteresting

pedigree 1. *n.* ancestry, blood, breed, derivation, descent, extraction, family, family tree, genealogy, heritage, line, lineage, race, stemma, stirps, stock 2. *adj.* full-blooded, purebred, thoroughbred

pedlar cheap-jack (*Inf.*), colporteur, door-to-door salesman, duffer (*Dialect*), hawker, huckster, seller, vendor

peek 1. *v.* glance, keek (*Scot.*), look, peep, peer, snatch a glimpse, sneak a look, spy, squinny, take *or* have a gander (*Inf.*), take a look 2. *n.* blink, gander (*Inf.*), glance, glim (*Scot.*), glimpse, keek (*Scot.*), look, look-see (*Sl.*), peep

peel 1. *v.* decorticate, desquamate, flake off, pare, scale, skin, strip off 2. *n.* epicarp, exocarp, peeling, rind, skin

peep[1] *v.* 1. keek (*Scot.*), look from hiding, look surreptitiously, peek, peer, sneak a look, spy, steal a look 2. appear briefly, emerge, peer out, show partially ~*n.* 3. gander (*Inf.*), glim (*Scot.*), glimpse, keek (*Scot.*), look, look-see (*Sl.*), peek

peep[2] *v./n.* cheep, chirp, chirrup, pipe, squeak, tweet, twitter

peephole aperture, chink, crack, crevice, fissure, hole, keyhole, opening, pinhole, slit, spyhole

peer[1] *n.* 1. aristocrat, baron, count, duke, earl, lord, marquess, marquis, noble, nobleman, viscount 2. coequal, compeer, equal, fellow, like, match

peer[2] *v.* 1. gaze, inspect, peep, scan, scrutinize, snoop, spy, squinny, squint 2. appear, become visible, emerge, peep out

peerage aristocracy, lords and ladies, nobility, peers, titled classes

peerless beyond compare, excellent, incomparable, matchless, nonpareil, outstanding, second to none, superlative, unequalled, unique, unmatched, unparalleled, unrivalled, unsurpassed

peeve 1. *v.* annoy, bother, bug (*Inf.*), exasperate, gall, get (*Inf.*), get one's goat (*Inf.*), irk, irritate, nettle, pique, provoke, rile, rub (up) the wrong way, vex 2. *n.* annoyance, bother, gripe (*Inf.*), nuisance, pest, sore point, vexation

peeved annoyed, exasperated, galled, irked, irritated, nettled, piqued, put out, riled, sore, upset, vexed

peevish acrimonious, cantankerous, captious, childish, churlish, crabbed, cross, crotchety (*Inf.*), crusty, fractious, fretful, grumpy, ill-natured, ill-tempered, irritable, pettish, petulant, querulous, ratty (*Brit. sl.*), short-tempered, snappy, splenetic, sulky, sullen, surly, testy, touchy, waspish, whingeing (*Inf.*)

peg *v.* 1. attach, fasten, fix, join, make fast, secure 2. *With* **along** *or* **away** apply oneself to, beaver away (*Brit. inf.*), keep at it, keep going, keep on, persist, plod along, plug away at (*Inf.*), stick to it, work at, work away 3. *Of prices, etc.* control, fix, freeze, limit, set

pejorative belittling, debasing, deprecatory, depreciatory, derogatory, detractive, detractory, disparaging, negative, slighting, uncomplimentary, unpleasant

pell-mell 1. *adv.* full tilt, hastily, heedlessly, helter-skelter, hurriedly, impetuously, posthaste, precipitously, rashly, recklessly 2. *adj.* chaotic, confused, disordered, disorganized, haphazard, tumultuous 3. *n.* anarchy, chaos, confusion, disarray, disorder, ferment, helter-skelter, pandemonium, tumult, turmoil, upheaval

pellucid 1. bright, clear, crystalline, glassy, limpid, translucent, transparent **2.** clear, comprehensible, limpid, lucid, perspicuous, plain, straightforward, unambiguous

pelt[1] *v.* **1.** assail, batter, beat, belabour, bombard, cast, hurl, pepper, pummel, shower, sling, strike, thrash, throw, wallop (*Inf.*) **2.** belt (*Sl.*), career, charge, dash, hurry, run fast, rush, shoot, speed, tear, whiz (*Inf.*) **3.** bucket down (*Inf.*), pour, rain cats and dogs (*Inf.*), rain hard, teem

pelt[2] *n.* coat, fell, hide, skin

pen[1] *v.* commit to paper, compose, draft, draw up, jot down, write

pen[2] **1.** *n.* cage, coop, enclosure, fold, hutch, sty **2.** *v.* cage, confine, coop up, enclose, fence in, hedge, hem in, hurdle, mew (up), shut up *or* in

penal corrective, disciplinary, penalizing, punitive, retributive

penalize award a penalty against (*Sport*), correct, discipline, handicap, impose a penalty on, inflict a handicap on, punish, put at a disadvantage

penalty disadvantage, fine, forfeit, forfeiture, handicap, mulct, price, punishment, retribution

penance 1. atonement, mortification, penalty, punishment, reparation, sackcloth and ashes **2. do penance** accept punishment, atone, make amends, make reparation, mortify oneself, show contrition, suffer

penchant affinity, bent, bias, disposition, fondness, inclination, leaning, liking, partiality, predilection, predisposition, proclivity, proneness, propensity, taste, tendency, turn

pendent *adj.* dangling, drooping, hanging, pendulous, suspended, swinging

pending awaiting, forthcoming, hanging fire, imminent, impending, in the balance, in the offing, undecided, undetermined, unsettled, up in the air

pendulous dangling, drooping, hanging, pendent, sagging, swaying, swinging

penetrable accessible, clear, comprehensible, fathomable, intelligible, open, passable, permeable, pervious, porous

penetrate 1. bore, enter, go through, perforate, pierce, prick, probe, stab **2.** diffuse, enter, get in, infiltrate, permeate, pervade, seep, suffuse **3.** *Fig.* affect, become clear, be understood, come

across, get through to, impress, touch **4.** *Fig.* comprehend, decipher, discern, fathom, figure out (*Inf.*), get to the bottom of, grasp, understand, unravel, work out

penetrating 1. biting, carrying, harsh, intrusive, pervasive, piercing, pungent, sharp, shrill, stinging, strong **2.** *Fig.* acute, astute, critical, discerning, discriminating, incisive, intelligent, keen, perceptive, perspicacious, profound, quick, sagacious, searching, sharp, sharp-witted, shrewd

penetration 1. entrance, entry, incision, inroad, invasion, perforation, piercing, puncturing **2.** acuteness, astuteness, discernment, insight, keenness, perception, perspicacity, sharpness, shrewdness, wit

penitence compunction, contrition, regret, remorse, repentance, ruefulness, self-reproach, shame, sorrow

penitent *adj.* abject, apologetic, atoning, conscience-stricken, contrite, regretful, remorseful, repentant, rueful, sorrowful, sorry

penmanship calligraphy, chirography, fist (*Inf.*), hand, handwriting, longhand, script, writing

pen name allonym, nom de plume, pseudonym

pennant banderole, banner, burgee (*Nautical*), ensign, flag, jack, pennon, streamer

penniless bankrupt, broke (*Inf.*), cleaned out (*Sl.*), destitute, impecunious, impoverished, indigent, moneyless, necessitous, needy, on one's uppers, penurious, poor, poverty-stricken, ruined, skint (*Brit. sl.*), stony-broke (*Brit. sl.*), strapped (*U.S. sl.*), without a penny to one's name

penny-pincher meany (*Inf.*), miser, niggard, pinchpenny, screw (*Sl.*), Scrooge, skinflint

penny-pinching *adj.* cheeseparing, close, frugal, mean, mingy (*Brit. inf.*), miserly, near (*Inf.*), niggardly, scrimping, Scroogelike, stingy, tightfisted

pennyworth bit, crumb, jot, little, mite, modicum, particle, scrap, small amount, tittle

pension allowance, annuity, benefit, superannuation

pensioner O.A.P., retired person, senior citizen

pensive blue (*Inf.*), cogitative, contemplative, dreamy, grave, in a brown study (*Inf.*), meditative, melancholy, mournful, musing, preoccupied, reflective, ruminative, sad, serious, sober, solemn, sorrowful, thoughtful, wistful

pent-up bottled up, bridled, checked, constrained, curbed, held back, inhibited, repressed, smothered, stifled, suppressed

penurious 1. cheeseparing, close, close-fisted, frugal, grudging, mean, miserly, near (*Inf.*), niggardly, parsimonious, skimping, stingy, tightfisted, ungenerous **2**. destitute, impecunious, impoverished, indigent, needy, penniless, poor, poverty-stricken **3**. beggarly, deficient, inadequate, meagre, miserable, miserly, paltry, poor, scanty

penury 1. beggary, destitution, indigence, need, pauperism, poverty, privation, straitened circumstances, want **2**. dearth, deficiency, lack, paucity, scantiness, scarcity, shortage, sparseness

people *n*. **1**. human beings, humanity, humans, mankind, men and women, mortals, persons **2**. citizens, clan, community, family, folk, inhabitants, nation, population, public, race, tribe **3**. commonalty, crowd, general public, grass roots, hoi polloi, masses, mob, multitude, plebs (*Brit. sl.*), populace, rabble, rank and file, the herd ~*v*. **4**. colonize, inhabit, occupy, populate, settle

pep 1. *n*. animation, energy, get-up-and-go (*Inf.*), gusto, high spirits, life, liveliness, spirit, verve, vigour, vim (*Sl.*), vitality, vivacity, zip (*Inf.*) **2**. *v. With* **up** animate, enliven, exhilarate, inspire, invigorate, jazz up (*Inf.*), quicken, stimulate, vitalize, vivify

pepper *v*. **1**. flavour, season, spice **2**. bespeckle, dot, fleck, spatter, speck, sprinkle, stipple, stud **3**. bombard, pelt, riddle, scatter, shower

peppery 1. fiery, highly seasoned, hot, piquant, pungent, spicy **2**. choleric, hot-tempered, irascible, irritable, quick-tempered, snappish, testy, touchy, waspish **3**. astringent, biting, caustic, incisive, sarcastic, sharp, stinging, trenchant

perceive 1. be aware of, behold, descry, discern, discover, distinguish, espy, make out, note, notice, observe, recognize, remark, see, spot **2**. appreciate, apprehend, comprehend, conclude, deduce, feel, gather, get (*Inf.*), grasp, know, learn, realize, see, sense, understand

perceptible apparent, appreciable, clear, conspicuous, detectable, discernible, distinct, evident, noticeable, observable, obvious, palpable, perceivable, recognizable, tangible, visible

perception apprehension, awareness, conception, consciousness, discernment, feeling, grasp, idea, impression, insight, notion, observation, recognition, sensation, sense, taste, understanding

perceptive acute, alert, astute, aware, discerning, insightful, intuitive, observant, penetrating, percipient, perspicacious, quick, responsive, sensitive, sharp

perch 1. *n*. branch, pole, post, resting place, roost **2**. *v*. alight, balance, land, rest, roost, settle, sit on

perchance by chance, for all one knows, haply (*Archaic*), maybe, mayhap (*Archaic*), peradventure (*Archaic*), perhaps, possibly, probably

percipience acuity, alertness, astuteness, awareness, discernment, insight, intuition, penetration, perception, perspicacity, sagacity, sensitivity, understanding

percipient alert, alive, astute, aware, discerning, discriminating, intelligent, penetrating, perceptive, perspicacious, quick-witted, sharp, wide-awake

percolate drain, drip, exude, filter, filtrate, leach, ooze, penetrate, perk (*of coffee, inf.*), permeate, pervade, seep, strain, transfuse

percussion blow, brunt, bump, clash, collision, concussion, crash, impact, jolt, knock, shock, smash, thump

perdition condemnation, damnation, destruction, doom, downfall, everlasting punishment, hell, hellfire, ruin

peregrination 1. expedition, exploration, journey, odyssey, tour, trek, trip, voyage **2**. globetrotting, roaming, roving, travelling, trekking, wandering, wayfaring

peremptory 1. absolute, binding, categorical, commanding, compelling, decisive, final, imperative, incontrovertible, irrefutable, obligatory, undeniable **2**. arbitrary, assertive, authoritative, autocratic, bossy (*Inf.*), dictatorial, dogmatic, domineering, high-handed, imperious, intolerant, overbearing

perennial 1. abiding, chronic, constant, continual, continuing, enduring, incessant, inveterate, lasting, lifelong, persistent, recurrent, unchanging **2**.

ceaseless, deathless, eternal, everlasting, immortal, imperishable, never-ending, permanent, perpetual, unceasing, undying, unfailing, uninterrupted

perfect *adj.* **1**. absolute, complete, completed, consummate, entire, finished, full, out-and-out, sheer, unadulterated, unalloyed, unmitigated, utter, whole **2**. blameless, excellent, faultless, flawless, ideal, immaculate, impeccable, pure, splendid, spotless, sublime, superb, superlative, supreme, unblemished, unmarred, untarnished **3**. accurate, close, correct, exact, faithful, precise, right, spot-on (*Brit. inf.*), strict, true, unerring **4**. accomplished, adept, experienced, expert, finished, masterly, polished, practised, skilful, skilled ~*v.* **5**. accomplish, achieve, carry out, complete, consummate, effect, finish, fulfil, perform, realize **6**. ameliorate, cultivate, develop, elaborate, hone, improve, polish, refine

perfection **1**. accomplishment, achievement, achieving, completion, consummation, evolution, fulfilment, realization **2**. completeness, exactness, excellence, exquisiteness, faultlessness, integrity, maturity, perfectness, precision, purity, sublimity, superiority, wholeness **3**. acme, crown, ideal, paragon

perfectionist formalist, precisian, precisionist, purist, stickler

perfectly **1**. absolutely, altogether, completely, consummately, entirely, fully, quite, thoroughly, totally, utterly, wholly **2**. admirably, exquisitely, faultlessly, flawlessly, ideally, impeccably, superbly, superlatively, supremely, to perfection, wonderfully

perfidious corrupt, deceitful, dishonest, disloyal, double-dealing, double-faced, faithless, false, recreant (*Archaic*), traitorous, treacherous, treasonous, two-faced, unfaithful, untrustworthy

perfidy betrayal, deceit, disloyalty, double-dealing, duplicity, faithlessness, falsity, infidelity, perfidiousness, treachery, treason

perforate bore, drill, hole, honeycomb, penetrate, pierce, punch, puncture

perforce by force of circumstances, by necessity, inevitably, necessarily, needs must, of necessity, unavoidably, willy-nilly, without choice

perform **1**. accomplish, achieve, act, bring about, carry out, complete, comply

with, discharge, do, effect, execute, fulfil, function, observe, pull off, satisfy, transact, work **2**. act, appear as, depict, enact, play, present, produce, put on, render, represent, stage

performance **1**. accomplishment, achievement, act, carrying out, completion, conduct, consummation, discharge, execution, exploit, feat, fulfilment, work **2**. acting, appearance, exhibition, gig (*Inf.*), interpretation, play, portrayal, presentation, production, representation, show **3**. action, conduct, efficiency, functioning, operation, practice, running, working **4**. *Inf.* act, behaviour, bother, business, carry-on (*Brit. inf.*), fuss, pother, rigmarole, to-do

performer actor, actress, artiste, play-actor, player, Thespian, trouper

perfume aroma, attar, balminess, bouquet, cologne, essence, fragrance, incense, odour, redolence, scent, smell, sweetness

perfunctory automatic, careless, cursory, heedless, inattentive, indifferent, mechanical, negligent, offhand, routine, sketchy, slipshod, slovenly, stereotyped, superficial, unconcerned, unthinking, wooden

perhaps as the case may be, conceivably, feasibly, for all one knows, it may be, maybe, perchance (*Archaic*), possibly

peril danger, exposure, hazard, insecurity, jeopardy, menace, pitfall, risk, uncertainty, vulnerability

perilous chancy (*Inf.*), dangerous, exposed, fraught with danger, hairy (*Sl.*), hazardous, parlous (*Archaic*), precarious, risky, threatening, unsafe, unsure, vulnerable

perimeter ambit, border, borderline, boundary, bounds, circumference, confines, edge, limit, margin, periphery

period **1**. interval, season, space, span, spell, stretch, term, time, while **2**. aeon, age, course, cycle, date, days, epoch, era, generation, season, stage, term, time, years

periodic at fixed intervals, cyclic, cyclical, every once in a while, every so often, infrequent, intermittent, occasional, periodical, recurrent, regular, repeated, seasonal, spasmodic, sporadic

periodical *n.* journal, magazine, monthly, organ, paper, publication, quarterly, review, serial, weekly

peripatetic ambulant, itinerant, migrant, mobile, nomadic, roaming, roving, travelling, vagabond, vagrant, wandering

peripheral 1. beside the point, borderline, incidental, inessential, irrelevant, marginal, minor, secondary, superficial, tangential, unimportant **2.** exterior, external, outer, outermost, outside, perimetric, surface

periphery ambit, border, boundary, brim, brink, circumference, edge, fringe, hem, outer edge, outskirts, perimeter, rim, skirt, verge

periphrastic circuitous, circumlocutory, pleonastic, prolix, roundabout, tautological, verbose, wordy

perish 1. be killed, be lost, decease, die, expire, lose one's life, pass away **2.** be destroyed, collapse, decline, disappear, fall, go under, vanish **3.** decay, decompose, disintegrate, moulder, rot, waste, wither

perishable decaying, decomposable, destructible, easily spoilt, liable to rot, short-lived, unstable

perjure (oneself) bear false witness, commit perjury, forswear, give false testimony, lie under oath, swear falsely

perjured deceitful, false, forsworn, lying, mendacious, perfidious, traitorous, treacherous, untrue, untruthful

perjury bearing false witness, false oath, false statement, false swearing, forswearing, giving false testimony, lying under oath, oath breaking, violation of an oath, wilful falsehood

perk benefit, bonus, dividend, extra, fringe benefit, perquisite, plus

perk up brighten, buck up (*Inf.*), cheer up, liven up, look up, pep up, rally, recover, recuperate, revive, take heart

perky animated, bouncy, bright, bright-eyed and bushy-tailed (*Inf.*), bubbly, buoyant, cheerful, cheery, gay, in fine fettle, jaunty, lively, spirited, sprightly, sunny, vivacious

permanence constancy, continuance, continuity, dependability, durability, duration, endurance, finality, fixedness, fixity, immortality, indestructibility, lastingness, perdurability (*Rare*), permanency, perpetuity, stability, survival

permanent abiding, constant, durable, enduring, everlasting, fixed, immutable, imperishable, indestructible, invariable, lasting, long-lasting, perennial, perpetual, persistent, stable, steadfast, unchanging, unfading

permeable absorbent, absorptive, penetrable, pervious, porous, spongy

permeate charge, diffuse throughout, fill, filter through, imbue, impregnate, infiltrate, pass through, penetrate, percolate, pervade, saturate, seep through, soak through, spread throughout

permissible acceptable, admissible, allowable, all right, authorized, kosher (*Inf.*), lawful, legal, legit (*Sl.*), legitimate, licit, O.K. (*Inf.*), permitted, proper, sanctioned

permission allowance, approval, assent, authorization, consent, dispensation, freedom, go-ahead (*Inf.*), green light, leave, liberty, licence, permit, sanction, sufferance, tolerance

permissive acquiescent, easy-going, forbearing, free, indulgent, latitudinarian, lax, lenient, liberal, open-minded, tolerant

permit 1. *v.* admit, agree, allow, authorize, consent, empower, enable, endorse, endure, give leave *or* permission, grant, let, license, sanction, suffer, tolerate, warrant **2.** *n.* authorization, liberty, licence, pass, passport, permission, sanction, warrant

permutation alteration, change, shift, transformation, transmutation, transposition

pernicious bad, baleful, baneful (*Archaic*), damaging, dangerous, deadly, deleterious, destructive, detrimental, evil, fatal, harmful, hurtful, injurious, maleficent, malevolent, malicious, malign, malignant, noisome, noxious, offensive, pestilent, poisonous, ruinous, venomous, wicked

pernickety 1. careful, carping, difficult to please, exacting, fastidious, finicky, fussy, hairsplitting, nice, nitpicking (*Inf.*), overprecise, painstaking, particular, punctilious **2.** detailed, exacting, fiddly, fine, tricky

peroration closing remarks, conclusion, recapitulation, recapping (*Inf.*), reiteration, summing-up

perpendicular at right angles to, on end, plumb, straight, upright, vertical

perpetrate be responsible for, bring about, carry out, commit, do, effect, enact, execute, inflict, perform, wreak

perpetual 1. abiding, endless, enduring, eternal, everlasting, immortal, infinite, lasting, never-ending, perennial, permanent, sempiternal (*Literary*), unchanging, undying, unending **2.** ceaseless, constant, continual, continuous, endless, incessant, interminable, never-ending, perennial, persistent, recurrent, repeated, unceasing, unfailing, uninterrupted, unremitting

perpetuate continue, eternalize, immortalize, keep alive, keep going, keep up, maintain, preserve, sustain

perplex 1. baffle, befuddle, beset, bewilder, confound, confuse, dumbfound, mix up, muddle, mystify, nonplus, puzzle, stump **2.** complicate, encumber, entangle, involve, jumble, mix up, snarl up, tangle, thicken

perplexing baffling, bewildering, complex, complicated, confusing, difficult, enigmatic, hard, inexplicable, intricate, involved, knotty, labyrinthine, mysterious, mystifying, paradoxical, puzzling, strange, taxing, thorny, unaccountable, weird

perplexity 1. bafflement, bewilderment, confusion, incomprehension, mystification, puzzlement, stupefaction **2.** complexity, difficulty, inextricability, intricacy, involvement, obscurity **3.** difficulty, dilemma, enigma, fix (*Inf.*), knotty problem, mystery, paradox, puzzle, snarl

perquisite benefit, bonus, dividend, extra, fringe benefit, perk (*Inf.*), plus

per se as such, by definition, by itself, by its very nature, essentially, in essence, in itself, intrinsically, of itself

persecute 1. afflict, distress, dragoon, harass, hound, hunt, ill-treat, injure, maltreat, martyr, molest, oppress, pursue, torment, torture, victimize **2.** annoy, badger, bait, bother, pester, tease, vex, worry

perseverance constancy, dedication, determination, diligence, doggedness, endurance, indefatigability, persistence, pertinacity, purposefulness, resolution, sedulity, stamina, steadfastness, tenacity

persevere be determined *or* resolved, carry on, continue, endure, go on, hang on, hold fast, hold on (*Inf.*), keep going, keep on *or* at, maintain, persist, plug away (*Inf.*), pursue, remain, stand firm, stick at *or* to

persiflage badinage, banter, chaff, frivolity, pleasantry, raillery, repartee, teasing, wit, wittiness, wordplay

persist 1. be resolute, continue, hold on (*Inf.*), insist, persevere, stand firm **2.**

abide, carry on, continue, endure, keep up, last, linger, remain

persistence constancy, determination, diligence, doggedness, endurance, grit, indefatigability, perseverance, pertinacity, pluck, resolution, stamina, steadfastness, tenacity, tirelessness

persistent 1. assiduous, determined, dogged, enduring, fixed, immovable, indefatigable, obdurate, obstinate, persevering, pertinacious, resolute, steadfast, steady, stubborn, tenacious, tireless, unflagging **2.** constant, continual, continuous, endless, incessant, interminable, never-ending, perpetual, relentless, repeated, unrelenting, unremitting

person 1. being, body, human, human being, individual, living soul, soul **2. in person** bodily, in the flesh, oneself, personally

persona assumed role, character, façade, face, front, mask, part, personality, public face, role

personable affable, agreeable, amiable, attractive, charming, good-looking, handsome, likable, nice, pleasant, pleasing, presentable, winning

personage big noise (*Brit. sl.*), big shot (*Sl.*), celebrity, dignitary, luminary, notable, personality, public figure, somebody, V.I.P., well-known person, worthy

personal 1. exclusive, individual, intimate, own, particular, peculiar, private, privy, special **2.** bodily, corporal, corporeal, exterior, material, physical **3.** derogatory, disparaging, insulting, nasty, offensive, pejorative, slighting

personality 1. character, disposition, identity, individuality, make-up, nature, psyche, temper, temperament, traits **2.** attraction, attractiveness, character, charisma, charm, dynamism, likableness, magnetism, pleasantness **3.** celebrity, famous name, household name, notable, personage, star, well-known face, well-known person

personally 1. alone, by oneself, independently, in person, in the flesh, on one's own, solely **2.** for oneself, for one's part, from one's own viewpoint, in one's own view **3.** individualistically, individually, privately, specially, subjectively

personate act, depict, do (*Inf.*), enact, feign, imitate, impersonate, play-act, portray, represent

personification embodiment, image, incarnation, likeness, portrayal, recreation, representation, semblance

personify body forth, embody, epitomize, exemplify, express, image (*Rare*), incarnate, mirror, represent, symbolize, typify

personnel employees, helpers, human resources, liveware, members, men and women, people, staff, workers, work force

perspective 1. angle, attitude, broad view, context, frame of reference, objectivity, outlook, overview, proportion, relation, relative importance, relativity, way of looking **2**. outlook, panorama, prospect, scene, view, vista

perspicacious acute, alert, astute, aware, clear-sighted, clever, discerning, keen, observant, penetrating, perceptive, percipient, sagacious, sharp, sharp-witted, shrewd

perspicacity acumen, acuteness, discernment, discrimination, insight, keenness, penetration, perceptiveness, percipience, perspicaciousness, perspicuity, sagaciousness, sagacity, sharpness, shrewdness, wit

perspicuity clarity, clearness, comprehensibility, distinctness, explicitness, intelligibility, limpidity, limpidness, lucidity, plainness, precision, straightforwardness, transparency

perspicuous clear, comprehensible, crystal-clear, distinct, easily understood, explicit, intelligible, limpid, lucid, obvious, plain, self-evident, straightforward, transparent, unambiguous, understandable

perspiration exudation, moisture, sweat, wetness

perspire be damp, be wet, drip, exude, glow, pour with sweat, secrete, sweat, swelter

persuade 1. actuate, advise, allure, bring round (*Inf.*), coax, counsel, entice, impel, incite, induce, influence, inveigle, prevail upon, prompt, sway, talk into, urge, win over **2**. cause to believe, convert, convince, satisfy

persuasion 1. blandishment, cajolery, conversion, enticement, exhortation, inducement, influencing, inveiglement, wheedling **2**. cogency, force, persuasiveness, potency, power, pull (*Inf.*) **3**. belief, certitude, conviction, credo, creed, faith, firm belief, fixed opinion, opinion, tenet, views **4**. camp, cult, denomination, fac-

tion, party, school, school of thought, sect, side

persuasive cogent, compelling, convincing, credible, effective, eloquent, forceful, impelling, impressive, inducing, influential, logical, moving, plausible, sound, telling, touching, valid, weighty, winning

pert 1. bold, brash, cheeky, flip (*Inf.*), flippant, forward, fresh (*Inf.*), impertinent, impudent, insolent, presumptuous, saucy, smart **2**. brisk, dapper, daring, dashing, gay, jaunty, lively, nimble, perky, smart, spirited, sprightly

pertain appertain, apply, be appropriate, bear on, befit, belong, be part of, be relevant, concern, refer, regard, relate

pertinacious bull-headed, determined, dogged, headstrong, inflexible, intractable, mulish, obdurate, obstinate, persevering, persistent, perverse, pig-headed, relentless, resolute, self-willed, strong-willed, stubborn, tenacious, unyielding, wilful

pertinent admissible, *ad rem*, applicable, apposite, appropriate, apropos, apt, fit, fitting, germane, material, pat, proper, relevant, suitable, to the point, to the purpose

pertness audacity, brashness, brass (*Inf.*), bumptiousness, cheek (*Inf.*), cheekiness, cockiness, effrontery, forwardness, impertinence, impudence, insolence, presumption, rudeness, sauciness

perturb 1. agitate, alarm, bother, discompose, disconcert, discountenance, disquiet, disturb, fluster, ruffle, trouble, unsettle, upset, vex, worry **2**. confuse, disarrange, disorder, muddle, unsettle

perturbed agitated, alarmed, anxious, disconcerted, disquieted, disturbed, fearful, flurried, flustered, ill at ease, nervous, restless, shaken, troubled, uncomfortable, uneasy, upset, worried

perusal browse, check, examination, inspection, look through, read, scrutiny, study

peruse browse, check, examine, inspect, look through, read, run one's eye over, scan, scrutinize, study

pervade affect, charge, diffuse, extend, fill, imbue, infuse, overspread, penetrate, percolate, permeate, spread through, suffuse

pervasive common, extensive, general, inescapable, omnipresent, permeating, pervading, prevalent, rife, ubiquitous, universal, widespread

perverse 1. abnormal, contradictory, contrary, delinquent, depraved, deviant, disobedient, froward, improper, incorrect, miscreant, rebellious, refractory, troublesome, unhealthy, unmanageable, unreasonable **2.** contrary, contumacious, cross-grained, dogged, headstrong, intractable, intransigent, obdurate, wilful, wrong-headed **3.** contrary, mulish, obstinate, pig-headed, stubborn, unyielding, wayward **4.** cantankerous, churlish, crabbed, cross, fractious, ill-natured, ill-tempered, peevish, petulant, spiteful, stroppy (*Brit. sl.*), surly

perversion 1. aberration, abnormality, debauchery, depravity, deviation, immorality, kink (*Brit. sl.*), kinkiness (*Sl.*), unnaturalness, vice, vitiation, wickedness **2.** corruption, distortion, falsification, misinterpretation, misrepresentation, misuse, twisting

perversity contradictiveness, contradictoriness, contrariness, contumacy, frowardness, intransigence, obduracy, refractoriness, waywardness, wrongheadedness

pervert *v.* **1.** abuse, distort, falsify, garble, misconstrue, misinterpret, misrepresent, misuse, twist, warp **2.** corrupt, debase, debauch, degrade, deprave, desecrate, initiate, lead astray, subvert ~*n.* **3.** debauchee, degenerate, deviant, weirdo (*Sl.*)

perverted aberrant, abnormal, corrupt, debased, debauched, depraved, deviant, distorted, evil, immoral, impaired, kinky (*Sl.*), misguided, sick, twisted, unhealthy, unnatural, vicious, vitiated, warped, wicked

pessimism cynicism, dejection, depression, despair, despondency, distrust, gloom, gloominess, gloomy outlook, glumness, hopelessness, melancholy

pessimist cynic, defeatist, doomster, gloom merchant (*Inf.*), kill-joy, melancholic, misanthrope, prophet of doom, wet blanket (*Inf.*), worrier

pessimistic bleak, cynical, dark, dejected, depressed, despairing, despondent, distrustful, downhearted, fatalistic, foreboding, gloomy, glum, hopeless, melancholy, misanthropic, morose, resigned, sad

pest 1. annoyance, bane, bore, bother, irritation, nuisance, pain (*Inf.*), pain in the neck (*Inf.*), thorn in one's flesh, trial, vexation **2.** bane, blight, bug, curse, epidemic, infection, pestilence, plague, scourge

pester annoy, badger, bedevil, bother, bug (*Inf.*), chivvy, disturb, drive one up the wall (*Sl.*), fret, get at, get on someone's nerves, harass, harry, hassle (*Inf.*), irk, nag, pick on, plague, ride (*Inf.*), torment, worry

pestilence 1. Black Death, epidemic, pandemic, plague, visitation **2.** affliction, bane, blight, cancer, canker, curse, scourge

pestilent 1. annoying, bothersome, galling, irksome, irritating, plaguy (*Inf.*), tiresome, vexing **2.** corrupting, deleterious, destructive, detrimental, evil, harmful, injurious, pernicious, ruinous, vicious **3.** catching, contagious, contaminated, diseased, disease-ridden, infected, infectious, plague-ridden, tainted

pestilential 1. annoying, dangerous, deleterious, destructive, detrimental, evil, foul, harmful, hazardous, injurious, pernicious, ruinous, troublesome **2.** catching, contagious, contaminated, deadly, disease-ridden, infectious, malignant, noxious, pestiferous, poisonous, venomous

pet[1] *n.* **1.** apple of one's eye, blue-eyed boy (*Inf.*), darling, favourite, idol, jewel, treasure ~*adj.* **2.** cherished, dearest, dear to one's heart, favoured, favourite, particular, preferred, special **3.** domesticated, house, house-broken, housetrained (*Brit.*), tame, trained ~*v.* **4.** baby, coddle, cosset, mollycoddle, pamper, spoil **5.** caress, fondle, pat, stroke **6.** *Inf.* canoodle (*Sl.*), cuddle, kiss, neck (*Inf.*), smooch (*Sl.*), snog (*Brit. sl.*)

pet[2] bad mood, huff, ill temper, miff (*Inf.*), paddy (*Brit. inf.*), paddywhack (*Brit. inf.*), pique, pout, sulk, sulks, tantrum, temper

peter out come to nothing, die out, dwindle, ebb, evaporate, fade, fail, give out, run dry, run out, stop, taper off, wane

petite dainty, delicate, dinky (*Brit. inf.*), elfin, little, slight, small

petition 1. *n.* address, appeal, application, entreaty, invocation, memorial, plea, prayer, request, round robin, solicitation, suit, supplication **2.** *v.* adjure, appeal, ask, beg, beseech, call upon, crave, entreat, plead, pray, press, solicit, sue, supplicate, urge

petrified 1. fossilized, ossified, rocklike 2. aghast, appalled, dazed, dumbfounded, frozen, horrified, numb, scared stiff, shocked, speechless, stunned, stupefied, terrified, terror-stricken

petrify 1. calcify, fossilize, harden, set, solidify, turn to stone 2. amaze, appal, astonish, astound, confound, dumbfound, horrify, immobilize, paralyse, stun, stupefy, terrify, transfix

pettifoggery cheating, corruption, deceit, deception, dishonesty, doubledealing, duplicity, fraud, gerrymandering, jobbery, swindling

pettifogging captious, casuistic, cavilling, equivocating, hairsplitting, insignificant, mean, niggling, nit-picking (*Inf.*), paltry, petty, piddling (*Inf.*), quibbling, sophistical, sophisticated, subtle

pettish cross, fractious, fretful, grumpy, huffy, ill-humoured, irritable, peevish, petulant, querulous, sulky, tetchy, thin-skinned, touchy, waspish

petty 1. contemptible, inconsiderable, inessential, inferior, insignificant, little, measly (*Inf.*), negligible, paltry, piddling (*Inf.*), slight, small, trifling, trivial, unimportant 2. cheap, grudging, mean, mean-minded, shabby, small-minded, spiteful, stingy, ungenerous 3. inferior, junior, lesser, lower, minor, secondary, subordinate

petulance bad temper, crabbiness, ill humour, irritability, peevishness, pettishness, pique, pouts, querulousness, spleen, sulkiness, sullenness, waspishness

petulant bad-tempered, captious, cavilling, crabbed, cross, crusty, faultfinding, fretful, ill-humoured, impatient, irritable, moody, peevish, perverse, pouting, querulous, snappish, sour, sulky, sullen, ungracious, waspish

phantasm 1. apparition, eidolon, ghost, phantom, revenant, shade (*Literary*), spectre, spirit, spook (*Inf.*), wraith 2. chimera, figment, figment of the imagination, hallucination, illusion, vision

phantasmagoric, phantasmagorical chimerical, dreamlike, hallucinatory, illusory, Kafkaesque, kaleidoscopic, nightmarish, phantasmal, psychedelic, surreal, unreal

phantasmal chimerical, delusory, fancied, fanciful, ghostlike, ghostly, illusory, imaginary, imagined, phantasmagoric, phantasmagorical, phantomlike, shadowy, spectral, unreal, wraithlike

phantasy see FANTASY

phantom 1. apparition, eidolon, ghost, phantasm, revenant, shade (*Literary*), spectre, spirit, spook (*Inf.*), wraith 2. chimera, figment, figment of the imagination, hallucination, illusion, vision

pharisaic, pharisaical canting, formal, goody-goody, holier-than-thou, hypocritical, insincere, Pecksniffian, pietistic, sanctimonious, self-righteous

pharisaism cant, false piety, hypocrisy, insincerity, lip service, pietism, religiosity, sanctimoniousness, self-righteousness

pharisee canter, dissembler, dissimulator, fraud, humbug, hypocrite, phoney (*Sl.*), pietist, whited sepulchre

phase aspect, chapter, condition, development, juncture, period, point, position, stage, state, step, time

phase out close, deactivate, dispose of gradually, ease off, eliminate, pull out, remove, replace, run down, taper off, terminate, wind down, wind up (*Inf.*), withdraw

phenomenal exceptional, extraordinary, fantastic, marvellous, miraculous, outstanding, prodigious, remarkable, sensational, singular, uncommon, unique, unparalleled, unusual, wondrous

phenomenon 1. circumstance, episode, event, fact, happening, incident, occurrence 2. exception, marvel, miracle, nonpareil, prodigy, rarity, sensation, sight, spectacle, wonder

philander coquet, court, dally, flirt, fool around (*Inf.*), toy, trifle, womanize (*Inf.*)

philanderer Casanova, dallier, Don Juan, flirt, gallant, gay dog, ladies' man, lady-killer (*Inf.*), Lothario, playboy, stud (*Sl.*), trifler, wolf (*Inf.*), womanizer (*Inf.*)

philanthropic alms-giving, altruistic, beneficent, benevolent, benignant, charitable, eleemosynary, gracious, humane, humanitarian, kind, kind-hearted, munificent, public-spirited

philanthropist alms-giver, altruist, benefactor, contributor, donor, giver, humanitarian, patron

philanthropy alms-giving, altruism, beneficence, benevolence, benignity, bounty, brotherly love, charitableness, charity, generosity, humanitarianism, kind-heartedness, liberality, munificence, open-handedness, patronage, public-spiritedness

philippic condemnation, denunciation, diatribe, fulmination, harangue, invective, obloquy, stream of abuse, tirade, vituperation

philistine 1. *n.* barbarian, boor, bourgeois, Goth, ignoramus, lout, lowbrow, vulgarian, yahoo **2.** *adj.* anti-intellectual, boorish, bourgeois, crass, ignorant, lowbrow, tasteless, uncultivated, uncultured, uneducated, unrefined

philosopher dialectician, logician, metaphysician, sage, seeker after truth, theorist, thinker, wise man

philosophical, philosophic 1. abstract, erudite, learned, logical, rational, sagacious, theoretical, thoughtful, wise **2.** calm, collected, composed, cool, impassive, imperturbable, patient, resigned, serene, stoical, tranquil, unruffled

philosophy 1. aesthetics, knowledge, logic, metaphysics, rationalism, reason, reasoning, thinking, thought, wisdom **2.** attitude to life, basic idea, beliefs, convictions, doctrine, ideology, principle, tenets, thinking, values, viewpoint, *Weltanschauung*, world-view **3.** composure, coolness, dispassion, equanimity, resignation, restraint, self-possession, serenity, stoicism

phlegmatic apathetic, bovine, cold, dull, frigid, heavy, impassive, indifferent, lethargic, listless, lymphatic, matter-of-fact, placid, sluggish, stoical, stolid, undemonstrative, unemotional, unfeeling

phobia aversion, detestation, dislike, distaste, dread, fear, hatred, horror, irrational fear, loathing, obsession, overwhelming anxiety, repulsion, revulsion, terror, thing (*Inf.*)

phone *n.* **1.** blower (*Inf.*), telephone **2.** bell (*Brit. sl.*), buzz (*Inf.*), call, ring, tinkle (*Brit. inf.*) ~*v.* **3.** buzz (*Inf.*), call, get on the blower (*Inf.*), give someone a bell (*Brit. sl.*), give someone a buzz (*Inf.*), give someone a call, give someone a ring, give someone a tinkle (*Brit. inf.*), make a call, ring, ring up, telephone

phoney 1. *adj.* affected, assumed, bogus, counterfeit, fake, false, forged, imitation, pseudo (*Inf.*), put-on, sham, spurious, trick **2.** *n.* counterfeit, fake, faker,

forgery, fraud, humbug, impostor, pretender, pseud (*Sl.*), sham

photograph 1. *n.* image, likeness, photo (*Inf.*), picture, print, shot, slide, snap (*Inf.*), snapshot, transparency **2.** *v.* capture on film, film, get a shot of, record, shoot, snap (*Inf.*), take, take a picture of, take (someone's) picture

photographic accurate, cinematic, detailed, exact, faithful, filmic, graphic, lifelike, minute, natural, pictorial, precise, realistic, retentive, visual, vivid

phrase 1. *n.* expression, group of words, idiom, locution, motto, remark, saying, tag, utterance, way of speaking **2.** *v.* couch, express, formulate, frame, present, put, put into words, say, term, utter, voice, word

phraseology choice of words, diction, expression, idiom, language, parlance, phrase, phrasing, speech, style, syntax, wording

physical 1. bodily, carnal, corporal, corporeal, earthly, fleshly, incarnate, mortal, somatic, unspiritual **2.** material, natural, palpable, real, sensible, solid, substantial, tangible, visible

physician doc (*Inf.*), doctor, doctor of medicine, general practitioner, G.P., healer, M.D., medic (*Inf.*), medical practitioner, medico (*Inf.*), sawbones (*Sl.*), specialist

physiognomy clock (*Brit. sl.*), countenance, dial (*Brit. sl.*), face, features, look, phiz (*Sl.*), phizog (*Sl.*), visage

physique body, build, constitution, figure, form, frame, make-up, shape, structure

pick *v.* **1.** choose, decide upon, elect, fix upon, hand-pick, mark out, opt for, select, settle upon, sift out, single out, sort out **2.** collect, cull, cut, gather, harvest, pluck, pull **3.** have no appetite, nibble, peck at, play *or* toy with, push the food round the plate **4.** foment, incite, instigate, provoke, start **5.** break into, break open, crack, force, jemmy, open, prise open **6. pick one's way** be tentative, find *or* make one's way, move cautiously, tread carefully, work through ~*n.* **7.** choice, choosing, decision, option, preference, selection **8.** choicest, *crème de la crème*, elect, elite, flower, pride, prize, the best, the cream, the tops (*Sl.*)

pick at carp, cavil, criticize, find fault, get at, nag, pick holes, pick to pieces, quibble

picket *n.* **1.** pale, paling, palisade, peg, post, stake, stanchion, upright **2.** demonstrator, picketer, protester **3.** guard, lookout, patrol, scout, sentinel, sentry, spotter, vedette (*Military*), watch ~*v.* **4.** blockade, boycott, demonstrate **5.** corral (*U.S.*), enclose, fence, hedge in, palisade, pen in, rail in, shut in, wall in

pickings booty, earnings, gravy (*U.S. sl.*), ill-gotten gains, loot, plunder, proceeds, profits, returns, rewards, spoils, yield

pickle *n.* **1.** *Inf.* bind (*Inf.*), difficulty, dilemma, fix (*Inf.*), hot water (*Inf.*), jam (*Inf.*), predicament, quandary, scrape (*Inf.*), spot (*Inf.*), tight spot **2.** *Brit. inf.* little horror, mischief, mischief maker, monkey, naughty child, rascal ~*v.* **3.** cure, keep, marinade, preserve, steep

pick-me-up bracer (*Inf.*), drink, pickup (*Sl.*), refreshment, restorative, roborant, shot in the arm (*Inf.*), stimulant, tonic

pick on badger, bait, blame, bully, goad, hector, tease, torment

pick out 1. choose, cull, hand-pick, select, separate the sheep from the goats, single out, sort out **2.** discriminate, distinguish, make distinct, make out, notice, perceive, recognize, tell apart

pick-up *n.* **1.** acceleration, response, revving (*Inf.*), speed-up **2.** change for the better, gain, improvement, rally, recovery, revival, strengthening, upswing, upturn

pick up *v.* **1.** gather, grasp, hoist, lift, raise, take up, uplift **2.** buy, come across, find, garner, happen upon, obtain, purchase, score (*Sl.*) **3.** gain, gain ground, get better, improve, make a comeback (*Inf.*), mend, perk up, rally, recover, take a turn for the better **4.** call for, collect, get, give someone a lift, go to get, uplift (*Scot.*) **5.** acquire, get the hang of (*Inf.*), learn, master **6.** *Sl.* apprehend, arrest, bust (*Inf.*), collar (*Inf.*), do (*Sl.*), nab (*Inf.*), nick (*Brit. sl.*), pinch (*Inf.*), pull in (*Brit. sl.*), run in (*Sl.*), take into custody

picky captious, carping, cavilling, choosy, critical, dainty, fastidious, fault-finding, finicky, fussy, nice, particular, pernickety (*Inf.*)

picnic 1. excursion, *fête champêtre*, outdoor meal, outing **2.** *Inf.* child's play (*Inf.*), cinch (*Sl.*), piece of cake (*Brit.*

inf.), pushover (*Sl.*), snap (*Inf.*), walkover (*Inf.*)

pictorial expressive, graphic, illustrated, picturesque, representational, scenic, striking, vivid

picture *n.* **1.** delineation, drawing, effigy, engraving, illustration, image, likeness, painting, photograph, portrait, portrayal, print, representation, similitude, sketch **2.** account, depiction, description, image, impression, re-creation, report **3.** carbon copy, copy, dead ringer (*Sl.*), double, duplicate, image, likeness, living image, lookalike, replica, ringer (*Sl.*), spit (*Inf.*), spit and image (*Inf.*), spitting image (*Inf.*), twin **4.** archetype, embodiment, epitome, essence, living example, perfect example, personification **5.** film, flick (*Sl.*), motion picture, movie (*U.S. inf.*) ~*v.* **6.** conceive of, envision, image, see, see in the mind's eye, visualize **7.** delineate, depict, describe, draw, illustrate, paint, photograph, portray, render, represent, show, sketch

picturesque attractive, beautiful, charming, colourful, graphic, pretty, quaint, scenic, striking, vivid

piddling derisory, fiddling, insignificant, little, measly (*Inf.*), Mickey Mouse (*Sl.*), paltry, petty, piffling, puny, trifling, trivial, unimportant, useless, worthless

piebald black and white, brindled, dappled, flecked, mottled, pied, speckled, spotted

piece *n.* **1.** allotment, bit, chunk, division, fraction, fragment, length, morsel, mouthful, part, portion, quantity, scrap, section, segment, share, shred, slice **2.** case, example, instance, occurrence, sample, specimen, stroke **3.** article, bit (*Sl.*), composition, creation, item, production, study, work, work of art **4. go to pieces** break down, crack up (*Inf.*), crumple, disintegrate, fall apart, lose control, lose one's head **5. in pieces** broken, bust (*Inf.*), damaged, disintegrated, in bits, in smithereens, ruined, shattered, smashed **6. of a piece** alike, analogous, consistent, identical, of the same kind, similar, the same, uniform ~*v.* **7.** *Often with* **together** assemble, compose, fix, join, mend, patch, repair, restore, unite

pièce de résistance *chef-d'oeuvre*, jewel, masterpiece, masterwork, showpiece

piecemeal 1. *adv.* at intervals, bit by bit, by degrees, by fits and starts, fitfully, intermittently, little by little, partially, slowly 2. *adj.* fragmentary, intermittent, interrupted, partial, patchy, spotty, unsystematic

pied dappled, flecked, irregular, motley, mottled, multicoloured, particoloured, piebald, spotted, streaked, varicoloured, variegated

pier *n.* 1. jetty, landing place, promenade, quay, wharf 2. buttress, column, pile, piling, pillar, post, support, upright

pierce 1. bore, drill, enter, penetrate, perforate, prick, probe, puncture, run through, spike, stab, stick into, transfix 2. comprehend, discern, discover, fathom, grasp, realize, see, understand 3. *Fig.* affect, cut, cut to the quick, excite, hurt, move, pain, rouse, sting, stir, strike, thrill, touch, wound

piercing 1. *Usually of sound* ear-splitting, high-pitched, loud, penetrating, sharp, shattering, shrill 2. alert, aware, keen, penetrating, perceptive, perspicacious, probing, quick-witted, searching, sharp, shrewd 3. *Usually of weather* arctic, biting, bitter, cold, freezing, frosty, keen, nipping, nippy, numbing, raw, wintry 4. acute, agonizing, excruciating, exquisite, fierce, intense, painful, powerful, racking, severe, sharp, shooting, stabbing

piety devotion, devoutness, dutifulness, duty, faith, godliness, grace, holiness, piousness, religion, reverence, sanctity, veneration

piffle balderdash, bunk (*Inf.*), bunkum, codswallop (*Brit. sl.*), drivel, guff (*Sl.*), hooey (*Sl.*), nonsense, poppycock (*Inf.*), rot, rubbish, tarradiddle, tosh (*Inf.*), trash, tripe (*Inf.*), twaddle

piffling derisory, fiddling, insignificant, little, measly (*Inf.*), Mickey Mouse (*Sl.*), paltry, petty, piddling (*Inf.*), puny, trifling, trivial, unimportant, useless, worthless

pig 1. boar, grunter, hog, piggy, piglet, porker, shoat, sow, swine 2. *Inf.* animal, beast, boor, brute, glutton, greedy guts (*Sl.*), guzzler, hog (*Inf.*), slob (*Sl.*), sloven, swine

pigeon 1. bird, culver (*Archaic*), cushat, dove, squab 2. *Sl.* dupe, fall guy (*Inf.*), gull (*Archaic*), mug (*Sl.*), sitting duck, sucker (*Sl.*), victim 3. *Brit. inf.*

baby (*Sl.*), business, concern, lookout (*Inf.*), responsibility, worry

pigeonhole *n.* 1. compartment, cubbyhole, cubicle, locker, niche, place, section 2. *Inf.* category, class, classification, slot (*Inf.*) ~*v.* 3. defer, file, postpone, put off, shelve 4. catalogue, characterize, classify, codify, compartmentalize, label, slot (*Inf.*), sort

piggish 1. boorish, crude, gluttonous, greedy, hoggish, piggy, rude, swinish, voracious 2. *Inf.* hoggish, mean, obstinate, pig-headed, possessive, selfish, stubborn

pig-headed bull-headed, contrary, cross-grained, dense, froward, inflexible, mulish, obstinate, perverse, self-willed, stiff-necked, stubborn, stupid, unyielding, wilful, wrong-headed

pigment colorant, colour, colouring, colouring matter, dye, dyestuff, paint, stain, tincture, tint

pile¹ *n.* 1. accumulation, assemblage, assortment, collection, heap, hoard, mass, mound, mountain, stack, stockpile 2. *Inf.* bomb (*Brit. sl.*), fortune, mint, money, packet (*Sl.*), pot, tidy sum (*Inf.*), wealth 3. *Often plural. Inf.* a lot, great deal, ocean, oodles (*Inf.*), quantity, stacks 4. building, edifice, erection, structure ~*v.* 5. accumulate, amass, assemble, collect, gather, heap, hoard, load up, mass, stack, store 6. charge, crowd, crush, flock, flood, jam, pack, rush, stream

pile² beam, column, foundation, pier, piling, pillar, post, support, upright

pile³ down, fibre, filament, fur, hair, nap, plush, shag, surface

piles haemorrhoids

pile-up accident, collision, crash, multiple collision, smash, smash-up (*Inf.*)

pilfer appropriate, embezzle, filch, knock off (*Sl.*), lift (*Inf.*), nick (*Brit. sl.*), pinch (*Inf.*), purloin, rifle, rob, snaffle (*Brit. inf.*), snitch (*Sl.*), steal, swipe (*Sl.*), take, thieve, walk off with

pilgrim crusader, hajji, palmer, traveller, wanderer, wayfarer

pilgrimage crusade, excursion, expedition, hajj, journey, mission, tour, trip

pill 1. bolus, capsule, pellet, pilule, tablet 2. **the pill** oral contraceptive 3. *Sl.* bore, drag (*Sl.*), nuisance, pain (*Inf.*), pain in the neck (*Inf.*), pest, trial

pillage *v.* 1. depredate (*Rare*), despoil,

freeboot, loot, maraud, plunder, raid, ransack, ravage, reive (*Dialect*), rifle, rob, sack, spoil (*Archaic*), spoliate, strip ~*n.* **2.** depredation, devastation, marauding, plunder, rapine, robbery, sack, spoliation **3.** booty, loot, plunder, spoils

pillar 1. column, pier, pilaster, piling, post, prop, shaft, stanchion, support, upright **2.** leader, leading light (*Inf.*), mainstay, rock, supporter, tower of strength, upholder, worthy

pillory *v.* brand, cast a slur on, denounce, expose to ridicule, heap *or* pour scorn on, hold up to shame, lash, show up, stigmatize

pilot 1. *n.* airman, aviator, captain, conductor, coxswain, director, flier, guide, helmsman, leader, navigator, steersman **2.** *v.* conduct, control, direct, drive, fly, guide, handle, lead, manage, navigate, operate, shepherd, steer **3.** *adj.* experimental, model, test, trial

pimp 1. *n.* bawd (*Archaic*), go-between, pander, panderer, procurer, white-slaver, whoremaster (*Archaic*) **2.** *v.* live off immoral earnings, procure, sell, solicit, tout

pimple boil, papule (*Pathol.*), plook (*Scot.*), pustule, spot, swelling

pin *v.* **1.** affix, attach, fasten, fix, join, secure **2.** fix, hold down, hold fast, immobilize, pinion, press, restrain

pinch *v.* **1.** compress, grasp, nip, press, squeeze, tweak **2.** chafe, confine, cramp, crush, hurt, pain **3.** afflict, be stingy, distress, economize, oppress, pinch pennies, press, scrimp, skimp, spare, stint **4.** *Inf.* filch, knock off (*Sl.*), lift (*Inf.*), nick (*Brit. sl.*), pilfer, purloin, rob, snaffle (*Brit. inf.*), snatch, snitch (*Sl.*), steal, swipe (*Sl.*) **5.** *Inf.* apprehend, arrest, bust (*Inf.*), collar (*Inf.*), do (*Sl.*), nab (*Inf.*), nick (*Brit. sl.*), pick up (*Sl.*), pull in (*Brit. sl.*), run in (*Sl.*), take into custody ~*n.* **6.** nip, squeeze, tweak **7.** bit, dash, jot, mite, small quantity, *soupçon*, speck, taste **8.** crisis, difficulty, emergency, exigency, hardship, necessity, oppression, pass, plight, predicament, pressure, strait, stress

pinchbeck 1. *n.* counterfeit, fake, imitation, paste, phoney (*Sl.*), sham **2.** *adj.* artificial, bogus, counterfeit, ersatz, fake, imitation, pseudo (*Inf.*), spurious

pinched careworn, drawn, gaunt, haggard, peaky, starved, thin, worn

pin down 1. compel, constrain, force,

make, press, pressurize **2.** designate, determine, home in on, identify, locate, name, pinpoint, specify **3.** bind, confine, constrain, fix, hold, hold down, immobilize, nail down, tie down

pine 1. *Often with* **for** ache, carry a torch for, covet, crave, desire, hanker, hunger for, long, lust after, sigh, thirst for, wish, yearn **2.** decay, decline, droop, dwindle, fade, flag, languish, peak, sicken, sink, waste, weaken, wilt, wither

pinion *v.* bind, chain, confine, fasten, fetter, immobilize, manacle, pin down, shackle, tie

pink¹ 1. *n.* acme, best, height, peak, perfection, summit **2.** *adj.* flesh, flushed, reddish, rose, roseate, rosy, salmon

pink² incise, notch, perforate, prick, punch, scallop, score

pinnacle 1. acme, apex, apogee, crest, crown, eminence, height, meridian, peak, summit, top, vertex, zenith **2.** belfry, cone, needle, obelisk, pyramid, spire, steeple

pinpoint define, distinguish, get a fix on, home in on, identify, locate, spot

pint ale, beer, jar (*Brit. inf.*), jug (*Brit. inf.*)

pint-size diminutive, little, midget, miniature, pocket, small, tiny, wee

pioneer *n.* **1.** colonist, colonizer, explorer, frontiersman, settler **2.** developer, founder, founding father, innovator, leader, trailblazer ~*v.* **3.** create, develop, discover, establish, initiate, instigate, institute, invent, launch, lay the groundwork, map out, open up, originate, prepare, show the way, start, take the lead

pious 1. dedicated, devoted, devout, God-fearing, godly, holy, religious, reverent, righteous, saintly, spiritual **2.** goody-goody, holier-than-thou, hypocritical, pietistic, religiose, sanctimonious, self-righteous, unctuous

pipe *n.* **1.** conduit, conveyor, duct, hose, line, main, passage, pipeline, tube **2.** briar, clay, meerschaum **3.** fife, horn, tooter, whistle, wind instrument ~*v.* **4.** cheep, peep, play, sing, sound, tootle, trill, tweet, twitter, warble, whistle **5.** bring in, channel, conduct, convey, siphon, supply, transmit

pipe down belt up (*Sl.*), be quiet, hold one's tongue, hush, quieten down, shush, shut one's mouth, shut up (*Inf.*), silence

pipe dream castle in the air, chimera,

daydream, delusion, dream, fantasy, notion, reverie, vagary

pipeline 1. conduit, conveyor, duct, line, passage, pipe, tube **2. in the pipeline** brewing, coming, getting ready, in process, in production, on the way, under way

pipe up have one's say, make oneself heard, put one's oar in, raise one's voice, speak, speak up, volunteer

pipsqueak creep (*Sl.*), nobody, nonentity, nothing (*Inf.*), squirt (*Inf.*), upstart, whippersnapper

piquancy 1. bite (*Inf.*), edge, flavour, kick (*Inf.*), pungency, relish, sharpness, spice, spiciness, tang, zest **2.** colour, excitement, interest, pep, pizazz (*Sl.*), raciness, spirit, vigour, vitality, zip (*Inf.*)

piquant 1. biting, highly-seasoned, peppery, pungent, savoury, sharp, spicy, stinging, tangy, tart, with a kick (*Inf.*), zesty **2.** interesting, lively, provocative, racy, salty, scintillating, sparkling, spirited, stimulating

pique *n.* **1.** annoyance, displeasure, grudge, huff, hurt feelings, irritation, miff (*Inf.*), offence, resentment, umbrage, vexation, wounded pride ~*v.* **2.** affront, annoy, displease, gall, get (*Inf.*), incense, irk, irritate, miff (*Inf.*), mortify, nettle, offend, peeve (*Inf.*), provoke, put out, put someone's nose out of joint (*Inf.*), rile, sting, vex, wound **3.** arouse, excite, galvanize, goad, kindle, provoke, rouse, spur, stimulate, stir, whet **4.** *With* **on** *or* **upon** *Of oneself* congratulate, flatter, plume, preen, pride

piracy buccaneering, freebooting, hijacking, infringement, plagiarism, rapine, robbery at sea, stealing, theft

pirate *n.* **1.** buccaneer, corsair, filibuster, freebooter, marauder, raider, rover, sea robber, sea rover, sea wolf **2.** cribber (*Inf.*), infringer, plagiarist, plagiarizer ~*v.* **3.** appropriate, borrow, copy, crib (*Inf.*), lift (*Inf.*), plagiarize, poach, reproduce, steal

piratical buccaneering, criminal, dishonest, felonious, fraudulent, lawless, pillaging, plundering, rapacious, thieving, unprincipled, wolfish

pirouette *n./v.* pivot, spin, turn, twirl, whirl

pit *n.* **1.** abyss, cavity, chasm, coal mine, crater, dent, depression, dimple, excavation, gulf, hole, hollow, indentation, mine, pockmark, pothole, trench ~*v.* **2.** *Often with* **against** match, oppose, put in opposition, set against **3.** dent, dint, gouge, hole, indent, mark, nick, notch, pockmark, scar

pitch *v.* **1.** bung (*Brit. sl.*), cast, chuck (*Inf.*), fling, heave, hurl, launch, lob (*Inf.*), sling, throw, toss **2.** erect, fix, locate, place, plant, put up, raise, settle, set up, station **3.** flounder, lurch, make heavy weather, plunge, roll, toss, wallow, welter **4.** dive, drop, fall headlong, stagger, topple, tumble ~*n.* **5.** angle, cant, dip, gradient, incline, slope, steepness, tilt **6.** degree, height, highest point, level, point, summit **7.** harmonic, modulation, sound, timbre, tone **8.** line, patter, sales talk, spiel (*Inf.*) **9.** field of play, ground, park (*Brit. inf.*), sports field

pitch-black dark, ebony, inky, jet, jet-black, pitch-dark, raven, sable, unlit

pitch-dark black, dark, pitch-black, pitchy, Stygian, unilluminated, unlit

pitch in 1. chip in (*Inf.*), contribute, cooperate, do one's bit, help, join in, lend a hand, participate **2.** begin, fall to, get busy, get cracking (*Inf.*), plunge into, set about, set to, tackle

pitch into assail, assault, attack, get stuck into (*Inf.*), lace into, light into (*Inf.*), sail into (*Inf.*), tear into (*Inf.*)

pitch on *or* **upon** choose, decide on, determine, elect, light on, opt for, pick, plump for, select, single out

pitchy black, coal-black, dark, ebony, inky, jet, jetty, moonless, pitch-black, raven, sable, unilluminated, unlighted

piteous affecting, deplorable, distressing, doleful, grievous, heartbreaking, heart-rending, lamentable, miserable, mournful, moving, pathetic, pitiable, pitiful, plaintive, poignant, sad, sorrowful, woeful, wretched

pitfall 1. catch, danger, difficulty, drawback, hazard, peril, snag, trap **2.** deadfall, downfall, pit, snare, trap

pith 1. core, crux, essence, gist, heart, heart of the matter, kernel, marrow, meat, nub, point, quintessence, salient point, the long and the short of it **2.** consequence, depth, force, import, importance, matter, moment, power, significance, strength, substance, value, weight

pithy brief, cogent, compact, concise, epigrammatic, expressive, finely honed, forceful, laconic, meaningful, pointed, short, succinct, terse, to the point, trenchant

pitiable deplorable, distressing, doleful, grievous, lamentable, miserable, mournful, pathetic, piteous, poor, sad, sorry, woeful, wretched

pitiful 1. deplorable, distressing, grievous, heartbreaking, heart-rending, lamentable, miserable, pathetic, piteous, pitiable, sad, woeful, wretched **2.** abject, base, beggarly, contemptible, despicable, inadequate, insignificant, low, mean, miserable, paltry, scurvy, shabby, sorry, vile, worthless

pitiless brutal, callous, cold-blooded, cold-hearted, cruel, hardhearted, harsh, heartless, implacable, inexorable, inhuman, merciless, relentless, ruthless, uncaring, unfeeling, unmerciful, unsympathetic

pittance allowance, chicken feed (*Sl.*), drop, mite, modicum, peanuts (*Sl.*), portion, ration, slave wages, trifle

pitted blemished, dented, eaten away, holey, indented, marked, pockmarked, pocky, potholed, riddled, rough, rutty, scarred, scratched

pity *n.* **1.** charity, clemency, commiseration, compassion, condolence, fellow feeling, forbearance, kindness, mercy, sympathy, tenderness, understanding **2.** crime (*Inf.*), crying shame, misfortune, regret, sad thing, shame, sin **3. take pity on** feel compassion for, forgive, have mercy on, melt, pardon, put out of one's misery, relent, reprieve, show mercy, spare ~*v.* **4.** bleed for, commiserate with, condole with, feel for, feel sorry for, grieve for, have compassion for, sympathize with, weep for

pivot *n.* **1.** axis, axle, fulcrum, spindle, swivel **2.** centre, focal point, heart, hinge, hub, kingpin ~*v.* **3.** revolve, rotate, spin, swivel, turn, twirl **4.** be contingent, depend, hang, hinge, rely, revolve round, turn

pivotal central, climactic, critical, crucial, decisive, determining, focal, vital

pixie brownie, elf, fairy, sprite

placard advertisement, *affiche*, bill, poster, public notice, sticker

placate appease, assuage, calm, conciliate, humour, mollify, pacify, propitiate, satisfy, soothe, win over

placatory appeasing, conciliatory, designed to please, pacificatory, peacemaking, propitiative

place *n.* **1.** area, location, locus, point, position, site, situation, spot, station, venue, whereabouts **2.** city, district, hamlet, locale, locality, neighbourhood, quarter, region, town, vicinity, village **3.** grade, position, rank, station, status **4.** appointment, berth (*Inf.*), billet (*Inf.*), employment, job, position, post **5.** abode, apartment, domicile, dwelling, flat, home, house, manor, mansion, pad (*Sl.*), property, residence, seat **6.** accommodation, room, space, stead **7.** affair, charge, concern, duty, function, prerogative, responsibility, right, role **8. in place of** as an alternative to, as a substitute for, in exchange for, in lieu of, instead of, taking the place of **9. put (someone) in his place** bring down, cut down to size, humble, humiliate, make (someone) eat humble pie, make (someone) swallow his pride, mortify, take down a peg (*Inf.*) **10. take place** befall, betide, come about, come to pass (*Archaic*), go on, happen, occur, transpire (*Inf.*) ~*v.* **11.** bung (*Inf.*), deposit, dispose, establish, fix, install, lay, locate, plant, position, put, rest, set, settle, situate, stand, station, stick (*Inf.*) **12.** arrange, class, classify, grade, group, order, rank, sort **13.** associate, identify, know, put one's finger on, recognize, remember, set in context **14.** allocate, appoint, assign, charge, commission, entrust, give

placement 1. arrangement, deployment, disposition, distribution, emplacement, installation, locating, location, ordering, positioning, stationing **2.** appointment, assignment, employment, engagement

placid calm, collected, composed, cool, equable, even, even-tempered, gentle, halcyon, imperturbable, mild, peaceful, quiet, self-possessed, serene, still, tranquil, undisturbed, unexcitable, unmoved, unruffled, untroubled

plagiarism appropriation, borrowing, copying, cribbing (*Inf.*), infringement, lifting (*Inf.*), piracy, theft

plagiarize appropriate, borrow, crib (*Inf.*), infringe, lift (*Inf.*), pirate, steal, thieve

plague *n.* **1.** contagion, disease, epidemic, infection, pandemic, pestilence **2.** *Fig.* affliction, bane, blight, calamity, cancer, curse, evil, scourge, torment, trial **3.** *Inf.* aggravation (*Inf.*), annoyance, bother, irritant, nuisance, pain (*Inf.*), pest, problem, thorn in one's flesh, vexation ~*v.* **4.** afflict, annoy, badger, bedevil, bother, disturb, fret, harass, harry, hassle (*Inf.*), haunt, molest, pain, persecute, pester, tease, torment, torture, trouble, vex

plaguy annoying, disagreeable, harassing, impossible, irksome, irritating, provoking, troublesome, trying, vexing, wretched

plain *adj.* **1.** apparent, clear, comprehensible, distinct, evident, legible, lucid, manifest, obvious, patent, transparent, unambiguous, understandable, unmistakable, visible **2.** artless, blunt, candid, direct, downright, forthright, frank, guileless, honest, ingenuous, open, outspoken, sincere, straightforward **3.** common, commonplace, everyday, frugal, homely, lowly, modest, ordinary, simple, unaffected, unpretentious, workaday **4.** austere, bare, basic, discreet, modest, muted, pure, restrained, severe, simple, Spartan, stark, unadorned, unembellished, unornamented, unpatterned, unvarnished **5.** ill-favoured, not beautiful, not striking, ordinary, ugly, unalluring, unattractive, unlovely, unprepossessing **6.** even, flat, level, plane, smooth ~*n.* **7.** flatland, grassland, lowland, open country, plateau, prairie, steppe, tableland

plain-spoken blunt, candid, direct, downright, explicit, forthright, frank, open, outright, outspoken, straightforward, unequivocal

plaintive disconsolate, doleful, grief-stricken, grievous, heart-rending, melancholy, mournful, pathetic, piteous, pitiful, rueful, sad, sorrowful, wistful, woebegone, woeful

plan *n.* **1.** contrivance, design, device, idea, method, plot, procedure, programme, project, proposal, proposition, scenario, scheme, strategy, suggestion, system **2.** blueprint, chart, delineation, diagram, drawing, illustration, layout, map, representation, scale drawing, sketch ~*v.* **3.** arrange, concoct, contrive, design, devise, draft, formulate, frame, invent, organize, outline, plot, prepare, represent, scheme, think out **4.** aim, contemplate, envisage, foresee, intend, mean, propose, purpose

plane *n.* **1.** flat surface, level surface **2.** condition, degree, footing, level, position, stratum **3.** aeroplane, aircraft, jet ~*adj.* **4.** even, flat, flush, horizontal, level, plain, regular, smooth, uniform ~*v.* **5.** glide, sail, skate, skim, volplane

planetary 1. earthly, mundane, sublunary, tellurian, terrene, terrestrial **2.** aberrant, erratic, journeying, moving, travelling, vacillating, variable, wandering

plangent clangorous, deep-toned, loud, mournful, plaintive, resonant, resounding, reverberating, ringing, sonorous

plant *n.* **1.** bush, flower, herb, shrub, vegetable, weed **2.** factory, foundry, mill, shop, works, yard **3.** apparatus, equipment, gear, machinery ~*v.* **4.** implant, put in the ground, scatter, seed, set out, sow, transplant **5.** establish, fix, found, imbed, insert, institute, lodge, root, set, settle

plaque badge, brooch, cartouche, medal, medallion, panel, plate, slab, tablet

plaster *n.* **1.** gypsum, mortar, plaster of Paris, stucco **2.** adhesive plaster, bandage, dressing, Elastoplast (*Trademark*), sticking plaster ~*v.* **3.** bedaub, besmear, coat, cover, daub, overlay, smear, spread

plastic *adj.* **1.** compliant, docile, easily influenced, impressionable, malleable, manageable, pliable, receptive, responsive, tractable **2.** ductile, fictile, flexible, mouldable, pliable, pliant, soft, supple **3.** *Sl.* artificial, false, meretricious, phoney (*Inf.*), pseudo (*Inf.*), sham, specious, spurious, superficial, synthetic

plasticity flexibility, malleability, pliability, pliableness, suppleness, tractability

plate *n.* **1.** dish, platter, trencher (*Archaic*) **2.** course, dish, helping, portion, serving **3.** layer, panel, sheet, slab **4.** illustration, lithograph, print ~*v.* **5.** anodize, coat, cover, electroplate, face, gild, laminate, nickel, overlay, platinize, silver

plateau 1. highland, mesa, table, tableland, upland **2.** level, levelling off, stability, stage

platform 1. dais, podium, rostrum, stage, stand **2.** manifesto, objective(s), party line, policy, principle, programme, tenet(s)

platitude 1. banality, bromide, cliché, commonplace, hackneyed saying, inanity, stereotype, trite remark, truism **2.** banality, dullness, inanity, insipidity, triteness, triviality, vapidity, verbiage

platitudinous banal, clichéd, commonplace, corny (*Sl.*), hack, hackneyed, overworked, set, stale, stereotyped, stock, tired, trite, truistic, vapid, well-worn

platonic *All of love* ideal, idealistic, intellectual, nonphysical, spiritual, transcendent

platoon company, group, outfit (*Inf.*), patrol, squad, squadron, team

platter charger, dish, plate, salver, tray, trencher (*Archaic*)

plaudit *Usually plural* acclaim, acclamation, applause, approbation, approval, clapping, commendation, congratulation, hand, kudos, ovation, praise, round of applause

plausible believable, colourable, conceivable, credible, fair-spoken, glib, likely, persuasive, possible, probable, reasonable, smooth, smooth-talking, smooth-tongued, specious, tenable

play *v.* 1. amuse oneself, caper, engage in games, entertain oneself, frisk, frolic, gambol, have fun, revel, romp, sport, trifle 2. be in a team, challenge, compete, contend against, participate, rival, take on, take part, vie with 3. act, act the part of, execute, impersonate, perform, personate, portray, represent, take the part of 4. bet, chance, gamble, hazard, punt (*Brit.*), risk, speculate, take, wager 5. **play ball** *Inf.* collaborate, cooperate, go along, play along, reciprocate, respond, show willing 6. **play by ear** ad lib, extemporize, improvise, rise to the occasion, take it as it comes 7. **play for time** delay, drag one's feet (*Inf.*), filibuster, hang fire, procrastinate, stall, temporize 8. **play the fool** act the goat (*Inf.*), clown, clown around, horse around (*Inf.*), lark (about) (*Inf.*), mess about, monkey around, skylark (*Inf.*) 9. **play the game** *Inf.* conform, follow the rules, go along with, keep in step, play by the rules, play fair, toe the line ~*n.* 10. comedy, drama, dramatic piece, entertainment, farce, masque, performance, piece, radio play, show, stage show, television drama, tragedy 11. amusement, caper, diversion, entertainment, frolic, fun, gambol, game, jest, pastime, prank, recreation, romp, sport 12. gambling, gaming 13. action, activity, elbowroom, exercise, give (*Inf.*), latitude, leeway, margin, motion, movement, operation, range, room, scope, space, sweep, swing 14. action, activity, employment, function, operation, transaction, working 15. foolery, fun, hu-

mour, jest, joking, lark (*Inf.*), prank, sport, teasing

play around dally, fool around, mess around, philander, take lightly, trifle, womanize

playboy gay dog, ladies' man, ladykiller (*Inf.*), lover boy (*Sl.*), man about town, philanderer, pleasure seeker, rake, roué, socialite, womanizer

play down gloss over, make light of, make little of, minimize, set no store by, soft-pedal (*Inf.*), underplay, underrate

player 1. competitor, contestant, participant, sportsman, sportswoman, team member 2. actor, actress, entertainer, performer, Thespian, trouper 3. artist, instrumentalist, musician, music maker, performer, virtuoso

playful 1. cheerful, coltish, frisky, frolicsome, gay, impish, joyous, kittenish, larkish (*Inf.*), lively, merry, mischievous, puckish, rollicking, spirited, sportive, sprightly, vivacious 2. arch, coy, flirtatious, good-natured, humorous, jesting, jokey, joking, roguish, teasing, tongue-in-cheek, waggish

playmate chum (*Inf.*), companion, comrade, friend, neighbour, pal (*Inf.*), playfellow

play on *or* **upon** abuse, capitalize on, exploit, impose on, milk, profit by, take advantage of, trade on, turn to account, utilize

plaything amusement, bauble, game, gewgaw, gimcrack, pastime, toy, trifle, trinket

play up 1. accentuate, bring to the fore, call attention to, emphasize, highlight, magnify, point up, stress, turn the spotlight on, underline 2. *Brit. inf.* be painful, be sore, bother, give one gyp (*Brit. sl.*), give one trouble, hurt, pain, trouble 3. *Brit. inf.* be awkward, be bolshie (*Brit. inf.*), be cussed (*Inf.*), be disobedient, be stroppy (*Brit. sl.*), give trouble, misbehave 4. *Brit. inf.* be on the blink (*Sl.*), be wonky (*Brit. sl.*), malfunction, not work properly 5. **play up to** *Inf.* bootlick (*Inf.*), butter up, curry favour, fawn, flatter, get in with, ingratiate oneself, suck up to (*Inf.*), toady

play with 1. amuse oneself with, flirt with, string along, toy with, trifle with 2. fiddle with, fidget with, fool around, interfere with, jiggle, mess about, waggle, wiggle

playwright dramatist, dramaturge, dramaturgist

plea 1. appeal, begging, entreaty, intercession, overture, petition, prayer, request, suit, supplication **2.** *Law* action, allegation, cause, suit **3.** apology, claim, defence, excuse, explanation, extenuation, justification, pretext, vindication

plead 1. appeal (to), ask, beg, beseech, crave, entreat, implore, importune, petition, request, solicit, supplicate **2.** adduce, allege, argue, assert, maintain, put forward, use as an excuse

pleasant 1. acceptable, agreeable, amusing, delectable, delightful, enjoyable, fine, gratifying, lovely, nice, pleasing, pleasurable, refreshing, satisfying, welcome **2.** affable, agreeable, amiable, charming, cheerful, cheery, congenial, engaging, friendly, genial, good-humoured, likable, nice

pleasantry badinage, banter, bon mot, good-natured remark, jest, joke, quip, sally, witticism

please 1. amuse, charm, cheer, content, delight, entertain, give pleasure to, gladden, gratify, humour, indulge, rejoice, satisfy, suit, tickle, tickle pink **2.** be inclined, choose, desire, like, opt, prefer, see fit, want, will, wish

pleased chuffed (*Brit. sl.*), contented, delighted, euphoric, glad, gratified, happy, in high spirits, over the moon (*Inf.*), pleased as punch (*Inf.*), satisfied, thrilled, tickled, tickled pink

pleasing agreeable, amiable, amusing, attractive, charming, delightful, engaging, enjoyable, entertaining, gratifying, likable, pleasurable, polite, satisfying, winning

pleasurable agreeable, congenial, delightful, diverting, enjoyable, entertaining, fun, good, gratifying, lovely, nice, pleasant, welcome

pleasure 1. amusement, bliss, comfort, contentment, delectation, delight, diversion, ease, enjoyment, gladness, gratification, happiness, joy, recreation, satisfaction, solace **2.** choice, command, desire, inclination, mind, option, preference, purpose, will, wish

plebeian 1. *adj.* base, coarse, common, ignoble, low, lowborn, lower-class, mean, non-U (*Brit. inf.*), proletarian, uncultivated, unrefined, vulgar, working-class **2.** *n.* commoner, common man, man in the street, peasant, pleb (*Brit. sl.*), prole (*Sl.*), proletarian

plebiscite ballot, poll, referendum, vote

pledge *n.* **1.** assurance, covenant, oath, promise, undertaking, vow, warrant, word, word of honour **2.** bail, bond, collateral, deposit, earnest, gage, guarantee, pawn, security, surety **3.** health, toast ~*v.* **4.** contract, engage, give one's oath (word, word of honour), promise, swear, undertake, vouch, vow **5.** bind, engage, gage (*Archaic*), guarantee, mortgage, plight **6.** drink the health of, drink to, toast

plenary 1. absolute, complete, full, sweeping, thorough, unconditional, unlimited, unqualified, unrestricted **2.** *Of assemblies, councils, etc.* complete, entire, full, general, open, whole

plenipotentiary ambassador, emissary, envoy, legate, minister

plenitude 1. abundance, bounty, copiousness, cornucopia, excess, plenteousness, plenty, plethora, profusion, wealth **2.** amplitude, completeness, fullness, repletion

plenteous 1. abundant, ample, bounteous (*Literary*), bountiful, copious, generous, inexhaustible, infinite, lavish, liberal, overflowing, plentiful, profuse **2.** bumper, fertile, fruitful, luxuriant, plentiful, productive, prolific

plentiful 1. abundant, ample, bounteous (*Literary*), bountiful, complete, copious, generous, inexhaustible, infinite, lavish, liberal, overflowing, plenteous, profuse **2.** bumper, fertile, fruitful, luxuriant, plenteous, productive, prolific

plenty 1. abundance, enough, fund, good deal, great deal, heap(s) (*Inf.*), lots (*Inf.*), mass, masses, mine, mountain(s), oodles (*Inf.*), pile(s) (*Inf.*), plethora, quantities, quantity, stack(s), store, sufficiency, volume **2.** abundance, affluence, copiousness, fertility, fruitfulness, luxury, opulence, plenitude, plenteousness, plentifulness, profusion, prosperity, wealth

pleonasm circuitousness, circumlocution, convolution, periphrasis, redundancy, repetition, tautology, verbiage, verbosity, wordiness

pleonastic circuitous, circumlocutory, convoluted, periphrastic, prolix, redundant, repetitious, superfluous, tautological, verbose, wordy

plethora excess, glut, overabundance, profusion, superabundance, superfluity, surfeit, surplus

pliability 1. bendability, ductility, elasticity, flexibility, malleability, mobility, plasticity, pliancy **2.** adaptability, amenability, compliance, docility, impressionableness, susceptibility, tractableness

pliable 1. bendable, bendy, ductile, flexible, limber, lithe, malleable, plastic, pliant, supple **2.** adaptable, compliant, docile, easily led, impressionable, influenceable, manageable, persuadable, pliant, receptive, responsive, susceptible, tractable, yielding

pliant 1. bendable, bendy, ductile, flexible, lithe, plastic, pliable, supple **2.** adaptable, biddable, compliant, easily led, impressionable, influenceable, manageable, persuadable, pliable, susceptible, tractable, yielding

plight[1] *n.* case, circumstances, condition, difficulty, dilemma, extremity, hole (*Sl.*), jam (*Inf.*), perplexity, pickle (*Inf.*), predicament, scrape (*Inf.*), situation, spot (*Inf.*), state, straits, trouble

plight[2] *v.* contract, covenant, engage, guarantee, pledge, promise, propose, swear, vouch, vow

plod 1. clump, drag, lumber, slog, stomp (*Inf.*), tramp, tread, trudge **2.** drudge, grind (*Inf.*), grub, labour, peg away, persevere, plough through, plug away (*Inf.*), slog, soldier on, toil

plot[1] *n.* **1.** cabal, conspiracy, covin (*Law*), intrigue, machination, plan, scheme, stratagem **2.** action, narrative, outline, scenario, story, story line, subject, theme, thread ~*v.* **3.** cabal, collude, conspire, contrive, hatch, intrigue, machinate, manoeuvre, plan, scheme **4.** calculate, chart, compute, draft, draw, locate, map, mark, outline **5.** brew, conceive, concoct, contrive, cook up (*Inf.*), design, devise, frame, hatch, imagine, lay, project

plot[2] *n.* allotment, area, ground, lot, parcel, patch, tract

plough *v.* **1.** break ground, cultivate, dig, furrow, ridge, till, turn over **2.** *Usually with* **through** cut, drive, flounder, forge, plod, plunge, press, push, stagger, surge, wade **3.** *With* **into** bulldoze, career, crash, hurtle, plunge, shove, smash

ploy contrivance, device, dodge, gambit, game, manoeuvre, move, ruse,

scheme, stratagem, subterfuge, tactic, trick, wile

pluck[1] *n.* backbone, boldness, bottle (*Brit. sl.*), bravery, courage, determination, grit, guts (*Inf.*), hardihood, heart, intrepidity, mettle, nerve, resolution, spirit, spunk (*Inf.*)

pluck[2] *v.* **1.** collect, draw, gather, harvest, pick, pull out *or* off **2.** catch, clutch, jerk, pull at, snatch, tug, tweak, yank **3.** finger, pick, plunk, strum, thrum, twang

plucky bold, brave, courageous, daring, doughty, game, gritty, gutsy (*Sl.*), hardy, heroic, intrepid, mettlesome, spirited, spunky (*Inf.*), undaunted, unflinching, valiant

plug *n.* **1.** bung, cork, spigot, stopper, stopple **2.** cake, chew, pigtail, quid, twist, wad **3.** *Inf.* advert (*Brit. inf.*), advertisement, good word, hype (*Sl.*), mention, publicity, puff, push ~*v.* **4.** block, bung, choke, close, cork, cover, fill, pack, seal, stop, stopper, stopple, stop up, stuff **5.** *Inf.* advertise, build up, hype (*Sl.*), mention, promote, publicize, puff, push, write up **6.** *Sl.* gun down, pick off, pop, pot, put a bullet in, shoot **7.** *With* **along** *or* **away** *Inf.* drudge, grind (*Inf.*), labour, peg away, plod, slog, toil

plum *Fig.* **1.** *n.* bonus, cream, find, pick, prize, treasure **2.** *adj.* best, choice, first-class, prize

plumb *n.* **1.** lead, plumb bob, plummet, weight ~*adv.* **2.** perpendicularly, up and down, vertically **3.** bang, exactly, precisely, slap, spot-on (*Brit. inf.*) ~*v.* **4.** delve, explore, fathom, gauge, go into, measure, penetrate, probe, search, sound, unravel

plume 1. *n.* aigrette, crest, feather, pinion, quill **2.** *v. With* **on** *or* **upon** congratulate oneself, pat oneself on the back, pique oneself, preen oneself, pride oneself

plummet crash, descend, dive, drop down, fall, nose-dive, plunge, stoop, swoop, tumble

plump[1] *adj.* beefy (*Inf.*), burly, buxom, chubby, corpulent, dumpy, fat, fleshy, full, obese, podgy, portly, roly-poly, rotund, round, stout, tubby, well-covered, well-upholstered (*Inf.*)

plump[2] *v.* **1.** drop, dump, fall, flop, sink, slump **2.** *With* **for** back, choose, come down in favour of, favour, opt for, side with, support ~*adj.* **3.** abrupt, direct, downright, forthright, plain, unqualified, unreserved

plunder 1. *v.* despoil, devastate, loot, pillage, raid, ransack, ravage, rifle, rob, sack, spoil, steal, strip **2.** *n.* booty, ill-gotten gains, loot, pillage, prey, prize, rapine, spoils, swag (*Sl.*)

plunge *v.* **1.** cast, descend, dip, dive, douse, drop, fall, go down, immerse, jump, nose-dive, pitch, plummet, sink, submerge, swoop, throw, tumble **2.** career, charge, dash, hurtle, lurch, rush, tear ~*n.* **3.** descent, dive, drop, fall, immersion, jump, submersion, swoop

plurality 1. diversity, multiplicity, numerousness, profusion, variety **2.** bulk, majority, mass, most, nearly all, overwhelming number, preponderance

plus 1. *prep.* added to, and, coupled with, with, with the addition of **2.** *adj.* added, additional, extra, positive, supplementary **3.** *n. Inf.* advantage, asset, benefit, bonus, extra, gain, good point, perk (*Inf.*), surplus

plush costly, de luxe, lavish, luxurious, luxury, opulent, palatial, rich, ritzy (*Sl.*), sumptuous

plutocrat capitalist, Croesus, Dives, fat cat (*Sl.*), magnate, millionaire, moneybags (*Sl.*), rich man, tycoon

ply[1] **1.** carry on, exercise, follow, practise, pursue, work at **2.** employ, handle, manipulate, swing, utilize, wield **3.** assail, beset, besiege, bombard, harass, importune, press, urge

ply[2] fold, layer, leaf, sheet, strand, thickness

poach appropriate, encroach, hunt *or* fish illegally, infringe, intrude, plunder, rob, steal, steal game, trespass

pock blemish, flaw, mark, pimple, pockmark, pustule, scar, spot

pocket *n.* **1.** bag, compartment, hollow, pouch, receptacle, sack ~*adj.* **2.** abridged, compact, concise, little, miniature, pint-size(d) (*Inf.*), portable, potted (*Inf.*), small ~*v.* **3.** appropriate, filch, help oneself to, lift (*Inf.*), pilfer, purloin, snaffle (*Brit. inf.*), steal, take **4.** accept, bear, brook, endure, put up with (*Inf.*), stomach, swallow, take, tolerate

pockmark blemish, pit, pock, scar

pod *n./v.* hull, husk, shell, shuck

podgy chubby, chunky, dumpy, fat, fleshy, plump, roly-poly, rotund, short and fat, squat, stout, stubby, stumpy, tubby

podium dais, platform, rostrum, stage

poem lyric, ode, rhyme, song, sonnet, verse

poet bard, lyricist, maker (*Archaic*), rhymer, versifier

poetic elegiac, lyric, lyrical, metrical, rhythmical, songlike

poetry metrical composition, poems, poesy (*Archaic*), rhyme, rhyming, verse

po-faced disapproving, humourless, narrow-minded, prim, prudish, puritanical, solemn, stolid, strait-laced

poignancy 1. emotion, emotionalism, evocativeness, feeling, pathos, piteousness, plaintiveness, sadness, sentiment, tenderness **2.** bitterness, intensity, keenness, piquancy, pungency, sharpness

poignant 1. affecting, agonizing, bitter, distressing, heartbreaking, heart-rending, intense, moving, painful, pathetic, sad, touching, upsetting **2.** acute, biting, caustic, keen, penetrating, piercing, pointed, sarcastic, severe **3.** acrid, piquant, pungent, sharp, stinging, tangy

point *n.* **1.** dot, full stop, mark, period, speck, stop **2.** location, place, position, site, spot, stage, station **3.** apex, end, nib, prong, sharp end, spike, spur, summit, tine, tip, top **4.** bill, cape, foreland, head, headland, ness (*Archaic*), promontory **5.** circumstance, condition, degree, extent, position, stage **6.** instant, juncture, moment, time, very minute **7.** aim, design, end, goal, intent, intention, motive, object, objective, purpose, reason, use, usefulness, utility **8.** burden, core, crux, drift, essence, gist, heart, import, main idea, marrow, matter, meaning, nub, pith, proposition, question, subject, text, theme, thrust **9.** aspect, detail, facet, feature, instance, item, nicety, particular **10.** aspect, attribute, characteristic, peculiarity, property, quality, respect, side, trait **11.** score, tally, unit **12. beside the point** immaterial, incidental, inconsequential, irrelevant, not to the purpose, off the subject, out of the way, pointless, unimportant, without connection **13. to the point** applicable, appropriate, apropos, apt, brief, fitting, germane, pertinent, pithy, pointed, relevant, short, suitable, terse ~*v.* **14.** bespeak, call attention to, denote, designate, direct, indicate, show, signify **15.** aim, bring to bear, direct, level, train **16.** barb, edge, sharpen, taper, whet

point-blank 1. *adj.* abrupt, blunt,

categorical, direct, downright, explicit, express, plain, straight-from-the-shoulder, unreserved **2.** *adv.* bluntly, brusquely, candidly, directly, explicitly, forthrightly, frankly, openly, plainly, straight, straightforwardly

pointed 1. acicular, acuminate, acute, barbed, cuspidate, edged, mucronate, sharp **2.** accurate, acute, biting, cutting, incisive, keen, penetrating, pertinent, sharp, telling, trenchant

pointer 1. guide, hand, indicator, needle **2.** advice, caution, hint, information, recommendation, suggestion, tip, warning

pointless absurd, aimless, fruitless, futile, inane, ineffectual, irrelevant, meaningless, nonsensical, senseless, silly, stupid, unavailing, unproductive, unprofitable, useless, vague, vain, worthless

point of view 1. angle, orientation, outlook, perspective, position, standpoint **2.** approach, attitude, belief, judgment, opinion, slant, view, viewpoint, way of looking at it

point out allude to, bring up, call attention to, identify, indicate, mention, remind, reveal, show, specify

point up accent, accentuate, emphasize, make clear, stress, underline

poise 1. *n.* aplomb, assurance, calmness, composure, cool (*Sl.*), coolness, dignity, elegance, equanimity, equilibrium, grace, presence, presence of mind, sangfroid, savoir-faire, self-possession, serenity **2.** *v.* balance, float, hang, hang in midair, hang suspended, hold, hover, position, support, suspend

poised 1. calm, collected, composed, dignified, graceful, nonchalant, self-confident, self-possessed, serene, suave, together (*Inf.*), unruffled, urbane **2.** all set, in the wings, on the brink, prepared, ready, standing by, waiting

poison *n.* **1.** bane, toxin, venom **2.** bane, blight, cancer, canker, contagion, contamination, corruption, malignancy, miasma, virus ~*v.* **3.** adulterate, contaminate, envenom, give (someone) poison, infect, kill, murder, pollute **4.** corrupt, defile, deprave, pervert, subvert, taint, undermine, vitiate, warp ~*adj.* **5.** deadly, lethal, poisonous, toxic, venomous

poisonous 1. baneful (*Archaic*), deadly, fatal, lethal, mephitic, mortal, noxious, toxic, venomous, virulent **2.** baleful, baneful (*Archaic*), corruptive, evil, malicious, noxious, pernicious, pestiferous, pestilential, vicious

poke *v.* **1.** butt, dig, elbow, hit, jab, nudge, prod, punch, push, shove, stab, stick, thrust **2.** butt in, interfere, intrude, meddle, nose, peek, poke one's nose into (*Inf.*), pry, snoop (*Inf.*), tamper **3. poke fun at** chaff, jeer, make a mock of, make fun of, mock, rib (*Inf.*), ridicule, send up (*Brit. inf.*), take the mickey (*Inf.*), tease ~*n.* **4.** butt, dig, hit, jab, nudge, prod, punch, thrust

poky confined, cramped, incommodious, narrow, small, tiny

polar 1. Antarctic, Arctic, cold, extreme, freezing, frozen, furthest, glacial, icy, terminal **2.** beacon-like, cardinal, guiding, leading, pivotal **3.** antagonistic, antipodal, antithetical, contradictory, contrary, diametric, opposed, opposite

polarity ambivalence, contradiction, contrariety, dichotomy, duality, opposition, paradox

pole[1] bar, mast, post, rod, shaft, spar, staff, standard, stick

pole[2] **1.** antipode, extremity, limit, terminus **2. poles apart** at opposite ends of the earth, at opposite extremes, incompatible, irreconcilable, miles apart, widely separated, worlds apart

polemic 1. *n.* argument, controversy, debate, dispute **2.** *adj.* argumentative, contentious, controversial, disputatious, polemical

polemics argument, argumentation, contention, controversy, debate, disputation, dispute

police *n.* **1.** boys in blue (*Inf.*), constabulary, fuzz (*Sl.*), law enforcement agency, police force, the law (*Inf.*), the Old Bill (*Sl.*) ~*v.* **2.** control, guard, keep in order, keep the peace, patrol, protect, regulate, watch **3.** *Fig.* check, monitor, observe, oversee, supervise

policeman bobby (*Inf.*), bogey (*Sl.*), constable, cop (*Sl.*), copper (*Sl.*), fuzz (*Sl.*), gendarme (*Sl.*), officer, peeler (*Obsolete Brit. sl.*), pig (*Sl.*), rozzer (*Sl.*)

policy 1. action, approach, code, course, custom, guideline, line, plan, practice, procedure, programme, protocol, rule, scheme, stratagem, theory **2.** discretion, good sense, prudence, sagacity, shrewdness, wisdom

polish *v.* **1.** brighten, buff, burnish, clean, furbish, rub, shine, smooth, wax **2.**

brush up, correct, cultivate, emend, enhance, finish, improve, perfect, refine, touch up ~n. **3**. brightness, brilliance, finish, glaze, gloss, lustre, sheen, smoothness, sparkle, veneer **4**. varnish, wax **5**. *Fig.* class (*Inf.*), elegance, finesse, finish, grace, politesse, refinement, style, suavity, urbanity

polished 1. bright, burnished, furbished, glassy, gleaming, glossy, shining, slippery, smooth **2**. *Fig.* accomplished, civilized, courtly, cultivated, elegant, finished, genteel, polite, refined, sophisticated, urbane, well-bred **3**. adept, expert, faultless, fine, flawless, impeccable, masterly, outstanding, professional, skilful, superlative

polish off 1. consume, down, eat up, finish, put away, shift (*Inf.*), swill, wolf **2**. bump off (*Inf.*), dispose of, do away with, do in (*Sl.*), eliminate, get rid of, kill, liquidate, murder

polite 1. affable, civil, complaisant, courteous, deferential, gracious, mannerly, obliging, respectful, well-behaved, well-mannered **2**. civilized, courtly, cultured, elegant, genteel, polished, refined, urbane, well-bred

politic 1. artful, astute, canny, crafty, cunning, designing, ingenious, intriguing, Machiavellian, scheming, shrewd, sly, subtle, unscrupulous **2**. advisable, diplomatic, discreet, expedient, in one's best interests, judicious, prudent, sagacious, sensible, tactful, wise

politician legislator, Member of Parliament, M.P., office bearer, politico (*Inf., chiefly U.S.*), public servant, statesman

politics 1. affairs of state, civics, government, government policy, political science, polity, statecraft, statesmanship **2**. Machiavellianism, machination, power struggle, *Realpolitik*

poll *n.* **1**. figures, returns, tally, vote, voting **2**. ballot, canvass, census, count, Gallup Poll, (public) opinion poll, sampling, survey ~*v.* **3**. register, tally **4**. ballot, canvass, interview, question, sample, survey

pollute 1. adulterate, befoul, contaminate, dirty, foul, infect, make filthy, mar, poison, soil, spoil, stain, taint **2**. besmirch, corrupt, debase, debauch, defile, deprave, desecrate, dishonour, profane, sully, violate

pollution adulteration, contamination, corruption, defilement, dirtying, foulness, impurity, taint, uncleanness, vitiation

poltroon caitiff (*Archaic*), chicken (*Sl.*), coward, craven, cur, dastard (*Archaic*), recreant (*Archaic*), skunk (*Inf.*), yellow-belly (*Sl.*)

polychromatic many-coloured, many-hued, multicoloured, of all the colours of the rainbow, polychrome, rainbow, varicoloured, variegated

pomp 1. ceremony, flourish, grandeur, magnificence, pageant, pageantry, parade, solemnity, splendour, state **2**. display, grandiosity, ostentation, pomposity, show, vainglory

pomposity 1. affectation, airs, arrogance, flaunting, grandiosity, haughtiness, pompousness, portentousness, presumption, pretension, pretentiousness, self-importance, vainglory, vanity **2**. bombast, fustian, grandiloquence, loftiness, magniloquence, rant, turgidity

pompous 1. affected, arrogant, bloated, grandiose, imperious, magisterial, ostentatious, overbearing, pontifical, portentous, pretentious, puffed up, self-important, showy, supercilious, vainglorious **2**. boastful, bombastic, flatulent, fustian, grandiloquent, high-flown, inflated, magniloquent, orotund, overblown, turgid, windy

pond dew pond, duck pond, fish pond, lochan (*Scot.*), millpond, pool, small lake, tarn

ponder brood, cerebrate, cogitate, consider, contemplate, deliberate, examine, excogitate, give thought to, meditate, mull over, muse, puzzle over, reflect, ruminate, study, think, weigh

ponderous 1. bulky, cumbersome, cumbrous, heavy, hefty, huge, massive, unwieldy, weighty **2**. awkward, clumsy, elephantine, graceless, heavy-footed, laborious, lumbering **3**. dreary, dull, heavy, laboured, lifeless, long-winded, pedantic, pedestrian, plodding, prolix, stilted, stodgy, tedious, verbose

poniard bodkin (*Archaic*), dagger, dirk, misericord (*Archaic*), stiletto

pontifical 1. apostolic, ecclesiastical, papal, prelatic **2**. bloated, condescending, dogmatic, imperious, magisterial, overbearing, pompous, portentous, pretentious, self-important

pontificate declaim, dogmatize, expound, hold forth, lay down the law, pontify, preach, pronounce, sound off

pooh-pooh belittle, brush aside, deride, disdain, dismiss, disregard, make little of, play down, scoff, scorn, slight, sneer, sniff at, spurn, turn up one's nose at (*Inf.*)

pool[1] 1. lake, mere, pond, puddle, splash, tarn 2. swimming bath, swimming pool

pool[2] *n.* 1. collective, combine, consortium, group, syndicate, team, trust 2. bank, funds, jackpot, kitty, pot, stakes ~*v.* 3. amalgamate, combine, join forces, league, merge, put together, share

poor 1. badly off, broke (*Inf.*), destitute, hard up (*Inf.*), impecunious, impoverished, indigent, in need, in want, necessitous, needy, on one's beam-ends, on one's uppers, on the rocks, penniless, penurious, poverty-stricken, skint (*Brit. sl.*), stony-broke (*Brit. sl.*) 2. deficient, exiguous, inadequate, incomplete, insufficient, lacking, meagre, miserable, niggardly, pitiable, reduced, scanty, skimpy, slight, sparse, straitened 3. below par, faulty, feeble, inferior, lowgrade, mediocre, rotten (*Inf.*), rubbishy, second-rate, shabby, shoddy, sorry, substandard, unsatisfactory, valueless, weak, worthless 4. bad, bare, barren, depleted, exhausted, fruitless, impoverished, infertile, sterile, unfruitful, unproductive 5. hapless, ill-fated, luckless, miserable, pathetic, pitiable, unfortunate, unhappy, unlucky, wretched 6. humble, insignificant, lowly, mean, modest, paltry, plain, trivial

poorly 1. *adv.* badly, crudely, inadequately, incompetently, inexpertly, inferiorly, insufficiently, meanly, shabbily, unsatisfactorily, unsuccessfully 2. *adj. Inf.* ailing, below par, ill, indisposed, off colour, out of sorts, rotten (*Inf.*), seedy (*Inf.*), sick, under the weather (*Inf.*), unwell

pop *v.* 1. bang, burst, crack, explode, go off, report, snap 2. *Often with* **in, out,** *etc. Inf.* appear, call, come *or* go suddenly, drop in (*Inf.*), leave quickly, nip in (*Brit. inf.*), nip out (*Brit. inf.*), visit 3. *Esp. of eyes* bulge, protrude, stick out 4. insert, push, put, shove, slip, stick, thrust, tuck ~*n.* 5. bang, burst, crack, explosion, noise, report 6. *Inf.* fizzy drink, lemonade, soda water, soft drink

pope Bishop of Rome, Holy Father, pontiff, Vicar of Christ

popinjay buck (*Archaic*), coxcomb (*Archaic*), dandy, fop, jackanapes, peacock, swell (*Inf.*)

poppycock babble, balderdash, baloney (*Inf.*), bunk (*Inf.*), bunkum, drivel, gibberish, gobbledegook (*Inf.*), guff (*Sl.*), hooey (*Sl.*), nonsense, rot, rubbish, tommyrot, tosh (*Inf.*), trash, twaddle

populace commonalty, crowd, general public, hoi polloi, inhabitants, masses, mob, multitude, people, rabble, throng

popular 1. accepted, approved, celebrated, famous, fashionable, favoured, favourite, in, in demand, in favour, liked, sought-after, well-liked 2. common, conventional, current, general, prevailing, prevalent, public, standard, stock, ubiquitous, universal, widespread

popularity acceptance, acclaim, adoration, approval, celebrity, currency, esteem, fame, favour, idolization, lionization, recognition, regard, renown, reputation, repute, vogue

popularize disseminate, familiarize, give currency to, give mass appeal, make available to all, simplify, spread, universalize

popularly commonly, conventionally, customarily, generally, ordinarily, regularly, traditionally, universally, usually, widely

populate colonize, inhabit, live in, occupy, people, settle

population citizenry, community, denizens, folk, inhabitants, natives, people, populace, residents, society

populous crowded, heavily populated, overpopulated, packed, populated, swarming, teeming, thronged

pore[1] *v.* brood, contemplate, dwell on, examine, go over, peruse, ponder, read, scrutinize, study

pore[2] *n.* hole, opening, orifice, outlet, stoma

pornographic blue, dirty, filthy, indecent, lewd, obscene, offensive, prurient, salacious, smutty

pornography dirt, erotica, filth, indecency, obscenity, porn (*Inf.*), porno (*Inf.*), smut

porous absorbent, absorptive, penetrable, permeable, pervious, spongy

port *Nautical* anchorage, harbour, haven, roads, roadstead, seaport

portable compact, convenient, easily carried, handy, light, lightweight, manageable, movable, portative

portal door, doorway, entrance, entrance way, entry, gateway, way in

portend adumbrate, augur, bespeak, betoken, bode, foreshadow, foretell, foretoken, forewarn, harbinger, herald, indicate, omen, point to, predict, presage, prognosticate, promise, threaten, warn of

portent augury, foreboding, foreshadowing, forewarning, harbinger, indication, omen, premonition, presage, presentiment, prognostic, prognostication, sign, threat, warning

portentous 1. alarming, crucial, fateful, important, menacing, minatory, momentous, ominous, significant, sinister, threatening **2.** amazing, astounding, awe-inspiring, extraordinary, miraculous, phenomenal, prodigious, remarkable **3.** bloated, elephantine, heavy, pompous, ponderous, pontifical, self-important, solemn

porter [1] baggage attendant, bearer, carrier

porter [2] caretaker, concierge, doorman, gatekeeper, janitor

portion *n.* **1.** bit, fraction, fragment, morsel, part, piece, scrap, section, segment **2.** allocation, allotment, allowance, division, lot, measure, parcel, quantity, quota, ration, share **3.** helping, piece, serving **4.** cup, destiny, fate, fortune, lot, luck ~*v.* **5.** allocate, allot, apportion, assign, deal, distribute, divide, divvy up (*Inf.*), dole out, parcel out, partition, share out

portly ample, beefy (*Inf.*), bulky, burly, corpulent, fat, fleshy, heavy, large, obese, overweight, plump, rotund, stout, tubby (*Inf.*)

portrait 1. image, likeness, painting, photograph, picture, portraiture, representation, sketch **2.** account, characterization, depiction, description, portrayal, profile, thumbnail sketch, vignette

portray 1. delineate, depict, draw, figure, illustrate, limn, paint, picture, render, represent, sketch **2.** characterize, depict, describe, paint a mental picture of, put in words **3.** act the part of, play, represent

portrayal characterization, delineation, depiction, description, impersonation, interpretation, performance, picture, rendering, representation

pose *v.* **1.** arrange, model, position, sit, sit for **2.** *Often with* **as** feign, impersonate, masquerade as, pass oneself off as, pretend to be, profess to be, sham **3.** affect, attitudinize, posture, put on airs, show off (*Inf.*), strike an attitude **4.** advance, posit, present, propound, put, put forward, set, state, submit ~*n.* **5.** attitude, bearing, mien (*Literary*), position, posture, stance **6.** act, affectation, air, attitudinizing, façade, front, mannerism, masquerade, posturing, pretence, role

poser brain-teaser (*Inf.*), conundrum, enigma, knotty point, problem, puzzle, question, riddle, tough one, vexed question

poseur attitudinizer, exhibitionist, impostor, mannerist, masquerader, poser, posturer, self-publicist, show-off (*Inf.*)

posh classy (*Sl.*), elegant, exclusive, fashionable, grand, high-class, la-di-da (*Inf.*), luxurious, luxury, ritzy (*Sl.*), smart, stylish, swanky (*Inf.*), swish (*Inf.*), upper-class

posit advance, assert, assume, postulate, predicate, presume, propound, put forward, state, submit

position *n.* **1.** area, bearings, locale, locality, location, place, point, post, reference, site, situation, spot, station, whereabouts **2.** arrangement, attitude, disposition, pose, posture, stance **3.** angle, attitude, belief, opinion, outlook, point of view, slant, stance, stand, standpoint, view, viewpoint **4.** circumstances, condition, pass, plight, predicament, situation, state, strait(s) **5.** caste, class, consequence, importance, place, prestige, rank, reputation, standing, station, stature, status **6.** berth (*Inf.*), billet (*Inf.*), capacity, duty, employment, function, job, occupation, office, place, post, role, situation ~*v.* **7.** arrange, array, dispose, fix, lay out, locate, place, put, set, settle, stand, stick (*Inf.*)

positive 1. absolute, actual, affirmative, categorical, certain, clear, clear-cut, conclusive, concrete, decisive, definite, direct, explicit, express, firm, incontrovertible, indisputable, real, unequivocal, unmistakable **2.** assured, certain, confident, convinced, sure **3.** assertive, cocksure, decided, dogmatic, emphatic, firm, forceful, opinionated, peremptory, resolute, stubborn **4.** beneficial, constructive, effective, efficacious, forward-looking, helpful, practical, productive, progressive, useful **5.** *Inf.* absolute, complete, consummate, out-and-out, perfect, rank, thorough, thoroughgoing, unmitigated, utter

positively absolutely, assuredly, categorically, certainly, definitely, emphatically, firmly, surely, undeniably, unequivocally, unmistakably, unquestionably, with certainty, without qualification

possess 1. be blessed with, be born with, be endowed with, enjoy, have, have to one's name, hold, own **2.** acquire, control, dominate, hold, occupy, seize, take over, take possession of **3.** bewitch, consume, control, dominate, enchant, fixate, influence, mesmerize, obsess, put under a spell

possessed bedevilled, berserk, bewitched, consumed, crazed, cursed, demented, enchanted, frenetic, frenzied, hag-ridden, haunted, maddened, obsessed, raving, under a spell

possession 1. control, custody, hold, occupancy, occupation, ownership, proprietorship, tenure, title **2.** *Plural* assets, belongings, chattels, effects, estate, goods and chattels, property, things, wealth **3.** colony, dominion, protectorate, province, territory

possessive acquisitive, controlling, covetous, dominating, domineering, grasping, jealous, overprotective, selfish

possibility 1. feasibility, likelihood, plausibility, potentiality, practicability, workableness **2.** chance, hazard, hope, liability, likelihood, odds, probability, prospect, risk **3.** *Often plural* capabilities, potential, potentiality, promise, prospects, talent

possible 1. conceivable, credible, hypothetical, imaginable, likely, potential **2.** attainable, doable, feasible, on (*Inf.*), practicable, realizable, viable, within reach, workable **3.** hopeful, likely, potential, probable, promising

possibly 1. God willing, haply (*Archaic*), maybe, mayhap (*Archaic*), peradventure (*Archaic*), perchance (*Archaic*), perhaps **2.** at all, by any chance, by any means, in any way

post¹ 1. *n.* column, newel, pale, palisade, picket, pillar, pole, shaft, stake, standard, stock, support, upright **2.** *v.* advertise, affix, announce, display, make known, pin up, proclaim, promulgate, publicize, publish, put up, stick up

post² n. 1. appointment, assignment, berth (*Inf.*), billet (*Inf.*), employment,

job, office, place, position, situation **2.** beat, place, position, station ~*v.* **3.** assign, establish, locate, place, position, put, situate, station

post³ n. 1. collection, delivery, mail, postal service ~*v.* **2.** dispatch, mail, send, transmit **3.** advise, brief, fill in on, inform, notify, report to

poster advertisement, *affiche*, announcement, bill, notice, placard, public notice, sticker

posterior *adj.* **1.** after, back, behind, hind, hinder, rear **2.** ensuing, following, later, latter, subsequent

posterity 1. children, descendants, family, heirs, issue, offspring, progeny, scions, seed **2.** future, future generations, succeeding generations

posthaste at once, before one can say Jack Robinson, directly, double-quick, full tilt, hastily, promptly, pronto (*Inf.*), quickly, speedily, straightaway, swiftly

postmortem *n.* analysis, autopsy, dissection, examination, necropsy

postpone adjourn, defer, delay, hold over, put back, put off, shelve, suspend, table

postponement adjournment, deferment, deferral, delay, moratorium, respite, stay, suspension

postscript addition, afterthought, afterword, appendix, P.S., supplement

postulate advance, assume, hypothesize, posit, predicate, presuppose, propose, put forward, suppose, take for granted, theorize

posture *n.* **1.** attitude, bearing, carriage, disposition, mien (*Literary*), pose, position, set, stance **2.** circumstance, condition, mode, phase, position, situation, state **3.** attitude, disposition, feeling, frame of mind, inclination, mood, outlook, point of view, stance, standpoint ~*v.* **4.** affect, attitudinize, do for effect, make a show, pose, put on airs, show off (*Inf.*), try to attract attention

posy bouquet, boutonniere, buttonhole, corsage, nosegay, spray

potbellied bloated, corpulent, distended, fat, obese, overweight, paunchy

potbelly beer belly (*Inf.*), corporation (*Brit. inf.*), gut, paunch, pot, spare tyre (*Brit. sl.*)

potency authority, capacity, control, effectiveness, efficacy, energy, force, influence, might, muscle, potential, power, puissance, strength, sway, vigour

potent 1. efficacious, forceful, mighty, powerful, puissant, strong, vigorous 2. cogent, compelling, convincing, effective, forceful, impressive, persuasive, telling 3. authoritative, commanding, dominant, dynamic, influential, powerful

potentate emperor, king, mogul, monarch, overlord, prince, ruler, sovereign

potential 1. *adj.* budding, dormant, embryonic, future, hidden, inherent, latent, likely, possible, promising, undeveloped, unrealized 2. *n.* ability, aptitude, capability, capacity, possibility, potentiality, power, the makings, what it takes (*Inf.*), wherewithal

potentiality ability, aptitude, capability, capacity, likelihood, potential, promise, prospect, the makings

pother bother, carry-on (*Brit. inf.*), commotion, disturbance, flap (*Inf.*), fuss, hoo-ha, lather (*Inf.*), ruction (*Inf.*), stew (*Inf.*), tizzy (*Inf.*), to-do

potion brew, concoction, cup, dose, draught, elixir, mixture, philtre, tonic

potpourri collection, combination, gallimaufry, hotchpotch, medley, *mélange*, miscellany, mixture, motley, pastiche, patchwork, salmagundi

potter dabble, fiddle (*Inf.*), footle (*Inf.*), fribble, fritter, mess about, poke along, tinker

pottery ceramics, earthenware, stoneware, terra cotta

potty 1. barmy (*Sl.*), crackers (*Brit. sl.*), crazy, daft (*Inf.*), dippy (*Sl.*), dotty (*Sl.*), eccentric, foolish, off one's chump (*Sl.*), silly, soft (*Inf.*), touched 2. footling (*Inf.*), insignificant, petty, piddling (*Inf.*), trifling, trivial

pouch bag, container, pocket, poke (*Dialect*), purse, sack

pounce 1. *v.* ambush, attack, bound onto, dash at, drop, fall upon, jump, leap at, snatch, spring, strike, swoop, take by surprise, take unawares 2. *n.* assault, attack, bound, jump, leap, spring, swoop

pound[1] 1. batter, beat, belabour, clobber (*Sl.*), hammer, pelt, pummel, strike, thrash, thump 2. bray (*Dialect*), bruise, comminute, crush, powder, pulverize, triturate 3. din into, drub into, drum into, hammer into 4. *With* **out** bang, beat, hammer, thump 5. clomp, march, stomp (*Inf.*), thunder, tramp 6. beat, palpitate, pitapat, pulsate, pulse, throb

pound[2] *n.* compound, enclosure, pen, yard

pour 1. decant, let flow, spill, splash 2. course, emit, flow, gush, run, rush, spew, spout, stream 3. bucket down (*Inf.*), come down in torrents, rain, rain cats and dogs (*Inf.*), rain hard *or* heavily, sheet, teem 4. crowd, stream, swarm, teem, throng

pout 1. *v.* glower, look petulant, look sullen, lower, make a *moue*, mope, pull a long face, purse one's lips, sulk, turn down the corners of one's mouth 2. *n.* glower, long face, *moue*, sullen look

pouting bad-tempered, cross, ill-humoured, long-faced, moody, moping, morose, peevish, petulant, sulky, sullen

poverty 1. beggary, destitution, distress, hand-to-mouth existence, hardship, indigence, insolvency, necessitousness, necessity, need, pauperism, pennilessness, penury, privation, want 2. dearth, deficiency, insufficiency, lack, paucity, scarcity, shortage 3. aridity, bareness, barrenness, deficiency, infertility, meagreness, poorness, sterility, unfruitfulness

poverty-stricken bankrupt, beggared, broke (*Inf.*), destitute, distressed, impecunious, impoverished, indigent, needy, on one's beam-ends, on one's uppers, penniless, penurious, poor, skint (*Brit. sl.*), stony-broke (*Brit. sl.*)

powder *n.* 1. dust, fine grains, loose particles, pounce, talc ~*v.* 2. crush, granulate, grind, pestle, pound, pulverize 3. cover, dredge, dust, scatter, sprinkle, strew

powdery chalky, crumbling, crumbly, dry, dusty, fine, friable, grainy, granular, loose, pulverized, sandy

power 1. ability, capability, capacity, competence, competency, faculty, potential 2. brawn, energy, force, forcefulness, intensity, might, muscle, potency, strength, vigour, weight 3. ascendancy, authority, command, control, dominance, domination, dominion, influence, mastery, rule, sovereignty, supremacy, sway 4. authority, authorization, licence, prerogative, privilege, right, warrant

powerful 1. energetic, mighty, potent, robust, stalwart, strapping, strong, sturdy, vigorous 2. authoritative, commanding, controlling, dominant, influential, prevailing, puissant, sovereign, supreme 3. cogent, compelling, convincing, effective, effectual, forceful, forcible, impressive, persuasive, telling, weighty

powerfully forcefully, forcibly, hard, mightily, strongly, vigorously, with might and main

powerless 1. debilitated, disabled, etiolated, feeble, frail, helpless, impotent, incapable, incapacitated, ineffectual, infirm, paralysed, prostrate, weak **2**. defenceless, dependent, disenfranchised, disfranchised, ineffective, subject, tied, unarmed, vulnerable

powwow 1. *n*. chinwag (*Brit. inf.*), confab (*Inf.*), confabulation, conference, consultation, council, discussion, gettogether (*Inf.*), huddle (*Inf.*), meeting, palaver, parley, talk **2**. *v*. confab (*Inf.*), confer, discuss, get together (*Inf.*), go into a huddle (*Inf.*), meet, palaver, parley, talk

practicability advantage, feasibility, operability, possibility, practicality, use, usefulness, value, viability, workability

practicable achievable, attainable, doable, feasible, performable, possible, viable, within the realm of possibility, workable

practical 1. applied, efficient, empirical, experimental, factual, functional, pragmatic, realistic, utilitarian **2**. businesslike, down-to-earth, everyday, hard-headed, matter-of-fact, mundane, ordinary, realistic, sensible, workaday **3**. doable, feasible, practicable, serviceable, sound, useful, workable **4**. accomplished, efficient, experienced, proficient, qualified, seasoned, skilled, trained, veteran, working

practically 1. all but, almost, basically, close to, essentially, fundamentally, in effect, just about, nearly, to all intents and purposes, very nearly, virtually, well-nigh **2**. clearly, matter-of-factly, rationally, realistically, reasonably, sensibly, unsentimentally, with common sense

practice 1. custom, habit, method, mode, praxis, routine, rule, system, tradition, usage, use, usual procedure, way, wont **2**. discipline, drill, exercise, preparation, rehearsal, repetition, study, training, work-out **3**. action, application, effect, exercise, experience, operation, use **4**. business, career, profession, vocation, work

practise 1. discipline, drill, exercise, go over, go through, polish, prepare, rehearse, repeat, study, train, warm up, work out **2**. apply, carry out, do, follow, live up to, observe, perform, put into practice **3**. carry on, engage in, ply, pursue, specialize in, undertake, work at

practised able, accomplished, experienced, expert, proficient, qualified, seasoned, skilled, trained, versed

pragmatic businesslike, down-to-earth, efficient, hard-headed, matter-of-fact, practical, realistic, sensible, utilitarian

praise *n*. **1**. acclaim, acclamation, accolade, applause, approbation, approval, cheering, commendation, compliment, congratulation, encomium, eulogy, good word, kudos, laudation, ovation, panegyric, plaudit, tribute **2**. adoration, devotion, glory, homage, thanks, worship ~*v*. **3**. acclaim, admire, applaud, approve, cheer, compliment, congratulate, cry up, eulogize, extol, honour, laud, pay tribute to, sing the praises of **4**. adore, bless, exalt, give thanks to, glorify, magnify (*Archaic*), pay homage to, worship

praiseworthy admirable, commendable, creditable, estimable, excellent, exemplary, fine, honourable, laudable, meritorious, worthy

prance 1. bound, caper, cavort, dance, frisk, gambol, jump, leap, romp, skip, spring **2**. parade, show off (*Inf.*), stalk, strut, swagger, swank (*Inf.*)

prank antic, caper, escapade, frolic, jape, lark (*Inf.*), practical joke, skylarking (*Inf.*), trick

prate babble, blather, boast, brag, chatter, drivel, gab (*Inf.*), gas (*Inf.*), go on and on, jaw (*Sl.*), shoot off one's mouth (*Sl.*), witter on (*Inf.*), yak (*Sl.*)

prattle babble, blather, blether, chatter, clack, drivel, gabble, jabber, patter, rattle on, run on, twitter, witter (*Inf.*)

pray 1. offer a prayer, recite the rosary, say one's prayers **2**. adjure, ask, beg, beseech, call upon, crave, cry for, entreat, implore, importune, invoke, petition, plead, request, solicit, sue, supplicate, urge

prayer 1. communion, devotion, invocation, litany, orison, supplication **2**. appeal, entreaty, petition, plea, request, suit, supplication

preach 1. address, deliver a sermon, evangelize, exhort, orate **2**. admonish, advocate, exhort, harangue, lecture, moralize, sermonize, urge

preacher clergyman, evangelist, minister, missionary, parson, revivalist

preachify drone on, go on and on, harangue, hold forth, lecture, moralize, prose, sermonize

preachy canting, didactic, edifying, holier-than-thou, homiletic, moralizing, pharisaic, pietistic, pontifical, religiose, sanctimonious, self-righteous

preamble exordium, foreword, introduction, opening statement *or* remarks, overture, preface, prelude, proem, prolegomenon

precarious chancy (*Inf.*), dangerous, dicey (*Sl.*), dodgy (*Brit. inf.*), doubtful, dubious, hairy (*Sl.*), hazardous, insecure, perilous, risky, shaky, slippery, touch and go, tricky, uncertain, unreliable, unsafe, unsettled, unstable, unsteady, unsure

precaution 1. insurance, preventative measure, protection, provision, safeguard, safety measure **2.** anticipation, care, caution, circumspection, foresight, forethought, providence, prudence, wariness

precede antecede, antedate, come first, forerun, go ahead of, go before, head, herald, introduce, lead, pave the way, preface, take precedence, usher

precedence antecedence, lead, preeminence, preference, primacy, priority, rank, seniority, superiority, supremacy

precedent *n.* antecedent, authority, criterion, example, exemplar, instance, model, paradigm, pattern, previous example, prototype, standard

preceding above, aforementioned, aforesaid, anterior, earlier, foregoing, former, past, previous, prior

precept 1. behest, canon, command, commandment, decree, direction, instruction, law, mandate, order, ordinance, principle, regulation, rule, statute **2.** axiom, byword, guideline, maxim, motto, principle, rule, saying

precinct 1. bound, boundary, confine, enclosure, limit **2.** area, district, quarter, section, sector, zone

precincts borders, bounds, confines, district, environs, limits, milieu, neighbourhood, purlieus, region, surrounding area

precious 1. adored, beloved, cherished, darling, dear, dearest, favourite, idolized, loved, prized, treasured, valued **2.** choice, costly, dear, expensive, exquisite, fine, high-priced, inestimable, invaluable, priceless, prized, rare,

recherché, valuable **3.** affected, alembicated, artificial, chichi, fastidious, overnice, overrefined, twee (*Brit. inf.*)

precipice bluff, brink, cliff, cliff face, crag, height, rock face, sheer drop, steep

precipitate *v.* **1.** accelerate, advance, bring on, dispatch, expedite, further, hasten, hurry, press, push forward, quicken, speed up, trigger **2.** cast, discharge, fling, hurl, launch, let fly, send forth, throw ~*adj.* **3.** breakneck, headlong, plunging, rapid, rushing, swift, violent **4.** frantic, harum-scarum, hasty, heedless, hurried, ill-advised, impetuous, impulsive, indiscreet, madcap, precipitous, rash, reckless **5.** abrupt, brief, quick, sudden, unexpected, without warning

precipitous 1. abrupt, dizzy, falling sharply, high, perpendicular, sheer, steep **2.** abrupt, careless, harum-scarum, hasty, heedless, hurried, ill-advised, precipitate, rash, reckless, sudden

précis 1. *n.* abridgment, abstract, *aperçu*, compendium, condensation, digest, outline, résumé, rundown, sketch, summary, synopsis **2.** *v.* abridge, abstract, compress, condense, outline, shorten, summarize, sum up

precise 1. absolute, accurate, actual, clear-cut, correct, definite, exact, explicit, express, fixed, literal, particular, specific, strict, unequivocal **2.** careful, ceremonious, exact, fastidious, finicky, formal, inflexible, meticulous, nice, particular, prim, punctilious, puritanical, rigid, scrupulous, stiff, strict

precisely absolutely, accurately, bang, correctly, exactly, just, just so, literally, neither more nor less, plumb (*Inf.*), slap (*Inf.*), smack (*Inf.*), square, squarely, strictly

precision accuracy, care, correctness, definiteness, exactitude, exactness, fidelity, meticulousness, nicety, particularity, preciseness, rigour

preclude check, debar, exclude, forestall, hinder, inhibit, make impossible, make impracticable, obviate, prevent, prohibit, put a stop to, restrain, rule out, stop

precocious advanced, ahead, bright, developed, forward, quick, smart

preconception bias, notion, preconceived idea *or* notion, predisposition, prejudice, prepossession, presumption, presupposition

precondition essential, must, necessity, prerequisite, requirement, *sine qua non*

precursor 1. forerunner, harbinger, herald, messenger, usher, vanguard **2.** antecedent, forebear, forerunner, originator, pioneer, predecessor

precursory antecedent, introductory, preceding, prefatory, preliminary, preparatory, previous, prior

predatory 1. carnivorous, hunting, predacious, rapacious, raptorial, ravening **2.** despoiling, greedy, marauding, pillaging, plundering, rapacious, ravaging, thieving, voracious, vulturine, vulturous

predecessor 1. antecedent, forerunner, precursor, previous (former, prior) job holder **2.** ancestor, antecedent, forebear, forefather

predestination destiny, doom, election (*Theology*), fate, foreordainment, foreordination, lot, necessity, predetermination

predestine doom, fate, foreordain, mean, predestinate, predetermine, preelect, preordain

predetermined agreed, arranged in advance, cut and dried (*Inf.*), decided beforehand, fixed, prearranged, preplanned, set, settled, set up

predicament corner, dilemma, emergency, fix (*Inf.*), hole (*Sl.*), jam (*Inf.*), mess, pickle (*Inf.*), pinch, plight, quandary, scrape (*Inf.*), situation, spot (*Inf.*), state

predicate 1. affirm, assert, aver, avouch, avow, contend, declare, maintain, proclaim, state **2.** connote, imply, indicate, intimate, signify, suggest **3.** *With* **on** *or* **upon** base, build, establish, found, ground, postulate, rest

predict augur, divine, forebode, forecast, foresee, foretell, portend, presage, prognosticate, prophesy, soothsay

predictable anticipated, calculable, certain, expected, foreseeable, foreseen, likely, reliable, sure, sure-fire (*Inf.*)

prediction augury, divination, forecast, prognosis, prognostication, prophecy, soothsaying

predilection bias, fancy, fondness, inclination, leaning, liking, love, partiality, penchant, predisposition, preference, proclivity, proneness, propensity, taste, tendency, weakness

predispose affect, bias, dispose, incline, induce, influence, lead, make (one)

of a mind to, prejudice, prepare, prime, prompt, sway

predisposed agreeable, amenable, given to, inclined, liable, minded, prone, ready, subject, susceptible, willing

predisposition bent, bias, disposition, inclination, likelihood, penchant, potentiality, predilection, proclivity, proneness, propensity, susceptibility, tendency, willingness

predominance ascendancy, control, dominance, dominion, edge, greater number, hold, leadership, mastery, paramountcy, preponderance, supremacy, sway, upper hand, weight

predominant ascendant, capital, chief, controlling, dominant, important, leading, main, paramount, preponderant, prevailing, prevalent, primary, prime, principal, prominent, ruling, sovereign, superior, supreme

predominate be most noticeable, carry weight, get the upper hand, hold sway, outweigh, overrule, overshadow, preponderate, prevail, reign, rule, tell

pre-eminence distinction, excellence, paramountcy, predominance, prestige, prominence, renown, superiority, supremacy, transcendence

pre-eminent chief, consummate, distinguished, excellent, foremost, incomparable, matchless, outstanding, paramount, peerless, predominant, renowned, superior, supreme, transcendent, unequalled, unrivalled, unsurpassed

pre-eminently above all, by far, conspicuously, eminently, emphatically, exceptionally, far and away, incomparably, inimitably, matchlessly, notably, *par excellence*, particularly, second to none, signally, singularly, strikingly, superlatively, supremely

pre-empt acquire, anticipate, appropriate, arrogate, assume, seize, take over, usurp

preen 1. *Of birds* clean, plume **2.** array, deck out, doll up (*Sl.*), dress up, prettify, primp, prink, spruce up, titivate, trim **3. preen oneself (on)** congratulate oneself, pique oneself, plume oneself, pride oneself

preface 1. *n.* exordium, foreword, introduction, preamble, preliminary, prelude, proem, prolegomenon, prologue **2.** *v.* begin, introduce, launch, lead up to, open, precede, prefix

prefatory antecedent, introductory,

opening, precursory, prefatorial, preliminary, prelusive, prelusory, preparatory, proemial, prolegomenal

prefer 1. adopt, be partial to, choose, desire, elect, fancy, favour, go for, incline towards, like better, opt for, pick, plump for, select, single out, wish, would rather, would sooner 2. file, lodge, place, present, press, put forward 3. advance, aggrandize, elevate, move up, promote, raise, upgrade

preferable best, better, choice, chosen, favoured, more desirable, more eligible, superior, worthier

preferably as a matter of choice, by choice, first, in *or* for preference, much rather, much sooner, rather, sooner, willingly

preference 1. choice, desire, election, favourite, first choice, option, partiality, pick, predilection, selection, top of the list 2. advantage, favoured treatment, favouritism, first place, precedence, pride of place, priority

preferential advantageous, better, favoured, partial, partisan, privileged, special, superior

preferment advancement, dignity, elevation, exaltation, promotion, rise, upgrading

prefigure 1. adumbrate, foreshadow, foretoken, indicate, intimate, portend, presage, shadow forth, suggest 2. consider, fancy, imagine, picture, presuppose

pregnancy gestation, gravidity

pregnant 1. big *or* heavy with child, enceinte, expectant, expecting (*Inf.*), gravid, in the club (*Brit. sl.*), in the family way (*Inf.*), in the pudding club (*Sl.*), preggers (*Brit. inf.*), with child 2. charged, eloquent, expressive, loaded, meaningful, pointed, significant, suggestive, telling, weighty 3. creative, imaginative, inventive, original, seminal 4. abounding in, abundant, fecund, fertile, fraught, fruitful, full, productive, prolific, replete, rich in, teeming

prehistoric 1. earliest, early, primeval, primitive, primordial 2. ancient, antediluvian, antiquated, archaic, out of date, out of the ark (*Inf.*)

prejudge anticipate, forejudge, jump to conclusions, make a hasty assessment, presume, presuppose

prejudice *n.* 1. bias, jaundiced eye, partiality, preconceived notion, preconception, prejudgment, warp 2. bigotry,

chauvinism, discrimination, injustice, intolerance, narrow-mindedness, racism, sexism, unfairness 3. damage, detriment, disadvantage, harm, hurt, impairment, loss, mischief ~*v.* 4. bias, colour, distort, influence, jaundice, poison, predispose, prepossess, slant, sway, warp 5. damage, harm, hinder, hurt, impair, injure, mar, spoil, undermine

prejudiced biased, bigoted, conditioned, discriminatory, influenced, intolerant, jaundiced, narrow-minded, onesided, opinionated, partial, partisan, prepossessed, unfair

prejudicial counterproductive, damaging, deleterious, detrimental, disadvantageous, harmful, hurtful, inimical, injurious, undermining, unfavourable

preliminary 1. *adj.* exploratory, first, initial, initiatory, introductory, opening, pilot, precursory, prefatory, preparatory, prior, qualifying, test, trial 2. *n.* beginning, first round, foundation, groundwork, initiation, introduction, opening, preamble, preface, prelims, prelude, preparation, start

prelude beginning, commencement, curtain-raiser, exordium, foreword, intro (*Inf.*), introduction, overture, preamble, preface, preliminary, preparation, proem, prolegomenon, prologue, start

premature 1. abortive, early, embryonic, forward, green, immature, incomplete, predeveloped, raw, undeveloped, unfledged, unripe, unseasonable, untimely 2. *Fig.* hasty, ill-considered, illtimed, impulsive, inopportune, overhasty, precipitate, previous (*Inf.*), rash, too soon, untimely

prematurely 1. before one's time, too early, too soon, untimely 2. at half-cock, half-cocked, overhastily, precipitately, rashly, too hastily, too soon

premeditated aforethought, calculated, conscious, considered, contrived, deliberate, intended, intentional, planned, prepense, studied, wilful

premeditation deliberation, design, determination, forethought, intention, malice aforethought, planning, plotting, prearrangement, predetermination, purpose

premier *n.* 1. chancellor, head of government, P.M., prime minister ~*adj.* 2. arch, chief, first, foremost, head, highest, leading, main, primary, prime, principal, top **3**. earliest, first, inaugural, initial, original

premiere debut, first night, first performance, first showing, opening

premise v. assume, hypothesize, posit, postulate, predicate, presuppose, state

premises building, establishment, place, property, site

premiss, premise argument, assertion, assumption, ground, hypothesis, postulate, postulation, presupposition, proposition, supposition, thesis

premium 1. bonus, boon, bounty, fee, percentage (Inf.), perk (Brit. inf.), perquisite, prize, recompense, remuneration, reward **2**. appreciation, regard, stock, store, value **3. at a premium** beyond one's means, costly, expensive, hard to come by, in great demand, in short supply, like gold dust, not to be had for love or money, rare, scarce, valuable

premonition apprehension, feeling, feeling in one's bones, foreboding, forewarning, funny feeling (Inf.), hunch, idea, intuition, misgiving, omen, portent, presage, presentiment, sign, suspicion, warning

preoccupation 1. absence of mind, absent-mindedness, absorption, abstraction, brown study, daydreaming, engrossment, immersion, inattentiveness, musing, oblivion, pensiveness, prepossession, reverie, woolgathering **2**. bee in one's bonnet, concern, fixation, hang-up (Inf.), hobbyhorse, idée fixe, obsession, pet subject

preoccupied absent-minded, absorbed, abstracted, caught up in, distracted, distrait, engrossed, faraway, heedless, immersed, in a brown study, intent, lost in, lost in thought, oblivious, rapt, taken up, unaware, wrapped up

preordain destine, doom, fate, map out in advance, predestine, predetermine

preparation 1. development, getting ready, groundwork, preparing, putting in order **2**. alertness, anticipation, expectation, foresight, precaution, preparedness, provision, readiness, safeguard **3**. Often plural arrangement, measure, plan, provision **4**. composition, compound, concoction, medicine, mixture, tincture **5**. homework, prep (Inf.), revision, schoolwork, study, swotting (Inf.)

preparatory 1. basic, elementary,

introductory, opening, prefatory, preliminary, preparative, primary **2. preparatory to** before, in advance of, in anticipation of, in preparation for, prior to

prepare 1. adapt, adjust, anticipate, arrange, coach, dispose, form, groom, make provision, make ready, plan, practise, prime, put in order, train, warm up **2**. brace, fortify, gird, ready, steel, strengthen **3**. assemble, concoct, construct, contrive, draw up, fashion, fix up, get up (Inf.), make, produce, put together, turn out **4**. accoutre, equip, fit, fit out, furnish, outfit, provide, supply

prepared 1. all set, arranged, fit, in order, in readiness, planned, primed, ready, set **2**. able, disposed, inclined, minded, of a mind, predisposed, willing

preparedness alertness, fitness, order, preparation, readiness

preponderance ascendancy, bulk, dominance, domination, dominion, extensiveness, greater numbers, greater part, lion's share, mass, power, predominance, prevalence, superiority, supremacy, sway, weight

preponderant ascendant, dominant, extensive, foremost, greater, important, larger, paramount, predominant, prevailing, prevalent, significant

preponderate dominate, hold sway, outnumber, predominate, prevail, reign supreme, rule

prepossessed biased, inclined, partial, partisan, predisposed, prejudiced

prepossessing alluring, amiable, appealing, attractive, beautiful, bewitching, captivating, charming, engaging, fair, fascinating, fetching, good-looking, handsome, inviting, likable, lovable, magnetic, pleasing, striking, taking, winning

prepossession 1. absorption, engrossment, preoccupation **2**. bias, inclination, liking, partiality, predilection, predisposition, prejudice

preposterous absurd, asinine, bizarre, crazy, excessive, exorbitant, extravagant, extreme, foolish, impossible, incredible, insane, irrational, laughable, ludicrous, monstrous, nonsensical, out of the question, outrageous, ridiculous, senseless, shocking, unreasonable, unthinkable

prerequisite 1. adj. called for, essential, imperative, indispensable, mandatory, necessary, needful, obligatory, of the essence, required, requisite, vital **2**.

n. condition, essential, imperative, must, necessity, precondition, qualification, requirement, requisite, *sine qua non*

prerogative advantage, authority, birthright, choice, claim, droit, due, exemption, immunity, liberty, perquisite, privilege, right, sanction, title

presage *n.* 1. augury, auspice, forecast, forewarning, harbinger, intimation, omen, portent, prediction, prognostic, prognostication, prophecy, sign, warning 2. apprehension, boding, feeling, foreboding, intuition, misgiving, premonition, presentiment ~*v.* 3. divine, feel, foresee, have a feeling, intuit, sense 4. adumbrate, augur, betoken, bode, forebode, foreshadow, foretoken, omen, point to, portend, signify, warn 5. forecast, foretell, forewarn, predict, prognosticate, prophesy, soothsay, vaticinate (*Rare*)

prescience clairvoyance, foreknowledge, foresight, precognition, prevision (*Rare*), second sight

prescient clairvoyant, discerning, divinatory, divining, far-sighted, foresighted, mantic, perceptive, prophetic, psychic

prescribe appoint, assign, command, decree, define, dictate, direct, enjoin, fix, impose, lay down, ordain, order, require, rule, set, specify, stipulate

prescript command, dictate, dictum, direction, directive, edict, instruction, law, mandate, order, ordinance, precept, regulation, requirement, rule

prescription 1. direction, formula, instruction, recipe 2. drug, medicine, mixture, preparation, remedy

prescriptive authoritarian, dictatorial, didactic, dogmatic, legislating, preceptive, rigid

presence 1. attendance, being, companionship, company, existence, habitation, inhabitance, occupancy, residence 2. closeness, immediate circle, nearness, neighbourhood, propinquity, proximity, vicinity 3. air, appearance, aspect, aura, bearing, carriage, comportment, demeanour, ease, mien (*Literary*), personality, poise, self-assurance 4. apparition, ghost, manifestation, revenant, shade (*Literary*), spectre, spirit, supernatural being, wraith

presence of mind alertness, aplomb, calmness, composure, cool (*Sl.*), coolness, imperturbability, level-headedness,

phlegm, quickness, sang-froid, self-assurance, self-command, self-possession, wits

present[1] *adj.* 1. contemporary, current, existent, existing, extant, immediate, instant, present-day 2. accounted for, at hand, available, here, in attendance, near, nearby, ready, there, to hand ~*n.* 3. here and now, now, present moment, the time being, this day and age, today 4. **at present** at the moment, just now, now, nowadays, right now 5. **for the present** for a while, for the moment, for the time being, in the meantime, not for long, provisionally, temporarily

present[2] *v.* 1. acquaint with, introduce, made known 2. demonstrate, display, exhibit, give, mount, put before the public, put on, show, stage 3. adduce, advance, declare, expound, extend, hold out, introduce, offer, pose, produce, proffer, put forward, raise, recount, relate, state, submit, suggest, tender 4. award, bestow, confer, donate, entrust, furnish, give, grant, hand over, offer, proffer, put at (someone's) disposal ~*n.* 5. benefaction, boon, bounty, donation, endowment, favour, gift, grant, gratuity, largess, offering, prezzie (*Inf.*)

presentable acceptable, becoming, decent, fit to be seen, good enough, not bad (*Inf.*), O.K. (*Inf.*), passable, proper, respectable, satisfactory, suitable, tolerable

presentation 1. award, bestowal, conferral, donation, giving, investiture, offering 2. appearance, arrangement, delivery, exposition, production, rendition, staging, submission 3. demonstration, display, exhibition, performance, production, representation, show 4. coming out, debut, introduction, launch, launching, reception

presentiment anticipation, apprehension, expectation, fear, feeling, foreboding, forecast, forethought, hunch, intuition, misgiving, premonition, presage

presently anon (*Archaic*), before long, by and by, in a minute, in a moment, in a short while, pretty soon (*Inf.*), shortly, soon

preservation conservation, defence, keeping, maintenance, perpetuation, protection, safeguarding, safekeeping, safety, salvation, security, storage, support, upholding

preserve *v.* 1. care for, conserve, defend, guard, keep, protect, safeguard, save, secure, shelter, shield **2**. continue, keep, keep up, maintain, perpetuate, retain, sustain, uphold **3**. conserve, keep, put up, save, store ~*n*. **4**. area, domain, field, realm, specialism, sphere **5**. *Often plural* confection, confiture, conserve, jam, jelly, marmalade, sweetmeat **6**. game reserve, reservation, reserve, sanctuary

preside administer, be at the head of, be in authority, chair, conduct, control, direct, govern, head, lead, manage, officiate, run, supervise

press *v*. **1**. bear down on, compress, condense, crush, depress, force down, jam, mash, push, reduce, squeeze, stuff **2**. calender, finish, flatten, iron, mangle, put the creases in, smooth, steam **3**. clasp, crush, embrace, encircle, enfold, fold in one's arms, hold close, hug, squeeze **4**. compel, constrain, demand, enforce, enjoin, force, insist on **5**. beg, entreat, exhort, implore, importune, petition, plead, pressurize, sue, supplicate, urge **6**. afflict, assail, beset, besiege, disquiet, harass, plague, torment, trouble, vex, worry **7**. **be pressed** be hard put, be pushed (hurried, rushed), be short of **8**. cluster, crowd, flock, gather, hasten, herd, hurry, mill, push, rush, seethe, surge, swarm, throng ~*n*. **9**. **the press a**. Fleet Street, fourth estate, journalism, news media, newspapers, the papers **b**. columnists, correspondents, gentlemen of the press, journalists, newsmen, photographers, pressmen, reporters **10**. bunch, crowd, crush, flock, herd, horde, host, mob, multitude, pack, push (*Inf.*), swarm, throng **11**. bustle, demand, hassle (*Inf.*), hurry, pressure, strain, stress, urgency

pressing burning, constraining, crucial, exigent, high-priority, imperative, important, importunate, serious, urgent, vital

pressure 1. compressing, compression, crushing, force, heaviness, squeezing, weight **2**. coercion, compulsion, constraint, force, influence, obligation, power, sway **3**. adversity, affliction, burden, demands, difficulty, distress, exigency, hassle (*Inf.*), heat, hurry, load, press, strain, stress, urgency

prestige authority, cachet, celebrity, credit, distinction, eminence, esteem, fame, honour, importance, influence, ku-

dos, regard, renown, reputation, standing, stature, status, weight

prestigious celebrated, eminent, esteemed, exalted, great, illustrious, important, imposing, impressive, influential, prominent, renowned, reputable, respected

presumably apparently, doubtless, doubtlessly, in all likelihood, in all probability, it would seem, likely, most likely, on the face of it, probably, seemingly

presume 1. assume, believe, conjecture, infer, posit, postulate, presuppose, suppose, surmise, take for granted, take it, think **2**. dare, go so far, have the audacity, make bold, make so bold, take the liberty, undertake, venture **3**. bank on, count on, depend, rely, trust

presumption 1. assurance, audacity, boldness, brass (*Inf.*), brass neck (*Inf.*), cheek (*Inf.*), effrontery, forwardness, gall (*Inf.*), impudence, insolence, nerve (*Inf.*), presumptuousness, temerity **2**. anticipation, assumption, belief, conjecture, guess, hypothesis, opinion, premiss, presupposition, supposition, surmise **3**. basis, chance, grounds, likelihood, plausibility, probability, reason

presumptive 1. assumed, believed, expected, hypothetical, inferred, supposed, understood **2**. believable, conceivable, credible, likely, plausible, possible, probable, reasonable

presumptuous arrogant, audacious, bigheaded (*Inf.*), bold, conceited, foolhardy, forward, insolent, overconfident, overfamiliar, overweening, presuming, pushy (*Inf.*), rash, too big for one's boots, uppish (*Brit. inf.*)

presuppose accept, assume, consider, imply, posit, postulate, presume, suppose, take as read, take for granted, take it

presupposition assumption, belief, hypothesis, preconceived idea, preconception, premiss, presumption, supposition, theory

pretence 1. acting, charade, deceit, deception, fabrication, fakery, faking, falsehood, feigning, invention, make-believe, sham, simulation, subterfuge, trickery **2**. affectation, appearance, artifice, display, façade, posing, posturing, pretentiousness, show, veneer **3**. claim, cloak, colour, cover, excuse, façade, garb, guise, mask, masquerade, pretext, ruse, semblance, show, veil, wile

pretend 1. affect, allege, assume, counterfeit, dissemble, dissimulate, fake, falsify, feign, impersonate, make out, pass oneself off as, profess, put on, sham, simulate 2. act, imagine, make believe, make up, play, play the part of, suppose 3. allege, aspire, claim, lay claim, profess, purport

pretended alleged, avowed, bogus, counterfeit, fake, false, feigned, fictitious, imaginary, ostensible, phoney (*Sl.*), pretend (*Inf.*), professed, pseudo (*Inf.*), purported, sham, so-called, spurious

pretender aspirant, claimant, claimer

pretension 1. aspiration, assertion, assumption, claim, demand, pretence, profession 2. affectation, airs, conceit, hypocrisy, ostentation, pomposity, pretentiousness, self-importance, show, showiness, snobbery, snobbishness, vainglory, vanity

pretentious affected, assuming, bombastic, conceited, exaggerated, extravagant, flaunting, grandiloquent, grandiose, highfalutin (*Inf.*), high-flown, high-sounding, hollow, inflated, magniloquent, mannered, ostentatious, overambitious, pompous, puffed up, showy, snobbish, specious, vainglorious

preternatural abnormal, anomalous, extraordinary, inexplicable, irregular, marvellous, miraculous, mysterious, odd, peculiar, strange, supernatural, unaccountable, unearthly, unnatural, unusual

pretext affectation, alleged reason, appearance, cloak, cover, device, excuse, guise, mask, ploy, pretence, red herring, ruse, semblance, show, simulation, veil

prettify adorn, deck out, decorate, doll up (*Sl.*), do up, embellish, garnish, gild, ornament, pretty up, tart up (*Brit. sl.*), titivate, trick out, trim

pretty *adj.* 1. appealing, attractive, beautiful, bonny, charming, comely, cute, fair, good-looking, graceful, lovely, personable 2. bijou, dainty, delicate, elegant, fine, neat, nice, pleasing, tasteful, trim ~*adv.* 3. *Inf.* fairly, kind of (*Inf.*), moderately, quite, rather, reasonably, somewhat

prevail 1. be victorious, carry the day, gain mastery, overcome, overrule, prove superior, succeed, triumph, win 2. abound, be current (prevalent, widespread), exist generally, obtain, predominate, preponderate 3. *Often with*

on *or* **upon** bring round, convince, dispose, incline, induce, influence, persuade, prompt, sway, talk into, win over

prevailing 1. common, current, customary, established, fashionable, general, in style, in vogue, ordinary, popular, prevalent, set, usual, widespread 2. dominant, influential, main, operative, predominating, preponderating, principal, ruling

prevalence 1. acceptance, commonness, common occurrence, currency, frequency, pervasiveness, popularity, profusion, regularity, ubiquity, universality 2. ascendancy, hold, mastery, predominance, preponderance, primacy, rule, sway

prevalent 1. accepted, common, commonplace, current, customary, established, everyday, extensive, frequent, general, habitual, popular, rampant, rife, ubiquitous, universal, usual, widespread 2. ascendant, compelling, dominant, governing, powerful, predominant, prevailing, successful, superior

prevaricate beat about the bush, beg the question, cavil, deceive, dodge, equivocate, evade, give a false colour to, hedge, lie, palter, quibble, shift, shuffle, stretch the truth, tergiversate

prevarication cavilling, deceit, deception, equivocation, evasion, falsehood, falsification, lie, misrepresentation, pretence, quibbling, tergiversation, untruth

prevaricator Ananias, deceiver, dissembler, dodger, equivocator, evader, fibber, hypocrite, liar, pettifogger, quibbler, sophist

prevent anticipate, avert, avoid, balk, bar, block, check, counteract, defend against, foil, forestall, frustrate, hamper, head off, hinder, impede, inhibit, intercept, nip in the bud, obstruct, obviate, preclude, restrain, stave off, stop, thwart, ward off

prevention 1. anticipation, avoidance, deterrence, elimination, forestalling, obviation, precaution, preclusion, prophylaxis, safeguard, thwarting 2. bar, check, deterrence, frustration, hindrance, impediment, interruption, obstacle, obstruction, stoppage

preventive, preventative *adj.* 1. hampering, hindering, impeding, obstructive 2. counteractive, deterrent, inhibitory, precautionary, prophylactic, protective, shielding ~*n.* 3. block, hindrance, impediment, obstacle, obstruction **4**. deterrent, neutralizer, prevention, prophylactic, protection, protective, remedy, safeguard, shield

previous 1. antecedent, anterior, earlier, erstwhile, ex-, foregoing, former, one-time, past, preceding, prior, quondam, sometime **2**. *Inf.* ahead of oneself, precipitate, premature, too early, too soon, untimely

previously at one time, a while ago, before, beforehand, earlier, formerly, heretofore, hitherto, in advance, in anticipation, in days *or* years gone by, in the past, once, then, until now

prey *n*. **1**. game, kill, quarry **2**. dupe, fall guy (*Inf.*), mark, mug (*Sl.*), target, victim ~*v*. **3**. devour, eat, feed upon, hunt, live off, seize **4**. blackmail, bleed (*Inf.*), bully, exploit, intimidate, take advantage of, terrorize, victimize **5**. burden, distress, hang over, haunt, oppress, trouble, weigh down, weigh heavily, worry

price *n*. **1**. amount, asking price, assessment, bill, charge, cost, damage (*Inf.*), estimate, expenditure, expense, face value, fee, figure, outlay, payment, rate, valuation, value, worth **2**. consequences, cost, penalty, sacrifice, toll **3**. bounty, compensation, premium, recompense, reward **4**. **at any price** anyhow, cost what it may, expense no object, no matter what the cost, regardless, whatever the cost **5**. **beyond price** inestimable, invaluable, of incalculable value, precious, priceless, treasured, without price ~*v*. **6**. assess, cost, estimate, evaluate, put a price on, rate, value

priceless 1. beyond price, cherished, costly, dear, expensive, incalculable, incomparable, inestimable, invaluable, irreplaceable, precious, prized, rare, rich, treasured, worth a king's ransom **2**. *Inf.* absurd, a hoot (*Brit. inf.*), amusing, a scream (*Inf.*), comic, droll, funny, hilarious, killing (*Inf.*), rib-tickling, ridiculous, riotous, side-splitting

pricey, pricy costly, dear, exorbitant, expensive, extortionate, high-priced, over the odds (*Brit. inf.*), steep (*Inf.*)

prick *v*. **1**. bore, jab, lance, perforate, pierce, pink, punch, puncture, stab **2**. bite, itch, prickle, smart, sting, tingle **3**. cut, distress, grieve, move, pain, stab, touch, trouble, wound **4**. *Usually with* **up** point, raise, rise, stand erect ~*n*. **5**.

cut, gash, hole, perforation, pinhole, puncture, wound **6**. gnawing, pang, prickle, smart, spasm, sting, twinge

prickle *n*. **1**. barb, needle, point, spike, spine, spur, thorn **2**. chill, formication, goose flesh, paraesthesia (*Medical*), pins and needles (*Inf.*), smart, tickle, tingle, tingling ~*v*. **3**. itch, smart, sting, tingle, twitch **4**. jab, nick, prick, stick

prickly 1. barbed, brambly, briery, bristly, spiny, thorny **2**. crawling, itchy, pricking, prickling, scratchy, sharp, smarting, stinging, tingling **3**. bad-tempered, cantankerous, edgy, fractious, grumpy, irritable, peevish, pettish, petulant, ratty (*Brit. sl.*), shirty (*Sl.*), snappish, stroppy (*Brit. sl.*), tetchy, touchy, waspish **4**. complicated, difficult, intricate, involved, knotty, thorny, ticklish, tricky, troublesome, trying

pride *n*. **1**. *amour-propre*, dignity, honour, self-esteem, self-respect, self-worth **2**. arrogance, bigheadedness (*Inf.*), conceit, egotism, haughtiness, hauteur, hubris, loftiness, *morgue*, presumption, pretension, pretentiousness, self-importance, self-love, smugness, snobbery, superciliousness, vainglory, vanity **3**. boast, gem, jewel, pride and joy, prize, treasure **4**. delight, gratification, joy, pleasure, satisfaction **5**. best, choice, cream, elite, flower, glory, pick ~*v*. **6**. be proud of, boast, brag, congratulate oneself, crow, exult, flatter oneself, glory in, pique, plume, preen, revel in, take pride, vaunt

priest churchman, clergyman, cleric, curate, divine, ecclesiastic, father, father confessor, holy man, man of God, man of the cloth, minister, padre (*Inf.*), vicar

priestly canonical, clerical, ecclesiastic, hieratic, pastoral, priestlike, sacerdotal

prig goody-goody (*Inf.*), Holy Joe (*Inf.*), Holy Willie (*Inf.*), Mrs Grundy, old maid (*Inf.*), pedant, prude, puritan, stuffed shirt (*Inf.*)

priggish goody-goody (*Inf.*), holier-than-thou, narrow-minded, pedantic, prim, prudish, puritanical, self-righteous, self-satisfied, smug, starchy (*Inf.*), stiff, stuffy

prim demure, fastidious, formal, fussy, old-maidish (*Inf.*), particular, precise, priggish, prissy (*Inf.*), proper, prudish, puritanical, schoolmarmish (*Brit. inf.*), starchy (*Inf.*), stiff, strait-laced

primacy ascendancy, command, dominance, dominion, leadership, pre-eminence, superiority, supremacy

prima donna diva, leading lady, star

primal 1. earliest, first, initial, original, primary, prime, primitive, primordial, pristine **2.** central, chief, first, greatest, highest, main, major, most important, paramount, prime, principal

primarily 1. above all, basically, chiefly, especially, essentially, for the most part, fundamentally, generally, mainly, mostly, on the whole, principally **2.** at first, at *or* from the start, first and foremost, initially, in the beginning, in the first place, originally

primary 1. best, capital, cardinal, chief, dominant, first, greatest, highest, leading, main, paramount, prime, principal, top **2.** aboriginal, earliest, initial, original, primal, primeval, primitive, primordial, pristine **3.** basic, beginning, elemental, essential, fundamental, radical, ultimate, underlying **4.** elementary, introductory, rudimentary, simple

prime *adj.* **1.** best, capital, choice, excellent, first-class, first-rate, grade A, highest, quality, select, selected, superior, top **2.** basic, earliest, fundamental, original, primary, underlying **3.** chief, leading, main, predominant, pre-eminent, primary, principal, ruling, senior ~*n.* **4.** best days, bloom, flower, full flowering, height, heyday, maturity, peak, perfection, zenith **5.** beginning, morning, opening, spring, start ~*v.* **6.** break in, coach, fit, get ready, groom, make ready, prepare, train **7.** brief, clue up, fill in (*Inf.*), gen up (*Brit. inf.*), give someone the lowdown (*Inf.*), inform, notify, tell

primeval, primaeval ancient, earliest, early, first, old, original, prehistoric, primal, primitive, primordial, pristine

primitive 1. earliest, early, elementary, first, original, primary, primeval, primordial, pristine **2.** barbarian, barbaric, crude, rough, rude, rudimentary, savage, simple, uncivilized, uncultivated, undeveloped, unrefined **3.** childlike, naive, simple, undeveloped, unsophisticated, untrained, untutored

primordial 1. earliest, first, prehistoric, primal, primeval, primitive, pristine **2.** basic, elemental, fundamental, original, radical

primp be in full fig (*Sl.*), deck out, doll up (*Sl.*), dress up, fig up (*Sl.*), gussy up (*Sl.*), prank, preen, prink, put on one's best bib and tucker (*Inf.*), put on one's gladrags (*Sl.*)

prince lord, monarch, potentate, ruler, sovereign

princely 1. bounteous, bountiful, generous, gracious, lavish, liberal, magnanimous, munificent, open-handed, rich **2.** august, dignified, grand, high-born, imperial, imposing, lofty, magnificent, majestic, noble, regal, royal, sovereign, stately

principal *adj.* **1.** capital, cardinal, chief, controlling, dominant, essential, first, foremost, highest, key, leading, main, most important, paramount, pre-eminent, primary, prime, strongest ~*n.* **2.** boss (*Inf.*), chief, director, head, leader, master, ruler, superintendent **3.** dean, director, head (*Inf.*), headmaster, headmistress, head teacher, master, rector **4.** assets, capital, capital funds, money **5.** first violin, lead, leader, star

principally above all, chiefly, especially, first and foremost, for the most part, in the main, mainly, mostly, particularly, predominantly, primarily

principle 1. assumption, axiom, canon, criterion, dictum, doctrine, dogma, ethic, formula, fundamental, golden rule, law, maxim, moral law, precept, proposition, rule, standard, truth, verity **2.** attitude, belief, code, credo, ethic, morality, opinion, tenet **3.** conscience, integrity, morals, probity, rectitude, scruples, sense of duty, sense of honour, uprightness **4. in principle** ideally, in essence, in theory, theoretically

principled conscientious, correct, decent, ethical, high-minded, honourable, just, moral, righteous, right-minded, scrupulous, upright, virtuous

prink adorn, deck, doll up (*Sl.*), dress to kill (*Inf.*), dress up, dress (up) to the nines (*Inf.*), fig up (*Sl.*), groom, gussy up (*Sl.*), prank, preen, primp, titivate, trick out

print *v.* **1.** engrave, go to press, impress, imprint, issue, mark, publish, put to bed (*Inf.*), run off, stamp ~*n.* **2.** book, magazine, newspaper, newsprint, periodical, printed matter, publication, typescript **3. in print a.** in black and white, on paper, on the streets, out, printed, published **b.** available, current, in the shops, obtainable, on the market, on the shelves **4**. **out of print** no longer published, o.p., unavailable, unobtainable **5**. copy, engraving, photo (*Inf.*), photograph, picture, reproduction **6**. characters, face, font (*Chiefly U.S.*), fount, lettering, letters, type, typeface

prior 1. aforementioned, antecedent, anterior, earlier, foregoing, former, preceding, pre-existent, pre-existing, previous **2**. **prior to** before, earlier than, preceding, previous to

priority first concern, greater importance, precedence, pre-eminence, preference, prerogative, rank, right of way, seniority, superiority, supremacy, the lead

priory abbey, cloister, convent, monastery, nunnery, religious house

prison can (*Sl.*), choky (*Sl.*), clink (*Sl.*), confinement, cooler (*Sl.*), dungeon, gaol, glasshouse (*Military inf.*), jail, jug (*Sl.*), lockup, penal institution, penitentiary (*U.S.*), quod (*Sl.*), stir (*Sl.*)

prisoner 1. con (*Sl.*), convict, jailbird, lag (*Sl.*) **2**. captive, detainee, hostage, internee

prissy fastidious, finicky, fussy, old-maidish (*Inf.*), overnice, precious, prim, prim and proper, prudish, schoolmarmish (*Brit. inf.*), squeamish, strait-laced

pristine 1. earliest, first, former, initial, original, primal, primary, primeval, primitive, primordial **2**. immaculate, new, pure, uncorrupted, undefiled, unspoiled, unsullied, untouched, virgin, virginal

privacy 1. isolation, privateness, retirement, retreat, seclusion, separateness, sequestration, solitude **2**. clandestineness, concealment, confidentiality, secrecy

private *adj*. **1**. clandestine, closet, confidential, hush-hush (*Inf.*), in camera, inside, off the record, privy (*Archaic*), secret, unofficial **2**. exclusive, individual, intimate, own, particular, personal, reserved, special **3**. independent, nonpublic **4**. concealed, isolated, not overlooked, retired, secluded, secret, separate, sequestered, solitary, withdrawn **5**. **in private** behind closed doors, confidentially, in camera, in secret, personally, privately ~*n*. **6**. enlisted man (*U.S.*), private soldier, squaddy (*Inf.*), tommy (*Brit. inf.*), Tommy Atkins (*Brit. inf.*)

privation destitution, distress, hardship, indigence, lack, loss, misery, necessity, need, neediness, penury, poverty, suffering, want

privilege advantage, benefit, birthright, claim, concession, due, entitlement, franchise, freedom, immunity, liberty, prerogative, right, sanction

privileged 1. advantaged, elite, entitled, favoured, honoured, indulged, powerful, ruling, special **2**. allowed, empowered, exempt, free, granted, licensed, sanctioned, vested **3**. *Of information* confidential, exceptional, inside, not for publication, off the record, privy, special

privy *adj*. **1**. **With to** apprised of, aware of, cognizant of, hip to (*Sl.*), informed, in on, in the know (*Inf.*), wise to (*Sl.*) **2**. *Archaic* confidential, hidden, hush-hush (*Inf.*), off the record, personal, private, secret ~*n*. **3**. bog (*Sl.*), closet, earth closet, latrine, lavatory, outside toilet

prize[1] *n*. **1**. accolade, award, honour, premium, reward, trophy **2**. haul, jackpot, purse, stakes, windfall, winnings **3**. aim, ambition, conquest, desire, gain, goal, hope **4**. booty, capture, loot, pickings, pillage, plunder, spoil(s), trophy ~*adj*. **5**. award-winning, best, champion, first-rate, outstanding, top, topnotch (*Inf.*), winning

prize[2] *v*. appreciate, cherish, esteem, hold dear, regard highly, set store by, treasure, value

prizefighter boxer, bruiser (*Inf.*), fighter, pug (*Sl.*), pugilist

prizefighting boxing, fighting, pugilism, the noble art *or* science, the prize ring, the ring

probability chance(s), expectation, liability, likelihood, likeliness, odds, presumption, prospect

probable apparent, credible, feasible, likely, most likely, odds-on, on the cards, ostensible, plausible, possible, presumable, presumed, reasonable, seeming

probably as likely as not, doubtless, in all likelihood, in all probability, likely, maybe, most likely, perchance (*Archaic*), perhaps, possibly, presumably

probation apprenticeship, examination, initiation, novitiate, test, trial, trial period

probe *v*. **1**. examine, explore, go into, investigate, look into, query, scrutinize, search, sift, sound, test, verify **2**. explore, feel around, poke, prod ~*n*. **3**. detection, examination, exploration, inquest, inquiry, investigation, research, scrutiny, study

probity equity, fairness, fidelity, goodness, honesty, honour, integrity, justice, morality, rectitude, righteousness, sincerity, trustworthiness, truthfulness, uprightness, virtue, worth

problem n. **1.** can of worms (Inf.), complication, difficulty, dilemma, disagreement, dispute, disputed point, doubt, hard nut to crack (Inf.), point at issue, predicament, quandary, trouble **2.** brain-teaser (Inf.), conundrum, enigma, poser, puzzle, question, riddle ~adj. **3.** delinquent, difficult, intractable, uncontrollable, unmanageable, unruly

problematic chancy (Inf.), debatable, doubtful, dubious, enigmatic, moot, open to doubt, problematical, puzzling, questionable, tricky, uncertain, unsettled

procedure action, conduct, course, custom, form, formula, method, modus operandi, operation, performance, plan of action, policy, practice, process, routine, scheme, step, strategy, system, transaction

proceed 1. advance, carry on, continue, get going, get on with, get under way with, go ahead, go on, make a start, move on, press on, progress, set in motion **2.** arise, come, derive, emanate, ensue, flow, follow, issue, originate, result, spring, stem

proceeding 1. act, action, course of action, deed, measure, move, occurrence, procedure, process, step, undertaking, venture **2.** Plural account, affairs, annals, archives, business, dealings, doings, matters, minutes, records, report, transactions

proceeds earnings, gain, income, produce, products, profit, receipts, returns, revenue, takings, yield

process n. **1.** action, course, course of action, manner, means, measure, method, mode, operation, performance, practice, procedure, proceeding, system, transaction **2.** advance, course, development, evolution, formation, growth, movement, progress, progression, stage, step, unfolding **3.** Law action, case, suit, trial ~v. **4.** deal with, dispose of, fulfil, handle, take care of **5.** alter, convert, prepare, refine, transform, treat

procession 1. cavalcade, column, cortege, file, march, motorcade, parade,

train **2.** course, cycle, run, sequence, series, string, succession, train

proclaim advertise, affirm, announce, blaze (abroad), blazon (abroad), circulate, declare, enunciate, give out, herald, indicate, make known, profess, promulgate, publish, shout from the housetops (Inf.), show, trumpet

proclamation announcement, declaration, decree, edict, manifesto, notice, notification, promulgation, pronouncement, pronunciamento, publication

proclivity bent, bias, disposition, facility, inclination, leaning, liableness, penchant, predilection, predisposition, proneness, propensity, tendency, weakness

procrastinate adjourn, be dilatory, dally, defer, delay, drag one's feet (Inf.), gain time, play a waiting game, play for time, postpone, prolong, protract, put off, retard, stall, temporize

procreate beget, breed, bring into being, engender, father, generate, mother, produce, propagate, reproduce, sire

procure acquire, appropriate, buy, come by, earn, effect, find, gain, get, get hold of, lay hands on, manage to get, obtain, pick up, purchase, secure, win

procurer bawd (Archaic), madam, pander, panderer, pimp, procuress, white-slaver, whoremaster (Archaic)

prod v. **1.** dig, drive, elbow, jab, nudge, poke, prick, propel, push, shove **2.** egg on, goad, impel, incite, motivate, move, prompt, rouse, spur, stimulate, stir up, urge ~n. **3.** boost, dig, elbow, jab, nudge, poke, push, shove **4.** goad, poker, spur, stick **5.** boost, cue, prompt, reminder, signal, stimulus

prodigal adj. **1.** excessive, extravagant, immoderate, improvident, intemperate, profligate, reckless, spendthrift, squandering, wanton, wasteful **2.** bounteous, bountiful, copious, exuberant, lavish, luxuriant, profuse, sumptuous, superabundant, teeming ~n. **3.** big spender, profligate, spendthrift, squanderer, wastrel

prodigality 1. abandon, dissipation, excess, extravagance, immoderation, intemperance, profligacy, recklessness, squandering, wantonness, waste, wastefulness **2.** abundance, amplitude, bounteousness, bounty, copiousness, cornucopia, exuberance, horn of plenty, lavishness, luxuriance, plenteousness, plenty, profusion, richness, sumptuousness

prodigious 1. colossal, enormous, giant, gigantic, huge, immeasurable, immense, inordinate, mammoth, massive, monstrous, monumental, stupendous, tremendous, vast **2.** abnormal, amazing, astounding, exceptional, extraordinary, fabulous, fantastic (*Inf.*), flabbergasting (*Inf.*), impressive, marvellous, miraculous, phenomenal, remarkable, staggering, startling, striking, stupendous, unusual, wonderful

prodigy 1. child genius, genius, mastermind, talent, whiz (*Inf.*), whiz kid (*Inf.*), wizard, wonder child, wunderkind **2.** marvel, miracle, one in a million, phenomenon, rare bird (*Inf.*), sensation, wonder **3.** abnormality, curiosity, freak, grotesque, monster, monstrosity, mutation, spectacle

produce *v.* **1.** compose, construct, create, develop, fabricate, invent, make, manufacture, originate, put together, turn out **2.** afford, bear, beget, breed, bring forth, deliver, engender, furnish, give, render, supply, yield **3.** bring about, cause, effect, generate, give rise to, make for, occasion, provoke, set off **4.** advance, bring forward, bring to light, demonstrate, exhibit, offer, present, put forward, set forth, show **5.** direct, do, exhibit, mount, present, put before the public, put on, show, stage **6.** *Geometry* extend, lengthen, prolong, protract ~*n.* **7.** crop, fruit and vegetables, greengrocery, harvest, product, yield

producer 1. director, impresario, *régisseur* **2.** farmer, grower, maker, manufacturer

product 1. artefact, commodity, concoction, creation, goods, invention, merchandise, produce, production, work **2.** consequence, effect, fruit, issue, legacy, offshoot, outcome, result, returns, spin-off, upshot, yield

production 1. assembly, construction, creation, fabrication, formation, making, manufacture, manufacturing, origination, preparation, producing **2.** direction, management, presentation, staging

productive 1. creative, dynamic, energetic, fecund, fertile, fruitful, generative, inventive, plentiful, producing, prolific, rich, teeming, vigorous **2.** advantageous, beneficial, constructive, effective, fruitful, gainful, gratifying, profitable, rewarding, useful, valuable, worthwhile

productivity abundance, mass production, output, production, productive capacity, productiveness, work rate, yield

profane *adj.* **1.** disrespectful, godless, heathen, idolatrous, impious, impure, irreligious, irreverent, pagan, sacrilegious, sinful, ungodly, wicked **2.** lay, secular, temporal, unconsecrated, unhallowed, unholy, unsanctified, worldly **3.** abusive, blasphemous, coarse, crude, filthy, foul, obscene, vulgar ~*v.* **4.** abuse, commit sacrilege, contaminate, debase, defile, desecrate, misuse, pervert, pollute, prostitute, violate, vitiate

profanity abuse, blasphemy, curse, cursing, execration, foul language, four-letter word, impiety, imprecation, irreverence, malediction, obscenity, profaneness, sacrilege, swearing, swearword

profess 1. acknowledge, admit, affirm, announce, assert, asseverate, aver, avow, certify, confess, confirm, declare, maintain, own, proclaim, state, vouch **2.** act as if, allege, call oneself, claim, dissemble, fake, feign, let on, make out, pretend, purport, sham

professed 1. avowed, certified, confirmed, declared, proclaimed, self-acknowledged, self-confessed **2.** alleged, apparent, ostensible, pretended, purported, self-styled, so-called, *soi-disant*, supposed, would-be

professedly 1. allegedly, apparently, by one's own account, falsely, ostensibly, purportedly, supposedly, under the pretext of **2.** admittedly, avowedly, by open declaration, confessedly

profession 1. business, calling, career, employment, line, line of work, métier, occupation, office, position, sphere, vocation, walk of life **2.** acknowledgment, affirmation, assertion, attestation, avowal, claim, confession, declaration, statement, testimony, vow

professional 1. *adj.* ace (*Inf.*), adept, competent, crack (*Sl.*), efficient, experienced, expert, finished, masterly, polished, practised, proficient, qualified, skilled, slick, trained **2.** *n.* adept, authority, dab hand (*Brit. inf.*), expert, maestro, master, past master, pro (*Inf.*), specialist, virtuoso, wizard

professor don (*Brit.*), fellow (*Brit.*), head of faculty, prof (*Inf.*)

proffer extend, hand, hold out, offer,

present, propose, propound, submit, suggest, tender, volunteer

proficiency ability, accomplishment, aptitude, competence, dexterity, expertise, expertness, facility, knack, know-how (*Inf.*), mastery, skilfulness, skill, talent

proficient able, accomplished, adept, apt, capable, clever, competent, conversant, efficient, experienced, expert, gifted, masterly, qualified, skilful, skilled, talented, trained, versed

profile *n.* **1.** contour, drawing, figure, form, outline, portrait, shape, side view, silhouette, sketch **2.** biography, characterization, character sketch, sketch, thumbnail sketch, vignette **3.** analysis, chart, diagram, examination, graph, review, study, survey, table

profit *n.* **1.** *Often plural* bottom line, earnings, emoluments, gain, percentage (*Inf.*), proceeds, receipts, return, revenue, surplus, takings, winnings, yield **2.** advancement, advantage, avail, benefit, gain, good, interest, use, value ~*v.* **3.** aid, avail, benefit, be of advantage to, better, contribute, gain, help, improve, promote, serve, stand in good stead **4.** capitalize on, cash in on (*Sl.*), exploit, learn from, make capital of, make good use of, make the most of, put to good use, reap the benefit of, take advantage of, turn to advantage *or* account, use, utilize **5.** clean up (*Inf.*), clear, earn, gain, make a good thing of (*Inf.*), make a killing (*Inf.*), make money

profitable **1.** commercial, cost-effective, fruitful, gainful, lucrative, money-making, paying, remunerative, rewarding, worthwhile **2.** advantageous, beneficial, fruitful, productive, rewarding, serviceable, useful, valuable, worthwhile

profiteer **1.** *n.* exploiter, racketeer **2.** *v.* exploit, fleece, make a quick buck (*Sl.*), make someone pay through the nose, overcharge, racketeer, sting (*Inf.*)

profitless bootless, fruitless, futile, idle, ineffective, ineffectual, pointless, thankless, to no purpose, unavailing, unproductive, unprofitable, unremunerative, useless, vain, worthless

profligacy **1.** abandon, corruption, debauchery, degeneracy, depravity, dissipation, dissoluteness, dolce vita, immorality, laxity, libertinism, licentiousness, promiscuity, unrestraint, wantonness **2.**

excess, extravagance, improvidence, lavishness, prodigality, recklessness, squandering, waste, wastefulness

profligate *adj.* **1.** abandoned, corrupt, debauched, degenerate, depraved, dissipated, dissolute, immoral, iniquitous, libertine, licentious, loose, promiscuous, shameless, unprincipled, vicious, vitiated, wanton, wicked, wild **2.** extravagant, immoderate, improvident, prodigal, reckless, spendthrift, squandering, wasteful ~*n.* **3.** debauchee, degenerate, dissipater, libertine, rake, reprobate, roué **4.** prodigal, spendthrift, squanderer, waster, wastrel

profound **1.** abstruse, deep, discerning, erudite, learned, penetrating, philosophical, recondite, sagacious, sage, serious, skilled, subtle, thoughtful, weighty, wise **2.** abysmal, bottomless, cavernous, deep, fathomless, yawning **3.** abject, acute, deeply felt, extreme, great, heartfelt, heartrending, hearty, intense, keen, sincere **4.** absolute, complete, consummate, exhaustive, extensive, extreme, far-reaching, intense, out-and-out, pronounced, thoroughgoing, total, utter

profoundly abjectly, acutely, deeply, extremely, from the bottom of one's heart, greatly, heartily, intensely, keenly, seriously, sincerely, thoroughly, very

profundity **1.** acuity, acumen, depth, erudition, insight, intelligence, learning, penetration, perceptiveness, perspicacity, perspicuity, sagacity, wisdom **2.** depth, extremity, intensity, seriousness, severity, strength

profuse **1.** abundant, ample, bountiful, copious, luxuriant, overflowing, plentiful, prolific, teeming **2.** excessive, extravagant, exuberant, fulsome, generous, immoderate, lavish, liberal, open-handed, prodigal, unstinting

profusion abundance, bounty, copiousness, cornucopia, excess, extravagance, exuberance, glut, lavishness, luxuriance, multitude, oversupply, plenitude, plethora, prodigality, quantity, riot, superabundance, superfluity, surplus, wealth

progenitor **1.** ancestor, begetter, forebear, forefather, parent, primogenitor, procreator **2.** antecedent, forerunner, instigator, originator, precursor, predecessor, source

progeny breed, children, descendants, family, issue, lineage, offspring, posterity, race, scions, seed, stock, young

prognosis diagnosis, expectation, forecast, prediction, prognostication, projection, speculation, surmise

prognostic 1. *adj.* diagnostic, foretelling, indicating, predicting, predictive, prophetic **2.** *n.* forecast, indication, omen, portent, preindication, sign, symptom, warning

prognosticate 1. divine, forecast, foretell, predict, presage, prophesy, soothsay **2.** augur, betoken, forebode, foreshadow, harbinger, herald, point to, portend, presage

prognostication expectation, forecast, prediction, prognosis, projection, prophecy, speculation, surmise

programme *n.* **1.** agenda, curriculum, line-up, list, listing, list of players, order of events, order of the day, plan, schedule, syllabus **2.** broadcast, performance, presentation, production, show **3.** design, order of the day, plan, plan of action, procedure, project, scheme ~*v.* **4.** arrange, bill, book, design, engage, formulate, itemize, lay on, line up, list, map out, plan, prearrange, schedule, work out

progress *n.* **1.** advance, course, movement, onward course, passage, progression, way **2.** advance, advancement, amelioration, betterment, breakthrough, development, gain, gaining ground, growth, headway, improvement, increase, progression, promotion, step forward **3. in progress** being done, going on, happening, occurring, proceeding, taking place, under way ~*v.* **4.** advance, come on, continue, cover ground, forge ahead, gain ground, gather way, get on, go forward, make headway, make one's way, make strides, move on, proceed, travel **5.** advance, ameliorate, better, blossom, develop, gain, grow, improve, increase, mature

progression 1. advance, advancement, furtherance, gain, headway, movement forward, progress **2.** chain, course, cycle, order, sequence, series, string, succession

progressive 1. accelerating, advancing, continuing, continuous, developing, escalating, growing, increasing, intensifying, ongoing **2.** advanced, avant-garde, dynamic, enlightened, enterprising, forward-looking, go-ahead, liberal, modern, radical, reformist, revolutionary, up-and-coming

prohibit 1. ban, debar, disallow, forbid, interdict, outlaw, proscribe, veto **2.** constrain, hamper, hinder, impede, make impossible, obstruct, preclude, prevent, restrict, rule out, stop

prohibited banned, barred, forbidden, not allowed, proscribed, taboo, *verboten*, vetoed

prohibition 1. constraint, exclusion, forbiddance, interdiction, negation, obstruction, prevention, restriction **2.** ban, bar, disallowance, embargo, injunction, interdict, proscription, veto

prohibitive 1. forbidding, prohibiting, proscriptive, repressive, restraining, restrictive, suppressive **2.** *Esp. of prices* beyond one's means, excessive, exorbitant, extortionate, high-priced, preposterous, sky-high, steep (*Inf.*)

project *n.* **1.** activity, assignment, design, enterprise, job, occupation, plan, programme, proposal, scheme, task, undertaking, venture, work ~*v.* **2.** contemplate, contrive, design, devise, draft, frame, map out, outline, plan, propose, purpose, scheme **3.** cast, discharge, fling, hurl, launch, make carry, propel, shoot, throw, transmit **4.** beetle, bulge, extend, jut, overhang, protrude, stand out, stick out **5.** calculate, estimate, extrapolate, forecast, gauge, predetermine, predict, reckon

projectile bullet, missile, rocket, shell

projection 1. bulge, eaves, jut, ledge, overhang, protrusion, protuberance, ridge, shelf, sill **2.** blueprint, diagram, map, outline, plan, representation **3.** calculation, computation, estimate, estimation, extrapolation, forecast, prediction, reckoning

proletarian 1. *adj.* cloth-cap (*Inf.*), common, plebeian, working-class **2.** *n.* commoner, Joe Bloggs (*Brit. inf.*), man of the people, pleb (*Sl.*), plebeian, prole (*Sl.*), worker

proletariat commonalty, commoners, hoi polloi, labouring classes, lower classes, lower orders, plebs, proles (*Sl.*), the common people, the great unwashed (*Derogatory*), the herd, the masses, the rabble, wage-earners, working class

proliferate breed, burgeon, escalate, expand, grow rapidly, increase, multiply, mushroom, run riot, snowball

proliferation build-up, concentration, escalation, expansion, extension, increase, intensification, multiplication, spread, step-up (*Inf.*)

prolific abundant, bountiful, copious, fecund, fertile, fruitful, generative, luxuriant, productive, profuse, rank, rich, teeming

prolix boring, diffuse, digressive, discursive, dragged out, full of verbiage, lengthy, long, long-drawn-out, long-winded, prolonged, protracted, rambling, spun out, tedious, tiresome, verbose, wordy

prolixity boringness, circuity, diffuseness, discursiveness, long-windedness, maundering, pleonasm, rambling, redundancy, tautology, tediousness, verbiage, verboseness, verbosity, wandering, wordiness

prologue exordium, foreword, introduction, preamble, preface, preliminary, prelude, proem

prolong carry on, continue, delay, drag out, draw out, extend, lengthen, make longer, perpetuate, protract, spin out, stretch

promenade *n.* 1. boulevard, esplanade, parade, prom, public walk, walkway 2. airing, constitutional, saunter, stroll, turn, walk ~*v.* 3. perambulate, saunter, stretch one's legs, stroll, take a walk, walk 4. flaunt, parade, strut, swagger

prominence 1. cliff, crag, crest, elevation, headland, height, high point, hummock, mound, pinnacle, projection, promontory, rise, rising ground, spur 2. bulge, jutting, projection, protrusion, protuberance, swelling 3. conspicuousness, markedness, outstandingness, precedence, salience, specialness, top billing, weight 4. celebrity, distinction, eminence, fame, greatness, importance, name, notability, pre-eminence, prestige, rank, reputation, standing

prominent 1. bulging, jutting, projecting, protruding, protrusive, protuberant, standing out 2. conspicuous, easily seen, eye-catching, in the foreground, noticeable, obtrusive, obvious, outstanding, pronounced, remarkable, salient, striking, to the fore, unmistakable 3. celebrated, chief, distinguished, eminent, famous, foremost, important, leading, main, noted, outstanding, popular, pre-eminent, renowned, respected, top, well-known, well-thought-of

promiscuity abandon, amorality, debauchery, depravity, dissipation, immorality, incontinence, laxity, laxness, lechery, libertinism, licentiousness, looseness, permissiveness, profligacy, promiscuousness, sleeping around (*Inf.*), wantonness

promiscuous 1. abandoned, debauched, dissipated, dissolute, fast, immoral, lax, libertine, licentious, loose, of easy virtue, profligate, unbridled, unchaste, wanton, wild 2. chaotic, confused, disordered, diverse, heterogeneous, ill-assorted, indiscriminate, intermingled, intermixed, jumbled, mingled, miscellaneous, mixed, motley 3. careless, casual, haphazard, heedless, indifferent, indiscriminate, irregular, irresponsible, random, slovenly, uncontrolled, uncritical, undiscriminating, unfastidious, unselective

promise *v.* 1. assure, contract, cross one's heart, engage, give an undertaking, give one's word, guarantee, pledge, plight, stipulate, swear, take an oath, undertake, vouch, vow, warrant 2. augur, bespeak, betoken, bid fair, denote, give hope of, hint at, hold a probability, hold out hopes of, indicate, lead one to expect, look like, seem likely to, show signs of, suggest ~*n.* 3. assurance, bond, commitment, compact, covenant, engagement, guarantee, oath, pledge, undertaking, vow, word, word of honour 4. ability, aptitude, capability, capacity, flair, potential, talent

promising 1. auspicious, bright, encouraging, favourable, full of promise, hopeful, likely, propitious, reassuring, rosy 2. able, gifted, likely, rising, talented, up-and-coming

promontory cape, foreland, head, headland, ness (*Archaic*), point, spur

promote 1. advance, aid, assist, back, boost, contribute to, develop, encourage, forward, foster, further, help, nurture, stimulate, support 2. aggrandize, dignify, elevate, exalt, honour, kick upstairs (*Inf.*), prefer, raise, upgrade 3. advocate, call attention to, champion, endorse, espouse, popularize, push for, recommend, speak for, sponsor, support, urge, work for 4. advertise, beat the drum for (*Inf.*), hype (*Sl.*), plug (*Inf.*), publicize, puff, push, sell

promotion 1. advancement, aggrandizement, elevation, ennoblement, exaltation, honour, move up, preferment, rise, upgrading **2**. advancement, advocacy, backing, boosting, cultivation, development, encouragement, espousal, furtherance, progress, support **3**. advertising, advertising campaign, ballyhoo (*Inf.*), hard sell, hype (*Sl.*), media hype (*Sl.*), plugging (*Inf.*), propaganda, publicity, puffery (*Inf.*), pushing

prompt *adj.* **1**. early, immediate, instant, instantaneous, on time, punctual, quick, rapid, speedy, swift, timely, unhesitating **2**. alert, brisk, eager, efficient, expeditious, quick, ready, responsive, smart, willing ~*adv.* **3**. *Inf.* exactly, on the dot, promptly, punctually, sharp ~*v.* **4**. cause, impel, incite, induce, inspire, instigate, motivate, move, provoke, spur, stimulate, urge **5**. assist, cue, help out, jog the memory, prod, refresh the memory, remind **6**. call forth, cause, elicit, evoke, give rise to, occasion, provoke ~*n.* **7**. cue, help, hint, jog, jolt, prod, reminder, spur, stimulus

prompter 1. autocue, idiot board (*Sl.*), Teleprompter (*Trademark*) **2**. agitator, catalyst, gadfly, inspirer, instigator, moving spirit, prime mover

prompting assistance, encouragement, hint, incitement, influence, jogging, persuasion, pressing, pressure, prodding, pushing, reminder, reminding, suggestion, urging

promptly at once, by return, directly, immediately, instantly, on the dot, on time, pronto (*Inf.*), punctually, quickly, speedily, swiftly, unhesitatingly

promptness alacrity, alertness, briskness, dispatch, eagerness, haste, promptitude, punctuality, quickness, readiness, speed, swiftness, willingness

promulgate advertise, announce, broadcast, circulate, communicate, declare, decree, disseminate, issue, make known, make public, notify, proclaim, promote, publish, spread

prone 1. face down, flat, horizontal, lying down, procumbent, prostrate, recumbent, supine **2**. apt, bent, disposed, given, inclined, liable, likely, predisposed, subject, susceptible, tending

proneness bent, bias, disposition, inclination, leaning, liability, proclivity, propensity, susceptibility, tendency, weakness

prong point, projection, spike, tine, tip

pronounce 1. accent, articulate,

enunciate, say, sound, speak, stress, utter, vocalize, voice **2**. affirm, announce, assert, declare, decree, deliver, judge, proclaim

pronounced broad, clear, conspicuous, decided, definite, distinct, evident, marked, noticeable, obvious, striking, strong, unmistakable

pronouncement announcement, declaration, decree, dictum, edict, judgment, manifesto, notification, proclamation, promulgation, pronunciamento, statement

pronunciation accent, accentuation, articulation, diction, elocution, enunciation, inflection, intonation, speech, stress

proof *n.* **1**. attestation, authentication, certification, confirmation, corroboration, demonstration, evidence, substantiation, testimony, verification **2**. *As in* **put to the proof** assay, examination, experiment, ordeal, scrutiny, test, trial **3**. *Printing* galley, galley proof, page proof, pull, slip, trial impression, trial print ~*adj.* **4**. impenetrable, impervious, repellent, resistant, strong, tight, treated **5**. **be proof against** hold out against, resist, stand firm against, stand up to, withstand

prop *v.* **1**. bolster, brace, buttress, hold up, maintain, shore, stay, support, sustain, truss, uphold **2**. lean, rest, set, stand ~*n.* **3**. brace, buttress, mainstay, stanchion, stay, support, truss

propaganda advertising, agitprop, ballyhoo (*Inf.*), brainwashing, disinformation, hype (*Sl.*), information, newspeak, promotion, publicity

propagandist advocate, evangelist, indoctrinator, pamphleteer, promoter, proponent, proselytizer, publicist

propagandize brainwash, convince, indoctrinate, instil, persuade, proselytize

propagate 1. beget, breed, engender, generate, increase, multiply, procreate, produce, proliferate, reproduce **2**. broadcast, circulate, diffuse, disseminate, make known, proclaim, promote, promulgate, publicize, publish, spread, transmit

propagation 1. breeding, generation, increase, multiplication, procreation, proliferation, reproduction **2**. circulation, communication, diffusion, dissemination, distribution, promotion, promulgation, spread, spreading, transmission

propel drive, force, impel, launch,

push, send, set in motion, shoot, shove, start, thrust

propensity aptness, bent, bias, disposition, inclination, leaning, liability, penchant, predisposition, proclivity, proneness, susceptibility, tendency, weakness

proper 1. appropriate, apt, becoming, befitting, fit, fitting, legitimate, meet (*Archaic*), right, suitable, suited **2**. *comme il faut*, decent, decorous, *de rigueur*, genteel, gentlemanly, ladylike, mannerly, polite, punctilious, refined, respectable, seemly **3**. accepted, accurate, conventional, correct, established, exact, formal, orthodox, precise, right **4**. characteristic, individual, own, particular, peculiar, personal, respective, special, specific

property 1. assets, belongings, building(s), capital, chattels, effects, estate, goods, holdings, house(s), means, possessions, resources, riches, wealth **2**. acres, estate, freehold, holding, land, real estate, real property, realty, title **3**. ability, attribute, characteristic, feature, hallmark, idiosyncrasy, mark, peculiarity, quality, trait, virtue

prophecy augury, divination, forecast, foretelling, prediction, prognosis, prognostication, revelation, second sight, soothsaying, vaticination (*Rare*)

prophesy augur, divine, forecast, foresee, foretell, forewarn, predict, presage, prognosticate, soothsay, vaticinate (*Rare*)

prophet augur, Cassandra, clairvoyant, diviner, forecaster, oracle, prognosticator, prophesier, seer, sibyl, soothsayer

prophetic augural, divinatory, fatidic (*Rare*), foreshadowing, mantic, oracular, predictive, presaging, prescient, prognostic, sibylline, vatic (*Rare*)

propinquity 1. adjacency, closeness, contiguity, nearness, neighbourhood, proximity, vicinity **2**. affiliation, affinity, blood, connection, consanguinity, kindred, kinship, relation, relationship, tie, ties of blood

propitiate appease, conciliate, make peace, mollify, pacify, placate, reconcile, satisfy

propitiation appeasement, conciliation, mollification, peacemaking, placation, reconciliation

propitiatory appeasing, assuaging, conciliatory, pacificatory, pacifying,

peacemaking, placative, placatory, propitiative, reconciliatory

propitious 1. advantageous, auspicious, bright, encouraging, favourable, fortunate, full of promise, happy, lucky, opportune, promising, prosperous, rosy, timely **2**. benevolent, benign, favourably inclined, friendly, gracious, kind, well-disposed

proponent advocate, apologist, backer, champion, defender, enthusiast, exponent, friend, partisan, patron, spokesman, spokeswoman, subscriber, supporter, upholder, vindicator

proportion 1. distribution, ratio, relationship, relative amount **2**. agreement, balance, congruity, correspondence, harmony, symmetry **3**. amount, cut (*Inf.*), division, fraction, measure, part, percentage, quota, segment, share **4**. *Plural* amplitude, breadth, bulk, capacity, dimensions, expanse, extent, magnitude, measurements, range, scope, size, volume

proportional, proportionate balanced, commensurate, comparable, compatible, consistent, correspondent, corresponding, equitable, equivalent, even, in proportion, just

proposal bid, design, motion, offer, overture, plan, presentation, proffer, programme, project, proposition, recommendation, scheme, suggestion, tender, terms

propose 1. advance, come up with, present, proffer, propound, put forward, submit, suggest, tender **2**. introduce, invite, name, nominate, present, put up, recommend **3**. aim, design, have every intention, have in mind, intend, mean, plan, purpose, scheme **4**. ask for someone's hand (in marriage), offer marriage, pay suit, pop the question (*Inf.*)

proposition 1. *n*. motion, plan, programme, project, proposal, recommendation, scheme, suggestion **2**. *v*. accost, make an improper suggestion, make an indecent proposal, solicit

propound advance, advocate, contend, lay down, postulate, present, propose, put forward, set forth, submit, suggest

proprietor, proprietress deed holder, freeholder, landlady, landlord, landowner, owner, possessor, titleholder

propriety 1. appropriateness, aptness, becomingness, correctness, fitness, rightness, seemliness, suitableness **2**. breeding, courtesy, decency, decorum, delicacy, etiquette, good form, good manners, manners, modesty, politeness, protocol, punctilio, rectitude, refinement, respectability, seemliness **3. the proprieties** accepted conduct, amenities, civilities, etiquette, niceties, rules of conduct, social code, social conventions, social graces, the done thing

propulsion drive, impetus, impulse, impulsion, momentum, motive power, power, pressure, propelling force, push, thrust

prosaic banal, boring, commonplace, dry, dull, everyday, flat, hackneyed, humdrum, matter-of-fact, mundane, ordinary, pedestrian, routine, stale, tame, trite, unimaginative, uninspiring, vapid, workaday

proscribe 1. ban, boycott, censure, condemn, damn, denounce, doom, embargo, forbid, interdict, prohibit, reject **2**. attaint (*Archaic*), banish, blackball, deport, exclude, excommunicate, exile, expatriate, expel, ostracize, outlaw

proscription 1. ban, boycott, censure, condemnation, damning, denunciation, dooming, embargo, interdict, prohibition, rejection **2**. attainder (*Archaic*), banishment, deportation, ejection, eviction, exclusion, excommunication, exile, expatriation, expulsion, ostracism, outlawry

prosecute 1. *Law* arraign, bring action against, bring suit against, bring to trial, do (*Sl.*), indict, litigate, prefer charges, put in the dock, put on trial, seek redress, sue, summon, take to court, try **2**. carry on, conduct, direct, discharge, engage in, manage, perform, practise, work at **3**. carry through, continue, follow through, persevere, persist, pursue, see through

proselyte catechumen, convert, initiate, neophyte, new believer, novice, tyro

proselytize bring into the fold, bring to God, convert, evangelize, make converts, persuade, propagandize, spread the gospel, win over

prospect *n*. **1**. anticipation, calculation, contemplation, expectation, future, hope, odds, opening, outlook, plan, presumption, probability, promise, proposal, thought **2**. landscape, outlook, panorama, perspective, scene, sight, spectacle, view, vision, vista **3. in prospect** in

sight, in store, in the offing, in the wind, in view, on the cards, on the horizon, planned, projected **4**. *Sometimes plural* chance, likelihood, possibility ~*v*. **5**. explore, go after, look for, search, seek, survey

prospective about to be, anticipated, approaching, awaited, coming, destined, eventual, expected, forthcoming, future, hoped-for, imminent, intended, likely, looked-for, possible, potential, soon-to-be, -to-be, to come

prospectus announcement, catalogue, conspectus, list, outline, plan, programme, scheme, syllabus, synopsis

prosper advance, be fortunate, bloom, do well, fare well, flourish, flower, get on, grow rich, make good, make it (*Inf.*), progress, succeed, thrive

prosperity affluence, boom, ease, fortune, good fortune, good times, life of luxury, life of Riley (*Inf.*), luxury, plenty, prosperousness, riches, success, the good life, wealth, well-being

prosperous 1. blooming, booming, doing well, flourishing, fortunate, lucky, on the up and up (*Brit.*), palmy, prospering, successful, thriving **2**. affluent, in clover (*Inf.*), in the money (*Inf.*), moneyed, opulent, rich, wealthy, well-heeled (*Sl.*), well-off, well-to-do **3**. advantageous, auspicious, bright, favourable, good, profitable, promising, propitious, timely

prostitute 1. *n*. bawd (*Archaic*), brass (*Sl.*), call girl, camp follower, cocotte, courtesan, fallen woman, *fille de joie*, harlot, hooker (*U.S. sl.*), hustler (*Sl.*), loose woman, moll (*Sl.*), pro (*Sl.*), streetwalker, strumpet, tart (*Inf.*), trollop, white slave, whore **2**. *v*. cheapen, debase, degrade, demean, devalue, misapply, pervert, profane

prostitution harlotry, harlot's trade, Mrs. Warren's profession, streetwalking, the game (*Sl.*), the oldest profession, vice, whoredom

prostrate *adj*. **1**. abject, bowed low, flat, horizontal, kowtowing, procumbent, prone **2**. at a low ebb, dejected, depressed, desolate, drained, exhausted, fagged out (*Inf.*), fallen, inconsolable, overcome, spent, worn out **3**. brought to one's knees, defenceless, disarmed, helpless, impotent, overwhelmed, paralysed, powerless, reduced ~*v*. **4**. *Of oneself* abase, bend the knee to, bow before, bow down to, cast oneself before, cringe, fall at (someone's) feet, fall on one's knees before, grovel, kneel, kowtow, submit **5.** bring low, crush, depress, disarm, lay low, overcome, overthrow, overturn, overwhelm, paralyse, reduce, ruin **6.** drain, exhaust, fag out (*Inf.*), fatigue, sap, tire, wear out, weary

prostration 1. abasement, bow, genuflection, kneeling, kowtow, obeisance, submission **2.** collapse, dejection, depression, depth of misery, desolation, despair, despondency, exhaustion, grief, helplessness, paralysis, weakness, weariness

prosy boring, commonplace, dull, flat, humdrum, long, long-drawn-out, longwinded, monotonous, overlong, pedestrian, prosaic, prosing, stale, tedious, tiresome, unimaginative, uninteresting, wordy

protagonist 1. central character, hero, heroine, lead, leading character, principal **2.** advocate, champion, exponent, leader, mainstay, moving spirit, prime mover, standard-bearer, supporter

protean changeable, ever-changing, many-sided, mercurial, multiform, mutable, polymorphous, variable, versatile, volatile

protect care for, chaperon, cover, cover up for, defend, foster, give sanctuary, guard, harbour, keep, keep safe, look after, mount *or* stand guard over, preserve, safeguard, save, screen, secure, shelter, shield, support, take under one's wing, watch over

protection 1. aegis, care, charge, custody, defence, guardianship, guarding, preservation, protecting, safeguard, safekeeping, safety, security **2.** armour, barrier, buffer, bulwark, cover, guard, refuge, safeguard, screen, shelter, shield

protective careful, covering, defensive, fatherly, insulating, jealous, maternal, motherly, paternal, possessive, protecting, safeguarding, sheltering, shielding, vigilant, warm, watchful

protector advocate, benefactor, bodyguard, champion, counsel, defender, guard, guardian, guardian angel, knight in shining armour, patron, safeguard, tower of strength

protégé, protégée charge, dependant, discovery, pupil, student, ward

protest *n.* **1.** complaint, declaration, demur, demurral, disapproval, dissent, formal complaint, objection, outcry, protestation, remonstrance ~*v.* **2.** complain, cry out, demonstrate, demur, disagree, disapprove, expostulate, express disapproval, kick (against) (*Inf.*), object, oppose, remonstrate, say no to, take exception **3.** affirm, argue, assert, asseverate, attest, avow, contend, declare, insist, maintain, profess, testify, vow

protestation 1. complaint, disagreement, dissent, expostulation, objection, outcry, protest, remonstrance, remonstration **2.** affirmation, asseveration, avowal, declaration, oath, pledge, profession, vow

protester agitator, demonstrator, dissenter, dissident, protest marcher, rebel

protocol 1. code of behaviour, conventions, courtesies, customs, decorum, etiquette, formalities, good form, manners, politesse, propriety, rules of conduct **2.** agreement, compact, concordat, contract, convention, covenant, pact, treaty

prototype archetype, example, first, mock-up, model, norm, original, paradigm, pattern, precedent, standard, type

protract continue, drag on *or* out, draw out, extend, keep going, lengthen, prolong, spin out, stretch out

protracted dragged out, drawn-out, extended, interminable, lengthy, long, long-drawn-out, never-ending, overlong, prolonged, spun out, time-consuming

protrude bulge, come through, extend, jut, obtrude, point, pop (*of eyes*), project, shoot out, stand out, start (from), stick out

protrusion bulge, bump, jut, lump, outgrowth, projection, protuberance, swelling

protuberance bulge, bump, excrescence, knob, lump, outgrowth, process, projection, prominence, protrusion, swelling, tumour

protuberant beetling, bulbous, bulging, gibbous, jutting, popping (*of eyes*), prominent, protruding, protrusive, proud (*Dialect*), swelling, swollen

proud 1. appreciative, content, contented, glad, gratified, honoured, pleased, satisfied, self-respecting, well-pleased **2.** arrogant, boastful, conceited, disdainful, egotistical, haughty, high and mighty (*Inf.*), imperious, lordly, narcissistic, orgulous (*Archaic*), overbearing, presumptuous, self-important, self-satisfied, snobbish, snooty (*Inf.*), stuck-up (*Inf.*), supercilious, toffee-nosed (*Sl.*), vain **3**. exalted, glorious, gratifying, illustrious, memorable, pleasing, red-letter, rewarding, satisfying **4**. august, distinguished, eminent, grand, great, illustrious, imposing, magnificent, majestic, noble, splendid, stately

provable attestable, demonstrable, evincible, testable, verifiable

prove 1. ascertain, attest, authenticate, bear out, confirm, corroborate, demonstrate, determine, establish, evidence, evince, justify, show, show clearly, substantiate, verify **2**. analyse, assay, check, examine, experiment, put to the test, put to trial, test, try **3**. be found to be, come out, end up, result, turn out

proven *adj*. accepted, attested, authentic, certified, checked, confirmed, definite, dependable, established, proved, reliable, tested, tried, trustworthy, undoubted, valid, verified

provenance birthplace, derivation, origin, source

provender 1. feed, fodder, forage **2**. comestibles, eatables, eats (*Sl*.), edibles, fare, food, foodstuffs, groceries, grub (*Sl*.), nosh (*Sl*.), provisions, rations, supplies, sustenance, victuals

proverb adage, aphorism, apophthegm, byword, dictum, gnome, maxim, saw, saying

proverbial accepted, acknowledged, archetypal, axiomatic, conventional, current, customary, famed, famous, legendary, notorious, self-evident, timehonoured, traditional, typical, unquestioned, well-known

provide 1. accommodate, cater, contribute, equip, furnish, outfit, provision, stock up, supply **2**. add, afford, bring, give, impart, lend, present, produce, render, serve, yield **3**. *With* **for** *or* **against** anticipate, arrange for, forearm, get ready, make arrangements, make plans, plan ahead, plan for, prepare for, take measures, take precautions **4**. *With* **for** care for, keep, look after, maintain, support, sustain, take care of **5**. determine, lay down, require, specify, state, stipulate

providence 1. destiny, divine intervention, fate, fortune, God's will, predestination **2**. care, caution, discretion, farsightedness, foresight, forethought, perspicacity, presence of mind, prudence

provident canny, careful, cautious, discreet, economical, equipped, far-

seeing, far-sighted, forearmed, foresighted, frugal, prudent, sagacious, shrewd, thrifty, vigilant, well-prepared, wise

providential fortuitous, fortunate, happy, heaven-sent, lucky, opportune, timely, welcome

provider 1. benefactor, donor, giver, source, supplier **2**. breadwinner, earner, mainstay, supporter, wage earner

providing, provided *conj*. as long as, contingent upon, given, if and only if, in case, in the event, on condition, on the assumption, subject to, upon these terms, with the proviso, with the understanding

province 1. colony, county, department, dependency, district, division, domain, region, section, territory, tract, zone **2**. *Fig*. area, business, capacity, charge, concern, duty, employment, field, function, line, orbit, part, pigeon (*Brit. inf*.), post, responsibility, role, sphere

provincial *adj*. **1**. country, homegrown, homespun, local, rural, rustic **2**. insular, inward-looking, limited, narrow, narrow-minded, parish-pump, parochial, small-minded, small-town (*U.S*.), uninformed, unsophisticated, upcountry ~*n*. **3**. country cousin, rustic, yokel

provincialism 1. insularity, lack of sophistication, narrow-mindedness, parochialism, sectionalism **2**. dialect, idiom, localism, patois, regionalism, vernacularism

provision 1. accoutrement, catering, equipping, fitting out, furnishing, providing, supplying, victualling **2**. arrangement, plan, prearrangement, precaution, preparation **3**. *Fig*. agreement, clause, condition, demand, proviso, requirement, specification, stipulation, term

provisional conditional, contingent, interim, limited, pro tem, provisory, qualified, stopgap, temporary, tentative, transitional

provisions comestibles, eatables, eats (*Sl*.), edibles, fare, food, foodstuff, groceries, grub (*Sl*.), provender, rations, stores, supplies, sustenance, viands, victuals

proviso clause, condition, limitation, provision, qualification, requirement, reservation, restriction, rider, stipulation, strings

provocation 1. *casus belli*, cause,

grounds, incitement, inducement, instigation, justification, motivation, reason, stimulus **2.** affront, annoyance, challenge, dare, grievance, indignity, injury, insult, offence, red rag, taunt, vexation

provocative 1. aggravating (*Inf.*), annoying, challenging, disturbing, galling, goading, incensing, insulting, offensive, outrageous, provoking, stimulating **2.** alluring, arousing, erotic, exciting, inviting, seductive, sexy (*Inf.*), stimulating, suggestive, tantalizing, tempting

provoke 1. affront, aggravate (*Inf.*), anger, annoy, chafe, enrage, exasperate, gall, get on one's nerves, incense, infuriate, insult, irk, irritate, madden, make one's blood boil, offend, pique, put out, rile, try one's patience, vex **2.** bring about, bring on *or* down, call forth, cause, draw forth, elicit, evoke, excite, fire, generate, give rise to, incite, induce, inflame, inspire, instigate, kindle, lead to, motivate, move, occasion, precipitate, produce, promote, prompt, rouse, stimulate, stir

provoking aggravating (*Inf.*), annoying, exasperating, galling, irking, irksome, irritating, maddening, obstructive, offensive, tiresome, vexatious, vexing

prow bow(s), fore, forepart, front, head, nose, sharp end (*Jocular*), stem

prowess 1. ability, accomplishment, adeptness, adroitness, aptitude, attainment, command, dexterity, excellence, expertise, expertness, facility, genius, mastery, skill, talent **2.** boldness, bravery, courage, daring, dauntlessness, doughtiness, fearlessness, gallantry, hardihood, heroism, intrepidity, mettle, valiance, valour

prowl cruise, hunt, lurk, move stealthily, nose around, patrol, range, roam, rove, scavenge, skulk, slink, sneak, stalk, steal

proximity adjacency, closeness, contiguity, juxtaposition, nearness, neighbourhood, propinquity, vicinity

proxy agent, attorney, delegate, deputy, factor, representative, substitute, surrogate

prude Grundy, old maid (*Inf.*), prig, puritan, schoolmarm (*Brit. inf.*)

prudence 1. canniness, care, caution, circumspection, common sense, discretion, good sense, heedfulness, judgment, judiciousness, sagacity, vigilance, wariness, wisdom **2.** careful budgeting,

economizing, economy, far-sightedness, foresight, forethought, frugality, good management, husbandry, planning, precaution, preparedness, providence, saving, thrift

prudent 1. canny, careful, cautious, circumspect, discerning, discreet, judicious, politic, sagacious, sage, sensible, shrewd, vigilant, wary, wise **2.** canny, careful, economical, far-sighted, frugal, provident, sparing, thrifty

prudery Grundyism, old-maidishness (*Inf.*), overmodesty, priggishness, primness, prudishness, puritanicalness, squeamishness, starchiness (*Inf.*), strictness, stuffiness

prudish demure, narrow-minded, old-maidish (*Inf.*), overmodest, overnice, priggish, prim, prissy (*Inf.*), proper, puritanical, schoolmarmish (*Brit. inf.*), squeamish, starchy (*Inf.*), strait-laced, stuffy, Victorian

prune clip, cut, cut back, dock, lop, pare down, reduce, shape, shorten, snip, trim

prurient 1. concupiscent, desirous, hankering, itching, lascivious, lecherous, libidinous, longing, lustful, salacious **2.** dirty, erotic, indecent, lewd, obscene, pornographic, salacious, smutty, voyeuristic

pry be a busybody, be inquisitive, be nosy (*Inf.*), ferret about, interfere, intrude, meddle, nose into, peep, peer, poke, poke one's nose in *or* into (*Inf.*), snoop (*Inf.*)

prying curious, eavesdropping, impertinent, inquisitive, interfering, intrusive, meddlesome, meddling, nosy (*Inf.*), snooping (*Inf.*), snoopy (*Inf.*), spying

psalm chant, hymn, paean, song of praise

pseud *n.* fraud, humbug, phoney (*Sl.*), poser (*Inf.*), trendy (*Brit. inf.*)

pseudo *adj.* artificial, bogus, counterfeit, ersatz, fake, false, imitation, mock, not genuine, phoney (*Sl.*), pretended, quasi-, sham, spurious

pseudonym alias, assumed name, false name, incognito, nom de guerre, nom de plume, pen name, professional name, stage name

psyche anima, essential nature, individuality, inner man, innermost self, mind, personality, pneuma (*Philos.*), self, soul, spirit, subconscious, true being

psychedelic 1. consciousness-expanding, hallucinatory, hallucinogenic, mind-bending (*Inf.*), mind-blowing (*Inf.*), mind-expanding, psychoactive, psychotomimetic, psychotropic **2**. *Inf.* crazy, freaky (*Sl.*), kaleidoscopic, multicoloured, wild

psychiatrist analyst, headshrinker (*Sl.*), psychoanalyser, psychoanalyst, psychologist, psychotherapist, shrink (*Sl.*), therapist

psychic 1. clairvoyant, extrasensory, mystic, occult, preternatural, supernatural, telekinetic, telepathic **2**. mental, psychogenic, psychological, spiritual

psychological 1. cerebral, cognitive, intellectual, mental **2**. all in the mind, emotional, imaginary, irrational, psychosomatic, subconscious, subjective, unconscious, unreal

psychology 1. behaviourism, science of mind, study of personality **2**. *Inf.* attitude, mental make-up, mental processes, thought processes, way of thinking, what makes one tick

psychopath insane person, lunatic, madman, maniac, mental case, nutcase (*Sl.*), nutter (*Brit. sl.*), psychotic, sociopath

psychotic *adj.* certifiable, demented, deranged, insane, lunatic, mad, mental, *non compos mentis*, off one's chump (head, rocker, trolley) (*Sl.*), psychopathic, unbalanced

pub or **public house** alehouse (*Archaic*), bar, boozer (*Inf.*), inn, local (*Brit. inf.*), roadhouse, tavern

puberty adolescence, awkward age, juvenescence, pubescence, teenage, teens, young adulthood

public *adj.* **1**. civic, civil, common, general, national, popular, social, state, universal, widespread **2**. accessible, communal, community, free to all, not private, open, open to the public, unrestricted **3**. acknowledged, exposed, in circulation, known, notorious, obvious, open, overt, patent, plain, published, recognized **4**. important, prominent, respected, well-known ~*n*. **5**. citizens, commonalty, community, country, electorate, everyone, hoi polloi, masses, multitude, nation, people, populace, population, society, voters **6**. audience, buyers, clientele, followers, following, patrons, supporters, those interested, trade **7**. **in public** *coram populo*, for all to see, in full view, openly, publicly

publication 1. advertisement, airing, announcement, appearance, broadcasting, declaration, disclosure, dissemination, notification, proclamation, promulgation, publishing, reporting **2**. book, booklet, brochure, handbill, issue, leaflet, magazine, newspaper, pamphlet, periodical

publicity advertising, attention, ballyhoo (*Sl.*), boost, build-up, hype (*Sl.*), plug (*Inf.*), press, promotion, public notice, puff, puffery (*Inf.*)

publicize advertise, beat the drum for (*Inf.*), bring to public notice, broadcast, give publicity to, hype (*Sl.*), make known, play up, plug (*Inf.*), promote, puff, push, spotlight, spread about, write up

public-spirited altruistic, charitable, community-minded, generous, humanitarian, philanthropic, unselfish

publish 1. bring out, issue, print, produce, put out **2**. advertise, announce, broadcast, circulate, communicate, declare, disclose, distribute, divulge, impart, leak, proclaim, promulgate, publicize, reveal, spread

pucker 1. *v.* compress, contract, crease, crinkle, crumple, draw together, furrow, gather, purse, ruckle, ruck up, ruffle, screw up, tighten, wrinkle **2**. *n.* crease, crinkle, crumple, fold, ruck, ruckle, wrinkle

puckish frolicsome, impish, mischievous, naughty, playful, roguish, sly, sportive, teasing, waggish, whimsical

pudding afters (*Brit. inf.*), dessert, last course, pud (*Inf.*), second course, sweet

puerile babyish, childish, foolish, immature, inane, infantile, irresponsible, jejune, juvenile, naive, petty, ridiculous, silly, trivial, weak

puff *n.* **1**. blast, breath, draught, emanation, flurry, gust, whiff **2**. drag (*Inf.*), pull, smoke **3**. bulge, bunching, swelling **4**. advertisement, commendation, favourable mention, good word, plug (*Inf.*), sales talk ~*v*. **5**. blow, breathe, exhale, gasp, gulp, pant, wheeze **6**. drag (*Sl.*), draw, inhale, pull at or on, smoke, suck **7**. *Usually with* **up** bloat, dilate, distend, expand, inflate, swell **8**. hype (*Sl.*), overpraise, plug (*Inf.*), praise, promote, publicize, push

puffed 1. done in (*Inf.*), exhausted, gasping, out of breath, panting, short of breath, spent, winded **2. puffed up** big-headed (*Inf.*), full of oneself, high and mighty (*Inf.*), proud, swollen-headed, too big for one's boots

puffy bloated, distended, enlarged, inflamed, inflated, puffed up, swollen

pugilism boxing, fighting, prize-fighting, the noble art *or* science, the prize ring, the ring

pugilist boxer, bruiser (*Inf.*), fighter, prizefighter, pug (*Sl.*)

pugnacious aggressive, antagonistic, argumentative, bellicose, belligerent, choleric, combative, contentious, disputatious, hot-tempered, irascible, irritable, petulant, quarrelsome

puke be nauseated, be sick, disgorge, heave, regurgitate, retch, spew, throw up (*Inf.*), vomit

pukka authentic, bona fide, genuine, official, proper, real

pull *v.* **1.** drag, draw, haul, jerk, tow, trail, tug, yank **2.** cull, draw out, extract, gather, pick, pluck, remove, take out, uproot, weed **3.** dislocate, rend, rip, sprain, strain, stretch, tear, wrench **4.** *Inf.* attract, draw, entice, lure, magnetize **5. pull apart** *or* **to pieces** attack, criticize, find fault, flay, lay into, pan (*Inf.*), pick holes in, run down, slam (*Sl.*), slate (*Inf.*) **6. pull oneself together** *Inf.* buck up (*Inf.*), get a grip on oneself, get over it, regain composure, snap out of it (*Inf.*) **7. pull strings** *Brit. inf.* influence, pull wires (*U.S.*), use one's influence **8. pull someone's leg** *Inf.* chaff, have (someone) on, joke, make fun of, poke fun at, rag, rib (*Inf.*), tease, twit ~*n.* **9.** jerk, tug, twitch, yank **10.** attraction, drawing power, effort, exertion, force, forcefulness, influence, lure, magnetism, power **11.** *Inf.* advantage, clout (*Inf.*), influence, leverage, muscle, weight **12.** drag (*Inf.*), inhalation, puff

pull down bulldoze, demolish, destroy, raze, remove

pull in 1. arrive, come in, draw in, draw up, reach, stop **2.** attract, bring in, draw **3.** *Brit. sl.* arrest, bust (*Inf.*), collar (*Inf.*), nab (*Inf.*), nail (*Inf.*), pinch (*Inf.*), run in (*Sl.*), take into custody **4.** clear, earn, gain, gross, make, net, pocket, take home

pull off 1. detach, doff, remove, rip off, tear off, wrench off **2.** accomplish, bring off, carry out, manage, score a success, secure one's object, succeed

pull out abandon, depart, evacuate, leave, quit, rat on, retreat, stop participating, withdraw

pull through come through, get better, get over, pull round, rally, recover, survive, weather

pull up 1. dig out, lift, raise, uproot **2.** brake, come to a halt, halt, reach a standstill, stop **3.** admonish, carpet (*Inf.*), castigate, dress down (*Inf.*), rebuke, reprimand, reprove, take to task, tell off (*Inf.*), tick off (*Inf.*)

pulp *n.* **1.** flesh, marrow, soft part **2.** mash, mush, pap, paste, pomace, semiliquid, semisolid, triturate ~*v.* **3.** crush, mash, pulverize, squash, triturate ~*adj.* **4.** cheap, lurid, mushy (*Inf.*), rubbishy, sensational, trashy

pulpy fleshy, mushy, pappy, soft, squashy, succulent

pulsate beat, hammer, oscillate, palpitate, pound, pulse, quiver, throb, thud, thump, tick, vibrate

pulse 1. *n.* beat, beating, oscillation, pulsation, rhythm, stroke, throb, throbbing, vibration **2.** *v.* beat, pulsate, throb, tick, vibrate

pulverize 1. bray, comminute, crush, granulate, grind, levigate (*Chem.*), mill, pestle, pound, triturate **2.** *Fig.* annihilate, crush, defeat, demolish, destroy, flatten, smash, vanquish, wreck

pummel bang, batter, beat, hammer, knock, pound, punch, rain blows upon, strike, thump

pump *v.* **1.** *With* **out** bail out, drain, draw off, drive out, empty, force out, siphon **2.** *With* **up** blow up, dilate, inflate **3.** drive, force, inject, pour, push, send, supply **4.** cross-examine, give (someone) the third degree, grill (*Inf.*), interrogate, probe, question closely, quiz, worm out of

pun double entendre, equivoque, paronomasia (*Rhetoric*), play on words, quip, witticism

punch[1] *v.* **1.** bash (*Inf.*), biff (*Sl.*), bop (*Inf.*), box, clout (*Inf.*), hit, plug (*Sl.*), pummel, slam, slug, smash, sock (*Sl.*), strike, wallop (*Inf.*) ~*n.* **2.** bash (*Inf.*), biff (*Sl.*), blow, bop (*Inf.*), clout (*Inf.*), hit, jab, knock, plug (*Sl.*), sock (*Sl.*), thump, wallop (*Inf.*) **3.** *Inf.* bite, drive, effectiveness, force, forcefulness, impact, point, verve, vigour

punch[2] *v.* bore, cut, drill, perforate, pierce, pink, prick, puncture, stamp

punch-drunk befuddled, confused, dazed, groggy (*Inf.*), in a daze, knocked silly, punchy (*Inf.*), reeling, slaphappy (*Inf.*), staggering, stupefied, unsteady, woozy (*Inf.*)

punch-up argument, battle royal, brawl, dingdong, dust-up (*Inf.*), fight, free-for-all (*Inf.*), row, scrap (*Inf.*), set-to (*Inf.*), shindy, stand-up fight (*Inf.*)

punchy aggressive, dynamic, effective, forceful, incisive, lively, spirited, vigorous

punctilio 1. exactitude, finickiness, meticulousness, particularity, precision, punctiliousness, scrupulousness, strictness **2.** convention, delicacy, distinction, fine point, formality, nicety, particular, refinement

punctilious careful, ceremonious, conscientious, exact, finicky, formal, fussy, meticulous, nice, particular, precise, proper, scrupulous, strict

punctual early, exact, in good time, on the dot, on time, precise, prompt, punctilious, seasonable, strict, timely

punctuality promptitude, promptness, readiness, regularity

punctuate 1. break, interject, interrupt, intersperse, pepper, sprinkle **2.** accentuate, emphasize, lay stress on, mark, point up, stress, underline

puncture *n.* **1.** break, cut, damage, hole, leak, nick, opening, perforation, rupture, slit **2.** flat, flat tyre ~*v.* **3.** bore, cut, nick, penetrate, perforate, pierce, prick, rupture **4.** deflate, go down, go flat **5.** deflate, discourage, disillusion, flatten, humble, take down a peg (*Inf.*)

pundit buff (*Inf.*), maestro, one of the cognoscenti, (self-appointed) authority *or* expert

pungent 1. acid, acrid, aromatic, bitter, highly flavoured, hot, peppery, piquant, seasoned, sharp, sour, spicy, stinging, strong, tangy, tart **2.** acrimonious, acute, barbed, biting, caustic, cutting, incisive, keen, mordant, penetrating, piercing, poignant, pointed, sarcastic, scathing, sharp, stinging, stringent, telling, trenchant

punish 1. beat, castigate, chasten, chastise, correct, discipline, flog, give a lesson to, give (someone) the works (*Sl.*), lash, penalize, rap someone's knuckles, scourge, sentence, slap someone's wrist, whip **2.** abuse, batter, give (someone) a going over (*Inf.*), harm, hurt, injure, knock about, maltreat, manhandle, misuse, oppress, rough up

punishable blameworthy, chargeable, convictable, criminal, culpable, indictable

punishing arduous, backbreaking, burdensome, demanding, exhausting, grinding, gruelling, hard, strenuous, taxing, tiring, uphill, wearing

punishment 1. chastening, chastisement, comeuppance (*Sl.*), correction, discipline, just deserts, penalty, penance, punitive measures, retribution, sanction, what for (*Inf.*) **2.** *Inf.* abuse, beating, hard work, maltreatment, manhandling, pain, rough treatment, slave labour, torture, victimization

punitive in reprisal, in retaliation, punitory, retaliative, retaliatory, revengeful, vindictive

punt *v.* **1.** back, bet, gamble, lay, stake, wager ~*n.* **2.** bet, gamble, stake, wager **3.** backer, better, gambler, punter

punter *n.* **1.** backer, better, gambler, punt **2.** *Inf.* bloke (*Brit. inf.*), fellow, guy (*Inf.*), man in the street, person **3.** *Inf.* client, customer

puny 1. diminutive, dwarfish, feeble, frail, little, pint-sized (*Inf.*), pygmy, sickly, stunted, tiny, underfed, undersized, undeveloped, weak, weakly **2.** inconsequential, inferior, insignificant, minor, paltry, petty, piddling (*Inf.*), trifling, trivial, worthless

pup *or* **puppy** *Fig.* braggart, cub, jackanapes, popinjay, whelp, whippersnapper, young dog

pupil beginner, catechumen, disciple, learner, neophyte, novice, scholar, schoolboy, schoolgirl, student, tyro

puppet 1. doll, marionette **2.** *Fig.* cat's-paw, creature, dupe, figurehead, gull (*Archaic*), instrument, mouthpiece, pawn, stooge, tool

purchasable 1. bribable, corrupt, corruptible, dishonest, having one's price, unscrupulous, venal **2.** available, for sale, in stock, obtainable, on sale, on the market, to be had

purchase *v.* **1.** acquire, buy, come by, gain, get, get hold of, invest in, make a purchase, obtain, pay for, pick up, procure, secure, shop for **2.** achieve, attain, earn, gain, realize, win ~*n.* **3.** acquisition, asset, buy, gain, investment, possession, property **4.** advantage, edge, foothold, footing, grasp, grip, hold, influence, lever, leverage, support, toehold

purchaser buyer, consumer, customer, vendee (*Law*)

pure 1. authentic, clear, flawless, genuine, natural, neat, perfect, real, simple, straight, true, unalloyed, unmixed **2.** clean, disinfected, germ-free, immaculate, pasteurized, sanitary, spotless, sterile, sterilized, unadulterated, unblemished, uncontaminated, unpolluted, untainted, wholesome **3.** blameless, chaste, guileless, honest, immaculate, innocent, maidenly, modest, true, uncorrupted, undefiled, unspotted, unstained, unsullied, upright, virgin, virginal, virtuous **4.** absolute, complete, mere, sheer, thorough, unmitigated, unqualified, utter **5.** abstract, academic, philosophical, speculative, theoretical

purebred blood, full-blooded, pedigree, thoroughbred

purely absolutely, completely, entirely, exclusively, just, merely, only, plainly, simply, solely, totally, wholly

purgative 1. *n.* aperient (*Medical*), cathartic, depurative, emetic, enema, evacuant, laxative, physic (*Rare*), purge **2.** *adj.* aperient (*Medical*), cleansing, depurative, evacuant, laxative, purging

purgatory *As used informally* agony, hell (*Inf.*), hell on earth, misery, murder (*Inf.*), the rack, torment, torture

purge *v.* **1.** clean out, dismiss, do away with, eject, eradicate, expel, exterminate, get rid of, kill, liquidate, oust, remove, rid of, rout out, sweep out, wipe out **2.** absolve, cleanse, clear, exonerate, expiate, forgive, pardon, purify, wash ~*n.* **3.** cleanup, crushing, ejection, elimination, eradication, expulsion, liquidation, reign of terror, removal, suppression, witch hunt **4.** aperient (*Medical*), cathartic, dose of salts, emetic, enema, laxative, physic (*Rare*), purgative (*Medical*)

purify 1. clarify, clean, cleanse, decontaminate, disinfect, filter, fumigate, refine, sanitize, wash **2.** absolve, cleanse, exculpate, exonerate, lustrate, redeem, sanctify, shrive

purist classicist, formalist, pedant, precisian, stickler

puritan 1. *n.* fanatic, moralist, pietist, prude, rigorist, zealot **2.** *adj.* ascetic, austere, hidebound, intolerant, moralistic, narrow, narrow-minded, prudish, puritanical, severe, strait-laced, strict

puritanical ascetic, austere, bigoted, disapproving, fanatical, forbidding, narrow, narrow-minded, prim, proper, prudish, puritan, rigid, severe, stiff, strait-laced, strict, stuffy

purity 1. brilliance, clarity, cleanliness, cleanness, clearness, faultlessness, fineness, genuineness, immaculateness, pureness, untaintedness, wholesomeness **2.** blamelessness, chasteness, chastity, decency, guilelessness, honesty, innocence, integrity, piety, rectitude, sincerity, virginity, virtue, virtuousness

purlieus 1. borders, confines, environs, fringes, limits, neighbourhood, outskirts, periphery, precincts, suburbs, vicinity **2.** *Sometimes singular* hang-out (*Inf.*), haunt, patch, resort, stamping ground, territory

purloin appropriate, filch, knock off (*Sl.*), lift (*Inf.*), nick (*Brit. sl.*), nobble (*Brit. sl.*), pilfer, pinch (*Inf.*), prig (*Brit. sl.*), rob, snaffle (*Brit. inf.*), snitch (*Sl.*), steal, swipe (*Sl.*), thieve, walk off with

purport *v.* **1.** allege, assert, claim, declare, maintain, pose as, pretend, proclaim, profess **2.** betoken, convey, denote, express, imply, import, indicate, intend, mean, point to, signify, suggest ~*n.* **3.** bearing, drift, gist, idea, implication, import, meaning, significance, spirit, tendency, tenor **4.** aim, design, intent, intention, object, objective, plan, purpose

purpose *n.* **1.** aim, design, function, idea, intention, object, point, principle, reason **2.** aim, ambition, aspiration, desire, end, goal, hope, intention, object, objective, plan, project, scheme, target, view, wish **3.** constancy, determination, firmness, persistence, resolution, resolve, single-mindedness, steadfastness, tenacity, will **4.** advantage, avail, benefit, effect, gain, good, outcome, profit, result, return, use, utility **5. on purpose** by design, deliberately, designedly, intentionally, knowingly, purposely, wilfully, wittingly ~*v.* **6.** aim, aspire, commit oneself, contemplate, decide, design, determine, have a mind to, intend, make up one's mind, mean, meditate, plan, propose, resolve, set one's sights on, think to, work towards

purposeful decided, deliberate, determined, firm, fixed, positive, resolute, resolved, settled, single-minded, steadfast, strong-willed, tenacious, unfaltering

purposeless aimless, empty, goalless,

motiveless, needless, pointless, senseless, uncalled-for, unnecessary, useless, vacuous, wanton

purposely by design, calculatedly, consciously, deliberately, designedly, expressly, intentionally, knowingly, on purpose, wilfully, with intent

purse n. **1**. money-bag, pouch, wallet **2**. coffers, exchequer, funds, means, money, resources, treasury, wealth, wherewithal **3**. award, gift, present, prize, reward ~v. **4**. close, contract, press together, pucker, tighten, wrinkle

pursuance bringing about, carrying out, discharge, doing, effecting, execution, following, performance, prosecution, pursuing

pursue **1**. accompany, attend, chase, dog, follow, give chase to, go after, harass, harry, haunt, hound, hunt, hunt down, plague, run after, shadow, stalk, tail, track **2**. aim for, aspire to, desire, have as one's goal, purpose, seek, strive for, try for, work towards **3**. adhere to, carry on, continue, cultivate, hold to, keep on, maintain, persevere in, persist in, proceed, see through **4**. apply oneself, carry on, conduct, engage in, perform, ply, practise, prosecute, tackle, wage, work at **5**. chase after, court, make up to (*Inf.*), pay attention to, pay court to, set one's cap at, woo

pursuit **1**. chase, hunt, hunting, inquiry, quest, search, seeking, tracking, trail, trailing **2**. activity, hobby, interest, line, occupation, pastime, pleasure, vocation

purvey **1**. cater, deal in, furnish, provide, provision, retail, sell, supply, trade in, victual **2**. communicate, make available, pass on, publish, retail, spread, transmit

purview **1**. ambit, compass, confine(s), extent, field, limit, orbit, province, range, reach, scope, sphere **2**. comprehension, ken, overview, perspective, range of view, understanding

push v. **1**. depress, drive, poke, press, propel, ram, shove, thrust **2**. elbow, jostle, make *or* force one's way, move, shoulder, shove, squeeze, thrust **3**. egg on, encourage, expedite, hurry, impel, incite, persuade, press, prod, speed (up), spur, urge **4**. advertise, boost, cry up, hype (*Sl.*), make known, plug (*Inf.*), promote, propagandize, publicize, puff **5**. browbeat, coerce, constrain, dragoon, en-

courage, exert influence on, influence, oblige ~n. **6**. butt, jolt, nudge, poke, prod, shove, thrust **7**. *Inf.* ambition, determination, drive, dynamism, energy, enterprise, get-up-and-go (*Inf.*), go (*Inf.*), gumption (*Inf.*), initiative, vigour, vitality **8**. *Inf.* advance, assault, attack, charge, effort, offensive, onset, thrust **9**. **the push** *Sl.* discharge, dismissal, marching orders (*Inf.*), one's books (*Inf.*), one's cards, the boot (*Sl.*), the sack (*Inf.*)

pushed *Often with* **for** hurried, in difficulty, pressed, rushed, short of, tight, under pressure, up against it (*Inf.*)

pushing **1**. ambitious, determined, driving, dynamic, enterprising, go-ahead, on the go, purposeful, resourceful **2**. assertive, bold, brash, bumptious, forward, impertinent, intrusive, presumptuous, pushy (*Inf.*), self-assertive

push off beat it (*Sl.*), depart, get lost (*Inf.*), go away, hit the road (*Sl.*), launch, leave, light out (*Inf.*), make oneself scarce (*Inf.*), shove off (*Inf.*), take off (*Inf.*)

pushover **1**. child's play (*Inf.*), cinch (*Sl.*), doddle (*Brit. sl.*), picnic (*Inf.*), piece of cake (*Brit. inf.*), walkover (*Inf.*) **2**. chump (*Inf.*), easy *or* soft mark, easy game (*Inf.*), mug (*Sl.*), soft touch (*Inf.*), stooge (*Sl.*), sucker (*Sl.*), walkover (*Inf.*)

pushy aggressive, ambitious, bold, brash, bumptious, forceful, loud, obnoxious, obtrusive, offensive, officious, presumptuous, pushing, self-assertive

pusillanimous chicken-hearted, cowardly, craven, faint-hearted, fearful, feeble, gutless (*Inf.*), lily-livered, recreant (*Archaic*), spineless, timid, timorous, weak, yellow (*Inf.*)

pussyfoot **1**. creep, prowl, slink, steal, tiptoe, tread warily **2**. beat about the bush, be noncommittal, equivocate, hedge, hum and haw, prevaricate, sit on the fence, tergiversate

pustule abscess, blister, boil, fester, gathering, pimple, ulcer

put **1**. bring, deposit, establish, fix, lay, place, position, rest, set, settle, situate **2**. commit, condemn, consign, doom, enjoin, impose, inflict, levy, subject **3**. assign, constrain, employ, force, induce, make, oblige, require, set, subject to **4**. express, phrase, pose, set, state, utter, word **5**. advance, bring forward, forward, offer, posit, present, propose, set before, submit, tender **6**. cast, fling, heave, hurl, lob, pitch, throw, toss

put across *or* **over** communicate, convey, explain, get across, get through, make clear, make oneself understood, spell out

put aside *or* **by 1**. cache, deposit, keep in reserve, lay by, salt away, save, squirrel away, stockpile, store, stow away **2**. bury, discount, disregard, forget, ignore

putative alleged, assumed, commonly believed, imputed, presumed, presumptive, reported, reputed, supposed

put away 1. put back, replace, return to (its) place, tidy away **2**. deposit, keep, lay in, put by, save, set aside, store away **3**. certify, commit, confine, institutionalize, lock up **4**. consume, devour, eat up, gobble, gulp down, wolf down **5**. destroy, do away with, put down, put out of its misery, put to sleep

put-down dig, disparagement, gibe, humiliation, knock (*Inf.*), one in the eye (*Inf.*), rebuff, sarcasm, slight, sneer, snub

put down 1. enter, inscribe, log, record, set down, take down, transcribe, write down **2**. crush, quash, quell, repress, silence, stamp out, suppress **3**. *With* **to** ascribe, attribute, impute, set down **4**. destroy, do away with, put away, put out of its misery, put to sleep **5**. *Sl.* condemn, crush, deflate, dismiss, disparage, humiliate, mortify, reject, shame, slight, snub

put forward advance, introduce, move, nominate, present, press, proffer, propose, recommend, submit, suggest, tender

put off 1. defer, delay, hold over, postpone, put back, reschedule **2**. abash, confuse, discomfit, disconcert, dismay, distress, nonplus, perturb, rattle (*Inf.*), throw (*Inf.*), unsettle **3**. discourage, dishearten, dissuade

put on 1. change into, don, dress, get dressed in, slip into **2**. affect, assume, fake, feign, make believe, play-act, pretend, sham, simulate **3**. do, mount, present, produce, show, stage **4**. add, gain, increase by **5**. back, bet, lay, place, wager

put out 1. anger, annoy, confound, disturb, exasperate, harass, irk, irritate, nettle, perturb, provoke, vex **2**. blow out, douse, extinguish, quench, smother, snuff out, stamp out **3**. bother, discomfit, discommode, discompose, disconcert, discountenance, disturb, embarrass, impose upon, incommode, inconvenience, put on the spot, trouble, upset **4**. bring out, broadcast, circulate, issue, make known, make public, publish, release

putrefy corrupt, decay, decompose, deteriorate, go bad, rot, spoil, stink, taint

putrescent decaying, decomposing, going bad, rotting, stinking

putrid bad, contaminated, corrupt, decayed, decomposed, fetid, foul, off, putrefied, rancid, rank, reeking, rotten, rotting, spoiled, stinking, tainted

put through accomplish, achieve, bring off, carry through, conclude, do, effect, execute, manage, pull off, realize

put up 1. build, construct, erect, fabricate, raise **2**. accommodate, board, entertain, give one lodging, house, lodge, take in **3**. float, nominate, offer, present, propose, put forward, recommend, submit **4**. advance, give, invest, pay, pledge, provide, supply **5**. **put up to** egg on, encourage, goad, incite, instigate, prompt, put the idea into one's head, urge **6**. **put up with** *Inf.* abide, bear, brook, endure, lump (*Inf.*), pocket, stand, stand for, stomach, suffer, swallow, take, tolerate

put-upon abused, beset, exploited, harried, imposed upon, inconvenienced, overworked, put-out, saddled, taken advantage of, taken for a fool, taken for granted, troubled

puzzle *v.* **1**. baffle, beat (*Sl.*), bewilder, confound, confuse, flummox, mystify, nonplus, perplex, stump **2**. ask oneself, brood, cudgel *or* rack one's brains, mull over, muse, ponder, study, think about, think hard, wonder **3**. *Usually with* **out** clear up, crack, crack the code, decipher, figure out, find the key, get it, get the answer, resolve, see, solve, sort out, think through, unravel, work out ~*n.* **4**. brainteaser (*Inf.*), conundrum, enigma, labyrinth, maze, mystery, paradox, poser, problem, question, question mark, riddle **5**. bafflement, bewilderment, confusion, difficulty, dilemma, perplexity, quandary, uncertainty

puzzled at a loss, at sea, baffled, beaten, bewildered, clueless, confused, doubtful, flummoxed, in a fog, lost, mixed up, mystified, nonplussed, perplexed, stuck, stumped, without a clue

puzzlement bafflement, bewilderment, confusion, disorientation, doubt, doubtfulness, mystification, perplexity, questioning, surprise, uncertainty, wonder

puzzling abstruse, ambiguous, baffling, bewildering, beyond one, enigmatic, full of surprises, hard, incomprehensible, inexplicable, involved, knotty, labyrinthine, misleading, mystifying, perplexing, unaccountable, unclear, unfathomable

pygmy *n*. **1**. dwarf, homunculus, Lilliputian, manikin, midget, shrimp (*Inf.*), Tom Thumb **2**. cipher, lightweight (*Inf.*), mediocrity, nobody, nonentity, pipsqueak (*Inf.*), small fry ~*adj*. **3**. baby, diminutive, dwarf, dwarfish, elfin, Lilliputian, midget, miniature, minuscule, pocket, pygmean, small, stunted, tiny, undersized, wee

pyromaniac arsonist, firebug (*Inf.*), fire raiser, incendiary

Q

quack 1. *n.* charlatan, fake, fraud, humbug, impostor, mountebank, phoney (*Sl.*), pretender, quacksalver (*Archaic*) **2.** *adj.* counterfeit, fake, fraudulent, phoney (*Sl.*), pretended, sham

quaff carouse, down, drink, gulp, guzzle, imbibe, swallow, swig (*Inf.*), tope

quaggy boggy, fenny, marshy, miry, muddy, mushy, paludal, soft, soggy, squelchy, swampy, yielding

quagmire 1. bog, fen, marsh, mire, morass, quicksand, slough, swamp **2.** difficulty, dilemma, entanglement, fix (*Inf.*), imbroglio, impasse, jam (*Inf.*), muddle, pass, pickle (*Inf.*), pinch, plight, predicament, quandary, scrape (*Inf.*)

quail blanch, blench, cower, cringe, droop, faint, falter, flinch, have cold feet (*Inf.*), quake, recoil, shake, shrink, shudder, tremble

quaint 1. bizarre, curious, droll, eccentric, fanciful, fantastic, odd, old-fashioned, original, peculiar, queer, singular, strange, unusual, whimsical **2.** antiquated, antique, artful, charming, gothic, ingenious, old-fashioned, old-world, picturesque

quake convulse, move, pulsate, quail, quiver, rock, shake, shiver, shudder, throb, totter, tremble, vibrate, waver, wobble

qualification 1. ability, accomplishment, aptitude, attribute, capability, capacity, eligibility, endowment(s), fitness, quality, skill, suitability, suitableness **2.** allowance, caveat, condition, criterion, exception, exemption, limitation, modification, objection, prerequisite, proviso, requirement, reservation, restriction, stipulation

qualified 1. able, accomplished, adept, capable, certificated, competent, efficient, equipped, experienced, expert, fit, knowledgeable, licensed, practised, proficient, skilful, talented, trained **2.** bounded, circumscribed, conditional, confined, contingent, equivocal, guarded, limited, modified, provisional, reserved, restricted

qualify 1. capacitate, certify, commission, condition, empower, endow, equip,

fit, ground, permit, prepare, ready, sanction, train **2.** abate, adapt, assuage, circumscribe, diminish, ease, lessen, limit, mitigate, moderate, modify, modulate, reduce, regulate, restrain, restrict, soften, temper, vary **3.** characterize, describe, designate, distinguish, modify, name

quality 1. aspect, attribute, characteristic, condition, feature, mark, peculiarity, property, trait **2.** character, constitution, description, essence, kind, make, nature, sort **3.** calibre, distinction, excellence, grade, merit, position, preeminence, rank, standing, status, superiority, value, worth **4.** *Obsolete* aristocracy, gentry, nobility, ruling class, upper class

qualm 1. anxiety, apprehension, compunction, disquiet, doubt, hesitation, misgiving, regret, reluctance, remorse, scruple, twinge *or* pang of conscience, uncertainty, uneasiness **2.** agony, attack, nausea, pang, queasiness, sickness, spasm, throe (*Rare*), twinge

quandary bewilderment, cleft stick, delicate situation, difficulty, dilemma, doubt, embarrassment, impasse, perplexity, plight, predicament, puzzle, strait, uncertainty

quantity 1. aggregate, allotment, amount, lot, number, part, portion, quota, sum, total **2.** bulk, capacity, expanse, extent, greatness, length, magnitude, mass, measure, size, volume

quarrel *n.* **1.** affray, altercation, argument, brawl, breach, broil, commotion, contention, controversy, difference (of opinion), disagreement, discord, disputation, dispute, dissension, dissidence, disturbance, feud, fight, fracas, fray, misunderstanding, row, scrap (*Inf.*), spat, squabble, strife, tiff, tumult, vendetta, wrangle ~*v.* **2.** altercate, argue, bicker, brawl, clash, differ, disagree, dispute, fall out (*Inf.*), fight, row, spar, squabble, wrangle **3.** carp, cavil, complain, decry, disapprove, find fault, object to, take exception to

quarrelsome argumentative, belligerent, cat-and-dog (*Inf.*), choleric, combative, contentious, cross, disputatious, fractious, ill-tempered, irascible, irritable, peevish, petulant, pugnacious, querulous

quarry aim, game, goal, objective, prey, prize, victim

quarter *n.* **1.** area, direction, district, locality, location, neighbourhood, part, place, point, position, province, region, side, spot, station, territory, zone **2.** clemency, compassion, favour, forgiveness, leniency, mercy, pity ~*v.* **3.** accommodate, billet, board, house, install, lodge, place, post, put up, station

quarters abode, accommodation, barracks, billet, cantonment (*Military*), chambers, digs (*Inf.*), domicile, dwelling, habitation, lodging, lodgings, post, residence, rooms, shelter, station

quash **1.** beat, crush, destroy, extinguish, extirpate, overthrow, put down, quell, quench, repress, squash, subdue, suppress **2.** annul, cancel, declare null and void, invalidate, nullify, overrule, overthrow, rescind, reverse, revoke, set aside, void

quasi- **1.** almost, apparently, partly, seemingly, supposedly **2.** apparent, fake, mock, near, nominal, pretended, pseudo-, seeming, semi-, sham, so-called, synthetic, virtual, would-be

quaver **1.** *v.* flicker, flutter, oscillate, pulsate, quake, quiver, shake, shudder, thrill, tremble, trill, twitter, vibrate, waver **2.** *n.* break, quiver, shake, sob, throb, tremble, trembling, tremor, trill, vibration, warble

queasy **1.** bilious, giddy, green around the gills (*Inf.*), groggy (*Inf.*), ill, indisposed, nauseated, off colour, queer, sick, sickish, squeamish, uncomfortable, unwell, upset **2.** anxious, concerned, fidgety, ill at ease, restless, troubled, uncertain, uneasy, worried

queen **1.** consort, monarch, ruler, sovereign **2.** diva, doyenne, ideal, idol, mistress, model, perfection, prima donna, star

queenly grand, imperial, majestic, noble, regal, royal, stately

queer *adj.* **1.** abnormal, anomalous, atypical, curious, disquieting, droll, eerie, erratic, extraordinary, funny, odd, outlandish, *outré*, peculiar, remarkable, singular, strange, uncanny, uncommon, unconventional, unnatural, unorthodox, unusual, weird **2.** doubtful, dubious,

fishy (*Inf.*), irregular, mysterious, puzzling, questionable, shady (*Inf.*), suspicious **3.** dizzy, faint, giddy, light-headed, queasy, reeling, uneasy **4.** crazy, demented, eccentric, idiosyncratic, irrational, mad, odd, touched, unbalanced, unhinged ~*v.* **5.** botch, endanger, harm, impair, imperil, injure, jeopardize, mar, ruin, spoil, thwart, wreck

quell **1.** conquer, crush, defeat, extinguish, overcome, overpower, put down, quash, squelch, stamp out, stifle, subdue, suppress, vanquish **2.** allay, alleviate, appease, assuage, calm, compose, deaden, dull, mitigate, moderate, mollify, pacify, quiet, silence, soothe

quench **1.** check, crush, destroy, douse, end, extinguish, put out, smother, snuff out, squelch, stifle, suppress **2.** allay, appease, cool, sate, satiate, satisfy, slake

querulous cantankerous, captious, carping, censorious, complaining, critical, cross, discontented, dissatisfied, fault-finding, fretful, grouchy (*Inf.*), grumbling, hard to please, irascible, irritable, murmuring, peevish, petulant, plaintive, sour, testy, touchy, waspish, whining

query *v.* **1.** ask, enquire, question **2.** challenge, disbelieve, dispute, distrust, doubt, mistrust, suspect ~*n.* **3.** demand, doubt, hesitation, inquiry, objection, problem, question, reservation, scepticism, suspicion

quest *n.* adventure, crusade, enterprise, expedition, exploration, hunt, journey, mission, pilgrimage, pursuit, search, voyage

question *v.* **1.** ask, catechize, cross-examine, enquire, examine, grill (*Inf.*), interrogate, interview, investigate, probe, pump (*Inf.*), quiz, sound out **2.** call into question, cast doubt upon, challenge, controvert, disbelieve, dispute, distrust, doubt, impugn, mistrust, oppose, query, suspect ~*n.* **3.** examination, inquiry, interrogation, investigation **4.** argument, confusion, contention, controversy, debate, difficulty, dispute, doubt, dubiety, misgiving, problem, query, uncertainty **5.** issue, motion, point, point at issue, proposal, proposition, subject, theme, topic **6.** **in question** at issue, in doubt, open to debate, under discussion **7.** **out of the question** impossible, inconceivable, not to be thought of, unthinkable

questionable arguable, controversial, controvertible, debatable, disputable, doubtful, dubious, dubitable, equivocal, fishy (*Inf.*), moot, paradoxical, problematical, shady (*Inf.*), suspect, suspicious, uncertain, unproven, unreliable

queue chain, concatenation, file, line, order, progression, sequence, series, string, succession, train

quibble 1. *v.* carp, cavil, equivocate, evade, pretend, prevaricate, shift, split hairs **2.** *n.* artifice, cavil, complaint, criticism, duplicity, equivocation, evasion, nicety, niggle, objection, pretence, prevarication, protest, quirk, shift, sophism, subterfuge, subtlety

quibbling ambiguous, carping, caviling, critical, equivocal, evasive, hair-splitting, jesuitical, niggling, nit-picking (*Inf.*), overnice, sophistical

quick 1. active, brief, brisk, cursory, expeditious, express, fast, fleet, hasty, headlong, hurried, perfunctory, prompt, rapid, speedy, sudden, swift **2.** agile, alert, animated, energetic, flying, keen, lively, nimble, spirited, sprightly, spry, vivacious, winged **3.** able, acute, adept, adroit, all there (*Inf.*), apt, astute, bright, clever, deft, dexterous, discerning, intelligent, nimble-witted, perceptive, quick on the uptake (*Inf.*), quick-witted, receptive, sharp, shrewd, skilful, smart **4.** abrupt, curt, excitable, hasty, impatient, irascible, irritable, passionate, petulant, testy, touchy **5.** *Archaic* alive, animate, existing, live, living, viable

quicken 1. accelerate, dispatch, expedite, hasten, hurry, impel, precipitate, speed **2.** activate, animate, arouse, energize, excite, galvanize, incite, inspire, invigorate, kindle, refresh, reinvigorate, resuscitate, revitalize, revive, rouse, stimulate, strengthen, vitalize, vivify

quickly abruptly, at a rate of knots (*Inf.*), at *or* on the double, at speed, briskly, expeditiously, fast, hastily, hell for leather, hurriedly, immediately, instantly, posthaste, promptly, quick, rapidly, soon, speedily, swiftly, with all speed

quick-tempered choleric, excitable, fiery, hot-tempered, impatient, impulsive, irascible, irritable, petulant, quarrelsome, shrewish, splenetic, testy, waspish

quick-witted alert, astute, clever, keen, perceptive, sharp, shrewd, smart

quid pro quo compensation, equivalent, exchange, interchange, reprisal, retaliation, substitution, tit for tat

quiescent calm, dormant, in abeyance, inactive, latent, motionless, peaceful, placid, quiet, resting, serene, silent, smooth, still, tranquil, unagitated, undisturbed, unmoving, unruffled

quiet *adj.* **1.** dumb, hushed, inaudible, low, low-pitched, noiseless, peaceful, silent, soft, soundless **2.** calm, contented, gentle, mild, motionless, pacific, peaceful, placid, restful, serene, smooth, tranquil, untroubled **3.** isolated, private, retired, secluded, secret, sequestered, undisturbed, unfrequented **4.** conservative, modest, plain, restrained, simple, sober, subdued, unassuming, unobtrusive, unpretentious **5.** collected, docile, even-tempered, gentle, imperturbable, meek, mild, phlegmatic, reserved, retiring, sedate, shy, unexcitable ~*n.* **6.** calmness, ease, peace, quietness, repose, rest, serenity, silence, stillness, tranquillity

quieten *v.* allay, alleviate, appease, assuage, blunt, calm, compose, deaden, dull, hush, lull, mitigate, mollify, muffle, mute, palliate, quell, quiet, shush (*Inf.*), silence, soothe, stifle, still, stop, subdue, tranquillize

quietly 1. confidentially, dumbly, in a low voice *or* whisper, in an undertone, inaudibly, in hushed tones, in silence, mutely, noiselessly, privately, secretly, silently, softly, without talking **2.** calmly, contentedly, dispassionately, meekly, mildly, patiently, placidly, serenely, undemonstratively **3.** coyly, demurely, diffidently, humbly, modestly, unassumingly, unobtrusively, unostentatiously, unpretentiously

quietness calm, calmness, hush, peace, placidity, quiescence, quiet, quietude, repose, rest, serenity, silence, still, stillness, tranquillity

quietus clincher (*Inf.*), coup de grâce, death, deathblow, demise, end, final blow, finish

quilt bedspread, comforter (*U.S.*), counterpane, coverlet, duvet, eiderdown

quintessence core, distillation, essence, extract, gist, heart, kernel, life-blood, marrow, pith, soul, spirit

quip n. badinage, bon mot, gibe, jest, joke, pleasantry, repartee, retort, riposte, sally, wisecrack (Inf.), witticism

quirk aberration, caprice, characteristic, eccentricity, fancy, fetish, foible, habit, idée fixe, idiosyncrasy, kink, mannerism, oddity, peculiarity, singularity, trait, vagary, whim

quisling betrayer, collaborator, fifth columnist, Judas, renegade, traitor, turncoat

quit v. 1. abandon, abdicate, decamp, depart, desert, exit, forsake, go, leave, pull out, relinquish, renounce, resign, retire, surrender, take off (Inf.), withdraw 2. abandon, cease, conclude, discontinue, drop, end, give up, halt, stop, suspend ~adj. 3. absolved, acquitted, clear, discharged, exculpated, exempt, exonerated, free, released, rid of

quite 1. absolutely, completely, considerably, entirely, fully, in all respects, largely, perfectly, precisely, totally, wholly, without reservation 2. fairly, moderately, rather, reasonably, relatively, somewhat, to a certain extent, to some degree 3. in fact, in reality, in truth, really, truly

quiver 1. v. agitate, convulse, oscillate, palpitate, pulsate, quake, quaver, shake, shiver, shudder, tremble, vibrate 2. n. convulsion, oscillation, palpitation, pulsation, shake, shiver, shudder, spasm, throb, tic, tremble, tremor, vibration

quixotic absurd, chimerical, chivalrous, dreamy, fanciful, fantastical, idealistic, imaginary, impracticable, impractical, impulsive, mad, romantic, unrealistic, unworldly, Utopian, visionary, wild

quiz 1. n. examination, investigation, questioning, test 2. v. ask, catechize, examine, grill (Inf.), interrogate, investigate, pump (Inf.), question

quizzical arch, bantering, curious, derisive, inquiring, mocking, questioning, sardonic, supercilious, teasing

quondam bygone, earlier, ex-, foregoing, former, late, one-time, past, previous, retired, sometime

quota allocation, allowance, assignment, cut (Inf.), part, portion, proportion, ration, share, slice, whack (Inf.)

quotation 1. citation, cutting, excerpt, extract, passage, quote (Inf.), reference, selection 2. Commerce bid price, charge, cost, estimate, figure, price, quote (Inf.), rate, tender

quote adduce, attest, cite, detail, extract, instance, name, paraphrase, proclaim, recall, recite, recollect, refer to, repeat, retell

quotidian 1. daily, diurnal 2. common, commonplace, customary, everyday, habitual, ordinary, regular, routine

R

rabble 1. *canaille,* crowd, herd, horde, mob, swarm, throng **2.** *Derogatory canaille,* commonalty, commoners, common people, crowd, dregs, hoi polloi, lower classes, masses, peasantry, populace, proletariat, riffraff, scum, the great unwashed (*Inf.*), trash

rabble-rouser agitator, demagogue, firebrand, incendiary, troublemaker

Rabelaisian bawdy, broad, coarse, earthy, extravagant, exuberant, gross, lusty, robust, satirical, uninhibited, unrestrained

rabid 1. hydrophobic, mad **2.** berserk, crazed, frantic, frenzied, furious, infuriated, mad, maniacal, raging, violent, wild **3.** bigoted, extreme, fanatical, fervent, intemperate, intolerant, irrational, narrow-minded, zealous

race[1] **1.** *n.* chase, competition, contention, contest, dash, pursuit, rivalry **2.** *v.* career, compete, contest, dart, dash, fly, gallop, hare (*Brit. inf.*), hasten, hurry, run, run like mad (*Inf.*), speed, tear, zoom

race[2] blood, breed, clan, ethnic group, family, folk, house, issue, kin, kindred, line, lineage, nation, offspring, people, progeny, seed (*Archaic*), stock, tribe, type

racial ethnic, ethnological, folk, genealogical, genetic, national, tribal

rack *n.* **1.** frame, framework, stand, structure **2.** affliction, agony, anguish, misery, pain, pang, persecution, suffering, torment, torture ~*v.* **3.** afflict, agonize, crucify, distress, excruciate, harass, harrow, oppress, pain, torment, torture **4.** force, pull, shake, strain, stress, stretch, tear, wrench

racket 1. babel, ballyhoo (*Inf.*), clamour, commotion, din, disturbance, fuss, hubbub, hullabaloo, noise, outcry, pandemonium, row, shouting, tumult, uproar **2.** criminal activity, fraud, illegal enterprise, scheme **3.** *Sl.* business, game (*Inf.*), line, occupation

rackety blaring, boisterous, clamorous, disorderly, noisy, rowdy, uproarious

racy 1. animated, buoyant, energetic, entertaining, exciting, exhilarating, heady, lively, sparkling, spirited, stimulating, vigorous, zestful **2.** distinctive, piquant, pungent, rich, sharp, spicy, strong, tangy, tart, tasty **3.** bawdy, blue, broad, immodest, indecent, indelicate, naughty, near the knuckle (*Inf.*), off colour, risqué, smutty, spicy (*Inf.*), suggestive

raddled broken-down, coarsened, dilapidated, dishevelled, haggard, run-down, tattered, the worse for wear, unkempt

radiance 1. brightness, brilliance, effulgence, glare, gleam, glitter, glow, incandescence, light, luminosity, lustre, resplendence, shine **2.** delight, gaiety, happiness, joy, pleasure, rapture, warmth

radiant 1. beaming, bright, brilliant, effulgent, gleaming, glittering, glorious, glowing, incandescent, luminous, lustrous, resplendent, shining, sparkling, sunny **2.** beaming, beatific, blissful, delighted, ecstatic, gay, glowing, happy, joyful, joyous, rapturous

radiate 1. diffuse, disseminate, emanate, emit, give off *or* out, gleam, glitter, pour, scatter, send out, shed, shine, spread **2.** branch out, diverge, issue, spread out

radiation emanation, emission, rays

radical *adj.* **1.** basic, constitutional, deep-seated, essential, fundamental, innate, native, natural, organic, profound, thoroughgoing **2.** complete, entire, excessive, extreme, extremist, fanatical, revolutionary, severe, sweeping, thorough, violent ~*n.* **3.** extremist, fanatic, militant, revolutionary

raffish 1. bohemian, careless, casual, dashing, devil-may-care, disreputable, jaunty, rakish, sporty, unconventional **2.** coarse, flash (*Inf.*), garish, gaudy, gross, loud, meretricious, showy, tasteless, tawdry, trashy, uncouth, vulgar

raffle draw, lottery, sweep, sweepstake

ragamuffin gamin, guttersnipe, scarecrow (*Inf.*), street arab, tatterdemalion (*Rare*), urchin

ragbag 1. confusion, hotchpotch, jumble, medley, miscellany, mixture, omnium-gatherum, potpourri **2.** *Inf.*

frump, scarecrow (*Inf.*), scruff (*Inf.*), slattern, sloven, slut, trollop

rage *n.* **1.** agitation, anger, frenzy, fury, high dudgeon, ire, madness, mania, obsession, passion, rampage, raving, vehemence, violence, wrath **2.** craze, enthusiasm, fad (*Inf.*), fashion, latest thing, mode, style, vogue ~*v.* **3.** be beside oneself, be furious, blow one's top, blow up (*Inf.*), chafe, foam at the mouth, fret, fume, rant and rave, rave, seethe, storm, throw a fit (*Inf.*) **4.** be at its height, be uncontrollable, rampage, storm, surge

ragged **1.** contemptible, down at heel, frayed, in holes, in rags, in tatters, mean, poor, rent, scraggy, shabby, shaggy, tattered, tatty, threadbare, torn, unkempt, worn-out **2.** crude, jagged, notched, poor, rough, rugged, serrated, uneven, unfinished **3.** broken, desultory, disorganized, fragmented, irregular, uneven

raging beside oneself, boiling mad (*Inf.*), doing one's nut (*Brit. sl.*), enraged, fit to be tied (*Sl.*), fizzing (*Scot.*), foaming at the mouth, frenzied, fuming, furious, incensed, infuriated, mad, raving, seething

rags **1.** castoffs, old clothes, tattered clothing, tatters **2. in rags** down at heel, out at elbow, ragged, seedy, shabby, tattered

raid **1.** *n.* attack, break-in, descent, foray, hit-and-run attack, incursion, inroad, invasion, irruption, onset, sally, seizure, sortie, surprise attack **2.** *v.* assault, attack, break into, descend on, fall upon, forage (*Military*), foray, invade, pillage, plunder, reive (*Dialect*), rifle, sack, sally forth, swoop down upon

raider attacker, forager (*Military*), invader, marauder, plunderer, reiver (*Dialect*), robber, thief

rail *v.* abuse, attack, castigate, censure, complain, criticize, fulminate, inveigh, revile, scold, upbraid, vituperate, vociferate

railing balustrade, barrier, fence, paling, rails

raillery badinage, banter, chaff, irony, jesting, joke, joking, kidding (*Inf.*), mockery, persiflage, pleasantry, repartee, ridicule, satire, sport, teasing

rain *n.* **1.** cloudburst, deluge, downpour, drizzle, fall, precipitation, raindrops, rainfall, showers **2.** deluge, flood, hail, shower, spate, stream, torrent, vol-

ley ~*v.* **3.** bucket down (*Inf.*), come down in buckets (*Inf.*), drizzle, fall, pour, rain cats and dogs (*Inf.*), shower, teem **4.** deposit, drop, fall, shower, sprinkle **5.** bestow, lavish, pour, shower

rainy damp, drizzly, showery, wet

raise **1.** build, construct, elevate, erect, exalt, heave, hoist, lift, move up, promote, put up, rear, set upright, uplift **2.** advance, aggravate, amplify, augment, boost, enhance, enlarge, escalate, exaggerate, heighten, hike (up) (*Inf.*), increase, inflate, intensify, jack up, magnify, put up, reinforce, strengthen **3.** advance, aggrandize, elevate, exalt, prefer, promote, upgrade **4.** activate, arouse, awaken, cause, evoke, excite, foment, foster, incite, instigate, kindle, motivate, provoke, set on foot, stir up, summon up, whip up **5.** bring about, cause, create, engender, give rise to, occasion, originate, produce, provoke, start **6.** advance, bring up, broach, introduce, moot, put forward, suggest **7.** assemble, collect, form, gather, get, levy, mass, mobilize, muster, obtain, rally, recruit **8.** breed, bring up, cultivate, develop, grow, nurture, produce, propagate, rear **9.** abandon, end, give up, lift, relieve, relinquish, remove, terminate

rake[1] *v.* **1.** collect, gather, remove, scrape up **2.** break up, harrow, hoe, scour, scrape, scratch **3. With up or together** assemble, collect, dig up, dredge up, gather, scrape together **4.** comb, examine, hunt, ransack, scan, scour, scrutinize, search **5.** graze, scrape, scratch **6.** enfilade, pepper, sweep

rake[2] *n.* debauchee, dissolute man, lecher, libertine, playboy, profligate, rakehell (*Archaic*), roué, sensualist, voluptuary

rakish[1] abandoned, debauched, depraved, dissipated, dissolute, immoral, lecherous, licentious, loose, prodigal, profligate, sinful, wanton

rakish[2] breezy, dapper, dashing, debonair, devil-may-care, flashy, jaunty, natty (*Inf.*), raffish, smart, snazzy (*Inf.*), sporty

rally[1] *v.* **1.** bring or come to order, reassemble, re-form, regroup, reorganize, unite ~*n.* **2.** regrouping, reorganization, reunion, stand ~*v.* **3.** assemble, bond together, bring or come together, collect, convene, gather, get together, marshal, mobilize, muster, organize, round up, summon, unite ~*n.* **4.** assembly, conference, congregation, convention, convocation, gathering, mass meeting, meeting, muster ~*v.* **5.** come round, get better, get one's second wind, improve, perk up, pick up, pull through, recover, recuperate, regain one's strength, revive, take a turn for the better ~*n.* **6.** comeback (*Inf.*), improvement, recovery, recuperation, renewal, resurgence, revival, turn for the better

rally² chaff, make fun of, mock, poke fun at, ridicule, send up (*Brit. inf.*), take the mickey out of (*Inf.*), taunt, tease, twit

ram *v.* **1.** butt, collide with, crash, dash, drive, force, hit, impact, run into, slam, smash, strike **2.** beat, cram, crowd, drum, force, hammer, jam, pack, pound, stuff, tamp, thrust

ramble *v.* **1.** amble, drift, perambulate, peregrinate, range, roam, rove, saunter, straggle, stravaig (*Scot.*), stray, stroll, traipse (*Inf.*), walk, wander **2.** meander, snake, twist and turn, wind, zigzag **3.** babble, chatter, digress, expatiate, maunder, rabbit on (*Brit. sl.*), rattle on, wander, witter on (*Inf.*) ~*n.* **4.** excursion, hike, perambulation, peregrination, roaming, roving, saunter, stroll, tour, traipse (*Inf.*), trip, walk

rambler drifter, hiker, roamer, rover, stroller, walker, wanderer, wayfarer

rambling 1. circuitous, desultory, diffuse, digressive, disconnected, discursive, disjointed, incoherent, irregular, long-winded, periphrastic, prolix, wordy **2.** irregular, sprawling, spreading, straggling, trailing

ramification 1. branch, development, divarication, division, excrescence, extension, forking, offshoot, outgrowth, subdivision **2.** complication, consequence, development, result, sequel, upshot

ramify 1. branch, divaricate, divide, fork, separate, split up **2.** become complicated, multiply, thicken

ramp grade, gradient, incline, inclined plane, rise, slope

rampage *v.* **1.** go berserk, rage, run amuck, run riot, run wild, storm, tear ~*n.* **2.** destruction, frenzy, fury, rage, storm, tempest, tumult, uproar, violence **3. on the rampage** amuck, berserk, destructive, out of control, raging, rampant, riotous, violent, wild

rampant 1. aggressive, dominant, excessive, flagrant, on the rampage, out of control, out of hand, outrageous, raging, rampaging, riotous, unbridled, uncontrollable, ungovernable, unrestrained, vehement, violent, wanton, wild **2.** epidemic, exuberant, luxuriant, prevalent, profuse, rank, rife, spreading like wildfire, unchecked, uncontrolled, unrestrained, widespread **3.** *Heraldry* erect, rearing, standing, upright

rampart barricade, bastion, breastwork, bulwark, defence, earthwork, embankment, fence, fort, fortification, guard, parapet, security, stronghold, wall

ramshackle broken-down, crumbling, decrepit, derelict, dilapidated, flimsy, jerry-built, rickety, shaky, tottering, tumbledown, unsafe, unsteady

rancid bad, fetid, foul, frowsty, fusty, musty, off, putrid, rank, rotten, sour, stale, strong-smelling, tainted

rancorous acrimonious, bitter, hostile, implacable, malevolent, malicious, malign, malignant, resentful, spiteful, splenetic, venomous, vindictive, virulent

rancour animosity, animus, antipathy, bad blood, bitterness, enmity, grudge, hate, hatred, hostility, ill feeling, ill will, malevolence, malice, malignity, resentfulness, resentment, spite, spleen, venom

random 1. accidental, adventitious, aimless, arbitrary, casual, chance, desultory, fortuitous, haphazard, hit or miss, incidental, indiscriminate, purposeless, spot, stray, unplanned, unpremeditated **2. at random** accidentally, adventitiously, aimlessly, arbitrarily, by chance, casually, haphazardly, indiscriminately, irregularly, purposelessly, randomly, unsystematically, willy-nilly

randy amorous, aroused, concupiscent, horny (*Sl.*), hot, lascivious, lecherous, lustful, raunchy (*U.S. sl.*), satyric, sexually excited, sexy (*Inf.*), turned-on (*Sl.*)

range *n.* **1.** amplitude, area, bounds, compass, confines, distance, domain, extent, field, latitude, limits, orbit, parameters (*Inf.*), province, purview, radius, reach, scope, span, sphere, sweep **2.** chain, file, line, rank, row, sequence, series, string, tier **3.** assortment, class, collection, gamut, kind, lot, order, selection, series, sort, variety ~*v.* **4.** align, arrange, array, dispose, draw up, line up, order **5.** arrange, bracket, catalogue, categorize, class, classify, file, grade, group, pigeon-hole, rank **6**. aim, align, direct, level, point, train **7**. cruise, explore, ramble, roam, rove, straggle, stray, stroll, sweep, traverse, wander **8**. extend, fluctuate, go, reach, run, stretch, vary between

rangy gangling, lanky, leggy, long-legged, long-limbed

rank¹ n. **1**. caste, class, classification, degree, dignity, division, echelon, grade, level, nobility, order, position, quality, sort, standing, station, status, stratum, type **2**. column, file, formation, group, line, range, row, series, tier ~v. **3**. align, arrange, array, class, classify, dispose, grade, line up, locate, marshal, order, position, range, sort

rank² **1**. abundant, dense, exuberant, flourishing, lush, luxuriant, productive, profuse, strong-growing, vigorous **2**. bad, disagreeable, disgusting, fetid, foul, fusty, gamy, mephitic, musty, noisome, noxious, off, offensive, pungent, putrid, rancid, revolting, stale, stinking, strong-smelling **3**. absolute, arrant, blatant, complete, downright, egregious, excessive, extravagant, flagrant, glaring, gross, rampant, sheer, thorough, total, undisguised, unmitigated, utter **4**. abusive, atrocious, coarse, crass, filthy, foul, gross, indecent, nasty, obscene, outrageous, scurrilous, shocking, vulgar

rank and file **1**. lower ranks, men, other ranks, private soldiers, soldiers, troops **2**. body, general public, majority, mass, masses

rankle anger, annoy, chafe, embitter, fester, gall, get one's goat (Inf.), irk, irritate, rile

ransack **1**. comb, explore, go through, rake, rummage, scour, search, turn inside out **2**. despoil, gut, loot, pillage, plunder, raid, ravage, rifle, sack, strip

ransom n. **1**. deliverance, liberation, redemption, release, rescue **2**. money, payment, payoff, price ~v. **3**. buy (someone) out (Inf.), buy the freedom of, deliver, liberate, obtain or pay for the release of, redeem, release, rescue, set free

rant **1**. v. bellow, bluster, cry, declaim, rave, roar, shout, spout (Inf.), vociferate, yell **2**. n. bluster, bombast, diatribe, fanfaronade (Rare), harangue, philippic, rhetoric, tirade, vociferation

rap v. **1**. crack, hit, knock, strike, tap **2**. bark, speak abruptly, spit **3**. Sl., chiefly U.S. chat, confabulate, converse,

discourse, talk **4**. castigate, censure, criticize, knock (Inf.), pan (Inf.), reprimand, scold, tick off (Inf.) ~n. **5**. blow, clout (Inf.), crack, knock, tap **6**. Sl., chiefly U.S. chat, colloquy, confabulation, conversation, dialogue, discourse, discussion, talk **7**. Sl. blame, censure, chiding, punishment, rebuke, responsibility, sentence

rapacious avaricious, extortionate, grasping, greedy, insatiable, marauding, plundering, predatory, preying, ravenous, usurious, voracious, wolfish

rapacity avarice, avidity, cupidity, graspingness, greed, greediness, insatiableness, predatoriness, rapaciousness, ravenousness, usury, voraciousness, voracity, wolfishness

rape n. **1**. outrage, ravishment, sexual assault, violation **2**. depredation, despoilment, despoliation, pillage, plundering, rapine, sack, spoliation **3**. abuse, defilement, desecration, maltreatment, perversion, violation ~v. **4**. outrage, ravish, sexually assault, violate **5**. despoil, loot, pillage, plunder, ransack, sack, spoliate

rapid brisk, expeditious, express, fast, fleet, flying, hasty, hurried, precipitate, prompt, quick, speedy, swift

rapidity alacrity, briskness, celerity, dispatch, expedition, fleetness, haste, hurry, precipitateness, promptitude, promptness, quickness, rush, speed, speediness, swiftness, velocity

rapidly at speed, briskly, expeditiously, fast, hastily, hurriedly, in a hurry, in a rush, in haste, like a shot, precipitately, promptly, quickly, speedily, swiftly, with dispatch

rapine depredation, despoilment, despoliation, looting, marauding, pillage, plunder, ransacking, rape, robbery, sack, seizure, spoliation, theft

rapport affinity, bond, empathy, harmony, interrelationship, link, relationship, sympathy, understanding

rapprochement détente, reconcilement, reconciliation, restoration of harmony, reunion, softening

rapscallion blackguard, black sheep, cad, disgrace, good-for-nothing, knave (Archaic), ne'er-do-well, rascal, rogue, scallywag (Inf.), scamp, scoundrel, wastrel

rapt **1**. absorbed, carried away, engrossed, enthralled, entranced, fascinated, gripped, held, intent, preoccupied, spellbound **2.** bewitched, blissful, captivated, charmed, delighted, ecstatic, enchanted, enraptured, rapturous, ravished, transported

rapture beatitude, bliss, cloud nine (*Inf.*), delectation, delight, ecstasy, enthusiasm, euphoria, exaltation, felicity, happiness, joy, ravishment, rhapsody, seventh heaven, spell, transport

rapturous blissful, delighted, ecstatic, enthusiastic, euphoric, exalted, happy, in seventh heaven, joyful, joyous, on cloud nine (*Inf.*), overjoyed, over the moon (*Inf.*), ravished, rhapsodic, transported

rare[1] **1.** exceptional, few, infrequent, out of the ordinary, recherché, scarce, singular, sparse, sporadic, strange, thin on the ground, uncommon, unusual **2.** admirable, choice, excellent, exquisite, extreme, fine, great, incomparable, peerless, superb, superlative **3.** invaluable, precious, priceless, rich

rare[2] bloody, half-cooked, half-raw, undercooked, underdone

rarefied 1. elevated, exalted, high, lofty, noble, spiritual, sublime **2.** clannish, cliquish, esoteric, exclusive, occult, private, select

rarefy attenuate, clarify, purify, refine, sublimate, subtilize, thin out

rarely 1. almost never, hardly, hardly ever, infrequently, little, once in a blue moon, once in a while, only now and then, on rare occasions, scarcely ever, seldom **2.** exceptionally, extraordinarily, finely, notably, remarkably, singularly, uncommonly, unusually

raring athirst, avid, champing at the bit (*Inf.*), desperate, eager, enthusiastic, impatient, keen, longing, ready, willing, yearning

rarity 1. curio, curiosity, find, gem, one-off, pearl, treasure **2.** infrequency, scarcity, shortage, singularity, sparseness, strangeness, uncommonness, unusualness **3.** choiceness, excellence, exquisiteness, fineness, incomparability, incomparableness, peerlessness, quality, superbness **4.** invaluableness, preciousness, pricelessness, richness, value, worth

rascal blackguard, caitiff (*Archaic*), devil, disgrace, good-for-nothing, imp, knave (*Archaic*), miscreant, ne'er-do-well, rake, rapscallion, reprobate, rogue, scallywag (*Inf.*), scamp, scoundrel, varmint (*Inf.*), villain, wastrel, wretch

rascally bad, base, crooked, dishonest, disreputable, evil, good-for-nothing, low, mean, reprobate, scoundrelly, unscrupulous, vicious, villainous, wicked

rash[1] adventurous, audacious, brash, careless, foolhardy, harebrained, harum-scarum, hasty, headlong, headstrong, heedless, helter-skelter, hot-headed, ill-advised, ill-considered, impetuous, imprudent, impulsive, incautious, indiscreet, injudicious, madcap, precipitate, premature, reckless, thoughtless, unguarded, unthinking, unwary, venturesome

rash[2] **1.** eruption, outbreak **2.** epidemic, flood, outbreak, plague, series, spate, succession, wave

rashness adventurousness, audacity, brashness, carelessness, foolhardiness, hastiness, heedlessness, indiscretion, precipitation, recklessness, temerity, thoughtlessness

rasp *n.* **1.** grating, grinding, scrape, scratch ~*v.* **2.** abrade, excoriate, file, grind, rub, sand, scour, scrape **3.** grate (upon), irk, irritate, jar (upon), rub (someone) up the wrong way, set one's teeth on edge, wear upon

rasping *or* **raspy** creaking, croaking, croaky, grating, gravelly, gruff, harsh, hoarse, husky, jarring, rough, scratchy

rate[1] *n.* **1.** degree, percentage, proportion, ratio, relation, scale, standard **2.** charge, cost, dues, duty, fee, figure, hire, price, tariff, tax, toll **3.** gait, measure, pace, speed, tempo, time, velocity **4.** class, classification, degree, grade, position, quality, rank, rating, status, value, worth **5. at any rate** anyhow, anyway, at all events, in any case, nevertheless ~*v.* **6.** adjudge, appraise, assess, class, classify, consider, count, esteem, estimate, evaluate, grade, measure, rank, reckon, regard, value, weigh **7.** be entitled to, be worthy of, deserve, merit **8.** *Sl.* admire, esteem, respect, think highly of, value

rate[2] bawl out (*Inf.*), berate, blame, castigate, censure, chew out (*U.S. inf.*), chide, criticize severely, haul over the coals (*Inf.*), rebuke, reprimand, reprove, roast (*Inf.*), scold, take to task, tear (someone) off a strip (*Inf.*), tell off (*Inf.*), tongue-lash, upbraid

rather 1. a bit, a little, fairly, kind of (*Inf.*), moderately, pretty (*Inf.*), quite, relatively, slightly, somewhat, sort of (*Inf.*), to some degree, to some extent **2.** a good bit, noticeably, significantly, very **3.** instead, more readily, more willingly, preferably, sooner

ratify affirm, approve, authenticate, authorize, bear out, bind, certify, confirm, consent to, corroborate, endorse, establish, sanction, sign, uphold, validate

rating[1] class, classification, degree, designation, estimate, evaluation, grade, order, placing, position, rank, rate, standing, status

rating[2] chiding, dressing down (*Inf.*), lecture, piece of one's mind (*Inf.*), rebuke, reprimand, reproof, roasting (*Inf.*), row (*Inf.*), scolding, telling-off (*Inf.*), ticking-off (*Inf.*), tongue-lashing, wigging (*Brit. sl.*)

ratio arrangement, correlation, correspondence, equation, fraction, percentage, proportion, rate, relation, relationship

ration *n.* **1.** allotment, allowance, dole, helping, measure, part, portion, provision, quota, share **2.** *Plural* commons (*Brit.*), food, provender, provisions, stores, supplies ~*v.* **3.** *With* **out** allocate, allot, apportion, deal, distribute, dole, give out, issue, measure out, mete, parcel out **4.** budget, conserve, control, limit, restrict, save

rational **1.** enlightened, intelligent, judicious, logical, lucid, realistic, reasonable, sagacious, sane, sensible, sound, wise **2.** cerebral, cognitive, ratiocinative, reasoning, thinking **3.** all there (*Inf.*), balanced, *compos mentis*, in one's right mind, lucid, normal, of sound mind, sane

rationale exposition, grounds, logic, motivation, philosophy, principle, *raison d'être*, reasons, theory

rationalize **1.** account for, excuse, explain away, extenuate, justify, make allowance for, make excuses for, vindicate **2.** apply logic to, elucidate, reason out, resolve, think through **3.** make cuts, make more efficient, streamline, trim

rattle *v.* **1.** bang, clatter, jangle **2.** bounce, jar, jiggle, jolt, jounce, shake, vibrate **3.** *With* **on** blether, cackle, chatter, gabble, gibber, jabber, prate, prattle, rabbit on (*Brit. sl.*), run on, witter (*Inf.*), yak (away) (*Sl.*) **4.** *Inf.* discomfit, discompose, disconcert, discountenance, disturb, faze (*U.S. inf.*), frighten, per-

turb, put (someone) off his stride, put (someone) out of countenance, scare, shake, upset **5.** *With* **off** list, recite, reel off, rehearse, run through, spiel off (*Inf.*)

ratty angry, annoyed, crabbed, cross, impatient, irritable, short-tempered, snappy, testy, touchy

raucous grating, harsh, hoarse, husky, loud, noisy, rasping, rough, strident

ravage **1.** *v.* demolish, desolate, despoil, destroy, devastate, gut, lay waste, leave in ruins, loot, pillage, plunder, ransack, raze, ruin, sack, shatter, spoil, wreak havoc on, wreck **2.** *n. Often plural* damage, demolition, depredation, desolation, destruction, devastation, havoc, pillage, plunder, rapine, ruin, ruination, spoliation, waste

rave *v.* **1.** babble, be delirious, fume, go mad, rage, rant, roar, run amuck, splutter, storm, talk wildly, thunder **2.** *With* **about** *Inf.* be delighted by, be mad about (*Inf.*), be wild about (*Inf.*), cry up, enthuse, gush, praise, rhapsodize ~*n.* **3.** *Inf.* acclaim, applause, encomium, praise **4.** *Also* **rave-up** *Brit. sl.* affair, bash (*Inf.*), blow-out (*Sl.*), celebration, do (*Inf.*), party **5.** *Brit. sl.* craze, fad, fashion, vogue ~*adj.* **6.** *Inf.* ecstatic, enthusiastic, excellent, favourable, laudatory

ravenous **1.** famished, starved, starving, very hungry **2.** avaricious, covetous, devouring, ferocious, gluttonous, grasping, greedy, insatiable, insatiate, predatory, rapacious, ravening, voracious, wolfish

ravine canyon, clough (*Dialect*), defile, flume, gap (*U.S.*), gorge, gulch (*U.S.*), gully, linn (*Scot.*), pass

raving berserk, crazed, crazy, delirious, frantic, frenzied, furious, hysterical, insane, irrational, mad, out of one's mind, rabid, raging, wild

ravish **1.** captivate, charm, delight, enchant, enrapture, entrance, fascinate, overjoy, spellbind, transport **2.** abuse, outrage, rape, sexually assault, violate

ravishing beautiful, bewitching, charming, dazzling, delightful, enchanting, entrancing, gorgeous, lovely, radiant, stunning (*Inf.*)

raw **1.** bloody (*of meat*), fresh, natural, uncooked, undressed, unprepared **2.** basic, coarse, crude, green, natural, organic, rough, unfinished, unprocessed, unrefined, unripe, untreated **3.** abraded, chafed, grazed, open, scratched, sensitive, skinned, sore, tender **4**. callow, green, ignorant, immature, inexperienced, new, undisciplined, unpractised, unseasoned, unskilled, untrained, untried **5**. bare, blunt, brutal, candid, frank, naked, plain, realistic, unembellished, unvarnished **6**. biting, bitter, bleak, chill, chilly, cold, damp, freezing, harsh, piercing, unpleasant, wet

ray 1. bar, beam, flash, gleam, shaft **2**. flicker, glimmer, hint, indication, scintilla, spark, trace

raze 1. bulldoze, demolish, destroy, flatten, knock down, level, pull down, remove, ruin, tear down, throw down **2**. delete, efface, erase, expunge, extinguish, extirpate, obliterate, rub out, scratch out, strike out, wipe out

re about, anent (*Scot.*), apropos, concerning, in respect of, on the subject of, regarding, respecting, with reference to, with regard to

reach v. **1**. arrive at, attain, get as far as, get to, land at, make **2**. contact, extend to, get (a) hold of, go as far as, grasp, stretch to, touch **3**. amount to, arrive at, attain, climb to, come to, drop, fall, move, rise, sink **4**. *Inf*. hand, hold out, pass, stretch **5**. communicate with, contact, establish contact with, find, get, get hold of, get in touch with, get through to, make contact with ~n. **6**. ambit, capacity, command, compass, distance, extension, extent, grasp, influence, jurisdiction, mastery, power, range, scope, spread, stretch, sweep

react 1. acknowledge, answer, reply, respond **2**. act, behave, conduct oneself, function, operate, proceed, work

reaction 1. acknowledgment, answer, feedback, reply, response **2**. compensation, counteraction, counterbalance, counterpoise, recoil **3**. conservatism, counter-revolution, obscurantism, the right

reactionary 1. *adj*. blimpish, conservative, counter-revolutionary, obscurantist, rightist **2**. *n*. Colonel Blimp, conservative, counter-revolutionary, diehard, obscurantist, rightist, right-winger

read 1. glance at, look at, peruse, pore over, refer to, run one's eye over, scan, study **2**. announce, declaim, deliver, recite, speak, utter **3**. comprehend, construe, decipher, discover, interpret, perceive the meaning of, see, understand **4**. display, indicate, record, register, show

readable 1. clear, comprehensible, decipherable, intelligible, legible, plain, understandable **2**. easy to read, enjoyable, entertaining, enthralling, gripping, interesting, pleasant, worth reading

readily 1. cheerfully, eagerly, freely, gladly, promptly, quickly, voluntarily, willingly, with good grace, with pleasure **2**. at once, easily, effortlessly, in no time, quickly, right away, smoothly, speedily, straight away, unhesitatingly, without delay, without demur, without difficulty, without hesitation

readiness 1. fitness, maturity, preparation, preparedness, ripeness **2**. aptness, eagerness, gameness (*Inf.*), inclination, keenness, willingness **3**. adroitness, dexterity, ease, facility, handiness, promptitude, promptness, quickness, rapidity, skill **4. in readiness** all set, at *or* on hand, at the ready, fit, prepared, primed, ready, set, waiting, waiting in the wings

reading 1. examination, inspection, perusal, review, scrutiny, study **2**. homily, lecture, lesson, performance, recital, rendering, rendition, sermon **3**. conception, construction, grasp, impression, interpretation, treatment, understanding, version **4**. book-learning, edification, education, erudition, knowledge, learning, scholarship

ready *adj*. **1**. all set, arranged, completed, fit, in readiness, organized, prepared, primed, ripe, set **2**. agreeable, apt, disposed, eager, game (*Inf.*), glad, happy, inclined, keen, minded, predisposed, prone, willing **3**. acute, adroit, alert, apt, astute, bright, clever, deft, dexterous, expert, handy, intelligent, keen, perceptive, prompt, quick, quick-witted, rapid, resourceful, sharp, skilful, smart **4**. about, close, in danger of, liable, likely, on the brink of, on the point of, on the verge of **5**. accessible, at *or* on hand, at one's fingertips, at the ready, available, close to hand, convenient, handy, near, on call, on tap (*Inf.*), present ~n. **6. at the ready** in readiness, poised, prepared, ready for action, waiting ~v. **7**. arrange, equip, fit out, get ready, make ready, order, organize, prepare, set

real absolute, actual, authentic, bona fide, certain, essential, existent, factual, genuine, heartfelt, honest, intrinsic, legitimate, positive, right, rightful, sincere, true, unaffected, unfeigned, valid, veritable

realistic 1. businesslike, commonsense, down-to-earth, hard-headed, level-headed, matter-of-fact, practical, pragmatic, rational, real, sensible, sober, unromantic, unsentimental 2. authentic, faithful, genuine, graphic, lifelike, natural, naturalistic, representational, true, true to life, truthful

reality 1. actuality, authenticity, certainty, corporeality, fact, genuineness, materiality, realism, truth, validity, verisimilitude, verity 2. **in reality** actually, as a matter of fact, in actuality, in fact, in point of fact, in truth, really

realization 1. appreciation, apprehension, awareness, cognizance, comprehension, conception, consciousness, grasp, imagination, perception, recognition, understanding 2. accomplishment, achievement, carrying-out, completion, consummation, effectuation, fulfilment

realize 1. appreciate, apprehend, be cognizant of, become aware of, become conscious of, catch on (*Inf.*), comprehend, conceive, grasp, imagine, recognize, take in, twig (*Brit. inf.*), understand 2. accomplish, actualize, bring about, bring off, bring to fruition, carry out *or* through, complete, consummate, do, effect, effectuate, fulfil, make concrete, make happen, perform, reify 3. acquire, bring *or* take in, clear, earn, gain, get, go for, make, net, obtain, produce, sell for

really absolutely, actually, assuredly, categorically, certainly, genuinely, in actuality, indeed, in, in fact, in reality, positively, surely, truly, undoubtedly, verily, without a doubt

realm 1. country, domain, dominion, empire, kingdom, land, monarchy, principality, province, state 2. area, branch, department, field, orbit, province, region, sphere, territory, world, zone

reap acquire, bring in, collect, cut, derive, gain, garner, gather, get, harvest, obtain, win

rear[1] 1. *n.* back, back end, end, rearguard, stern, tail, tail end 2. *adj.* aft, after (*Nautical*), back, following, hind, hindmost, last

rear[2] *v.* 1. breed, bring up, care for, cultivate, educate, foster, grow, nurse, nurture, raise, train 2. elevate, hoist, hold up, lift, raise, set upright 3. build,

construct, erect, fabricate, put up 4. loom, rise, soar, tower

reason *n.* 1. apprehension, brains, comprehension, intellect, judgment, logic, mentality, mind, ratiocination, rationality, reasoning, sanity, sense(s), sound mind, soundness, understanding 2. aim, basis, cause, design, end, goal, grounds, impetus, incentive, inducement, intention, motive, object, occasion, purpose, target, warrant, why and wherefore (*Inf.*) 3. apologia, apology, argument, case, defence, excuse, explanation, exposition, ground, justification, rationale, vindication 4. bounds, limits, moderation, propriety, reasonableness, sense, sensibleness, wisdom 5. **in** *or* **within reason** in moderation, proper, reasonable, sensible, warrantable, within bounds, within limits ~*v.* 6. conclude, deduce, draw conclusions, infer, make out, ratiocinate, resolve, solve, syllogize, think, work out 7. *With* **with** argue, bring round (*Inf.*), debate, dispute, dissuade, expostulate, move, persuade, prevail upon, remonstrate, show (someone) the error of his ways, talk into *or* out of, urge, win over

reasonable 1. advisable, arguable, believable, credible, intelligent, judicious, justifiable, logical, plausible, practical, rational, reasoned, sane, sensible, sober, sound, tenable, well-advised, well thought-out, wise 2. acceptable, average, equitable, fair, fit, honest, inexpensive, just, moderate, modest, O.K. (*Inf.*), proper, right, tolerable, within reason

reasoned clear, judicious, logical, sensible, systematic, well expressed, well presented, well thought-out

reasoning 1. analysis, cogitation, deduction, logic, ratiocination, reason, thinking, thought 2. argument, case, exposition, hypothesis, interpretation, proof, train of thought

reassure bolster, buoy up, cheer up, comfort, encourage, hearten, inspirit, put *or* set one's mind at rest, relieve (someone) of anxiety, restore confidence to

rebate allowance, bonus, deduction, discount, reduction, refund

rebel *v.* 1. man the barricades, mutiny, resist, revolt, rise up, take to the streets, take up arms 2. come out against, defy, disobey, dissent, refuse to obey 3. flinch, recoil, show repugnance, shrink, shy away ~n. **4**. insurgent, insurrectionary, mutineer, resistance fighter, revolutionary, revolutionist, secessionist **5**. apostate, dissenter, heretic, nonconformist, schismatic ~adj. **6**. insubordinate, insurgent, insurrectionary, mutinous, rebellious, revolutionary

rebellion 1. insurgence, insurgency, insurrection, mutiny, resistance, revolt, revolution, rising, uprising **2**. apostasy, defiance, disobedience, dissent, heresy, insubordination, nonconformity, schism

rebellious 1. contumacious, defiant, disaffected, disloyal, disobedient, disorderly, insubordinate, insurgent, insurrectionary, intractable, mutinous, rebel, recalcitrant, revolutionary, seditious, turbulent, ungovernable, unruly **2**. difficult, incorrigible, obstinate, recalcitrant, refractory, resistant, unmanageable

rebirth new beginning, regeneration, reincarnation, renaissance, renascence, renewal, restoration, resurgence, resurrection, revitalization, revival

rebound v. **1**. bounce, recoil, resound, return, ricochet, spring back **2**. backfire, boomerang, misfire, recoil ~n. **3**. bounce, comeback, kickback, repercussion, return, ricochet

rebuff 1. v. brush off (*Sl.*), check, cold-shoulder, cut, decline, deny, discourage, put off, refuse, reject, repulse, resist, slight, snub, spurn, turn down **2**. n. brushoff (*Sl.*), check, cold shoulder, defeat, denial, discouragement, opposition, refusal, rejection, repulse, slight, snub, thumbs down

rebuke 1. v. admonish, bawl out (*Inf.*), berate, blame, carpet (*Inf.*), castigate, censure, chide, dress down (*Inf.*), haul (someone) over the coals (*Inf.*), lecture, reprehend, reprimand, reproach, reprove, scold, take to task, tear (someone) off a strip (*Inf.*), tell off (*Inf.*), tick off (*Inf.*), upbraid **2**. n. admonition, blame, castigation, censure, dressing down (*Inf.*), lecture, reprimand, reproach, reproof, reproval, row, telling-off (*Inf.*), ticking-off (*Inf.*), tongue-lashing, wigging (*Brit. sl.*)

rebut confute, defeat, disprove, invalidate, negate, overturn, prove wrong, quash, refute

rebuttal confutation, defeat, disproof, invalidation, negation, refutation

recalcitrant contrary, contumacious, defiant, disobedient, insubordinate, intractable, obstinate, refractory, stubborn, uncontrollable, ungovernable, unmanageable, unruly, unwilling, wayward, wilful

recall v. **1**. bring or call to mind, call or summon up, evoke, look or think back to, mind (*Dialect*), recollect, remember, reminisce about **2**. abjure, annul, call back, call in, cancel, countermand, nullify, repeal, rescind, retract, revoke, take back, withdraw ~n. **3**. annulment, cancellation, nullification, recision, repeal, rescindment, rescission, retraction, revocation, withdrawal **4**. memory, recollection, remembrance

recant abjure, apostatize, deny, disavow, disclaim, disown, forswear, recall, renounce, repudiate, retract, revoke, take back, unsay, withdraw

recapitulate epitomize, go over again, outline, recap (*Inf.*), recount, reiterate, repeat, restate, review, run over, run through again, summarize, sum up

recede 1. abate, draw back, ebb, fall back, go back, regress, retire, retreat, retrogress, return, subside, withdraw **2**. decline, diminish, dwindle, fade, lessen, shrink, sink, wane

receipt 1. acknowledgment, counterfoil, proof of purchase, sales slip, stub, voucher **2**. acceptance, delivery, receiving, reception, recipience **3**. *Plural* gains, gate, income, proceeds, profits, return, takings

receive 1. accept, accept delivery of, acquire, be given, be in receipt of, collect, derive, get, obtain, pick up, take **2**. apprehend, be informed of, be told, gather, hear, perceive **3**. bear, be subjected to, encounter, experience, go through, meet with, suffer, sustain, undergo **4**. accommodate, admit, be at home to, entertain, greet, meet, take in, welcome

recent contemporary, current, fresh, late, latter, latter-day, modern, new, novel, present-day, up-to-date, young

recently currently, freshly, lately, newly, not long ago, of late

receptacle container, holder, repository

reception 1. acceptance, admission, receipt, receiving, recipience **2**. acknowledgment, greeting, reaction, recognition, response, treatment, welcome **3**. do (*Inf.*), entertainment, function, levee, party, soirée

receptive 1. alert, bright, perceptive,

quick on the uptake (*Inf.*), responsive, sensitive **2.** accessible, amenable, approachable, favourable, friendly, hospitable, interested, open, open-minded, open to suggestions, susceptible, sympathetic, welcoming

recess 1. alcove, bay, cavity, corner, depression, hollow, indentation, niche, nook, oriel **2.** *Plural* bowels, depths, heart, innards (*Inf.*), innermost parts, penetralia, reaches, retreats, secret places **3.** break, cessation of business, closure, holiday, intermission, interval, respite, rest, vacation

recession decline, depression, downturn, slump

recherché arcane, choice, esoteric, exotic, far-fetched, rare, refined

recipe 1. directions, ingredients, instructions, receipt (*Obsolete*) **2.** formula, method, modus operandi, prescription, procedure, process, programme, technique

reciprocal alternate, complementary, correlative, corresponding, equivalent, exchanged, give-and-take, interchangeable, interdependent, mutual, reciprocative, reciprocatory

reciprocate 1. barter, exchange, feel in return, interchange, reply, requite, respond, return, return the compliment, swap, trade **2.** be equivalent, correspond, equal, match

recital account, description, detailing, enumeration, narration, narrative, performance, reading, recapitulation, recitation, rehearsal, relation, rendering, repetition, statement, story, tale, telling

recitation lecture, narration, passage, performance, piece, reading, recital, rendering, telling

recite declaim, deliver, describe, detail, do one's party piece (*Inf.*), enumerate, itemize, narrate, perform, recapitulate, recount, rehearse, relate, repeat, speak, tell

reckless careless, daredevil, devil-may-care, foolhardy, harebrained, harum-scarum, hasty, headlong, heedless, ill-advised, imprudent, inattentive, incautious, indiscreet, irresponsible, madcap, mindless, negligent, overventuresome, precipitate, rash, regardless, thoughtless, wild

reckon 1. add up, calculate, compute, count, enumerate, figure, number, tally, total **2.** account, appraise, consider,

count, deem, esteem, estimate, evaluate, gauge, hold, judge, look upon, rate, regard, think of **3.** assume, believe, be of the opinion, conjecture, expect, fancy, guess (*Inf.*), imagine, suppose, surmise, think **4.** *With* **with** cope, deal, face, handle, settle accounts, treat **5.** *With* **with** anticipate, bargain for, bear in mind, be prepared for, expect, foresee, plan for, take cognizance of, take into account **6.** *With* **on** *or* **upon** bank, calculate, count, depend, hope for, rely, take for granted, trust in **7. to be reckoned with** consequential, considerable, important, influential, powerful, significant, strong, weighty

reckoning 1. adding, addition, calculation, computation, count, counting, estimate, summation, working **2.** account, bill, charge, due, score, settlement **3.** doom, judgment, last judgment, retribution

reclaim get *or* take back, recapture, recover, redeem, reform, regain, regenerate, reinstate, rescue, restore, retrieve, salvage

recline be recumbent, lay (something) down, lean, lie (down), loll, lounge, repose, rest, sprawl, stretch out

recluse 1. *n.* anchoress, anchorite, ascetic, eremite, hermit, monk, solitary **2.** *adj.* cloistered, isolated, reclusive, retiring, secluded, sequestered, solitary, withdrawn

reclusive ascetic, cloistered, eremitic, hermitic, hermit-like, isolated, monastic, recluse, retiring, secluded, sequestered, solitary, withdrawn

recognition 1. detection, discovery, identification, recall, recollection, remembrance **2.** acceptance, acknowledgment, admission, allowance, appreciation, avowal, awareness, cognizance, concession, confession, notice, perception, realization, respect, understanding **3.** acknowledgment, appreciation, approval, gratitude, greeting, honour, salute

recognize 1. identify, know, know again, make out, notice, place, recall, recollect, remember, spot **2.** accept, acknowledge, admit, allow, appreciate, avow, be aware of, concede, confess, grant, own, perceive, realize, respect, see, understand **3.** acknowledge, appreciate, approve, greet, honour, salute

recoil *v.* **1.** jerk back, kick, react, rebound, resile, spring back **2.** balk at, draw back, falter, flinch, quail, shrink, shy away **3.** backfire, boomerang, go wrong, misfire, rebound ~*n.* **4.** backlash, kick, reaction, rebound, repercussion

recollect call to mind, mind (*Dialect*), place, recall, remember, reminisce, summon up

recollection impression, memory, mental image, recall, remembrance, reminiscence

recommend 1. advance, advise, advocate, counsel, enjoin, exhort, propose, put forward, suggest, urge **2.** approve, commend, endorse, praise, put in a good word for, speak well of, vouch for **3.** make attractive (acceptable, appealing, interesting)

recommendation 1. advice, counsel, proposal, suggestion, urging **2.** advocacy, approbation, approval, blessing, commendation, endorsement, favourable mention, good word, plug (*Inf.*), praise, reference, sanction, testimonial

recompense *v.* **1.** pay, remunerate, reward **2.** compensate, indemnify, make amends for, make good, make restitution for, make up for, pay for, redress, reimburse, repay, requite, satisfy ~*n.* **3.** amends, compensation, damages, emolument, indemnification, indemnity, pay, payment, remuneration, reparation, repayment, requital, restitution, return, reward, satisfaction, wages

reconcilable 1. compatible, congruous, consistent **2.** appeasable, conciliatory, forgiving, peaceable, placable

reconcile 1. accept, accommodate, get used, make the best of, put up with (*Inf.*), resign, submit, yield **2.** appease, bring to terms, conciliate, make peace between, pacify, placate, propitiate, re-establish friendly relations between, restore harmony between, reunite **3.** adjust, compose, harmonize, patch up, put to rights, rectify, resolve, settle, square

reconciliation 1. appeasement, conciliation, détente, pacification, propitiation, *rapprochement*, reconcilement, reunion, understanding **2.** accommodation, adjustment, compromise, harmony, rectification, settlement

recondite abstruse, arcane, cabbalistic, concealed, dark, deep, difficult, esoteric, hidden, involved, mysterious, mystical, obscure, occult, profound, secret

recondition do up (*Inf.*), fix up (*Inf.*, *chiefly U.S.*), overhaul, remodel, renew,

renovate, repair, restore, revamp

reconnaissance exploration, inspection, investigation, observation, patrol, recce (*Sl.*), reconnoitring, scan, scouting, scrutiny, survey

reconnoitre explore, get the lie of the land, inspect, investigate, make a reconnaissance (of), observe, patrol, recce (*Sl.*), scan, scout, scrutinize, see how the land lies, spy out, survey

reconsider change one's mind, have second thoughts, reassess, re-evaluate, re-examine, rethink, review, revise, take another look at, think again, think better of, think once more, think twice

reconstruct 1. reassemble, rebuild, recreate, re-establish, reform, regenerate, remake, remodel, renovate, reorganize, restore **2.** build up, build up a picture of, deduce, piece together

record *n.* **1.** account, annals, archives, chronicle, diary, document, entry, file, journal, log, memoir, memorandum, memorial, minute, register, report **2.** documentation, evidence, memorial, remembrance, testimony, trace, witness **3.** background, career, curriculum vitae, history, performance, track record (*Inf.*) **4.** album, disc, EP, forty-five, gramophone record, LP, platter (*U.S. sl.*), recording, release, single **5. off the record** confidential, confidentially, in confidence, in private, not for publication, private, sub rosa, under the rose, unofficial, unofficially ~*v.* **6.** chalk up (*Inf.*), chronicle, document, enrol, enter, inscribe, log, minute, note, preserve, put down, put on file, put on record, register, report, set down, take down, transcribe, write down **7.** contain, give evidence of, indicate, read, register, say, show **8.** cut, lay down (*Sl.*), make a recording of, put on wax (*Inf.*), tape, tape-record, video, video-tape, wax (*Inf.*)

recorder annalist, archivist, chronicler, clerk, diarist, historian, registrar, scorekeeper, scorer, scribe

recording cut (*Inf.*), disc, gramophone record, record, tape, video

recount delineate, depict, describe, detail, enumerate, give an account of, narrate, portray, recite, rehearse, relate, repeat, report, tell, tell the story of

recoup 1. make good, recover, redeem, regain, retrieve, win back **2.** compensate, make redress for, make up for, refund, reimburse, remunerate, repay, requite, satisfy

recourse alternative, appeal, choice, expedient, option, refuge, remedy, resort, resource, way out

recover 1. find again, get back, make good, recapture, reclaim, recoup, redeem, regain, repair, repossess, restore, retake, retrieve, take back, win back **2.** bounce back, come round, convalesce, feel oneself again, get back on one's feet, get better, get well, heal, improve, mend, pick up, pull through, rally, recuperate, regain one's health *or* strength, revive, take a turn for the better

recovery 1. convalescence, healing, improvement, mending, rally, recuperation, return to health, revival, turn for the better **2.** amelioration, betterment, improvement, rally, rehabilitation, restoration, revival, upturn **3.** recapture, reclamation, redemption, repair, repossession, restoration, retrieval

recreation amusement, distraction, diversion, enjoyment, entertainment, exercise, fun, hobby, leisure activity, pastime, play, pleasure, refreshment, relaxation, relief, sport

recrimination bickering, counterattack, countercharge, mutual accusation, name-calling, quarrel, retaliation, retort, squabbling

recruit *v.* **1.** draft, enlist, enrol, impress, levy, mobilize, muster, raise, strengthen **2.** engage, enrol, gather, obtain, procure, proselytize, round up, take on, win (over) **3.** augment, build up, refresh, reinforce, renew, replenish, restore, strengthen, supply ~*n.* **4.** apprentice, beginner, convert, greenhorn (*Inf.*), helper, initiate, learner, neophyte, novice, proselyte, rookie (*Inf.*), trainee, tyro

rectify 1. adjust, amend, correct, emend, fix, improve, make good, mend, put right, redress, reform, remedy, repair, right, square **2.** *Chem.* distil, purify, refine, separate

rectitude 1. correctness, decency, equity, goodness, honesty, honour, incorruptibility, integrity, justice, morality, principle, probity, righteousness, scrupulousness, uprightness, virtue **2.** accuracy, correctness, exactness, justice, precision, rightness, soundness, verity

recumbent flat, flat on one's back, horizontal, leaning, lying, lying down,

prone, prostrate, reclining, resting, stretched out, supine

recuperate convalesce, get back on one's feet, get better, improve, mend, pick up, recover, regain one's health

recur 1. come again, come and go, come back, happen again, persist, reappear, repeat, return, revert **2.** be remembered, come back, haunt one's thoughts, return to mind, run through one's mind

recurrent continued, cyclical, frequent, habitual, periodic, recurring, regular, repeated, repetitive

recycle reclaim, reprocess, reuse, salvage, save

red *adj.* **1.** cardinal, carmine, cherry, coral, crimson, gules (*Heraldry*), maroon, pink, rose, ruby, scarlet, vermeil, vermilion, wine **2.** bay, carroty, chestnut, flame-coloured, flaming, foxy, reddish, sandy, titian **3.** blushing, embarrassed, florid, flushed, rubicund, shamefaced, suffused **4.** blooming, glowing, healthy, roseate, rosy, ruddy **5.** bloodshot, inflamed, red-rimmed **6.** bloodstained, bloody, ensanguined (*Literary*), gory, sanguine ~*n.* **7.** colour, redness **8. in the red** *Inf.* bankrupt, in arrears, in debit, in debt, in deficit, insolvent, on the rocks, overdrawn, owing money, showing a loss **9. see red** *Inf.* be *or* get very angry, be beside oneself with rage (*Inf.*), become enraged, blow one's top, boil, go mad (*Inf.*), go off one's head (*Sl.*), lose one's rag (*Sl.*), lose one's temper, seethe

red-blooded hearty, lusty, manly, robust, strong, vigorous, virile, vital

redden blush, colour (up), crimson, flush, go red, suffuse

redeem 1. buy back, reclaim, recover, recover possession of, regain, repossess, repurchase, retrieve, win back **2.** cash (in), change, exchange, trade in **3.** abide by, acquit, adhere to, be faithful to, carry out, discharge, fulfil, hold to, keep, keep faith with, make good, meet, perform, satisfy **4.** absolve, rehabilitate, reinstate, restore to favour **5.** atone for, compensate for, defray, make amends for, make good, make up for, offset, outweigh, redress, save **6.** buy the freedom of, deliver, emancipate, extricate, free, liberate, pay the ransom of, ransom, rescue, save, set free

redemption 1. reclamation, recovery, repossession, repurchase, retrieval **2.**

discharge, exchange, fulfilment, performance, quid pro quo, trade-in **3.** amends, atonement, compensation, expiation, reparation **4.** deliverance, emancipation, liberation, ransom, release, rescue, salvation

red-handed (in) flagrante delicto, in the act, with one's fingers *or* hand in the till (*Inf.*)

redolent 1. aromatic, fragrant, odorous, perfumed, scented, sweet-smelling **2.** evocative, remindful, reminiscent, suggestive

redoubtable awful, doughty, dreadful, fearful, fearsome, formidable, mighty, powerful, resolute, strong, terrible, valiant

redound 1. conduce, contribute, effect, lead to, militate for, tend **2.** accrue, come back, ensue, rebound, recoil, reflect, result

redress *v.* **1.** compensate for, make amends (reparation, restitution) for, make up for, pay for, put right, recompense for **2.** adjust, amend, balance, correct, ease, even up, mend, put right, rectify, reform, regulate, relieve, remedy, repair, restore the balance, square ~*n.* **3.** aid, assistance, correction, cure, ease, help, justice, rectification, relief, remedy, satisfaction **4.** amends, atonement, compensation, payment, quittance, recompense, reparation, requital, restitution

reduce 1. abate, abridge, contract, curtail, cut down, debase, decrease, depress, dilute, diminish, impair, lessen, lower, moderate, shorten, slow down, tone down, truncate, turn down, weaken, wind down **2.** bankrupt, break, impoverish, pauperize, ruin **3.** bring, bring to the point of, conquer, drive, force, master, overpower, subdue, vanquish **4.** be *or* go on a diet, diet, lose weight, shed weight, slenderize (*Chiefly U.S.*), slim, trim **5.** bring down the price of, cheapen, cut, discount, lower, mark down, slash **6.** break, bring low, degrade, demote, downgrade, humble, humiliate, lower in rank, lower the status of, take down a peg (*Inf.*)

redundant 1. *de trop*, excessive, extra, inessential, inordinate, supererogatory, superfluous, supernumerary, surplus, unnecessary, unwanted **2.** diffuse, padded, periphrastic, pleonastic, prolix, repetitious, tautological, verbose, wordy

reek *v.* **1.** hum (*Sl.*), pong (*Brit. inf.*), smell, smell to high heaven, stink **2.** be characterized by, be permeated by, be redolent of **3.** *Dialect* fume, give off smoke *or* fumes, smoke, steam ~*n.* **4.** effluvium, fetor, mephitis, odour, pong (*Brit. inf.*), smell, stench, stink **5.** *Dialect* exhalation, fumes, smoke, steam, vapour

reel 1. falter, lurch, pitch, rock, roll, stagger, stumble, sway, totter, waver, wobble **2.** go round and round, revolve, spin, swim, swirl, twirl, whirl

refer 1. advert, allude, bring up, cite, hint, invoke, make mention of, make reference, mention, speak of, touch on **2.** direct, guide, point, recommend, send **3.** apply, consult, go, have recourse to, look up, seek information from, turn to **4.** apply, be directed to, belong, be relevant to, concern, pertain, relate **5.** accredit, ascribe, assign, attribute, credit, impute, put down to **6.** commit, consign, deliver, hand over, pass on, submit, transfer, turn over

referee 1. *n.* adjudicator, arbiter, arbitrator, judge, ref (*Inf.*), umpire **2.** *v.* adjudicate, arbitrate, judge, umpire

reference 1. allusion, citation, mention, note, quotation, remark **2.** applicability, bearing, concern, connection, consideration, regard, relation, respect **3.** certification, character, credentials, endorsement, good word, recommendation, testimonial

referendum plebiscite, popular vote, public vote

refine 1. clarify, cleanse, distil, filter, process, purify, rarefy **2.** civilize, cultivate, elevate, hone, improve, perfect, polish, temper

refined 1. civil, civilized, courtly, cultivated, cultured, elegant, genteel, gentlemanly, gracious, ladylike, polished, polite, sophisticated, urbane, well-bred, well-mannered **2.** cultured, delicate, discerning, discriminating, exact, fastidious, fine, nice, precise, punctilious, sensitive, sublime, subtle **3.** clarified, clean, distilled, filtered, processed, pure, purified

refinement 1. clarification, cleansing, distillation, filtering, processing, purification, rarefaction, rectification **2.** fine point, fine tuning, nicety, nuance, subtlety **3.** civility, civilization, courtesy, courtliness, cultivation, culture, delicacy, discrimination, elegance, fastidiousness, fineness, finesse, finish, gentility, good breeding, good manners, grace, graciousness, polish, politeness, politesse, precision, sophistication, style, taste, urbanity

reflect 1. echo, give back, imitate, mirror, reproduce, return, throw back **2.** bear out, bespeak, communicate, demonstrate, display, evince, exhibit, express, indicate, manifest, reveal, show **3.** cogitate, consider, contemplate, deliberate, meditate, mull over, muse, ponder, ruminate, think, wonder

reflection 1. counterpart, echo, image, mirror image **2.** cerebration, cogitation, consideration, contemplation, deliberation, idea, impression, meditation, musing, observation, opinion, pondering, rumination, study, thinking, thought, view **3.** aspersion, censure, criticism, derogation, imputation, reproach, slur

reflective cogitating, contemplative, deliberative, meditative, pensive, pondering, reasoning, ruminative, thoughtful

reform v. **1.** ameliorate, amend, better, correct, emend, improve, mend, rebuild, reclaim, reconstitute, reconstruct, rectify, regenerate, rehabilitate, remodel, renovate, reorganize, repair, restore, revolutionize **2.** get back on the straight and narrow (*Inf.*), go straight (*Inf.*), mend one's ways, turn over a new leaf ~n. **3.** amelioration, amendment, betterment, correction, improvement, rectification, rehabilitation, renovation

refractory cantankerous, contentious, contumacious, difficult, disobedient, disputatious, headstrong, intractable, mulish, obstinate, perverse, recalcitrant, stubborn, uncontrollable, uncooperative, unmanageable, unruly, wilful

refrain¹ v. abstain, avoid, cease, desist, do without, eschew, forbear, give up, leave off, renounce, stop

refrain² n. burden, chorus, melody, song, tune

refresh 1. brace, breathe new life into, cheer, cool, enliven, freshen, inspirit, reanimate, reinvigorate, rejuvenate, revitalize, revive, revivify, stimulate **2.** brush up (*Inf.*), jog, prod, prompt, renew, stimulate **3.** renew, renovate, repair, replenish, restore, top up

refreshing bracing, cooling, different, fresh, inspiriting, invigorating, new, novel, original, revivifying, stimulating, thirst-quenching

refreshment 1. enlivenment, freshening, reanimation, renewal, renovation, repair, restoration, revival, stimulation **2.** *Plural* drinks, food and drink, snacks, titbits

refrigerate chill, cool, freeze, keep cold

refuge asylum, bolt hole, harbour, haven, hide-out, protection, resort, retreat, sanctuary, security, shelter

refugee displaced person, émigré, escapee, exile, fugitive, runaway

refulgent bright, brilliant, gleaming, irradiant, lambent, lustrous, radiant, resplendent, shining

refund 1. v. give back, make good, pay back, reimburse, repay, restore, return **2.** n. reimbursement, repayment, return

refurbish clean up, do up (*Inf.*), fix up (*Inf., chiefly U.S.*), mend, overhaul, reequip, refit, remodel, renovate, repair, restore, revamp, set to rights, spruce up

refusal 1. defiance, denial, knockback (*Sl.*), negation, no, rebuff, rejection, repudiation, thumbs down **2.** choice, consideration, opportunity, option

refuse¹ v. decline, deny, reject, repel, repudiate, say no, spurn, turn down, withhold

refuse² n. dregs, dross, garbage, junk, leavings, lees, litter, offscourings, rubbish, scum, sediment, sweepings, trash, waste

refute confute, counter, discredit, disprove, give the lie to, negate, overthrow, prove false, rebut, silence

regain 1. get back, recapture, recoup, recover, redeem, repossess, retake, retrieve, take back, win back **2.** get back to, reach again, reattain, return to

regal fit for a king *or* queen, kingly, magnificent, majestic, noble, princely, proud, queenly, royal, sovereign

regale amuse, delight, divert, entertain, feast, gratify, ply, refresh, serve

regard v. **1.** behold, eye, gaze at, look closely at, mark, notice, observe, remark, scrutinize, view, watch **2.** account, adjudge, believe, consider, deem, esteem, estimate, hold, imagine, judge, look upon, rate, see, suppose, think, treat, value, view **3.** apply to, be relevant to, concern, have a bearing on, have to do with, interest, pertain to, relate to **4.** attend, heed, listen to, mind, note, pay attention to, respect, take into consideration, take notice of ~*n.* **5.** attention, heed, mind, notice **6.** account, affection, attachment, care, concern, consideration, deference, esteem, honour, love, note, reputation, repute, respect, store, sympathy, thought **7.** aspect, detail, feature, item, matter, particular, point, respect **8.** gaze, glance, look, scrutiny, stare **9.** bearing, concern, connection, reference, relation, relevance **10.** *Plural* best wishes, compliments, devoirs, good wishes, greetings, respects, salutations

regardful attentive, aware, careful, considerate, dutiful, heedful, mindful, observant, respectful, thoughtful, watchful

regarding about, apropos, as regards, as to, concerning, in *or* with regard to, in re, in respect of, in the matter of, on the subject of, re, respecting, with reference to

regardless 1. *adj.* disregarding, heedless, inattentive, inconsiderate, indifferent, neglectful, negligent, rash, reckless, remiss, unconcerned, unmindful **2.** *adv.* anyway, come what may, despite everything, for all that, in any case, in spite of everything, nevertheless, no matter what, nonetheless

regenerate breathe new life into, change, inspirit, invigorate, reawaken, reconstruct, re-establish, reinvigorate, rejuvenate, renew, renovate, reproduce, restore, revive, revivify, uplift

regime administration, establishment, government, leadership, management, reign, rule, system

regiment *v.* bully, control, discipline, order, organize, regulate, systematize

region 1. area, country, district, division, expanse, land, locality, part, place, province, quarter, section, sector, territory, tract, zone **2.** domain, field, province, realm, sphere, world **3.** area, locality, neighbourhood, range, scope, vicinity

regional district, local, parochial, provincial, sectional, zonal

register *n.* **1.** annals, archives, catalogue, chronicle, diary, file, ledger, list, log, memorandum, record, roll, roster, schedule ~*v.* **2.** catalogue, check in, chronicle, enlist, enrol, enter, inscribe, list, note, record, set down, sign on *or* up, take down **3.** be shown, bespeak, betray, display, exhibit, express, indicate, mani-

fest, mark, read, record, reflect, reveal, say, show **4.** *Inf.* come home, dawn on, get through, have an effect, impress, make an impression, sink in, tell

regress backslide, degenerate, deteriorate, ebb, fall away *or* off, fall back, go back, lapse, lose ground, recede, relapse, retreat, retrogress, return, revert, wane

regret 1. *v.* bemoan, be upset, bewail, deplore, feel remorse for, feel sorry for, grieve, lament, miss, mourn, repent, rue, weep over **2.** *n.* bitterness, compunction, contrition, disappointment, grief, lamentation, pang of conscience, penitence, remorse, repentance, ruefulness, self-reproach, sorrow

regretful apologetic, ashamed, contrite, disappointed, mournful, penitent, remorseful, repentant, rueful, sad, sorrowful, sorry

regrettable deplorable, disappointing, distressing, ill-advised, lamentable, pitiable, sad, shameful, unfortunate, unhappy, woeful, wrong

regular 1. common, commonplace, customary, daily, everyday, habitual, normal, ordinary, routine, typical, unvarying, usual **2.** consistent, constant, established, even, fixed, ordered, periodic, rhythmic, set, stated, steady, systematic, uniform **3.** dependable, efficient, formal, methodical, orderly, standardized, steady, systematic **4.** balanced, even, flat, level, smooth, straight, symmetrical, uniform **5.** approved, bona fide, classic, correct, established, formal, official, orthodox, prevailing, proper, sanctioned, standard, time-honoured, traditional

regulate adjust, administer, arrange, balance, conduct, control, direct, fit, govern, guide, handle, manage, moderate, modulate, monitor, order, organize, oversee, rule, run, settle, superintend, supervise, systematize, tune

regulation *n.* **1.** adjustment, administration, arrangement, control, direction, governance, government, management, modulation, supervision, tuning **2.** commandment, decree, dictate, direction, edict, law, order, ordinance, precept, procedure, requirement, rule, standing order, statute ~*adj.* **3.** customary, mandatory, normal, official, prescribed, required, standard, usual

regurgitate disgorge, puke (*Sl.*), spew (up), throw up (*Inf.*), vomit

rehabilitate 1. adjust, redeem, reform,

reintegrate, save 2. clear, convert, fix up, make good, mend, rebuild, recondition, reconstitute, reconstruct, re-establish, reinstate, reinvigorate, renew, renovate, restore

rehash 1. *v.* alter, change, make over, rearrange, refashion, rejig (*Inf.*), reshuffle, reuse, rework, rewrite 2. *n.* new version, rearrangement, reworking, rewrite

rehearsal 1. drill, going-over, practice, practice session, preparation, reading, rehearsing, run-through 2. account, catalogue, description, enumeration, list, narration, recital, recounting, relation, telling

rehearse 1. act, drill, go over, practise, prepare, ready, recite, repeat, run through, study, train, try out 2. delineate, depict, describe, detail, enumerate, go over, list, narrate, recite, recount, relate, review, run through, spell out, tell, trot out (*Inf.*)

reign *n.* 1. ascendancy, command, control, dominion, empire, hegemony, influence, monarchy, power, rule, sovereignty, supremacy, sway ~*v.* 2. administer, be in power, command, govern, hold sway, influence, occupy *or* sit on the throne, rule, wear the crown, wield the sceptre 3. be rampant, be rife, be supreme, hold sway, obtain, predominate, prevail

reimburse compensate, indemnify, pay back, recompense, refund, remunerate, repay, restore, return, square up

rein *n.* 1. brake, bridle, check, control, curb, harness, hold, restraint, restriction 2. **give (a) free rein (to)** free, give a free hand, give carte blanche, give (someone) his head, give way to, indulge, let go, remove restraints ~*v.* 3. bridle, check, control, curb, halt, hold, hold back, limit, restrain, restrict, slow down

reincarnation metempsychosis, rebirth, transmigration of souls

reinforce augment, bolster, buttress, emphasize, fortify, harden, increase, prop, shore up, stiffen, strengthen, stress, supplement, support, toughen, underline

reinforcement 1. addition, amplification, augmentation, enlargement, fortification, increase, strengthening, supplement 2. brace, buttress, prop, shore, stay, support 3. *Plural* additional *or* fresh troops, auxiliaries, reserves, support

reinstate bring back, recall, re-establish, rehabilitate, replace, restore, return

reiterate do again, iterate, recapitulate, repeat, restate, retell, say again

reject 1. *v.* cast aside, decline, deny, despise, disallow, discard, eliminate, exclude, jettison, jilt, rebuff, refuse, renounce, repel, repudiate, repulse, say no to, scrap, spurn, throw away *or* out, turn down, veto 2. *n.* castoff, discard, failure, flotsam, second

rejection brushoff (*Sl.*), denial, dismissal, elimination, exclusion, rebuff, refusal, renunciation, repudiation, thumbs down, veto

rejoice be glad (happy, overjoyed), celebrate, delight, exult, glory, joy, jump for joy, make merry, revel, triumph

rejoicing celebration, cheer, delight, elation, exultation, festivity, gaiety, gladness, happiness, joy, jubilation, merrymaking, revelry, triumph

rejoin answer, come back with, reply, respond, retort, return, riposte

rejoinder answer, comeback (*Inf.*), counter, reply, response, retort, riposte

rejuvenate breathe new life into, give new life to, make young again, reanimate, refresh, regenerate, reinvigorate, renew, restore, restore vitality to, revitalize, revivify

relapse *v.* 1. backslide, degenerate, fail, fall back, lapse, regress, retrogress, revert, slip back, weaken 2. deteriorate, fade, fail, sicken, sink, weaken, worsen ~*n.* 3. backsliding, fall from grace, lapse, recidivism, regression, retrogression, reversion 4. deterioration, recurrence, setback, turn for the worse, weakening, worsening

relate 1. chronicle, describe, detail, give an account of, impart, narrate, present, recite, recount, rehearse, report, set forth, tell 2. ally, associate, connect, coordinate, correlate, couple, join, link 3. appertain, apply, bear upon, be relevant to, concern, have reference to, have to do with, pertain, refer

related 1. accompanying, affiliated, agnate, akin, allied, associated, cognate, concomitant, connected, correlated, interconnected, joint, linked 2. agnate, akin, cognate, consanguineous, kin, kindred

relation 1. affiliation, affinity, consanguinity, kindred, kinship, propinquity, relationship **2**. kin, kinsman, kinswoman, relative **3**. application, bearing, bond, comparison, connection, correlation, interdependence, link, pertinence, reference, regard, similarity, tie-in **4**. account, description, narration, narrative, recital, recountal, report, story, tale

relations 1. affairs, associations, communications, connections, contact, dealings, interaction, intercourse, liaison, meetings, rapport, relationship, terms **2**. clan, family, kin, kindred, kinsmen, relatives, tribe

relationship affair, association, bond, communications, conjunction, connection, correlation, exchange, kinship, liaison, link, parallel, proportion, rapport, ratio, similarity, tie-up

relative adj. **1**. allied, associated, comparative, connected, contingent, corresponding, dependent, proportionate, reciprocal, related, respective **2**. applicable, apposite, appropriate, appurtenant, apropos, germane, pertinent, relevant **3**. With **to** corresponding to, in proportion to, proportional to ~n. **4**. connection, kinsman, kinswoman, member of one's or the family, relation

relatively comparatively, in or by comparison, rather, somewhat, to some extent

relax 1. abate, diminish, ease, ebb, lessen, let up, loosen, lower, mitigate, moderate, reduce, relieve, slacken, weaken **2**. be or feel at ease, calm, laze, let oneself go (Inf.), let one's hair down (Inf.), loosen up, put one's feet up, rest, soften, take it easy (Inf.), take one's ease, tranquillize, unbend, unwind

relaxation 1. amusement, enjoyment, entertainment, fun, leisure, pleasure, recreation, refreshment, rest **2**. abatement, diminution, easing, lessening, letup (Inf.), moderation, reduction, slackening, weakening

relay n. **1**. relief, shift, turn **2**. communication, dispatch, message, transmission ~v. **3**. broadcast, carry, communicate, hand on, pass on, send, spread, transmit

release v. **1**. deliver, discharge, disengage, drop, emancipate, extricate, free, let go, let out, liberate, loose, manumit, set free, turn loose, unchain, undo, unfasten, unfetter, unloose, unshackle, un-

tie **2**. absolve, acquit, dispense, excuse, exempt, exonerate, let go, let off **3**. break, circulate, disseminate, distribute, issue, launch, make known, make public, present, publish, put out, unveil ~n. **4**. acquittal, deliverance, delivery, discharge, emancipation, freedom, liberation, liberty, manumission, relief **5**. absolution, acquittance, dispensation, exemption, exoneration, let-off (Inf.) **6**. announcement, issue, offering, proclamation, publication

relegate 1. demote, downgrade **2**. assign, consign, delegate, entrust, pass on, refer, transfer **3**. banish, deport, eject, exile, expatriate, expel, throw out

relent 1. acquiesce, be merciful, capitulate, change one's mind, come round, forbear, give in, give quarter, give way, have pity, melt, show mercy, soften, unbend, yield **2**. die down, drop, ease, fall, let up, relax, slacken, slow, weaken

relentless 1. cruel, fierce, grim, hard, harsh, implacable, inexorable, inflexible, merciless, pitiless, remorseless, ruthless, uncompromising, undeviating, unforgiving, unrelenting, unstoppable, unyielding **2**. incessant, nonstop, persistent, punishing, sustained, unabated, unbroken, unfaltering, unflagging, unrelenting, unrelieved, unremitting, unstoppable

relevant admissible, ad rem, applicable, apposite, appropriate, appurtenant, apt, fitting, germane, material, pertinent, proper, related, relative, significant, suited, to the point, to the purpose

reliable certain, dependable, faithful, honest, predictable, regular, responsible, safe, sound, stable, sure, tried and true, true, trustworthy, trusty, unfailing, upright

reliance assurance, belief, confidence, credence, credit, dependence, faith, trust

relic fragment, keepsake, memento, remembrance, remnant, scrap, souvenir, survival, token, trace, vestige

relief 1. abatement, alleviation, assuagement, balm, comfort, cure, deliverance, ease, easement, mitigation, palliation, release, remedy, solace **2**. aid, assistance, help, succour, support, sustenance **3**. break, breather (Inf.), diversion, letup (Inf.), refreshment, relaxation, remission, respite, rest

relieve 1. abate, alleviate, appease, assuage, calm, comfort, console, cure, diminish, dull, ease, mitigate, mollify, pal-

liate, relax, salve, soften, solace, soothe
2. aid, assist, bring aid to, help, succour,
support, sustain **3**. give (someone) a
break *or* rest, stand in for, substitute for,
take over from, take the place of **4**. deliver, discharge, disembarrass, disencumber, exempt, free, release, unburden **5**.
break, brighten, interrupt, let up on
(*Inf.*), lighten, slacken, vary

religious 1. churchgoing, devotional,
devout, divine, doctrinal, faithful, godfearing, godly, holy, pious, pure, reverent, righteous, sacred, scriptural, sectarian, spiritual, theological **2**. conscientious, exact, faithful, fastidious, meticulous, punctilious, rigid, rigorous, scrupulous, unerring, unswerving

relinquish abandon, abdicate, cast off,
cede, desert, drop, forgo, forsake, give
up, hand over, lay aside, leave, let go,
quit, release, renounce, repudiate, resign, retire from, surrender, vacate,
waive, withdraw from, yield

relish *v.* **1**. appreciate, delight in, enjoy, fancy, like, look forward to, luxuriate in, prefer, revel in, savour, taste ~*n.*
2. appetite, appreciation, enjoyment,
fancy, fondness, gusto, liking, love, partiality, penchant, predilection, stomach,
taste, zest **3**. appetizer, condiment,
sauce, seasoning **4**. flavour, piquancy, savour, smack, spice, tang, taste, trace

reluctance aversion, backwardness,
disinclination, dislike, disrelish, distaste,
hesitancy, indisposition, loathing, repugnance, unwillingness

reluctant averse, backward, disinclined, grudging, hesitant, indisposed,
loath, recalcitrant, slow, unenthusiastic,
unwilling

rely bank, be confident of, be sure of,
bet, count, depend, have confidence in,
lean, reckon, repose trust in, swear by,
trust

remain abide, be left, cling, continue,
delay, dwell, endure, go on, last, linger,
persist, prevail, rest, stand, stay, stay behind, stay put (*Inf.*), survive, tarry, wait

remainder balance, dregs, excess,
leavings, relic, remains, remnant, residue, residuum, rest, surplus, trace, vestige(s)

remaining abiding, extant, lasting,
left, lingering, outstanding, persisting,
residual, surviving, unfinished

remains 1. balance, crumbs, debris,
detritus, dregs, fragments, leavings, left-

overs, oddments, odds and ends, pieces,
relics, remainder, remnants, residue,
rest, scraps, traces, vestiges **2**. body, cadaver, carcass, corpse

remark *v.* **1**. animadvert, comment,
declare, mention, observe, pass comment, reflect, say, state **2**. espy, heed,
make out, mark, note, notice, observe,
perceive, regard, see, take note *or* notice
of ~*n.* **3**. assertion, comment, declaration, observation, opinion, reflection,
statement, thought, utterance, word **4**.
acknowledgment, attention, comment,
consideration, heed, mention, notice, observation, recognition, regard, thought

remarkable conspicuous, distinguished, extraordinary, famous, impressive, miraculous, notable, noteworthy,
odd, outstanding, phenomenal, preeminent, prominent, rare, signal, singular, strange, striking, surprising, uncommon, unusual, wonderful

remediable corrigible, curable, medicable, repairable, soluble, solvable, treatable

remedy *n.* **1**. antidote, counteractive,
cure, medicament, medicine, nostrum,
panacea, physic (*Rare*), relief, restorative, specific, therapy, treatment **2**. antidote, corrective, countermeasure, panacea, redress, relief, solution ~*v.* **3**. alleviate, assuage, control, cure, ease, heal,
help, mitigate, palliate, relieve, restore,
soothe, treat **4**. ameliorate, correct, fix,
put right, rectify, redress, reform, relieve, repair, set to rights, solve

remember bear in mind, call to mind,
call up, commemorate, keep in mind,
look back (on), recall, recognize, recollect, reminisce, retain, summon up,
think back

remembrance 1. anamnesis, memory,
mind, recall, recognition, recollection,
regard, reminiscence, retrospect,
thought **2**. commemoration, keepsake,
memento, memorial, monument, relic,
remembrancer (*Archaic*), reminder, souvenir, testimonial, token

remind awaken memories of, bring
back to, bring to mind, call to mind, call
up, jog one's memory, make (someone)
remember, prompt, put in mind, refresh
one's memory

reminisce go over in the memory,
hark back, live in the past, look back, recall, recollect, remember, review, think
back

reminiscence anecdote, memoir, memory, recall, recollection, reflection, remembrance, retrospection, review

reminiscent evocative, redolent, reminding, similar, suggestive

remiss careless, culpable, delinquent, derelict, dilatory, forgetful, heedless, inattentive, indifferent, lackadaisical, lax, neglectful, negligent, regardless, slack, slipshod, sloppy (*Inf.*), slothful, slow, tardy, thoughtless, unmindful

remission 1. absolution, acquittal, amnesty, discharge, excuse, exemption, exoneration, forgiveness, indulgence, pardon, release, reprieve **2.** abatement, abeyance, alleviation, amelioration, decrease, diminution, ebb, lessening, let-up (*Inf.*), lull, moderation, reduction, relaxation, respite, suspension

remit *v.* **1.** dispatch, forward, mail, post, send, transmit **2.** cancel, desist, forbear, halt, repeal, rescind, stop **3.** abate, alleviate, decrease, diminish, dwindle, ease up, fall away, mitigate, moderate, reduce, relax, sink, slacken, soften, wane, weaken **4.** defer, delay, postpone, put off, shelve, suspend ~*n.* **5.** authorization, brief, guidelines, instructions, orders, terms of reference

remittance allowance, consideration, fee, payment

remnant balance, bit, end, fragment, hangover, leftovers, piece, remainder, remains, residue, residuum, rest, rump, scrap, shred, survival, trace, vestige

remonstrance complaint, expostulation, grievance, objection, petition, protest, protestation, reprimand, reproof

remonstrate argue, challenge, complain, dispute, dissent, expostulate, object, protest, take exception, take issue

remorse anguish, bad *or* guilty conscience, compassion, compunction, contrition, grief, guilt, pangs of conscience, penitence, pity, regret, repentance, ruefulness, self-reproach, shame, sorrow

remorseful apologetic, ashamed, chastened, conscience-stricken, contrite, guilt-ridden, guilty, penitent, regretful, repentant, rueful, sad, self-reproachful, sorrowful, sorry

remorseless 1. inexorable, relentless, unrelenting, unremitting, unstoppable **2.** callous, cruel, hard, hardhearted, harsh, implacable, inhumane, merciless, pitiless, ruthless, savage, uncompassionate, unforgiving, unmerciful

remote 1. backwoods, distant, far, faraway, far-off, godforsaken, inaccessible, isolated, lonely, off the beaten track, outlying, out-of-the-way, secluded **2.** alien, extraneous, extrinsic, foreign, immaterial, irrelevant, outside, removed, unconnected, unrelated **3.** doubtful, dubious, faint, implausible, inconsiderable, meagre, negligible, outside, poor, slender, slight, slim, small, unlikely **4.** abstracted, aloof, cold, detached, distant, faraway, indifferent, introspective, introverted, removed, reserved, standoffish, unapproachable, uncommunicative, uninterested, uninvolved, withdrawn

removal 1. abstraction, dislodgment, dismissal, displacement, dispossession, ejection, elimination, eradication, erasure, expulsion, expunction, extraction, purging, stripping, subtraction, taking off, uprooting, withdrawal **2.** departure, flitting (*Scot., & northern English dialect*), move, relocation, transfer

remove 1. abolish, abstract, amputate, carry off *or* away, delete, depose, detach, dethrone, discharge, dislodge, dismiss, displace, do away with, doff, efface, eject, eliminate, erase, expel, expunge, extract, get rid of, move, oust, purge, relegate, shed, strike out, take away, take off, take out, throw out, transfer, transport, unseat, wipe out, withdraw **2.** depart, flit (*Scot., & northern English dialect*), move, move away, quit, relocate, shift, transfer, transport, vacate **3.** *Fig.* assassinate, bump off (*Sl.*), dispose of, do away with, do in (*Sl.*), eliminate, execute, get rid of, kill, liquidate, murder

remunerate compensate, indemnify, pay, recompense, redress, reimburse, repay, requite, reward

remuneration compensation, earnings, emolument, fee, income, indemnity, pay, payment, profit, recompense, reimbursement, reparation, repayment, retainer, return, reward, salary, stipend, wages

remunerative gainful, lucrative, moneymaking, paying, profitable, recompensing, rewarding, rich, worthwhile

renaissance, renascence awakening, new birth, new dawn, reappearance, reawakening, rebirth, re-emergence, regeneration, renewal, restoration, resurgence, resurrection, revival

renascent reanimated, reawakening, reborn, redivivus (*Rare*), re-emerging, renewed, resurgent, resurrected, reviving

rend 1. break, burst, cleave, crack, dissever, disturb, divide, fracture, lacerate, pierce, pull, rip, rive, rupture, separate, sever, shatter, smash, splinter, split, sunder (*Literary*), tear, tear to pieces, wrench **2.** afflict, anguish, break, distress, hurt, lacerate, pain, pierce, stab, torment, wound, wring

render 1. contribute, deliver, furnish, give, make available, pay, present, provide, show, submit, supply, tender, turn over, yield **2.** display, evince, exhibit, manifest, show **3.** exchange, give, return, swap, trade **4.** cause to become, leave, make **5.** act, depict, do, give, interpret, perform, play, portray, present, represent **6.** construe, explain, interpret, put, reproduce, restate, transcribe, translate **7.** cede, deliver, give, give up, hand over, relinquish, surrender, turn over, yield **8.** give back, make restitution, pay back, repay, restore, return

rendezvous *n.* **1.** appointment, assignation, date, engagement, meeting, tryst (*Archaic*) **2.** gathering point, meeting place, place of assignation, trysting-place (*Archaic*), venue ~*v.* **3.** assemble, be reunited, collect, come together, converge, gather, get together, join up, meet, muster, rally

rendition 1. arrangement, delivery, depiction, execution, interpretation, performance, portrayal, presentation, reading, rendering, version **2.** construction, explanation, interpretation, reading, transcription, translation, version

renegade 1. *n.* apostate, backslider, betrayer, defector, deserter, dissident, mutineer, outlaw, rebel, recreant (*Archaic*), runaway, traitor, turncoat **2.** *adj.* apostate, backsliding, disloyal, dissident, mutinous, outlaw, rebel, rebellious, recreant (*Archaic*), runaway, traitorous, unfaithful

renege, renegue back out, break a promise, break one's word, default, go back, repudiate, welsh (*Sl.*)

renew begin again, breathe new life into, bring up to date, continue, extend, fix up (*Inf., chiefly U.S.*), mend, modernize, overhaul, prolong, reaffirm, recommence, recreate, re-establish, refit, refresh, refurbish, regenerate, rejuvenate, renovate, reopen, repair, repeat, replace, replenish, restate, restock, restore, resume, revitalize, transform

renounce abandon, abdicate, abjure, abnegate, abstain from, cast off, decline, deny, discard, disclaim, disown, eschew, forgo, forsake, forswear, give up, leave off, quit, recant, reject, relinquish, repudiate, resign, spurn, swear off, throw off, waive, wash one's hands of

renovate do up (*Inf.*), fix up (*Inf., chiefly U.S.*), modernize, overhaul, recondition, reconstitute, recreate, refit, reform, refurbish, rehabilitate, remodel, renew, repair, restore, revamp

renown acclaim, celebrity, distinction, eminence, fame, glory, honour, illustriousness, lustre, mark, note, reputation, repute, stardom

renowned acclaimed, celebrated, distinguished, eminent, esteemed, famed, famous, illustrious, notable, noted, well-known

rent[1] **1.** *n.* fee, hire, lease, payment, rental, tariff **2.** *v.* charter, hire, lease, let

rent[2] **1.** breach, break, chink, crack, flaw, gash, hole, opening, perforation, rip, slash, slit, split, tear **2.** breach, break, cleavage, discord, dissension, disunity, division, faction, rift, rupture, schism, split

renunciation abandonment, abdication, abjuration, abnegation, abstention, denial, disavowal, disclaimer, eschewal, forswearing, giving up, rejection, relinquishment, repudiation, resignation, spurning, surrender, waiver

repair[1] *v.* **1.** compensate for, fix, heal, make good, make up for, mend, patch, patch up, put back together, put right, recover, rectify, redress, renew, renovate, restore, restore to working order, retrieve, square ~*n.* **2.** adjustment, darn, mend, overhaul, patch, restoration **3.** condition, fettle, form, nick (*Inf.*), shape (*Inf.*), state

repair[2] **1.** betake oneself, go, head for, leave for, move, remove, retire, set off for, withdraw **2.** have recourse, resort, turn

reparable corrigible, curable, recoverable, rectifiable, remediable, restorable, retrievable, salvageable

reparation amends, atonement, compensation, damages, indemnity, propitiation, recompense, redress, renewal, repair, requital, restitution, satisfaction

repartee badinage, banter, bon mot, persiflage, pleasantry, raillery, riposte, sally, wit, witticism, wittiness, wordplay

repast collation, food, meal, nourishment, refection, spread, victuals

repay 1. compensate, make restitution, pay back, recompense, refund, reimburse, remunerate, requite, restore, return, reward, settle up with, square **2.** avenge, even *or* settle the score with, get back at (*Inf.*), get even with (*Inf.*), get one's own back on (*Inf.*), make reprisal, reciprocate, retaliate, return the compliment, revenge

repeal 1. *v.* abolish, abrogate, annul, cancel, countermand, declare null and void, invalidate, nullify, recall, rescind, reverse, revoke, set aside, withdraw **2.** *n.* abolition, abrogation, annulment, cancellation, invalidation, nullification, rescinding, rescindment, rescission, revocation, withdrawal

repeat 1. *v.* duplicate, echo, iterate, quote, recapitulate, recite, redo, rehearse, reiterate, relate, renew, replay, reproduce, rerun, reshow, restate, retell **2.** *n.* duplicate, echo, recapitulation, reiteration, repetition, replay, reproduction, rerun, reshowing

repeatedly again and again, frequently, many a time and oft, many times, often, over and over, time after time, time and (time) again

repel 1. beat off, check, confront, decline, drive off, fight, hold off, keep at arm's length, oppose, parry, put to flight, rebuff, refuse, reject, repulse, resist, ward off **2.** disgust, give one the creeps (*Inf.*), make one shudder, make one sick, nauseate, offend, put one off, revolt, sicken, turn one off (*Inf.*), turn one's stomach

repellent 1. abhorrent, abominable, discouraging, disgusting, distasteful, hateful, horrid, loathsome, nauseating, noxious, obnoxious, odious, offensive, off-putting (*Brit. inf.*), repugnant, repulsive, revolting, sickening **2.** impermeable, proof, repelling, resistant

repent atone, be ashamed, be contrite, be sorry, deplore, feel remorse, lament, regret, relent, reproach oneself, rue, see the error of one's ways, show penitence, sorrow

repentance compunction, contrition, grief, guilt, penitence, regret, remorse, sackcloth and ashes, self-reproach, sorriness, sorrow

repentant apologetic, ashamed, chastened, contrite, penitent, regretful, re-

morseful, rueful, self-reproachful, sorry

repercussion backlash, consequence, echo, rebound, recoil, result, reverberation, side effect

repertory collection, list, range, repertoire, repository, stock, store, supply

repetition duplication, echo, iteration, reappearance, recapitulation, recital, recurrence, redundancy, rehearsal, reiteration, relation, renewal, repeat, repetitiousness, replication, restatement, return, tautology

repetitious long-winded, pleonastic, prolix, redundant, tautological, tedious, verbose, windy, wordy

repetitive boring, dull, mechanical, monotonous, recurrent, samey (*Inf.*), tedious, unchanging, unvaried

rephrase paraphrase, put differently, recast, reword, say in other words

repine brood, complain, fret, grieve, grumble, lament, languish, moan, mope, murmur, sulk

replace follow, oust, put back, reestablish, reinstate, restore, stand in lieu of, substitute, succeed, supersede, supplant, supply, take over from, take the place of

replacement double, fill-in, proxy, stand-in, substitute, successor, surrogate, understudy

replenish fill, furnish, make up, provide, refill, reload, renew, replace, restock, restore, stock, supply, top up

replete abounding, brimful, brimming, charged, chock-full, crammed, filled, full, full to bursting, full up, glutted, gorged, jammed, jam-packed, sated, satiated, stuffed, teeming, well-provided, well-stocked

repletion completeness, fullness, glut, overfullness, satiation, satiety, superfluity, surfeit

replica carbon copy, copy, duplicate, facsimile, imitation, model, reproduction

replicate ape, copy, duplicate, follow, mimic, recreate, reduplicate, repeat, reproduce

reply 1. *v.* acknowledge, answer, come back, counter, echo, make answer, react, reciprocate, rejoin, respond, retaliate, retort, return, riposte, write back **2.** *n.* acknowledgment, answer, comeback (*Inf.*), counter, echo, reaction, reciprocation, rejoinder, response, retaliation, retort, return, riposte

report *n.* **1.** account, announcement,

article, communication, communiqué, declaration, description, detail, dispatch, information, message, narrative, news, note, paper, piece, recital, record, relation, statement, story, summary, tale, tidings, version, word, write-up **2**. gossip, hearsay, rumour, talk **3**. character, esteem, fame, regard, reputation, repute **4**. bang, blast, boom, crack, crash, detonation, discharge, explosion, noise, reverberation, sound ~*v.* **5**. air, announce, bring word, broadcast, circulate, communicate, cover, declare, describe, detail, document, give an account of, inform of, mention, narrate, note, notify, pass on, proclaim, publish, recite, record, recount, relate, relay, state, tell, write up **6**. appear, arrive, be present, clock in *or* on, come, present oneself, show up (*Inf.*), turn up

reporter announcer, correspondent, hack (*Derogatory*), journalist, newscaster, newshound (*Inf.*), newspaperman, newspaperwoman, pressman, writer

repose[1] *n*. **1**. ease, inactivity, peace, quiet, quietness, quietude, relaxation, respite, rest, restfulness, sleep, slumber, stillness, tranquillity **2**. aplomb, calmness, composure, dignity, equanimity, peace of mind, poise, self-possession, serenity, tranquillity ~*v*. **3**. lay down, lie, lie down, lie upon, recline, relax, rest, rest upon, sleep, slumber, take it easy (*Inf.*), take one's ease

repose[2] confide, deposit, entrust, invest, lodge, place, put, store

repository archive, depository, depot, emporium, magazine, receptacle, store, storehouse, treasury, vault, warehouse

reprehensible bad, blameworthy, censurable, condemnable, culpable, delinquent, discreditable, disgraceful, errant, erring, ignoble, objectionable, opprobrious, remiss, shameful, unworthy

represent 1. act for, be, betoken, correspond to, equal, equate with, express, mean, serve as, speak for, stand for, substitute for, symbolize **2**. embody, epitomize, exemplify, personify, symbolize, typify **3**. delineate, denote, depict, describe, designate, evoke, express, illustrate, outline, picture, portray, render, reproduce, show, sketch **4**. describe as, make out to be, pass off as, pose as, pretend to be **5**. act, appear as, assume the role of, enact, exhibit, perform, play the

part of, produce, put on, show, stage

representation 1. account, delineation, depiction, description, illustration, image, likeness, model, narration, narrative, picture, portrait, portrayal, relation, resemblance, sketch **2**. body of representatives, committee, delegates, delegation, embassy **3**. exhibition, performance, play, production, show, sight, spectacle **4**. *Often plural* account, argument, explanation, exposition, expostulation, remonstrance, statement

representative *n*. **1**. agent, commercial traveller, rep, salesman, traveller **2**. archetype, embodiment, epitome, exemplar, personification, type, typical example **3**. agent, commissioner, councillor, delegate, depute (*Scot.*), deputy, member, member of parliament, M.P., proxy, spokesman, spokeswoman ~*adj*. **4**. archetypal, characteristic, emblematic, evocative, exemplary, illustrative, symbolic, typical **5**. chosen, delegated, elected, elective

repress bottle up, chasten, check, control, crush, curb, hold back, hold in, inhibit, keep in check, master, muffle, overcome, overpower, quash, quell, restrain, silence, smother, stifle, subdue, subjugate, suppress, swallow

repression authoritarianism, censorship, coercion, constraint, control, despotism, domination, inhibition, restraint, subjugation, suppression, tyranny

repressive absolute, authoritarian, coercive, despotic, dictatorial, harsh, oppressive, severe, tough, tyrannical

reprieve *v*. **1**. grant a stay of execution to, let off the hook (*Sl.*), pardon, postpone *or* remit the punishment of **2**. abate, allay, alleviate, mitigate, palliate, relieve, respite ~*n*. **3**. abeyance, amnesty, deferment, pardon, postponement, remission, stay of execution, suspension **4**. abatement, alleviation, let-up (*Inf.*), mitigation, palliation, relief, respite

reprimand 1. *n*. admonition, blame, castigation, censure, dressing-down (*Inf.*), flea in one's ear (*Inf.*), lecture, rebuke, reprehension, reproach, reproof, row, talking-to (*Inf.*), telling-off (*Inf.*), ticking-off (*Inf.*), tongue-lashing, wigging (*Brit. sl.*) **2**. *v*. admonish, blame, castigate, censure, check, chide, dress down (*Inf.*), give (someone) a row (*Inf.*), haul over the coals (*Inf.*), lecture, rap over the knuckles (*Inf.*), rebuke, reprehend, reproach, reprove, scold, send one away with a flea in one's ear (*Inf.*), take to task, tell off (*Inf.*), tick off (*Inf.*), tongue-lash, upbraid

reprisal an eye for an eye, counterstroke, requital, retaliation, retribution, revenge, vengeance

reproach 1. *v.* abuse, blame, censure, chide, condemn, criticize, defame, discredit, disparage, find fault with, rebuke, reprehend, reprimand, reprove, scold, take to task, upbraid 2. *n.* abuse, blame, blemish, censure, condemnation, contempt, disapproval, discredit, disgrace, dishonour, disrepute, ignominy, indignity, obloquy, odium, opprobrium, scorn, shame, slight, slur, stain, stigma

reproachful abusive, admonitory, castigatory, censorious, condemnatory, contemptuous, critical, disappointed, disapproving, fault-finding, reproving, scolding, upbraiding

reprobate 1. *adj.* abandoned, bad, base, corrupt, damned, degenerate, depraved, dissolute, hardened, immoral, incorrigible, profligate, shameless, sinful, unprincipled, vile, wicked 2. *n.* blackguard, degenerate, evildoer, miscreant, ne'er-do-well, outcast, pariah, profligate, rake, rakehell (*Archaic*), rascal, roué, scoundrel, sinner, villain, wastrel, wretch, wrongdoer 3. *v.* condemn, damn, denounce, disapprove of, frown upon, reprehend, vilify

reproduce 1. copy, duplicate, echo, emulate, imitate, match, mirror, parallel, print, recreate, repeat, replicate, represent, transcribe 2. breed, generate, multiply, procreate, produce young, proliferate, propagate, spawn

reproduction 1. breeding, generation, increase, multiplication, procreation, proliferation, propagation 2. copy, duplicate, facsimile, imitation, picture, print, replica

reproof admonition, blame, castigation, censure, chiding, condemnation, criticism, dressing-down (*Inf.*), rebuke, reprehension, reprimand, reproach, reproval, scolding, ticking-off (*Inf.*), tongue-lashing, upbraiding

reprove abuse, admonish, berate, blame, censure, check, chide, condemn, rebuke, reprehend, reprimand, scold, take to task, tell off (*Inf.*), tick off (*Inf.*), upbraid

repudiate abandon, abjure, cast off, cut off, deny, desert, disavow, discard, disclaim, disown, forsake, reject, renounce, rescind, retract, reverse, revoke, turn one's back on, wash one's hands of

repugnance abhorrence, antipathy, aversion, disgust, dislike, disrelish, distaste, hatred, loathing, reluctance, repulsion, revulsion

repugnant 1. abhorrent, abominable, disgusting, distasteful, foul, hateful, horrid, loathsome, nauseating, objectionable, obnoxious, odious, offensive, repellent, revolting, sickening, vile 2. adverse, antagonistic, antipathetic, averse, contradictory, hostile, incompatible, inconsistent, inimical, opposed

repulse *v.* 1. beat off, check, defeat, drive back, fight off, rebuff, repel, throw back, ward off 2. disdain, disregard, give the cold shoulder to, rebuff, refuse, reject, snub, spurn, turn down ~*n.* 3. check, defeat, disappointment, failure, reverse 4. cold shoulder, rebuff, refusal, rejection, snub, spurning

repulsion abhorrence, aversion, detestation, disgust, disrelish, distaste, hatred, loathing, repugnance, revulsion

repulsive abhorrent, abominable, disagreeable, disgusting, distasteful, forbidding, foul, hateful, hideous, horrid, loathsome, nauseating, objectionable, obnoxious, odious, offensive, repellent, revolting, sickening, ugly, unpleasant, vile

reputable creditable, estimable, excellent, good, honourable, honoured, legitimate, of good repute, reliable, respectable, trustworthy, upright, well-thought-of, worthy

reputation character, credit, distinction, esteem, estimation, fame, honour, name, opinion, renown, repute, standing, stature

repute celebrity, distinction, esteem, estimation, fame, name, renown, reputation, standing, stature

reputed accounted, alleged, believed, considered, deemed, estimated, held, ostensible, putative, reckoned, regarded, rumoured, said, seeming, supposed, thought

reputedly allegedly, apparently, ostensibly, seemingly, supposedly

request 1. *v.* appeal for, apply for, ask (for), beg, beseech, call for, demand, desire, entreat, petition, pray, put in for, requisition, seek, solicit, sue for, suppli-cate 2. *n.* appeal, application, asking, begging, call, demand, desire, entreaty, petition, prayer, requisition, solicitation, suit, supplication

require 1. crave, depend upon, desire, have need of, lack, miss, need, stand in need of, want, wish **2.** ask, beg, beseech, bid, call upon, command, compel, con-strain, demand, direct, enjoin, exact, in-sist upon, instruct, oblige, order, request **3.** call for, demand, involve, necessitate, take

required called for, compulsory, de-manded, essential, mandatory, neces-sary, needed, obligatory, prescribed, rec-ommended, requisite, set, unavoidable, vital

requirement demand, desideratum, essential, lack, must, necessity, need, precondition, prerequisite, qualification, requisite, *sine qua non*, specification, stipulation, want

requisite 1. *adj.* called for, essential, indispensable, mandatory, necessary, needed, needful, obligatory, prerequi-site, required, vital **2.** *n.* condition, de-sideratum, essential, must, necessity, need, precondition, prerequisite, re-quirement, *sine qua non*

requisition *n.* **1.** application, call, de-mand, request, summons **2.** appropria-tion, commandeering, occupation, sei-zure, takeover ~*v.* **3.** apply for, call for, demand, put in for, request **4.** appropri-ate, commandeer, occupy, seize, take over, take possession of

requital amends, compensation, pay-ment, recompense, redress, reimburse-ment, remuneration, repayment, restitu-tion, return, reward

requite compensate, give in return, give tit for tat, make amends, make good, make restitution, pay, reciprocate, recompense, redress, reimburse, remu-nerate, repay, respond, retaliate, return, return like for like, reward, satisfy

rescind abrogate, annul, cancel, countermand, declare null and void, in-validate, overturn, quash, recall, repeal, retract, reverse, revoke, set aside, void

rescission abrogation, annulment, cancellation, invalidation, recall, repeal, rescindment, retraction, reversal, revoca-tion, setting aside, voidance

rescue 1. *v.* deliver, extricate, free, get out, liberate, recover, redeem, release,

salvage, save, save the life of, set free **2.** *n.* deliverance, extrication, liberation, re-covery, redemption, release, relief, sal-vage, salvation, saving

research 1. *n.* analysis, delving, ex-amination, experimentation, explora-tion, fact-finding, groundwork, inquiry, investigation, probe, scrutiny, study **2.** *v.* analyse, consult the archives, do tests, examine, experiment, explore, investi-gate, look into, make inquiries, probe, scrutinize, study

resemblance affinity, analogy, close-ness, comparability, comparison, con-formity, correspondence, counterpart, facsimile, image, kinship, likeness, paral-lel, parity, sameness, semblance, similar-ity, similitude

resemble bear a resemblance to, be like, be similar to, duplicate, echo, fa-vour (*Inf.*), look like, mirror, parallel, put one in mind of, remind one of, take after

resent be angry about, bear a grudge about, begrudge, be in a huff about, be offended by, dislike, feel bitter about, grudge, harbour a grudge against, have hard feelings about, object to, take amiss, take as an insult, take exception to, take offence at, take umbrage at

resentful aggrieved, angry, bitter, em-bittered, exasperated, grudging, huffish, huffy, hurt, in a huff, incensed, indig-nant, in high dudgeon, irate, jealous, miffed (*Inf.*), offended, peeved (*Inf.*), piqued, put out, revengeful, unforgiving, wounded

resentment anger, animosity, bitter-ness, displeasure, fury, grudge, huff, hurt, ill feeling, ill will, indignation, ire, irritation, malice, pique, rage, rancour, umbrage, vexation, wrath

reservation 1. condition, demur, doubt, hesitancy, proviso, qualification, scepticism, scruple, stipulation **2.** en-clave, homeland, preserve, reserve, sanc-tuary, territory, tract

reserve *v.* **1.** conserve, hang on to, hoard, hold, husband, keep, keep back, lay up, preserve, put by, retain, save, set aside, stockpile, store, withhold **2.** be-speak, book, engage, prearrange, pre-engage, retain, secure **3.** defer, delay, keep back, postpone, put off, withhold ~*n.* **4.** backlog, cache, capital, fund, hoard, reservoir, savings, stock, stock-pile, store, supply **5.** park, preserve, reservation, sanctuary, tract **6**. aloofness, constraint, coolness, formality, modesty, reluctance, reservation, restraint, reticence, secretiveness, shyness, silence, taciturnity ~*adj*. **7**. alternate, auxiliary, extra, secondary, spare, substitute

reserved 1. booked, engaged, held, kept, restricted, retained, set aside, spoken for, taken **2**. aloof, cautious, closemouthed, cold, cool, demure, formal, modest, prim, restrained, reticent, retiring, secretive, shy, silent, standoffish, taciturn, unapproachable, uncommunicative, undemonstrative, unforthcoming, unresponsive, unsociable **3**. bound, destined, fated, intended, meant, predestined

reservoir 1. basin, lake, pond, tank **2**. container, holder, receptacle, repository, store, tank **3**. accumulation, fund, pool, reserves, source, stock, stockpile, store, supply

reshuffle 1. *n*. change, interchange, realignment, rearrangement, redistribution, regrouping, reorganization, restructuring, revision, shake-up (*Inf.*) **2**. *v*. change around, change the line-up of, interchange, realign, rearrange, redistribute, regroup, reorganize, restructure, revise, shake up (*Inf.*)

reside 1. abide, dwell, hang out (*Inf.*), have one's home, inhabit, live, lodge, remain, settle, sojourn, stay **2**. abide, be intrinsic to, be vested, consist, dwell, exist, inhere, lie, rest with

residence 1. abode, domicile, dwelling, habitation, home, house, household, lodging, pad (*Sl.*), place, quarters **2**. hall, manor, mansion, palace, seat, villa **3**. occupancy, occupation, sojourn, stay, tenancy

resident 1. *n*. citizen, denizen, indweller, inhabitant, local, lodger, occupant, tenant **2**. *adj*. dwelling, inhabiting, living, local, neighbourhood, settled

residual leftover, net, nett, remaining, unconsumed, unused, vestigial

residue balance, dregs, excess, extra, leftovers, remainder, remains, remnant, residuum, rest, surplus

resign 1. abandon, abdicate, cede, forgo, forsake, give in one's notice, give up, hand over, leave, quit, relinquish, renounce, surrender, turn over, vacate, yield **2**. **resign oneself** accept, acquiesce, bow, give in, give up, reconcile, submit, yield

resignation 1. abandonment, abdication, departure, leaving, notice, relinquishment, renunciation, retirement, surrender **2**. acceptance, acquiescence, compliance, endurance, forbearing, fortitude, nonresistance, passivity, patience, submission, sufferance

resigned acquiescent, compliant, long-suffering, patient, stoical, subdued, submissive, unprotesting, unresisting

resilient 1. bouncy, elastic, flexible, plastic, pliable, rubbery, springy, supple, whippy **2**. bouncy, buoyant, hardy, irrepressible, quick to recover, strong, tough

resist 1. battle, be proof against, check, combat, confront, contend with, counteract, countervail, curb, defy, dispute, fight back, hinder, hold out against, oppose, put up a fight (against), refuse, repel, stand up to, struggle against, thwart, weather, withstand **2**. abstain from, avoid, forbear, forgo, keep from, leave alone, prevent oneself from, refrain from, refuse, turn down

resistance battle, combat, contention, counteraction, defiance, fight, fighting, hindrance, impediment, intransigence, obstruction, opposition, refusal, struggle

Resistance freedom fighters, guerrillas, irregulars, maquis, partisans, underground

resistant 1. hard, impervious, insusceptible, proof against, strong, tough, unaffected by, unyielding **2**. antagonistic, combative, defiant, dissident, hostile, intractable, intransigent, opposed, recalcitrant, unwilling

resolute bold, constant, determined, dogged, firm, fixed, inflexible, obstinate, persevering, purposeful, relentless, set, staunch, steadfast, strong-willed, stubborn, tenacious, unbending, undaunted, unflinching, unshakable, unshaken, unwavering

resolution 1. boldness, constancy, courage, dedication, determination, doggedness, earnestness, energy, firmness, fortitude, obstinacy, perseverance, purpose, relentlessness, resoluteness, resolve, sincerity, staunchness, staying power, steadfastness, stubbornness, tenacity, willpower **2**. aim, decision, declaration, determination, intent, intention, judgment, motion, purpose, resolve, verdict **3**. answer, end, finding, outcome, settlement, solution, solving, sorting out, unravelling, upshot, working out

resolve v. 1. agree, conclude, decide, design, determine, fix, intend, make up one's mind, purpose, settle, undertake 2. answer, clear up, crack, elucidate, fathom, find the solution to, work out 3. banish, clear up, dispel, explain, remove 4. analyse, anatomize, break down, clear, disentangle, disintegrate, dissect, dissolve, liquefy, melt, reduce, separate, solve, split up, unravel 5. alter, change, convert, metamorphose, transform, transmute ~n. 6. conclusion, decision, design, intention, objective, project, purpose, resolution, undertaking 7. boldness, courage, determination, earnestness, firmness, resoluteness, resolution, steadfastness, willpower

resonant booming, echoing, full, resounding, reverberant, reverberating, rich, ringing, sonorous, vibrant

resort v. 1. avail oneself of, bring into play, employ, exercise, fall back on, have recourse to, look to, make use of, turn to, use, utilize 2. frequent, go, haunt, head for, repair, visit ~n. 3. haunt, holiday centre, refuge, retreat, spot, tourist centre, watering place (*Brit.*) 4. alternative, chance, course, expedient, hope, possibility, recourse, reference

resound echo, fill the air, re-echo, resonate, reverberate, ring

resounding booming, echoing, full, powerful, resonant, reverberating, rich, ringing, sonorous, sounding, vibrant

resource 1. ability, capability, cleverness, ingenuity, initiative, inventiveness, quick-wittedness, resourcefulness, talent 2. hoard, reserve, source, stockpile, supply 3. appliance, contrivance, course, device, expedient, means, resort

resourceful able, bright, capable, clever, creative, imaginative, ingenious, inventive, quick-witted, sharp, talented

resources assets, capital, funds, holdings, materials, means, money, property, reserves, riches, supplies, wealth, wherewithal

respect n. 1. admiration, appreciation, approbation, consideration, deference, esteem, estimation, honour, recognition, regard, reverence, veneration 2. aspect, characteristic, detail, facet, feature, matter, particular, point, sense, way 3. bearing, connection, reference, regard, relation 4. *Plural* compliments, devoirs, good wishes, greetings, regards, salutations ~v. 5. admire, adore, appreciate,

defer to, esteem, have a good *or* high opinion of, honour, look up to, recognize, regard, revere, reverence, set store by, show consideration for, think highly of, value, venerate 6. abide by, adhere to, attend, comply with, follow, heed, honour, notice, obey, observe, pay attention to, regard, show consideration for

respectable 1. admirable, decent, decorous, dignified, estimable, good, honest, honourable, proper, reputable, respected, upright, venerable, worthy 2. ample, appreciable, considerable, decent, fair, fairly good, goodly, presentable, reasonable, sizable, substantial, tidy (*Inf.*), tolerable

respectful civil, courteous, courtly, deferential, dutiful, gracious, humble, mannerly, obedient, polite, regardful, reverent, reverential, self-effacing, solicitous, submissive, well-mannered

respective corresponding, individual, own, particular, personal, relevant, separate, several, specific, various

respite 1. break, breather (*Inf.*), breathing space, cessation, halt, hiatus, intermission, interruption, interval, let-up (*Inf.*), lull, pause, recess, relaxation, relief, rest 2. adjournment, delay, moratorium, postponement, reprieve, stay, suspension

resplendent beaming, bright, brilliant, dazzling, effulgent, gleaming, glittering, glorious, irradiant, luminous, lustrous, radiant, refulgent (*Literary*), shining, splendid

respond acknowledge, act in response, answer, come back, counter, react, reciprocate, rejoin, reply, retort, return

response acknowledgment, answer, comeback (*Inf.*), counterblast, feedback, reaction, rejoinder, reply, retort, return, riposte

responsibility 1. accountability, amenability, answerability, care, charge, duty, liability, obligation, onus, trust 2. authority, importance, power 3. blame, burden, culpability, fault, guilt 4. conscientiousness, dependability, level-headedness, maturity, rationality, reliability, sensibleness, soberness, stability, trustworthiness

responsible 1. at the helm, carrying the can (*Inf.*), in authority, in charge, in control 2. accountable, amenable, answerable, bound, chargeable, duty-bound, liable, subject, under obligation

3. authoritative, decision-making, executive, high, important **4.** at fault, culpable, guilty, to blame **5.** adult, conscientious, dependable, level-headed, mature, rational, reliable, sensible, sober, sound, stable, trustworthy

responsive alive, awake, aware, forthcoming, impressionable, open, perceptive, quick to react, reactive, receptive, sensitive, sharp, susceptible, sympathetic

rest[1] *n.* **1.** calm, doze, forty winks (*Inf.*), idleness, inactivity, leisure, lie-down, motionlessness, nap, refreshment, relaxation, relief, repose, siesta, sleep, slumber, snooze (*Inf.*), somnolence, standstill, stillness, tranquillity **2. at rest** asleep, at a standstill, at peace, calm, dead, motionless, peaceful, resting, sleeping, still, stopped, tranquil, unmoving **3.** break, breather (*Inf.*), breathing space, cessation, halt, holiday, interlude, intermission, interval, lull, pause, stop, time off, vacation **4.** haven, lodging, refuge, retreat, shelter **5.** base, holder, prop, shelf, stand, support, trestle ~*v.* **6.** be at ease, be calm, doze, have a snooze (*Inf.*), have forty winks (*Inf.*), idle, laze, lie down, lie still, nap, put one's feet up, refresh oneself, relax, sit down, sleep, slumber, snooze (*Inf.*), take a nap, take it easy (*Inf.*), take one's ease **7.** be supported, lay, lean, lie, prop, recline, repose, sit, stand, stretch out **8.** break off, cease, come to a standstill, desist, discontinue, halt, have a break, knock off (*Inf.*), stay, stop, take a breather (*Inf.*) **9.** base, be based, be founded, depend, found, hang, hinge, lie, rely, reside, turn

rest[2] **1.** *n.* balance, excess, leftovers, others, remainder, remains, remnants, residue, residuum, rump, surplus **2.** *v.* be left, continue being, go on being, keep, remain, stay

restful calm, calming, comfortable, languid, pacific, peaceful, placid, quiet, relaxed, relaxing, serene, sleepy, soothing, tranquil, tranquillizing, undisturbed, unhurried

restitution amends, compensation, indemnification, indemnity, recompense, redress, refund, reimbursement, remuneration, reparation, repayment, requital, restoration, return, satisfaction

restive agitated, edgy, fidgety, fractious, fretful, ill at ease, impatient, jittery (*Inf.*), jumpy, nervous, on edge, re-

calcitrant, refractory, restless, uneasy, unquiet, unruly

restless 1. active, bustling, changeable, footloose, hurried, inconstant, irresolute, moving, nomadic, roving, transient, turbulent, unsettled, unstable, unsteady, wandering **2.** agitated, anxious, disturbed, edgy, fidgeting, fidgety, fitful, fretful, ill at ease, jumpy, nervous, on edge, restive, sleepless, tossing and turning, troubled, uneasy, unquiet, unruly, unsettled, worried

restlessness 1. activity, bustle, hurry, hurry-scurry, inconstancy, instability, movement, transience, turbulence, turmoil, unrest, unsettledness **2.** agitation, ants in one's pants (*Sl.*), anxiety, disquiet, disturbance, edginess, fitfulness, fretfulness, heebie-jeebies (*Sl.*), inquietude, insomnia, jitters (*Inf.*), jumpiness, nervousness, restiveness, uneasiness, worriedness

restoration 1. reconstruction, recovery, refreshment, refurbishing, rehabilitation, rejuvenation, renewal, renovation, repair, revitalization, revival **2.** recovery, re-establishment, reinstallation, reinstatement, replacement, restitution, return

restore 1. fix, mend, rebuild, recondition, reconstruct, recover, refurbish, rehabilitate, renew, renovate, repair, retouch, set to rights, touch up **2.** bring back to health, build up, reanimate, refresh, rejuvenate, revitalize, revive, revivify, strengthen **3.** bring back, give back, hand back, recover, re-establish, reinstate, replace, return, send back **4.** reconstitute, re-enforce, reimpose, reinstate, reintroduce

restrain 1. bridle, check, confine, constrain, contain, control, curb, curtail, debar, govern, hamper, handicap, harness, hinder, hold, hold back, inhibit, keep, keep under control, limit, muzzle, prevent, repress, restrict, subdue, suppress **2.** arrest, bind, chain, confine, detain, fetter, hold, imprison, jail, lock up, manacle, pinion, tie up

restrained 1. calm, controlled, mild, moderate, muted, reasonable, reticent, self-controlled, soft, steady, temperate, undemonstrative **2.** discreet, quiet, subdued, tasteful, unobtrusive

restraint 1. coercion, command, compulsion, confines, constraint, control, curtailment, grip, hindrance, hold, inhibition, limitation, moderation, prevention, restriction, self-control, self-discipline, self-possession, self-restraint, suppression **2**. arrest, bondage, bonds, captivity, chains, confinement, detention, fetters, imprisonment, manacles, pinions, straitjacket **3**. ban, bridle, check, curb, embargo, interdict, limit, limitation, rein, taboo

restrict bound, circumscribe, confine, contain, cramp, demarcate, hamper, handicap, hem in, impede, inhibit, keep within bounds or limits, limit, regulate, restrain

restriction check, condition, confinement, constraint, containment, control, curb, demarcation, handicap, inhibition, limitation, regulation, restraint, rule, stipulation

result n. **1**. conclusion, consequence, decision, development, effect, end, event, fruit, issue, outcome, product, reaction, sequel, termination, upshot ~v. **2**. appear, arise, derive, develop, emanate, ensue, eventuate, flow, follow, happen, issue, spring, stem, turn out **3**. With in culminate, end, finish, terminate, wind up (Inf.)

resume 1. begin again, carry on, continue, go on, proceed, recommence, reinstitute, reopen, restart, take up or pick up where one left off **2**. assume again, occupy again, reoccupy, take back, take up again

résumé abstract, digest, epitome, précis, recapitulation, review, rundown, summary, synopsis

resumption carrying on, continuation, fresh outbreak, new beginning, reestablishment, renewal, reopening, restart, resurgence

resurgence rebirth, recrudescence, reemergence, renaissance, renascence, resumption, resurrection, return, revival

resurrect breathe new life into, bring back, raise from the dead, reintroduce, renew, restore to life, revive

resurrection comeback (Inf.), raising or rising from the dead, reappearance, rebirth, renaissance, renascence, renewal, restoration, resurgence, resuscitation, return, return from the dead, revival

resuscitate breathe new life into, bring round, bring to life, give artificial respiration to, give the kiss of life (Inf.), quicken, reanimate, renew, rescue, re-store, resurrect, revitalize, revive, revivify, save

retain 1. absorb, contain, detain, grasp, grip, hang or hold onto, hold, hold back, hold fast, keep, keep possession of, maintain, preserve, reserve, restrain, save **2**. bear in mind, impress on the memory, keep in mind, memorize, recall, recollect, remember **3**. commission, employ, engage, hire, pay, reserve

retainer 1. attendant, dependant, domestic, flunky, footman, lackey, servant, supporter, valet, vassal **2**. advance, deposit, fee

retaliate even the score, exact retribution, get back at (Inf.), get even with (Inf.), get one's own back (Inf.), give as good as one gets (Inf.), give one a taste of one's own medicine, give tit for tat, make reprisal, pay one back in one's own coin, reciprocate, return like for like, strike back, take an eye for an eye, take revenge, wreak vengeance

retaliation an eye for an eye, a taste of one's own medicine, counterblow, counterstroke, reciprocation, repayment, reprisal, requital, retribution, revenge, tit for tat, vengeance

retard arrest, brake, check, clog, decelerate, defer, delay, detain, encumber, handicap, hinder, hold back or up, impede, obstruct, set back, slow down, stall

retch be sick, disgorge, gag (Sl.), heave, puke (Sl.), regurgitate, spew, throw up (Inf.), vomit

reticence quietness, reserve, restraint, secretiveness, silence, taciturnity, uncommunicativeness, unforthcomingness

reticent close-mouthed, mum, quiet, reserved, restrained, secretive, silent, taciturn, tight-lipped, uncommunicative, unforthcoming, unspeaking

retinue aides, attendants, cortege, entourage, escort, followers, following, servants, suite, train

retire 1. be pensioned off, (be) put out to grass (Inf.), give up work, stop working **2**. absent oneself, betake oneself, depart, exit, go away, leave, remove, withdraw **3**. go to bed, go to one's room, go to sleep, hit the sack (Sl.), kip down (Brit. sl.), turn in (Inf.) **4**. decamp, ebb, fall back, give ground, give way, pull back, pull out, recede, retreat, withdraw

retirement loneliness, obscurity, privacy, retreat, seclusion, solitude, withdrawal

retiring bashful, coy, demure, diffident, humble, meek, modest, quiet, reclusive, reserved, reticent, self-effacing, shrinking, shy, timid, timorous, unassertive, unassuming

retort 1. *v.* answer, answer back, come back with, counter, rejoin, reply, respond, retaliate, return, riposte **2.** *n.* answer, comeback (*Inf.*), rejoinder, reply, response, riposte

retouch brush up, correct, finish, improve, recondition, renovate, restore, touch up

retract 1. draw in, pull back, pull in, reel in, sheathe **2.** abjure, cancel, deny, disavow, disclaim, disown, recall, recant, renounce, repeal, repudiate, rescind, reverse, revoke, take back, unsay, withdraw **3.** back out of, go back on, renege on

retreat *v.* **1.** back away, depart, draw back, ebb, fall back, give ground, go back, leave, pull back, recede, recoil, retire, shrink, turn tail, withdraw ~*n.* **2.** departure, ebb, evacuation, flight, retirement, withdrawal **3.** asylum, den, haunt, haven, hideaway, privacy, refuge, resort, retirement, sanctuary, seclusion, shelter

retrench curtail, cut, cut back, decrease, diminish, economize, husband, lessen, limit, make economies, pare, prune, reduce, save, tighten one's belt, trim

retrenchment contraction, cost-cutting, curtailment, cut, cutback, economy, pruning, reduction, rundown, tightening one's belt

retribution an eye for an eye, compensation, justice, Nemesis, punishment, reckoning, recompense, redress, repayment, reprisal, requital, retaliation, revenge, reward, satisfaction, vengeance

retrieve fetch back, get back, recall, recapture, recoup, recover, redeem, regain, repair, repossess, rescue, restore, salvage, save, win back

retrograde 1. *adj.* backward, declining, degenerative, deteriorating, downward, inverse, negative, regressive, relapsing, retreating, retrogressive, reverse, waning, worsening **2.** *v.* backslide, decline, degenerate, deteriorate, go downhill (*Inf.*), regress, relapse, retreat, retrogress, revert, wane, worsen

retrogress 1. backslide, decline, deteriorate, go back, go downhill (*Inf.*), regress, relapse, retrograde, return, revert,

worsen **2.** drop, ebb, fall, go back, lose ground, recede, retire, retreat, sink, wane, withdraw

retrospect afterthought, hindsight, recollection, re-examination, remembrance, reminiscence, review, survey

return *v.* **1.** come back, come round again, go back, reappear, rebound, recoil, recur, repair, retreat, revert, turn back **2.** carry back, convey, give back, put back, re-establish, reinstate, remit, render, replace, restore, send, send back, take back, transmit **3.** give back, pay back, reciprocate, recompense, refund, reimburse, repay, requite **4.** bring in, earn, make, net, repay, yield **5.** answer, come back (with), communicate, rejoin, reply, respond, retort **6.** choose, elect, pick, vote in **7.** announce, arrive at, bring in, come to, deliver, render, report, submit ~*n.* **8.** homecoming, reappearance, rebound, recoil, recrudescence, recurrence, retreat, reversion **9.** re-establishment, reinstatement, replacement, restoration **10.** advantage, benefit, gain, income, interest, proceeds, profit, revenue, takings, yield **11.** compensation, reciprocation, recompense, reimbursement, reparation, repayment, requital, retaliation, reward **12.** account, form, list, report, statement, summary **13.** answer, comeback (*Inf.*), rejoinder, reply, response, retort, riposte

revamp do up (*Inf.*), fix up (*Inf.*, chiefly U.S.*), give a face-lift to, overhaul, patch up, recondition, refit, refurbish, rehabilitate, renovate, repair, restore

reveal 1. announce, betray, broadcast, communicate, disclose, divulge, give away, give out, impart, leak, let on, let out, let slip, make known, make public, proclaim, publish, tell **2.** bare, bring to light, display, exhibit, expose to view, lay bare, manifest, open, show, uncover, unearth, unmask, unveil

revel *v.* **1.** *With* in bask, crow, delight, gloat, indulge, joy, lap up, luxuriate, rejoice, relish, savour, take pleasure, thrive on, wallow **2.** carouse, celebrate, go on a spree, live it up (*Inf.*), make merry, paint the town red (*Inf.*), push the boat out (*Brit. inf.*), rave (*Brit. sl.*), roister, whoop it up (*Inf.*) ~*n.* **3.** *Often plural* bacchanal, carousal, carouse, celebration, debauch, festivity, gala, jollification, merrymaking, party, saturnalia, spree

revelation announcement, betrayal, broadcasting, communication, disclosure, discovery, display, exhibition, exposé, exposition, exposure, giveaway, leak, manifestation, news, proclamation, publication, telling, uncovering, unearthing, unveiling

reveller carouser, celebrator, merrymaker, partygoer, pleasure-seeker, roisterer

revelry carousal, carouse, celebration, debauch, debauchery, festivity, fun, jollification, jollity, merrymaking, party, roistering, saturnalia, spree

revenge 1. *n.* an eye for an eye, reprisal, requital, retaliation, retribution, satisfaction, vengeance, vindictiveness **2**. *v.* avenge, even the score for, get one's own back for (*Inf.*), make reprisal for, repay, requite, retaliate, take an eye for an eye for, take revenge for, vindicate

revengeful bitter, implacable, malevolent, malicious, malignant, merciless, pitiless, resentful, spiteful, unforgiving, unmerciful, vengeful, vindictive

revenue gain, income, interest, proceeds, profits, receipts, returns, rewards, takings, yield

reverberate echo, rebound, recoil, re-echo, resound, ring, vibrate

reverberation 1. echo, rebound, recoil, re-echoing, reflection, resonance, resounding, ringing, vibration **2**. *Fig. Usually plural* consequences, effects, repercussions, results

revere adore, be in awe of, defer to, exalt, have a high opinion of, honour, look up to, put on a pedestal, respect, reverence, think highly of, venerate, worship

reverence 1. *n.* admiration, adoration, awe, deference, devotion, high esteem, homage, honour, respect, veneration, worship **2**. *v.* admire, adore, be in awe of, hold in awe, honour, pay homage to, respect, revere, venerate, worship

reverent adoring, awed, decorous, deferential, devout, humble, loving, meek, pious, respectful, reverential, solemn, submissive

reverie absent-mindedness, abstraction, brown study, castles in the air *or* Spain, daydream, daydreaming, inattention, musing, preoccupation, trance, woolgathering

reverse *v.* **1**. invert, transpose, turn back, turn over, turn round, turn upside down, upend **2**. alter, annul, cancel, change, countermand, declare null and void, invalidate, negate, overrule, overset, overthrow, overturn, quash, repeal, rescind, retract, revoke, set aside, undo, upset **3**. back, backtrack, back up, go backwards, move backwards, retreat ~*n.* **4**. antithesis, contradiction, contrary, converse, inverse, opposite **5**. back, flip side, other side, rear, underside, verso, wrong side **6**. adversity, affliction, blow, check, defeat, disappointment, failure, hardship, misadventure, misfortune, mishap, repulse, reversal, setback, trial, vicissitude ~*adj.* **7**. back to front, backward, contrary, converse, inverse, inverted, opposite

revert backslide, come back, go back, hark back, lapse, recur, regress, relapse, resume, return, take up where one left off

review *v.* **1**. go over again, look at again, reassess, recapitulate, reconsider, re-evaluate, re-examine, rethink, revise, run over, take another look at, think over **2**. call to mind, look back on, recall, recollect, reflect on, remember, summon up **3**. assess, criticize, discuss, evaluate, examine, give one's opinion of, inspect, judge, read through, scrutinize, study, weigh, write a critique of ~*n.* **4**. analysis, examination, report, scrutiny, study, survey **5**. commentary, critical assessment, criticism, critique, evaluation, judgment, notice, study **6**. journal, magazine, periodical **7**. another look, fresh look, reassessment, recapitulation, reconsideration, re-evaluation, re-examination, rethink, retrospect, revision, second look **8**. *Military* display, inspection, march past, parade, procession

reviewer arbiter, commentator, connoisseur, critic, essayist, judge

revile abuse, calumniate, defame, denigrate, libel, malign, reproach, run down, scorn, slander, smear, traduce, vilify, vituperate

revise 1. alter, amend, change, correct, edit, emend, modify, reconsider, redo, re-examine, revamp, review, rework, rewrite, update **2**. go over, memorize, reread, run through, study, swot up (*Brit. inf.*)

revision 1. alteration, amendment, change, correction, editing, emendation, modification, re-examination, review, rewriting, updating 2. homework, memorizing, rereading, studying, swotting (*Brit. inf.*)

revitalize breathe new life into, bring back to life, reanimate, refresh, rejuvenate, renew, restore, resurrect, revivify

revival awakening, quickening, reanimation, reawakening, rebirth, recrudescence, renaissance, renascence, renewal, restoration, resurgence, resurrection, resuscitation, revitalization, revivification

revive animate, awaken, breathe new life into, bring back to life, bring round, cheer, come round, comfort, invigorate, quicken, rally, reanimate, recover, refresh, rekindle, renew, renovate, restore, resuscitate, revitalize, rouse, spring up again

revivify breathe new life into, give new life to, inspirit, invigorate, reanimate, refresh, renew, restore, resuscitate, revive

revoke abolish, abrogate, annul, call back, cancel, countermand, declare null and void, disclaim, invalidate, negate, nullify, quash, recall, recant, renounce, repeal, repudiate, rescind, retract, reverse, set aside, take back, withdraw

revolt *n.* **1.** defection, insurgency, insurrection, mutiny, putsch, rebellion, revolution, rising, sedition, uprising ~*v.* **2.** defect, mutiny, rebel, resist, rise, take to the streets, take up arms (against) **3.** disgust, give one the creeps (*Sl.*), make one's flesh creep, nauseate, offend, repel, repulse, shock, sicken, turn off (*Inf.*), turn one's stomach

revolting abhorrent, abominable, appalling, disgusting, distasteful, foul, horrible, horrid, loathsome, nasty, nauseating, nauseous, noisome, obnoxious, obscene, offensive, repellent, repugnant, repulsive, shocking, sickening

revolution *n.* **1.** coup, coup d'état, insurgency, mutiny, putsch, rebellion, revolt, rising, uprising **2.** drastic *or* radical change, innovation, metamorphosis, reformation, sea change, shift, transformation, upheaval **3.** circle, circuit, cycle, gyration, lap, orbit, rotation, round, spin, turn, wheel, whirl

revolutionary *n.* **1.** insurgent, insurrectionary, insurrectionist, mutineer, rebel, revolutionist ~*adj.* **2.** extremist, insurgent, insurrectionary, mutinous, radical, rebel, seditious, subversive **3.** avant-garde, different, drastic, experimental,

fundamental, innovative, new, novel, progressive, radical, thoroughgoing

revolve **1.** circle, go round, gyrate, orbit, rotate, spin, turn, twist, wheel, whirl **2.** consider, deliberate, meditate, mull over, ponder, reflect, ruminate, study, think about, think over, turn over (in one's mind)

revulsion abhorrence, abomination, aversion, detestation, disgust, distaste, loathing, recoil, repugnance, repulsion

reward *n.* **1.** benefit, bonus, bounty, compensation, gain, honour, merit, payment, premium, prize, profit, recompense, remuneration, repayment, requital, return, wages **2.** comeuppance (*Sl.*), desert, just deserts, punishment, requital, retribution ~*v.* **3.** compensate, honour, make it worth one's while, pay, recompense, remunerate, repay, requite

rewarding advantageous, beneficial, edifying, enriching, fruitful, fulfilling, gainful, gratifying, pleasing, productive, profitable, remunerative, satisfying, valuable, worthwhile

reword express differently, paraphrase, put another way, put in other words, recast, rephrase

rewrite correct, edit, emend, recast, redraft, revise, touch up

rhetoric **1.** eloquence, oratory **2.** bombast, fustian, grandiloquence, hot air (*Inf.*), hyperbole, magniloquence, pomposity, rant, verbosity, wordiness

rhetorical **1.** bombastic, declamatory, flamboyant, flashy, florid, flowery, grandiloquent, high-flown, high-sounding, hyperbolic, magniloquent, oratorical, pompous, pretentious, showy, silver-tongued, verbose, windy **2.** linguistic, oratorical, stylistic, verbal

rhyme *n.* **1.** ode, poem, poetry, song, verse **2. rhyme or reason** logic, meaning, method, plan, sense ~*v.* **3.** chime, harmonize, sound like

rhythm accent, beat, cadence, flow, lilt, measure (*Prosody*), metre, movement, pattern, periodicity, pulse, swing, tempo, time

rhythmic, rhythmical cadenced, flowing, harmonious, lilting, melodious, metrical, musical, periodic, pulsating, throbbing

ribald bawdy, blue, broad, coarse, earthy, filthy, gross, indecent, licentious, naughty, near the knuckle (*Inf.*), obscene, off colour, Rabelaisian, racy, risqué, rude, scurrilous, smutty, vulgar

ribaldry bawdiness, billingsgate, coarseness, earthiness, filth, grossness, indecency, licentiousness, naughtiness, obscenity, raciness, rudeness, scurrility, smut, smuttiness, vulgarity

rich 1. affluent, filthy rich (*Inf.*), flush (*Inf.*), loaded (*Sl.*), made of money (*Inf.*), moneyed, opulent, propertied, prosperous, rolling (*Sl.*), stinking rich (*Inf.*), wealthy, well-heeled (*Sl.*), well-off, well-to-do **2.** abounding, full, productive, well-endowed, well-provided, well-stocked, well-supplied **3.** abounding, abundant, ample, copious, exuberant, fecund, fertile, fruitful, full, lush, luxurious, plenteous, plentiful, productive, prolific **4.** beyond price, costly, elaborate, elegant, expensive, exquisite, fine, gorgeous, lavish, palatial, precious, priceless, splendid, sumptuous, superb, valuable **5.** creamy, delicious, fatty, flavoursome, full-bodied, heavy, highly-flavoured, juicy, luscious, savoury, spicy, succulent, sweet, tasty **6.** bright, deep, gay, intense, strong, vibrant, vivid, warm **7.** deep, dulcet, full, mellifluous, mellow, resonant **8.** amusing, comical, funny, hilarious, humorous, laughable, ludicrous, ridiculous, risible, side-splitting

riches abundance, affluence, assets, fortune, gold, money, opulence, plenty, property, resources, richness, substance, treasure, wealth

richly 1. elaborately, elegantly, expensively, exquisitely, gorgeously, lavishly, luxuriously, opulently, palatially, splendidly, sumptuously **2.** amply, appropriately, fully, in full measure, properly, suitably, thoroughly, well

rickety broken, broken-down, decrepit, derelict, dilapidated, feeble, flimsy, frail, imperfect, infirm, insecure, jerry-built, precarious, ramshackle, shaky, tottering, unsound, unsteady, weak, wobbly

rid 1. clear, deliver, disabuse, disburden, disembarrass, disencumber, free, make free, purge, relieve, unburden **2. get rid of** dispense with, dispose of, do away with, dump, eject, eliminate, expel, jettison, remove, shake off, throw away *or* out, unload, weed out

riddance clearance, clearing out, deliverance, disposal, ejection, elimination, expulsion, freedom, release, relief, removal

riddle¹ brain-teaser (*Inf.*), Chinese puzzle, conundrum, enigma, mystery, poser, problem, puzzle, rebus

riddle² *v.* **1.** honeycomb, pepper, perforate, pierce, puncture **2.** corrupt, damage, fill, impair, infest, mar, permeate, pervade, spoil **3.** bolt, filter, screen, sieve, sift, strain, winnow ~*n.* **4.** filter, screen, sieve, strainer

ride *v.* **1.** control, handle, manage, sit on **2.** be borne (carried, supported), float, go, journey, move, progress, sit, travel **3.** dominate, enslave, grip, haunt, oppress, tyrannize over ~*n.* **4.** drive, jaunt, journey, lift, outing, spin (*Inf.*), trip, whirl (*Inf.*)

ridicule 1. *n.* banter, chaff, derision, gibe, irony, jeer, laughter, mockery, raillery, sarcasm, satire, scorn, sneer, taunting **2.** *v.* banter, caricature, chaff, deride, humiliate, jeer, lampoon, laugh at, laugh out of court, laugh to scorn, make a fool of, make fun of, make one a laughing stock, mock, parody, poke fun at, pooh-pooh, satirize, scoff, send up (*Brit. inf.*), sneer, take the mickey out of (*Inf.*), taunt

ridiculous absurd, comical, contemptible, derisory, farcical, foolish, funny, hilarious, incredible, laughable, ludicrous, nonsensical, outrageous, preposterous, risible, silly, stupid, unbelievable

rife abundant, common, current, epidemic, frequent, general, plentiful, prevailing, prevalent, raging, rampant, teeming, ubiquitous, universal, widespread

riffraff canaille, dregs of society, hoi polloi, rabble, ragtag and bobtail, scum, undesirables

rifle *v.* burgle, despoil, go through, gut, loot, pillage, plunder, ransack, rob, rummage, sack, strip

rift 1. breach, break, chink, cleavage, cleft, crack, cranny, crevice, fault, fissure, flaw, fracture, gap, opening, space, split **2.** alienation, breach, difference, disagreement, division, estrangement, falling out (*Inf.*), quarrel, schism, separation, split

rig *v.* **1.** accoutre, equip, fit out, furnish, kit out, outfit, provision, supply, turn out **2.** arrange, doctor, engineer, fake, falsify, fiddle with (*Inf.*), fix (*Inf.*), gerrymander, juggle, manipulate, tamper with, trump up ~*n.* **3.** accoutrements, apparatus, equipage, equipment, fitments, fittings, fixtures, gear, machinery, outfit, tackle

right *adj.* **1.** equitable, ethical, fair, good, honest, honourable, just, lawful, moral, proper, righteous, true, upright, virtuous **2.** accurate, admissible, authentic, correct, exact, factual, genuine, precise, satisfactory, sound, spot-on (*Brit. inf.*), true, unerring, valid, veracious **3.** advantageous, appropriate, becoming, *comme il faut*, convenient, deserved, desirable, done, due, favourable, fit, fitting, ideal, opportune, proper, propitious, rightful, seemly, suitable **4.** all there (*Inf.*), balanced, *compos mentis*, fine, fit, healthy, in good health, in the pink, lucid, normal, rational, reasonable, sane, sound, unimpaired, up to par, well **5.** conservative, reactionary, Tory **6.** absolute, complete, out-and-out, real, thorough, thoroughgoing, utter ~*adv.* **7.** accurately, aright, correctly, exactly, factually, genuinely, precisely, truly **8.** appropriately, aptly, befittingly, fittingly, properly, satisfactorily, suitably **9.** directly, immediately, instantly, promptly, quickly, straight, straightaway, without delay **10.** bang, exactly, precisely, slapbang (*Inf.*), squarely **11.** absolutely, all the way, altogether, completely, entirely, perfectly, quite, thoroughly, totally, utterly, wholly **12.** ethically, fairly, honestly, honourably, justly, morally, properly, righteously, virtuously **13.** advantageously, beneficially, favourably, for the better, fortunately, to advantage, well ~*n.* **14.** authority, business, claim, due, freedom, interest, liberty, licence, permission, power, prerogative, privilege, title **15.** equity, good, goodness, honour, integrity, justice, lawfulness, legality, morality, propriety, reason, rectitude, righteousness, truth, uprightness, virtue **16. by rights** equitably, in fairness, justly, properly **17. to rights** arranged, in order, straight, tidy ~*v.* **18.** compensate for, correct, fix, put right, rectify, redress, repair, settle, set upright, sort out, straighten, vindicate

right away at once, directly, forthwith, immediately, instantly, now, promptly, right off, straightaway, straight off (*Inf.*), this instant, without delay, without hesitation

righteous blameless, equitable, ethical, fair, good, honest, honourable, just, law-abiding, moral, pure, upright, virtuous

righteousness blamelessness, equity, ethicalness, faithfulness, goodness, honesty, honour, integrity, justice, morality, probity, purity, rectitude, uprightness, virtue

rightful authorized, bona fide, de jure, due, just, lawful, legal, legitimate, proper, real, suitable, true, valid

rigid adamant, austere, exact, fixed, harsh, inflexible, intransigent, invariable, rigorous, set, severe, stern, stiff, strict, stringent, unalterable, unbending, uncompromising, undeviating, unrelenting, unyielding

rigmarole balderdash, bother, carry-on (*Inf.*), gibberish, hassle (*Inf.*), jargon, nonsense, palaver, performance (*Inf.*), red tape, to-do, trash, twaddle

rigorous 1. austere, challenging, demanding, exacting, firm, hard, harsh, inflexible, rigid, severe, stern, strict, stringent, tough **2.** accurate, conscientious, exact, meticulous, nice, painstaking, precise, punctilious, scrupulous, thorough **3.** bad, bleak, extreme, harsh, inclement, inhospitable, severe

rigour 1. asperity, austerity, firmness, hardness, hardship, harshness, inflexibility, ordeal, privation, rigidity, sternness, strictness, stringency, suffering, trial **2.** accuracy, conscientiousness, exactitude, exactness, meticulousness, preciseness, precision, punctiliousness, thoroughness

rig-out apparel, clobber (*Brit. sl.*), clothing, costume, dress, garb, gear (*Sl.*), get-up (*Inf.*), habit, outfit, raiment, togs

rig out 1. accoutre, equip, fit, furnish, kit out, outfit, set up **2.** array, attire, clothe, costume, dress, kit out

rig up arrange, assemble, build, cobble together, construct, erect, fix up, improvise, put together, put up, set up, throw together

rile anger, annoy, bug (*Inf.*), gall, get one's back up (*Inf.*), get one's goat (*Inf.*), get under one's skin (*Inf.*), irk, irritate, nark (*Sl.*), nettle, peeve (*Inf.*), pique, provoke, rub one up the wrong way, try one's patience, upset, vex

rim border, brim, brink, circumference, edge, lip, margin, verge

rind crust, epicarp, husk, integument, outer layer, peel, skin

ring[1] *n.* **1.** band, circle, circuit, halo, hoop, loop, round **2.** arena, circus, enclosure, rink **3.** association, band, cabal, cartel, cell, circle, clique, combine, coterie, crew (*Inf.*), gang, group, junto, knot, mob, organization, syndicate ~*v.* **4.** circumscribe, encircle, enclose, encompass, gird, girdle, hem in, seal off, surround

ring[2] *v.* **1.** chime, clang, peal, resonate, resound, reverberate, sound, toll **2.** buzz (*Inf.*), call, phone, telephone ~*n.* **3.** chime, knell, peal **4.** buzz (*Inf.*), call, phone call

rinse 1. *v.* bathe, clean, cleanse, dip, splash, wash, wash out, wet **2.** *n.* bath, dip, splash, wash, wetting

riot *n.* **1.** anarchy, commotion, confusion, disorder, disturbance, donnybrook, fray, lawlessness, mob violence, quarrel, row, street fighting, strife, tumult, turbulence, turmoil, uproar **2.** boisterousness, carousal, excess, festivity, frolic, high jinks, jollification, merrymaking, revelry, romp **3.** display, extravaganza, flourish, show, splash **4. run riot a.** be out of control, break *or* cut loose, go wild, let oneself go, raise hell, rampage, throw off all restraint **b.** grow like weeds, grow profusely, luxuriate, spread like wildfire ~*v.* **5.** fight in the streets, go on the rampage, raise an uproar, rampage, run riot, take to the streets **6.** carouse, cut loose, frolic, go on a binge *or* spree, make merry, paint the town red (*Inf.*), revel, roister, romp

riotous 1. anarchic, disorderly, insubordinate, lawless, mutinous, rampageous, rebellious, refractory, rowdy, tumultuous, ungovernable, unruly, uproarious, violent **2.** boisterous, loud, luxurious, noisy, orgiastic, rambunctious (*Inf.*), roisterous, rollicking, saturnalian, side-splitting, unrestrained, uproarious, wanton, wild

rip 1. *v.* be rent, burst, claw, cut, gash, hack, lacerate, rend, score, slash, slit, split, tear **2.** *n.* cleavage, cut, gash, hole, laceration, rent, slash, slit, split, tear

ripe 1. fully developed, fully grown, mature, mellow, ready, ripened, seasoned **2.** accomplished, complete, finished, in readiness, perfect, prepared, ready **3.** auspicious, favourable, ideal, opportune, right, suitable, timely

ripen burgeon, come of age, come to fruition, develop, get ready, grow ripe, make ripe, mature, prepare, season

rip-off cheat, con (*Sl.*), con trick (*Inf.*),

daylight robbery (*Inf.*), exploitation, fraud, robbery, swindle, theft

rip off cheat, con (*Sl.*), defraud, dupe, filch, fleece, gyp (*Sl.*), knock off (*Sl.*), lift (*Inf.*), pilfer, pinch (*Inf.*), rob, steal from, swindle, swipe (*Sl.*), thieve, trick

riposte 1. *n.* answer, comeback (*Inf.*), rejoinder, repartee, reply, response, retort, return, sally **2.** *v.* answer, come back, reciprocate, rejoin, reply, respond, retort, return

rise *v.* **1.** arise, get out of bed, get to one's feet, get up, rise and shine, stand up, surface **2.** arise, ascend, climb, enlarge, go up, grow, improve, increase, intensify, levitate, lift, mount, move up, soar, swell, wax **3.** advance, be promoted, climb the ladder, get on, get somewhere, go places (*Inf.*), progress, prosper, work one's way up **4.** appear, become apparent, crop up, emanate, emerge, eventuate, flow, happen, issue, occur, originate, spring, turn up **5.** mount the barricades, mutiny, rebel, resist, revolt, take up arms **6.** ascend, climb, get steeper, go uphill, mount, slope upwards ~*n.* **7.** advance, ascent, climb, improvement, increase, upsurge, upswing, upturn, upward turn **8.** advancement, aggrandizement, climb, progress, promotion **9.** acclivity, ascent, elevation, hillock, incline, rising ground, upward slope **10.** increment, pay increase, raise (*U.S.*) **11. give rise to** bring about, bring on, cause, effect, produce, provoke, result in

risible absurd, amusing, comical, droll, farcical, funny, hilarious, humorous, laughable, ludicrous, rib-tickling (*Inf.*), ridiculous, side-splitting

risk 1. *n.* chance, danger, gamble, hazard, jeopardy, peril, possibility, speculation, uncertainty, venture **2.** *v.* chance, dare, endanger, expose to danger, gamble, hazard, imperil, jeopardize, put in jeopardy, take a chance on, venture

risky chancy (*Inf.*), dangerous, dicey (*Sl.*), dodgy (*Brit. inf.*), fraught with danger, hazardous, perilous, precarious, touch-and-go, tricky, uncertain, unsafe

risqué bawdy, blue, daring, immodest, improper, indelicate, naughty, near the knuckle (*Inf.*), off colour, Rabelaisian, racy, ribald, suggestive

rite act, ceremonial, ceremony, communion, custom, form, formality, liturgy, mystery, observance, ordinance, practice, procedure, ritual, sacrament, service, solemnity, usage

ritual n. **1.** ceremonial, ceremony, communion, liturgy, mystery, observance, rite, sacrament, service, solemnity **2.** convention, custom, form, formality, habit, ordinance, practice, prescription, procedure, protocol, red tape, routine, stereotype, usage ~adj. **3.** ceremonial, ceremonious, conventional, customary, formal, habitual, prescribed, procedural, routine, stereotyped

rival n. **1.** adversary, antagonist, challenger, competitor, contender, contestant, emulator, opponent **2.** compeer, equal, equivalent, fellow, match, peer ~adj. **3.** competing, competitive, conflicting, emulating, opposed, opposing ~v. **4.** be a match for, bear comparison with, come up to, compare with, compete, contend, emulate, equal, match, measure up to, oppose, seek to displace, vie with

rivalry antagonism, competition, competitiveness, conflict, contention, contest, duel, emulation, opposition, struggle, vying

riveting absorbing, arresting, captivating, engrossing, enthralling, fascinating, gripping, hypnotic, spellbinding

road **1.** avenue, course, direction, highway, lane, motorway, path, pathway, roadway, route, street, thoroughfare, track, way **2.** *Nautical* anchorage, roadstead

roam drift, meander, peregrinate, prowl, ramble, range, rove, stravaig (*Scot.*), stray, stroll, travel, walk, wander

roar v. **1.** bawl, bay, bellow, clamour, crash, cry, howl, rumble, shout, thunder, vociferate, yell **2.** guffaw, hoot, laugh heartily, split one's sides (*Inf.*) ~n. **3.** bellow, clamour, crash, cry, howl, outcry, rumble, shout, thunder, yell **4.** belly laugh (*Inf.*), guffaw, hoot

rob bereave, burgle, cheat, con (*Sl.*), defraud, deprive, despoil, dispossess, do out of (*Inf.*), gyp (*Sl.*), hold up, loot, pillage, plunder, raid, ransack, rifle, rip off (*Inf.*), sack, strip, swindle

robber bandit, brigand, burglar, cheat, con man (*Inf.*), fraud, highwayman, looter, pirate, plunderer, raider, stealer, swindler, thief

robbery burglary, depredation, embezzlement, filching, fraud, hold-up, larceny, pillage, plunder, raid, rapine, rip-

off (*Inf.*), spoliation, stealing, stick-up (*U.S. sl.*), swindle, theft, thievery

robe n. **1.** costume, gown, habit, vestment **2.** bathrobe, dressing gown, housecoat, peignoir, wrapper ~v. **3.** apparel (*Archaic*), attire, clothe, drape, dress, garb

robot android, automaton, machine, mechanical man

robust **1.** able-bodied, athletic, brawny, fit, hale, hardy, healthy, hearty, husky (*Inf.*), in fine fettle, in good health, lusty, muscular, powerful, rude, rugged, sinewy, sound, staunch, stout, strapping, strong, sturdy, tough, vigorous, well **2.** boisterous, coarse, earthy, indecorous, raw, roisterous, rollicking, rough, rude, unsubtle **3.** commonsensical, down-to-earth, hard-headed, practical, pragmatic, realistic, sensible, straightforward

rock[1] **1.** boulder, stone **2.** anchor, bulwark, cornerstone, foundation, mainstay, protection, support, tower of strength

rock[2] **1.** lurch, pitch, reel, roll, sway, swing, toss, wobble **2.** astonish, astound, daze, dumbfound, jar, set one back on one's heels (*Inf.*), shake, shock, stagger, stun, surprise

rocky[1] **1.** boulder-strewn, craggy, pebbly, rough, rugged, stony **2.** adamant, firm, flinty, hard, rocklike, rugged, solid, steady, tough, unyielding

rocky[2] **1.** doubtful, rickety, shaky, uncertain, undependable, unreliable, unstable, unsteady, weak, wobbly **2.** *Inf.* dizzy, ill, sick, sickly, staggering, tottering, unsteady, unwell, weak, wobbly

rod bar, baton, birch, cane, dowel, mace, pole, sceptre, shaft, staff, stick, switch, wand

rogue blackguard, charlatan, cheat, con man (*Inf.*), crook (*Inf.*), deceiver, devil, fraud, knave (*Archaic*), mountebank, ne'er-do-well, rapscallion, rascal, reprobate, scamp, scoundrel, sharper, swindler, villain

roguish **1.** criminal, crooked, deceitful, deceiving, dishonest, fraudulent, knavish, raffish, rascally, shady (*Inf.*), swindling, unprincipled, unscrupulous, villainous **2.** arch, cheeky, coquettish, frolicsome, impish, mischievous, playful, puckish, sportive, waggish

roister **1.** carouse, celebrate, frolic, go on a spree, live it up (*Inf.*), make merry, paint the town red (*Inf.*), push the boat out (*Brit. inf.*), rave (*Sl.*), revel, rollick, romp, whoop it up (*Inf.*) **2.** bluster, boast, brag, show off (*Inf.*), strut, swagger

role 1. character, impersonation, part, portrayal, representation **2.** capacity, duty, function, job, part, position, post, task

roll *v.* **1.** elapse, flow, go past, go round, gyrate, pass, pivot, reel, revolve, rock, rotate, run, spin, swivel, trundle, turn, twirl, undulate, wheel, whirl **2.** bind, coil, curl, enfold, entwine, envelop, furl, swathe, twist, wind, wrap **3.** even, flatten, level, press, smooth, spread **4.** boom, drum, echo, grumble, resound, reverberate, roar, rumble, thunder **5.** billow, lurch, reel, rock, sway, swing, toss, tumble, wallow, welter **6.** lumber, lurch, reel, stagger, swagger, sway, waddle ∼*n.* **7.** cycle, gyration, reel, revolution, rotation, run, spin, turn, twirl, undulation, wheel, whirl **8.** ball, bobbin, cylinder, reel, scroll, spool **9.** annals, catalogue, census, chronicle, directory, index, inventory, list, record, register, roster, schedule, scroll, table **10.** billowing, lurching, pitching, rocking, rolling, swell, tossing, undulation, wallowing, waves **11.** boom, drumming, growl, grumble, resonance, reverberation, roar, rumble, thunder

rollick caper, cavort, frisk, galumph (*Inf.*), gambol, make merry, revel, romp

rollicking[1] *adj.* boisterous, carefree, cavorting, devil-may-care, exuberant, frisky, frolicsome, hearty, jaunty, jovial, joyous, lively, merry, playful, rip-roaring (*Inf.*), romping, spirited, sportive, sprightly, swashbuckling

rollicking[2] *n.* dressing-down (*Inf.*), lecture, reprimand, roasting (*Inf.*), scolding, telling-off (*Inf.*), ticking off (*Inf.*), tongue-lashing, wigging (*Brit. sl.*)

roly-poly buxom, chubby, fat, overweight, plump, podgy, pudgy, rotund, rounded, tubby

romance *n.* **1.** affair, *affaire* (*du coeur*), affair of the heart, amour, attachment, intrigue, liaison, love affair, passion, relationship **2.** adventure, charm, colour, excitement, exoticness, fascination, glamour, mystery, nostalgia, sentiment **3.** fairy tale, fantasy, fiction, idyll, legend, love story, melodrama, novel, story, tale, tear-jerker (*Inf.*) **4.** absurdity, exaggeration, fabrication, fairy tale,

falsehood, fiction, flight of fancy, invention, lie, tall story (*Inf.*), trumped-up story ∼*v.* **5.** exaggerate, fantasize, let one's imagination run away with one, lie, make up stories, stretch the truth, tell stories

romantic *adj.* **1.** amorous, fond, lovey-dovey, loving, mushy (*Inf.*), passionate, sentimental, sloppy (*Inf.*), soppy (*Brit. inf.*), tender **2.** charming, colourful, exciting, exotic, fascinating, glamorous, mysterious, nostalgic, picturesque **3.** dreamy, high-flown, idealistic, impractical, quixotic, starry-eyed, unrealistic, utopian, visionary, whimsical **4.** chimerical, exaggerated, extravagant, fabulous, fairy-tale, fanciful, fantastic, fictitious, idyllic, imaginary, imaginative, improbable, legendary, made-up, unrealistic, wild ∼*n.* **5.** Don Quixote, dreamer, idealist, romancer, sentimentalist, utopian, visionary

romp *v.* **1.** caper, cavort, cut capers, frisk, frolic, gambol, have fun, make merry, revel, roister, rollick, skip, sport **2. romp home** *or* **in** run away with it, walk it (*Inf.*), win by a mile (*Inf.*), win easily, win hands down ∼*n.* **3.** caper, frolic, lark (*Inf.*)

rook bilk, cheat, clip (*Sl.*), defraud, diddle (*Inf.*), do (*Sl.*), fleece, gyp (*Sl.*), mulct, overcharge, rip off (*Sl.*), sting (*Inf.*), swindle

room 1. allowance, area, capacity, compass, elbowroom, expanse, extent, latitude, leeway, margin, play, range, scope, space, territory, volume **2.** apartment, chamber, office **3.** chance, occasion, opportunity, scope

roomy ample, broad, capacious, commodious, extensive, generous, large, sizable, spacious, wide

root[1] *n.* **1.** radicle, radix, rhizome, stem, tuber **2.** base, beginnings, bottom, cause, core, crux, derivation, essence, foundation, fountainhead, fundamental, germ, heart, mainspring, nub, nucleus, occasion, origin, seat, seed, source, starting point **3.** *Plural* birthplace, cradle, family, heritage, home, origins, sense of belonging **4. root and branch** completely, entirely, finally, radically, thoroughly, totally, to the last man, utterly, wholly, without exception ∼*v.* **5.** anchor, become established, become settled, embed, entrench, establish, fasten, fix, ground, implant, moor, set, stick, take root

root[2] burrow, delve, dig, ferret, forage, hunt, nose, poke, pry, rootle, rummage

rooted confirmed, deep, deeply felt, deep-seated, entrenched, established, firm, fixed, ingrained, radical, rigid

root out 1. *Also* **root up** abolish, cut out, destroy, dig up by the roots, do away with, efface, eliminate, eradicate, erase, exterminate, extirpate, get rid of, remove, tear out by the roots, uproot, weed out **2.** bring to light, dig out, discover, dredge up, produce, turn up, unearth

rope n. **1.** cable, cord, hawser, line, strand **2. the rope** capital punishment, halter, hanging, lynching, noose **3. know the ropes** be an old hand, be experienced, be knowledgeable, know all the ins and outs, know one's way around, know the score (*Inf.*), know what's what ~v. **4.** bind, fasten, hitch, lash, lasso, moor, pinion, tether, tie

rope in drag in, engage, enlist, inveigle, involve, persuade, talk into

ropy, ropey 1. deficient, inadequate, indifferent, inferior, mediocre, of poor quality, poor, sketchy, substandard **2.** *Inf.* below par, off colour, poorly (*Inf.*), rough (*Inf.*), sickish, under the weather (*Inf.*), unwell

roseate 1. blooming, blushing, pink, pinkish, red, rose-coloured, rosy, rubicund, ruddy **2.** idealistic, overoptimistic, rose-coloured, unrealistic, utopian

roster agenda, catalogue, inventory, list, listing, register, roll, rota, schedule, scroll, table

rostrum dais, platform, podium, stage

rosy 1. pink, red, roseate, rose-coloured **2.** blooming, blushing, fresh, glowing, healthy-looking, reddish, roseate, rubicund, ruddy **3.** auspicious, bright, cheerful, encouraging, favourable, hopeful, optimistic, promising, reassuring, roseate, rose-coloured, sunny

rot v. **1.** corrode, corrupt, crumble, decay, decompose, degenerate, deteriorate, disintegrate, fester, go bad, moulder, perish, putrefy, spoil, taint **2.** decline, degenerate, deteriorate, languish, waste away, wither away ~n. **3.** blight, canker, corrosion, corruption, decay, decomposition, deterioration, disintegration, mould, putrefaction, putrescence **4.** balderdash, bosh (*Inf.*), bunk (*Inf.*), bun-

kum, claptrap (*Inf.*), codswallop (*Brit. sl.*), drivel, flapdoodle (*Sl.*), guff (*Sl.*), hogwash, moonshine, nonsense, poppycock (*Inf.*), rubbish, stuff and nonsense, tommyrot, tosh (*Inf.*), twaddle

rotary gyratory, revolving, rotating, rotational, rotatory, spinning, turning

rotate 1. go round, gyrate, pirouette, pivot, reel, revolve, spin, swivel, turn, wheel **2.** alternate, follow in sequence, interchange, switch, take turns

rotation 1. gyration, orbit, pirouette, reel, revolution, spin, spinning, turn, turning, wheel **2.** alternation, cycle, interchanging, sequence, succession, switching

rotten 1. bad, corroded, corrupt, crumbling, decayed, decaying, decomposed, decomposing, disintegrating, festering, fetid, foul, mouldering, mouldy, perished, putrescent, putrid, rank, sour, stinking, tainted, unsound **2.** bent (*Sl.*), corrupt, crooked (*Inf.*), deceitful, degenerate, dishonest, dishonourable, disloyal, faithless, immoral, mercenary, perfidious, treacherous, untrustworthy, venal, vicious **3.** *Inf.* base, contemptible, despicable, dirty, disagreeable, filthy, mean, nasty, scurrilous, unpleasant, vile, wicked **4.** *Inf.* bad, deplorable, disappointing, regrettable, unfortunate, unlucky **5.** *Inf.* crummy (*Sl.*), ill-considered, ill thought-out, inadequate, inferior, lousy (*Sl.*), low-grade, poor, punk, ropy (*Inf.*), sorry, substandard, unacceptable, unsatisfactory **6.** *Inf.* bad, below par, ill, off colour, poorly (*Inf.*), ropy (*Inf.*), rough (*Inf.*), sick, under the weather (*Inf.*), unwell

rotter bad lot, blackguard, blighter (*Brit. inf.*), bounder (*Inf.*), cad (*Brit. inf.*), cur, louse (*Sl.*), rat (*Sl.*), stinker (*Sl.*), swine

rotund 1. bulbous, globular, orbicular, round, rounded, spherical **2.** chubby, corpulent, fat, fleshy, heavy, obese, plump, podgy, portly, roly-poly, rounded, stout, tubby **3.** full, grandiloquent, magniloquent, orotund, resonant, rich, round, sonorous

roué debauchee, dirty old man (*Sl.*), lecher, libertine, profligate, rake, sensualist, wanton

rough adj. **1.** broken, bumpy, craggy, irregular, jagged, rocky, rugged, stony, uneven **2.** bristly, bushy, coarse, dishevelled, disordered, fuzzy, hairy, shaggy, tangled, tousled, uncut, unshaven, unshorn **3.** agitated, boisterous, choppy, inclement, squally, stormy, tempestuous, turbulent, wild **4.** bearish, bluff, blunt, brusque, churlish, coarse, curt, discourteous, ill-bred, ill-mannered, impolite, inconsiderate, indelicate, loutish, rude, unceremonious, uncivil, uncouth, uncultured, ungracious, unmannerly, unpolished, unrefined, untutored **5.** boisterous, cruel, curt, drastic, extreme, hard, harsh, nasty, rowdy, severe, sharp, tough, unfeeling, unjust, unpleasant, violent **6.** *Inf.* below par, ill, not a hundred per cent (*Inf.*), off colour, poorly (*Inf.*), ropy (*Inf.*), rotten (*Inf.*), sick, under the weather (*Inf.*), unwell, upset **7.** cacophonous, discordant, grating, gruff, harsh, husky, inharmonious, jarring, rasping, raucous, unmusical **8.** arduous, austere, hard, rugged, spartan, tough, uncomfortable, unpleasant, unrefined **9.** basic, crude, cursory, formless, hasty, imperfect, incomplete, quick, raw, rough-and-ready, rough-hewn, rudimentary, shapeless, sketchy, unfinished, unpolished, unrefined, untutored **10.** crude, raw, rough-hewn, uncut, undressed, unhewn, unpolished, unprocessed, unwrought **11.** amorphous, approximate, estimated, foggy, general, hazy, imprecise, inexact, sketchy, vague ~*n.* **12.** draft, mock-up, outline, preliminary sketch, suggestion **13.** *Inf.* bruiser, bully boy, roughneck (*Sl.*), rowdy, ruffian, thug, tough ~*v.* **14.** **rough out** adumbrate, block out, delineate, draft, outline, plan, sketch, suggest **15. rough up** bash up (*Sl.*), batter, beat up, do over (*Sl.*), knock about, maltreat, manhandle, mistreat, thrash

rough-and-ready adequate, cobbled together, crude, improvised, makeshift, provisional, sketchy, stopgap, thrown together, unpolished, unrefined

rough-and-tumble 1. *n.* affray (*Law*), brawl, donnybrook, dust-up, (*Inf.*), fight, fracas, melee, punch-up (*Brit. sl.*), roughhouse (*Sl.*), scrap (*Inf.*), scuffle, struggle **2.** *adj.* boisterous, disorderly, haphazard, indisciplined, irregular, rough, rowdy, scrambled, scrambling

roughhouse 1. *n.* boisterousness, brawl, brawling, disorderliness, disturbance, horseplay, rough behaviour, row, rowdiness, rowdyism, skylarking (*Inf.*) **2.** *v.* brawl, handle roughly, ill-treat, kick up a row (*Inf.*), knock about, maltreat, manhandle, mistreat, paw, skylark (*Inf.*)

roughneck bruiser (*Inf.*), bully boy, rough (*Inf.*), rowdy, ruffian, thug, tough

round *adj.* **1.** annular, ball-shaped, bowed, bulbous, circular, curved, curvilinear, cylindrical, discoid, disc-shaped, globular, orbicular, ring-shaped, rotund, rounded, spherical **2.** complete, entire, full, solid, unbroken, undivided, whole **3.** ample, bounteous, bountiful, considerable, generous, great, large, liberal, substantial **4.** ample, fleshy, full, full-fleshed, plump, roly-poly, rotund, rounded **5.** full, mellifluous, orotund, resonant, rich, rotund, sonorous **6.** blunt, candid, direct, frank, outspoken, plain, straightforward, unmodified ~*n.* **7.** ball, band, circle, disc, globe, orb, ring, sphere **8.** bout, cycle, sequence, series, session, succession **9.** division, lap, level, period, session, stage, turn **10.** ambit, beat, circuit, compass, course, routine, schedule, series, tour, turn **11.** bullet, cartridge, discharge, shell, shot ~*v.* **12.** bypass, circle, circumnavigate, encircle, flank, go round, skirt, turn

roundabout *adj.* circuitous, circumlocutory, devious, discursive, evasive, indirect, meandering, oblique, periphrastic, tortuous

roundly bitterly, bluntly, fiercely, frankly, intensely, outspokenly, rigorously, severely, sharply, thoroughly, vehemently, violently

round off bring to a close, cap, close, complete, conclude, crown, finish off, put the finishing touch to, settle

round on abuse, attack, bite (someone's) head off (*Inf.*), have a go at (*Brit. sl.*), lose one's temper with, retaliate, snap at, turn on, wade into

roundup 1. assembly, collection, gathering, herding, marshalling, muster, rally **2.** *Inf.* collation, summary, survey

round up assemble, bring together, collect, drive, gather, group, herd, marshal, muster, rally

rouse 1. arouse, awaken, call, get up, rise, wake, wake up **2.** agitate, anger, animate, arouse, bestir, disturb, excite, exhilarate, galvanize, get going, incite, inflame, instigate, move, provoke, startle, stimulate, stir, whip up

rousing brisk, electrifying, exciting, exhilarating, inflammatory, inspiring, lively, moving, spirited, stimulating, stirring, vigorous

rout 1. *n.* beating, debacle, defeat, disorderly retreat, drubbing, headlong flight, hiding (*Inf.*), licking (*Inf.*), overthrow, overwhelming defeat, ruin, shambles, thrashing 2. *v.* beat, chase, conquer, crush, cut to pieces, defeat, destroy, dispel, drive off, drub, lick (*Inf.*), overpower, overthrow, put to flight, put to rout, scatter, thrash, throw back in confusion, worst

route 1. *n.* avenue, beat, circuit, course, direction, itinerary, journey, passage, path, road, round, run, way 2. *v.* convey, direct, dispatch, forward, send, steer

routine *n.* 1. custom, formula, grind (*Inf.*), groove, method, order, pattern, practice, procedure, programme, usage, way, wont 2. *Inf.* act, bit (*Inf.*), line, performance, piece, spiel (*Inf.*) ~*adj.* 3. conventional, customary, everyday, familiar, habitual, normal, ordinary, standard, typical, usual, wonted, workaday 4. boring, clichéd, dull, hackneyed, humdrum, predictable, run-of-the-mill, tedious, tiresome, unimaginative, uninspired, unoriginal

rove cruise, drift, gad about, gallivant, meander, ramble, range, roam, stravaig (*Scot.*), stray, stroll, traipse (*Inf.*), wander

rover bird of passage, drifter, gadabout (*Inf.*), gypsy, itinerant, nomad, rambler, ranger, rolling stone, stroller, transient, traveller, vagrant, wanderer

row[1] bank, column, file, line, queue, range, rank, sequence, series, string, tier

row[2] *n.* 1. altercation, brawl, commotion, controversy, dispute, disturbance, falling-out (*Inf.*), fracas, fray, fuss, noise, quarrel, racket, ruckus (*Inf.*), ruction (*Inf.*), rumpus, scrap (*Inf.*), shouting match (*Inf.*), slanging match (*Brit.*), squabble, tiff, trouble, tumult, uproar 2. castigation, dressing-down (*Inf.*), flea in one's ear (*Inf.*), lecture, reprimand, reproof, rollicking (*Brit. inf.*), talking-to (*Inf.*), telling-off (*Inf.*), ticking-off (*Inf.*), tongue-lashing ~*v.* 3. argue, brawl, dispute, fight, scrap (*Inf.*), squabble, wrangle

rowdy 1. *adj.* boisterous, disorderly, loud, loutish, noisy, obstreperous, rough, unruly, uproarious, wild 2. *n.* brawler, hooligan, lout, rough (*Inf.*), ruffian, tearaway (*Brit.*), tough, troublemaker, yahoo

royal 1. imperial, kinglike, kingly, monarchical, princely, queenly, regal, sover-

eign 2. august, grand, impressive, magnificent, majestic, splendid, stately, superb, superior

rub *v.* 1. abrade, caress, chafe, clean, fray, grate, knead, massage, polish, scour, scrape, shine, smooth, stroke, wipe 2. apply, put, smear, spread 3. **rub up the wrong way** anger, annoy, bug (*Inf.*), get one's goat (*Inf.*), get under one's skin (*Inf.*), irk, irritate, peeve (*Inf.*), vex ~*n.* 4. caress, kneading, massage, polish, shine, stroke, wipe 5. catch, difficulty, drawback, hindrance, hitch, impediment, obstacle, problem, snag, trouble

rubbish 1. debris, dregs, dross, flotsam and jetsam, garbage, junk, litter, lumber, offal, offscourings, refuse, scrap, trash, waste 2. balderdash, bosh (*Inf.*), bunkum, claptrap (*Inf.*), codswallop (*Brit. sl.*), drivel, flapdoodle (*Sl.*), gibberish, guff (*Sl.*), havers (*Scot.*), hogwash, moonshine, nonsense, piffle (*Inf.*), poppycock (*Inf.*), rot, stuff and nonsense, tommyrot, tosh (*Inf.*), twaddle

rubbishy brummagem, cheap, gimcrack, paltry, shoddy, tatty, tawdry, throwaway, trashy, twopenny, twopenny-halfpenny, valueless, worthless

rubicund blushing, florid, flushed, pink, reddish, roseate, rosy, ruddy

rub out cancel, delete, efface, erase, expunge, obliterate, remove, wipe out

ruction altercation, brawl, commotion, dispute, disturbance, fracas, fuss, quarrel, racket, row, rumpus, scrap (*Inf.*), storm, to-do, trouble, uproar

ruddy 1. blooming, blushing, florid, flushed, fresh, glowing, healthy, red, reddish, rosy, rosy-cheeked, rubicund, sanguine, sunburnt 2. crimson, pink, red, reddish, roseate, ruby, scarlet

rude 1. abrupt, abusive, blunt, brusque, cheeky, churlish, curt, discourteous, disrespectful, ill-mannered, impertinent, impolite, impudent, inconsiderate, insolent, insulting, offhand, peremptory, short, uncivil, unmannerly 2. barbarous, boorish, brutish, coarse, crude, graceless, gross, ignorant, illiterate, loutish, low, oafish, obscene, rough, savage, scurrilous, uncivilised, uncouth, uncultured, uneducated, ungracious, unpolished, unrefined, untutored, vulgar 3. artless, crude, inartistic, inelegant, makeshift, primitive, raw, rough, rough-hewn, roughly-made, simple **4**. abrupt, harsh, sharp, startling, sudden, unpleasant, violent

rudimentary basic, early, elementary, embryonic, fundamental, immature, initial, introductory, primary, primitive, undeveloped, vestigial

rudiments basics, beginnings, elements, essentials, first principles, foundation, fundamentals

rue bemoan, be sorry for, bewail, deplore, grieve, kick oneself for, lament, mourn, regret, repent, reproach oneself for, sorrow for, weep over

rueful conscience-stricken, contrite, dismal, doleful, grievous, lugubrious, melancholy, mournful, penitent, pitiable, pitiful, plaintive, regretful, remorseful, repentant, sad, self-reproachful, sorrowful, sorry, woebegone, woeful

ruffian bruiser (*Inf.*), brute, bully, bully boy, hoodlum, hooligan, miscreant, rascal, rogue, rough (*Inf.*), roughneck (*Sl.*), rowdy, scoundrel, thug, tough, villain, wretch

ruffle 1. derange, disarrange, discompose, dishevel, disorder, mess up, rumple, tousle, wrinkle **2**. agitate, annoy, confuse, disconcert, disquiet, disturb, fluster, harass, irritate, nettle, peeve (*Inf.*), perturb, put out, rattle (*Inf.*), shake up (*Inf.*), stir, torment, trouble, unsettle, upset, vex, worry

rugged 1. broken, bumpy, craggy, difficult, irregular, jagged, ragged, rocky, rough, stark, uneven **2**. furrowed, leathery, lined, rough-hewn, strong-featured, weather-beaten, weathered, worn, wrinkled **3**. austere, crabbed, dour, gruff, hard, harsh, rough, rude, severe, sour, stern, surly **4**. barbarous, blunt, churlish, crude, graceless, rude, uncouth, uncultured, unpolished, unrefined **5**. arduous, demanding, difficult, exacting, hard, harsh, laborious, rigorous, stern, strenuous, taxing, tough, trying, uncompromising **6**. beefy (*Inf.*), brawny, burly, hale, hardy, husky (*Inf.*), muscular, robust, strong, sturdy, tough, vigorous, well-built

ruin *n.* **1**. bankruptcy, breakdown, collapse, crackup (*Inf.*), crash, damage, decay, defeat, destitution, destruction, devastation, disintegration, disrepair, dissolution, downfall, failure, fall, havoc, insolvency, nemesis, overthrow, ruina-

tion, subversion, the end, undoing, Waterloo, wreck, wreckage ~*v.* **2**. bankrupt, break, bring down, bring to nothing, bring to ruin, crush, defeat, demolish, destroy, devastate, impoverish, lay in ruins, lay waste, overthrow, overturn, overwhelm, pauperize, raze, shatter, smash, wreak havoc upon, wreck **3**. botch, damage, disfigure, injure, make a mess of, mangle, mar, mess up, spoil

ruinous 1. baleful, baneful (*Archaic*), calamitous, catastrophic, crippling, deadly, deleterious, destructive, devastating, dire, disastrous, extravagant, fatal, immoderate, injurious, murderous, noxious, pernicious, shattering, wasteful, withering **2**. broken-down, decrepit, derelict, dilapidated, in ruins, ramshackle, ruined

rule *n.* **1**. axiom, canon, criterion, decree, direction, guide, guideline, law, maxim, order, ordinance, precept, principle, regulation, ruling, standard, tenet **2**. administration, ascendancy, authority, command, control, direction, domination, dominion, empire, government, influence, jurisdiction, leadership, mastery, power, regime, reign, supremacy, sway **3**. condition, convention, custom, form, habit, order *or* way of things, practice, procedure, routine, wont **4**. course, formula, method, policy, procedure, way **5. as a rule** customarily, for the most part, generally, mainly, normally, on the whole, ordinarily, usually ~*v.* **6**. administer, be in authority, be in power, be number one (*Inf.*), command, control, direct, dominate, govern, guide, hold sway, lead, manage, preside over, regulate, reign, wear the crown **7**. adjudge, adjudicate, decide, decree, determine, establish, find, judge, lay down, pronounce, resolve, settle **8**. be customary (pre-eminent, prevalent, superior), hold sway, obtain, predominate, preponderate, prevail

rule out ban, debar, dismiss, eliminate, exclude, forbid, leave out, obviate, preclude, prevent, prohibit, proscribe, reject

ruler 1. commander, controller, crowned head, emperor, empress, governor, head of state, king, leader, lord, monarch, potentate, prince, princess, queen, sovereign **2**. measure, rule, straight edge, yardstick

ruling *n.* **1**. adjudication, decision, decree, finding, judgment, pronouncement, resolution, verdict ~*adj.* **2.** commanding, controlling, dominant, governing, leading, regnant, reigning, upper **3.** chief, current, dominant, main, predominant, pre-eminent, preponderant, prevailing, prevalent, principal, regnant, supreme

rum curious, funny, odd, peculiar, queer, singular, strange, suspect, suspicious, unusual, weird

rumbustious boisterous, clamorous, disorderly, exuberant, loud, noisy, obstreperous, refractory, robust, rough, rowdy, unmanageable, unruly, uproarious, wayward, wild, wilful

ruminate brood, chew over, cogitate, consider, contemplate, deliberate, meditate, mull over, muse, ponder, reflect, revolve, think, turn over in one's mind

rummage delve, examine, explore, hunt, ransack, root, rootle, search

rumour 1. *n.* bruit (*Archaic or U.S.*), buzz, canard, gossip, hearsay, news, report, story, talk, tidings, whisper, word **2.** *v.* bruit (*Archaic or U.S.*), circulate, gossip, noise abroad, pass around, publish, put about, report, say, tell, whisper

rump backside (*Inf.*), bottom, buttocks, croup, haunch, hindquarters, posterior, rear, rear end, seat

rumple crease, crinkle, crumple, crush, derange, dishevel, disorder, mess up, pucker, ruffle, screw up, scrunch, tousle, wrinkle

rumpus brouhaha, commotion, confusion, disruption, disturbance, furore, fuss, kerfuffle (*Inf.*), noise, row, shindig (*Sl.*), shindy (*Sl.*), tumult, uproar

run *v.* **1.** bolt, career, dart, dash, gallop, hare (*Brit. inf.*), hasten, hie, hotfoot, hurry, jog, leg it (*Inf.*), lope, race, rush, scamper, scramble, scud, scurry, speed, sprint **2.** abscond, beat a retreat, beat it (*Sl.*), bolt, clear out, cut and run (*Inf.*), decamp, depart, escape, flee, leg it (*Inf.*), make a run for it, make off, scarper (*Brit. sl.*), show a clean pair of heels, skedaddle (*Inf.*), take flight, take off (*Inf.*), take to one's heels **3.** course, glide, go, move, pass, roll, skim, slide **4.** bear, carry, convey, drive, give a lift to, manoeuvre, operate, propel, transport **5.** go, operate, ply **6.** function, go, operate, perform, tick, work **7.** administer, be in charge of, boss (*Inf.*), carry on, conduct, control, coordinate, direct, head, lead,

look after, manage, mastermind, operate, oversee, own, regulate, superintend, supervise, take care of **8.** continue, extend, go, last, lie, proceed, range, reach, stretch **9.** cascade, discharge, flow, go, gush, issue, leak, move, pour, proceed, spill, spout, stream **10.** dissolve, fuse, go soft, liquefy, melt, turn to liquid **11.** be diffused, bleed, lose colour, mix, spread **12.** come apart, come undone, ladder, tear, unravel **13.** be current, circulate, climb, creep, go round, spread, trail **14.** display, feature, print, publish **15.** be a candidate, challenge, compete, contend, put oneself up for, stand, take part **16.** bootleg, deal in, ship, smuggle, sneak, traffic in **17. run for it** abscond, bolt, cut and run (*Inf.*), do a bunk (*Brit. inf.*), escape, flee, fly, make a break for it, make off, scarper (*Brit. sl.*), scram (*Inf.*), show a clean pair of heels, skedaddle (*Inf.*), take flight, take off ~*n.* **18.** dash, gallop, jog, race, rush, sprint, spurt **19.** drive, excursion, jaunt, journey, joy ride (*Inf.*), lift, outing, ride, round, spin (*Inf.*), trip **20.** chain, course, cycle, passage, period, round, season, sequence, series, spell, streak, stretch, string **21.** category, class, kind, order, sort, type, variety **22.** application, demand, pressure, rush **23.** ladder, rip, snag, tear **24.** course, current, direction, drift, flow, motion, movement, passage, path, progress, stream, tendency, tenor, tide, trend, way **25.** coop, enclosure, pen **26. in the long run** at the end of the day, eventually, in the end, in the final analysis, in time, ultimately, when all is said and done **27. on the run a.** at liberty, escaping, fugitive, in flight, on the lam (*U.S. sl.*), on the loose **b.** defeated, falling back, fleeing, in flight, in retreat, retreating, running away **c.** at speed, hastily, hurriedly, hurrying, in a hurry, in a rush, in haste

run across bump into, chance upon, come across, come upon, encounter, meet, meet with, run into

run after chase, follow, give chase, pursue

runaway *n.* **1.** absconder, deserter, escapee, escaper, fugitive, refugee, truant ~*adj.* **2.** escaped, fleeing, fugitive, loose, out of control, uncontrolled, wild **3.** easily won, easy, effortless

run away 1. abscond, beat it (*Sl.*), bolt, clear out, cut and run (*Inf.*), decamp, do a bunk (*Brit. inf.*), escape, flee, make a run for it, run off, scarper (*Brit. sl.*), scram (*Inf.*), show a clean pair of heels, skedaddle (*Inf.*), take flight, take off, take to one's heels **2**. *With* **with a**. abduct, abscond, elope **b**. abscond, make off, pinch (*Inf.*), run off, snatch, steal **c**. romp home, walk it (*Inf.*), win by a mile (*Inf.*), win easily, win hands down

rundown briefing, outline, précis, recap (*Inf.*), résumé, review, run-through, sketch, summary, synopsis

run-down 1. below par, debilitated, drained, enervated, exhausted, fatigued, out of condition, peaky, tried, under the weather (*Inf.*), unhealthy, weak, weary, worn-out **2**. broken-down, decrepit, dilapidated, dingy, ramshackle, seedy, shabby, tumble-down, worn-out

run down 1. curtail, cut, cut back, decrease, drop, pare down, reduce, trim **2**. debilitate, exhaust, sap the strength of, tire, undermine the health of, weaken **3**. belittle, criticize adversely, decry, defame, denigrate, disparage, knock (*Inf.*), revile, speak ill of, vilify **4**. hit, knock down, knock over, run into, run over, strike

run-in altercation, argument, brush, confrontation, contretemps, dispute, dust-up (*Inf.*), encounter, fight, quarrel, set-to (*Inf.*), skirmish, tussle

run in 1. break in gently, run gently **2**. *Sl.* apprehend, arrest, bust (*Inf.*), collar (*Inf.*), jail, nab (*Inf.*), pick up, pinch (*Inf.*), pull in (*Brit. sl.*), take into custody, take to jail, throw in jail

run into 1. bump into, collide with, crash into, dash against, hit, ram, strike **2**. be beset by, be confronted by, bump into, chance upon, come across, come upon, encounter, meet, meet with, run across

runner 1. athlete, harrier, jogger, miler, sprinter **2**. courier, dispatch bearer, errand boy, messenger **3**. offshoot, shoot, sprig, sprout, stem, stolon (*Bot.*), tendril

running *adj.* **1**. constant, continuous, incessant, in succession, on the trot (*Inf.*), perpetual, together, unbroken, unceasing, uninterrupted **2**. flowing, moving, streaming ~*n*. **3**. administration, charge, conduct, control, coordination, direction, leadership, management, organization, regulation, superintendency, supervision **4**. functioning, maintenance, operation, performance, working **5**. competition, contention, contest

runny diluted, flowing, fluid, liquefied, liquid, melted, streaming, watery

run off 1. bolt, clear out, cut and run (*Inf.*), decamp, escape, flee, make off, run away, scarper (*Brit. sl.*), show a clean pair of heels, skedaddle (*Inf.*), take flight, take to one's heels **2**. churn out (*Inf.*), duplicate, print, produce **3**. bleed, drain, flow away, siphon, tap **4**. *With* **with a**. lift (*Inf.*), make off, pinch (*Inf.*), purloin, run away, steal, swipe (*Sl.*) **b**. abscond, elope, run away

run-of-the-mill average, common, commonplace, fair, mediocre, middling, modest, ordinary, passable, tolerable, undistinguished, unexceptional, unexciting, unimpressive

run out 1. be exhausted, cease, close, come to a close, dry up, end, expire, fail, finish, give out, peter out, terminate **2**. *With* **of** be cleaned out, be out of, exhaust one's supply of, have no more of, have none left, have no remaining **3**. *With* **on** *Inf.* abandon, desert, forsake, leave high and dry, leave holding the baby, leave in the lurch, rat, run away from

run over 1. hit, knock down, knock over, run down, strike **2**. brim over, overflow, spill, spill over **3**. check, examine, go over, go through, rehearse, reiterate, review, run through, survey

run through 1. pierce, spit, stab, stick, transfix **2**. blow (*Sl.*), dissipate, exhaust, fritter away, spend like water, squander, throw away, waste **3**. go over, practise, read, rehearse, run over **4**. check, examine, go through, look over, review, run over, survey

rupture *n*. **1**. breach, break, burst, cleavage, cleft, crack, fissure, fracture, rent, split, tear **2**. altercation, breach, break, bust-up (*Inf.*), contention, disagreement, disruption, dissolution, estrangement, falling-out (*Inf.*), feud, hostility, quarrel, rift, schism, split **3**. *Medical* hernia ~*v*. **4**. break, burst, cleave, crack, fracture, puncture, rend, separate, sever, split, tear **5**. break off, cause a breach, come between, disrupt, dissever, divide, split

rural agrarian, agricultural, Arcadian, bucolic, countrified, country, pastoral, rustic, sylvan, upcountry

ruse artifice, blind, deception, device, dodge, hoax, imposture, manoeuvre, ploy, sham, stratagem, subterfuge, trick, wile

rush v. **1.** accelerate, bolt, career, dart, dash, dispatch, expedite, fly, hasten, hotfoot, hurry, hustle, lose no time, make haste, make short work of, press, push, quicken, race, run, scramble, scurry, shoot, speed, speed up, sprint, tear ~n. **2.** charge, dash, dispatch, expedition, haste, hurry, race, scramble, speed, surge, swiftness, urgency ~v. **3.** attack, capture, charge, overcome, storm, take by storm ~n. **4.** assault, charge, onslaught, push, storm, surge ~adj. **5.** brisk, cursory, emergency, expeditious, fast, hasty, hurried, prompt, quick, rapid, swift, urgent

rust n. **1.** corrosion, oxidation ~v. **2.** corrode, oxidize ~n. **3.** blight, mildew, mould, must, rot ~v. **4.** atrophy, decay, decline, deteriorate, go stale, stagnate, tarnish

rustic adj. **1.** Arcadian, bucolic, countrified, country, pastoral, rural, sylvan, upcountry **2.** artless, homely, homespun, plain, simple, unaffected, unpolished, unrefined, unsophisticated **3.** awkward, boorish, churlish, cloddish, clodhopping (Inf.), clownish, coarse, crude, graceless, loutish, lumpish, maladroit, rough, uncouth, uncultured, unmannerly ~n. **4.** boor, bumpkin, clod, clodhopper (Inf.), clown, country boy, country cousin, countryman, countrywoman, hillbilly,

Hodge, peasant, son of the soil, swain (Archaic), yokel

rustle 1. v. crackle, crepitate, crinkle, susurrate (Literary), swish, whish, whisper, whoosh **2.** n. crackle, crepitation, crinkling, susurration or susurrus (Literary), rustling, whisper

rusty 1. corroded, oxidized, rustcovered, rusted **2.** chestnut, coppery, reddish, reddish-brown, russet, rustcoloured **3.** cracked, creaking, croaking, croaky, hoarse **4.** ancient, antiquated, antique, dated, old-fashioned, outmoded, out of date, passé **5.** deficient, impaired, not what it was, out of practice, sluggish, stale, unpractised, weak

rut n. **1.** furrow, gouge, groove, indentation, pothole, score, track, trough, wheelmark **2.** dead end, groove, habit, humdrum existence, pattern, routine, system ~v. **3.** cut, furrow, gouge, groove, hole, indent, mark, score

ruthless adamant, barbarous, brutal, callous, cruel, ferocious, fierce, hard, hard-hearted, harsh, heartless, inexorable, inhuman, merciless, pitiless, relentless, remorseless, savage, severe, stern, unfeeling, unmerciful, unpitying, unrelenting, without pity

ruttish 1. in heat, in rut, in season, sexually excited **2.** aroused, horny (Sl.), lascivious, lecherous, lewd, libidinous, lustful, randy (Sl.), salacious

S

sable *adj.* black, dark, dusty, ebon (*Poetic*), ebony, jet, jetty, raven, sombre

sabotage 1. *v.* cripple, damage, destroy, disable, disrupt, incapacitate, sap the foundations of, subvert, throw a spanner in the works (*Inf.*), undermine, vandalize, wreck 2. *n.* damage, destruction, disruption, subversion, treachery, treason, wrecking

sac bag, bladder, bursa, cyst, pocket, pod, pouch, vesicle

saccharine cloying, honeyed, maudlin, mawkish, nauseating, oversweet, sentimental, sickly, soppy (*Brit. inf.*), sugary, syrupy (*Inf.*)

sack[1] 1. *v.* axe (*Inf.*), discharge, dismiss, fire (*Inf.*), give (someone) his cards, give (someone) his marching orders, give (someone) the boot (*Sl.*), kick out (*Inf.*) 2. *n.* the sack discharge, dismissal, termination of employment, the axe (*Inf.*), the boot (*Sl.*), the chop (*Brit. sl.*), the push (*Sl.*)

sack[2] 1. *v.* demolish, depredate (*Rare*), despoil, destroy, devastate, lay waste, loot, maraud, pillage, plunder, raid, ravage, rifle, rob, ruin, spoil, strip 2. *n.* depredation, despoliation, destruction, devastation, looting, pillage, plunder, plundering, rape, rapine, ravage, ruin, waste

sack[3] *n.* **hit the sack** bed down, go to bed, hit the hay (*Inf.*), retire, turn in (*Inf.*)

sackcloth and ashes compunction, contrition, grief, hair shirt, mortification, mourning, penitence, remorse, repentance

sacred 1. blessed, consecrated, divine, hallowed, holy, revered, sanctified, venerable 2. inviolable, inviolate, invulnerable, protected, sacrosanct, secure 3. holy, religious, solemn

sacrifice 1. *v.* forego, forfeit, give up, immolate, let go, lose, offer, offer up, surrender 2. *n.* burnt offering, destruction, hecatomb, immolation, loss, oblation, renunciation, surrender

sacrificial atoning, expiatory, oblatory, propitiatory, reparative

sacrilege blasphemy, desecration, heresy, impiety, irreverence, mockery, profanation, profaneness, profanity, violation

sacrilegious blasphemous, desecrating, godless, impious, irreligious, irreverent, profane, ungodly, unholy

sacrosanct hallowed, inviolable, inviolate, sacred, sanctified, set apart, untouchable

sad 1. blue, cheerless, dejected, depressed, disconsolate, dismal, doleful, down, downcast, down in the dumps (*Inf.*), down in the mouth (*Inf.*), gloomy, glum, grief-stricken, grieved, heavy-hearted, low, low-spirited, lugubrious, melancholy, mournful, pensive, sick at heart, sombre, triste (*Archaic*), unhappy, wistful, woebegone 2. calamitous, dark, depressing, disastrous, dismal, grievous, heart-rending, lachrymose, moving, pathetic, pitiable, pitiful, poignant, sorry, tearful, tragic, upsetting 3. bad, deplorable, dismal, distressing, grave, lamentable, miserable, regrettable, serious, shabby, sorry, to be deplored, unfortunate, unhappy, unsatisfactory, wretched

sadden bring tears to one's eyes, cast a gloom upon, cast down, dash, deject, depress, desolate, dispirit, distress, grieve, make blue, make one's heart bleed, upset

saddle *v.* burden, charge, encumber, load, lumber (*Brit. inf.*), task, tax

sadistic barbarous, brutal, cruel, fiendish, perverse, perverted, ruthless, vicious

sadness bleakness, cheerlessness, dejection, depression, despondency, dolefulness, dolour (*Poetic*), gloominess, grief, heavy heart, melancholy, misery, mournfulness, poignancy, sorrow, sorrowfulness, the blues, the dumps (*Inf.*), unhappiness

safe 1. free from harm, guarded, impregnable, in safety, intact, O.K. or okay (*Inf.*), out of danger, out of harm's way, protected, safe and sound, secure, undamaged, unharmed, unhurt, unscathed 2. harmless, innocuous, nonpoisonous, nontoxic, pure, tame, unpolluted, wholesome 3. cautious, circumspect, conservative, dependable, discreet, on the safe side, prudent, realistic, reliable, sure, tried and true, trustworthy, unadventurous **4**. certain, impregnable, risk-free, riskless, secure, sound ~*n*. **5**. coffer, deposit box, repository, safe-deposit box, strongbox, vault

safe-conduct authorization, licence, pass, passport, permit, safeguard, warrant

safeguard 1. *v*. defend, guard, look after, preserve, protect, screen, shield, watch over **2**. *n*. aegis, armour, bulwark, convoy, defence, escort, guard, protection, security, shield, surety

safekeeping care, charge, custody, guardianship, keeping, protection, supervision, surveillance, trust, tutelage, ward

safely in one piece, in safety, safe and sound, securely, with impunity, without risk, with safety

safety assurance, cover, immunity, impregnability, protection, refuge, sanctuary, security, shelter

sag *v*. **1**. bag, bulge, cave in, dip, droop, drop, fall, fall unevenly, give way, hang loosely, seat (*of skirts, etc.*), settle, sink, slump, swag **2**. decline, droop, fall, flag, slide, slip, slump, wane, weaken, wilt ~*n*. **3**. decline, depression, dip, downturn, drop, fall, slip, slump

saga adventure, chronicle, epic, narrative, *roman-fleuve*, soap opera, story, tale, yarn

sagacious able, acute, apt, astute, canny, clear-sighted, discerning, downy (*Brit. sl.*), far-sighted, fly (*Sl.*), insightful, intelligent, judicious, knowing, longheaded, perceptive, perspicacious, sage, sharp, sharp-witted, shrewd, smart, wise

sagacity acuteness, astuteness, canniness, discernment, foresight, insight, judiciousness, knowingness, penetration, perspicacity, prudence, sapience, sense, sharpness, shrewdness, understanding, wisdom

sage 1. *adj*. acute, canny, discerning, intelligent, judicious, learned, perspicacious, politic, prudent, sagacious, sapient, sensible, wise **2**. *n*. authority, elder, expert, guru, man of learning, master, Nestor, philosopher, pundit, savant, Solomon, Solon, wise man

sail *v*. **1**. cast *or* weigh anchor, embark, get under way, hoist the blue peter, put to sea, set sail **2**. captain, cruise, go by water, navigate, pilot, ride the waves, skipper, steer, voyage **3**. drift, float, fly, glide, scud, shoot, skim, skirr, soar, sweep, wing **4**. *Inf. With* **in** *or* **into** assault, attack, begin, belabour, fall upon, get going, get to work on, lambaste, set about, tear into (*Inf.*)

sailor hearty (*Inf.*), Jack Tar, lascar, leatherneck (*Sl.*), marine, mariner, matelot (*Sl.*), navigator, salt, sea dog, seafarer, seafaring man, seaman, tar (*Inf.*)

saintly angelic, beatific, blameless, blessed, devout, full of good works, godfearing, godly, holy, pious, religious, righteous, sainted, saintlike, sinless, virtuous, worthy

sake 1. account, advantage, behalf, benefit, consideration, gain, good, interest, profit, regard, respect, welfare, wellbeing **2**. aim, cause, end, motive, objective, principle, purpose, reason

salacious bawdy, blue, carnal, concupiscent, erotic, indecent, lascivious, lecherous, lewd, libidinous, lickerish (*Archaic*), lustful, obscene, pornographic, prurient, ribald, ruttish, smutty, wanton

salary earnings, emolument, income, pay, remuneration, stipend

sale 1. deal, disposal, marketing, selling, transaction, vending **2**. buyers, consumers, customers, demand, market, outlet, purchasers **3. for sale** available, in stock, obtainable, on offer, on sale, on the market

salient arresting, conspicuous, important, jutting, marked, noticeable, outstanding, projecting, prominent, pronounced, protruding, remarkable, signal, striking

sallow anaemic, bilious, jaundiced-looking, pale, pallid, pasty, sickly, unhealthy, wan, yellowish

sally *v*. **1**. erupt, go forth, issue, rush, set out, surge ~*n*. **2**. *Military* foray, incursion, offensive, raid, sortie, thrust **3**. *Fig*. bon mot, crack (*Inf.*), jest, joke, quip, retort, riposte, smart remark, wisecrack (*Inf.*), witticism **4**. escapade, excursion, frolic, jaunt, trip

salt *n*. **1**. flavour, relish, savour, seasoning, taste **2. with a grain** *or* **pinch of salt** cynically, disbelievingly, doubtfully, sceptically, suspiciously, with reservations **3**. *Fig*. Attic wit, bite, dry humour, liveliness, piquancy, punch, pungency, sarcasm, sharpness, wit, zest, zip (*Inf.*)

4. mariner, sailor, sea dog, seaman, tar (*Inf.*) ~*adj.* **5**. brackish, briny, saline, salted, salty

salt away accumulate, amass, bank, cache, hide, hoard up, lay by, lay in, lay up, put by, save, save for a rainy day, stash away (*Inf.*), stockpile

salty 1. brackish, briny, over-salted, saline, salt, salted **2**. colourful, humorous, lively, piquant, pungent, racy, sharp, snappy (*Inf.*), spicy, tangy, tart, witty, zestful

salubrious beneficial, good for one, healthful, health-giving, healthy, invigorating, salutary, wholesome

salutary 1. advantageous, beneficial, good, good for one, helpful, practical, profitable, timely, useful, valuable **2**. healthful, healthy, salubrious

salutation address, greeting, obeisance, salute, welcome

salute *v.* **1**. accost, acknowledge, address, doff one's cap to, greet, hail, kiss, pay one's respects to, salaam, welcome **2**. acknowledge, honour, pay tribute *or* homage to, present arms, recognize, take one's hat off to (*Inf.*) ~*n.* **3**. address, greeting, kiss, obeisance, recognition, salaam, salutation, tribute

salvage *v.* glean, recover, redeem, rescue, restore, retrieve, save

salvation deliverance, escape, lifeline, preservation, redemption, rescue, restoration, saving

salve *n.* balm, cream, dressing, emollient, liniment, lotion, lubricant, medication, ointment, unguent

same *adj.* **1**. aforementioned, aforesaid, selfsame, very **2**. alike, corresponding, duplicate, equal, equivalent, identical, indistinguishable, interchangeable, synonymous, twin **3**. changeless, consistent, constant, invariable, unaltered, unchanged, unfailing, uniform, unvarying **4. all the same a.** after all, anyhow, be that as it may, in any event, just the same, nevertheless, nonetheless, still **b.** immaterial, not worth mentioning, of no consequence, unimportant

sameness identicalness, identity, indistinguishability, lack of variety, likeness, monotony, oneness, predictability, repetition, resemblance, similarity, standardization, tedium, uniformity

sample 1. *n.* cross section, example, exemplification, illustration, indication, instance, model, pattern, representative,

sign, specimen **2**. *v.* experience, inspect, partake of, taste, test, try **3**. *adj.* illustrative, pilot, representative, specimen, test, trial

sanctify absolve, anoint, bless, cleanse, consecrate, hallow, purify, set apart

sanctimonious canting, false, goody-goody (*Inf.*), holier-than-thou, hypocritical, pharisaical, pi (*Brit. sl.*), pietistic, pious, self-righteous, self-satisfied, smug, Tartuffian *or* Tartufian, too good to be true, unctuous

sanction *n.* **1**. allowance, approbation, approval, authority, authorization, backing, confirmation, countenance, endorsement, O.K. *or* okay (*Inf.*), ratification, stamp *or* seal of approval, support **2**. *Often plural* ban, boycott, coercive measures, embargo, penalty ~*v.* **3**. allow, approve, authorize, back, countenance, endorse, lend one's name to, permit, support, vouch for **4**. confirm, ratify, warrant

sanctity 1. devotion, godliness, goodness, grace, holiness, piety, purity, religiousness, righteousness, sanctitude, spirituality **2**. inviolability, sacredness, solemnity

sanctuary 1. altar, church, Holy of Holies, sanctum, shrine, temple **2**. asylum, haven, protection, refuge, retreat, shelter **3**. conservation area, national park, nature reserve, reserve

sanctum 1. Holy of Holies, sanctuary, shrine **2**. den, private room, refuge, retreat, study

sane 1. all there (*Inf.*), *compos mentis*, in one's right mind, in possession of all one's faculties, lucid, mentally sound, normal, of sound mind, rational **2**. balanced, judicious, level-headed, moderate, reasonable, sensible, sober, sound

sang-froid aplomb, calmness, composure, cool (*Sl.*), cool-headedness, coolness, equanimity, imperturbability, indifference, nonchalance, phlegm, poise, self-possession, unflappability (*Inf.*)

sanguinary bloodied, bloodthirsty, bloody, cruel, fell (*Archaic*), flowing with blood, gory, grim, merciless, murderous, pitiless, ruthless, savage

sanguine 1. animated, assured, buoyant, cheerful, confident, hopeful, in good heart, lively, optimistic, spirited **2**. florid, red, rubicund, ruddy

sanitary clean, germ-free, healthy, hygienic, salubrious, unpolluted, whole-some

sanity 1. mental health, normality, rationality, reason, right mind (*Inf.*), saneness, stability 2. common sense, good sense, judiciousness, level-headedness, rationality, sense, soundness of judgment

sap[1] *n.* 1. animating force, essence, lifeblood, vital fluid 2. *Inf.* charlie (*Brit. inf.*), chump (*Inf.*), drip (*Inf.*), fool, gull (*Archaic*), idiot, jerk (*Sl.*), muggins (*Brit. sl.*), nincompoop, ninny, nitwit, noddy, noodle, Simple Simon, simpleton, twit (*Inf.*), weakling, wet (*Inf.*)

sap[2] *v.* bleed, deplete, devitalize, drain, enervate, erode, exhaust, rob, undermine, weaken, wear down

sapience acuity, acuteness, discernment, insight, mother wit, nous (*Brit. sl.*), perspicacity, sagacity, sense, shrewdness, understanding, wisdom

sapient acute, canny, discerning, discriminating, intelligent, judicious, knowing, long-headed, perspicacious, sagacious, sage, shrewd, wise, would-be-wise

sarcasm bitterness, causticness, contempt, cynicism, derision, irony, mockery, mordancy, satire, scorn, sneering

sarcastic acerbic, acrimonious, backhanded, biting, caustic, contemptuous, cutting, cynical, derisive, disparaging, ironical, mocking, mordant, sardonic, sarky (*Brit. inf.*), satirical, sharp, sneering, taunting

sardonic bitter, cynical, derisive, dry, ironical, jeering, malevolent, malicious, malignant, mocking, mordant, sarcastic, wry

Satan Apollyon, Beelzebub, Lord of the Flies, Lucifer, Mephistopheles, Old Nick, Prince of Darkness, The Devil, The Evil One

satanic accursed, black, demoniac, demoniacal, demonic, devilish, diabolic, evil, fiendish, hellish, infernal, inhuman, iniquitous, malevolent, malignant, wicked

sate 1. indulge to the full, satiate, satisfy, slake 2. cloy, glut, gorge, overfill, saturate, sicken, surfeit, weary

satellite *n.* 1. communications satellite, moon, sputnik 2. *Fig.* attendant, dependant, follower, hanger-on, lackey, minion, parasite, retainer, sidekick (*Sl.*), sycophant, vassal ~*adj.* 3. *Fig.* client,

dependent, puppet, subordinate, tributary, vassal

satiate 1. cloy, glut, gorge, jade, nauseate, overfill, stuff 2. sate, satisfy, slake, surfeit

satiety 1. overindulgence, saturation, surfeit 2. fullness, gratification, repletion, satiation, satisfaction

satire burlesque, caricature, irony, lampoon, parody, pasquinade, raillery, ridicule, sarcasm, send-up (*Brit. inf.*), skit, spoof (*Inf.*), takeoff (*Inf.*), travesty, wit

satirical, satiric biting, bitter, burlesque, caustic, censorious, cutting, cynical, incisive, ironical, mocking, mordant, pungent, Rabelaisian, sarcastic, sardonic, taunting

satirize abuse, burlesque, censure, criticize, deride, hold up to ridicule, lampoon, lash, parody, ridicule, send up (*Brit. inf.*), take off (*Inf.*), travesty

satisfaction 1. comfort, complacency, content, contentedness, contentment, ease, enjoyment, gratification, happiness, peace of mind, pleasure, pride, repletion, satiety, well-being 2. achievement, appeasing, assuaging, fulfilment, gratification, resolution, settlement 3. amends, atonement, compensation, damages, indemnification, justice, recompense, redress, reimbursement, remuneration, reparation, requital, restitution, settlement, vindication

satisfactory acceptable, adequate, all right, average, competent, fair, good enough, passable, sufficient, suitable, up to standard, up to the mark

satisfied at ease, complacent, content, contented, convinced, easy in one's mind, happy, like the cat that swallowed the canary (*Inf.*), pacified, positive, smug, sure

satisfy 1. appease, assuage, content, fill, gratify, indulge, mollify, pacify, please, quench, sate, satiate, slake, surfeit 2. answer, be enough (adequate, sufficient), come up to expectations, do, fill the bill (*Inf.*), fulfil, meet, qualify, serve, serve the purpose, suffice 3. assure, convince, dispel (someone's) doubts, persuade, put (someone's) mind at rest, quiet, reassure 4. answer, comply with, discharge, fulfil, meet, pay (off), settle, square up 5. atone, compensate, indemnify, make good, make reparation for, recompense, remunerate, requite, reward

satisfying cheering, convincing, filling, gratifying, pleasing, pleasurable, satisfactory

saturate douse, drench, drouk (*Scot.*), imbue, impregnate, ret (*used of flax, etc.*), soak, souse, steep, suffuse, waterlog, wet through

saturated drenched, dripping, droukit (*Scot.*), soaked, soaked to the skin, soaking (wet), sodden, sopping (wet), wet through, wringing wet

saturnine dour, dull, gloomy, glum, grave, heavy, morose, phlegmatic, sedate, sluggish, sombre, taciturn, uncommunicative

sauce n. backchat (*Inf.*), brass (*Inf.*), cheek (*Inf.*), cheekiness, disrespectfulness, impertinence, impudence, insolence, lip (*Sl.*), nerve (*Inf.*), rudeness

sauciness backchat (*Inf.*), brass (*Inf.*), brazenness, cheek (*Inf.*), flippancy, impertinence, impudence, insolence, lip (*Sl.*), pertness, rudeness, sauce (*Inf.*)

saucy 1. cheeky (*Inf.*), disrespectful, flip (*Inf.*), flippant, forward, fresh (*Inf.*), impertinent, impudent, insolent, pert, presumptuous, rude, smart-alecky (*Inf.*) **2.** dashing, gay, jaunty, natty (*Inf.*), perky, rakish, sporty

saunter 1. v. amble, dally, linger, loiter, meander, mosey (*Inf.*), ramble, roam, rove, stravaig (*Scot. & Northern English dialect*), stroll, take a stroll, tarry, wander **2.** n. airing, amble, constitutional, promenade, ramble, stroll, turn, walk

savage adj. **1.** feral, rough, rugged, uncivilized, uncultivated, undomesticated, untamed, wild **2.** barbarous, beastly, bestial, bloodthirsty, bloody, brutal, brutish, cruel, devilish, diabolical, ferocious, fierce, harsh, inhuman, merciless, murderous, pitiless, ravening, ruthless, sadistic, vicious **3.** in a state of nature, nonliterate, primitive, rude, unspoilt ~n. **4.** aboriginal, aborigine, autochthon, barbarian, heathen, indigene, native, primitive **5.** barbarian, bear, boor, roughneck (*Sl.*), yahoo, yobbo (*Brit. sl.*) **6.** beast, brute, fiend, monster ~v. **7.** attack, lacerate, mangle, maul, tear into (*Inf.*)

savagery barbarity, bestiality, bloodthirstiness, brutality, cruelty, ferocity,

fierceness, inhumanity, ruthlessness, sadism, viciousness

savant authority, intellectual, master, mastermind, philosopher, sage, scholar

save 1. bail (someone) out, come to (someone's) rescue, deliver, free, liberate, recover, redeem, rescue, salvage, set free **2.** be frugal, be thrifty, collect, economize, gather, hide away, hoard, hold, husband, keep, keep up one's sleeve (*Inf.*), lay by, put aside for a rainy day, put by, reserve, retrench, salt away, set aside, store, tighten one's belt (*Inf.*), treasure up **3.** conserve, guard, keep safe, look after, preserve, protect, safeguard, screen, shield, take care of **4.** hinder, obviate, prevent, rule out, spare

saving 1. adj. compensatory, extenuating, qualifying, redeeming **2.** n. bargain, discount, economy, reduction

savings fund, nest egg, provision for a rainy day, reserves, resources, store

saviour defender, deliverer, friend in need, Good Samaritan, guardian, knight in shining armour, liberator, preserver, protector, rescuer, salvation

Saviour Our or **The** Christ, Jesus, Messiah, Redeemer

savoir-faire accomplishment, address, diplomacy, discretion, finesse, poise, social graces, social know-how (*Inf.*), tact, urbanity

savour n. **1.** flavour, piquancy, relish, smack, smell, tang, taste **2.** distinctive quality, excitement, flavour, interest, salt, spice, zest ~v. **3.** *Often with* of bear the hallmarks, be indicative, be suggestive, partake, show signs, smack, suggest, verge on **4.** appreciate, delight in, enjoy, enjoy to the full, gloat over, like, luxuriate in, partake, relish, revel in, smack one's lips over

savoury 1. agreeable, appetizing, dainty, delectable, delicious, full-flavoured, good, luscious, mouthwatering, palatable, piquant, rich, scrumptious (*Inf.*), spicy, tangy, tasty, toothsome **2.** decent, edifying, honest, reputable, respectable, wholesome

saw adage, aphorism, apophthegm, axiom, byword, dictum, gnome, maxim, proverb, saying

saw-toothed crenate (*Bot., Zool.*), dentate, denticulate (*Biol.*), notched, serrate, serrated

say v. **1.** add, affirm, announce, assert, come out with (*Inf.*), declare, give voice *or* utterance to, maintain, mention, pronounce, put into words, remark, speak, state, utter, voice **2.** answer, disclose, divulge, give as one's opinion, make known, reply, respond, reveal, tell **3.** allege, bruit (*Archaic or U.S.*), claim, noise abroad, put about, report, rumour, suggest **4.** deliver, do, orate, perform, read, recite, rehearse, render, repeat **5.** assume, conjecture, dare say, estimate, guess, hazard a guess, imagine, judge, presume, suppose, surmise **6.** communicate, convey, express, give the impression that, imply **7. go without saying** be accepted, be a matter of course, be obvious, be self-evident, be taken as read, be taken for granted, be understood **8. to say the least** at the very least, to put it mildly, without any exaggeration ~*n.* **9.** crack (*Inf.*), turn (chance, opportunity) to speak, voice, vote **10.** authority, clout (*Inf.*), influence, power, sway, weight

saying adage, aphorism, apophthegm, axiom, byword, dictum, gnome, maxim, proverb, saw

say-so 1. assertion, asseveration, assurance, dictum, guarantee, word **2.** agreement, authority, authorization, consent, O.K. *or* okay (*Inf.*), permission, sanction

scalding blistering, boiling, burning, piping hot, searing

scale[1] *n.* **1.** calibration, degrees, gamut, gradation, graduated system, graduation, hierarchy, ladder, pecking order (*Inf.*), progression, ranking, register, seniority system, sequence, series, spectrum, spread, steps **2.** proportion, ratio **3.** degree, extent, range, reach, scope, way ~*v.* **4.** ascend, clamber, climb, escalade, mount, surmount **5.** adjust, proportion, prorate (*Chiefly U.S.*), regulate

scale[2] *n.* flake, lamina, layer, plate, squama (*Biol.*)

scaly flaky, furfuraceous (*Medical*), scabrous, scurfy, squamous *or* squamose (*Biol.*), squamulose

scamp devil, imp, knave (*Archaic*), mischief-maker, monkey, prankster, rascal, rogue, scallywag (*Inf.*), scapegrace, tyke (*Inf.*), wretch

scamper dart, dash, fly, hasten, hie (*Archaic*), hurry, romp, run, scoot, scurry, scuttle, sprint

scan check, con (*Archaic*), examine, glance over, investigate, look one up and down, look through, run one's eye over, run over, scour, scrutinize, search, size up (*Inf.*), skim, survey, sweep, take stock of

scandal 1. crime, crying shame (*Inf.*), disgrace, embarrassment, offence, sin, wrongdoing **2.** calumny, defamation, detraction, discredit, disgrace, dishonour, ignominy, infamy, obloquy, offence, opprobrium, reproach, shame **3.** abuse, aspersion, backbiting, dirt, dirty linen (*Inf.*), gossip, rumours, skeleton in the cupboard, slander, talk, tattle

scandalize affront, appal, cause a few raised eyebrows (*Inf.*), disgust, horrify, offend, outrage, shock

scandalmonger calumniator, defamer, destroyer of reputations, gossip, muckraker, tattle, tattler, traducer

scandalous 1. atrocious, disgraceful, disreputable, highly improper, infamous, monstrous, odious, opprobrious, outrageous, shameful, shocking, unseemly **2.** defamatory, gossiping, libellous, scurrilous, slanderous, untrue

scant bare, barely sufficient, deficient, inadequate, insufficient, limited, little, minimal, sparse

scanty bare, deficient, exiguous, inadequate, insufficient, meagre, narrow, poor, restricted, scant, short, skimpy, slender, sparing, sparse, thin

scapegoat fall guy (*Inf.*), whipping boy

scapegrace bad lot (*Inf.*), good-for-nothing, limb of Satan, ne'er-do-well, rascal, rogue, scallywag (*Inf.*), scamp, the despair of

scar 1. *n.* blemish, cicatrix, injury, mark, wound **2.** *v.* brand, damage, disfigure, mark, traumatize

scarce at a premium, deficient, few, few and far between, infrequent, in short supply, insufficient, rare, seldom met with, uncommon, unusual, wanting

scarcely 1. barely, hardly, only just, scarce (*Archaic*) **2.** by no means, definitely not, hardly, not at all, on no account, under no circumstances

scarcity dearth, deficiency, infrequency, insufficiency, lack, paucity, poverty, rareness, shortage, undersupply, want

scare 1. *v.* affright (*Archaic*), alarm, daunt, dismay, frighten, give (someone) a fright, give (someone) a turn (*Inf.*), intimidate, panic, put the wind up (someone) (*Inf.*), shock, startle, terrify, terrorize **2.** *n.* alarm, alert, fright, panic, shock, start, terror

scared fearful, frightened, panicky, panic-stricken, petrified, shaken, startled, terrified

scaremonger alarmist, Calamity Jane, doom merchant (*Inf.*), prophet of doom, spreader of despair and despondency

scarper beat a hasty retreat, beat it (*Sl.*), clear off (*Inf.*), cut and run (*Inf.*), decamp, depart, disappear, do a bunk (*Brit. sl.*), flee, go, make off, make oneself scarce (*Inf.*), run away, run for it, scram (*Inf.*), skedaddle (*Inf.*), take flight, take oneself off, take to one's heels, vamoose (*Sl., chiefly U.S.*)

scary alarming, bloodcurdling, chilling, creepy (*Inf.*), frightening, hairraising, hairy (*Sl.*), horrendous, horrifying, intimidating, shocking, spinechilling, spooky (*Inf.*), terrifying, unnerving

scathing belittling, biting, brutal, caustic, critical, cutting, harsh, mordant, sarcastic, scornful, searing, trenchant, withering

scatter 1. broadcast, diffuse, disseminate, fling, litter, shower, sow, spread, sprinkle, strew **2.** disband, dispel, disperse, dissipate, disunite, put to flight, separate

scatterbrain bird-brain (*Inf.*), butterfly, featherbrain, flibbertigibbet, grasshopper mind, madcap

scatterbrained bird-brained (*Inf.*), careless, empty-headed, featherbrained, forgetful, frivolous, giddy, inattentive, irresponsible, madcap, scatty (*Brit. inf.*), silly, slaphappy (*Inf.*), thoughtless

scattering few, handful, scatter, smatter, smattering, sprinkling

scenario master plan, outline, résumé, rundown, scheme, sequence of events, sketch, story line, summary, synopsis

scene 1. display, exhibition, pageant, picture, representation, show, sight, spectacle, tableau **2.** area, locality, place, position, setting, site, situation, spot, whereabouts **3.** backdrop, background, location, *mise en scène*, set, setting **4.** act, division, episode, incident, part, stage **5.** carry-on (*Brit. inf.*), commotion, confrontation, display of emotion, exhibition, fuss, performance, row, tantrum, to-do, upset **6.** landscape, panorama, prospect, view, vista **7.** *Inf.* arena, busi-

ness, environment, field of interest, milieu, world

scenery 1. landscape, surroundings, terrain, view, vista **2.** *Theatre* backdrop, décor, flats, *mise en scène*, set, setting, stage set

scenic beautiful, breathtaking, grand, impressive, panoramic, picturesque, spectacular, striking

scent *n.* **1.** aroma, bouquet, fragrance, odour, perfume, redolence, smell **2.** spoor, track, trail ~*v.* **3.** be on the track *or* trail of, detect, discern, get wind of, nose out, recognize, sense, smell, sniff, sniff out

scented aromatic, fragrant, perfumed, sweet-smelling

sceptic agnostic, cynic, disbeliever, doubter, doubting Thomas, Pyrrhonist, scoffer

sceptical cynical, disbelieving, doubtful, doubting, dubious, hesitating, incredulous, mistrustful, questioning, quizzical, scoffing, unbelieving, unconvinced

scepticism cynicism, disbelief, doubt, incredulity, Pyrrhonism, suspicion

schedule 1. *n.* agenda, calendar, catalogue, inventory, itinerary, list, list of appointments, plan, programme, timetable **2.** *v.* appoint, arrange, be due, book, organize, plan, programme, time

schematic diagrammatic, diagrammatical, graphic, illustrative, representational

schematize arrange, catalogue, categorize, classify, file, grade, methodize, order, pigeonhole, put into order, regulate, sort, standardize, systematize, systemize, tabulate

scheme *n.* **1.** contrivance, course of action, design, device, plan, programme, project, proposal, strategy, system, tactics, theory **2.** arrangement, blueprint, chart, codification, diagram, disposition, draft, layout, outline, pattern, schedule, schema, system **3.** conspiracy, dodge, game (*Inf.*), intrigue, machinations, manoeuvre, plot, ploy, ruse, shift, stratagem, subterfuge ~*v.* **4.** contrive, design, devise, frame, imagine, lay plans, plan, project, work out **5.** collude, conspire, intrigue, machinate, manoeuvre, plot, wheel and deal (*Inf.*)

schemer conniver, deceiver, intriguer, Machiavelli, plotter, slyboots (*Inf.*), wangler (*Inf.*), wheeler-dealer (*Inf.*)

scheming artful, calculating, conniving, cunning, deceitful, designing, duplicitous, foxy, Machiavellian, slippery, sly, tricky, underhand, wily

schism breach, break, discord, disunion, division, rift, rupture, separation, splintering, split

schismatic, schismatical *adj.* discordant, dissentient, dissenting, dissident, heretical, heterodox, seceding, separatist, splinter

scholar 1. academic, bookworm, egghead (*Inf.*), intellectual, man of letters, savant 2. disciple, learner, pupil, schoolboy, schoolgirl, student

scholarly academic, bookish, erudite, intellectual, learned, lettered

scholarship 1. accomplishments, attainments, book-learning, education, erudition, knowledge, learning, lore 2. bursary, exhibition, fellowship

scholastic 1. academic, bookish, learned, lettered, literary, scholarly 2. pedagogic, pedantic, precise

school *n.* 1. academy, alma mater, college, department, discipline, faculty, institute, institution, seminary 2. adherents, circle, class, clique, denomination, devotees, disciples, faction, followers, following, group, pupils, sect, set 3. creed, faith, outlook, persuasion, school of thought, stamp, way of life ~*v.* 4. coach, discipline, drill, educate, indoctrinate, instruct, prepare, prime, train, tutor, verse

schooling 1. book-learning, education, formal education, teaching, tuition 2. coaching, drill, grounding, guidance, instruction, preparation, training

schoolteacher dominie (*Scot.*), instructor, pedagogue, schoolmarm (*Inf.*), schoolmaster, schoolmistress

science 1. body of knowledge, branch of knowledge, discipline 2. art, skill, technique

scientific accurate, controlled, exact, mathematical, precise, systematic

scintillate coruscate, flash, give off sparks, gleam, glint, glisten, glitter, sparkle, twinkle

scintillating animated, bright, brilliant, dazzling, ebullient, exciting, glittering, lively, sparkling, stimulating, witty

scion 1. child, descendant, heir, offspring, successor 2. branch, graft, offshoot, shoot, slip, sprout, twig

scoff[1] belittle, deride, despise, flout, gibe, jeer, knock (*Inf.*), laugh at, make light of, make sport of, mock, poke fun at, pooh-pooh, revile, ridicule, scorn, scout (*Archaic*), sneer, taunt, twit

scoff[2] 1. *v.* bolt, cram, devour, gobble (up), gollop, gorge (cram, stuff) oneself on, gulp down, guzzle, make a pig of oneself on (*Inf.*), put away, wolf 2. *n.* chow (*Inf.*), eats (*Sl.*), fare, feed, food, grub (*Sl.*), meal, nosh (*Sl.*), nosh-up (*Brit. sl.*), rations

scold 1. *v.* bawl out (*Inf.*), berate, blame, bring (someone) to book, castigate, censure, chide, find fault with, give (someone) a dressing-down (row, talking-to) (*Inf.*), go on at (*Inf.*), haul (someone) over the coals (*Inf.*), have (someone) on the carpet (*Inf.*), lecture, nag, rate, rebuke, remonstrate with, reprimand, reproach, reprove, take (someone) to task, tell off (*Inf.*), tick off (*Inf.*), upbraid, vituperate 2. *n.* nag, shrew, termagant (*Rare*), Xanthippe

scolding dressing-down (*Inf.*), (good) talking-to (*Inf.*), lecture, piece of one's mind (*Inf.*), rebuke, row, telling-off (*Inf.*), ticking-off (*Inf.*), tongue-lashing, wigging (*Brit. sl.*)

scoop *n.* 1. dipper, ladle, spoon 2. exclusive, exposé, inside story, revelation, sensation ~*v.* 3. *Often with* up clear away, gather up, lift, pick up, remove, sweep up *or* away, take up 4. bail, dig, dip, empty, excavate, gouge, hollow, ladle, scrape, shovel

scoot bolt, dart, dash, run, scamper, scurry, scuttle, skedaddle (*Inf.*), skirr, skitter, sprint, zip

scope area, capacity, compass, confines, elbowroom, extent, field of reference, freedom, latitude, liberty, opportunity, orbit, outlook, purview, range, reach, room, space, span, sphere

scorch blacken, blister, burn, char, parch, roast, sear, shrivel, singe, wither

scorching baking, boiling, broiling, burning, fiery, flaming, red-hot, roasting, searing, sizzling, sweltering, torrid, tropical, unbearably hot

score *n.* 1. grade, mark, outcome, points, record, result, total 2. **the score** *Inf.* the facts, the reality, the setup (*Inf.*), the situation, the truth 3. *Plural* a flock, a great number, an army, a throng, crowds, droves, hosts, hundreds, legions, lots, masses, millions, multitudes, myriads, swarms, very many **4**. account, basis, cause, ground, grounds, reason **5**. a bone to pick, grievance, grudge, injury, injustice, wrong **6**. **pay off old scores** avenge, get even with (*Inf.*), get one's own back (*Inf.*), give an eye for an eye, give like for like *or* tit for tat, give (someone) a taste of his own medicine, pay (someone) back (in his own coin), repay, requite, retaliate **7**. account, amount due, bill, charge, debt, obligation, reckoning, tab (*U.S. inf.*), tally, total ~*v*. **8**. achieve, amass, chalk up (*Inf.*), gain, make, notch up (*Inf.*), win **9**. count, keep a tally of, keep count, record, register, tally **10**. crosshatch, cut, deface, gouge, graze, indent, mar, mark, nick, notch, scrape, scratch, slash **11**. *With* **out** *or* **through** cancel, cross out, delete, obliterate, put a line through, strike out **12**. *Music* adapt, arrange, orchestrate, set **13**. gain an advantage, go down well with (someone), impress, make a hit (*Inf.*), make an impact *or* impression, make a point, put oneself across, triumph

score off be one up on (*Inf.*), get the better of, have the laugh on, humiliate, make a fool of, make (someone) look silly, worst

scorn 1. *n*. contempt, contemptuousness, contumely, derision, despite, disdain, disparagement, mockery, sarcasm, scornfulness, slight, sneer **2**. *v*. be above, consider beneath one, contemn, curl one's lip at, deride, disdain, flout, hold in contempt, look down on, make fun of, reject, scoff at, scout (*Archaic*), slight, sneer at, spurn, turn up one's nose at (*Inf.*)

scornful contemptuous, contumelious, defiant, derisive, disdainful, haughty, insolent, insulting, jeering, mocking, sarcastic, sardonic, scathing, scoffing, slighting, sneering, supercilious, withering

scornfully contemptuously, disdainfully, dismissively, scathingly, slightingly, with a sneer, with contempt, with disdain, witheringly, with lip curled

scot-free clear, safe, scatheless (*Archaic*), undamaged, unharmed, unhurt, uninjured, unpunished, unscathed, without a scratch

Scots Caledonian, Scottish

scoundrel blackguard, caitiff (*Archaic*), cheat, dastard (*Archaic*), good-for-nothing, heel (*Sl.*), incorrigible, knave

(*Archaic*), miscreant, ne'er-do-well, rascal, reprobate, rogue, rotter (*Sl.*), scamp, scapegrace, vagabond, villain, wretch

scour[1] abrade, buff, burnish, clean, cleanse, flush, furbish, polish, purge, rub, scrub, wash, whiten

scour[2] beat, comb, forage, go over with a fine-tooth comb, hunt, look high and low, rake, ransack, search

scourge *n*. **1**. affliction, bane, curse, infliction, misfortune, penalty, pest, plague, punishment, terror, torment, visitation **2**. cat, cat-o'-nine-tails, lash, strap, switch, thong, whip ~*v*. **3**. beat, belt, cane, castigate, chastise, discipline, flog, horsewhip, lash, lather (*Inf.*), leather, punish, take a strap to, tan (someone's) hide (*Sl.*), thrash, trounce, wallop (*Inf.*), whale, whip **4**. afflict, curse, excoriate, harass, plague, terrorize, torment

scout *v*. **1**. case (*Sl.*), check out, investigate, make a reconnaissance, observe, probe, reconnoitre, see how the land lies, spy, spy out, survey, watch **2**. *Often with* **out, up,** *or* **around** cast around for, ferret out, hunt for, look for, rustle up, search for, search out, seek, track down ~*n*. **3**. advance guard, escort, lookout, outrider, precursor, reconnoitrer, vanguard **4**. recruiter, talent scout

scowl 1. *v*. frown, glower, look daggers at, lower **2**. *n*. black look, dirty look, frown, glower

scrabble clamber, claw, dig, grope, paw, scramble, scrape, scratch

scraggy 1. angular, bony, emaciated, gangling, gaunt, lanky, lean, rawboned, scrawny, skinny, undernourished **2**. draggletailed (*Archaic*), grotty (*Brit. sl.*), lank, meagre, rough, scanty, scruffy, tousled, unkempt

scram beat it (*Sl.*), clear off (*Inf.*), depart, disappear, get lost (*Inf.*), go away, leave, make oneself scarce (*Inf.*), make tracks, quit, scarper (*Brit. sl.*), scoot, skedaddle (*Inf.*), take oneself off, vamoose (*Sl., chiefly U.S.*)

scramble *v*. **1**. clamber, climb, crawl, move with difficulty, push, scrabble, struggle, swarm **2**. contend, hasten, jockey for position, jostle, look lively *or* snappy (*Inf.*), make haste, push, run, rush, strive, vie ~*n*. **3**. climb, trek **4**. commotion, competition, confusion, free-for-all (*Inf.*), hassle (*Inf.*), hustle, melee, muddle, race, rat race, rush, struggle, tussle

scrap[1] *n*. **1**. atom, bit, bite, crumb,

fragment, grain, iota, mite, modicum, morsel, mouthful, part, particle, piece, portion, sliver, snatch, snippet, trace **2.** junk, off cuts, waste **3. on the scrap heap** discarded, ditched (*Sl.*), jettisoned, put out to grass (*Inf.*), redundant, written off **4.** *Plural* bits, leavings, leftovers, remains, scrapings ~*v.* **5.** abandon, break up, demolish, discard, dispense with, ditch (*Sl.*), drop, get rid of, jettison, junk (*Inf.*), shed, throw away *or* out, throw on the scrapheap, toss out, write off

scrap² **1.** *n.* argument, battle, brawl, disagreement, dispute, dust-up (*Inf.*), fight, quarrel, row, scuffle, set-to (*Inf.*), squabble, tiff, wrangle **2.** *v.* argue, bicker, come to blows, fall out (*Inf.*), fight, have a shouting match (*Inf.*), have words, row, squabble, wrangle

scrape *v.* **1.** abrade, bark, graze, rub, scratch, scuff, skin **2.** grate, grind, rasp, scratch, screech, set one's teeth on edge, squeak **3.** clean, erase, file, remove, rub, scour **4.** pinch, save, scrimp, skimp, stint **5. scrape by, in, through** barely make it, cut it fine (*Inf.*), get by (*Inf.*), have a close shave (*Inf.*), struggle ~*n.* **6.** *Inf.* awkward *or* embarrassing situation, difficulty, dilemma, distress, fix (*Inf.*), mess, plight, predicament, pretty pickle (*Inf.*), tight spot (*Inf.*), trouble

scrape together amass, dredge up, get hold of, glean, hoard, muster, rake up *or* together, save

scrappy bitty, disjointed, fragmentary, incomplete, perfunctory, sketchy, thrown together

scratch *v.* **1.** claw, cut, damage, etch, grate, graze, incise, lacerate, make a mark on, mark, rub, score, scrape **2.** annul, cancel, delete, eliminate, erase, pull out, stand down, strike off, withdraw ~*n.* **3.** blemish, claw mark, gash, graze, laceration, mark, scrape **4. up to scratch** acceptable, adequate, capable, competent, satisfactory, sufficient, up to snuff (*Inf.*), up to standard ~*adj.* **5.** haphazard, hastily prepared, impromptu, improvised, rough, rough-and-ready

scrawl doodle, scrabble, scratch, scribble, squiggle

scrawny angular, bony, gaunt, lanky, lean, rawboned, scraggy, skeletal, skin-and-bones, skinny, thin, undernourished

scream *v.* **1.** bawl, cry, holler (*Inf.*), screech, shriek, shrill, sing out, squeal, yell **2.** *Fig.* be conspicuous, clash, jar,

shriek ~*n.* **3.** howl, outcry, screech, shriek, wail, yell, yelp **4.** *Inf.* card (*Inf.*), caution (*Inf.*), character (*Inf.*), comedian, comic, entertainer, hoot (*Brit. inf.*), joker, laugh, riot (*Sl.*), sensation, wit

screech cry, scream, shriek, squawk, squeal, yelp

screen *v.* **1.** cloak, conceal, cover, hide, mask, shade, shroud, shut out, veil **2.** defend, guard, protect, safeguard, shelter, shield **3.** cull, evaluate, examine, filter, gauge, grade, process, riddle, scan, sieve, sift, sort, vet **4.** broadcast, present, put on, show ~*n.* **5.** awning, canopy, cloak, concealment, cover, guard, hedge, mantle, shade, shelter, shield, shroud **6.** mesh, net, partition, room divider

screw *v.* **1.** tighten, turn, twist, work in **2.** contort, contract, crumple, distort, pucker, wrinkle **3.** *Inf.* bring pressure to bear on, coerce, constrain, force, hold a knife to (someone's) throat, oppress, pressurize, put the screws on (*Inf.*), squeeze **4.** *Inf. Often with* **out of** bleed, extort, extract, wrest, wring

screwed up anxious, apprehensive, confused, edgy, in a mess, keyed up, mixed up, nervous, neurotic, on edge, strung up (*Inf.*), tense, uptight (*Sl.*), worked up, worried

screw up 1. contort, contract, crumple, distort, knot, pucker, wrinkle **2.** *Inf.* bitch (up) (*Sl.*), botch, bungle, louse up (*Sl.*), make a hash of (*Inf.*), make a mess *or* muck-up of (*Sl.*), mess up, mishandle, mismanage, queer (*Inf.*), spoil

screwy batty (*Sl.*), cracked (*Sl.*), crackers (*Brit. sl.*), crazy, dotty (*Sl.*), eccentric, nutty (*Sl.*), odd, queer, round the bend (*Brit. sl.*), weird

scribble *v.* dash off, doodle, jot, pen, scratch, scrawl, write

scribe amanuensis, clerk, copyist, notary (*Archaic*), penman (*Rare*), scrivener (*Archaic*), secretary, writer

scrimmage affray (*Law*), bovver (*Brit. sl.*), brawl, disturbance, dust-up (*Inf.*), fight, fray, free-for-all (*Inf.*), melee, riot, row, scrap (*Inf.*), scuffle, set-to (*Inf.*), shindy (*Sl.*), skirmish, squabble, struggle

scrimp be frugal, curtail, economize, limit, pinch, pinch pennies, reduce, save, scrape, shorten, skimp, stint, straiten

script **1.** calligraphy, hand, handwriting, letters, longhand, penmanship, writing **2.** book, copy, dialogue, libretto, lines, manuscript, text, words

Scripture Holy Bible, Holy Scripture, Holy Writ, The Bible, The Book of Books, The Good Book, The Gospels, The Scriptures, The Word, The Word of God

scroll inventory, list, parchment, roll

Scrooge meanie (*Inf.*), miser, money-grubber (*Inf.*), niggard, penny-pincher (*Inf.*), skinflint, tightwad (*U.S. sl.*)

scrounge beg, bum (*Inf., chiefly U.S.*), cadge, forage for, freeload (*U.S. sl.*), hunt around (for), sorn (*Scot.*), sponge (*Inf.*), wheedle

scrounger cadger, freeloader (*U.S. sl.*), parasite, sorner (*Scot.*), sponger (*Inf.*)

scrub v. 1. clean, cleanse, rub, scour 2. *Inf.* abandon, abolish, call off, cancel, delete, discontinue, do away with, drop, forget about, give up

scrubby insignificant, meagre, paltry, scrawny, spindly, stunted, underdeveloped, undersized

scruff 1. nape, scrag (*Inf.*) 2. *Inf.* ragamuffin, ragbag (*Inf.*), scarecrow, sloven, tatterdemalion (*Rare*), tramp

scruffy disreputable, draggletailed (*Archaic*), frowzy, ill-groomed, mangy, messy, ragged, run-down, scrubby (*Brit. inf.*), seedy, shabby, slatternly, slovenly, sluttish, squalid, tattered, ungroomed, unkempt, untidy

scrumptious appetizing, delectable, delicious, exquisite, inviting, luscious, magnificent, moreish (*Inf.*), mouth-watering, succulent, yummy (*Sl.*)

scrunch champ, chew, crumple, crunch, crush, mash, ruck up, squash

scruple 1. v. balk at, be loath, be reluctant, demur, doubt, falter, have misgivings about, have qualms about, hesitate, stick at, think twice about, vacillate, waver 2. n. caution, compunction, difficulty, doubt, hesitation, misgiving, perplexity, qualm, reluctance, second thoughts, squeamishness, twinge of conscience, uneasiness

scrupulous careful, conscientious, exact, fastidious, honourable, meticulous, minute, moral, nice, painstaking, precise, principled, punctilious, rigorous, strict, upright

scrutinize analyse, dissect, examine, explore, inquire into, inspect, investigate, peruse, pore over, probe, scan, search, sift, study

scrutiny analysis, close study, examination, exploration, inquiry, inspection, investigation, perusal, search, sifting, study

scud blow, fly, haste, hasten, race, sail, shoot, skim, speed

scuffle 1. v. clash, come to blows, contend, exchange blows, fight, grapple, jostle, struggle, tussle 2. n. affray (*Law*), brawl, commotion, disturbance, fight, fray, ruck (*Sl.*), ruckus (*Inf.*), ruction (*Inf.*), rumpus, scrap (*Inf.*), set-to (*Inf.*), tussle

sculpture v. carve, chisel, cut, fashion, form, hew, model, mould, sculp, sculpt, shape

scum 1. algae, crust, dross, film, froth, impurities, offscourings, scruff 2. *Fig. canaille*, dregs of society, lowest of the low, rabble, ragtag and bobtail, riffraff, rubbish, trash (*Chiefly U.S.*)

scupper defeat, demolish, destroy, disable, discomfit, overthrow, overwhelm, put paid to, ruin, torpedo, wreck

scurrility abusiveness, billingsgate, coarseness, grossness, indecency, infamousness, invective, obloquy, obscenity, offensiveness, scurrilousness, vituperation

scurrilous abusive, coarse, defamatory, foul, foul-mouthed, gross, indecent, infamous, insulting, low, obscene, offensive, Rabelaisian, ribald, salacious, scabrous, scandalous, slanderous, vituperative, vulgar

scurry 1. v. dart, dash, fly, hurry, race, scamper, scoot, scud, scuttle, skim, sprint, whisk 2. n. bustle, flurry, scampering, whirl

scurvy adj. abject, bad, base, contemptible, despicable, dishonourable, ignoble, low, low-down (*Inf.*), mean, pitiful, rotten, scabby (*Inf.*), shabby, sorry, vile, worthless

scuttle bustle, hare (*Brit. inf.*), hasten, hurry, run, rush, scamper, scoot, scramble, scud, scurry, scutter (*Brit. inf.*)

sea n. 1. main, ocean, the briny (*Inf.*), the deep, the drink (*Inf.*), the waves 2. *Fig.* abundance, expanse, mass, multitude, plethora, profusion, sheet, vast number 3. **at sea** adrift, astray, at a loss, at sixes and sevens, baffled, bewildered, confused, disoriented, lost, mystified, puzzled, upset ~adj. 4. aquatic, briny, marine, maritime, ocean, ocean-going, oceanic, pelagic, salt, saltwater, seagoing

seafaring marine, maritime, nautical, naval, oceanic

seal v. **1.** close, cork, enclose, fasten, make airtight, plug, secure, shut, stop, stopper, stop up, waterproof **2.** assure, attest, authenticate, confirm, establish, ratify, stamp, validate **3.** clinch, conclude, consummate, finalize, settle, shake hands on (*Inf.*) **4.** *With* **off** board up, fence off, isolate, put out of bounds, quarantine, segregate ~n. **5.** assurance, attestation, authentication, confirmation, imprimatur, insignia, notification, ratification, stamp

seam n. **1.** closure, joint, suture (*Surgery*) **2.** layer, lode, stratum, vein **3.** furrow, line, ridge, scar, wrinkle

seamy corrupt, dark, degraded, disagreeable, disreputable, low, nasty, rough, sordid, squalid, unpleasant, unwholesome

sear blight, brand, burn, cauterize, desiccate, dry up *or* out, scorch, seal, shrivel, sizzle, wilt, wither

search v. **1.** cast around, check, comb, examine, explore, ferret, frisk (*Inf.*), go over with a fine-tooth comb, inquire, inspect, investigate, leave no stone unturned, look, look high and low, probe, pry, ransack, rifle through, rummage through, scour, scrutinize, seek, sift, turn inside out, turn upside down ~n. **2.** examination, exploration, going-over (*Inf.*), hunt, inquiry, inspection, investigation, pursuit, quest, researches, rummage, scrutiny **3. in search of** hunting for, in need of, in pursuit of, looking for, making enquiries concerning, on the lookout for, on the track of, seeking

searching adj. close, intent, keen, minute, penetrating, piercing, probing, quizzical, severe, sharp, thorough

seasickness *mal de mer*

season n. **1.** division, interval, juncture, occasion, opportunity, period, spell, term, time, time of year ~v. **2.** colour, enliven, flavour, lace, leaven, pep up, salt, salt and pepper, spice **3.** acclimatize, accustom, anneal, discipline, habituate, harden, inure, mature, prepare, toughen, train **4.** mitigate, moderate, qualify, temper

seasonable appropriate, convenient, fit, opportune, providential, suitable, timely, welcome, well-timed

seasoned battle-scarred, experienced, hardened, long-serving, mature, old, practised, time-served, veteran, weathered, well-versed

seasoning condiment, dressing, flavouring, relish, salt and pepper, sauce, spice

seat n. **1.** bench, chair, pew, settle, stall, stool **2.** axis, capital, centre, cradle, headquarters, heart, hub, location, place, site, situation, source, station **3.** base, bed, bottom, cause, footing, foundation, ground, groundwork **4.** abode, ancestral hall, house, mansion, residence **5.** chair, constituency, incumbency, membership, place ~v. **6.** accommodate, cater for, contain, have room *or* capacity for, hold, sit, take **7.** deposit, fix, install, locate, place, set, settle, sit

seating accommodation, chairs, places, room, seats

secede apostatize, break with, disaffiliate, leave, pull out, quit, resign, retire, separate, split from, withdraw

secession apostasy, break, defection, disaffiliation, seceding, split, withdrawal

secluded cloistered, cut off, isolated, lonely, off the beaten track, out-of-the-way, private, reclusive, remote, retired, sequestered, sheltered, solitary, tucked away, unfrequented

seclusion concealment, hiding, isolation, privacy, remoteness, retirement, retreat, shelter, solitude

second[1] adj. **1.** following, next, subsequent, succeeding **2.** additional, alternative, extra, further, other, repeated **3.** inferior, lesser, lower, secondary, subordinate, supporting **4.** double, duplicate, reproduction, twin ~n. **5.** assistant, backer, helper, supporter ~v. **6.** advance, aid, approve, assist, back, encourage, endorse, forward, further, give moral support to, go along with, help, promote, support

second[2] n. flash, instant, jiffy (*Inf.*), minute, moment, sec (*Inf.*), split second, tick (*Brit. inf.*), trice, twinkling, twinkling of an eye, two shakes of a lamb's tail (*Inf.*)

secondary **1.** derivative, derived, indirect, resultant, resulting, second-hand **2.** consequential, contingent, inferior, lesser, lower, minor, second-rate, subordinate, unimportant **3.** alternate, auxiliary, backup, extra, relief, reserve, second, subsidiary, supporting

second childhood caducity, dotage, senility

second class *adj.* déclassé, indifferent, inferior, mediocre, outclassed, second-best, second-rate, undistinguished, uninspiring

second-hand 1. *adj.* handed down, hand-me-down (*Inf.*), nearly new, reach-me-down (*Inf.*), used **2.** *adv.* at second-hand, indirectly, on the grapevine (*Inf.*)

second in command depute (*Scot.*), deputy, number two, right-hand man, successor designate

secondly in the second place, next, second

second-rate cheap, cheap and nasty (*Inf.*), commonplace, inferior, low-grade, low-quality, mediocre, poor, rubbishy, shoddy, substandard, tacky (*Inf.*), tawdry

secrecy 1. concealment, confidentiality, huggermugger (*Rare*), mystery, privacy, retirement, seclusion, silence, solitude, surreptitiousness **2.** clandestineness, covertness, furtiveness, secretiveness, stealth

secret *adj.* **1.** backstairs, camouflaged, cloak-and-dagger, close, closet (*Inf.*), concealed, conspiratorial, covered, covert, disguised, furtive, hidden, hole-and-corner (*Inf.*), hush-hush (*Inf.*), reticent, shrouded, undercover, underground, under wraps, undisclosed, unknown, unpublished, unrevealed, unseen **2.** abstruse, arcane, cabbalistic, clandestine, classified, cryptic, esoteric, mysterious, occult, recondite **3.** hidden, out-of-the-way, private, retired, secluded, unfrequented, unknown **4.** close, deep, discreet, reticent, secretive, sly, stealthy, underhand ~*n.* **5.** code, confidence, enigma, formula, key, mystery, recipe, skeleton in the cupboard **6. in secret** behind closed doors, by stealth, huggermugger (*Archaic*), in camera, incognito, secretly, slyly, surreptitiously

secret agent cloak-and-dagger man, spook (*U.S. sl.*), spy, undercover agent

secrete[1] bury, cache, conceal, cover, disguise, harbour, hide, screen, secure, shroud, stash away (*Inf.*), stow, veil

secrete[2] emanate, emit, extravasate (*Medical*), extrude, exude, give off

secretion discharge, emission, excretion, extravasation (*Medical*), exudation

secretive cagey (*Inf.*), clamlike, close, cryptic, deep, enigmatic, playing one's cards close to one's chest, reserved, reticent, tight-lipped, uncommunicative, unforthcoming, withdrawn

secretly behind closed doors, behind (someone's) back, clandestinely, confidentially, covertly, furtively, in camera, in confidence, in one's heart, in one's inmost thoughts, in secret, on the q.t. (*Inf.*), on the sly, privately, quietly, stealthily, surreptitiously, unobserved

sect camp, denomination, division, faction, group, party, school, school of thought, splinter group, wing

sectarian 1. *adj.* bigoted, clannish, cliquish, doctrinaire, dogmatic, exclusive, factional, fanatic, fanatical, hidebound, insular, limited, narrow-minded, parochial, partisan, rigid **2.** *n.* adherent, bigot, disciple, dogmatist, extremist, fanatic, partisan, true believer, zealot

section *n.* **1.** component, cross section, division, fraction, fragment, instalment, part, passage, piece, portion, sample, segment, slice, subdivision **2.** *Chiefly U.S.* area, department, district, region, sector, zone

sectional divided, exclusive, factional, local, localized, partial, regional, separate, separatist

sector area, category, district, division, part, quarter, region, stratum, subdivision, zone

secular civil, earthly, laic, laical, lay, nonspiritual, profane, state, temporal, worldly

secure *adj.* **1.** immune, impregnable, out of harm's way, protected, safe, sheltered, shielded, unassailable, undamaged, unharmed **2.** dependable, fast, fastened, firm, fixed, fortified, immovable, stable, steady, tight **3.** assured, certain, confident, easy, reassured, sure **4.** absolute, conclusive, definite, in the bag (*Inf.*), reliable, solid, steadfast, tried and true, well-founded ~*v.* **5.** acquire, come by, gain, get, get hold of, land (*Inf.*), make sure of, obtain, pick up, procure, win possession of **6.** attach, batten down, bolt, chain, fasten, fix, lash, lock, lock up, make fast, moor, padlock, rivet, tie up **7.** assure, ensure, guarantee, insure

security 1. asylum, care, cover, custody, immunity, preservation, protection, refuge, retreat, safekeeping, safety, sanctuary **2.** defence, guards, precautions, protection, safeguards, safety measures, surveillance **3.** assurance, certainty, confidence, conviction, ease of mind, freedom from doubt, positiveness, reliance, sureness **4.** collateral, gage, guarantee, hostage, insurance, pawn, pledge, surety

sedate calm, collected, composed, cool, decorous, deliberate, demure, dignified, earnest, grave, imperturbable, middle-aged, placid, proper, quiet, seemly, serene, serious, slow-moving, sober, solemn, staid, tranquil, unflappable (*Inf.*), unruffled

sedative 1. *adj.* allaying, anodyne, calmative, calming, lenitive, relaxing, sleep-inducing, soothing, soporific, tranquillizing **2.** *n.* anodyne, calmative, downer *or* down (*Sl.*), narcotic, opiate, sleeping pill, tranquillizer

sedentary desk, desk-bound, inactive, motionless, seated, sitting, torpid

sediment deposit, dregs, grounds, lees, precipitate, residuum, settlings

sedition agitation, disloyalty, incitement to riot, rabble-rousing, subversion, treason

seditious disloyal, dissident, insubordinate, mutinous, rebellious, refractory, revolutionary, subversive, treasonable

seduce 1. betray, corrupt, debauch, deflower, deprave, dishonour, ruin (*Archaic*) **2.** allure, attract, beguile, deceive, decoy, ensnare, entice, inveigle, lead astray, lure, mislead, tempt

seduction 1. corruption, defloration, ruin (*Archaic*) **2.** allure, enticement, lure, snare, temptation

seductive alluring, attractive, beguiling, bewitching, captivating, come-hither (*Inf.*), enticing, flirtatious, inviting, irresistible, provocative, ravishing, sexy (*Inf.*), siren, specious, tempting

seductress Circe, enchantress, *femme fatale*, Lorelei, siren, temptress, vamp (*Inf.*)

sedulous assiduous, busy, conscientious, constant, diligent, industrious, laborious, painstaking, persevering, persistent, tireless, unflagging, unremitting

see[1] *v.* **1.** behold, catch a glimpse of, catch sight of, descry, discern, distinguish, espy, get a load of (*Sl.*), glimpse, heed, identify, lay *or* clap eyes on (*Inf.*), look, make out, mark, note, notice, observe, perceive, recognize, regard, sight, spot, view, witness **2.** appreciate, catch on (*Inf.*), comprehend, fathom, feel, follow, get, get the drift of, get the hang of (*Inf.*), grasp, know, make out, realize, take in, understand **3.** ascertain, deter-

mine, discover, find out, investigate, learn, make enquiries, refer to **4.** ensure, guarantee, make certain, make sure, mind, see to it, take care **5.** consider, decide, deliberate, give some thought to, judge, make up one's mind, mull over, reflect, think over **6.** confer with, consult, encounter, interview, meet, receive, run into, speak to, visit **7.** accompany, attend, escort, lead, show, usher, walk **8.** consort *or* associate with, court, date (*Inf., chiefly U.S.*), go out with, go steady with (*Inf.*), keep company with, walk out with (*Obsolete*) **9.** anticipate, divine, envisage, foresee, foretell, imagine, picture, visualize

see[2] *n.* bishopric, diocese

see about 1. attend to, consider, deal with, give some thought to, look after, see to, take care of **2.** investigate, look into, make enquiries

seed 1. egg, egg cell, embryo, germ, grain, kernel, ovule, ovum, spore **2.** beginning, germ, inkling, nucleus, source, start, suspicion **3.** *Fig.* children, descendants, heirs, issue, offspring, progeny, race, scions, spawn, successors **4. go** *or* **run to seed** decay, decline, degenerate, deteriorate, go downhill (*Inf.*), go to pieces, go to pot, go to rack and ruin, go to waste, let oneself go

seedy 1. crummy (*Sl.*), decaying, dilapidated, down at heel, faded, grubby, mangy, manky (*Scot. dialect*), old, run-down, scruffy (*Brit. inf.*), shabby, sleazy, slovenly, squalid, tatty, unkempt, worn **2.** *Inf.* ailing, ill, off colour, out of sorts, poorly (*Inf.*), sickly, under the weather (*Inf.*), unwell

seeing *conj.* as, inasmuch as, in view of the fact that, since

seek 1. be after, follow, go gunning for, go in pursuit (quest, search) of, hunt, inquire, look for, pursue, search for **2.** aim, aspire to, attempt, endeavour, essay, have a go (*Inf.*), strive, try **3.** ask, beg, entreat, inquire, invite, petition, request, solicit

seem appear, assume, give the impression, have the *or* every appearance of, look, look as if, look to be, pretend, sound like, strike one as being

seeming *adj.* apparent, appearing, illusory, ostensible, outward, quasi-, specious, surface

seemingly apparently, as far as anyone could tell, on the face of it, on the surface, ostensibly, outwardly, to all appearances, to all intents and purposes

seemly appropriate, becoming, befitting, *comme il faut*, decent, decorous, fit, fitting, in good taste, meet (*Archaic*), nice, proper, suitable, suited, the done thing

see over inspect, look round, see round, tour

seep bleed, leach, leak, ooze, percolate, permeate, soak, trickle, weep, well

seepage exudation, leak, leakage, oozing, percolation

seer augur, predictor, prophet, sibyl, soothsayer

seesaw *v.* alternate, fluctuate, go from one extreme to the other, oscillate, pitch, swing, teeter

seethe 1. boil, bubble, churn, ferment, fizz, foam, froth 2. be in a state (*Inf.*), be livid (furious, incensed), breathe fire and slaughter, foam at the mouth, fume, get hot under the collar (*Inf.*), rage, simmer, storm 3. be alive with, swarm, teem

seethrough diaphanous, filmy, gauzy, gossamer, sheer, translucent, transparent

see through 1. be undeceived by, be wise to, fathom, get to the bottom of, have (someone's) number (*Inf.*), not fall for, penetrate 2. **see (something** or **someone) through** help out, keep at, persevere (with), persist, see out, stay to the bitter end, stick by, stick out (*Inf.*), support

see to arrange, attend to, be responsible for, do, look after, manage, organize, sort out, take care of, take charge of

segment bit, compartment, division, part, piece, portion, section, slice, wedge

segregate discriminate against, dissociate, isolate, separate, set apart, single out

segregation apartheid (*in South Africa*), discrimination, isolation, separation

seize 1. clutch, collar (*Inf.*), fasten, grab, grasp, grip, lay hands on, snatch, take 2. apprehend, catch, get, grasp 3. abduct, annex, appropriate, arrest, capture, commandeer, confiscate, hijack, impound, take by storm, take captive, take possession of

seizure 1. abduction, annexation, apprehension, arrest, capture, commandeering, confiscation, grabbing, taking 2. attack, convulsion, fit, paroxysm, spasm

seldom hardly ever, infrequently, not often, occasionally, once in a blue moon (*Inf.*), rarely, scarcely ever

select *v.* 1. choose, opt for, pick, prefer, single out, sort out ~*adj.* 2. choice, excellent, first-class, first-rate, hand-picked, picked, posh (*Inf.*), preferable, prime, rare, recherché, selected, special, superior, topnotch (*Inf.*) 3. cliquish, elite, exclusive, limited, privileged

selection 1. choice, choosing, option, pick, preference 2. anthology, assortment, choice, collection, line-up, medley, miscellany, potpourri, range, variety

selective careful, discerning, discriminating, discriminatory, eclectic, particular

self-assurance assertiveness, confidence, positiveness, self-confidence

self-centred egotistic, inward looking, narcissistic, self-absorbed, selfish, self-seeking, wrapped up in oneself

self-confidence aplomb, confidence, high morale, nerve, poise, self-assurance, self-reliance, self-respect

self-confident assured, fearless, poised, secure, self-assured, self-reliant, sure of oneself

self-conscious affected, awkward, bashful, diffident, embarrassed, ill at ease, insecure, nervous, out of countenance, shamefaced, sheepish, uncomfortable

self-control restraint, self-discipline, self-mastery, self-restraint, strength of mind or will, willpower

self-denial abstemiousness, asceticism, renunciation, self-abnegation, selflessness, self-sacrifice, unselfishness

self-esteem *amour-propre*, confidence, faith in oneself, pride, self-assurance, self-regard, self-respect, vanity

self-evident axiomatic, clear, incontrovertible, inescapable, manifestly or patently true, obvious, undeniable, written all over (something)

self-government autonomy, home rule, independence, self-determination, self-rule, sovereignty

self-important arrogant, conceited, overbearing, pompous, presumptuous, pushy (*Inf.*), strutting, swaggering, swollen-headed

self-indulgence dissipation, excess, extravagance, incontinence, intemperance, self-gratification, sensualism

selfish egoistic, egoistical, egotistic,

egotistical, greedy, looking out for number one (*Inf.*), mean, mercenary, narrow,
self-centred, self-interested, self-seeking,
ungenerous

selfless altruistic, generous, magnanimous, self-denying, self-sacrificing, ungrudging, unselfish

self-possessed collected, confident,
cool, cool as a cucumber (*Inf.*), poised,
self-assured, sure of oneself, together
(*Sl.*), unruffled

self-possession aplomb, composure,
confidence, cool (*Sl.*), poise, sang-froid,
self-command, unflappability (*Inf.*)

self-reliant able to stand on one's own
two feet (*Inf.*), capable, independent,
self-sufficient

self-respect *amour-propre*, dignity,
faith in oneself, morale, one's own image,
pride, self-esteem

self-restraint abstemiousness, forbearance, patience, self-command, self-
control, self-discipline, willpower

self-righteous complacent, goody-
goody (*Inf.*), holier-than-thou, hypocritical, pharisaic, pi (*Brit. sl.*), pietistic, pious, priggish, sanctimonious, self-
satisfied, smug, superior, too good to be
true

self-sacrifice altruism, generosity,
self-abnegation, self-denial, selflessness

self-satisfaction complacency, contentment, ease of mind, flush of success,
glow of achievement, pride, self-
approbation, self-approval, smugness

self-satisfied complacent, flushed
with success, like a cat that has swallowed the cream *or* the canary, pleased
with oneself, proud of oneself, puffed up,
self-congratulatory, smug, well-pleased

self-seeking *adj.* acquisitive, calculating, careerist, fortune-hunting, gold-
digging, lookin out for number one
(*Inf.*), mercenary, on the make (*Sl.*), op-
portunistic, out for what one can get,
self-interested, selfish, self-serving

self-styled *soi-disant*, professed,
quasi-, self-appointed, so-called, would-
be

self-willed cussed (*Inf.*), headstrong,
intractable, obstinate, opinionated, pig-
headed, refractory, stiff-necked, stubborn, stubborn as a mule, ungovernable,
wilful

sell 1. barter, dispose of, exchange, put
up for sale, trade **2.** be in the business of,
deal in, handle, hawk, market, merchan-

dise, peddle, retail, stock, trade in, traffic
in, vend **3.** gain acceptance for, promote,
put across **4.** *Inf.* With **on** convert to,
convince of, get (someone) hooked on
(*Inf.*), persuade of, talk (someone) into,
win (someone) over to **5.** betray, deliver
up, give up, sell down the river (*Inf.*), sell
out (*Inf.*), surrender

seller agent, dealer, merchant, rep,
representative, retailer, salesman, sales-
woman, shopkeeper, tradesman, traveller, vendor

selling 1. business, commercial transactions, dealing, trading, traffic **2.** marketing, merchandising, promotion, salesmanship

sell out 1. be out of stock of, dispose
of, get rid of, run out of, sell up **2.** *Inf.*
betray, break faith with, double-cross
(*Inf.*), fail, give away, play false, rat on,
sell down the river (*Inf.*), stab in the
back

semblance air, appearance, aspect,
bearing, façade, figure, form, front,
guise, image, likeness, mask, mien, pretence, resemblance, show, similarity, veneer

semidarkness dusk, gloaming, gloom,
half-light, murk, twilight, waning light

seminal *Fig.* creative, formative, imaginative, important, influential, innovative, original, productive

seminary academy, college, high
school, institute, institution, school

send 1. communicate, consign, convey,
direct, dispatch, forward, remit, transmit **2.** cast, deliver, fire, fling, hurl, let
fly, propel, shoot **3.** *With* **off, out,** *etc.*
broadcast, discharge, emit, exude, give
off, radiate **4.** *Sl.* charm, delight, electrify, enrapture, enthrall, excite, intoxicate,
move, please, ravish, stir, thrill, titillate,
turn (someone) on (*Sl.*) **5. send (someone) packing** discharge, dismiss, give
(someone) the bird (*Inf.*), give (someone)
the brushoff (*Sl.*), send away, send
(someone) about his *or* her business,
send (someone) away with a flea in his *or*
her ear (*Inf.*)

send for call for, order, request, summon

sendoff departure, farewell, going-
away party, leave-taking, start, valediction

send-up imitation, mockery, parody,
satire, skit, spoof (*Inf.*), take-off (*Inf.*)

send up burlesque, imitate, lampoon,

make fun of, mimic, mock, parody, satirize, spoof (*Inf.*), take off (*Inf.*), take the mickey out of (*Inf.*)

senile decrepit, doddering, doting, failing, imbecile, in one's dotage, in one's second childhood

senility caducity, decrepitude, dotage, infirmity, loss of one's faculties, second childhood, senescence, senile dementia

senior *adj.* elder, higher ranking, major (*Brit.*), older, superior

senior citizen elder, O.A.P., old *or* elderly person, old age pensioner, pensioner, retired person

seniority eldership, longer service, precedence, priority, rank, superiority

sensation 1. awareness, consciousness, feeling, impression, perception, sense, tingle **2.** agitation, commotion, crowd puller (*Inf.*), excitement, furore, hit (*Inf.*), scandal, stir, surprise, thrill, wow (*Sl., chiefly U.S.*)

sensational 1. amazing, astounding, breathtaking, dramatic, electrifying, exciting, hair-raising, horrifying, lurid, melodramatic, revealing, scandalous, sensationalistic, shocking, spectacular, staggering, startling, thrilling, yellow (*of the press*) **2.** *Inf.* excellent, exceptional, fabulous (*Inf.*), first class, impressive, marvellous, mind-blowing (*Inf.*), out of this world (*Inf.*), smashing (*Inf.*), superb

sense *n.* **1.** faculty, feeling, sensation, sensibility **2.** appreciation, atmosphere, aura, awareness, consciousness, feel, impression, intuition, perception, premonition, presentiment, sentiment **3.** definition, denotation, drift, gist, implication, import, interpretation, meaning, message, nuance, purport, significance, signification, substance **4.** *Sometimes plural* brains (*Inf.*), clear-headedness, cleverness, common sense, discernment, discrimination, gumption (*Brit. inf.*), intelligence, judgment, mother wit, nous (*Brit. sl.*), quickness, reason, sagacity, sanity, sharpness, tact, understanding, wisdom, wit(s) **5.** advantage, good, logic, point, purpose, reason, use, value, worth ~*v.* **6.** appreciate, apprehend, be aware of, discern, divine, feel, get the impression, grasp, have a feeling in one's bones (*Inf.*), have a funny feeling (*Inf.*), have a hunch, just know, notice, observe, perceive, pick up, realize, suspect, understand

senseless 1. absurd, asinine, crazy,

daft (*Inf.*), fatuous, foolish, halfwitted, idiotic, illogical, imbecilic, inane, incongruous, inconsistent, irrational, ludicrous, mad, meaningless, mindless, moronic, nonsensical, pointless, ridiculous, silly, simple, stupid, unintelligent, unreasonable, unwise **2.** anaesthetized, cold, deadened, insensate, insensible, numb, numbed, out, out cold, stunned, unconscious, unfeeling

sensibility 1. responsiveness, sensitiveness, sensitivity, susceptibility **2.** *Often plural* emotions, feelings, moral sense, sentiments, susceptibilities **3.** appreciation, awareness, delicacy, discernment, insight, intuition, perceptiveness, taste

sensible 1. canny, discreet, discriminating, down-to-earth, far-sighted, intelligent, judicious, matter-of-fact, practical, prudent, rational, realistic, reasonable, sagacious, sage, sane, shrewd, sober, sound, well-reasoned, well-thought-out, wise **2.** *Usually with* of acquainted with, alive to, aware, conscious, convinced, mindful, observant, sensitive to, understanding **3.** appreciable, considerable, discernable, noticeable, palpable, perceptible, significant, tangible, visible

sensitive 1. acute, delicate, easily affected, fine, impressionable, keen, perceptive, precise, reactive, responsive, sentient, susceptible **2.** delicate, easily upset (hurt, offended), irritable, temperamental, tender, thin-skinned, touchy, umbrageous (*Rare*)

sensitivity delicacy, reactiveness, reactivity, receptiveness, responsiveness, sensitiveness, susceptibility

sensual 1. animal, bodily, carnal, epicurean, fleshly, luxurious, physical, unspiritual, voluptuous **2.** erotic, lascivious, lecherous, lewd, libidinous, licentious, lustful, randy (*Sl.*), raunchy (*U.S. sl.*), sexual, sexy (*Inf.*), unchaste

sensualist *bon vivant*, bon viveur, epicure, epicurean, hedonist, pleasure-lover, sybarite, voluptuary

sensuality animalism, carnality, eroticism, lasciviousness, lecherousness, lewdness, libidinousness, licentiousness, prurience, salaciousness, sexiness (*Inf.*), voluptuousness

sensuous epicurean, gratifying, hedonistic, lush, pleasurable, rich, sensory, sumptuous, sybaritic

sentence 1. *n.* condemnation, decision, decree, doom, judgment, order, pronouncement, ruling, verdict **2.** *v.* condemn, doom, mete out justice to, pass judgment on, penalize

sententious 1. aphoristic, axiomatic, brief, compact, concise, epigrammatic, gnomic, laconic, pithy, pointed, short, succinct, terse **2.** canting, judgmental, moralistic, pompous, ponderous, preachifying (*Inf.*), sanctimonious

sentient conscious, live, living, reactive, sensitive

sentiment 1. emotion, sensibility, soft-heartedness, tender feeling, tenderness **2.** *Often plural* attitude, belief, feeling, idea, judgment, opinion, persuasion, saying, thought, view, way of thinking **3.** emotionalism, mawkishness, overemotionalism, romanticism, sentimentality, slush (*Inf.*)

sentimental corny (*Sl.*), dewy-eyed, drippy (*Inf.*), emotional, gushy (*Inf.*), impressionable, maudlin, mawkish, mushy (*Inf.*), nostalgic, overemotional, pathetic, romantic, schmaltzy (*Sl.*), simpering, sloppy (*Inf.*), slushy (*Inf.*), softhearted, tearful, tear-jerking (*Inf.*), tender, touching, weepy (*Inf.*)

sentimentality bathos, corniness (*Sl.*), emotionalism, gush (*Inf.*), mawkishness, mush (*Inf.*), nostalgia, play on the emotions, romanticism, schmaltz (*Sl.*), sloppiness (*Inf.*), slush (*Inf.*), sob stuff (*Inf.*), tenderness

sentinel *or* **sentry** guard, lookout, picket, watch, watchman

separable detachable, distinguishable, divisible, scissile, severable

separate *v.* **1.** break off, cleave, come apart, come away, come between, detach, disconnect, disentangle, disjoin, divide, keep apart, remove, sever, split, sunder, uncouple **2.** discriminate between, isolate, put on one side, segregate, single out, sort out **3.** bifurcate, break up, disunite, diverge, divorce, estrange, go different ways, part, part company, set at variance *or* at odds, split up ∼*adj.* **4.** detached, disconnected, discrete, disjointed, divided, divorced, isolated, unattached, unconnected **5.** alone, apart, autonomous, distinct, independent, individual, particular, single, solitary

separated apart, broken up, disassociated, disconnected, disunited, divided, living apart, parted, put asunder, separate, split up, sundered

separately alone, apart, independently, individually, one at a time, one by one, personally, severally, singly

separation 1. break, detachment, disconnection, disengagement, disjunction, dissociation, disunion, division, gap, segregation, severance **2.** break-up, divorce, estrangement, farewell, leave-taking, parting, rift, split, split-up

septic festering, infected, poisoned, pussy, putrefactive, putrefying, putrid, toxic

sepulchral 1. cheerless, dismal, funereal, gloomy, grave, lugubrious, melancholy, morbid, mournful, sad, sombre, Stygian, woeful **2.** deep, hollow, lugubrious, reverberating, sonorous

sepulchre burial place, grave, tomb, vault

sequel conclusion, consequence, continuation, development, end, follow-up, issue, outcome, payoff (*Inf.*), result, upshot

sequence arrangement, chain, course, cycle, order, procession, progression, series, succession

sequestered cloistered, isolated, lonely, out-of-the-way, private, quiet, remote, retired, secluded, unfrequented

seraphic angelic, beatific, blissful, celestial, divine, heavenly, holy, pure, sublime

serene 1. calm, composed, imperturbable, peaceful, placid, tranquil, undisturbed, unruffled, untroubled **2.** bright, clear, cloudless, fair, halcyon, unclouded

serenity 1. calm, calmness, composure, peace, peacefulness, peace of mind, placidity, quietness, quietude, stillness, tranquillity **2.** brightness, clearness, fairness

serf bondsman, helot, servant, slave, thrall, villein

series arrangement, chain, course, line, order, progression, run, sequence, set, string, succession, train

serious 1. grave, humourless, long-faced, pensive, sedate, sober, solemn, stern, thoughtful, unsmiling **2.** deliberate, determined, earnest, genuine, honest, in earnest, resolute, resolved, sincere **3.** crucial, deep, difficult, far-reaching, fateful, grim, important, momentous, no laughing matter, of moment *or* consequence, pressing, significant, urgent, weighty, worrying **4.** acute, alarming, critical, dangerous, grave, severe

seriously 1. all joking aside, earnestly, gravely, in all conscience, in earnest, no joking (*Inf.*), sincerely, solemnly, thoughtfully, with a straight face **2.** acutely, badly, critically, dangerously, distressingly, gravely, grievously, severely, sorely

seriousness 1. earnestness, gravity, humourlessness, sedateness, sobriety, solemnity, staidness, sternness **2.** danger, gravity, importance, moment, significance, urgency, weight

sermon 1. address, exhortation, homily **2.** dressing-down (*Inf.*), harangue, lecture, talking-to (*Inf.*)

serpentine coiling, crooked, meandering, sinuous, snaking, snaky, tortuous, twisting, winding

serrated notched, sawlike, sawtoothed, serrate, serriform (*Biol.*), serrulate, toothed

serried assembled, close, compact, dense, massed, phalanxed

servant attendant, domestic, drudge, help, helper, lackey, maid, menial, retainer, servitor (*Archaic*), slave, vassal

serve 1. aid, assist, attend to, be in the service of, be of assistance, be of use, help, minister to, oblige, succour, wait on, work for **2.** act, attend, complete, discharge, do, fulfil, go through, observe, officiate, pass, perform **3.** answer, answer the purpose, be acceptable, be adequate, be good enough, content, do, do duty as, do the work of, fill the bill (*Inf.*), function as, satisfy, suffice, suit **4.** arrange, deal, deliver, dish up, distribute, handle, present, provide, set out, supply

service *n.* **1.** advantage, assistance, avail, benefit, help, ministrations, supply, use, usefulness, utility **2.** check, maintenance, overhaul, servicing **3.** business, duty, employ, employment, labour, office, work **4.** ceremony, function, observance, rite, worship ~*v.* **5.** check, fine .tune, go over, maintain, overhaul, recondition, repair, tune (up)

serviceable advantageous, beneficial, convenient, dependable, durable, efficient, functional, hard-wearing, helpful, operative, practical, profitable, usable, useful, utilitarian

servile abject, base, bootlicking (*Inf.*), craven, cringing, fawning, grovelling, humble, low, mean, menial, obsequious, slavish, submissive, subservient, sycophantic, toadying, toadyish, unctuous

servility abjection, baseness, bootlicking (*Inf.*), fawning, grovelling, meanness, obsequiousness, self-abasement, slavishness, submissiveness, subservience, sycophancy, toadyism, unctuousness

serving *n.* helping, plateful, portion

servitude bondage, bonds, chains, enslavement, obedience, serfdom, slavery, subjugation, thraldom, thrall, vassalage

session assembly, conference, discussion, get-together (*Inf.*), hearing, meeting, period, sitting, term

set¹ *v.* **1.** aim, apply, deposit, direct, embed, fasten, fix, install, lay, locate, lodge, mount, park, place, plant, plonk, plump, position, put, rest, seat, situate, station, stick, turn **2.** agree upon, allocate, appoint, arrange, assign, conclude, decide (upon), designate, determine, establish, fix, fix up, name, ordain, regulate, resolve, schedule, settle, specify **3.** arrange, lay, make ready, prepare, spread **4.** adjust, coordinate, rectify, regulate, synchronize **5.** cake, condense, congeal, crystallize, gelatinize, harden, jell, solidify, stiffen, thicken **6.** allot, decree, impose, lay down, ordain, prescribe, specify **7.** decline, dip, disappear, go down, sink, subside, vanish ~*n.* **8.** attitude, bearing, carriage, fit, hang, position, posture, turn **9.** *mise-en-scène*, scene, scenery, setting, stage set, stage setting ~*adj.* **10.** agreed, appointed, arranged, customary, decided, definite, established, firm, fixed, prearranged, predetermined, prescribed, regular, scheduled, settled, usual **11.** artificial, conventional, formal, hackneyed, rehearsed, routine, standard, stereotyped, stock, traditional, unspontaneous **12.** entrenched, firm, hard and fast, hardened, hidebound, immovable, inflexible, rigid, strict, stubborn **13.** *With* **on** *or* **upon** bent, determined, intent, resolute

set² *n.* **1.** band, circle, class, clique, company, coterie, crew (*Inf.*), crowd, faction, gang, group, outfit (*Inf.*), sect **2.** assemblage, assortment, batch, collection, compendium, coordinated group, kit, outfit, series

set about 1. address oneself to, attack, begin, get cracking (*Inf.*), get down to (*Inf.*), get to work, get weaving (*Inf.*), make a start on, put one's shoulder to the wheel (*Inf.*), roll up one's sleeves, sail into (*Inf.*), set to, start, tackle, take the first step, wade into **2.** assail, assault, at-

tack, belabour, lambaste, sail into (Inf.)
set against 1. balance, compare, contrast, juxtapose, weigh **2.** alienate, disunite, divide, drive a wedge between, estrange, make bad blood, make mischief, oppose, set at cross purposes, set at odds, set by the ears (Inf.), sow dissension
set aside 1. keep, keep back, put on one side, reserve, save, select, separate, set apart, single out **2.** abrogate, annul, cancel, discard, dismiss, nullify, overrule, overturn, quash, reject, render null and void, repudiate, reverse
setback bit of trouble, blow, check, defeat, disappointment, hitch, hold-up, misfortune, rebuff, reverse, upset
set back delay, hinder, hold up, impede, retard, slow
set off 1. depart, embark, leave, sally forth, set out, start out **2.** detonate, explode, ignite, light, set in motion, touch off **3.** bring out the highlights in, enhance, show off, throw into relief
set on assail, assault, attack, fall upon, fly at, go for, incite, instigate, let fly at, pitch into, pounce on, sail into (Inf.), set about, sic, spur on, urge
set out 1. arrange, array, describe, detail, display, dispose, elaborate, elucidate, exhibit, explain, expose to view, lay out, present, set forth **2.** begin, embark, get under way, hit the road (Sl.), sally forth, set off, start out, take to the road
setting backdrop, background, context, frame, locale, location, mise en scène, mounting, perspective, scene, scenery, set, site, surround, surroundings
settle 1. adjust, dispose, order, put into order, regulate, set to rights, straighten out, work out **2.** choose, clear up, complete, conclude, decide, dispose of, put an end to, reconcile, resolve **3.** Often with **on** or **upon** agree, appoint, arrange, choose, come to an agreement, confirm, decide, determine, establish, fix **4.** calm, compose, lull, pacify, quell, quiet, quieten, reassure, relax, relieve, sedate, soothe, tranquillize **5.** alight, bed down, come to rest, descend, land, light, make oneself comfortable **6.** dwell, inhabit, live, make one's home, move to, put down roots, reside, set up home, take up residence **7.** colonize, found, people, pioneer, plant, populate **8.** acquit oneself of, clear, discharge, liquidate, pay, quit, square (up) **9.** decline, fall, sink, subside

settlement 1. adjustment, agreement, arrangement, completion, conclusion, confirmation, disposition, establishment, resolution, termination, working out **2.** clearance, clearing, defrayal, discharge, liquidation, payment, satisfaction **3.** colonization, colony, community, encampment, hamlet, outpost, peopling
settler colonist, colonizer, frontiersman, immigrant, pioneer, planter
set-to argument, argy-bargy (Brit. inf.), barney (Inf.), brush, disagreement, dust-up (Inf.), fight, quarrel, row, scrap (Inf.), slanging match (Brit.), spat, squabble, wrangle
setup arrangement, circumstances, conditions, organization, regime, structure, system
set up 1. arrange, begin, compose, establish, found, initiate, install, institute, make provision for, organize, prearrange, prepare **2.** back, build up, establish, finance, promote, put some beef into (Inf.), strengthen, subsidize **3.** assemble, build, construct, elevate, erect, put together, put up, raise
set upon ambush, assail, assault, attack, beat up, fall upon, go for, lay into, mug (Inf.), set about, turn on
sever 1. bisect, cleave, cut, cut in two, detach, disconnect, disjoin, disunite, divide, part, rend, separate, split, sunder **2.** abandon, break off, dissociate, dissolve, put an end to, terminate
several adj. assorted, different, disparate, distinct, divers (Archaic), diverse, indefinite, individual, many, particular, respective, single, some, sundry, various
severe 1. austere, cruel, Draconian, hard, harsh, inexorable, iron-handed, oppressive, pitiless, relentless, rigid, strict, unbending, unrelenting **2.** cold, disapproving, dour, flinty, forbidding, grave, grim, serious, sober, stern, strait-laced, tight-lipped, unsmiling **3.** acute, bitter, critical, dangerous, distressing, extreme, fierce, grinding, inclement, intense, violent **4.** ascetic, austere, chaste, classic, forbidding, functional, plain, restrained, simple, Spartan, unadorned, unembellished, unfussy **5.** arduous, demanding, difficult, exacting, fierce, hard, punishing, rigorous, stringent, taxing, tough, unrelenting **6.** astringent, biting, caustic, cutting, harsh, satirical, scathing, unsparing

severely 1. harshly, rigorously, sharply, sternly, strictly, with an iron hand, with a rod of iron **2**. acutely, badly, critically, dangerously, extremely, gravely, hard, sorely

severity austerity, gravity, hardness, harshness, plainness, rigour, seriousness, severeness, sternness, strictness, stringency, toughness

sex 1. gender **2**. *Inf*. coition, coitus, copulation, fornication, going to bed (with someone), intimacy, lovemaking, (sexual) intercourse, sexual relations **3**. desire, facts of life, libido, reproduction, sexuality, the birds and the bees (*Inf.*)

sex appeal allure, desirability, glamour, it (*Inf.*), magnetism, oomph (*Inf.*), seductiveness, sensuality, sexiness (*Inf.*), voluptuousness

sexless androgynous, asexual, epicene, hermaphrodite, neuter, nonsexual, parthenogenetic

sexual 1. carnal, erotic, intimate, of the flesh, sensual **2**. genital, procreative, reproductive, sex, venereal

sexual intercourse carnal knowledge, coition, coitus, commerce (*Archaic*), congress, copulation, coupling, mating, union

sexuality bodily appetites, carnality, desire, eroticism, lust, sensuality, sexiness (*Inf.*), voluptuousness

sexy arousing, beddable, bedroom, come-hither (*Inf.*), cuddly, erotic, flirtatious, inviting, kissable, naughty, provocative, provoking, seductive, sensual, sensuous, slinky, suggestive, titillating, voluptuous

shabby 1. dilapidated, down at heel, faded, frayed, having seen better days, mean, neglected, poor, ragged, rundown, scruffy, seedy, tattered, tatty, the worse for wear, threadbare, worn, worn-out **2**. cheap, contemptible, despicable, dirty, dishonourable, ignoble, low, low-down (*Inf.*), mean, rotten (*Inf.*), scurvy, shameful, shoddy, ungentlemanly, unworthy

shack cabin, dump (*Inf.*), hovel, hut, lean-to, shanty, shiel (*Scot.*), shieling (*Scot.*)

shackle *n*. **1**. *Often plural* bond, chain, fetter, gyve (*Archaic*), handcuff, hobble, iron, leg-iron, manacle, rope, tether ~*v*. **2**. bind, chain, fetter, handcuff, hobble, manacle, pinion, put in irons, secure, tether, tie, trammel **3**. con-

strain, embarrass, encumber, hamper, hamstring, impede, inhibit, limit, obstruct, restrain, restrict, tie (someone's) hands

shade *n*. **1**. coolness, dimness, dusk, gloom, gloominess, obscurity, screen, semidarkness, shadiness, shadow, shadows **2**. **put into the shade** eclipse, make pale by comparison, outclass, outshine, overshadow **3**. blind, canopy, cover, covering, curtain, screen, shield, veil **4**. colour, hue, stain, tinge, tint, tone **5**. amount, dash, degree, difference, gradation, hint, nuance, semblance, suggestion, suspicion, trace, variety **6**. apparition, ghost, manes, phantom, shadow, spectre, spirit ~*v*. **7**. cast a shadow over, cloud, conceal, cover, darken, dim, hide, mute, obscure, protect, screen, shadow, shield, shut out the light, veil

shadow *n*. **1**. cover, darkness, dimness, dusk, gathering darkness, gloaming, gloom, obscurity, protection, shade, shelter **2**. hint, suggestion, suspicion, trace **3**. ghost, image, phantom, remnant, representation, spectre, vestige **4**. blight, cloud, gloom, sadness ~*v*. **5**. cast a shadow over, darken, overhang, screen, shade, shield **6**. dog, follow, spy on, stalk, tail (*Inf.*), trail

shadowy 1. crepuscular, dark, dim, dusky, gloomy, indistinct, murky, obscure, shaded, shady, tenebrious, tenebrous **2**. dim, dreamlike, faint, ghostly, illusory, imaginary, impalpable, intangible, nebulous, obscure, phantom, spectral, undefined, unreal, unsubstantial, vague, wraithlike

shady 1. bosky (*Literary*), bowery, cool, dim, leafy, shaded, shadowy, umbrageous **2**. *Inf*. crooked, disreputable, dubious, fishy (*Inf.*), questionable, shifty, slippery, suspect, suspicious, unethical, unscrupulous, untrustworthy

shaft 1. handle, pole, rod, shank, stem, upright **2**. beam, gleam, ray, streak **3**. barb, cut, dart, gibe, sting, thrust

shaggy hairy, hirsute, long-haired, rough, unkempt, unshorn

shake *v*. **1**. bump, fluctuate, jar, joggle, jolt, jounce, oscillate, quake, quiver, rock, shiver, shudder, sway, totter, tremble, vibrate, waver, wobble **2**. brandish, flourish, wave **3**. *Often with* **up** agitate, churn, convulse, rouse, stir **4**. discompose, distress, disturb, frighten, intimidate, move, rattle (*Inf.*), shock, unnerve, upset **5**. impair, pull the rug out from under (*Inf.*), undermine, weaken ~*n.* **6**. agitation, convulsion, disturbance, jar, jerk, jolt, jounce, pulsation, quaking, shiver, shock, shudder, trembling, tremor, vibration **7**. *Inf.* instant, jiffy (*Inf.*), moment, second, tick (*Brit. inf.*), trice

shake off dislodge, elude, get away from, get rid of, get shot of (*Sl.*), give the slip, leave behind, lose, rid oneself of, throw off

shake up agitate, churn (up), disturb, mix, overturn, reorganize, shock, stir (up), turn upside down, unsettle, upset

shaky 1. all of a quiver (*Inf.*), faltering, insecure, precarious, quivery, rickety, tottering, trembling, tremulous, unstable, unsteady, weak, wobbly **2**. dubious, questionable, suspect, uncertain, undependable, unreliable, unsound, unsupported

shallow 1. *adj. Fig.* empty, flimsy, foolish, frivolous, idle, ignorant, meaningless, puerile, simple, skin-deep, slight, superficial, surface, trivial, unintelligent **2**. *n. Often plural* bank, flat, sandbank, sand bar, shelf, shoal

sham 1. *n.* counterfeit, feint, forgery, fraud, hoax, humbug, imitation, impostor, imposture, phoney (*Sl.*), pretence, pretender, pseud (*Sl.*), wolf in sheep's clothing **2**. *adj.* artificial, bogus, counterfeit, ersatz, false, feigned, imitation, mock, phoney (*Sl.*), pretended, pseud (*Sl.*), pseudo (*Inf.*), simulated, spurious, synthetic **3**. *v.* affect, assume, counterfeit, fake, feign, imitate, play possum, pretend, put on, simulate

shambles anarchy, chaos, confusion, disarray, disorder, disorganization, havoc, madhouse, mess, muddle

shambling awkward, clumsy, lumbering, lurching, shuffling, ungainly, unsteady

shambolic anarchic, at sixes and sevens, chaotic, confused, disordered, disorganized, inefficient, in total disarray, muddled, topsy-turvy, unsystematic

shame *n.* **1**. blot, contempt, degradation, derision, disgrace, dishonour, disrepute, ill repute, infamy, obloquy, odium, opprobrium, reproach, scandal, skeleton in the cupboard, smear **2**. abashment, chagrin, compunction, embarrassment, humiliation, ignominy, loss of face, mortification, shamefacedness **3**. **put to shame** disgrace, eclipse, outclass, outdo,

outstrip, show up, surpass ~*v.* **4**. abash, confound, disconcert, disgrace, embarrass, humble, humiliate, mortify, reproach, ridicule, take (someone) down a peg (*Inf.*) **5**. blot, debase, defile, degrade, discredit, dishonour, smear, stain

shamefaced 1. bashful, blushing, diffident, hesitant, modest, shrinking, shy, timid **2**. abashed, ashamed, chagrined, conscience-stricken, contrite, discomfited, embarrassed, humiliated, mortified, red-faced, remorseful, sheepish

shameful 1. atrocious, base, dastardly, degrading, disgraceful, dishonourable, ignominious, indecent, infamous, low, mean, outrageous, reprehensible, scandalous, unbecoming, unworthy, vile, wicked **2**. blush-making (*Inf.*), degrading, embarrassing, humiliating, mortifying, shaming

shameless abandoned, audacious, barefaced, brash, brazen, corrupt, depraved, dissolute, flagrant, hardened, immodest, improper, impudent, incorrigible, indecent, insolent, profligate, reprobate, unabashed, unashamed, unblushing, unprincipled, wanton

shanty cabin, hovel, hut, lean-to, shack, shed, shiel (*Scot.*), shieling (*Scot.*)

shape *n.* **1**. build, configuration, contours, cut, figure, form, lines, make, outline, profile, silhouette **2**. frame, model, mould, pattern **3**. appearance, aspect, form, guise, likeness, semblance **4**. condition, fettle, health, kilter, state, trim ~*v.* **5**. create, fashion, form, make, model, mould, produce **6**. accommodate, adapt, define, develop, devise, frame, guide, modify, plan, prepare, regulate, remodel

shapeless amorphous, asymmetrical, battered, embryonic, formless, indeterminate, irregular, misshapen, nebulous, undeveloped, unstructured

shapely comely, curvaceous, elegant, graceful, neat, sightly, trim, well-formed, well-proportioned, well-turned

shape up be promising, come on, develop, look good, proceed, progress, turn out

share 1. *v.* apportion, assign, distribute, divide, go Dutch (*Inf.*), go fifty-fifty (*Inf.*), go halves, parcel out, partake, participate, receive, split, use in common **2**. *n.* allotment, allowance, contribution, cut (*Inf.*), division, due, lot, part, portion, proportion, quota, ration, whack (*Inf.*)

sharp *adj.* **1.** acute, cutting, honed, jagged, keen, knife-edged, knifelike, pointed, razor-sharp, serrated, sharpened, spiky **2.** abrupt, distinct, extreme, marked, sudden **3.** alert, apt, astute, bright, clever, discerning, knowing, longheaded, observant, penetrating, perceptive, quick, quick-witted, ready, subtle **4.** artful, crafty, cunning, dishonest, fly (*Sl.*), shrewd, sly, smart, unscrupulous, wily **5.** acute, distressing, excruciating, fierce, intense, painful, piercing, severe, shooting, sore, stabbing, stinging, violent **6.** clear, clear-cut, crisp, distinct, welldefined **7.** *Inf.* chic, classy (*Sl.*), dressy, fashionable, natty (*Inf.*), smart, snappy, stylish **8.** acrimonious, barbed, biting, bitter, caustic, cutting, harsh, hurtful, sarcastic, sardonic, scathing, severe, trenchant, vitriolic **9.** acerbic, acid, acrid, burning, hot, piquant, pungent, sour, tart, vinegary ~*adv.* **10.** exactly, on the dot, on time, precisely, promptly, punctually **11.** abruptly, suddenly, unexpectedly, without warning

sharpen edge, grind, hone, put an edge on, strop, whet

shatter **1.** break, burst, crack, crush, crush to smithereens, demolish, explode, implode, pulverize, shiver, smash, split **2.** blast, blight, bring to nought, demolish, destroy, disable, exhaust, impair, overturn, ruin, torpedo, wreck **3.** break (someone's) heart, crush, devastate, dumbfound, knock the stuffing out of (someone) (*Inf.*), upset

shattered all in (*Sl.*), crushed, dead beat (*Inf.*), devastated, dog-tired (*Inf.*), done in (*Inf.*), exhausted, ready to drop, tired out, worn out

shattering crushing, devastating, overwhelming, paralysing, severe, stunning

shave *v.* **1.** crop, pare, plane, shear, trim **2.** brush, graze, touch

shed *v.* **1.** afford, cast, diffuse, drop, emit, give, give forth, pour forth, radiate, scatter, shower, spill, throw **2.** cast off, discard, exuviate, moult, slough

sheen brightness, burnish, gleam, gloss, lustre, patina, polish, shine, shininess

sheepish abashed, chagrined, embarrassed, foolish, mortified, self-conscious, shamefaced, silly, uncomfortable

sheer **1.** abrupt, headlong (*Archaic*), perpendicular, precipitous, steep **2.** absolute, arrant, complete, downright, outand-out, pure, rank, thoroughgoing, total, unadulterated, unalloyed, unmitigated, unqualified, utter **3.** *Of fabrics* diaphanous, fine, gauzy, gossamer, seethrough, thin, transparent

sheet **1.** coat, film, folio, lamina, layer, leaf, membrane, overlay, pane, panel, piece, plate, slab, stratum, surface, veneer **2.** area, blanket, covering, expanse, stretch, sweep

shell *n.* **1.** carapace, case, husk, pod ~*v.* **2.** husk, shuck **3.** attack, barrage, blitz, bomb, bombard, strafe, strike ~*n.* **4.** chassis, frame, framework, hull, skeleton, structure

shell out ante up (*Inf.*, *chiefly U.S.*), disburse, expend, fork out (*Sl.*), give, hand over, lay out (*Inf.*), pay out

shelter **1.** *v.* cover, defend, guard, harbour, hide, protect, safeguard, seek refuge, shield, take in, take shelter **2.** *n.* asylum, cover, covert, defence, guard, haven, protection, refuge, retreat, roof over one's head, safety, sanctuary, screen, security, shiel (*Scot.*), umbrella

sheltered cloistered, conventual, ensconced, hermitic, isolated, protected, quiet, reclusive, retired, screened, secluded, shaded, shielded, withdrawn

shelve defer, dismiss, freeze, hold in abeyance, hold over, lay aside, mothball, pigeonhole, postpone, put aside, put off, put on ice, table (*U.S.*)

shepherd *v.* conduct, convoy, guide, herd, marshal, steer, usher

shield *n.* **1.** buckler, escutcheon (*Heraldry*), targe (*Archaic*) **2.** aegis, bulwark, cover, defence, guard, protection, rampart, safeguard, screen, shelter, ward (*Archaic*) ~*v.* **3.** cover, defend, guard, protect, safeguard, screen, shelter, ward off

shift *v.* **1.** alter, budge, change, displace, fluctuate, move, move around, rearrange, relocate, remove, reposition, swerve, switch, transfer, transpose, vary, veer **2.** *As in* shift for oneself assume responsibility, contrive, devise, fend, get along, look after, make do, manage, plan, scheme, take care of ~*n.* **3.** about-turn, alteration, change, displacement, fluctuation, modification, move, permutation, rearrangement, removal, shifting, switch, transfer, veering **4.** artifice, contrivance, craft, device, dodge, equivocation, evasion, expedient, move, resource, ruse, stratagem, subterfuge, trick, wile

shiftless aimless, good-for-nothing, idle, incompetent, indolent, inefficient, inept, irresponsible, lackadaisical, lazy, slothful, unambitious, unenterprising

shifty contriving, crafty, deceitful, devious, duplicitous, evasive, fly-by-night (*Inf.*), furtive, scheming, slippery, tricky, underhand, unprincipled, untrustworthy, wily

shillyshally v. be irresolute *or* indecisive, dilly-dally (*Inf.*), dither, falter, fluctuate, haver (*Brit.*), hem and haw, hesitate, seesaw, swither (*Scot. dialect*), vacillate, waver, yo-yo (*Inf.*)

shimmer 1. v. dance, gleam, glisten, phosphoresce, scintillate, twinkle 2. n. diffused light, gleam, glimmer, glow, incandescence, iridescence, lustre, phosphorescence, unsteady light

shin v. ascend, clamber, climb, scale, scramble, swarm

shine v. 1. beam, emit light, flash, give off light, glare, gleam, glimmer, glisten, glitter, glow, radiate, scintillate, shimmer, sparkle, twinkle 2. be conspicuous (distinguished, outstanding, preeminent), excel, stand out, stand out in a crowd, star 3. brush, buff, burnish, polish, rub up ~n. 4. brightness, glare, gleam, lambency, light, luminosity, radiance, shimmer, sparkle 5. glaze, gloss, lustre, patina, polish, sheen

shining 1. beaming, bright, brilliant, effulgent, gleaming, glistening, glittering, luminous, radiant, resplendent, shimmering, sparkling 2. *Fig.* brilliant, celebrated, conspicuous, distinguished, eminent, glorious, illustrious, leading, outstanding, splendid

shiny agleam, bright, burnished, gleaming, glistening, glossy, lustrous, nitid (*Poetic*), polished, satiny, sheeny

shipshape Bristol fashion, businesslike, neat, orderly, spick-and-span, tidy, trig (*Archaic*), trim, uncluttered, well-ordered, well-organized, well-regulated

shirk avoid, dodge, duck (out of) (*Inf.*), evade, get out of, scrimshank (*Brit. military sl.*), shun, sidestep, skive (*Brit. sl.*), slack

shirker clock-watcher, dodger, gold brick (*U.S. sl.*), idler, malingerer, quitter, scrimshanker (*Brit. military sl.*), shirk, skiver (*Brit. sl.*), slacker

shiver[1] v. 1. palpitate, quake, quiver, shake, shudder, tremble ~n. 2. flutter, *frisson*, quiver, shudder, thrill, tremble, trembling, tremor 3. **the shivers** chattering teeth, chill, goose flesh, goose pimples, the shakes (*Inf.*)

shiver[2] v. break, crack, fragment, shatter, smash, smash to smithereens, splinter

shivery chilled, chilly, cold, quaking, quivery, shaking, trembly

shoal sandbank, sand bar, shallow, shelf

shock v. 1. agitate, appal, astound, disgust, disquiet, give (someone) a turn (*Inf.*), horrify, jar, jolt, nauseate, numb, offend, outrage, paralyse, revolt, scandalize, shake, shake out of one's complacency, shake up (*Inf.*), sicken, stagger, stun, stupefy, traumatize, unsettle ~n. 2. blow, bolt from the blue, bombshell, breakdown, collapse, consternation, distress, disturbance, prostration, state of shock, stupefaction, stupor, trauma, turn (*Inf.*), upset 3. blow, clash, collision, encounter, impact, jarring, jolt

shocking abominable, appalling, atrocious, detestable, disgraceful, disgusting, disquieting, distressing, dreadful, foul, frightful, ghastly, hideous, horrible, horrifying, loathsome, monstrous, nauseating, odious, offensive, outrageous, repulsive, revolting, scandalous, sickening, stupefying, unspeakable

shoddy cheap-jack (*Inf.*), inferior, junky, poor, rubbishy, second-rate, slipshod, tacky (*Inf.*), tatty, tawdry, trashy

shoemaker bootmaker, cobbler, souter (*Scot.*)

shoot[1] v. 1. bag, blast (*Sl.*), bring down, hit, kill, open fire, pick off, plug (*Sl.*), pump full of lead (*Sl.*), zap (*Sl.*) 2. discharge, emit, fire, fling, hurl, launch, let fly, project, propel 3. bolt, charge, dart, dash, flash, fly, hurtle, race, rush, scoot, speed, spring, streak, tear, whisk, whiz (*Inf.*)

shoot[2] 1. n. branch, bud, offshoot, scion, slip, sprig, sprout, twig 2. v. bud, burgeon, germinate, put forth new growth, sprout

shore 1. n. beach, coast, foreshore, lakeside, sands, seaboard (*Chiefly U.S.*), seashore, strand (*Poetic*), waterside 2. adj. littoral

shore (**up**) brace, buttress, hold, prop, reinforce, strengthen, support, underpin

short *adj.* **1.** abridged, brief, compendious, compressed, concise, curtailed, laconic, pithy, sententious, succinct, summary, terse **2.** diminutive, dumpy, little, low, petite, small, squat, wee **3.** brief, fleeting, momentary, short-lived, short-term **4.** *Often with* **of** deficient, inadequate, insufficient, lacking, limited, low (on), meagre, poor, scant, scanty, scarce, short-handed, slender, slim, sparse, tight, wanting **5.** abrupt, blunt, brusque, crusty, curt, discourteous, gruff, impolite, offhand, sharp, terse, testy, uncivil **6.** direct, straight **7.** *Of pastry* brittle, crisp, crumbly, friable ~*adv.* **8.** abruptly, by surprise, suddenly, unaware, without warning **9. cut short** abbreviate, arrest, butt in, curtail, cut in on, dock, halt, interrupt, reduce, stop, terminate **10. fall short** be inadequate, disappoint, fail, fall down on (*Inf.*), not come up to expectations *or* scratch (*Inf.*) **11. in short** briefly, in a nutshell, in a word, in essence, to come to the point, to cut a long story short, to put it briefly **12. short of a.** apart from, except, other than, unless **b.** deficient in, in need of, lacking, low (on), missing, wanting

shortage dearth, deficiency, deficit, failure, inadequacy, insufficiency, lack, leanness, paucity, poverty, scarcity, shortfall, want

shortcoming defect, drawback, failing, fault, flaw, frailty, imperfection, weakness, weak point

shorten abbreviate, abridge, curtail, cut, cut back, cut down, decrease, diminish, dock, lessen, reduce, trim, turn up

short-lived brief, ephemeral, fleeting, impermanent, passing, short, temporary, transient, transitory

shortly 1. anon (*Archaic*), any minute now, before long, in a little while, presently, soon **2.** abruptly, curtly, sharply, tartly, tersely **3.** briefly, concisely, in a few words, succinctly

short-sighted 1. myopic, near-sighted **2.** careless, ill-advised, ill-considered, impolitic, impractical, improvident, imprudent, injudicious, unthinking

short-staffed below strength, short-handed, undermanned, understaffed

short-tempered choleric, fiery, hot-tempered, impatient, irascible, peppery, quick-tempered, ratty (*Brit. sl.*), testy, touchy

shot¹ *n.* **1.** discharge, lob, pot shot, throw **2.** ball, bullet, lead, pellet, projectile, slug **3.** marksman, shooter **4.** *Inf.* attempt, chance, conjecture, crack (*Inf.*), effort, endeavour, essay, go, guess, opportunity, stab, surmise, try, turn **5. by a long shot a.** by far, easily, far and away, indubitably, undoubtedly, without doubt **b.** by any means, in any circumstances, on any account **6. have a shot** *Inf.* attempt, have a go (bash (*Inf.*), crack (*Inf.*), stab), tackle, try, try one's luck **7. like a shot** at once, eagerly, immediately, like a flash, quickly, unhesitatingly **8. shot in the arm** *Inf.* boost, encouragement, fillip, impetus, lift, stimulus

shot² *adj.* iridescent, moiré, watered

shoulder *n.* **1. give (someone) the cold shoulder** cut (*Inf.*), ignore, ostracize, rebuff, shun, snub **2. put one's shoulder to the wheel** *Inf.* apply oneself, buckle down to (*Inf.*), exert oneself, get down to, make every effort, set to work, strive **3. rub shoulders with** *Inf.* associate with, consort with, fraternize with, hobnob with, mix with, socialize with **4. shoulder to shoulder** as one, in cooperation, in partnership, in unity, jointly, side by side, together, united **5. straight from the shoulder** candidly, directly, frankly, man to man, outright, plainly, pulling no punches (*Inf.*), straight, unequivocally, with no holds barred ~*v.* **6.** accept, assume, bear, be responsible for, carry, take on, take upon oneself **7.** elbow, jostle, press, push, shove, thrust

shoulder blade scapula

shout 1. *n.* bellow, call, cry, roar, scream, yell **2.** *v.* bawl, bay, bellow, call (out), cry (out), holler (*Inf.*), hollo, raise one's voice, roar, scream, yell

shout down drown, drown out, overwhelm, silence

shove *v.* crowd, drive, elbow, impel, jostle, press, propel, push, shoulder, thrust

shovel *v.* convey, dredge, heap, ladle, load, move, scoop, shift, spoon, toss

shove off clear off (*Inf.*), depart, go away, leave, push off (*Inf.*), scram (*Inf.*), take oneself off, vamoose (*Inf., chiefly U.S.*)

show *v.* **1.** appear, be visible, disclose, display, divulge, evidence, evince, exhibit, indicate, make known, manifest, present, register, reveal, testify to **2.** assert, clarify, demonstrate, elucidate, evince, explain, instruct, point out, present, prove, teach **3.** accompany, attend, conduct, escort, guide, lead **4.** accord, act with, bestow, confer, grant ~*n.* **5.** array, demonstration, display, exhibition, expo (*Inf.*), exposition, fair, manifestation, pageant, pageantry, parade, representation, sight, spectacle, view **6.** affectation, air, appearance, display, illusion, likeness, ostentation, parade, pose, pretence, pretext, profession, semblance **7.** entertainment, presentation, production

showdown breaking point, clash, climax, confrontation, crisis, culmination, exposé, moment of truth

shower *n.* **1.** *Fig.* barrage, deluge, fusillade, plethora, rain, stream, torrent, volley **2.** *Brit. sl.* bunch of layabouts, crew, rabble ~*v.* **3.** deluge, heap, inundate, lavish, load, pour, rain, spray, sprinkle

showing *n.* **1.** display, exhibition, presentation, staging **2.** account of oneself, appearance, impression, performance, show, track record **3.** evidence, representation, statement

showman entertainer, impresario, performer, publicist, stage manager

show-off boaster, braggadocio, braggart, egotist, exhibitionist, swaggerer

show off **1.** advertise, demonstrate, display, exhibit, flaunt, parade, spread out **2.** boast, brag, make a spectacle of oneself, shoot a line (*Inf.*), swagger

show up **1.** expose, highlight, lay bare, pinpoint, put the spotlight on, reveal, unmask **2.** appear, be conspicuous, be visible, catch the eye, leap to the eye, stand out **3.** *Inf.* embarrass, let down, mortify, put to shame, shame, show in a bad light **4.** *Inf.* appear, arrive, come, make an appearance, put in an appearance, turn up

showy flamboyant, flash (*Inf.*), flashy, garish, gaudy, loud, ostentatious, pompous, pretentious, splashy (*Inf.*), tawdry, tinselly

shred *n.* **1.** bit, fragment, piece, rag, ribbon, scrap, sliver, snippet, tatter **2.** *Fig.* atom, grain, iota, jot, particle, scrap, trace, whit

shrew dragon (*Inf.*), fury, harridan, nag, scold, spitfire, termagant (*Rare*), virago, vixen, Xanthippe

shrewd acute, artful, astute, calculated, calculating, canny, clever, crafty, cunning, discerning, discriminating, far-

seeing, far-sighted, fly (*Sl.*), intelligent, keen, knowing, long-headed, perceptive, perspicacious, sagacious, sharp, sly, smart, wily

shrewdly artfully, astutely, cannily, cleverly, far-sightedly, knowingly, perceptively, perspicaciously, sagaciously, with all one's wits about one, with consummate skill

shrewdness acumen, acuteness, astuteness, canniness, discernment, grasp, judgment, penetration, perspicacity, quick wits, sagacity, sharpness, smartness

shrewish bad-tempered, complaining, discontented, fault-finding, ill-humoured, ill-natured, ill-tempered, nagging, peevish, petulant, quarrelsome, scolding, sharp-tongued, vixenish

shriek *v./n.* cry, howl, scream, screech, squeal, wail, whoop, yell

shrill acute, ear-piercing, ear-splitting, high, high-pitched, penetrating, piercing, piping, screeching, sharp

shrink **1.** contract, decrease, deflate, diminish, drop off, dwindle, fall off, grow smaller, lessen, narrow, shorten, shrivel, wither, wrinkle **2.** cower, cringe, draw back, flinch, hang back, quail, recoil, retire, shy away, wince, withdraw

shrivel **1.** burn, dry (up), parch, scorch, sear **2.** dehydrate, desiccate, dwindle, shrink, wilt, wither, wizen, wrinkle

shrivelled desiccated, dried up, dry, sere (*Archaic*), shrunken, withered, wizened, wrinkled

shroud *v.* **1.** blanket, cloak, conceal, cover, envelop, hide, screen, swathe, veil ~*n.* **2.** cerecloth, cerement, covering, grave clothes, winding sheet **3.** cloud, mantle, pall, screen, veil

shudder **1.** *v.* convulse, quake, quiver, shake, shiver, tremble **2.** *n.* convulsion, quiver, spasm, trembling, tremor

shuffle **1.** drag, scrape, scuff, scuffle, shamble **2.** confuse, disarrange, disorder, intermix, jumble, mix, rearrange, shift **3.** *Usually with* **off** *or* **out of** beat about the bush, beg the question, cavil, dodge, equivocate, evade, gloss over, hedge, prevaricate, pussyfoot (*Inf.*), quibble

shun avoid, cold-shoulder, elude, eschew, evade, fight shy of, give (someone or something) a wide berth, have no part in, keep away from, shy away from, steer clear of

shut 1. bar, close, draw to, fasten, push to, seal, secure, slam 2. *With* **in, out,** *etc.* cage, confine, enclose, exclude, imprison, wall off *or* up

shut down cease, cease operating, close, discontinue, halt, shut up, stop, switch off

shut out 1. bar, debar, exclude, keep out, lock out, ostracize 2. block out, conceal, cover, hide, mask, screen, veil

shuttle *v.* alternate, commute, ply, seesaw, shunt

shut up 1. bottle up, box in, cage, confine, coop up, immure, imprison, incarcerate, intern, keep in 2. *Inf.* be quiet, fall silent, gag, hold one's tongue, hush, keep one's trap shut (*Sl.*), muzzle, pipe down (*Sl.*), silence

shy 1. *adj.* backward, bashful, cautious, chary, coy, diffident, distrustful, hesitant, modest, mousy, nervous, reserved, reticent, retiring, self-conscious, self-effacing, shrinking, suspicious, timid, wary 2. *v. Sometimes with* **off** *or* **away** balk, buck, draw back, flinch, quail, rear, recoil, start, swerve, take fright, wince

shyness bashfulness, diffidence, lack of confidence, modesty, mousiness, nervousness, reticence, self-consciousness, timidity, timidness, timorousness

sibyl Cassandra, oracle, prophetess, Pythia, pythoness, seer

sick 1. green around the gills (*Inf.*), ill, nauseated, puking (*Sl.*), qualmish, queasy 2. ailing, diseased, feeble, indisposed, laid up (*Inf.*), on the sick list (*Inf.*), poorly (*Inf.*), under the weather (*Inf.*), unwell, weak 3. *Inf.* black, ghoulish, macabre, morbid, sadistic 4. *Inf. Often with* **of** blasé, bored, disgusted, displeased, fed up, jaded, revolted, satiated, tired, weary

sicken 1. disgust, make one's gorge rise, nauseate, repel, revolt, turn one's stomach 2. be stricken by, contract, fall ill, go down with (*Brit.*), show symptoms of, take sick

sickening disgusting, distasteful, foul, loathsome, nauseating, nauseous, noisome, offensive, putrid, repulsive, revolting, stomach-turning (*Inf.*), vile

sickly 1. ailing, bilious, bloodless, delicate, faint, feeble, indisposed, infirm, in poor health, lacklustre, languid, pallid, peaky, pining, unhealthy, wan, weak 2. bilious (*Inf.*), cloying, mawkish, nauseating, revolting (*Inf.*), syrupy (*Inf.*)

sickness 1. nausea, queasiness, (the) collywobbles (*Sl.*), vomiting 2. affliction, ailment, bug (*Inf.*), complaint, disease, disorder, illness, indisposition, infirmity, malady

side *n.* 1. border, boundary, division, edge, limit, margin, part, perimeter, periphery, rim, sector, verge 2. aspect, face, facet, flank, hand, part, surface, view 3. angle, light, opinion, point of view, position, slant, stand, standpoint, viewpoint 4. camp, cause, faction, party, sect, team 5. *Brit. sl.* airs, arrogance, insolence, pretentiousness ~*adj.* 6. flanking, lateral 7. ancillary, incidental, indirect, lesser, marginal, minor, oblique, roundabout, secondary, subordinate, subsidiary ~*v.* 8. *Usually with* **with** ally with, associate oneself with, befriend, favour, go along with (*Inf.*), join with, second, support, take the part of, team up with (*Inf.*)

sidelong *adj.* covert, indirect, oblique, sideways

side-splitting farcical, hilarious, hysterical, rollicking, uproarious

sidestep avoid, bypass, circumvent, dodge, duck (*Inf.*), elude, evade, skip, skirt

sidetrack deflect, distract, divert, lead off the subject

sideways 1. *adv.* crabwise, edgeways, laterally, obliquely, sidelong, sidewards, to the side 2. *adj.* oblique, side, sidelong, slanted

sidle creep, edge, inch, slink, sneak, steal

siesta catnap, doze, forty winks (*Inf.*), nap, rest, sleep, snooze (*Inf.*)

sieve 1. *n.* colander, riddle, screen, sifter, strainer, tammy cloth 2. *v.* bolt, remove, riddle, separate, sift, strain

sift 1. bolt, filter, pan, part, riddle, separate, sieve 2. analyse, examine, fathom, go through, investigate, pore over, probe, screen, scrutinize

sigh *v.* 1. breathe, complain, grieve, lament, moan, sorrow, sough, suspire (*Archaic*) 2. *Often with* **for** languish, long, mourn, pine, yearn

sight *n.* 1. eye, eyes, eyesight, seeing, vision 2. appearance, apprehension, eyeshot, field of vision, ken, perception, range of vision, view, viewing, visibility 3. display, exhibition, pageant, scene, show, spectacle, vista 4. *Inf.* blot on the landscape (*Inf.*), eyesore, fright (*Inf.*), mess, monstrosity, spectacle 5. **catch**

sight of descry, espy, glimpse, recognize, spot, view ~v. **6.** behold, discern, distinguish, make out, observe, perceive, see, spot

sign n. **1.** clue, evidence, gesture, giveaway, hint, indication, manifestation, mark, note, proof, signal, spoor, suggestion, symptom, token, trace, vestige **2.** board, notice, placard, warning **3.** badge, character, cipher, device, emblem, ensign, figure, logo, mark, representation, symbol **4.** augury, auspice, foreboding, forewarning, omen, portent, presage, warning, writing on the wall ~v. **5.** autograph, endorse, initial, inscribe, set one's hand to, subscribe **6.** beckon, gesticulate, gesture, indicate, signal, use sign language, wave

signal 1. n. beacon, cue, gesture, goahead (Inf.), green light, indication, indicator, mark, sign, token **2.** adj. conspicuous, distinguished, eminent, exceptional, extraordinary, famous, memorable, momentous, notable, noteworthy, outstanding, remarkable, significant, striking **3.** v. beckon, communicate, gesticulate, gesture, give a sign to, indicate, motion, nod, sign, wave

sign away abandon, dispose of, forgo, give up all claim to, lose, relinquish, renounce, surrender, transfer, waive

significance 1. force, implication(s), import, meaning, message, point, purport, sense, signification **2.** consequence, consideration, importance, impressiveness, matter, moment, relevance, weight

significant 1. denoting, eloquent, expressing, expressive, indicative, knowing, meaning, meaningful, pregnant, suggestive **2.** critical, important, material, momentous, noteworthy, serious, vital, weighty

signify 1. announce, be a sign of, betoken, communicate, connote, convey, denote, evidence, exhibit, express, imply, indicate, intimate, matter, mean, portend, proclaim, represent, show, stand for, suggest, symbolize **2.** Inf. be of importance or significance, carry weight, count, matter

sign on or **up 1.** contract with, enlist, enrol, join, join up, register, volunteer **2.** employ, engage, hire, put on the payroll, recruit, take into service, take on, take on board (Inf.)

silence n. **1.** calm, hush, lull, noiselessness, peace, quiescence, quiet, stillness

2. dumbness, muteness, reticence, speechlessness, taciturnity, uncommunicativeness ~v. **3.** cut off, cut short, deaden, extinguish, gag, muffle, quell, quiet, quieten, stifle, still, strike dumb, subdue, suppress

silent 1. hushed, muted, noiseless, quiet, soundless, still, stilly (Poetic) **2.** dumb, mum, mute, nonvocal, not talkative, speechless, struck dumb (Inf.), taciturn, tongue-tied, uncommunicative, unspeaking, voiceless, wordless **3.** aphonic (Phonetics), implicit, implied, tacit, understood, unexpressed, unpronounced, unspoken

silently as quietly as a mouse (Inf.), dumbly, in silence, mutely, noiselessly, quietly, soundlessly, speechlessly, without a sound, wordlessly

silhouette 1. n. delineation, form, outline, profile, shape **2.** v. delineate, etch, outline, stand out

silky silken, sleek, smooth, velvety

silly adj. **1.** absurd, asinine, brainless, childish, fatuous, foolhardy, foolish, frivolous, giddy, idiotic, immature, imprudent, inane, inappropriate, irresponsible, meaningless, pointless, preposterous, puerile, ridiculous, senseless, stupid, unwise, witless **2.** Inf. benumbed, dazed, groggy (Inf.), in a daze, muzzy, stunned, stupefied ~n. **3.** Inf. clot (Brit. sl.), duffer (Inf.), goose (Inf.), ignoramus, ninny, silly-billy (Inf.), simpleton, twit (Inf.)

silt 1. n. alluvium, deposit, ooze, residue, sediment, sludge **2.** v. Usually with **up** choke, clog, congest, dam

silver 1. adj. argent (Poetic), pearly, silvered, silvery **2.** n. silver plate, silverware

similar alike, comparable, congruous, corresponding, in agreement, much the same, resembling, uniform

similarity affinity, agreement, analogy, closeness, comparability, concordance, congruence, correspondence, likeness, point of comparison, relation, resemblance, sameness, similitude

similarly by the same token, correspondingly, in like manner, likewise

simmer v. Fig. be angry (agitated, tense, uptight (Inf.)), boil, burn, fume, rage, seethe, smart, smoulder

simmer down calm down, collect oneself, contain oneself, control oneself, cool off or down, get down off one's high horse (*Inf.*), grow quieter, unwind (*Inf.*)

simper grimace, smile affectedly (coyly, self-consciously), smirk, titter

simpering *adj.* affected, coy, self-conscious

simple 1. clear, easy, elementary, intelligible, lucid, manageable, plain, straightforward, uncomplicated, understandable, uninvolved **2.** classic, clean, natural, plain, Spartan, unadorned, uncluttered, unembellished, unfussy **3.** elementary, pure, single, unalloyed, unblended, uncombined, undivided, unmixed **4.** artless, childlike, frank, green, guileless, ingenuous, innocent, naive, natural, sincere, unaffected, unpretentious, unsophisticated **5.** bald, basic, direct, frank, honest, naked, plain, sincere, stark, undeniable, unvarnished **6.** homely, humble, lowly, modest, rustic, unpretentious **7.** brainless, credulous, dense, dumb (*Inf.*), feeble, feeble-minded, foolish, half-witted, moronic, obtuse, shallow, silly, slow, stupid, thick

simple-minded 1. a bit lacking (*Inf.*), addle-brained, backward, brainless, dead from the neck up (*Sl.*), dim-witted, feeble-minded, foolish, idiot, idiotic, moronic, retarded, simple, stupid **2.** artless, natural, unsophisticated

simpleton blockhead, booby, dolt, dope (*Sl.*), dullard, dunce, fool, goose (*Inf.*), greenhorn (*Inf.*), idiot, imbecile (*Inf.*), jackass, moron, nincompoop, ninny, numskull, Simple Simon, stupid (*Inf.*), twerp (*Inf.*)

simplicity 1. absence of complications, clarity, clearness, ease, easiness, elementariness, obviousness, straightforwardness **2.** clean lines, lack of adornment, modesty, naturalness, plainness, purity, restraint **3.** artlessness, candour, directness, guilelessness, innocence, lack of sophistication, naivety, openness

simplify abridge, decipher, disentangle, facilitate, make intelligible, reduce to essentials, streamline

simplistic naive, oversimplified

simply 1. clearly, directly, easily, intelligibly, modestly, naturally, plainly, straightforwardly, unaffectedly, unpretentiously, without any elaboration **2.** just, merely, only, purely, solely **3.** absolutely, altogether, completely, really, totally, unreservedly, utterly, wholly

simulate act, affect, assume, counterfeit, fabricate, feign, imitate, make be-

lieve, pretend, put on, reproduce, sham

simulated 1. artificial, fake, imitation, man-made, mock, pseudo (*Inf.*), sham, substitute, synthetic **2.** artificial, assumed, feigned, insincere, make-believe, phoney (*Sl.*), pretended, put-on

simultaneous at the same time, coincident, coinciding, concurrent, contemporaneous, synchronous

simultaneously all together, at the same time, concurrently, in chorus, in concert, in the same breath, in unison, together

sin 1. *n.* crime, damnation, error, evil, guilt, iniquity, misdeed, offence, sinfulness, transgression, trespass, ungodliness, unrighteousness, wickedness, wrong, wrongdoing **2.** *v.* err, fall, fall from grace, go astray, lapse, offend, transgress, trespass (*Archaic*)

sincere artless, bona fide, candid, earnest, frank, genuine, guileless, heartfelt, honest, natural, no-nonsense, open, real, serious, straightforward, true, unaffected, unfeigned, wholehearted

sincerely earnestly, genuinely, honestly, in all sincerity, in good faith, really, seriously, truly, wholeheartedly

sincerity artlessness, bona fides, candour, frankness, genuineness, good faith, guilelessness, honesty, probity, seriousness, straightforwardness, truth, wholeheartedness

sinecure cushy number (*Sl.*), gravy train (*Sl., chiefly U.S.*), money for jam or old rope (*Inf.*), soft job (*Inf.*), soft option

sinewy athletic, brawny, lusty, muscular, powerful, robust, strong, sturdy, vigorous, wiry

sinful bad, corrupt, criminal, depraved, erring, guilty, immoral, iniquitous, irreligious, morally wrong, ungodly, unholy, unrighteous, wicked

sing 1. carol, chant, chirp, croon, make melody, pipe, trill, vocalize, warble, yodel **2.** *Sl., chiefly U.S.* betray, blow the whistle (on) (*Inf.*), fink (on) (*Sl., chiefly U.S.*), grass (*Brit. sl.*), inform (on), peach (*Sl.*), rat (on), spill the beans (*Inf.*), squeal (*Sl.*), turn in (*Inf.*) **3.** buzz, hum, purr, whine, whistle

singe burn, char, scorch, sear

singer chanteuse (*Fem.*), chorister, crooner, minstrel, songster, vocalist

single *adj.* **1.** distinct, individual, lone, one, only, particular, separate, singular, sole, solitary, unique 2. free, unattached, unmarried, unwed 3. exclusive, individual, separate, simple, unblended, uncompounded, undivided, unmixed, unshared ~v. 4. *Usually with* **out** choose, cull, distinguish, fix on, pick, pick on *or* out, put on one side, select, separate, set apart, winnow

single-handed alone, by oneself, independently, on one's own, solo, unaided, unassisted, without help

single-minded dedicated, determined, dogged, fixed, monomaniacal, steadfast, stubborn, tireless, undeviating, unswerving, unwavering

singly individually, one at a time, one by one, separately

sing out call (out), cooee, cry (out), halloo, holler (*Inf.*), make oneself heard, shout, shout ahoy, yell

singsong adj. droning, monotone, monotonous, repetitious, toneless

singular 1. conspicuous, eminent, exceptional, noteworthy, outstanding, prodigious, rare, remarkable, uncommon, unique, unparalleled 2. atypical, curious, eccentric, extraordinary, odd, out-of-the-way, peculiar, puzzling, queer, strange, unusual, 3. individual, separate, single, sole

singularity 1. abnormality, curiousness, extraordinariness, irregularity, oddness, peculiarity, queerness, strangeness 2. eccentricity, idiosyncrasy, oddity, particularity, peculiarity, quirk, twist

singularly conspicuously, especially, exceptionally, extraordinarily, notably, outstandingly, particularly, prodigiously, remarkably, surprisingly, uncommonly, unusually

sinister dire, disquieting, evil, injurious, malevolent, malign, malignant, menacing, ominous, threatening

sink v. 1. cave in, decline, descend, dip, disappear, droop, drop, drown, ebb, engulf, fall, founder, go down, go under, lower, merge, plummet, plunge, sag, slope, submerge, subside 2. abate, collapse, drop, fall, lapse, relapse, retrogress, slip, slump, subside 3. decay, decline, decrease, degenerate, depreciate, deteriorate, die, diminish, dwindle, fade, fail, flag, go downhill (*Inf.*), lessen, weaken, worsen 4. bore, dig, drill, drive, excavate, lay, put down 5. be the ruin of, defeat, destroy, finish, overwhelm, ruin, scupper (*Brit. sl.*), seal the doom of 6. be

reduced to, debase oneself, lower oneself, stoop, succumb

sink in be understood, get through to, make an impression, penetrate, register (*Inf.*), take hold of

sinless faultless, guiltless, immaculate, innocent, pure, unblemished, uncorrupted, undefiled, unsullied, virtuous, without fault, without sin

sinner evildoer, miscreant, offender, reprobate, transgressor, trespasser (*Archaic*), wrongdoer

sinuous coiling, crooked, curved, curvy, lithe, mazy, meandering, serpentine, supple, tortuous, undulating, winding

sip 1. v. sample, sup, taste 2. n. drop, swallow, taste, thimbleful

siren charmer, Circe, *femme fatale*, Lorelei, seductress, temptress, vamp (*Inf.*), witch

sissy 1. n. baby, coward, milksop, milquetoast (*U.S.*), mollycoddle, mummy's boy, namby-pamby, sisspot (*Inf.*), softy (*Inf.*), weakling, wet (*Brit. inf.*) 2. adj. cowardly, effeminate, feeble, namby-pamby, sissified (*Inf.*), soft (*Inf.*), unmanly, weak, wet (*Brit. inf.*)

sit 1. be seated, perch, rest, settle, take a seat, take the weight off one's feet 2. assemble, be in session, convene, deliberate, meet, officiate, preside 3. accommodate, contain, have space for, hold, seat

site 1. n. ground, location, place, plot, position, spot 2. v. install, locate, place, position, set, situate

sitting n. consultation, get-together (*Inf.*), hearing, meeting, period, session

situation 1. locale, locality, location, place, position, seat, setting, site, spot 2. ball game (*Inf.*), case, circumstances, condition, kettle of fish (*Inf.*), plight, state, state of affairs, status quo, the picture (*Inf.*) 3. rank, sphere, station, status 4. berth (*Inf.*), employment, job, office, place, position, post

sixth sense clairvoyance, feyness, intuition, second sight

sizable considerable, decent, decent-sized, goodly, large, largish, respectable, substantial, tidy (*Inf.*)

size amount, bigness, bulk, dimensions, extent, greatness, hugeness, immensity, largeness, magnitude, mass, measurement(s), proportions, range, vastness, volume

size up appraise, assess, evaluate, get

(something) taped (*Brit. inf.*), get the measure of, take stock of

sizzle crackle, frizzle, fry, hiss, spit, sputter

skedaddle beat a hasty retreat, bolt, decamp, disappear, do a bunk (*Inf.*), flee, hop it (*Brit. sl.*), run away, scarper (*Brit. sl.*), scoot, scram (*Inf.*), scurry away, scuttle away, vamoose (*Sl., chiefly U.S.*)

skeletal cadaverous, emaciated, fleshless, gaunt, hollow-cheeked, lantern-jawed, skin-and-bone (*Inf.*), wasted, worn to a shadow

skeleton *Fig.* bare bones, bones, draft, frame, framework, outline, sketch, structure

sketch 1. *v.* block out, delineate, depict, draft, draw, outline, paint, plot, portray, represent, rough out **2.** *n.* delineation, design, draft, drawing, outline, plan, skeleton

sketchily cursorily, hastily, imperfectly, incompletely, patchily, perfunctorily, roughly

sketchy bitty, cobbled together, crude, cursory, inadequate, incomplete, outline, perfunctory, rough, scrappy, skimpy, slight, superficial, unfinished, vague

skewwhiff askew, aslant, cockeyed (*Inf.*), crooked, out of true, squint (*Inf.*), tilted

skilful able, accomplished, adept, adroit, apt, clever, competent, dexterous, experienced, expert, handy, masterly, practised, professional, proficient, quick, ready, skilled, trained

skill ability, accomplishment, adroitness, aptitude, art, cleverness, competence, dexterity, experience, expertise, expertness, facility, finesse, handiness, ingenuity, intelligence, knack, proficiency, quickness, readiness, skilfulness, talent, technique

skilled able, accomplished, a dab hand at (*Brit. inf.*), experienced, expert, masterly, practised, professional, proficient, skilful, trained

skim 1. cream, separate **2.** brush, coast, dart, float, fly, glide, sail, soar **3.** *Usually with* **through** glance, run one's eye over, scan, skip (*Inf.*), thumb *or* leaf through

skimp be mean with, be niggardly, be sparing with, pinch, scamp, scant, scrimp, stint, withhold

skimpy exiguous, inadequate, insufficient, meagre, miserly, niggardly, scanty, short, sparse, thin, tight

skin *n.* **1.** fell, hide, integument, pelt, tegument **2.** casing, coating, crust, film, husk, membrane, outside, peel, rind **3. by the skin of one's teeth** by a hair's-breadth, by a narrow margin, by a whisker (*Inf.*), narrowly, only just **4. get under one's skin** annoy, grate on, irk, irritate, needle (*Inf.*), nettle, rub up the wrong way ~*v.* **5.** abrade, bark, excoriate, flay, graze, peel, scrape

skin-deep artificial, external, meaningless, on the surface, shallow, superficial, surface

skinflint miser, niggard, penny-pincher (*Inf.*), Scrooge, tightwad (*U.S. sl.*)

skinny emaciated, lean, scraggy, skeletal, skin-and-bone (*Inf.*), thin, twiggy, undernourished

skip *v.* **1.** bob, bounce, caper, cavort, dance, flit, frisk, gambol, hop, prance, trip **2.** eschew, give (something) a miss, leave out, miss out, omit, pass over, skim over **3.** *Inf.* cut (*Inf.*), dog it *or* dog off (*Dialect*), miss, play truant from, twag (*Dialect*)

skirmish 1. *n.* affair, affray (*Law*), battle, brush, clash, combat, conflict, contest, dust-up (*Inf.*), encounter, engagement, fracas, incident, scrap (*Inf.*), scrimmage, set-to (*Inf.*), spat, tussle **2.** *v.* clash, collide, come to blows, scrap (*Inf.*), tussle

skirt *v.* **1.** border, edge, flank, lie alongside **2.** *Often with* **around** *or* **round** avoid, bypass, circumvent, detour, evade, steer clear of ~*n.* **3.** *Often plural* border, edge, fringe, hem, margin, outskirts, periphery, purlieus, rim

skit burlesque, parody, sketch, spoof (*Inf.*), takeoff (*Inf.*), travesty, turn

skittish excitable, fickle, fidgety, frivolous, highly strung, jumpy, lively, nervous, playful, restive

skive dodge, gold-brick (*U.S. sl.*), idle, scrimshank (*Brit. military sl.*), shirk, skulk, slack

skiver dodger, do-nothing, gold brick (*U.S. sl.*), idler, loafer, scrimshanker (*Brit. military sl.*), shirker, slacker

skulduggery double-dealing, duplicity, fraudulence, machinations, shenanigan(s) (*Inf.*), swindling, trickery, underhandedness, unscrupulousness

skulk creep, lie in wait, loiter, lurk, pad, prowl, slink, sneak

sky n. **1.** azure (*Poetic*), empyrean (*Poetic*), firmament, heavens, upper atmosphere, vault of heaven, welkin (*Archaic*) **2. to the skies** excessively, extravagantly, fulsomely, highly, immoderately, inordinately, profusely

slab chunk, hunk, lump, piece, portion, slice, wedge, wodge (*Brit. inf.*)

slack adj. **1.** baggy, easy, flaccid, flexible, lax, limp, loose, not taut, relaxed **2.** asleep on the job (*Inf.*), easy-going, idle, inactive, inattentive, lax, lazy, neglectful, negligent, permissive, remiss, tardy **3.** dull, inactive, quiet, slow, slow-moving, sluggish ~n. **4.** excess, give (*Inf.*), leeway, looseness, play, room ~v. **5.** dodge, flag, idle, neglect, relax, shirk, skive (*Brit. sl.*), slacken

slacken (off) abate, decrease, diminish, drop (off), ease (off), lessen, let up, loosen, moderate, reduce, relax, release, slack off, slow down, tire

slacker dodger, do-nothing, gold brick (*U.S. sl.*), good-for-nothing, idler, loafer, passenger, scrimshanker (*Brit. military sl.*), shirker, skiver (*Brit. sl.*)

slake assuage, gratify, quench, sate, satiate, satisfy

slam 1. bang, crash, dash, fling, hurl, smash, throw, thump **2.** *Sl.* attack, castigate, criticize, damn, excoriate, lambaste, pan (*Inf.*), pillory, shoot down (*Inf.*), slate (*Inf.*), vilify

slander 1. n. aspersion, backbiting, calumny, defamation, detraction, libel, misrepresentation, muckraking, obloquy, scandal, smear **2.** v. backbite, blacken (someone's) name, calumniate, decry, defame, detract, disparage, libel, malign, muckrake, slur, smear, traduce, vilify

slanderous abusive, calumnious, damaging, defamatory, libellous, malicious

slang v. abuse, berate, call names, hurl insults at, insult, inveigh against, malign, rail against, revile, vilify, vituperate

slanging match altercation, argument, argy-bargy (*Brit. inf.*), barney (*Inf.*), battle of words, ding-dong, quarrel, row, set-to (*Inf.*), spat

slant v. **1.** angle off, bend, bevel, cant, incline, lean, list, shelve, skew, slope, tilt ~n. **2.** camber, declination, diagonal, gradient, incline, pitch, rake, ramp, slope, tilt ~v. **3.** angle, bias, colour, distort, twist, weight ~n. **4.** angle, attitude,

bias, emphasis, leaning, one-sidedness, point of view, prejudice, viewpoint

slanting angled, aslant, asymmetrical, at an angle, bent, canted, cater-cornered (*U.S. inf.*), diagonal, inclined, oblique, on the bias, sideways, slanted, slantwise, sloping, tilted, tilting

slap n. **1.** bang, blow, clout (*Inf.*), cuff, smack, spank, wallop (*Inf.*), whack **2. a slap in the face** blow, humiliation, insult, put-down, rebuff, rebuke, rejection, repulse, snub ~v. **3.** bang, clap, clout (*Inf.*), cuff, hit, spank, strike, whack **4.** *Inf.* daub, plaster, plonk, spread ~adv. **5.** *Inf.* bang, directly, exactly, plumb (*Inf.*), precisely, slap-bang (*Inf.*), smack (*Inf.*)

slapdash careless, clumsy, disorderly, haphazard, hasty, hurried, last-minute, messy, negligent, perfunctory, slipshod, sloppy (*Inf.*), slovenly, thoughtless, thrown-together, untidy

slap down bring to heel, put (someone) in his place, rebuke, reprimand, restrain, squash

slaphappy 1. casual, haphazard, happy-go-lucky, hit-or-miss (*Inf.*), irresponsible, nonchalant **2.** dazed, giddy, punch-drunk, reeling, woozy (*Inf.*)

slapstick n. buffoonery, farce, horseplay, knockabout comedy

slap-up elaborate, excellent, first-rate, fit for a king, lavish, luxurious, magnificent, no-expense-spared, princely, splendid, sumptuous, superb

slash v. **1.** cut, gash, hack, lacerate, rend, rip, score, slit ~n. **2.** cut, gash, incision, laceration, rent, rip, slit ~v. **3.** cut, drop, lower, reduce

slashing aggressive, biting, brutal, harsh, savage, searing, vicious

slate v. berate, blame, castigate, censure, criticize, haul over the coals (*Inf.*), lambaste, lay into (*Inf.*), pan (*Inf.*), pitch into, rail against, rap (someone's) knuckles (*Inf.*), rebuke, roast (*Inf.*), scold, slam (*Sl.*), slang, take to task, tear (someone) off a strip (*Inf.*)

slattern drab (*Archaic*), sloven, slut, trollop

slatternly bedraggled, dirty, draggle-tailed (*Archaic*), frowzy, slipshod, sloppy (*Inf.*), slovenly, sluttish, unclean, unkempt, untidy

slaughter n. **1.** blood bath, bloodshed, butchery, carnage, extermination, killing, liquidation, massacre, murder, slaying ~v. **2.** butcher, destroy, do to death, exterminate, kill, liquidate, massacre, murder, put to the sword, slay **3.** *Inf.* crush, defeat, hammer (*Inf.*), overwhelm, rout, thrash, trounce, vanquish, wipe the floor with (*Inf.*)

slaughterhouse abattoir, butchery, shambles

slave 1. *n.* bondservant, bondsman, drudge, scullion (*Archaic*), serf, servant, skivvy, slavey (*Brit. inf.*), vassal, villein **2.** *v.* drudge, grind (*Inf.*), skivvy (*Brit.*), slog, toil, work one's fingers to the bone

slaver dribble, drool, salivate, slobber

slavery bondage, captivity, enslavement, serfdom, servitude, subjugation, thraldom, thrall, vassalage

slavish 1. abject, base, cringing, despicable, fawning, grovelling, low, mean, menial, obsequious, servile, submissive, sycophantic **2.** conventional, imitative, second-hand, unimaginative, uninspired, unoriginal

slay 1. annihilate, assassinate, butcher, destroy, dispatch, do away with, eliminate, exterminate, kill, massacre, mow down, murder, rub out (*U.S. sl.*), slaughter **2.** *Inf.* amuse, be the death of (*Inf.*), impress, make a hit with (*Inf.*), wow (*Sl., chiefly U.S.*)

sleazy disreputable, low, seedy, sordid, squalid

sleek glossy, lustrous, shiny, smooth, well-fed, well-groomed

sleep 1. *v.* be in the land of Nod, catnap, doze, drop off (*Inf.*), drowse, hibernate, nod off (*Inf.*), rest in the arms of Morpheus, slumber, snooze (*Inf.*), snore, take a nap, take forty winks (*Inf.*) **2.** *n.* beauty sleep (*Inf.*), dormancy, doze, forty winks (*Inf.*), hibernation, nap, repose, rest, shuteye (*Sl.*), siesta, slumber(s), snooze (*Inf.*)

sleepiness doziness, drowsiness, heaviness, lethargy, somnolence, torpor

sleepless 1. disturbed, insomniac, restless, unsleeping, wakeful **2.** alert, unsleeping, vigilant, watchful, wide awake

sleeplessness insomnia, wakefulness

sleepwalker noctambulist, somnambulist

sleepwalking noctambulation, noctambulism, somnambulation, somnambulism

sleepy 1. drowsy, dull, heavy, inactive, lethargic, sluggish, slumbersome, somnolent, torpid **2.** dull, hypnotic, inactive,

quiet, sleep-inducing, slow, slumberous, somnolent, soporific

sleight of hand adroitness, artifice, dexterity, legerdemain, manipulation, prestidigitation, skill

slender 1. lean, narrow, slight, slim, svelte, sylphlike, willowy **2.** inadequate, inconsiderable, insufficient, little, meagre, scanty, small, spare **3.** faint, feeble, flimsy, fragile, poor, remote, slight, slim, tenuous, thin, weak

sleuth detective, dick (*U.S. sl.*), gumshoe (*U.S. sl.*), private eye (*Inf.*), (private) investigator, sleuthhound (*Inf.*), tail (*Inf.*)

slice 1. *n.* cut, helping, piece, portion, segment, share, sliver, wedge **2.** *v.* carve, cut, divide, sever

slick *adj.* **1.** glib, meretricious, plausible, polished, smooth, sophistical, specious **2.** adroit, deft, dextrous, polished, professional, sharp, skilful ~v. **3.** make glossy, plaster down, sleek, smarm down (*Brit. inf.*), smooth

slide *v.* **1.** coast, glide, glissade, skim, slip, slither, toboggan, veer **2. let slide** forget, gloss over, ignore, let ride, neglect, pass over, push to the back of one's mind, turn a blind eye to

slight *adj.* **1.** feeble, inconsiderable, insignificant, insubstantial, meagre, minor, modest, negligible, paltry, scanty, small, superficial, trifling, trivial, unimportant, weak **2.** delicate, feeble, fragile, lightly-built, slim, small, spare ~v. **3.** affront, cold-shoulder, despise, disdain, disparage, give offence *or* umbrage to, ignore, insult, neglect, scorn, show disrespect for, snub, treat with contempt ~n. **4.** affront, contempt, discourtesy, disdain, disregard, disrespect, inattention, indifference, insult, neglect, rebuff, slap in the face (*Inf.*), snub, (the) cold shoulder

slighting belittling, derogatory, disdainful, disparaging, disrespectful, insulting, offensive, scornful, supercilious, uncomplimentary

slightly a little, marginally, on a small scale, somewhat, to some extent *or* degree

slim *adj.* **1.** lean, narrow, slender, slight, svelte, sylphlike, thin, trim **2.** faint, poor, remote, slender, slight ~v. **3.** diet, lose weight, reduce, slenderize (*Chiefly U.S.*)

slimy 1. clammy, glutinous, miry, mucous, muddy, oozy, viscous **2.** creeping, grovelling, obsequious, oily, servile, smarmy (*Brit. inf.*), soapy (*Sl.*), sycophantic, toadying, unctuous

sling *v.* **1.** cast, chuck (*Inf.*), fling, heave, hurl, lob (*Inf.*), shy, throw, toss **2.** dangle, hang, suspend, swing

slink creep, prowl, pussyfoot (*Inf.*), skulk, slip, sneak, steal

slinky clinging, feline, figure-hugging, sinuous, skintight, sleek

slip¹ *v.* **1.** glide, skate, slide, slither **2.** fall, lose one's balance, miss *or* lose one's footing, skid, trip (over) **3.** conceal, creep, hide, insinuate oneself, sneak, steal **4.** *Sometimes with* **up** blunder, boob (*Brit. sl.*), err, go wrong, make a mistake, miscalculate, misjudge, mistake **5.** break away from, break free from, disappear, escape, get away, get clear of, take French leave **6. let slip** blurt out, come out with (*Inf.*), disclose, divulge, give away, leak, let out (*Inf.*), let the cat out of the bag, reveal ~*n.* **7.** bloomer (*Brit. inf.*), blunder, boob (*Brit. sl.*), error, failure, fault, imprudence, indiscretion, mistake, omission, oversight, slip of the tongue, slip-up (*Inf.*) **8. give (someone) the slip** dodge, elude, escape from, evade, get away from, lose (someone), outwit, shake (someone) off

slip² *n.* **1.** piece, sliver, strip **2.** cutting, offshoot, runner, scion, shoot, sprig, sprout

slippery 1. glassy, greasy, icy, lubricious (*Rare*), perilous, skiddy (*Inf.*), slippy (*Inf.*), smooth, unsafe, unstable, unsteady **2.** crafty, cunning, devious, dishonest, duplicitous, evasive, false, foxy, shifty, sneaky, treacherous, tricky, two-faced, unpredictable, unreliable, untrustworthy

slipshod careless, loose, slapdash, sloppy (*Inf.*), slovenly, unsystematic, untidy

slit 1. *v.* cut (open), gash, knife, lance, pierce, rip, slash, split open **2.** *n.* cut, fissure, gash, incision, opening, rent, split, tear

slither *v.* glide, skitter, slide, slink, slip, snake, undulate

sliver *n.* flake, fragment, paring, shaving, shred, slip, splinter

slob boor, churl, lout, oaf, yahoo, yob (*Brit. sl.*)

slobber *v.* dribble, drivel, drool, sali-

vate, slabber (*Dialect*), slaver, water at the mouth

slog *v.* **1.** hit, hit for six, slosh (*Brit. sl.*), slug, sock (*Sl.*), strike, thump, wallop (*Inf.*) **2.** apply oneself to, labour, peg away at, persevere, plod, plough through, slave, toil, tramp, trek, trudge, work ~*n.* **3.** effort, exertion, hike, labour, struggle, tramp, trek, trudge

slogan catchword, jingle, motto, rallying cry

slop *v.* overflow, slosh (*Inf.*), spatter, spill, splash, splatter

slop around *or* **about** flop, loaf, lollop, lounge, shamble, shuffle, slouch, slump, sprawl

slope *v.* **1.** drop away, fall, incline, lean, pitch, rise, slant, tilt ~*n.* **2.** brae (*Scot.*), declination, declivity, descent, downgrade (*Chiefly U.S.*), gradient, inclination, incline, ramp, rise, scarp, slant, tilt ~*v.* **3.** *With* **off, away,** *etc.* creep, make oneself scarce, skulk, slink, slip, steal

sloping bevelled, cant, inclined, inclining, leaning, oblique, slanting

sloppy 1. sludgy, slushy, splashy, watery, wet **2.** *Inf.* amateurish, careless, clumsy, hit-or-miss (*Inf.*), inattentive, messy, slipshod, slovenly, unkempt, untidy, weak **3.** banal, gushing, mawkish, mushy (*Inf.*), overemotional, sentimental, slushy (*Inf.*), soppy (*Brit. inf.*), trite, wet (*Brit. inf.*)

slosh *v.* **1.** flounder, plash, pour, shower, slap, slop, splash, spray, swash, wade **2.** *Brit. sl.* bash (*Sl.*), biff (*Sl.*), hit, punch, slog, slug, sock (*Sl.*), strike, swipe, thwack, wallop (*Inf.*)

slot *n.* **1.** aperture, channel, groove, hole, slit **2.** *Inf.* niche, opening, place, position, space, time, vacancy ~*v.* **3.** adjust, assign, fit, fit in, insert, pigeonhole

sloth faineance, idleness, inactivity, indolence, inertia, laziness, slackness, slothfulness, sluggishness, torpor

slothful do-nothing (*Inf.*), fainéant, idle, inactive, indolent, inert, lazy, skiving (*Brit. inf.*), slack, sluggish, torpid, workshy

slouch *v.* droop, loll, slump, stoop

slouching awkward, loutish, lumbering, shambling, uncouth, ungainly

slovenly careless, disorderly, heedless, loose, negligent, slack, slapdash, slatternly, slipshod, sloppy (*Inf.*), unkempt, untidy

slow *adj.* **1.** creeping, dawdling, deliberate, easy, lackadaisical, laggard, lagging, lazy, leaden, leisurely, loitering, measured, plodding, ponderous, slow-moving, sluggardly, sluggish, tortoise-like, unhurried **2.** backward, behind, behindhand, delayed, dilatory, late, long-delayed, tardy, unpunctual **3.** gradual, lingering, long-drawn-out, prolonged, protracted, time-consuming **4.** behind the times, boring, conservative, dead, dead-and-alive (*Brit.*), dull, inactive, one-horse (*Inf.*), quiet, slack, sleepy, sluggish, stagnant, tame, tedious, uneventful, uninteresting, unproductive, unprogressive, wearisome **5.** blockish, bovine, dense, dim, dull, dull-witted, dumb (*Inf.*), obtuse, retarded, slow on the uptake (*Inf.*), slow-witted, stupid, thick, unresponsive **6.** *With* **to** averse, disinclined, hesitant, indisposed, loath, reluctant, unwilling ~*v.* **7.** *Often with* **up** *or* **down** brake, check, curb, decelerate, delay, detain, handicap, hold up, lag, reduce speed, rein in, relax, restrict, retard, slacken (off), spin out

slowly at a snail's pace, at one's leisure, by degrees, gradually, inchmeal, in one's own (good) time, leisurely, ploddingly, steadily, taking one's time, unhurriedly, with leaden steps

sludge dregs, mire, muck, mud, ooze, residue, sediment, silt, slime, slop, slush

sluggish dull, heavy, inactive, indolent, inert, lethargic, lifeless, listless, phlegmatic, slothful, slow, slow-moving, torpid, unresponsive

sluggishness apathy, drowsiness, dullness, heaviness, indolence, inertia, languor, lassitude, lethargy, listlessness, slothfulness, somnolence, stagnation, torpor

sluice *v.* cleanse, drain, drench, flush, irrigate, wash down, wash out

slumber *v.* be inactive, doze, lie dormant, nap, repose, sleep, snooze (*Inf.*)

slummy decayed, overcrowded, run-down, seedy, sleazy, sordid, squalid, wretched

slump *v.* **1.** collapse, crash, decline, deteriorate, fall, fall off, go downhill (*Inf.*), plummet, plunge, reach a new low, sink, slip ~*n.* **2.** collapse, crash, decline, depreciation, depression, downturn, failure, fall, falling-off, low, recession, reverse, stagnation, trough ~*v.* **3.** bend, droop, hunch, loll, sag, slouch

slur *n.* affront, aspersion, blot, brand, calumny, discredit, disgrace, innuendo, insinuation, insult, reproach, smear, stain, stigma

slut drab (*Archaic*), slattern, sloven, trollop

sly *adj.* **1.** artful, astute, clever, conniving, covert, crafty, cunning, devious, foxy, furtive, guileful, insidious, scheming, secret, shifty, stealthy, subtle, underhand, wily **2.** arch, impish, knowing, mischievous, roguish ~*n.* **3. on the sly** behind (someone's) back, covertly, like a thief in the night, on the q.t. (*Inf.*), on the quiet, privately, secretly, surreptitiously, underhandedly, under the counter (*Inf.*)

smack *v.* **1.** box, clap, cuff, hit, pat, slap, sock (*Sl.*), spank, strike, tap ~*n.* **2.** blow, crack, slap **3. smack in the eye** blow, rebuff, repulse, setback, slap in the face, snub ~*adv.* **4.** *Inf.* directly, exactly, plumb, point-blank, precisely, right, slap (*Inf.*), squarely, straight

smack of bear the stamp of, be redolent of, be suggestive *or* indicative of, betoken, have all the hallmarks of, reek of, smell of, suggest, testify to

small 1. diminutive, immature, little, mini, miniature, minute, petite, pint-sized (*Inf.*), pocket-sized, puny, slight, tiny, undersized, wee, young **2.** insignificant, lesser, minor, negligible, paltry, petty, trifling, trivial, unimportant **3.** inadequate, inconsiderable, insufficient, limited, meagre, scanty **4.** humble, modest, small-scale, unpretentious **5.** base, grudging, illiberal, mean, narrow, petty, selfish **6. make (someone) feel small** chagrin, disconcert, humble, humiliate, make (someone) look foolish, mortify, put down (*Sl.*), show up (*Inf.*), take down a peg or two (*Inf.*)

small-minded bigoted, envious, grudging, hidebound, intolerant, mean, narrow-minded, petty, rigid, ungenerous

small-time insignificant, minor, no-account (*U.S. inf.*), of no account, of no consequence, petty, unimportant

smarmy bootlicking (*Inf.*), crawling, greasy, ingratiating, oily, servile, smooth, soapy (*Sl.*), suave, sycophantic, toadying, unctuous

smart[1] *adj.* **1.** acute, adept, agile, apt, astute, bright, brisk, canny, clever, ingenious, intelligent, keen, nimble, quick, quick-witted, ready, sharp, shrewd **2.**

chic, elegant, fashionable, fine, modish, natty (*Inf.*), neat, snappy, spruce, stylish, trim, well turned-out **3.** effective, impertinent, nimble-witted, pointed, ready, saucy, smart-alecky (*Inf.*), witty **4.** brisk, cracking (*Inf.*), jaunty, lively, quick, spanking, spirited, vigorous

smart² **1.** *v.* burn, hurt, pain, sting, throb, tingle **2.** *adj.* hard, keen, painful, piercing, resounding, sharp, stinging **3.** *n.* burning sensation, pain, pang, smarting, soreness, sting

smart aleck clever Dick (*Inf.*), know-all (*Inf.*), smarty boots (*Inf.*), smarty pants (*Inf.*), wise guy (*Inf.*)

smarten beautify, groom, put in order, put to rights, spruce up, tidy

smash *v.* **1.** break, collide, crash, crush, demolish, disintegrate, pulverize, shatter, shiver ~*n.* **2.** accident, collision, crash, pile-up (*Inf.*), smash-up (*Inf.*) ~*v.* **3.** defeat, destroy, lay waste, overthrow, ruin, wreck ~*n.* **4.** collapse, defeat, destruction, disaster, downfall, failure, ruin, shattering

smashing excellent, exhilarating, fab (*Sl.*), fabulous (*Inf.*), fantastic (*Inf.*), first-class, first-rate, great (*Inf.*), magnificent, marvellous, out of this world (*Inf.*), sensational, stupendous, super (*Inf.*), superb, superlative, terrific (*Inf.*), wonderful

smattering bit, dash, elements, modicum, rudiments, smatter, sprinkling

smear *v.* **1.** bedaub, bedim, besmirch, blur, coat, cover, daub, dirty, patch, plaster, rub on, smudge, soil, spread over, stain, sully ~*n.* **2.** blot, blotch, daub, smudge, splotch, streak ~*v.* **3.** asperse, besmirch, blacken, calumniate, drag (someone's) name through the mud (*Inf.*), malign, sully, tarnish, traduce, vilify ~*n.* **4.** calumny, defamation, libel, mudslinging, slander, vilification, whispering campaign

smell *n.* **1.** aroma, bouquet, fragrance, odour, perfume, redolence, scent, whiff ~*v.* **2.** get a whiff of (*Brit. sl.*), nose, scent, sniff ~*n.* **3.** fetor, pong (*Brit. inf.*), stench, stink ~*v.* **4.** be malodorous, hum (*Sl.*), pong (*Brit. inf.*), reek, stink, stink to high heaven (*Inf.*), whiff (*Brit. sl.*)

smelly evil-smelling, fetid, foul, foul-smelling, high, malodorous, mephitic, noisome, pongy (*Brit. inf.*), putrid, reeking, stinking, strong, strong-smelling, whiffy (*Brit. sl.*)

smirk *n.* grin, leer, simper, smug look, sneer

smitten **1.** afflicted, beset, laid low, plagued, struck **2.** beguiled, bewitched, bowled over (*Inf.*), captivated, charmed, enamoured, infatuated, swept off one's feet

smoky begrimed, black, caliginous (*Archaic*), grey, grimy, hazy, murky, reeky, smoke-darkened, sooty, thick

smooth *adj.* **1.** even, flat, flush, horizontal, level, plain, plane, unwrinkled **2.** glossy, polished, shiny, silky, sleek, soft, velvety **3.** calm, equable, glassy, mirror-like, peaceful, serene, tranquil, undisturbed, unruffled **4.** agreeable, bland, mellow, mild, pleasant, soothing **5.** facile, glib, ingratiating, persuasive, silky, slick, smarmy (*Brit. inf.*), suave, unctuous, urbane **6.** easy, effortless, flowing, fluent, frictionless, regular, rhythmic, steady, unbroken, uneventful, uniform, uninterrupted, untroubled, well-ordered ~*v.* **7.** flatten, iron, level, plane, polish, press **8.** allay, alleviate, appease, assuage, calm, ease, extenuate, facilitate, iron out the difficulties of, mitigate, mollify, palliate, pave the way, soften

smoothness **1.** evenness, flushness, levelness, regularity, unbrokenness **2.** silkiness, sleekness, smooth texture, softness, velvetiness **3.** calmness, glassiness, placidity, serenity, stillness, unruffled surface **4.** glibness, oiliness, smarminess (*Brit. inf.*), suavity, urbanity **5.** ease, efficiency, effortlessness, felicity, finish, flow, fluency, polish, rhythm, slickness, smooth running

smother *v.* **1.** choke, extinguish, snuff, stifle, strangle, suffocate **2.** conceal, hide, keep back, muffle, repress, stifle, suppress **3.** be swimming in, cocoon, cover, envelop, heap, inundate, overwhelm, shower, shroud, surround ~*n.* **4.** fug (*Chiefly Brit.*), smog

smoulder *Fig.* be resentful, boil, burn, fester, fume, rage, seethe, simmer, smart under

smudge **1.** *v.* blacken, blur, daub, dirty, mark, smear, smirch, soil **2.** *n.* blemish, blot, blur, smear, smut, smutch

smug complacent, conceited, holier-than-thou, priggish, self-opinionated, self-righteous, self-satisfied, superior

smuggler bootlegger, contrabandist,

gentleman, moonshiner (*U.S.*), rum-runner, runner, wrecker

smutty bawdy, blue, coarse, crude, dirty, filthy, improper, indecent, indelicate, lewd, obscene, off colour, pornographic, prurient, racy, raunchy (*U.S. sl.*), risqué, salacious, suggestive, vulgar

snack bite, bite to eat, break, elevenses (*Brit. inf.*), light meal, nibble, refreshment(s), titbit

snag 1. *n.* catch, complication, difficulty, disadvantage, drawback, hitch, inconvenience, obstacle, problem, stumbling block, the rub **2**. *v.* catch, hole, rip, tear

snaky 1. convoluted, serpentine, sinuous, tortuous, twisting, writhing **2**. crafty, insidious, perfidious, sly, treacherous, venomous

snap *v.* **1**. break, come apart, crack, give way, separate **2**. bite, bite at, catch, grip, nip, seize, snatch **3**. bark, flare out, flash, fly off the handle at (*Inf.*), growl, jump down (someone's) throat (*Inf.*), lash out at, retort, snarl, speak sharply **4**. click, crackle, pop **5**. **snap one's fingers at** cock a snook at (*Brit.*), defy, flout, pay no attention to, scorn, set at naught, wave two fingers at (*Sl.*) **6**. **snap out of it** cheer up, get a grip on oneself, get over, liven up, perk up, pull oneself together (*Inf.*), recover ~*n.* **7**. crackle, fillip, flick, pop **8**. bite, grab, nip **9**. *Inf.* energy, get-up-and-go (*Inf.*), go (*Inf.*), liveliness, pizazz (*Inf.*), vigour, zip (*Inf.*) ~*adj.* **10**. abrupt, immediate, instant, on-the-spot, sudden, unpremeditated

snappy 1. apt to fly off the handle (*Inf.*), cross, edgy, hasty, irritable, like a bear with a sore head (*Inf.*), quick-tempered, snappish, tart, testy, touchy, waspish **2**. chic, dapper, fashionable, modish, natty (*Inf.*), smart, stylish, trendy (*Brit. inf.*), up-to-the-minute **3**. **look snappy** be quick, buck up (*Inf.*), get a move on (*Inf.*), get one's skates on, hurry (up), look lively, make haste

snap up avail oneself of, grab, grasp, nab (*Inf.*), pounce upon, seize, swoop down on, take advantage of

snare 1. *v.* catch, entrap, net, seize, springe, trap, trepan (*Archaic*), wire **2**. *n.* catch, gin net, noose, pitfall, springe, trap, wire

snarl[1] *v.* complain, growl, grumble, mumble, murmur, show its teeth (*of an animal*)

snarl[2] *v.* Often with **up** complicate, confuse, embroil, enmesh, entangle, entwine, muddle, ravel, tangle

snarl-up confusion, entanglement, muddle, tangle, (traffic) jam

snatch 1. *v.* clutch, gain, grab, grasp, grip, make off with, pluck, pull, rescue, seize, take, win, wrench, wrest **2**. *n.* bit, fragment, part, piece, smattering, snippet, spell

snazzy attractive, dashing, flamboyant, flashy, jazzy (*Inf.*), raffish, ritzy (*Sl.*), showy, smart, sophisticated, sporty, stylish, swinging (*Sl.*), with-it (*Inf.*)

sneak *v.* **1**. cower, lurk, pad, sidle, skulk, slink, slip, smuggle, spirit, steal **2**. *Inf.* grass on (*Brit. inf.*), inform on, peach (*Sl.*), tell on (*Inf.*), tell tales ~*n.* **3**. informer, snake in the grass, telltale ~*adj.* **4**. clandestine, furtive, quick, secret, stealthy, surprise

sneaking 1. hidden, private, secret, suppressed, unavowed, unconfessed, undivulged, unexpressed, unvoiced **2**. intuitive, nagging, niggling, persistent, uncomfortable, worrying **3**. contemptible, furtive, mean, sly, sneaky, surreptitious, two-faced, underhand

sneaky base, contemptible, cowardly, deceitful, devious, dishonest, disingenuous, double-dealing, furtive, low, malicious, mean, nasty, shifty, slippery, sly, snide, unreliable, unscrupulous, untrustworthy

sneer 1. *v.* curl one's lip, deride, disdain, gibe, hold in contempt, hold up to ridicule, jeer, laugh, look down on, mock, ridicule, scoff, scorn, sniff at, snigger, turn up one's nose (*Inf.*) **2**. *n.* derision, disdain, gibe, jeer, mockery, ridicule, scorn, snidery, snigger

snide cynical, disparaging, hurtful, ill-natured, insinuating, malicious, mean, nasty, sarcastic, scornful, sneering, spiteful, unkind

sniff *v.* breathe, inhale, smell, snuff, snuffle

sniffy condescending, contemptuous, disdainful, haughty, supercilious, superior

snigger giggle, laugh, smirk, sneer, snicker, titter

snip *v.* **1**. clip, crop, cut, nick, nip off, notch, shave, trim ~*n.* **2**. bit, clipping, fragment, piece, scrap, shred, snippet **3**. *Inf.* bargain, giveaway, good buy

snippet fragment, part, particle, piece, scrap, shred, snatch

snivel blubber, cry, girn (*Dialect*), gripe (*Inf.*), grizzle (*Inf.*), mewl, moan, sniffle, snuffle, weep, whimper, whine, whinge (*Inf.*)

snobbery arrogance, condescension, pretension, pride, side (*Brit. sl.*), snobbishness, snootiness (*Inf.*) airs, uppishness (*Brit. inf.*)

snobbish arrogant, condescending, high and mighty (*Inf.*), high-hat (*Inf., chiefly U.S.*), hoity-toity (*Inf.*), patronizing, pretentious, snooty (*Inf.*), stuck-up (*Inf.*), superior, toffee-nosed (*Sl.*), uppish (*Brit. inf.*)

snoop interfere, poke one's nose in (*Inf.*), pry, spy

snooper busybody, meddler, nosy parker (*Inf.*), Paul Pry, pry, snoop (*Inf.*), stickybeak (*Aust. inf.*)

snooze 1. *v.* catnap, doze, drop off (*Inf.*), drowse, kip (*Brit. sl.*), nap, nod off (*Inf.*), take forty winks (*Inf.*) 2. *n.* catnap, doze, forty winks (*Inf.*), kip (*Brit. sl.*), nap, siesta

snub 1. *v.* cold-shoulder, cut (*Inf.*), cut dead (*Inf.*), give (someone) the brush-off (*Sl.*), give (someone) the cold shoulder, humble, humiliate, mortify, rebuff, shame, slight 2. *n.* affront, brushoff (*Sl.*), humiliation, insult, put-down, slap in the face

snug 1. comfortable, comfy (*Inf.*), cosy, homely, intimate, sheltered, warm 2. close, compact, neat, trim

snuggle cuddle, nestle, nuzzle

soak *v.* 1. bathe, damp, drench, immerse, infuse, marinate (*Cookery*), moisten, penetrate, permeate, saturate, steep, wet 2. *With up* absorb, assimilate, drink in, take up *or* in

soaking drenched, dripping, drookit (*Scot.*), saturated, soaked, soaked to the skin, sodden, sopping, streaming, waterlogged, wet through, wringing wet

soar 1. ascend, fly, mount, rise, tower, wing 2. climb, escalate, rise, rocket, shoot up

sob *v.* bawl, blubber, boohoo, cry, greet (*Dialect*), howl, shed tears, snivel, weep

sober *adj.* 1. abstemious, abstinent, moderate, on the wagon (*Inf.*), temperate 2. calm, clear-headed, cold, composed, cool, dispassionate, grave, level-headed, lucid, peaceful, practical, rational, realistic, reasonable, sedate, serene,

serious, solemn, sound, staid, steady, unexcited, unruffled 3. dark, drab, plain, quiet, severe, sombre, subdued ~*v.* 4. *Usually with* **up** bring (someone) back to earth, calm down, clear one's head, come *or* bring to one's senses, give (someone) pause for thought, make (someone) stop and think

sobriety 1. abstemiousness, abstinence, moderation, nonindulgence, self-restraint, soberness, temperance 2. calmness, composure, coolness, gravity, level-headedness, reasonableness, restraint, sedateness, seriousness, solemnity, staidness, steadiness

so-called soi-disant, alleged, ostensible, pretended, professed, self-styled, supposed

sociability affability, companionability, congeniality, conviviality, cordiality, friendliness, gregariousness, neighbourliness

sociable accessible, affable, approachable, companionable, conversable, convivial, cordial, familiar, friendly, genial, gregarious, neighbourly, outgoing, social, warm

social *adj.* 1. collective, common, communal, community, general, group, organized, public, societal 2. companionable, friendly, gregarious, neighbourly, sociable ~*n.* 3. do (*Inf.*), gathering, get-together (*Inf.*)

socialize be a good mixer, entertain, fraternize, get about *or* around, get together, go out, mix

society 1. civilization, culture, humanity, mankind, people, population, social order, the community, the general public, the public, the world at large 2. camaraderie, companionship, company, fellowship, friendship 3. association, brotherhood, circle, club, corporation, fellowship, fraternity, group, guild, institute, league, organization, sisterhood, union 4. beau monde, elite, gentry, *haut monde*, high society, polite society, the country set, the nobs (*Sl.*), the smart set, the swells (*Inf.*), the toffs (*Brit. sl.*), the top drawer, upper classes, upper crust (*Inf.*)

sodden boggy, drenched, drookit (*Scot.*), marshy, miry, saturated, soaked, soggy, sopping, waterlogged

soft 1. creamy, cushioned, cushiony, doughy, elastic, gelatinous, pulpy, quaggy, spongy, squashy, swampy, yielding 2.

bendable, ductile (*of metals*), elastic, flexible, impressible, malleable, mouldable, plastic, pliable, supple **3**. downy, feathery, fleecy, flowing, fluid, furry, like a baby's bottom (*Inf.*), rounded, silky, smooth, velvety **4**. balmy, bland, caressing, delicate, diffuse, dim, dimmed, dulcet, faint, gentle, light, low, mellifluous, mellow, melodious, mild, murmured, muted, pale, pastel, pleasing, quiet, restful, shaded, soft-toned, soothing, subdued, sweet, temperate, twilight, understated, whispered **5**. compassionate, gentle, kind, pitying, sensitive, sentimental, sympathetic, tender, tenderhearted **6**. easy-going, indulgent, lax, lenient, liberal, overindulgent, permissive, spineless, weak **7**. *Inf.* comfortable, cushy (*Sl.*), easy, undemanding **8**. effeminate, flabby, flaccid, limp, namby-pamby, out of condition, out of training, overindulged, pampered, podgy, weak **9**. *Inf.* a bit lacking (*Inf.*), daft (*Inf.*), feeble-minded, foolish, silly, simple, soft in the head (*Inf.*), soppy (*Brit. inf.*)

soften abate, allay, alleviate, appease, assuage, calm, cushion, diminish, ease, lessen, lighten, lower, melt, mitigate, moderate, modify, mollify, muffle, palliate, quell, relax, soothe, still, subdue, temper, tone down, turn down

soften up conciliate, disarm, melt, soft-soap (*Inf.*), weaken, win over, work on

softhearted charitable, compassionate, generous, indulgent, kind, sentimental, sympathetic, tender, tenderhearted, warm-hearted

soft pedal de-emphasize, go easy (*Inf.*), moderate, play down, tone down

soft spot fondness, liking, partiality, weakness

soggy dripping, heavy, moist, mushy, pulpy, saturated, soaked, sodden, sopping, spongy, waterlogged

soil[1] *n.* **1**. clay, dirt, dust, earth, ground, loam **2**. country, land, region, terra firma

soil[2] *v.* bedraggle, befoul, begrime, besmirch, defile, dirty, foul, maculate (*Literary*), muddy, pollute, smear, spatter, spot, stain, sully, tarnish

sojourn 1. *n.* rest, stay, stop, stopover, visit **2**. *v.* abide, dwell, lodge, reside, rest, stay, stop, tarry

solace 1. *n.* alleviation, assuagement, comfort, consolation, relief **2**. *v.* allay, al-leviate, comfort, console, mitigate, soften, soothe

soldier enlisted man (*U.S.*), fighter, GI (*U.S. inf.*), man-at-arms, military man, redcoat, serviceman, squaddy (*Brit. inf.*), Tommy (*Brit.*), trooper, warrior

sole alone, exclusive, individual, one, one and only, only, single, singular, solitary

solecism blunder, boo-boo (*Inf.*), breach of etiquette, cacology, faux pas, gaffe, gaucherie, impropriety, incongruity, indecorum, lapse, mistake

solely alone, completely, entirely, exclusively, merely, only, single-handedly, singly

solemn 1. earnest, glum, grave, portentous, sedate, serious, sober, staid, thoughtful **2**. august, awe-inspiring, ceremonial, ceremonious, dignified, formal, grand, grave, imposing, impressive, majestic, momentous, stately **3**. devotional, hallowed, holy, religious, reverential, ritual, sacred, sanctified, venerable

solemnity 1. earnestness, grandeur, gravity, impressiveness, momentousness, portentousness, sacredness, sanctity, seriousness **2**. *Often plural* celebration, ceremonial, ceremony, formalities, observance, proceedings, rite, ritual

solemnize celebrate, commemorate, honour, keep, observe

solicit ask, beg, beseech, canvass, crave, entreat, implore, importune, petition, plead for, pray, seek, supplicate

solicitous anxious, apprehensive, attentive, careful, caring, concerned, eager, earnest, troubled, uneasy, worried, zealous

solicitude anxiety, attentiveness, care, concern, considerateness, consideration, regard, worry

solid *adj.* **1**. compact, concrete, dense, firm, hard, massed, stable, strong, sturdy, substantial, unshakable **2**. genuine, good, pure, real, reliable, sound **3**. agreed, complete, continuous, unalloyed, unanimous, unbroken, undivided, uninterrupted, united, unmixed **4**. constant, decent, dependable, estimable, lawabiding, level-headed, reliable, sensible, serious, sober, trusty, upright, upstanding, worthy

solidarity accord, camaraderie, cohesion, community of interest, concordance, esprit de corps, harmony, likemindedness, singleness of purpose,

soundness, stability, team spirit, unanimity, unification, unity

solidify cake, coagulate, cohere, congeal, harden, jell, set

solitary adj. 1. desolate, hidden, isolated, lonely, out-of-the-way, remote, retired, secluded, sequestered, unfrequented, unvisited 2. alone, lone, single, sole
3. cloistered, companionless, friendless,
hermitical, lonely, lonesome, reclusive,
unsociable, unsocial ~n. 4. hermit,
introvert, loner (Inf.), lone wolf, recluse

solitude 1. isolation, loneliness, privacy, reclusiveness, retirement, seclusion
2. Poetic desert, emptiness, waste,
wasteland, wilderness

solution 1. answer, clarification, elucidation, explanation, explication, key,
resolution, result, solving, unfolding, unravelling 2. blend, compound, emulsion,
mix, mixture, solvent, suspension
(Chem.) 3. disconnection, dissolution,
liquefaction, melting

solve answer, clarify, clear up, crack,
decipher, disentangle, elucidate, explain,
expound, get to the bottom of, interpret,
resolve, unfold, unravel, work out

sombre dark, dim, dismal, doleful,
drab, dull, dusky, funereal, gloomy,
grave, joyless, lugubrious, melancholy,
mournful, obscure, sad, sepulchral, shadowy, shady, sober

somebody n. big noise (Brit. sl.), big
shot (Sl.), big wheel (Sl.), bigwig (Sl.),
celebrity, dignitary, heavyweight (Inf.),
household name, luminary, name, notable, personage, person of note, public figure, star, superstar, V.I.P.

someday eventually, one day, one of
these (fine) days, sooner or later, ultimately

somehow by fair means or foul, by
hook or (by) crook, by some means or
other, come hell or high water (Inf.),
come what may, one way or another

sometimes at times, every now and
then, every so often, from time to time,
now and again, now and then, occasionally, off and on, once in a while, on occasion

somnolent comatose, dozy, drowsy,
half-awake, heavy-eyed, nodding off
(Inf.), sleepy, soporific, torpid

song air, anthem, ballad, canticle, canzonet, carol, chant, chorus, ditty, hymn,
lay, lyric, melody, number, pop song,
psalm, shanty, strain, tune

song and dance ado, commotion, flap
(Inf.), fuss, hoo-ha, kerfuffle (Inf.), performance (Inf.), pother, shindig (Sl.),
shindy (Sl.), stir, to-do

sonorous full, grandiloquent, high-
flown, high-sounding, loud, orotund,
plangent, resonant, resounding, rich,
ringing, rounded, sounding

soon anon (Archaic), any minute now,
before long, betimes (Archaic), in a little
while, in a minute, in a short time, in the
near future, shortly

soothe allay, alleviate, appease, assuage, calm, calm down, compose, ease,
hush, lull, mitigate, mollify, pacify, quiet, relieve, settle, smooth down, soften,
still, tranquillize

soothing balsamic, calming, demulcent, easeful, emollient, lenitive, palliative, relaxing, restful

soothsayer augur, diviner, foreteller,
prophet, seer, sibyl

sophisticated 1. blasé, citified, cosmopolitan, cultivated, cultured, jet-set,
refined, seasoned, urbane, worldly,
worldly-wise, world-weary 2. advanced,
complex, complicated, delicate, elaborate, highly-developed, intricate, multifaceted, refined, subtle

sophistication finesse, poise, savoir-
faire, savoir-vivre, urbanity, worldliness,
worldly wisdom

sophistry casuistry, fallacy, quibble,
sophism

soporific 1. adj. hypnotic, sedative,
sleep-inducing, sleepy, somniferous
(Rare), somnolent, tranquillizing 2. n.
anaesthetic, hypnotic, narcotic, opiate,
sedative, tranquillizer

soppy corny (Inf.), daft (Inf.), drippy
(Inf.), gushy (Inf.), lovey-dovey, mawkish, overemotional, schmaltzy (Sl.), sentimental, silly, slushy (Inf.), soft (Inf.),
weepy (Inf.)

sorcerer enchanter, mage (Archaic),
magician, magus, necromancer, sorceress, warlock, witch, wizard

sorcery black art, black magic, charm,
divination, enchantment, incantation,
magic, necromancy, spell, witchcraft,
witchery, wizardry

sordid 1. dirty, filthy, foul, mean,
seamy, seedy, sleazy, slovenly, slummy,
squalid, unclean, wretched 2. backstreet,
base, debauched, degenerate, degraded,
despicable, disreputable, low, shabby,
shameful, vicious, vile 3. avaricious, cor-

rupt, covetous, grasping, mercenary, miserly, niggardly, selfish, self-seeking, ungenerous, venal

sore *adj.* **1.** angry, burning, chafed, inflamed, irritated, painful, raw, reddened, sensitive, smarting, tender **2.** annoying, distressing, grievous, harrowing, severe, sharp, troublesome **3.** acute, critical, desperate, dire, extreme, pressing, urgent **4.** afflicted, aggrieved, angry, annoyed, grieved, hurt, irked, irritated, pained, peeved (*Inf.*), resentful, stung, upset, vexed ~*n.* **5.** abscess, boil, chafe, gathering, inflammation, ulcer

sorrow *n.* **1.** affliction, anguish, distress, grief, heartache, heartbreak, misery, mourning, regret, sadness, unhappiness, woe **2.** affliction, blow, hardship, misfortune, trial, tribulation, trouble, woe, worry ~*v.* **3.** agonize, bemoan, be sad, bewail, grieve, lament, moan, mourn, weep

sorrowful affecting, afflicted, dejected, depressed, disconsolate, distressing, doleful, grievous, heartbroken, heartrending, heavy-hearted, lamentable, lugubrious, melancholy, miserable, mournful, painful, piteous, rueful, sad, sick at heart, sorry, tearful, unhappy, woebegone, woeful, wretched

sorry **1.** apologetic, conscience-stricken, contrite, guilt-ridden, in sackcloth and ashes, penitent, regretful, remorseful, repentant, self-reproachful, shamefaced **2.** disconsolate, distressed, grieved, melancholy, mournful, sad, sorrowful, unhappy **3.** commiserative, compassionate, full of pity, moved, pitying, sympathetic **4.** abject, base, deplorable, dismal, distressing, mean, miserable, paltry, pathetic, piteous, pitiable, pitiful, poor, sad, shabby, vile, wretched

sort *n.* **1.** brand, breed, category, character, class, denomination, description, family, genus, group, ilk, kind, make, nature, order, quality, race, species, stamp, style, type, variety **2. out of sorts** crotchety, down in the dumps (*Inf.*), down in the mouth (*Inf.*), grouchy (*Inf.*), in low spirits, mopy, not up to par, not up to snuff (*Inf.*), off colour, poorly (*Inf.*), under the weather (*Inf.*) **3. sort of** as it were, in part, moderately, rather, reasonably, slightly, somewhat, to some extent ~*v.* **4.** arrange, assort, catalogue, categorize, choose, class, classify, distribute, divide, file, grade, group, order, put in or-

der, rank, select, separate, systematize

sort out **1.** clarify, clear up, organize, put *or* get straight, resolve, tidy up **2.** pick out, put on one side, segregate, select, separate, sift

so-so *adj.* adequate, average, fair, fair to middling (*Inf.*), indifferent, middling, moderate, not bad (*Inf.*), O.K. (*Inf.*), ordinary, passable, respectable, run-of-the-mill, tolerable, undistinguished

soul **1.** animating principle, essence, intellect, life, mind, psyche, reason, spirit, vital force **2.** being, body, creature, individual, man, mortal, person, woman **3.** embodiment, essence, incarnation, personification, quintessence, type **4.** animation, ardour, courage, energy, feeling, fervour, force, inspiration, nobility, vitality, vivacity

soulful eloquent, expressive, heartfelt, meaningful, mournful, moving, profound, sensitive

soulless **1.** callous, cold, cruel, inhuman, unfeeling, unkind, unsympathetic **2.** dead, lifeless, mechanical, soul-destroying, spiritless, uninteresting

sound[1] *n.* **1.** din, noise, report, resonance, reverberation, tone, voice **2.** drift, idea, implication(s), impression, look, tenor **3.** earshot, hearing, range ~*v.* **4.** echo, resonate, resound, reverberate **5.** appear, give the impression of, look, seem, strike one as being **6.** announce, articulate, declare, enunciate, express, pronounce, signal, utter

sound[2] *adj.* **1.** complete, entire, firm, fit, hale, hale and hearty, healthy, intact, perfect, robust, solid, sturdy, substantial, undamaged, unhurt, unimpaired, uninjured, vigorous, well-constructed, whole **2.** correct, fair, just, level-headed, logical, orthodox, proper, prudent, rational, reasonable, reliable, responsible, right, right-thinking, sensible, true, trustworthy, valid, well-founded, well-grounded, wise **3.** established, orthodox, proven, recognized, reliable, reputable, safe, secure, solid, solvent, stable, tried-and-true **4.** deep, peaceful, unbroken, undisturbed, untroubled

sound[3] *v.* **1.** fathom, plumb, probe **2.** examine, inspect, investigate, test

sound[4] *n.* **1.** channel, passage, strait **2.** arm of the sea, fjord, inlet, voe

sound out canvass, examine, probe, pump, question, see how the land lies

sour *adj.* **1.** acetic, acid, acidulated,

bitter, pungent, sharp, tart, unpleasant **2.** bad, curdled, fermented, gone off, rancid, turned, unsavoury, unwholesome **3.** acrid, acrimonious, churlish, crabbed, cynical, disagreeable, discontented, embittered, grouchy (*Inf.*), grudging, ill-natured, ill-tempered, jaundiced, peevish, tart, ungenerous, waspish ~v. **4.** alienate, disenchant, embitter, envenom, exacerbate, exasperate, turn off (*Inf.*)

source 1. author, begetter, beginning, cause, commencement, derivation, fountainhead, origin, originator, rise, spring, wellspring **2.** authority, informant

sourpuss crosspatch (*Inf.*), grouser, grump (*Inf., chiefly U.S.*), killjoy, misery (*Brit. inf.*), shrew

souse drench, dunk, immerse, marinate (*Cookery*), pickle, soak, steep

souvenir keepsake, memento, relic, remembrancer (*Archaic*), reminder, token

sovereign n. **1.** chief, emperor, empress, king, monarch, potentate, prince, queen, ruler, shah, supreme ruler, tsar ~adj. **2.** absolute, chief, dominant, imperial, kingly, monarchal, paramount, predominant, principal, queenly, regal, royal, ruling, supreme, unlimited **3.** effectual, efficacious, efficient, excellent

sovereignty ascendancy, domination, kingship, primacy, supremacy, supreme power, suzerainty, sway

sow broadcast, disseminate, implant, inseminate, lodge, plant, scatter, seed

space 1. amplitude, capacity, elbow-room, expanse, extension, extent, leeway, margin, play, room, scope, spaciousness, volume **2.** blank, distance, gap, interval, lacuna, omission **3.** duration, interval, period, span, time, while **4.** accommodation, berth, place, seat

spaceman *or* **spacewoman** astronaut, cosmonaut

spacious ample, broad, capacious, comfortable, commodious, expansive, extensive, huge, large, roomy, sizable, uncrowded, vast

spadework donkey-work, ground-work, labour, preparation

span n. **1.** amount, distance, extent, length, reach, spread, stretch **2.** duration, period, spell, term ~v. **3.** arch across, bridge, cover, cross, extend across, link, range over, traverse, vault

spank v. belt (*Sl.*), cuff, give (some-

one) a hiding (*Inf.*), put (someone) over one's knee, slap, slipper (*Inf.*), smack, tan (*Sl.*), wallop (*Inf.*)

spanking adj. **1.** brisk, energetic, fast, invigorating, lively, quick, smart, snappy, vigorous **2.** *Inf.* brand-new, fine, gleaming, smart

spar v. argue, bicker, dispute, exchange blows, fall out (*Inf.*), have a tiff, lead a cat-and-dog life, scrap (*Inf.*), skirmish, spat (*U.S.*), squabble, wrangle, wrestle

spare adj. **1.** additional, emergency, extra, free, going begging (*Inf.*), in excess, in reserve, leftover, odd, over, superfluous, supernumerary, surplus, unoccupied, unused, unwanted **2.** gaunt, lank, lean, meagre, slender, slight, slim, wiry **3.** economical, frugal, meagre, modest, scanty, sparing **4. go spare** *Brit. sl.* become angry (distracted, distraught, enraged, mad (*Inf.*), upset), blow one's top (*Inf.*), do one's nut (*Brit. sl.*), go up the wall (*Sl.*), have *or* throw a fit (*Inf.*) ~v. **5.** afford, allow, bestow, dispense with, do without, give, grant, let (someone) have, manage without, part with, relinquish **6.** be merciful to, deal leniently with, go easy on (*Inf.*), have mercy on, leave, let off (*Inf.*), pardon, refrain from, release, relieve from, save from

spare time free time, leisure, odd moments, time on one's hands, time to kill

sparing careful, chary, cost-conscious, economical, frugal, money-conscious, prudent, saving, thrifty

spark n. **1.** flare, flash, flicker, gleam, glint, scintillation, spit **2.** atom, hint, jot, scintilla, scrap, trace, vestige ~v. **3.** *Often with* **off** animate, excite, inspire, kindle, precipitate, provoke, set in motion, set off, start, stimulate, stir, touch off, trigger (off)

sparkle v. **1.** beam, coruscate, dance, flash, gleam, glint, glisten, glister (*Archaic*), glitter, glow, scintillate, shimmer, shine, spark, twinkle, wink **2.** bubble, effervesce, fizz, fizzle ~n. **3.** brilliance, coruscation, dazzle, flash, flicker, gleam, glint, radiance, spark, twinkle **4.** animation, dash, élan, gaiety, life, panache, spirit, vim (*Sl.*), vitality, vivacity, zip (*Inf.*)

sparse few and far between, meagre, scanty, scarce, scattered

spartan 1. abstemious, ascetic, austere, bleak, disciplined, extreme, frugal, plain, rigorous, self-denying, severe, stern, strict, stringent 2. bold, brave, courageous, daring, dauntless, doughty, fearless, hardy, heroic, intrepid, resolute, unflinching, valorous

spasm 1. contraction, convulsion, paroxysm, throe (*Rare*), twitch 2. access, burst, eruption, fit, frenzy, outburst, seizure

spasmodic convulsive, erratic, fitful, intermittent, irregular, jerky, sporadic

spate deluge, flood, flow, outpouring, rush, torrent

spatter bespatter, bestrew, daub, dirty, scatter, soil, speckle, splash, splodge, spray, sprinkle

speak 1. articulate, communicate, converse, discourse, enunciate, express, make known, pronounce, say, state, talk, tell, utter, voice 2. address, argue, declaim, deliver an address, descant, discourse, harangue, hold forth, lecture, plead, speechify, spiel (*Inf.*) 3. *With* of advert to, allude to, comment on, deal with, discuss, make reference to, mention, refer to

speaker lecturer, mouthpiece, orator, public speaker, spieler (*Inf.*), spokesman, spokesperson, spokeswoman, wordspinner

speak for act for *or* on behalf of, appear for, hold a brief for, hold a mandate for, represent

speaking *adj.* eloquent, expressive, moving, noticeable, striking

speak out *or* **up** 1. make oneself heard, say it loud and clear, speak loudly 2. have one's say, make one's position plain, sound off, speak one's mind, stand up and be counted

speak to 1. accost, address, apostrophize, direct one's words at, talk to 2. admonish, bring to book, dress down (*Inf.*), lecture, rebuke, reprimand, scold, tell off (*Inf.*), tick off (*Inf.*), warn

spearhead *v.* be in the van, blaze the trail, head, initiate, launch, lay the first stone, lead, lead the way, pioneer, set in motion, set off

special 1. distinguished, especial, exceptional, extraordinary, festive, gala, important, memorable, momentous, out of the ordinary, red-letter, significant, uncommon, unique, unusual 2. appropriate, certain, characteristic, distinctive, especial, individual, particular, peculiar, precise, specialized, specific 3. chief,

main, major, particular, primary

specialist *n.* authority, connoisseur, consultant, expert, master, professional

speciality claim to fame, distinctive *or* distinguishing feature, forte, *pièce de résistance*, special, specialty

species breed, category, class, collection, description, group, kind, sort, type, variety

specific *adj.* 1. clear-cut, definite, exact, explicit, express, limited, particular, precise, unambiguous, unequivocal 2. characteristic, distinguishing, especial, peculiar, special

specification condition, detail, item, particular, qualification, requirement, stipulation

specify be specific about, cite, define, designate, detail, enumerate, indicate, individualize, itemize, mention, name, particularize, spell out, stipulate

specimen copy, embodiment, example, exemplar, exemplification, exhibit, individual, instance, model, pattern, proof, representative, sample, type

specious casuistic, deceptive, fallacious, misleading, plausible, sophistic, sophistical, unsound

speck 1. blemish, blot, defect, dot, fault, flaw, fleck, mark, mote, speckle, spot, stain 2. atom, bit, dot, grain, iota, jot, mite, modicum, particle, shred, tittle, whit

speckled brindled, dappled, dotted, flecked, freckled, mottled, speckledy, spotted, spotty, sprinkled, stippled

spectacle 1. display, event, exhibition, extravaganza, pageant, parade, performance, show, sight 2. curiosity, laughing stock, marvel, phenomenon, scene, sight, wonder

spectacular 1. *adj.* breathtaking, daring, dazzling, dramatic, eye-catching, fantastic (*Inf.*), grand, impressive, magnificent, marked, remarkable, sensational, splendid, staggering, striking, stunning (*Inf.*) 2. *n.* display, extravaganza, show, spectacle

spectator beholder, bystander, eyewitness, looker-on, observer, onlooker, viewer, watcher, witness

spectral eerie, ghostly, incorporeal, insubstantial, phantom, shadowy, spooky (*Inf.*), supernatural, uncanny, unearthly, weird, wraithlike

spectre apparition, ghost, phantom,

presence, shade (*Literary*), shadow, spirit, vision, wraith

speculate 1. cogitate, conjecture, consider, contemplate, deliberate, hypothesize, meditate, muse, scheme, suppose,
surmise, theorize, wonder **2.** gamble,
have a flutter (*Inf.*), hazard, play the
market, risk, take a chance with, venture

speculation 1. conjecture, consideration, contemplation, deliberation, guess,
guesswork, hypothesis, opinion, supposition, surmise, theory **2.** gamble, gambling, hazard, risk

speculative 1. abstract, academic,
conjectural, hypothetical, notional, suppositional, tentative, theoretical **2.**
chancy (*Inf.*), dicey (*Sl.*), hazardous,
risky, uncertain, unpredictable

speech 1. communication, conversation, dialogue, discussion, intercourse,
talk **2.** address, discourse, disquisition,
harangue, homily, lecture, oration, spiel
(*Inf.*) **3.** articulation, dialect, diction,
enunciation, idiom, jargon, language, lingo (*Inf.*), parlance, tongue, utterance,
voice

speechless 1. dumb, inarticulate,
mum, mute, silent, tongue-tied, unable
to get a word out (*Inf.*), wordless **2.** *Fig.*
aghast, amazed, astounded, dazed,
dumbfounded, dumbstruck, shocked,
thunderstruck

speed *n.* **1.** acceleration, celerity,
expedition, fleetness, haste, hurry, momentum, pace, precipitation, quickness,
rapidity, rush, swiftness, velocity ~*v.* **2.**
belt (along) (*Sl.*), bomb (along), bowl
along, career, dispatch, exceed the speed
limit, expedite, flash, gallop, get a move
on (*Inf.*), go hell for leather (*Inf.*), go like
a bat out of hell (*Inf.*), go like the wind,
hasten, hurry, lose no time, make haste,
press on, put one's foot down (*Inf.*),
quicken, race, rush, sprint, step on it
(*Inf.*), tear, urge, zoom **3.** advance, aid,
assist, boost, expedite, facilitate, further,
help, impel, promote

speed up accelerate, gather momentum, get moving, get under way, increase, increase the tempo, open up the
throttle, put one's foot down (*Inf.*), put
on speed

speedy expeditious, express, fast,
fleet, fleet of foot, hasty, headlong, hurried, immediate, nimble, precipitate,
prompt, quick, rapid, summary, swift,
winged

spell[1] *n.* bout, course, interval, patch,
period, season, stint, stretch, term, time,
tour of duty, turn

spell[2] *n.* **1.** abracadabra, charm, conjuration, exorcism, incantation, sorcery,
witchery **2.** allure, bewitchment, enchantment, fascination, glamour, magic,
trance

spell[3] *v.* amount to, augur, herald, imply, indicate, mean, point to, portend,
presage, promise, signify, suggest

spellbound bemused, bewitched, captivated, charmed, enthralled, entranced,
fascinated, gripped, hooked (*Inf.*), mesmerized, possessed, rapt, transfixed,
transported, under a spell

spelling orthography

spell out 1. clarify, elucidate, make
clear *or* plain, make explicit, specify **2.**
discern, make out, puzzle out

spend 1. disburse, expend, fork out
(*Sl.*), lay out, pay out, shell out (*Inf.*),
splash out (*Brit. inf.*) **2.** blow (*Sl.*), consume, deplete, dispense, dissipate, drain,
empty, exhaust, fritter away, run
through, squander, use up, waste **3.** apply, bestow, concentrate, devote, employ, invest, lavish, put in, use **4.** fill, occupy, pass, while away

spendthrift 1. *n.* big spender, prodigal, profligate, spender, squanderer,
waster, wastrel **2.** *adj.* extravagant, improvident, prodigal, profligate, wasteful

spent *adj.* **1.** all in (*Sl.*), burnt out,
bushed (*U.S. inf.*), dead beat (*Inf.*), debilitated, dog-tired (*Inf.*), done in *or* up
(*Inf.*), drained, exhausted, fagged (out)
(*Inf.*), knackered (*Sl.*), played out (*Inf.*),
prostrate, ready to drop (*Inf.*), shattered
(*Inf.*), tired out, weakened, wearied, weary, whacked (*Brit. inf.*), worn out **2.** consumed, expended, finished, gone, used
up

spew belch forth, disgorge, puke (*Sl.*),
regurgitate, spit out, throw up (*Inf.*),
vomit

sphere 1. ball, circle, globe, globule,
orb **2.** capacity, compass, department,
domain, employment, field, function,
pale, province, range, rank, realm, scope,
station, stratum, territory, walk of life

spherical globe-shaped, globular, orbicular, rotund, round

spice *n.* **1.** relish, savour, seasoning **2.**
colour, excitement, gusto, kick (*Inf.*),
pep, piquancy, tang, zap (*Sl.*), zest, zip
(*Inf.*)

spick-and-span clean, fresh as paint, immaculate, in apple-pie order (*Inf.*), neat as a new pin, shipshape, spotless, spruce, tidy, trim

spicy 1. aromatic, flavoursome, hot, piquant, pungent, savoury, seasoned, tangy 2. *Inf.* broad, hot (*Inf.*), improper, indecorous, indelicate, off-colour, racy, ribald, risqué, scandalous, sensational, suggestive, titillating, unseemly

spiel 1. *v.* expatiate on, hold forth, lecture, recite, speechify, spout (*Inf.*) 2. *n.* harangue, patter, pitch, recital, sales patter, sales talk, speech

spike *n.* 1. barb, point, prong, spine ~*v.* 2. impale, spear, spit, stick 3. block, foil, frustrate, render ineffective, thwart

spill *v.* 1. discharge, disgorge, overflow, overturn, scatter, shed, slop over, spill *or* run over, throw off, upset 2. **spill the beans** *Inf.* betray a secret, blab, blow the gaff (*Brit. sl.*), give the game away, inform, let the cat out of the bag, split (*Sl.*), squeal (*Sl.*), talk out of turn, tattle ~*n.* 3. *Inf.* accident, cropper (*Inf.*), fall, tumble

spin *v.* 1. gyrate, pirouette, reel, revolve, rotate, turn, twirl, twist, wheel, whirl 2. concoct, develop, invent, narrate, recount, relate, tell, unfold 3. be giddy, be in a whirl, grow dizzy, reel, swim, whirl ~*n.* 4. gyration, revolution, roll, twist, whirl 5. **(flat) spin** *Inf.* agitation, commotion, flap (*Inf.*), panic, state (*Inf.*), tiz-woz (*Inf.*), tizzy (*Inf.*) 6. *Inf.* drive, hurl (*Scot.*), joy ride (*Inf.*), ride, turn, whirl

spindly attenuated, gangling, gangly, lanky, leggy, spidery, spindle-shanked, twiggy

spine 1. backbone, spinal column, vertebrae, vertebral column 2. barb, needle, quill, rachis, ray, spike, spur

spine-chilling bloodcurdling, eerie, frightening, hair-raising, horrifying, scary (*Inf.*), spooky (*Inf.*), terrifying

spineless cowardly, faint-hearted, feeble, gutless (*Inf.*), inadequate, ineffective, irresolute, lily-livered, soft, spiritless, squeamish, submissive, vacillating, weak, weak-kneed (*Inf.*), weak-willed, without a will of one's own, yellow (*Inf.*)

spin out amplify, delay, drag out, draw out, extend, lengthen, pad out, prolong, prolongate, protract

spiral 1. *adj.* circular, cochlear, cochleate (*Biol.*), coiled, corkscrew, helical, scrolled, voluted, whorled, winding 2. *n.* coil, corkscrew, curlicue, gyre (*Literary*), helix, screw, volute, whorl

spirit *n.* 1. air, breath, life, life force, psyche, soul, vital spark 2. attitude, character, complexion, disposition, essence, humour, outlook, quality, temper, temperament 3. animation, ardour, backbone, courage, dauntlessness, earnestness, energy, enterprise, enthusiasm, fire, force, gameness, grit, guts (*Inf.*), life, liveliness, mettle, resolution, sparkle, spunk (*Inf.*), stoutheartedness, vigour, warmth, zest 4. motivation, resolution, resolve, will, willpower 5. atmosphere, feeling, gist, humour, tenor, tone 6. essence, intent, intention, meaning, purport, purpose, sense, substance 7. *Plural* feelings, frame of mind, humour, mood, morale 8. apparition, ghost, phantom, shade (*Literary*), shadow, spectre, spook (*Inf.*), sprite, vision ~*v.* 9. *With* **away** *or* **off** abduct, abstract, carry, convey, make away with, purloin, remove, seize, snaffle (*Brit. inf.*), steal, whisk

spirited active, animated, ardent, bold, courageous, energetic, game, high-spirited, lively, mettlesome, plucky, sparkling, sprightly, spunky (*Inf.*), vigorous, vivacious

spiritless apathetic, dejected, depressed, despondent, dispirited, droopy, dull, lacklustre, languid, lifeless, listless, low (*Inf.*), melancholic, melancholy, mopy, torpid, unenthusiastic, unmoved

spirits alcohol, firewater, liquor, strong liquor, the hard stuff (*Inf.*)

spiritual devotional, divine, ethereal, ghostly, holy, immaterial, incorporeal, nonmaterial, otherworldly, pure, religious, sacred

spit 1. *v.* discharge, eject, expectorate, hiss, spew, splutter, sputter, throw out 2. *n.* dribble, drool, saliva, slaver, spittle, sputum

spite *n.* 1. animosity, bitchiness (*Sl.*), gall, grudge, hate, hatred, ill will, malevolence, malice, malignity, pique, rancour, spitefulness, spleen, venom 2. **in spite of** despite, in defiance of, notwithstanding, regardless of ~*v.* 3. annoy, discomfit, gall, harm, hurt, injure, needle (*Inf.*), nettle, offend, pique, provoke, put out, put (someone's) nose out of joint (*Inf.*), vex

spiteful barbed, bitchy (*Inf.*), catty (*Inf.*), cruel, ill-disposed, ill-natured, malevolent, malicious, malignant, rancorous, snide, splenetic, venomous, vindictive

spitting image clone, (dead) ringer (*Sl.*), double, likeness, living image, lookalike, picture, replica, spit (*Inf.*), spit and image (*Inf.*)

splash *v.* **1.** bespatter, shower, slop, slosh (*Inf.*), spatter, splodge, spray, spread, sprinkle, squirt, strew, wet **2.** bathe, dabble, paddle, plunge, wade, wallow **3.** batter, break, buffet, dash, plash, plop, smack, strike, surge, wash **4.** blazon, broadcast, flaunt, headline, plaster, publicize, tout, trumpet ~*n.* **5.** burst, dash, patch, spattering, splodge, touch **6.** *Inf.* display, effect, impact, sensation, splurge, stir **7. make a splash** be ostentatious, cause a stir, cut a dash, go overboard (*Inf.*), go to town (*Inf.*), splurge

splash out be extravagant, lash out (*Inf.*), push the boat out (*Brit. inf.*), spare no expense, spend, splurge

spleen acrimony, anger, animosity, animus, bad temper, bile, bitterness, gall, hatred, hostility, ill humour, ill will, malevolence, malice, malignity, peevishness, pique, rancour, resentment, spite, spitefulness, venom, vindictiveness, wrath

splendid **1.** admirable, brilliant, exceptional, glorious, grand, heroic, illustrious, magnificent, outstanding, rare, remarkable, renowned, sterling, sublime, superb, supreme **2.** costly, dazzling, gorgeous, imposing, impressive, lavish, luxurious, magnificent, ornate, resplendent, rich, sumptuous, superb **3.** excellent, fantastic (*Inf.*), fine, first-class, glorious, great (*Inf.*), marvellous, wonderful **4.** beaming, bright, brilliant, glittering, glowing, lustrous, radiant, refulgent

splendour brightness, brilliance, ceremony, dazzle, display, effulgence, glory, gorgeousness, grandeur, lustre, magnificence, majesty, pomp, radiance, refulgence, renown, resplendence, richness, show, solemnity, spectacle, stateliness, sumptuousness

splenetic acid, bitchy (*Inf.*), choleric, churlish, crabbed, crabby, cross, envenomed, fretful, irascible, irritable, morose, peevish, petulant, rancorous, sour, spiteful, sullen, testy, touchy

splice *v.* braid, entwine, graft, interlace, intertwine, intertwist, interweave, join, knit, marry, mesh, plait, unite, wed, yoke

splinter **1.** *n.* chip, flake, fragment, needle, paring, shaving, sliver **2.** *v.* break into smithereens, disintegrate, fracture, shatter, shiver, split

split *v.* **1.** bifurcate, branch, break, break up, burst, cleave, come apart, come undone, crack, disband, disunite, diverge, fork, gape, give way, go separate ways, open, part, pull apart, rend, rip, separate, slash, slit, snap, splinter **2.** allocate, allot, apportion, carve up, distribute, divide, divvy up (*Inf.*), dole out, halve, parcel out, partition, share out, slice up **3.** *With* **on** *Sl.* betray, give away, grass (*Brit. sl.*), inform on, peach (*Sl.*), squeal (*Sl.*) ~*n.* **4.** breach, crack, damage, division, fissure, gap, rent, rip, separation, slash, slit, tear **5.** breach, break, break-up, difference, discord, disruption, dissension, disunion, divergence, division, estrangement, partition, rift, rupture, schism ~*adj.* **6.** ambivalent, bisected, broken, cleft, cracked, divided, dual, fractured, ruptured, twofold

split up break up, disband, divorce, go separate ways, part, part company, separate

spoil *v.* **1.** blemish, damage, debase, deface, destroy, disfigure, harm, impair, injure, mar, mess up, ruin, upset, wreck **2.** baby, cocker (*Rare*), coddle, cosset, indulge, kill with kindness, mollycoddle, overindulge, pamper, spoon-feed **3.** addle, become tainted, curdle, decay, decompose, go bad, go off (*Brit. inf.*), mildew, putrefy, rot, turn **4. spoiling for** bent upon, desirous of, eager for, enthusiastic about, keen to, looking for, out to get (*Inf.*), raring to

spoils boodle (*Sl., chiefly U.S.*), booty, gain, loot, pickings, pillage, plunder, prey, prizes, rapine, swag (*Sl.*)

spoilsport damper, dog in the manger, kill-joy, misery (*Brit. inf.*), party-pooper (*U.S. sl.*), wet blanket (*Inf.*)

spoken expressed, oral, phonetic, put into words, said, told, unwritten, uttered, verbal, viva voce, voiced, by word of mouth

sponger bloodsucker (*Inf.*), cadge (*Brit.*), cadger, freeloader (*U.S. sl.*), hanger-on, leech, parasite, scrounger (*Inf.*)

spongy absorbent, cushioned, cushiony, elastic, light, porous, springy

sponsor 1. *n.* angel (*Inf.*), backer, god-parent, guarantor, patron, promoter 2. *v.* back, finance, fund, guarantee, lend one's name to, patronize, promote, put up the money for, subsidize

spontaneous extempore, free, impromptu, impulsive, instinctive, natural, unbidden, uncompelled, unconstrained, unforced, unpremeditated, unprompted, voluntary, willing

spontaneously extempore, freely, impromptu, impulsively, instinctively, off one's own bat, off the cuff (*Inf.*), of one's own accord, on impulse, quite unprompted, voluntarily

spoof *n.* 1. burlesque, caricature, lampoon, mockery, parody, satire, send-up (*Brit. inf.*), take-off (*Inf.*), travesty 2. bluff, deception, game, hoax, joke, leg-pull (*Brit. inf.*), prank, trick

spooky chilling, creepy (*Inf.*), eerie, frightening, ghostly, mysterious, scary (*Inf.*), spine-chilling, supernatural, uncanny, unearthly, weird

spoon-feed baby, cosset, featherbed, mollycoddle, overindulge, overprotect, spoil, wrap up in cotton wool (*Inf.*)

sporadic infrequent, intermittent, irregular, isolated, occasional, on and off, random, scattered, spasmodic

sport *n.* 1. amusement, diversion, entertainment, exercise, game, pastime, physical activity, play, recreation 2. badinage, banter, frolic, fun, jest, joking, kidding (*Inf.*), merriment, mirth, raillery, teasing 3. buffoon, butt, derision, fair game, game, laughing stock, mockery, plaything, ridicule ~*v.* 4. *With* with amuse oneself, dally, flirt, play, take advantage of, toy, treat lightly *or* cavalierly, trifle 5. *Inf.* display, exhibit, show off, wear 6. caper, disport, frolic, gambol, play, romp

sporting fair, game (*Inf.*), gentlemanly, sportsman-like

sportive coltish, frisky, frolicsome, full of beans (*Inf.*), full of fun, gamesome, gay, joyous, kittenish, lively, merry, playful, prankish, rollicking, skittish, sprightly

sporty 1. casual, flashy, gay, informal, jaunty, jazzy (*Inf.*), loud, raffish, rakish, showy, snazzy (*Inf.*), stylish, trendy 2. athletic, energetic, hearty, outdoor

spot *n.* 1. blemish, blot, blotch, daub, discoloration, flaw, mark, pimple, plook (*Scot.*), pustule, smudge, speck, stain, taint 2. locality, location, place, point, position, scene, site, situation 3. *Inf.* bit, little, morsel, splash 4. *Inf.* difficulty, mess, plight, predicament, quandary, trouble ~*v.* 5. catch sight of, descry, detect, discern, espy, identify, make out, observe, pick out, recognize, see, sight 6. besmirch, blot, dirty, dot, fleck, mark, mottle, soil, spatter, speckle, splodge, splotch, stain, sully, taint, tarnish

spotless above reproach, blameless, chaste, faultless, flawless, gleaming, immaculate, innocent, irreproachable, pure, shining, snowy, unblemished, unimpeachable, unstained, unsullied, untarnished, virgin, virginal, white

spotlight *Fig.* 1. *v.* accentuate, draw attention to, feature, focus attention on, give prominence to, highlight, illuminate, point up, throw into relief 2. *n.* attention, fame, interest, limelight, notoriety, public attention, public eye

spot-on accurate, correct, exact, hitting the nail on the head (*Inf.*), on the bull's-eye (*Inf.*), precise, punctual (to the minute), right, unerring

spotted dappled, dotted, flecked, mottled, pied, polka-dot, specked, speckled

spotty 1. blotchy, pimpled, pimply, plooky-faced (*Scot.*), poor-complexioned 2. erratic, fluctuating, irregular, patchy, sporadic, uneven

spouse better half (*Inf.*), companion, consort, helpmate, husband, mate, partner, wife

spout *v.* 1. discharge, emit, erupt, gush, jet, shoot, spray, spurt, squirt, stream, surge 2. *Inf.* declaim, expatiate, go on (*Inf.*), hold forth, orate, pontificate, rabbit on (*Brit. sl.*), ramble (on), rant, speechify, spiel (*Inf.*), talk

sprawl *v.* flop, loll, lounge, ramble, slouch, slump, spread, straggle, trail

spray[1] *v.* 1. atomize, diffuse, scatter, shower, sprinkle ~*n.* 2. drizzle, droplets, fine mist, moisture, spindrift, spoondrift 3. aerosol, atomizer, sprinkler

spray[2] *n.* bough, branch, corsage, floral arrangement, shoot, sprig

spread *v.* 1. be displayed, bloat, broaden, dilate, expand, extend, fan out, open, open out, sprawl, stretch, swell, unfold, unfurl, unroll, widen 2. escalate, multiply, mushroom, proliferate 3. advertise, blazon, broadcast, bruit, cast, circulate, cover, diffuse, disseminate, distribute, make known, make public, proclaim, promulgate, propagate, publicize, publish, radiate, scatter, shed, strew, transmit **4.** arrange, array, cover, furnish, lay, prepare, set ~*n.* **5.** advance, advancement, development, diffusion, dispersion, dissemination, escalation, expansion, increase, proliferation, spreading, suffusion, transmission **6.** compass, extent, period, reach, span, stretch, sweep, term **7.** *Inf.* array, banquet, blowout (*Sl.*), feast, repast

spree bacchanalia, bender (*Inf.*), binge (*Inf.*), carouse, debauch, fling, jag (*Sl.*), junketing, orgy, revel, splurge

sprightly active, agile, airy, alert, animated, blithe, brisk, cheerful, energetic, frolicsome, gay, jaunty, joyous, lively, nimble, perky, playful, spirited, sportive, spry, vivacious

spring *v.* **1.** bounce, bound, hop, jump, leap, rebound, recoil, vault **2.** *Often with* **from** arise, be derived, be descended, come, derive, descend, emanate, emerge, grow, issue, originate, proceed, start, stem **3.** *With* **up** appear, burgeon, come into existence *or* being, develop, mushroom, shoot up ~*n.* **4.** bound, buck, hop, jump, leap, saltation, vault **5.** bounce, bounciness, buoyancy, elasticity, flexibility, give (*Inf.*), recoil, resilience, springiness **6.** beginning, cause, fountainhead, origin, root, source, well, wellspring ~*adj.* **7.** *Of the season* springlike, vernal

springy bouncy, buoyant, elastic, flexible, resilient, rubbery, spongy

sprinkle *v.* dredge, dust, pepper, powder, scatter, shower, spray, strew

sprinkling admixture, dash, dusting, few, handful, scatter, scattering, smattering, sprinkle

sprint *v.* dart, dash, go at top speed, hare (*Brit. inf.*), hotfoot, put on a burst of speed, race, scamper, shoot, tear, whiz (*Inf.*)

sprite apparition, brownie, dryad, elf, fairy, goblin, imp, leprechaun, naiad, nymph, pixie, spirit, sylph

sprout *v.* bud, develop, germinate, grow, push, shoot, spring, vegetate

spruce as if one had just stepped out of a bandbox, dainty, dapper, elegant, natty (*Inf.*), neat, smart, trig (*Archaic*), trim, well-groomed, well turned out

spruce up groom, have a wash and brush-up (*Brit.*), smarten up, tidy, titivate

spry active, agile, alert, brisk, nimble, nippy (*Brit. inf.*), quick, ready, sprightly, supple

spunk backbone, bottle (*Brit. sl.*), courage, gameness, grit, gumption (*Inf.*), guts (*Inf.*), mettle, nerve, pluck, resolution, spirit, toughness

spur *v.* **1.** animate, drive, goad, impel, incite, press, prick, prod, prompt, stimulate, urge ~*n.* **2.** goad, prick, rowel **3.** impetus, impulse, incentive, incitement, inducement, motive, stimulus **4. on the spur of the moment** impetuously, impromptu, impulsively, on impulse, on the spot, unpremeditatedly, unthinkingly, without planning, without thinking

spurious artificial, bogus, contrived, counterfeit, deceitful, fake, false, feigned, forged, imitation, mock, phoney (*Sl.*), pretended, pseudo (*Inf.*), sham, simulated, specious, unauthentic

spurn cold-shoulder, contemn, despise, disdain, disregard, rebuff, reject, repulse, scorn, slight, snub, turn one's nose up at (*Inf.*)

spurt 1. *v.* burst, erupt, gush, jet, shoot, spew, squirt, surge **2.** *n.* access, burst, fit, rush, spate, surge

spy *n.* **1.** double agent, fifth columnist, foreign agent, mole, secret agent, secret service agent, undercover agent ~*v.* **2.** *Usually with* **on** follow, keep under surveillance, keep watch on, shadow, tail (*Inf.*), trail, watch **3.** catch sight of, descry, espy, glimpse, notice, observe, set eyes on, spot

spying *n.* espionage, secret service

squabble 1. *v.* argue, bicker, brawl, clash, dispute, fall out (*Inf.*), fight, have words, quarrel, row, scrap (*Inf.*), wrangle **2.** *n.* argument, barney (*Inf.*), difference of opinion, disagreement, dispute, fight, row, scrap (*Inf.*), set-to (*Inf.*), spat, tiff

squad band, company, crew, force, gang, group, team, troop

squalid broken-down, decayed, dirty, disgusting, fetid, filthy, foul, low, nasty, poverty-stricken, repulsive, run-down, seedy, sleazy, slovenly, slummy, sordid, unclean

squally blustery, gusty, rough, stormy, tempestuous, turbulent, wild, windy

squalor decay, filth, foulness, meanness, sleaziness, slumminess, squalidness, wretchedness

squander be prodigal with, blow (*Sl.*), consume, dissipate, expend, fritter away, frivol away, lavish, misspend, misuse, run through, scatter, spend, spend like water, throw away, waste

square *Fig. v.* **1.** *Often with* **with** accord, agree, conform, correspond, fit, harmonize, match, reconcile, tally **2.** *Sometimes with* **up** balance, clear (up), discharge, liquidate, make even, pay off, quit, satisfy, settle **3.** accommodate, adapt, adjust, align, even up, level, regulate, suit, tailor, true (up) **4.** *Sl.* bribe, buy off, corrupt, fix (*Inf.*), rig, suborn ~*adj.* **5.** aboveboard, decent, equitable, ethical, fair, fair and square, genuine, honest, just, on the level (*Inf.*), straight, straightforward, upright **6.** *Inf.* behind the times (*Inf.*), bourgeois, conservative, conventional, old-fashioned, out of date, straight (*Sl.*), strait-laced, stuffy ~*n.* **7.** *Inf.* antediluvian, back number (*Inf.*), conservative, die-hard, fuddy-duddy (*Inf.*), old buffer (*Brit. inf.*), (old) fogy, stick-in-the-mud (*Inf.*), traditionalist

squash *v.* **1.** compress, crush, distort, flatten, mash, pound, press, pulp, smash, stamp on, trample down **2.** annihilate, crush, humiliate, put down (*Sl.*), put (someone) in his (*or her*) place, quash, quell, silence, sit on (*Inf.*), suppress

squashy mushy, pappy, pulpy, soft, spongy, yielding

squawk *v.* **1.** cackle, crow, cry, hoot, screech, yelp **2.** *Inf.* complain, kick up a fuss (*Inf.*), protest, raise Cain (*Sl.*), squeal (*Inf.*)

squeak *v.* peep, pipe, shrill, squeal, whine, yelp

squeal *n.* **1.** scream, screech, shriek, wail, yell, yelp, yowl ~*v.* **2.** scream, screech, shout, shriek, shrill, wail, yelp **3.** *Sl.* betray, blab, grass (*Brit. sl.*), inform on, peach (*Sl.*), rat on, sell (someone) down the river (*Inf.*), sing (*Sl.*), snitch (*Sl.*) **4.** *Inf.* complain, kick up a fuss (*Inf.*), moan, protest, squawk (*Inf.*)

squeamish **1.** delicate, fastidious, finicky, nice (*Rare*), particular, prissy (*Inf.*), prudish, punctilious, scrupulous, strait-laced **2.** nauseous, qualmish, queasy, queer, sick, sickish

squeeze *v.* **1.** clutch, compress, crush, grip, nip, pinch, press, squash, wring **2.** cram, crowd, force, jam, jostle, pack, press, ram, stuff, thrust, wedge **3.** clasp, cuddle, embrace, enfold, hold tight, hug **4.** bleed (*Inf.*), bring pressure to bear on, extort, lean on (*Inf.*), milk, oppress,

pressurize, put the screws on (*Inf.*), put the squeeze on (*Inf.*), wrest ~*n.* **5.** clasp, embrace, handclasp, hold, hug **6.** congestion, crowd, crush, jam, press, squash

squire *v.* accompany, attend, companion, escort

squirm agonize, fidget, flounder, shift, twist, wiggle, wriggle, writhe

stab *v.* **1.** bayonet, cut, gore, injure, jab, knife, pierce, puncture, run through, spear, stick, thrust, transfix, wound **2.** **stab in the back** betray, break faith with, deceive, do the dirty on (*Brit. sl.*), double-cross (*Inf.*), give the Judas kiss to, inform on, let down, play false, sell, sell out (*Inf.*), slander ~*n.* **3.** gash, incision, jab, puncture, rent, thrust, wound **4.** ache, pang, prick, twinge **5.** **make a stab at** attempt, endeavour, essay, have a go (crack, shot) (*Inf.*), try, try one's hand at, venture

stability constancy, durability, firmness, permanence, solidity, soundness, steadfastness, steadiness, strength

stable abiding, constant, deep-rooted, durable, enduring, established, fast, firm, fixed, immutable, invariable, lasting, permanent, reliable, secure, sound, steadfast, steady, strong, sturdy, sure, unalterable, unchangeable, unwavering, well-founded

stack **1.** *n.* clamp (*Brit. agriculture*), cock, heap, hoard, load, mass, mound, mountain, pile **2.** *v.* accumulate, amass, assemble, bank up, heap up, load, pile, stockpile

staff *n.* **1.** employees, lecturers, officers, organization, personnel, teachers, team, workers, work force **2.** cane, pole, prop, rod, stave, wand

stage **1.** *n.* division, juncture, lap, leg, length, level, period, phase, point, step **2.** *v.* arrange, do, engineer, give, lay on, mount, orchestrate, organize, perform, play, present, produce, put on

stagger *v.* **1.** falter, hesitate, lurch, reel, sway, teeter, totter, vacillate, waver, wobble **2.** amaze, astonish, astound, bowl over (*Inf.*), confound, dumbfound, flabbergast, give (someone) a shock, nonplus, overwhelm, shake, shock, strike (someone) dumb (*Inf.*), stun, stupefy, surprise, take (someone) aback, take (someone's) breath away, throw off balance **3.** alternate, overlap, step, zigzag

stagnant brackish, motionless, quiet, sluggish, stale, standing, still

stagnate decay, decline, deteriorate, fester, go to seed, idle, languish, lie fallow, rot, rust, stand still, vegetate

staid calm, composed, decorous, demure, grave, quiet, sedate, self-restrained, serious, sober, solemn, steady

stain *v.* **1.** blemish, blot, colour, dirty, discolour, dye, mark, soil, spot, tarnish, tinge **2.** besmirch, blacken, contaminate, corrupt, defile, deprave, disgrace, drag through the mud, sully, taint ~*n.* **3.** blemish, blot, discoloration, dye, spot, tint **4.** blemish, blot on the escutcheon, disgrace, dishonour, infamy, reproach, shame, slur, stigma

stake[1] *n.* **1.** pale, paling, picket, pole, post, spike, stave, stick ~*v.* **2.** brace, prop, secure, support, tether, tie up **3.** *Often with* **out** define, delimit, demarcate, lay claim to, mark out, outline, reserve

stake[2] *n.* **1.** ante, bet, chance, hazard, peril, pledge, risk, venture, wager **2.** claim, concern, interest, investment, involvement, share ~*v.* **3.** bet, chance, gamble, hazard, imperil, jeopardize, pledge, put on, risk, venture, wager

stale **1.** decayed, dry, faded, fetid, flat, fusty, hard, insipid, musty, old, sour, stagnant, tasteless **2.** antiquated, banal, cliché-ridden, common, commonplace, drab, effete, flat, hackneyed, insipid, old hat, overused, platitudinous, repetitious, stereotyped, threadbare, trite, unoriginal, worn-out

stalemate deadlock, draw, impasse, standstill, tie

stalk *v.* **1.** creep up on, follow, haunt, hunt, pursue, shadow, tail (*Inf.*), track **2.** flounce, march, pace, stride, strut

stall *v.* beat about the bush (*Inf.*), equivocate, hedge, play for time, prevaricate, stonewall, temporize

stalwart athletic, beefy (*Inf.*), brawny, daring, dependable, hefty (*Inf.*), husky (*Inf.*), indomitable, intrepid, lusty, manly, muscular, redoubtable, robust, rugged, sinewy, staunch, stout, strapping, strong, sturdy, valiant, vigorous

stamina energy, force, grit (*Inf.*), indefatigability, lustiness, power, power of endurance, resilience, resistance, staying power, strength, vigour

stammer *v.* falter, hem and haw, hesitate, pause, splutter, stumble, stutter

stamp *v.* **1.** beat, crush, trample **2.** engrave, fix, impress, imprint, inscribe, mark, mould, print **3.** betray, brand, categorize, exhibit, identify, label, mark, pronounce, reveal, show to be, typecast ~*n.* **4.** brand, cast, earmark, hallmark, imprint, mark, mould, signature **5.** breed, cast, character, cut, description, fashion, form, kind, sort, type

stamp collecting philately

stampede *n.* charge, flight, rout, rush, scattering

stamp out crush, destroy, eliminate, eradicate, extinguish, extirpate, put down, put out, quell, quench, scotch, suppress

stance **1.** bearing, carriage, deportment, posture **2.** attitude, position, stand, standpoint, viewpoint

stanch, staunch arrest, check, dam, halt, plug, stay, stem, stop

stand *v.* **1.** be upright, be vertical, erect, mount, place, position, put, rank, rise, set **2.** be in force, belong, be situated *or* located, be valid, continue, exist, halt, hold, obtain, pause, prevail, remain, rest, stay, stop **3.** abide, allow, bear, brook, cope with, countenance, endure, experience, handle, put up with (*Inf.*), stomach, submit to, suffer, support, sustain, take, thole (*Dialect*), tolerate, undergo, wear (*Brit. sl.*), weather, withstand ~*n.* **4.** halt, rest, standstill, stay, stop, stopover **5.** attitude, determination, firm stand, opinion, position, stance, standpoint **6.** base, booth, bracket, dais, frame, grandstand, place, platform, rack, rank, stage, staging, stall, stance (*Chiefly Scot.*), support, table

standard[1] *n.* **1.** average, benchmark, canon, criterion, example, gauge, grade, guide, guideline, measure, model, norm, pattern, principle, requirement, rule, sample, specification, touchstone, type, yardstick **2.** *Often plural* code of honour, ethics, ideals, moral principles, morals, principles ~*adj.* **3.** accepted, average, basic, customary, normal, orthodox, popular, prevailing, regular, set, staple, stock, typical, usual **4.** approved, authoritative, classic, definitive, established, official, recognized

standard[2] *n.* banner, colours, ensign, flag, pennant, pennon, streamer

standardize assimilate, bring into line, institutionalize, mass-produce, regiment, stereotype

stand by 1. back, befriend, be loyal to, champion, defend, stick up for (*Inf.*), support, take (someone's) part, uphold **2**. be prepared, wait, wait in the wings

stand for 1. betoken, denote, exemplify, indicate, mean, represent, signify, symbolize **2**. *Inf*. bear, brook, endure, lie down under (*Inf*.), put up with, suffer, tolerate, wear (*Brit. inf*.)

stand in for cover for, deputize for, do duty for, hold the fort for, replace, take the place of, understudy

standing *n*. **1**. condition, credit, eminence, estimation, footing, position, rank, reputation, repute, station, status **2**. continuance, duration, existence, experience ~*adj*. **3**. fixed, lasting, permanent, perpetual, regular, repeated **4**. erect, perpendicular, rampant (*Heraldry*), upended, upright, vertical

standoffish aloof, cold, distant, haughty, remote, reserved, unapproachable, unsociable

stand out attract attention, be highlighted, be prominent (conspicuous, distinct, striking), be thrown into relief, bulk large, catch the eye, leap to the eye, project, stare one in the face (*Inf*.), stick out a mile (*Inf*.)

standpoint angle, point of view, position, post, stance, station, vantage point, viewpoint

stand up for champion, come to the defence of, defend, side with, stick up for (*Inf*.), support, uphold

stand up to brave, confront, defy, endure, oppose, resist, withstand

staple *adj*. basic, chief, essential, fundamental, key, main, predominant, primary, principle

star 1. *n*. celebrity, draw (*Inf*.), idol, lead, leading man *or* lady, luminary, main attraction, name **2**. *adj*. brilliant, celebrated, illustrious, leading, major, paramount, principal, prominent, talented, well-known

starchy ceremonious, conventional, formal, precise, prim, punctilious, stiff, stuffy

stare *v*. gape, gawk, gawp (*Brit. sl*.), gaze, goggle, look, rubberneck (*Sl*.), watch

stark *adj*. **1**. absolute, arrant, bald, bare, blunt, consummate, downright, entire, flagrant, out-and-out, palpable, patent, pure, sheer, simple, unalloyed, unmitigated, utter **2**. austere, bare, barren, bleak, cold, depressing, desolate, drear (*Literary*), dreary, forsaken, grim, harsh,

plain, severe, solitary, unadorned ~*adv*. **3**. absolutely, altogether, clean, completely, entirely, quite, utterly, wholly

stark-naked in a state of nature, in one's birthday suit (*Inf*.), in the altogether (*Inf*.), in the buff (*Inf*.), in the raw (*Inf*.), naked, nude, stark, starkers (*Inf*.), stripped, unclad, undressed, without a stitch on (*Inf*.)

start *v*. **1**. appear, arise, begin, come into being, come into existence, commence, depart, first see the light of day, get on the road, get under way, go ahead (*Inf*.), hit the road (*Inf*.), issue, leave, originate, pitch in (*Inf*.), sally forth, set off, set out **2**. activate, embark upon, engender, enter upon, get going, initiate, instigate, kick off (*Inf*.), make a beginning, open, originate, put one's hand to the plough (*Inf*.), set about, set in motion, start the ball rolling, take the first step, take the plunge (*Inf*.), turn on **3**. begin, create, establish, father, found, inaugurate, initiate, institute, introduce, launch, lay the foundations of, pioneer, set up **4**. blench, flinch, jerk, jump, recoil, shy, twitch ~*n*. **5**. beginning, birth, commencement, dawn, first step(s), foundation, inauguration, inception, initiation, kickoff (*Inf*.), onset, opening, outset **6**. advantage, edge, head start, lead **7**. backing, break (*Inf*.), chance, helping hand, introduction, opening, opportunity, sponsorship **8**. convulsion, jar, jump, spasm, twitch

startle agitate, alarm, amaze, astonish, astound, frighten, give (someone) a turn (*Inf*.), make (someone) jump, scare, shock, surprise, take (someone) aback

startling alarming, astonishing, astounding, extraordinary, shocking, staggering, sudden, surprising, unexpected, unforeseen

starving faint from lack of food, famished, hungering, hungry, ravenous, ready to eat a horse (*Inf*.), sharp-set, starved

stash *v*. cache, hide, hoard, lay up, put aside for a rainy day, salt away, save up, secrete, stockpile, stow

state[1] *v*. **1**. affirm, articulate, assert, asseverate, aver, declare, enumerate, explain, expound, express, present, propound, put, report, say, specify, voice ~*n*. **2**. case, category, circumstances, condition, mode, pass, plight, position, predicament, shape, situation, state of affairs **3.** attitude, frame of mind, humour, mood, spirits **4.** ceremony, dignity, display, glory, grandeur, majesty, pomp, splendour, style **5.** *Inf.* bother, flap (*Inf.*), panic, pother, tiz-woz (*Inf.*), tizzy (*Inf.*) **6. in a state** *Inf.* agitated, all steamed up (*Sl.*), anxious, distressed, disturbed, flustered, het up, panic-stricken, ruffled, upset

state[2] *n.* body politic, commonwealth, country, federation, government, kingdom, land, nation, republic, territory

stately august, ceremonious, deliberate, dignified, elegant, grand, imperial, imposing, impressive, lofty, majestic, measured, noble, pompous, regal, royal, solemn

statement account, announcement, communication, communiqué, declaration, explanation, proclamation, recital, relation, report, testimony, utterance

static changeless, constant, fixed, immobile, inert, motionless, stagnant, stationary, still, unmoving, unvarying

station *n.* **1.** base, depot, headquarters, location, place, position, post, seat, situation **2.** appointment, business, calling, employment, grade, occupation, position, post, rank, situation, sphere, standing, status ~*v.* **3.** assign, establish, fix, garrison, install, locate, post, set

stationary at a standstill, fixed, inert, moored, motionless, parked, standing, static, stock-still, unmoving

statuesque dignified, imposing, Junoesque, majestic, regal, stately

stature consequence, eminence, high station, importance, prestige, prominence, rank, size, standing

status condition, consequence, degree, distinction, eminence, grade, position, prestige, rank, standing

statute act, decree, edict, enactment, ordinance, regulation, rule

staunch constant, dependable, faithful, firm, loyal, reliable, resolute, sound, steadfast, stout, strong, sure, tried and true, true, true-blue, trustworthy, trusty

stave off avert, evade, fend off, foil, hold off, keep at arm's length, keep at bay, parry, ward off

stay[1] *v.* **1.** abide, continue, delay, establish oneself, halt, hang around (*Inf.*), hover, linger, loiter, pause, put down roots, remain, reside, settle, sojourn, stand, stay put, stop, tarry, wait **2.** *Often with* **at** be accommodated at, lodge, put

up at, sojourn, visit **3.** adjourn, defer, discontinue, hold in abeyance, hold over, prorogue, put off, suspend **4.** *Archaic* arrest, check, curb, delay, detain, hinder, hold, impede, obstruct, prevent ~*n.* **5.** holiday, sojourn, stop, stopover, visit **6.** deferment, delay, halt, pause, postponement, remission, reprieve, stopping, suspension

stay[2] *n.* brace, buttress, prop, reinforcement, shoring, stanchion, support

staying power endurance, stamina, strength, toughness

steadfast constant, dedicated, dependable, established, faithful, fast, firm, fixed, intent, loyal, persevering, reliable, resolute, single-minded, stable, staunch, steady, unfaltering, unflinching, unswerving, unwavering

steady *adj.* **1.** firm, fixed, immovable, safe, stable, substantial, unchangeable, uniform **2.** balanced, calm, dependable, equable, having both feet on the ground, imperturbable, level-headed, reliable, sedate, sensible, sober, serene, serious-minded, settled, sober, staid, steadfast **3.** ceaseless, confirmed, consistent, constant, continuous, even, faithful, habitual, incessant, nonstop, persistent, regular, rhythmic, unbroken, unfaltering, unfluctuating, uninterrupted, unremitting, unvarying, unwavering ~*v.* **4.** balance, brace, secure, stabilize, support **5.** compose *or* calm oneself, cool down, sober (up), get a grip on oneself (*Inf.*)

steal 1. appropriate, be light-fingered, embezzle, filch, half-inch (*Inf.*), heist (*U.S. sl.*), lift (*Inf.*), misappropriate, nick (*Sl.*), peculate, pilfer, pinch (*Inf.*), pirate, plagiarize, poach, prig (*Brit. sl.*), purloin, shoplift, snitch (*Sl.*), swipe (*Sl.*), take, thieve, walk *or* make off with **2.** creep, flit, insinuate oneself, slink, slip, sneak, tiptoe

stealing embezzlement, larceny, misappropriation, pilferage, pilfering, plagiarism, robbery, shoplifting, theft, thievery, thieving

stealth furtiveness, secrecy, slyness, sneakiness, stealthiness, surreptitiousness, unobtrusiveness

stealthy clandestine, covert, furtive, secret, secretive, skulking, sly, sneaking, sneaky, surreptitious, underhand

steel *v.* brace, fortify, grit one's teeth, harden, make up one's mind

steep[1] *adj.* **1.** abrupt, headlong, precipitous, sheer 2. *Inf.* excessive, exorbitant, extortionate, extreme, high, overpriced, stiff, uncalled-for, unreasonable

steep[2] *v.* 1. damp, drench, imbrue (*Rare*), immerse, macerate, marinate (*Cookery*), moisten, soak, souse, submerge 2. fill, imbue, infuse, permeate, pervade, saturate, suffuse

steer 1. be in the driver's seat, conduct, control, direct, govern, guide, pilot 2. **steer clear of** avoid, circumvent, eschew, evade, give a wide berth to, sheer off, shun

steersman cox, coxswain, helmsman, pilot, wheelman (*U.S.*)

stem[1] 1. *n.* axis, branch, peduncle, shoot, stalk, stock, trunk 2. *v. Usually with* **from** arise, be caused (bred, brought about, generated) by, derive, develop, emanate, flow, issue, originate

stem[2] *v.* bring to a standstill, check, contain, curb, dam, hold back, oppose, resist, restrain, stanch, stay (*Archaic*), stop, withstand

stench foul odour, mephitis, noisomeness, pong (*Brit. inf.*), reek, stink

step *n.* 1. footfall, footprint, footstep, gait, impression, pace, print, stride, trace, track, walk 2. act, action, deed, expedient, manoeuvre, means, measure, move, procedure, proceeding 3. **take steps** act, intervene, move in, prepare, take action, take measures, take the initiative 4. advance, advancement, move, phase, point, process, progression, stage 5. degree, level, rank, remove 6. doorstep, round, rung, stair, tread 7. **in step** coinciding, conforming, in harmony (agreement, conformity, unison), in line 8. **out of step** erratic, incongruous, in disagreement, out of harmony, out of line, out of phase, pulling different ways 9. **watch one's step** be discreet (canny, careful, cautious), be on one's guard, have one's wits about one, look out, mind how one goes, mind one's p's and q's, take care, take heed, tread carefully ~*v.* 10. move, pace, tread, walk

step down abdicate, bow out, give up, hand over, leave, pull out, quit, resign, retire

step in become involved, chip in (*Inf.*), intercede, intervene, take action, take a hand

step up accelerate, augment, boost, escalate, increase, intensify, raise, speed up, up

stereotype 1. *n.* formula, mould, pattern, received idea 2. *v.* categorize, conventionalize, dub, pigeonhole, standardize, take to be, typecast

stereotyped banal, cliché-ridden, conventional, corny (*Inf.*), hackneyed, mass-produced, overused, platitudinous, played out, stale, standard, standardized, stock, threadbare, tired, trite, unoriginal

sterile 1. abortive, bare, barren, dry, empty, fruitless, infecund, unfruitful, unproductive, unprofitable, unprolific 2. antiseptic, aseptic, disinfected, germ-free, sterilized

sterilize autoclave, disinfect, fumigate, purify

sterling authentic, excellent, first-class, genuine, pure, real, sound, standard, substantial, superlative, true

stern austere, authoritarian, bitter, cruel, flinty, forbidding, frowning, grim, hard, harsh, inflexible, relentless, rigid, rigorous, serious, severe, steely, strict, unrelenting, unsparing, unyielding

stick[1] *v.* 1. adhere, affix, attach, bind, bond, cement, cleave, cling, fasten, fix, fuse, glue, hold, hold on, join, paste, weld 2. dig. gore, insert, jab, penetrate, pierce, pin, poke, prod, puncture, spear, stab, thrust, transfix 3. *With* **out, up** *etc.* bulge, extend, jut, obtrude, poke, project, protrude, show 4. *Inf.* deposit, drop, fix, install, lay, place, plant, plonk, position, put, set, store, stuff 5. be bogged down, become immobilized, be embedded, catch, clog, come to a standstill, jam, lodge, snag, stop 6. linger, persist, remain, stay 7. *Sl.* abide, bear up under, endure, get on with, stand, stomach, take, tolerate 8. **stick it out** *Inf.* bear, endure, grin and bear it (*Inf.*), last out, put up with (*Inf.*), see it through, see through to the bitter end, soldier on, take it (*Inf.*), weather 9. **stick up for** *Inf.* champion, defend, stand up for, support, take the part *or* side of, uphold

stick[2] *n.* 1. baton, birch, cane, pole, rod, staff, stake, switch, twig, wand 2. *Inf.* fuddy-duddy (*Inf.*), (old) fogy, pain (*Inf.*), prig, stick-in-the-mud (*Inf.*) 3. *Brit. sl.* abuse, blame, criticism, flak (*Inf.*), hostility, punishment

stick at 1. continue, keep at, persevere in, persist, plug away at (*Inf.*), see (something) through 2. balk, be conscience-stricken, be deterred by, demur, doubt, hesitate, pause, recoil, scruple, shrink from, stop at

stick-in-the-mud Colonel Blimp, conservative, die-hard, fuddy-duddy (*Inf.*), (old) fogy, reactionary, sobersides, stick (*Inf.*)

stickler fanatic, fusspot (*Brit. inf.*), hard taskmaster, maniac (*Inf.*), martinet, nut (*Sl.*), pedant, perfectionist, purist

stick to adhere to, cleave to, continue in, honour, keep, persevere in, remain loyal (faithful, true), stick at

sticky 1. adhesive, claggy (*Dialect*), clinging, gluey, glutinous, gooey (*Inf.*), gummy, syrupy, tacky, tenacious, viscid, viscous **2.** *Inf.* awkward, delicate, difficult, discomforting, embarrassing, hairy (*Sl.*), nasty, painful, thorny, tricky, unpleasant **3.** clammy, close, humid, muggy, oppressive, sultry, sweltering

stiff 1. brittle, firm, hard, hardened, inelastic, inflexible, rigid, solid, solidified, taut, tense, tight, unbending, unyielding **2.** artificial, austere, ceremonious, chilly, cold, constrained, forced, formal, laboured, mannered, pompous, priggish, prim, punctilious, standoffish, starchy (*Inf.*), stilted, uneasy, unnatural, unrelaxed, wooden **3.** arthritic, awkward, clumsy, creaky (*Inf.*), crude, graceless, inelegant, jerky, rheumaticky (*Inf.*), ungainly, ungraceful, unsupple **4.** arduous, difficult, exacting, fatiguing, formidable, hard, laborious, tough, trying, uphill **5.** austere, cruel, drastic, extreme, great, hard, harsh, heavy, inexorable, oppressive, pitiless, rigorous, severe, sharp, strict, stringent **6.** brisk, fresh, powerful, strong, vigorous

stiffen brace, coagulate, congeal, crystallize, harden, jell, reinforce, set, solidify, starch, tauten, tense, thicken

stiff-necked boneheaded (*Inf.*), contumacious, haughty, obstinate, opinionated, stubborn, uncompromising, unreceptive

stifle 1. asphyxiate, choke, smother, strangle, suffocate **2.** check, choke back, cover up, curb, extinguish, hush, muffle, prevent, repress, restrain, silence, smother, stop, suppress

stigma blot, brand, disgrace, dishonour, imputation, mark, reproach, shame, slur, smirch, spot, stain

stigmatize brand, cast a slur upon, defame, denounce, discredit, label, mark, pillory

still 1. *adj.* at rest, calm, hushed, inert, lifeless, motionless, noiseless, pacific, peaceful, placid, quiet, restful, serene, silent, smooth, stationary, stilly (*Poetic*), tranquil, undisturbed, unruffled, unstirring **2.** *v.* allay, alleviate, appease, calm, hush, lull, pacify, quiet, quieten, settle, silence, smooth, smooth over, soothe, subdue, tranquillize **3.** *conj.* but, for all that, however, nevertheless, notwithstanding, yet **4.** *n. Poetic* hush, peace, quiet, silence, stillness, tranquillity

stilted artificial, bombastic, constrained, forced, grandiloquent, highflown, high-sounding, inflated, laboured, pedantic, pompous, pretentious, stiff, unnatural, wooden

stimulant analeptic, bracer (*Inf.*), energizer, excitant, pep pill (*Inf.*), pick-me-up (*Inf.*), restorative, reviver, tonic, upper (*Sl.*)

stimulate animate, arouse, encourage, fan, fire, foment, goad, impel, incite, inflame, instigate, prompt, provoke, quicken, rouse, spur, turn on (*Inf.*), urge, whet

stimulating exciting, exhilarating, galvanic, inspiring, intriguing, provocative, provoking, rousing, stirring, thought-provoking

stimulus encouragement, fillip, goad, incentive, incitement, inducement, provocation, shot in the arm (*Inf.*), spur

sting *v.* **1.** burn, hurt, pain, smart, tingle, wound **2.** anger, gall, incense, inflame, infuriate, nettle, pique, provoke, rile **3.** *Inf.* cheat, defraud, do (*Sl.*), fleece, overcharge, rip off (*Sl.*), swindle, take for a ride (*Inf.*)

stingy 1. avaricious, cheeseparing, close-fisted, covetous, illiberal, mean, mingy (*Brit. inf.*), miserly, near, niggardly, parsimonious, penny-pinching (*Inf.*), penurious, scrimping, tightfisted, ungenerous **2.** inadequate, insufficient, meagre, measly (*Inf.*), mouldy (*Inf.*), on the small side, scanty, small

stink *v.* **1.** offend the nostrils, pong (*Brit. inf.*), reek, stink to high heaven (*Inf.*), whiff (*Brit. sl.*) **2.** *Sl.* be held in disrepute, be no good, be offensive, be rotten (abhorrent, bad, detestable), have a bad name ~*n.* **3.** fetor, foulness, foul odour, malodour, noisomeness, pong (*Brit. inf.*), stench **4.** *Sl.* brouhaha, commotion, deal of trouble (*Inf.*), disturbance, fuss, hubbub, row, rumpus, scandal, stir, to-do, uproar, upset

stinker 1. bounder (*Inf.*), cad (*Brit. inf.*), cur, dastard (*Archaic*), heel, nasty piece of work (*Inf.*), rotter (*Sl.*), scab, scoundrel, sod (*Sl.*), swine **2**. affliction, beast, difficulty, fine how-do-you-do (*Inf.*), horror, impediment, plight, poser, predicament, problem, shocker

stinking 1. fetid, foul-smelling, ill-smelling, malodorous, mephitic, noisome, pongy (*Brit. inf.*), reeking, smelly, whiffy (*Brit. sl.*) **2**. *Inf.* contemptible, disgusting, low, low-down (*Inf.*), mean, rotten, unpleasant, vile, wretched **3**. *Sl.* boozed, canned (*Sl.*), drunk, drunk as a lord, intoxicated, plastered (*Sl.*), smashed (*Sl.*), sozzled (*Inf.*), stewed (*Sl.*), stoned (*Sl.*)

stint 1. *n*. assignment, bit, period, quota, share, shift, spell, stretch, term, time, tour, turn **2**. *v*. begrudge, be sparing (frugal, mingy (*Brit. inf.*), parsimonious), economize, hold back, save, scrimp, skimp on, spoil the ship for a ha'porth of tar, withhold

stipulate agree, contract, covenant, engage, guarantee, insist upon, lay down, lay down *or* impose conditions, make a point of, pledge, postulate, promise, require, settle, specify

stipulation agreement, clause, condition, contract, engagement, precondition, prerequisite, provision, proviso, qualification, requirement, restriction, settlement, *sine qua non*, specification, term

stir *v*. **1**. agitate, beat, disturb, flutter, mix, move, quiver, rustle, shake, tremble **2**. *Often with* **up** animate, arouse, awaken, excite, incite, inflame, instigate, kindle, prompt, provoke, quicken, raise, spur, stimulate, urge **3**. affect, electrify, excite, fire, inspire, move, thrill, touch **4**. bestir, be up and about (*Inf.*), budge, exert oneself, get a move on (*Inf.*), get moving (*Inf.*), hasten, look lively (*Inf.*), make an effort, mill about, move, shake a leg (*Inf.*) ~*n*. **5**. activity, ado, agitation, bustle, commotion, disorder, disturbance, excitement, ferment, flurry, fuss, movement, to-do, tumult, uproar

stirring animating, dramatic, emotive, exciting, exhilarating, heady, impassioned, inspiring, intoxicating, lively, moving, rousing, spirited, stimulating, thrilling

stock *n*. **1**. array, assets, assortment, cache, choice, commodities, fund, goods, hoard, inventory, merchandise, range, reserve, reservoir, selection, stockpile, store, supply, variety, wares **2**. *Animals* beasts, cattle, domestic animals, flocks, herds, horses, livestock, sheep **3**. ancestry, background, breed, descent, extraction, family, forebears, house, line, lineage, line of descent, parentage, pedigree, race, strain, type, variety **4**. *Money* capital, funds, investment, property **5**. **take stock** appraise, estimate, review the situation, see how the land lies, size up (*Inf.*), weigh up ~*adj.* **6**. banal, basic, commonplace, conventional, customary, formal, hackneyed, ordinary, overused, regular, routine, run-of-the-mill, set, standard, staple, stereotyped, traditional, trite, usual, worn-out ~*v*. **7**. deal in, handle, keep, sell, supply, trade in **8**. *With* **up** accumulate, amass, buy up, gather, hoard, lay in, put away, replenish, save, store (up), supply **9**. equip, fill, fit out, furnish, kit out, provide with, provision, supply

stocky chunky, dumpy, mesomorphic, solid, stubby, stumpy, sturdy, thickset

stodgy 1. filling, heavy, leaden, starchy, substantial **2**. boring, dull, dull as ditchwater, formal, fuddy-duddy (*Inf.*), heavy going, laboured, staid, stuffy, tedious, turgid, unexciting, unimaginative, uninspired

stoical calm, cool, dispassionate, impassive, imperturbable, indifferent, long-suffering, philosophic, phlegmatic, resigned, stoic, stolid

stoicism acceptance, calmness, dispassion, fatalism, forbearance, fortitude, impassivity, imperturbability, indifference, long-suffering, patience, resignation, stolidity

stolid apathetic, bovine, doltish, dull, heavy, lumpish, obtuse, slow, stupid, unemotional, wooden

stomach *n*. **1**. abdomen, belly, breadbasket (*Sl.*), gut (*Inf.*), inside(s) (*Inf.*), paunch, pot, potbelly, spare tyre (*Inf.*), tummy (*Inf.*) **2**. appetite, desire, inclination, mind, relish, taste ~*v*. **3**. abide, bear, endure, put up with (*Inf.*), reconcile *or* resign oneself to, submit to, suffer, swallow, take, tolerate

stony *Fig.* adamant, blank, callous, chilly, expressionless, frigid, hard, heartless, hostile, icy, indifferent, inexorable, merciless, obdurate, pitiless, unfeeling, unforgiving, unresponsive

stooge 1. *n.* butt, dupe, fall guy (*Inf.*, *chiefly U.S.*), foil, henchman, lackey, patsy (*U.S. sl.*), pawn, puppet **2.** *v. Inf.* flit, fly, hang about (*Inf.*), meander, mooch (*Sl.*), mosey (*Inf.*), move, wander

stoop *v.* **1.** be bowed *or* round-shouldered, bend, bow, crouch, descend, duck, hunch, incline, kneel, lean, squat **2.** *Often with* **to** condescend, deign, demean oneself, descend, lower oneself, resort, sink, vouchsafe ~*n.* **3.** bad posture, droop, round-shoulderedness, sag, slouch, slump

stop *v.* **1.** be over, break off, bring *or* come to a halt, bring *or* come to a standstill, call it a day (*Inf.*), cease, come to an end, conclude, cut out (*Inf.*), cut short, desist, discontinue, draw up, end, finish, halt, leave off, pack in (*Brit. inf.*), pause, peter out, pull up, put an end to, quit, refrain, run down, run its course, shut down, stall, terminate **2.** arrest, bar, block, break, check, close, forestall, frustrate, hinder, hold back, impede, intercept, interrupt, obstruct, plug, prevent, rein in, repress, restrain, seal, silence, staunch, stem, suspend **3.** break one's journey, lodge, put up, rest, sojourn, stay, tarry ~*n.* **4.** cessation, conclusion, discontinuance, end, finish, halt, standstill **5.** break, rest, sojourn, stay, stopover, visit **6.** bar, block, break, check, control, hindrance, impediment, plug, stoppage **7.** depot, destination, halt, stage, station, termination, terminus

stopgap 1. *n.* improvisation, makeshift, resort, shift, substitute, temporary expedient **2.** *adj.* emergency, impromptu, improvised, makeshift, provisional, rough-and-ready, temporary

stoppage 1. abeyance, arrest, close, closure, cutoff, deduction, discontinuance, halt, hindrance, lay-off, shutdown, standstill, stopping **2.** blockage, check, curtailment, interruption, obstruction, occlusion, stopping up

store *v.* **1.** accumulate, deposit, garner, hoard, husband, keep, keep in reserve, lay by *or* in, lock away, put aside, put aside for a rainy day, put by, put in storage, reserve, salt away, save, stash (*Inf.*), stock, stockpile ~*n.* **2.** abundance, accumulation, cache, fund, hoard, lot, mine, plenty, plethora, provision, quantity, reserve, reservoir, stock, stockpile, supply,

wealth **3.** chain store, department store, emporium, market, mart, outlet, shop, supermarket **4.** depository, repository, storehouse, storeroom, warehouse **5. set store by** appreciate, esteem, hold in high regard, prize, think highly of, value

storm *n.* **1.** blast, blizzard, cyclone, gale, gust, hurricane, squall, tempest, tornado, whirlwind **2.** *Fig.* agitation, anger, clamour, commotion, disturbance, furore, hubbub, outbreak, outburst, outcry, passion, roar, row, rumpus, stir, strife, tumult, turmoil, violence ~*v.* **3.** assail, assault, beset, charge, rush, take by storm ~*n.* **4.** assault, attack, blitz, blitzkrieg, offensive, onset, onslaught, rush ~*v.* **5.** bluster, complain, fly off the handle (*Inf.*), fume, rage, rant, rave, scold, thunder **6.** flounce, fly, rush, stalk, stamp, stomp (*Inf.*)

stormy blustering, blustery, boisterous, dirty, foul, gusty, raging, rough, squally, tempestuous, turbulent, wild, windy

story 1. account, anecdote, chronicle, fictional account, history, legend, narration, narrative, novel, recital, record, relation, romance, tale, version, yarn **2.** *Inf.* falsehood, fib, fiction, lie, untruth, white lie **3.** article, feature, news, news item, report, scoop

storyteller anecdotist, author, bard, chronicler, fabulist, narrator, novelist, raconteur, romancer, spinner of yarns

stout 1. big, bulky, burly, corpulent, fat, fleshy, heavy, obese, on the large *or* heavy side, overweight, plump, portly, rotund, substantial, tubby **2.** ablebodied, athletic, beefy (*Inf.*), brawny, hardy, hulking, husky (*Inf.*), lusty, muscular, robust, stalwart, strapping, strong, sturdy, substantial, tough, vigorous **3.** bold, brave, courageous, dauntless, doughty, fearless, gallant, intrepid, lionhearted, manly, plucky, resolute, valiant, valorous

stouthearted bold, brave, courageous, dauntless, doughty, fearless, greathearted, gutsy (*Sl.*), heroic, indomitable, intrepid, lion-hearted, plucky, spirited, stalwart, valiant, valorous

stow bundle, cram, deposit, jam, load, pack, put away, secrete, stash (*Inf.*), store, stuff, tuck

straggle drift, lag, loiter, ramble, range, roam, rove, spread, stray, string out, trail, wander

straggly aimless, disorganized, drifting, irregular, loose, rambling, random, spreading, spread out, straggling, straying, untidy

straight *adj.* **1.** direct, near, short, undeviating, unswerving **2.** aligned, erect, even, horizontal, in line, level, perpendicular, plumb, right, smooth, square, true, upright, vertical **3.** blunt, candid, forthright, frank, honest, outright, plain, point-blank, straightforward, unqualified **4.** above board, accurate, authentic, decent, equitable, fair, fair and square, honest, honourable, just, law-abiding, reliable, respectable, trustworthy, upright **5.** arranged, in order, neat, orderly, organized, put to rights, shipshape, sorted out, tidy **6.** consecutive, continuous, nonstop, running, solid, successive, sustained, through, uninterrupted, unrelieved **7.** *Sl.* bourgeois, conservative, conventional, orthodox, square (*Inf.*), traditional **8.** neat, pure, unadulterated, undiluted, unmixed ~*adj.* **9.** as the crow flies, at once, directly, immediately, instantly **10.** candidly, frankly, honestly, in plain English, point-blank, pulling no punches (*Inf.*), with no holds barred

straightaway at once, directly, immediately, instantly, now, on the spot, right away, straightway (*Archaic*), there and then, this minute, without any delay, without more ado

straighten arrange, neaten, order, put in order, set *or* put to rights, smarten up, spruce up, tidy (up)

straighten out become clear, clear up, correct, disentangle, put right, rectify, regularize, resolve, settle, sort out, unsnarl, work out

straightforward 1. above board, candid, direct, forthright, genuine, guileless, honest, open, sincere, truthful **2.** clearcut, easy, elementary, routine, simple, uncomplicated, undemanding

strain[1] *v.* **1.** distend, draw tight, extend, stretch, tauten, tighten **2.** drive, exert, fatigue, injure, overexert, overtax, overwork, pull, push to the limit, sprain, tax, tear, tire, twist, weaken, wrench **3.** endeavour, go all out for (*Inf.*), labour, make a supreme effort, strive, struggle **4.** filter, percolate, purify, riddle, screen, seep, separate, sieve, sift ~*n.* **5.** effort, exertion, force, injury, pull, sprain, struggle, tautness, tension, tensity (*Rare*), wrench **6.** anxiety, burden, pressure, stress, tension **7.** *Often plural* air, lay, measure (*Poetic*), melody, song, theme, tune

strain[2] *n.* **1.** ancestry, blood, descent, extraction, family, lineage, pedigree, race, stock **2.** streak, suggestion, suspicion, tendency, trace, trait **3.** humour, manner, spirit, style, temper, tone, vein, way

strained artificial, awkward, constrained, difficult, embarrassed, false, forced, laboured, put on, self-conscious, stiff, tense, uncomfortable, uneasy, unnatural, unrelaxed

straitened difficult, distressed, embarrassed, limited, reduced, restricted

strait-laced moralistic, narrow, narrow-minded, of the old school, old-maidish (*Inf.*), overscrupulous, prim, proper, prudish, puritanical, strict, Victorian

straits *n. Sometimes singular* **1.** crisis, difficulty, dilemma, distress, embarrassment, emergency, extremity, hardship, hole (*Sl.*), mess, pass, perplexity, plight, predicament, pretty *or* fine kettle of fish (*Inf.*) **2.** channel, narrows, sound

strand *n.* fibre, filament, length, lock, rope, string, thread, tress, twist

stranded 1. aground, ashore, beached, cast away, grounded, marooned, wrecked **2.** *Fig.* abandoned, helpless, high and dry, homeless, left in the lurch, penniless

strange 1. abnormal, astonishing, bizarre, curious, eccentric, exceptional, extraordinary, fantastic, funny, irregular, marvellous, mystifying, odd, out-of-the-way, peculiar, perplexing, queer, rare, remarkable, singular, unaccountable, uncanny, uncommon, unheard of, weird, wonderful **2.** alien, exotic, foreign, new, novel, outside one's experience, remote, unexplored, unfamiliar, unknown, untried **3.** *Often with* to a stranger to, ignorant of, inexperienced, new to, unaccustomed, unpractised, unseasoned, unused, unversed in **4.** awkward, bewildered, disoriented, ill at ease, lost, out of place, uncomfortable

stranger alien, foreigner, guest, incomer, new arrival, newcomer, outlander, unknown, visitor

strangle 1. asphyxiate, choke, garrotte, smother, strangulate, suffocate, throttle **2.** gag (*Inf.*), inhibit, repress, stifle, suppress

strap *n.* **1.** belt, leash, thong, tie ~*v.* **2.**

bind, buckle, fasten, lash, secure, tie, truss **3**. beat, belt, flog, lash, scourge, whip

strapping beefy (*Inf.*), big, brawny, burly, hefty (*Inf.*), hulking, husky (*Inf.*), powerful, robust, stalwart, sturdy, well-built, well set-up

stratagem artifice, device, dodge, feint, intrigue, manoeuvre, plan, plot, ploy, ruse, scheme, subterfuge, trick, wile

strategic 1. cardinal, critical, crucial, decisive, key, vital **2**. calculated, deliberate, diplomatic, planned, politic

strategy approach, grand design, manoeuvring, plan, planning, policy, procedure, programme, scheme

stratum 1. bed, layer, level, lode, seam, stratification, table, tier, vein **2**. bracket, caste, category, class, estate, grade, group, level, rank, station

stray *v*. **1**. deviate, digress, diverge, get off the point, get sidetracked, go off at a tangent, ramble **2**. be abandoned *or* lost, drift, err, go astray, lose one's way, meander, range, roam, rove, straggle, wander ~*adj*. **3**. abandoned, homeless, lost, roaming, vagrant **4**. accidental, chance, erratic, freak, odd, random, scattered

streak *n*. **1**. band, layer, line, slash, smear, strip, stripe, stroke, vein **2**. dash, element, strain, touch, trace, vein ~*v*. **3**. band, daub, fleck, slash, smear, striate, stripe **4**. dart, flash, fly, hurtle, move like greased lightning (*Inf.*), speed, sprint, sweep, tear, whistle, whiz (*Inf.*), zoom

stream 1. *n*. beck, brook, burn, course, creek (*U.S.*), current, drift, flow, freshet, outpouring, rill, river, rivulet, run, rush, surge, tide, torrent, tributary **2**. *v*. cascade, course, emit, flood, flow, glide, gush, issue, pour, run, shed, spill, spout

streamer banner, colours, ensign, flag, gonfalon, pennant, pennon, ribbon, standard

streamlined efficient, modernized, organized, rationalized, sleek, slick, smooth, smooth-running, time-saving, well-run

street 1. avenue, boulevard, lane, road, roadway, row, terrace, thoroughfare **2**. (**right**) **up one's street** acceptable, compatible, congenial, familiar, one's cup of tea (*Inf.*), pleasing, suitable, to one's liking, to one's taste

strength 1. backbone, brawn, brawniness, courage, firmness, fortitude, health,

lustiness, might, muscle, robustness, sinew, stamina, stoutness, sturdiness, toughness **2**. cogency, concentration, effectiveness, efficacy, energy, force, intensity, potency, power, resolution, spirit, vehemence, vigour, virtue (*Archaic*) **3**. advantage, anchor, asset, mainstay, security, strong point, succour, tower of strength

strengthen 1. animate, brace up, consolidate, encourage, fortify, give new energy to, harden, hearten, invigorate, nerve, nourish, rejuvenate, restore, stiffen, toughen **2**. bolster, brace, build up, buttress, confirm, corroborate, enhance, establish, give a boost to, harden, heighten, increase, intensify, justify, reinforce, steel, substantiate, support

strenuous 1. arduous, demanding, exhausting, hard, Herculean, laborious, taxing, toilsome, tough, tough going, unrelaxing, uphill **2**. active, bold, determined, eager, earnest, energetic, persistent, resolute, spirited, strong, tireless, vigorous, zealous

stress *n*. **1**. emphasis, force, importance, significance, urgency, weight **2**. anxiety, burden, hassle (*Inf.*), nervous tension, oppression, pressure, strain, tautness, tension, trauma, worry **3**. accent, accentuation, beat, emphasis ~*v*. **4**. accentuate, belabour, dwell on, emphasize, harp on, lay emphasis upon, point up, repeat, rub in, underline, underscore

stretch *v*. **1**. cover, extend, put forth, reach, spread, unfold, unroll **2**. distend, draw out, elongate, expand, inflate, lengthen, pull, pull out of shape, rack, strain, swell, tighten ~*n*. **3**. area, distance, expanse, extent, spread, sweep, tract **4**. bit, period, run, space, spell, stint, term, time

strew bestrew, disperse, litter, scatter, spread, sprinkle, toss

stricken affected, afflicted, hit, injured, laid low, smitten, struck, struck down

strict 1. austere, authoritarian, firm, harsh, no-nonsense, rigid, rigorous, severe, stern, stringent **2**. accurate, close, exact, faithful, meticulous, particular, precise, religious, scrupulous, true **3**. absolute, complete, perfect, total, utter

stricture animadversion, bad press, blame, censure, criticism, flak (*Inf.*), rebuke

strident clamorous, clashing, discordant, grating, harsh, jangling, jarring, rasping, raucous, screeching, shrill, stridulant, stridulous, unmusical, vociferous

strife animosity, battle, bickering, clash, clashes, combat, conflict, contention, contest, controversy, discord, dissension, friction, quarrel, rivalry, row, squabbling, struggle, warfare, wrangling

strike v. **1.** bang, beat, box, buffet, chastise, clobber (Sl.), clout (Inf.), clump (Sl.), cuff, hammer, hit, knock, lay a finger on (Inf.), pound, punish, slap, smack, smite, sock (Sl.), thump, wallop (Inf.) **2.** be in collision with, bump into, clash, collide with, come into contact with, dash, hit, knock into, run into, smash into, touch **3.** drive, force, hit, impel, thrust **4.** affect, come to, come to the mind of, dawn on or upon, hit, impress, make an impact on, occur to, reach, register (Inf.), seem **5.** Sometimes with **upon** come upon or across, discover, encounter, find, happen or chance upon, hit upon, light upon, reach, stumble upon or across, turn up, uncover, unearth **6.** affect, assail, assault, attack, deal a blow to, devastate, fall upon, hit, invade, set upon, smite **7.** achieve, arrange, arrive at, attain, effect, reach **8.** down tools, mutiny, revolt, walk out

strike down afflict, bring low, deal a deathblow to, destroy, kill, ruin, slay, smite

strike out **1.** Also **strike off, strike through** cancel, cross out, delete, efface, erase, expunge, remove, score out **2.** begin, get under way, set out, start out

striking astonishing, conspicuous, dazzling, extraordinary, forcible, impressive, memorable, noticeable, out of the ordinary, outstanding, stunning (Inf.), wonderful

string n. **1.** cord, fibre, twine **2.** chain, file, line, procession, queue, row, sequence, series, strand, succession ~v. **3.** festoon, hang, link, loop, sling, stretch, suspend, thread **4.** With **out** disperse, extend, fan out, lengthen, protract, space out, spread out, straggle

string along **1.** Often with **with** agree, assent, collaborate, go along with **2.** Also **string on** bluff, deceive, dupe, fool, hoax, play fast and loose with (someone) (Inf.), play (someone) false, put one over on (someone) (Inf.), take (someone) for a ride (Inf.)

stringent binding, demanding, exacting, inflexible, rigid, rigorous, severe, strict, tight, tough

strings Fig. catches (Inf.), complications, conditions, obligations, prerequisites, provisos, qualifications, requirements, stipulations

stringy chewy, fibrous, gristly, sinewy, tough, wiry

strip¹ v. **1.** bare, denude, deprive, despoil, dismantle, divest, empty, gut, lay bare, loot, peel, pillage, plunder, ransack, rob, sack, skin, spoil **2.** disrobe, unclothe, uncover, undress

strip² n. band, belt, bit, fillet, piece, ribbon, shred, slip, swathe, tongue

striped banded, barred, striated, stripy

stripling adolescent, boy, fledgling, hobbledehoy (Archaic), lad, shaver (Inf.), young fellow, youngster, youth

strive attempt, compete, contend, do all one can, do one's best, do one's utmost, endeavour, exert oneself, fight, go all out (Inf.), labour, leave no stone unturned, make every effort, strain, struggle, toil, try, try hard

stroke n. **1.** accomplishment, achievement, blow, feat, flourish, hit, knock, move, movement, pat, rap, thump **2.** apoplexy, attack, collapse, fit, seizure, shock ~v. **3.** caress, fondle, pat, pet, rub

stroll **1.** v. amble, make one's way, mooch (Inf.), mosey (Inf.), promenade, ramble, saunter, stooge (Inf.), stretch one's legs, take a turn, toddle, wander **2.** n. airing, breath of air, constitutional, excursion, promenade, ramble, turn, walk

strong **1.** athletic, beefy (Inf.), brawny, burly, capable, hale, hardy, healthy, Herculean, lusty, muscular, powerful, robust, sinewy, sound, stalwart, stout, strapping, sturdy, tough, virile **2.** aggressive, brave, courageous, determined, firm in spirit, forceful, hard as nails, hard-nosed (Inf.), high-powered, plucky, resilient, resolute, resourceful, self-assertive, steadfast, stouthearted, tenacious, tough, unyielding **3.** acute, dedicated, deep, deep-rooted, eager, fervent, fervid, fierce, firm, intense, keen, severe, staunch, vehement, violent, zealous **4.** clear, clear-cut, cogent, compelling, convincing, distinct, effective, formidable, great, marked, overpowering, persuasive, potent, redoubtable, sound, telling, trenchant, unmistakable, urgent, weighty, well-established, well-founded **5.** Draconian, drastic, extreme, forceful, severe **6.** durable, hard-wearing, heavy-duty, on a firm foundation, reinforced, sturdy, substantial, well-armed, well-built, well-protected **7.** bold, bright, brilliant, dazzling, glaring, loud, stark **8.** biting, concentrated, heady, highly-flavoured, highly-seasoned, hot, intoxicating, piquant, pungent, pure, sharp, spicy, undiluted

strong-arm *adj.* aggressive, bullying, coercive, forceful, high-pressure, terror, terrorizing, threatening, thuggish, violent

stronghold bastion, bulwark, castle, citadel, fastness, fort, fortress, keep, refuge

strong-minded determined, firm, independent, iron-willed, resolute, strong-willed, unbending, uncompromising

strong point advantage, asset, forte, long suit (*Inf.*), métier, speciality, strength, strong suit

stroppy awkward, bloody-minded (*Brit. inf.*), cantankerous, destructive, difficult, obstreperous, perverse, quarrelsome, uncooperative, unhelpful

structure *n.* **1.** arrangement, configuration, conformation, construction, design, fabric, form, formation, interrelation of parts, make, make-up, organization **2.** building, construction, edifice, erection, pile ~*v.* **3.** arrange, assemble, build up, design, organize, put together, shape

struggle *v.* **1.** exert oneself, go all out (*Inf.*), labour, make every effort, strain, strive, toil, work, work like a Trojan ~*n.* **2.** effort, exertion, grind (*Inf.*), labour, long haul, pains, scramble, toil, work ~*v.* **3.** battle, compete, contend, fight, grapple, lock horns, scuffle, wrestle ~*n.* **4.** battle, brush, clash, combat, conflict, contest, encounter, hostilities, skirmish, strife, tussle

strung up a bundle of nerves (*Inf.*), edgy, jittery (*Inf.*), keyed up, nervous, on edge, on tenterhooks, tense, under a strain, uptight (*Inf.*)

strut *v.* parade, peacock, prance, stalk, swagger

stub *n.* butt, counterfoil, dog-end

(*Inf.*), end, fag end (*Inf.*), remnant, stump, tail, tail end

stubborn bull-headed, contumacious, cross-grained, dogged, dour, fixed, headstrong, inflexible, intractable, mulish, obdurate, obstinate, opinionated, persistent, pig-headed, recalcitrant, refractory, self-willed, stiff-necked, tenacious, unbending, unmanageable, unshakable, unyielding, wilful

stubby **1.** chunky, dumpy, short, squat, stocky, stumpy, thickset **2.** bristling, bristly, prickly, rough, stubbly

stuck **1.** cemented, fast, fastened, firm, fixed, glued, joined **2.** *Inf.* at a loss, at a standstill, at one's wits' end, baffled, beaten, bereft of ideas, nonplussed, stumped, up against a brick wall (*Inf.*) **3.** *Sl.* With **on** enthusiastic about, hung up on (*Sl.*), infatuated, keen, mad, obsessed with, wild about (*Inf.*) **4. get stuck into** *Inf.* get down to, make a start on, set about, tackle

stuck-up arrogant, big-headed (*Inf.*), conceited, condescending, haughty, high and mighty (*Inf.*), hoity-toity (*Inf.*), patronizing, proud, snobbish, snooty (*Inf.*), swollen-headed, toffee-nosed (*Sl.*), uppish (*Brit. inf.*), uppity (*Inf.*)

stud *v.* bejewel, bespangle, dot, fleck, ornament, spangle, speckle, spot, sprinkle

student apprentice, disciple, learner, observer, pupil, scholar, undergraduate

studied calculated, conscious, deliberate, intentional, planned, premeditated, purposeful, well-considered, wilful

studio atelier, workshop

studious academic, assiduous, attentive, bookish, careful, diligent, eager, earnest, hard-working, intellectual, meditative, reflective, scholarly, sedulous, serious, thoughtful

study *v.* **1.** apply oneself (to), bone up (on) (*Inf.*), burn the midnight oil, cogitate, con (*Archaic*), consider, contemplate, cram (*Inf.*), examine, go into, hammer away at, learn, lucubrate (*Rare*), meditate, mug up (*Brit. sl.*), ponder, pore over, read, read up, swot (up) (*Brit. inf.*) **2.** analyse, deliberate, examine, investigate, look into, peruse, research, scrutinize, survey ~*n.* **3.** academic work, application, book work, cramming (*Inf.*), learning, lessons, reading, research, school work, swotting (*Brit. inf.*), thought **4.** analysis, attention, cogitation, consideration, contemplation, examination, inquiry, inspection, investigation, review, scrutiny, survey

stuff *v.* 1. compress, cram, crowd, fill, force, jam, load, pack, pad, push, ram, shove, squeeze, stow, wedge 2. gobble, gorge, gormandize, guzzle, make a pig of oneself (*Inf.*), overindulge, sate, satiate ~*n.* 3. belongings, bits and pieces, clobber (*Brit. sl.*), effects, equipment, gear, goods and chattels, impedimenta, junk, kit, luggage, materials, objects, paraphernalia, possessions, tackle, things, trappings 4. cloth, fabric, material, raw material, textile 5. essence, matter, pith, quintessence, staple, substance 6. balderdash, baloney (*Inf.*), bosh (*Inf.*), bunk (*Inf.*), bunkum, claptrap (*Inf.*), foolishness, humbug, nonsense, poppycock (*Inf.*), rot, rubbish, stuff and nonsense, tommyrot, tripe (*Inf.*), twaddle, verbiage

stuffing 1. filler, kapok, packing, quilting, wadding 2. farce, farcemeat, forcemeat

stuffy 1. airless, close, fetid, frowsty, fuggy, heavy, muggy, oppressive, stale, stifling, suffocating, sultry, unventilated 2. conventional, deadly, dreary, dull, fusty, humourless, musty, old-fashioned, old-fogyish, pompous, priggish, prim, prim and proper, staid, stilted, stodgy, strait-laced, uninteresting

stumble 1. blunder about, come a cropper (*Inf.*), fall, falter, flounder, hesitate, lose one's balance, lurch, reel, slip, stagger, trip 2. *With* **on** *or* **upon** blunder upon, chance upon, come across, discover, encounter, find, happen upon, light upon, run across, turn up 3. falter, fluff (*Inf.*), stammer, stutter

stumbling block bar, barrier, difficulty, hindrance, hurdle, impediment, obstacle, obstruction, snag

stump *v.* 1. baffle, bewilder, bring (someone) up short, confound, confuse, dumbfound, flummox, foil, mystify, outwit, perplex, puzzle, stop, stymie 2. clomp, clump, lumber, plod, stamp, stomp (*Inf.*), trudge

stumped at a loss, at one's wits' end, at sea, baffled, brought to a standstill, floored (*Inf.*), flummoxed, in despair, perplexed, stymied, uncertain which way to turn

stump up chip in (*Inf.*), come across

with (*Inf.*), contribute, cough up (*Inf.*), donate, fork out (*Sl.*), hand over, pay, shell out (*Inf.*)

stumpy chunky, dumpy, heavy, short, squat, stocky, stubby, thick, thickset

stun *Fig.* amaze, astonish, astound, bewilder, confound, confuse, daze, dumbfound, flabbergast (*Inf.*), hit (someone) like a ton of bricks (*Inf.*), knock out, knock (someone) for six (*Inf.*), overcome, overpower, shock, stagger, strike (someone) dumb (*Inf.*), stupefy, take (someone's) breath away

stung angered, exasperated, goaded, hurt, incensed, nettled, piqued, resentful, roused, wounded

stunned *Fig.* astounded, at a loss for words, bowled over (*Inf.*), dazed, devastated, dumbfounded, flabbergasted (*Inf.*), numb, shocked, staggered, struck dumb (*Inf.*)

stunner beauty, charmer, dazzler, dish (*Sl.*), dolly (*Sl.*), eyeful (*Inf.*), glamour puss, good-looker, heart-throb, honey (*Inf.*), knockout (*Inf.*), looker (*Inf., chiefly U.S.*), lovely (*Sl.*), peach (*Inf.*), sensation, smasher (*Inf.*), wow (*Sl., chiefly U.S.*)

stunning beautiful, brilliant, dazzling, devastating (*Inf.*), gorgeous, great (*Inf.*), heavenly, impressive, lovely, marvellous, out of this world (*Inf.*), ravishing, remarkable, sensational, smashing (*Inf.*), spectacular, striking, wonderful

stunt *n.* act, deed, exploit, feat, feature, gest (*Archaic*), *tour de force*, trick

stunted diminutive, dwarfed, dwarfish, little, small, tiny, undersized

stupefaction amazement, astonishment, awe, wonder, wonderment

stupefy amaze, astound, bewilder, confound, daze, dumbfound, knock senseless, numb, shock, stagger, stun

stupendous amazing, astounding, breathtaking, colossal, enormous, fabulous (*Inf.*), fantastic (*Inf.*), gigantic, huge, marvellous, mind-blowing (*Sl.*), mind-boggling (*Inf.*), out of this world (*Inf.*), overwhelming, phenomenal, prodigious, staggering, stunning (*Inf.*), superb, surpassing belief, surprising, tremendous (*Inf.*), vast, wonderful

stupid 1. Boeotian, brainless, cretinous, deficient, dense, dim, doltish, dopey (*Sl.*), dozy (*Brit. inf.*), dull, dumb (*Inf., chiefly U.S.*), foolish, gullible, half-witted, moronic, naive, obtuse, simple,

simple-minded, slow, slow on the uptake (*Inf.*), slow-witted, sluggish, stolid, thick, thickheaded, unintelligent, witless, woodenheaded (*Inf.*) **2.** crackbrained, futile, half-baked (*Inf.*), idiotic, ill-advised, imbecilic, inane, indiscreet, irrelevant, irresponsible, laughable, ludicrous, meaningless, mindless, nonsensical, pointless, puerile, rash, senseless, short-sighted, trivial, unintelligent, unthinking **3.** dazed, groggy, in a daze, insensate, punch-drunk, semiconscious, senseless, stunned, stupefied

stupidity 1. asininity, brainlessness, denseness, dimness, dopiness (*Sl.*), doziness (*Brit. inf.*), dullness, dumbness (*Inf., chiefly U.S.*), feeble-mindedness, imbecility, lack of brain, lack of intelligence, naivety, obtuseness, puerility, simplicity, slowness, thickheadedness, thickness **2.** absurdity, fatuity, fatuousness, folly, foolhardiness, foolishness, futility, idiocy, impracticality, inanity, indiscretion, ineptitude, irresponsibility, ludicrousness, lunacy, madness, pointlessness, rashness, senselessness, silliness

stupor coma, daze, inertia, insensibility, lethargy, numbness, stupefaction, torpor, trance, unconsciousness

sturdy athletic, brawny, built to last, determined, durable, firm, flourishing, hardy, hearty, lusty, muscular, powerful, resolute, robust, secure, solid, stalwart, staunch, steadfast, stouthearted, substantial, vigorous, well-built, well-made

stutter *v.* falter, hesitate, speak haltingly, splutter, stammer, stumble

Stygian black, caliginous (*Archaic*), dark, dreary, gloomy, Hadean, hellish, infernal, sombre, Tartarean, tenebrous

style *n.* **1.** cut, design, form, hand, manner, technique **2.** fashion, mode, rage, trend, vogue **3.** approach, custom, manner, method, mode, way **4.** *bon ton*, chic, cosmopolitanism, dash, dressiness (*Inf.*), élan, elegance, fashionableness, flair, grace, panache, polish, refinement, savoir-faire, smartness, sophistication, stylishness, taste, urbanity **5.** affluence, comfort, ease, elegance, gracious living, grandeur, luxury **6.** appearance, category, characteristic, genre, kind, pattern, sort, spirit, strain, tenor, tone, type, variety **7.** diction, expression, mode of expression, phraseology, phrasing, treatment, turn of phrase, vein, wording ~*v.* **8.** adapt, arrange, cut, design, dress,

fashion, shape, tailor **9.** address, call, christen, denominate, designate, dub, entitle, label, name, term

stylish à la mode, chic, classy (*Sl.*), dapper, dressy (*Inf.*), fashionable, in fashion, in vogue, modish, natty (*Inf.*), polished, smart, snappy, snazzy (*Inf.*), trendy (*Brit. inf.*), urbane, voguish, well turned-out

stymie balk, confound, defeat, flummox, foil, frustrate, hinder, mystify, nonplus, puzzle, snooker, spike (someone's) guns, stump, throw a spanner in the works (*Inf.*), thwart

suave affable, agreeable, bland, charming, civilized, courteous, diplomatic, gracious, obliging, pleasing, polite, smooth, smooth-tongued, sophisticated, svelte, urbane, worldly

subconscious *adj.* hidden, inner, innermost, intuitive, latent, repressed, subliminal, suppressed

subdue 1. beat down, break, conquer, control, crush, defeat, discipline, gain ascendancy over, get the better of, get the upper hand over, get under control, humble, master, overcome, overpower, overrun, put down, quell, tame, trample, triumph over, vanquish **2.** check, control, mellow, moderate, quieten down, repress, soften, suppress, tone down

subdued 1. chastened, crestfallen, dejected, downcast, down in the mouth, grave, out of spirits, quiet, repentant, repressed, restrained, sad, sadder and wiser, serious, sobered, solemn **2.** dim, hushed, low-key, muted, quiet, shaded, sober, soft, subtle, toned down, unobtrusive

subject *n.* **1.** affair, business, field of enquiry *or* reference, issue, matter, object, point, question, subject matter, substance, theme, topic **2.** case, client, guinea pig (*Inf.*), participant, patient, victim **3.** citizen, dependant, liegeman, national, subordinate, vassal ~*adj.* **4.** at the mercy of, disposed, exposed, in danger of, liable, open, prone, susceptible, vulnerable **5.** conditional, contingent, dependent **6.** answerable, bound by, captive, dependent, enslaved, inferior, obedient, satellite, subjugated, submissive, subordinate, subservient ~*v.* **7.** expose, lay open, make liable, put through, submit, treat

subjective biased, emotional, idiosyncratic, instinctive, intuitive, nonobjective, personal, prejudiced

subjugate bring (someone) to his knees, bring to heel, bring under the yoke, conquer, crush, defeat, enslave, hold sway over, master, overcome, overpower, overthrow, put down, quell, reduce, rule over, subdue, suppress, tame, vanquish

sublimate 1. channel, divert, redirect, transfer, turn 2. elevate, exalt, heighten, refine

sublime elevated, eminent, exalted, glorious, grand, great, high, imposing, lofty, magnificent, majestic, noble, transcendent

submerge deluge, dip, drown, duck, dunk, engulf, flood, immerse, inundate, overflow, overwhelm, plunge, sink, swamp

submerged drowned, immersed, subaquatic, subaqueous, submarine, submersed, sunk, sunken, undersea, underwater

submission 1. acquiescence, assent, capitulation, giving in, surrender, yielding 2. compliance, deference, docility, meekness, obedience, passivity, resignation, submissiveness, tractability, unassertiveness 3. argument, contention, proposal 4. entry, handing in, presentation, submitting, tendering

submissive abject, accommodating, acquiescent, amenable, biddable, bootlicking (*Inf.*), compliant, deferential, docile, dutiful, humble, ingratiating, lowly, malleable, meek, obedient, obeisant, obsequious, passive, patient, pliant, resigned, subdued, tractable, uncomplaining, unresisting, yielding

submit 1. accede, acquiesce, agree, bend, bow, capitulate, comply, defer, endure, give in, hoist the white flag, knuckle under, lay down arms, put up with (*Inf.*), resign oneself, stoop, succumb, surrender, throw in the sponge, toe the line, tolerate, yield 2. commit, hand in, present, proffer, put forward, refer, table, tender 3. advance, argue, assert, claim, contend, move, propose, propound, put, state, suggest, volunteer

subordinate *adj.* 1. dependent, inferior, junior, lesser, lower, minor, secondary, subject, subservient 2. ancillary, auxiliary, subsidiary, supplementary ~*n.* 3. aide, assistant, attendant, dependant, inferior, junior, second, subaltern, underling

subordination inferior *or* secondary status, inferiority, servitude, subjection, submission

sub rosa behind closed doors, in camera, in secret, in strict confidence, secretly

subscribe 1. chip in (*Inf.*), contribute, donate, give, offer, pledge, promise 2. acquiesce, advocate, agree, consent, countenance, endorse, support

subscription annual payment, contribution, donation, dues, gift, membership fee, offering

subsequent after, consequent, consequential, ensuing, following, later, succeeding, successive

subsequently afterwards, at a later date, consequently, in the aftermath (of), in the end, later

subservient 1. abject, bootlicking (*Inf.*), deferential, inferior, obsequious, servile, slavish, subject, submissive, sycophantic, truckling 2. accessory, ancillary, auxiliary, conducive, helpful, instrumental, serviceable, subordinate, subsidiary, useful

subside 1. abate, decrease, deescalate, diminish, dwindle, ease, ebb, lessen, let up, level off, melt away, moderate, peter out, quieten, recede, slacken, wane 2. cave in, collapse, decline, descend, drop, ebb, lower, settle, sink

subsidence 1. decline, descent, ebb, settlement, settling, sinking 2. abatement, decrease, de-escalation, diminution, easing off, lessening, slackening

subsidiary aiding, ancillary, assistant, auxiliary, contributory, cooperative, helpful, lesser, minor, secondary, serviceable, subordinate, subservient, supplemental, supplementary, useful

subsidize finance, fund, promote, put up the money for, sponsor, support, underwrite

subsidy aid, allowance, assistance, contribution, financial aid, grant, help, subvention, support

subsist be, continue, eke out an existence, endure, exist, keep going, last, live, make ends meet, remain, stay alive, survive, sustain oneself

subsistence aliment, existence, food, keep, livelihood, living, maintenance, provision, rations, support, survival, sustenance, upkeep, victuals

substance 1. body, element, fabric, material, stuff, texture **2.** burden, essence, gist, gravamen (*Law*), import, main point, matter, meaning, pith, significance, subject, sum and substance, theme **3.** actuality, concreteness, entity, force, reality **4.** affluence, assets, estate, means, property, resources, wealth

substandard damaged, imperfect, inadequate, inferior, second-rate, shoddy, unacceptable

substantial 1. ample, big, considerable, generous, goodly, important, large, significant, sizable, tidy (*Inf.*), worthwhile **2.** bulky, durable, firm, hefty, massive, solid, sound, stout, strong, sturdy, well-built **3.** actual, existent, material, positive, real, true, valid, weighty

substantially essentially, in essence, in essentials, in substance, in the main, largely, materially, to a large extent

substantiate affirm, attest to, authenticate, bear out, confirm, corroborate, establish, prove, support, validate, verify

substitute *v.* **1.** change, commute, exchange, interchange, replace, swap (*Inf.*), switch **2.** *With* **for** act for, be in place of, cover for, deputize, double for, fill in for, hold the fort for, relieve, stand in for, take over ~*n.* **3.** agent, depute (*Chiefly Scot.*), deputy, equivalent, expedient, locum, locum tenens, makeshift, proxy, relief, replacement, representative, reserve, stand-by, stopgap, sub, supply, surrogate, temp (*Inf.*), temporary ~*adj.* **4.** acting, additional, alternative, proxy, replacement, reserve, second, surrogate, temporary

substitution change, exchange, interchange, replacement, swap (*Inf.*), switch

subterfuge artifice, deception, deviousness, dodge, duplicity, evasion, excuse, machination, manoeuvre, ploy, pretence, pretext, quibble, ruse, shift, stall, stratagem, trick

subtle 1. deep, delicate, discriminating, ingenious, nice, penetrating, profound, refined, sophisticated **2.** delicate, faint, implied, indirect, insinuated, slight, understated **3.** artful, astute, crafty, cunning, designing, devious, intriguing, keen, Machiavellian, scheming, shrewd, sly, wily

subtlety 1. acumen, acuteness, cleverness, delicacy, discernment, fine point, intricacy, nicety, refinement, sagacity, skill, sophistication **2.** discernment, dis-

crimination, finesse, penetration **3.** artfulness, astuteness, craftiness, cunning, deviousness, guile, slyness, wiliness

subtract deduct, detract, diminish, remove, take away, take from, take off, withdraw

suburbs dormitory area (*Brit.*), environs, faubourgs, neighbourhood, outskirts, precincts, purlieus, residential areas, suburbia

subversive 1. *adj.* destructive, incendiary, inflammatory, insurrectionary, overthrowing, perversive, riotous, seditious, treasonous, underground, undermining **2.** *n.* deviationist, dissident, fifth columnist, insurrectionary, quisling, saboteur, seditionary, seditionist, terrorist, traitor

subvert 1. demolish, destroy, invalidate, overturn, raze, ruin, sabotage, undermine, upset, wreck **2.** confound, contaminate, corrupt, debase, demoralize, deprave, pervert, poison, vitiate

succeed 1. arrive (*Inf.*), be successful, come off (*Inf.*), do all right for oneself (*Inf.*), do the trick (*Inf.*), flourish, gain one's end, get to the top (*Inf.*), make good, make it (*Inf.*), prosper, thrive, triumph, turn out well, work **2.** be subsequent, come next, ensue, follow, result, supervene **3.** *Usually with* **to** accede, assume the office of, come into, come into possession of, enter upon, inherit, replace, take over

succeeding ensuing, following, next, subsequent, successive

success 1. ascendancy, eminence, fame, favourable outcome, fortune, happiness, hit (*Inf.*), luck, prosperity, triumph **2.** best seller, big name, celebrity, hit (*Inf.*), market leader, sensation, smash hit (*Inf.*), somebody, star, V.I.P., winner

successful acknowledged, at the top of the tree, best-selling, booming, efficacious, favourable, flourishing, fortunate, fruitful, lucky, lucrative, moneymaking, out in front (*Inf.*), paying, profitable, prosperous, rewarding, thriving, top, unbeaten, victorious, wealthy

successfully famously (*Inf.*), favourably, in triumph, swimmingly, victoriously, well, with flying colours

succession 1. chain, continuation, course, cycle, flow, order, procession, progression, run, sequence, series, train **2. in succession** consecutively, one after the other, one behind the other, on the trot (*Inf.*), running, successively **3**. accession, assumption, elevation, entering upon, inheritance, taking over **4**. descendants, descent, line, lineage, race

successive consecutive, following, in a row, in succession, sequent, succeeding

succinct brief, compact, compendious, concise, condensed, gnomic, in a few well-chosen words, laconic, pithy, summary, terse, to the point

succour 1. *v*. aid, assist, befriend, comfort, encourage, foster, give aid and encouragement to, help, minister to, nurse, relieve, render assistance to, support **2**. *n*. aid, assistance, comfort, help, relief, support

succulent juicy, luscious, lush, mellow, moist, mouthwatering, rich

succumb capitulate, die, fall, fall victim to, give in, give way, go under, knuckle under, submit, surrender, yield

sucker butt, cat's paw, dupe, easy game or mark (*Inf.*), fool, mug (*Sl.*), pushover (*Sl.*), sap (*Sl.*), sitting duck (*Inf.*), victim

suck up to butter up, curry favour with, dance attendance on, fawn on, flatter, get on the right side of, ingratiate oneself with, keep in with (*Inf.*), lick (someone's) boots, play up to (*Inf.*), toady, truckle, worm oneself into (someone's) favour

sudden abrupt, hasty, hurried, impulsive, quick, rapid, rash, swift, unexpected, unforeseen, unusual

suddenly abruptly, all at once, all of a sudden, on the spur of the moment, out of the blue (*Inf.*), unexpectedly, without warning

sue 1. *Law* bring an action against (someone), charge, have the law on (someone) (*Inf.*), indict, institute legal proceedings against (someone), prefer charges against (someone), prosecute, summon, take (someone) to court **2**. appeal for, beg, beseech, entreat, petition, plead, solicit, supplicate

suffer 1. ache, agonize, be affected, be in pain, be racked, feel wretched, go through a lot (*Inf.*), grieve, have a thin *or* bad time, hurt **2**. bear, endure, experience, feel, go through, put up with (*Inf.*), support, sustain, tolerate, undergo **3**. appear in a poor light, be handicapped, be impaired, deteriorate, fall off, show to

disadvantage **4**. *Archaic* allow, let, permit

suffering *n*. affliction, agony, anguish, discomfort, distress, hardship, martyrdom, misery, ordeal, pain, torment, torture

suffice answer, be sufficient (adequate, enough), content, do, fill the bill (*Inf.*), meet requirements, satisfy, serve

sufficient adequate, competent, enough, enow (*Archaic*), satisfactory

suffocate asphyxiate, choke, smother, stifle, strangle

suffrage ballot, consent, franchise, right to vote, voice (*Fig.*), vote

suffuse bathe, cover, flood, imbue, infuse, mantle, overspread, permeate, pervade, spread over, steep, transfuse

suggest 1. advise, advocate, move, offer a suggestion, propose, put forward, recommend **2**. bring to mind, connote, evoke, put one in mind of **3**. hint, imply, indicate, insinuate, intimate, lead one to believe

suggestion 1. motion, plan, proposal, proposition, recommendation **2**. breath, hint, indication, insinuation, intimation, suspicion, trace, whisper

suggestive 1. *With of* evocative, expressive, indicative, redolent, reminiscent **2**. bawdy, blue, immodest, improper, indecent, indelicate, off colour, provocative, prurient, racy, ribald, risqué, rude, smutty, spicy (*Inf.*), titillating, unseemly

suit *v*. **1**. agree, agree with, answer, be acceptable to, become, befit, be seemly, conform to, correspond, do, go with, gratify, harmonize, match, please, satisfy, tally **2**. accommodate, adapt, adjust, fashion, fit, modify, proportion, tailor ~*n*. **3**. addresses, appeal, attentions, courtship, entreaty, invocation, petition, prayer, request **4**. *Law* action, case, cause, lawsuit, proceeding, prosecution, trial **5**. clothing, costume, dress, ensemble, habit, outfit **6**. **follow suit** accord with, copy, emulate, run with the herd, take one's cue from

suitability appropriateness, aptness, fitness, opportuneness, rightness, timeliness

suitable acceptable, applicable, apposite, appropriate, apt, becoming, befitting, convenient, cut out for, due, fit, fitting, in character, in keeping, opportune, pertinent, proper, relevant, right, satisfactory, seemly, suited

suite 1. apartment, collection, furniture, rooms, series, set 2. attendants, entourage, escort, followers, retainers, retinue, train

suitor admirer, beau, follower (*Obsolete*), swain (*Archaic*), wooer

sulk be in a huff, be put out, brood, have the hump (*Brit. inf.*), look sullen, pout

sulky aloof, churlish, cross, disgruntled, ill-humoured, in the sulks, moody, morose, perverse, petulant, put out, querulous, resentful, sullen, vexed

sullen brooding, cheerless, cross, dismal, dull, gloomy, glowering, heavy, moody, morose, obstinate, out of humour, perverse, silent, sombre, sour, stubborn, surly, unsociable

sullenness glumness, heaviness, ill humour, moodiness, moroseness, sourness, sulkiness, sulks

sully befoul, besmirch, blemish, contaminate, darken, defile, dirty, disgrace, dishonour, pollute, spoil, spot, stain, taint, tarnish

sultry 1. close, hot, humid, muggy, oppressive, sticky, stifling, stuffy, sweltering 2. come-hither (*Inf.*), erotic, passionate, provocative, seductive, sensual, sexy (*Inf.*), voluptuous

sum aggregate, amount, entirety, quantity, reckoning, score, sum total, tally, total, totality, whole

summarily arbitrarily, at short notice, expeditiously, forthwith, immediately, on the spot, peremptorily, promptly, speedily, swiftly, without delay, without wasting words

summarize abridge, condense, encapsulate, epitomize, give a rundown of, give the main points of, outline, précis, put in a nutshell, review, sum up

summary 1. *n.* abridgment, abstract, compendium, digest, epitome, essence, extract, outline, précis, recapitulation, résumé, review, rundown, summing-up, synopsis 2. *adj.* arbitrary, brief, compact, compendious, concise, condensed, cursory, hasty, laconic, perfunctory, pithy, succinct

summit acme, apex, crown, crowning point, culmination, head, height, peak, pinnacle, top, zenith

summon 1. arouse, assemble, bid, call, call together, cite, convene, convoke, invite, rally, rouse, send for 2. *Often with* **up** call into action, draw on, gather, invoke, mobilize, muster

sumptuous costly, dear, de luxe, expensive, extravagant, gorgeous, grand, lavish, luxurious, magnificent, opulent, plush (*Inf.*), posh (*Inf.*), rich, ritzy (*Sl.*), splendid, superb

sum up 1. close, conclude, put in a nutshell, recapitulate, review, summarize 2. estimate, form an opinion of, get the measure of, size up (*Inf.*)

sun 1. *n.* daystar (*Poetic*), eye of heaven, Helios (*Greek myth*), Phoebus (*Greek myth*), Phoebus Apollo (*Greek myth*), Sol (*Roman myth*) 2. *v.* bake, bask, sunbathe, tan

sunburnt bronzed, brown, brown as a berry, burnt, like a lobster, peeling, red, ruddy, scarlet, tanned

sundry assorted, different, divers (*Archaic*), miscellaneous, several, some, varied, various

sunk all washed up (*Inf.*), done for (*Inf.*), finished, lost, on the rocks, ruined

sunken 1. concave, drawn, haggard, hollow, hollowed 2. at a lower level, below ground, buried, depressed, immersed, lower, recessed, submerged

sunless bleak, cheerless, cloudy, dark, depressing, gloomy, grey, hazy, overcast, sombre

sunny 1. bright, brilliant, clear, fine, luminous, radiant, summery, sunlit, sunshiny, unclouded, without a cloud in the sky 2. *Fig.* beaming, blithe, buoyant, cheerful, cheery, genial, happy, joyful, light-hearted, optimistic, pleasant, smiling

sunrise aurora (*Poetic*), break of day, cockcrow, dawn, daybreak, daylight, dayspring (*Poetic*), sunup

sunset close of (the) day, dusk, eventide, gloaming, nightfall, sundown

super excellent, glorious, incomparable, magnificent, marvellous, matchless, out of this world (*Inf.*), outstanding, peerless, sensational, smashing (*Inf.*), superb, terrific (*Inf.*), topnotch (*Inf.*), wonderful

superannuated aged, antiquated, decrepit, discharged, obsolete, old, past it (*Inf.*), pensioned off, put out to grass (*Inf.*), retired, senile, unfit

superb admirable, breathtaking, choice, excellent, exquisite, fine, first-rate, gorgeous, grand, magnificent, marvellous, of the first water, splendid, superior, unrivalled

supercilious arrogant, condescending, contemptuous, disdainful, haughty, high and mighty (*Inf.*), hoity-toity (*Inf.*), imperious, insolent, lofty, lordly, overbearing, patronizing, proud, scornful, snooty (*Inf.*), stuck-up (*Inf.*), toffee-nosed (*Sl.*), uppish (*Brit. inf.*), vainglorious

superficial 1. exterior, external, on the surface, peripheral, shallow, skin-deep, slight, surface **2.** casual, cosmetic, cursory, desultory, hasty, hurried, inattentive, nodding, passing, perfunctory, sketchy, slapdash **3.** empty, empty-headed, frivolous, lightweight, shallow, silly, trivial **4.** apparent, evident, ostensible, outward, seeming

superficiality emptiness, lack of depth, lack of substance, shallowness, triviality

superficially apparently, at first glance, externally, on the surface, ostensibly, to the casual eye

superfluity excess, exuberance, glut, plethora, redundancy, superabundance, surfeit, surplus

superfluous excess, excessive, extra, in excess, left over, needless, on one's hands, pleonastic (*Rhetoric*), redundant, remaining, residuary, spare, superabundant, supererogatory, supernumerary, surplus, surplus to requirements, uncalled-for, unnecessary, unneeded, unrequired

superhuman 1. herculean, heroic, phenomenal, prodigious, stupendous, valiant **2.** divine, paranormal, preternatural, supernatural

superintend administer, control, direct, inspect, look after, manage, overlook, oversee, run, supervise

superintendence care, charge, control, direction, government, guidance, inspection, management, supervision, surveillance

superintendent administrator, chief, conductor, controller, director, governor, inspector, manager, overseer, supervisor

superior adj. **1.** better, grander, greater, higher, more advanced (expert, extensive, skilful), paramount, predominant, preferred, prevailing, surpassing, unrivalled **2.** a cut above (*Inf.*), admirable, choice, de luxe, distinguished, excellent, exceptional, exclusive, fine, first-class, first-rate, good, good quality, high

calibre, high-class, of the first order **3.** airy, condescending, disdainful, haughty, lofty, lordly, patronizing, pretentious, snobbish, stuck-up (*Inf.*), supercilious ~*n.* **4.** boss (*Inf.*), chief, director, manager, principal, senior, supervisor

superiority advantage, ascendancy, excellence, lead, predominance, preeminence, preponderance, prevalence, supremacy

superlative adj. consummate, crack (*Sl.*), excellent, greatest, highest, magnificent, matchless, of the first water, of the highest order, outstanding, peerless, supreme, surpassing, transcendent, unparalleled, unrivalled, unsurpassed

supernatural abnormal, dark, ghostly, hidden, miraculous, mysterious, mystic, occult, paranormal, phantom, preternatural, psychic, spectral, supranatural, uncanny, unearthly, unnatural

supernumerary excess, excessive, extra, in excess, odd, redundant, spare, superfluous, surplus, unrequired

supersede annul, displace, oust, overrule, remove, replace, set aside, supplant, supplement, suspend, take over, take the place of, usurp

supervise administer, be on duty at, be responsible for, conduct, control, direct, handle, have *or* be in charge of, inspect, keep an eye on, look after, manage, oversee, preside over, run, superintend

supervision administration, auspices, care, charge, control, direction, guidance, instruction, management, oversight, stewardship, superintendence, surveillance

supervisor administrator, boss (*Inf.*), chief, foreman, inspector, manager, overseer, steward, superintendent

supervisory administrative, executive, managerial, overseeing, superintendent

supine 1. flat, flat on one's back, horizontal, prone, prostrate, recumbent **2.** apathetic, careless, heedless, idle, incurious, indifferent, indolent, inert, languid, lazy, lethargic, listless, lymphatic, negligent, passive, slothful, sluggish, spineless, spiritless, torpid, uninterested

supplant displace, oust, overthrow, remove, replace, supersede, take over, take the place of, undermine, unseat

supple bending, elastic, flexible, limber, lithe, plastic, pliable, pliant

supplement 1. *n.* added feature, addendum, addition, appendix, codicil, complement, extra, insert, postscript, pull-out, sequel **2.** *v.* add, augment, complement, extend, fill out, reinforce, supply, top up

supplementary accompanying, additional, ancillary, auxiliary, complementary, extra, secondary, supplemental

suppliant 1. *adj.* begging, beseeching, craving, entreating, imploring, importunate, on bended knee **2.** *n.* applicant, petitioner, suitor, supplicant

supplication appeal, entreaty, invocation, petition, plea, pleading, prayer, request, solicitation, suit

supply *v.* **1.** afford, cater to *or* for, come up with, contribute, endow, fill, furnish, give, grant, minister, outfit, produce, provide, purvey, replenish, satisfy, stock, store, victual, yield ~*n.* **2.** cache, fund, hoard, quantity, reserve, reservoir, source, stock, stockpile, store **3.** *Usually plural* equipment, food, foodstuff, items, materials, necessities, provender, provisions, rations, stores

support *v.* **1.** bear, bolster, brace, buttress, carry, hold, hold up, prop, reinforce, shore up, sustain, underpin, uphold **2.** be a source of strength to, buoy up, cherish, finance, foster, fund, keep, look after, maintain, nourish, provide for, strengthen, subsidize, succour, sustain, take care of, underwrite **3.** advocate, aid, assist, back, boost (someone's) morale, champion, defend, forward, go along with, help, promote, second, side with, stand behind, stand up for, stick up for (*Inf.*), take (someone's) part, take up the cudgels for, uphold **4.** attest to, authenticate, bear out, confirm, corroborate, document, endorse, lend credence to, substantiate, verify **5.** bear, brook, countenance, endure, put up with (*Inf.*), stand (for), stomach, submit, suffer, thole (*Dialect*), tolerate, undergo ~*n.* **6.** abutment, back, brace, foundation, lining, pillar, post, prop, shore, stanchion, stay, stiffener, underpinning **7.** aid, approval, assistance, backing, blessing, championship, comfort, encouragement, friendship, furtherance, help, loyalty, moral support, patronage, protection, relief, succour, sustenance **8.** keep, livelihood, maintenance, subsistence, sustenance, upkeep **9.** backbone, backer, com-

forter, mainstay, prop, second, stay, supporter, tower of strength

supporter adherent, advocate, ally, apologist, champion, co-worker, defender, fan, follower, friend, helper, patron, sponsor, upholder, well-wisher

supportive caring, encouraging, helpful, reassuring, sympathetic, understanding

suppose 1. assume, calculate (*U.S. dialect*), conjecture, dare say, expect, guess (*Inf.*), imagine, infer, judge, opine, presume, presuppose, surmise, take as read, take for granted, think **2.** believe, conceive, conclude, conjecture, consider, fancy, hypothesize, imagine, postulate, pretend

supposed 1. accepted, alleged, assumed, hypothetical, presumed, presupposed, professed, putative, reputed, rumoured **2.** *With* **to** expected, meant, obliged, ought, required

supposedly allegedly, at a guess, avowedly, by all accounts, hypothetically, ostensibly, presumably, professedly, purportedly, theoretically

supposition conjecture, doubt, guess, guesswork, hypothesis, idea, notion, postulate, presumption, speculation, surmise, theory

suppress 1. beat down, check, clamp down on, conquer, crack down on, crush, drive underground, extinguish, overpower, overthrow, put an end to, quash, quell, quench, snuff out, stamp out, stop, subdue, trample on **2.** censor, conceal, contain, cover up, curb, hold in *or* back, hold in check, keep secret, muffle, muzzle, repress, restrain, silence, smother, stifle, withhold

suppression check, clampdown, crackdown, crushing, dissolution, elimination, extinction, inhibition, prohibition, quashing, smothering, termination

suppurate discharge, fester, gather, maturate, ooze, weep

supremacy absolute rule, ascendancy, dominance, domination, dominion, lordship, mastery, paramountcy, predominance, pre-eminence, primacy, sovereignty, supreme authority, sway

supreme cardinal, chief, crowning, culminating, extreme, final, first, foremost, greatest, head, highest, incomparable, leading, matchless, paramount, peerless, predominant, pre-eminent, prevailing, prime, principal, sovereign, superlative, surpassing, top, ultimate, unsurpassed, utmost

sure 1. assured, certain, clear, confident, convinced, decided, definite, free from doubt, persuaded, positive, satisfied **2.** accurate, dependable, effective, foolproof, honest, indisputable, infallible, never-failing, precise, reliable, sure-fire (*Inf.*), tried and true, trustworthy, trusty, undeniable, undoubted, unerring, unfailing, unmistakable, well-proven **3.** assured, bound, guaranteed, ineluctable, inescapable, inevitable, irrevocable **4.** fast, firm, fixed, safe, secure, solid, stable, steady

surely assuredly, beyond the shadow of a doubt, certainly, come what may, definitely, doubtlessly, for certain, indubitably, inevitably, inexorably, undoubtedly, unquestionably, without doubt, without fail

surety 1. bail, bond, deposit, guarantee, indemnity, insurance, pledge, safety, security, warranty **2.** bondsman, guarantor, hostage, mortgagor, sponsor

surface *n.* **1.** covering, exterior, façade, face, facet, outside, plane, side, skin, superficies (*Rare*), top, veneer **2. on the surface** apparently, at first glance, ostensibly, outwardly, superficially, to all appearances, to the casual eye ~*adj.* **3.** apparent, exterior, external, outward, superficial ~*v.* **4.** appear, come to light, come up, crop up (*Inf.*), emerge, materialize, rise, transpire

surfeit 1. *n.* excess, glut, overindulgence, plethora, satiety, superabundance, superfluity **2.** *v.* cram, fill, glut, gorge, overfeed, overfill, satiate, stuff

surge 1. *v.* billow, eddy, gush, heave, rise, roll, rush, swell, swirl, tower, undulate, well forth **2.** *n.* billow, breaker, efflux, flood, flow, gush, intensification, outpouring, roller, rush, swell, uprush, upsurge, wave

surly bearish, brusque, churlish, crabbed, cross, crusty, curmudgeonly, grouchy (*Inf.*), gruff, ill-natured, morose, perverse, sulky, sullen, testy, uncivil, ungracious

surmise 1. *v.* come to the conclusion, conclude, conjecture, consider, deduce, fancy, guess, hazard a guess, imagine, infer, opine, presume, speculate, suppose, suspect **2.** *n.* assumption, conclusion, conjecture, deduction, guess, hypothesis, idea, inference, notion, possibility, presumption, speculation, supposition, suspicion, thought

surmount conquer, exceed, master, overcome, overpower, overtop, pass, prevail over, surpass, triumph over, vanquish

surpass beat, best, eclipse, exceed, excel, go one better than (*Inf.*), outdo, outshine, outstrip, override, overshadow, top, tower above, transcend

surpassing exceptional, extraordinary, incomparable, matchless, outstanding, phenomenal, rare, supreme, transcendent, unrivalled

surplus 1. *n.* balance, excess, remainder, residue, superabundance, superfluity, surfeit **2.** *adj.* excess, extra, in excess, left over, odd, remaining, spare, superfluous, unused

surprise *v.* **1.** amaze, astonish, astound, bewilder, bowl over (*Inf.*), confuse, disconcert, flabbergast (*Inf.*), leave open-mouthed, nonplus, stagger, stun, take aback **2.** burst in on, catch in the act *or* red-handed, catch napping, catch unawares *or* off-guard, come down on like a bolt from the blue, discover, spring upon, startle ~*n.* **3.** amazement, astonishment, bewilderment, incredulity, stupefaction, wonder **4.** bolt from the blue, bombshell, eye-opener (*Inf.*), jolt, revelation, shock, start (*Inf.*)

surprised amazed, astonished, at a loss, caught on the hop (*Brit. inf.*), caught on the wrong foot (*Inf.*), disconcerted, incredulous, nonplussed, open-mouthed, speechless, startled, taken aback, taken by surprise, thunderstruck, unable to believe one's eyes

surprising amazing, astonishing, astounding, extraordinary, incredible, marvellous, remarkable, staggering, startling, unexpected, unlooked-for, unusual, wonderful

surrender *v.* **1.** abandon, cede, concede, deliver up, forego, give up, part with, relinquish, renounce, resign, waive, yield **2.** capitulate, give in, give oneself up, give way, lay down arms, quit, show the white flag, submit, succumb, throw in the towel, yield ~*n.* **3.** capitulation, delivery, relinquishment, renunciation, resignation, submission, yielding

surreptitious clandestine, covert, fraudulent, furtive, secret, sly, sneaking, stealthy, unauthorized, underhand, veiled

surrogate *n*. deputy, proxy, representative, stand-in, substitute

surround 1. close in on, encircle, enclose, encompass, envelop, environ, fence in, girdle, hem in, ring **2.** *Military* besiege, invest (*Rare*), lay siege to

surrounding nearby, neighbouring

surroundings background, environment, environs, location, milieu, neighbourhood, setting

surveillance care, control, direction, inspection, observation, scrutiny, superintendence, supervision, vigilance, watch

survey *v*. **1.** contemplate, examine, inspect, look over, observe, reconnoitre, research, review, scan, scrutinize, study, supervise, view **2.** appraise, assess, estimate, measure, plan, plot, prospect, size up, take stock of, triangulate ~*n*. **3.** examination, inquiry, inspection, overview, perusal, random sample, review, scrutiny, study

survive be extant, endure, exist, hold out, keep body and soul together (*Inf*.), last, live, live on, outlast, outlive, pull through, remain alive, subsist

susceptibility liability, predisposition, proneness, propensity, responsiveness, sensitivity, suggestibility, vulnerability, weakness

susceptible 1. *Usually with to* disposed, given, inclined, liable, open, predisposed, prone, subject, vulnerable **2.** alive to, easily moved, impressionable, receptive, responsive, sensitive, suggestible, tender

suspect *v*. **1.** distrust, doubt, harbour suspicions about, have one's doubts about, mistrust, smell a rat (*Inf*.) **2.** believe, conclude, conjecture, consider, fancy, feel, guess, have a sneaking suspicion, hazard a guess, speculate, suppose, surmise, think probable ~*adj*. **3.** doubtful, dubious, fishy (*Inf*.), open to suspicion, questionable

suspend 1. append, attach, dangle, hang, swing **2.** adjourn, arrest, cease, cut short, debar, defer, delay, discontinue, hold off, interrupt, lay aside, pigeonhole, postpone, put off, shelve, stay, withhold

suspense 1. anticipation, anxiety, apprehension, doubt, expectancy, expectation, indecision, insecurity, irresolution, tension, uncertainty, wavering **2. in suspense** anxious, in an agony of doubt, keyed up, on edge, on tenterhooks

suspenseful cliffhanging, exciting, gripping, hair-raising, spine-chilling, thrilling

suspension abeyance, adjournment, break, breaking off, deferment, delay, disbarment, discontinuation, interruption, moratorium, postponement, remission, respite, stay

suspicion 1. bad vibes (*Inf*.), chariness, distrust, doubt, funny feeling (*Inf*.), jealousy, lack of confidence, misgiving, mistrust, qualm, scepticism, wariness **2. above suspicion** above reproach, blameless, honourable, like Caesar's wife, pure, sinless, unimpeachable, virtuous **3.** conjecture, guess, gut feeling (*Inf*.), hunch, idea, impression, notion, supposition, surmise **4.** glimmer, hint, shade, shadow, *soupçon*, strain, streak, suggestion, tinge, touch, trace

suspicious 1. apprehensive, distrustful, doubtful, jealous, mistrustful, sceptical, suspecting, unbelieving, wary **2.** doubtful, dubious, fishy (*Inf*.), funny, irregular, of doubtful honesty, open to doubt *or* misconstruction, queer, questionable, shady (*Inf*.), suspect

sustain 1. bear, carry, keep from falling, keep up, support, uphold **2.** bear, bear up under, endure, experience, feel, suffer, undergo, withstand **3.** aid, assist, comfort, foster, help, keep alive, nourish, nurture, provide for, relieve **4.** approve, confirm, continue, keep alive, keep going, keep up, maintain, prolong, protract, ratify **5.** endorse, uphold, validate, verify

sustained constant, continuous, nonstop, perpetual, prolonged, steady, unremitting

sustenance 1. aliment, comestibles, daily bread, eatables, edibles, food, nourishment, provender, provisions, rations, refection, refreshments, victuals **2.** livelihood, maintenance, subsistence, support

svelte 1. graceful, lissom, lithe, slender, slinky, sylphlike, willowy **2.** polished, smooth, sophisticated, urbane

swagger 1. *v*. bluster, boast, brag, bully, gasconade (*Rare*), hector, parade, prance, show off (*Inf*.), strut, swank (*Inf*.) **2.** *n*. arrogance, bluster, braggadocio, display, gasconade (*Rare*), ostentation, pomposity, show, showing off (*Inf*.), swank (*Inf*.), swashbuckling

swallow *v*. **1.** absorb, consume, devour, down (*Inf*.), drink, eat, gulp, ingest, swig (*Inf*.), swill, wash down **2.** *Of-*

ten with **up** absorb, assimilate, consume, engulf, envelop, overrun, overwhelm, use up, waste **3**. choke back, hold in, repress **4**. *Inf*. accept, believe, buy (*Inf*.), fall for

swamp *n*. **1**. bog, everglade(s) (*U.S.*), fen, marsh, mire, morass, moss (*Scot., & northern English dialect*), quagmire, slough ~*v*. **2**. capsize, drench, engulf, flood, inundate, overwhelm, sink, submerge, swallow up, upset, wash over, waterlog **3**. beset, besiege, deluge, flood, inundate, overload, overwhelm, snow under

swampy boggy, fenny, marish (*Obsolete*), marshy, miry, quaggy, waterlogged, wet

swank *v*. **1**. give oneself airs, posture, put on side (*Brit. sl.*), show off (*Inf*.), swagger ~*n*. **2**. attitudinizer, braggadocio, poser, show-off (*Inf*.), swankpot (*Inf*.), swashbuckler **3**. boastfulness, display, ostentation, show, swagger, vainglory

swanky de luxe, exclusive, expensive, fancy, fashionable, flashy, glamorous, grand, lavish, luxurious, ostentatious, plush (*Inf*.), plushy (*Inf*.), posh (*Inf*.), rich, ritzy (*Sl*.), showy, smart, stylish, sumptuous, swank (*Inf*.), swish (*Inf*.)

swap, swop *v*. bandy, barter, exchange, interchange, switch, trade, traffic

swarm *n*. **1**. army, bevy, concourse, crowd, drove, flock, herd, horde, host, mass, multitude, myriad, shoal, throng ~*v*. **2**. congregate, crowd, flock, mass, stream, throng **3**. *With* **with** abound, be alive (infested, overrun), bristle, crawl, teem

swarthy black, brown, dark, dark-complexioned, dark-skinned, dusky, swart (*Archaic*), tawny

swashbuckling bold, daredevil, dashing, flamboyant, gallant, mettlesome, roisterous, spirited, swaggering

swastika fylfot

swathe bandage, bind, bundle up, cloak, drape, envelop, enwrap, fold, furl, lap, muffle up, sheathe, shroud, swaddle, wrap

sway *v*. **1**. bend, fluctuate, incline, lean, lurch, oscillate, rock, roll, swing, wave **2**. affect, control, direct, dominate, govern, guide, induce, influence, persuade, prevail on, win over ~*n*. **3**. ascendency, authority, clout (*Inf*.), command, control, dominion, government, influence, jurisdiction, power, predominance, rule, sovereignty **4**. **hold sway** predominate, prevail, reign, rule, run

swear **1**. affirm, assert, attest, avow, declare, depose, give one's word, pledge oneself, promise, state under oath, take an oath, testify, vow, warrant **2**. be foul-mouthed, blaspheme, curse, cuss (*Inf*.), imprecate, take the Lord's name in vain, turn the air blue, utter profanities **3**. *With* **by** depend on, have confidence in, rely on, trust

swearing bad language, blasphemy, cursing, cussing (*Inf*.), foul language, imprecations, malediction, profanity

swearword curse, cuss (*Inf*.), expletive, four-letter word, oath, obscenity, profanity

sweat *n*. **1**. diaphoresis (*Medical*), exudation, perspiration, sudor (*Medical*) **2**. *Inf*. agitation, anxiety, distress, flap (*Inf*.), panic, strain, worry **3**. *Inf*. back-breaking task, chore, drudgery, effort, labour ~*v*. **4**. break out in a sweat, exude moisture, glow, perspire **5**. *Inf*. agonize, be on pins and needles (*Inf*.), be on tenterhooks, chafe, fret, lose sleep over, suffer, torture oneself, worry **6**. **sweat it out** *Inf*. endure, see (something) through, stay the course, stick it out (*Inf*.)

sweaty clammy, drenched (bathed, soaked) in perspiration, glowing, perspiring, sticky, sweating

sweep *v*. **1**. brush, clean, clear, remove **2**. career, flounce, fly, glance, glide, hurtle, pass, sail, scud, skim, tear, zoom ~*n*. **3**. arc, bend, curve, gesture, move, movement, stroke, swing **4**. compass, extent, range, scope, span, stretch, vista

sweeping **1**. all-embracing, all-inclusive, bird's-eye, broad, comprehensive, extensive, global, radical, thoroughgoing, wide, wide-ranging **2**. across-the-board, blanket, exaggerated, indiscriminate, overdrawn, overstated, unqualified, wholesale

sweet *adj*. **1**. cloying, honeyed, luscious, melting, saccharine, sugary, sweetened, syrupy, toothsome **2**. affectionate, agreeable, amiable, appealing, attractive, beautiful, charming, delightful, engaging, fair, gentle, kind, lovable, sweet-tempered, taking, tender, unselfish, winning, winsome **3**. beloved, cherished, darling, dear, dearest, pet, precious, treasured **4**. aromatic, balmy, clean, fragrant, fresh, new, perfumed, pure, redolent, sweet-smelling, wholesome **5.** dulcet, euphonic, euphonious, harmonious, mellow, melodious, musical, silvertoned, silvery, soft, sweet-sounding, tuneful **6. sweet on** enamoured of, gone on (*Sl.*), head over heels in love with, infatuated by, in love with, keen on, obsessed *or* bewitched by, taken with, wild *or* mad about (*Inf.*) ~*n.* **7.** afters (*Brit. inf.*), dessert, pudding, sweet course **8.** *Usually plural* bonbon, candy (*U.S.*), confectionery, sweetie, sweetmeats

sweeten 1. honey, sugar, sugar-coat **2.** alleviate, appease, mollify, pacify, soften up, soothe, sugar the pill

sweetheart admirer, beau, beloved, boyfriend, darling, dear, flame (*Inf.*), follower (*Obsolete*), girlfriend, inamorata, inamorato, love, lover, steady (*Inf.*), suitor, swain (*Archaic*), sweetie (*Inf.*), truelove, valentine

sweet-scented ambrosial, aromatic, fragrant, perfumed, sweet-smelling

swell *v.* **1.** balloon, become bloated *or* distended, become larger, be inflated, belly, billow, bloat, bulge, dilate, distend, enlarge, expand, extend, fatten, grow, increase, protrude, puff up, rise, round out, tumefy, well up **2.** add to, aggravate, augment, enhance, heighten, intensify, mount, surge ~*n.* **3.** billow, rise, surge, undulation, wave **4.** *Inf.* beau, blade (*Archaic*), cockscomb (*Inf.*), dandy, fashion plate, fop, nob (*Sl.*), toff (*Brit. sl.*) ~*adj.* **5.** *Inf.* de luxe, exclusive, fashionable, grand, plush *or* plushy (*Inf.*), posh (*Inf.*), ritzy (*Sl.*), smart, stylish

swelling *n.* blister, bruise, bulge, bump, dilation, distension, enlargement, inflammation, lump, protuberance, puffiness, tumescence

sweltering airless, baking, burning, hot, humid, oppressive, scorching, stifling, sultry, torrid

swerve *v.* bend, deflect, depart from, deviate, diverge, incline, sheer off, shift, skew, stray, swing, turn, turn aside, veer, wander, wind

swift abrupt, expeditious, express, fast, fleet, fleet-footed, flying, hurried, nimble, nippy (*Brit. inf.*), prompt, quick, rapid, ready, short, short-lived, spanking, speedy, sudden, winged

swiftly as fast as one's legs can carry one, (at) full tilt, double-quick, fast, hot-

foot, hurriedly, in less than no time, nippily (*Brit. inf.*), posthaste, promptly, rapidly, speedily, without losing time

swiftness alacrity, celerity, dispatch, expedition, fleetness, promptness, quickness, rapidity, speed, speediness, velocity

swill *v.* **1.** consume, drain, drink (down), gulp, guzzle, imbibe, pour down one's gullet, quaff, swallow, swig (*Inf.*), toss off **2.** *Often with* out drench, flush, rinse, sluice, wash down, wash out ~*n.* **3.** hogwash, mash, mush, pigswill, scourings, slops, waste

swimmingly as planned, cosily, effortlessly, like a dream, like clockwork, smoothly, successfully, very well, with no trouble, without a hitch

swindle 1. *v.* bamboozle (*Inf.*), bilk (of), cheat, con (*Sl.*), deceive, defraud, diddle (*Inf.*), do (*Sl.*), dupe, fleece, hornswoggle (*Sl.*), overcharge, pull a fast one (on someone) (*Inf.*), put one over on (someone) (*Inf.*), rip (someone) off (*Sl.*), rook (*Sl.*), take (someone) for a ride (*Inf.*), take to the cleaners (*Inf.*), trick **2.** *n.* con trick (*Inf.*), deceit, deception, double-dealing, fiddle (*Brit. inf.*), fraud, imposition, knavery, racket, rip-off (*Sl.*), roguery, sharp practice, swizz (*Brit. inf.*), swizzle (*Brit. inf.*), trickery

swindler charlatan, cheat, confidence man, con man (*Sl.*), fraud, impostor, knave (*Archaic*), mountebank, rascal, rogue, rook (*Sl.*), shark, sharper, trickster

swing *v.* **1.** be pendent, be suspended, dangle, hang, move back and forth, suspend **2.** fluctuate, oscillate, rock, sway, vary, veer, vibrate, wave **3.** *Usually with* round curve, pivot, rotate, swivel, turn, turn on one's heel, wheel ~*n.* **4.** fluctuation, oscillation, stroke, sway, swaying, vibration **5. in full swing** animated, at its height, lively, on the go (*Inf.*), under way

swingeing daunting, Draconian, drastic, excessive, exorbitant, harsh, heavy, huge, oppressive, punishing, severe, stringent

swinging dynamic, fashionable, full of go *or* pep (*Inf.*), groovy (*Sl.*), hip (*Sl.*), in the swim (*Inf.*), lively, trendy (*Brit. inf.*), up-to-date, up to the minute, with it (*Inf.*)

swipe *v.* **1.** clip (*Inf.*), fetch (someone) a blow, hit, lash out at, slap, slosh (*Brit. sl.*), sock (*Sl.*), strike, wallop (*Inf.*) ~*n.*

2. blow, clip (*Inf.*), clout (*Inf.*), clump (*Sl.*), cuff, slap, smack, wallop (*Inf.*) ~*v.* **3.** *Sl.* appropriate, filch, lift (*Inf.*), make off with, nick (*Sl.*), pilfer, pinch (*Inf.*), purloin, snaffle (*Brit. inf.*), steal

swirl *v.* agitate, boil, churn, eddy, spin, surge, twirl, twist, whirl

swish *adj.* de luxe, elegant, exclusive, fashionable, grand, plush *or* plushy (*Inf.*), posh (*Inf.*), ritzy (*Sl.*), smart, sumptuous, swell (*Inf.*)

switch *v.* **1.** change, change course, deflect, deviate, divert, exchange, interchange, rearrange, replace by, shift, substitute, swap (*Inf.*), trade, turn aside ~*n.* **2.** about-turn, alteration, change, change of direction, exchange, reversal, shift, substitution, swap (*Inf.*) ~*v.* **3.** lash, swish, twitch, wave, whip

swivel *v.* pirouette, pivot, revolve, rotate, spin, swing round, turn

swollen bloated, distended, dropsical, enlarged, inflamed, puffed up, puffy, tumescent, tumid

swollen-headed bigheaded (*Inf.*), bumptious, cocky, full of oneself, proud, puffed up, self-important, too big for one's boots, vain, vainglorious

swoop 1. *v.* descend, dive, pounce, rush, stoop, sweep **2.** *n.* descent, drop, lunge, plunge, pounce, rush, stoop, sweep

swop *see* SWAP

sword 1. blade, brand (*Archaic*), trusty steel **2. cross swords** argue, come to blows, dispute, fight, spar, wrangle **3. the sword** aggression, arms, butchery, death, massacre, military might, murder, slaying, violence, war

swot *v.* apply oneself to, bone up (on) (*Inf.*), burn the midnight oil, cram (*Inf.*), get up (*Inf.*), lucubrate (*Rare*), mug up (*Brit. sl.*), pore over, revise, study, toil over, work

sybarite epicure, epicurean, hedonist, playboy, sensualist, voluptuary

sybaritic epicurean, hedonistic, Lucullan, luxurious, luxury-loving, pleasure-loving, self-indulgent, sensual, voluptuous

sycophancy adulation, bootlicking (*Inf.*), cringing, fawning, flattery, grovelling, kowtowing, obsequiousness, servility, slavishness, toadyism, truckling

sycophant apple polisher (*U.S. sl.*), bootlicker (*Inf.*), cringer, fawner, flatterer, hanger-on, lickspittle, parasite, slave,

sponger, toadeater (*Rare*), toady, truckler, yes man

sycophantic all over (someone) (*Inf.*), bootlicking (*Inf.*), cringing, fawning, flattering, grovelling, ingratiating, obsequious, parasitical, servile, slavish, slimy, smarmy (*Brit. inf.*), timeserving, toadying, unctuous

syllabus course of study, curriculum

sylphlike graceful, lithe, slender, svelte, willowy

symbol badge, emblem, figure, image, logo, mark, representation, sign, token, type

symbolic, symbolical allegorical, emblematic, figurative, representative, significant, token, typical

symbolize betoken, body forth, connote, denote, exemplify, mean, personify, represent, signify, stand for, typify

symmetrical balanced, in proportion, proportional, regular, well-proportioned

symmetry agreement, balance, correspondence, evenness, form, harmony, order, proportion, regularity

sympathetic 1. affectionate, caring, commiserating, compassionate, concerned, condoling, feeling, interested, kind, kindly, pitying, responsive, supportive, tender, understanding, warm, warm-hearted **2.** *Often with* **to** agreeable, approving, encouraging, favourably disposed, friendly, in sympathy with, pro, well-disposed **3.** agreeable, appreciative, companionable, compatible, congenial, friendly, like-minded, responsive, well-intentioned

sympathetically appreciatively, feelingly, kindly, perceptively, responsively, sensitively, understandingly, warmheartedly, warmly, with compassion, with feeling, with interest

sympathize 1. bleed for, commiserate, condole, empathize, feel for, feel one's heart go out to, grieve with, have compassion, offer consolation, pity, share another's sorrow **2.** agree, be in accord, be in sympathy, go along with, identify with, side with, understand

sympathizer condoler, fellow traveller, partisan, supporter, well-wisher

sympathy 1. commiseration, compassion, condolence(s), empathy, pity, tenderness, thoughtfulness, understanding **2.** affinity, agreement, congeniality, correspondence, fellow feeling, harmony, rapport, union, warmth

symptom expression, indication, mark, note, sign, syndrome, token, warning

symptomatic characteristic, indicative, suggestive

synonymous equal, equivalent, identical, identified, interchangeable, one and the same, similar, tantamount, the same

synopsis abridgment, abstract, *aperçu*, compendium, condensation, conspectus, digest, epitome, outline, outline sketch, précis, résumé, review, rundown, summary

synthesis 1. amalgamation, coalescence, combination, integration, unification, welding 2. amalgam, blend, combination, composite, compound, fusion, union

synthetic artificial, ersatz, fake, manmade, manufactured, mock

system 1. arrangement, classification, combination, coordination, organization, scheme, setup (*Sl.*), structure 2. fixed order, frame of reference, method, methodology, modus operandi, practice, procedure, routine, technique, theory, usage 3. definite plan, logical process, method, methodicalness, orderliness, regularity, systematization

systematic businesslike, efficient, methodical, orderly, organized, precise, standardized, systematized, well-ordered

systematize dispose, make uniform, methodize, organize, put in order, rationalize, regulate, schematize, standardize

T

tab flag, flap, label, marker, sticker, tag, ticket

tabby banded, brindled, streaked, striped, stripy, wavy

table n. **1.** bench, board, counter, slab, stand **2.** board, diet, fare, food, spread (*Inf.*), victuals **3.** flat, flatland, plain, plateau, tableland **4.** agenda, catalogue, chart, diagram, digest, graph, index, inventory, list, plan, record, register, roll, schedule, synopsis, tabulation ~v. **5.** enter, move, propose, put forward, submit, suggest

tableau picture, representation, scene, spectacle

tableland flat, flatland, plain, plateau, table

taboo **1.** *adj.* anathema, banned, beyond the pale, disapproved of, forbidden, frowned on, not allowed, not permitted, outlawed, prohibited, proscribed, ruled out, unacceptable, unmentionable, unthinkable **2.** *n.* anathema, ban, disapproval, interdict, prohibition, proscription, restriction

tabulate arrange, catalogue, categorize, chart, classify, codify, index, list, order, range, systematize, tabularize

tacit implicit, implied, inferred, silent, taken for granted, undeclared, understood, unexpressed, unspoken, unstated, wordless

taciturn aloof, antisocial, close-lipped, cold, distant, dumb, mute, quiet, reserved, reticent, silent, tight-lipped, uncommunicative, unforthcoming, withdrawn

tack n. **1.** drawing pin, nail, pin, staple, thumbtack (*U.S.*), tintack **2.** approach, bearing, course, direction, heading, line, method, path, plan, procedure, tactic, way ~v. **3.** affix, attach, fasten, fix, nail, pin, staple **4.** baste, stitch **5.** add, annex, append, attach, tag

tackle n. **1.** accoutrements, apparatus, equipment, gear, implements, outfit, paraphernalia, rig, rigging, tools, trappings **2.** block, challenge, stop ~v. **3.** apply oneself to, attempt, begin, come or get to grips with, deal with, embark upon, engage in, essay, get stuck into

(*Inf.*), have a go at (*Inf.*), set about, take on, try, turn one's hand to, undertake **4.** block, bring down, challenge, clutch, confront, grab, grasp, halt, intercept, seize, stop, take hold of, throw

tacky **1.** adhesive, gluey, gummy, sticky, wet **2.** cheap, messy, nasty, seedy, shabby, shoddy, sleazy, tasteless, tatty, vulgar

tact address, adroitness, consideration, delicacy, diplomacy, discretion, finesse, judgment, perception, savoir-faire, sensitivity, skill, thoughtfulness, understanding

tactful careful, considerate, delicate, diplomatic, discreet, judicious, perceptive, polished, polite, politic, prudent, sensitive, subtle, thoughtful, understanding

tactic **1.** approach, course, device, line, manoeuvre, means, method, move, ploy, policy, scheme, stratagem, tack, trick, way **2.** *Plural* campaign, generalship, manoeuvres, plans, strategy

tactical adroit, artful, clever, cunning, diplomatic, politic, shrewd, skilful, smart, strategic

tactician brain (*Inf.*), campaigner, coordinator, director, general, mastermind, planner, strategist

tactless blundering, boorish, careless, clumsy, discourteous, gauche, harsh, impolite, impolitic, imprudent, inconsiderate, indelicate, indiscreet, inept, injudicious, insensitive, maladroit, rough, rude, sharp, thoughtless, uncivil, undiplomatic, unfeeling, unkind, unsubtle

tag n. **1.** docket, flap, identification, label, mark, marker, note, slip, sticker, tab, ticket ~v. **2.** earmark, identify, label, mark, ticket **3.** add, adjoin, affix, annex, append, fasten, tack **4.** *With on or along* accompany, attend, dog, follow, shadow, tail, trail **5.** call, christen, dub, label, name, nickname, style, term

tail n. **1.** appendage, conclusion, empennage, end, extremity, rear end, tailpiece, train **2.** file, line, queue, tailback, train **3.** *Of hair* braid, pigtail, plait, ponytail, tress **4.** *Inf.* backside (*Inf.*), behind (*Inf.*), bottom, buttocks, croup, posterior, rear (*Inf.*), rear end, rump **5.** **turn tail** cut and run, escape, flee, make off, retreat, run away, run for it (*Inf.*), run off, scarper (*Brit. sl.*), show a clean pair of heels, skedaddle (*Inf.*), take off (*Inf.*), take to one's heels ~*v.* **6.** *Inf.* dog the footsteps of, follow, keep an eye on, shadow, stalk, track, trail

tail off *or* **away** decrease, die out, drop, dwindle, fade, fall away, peter out, wane

tailor 1. *n.* clothier, costumier, couturier, dressmaker, garment maker, outfitter, seamstress **2.** *v.* accommodate, adapt, adjust, alter, convert, cut, fashion, fit, modify, mould, shape, style, suit

tailor-made 1. cut to fit, fitted, made-to-measure, made to order **2.** custom-made, ideal, just right, perfect, right, right up one's street (*Inf.*), suitable

taint *v.* **1.** adulterate, blight, contaminate, corrupt, dirty, foul, infect, poison, pollute, soil, spoil **2.** besmirch, blacken, blemish, blot, brand, damage, defile, disgrace, dishonour, muddy, ruin, shame, smear, stain, stigmatize, sully, tarnish, vitiate ~*n.* **3.** black mark, blemish, blot, blot on one's escutcheon, defect, disgrace, dishonour, fault, flaw, shame, smear, spot, stain, stigma **4.** contagion, contamination, infection, pollution

take *v.* **1.** abduct, acquire, arrest, capture, carry off, catch, clutch, ensnare, entrap, gain possession of, get, get hold of, grasp, grip, have, help oneself to, lay hold of, obtain, receive, secure, seize, win **2.** abstract, appropriate, carry off, filch, misappropriate, nick (*Brit. sl.*), pinch (*Inf.*), pocket, purloin, run off with, steal, swipe (*Sl.*), walk off with **3.** book, buy, engage, hire, lease, pay for, pick, purchase, rent, reserve, select **4.** abide, bear, brave, brook, endure, go through, pocket, put up with (*Inf.*), stand, stomach, submit to, suffer, swallow, thole (*Scot.*), tolerate, undergo, weather, withstand **5.** consume, drink, eat, imbibe, ingest, inhale, swallow **6.** accept, adopt, assume, enter upon, undertake **7.** do, effect, execute, have, make, perform **8.** assume, believe, consider, deem, hold, interpret as, perceive, presume, receive, regard, see as, think of as, understand **9.** be efficacious, do the trick (*Inf.*), have effect, operate, succeed, work **10.** bear, bring, carry, cart, convey, ferry, fetch, haul, tote (*Inf.*), transport **11.** accompa-

ny, bring, conduct, convoy, escort, guide, lead, usher **12.** attract, become popular, captivate, charm, delight, enchant, fascinate, please, win favour **13.** call for, demand, necessitate, need, require **14.** deduct, eliminate, remove, subtract **15.** accept, accommodate, contain, have room for, hold **16.** *Sl.* bilk, cheat, con (*Inf.*), deceive, defraud, do (*Sl.*), dupe, fiddle (*Inf.*), gull (*Archaic*), pull a fast one on (*Inf.*), swindle ~*n.* **17.** catch, gate, haul, proceeds, profits, receipts, return, revenue, takings, yield

take aback astonish, astound, bewilder, disconcert, flabbergast (*Inf.*), floor (*Inf.*), nonplus, stagger, startle, stun, surprise

take back 1. disavow, disclaim, recant, renounce, retract, unsay, withdraw **2.** get back, recapture, reclaim, reconquer, regain, repossess, retake **3.** accept back, exchange, give one a refund for

take down 1. make a note of, minute, note, put on record, record, set down, transcribe, write down **2.** depress, drop, haul down, let down, lower, pull down, remove, take off **3.** demolish, disassemble, dismantle, level, raze, take apart, take to pieces, tear down **4.** deflate, humble, humiliate, mortify, put down (*Sl.*)

take in 1. absorb, assimilate, comprehend, digest, grasp, understand **2.** comprise, contain, cover, embrace, encompass, include **3.** accommodate, admit, let in, receive **4.** *Inf.* bilk, cheat, con (*Inf.*), deceive, do (*Sl.*), dupe, fool, gull (*Archaic*), hoodwink, mislead, pull the wool over (someone's) eyes (*Inf.*), swindle, trick

takeoff 1. departure, launch, liftoff **2.** *Inf.* caricature, imitation, lampoon, mocking, parody, satire, send-up (*Brit. inf.*), spoof (*Inf.*), travesty

take off 1. discard, divest oneself of, doff, drop, peel off, remove, strip off **2.** become airborne, leave the ground, lift off, take to the air **3.** *Inf.* beat it (*Sl.*), decamp, depart, disappear, go, hit the road (*Sl.*), leave, set out, split (*Sl.*), strike out **4.** *Inf.* caricature, hit off, imitate, lampoon, mimic, mock, parody, satirize, send up (*Brit. inf.*), spoof (*Inf.*), travesty

take on 1. employ, engage, enlist, enrol, hire, retain **2.** acquire, assume, come to have **3.** accept, address oneself to, agree to do, have a go at (*Inf.*), tackle, undertake **4**. compete against, contend with, enter the lists against, face, fight, match oneself against, oppose, pit oneself against, vie with **5**. *Inf.* break down, get excited, get upset (*Inf.*), give way, make a fuss

takeover change of leadership, coup, incorporation, merger

take over assume control of, become leader of, come to power, gain control of, succeed to, take command of

take to 1. flee to, head for, make for, man, run for **2**. become friendly, be pleased by, be taken with, conceive an affection for, get on with, like, warm to **3**. have recourse to, make a habit of, resort to

take up 1. adopt, assume, become involved in, engage in, start **2**. begin again, carry on, continue, follow on, go on, pick up, proceed, recommence, restart, resume **3**. absorb, consume, cover, extend over, fill, occupy, use up

taking *adj.* **1**. attractive, beguiling, captivating, charming, compelling, delightful, enchanting, engaging, fascinating, fetching (*Inf.*), intriguing, pleasing, prepossessing, winning **2**. *Inf.* catching, contagious, infectious ~*n.* **3**. *Plural* earnings, gain, gate, income, pickings, proceeds, profits, receipts, returns, revenue, take, yield

tale 1. account, anecdote, *conte*, fable, fiction, legend, narration, narrative, novel, relation, report, romance, saga, short story, story, yarn (*Inf.*) **2**. cock-and-bull story (*Inf.*), fabrication, falsehood, fib, lie, rigmarole, rumour, spiel (*Inf.*), tall story (*Inf.*), untruth

talent ability, aptitude, bent, capacity, endowment, faculty, flair, forte, genius, gift, knack, parts, power

talented able, artistic, brilliant, gifted, well-endowed

talisman amulet, charm, fetish, juju, lucky charm, mascot, periapt (*Rare*)

talk *v.* **1**. articulate, chat, chatter, communicate, converse, crack (*Scot.*), express oneself, gab (*Inf.*), give voice to, gossip, natter, prate, prattle, rap (*Sl.*), say, speak, utter, verbalize, witter (*Inf.*) **2**. chew the rag (*Inf.*), confabulate, confer, have a confab (*Inf.*), hold discussions, negotiate, palaver, parley **3**. blab, crack, give the game away, grass (*Sl.*), inform, reveal information, sing (*Inf.*), spill the beans (*Inf.*), squeak (*Inf.*),

squeal (*Sl.*) ~*n.* **4**. address, discourse, disquisition, dissertation, harangue, lecture, oration, sermon, speech **5**. blather, blether, chat, chatter, chitchat, conversation, crack (*Scot.*), gab (*Inf.*), gossip, hearsay, jaw (*Sl.*), natter, rap (*Sl.*), rumour, tittle-tattle **6**. colloquy, conclave, confab (*Inf.*), confabulation, conference, consultation, dialogue, discussion, meeting, negotiation, palaver, parley, seminar, symposium **7**. argot, dialect, jargon, language, lingo (*Inf.*), patois, slang, speech, words

talkative big-mouthed (*Sl.*), chatty, effusive, gabby (*Inf.*), garrulous, gossipy, long-winded, loquacious, mouthy, prolix, verbose, voluble, wordy

talk big bluster, boast, brag, crow, exaggerate, vaunt

talker conversationalist, lecturer, orator, speaker, speechmaker

talking-to criticism, dressing-down (*Inf.*), lecture, rap on the knuckles (*Inf.*), rebuke, reprimand, reproach, reproof, row, scolding, slating (*Inf.*), telling-off (*Inf.*), ticking-off (*Inf.*), wigging (*Brit. sl.*)

talk into bring round (*Inf.*), convince, persuade, prevail on *or* upon, sway, win over

tall 1. big, elevated, giant, high, lanky, lofty, soaring, towering **2**. *Inf.* absurd, embellished, exaggerated, far-fetched, implausible, incredible, overblown, preposterous, steep (*Brit. inf.*), unbelievable **3**. *Inf.* demanding, difficult, exorbitant, hard, unreasonable, well-nigh impossible

tally *v.* **1**. accord, agree, coincide, concur, conform, correspond, fit, harmonize, jibe (*Inf.*), match, parallel, square, suit **2**. compute, count up, keep score, mark, reckon, record, register, total ~*n.* **3**. count, mark, reckoning, record, running total, score, total **4**. counterfoil, counterpart, duplicate, match, mate, stub

tame *adj.* **1**. amenable, broken, cultivated, disciplined, docile, domesticated, gentle, obedient, tractable **2**. fearless, unafraid, used to human contact **3**. compliant, docile, manageable, meek, obedient, spiritless, subdued, submissive, unresisting **4**. bland, boring, dull, flat, humdrum, insipid, lifeless, prosaic, tedious, unexciting, uninspiring, uninteresting, vapid, wearisome ~*v.* **5**. break in, domesticate, gentle, house-train, make tame, pacify, train **6**. break the spirit of,

bridle, bring to heel, conquer, curb, discipline, enslave, humble, master, repress, subdue, subjugate, suppress **7**. mitigate, mute, soften, soft-pedal (*Inf.*), subdue, temper, tone down, water down
tamper 1. alter, damage, fiddle (*Inf.*), fool about (*Inf.*), interfere, intrude, meddle, mess about, monkey around, muck about (*Brit. sl.*), poke one's nose into (*Inf.*), tinker **2**. bribe, corrupt, fix (*Inf.*), get at, influence, manipulate, rig
tang 1. aroma, bite, flavour, odour, piquancy, reek, savour, scent, smack, smell, taste **2**. hint, suggestion, tinge, touch, trace, whiff
tangible actual, concrete, corporeal, definite, discernible, evident, manifest, material, objective, palpable, perceptible, physical, positive, real, solid, substantial, tactile, touchable
tangle *n*. **1**. coil, confusion, entanglement, jam, jungle, knot, mass, mat, mesh, snarl, twist, web **2**. complication, entanglement, fix (*Inf.*), imbroglio, labyrinth, maze, mess, mix-up ~*v*. **3**. coil, confuse, entangle, interlace, interlock, intertwist, interweave, jam, kink, knot, mat, mesh, snarl, twist **4**. *Often with* **with** come into conflict, come up against, contend, contest, cross swords, dispute, lock horns **5**. catch, drag into, embroil, enmesh, ensnare, entangle, entrap, implicate, involve
tangled 1. entangled, jumbled, knotted, knotty, matted, messy, scrambled, snarled, tousled, twisted **2**. complex, complicated, confused, convoluted, involved, knotty, messy, mixed-up
tangy biting, briny, fresh, piquant, pungent, sharp, spicy, tart
tantalize baffle, balk, disappoint, entice, frustrate, keep (someone) hanging on, lead on, make (someone's) mouth water, provoke, taunt, tease, thwart, titillate, torment, torture
tantamount as good as, commensurate, equal, equivalent, synonymous, the same as
tantrum fit, flare-up, hysterics, ill humour, outburst, paddy (*Brit. inf.*), storm, temper, wax (*Inf.*)
tap¹ 1. *v*. beat, drum, knock, pat, rap, strike, touch **2**. *n*. beat, knock, light blow, pat, rap, touch
tap² *n*. 1. faucet (*U.S.*), spigot, spout, stopcock, valve **2**. bung, plug, spile, stopper **3**. bug (*Inf.*), listening device **4**. on

tap a. *Inf.* at hand, available, in reserve, on hand, ready **b**. on draught ~*v*. **5**. bleed, broach, drain, draw off, open, pierce, siphon off, unplug **6**. draw on, exploit, make use of, milk, mine, put to use, turn to account, use, utilize **7**. bug (*Inf.*), eavesdrop on, listen in on
tape *n*. 1. band, ribbon, strip ~*v*. **2**. bind, seal, secure, stick, wrap **3**. record, tape-record, video
taper 1. come to a point, narrow, thin **2**. *With* **off** decrease, die away, die out, dwindle, fade, lessen, reduce, subside, thin out, wane, weaken, wind down
tardiness belatedness, delay, dilatoriness, lateness, procrastination, slowness, unpunctuality
tardy backward, behindhand, belated, dawdling, dilatory, late, loitering, overdue, procrastinating, retarded, slack, slow, sluggish, unpunctual
target 1. aim, ambition, bull's-eye, end, goal, intention, mark, object, objective **2**. butt, quarry, scapegoat, victim
tariff 1. assessment, duty, excise, impost, levy, rate, tax, toll **2**. bill of fare, charges, menu, price list, schedule
tarnish 1. *v*. befoul, blacken, blemish, blot, darken, dim, discolour, drag through the mud, dull, lose lustre *or* shine, rust, soil, spot, stain, sully, taint **2**. *n*. blackening, black mark, blemish, blot, discoloration, rust, spot, stain, taint
tarry abide, bide, dally, dawdle, delay, dwell, hang around (*Inf.*), linger, lodge, loiter, lose time, pause, remain, rest, sojourn, stay, take one's time, wait
tart¹ 1. pastry, pie, tartlet **2**. call girl, fallen woman, fille de joie, floozy (*Sl.*), harlot, hooker (*U.S. sl.*), loose woman, prostitute, slut, streetwalker, strumpet, trollop, whore, woman of easy virtue
tart² 1. acid, acidulous, astringent, bitter, piquant, pungent, sharp, sour, tangy, vinegary **2**. acrimonious, astringent, barbed, biting, caustic, crusty, cutting, harsh, nasty, scathing, sharp, short, snappish, testy, trenchant, wounding
task *n*. 1. assignment, business, charge, chore, duty, employment, enterprise, exercise, job, labour, mission, occupation, toil, undertaking, work **2. take to task** blame, censure, criticize, lecture, reprimand, reproach, reprove, scold, tell off (*Inf.*), upbraid ~*v*. **3**. assign to, charge, entrust **4**. burden, exhaust, load, lumber (*Brit. inf*), oppress, overload,

push, saddle, strain, tax, test, weary

taste n. 1. flavour, relish, savour, smack, tang 2. bit, bite, dash, drop, morsel, mouthful, nip, sample, sip, *soupçon*, spoonful, swallow, titbit, touch 3. appetite, bent, desire, fancy, fondness, inclination, leaning, liking, palate, partiality, penchant, predilection, preference, relish 4. appreciation, cultivation, culture, discernment, discrimination, elegance, grace, judgment, perception, polish, refinement, style 5. correctness, decorum, delicacy, discretion, nicety, politeness, propriety, restraint, tact, tactfulness ~v. 6. differentiate, discern, distinguish, perceive 7. assay, nibble, relish, sample, savour, sip, test, try 8. have a flavour of, savour of, smack 9. come up against, encounter, experience, feel, have knowledge of, know, meet with, partake of, undergo

tasteful aesthetically pleasing, artistic, beautiful, charming, cultivated, cultured, delicate, discriminating, elegant, exquisite, fastidious, graceful, handsome, harmonious, in good taste, polished, refined, restrained, smart, stylish

tasteless 1. bland, boring, dull, flat, flavourless, insipid, mild, stale, tame, thin, uninspired, uninteresting, vapid, watered-down, weak 2. cheap, coarse, crass, crude, flashy, garish, gaudy, graceless, gross, impolite, improper, indecorous, indelicate, indiscreet, inelegant, low, rude, tactless, tawdry, uncouth, unseemly, vulgar

tasty appetizing, delectable, delicious, flavourful, flavoursome, full-flavoured, good-tasting, luscious, palatable, sapid, savoury, scrumptious (*Inf.*), toothsome, yummy (*Sl.*)

tatter 1. bit, piece, rag, scrap, shred 2. **in tatters** down at heel, in rags, in shreds, ragged, ripped, tattered, threadbare, torn

tattle 1. v. babble, blab, blather, blether, chat, chatter, gossip, jabber, natter, prate, prattle, spread rumours, talk idly, tell tales, tittle-tattle, yak (*Sl.*) 2. n. babble, blather, blether, chat, chatter, chitchat, gossip, hearsay, idle talk, jabber, prattle, small talk, tittle-tattle, yak (*Sl.*), yap (*Inf.*)

tattler bigmouth (*Sl.*), gossip, quidnunc, rumourmonger, scandalmonger, talebearer, taleteller, telltale

taunt 1. v. deride, flout, gibe, guy (*Inf.*), insult, jeer, mock, provoke, reproach, revile, ridicule, sneer, tease, torment, twit, upbraid 2. n. barb, censure, cut, derision, dig, gibe, insult, jeer, provocation, reproach, ridicule, sarcasm, teasing

taut 1. flexed, rigid, strained, stressed, stretched, tense, tight 2. *Nautical* in good order, neat, orderly, shipshape, spruce, tidy, tight, trim, well-ordered, well-regulated

tautological iterative, pleonastic, prolix, redundant, repetitious, repetitive, verbose

tautology iteration, pleonasm, prolixity, redundancy, repetition, repetitiousness, repetitiveness, verbiage, verbosity

tavern alehouse (*Archaic*), bar, boozer (*Brit. inf.*), hostelry, inn, pub (*Brit. inf.*), public house

tawdry brummagem, cheap, cheapjack (*Inf.*), flashy, gaudy, gimcrack, glittering, meretricious, plastic (*Sl.*), raffish, showy, tacky, tasteless, tatty, tinsel, tinselly, vulgar

tax n. 1. assessment, charge, contribution, customs, duty, excise, imposition, impost, levy, rate, tariff, tithe, toll, tribute 2. burden, demand, drain, load, pressure, strain, weight ~v. 3. assess, charge, demand, exact, extract, impose, levy a tax on, rate, tithe 4. burden, drain, enervate, exhaust, load, make heavy demands on, overburden, push, put pressure on, sap, strain, stretch, task, try, weaken, wear out, weary, weigh heavily on 5. accuse, arraign, blame, charge, impeach, impugn, incriminate, lay at one's door

taxing burdensome, demanding, enervating, exacting, heavy, onerous, punishing, sapping, stressful, tiring, tough, trying, wearing, wearisome

teach advise, coach, demonstrate, direct, discipline, drill, edify, educate, enlighten, give lessons in, guide, impart, implant, inculcate, inform, instil, instruct, school, show, train, tutor

teacher coach, dominie (*Scot.*), don, educator, guide, guru, instructor, lecturer, master, mentor, mistress, pedagogue, professor, schoolmaster, schoolmistress, schoolteacher, trainer, tutor

team n. 1. band, body, bunch, company, crew, gang, group, line-up, set, side, squad, troupe 2. pair, span, yoke ~v. 3. *Often with* **up** band together, cooperate, couple, get together, join, link, unite, work together, yoke

teamwork collaboration, concert, co-operation, coordination, esprit de corps, fellowship, harmony, joint action, unity

tear v. 1. claw, divide, lacerate, mangle, mutilate, pull apart, rend, rip, rive, run, rupture, scratch, sever, shred, split, sunder 2. belt (Sl.), bolt, career, charge, dart, dash, fly, gallop, hurry, race, run, rush, shoot, speed, sprint, zoom 3. grab, pluck, pull, rip, seize, snatch, wrench, wrest, yank ~n. 4. hole, laceration, mutilation, rent, rip, run, rupture, scratch, split

tearaway daredevil, delinquent, good-for-nothing, hooligan, madcap, rough (Inf.), roughneck (Sl.), rowdy, ruffian, tough

tearful 1. blubbering, crying, in tears, lachrymose, sobbing, weeping, weepy (Inf.), whimpering 2. distressing, dolorous, lamentable, mournful, pathetic, pitiable, pitiful, poignant, sad, sorrowful, upsetting, woeful

tears 1. blubbering, crying, distress, lamentation, mourning, pain, regret, sadness, sobbing, sorrow, wailing, weeping, whimpering, woe 2. **in tears** blubbering, crying, distressed, sobbing, visibly moved, weeping, whimpering

tease aggravate (Inf.), annoy, badger, bait, bedevil, chaff, gibe, goad, guy (Inf.), lead on, mock, needle, pester, plague (Inf.), provoke, rag, rib (Inf.), ridicule, tantalize, taunt, torment, twit, vex, worry

technique 1. approach, course, fashion, manner, means, method, mode, modus operandi, procedure, style, system, way 2. address, adroitness, art, artistry, craft, craftsmanship, delivery, execution, facility, knack, know-how (Inf.), performance, proficiency, skill, touch

tedious annoying, banal, boring, deadly dull, drab, dreary, dull, fatiguing, humdrum, irksome, laborious, lifeless, long-drawn-out, monotonous, prosaic, prosy, soporific, tiring, unexciting, uninteresting, vapid, wearisome

tedium banality, boredom, deadness, drabness, dreariness, dullness, ennui, lifelessness, monotony, routine, sameness, tediousness, the doldrums

teem[1] abound, be abundant, bear, be crawling with, be full of, be prolific, brim, bristle, burst at the seams, over-

flow, produce, pullulate, swarm

teem[2] belt (Sl.), bucket down (Inf.), lash, pelt, pour, rain cats and dogs (Inf.), sheet, stream

teeming[1] abundant, alive, brimful, brimming, bristling, bursting, chock-a-block, chock-full, crawling, fruitful, full, numerous, overflowing, packed, replete, swarming, thick

teeming[2] belting (Sl.), bucketing down (Inf.), lashing, pelting, pouring, sheeting, streaming

teenage adolescent, immature, juvenile, youthful

teenager adolescent, boy, girl, juvenile, minor, youth

teeny diminutive, microscopic, miniature, minuscule, minute, teensy-weensy, teeny-weeny, tiny, wee

teeter balance, pivot, rock, seesaw, stagger, sway, totter, tremble, waver, wobble

teetotaller abstainer, nondrinker, Rechabite

telegram cable, radiogram, telegraph, telex, wire (Inf.)

telegraph n. 1. tape machine (Stock Exchange), teleprinter, telex 2. cable, radiogram, telegram, telex, wire (Inf.) ~v. 3. cable, send, telex, transmit, wire (Inf.)

telepathy mind-reading, sixth sense, thought transference

telephone 1. n. blower (Inf.), handset, line, phone 2. v. buzz (Inf.), call, call up, dial, get on the blower (Inf.), give (someone) a buzz (Inf.), give (someone) a call, give (someone) a ring (Brit.), give someone a tinkle (Brit. inf.), phone, put a call through to, ring (Brit.)

telescope n. 1. glass, spyglass ~v. 2. concertina, crush, squash 3. abbreviate, abridge, compress, condense, consolidate, contract, curtail, cut, shorten, shrink, trim, truncate

television gogglebox (Brit. sl.), idiot box (Sl.), receiver, small screen (Inf.), telly (Brit. inf.), the box (Brit. inf.), the tube (Sl.), TV, TV set

tell v. 1. acquaint, announce, apprise, communicate, confess, disclose, divulge, express, impart, inform, let know, make known, mention, notify, proclaim, reveal, say, speak, state, utter 2. authorize, bid, call upon, command, direct, enjoin, instruct, order, require, summon 3. chronicle, depict, describe, give an account of, narrate, portray, recount, re-hearse, relate, report **4**. comprehend, discern, discover, make out, see, under-stand **5**. differentiate, discern, discrimi-nate, distinguish, identify **6**. carry weight, count, have *or* take effect, have force, make its presence felt, register, take its toll, weigh **7**. calculate, compute, count, enumerate, number, reckon, tally

telling considerable, decisive, effec-tive, effectual, forceful, forcible, impres-sive, influential, marked, potent, power-ful, significant, solid, striking, trenchant, weighty

tell off berate, censure, chide, give (someone) a piece of one's mind (*Inf.*), haul over the coals (*Inf.*), lecture, re-buke, reprimand, reproach, reprove, scold, take to task, tear off a strip (*Inf.*), tick off (*Inf.*), upbraid

temerity assurance, audacity, bold-ness, brass neck (*Inf.*), effrontery, fool-hardiness, forwardness, gall (*Inf.*), heed-lessness, impudence, impulsiveness, in-trepidity, nerve (*Inf.*), pluck, rashness, recklessness

temper *n.* **1**. attitude, character, con-stitution, disposition, frame of mind, hu-mour, mind, mood, nature, tempera-ment, tenor, vein **2**. bad mood, fit of pique, fury, paddy (*Brit. inf.*), passion, rage, tantrum, wax (*Inf.*) **3**. anger, an-noyance, heat, hot-headedness, ill hu-mour, irascibility, irritability, irritation, passion, peevishness, petulance, resent-ment, surliness **4**. calm, calmness, com-posure, cool (*Sl.*), coolness, equanimity, good humour, moderation, self-control, tranquillity ~*v.* **5**. abate, admix, allay, assuage, calm, lessen, mitigate, moder-ate, mollify, palliate, restrain, soften, soft-pedal (*Inf.*), soothe, tone down **6**. anneal, harden, strengthen, toughen

temperament 1. bent, cast of mind, character, complexion, constitution, dis-position, frame of mind, humour, make-up, mettle, nature, outlook, personality, quality, soul, spirit, stamp, temper, ten-dencies, tendency **2**. anger, excitability, explosiveness, hot-headedness, impa-tience, mercurialness, moodiness, moods, petulance, volatility

temperamental 1. capricious, easily upset, emotional, erratic, excitable, ex-plosive, fiery, highly strung, hot-headed, hypersensitive, impatient, irritable, mer-curial, moody, neurotic, passionate,

petulant, sensitive, touchy, volatile **2**. congenital, constitutional, inborn, in-grained, inherent, innate, natural **3**. er-ratic, inconsistent, undependable, un-predictable, unreliable

temperance 1. continence, discretion, forbearance, moderation, restraint, self-control, self-discipline, self-restraint **2**. abstemiousness, abstinence, prohibition, sobriety, teetotalism

temperate 1. agreeable, balmy, calm, clement, cool, fair, gentle, mild, moder-ate, pleasant, soft **2**. calm, composed, dispassionate, equable, even-tempered, mild, moderate, reasonable, self-controlled, self-restrained, sensible, sta-ble **3**. abstemious, abstinent, continent, moderate, sober

tempest 1. cyclone, gale, hurricane, squall, storm, tornado, typhoon **2**. com-motion, disturbance, ferment, furore, storm, tumult, upheaval, uproar

tempestuous 1. agitated, blustery, boisterous, breezy, gusty, raging, squally, stormy, turbulent, windy **2**. agitated, boisterous, emotional, excited, feverish, furious, heated, hysterical, impassioned, intense, passionate, stormy, turbulent, uncontrolled, violent, wild

temple church, holy place, place of worship, sanctuary, shrine

tempo beat, cadence, measure, metre, pace, pulse, rate, rhythm, speed, time

temporal 1. carnal, civil, earthly, fleshly, lay, material, mortal, mundane, profane, secular, sublunary, terrestrial, worldly **2**. evanescent, fleeting, fuga-cious, fugitive, impermanent, momen-tary, passing, short-lived, temporary, transient, transitory

temporarily briefly, fleetingly, for a little while, for a moment, for a short time, for a short while, for the moment, for the time being, momentarily, pro tem

temporary brief, ephemeral, evanes-cent, fleeting, fugacious, fugitive, here today and gone tomorrow, impermanent, interim, momentary, passing, pro tem, *pro tempore*, provisional, short-lived, transient, transitory

temporize be evasive, delay, equivo-cate, gain time, hum and haw, play a waiting game, play for time, procrasti-nate, stall, tergiversate

tempt 1. allure, appeal to, attract, coax, decoy, draw, entice, inveigle, in-vite, lead on, lure, make one's mouth water, seduce, tantalize, whet the appetite of, woo **2.** bait, dare, fly in the face of, provoke, risk, test, try

temptation allurement, appeal, attraction, attractiveness, bait, blandishments, coaxing, come-on (*Inf.*), decoy, draw, enticement, inducement, invitation, lure, pull, seduction, snare, tantalization

tempting alluring, appetizing, attractive, enticing, inviting, mouthwatering, seductive, tantalizing

tenable arguable, believable, defendable, defensible, justifiable, maintainable, plausible, rational, reasonable, sound, viable

tenacious 1. clinging, fast, firm, forceful, iron, strong, tight, unshakable **2.** retentive, unforgetful **3.** adamant, determined, dogged, firm, inflexible, intransigent, obdurate, obstinate, persistent, pertinacious, resolute, staunch, steadfast, strong-willed, stubborn, sure, unswerving, unyielding **4.** coherent, cohesive, solid, strong, tough **5.** adhesive, clinging, gluey, glutinous, mucilaginous, sticky

tenacity 1. fastness, firmness, force, forcefulness, power, strength **2.** firm grasp, retention, retentiveness **3.** application, determination, diligence, doggedness, firmness, inflexibility, intransigence, obduracy, obstinacy, perseverance, persistence, pertinacity, resoluteness, resolution, resolve, staunchness, steadfastness, strength of purpose, strength of will, stubbornness **4.** coherence, cohesiveness, solidity, solidness, strength, toughness **5.** adhesiveness, clingingness, stickiness

tenancy 1. holding, lease, occupancy, occupation, possession, renting, residence **2.** incumbency, period of office, tenure, time in office

tenant holder, inhabitant, leaseholder, lessee, occupant, occupier, renter, resident

tend[1] **1.** be apt, be biased, be disposed, be inclined, be liable, be likely, gravitate, have a leaning, have an inclination, have a tendency, incline, lean, trend **2.** aim, bear, be conducive, conduce, contribute, go, head, influence, lead, make for, move, point

tend[2] attend, care for, cater to, control, cultivate, feed, guard, handle, keep, keep an eye on, look after, maintain, manage, minister to, nurse, nurture, protect, see to, serve, take care of, wait on, watch, watch over

tendency 1. bent, disposition, inclination, leaning, liability, partiality, penchant, predilection, predisposition, proclivity, proneness, propensity, readiness, susceptibility **2.** bearing, bias, course, direction, drift, drive, heading, movement, purport, tenor, trend, turning

tender[1] **1.** breakable, delicate, feeble, fragile, frail, soft, weak **2.** callow, green, immature, impressionable, inexperienced, new, raw, sensitive, unripe, vulnerable, wet behind the ears (*Inf.*), young, youthful **3.** affectionate, amorous, benevolent, caring, compassionate, considerate, fond, gentle, humane, kind, loving, merciful, pitiful, sentimental, softhearted, sympathetic, tenderhearted, warm, warm-hearted **4.** emotional, evocative, moving, poignant, romantic, touching **5.** complicated, dangerous, difficult, risky, sensitive, ticklish, touchy, tricky **6.** aching, acute, bruised, inflamed, irritated, painful, raw, sensitive, smarting, sore

tender[2] *v.* **1.** extend, give, hand in, offer, present, proffer, propose, put forward, submit, suggest, volunteer ∼*n.* **2.** bid, estimate, offer, proffer, proposal, submission, suggestion **3.** currency, medium, money, payment, specie

tenderhearted affectionate, benevolent, benign, caring, compassionate, considerate, fond, gentle, humane, kind, kind-hearted, kindly, loving, merciful, mild, responsive, sensitive, sentimental, softhearted, sympathetic, warm, warmhearted

tenderness 1. delicateness, feebleness, fragility, frailness, sensitiveness, sensitivity, softness, vulnerability, weakness **2.** callowness, greenness, immaturity, impressionableness, inexperience, newness, rawness, sensitivity, vulnerability, youth, youthfulness **3.** affection, amorousness, attachment, benevolence, care, compassion, consideration, devotion, fondness, gentleness, humaneness, humanity, kindness, liking, love, mercy, pity, sentimentality, softheartedness, sympathy, tenderheartedness, warmheartedness, warmth **4.** ache, aching, bruising, inflammation, irritation, pain, painfulness, rawness, sensitiveness, sensitivity, smart, soreness

tenebrous dark, dim, dingy, dusky, gloomy, murky, obscure, shadowy, shady, sombre, Stygian, sunless, unlit

tenet article of faith, belief, canon, conviction, creed, doctrine, dogma, maxim, opinion, precept, principle, rule, teaching, thesis, view

tenor aim, burden, course, direction, drift, evolution, intent, meaning, path, purport, purpose, sense, substance, tendency, theme, trend, way

tense adj. **1.** rigid, strained, stretched, taut, tight **2.** anxious, apprehensive, edgy, fidgety, jittery (*Inf.*), jumpy, keyed up, nervous, on edge, overwrought, restless, strained, strung up (*Inf.*), under pressure, uptight (*Sl.*), wound up (*Inf.*), wrought up **3.** exciting, moving, nerveracking, stressful, worrying ~v. **4.** brace, flex, strain, stretch, tauten, tighten

tension 1. pressure, rigidity, stiffness, straining, stress, stretching, tautness, tightness **2.** anxiety, apprehension, edginess, hostility, ill feeling, nervousness, pressure, restlessness, strain, stress, suspense, the jitters (*Inf.*), unease

tentative 1. conjectural, experimental, indefinite, provisional, speculative, unconfirmed, unsettled **2.** backward, cautious, diffident, doubtful, faltering, hesitant, timid, uncertain, undecided, unsure

tenuous 1. doubtful, dubious, flimsy, insignificant, insubstantial, nebulous, questionable, shaky, sketchy, slight, weak **2.** attenuated, delicate, fine, gossamer, slim

tenure holding, incumbency, occupancy, occupation, possession, proprietorship, residence, tenancy, term, time

tepid 1. lukewarm, slightly warm, warmish **2.** apathetic, cool, half-hearted, indifferent, lukewarm, unenthusiastic

tergiversate 1. apostatize, change sides, defect, desert, go over to the other side, renege, turn traitor **2.** beat about the bush, blow hot and cold (*Inf.*), dodge, equivocate, fence, hedge, prevaricate, pussyfoot (*Inf.*), vacillate

term n. **1.** appellation, denomination, designation, expression, locution, name, phrase, title, word **2.** duration, interval, period, season, space, span, spell, time, while **3.** course, session **4.** bound, boundary, close, conclusion, confine, culmination, end, finish, fruition, limit, terminus ~v. **5.** call, denominate, desig-

nate, dub, entitle, label, name, style

terminal adj. **1.** bounding, concluding, extreme, final, last, limiting, ultimate, utmost **2.** deadly, fatal, incurable, killing, lethal, mortal ~n. **3.** boundary, end, extremity, limit, termination, terminus **4.** depot, end of the line, station, terminus

terminate abort, bring or come to an end, cease, close, complete, conclude, cut off, discontinue, end, expire, finish, issue, lapse, put an end to, result, run out, stop, wind up

termination abortion, cessation, close, completion, conclusion, consequence, cut-off point, discontinuation, effect, end, ending, expiry, finale, finis, finish, issue, result, wind-up (*Inf.*)

terminology argot, cant, jargon, language, lingo (*Inf.*), nomenclature, patois, phraseology, terms, vocabulary

terminus 1. boundary, close, end, extremity, final point, goal, limit, target, termination **2.** depot, end of the line, garage, last stop, station

terms 1. language, manner of speaking, phraseology, terminology **2.** conditions, particulars, premises (*Law*), provisions, provisos, qualifications, specifications, stipulations **3.** charges, fee, payment, price, rates **4.** footing, position, relations, relationship, standing, status **5. come to terms** be reconciled, come to an agreement, come to an understanding, conclude agreement, learn to live with, reach acceptance, reach agreement

terrain country, going, ground, land, landscape, topography

terrestrial 1. adj. earthly, global, mundane, sublunary, tellurian, terrene, worldly **2.** n. earthling, earthman, earthwoman, human

terrible 1. bad, dangerous, desperate, extreme, serious, severe **2.** *Inf.* abhorrent, awful, bad, beastly (*Inf.*), dire, dreadful, duff (*Brit. sl.*), foul, frightful, hateful, hideous, loathsome, obnoxious, odious, offensive, poor, repulsive, revolting, rotten (*Inf.*), unpleasant, vile **3.** appalling, awful, dread, dreaded, dreadful, fearful, frightful, gruesome, harrowing, horrendous, horrible, horrid, horrifying, monstrous, shocking

terribly awfully (*Inf.*), decidedly, desperately, exceedingly, extremely, gravely, greatly, much, seriously, thoroughly, very

terrific 1. awesome, awful, dreadful, enormous, excessive, extreme, fearful, fierce, gigantic, great, harsh, horrific, huge, intense, monstrous, severe, terrible, tremendous **2**. *Inf.* ace (*Inf.*), amazing, breathtaking, excellent, fabulous (*Inf.*), fantastic (*Inf.*), fine, great (*Inf.*), magnificent, marvellous, outstanding, sensational (*Inf.*), smashing (*Inf.*), stupendous, super (*Inf.*), superb, very good, wonderful

terrified alarmed, appalled, awed, dismayed, frightened, frightened out of one's wits, horrified, horror-struck, intimidated, panic-stricken, petrified, scared, scared stiff, scared to death, shocked, terror-stricken

terrify alarm, appal, awe, dismay, fill with terror, frighten, frighten out of one's wits, horrify, intimidate, make one's blood run cold, make one's flesh creep, make one's hair stand on end, petrify, put the fear of God into, scare, scare to death, shock, terrorize

territory area, bailiwick, country, district, domain, land, province, region, sector, state, terrain, tract, zone

terror 1. alarm, anxiety, awe, consternation, dismay, dread, fear, fear and trembling, fright, horror, intimidation, panic, shock **2**. bogeyman, bugbear, devil, fiend, monster, scourge

terrorize 1. browbeat, bully, coerce, intimidate, menace, oppress, strong-arm (*Inf.*), threaten **2**. alarm, appal, awe, dismay, fill with terror, frighten, frighten out of one's wits, horrify, inspire panic in, intimidate, make one's blood run cold, make one's flesh creep, make one's hair stand on end, petrify, put the fear of God into, scare, scare to death, shock, strike terror into, terrify

terse 1. aphoristic, brief, clipped, compact, concise, condensed, crisp, elliptical, epigrammatic, gnomic, incisive, laconic, neat, pithy, sententious, short, succinct, summary, to the point **2**. abrupt, brusque, curt, short, snappy

test 1. *v.* analyse, assay, assess, check, examine, experiment, investigate, prove, put to the proof, put to the test, try, try out, verify **2**. *n.* analysis, assessment, attempt, catechism, check, evaluation, examination, investigation, ordeal, probation, proof, trial

testament 1. last wishes, will **2**. attestation, demonstration, earnest, evidence,

exemplification, proof, testimony, tribute, witness

testify affirm, assert, attest, bear witness, certify, corroborate, declare, depone (*Scots Law*), depose (*Law*), evince, give testimony, show, state, swear, vouch, witness

testimonial certificate, character, commendation, credential, endorsement, recommendation, reference, tribute

testimony 1. affidavit, affirmation, attestation, avowal, confirmation, corroboration, declaration, deposition, evidence, information, profession, statement, submission, witness **2**. corroboration, demonstration, evidence, indication, manifestation, proof, support, verification

testy bad-tempered, cantankerous, captious, crabbed, cross, fretful, grumpy, impatient, irascible, irritable, peevish, peppery, petulant, quarrelsome, quick-tempered, short-tempered, snappish, snappy, splenetic, sullen, tetchy, touchy, waspish

tetchy bad-tempered, cantankerous, captious, crabbed, cross, fretful, grumpy, impatient, irascible, irritable, peevish, peppery, petulant, quarrelsome, quick-tempered, short-tempered, snappish, snappy, splenetic, sullen, testy, touchy, waspish

tête-à-tête 1. *n.* chat, confab (*Inf.*), cosy chat, parley, private conversation, private word, talk **2**. *adv.* in private, intimately, privately

tether *n.* **1**. bond, chain, fastening, fetter, halter, lead, leash, restraint, rope, shackle **2. at the end of one's tether** at one's wits' end, at the limit of one's endurance, exasperated, exhausted, finished, out of patience ~*v.* **3**. bind, chain, fasten, fetter, leash, manacle, picket, restrain, rope, secure, shackle, tie

text 1. body, contents, main body, matter **2**. wording, words **3**. *Bible* paragraph, passage, sentence, verse **4**. argument, matter, motif, subject, theme, topic **5**. reader, reference book, source, textbook

texture character, composition, consistency, constitution, fabric, feel, grain, make, quality, structure, surface, tissue, weave

thank express gratitude, say thank you, show gratitude, show one's appreciation

thankful appreciative, beholden,

grateful, indebted, obliged, pleased, relieved

thankless 1. fruitless, unappreciated, unprofitable, unrequited, unrewarding, useless **2.** inconsiderate, unappreciative, ungracious, ungrateful, unmindful, unthankful

thanks 1. acknowledgment, appreciation, credit, gratefulness, gratitude, recognition, thanksgiving **2. thanks to** as a result of, because of, by reason of, due to, owing to, through

thaw defrost, dissolve, liquefy, melt, soften, unfreeze, warm

theatrical 1. dramatic, dramaturgic, melodramatic, scenic, Thespian **2.** affected, artificial, ceremonious, dramatic, exaggerated, hammy (*Inf.*), histrionic, mannered, ostentatious, overdone, pompous, showy, stagy, stilted, unreal

theft embezzlement, fraud, larceny, pilfering, purloining, rip-off (*Sl.*), robbery, stealing, swindling, thievery, thieving

theme 1. argument, burden, idea, keynote, matter, subject, subject matter, text, thesis, topic **2.** leitmotiv, motif, recurrent image, unifying idea **3.** composition, dissertation, essay, exercise, paper

theological divine, doctrinal, ecclesiastical, religious

theorem deduction, dictum, formula, hypothesis, principle, proposition, rule, statement

theoretical abstract, academic, conjectural, hypothetical, ideal, impractical, pure, speculative

theorize conjecture, formulate, guess, hypothesize, project, propound, speculate, suppose

theory 1. assumption, conjecture, guess, hypothesis, presumption, speculation, supposition, surmise, thesis **2.** philosophy, plan, proposal, scheme, system

therapeutic ameliorative, analeptic, beneficial, corrective, curative, good, healing, remedial, restorative, salubrious, salutary, sanative

therapy cure, healing, remedial treatment, remedy, treatment

therefore accordingly, as a result, consequently, ergo, for that reason, hence, so, then, thence, thus, whence

thesaurus dictionary, encyclopedia, repository, storehouse, treasury, wordbook

thesis 1. composition, disquisition,

dissertation, essay, monograph, paper, treatise **2.** contention, hypothesis, idea, line of argument, opinion, proposal, proposition, theory, view **3.** area, subject, theme, topic **4.** assumption, postulate, premiss, proposition, statement, supposition, surmise

thick *adj.* **1.** broad, bulky, deep, fat, solid, substantial, wide **2.** close, clotted, coagulated, compact, concentrated, condensed, crowded, deep, dense, heavy, impenetrable, opaque **3.** abundant, brimming, bristling, bursting, chock-a-block, chock-full, covered, crawling, frequent, full, numerous, packed, replete, swarming, teeming **4.** blockheaded, brainless, dense, dim-witted (*Inf.*), dopey (*Sl.*), dull, insensitive, moronic, obtuse, slow, slow-witted, stupid, thickheaded **5.** dense, heavy, impenetrable, soupy **6.** distorted, guttural, hoarse, husky, inarticulate, indistinct, throaty **7.** broad, decided, distinct, marked, pronounced, rich, strong **8.** *Inf.* chummy (*Inf.*), close, confidential, devoted, familiar, friendly, hand in glove, inseparable, intimate, matey (*Brit. inf.*), on good terms, pally (*Inf.*), well in (*Inf.*) **9. a bit thick** excessive, over the score (*Inf.*), too much, unfair, unjust, unreasonable ~*n.* **10.** centre, heart, middle, midst

thicken cake, clot, coagulate, condense, congeal, deepen, gel, inspissate (*Archaic*), jell, set

thicket brake, clump, coppice, copse, covert, grove, spinney (*Brit.*), wood, woodland

thickhead blockhead, bonehead (*Sl.*), clot (*Brit. sl.*), dimwit (*Inf.*), dolt, dope (*Sl.*), dummy (*Sl.*), dunce, dunderhead, fathead (*Inf.*), fool, idiot, imbecile, moron, numskull, pinhead (*Sl.*)

thickheaded blockheaded, brainless, dense, dim-witted (*Inf.*), doltish, dopey (*Sl.*), idiotic, moronic, obtuse, slow, slow-witted, stupid, thick

thickset 1. beefy (*Inf.*), brawny, bulky, burly, heavy, muscular, powerfully built, stocky, strong, stubby, sturdy, well-built **2.** closely packed, dense, densely planted, solid, thick

thick-skinned callous, case-hardened, hard-boiled (*Inf.*), hardened, impervious, insensitive, stolid, tough, unfeeling, unsusceptible

thief bandit, burglar, cheat, cracksman (*Sl.*), crook (*Inf.*), embezzler, housebreaker, larcenist, mugger (*Inf.*), pick-pocket, pilferer, plunderer, purloiner, robber, shoplifter, stealer, swindler

thieve cheat, embezzle, filch, half-inch (*Inf.*), knock off (*Sl.*), lift (*Inf.*), misappropriate, nick (*Brit. sl.*), peculate, pilfer, pinch (*Inf.*), plunder, poach, purloin, rip off (*Sl.*), rob, run off with, snitch (*Sl.*), steal, swindle, swipe (*Sl.*)

thievery banditry, burglary, crookedness (*Inf.*), embezzlement, larceny, mugging (*Inf.*), pilfering, plundering, robbery, shoplifting, stealing, theft, thieving

thievish crooked (*Inf.*), dishonest, fraudulent, larcenous, light-fingered, predatory, rapacious, sticky-fingered (*Inf.*), thieving

thimbleful capful, dab, dash, dram, drop, jot, modicum, nip, pinch, sip, *soupçon*, spoonful, spot, taste, toothful

thin *adj.* **1.** attenuate, attenuated, fine, narrow, threadlike **2.** delicate, diaphanous, filmy, fine, flimsy, gossamer, seethrough, sheer, translucent, transparent, unsubstantial **3.** bony, emaciated, lank, lanky, lean, light, meagre, scraggy, scrawny, skeletal, skinny, slender, slight, slim, spare, spindly, thin as a rake, undernourished, underweight **4.** deficient, meagre, scanty, scarce, scattered, skimpy, sparse, wispy **5.** dilute, diluted, rarefied, runny, watery, weak, wishy-washy (*Inf.*) **6.** feeble, flimsy, inadequate, insufficient, lame, poor, scant, scanty, shallow, slight, superficial, unconvincing, unsubstantial, weak ~*v.* **7.** attenuate, cut back, dilute, diminish, emaciate, prune, rarefy, reduce, refine, trim, water down, weaken, weed out

thing 1. affair, article, being, body, circumstance, concept, entity, fact, matter, object, part, portion, something, substance **2.** act, deed, event, eventuality, feat, happening, incident, occurrence, phenomenon, proceeding **3.** apparatus, contrivance, device, gadget, implement, instrument, machine, means, mechanism, tool **4.** aspect, detail, facet, factor, feature, item, particular, point, statement, thought **5.** *Plural* baggage, belongings, bits and pieces, clobber (*Brit. sl.*), clothes, effects, equipment, gear (*Inf.*), goods, impedimenta, luggage, odds and ends, paraphernalia, possessions, stuff **6.** *Inf.* attitude, bee in one's bonnet, fetish, fixation, hang-up (*Inf.*), *idée fixe*, mania, obsession, phobia, preoccupation, quirk

think *v.* **1.** believe, conceive, conclude, consider, deem, determine, esteem, estimate, hold, imagine, judge, reckon, regard, suppose, surmise **2.** brood, cerebrate, chew over (*Inf.*), cogitate, consider, contemplate, deliberate, have in mind, meditate, mull over, muse, ponder, reason, reflect, revolve, ruminate, turn over in one's mind, weigh up **3.** call to mind, recall, recollect, remember **4.** anticipate, envisage, expect, foresee, imagine, plan for, presume, suppose **5.** **think better of** change one's mind about, decide against, go back on, have second thoughts about, reconsider, repent, think again, think twice about **6.** **think much of** admire, attach importance to, esteem, have a high opinion of, hold in high regard, rate (*Sl.*), respect, set store by, think highly of, value **7.** **think nothing of** consider unimportant, have no compunction about, have no hesitation about, regard as routine, set no store by, take in one's stride ~*n.* **8.** assessment, consideration, contemplation, deliberation, look, reflection

thinkable conceivable, feasible, imaginable, likely, possible, reasonable, within the bounds of possibility

thinker brain (*Inf.*), intellect (*Inf.*), mastermind, philosopher, sage, theorist, wise man

thinking 1. *n.* assessment, conclusions, conjecture, idea, judgment, opinion, outlook, philosophy, position, reasoning, theory, thoughts, view **2.** *adj.* contemplative, cultured, intelligent, meditative, philosophical, ratiocinative, rational, reasoning, reflective, sophisticated, thoughtful

think over chew over (*Inf.*), consider, consider the pros and cons of, contemplate, give thought to, mull over, ponder, reflect upon, turn over in one's mind, weigh up

think up come up with, concoct, contrive, create, devise, dream up, imagine, improvise, invent, visualize

thin-skinned easily hurt, hypersensitive, quick to take offence, sensitive, soft, susceptible, tender, touchy, vulnerable

third-rate bad, duff (*Brit. sl.*), indifferent, inferior, low-grade, mediocre, poor, poor-quality, ropy (*Brit. inf.*), shoddy

thirst *n.* **1.** craving to drink, drought,

dryness, thirstiness 2. appetite, craving, desire, eagerness, hankering, hunger, keenness, longing, lust, passion, yearning, yen (*Inf.*)

thirsty 1. arid, dehydrated, dry, parched 2. athirst, avid, burning, craving, desirous, dying, eager, greedy, hankering, hungry, itching, longing, lusting, thirsting, yearning

thorn 1. barb, prickle, spike, spine 2. affliction, annoyance, bane, bother, curse, irritant, irritation, nuisance, pest, plague, scourge, torment, torture, trouble

thorny 1. barbed, bristling with thorns, bristly, pointed, prickly, sharp, spiky, spinous, spiny 2. awkward, difficult, harassing, hard, irksome, problematic, sticky (*Inf.*), ticklish, tough, troublesome, trying, unpleasant, upsetting, vexatious, worrying

thorough *or* **thoroughgoing** 1. all-embracing, all-inclusive, assiduous, careful, complete, comprehensive, conscientious, efficient, exhaustive, full, in-depth, intensive, leaving no stone unturned, meticulous, painstaking, scrupulous, sweeping 2. absolute, arrant, complete, downright, entire, out-and-out, perfect, pure, sheer, total, unmitigated, unqualified, utter

thoroughbred blood, full-blooded, of unmixed stock, pedigree, pure-blooded, purebred

thoroughfare access, avenue, highway, passage, passageway, road, roadway, street, way

thoroughly 1. assiduously, carefully, completely, comprehensively, conscientiously, efficiently, exhaustively, from top to bottom, fully, inside out, intensively, leaving no stone unturned, meticulously, painstakingly, scrupulously, sweepingly, through and through, throughout 2. absolutely, completely, downright, entirely, perfectly, quite, totally, to the full, utterly, without reservation

though 1. *conj.* albeit, allowing, although, despite the fact that, even if, even supposing, granted, notwithstanding, while 2. *adv.* all the same, for all that, however, nevertheless, nonetheless, notwithstanding, still, yet

thought 1. brainwork, cerebration, cogitation, consideration, contemplation, deliberation, introspection, meditation, musing, reflection, regard, rumination, thinking 2. assessment, belief, concept, conception, conclusion, conjecture, conviction, estimation, idea, judgment, notion, opinion, thinking, view 3. attention, consideration, heed, regard, scrutiny, study 4. aim, design, idea, intention, notion, object, plan, purpose 5. anticipation, aspiration, dream, expectation, hope, prospect 6. dash, jot, little, small amount, *soupçon*, touch, trifle, whisker (*Inf.*) 7. anxiety, attentiveness, care, compassion, concern, kindness, regard, solicitude, sympathy, thoughtfulness

thoughtful 1. attentive, caring, considerate, helpful, kind, kindly, solicitous, unselfish 2. astute, canny, careful, cautious, circumspect, deliberate, discreet, heedful, mindful, prudent, wary, well thought-out 3. contemplative, deliberative, in a brown study, introspective, lost in thought, meditative, musing, pensive, rapt, reflective, ruminative, serious, studious, thinking, wistful

thoughtless 1. impolite, inconsiderate, indiscreet, insensitive, rude, selfish, tactless, uncaring, undiplomatic, unkind 2. absent-minded, careless, foolish, heedless, ill-considered, imprudent, inadvertent, inattentive, injudicious, mindless, neglectful, negligent, rash, reckless, regardless, remiss, silly, stupid, unmindful, unobservant, unthinking

thraldom bondage, enslavement, serfdom, servitude, slavery, subjection, subjugation, thrall, vassalage

thrall 1. bondage, enslavement, serfdom, servitude, slavery, subjection, subjugation, thraldom, vassalage 2. bondservant, bondsman, serf, slave, subject, vassal

thrash 1. beat, belt, birch, cane, chastise, drub, flagellate, flog, give (someone) a (good) hiding (*Inf.*), hide (*Inf.*), horsewhip, lambaste, leather, paste (*Sl.*), punish, scourge, spank, take a stick to, tan (*Sl.*), whip 2. beat, beat (someone) hollow (*Brit. inf.*), clobber (*Brit. sl.*), crush, defeat, drub, hammer (*Inf.*), maul, overwhelm, paste (*Sl.*), rout, slaughter (*Inf.*), trounce, wipe the floor with (*Inf.*) 3. flail, heave, jerk, plunge, squirm, thresh, toss, toss and turn, writhe

thrashing 1. beating, belting, caning, chastisement, drubbing, flogging, hiding (*Inf.*), lashing, pasting (*Sl.*), punishment, tanning (*Sl.*), whipping 2. beating, defeat, drubbing, hammering (*Inf.*), hiding (*Inf.*), mauling, pasting (*Sl.*), rout, trouncing

thrash out argue out, debate, discuss, have out, resolve, settle, solve, talk over

thread *n.* **1.** cotton, fibre, filament, line, strand, string, yarn **2.** course, direction, drift, motif, plot, story line, strain, tenor, theme, train of thought ~*v.* **3.** ease, inch, loop, meander, pass, pick (one's way), squeeze through, string, wind

threadbare 1. down at heel, frayed, old, ragged, scruffy, shabby, tattered, tatty, used, worn, worn-out **2.** clichéd, cliché-ridden, common, commonplace, conventional, corny (*Inf.*), familiar, hackneyed, overused, stale, stereotyped, stock, tired, trite, well-worn

threat 1. commination, intimidatory remark, menace, threatening remark, warning **2.** foreboding, foreshadowing, omen, portent, presage, warning, writing on the wall **3.** danger, hazard, menace, peril, risk

threaten 1. endanger, imperil, jeopardize, put at risk, put in jeopardy **2.** be imminent, be in the air, be in the offing, forebode, foreshadow, hang over, impend, loom over, portend, presage, warn **3.** browbeat, bully, cow, intimidate, lean on (*Sl.*), make threats to, menace, pressurize, terrorize, warn

threatening 1. bullying, cautionary, comminatory, intimidatory, menacing, minatory, terrorizing, warning **2.** baleful, grim, inauspicious, ominous, sinister

threesome triad, trilogy, trine, trinity, trio, triple, triplet, triplex, triptych, triumvirate, triune, troika

threnody coronach (*Scot., Irish*), dirge, elegy, funeral ode, keen, lament, monody, requiem

threshold 1. door, doorsill, doorstep, doorway, entrance, sill **2.** beginning, brink, dawn, inception, opening, outset, start, starting point, verge **3.** lower limit, minimum

thrift carefulness, economy, frugality, good husbandry, parsimony, prudence, saving, thriftiness

thriftless extravagant, improvident, imprudent, lavish, prodigal, profligate, spendthrift, unthrifty, wasteful

thrifty careful, economical, frugal, parsimonious, provident, prudent, saving, sparing

thrill *n.* **1.** adventure, buzz (*Sl.*), charge (*Sl.*), flush of excitement, glow, kick (*Inf.*), pleasure, sensation, stimulation, tingle, titillation **2.** flutter, fluttering, quiver, shudder, throb, tremble, tremor, vibration ~*v.* **3.** arouse, electrify, excite, flush, get a charge (*Sl.*), get a kick (*Inf.*), glow, move, send (*Sl.*), stimulate, stir, tingle, titillate **4.** flutter, quake, quiver, shake, shudder, throb, tremble, vibrate

thrilling 1. electrifying, exciting, gripping, hair-raising, rip-roaring (*Inf.*), riveting, rousing, sensational, stimulating, stirring **2.** quaking, shaking, shivering, shuddering, trembling, vibrating

thrive advance, bloom, boom, burgeon, develop, do well, flourish, get on, grow, grow rich, increase, prosper, succeed, wax

thriving blooming, booming, burgeoning, developing, doing well, flourishing, going strong (*Inf.*), growing, healthy, prosperous, successful, wealthy, well

throaty deep, gruff, guttural, hoarse, husky, low, thick

throb 1. *v.* beat, palpitate, pound, pulsate, pulse, thump, vibrate **2.** *n.* beat, palpitation, pounding, pulsating, pulse, thump, thumping, vibration

throe 1. convulsion, fit, pain, pang, paroxysm, spasm, stab **2.** *Plural* agony, anguish, pain, suffering, torture, travail **3. in the throes of** agonized by, anguished by, in the midst of, in the pangs of, in the process of, struggling with, suffering from, toiling with, wrestling with

throng 1. *n.* assemblage, concourse, congregation, crowd, crush, horde, host, jam, mass, mob, multitude, pack, press, swarm **2.** *v.* bunch, congregate, converge, cram, crowd, fill, flock, hem in, herd, jam, mill around, pack, press, swarm around, troop

throttle *v.* **1.** choke, garrotte, strangle, strangulate **2.** control, gag (*Inf.*), inhibit, silence, stifle, suppress

through *prep.* **1.** between, by, from end to end of, from one side to the other of, in and out of, past **2.** as a consequence or result of, because of, by means of, by virtue of, by way of, using, via, with the help of **3.** during, in, in the middle of, throughout **4.** *With* **with** at the end of, done, finished, having completed, having had enough of ~*adj.* **5.** completed, done, ended, finished, terminated, washed up (*Inf.*) ~*adv.* **6. through and through** altogether, completely, entirely, fully, thoroughly, totally, to the core, unreservedly, utterly, wholly

throughout all over, all the time, all through, during the whole of, everywhere, for the duration of, from beginning to end, from end to end, from start to finish, from the start, over the length and breadth of, right through, the whole time, through the whole of

throw *v.* **1.** cast, chuck (*Inf.*), fling, heave, hurl, launch, lob (*Inf.*), pitch, project, propel, put, send, shy, sling, toss **2.** *Inf.* astonish, baffle, confound, confuse, disconcert, dumbfound, put one off one's stroke, throw off, throw one off one's stride, throw out **3.** bring down, dislodge, fell, floor, hurl to the ground, overturn, unseat, upset ~*n.* **4.** cast, fling, heave, lob (*Inf.*), pitch, projection, put, shy, sling, toss **5.** *Inf.* attempt, chance, essay, gamble, hazard, try, venture, wager

throwaway *adj.* careless, casual, offhand, passing, understated

throw away 1. cast off, discard, dispense with, dispose of, ditch (*Sl.*), dump (*Inf.*), get rid of, jettison, reject, scrap, throw out **2.** blow (*Sl.*), fail to exploit, fritter away, lose, make poor use of, squander, waste

throw off 1. abandon, cast off, discard, drop, free oneself of, rid oneself of, shake off **2.** elude, escape from, evade, get away from, give (someone) the slip, leave behind, lose, outdistance, outrun, shake off, show a clean pair of heels to **3.** confuse, disconcert, disturb, put one off one's stroke, throw (*Inf.*), throw one off one's stride, unsettle, upset

throw out 1. cast off, discard, dismiss, dispense with, ditch (*Sl.*), dump (*Inf.*), eject, evict, expel, get rid of, jettison, kick out (*Inf.*), reject, scrap, show the door to, throw away, turf out (*Brit. inf.*), turn down **2.** confuse, disconcert, disturb, put one off one's stroke, throw (*Inf.*), throw one off one's stride, unsettle, upset **3.** diffuse, disseminate, emit, give off, put forth, radiate

throw over abandon, break with, chuck (*Inf.*), desert, discard, drop (*Inf.*), finish with, forsake, jilt, leave, quit, split up with, walk out on (*Inf.*)

throw up 1. abandon, chuck (*Inf.*),

give up, jack in, leave, quit, relinquish, renounce, resign **2.** bring forward, bring to light, bring to notice, bring to the surface, produce, reveal **3.** *Inf.* be sick, bring up, disgorge, heave, puke (*Sl.*), regurgitate, retch, spew, vomit **4.** jerrybuild, run up, slap together, throw together

thrust *v.* **1.** butt, drive, elbow *or* shoulder one's way, force, impel, jam, plunge, poke, press, prod, propel, push, ram, shove, urge **2.** jab, lunge, pierce, stab, stick ~*n.* **3.** drive, lunge, poke, prod, push, shove, stab **4.** impetus, momentum, motive force, motive power, propulsive force

thud *n./v.* clonk, clump, clunk, crash, knock, smack, thump, wallop (*Inf.*)

thug assassin, bandit, bruiser (*Inf.*), bully boy, cutthroat, gangster, hooligan, killer, mugger (*Inf.*), murderer, robber, ruffian, tough

thumb *n.* **1.** pollex **2. all thumbs** butterfingered (*Inf.*), cack-handed (*Inf.*), clumsy, ham-fisted (*Inf.*), inept, maladroit **3. thumbs down** disapproval, negation, no, rebuff, refusal, rejection **4. thumbs up** acceptance, affirmation, approval, encouragement, go-ahead (*Inf.*), green light, O.K. (*Inf.*), yes ~*v.* **5.** hitch (*Inf.*), hitchhike **6.** *Often with* **through** browse through, flick through, flip through, glance at, leaf through, riffle through, run one's eye over, scan the pages of, skim through, turn over **7.** dogear, finger, handle, mark **8. thumb one's nose at** be contemptuous of, cock a snook at, deride, flout, jeer at, laugh at, laugh in the face of, mock, ridicule, show contempt for, show disrespect to

thumbnail *adj.* brief, compact, concise, pithy, quick, short, succinct

thump 1. *n.* bang, blow, clout (*Inf.*), clunk, crash, knock, rap, smack, thud, thwack, wallop (*Inf.*), whack **2.** *v.* bang, batter, beat, belabour, clout (*Inf.*), crash, hit, knock, lambaste (*Sl.*), pound, rap, smack, strike, thrash, throb, thud, thwack, wallop (*Inf.*), whack

thumping colossal, enormous, excessive, exorbitant, gargantuan, gigantic, great, huge, impressive, mammoth, massive, monumental, terrific, thundering (*Sl.*), titanic, tremendous, whopping (*Inf.*)

thunder *n.* **1.** boom, booming, cracking, crash, crashing, detonation, explosion, pealing, rumble, rumbling ~v. **2.** blast, boom, clap, crack, crash, detonate, explode, peal, resound, reverberate, roar, rumble **3.** bark, bellow, declaim, roar, shout, yell **4.** curse, denounce, fulminate, rail, threaten, utter threats

thundering decided, enormous, excessive, great, monumental, remarkable, unmitigated, utter

thunderous booming, deafening, ear-splitting, loud, noisy, resounding, roaring, tumultuous

thunderstruck aghast, amazed, astonished, astounded, bowled over (*Inf.*), dazed, dumbfounded, flabbergasted (*Inf.*), floored (*Inf.*), knocked for six (*Inf.*), left speechless, nonplussed, open-mouthed, paralysed, petrified, rooted to the spot, shocked, staggered, struck dumb, stunned, taken aback

thus 1. as follows, in this fashion (manner, way), like so, like this, so, to such a degree **2.** accordingly, consequently, ergo, for this reason, hence, on that account, so, then, therefore

thwack 1. *v.* bash (*Inf.*), beat, clout (*Inf.*), flog, hit, smack, thump, wallop (*Inf.*), whack **2.** *n.* bash (*Inf.*), blow, clout (*Inf.*), smack, thump, wallop (*Inf.*), whack

thwart baffle, balk, check, defeat, foil, frustrate, hinder, impede, obstruct, oppose, outwit, prevent, stop, stymie

tic jerk, spasm, twitch

tick¹ *n.* **1.** clack, click, clicking, tap, tapping, ticktock **2.** *Brit. inf.* flash, half a mo (*Brit. inf.*), instant, jiffy (*Inf.*), minute, moment, sec (*Inf.*), second, shake (*Inf.*), split second, trice, twinkling, two shakes of a lamb's tail (*Inf.*) **3.** dash, mark, stroke ~v. **4.** clack, click, tap, ticktock **5.** check off, choose, indicate, mark, mark off, select **6. what makes someone tick** drive, motivation, motive, *raison d'être*

tick² account, credit, deferred payment, the slate (*Brit. inf.*)

ticket 1. card, certificate, coupon, pass, slip, token, voucher **2.** card, docket, label, marker, slip, sticker, tab, tag

tickle *Fig.* amuse, delight, divert, entertain, excite, gratify, please, thrill, titillate

ticklish awkward, critical, delicate, difficult, nice, risky, sensitive, thorny, touchy, tricky, uncertain, unstable, unsteady

tick off 1. check off, mark off, put a tick at **2.** *Inf.* berate, censure, chide, haul over the coals (*Inf.*), lecture, rebuke, reprimand, reproach, reprove, scold, take to task, tear off a strip (*Inf.*), tell off (*Inf.*), upbraid

tide 1. course, current, ebb, flow, stream **2.** course, current, direction, drift, movement, tendency, trend

tide over aid, assist, bridge the gap, help, keep one going, keep one's head above water, keep the wolf from the door, see one through

tidings advice, bulletin, communication, greetings, information, intelligence, message, news, report, word

tidy *adj.* **1.** businesslike, clean, cleanly, methodical, neat, ordered, orderly, shipshape, spick-and-span, spruce, systematic, trim, well-groomed, well-kept, well-ordered **2.** *Inf.* ample, considerable, fair, generous, good, goodly, handsome, healthy, large, largish, respectable, sizable, substantial ~v. **3.** clean, groom, neaten, order, put in order, put in trim, put to rights, spruce up, straighten

tie *v.* **1.** attach, bind, connect, fasten, interlace, join, knot, lash, link, make fast, moor, rope, secure, tether, truss, unite **2.** bind, confine, hamper, hinder, hold, limit, restrain, restrict **3.** be even, be neck and neck, draw, equal, match ~n. **4.** band, bond, connection, cord, fastening, fetter, joint, knot, ligature, link, rope, string **5.** affiliation, allegiance, bond, commitment, connection, duty, kinship, liaison, obligation, relationship **6.** encumbrance, hindrance, limitation, restraint, restriction **7.** dead heat, deadlock, draw, stalemate **8.** *Brit.* contest, fixture, game, match

tie-in association, connection, coordination, hook-up, liaison, link, relation, relationship, tie-up

tie in be relevant, come in, connect, coordinate, fit in, have bearing, link, relate

tier bank, echelon, file, layer, level, line, order, rank, row, series, storey, stratum

tie-up association, connection, coordination, hook-up, liaison, link, link-up, relation, relationship, tie-in

tie up 1. attach, bind, pinion, restrain, tether, truss **2.** lash, make fast, moor, rope, secure **3.** engage, engross, keep busy, occupy **4.** bring to a close, conclude, end, finish off, settle, terminate, wind up, wrap up (*Inf.*)

tiff 1. difference, disagreement, dispute, falling-out (*Inf.*), petty quarrel, quarrel, row, scrap (*Inf.*), squabble, words 2. bad mood, fit of ill humour, fit of pique, huff, ill humour, pet, sulk, tantrum, temper

tight 1. close, close-fitting, compact, constricted, cramped, fast, firm, fixed, narrow, rigid, secure, snug, stiff, stretched, taut, tense 2. hermetic, impervious, proof, sealed, sound, watertight 3. harsh, inflexible, rigid, rigorous, severe, stern, strict, stringent, tough, uncompromising, unyielding 4. close, grasping, mean, miserly, niggardly, parsimonious, penurious, sparing, stingy, tightfisted 5. dangerous, difficult, hazardous, perilous, precarious, problematic, sticky (*Inf.*), ticklish, tough, tricky, troublesome, worrisome 6. close, even, evenly-balanced, near, well-matched 7. *Inf.* drunk, half cut (*Brit. sl.*), half seas over (*Brit. inf.*), inebriated, in one's cups, intoxicated, pickled (*Inf.*), pie-eyed (*Sl.*), plastered (*Sl.*), smashed (*Sl.*), sozzled (*Inf.*), stewed (*Sl.*), stoned (*Sl.*), three sheets in the wind (*Sl.*), tiddly (*Brit. sl.*), tipsy, under the influence (*Inf.*)

tighten close, constrict, cramp, fasten, fix, narrow, rigidify, screw, secure, squeeze, stiffen, stretch, tauten, tense

tightfisted close, close-fisted, grasping, mean, mingy (*Brit. inf.*), miserly, niggardly, parsimonious, penurious, sparing, stingy, tight

tight-lipped close-lipped, close-mouthed, mum, mute, quiet, reserved, reticent, secretive, silent, taciturn, uncommunicative, unforthcoming

till¹ cultivate, dig, plough, turn over, work

till² cash box, cash drawer, cash register

tilt *v.* 1. cant, incline, lean, list, slant, slope, tip 2. attack, break a lance, clash, contend, cross swords, duel, encounter, fight, joust, overthrow, spar ∼*n.* 3. angle, cant, inclination, incline, list, pitch, slant, slope 4. *Medieval history* clash, combat, duel, encounter, fight, joust, lists, set-to (*Inf.*), tournament, tourney 5. (**at**) **full tilt** for dear life, full force, full speed, headlong, like a bat out of hell (*Inf.*), like the clappers (*Brit. inf.*)

timber beams, boards, forest, logs, planks, trees, wood

timbre colour, quality of sound, resonance, ring, tonality, tone, tone colour

time *n.* 1. age, chronology, date, duration, epoch, era, generation, hour, interval, period, season, space, span, spell, stretch, term, while 2. instance, juncture, occasion, point, stage 3. allotted span, day, duration, life, life span, lifetime, season 4. heyday, hour, peak 5. *Mus.* beat, measure, metre, rhythm, tempo 6. **all the time** always, at all times, constantly, continually, continuously, ever, for the duration, perpetually, throughout 7. **at one time a.** for a while, formerly, hitherto, once, once upon a time, previously **b.** all at once, at the same time, simultaneously, together 8. **at times** every now and then, every so often, from time to time, now and then, occasionally, once in a while, on occasion, sometimes 9. **behind the times** antiquated, dated, obsolete, old-fashioned, old hat, outdated, outmoded, out of date, out of fashion, out of style, passé, square (*Inf.*) 10. **for the time being** for now, for the moment, for the present, in the meantime, meantime, meanwhile, pro tem, temporarily 11. **from time to time** at times, every now and then, every so often, now and then, occasionally, once in a while, on occasion, sometimes 12. **in good time a.** early, on time, with time to spare **b.** quickly, rapidly, speedily, swiftly, with dispatch 13. **in no time** before one knows it, before you can say Jack Robinson, in an instant, in a trice (flash, jiffy, moment), in two shakes of a lamb's tail (*Inf.*), quickly, rapidly, speedily, swiftly 14. **in time a.** at the appointed time, early, in good time, on schedule, on time, with time to spare **b.** by and by, eventually, one day, someday, sooner or later, ultimately 15. **on time** in good time, on the dot, punctually 16. **time and again** frequently, many times, often, on many occasions, over and over again, repeatedly, time after time ∼*v.* 17. clock, control, count, judge, measure, regulate, schedule, set

time-honoured age-old, ancient, conventional, customary, established, fixed, long-established, old, traditional, usual, venerable

timeless abiding, ageless, ceaseless, changeless, deathless, endless, enduring, eternal, everlasting, immortal, immutable, imperishable, indestructible, lasting, permanent, persistent, undying

timely appropriate, at the right time, convenient, judicious, opportune, prompt, propitious, punctual, seasonable, suitable, well-timed

timeserver hypocrite, opportunist, self-seeker, trimmer, Vicar of Bray, weathercock

timetable agenda, calendar, curriculum, diary, list, order of the day, programme, schedule

timeworn 1. aged, ancient, brokendown, decrepit, dog-eared, lined, ragged, run-down, shabby, the worse for wear, weathered, worn, wrinkled **2.** ancient, clichéd, dated, hackneyed, hoary, old hat, out of date, outworn, passé, stale, stock, threadbare, tired, trite, well-worn

timid afraid, apprehensive, bashful, cowardly, coy, diffident, faint-hearted, fearful, irresolute, modest, mousy, nervous, pusillanimous, retiring, shrinking, shy, timorous

timorous afraid, apprehensive, bashful, cowardly, coy, diffident, fainthearted, fearful, frightened, irresolute, mousy, nervous, pusillanimous, retiring, shrinking, shy, timid, trembling

tincture 1. *n.* aroma, colour, dash, flavour, hint, hue, seasoning, shade, smack, *soupçon*, stain, suggestion, tinge, tint, touch, trace **2.** *v.* colour, dye, flavour, scent, season, stain, tinge, tint

tinge *n.* **1.** cast, colour, dye, shade, stain, tincture, tint, wash **2.** bit, dash, drop, pinch, smack, smattering, *soupçon*, sprinkling, suggestion, touch, trace ~*v.* **3.** colour, dye, imbue, shade, stain, suffuse, tinge, tint

tingle 1. *v.* have goose pimples, itch, prickle, sting, tickle **2.** *n.* goose pimples, itch, itching, pins and needles (*Inf.*), prickling, quiver, shiver, stinging, thrill, tickle, tickling

tinker *v.* dabble, fiddle (*Inf.*), meddle, mess about, monkey, muck about (*Brit. sl.*), play, potter, toy

tinsel *adj.* brummagem, cheap, flashy, gaudy, meretricious, ostentatious, pinchbeck, sham, showy, specious, superficial, tawdry, trashy

tint *n.* **1.** cast, colour, hue, shade, tone **2.** dye, rinse, stain, tincture, tinge, wash **3.** hint, shade, suggestion, tinge, touch, trace ~*v.* **4.** colour, dye, rinse, stain,

tincture, tinge **5.** affect, colour, influence, taint, tinge

tiny diminutive, dwarfish, infinitesimal, insignificant, Lilliputian, little, microscopic, mini, miniature, minute, negligible, petite, pint-sized (*Inf.*), puny, pygmy, slight, small, trifling, wee

tip¹ 1. *n.* apex, cap, crown, end, extremity, head, peak, point, summit, top **2.** *v.* cap, crown, finish, surmount, top

tip² 1. cant, capsize, incline, lean, list, overturn, slant, spill, tilt, topple over, upend, upset **2.** *Brit.* ditch (*Sl.*), dump, empty, pour out, unload ~*n.* **3.** *Brit.* dump, midden (*Dialect*), refuse heap, rubbish heap

tip³ *n.* **1.** baksheesh, gift, gratuity, perquisite, *pourboire* **2.** *Also* **tip-off** clue, forecast, gen (*Brit. inf.*), hint, information, inside information, pointer, suggestion, warning, word, word of advice ~*v.* **3.** remunerate, reward **4.** *Also* **tip off** advise, caution, forewarn, give a clue, give a hint, suggest, tip (someone) the wink (*Brit. inf.*), warn

tipple 1. *v.* bend the elbow (*Inf.*), drink, imbibe, indulge (*Inf.*), quaff, swig, take a drink, tope **2.** *n.* alcohol, booze (*Inf.*), drink, John Barleycorn, liquor, poison (*Inf.*)

tippler bibber, boozer (*Inf.*), drinker, drunk, drunkard, inebriate, soak (*Sl.*), sot, sponge (*Inf.*), toper

tipsy elevated (*Inf.*), fuddled, happy (*Inf.*), mellow, merry (*Brit. inf.*), slightly drunk, tiddly (*Brit. sl.*), woozy (*Inf.*)

tirade abuse, denunciation, diatribe, fulmination, harangue, invective, lecture, outburst, philippic

tire 1. drain, droop, enervate, exhaust, fag (*Inf.*), fail, fatigue, flag, jade, knacker (*Sl.*), sink, take it out of (*Inf.*), wear down, wear out, weary, whack (*Brit. inf.*) **2.** annoy, bore, exasperate, harass, irk, irritate, weary

tired 1. all in (*Sl.*), asleep *or* dead on one's feet, dead beat (*Inf.*), dog-tired (*Inf.*), done in (*Inf.*), drained, drooping, drowsy, enervated, exhausted, fagged (*Inf.*), fatigued, flagging, jaded, knackered (*Sl.*), ready to drop, sleepy, spent, weary, whacked (*Brit. inf.*), worn out **2.** *With* of annoyed with, bored with, exasperated by, fed up with, irked by, irritated by, sick of, weary of **3.** clichéd, conventional, corny (*Inf.*), familiar, hackneyed, old, outworn, stale, stock, thread-bare, trite, well-worn

tireless determined, energetic, inde-fatigable, industrious, resolute, unflag-ging, untiring, unwearied, vigorous

tiresome annoying, boring, dull, exas-perating, flat, irksome, irritating, labo-rious, monotonous, tedious, trying, unin-teresting, vexatious, wearing, wearisome

tiring arduous, demanding, enerva-tive, exacting, exhausting, fatiguing, la-borious, strenuous, tough, wearing, wea-rying

tiro *see* TYRO

tissue 1. fabric, gauze, mesh, struc-ture, stuff, texture, web 2. paper, paper handkerchief, wrapping paper 3. accu-mulation, chain, collection, combination, concatenation, conglomeration, fabrica-tion, mass, network, pack, series, web

titan colossus, giant, leviathan, super-man

titanic Brobdingnagian, colossal, enor-mous, giant, gigantic, herculean, huge, immense, jumbo (*Inf.*), mammoth, mas-sive, mighty, monstrous, mountainous, prodigious, stupendous, towering, vast

titbit *bonne bouche*, choice item, dain-ty, delicacy, goody (*Inf.*), juicy bit, mor-sel, scrap, snack, treat

tit for tat an eye for an eye, as good as one gets, a tooth for a tooth, blow for blow, like for like, measure for measure, retaliation

tithe *n.* 1. assessment, duty, impost, levy, tariff, tax, tenth, toll, tribute ~*v.* 2. assess, charge, levy, rate, tax 3. give up, pay, pay a tithe on, render, surrender, turn over

titillate arouse, excite, interest, pro-voke, stimulate, tantalize, tease, thrill, tickle, turn on (*Sl.*)

titillating arousing, exciting, interest-ing, lewd, lurid, provocative, sensational, stimulating, suggestive, teasing, thrilling

titivate doll up (*Sl.*), do up (*Inf.*), make up, prank, preen, primp, prink, re-furbish, smarten up, tart up (*Brit. sl.*), touch up

title *n.* 1. caption, heading, inscription, label, legend, name, style 2. appellation, denomination, designation, epithet, han-dle (*Sl.*), moniker (*Inf.*), name, nick-name, nom de plume, pseudonym, sobri-quet, term 3. championship, crown, lau-rels 4. claim, entitlement, ownership, prerogative, privilege, right ~*v.* 5. call,

designate, label, name, style, term

titter chortle (*Inf.*), chuckle, giggle, laugh, snigger, te-hee

tittle atom, bit, dash, drop, grain, iota, jot, mite, particle, scrap, shred, speck, whit

tittle-tattle 1. *n.* babble, blather, blether, cackle, chatter, chitchat, clish-maclaver (*Scot.*), gossip, hearsay, idle chat, jaw (*Sl.*), natter, prattle, rumour, twaddle, yackety-yak (*Sl.*), yatter (*Inf.*) 2. *v.* babble, blather, blether, cackle, chat, chatter, chitchat, gossip, jaw (*Sl.*), natter, prattle, witter (*Inf.*), yak (*Sl.*), yatter (*Inf.*)

titular honorary, in name only, nomi-nal, puppet, putative, so-called, theoreti-cal, token

toady 1. *n.* apple polisher (*U.S. sl.*), bootlicker (*Inf.*), crawler (*Sl.*), creep (*Sl.*), fawner, flatterer, flunkey, groveller, hanger-on, jackal, lackey, lickspittle, minion, parasite, spaniel, sycophant, truckler, yes man 2. *v.* be obsequious to, bow and scrape, butter up, crawl, creep, cringe, curry favour with, fawn on, flat-ter, grovel, kiss the feet of, kowtow to, lick the boots of (*Inf.*), suck up to (*Inf.*)

toast[1] *v.* brown, grill, heat, roast, warm

toast[2] *n.* 1. compliment, drink, health, pledge, salutation, salute, tribute 2. dar-ling, favourite, heroine ~*v.* 3. drink to, drink (to) the health of, pledge, salute

to-do agitation, bother, brouhaha, bus-tle, commotion, disturbance, excitement, flap (*Inf.*), furore, fuss, hoo-ha, perfor-mance (*Inf.*), quarrel, ruction (*Inf.*), rumpus, stir, tumult, turmoil, unrest, uproar

together *adv.* 1. as a group, as one, cheek by jowl, closely, collectively, hand in glove, hand in hand, in a body, in con-cert, in cooperation, in unison, jointly, mutually, shoulder to shoulder, side by side 2. all at once, as one, at one fell swoop, at the same time, concurrently, contemporaneously, en masse, in unison, simultaneously, with one accord 3. con-secutively, continuously, in a row, in suc-cession, one after the other, on end, suc-cessively, without a break, without inter-ruption 4. *Inf.* arranged, fixed, ordered, organized, settled, sorted out, straight, to rights ~*adj.* 5. *Sl.* calm, composed, cool, stable, well-adjusted, well-balanced, well-organized

toil 1. *n.* application, donkey-work,

drudgery, effort, elbow grease (*Inf.*), exertion, graft (*Inf.*), hard work, industry, labour, pains, slog, sweat, travail **2.** *v.* drag oneself, drudge, graft (*Inf.*), grind (*Inf.*), grub, knock oneself out, labour, push oneself, slave, slog, strive, struggle, sweat (*Inf.*), work, work like a dog, work like a Trojan, work one's fingers to the bone

toilet 1. ablutions (*Military inf.*), bathroom, bog (*Brit. sl.*), closet, convenience, gents (*Brit. inf.*), ladies' room, latrine, lavatory, loo (*Brit. inf.*), outhouse, powder room, privy, urinal, washroom, water closet, W.C. **2.** ablutions, bathing, dressing, grooming, toilette

toilsome arduous, backbreaking, difficult, fatiguing, hard, herculean, laborious, painful, severe, strenuous, taxing, tedious, tiresome, tough, wearisome

token *n.* **1.** badge, clue, demonstration, earnest, evidence, expression, index, indication, manifestation, mark, note, proof, representation, sign, symbol, warning **2.** keepsake, memento, memorial, remembrance, reminder, souvenir ~*adj.* **3.** hollow, minimal, nominal, perfunctory, superficial, symbolic

tolerable 1. acceptable, allowable, bearable, endurable, sufferable, supportable **2.** acceptable, adequate, all right, average, fair, fairly good, fair to middling, good enough, indifferent, mediocre, middling, not bad (*Inf.*), O.K. (*Inf.*), ordinary, passable, run-of-the-mill, so-so (*Inf.*), unexceptional

tolerance 1. broad-mindedness, charity, forbearance, indulgence, lenity, magnanimity, open-mindedness, patience, permissiveness, sufferance, sympathy **2.** endurance, fortitude, hardiness, hardness, resilience, resistance, stamina, staying power, toughness **3.** fluctuation, play, swing, variation

tolerant 1. broad-minded, catholic, charitable, fair, forbearing, latitudinarian, liberal, long-suffering, magnanimous, open-minded, patient, sympathetic, unbigoted, understanding, unprejudiced **2.** complaisant, easy-going, free and easy, indulgent, kind-hearted, lax, lenient, permissive, soft

tolerate abide, accept, admit, allow, bear, brook, condone, countenance, endure, indulge, permit, pocket, put up with (*Inf.*), receive, sanction, stand, stomach, submit to, suffer, swallow,

take, thole (*Scot.*), turn a blind eye to, undergo, wink at

toleration 1. acceptance, allowance, condonation, endurance, indulgence, permissiveness, sanction, sufferance **2.** freedom of conscience, freedom of worship, religious freedom

toll[1] *v.* **1.** chime, clang, knell, peal, ring, sound, strike **2.** announce, call, signal, summon, warn ~*n.* **3.** chime, clang, knell, peal, ring, ringing, tolling

toll[2] **1.** assessment, charge, customs, demand, duty, fee, impost, levy, payment, rate, tariff, tax, tribute **2.** cost, damage, inroad, loss, penalty

tomb burial chamber, catacomb, crypt, grave, mausoleum, sepulchre, vault

tombstone gravestone, headstone, marker, memorial, monument

tome book, volume, work

tomfool 1. *n.* ass, blockhead, chump (*Inf.*), clown, dolt, fool, idiot, nincompoop, ninny, nitwit, simpleton, twit (*Brit. inf.*) **2.** *adj.* crackbrained, crazy, daft (*Inf.*), foolish, halfwitted, harebrained, idiotic, rash, senseless, silly, stupid

tomfoolery 1. buffoonery, childishness, clowning, fooling around (*Inf.*), foolishness, horseplay, idiocy, larks (*Inf.*), messing around (*Inf.*), shenanigans (*Inf.*), silliness, skylarking (*Inf.*), stupidity **2.** balderdash, baloney (*Inf.*), bilge (*Inf.*), bosh (*Inf.*), bunk (*Inf.*), bunkum, claptrap (*Inf.*), hogwash, hooey (*Sl.*), inanity, nonsense, poppycock (*Inf.*), rot, rubbish, stuff and nonsense, tommyrot, tosh, trash, twaddle

tone *n.* **1.** accent, emphasis, force, inflection, intonation, modulation, pitch, strength, stress, timbre, tonality, volume **2.** air, approach, aspect, attitude, character, drift, effect, feel, frame, grain, manner, mood, note, quality, spirit, style, temper, tenor, vein **3.** cast, colour, hue, shade, tinge, tint ~*v.* **4.** blend, go well with, harmonize, match, suit

tone down dampen, dim, mitigate, moderate, modulate, play down, reduce, restrain, soften, soft-pedal (*Inf.*), subdue, temper

tone up freshen, get in shape, get into condition, invigorate, limber up, shape up, sharpen up, trim, tune up

tongue 1. argot, dialect, idiom, language, lingo (*Inf.*), parlance, patois, speech, talk, vernacular **2.** articulation, speech, utterance, verbal expression, voice

tongue-lashing dressing-down (*Inf.*), lecture, rebuke, reprimand, reproach, reproof, scolding, slating (*Inf.*), talking-to (*Inf.*), telling-off (*Inf.*), ticking-off (*Inf.*), wigging (*Brit. sl.*)

tongue-tied at a loss for words, dumb, dumbstruck, inarticulate, mute, speechless, struck dumb

tonic analeptic, boost, bracer (*Inf.*), cordial, fillip, livener, pick-me-up (*Inf.*), refresher, restorative, roborant, shot in the arm (*Inf.*), stimulant

too 1. also, as well, besides, further, in addition, into the bargain, likewise, moreover, to boot **2.** excessively, exorbitantly, extremely, immoderately, inordinately, over-, overly, unduly, unreasonably, very

tool *n.* **1.** apparatus, appliance, contraption, contrivance, device, gadget, implement, instrument, machine, utensil **2.** agency, agent, intermediary, means, medium, vehicle, wherewithal **3.** cat's-paw, creature, dupe, flunkey, hireling, jackal, lackey, minion, pawn, puppet, stooge (*Sl.*) ~*v.* **4.** chase, cut, decorate, ornament, shape, work

toothsome agreeable, appetizing, dainty, delectable, delicious, luscious, mouthwatering, nice, palatable, savoury, scrumptious (*Inf.*), sweet, tasty, tempting, yummy (*Sl.*)

top *n.* **1.** acme, apex, apogee, crest, crown, culmination, head, height, high point, meridian, peak, pinnacle, summit, vertex, zenith **2.** cap, cork, cover, lid, stopper **3.** first place, head, highest rank, lead **4. blow one's top** *Inf.* blow up (*Inf.*), do one's nut (*Brit. sl.*), explode, fly into a temper, fly off the handle (*Inf.*), go spare (*Brit. sl.*), have a fit (*Inf.*), lose one's temper, see red (*Inf.*), throw a tantrum **5. over the top** a bit much (*Inf.*), excessive, going too far, immoderate, inordinate, over the limit, too much, uncalled-for ~*adj.* **6.** best, chief, crack (*Inf.*), crowning, culminating, dominant, elite, finest, first, foremost, greatest, head, highest, lead, leading, pre-eminent, prime, principal, ruling, sovereign, superior, topmost, upper, uppermost ~*v.* **7.** cap, cover, crown, finish, garnish, roof, tip **8.** ascend, climb, crest, reach the top of, scale, surmount **9.** be first, be in charge of, command, head, lead, rule **10.** beat, best, better, eclipse, exceed, excel, go beyond, outdo, outshine, outstrip, surpass, transcend

topic issue, matter, point, question, subject, subject matter, text, theme, thesis

topical 1. contemporary, current, newsworthy, popular, up-to-date, up-to-the-minute **2.** local, parochial, regional, restricted

topmost dominant, foremost, highest, leading, loftiest, paramount, principal, supreme, top, upper, uppermost

topple 1. capsize, collapse, fall, fall headlong, fall over, keel over, knock down, knock over, overbalance, overturn, tip over, totter, tumble, upset **2.** bring down, bring low, oust, overthrow, overturn, unseat

topsy-turvy chaotic, confused, disarranged, disorderly, disorganized, inside-out, jumbled, messy, mixed-up, untidy, upside-down

torment *v.* **1.** afflict, agonize, crucify, distress, excruciate, harrow, pain, rack, torture **2.** annoy, bedevil, bother, chivvy, devil (*Inf.*), harass, harry, hound, irritate, nag, persecute, pester, plague, provoke, tease, trouble, vex, worry ~*n.* **3.** agony, anguish, distress, hell, misery, pain, suffering, torture **4.** affliction, annoyance, bane, bother, harassment, irritation, nag, nagging, nuisance, pain in the neck (*Inf.*), persecution, pest, plague, provocation, scourge, thorn in one's flesh, trouble, vexation, worry

torn *adj.* **1.** cut, lacerated, ragged, rent, ripped, slit, split **2.** divided, in two minds (*Inf.*), irresolute, split, uncertain, undecided, unsure, vacillating, wavering

tornado cyclone, gale, hurricane, squall, storm, tempest, twister (*U.S. inf.*), typhoon, whirlwind, windstorm

torpid apathetic, benumbed, dormant, drowsy, dull, fainéant, inactive, indolent, inert, lackadaisical, languid, languorous, lazy, lethargic, listless, lymphatic, motionless, numb, passive, slothful, slow, slow-moving, sluggish, somnolent, stagnant

torpor accidie, acedia, apathy, dormancy, drowsiness, dullness, inactivity, inanition, indolence, inertia, inertness, languor, laziness, lethargy, listlessness, numbness, passivity, sloth, sluggishness, somnolence, stagnancy, stupor, torpidity

torrent cascade, deluge, downpour, effusion, flood, flow, gush, outburst, rush, spate, stream, tide

torrid 1. arid, blistering, boiling, broiling, burning, dried, dry, fiery, hot, parched, parching, scorched, scorching, sizzling, stifling, sultry, sweltering, tropical **2.** ardent, erotic, fervent, hot, intense, passionate, sexy (*Inf.*), steamy (*Inf.*)

tortuous 1. bent, circuitous, convoluted, crooked, curved, indirect, mazy, meandering, serpentine, sinuous, twisted, twisting, winding, zigzag **2.** ambiguous, complicated, convoluted, cunning, deceptive, devious, indirect, involved, mazy, misleading, roundabout, tricky

torture 1. *v.* afflict, agonize, crucify, distress, excruciate, harrow, lacerate, martyr, pain, persecute, put on the rack, rack, torment **2.** *n.* affliction, agony, anguish, distress, hell, laceration, martyrdom, misery, pain, pang(s), persecution, rack, suffering, torment

toss *v.* **1.** cast, chuck (*Inf.*), fling, flip, hurl, launch, lob (*Inf.*), pitch, project, propel, shy, sling, throw **2.** agitate, disturb, jiggle, joggle, jolt, rock, roll, shake, thrash, tumble, wriggle, writhe **3.** heave, labour, lurch, pitch, roll, wallow ~*n.* **4.** cast, fling, lob (*Inf.*), pitch, shy, throw

tot¹ *n.* **1.** baby, child, infant, little one, mite, toddler, wean (*Scot.*) **2.** dram, finger, measure, nip, shot (*Inf.*), slug, snifter (*Inf.*), toothful

tot² *v.* add up, calculate, count up, reckon, sum (up), tally, total

total 1. *n.* aggregate, all, amount, entirety, full amount, mass, sum, totality, whole **2.** *adj.* absolute, all-out, complete, comprehensive, consummate, downright, entire, full, gross, integral, out-and-out, outright, perfect, sheer, sweeping, thorough, thoroughgoing, unconditional, undisputed, undivided, unmitigated, unqualified, utter, whole **3.** *v.* add up, amount to, come to, mount up to, reach, reckon, sum up, tot up

totalitarian authoritarian, despotic, dictatorial, monolithic, one-party, oppressive, tyrannous, undemocratic

totality 1. aggregate, all, entirety, everything, sum, total, whole **2.** completeness, entireness, fullness, wholeness

totally absolutely, completely, comprehensively, consummately, entirely, fully, perfectly, quite, thoroughly, un-

conditionally, unmitigatedly, utterly, wholeheartedly, wholly

totter falter, lurch, quiver, reel, rock, shake, stagger, stumble, sway, teeter, tremble, walk unsteadily, waver

touch *n.* **1.** feel, feeling, handling, palpation, physical contact, tactility **2.** blow, brush, caress, contact, fondling, hit, pat, push, stroke, tap **3.** bit, dash, detail, drop, hint, intimation, jot, pinch, smack, small amount, smattering, soupçon, speck, spot, suggestion, suspicion, taste, tincture, tinge, trace, whiff **4.** direction, effect, hand, influence **5.** approach, characteristic, handiwork, manner, method, style, technique, trademark, way **6.** ability, adroitness, art, artistry, command, deftness, facility, flair, knack, mastery, skill, virtuosity **7.** acquaintance, awareness, communication, contact, correspondence, familiarity, understanding ~*v.* **8.** brush, caress, contact, feel, finger, fondle, graze, handle, hit, lay a finger on, palpate, pat, push, strike, stroke, tap **9.** abut, adjoin, be in contact, border, brush, come together, contact, converge, graze, impinge upon, meet **10.** affect, disturb, get through to, get to (*Inf.*), have an effect on, impress, influence, inspire, make an impression on, mark, melt, move, soften, stir, strike, upset **11.** be a party to, concern oneself with, consume, deal with, drink, eat, get involved in, handle, have to do with, partake of, use, utilize **12.** *With* **on** allude to, bring in, cover, deal with, mention, refer to, speak of **13.** bear upon, concern, have to do with, interest, pertain to, regard **14.** be a match for, be in the same league as, be on a par with, come near, come up to, compare with, equal, hold a candle to (*Inf.*), match, parallel, rival **15.** arrive at, attain, come to, reach

touch-and-go close, critical, dangerous, hairy (*Sl.*), hazardous, near, nerve-racking, parlous, perilous, precarious, risky, sticky (*Inf.*), tricky

touched 1. affected, disturbed, impressed, melted, moved, softened, stirred, swayed, upset **2.** barmy (*Sl.*), batty (*Sl.*), bonkers (*Brit. sl.*), crazy, cuckoo (*Inf.*), daft (*Inf.*), not all there, not right in the head, nuts (*Sl.*), nutty (*Sl.*), nutty as a fruitcake (*Sl.*), off one's rocker (*Sl.*), soft in the head (*Inf.*)

touchiness bad temper, crabbedness, fretfulness, grouchiness, irascibility, irritability, peevishness, pettishness, petulance, surliness, testiness, tetchiness, ticklishness

touching affecting, emotive, heartbreaking, melting, moving, pathetic, piteous, pitiable, pitiful, poignant, sad, stirring, tender

touch off 1. fire, ignite, light, put a match to, set off **2.** arouse, begin, cause, foment, give rise to, initiate, provoke, set in motion, spark off, trigger (off)

touchstone criterion, gauge, measure, norm, standard, yardstick

touch up 1. finish off, perfect, put the finishing touches to, round off **2.** brush up, enhance, fake (up), falsify, give a face-lift to, gloss over, improve, patch up, polish up, renovate, retouch, revamp, titivate, whitewash (*Inf.*)

touchy bad-tempered, captious, crabbed, cross, easily offended, grouchy, grumpy, irascible, irritable, oversensitive, peevish, pettish, petulant, querulous, quick-tempered, splenetic, surly, testy, tetchy, thin-skinned, ticklish

tough *adj.* **1.** cohesive, durable, firm, hard, inflexible, leathery, resilient, resistant, rigid, rugged, solid, stiff, strong, sturdy, tenacious **2.** brawny, fit, hard as nails, hardened, hardy, resilient, seasoned, stalwart, stout, strapping, strong, sturdy, vigorous **3.** hard-bitten, pugnacious, rough, ruffianly, ruthless, vicious, violent **4.** adamant, callous, exacting, firm, hard, hard-boiled (*Inf.*), hardnosed (*Sl.*), inflexible, intractable, merciless, obdurate, obstinate, refractory, resolute, severe, stern, strict, stubborn, unbending, unforgiving, unyielding **5.** arduous, baffling, difficult, exacting, exhausting, hard, intractable, irksome, knotty, laborious, perplexing, puzzling, strenuous, thorny, troublesome, uphill **6.** *Inf.* bad, hard cheese (*Brit. sl.*), hard lines (*Brit. inf.*), hard luck, lamentable, regrettable, too bad (*Inf.*), unfortunate, unlucky ~*n.* **7.** bravo, bruiser (*Inf.*), brute, bully, bully boy, hooligan, rough (*Inf.*), roughneck (*Sl.*), rowdy, ruffian, thug

tour *n.* **1.** excursion, expedition, jaunt, journey, outing, peregrination, progress, trip **2.** circuit, course, round ~*v.* **3.** explore, go on the road, go round, holiday in, journey, sightsee, travel round, travel through, visit

tourist excursionist, globetrotter, holiday-maker, journeyer, sightseer, traveller, tripper, voyager

tournament 1. competition, contest, event, match, meeting, series **2.** *Medieval* joust, the lists, tourney

tousle disarrange, disarray, dishevel, disorder, mess up, ruffle, rumple, tangle

tow *v.* drag, draw, haul, lug, pull, trail, trawl, tug

towards 1. en route for, for, in the direction of, in the vicinity of, on the road to, on the way to, to **2.** about, concerning, for, regarding, with regard to, with respect to **3.** almost, close to, coming up to, getting on for, just before, nearing, nearly, not quite, shortly before

tower *n.* **1.** belfry, column, obelisk, pillar, skyscraper, steeple, turret **2.** castle, citadel, fort, fortification, fortress, keep, refuge, stronghold ~*v.* **3.** ascend, be head and shoulders above, dominate, exceed, loom, mount, overlook, overtop, rear, rise, soar, surpass, top, transcend

towering 1. colossal, elevated, extraordinary, gigantic, great, high, imposing, impressive, lofty, magnificent, outstanding, paramount, prodigious, soaring, sublime, superior, supreme, surpassing, tall, transcendent **2.** burning, excessive, extreme, fiery, immoderate, inordinate, intemperate, intense, mighty, passionate, vehement, violent

toxic baneful (*Archaic*), deadly, harmful, lethal, noxious, pernicious, pestilential, poisonous, septic

toy *n.* **1.** doll, game, plaything **2.** bauble, gewgaw, knick-knack, trifle, trinket ~*v.* **3.** amuse oneself, dally, fiddle (*Inf.*), flirt, play, sport, trifle, wanton

trace *n.* **1.** evidence, indication, mark, record, relic, remains, remnant, sign, survival, token, vestige **2.** bit, dash, drop, hint, iota, jot, shadow, *soupçon*, suggestion, suspicion, tincture, tinge, touch, trifle, whiff **3.** footmark, footprint, footstep, path, slot, spoor, track, trail ~*v.* **4.** ascertain, detect, determine, discover, ferret out, find, follow, hunt down, pursue, search for, seek, shadow, stalk, track, trail, unearth **5.** chart, copy, delineate, depict, draw, map, mark out, outline, record, show, sketch

track *n.* **1.** footmark, footprint, footstep, mark, path, scent, slot, spoor, trace, trail, wake **2.** course, flight path, line, orbit, path, pathway, road, track, trajectory, way **3.** line, permanent way, rail, rails **4. keep track of** follow, keep an eye on, keep in sight, keep in touch with, keep up to date with, keep up with, monitor, oversee, watch **5. lose track of** lose, lose sight of, misplace ~*v.* **6.** chase, dog, follow, follow the trail of, hunt down, pursue, shadow, stalk, tail (*Inf.*), trace, trail

track down apprehend, bring to light, capture, catch, dig up, discover, expose, ferret out, find, hunt down, run to earth, sniff out, trace, unearth

trackless empty, pathless, solitary, uncharted, unexplored, unfrequented, untrodden, unused, virgin

tracks 1. footprints, impressions, imprints, tyremarks, tyreprints, wheelmarks **2. make tracks** beat it (*Sl.*), depart, disappear, get going, get moving, go, head off, hit the road (*Sl.*), leave, set out, split (*Sl.*), take off (*Inf.*) **3. stop in one's tracks** bring to a standstill, freeze, immobilize, petrify, rivet to the spot, stop dead, transfix

tract[1] area, district, estate, expanse, extent, lot, plot, quarter, region, stretch, territory, zone

tract[2] booklet, brochure, disquisition, dissertation, essay, homily, leaflet, monograph, pamphlet, tractate, treatise

tractable 1. amenable, biddable, compliant, controllable, docile, governable, manageable, obedient, persuadable, submissive, tame, willing, yielding **2.** ductile, fictile, malleable, plastic, pliable, pliant, tractile, workable

traction adhesion, drag, draught, drawing, friction, grip, haulage, pull, pulling, purchase, resistance

trade *n.* **1.** barter, business, buying and selling, commerce, dealing, exchange, traffic, transactions, truck **2.** avocation, business, calling, craft, employment, job, line, line of work, métier, occupation, profession, pursuit, skill **3.** deal, exchange, interchange, swap **4.** clientele, custom, customers, market, patrons, public ~*v.* **5.** bargain, barter, buy and sell, deal, do business, exchange, have dealings, peddle, traffic, transact, truck **6.** barter, exchange, swap, switch

trader broker, buyer, dealer, marketer, merchandiser, merchant, seller

tradesman 1. dealer, merchant, retailer, seller, shopkeeper, vendor **2.** artisan, craftsman, journeyman, skilled worker, workman

tradition convention, custom, customs, established practice, folklore, habit, institution, lore, praxis, ritual, unwritten law, usage

traditional accustomed, ancestral, conventional, customary, established, fixed, folk, historic, long-established, old, oral, time-honoured, transmitted, unwritten, usual

traduce abuse, asperse, blacken, calumniate, decry, defame, denigrate, deprecate, depreciate, detract, disparage, drag through the mud, malign, misrepresent, revile, run down, slander, smear, speak ill of, vilify

traducer abuser, asperser, calumniator, defamer, denigrator, deprecator, detractor, disparager, slanderer, smearer, vilifier

traffic *n.* **1.** coming and going, freight, movement, passengers, transport, transportation, vehicles **2.** barter, business, buying and selling, commerce, communication, dealing, dealings, doings, exchange, intercourse, peddling, relations, trade, truck ~*v.* **3.** bargain, barter, buy and sell, deal, do business, exchange, have dealings, have transactions, market, peddle, trade, truck

tragedy adversity, affliction, calamity, catastrophe, disaster, grievous blow, misfortune

tragic anguished, appalling, awful, calamitous, catastrophic, deadly, dire, disastrous, doleful, dreadful, fatal, grievous, heartbreaking, heart-rending, ill-fated, ill-starred, lamentable, miserable, mournful, pathetic, pitiable, ruinous, sad, shocking, sorrowful, unfortunate, woeful, wretched

trail *v.* **1.** dangle, drag, draw, hang down, haul, pull, stream, tow **2.** chase, follow, hunt, pursue, shadow, stalk, tail (*Inf.*), trace, track **3.** bring up the rear, dawdle, drag oneself, fall behind, follow, hang back, lag, linger, loiter, straggle, traipse (*Inf.*) **4.** dangle, droop, extend, hang, straggle ~*n.* **5.** footprints, footsteps, mark, marks, path, scent, spoor, trace, track, wake **6.** beaten track, footpath, path, road, route, track, way **7.** appendage, stream, tail, train

trail away *or* **off** decrease, die away, diminish, dwindle, fade away *or* out, fall away, grow faint, grow weak, lessen, peter out, shrink, sink, subside, tail off, taper off, weaken

train v. **1.** coach, discipline, drill, educate, guide, improve, instruct, prepare, rear, rehearse, school, teach, tutor **2.** exercise, improve, prepare, work out **3.** aim, bring to bear, direct, focus, level, line up, point ~n. **4.** chain, concatenation, course, order, progression, sequence, series, set, string, succession **5.** caravan, column, convoy, file, procession **6.** appendage, tail, trail **7.** attendants, cortege, court, entourage, followers, following, household, retinue, staff, suite

trainer coach

training 1. coaching, discipline, education, grounding, guidance, instruction, schooling, teaching, tuition, tutelage, upbringing **2.** body building, exercise, practice, preparation, working-out

traipse 1. v. drag oneself, footslog, slouch, trail, tramp, trudge **2.** n. long walk, slog, tramp, trek, trudge

trait attribute, characteristic, feature, idiosyncrasy, lineament, mannerism, peculiarity, quality, quirk

traitor apostate, back-stabber, betrayer, deceiver, defector, deserter, double-crosser (*Inf.*), fifth columnist, informer, Judas, miscreant, quisling, rebel, renegade, snake in the grass (*Inf.*), turncoat

traitorous apostate, disloyal, double-crossing (*Inf.*), double-dealing, faithless, false, perfidious, renegade, seditious, treacherous, treasonable, unfaithful, untrue

trajectory course, flight, flight path, line, path, route, track

trammel 1. n. bar, block, bond, chain, check, clog, curb, fetter, handicap, hindrance, impediment, obstacle, rein, shackle, stumbling block **2.** v. bar, block, capture, catch, check, clog, curb, enmesh, ensnare, entrap, fetter, hamper, handicap, hinder, impede, net, restrain, restrict, snag, tie

tramp v. **1.** footslog, hike, march, ramble, range, roam, rove, slog, trek, walk, yomp **2.** march, plod, stamp, stump, toil, traipse (*Inf.*), trudge, walk heavily **3.** crush, stamp, stomp (*Inf.*), trample, tread, walk over ~n. **4.** derelict, dosser (*Brit. sl.*), down-and-out, drifter, hobo (*Chiefly U.S.*), vagabond, vagrant **5.** hike, march, ramble, slog, trek **6.** footfall, footstep, stamp, tread

trample 1. crush, flatten, run over, squash, stamp, tread, walk over **2.** do violence to, encroach upon, hurt, in-

fringe, ride roughshod over, show no consideration for, violate

trance abstraction, daze, dream, ecstasy, hypnotic state, muse, rapture, reverie, spell, stupor, unconsciousness

tranquil at peace, calm, composed, cool, pacific, peaceful, placid, quiet, restful, sedate, serene, still, undisturbed, unexcited, unperturbed, unruffled, untroubled

tranquillity ataraxia, calm, calmness, composure, coolness, equanimity, hush, imperturbability, peace, peacefulness, placidity, quiet, quietness, quietude, repose, rest, restfulness, sedateness, serenity, stillness

tranquillize calm, compose, lull, pacify, quell, quiet, relax, sedate, settle one's nerves, soothe

tranquillizer barbiturate, bromide, downer (*Sl.*), opiate, red (*Sl.*), sedative

transact accomplish, carry on, carry out, conclude, conduct, discharge, do, enact, execute, handle, manage, negotiate, perform, prosecute, see to, settle, take care of

transaction 1. action, affair, bargain, business, coup, deal, deed, enterprise, event, matter, negotiation, occurrence, proceeding, undertaking **2.** *Plural* affairs, annals, doings, goings-on (*Inf.*), minutes, proceedings, record

transcend eclipse, exceed, excel, go above, go beyond, leave behind, leave in the shade (*Inf.*), outdo, outrival, outshine, outstrip, outvie, overstep, rise above, surpass

transcendence, transcendency ascendancy, excellence, greatness, incomparability, matchlessness, paramountcy, pre-eminence, sublimity, superiority, supremacy

transcendent consummate, exceeding, extraordinary, incomparable, matchless, peerless, pre-eminent, second to none, sublime, superior, transcendental, unequalled, unique, unparalleled, unrivalled

transcribe 1. copy out, engross, note, reproduce, rewrite, set out, take down, transfer, write out **2.** interpret, render, translate, transliterate **3.** record, tape, tape-record

transcript carbon, carbon copy, copy, duplicate, manuscript, note, notes, record, reproduction, transcription, translation, transliteration, version

transfer 1. *v.* carry, change, consign, convey, displace, hand over, make over, move, pass on, relocate, remove, shift, translate, transmit, transplant, transport, transpose, turn over **2.** *n.* change, displacement, handover, move, relocation, removal, shift, transference, translation, transmission, transposition

transfigure alter, apotheosize, change, convert, exalt, glorify, idealize, metamorphose, transform, transmute

transfix 1. engross, fascinate, halt *or* stop in one's tracks, hold, hypnotize, mesmerize, paralyse, petrify, rivet the attention of, root to the spot, spellbind, stop dead, stun **2.** fix, impale, pierce, puncture, run through, skewer, spear, spit, transpierce

transform alter, change, convert, make over, metamorphose, reconstruct, remodel, renew, revolutionize, transfigure, translate, transmogrify (*Jocular*), transmute

transformation alteration, change, conversion, metamorphosis, radical change, renewal, revolution, revolutionary change, sea change, transfiguration, transmogrification (*Jocular*), transmutation

transfuse permeate, pervade, spread over, suffuse

transgress break, break the law, contravene, defy, disobey, do *or* go wrong, encroach, err, exceed, fall from grace, go astray, go beyond, infringe, lapse, misbehave, offend, overstep, sin, trespass, violate

transgression breach, contravention, crime, encroachment, error, fault, infraction, infringement, iniquity, lapse, misbehaviour, misdeed, misdemeanour, offence, sin, trespass, violation, wrong, wrongdoing

transgressor criminal, culprit, delinquent, evildoer, felon, lawbreaker, malefactor, miscreant, offender, sinner, trespasser, villain, wrongdoer

transience brevity, briefness, ephemerality, evanescence, fleetingness, fugacity, fugitiveness, impermanence, momentariness, shortness, transitoriness

transient brief, ephemeral, evanescent, fleeting, flying, fugacious, fugitive, here today and gone tomorrow, impermanent, momentary, passing, short, short-lived, short-term, temporary, transitory

transit *n.* **1.** carriage, conveyance, crossing, motion, movement, passage, portage, shipment, transfer, transport, transportation, travel, traverse **2.** alteration, change, changeover, conversion, shift, transition **3.** **in transit** during passage, en route, on the journey, on the move, on the road, on the way, while travelling ∼*v.* **4.** cross, journey, move, pass, travel, traverse

transition alteration, change, changeover, conversion, development, evolution, flux, metamorphosis, metastasis, passage, passing, progression, shift, transit, transmutation, upheaval

transitional changing, developmental, fluid, intermediate, passing, provisional, temporary, transitionary, unsettled

transitory brief, ephemeral, evanescent, fleeting, flying, fugacious, here today and gone tomorrow, impermanent, momentary, passing, short, short-lived, short-term, temporary, transient

translate 1. construe, convert, decipher, decode, interpret, paraphrase, render, transcribe, transliterate **2.** elucidate, explain, make clear, paraphrase, put in plain English, simplify, spell out, state in layman's language **3.** alter, change, convert, metamorphose, transfigure, transform, transmute, turn **4.** carry, convey, move, remove, send, transfer, transplant, transport, transpose

translation 1. construction, decoding, gloss, interpretation, paraphrase, rendering, rendition, transcription, transliteration, version **2.** elucidation, explanation, paraphrase, rephrasing, rewording, simplification **3.** alteration, change, conversion, metamorphosis, transfiguration, transformation, transmutation **4.** conveyance, move, removal, transference, transposition

translator interpreter, linguist, metaphrast, paraphrast

translucent clear, diaphanous, limpid, lucent, pellucid, semitransparent

transmigration journey, metempsychosis, migration, movement, passage, rebirth, reincarnation, travel

transmission 1. carriage, communication, conveyance, diffusion, dispatch, dissemination, remission, sending, shipment, spread, transfer, transference, transport **2.** broadcasting, dissemination, putting out, relaying, sending, showing **3.** broadcast, programme, show

transmit 1. bear, carry, communicate, convey, diffuse, dispatch, disseminate, forward, hand down, hand on, impart, pass on, remit, send, spread, take, transfer, transport **2**. broadcast, disseminate, put on the air, radio, relay, send, send out

transmute alchemize, alter, change, convert, metamorphose, remake, transfigure, transform

transparency 1. clarity, clearness, diaphaneity, diaphanousness, filminess, gauziness, limpidity, limpidness, pellucidity, pellucidness, sheerness, translucence, translucency, transparence **2**. apparentness, distinctness, explicitness, obviousness, patentness, perspicuousness, plainness, unambiguousness, visibility **3**. candidness, directness, forthrightness, frankness, openness, straightforwardness **4**. photograph, slide

transparent 1. clear, crystal clear, crystalline, diaphanous, filmy, gauzy, limpid, lucent, lucid, pellucid, seethrough, sheer, translucent, transpicuous **2**. apparent, as plain as the nose on one's face (*Inf.*), distinct, easy, evident, explicit, manifest, obvious, patent, perspicuous, plain, recognizable, unambiguous, understandable, undisguised, visible **3**. candid, direct, forthright, frank, open, plain-spoken, straight, straightforward, unambiguous, unequivocal

transpire 1. *Inf.* arise, befall, chance, come about, come to pass (*Archaic*), happen, occur, take place, turn up **2**. become known, be disclosed, be discovered, be made public, come out, come to light, emerge

transplant displace, relocate, remove, resettle, shift, transfer, uproot

transport *v.* **1**. bear, bring, carry, convey, fetch, haul, move, remove, run, ship, take, transfer **2**. banish, deport, exile, sentence to transportation **3**. captivate, carry away, delight, electrify, enchant, enrapture, entrance, move, ravish, spellbind ~*n.* **4**. conveyance, transportation, vehicle **5**. carriage, conveyance, removal, shipment, shipping, transference, transportation **6**. cloud nine (*Inf.*), enchantment, euphoria, heaven, rapture, seventh heaven **7**. bliss, delight, ecstasy, happiness, ravishment

transpose alter, change, exchange, interchange, move, rearrange, relocate,

reorder, shift, substitute, swap (*Inf.*), switch, transfer

transverse athwart, crossways, crosswise, diagonal, oblique

trap *n.* **1**. ambush, gin, net, noose, pitfall, snare, springe, toils **2**. ambush, artifice, deception, device, ruse, stratagem, subterfuge, trick, wile ~*v.* **3**. catch, corner, enmesh, ensnare, entrap, snare, take **4**. ambush, beguile, deceive, dupe, ensnare, inveigle, trick

trapped ambushed, at bay, beguiled, caught, cornered, cut off, deceived, duped, ensnared, in a tight corner, in a tight spot, inveigled, netted, snared, stuck (*Inf.*), surrounded, tricked, with one's back to the wall

trappings accoutrements, adornments, decorations, dress, equipment, finery, fittings, fixtures, fripperies, furnishings, gear, livery, ornaments, panoply, paraphernalia, raiment (*Archaic*), things, trimmings

trash 1. balderdash, drivel, foolish talk, hogwash, inanity, nonsense, rot, rubbish, tripe (*Inf.*), trumpery, twaddle **2**. dregs, dross, garbage, junk, litter, offscourings, refuse, rubbish, sweepings, waste

trashy brummagem, catchpenny, cheap, cheap-jack (*Inf.*), flimsy, inferior, meretricious, rubbishy, shabby, shoddy, tawdry, thrown together, tinsel, worthless

trauma agony, anguish, damage, disturbance, hurt, injury, jolt, ordeal, pain, shock, strain, suffering, torture, upheaval, upset, wound

traumatic agonizing, damaging, disturbing, hurtful, injurious, painful, scarring, shocking, upsetting, wounding

travail *n.* **1**. distress, drudgery, effort, exertion, grind (*Inf.*), hardship, hard work, labour, pain, slavery, slog, strain, stress, suffering, sweat, tears, toil **2**. birth pangs, childbirth, labour, labour pains ~*v.* **3**. drudge, grind (*Inf.*), labour, slave, slog, suffer, sweat, toil

travel *v.* **1**. cross, go, journey, make a journey, make one's way, move, proceed, progress, ramble, roam, rove, take a trip, tour, traverse, trek, voyage, walk, wander, wend **2**. be transmitted, carry, get through, move ~*n.* **3**. *Usually plural* excursion, expedition, globetrotting, journey, movement, passage, peregrination, ramble, tour, touring, trip, voyage, walk, wandering

traveller 1. excursionist, explorer, globetrotter, gypsy, hiker, holiday-maker, journeyer, migrant, nomad, passenger, tourist, tripper, voyager, wanderer, wayfarer 2. agent, commercial traveller, rep, representative, salesman, travelling salesman

travelling adj. itinerant, migrant, migratory, mobile, moving, nomadic, peripatetic, restless, roaming, roving, touring, unsettled, wandering, wayfaring

traverse 1. bridge, cover, cross, cut across, go across, go over, make one's way across, negotiate, pass over, ply, range, roam, span, travel over, wander 2. balk, contravene, counter, counteract, deny, frustrate, go against, hinder, impede, obstruct, oppose, thwart 3. check, consider, examine, eye, inspect, investigate, look into, look over, pore over, range over, review, scan, scrutinize, study

travesty 1. n. burlesque, caricature, distortion, lampoon, mockery, parody, perversion, send-up (Brit. inf.), sham, spoof (Inf.), takeoff (Inf.) 2. v. burlesque, caricature, deride, distort, lampoon, make a mockery of, make fun of, mock, parody, pervert, ridicule, send up (Brit. inf.), sham, spoof (Inf.), take off (Inf.)

treacherous 1. deceitful, disloyal, double-crossing (Inf.), double-dealing, duplicitous, faithless, false, perfidious, recreant (Archaic), traitorous, treasonable, unfaithful, unreliable, untrue, untrustworthy 2. dangerous, deceptive, hazardous, icy, perilous, precarious, risky, slippery, slippy (Inf.), tricky, unreliable, unsafe, unstable

treachery betrayal, disloyalty, double-cross (Inf.), double-dealing, duplicity, faithlessness, infidelity, perfidiousness, perfidy, stab in the back, treason

tread v. 1. hike, march, pace, plod, stamp, step, stride, tramp, trudge, walk 2. crush underfoot, squash, trample 3. bear down, crush, oppress, quell, repress, ride roughshod over, subdue, subjugate, suppress 4. **tread on someone's toes** affront, annoy, bruise, disgruntle, get someone's back up (Sl.), hurt, hurt someone's feelings, infringe, injure, irk, offend, vex ~n. 5. footfall, footstep, gait, pace, step, stride, walk

treason disaffection, disloyalty, duplicity, lese-majesty, mutiny, perfidy, sedition, subversion, traitorousness, treachery

treasonable disloyal, false, mutinous, perfidious, seditious, subversive, traitorous, treacherous, treasonous

treasure n. 1. cash, fortune, funds, gold, jewels, money, riches, valuables, wealth 2. apple of one's eye, darling, gem, jewel, nonpareil, paragon, pearl, precious, pride and joy, prize ~v. 3. adore, cherish, dote upon, esteem, hold dear, idolize, love, prize, revere, value, venerate, worship 4. accumulate, cache, collect, garner, hoard, husband, lay up, salt away, save, stash (away) (Inf.), store up

treasury 1. bank, cache, hoard, repository, store, storehouse, vault 2. assets, capital, coffers, exchequer, finances, funds, money, resources, revenues

treat n. 1. banquet, celebration, entertainment, feast, gift, party, refreshment 2. delight, enjoyment, fun, gratification, joy, pleasure, satisfaction, surprise, thrill ~v. 3. act towards, behave towards, consider, deal with, handle, look upon, manage, regard, use 4. apply treatment to, attend to, care for, doctor, medicate, nurse 5. buy for, entertain, feast, foot or pay the bill, give, lay on, pay for, provide, regale, stand (Inf.), take out, wine and dine 6. be concerned with, contain, deal with, discourse upon, discuss, go into, touch upon 7. bargain, come to terms, confer, have talks, make terms, negotiate, parley

treatise disquisition, dissertation, essay, exposition, monograph, pamphlet, paper, study, thesis, tract, work, writing

treatment 1. care, cure, healing, medication, medicine, remedy, surgery, therapy 2. action towards, behaviour towards, conduct, dealing, handling, management, manipulation, reception, usage

treaty agreement, alliance, bargain, bond, compact, concordat, contract, convention, covenant, entente, pact

trek 1. n. expedition, footslog, hike, journey, long haul, march, odyssey, slog, tramp 2. v. footslog, hike, journey, march, plod, range, roam, rove, slog, traipse (Inf.), tramp, trudge, yomp

tremble 1. v. oscillate, quake, quiver, rock, shake, shake in one's shoes, shiver, shudder, teeter, totter, vibrate, wobble

2. *n.* oscillation, quake, quiver, shake, shiver, shudder, tremor, vibration, wobble

tremendous 1. appalling, awesome, awful, colossal, deafening, dreadful, enormous, fearful, formidable, frightful, gargantuan, gigantic, great, huge, immense, mammoth, monstrous, prodigious, stupendous, terrible, terrific, titanic, towering, vast, whopping (*Inf.*) **2.** *Inf.* ace (*Inf.*), amazing, excellent, exceptional, extraordinary, fabulous (*Inf.*), fantastic (*Inf.*), great, incredible, marvellous, super (*Inf.*), terrific (*Inf.*), wonderful

tremor 1. agitation, quaking, quaver, quiver, quivering, shake, shaking, shiver, tremble, trembling, trepidation, vibration, wobble **2.** earthquake, quake (*Inf.*), shock

tremulous aflutter, afraid, agitated, agog, anxious, aquiver, excited, fearful, frightened, jittery (*Inf.*), jumpy, nervous, quavering, quivering, quivery, scared, shaking, shivering, timid, trembling, vibrating, wavering

trench channel, cut, ditch, drain, earthwork, entrenchment, excavation, fosse, furrow, gutter, pit, trough, waterway

trenchant 1. acerbic, acid, acidulous, acute, astringent, biting, caustic, cutting, hurtful, incisive, keen, mordant, penetrating, piquant, pointed, pungent, sarcastic, scathing, severe, sharp, tart **2.** driving, effective, effectual, emphatic, energetic, forceful, potent, powerful, strong, vigorous **3.** clear, clear-cut, crisp, distinct, distinctly defined, explicit, salient, unequivocal, well-defined

trend *n.* **1.** bias, course, current, direction, drift, flow, inclination, leaning, tendency **2.** craze, fad (*Inf.*), fashion, look, mode, rage, style, thing, vogue ~*v.* **3.** bend, flow, head, incline, lean, run, stretch, swing, tend, turn, veer

trendsetter arbiter of taste, avant-gardist, leader of fashion, pacemaker, pacesetter

trendy 1. *adj.* fashionable, flash (*Inf.*), in (*Sl.*), in fashion, in vogue, latest, modish, now (*Inf.*), stylish, up to the minute, voguish, with it (*Inf.*) **2.** *n.* poser (*Inf.*), pseud (*Sl.*)

trepidation agitation, alarm, anxiety, apprehension, blue funk (*Inf.*), butterflies (*Inf.*), cold feet (*Inf.*), cold sweat (*Inf.*), consternation, dismay, disquiet, disturbance, dread, emotion, excitement, fear, fright, jitters (*Inf.*), nervousness, palpitation, perturbation, quivering, shaking, the heebie-jeebies (*Sl.*), trembling, tremor, uneasiness, worry

trespass *v.* **1.** encroach, infringe, intrude, invade, obtrude, poach **2.** *Archaic* offend, sin, transgress, violate, wrong ~*n.* **3.** encroachment, infringement, intrusion, invasion, poaching, unlawful entry, wrongful entry **4.** breach, crime, delinquency, error, evildoing, fault, infraction, iniquity, injury, misbehaviour, misconduct, misdeed, misdemeanour, offence, sin, transgression, wrongdoing

trespasser 1. infringer, interloper, intruder, invader, poacher, unwelcome visitor **2.** *Archaic* criminal, delinquent, evildoer, malefactor, offender, sinner, transgressor, wrongdoer

tress braid, curl, lock, plait, ringlet

triad threesome, trilogy, trine, trinity, trio, triple, triplet, triptych, triumvirate, triune

trial *n.* **1.** assay, audition, check, dry run (*Inf.*), examination, experience, experiment, probation, proof, test, testing, test-run **2.** contest, hearing, judicial examination, litigation, tribunal **3.** attempt, crack (*Inf.*), effort, endeavour, go, shot (*Inf.*), stab, try, venture, whack (*Inf.*) **4.** adversity, affliction, burden, cross to bear, distress, grief, hardship, hard times, load, misery, ordeal, pain, suffering, tribulation, trouble, unhappiness, vexation, woe, wretchedness **5.** bane, bother, hassle (*Inf.*), irritation, nuisance, pain in the neck (*Inf.*), pest, plague (*Inf.*), thorn in one's flesh, vexation ~*adj.* **6.** experimental, exploratory, pilot, probationary, provisional, testing

tribe blood, caste, clan, class, division, dynasty, ethnic group, family, gens, house, people, race, seed, sept, stock

tribulation adversity, affliction, bad luck, blow, burden, care, cross to bear, curse, distress, grief, heartache, ill fortune, misery, misfortune, ordeal, pain, reverse, sorrow, suffering, trial, trouble, unhappiness, vexation, woe, worry, wretchedness

tribunal bar, bench, court, hearing, judgment seat, judicial examination, trial

tribute 1. accolade, acknowledgment, applause, commendation, compliment, encomium, esteem, eulogy, gift, gratitude, honour, laudation, panegyric, praise, recognition, respect, testimonial **2.** charge, contribution, customs, duty, excise, homage, impost, offering, payment, ransom, subsidy, tax, toll

trice flash, instant, jiffy (*Inf.*), minute, moment, second, shake (*Inf.*), split second, tick (*Brit. inf.*), twinkling, twinkling of an eye, two shakes of a lamb's tail (*Inf.*)

trick *n.* **1.** artifice, con (*Sl.*), deceit, deception, device, dodge, feint, fraud, gimmick, hoax, imposition, imposture, manoeuvre, ploy, ruse, stratagem, subterfuge, swindle, trap, wile **2.** antic, cantrip (*Scot.*), caper, device, feat, frolic, gag (*Sl.*), gambol, jape, joke, juggle, legerdemain, leg-pull (*Brit. inf.*), practical joke, prank, put-on (*Sl.*), sleight of hand, stunt **3.** art, command, craft, device, expertise, gift, hang (*Inf.*), knack, know-how (*Inf.*), secret, skill, technique **4.** characteristic, crotchet, foible, habit, idiosyncrasy, mannerism, peculiarity, practice, quirk, trait **5. do the trick** *Inf.* be effective *or* effectual, have effect, produce the desired result, work ~*v.* **6.** bamboozle (*Inf.*), cheat, con (*Sl.*), deceive, defraud, delude, dupe, fool, gull (*Archaic*), have (someone) on, hoax, hoodwink, impose upon, mislead, pull the wool over (someone's) eyes, put one over on (someone) (*Inf.*), swindle, take in (*Inf.*), trap

trickery cheating, chicanery, con (*Sl.*), deceit, deception, dishonesty, double-dealing, fraud, funny business, guile, hanky-panky (*Inf.*), hoax, imposture, jiggery-pokery (*Inf.*), monkey business (*Inf.*), pretence, skulduggery (*Inf.*), swindling

trickle **1.** *v.* crawl, creep, dribble, drip, drop, exude, ooze, percolate, run, seep, stream **2.** *n.* dribble, drip, seepage

trick out *or* **up** adorn, array, attire, bedeck, deck out, doll up (*Sl.*), do up (*Inf.*), dress up, get up (*Inf.*), ornament, prank, prink

trickster cheat, con man (*Inf.*), deceiver, fraud, hoaxer, impostor, joker, practical joker, pretender, swindler

tricky **1.** complicated, delicate, difficult, knotty, problematic, risky, sticky (*Inf.*), thorny, ticklish, touch-and-go **2.** artful, crafty, cunning, deceitful, decep-

tive, devious, foxy, scheming, slippery, sly, subtle, wily

trifle *n.* **1.** bagatelle, bauble, child's play, gewgaw, knick-knack, nothing, plaything, toy, triviality **2.** bit, dash, drop, jot, little, pinch, spot, touch, trace ~*v.* **3.** amuse oneself, coquet, dally, dawdle, flirt, fritter, idle, mess about, palter, play, toy, wanton, waste, waste time

trifler dilettante, good-for-nothing, idler, layabout, loafer, ne'er-do-well, waster

trifling empty, frivolous, idle, inconsiderable, insignificant, minuscule, negligible, paltry, petty, piddling (*Inf.*), puny, shallow, silly, slight, small, tiny, trivial, unimportant, valueless, worthless

trigger *v.* activate, bring about, cause, elicit, generate, give rise to, produce, prompt, provoke, set in motion, set off, spark off, start

trim **1.** compact, dapper, natty (*Inf.*), neat, nice, orderly, shipshape, smart, soigné, soignée, spick-and-span, spruce, tidy, well-groomed, well-ordered, well turned-out **2.** fit, shapely, sleek, slender, slim, streamlined, svelte, willowy ~*v.* **3.** barber, clip, crop, curtail, cut, cut back, dock, even up, lop, pare, prune, shave, shear, tidy **4.** adorn, array, beautify, bedeck, deck, deck out, decorate, dress, embellish, embroider, garnish, ornament, trick out **5.** adjust, arrange, balance, distribute, order, prepare, settle ~*n.* **6.** adornment, border, decoration, edging, embellishment, frill, fringe, garnish, ornamentation, piping, trimming **7.** condition, fettle, fitness, form, health, order, repair, shape (*Inf.*), situation, state **8.** clipping, crop, cut, pruning, shave, shearing, tidying up, trimming **9.** array, attire, dress, equipment, gear, trappings

trimming **1.** adornment, border, braid, decoration, edging, embellishment, frill, fringe, garnish, ornamentation, piping **2.** *Plural* accessories, accompaniments, appurtenances, extras, frills, garnish, ornaments, paraphernalia, trappings **3.** *Plural* brash, clippings, cuttings, ends, parings, shavings

trinity threesome, triad, trilogy, trine, trio, triple, triplet, triptych, triumvirate, triune

trinket bagatelle, bauble, bibelot, gewgaw, gimcrack, kickshaw, knick-knack, nothing, ornament, piece of bric-a-brac, toy, trifle

trio threesome, triad, trilogy, trine, trinity, triple, triplet, triptych, triumvirate, triune

trip n. **1.** errand, excursion, expedition, foray, jaunt, journey, outing, ramble, run, tour, travel, voyage **2.** blunder, boob (*Brit. sl.*), error, fall, false move, false step, faux pas, indiscretion, lapse, misstep, slip, stumble ~v. **3.** blunder, boob (*Brit. sl.*), err, fall, go wrong, lapse, lose one's balance, lose one's footing, make a false move, make a faux pas, miscalculate, misstep, slip, slip up (*Inf.*), stumble, tumble **4.** catch out, confuse, disconcert, put off one's stride, throw off, trap, unsettle **5.** go, ramble, tour, travel, voyage **6.** caper, dance, flit, frisk, gambol, hop, skip, spring, tread lightly **7.** *Inf.* get high (*Inf.*), get stoned (*Sl.*), take drugs, turn on (*Sl.*) **8.** activate, engage, flip, pull, release, set off, switch on, throw, turn on

tripe balderdash, bunkum, claptrap (*Inf.*), drivel, foolish talk, garbage, guff (*Sl.*), hogwash, inanity, nonsense, poppycock (*Inf.*), rot, rubbish, trash, trumpery, twaddle

triple **1.** *adj.* threefold, three times as much, three-way, tripartite **2.** *n.* threesome, triad, trilogy, trine, trinity, trio, triplet, triumvirate, triune **3.** *v.* increase threefold, treble, triplicate

triplet threesome, triad, trilogy, trine, trinity, trio, triple, triumvirate, triune

tripper excursionist, holiday-maker, journeyer, sightseer, tourist, voyager

trite banal, bromidic, clichéd, common, commonplace, corny (*Sl.*), dull, hack, hackneyed, ordinary, pedestrian, routine, run-of-the-mill, stale, stereotyped, stock, threadbare, tired, uninspired, unoriginal, worn

triturate beat, bray, bruise, comminute, crush, grind, masticate, pound, powder, pulverize

triumph n. **1.** elation, exultation, happiness, joy, jubilation, pride, rejoicing **2.** accomplishment, achievement, ascendancy, attainment, conquest, coup, feat, hit (*Inf.*), mastery, sensation, smash (*Inf.*), smash-hit (*Inf.*), success, *tour de force*, victory, walkover (*Inf.*) ~v. **3.** *Often with* **over** best, carry the day, come out on top (*Inf.*), dominate, flourish, get the better of, overcome, overwhelm, prevail, prosper, subdue, succeed, take the honours, thrive, vanquish, win **4.** cel-

ebrate, crow, exult, gloat, glory, jubilate, rejoice, revel, swagger

triumphant boastful, celebratory, cock-a-hoop, conquering, dominant, elated, exultant, glorious, jubilant, proud, rejoicing, successful, swaggering, triumphal, undefeated, victorious, winning

trivia details, minutiae, petty details, trifles, trivialities

trivial commonplace, everyday, frivolous, incidental, inconsequential, inconsiderable, insignificant, little, meaningless, minor, negligible, paltry, petty, puny, slight, small, trifling, trite, unimportant, valueless, worthless

triviality **1.** frivolity, inconsequentiality, insignificance, littleness, meaninglessness, negligibility, paltriness, pettiness, slightness, smallness, triteness, unimportance, valuelessness, worthlessness **2.** detail, no big thing, no great matter, nothing, petty detail, technicality, trifle

trivialize belittle, laugh off, make light of, minimize, play down, scoff at, underestimate, underplay, undervalue

trollop fallen woman, floozy (*Sl.*), harlot, hussy, loose woman, prostitute, slattern, slut, streetwalker, strumpet, tart (*Inf.*), wanton, whore

troop n. **1.** assemblage, band, body, bunch (*Inf.*), company, contingent, crew (*Inf.*), crowd, drove, flock, gang, gathering, group, herd, horde, multitude, pack, squad, swarm, team, throng, unit **2.** *Plural* armed forces, army, fighting men, men, military, servicemen, soldiers, soldiery ~v. **3.** crowd, flock, march, parade, stream, swarm, throng, traipse (*Inf.*)

trophy award, bays, booty, cup, laurels, memento, prize, souvenir, spoils

tropical hot, humid, lush, steamy, stifling, sultry, sweltering, torrid

trot v. **1.** canter, go briskly, jog, lope, run, scamper ~n. **2.** brisk pace, canter, jog, lope, run **3. on the trot** *Inf.* consecutively, in a row, in succession, one after the other, without break, without interruption

trot out bring forward, bring up, come out with, drag up, exhibit, recite, rehearse, reiterate, relate, repeat

troubadour balladeer, jongleur, lyric poet, minstrel, poet, singer

trouble n. **1.** agitation, annoyance, anxiety, disquiet, distress, grief, heartache, irritation, misfortune, pain, sorrow, suffering, torment, tribulation, vexation, woe, worry **2.** agitation, bother (*Inf.*), commotion, discontent, discord, disorder, dissatisfaction, disturbance, row, strife, tumult, unrest **3.** ailment, complaint, defect, disability, disease, disorder, failure, illness, malfunction, upset **4.** bother, concern, danger, difficulty, dilemma, dire straits, hot water (*Inf.*), mess, nuisance, pest, pickle (*Inf.*), predicament, problem, scrape (*Inf.*), spot (*Inf.*) **5.** attention, bother, care, effort, exertion, inconvenience, labour, pains, struggle, thought, work ~*v.* **6.** afflict, agitate, annoy, bother, discompose, disconcert, disquiet, distress, disturb, fret, grieve, harass, inconvenience, pain, perplex, perturb, pester, plague, sadden, torment, upset, vex, worry **7.** be concerned, bother, burden, discomfort, discommode, disturb, impose upon, incommode, inconvenience, put out **8.** exert oneself, go to the effort of, make an effort, take pains, take the time

troublemaker *agent provocateur*, agitator, firebrand, incendiary, instigator, meddler, mischief-maker, rabble-rouser, stormy petrel

troublesome 1. annoying, arduous, bothersome, burdensome, demanding, difficult, harassing, hard, importunate, inconvenient, irksome, irritating, laborious, oppressive, pestilential, plaguy (*Inf.*), taxing, tiresome, tricky, trying, upsetting, vexatious, wearisome, worrisome, worrying **2.** disorderly, insubordinate, rebellious, recalcitrant, refractory, rowdy, turbulent, uncooperative, undisciplined, unruly, violent

trough 1. crib, manger, water trough **2.** canal, channel, depression, ditch, duct, flume, furrow, gully, gutter, trench, watercourse

trounce beat, clobber (*Brit. sl.*), crush, defeat heavily *or* utterly, drub, give a hiding (*Inf.*), give a pasting (*Sl.*), hammer (*Inf.*), lick (*Inf.*), make mincemeat of, overwhelm, paste (*Sl.*), rout, slaughter (*Inf.*), thrash, walk over (*Inf.*), wipe the floor with (*Inf.*)

troupe band, cast, company

trouper actor, artiste, entertainer, performer, player, theatrical, thespian

truancy absence, absence without leave, malingering, shirking, skiving (*Brit. sl.*)

truant *n.* **1.** absentee, delinquent, deserter, dodger, malingerer, runaway, shirker, skiver (*Brit. sl.*), straggler **2.** *adj.* absent, absent without leave, A.W.O.L., missing, skiving (*Brit. sl.*) ~*v.* **3.** absent oneself, desert, dodge, go missing, malinger, play truant, run away, shirk, skive (*Brit. sl.*), twag (*Dialect*)

truce armistice, break, ceasefire, cessation, cessation of hostilities, intermission, interval, let-up (*Inf.*), lull, moratorium, peace, respite, rest, stay, treaty

truck *n.* **1.** commercial goods, commodities, goods, merchandise, stock, stuff, wares **2.** barter, business, buying and selling, commerce, communication, connection, contact, dealings, exchange, relations, trade, traffic ~*v.* **3.** bargain, barter, buy and sell, deal, do business, exchange, have dealings, negotiate, swap, trade, traffic, transact business

truckle bend the knee, bow and scrape, concede, cringe, crouch, defer, fawn, give in, give way, knuckle under, kowtow, lick the boots of (*Inf.*), stoop, submit, toady, yield

truculent aggressive, antagonistic, bad-tempered, bellicose, belligerent, combative, contentious, cross, defiant, fierce, hostile, ill-tempered, itching *or* spoiling for a fight (*Inf.*), obstreperous, pugnacious, scrappy (*Inf.*), sullen, violent

trudge 1. *v.* clump, drag oneself, footslog, hike, lumber, march, plod, slog, stump, traipse (*Inf.*), tramp, trek, walk heavily, yomp **2.** *n.* footslog, haul, hike, march, slog, traipse (*Inf.*), tramp, trek, yomp

true *adj.* **1.** accurate, actual, authentic, bona fide, correct, exact, factual, genuine, legitimate, natural, precise, pure, real, right, truthful, valid, veracious, veritable **2.** confirmed, constant, dedicated, devoted, dutiful, faithful, fast, firm, honest, honourable, loyal, pure, sincere, staunch, steady, true-blue, trustworthy, trusty, unswerving, upright **3.** accurate, correct, exact, on target, perfect, precise, proper, spot-on (*Brit. inf.*), unerring ~*adv.* **4.** honestly, rightly, truthfully, veraciously, veritably **5.** accurately, correctly, on target, perfectly, precisely, properly, unerringly **6. come true** become reality, be granted, be realized, come to pass, happen, occur

true-blue confirmed, constant, dedicated, devoted, dyed-in-the-wool, faithful, loyal, orthodox, staunch, trusty, uncompromising, unwavering

truism axiom, bromide, cliché, commonplace, platitude, stock phrase, trite saying

truly 1. accurately, authentically, beyond doubt, beyond question, correctly, exactly, factually, genuinely, in actuality, in fact, in reality, in truth, legitimately, precisely, really, rightly, truthfully, veraciously, veritably, without a doubt **2.** confirmedly, constantly, devotedly, dutifully, faithfully, firmly, honestly, honourably, loyally, sincerely, staunchly, steadily, with all one's heart, with dedication, with devotion **3.** exceptionally, extremely, greatly, indeed, of course, really, to be sure, verily, very

trumped-up concocted, contrived, cooked-up (*Inf.*), fabricated, fake, false, falsified, invented, made-up, phoney (*Sl.*), untrue

trumpery *n.* **1.** balderdash, bilge (*Inf.*), bunkum, claptrap (*Inf.*), drivel, foolishness, foolish talk, garbage, guff (*Sl.*), hogwash, idiocy, inanity, nonsense, poppycock (*Inf.*), rot, rubbish, stuff, trash, tripe (*Inf.*), twaddle **2.** bagatelle, bauble, gewgaw, kickshaw, knick-knack, toy, trifle, trinket ~*adj.* **3.** brummagem, cheap, flashy, meretricious, nasty, rubbishy, shabby, shoddy, tawdry, trashy, trifling, useless, valueless, worthless

trumpet *n.* **1.** bugle, clarion, horn **2.** bay, bellow, call, cry, roar **3. blow one's own trumpet** boast, brag, crow, sing one's own praises, vaunt ~*v.* **4.** advertise, announce, broadcast, extol, noise abroad, proclaim, publish, shout from the rooftops, sound loudly, tout (*Inf.*)

trump up concoct, contrive, cook up (*Inf.*), create, fabricate, fake, invent, make up

truncate abbreviate, clip, crop, curtail, cut, cut short, lop, pare, prune, shorten, trim

truncheon baton, club, cudgel, staff

trunk 1. bole, stalk, stem, stock **2.** body, torso **3.** proboscis, snout **4.** bin, box, case, chest, coffer, crate, kist (*Scot.*), locker, portmanteau

truss *v.* **1.** bind, bundle, fasten, make fast, pack, pinion, secure, strap, tether, tie ~*n.* **2.** beam, brace, buttress, joist, prop, shore, stanchion, stay, strut, support **3.** *Medical* bandage, support **4.** bale, bundle, package, packet

trust *n.* **1.** assurance, belief, certainty, certitude, confidence, conviction, credence, credit, expectation, faith, hope, reliance **2.** duty, obligation, responsibility **3.** care, charge, custody, guard, guardianship, protection, safekeeping, trusteeship ~*v.* **4.** assume, believe, expect, hope, presume, suppose, surmise, think likely **5.** bank on, believe, count on, depend on, have faith in, lean on, pin one's faith on, place confidence in, place one's trust in, place reliance on, rely upon, swear by, take at face value **6.** assign, command, commit, confide, consign, delegate, entrust, give, put into the hands of, sign over, turn over

trustful, trusting confiding, credulous, gullible, innocent, naive, optimistic, simple, unguarded, unsuspecting, unsuspicious, unwary

trustworthy dependable, ethical, honest, honourable, level-headed, mature, principled, reliable, responsible, righteous, sensible, steadfast, to be trusted, true, trusty, truthful, upright

trusty dependable, faithful, firm, honest, reliable, responsible, solid, staunch, steady, straightforward, strong, true, trustworthy, upright

truth 1. accuracy, actuality, exactness, fact, factuality, factualness, genuineness, legitimacy, precision, reality, truthfulness, validity, veracity, verity **2.** candour, constancy, dedication, devotion, dutifulness, faith, faithfulness, fidelity, frankness, honesty, integrity, loyalty, naturalism, realism, uprightness **3.** axiom, certainty, fact, law, maxim, proven principle, reality, truism, verity

truthful accurate, candid, correct, exact, faithful, forthright, frank, honest, literal, naturalistic, plain-spoken, precise, realistic, reliable, sincere, straight, straightforward, true, trustworthy, veracious, veritable

truthless deceitful, deceptive, dishonest, faithless, false, fraudulent, insincere, lying, mendacious, perjured, treacherous, untrue, untrustworthy

try *v.* **1.** aim, attempt, do one's best, do one's damnedest (*Inf.*), endeavour, essay, exert oneself, have a go (crack, shot, stab, whack), make an attempt, make an effort, seek, strive, struggle, undertake **2.** appraise, check out, evaluate, examine, experiment, inspect, investigate, prove, put to the test, sample, taste, test **3.**

afflict, annoy, inconvenience, irk, irritate, pain, plague, strain, stress, tax, tire, trouble, upset, vex, weary **4.** adjudge, adjudicate, examine, hear ~*n.* **5.** attempt, crack (*Inf.*), effort, endeavour, essay, go, shot (*Inf.*), stab, whack (*Inf.*) **6.** appraisal, evaluation, experiment, inspection, sample, taste, test, trial

trying aggravating (*Inf.*), annoying, arduous, bothersome, difficult, exasperating, fatiguing, hard, irksome, irritating, stressful, taxing, tiresome, tough, troublesome, upsetting, vexing, wearisome

try out appraise, check out, evaluate, experiment with, inspect, put into practice, put to the test, sample, taste, test

tsar, czar autocrat, despot, emperor, head, leader, overlord, ruler, sovereign, tyrant

tubby chubby, corpulent, fat, obese, overweight, paunchy, plump, podgy, portly, roly-poly, stout

tuck *v.* **1.** fold, gather, insert, push ~*n.* **2.** fold, gather, pinch, pleat **3.** *Inf.* comestibles, eats (*Sl.*), food, grub (*Sl.*), nosh (*Sl.*), scoff (*Sl.*), victuals

tuck in 1. bed down, enfold, fold under, make snug, put to bed, swaddle, wrap up **2.** eat heartily, get stuck in (*Sl.*)

tuft bunch, clump, cluster, collection, knot, shock, topknot, tussock

tug 1. *v.* drag, draw, haul, heave, jerk, lug, pull, tow, wrench, yank **2.** *n.* drag, haul, heave, jerk, pull, tow, traction, wrench, yank

tuition education, instruction, lessons, schooling, teaching, training, tutelage, tutoring

tumble 1. *v.* drop, fall, fall end over end, fall headlong, fall head over heels, flop, lose one's footing, pitch, plummet, roll, stumble, topple, toss, trip up **2.** *n.* collapse, drop, fall, flop, headlong fall, plunge, roll, spill, stumble, toss, trip

tumble-down crumbling, decrepit, dilapidated, disintegrating, falling to pieces, ramshackle, rickety, ruined, shaky, tottering

tumid 1. bloated, bulging, distended, enlarged, inflated, protuberant, puffed up, puffy, swollen, tumescent **2.** bombastic, flowery, fulsome, fustian, grandiloquent, grandiose, high-flown, inflated, magniloquent, orotund, overblown, pompous, pretentious, sesquipedalian, stilted, turgid

tumour cancer, carcinoma (*Medical*), growth, lump, neoplasm (*Medical*), sarcoma (*Medical*), swelling

tumult ado, affray (*Law*), agitation, altercation, bedlam, brawl, brouhaha, clamour, commotion, din, disorder, disturbance, excitement, fracas, hubbub, hullabaloo, outbreak, pandemonium, quarrel, racket, riot, row, ruction (*Inf.*), stir, strife, turmoil, unrest, upheaval, uproar

tumultuous agitated, boisterous, clamorous, confused, disorderly, disturbed, excited, fierce, hectic, irregular, lawless, noisy, obstreperous, passionate, raging, restless, riotous, rowdy, rumbustious, stormy, turbulent, unrestrained, unruly, uproarious, violent, vociferous, wild

tune *n.* **1.** air, melody, melody line, motif, song, strain, theme **2.** agreement, concert, concord, consonance, euphony, harmony, pitch, sympathy, unison **3.** attitude, demeanour, disposition, frame of mind, mood **4. call the tune** be in charge (command, control), call the shots (*Sl.*), command, dictate, govern, lead, rule, rule the roost **5. change one's tune** change one's mind, do an about-face, have a change of heart, reconsider, take a different tack, think again ~*v.* **6.** adapt, adjust, attune, bring into harmony, harmonize, pitch, regulate

tuneful catchy, consonant (*Music*), easy on the ear (*Inf.*), euphonious, harmonious, mellifluous, melodic, melodious, musical, pleasant, symphonic

tuneless atonal, cacophonous, clashing, discordant, dissonant, harsh, unmelodic, unmelodious, unmusical

tunnel 1. *n.* burrow, channel, hole, passage, passageway, shaft, subway, underpass **2.** *v.* burrow, dig, dig one's way, excavate, mine, penetrate, scoop out, undermine

turbid clouded, cloudy, confused, dense, dim, dreggy, foggy, foul, fuzzy, hazy, impure, incoherent, muddled, muddy, murky, opaque, roiled, thick, unclear, unsettled

turbulence agitation, boiling, commotion, confusion, disorder, instability, pandemonium, roughness, storm, tumult, turmoil, unrest, upheaval

turbulent 1. agitated, blustery, boiling, choppy, confused, disordered, foaming, furious, raging, rough, tempestuous, tumultuous, unsettled, unstable **2.** agitated, anarchic, boisterous, disorderly, insubordinate, lawless, mutinous, obstreperous, rebellious, refractory, riotous, rowdy, seditious, tumultuous, unbridled, undisciplined, ungovernable, unruly, uproarious, violent, wild

turf 1. clod, divot, grass, green, sod, sward 2. **the turf** horse-racing, racecourse, racetrack, racing, the flat

turf out banish, bounce (*Sl.*), cast out, chuck out (*Inf.*), discharge, dismiss, dispossess, eject, evict, expel, fire (*Inf.*), fling out, give one the sack (*Inf.*), kick out (*Inf.*), oust, sack (*Inf.*), show (someone) the door, throw out

turgid 1. bloated, bulging, congested, distended, inflated, protuberant, puffed up, puffy, swollen, tumescent, tumid 2. bombastic, flowery, fulsome, fustian, grandiloquent, grandiose, high-flown, inflated, magniloquent, orotund, ostentatious, overblown, pompous, pretentious, sesquipedalian, stilted, tumid, windy

turmoil agitation, bedlam, brouhaha, bustle, chaos, commotion, confusion, disorder, disturbance, ferment, flurry, hubbub, noise, pandemonium, row, stir, strife, trouble, tumult, turbulence, uproar, violence

turn v. 1. circle, go round, gyrate, move in a circle, pivot, revolve, roll, rotate, spin, swivel, twirl, twist, wheel, whirl 2. change course, change position, go back, move, return, reverse, shift, swerve, switch, veer, wheel 3. arc, come round, corner, go round, negotiate, pass, pass around, take a bend 4. adapt, alter, become, change, convert, divert, fashion, fit, form, metamorphose, mould, mutate, remodel, shape, transfigure, transform, transmute 5. become rancid, curdle, go bad, go off (*Brit. inf.*), go sour, make rancid, sour, spoil, taint 6. appeal, apply, approach, go, have recourse, look, resort 7. nauseate, sicken, upset 8. apostatize, bring round (*Inf.*), change one's mind, change sides, defect, desert, go over, influence, persuade, prejudice, prevail upon, renege, retract, talk into 9. construct, deliver, execute, fashion, frame, make, mould, perform, shape, write 10. **turn tail** beat a hasty retreat, bolt, cut and run (*Inf.*), flee, run away, run off, show a clean pair of heels, take off (*Inf.*), take to one's heels ~n. 11. bend, change, circle, curve, cycle, gyration, pivot, reversal, revolution, rotation, spin,

swing, turning, twist, whirl 12. bias, direction, drift, heading, tendency, trend 13. bend, change of course, change of direction, curve, departure, deviation, shift 14. chance, crack (*Inf.*), fling, go, opportunity, period, round, shift, shot (*Inf.*), spell, stint, succession, time, try, whack (*Inf.*) 15. airing, circuit, constitutional, drive, excursion, jaunt, outing, promenade, ride, saunter, spin (*Inf.*), stroll, walk 16. affinity, aptitude, bent, bias, flair, gift, inclination, knack, leaning, propensity, talent 17. cast, fashion, form, format, guise, make-up, manner, mode, mould, shape, style, way 18. act, action, deed, favour, gesture, service 19. bend, distortion, twist, warp 20. *Inf.* fright, scare, shock, start, surprise 21. **by turns** alternately, in succession, one after another, reciprocally, turn and turn about 22. **to a turn** correctly, exactly, just right, perfectly, precisely

turncoat apostate, backslider, defector, deserter, rat (*Inf.*), recreant (*Archaic*), renegade, seceder, tergiversator, traitor

turn down 1. diminish, lessen, lower, muffle, mute, quieten, reduce the volume of, soften 2. decline, rebuff, refuse, reject, repudiate, say no to, spurn, throw out

turn in 1. go to bed, go to sleep, hit the sack (*Sl.*), retire for the night 2. deliver, give back, give up, hand in, hand over, return, submit, surrender, tender

turning bend, crossroads, curve, junction, side road, turn, turn-off

turning point change, climacteric, crisis, critical moment, crossroads, crux, decisive moment, moment of decision, moment of truth

turn-off branch, exit, side road, turn, turning

turn off 1. branch off, change direction, depart from, deviate, leave, quit, take another road, take a side road 2. cut out, kill, put out, shut down, stop, switch off, turn out, unplug 3. *Inf.* alienate, bore, disenchant, disgust, displease, irritate, lose one's interest, nauseate, offend, put off, repel, sicken

turn on 1. activate, energize, ignite, put on, set in motion, start, start up, switch on 2. balance, be contingent on, be decided by, depend, hang, hinge, pivot, rest 3. assail, assault, attack, fall on, lose one's temper with, round on 4. *Sl.*

arouse, arouse one's desire, attract, excite, please, stimulate, thrill, titillate, work up **5.** *Sl.* get high (*Inf.*), get stoned (*Sl.*), take drugs, trip (*Inf.*) **6.** *Sl.* expose, get one started with, inform, initiate, introduce, show

turnout 1. assemblage, assembly, attendance, audience, congregation, crowd, gate, number, throng **2.** amount produced, output, outturn (*Rare*), production, production quota, productivity, turnover, volume, yield **3.** array, attire, costume, dress, equipage, equipment, gear, get-up (*Inf.*), outfit, rigout (*Inf.*)

turn out 1. put out, switch off, turn off, unplug **2.** bring out, fabricate, finish, make, manufacture, process, produce, put out **3.** axe (*Inf.*), banish, cashier, cast out, deport, discharge, dismiss, dispossess, drive out, drum out, evict, expel, fire (*Inf.*), give one the sack (*Inf.*), kick out (*Inf.*), oust, put out, sack (*Inf.*), throw out, turf out (*Brit. inf.*), unseat **4.** clean out, clear, discharge, empty, take out the contents of **5.** become, come about, come to be, come to light, crop up (*Inf.*), develop, emerge, end up, eventuate, evolve, happen, prove to be, result, transpire (*Inf.*), work out **6.** accoutre, apparel (*Archaic*), attire, clothe, dress, fit, outfit, rig out **7.** appear, assemble, attend, be present, come, gather, go, put in an appearance, show up (*Inf.*), turn up

turnover 1. business, flow, output, outturn (*Rare*), production, productivity, volume, yield **2.** change, coming and going, movement, replacement

turn over 1. capsize, flip over, keel over, overturn, reverse, tip over, upend, upset **2.** activate, crank, press the starter button, set going, set in motion, start up, switch on, switch on the ignition, warm up **3.** assign, commend, commit, deliver, give over, give up, hand over, pass on, render, surrender, transfer, yield **4.** consider, contemplate, deliberate, give thought to, mull over, ponder, reflect on, revolve, ruminate about, think about, think over, wonder about **5.** break up, dig, plough

turn up 1. appear, arrive, attend, come, put in an appearance, show (*Sl.*), show one's face, show up (*Inf.*) **2.** appear, become known, be found, bring to light, come to light, come to pass, come up with, crop up (*Inf.*), dig up, disclose, discover, expose, find, pop up, reveal,

transpire, unearth **3.** amplify, boost, enhance, increase, increase the volume of, intensify, make louder, raise

turpitude badness, baseness, corruption, criminality, degeneracy, depravity, evil, foulness, immorality, iniquity, nefariousness, sinfulness, viciousness, vileness, villainy, wickedness

tussle 1. *v.* battle, brawl, contend, fight, grapple, scrap (*Inf.*), scuffle, struggle, vie, wrestle **2.** *n.* battle, bout, brawl, competition, conflict, contention, contest, fight, fracas, fray, punch-up (*Inf.*), scrap (*Inf.*), scuffle, set-to (*Inf.*), struggle

tutelage care, charge, custody, dependence, education, guardianship, guidance, instruction, patronage, preparation, protection, schooling, teaching, tuition, wardship

tutor 1. *n.* coach, educator, governor, guardian, guide, guru, instructor, lecturer, master, mentor, preceptor, schoolmaster, teacher **2.** *v.* coach, direct, discipline, drill, edify, educate, guide, instruct, lecture, school, teach, train

tutorial 1. *n.* individual instruction, lesson, seminar **2.** *adj.* coaching, guiding, instructional, teaching

TV gogglebox (*Brit. sl.*), idiot box (*Sl.*), receiver, small screen (*Inf.*), television, television set, telly (*Brit. inf.*), the box (*Brit. inf.*), the tube (*Sl.*), TV set

twaddle 1. *n.* balderdash, blather, bunkum, chatter, claptrap (*Inf.*), drivel, foolish talk, gabble, garbage, gobbledegook (*Inf.*), gossip, guff (*Sl.*), hogwash, hot air (*Inf.*), inanity, nonsense, piffle (*Inf.*), poppycock (*Inf.*), rigmarole, rot, rubbish, tattle, trash, trumpery, verbiage, waffle (*Inf.*) **2.** *v.* blather, chatter, gabble, gossip, prattle, rattle on, talk nonsense, talk through one's hat, tattle, waffle (*Inf.*)

tweak *v./n.* jerk, nip, pinch, pull, squeeze, twist, twitch

twee bijou, cute, dainty, precious, pretty, quaint, sentimental, sweet

twiddle 1. adjust, fiddle, finger, jiggle, juggle, monkey with (*Inf.*), play with, twirl, wiggle **2. twiddle one's thumbs** be idle, be unoccupied, do nothing, have nothing to do, malinger, mark time, sit around

twig[1] branch, offshoot, shoot, spray, sprig, stick, withe

twig[2] catch on (*Inf.*), comprehend, fathom, find out, get, grasp, make out, rumble (*Sl.*), see, tumble to (*Inf.*), understand

twilight *n.* **1.** dimness, dusk, evening, gloaming (*Scot.*), half-light, sundown, sunset **2.** decline, ebb, last phase ~*adj.* **3.** crepuscular, darkening, dim, evening **4.** declining, dying, ebbing, final, last

twin **1.** *n.* clone, corollary, counterpart, double, duplicate, fellow, likeness, lookalike, match, mate, ringer (*Sl.*) **2.** *adj.* corresponding, double, dual, duplicate, geminate, identical, matched, matching, paired, parallel, twofold **3.** *v.* couple, join, link, match, pair, yoke

twine *n.* **1.** cord, string, yarn **2.** coil, convolution, interlacing, twist, whorl **3.** knot, snarl, tangle ~*v.* **4.** braid, entwine, interlace, interweave, knit, plait, splice, twist, twist together, weave **5.** bend, coil, curl, encircle, loop, meander, spiral, surround, twist, wind, wrap, wreathe

twinge bite, gripe, pain, pang, pinch, prick, sharp pain, spasm, stab, stitch, throb, throe (*Rare*), tic, tweak, twist, twitch

twinkle *v.* **1.** blink, coruscate, flash, flicker, gleam, glint, glisten, glitter, scintillate, shimmer, shine, sparkle, wink ~*n.* **2.** blink, coruscation, flash, flicker, gleam, glimmer, glistening, glittering, light, scintillation, shimmer, shine, spark, sparkle, wink **3.** flash, instant, jiffy (*Inf.*), moment, second, shake (*Inf.*), split second, tick (*Inf.*), trice, twinkling, two shakes of a lamb's tail (*Inf.*)

twinkling **1.**, blink, coruscation, flash, flashing, flicker, gleam, glimmer, glistening, glittering, scintillation, shimmer, shining, sparkle, twinkle, wink **2.** flash, instant, jiffy (*Inf.*), moment, second, shake (*Inf.*), split second, tick (*Inf.*), trice, twinkle, two shakes of a lamb's tail (*Inf.*)

twirl *v.* **1.** gyrate, pirouette, pivot, revolve, rotate, spin, turn, turn on one's heel, twiddle, twist, wheel, whirl, wind ~*n.* **2.** gyration, pirouette, revolution, rotation, spin, turn, twist, wheel, whirl **3.** coil, spiral, twist

twist *v.* **1.** coil, corkscrew, curl, encircle, entwine, intertwine, screw, spin, swivel, twine, weave, wind, wrap, wreathe, wring **2.** contort, distort, screw up **3.** rick, sprain, turn, wrench **4.** alter, change, distort, falsify, garble, misquote, misrepresent, pervert, warp **5.** squirm, wriggle, writhe **6. twist someone's arm**

bully, coerce, force, persuade, pressurize, talk into ~*n.* **7.** coil, curl, spin, swivel, twine, wind **8.** braid, coil, curl, hank, plug, quid, roll **9.** change, development, revelation, slant, surprise, turn, variation **10.** arc, bend, convolution, curve, meander, turn, undulation, zigzag **11.** defect, deformation, distortion, flaw, imperfection, kink, warp **12.** jerk, pull, sprain, turn, wrench **13.** aberration, bent, characteristic, crotchet, eccentricity, fault, foible, idiosyncrasy, oddity, peculiarity, proclivity, quirk, trait **14.** confusion, entanglement, kink, knot, mess, mix-up, snarl, tangle **15. round the twist** *Brit. sl.* barmy (*Sl.*), batty (*Sl.*), bonkers (*Brit. sl.*), crazy, cuckoo (*Inf.*), daft (*Inf.*), insane, mad, not all there, not right in the head, nuts (*Sl.*), nutty (*Sl.*), nutty as a fruitcake (*Sl.*), off one's rocker (*Sl.*)

twister cheat, con man (*Inf.*), crook (*Inf.*), deceiver, fraud, rogue, swindler, trickster

twit[1] *v.* banter, berate, blame, censure, deride, jeer, make fun of, scorn, taunt, tease, upbraid

twit[2] ass, blockhead, chump (*Inf.*), clown, dope (*Sl.*), fool, halfwit, idiot, juggins (*Brit. inf.*), nincompoop, ninny, nitwit, silly-billy (*Inf.*), simpleton, twerp (*Inf.*)

twitch **1.** *v.* blink, flutter, jerk, jump, pluck, pull, snatch, squirm, tug, yank **2.** *n.* blink, flutter, jerk, jump, pull, spasm, tic, tremor, twinge

twitter *v.* **1.** chatter, cheep, chirp, chirrup, trill, tweet, warble, whistle **2.** chatter, giggle, prattle, simper, snigger, titter ~*n.* **3.** call, chatter, cheep, chirp, chirrup, cry, song, trill, tweet, warble, whistle **4.** agitation, anxiety, bustle, dither, excitement, flurry, fluster, flutter, nervousness, tizzy (*Inf.*), whirl

two-edged ambiguous, ambivalent, backhanded, double-edged, equivocal

two-faced deceitful, deceiving, dissembling, double-dealing, duplicitous, false, hypocritical, insincere, Janus-faced, perfidious, treacherous, untrustworthy

tycoon baron, big cheese (*Sl.*), big noise (*Sl.*), capitalist, captain of industry, fat cat (*Sl.*), financier, industrialist, magnate, merchant prince, mogul, plutocrat, potentate, wealthy businessman

type **1.** breed, category, class, classification, form, genre, group, ilk, kidney, kind, order, sort, species, strain, subdivision, variety **2**. case, characters, face, fount, print, printing **3**. archetype, epitome, essence, example, exemplar, model, original, paradigm, pattern, personification, prototype, quintessence, specimen, standard

typhoon cyclone, squall, storm, tempest, tornado, tropical storm

typical archetypal, average, characteristic, classic, conventional, essential, illustrative, in character, indicative, in keeping, model, normal, orthodox, representative, standard, stock, true to type, usual

typify characterize, embody, epitomize, exemplify, illustrate, incarnate, personify, represent, sum up, symbolize

tyrannical absolute, arbitrary, authoritarian, autocratic, coercive, cruel, despotic, dictatorial, domineering, high-handed, imperious, inhuman, magiste-rial, oppressive, overbearing, overweening, peremptory, severe, tyrannous, unjust, unreasonable

tyrannize browbeat, bully, coerce, dictate, domineer, enslave, have (someone) under one's thumb, intimidate, oppress, ride roughshod over, rule with an iron hand, subjugate, terrorize

tyranny absolutism, authoritarianism, autocracy, coercion, cruelty, despotism, dictatorship, harsh discipline, high-handedness, imperiousness, oppression, peremptoriness, reign of terror, unreasonableness

tyrant absolutist, authoritarian, autocrat, bully, despot, dictator, Hitler, martinet, oppressor, slave-driver

tyro apprentice, beginner, catechumen, greenhorn (*Inf.*), initiate, learner, neophyte, novice, novitiate, pupil, student, trainee

u

ubiquitous all-over, ever-present, everywhere, omnipresent, pervasive, universal

ugly 1. hard-favoured, hard-featured, homely (*Chiefly U.S.*), ill-favoured, misshapen, not much to look at, plain, unattractive, unlovely, unprepossessing, unsightly **2.** disagreeable, disgusting, distasteful, frightful, hideous, horrid, monstrous, objectionable, offensive, repugnant, repulsive, revolting, shocking, terrible, unpleasant, vile **3.** dangerous, forbidding, menacing, ominous, sinister, threatening **4.** angry, bad-tempered, dark, evil, malevolent, nasty, spiteful, sullen, surly

ulcer abscess, boil, fester, gathering, gumboil, peptic ulcer, pustule, sore

ulcerous cankered, cankerous, festering, furunculous (*Medical*), suppurative, ulcerative

ulterior concealed, covert, hidden, personal, secondary, secret, selfish, undisclosed, unexpressed

ultimate *adj.* **1.** conclusive, decisive, end, eventual, extreme, final, furthest, last, terminal **2.** extreme, greatest, highest, maximum, most significant, paramount, superlative, supreme, topmost, utmost **3.** basic, elemental, fundamental, primary, radical ~*n.* **4.** culmination, epitome, extreme, greatest, height, peak, perfection, summit, the last word

ultimately after all, at last, basically, eventually, finally, fundamentally, in due time, in the end, sooner or later

ultra *adj.* excessive, extreme, fanatical, immoderate, rabid, radical, revolutionary

ultramodern advanced, ahead of its time, avant-garde, futuristic, modernistic, neoteric (*Rare*), progressive, way-out (*Inf.*)

ululate cry, howl, keen, lament, moan, mourn, sob, wail, weep

umbrage anger, chagrin, displeasure, grudge, high dudgeon, huff, indignation, offence, pique, resentment, sense of injury

umbrella 1. brolly (*Brit. inf.*), gamp (*Brit. inf.*) **2.** aegis, agency, cover, patronage, protection

umpire 1. *n.* adjudicator, arbiter, arbitrator, judge, moderator, ref (*Inf.*), referee **2.** *v.* adjudicate, arbitrate, call (*Sport*), judge, moderate, referee

umpteen a good many, a thousand and one, considerable, countless, ever so many, millions, n, numerous, very many

unabashed blatant, bold, brazen, confident, unawed, unblushing, unconcerned, undaunted, undismayed, unembarrassed

unable impotent, inadequate, incapable, ineffectual, no good, not able, not equal to, not up to, powerless, unfit, unfitted, unqualified

unabridged complete, full-length, uncondensed, uncut, unexpurgated, unshortened, whole

unacceptable disagreeable, displeasing, distasteful, improper, inadmissible, insupportable, objectionable, offensive, undesirable, unpleasant, unsatisfactory, unwelcome

unaccompanied a cappella (*Music*), alone, by oneself, lone, on one's own, solo, unescorted

unaccomplished 1. incomplete, unachieved, uncompleted, undone, unfinished, unperformed **2.** inexpert, lacking finesse, uncultivated, unskilful, unskilled

unaccountable 1. baffling, incomprehensible, inexplicable, inscrutable, mysterious, odd, peculiar, puzzling, strange, unexplainable, unfathomable, unintelligible **2.** astonishing, extraordinary, uncommon, unheard-of, unusual, unwonted **3.** clear, exempt, free, not answerable, not responsible, unliable

unaccounted-for lost, missing, not explained, not taken into consideration, not understood, unexplained

unaccustomed 1. *With* to a newcomer to, a novice at, green, inexperienced, not given to, not used to, unfamiliar with, unpractised, unused to, unversed in **2.** new, out of the ordinary, remarkable, special, strange, surprising, uncommon, unexpected, unfamiliar, unprecedented, unusual, unwonted

unadorned plain, restrained, severe, simple, stark, straightforward, unembellished, unornamented, unvarnished

unadvised 1. careless, hasty, heedless, ill-advised, imprudent, inadvisable, indiscreet, injudicious, rash, reckless, unwary, unwise 2. ignorant, in the dark, unaware, uninformed, unknowing, unsuspecting, unwarned

unaffected[1] artless, genuine, honest, ingenuous, naive, natural, plain, simple, sincere, straightforward, unassuming, unpretentious, unsophisticated, unspoilt, unstudied, without airs

unaffected[2] aloof, impervious, not influenced, proof, unaltered, unchanged, unimpressed, unmoved, unresponsive, unstirred, untouched

unafraid confident, daring, dauntless, fearless, intrepid, unfearing, unshakable

unalterable fixed, fixed as the laws of the Medes and the Persians, immutable, invariable, permanent, steadfast, unchangeable, unchanging

unanimity accord, agreement, chorus, concert, concord, concurrence, consensus, harmony, like-mindedness, one mind, unison, unity

unanimous agreed, agreeing, at one, common, concerted, concordant, harmonious, in agreement, in complete accord, like-minded, of one mind, united

unanimously by common consent, nem. con., unitedly, unopposed, with one accord, without exception, without opposition

unanswerable 1. absolute, conclusive, incontestable, incontrovertible, indisputable, irrefutable, unarguable, undeniable 2. insoluble, insolvable, unascertainable, unexplainable, unresolvable

unanswered disputed, ignored, in doubt, open, undecided, undenied, unnoticed, unrefuted, unresolved, unsettled, up in the air, vexed

unappetizing distasteful, insipid, off-putting (*Brit. inf.*), tasteless, unappealing, unattractive, uninteresting, uninviting, unpalatable, unpleasant, unsavoury, vapid

unapproachable 1. aloof, chilly, cool, distant, frigid, offish (*Inf.*), remote, reserved, standoffish, unfriendly, unsociable, withdrawn 2. inaccessible, out of reach, out-of-the-way, remote, un-get-at-able (*Inf.*), unreachable

unapt 1. inapplicable, inapposite, in-apt, out of character, out of keeping, out of place, unappropriate, unfit, unfitted, unsuitable 2. backward, dim, dim-witted (*Inf.*), dull, incompetent, slow, stupid, thick 3. averse, disinclined, loath, not prone, reluctant, undisposed, unlikely, unwilling

unarmed assailable, defenceless, exposed, helpless, open, open to attack, unarmoured, unprotected, weak, weaponless, without arms

unasked 1. gratuitous, spontaneous, unbidden, undemanded, undesired, uninvited, unprompted, unrequested, unsought, unwanted 2. off one's own bat, of one's own accord, voluntarily, without prompting

unassailable 1. impregnable, invincible, invulnerable, secure, well-defended 2. absolute, conclusive, incontestable, incontrovertible, indisputable, irrefutable, positive, proven, sound, undeniable

unassertive backward, bashful, diffident, meek, mousy, retiring, self-effacing, timid, timorous, unassuming

unassuming diffident, humble, meek, modest, quiet, reserved, retiring, self-effacing, simple, unassertive, unobtrusive, unostentatious, unpretentious

unattached 1. autonomous, free, independent, nonaligned, unaffiliated, uncommitted 2. a free agent, available, by oneself, footloose and fancy-free, not spoken for, on one's own, single, unengaged, unmarried

unattended 1. abandoned, disregarded, ignored, left alone, not cared for, unguarded, unwatched 2. alone, on one's own, unaccompanied, unescorted

unauthorized illegal, unapproved, unconstitutional, unlawful, unofficial, unsanctioned, unwarranted

unavailing abortive, bootless, fruitless, futile, idle, ineffective, ineffectual, of no avail, pointless, to no purpose, unproductive, unsuccessful, useless, vain

unavoidable bound to happen, certain, compulsory, fated, ineluctable, inescapable, inevitable, inexorable, necessary, obligatory, sure

unaware heedless, ignorant, incognizant, oblivious, unconscious, unenlightened, uninformed, unknowing, unmindful, unsuspecting

unawares 1. aback, abruptly, by surprise, off guard, on the hop (*Brit. inf.*), suddenly, unexpectedly, unprepared, without warning **2.** accidentally, by accident, by mistake, inadvertently, mistakenly, unconsciously, unintentionally, unknowingly, unwittingly

unbalanced 1. asymmetrical, irregular, lopsided, not balanced, shaky, unequal, uneven, unstable, unsymmetrical, wobbly **2.** crazy, demented, deranged, disturbed, eccentric, erratic, insane, irrational, lunatic, mad, *non compos mentis*, not all there, touched, unhinged, unsound, unstable **3.** biased, inequitable, one-sided, partial, partisan, prejudiced, unfair, unjust

unbearable insufferable, insupportable, intolerable, oppressive, too much (*Inf.*), unacceptable, unendurable

unbeatable indomitable, invincible, more than a match for, unconquerable, unstoppable, unsurpassable

unbeaten 1. triumphant, unbowed, undefeated, unsubdued, unsurpassed, unvanquished, victorious, winning **2.** new, untouched, untried, untrodden, virgin

unbecoming 1. ill-suited, inappropriate, incongruous, unattractive, unbefitting, unfit, unflattering, unsightly, unsuitable, unsuited **2.** discreditable, improper, indecorous, indelicate, offensive, tasteless, unseemly

unbelief atheism, disbelief, distrust, doubt, incredulity, scepticism

unbelievable astonishing, beyond belief, far-fetched, implausible, impossible, improbable, inconceivable, incredible, outlandish, preposterous, questionable, staggering, unconvincing, unimaginable, unthinkable

unbeliever agnostic, atheist, disbeliever, doubting Thomas, infidel, sceptic

unbelieving disbelieving, distrustful, doubtful, doubting, dubious, incredulous, sceptical, suspicious, unconvinced

unbend 1. be informal, calm down, cool it (*Sl.*), ease up, let it all hang out (*Sl.*), let oneself go, let up, loosen up, relax, slacken, slow down, take it easy (*Inf.*), unbutton (*Inf.*), unwind **2.** put straight, straighten, uncoil, uncurl

unbending 1. aloof, distant, formal, inflexible, reserved, rigid, stiff, uptight (*Sl.*) **2.** firm, hard-line, intractable, resolute, severe, strict, stubborn, tough, uncompromising, unyielding

unbiased disinterested, dispassionate, equitable, even-handed, fair, impartial, just, neutral, objective, open-minded, unprejudiced

unbidden 1. free, spontaneous, unforced, unprompted, voluntary, willing **2.** unasked, uninvited, unwanted, unwelcome

unbind free, loosen, release, set free, unchain, undo, unfasten, unfetter, unloose, unshackle, untie, unyoke

unblemished flawless, immaculate, perfect, pure, spotless, unflawed, unspotted, unstained, unsullied, untarnished

unblinking 1. calm, cool, emotionless, impassive, unemotional, unfaltering, unwavering **2.** fearless, steady, unafraid, unflinching, unshrinking

unblushing amoral, bold, brazen, forward, immodest, shameless, unabashed, unashamed, unembarrassed

unborn 1. awaited, embryonic, expected, *in utero* **2.** coming, future, hereafter, latter, subsequent, to come

unbosom admit, confess, confide, disburden, disclose, divulge, get (something) off one's chest (*Inf.*), get (something) out of one's system, lay bare, let out, reveal, tell, unburden

unbounded absolute, boundless, endless, immeasurable, infinite, limitless, unbridled, unchecked, unconstrained, uncontrolled, unlimited, unrestrained, vast

unbreakable armoured, durable, indestructible, infrangible, lasting, nonbreakable, resistant, rugged, shatterproof, solid, strong, toughened

unbridled excessive, intemperate, licentious, rampant, riotous, unchecked, unconstrained, uncontrolled, uncurbed, ungovernable, ungoverned, unrestrained, unruly, violent, wanton

unbroken 1. complete, entire, intact, solid, total, unimpaired, whole **2.** ceaseless, constant, continuous, endless, incessant, progressive, serried, successive, uninterrupted, unremitting **3.** deep, fast, profound, sound, undisturbed, unruffled, untroubled **4.** unbowed, unsubdued, untamed

unburden 1. disburden, discharge, disencumber, ease the load, empty, lighten, relieve, unload **2.** come clean (*Inf.*), confess, confide, disclose, get (something) off one's chest (*Inf.*), lay bare, make a clean breast of, reveal, tell all, unbosom

uncalled-for gratuitous, inappropriate, needless, undeserved, unjust, unjustified, unnecessary, unprovoked, unwarranted, unwelcome

uncanny 1. creepy (*Inf.*), eerie, eldritch (*Poetic*), mysterious, preternatural, queer, spooky (*Inf.*), strange, supernatural, unearthly, unnatural, weird **2.** astonishing, astounding, exceptional, extraordinary, fantastic, incredible, inspired, miraculous, prodigious, remarkable, singular, unheard-of, unusual

uncaring indifferent, negligent, unconcerned, unfeeling, uninterested, unmoved, unresponsive, unsympathetic

unceasing ceaseless, constant, continual, continuing, continuous, endless, incessant, never-ending, nonstop, perpetual, persistent, unending, unfailing, unremitting

uncertain 1. ambiguous, chancy, conjectural, doubtful, incalculable, indefinite, indeterminate, indistinct, questionable, risky, speculative, undetermined, unforeseeable, unpredictable **2.** ambivalent, doubtful, dubious, hazy, in two minds, irresolute, unclear, unconfirmed, undecided, undetermined, unfixed, unresolved, unsettled, unsure, up in the air, vacillating, vague **3.** changeable, erratic, fitful, hesitant, inconstant, insecure, irregular, precarious, unpredictable, unreliable, vacillating, variable, wavering

uncertainty ambiguity, bewilderment, confusion, dilemma, doubt, hesitancy, hesitation, inconclusiveness, indecision, irresolution, lack of confidence, misgiving, mystification, perplexity, puzzlement, qualm, quandary, scepticism, state of suspense, unpredictability, vagueness

unchangeable changeless, constant, fixed, immutable, inevitable, invariable, irreversible, permanent, stable, steadfast, strong, unalterable

unchanging abiding, changeless, constant, continuing, enduring, eternal, immutable, imperishable, lasting, permanent, perpetual, unchanged, unfading, unvarying

uncharitable cruel, hardhearted, insensitive, mean, merciless, stingy, unchristian, unfeeling, unforgiving, unfriendly, ungenerous, unkind, unsympathetic

uncharted not mapped, strange, un-

discovered, unexplored, unfamiliar, unknown, unplumbed, virgin

unchaste depraved, dissolute, fallen, immodest, immoral, impure, lewd, loose, promiscuous, unvirtuous, wanton

uncivil bad-mannered, bearish, boorish, brusque, churlish, discourteous, disrespectful, gruff, ill-bred, ill-mannered, impolite, rude, surly, uncouth, unmannerly

uncivilized 1. barbarian, barbaric, barbarous, illiterate, primitive, savage, wild **2.** beyond the pale, boorish, brutish, churlish, coarse, gross, philistine, uncouth, uncultivated, uncultured, uneducated, unmannered, unpolished, unsophisticated, vulgar

unclad bare, in one's birthday suit (*Inf.*), in the altogether (*Inf.*), in the buff (*Inf.*), naked, nude, starkers (*Inf.*), stripped, unclothed, undressed, with nothing on, without a stitch on

unclean contaminated, corrupt, defiled, dirty, evil, filthy, foul, impure, nasty, polluted, soiled, spotted, stained, sullied, tainted

uncomfortable 1. awkward, causing discomfort, cramped, disagreeable, hard, ill-fitting, incommodious, irritating, painful, rough, troublesome **2.** awkward, confused, discomfited, disquieted, distressed, disturbed, embarrassed, ill at ease, out of place, self-conscious, troubled, uneasy

uncommitted floating, free, freefloating, neutral, nonaligned, nonpartisan, not involved, (sitting) on the fence, unattached, uninvolved

uncommon 1. bizarre, curious, few and far between, infrequent, novel, odd, out of the ordinary, peculiar, queer, rare, scarce, singular, strange, unfamiliar, unusual **2.** distinctive, exceptional, extraordinary, incomparable, inimitable, notable, noteworthy, outstanding, rare, remarkable, singular, special, superior, unparalleled, unprecedented

uncommonly 1. hardly ever, infrequently, not often, occasionally, only now and then, rarely, scarcely ever, seldom **2.** exceptionally, extremely, particularly, peculiarly, remarkably, strangely, unusually, very

uncommunicative close, curt, guarded, reserved, reticent, retiring, secretive, short, shy, silent, taciturn, tight-lipped, unforthcoming, unresponsive, unsociable, withdrawn

uncompromising decided, firm, hard-line, inexorable, inflexible, intransigent, obdurate, obstinate, rigid, steadfast, strict, stubborn, tough, unbending, unyielding

unconcern aloofness, apathy, detachment, indifference, insouciance, lack of interest, nonchalance, remoteness, uninterest, uninterestedness

unconcerned 1. aloof, apathetic, cool, detached, dispassionate, distant, incurious, indifferent, oblivious, uninterested, uninvolved, unmoved, unsympathetic **2.** blithe, carefree, careless, easy, insouciant, nonchalant, not bothered, relaxed, serene, unperturbed, unruffled, untroubled, unworried

unconditional absolute, categorical, complete, downright, entire, explicit, full, out-and-out, outright, plenary, positive, thoroughgoing, total, unlimited, unqualified, unreserved, unrestricted, utter

uncongenial antagonistic, antipathetic, disagreeable, discordant, displeasing, distasteful, incompatible, not one's cup of tea (*Inf.*), unharmonious, uninviting, unpleasant, unsuited, unsympathetic

unconnected 1. detached, disconnected, divided, independent, separate **2.** disconnected, disjointed, illogical, incoherent, irrelevant, meaningless, nonsensical, not related, unrelated

unconquerable 1. indomitable, invincible, unbeatable, undefeatable, unyielding **2.** enduring, ingrained, innate, insurmountable, inveterate, irrepressible, irresistible, overpowering

unconscionable 1. amoral, criminal, unethical, unfair, unjust, unprincipled, unscrupulous **2.** excessive, exorbitant, extravagant, extreme, immoderate, inordinate, outrageous, preposterous, unreasonable

unconscious 1. blacked out (*Inf.*), comatose, dead to the world, insensible, knocked out, numb, out, out cold, senseless, stunned **2.** blind to, deaf to, heedless, ignorant, in ignorance, lost to, oblivious, unaware, unknowing, unmindful, unsuspecting **3.** accidental, inadvertent, unintended, unintentional, unpremeditated, unwitting **4.** automatic, gut (*Inf.*), inherent, innate, instinctive, involuntary, latent, reflex, repressed, sub-

conscious, subliminal, suppressed, unrealized

uncontrollable beside oneself, carried away, frantic, furious, irrepressible, irresistible, like one possessed, mad, strong, ungovernable, unmanageable, unruly, violent, wild

uncontrolled boisterous, furious, lacking self-control, out of control, out of hand, rampant, riotous, running wild, unbridled, unchecked, uncurbed, undisciplined, ungoverned, unrestrained, unruly, unsubmissive, untrammelled, violent

unconventional atypical, bizarre, bohemian, different, eccentric, far-out (*Sl.*), freakish (*Inf.*), idiosyncratic, individual, individualistic, informal, irregular, nonconformist, odd, offbeat, original, out of the ordinary, uncustomary, unorthodox, unusual, way-out (*Inf.*)

unconvincing dubious, feeble, fishy (*Inf.*), flimsy, hard to believe, implausible, improbable, inconclusive, lame, questionable, specious, suspect, thin, unlikely, unpersuasive, weak

uncoordinated all thumbs, awkward, bumbling, bungling, butterfingered (*Inf.*), clodhopping (*Inf.*), clumsy, graceless, heavy-footed, inept, lumbering, maladroit, ungainly, ungraceful

uncounted countless, infinite, innumerable, legion, multitudinous, myriad, numberless, unnumbered, untold

uncouth awkward, barbaric, boorish, clownish, clumsy, coarse, crude, gawky, graceless, gross, ill-mannered, loutish, lubberly, oafish, rough, rude, rustic, uncivilized, uncultivated, ungainly, unrefined, unseemly, vulgar

uncover 1. bare, lay open, lift the lid, open, show, strip, take the wraps off, unwrap **2.** bring to light, disclose, discover, divulge, expose, lay bare, make known, reveal, unearth, unmask

uncritical easily pleased, indiscriminate, undiscerning, undiscriminating, unexacting, unfussy, unperceptive, unselective, unthinking

unctuous 1. fawning, glib, gushing, ingratiating, insincere, obsequious, oily, plausible, slick, smarmy (*Brit. inf.*), smooth, suave, sycophantic **2.** greasy, oily, oleaginous, slippery, slithery

undaunted bold, brave, courageous, dauntless, fearless, gallant, indomitable, intrepid, not discouraged, nothing daunted, not put off, resolute, steadfast, undeterred, undiscouraged, undismayed, unfaltering, unflinching, unshrinking

undeceive be honest with, correct, disabuse, disillusion, enlighten, open (someone's) eyes (to), put (someone) right, set (someone) straight, shatter (someone's) illusions

undecided 1. ambivalent, dithering, doubtful, dubious, hesitant, in two minds, irresolute, swithering (*Scot.*), torn, uncertain, uncommitted, unsure, wavering **2.** debatable, indefinite, in the balance, moot, open, pending, tentative, unconcluded, undetermined, unsettled, up in the air, vague

undecipherable crabbed, cryptic, hieroglyphic, illegible, impenetrable, incomprehensible, indecipherable, indistinct, undistinguishable, unreadable, unrecognizable

undefended defenceless, exposed, naked, open to attack, unarmed, unfortified, unguarded, unprotected, vulnerable, wide open

undefiled chaste, clean, clear, flawless, immaculate, pure, sinless, spotless, unblemished, unsoiled, unspotted, unstained, unsullied, virginal

undefined 1. formless, hazy, indefinite, indistinct, shadowy, tenuous, vague **2.** imprecise, indeterminate, inexact, unclear, unexplained, unspecified

undemonstrative aloof, cold, contained, distant, formal, impassive, reserved, restrained, reticent, stiff, stolid, unaffectionate, uncommunicative, unemotional, unresponsive, withdrawn

undeniable beyond (a) doubt, beyond question, certain, clear, evident, incontestable, incontrovertible, indisputable, indubitable, irrefutable, manifest, obvious, patent, proven, sound, sure, unassailable, undoubted, unquestionable

undependable capricious, changeable, erratic, fickle, inconsistent, inconstant, irresponsible, treacherous, uncertain, unpredictable, unreliable, unstable, untrustworthy, variable

under *prep.* **1.** below, beneath, on the bottom of, underneath **2.** directed by, governed by, inferior to, junior to, reporting to, secondary to, subject to, subordinate to, subservient to **3.** belonging to, comprised in, included in, subsumed under ~*adv.* **4.** below, beneath, down, downward, lower, to the bottom

underclothes lingerie, smalls (*Inf.*), underclothing, undergarments, underlinen, underthings (*Inf.*), underwear, undies (*Inf.*)

undercover clandestine, concealed, confidential, covert, hidden, hush-hush (*Inf.*), intelligence, private, secret, spy, surreptitious, underground

undercurrent 1. crosscurrent, rip, rip current, riptide, underflow, undertow **2.** atmosphere, aura, drift, feeling, flavour, hidden feeling, hint, murmur, overtone, sense, suggestion, tendency, tenor, tinge, trend, undertone, vibes (*Inf.*), vibrations

undercut 1. sacrifice, sell at a loss, sell cheaply, undercharge, underprice, undersell **2.** cut away, cut out, excavate, gouge out, hollow out, mine, undermine

underdog fall guy (*Inf.*), little fellow (*Inf.*), loser, victim, weaker party

underestimate belittle, hold cheap, minimize, miscalculate, misprize, not do justice to, rate too low, sell short (*Inf.*), set no store by, think too little of, underrate, undervalue

undergo bear, be subjected to, endure, experience, go through, stand, submit to, suffer, sustain, weather, withstand

underground *adj.* **1.** below ground, below the surface, buried, covered, subterranean **2.** clandestine, concealed, covert, hidden, secret, surreptitious, undercover **3.** alternative, avant-garde, experimental, radical, revolutionary, subversive ~*n.* **the underground 4.** the metro, the subway, the tube (*Brit.*) **5.** the Maquis, partisans, the Resistance

undergrowth bracken, brambles, briars, brush, brushwood, scrub, underbrush, underbush, underwood

underhand clandestine, crafty, crooked (*Inf.*), deceitful, deceptive, devious, dishonest, dishonourable, fraudulent, furtive, secret, secretive, sly, sneaky, stealthy, surreptitious, treacherous, underhanded, unethical, unscrupulous

underline 1. italicize, mark, rule a line under, underscore **2.** accentuate, bring home, call *or* draw attention to, emphasize, give emphasis to, highlight, point up, stress

underling flunky, hireling, inferior, lackey, menial, minion, nonentity, retainer, servant, slave, subordinate, understrapper

underlying 1. concealed, hidden, latent, lurking, veiled **2.** basal, basic, elementary, essential, fundamental, intrinsic, primary, prime, root

undermine 1. dig out, eat away at, erode, excavate, mine, tunnel, undercut, wear away **2.** debilitate, disable, impair, sabotage, sap, subvert, threaten, weaken

underpinning 1. base, footing, foundation, groundwork, substructure, support **2.** *Plural* backbone, basis, foundation, ground, support

underprivileged badly off, deprived, destitute, disadvantaged, impoverished, in need, in want, needy, poor

underrate belittle, discount, disparage, fail to appreciate, misprize, not do justice to, set (too) little store by, underestimate, undervalue

undersell 1. cut, mark down, reduce, slash, undercharge, undercut **2.** play down, understate

undersized atrophied, dwarfish, miniature, pygmy, runtish, runty, small, squat, stunted, tiny, underdeveloped, underweight

understand 1. appreciate, apprehend, be aware, catch on (*Inf.*), comprehend, conceive, cotton on (*Inf.*), discern, fathom, follow, get, get the hang of (*Inf.*), get to the bottom of, grasp, know, make head or tail of (*Inf.*), make out, penetrate, perceive, realize, recognize, savvy (*Sl.*), see, take in, tumble to (*Inf.*), twig (*Brit. inf.*) **2.** assume, be informed, believe, conclude, gather, hear, learn, presume, suppose, take it, think **3.** accept, appreciate, be able to see, commiserate, show compassion for, sympathize with, tolerate

understanding *n.* **1.** appreciation, awareness, comprehension, discernment, grasp, insight, intelligence, judgment, knowledge, penetration, perception, sense **2.** belief, conclusion, estimation, idea, interpretation, judgment, notion, opinion, perception, view, viewpoint **3.** accord, agreement, common view, gentlemen's agreement, meeting of minds, pact ~*adj.* **4.** accepting, compassionate, considerate, discerning, forbearing, forgiving, kind, kindly, patient, perceptive, responsive, sensitive, sympathetic, tolerant

understood 1. implicit, implied, inferred, tacit, unspoken, unstated **2.** accepted, assumed, axiomatic, presumed, taken for granted

understudy *n.* double, fill-in, replacement, reserve, stand-in, sub, substitute

undertake 1. agree, bargain, commit oneself, contract, covenant, engage, guarantee, pledge, promise, stipulate, take upon oneself **2.** attempt, begin, commence, embark on, endeavour, enter upon, set about, tackle, take on, try

undertaker funeral director, mortician (*U.S.*)

undertaking 1. affair, attempt, business, effort, endeavour, enterprise, game, operation, project, task, venture **2.** assurance, commitment, pledge, promise, solemn word, vow, word, word of honour

undertone 1. low tone, murmur, subdued voice, whisper **2.** atmosphere, feeling, flavour, hint, suggestion, tinge, touch, trace, undercurrent

undervalue depreciate, hold cheap, look down on, make light of, minimize, misjudge, misprize, set no store by, underestimate, underrate

underwater submarine, submerged, sunken, undersea

under way afoot, begun, going on, in motion, in operation, in progress, started

underwear lingerie, smalls (*Inf.*), underclothes, underclothing, undergarments, underlinen, undies (*Inf.*), unmentionables

underweight half-starved, puny, skin and bone, skinny, undernourished, undersized

underworld 1. criminal element, criminals, gangland (*Inf.*), gangsters, organized crime **2.** abode of the dead, Hades, hell, infernal region, nether regions, nether world, the inferno

underwrite 1. back, finance, fund, guarantee, insure, provide security, sponsor, subsidize **2.** countersign, endorse, initial, sign, subscribe **3.** agree to, approve, consent, okay (*Inf.*), sanction

undesigned accidental, fortuitous, inadvertent, not meant, unintended, unintentional, unpremeditated

undesirable disagreeable, disliked, distasteful, dreaded, objectionable, obnoxious, offensive, out of place, repugnant, (to be) avoided, unacceptable, unattractive, unpleasing, unpopular, unsavoury, unsuitable, unwanted, unwelcome, unwished-for

undeveloped embryonic, immature, inchoate, in embryo, latent, potential, primordial (*Biol.*)

undignified beneath one, beneath

one's dignity, improper, inappropriate, indecorous, inelegant, infra dig (*Inf.*), lacking dignity, unbecoming, ungentlemanly, unladylike, unrefined, unseemly, unsuitable

undisciplined disobedient, erratic, fitful, obstreperous, uncontrolled, unpredictable, unreliable, unrestrained, unruly, unschooled, unsteady, unsystematic, untrained, wayward, wild, wilful

undisguised complete, evident, explicit, genuine, manifest, obvious, open, out-and-out, overt, patent, thoroughgoing, transparent, unconcealed, unfeigned, unmistakable, utter, wholehearted

undisputed accepted, acknowledged, beyond question, certain, conclusive, freely admitted, incontestable, incontrovertible, indisputable, irrefutable, not disputed, recognized, sure, unchallenged, uncontested, undeniable, undoubted, unquestioned

undistinguished commonplace, everyday, indifferent, mediocre, no great shakes (*Inf.*), nothing to write home about (*Inf.*), ordinary, pedestrian, prosaic, run-of-the-mill, so-so (*Inf.*), unexceptional, unexciting, unimpressive, unremarkable

undisturbed 1. not moved, quiet, uninterrupted, untouched, without interruption 2. calm, collected, composed, equable, even, motionless, placid, serene, tranquil, unagitated, unbothered, unperturbed, unruffled, untroubled

undivided combined, complete, concentrated, concerted, entire, exclusive, full, solid, thorough, unanimous, undistracted, united, whole, wholehearted

undo 1. disengage, disentangle, loose, loosen, open, unbutton, unfasten, unlock, untie, unwrap 2. annul, cancel, invalidate, neutralize, nullify, offset, reverse, wipe out 3. bring to naught, defeat, destroy, impoverish, invalidate, mar, overturn, quash, ruin, shatter, subvert, undermine, upset, wreck

undoing 1. collapse, defeat, destruction, disgrace, downfall, humiliation, overthrow, overturn, reversal, ruin, ruination, shame 2. affliction, blight, curse, fatal flaw, misfortune, the last straw, trial, trouble, weakness

undone[1] incomplete, left, neglected, not completed, not done, omitted, outstanding, passed over, unattended to,

unfinished, unfulfilled, unperformed

undone[2] betrayed, destroyed, forlorn, hapless, overcome, prostrate, ruined, wretched

undoubted acknowledged, certain, definite, evident, incontrovertible, indisputable, indubitable, obvious, sure, undisputed, unquestionable, unquestioned

undoubtedly assuredly, beyond a shadow of (a) doubt, beyond question, certainly, definitely, doubtless, of course, surely, undeniably, unmistakably, unquestionably, without doubt

undreamed of astonishing, inconceivable, incredible, miraculous, undreamt, unexpected, unforeseen, unheard-of, unimagined, unsuspected, unthought-of

undress 1. *v.* disrobe, divest oneself of, peel off (*Sl.*), shed, strip, take off one's clothes 2. *n.* disarray, dishabille, nakedness, nudity

undue disproportionate, excessive, extravagant, extreme, immoderate, improper, inordinate, intemperate, needless, overmuch, too great, too much, uncalled-for, undeserved, unnecessary, unseemly, unwarranted

undulate billow, heave, ripple, rise and fall, roll, surge, swell, wave

unduly disproportionately, excessively, extravagantly, immoderately, improperly, inordinately, out of all proportion, overly, overmuch, unjustifiably, unnecessarily, unreasonably

undying constant, continuing, deathless, eternal, everlasting, immortal, imperishable, indestructible, inextinguishable, infinite, perennial, permanent, perpetual, sempiternal (*Literary*), undiminished, unending, unfading

unearth 1. dig up, disinter, dredge up, excavate, exhume 2. bring to light, discover, expose, ferret out, find, reveal, root up, turn up, uncover

unearthly 1. eerie, eldritch (*Poetic*), ghostly, haunted, nightmarish, phantom, spectral, spooky (*Inf.*), strange, uncanny, weird 2. ethereal, heavenly, not of this world, preternatural, sublime, supernatural 3. abnormal, absurd, extraordinary, ridiculous, strange, ungodly (*Inf.*), unholy (*Inf.*), unreasonable

uneasiness agitation, alarm, anxiety, apprehension, apprehensiveness, disquiet, doubt, misgiving, nervousness, perturbation, qualms, suspicion, worry

uneasy 1. agitated, anxious, apprehensive, discomposed, disturbed, edgy, ill at ease, impatient, jittery (*Inf.*), nervous, on edge, perturbed, restive, restless, troubled, uncomfortable, unsettled, upset, worried **2**. awkward, constrained, insecure, precarious, shaky, strained, tense, uncomfortable, unstable **3**. bothering, dismaying, disquieting, disturbing, troubling, upsetting, worrying

uneconomic loss-making, nonpaying, non-profit-making, nonviable, unprofitable

uneducated 1. ignorant, illiterate, unlettered, unread, unschooled, untaught **2**. benighted, lowbrow, uncultivated, uncultured

unembellished austere, bald, bare, functional, modest, plain, severe, simple, stark, unadorned, unornamented, unvarnished

unemotional apathetic, cold, cool, impassive, indifferent, listless, passionless, phlegmatic, reserved, undemonstrative, unexcitable, unfeeling, unimpressionable, unresponsive

unemployed idle, jobless, laid off, on the dole (*Brit. inf.*), out of a job, out of work, redundant, resting (*of an actor*), workless

unending ceaseless, constant, continual, endless, eternal, everlasting, incessant, interminable, never-ending, perpetual, unceasing, unremitting

unendurable insufferable, insupportable, intolerable, more than flesh and blood can stand, unbearable

unenthusiastic apathetic, blasé, bored, half-hearted, indifferent, lukewarm, neutral, nonchalant, unimpressed, uninterested, unmoved, unresponsive

unenviable disagreeable, painful, thankless, uncomfortable, undesirable, unpleasant

unequal 1. different, differing, disparate, dissimilar, not uniform, unlike, unmatched, variable, varying **2**. *With* **to** found wanting, inadequate, insufficient, not up to **3**. asymmetrical, disproportionate, ill-matched, irregular, unbalanced, uneven

unequalled beyond compare, incomparable, inimitable, matchless, nonpareil, paramount, peerless, pre-eminent, second to none, supreme, transcendent, unmatched, unparalleled, unrivalled, unsurpassed, without equal

unequivocal absolute, certain, clear, clear-cut, decisive, definite, direct, evident, explicit, incontrovertible, indubitable, manifest, plain, positive, straight, unambiguous, uncontestable, unmistakable

unerring accurate, certain, exact, faultless, impeccable, infallible, perfect, sure, unfailing

unethical dirty, dishonest, dishonourable, disreputable, illegal, immoral, improper, shady (*Inf.*), underhand, unfair, unprincipled, unprofessional, unscrupulous, wrong

uneven 1. bumpy, not flat, not level, not smooth, rough **2**. broken, changeable, fitful, fluctuating, intermittent, irregular, jerky, patchy, spasmodic, unsteady, variable **3**. asymmetrical, lopsided, not parallel, odd, out of true, unbalanced **4**. disparate, ill-matched, onesided, unequal, unfair

uneventful boring, commonplace, dull, humdrum, monotonous, ordinary, quiet, routine, tedious, unexceptional, unexciting, uninteresting, unmemorable, unremarkable, unvaried

unexampled unequalled, unheard-of, unique, unmatched, unparalleled, unprecedented

unexceptional common or garden (*Inf.*), commonplace, conventional, insignificant, mediocre, normal, ordinary, pedestrian, run-of-the-mill, undistinguished, unimpressive, unremarkable, usual

unexpected abrupt, accidental, astonishing, chance, fortuitous, not bargained for, out of the blue, startling, sudden, surprising, unanticipated, unforeseen, unlooked-for, unpredictable

unexpressive blank, emotionless, expressionless, impassive, inexpressive, inscrutable, vacant

unfailing 1. bottomless, boundless, ceaseless, continual, continuous, endless, inexhaustible, never-failing, persistent, unflagging, unlimited **2**. certain, constant, dependable, faithful, infallible, loyal, reliable, staunch, steadfast, sure, tried and true, true

unfair 1. arbitrary, biased, bigoted, discriminatory, inequitable, one-sided, partial, partisan, prejudiced, unjust **2**. crooked (*Inf.*), dishonest, dishonourable, uncalled-for, unethical, unprincipled, unscrupulous, unsporting, unwarranted, wrongful

unfaithful 1. deceitful, disloyal, faithless, false, false-hearted, perfidious, recreant (*Archaic*), traitorous, treacherous, treasonable, unreliable, untrustworthy **2**. adulterous, faithless, fickle, inconstant, two-timing (*Inf.*), unchaste, untrue **3**. distorted, erroneous, imperfect, imprecise, inaccurate, inexact, unreliable, untrustworthy

unfaltering firm, indefatigable, persevering, resolute, steadfast, steady, tireless, unfailing, unflagging, unflinching, unswerving, untiring, unwavering

unfamiliar 1. alien, curious, different, little known, new, novel, out-of-the-way, strange, unaccustomed, uncommon, unknown, unusual **2**. *With* **with** a stranger to, inexperienced in, unaccustomed to, unacquainted, unconversant, uninformed about, uninitiated in, unpractised in, unskilled at, unversed in

unfashionable antiquated, behind the times, dated, obsolete, old-fashioned, old hat, out, outmoded, out of date, out of fashion, passé, unpopular

unfasten detach, disconnect, let go, loosen, open, separate, uncouple, undo, unlace, unlock, untie

unfathomable 1. bottomless, immeasurable, unmeasured, unplumbed, unsounded **2**. abstruse, baffling, deep, esoteric, impenetrable, incomprehensible, indecipherable, inexplicable, profound, unknowable

unfavourable 1. adverse, bad, contrary, disadvantageous, hostile, ill-suited, infelicitous, inimical, low, negative, poor, unfortunate, unfriendly, unsuited **2**. inauspicious, inopportune, ominous, threatening, unlucky, unpromising, unpropitious, unseasonable, untimely, untoward

unfeeling 1. apathetic, callous, cold, cruel, hardened, hardhearted, heartless, inhuman, insensitive, pitiless, stony, uncaring, unsympathetic **2**. insensate, insensible, numb, sensationless

unfeigned genuine, heartfelt, natural, pure, real, sincere, unaffected, unforced, wholehearted

unfettered free, unbridled, unchecked, unconfined, unconstrained, unrestrained, unshackled, untrammelled

unfinished 1. deficient, half-done, imperfect, incomplete, in the making, lacking, unaccomplished, uncompleted, undone, unfulfilled, wanting **2**. bare, crude,

natural, raw, rough, sketchy, unpolished, unrefined, unvarnished

unfit 1. ill-equipped, inadequate, incapable, incompetent, ineligible, no good, not cut out for, not equal to, not up to, unprepared, unqualified, untrained, useless **2**. ill-adapted, inadequate, inappropriate, ineffective, not designed, not fit, unsuitable, unsuited, useless **3**. debilitated, decrepit, feeble, flabby, in poor condition, out of kelter, out of shape, out of trim, unhealthy

unflagging constant, fixed, indefatigable, persevering, persistent, staunch, steady, tireless, unceasing, undeviating, unfailing, unfaltering, unremitting, untiring, unwearied

unflappable calm, collected, composed, cool, impassive, imperturbable, level-headed, not given to worry, self-possessed, unruffled

unflattering 1. blunt, candid, critical, honest, uncomplimentary, warts and all **2**. not shown in the best light, not shown to advantage, plain, unattractive, unbecoming, unprepossessing

unfledged callow, green, immature, inexperienced, raw, undeveloped, untried, young

unflinching bold, constant, determined, firm, resolute, stalwart, staunch, steadfast, steady, unfaltering, unshaken, unshrinking, unswerving, unwavering

unfold 1. disentangle, expand, flatten, open, spread out, straighten, stretch out, undo, unfurl, unravel, unroll, unwrap **2**. *Fig.* clarify, describe, disclose, divulge, explain, illustrate, make known, present, reveal, show, uncover **3**. bear fruit, develop, evolve, expand, grow, mature

unforeseen abrupt, accidental, out of the blue, startling, sudden, surprise, surprising, unanticipated, unexpected, unlooked-for, unpredicted

unforgettable exceptional, extraordinary, fixed in the mind, impressive, memorable, never to be forgotten, notable

unforgivable deplorable, disgraceful, indefensible, inexcusable, shameful, unjustifiable, unpardonable, unwarrantable

unfortunate 1. adverse, calamitous, disastrous, ill-fated, ill-starred, inopportune, ruinous, unfavourable, untoward **2**. cursed, doomed, hapless, hopeless, luckless, out of luck, poor, star-crossed, unhappy, unlucky, unprosperous, unsuccessful, wretched **3**. deplorable, ill-advised, inappropriate, infelicitous, lamentable, regrettable, unbecoming, unsuitable

unfounded baseless, fabricated, false, groundless, idle, spurious, trumped up, unjustified, unproven, unsubstantiated, vain, without basis, without foundation

unfrequented deserted, godforsaken, isolated, lone, lonely, off the beaten track, remote, sequestered, solitary, uninhabited, unvisited

unfriendly 1. aloof, antagonistic, chilly, cold, disagreeable, distant, hostile, ill-disposed, inhospitable, not on speaking terms, quarrelsome, sour, surly, uncongenial, unneighbourly, unsociable **2**. alien, hostile, inauspicious, inhospitable, inimical, unfavourable, unpropitious

unfruitful barren, fruitless, infecund, infertile, sterile, unproductive, unprofitable, unprolific, unrewarding

ungainly awkward, clumsy, gangling, gawky, inelegant, loutish, lubberly, lumbering, slouching, uncoordinated, uncouth, ungraceful

ungodly 1. blasphemous, corrupt, depraved, godless, immoral, impious, irreligious, profane, sinful, vile, wicked **2.** *Inf.* dreadful, horrendous, intolerable, outrageous, unearthly, unholy (*Inf.*), unreasonable, unseemly

ungovernable rebellious, refractory, uncontrollable, unmanageable, unrestrainable, unruly, wild

ungracious bad-mannered, churlish, discourteous, ill-bred, impolite, offhand, rude, uncivil, unmannerly

ungrateful heedless, ingrate (*Archaic*), selfish, thankless, unappreciative, unmindful, unthankful

unguarded 1. careless, foolhardy, heedless, ill-considered, impolitic, imprudent, incautious, indiscreet, rash, thoughtless, uncircumspect, undiplomatic, unthinking, unwary **2**. defenceless, open to attack, undefended, unpatrolled, unprotected, vulnerable **3**. artless, candid, direct, frank, guileless, open, straightforward

unhallowed 1. not sacred, unblessed, unconsecrated, unholy, unsanctified **2.** damnable, evil, godless, irreverent, profane, sinful, wicked

unhandy 1. awkward, bumbling, bungling, clumsy, fumbling, heavy-handed, incompetent, inept, inexpert, maladroit,

unskilful **2**. awkward, cumbersome, hampering, ill-arranged, ill-contrived, inconvenient, unwieldy

unhappy 1. blue, crestfallen, dejected, depressed, despondent, disconsolate, dispirited, down, downcast, gloomy, long-faced, melancholy, miserable, mournful, sad, sorrowful **2**. cursed, hapless, ill-fated, ill-omened, luckless, unfortunate, unlucky, wretched **3**. awkward, clumsy, gauche, ill-advised, ill-timed, inappropriate, inept, infelicitous, injudicious, malapropos, tactless, unsuitable, untactful

unharmed in one piece (*Inf.*), intact, safe, safe and sound, sound, undamaged, unhurt, uninjured, unscarred, unscathed, untouched, whole, without a scratch

unhealthy 1. ailing, delicate, feeble, frail, infirm, in poor health, invalid, poorly (*Inf.*), sick, sickly, unsound, unwell, weak **2**. deleterious, detrimental, harmful, insalubrious, insanitary, noisome, noxious, unwholesome **3**. bad, baneful (*Archaic*), corrupt, corrupting, degrading, demoralizing, morbid, negative, undesirable

unheard-of 1. little known, obscure, undiscovered, unfamiliar, unknown, unregarded, unremarked, unsung **2**. inconceivable, never before encountered, new, novel, singular, unbelievable, undreamed of, unexampled, unique, unprecedented, unusual **3**. disgraceful, extreme, offensive, outlandish, outrageous, preposterous, shocking, unacceptable, unthinkable

unheeded disobeyed, disregarded, forgotten, ignored, neglected, overlooked, unfollowed, unnoticed, unobserved, untaken

unheralded out of the blue, surprise, unacclaimed, unannounced, unexpected, unforeseen, unnoticed, unproclaimed, unpublicized, unrecognized, unsung

unhesitating 1. implicit, resolute, steadfast, unfaltering, unquestioning, unreserved, unswerving, unwavering, wholehearted **2**. immediate, instant, instantaneous, prompt, ready, without delay

unhinge 1. confound, confuse, craze, derange, disorder, distemper (*Archaic*), drive out of one's mind, madden, unbalance, unsettle **2**. detach, disconnect, disjoint, dislodge, remove

unholy 1. base, corrupt, depraved, dishonest, evil, heinous, immoral, iniquitous, irreligious, profane, sinful, ungodly, vile, wicked 2. *Inf.* appalling, awful, dreadful, horrendous, outrageous, shocking, unearthly, ungodly (*Inf.*), unnatural, unreasonable

unhoped-for beyond one's wildest dreams, incredible, like a dream come true, out of the blue, surprising, unanticipated, unbelievable, undreamed of, unexpected, unimaginable, unlooked-for

unhurried calm, deliberate, easy, easy-going, leisurely, sedate, slow, slow and steady, slow-paced

unidentified anonymous, mysterious, nameless, unclassified, unfamiliar, unknown, unmarked, unnamed, unrecognized, unrevealed

unification alliance, amalgamation, coalescence, coalition, combination, confederation, federation, fusion, merger, union, uniting

uniform *n.* 1. costume, dress, garb, habit, livery, outfit, regalia, regimentals, suit ~*adj.* 2. consistent, constant, equable, even, regular, smooth, unbroken, unchanging, undeviating, unvarying 3. alike, equal, identical, like, same, selfsame, similar

uniformity 1. constancy, evenness, homogeneity, invariability, regularity, sameness, similarity 2. drabness, dullness, flatness, lack of diversity, monotony, sameness, tedium

unify amalgamate, bind, bring together, combine, confederate, consolidate, federate, fuse, join, merge, unite

unimaginable beyond one's wildest dreams, fantastic, impossible, inconceivable, incredible, indescribable, ineffable, mind-boggling (*Inf.*), unbelievable, unheard-of, unthinkable

unimaginative barren, commonplace, derivative, dry, dull, hackneyed, lifeless, matter-of-fact, ordinary, pedestrian, predictable, prosaic, routine, tame, uncreative, uninspired, unoriginal, unromantic, usual

unimpassioned calm, collected, composed, controlled, cool, dispassionate, impassive, moderate, rational, sedate, temperate, tranquil, undemonstrative, unemotional, unmoved

unimpeachable above reproach, beyond criticism, beyond question, blameless, faultless, impeccable, irreproachable, perfect, unassailable, unblemished, unchallengeable, unexceptionable, unquestionable

unimpeded free, open, unblocked, unchecked, unconstrained, unhampered, unhindered, unrestrained, untrammelled

unimportant immaterial, inconsequential, insignificant, irrelevant, low-ranking, minor, not worth mentioning, nugatory, of no account, of no consequence, of no moment, paltry, petty, slight, trifling, trivial, worthless

uninhabited abandoned, barren, desert, deserted, desolate, empty, unoccupied, unpopulated, unsettled, untenanted, vacant, waste

uninhibited 1. candid, frank, free, free and easy, informal, instinctive, liberated, natural, open, relaxed, spontaneous, unrepressed, unreserved, unselfconscious 2. free, unbridled, unchecked, unconstrained, uncontrolled, uncurbed, unrestrained, unrestricted

uninspired commonplace, dull, humdrum, indifferent, ordinary, prosaic, stale, stock, unexciting, unimaginative, uninspiring, uninteresting, unoriginal

unintelligent brainless, dense, dull, empty-headed, foolish, gormless (*Brit. inf.*), obtuse, slow, stupid, thick, unreasoning, unthinking

unintelligible double Dutch (*Brit. inf.*), illegible, inarticulate, incoherent, incomprehensible, indecipherable, indistinct, jumbled, meaningless, muddled, unfathomable

unintentional accidental, casual, fortuitous, inadvertent, involuntary, unconscious, undesigned, unintended, unpremeditated, unthinking, unwitting

uninterested apathetic, blasé, bored, distant, impassive, incurious, indifferent, listless, unconcerned, uninvolved, unresponsive

uninteresting boring, commonplace, drab, dreary, dry, dull, flat, humdrum, monotonous, tedious, tiresome, unenjoyable, uneventful, unexciting, uninspiring, wearisome

uninterrupted constant, continual, continuous, nonstop, peaceful, steady, sustained, unbroken, undisturbed, unending

uninvited not asked, not invited, unasked, unbidden, unwanted, unwelcome

uninviting disagreeable, offensive, off-putting (*Brit. inf.*), repellent, repulsive, unappealing, unappetizing, unattractive, undesirable, unpleasant, untempting, unwelcoming

union 1. amalgam, amalgamation, blend, combination, conjunction, fusion, junction, mixture, synthesis, uniting **2.** alliance, association, Bund, coalition, confederacy, confederation, federation, league **3.** accord, agreement, concord, concurrence, harmony, unanimity, unison, unity **4.** coition, coitus, copulation, coupling, intercourse, marriage, matrimony, wedlock

unique 1. lone, one and only, only, single, solitary, sui generis **2.** incomparable, inimitable, matchless, nonpareil, peerless, unequalled, unexampled, unmatched, unparalleled, unrivalled, without equal

unison accord, accordance, agreement, concert, concord, cooperation, harmony, unanimity, unity

unit 1. assembly, detachment, entity, group, section, system, whole **2.** component, constituent, element, item, member, module, part, piece, portion, section, segment **3.** measure, measurement, module, quantity

unite 1. amalgamate, blend, coalesce, combine, confederate, consolidate, couple, fuse, incorporate, join, link, marry, merge, unify, wed **2.** ally, associate, band, close ranks, club together, cooperate, join forces, join together, league, pool, pull together

united 1. affiliated, allied, banded together, collective, combined, concerted, in partnership, leagued, pooled, unified **2.** agreed, in accord, in agreement, likeminded, of like mind, of one mind, of the same opinion, one, unanimous

unity 1. entity, integrity, oneness, singleness, undividedness, unification, union, wholeness **2.** accord, agreement, concord, concurrence, consensus, harmony, peace, solidarity, unanimity

universal all-embracing, catholic, common, ecumenical, entire, general, omnipresent, total, unlimited, whole, widespread, worldwide

universality all-inclusiveness, completeness, comprehensiveness, entirety, generality, generalization, totality, ubiquity

universally always, everywhere, in all cases, in every instance, invariably, uniformly, without exception

universe cosmos, creation, everything, macrocosm, nature, the natural world

unjust biased, inequitable, one-sided, partial, partisan, prejudiced, undeserved, unfair, unjustified, unmerited, wrong, wrongful

unjustifiable indefensible, inexcusable, outrageous, unacceptable, unforgivable, unjust, unpardonable, unwarrantable, wrong

unkempt bedraggled, blowzy, disarranged, dishevelled, disordered, frowzy, messy, rumpled, scruffy, shabby, shaggy, slatternly, sloppy (*Inf.*), slovenly, sluttish, tousled, uncombed, ungroomed, untidy

unkind cruel, hardhearted, harsh, inconsiderate, inhuman, insensitive, malicious, mean, nasty, spiteful, thoughtless, uncaring, uncharitable, unchristian, unfeeling, unfriendly, unsympathetic

unknown 1. alien, concealed, dark, hidden, mysterious, new, secret, strange, unrecognized, unrevealed, untold **2.** anonymous, nameless, uncharted, undiscovered, unexplored, unidentified, unnamed **3.** humble, little known, obscure, undistinguished, unfamiliar, unheard-of, unrenowned, unsung

unladylike coarse, ill-bred, impolite, indelicate, rude, uncivil, ungracious, unmannerly, unrefined

unlamented unbemoaned, unbewailed, undeplored, unmissed, unmourned, unregretted, unwept

unlawful actionable, against the law, banned, criminal, forbidden, illegal, illegitimate, illicit, outlawed, prohibited, unauthorized, unlicensed

unleash free, let go, let loose, release, unloose, untie

unlettered ignorant, illiterate, uneducated, unlearned, unschooled, untaught, untutored

unlike contrasted, different, dissimilar, distinct, divergent, diverse, illmatched, incompatible, not alike, opposite, unequal, unrelated

unlikely 1. doubtful, faint, improbable, not likely, remote, slight, unimaginable **2.** implausible, incredible, questionable, unbelievable, unconvincing

unlimited 1. boundless, countless, endless, extensive, great, illimitable, immeasurable, immense, incalculable, infinite, limitless, unbounded, vast **2.** absolute, all-encompassing, complete, full, total, unconditional, unconstrained, unfettered, unqualified, unrestricted

unload disburden, discharge, dump, empty, off-load, relieve, unburden, unlade, unpack

unlock free, let loose, open, release, unbar, unbolt, undo, unfasten, unlatch

unlooked-for chance, fortuitous, out of the blue, surprise, surprising, unanticipated, undreamed of, unexpected, unforeseen, unhoped-for, unpredicted, unthought-of

unloved disliked, forsaken, loveless, neglected, rejected, spurned, uncared-for, uncherished, unpopular, unwanted

unlucky 1. cursed, disastrous, hapless, luckless, miserable, unfortunate, unhappy, unsuccessful, wretched **2.** doomed, ill-fated, ill-omened, ill-starred, inauspicious, ominous, unfavourable, untimely

unman daunt, demoralize, discourage, dispirit, emasculate, enervate, enfeeble, intimidate, unnerve, weaken

unmanageable 1. awkward, bulky, cumbersome, difficult to handle, inconvenient, unhandy, unwieldy **2.** difficult, fractious, intractable, obstreperous, out of hand, refractory, stroppy (*Brit. sl.*), uncontrollable, unruly, wild

unmanly 1. effeminate, feeble, sissy, soft (*Inf.*), weak, womanish **2.** chicken-hearted, cowardly, craven, dishonourable, ignoble, weak-kneed (*Inf.*), yellow (*Inf.*)

unmannerly badly behaved, bad-mannered, discourteous, disrespectful, ill-bred, ill-mannered, impolite, misbehaved, rude, uncivil, uncouth

unmarried bachelor, celibate, maiden, single, unattached, unwed, unwedded, virgin

unmask bare, bring to light, disclose, discover, expose, lay bare, reveal, show up, uncloak, uncover, unveil

unmatched beyond compare, consummate, incomparable, matchless, paramount, peerless, second to none, supreme, unequalled, unparalleled, unrivalled, unsurpassed

unmentionable disgraceful, disreputable, forbidden, frowned on, immodest, indecent, scandalous, shameful, shocking, taboo, unspeakable, unutterable

unmerciful brutal, cruel, hard, heartless, implacable, merciless, pitiless, relentless, remorseless, ruthless, uncaring, unfeeling, unsparing

unmethodical confused, desultory, disorderly, haphazard, irregular, muddled, orderless, random, systemless, unorganized, unsystematic

unmindful careless, forgetful, heedless, inattentive, indifferent, lax, neglectful, negligent, oblivious, remiss, slack, unheeding

unmistakable certain, clear, conspicuous, decided, distinct, evident, glaring, indisputable, manifest, obvious, palpable, patent, plain, positive, pronounced, sure, unambiguous, unequivocal

unmitigated 1. grim, harsh, intense, oppressive, persistent, relentless, unabated, unalleviated, unbroken, undiminished, unmodified, unqualified, unredeemed, unrelieved **2.** absolute, arrant, complete, consummate, downright, out-and-out, outright, perfect, rank, sheer, thorough, thoroughgoing, utter

unmoved 1. fast, firm, in place, in position, steady, unchanged, untouched **2.** cold, dry-eyed, impassive, indifferent, unaffected, unfeeling, unimpressed, unresponsive, unstirred, untouched **3.** determined, firm, inflexible, resolute, resolved, steadfast, undeviating, unshaken, unwavering

unnatural 1. aberrant, abnormal, anomalous, irregular, odd, perverse, perverted, unusual **2.** bizarre, extraordinary, freakish, outlandish, queer, strange, supernatural, unaccountable, uncanny **3.** affected, artificial, assumed, contrived, factitious, false, feigned, forced, insincere, laboured, mannered, phoney (*Sl.*), self-conscious, stagy, stiff, stilted, strained, studied, theatrical **4.** brutal, callous, cold-blooded, evil, fiendish, heartless, inhuman, monstrous, ruthless, savage, unfeeling, wicked

unnecessary dispensable, expendable, inessential, needless, nonessential, redundant, supererogatory, superfluous, surplus to requirements, uncalled-for, unneeded, unrequired, useless

unnerve confound, daunt, demoralize, disarm, disconcert, discourage, dishearten, dismay, dispirit, fluster, frighten, intimidate, rattle (*Inf.*), shake, throw off balance, unhinge, unman, upset

unnoticed disregarded, ignored, neglected, overlooked, undiscovered, unheeded, unobserved, unperceived, unrecognized, unremarked, unseen

unobtrusive humble, inconspicuous, keeping a low profile, low-key, meek, modest, quiet, restrained, retiring, self-effacing, subdued, unassuming, unnoticeable, unostentatious, unpretentious

unoccupied 1. empty, tenantless, uninhabited, untenanted, vacant 2. at leisure, disengaged, idle, inactive, unemployed

unofficial informal, personal, private, unauthorized, unconfirmed, wildcat

unorthodox abnormal, heterodox, irregular, unconventional, uncustomary, unusual, unwonted

unpaid 1. due, not discharged, outstanding, overdue, owing, payable, unsettled 2. honorary, unsalaried, voluntary

unpalatable bitter, disagreeable, displeasing, distasteful, offensive, repugnant, unappetizing, unattractive, uneatable, unpleasant, unsavoury

unparalleled beyond compare, consummate, exceptional, incomparable, matchless, peerless, rare, singular, superlative, unequalled, unique, unmatched, unprecedented, unrivalled, unsurpassed, without equal

unpardonable deplorable, disgraceful, indefensible, inexcusable, outrageous, scandalous, shameful, unforgivable, unjustifiable

unperturbed calm, collected, composed, cool, placid, poised, self-possessed, tranquil, undismayed, unflustered, unruffled, untroubled, unworried

unpleasant abhorrent, bad, disagreeable, displeasing, distasteful, ill-natured, irksome, nasty, objectionable, obnoxious, repulsive, troublesome, unattractive, unlikable, unlovely, unpalatable

unpolished 1. crude, rough, rude, sketchy, unfashioned, unfinished, unworked 2. uncivilized, uncouth, uncultivated, uncultured, unrefined, unsophisticated, vulgar

unpopular avoided, detested, disliked, not sought out, out in the cold, out of favour, rejected, shunned, unattractive, undesirable, unloved, unwanted, unwelcome

unprecedented abnormal, exceptional, extraordinary, freakish, new, novel, original, remarkable, singular, unexam-

pled, unheard-of, unparalleled, unrivalled, unusual

unpredictable chance, changeable, doubtful, erratic, fickle, fluky (*Inf.*), iffy, inconstant, random, unforeseeable, unreliable, unstable, variable

unprejudiced balanced, even-handed, fair, fair-minded, impartial, just, nonpartisan, objective, open-minded, unbiased, uninfluenced

unpremeditated extempore, impromptu, impulsive, offhand, off the cuff (*Inf.*), spontaneous, spur-of-the-moment, unplanned, unprepared

unprepared 1. half-baked (*Inf.*), ill-considered, incomplete, not thought out, unfinished, unplanned 2. caught napping, caught on the hop (*Brit. inf.*), surprised, taken aback, taken off guard, unaware, unready, unsuspecting 3. ad-lib, extemporaneous, improvised, off the cuff (*Inf.*), spontaneous

unpretentious homely, honest, humble, modest, plain, simple, straightforward, unaffected, unassuming, unimposing, unobtrusive, unostentatious, unspoiled

unprincipled amoral, corrupt, crooked, deceitful, devious, dishonest, immoral, tricky, unconscionable, underhand, unethical, unprofessional, unscrupulous

unproductive 1. bootless, fruitless, futile, idle, ineffective, inefficacious, otiose, unavailing, unprofitable, unremunerative, unrewarding, useless, vain, valueless, worthless 2. barren, dry, fruitless, sterile, unprolific

unprofessional 1. improper, lax, negligent, unethical, unfitting, unprincipled, unseemly, unworthy 2. amateur, amateurish, incompetent, inefficient, inexperienced, inexpert, untrained

unpromising adverse, discouraging, doubtful, gloomy, inauspicious, infelicitous, ominous, unfavourable, unpropitious

unprotected defenceless, exposed, helpless, naked, open, open to attack, pregnable, unarmed, undefended, unguarded, unsheltered, unshielded, vulnerable

unqualified 1. ill-equipped, incapable, incompetent, ineligible, not equal to, not up to, unfit, unprepared 2. categorical, downright, outright, unconditional, unmitigated, unreserved, unrestricted, without reservation 3. absolute, complete, consummate, downright, out-and-out, thorough, thoroughgoing, total, utter

unquestionable absolute, beyond a shadow of doubt, certain, clear, conclusive, definite, faultless, flawless, incontestable, incontrovertible, indisputable, indubitable, irrefutable, manifest, patent, perfect, self-evident, sure, undeniable, unequivocal, unmistakable

unravel 1. disentangle, extricate, free, separate, straighten out, undo, unknot, untangle, unwind **2.** clear up, explain, figure out (*Inf.*), get straight, get to the bottom of, interpret, make out, puzzle out, resolve, solve, work out

unreadable 1. crabbed, illegible, undecipherable **2.** badly written, dry as dust, heavy going, turgid

unreal 1. chimerical, dreamlike, fabulous, fanciful, fictitious, illusory, imaginary, make-believe, phantasmagoric, storybook, visionary **2.** hypothetical, immaterial, impalpable, insubstantial, intangible, mythical, nebulous **3.** artificial, fake, false, insincere, mock, ostensible, pretended, seeming, sham

unrealistic 1. half-baked (*Inf.*), impracticable, impractical, improbable, quixotic, romantic, starry-eyed, theoretical, unworkable **2.** non-naturalistic, unauthentic, unlifelike, unreal

unreasonable 1. excessive, exorbitant, extortionate, extravagant, immoderate, steep (*Brit. inf.*), too great, uncalled-for, undue, unfair, unjust, unwarranted **2.** arbitrary, biased, blinkered, capricious, erratic, headstrong, inconsistent, opinionated, quirky **3.** absurd, far-fetched, foolish, illogical, irrational, mad, nonsensical, preposterous, senseless, silly, stupid

unrefined 1. crude, raw, unfinished, unpolished, unpurified, untreated **2.** boorish, coarse, inelegant, rude, uncultured, unsophisticated, vulgar

unregenerate 1. godless, impious, profane, sinful, unconverted, unreformed, unrepentant, wicked **2.** hardened, intractable, obdurate, obstinate, recalcitrant, refractory, self-willed, stubborn

unrelated 1. different, dissimilar, not kin, not kindred, not related, unconnected, unlike **2.** beside the point, extraneous, inapplicable, inappropriate, irrelevant, not germane, unassociated, unconnected

unrelenting 1. cruel, implacable, inexorable, intransigent, merciless, pitiless, relentless, remorseless, ruthless, stern, tough, unsparing **2.** ceaseless, constant, continual, continuous, endless, incessant, perpetual, steady, unabated, unbroken, unremitting, unwavering

unreliable 1. disreputable, irresponsible, not conscientious, treacherous, undependable, unstable, untrustworthy **2.** deceptive, delusive, erroneous, fake, fallible, false, implausible, inaccurate, mistaken, specious, uncertain, unconvincing, unsound

unremitting assiduous, constant, continual, continuous, diligent, incessant, indefatigable, perpetual, relentless, remorseless, sedulous, unabated, unbroken, unceasing, unwavering, unwearied

unrepentant abandoned, callous, hardened, impenitent, incorrigible, not contrite, obdurate, shameless, unregenerate, unremorseful, unrepenting

unreserved 1. demonstrative, extrovert, forthright, frank, free, open, openhearted, outgoing, outspoken, uninhibited, unrestrained, unreticent **2.** absolute, complete, entire, full, total, unconditional, unlimited, unqualified, wholehearted, without reservation

unresolved doubtful, moot, open to question, pending, problematical, unanswered, undecided, undetermined, unsettled, unsolved, up in the air, vague, yet to be decided

unrest 1. agitation, disaffection, discontent, discord, dissatisfaction, dissension, protest, rebellion, sedition, strife, tumult, turmoil **2.** agitation, anxiety, disquiet, distress, perturbation, restlessness, uneasiness, worry

unrestrained abandoned, boisterous, free, immoderate, inordinate, intemperate, natural, unbounded, unbridled, unchecked, unconstrained, uncontrolled, unhindered, uninhibited, unrepressed

unrestricted 1. absolute, free, free-for-all (*Inf.*), freewheeling (*Inf.*), open, unbounded, uncircumscribed, unhindered, unlimited, unregulated **2.** clear, open, public, unobstructed, unopposed

unrivalled beyond compare, incomparable, matchless, nonpareil, peerless, supreme, unequalled, unexcelled, unmatched, unparalleled, unsurpassed, without equal

unruffled 1. calm, collected, composed, cool, peaceful, placid, serene, tranquil, undisturbed, unflustered, unmoved, unperturbed 2. even, flat, level, smooth, unbroken

unruly disobedient, disorderly, fractious, headstrong, insubordinate, intractable, lawless, mutinous, obstreperous, rebellious, refractory, riotous, rowdy, turbulent, uncontrollable, ungovernable, unmanageable, wayward, wild, wilful

unsafe dangerous, hazardous, insecure, perilous, precarious, risky, threatening, treacherous, uncertain, unreliable, unsound, unstable

unsaid left to the imagination, tacit, undeclared, unexpressed, unspoken, unstated, unuttered, unvoiced

unsanitary dirty, filthy, germ-ridden, infected, insalubrious, insanitary, sordid, squalid, unclean, unhealthy, unhygienic

unsatisfactory deficient, disappointing, displeasing, inadequate, insufficient, mediocre, not good enough, not up to par, not up to scratch (*Inf.*), poor, unacceptable, unsuitable, unworthy, weak

unsavoury 1. distasteful, nasty, objectionable, obnoxious, offensive, repellent, repugnant, repulsive, revolting, unpleasant 2. disagreeable, distasteful, nauseating, sickening, unappetizing, unpalatable

unscathed in one piece, safe, sound, unharmed, unhurt, uninjured, unmarked, unscarred, unscratched, untouched, whole

unscrupulous conscienceless, corrupt, crooked (*Inf.*), dishonest, dishonourable, exploitative, immoral, improper, knavish, roguish, ruthless, unconscientious, unconscionable, unethical, unprincipled

unseasonable ill-timed, inappropriate, inopportune, mistimed, out of keeping, unsuitable, untimely

unseat 1. throw, unhorse, unsaddle 2. depose, dethrone, discharge, dismiss, displace, oust, overthrow, remove

unseemly discreditable, disreputable, improper, inappropriate, indecorous, indelicate, in poor taste, out of keeping, out of place, unbecoming, unbefitting, undignified, unrefined, unsuitable

unseen concealed, hidden, invisible, lurking, obscure, undetected, unnoticed, unobserved, unobtrusive, unperceived, veiled

unselfish altruistic, charitable, devoted, disinterested, generous, humanitarian, kind, liberal, magnanimous, noble, self-denying, selfless, self-sacrificing

unsettle agitate, bother, confuse, discompose, disconcert, disorder, disturb, fluster, perturb, rattle (*Inf.*), ruffle, throw (*Inf.*), throw into confusion (disorder, uproar), throw off balance, trouble, unbalance, upset

unsettled 1. disorderly, insecure, shaky, unstable, unsteady 2. changeable, changing, inconstant, uncertain, unpredictable, variable 3. agitated, anxious, confused, disturbed, flustered, on edge, perturbed, restive, restless, shaken, tense, troubled, uneasy, unnerved 4. debatable, doubtful, moot, open, undecided, undetermined, unresolved 5. due, in arrears, outstanding, owing, payable, pending 6. uninhabited, unoccupied, unpeopled, unpopulated

unshakable absolute, constant, firm, fixed, resolute, staunch, steadfast, sure, unassailable, unswerving, unwavering, well-founded

unshaken calm, collected, composed, impassive, unaffected, unalarmed, undaunted, undismayed, undisturbed, unmoved, unperturbed, unruffled

unsheltered exposed, open, out in the open, unprotected, unscreened, unshielded

unsightly disagreeable, hideous, horrid, repulsive, revolting (*Inf.*), ugly, unattractive, unpleasant, unprepossessing

unskilful awkward, bungling, clumsy, fumbling, incompetent, inept, inexpert, maladroit, unhandy, unpractised, unworkmanlike

unskilled amateurish, inexperienced, uneducated, unprofessional, unqualified, untalented, untrained

unsociable chilly, cold, distant, hostile, inhospitable, introverted, reclusive, retiring, standoffish, uncongenial, unforthcoming, unfriendly, unneighbourly, unsocial, withdrawn

unsolicited free-will, gratuitous, spontaneous, unasked for, uncalled-for, unforced, uninvited, unrequested, unsought, unwelcome, voluntary, volunteered

unsophisticated 1. artless, childlike, guileless, inexperienced, ingenuous, innocent, naive, natural, unaffected, untutored, unworldly **2.** plain, simple, straightforward, uncomplex, uncomplicated, uninvolved, unrefined, unspecialized **3.** genuine, not artificial, pure, unadulterated

unsound 1. ailing, defective, delicate, deranged, diseased, frail, ill, in poor health, unbalanced, unhealthy, unhinged, unstable, unwell, weak **2.** defective, erroneous, fallacious, false, faulty, flawed, ill-founded, illogical, invalid, shaky, specious, unreliable, weak **3.** flimsy, insecure, not solid, rickety, shaky, tottering, unreliable, unsafe, unstable, unsteady, wobbly

unsparing 1. abundant, bountiful, generous, lavish, liberal, munificent, open-handed, plenteous, profuse, ungrudging, unstinting **2.** cold-blooded, hard, harsh, implacable, inexorable, relentless, rigorous, ruthless, severe, stern, stringent, uncompromising, unforgiving, unmerciful

unspeakable 1. beyond description, beyond words, inconceivable, indescribable, ineffable, inexpressible, overwhelming, unbelievable, unimaginable, unutterable, wonderful **2.** abominable, appalling, awful, bad, dreadful, evil, execrable, frightful, heinous, horrible, loathsome, monstrous, odious, repellent, shocking, too horrible for words

unspoiled, unspoilt 1. intact, perfect, preserved, unaffected, unblemished, unchanged, undamaged, unharmed, unimpaired, untouched **2.** artless, innocent, natural, unaffected, unassuming, unstudied, wholesome

unspoken 1. assumed, implicit, implied, left to the imagination, not put into words, not spelt out, tacit, taken for granted, undeclared, understood, unexpressed, unspoken, unstated **2.** mute, silent, unsaid, unuttered, voiceless, wordless

unstable 1. insecure, not fixed, precarious, rickety, risky, shaky, tottering, unsettled, unsteady, wobbly **2.** capricious, changeable, erratic, fitful, fluctuating, inconsistent, inconstant, irrational, unpredictable, unsteady, untrustworthy, vacillating, variable, volatile

unsteady 1. infirm, insecure, precarious, reeling, rickety, shaky, tottering, treacherous, unsafe, unstable, wobbly **2.** changeable, erratic, flickering, flighty, fluctuating, inconstant, irregular, unreliable, unsettled, vacillating, variable, volatile, wavering

unstinted abundant, ample, bountiful, full, generous, large, lavish, liberal, plentiful, prodigal, profuse

unsubstantial 1. airy, flimsy, fragile, frail, inadequate, light, slight, thin **2.** erroneous, full of holes, ill-founded, superficial, tenuous, unsound, unsupported, weak **3.** dreamlike, fanciful, illusory, imaginary, immaterial, impalpable, visionary

unsubstantiated open to question, unattested, unconfirmed, uncorroborated, unestablished, unproven, unsupported

unsuccessful 1. abortive, bootless, failed, fruitless, futile, ineffective, unavailing, unproductive, useless, vain **2.** balked, defeated, foiled, frustrated, hapless, ill-starred, losing, luckless, unfortunate, unlucky

unsuitable improper, inapposite, inappropriate, inapt, incompatible, incongruous, ineligible, infelicitous, out of character, out of keeping, out of place, unacceptable, unbecoming, unbefitting, unfitting, unseasonable, unseemly, unsuited

unsullied clean, immaculate, pristine, pure, spotless, stainless, unblackened, unblemished, uncorrupted, undefiled, unsoiled, untainted, untarnished, untouched

unsung anonymous, disregarded, neglected, unacclaimed, unacknowledged, uncelebrated, unhailed, unhonoured, unknown, unnamed, unrecognized

unsure 1. insecure, lacking in confidence, unassured, unconfident **2.** distrustful, doubtful, dubious, hesitant, in a quandary, irresolute, mistrustful, sceptical, suspicious, unconvinced, undecided

unsurpassed consummate, exceptional, incomparable, matchless, nonpareil, paramount, peerless, second to none, superlative, supreme, transcendent, unequalled, unexcelled, unparalleled, unrivalled, without an equal

unsuspecting confiding, credulous, gullible, inexperienced, ingenuous, innocent, naive, off guard, trustful, trusting, unconscious, unsuspicious, unwarned, unwary

unswerving constant, dedicated, devoted, direct, firm, resolute, single-minded, staunch, steadfast, steady, true, undeviating, unfaltering, unflagging, untiring, unwavering

unsympathetic apathetic, callous, cold, compassionless (*Rare*), cruel, hard, harsh, heartless, indifferent, insensitive, soulless, stony-hearted, uncompassionate, unconcerned, unfeeling, unkind, unmoved, unpitying, unresponsive

unsystematic chaotic, confused, disorderly, disorganized, haphazard, irregular, jumbled, muddled, random, slapdash, unmethodical, unorganized, unplanned, unsystematized

untamed barbarous, feral, fierce, not broken in, savage, unbroken, uncontrollable, undomesticated, untameable, wild

untangle clear up, disentangle, explain, extricate, solve, straighten out, unravel, unsnarl

untarnished bright, burnished, clean, glowing, immaculate, impeccable, polished, pure, shining, spotless, unblemished, unimpeachable, unsoiled, unspotted, unstained, unsullied

untenable fallacious, flawed, groundless, illogical, indefensible, insupportable, shaky, unreasonable, unsound, unsustainable, weak

unthinkable 1. absurd, illogical, impossible, improbable, not on (*Inf.*), out of the question, preposterous, unlikely, unreasonable **2.** beyond belief, beyond the bounds of possibility, implausible, inconceivable, incredible, insupportable, unbelievable, unimaginable

unthinking 1. blundering, inconsiderate, insensitive, rude, selfish, tactless, thoughtless, undiplomatic **2.** careless, heedless, impulsive, inadvertent, instinctive, mechanical, negligent, oblivious, rash, senseless, unconscious, unmindful, vacant, witless

untidy bedraggled, chaotic, cluttered, disorderly, higgledy-piggledy (*Inf.*), jumbled, littered, messy, muddled, muddly, mussy (*U.S. inf.*), rumpled, slatternly, slipshod, sloppy (*Inf.*), slovenly, topsyturvy, unkempt

untie free, loosen, release, unbind, undo, unfasten, unknot, unlace

untimely awkward, badly timed, early, ill-timed, inappropriate, inauspicious, inconvenient, inopportune, mistimed, premature, unfortunate, unseasonable, unsuitable

untiring constant, dedicated, deter-

mined, devoted, dogged, incessant, indefatigable, patient, persevering, persistent, staunch, steady, tireless, unfaltering, unflagging, unremitting, unwearied

untold 1. indescribable, inexpressible, undreamed of, unimaginable, unspeakable, unthinkable, unutterable **2.** countless, incalculable, innumerable, measureless, myriad, numberless, uncountable, uncounted, unnumbered **3.** hidden, private, secret, undisclosed, unknown, unpublished, unrecounted, unrelated, unrevealed

untouched 1. intact, safe and sound, undamaged, unharmed, unhurt, uninjured, unscathed, without a scratch **2.** dry-eyed, indifferent, unaffected, unconcerned, unimpressed, unmoved, unstirred

untoward 1. annoying, awkward, disastrous, ill-timed, inconvenient, inimical, irritating, troublesome, unfortunate, vexatious **2.** adverse, contrary, inauspicious, inopportune, unfavourable, unlucky, untimely **3.** improper, inappropriate, indecorous, out of place, unbecoming, unfitting, unseemly, unsuitable

untrained amateur, green, inexperienced, raw, uneducated, unpractised, unqualified, unschooled, unskilled, untaught, untutored

untried in the experimental stage, new, novel, unattempted, unessayed, unproved, untested

untroubled calm, composed, cool, peaceful, placid, serene, steady, tranquil, unagitated, unconcerned, undisturbed, unflappable (*Inf.*), unflustered, unperturbed, unruffled, unstirred, unworried

untrue 1. deceptive, dishonest, erroneous, fallacious, false, inaccurate, incorrect, lying, misleading, mistaken, sham, spurious, untruthful, wrong **2.** deceitful, disloyal, faithless, false, forsworn, inconstant, perfidious, traitorous, treacherous, two-faced, unfaithful, untrustworthy **3.** deviant, distorted, inaccurate, off, out of line, out of true, wide

untrustworthy capricious, deceitful, devious, dishonest, disloyal, fairweather, faithless, false, fickle, fly-by-night (*Inf.*), not to be depended on, slippery, treacherous, tricky, two-faced, undependable, unfaithful, unreliable, untrue, untrusty

untruth 1. deceitfulness, duplicity, falsity, inveracity (*Rare*), lying, mendacity, perjury, truthlessness, untruthfulness **2**. deceit, fabrication, falsehood, falsification, fib, fiction, lie, prevarication, story, tale, trick, whopper (*Inf.*)

untruthful crooked (*Inf.*), deceitful, deceptive, dishonest, dissembling, false, fibbing, hypocritical, lying, mendacious

untutored 1. ignorant, illiterate, uneducated, unlearned, unschooled, untrained, unversed **2**. artless, inexperienced, simple, unpractised, unrefined, unsophisticated

unused 1. fresh, intact, new, pristine, untouched **2**. *With* to a stranger to, inexperienced in, new to, not ready for, not up to, unaccustomed to, unfamiliar with, unhabituated to **3**. available, extra, left, leftover, remaining, unconsumed, unexhausted, unutilized

unusual abnormal, atypical, bizarre, curious, different, exceptional, extraordinary, odd, out of the ordinary, phenomenal, queer, rare, remarkable, singular, strange, surprising, uncommon, unconventional, unexpected, unfamiliar, unwonted

unutterable beyond words, extreme, indescribable, ineffable, overwhelming, unimaginable, unspeakable

unvarnished bare, candid, frank, honest, naked, plain, pure, pure and simple, simple, sincere, stark, straightforward, unadorned, unembellished

unveil bare, bring to light, disclose, divulge, expose, lay bare, lay open, make known, make public, reveal, uncover

unwanted *de trop*, going begging, outcast, rejected, superfluous, surplus to requirements, unasked, undesired, uninvited, unneeded, unsolicited, unwelcome, useless

unwarranted gratuitous, groundless, indefensible, inexcusable, uncalled-for, unjust, unjustified, unprovoked, unreasonable, wrong

unwary careless, hasty, heedless, imprudent, incautious, indiscreet, rash, reckless, thoughtless, uncircumspect, unguarded, unwatchful

unwavering consistent, dedicated, determined, resolute, single-minded, staunch, steadfast, steady, undeviating, unfaltering, unflagging, unshakable, unshaken, unswerving, untiring

unwelcome 1. excluded, rejected, unacceptable, undesirable, uninvited, unpopular, unwanted, unwished for **2**. disagreeable, displeasing, distasteful, thankless, undesirable, unpleasant

unwell ailing, ill, indisposed, in poor health, off colour, out of sorts, poorly (*Inf.*), sick, sickly, under the weather (*Inf.*), unhealthy

unwholesome 1. deleterious, harmful, insalubrious, junk (*Inf.*), noxious, poisonous, tainted, unhealthy, unnourishing **2**. bad, corrupting, degrading, demoralizing, depraving, evil, immoral, perverting, wicked **3**. anaemic, pale, pallid, pasty, sickly, wan

unwieldy 1. awkward, burdensome, cumbersome, inconvenient, unhandy, unmanageable **2**. bulky, clumsy, hefty, massive, ponderous, ungainly, weighty

unwilling averse, demurring, disinclined, grudging, indisposed, laggard (*Rare*), loath, not in the mood, opposed, reluctant, resistant, unenthusiastic

unwind 1. disentangle, slacken, uncoil, undo, unravel, unreel, unroll, untwine, untwist **2**. calm down, let oneself go, loosen up, quieten down, relax, sit back, slow down, take a break, take it easy (*Inf.*), wind down

unwise foolhardy, foolish, ill-advised, ill-considered, ill-judged, impolitic, improvident, imprudent, inadvisable, indiscreet, injudicious, irresponsible, rash, reckless, senseless, short-sighted, silly, stupid

unwitting 1. ignorant, innocent, unaware, unconscious, unknowing, unsuspecting **2**. accidental, chance, inadvertent, involuntary, undesigned, unintended, unintentional, unmeant, unplanned

unwonted atypical, extraordinary, infrequent, out of the ordinary, peculiar, rare, seldom seen, singular, unaccustomed, uncommon, uncustomary, unexpected, unfamiliar, unheard-of, unusual

unworldly 1. abstract, celestial, metaphysical, nonmaterialistic, religious, spiritual, transcendental **2**. green, idealistic, inexperienced, innocent, naive, raw, trusting, unsophisticated **3**. ethereal, extraterrestrial, otherworldly, unearthly

unworthy 1. *With* of beneath the dignity of, improper, inappropriate, out of character, out of place, unbecoming, unbefitting, unfitting, unseemly, unsuitable **2**. base, contemptible, degrading, discreditable, disgraceful, dishonourable, disreputable, ignoble, shameful **3**. ineligible, not deserving of, not fit for, not good enough, not worth, undeserving

unwritten 1. oral, unrecorded, vocal, word-of-mouth 2. accepted, conventional, customary, tacit, traditional, understood, unformulated

unyielding adamant, determined, firm, hardline, immovable, inexorable, inflexible, intractable, obdurate, obstinate, relentless, resolute, rigid, staunch, steadfast, stubborn, tough, unbending, uncompromising, unwavering

up-and-coming ambitious, eager, go-getting (*Inf.*), on the make (*Sl.*), promising, pushing

upbeat *adj.* buoyant, cheerful, cheery, encouraging, favourable, forward-looking, heartening, hopeful, looking up, optimistic, positive, promising, rosy

upbraid admonish, berate, blame, carpet (*Inf.*), castigate, censure, chide, condemn, dress down (*Inf.*), lecture, rebuke, reprimand, reproach, reprove, scold, take to task, tell off (*Inf.*), tick off (*Inf.*)

upbringing breeding, bringing-up, care, cultivation, education, nurture, raising, rearing, tending, training

update amend, bring up to date, modernize, renew, revise

upgrade advance, ameliorate, better, elevate, enhance, improve, promote, raise

upheaval cataclysm, disorder, disruption, disturbance, eruption, overthrow, revolution, turmoil, violent change

uphill *adj.* 1. ascending, climbing, mounting, rising 2. arduous, difficult, exhausting, gruelling, hard, laborious, punishing, Sisyphean, strenuous, taxing, tough, wearisome

uphold advocate, aid, back, champion, defend, encourage, endorse, hold to, justify, maintain, promote, stand by, support, sustain, vindicate

upkeep 1. conservation, keep, maintenance, preservation, repair, running, subsistence, support, sustenance 2. expenditure, expenses, oncosts (*Brit.*), operating costs, outlay, overheads, running costs

uplift *v.* 1. elevate, heave, hoist, lift up, raise 2. advance, ameliorate, better, civilize, cultivate, edify, improve, inspire, raise, refine, upgrade ~*n.* 3. advancement, betterment, cultivation, edification, enhancement, enlightenment, enrichment, improvement, refinement

upper 1. high, higher, loftier, top, topmost 2. elevated, eminent, greater, important, superior

upper-class aristocratic, blue-blooded, highborn, high-class, noble, patrician, top-drawer, well-bred

upper hand advantage, ascendancy, control, dominion, edge, mastery, superiority, supremacy, sway, whip hand

uppermost 1. highest, loftiest, most elevated, top, topmost, upmost 2. chief, dominant, foremost, greatest, leading, main, paramount, predominant, preeminent, primary, principal, supreme

uppish affected, arrogant, conceited, high and mighty (*Inf.*), hoity-toity (*Inf.*), overweening, presumptuous, putting on airs, self-important, snobbish, stuck-up (*Inf.*), supercilious, toffee-nosed (*Sl.*), uppity (*Inf.*)

uppity bigheaded (*Inf.*), bumptious, cocky, conceited, full of oneself, impertinent, on one's high horse (*Inf.*), overweening, self-important, swanky (*Inf.*), uppish (*Brit. inf.*)

upright 1. erect, on end, perpendicular, straight, vertical 2. *Fig.* above board, conscientious, ethical, faithful, good, high-minded, honest, honourable, incorruptible, just, principled, righteous, straightforward, true, trustworthy, unimpeachable, virtuous

uprightness fairness, faithfulness, goodness, high-mindedness, honesty, incorruptibility, integrity, justice, probity, rectitude, righteousness, straightforwardness, trustworthiness, virtue

uprising disturbance, insurgence, insurrection, mutiny, outbreak, putsch, rebellion, revolt, revolution, rising, upheaval

uproar brawl, brouhaha, clamour, commotion, confusion, din, furore, hubbub, hullabaloo, hurly-burly, mayhem, noise, outcry, pandemonium, racket, riot, ruckus (*Inf.*), ruction (*Inf.*), rumpus, turbulence, turmoil

uproarious 1. clamorous, confused, disorderly, loud, noisy, riotous, rowdy, tempestuous, tumultuous, turbulent, wild 2. convulsive (*Inf.*), hilarious, hysterical, killing (*Inf.*), rib-tickling, rip-roaring (*Inf.*), screamingly funny, side-splitting, very funny 3. boisterous, gleeful, loud, rollicking, unrestrained

uproot 1. deracinate, dig up, extirpate, grub up, pull out by the roots, pull up, rip up, root out, weed out **2.** deracinate, disorient, displace, exile **3.** destroy, do away with, eliminate, eradicate, extirpate, remove, wipe out

ups and downs changes, ebb and flow, fluctuations, moods, vicissitudes, wheel of fortune

upset v. **1.** capsize, knock over, overturn, spill, tip over, topple over **2.** change, disorder, disorganize, disturb, mess up, mix up, put out of order, spoil, turn topsy-turvy **3.** agitate, bother, discompose, disconcert, dismay, disquiet, distress, disturb, fluster, grieve, perturb, ruffle, throw (someone) off balance, trouble **4.** be victorious over, conquer, defeat, get the better of, overcome, overthrow, triumph over, win against the odds ~n. **5.** defeat, reverse, shake-up (*Inf.*), sudden change, surprise **6.** bug (*Inf.*), complaint, disorder, disturbance, illness, indisposition, malady, queasiness, sickness **7.** agitation, bother, discomposure, disquiet, distress, disturbance, shock, trouble, worry ~adj. **8.** capsized, overturned, spilled, tipped over, toppled, tumbled, upside down **9.** disordered, disturbed, gippy (*Sl.*), ill, poorly (*Inf.*), queasy, sick **10.** agitated, bothered, confused, disconcerted, dismayed, disquieted, distressed, disturbed, frantic, grieved, hurt, overwrought, put out, ruffled, troubled, worried **11.** at sixes and sevens, chaotic, confused, disordered, in disarray *or* disorder, messed up, muddled, topsy-turvy **12.** beaten, conquered, defeated, overcome, overthrown, vanquished

upshot conclusion, consequence, culmination, end, end result, event, finale, issue, outcome, payoff (*Inf.*), result

upside down 1. bottom up, inverted, on its head, overturned, upturned, wrong side up **2.** *Inf.* chaotic, confused, disordered, higgledy-piggledy (*Inf.*), in confusion (chaos, disarray, disorder), jumbled, muddled, topsy-turvy

upstanding 1. ethical, good, honest, honourable, incorruptible, moral, principled, true, trustworthy, upright **2.** firm, hale and hearty, hardy, healthy, robust, stalwart, strong, sturdy, upright, vigorous

upstart arriviste, nobody, *nouveau riche*, parvenu, social climber, status seeker

uptight anxious, edgy, nervy (*Brit.*

inf.), on edge, on the defensive, prickly, tense, uneasy, withdrawn

up-to-date all the rage, current, fashionable, in, in vogue, modern, newest, now (*Inf.*), stylish, trendy (*Brit. inf.*), up-to-the-minute, with it (*Inf.*)

upturn n. advancement, boost, improvement, increase, recovery, revival, upsurge, upswing

urban city, civic, inner-city, metropolitan, municipal, oppidan (*Rare*), town

urbane civil, civilized, cosmopolitan, courteous, cultivated, cultured, debonair, elegant, mannerly, polished, refined, smooth, sophisticated, suave, well-bred, well-mannered

urbanity charm, civility, courtesy, culture, elegance, grace, mannerliness, polish, refinement, sophistication, suavity, worldliness

urchin brat, gamin, guttersnipe, mudlark (*Sl.*), ragamuffin, street Arab, waif, young rogue

urge v. **1.** appeal to, beg, beseech, entreat, exhort, implore, plead, press, solicit **2.** advise, advocate, champion, counsel, insist on, push for, recommend, support **3.** compel, constrain, drive, egg on, encourage, force, goad, hasten, impel, incite, induce, instigate, press, propel, push, spur, stimulate ~n. **4.** compulsion, desire, drive, fancy, impulse, itch, longing, wish, yearning, yen (*Inf.*)

urgency exigency, extremity, gravity, hurry, imperativeness, importance, importunity, necessity, need, pressure, seriousness, stress

urgent 1. compelling, critical, crucial, immediate, imperative, important, instant, not to be delayed, pressing, top-priority **2.** clamorous, earnest, importunate, insistent, intense, persistent, persuasive

urinate leak (*Sl.*), make water, micturate, pass water, pee (*Sl.*), spend a penny (*Brit. inf.*), tinkle (*Brit. inf.*), wee (*Inf.*), wee-wee (*Inf.*)

usable at one's disposal, available, current, fit for use, functional, in running order, practical, ready for use, serviceable, utilizable, valid, working

usage 1. control, employment, handling, management, operation, regulation, running, treatment, use **2.** convention, custom, form, habit, matter of course, method, mode, practice, procedure, regime, routine, rule, tradition, wont

use v. **1.** apply, avail oneself of, bring into play, employ, exercise, find a use for, make use of, operate, ply, practise, profit by, put to use, turn to account, utilize, wield, work **2.** act towards, behave towards, deal with, exploit, handle, manipulate, misuse, take advantage of, treat **3.** consume, exhaust, expend, run through, spend, waste ~n. **4.** application, employment, exercise, handling, operation, practice, service, treatment, usage, wear and tear **5.** advantage, application, avail, benefit, good, help, mileage (*Inf.*), point, profit, service, usefulness, utility, value, worth **6.** custom, habit, practice, usage, way, wont **7.** call, cause, end, necessity, need, object, occasion, point, purpose, reason

used cast-off, hand-me-down (*Inf.*), nearly new, not new, reach-me-down (*Inf.*), second-hand, shopsoiled, worn

used to accustomed to, at home in, attuned to, familiar with, given to, habituated to, hardened to, in the habit of, inured to, tolerant of, wont to

useful advantageous, all-purpose, beneficial, effective, fruitful, general-purpose, helpful, of help, of service, of use, practical, profitable, salutary, serviceable, valuable, worthwhile

useless 1. bootless, disadvantageous, fruitless, futile, hopeless, idle, impractical, ineffective, ineffectual, of no use, pointless, profitless, unavailing, unproductive, unworkable, vain, valueless, worthless **2.** *Inf.* hopeless, incompetent, ineffectual, inept, no good, stupid, weak

use up absorb, burn up, consume, deplete, devour, drain, exhaust, finish, fritter away, run through, squander, swallow up, waste

usher n. **1.** attendant, doorkeeper, escort, guide, usherette ~v. **2.** conduct, direct, escort, guide, lead, pilot, show in *or* out, steer **3.** *Usually with* in bring in, herald, inaugurate, initiate, introduce, launch, open the door to, pave the way for, precede, ring in

usual accustomed, common, constant, customary, everyday, expected, familiar, fixed, general, habitual, normal, ordinary, regular, routine, standard, stock, typical, wonted

usually as a rule, as is the custom, as is usual, by and large, commonly, for the most part, generally, habitually, in the main, mainly, mostly, most often, normally, on the whole, ordinarily, regularly, routinely

usurp appropriate, arrogate, assume, commandeer, infringe upon, lay hold of, seize, take, take over, wrest

utensil apparatus, contrivance, device, gadget, implement, instrument, tool

utilitarian down-to-earth, effective, efficient, functional, practical, pragmatic, sensible, serviceable, useful

utility advantageousness, avail, benefit, convenience, efficacy, fitness, point, practicality, profit, service, serviceableness, use, usefulness

utilize appropriate, avail oneself of, employ, have recourse to, make the most of, make use of, profit by, put to use, resort to, take advantage of, turn to account, use

utmost adj. **1.** chief, extreme, greatest, highest, maximum, paramount, pre-eminent, supreme **2.** extreme, farthest, final, last, most distant, outermost, remotest, uttermost ~n. **3.** best, greatest, most hardest, highest, most

Utopia bliss, Eden, Erewhon, Garden of Eden, heaven, ideal life, paradise, perfect place, seventh heaven, Shangri-la

Utopian 1. adj. airy, chimerical, dream, fanciful, fantasy, ideal, idealistic, illusory, imaginary, impractical, perfect, romantic, visionary **2.** n. Don Quixote, dreamer, idealist, romanticist, visionary

utter[1] v. **1.** articulate, enunciate, express, pronounce, put into words, say, speak, verbalize, vocalize, voice **2.** declare, divulge, give expression to, make known, proclaim, promulgate, publish, reveal, state

utter[2] adj. absolute, arrant, complete, consummate, downright, entire, out-and-out, perfect, sheer, stark, thorough, thoroughgoing, total, unmitigated, unqualified

utterance 1. announcement, declaration, expression, opinion, remark, speech, statement, words **2.** articulation, delivery, ejaculation, expression, verbalization, vocalization, vociferation

utterly absolutely, completely, entirely, extremely, fully, perfectly, thoroughly, totally, to the core, wholly

uttermost extreme, farthest, final, last, outermost, remotest, utmost

V

vacancy 1. job, opening, opportunity, position, post, room, situation 2. absent-mindedness, abstraction, blankness, inanity, inattentiveness, incomprehension, incuriousness, lack of interest, vacuousness 3. emptiness, gap, space, vacuum, void

vacant 1. available, disengaged, empty, free, idle, not in use, to let, unemployed, unengaged, unfilled, unoccupied, untenanted, void 2. absent-minded, abstracted, blank, dreaming, dreamy, expressionless, idle, inane, incurious, thoughtless, unthinking, vacuous

vacate depart, evacuate, give up, go away, leave, leave empty, move out of, quit, relinquish possession of, withdraw

vacillate be irresolute or indecisive, blow hot and cold (*Inf.*), fluctuate, haver, hesitate, keep changing one's mind, oscillate, reel, rock, shillyshally (*Inf.*), sway, swither (*Scot. dialect*), waver

vacillating hesitant, in two minds (*Inf.*), irresolute, oscillating, shillyshallying (*Inf.*), uncertain, unresolved, wavering

vacillation fluctuation, hesitation, inconstancy, indecisiveness, irresoluteness, irresolution, shillyshallying (*Inf.*), unsteadiness, wavering

vacuity 1. blankness, emptiness, inanity, incognizance, incomprehension, vacuousness 2. emptiness, nothingness, space, vacuum, void

vacuous 1. blank, inane, stupid, uncomprehending, unintelligent, vacant 2. empty, unfilled, vacant, void

vacuum emptiness, free space, gap, nothingness, space, vacuity, void

vagabond 1. *n.* beggar, bum (*U.S. inf.*), down-and-out, hobo (*U.S.*), itinerant, knight of the road, migrant, nomad, outcast, rascal, rover, tramp, vagrant, wanderer, wayfarer 2. *adj.* destitute, down and out, drifting, fly-by-night (*Inf.*), footloose, homeless, idle, itinerant, journeying, nomadic, rootless, roving, shiftless, vagrant, wandering

vagary caprice, crotchet, fancy, humour, megrim (*Archaic*), notion, whim, whimsy

vagrant 1. *n.* beggar, bird of passage, bum (*U.S. inf.*), hobo (*U.S.*), itinerant, person of no fixed address, rolling stone, tramp, wanderer 2. *adj.* itinerant, nomadic, roaming, rootless, roving, unsettled, vagabond

vague amorphous, blurred, dim, doubtful, fuzzy, generalized, hazy, ill-defined, imprecise, indefinite, indeterminate, indistinct, lax, loose, nebulous, obscure, shadowy, uncertain, unclear, unknown, unspecified, woolly

vaguely absent-mindedly, dimly, evasively, imprecisely, in a general way, obscurely, slightly, through a glass darkly, vacantly

vagueness ambiguity, impreciseness, inexactitude, lack of preciseness, looseness, obscurity

vain 1. arrogant, bigheaded (*Inf.*), cocky, conceited, egotistical, inflated, narcissistic, ostentatious, overweening, peacockish, pleased with oneself, proud, self-important, stuck-up (*Inf.*), swaggering, swanky (*Inf.*), swollen-headed (*Inf.*), vainglorious 2. abortive, empty, fruitless, futile, hollow, idle, nugatory, pointless, senseless, time-wasting, trifling, trivial, unavailing, unimportant, unproductive, unprofitable, useless, worthless 3. **be vain** have a high opinion of oneself, have a swelled head (*Inf.*), have one's head turned, think a lot of oneself, think oneself it (*Inf.*), think oneself the cat's whiskers or pyjamas (*Sl.*) 4. **in vain** bootless, fruitless(ly), ineffectual(ly), to no avail, to no purpose, unsuccessful(ly), useless(ly), vain(ly), wasted, without success

valediction adieu, farewell, goodbye, leave-taking, sendoff (*Inf.*), *vale*

valedictory *adj.* farewell, final, parting

valetudinarian *adj.* delicate, feeble, frail, hypochondriac, infirm, in poor health, invalid, sickly, weakly

valiant bold, brave, courageous, dauntless, doughty, fearless, gallant, heroic, indomitable, intrepid, lion-hearted, plucky, redoubtable, stouthearted, valorous, worthy

valid 1. binding, cogent, conclusive, convincing, efficacious, efficient, good, just, logical, powerful, sound, substantial, telling, weighty, well-founded, well-grounded 2. authentic, bona fide, genuine, in force, lawful, legal, legally binding, legitimate, official

validate authenticate, authorize, certify, confirm, corroborate, endorse, legalize, make legally binding, ratify, set one's seal on *or* to, substantiate

validity 1. cogency, force, foundation, grounds, point, power, soundness, strength, substance, weight 2. authority, lawfulness, legality, legitimacy, right

valley coomb, cwm (*Welsh*), dale, dell, depression, dingle, glen, hollow, strath (*Scot.*), vale

valorous bold, brave, courageous, dauntless, doughty, fearless, gallant, heroic, intrepid, lion-hearted, plucky, valiant

valour boldness, bravery, courage, derring-do (*Archaic*), doughtiness, fearlessness, gallantry, heroism, intrepidity, lion-heartedness, spirit

valuable *adj.* 1. costly, dear, expensive, high-priced, precious 2. beneficial, cherished, esteemed, estimable, held dear, helpful, important, prized, profitable, serviceable, treasured, useful, valued, worthwhile, worthy ~*n.* 3. *Usually plural* heirloom, treasure(s)

value *n.* 1. cost, equivalent, market price, monetary worth, rate 2. advantage, benefit, desirability, help, importance, merit, profit, serviceableness, significance, use, usefulness, utility, worth 3. *Plural* code of behaviour, ethics, (moral) standards, principles ~*v.* 4. account, appraise, assess, compute, estimate, evaluate, price, put a price on, rate, set at, survey 5. appreciate, cherish, esteem, hold dear, hold in high regard *or* esteem, prize, regard highly, respect, set store by, treasure

valued cherished, dear, esteemed, highly regarded, loved, prized, treasured

valueless miserable, no good, of no earthly use, of no value, unsaleable, useless, worthless

vamoose clear off (*Inf.*), decamp, do a bunk (*Inf.*), go away, make off, make oneself scarce (*Inf.*), run away, scarper (*Brit. sl.*), scram (*Inf.*), skedaddle (*Inf.*), take flight, take oneself off

vanguard advance guard, forefront, forerunners, front, front line, front rank, leaders, spearhead, trailblazers, trendsetters, van

vanish become invisible, be lost to sight, die out, disappear, disappear from sight *or* from the face of the earth, dissolve, evanesce, evaporate, exit, fade (away), melt (away)

vanity 1. affected ways, airs, arrogance, bigheadedness (*Inf.*), conceit, conceitedness, egotism, narcissism, ostentation, pretension, pride, self-admiration, self-love, showing off (*Inf.*), swollen-headedness (*Inf.*), vainglory 2. emptiness, frivolity, fruitlessness, futility, hollowness, inanity, pointlessness, profitlessness, triviality, unproductiveness, unreality, unsubstantiality, uselessness, worthlessness

vanquish beat, conquer, crush, defeat, get the upper hand over, master, overcome, overpower, overwhelm, put down, put to flight, put to rout, quell, reduce, repress, rout, subdue, subjugate, triumph over

vapid 1. bland, dead, flat, flavourless, insipid, lifeless, milk-and-water, stale, tasteless, unpalatable, watery, weak, wishy-washy (*Inf.*) 2. boring, colourless, dull, flat, limp, tame, tedious, tiresome, uninspiring, uninteresting

vapour breath, dampness, exhalation, fog, fumes, haze, miasma, mist, smoke, steam

variable capricious, chameleonic, changeable, fickle, fitful, flexible, fluctuating, inconstant, mercurial, mutable, protean, shifting, temperamental, unstable, unsteady, vacillating, wavering

variance 1. difference, difference of opinion, disagreement, discord, discrepancy, dissension, dissent, divergence, inconsistency, lack of harmony, strife, variation 2. **at variance** at loggerheads, at odds, at sixes and sevens (*Inf.*), conflicting, in disagreement, in opposition, out of harmony, out of line

variant 1. *adj.* alternative, derived, different, divergent, exceptional, modified 2. *n.* alternative, derived form, development, modification, sport (*Biol.*), variation

variation alteration, break in routine, change, departure, departure from the norm, deviation, difference, discrepancy, diversification, diversity, innovation, modification, novelty, variety

varied assorted, different, diverse, heterogeneous, miscellaneous, mixed, motley, sundry, various

variegated diversified, many-coloured, motley, mottled, parti-coloured, pied, streaked, varicoloured

variety 1. change, difference, discrepancy, diversification, diversity, many-sidedness, multifariousness, variation **2.** array, assortment, collection, cross section, intermixture, medley, miscellany, mixture, multiplicity, range **3.** brand, breed, category, class, kind, make, order, sort, species, strain, type

various assorted, different, differing, disparate, distinct, divers (*Archaic*), diverse, diversified, heterogeneous, many, many-sided, miscellaneous, several, sundry, varied, variegated

varnish *v.* adorn, decorate, embellish, gild, glaze, gloss, japan, lacquer, polish, shellac

vary alter, alternate, be unlike, change, depart, differ, disagree, diverge, diversify, fluctuate, intermix, modify, permutate, reorder, transform

varying changing, different, distinct, distinguishable, diverse, fluctuating, inconsistent

vassal bondman, bondservant, bondsman, retainer, serf, slave, subject, thrall

vassalage bondage, dependence, serfdom, servitude, slavery, subjection, thraldom

vast astronomical, boundless, colossal, enormous, extensive, gigantic, great, huge, illimitable, immeasurable, immense, limitless, mammoth, massive, measureless, monstrous, monumental, never-ending, prodigious, sweeping, tremendous, unbounded, unlimited, vasty (*Archaic*), voluminous, wide

vault¹ *v.* bound, clear, hurdle, jump, leap, spring

vault² *n.* **1.** arch, ceiling, roof, span **2.** catacomb, cellar, crypt, mausoleum, tomb, undercroft **3.** depository, repository, strongroom ~*v.* **4.** arch, bend, bow, curve, overarch, span

vaulted arched, cavernous, domed, hemispheric

vaunt boast about, brag about, crow about, exult in, flaunt, give oneself airs about, make a display of, make much of, parade, prate about, show off, talk big about (*Inf.*)

veer be deflected, change, change course, change direction, sheer, shift, swerve, tack, turn

vegetate 1. be inert, deteriorate, exist, go to seed, idle, languish, loaf, moulder, stagnate **2.** burgeon, germinate, grow, shoot, spring, sprout, swell

vehemence ardour, eagerness, earnestness, emphasis, energy, enthusiasm, fervency, fervour, fire, force, forcefulness, heat, impetuosity, intensity, keenness, passion, verve, vigour, violence, warmth, zeal

vehement ardent, eager, earnest, emphatic, enthusiastic, fervent, fervid, fierce, forceful, forcible, impassioned, impetuous, intense, passionate, powerful, strong, violent, zealous

vehicle *Fig.* apparatus, channel, means, means of expression, mechanism, medium, organ

veil 1. *v.* cloak, conceal, cover, dim, disguise, hide, mantle, mask, obscure, screen, shield **2.** *n.* blind, cloak, cover, curtain, disguise, film, mask, screen, shade, shroud

veiled concealed, covert, disguised, hinted at, implied, masked, suppressed

vein 1. blood vessel, course, current, lode, seam, stratum, streak, stripe **2.** dash, hint, strain, streak, thread, trait **3.** attitude, bent, character, faculty, humour, mode, mood, note, style, temper, tenor, tone, turn

velocity celerity, fleetness, impetus, pace, quickness, rapidity, speed, swiftness

velvety delicate, downy, mossy, smooth, soft, velutinous, velvet-like

venal bent (*Sl.*), corrupt, corruptible, crooked (*Inf.*), dishonourable, grafting, mercenary, prostituted, purchasable, rapacious, simoniacal, sordid, unprincipled

vendetta bad blood, blood feud, feud, quarrel

veneer *n. Fig.* appearance, façade, false front, finish, front, gloss, guise, mask, pretence, semblance, show

venerable august, esteemed, grave, honoured, respected, revered, reverenced, sage, sedate, wise, worshipped

venerate adore, esteem, hold in awe, honour, look up to, respect, revere, reverence, worship

veneration adoration, awe, deference, esteem, respect, reverence, worship

vengeance 1. an eye for an eye, avenging, lex talionis, reprisal, requital, retaliation, retribution, revenge, settling of scores 2. **with a vengeance a.** forcefully, furiously, vehemently, violently **b.** and no mistake, extremely, greatly, to the full, to the utmost, with no holds barred

vengeful avenging, implacable, punitive, rancorous, relentless, retaliatory, revengeful, spiteful, thirsting for revenge, unforgiving, vindictive

venial allowable, excusable, forgivable, insignificant, minor, pardonable, slight, trivial

venom 1. bane, poison, toxin **2.** acidity, acrimony, bitterness, gall, grudge, hate, ill will, malevolence, malice, maliciousness, malignity, rancour, spite, spitefulness, spleen, virulence

venomous 1. baneful (*Archaic*), envenomed, mephitic, noxious, poison, poisonous, toxic, virulent **2.** baleful, hostile, malicious, malignant, rancorous, savage, spiteful, vicious, vindictive, virulent

vent 1. *n.* aperture, duct, hole, opening, orifice, outlet, split **2.** *v.* air, come out with, discharge, emit, empty, express, give expression to, give vent to, pour out, release, utter, voice

ventilate *Fig.* air, bring out into the open, broadcast, debate, discuss, examine, make known, scrutinize, sift, talk about

venture *v.* **1.** chance, endanger, hazard, imperil, jeopardize, put in jeopardy, risk, speculate, stake, wager **2.** advance, dare, dare say, hazard, make bold, presume, stick one's neck out (*Inf.*), take the liberty, volunteer **3.** *With* out, forth, *etc.* embark on, go, plunge into, set out ~*n.* **4.** adventure, chance, endeavour, enterprise, fling, gamble, hazard, jeopardy, project, risk, speculation, undertaking

venturesome adventurous, bold, courageous, daredevil, daring, doughty, enterprising, fearless, intrepid, plucky, spirited

veracious accurate, credible, dependable, ethical, factual, faithful, frank, genuine, high-principled, honest, reliable, straightforward, true, trustworthy, truthful, veridical

veracity accuracy, candour, credibility, exactitude, frankness, honesty, integrity, precision, probity, rectitude, trustworthiness, truth, truthfulness, uprightness

verbal literal, oral, spoken, unwritten, verbatim, word-of-mouth

verbally by word of mouth, orally

verbatim exactly, precisely, to the letter, word for word

verbiage circumlocution, periphrasis, pleonasm, prolixity, redundancy, repetition, tautology, verbosity

verbose circumlocutory, diffuse, garrulous, long-winded, periphrastic, pleonastic, prolix, tautological, windy, wordy

verbosely at great length, at undue length, long-windedly, wordily

verbosity garrulity, logorrhoea, long-windedness, loquaciousness, prolixity, rambling, verbiage, verboseness, windiness, wordiness

verdant flourishing, fresh, grassy, green, leafy, lush

verdict adjudication, conclusion, decision, finding, judgment, opinion, sentence

verge 1. *n.* border, boundary, brim, brink, edge, extreme, limit, lip, margin, roadside, threshold **2.** *v.* approach, border, come near

verification authentication, confirmation, corroboration, proof, substantiation, validation

verify attest, attest to, authenticate, bear out, check, confirm, corroborate, prove, substantiate, support, validate

verisimilitude authenticity, colour, credibility, likeliness, likeness, plausibility, realism, resemblance, semblance, show of

verminous alive, crawling, flea-ridden, lousy, rat-infested

vernacular 1. *adj.* colloquial, common, indigenous, informal, local, mother, native, popular, vulgar **2.** *n.* argot, cant, dialect, idiom, jargon, native language, parlance, patois, speech, vulgar tongue

versatile adaptable, adjustable, all-purpose, all-round, flexible, functional, handy, many-sided, multifaceted, protean, resourceful, variable

versed accomplished, acquainted, competent, conversant, experienced, familiar, knowledgeable, practised, proficient, qualified, seasoned, skilled, well informed, well up in (*Inf.*)

version 1. account, adaptation, exercise, interpretation, portrayal, reading, rendering, side, translation **2.** design, form, kind, model, style, type, variant

vertex acme, apex, apogee, crown, culmination, extremity, height, pinnacle, summit, top, zenith

vertical erect, on end, perpendicular, upright

vertigo dizziness, giddiness, lightheadedness, loss of equilibrium, swimming of the head

verve animation, brio, dash, élan, energy, enthusiasm, force, get-up-and-go (*Inf.*), gusto, life, liveliness, punch (*Inf.*), sparkle, spirit, vigour, vim (*Sl.*), vitality, vivacity, zeal, zip (*Inf.*)

very *adv.* 1. absolutely, acutely, awfully (*Inf.*), decidedly, deeply, eminently, exceedingly, excessively, extremely, greatly, highly, jolly (*Brit.*), noticeably, particularly, profoundly, really, remarkably, superlatively, surpassingly, terribly, truly, uncommonly, unusually, wonderfully ~*adj.* 2. actual, appropriate, exact, express, identical, perfect, precise, real, same, selfsame, unqualified 3. bare, mere, plain, pure, sheer, simple

vessel 1. barque (*Poetic*), boat, craft, ship 2. container, pot, receptacle, utensil

vest *v.* 1. *With* **in** or **with** authorize, be devolved upon, bestow, confer, consign, empower, endow, entrust, furnish, invest, lodge, place, put in the hands of, settle 2. apparel, bedeck, clothe, cover, dress, envelop, garb, robe

vestibule anteroom, entrance hall, foyer, hall, lobby, porch, portico

vestige evidence, glimmer, hint, indication, relic, remainder, remains, remnant, residue, scrap, sign, suspicion, token, trace, track

vestigial imperfect, incomplete, nonfunctional, rudimentary, surviving, undeveloped

vet *v.* appraise, check, check out, examine, give (someone *or* something) the once-over (*Inf.*), investigate, look over, pass under review, review, scan, scrutinize, size up (*Inf.*)

veteran 1. *n.* master, old hand, old stager, old-timer, past master, past mistress, pro (*Inf.*), trouper, warhorse (*Inf.*) 2. *adj.* adept, battle-scarred, expert, long-serving, old, proficient, seasoned

veto 1. *v.* ban, disallow, forbid, give the thumbs down to, interdict, kill (*Inf.*), negative, prohibit, put the kibosh on (*Sl.*), refuse permission, reject, rule out, turn down 2. *n.* ban, embargo, interdict, nonconsent, prohibition

vex afflict, aggravate (*Inf.*), agitate, annoy, bother, bug (*Inf.*), displease, distress, disturb, exasperate, fret, gall, grate on, harass, irritate, molest, needle (*Inf.*), nettle, offend, peeve (*Inf.*), perplex, pester, pique, plague, provoke, put out, rile, tease, torment, trouble, upset, worry

vexation 1. aggravation (*Inf.*), annoyance, displeasure, dissatisfaction, exasperation, frustration, irritation, pique 2. bother, difficulty, headache (*Inf.*), irritant, misfortune, nuisance, problem, thorn in one's flesh, trouble, upset, worry

vexatious afflicting, aggravating (*Inf.*), annoying, bothersome, burdensome, disagreeable, disappointing, distressing, exasperating, harassing, irksome, irritating, nagging, plaguy (*Archaic*), provoking, teasing, tormenting, troublesome, trying, unpleasant, upsetting, worrisome, worrying

vexed 1. afflicted, aggravated (*Inf.*), agitated, annoyed, bothered, confused, displeased, distressed, disturbed, exasperated, fed up, harassed, irritated, miffed (*Inf.*), nettled, out of countenance, peeved (*Inf.*), perplexed, provoked, put out, riled, ruffled, tormented, troubled, upset, worried 2. contested, controversial, disputed, moot, much debated

viable applicable, feasible, operable, practicable, usable, within the bounds of possibility, workable

vibes atmosphere, aura, emanation, emotions, feelings, reaction, response, vibrations

vibrant 1. aquiver, oscillating, palpitating, pulsating, quivering, trembling 2. alive, animated, colourful, dynamic, electrifying, full of pep (*Inf.*), responsive, sensitive, sparkling, spirited, vivacious, vivid

vibrate fluctuate, judder (*Inf.*), oscillate, pulsate, pulse, quiver, resonate, reverberate, shake, shiver, sway, swing, throb, tremble, undulate

vibration juddering (*Inf.*), oscillation, pulsation, pulse, quiver, resonance, reverberation, shaking, throb, throbbing, trembling, tremor

vicarious acting, at one remove, commissioned, delegated, deputed, empathetic, indirect, substituted, surrogate

vice 1. corruption, degeneracy, depravity, evil, evildoing, immorality, iniquity, profligacy, sin, venality, wickedness 2. blemish, defect, failing, fault, imperfection, shortcoming, weakness

vice versa contrariwise, conversely, in reverse, the other way round

vicinity area, district, environs, locality, neck of the woods (*Inf.*), neighbourhood, precincts, propinquity, proximity, purlieus

vicious 1. abandoned, abhorrent, atrocious, bad, barbarous, corrupt, cruel, dangerous, debased, degenerate, degraded, depraved, diabolical, ferocious, fiendish, foul, heinous, immoral, infamous, monstrous, profligate, savage, sinful, unprincipled, vile, violent, wicked, worthless, wrong 2. backbiting, bitchy (*Sl.*), cruel, defamatory, malicious, mean, rancorous, slanderous, spiteful, venomous, vindictive

viciousness 1. badness, corruption, cruelty, depravity, ferocity, immorality, profligacy, savagery, wickedness 2. bitchiness (*Sl.*), malice, rancour, spite, spitefulness, venom

vicissitude alteration, alternation, change, fluctuation of fortune, mutation, one of life's ups and downs (*Inf.*), revolution, shift, variation

victim 1. casualty, fatality, injured party, martyr, sacrifice, scapegoat, sufferer 2. dupe, easy prey, fall guy (*Inf.*), gull (*Archaic*), innocent, sitting target, sucker (*Sl.*)

victimize 1. discriminate against, have a down on (someone) (*Inf.*), have it in for (someone) (*Inf.*), have one's knife into (someone), persecute, pick on 2. cheat, deceive, defraud, dupe, exploit, fool, gull (*Archaic*), hoodwink, prey on, swindle, take advantage of, use

victor champ (*Inf.*), champion, conquering hero, conqueror, first, prizewinner, top dog (*Inf.*), vanquisher, winner

victorious champion, conquering, first, prizewinning, successful, triumphant, vanquishing, winning

victory conquest, laurels, mastery, success, superiority, the palm, the prize, triumph, win

victuals bread, comestibles, eatables, eats (*Sl.*), edibles, food, grub (*Sl.*), meat, nosh (*Sl.*), provisions, rations, stores, supplies, viands, vittles (*Obsolete*)

vie be rivals, compete, contend, contest, match oneself against, strive, struggle

view *n.* **1.** aspect, landscape, outlook, panorama, perspective, picture, prospect, scene, spectacle, vista 2. range *or* field of vision, sight, vision 3. *Sometimes plural* attitude, belief, conviction, feeling, impression, judgment, notion, opinion, point of view, sentiment, thought, way of thinking 4. contemplation, display, examination, inspection, look, scan, scrutiny, sight, survey, viewing 5. **with a view to** in order to, in the hope of, so as to, with the aim *or* intention of ~*v.* **6.** behold, contemplate, examine, explore, eye, gaze at, inspect, look at, observe, regard, scan, spectate, stare at, survey, watch, witness 7. consider, deem, judge, look on, regard, think about

viewer observer, one of an audience, onlooker, spectator, TV watcher, watcher

viewpoint angle, frame of reference, perspective, point of view, position, slant, stance, standpoint, vantage point, way of thinking

vigilance alertness, attentiveness, carefulness, caution, circumspection, observance, watchfulness

vigilant alert, Argus-eyed, attentive, careful, cautious, circumspect, keeping one's eyes peeled *or* skinned (*Inf.*), on one's guard, on one's toes, on the alert, on the lookout, on the qui vive, on the watch, sleepless, unsleeping, wakeful, watchful, wide awake

vigorous active, brisk, dynamic, effective, efficient, energetic, enterprising, flourishing, forceful, forcible, full of energy, hale, hale and hearty, hardy, healthy, intense, lively, lusty, powerful, red-blooded, robust, sound, spanking, spirited, strenuous, strong, virile, vital, zippy (*Inf.*)

vigorously all out, eagerly, energetically, forcefully, hammer and tongs, hard, like mad (*Sl.*), lustily, strenuously, strongly, with a vengeance, with might and main

vigour activity, animation, dash, dynamism, energy, force, forcefulness, gusto, health, liveliness, might, oomph (*Inf.*), pep, power, punch (*Inf.*), robustness, snap (*Inf.*), soundness, spirit, strength, verve, vim (*Sl.*), virility, vitality, zip (*Inf.*)

vile 1. abandoned, abject, appalling, bad, base, coarse, contemptible, corrupt, debased, degenerate, degrading, depraved, despicable, disgraceful, evil, humiliating, ignoble, impure, loathsome, low, mean, miserable, nefarious, perverted, shocking, sinful, ugly, vicious, vulgar, wicked, worthless, wretched **2**. disgusting, foul, horrid, loathsome, nasty, nauseating, noxious, offensive, repellent, repugnant, repulsive, revolting, sickening

vileness coarseness, corruption, degeneracy, depravity, dreadfulness, enormity, evil, foulness, heinousness, noxiousness, offensiveness, outrage, profanity, ugliness, wickedness

vilification abuse, aspersion, calumniation, calumny, contumely, defamation, denigration, disparagement, invective, mudslinging, scurrility, vituperation

vilify abuse, asperse, bad-mouth (*U.S. sl.*), berate, calumniate, debase, decry, defame, denigrate, disparage, malign, pull to pieces (*Inf.*), revile, run down, slander, smear, speak ill of, traduce, vilipend (*Rare*), vituperate

villain 1. blackguard, caitiff (*Archaic*), criminal, evildoer, knave (*Archaic*), libertine, malefactor, miscreant, profligate, rapscallion, reprobate, rogue, scoundrel, wretch **2**. antihero, baddy (*Inf.*) **3**. devil, monkey, rascal, rogue, scallywag (*Inf.*), scamp

villainous atrocious, bad, base, blackguardly, criminal, cruel, debased, degenerate, depraved, detestable, diabolical, evil, fiendish, hateful, heinous, ignoble, infamous, inhuman, mean, nefarious, outrageous, ruffianly, scoundrelly, sinful, terrible, thievish, vicious, vile, wicked

villainy atrocity, baseness, crime, criminality, delinquency, depravity, devilry, iniquity, knavery, rascality, sin, turpitude, vice, wickedness

vindicate 1. absolve, acquit, clear, defend, do justice to, exculpate, excuse, exonerate, free from blame, justify, rehabilitate **2**. advocate, assert, establish, maintain, support, uphold

vindication apology, assertion, defence, exculpating, exculpation, excuse, exoneration, justification, maintenance, plea, rehabilitation, substantiation, support

vindictive full of spleen, implacable, malicious, malignant, rancorous, relentless, resentful, revengeful, spiteful, unforgiving, unrelenting, vengeful, venomous

vintage 1. *n.* collection, crop, epoch, era, generation, harvest, origin, year **2**.

adj. best, choice, classic, mature, prime, rare, ripe, select, superior, venerable

violate 1. break, contravene, disobey, disregard, encroach upon, infract, infringe, transgress **2**. abuse, assault, befoul, debauch, defile, desecrate, dishonour, invade, outrage, pollute, profane, rape, ravish

violation 1. abuse, breach, contravention, encroachment, infraction, infringement, transgression, trespass **2**. defilement, desecration, profanation, sacrilege, spoliation

violence 1. bestiality, bloodshed, bloodthirstiness, brutality, brute force, cruelty, destructiveness, ferocity, fierceness, fighting, force, frenzy, fury, murderousness, passion, rough handling, savagery, strong-arm tactics (*Inf.*), terrorism, thuggery, vehemence, wildness **2**. boisterousness, power, raging, roughness, storminess, tumult, turbulence, wildness **3**. abandon, acuteness, fervour, force, harshness, intensity, severity, sharpness, vehemence

violent 1. berserk, bloodthirsty, brutal, cruel, destructive, fiery, forcible, furious, headstrong, homicidal, hotheaded, impetuous, intemperate, maddened, maniacal, murderous, passionate, powerful, raging, riotous, rough, savage, strong, uncontrollable, ungovernable, unrestrained, vehement, vicious, wild **2**. blustery, boisterous, devastating, full of force, gale force, powerful, raging, ruinous, strong, tempestuous, tumultuous, turbulent, wild **3**. acute, agonizing, biting, excruciating, extreme, harsh, inordinate, intense, outrageous, painful, severe, sharp

V.I.P. big name, big noise (*Brit. sl.*), big shot (*Sl.*), bigwig (*Inf.*), celebrity, leading light (*Inf.*), lion, luminary, man or woman of the hour, notable, personage, public figure, somebody, star

virago battle-axe (*Inf.*), fury, harridan, scold, shrew, termagant (*Rare*), vixen, Xanthippe

virgin 1. *n.* damsel (*Archaic*), girl, maid (*Archaic*), maiden (*Archaic*), vestal, virgo intacta **2**. *adj.* chaste, fresh, immaculate, maidenly, modest, new, pristine, pure, snowy, uncorrupted, undefiled, unsullied, untouched, unused, vestal, virginal

virginal celibate, chaste, fresh, immaculate, maidenly, pristine, pure, snowy, spotless, uncorrupted, undefiled, undisturbed, untouched, virgin, white

virginity chastity, maidenhead, maidenhood

virile forceful, lusty, macho, male, manlike, manly, masculine, potent, red-blooded, robust, strong, vigorous

virility machismo, manhood, masculinity, potency, vigour

virtual essential, implicit, implied, in all but name, indirect, potential, practical, tacit, unacknowledged

virtually as good as, effectually, for all practical purposes, in all but name, in effect, in essence, nearly, practically, to all intents and purposes

virtue 1. ethicalness, excellence, goodness, high-mindedness, incorruptibility, integrity, justice, morality, probity, quality, rectitude, righteousness, uprightness, worth, worthiness 2. advantage, asset, attribute, credit, good point, good quality, merit, plus (*Inf.*), strength 3. chastity, honour, innocence, morality, purity, virginity 4. **by virtue of** as a result of, by dint of, by reason of, in view of, on account of, owing to, thanks to

virtuosity brilliance, éclat, expertise, finish, flair, mastery, panache, polish, skill

virtuoso 1. *n.* artist, genius, maestro, magician, master, master hand 2. *adj.* bravura (*Music*), brilliant, dazzling, masterly

virtuous 1. blameless, ethical, excellent, exemplary, good, high-principled, honest, honourable, incorruptible, moral, praiseworthy, pure, righteous, upright, worthy 2. celibate, chaste, clean-living, innocent, pure, spotless, virginal

virulence 1. deadliness, harmfulness, hurtfulness, infectiousness, injuriousness, malignancy, noxiousness, poisonousness, toxicity, virulency 2. acrimony, antagonism, bitterness, hatred, hostility, ill will, malevolence, malice, poison, rancour, resentment, spite, spleen, venom, viciousness, vindictiveness

virulent 1. baneful (*Archaic*), deadly, infective, injurious, lethal, malignant, pernicious, poisonous, septic, toxic, venomous 2. acrimonious, bitter, envenomed, hostile, malevolent, malicious, rancorous, resentful, spiteful, splenetic, venomous, vicious, vindictive

viscous adhesive, clammy, gelatinous, gluey, glutinous, gooey (*Inf.*), gummy, mucilaginous, sticky, syrupy, tenacious, thick, treacly, viscid

visible anywhere to be seen, apparent, clear, conspicuous, detectable, discernible, discoverable, distinguishable, evident, in sight, in view, manifest, not hidden, noticeable, observable, obvious, palpable, patent, perceivable, perceptible, plain, to be seen, unconcealed, unmistakable

vision 1. eyes, eyesight, perception, seeing, sight, view 2. breadth of view, discernment, farsightedness, foresight, imagination, insight, intuition, penetration, prescience 3. castle in the air, concept, conception, daydream, dream, fantasy, idea, ideal, image, mental picture, pipe dream 4. apparition, chimera, delusion, ghost, hallucination, illusion, mirage, phantasm, phantom, revelation, spectre, wraith 5. dream, feast for the eyes, perfect picture, picture, sight, sight for sore eyes, spectacle

visionary *adj.* 1. dreaming, dreamy, idealistic, quixotic, romantic, starry-eyed, with one's head in the clouds 2. chimerical, delusory, fanciful, fantastic, ideal, idealized, illusory, imaginary, impractical, prophetic, speculative, unreal, unrealistic, unworkable, utopian ~*n.* 3. daydreamer, Don Quixote, dreamer, enthusiast (*Archaic*), idealist, mystic, prophet, romantic, seer, theorist, utopian, zealot

visit *v.* 1. be the guest of, call in, call on, drop in on (*Inf.*), go to see, inspect, look (someone) up, pay a call on, pop in (*Inf.*), stay at, stay with, stop by, take in (*Inf.*) 2. afflict, assail, attack, befall, descend upon, haunt, smite, trouble 3. *With* **on** *or* **upon** bring down upon, execute, impose, inflict, wreak ~*n.* 4. call, sojourn, stay, stop

visitation 1. examination, inspection, visit 2. bane, blight, calamity, cataclysm, catastrophe, disaster, infliction, ordeal, punishment, scourge, trial

visitor caller, company, guest, visitant

vista panorama, perspective, prospect, view

visual 1. ocular, optic, optical 2. discernible, observable, perceptible, visible

visualize conceive of, conjure up a mental picture of, envisage, imagine, picture, see in the mind's eye

vital 1. basic, cardinal, essential, fundamental, imperative, indispensable, necessary, requisite **2**. critical, crucial, decisive, important, key, life-or-death, significant, urgent **3**. animated, dynamic, energetic, forceful, full of the joy of living, lively, spirited, vibrant, vigorous, vivacious, zestful **4**. alive, animate, generative, invigorative, life-giving, live, living, quickening

vitality animation, energy, exuberance, go (*Inf.*), life, liveliness, lustiness, pep, robustness, sparkle, stamina, strength, vigour, vim (*Sl.*), vivaciousness, vivacity

vitiate 1. blemish, devalue, harm, impair, injure, invalidate, mar, spoil, undermine, water down **2**. blight, contaminate, corrupt, debase, defile, deprave, deteriorate, pervert, pollute, sully, taint

vitiation 1. deterioration, devaluation, dilution, impairment, marring, reduction, spoiling, undermining **2**. adulteration, contamination, corruption, debasement, degradation, perversion, pollution, sullying

vitriolic *Fig.* acerbic, acid, bitchy (*Sl.*), bitter, caustic, destructive, dripping with malice, envenomed, sardonic, scathing, venomous, virulent, withering

vituperate abuse, berate, blame, castigate, censure, cry down, denounce, find fault with, rail against, rate, reproach, revile, run down, slang, slate (*Inf.*), tear into (*Inf.*), upbraid, vilify

vituperation abuse, billingsgate, blame, castigation, censure, faultfinding, flak (*Inf.*), invective, obloquy, rebuke, reprimand, reproach, scurrility, tongue-lashing, vilification

vituperative abusive, belittling, calumniatory, censorious, defamatory, denunciatory, derogatory, harsh, insulting, malign, opprobrious, sardonic, scurrilous, withering

vivacious animated, bubbling, cheerful, ebullient, effervescent, frolicsome, full of life, gay, high-spirited, jolly, lighthearted, lively, merry, scintillating, sparkling, spirited, sportive, sprightly, vital

vivacity animation, ebullience, effervescence, energy, gaiety, high spirits, life, liveliness, pep, quickness, sparkle, spirit, sprightliness

vivid 1. bright, brilliant, clear, colourful, glowing, intense, rich **2**. distinct, dramatic, graphic, highly-coloured, lifelike, memorable, powerful, realistic, sharp, sharply-etched, stirring, strong, telling, true to life **3**. active, animated, dynamic, energetic, expressive, flamboyant, lively, quick, spirited, striking, strong, vigorous

vividness 1. brightness, brilliancy, glow, life, radiance, resplendence, sprightliness **2**. clarity, distinctness, graphicness, immediacy, intensity, realism, sharpness, strength

vixen *Fig.* fury, harpy, harridan, hellcat, scold, shrew, spitfire, termagant (*Rare*), virago, Xanthippe

viz. namely, that is to say, to wit, videlicet

vocabulary dictionary, glossary, language, lexicon, wordbook, word hoard, words, word stock

vocal *adj.* **1**. articulate, articulated, oral, put into words, said, spoken, uttered, voiced **2**. articulate, blunt, clamorous, eloquent, expressive, forthright, frank, free-spoken, noisy, outspoken, plain-spoken, strident, vociferous

vocation business, calling, career, employment, job, life's work, life work, métier, mission, office, post, profession, pursuit, role, trade

vociferous clamant, clamorous, loud, loudmouthed (*Inf.*), noisy, obstreperous, ranting, shouting, strident, uproarious, vehement

vogue *n.* **1**. craze, custom, *dernier cri*, fashion, last word, mode, style, the latest, the rage, the thing (*Inf.*), trend, way **2**. acceptance, currency, fashionableness, favour, popularity, prevalence, usage, use ~*adj.* **3**. fashionable, in, modish, now (*Inf.*), popular, prevalent, trendy (*Brit. inf.*), up-to-the-minute, voguish, with it (*Inf.*)

voice *n.* **1**. articulation, language, power of speech, sound, tone, utterance, words **2**. decision, expression, part, say, view, vote, will, wish **3**. agency, instrument, medium, mouthpiece, organ, spokesman, spokesperson, spokeswoman, vehicle ~*v.* **4**. air, articulate, assert, come out with (*Inf.*), declare, divulge, enunciate, express, give expression or utterance to, put into words, say, utter, ventilate

void *adj.* **1**. bare, clear, drained, emptied, empty, free, tenantless, unfilled, unoccupied, vacant **2**. *With* of destitute, devoid, lacking, without **3**. dead, ineffective, ineffectual, inoperative, invalid, nonviable, nugatory, null and void, unenforceable, useless, vain, worthless ~n. **4**. blank, blankness, emptiness, gap, lack, opening, space, vacuity, vacuum, want ~v. **5**. discharge, drain, eject, eliminate (*Physiol.*), emit, empty, evacuate **6**. abnegate, cancel, invalidate, nullify, rescind

volatile airy, changeable, erratic, explosive, fickle, flighty, gay, giddy, inconstant, lively, mercurial, sprightly, unsettled, unstable, unsteady, up and down (*Inf.*), variable, whimsical

volition choice, choosing, determination, discretion, election, free will, option, preference, purpose, resolution, will

volley *n*. barrage, blast, bombardment, burst, cannonade, discharge, explosion, fusillade, hail, salvo, shower

volubility fluency, garrulity, gift of the gab (*Inf.*), glibness, loquaciousness, loquacity

voluble articulate, blessed with the gift of the gab (*Inf.*), fluent, forthcoming, glib, loquacious, talkative

volume 1. aggregate, amount, body, bulk, capacity, compass, cubic content, dimensions, mass, quantity, total **2**. book, publication, tome, treatise

voluminous ample, big, billowing, bulky, capacious, cavernous, copious, full, large, massive, prolific, roomy, vast

voluntarily by choice, freely, of one's own accord, of one's own free will, on one's own initiative, willingly, without being asked, without prompting

voluntary discretional, free, gratuitous, honorary, intended, intentional, optional, spontaneous, uncompelled, unconstrained, unforced, unpaid, volunteer, willing

volunteer *v*. advance, let oneself in for (*Inf.*), need no invitation, offer, offer one's services, present, proffer, propose, put forward, put oneself at (someone's) disposal, step forward, suggest, tender

voluptuary *n*. bon vivant, epicurean, hedonist, luxury-lover, playboy, pleasure seeker, profligate, sensualist, sybarite

voluptuous 1. epicurean, hedonistic, licentious, luxurious, pleasure-loving, self-indulgent, sensual, sybaritic **2**. ample, buxom, curvaceous (*Inf.*), enticing, erotic, full-bosomed, provocative, seductive, shapely, well-stacked (*Brit. sl.*)

voluptuousness carnality, curvaceousness (*Inf.*), licentiousness, opulence, seductiveness, sensuality, shapeliness

vomit *v*. belch forth, be sick, bring up, disgorge, eject, emit, heave, puke (*Sl.*), regurgitate, retch, sick up (*Inf.*), spew out *or* up, throw up (*Inf.*)

voracious avid, devouring, gluttonous, greedy, hungry, insatiable, omnivorous, prodigious, rapacious, ravening, ravenous, uncontrolled, unquenchable

voracity avidity, eagerness, greed, hunger, rapacity, ravenousness

vortex eddy, maelstrom, whirlpool

votary adherent, aficionado, believer, devotee, disciple, follower

vote *n*. **1**. ballot, franchise, plebiscite, poll, referendum, right to vote, show of hands, suffrage ~v. **2**. ballot, cast one's vote, elect, go to the polls, opt, return **3**. *Inf.* declare, judge, pronounce, propose, recommend, suggest

vouch *Usually with* **for** affirm, answer for, assert, asseverate, attest to, back, certify, confirm, give assurance of, go bail for, guarantee, stand witness, support, swear to, uphold

vouchsafe accord, cede, condescend to give, confer, deign, favour (someone) with, grant, yield

vow 1. *v*. affirm, consecrate, dedicate, devote, pledge, promise, swear, undertake solemnly **2**. *n*. oath, pledge, promise, troth (*Archaic*)

voyage *n*. crossing, cruise, journey, passage, travels, trip

vulgar 1. blue, boorish, cheap and nasty, coarse, common, crude, dirty, flashy, gaudy, gross, ill-bred, impolite, improper, indecent, indecorous, indelicate, low, nasty, naughty, off colour, ribald, risqué, rude, suggestive, tasteless, tawdry, uncouth, unmannerly, unrefined **2**. general, native, ordinary, unrefined, vernacular

vulgarian arriviste, boor, churl, nouveau riche, parvenu, philistine, upstart

vulgarity bad taste, coarseness, crudeness, crudity, gaudiness, grossness, indecorum, indelicacy, lack of refinement, ribaldry, rudeness, suggestiveness, tastelessness, tawdriness

vulnerable accessible, assailable, defenceless, exposed, open to attack, sensitive, susceptible, tender, thin-skinned, unprotected, weak, wide open

W

wacky crazy, daft (*Inf.*), eccentric, erratic, irrational, loony (*Sl.*), nutty (*Sl.*), odd, screwy (*Inf.*), silly, unpredictable, wild, zany

wad ball, block, bundle, chunk, hunk, lump, mass, plug, roll

wadding filler, lining, packing, padding, stuffing

waddle rock, shuffle, sway, toddle, totter, wobble

wade 1. ford, paddle, splash, walk through 2. *With* **through** drudge, labour, peg away, plough through, toil, work one's way 3. *With* **in** *or* **into** assail, attack, get stuck in (*Sl.*), go for, launch oneself at, light into (*Inf.*), set about, tackle, tear into (*Inf.*)

waffle 1. *v.* blather, jabber, prate, prattle, rabbit on (*Brit. sl.*), verbalize, witter on (*Inf.*) 2. *n.* blather, jabber, padding, prating, prattle, prolixity, verbiage, verbosity, wordiness

waft 1. *v.* bear, be carried, carry, convey, drift, float, ride, transmit, transport 2. *n.* breath, breeze, current, draught, puff, whiff

wag[1] 1. *v.* bob, flutter, nod, oscillate, quiver, rock, shake, stir, vibrate, waggle, wave, wiggle 2. *n.* bob, flutter, nod, oscillation, quiver, shake, toss, vibration, waggle, wave, wiggle

wag[2] *n.* card (*Inf.*), clown, comedian, comic, humorist, jester, joker, wit

wage 1. *n. Also* **wages** allowance, compensation, earnings, emolument, fee, hire, pay, payment, recompense, remuneration, reward, stipend 2. *v.* carry on, conduct, engage in, practise, proceed with, prosecute, pursue, undertake

wager 1. *n.* bet, flutter (*Brit. inf.*), gamble, pledge, punt, stake, venture 2. *v.* bet, chance, gamble, hazard, lay, pledge, punt, put on, risk, speculate, stake, venture

waggish amusing, comical, droll, facetious, funny, humorous, impish, jesting, jocose, jocular, merry, mischievous, playful, puckish, risible, sportive, witty

waggle 1. *v.* flutter, oscillate, shake, wag, wave, wiggle, wobble 2. *n.* flutter, oscillation, shake, wag, wave, wiggle, wobble

waif foundling, orphan, stray

wail 1. *v.* bemoan, bewail, cry, deplore, grieve, howl, keen, lament, ululate, weep, yowl 2. *n.* complaint, cry, grief, howl, keen, lament, lamentation, moan, ululation, weeping, yowl

wait 1. *v.* abide, bide one's time, cool one's heels, dally, delay, hang fire, hold back, hold on (*Inf.*), linger, mark time, pause, remain, rest, stand by, stay, tarry 2. *n.* delay, halt, hold-up, interval, pause, rest, stay

waiter, waitress attendant, server, steward, stewardess

wait on *or* **upon** attend, minister to, serve, tend

waive abandon, defer, dispense with, forgo, give up, postpone, put off, refrain from, relinquish, remit, renounce, resign, set aside, surrender

waiver abandonment, abdication, disclaimer, giving up, relinquishment, remission, renunciation, resignation, setting aside, surrender

wake[1] *v.* 1. arise, awake, awaken, bestir, come to, get up, rouse, rouse from sleep, stir 2. activate, animate, arouse, awaken, enliven, excite, fire, galvanize, kindle, provoke, quicken, stimulate, stir up ~*n.* 3. deathwatch, funeral, vigil, watch

wake[2] aftermath, backwash, path, track, trail, train, wash, waves

wakeful 1. insomniac, restless, sleepless, unsleeping 2. alert, alive, attentive, heedful, observant, on guard, on the alert, on the lookout, on the qui vive, unsleeping, vigilant, wary, watchful

waken activate, animate, arouse, awake, awaken, be roused, come awake, come to, enliven, fire, galvanize, get up, kindle, quicken, rouse, stimulate, stir

wale contusion, mark, scar, streak, stripe, weal, welt, wheal

walk *v.* 1. advance, amble, foot it, go, go by shanks's pony (*Inf.*), go on foot, hike, hoof it (*Sl.*), march, move, pace, perambulate, promenade, saunter, step, stride, stroll, traipse (*Inf.*), tramp, travel on foot, trek, trudge 2. accompany, convoy, escort, take ~n. 3. constitutional, hike, march, perambulation, promenade, ramble, saunter, stroll, traipse (*Inf.*), tramp, trek, trudge, turn 4. carriage, gait, manner of walking, pace, step, stride 5. aisle, alley, avenue, esplanade, footpath, lane, path, pathway, pavement, promenade, sidewalk, trail 6. area, arena, calling, career, course, field, line, métier, profession, sphere, trade, vocation

walker footslogger, hiker, pedestrian, rambler, wayfarer

walkout industrial action, protest, stoppage, strike

walk out 1. flounce out, get up and go, leave suddenly, storm out, take off (*Inf.*) 2. down tools, go on strike, stop work, strike, take industrial action, withdraw one's labour 3. *With* **on** abandon, chuck (*Inf.*), desert, forsake, jilt, leave, leave in the lurch, pack in (*Inf.*), run away from, throw over

walkover child's play (*Inf.*), doddle (*Brit. sl.*), easy victory, picnic (*Inf.*), piece of cake (*Inf.*), pushover (*Sl.*), snap (*Inf.*)

wall 1. divider, enclosure, panel, partition, screen 2. barricade, breastwork, bulwark, embankment, fortification, palisade, parapet, rampart, stockade 3. barrier, block, fence, hedge, impediment, obstacle, obstruction 4. **go to the wall** *Inf.* be ruined, collapse, fail, fall, go bust (*Inf.*), go under 5. **drive up the wall** *Sl.* annoy, dement, derange, drive crazy, drive insane, exasperate, infuriate, irritate, madden, send off one's head (*Sl.*), try

wallet case, holder, notecase, pocketbook, pouch, purse

wallop *v.* 1. batter, beat, belt (*Sl.*), buffet, clobber (*Inf.*), hit, lambaste, paste (*Sl.*), pound, pummel, punch, slug, smack, strike, thrash, thump, whack 2. beat, best, clobber (*Inf.*), crush, defeat, drub, hammer (*Inf.*), lick (*Inf.*), rout, thrash, trounce, vanquish, wipe the floor with (*Inf.*), worst ~n. 3. bash, belt (*Inf.*), blow, haymaker (*Sl.*), kick, punch, slug, smack, thump, thwack, whack

wallow 1. lie, roll about, splash around, tumble, welter 2. flounder, lurch, stagger, stumble, wade 3. bask, delight, glory, indulge oneself, luxuriate, relish, revel, take pleasure

wan 1. anaemic, ashen, bloodless, cadaverous, colourless, discoloured, ghastly, livid, pale, pallid, pasty, sickly, washed out, waxen, wheyfaced, white 2. dim, faint, feeble, pale, weak

wand baton, rod, sprig, stick, twig, withe, withy

wander *v.* 1. cruise, drift, knock about, knock around, meander, mooch around (*Sl.*), peregrinate, ramble, range, roam, rove, straggle, stravaig (*Scot.*), stray, stroll, traipse (*Inf.*) 2. depart, deviate, digress, divagate (*Rare*), diverge, err, get lost, go astray, go off at a tangent, go off course, lapse, lose concentration, lose one's train of thought, lose one's way, swerve, veer 3. babble, be delirious, be incoherent, ramble, rave, speak incoherently, talk nonsense ~n. 4. cruise, excursion, meander, peregrination, ramble, traipse (*Inf.*)

wanderer bird of passage, drifter, gypsy, itinerant, nomad, rambler, ranger, rolling stone, rover, stroller, traveller, vagabond, vagrant, voyager

wandering drifting, homeless, itinerant, migratory, nomadic, peripatetic, rambling, rootless, roving, strolling, travelling, vagabond, vagrant, voyaging, wayfaring

wanderlust itchy feet (*Inf.*), restlessness, urge to travel

wane *v.* 1. abate, atrophy, decline, decrease, die out, dim, diminish, draw to a close, drop, dwindle, ebb, fade, fade away, fail, lessen, sink, subside, taper off, weaken, wind down, wither ~n. 2. abatement, atrophy, decay, declension, decrease, diminution, drop, dwindling, ebb, fading, failure, fall, falling off, lessening, sinking, subsidence, tapering off, withering 3. **on the wane** at its lowest ebb, declining, dropping, dwindling, dying out, ebbing, fading, lessening, obsolescent, on its last legs, on the decline, on the way out, subsiding, tapering off, weakening, withering

wangle arrange, bring off, contrive, engineer, fiddle (*Inf.*), finagle (*Inf.*), fix (*Inf.*), manipulate, manoeuvre, pull off, scheme, work (*Inf.*)

want *v.* 1. covet, crave, desire, feel a need for, hanker after, have a fancy for, have a yen for (*Inf.*), hunger for, long for, need, pine for, require, thirst for, wish, yearn for 2. be able to do with, be deficient in, be short of, be without, call for, demand, fall short in, have need of, lack, miss, need, require, stand in need of ~n. **3.** appetite, craving, demand, desire, fancy, hankering, hunger, longing, necessity, need, requirement, thirst, wish, yearning, yen (*Inf.*) **4.** absence, dearth, default, deficiency, famine, insufficiency, lack, paucity, scantiness, scarcity, shortage **5.** destitution, indigence, need, neediness, pauperism, penury, poverty, privation

wanting 1. absent, incomplete, lacking, less, missing, short, shy **2.** defective, deficient, disappointing, faulty, imperfect, inadequate, inferior, leaving much to be desired, not good enough, not up to expectations, not up to par, patchy, poor, sketchy, substandard, unsound

wanton *adj.* **1.** abandoned, dissipated, dissolute, fast, immoral, lecherous, lewd, libertine, libidinous, licentious, loose, lustful, of easy virtue, promiscuous, rakish, shameless, unchaste **2.** arbitrary, cruel, evil, gratuitous, groundless, malevolent, malicious, motiveless, needless, senseless, spiteful, uncalled-for, unjustifiable, unjustified, unprovoked, vicious, wicked, wilful **3.** careless, devil-may-care, extravagant, heedless, immoderate, intemperate, lavish, outrageous, rash, reckless, unrestrained, wild ~n. **4.** Casanova, debauchee, Don Juan, harlot, lecher, libertine, loose woman, profligate, prostitute, rake, roué, slut, strumpet, tart (*Inf.*), trollop, voluptuary, whore, woman of easy virtue ~v. **5.** debauch, dissipate, revel, riot, sleep around (*Inf.*), wench (*Archaic*), whore **6.** fritter away, misspend, squander, throw away, waste

war 1. *n.* armed conflict, battle, bloodshed, combat, conflict, contention, contest, enmity, fighting, hostilities, hostility, strife, struggle, warfare **2.** *v.* battle, campaign against, carry on hostilities, clash, combat, conduct a war, contend, contest, fight, make war, strive, struggle, take up arms, wage war

warble 1. *v.* chirp, chirrup, quaver, sing, trill, twitter **2.** *n.* call, chirp, chirrup, cry, quaver, song, trill, twitter

war cry battle cry, rallying cry, slogan, war whoop

ward 1. area, district, division, precinct, quarter, zone **2.** apartment, cubicle, room **3.** charge, dependant, minor, protégé, pupil **4.** care, charge, custody,

guardianship, keeping, protection, safekeeping

warden administrator, caretaker, curator, custodian, guardian, janitor, keeper, ranger, steward, superintendent, warder, watchman

warder, wardress custodian, gaoler, guard, jailer, keeper, prison officer, screw (*Sl.*), turnkey (*Archaic*)

ward off avert, avoid, beat off, block, deflect, fend off, forestall, keep at arm's length, keep at bay, parry, repel, stave off, thwart, turn aside, turn away

wardrobe 1. closet, clothes cupboard, clothes-press **2.** apparel, attire, clothes, collection of clothes, outfit

warehouse depository, depot, stockroom, store, storehouse

wares commodities, goods, lines, manufactures, merchandise, produce, products, stock, stuff

warfare armed conflict, armed struggle, arms, battle, blows, campaigning, clash of arms, combat, conflict, contest, discord, fighting, hostilities, passage of arms, strategy, strife, struggle, war

warily cagily (*Inf.*), carefully, cautiously, charily, circumspectly, distrustfully, gingerly, guardedly, suspiciously, vigilantly, watchfully, with care

wariness alertness, attention, caginess (*Inf.*), care, carefulness, caution, circumspection, discretion, distrust, foresight, heedfulness, mindfulness, prudence, suspicion, vigilance, watchfulness

warlike aggressive, bellicose, belligerent, bloodthirsty, combative, hawkish, hostile, inimical, jingoistic, martial, militaristic, military, pugnacious, sabrerattling, unfriendly, warmongering

warlock conjurer, enchanter, magician, necromancer, sorcerer, witch, wizard

warm *adj.* **1.** balmy, heated, lukewarm, moderately hot, pleasant, sunny, tepid, thermal **2.** affable, affectionate, amiable, amorous, cheerful, cordial, friendly, genial, happy, hearty, hospitable, kindly, loving, pleasant, tender **3.** animated, ardent, cordial, earnest, effusive, emotional, enthusiastic, excited, fervent, glowing, heated, intense, keen, lively, passionate, spirited, stormy, vehement, vigorous, violent, zealous **4.** irascible, irritable, passionate, quick, sensitive, short, touchy **5.** *Inf.* dangerous, disagreeable, hazardous, perilous, tricky, uncomfortable, unpleasant ~v. 6. heat, heat up, melt, thaw, warm up 7. animate, awaken, excite, get going (*Inf.*), interest, make enthusiastic, put some life into, rouse, stimulate, stir, turn on (*Sl.*)

warm-blooded ardent, earnest, emotional, enthusiastic, excitable, fervent, impetuous, lively, passionate, rash, spirited, vivacious

warm-hearted affectionate, compassionate, cordial, generous, kind-hearted, kindly, loving, sympathetic, tender, tender-hearted

warmonger belligerent, hawk, jingo, militarist, sabre-rattler

warmth 1. heat, hotness, warmness 2. animation, ardour, eagerness, earnestness, effusiveness, enthusiasm, excitement, fervency, fervour, fire, heat, intensity, passion, spirit, transport, vehemence, vigour, violence, zeal, zest 3. affability, affection, amorousness, cheerfulness, cordiality, happiness, heartiness, hospitableness, kindliness, love, tenderness

warn admonish, advise, alert, apprise, caution, forewarn, give fair warning, give notice, inform, make (someone) aware, notify, put one on one's guard, summon, tip off

warning 1. *n.* admonition, advice, alarm, alert, augury, caution, caveat, foretoken, hint, notice, notification, omen, premonition, presage, sign, signal, threat, tip, tip-off, token, word, word to the wise 2. *adj.* admonitory, cautionary, monitory, ominous, premonitory, threatening

warp 1. *v.* bend, contort, deform, deviate, distort, misshape, pervert, swerve, turn, twist 2. *n.* bend, bent, bias, contortion, deformation, deviation, distortion, kink, perversion, quirk, turn, twist

warrant *n.* 1. assurance, authority, authorization, carte blanche, commission, guarantee, licence, permission, permit, pledge, sanction, security, warranty ~v. 2. affirm, answer for, assure, attest, avouch, certify, declare, guarantee, pledge, secure, stand behind, underwrite, uphold, vouch for 3. approve, authorize, call for, commission, demand, empower, entitle, excuse, give ground for, justify, license, necessitate, permit, require, sanction

warrantable accountable, allowable, defensible, justifiable, lawful, necessary,

permissible, proper, reasonable, right

warranty assurance, bond, certificate, contract, covenant, guarantee, pledge

warring at daggers drawn, at war, belligerent, combatant, conflicting, contending, embattled, fighting, hostile, opposed

warrior champion, combatant, fighter, fighting man, man-at-arms, soldier

wary alert, attentive, cagey (*Inf.*), careful, cautious, chary, circumspect, distrustful, guarded, heedful, leery (*Sl.*), on one's guard, on the lookout, on the qui vive, prudent, suspicious, vigilant, watchful, wide-awake

wash *v.* 1. bath, bathe, clean, cleanse, launder, moisten, rinse, scrub, shampoo, shower, wet 2. *With* away bear away, carry off, erode, move, sweep away, wash off 3. *Inf.* bear scrutiny, be convincing, be plausible, carry weight, hold up, hold water, stand up, stick 4. **wash one's hands of** abandon, accept no responsibility for, give up on, have nothing to do with, leave to one's own devices ~n. 5. ablution, bath, bathe, cleaning, cleansing, laundering, rinse, scrub, shampoo, shower, washing 6. ebb and flow, flow, roll, surge, sweep, swell, wave 7. coat, coating, film, layer, overlay, screen, stain, suffusion

washed out 1. blanched, bleached, colourless, etiolated, faded, flat, lacklustre, mat, pale 2. all in (*Sl.*), dead on one's feet, dog-tired (*Inf.*), done in (*Inf.*), drained, drawn, exhausted, fatigued, haggard, knackered (*Sl.*), pale, spent, tired-out, wan, weary, worn-out

washout 1. disappointment, disaster, dud (*Inf.*), failure, fiasco, flop (*Inf.*), mess 2. failure, incompetent, loser

washy attenuated, diluted, feeble, insipid, overdiluted, thin, watered-down, watery, weak, wishy-washy (*Inf.*)

waspish bad-tempered, cantankerous, captious, crabbed, crabby, cross, crotchety (*Inf.*), fretful, grumpy, ill-tempered, irascible, irritable, peevish, peppery, pettish, petulant, snappish, splenetic, testy, touchy, waxy (*Brit. sl.*)

waste *v.* 1. blow (*Sl.*), dissipate, fritter away, frivol away (*Inf.*), lavish, misuse, run through, squander, throw away 2. atrophy, consume, corrode, crumble, debilitate, decay, decline, deplete, disable, drain, dwindle, eat away, ebb, emaciate, enfeeble, exhaust, fade, gnaw, perish, sap the strength of, sink, undermine, wane, wear out, wither **3.** despoil, destroy, devastate, lay waste, pillage, rape, ravage, raze, ruin, sack, spoil, wreak havoc upon ~*n.* **4.** dissipation, expenditure, extravagance, frittering away, loss, lost opportunity, misapplication, misuse, prodigality, squandering, unthriftiness, wastefulness **5.** desolation, destruction, devastation, havoc, ravage, ruin **6.** debris, dregs, dross, garbage, leavings, leftovers, litter, offal, offscourings, refuse, rubbish, scrap, sweepings, trash **7.** desert, solitude, void, wasteland, wild, wilderness ~*adj.* **8.** leftover, superfluous, supernumerary, unused, unwanted, useless, worthless **9.** bare, barren, desolate, devastated, dismal, dreary, empty, uncultivated, uninhabited, unproductive, wild **10.** lay waste deprecate (*Rare*), despoil, destroy, devastate, pillage, rape, ravage, raze, ruin, sack, spoil, wreak havoc upon

wasteful extravagant, improvident, lavish, prodigal, profligate, ruinous, spendthrift, thriftless, uneconomical, unthrifty

wasteland desert, void, waste, wild, wilderness

waster drone, good-for-nothing, idler, layabout, loafer, loser, malingerer, ne'er-do-well, shirker, skiver (*Brit. sl.*), wastrel

wastrel 1. prodigal, profligate, spendthrift, squanderer **2.** drone, good-for-nothing, idler, layabout, loafer, loser, malingerer, ne'er-do-well, shirker, waster

watch *v.* **1.** contemplate, eye, gaze at, look, look at, look on, mark, note, observe, pay attention, peer at, regard, see, stare at, view **2.** attend, be on the alert, be on the lookout, be vigilant, be wary, be watchful, keep an eye open (*Inf.*), look out, take heed, wait **3.** guard, keep, look after, mind, protect, superintend, take care of, tend ~*n.* **4.** chronometer, clock, pocket watch, timepiece, wristwatch **5.** alertness, attention, eye, heed, inspection, lookout, notice, observation, supervision, surveillance, vigil, vigilance, watchfulness

watchdog 1. guard dog **2.** custodian, guardian, inspector, monitor, protector, scrutineer

watcher looker-on, lookout, observer, onlooker, spectator, spy, viewer, witness

watchful alert, attentive, circumspect, guarded, heedful, observant, on one's guard, on the lookout, on the qui vive, on the watch, suspicious, vigilant, wary, wide awake

watchfulness alertness, attention, attentiveness, caution, cautiousness, circumspection, heedfulness, vigilance, wariness

watchman caretaker, custodian, guard, security guard, security man

watch out be alert, be careful, be on one's guard, be on the alert, be on (the) watch, be vigilant, be watchful, have a care, keep a sharp lookout, keep a weather eye open, keep one's eyes open, keep one's eyes peeled *or* skinned (*Inf.*), look out, mind out, watch oneself

watch over defend, guard, keep safe, look after, preserve, protect, shelter, shield, stand guard over

watchword 1. countersign, magic word, password, shibboleth **2.** battle cry, byword, catch phrase, catchword, maxim, motto, rallying cry, slogan

water *n.* **1.** Adam's ale *or* wine, aqua, H_2O **2.** hold water bear examination *or* scrutiny, be credible (logical, sound), make sense, pass the test, ring true, work **3.** of the first water excellent, of the best, of the best quality, of the finest quality, of the highest degree, of the highest grade ~*v.* **4.** damp, dampen, douse, drench, flood, hose, irrigate, moisten, soak, souse, spray, sprinkle **5.** add water to, adulterate, dilute, put water in, thin, water down, weaken

water down 1. add water to, adulterate, dilute, put water in, thin, water, weaken **2.** adulterate, mitigate, qualify, soften, tone down, weaken

waterfall cascade, cataract, chute, fall, force (*Northern Brit.*), linn (*Scot.*)

watertight 1. sound, waterproof **2.** airtight, firm, flawless, foolproof, impregnable, incontrovertible, sound, unassailable

watery 1. aqueous, damp, fluid, humid, liquid, marshy, moist, soggy, squelchy, wet **2.** rheumy, tear-filled, tearful, weepy **3.** adulterated, dilute, diluted, flavourless, insipid, runny, tasteless, thin, washy, watered-down, waterish, weak, wishy-washy (*Inf.*)

wave *v.* **1.** brandish, flap, flourish, flutter, move to and fro, oscillate, quiver, ripple, shake, stir, sway, swing, undulate, wag, waver, wield **2.** beckon, direct, gesticulate, gesture, indicate, sign, signal ~n. **3**. billow, breaker, comber, ridge, ripple, roller, sea surf, swell, undulation, unevenness **4**. current, drift, flood, ground swell, movement, outbreak, rash, rush, stream, surge, sweep, tendency, trend, upsurge

waver 1. be indecisive, be irresolute, be unable to decide, be unable to make up one's mind, blow hot and cold (*Inf.*), dither, falter, fluctuate, hesitate, hum and haw, seesaw, shillyshally (*Inf.*), swither (*Scot.*), vacillate **2**. flicker, fluctuate, quiver, reel, shake, sway, totter, tremble, undulate, vary, wave, weave, wobble

wax *v*. become fuller, become larger, develop, dilate, enlarge, expand, fill out, get bigger, grow, increase, magnify, mount, rise, swell

waxen anaemic, ashen, bloodless, colourless, ghastly, pale, pallid, wan, white, whitish

way 1. approach, course of action, fashion, manner, means, method, mode, plan, practice, procedure, process, scheme, system, technique **2**. access, avenue, channel, course, direction, highway, lane, path, pathway, road, route, street, thoroughfare, track, trail **3**. elbowroom, opening, room, space **4**. distance, journey, length, stretch, trail **5**. advance, approach, journey, march, passage, progress **6**. characteristic, conduct, custom, habit, idiosyncrasy, manner, nature, personality, practice, style, trait, usage, wont **7**. aspect, detail, feature, particular, point, respect, sense **8**. aim, ambition, choice, demand, desire, goal, pleasure, will, wish **9**. *Inf.* circumstance, condition, fettle, shape (*Inf.*), situation, state, status **10**. forward motion, headway, movement, passage, progress **11. by the way** by the bye, en passant, incidentally, in parenthesis, in passing **12. give way a**. break down, cave in, collapse, crack, crumple, fall, fall to pieces, give, go to pieces, subside **b**. accede, acknowledge defeat, acquiesce, back down, concede, make concessions, withdraw, yield **13. under way** afoot, begun, going, in motion, in progress, moving, on the go (*Inf.*), on the move, started

wayfarer bird of passage, globetrotter, Gypsy, itinerant, journeyer, nomad, rover, traveller, trekker, voyager, walker, wanderer

wayfaring *adj.* drifting, itinerant, journeying, nomadic, peripatetic, rambling, roving, travelling, voyaging, walking, wandering

waylay accost, ambush, attack, catch, hold up, intercept, lie in wait for, pounce on, set upon, surprise, swoop down on

way-out 1. advanced, avant-garde, bizarre, crazy, eccentric, experimental, farout (*Sl.*), freaky (*Sl.*), offbeat, outlandish, progressive, unconventional, unorthodox, weird, wild **2**. amazing, excellent, fantastic (*Inf.*), great (*Inf.*), marvellous, tremendous (*Inf.*), wonderful

ways and means ability, capability, capacity, course, funds, methods, procedure, reserves, resources, tools, way, wherewithal

wayward capricious, changeable, contrary, contumacious, cross-grained, disobedient, erratic, fickle, flighty, froward, headstrong, inconstant, incorrigible, insubordinate, intractable, mulish, obdurate, obstinate, perverse, rebellious, refractory, self-willed, stubborn, undependable, ungovernable, unmanageable, unpredictable, unruly, wilful

weak 1. anaemic, debilitated, decrepit, delicate, effete, enervated, exhausted, faint, feeble, fragile, frail, infirm, languid, puny, shaky, sickly, spent, tender, unsound, unsteady, wasted, weakly **2**. cowardly, impotent, indecisive, ineffectual, infirm, irresolute, namby-pamby, powerless, soft, spineless, timorous, weak-kneed (*Inf.*) **3**. distant, dull, faint, imperceptible, low, muffled, poor, quiet, slight, small, soft **4**. deficient, faulty, inadequate, lacking, poor, substandard, under-strength, wanting **5**. feeble, flimsy, hollow, inconclusive, invalid, lame, pathetic, shallow, slight, unconvincing, unsatisfactory **6**. defenceless, exposed, helpless, unguarded, unprotected, unsafe, untenable, vulnerable, wide open **7**. diluted, insipid, milk-and-water, runny, tasteless, thin, under-strength, waterish, watery, wishy-washy (*Inf.*)

weaken 1. abate, debilitate, depress, diminish, droop, dwindle, ease up, enervate, fade, fail, flag, give way, impair, invalidate, lessen, lower, mitigate, moderate, reduce, sap, sap the strength of, soften up, temper, tire, undermine, wane **2**. adulterate, cut, debase, dilute, thin, thin out, water down

weakling coward, doormat (*Sl.*), drip

(*Inf.*), jellyfish (*Inf.*), milksop, mouse, sissy, wet (*Brit. inf.*), wimp (*Inf.*)

weakness 1. debility, decrepitude, enervation, faintness, feebleness, fragility, frailty, impotence, infirmity, irresolution, powerlessness, vulnerability **2.** Achilles heel, blemish, chink in one's armour, defect, deficiency, failing, fault, flaw, imperfection, lack, shortcoming **3.** fondness, inclination, liking, passion, penchant, predilection, proclivity, proneness, soft spot

weal contusion, mark, ridge, scar, streak, stripe, wale, welt, wheal

wealth 1. affluence, assets, capital, cash, estate, fortune, funds, goods, lucre, means, money, opulence, pelf, possessions, property, prosperity, resources, riches, substance **2.** abundance, bounty, copiousness, cornucopia, fullness, plenitude, plenty, profusion, richness, store

wealthy affluent, comfortable, filthy rich (*Sl.*), flush (*Inf.*), in the money (*Inf.*), loaded (*Sl.*), made of money (*Inf.*), moneyed, on easy street (*Sl.*), opulent, prosperous, quids in (*Sl.*), rich, rolling in it (*Sl.*), stinking rich (*Sl.*), well-heeled (*Sl.*), well-off, well-to-do

wear *v.* **1.** bear, be clothed in, be dressed in, carry, clothe oneself, don, dress in, have on, put on, sport **2.** display, exhibit, fly, show **3.** abrade, consume, corrode, deteriorate, erode, fray, grind, impair, rub, use, wash away, waste **4.** bear up, be durable, endure, hold up, last, stand up **5.** annoy, drain, enervate, exasperate, fatigue, harass, irk, pester, tax, undermine, vex, weaken, weary **6.** *Brit. sl.* accept, allow, brook, countenance, fall for, permit, put up with (*Inf.*), stand for, stomach, swallow (*Inf.*), take ~*n.* **7.** employment, mileage (*Inf.*), service, use, usefulness, utility **8.** apparel, attire, clothes, costume, dress, garb, garments, gear, habit, outfit, things **9.** abrasion, attrition, corrosion, damage, depreciation, deterioration, erosion, friction, use, wear and tear

wear down 1. abrade, be consumed, consume, corrode, erode, grind down, rub away **2.** chip away at (*Inf.*), fight a war of attrition against, overcome gradually, reduce, undermine

weariness drowsiness, enervation, exhaustion, fatigue, languor, lassitude, lethargy, listlessness, prostration, tiredness

wearing exasperating, exhausting, fatiguing, irksome, oppressive, taxing, tiresome, tiring, trying, wearisome

wearisome annoying, boring, bothersome, burdensome, dull, exasperating, exhausting, fatiguing, humdrum, irksome, monotonous, oppressive, pestiential, prosaic, tedious, troublesome, trying, uninteresting, vexatious, wearing

wear off 1. abate, decrease, diminish, disappear, dwindle, ebb, fade, lose effect, lose strength, peter out, subside, wane, weaken **2.** abrade, disappear, efface, fade, rub away

wear out 1. become useless, become worn, consume, deteriorate, erode, fray, impair, use up, wear through **2.** enervate, exhaust, fag out (*Inf.*), fatigue, frazzle (*Inf.*), knacker (*Brit. sl.*), prostrate, sap, tire, weary

weary *adj.* **1.** all in (*Sl.*), asleep *or* dead on one's feet (*Inf.*), dead beat (*Inf.*), dog-tired (*Inf.*), done in (*Inf.*), drained, drooping, drowsy, enervated, exhausted, fagged (*Inf.*), fatigued, flagging, jaded, knackered (*Sl.*), ready to drop, sleepy, spent, tired, wearied, whacked (*Brit. inf.*), worn out **2.** arduous, enervative, irksome, laborious, taxing, tiresome, tiring, wearing, wearisome **3.** bored, browned-off (*Inf.*), discontented, fed up, impatient, indifferent, jaded, sick (*Inf.*), sick and tired (*Inf.*) ~*v.* **4.** burden, debilitate, drain, droop, enervate, fade, fag (*Inf.*), fail, fatigue, grow tired, sap, take it out of (*Inf.*), tax, tire, tire out, wear out **5.** annoy, become bored, bore, exasperate, have had enough, irk, jade, make discontented, plague, sicken, try the patience of, vex

weather *n.* **1.** climate, conditions **2. under the weather** *a.* ailing, below par, ill, indisposed, nauseous, not well, off-colour, out of sorts, poorly (*Inf.*), seedy (*Inf.*), sick **b.** crapulent, crapulous, drunk, groggy (*Inf.*), hung over (*Inf.*), inebriated, intoxicated, one over the eight (*Sl.*), the worse for drink, three sheets in the wind (*Inf.*), under the influence (*Inf.*) ~*v.* **3.** expose, harden, season, toughen **4.** bear up against, brave, come through, endure, get through, live through, make it (*Inf.*), overcome, pull through, resist, ride out, rise above, stand, stick it out (*Inf.*), suffer, surmount, survive, withstand

weave 1. blend, braid, entwine, fuse,

incorporate, interlace, intermingle, intertwine, introduce, knit, mat, merge, plait, twist, unite **2**. build, construct, contrive, create, fabricate, make, make up, put together, spin **3**. crisscross, move in and out, weave one's way, wind, zigzag **4**. **get weaving** *Inf*. get a move on, get going, get one's finger out (*Brit. inf.*), get under way, hurry, make a start, shake a leg (*Sl.*), start

web 1. cobweb, spider's web **2**. interlacing, lattice, mesh, net, netting, network, screen, tangle, toils, weave, webbing

wed 1. become man and wife, be married to, espouse, get hitched (*Inf.*), get married, join, make one, marry, splice (*Inf.*), take as one's husband, take as one's wife, take to wife, tie the knot (*Inf.*), unite **2**. ally, blend, coalesce, combine, commingle, dedicate, fuse, interweave, join, link, marry, merge, unify, unite, yoke

wedding espousals, marriage, marriage ceremony, nuptial rite, nuptials, wedlock

wedge 1. *n*. block, chock, chunk, lump, wodge (*Brit. inf.*) **2**. *v*. block, cram, crowd, force, jam, lodge, pack, ram, split, squeeze, stuff, thrust

wedlock marriage, matrimony

wee diminutive, insignificant, itsybitsy (*Inf.*), Lilliputian, little, microscopic, miniature, minuscule, minute, negligible, small, teeny, teeny-weeny, tiny

weed out dispense with, eliminate, eradicate, extirpate, get rid of, remove, root out, separate out, shed, uproot

weedy feeble, frail, ineffectual, namby-pamby, puny, skinny, thin, undersized, weak, weak-kneed (*Inf.*)

weekly by the week, every week, hebdomadal, hebdomadally, hebdomadary, once a week

weep bemoan, bewail, blub (*Sl.*), blubber, boohoo, complain, cry, greet (*Dialect*), keen, lament, moan, mourn, shed tears, snivel, sob, ululate, whimper, whinge (*Inf.*)

weepy 1. *adj*. blubbering, close to tears, crying, lachrymose, on the verge of tears, sobbing, tearful, weeping, whimpering **2**. *n*. tear-jerker (*Inf.*)

weigh 1. have a weight of, measure the weight of, put on the scales, tip the scales at (*Inf.*) **2**. apportion, deal out, dole out, measure **3**. consider, contem-plate, deliberate upon, evaluate, examine, give thought to, meditate upon, mull over, ponder, reflect upon, study, think over **4**. be influential, carry weight, count, cut any ice (*Inf.*), have influence, impress, matter, tell **5**. bear down, burden, oppress, prey

weigh down bear down, burden, depress, get down, oppress, overburden, overload, press down, trouble, weigh upon, worry

weight *n*. **1**. avoirdupois, burden, gravity, heaviness, heft (*Inf.*), load, mass, poundage, pressure, tonnage **2**. ballast, heavy object, load, mass **3**. burden, load, millstone, oppression, pressure, strain **4**. greatest force, main force, onus, preponderance **5**. authority, clout (*Inf.*), consequence, consideration, efficacy, emphasis, impact, import, importance, influence, moment, persuasiveness, power, significance, substance, value ~*v*. **6**. add weight to, ballast, charge, freight, increase the load on, increase the weight of, load, make heavier **7**. burden, encumber, handicap, impede, oppress, overburden, weigh down **8**. bias, load, unbalance

weighty 1. burdensome, cumbersome, dense, heavy, hefty (*Inf.*), massive, ponderous **2**. consequential, considerable, critical, crucial, forcible, grave, important, momentous, portentous, serious, significant, solemn, substantial **3**. backbreaking, burdensome, crushing, demanding, difficult, exacting, onerous, oppressive, taxing, worrisome, worrying

weird bizarre, creepy (*Inf.*), eerie, eldritch (*Poetic*), far-out (*Sl.*), freakish, ghostly, grotesque, mysterious, odd, outlandish, queer, spooky (*Inf.*), strange, supernatural, uncanny, unearthly, unnatural

weirdie, weirdo crackpot (*Inf.*), crank (*Inf.*), eccentric, freak (*Sl.*), loony (*Sl.*), nut (*Sl.*), nutcase (*Sl.*), nutter (*Brit. sl.*), oddball (*Inf.*), queer fish (*Inf.*)

welcome *adj*. **1**. acceptable, accepted, agreeable, appreciated, delightful, desirable, gladly received, gratifying, pleasant, pleasing, pleasurable, refreshing, wanted **2**. at home, free, invited, under no obligation ~*n*. **3**. acceptance, entertainment, greeting, hospitality, reception, salutation ~*v*. **4**. accept gladly, bid welcome, embrace, greet, hail, meet, offer hospitality to, receive, receive with open arms, roll out the red carpet for, usher in

weld 1. *v.* bind, bond, braze, cement, connect, fuse, join, link, solder, unite 2. *n.* bond, joint, juncture, seam

welfare advantage, benefit, good, happiness, health, interest, profit, prosperity, success, wellbeing

well[1] *adv.* 1. agreeably, capitally, famously (*Inf.*), happily, in a satisfactory manner, nicely, pleasantly, satisfactorily, smoothly, splendidly, successfully 2. ably, adeptly, adequately, admirably, conscientiously, correctly, effectively, efficiently, expertly, proficiently, properly, skilfully, with skill 3. accurately, attentively, carefully, closely 4. comfortably, flourishingly, prosperously 5. correctly, easily, fairly, fittingly, in all fairness, justly, properly, readily, rightly, suitably 6. closely, completely, deeply, fully, intimately, personally, profoundly, thoroughly 7. approvingly, favourably, glowingly, graciously, highly, kindly, warmly 8. abundantly, amply, completely, considerably, fully, greatly, heartily, highly, substantially, sufficiently, thoroughly, very much 9. **as well** also, besides, in addition, into the bargain, to boot, too 10. **as well as** along with, at the same time as, in addition to, including, over and above ~*adj.* 11. able-bodied, fit, hale, healthy, hearty, in fine fettle, in good health, robust, sound, strong, up to par 12. advisable, agreeable, bright, fine, fitting, flourishing, fortunate, good, happy, lucky, pleasing, profitable, proper, prudent, right, satisfactory, thriving, useful

well[2] *n.* 1. fountain, pool, source, spring, waterhole 2. bore, hole, pit, shaft 3. fount, mine, repository, source, wellspring ~*v.* 4. flow, gush, jet, ooze, pour, rise, run, seep, spout, spring, spurt, stream, surge, trickle

well-balanced 1. graceful, harmonious, proportional, symmetrical, well-proportioned 2. judicious, level-headed, rational, reasonable, sane, sensible, sober, sound, together (*Sl.*), well-adjusted

well-bred 1. aristocratic, blue-blooded, gentle, highborn, noble, patrician, well-born 2. civil, courteous, courtly, cultivated, cultured, gallant, genteel, gentlemanly, ladylike, mannerly, polished, polite, refined, urbane, well-brought-up, well-mannered

well-favoured attractive, beautiful, bonny, comely, fair, good-looking, handsome, lovely, nice-looking, pretty

well-fed 1. healthy, in good condition, well-nourished 2. chubby, fat, fleshy, plump, podgy, portly, rotund, rounded, stout

well-groomed dapper, neat, smart, spruce, tidy, trim, well-dressed, well turned out

well-known celebrated, familiar, famous, illustrious, notable, noted, popular, renowned, widely known

well-nigh all but, almost, just about, more or less, nearly, next to, practically, virtually

well-off 1. comfortable, flourishing, fortunate, lucky, successful, thriving 2. affluent, comfortable, flush (*Inf.*), loaded (*Sl.*), moneyed, prosperous, rich, wealthy, well-heeled (*Sl.*), well-to-do

wellspring 1. fount, fountainhead, origin, source, wellhead 2. fund, mine, repository, reserve, reservoir, source, supply, well

well-thought-of admired, esteemed, highly regarded, of good repute, reputable, respected, revered, venerated

well-to-do affluent, comfortable, flush (*Inf.*), loaded (*Sl.*), moneyed, prosperous, rich, wealthy, well-heeled (*Sl.*), well-off

well-worn commonplace, hackneyed, overused, stale, stereotyped, threadbare, timeworn, tired, trite

welt contusion, mark, ridge, scar, streak, stripe, wale, weal, wheal

welter *v.* 1. flounder, lie, roll, splash, tumble, wade, wallow, writhe 2. billow, heave, pitch, roll, surge, swell, toss ~*n.* 3. confusion, hotchpotch, jumble, mess, muddle, tangle, web

wend direct one's course, go, make for, move, proceed, progress, travel

wet *adj.* 1. aqueous, damp, dank, drenched, dripping, humid, moist, moistened, saturated, soaked, soaking, sodden, soggy, sopping, waterlogged, watery, wringing wet 2. clammy, dank, drizzling, humid, misty, pouring, raining, rainy, showery, teeming 3. *Brit. inf.* effete, feeble, foolish, ineffectual, irresolute, namby-pamby, silly, soft, spineless, timorous, weak, weedy (*Inf.*) 4. **wet behind the ears** *Inf.* born yesterday, callow, green, immature, inexperienced, innocent, naive, new, raw ~*n.* 5. clamminess, condensation, damp, dampness, humidity, liquid, moisture, water, wetness **6.** damp weather, drizzle, rain, rains, rainy season, rainy weather **7.** *Brit. inf.* drip (*Inf.*), milksop, weakling, weed (*Inf.*), wimp (*Inf.*) ~*v.* **8.** damp, dampen, dip, douse, drench, humidify, irrigate, moisten, saturate, soak, splash, spray, sprinkle, steep, water

wetness clamminess, condensation, damp, dampness, humidity, liquid, moisture, sogginess, water, wet

whack *v.* **1.** bang, bash (*Inf.*), beat, belabour, belt (*Sl.*), box, buffet, clobber (*Sl.*), clout (*Inf.*), cuff, hit, lambaste, rap, slap, slug, smack, sock (*Sl.*), strike, thrash, thump, thwack, wallop (*Inf.*) ~*n.* **2.** bang, bash (*Inf.*), belt (*Sl.*), blow, box, buffet, clout (*Inf.*), cuff, hit, rap, slap, slug, smack, sock (*Sl.*), stroke, thump, thwack, wallop (*Inf.*), wham **3.** *Inf.* allotment, bit, cut (*Inf.*), part, portion, quota, share **4.** *Inf.* attempt, bash (*Inf.*), crack (*Inf.*), go, shot (*Inf.*), stab, try, turn

whacking big, enormous, extraordinary, giant, gigantic, great, huge, large, mammoth, monstrous, prodigious, tremendous, whopping (*Inf.*)

wham bang, bash (*Inf.*), blow, concussion, impact, slam, smack, thump, thwack, wallop (*Inf.*), whack, whang

wharf dock, jetty, landing stage, pier, quay

wheal contusion, mark, ridge, scar, streak, stripe, wale, weal

wheedle butter up, cajole, charm, coax, court, draw, entice, flatter, inveigle, persuade, talk into, worm

wheel *n.* **1.** circle, gyration, pivot, revolution, roll, rotation, spin, turn, twirl, whirl **2. at the wheel** at the helm, driving, in charge, in command, in control, in the driving seat, steering ~*v.* **3.** circle, gyrate, orbit, pirouette, revolve, roll, rotate, spin, swing, swivel, turn, twirl, whirl

wheeze *v.* **1.** breathe roughly, catch one's breath, cough, gasp, hiss, rasp, whistle ~*n.* **2.** cough, gasp, hiss, rasp, whistle **3.** *Brit. sl.* expedient, idea, plan, ploy, ruse, scheme, stunt, trick, wrinkle (*Inf.*) **4.** *Inf.* anecdote, chestnut (*Inf.*), crack (*Sl.*), gag (*Sl.*), joke, old joke, one-liner (*Sl.*), story

whereabouts location, position, site, situation

wherewithal capital, equipment, essentials, funds, means, money, ready (*Inf.*), ready money, resources, supplies

whet 1. edge, file, grind, hone, sharpen, strop **2.** animate, arouse, awaken, enhance, excite, incite, increase, kindle, pique, provoke, quicken, rouse, stimulate, stir

whiff *n.* **1.** aroma, blast, breath, draught, gust, hint, odour, puff, scent, smell, sniff ~*v.* **2.** breathe, inhale, puff, smell, smoke, sniff, waft **3.** *Brit. sl.* hum (*Sl.*), pong (*Brit. inf.*), reek, stink

whim caprice, conceit, craze, crotchet, fad (*Inf.*), fancy, freak, humour, impulse, notion, passing thought, quirk, sport, sudden notion, urge, vagary, whimsy

whimper 1. *v.* blub (*Sl.*), blubber, cry, grizzle (*Inf.*), mewl, moan, pule, snivel, sob, weep, whine, whinge (*Inf.*) **2.** *n.* moan, snivel, sob, whine

whimsical capricious, chimerical, crotchety, curious, droll, eccentric, fanciful, fantastic, fantastical, freakish, funny, mischievous, odd, peculiar, playful, quaint, queer, singular, unusual, waggish, weird

whine *n.* **1.** cry, moan, plaintive cry, sob, wail, whimper **2.** beef (*Sl.*), complaint, gripe (*Inf.*), grouse, grumble, moan ~*v.* **3.** beef (*Sl.*), bellyache (*Sl.*), carp, complain, cry, gripe (*Inf.*), grizzle (*Inf.*), grouse, grumble, moan, sob, wail, whimper, whinge (*Inf.*)

whiner complainer, fault-finder, grouch (*Inf.*), grouser, grumbler, malcontent, moaner, whinger (*Inf.*)

whip *v.* **1.** beat, birch, cane, castigate, flagellate, flog, give a hiding (*Inf.*), lash, leather, punish, scourge, spank, strap, switch, tan (*Sl.*), thrash **2.** exhibit, flash, jerk, produce, pull, remove, seize, show, snatch, whisk **3.** *Inf.* dart, dash, dive, flit, flounce, fly, rush, shoot, tear, whisk **4.** *Inf.* beat, best, clobber (*Sl.*), conquer, defeat, drub, hammer (*Inf.*), lick (*Inf.*), outdo, overcome, overpower, overwhelm, rout, take apart (*Sl.*), thrash, trounce, wipe the floor with (*Inf.*), worst **5.** agitate, compel, drive, foment, goad, hound, incite, instigate, prick, prod, provoke, push, spur, stir, urge, work up **6.** beat, whisk ~*n.* **7.** birch, bullwhip, cane, cat-o'-nine-tails, crop, horsewhip, knout, lash, rawhide, riding crop, scourge, switch, thong

whipping beating, birching, caning,

castigation, flagellation, flogging, hiding (*Inf.*), lashing, leathering, punishment, spanking, tanning (*Sl.*), the strap, thrashing

whip up agitate, arouse, excite, foment, incite, inflame, instigate, kindle, provoke, stir up, work up

whirl *v.* **1.** circle, gyrate, pirouette, pivot, reel, revolve, roll, rotate, spin, swirl, turn, twirl, twist, wheel **2.** feel dizzy, reel, spin ~*n.* **3.** birl (*Scot.*), circle, gyration, pirouette, reel, revolution, roll, rotation, spin, swirl, turn, twirl, twist, wheel **4.** confusion, daze, dither, flurry, giddiness, spin **5.** flurry, merry-go-round, round, series, succession **6.** agitation, bustle, commotion, confusion, flurry, hurly-burly, stir, tumult, uproar **7. give (something) a whirl** *Inf.* attempt, have a bash (crack, go, shot, stab, whack) (*Inf.*), try

whirlwind **1.** *n.* dust devil, tornado, waterspout **2.** *adj.* hasty, headlong, impetuous, impulsive, lightning, quick, rapid, rash, short, speedy, swift

whisk *v.* **1.** brush, flick, sweep, whip, wipe **2.** dart, dash, fly, hasten, hurry, race, rush, shoot, speed, sweep, tear **3.** beat, fluff up, whip ~*n.* **4.** brush, flick, sweep, whip, wipe **5.** beater

whisky barley-bree (*Scot.*), bourbon, John Barleycorn, malt, rye, Scotch, usquebaugh

whisper *v.* **1.** breathe, murmur, say softly, speak in hushed tones, utter under the breath **2.** gossip, hint, insinuate, intimate, murmur, spread rumours **3.** hiss, murmur, rustle, sigh, sough, susurrate (*Literary*), swish ~*n.* **4.** hushed tone, low voice, murmur, soft voice, undertone **5.** hiss, murmur, rustle, sigh, sighing, soughing, susurration *or* susurrus (*Literary*), swish **6.** breath, fraction, hint, shadow, suggestion, suspicion, tinge, trace, whiff **7.** *Inf.* buzz, gossip, innuendo, insinuation, report, rumour, word

whit atom, bit, crumb, dash, drop, fragment, grain, iota, jot, least bit, little, mite, modicum, particle, piece, pinch, scrap, shred, speck, trace

white **1.** ashen, bloodless, ghastly, grey, pale, pallid, pasty, wan, waxen, wheyfaced **2.** grey, grizzled, hoary, silver, snowy **3.** clean, immaculate, innocent, pure, spotless, stainless, unblemished, unsullied

white-collar clerical, executive, nonmanual, office, professional, salaried

whiten blanch, bleach, blench, etiolate, fade, go white, pale, turn pale

whitewash **1.** *n.* camouflage, concealment, cover-up, deception, extenuation **2.** *v.* camouflage, conceal, cover up, extenuate, gloss over, make light of, suppress

whittle **1.** carve, cut, hew, pare, shape, shave, trim **2.** consume, destroy, eat away, erode, reduce, undermine, wear away

whole *adj.* **1.** complete, entire, full, in one piece, integral, total, unabridged, uncut, undivided **2.** faultless, flawless, good, in one piece, intact, inviolate, mint, perfect, sound, unbroken, undamaged, unharmed, unhurt, unimpaired, uninjured, unmutilated, unscathed, untouched **3.** able-bodied, better, cured, fit, hale, healed, healthy, in fine fettle, in good health, recovered, robust, sound, strong, well ~*adv.* **4.** in one, in one piece ~*n.* **5.** aggregate, all, everything, lot, sum total, the entire amount, total **6.** ensemble, entirety, entity, fullness, piece, totality, unit, unity **7. on the whole a.** all in all, all things considered, by and large, taking everything into consideration **b.** as a rule, for the most part, generally, in the main, in general, mostly, predominantly

wholehearted committed, complete, dedicated, determined, devoted, earnest, emphatic, enthusiastic, genuine, heartfelt, hearty, real, sincere, true, unfeigned, unqualified, unreserved, unstinting, warm, zealous

wholesale **1.** *adj.* all-inclusive, broad, comprehensive, extensive, far-reaching, indiscriminate, mass, sweeping, wideranging **2.** *adv.* all at once, comprehensively, extensively, indiscriminately, on a large scale, without exception

wholesome **1.** beneficial, good, healthful, health-giving, healthy, helpful, hygienic, invigorating, nourishing, nutritious, salubrious, salutary, sanitary, strengthening **2.** clean, decent, edifying, ethical, exemplary, honourable, improving, innocent, moral, nice, pure, respectable, righteous, uplifting, virtuous, worthy

wholly **1.** all, altogether, completely, comprehensively, entirely, fully, heart and soul, in every respect, one hundred per cent (*Inf.*), perfectly, thoroughly, totally, utterly 2. exclusively, only, solely, without exception

whoop cheer, cry, halloo, holler (*Inf.*), hoot, hurrah, scream, shout, shriek, yell

whopper 1. colossus, crackerjack (*Inf.*), giant, jumbo (*Inf.*), leviathan, mammoth, monster 2. big lie, fable, fabrication, falsehood, tall story (*Inf.*), untruth

whopping big, enormous, extraordinary, giant, gigantic, great, huge, large, mammoth, massive, monstrous, prodigious, tremendous, whacking (*Inf.*)

whore *n.* 1. brass (*Sl.*), call girl, cocotte, courtesan, demimondaine, demirep (*Rare*), fallen woman, *fille de joie*, harlot, hooker (*U.S. sl.*), hustler (*U.S. sl.*), lady of the night, loose woman, prostitute, streetwalker, strumpet, tart (*Inf.*), trollop, woman of easy virtue, woman of ill repute ~*v.* 2. be on the game (*Sl.*), hustle (*U.S. sl.*), prostitute oneself, sell one's body, sell oneself, solicit, walk the streets 3. fornicate, lech (*Inf.*), sleep around (*Inf.*), wanton, wench (*Archaic*), womanize

whorehouse bagnio, bordello, brothel, cathouse (*U.S. sl.*), disorderly house, house of ill fame *or* repute, house of prostitution, knocking-shop (*Brit. sl.*)

whorl coil, corkscrew, helix, spiral, swirl, twist, vortex

wicked 1. abandoned, abominable, amoral, atrocious, bad, black-hearted, corrupt, debased, depraved, devilish, dissolute, egregious, evil, fiendish, flagitious, foul, guilty, heinous, immoral, impious, iniquitous, irreligious, nefarious, scandalous, shameful, sinful, unprincipled, unrighteous, vicious, vile, villainous, worthless 2. arch, impish, incorrigible, mischievous, naughty, rascally, roguish 3. acute, agonizing, awful, crashing, destructive, dreadful, fearful, fierce, harmful, injurious, intense, mighty, painful, severe, terrible 4. bothersome, difficult, distressing, galling, offensive, troublesome, trying, unpleasant 5. *Sl.* adept, adroit, deft, expert, masterly, mighty, outstanding, powerful, skilful, strong

wide *adj.* 1. ample, broad, catholic, comprehensive, distended, encyclopedic, expanded, expansive, extensive, far-reaching, general, immense, inclusive, large, sweeping, vast 2. away, distant,

off, off course, off target, remote 3. dilated, distended, expanded, fully open, outspread, outstretched 4. ample, baggy, capacious, commodious, full, loose, roomy, spacious ~*adv.* 5. as far as possible, completely, fully, right out, to the furthest extent 6. astray, nowhere near, off course, off target, off the mark, out

wide-awake 1. conscious, fully awake, roused, wakened 2. alert, aware, heedful, keen, observant, on one's toes, on the alert, on the ball (*Inf.*), on the qui vive, vigilant, wary, watchful

wide-eyed credulous, green, impressionable, ingenuous, innocent, naive, simple, trusting, unsophisticated, unsuspicious, wet behind the ears (*Inf.*)

widen broaden, dilate, enlarge, expand, extend, open out *or* up, open wide, spread, stretch

wide-open 1. fully extended, fully open, gaping, outspread, outstretched, splayed, spread 2. at risk, defenceless, exposed, in danger, in peril, open, susceptible, unprotected, vulnerable 3. anybody's guess (*Inf.*), indeterminate, uncertain, unpredictable, unsettled, up for grabs (*Inf.*)

widespread broad, common, epidemic, extensive, far-flung, far-reaching, general, pervasive, popular, prevalent, rife, sweeping, universal, wholesale

width breadth, compass, diameter, extent, girth, measure, range, reach, scope, span, thickness, wideness

wield 1. brandish, employ, flourish, handle, manage, manipulate, ply, swing, use 2. apply, be possessed of, command, control, exercise, exert, have, have at one's disposal, hold, maintain, make use of, manage, possess, put to use, utilize

wife better half (*Humorous*), bride, helpmate, helpmeet, little woman (*Inf.*), mate, old lady (*Inf.*), old woman (*Inf.*), partner, spouse, (the) missis *or* missus (*Inf.*), woman (*Inf.*)

wiggle *v./n.* jerk, jiggle, shake, shimmy, squirm, twitch, wag, waggle, writhe

wild *adj.* 1. feral, ferocious, fierce, savage, unbroken, undomesticated, untamed 2. free, indigenous, native, natural, uncultivated 3. desert, deserted, desolate, empty, godforsaken, trackless, uncivilized, uncultivated, uninhabited, unpopulated, virgin 4. barbaric, barbarous, brutish, ferocious, fierce, primitive, rude, savage, uncivilized 5. boisterous, chaotic, disorderly, impetuous, lawless, noisy, riotous, rough, rowdy, self-willed, turbulent, unbridled, uncontrolled, undisciplined, unfettered, ungovernable, unmanageable, unrestrained, unruly, uproarious, violent, wayward **6.** blustery, choppy, furious, howling, intense, raging, rough, tempestuous, violent **7.** dishevelled, disordered, straggly, tousled, unkempt, untidy, windblown **8.** at one's wits' end, berserk, beside oneself, crazed, crazy, delirious, demented, excited, frantic, frenzied, hysterical, irrational, mad, maniacal, rabid, raving **9.** extravagant, fantastic, flighty, foolhardy, foolish, giddy, ill-considered, impracticable, imprudent, madcap, outrageous, preposterous, rash, reckless **10.** *Inf.* agog, avid, crazy (*Inf.*), daft (*Inf.*), eager, enthusiastic, excited, mad (*Inf.*), nuts (*Sl.*), potty (*Inf.*) ~*adv.* **11. run wild a.** grow unchecked, ramble, spread, straggle **b.** abandon all restraint, cut loose, go on the rampage, kick over the traces, rampage, run free, run riot, stray ~*n.* **12.** Often plural back of beyond (*Inf.*), desert, middle of nowhere (*Inf.*), uninhabited area, wasteland, wilderness

wilderness 1. desert, jungle, waste, wasteland, wild **2.** clutter, confused mass, confusion, congeries, jumble, maze, muddle, tangle, welter

wildlife flora and fauna

wile 1. artfulness, artifice, cheating, chicanery, craft, craftiness, cunning, fraud, guile, slyness, trickery **2.** *Usually plural* artifice, contrivance, device, dodge, imposition, lure, manoeuvre, ploy, ruse, stratagem, subterfuge, trick

wilful 1. adamant, bull-headed, determined, dogged, froward, headstrong, inflexible, intractable, intransigent, mulish, obdurate, obstinate, persistent, perverse, pig-headed, refractory, self-willed, stubborn, uncompromising, unyielding **2.** conscious, deliberate, intended, intentional, purposeful, volitional, voluntary, willed

will *n.* **1.** choice, decision, determination, discretion, option, prerogative, volition **2.** declaration, last wishes, testament **3.** choice, decision, decree, desire, fancy, inclination, mind, pleasure, preference, wish **4.** aim, determination, intention, purpose, resolution, resolve, willpower **5.** attitude, disposition, feeling **6. at will** as one pleases, as one thinks fit,

as one wishes, at one's desire (discretion, inclination, pleasure, whim, wish) ~*v.* **7.** bid, bring about, cause, command, decree, determine, direct, effect, ordain, order, resolve **8.** choose, desire, elect, opt, prefer, see fit, want, wish **9.** bequeath, confer, give, leave, pass on, transfer

willing agreeable, amenable, compliant, consenting, content, desirous, disposed, eager, enthusiastic, favourable, game (*Inf.*), happy, inclined, in favour, in the mood, nothing loath, pleased, prepared, ready, so-minded

willingly by choice, cheerfully, eagerly, freely, gladly, happily, of one's own accord, of one's own free will, readily, voluntarily, with all one's heart, without hesitation, with pleasure

willingness agreeableness, agreement, consent, desire, disposition, enthusiasm, favour, good will, inclination, volition, will, wish

willowy graceful, limber, lissom, lithe, slender, slim, supple, svelte, sylphlike

willpower determination, drive, firmness of purpose or will, fixity of purpose, force or strength of will, grit, resolution, resolve, self-control, self-discipline, single-mindedness

willy-nilly 1. *adv.* necessarily, *nolens volens*, of necessity, perforce, whether desired or not, whether one likes it or not, whether or no **2.** *adj.* inevitable, irrespective of one's wishes, necessary, unavoidable

wilt 1. become limp or flaccid, droop, sag, shrivel, wither **2.** diminish, dwindle, ebb, fade, fail, flag, languish, lose courage, melt away, sag, sink, wane, weaken, wither

wily arch, artful, astute, cagey (*Inf.*), crafty, crooked, cunning, deceitful, deceptive, designing, fly (*Sl.*), foxy, guileful, intriguing, scheming, sharp, shifty, shrewd, sly, tricky, underhand

win *v.* **1.** achieve first place, achieve mastery, be victorious, carry all before one, carry the day, come first, conquer, finish first, gain victory, overcome, prevail, succeed, take the prize, triumph **2.** accomplish, achieve, acquire, attain, bag (*Inf.*), catch, collect, come away with, earn, gain, get, net, obtain, pick up, procure, receive, secure **3.** *Often with* **over** allure, attract, bring or talk round, carry, charm, convert, convince, disarm, induce, influence, persuade, prevail upon, sway ~n. **4.** *Inf.* conquest, success, triumph, victory

wince 1. *v.* blench, cower, cringe, draw back, flinch, quail, recoil, shrink, start **2.** *n.* cringe, flinch, start

wind[1] **1.** *n.* air, air-current, blast, breath, breeze, current of air, draught, gust, zephyr **2.** *Inf.* clue, hint, inkling, intimation, notice, report, rumour, suggestion, tidings, warning, whisper **3.** babble, blather, bluster, boasting, empty talk, gab (*Inf.*), hot air, humbug, idle talk, talk, verbalizing **4.** breath, puff, respiration **5.** *Inf.* flatulence, flatus, gas **6. get** *or* **have the wind up** *Inf.* be afraid (alarmed, frightened, scared), fear, take fright **7. in the wind** about to happen, approaching, close at hand, coming, imminent, impending, in the offing, near, on the cards (*Inf.*), on the way **8. put the wind up** *Inf.* alarm, discourage, frighten, frighten off, scare, scare off

wind[2] *v.* **1.** coil, curl, encircle, furl, loop, reel, roll, spiral, turn around, twine, twist, wreathe **2.** bend, curve, deviate, meander, ramble, snake, turn, twist, zigzag ~n. **3.** bend, curve, meander, turn, twist, zigzag

windbag bigmouth (*Sl.*), blether (*Scot.*), blowhard (*Inf.*), boaster, bore, braggart, gasbag (*Sl.*), gossip, prattler

wind down cool off, decline, diminish, dwindle, lessen, reduce, relax, slacken, subside, taper off, unwind

winded breathless, gasping for breath, out of breath, out of puff, panting, puffed, puffed out

windfall bonanza, find, godsend, jackpot, manna from heaven, stroke of luck

winding 1. *n.* bend, convolution, curve, meander, turn, twist, undulation **2.** *adj.* anfractuous, bending, circuitous, convoluted, crooked, curving, flexuous, indirect, meandering, roundabout, serpentine, sinuous, spiral, tortuous, turning, twisting

wind-up close, conclusion, culmination, dénouement, end, finale, finish, termination

wind up 1. bring to a close, close, close down, conclude, end, finalize, finish, liquidate, settle, terminate, tie up the loose ends (*Inf.*), wrap up **2.** *Inf.* excite, make nervous, make tense, put on edge, work up **3.** *Inf.* be left, end one's days, end up, find oneself, finish up

windy 1. blowy, blustering, blustery,

boisterous, breezy, gusty, squally, stormy, tempestuous, wild, windswept **2.** boastful, bombastic, diffuse, empty, garrulous, long-winded, loquacious, meandering, pompous, prolix, rambling, turgid, verbose, wordy **3.** *Sl.* afraid, chicken (*Sl.*), cowardly, fearful, frightened, nervous, scared, timid

wing *n.* **1.** organ of flight, pennon (*Poetic*), pinion (*Poetic*) **2.** arm, branch, circle, clique, coterie, faction, group, grouping, section, segment, set, side **3.** adjunct, annexe, ell, extension ~v. **4.** fly, glide, soar **5.** fleet, fly, hasten, hurry, race, speed, zoom **6.** clip, hit, nick, wound

wink *v.* **1.** bat, blink, flutter, nictate, nictitate **2.** flash, gleam, glimmer, sparkle, twinkle ~n. **3.** blink, flutter, nictation **4.** flash, gleam, glimmering, sparkle, twinkle **5.** instant, jiffy (*Inf.*), moment, second, split second, twinkling

wink at allow, blink at, condone, connive at, disregard, ignore, overlook, pretend not to notice, put up with (*Inf.*), shut one's eyes to, tolerate, turn a blind eye to

winkle out dig out, dislodge, draw out, extract, extricate, force out, prise out, smoke out, worm out

winner champ (*Inf.*), champion, conquering hero, conqueror, first, master, vanquisher, victor

winning 1. alluring, amiable, attractive, bewitching, captivating, charming, delectable, delightful, disarming, enchanting, endearing, engaging, fascinating, fetching, lovely, pleasing, prepossessing, sweet, taking, winsome **2.** conquering, successful, triumphant, victorious

winnings booty, gains, prize(s), proceeds, profits, spoils, takings

winnow comb, cull, divide, fan, part, screen, select, separate, separate the wheat from the chaff, sift, sort out

winsome agreeable, alluring, amiable, attractive, bewitching, captivating, charming, comely, delectable, disarming, enchanting, endearing, engaging, fair, fascinating, fetching, pleasant, pleasing, pretty, sweet, taking, winning

wintry 1. brumal, chilly, cold, freezing, frosty, frozen, harsh, hibernal, hiemal, icy, snowy **2.** bleak, cheerless, cold, desolate, dismal

wipe *v.* **1.** brush, clean, dry, dust, mop,

rub, sponge, swab **2.** clean off, erase, get rid of, remove, rub off, take away, take off ~n. **3.** brush, lick, rub, swab

wipe out annihilate, blot out, destroy, efface, eradicate, erase, expunge, exterminate, extirpate, kill to the last man, massacre, obliterate

wiry 1. lean, sinewy, strong, tough **2.** bristly, kinky, stiff

wisdom astuteness, circumspection, comprehension, discernment, enlightenment, erudition, foresight, insight, intelligence, judgment, judiciousness, knowledge, learning, penetration, prudence, reason, sagacity, sapience, sense, sound judgment, understanding

wise 1. aware, clever, discerning, enlightened, erudite, informed, intelligent, judicious, knowing, perceptive, politic, prudent, rational, reasonable, sagacious, sage, sapient, sensible, shrewd, sound, understanding, well-advised, well-informed **2. put wise** *Sl.* alert, apprise, clue in *or* up, inform, let (someone) into the secret, notify, tell, tip off, warn

wisecrack 1. *n.* barb, funny (*Inf.*), gag (*Sl.*), jest, jibe, joke, pithy remark, quip, sardonic remark, smart remark, witticism **2.** *v.* be facetious, jest, jibe, joke, quip, tell jokes

wish *v.* **1.** aspire, covet, crave, desiderate, desire, hanker, hope, hunger, long, need, set one's heart on, sigh for, thirst, want, yearn **2.** bid, greet with **3.** ask, bid, command, desire, direct, instruct, order, require ~n. **4.** aspiration, desire, hankering, hope, hunger, inclination, intention, liking, longing, thirst, urge, want, whim, will, yearning **5.** bidding, command, desire, order, request, will

wishy-washy bland, feeble, flat, ineffective, ineffectual, insipid, jejune, tasteless, thin, vapid, watered-down, watery, weak

wisp piece, shred, snippet, strand, thread, twist

wispy attenuate, attenuated, delicate, diaphanous, ethereal, faint, fine, flimsy, fragile, frail, gossamer, insubstantial, light, thin, wisplike

wistful contemplative, disconsolate, dreaming, dreamy, forlorn, longing, meditative, melancholy, mournful, musing, pensive, reflective, sad, thoughtful, yearning

wit 1. badinage, banter, drollery, facetiousness, fun, humour, jocularity, levity, pleasantry, raillery, repartee, wordplay **2.** card (*Inf.*), comedian, epigrammatist, *farceur*, humorist, joker, punster, wag **3.** acumen, brains, cleverness, common sense, comprehension, discernment, ingenuity, insight, intellect, judgment, mind, nous (*Brit. sl.*), perception, practical intelligence, reason, sense, understanding, wisdom

witch enchantress, magician, necromancer, occultist, sorceress

witchcraft enchantment, incantation, magic, necromancy, occultism, sorcery, sortilege, spell, the black art, the occult, voodoo, witchery, witching, wizardry

withdraw 1. draw back, draw out, extract, pull out, remove, take away, take off **2.** abjure, disavow, disclaim, recall, recant, rescind, retract, revoke, take back, unsay **3.** absent oneself, back out, depart, detach oneself, disengage, drop out, fall back, go, leave, make oneself scarce (*Inf.*), pull back, pull out, retire, retreat, secede

withdrawal 1. extraction, removal **2.** abjuration, disavowal, disclaimer, recall, recantation, repudiation, rescission, retraction, revocation **3.** departure, disengagement, exit, exodus, retirement, retreat, secession

withdrawn 1. aloof, detached, distant, introverted, quiet, reserved, retiring, shrinking, shy, silent, taciturn, timorous, uncommunicative, unforthcoming **2.** hidden, isolated, out-of-the-way, private, remote, secluded, solitary

wither 1. blast, blight, decay, decline, desiccate, disintegrate, droop, dry, fade, languish, perish, shrink, shrivel, wane, waste, wilt **2.** abash, blast, humiliate, mortify, put down (*Sl.*), shame, snub

withering 1. blasting, blighting, devastating, humiliating, hurtful, mortifying, scornful, snubbing **2.** deadly, death-dealing, destructive, devastating, killing, murderous, slaughterous

withhold 1. check, conceal, deduct, hide, hold back, keep, keep back, keep secret, refuse, repress, reserve, resist, restrain, retain, sit on (*Inf.*), suppress **2.** *With* **from** forbear, keep oneself, refrain, stop oneself

with it fashionable, in (*Inf.*), latest (*Inf.*), modern, modish, progressive, stylish, swinging (*Sl.*), trendy (*Brit. inf.*), up-to-date, up-to-the-minute, vogue

withstand 1. bear, brave, combat,

confront, cope with, defy, endure, face, grapple with, hold off, hold out against, oppose, put up with (*Inf.*), resist, stand up to, suffer, take, take on, thwart, tolerate, weather **2.** endure, hold *or* stand one's ground, hold out, remain firm, stand, stand fast, stand firm

witless crazy, daft (*Inf.*), dull, empty-headed, foolish, halfwitted, idiotic, imbecilic, inane, moronic, obtuse, rattle-brained (*Sl.*), senseless, silly, stupid, unintelligent

witness *n.* **1.** beholder, bystander, eye-witness, looker-on, observer, onlooker, spectator, viewer, watcher **2.** attestant, corroborator, deponent, testifier **3. bear witness a.** depone, depose, give evidence, give testimony, testify **b.** attest to, bear out, be evidence of, be proof of, betoken, confirm, constitute proof of, corroborate, demonstrate, evince, prove, show, testify to, vouch for ~*v.* **4.** attend, be present at, look on, mark, note, notice, observe, perceive, see, view, watch **5.** attest, authenticate, bear out,· bear witness, confirm, corroborate, depone, depose, give evidence, give testimony, testify **6.** countersign, endorse, sign

wits 1. acumen, astuteness, brains (*Inf.*), cleverness, comprehension, faculties, ingenuity, intelligence, judgment, nous (*Brit. sl.*), reason, sense, understanding **2. at one's wits' end** at a loss, at the end of one's tether, baffled, bewildered, in despair, lost, stuck (*Inf.*), stumped

witticism bon mot, clever remark, epigram, one-liner (*Sl.*), play on words, pleasantry, pun, quip, repartee, riposte, sally, witty remark

witty amusing, brilliant, clever, droll, epigrammatic, facetious, fanciful, funny, gay, humorous, ingenious, jocular, lively, original, piquant, sparkling, waggish, whimsical

wizard 1. conjurer, enchanter, mage (*Archaic*), magician, magus, necromancer, occultist, shaman, sorcerer, thaumaturge (*Rare*), warlock, witch **2.** ace (*Inf.*), adept, expert, genius, hotshot (*Inf.*), maestro, master, prodigy, star, virtuoso, whiz (*Inf.*), whizz kid (*Inf.*), wiz (*Inf.*)

wizardry conjuration, enchantment, magic, necromancy, occultism, sorcery, sortilege, the black art, voodoo, witchcraft, witchery, witching

wizened dried up, gnarled, lined, sere

(*Archaic*), shrivelled, shrunken, withered, worn, wrinkled

wobble *v.* **1.** quake, rock, seesaw, shake, sway, teeter, totter, tremble, vibrate, waver **2.** be unable to make up one's mind, be undecided, dither, fluctuate, hesitate, shillyshally (*Inf.*), swither (*Scot.*), vacillate, waver ~*n.* **3.** quaking, shake, tremble, tremor, unsteadiness, vibration

wobbly rickety, shaky, teetering, tottering, unbalanced, uneven, unsafe, unstable, unsteady, wonky (*Brit. sl.*)

woe adversity, affliction, agony, anguish, burden, curse, dejection, depression, disaster, distress, gloom, grief, hardship, heartache, heartbreak, melancholy, misery, misfortune, pain, sadness, sorrow, suffering, trial, tribulation, trouble, unhappiness, wretchedness

woebegone blue, chapfallen, cheerless, crestfallen, dejected, disconsolate, doleful, downcast, downhearted, down in the mouth (*Inf.*), forlorn, gloomy, grief-stricken, hangdog, long-faced, lugubrious, miserable, mournful, sad, sorrowful, troubled, wretched

woeful 1. afflicted, agonized, anguished, calamitous, catastrophic, cruel, deplorable, disastrous, disconsolate, distressing, doleful, dreadful, gloomy, grieving, grievous, heartbreaking, heart-rending, lamentable, miserable, mournful, pathetic, piteous, pitiable, pitiful, plaintive, sad, sorrowful, tragic, unhappy, wretched **2.** appalling, awful, bad, deplorable, disappointing, disgraceful, dreadful, duff (*Brit. Sl.*), feeble, hopeless, inadequate, lousy (*Inf.*), mean, miserable, paltry, pathetic, pitiable, pitiful, poor, rotten (*Inf.*), shocking, sorry, terrible, wretched

wolf *n.* **1.** *Fig.* devil, fiend, killer, mercenary, pirate, predator, robber, savage, shark **2.** *Inf.* Casanova, Don Juan, lady-killer, lecher, Lothario, philanderer, seducer, womanizer ~*v.* **3.** *With* **down** bolt, cram, devour, gobble, gollop, gorge, gulp, pack away (*Inf.*), scoff (*Sl.*), stuff

wolfish avaricious, fierce, gluttonous, greedy, insatiable, predatory, rapacious, ravenous, savage, voracious

woman 1. bird (*Sl.*), chick (*Sl.*), dame (*Sl.*), female, girl, lady, lass, lassie, maid (*Archaic*), maiden (*Archaic*), miss, she **2.** chambermaid, char (*Inf.*), charwoman, domestic, female servant, handmaiden, housekeeper, lady-in-waiting, maid, maidservant **3**. *Inf.* bride, girl, girlfriend, ladylove, mate, mistress, old lady (*Inf.*), partner, spouse, sweetheart, wife

womanizer Casanova, Don Juan, lady-killer, lecher, Lothario, philanderer, seducer, wolf (*Inf.*)

womanly female, feminine, ladylike, matronly, motherly, tender, warm

wonder *n*. **1**. admiration, amazement, astonishment, awe, bewilderment, curiosity, fascination, stupefaction, surprise, wonderment **2**. curiosity, marvel, miracle, nonpareil, phenomenon, portent, prodigy, rarity, sight, spectacle, wonderment ~*v*. **3**. ask oneself, be curious, be inquisitive, conjecture, cudgel one's brains (*Inf.*), doubt, inquire, meditate, ponder, puzzle, query, question, speculate, think **4**. be amazed (astonished, awed, dumbstruck), be flabbergasted (*Inf.*), boggle, gape, gawk, marvel, stand amazed, stare

wonderful 1. amazing, astonishing, astounding, awe-inspiring, awesome, extraordinary, fantastic, incredible, marvellous, miraculous, odd, peculiar, phenomenal, remarkable, staggering, startling, strange, surprising, unheard-of, wondrous **2**. ace (*Inf.*), admirable, brilliant, excellent, fabulous (*Inf.*), fantastic (*Inf.*), great (*Inf.*), magnificent, marvellous, outstanding, sensational, smashing (*Inf.*), stupendous, super (*Inf.*), superb, terrific, tiptop, tremendous

wonky 1. groggy (*Inf.*), infirm, shaky, unsteady, weak, wobbly, woozy (*Inf.*) **2**. askew, awry, out of alignment, skewwhiff (*Brit. inf.*), squint (*Inf.*)

wont 1. *adj.* accustomed, given, in the habit of, used **2**. *n.* custom, habit, practice, rule, use, way

wonted 1. accustomed, given, habituated, in the habit of, used **2**. accustomed, common, conventional, customary, familiar, frequent, habitual, normal, regular, usual

woo chase, court, cultivate, importune, pay court to, pay one's addresses to, pay suit to, press one's suit with, pursue, seek after, seek the hand of, seek to win, solicit the good will of, spark (*Rare*)

wood 1. *Also* **woods** coppice, copse, forest, grove, thicket, trees, woodland **2**. **out of the wood(s)** clear, home and dry (*Brit. sl.*), in the clear, out of danger, safe, safe and sound, secure **3**. planks, timber

wooded forested, sylvan (*Poetic*), timbered, tree-clad, tree-covered, woody

wooden 1. ligneous, made of wood, of wood, timber, woody **2**. awkward, clumsy, gauche, gawky, graceless, inelegant, maladroit, rigid, stiff, ungainly **3**. blank, colourless, deadpan, dull, emotionless, empty, expressionless, glassy, lifeless, spiritless, unemotional, unresponsive, vacant **4**. inflexible, obstinate, rigid, stiff, unbending, unyielding **5**. dense, dim, dim-witted (*Inf.*), dull, dull-witted, obtuse, slow, stupid, thick, witless, woodenheaded (*Inf.*) **6**. dull, muffled

wool 1. fleece, hair, yarn **2**. **dyed in the wool** confirmed, diehard, fixed, hardened, inflexible, inveterate, settled, unchangeable, uncompromising, unshakable **3**. **pull the wool over someone's eyes** bamboozle (*Inf.*), con (*Sl.*), deceive, delude, dupe, fool, hoodwink, lead (someone) up the garden path (*Inf.*), pull a fast one (on someone) (*Inf.*), put one over on (*Sl.*), take in (*Inf.*), trick

woolgathering absent-mindedness, abstraction, building castles in the air, daydreaming, dreaming, inattention, musing, preoccupation, reverie

woolly *adj.* **1**. fleecy, flocculent, hairy, made of wool, shaggy, woollen **2**. blurred, clouded, confused, foggy, fuzzy, hazy, ill-defined, indefinite, indistinct, muddled, nebulous, unclear, vague

woozy befuddled, bemused, confused, dazed, dizzy, nauseated, rocky (*Inf.*), tipsy, unsteady, wobbly

word *n*. **1**. brief conversation, chat, chitchat, colloquy, confab (*Inf.*), confabulation, consultation, discussion, talk, tête-à-tête **2**. brief statement, comment, declaration, expression, remark, utterance **3**. expression, locution, name, term, vocable **4**. account, advice, bulletin, communication, communiqué, dispatch, gen (*Brit. inf.*), information, intelligence, intimation, message, news, notice, report, tidings **5**. command, go-ahead (*Inf.*), green light, order, signal **6**. affirmation, assertion, assurance, guarantee, oath, parole, pledge, promise, solemn oath, solemn word, undertaking, vow, word of honour **7**. bidding, command, commandment, decree, edict, mandate, order, ukase (*Rare*), will **8**. countersign, password, slogan, watchword **9. in a word** briefly, concisely, in a nutshell, in short, succinctly, to put it briefly, to sum up ~*v.* **10.** couch, express, phrase, put, say, state, utter

wording choice of words, language, mode of expression, phraseology, phrasing, terminology, words

wordplay punning, puns, repartee, wit, witticisms

words 1. lyrics, text **2.** altercation, angry exchange, angry speech, argument, barney (*Inf.*), bickering, disagreement, dispute, falling-out (*Inf.*), quarrel, row, run-in (*Inf.*), set-to (*Inf.*), squabble

wordy diffuse, discursive, garrulous, long-winded, loquacious, pleonastic, prolix, rambling, verbose, windy

work *n.* **1.** drudgery, effort, elbow grease (*Inf.*), exertion, grind (*Inf.*), industry, labour, slog, sweat, toil, travail (*Literary*) **2.** business, calling, craft, duty, employment, job, line, livelihood, métier, occupation, office, profession, pursuit, trade **3.** assignment, chore, commission, duty, job, stint, task, undertaking **4.** achievement, composition, creation, handiwork, *oeuvre*, opus, performance, piece, production **5.** art, craft, skill, workmanship **6. out of work** idle, jobless, on the dole (*Brit. inf.*), on the street, out of a job, unemployed ~*v.* **7.** drudge, exert oneself, labour, peg away, slave, slog (away), sweat, toil **8.** be employed, be in work, do business, earn a living, have a job **9.** act, control, direct, drive, handle, manage, manipulate, move, operate, ply, use, wield **10.** function, go, operate, perform, run **11.** cultivate, dig, farm, till **12.** fashion, form, handle, knead, make, manipulate, mould, process, shape **13.** be agitated, convulse, move, twitch, writhe **14.** *Often with* **up** arouse, excite, move, prompt, provoke, rouse, stir **15.** accomplish, achieve, bring about, carry out, cause, contrive, create, effect, encompass, execute, implement **16.** force, make one's way, manoeuvre, move, progress **17.** *Inf.* arrange, bring off, contrive, exploit, fiddle (*Inf.*), fix (*Inf.*), handle, manipulate, pull off, swing (*Inf.*)

workable doable, feasible, possible, practicable, practical, viable

workaday common, commonplace, everyday, familiar, humdrum, mundane, ordinary, practical, prosaic, routine

worker artisan, craftsman, employee, hand, labourer, proletarian, tradesman, wage earner, working man, working woman, workman

working *n.* **1.** action, functioning, manner, method, mode of operation, operation, running **2.** *Plural* diggings, excavations, mine, pit, quarry, shaft ~*adj.* **3.** active, employed, in a job, in work, labouring **4.** functioning, going, operative, running **5.** effective, practical, useful, viable

workman artificer, artisan, craftsman, employee, hand, journeyman, labourer, mechanic, operative, tradesman, worker

workmanlike, workmanly adept, careful, efficient, expert, masterly, painstaking, professional, proficient, satisfactory, skilful, skilled, thorough

workmanship art, artistry, craft, craftsmanship, execution, expertise, handicraft, handiwork, manufacture, skill, technique, work

work-out drill, exercise, exercise session, practice session, training, training session, warm-up

work out 1. accomplish, achieve, attain, win **2.** calculate, clear up, figure out, find out, puzzle out, resolve, solve **3.** arrange, construct, contrive, develop, devise, elaborate, evolve, form, formulate, plan, put together **4.** be effective, flourish, go as planned, go well, prosper, prove satisfactory, succeed **5.** come out, develop, evolve, go, happen, pan out (*Inf.*), result, turn out **6.** do exercises, drill, exercise, practise, train, warm up **7.** add up to, amount to, come to, reach, reach a total of

works 1. factory, mill, plant, shop, workshop **2.** canon, *oeuvre*, output, productions, writings **3.** actions, acts, deeds, doings **4.** action, guts (*Sl.*), innards (*Inf.*), insides (*Inf.*), machinery, mechanism, movement, moving parts, parts, workings

workshop 1. atelier, factory, mill, plant, shop, studio, workroom, works **2.** class, discussion group, seminar, study group

work up agitate, animate, arouse, enkindle, excite, foment, generate, get (someone) all steamed up (*Sl.*), incite, inflame, instigate, move, rouse, spur, stir up, wind up (*Inf.*)

world 1. earth, earthly sphere, globe **2.** everybody, everyone, humanity, humankind, human race, man, mankind, men, the public, the race of man **3.** cosmos, creation, existence, life, nature, universe **4.** heavenly body, planet, star **5.** area, domain, environment, field, kingdom, province, realm, sphere, system **6.** age, days, epoch, era, period, times **7. for all the world** exactly, in every respect, in every way, just as if, just like, precisely, to all intents and purposes **8. on top of the world** *Inf.* beside oneself with joy, ecstatic, elated, exultant, happy, in raptures, on cloud nine (*Inf.*), overjoyed, over the moon (*Inf.*) **9. out of this world** *Inf.* excellent, fabulous (*Inf.*), fantastic (*Inf.*), great (*Inf.*), incredible, indescribable, marvellous, superb, unbelievable, wonderful

worldly 1. carnal, earthly, fleshly, lay, mundane, physical, profane, secular, sublunary, temporal, terrestrial **2.** avaricious, covetous, grasping, greedy, materialistic, selfish, worldly-minded **3.** blasé, cosmopolitan, experienced, knowing, politic, sophisticated, urbane, well versed in the ways of the world, worldly-wise

worldwide general, global, international, omnipresent, pandemic, ubiquitous, universal

worn 1. frayed, ragged, shabby, shiny, tattered, tatty, the worse for wear, threadbare **2.** careworn, drawn, haggard, lined, pinched, wizened **3.** exhausted, fatigued, jaded, played-out (*Inf.*), spent, tired, tired out, wearied, weary, worn-out

worn-out 1. broken-down, clapped-out (*Brit. inf.*), decrepit, done, frayed, on its last legs, ragged, run-down, shabby, tattered, tatty, threadbare, used, used-up, useless, worn **2.** all in (*Sl.*), dead *or* out on one's feet (*Inf.*), dog-tired (*Inf.*), done in (*Inf.*), exhausted, fatigued, fit to drop, jiggered (*Dialect*), knackered (*Brit. sl.*), played-out, prostrate, spent, tired, tired out, weary

worried afraid, anxious, apprehensive, bothered, concerned, distracted, distraught, distressed, disturbed, fearful, fretful, frightened, ill at ease, nervous, on edge, overwrought, perturbed, tense, tormented, troubled, uneasy, unquiet, upset

worrisome 1. bothersome, disquieting, distressing, disturbing, irksome, perturbing, troublesome, upsetting, vexing, worrying **2.** anxious, apprehensive, fret-

ful, insecure, jittery (*Inf.*), nervous, uneasy

worry *v.* **1.** agonize, annoy, badger, be anxious, bother, brood, disquiet, distress, disturb, feel uneasy, fret, harass, harry, hassle (*Inf.*), hector, importune, irritate, make anxious, perturb, pester, plague, tantalize, tease, torment, trouble, unsettle, upset, vex **2.** attack, bite, gnaw at, go for, harass, harry, kill, lacerate, savage, tear ~*n.* **3.** annoyance, care, irritation, pest, plague, problem, torment, trial, trouble, vexation **4.** annoyance, anxiety, apprehension, care, concern, disturbance, fear, irritation, misery, misgiving, perplexity, torment, trouble, unease, vexation, woe

worsen aggravate, damage, decay, decline, degenerate, deteriorate, exacerbate, get worse, go downhill (*Inf.*), go from bad to worse, retrogress, sink, take a turn for the worse

worship 1. *v.* adore, adulate, deify, exalt, glorify, honour, idolize, laud, love, praise, pray to, put on a pedestal, respect, revere, reverence, venerate **2.** *n.* adoration, adulation, deification, devotion, exaltation, glorification, glory, homage, honour, laudation, love, praise, prayer(s), regard, respect, reverence

worst *v.* beat, best, conquer, crush, defeat, gain the advantage over, get the better of, master, overcome, overpower, overthrow, subdue, subjugate, vanquish

worth 1. aid, assistance, avail, benefit, credit, desert(s), estimation, excellence, goodness, help, importance, merit, quality, usefulness, utility, value, virtue, worthiness **2.** cost, price, rate, valuation, value

worthless 1. futile, ineffectual, insignificant, inutile, meaningless, miserable, no use, nugatory, paltry, pointless, poor, rubbishy, trashy, trifling, trivial, unavailing, unimportant, unusable, useless, valueless, wretched **2.** abandoned, abject, base, contemptible, depraved, despicable, good-for-nothing, ignoble, useless, vile

worthwhile beneficial, constructive, gainful, good, helpful, justifiable, productive, profitable, useful, valuable, worthy

worthy 1. *adj.* admirable, commendable, creditable, decent, dependable, deserving, estimable, excellent, good, honest, honourable, laudable, meritorious, praiseworthy, reliable, reputable, respectable, righteous, upright, valuable, virtuous, worthwhile **2.** *n.* big shot (*Sl.*), bigwig (*Sl.*), dignitary, luminary, notable, personage

wound *n.* **1.** cut, damage, gash, harm, hurt, injury, laceration, lesion, slash **2.** anguish, distress, grief, heartbreak, injury, insult, offence, pain, pang, sense of loss, shock, slight, torment, torture, trauma ~*v.* **3.** cut, damage, gash, harm, hit, hurt, injure, irritate, lacerate, pierce, slash, wing **4.** annoy, cut (someone) to the quick, distress, grieve, hurt, hurt the feelings of, mortify, offend, pain, shock, sting, traumatize

wraith apparition, ghost, phantom, revenant, shade (*Literary*), spectre, spirit, spook (*Inf.*)

wrangle 1. *v.* altercate, argue, bicker, brawl, contend, disagree, dispute, fall out (*Inf.*), fight, have words, quarrel, row, scrap, squabble **2.** *n.* altercation, angry exchange, argy-bargy (*Brit. inf.*), barney (*Inf.*), bickering, brawl, clash, contest, controversy, dispute, falling-out (*Inf.*), quarrel, row, set-to (*Inf.*), slanging match (*Brit.*), squabble, tiff

wrap 1. *v.* absorb, bind, bundle up, cloak, cover, encase, enclose, enfold, envelop, fold, immerse, muffle, pack, package, roll up, sheathe, shroud, surround, swathe, wind **2.** *n.* cape, cloak, mantle, shawl, stole

wrapper case, cover, envelope, jacket, packaging, paper, sheath, sleeve, wrapping

wrap up 1. bundle up, enclose, enwrap, giftwrap, pack, package **2.** dress warmly, muffle up, put warm clothes on, wear something warm **3.** *Sl.* be quiet, be silent, hold one's tongue, put a sock in it (*Brit. sl.*), shut one's face (*Brit. sl.*), shut one's mouth (*Sl.*), shut one's trap (*Sl.*), shut up **4.** *Inf.* bring to a close, conclude, end, finish off, polish off, round off, terminate, tidy up, wind up

wrath anger, choler, displeasure, exasperation, fury, indignation, ire, irritation, passion, rage, resentment, temper

wrathful angry, beside oneself with rage, displeased, enraged, furious, incensed, indignant, infuriated, irate, on the warpath (*Inf.*), raging, wroth (*Archaic*)

wreak 1. bring about, carry out, cause, create, effect, execute, exercise, inflict,

visit, work **2.** express, give free rein to, give vent to, gratify, indulge, unleash, vent

wreath band, chaplet, coronet, crown, festoon, garland, loop, ring

wreathe adorn, coil, crown, encircle, enfold, entwine, envelop, enwrap, festoon, intertwine, interweave, surround, twine, twist, wind, wrap, writhe

wreck *v.* **1.** break, dash to pieces, demolish, destroy, devastate, mar, play havoc with, ravage, ruin, shatter, smash, spoil **2.** founder, go *or* run aground, run onto the rocks, shipwreck, strand ~*n.* **3.** derelict, hulk, shipwreck, sunken vessel **4.** desolation, destruction, devastation, disruption, mess, overthrow, ruin, undoing

wreckage debris, fragments, hulk, pieces, remains, rubble, ruin, wrack

wrench *v.* **1.** force, jerk, pull, rip, tear, tug, twist, wrest, wring, yank **2.** distort, rick, sprain, strain ~*n.* **3.** jerk, pull, rip, tug, twist, yank **4.** sprain, strain, twist **5.** ache, blow, pain, pang, shock, upheaval, uprooting **6.** adjustable spanner, shifting spanner, spanner

wrest extract, force, pull, seize, strain, take, twist, win, wrench, wring

wrestle battle, combat, contend, fight, grapple, scuffle, strive, struggle, tussle

wretch 1. blackguard, cur, good-for-nothing, miscreant, outcast, profligate, rascal, rat (*Inf.*), rogue, rotter (*Sl.*), ruffian, scoundrel, swine, vagabond, villain, worm **2.** poor thing, unfortunate

wretched 1. abject, brokenhearted, cheerless, comfortless, crestfallen, dejected, deplorable, depressed, disconsolate, distressed, doleful, downcast, forlorn, gloomy, hapless, hopeless, melancholy, miserable, pathetic, pitiable, pitiful, poor, sorry, unfortunate, unhappy, woebegone, woeful, worthless **2.** calamitous, deplorable, inferior, miserable, paltry, pathetic, poor, sorry, worthless **3.** base, contemptible, despicable, low, low-down (*Inf.*), mean, paltry, scurvy, shabby, shameful, vile

wriggle *v.* **1.** jerk, jiggle, squirm, turn, twist, wag, waggle, wiggle, writhe **2.** crawl, slink, snake, twist and turn, worm, zigzag **3.** crawl, dodge, extricate oneself, manoeuvre, sneak, talk one's way out, worm ~*n.* **4.** jerk, jiggle, squirm, turn, twist, wag, waggle, wiggle

wring 1. coerce, extort, extract, force,

screw, squeeze, twist, wrench, wrest **2.** distress, hurt, lacerate, pain, pierce, rack, rend, stab, tear at, wound

wrinkle[1] **1.** *n.* corrugation, crease, crinkle, crow's-foot, crumple, fold, furrow, gather, line, pucker, rumple **2.** *v.* corrugate, crease, crinkle, crumple, fold, furrow, gather, line, pucker, ruck, rumple

wrinkle[2] device, dodge, gimmick, idea, plan, ploy, ruse, scheme, stunt, tip, trick, wheeze (*Brit. sl.*)

writ court order, decree, document, summons

write author (*Nonstandard*), commit to paper, compose, copy, correspond, create, draft, draw up, indite, inscribe, jot down, pen, put down in black and white, put in writing, record, scribble, set down, take down, tell, transcribe

write off 1. cancel, cross out, disregard, forget about, give up for lost, score out, shelve **2.** *Inf.* crash, damage beyond repair, destroy, smash up, total (*U.S. sl.*), wreck

writer author, columnist, essayist, hack, littérateur, man of letters, novelist, penman, penny-a-liner (*Rare*), penpusher, scribbler, scribe, wordsmith

writhe contort, distort, jerk, squirm, struggle, thrash, thresh, toss, twist, wiggle, wriggle

writing 1. calligraphy, chirography, hand, handwriting, penmanship, print, scrawl, scribble, script **2.** book, composition, document, letter, opus, publication, work **3.** belles-lettres, letters, literature

wrong *adj.* **1.** erroneous, fallacious, false, faulty, inaccurate, incorrect, in error, mistaken, off beam (*Inf.*), off target, out, unsound, untrue, wide of the mark **2.** bad, blameworthy, criminal, crooked, dishonest, dishonourable, evil, felonious, illegal, illicit, immoral, iniquitous, reprehensible, sinful, unethical, unfair, unjust, unlawful, wicked, wrongful **3.** funny, improper, inappropriate, inapt, incongruous, incorrect, indecorous, infelicitous, malapropos, not done, unacceptable, unbecoming, unconventional, undesirable, unfitting, unhappy, unseemly, unsuitable **4.** amiss, askew, awry, defective, faulty, not working, out of commission, out of order **5.** inside, inverse, op-posite, reverse ~*adv.* **6.** amiss, askew, astray, awry, badly, erroneously, inaccurately, incorrectly, mistakenly, wrongly **7. go wrong a.** come to grief (*Inf.*), come to nothing, fail, fall through, flop (*Inf.*), miscarry, misfire **b.** boob (*Brit. sl.*), err, go astray, make a mistake, slip up (*Inf.*), **c.** break down, cease to function, conk out (*Inf.*), fail, go kaput (*Inf.*), go on the blink (*Sl.*), go phut (*Inf.*), malfunction, misfire **d.** err, fall from grace, go astray, go off the straight and narrow (*Inf.*), go to the bad, lapse, sin ~*n.* **8.** abuse, bad *or* evil deed, crime, error, grievance, immorality, iniquity, infraction, infringement, injury, injustice, misdeed, offence, sin, sinfulness, transgression, trespass, unfairness, wickedness **9. in the wrong** at fault, blameworthy, guilty, in error, mistaken, off beam (*Inf.*), off course, off target, to be blamed ~*v.* **10.** abuse, cheat, discredit, dishonour, harm, hurt, ill-treat, ill-use, impose upon, injure, malign, maltreat, misrepresent, mistreat, oppress, take advantage of

wrongdoer criminal, culprit, delinquent, evildoer, lawbreaker, malefactor, miscreant, offender, sinner, transgressor, trespasser (*Archaic*)

wrongful blameworthy, criminal, dishonest, dishonourable, evil, felonious, illegal, illegitimate, illicit, immoral, improper, reprehensible, unethical, unfair, unjust, unlawful, wicked

wrong-headed 1. bull-headed, contrary, cross-grained, dogged, froward, inflexible, intransigent, mulish, obdurate, obstinate, perverse, pig-headed, refractory, self-willed, stubborn, wilful **2.** erroneous, fallacious, false, faulty, incorrect, in error, misguided, mistaken, off target, unsound, wrong

wrought-up agitated, animated, aroused, at fever pitch, beside oneself, excited, inflamed, keyed up, moved, overwrought, roused, stirred, strung up (*Inf.*), worked-up, wound up (*Inf.*)

wry 1. askew, aslant, awry, contorted, crooked, deformed, distorted, off the level, twisted, uneven, warped **2.** droll, dry, ironic, mocking, pawky (*Scot.*), sarcastic, sardonic

X · Y · Z

Xmas Christmas, Christmastide, festive season, Noel, Yule (*Archaic*), Yuletide (*Archaic*)

X-rays Röntgen rays (*Old name*)

yahoo barbarian, beast, boor, brute, churl, lout, philistine, roughneck (*Sl.*), rowdy, savage, yob *or* yobbo (*Brit. sl.*)

yak 1. *v.* blather, chatter, gab (*Inf.*), gossip, jabber, jaw (*Sl.*), run on, tattle, witter on (*Inf.*), yap (*Inf.*) **2.** *n.* blather, chat, chinwag (*Brit. inf.*), confab (*Inf.*), gossip, hot air (*Inf.*), jaw (*Sl.*), yackety-yak (*Sl.*), yammer (*Inf.*)

yank *v./n.* hitch, jerk, pull, snatch, tug, wrench

yap *v.* **1.** yammer (*Inf.*), yelp, yip (*Chiefly U.S.*) **2.** *Inf.* babble, blather, chatter, go on (*Inf.*), gossip, jabber, jaw (*Sl.*), prattle, talk, tattle

yardstick benchmark, criterion, gauge, measure, standard, touchstone

yarn *n.* **1.** fibre, thread **2.** *Inf.* anecdote, cock-and-bull story (*Inf.*), fable, story, tale, tall story

yawning cavernous, chasmal, gaping, vast, wide, wide-open

yearly annual, annually, every year, once a year, per annum

yearn ache, covet, crave, desire, hanker, have a yen for (*Inf.*), hunger, itch, languish, long, lust, pant, pine, set one's heart upon

years 1. age, dotage, old age, second childhood, senescence, senility **2.** days, generation(s), lifetime, span, time

yell 1. *v.* bawl, holler (*Inf.*), howl, scream, screech, shout, shriek, squeal **2.** *n.* cry, howl, scream, screech, shriek, whoop

yelp cry, yammer (*Inf.*), yap, yip (*Chiefly U.S.*), yowl

yen *n.* craving, desire, hankering, hunger, itch, longing, passion, yearning

yes man bootlicker (*Inf.*), bosses' lackey, company man, crawler (*Sl.*), creature, minion, sycophant, timeserver, toady

yet 1. as yet, so far, thus far, until now, up to now **2.** however, nevertheless, notwithstanding, still **3.** additionally, as well, besides, further, in addition, into the bargain, moreover, over and above, still, to boot **4.** already, just now, now, right now, so soon

yield *v.* **1.** afford, bear, bring forth, bring in, earn, furnish, generate, give, net, pay, produce, provide, return, supply ~*n.* **2.** crop, earnings, harvest, income, output, produce, profit, return, revenue, takings ~*v.* **3.** abandon, abdicate, admit defeat, bow, capitulate, cave in (*Inf.*), cede, cry quits, give in, give up the struggle, give way, knuckle under, lay down one's arms, part with, raise the white flag, relinquish, resign, resign oneself, submit, succumb, surrender, throw in the towel **4.** accede, agree, allow, bow, comply, concede, consent, go along with, grant, permit

yielding 1. accommodating, acquiescent, biddable, compliant, docile, easy, flexible, obedient, pliant, submissive, tractable **2.** elastic, pliable, quaggy, resilient, soft, spongy, springy, supple, unresisting

yob, yobbo hoodlum, hooligan, lout, rough (*Inf.*), roughneck (*Sl.*), rowdy, ruffian, thug, tough, yahoo

yoke *n.* **1.** bond, chain, coupling, ligament, link, tie **2.** bondage, burden, enslavement, helotry, oppression, serfdom, service, servility, servitude, slavery, thraldom, vassalage ~*v.* **3.** bracket, connect, couple, harness, hitch, join, link, tie, unite

yokel boor, bucolic, clodhopper (*Inf.*), (country) bumpkin, country cousin, countryman, hick (*Inf., chiefly U.S.*), hillbilly, hind (*Obsolete*), peasant (*Inf.*), rustic

young *adj.* **1.** adolescent, callow, green, growing, immature, infant, in the springtime of life, junior, juvenile, little, unfledged, youthful **2.** at an early stage, early, fledgling, new, newish, not far advanced, recent, undeveloped ~*n.* **3.** babies, brood, family, issue, litter, little ones, offspring, progeny

youngster boy, cub, girl, juvenile, kid (*Inf.*), lad, lass, pup (*Inf.*), teenager, teenybopper (*Sl.*), urchin, young adult, young hopeful, young person, young

youth

youth 1. adolescence, boyhood, early life, girlhood, immaturity, juvenescence, salad days, young days **2.** adolescent, boy, kid (*Inf.*), lad, shaveling (*Archaic*), stripling, teenager, young man, young shaver (*Inf.*), youngster **3.** teenagers, the rising generation, the young, younger generation, young people

youthful 1. boyish, childish, girlish, immature, inexperienced, juvenile, pubescent, puerile, young **2.** active, fresh, spry, vigorous, young at heart, young looking

yowl *v.* bay, caterwaul, cry, give tongue, howl, screech, squall, ululate, wail, yell

yukky, yucky beastly, dirty, disgusting, foul, grotty (*Brit. sl.*), horrible, messy, mucky, revolting (*Inf.*), unpleasant

zany 1. *adj.* clownish, comical, crazy, eccentric, funny, goofy (*Inf.*), kooky (*U.S. inf.*), loony (*Inf.*), madcap, nutty (*Sl.*), wacky (*Sl.*) **2.** *n.* buffoon, clown, comedian, jester, joker, merry-andrew, nut (*Sl.*), screwball (*U.S. sl.*), wag

zeal ardour, devotion, eagerness, earnestness, enthusiasm, fanaticism, fervency, fervour, fire, gusto, keenness, militancy, passion, spirit, verve, warmth, zest

zealot bigot, enthusiast, extremist, fanatic, fiend (*Inf.*), maniac, militant

zealous afire, ardent, burning, devoted, eager, earnest, enthusiastic, fanatical, fervent, fervid, impassioned, keen, militant, passionate, rabid, spirited

zenith acme, apex, apogee, climax, height, high noon, high point, meridian, peak, pinnacle, summit, top, vertex

zero 1. cipher, naught, nil, nothing, nought **2.** bottom, lowest point *or* ebb, nadir, nothing, rock bottom

zero hour appointed hour, crisis, moment of decision, moment of truth, turning point, vital moment

zero in (on) aim, bring to bear, concentrate, converge, direct, focus, home in, level, pinpoint, train

zest 1. appetite, delectation, enjoyment, gusto, keenness, relish, zeal, zing (*Inf.*) **2.** charm, flavour, interest, kick (*Inf.*), piquancy, pungency, relish, savour, smack, spice, tang, taste

zing animation, brio, dash, energy, go (*Inf.*), life, liveliness, oomph (*Inf.*), pizazz (*Sl.*), spirit, vigour, vitality, zest, zip (*Inf.*)

zip 1. *n. Fig.* brio, drive, energy, get-up-and-go (*Inf.*), go (*Inf.*), gusto, life, liveliness, oomph (*Inf.*), pep, pizazz (*Sl.*), punch (*Inf.*), sparkle, spirit, verve, vigour, vim (*Sl.*), vitality, zest, zing (*Inf.*) **2.** *v.* dash, flash, fly, hurry, rush, shoot, speed, tear, whiz (*Inf.*), zoom

zone area, belt, district, region, section, sector, sphere

zoom *v.* buzz, dash, dive, flash, fly, hare (*Brit. inf.*), hum (*Sl.*), hurtle, pelt, rip (*Inf.*), rush, shoot, speed, streak, tear, whirl, whiz (*Inf.*), zip